NEWSWORTHY

WORLD VIEW

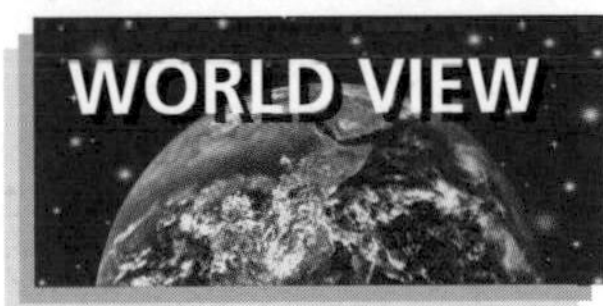

See the inside back cover for more examples of exciting features.

BUSINESS LAW

For A New Century

2nd Edition

Jeffrey F. Beatty
Boston University

Susan S. Samuelson
Boston University

WEST WEST LEGAL STUDIES IN BUSINESS
Thomson Learning™

Australia • Canada • Denmark • Japan • Mexico • New Zealand • Philippines
Puerto Rico • Singapore • South Africa • Spain • United Kingdom • United States

For Annabel, *semper laetans*
j.f.b.

For Bill, *valens atque benevolus*
s.s.s.

Business Law For A New Century, 2nd edition by Jeffrey F. Beatty and Susan S. Samuelson
Vice President and Publisher: Jack W. Calhoun
Senior Acquisitions Editor: Rob Dewey
Acquisitions Editor: Scott D. Person
Developmental Editor: Bob Sandman
Marketing Manager: Michael Worls
Production Editor: Peggy K. Buskey
Advertising Coordinator: Sally Kolks
Manufacturing Coordinator: Charlene Taylor
Editorial Assistant: Alana O'Koon
Internal Design: Carol Rose
Part and Chapter Illustrations: Ashley Van Etten
Cover Design: Imbue Design, Cincinnati, Ohio
Cover Photography: Foreground © Bruce Forster/Tony Stone Images, Background © Photodisc
Photography Manager: Cary Benbow
Photo Research: Susan Van Etten
Production Manager: Peggy Williams of Litten Editing And Production
Compositors: Texterity, Inc.; Thompson Steele, Inc.; and GGS Information Services
Printer: Von Hoffmann

Printed in the United States of America
1 2 3 4 5 03 02 01 00

For more information contact West Legal Studies in Business, South-Western College Publishing, 5101 Madison Road, Cincinnati, Ohio, 45227 or find us on the Internet at: http://www.westbuslaw.com

For permission to use material from this text or product, contact us by
- **telephone: 1-800-730-2214**
- **fax: 1-800-730-2215**
- **web: http://www.thomsonrights.com**

Library of Congress Cataloging-in-Publication Data
Beatty, Jeffrey F.
Business law for a new century / Jeffrey F. Beatty, Susan S. Samuelson.—2nd ed.
p. cm.
Includes bibliographical references and index.
ISBN 0-324-00350-1 (hc)
1. Commercial law—United States. 2. Commercial law—United States—Cases. I. Samuelson, Susan S. II. Title.

KF888 .B37 2000
346.7307—dc21 99-086716

This book is printed on acid-free paper.

WITNESS THE DIFFERENCE

WITH BEATTY AND SAMUELSON'S BUSINESS LAW FOR A NEW CENTURY, SECOND EDITION

THREE GREAT REASONS WHY BEATTY IS A WINNER:

- AUTHORITATIVE
- FULL OF HUMAN DRAMA
- HOLDS YOUR ATTENTION

ear Students:

For most of our adult lives, we have studied, practiced and written about the law. It is an endlessly fascinating and a moving subject that provides unparalleled insight into the human condition. In no area of study can you learn more about the inspirations and fears of men and women the world over. We have written a law textbook that reflects the power and excitement of this subject.

We have taught from this book, in both manuscript and printed form, for the better part of a decade. Over and over, we have heard from students at our school, and faculty and students at other institutions, that this book is indeed different from any other law text.

Witness the difference:

- This book is authoritative.
- It is a pleasure to read, full of law's human drama.
- It will hold your attention and make you eager to question and discuss.

Our best wishes as you embark on this great expedition.

Sincerely,

Jeffrey F. Beatty

Susan S. Samuelson

AUTHORITATIVE COVERAGE

THIS BOOK IS ONE YOU CAN RELY ON—IT IS THE RESULT OF EXHAUSTIVE RESEARCH AND METICULOUS PRESENTATION.

MODERN & CLASSIC
Many of the cases are from the 1990s but the classics are here, too—you'll find both *Jones v. Clinton* (p. 40) and *Palsgraf* (p. 132).

872

UNIT 5 • BUSINESS ORGANIZATIONS

IN RE **THE WALT DISNEY COMPANY DERIVATIVE LITIGATION**
1998 Del. Ch. LEXIS 186
Court of Chancery of Delaware, New Castle, 1998

Facts: As head of Creative Artists Agency (CAA), a major talent agency, Michael Ovitz was often called the "Most Powerful Man in Hollywood." Disney hired Ovitz to be its president. After 14 months, all parties agreed that the experiment had failed, so Ovitz left Disney—but not empty-handed. Under his employment contract, he was entitled to $140 million in severance pay. The court described this severance payment as "larger than almost anyone anywhere will receive in the lifetime of any of the parties, and perhaps larger than any ever paid."[8] Shareholders of Disney sued to prevent payment. Disney filed a motion to dismiss the lawsuit.

Issue: Did the Disney directors have the right to pay $140 million to an employee who had worked at the company unsuccessfully and for only 14 months?

Excerpts from Judge Chandler's Decision: Just as the 85,000-ton cruise ships Disney Magic and Disney Wonder are forced by science to obey the same laws of buoyancy as Disneyland's significantly smaller Jungle Cruise ships, so is a corporate board's extraordinary decision to award a $140 million severance package governed by the same corporate law principles as its everyday decision to authorize a loan. When the laws of buoyancy are followed, the Disney Magic can stay afloat as well as the Jungle Cruise vessels. When the Delaware General Corporation Law is followed, a large severance package is just as valid as an authorization to borrow. Nature does not sink a ship merely because of its size, and neither do courts overrule a board's decision to approve and later honor a severance package, merely because of its size. Unless Plaintiffs can plead with specificity facts

HIGH INTEREST
Cases were chosen because they are interesting—this one is about a Hollywood dispute. (p. 872)

ON POINT
All cases are on point—and are carefully edited to focus on one or two issues.

TOUGH ISSUES
Executive compensation is a contentious issue—why not discuss it in business school?

EXCERPTED CASES
Cases are in the "language of the court" so you can hear the individual voices of judges.

LEGAL RULES

Legal rules are in bold print, followed by clear explanations.

P. 231

CONTRACTS

THE PURPOSE OF A CONTRACT

Throughout this unit on contracts, we will consider issues like those raised in the Cassandra–Hard Body story. This long chain of mutually dependent people and companies exemplifies not only the law of contracts but the *purpose* of contracts. Parties enter into contracts attempting to control their future. **Contracts exist to make business matters more predictable.** Most contracts work out precisely as the parties intended because the parties fulfill their obligations. Most—but not all. In this unit we will study contracts that have gone wrong. We look at these errant deals to learn how to avoid the problems they manifest.

P. 273

A BARGAIN AND AN EXCHANGE

Consideration is a required element of any contract. **Consideration means that there must be bargaining that leads to an exchange between the parties.** "Bargaining" indicates that each side is obligating itself in some way *to induce the other side to agree.* Generally, a court will enforce one party's promise only if the other party did something or promised something in exchange. Without an exchange of mutual obligations, there is usually no deal.

How would the four Parsley examples in the introduction work out? In the

P. 385

Substantial Performance

Daniel, the house builder, won his case against Caitlin because he fulfilled most of his obligations, even though he did an imperfect job. Courts often rely on the substantial performance doctrine, especially in cases involving services as opposed to those concerning the sale of goods or land. **In a contract for services, a party that substantially performs its obligations will receive the full contract price, minus**

"I have never seen the complexity of contract law made this readable."
– Robert Fidrych, University of Wisconsin

STRONG NARRATIVE

THE LAW IS FULL OF GREAT STORIES, AND WE USE THEM.

P. 24
Was it an accident or was it a suicide? Will the right answer be revealed at trial?

Tony Caruso hadn't returned for dinner. His wife, Karen, was nervous. She put on some sandals and hurried across the dunes, a half mile to the ocean shore. She soon came upon Tony's dog, Blue, tied to an old picket fence. Tony's shoes and clothing were piled neatly nearby. Karen and friends searched frantically throughout the evening. A little past midnight, Tony's body washed ashore, his lungs filled with water. A local doctor concluded he had accidentally drowned. Karen and her

P. 250
Is it a contract or isn't it? Read the scene between the actress and the director to decide.

Interior. A glitzy cafe, New York. Evening. Bob, a famous director, and Katrina, a glamorous actress, sit at a table, near a wall of glass looking onto a New York sidewalk that is filled with life and motion. Bob sips a margarita while carefully eyeing Katrina. Katrina stares at her wine glass.

P. 545
Producing a rock video seemed like a golden opportunity until checks started bouncing.

Willie groaned under his breath. How had he ever gotten into this mess? Producing a rock video for the Hot Tamales had seemed a golden opportunity. He loved the music, and he didn't even mind living in a trailer on location, but the business end was driving him to despair. That morning, he had glanced out his trailer window and seen Vidalia slinking across the set. How could he have been so stupid as to let her finance the video? "Willie, darling," she had purred, as a circle of smoke from her cigarette caught in his throat, "I know that your promissory note for $50,000 isn't due 'til next month, but I simply do not like the music in this video, and I cannot support what I do not like. It would be so bad for my karma. But, take your time, dearest one, my driver will be back

P. 780
What happens when partners disagree? All students need to know the rules on business organizations.

Bailey was Chase's choice for the interior design; she could create the sleek, warm look he sought. With Zack's landscape plan, the house would appear to be a natural part of the site. At their first meeting, all three designers committed to the project and rapidly agreed to a deal: Chase would receive 50 percent of the profits, Bailey and Zack 25 percent each. All three would have veto

When you care about the material, you read it more eagerly.

P. 961
Full coverage of the Microsoft case, in easily understood language.

961

CHAPTER 41 • ANTITRUST: LAW AND COMPETITIVE STRATEGY, PART II

Does Microsoft Control a Market?

Ninety percent of the world's PCs use Windows, the Microsoft operating system. Microsoft also has 93 percent of the world market for office suites,[5] 45 percent of global software sales, and 1 percent of the computer industry. The company's market share suggests that it may have a monopoly in both operating systems and office suites. However, the *Syufy* case says that a large market share is not sufficient proof of a monopoly. There must also be evidence that the company can control prices or exclude competitors. During a five-year period, the average

P. 555
Liability rules for negotiable instruments are typically difficult to understand. Our presentation of these rules is the clearest you will ever see.

WARRANTY LIABILITY

Warranty liability rules apply when someone receives payment on an instrument that is invalid because it has been forged, altered, or stolen.

BASIC RULES OF WARRANTY LIABILITY

1. **The culprit is always liable.** If a forger signs someone else's name to an instrument, that signature counts as the *forger's*, not as that of the person whose name she signed. The forger is liable for the value of the instrument plus any other expenses or lost interest that subsequent parties may experience because of the forgery. If Hope signs David's name on one of his checks,

P. 124
Diagrams that are rich in color and content elucidate complex issues.

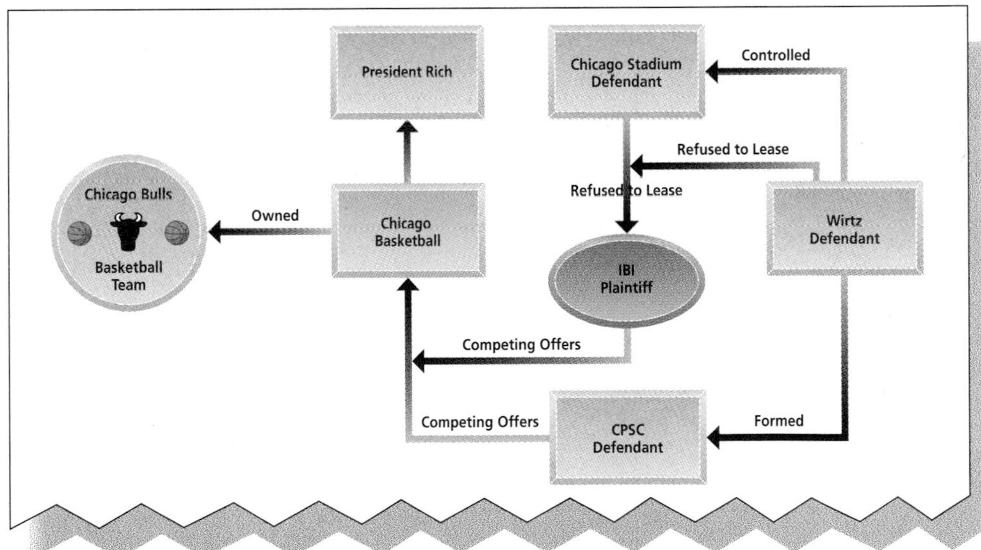

"I highly recommend this book to anyone interested in understanding the important legal issues surrounding business transactions. It is well organized, timely, interesting, and most of all, useful to both the student and professional. A well-done resource that I value immensely."
– Brian Plumb, Senior Financial Analyst, NEES Companies

SEE THE RELEVANCE

IT'S EASIER TO LEARN SOMETHING WHEN YOU CAN SEE WHY IT IS IMPORTANT.

YOU BE THE JUDGE

Think independently. Consider two sides of an argument. See pages 403, 503, and **849**.

care? You be the judge. It is a long and complex ca

SMITH v. VAN GORKOM
488 A.2d 858, 1985 Del. LEXIS 590
Supreme Court of Delaware, 1985

Facts: Trans Union was a publicly traded company in the railcar leasing business. Jerome Van Gorkom had been its chief executive officer for more than 17 years. He was nearing the mandatory retirement age of 65 and was concerned about maximizing the value of his 75,000 shares of Trans Union stock. In the pre-

Gorkom suggested to
(LBO) could be done
acquiring company b
using a loan secure
Thursday, September
Trans Union's stock
expired three days lat
On Saturday, Va
senior managers and
Salomon Brothers, th
was not invited to
Gorkom disclosed th

Argument for the Shareholders: The whole procedure for this sale was shockingly casual. Van Gorkom signed the final agreement at a social function. When the directors voted to sell the company,

the offer, they w
Alden Smi
reason to hold t
rule is meant t
faith decision.

Argument for the Board of Directors: Pritzker paid a fair price for the Trans Union stock. It represented a premium of (1) 62 percent over the average of the high and low price in the prior year, (2) 48 percent over the last closing price, and (3) 39 percent over the

NEWSWORTHY

See that the law touches us every day. See pages 411, 656, and **786**.

For 20 years, William Moses Kunstler, the shaman and showman lawyer of the radical left, started his mornings by climbing upstairs to the second floor of his Greenwich Village brownstone, taking coffee to the bedside of his wife, Margaret Ratner. After breakfast, Mr. Kunstler would commute to work simply by tromping downstairs to the brownstone's ground-floor office. There, for the last 11 years of his life, he fought the government in hundreds of cases with his acolyte and side-

WORLDVIEW
Connect with the world. Now the Internet makes international issues even more vital. See pages 362, 489, and **897**.

In its transition to a market economy, Russia is developing a securities market. To date, this market has tended to be underregulated and overhyped. The Russian government began by issuing privatization vouchers to all its citizens. These vouchers could be used to invest in newly privatized companies. Investment options varied widely. At a "privatization festival" in a Moscow exhibition hall, young men and women with neat business suits and alarmingly friendly smiles waved photocopies of their factories' business plans. Shares in these enterprises have since turned out to be worthless.

Because investing in legitimate enterprises proved so difficult, millions of

CYBERLAW
Master the present and anticipate the future. How does current law govern new technology? See pages 351, **481**, and 1029.

Rich and Enza Hill bought a computer from Gateway 2000, using a credit card to make the purchase over the phone. The Hills complained that their computer was defective and eventually filed suit. The court, however, dismissed their case. Why? The box that arrived at their doorstep contained not only their chosen hardware but a contract from Gateway. The contract stated that the buyer agreed to all of its terms unless she returned the computer within 30 days. One of the terms obligated the buyer to arbitrate any disputes, rather than litigate. The arbitration had to take place in Chicago and be conducted according to the rules of French

RIGHT & WRONG
Make ethics real. It's not just for philosophers any more. See pages **275**, 660, and 910.

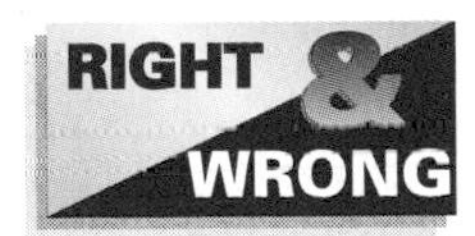

Because Kelsoe had given no consideration, International Wood was legally permitted to escape from its promise. But was that ethical? Should a corporation honor all commitments to employees? What policy would create the best workforce? What harm might befall a company that fulfilled all promises? What decision would you have made if you were Hernandez's boss and had the power to award the stock to Kelsoe or deny it?

When trying to enforce a defendant's promise, the plaintiff must show that

PREVENTIVE LAW
Stay out of court. Tips for keeping on the right side of the law. See pages **162**, 460, and 1044.

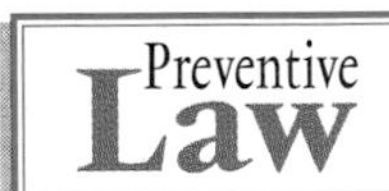

Experts point out that much fraud and embezzlement are readily apparent and can be avoided, if corporate leaders will only open their eyes. Here are a few warning signs:

- An employee with extremely high expense accounts.
- Purchase orders significantly above those of other departments or previous job holders.

"The textbook is awesome. A lot of the time I read more than what was assigned—I just didn't want to stop."
– An undergraduate at Boston University

CONTENTS: OVERVIEW

UNIT 5

CONTENTS

Tort= civil wrong

CHAPTER 7

CHAPTER 8

CHAPTER 9

UNIT 2

CHAPTER 10

end

PREFACE

We wrote this book to convey our passion for an exciting and profoundly important discipline. Business law is notoriously complex, and as authors we are obsessed with accuracy. Yet this intriguing subject also abounds with human conflict and hard-earned wisdom, forces that can make a law book sparkle. As this second edition is published, we are grateful to the faculty who tell us that this business law textbook is precise and authoritative *yet a pleasure to read*. Here are some of the book's key features:

Authoritative. We insist, as you do, on a lawbook that is indisputably accurate. A professor must teach with assurance, confident that every paragraph is the result of exhaustive research and meticulous presentation. Dozens of tough-minded people spent thousands of hours reviewing both editions of this book, and we are delighted with the stamp of approval we have received from trial and appellate judges, working attorneys, scholars and teachers.

We reject the cloudy definitions and fuzzy explanations that can invade judicial opinions and legal scholarship. To highlight the most important rules, we use bold print, and then follow with vivacious examples written in clear, forceful English. (See, for example, the description of assault, on page 115.) We cheerfully venture into contentious areas, relying on very recent appellate decisions. (Can computer software be patented? See page 1028.) Where there is doubt about the current (or future) status of a doctrine, we say so. In areas of particularly heated debate, we footnote our work: we want you to have absolute trust in this book.

Strong Narrative. The law is full of great stories, and we use them. Your students and ours should come to class excited. In Chapter 2, on dispute resolution (page 24), we explain litigation by tracking a double-indemnity lawsuit. An executive is dead. Did he drown accidentally, obligating the insurance company to pay? Or did the businessman commit suicide, voiding the policy? The student follows the action from the discovery of the body, through each step of the lawsuit, to the final appeal. The chapter offers a detailed discussion of dispute resolution, but it does so by exploiting the human drama that underlies litigation.

Students read stories and remember them. Strong narratives provide a rich context for the remarkable quantity of legal material presented. When students care about the material they are reading, they persevere. We have been delighted to find that they also arrive in class eager to question, discuss and learn.

Precise. The great joy of using English accurately is the power it gives us to attack and dissect difficult issues, rendering them comprehensible to any lay reader. This text takes on the most complex legal topics of the day, yet it is appropriate for *all college and graduate level students*. Accessible prose goes hand in hand with legal precision. We take great pride in walking our readers through the most serpentine mazes this tough subject can offer. UCC section 2-207, on "battle of forms" conflicts, is hardly sexy material, but it is important. We spotlight the real-world need for section 2-207, and then use pin-point directions to guide our readers through its many switchbacks, arriving at a full understanding with sanity and good humor intact. (See page 262.)

As we explore this extraordinary discipline, we lure readers along with quirky anecdotes and colorful diagrams. (Notice that the color display on page 615 clarifies one of the more complex transactions in Article 9 of the UCC.) However, before the trip is over we insist that students:

- gauge policy and political considerations,
- grapple with legal and social history,
- spot the nexus between disparate doctrines, and
- confront tough moral choices.

Beyond that, we demand that students incorporate all of these ideas in preventive law analyses, figuring out how to avoid the very problems that have generated our law.

Comprehensive. Staying comprehensive means staying current. Look, for example, at the important field of corporate governance. All texts cover cumulative voting, and so do we. Yet a future executive is far likelier to face conflicts over board composition, executive compensation, and shareholder proposals. We present a clear path through this thicket of new issues, including the latest recommendations from the National Association of Corporate Directors (page 862). We want tomorrow's business leaders to anticipate the challenges that await them and then use their knowledge to avert problems.

We have greatly rewritten many chapters for this second edition, to insure full coverage of rapidly evolving issues such as cyberlaw, international law, UCC revisions, and countless other topics. However, we have kept the strong narrative flow from the earlier edition. Like you, we are here to teach. We do not use boxes because, in our experience, they disrupt the flow of the text. Students inform us that a box indicates peripheral material, that is, material they routinely skip; we prefer to give them an uncluttered whole. Each chapter now contains several **Internet addresses**, offering students a quick link to additional knowledge. These addresses, however, are woven into the body of the text, to reinforce the point that new technology and research methods are an integral part of a lively discipline. For example on page 252, in the chapter on contract agreement, we provide a Web site that enables students to research and negotiate a home improvement contract. We believe that a well-written chapter is seamless and cohesive.

A Book for Students. We have written this book as if we were speaking directly to our students. We provide black letter law, but we also explain concepts in terms that hook students. Over the years, we have learned how much more successfully we can teach when our students are intrigued. No matter what kind of a show we put on in class, *they are only learning when they want to learn.*

Every chapter begins with a story, either fictional or real, to illustrate the issues in the chapter and provide context. Chapter 6, on negligence (page 131), opens with a drunken student who staggers from a fraternity party and causes a serious automobile accident while driving home. The intoxicated student is obviously liable. Are other fraternity members? Students want to know—right away.

Most of today's students were not yet born when Gerald Ford was president. They come to college with varying levels of preparation; many now arrive from foreign countries. We have found that to teach business law most effectively we must provide its context. The chapter on securities law begins with a brief but graphic description of the 1929 stock market crash and the Great Depression (page 886). Only with this background do students grasp the importance and impact of our securities laws.

At the same time, we enjoy offering "nuts and bolts" information that grab students: how much money corporate directors earn; how scam artists create car accidents in order to file fraudulent insurance claim; how to register an Internet domain name. In Chapter 42, on consumer law, we bring home the issue of credit history by providing phone numbers and Web sites that students can use to check their own credit reports (page 990).

Students respond enthusiastically to this approach. Along with other professors, we have used this text in courses for undergraduates, MBAs and executive MBAs, the students ranging in age from 18 to 55. The book works, as some unsolicited comments indicate:

- An undergraduate wrote, "This is the best textbook I have had in college, on any subject."
- A business law professor stated that the "clarity of presentation is superlative. I have never seen the complexity of contract law made this readable."
- An MBA student commented, "I think the textbook is great. The book is relevant, easy to understand and interesting."
- A state supreme court justice wrote that the book is "a valuable blend of rich scholarship and easy readability. Students and professors should rejoice with this publication."
- A Fortune 500 vice-president, enrolled in an Executive MBA program, commented, "I really liked the chapters. They were crisp, organized and current. The information was easy to understand and enjoyable."
- An undergraduate wrote, "The textbook is awesome. A lot of the time I read more than what is assigned—I just don't want to stop."

Humor. Throughout the text we use humor—judiciously—to lighten and enlighten. Not surprisingly, students have applauded—but is wit appropriate? How dare we employ levity in this venerable discipline? We offer humor because we take law seriously. We revere the law for its ancient traditions, its dazzling intricacy, its relentless though imperfect attempt to give order and decency to our world. Because we are confident of our respect for the law, we are not afraid to employ some levity. Leaden prose masquerading as legal scholarship does no honor to the field.

Humor also helps retention. We have found that students remember a contract problem described in a fanciful setting, and from that setting recall the underlying principle. By contrast, one widget is hard to distinguish from another.

FEATURES

We chose the features for our book with great care. As mentioned above, all features are considered an essential part of the text, and are woven into its body. Also, each feature responds to an essential pedagogical goal. Here are some of those goals, and the matching feature.

You Be The Judge

GOAL: Get them thinking independently. When reading case opinions, students tend to accept the court's "answer." Judges, of course, try to write decisions that appear indisputable, when in reality they may be controversial—or wrong. From time to time we want students to think through the problem and reach their own answer. Virtually every chapter contains a *You Be The Judge* feature, providing the facts of the case and conflicting appellate arguments. The court's decision, however, appears only in the Instructor's Manual.

Since students do not know the result, discussions tend to be more free-flowing. For instance, many commentators feel that *Smith v. Van Gorkom*, the landmark case on the business judgment rule, was wrongly decided. However, when students read the court's opinion they rarely consider the opposing side. Now, with the case presented as *You Be the Judge* in Chapter 36 (page 849), the students disagree with the court at least half the time. They are thinking.

Newsworthy

GOAL: Prove that the law touches each of us every day. Students are intrigued to see the relevancy of what they are learning. Each chapter contains at least one Newsworthy feature—a newspaper or magazine article illustrating the legal issue under discussion. Thus, in Chapter 28 on agency law (page 656), an article about an American diplomat killed by terrorists demonstrates that an agency relationship exists only when the principal has control over its agent.

Cyberlaw

GOAL: Master the present and anticipate the future. The computer has changed all of our lives forever, and the courts and statute books are full of fascinating cyberlaw issues. Do employers have the right to read workers' e-mail? When does an electronic signature satisfy the statute of frauds? May the government halt the export of encryption technology? Cyberlaw discussions are woven throughout the chapters, highlighted with an icon.

Preventive Law

GOAL: Help managers stay out of court. As every lawyer knows, the best lawsuit is the one that never happens. Some of our students are already in the workforce, and the rest soon will be, so we offer ideas on avoiding legal disputes. Sometimes we provide detailed methods to avoid the particular problem; other times we challenge the students to formulate their own approach to dispute prevention. (See, for example, page 162.)

Right & Wrong

GOAL: Make ethics real. We ask ethical questions about cases, legal issues and commercial practices. Is it fair for one party to void a contract by arguing, months after the fact, that there was no consideration? How much hospitality should an auditor accept from clients? Do managers have ethical obligations to older workers for whom employment opportunities may be limited? What is wrong with bribery? What should a young executive do if her company sells goods manufactured by underpaid foreign workers? We do not have definitive answers but believe that asking the questions, and encouraging discussion, reminds students that ethics is an essential element of justice, and of a satisfying life.

World View

GOAL: Bring the world into the classroom. Business is now global. We offer illustrations of how other countries and cultures treat legal issues. For example, the securities regulation chapter, at page 897, discusses the development of a securities market in modern Russia. Students can glimpse the vital role that securities regulation plays in the economic life of a nation, and have a chance to explore alternatives to our system.

Cases

GOAL: Let the judges speak. Each case begins with a summary of the facts and a statement of the issue. Next comes a tightly edited version of the decision, in the court's own language, so that students "hear" the law developing in the diverse voices of our many judges. We cite cases using a modified bluebook form. In the principal cases in each chapter, we provide the state or federal citation, the regional citation, and the LEXIS citation. We also give students a brief description of the court. Because many of our cases are so recent, some will have only a regional reporter and a LEXIS citation.

Practice Tests

GOAL: Encourage students to practice! At the end of the chapters we challenge the students with ten or more problems, including the following:

- *Internet Research Problem*. This question sends students to an Internet address where they can explore issues from the chapter.
- *You Be The Judge Writing Problem.* The students are given appellate arguments on both sides of the question, and must prepare a written opinion.
- *Right and Wrong*. This question highlights the ethical issues of a dispute, and calls upon the student to formulate a specific, reasoned response.
- *CPA Questions*. For topics covered by the CPA exam, administered by the American Institute of Certified Public Accountants, the practice tests include questions from previous CPA exams.

Answers to the *odd-numbered* questions appear at the back of the book, and here is why. Students often ask us how to study for exams. Reviewing the problems in the end-of-chapter practice tests is helpful, but without the answers students have no way of being sure they are on the right track. The answers to the *even-numbered* questions appear only in the Instructor's Manual, so that faculty can assign them for written or oral presentation.

TEACHING MATERIALS

For more information about any of these ancillaries, contact your ITP/South-Western Sales Representative for more details, or visit the Beatty *Business Law for a New Century* Web site at **http://beatty.westbuslaw.com/**.

Student Study Guide. (ISBN: 0-324-00354-4) Students may purchase a study guide that includes a chapter outline, chapter objectives, and practice questions. Students can find further practice problems in the Online Quiz at **http://beatty.westbuslaw.com**.

Instructor's Manual. (ISBN: 0-324-00351-X) We care about teaching, and wrote this manual ourselves. We have included special features to enhance class discussion and student progress:

- Dialogues. These are a series of questions-and-answers on pivotal cases and topics. The questions provide enough material to teach a full session. In a pinch, you could walk into class with nothing but the manual and use the Dialogues to conduct an exciting class.
- Action learning ideas: interviews, quick research projects, drafting exercises, classroom activities, commercial analyses and other suggested assignments that get students out of their chairs and into the diverse settings of business law.
- Skits. Various chapters have lively skits that students can perform in class, with no rehearsal, to put legal doctrine in a real-life context.
- A chapter theme and a quote of the day.
- Updates of text material.
- New cases and examples.
- Answers to You Be the Judge cases from the text, and to the Practice Test questions found at the end of each chapter.

Test Bank. (ISBN: 0-324-00352-8) The test bank offers hundreds of essay, short answer and multiple choice problems, and may be obtained in hard copy or electronic format.

Thomson Learning Testing Tools—Computerized Testing Software. (ISBN: 0-324-00353-6) This testing software contains all of the questions in the printed test bank. This program is an easy-to-use test creation software compatible with Microsoft Windows. Instructors can add or edit questions, instructions, and answers; and select questions by previewing them on the screen, selecting them randomly, or selecting them by number. Instructors can also create and administer quizzes online, whether over the Internet, a local area network (LAN), or a wide area network (WAN).

Microsoft PowerPoint Lecture Review Slides. PowerPoint slides are available for use by students as an aid to note-taking and by instructors for enhancing their lectures. Download these slides at http://beatty.westbuslaw.com/.

Transparency Masters. (ISBN: 0-324-04251-5) A book of blackline masters of the PowerPoint slides is available. Instructors can use the masters to make acetate transparencies.

Videos. Qualified adopters using this text have access to the entire library of West videos, a vast selection of videos covering most business law issues. There are some restrictions, and if you have questions, please contact your West representative.

Interaction with the Authors. This is our standard: Every professor who adopts this book must have a superior experience. We are available to help in any way we can. Adopters of this text often call us or E-mail us to ask questions, obtain a syllabus, offer suggestions, share pedagogical concerns or inquire about ancillaries. One of the pleasures of working on this project has been our discovery that the text provides a link to so many colleagues around the country. We value those connections, are eager to respond, and would be happy to hear from you.

To the Student

One other tip: Each chapter contains several Internet addresses, offering a resource for further learning. The Practice Test at the end of each chapter also includes an Internet research problem. Sometimes your web browser might not be able to find the entire address, but can find part of it. For example, if you receive an error message when you look for **http://www.ljx.com/practice/corporate/**, you might try looking first at **http://www.ljx.com** and then adding the other parts of the address.

Acknowledgments

We are grateful to the following reviewers who gave such helpful comments on the first edition and on the manuscript for the second edition of this book:

Thomas Higgins
Illinois Central College

Mary Kay Finn
The University of Akron

Dexter R. Woods
Ohio Northern University

Julia Derrick
Brevard Community College

Weldon Blake
Bethune Cookman College

Vivica Pierre
California State University Long Beach

Linda Moran
Santa Rosa Jr. College

Linda Samuels
The University of Akron

Cynthia Phillips
Moorehead State University

Scott A. White
University of Wisconsin - Platteville

Lara Short
Middle Tennessee State University

Minna Schiller
Bellevue Community College

Karl Boedecker
University of San Francisco

Edward Gac
University of Colorado

Jeffrey F. Beatty
Phone: (617) 353-6397
E-mail: jfbeatty@bu.edu

Susan S. Samuelson
Phone: (617) 353-2033
E-mail: ssamuels@bu.edu

Boston, Massachusetts
February 2000

UNIT 1

THE LEGAL ENVIRONMENT

CHAPTER 1

INTRODUCTION TO LAW

Law is powerful. Law is essential. And law is fascinating. We hope this book will persuade you of all three ideas.

THREE IMPORTANT IDEAS ABOUT LAW

POWER

The law displays its muscle every day, to corporate executives, homeless people—and presidents. A driver dies in an automobile accident and the jury concludes that the car had a design defect. The jurors award $8 million to the victim's family. A senior vice-president congratulates himself on a cagey stock purchase but is horrified to receive, not profits, but a prison sentence. A homeless person, ordered by local police to stop panhandling, ambles into court and walks out with an order permitting him to beg on the city's streets. A criminal inquiry spreads until a grand jury hears testimony from an unprecedented source—a sitting president of the United States. The strong reach of the law touches us all. To understand something that is powerful is itself power.

Suppose, some years after graduation, you are a mid-level manager at Sublime Corp., which manufactures and distributes video games and related hardware and software. You are delighted with this important position in an excellent company—and especially glad you bring legal knowledge to the job. Sarah, an expert at computer-generated imagery, complains that Rob, her boss, is constantly touching her and making lewd comments. That is sexual harassment and your knowledge of *employment law* helps you respond promptly and carefully. You have dinner with Jake, who has his own software company. Jake wants to manufacture an exciting new video game in cooperation with Sublime, but you are careful not to create a binding deal. (*Contract law.*) Jake mentions that a similar game is already on the market. Do you have the right to market one like it? That answer you already know. (*Intellectual property law.*)

The next day a letter from the Environmental Protection Agency asks how your company disposes of toxic chemicals used to manufacture computer drives. You can discuss it efficiently with in-house counsel, because you have a working knowledge of *environmental law* and *administrative law*. You may think your corporation is about to surge ahead in its field, and you would like to invest in its stock. But wait! Are you engaging in "insider trading"? Your training in *securities law* will distinguish the intelligent investment from the felony. LuYu, your personnel manager, reports that a silicon chip worker often seems drowsy; she suspects drug use. Does she have the right to test him? (*Constitutional law* and *employment law.*) On the other hand, if she fails to test him, could Sublime Corp. be liable for any harm the worker does? (*Tort law* and *agency law.*)

In a mere week you might use your legal training a dozen times, helping Sublime to steer clear of countless dangers. During the coming year you encounter many other legal issues, and you and your corporation benefit from your skills.

It is not only as a corporate manager that you will confront the law. As a voter, investor, juror, entrepreneur, and community member, you will influence and be affected by the law. Whenever you take a stance about a legal issue, whether in the corporate office, the voting booth, or as part of local community groups, you help to create the social fabric of our nation. Your views are vital. This book will offer you knowledge and ideas from which to form and continually reassess your legal opinions and values.

IMPORTANCE

Law is also essential. Every society of which we have any historical record has had some system of laws. Naturally, the systems have varied enormously.

An extraordinary example of a detailed written law comes from the Visigoths, a nomadic European people who overran much of present-day France and Spain during the fifth and sixth centuries A.D. Their code admirably required judges to be "quick of perception, clear in judgment, and lenient in the infliction of penalties." It detailed dozens of crimes. For example, a freeman who kidnapped the slave of another had to repay the owner with four slaves and suffer 100 lashes. If he did not have four slaves to give, the kidnapper was himself reduced to slavery. Sadly, the code explicitly permitted torture of slaves and lower-class freemen, while prohibiting it for nobles.[1]

The Iroquois Native Americans, disregarded by many historians, in fact played a role in the creation of our own government. Five major nations made up the Iroquois group: the Mohawk, Cayuga, Oneida, Onondaga, and Seneca. Each nation governed itself as to domestic issues. But each nation also elected "sachems" to a League of the Iroquois. The league had authority over any matters that were common to all, such as relations with outsiders. Thus, by the fifteenth century, the Iroquois had solved the problem of *federalism*: how to have two levels of government, each with specified powers. Their system impressed Benjamin Franklin and others and influenced the drafting of our Constitution, with its powers divided between state and federal governments.[2] As European nations today seek to create a more united Europe, they struggle with the same problem.

The greatest of all Chinese lawgivers disliked written law altogether. Confucius, who lived from 551 to 479 B.C., understood law within a broader social perspective. He considered good rulers, strong family ties, and an enlightened nobility to be the surest methods to a good society. "As a judge, I decide disputes, for that is my duty; but the best thing that could happen would be to eliminate the causes for litigation!" Although he spoke 2,500 years ago, the distinction Confucius described is still critically important in our society: Which do we trust more—a written law or the people who enforce it?

FASCINATION

Law is intriguing. When the jury awarded $8 million against an auto manufacturer for a defective car design, it certainly demonstrated the law's power. But was the jury's decision right? Should a company have to pay that much for one car accident? Maybe the jury was reacting emotionally. Or perhaps the anger caused by terrible trauma *should* be part of a court case. What about the government's role in auto safety? Would we prefer that a federal agency or a jury make decisions about car design? These are not abstract speculations for philosophers. Verdicts such as this may cause each of us to pay more for our next automobile. Then again, we may be driving safer cars. Legal issues can be complex, but they are never *theoretical*. The law affects us and we know it.

In 1835, the young French aristocrat Alexis de Tocqueville traveled through the United States, observing the newly democratic people and the qualities that made them unique. One of the things that struck de Tocqueville most forcefully was the American tendency to file suit: "Scarcely any political question arises in the United States that is not resolved, sooner or later, into a judicial question."[3] De Tocqueville got it right: for better or worse, we do expect courts to solve many problems. If you wonder about the accuracy of the Frenchman's comment, ask President Bill Clinton, who developed a rich understanding of the relationship between public affairs and judicial matters.

Not only do Americans litigate, but they watch each other do it. Almost all of the states permit live television coverage of trials, although federal courts do not. The most heavily viewed event in the history of television was the O. J. Simpson

---

1 S. P. Scott, *Visigothic Code (Forum Judicum)* (Littleton, CO: Fred B. Rothman & Co., 1982), pp. 3, 45.

2 Jack Weatherford, *Indian Givers* (New York: Fawcett Columbine, 1988), pp. 133–150.

3 Alexis de Tocqueville, *Democracy in America* (1835), Vol. 1, Ch. 16.

murder trial. Commentators from other countries, including Britain, harshly criticize live trial coverage. Nevertheless, when English nanny Louise Woodward went on trial in Massachusetts for the homicide of an infant, the British were glued to their television sets.

(From time to time we will present issues and views from other countries to give a broader perspective on legal affairs.) Although most nations bar television cameras from the courtroom, a small but growing list of countries permits limited coverage: Australia, Canada, France, Israel, Italy, the Netherlands, Norway, and Spain. British lawyers periodically—and hotly—debate the issue. Proponents of live coverage argue that some famous miscarriages of justice would never have occurred if the public had realized what was happening in the courtroom. For example, prosecutorial deceit led British courts to convict innocent people of terrorism in Northern Ireland. Advocates believe that television cameras would prevent a recurrence. The theory is that a witness would not lie under oath if millions of people were watching.

Opponents contend that television cameras unfairly subject the defendants to a second trial—by popular opinion. The evidence may taint a defendant forever, even one who is ultimately acquitted. Others point to American televised trials and argue that cameras transform what should be a dignified proceeding into frenzied entertainment, causing lawyers and even judges to play roles that are unbecoming and unethical. British barristers—lawyers who are specially trained to appear in court—enjoy wide respect, and many turn up their noses at what they see as American showboating. Thus far, the British have rejected live coverage.

Regardless of where we allow cameras, it is an undeniable benefit of the electronic age that we can obtain information so quickly. From time to time we will mention Web sites of interest. Some of these are for nonprofit groups while others are commercial sites. We do not endorse or advocate on behalf of any group or company, but simply wish to alert you to what is out there. The commercial site of a cable television company devoted to trial broadcasts, **http://www.courttv.com/**, includes up-to-the-minute information on current cases, often including trial testimony, appeal briefs, and other timely data.

The law is a big part of our lives, and it is wise to know something about it. Within a few weeks, you will probably find yourself following legal events in the news with keener interest and deeper understanding. In this chapter we develop the background for our study. We look at where law comes from: its history and its present-day institutions. In the section on jurisprudence, we examine different theories about what "law" really means. And finally we see how courts—and students—analyze a case.

ORIGINS OF OUR LAW

It would be nice if we could look up "the law" in one book, memorize it, and then apply it. But the law is not that simple, and *cannot* be that simple, because it reflects the complexity of contemporary life. In truth, there is no such thing as "the law." Principles and rules of law actually come from many different sources. Why is this so? In part because we inherited a complex structure of laws from England. We will see that by the time of the American Revolution, English law was already an intricate system.

Additionally, ours is a nation born in revolution and created, in large part, to protect the rights of its people from the government. The Founding Fathers created a national government but insisted that the individual states maintain control in many areas. As a result, each state has its own government with exclusive power over many important areas of our lives. To top it off, the Founders guaranteed many rights to the people alone, ordering national *and* state governments to keep clear. This has worked, but it has caused a multilayered system, with 50 state governments and one federal government all creating and enforcing law.

A summary of English legal history will show the origin of our legal institutions. This brisk summary will also demonstrate that certain problems never go away. Anglo-Saxon England, about 1,000 years ago, was a world utterly different from our own. Yet we can see uncanny foreshadowings of our own unfinished efforts to create a peaceful world.

ENGLISH ROOTS

England in the tenth century was a rustic agricultural community with a tiny population and very little law or order. Danes and Swedes invaded repeatedly, terrorizing the Anglo-Saxon peoples. Criminals were hard to catch in the heavily forested, sparsely settled nation. The king used a primitive legal system to maintain a tenuous control over his people.

England was divided into shires, and daily administration was carried out by a "shire reeve," later called a sheriff. The shire reeve collected taxes and did what he could to keep peace, apprehending criminals and acting as mediator between feuding families. Two or three times a year, a shire court met; lower courts met more frequently.

Contemporary law: Mediation lives on. As we discuss in Chapter 2, on dispute resolution, lawsuits have grown ever more costly. Increasingly, companies are turning to mediation to settle disputes. The humble shire reeve's work is back in vogue.

Because there were so few officers to keep the peace, Anglo-Saxon society created an interesting method of ensuring public order. Every freeman (nonslave) belonged to a group of 10 freemen known as a "tithing," headed by a "tithingman." If anyone injured a person outside his tithing or interfered with the king's property, all 10 men of the tithing could be forced to pay.

Contemporary law: Today, we still use this idea of collective responsibility. In a business partnership, all partners are personally responsible for the debts of the partnership. They could potentially lose their homes and all assets because of the irresponsible conduct of one partner.

When cases did come before an Anglo-Saxon court, the parties would often be represented either by a clergyman, by a nobleman, or by themselves. There were few professional lawyers. Each party produced "oath helpers," usually 12, who would swear that one version of events was correct. The court explicitly gave greater credence to oath helpers from the nobility.

Medieval *tenants in demesne* harrowing, plowing, and seeding a field.

Contemporary law: The Anglo-Saxon oath helpers are probably forerunners of our modern jury of 12 persons. But as to who is telling the truth, that is a question that will never disappear. We deny giving a witness greater credence because of his or her status. But is that accurate? Some commentators believe that jurors are overly impressed with "expert witnesses," such as doctors or engineers, and ignore their own common sense when faced with such "pedigreed" people.

In 1066, the Normans conquered England. William the Conqueror made a claim never before made in England: that he owned all of the land. The king then granted sections of his lands to his favorite noblemen, as his tenants in chief, creating the system of feudalism. These tenants in chief then granted parts of their land to *tenants in demesne*, who actually occupied a particular estate. Each tenant in demesne owed fidelity to his lord (hence "landlord"). So what? Just this: land became the most valuable commodity in all of England, and our law still reflects that.

Contemporary law: Nine hundred years later, American law still regards land as special. The statute of frauds, which we study in the section on contracts, demands that contracts for the sale or lease of property be in writing. And landlord-tenant law, vital to students and many others, still reflects its ancient roots. Some of a landlord's rights are based on the 1,000-year-old tradition that land is uniquely valuable.

In 1250, Henry de Bracton (d. 1268) wrote a legal treatise that still influences us. *De Legibus et Consuetudinibus Angliae (On the Laws and Customs of England)*, written in Latin, summarized many of the legal rulings in cases since the Norman Conquest. De Bracton was teaching judges to rule based on previous cases. He was helping to establish the idea of *precedent*. **The doctrine of precedent, which developed gradually over centuries, requires that judges decide current cases based on previous rulings.**

Contemporary law: This vital principle is the heart of American common law. Precedent ensures predictability. Suppose a 17-year-old student promises to lease an apartment from a landlord, but then changes her mind. The landlord sues to enforce the lease. The student claims that she cannot be held to the agreement because she is a minor. The judge will look for precedent, i.e., older cases dealing with the same issue, and he will find many holding that a contract generally may not be enforced against a minor. That precedent is binding on this case, and the student wins. The accumulation of precedent, based on case after case, makes up the **common law**.

During the next few centuries, judges and lawyers acquired special training and skills. Some lawyers began to plead cases full-time and gained unique skill—and power. They represented only those who could pay well.

Parliament passed an ever greater number of laws, generally called **statutes**, the word we still use to mean a law passed by a legislative body. Parliament's statutes swelled in number and complexity until they were unfathomable to anyone but a lawyer.

Contemporary law: Our society still struggles with unequal access to legal talent. Rich people often fare better in court than poor. And many Americans regard law as Byzantine and incomprehensible. A primary purpose of this text is to remove the mystique from the law and to empower you to participate in legal matters.

As lawyers became more highly skilled, they searched ever wider for ways to defeat the other side. One method was by attacking the particular writ in the case. The party bringing the case was called the plaintiff. His first task was to obtain a **writ**, which was was a letter from the central government ordering a court to hear the case. Each type of lawsuit required a different writ. For example, a landlord's lawsuit against a tenant required one kind of writ, while a claim of assault needed a different one. If a court decided that the plaintiff's lawyer had used the wrong writ, it would dismiss the lawsuit. This encouraged lawyers for the defendant to attack the writ itself, claiming it was inappropriate. By doing that, they could perhaps defeat the case without ever answering who did what to whom.

Contemporary law: This is the difference between procedure and substance, which will become clear during the course. **Substantive** rules of law state the rights of the parties. For example, it is substantive law that if you have paid the purchase price of land and accepted the deed, you are entitled to occupy the property. **Procedural** rules tell how a court should go about settling disputes. For example, what evidence can be used to establish that you *did* pay for the property? How much evidence is necessary? Who may testify about whether you paid? Those are all issues of procedural law. To this day, lawyers attack procedural aspects of an opponent's case before dealing with the substantive rights.

Here is an actual case from more than six centuries ago, in the court's own language. The dispute illustrates that some things have changed but others never do. The plaintiff claims that he asked the defendant to heal his eye with "herbs and other medicines." He says the defendant did it so badly that he blinded the plaintiff in that eye.

THE OCULIST'S CASE (1329)
LI MS. Hale 137 (1), fo. 150, Nottingham[4]

Attorney Launde [for defendant]: Sir, you plainly see how [the plaintiff claims] that he had submitted himself to [the defendant's] medicines and his care; and after that he can assign no trespass in his person, inasmuch as he submitted himself to his care: but this action, if he has any, sounds naturally in breach of covenant. We demand [that the case be dismissed].

Excerpts from Judge Denum's Decision: I saw a Newcastle man arraigned before my fellow justice and me for the death of a man. I asked the reason for the indictment, and it was said that he had slain a man under his care, who died within four days afterwards. And because I saw that he was a [doctor] and that he had not done the thing feloniously but [accidentally] I ordered him to be discharged. And suppose a blacksmith, who is a man of skill, injures your horse with a nail, whereby you lose your horse: you shall never have recovery against him. No more shall you here.

Afterwards the plaintiff did not wish to pursue his case any more.

This case from 1329 is an ancient medical malpractice case. Defendant's lawyer makes a procedural argument. Attorney Launde does not deny that his client blinded the plaintiff. He claims that the plaintiff has brought the wrong kind of lawsuit. Launde argues that the plaintiff should have brought a case of "covenant," i.e., a lawsuit about a contract.

Judge Denum decides the case on a different principle. He gives judgment to the defendant because the plaintiff voluntarily sought medical care. He implies that the defendant would lose only if he had attacked the plaintiff. As we will see when we study negligence law, this case might have a different outcome today. Note also the informality of the judge's ruling. He rather casually mentions that he came across a related case once before and that he would stand by that outcome. The idea of precedent is just beginning to take hold.

Sometimes a judge refused to hear a case, ruling that no such claims were legal. The injured party might then take his case to the Chancellor, in London, whose status in the king's council gave him unique, flexible powers. This *Court of Chancery* had no jury. The court's duty was to accomplish what "good conscience" required, that is, an *equitable* result, and so this more creative use of a court's power became known as **equity**.

Contemporary law: In present-day America, judges still exercise equity powers, based on those cases the Chancery court accepted. For example, a court today might issue an injunction requiring a factory owner to stop polluting the air. The injunction (order to stop) is an equitable remedy. Only a judge can exercise equitable powers because, historically, Chancery had no jury. If a judge grants an injunction, she is said to be exercising equitable powers.

Parliament added statutes on more and more matters, at times conflicting with common law rulings of the various judges. What should a court do when faced with a statute that contradicts well-established precedent? In the seventeenth century, one of England's greatest judges, Lord Coke, addressed the problem. In *Dr. Bonham's Case*,[5] Lord Coke ruled that "when an Act of Parliament is against Common right and reason, or repugnant, or impossible to be performed, the Common Law will control it and adjudge such Act to be void."

Audacious man! In a decision of breathtaking strength, Lord Coke declared that a single judge could overrule the entire Parliament, based on what the judge might consider "common right and reason." This same tension carries on today

[4] J. Baker and S. Milsom, *Sources of English Legal History* (London: Butterworth & Co., 1986).

[5] Eng. Rep. 638 (C.P. 1610).

between elected officials, such as state legislators, and courts, which sometimes declare acts of the legislatures void.

Of course, by the time Lord Coke was on the bench, in the seventeenth century, English common law had also spread across the ocean to the newly created colonies. We will pick up the story in America.

Law in the United States

The colonists brought with them a basic knowledge of English law, some of which they were content to adopt as their own. Other parts, such as religious restrictions, were abhorrent to them. Many had made the dangerous trip to America precisely to escape persecution, and they were not interested in re-creating their difficulties in a new land. Finally, some laws were simply irrelevant or unworkable in a world that was socially and geographically so different. American law ever since has been a whitewater river created from two strong currents: one carries the ancient principles of English common law, the other, a zeal and determination for change.

During the nineteenth century, the United States changed from a weak, rural nation into one of vast size and potential power. Cities grew, factories appeared, and sweeping movements of social migration changed the population. Changing conditions raised new legal questions. Did workers have a right to form industrial unions? To what extent should a manufacturer be liable if its product injured someone? Could a state government invalidate an employment contract that required 16-hour workdays? Should one company be permitted to dominate an entire industry?

In the twentieth century, the rate of social and technological change increased, creating new legal puzzles. Were some products, such as automobiles, so inherently dangerous that the seller should be responsible for injuries even if no mistakes were made in manufacturing? Who should clean up toxic waste if the company that had caused the pollution no longer existed? If a consumer signed a contract with a billion dollar corporation, should the agreement be enforced even if the consumer never understood it? Before we can begin to examine the answers to these questions, we need to understand the sources of contemporary law.

Sources of Contemporary Law

During the colonial period there were few trained lawyers and fewer lawbooks in America. After the Revolution that changed, and law became a serious, professional career. The first great legal achievement was the adoption of the United States Constitution.

Constitutions

United States Constitution

The United States Constitution, adopted in 1789 by the original 13 colonies, is the supreme law of the land.[6] Any law that conflicts with it is void. This Federal Constitution, as it is also known, does three basic things. First, it establishes the national government of the United States, with its three branches. The Constitution creates the Congress, with a Senate and a House of Representatives, and prescribes

---

[6] The complete text of the Constitution appears in Appendix A.

what laws Congress may pass. The same document establishes the office of the president and the duties that go with it. And it creates the third branch of government, the federal courts, describing what cases they may hear.

Second, the Constitution ensures that the states retain all power not given to the national government. This simple idea has meant that state governments play an important role in all of our lives. Major issues of family law, criminal law, property law, and many other areas are regulated predominantly by the various states.

Third, the Constitution guarantees many basic rights to the American people. Most of these rights are found in the amendments to the Constitution. The First Amendment guarantees the rights of free speech, free press, and the free exercise of religion. The Fourth, Fifth, and Sixth Amendments protect the rights of any person accused of a crime. Other amendments ensure that the government treats all people equally and that it pays for any property it takes from a citizen. Merely by creating a limited government of three branches and guaranteeing basic liberties to all citizens, the Constitution became one of the most important documents ever written.

State Constitutions

In addition to the Federal Constitution, each state has a constitution that establishes its own government. All states have an executive (the governor), a legislature, and a court system. Thus there are two entire systems of government affecting each of us: a federal government, with power over the entire country, and a state government, exercising those powers that the United States Constitution did not grant to the federal government. This is federalism at work.

STATUTES

The second important source of law is statutory law. The Constitution gave to the United States Congress the power to pass laws on various subjects. These laws are statutes, like those passed by the English Parliament. For example, the Constitution allows Congress to pass statutes about the military: to appropriate money, reorganize divisions, and close bases. You can find any federal statute, on any subject, at the Web site of the United States House of Representatives, which is **http://www.house.gov/**.

State legislatures also pass statutes. Each state constitution allows the legislature to pass laws on a wide variety of subjects. All state legislatures, for example, may pass statutes about family law issues such as divorce and child custody.

COMMON LAW

As we have seen, the common law originated in England as lawyers began to record decisions and urge judges to follow earlier cases. As judges started to do that, the earlier cases, called *precedent*, took on steadily greater importance. Eventually, judges were *obligated* to follow precedent. **The principle that precedent is binding on later cases is *stare decisis*, which means "let the decision stand."** *Stare decisis* makes the law predictable, and this in turn enables businesses and private citizens to plan intelligently.

Equity

Principles of equity, created by the Chancellor in England, traveled to the colonies along with the common law rules. All states permit courts to use equitable powers. An example of a contemporary equitable power is an *injunction*, a court order that someone stop doing something. Suppose a music company is about to issue a

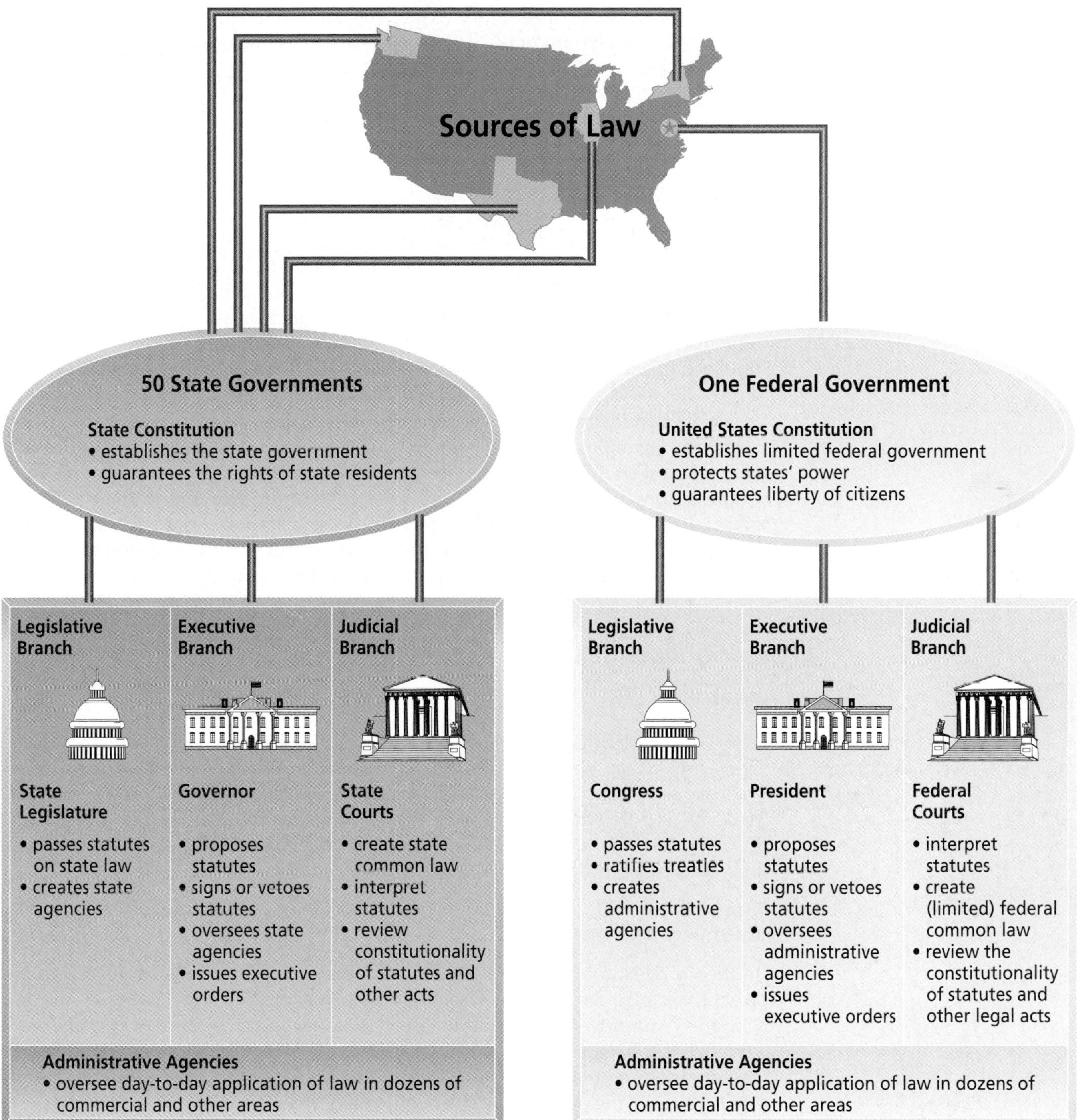

Federal Form of Government. **Principles and rules of law come from many sources. The government in Washington creates and enforces law throughout the nation. But 50 state governments exercise great power in local affairs. And citizens enjoy constitutional protection from both state and federal government. The Founding Fathers wanted this balance of power and rights, but the overlapping authority creates legal complexity.**

new compact disc by a well-known singer, but a composer claims that the recording artist has stolen his song. The composer, claiming copyright violation, could seek an injunction to prevent the company from issuing the compact disc. Every state has a trial court that can issue injunctions and carry out other equitable relief. As was true in medieval England, there is no jury in an equity case.

ADMINISTRATIVE LAW

In a society as large and diverse as ours, the executive and legislative branches of government cannot oversee all aspects of commerce. Congress passes statutes about air safety, but U.S. senators do not stand around air traffic towers, serving coffee to keep everyone awake. The executive branch establishes rules concerning how foreign nationals enter the United States, but presidents are reluctant to sit on the dock of the bay, watching the ships come in. **Administrative agencies** do this day-to-day work.

Most administrative agencies are created by Congress or by a state legislature. Familiar examples at the federal level are the Federal Communications Commission (FCC), which regulates most telecommunications; the Federal Trade Commission (FTC), which oversees interstate trade; and the Immigration and Naturalization Service (INS), which controls our nation's borders. At the state level, regulators set insurance rates for all companies in the state, control property development and land use, and regulate many other issues.

OTHER SOURCES OF LAW

Treaties

The Constitution authorizes the president to make treaties with foreign nations. These must then be ratified by the United States Senate. When they are ratified, they are as binding upon all citizens as any federal statute. In 1994 the Senate ratified the North American Free Trade Agreement (NAFTA) with Mexico and Canada. NAFTA was controversial then and is perhaps more so today—but it is now the law of the land.

Executive Orders

In theory all statutes must originate in Congress or a state legislature. But in fact executives also legislate by issuing executive orders. For example, in 1970 Congress authorized President Nixon to issue wage-price controls in an effort to stabilize the economy. This was a colossal grant of power, allowing the president personally to regulate the nation's economy. Critics charge that Congress should not give away the powers that the people have granted to it, and such delegations of authority have led to extensive lawsuits.

CLASSIFICATIONS OF LAW

We have seen where law comes from. Now we need to classify the law into different types. There are three main classifications that we use throughout the book: criminal and civil law, substantive and procedural law, and public and private law.

Criminal and Civil Law

It is a crime to embezzle money from a bank, to steal a car, to sell cocaine. **Criminal law concerns behavior so threatening that society outlaws it altogether.** Most criminal laws are statutes, passed by Congress or a state legislature. The government itself prosecutes the wrongdoer, regardless of what the bank president or car owner wants. A district attorney, paid by the government, brings the case to court. The injured party, for example the owner of the stolen car, is not in charge of the case, although she may appear as a witness. The government will seek to punish the defendant with a prison sentence, a fine, or both. If there is a fine, the money goes to the state, not to the injured party.

Civil law is different, and most of this book is about civil law. **The civil law regulates the rights and duties between parties.** Tracy agrees in writing to lease you a 30,000-square-foot store in her shopping mall. She now has a *legal duty* to make the space available. But then another tenant offers her more money, and she refuses to let you move in. Tracy has violated her duty, but she has not committed a crime. The government will not prosecute the case. It is up to you to file a civil lawsuit. Your case will be based on the common law of contract. You will also seek equitable relief, namely an injunction ordering Tracy not to lease to anyone else. You should win the suit, and you will get your injunction and some money damages. But Tracy will not go to jail.

Some conduct involves both civil and criminal law. Suppose Tracy is so upset over losing the court case that she becomes drunk and causes a serious car accident. She has committed the crime of driving while intoxicated, and the state will prosecute. She has also committed negligence, and the injured party will file a lawsuit against her, seeking money.

Substantive and Procedural Law

We saw this distinction in *The Oculist's Case* and it remains important today. **Substantive law defines the rights of people.** Substantive law requires that a landlord who has signed a lease must deliver the store to her tenant. Most of this book concerns substantive law. **Procedural law establishes the processes for settling disputes.** Procedural law requires that, to get an injunction against Tracy, you must first notify her in writing of your claims and the time and place of the hearing on the injunction.

Public and Private Law

Public law refers to the rights and obligations of governments as they deal with the nation's citizens. For example, when the Federal Trade Commission prohibits deceptive advertising, that is public law. **Private law** regulates the duties between individuals. Landlord-tenant law is private law.

Jurisprudence

We have had a glimpse of legal history and a summary of the present-day sources of American law. But what *is* law? That question is the basis of a field known as **jurisprudence**. How do we distinguish a moral rule from a legal rule? What is the real nature of law? Can there be such a thing as an "illegal" law?

Law and Morality

Law is different from morality, yet the two are obviously linked. There are many instances when the law duplicates what all of us would regard as a moral position. It is negligence to drive too fast in a school district, and few would dispute the moral value of that law. And similarly with contract law: if the owner of land agrees in writing to sell property to a buyer at a stated price, the seller must go through with the deal, and the legal outcome matches our moral expectations.

On the other hand, we have had laws that we now clearly regard as immoral. At the turn of the century, a factory owner could typically fire a worker for any reason at all—including, for example, his religious or political views. Today, we would say it is immoral to fire a worker because she is Jewish—and the law invariably prohibits it.

Finally, there are legal issues where the morality is not so clear. You are walking down a country lane and notice a three-year-old child playing with matches near a barn filled with hay. Are you obligated to intervene? No, says the law, though many think that is preposterous. (See Chapter 3, on common law, for details.) A company buys property and then discovers, buried under the ground, toxic waste that will cost $300,000 to clean up. The original owner has gone bankrupt. Should the new owner be forced to pay for the cleanup? If the new owner fails to pay for the job, who will? (See Chapter 43, on environmental law.)

Legal Positivism

This philosophy can be simply stated: law is what the sovereign says it is. The **sovereign** is the recognized political power whom citizens obey, so in the United States, both state and federal governments are sovereign. A legal positivist holds that whatever the sovereign declares to be the law *is* the law, whether it is right or wrong.

The primary criticism of legal positivism is that it seems to leave no room for questions of morality. A law permitting a factory owner to fire a worker because she is Catholic is surely different from a law prohibiting arson. Do citizens in a democracy have a duty to consider such differences?

Most states allow citizens to pass laws directly at the ballot box, a process called voter referendum. California voters often do this, and during the 1990s, they passed one of the state's most controversial laws. Proposition 187 was designed to curb illegal immigration into the state by eliminating social spending for undocumented aliens. Citizens debated the measure fiercely but passed it by a large margin. One section of the new law forbade public schools from educating illegal immigrants. The law obligated a principal to inquire into the immigration status of all children enrolled in the school and to report undocumented students to immigration authorities. Several San Diego school principals rejected the new rules, stating that they would neither inquire into immigration status nor report undocumented aliens. Their statements produced a heated response. Some San Diego residents castigated the school officials as lawbreakers, claiming that:

- A school officer who knowingly disobeyed a law was setting a terrible example for students, who would assume they were free to do the same
- The principals were advocating permanent residence and a free education for anyone able to evade our immigration laws; and

- The officials were scorning grass-roots democracy by disregarding a law passed by popular referendum.

Others applauded the principals' position, asserting that:

- The referendum's rules would transform school officials from educators into border police, forcing them to cross-examine young children and parents
- The new law was foolish because it punished innocent children for violations committed by their parents; and
- Our nation has long respected civil disobedience based on humanitarian ideals, and these officials were providing moral leadership to the whole community.

Ultimately, no one had to decide whether to obey Proposition 187. A federal judge ruled that only Congress had the power to regulate immigration and that California's attempt was unconstitutional and void. The debate over immigration reform—and ethics—did not end, however. California's governor announced that he would appeal the court's decision, and Congress considered various proposals for cutting off social benefits to illegal immigrants.

NATURAL LAW

St. Thomas Aquinas (1225–1274) answered the legal positivists even before they had spoken. In his *Summa Theologica*, he argued that an unjust law is no law at all and need not be obeyed. It is not enough that a sovereign makes a command. The law must have a moral basis.

Where do we find the moral basis that would justify a law? Aquinas says that "good is that which all things seek after." Therefore, the fundamental rule of all laws is that "good is to be done and promoted, and evil is to be avoided." This sounds appealing, but also vague. Exactly which laws promote good and which do not? Is it better to have a huge corporation dominate a market or many smaller companies competing? Did the huge company get that way by being better than its competitors? If Wal-Mart moves into a rural area, establishes a mammoth store, and sells inexpensive products, is that "good"? Yes, if you are a consumer who cares only about prices. No, if you are the owner of a Main Street store driven into bankruptcy. Maybe, if you are a resident who values small town life but wants lower prices.

Natural law is often in the news. Look at one of the most violently contested issues in the history of American law: abortion. In the landmark case of *Roe v. Wade*,[7] the United States Supreme Court ruled that the Constitution protects the right to an abortion, though with some important limitations. The Supreme Court hoped this ruling would settle the issue. It did not. Abortion has reappeared many times before the Supreme Court and dozens of times before lower courts. Does the idea of "natural law" help to settle the debate?

When President Bush nominated Judge Clarence Thomas for a seat on the United States Supreme Court in 1991, one of the first controversies to arise concerned writings and conversations in which it appeared that Judge Thomas had strongly supported natural law. In particular, his statements indicated that he viewed natural law as a reason for outlawing abortion. During his confirmation hearings before the Senate Judiciary Committee, Judge Thomas said that his

[7] 410 U.S. 113, 93 S. Ct. 705, 1973 U.S. LEXIS 159 (1973).

earlier statements were insignificant and that natural law would not influence his thinking about abortion or other issues.

What does natural law tell us about abortion? Abortion supporters, or those advocating free choice, will say that natural law protects a woman's reproductive rights and that it is violent and unnatural for any government to tell a woman what to do with her body. Opponents of abortion reach the opposite conclusion, arguing that no good can come from terminating the life of a fetus and that a law permitting abortion is no law at all. What do you think?

LEGAL REALISM

Legal realists take a very different tack. They claim it does not matter what is written as law. What counts is who enforces that law and by what process. All of us are biased by issues such as income, education, family background, race, religion, and many other factors. These personal characteristics, they say, determine which contracts will be enforced and which ignored, why some criminals receive harsh sentences while others get off lightly, and so on.

Judge Jones hears a multimillion dollar lawsuit involving an airplane crash. Was the airline negligent? The law is the same everywhere, but legal realists say that Jones's background will determine the outcome. If she spent 20 years representing insurance companies, she will tend to favor the airline. If her law practice consisted of helping the "little guy," she will favor the plaintiff.

Other legal realists argue, more aggressively, that those in power use the machinery of the law to perpetuate their control. The outcome of a given case will be determined by the needs of those with money and political clout. A court puts "window dressing" on a decision, they say, so that society thinks there are principles behind the law. A problem with legal realism, however, is its denial that any lawmaker can overcome personal bias. Yet clearly some do act unselfishly.

Summary of Jurisprudence

Legal Positivism	Law is what the sovereign says.
Natural Law	An unjust law is no law at all.
Legal Realism	*Who* enforces the law counts more than *what* is in writing.

No one school of jurisprudence is likely to seem perfect. We urge you to keep the different schools of thought in mind as you read cases in the book. Ask yourself which school of thought is the best fit for you.

ANALYZING A CASE

Cases are the heart of the law and an important part of this book. Reading them effectively takes practice. The following case is a good place to start. This lawsuit begins, as a certain number do, with a tragedy: the death of a 12-year-old child. Not all lawsuits in the book will be so unhappy, but we offer a fair number of dramatic cases for one reason: when the stakes are high, people care.

Gayle Quigley, the boy's mother, sued a church that relied on prayer rather than traditional medical assistance. Notice the narrow legal issue that the court had to decide: whether the church had a legal duty to summon medical help. To rephrase the point, this case was *not* about whether the death was a tragic loss (it was), or whether it was avoidable (it probably was), or whether church members grieved over the death (they did), or whether the father and nurses *morally* ought to have sought help (you decide).

QUIGLEY v. FIRST CHURCH OF CHRIST, SCIENTIST
65 Cal. App. 4th 1027, 76 Cal. Rptr. 2d 792, 1998 Cal. App. LEXIS 677
California Court of Appeal, 1998

Facts: Gayle Quigley and James Wantland had divorced. They had joint custody of their 12-year-old son, Andrew, who lived with his father. James was a member of the Christian Science church, a religion that regards disease as an "error of the mind" and discourages the use of traditional medicine. Members of the faith rely on Christian Science practitioners, who offer prayer for patients, and nurses, who are trained to provide only practical care, such as bathing and feeding.

On December 16 Andrew complained of feeling ill. James telephoned a Christian Science practitioner, who provided prayer and counseling over the telephone. Andrew's health declined. On December 20, Laura Armstrong, a Christian Science nurse, visited the Wantlands, having been told there was a "very sick" boy there. When Armstrong arrived, she asked James to sign a form stating that the parents agreed to rely on Christian Science treatment. The document provided a space for both parents to sign, but no one telephoned Gayle Quigley or informed her of her son's illness. Armstrong observed that Andrew was not talking or responding to people and that his breathing was quick and abnormal. The nurse was concerned that she could not help Andrew and called a second nurse, who arrived later in the afternoon. Later that day, James telephoned "911" and summoned an ambulance. On arrival at the hospital, Andrew was pronounced dead of what later turned out to be juvenile diabetes.

Gayle Quigley sued the Christian Science church, the practitioner, and the nurses who had participated in Andrew's treatment. She also sued her ex-husband, but this case does not concern him. Quigley alleged that the defendants' refusal to call medical help was *negligence,* meaning a failure to behave the way a reasonable person would. To win a negligence case, a plaintiff must first show that the defendant had a *duty* to the injured person. The defendants asked the court to dismiss the case without a trial, arguing that they had no duty to summon help. The trial court dismissed the case, and Quigley appealed.

Issue: Did the defendants have a duty to summon medical help for Andrew?

Excerpts from Judge Bedsworth's Decision: [The judge began by mentioning an earlier California case, in which the state's highest court ruled that one person generally has no duty to protect another from harm, unless there is a special relationship between the two, such as custody or control. That case also warned that obligating religious counselors to summon outside help might discourage such workers from offering their services at all.]

Quigley [argues] that imposing a duty on Christian Science healers to refer patients to medical care would not have a chilling effect on religious freedom. We disagree. Quigley's own complaint alleges that medical treatment is inconsistent with the tenets of the Christian Science faith, and it is considered "unethical" to provide Christian Science treatment to any patient receiving medical care. Under those circumstances, imposing any duty upon Christian Science healers which required them to encourage patients to seek medical care would directly interfere with their own religious practices. We can hardly conceive of a more chilling effect.

Finally, Quigley [claims that the] defendants voluntarily assumed a duty of due care regarding Andrew's illness, because "Andrew's physical well-being was entrusted to defendants' nationally coordinated system for treating seriously ill children." That contention, however, reveals the most fundamental flaw in Quigley's analysis. As Quigley expressly acknowledges in her complaint,

Christian Science treatment is intended to address only a spiritual problem, not a physical one, since Christian Science perceives disease to be an "error of the mind." Indeed, Quigley specifically alleges that Christian Science healers are trained "to not see the reality of the physical symptoms and to see the patient as healed." In this case, the fact that Andrew's problem turned out not to be spiritual, but was instead physical in nature, i.e., juvenile diabetes, does not change the fact that the defendants undertook no responsibility to evaluate the severity of, or otherwise address Andrew's physical condition or medical needs. Indeed, given their particular beliefs, Christian Science healers are perhaps the group least qualified to carry out such a duty and least likely to assume it.

[Affirmed.]

ANALYSIS

Let's take it from the top. The case is called *Quigley v. First Church of Christ, Scientist.* Gayle Quigley is the plaintiff, the person who is suing. The church, the practitioner, and the nurses are all defendants, the ones being sued. A case generally names only the first plaintiff and the first defendant. In this example, the plaintiff's name happens to appear first but that is not always true. When a defendant loses a trial and files an appeal, *some* courts reverse the names of the parties.

The next lines give the legal citation, which indicates where to find the case in a law library. We explain in the footnote how to locate a book if you plan to do research.[8] The last line informs us that the California Court of Appeal decided the case in 1998.

The *Facts* section provides a background to the lawsuit, written by the authors of this text. The court's own explanation of the facts is often many pages long and may involve complex matters irrelevant to the subject covered in this book, so we relate only what is necessary.

The *Issue* section is very important. It tells you what the court had to decide—and also why you are reading the case. In giving its decision, a court may digress. If you keep in mind the issue and relate the court's discussion to it, you will not get lost.

Excerpts from Judge Bedsworth's Decision is where the court's decision begins. This is called the *holding*, meaning a statement of who wins and who loses. The holding also includes the court's *rationale*, which is the reasoning behind the decision.

The holding that we provide is an edited version of the court's own language. Some judges write clear, forceful prose, others do not. Either way, their words give you an authentic feel of how judges think and rule, so we bring the decision to you in the original. We occasionally use brackets [] to substitute our language for that of the court, either to condense or to clarify. Notice the brackets at the beginning of

---

[8] Because the *Quigley* case is so recent, its citation is unusually short. We will explain how to read and use a more typical citation. Consider this one:

Academy Chicago Publishers v. Cheever
144 Ill. 2d 24, 578 N.E.2d 981, 1991 Ill. LEXIS 47

This citation provides three different places to find the full text of this case. The first citation is to "Ill. 2d," which means the official court reporter of the state of Illinois, second set. Illinois, like most states, reports its law cases in a series of numbered volumes. After the volumes reach number 999, most reporters start over with a second set of volumes. So this case appears in volume 144 of the second set of Illinois reporters. If you went to a law library and found that volume, you could then turn to page 24 and find the case. The same case is reported in another set of volumes, called the regional reporters. This group of law reports is grouped by geographic region. Illinois is included in the northeast region, so this case appears in volume 578 of the second set of the northeast regional reports, at page 981. Finally, most cases are now also available online through computer law libraries. The third citation is to the online law library operated by LEXIS. Typing "1991 Ill. LEXIS 47" would bring up the same case on the computer.

the *Quigley* decision, in which we summarize the court's discussion of an earlier case. We also leave out a great deal. A court's opinion may be 3 pages or it may be 75. We want to keep the reading manageable. We do not use ellipsis dots (. . .) to indicate these deletions because more is taken out than is kept in, and we want the text to be clean. If you are curious about the full holding, you can always look it up.

Let us look at a few of Judge Bedsworth's points. The holding begins with mention of an earlier case from the California Supreme Court. The earlier decision is *precedent*, and this court is bound to follow it. The previous suit dealt with religious counselors. That holding included a general rule, that one person owes no duty to protect another, and a more specific one, that religious counselors probably need special protection from legal burdens. Right away, we can sense that Gayle Quigley is going to lose unless this court concludes that her case is different from the earlier one.

The next topic is religious freedom, one of the founding principles of this nation. The plaintiff has urged this court to impose on Christian Science nurses the duty to summon traditional medical care, but the court declares that such an obligation would infringe on the church's basic beliefs. The court is considering *public policy*, that is, the long-term interests of society generally. Judges understand that they not only follow precedent, they help to make it. This court is determined not to interfere with religious freedom—a second reason to dismiss the case. Judges try hard to make their decisions persuasive, and you will often find a court offering two or more reasons to support a ruling.

Finally, the court responds to Quigley's argument that the church here was not a casual stranger to Andrew's suffering. The mother argues that the Christian Science practitioners had voluntarily undertaken Andrew's care and thereby *assumed a duty to provide reasonable care*. In other words, the plaintiff is arguing that even if most people owe no duty to each other, *these defendants* owed a duty because they chose to get involved. The court rejects the argument, ruling that the healers undertook to care only for Andrew's spiritual needs and lacked any training or inclination to administer to physical ailments.

For those three reasons, the court *affirms* the trial court's decision, meaning that it approves the decision and upholds the outcome. If the court had disagreed with the trial court, it might have *reversed* the decision, meaning to undo the result. Judge Bedsworth would then have *remanded* the case, that is, sent it back down to a lower court. The plaintiff would then have received her trial.

Finally, notice what this case was *not* about: whether the defendants did the "right" thing. Judge Bedsworth does not applaud the nurses' conduct. Elsewhere in the decision he suggests that the first nurse should have called an ambulance immediately—but had no *legal duty* to do so.

One of the best reasons to read about legal disputes is so you can avoid them. In *Preventive Law*, we focus on how to anticipate problems and steer clear of them. The *Quigley* case raises unusual issues that will not personally affect many people. Yet it is worth asking ourselves how Gayle Quigley might have prevented this tragedy. How could she have done that?

"YOU BE THE JUDGE"

Many cases involve difficult decisions for juries and judges. Often both parties have legitimate, opposing arguments. Most chapters in this book will have a feature called "You Be The Judge," in which we present the facts of a case but not the court's holding. We offer you two opposing arguments based on the kinds of claims the lawyers would have made in court. We leave it up to you to debate and decide which position is stronger or to add your own arguments to those given. The following case is another negligence lawsuit, though with a different issue than in *Quigley.* A suicide caused a distraught family to sue a rock singer and music producer. Once again the defendants asked the judge to dismiss the case. They pointed out, correctly, that a negligence case requires a plaintiff to prove not only duty (as in *Quigley*), but also *foreseeability*. The plaintiff must show that the defendant *could have foreseen the type of harm that occurred.* Could Ozzy Osbourne have foreseen this sad outcome to one of his songs? You be the judge.

McCOLLUM v. CBS, INC.
202 Cal. App. 3d 989, 249 Cal. Rptr. 187, 1988 Cal. App. LEXIS 909
California Court of Appeal, 1988

Facts: John McCollum, 19 years old, was an alcoholic with serious emotional problems. He listened over and over to music recorded by Ozzy Osbourne on CBS records, particularly two albums called *Blizzard of Oz* and *Diary of a Madman*. He usually listened to the music on the family stereo in the living room because the sound was most intense there. One Friday evening, though, he went to his bedroom and lay on his bed, listening to more Osbourne music. He placed a loaded .22-caliber handgun to his right temple and pulled the trigger.

McCollum's parents sued Osbourne and CBS records, claiming that they negligently aided and encouraged John to commit suicide. The parents' argument was that Osbourne's songs were designed to appeal to unstable youths and that the message of some of his music explicitly urged death. One of the songs John had listened to before his death was "Suicide Solution," which included these lyrics:

> Wine is fine but whiskey's quicker
> Suicide is slow with liquor
> Take a bottle drown your sorrows
> Then it floods away tomorrows
>
> Now you live inside a bottle
> The reaper's travelling at full throttle
>
> It's catching you but you don't see
> The reaper is you and the reaper is me
>
> Breaking law, knocking doors
> But there's no one at home
> Made your bed, rest your head
> But you lie there and moan
> Where to hide, Suicide is the only way out
> Don't you know what it's really about.[9]

The trial court dismissed the lawsuit, ruling that the plaintiff had not made out a valid negligence claim. The court ruled that the First Amendment's free speech provision protected the rights of Osbourne and CBS to publish any music they wanted. In addition, the court found that the defendants could not have foreseen that anyone would respond to the lyrics by taking his own life. With no foreseeability, the court ruled, the plaintiffs' case must fail. The parents appealed, arguing, among other things, that their son's suicide *was* foreseeable.

You Be the Judge: Was McCollum's suicide foreseeable?

Argument for the Parents: Your honors, for years Ozzy Osbourne has been well known as the "madman" of rock and roll. The words and music of his songs revolve around bizarre, antisocial beliefs, emphasizing death and satanic worship. Many of his songs suggest that life is hopeless and that suicide is not only acceptable but desirable. Now one of his devoted fans has acted on Osbourne's advice and killed himself. The defendants share responsibility for this tragic death.

Osbourne and CBS knew that many of Osbourne's fans struggled with self-identity, alienation, and substance abuse. Both defendants aggressively targeted this market and reaped enormous profits. They knew that Osbourne was a cult figure to his young fans and had great influence in their lives. They realized that the confused youths who adored Osbourne were precisely those most vulnerable to vicious advice. Yet in spite of their knowledge, both defendants churned out songs such as "Suicide Solution," urging troubled, chemically addicted young people to kill themselves. Not only was it *foreseeable* that one of Osbourne's fans would sooner or later take his life, it was *inevitable*. It is sheer hypocrisy for the defendants, their pockets filled with money taken from McCollum and countless others like him, to pretend surprise. The surprise is that this didn't happen earlier. The only way to ensure that this doesn't occur again is to permit a jury to hear the parents' case and, if it is persuaded by the evidence, to award the grieving parents damages.

Argument for Osbourne and CBS: Your honors, we all agree that this death was tragic and unneces-

[9] Words and music by John Osbourne, Robert Daisley and Randy Rhoads. TRO © Copyright 1981 Essex Music International, Inc., New York, New York and Kord Music Publishers, London England. Used by permission.

sary. But the plaintiffs delude themselves if they think that Mr. Osbourne and CBS bear any responsibility. The fact is that John McCollum was deeply troubled and alcoholic. He was responsible for his life—and for his own death. Next to the young man himself, of course, those who bear the greatest responsibility for his sad life and gruesome end are his parents, the plaintiffs in this case. Mr. Osbourne and CBS sympathize with the parents' bereavement, but not with their attempt to foist responsibility onto others.

If the plaintiffs' far-fetched foreseeability argument were the law—which it is not—every singer, writer, film and television producer would be at risk of several thousand lawsuits every year. Under their theory, a producer who made a bank robbery movie would be liable for every robbery that took place afterward, as would every author or singer who ever mentioned the subject. And, of course, there would be no more movies with bank robberies—or murders, assaults, or even fistfights. There would be no more books or articles on such subjects either. The First Amendment was written to ensure that we *do* have access to arts and entertainment, and to prohibit efforts at silencing artists with outlandish lawsuits. This death was never foreseeable and no jury should ever hear the case.

Foreseeability arises in countless cases, as we will see in the chapter on negligence. Suppose a clerk in a store is assaulted by a criminal. The clerk may sue not only the criminal (who will not have any money) but also the owner of the store. Whether the owner is found liable or not will depend upon whether the owner should have foreseen the assault. Similarly, if a tenant is harmed by defective property, the landlord's liability will be determined in part by foreseeability.

CHAPTER CONCLUSION

We depend upon the law to give us a stable nation and economy, a fair society, a safe place to live and work. These worthy goals have occupied Anglo-Saxon kings and twenty-first-century lawmakers alike. But while law is a vital tool for crafting the society we want, there are no easy answers about how to create it. In a democracy, we all participate in the crafting. Legal rules control us, yet we create *them*. A working knowledge of the law can help build a successful career—and a solid democracy.

CHAPTER REVIEW

1. There is no one source of the law. Our federal system of government means that law comes from a national government in Washington, D.C., and from 50 state governments.
2. The history of law foreshadows many current legal issues, including mediation, partnership liability, the jury system, the role of witnesses, the special value placed on land, the idea of precedent, and the difference between substantive and procedural law.
3. The primary sources of contemporary law are:
   - United States Constitution and state constitutions
   - Statutes, which are drafted by legislatures
   - Common law, which is the body of cases decided by judges, as they follow earlier cases, known as precedent; and
   - Administrative law, the rules and decisions made by federal and state administrative agencies.

4. Other sources of contemporary law include:
    - Treaties
    - Executive orders
5. Criminal law concerns behavior so threatening to society that it is outlawed altogether. Civil law deals with duties and disputes between parties, not outlawed behavior.
6. Substantive law defines the rights of people. Procedural law describes the processes for settling disputes.
7. Jurisprudence is concerned with the basic nature of law. Three theories of jurisprudence are:
    - Legal positivism: The law is what the sovereign says it is.
    - Natural law: An unjust law is no law at all.
    - Legal realism: Who enforces the law is more important than what the law says.

PRACTICE TEST

1. Can one person really understand all of the legal issues mentioned at the beginning of this chapter? For example, can a business executive know about insider trading and employment law and environmental law and tort law and all of the others? Will a court really hold one person to such knowledge?

2. Why does our law come from so many different sources?

3. The stock market crash of 1929 and the Great Depression that followed were caused in part because so many investors blindly put their money into stocks they knew nothing about. During the 1920s it was often impossible for an investor to find out what a corporation was planning to do with its money, who was running the corporation, and many other vital things. Congress responded by passing the Securities Act of 1933, which required a corporation to divulge more information about itself before it could seek money for a new stock issue. What *kind* of law did the Congress create? Explain the relationship between voters, Congress, and the law.

4. Union organizers at a hospital wanted to distribute leaflets to potential union members, but hospital rules prohibited leafletting in areas of patient care, hallways, cafeterias, and any areas open to the public. The National Labor Relations Board (NLRB) ruled that these restrictions violated the law and ordered the hospital to permit the activities in the cafeteria and coffee shop. The NLRB may not create common law or statutory law. What kind of law *was* it creating?

5. Leslie Bergh and his two brothers, Milton and Raymond, formed a partnership to help build a fancy saloon and dance hall in Evanston, Wyoming. Later, Leslie met with his friend and drinking buddy, John Mills, and tricked Mills into investing in the saloon. Leslie did not tell Mills that no one else was investing cash or that the entire enterprise was already insolvent. Mills mortgaged his home, invested $150,000 in the saloon—and lost every penny of it. Mills sued all three partners for fraud. Milton and Raymond defended on the ground that they didn't commit the fraud, only Leslie did. The defendants lost. Was that fair? By holding them liable, what general idea did the court rely on? What Anglo-Saxon legal custom did the ruling resemble?

6. RIGHT & WRONG Confucius did not esteem written laws, believing instead that good rulers were the best guarantee of justice. Does our legal system rely primarily on the rule of law or the rule of people? Which do you instinctively trust more? Legal realists argue that the "rule of law" is a misleading term. What point are they making, and how does it relate to Confucius's principles? Confucius himself was an extraordinarily wise man, full of wisdom about life and compassion for his fellow citizens. Since he was extraordinary, what does that tell us about other rulers by contrast? How does that affect Confucius's own views?

7. Tommy Parker may have been involved in some unsavory activities as an officer in a failed savings and loan institution. A federal agency, the Office of Thrift Supervision (OTS), ordered Tommy not to spend or waste any of his own assets while it was investigating him. Later, Tommy and his wife, Billie, got divorced and divided their property. On February 18, the OTS filed papers in court asking for an order that *Billie* not spend any of her assets. Billie received a copy of the papers on February 20, and the hearing took place on February 24, without Billie in attendance. The court ordered Billie not to spend any assets except for essential living expenses. Billie appealed, claiming that under court rules she was entitled to five days' notice before the hearing took place and that weekend days are not counted. She had had only two business days' notice. Assume that her counting of the days was correct (which it was). Explain the difference between procedural law and substantive law. Which type of law was Billie relying on? Should her appeal be granted?

8. Plaintiff Miss Universe, Inc. owns the trademark "*Miss U.S.A.*" For decades, the company has produced the Miss U.S.A. beauty pageant, seen by many millions of people in the United States. William Flesher and Treehouse Fun Ranch began to hold a nude beauty pageant in California. They called this the "Miss Nude U.S.A." pageant. Most of the contestants were from California; the majority of states were not represented in the contest. Miss Universe sued Flesher and Treehouse, claiming that the public would be confused and misled by the similar names. The company sought an *equitable remedy* in this lawsuit. What does "equitable" mean? What equitable remedy did Miss Universe seek? Should it win?

9. Jack and Jill go up a hill to fetch a pail of water. Jill heads back down with the water. Jack meets a stranger, who introduces herself as Katrina. Jack sells a kilo of cocaine to Katrina, who then mentions that she enjoys her job at the Drug Enforcement Agency. Jill, halfway down the hill, meets Freddy, a motorist whose car has overheated. Freddy is late for a meeting where he expects to make a $3 million profit; he's desperate for water for his car. He promises to pay Jill $500 tomorrow if she will give him the pail of water, which she does. The next day, Jack is in jail and Freddy refuses to pay for Jill's water. Explain the criminal law/civil law distinction and what it means to Jack and Jill. Who will do what to whom, with what results?

10. YOU BE THE JUDGE WRITING PROBLEM Should trials be televised? Here are a few arguments to add to those in the chapter. You be the judge. **Argument against Live Television Coverage:** We have tried this experiment and it has failed. Trials fall into two categories: those that create great public interest and those that do not. No one watches dull trials, so we do not need to broadcast them. The few that are interesting have all become circuses. Judges and lawyers have shown that they cannot resist the temptation to play to the camera. Trials are supposed to be about justice, not entertainment. If a citizen seriously wants to follow a case, she can do it by reading the daily newspaper. **Argument for Live Television Coverage:** It is true that some televised trials have been unseemly affairs, but that is the fault of the presiding judges, not the media. Indeed, one of the virtues of television coverage is that millions of people now understand that we have a lot of incompetent people running our courtrooms. The proper response is to train judges to run a tight trial by prohibiting the grandstanding in which some lawyers may engage. Access to accurate information is the foundation on which a democracy is built and we must not eliminate a source of valuable data just because some judges are ill-trained.

11. In his most famous novel, *The Red and the Black*, the French author Stendhal (1783–1842) wrote: "There is no such thing as 'natural law': this expression is nothing but old nonsense. Prior to laws, what is natural is only the strength of the lion, or the need of the creature suffering from hunger or cold, in short, need." What do you think?

INTERNET RESEARCH PROBLEM

Take a look at **http:\\www.courttv.com**. Find two current cases that interest you: one civil, one criminal. Explain the different roles played by each type of law, and summarize the issues in the respective cases.

You can find further practice problems in the Online Quiz at http://beatty.westbuslaw.com or in the Study Guide that accompanies this text.

CHAPTER 2

DISPUTE RESOLUTION

Tony Caruso hadn't returned for dinner. His wife, Karen, was nervous. She put on some sandals and hurried across the dunes, a half mile to the ocean shore. She soon came upon Tony's dog, Blue, tied to an old picket fence. Tony's shoes and clothing were piled neatly nearby. Karen and friends searched frantically throughout the evening. A little past midnight, Tony's body washed ashore, his lungs filled with water. A local doctor concluded he had accidentally drowned.

Karen and her friends were not the only ones distraught. Tony had been partners with Beth Smiles in an environmental consulting business, Enviro-Vision. They were good friends, and Beth was emotionally devastated. When she was able to focus on business issues, Beth filed an insurance claim with the Coastal Insurance Group. Beth hated to think about Tony's death in financial terms, but she was relieved that the struggling business would receive $2 million on the life insurance policy.

Several months after filing the claim, Beth received this reply from Coastal: "Under the policy issued to Enviro-Vision, we are conditionally liable in the amount of $1 million in the event of Mr. Caruso's death. If his death is accidental, we are conditionally liable to pay double indemnity of $2 million. But pursuant to section H(5) death by suicide is not covered. After a thorough investigation, we have concluded that Anthony

Caruso's death was an act of suicide, as defined in section B(11) of the policy. Your claim is denied in its entirety." Beth was furious. She was convinced Tony was incapable of suicide. And her company could not afford the $2 million loss. She decides to consult her lawyer, Chris Pruitt.

THREE FUNDAMENTAL AREAS OF LAW

This case is a fictionalized version of several real cases based on double indemnity insurance policies. In this chapter we follow Beth's dispute with Coastal from initial interview through appeal, using it to examine three fundamental areas of law: alternative dispute resolution, the structure of our court systems, and civil lawsuits. But first we need to look at the one good kind of dispute—the one that is prevented.

DISPUTE PREVENTION

Over the years, one of the important services attorney Chris Pruitt has done for Enviro-Vision is *prevent disputes*. It is vital to understand and apply this concept in business and professional work and in everyday life. There is an old saying that you have a chance to go broke twice in your life: once when you lose a lawsuit, the other time when you win. The financial and emotional costs of litigation are extraordinarily high.

You can avoid disputes in many different ways. Throughout the text we specify an array of preventive steps as they relate to the different legal problems posed. Here we can mention a few of the potential disputes Enviro-Vision avoided by thinking ahead.

When Beth and Tony started Enviro-Vision, Chris pointed out that, as business partners, the best way to protect both their friendship and their business was with a detailed partnership agreement. Although Beth and Tony found it tedious to create, the agreement helped them avoid problems such as those concerning capital contributions to the partnership, about who owns what, and about hiring and firing employees. Further, Enviro-Vision avoids unjustified firings by giving all employees written job descriptions. It educates employees about sexual harassment. When drafting a contract, Beth has learned to be sure that the client knows exactly what it is getting, when the work is due, what the risks are, and how much it will cost. Each of these practices has prevented potential lawsuits.

When Beth Smiles meets with her lawyer, Chris Pruitt brings a second attorney from his firm, Janet Booker, who is an experienced litigator. If they file a lawsuit, Janet will be in charge, so Chris wants her there for the first meeting. Janet probes about Tony's home life, the status of the business, his personal finances, everything. Beth becomes upset that Janet doesn't seem sympathetic, but Chris explains that Janet is doing her job: she needs all the information, good and bad.

LITIGATION VERSUS ALTERNATIVE DISPUTE RESOLUTION

Janet starts thinking about the two methods of dispute resolution: litigation and alternative dispute resolution. **Litigation** refers to lawsuits, the process of filing claims in court, and ultimately going to trial. **Alternative dispute resolution** is any other formal or informal process used to settle disputes without resorting to a trial. It is increasingly popular with corporations and individuals alike because it is generally cheaper and faster than litigation.

ALTERNATIVE DISPUTE RESOLUTION

Janet Booker knows that even after expert legal help, vast expense, and years of work, litigation may leave clients unsatisfied. If she can use alternative dispute resolution (ADR) to create a mutually satisfactory solution in a few months, for a fraction of the cost, she is glad to do it. We will look at different types of ADR and analyze their strengths and weaknesses.

NEGOTIATION

In most cases the parties negotiate, whether personally or through lawyers. Fortunately, the great majority of disputes are resolved this way. Negotiation often begins as soon as a dispute arises and may last a few days or several years.

MEDIATION

Mediation is the fastest growing method of dispute resolution in the United States. Here, a neutral person, called a mediator, attempts to coax the two disputing parties toward a voluntary settlement. (In some cases, there may be two or more mediators, but we will use the singular.) Generally, the two disputants voluntarily enter mediation, although some judges order the parties to try this form of ADR before allowing a case to go to trial.

A mediator does not render a decision in the dispute, but uses a variety of skills to prod the parties toward agreement. Often a mediator will shuttle between the antagonists, hearing their arguments, sorting out the serious issues from the less important, prompting the parties and lawyers alike to consider new perspectives, and looking for areas of agreement. Mediators must earn the trust of both parties, listen closely, try to diffuse anger and fear, and build the will to settle. Good mediators do not need a law degree, but they must have a sense of humor and low blood pressure.

Mediation has several major advantages. Because the parties maintain control of the process, the two antagonists can speak freely. They need not fear conceding too much, because no settlement takes effect until both parties sign. All discussions are confidential, further encouraging candid talk. This is particularly helpful in cases involving proprietary information that might be revealed during a trial.

Of all forms of dispute resolution, mediation probably offers the strongest "win-win" potential. Since the goal is voluntary settlement, neither party needs to fear that it will end up the loser. This is in sharp contrast to litigation, where one party is very likely to lose. Removing the fear of defeat often encourages thinking and talking that are more open and realistic than negotiations held in the midst of a lawsuit. Studies show that over 75 percent of mediated cases do reach a voluntary settlement. Such an agreement is particularly valuable to parties that wish to preserve a long-term relationship. Consider two companies that have done business successfully for 10 years but now are in the midst of a million dollar trade dispute. A lawsuit could last three or more years and destroy any chance of future trade. However, if the parties mediate the disagreement, they might reach an amicable settlement within a month or two and could quickly resume their mutually profitable business.

This form of ADR works for disputes both big and small. Two college roommates who cannot get along may find that a three-hour mediation session restores tranquillity in the apartment. On a larger scale, consider the work of former United States Senator George Mitchell, who mediated the Anglo-Irish peace agreement, setting Northern Ireland on the path to peace for the first time in three centuries. Like most good mediators, Mitchell was remarkably patient. In an early session, Mitchell permitted the head of one militant party to speak without interruption—for seven straight hours. The diatribe yielded no quick results, but Mitchell believed that after Northern Ireland's tortured history, any nonviolent discussions represented progress.

ARBITRATION

In this form of ADR, the parties agree to bring in a neutral third party, but with a major difference: the arbitrator has the power to impose an award. The arbitrator allows each side equal time to present its case and, after deliberation, issues a binding decision, generally without giving reasons. Unlike mediation, arbitration ensures that there will be a final result, although the parties lose control of the outcome. Arbitration is always faster and cheaper than litigation.

Parties in arbitration give up many rights that litigants retain, including discovery and class action. *Discovery*, as we see below, allows the two sides in a lawsuit to obtain, before trial, documentary and other evidence from the opponent. Arbitration permits both sides to keep secret many files that would have to be divulged in a court case, potentially depriving a party of valuable evidence. A party may have a stronger case than it realizes, and the absence of discovery may permanently deny it that knowledge. A *class action* is a suit in which one injured party represents a large group of people who have suffered similar harm. For example, in an employment discrimination case, a large group of employees who claim similar injury might band together to bring the case, giving themselves much greater clout. Arbitration eliminates this possibility, since injured employees face the employer one at a time. Finally, the fact that an arbitrator may not provide a written, public decision bars other plaintiffs, and society generally, from learning what happened.

Mandatory Arbitration

This variation contains one big difference: the parties agree *in advance* to arbitrate any disputes that may arise. For example, a consumer who purchases a computer or hires a real estate agent may sign an agreement requiring arbitration of any disputes; a customer opening an account with a stockbroker or bank—or health plan—may sign a similar form, often without realizing it. The good news is fewer lawsuits; the bad news is you might be the person kept out of court.

Assume that you live in Miami. Using the Internet, you order a $2,000 ThinkLite laptop computer, which arrives in a carton, loaded with six fat instructional manuals and many small leaflets. You read some of the documents and ignore others. For four weeks you struggle to make your computer work, to no avail. Finally, you telephone ThinkLite and demand a refund, but the company refuses. You file suit in your local court, at which time the company points out that buried among the hundreds of pages it mailed you was a *mandatory arbitration form*. This document prohibits you from filing suit against the company and states that, if you have any complaint with the company, you must fly to Chicago; pay a $2,000 arbitrator's fee; plead your case before an arbitrator selected by the Laptop Trade Association of America; and, in the event you lose, pay ThinkLite's attorney's fees, which could be several thousand dollars. Is that mandatory arbitration provision valid? It is too early to say with finality, but thus far the courts that have faced such clauses have ruled them valid.[1]

OTHER FORMS OF ADR

Several hybrid forms of ADR offer advantages in particular kinds of disputes. In a *mini-trial*, the parties agree to stage a short trial before a panel of three "judges." Two of the "judges" are actually executives of the corporate parties; the third is a neutral adviser. Lawyers present shortened versions of their cases. The "judges" then discuss settlement, with the corporate officers relying on the neutral party to act as mediator. This method is useful in commercial disputes where the respective executives interpret the facts very differently.

A *summary jury trial* is initiated and supervised by a court. When a case between two corporations is nearly ready for trial, the judge chooses a mock jury of perhaps six people. With the judge presiding, each lawyer summarizes what the witnesses would say in a real trial. A trial that might take two months can be summarized in a day or two. The "jury" then deliberates. They are asked to reach a consensus if possible, but they may make individual decisions if unavoidable. Each juror fills out a form explaining his impression of the case. The assumption is that once all parties and lawyers learn how jurors might react, their views of the lawsuit should converge, leading to settlement. If this doesn't happen, the parties proceed to a real trial.

Critics argue that summary jury trials can be misleading because juries do not see real witnesses. A lawyer's *summary* of a corporate officer's testimony might sound convincing, but the executive himself might be unpersuasive on the witness stand.

Alternative dispute resolution is controversial, but its surging popularity demonstrates great dissatisfaction with ordinary litigation. A corporate executive faced with a serious legal issue must at least consider the options available. Whatever route she chooses, she should be able to justify the choice in terms of time, cost, and likely satisfaction. Information about ADR is readily available on the Internet; a good place to begin a search is **http://www.findlaw.com/01topics/11disputeres/**.

To return to our hypothetical case, Janet Booker proposes to Coastal Insurance that they use ADR to expedite a decision in their dispute. Coastal rejects the offer. Coastal's lawyer, Rich Stewart, says that suicide is apparent. He does not want a neutral party to split the difference and award $1 million to Enviro-Vision. Janet reports this explanation to Beth, but adds that she does not believe it. She thinks that Coastal wants the case to drag on as long as possible in the hopes that Enviro-Vision will ultimately settle cheap.

It is a long way to go before trial, but Janet has to prepare her case. The first thing she thinks about is where to file the lawsuit.

COURT SYSTEMS

The United States has two *complete systems* of courts, state and federal. They are in different buildings, have different judges, and hear different kinds of cases. Each has special powers and certain limitations.

---

[1] See, e.g., *Hill v. Gateway 2000*, 105 F.3d 1147, 1997 U.S. App. LEXIS 1877 (7th Cir. 1997), upholding a similar clause.

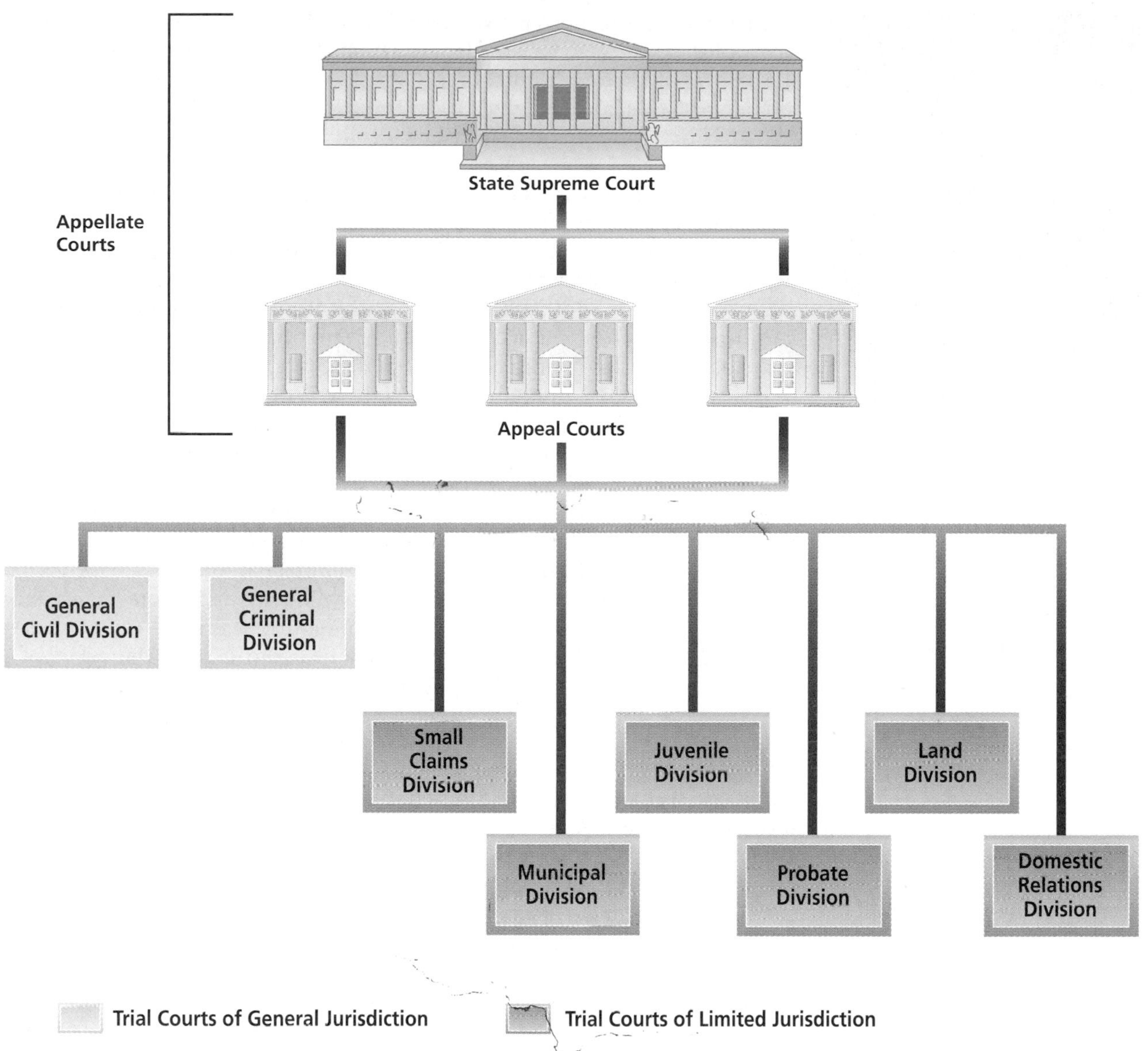

Exhibit 2.1

STATE COURTS

The typical state court system forms a pyramid, as Exhibit 2.1 shows.

Trial Courts

Almost all cases start in trial courts, the ones endlessly portrayed on television and film. There is one judge and there will often (but not always) be a jury. This is the only court to hear testimony from witnesses and receive evidence. **Trial courts determine the facts of a particular dispute and apply to those facts the law given by earlier appellate court decisions.**

In the Enviro-Vision dispute, the trial court will decide all important facts that are in dispute. Did Tony Caruso die? Did he drown? Assuming he drowned, was his death accidental or suicide? Once the jury has decided the facts, it will apply the law to those facts. If Tony Caruso died accidentally, contract law provides that Beth Smiles is entitled to double indemnity benefits. If the jury decides he killed himself, the law provides that Beth gets nothing.

A trial court determines facts, while an appeal court ensures that the lower court correctly applied the law to those facts.

Facts are critical. That may sound obvious, but in a course devoted to legal principles, it is easy to lose track of the key role that factual determinations play in the resolution of any dispute. In the Enviro-Vision case, we will see that one bit of factual evidence goes undetected, with costly consequences.

Jurisdiction refers to a court's power to hear a case. In state or federal court, a plaintiff may start a lawsuit only in a court that has jurisdiction over that kind of case. Some courts have very limited jurisdiction, while others have the power to hear almost any case.

Trial Courts of Limited Jurisdiction. These courts may hear only certain types of cases. Small Claims Court has jurisdiction only over civil lawsuits involving a maximum of, say, $2,500 (the amount varies from state to state). Municipal Court has jurisdiction over traffic citations and minor criminal matters. A Juvenile Court hears only cases involving minors. Probate Court is devoted to settling the estates of deceased persons, though in some states it will hear certain other cases as well. Land Court focuses on disputes about title to land and other real property issues. Domestic Relations Court resolves marital disputes and child custody issues.

Trial Courts of General Jurisdiction. Trial courts of general jurisdiction, however, can hear a very broad range of cases. The most important court, for our purposes, is the General Civil Division. This court may hear virtually any civil lawsuit. In one day it might hear a $450 million shareholders' derivative lawsuit, an employment issue involving freedom of religion, and a foreclosure on a mortgage. Most of the cases we study start in this court.[2] If Enviro-Vision's case against Coastal goes to trial in a state court, it will begin in the trial court of general jurisdiction.

Appellate Courts

Appellate courts are entirely different from trial courts. Three or more judges hear the case. There are no juries, ever. These courts do not hear witnesses or take new evidence. They hear appeals of cases already tried below. **Appeal courts generally accept the facts given to them by trial courts and review the trial record to see if the court made errors of law.**

Generally, an appeal court will accept a factual finding unless there was *no evidence at all* to support it. If the jury decides that Tony Caruso committed suicide, the appeal court will normally accept that fact, even though the appeal judges consider the jury's conclusion dubious. On the other hand, if a jury concluded that Tony had been murdered, an appeal court would overturn that finding if neither side had introduced any evidence of murder during the trial.

An appeal court reviews the trial record to make sure that the lower court correctly applied the law to the facts. If the trial court made an **error of law**, the appeal court may require a new trial. Suppose the jury concludes that Tony Caruso committed suicide, but votes to award Enviro-Vision $1 million because it feels sorry for Beth Smiles. That is an error of law: if Tony committed suicide, Beth is entitled to nothing. An appellate court will reverse the decision. Or suppose that the trial judge permitted a friend of Tony's to state that he was certain Tony would never commit suicide. Normally, such opinions are not permissible in trial, and it was a legal error for the judge to allow the jury to hear it.

Court of Appeals. The party that loses at the trial court may appeal to the intermediate court of appeals. The party filing the appeal is the **appellant**. The party opposing the appeal (because it won at trial) is the **appellee**.

[2] Note that the actual name of the court will vary from state to state. In many states it is called Superior Court, because it has power superior to the courts of limited jurisdiction. In New York it is called Supreme Court (anything to confuse the layperson); in some states it is called Court of Common Pleas; in Oregon and other states it is a Circuit Court. They are all civil trial courts of general jurisdiction.

This court allows both sides to submit written arguments on the case, called **briefs**. Each side then appears for oral argument, usually before a panel of three judges. The appellant's lawyer has about 15 minutes to convince the judges that the trial court made serious errors of law, and that the decision should be **reversed**, that is, nullified. The appellee's lawyer has the same time to persuade the court that the trial court acted correctly, and that the result should be **affirmed**, that is, permitted to stand.

State Supreme Court. This is the highest court in the state, and it accepts some appeals from the court of appeals. In most states, there is no absolute right to appeal to the Supreme Court. If the high court regards a legal issue as important, it accepts the case. It then takes briefs and hears oral argument just as the appeal court did. If it considers the matter unimportant, it refuses to hear the case, meaning that the court of appeals's ruling is the final word on the case.[3]

In most states seven judges, or justices, sit on the Supreme Court. They have the final word on state law.

FEDERAL COURTS

As discussed in Chapter 1, federal courts are established by the United States Constitution, which limits what kinds of cases can be brought in any federal court. See Exhibit 2.2. For our purposes, there are two kinds of civil lawsuits permitted in federal court: federal question cases and diversity cases.

Federal Question Cases

A claim based on the United States Constitution, a federal statute, or a federal treaty is called a federal question case. Federal courts have jurisdiction over these cases. If the Environmental Protection Agency orders Logging Company not to cut in a particular forest, and Logging Company claims that the agency has wrongly deprived it of its property, that suit is based on a federal statute and is thus a federal question. If Little Retailer sues Mega Retailer, claiming that Mega has established a monopoly, that claim is also based on a statute—the Sherman Antitrust Act—and creates federal question jurisdiction. Enviro-Vision's potential suit merely concerns an insurance contract. The federal district court has no federal question jurisdiction over the case.

Diversity Cases

Even if no federal law is at issue, federal courts have jurisdiction when (1) the plaintiff and defendant are citizens of different states *and* (2) the amount in dispute exceeds $75,000. The theory behind diversity jurisdiction is that courts of one state might be biased against citizens of another state. To ensure fairness, the parties have the option of federal court.

Enviro-Vision is located in Oregon and Coastal Insurance is incorporated in Georgia.[4] They are citizens of different states and the amount in dispute far exceeds $75,000. Janet could file this case in United States District Court based on diversity jurisdiction.

---

[3] In some states with smaller populations, there is no intermediate appeals court. All appeals from trial courts go directly to the State Supreme Court.

[4] For diversity purposes, a corporation is a citizen of the state in which it is incorporated and the state in which it has its principal place of business.

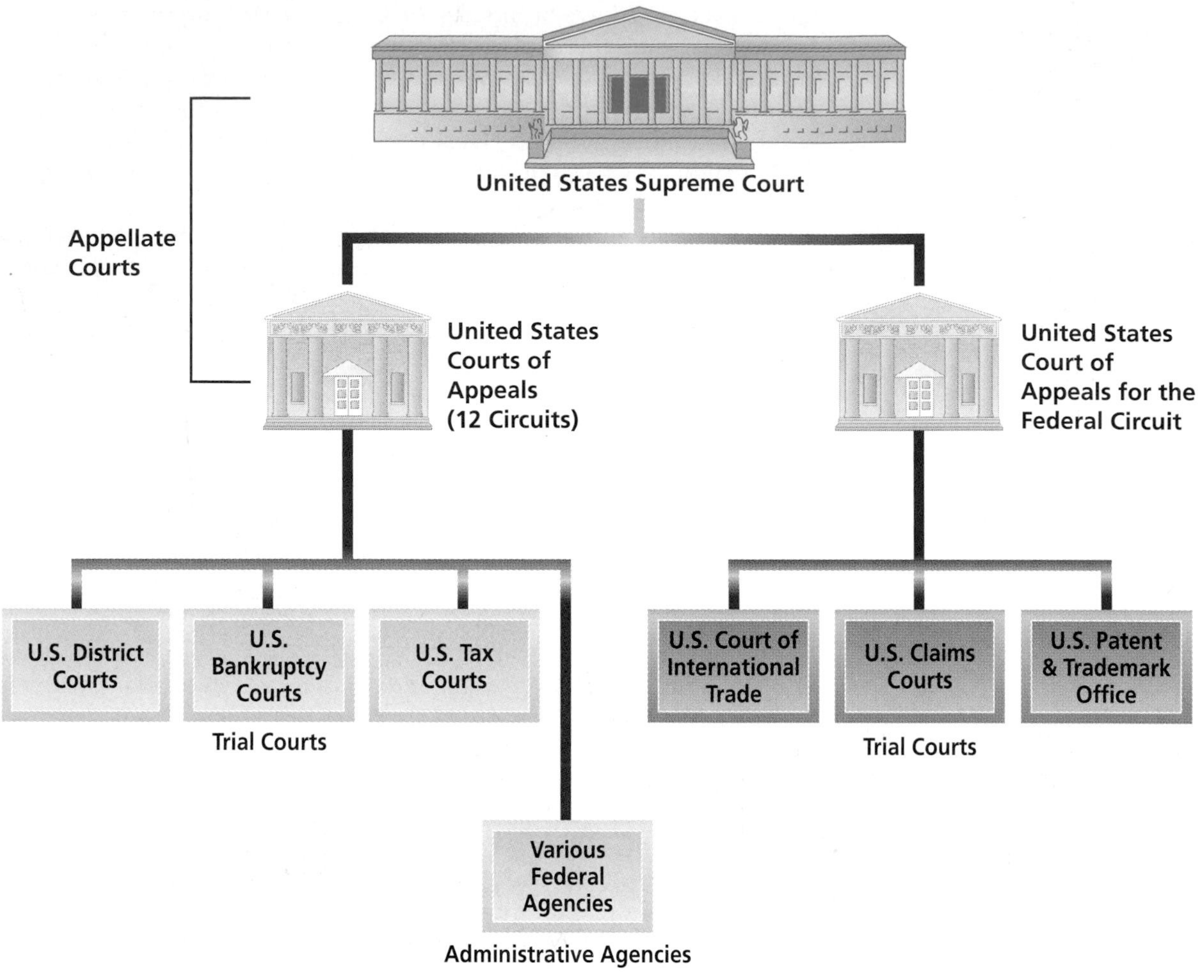

United States Supreme Court

Appellate Courts

United States Courts of Appeals (12 Circuits)

United States Court of Appeals for the Federal Circuit

U.S. District Courts

U.S. Bankruptcy Courts

U.S. Tax Courts

Trial Courts

U.S. Court of International Trade

U.S. Claims Courts

U.S. Patent & Trademark Office

Trial Courts

Various Federal Agencies

Administrative Agencies

Exhibit 2.2

Trial Courts

United States District Court. This is the primary trial court in the federal system. The nation is divided into about 96 districts, and each has a district court. States with smaller populations have one district. States with larger populations have several districts; Texas is divided geographically into four districts.

Other Trial Courts. There are other, specialized trial courts in the federal system. Bankruptcy Court, Tax Court, and the United States Court of International Trade all handle name-appropriate cases. The United States Claims Court hears cases brought against the United States, typically on contract disputes.

Judges. The president of the United States nominates all federal court judges, from district court to Supreme Court. The nominees must be confirmed by the Senate.

Appellate Courts

United States Courts of Appeals. These are the intermediate Courts of Appeals. As the map on the next page shows, they are divided into "circuits," which are geographical areas. There are 11 numbered circuits, hearing appeals from district courts. For example, an appeal from the Northern District of Illinois would go to the Court of Appeals for the Seventh Circuit.

A twelfth court, the Court of Appeals for the District of Columbia, hears appeals only from the district court of Washington, D.C. This is a particularly powerful court because so many suits about federal statutes begin in the district court for the District of Columbia. Also in Washington is the thirteenth Court of Appeals, known as the Federal Circuit. It hears appeals from specialized trial courts, as shown in Exhibit 2.2.

Within one circuit there are many circuit judges, up to about 30 judges in the largest circuit, the Ninth. When a case is appealed, three judges hear the appeal, taking briefs and hearing oral argument.

United States Supreme Court. This is the highest court in the country. There are nine justices on the Court. One justice is the Chief Justice and the other eight are Associate Justices. When they decide a case, each justice casts an equal vote. The Chief Justice's special power comes from his authority to assign opinions to a given justice. The justice assigned to write an opinion has an opportunity to control the precise language and thus to influence the voting by other justices. For a face-to-face meeting with Supreme Court justices, past and present, introduce yourself to http://oyez.nwu.edu/justices/justices.cgi.

The Supreme Court has the power to hear appeals in any federal case and in certain cases that began in state courts. Generally, it is up to the Court whether or not it will accept a case. A party that wants the Supreme Court to review a lower court ruling must file a **writ of certiorari**, asking the Court to hear the case. The

Court receives about 7,500 of these writs every year but currently accepts fewer than 100. Most cases accepted involve either an important issue of constitutional law or an interpretation of a major federal statute.

LITIGATION

Janet Booker decides to file the Enviro-Vision suit in the Oregon trial court. She thinks that a state court judge may take the issue more seriously than a federal district court judge.

PLEADINGS

The documents that begin a lawsuit are called the **pleadings**. These consist of the complaint, the answer, and sometimes a reply.

Complaint

The plaintiff files in court a **complaint**, which is a short, plain statement of the facts she is alleging and the legal claims being made. The purpose of the complaint is to inform the defendant of the general nature of the claims and the need to come into court and protect his interests.

Janet Booker files the complaint, as shown below. Since Enviro-Vision is a partnership, she files the suit on behalf of Beth, personally.

STATE OF OREGON
CIRCUIT COURT

Multnomah County — Civil Action No. ________

Elizabeth Smiles,
Plaintiff

JURY TRIAL DEMANDED

v.
Coastal Insurance Company, Inc.,
Defendant

COMPLAINT

Plaintiff Elizabeth Smiles states that:

1. She is a citizen of Multnomah County, Oregon.
2. Defendant Coastal Insurance Company, Inc. is incorporated under the laws of Georgia and has as its usual place of business 148 Thrift Street, Savannah, Georgia.
3. On or about July 5, 2000, plaintiff Smiles ("Smiles"), Defendant Coastal Insurance Co, Inc. ("Coastal") and Anthony Caruso entered into an insurance contract ("the contract"), a copy of which is annexed hereto as Exhibit "A." This contract was signed by all parties or their authorized agents, in Multnomah County, Oregon.
4. The contract obligates Coastal to pay to Smiles the sum of two million dollars ($2 million) if Anthony Caruso should die accidentally.
5. On or about September 18, 2000, Anthony Caruso accidentally drowned and died while swimming.
6. Coastal has refused to pay any sum pursuant to the contract.
7. Coastal has knowingly, willingly and unreasonably refused to honor its obligations under the contract.

WHEREFORE, plaintiff Elizabeth Smiles demands judgment against defendant Coastal for all monies due under the contract; demands triple damages for Coastal's knowing, willing, and unreasonable refusal to honor its obligations; and demands all costs and attorney's fees, with interest.

ELIZABETH SMILES,
By her attorney,
[Signed]
Janet Booker
Pruitt, Booker & Bother
983 Joy Avenue
Portland, OR
October 18, 2000

Service

When she files the complaint in court, Janet gets a summons, which is a paper ordering the defendant to answer the complaint within 20 days. A sheriff or constable then *serves* the two papers by delivering them to the defendant. Coastal's headquarters are in Georgia, so the state of Oregon has required Coastal to specify someone as its agent for receipt of service in Oregon.

Answer

Once the complaint and summons are served, Coastal has 20 days in which to file an answer. Coastal's answer, shown below, is a brief reply to each of the allegations in the complaint. The answer tells the court and the plaintiff exactly what issues are in dispute. Since Coastal admits that the parties entered into the contract that Beth claims they did, there is no need for her to prove that in court. The court can focus its attention on the disputed issue: whether Tony Caruso died accidentally.

STATE OF OREGON
CIRCUIT COURT

Multnomah County — Civil Action No. 00-5626

Elizabeth Smiles,
Plaintiff
v.
Coastal Insurance Company, Inc.,
Defendant

ANSWER

Defendant Coastal Insurance Company, Inc, answers the complaint as follows:

1. Admit.
2. Admit.
3. Admit.
4. Admit.
5. Deny.
6. Admit.
7. Deny.

COASTAL INSURANCE COMPANY, INC.,
By its attorney,
[Signed]
Richard B. Stewart
Kiley, Robbins, Stewart & Glote
333 Victory Boulevard
Portland, OR
October 30, 2000

If the defendant fails to answer in time, the plaintiff will ask for a **default judgment**, which a court will issue if one party fails to appear in court or to answer a pleading.

Counter-Claim

Sometimes a defendant does more than merely answer a complaint, and files a **counter-claim**, meaning a second lawsuit by the defendant against the plaintiff. Suppose that after her complaint was filed in court, Beth had written a letter to the newspaper, calling Coastal a bunch of "thieves and scoundrels who spend their days mired in fraud and larceny." Coastal would not have found that amusing. The company's answer would have included a counter-claim against Beth for libel, claiming that she falsely accused the insurer of serious criminal acts. Coastal would have demanded money damages.

If Coastal counter-claimed, Beth would have to file a **reply**, which is simply an answer to a counter-claim. Beth's reply would be similar to Coastal's answer, admitting or denying the various allegations.

Class Actions

Suppose Janet uncovers evidence that Coastal denies 80 percent of all life insurance claims, calling them suicide. She could ask the court to permit a **class action**. If the court granted her request, she would represent the entire group of plaintiffs, including those who are unaware of the lawsuit or even unaware they were harmed. Class actions can give the plaintiffs much greater leverage, since the defendant's potential liability is vastly increased. In the back of her mind, Janet has thoughts of a class action, *if* she can uncover evidence that Coastal has used a claim of suicide to deny coverage to a large number of claimants.

Judgment on the Pleadings

A party can ask the court for a judgment based simply on the pleadings themselves, by filing a motion to dismiss. A **motion is a formal request to the court** that the court take some step or issue some order. During a lawsuit the parties file many motions. A **motion to dismiss** is a request that the court terminate a case without permitting it to go further. Suppose that a state law requires claims on life insurance contracts to be filed within three years, and Beth files her claim four years after Tony's death. Coastal would move to dismiss based on this late filing. The court might well agree, and Beth would never get into court.

Discovery

Few cases are dismissed on the pleadings. Most proceed quickly to the next step. **Discovery is the critical, pre-trial opportunity for both parties to learn the strengths and weaknesses of the opponent's case.**

The theory behind civil litigation is that the best outcome is a negotiated settlement and that parties will move toward agreement if they understand the opponent's case. That is likeliest to occur if both sides have an opportunity to examine most of the evidence the other side will bring to trial. Further, if a case does go all the way to trial, efficient and fair litigation cannot take place in a courtroom filled, like a piñata, with surprises. On television dramas, witnesses say astonishing things that amaze the courtroom (and keep viewers hooked through the next commercial). In real trials the lawyers know in advance the answers to practically all the questions asked because discovery has allowed them to see the opponent's documents and question its witnesses. The following are the most important forms of discovery.

Interrogatories. These are written questions that the opposing party must answer, in writing, under oath.

Depositions. These provide a chance for one party's lawyer to question the other party, or a potential witness, under oath. The person being questioned is the **deponent**. Lawyers for both parties are present. During depositions, and in trial, good lawyers choose words carefully and ask questions calculated to advance their cause. A fine line separates ethical, probing questions from those that are tricky, and a similar line divides answers that are merely unhelpful from perjury. For a look at some of the dangers inherent in deposition questions, visit http://www.helpquick.com/tricks.htm—but make sure your lawyer is with you.

Production of Documents and Things. Each side may ask the other side to produce relevant documents for inspection and copying; to produce physical objects, such as part of a car alleged to be defective; and for permission to enter on land to make an inspection, for example, at the scene of an accident.

Physical and Mental Examination. A party may ask the court to order an examination of the other party, if his physical or mental condition is relevant, for example, in a case of medical malpractice.

Requests for Admission. Either party can insist that the opposing party admit or deny certain facts, to avoid wasting time on points not in dispute. In a medical malpractice case, the plaintiff would request that the doctor admit he performed the surgery and admit what would be the normal level of care a surgeon would provide for such a case (while not expecting the surgeon to admit that he erred).

Janet Booker begins her discovery with interrogatories. Her goal is to learn Coastal's basic position and factual evidence and then follow up with more detailed questioning during depositions. Her interrogatories ask for every fact Coastal relied on in denying the claim. She asks for the names of all witnesses, the identity of all documents, the description of all things or objects that they considered. She requests the names of all corporate officers who played any role in the decision and of any expert witnesses Coastal plans to call. Interrogatory No. 18 demands extensive information on all *other* claims in the past three years that Coastal has denied based on alleged suicide. Janet is looking for evidence that would support a class action.

Beth remarks on how thorough the interrogatories are. "This will tell us what their case is." Janet frowns and looks less optimistic: she's done this before.

Coastal has 30 days to answer Janet's interrogatories. Before it responds, Coastal mails to Janet a notice of deposition, stating its intention to depose Beth Smiles. Beth and Janet will go to the office of Coastal's lawyer, and Beth will answer questions under oath. But at the same time Coastal sends this notice, it sends *25 other notices of deposition*. It will depose Karen Caruso as soon as Beth's deposition is over. Coastal also plans to depose all seven employees of EnviroVision; three neighbors who lived near Tony and Karen's beach house; two policemen who participated in the search; the doctor and two nurses involved in the case; Tony's physician; Jerry Johnson, Tony's tennis partner; Craig Bergson, a college roommate; a couple who had dinner with Tony and Karen a week before his death; and several other people.

Beth is appalled. Janet explains that some of these people might have relevant information. But there may be another reason that Coastal is doing this: the company wants to make this litigation hurt. Janet will have to attend every one of these depositions. Costs will skyrocket.

Janet files a **motion for a protective order**. This is a request that the court limit Coastal's discovery by decreasing the number of depositions. Janet also calls Rich Stewart and suggests that they discuss what depositions are really necessary. Rich insists that all of the depositions are important. This is a $2 million case and Coastal is entitled to protect itself.

Before Beth's deposition date arrives, Rich sends Coastal's answers to EnviroVision's interrogatories. The answers contain no useful information whatsoever. For example, Interrogatory No. 10 asked, "If you claim that Anthony Caruso committed suicide, describe every fact upon which you rely in reaching that conclusion." Coastal's answer simply says, "His state of mind, his poor business affairs, and the circumstances of his death all indicate suicide."

Janet calls Rich and complains that the interrogatory answers are a bad joke. Rich disagrees, saying that it is the best information they have so early in the case.

After they debate it for 20 minutes, Rich offers to settle the case for $100,000. Janet refuses and makes no counteroffer.

Janet files a **motion to compel answers to interrogatories,** in other words, a formal request that the court order Coastal to supply more complete answers. Janet submits a **memorandum** with the motion, which is a supporting argument. Although it is only a few pages long, the memorandum takes several hours of library research and writing to prepare—more costs. Janet also informs Rich Stewart that Beth will not appear for the deposition, since Coastal's interrogatory answers are inadequate.

Rich now files *his* motion to compel, asking the court to order Beth Smiles to appear for her deposition. The court hears all of the motions together. Beth argues that Coastal's interrogatory answers are hopelessly uninformative and defeat the whole purpose of discovery. She claims that Coastal's large number of depositions creates a huge and unfair expense for a small firm.

Rich claims that the interrogatory answers are the best that Coastal can do thus far and that Coastal will supplement the answers when more information becomes available. He argues against Interrogatory No. 18, the one in which Janet asked for the names of other policyholders whom Coastal considered suicides. He claims that Janet is engaging in a fishing expedition that would violate the privacy of Coastal's insurance customers and provide no information relevant to this case. He demands that Janet make Beth available for a deposition.

These discovery rulings are critical because they will color the entire lawsuit. A trial judge has to make many discovery decisions before a case reaches trial. At times the judge must weigh the need of one party to see documents against the other side's need for privacy. One device a judge can use in reaching a discovery ruling is an **in camera inspection**, meaning that the judge views the requested documents alone, with no lawyers present, and decides whether the other side is entitled to view them. The following case illustrates how the cost of discovery can easily surpass the value of the lawsuit, particularly when the plaintiff claims that the defendant has similarly injured many other people.

EX PARTE **AMERICAN CARPET SALES, INC.**
703 So. 2d 950, 1997 Ala. LEXIS 490
Supreme Court of Alabama, 1997

Facts: Kerry and Angela Platt bought flooring for their home from American Carpet. When they got the company's bill, they filed suit, claiming that American Carpet had fraudulently increased the invoice price from the original price of $2,165 to $2,408. The couple also alleged that American Carpet had similarly cheated many other customers. The Platts served discovery requests on American Carpet. The company objected, claiming that the discovery requests were too broad; the trial judge ordered the defendant to furnish the information; and American Carpet appealed.

Issue: Must American Carpet furnish the requested information?

Excerpts from Justice Maddox's Decision: American Carpet objected to production of the following items:

> A copy of all buyer's orders and/or purchase agreements between [American Carpet] and any purchaser in the state of Alabama entered into over the past five years where [American Carpet] charged additional monies to the purchaser after the agreement had been entered into.

American Carpet states that it does not keep a separate list of purchase orders that have been adjusted within the past five years; that its invoices for each year are filed alphabetically by purchaser in individual file folders, with no notation on the folders to indicate which invoices have been adjusted; that within the past five years it has generated approximately 6,000 to 9,000 invoices each year for purchases of carpeting and flooring; and that to provide the information requested, it would have to review manually each one of those files. American Carpet says that in order for it to comply with the request, at a minimum someone would have to review approximately 30,000 invoices and that to do so would require approximately 1,500 man-hours, or 37.5 weeks, for one of its employees. American Carpet also says that the production of those invoices would invade the privacy of its customers by revealing their names and addresses and purchases, and it says that producing those invoices would mean releasing business secrets (specifically its customers' identities).

It is well established that the rules regarding discovery are to be broadly and liberally construed, to ensure that the spirit of the rules is carried out. This Court has held that if there is any likelihood that the information sought by a party will aid that party in pursuing a claim or in defending a claim, then discovery should be allowed. The Court has also said that the particular details of the discovery process must necessarily be left to the sound discretion of the trial court.

Considering the evidence before us, we hold that the trial judge did abuse his discretion in compelling the discovery for a period of five years; consequently, we issue a writ directing the trial court to limit its order compelling discovery, so as to require production only as to a two-year period.

The judge rules that Coastal must furnish more complete answers to the interrogatories, especially as to the factual basis of its denial. However, he rules against Interrogatory No. 18, the one concerning other claims Coastal has denied. This simple ruling kills Janet's hope of making a class action of the case. He orders Beth to appear for the deposition. As to future depositions, Coastal may take any 10, but then may take additional depositions only by demonstrating to the court that the deponents have useful information.

Rich proceeds to take Beth's deposition. It takes two full days. He asks about Enviro-Vision's past and present. He learns that Tony appeared to have won their biggest contract ever from Rapid City, Oregon, but that he then lost it when he had a fight with Rapid City's mayor. He inquires into Tony's mood, learns that he was depressed, and probes in every direction he can to find evidence of suicidal motivation. Janet and Rich argue frequently over questions and whether Beth should have to answer them. At times Janet is persuaded and permits Beth to answer; other times she instructs Beth not to answer. For example, toward the end of the second day, Rich asks Beth whether she and Tony had been sexually involved. Janet instructs Beth not to answer. This fight necessitates another trip into court to determine whether Beth must answer. The judge rules that Beth must discuss Tony's romantic life only if Coastal has some evidence that he was involved with someone outside his marriage. It does not have such evidence.

Crucial Clue. Now limited to 10 depositions, Rich selects his nine other deponents carefully. For example, he decides to depose only one of the two nurses; he chooses to question Jerry Johnson, the tennis partner, but not Craig Bergson, the former roommate; and so forth. When we look at the many legal issues this case raises, his choices seem minor. In fact, unbeknownst to Rich or anyone else, his choices may determine the outcome of the case. As we will see later, Craig Bergson has evidence that is possibly crucial to the lawsuit. If Rich decides not to depose him, neither side will ever learn the evidence and the jury will never hear it. A jury can only decide a case based on the evidence presented to it. *Facts are elusive—and often controlling.*

In each deposition, Rich carefully probes with his questions, sometimes trying to learn what he actually does not know, sometimes trying to pin down the witness to a specific version of facts so that Rich knows how the witness will testify at trial. Neighbors at the beach testify that Tony seemed tense; one testifies about seeing Tony, unhappy, on the beach with his dog. Another testifies he had never before seen Blue tied up on the beach. Karen Caruso admits that Tony had been somewhat tense and unhappy the last couple of months. She reluctantly discusses their marriage, admitting there were problems.

Other Discovery. Rich sends Requests to Produce Documents, seeking medical records about Tony. Once again, the parties fight over which records are relevant, but Rich gets most of what he wants. Rich sends Requests for Admission, forcing Beth to commit herself to certain positions, for example, that Tony had lost the Rapid City contract and had been depressed about it.

Plaintiff's Discovery. Janet does less discovery than Rich because most of the witnesses she will call are friendly witnesses. She can interview them privately without giving any information to Coastal. With the help of Beth and Karen, Janet builds her case just as carefully as Rich, choosing the witnesses who will bolster the view that Tony was in good spirits and died accidentally.

She deposes all of the officers of Coastal who participated in the decision to deny insurance coverage, pinning them down as to the limited information they had when they denied Beth's claim.

Summary Judgment

When discovery is completed, both sides may consider seeking summary judgment. **Summary judgment is a ruling by the court that no trial is necessary because there are no *essential* facts in dispute.** The purpose of a trial is to determine the facts of the case, that is, to decide who did what to whom, why, when, and with what consequences. If there are no relevant facts in dispute, then there is no need for a trial.

Suppose Joe sues EZBuck Films, claiming that the company's new movie, *Lover Boy*, violates the copyright of a screenplay that he wrote, called *Love Man*. Discovery establishes that the two stories are suspiciously similar. But EZBuck's lawyer also learns that Joe sold the copyright for *Love Man* to HotShot Pix. EZBuck may or may not have violated a copyright, but there is no need for a trial because Joe *cannot win* even if there is a copyright violation. He does not own the copyright. The court will grant summary judgment for EZBuck.

In the following case, the defendant won summary judgment, meaning that the case never went to trial. And yet, this was only the beginning of trouble for that defendant, William Jefferson Clinton.

JONES v. CLINTON

990 F. Supp. 657, 1998 U.S. Dist. LEXIS 3902
United States District Court for the Eastern District of Arkansas, 1998

Facts: In 1991, Bill Clinton was Governor of Arkansas. Paula Jones worked for a state agency, the Arkansas Industrial Development Commission (AIDC). When Clinton became President, Jones sued him, claiming that he had sexually harassed her. She alleged that, in May 1991, the Governor arranged for her to meet him in a hotel room in Little Rock, Arkansas. When they were alone, he put his hand on her leg and slid it toward her pelvis. She escaped from his grasp, exclaimed, "What are you doing?" and said she was "not that kind of girl." She was upset and confused, and sat on a sofa near the door. She claimed that Clinton approached her, "lowered his trousers and underwear, exposed his penis and told her to kiss it." Jones was horrified, jumped up and said she had to leave. Clinton responded by saying, "Well, I don't want to make you do anything you don't want to do," and pulled his pants up. He added that if she got in trouble for leaving work, Jones should "have Dave call me immediately and I'll take care of it." He also said, "You are smart. Let's keep this between ourselves." Jones remained at AIDC until February 1993, when she moved to California because of her husband's job transfer.

President Clinton denied all of the allegations. He also filed for summary judgment, claiming that Jones had not alleged facts that justified a trial. Jones opposed the motion for summary judgment.

Issue: Was Clinton entitled to summary judgment or was Jones entitled to a trial?

Excerpts from Judge Wright's Decision: [To establish this type of a sexual harassment case, a plaintiff must show that her refusal to submit to unwelcome sexual advances resulted in a tangible job detriment, meaning that she suffered a specific loss. Jones claims that she was denied promotions, given a job with fewer responsibilities, isolated physically, required to sit at a workstation with no work to do, and singled out as the only female employee not to be given flowers on Secretary's Day.]

There is no record of plaintiff ever applying for another job within AIDC, however, and the record shows that not only was plaintiff never downgraded, her position was reclassified upward from a Grade 9 classification to a Grade 11 classification, thereby increasing her annual salary. Indeed, it is undisputed that plaintiff received every merit increase and cost-of-living allowance for which she was eligible during her nearly two-year tenure with the AIDC and consistently received satisfactory job evaluations.

It is plaintiff's burden to come forward with specific facts showing that there is a genuine issue for trial, and the Court finds that her testimony on this point, being of a most general and non-specific nature (and in some cases contradictory to the record), simply does not suffice to create a genuine issue of fact regarding any tangible job detriment as a result of her having allegedly been discouraged from seeking more attractive jobs and reclassification.

Although plaintiff states that her job title upon returning from maternity leave was no longer that of purchasing assistant and that this change in title impaired her potential for promotion, her job duties prior to taking maternity leave and her job duties upon returning to work both involved data input; the difference being that instead of responsibility for data entry of AIDC purchase orders and driving records, she was assigned data entry responsibilities for employment applications. That being so, plaintiff cannot establish a tangible job detriment. A transfer that does not involve a demotion in form or substance and involves only minor changes in working conditions, with no reduction in pay or benefits, will not constitute an adverse employment action, otherwise every trivial personnel action that an irritable employee did not like would form the basis of a discrimination suit.

Finally, the Court rejects plaintiff's claim that she was subjected to hostile treatment having tangible effects when she was isolated physically, made to sit in a location from which she was constantly watched, made to sit at her workstation with no work to do, and singled out as the only female employee not to be given flowers on Secretary's Day. Plaintiff may well have perceived hostility and animus on the part of her supervisors, but these perceptions are merely conclusory in nature and do not, without more, constitute a tangible job detriment.

Similarly, plaintiff's allegations regarding her work station being moved so that she had to sit directly outside Pennington's office and, at times, not having work to do, describe nothing more than minor or de minimis personnel matters which, again without more, are insufficient to constitute a tangible job detriment or adverse employment action.

Although it is not clear why plaintiff failed to receive flowers on Secretary's Day in 1992, such an omission does not give rise to a federal cause of action in the absence of evidence of some more tangible change in duties or working conditions that constitute a material employment disadvantage.

In sum, the Court finds that a showing of a tangible job detriment or adverse employment action is an essential element of plaintiff's § 1983 quid pro quo sexual harassment claim and that plaintiff has not demonstrated any tangible job detriment or adverse employment action for her refusal to submit to the Governor's alleged advances. The President is therefore entitled to summary judgment [on this claim].

In other words, the court acknowledged that there were factual disputes, but concluded that even if Jones proved each of her allegations, she would *still* lose the case, because her allegations fell short of a legitimate case of sexual harassment. Jones appealed the case. Later the same year, as the appeal was pending and the House of Representatives was considering whether to impeach President Clinton, the parties settled the dispute. Clinton, without acknowledging any of the allegations, agreed to pay Jones $850,000 to drop the suit.

Janet and Rich each consider moving for summary judgment, but both correctly decide that they would lose. There is one major fact in dispute: Did Tony Caruso commit suicide? Only a jury may decide that issue. As long as there is *some evidence* supporting each side of a key factual dispute, the court may not grant summary judgment.

Final Preparation

The vast majority of litigation never proceeds to this stage. Well over 90 percent of all lawsuits are settled before trial. But the parties in the Enviro-Vision dispute cannot seem to compromise, so each side gears up for trial. The attorneys make lists of all witnesses they will call. They then prepare each witness very carefully, rehearsing the questions they will ask. It is considered ethical and proper to rehearse the questions, provided the answers are honest and come from the witness. It is unethical and illegal for a lawyer to tell a witness what to say. The lawyers also have colleagues cross-examine each witness, so that the witnesses are ready for the questions the other side's lawyer will ask.

This preparation takes hours and hours, for many days. Beth is frustrated that she cannot do the work she needs to for Enviro-Vision, because she is spending so much time preparing the case. Other employees have to prepare as well, especially for cross-examination by Rich Stewart, and it is a terrible drain on the small firm. More than a year after Janet filed her complaint, they are ready to begin trial.

TRIAL

ADVERSARY SYSTEM

Our system of justice assumes that the best way to bring out the truth is for the two contesting sides to present the strongest case possible to a neutral factfinder. Each side presents its witnesses and then the opponent has a chance to cross-examine. The adversary system presumes that by putting a witness on the stand and letting both lawyers "go at" her, the truth will emerge.

The judge runs the trial. Each lawyer sits at a large table near the front. Beth, looking tense and unhappy, sits with Janet. Rich Stewart sits with a Coastal executive. In the back of the courtroom are benches for the public. On one bench sits Craig Bergson. He will watch the entire proceeding with intense interest and a strange feeling of unease. He is convinced he knows what really happened.

Janet has demanded a jury trial for Beth's case, and Judge Rowland announces that they will now impanel the jury.

RIGHT TO JURY TRIAL

Not all cases are tried to a jury. As a general rule, both plaintiff and defendant have a right to demand a jury trial when the lawsuit is one for money damages. For example, in a typical contract lawsuit, such as Beth's insurance claim, both plaintiff and defendant have a jury trial right whether they are in state or federal court. Even in such a case, though, the parties may *waive* the jury right, meaning they agree to try the case to a judge.

If the plaintiff is seeking an equitable remedy, such as an injunction, there is no jury right for either party. Equitable rights come from the old Court of Chancery in England, where there was never a jury. Even today, only a judge may give an equitable remedy.

VOIR DIRE

The process of selecting a jury is called ***voir dire***, which means "to speak the truth."[5] The court's goal is to select an impartial jury; the lawyers will each try to get a jury as favorable to their side as possible.

Potential jurors are questioned individually, sometimes by the judge, and sometimes by the two lawyers as each side tries to ferret out potential bias. Each lawyer may make any number of **challenges for cause**, claiming that a juror has demonstrated probable bias. For example, if a prospective juror in the Enviro-Vision case works for an insurance company, the judge will excuse her on the assumption that she would be biased in favor of Coastal. If the judge perceives no bias, the lawyer may still make a limited number of **peremptory challenges**, entitling him to excuse that juror for virtually any reason, which need not be stated in court. For example, if Rich Stewart believes that a juror seems hostile to him personally, he will use a peremptory challenge to excuse that juror, even if the judge sensed no animosity. The process continues until 14 jurors are seated. Twelve will comprise the jury; the other two are alternates who hear the case and remain available in the event one of the impaneled jurors is taken ill. For a discussion of the jury's responsibility, see **http://www.placer.ca.gov/courts/** and click on "Jury Duty: An American Responsibility."

Although jury selection for a case can sometimes take many days, in the Enviro-Vision case the first day of the hearing ends with the jury selected. In the hallway outside the court, Rich offers Janet $200,000 to settle. Janet reports the offer to Beth and they agree to reject it. Craig Bergson drives home, emotionally confused. Only three weeks before his death, Tony had accidentally met his old roommate and they had had several drinks. Craig believes that what Tony told him answers the riddle of this case.

OPENING STATEMENTS

The next day, each attorney makes an opening statement to the jury, summarizing the proof he or she expects to offer, with the plaintiff going first. Janet focuses on Tony's successful life, his business and strong marriage, and the tragedy of his accidental death.[6]

---

[5] Students of French note that *voir* means "to *see*" and assume that *voir dire* should translate, "to see, to speak." However, the legal term is centuries old and derives not from modern French but from *Old* French, in which *voir* meant "truth."

[6] Janet Booker has dropped her claim for triple damages against Coastal. To have any hope of such a verdict, she would have to show that Coastal had no legitimate reason at all for denying the claim. Discovery has convinced her that Coastal will demonstrate some rational reasons for what it did.

Rich works hard to establish a friendly rapport with the jury. He expresses regret about the death. Nonetheless, suicide is a clear exclusion from the policy. If insurance companies are forced to pay claims they didn't bargain for, everyone's insurance rates will go up.

BURDEN OF PROOF

In civil cases, the plaintiff has the burden of proof. That means that the plaintiff must convince the jury that its version of the case is correct; the defendant is not obligated to disprove the allegations.

The plaintiff's burden in a civil lawsuit is to prove its case by a **preponderance of the evidence**. It must convince the jury that its version of the facts is at least *slightly more likely* than the defendant's version. Some courts describe this as a "51–49" persuasion, that is, that plaintiff's proof must "just tip" credibility in its favor. By contrast, in a criminal case, the prosecution must demonstrate **beyond a reasonable doubt** that the defendant is guilty. The burden of proof in a criminal case is much tougher because the likely consequences are, too. See Exhibit 2.3.

PLAINTIFF'S CASE

Since the plaintiff has the burden of proof, Janet puts in her case first. She wants to prove two things. First, that Tony died. That is easy, since the death certificate clearly demonstrates it and since Coastal does not seriously contest it. Second, in order to win double indemnity damages, she must show that the death was accidental. She will do this with the testimony of the witnesses she calls, one after the other. Her first witness is Beth. When a lawyer asks questions of her own witness, it is **direct examination**. Janet brings out all the evidence she wants the jury to hear: that the business was basically sound, though temporarily troubled, that Tony was a hard worker, why the company took out life insurance policies, and so forth.

Then Rich has a chance to **cross-examine** Beth, which means to ask questions of an opposing witness. He will try to create doubt in the jury's mind. He asks Beth only questions for which he is certain of the answers, based on discovery. Rich gets Beth to admit that the firm was not doing well the year of Tony's death; that Tony had lost the best client the firm ever had; that Beth had reduced salaries; and that Tony had been depressed about business.

RULES OF EVIDENCE

The lawyers are not free simply to ask any question they want. The law of **evidence** determines what questions a lawyer may ask and how the questions are to be phrased, what answers a witness may give, and what documents may be introduced. The goal is to get the best evidence possible before the jurors so they can

Exhibit 2.3
Burden of Proof. **In a civil lawsuit, a plaintiff wins with a mere preponderance of the evidence. But the prosecution must persuade a jury beyond a reasonable doubt in order to win a criminal conviction.**

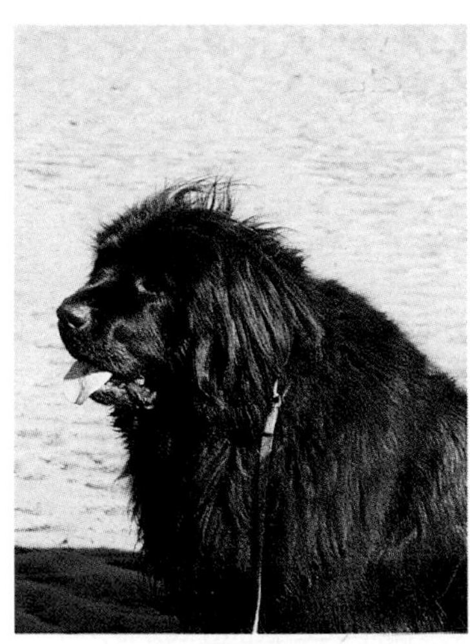
Is the pedigree relevant?

decide what really happened. In general, witnesses may only testify about things they saw or heard.

These rules are complex, and a thorough explication of them is beyond the scope of this chapter; however, they can be just as important in resolving a dispute as the underlying substantive law. Suppose a plaintiff's case depends upon the jury hearing about a certain conversation, but the rules of evidence prevent the lawyer from asking about it. That conversation might just as well never have occurred.

Janet calls an expert witness, a marine geologist, who testifies about the tides and currents in the area where Tony's body was found. The expert testifies that even experienced swimmers can be overwhelmed by a sudden shift in currents. Rich objects strenuously that this is irrelevant, because there is no testimony that there *was* such a current at the time of Tony's death. The judge permits the testimony.

Karen Caruso testifies that Tony was in "reasonably good" spirits the day of his death, and that he often took Blue for walks along the beach. Karen testifies that Blue was part Newfoundland. Rich objects that testimony about Blue's pedigree is irrelevant, but Janet insists it will show why Blue was tied up. The judge allows the testimony. Karen says that whenever Blue saw them swim he would instinctively go into the water and pull them to shore. Does that explain why Blue was tied up? Only the jury can answer.

Cross-examination is grim for Karen. Rich slowly but methodically questions her about Tony's state of mind and brings out the problems with the company, his depression, and tension within the marriage. Janet's other witnesses testify essentially as they did during their depositions.

MOTION FOR DIRECTED VERDICT

At the close of the plaintiff's case, Rich moves for a **directed verdict**, that is, a ruling that the plaintiff has entirely failed to prove some aspect of her case. Rich is seeking to win without even putting in his own case. He argues that it was Beth's burden to prove that Tony died accidentally and that she has entirely failed to do that.

A directed verdict is permissible only if the evidence so clearly favors the defendant that reasonable minds could not disagree on it. If reasonable minds could disagree, the motion must be denied. Here, Judge Rowland rules that the plaintiff has put in enough evidence of accidental death that a reasonable person could find in Beth's favor. The motion is denied.

DEFENDANT'S CASE

Rich now puts in his case, exactly as Janet did, except that he happens to have fewer witnesses. He calls the examining doctor, who admits that Tony could have committed suicide by swimming out too far. On cross-examination, Janet gets the doctor to acknowledge that he has no idea whether Tony intentionally drowned. Rich also questions several neighbors as to how depressed Tony had seemed and how unusual it was that Blue was tied up. Some of the witnesses Rich deposed, such as the tennis partner Jerry Johnson, have nothing helpful to Coastal's case, so he does not call them.

Craig Bergson, sitting in the back of the courtroom, thinks how different the trial would have been had he been called as a witness. When he and Tony had the fateful drink, Tony had been distraught: business was terrible, he was involved in an extramarital affair that he could not end, and he saw no way out of his problems. He had no one to talk to and had been hugely relieved to speak with Craig. Several times Tony had said, "I just can't go on like this. I don't want to, anymore."

Craig thought Tony seemed suicidal and urged him to see a therapist Craig knew and trusted. Tony had said that it was good advice, but Craig is unsure whether Tony sought any help.

This evidence would have affected the case. Had Rich Stewart known of the conversation, he would have deposed Craig and the therapist. Coastal's case would have been far stronger, perhaps overwhelming. But Craig's evidence will never be heard. Facts are critical. Rich's decision to depose other witnesses and omit Craig may influence the verdict more than any rule of law.

CLOSING ARGUMENT

Both lawyers sum up their case to the jury, explaining how they hope the jury will interpret what they have heard. Janet summarizes the plaintiff's version of the facts, claiming that Blue was tied up so that Tony could swim without worrying about him. Rich claims that business and personal pressures had overwhelmed Tony. He tied up his dog, neatly folded his clothes, and took his own life.

JURY INSTRUCTIONS

Judge Rowland instructs the jury as to its duty. He tells them that they are to evaluate the case based only on the evidence they heard at trial, relying on their own experience and common sense.

He explains the law and the burden of proof, telling the jury that it is Beth's obligation to prove that Tony died. If Beth has proven that Tony died, she is entitled to $1 million; if she has proven that his death was accidental, she is entitled to $2 million. However, if Coastal has proven suicide, Beth receives nothing. Finally, he states that if they are unable to decide between accidental death and suicide, there is a legal presumption that it was accidental. Rich asks Judge Rowland to rephrase the "legal presumption" part but the judge declines.

VERDICT

The jury deliberates informally, with all jurors entitled to voice their opinion. Some deliberations take two hours; some take two weeks. Many states require a unanimous verdict; others require only, for example, a 10–2 vote in civil cases.

This case presents a close call. No one saw Tony die. Yet even though they cannot know with certainty, the jury's decision will probably be the final word on whether he took his own life. After a day and a half of deliberating, the jury notifies the judge that it has reached a verdict. Rich Stewart quickly makes a new offer: $350,000. Beth hesitates but turns it down.

The judge summons the lawyers to court, and Beth goes as well. The judge asks the foreman if the jury has reached a decision. He states that it has: the jury finds that Tony Caruso drowned accidentally, and awards Beth Smiles $2 million.

MOTIONS AFTER THE VERDICT

Rich immediately moves for a **judgment** ***non obstante veredicto*** (judgment n.o.v.), meaning a judgment notwithstanding the jury's verdict. He is asking the judge to overturn the jury's verdict. Rich argues that the jury's decision went against all of the evidence. He also claims that the judge's instructions were wrong and misled the jury.

Judge Rowland denies the judgment n.o.v. Rich immediately moves for a new trial, making the same claim, and the judge denies the motion. Beth is elated that the case is finally over—until Janet says she expects an appeal. Craig Bergson, leaving the courtroom, wonders if he did the right thing. He felt sympathy for Beth and none for Coastal. Yet now he is neither happy nor proud.

APPEALS

Two days later, Rich files an appeal to the court of appeal. The same day, he phones Janet and increases his settlement offer to $425,000. Beth is tempted but wants Janet's advice. Janet says the risks of an appeal are that the court will order a new trial, and they would start all over. But to accept this offer is to forfeit over $1.5 million. Beth is unsure what to do. The firm desperately needs cash now. Janet suggests they wait until oral argument, another eight months.

Rich files a brief arguing that there were two basic errors at the trial: first, that the jury's verdict is clearly contrary to the evidence; and second, that the judge gave the wrong instructions to the jury. Janet files a reply brief, opposing Rich on both issues. In her brief, Janet cites many cases that she claims are **precedent**: earlier decisions by the state supreme court on similar or identical issues. Although the following case is from a different jurisdiction, it is an example of the kind of case that she will rely on.

DAKA, INC. v. BREINER
711 A. 2d 86, 1998 D.C. App. LEXIS 86
District of Columbia Court of Appeals, 1998

Facts: Daka was a contract food service provider for various famous museums in Washington. Daka hired James Breiner, aged fifty-four, to supervise service at the Museum of Natural History and five months later transferred him to the Museum of American History, a more demanding position for which he received a raise. A little more than a year later, Daka fired Breiner, claiming that his job performance had rapidly deteriorated after the transfer. Breiner filed suit, seeking damages for age discrimination. He alleged that his supervisors and co-workers made frequent, crude comments about his age, calling him "over the hill," an "old fogey," an "old fart," and someone who "could not get it up any more."

The jury awarded Breiner $10,000 in compensatory damages and $390,000 in punitive damages. Daka moved for a judgment notwithstanding the verdict (n.o.v.), which the trial court denied. Daka appealed.

Issue: Should the trial court have granted Daka a judgment n.o.v.?

Excerpts from Judge Terry's Decision: Daka contends that its motion for judgment n.o.v. should have been granted. Because a judgment notwithstanding the verdict is proper only in extreme cases, we review the denial of such a motion deferentially. Reversal is warranted only if no reasonable person, viewing the evidence in the light most favorable to the prevailing party, could reach a verdict in favor of that party. In this case Breiner had to prove that he was subjected to unwelcome harassment based on his age, and that this harassment was so severe or pervasive as to alter the conditions of his employment by creating a hostile or abusive working environment. We hold that the evidence was sufficient to meet this burden of proof.

Daka's strongest argument is that the evidence at trial showed that Breiner welcomed comments about his age. "Unwelcome" conduct is conduct which the employee did not solicit or invite and which the employee regarded as undesirable or offensive. It is true, as Daka says, that much of the evidence on this issue was controverted. The record reveals that Breiner sometimes referred to himself in relatively mild age-related terms such as "old man" or "old school," but it is less clear who initiated these remarks. What is obvious, however, is that even if Breiner did invite innocuous epithets such as "old man" or "old school," the subsequent ridicule he received was much more egregious and offensive. It is also evident that Breiner sought to discourage this behavior by making it well known, especially to Mr. Sakell, that he found these insults inappropriate. On three separate occasions Breiner approached Sakell and told him his comments were "against the law" or "illegal." But Sakell was undeterred by these complaints and, if anything, became more abusive toward Breiner. Not only did he insult Breiner in front of, and directly to, Breiner's subordinates, but he also condoned Reeves' improper conduct. Viewing the evidence in the light most favorable to Breiner, as we must, we conclude that there was sufficient evidence that the age-related comments were unwelcome, notwithstanding Daka's evidence to the contrary. On this point there was clearly an issue for the jury to resolve.

Affirmed.

Eight months later, the lawyers representing Coastal and Enviro-Vision appear in the court of appeal to argue their case. Rich, the appellant, goes first. The judges frequently interrupt his argument with questions. Relying on decisions like *Daka*, they show little sympathy for his claim that the verdict was against the facts. They seem more sympathetic with his second point, that the instructions were wrong.

When Janet argues, all of their questions concern the judge's instructions. It appears they believe the instructions were in error. The judges take the case under advisement, meaning they will decide some time in the future—maybe in two weeks, maybe in five months.

APPEAL COURT OPTIONS

The court of appeal can **affirm** the trial court, allowing the decision to stand. The court may **modify** the decision, for example, by affirming that the plaintiff wins but decreasing the size of the award. (That is unlikely here; Beth is entitled to $2 million or nothing.) The court might **reverse and remand,** nullifying the lower court's decision and returning the case to the trial court. Or it could simply **reverse**, turning the loser (Coastal) into the winner, with no new trial.

What will it do here? On the factual issue it will probably rule in Beth's favor. There *was* evidence from which a jury could conclude that Tony died accidentally. It is true that there was also considerable evidence to support Coastal's position, but that is probably not enough to overturn the verdict. As we saw in the *Daka* case, if reasonable people could disagree on what the evidence proves, an appellate court generally refuses to change the jury's factual findings. The court of appeal is likely to rule that a reasonable jury *could* have found accidental death, even if the appellate judges personally suspect that Tony may have killed himself.

The judge's instructions raise a more difficult problem. Some states would require a more complex statement about "presumptions."[7]

What does a court of appeal do if it decides the trial court's instructions were wrong? If it believes the error rendered the trial and verdict unfair, it will remand the case, that is, send it back to the lower court for a new trial. However, the court may conclude that the mistake was **harmless error**. A trial judge cannot do a perfect job, and not every error is fatal. The court may decide the verdict was fair in spite of the mistake.

Janet and Beth talk. Beth is very anxious and wants to settle. She does not want to wait four or five months, only to learn that they must start all over. Janet urges that they wait a few weeks to hear from Rich: they don't want to seem too eager.

A week later, Rich telephones and offers $500,000. Janet turns it down, but says she will ask Beth if she wants to make a counter-offer. She and Beth talk. They

---

[7] Judge Rowland probably should have said, "The law presumes that death is accidental, not suicide. So if there were no evidence either way, the plaintiff would win because we presume accident. But if there is competing evidence, the presumption becomes irrelevant. If you think that Coastal Insurance has introduced some evidence of suicide, then forget the legal presumption. You must then decide what happened based on what you have seen and heard in court, and on any inferences you choose to draw." Note that the judge's instructions were different, though similar.

agree that they will settle for $1 million. Janet then calls Rich and offers to settle for $1.7 million. Rich and Janet debate the merits of the case. Rich later calls back and offers $750,000, saying he doubts that he can go any higher. Janet counters with $1.4 million, saying she doubts she can go any lower. They argue, both predicting that they will win on appeal.

Rich calls, offers $900,000 and says, "That's it. No more." Janet argues for $1.2 million, expecting to nudge Rich up to $1 million. He doesn't nudge, instead saying, "Take it or leave it." Janet and Beth talk it over. Janet telephones Rich and accepts $900,000 to settle the case.

If they had waited for the court of appeal decision, would Beth have won? It is impossible to know. It is certain, though, that whoever lost would have appealed. Months would have passed waiting to learn if the state Supreme Court would accept the case. If that court had agreed to hear the appeal, Beth would have endured another year of waiting, brief writing, oral argument, and tense hoping. The high court has all of the options discussed: to affirm, modify, reverse and remand, or simply reverse.

CHAPTER CONCLUSION

No one will ever know for sure whether Tony took his own life. Craig Bergson's evidence might have tipped the scales in favor of Coastal. But even that is uncertain, since the jury could have found him unpersuasive. After two years, the case ends with a settlement and uncertainty—both typical lawsuit results. The missing witness is less common but not extraordinary. The vaguely unsatisfying feeling about it all is only too common and indicates why litigation is best avoided—by dispute prevention.

CHAPTER REVIEW

1. Alternative dispute resolution (ADR) is any formal or informal process to settle disputes without a trial. Mediation, arbitration, and other forms of ADR are growing in popularity.
2. There are two *systems* of courts, one federal and one in each state. A federal court will hear a case only if it involves a federal question or diversity jurisdiction.
3. Trial courts determine facts and apply the law to the facts; appeal courts generally accept the facts found by the trial court and review the trial record for errors of law.
4. A complaint and an answer are the two most important pleadings, that is, documents that start a lawsuit.
5. Discovery is the critical pre-trial opportunity for both parties to learn the strengths and weaknesses of the opponent's case. Important forms of discovery include interrogatories, depositions, production of documents and objects, physical and mental examinations, and requests for admission.
6. A motion is a formal request to the court.
7. Summary judgment is a ruling by the court that no trial is necessary because there are no essential facts in dispute.

8. Generally, both plaintiff and defendant may demand a jury in any lawsuit for money damages.

9. *Voir dire* is the process of selecting jurors in order to obtain an impartial panel.

10. The plaintiff's burden of proof in a civil lawsuit is preponderance of the evidence, meaning that its version of the facts must be at least slightly more persuasive than the defendant's. In a criminal prosecution, the government must offer proof beyond a reasonable doubt in order to win a conviction.

11. The rules of evidence determine what questions may be asked during trial, what testimony may be given, and what documents may be introduced.

12. The verdict is the jury's decision in a case. The losing party may ask the trial judge to overturn the verdict, seeking a judgment *non obstante veredicto* or a new trial. Judges seldom grant either.

13. An appeal court has many options. The court may affirm, upholding the lower court's decision; modify, changing the verdict but leaving the same party victorious; reverse, transforming the loser into the winner; and/or remand, sending the case back to the lower court.

PRACTICE TEST

1. You plan to open a store in Chicago, specializing in beautiful rugs imported from Turkey. You will work with a native Turk who will purchase and ship the rugs to your store. You are wise enough to insist on a contract establishing the rights and obligations of both parties and would prefer an ADR clause. But you want to be sensitive to different cultures and do not want a clause that will magnify a problem or alienate the parties. Is there some way you can accomplish all of this?

2. Solo Serve Corp. signed a lease for space in a shopping center. The lease contained this clause: "Neither Landlord nor tenant shall engage in or permit any activity at or around the Demised Premises which violates any applicable law, constitutes a nuisance, or is likely to bring discredit upon the Shopping Center, or discourage customers from patronizing other occupants of the Shopping Center by other than activities customarily engaged in by reputable businesses." Westowne Associates, the landlord, later leased other space in the center to The Finish Line, an off-track betting business that also had a license to sell food and liquor. Solo Serve sued, claiming that Westowne had breached the lease. Solo Serve requested either a permanent injunction barring The Finish Line from using the center or that The Finish Line pay the cost of relocating its own business.

The case raises two questions. The minor one is, did Westowne violate the lease? The major one is, how could this dispute have been prevented? It ultimately went to the United States Court of Appeals, costing both sides much time and money.

3. State which court(s) have jurisdiction as to each of these lawsuits:

(a) Pat wants to sue his next-door neighbor Dorothy, claiming that Dorothy promised to sell him the house next door.

(b) Paula, who lives in New York City, wants to sue Dizzy Movie Theatres, whose principal place of business is Dallas. She claims that while she was in Texas on holiday, she was injured by their negligent maintenance of a stairway. She claims damages of $30,000.

(c) Phil lives in Tennessee. He wants to sue Dick, who lives in Ohio. Phil claims that Dick agreed to sell him 3,000 acres of farmland in Ohio, worth over $2 million.

(d) Pete, incarcerated in a federal prison in Kansas, wants to sue the United States government. He claims that his treatment by prison authorities violates three federal statutes.

4. Probationary schoolteachers sued the New Madrid, Missouri, school district, claiming that the school district refused to give them permanent jobs because of their union organizing activity. The defendant school district claimed that each plaintiff was refused a permanent job because of inferior teaching. During discovery, the plaintiffs asked for the personnel files of probationary teachers who *had* been offered permanent jobs. The school district refused to provide them, arguing that the personnel files did not indicate the union status of the teachers and therefore would not help the plaintiffs. The trial court ruled that the school district need not release the files. On appeal, the plaintiffs argue that this hindered their ability to prove the real reasons they had been fired. How should the appeal court rule?

5. Students are now suing schools for sexual harassment. The cases raise important issues about the limits of discovery. In a case in Petaluma, California, a girl claimed that she was harassed for years and that the school knew about it and failed to act. According to press reports, she alleges that a boy stood up in class and asked, "I have a question. I want to know if [Jane Doe] has sex with hot dogs." In discovery, the school district sought the parents' therapy records, the girl's diary, and a psychological evaluation of the girl. Should they get those things?

6. British discovery practice differs from that in the United States. Most discovery in Britain concerns documents. The lawyers for the two sides, called solicitors, must deliver to the opposing side a list of all relevant documents in their possession. Each side may then request to look at and copy those it wishes. Depositions are rare. What advantages and disadvantages are there to the British practice?

7. **RIGHT & WRONG** Trial practice also is dramatically different in Britain. The parties' solicitors do not go into court. Courtroom work is done by different lawyers, called barristers. The barristers are not permitted to interview any witnesses before trial. They know the substance of what each witness intends to say, but do not rehearse questions and answers, as in the United States. Which approach do you consider more effective? More ethical? What is the purpose of a trial? Of pre-trial preparation?

8. Claus Scherer worked for Rockwell International and was paid over $300,000 per year. Rockwell fired Scherer for alleged sexual harassment of several workers, including his secretary, Terry Pendy. Scherer sued in United States District Court, alleging that Rockwell's real motive in firing him was his high salary.

Rockwell moved for summary judgment, offering deposition transcripts of various employees. Pendy's deposition detailed instances of harassment, including comments about her body, instances of unwelcome touching, and discussions of extramarital affairs. Another deposition, from a Rockwell employee who investigated the allegations, included complaints by other employees as to Scherer's harassment. In his own deposition, which he offered to oppose summary judgment, Scherer testified that he could not recall the incidents alleged by Pendy and others. He denied generally that he had sexually harassed anyone. The district court granted summary judgment for Rockwell. Was its ruling correct?

9. Lloyd Dace worked for ACF Industries as a supervisor in the punchpress department of a carburetor factory. ACF demoted Dace to an hourly job on the assembly line, and Dace sued, claiming that ACF discriminated on the basis of age. At trial, Dace showed that he had been 53 years old when demoted and had been replaced by a man aged 40. He offered evidence that ACF's benefits supervisor had attended the meeting at which his demotion was decided, and that the benefits supervisor was aware of the cost savings of replacing Dace with a younger man.

At the end of Dace's case, ACF moved for a directed verdict and the trial court granted it. The judge reasoned that Dace's entire case was based on circumstantial evidence. He held that it was too speculative for the jury to infer age discrimination from the few facts that Dace had offered. Was the trial court correct?

10. **YOU BE THE JUDGE WRITING PROBLEM** Apache Corp. and El Paso Exploration Co. operated a Texas gas well that exploded, burning out of control for over a year. More than 100 plaintiffs sued the two owners, claiming damage to adjoining gas fields. The plaintiffs also sued Axelson, Inc., which manufactured a valve whose failure may have contributed to the explosion. Axelson, in turn, sued Apache and El Paso. Axelson sought discovery from both companies about an internal investigation they had conducted, before the blowout, concerning kickbacks (illegal payments) at the gas field. Axelson claimed that the investigation could shed light on what caused the explosion, but the trial court ruled that the material was irrelevant, and denied discovery. Axelson appealed. Is the investigation discoverable? **Argument for Axelson:** If the companies investigated kickbacks, they were concerned about corruption and mismanagement—both of which can cause employees to cut corners, ignore safety concerns, fabricate reports, and so forth. All of those activities have the potential to cause a serious accident. All parties are entitled to discover material that may lead to relevant evidence, and that could easily happen here. **Argument for Apache and El Paso:** This is a fishing expedition. The investigation was completed before the explosion and is completely unrelated. Any internal investigation has the potential (a) to reveal valuable business or trade secrets and (b) to prove embarrassing to the companies investigated. Axelson's motive is to force the two owners to settle in order to avoid such revelations. Discovery is not supposed to be a weapon.

11. Imogene Williams sued the U.S. Elevator Corp. She claimed that when she entered one of the company's elevators, it went up three floors but failed to open, fell several floors, stopped, and then continued to erratically rise and fall for about 40 minutes. She claimed physical injuries and emotional distress. At trial, U.S. Elevator disputed every allegation. When the judge instructed the jury, he asked them to decide whether the company had been negligent. If it had, the jury was to decide what physical injuries Williams had suffered. The judge also instructed them that she could receive money for emotional damages only if the emotional damages resulted from her physical injury. The jury found for U.S. Elevator, deciding that it had not been negligent.

On appeal, Williams argues that the judge was wrong in stating that the emotional injuries had to result from the physical injuries. The court of appeal agreed that the instruction was incorrect. There could be emotional damages even if there were no physical injuries. What appellate remedy is appropriate?

INTERNET RESEARCH PROBLEM

You may be called for jury duty before long. Read the summary of the juror's responsibilities at http://www.placer.ca.gov/courts/jury.htm. Some people try hard to get out of jury duty. Why is that a problem in a democratic society?

You can find further practice problems in the Online Quiz at http://beatty.westbuslaw.com or in the Study Guide that accompanies this text.

CHAPTER 3

COMMON LAW, STATUTORY LAW, AND ADMINISTRATIVE LAW

Jason observes a toddler wander onto the railroad tracks and hears a train approaching. He has plenty of time to pull the child from the tracks with no risk to himself, but chooses to do nothing. The youngster is killed. The child's family sues Jason for his callous behavior, and a court determines that Jason owes—nothing.

"Why can't they just fix the law?" students and professionals often ask, in response to Jason's impunity and countless other legal oddities. Their exasperation is understandable. This chapter cannot guarantee intellectual tranquillity, but it should diminish the sense of bizarreness that law can instill. We will look at three sources of law: common law, statutory law, and administrative law. Most of the law you learn in the course comes from one of these sources. The substantive law will make more sense when you have a solid feel for *how* it was created.

COMMON LAW

Jason and the toddler present a classic legal puzzle: What, if anything, must a bystander do when he sees someone in danger? We will examine this issue to see how the common law works.

The common law is judge-made law. It is the sum total of all the cases decided by appellate courts. The common law of Pennsylvania consists of all cases decided by appellate courts in that state. The Illinois common law of bystander liability is all of the cases on that subject decided by Illinois appellate courts. Two hundred years ago, almost all of the law was common law. Today, most new law is statutory. But common law still predominates in tort, contract, and agency law, and it is very important in property, employment, and some other areas.

We focus on appellate courts because they are the only ones to make rulings of *law*, as discussed in Chapter 2. In a bystander case, it is the job of the state's highest court to say what legal obligations, if any, a bystander has. The trial court, on the other hand, must decide *facts:* Was this defendant able to see what was happening? Was the plaintiff really in trouble? Could the defendant have assisted without peril to himself?

STARE DECISIS

Nothing perks up a course like Latin. ***Stare decisis*** means "let the decision stand." It is the essence of the common law. The phrase indicates that once a court has decided a particular issue, it will generally apply the same rule in future cases. Suppose the highest court of Arizona must decide whether a contract for a new car, signed by a 16-year-old, can be enforced against him. The court will look to see if there is **precedent**, that is, whether the high court of Arizona has already decided a similar case. The Arizona court looks and finds several earlier cases, all holding that such contracts may not be enforced against a minor. The court will apply that precedent and refuse to enforce the contract in this case. Courts do not always follow precedent but they generally do: *stare decisis.*

Two words explain why the common law is never as easy as we might like: *predictability* and *flexibility*. The law is trying to accommodate both goals. The need for predictability is apparent: people must know what the law is. If contract law changed daily, an entrepreneur who leased factory space and then started buying machinery would be uncertain if the factory would actually be available when she was ready to move in. Will the landlord slip out of the lease? Will the machinery be ready on time? The need for predictability created the doctrine of *stare decisis.*

Yet there must also be flexibility in the law, some means to respond to new problems and changing social mores. As we enter a new millennium, we cannot be encumbered by ironclad rules established before electricity was discovered. These two ideas may be obvious but they also conflict: the more flexibility we permit, the less predictability we enjoy. We will watch the conflict play out in the bystander cases.

BYSTANDER CASES

This country inherited from England a simple rule about a bystander's obligations: you have no duty to assist someone in peril unless you created the danger. In *Union Pacific Railway Co. v. Cappier,*[1] through no fault of the railroad, a train struck a man, severing an arm and a leg. Railroad employees saw the incident happen but did nothing to assist him. By the time help arrived, the victim had

1 66 Kan. 649, 72 P. 281 (1903).

died. In this 1903 case the court held that the railroad had no duty to help the injured man:

> With the humane side of the question courts are not concerned. It is the omission or negligent discharge of legal duties only which come within the sphere of judicial cognizance. For withholding relief from the suffering, for failure to respond to the calls of worthy charity, or for faltering in the bestowment of brotherly love on the unfortunate, penalties are found not in the laws of men but in [the laws of God].

As harsh as this judgment might seem, it was an accurate statement of the law at that time in both England and the United States: bystanders need do nothing. Contemporary writers found the rule inhumane and cruel, and even judges criticized it. But—*stare decisis*—they followed it. With a rule this old and well established, no court was willing simply to scuttle it. What courts did do was seek openings for small changes.

Eighteen years after the Kansas case of *Cappier*, the court in nearby Iowa found the basis for one exception. Ed Carey was a farm laborer, working for Frank Davis. While in the fields, Carey fainted from sunstroke and remained unconscious. Davis simply hauled him to a nearby wagon and left him in the sun for an additional four hours, causing serious permanent injury. The court's response:

> It is unquestionably the well-settled rule that the master is under no legal duty to care for a sick or injured servant for whose illness or injury he is not at fault. Though not unjust in principle, this rule, if carried unflinchingly and without exception to its logical extreme, is sometimes productive of shocking results. To avoid this criticism [we hold that where] a servant suffers serious injury, or is suddenly stricken down in a manner indicating the immediate and emergent need of aid to save him from death or serious harm, the master, if present is in duty bound to take such reasonable measures as may be practicable to relieve him, even though such master be not chargeable with fault in bringing about the emergency.[2]

If this tranquil canoe trip turns perilous, a bystander has no obligation to respond. Is the common law rule a moral one?

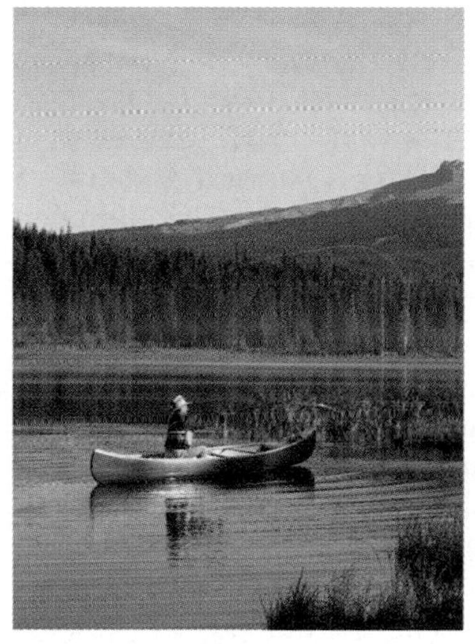

And this is how the common law changes: bit by tiny bit. In Iowa, a bystander could now be liable *if* he was the employer and *if* the worker was suddenly stricken and *if* it was an emergency and *if* the employer was present. That is a small change but an important one.

For the next 50 years, changes in bystander law came very slowly. Consider *Osterlind v. Hill*, a case from 1928.[3] Osterlind rented a canoe from Hill's boatyard, paddled into the lake, and promptly fell into the water. For *30 minutes* he clung to the side of the canoe and shouted for help. Hill heard the cries but did nothing; Osterlind drowned. Was Hill liable? No, said the court: a bystander has no liability. Not until half a century later did that same state supreme court reverse its position and begin to require assistance in extreme cases—a long time for Osterlind to hold on.[4]

In the 1970s, changes came more quickly.

TARASOFF v. REGENTS OF THE UNIVERSITY OF CALIFORNIA
17 Cal. 3d 425, 551 P.2d 334, 131 Cal. Rptr. 14
Supreme Court of California, 1976

Facts: On October 27, 1969, Prosenjit Poddar killed Tatiana Tarasoff. Tatiana's parents claimed that two months earlier Poddar had confided his intention to kill Tatiana to Dr. Lawrence Moore, a psychologist employed by the University of California at Berkeley. They sued the University, claiming that Dr. Moore should have warned Tatiana and/or should have arranged for Poddar's confinement.

Issue: Did Dr. Moore have a duty to Tatiana Tarasoff, and did he breach that duty?

---

2 *Carey v. Davis*, 190 Iowa 720, 180 N.W. 889 (1921).

3 263 Mass. 73, 160 N.E. 301 (1928).

4 *Pridgen v. Boston Housing Authority*, 364 Mass. 696, 308 N.E.2d 467 (1974).

Excerpts from Justice Tobriner's Decision: Although under the common law, as a general rule, one person owed no duty to control the conduct of another, nor to warn those endangered by such conduct, the courts have carved out an exception to this rule in cases in which the defendant stands in some special relationship to either the person whose conduct needs to be controlled or in a relationship to the foreseeable victim of that conduct. Applying this exception to the present case, we note that a relationship of defendant therapists to either Tatiana or Poddar will suffice to establish a duty of care.

We recognize the difficulty that a therapist encounters in attempting to forecast whether a patient presents a serious danger of violence. Obviously we do not require that the therapist, in making that determination, render a perfect performance; the therapist need only exercise that reasonable degree of skill, knowledge, and care ordinarily possessed and exercised by members of [the field] under similar circumstances.

In the instant case, however, the pleadings do not raise any question as to failure of defendant therapists to predict that Poddar presented a serious danger of violence. On the contrary, the present complaints allege that defendant therapists did in fact predict that Poddar would kill, but were negligent in failing to warn.

In our view, once a therapist does in fact determine, or under applicable professional standards reasonably should have determined, that a patient poses a serious danger of violence to others, he bears a duty to exercise reasonable care to protect the foreseeable victim of that danger.

[The Tarasoffs have stated a legitimate claim against Dr. Moore.]

The *Tarasoff* exception applies when there is some special relationship, such as therapist-patient. What if there is no such relationship? The 1983 case of *Soldano v. O'Daniels*[5] arose when a patron in Happy Jack's bar saw Villanueva threaten Soldano with a gun. The patron dashed next door, into the Circle Inn bar, told the bartender what was happening, and urged him to call the police. The bartender refused. The witness then asked to use the phone to call the police himself, but the bartender again refused. Tragically, the delay permitted Villanueva to kill Soldano.

As in the earlier cases we have seen, this case presented an emergency. But the exception created in *Carey v. Davis* applied only if the bystander was an employer, and that in *Tarasoff* only for a doctor. In *Soldano* the bystander was neither. Should the law require him to act, that is, should it carve a new exception? Here is what the California court decided:

> Many citizens simply "don't want to get involved." No rule should be adopted [requiring] a citizen to open up his or her house to a stranger so that the latter may use the telephone to call for emergency assistance. As Mrs. Alexander in Anthony Burgess' *A Clockwork Orange* learned to her horror, such an action may be fraught with danger. It does not follow, however, that use of a telephone in a public portion of a business should be refused for a legitimate emergency call.
>
> We conclude that the bartender owed a duty to [Soldano] to permit the patron from Happy Jack's to place a call to the police or to place the call himself. It bears emphasizing that the duty in this case does not require that one must go to the aid of another. That is not the issue here. The employee was not the good samaritan intent on aiding another. The patron was.

Do these exceptions mean that the bystander rule is gone? *Parra v. Tarasco*[6] provides a partial answer. Ernesto Parra was a customer at the Jiminez Restaurant

---

[5] 141 Cal. App. 3d 443, 190 Cal. Rptr. 310, 1983 Cal. App. LEXIS 1539 (1983).

[6] 9230 Ill. App. 3d 819, 595 N.E.2d 1186, 1992 Ill. App. LEXIS 935 (1992).

when food became lodged in his throat. The employees did not use the Heimlich maneuver or any other method to try to save him. Parra choked to death. Was the restaurant liable? No, said the Illinois Appeals Court. The restaurant had no obligation to do anything.

The bystander rule, that hardy oak, is alive and well. Various initials have been carved into its bark—the exceptions we have seen and a variety of others—but the trunk is strong and the leaves green. Perhaps someday the proliferating exceptions will topple it, but the process of the common law is slow and that day is nowhere in sight. Indeed, the following article demonstrates that new forces make bystanders even less likely to get involved.

In the past, emergency medical technician Angela Favors often asked bystanders to step aside at accident scenes so she could take over life-saving procedures they had initiated. But in the last year or so, the Grady Memorial Hospital emergency worker has rarely had that problem.

"Now we don't have to worry about telling anyone to move back," said Ms. Favors, a five-year employee. "I've seen times lately when the person has bled out and is by themselves. Everybody standing around can tell you what happened, but nobody has helped." Fewer good Samaritans are stepping forward to assist at accidents or other emergencies—apparently because of a growing fear of AIDS and Hepatitis B, metro Atlanta emergency medical personnel say.

The HIV virus, which causes AIDS, and Hepatitis B are blood-borne diseases that are contracted through intimate contact, primarily sexual. Both viruses have been found in saliva, although there are no documented cases of anyone contracting AIDS through saliva. One can contract Hepatitis B through saliva, however, health officials say.

During one recent accident in Doraville, bystanders discouraged others from helping a bloodied, dying victim until paramedics arrived, because of the fear of AIDS, according to one witness.[7]

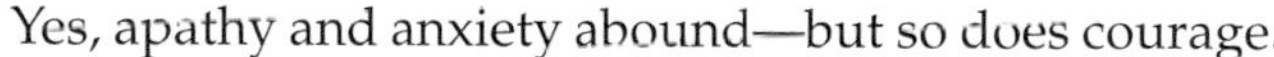

Yes, apathy and anxiety abound—but so does courage.

As the freight train rumbled through rural Indiana, conductor Robert Mohr looked ahead and saw what seemed to be a puppy. Then the "puppy" sat up straight and shook her blond curls. Nineteen-month-old Emily Marshall had wandered away from her mother and was playing on the tracks, dead ahead. Engineer Rodney Lindley jammed on the brakes, but could not possibly stop the 96-car, 6,000-ton train. There was no time to jump off and sprint ahead to the girl. Mohr, aged 49, hustled onto the engine's catwalk and clambered forward, as Lindley slowed the train to 10 miles per hour. Gripping a guard rail, Mohr leaned perilously far forward, waited until the engine loomed directly above the child—and deftly booted her to safety. Emily bounced up with nothing worse than a chipped tooth and forehead cuts, and Mohr, the merrier, was a Hoosier hero.

STATUTORY LAW

Most new law is statutory law. Statutes affect each of us every day, in our business, professional, and personal lives. When the system works correctly, this is the one part of the law over which we the people have control. We elect the local legislators who pass state statutes; we vote for the senators and representatives who create

[7] Susan Laccetti, "AIDS Awareness," *Atlanta Journal and Constitution,* Nov. 12, 1991, §C, p. 4. Reprinted with permission from The Atlanta Journal and The Atlanta Constitution.

federal statutes. If we understand the system, we can affect the largest source of contemporary law. If we live in ignorance of its strengths and pitfalls, we delude ourselves that we participate in a democracy.

As we saw in Chapter 1, there are two systems of government operating in the United States: a national government and 50 state governments. Each level of government has a legislative body. In Washington, D.C., Congress is our national legislature. Congress passes the statutes that govern the nation. In addition, each state has a legislature, which passes statutes for that state only. In this section we look at how Congress does its work creating statutes. State legislatures operate similarly, but the work of Congress is better documented and obviously of national importance.[8]

BILLS

Congress is organized into two houses, the House of Representatives and the Senate. Either house may originate a proposed statute, which is called a **bill**. The bill must be voted on and approved by both houses. Once both houses pass it, they will send it to the president. If the president signs the bill, it becomes law and is then a statute. If the president opposes the bill, he will veto it, in which case it is not law.[9]

Committee Work

If you visit either house of Congress, you will probably find half a dozen legislators on the floor, with one person talking and no one listening. This is because most of the work is done in committees. Both houses are organized into dozens of committees, each with special functions. The House currently has about 27 committees (further divided into about 150 subcommittees) and the Senate has approximately 20 committees (with about 86 subcommittees). For example, the armed services committee of each house oversees the huge defense budget and the workings of the armed forces. Labor committees handle legislation concerning organized labor and working conditions. Banking committees develop expertise on financial institutions. Judiciary committees review nominees to the federal courts. There are dozens of other committees, some very powerful, because they control vast amounts of money, and some relatively weak.

When a bill is proposed in either house, it is referred to the committee that specializes in that subject. Why are bills proposed in the first place? For any of several reasons:

- *New Issue, New Worry*. If society begins to focus on a new issue, Congress may respond with legislation. We consider below, for example, the congressional response to employment discrimination.

---

[8] See the chart of state and federal governments in Chapter 1. A vast amount of information about Congress is available on the Internet. The House of Representatives has a Web page at http://www.house.gov/. The Senate's site appears at http://www.senate.gov. Each page provides links to current law, pending legislation, votes, committees, and more. If you do not know the name of your representative or senator (shame!), the Web page will provide that information. Most state legislatures have Web sites, which you can reach from links found at http://www.ncsl.org/public/sitesleg.htm. These sites typically permit you to read statutes, research legislative history, examine the current calendar, and note upcoming events. For example, the Web site http://housegop.state.il.us/ brings you to the Republican caucus in the Illinois House of Representatives, while the site http://www.housedem.state.il.us/ will take you to the same body's Democratic caucus. Many of these Web sites enable you to e-mail your local representatives.

[9] Congress may, however, attempt to override the veto. See the discussion below.

- *Unpopular Judicial Ruling*. If a court makes a ruling that Congress disagrees with, the legislators may pass a statute "undoing" the court decision.
- *Criminal Law*. Statutory law, unlike common law, is prospective. Legislators are hoping to control the future. And that is why almost all criminal law is statutory. A court cannot retroactively announce that it *has been* a crime for a retailer to accept kickbacks from a wholesaler. Everyone must know the rules in advance because the consequences—prison, a felony record—are so harsh.

DISCRIMINATION: CONGRESS AND THE COURTS

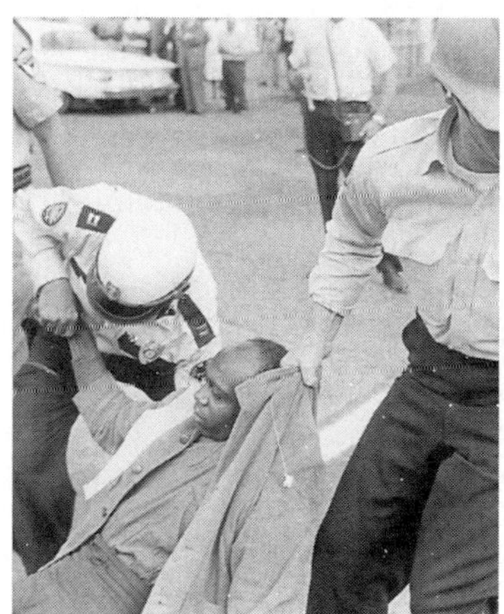

A civil rights demonstrator being arrested by the police.

The civil rights movement of the 1950s and 1960s convinced most Americans that African Americans continued to suffer relentless discrimination in jobs, housing, voting, schools, and other basic areas of life. Demonstrations and boycotts, marches and counter-marches, church bombings and killings persuaded the nation that the problem was vast and urgent.

In 1963 President Kennedy proposed legislation to guarantee equal rights to African Americans in these areas. The bill went to the House Judiciary Committee, which heard testimony for weeks. Witnesses testified that blacks were often unable to vote because of their race, that landlords and home sellers adamantly refused to sell or rent to blacks, that education was still grossly unequal, and that blacks were routinely denied good jobs in many industries. Eventually, the Judiciary Committee approved the bill and sent it to the full House.

The bill was dozens of pages long and divided into "titles," with each title covering a major issue. Title VII concerned employment. We will consider the progress of Title VII in Congress and in the courts. Here is one section of Title VII, as reported to the House floor:[10]

> Sec. 703(a). It shall be an unlawful employment practice for an employer—
>
> (1) to fail or refuse to hire or to discharge any individual, or otherwise to discriminate against any individual with respect to his compensation, terms, conditions, or privileges of employment, because of such individual's race, color, religion, or national origin; or
>
> (2) to limit, segregate, or classify his employees in any way which would deprive or tend to deprive any individual of employment opportunities or otherwise adversely affect his status as an employee, because of such individual's race, color, religion, or national origin.

DEBATE

The proposed bill was intensely controversial and sparked angry argument throughout Congress. Here are some excerpts from one day's debate on the House floor, on February 8, 1964:[11]

> MR. WAGGONNER. I speak to you in all sincerity and ask for the right to discriminate if I so choose because I think it is my right. I think it is my right to choose my social companions. I think it is my right if I am a businessman to run it as I please, to do with my own as I will. I think that is a right the Constitution gives to every man. I want the continued right to discriminate and I want the other man to have the right to continue to discriminate against me, because I am discriminated against every day. I do not feel inferior about it.

---

[10] The section number in the House bill was actually 704(a); we use 703 here because that is the number of the section when the bill became law and the number to which the Supreme Court refers in later litigation.

[11] The order of speakers is rearranged, and the remarks are edited.

> I ask you to forget about politics, forget about everything except the integrity of the individual, leaving to the people of this country the right to live their lives in the manner they choose to live. Do not destroy this democracy for a Socialist government. A vote for this bill is no less.

> MR. CONTE. If the serious cleavage which pitted brother against brother and citizen against citizen during the tragedy of the Civil War is ever to be justified, it can be justified in this House and then in the other body with the passage of this legislation which can and must reaffirm the rights to all individuals which are inherent in our Constitution.
>
> The distinguished poet Mark Van Doren has said that "equality is absolute or no, nothing between can stand," and nothing should now stand between us and the passage of strong and effective civil rights legislation. It is to this that we are united in a strong bipartisan coalition today, and when the laws of the land proclaim that the 88th Congress acted effectively, judiciously, and wisely, we can take pride in our accomplishments as free men.

Other debate was less rhetorical and aimed more at getting information. The following exchange anticipates a 30-year controversy on quotas:

> MR. JOHANSEN. I have asked for this time to raise a question and I would ask particularly for the attention of the gentleman from New York [MR. GOODELL] because of a remark he made—and I am not quarreling with it. I understood him to say there is no plan for balanced employment or for quotas in this legislation. . . . I am raising a question as to whether in the effort to eliminate discrimination—and incidentally that is an undefined term in the bill—we may get to a situation in which employers and conceivably union leaders, will insist on legislation providing for a quota system as a matter of self-protection.
>
> Now let us suppose this hypothetical situation exists with 100 jobs to be filled. Let us say 150 persons apply and suppose 75 of them are Negro and 75 of them are white. Supposing the employer . . . hires 75 white men and 25 Negroes. Do the other 50 Negroes or anyone of them severally have a right to claim they have been discriminated against on the basis of color?

> MR. GOODELL. It is the intention of the legislation that if applicants are equal in all other respects there will be no restriction. One may choose from among equals. So long as there is no distinction on the basis of race, creed, or color it will not violate the act.

The debate on racial issues carried on. Later in the day, Congressman Smith of Virginia offered an amendment that could scarcely have been smaller—or more important:

> Amendment offered by MR. SMITH of Virginia: On page 68, line 23, after the word "religion," insert the word "sex."

In other words, Smith was asking that discrimination on the basis of sex also be outlawed, along with the existing grounds of race, color, national origin, and religion. Congressman Smith's proposal produced the following comments:

> MR. CELLER. You know, the French have a phrase for it when they speak of women and men. They say "vive la difference." I think the French are right. Imagine the upheaval that would result from adoption of blanket language requiring total equality. Would male citizens be justified in insisting that women share with them the burdens of compulsory military service? What would become of traditional family relationships? What about alimony? What would become of the crimes of rape and statutory rape? I think the amendment seems illogical, ill timed, ill placed, and improper.

> MRS. ST. GEORGE. Mr. Chairman, I was somewhat amazed when I came on the floor this afternoon to hear the very distinguished chairman of the Committee on the Judiciary [MR. CELLER] make the remark that he considered the amendment at this point illogical. I can think of nothing more logical than this amendment at this point.
>
> There are still many States where women cannot serve on juries. There are still many States where women do not have equal educational opportunities. In most States

> and, in fact, I figure it would be safe to say, in all States—women do not get equal pay for equal work. That is a very well known fact. And to say that this is illogical. What is illogical about it? All you are doing is simply correcting something that goes back, frankly to the Dark Ages.

The debate continued. Some supported the "sex" amendment because they were determined to end sexual bias. But politics are complex. Some *opponents* of civil rights supported the amendment because they believed that it would make the legislation less popular and cause Congress to defeat the entire Civil Rights bill.

That strategy did not work. The amendment passed, and sex was added as a protected trait. And, after more debate and several votes, the entire bill passed the House. It went to the Senate, where it followed a similar route from Judiciary Committee to full Senate. Much of the Senate debate was similar to what we have seen. But some senators raised a new issue, concerning §703(2), which prohibited *segregating or classifying* employees based on any of the protected categories (race, color, national origin, religion, or sex). Senator Tower was concerned that §703(2) meant that an employee in a protected category could never be given any sort of job test. So the Senate amended §703 to include a new subsection:

> Sec. 703(h). Notwithstanding any other provision of this title, it shall not be an unlawful employment practice for an employer . . . to give and to act upon the results of any professionally developed ability test provided that such test . . . is not designed, intended or used to discriminate because of race, color, religion, sex or national origin.

With that amendment, and many others, the bill passed the Senate.

Conference Committee

Civil Rights legislation had now passed both houses, but the bills were no longer the same due to the many amendments. This is true with most legislation. The next step is for the two houses to send representatives to a House-Senate Conference Committee. This committee examines all of the differences between the two bills and tries to reach a compromise. With the Civil Rights bill, Senator Tower's amendment was left in; other Senate amendments were taken out. When the Conference Committee had settled every difference between the two versions, the new, modified bill was sent back to each house for a new vote.

The House of Representatives and the Senate again angrily debated the compromise language reported from the Conference Committee. Finally, after years of violent public demonstrations and months of debate, each house passed the same bill. President Johnson promptly signed it. The Civil Rights Act of 1964 was law. See Exhibit 3.1.

Title VII of the Civil Rights Act obviously prohibited an employer from saying to a job applicant, "We don't hire blacks." In some parts of the country, that had been common practice; after the Civil Rights Act passed, it became rare. Employers who routinely hired whites only, or promoted only whites, found themselves losing lawsuits.

A new group of cases arose, those in which some job standard was set that appeared to be racially neutral, yet had a discriminatory effect. In North Carolina, the Duke Power Co. required that applicants for higher paying, promotional positions meet two requirements: they must have a high school diploma, and they must pass a standardized written test. There was no evidence that either requirement related to successful job performance. Blacks met the requirements in lower percentages than whites, and consequently whites obtained a disproportionate share of the good jobs.

Title VII did not precisely address this kind of case. It clearly outlawed overt discrimination. Was Duke Power's policy overt discrimination, or was it protected

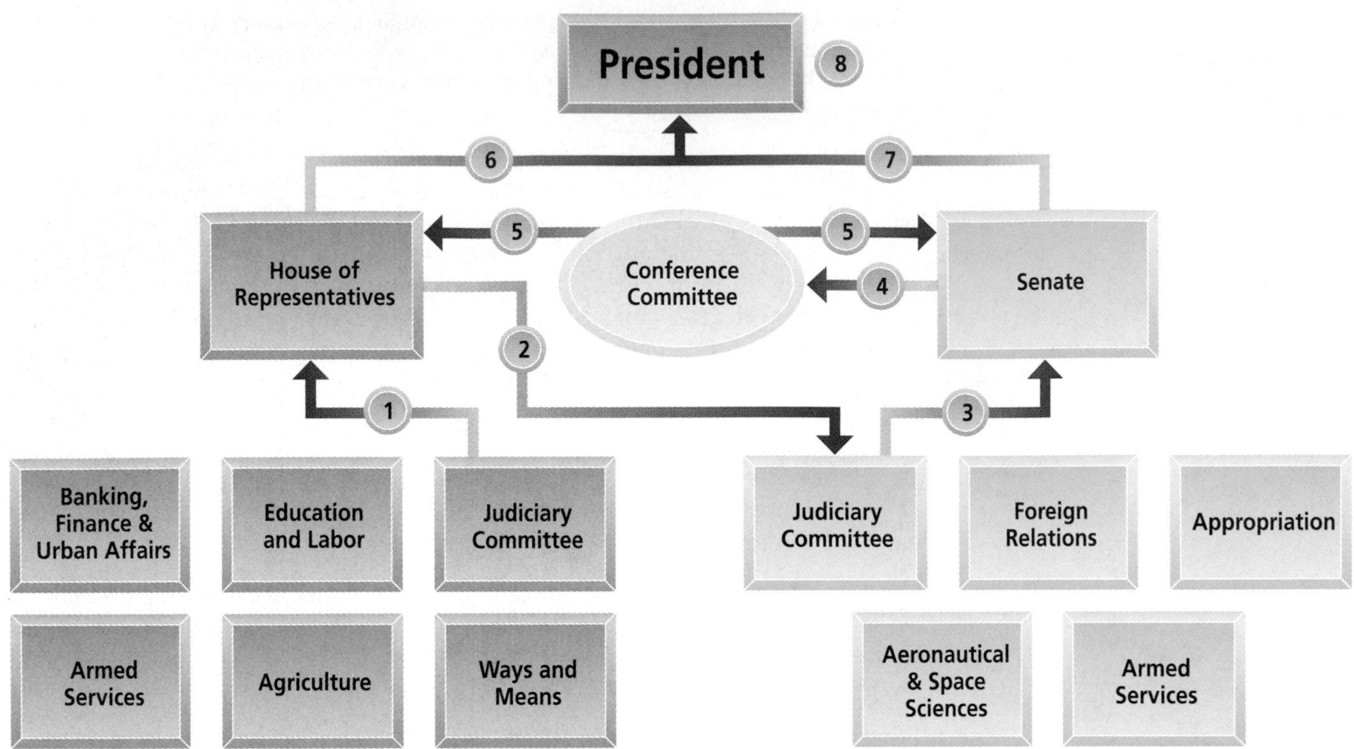

Exhibit 3.1
The two houses of Congress are organized into dozens of committees, a few of which are shown here. The path of the 1964 Civil Rights Act (somewhat simplified) was as follows: (1) The House Judiciary Committee approved the bill and sent it to the full House; (2) the full House passed the bill and sent it to the Senate, where it was assigned to the Senate Judiciary Committee; (3) the Senate Judiciary Committee passed an amended version of the bill and sent it to the full Senate; (4) the full Senate passed the bill with additional amendments. Since the Senate version was now different from the bill the House passed, the bill went to a Conference Committee. The Conference Committee (5) reached a compromise and sent the new version of the bill back to both houses. Each house passed the compromise bill (6 and 7) and sent it to the president, who signed it into law (8).

by Senator Tower's amendment, §703(h)? The case went all the way to the Supreme Court, where the Court had to interpret the new law.

STATUTORY INTERPRETATION

Courts are often called upon to interpret a statute, that is, to explain precisely what the language means and how it applies in a given case. There are three primary steps in a court's statutory interpretation:

- *Plain Meaning Rule*. When a statute's words have ordinary, everyday significance, the court will simply apply those words. Section 703(a)(1) of the Civil Rights Act prohibits firing someone because of her religion. Could an employer who had fired a Catholic because of her religion argue that Catholicism is not really a religion, but more of a social group? No. The word "religion" has a plain meaning and courts apply its commonsense definition.

- *Legislative History and Intent*. If the language is unclear, the court must look deeper. Section 703(a)(2) prohibits classifying employees in ways that are discriminatory. Does that section prevent an employer from requiring high school diplomas, as Duke Power did? The explicit language of the statute does not answer the question. The court will look at the law's history to determine the *intent* of the legislature. The court will examine committee hearings, reports, and the floor debates that we have seen.

- *Public Policy*. If the legislative history is unclear, courts will rely on general public policies, such as reducing crime, creating equal opportunity, and so forth. They may include in this examination some of their own prior decisions. Courts assume that the legislature is aware of prior judicial decisions, and if the legislature did not change those decisions, the statute will be interpreted to incorporate them.

Here is how the Supreme Court interpreted the 1964 Civil Rights Act.

GRIGGS v. DUKE POWER CO.
401 U.S. 424, 91 S. Ct. 849, 1971 U.S. LEXIS 134
United States Supreme Court, 1971

Excerpts from Mr. Chief Justice Burger's Decision: The objective of Congress in the enactment of Title VII is plain from the language of the statute. It was to achieve equality of employment opportunities and remove barriers that have operated in the past to favor an identifiable group of white employees over other employees. Under the Act, practices, procedures, or tests neutral on their face, and even neutral in terms of intent, cannot be maintained if they operate to "freeze" the status quo of prior discriminatory employment practices.

The Act proscribes not only overt discrimination but also practices that are fair in form, but discriminatory in operation. The touchstone is business necessity. If an employment practice which operates to exclude Negroes cannot be shown to be related to job performance, the practice is prohibited.

On the record before us, neither the high school completion requirement nor the general intelligence test is shown to bear a demonstrable relationship to successful performance of the jobs for which it was used.

Senator Tower offered an amendment which was adopted verbatim and is now the testing provision of section 703(h). Speaking for the supporters of Title VII, Senator Humphrey endorsed the amendment, stating: "Senators on both sides of the aisle who were deeply interested in Title VII have examined the text of this amendment and have found it to be in accord with the intent and purpose of that title." The amendment was then adopted. From the sum of the legislative history relevant in this case, the conclusion is inescapable that the . . . requirement that employment tests be job related comports with congressional intent.

And so the highest Court ruled that if a job requirement had a discriminatory impact, the employer could use that requirement only if it was related to job performance. Many more cases arose. For almost two decades courts held that, once workers showed that a job requirement had a discriminatory effect, the employer had the burden to prove that the requirement was necessary for the business. The requirement had to be essential to achieve an important goal. If there was any way to achieve that goal without discriminatory impact, the employer had to use it.

Changing Times

But things changed. In 1989, a more conservative Supreme Court decided *Wards Cove Packing Co. v. Atonio.*[12] The plaintiffs were nonwhite workers in salmon canneries in Alaska. The canneries had two types of jobs, skilled and unskilled. Nonwhites (Filipinos and native Alaskans) invariably worked as low-paid, unskilled workers, canning the fish. The higher paid, skilled positions were filled almost entirely with white workers, who were hired during the off-season in Washington and Oregon.

There was no overt discrimination. But plaintiffs claimed that various practices led to the racial imbalances. The practices included failing to promote from within the company, hiring through separate channels (cannery jobs were done through a union hall, skilled positions were filled out of state), nepotism, and an English language requirement. Once again the case reached the Supreme Court, where Justice White wrote the Court's opinion.

If the plaintiffs succeeded in showing that the job requirements led to racial imbalance, said the Court, the employer now only had to demonstrate that the requirement or practice "serves, in a significant way, the legitimate employment goals of the employer. . . . [T]here is no requirement that the challenged practice be 'essential' or 'indispensable' to the employer's business." In other words, the Court removed the "business necessity" requirement of *Griggs* and replaced it with "legitimate employment goals."

Voters' Role

The response to *Wards Cove* was quick. Liberals decried it; conservatives hailed it. Everyone agreed that it was a major change that would make it substantially harder for plaintiffs to bring successful discrimination cases. Why had the Court changed its interpretation? Because the *Court* was different. The Court of the 1980s was more conservative, with a majority of justices appointed by Presidents Nixon and Reagan. And so, the voters' political preference had affected the high Court, which in turn changed the interpretation of a statute passed in response to voter concerns of the 1960s. See Exhibit 3.2.

Democrats introduced bills to reverse the interpretation of *Wards Cove.* President Bush strongly opposed any new bill. He said it would lead to "quotas," that is, that employers would feel obligated to hire a certain percentage of workers from all racial categories to protect themselves from suits. This was the issue that Congressman Johansen had raised in the original House debate in 1964, but it had not been mentioned since.

Both houses passed bills restoring the "business necessity" holding of *Griggs.* Again there were differences, and a Conference Committee resolved them. After acrimonious debate, both houses passed the compromise bill in October 1990. Was it therefore law? No. President Bush immediately vetoed the bill. He said it would compel employers to adopt quotas.

Congressional Override

When the president vetoes a bill, Congress has one last chance to make it law: an override. If both houses repass the bill, each by a two-thirds margin, it becomes law over the president's veto. Congress attempted to pass the 1990 Civil Rights bill over the Bush veto, but it fell short in the Senate by one vote.

---

12 490 U.S. 642, 109 S. Ct. 2115, 1989 U.S. LEXIS 2794 (1989).

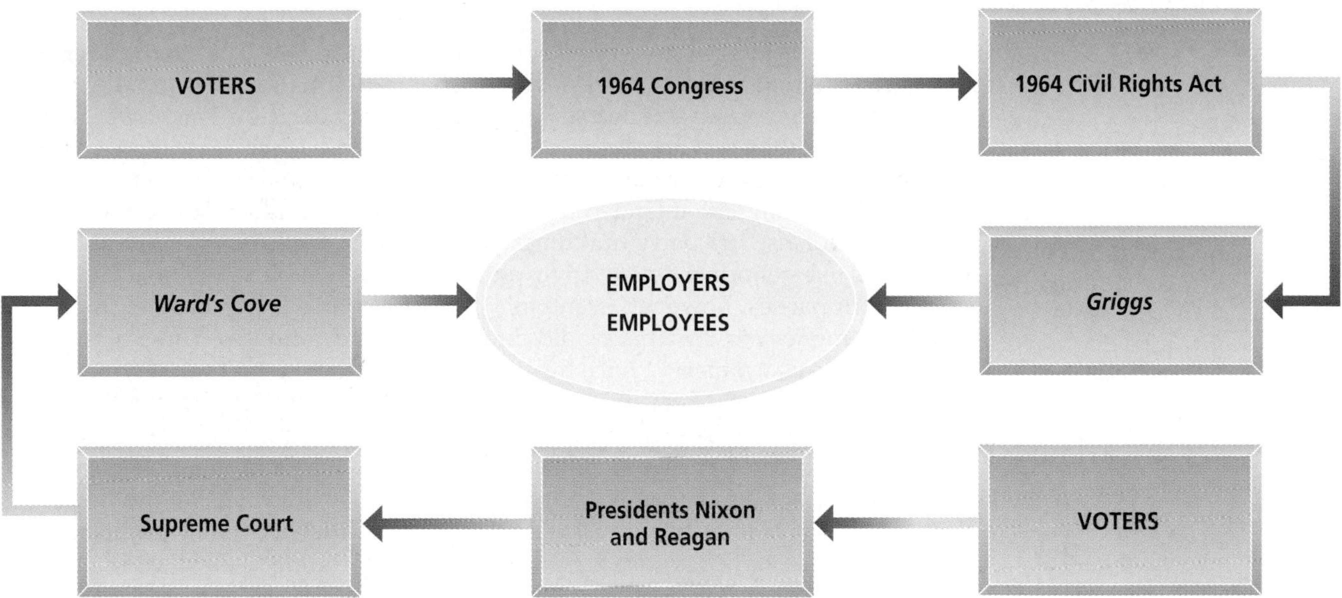

Exhibit 3.2
Statutory interpretation can be just as volatile as the common law, because voters, politicians, and courts all change over time.

Civil rights advocates tried again, in January 1991, introducing a new bill to reverse the *Wards Cove* rule. Again both houses debated and bargained. The new bill stated that, once an employee proves that a particular employment practice causes a discriminatory impact, the employer must "demonstrate that the challenged practice is job related for the position in question and consistent with business necessity."

Now the two sides fought over the exact meanings of two terms: "job related" and "business necessity." Each side offered definitions, but they could not reach agreement. It appeared that the entire bill would founder over those terms. So Congress did what it often does when faced with a problem of definition: it dropped the issue. Liberals and conservatives agreed not to define the troublesome terms. They would leave that task to courts to perform through statutory interpretation.

With the definitions left out, the new bill passed both houses. In November 1991, President Bush signed the bill into law. The president stated that the new bill had been improved and no longer threatened to create racial quotas. His opponents charged he had reversed course for political reasons, anticipating the 1992 presidential election.

And so, the Congress restored the "business necessity" interpretation to its own 1964 Civil Rights Act. No one would say, however, that it had been a simple process.

THE OTHER PLAYER: MONEY

No description of the legislative process would be complete, or even realistic, without mentioning money. Congress has made a few attempts to limit campaign contributions and spending, but to date the efforts are a failure—and a scandal. In 1971, Congress passed the Federal Election Campaign Act (FECA), which limited how much of his own money a federal candidate could spend. Three years later, the statute was amended to place two more limitations on federal campaigns: how much a campaign as a whole could spend, and how much anyone *else* could spend to promote a candidate. One goal was to reduce the power and influence of donors, who gave money expecting favors in return; another purpose was to permit candidates of modest means to compete with millionaire office seekers.

In 1976, the Supreme Court unsettled things in *Buckley v. Valeo*,[13] by ruling that mandatory *spending* limits violate the First Amendment. The Court permitted Congress to limit campaign *contributions*, from individuals and groups, but not to cap the amount that a candidate could spend. This decision was a windfall for wealthy candidates, who could now spend as much of their own money as they chose. It is no coincidence that most members of Congress are very rich.

In 1979, Congress amended the FECA to permit unlimited donations to *political parties* for use in "party building." Initially, party building meant only minor activities like get-out-the-vote drives and distribution of bumper stickers and buttons. Both parties, however, eventually discovered that it was easy to use party-building money in ways that would directly benefit candidates. These funds came to be known as *soft money*. Since the law placed no limit on soft money, the parties went after it feverishly, raising and spending hundreds of millions of dollars every election, effectively destroying any distinction between party building and campaigning. No one writes a $1 million check just to buy bumper stickers, and the influence of donors has grown apace with their contributions. Before the parties can spend the money, they must raise it, and all politicians, both incumbents and outsiders alike, now devote a high percentage of their time to fund-raising.

What do donors expect for their contributions? Access. Corporations, unions, advocacy groups, and rich individuals make large political donations on the assumption that they will later be able to speak directly with powerful politicians about issues that interest them. A corporation seeking to build an oil pipeline in Central Asia might give heavily to a senator with influence in foreign affairs, counting on the contribution to smooth international negotiations. A labor union trying to protect American manufacturing jobs could write a large check, expecting to earn opportunities to speak personally with powerful members of Congress.

A newer route for money to enter politics is through *issue ads*. Increasingly, businesses, labor unions, and advocacy groups run their own political campaigns, creating television and radio ads designed to support or oppose a given position. As long as the ads do not specifically endorse the election or defeat of a candidate, they are arguably outside the statutory limits on contributions.

Between the candidate's own assets, soft money, and issue ads, it is safe to say that giving and spending on many elections are largely uncontrolled. Some states have passed reform legislation, designed to limit contributions and spending by candidates for statewide office, but Congress has refused to reform federal elections. Various nonprofit, nonpartisan groups vigorously oppose the corrosive effect of campaign money. The nonprofit Center for Public Integrity has brought to light many money scandals in Washington. To see what a sharp spotlight will reveal, glance at the Center's Web page **http://www.publicintegrity.org/main.html**. Common Cause, which you can visit at **http://www.commoncause.org**, works hard for campaign finance reform. The Center for Responsive Politics, at **http://www.crp.org/**, includes in its Web site a dollar-by-dollar description of recent elections, demonstrating which candidates took how much from whom.

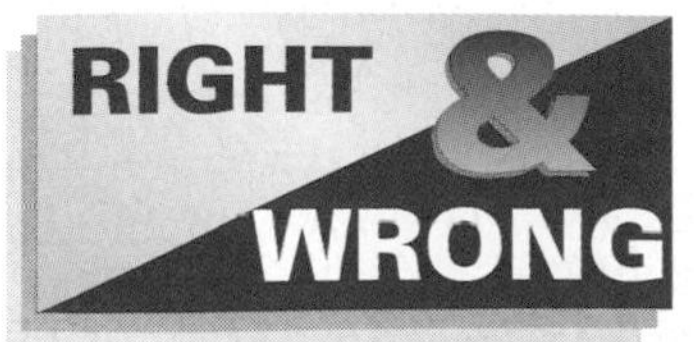

As described above, campaign law currently permits wealthy individuals, unions, corporations, and interest groups to funnel large sums of money to political campaigns. Are the contributions ethical? Suppose that you work for a corporation, union, or interest group that contributes heavily. Would you participate in that effort? Would you expect greater access to a politician because of campaign donations? What is the dividing line between legitimate contributions and bribes?

[13] 424 U.S. 1, 96 S. Ct. 612, 1976 U.S. LEXIS 16 (1976).

ADMINISTRATIVE LAW

Before beginning this section, please return your seat to its upright position. Stow the tray firmly in the seatback in front of you. Turn off any radios, CD players, or other electronic equipment. Sound familiar? Administrative agencies affect each of us every day in hundreds of ways. They have become the fourth branch of government. Supporters believe that they provide unique expertise in complex areas; detractors regard them as unelected government run amok.

Many administrative agencies are familiar. The Federal Aviation Agency, which requires all airlines to ensure that your seats are upright before takeoff and landing, is an administrative agency. The Internal Revenue Service haunts us every April 15. The Environmental Protection Agency regulates the water quality of the river in your town. The Federal Trade Commission oversees the commercials that shout at you from your television set.

Other agencies are less familiar. You may never have heard of the Bureau of Land Management, but if you go into the oil and gas industry, you will learn that this powerful agency has more control over your land than you do. If you develop real estate in Palos Hills, Illinois, you will tremble every time the Appearance Commission of the City of Palos Hills speaks, since you cannot construct a new building without its approval. If your software corporation wants to hire an Argentine expert on databases, you will get to know the complex workings of the Immigration and Naturalization Service: no one lawfully enters this country without its nod of approval.

BACKGROUND

By the 1880s, the amazing iron horse criss-crossed America. But this technological miracle became an economic headache. Congress worried that the railroads' economic muscle enabled a few powerful corporations to reap unfair profits. The railroad industry needed closer regulation. Who would do it? Courts decide individual cases, they do not regulate industries. Congress itself passes statutes, but it has no personnel to oversee the day-to-day working of a huge industry. For example, Congress lacks the expertise to establish rates for freight passing from Kansas City to Chicago, and it has no personnel to enforce rates once they are set.

A new entity was needed. Congress passed the Interstate Commerce Act, creating the Interstate Commerce Commission (ICC), the first administrative agency. The ICC began regulating freight and passenger transportation over the growing rail system and continued to do so for over 100 years. Congress gave the ICC power to regulate rates and investigate harmful practices, to hold hearings, issue orders, and punish railroads that did not comply.

The ICC was able to hire and develop a staff that was expert in the issues that Congress wanted controlled. The agency had enough flexibility to deal with the problems in a variety of ways: by regulating, investigating, and punishing. And that is what has made administrative agencies an attractive solution for Congress: one entity, focusing on one industry, can combine expertise and flexibility. However, the ICC also developed great power, which voters could not reach, and thereby started the great and lasting conflict over the role of agencies.

During the Great Depression of the 1930s, the Roosevelt administration and Congress created dozens of new agencies. Many were based on social demands, such as the need of the elderly population for a secure income. Political and social conditions dominated again in the 1960s, as Congress created agencies, such as the Equal Employment Opportunity Commission, to combat discrimination.

Then during the 1980s the Reagan administration made an effort to decrease the number and strength of the agencies. For several years some agencies declined in influence, though others did not. As we begin a new century, there is still controversy about how much power agencies should have, but there is no doubt that administrative agencies are a permanent part of our society.

CLASSIFICATION OF AGENCIES

Agencies exist at the federal, state, and local level. We will focus on federal agencies because they have national impact and great power. Most of the principles discussed apply to state and local agencies as well. Virtually any business or profession you choose to work in will be regulated by at least one administrative agency, and it may be regulated by several.

Executive-Independent

Some federal agencies are part of the executive branch while others are independent agencies. This is a major distinction. The president has much greater control of executive agencies for the simple reason that he can fire the agency head at any time. An executive agency will seldom diverge far from the president's preferred policies. Some familiar executive agencies are the Internal Revenue Service (part of the Treasury Department); the Federal Bureau of Investigation (Department of Justice); the Food and Drug Administration (Department of Health and Human Services); and the Nuclear Regulatory Commission (Department of Energy).

The president has no such removal power over independent agencies. The Federal Communications Commission (FCC) is an independent agency. For many corporations involved in broadcasting, the FCC has more day-to-day influence on their business than Congress, the courts, and the president combined. Other powerful independent agencies are the Federal Trade Commission, the Securities and Exchange Commission, the National Labor Relations Board, and the Environmental Protection Agency.

Enabling Legislation

Congress creates a federal agency by passing **enabling legislation**. The Interstate Commerce Act was the enabling legislation that established the ICC. Typically, the enabling legislation describes the problems that Congress believes need regulation, establishes an agency to do it, and defines the agency's powers.

Critics argue that Congress is delegating to another body powers that only the legislature or courts are supposed to exercise. This puts administrative agencies above the voters. But legal attacks on administrative agencies invariably fail. Courts acknowledge that agencies have become an integral part of a complex economy. As long as there are some limits on an agency's discretion, a court will uphold its powers.

The Administrative Procedure Act

This Act is a major limitation on how agencies do their work. Congress passed the Administrative Procedure Act (APA) in 1946 in an effort to bring uniformity and control to the many federal agencies. The APA regulates how federal agencies make rules, conduct investigations, hold meetings and hearings, reach decisions, and obtain and release information. How much power should agencies have? How much control should we impose on them? These are two of the major questions that businesses and courts face as we enter a new century.

POWER OF AGENCIES

Administrative agencies use three kinds of power to do the work assigned to them: they make rules, they investigate, and they adjudicate.

Rulemaking

One of the most important functions of an administrative agency is to make rules. In doing this, the agency attempts, prospectively, to establish fair and uniform behavior for all businesses in the affected area. **To create a new rule is to promulgate it.** Agencies promulgate two types of rules: legislative and interpretive.

Legislative Rules. These are the most important agency rules, and they are much like statutes. Here, an agency is changing the law by requiring businesses or private citizens to act in a certain way. For example, the Federal Communications Commission promulgated a rule requiring all cable television systems with more than 3,500 subscribers to develop the capacity to carry at least 20 channels and to make some of those channels available to local community stations. This legislative rule has a heavy financial impact on many cable systems. As far as a cable company is concerned, it is more important than most statutes passed by Congress. Legislative rules have the full effect of a statute.

An agency's interpretation of an environmental statute may be obscure, but the consequences affect us all.

Interpretive Rules. These rules do not change the law. They are the agency's interpretation of what the law already requires. But they can still affect all of us.

In 1977, Congress passed the Clean Air Act in an attempt to reduce pollution from factories. The Act required the Environmental Protection Agency (EPA) to impose emission standards on certain "stationary sources" of pollution. The definition of "stationary source" became critical. This is about as technical and unsexy as law can get, yet the outcome is critical: it will determine what air goes into our lungs every time we breathe. Environmentalists wanted the term defined to include every smokestack in a factory so that the EPA could regulate each one. The EPA, however, developed the "bubble concept," ruling that "stationary source" meant an entire factory, but not the individual smokestacks. As a result, polluters could shift emission among smokestacks in a single factory to avoid EPA regulation. Environmentalists howled that this gutted the purpose of the statute, but to no avail. The agency had spoken, merely by interpreting a statute.[14]

How Rules Are Made. Corporations fight many a court battle over whether an agency has the right to issue a particular rule and whether it was promulgated properly. The critical issue is this: How much participation is the public entitled to before an agency issues a rule? There are two basic methods of rulemaking.[15]

Informal Rulemaking. On many issues, agencies may use a simple "notice and comment" method of rulemaking. The agency must publish a proposed rule in advance and permit the public a comment period. During this period, the public may submit any objections and arguments, with supporting data. The agency will make its decision and publish the final rule.

For example, the Department of Transportation may use the informal rulemaking procedure to require safety features for all new automobiles. The agency must listen to objections from interested parties, notably car manufacturers, and it must give a written response to the objections. The agency is required to have rational reasons for the final choices it makes. However, it is not obligated to satisfy all parties or do their bidding.

Formal Rulemaking. In the enabling legislation, Congress may require that an agency hold a hearing before promulgating rules. Congress does this to make the agency more accountable to the public. After the agency publishes its proposed rule, it must hold a public hearing. Opponents of the rule, typically affected businesses, may cross-examine the agency experts about the need for the rule and may

[14] An agency's interpretation can be challenged in court, and this one was.

[15] Certain rules may be made with no public participation at all. For example, an agency's internal business affairs and procedures can be regulated without public comment, as can its general policy statements. None of these directly affect the public, and the public has no right to participate.

testify against it. When the agency makes its final decision about the rule, it must prepare a formal, written response to everything that occurred at the hearing.

When used responsibly, these hearings give the public access to the agency and can help formulate sound policy. When used irresponsibly, hearings can be manipulated to stymie needed regulation. The most famous example concerns peanut butter. The Food and Drug Administration (FDA) began investigating peanut butter content in 1958. It found, for example, that Jif peanut butter, made by Procter & Gamble, had only 75 percent peanuts and 20 percent of a Crisco-type of base. P&G fought the investigation, and any changes, for years. Finally, in 1965, the FDA proposed a minimum of 90 percent peanuts in peanut butter; P&G wanted 87 percent. The FDA wanted no more than 3 percent hydrogenated vegetable oil; P&G wanted no limit.

The hearings dragged on for months. One day, the P&G lawyer objected to the hearing going forward because he needed to vote that day. Another time, when an FDA official testified that consumer letters indicated the public wanted to know what was really in peanut butter, the P&G attorney demanded that the official bring in and identify the letters—all 20,000 of them. Finally, in 1968, a decade after beginning its investigation, the FDA promulgated final rules requiring 90 percent peanuts but eliminating the 3 percent cap on vegetable oil.[16]

Hybrid Rulemaking. In an effort to avoid the agency paralysis made famous in the peanut butter case, some agencies use hybrid rulemaking, following the informal model but adding a few elements of the formal. The agency may give notice and a comment period, deny the right to a full hearing, but allow limited cross-examination on one or two key issues.

Investigation

Agencies do an infinite variety of work, but they all need broad factual knowledge of the field they govern. Some companies cooperate with an agency, furnishing information and even voluntarily accepting agency recommendations. For example, the United States Product Safety Commission investigates hundreds of consumer products every year and frequently urges companies to recall goods that the agency considers defective. Many firms comply. (For an up-to-the-minute report on dangerous products and company compliance, proceed carefully to **http://www.cpsc.gov/index.html**.)

Other companies, however, jealously guard information, often because corporate officers believe that disclosure would lead to adverse rules. To obtain this information, agencies use *subpoenas* and *searches.*

Subpoenas. A **subpoena** is an order to appear at a particular time and place to provide evidence. A **subpoena *duces tecum*** requires the person to appear and bring specified documents. Businesses and other organizations intensely dislike subpoenas and resent government agents plowing through records and questioning employees. What are the limits on an agency's investigation? The information sought:

- Must be *relevant* to a lawful agency investigation. The FCC is clearly empowered to investigate the safety of broadcasting towers, and any documents about tower construction are obviously relevant. Documents about employee racial statistics might indicate discrimination, but the FCC lacks jurisdiction on that issue and thus may not obtain such documents.
- Must not be *unreasonably burdensome.* A court will compare the agency's need for the information with the intrusion on the corporation.

---

[16] For an excellent account of this high-fat hearing, see Mark J. Green, *The Other Government* (New York: W. W. Norton & Co., 1978), pp. 136–150.

- Must not be *privileged*. The Fifth Amendment privilege against self-incrimination means that a corporate officer accused of criminal securities violations may not be compelled to testify about his behavior.

In the following case, a federal agency investigating a married couple demands thousands of documents from their children and over a *million* documents from hospitals where the couple work. Is the agency entitled to the information?

FEDERAL DEPOSIT INSURANCE CORPORATION v. GARNER
126 F.3d 1138, 1997 U.S. App. LEXIS 25268
Ninth Circuit Court of Appeals, 1997

Facts: The American Commerce National Bank was dangerously close to default, prompting the Federal Deposit Insurance Corporation to investigate. The FDIC concluded that bank directors might have made illegal loans to friends and relatives, causing millions of dollars in losses. The FDIC issued broad subpoenas *duces tecum* to Gerald Garner and his wife, Joan, both of whom were bank directors, seeking personal financial information. The FDIC also subpoenaed the Garners' children, whose trust funds had allegedly benefited from illegal bank practices, and several hospitals where the Garners were corporate officers. To support its subpoenas, the FDIC submitted a declaration from its senior attorney, Playdon, explaining the evidence accumulated thus far. The Playdon Declaration stated that the subpoenas were intended to discover whether the Garners or others had made illegal loans or fraudulent transfers, and whether the Garners had sufficient assets to make litigation cost effective.

The Garners and the hospitals refused to furnish much of the information requested, claiming that the subpoenas were overbroad, and that they invaded the privacy of family members who were not targets of the investigation. The FDIC petitioned the United States District Court, which issued an order enforcing the subpoenas. The Garners appealed.

Issue: Were the FDIC's subpoenas valid?

Excerpts from Judge Brunetti's Decision: Appellants contend that the document requests are overbroad and unduly burdensome. They complain that the subpoenas require the individuals to provide thousands of financial documents and demand over one million documents from Coast Plaza Doctors Hospital. We have held that once an agency establishes that it has properly issued a subpoena, it "should be enforced unless the party being investigated proves the inquiry is unreasonable because it is overbroad or unduly burdensome." Appellants also cite to Federal Rule of Civil Procedure 45(c)(1), which prohibits a party from "imposing undue burden or expense on a person subject" to a subpoena.

Appellants fail to demonstrate that the subpoenas are overbroad or unduly burdensome. They cite to numerous cases which reject burdensome subpoenas. An administrative subpoena may not be so broad so as to be in the nature of a "fishing expedition." What Appellants fail to do is to enunciate how these subpoenas constitute a "fishing expedition," in light of the FDIC's specific and serious allegations of misconduct. Although the FDIC's requests are extensive, we cannot hold that the subpoenas are overbroad or unduly burdensome absent a showing by Appellants of additional support for this position.

We affirm the district court's decision to enforce the subpoenas duces tecum against all parties.

Search and Seizure. At times an agency will want to conduct a surprise **search** of an enterprise and **seize** any evidence of wrongdoing. May an agency do that? Yes, although there are limitations. When a particular industry is *comprehensively* *regulated*, courts will assume that companies know they are subject to periodic, unannounced inspections. In those industries, an administrative agency may conduct a search without a warrant and seize evidence of violations. For example, the mining industry is minutely regulated, with strict rules covering equipment, mining depths, transport and safety structures, air quality, and countless other things. Mining executives know that they are closely watched, and for good reason: mine safety is a matter of life and death, and surprise is an essential element of effective inspection. Accordingly, the Bureau of Mines may make unannounced, warrantless searches to ensure safety.[17] Today, it is a rare case that finds a warrantless search by an administrative agency to have been illegal.

Adjudication

To **adjudicate** a case is to hold a hearing about an issue and then decide it. Agencies adjudicate countless cases. The FCC adjudicates which applicant for a new television license is best qualified. The Occupational Safety and Health Administration (OSHA) holds adversarial hearings to determine whether a manufacturing plant is dangerous.

Most adjudications begin with a hearing before an **administrative law judge** (ALJ). There is no jury. An ALJ is an employee of the agency but is expected to be impartial in her rulings. All parties are represented by counsel. The rules of evidence are informal, and an ALJ may receive any testimony or documents that will help resolve the dispute.

After all evidence is taken, the ALJ makes a decision. The losing party has a right to appeal to an appellate board within the agency. The appellate board has the power to make a ***de novo* decision,** meaning it may ignore the ALJ's decision. A party unhappy with that decision may appeal to federal court.

LIMITS ON AGENCY POWER

There are four primary methods of reining in these powerful creatures: statutory, political, judicial, and informational.

STATUTORY CONTROL

As discussed, the enabling legislation of an agency provides some limits. It may require that the agency use formal rulemaking or investigate only certain issues. The APA imposes additional controls by requiring basic fairness in areas not regulated by the enabling legislation.

POLITICAL CONTROL

The president's influence is greatest with executive agencies. Congress, though, controls the purse. No agency, executive or independent, can spend money it does not have. An agency that angers Congress risks having a particular program defunded or its entire budget cut. Further, Congress may decide to defund an agency as a cost-cutting measure. In its effort to balance the budget, Congress abolished the Interstate Commerce Commission, transferring its functions to the Transportation Department.

---

[17] *Donovan v. Dewey*, 452 U.S. 594, 101 S. Ct. 2534, 1980 U.S. LEXIS 58 (1981).

Congress has additional control because it must approve presidential nominees to head agencies. Before approving a nominee, Congress will attempt to determine her intentions. And, finally, Congress may amend an agency's enabling legislation, limiting its power.

JUDICIAL REVIEW

An individual or corporation directly harmed by an administrative rule, investigation, or adjudication may generally have that action reviewed in federal court.[18] The party seeking review, for example, a corporation, must have suffered direct harm; the courts will not listen to theoretical complaints about an agency action.[19] And that party must first have taken all possible appeals within the agency itself.[20]

Standard on Review. Suppose OSHA promulgates a new rule limiting the noise level within steel mills. Certain mill operators are furious because they will have to retool their mills in order to comply. After exhausting their administrative appeals, they file suit seeking to force OSHA to withdraw the new rule. How does a court decide the case? Or, in legal terms, what standard does a court use in reviewing the case? Does it simply substitute its own opinion for that of the agency? No, it does not. The standard a court uses must take into account:

- *Facts.* Courts generally defer to an agency's factfinding. If OSHA finds that human hearing starts to suffer when decibels reach a particular level, a court will probably accept that as final. The agency is presumed to have expertise on such subjects. As long as there is *substantial evidence* to support the fact decision, it will be respected.
- *Law.* Courts often—but not always—defer to an agency's interpretation of the law, as the following case illustrates.

HOLLY FARMS CORP. v. NATIONAL LABOR RELATIONS BOARD
517 U.S. 392, 116 S. Ct. 1396, 1996 U.S. LEXIS 2801
United States Supreme Court, 1996

Facts: Holly Farms was a vertically integrated poultry producer, meaning that the company performed many different operations to produce commercial chicken. The company hatched broiler chicks and delivered them to independent farms, where they were raised. When the broilers were seven weeks old, the company sent its live-haul crews to reclaim the birds. The crew included chicken catchers, forklift operators, and "live-haul" drivers. At the farms, the chicken catchers entered the coops, manually captured the broilers, and loaded them into cages. The forklift operator lifted the caged chickens onto the bed of the truck, and the live-haul driver returned the truck, with the loaded cases and the crew, to Holly Farms' processing plant. After that, the chickens . . . well, never mind.

A group of Holly Farms workers organized a union, and the National Labor Relations Board permitted the union to include the company's "live-haul"

---

18 In two narrow groups of cases, a court may *not* review an agency action. In a few cases, courts hold that a decision is "committed to agency discretion," a formal way of saying that courts will keep hands off. This happens only with politically sensitive issues, such as international air routes. In some cases, the enabling legislation makes it absolutely clear that Congress wanted no court to review certain decisions. Courts will honor that.

19 The law describes this requirement by saying that a party must have *standing* to bring a case. A college student who has a theoretical belief that the EPA should not interfere with the timber industry has no standing to challenge an EPA rule that prohibits logging in a national forest. A lumber company that was ready to log that area has suffered a direct economic injury: it has standing to sue.

20 This is the doctrine of **exhaustion of remedies**. A lumber company may not go into court the day after the EPA publishes a proposed ban on logging. It must first *exhaust* its administrative remedies by participating in the administrative hearing and then pursuing appeals within the agency before venturing into court.

employees. Holly Farms objected to the new union, claiming that these laborers were actually agricultural workers, who by law were outside the Board's authority.

Labor law defines agriculture this way:

> Agriculture includes . . . the raising of livestock, bees, fur-bearing animals, or poultry, and any practices performed by a farmer or on a farm as an incident to or in conjunction with such farming operations, including preparation for market, delivery to storage or to market or to carriers for transportation to market.

Several United States Courts of Appeals had split over the issue of whether the NLRB's jurisdiction reached live-haul workers, and the dispute reached the United States Supreme Court.

Issue: Did the NLRB accurately interpret labor law by ruling that live-haul workers were employees rather than agricultural workers?

Excerpts from Justice Ginsburg's Decision: Holly Farms argues that under the plain language of the statute, the catching and loading of broilers qualifies as work performed "on a farm as an incident to" the raising of poultry. The corporation emphasizes that [the definition] enumerates "preparation for market" and "delivery to storage or to market" among activities that count as "agriculture." The live-haul employees' work, Holly Farms concludes, enjoys no NLRA protection.

We find Holly Farms' position to be a plausible, but not an inevitable, construction of [this definition]. Hence, we turn to the Board's position, examining only its reasonableness as an interpretation of the governing legislation.

While agreeing that the chicken catchers and forklift operators work "on a farm," the Board contends that their catch and cage work is not incidental to farming operations. Rather, the work is tied to Holly Farms' slaughtering and processing operations, activities that do not constitute "farming" under the statute. We conclude, as we next explain, that the Board's position is based on a reasonable interpretation of the statute, is consistent with the Board's prior holdings, and is supported by the Secretary of Labor's construction of [the definition].

We find the Board's answer reasonable. Once the broilers have grown on the farm for seven weeks, the growers' contractual obligation to raise the birds ends, and the work of the live-haul crew begins. The record reflects minimal overlap between the work of the live-haul crew and the independent growers' raising activities. The growers do not assist the live-haul crews in catching or loading the chickens; their only responsibilities are to move certain equipment from the chicken coops prior to the crews' arrival, and to be present when the crews are on the farms.

In sum, we find persuasive the Board's conclusion that the collection of broilers for slaughter was an activity serving Holly Farms' processing operations, and not Holly Farms' own or the independent growers' farming operations. Again, we stress that the reviewing court's function is limited. For the Board to prevail, it need not show that its construction is the best way to read the statute; rather, courts must respect the Board's judgment so long as its reading is a reasonable one. Regardless of how we might have resolved the question as an initial matter, the Board's decision here reflects a reasonable interpretation of the law and, therefore, merits our approbation. The judgment of the Court of Appeals is accordingly

Affirmed.

Excerpts from Justice O'Connor's Dissenting Opinion: As we said in *Chevron U.S.A. Inc. v. Natural Resources Defense Council, Inc.* [a 1984 case], "First, always, is the question whether Congress has directly spoken to the precise question at issue. If the intent of Congress is clear, that is the end of the matter; for the court, as well as the agency, must give effect to the unambiguously expressed intent of Congress." None of our precedents sanction blind adherence to the Board's position when it is directly contrary to the plain language of the relevant statute.

[Labor law] defines agriculture as "farming in all its branches," including "the raising of . . . poultry," as well as "any practices . . . performed by a farmer or on a farm as an incident to or in conjunction with such farming operations." The coverage intended by Congress is best determined by consulting the language of the statute at issue. Because the relevant portions are perfectly plain and directly speak to the precise question at issue, I would hold that the chicken catchers and forklift operators are agricultural laborers and that the Board's contrary conclusion does not deserve deference.

INFORMATIONAL CONTROL AND THE PUBLIC

We started this section describing the pervasiveness of administrative agencies. We should end it by noting one way in which all of us have some direct control over these ubiquitous authorities: information.

> A popular government, without popular information, or the means of acquiring it, is but a Prologue to a Farce or a Tragedy—or perhaps both. Knowledge will forever govern ignorance, and a people who mean to be their own Governors must arm themselves with the power which knowledge gives.
>
> *James Madison*, President, 1809–1817

Two federal statutes arm us with the power of knowledge.

Freedom of Information Act

Congress passed this landmark statute (known as "FOIA") in 1966. It is designed to give all of us, citizens, businesses, and organizations alike, access to the information that federal agencies are using. The idea is to avoid government by secrecy.

Any citizen or executive may make a "FOIA request" to any federal government agency. It is simply a written request that the agency furnish whatever information it has on the subject specified. Two types of data are available under FOIA. Anyone is entitled to information about how the agency operates, how it spends its money, and what statistics and other information it has collected on a given subject. People routinely obtain records about agency policies, environmental hazards, consumer product safety, taxes and spending, purchasing decisions, and agency forays into foreign affairs. A corporation that believes that OSHA is making more inspections of its textile mills than it makes of the competition could demand all relevant information, including OSHA's documents on the mill itself, comparative statistics on different inspections, OSHA's policies on choosing inspection sites, and so forth.

Second, all citizens are entitled to any records the government has *about them*. You are entitled to information that the Internal Revenue Service, or the Federal Bureau of Investigation, has collected about you.

FOIA does not apply to Congress, the federal courts, or the executive staff at the White House. Note also that, since FOIA applies to federal government agencies, you may not use it to obtain information from state or local governments or private businesses. For a step-by-step guide explaining how to make a FOIA request, see **http://www.aclu.org/library/foia.html**. For dramatic proof of FOIA's power, see **http://www.gwu.edu/~nsarchiv**, a Web site devoted to government documents that have been declassified as a result of FOIA requests.

Exemptions. An agency officially has 10 days to respond to the request. In reality, most agencies are unable to meet the deadline but are obligated to make good faith efforts. FOIA exempts altogether nine categories from disclosure. The most important exemptions permit an agency to keep confidential information that relates to national security, criminal investigations, internal agency matters such as personnel or policy discussions, trade secrets or financial institutions, or an individual's private life.

Privacy Act

This 1974 statute prohibits federal agencies from giving information about an individual to other agencies or organizations without written consent. There are exceptions, but overall this Act has reduced the government's exchange of information about us "behind our back."

CHAPTER CONCLUSION

"W**hy can't they just fix the law?"** They can, and sometimes they do—but it is a difficult and complex task. "They" includes a great many people and forces, from common law courts to members of Congress to campaign donors to administrative agencies. The courts have made the bystander rule slightly more humane, but it has been a long and bumpy road. Congress managed to restore the legal interpretation of its own 1964 Civil Rights Act, but it took months of debate and compromising. The FDA squeezed more peanuts into a jar of Jif, but it took nearly a decade to get the lid on.

A study of law is certain to create some frustrations. This chapter cannot prevent them all. However, an understanding of how law is made is the first step toward controlling that law.

CHAPTER REVIEW

1. *Stare decisis* means "let the decision stand," and indicates that once a court has decided a particular issue, it will generally apply the same rule in future cases.
2. The common law evolves in awkward fits and starts because courts attempt to achieve two contradictory purposes: predictability and flexibility.
3. The common law bystander rule holds that, generally, no one has a duty to assist someone in peril unless the bystander himself created the danger. Courts have carved some exceptions during the last 100 years, but the basic rule still stands.
4. Bills originate in congressional committees and go from there to the full House of Representatives or Senate. If both houses pass the bill, the legislation normally must go to a Conference Committee to resolve differences between the two versions. The compromise version then goes from the Conference Committee back to both houses, and if passed by both, to the president. If the president signs the bill, it becomes a statute; if he vetoes it, Congress can pass it over his veto with a two-thirds majority in each house.

5. Courts interpret a statute by using the plain meaning rule; then, if necessary, legislative history and intent; and finally, if necessary, public policy.
6. Campaign contributions and spending are largely uncontrolled.
7. Congress creates federal administrative agencies with enabling legislation. The Administrative Procedure Act controls how agencies do their work.
8. Agencies may promulgate legislative rules, which generally have the effect of statutes, or interpretive rules, which merely interpret existing statutes.
9. Agencies have broad investigatory powers and may use subpoenas and, in some cases, warrantless searches to obtain information.
10. Agencies adjudicate cases, meaning that they hold hearings and decide issues. Adjudication generally begins with a hearing before an administrative law judge and may involve an appeal to the full agency or ultimately to federal court.
11. The four most important limitations on the power of federal agencies are statutory control in the enabling legislation and the APA; political control by Congress and the president; judicial review; and the informational control created by the Freedom of Information Act and the Privacy Act.

PRACTICE TEST

1. **RIGHT & WRONG** Suppose you were on a state supreme court and faced with a restaurant-choking case. Should you require restaurant employees to know and employ the Heimlich maneuver to assist a choking victim? If they do a bad job, they could cause additional injury. Should you permit them to do nothing at all? Is there a compromise position? What social policies are most important?

2. **YOU BE THE JUDGE WRITING PROBLEM** An off-duty, out-of-uniform police officer and his son purchased some food from a 7-11 store and were still in the parking lot when a carload of teenagers became rowdy. The officer went to speak to them and the teenagers assaulted him. The officer shouted to his son to get the 7-11 clerk to call for help. The son entered the store, told the clerk that a police officer needed help, and told the clerk to call the police. He returned 30 seconds later and repeated the request, urging the clerk to say it was a Code 13. The son claimed that the clerk laughed at him and refused to do it. The policeman sued the store. **Argument for the Store:** We sympathize with the policeman and his family, but the store has no liability. A bystander is not obligated to come to the aid of anyone in distress unless the bystander created the peril, and obviously the store did not do so. The policeman should prosecute *and* sue those who attacked him. **Argument for the Policeman:** We agree that in general a bystander has no obligation to come to the aid of one in distress. However, when a business that is open to the public receives an urgent request to call the police, the business should either make the call or permit someone else to do it.

3. You sign a two-year lease with a landlord for an apartment. The rent will be $1,000 per month. A clause in the lease requires payment on the first of every month. The clause states that the landlord has the right to evict you if you are even one day late with the payment. You forget to pay on time and deliver your check to the landlord on the third day of the month. He starts an eviction case against you. Who should win? If we enforce the contract, what social result does that have? If we ignore the clause, what effect does that have on contract law?

4. Federal antitrust statutes are complex, but the basic goal is straightforward: to prevent a major industry from being so dominated by a small group of corporations that they destroy competition and injure consumers. Does major league baseball violate the antitrust laws? Many observers say that it does. A small group of owners not only dominate the industry, but actually *own* it, controlling the entry of new owners into the game. This issue went to the United States Supreme Court in 1922. Justice Holmes ruled, perhaps

surprisingly, that baseball is exempt from the antitrust laws, holding that baseball is not "trade or commerce." Suppose that a congressman dislikes this ruling and dislikes the current condition of baseball. What could he do?

5. Until recently, every state had a statute outlawing the burning of American flags. But in *Texas v. Johnson*,[21] the Supreme Court declared such statutes unconstitutional, saying that flag burning is symbolic speech, protected by the First Amendment. Does Congress have the power to overrule the Court's ruling?

6. Whitfield, who was black, worked for Ohio Edison. Edison fired him, but then later offered to rehire him. At about that time, another employee, representing Whitfield, argued that Edison's original termination of Whitfield had been race discrimination. Edison rescinded its offer to rehire Whitfield. Whitfield sued Edison, claiming that the rescission of the offer to rehire was in retaliation for the other employee's opposition to discrimination. Edison defended by saying that Title VII of the 1964 Civil Rights Act did not protect in such cases. Title VII prohibits, among other things, an employer from retaliating against *an employee who has opposed* illegal discrimination. But it does not explicitly prohibit an employer from retaliating against one employee based on *another employee's* opposition to discrimination. Edison argued that the statute did not protect Whitfield. Outcome?

Background for Questions 7 through 9. The following three questions begin with a deadly explosion. In 1988, terrorists bombed Pan Am flight 103 over Lockerbie, Scotland, killing all passengers on board. Congress sought to remedy security shortcomings by passing the Aviation Security Improvement Act of 1990, which, among other things, ordered the Federal Aviation Authority (FAA) to prescribe minimum training requirements and minimum staffing levels for airport security. The FAA promulgated rules according to the informal rulemaking process. However, the FAA refused to disclose certain rules, concerning training at specific airports. *Public Citizen, Inc. v. FAA*.[22]

7. Explain what "promulgated rules according to the informal rulemaking process" means.

8. A public interest group called Public Citizen, Inc., along with family members of those who had died at Lockerbie, wanted to know the details of airport security. What steps should they take to obtain the information? Are they entitled to obtain it?

9. The Aviation Security Improvement Act (ASIA) states that the FAA can refuse to divulge information about airport security. The FAA interprets this to mean that it can withhold the data in spite of FOIA. Public Citizen and the Lockerbie family members interpret FOIA as being the controlling statute, requiring disclosure. Is the FAA interpretation binding?

10. Hiller Systems, Inc. was performing a safety inspection on board the M/V *Cape Diamond*, an ocean-going vessel, when an accident occurred involving the fire extinguishing equipment. Two men were killed. The Occupational Safety and Health Administration (OSHA), a federal agency, attempted to investigate, but Hiller refused to permit any of its employees to speak to OSHA investigators. What could OSHA do to pursue the investigation? What limits were there on what OSHA could do?

INTERNET RESEARCH PROBLEM

Research some pending legislation in Congress. Go to http://www.senate.gov, and click on *bills*. Choose some key words that interest you, and see what your government is doing. Read the summary of the bill, if one is provided, or go to the text of the bill, and scan the introduction. What do the sponsors of this bill hope to accomplish? Do you agree or disagree with their goals?

You can find further practice problems in the Online Quiz at http://beatty.westbuslaw.com or in the Study Guide that accompanies this text.

---

[21] 491 U.S. 397, 109 S. Ct. 2533, 1989 U.S. LEXIS 3115 (1989).

[22] 988 F.2d 186, 1993 U.S. App. LEXIS 6024 (D.C. Cir. 1993).

CHAPTER 4

CONSTITUTIONAL LAW

Suppose you want to dance naked in front of 75 strangers. Do you have the *right* to do it? May the police interrupt your show and insist that you don a few garments? You may consider these odd questions, as relatively few business law students contemplate a career as a nude dancer. Yet the answers to these questions will affect you every day of your life, even if you choose a more prosaic line such as investments or retailing (it is good to have a backup plan).

Consider a very different—yet related—question. A state government wants to reduce the consumption of alcohol by making it expensive. On the theory that competitive ads drive prices down and make drinking more affordable, the legislators pass a statute prohibiting liquor stores from publishing their prices. The new law might have the desired effect—but is it fair? May a state forbid any conduct that it regards as harmful to its citizens? What if the same state passes a law preventing new construction along the coastline? This measure will protect the environment, but in the process it may render some very expensive beachfront property worthless. Whose interest is more important, that of the public or the property owners? Finally, suppose the state chooses to give certain summer camps a tax break because all of their campers come from within the state. May the state do that?

These seemingly unrelated questions all involve the same critical issue: power. Does your state have the *power* to prohibit nude dancing? If so, does that mean it could outlaw a campaign poster on your front lawn? Prohibit political protest? Is the state entitled to abolish liquor ads, for a well-intended purpose? Outlaw beachfront development? May it give tax breaks to organizations that benefit in-state residents?

Questions about regulating nude dancing affect all of us because the answers reveal how much control the government may exercise. Constitutional law is a series of variations on one vital theme: government power.

GOVERNMENT POWER

ONE IN A MILLION

The Constitution of the United States is the greatest legal document ever written. No other written constitution has lasted so long, governed so many, or withstood such challenge. This amazing work was drafted in 1787, when two weeks were needed to make the horseback ride from Boston to Philadelphia, a pair of young cities in a weak and disorganized nation. Yet today, when that trip requires less than two hours by jet, the same Constitution successfully governs the most powerful country on earth. This longevity is a tribute to the wisdom and idealism of the Founding Fathers.

The Constitution is not perfect. The original document contained provisions that were racist.[1] Other sections were unclear, and some needed early amendment. Overall, however, the Constitution has worked astonishingly well and has become the model for many constitutions around the world.

The Constitution is short and relatively easy to read. This brevity is potent. The Founding Fathers, also called the Framers, wanted it to last for centuries, and they understood that would happen only if the document permitted interpretation and "fleshing out" by later generations. The Constitution's versatility is striking, as we can see from the fact that the document can be used to resolve the crazy quilt of questions posed above. The *First Amendment* governs the two issues of nude dancing and liquor advertising. The *Commerce Clause* will resolve whether a state may give tax breaks to summer camps that benefit local residents. Courts will use the *Takings Clause* to decide when a state's efforts to protect the environment have unfairly injured property owners.

When the House of Representatives debated whether to impeach President Clinton for perjury and obstruction of justice, some Republicans and Democrats alike predicted that hearings based on a tawdry sex scandal would undermine the very structure of the federal government. They underestimated the Constitution. A stormy, intensely political inquiry in the House gave way to a comparatively decorous trial in the Senate. The evidence shamed the president yet also secured his acquittal—precisely the result most citizens wanted. The Framers could

---

[1] Two provisions explicitly endorsed slavery, belying the proposition that all people are created equal. The "Three-Fifths Clause," in Article I, section 2, required that for purposes of taxation and representation, a slave must be counted as three-fifths of a person. Article I, section 9 ensured that southern states would be permitted to continue importing slaves into the country at least until 1808.

scarcely have envisioned a "special prosecutor" reporting graphic sexual evidence, or media that, with frenzied glee, broadcast to the entire world every salacious word of accusation and denial. Yet the document that the Founding Fathers created reaffirmed their genius: both sides got their day in "court," and a Republican-controlled Senate voted not to oust a Democratic president.

This chapter is organized around the issue of power. The first part provides an overview of the Constitution, discussing how it came to be and how it is organized. The second part describes the power given to the three branches of government. The third part is the flip side of power, explaining what individual rights the Constitution guarantees to citizens.

OVERVIEW

Thirteen American colonies gained independence from Great Britain in 1783. The new status was exhilarating. This was the first nation in modern history founded on the idea that the people could govern themselves, democratically. The idea was daring, brilliant, and fraught with difficulties. The states were governing themselves under the Articles of Confederation, but these Articles gave the central government no real power. The government could not tax any state or its citizens and had no way to raise money. A government without the ability to raise money does not govern, it panhandles. The national government also lacked the power to regulate commerce between the states or between foreign nations and any state. This was disastrous. States began to impose taxes on goods entering from other states. The young "nation" was a collection of poor relations, threatening to squabble themselves to death.

By 1787 the Articles were largely deemed a failure, and the states sent a group of 55 delegates to Philadelphia to amend them. These delegates—the Framers of our Constitution—were not a true cross section of the populace. There were no women or blacks, artisans or small farmers. Most were wealthy; all were powerful within their states.

Rather than amend the old document, the Framers set out to draft a new one, to create a government that had never existed before. It was hard going. What structure should the government have? How much power? Representatives like Alexander Hamilton urged a strong central government. They were the *federalists*. The new government must be able to tax and spend, regulate commerce, control the borders, and do all things that national governments routinely do. But Patrick Henry and other *anti-federalists* feared a powerful central government. They had fought a bitter war precisely to get rid of autocratic rulers; they had seen the evil that a distant government could inflict. The anti-federalists insisted that the states retain maximum authority, keeping political control closer to home.

Another critical question was how much power the *people* should have. Most of the aristocratic delegates had little love for the common people and feared that extending this idea of democracy too far would lead to mob rule. Anti-federalists again disagreed. The British had been thrown out, they insisted, to guarantee individual liberty and a chance to participate in the government. Power corrupted. It must be dispersed amongst the people to avoid its abuse.

How to settle these basic differences? By compromise, of course. **The Constitution is a series of compromises about power.** We will see many provisions granting power to one branch of the government while at the same time limiting the power given.

SEPARATION OF POWERS

One method of limiting power was to create a national government divided into three branches, each independent and equal. Each branch would act as a check on the power of the other two, avoiding the despotic rule that had come from London. Article I of the Constitution created a Congress, which was to have legislative power. Article II created the office of president, defining the scope of executive power. Article III established judicial power by creating the Supreme Court and permitting additional federal courts.

Consider how the three separate powers balance one another: Congress was given the power to pass statutes, a major grant of power. But the president was permitted to veto legislation, a nearly equal grant. Congress, in turn, had the right to override the veto, ensuring that the president would not become a dictator. The president was allowed to appoint federal judges and members of his cabinet, but only with a consenting vote from the Senate.

FEDERALISM

The national government was indeed to have considerable power, but it would still be *limited power*. Article I, section 8 enumerates those issues on which Congress may pass statutes. If an issue is not on the list, Congress has no power to legislate. Thus Congress may create and regulate a post office because postal service is on the list. But Congress may not pass statutes regulating child custody in a divorce: that issue is not on the list. Only the states may legislate child custody issues.

INDIVIDUAL RIGHTS

The original Constitution was silent about the rights of citizens. This alarmed many citizens, who feared that the new federal government would have unlimited power over their lives. So in 1791 the first 10 amendments, known as the Bill of Rights, were added to the Constitution, guaranteeing many liberties directly to individual citizens.

In the next two sections, we look in more detail at the two sides of the great series of compromises: power granted and rights protected.

POWER GRANTED

CONGRESSIONAL POWER

Article I of the Constitution creates the Congress with its two houses. Representation in the House of Representatives is proportionate with a state's population, but each state elects two senators. The article establishes who is qualified to serve in Congress, setting only three requirements: age, citizenship, and residence. This obscure provision controls a major contemporary debate.

Term Limits

Toward the end of the twentieth century, many states passed laws limiting the number of terms elected officials could serve, both in state governments and in Congress. Citizens who favored limiting federal terms believed that, over the years, their representatives became ideologically remote from them, members of a Washington power culture rather than servants of the people. We will never know the wisdom of this view because the United States Supreme Court nullified federal term limits. The Framers envisioned a uniform national legislature, ruled the Court, with the people free to choose any representatives who met the minimum qualifications specified in the Constitution. No state government had the power to rewrite those qualifications. The states could limit the years someone might serve in the *state* government, but any attempt to put such a limit on federal officeholders was null and void.[2]

Legislation

One of the most important functions that Article I gives Congress is the power to pass legislation. (For a description of how Congress goes about creating new law, see Chapter 3.) The president has the right to propose a new law and to veto a bill, but only Congress may *enact* one. When legislators have attempted to yield some of this power, they have failed. Congress passed the "line-item veto" bill, granting the president the right to eliminate sections of a spending law that he disliked. This permitted the president, for example, to sign a health care bill into law, providing funds for cancer research and medical training, while striking out money intended for new hospital construction. The goal—and the effect—was to reduce federal spending. The Supreme Court invalidated the law. To eliminate some sections of a bill, said the Court, was essentially to draft new legislation—a power that Article I gave only to Congress.[3]

Interstate Commerce

"The Congress shall have power to regulate commerce with foreign nations, and among the several states." This is the **Commerce Clause**, and it is one of the most important powers granted to Congress. With it, the Framers were accomplishing several things in response to the commercial chaos that existed under the Articles of Confederation:

1. *International Commerce—Exclusive Power.* As to international commerce, the Commerce Clause is clear: only the federal government may regulate it. The federal government must speak with one voice when regulating commercial relations with foreign governments.[4]

2. *Domestic Commerce—Concurrent Power.* As to domestic commerce, the clause gives *concurrent power*, meaning that both Congress and the states may regulate it. Congress is authorized to regulate trade between states; each state regulates business within its own borders. Conflicts are inevitable, and they are important to all of us: *how* business is regulated depends upon *who* does it.

   - **Positive Aspect: Congressional Power.** The Framers wanted to give power to Congress to bring coordination and fairness to trade between the states. This is the positive aspect of the Commerce Clause: **Congress is authorized to regulate interstate commerce.**

---

[2] *U.S. Term Limits, Inc. v. Thornton*, 514 U.S. 779, 115 S. Ct. 1842, 1995 U.S. LEXIS 3487 (1995).

[3] *Clinton v. City of New York*, 524 U.S. 417, 118 S. Ct. 2091, 1998 U.S. LEXIS 4215 (1998).

[4] *Michelin Tire Corp. v. Wages, Tax Commissioner*, 423 U.S. 276, 96 S. Ct. 535, 1976 U.S. LEXIS 120 (1976).

- **Negative or Dormant Aspect: A Limit on the States.** The Framers also wanted to stop the states from imposing the taxes and regulations that were wrecking the nation's domestic trade. This is the negative, or dormant, aspect of the Commerce Clause: **The power of the states to regulate interstate commerce is severely restricted.**

Substantial Effect Rule

An early test of the Commerce Clause's positive aspect came in the depression years of the 1930s, in *Wickard v. Filburn*.[5] The price of wheat and other grains had fluctuated wildly, severely harming farmers and the national food market. Congress sought to stabilize prices by limiting the bushels per acre that a farmer could grow. Filburn grew more wheat than federal law allowed and was fined. In defense, he claimed that Congress had no right to regulate him. None of his wheat went into interstate commerce. He sold some locally and used the rest on his own farm as food for livestock and as seed. The Commerce Clause, Filburn claimed, gave Congress no authority to limit what he could do.

The Supreme Court disagreed and held that **Congress may regulate any activity that has a substantial economic effect on interstate commerce.** Filburn's wheat affected interstate commerce because the more he grew for use on his own farm, the less he would need to buy in the open market of interstate commerce. Congress could regulate his farm. Since this ruling, most federal statutes based on the Commerce Clause have been upheld. Congress has used the Commerce Clause to regulate such diverse issues as the working conditions in a factory, discrimination in a motel, and the environmental aspects of coal mining.[6] Each of these has substantial effect on interstate commerce.

In *United States v. Lopez*,[7] however, the Supreme Court ruled that Congress had exceeded its power under the Commerce Clause. Congress had passed a criminal statute called the "Gun-Free School Zones Act," which forbade any individual from possessing a firearm in a school zone. The goal of the statute was obvious: to keep schools safe. Lopez was convicted of violating the Act and appealed his conviction all the way to the high Court, claiming that Congress had no power to pass such a law. The government argued that the Commerce Clause gave it the power to pass the law, but the Supreme Court was unpersuaded.

> The possession of a gun in a local school zone is in no sense an economic activity that might, through repetition elsewhere, substantially affect any sort of interstate commerce. [Lopez] was a local student at a local school; there is no indication that he had recently moved in interstate commerce, and there is no requirement that his possession of the firearm have any concrete tie to interstate commerce. To uphold the Government's contentions here, we would have to pile inference upon inference in a manner that would bid fair to convert congressional authority under the Commerce Clause to a general police power of the sort retained by the States. [The statute was unconstitutional and void.]

Congress's power is great—but still limited.

---

[5] 317 U.S. 111, 63 S. Ct. 82, 1942 U.S. LEXIS 1046 (1942).

[6] *Maryland v. Wirts*, 392 U.S. 183, 88 S. Ct. 2017, 1968 U.S. LEXIS 2981 (1968); *Heart of Atlanta Motel v. United States*, 379 U.S. 241, 85 S. Ct. 348, 1964 U.S. LEXIS 2187 (1964); *Hodel v. Indiana*, 452 U.S. 314, 101 S. Ct. 2376, 1981 U.S. LEXIS 34 (1981).

[7] 514 U.S. 549, 115 S. Ct. 1624, 1995 U.S. LEXIS 3039 (1995).

State Legislative Power

The "dormant" or "negative" aspect of the Commerce Clause governs state efforts to regulate interstate commerce. **The dormant aspect holds that a state statute that discriminates against interstate commerce is invariably unconstitutional.** The following case illustrates the dormant aspect at work.

CAMPS NEWFOUND/ OWATONNA, INC. v. TOWN OF HARRISON, MAINE

520 U.S. 564, 117 S. Ct. 1590, 1997 U.S. LEXIS 3227
United States Supreme Court, 1997

Facts: Under a Maine statute, charitable institutions incorporated in that state were potentially exempt from real estate taxes. However, if the charitable organization operated principally for the benefit of nonresidents of the state, it only qualified for a limited tax break; further, if the organization charged more than $30 per week for its services, it had to pay full real estate taxes. Camps Newfound and Owatonna were Christian Science organizations that operated summer camps in Maine for children of that faith. The campers paid fees of $400 per week, and about 95 percent of them came from out of state. As a result, Maine law required Newfound and Owatonna to pay full real estate taxes.

The camps filed suit, claiming that Maine's tax laws violated the dormant aspect of the Commerce Clause by favoring intrastate institutions over those that engaged in interstate commerce. The Maine trial court agreed with the camps but the Maine Supreme Court reversed, noting that the statute treated all Maine nonprofit companies alike, and that all had an opportunity to qualify for a tax exemption by dispensing their charities in-state. The camps appealed to the United States Supreme Court.

Issue: Did the Maine statute violate the dormant aspect of the Commerce Clause?

Excerpts from Justice Stevens's Decision: During the first years of our history as an independent confederation, the National Government lacked the power to regulate commerce among the States. Because each State was free to adopt measures fostering its own local interests without regard to possible prejudice to nonresidents, what Justice Johnson [in an 1824 case] characterized as a "conflict of commercial regulations, destructive to the harmony of the States" ensued. In his view, this "was the immediate cause that led to the forming of a [constitutional] convention."

It is not necessary to look beyond the text of this statute to determine that it discriminates against interstate commerce. The Maine law expressly distinguishes between entities that serve a principally interstate clientele and those that primarily serve an intrastate market, singling out camps that serve mostly in-staters for beneficial tax treatment, and penalizing those camps that do a principally interstate business. As a practical matter, the statute encourages affected entities to limit their out-of-state clientele, and penalizes the principally nonresident customers of businesses catering to a primarily interstate market.

If such a policy were implemented by a statutory prohibition against providing camp services to nonresidents, the statute would almost certainly be invalid. We have consistently held that the Commerce Clause precludes a state from mandating that its residents be given a preferred right of access, over out-of-state consumers, to natural resources located within its borders or to the products derived therefrom.

Avoiding this sort of "economic Balkanization," and the retaliatory acts of other States that may follow, is one of the central purposes of our negative Commerce Clause jurisprudence. And, as we noted in [an earlier case:] "Economic protectionism is not limited to attempts to convey advantages on local merchants; it may include attempts to give local consumers an advantage over consumers in other States." By encouraging economic isolationism, prohibitions on out-of-state access to in-state resources serve the very evil that the dormant Commerce Clause was designed to prevent.

The judgment of the Maine Supreme Judicial Court is reversed.

Supremacy Clause

What happens when both the federal and state governments pass regulations that are permissible, but conflicting? For example, Congress passed the Federal Occupational Safety and Health Act (OSHA) establishing many job safety standards, including those for training workers who handle hazardous waste. Congress had the power to do so under the Commerce Clause. Later, Illinois passed its own hazardous waste statutes, seeking to protect both the general public and workers. The state statute did not violate the Commerce Clause because it imposed no restriction on interstate commerce.

Each statute specified worker training and employer licensing. But the requirements differed. Which statute did Illinois corporations have to obey? Article VI of the Constitution contains the answer. **The Supremacy Clause states that the Constitution, and federal statutes and treaties, shall be the supreme law of the land.**

- If there is a conflict between federal and state statutes, the federal law **preempts** the field, meaning it controls the issue. The state law is void.
- Even in cases where there is no conflict, if Congress demonstrates that it intends to exercise exclusive control over an issue, federal law preempts.

Thus state law controls only when there is no conflicting federal law *and* Congress has not intended to dominate the issue. In the Illinois case, the Supreme Court concluded that Congress intended to regulate the issue exclusively. Federal law therefore preempted the field, and local employers were obligated to obey only the federal regulations.

EXECUTIVE POWER

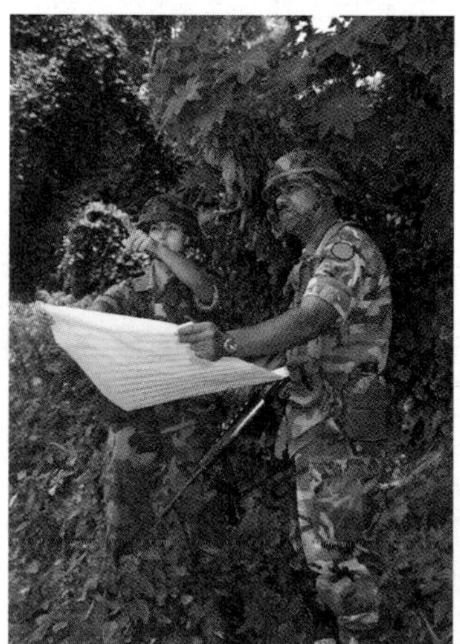

Several presidents have been criticized for using troops in combat without a declaration of war from Congress.

Article II of the Constitution defines the executive power. Once again the Constitution gives powers in general terms. The basic job of the president is to enforce the nation's laws. Three of his key powers concern appointment, legislation, and foreign policy.

Appointment

Administrative agencies play a powerful role in business regulation, and the president nominates the heads of most of them. These choices dramatically influence what issues the agencies choose to pursue and how aggressively they do it.[8]

Legislation

The president and his advisers propose bills to Congress. During the last 50 years, a vast number of newly proposed bills have come from the executive branch. Some argue that *too many* proposals come from the president and that Congress has become overly passive. The president, of course, also has the power to veto bills.[9]

---

[8] For a discussion of administrative agency power, see Chapter 3, on administrative law.

[9] For a discussion of the president's veto power and Congress's power to override a veto, see Chapter 3, on statutory law.

Foreign Policy

The president conducts the nation's foreign affairs, coordinating international efforts, negotiating treaties, and so forth. The president is also the commander in chief of the armed forces, meaning that he heads the military. But Article II does not give him the right to declare war—only the Senate may do that. Thus a continuing tension between president and Congress has resulted from the president's use of troops overseas *without* a formal declaration of war. Once again, the Founding Fathers' desire to create a balanced government leads to uncertain application of the law.

JUDICIAL POWER

Article III of the Constitution creates the Supreme Court and permits Congress to establish lower courts within the federal court system.[10] Federal courts have two key functions: adjudication and judicial review.

Adjudicating Cases

The federal court system hears criminal and civil cases. All prosecutions of federal crimes begin in United States District Court. That same court has limited jurisdiction to hear civil lawsuits, a subject discussed in Chapter 2, on dispute resolution.

Judicial Review

One of the greatest "constitutional" powers appears nowhere in the Constitution. In 1803 the Supreme Court decided *Marbury v. Madison.*[11] Congress had passed a relatively minor statute that gave certain powers to the Supreme Court, and Marbury wanted the Court to use those powers. The Court refused. In an opinion written by Chief Justice John Marshall, the Court held that the statute violated the Constitution because Article III of the Constitution did not grant the Court those powers. The details of the case were insignificant, but the ruling was profound: because the statute violated the Constitution, said the Court, it was void. **Judicial review refers to the power of federal courts to declare a statute or governmental action unconstitutional and void.**

This formidable grab of power has produced two centuries of controversy. The Court was declaring that it alone had the right to evaluate acts of the other two branches of government—the Congress and the executive—and to decide which were valid and which void. The Constitution nowhere grants this power. Undaunted, Marshall declared that "[I]t is emphatically the province and duty of the judicial department to say what the law is." In later cases, the Supreme Court expanded on the idea, holding that it could also nullify state statutes, rulings by state courts, and actions by federal and state officials. In this chapter we have already encountered examples of judicial review, for example, in the *Camps Newfound/Owatonna* case, in which the Supreme Court prohibited the state of Maine from giving preferential tax treatment to summer camps that benefited local residents, and in the *Lopez* case, where the justices declared that Congress lacked the power to pass local gun regulations.

Is judicial review good for the nation? Those who oppose it argue that federal court judges are all appointed, not elected, and that we should not permit judges to nullify a statute passed by elected officials because that diminishes the people's role in their government. Those who favor judicial review insist that there must be

---

[10] For a discussion of the federal court system, see Chapter 2, on dispute resolution.

[11] 5 U.S. (1 Cranch) 137 (1803).

one cohesive interpretation of the Constitution and the judicial branch is the logical one to provide it. This dispute about power simmers continuously beneath the surface and occasionally comes to the boil.

YOUNGSTOWN SHEET & TUBE CO. v. SAWYER
343 U.S. 579, 72 S. Ct. 863, 1952 U.S. LEXIS 2625
United States Supreme Court, 1952

Facts: During the Korean War, steel companies and the unions were unable to reach a contract. The union notified the companies that they would strike, beginning April 9, 1952. President Truman declared steel essential to the war effort and ordered his Secretary of Commerce, Sawyer, to take control of the steel mills and keep them running. Sawyer immediately ordered the presidents of the various companies to serve as operating managers for the United States.

On April 30, the federal district court issued an injunction to stop Sawyer from running the mills. That same day the United States Court of Appeals "stayed" the injunction, i.e., it permitted Sawyer to keep operating the mills. The Supreme Court quickly granted *certiorari*, heard argument May 12, and issued its decision June 2 (at least five years faster than most cases reach final decision).

Issue: **Did President Truman have the constitutional power to seize the steel mills?**

Excerpts from Justice Black's Decision: It is clear that if the President had authority to issue the order he did, it must be found in some provision of the Constitution. And it is not claimed that express constitutional language grants this power to the President. The contention is that presidential power should be implied from the aggregate of his powers under the Constitution [including the clauses stating that "the executive power shall be vested in a President," that "he shall take care that the laws be faithfully executed," and that he "shall be Commander in Chief."]

The order cannot properly be sustained as an exercise of the President's military power as Commander in Chief. We cannot with faithfulness to our constitutional system hold that the Commander in Chief has the ultimate power as such to take possession of private property in order to keep labor disputes from stopping production. This is a job for the Nation's lawmakers, not for its military authorities.

Nor can the seizure order be sustained because of the several constitutional provisions that grant executive power to the President. In the framework of our Constitution, the President's power to see that the laws are faithfully executed refutes the idea that he is to be a lawmaker. The Constitution limits his functions in the lawmaking process to the recommending of laws he thinks wise and the vetoing of laws he thinks bad. And the Constitution is neither silent nor equivocal about who shall make laws which the President is to execute. The first section of the first article says that "All legislative powers herein granted shall be vested in a Congress of the United States." The Constitution did not subject this lawmaking power of Congress to presidential or military supervision or control.

The Founders of this Nation entrusted the lawmaking power to the Congress alone in both good and bad times. It would do no good to recall the historical events, the fears of power and the hopes for freedom that lay behind their choice. Such a review would but confirm our holding that this seizure order cannot stand.

[The district court's injunction is *affirmed*.]

President Truman disliked anyone telling him what to do, and he disliked even more having the Supreme Court limit his powers during wartime. But he obeyed the Court's order.

Judicial Activism/Judicial Restraint. The power of judicial review is potentially dictatorial. The Supreme Court nullifies statutes passed by Congress (*Marbury v. Madison, United States v. Lopez*) and executive actions (*Youngstown Sheet & Tube*). May it strike down any law it dislikes? In theory, no. The Court should nullify only laws that violate the Constitution. But of course that is circular, since it is the Court that will tell us which laws are violative.

Judicial activism refers to a court's willingness, or even eagerness, to become involved in major issues and to decide cases on constitutional grounds. **Judicial restraint** is the opposite, an attitude that courts should leave lawmaking to legislators and nullify a law only when it unquestionably violates the Constitution.

From the 1950s through the 1970s, the Supreme Court took an active role, deciding many major social issues on constitutional grounds. The landmark 1954 decision in *Brown v. Board of Education*[12] ordered an end to racial segregation in public schools, not only changing the nation's educational systems but altering forever its expectations about race. The Court also struck down many state laws that denied minorities the right to vote. Beginning with *Miranda v. Arizona*,[13] the Court began a sweeping reappraisal of the police power of the state and the rights of criminal suspects during searches, interrogations, trials, and appeals. And in *Roe v. Wade*[14] the Supreme Court established certain rights to abortion, most of which remain after 30 years of continuous litigation and violence.

Beginning in the late 1970s, and lasting to the present, the Court has pulled back from its activism. Some justices believe that the Founding Fathers never intended the judicial branch to take so prominent a role in sculpting the nation's laws and its social vision. Simple numbers tell part of the story of a changing Court. Every year roughly 7,500 requests for review are made to the Court. In the early 1970s, the Supreme Court accepted almost 200 of these cases, but by the new century, it was taking fewer than 100. The Court's practice of judicial restraint means that major social issues will increasingly be left to state legislatures and Congress. The Court is diminishing its own power. Interestingly, while the Court has reduced its own volume of work, it has emphatically denied to other branches of government the power to interpret the Constitution. When Congress attempted to limit the ability of the states to restrict religious practices, the Court ruled that the legislators had no such power. Congress may *enforce* constitutional rights, but only the courts may *define* them.[15] For a look at the current justices, the full text of famous cases, and a calendar of pending cases, see http://supct.law.cornell.edu/supct/. You can tour the Court itself and even hear some of the justices read their opinions at http://court.it-services.nwu.edu/oyez/.

Exhibit 4.1 illustrates the balance among Congress, the president, and the Court.

PROTECTED RIGHTS

The amendments to the Constitution protect the people of this nation from the power of state and federal government. The First Amendment guarantees rights of free speech, free press, and religion; the Fourth Amendment protects against illegal searches; the Fifth Amendment ensures due process; the Sixth Amendment demands fair treatment for defendants in criminal prosecutions; and the

12 347 U.S. 483, 74 S. Ct. 686, 1954 U.S. LEXIS 2094 (1954).

13 384 U.S. 436, 86 S. Ct. 1602, 1966 U.S. LEXIS 2817 (1966).

14 410 U.S. 113, 93 S. Ct. 705, 1973 U.S. LEXIS 159 (1973).

15 *City of Boerne v. Flores*, 521 U.S. 507, 117 S. Ct. 2157, 1997 U.S. LEXIS 4035 (1997).

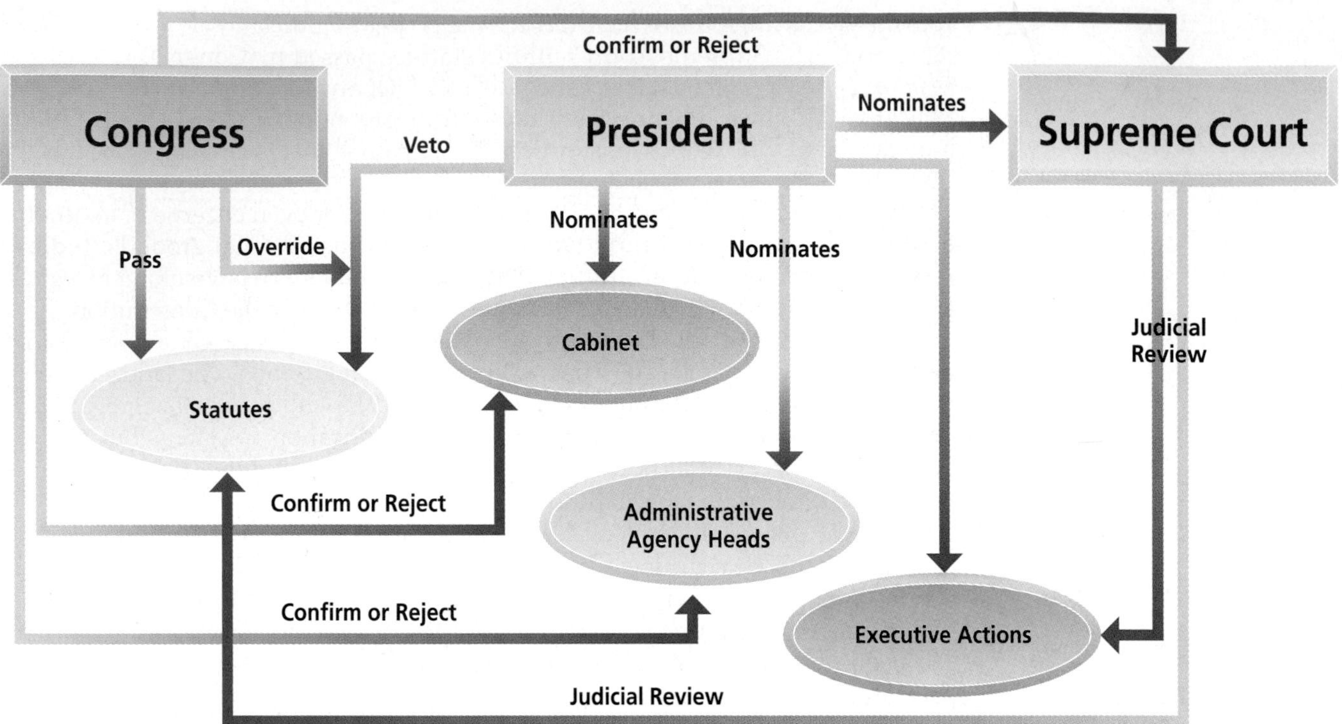

Exhibit 4.1

The Constitution established a federal government of checks and balances. Congress may pass statutes; the president may veto them; and Congress may override the veto. The president nominates cabinet officers, administrative heads, and Supreme Court justices, but the Senate must confirm his nominees. Finally, the Supreme Court (and lower federal courts) exercise judicial review over statutes and executive actions. Unlike the other checks and balances, judicial review is not provided for in the Constitution, but is a creation of the Court itself in *Marbury v. Madison*.

Fourteenth Amendment guarantees equal protection of the law. We consider the First, Fifth, and Fourteenth Amendments in this chapter and the Fourth, Fifth, and Sixth Amendments in Chapter 7, on crime.

The "people" who are protected include citizens and, for most purposes, corporations. Corporations are considered persons and receive most of the same protections. The great majority of these rights also extend to citizens of other countries who are in the United States.

Constitutional rights generally protect only against governmental acts. The Constitution generally does not protect us from the conduct of private parties, such as corporations or other citizens.

INCORPORATION

Constitutional protections apply to federal, state, and local governments. Yet that is not what the Bill of Rights explicitly states. The First Amendment declares that *Congress* shall not abridge the right of free speech. The Fourteenth Amendment explicitly limits the power only of *state* governments. But a series of Supreme Court cases has extended virtually all of the important constitutional protections to all levels of national, state, and local government. This process is called **incorporation** because rights explicitly guaranteed at one level are incorporated into rights that apply at other levels.

FIRST AMENDMENT: FREE SPEECH

The First Amendment states that "Congress shall make no law ... abridging the freedom of speech. . . ." In general, we expect our government to let people speak and hear whatever they choose. The Founding Fathers believed democracy would only work if the members of the electorate were free to talk, argue, listen, and exchange viewpoints in any way they wanted. The people could only cast informed ballots if they were informed. "Speech" also includes symbolic conduct, as the following case flamingly illustrates.

TEXAS v. JOHNSON

491 U.S. 397, 109 S. Ct. 2533, 1989 U.S. LEXIS 3115
United States Supreme Court, 1989

Facts: Outside the Republican National Convention in Dallas, Gregory Johnson participated in a protest against policies of the Reagan administration. Participants gave speeches and handed out leaflets. Johnson burned an American flag. He was arrested and convicted under a Texas statute that prohibited desecrating the flag, but the Texas Court of Criminal Appeals reversed on the grounds that the conviction violated the First Amendment. Texas appealed to the United States Supreme Court.

Issue: **Does the First Amendment protect flag burning?**

Excerpts from Justice Brennan's Decision: The First Amendment literally forbids the abridgment only of "speech," but we have long recognized that its protection does not end at the spoken or written word. While we have rejected the view that an apparently limitless variety of conduct can be labeled "speech," we have acknowledged that conduct may be sufficiently imbued with elements of communication to fall within the scope of the First and Fourteenth Amendments.

In deciding whether particular conduct possesses sufficient communicative elements to bring the First Amendment into play, we have asked whether an intent to convey a particularized message was present, and [whether] the likelihood was great that the message would be understood by those who viewed it. Hence, we have recognized the expressive nature of students' wearing of black armbands to protest American military involvement in Vietnam; of a sit-in by blacks in a "whites only" area to protest segregation; of the wearing of American military uniforms in a dramatic presentation criticizing American involvement in Vietnam; and of picketing about a wide variety of causes.

[The Court concluded that burning the flag was in fact symbolic speech.]

It remains to consider whether the State's interest in reserving the flag as a symbol of nationhood and national unity justifies Johnson's conviction. Johnson was prosecuted because he knew that his politically charged expression would cause "serious offense."

If there is a bedrock principle underlying the First Amendment, it is that the Government may not prohibit the expression of an idea simply because society finds the idea itself offensive or disagreeable. Nothing in our precedents suggests that a State may foster its own view of the flag by prohibiting expressive conduct relating to it.

Could the Government, on this theory, prohibit the burning of state flags? Of copies of the Presidential seal? Of the Constitution? In evaluating these choices under the First Amendment, how would we decide which symbols were sufficiently special to warrant this unique status? To do so, we would be forced to consult our own political preferences, and impose them on the citizenry, in the very way that the First Amendment forbids us to do.

A flag burner.

The way to preserve the flag's special role is not to punish those who feel differently about these matters. It is to persuade them that they are wrong. We can imagine no more appropriate response to burning a flag than waving one's own, no better way to counter a flagburner's message than by saluting the flag that burns, no surer means of preserving the dignity even of the flag that burned than by—as one witness here did—according its remains a respectful burial. We do not consecrate the flag by punishing its desecration, for in doing so we dilute the freedom that this cherished emblem represents.

The judgment of the Texas Court of Criminal Appeals is therefore *affirmed*.

Flag burning is an issue that will not go away. For additional thoughts on the subject, ignite http://www.esquilax.com/flag/, an irreverent page that strongly supports the rights of free speech. In the spirit of fair play, that page provides links to several strongly worded replies that decry flag burning. Extinguish all matches and go to http://www.indirect.com/user/warren/challenge/chal2.html.

Political Speech

Because the Framers were primarily concerned with enabling democracy to function, political speech has been given an especially high degree of protection. Such speech may not be barred even when it is offensive or outrageous. A speaker, for example, could accuse a U.S. senator of being insane and could use crude, violent language to describe him. The speech is still protected. The speech lacks protection only if it is *intended and likely to create imminent lawless action*.[16] For example, suppose the speaker said, "The senator is inside that restaurant. Let's get some matches and burn the place down." Speech of this sort is not protected. The speaker could be arrested for attempted arson or attempted murder.

Time, Place, and Manner

Even when speech is protected, the government may regulate the *time, place*, and *manner* of such speech. A town may require a group to apply for a permit before using a public park for a political demonstration. The town may insist that the demonstration take place during daylight hours and that there be adequate police supervision and sanitation provided. However, the town may not prohibit such demonstrations outright.

The Supreme Court is frequently called upon to balance the rights of the general public with the rights of those seeking to publicize their causes. In *Madsen v. Women's Health Center, Inc.*,[17] the Court ruled that a local judge could limit protesters' access to a family planning clinic. The protesters, opposed to abortion, had repeatedly blocked access to the clinic, harassed patients and doctors at the clinic and at their homes, and paraded with graphic signs and bullhorns. The Court upheld the order prohibiting the protesters from coming within 36 feet of the clinic and also the order that prohibited excessive noise. But the Court overturned a part of the order that had forbidden protesters from displaying graphic images that could be seen inside the clinic. The Court said that the proper remedy was for the clinic to close its curtains.

Morality and Obscenity

The regulation of morality and obscenity presents additional problems. Obscenity has never received constitutional protection. The Supreme Court has consistently held that it does not play a valued role in our society and has refused to give protection to obscene works. That is well and good, but it merely forces the question:

---

[16] *Brandenburg v. Ohio*, 395 U.S. 444, 89 S. Ct. 1827, 1969 U.S. LEXIS 1367 (1969).

[17] 511 U.S. 1016, 114 S. Ct. 1395, 1994 U.S. LEXIS 2671 (1994).

What is obscene? (For a list of books that have been—and in some cases still are—banned by local, state, or foreign governments, see **http://www.cs.cmu.edu/people/spok/banned-books.html**.)

In *Miller v. California*,[18] the Court created a three-part test to determine if a creative work is obscene. The basic guidelines for the factfinder are:

- Whether the average person, applying contemporary community standards, would find that the work, taken as a whole, appeals to the prurient interest
- Whether the work depicts or describes, in a patently offensive way, sexual conduct specifically defined by the applicable state law; and
- Whether the work, taken as a whole, lacks serious literary, artistic, political, or scientific value.

If the trial court finds that the answer to all three of those questions is "yes," it may judge the material obscene; the state may then prohibit the work. If the state fails to prove any one of the three criteria, though, the work is not obscene. A United States District Court ruled that "As Nasty As They Wanna Be," recorded by 2 Live Crew, was obscene. The appeals court, however, reversed, finding that the state had failed to prove lack of artistic merit.[19]

What if sexual conduct is not obscene? Let's go back to the chapter's starting point, nude dancing.

BARNES v. GLEN THEATRE, INC.
501 U.S. 560, 111 S. Ct. 2456, 1991 U.S. LEXIS 3633
United States Supreme Court, 1991

Facts: Indiana's public indecency statute prohibits any person from appearing nude in a public place. State courts have interpreted this to mean that a dancer in a theater or bar must wear pasties and a G-string. A nightclub called the Kitty Kat Lounge and several dancers who wished to perform nude filed suit, seeking an order that the statute was unconstitutional. The United States District Court ruled that the dancing was not expressive conduct and therefore was not entitled to First Amendment protection. The Court of Appeals reversed, declaring that it was nonobscene expressive conduct and thus protected by the First Amendment.

Indiana did not argue that the dancing was obscene. (If that were the issue, the *Miller* test would have determined the outcome.) Instead, Indiana claimed that its general police powers, including the power to protect social order, allowed it to enforce such a statute.

You Be the Judge: Does Indiana's public indecency statute violate the First Amendment?

Argument for Indiana: Your honors, the State of Indiana has no wish to suppress ideas or censor speech. We are not trying to outlaw eroticism or any other legitimate form of expression. We are simply prohibiting nudity in public. We have outlawed all public nudity, not just nightclub performances. Nudity on the beach, in the park, or anywhere in public is prohibited.

We do this to protect societal order, to foster a stable morality. It is well established that the police power of the state includes the right to regulate the public health, safety, and morals. Our citizens disapprove of people appearing in the nude in public places. The citizens of virtually all states feel the same. Decent dress has been a part of good society since time immemorial. Our voting public is entitled to have that standard upheld.

We also enforce this statute because experience has shown that nightclubs such as these are often associated with criminal behavior. Prostitution, illegal drugs, and violence appear too frequently in the vicinity. It is a reasonable step for the State to maintain control over the performances and the people they will attract.

Argument for Kitty Kat: It is apparent beyond debate that dance is expressive conduct. As an art form it has existed for at least several thousand years. Eroticism, also, is not exactly news. Erotic dance is clearly

[18] 413 U.S. 15, 93 S. Ct. 2607, 1973 U.S. LEXIS 149 (1973).

[19] *Luke Records, Inc. v. Navarro*, 960 F.2d 134, 1992 U.S. App. LEXIS 9592 (11th Cir. 1992).

expressive conduct. Indeed, the present dancing derives its strength from its eroticism. If the State did not consider it erotic, doubtless it would have left the dancers alone. This dancing is expressive conduct and deserves the full protection of the First Amendment.

Indiana is choosing a certain type of expression and outlawing it. The state has not outlawed all nudity, since quite obviously nudity in private is beyond the State's reach. Nor has it prohibited all nude performances. Testimony of police at trial indicated that no arrests have ever been made for nudity as part of a play or ballet. Nudity is no longer anything novel in musicals, ballets, stage plays, or film. Indiana permits nudity in all of them and enforces its moralizing law only against nightclubs.

This is an obvious value judgment on the part of the State. The State is saying that if you can afford to pay for a Broadway show that happens to have nudity, you are free to enjoy it; if your taste or pocketbook leads you to the Kitty Kat Lounge, we deny your right to witness nudity. If the State is allowed to make that appraisal, then it is free to censor any expression—artistic, political, or any other—that it finds inferior. It was *precisely* to prevent states from outlawing unpopular expression that the Founding Fathers added the First Amendment.

Concerned that pornography on the Internet was easily available to minors, Congress passed the Communications Decency Act (CDA), making it illegal for any person or company to send "obscene or indecent" communications to anyone under 18. Various plaintiffs, including library associations, booksellers, Internet service providers, and others, filed suit, claiming that the law would diminish the extraordinary opportunities for research and education that the Internet provides. The Supreme Court agreed, striking down the law as a violation of the First Amendment. The justices declared that the law failed to define "indecent." The CDA ignored the obscenity standard provided in *Miller v. California* and outlawed material that *did* have socially redeeming value. The Court noted that the law would deny adults access to a vast amount of material that they were legally entitled to obtain. Finally, the Court pointed out that concerned parents could purchase software to screen out objectionable items, avoiding the need for such far-reaching censorship.[20]

Commercial Speech

This refers to speech that has a **dominant theme to propose a commercial transaction.** For example, most advertisements on television and in the newspapers are commercial speech. This sort of speech is protected by the First Amendment, but the government is permitted to regulate it more closely than other forms of speech. **Commercial speech that is false or misleading may be outlawed altogether.** However, regulations on commercial speech must be reasonable and directed to a legitimate goal, as the following case shows.

---

44 LIQUORMART, INC. v. RHODE ISLAND

517 U.S. 484, 116 S. Ct. 1495, 1996 U.S. LEXIS 3020
United States Supreme Court, 1996

Facts: Rhode Island passed a statute that prohibited liquor stores from advertising prices, and a second law that barred the media from publicizing such ads. The legislature's goal was to reduce drinking by eliminating the competitive advertising that decreased prices and made alcohol more easily available. Liquor stores filed suit, claiming that the prohibition violated the First Amendment. The United States District Court declared that the laws violated the First Amendment, but the Court of Appeals reversed, holding that the state's theory was logical. The case reached the highest court.

Issue: Did Rhode Island violate the First Amendment by banning advertisements containing liquor prices?

---

[20] *Reno v. American Civil Liberties Union*, 521 U.S. 844, 117 S. Ct. 2329, 1997 U.S. LEXIS 4037 (1997).

Excerpts from Justice Stevens's Decision: It is the State's interest in protecting consumers from commercial harms that provides the typical reason why commercial speech can be subject to greater governmental regulation than noncommercial speech. Yet bans that target truthful, nonmisleading commercial messages rarely protect consumers from such harms. Instead, such bans often serve only to obscure an underlying governmental policy that could be implemented without regulating speech. In this way, these commercial speech bans not only hinder consumer choice, but also impede debate over central issues of public policy.

Precisely because bans against truthful, nonmisleading commercial speech rarely seek to protect consumers from either deception or overreaching, they usually rest solely on the offensive assumption that the public will respond "irrationally" to the truth. The First Amendment directs us to be especially skeptical of regulations that seek to keep people in the dark for what the government perceives to be their own good.

In evaluating the ban's effectiveness in advancing the State's interest, we note that a commercial speech regulation "may not be sustained if it provides only ineffective or remote support for the government's purpose." For that reason, the State bears the burden of showing not merely that its regulation will advance its interest, but also that it will do so "to a material degree."

Without any findings of fact, or indeed any evidentiary support whatsoever, we cannot agree with the assertion that the price advertising ban will significantly advance the State's interest in promoting temperance.

The State also cannot satisfy the requirement that its restriction on speech be no more extensive than necessary. It is perfectly obvious that alternative forms of regulation that would not involve any restriction on speech would be more likely to achieve the State's goal of promoting temperance. As the State's own expert conceded, higher prices can be maintained either by direct regulation or by increased taxation. Per capita purchases could be limited as is the case with prescription drugs. Even educational campaigns focused on the problems of excessive, or even moderate, drinking might prove to be more effective.

As a result, even under the less than strict standard that generally applies in commercial speech cases, the State has failed to establish a "reasonable fit" between its abridgment of speech and its temperance goal.

The judgment of the Court of Appeals is therefore reversed.

FIFTH AMENDMENT: DUE PROCESS AND THE TAKINGS CLAUSE

You are a third-year student in a combined business/law program at a major state university. You feel great about a difficult securities exam you took in Professor Watson's class. The Dean's Office sends for you, and you enter curiously, wondering if your exam was so good that the Dean is awarding you a prize. Not quite. The exam proctor has accused you of cheating. Based on the accusation, Watson has flunked you. You protest that you are innocent and demand to know what the accusation is. The Dean says that you will learn the details at a hearing, if you wish to have one. She reminds you that if you lose the hearing you will be expelled from the university. Three years of work and your entire career are suddenly on the line.

The hearing is run by Professor Holmes, who will make the final decision. Holmes is a junior faculty member in Watson's department. (Next year, Watson will decide Holmes's tenure application.) At the hearing the proctor accuses you of copying from a student sitting in front of you. Both Watson and Holmes have already compared the two papers and concluded that they are strongly similar. Holmes tells you that you must convince him the charge is wrong. You examine the papers, acknowledge that there are similarities, but plead as best you can that you never copied. Holmes doesn't buy it. The university expels you, placing on your transcript a notation of cheating.

Have you received fair treatment? To answer that, we must look to the Fifth Amendment, which provides several vital protections. We here consider two related provisions, the Due Process Clause and the Takings Clause. Together, they state: "No person shall be . . . deprived of life, liberty, or property without due process of law; nor shall private property be taken for public use, without just compensation." These clauses prevent the government from arbitrarily taking the most valuable possessions of a citizen or corporation. Here we discuss the civil law aspects of these clauses, but due process also applies to criminal law. The reference to "life" refers to capital punishment. The criminal law issues of this subject are discussed in Chapter 7, on crime.

In civil law proceedings, the government does have the right to take a person's liberty or property. But there are three important limitations:

- *Procedural Due Process*. Before depriving anyone of liberty or property, the government must go through certain procedures to ensure that the result is fair.
- *The Takings Clause*. When the government takes property for public use, such as to build a new highway, it has to pay a fair price.
- *Substantive Due Process*. Some rights are so fundamental that the government may not take them from us at all.

Procedural Due Process

The government deprives citizens or corporations of their property in a variety of ways. The Internal Revenue Service may fine a corporation for late payment of taxes. The Customs Service may seize goods at the border. As to liberty, the government may take it by confining someone in a mental institution or by taking a child out of the home because of parental neglect. **The purpose of procedural due process is to ensure that before the government takes liberty or property, the affected person has a fair chance to oppose the action.**

There are two steps in analyzing a procedural due process case:

- Is the government attempting to take liberty or property?
- If so, how much process is due? (If the government is *not* attempting to take liberty or property, there is no due process issue.)

Is the Government Attempting to Take Liberty or Property? Liberty interests are generally easy to spot: confining someone in a mental institution and taking a child from her home are both deprivations of liberty. A property interest may be obvious. Suppose that, during a civil lawsuit, the court **attaches** a defendant's house, meaning it bars the defendant from selling the property at least until the case is decided. This way, if the plaintiff wins, the defendant will have assets to pay the judgment. The court has clearly deprived the defendant of an important interest in his house, and the defendant is entitled to due process. However, a property interest may be subtler than that. A woman holding a job with a government agency has a "property interest" in that job, because her employer has agreed not to fire her without cause, and she can rely on it for income. If the government does fire her, it is taking away that property interest, and she is entitled to due process. A student attending any public school has a property interest in that education. If a public university suspends a law/business student, as described above, it is taking her property, and she, too, should receive due process.

How Much Process Is Due? Assuming that a liberty or property interest is affected, a court must decide how much process is due. Does the person get a formal trial, or an informal hearing, or merely a chance to reply in writing to the charges against her? If she gets a hearing, must it be held before the government deprives her of her property, or is it enough that she can be heard shortly thereafter? **What sort of hearing the government must offer depends upon how important the property or liberty interest is and on whether the government has a competing need for efficiency.** The more important the interest, the more formal the procedures must be.

Neutral Factfinder. Regardless of how formal the hearing, one requirement is constant: the factfinder must be neutral. Whether it is a superior court judge deciding a multimillion dollar contract suit or an employment supervisor deciding the fate of a government employee, the factfinder must have no personal interest in the outcome. In *Ward v. Monroeville,*[21] the plaintiff was a motorist who had been stopped for traffic offenses in a small town. He protested his innocence and received a judicial hearing. But the "judge" at the hearing was the town mayor. Traffic fines were a significant part of the town's budget. The motorist argued that the town was depriving him of procedural due process because the mayor had a financial interest in the outcome of the case. The United States Supreme Court agreed and reversed his conviction.

Attachment of Property. As described above, a plaintiff in a civil lawsuit often seeks to *attach* the defendant's property. This protects the plaintiff, but it may also harm the defendant if, for example, he is about to close a profitable real estate deal. Attachments used to be routine. In *Connecticut v. Doehr,* the Supreme Court required more caution.[22] Based on *Doehr,* when a plaintiff seeks to attach at the beginning of the trial, a court must look at the plaintiff's likelihood of winning. Generally, the court must grant the defendant a hearing *before* attaching the property. The defendant, represented by a lawyer, may offer evidence as to how attachment would harm him and why it should be denied.

Government Employment. A government employee must receive due process before being fired. Generally, this means some kind of hearing, but not necessarily a formal court hearing. The employee is entitled to know the charges against him, to hear the employer's evidence, and to have an opportunity to tell his side of the story. He is not entitled to have a lawyer present. The hearing "officer" need only be a neutral employee. Further, in an emergency, where the employee is a danger to the public or the organization, the government may suspend with pay, before holding a hearing. It then must provide a hearing before the decision becomes final.

Academic Suspension. There is still a property interest here, but it is the least important of those discussed. When a public school concludes that a student has failed to meet its normal academic standards, such as by failing too many courses, it may dismiss him without a hearing. Due process is served if the student receives notice of the reason and has some opportunity to respond, such as by writing a letter contradicting the school's claims.

In cases of disciplinary suspension or expulsion, courts generally require schools to provide a higher level of due process. In the hypothetical at the beginning of this section, the university has failed to provide adequate due process.[23] The school has accused the student of a serious infraction. The school must promptly provide details of the charge and cannot wait until the hearing to do so. The student should see the two papers and have a chance to rebut the charge. Moreover, Professor Holmes has demonstrated bias. He appears to have made up his mind in advance. He has placed the burden on the student to disprove the charges. And he probably feels obligated to support Watson's original conclusion, since Watson will be deciding his tenure case next year.

---

21 409 U.S. 57, 93 S. Ct. 80, 1972 U.S. LEXIS 11 (1972).

22 501 U.S. 1, 111 S. Ct. 2105, 1991 U.S. LEXIS 3317 (1991).

23 See, e.g., *University of Texas Medical School at Houston v. Than,* 901 S.W.2d 926, 1995 Tex. LEXIS 105 (Tex. 1995).

The Takings Clause

Florence Dolan ran a plumbing store in Tigard, Oregon. She and her husband wanted to enlarge it on land they already owned. But the city government said that they could expand only if they dedicated some of their own land for use as a public bicycle path and for other public use. Does the city have the right to make them do that? For an answer we must look to a different part of the Fifth Amendment.

The Takings Clause is closely related to the Due Process Clause. **The Takings Clause prohibits a state from taking private property for public use without just compensation.** A town wishing to build a new football field may boot you out of your house. But the town must compensate you. The government takes your land through the power of *eminent domain*. Officials must notify you of their intentions and give you an opportunity to oppose the project and to challenge the amount the town offers to pay. But when the hearings are done, the town may write you a check and grind your house into goalposts, whether you like it or not.

More controversial issues arise when a local government does not physically take the property but requires an owner to dedicate some part of the land to public use. Tigard is a city of 30,000 in Oregon. The city developed a comprehensive land use plan for its downtown area in order to preserve green space, to encourage transportation other than autos, and to reduce its flooding problems. Under the plan, when a property owner sought permission to build in the downtown section, the city could require some of her land to be used for public purposes. This has become a standard method of land use planning throughout the nation. States have used it to preserve coastline, urban green belts, and many environmental features.

When Florence Dolan applied for permission to expand, the city required that she dedicate a 15-foot strip of her property to the city as a bicycle pathway and that she preserve, as greenway, a portion of her land within a floodplain. She sued, and though she lost in the Oregon courts, she won in the United States Supreme Court. The Court held that Tigard City's method of routinely forcing all owners to dedicate land to public use violated the Takings Clause. The city was taking the land, even though title never changed hands.[24]

The Court did not outlaw all such requirements. What it required was that, **before a government may require an owner to dedicate land to a public use, it must show that this owner's proposed building requires this dedication of land.** In other words, it is not enough for Tigard to have a general plan, such as a bicycle pathway, and to make all owners participate in it. Tigard must show that it needs *Dolan's* land *specifically for a bike path and greenway*. This will be much harder for local governments to demonstrate than merely showing a city-wide plan. Some observers consider the decision a major advance for the interests of private property. They say that now the government cannot so easily demand that you give up land for public use. Property you have purchased with hard-earned money should truly be yours. Others decry the Court's ruling. In their view it harms our nation's effort to preserve the environment and gives a freer hand to those who value short-term profit over long-term planning.

Substantive Due Process

This doctrine is part of the Due Process Clause, but it is entirely different from procedural due process and from government taking. During the first third of the twentieth century, the Supreme Court frequently nullified state and federal laws, asserting that they interfered with basic rights. For example, in a famous 1905 case, *Lochner v. New York*,[25] the Supreme Court invalidated a New York statute that

---

[24] *Dolan v. City of Tigard*, 512 U.S. 374, 114 S. Ct. 2309, 1994 U.S. LEXIS 4826 (1994).

[25] 198 U.S. 45, 25 S. Ct. 539, 1905 U.S. LEXIS 1153 (1905).

had limited the number of hours that bakers could work in a week. New York had passed the law to protect employee health. But the Court declared that private parties had a basic constitutional right to contract. In this case, the statute interfered with the rights of the employer and the baker to make any bargain they wished. Over the next three decades, the Court struck down dozens of state and federal laws that were aimed at working conditions, union rights, and social welfare generally. This was called **substantive due process** because the Court was looking at the substantive rights being affected, such as the right to contract, not at any procedures.

Critics complained that the Court was interfering with the desires of the voting public by nullifying laws that the justices personally disliked (judicial activism). During the Great Depression, however, things changed. Beginning in 1934, the Court completely reversed itself and began to uphold the types of laws it earlier had struck down. How does the Court now regard substantive due process issues? It treats economic and social regulations differently from cases involving fundamental rights.

Economic and Social Regulations. Generally speaking, the Court will now *presume valid* any statute that regulates economic or social conditions. If the *Lochner* case were heard today, the legislation would be upheld. State or federal laws regulating wages, working conditions, discrimination, union rights, and any similar topics are presumed valid. The Court will invalidate such a law only if it is *arbitrary or irrational*. Almost all statutes have some minimal rationality, and most are now upheld.

Fundamental Rights. The standard of review is different for laws that affect **fundamental rights**. The Constitution expressly provides some of these rights, such as the right of free speech, the right to vote, and the right to travel. Other rights do not explicitly appear in the Constitution, but the Supreme Court has determined that they are implied. One of the most important of these is the right to privacy. The Court has decided that the Bill of Rights, taken together, implies a right of privacy for all persons. This includes the right to contraception, to marriage, and, most controversially, to abortion.

Any law that infringes upon a fundamental right is presumed invalid and will be struck down unless it is necessary to a compelling government interest. For example, because it is a fundamental right, no state may outlaw abortion altogether. But the state may require a minor to obtain the consent of a parent or a judge. Although this infringes upon a fundamental right, the government has a compelling interest in regulating the welfare of minors, and this regulation is necessary to achieve that goal.

FOURTEENTH AMENDMENT: EQUAL PROTECTION CLAUSE

Shannon Faulkner wanted to attend The Citadel, a state-supported military college in South Carolina. She was a fine student who met every admission requirement that The Citadel set except one: she was not a male. The Citadel argued that its long and distinguished history demanded that it remain all male. The state government claimed that Ms. Faulkner had no need to attend this particular school. Faulkner responded that she was a citizen of the state and ought to receive the benefits that others got, including the right to a military education. Could the school exclude her on the basis of gender?

The Fourteenth Amendment provides that "No State shall . . . deny to any person within its jurisdiction the equal protection of the laws." This is the **Equal Protection Clause**, and it means that, generally speaking, **governments must treat people equally.** Unfair classifications among people or corporations will not be

The Citadel.

permitted. A notorious example of unfair classification would be race discrimination: permitting only white children to attend a public school violates the Equal Protection Clause.

Yet clearly, governments do make classifications every day. Rich people pay a higher tax rate than poor people; some corporations are permitted to deal in securities, others are not. To determine which classifications are constitutionally permissible, we need to know what is being classified. There are three major groups of classifications. The outcome of a case can generally be predicted by knowing which group it is in.

- *Minimal Scrutiny: Economic and Social Relations.* Government actions that classify people or corporations on these bases are almost always upheld.

- *Intermediate Scrutiny: Gender.* Government classifications are sometimes upheld.

- *Strict Scrutiny: Race, Ethnicity, and Fundamental Rights.* Classifications based on any of these are almost never upheld.

Minimal Scrutiny: Economic and Social Regulation

Just as with the Due Process Clause, laws that regulate economic or social issues are presumed valid. They will be upheld if they are *rationally related to a legitimate goal*. This means a statute may classify corporations and/or people and the classifications will be upheld if they make any sense at all. The New York City Transit Authority excluded all methadone users from any employment. The United States District Court concluded that this violated the Equal Protection Clause by unfairly excluding all those who were on methadone. The court noted that even those who tested free of any illegal drugs and were seeking non-safety-sensitive jobs, such as clerks, were turned away. That, said the district court, was irrational.

Not so, said the United States Supreme Court. The Court admitted that the policy might not be the wisest. It would probably make more sense to test individually for illegal drugs rather than automatically exclude methadone users. But, said the Court, it was not up to the justices to choose the best policy. They were only to decide if the policy was rational. Excluding methadone users related rationally to the safety of public transport and therefore did not violate the Equal Protection Clause.[26]

Intermediate Scrutiny: Gender

Classifications based on sex must meet a tougher test than those resulting from economic or social regulation. Such laws must *substantially relate to important government objectives*. Courts have increasingly nullified government sex classifications as societal concern with gender equality has grown.

At about the same time Shannon Faulkner began her campaign to enter The Citadel, another woman sought admission to the Virginia Military Institute, an all-male state school. The Supreme Court held that Virginia had violated the Equal Protection Clause by excluding women from VMI. The Court ruled that gender-based government discrimination requires an "exceedingly persuasive justification," and that Virginia had failed that standard of proof. The Citadel promptly

---

[26] *New York City Transit Authority v. Beazer*, 440 U.S. 568, 99 S. Ct. 1355, 1979 U.S. LEXIS 77 (1979).

opened its doors to women, while VMI alumni contemplated purchasing the school, to escape altogether the reaches of the Equal Protection Clause.[27]

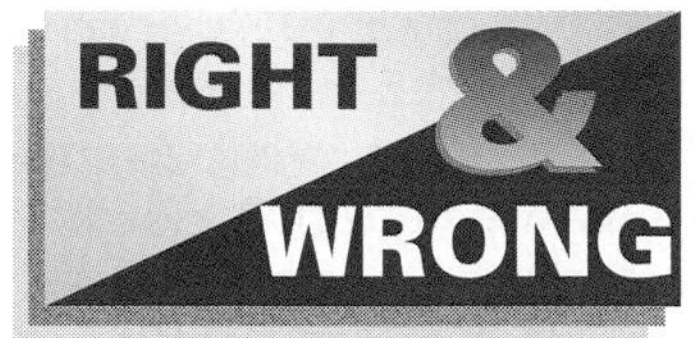

Today over 800 high school girls wrestle competitively. Some join female clubs but others have no such opportunity and compete with boys—or seek to. Some schools allow girls to join the boys' wrestling team, but others refuse, citing moral reasons, concern for the girls' safety, and the possibility of sexual harassment. If a particular school has no female team, should girls be permitted to wrestle boys? Do they have an equal protection right to do so?

Strict Scrutiny: Race, Ethnicity, and Fundamental Rights

Any government action that intentionally discriminates against racial or ethnic minorities, or interferes with a fundamental right, is presumed invalid. In such cases, courts will look at the statute or policy with *strict scrutiny*; that is, courts will examine it very closely to determine whether there is compelling justification for it. The law will be upheld only if it is *necessary to promote a compelling state interest*. Very few meet that test.

- *Racial and Ethnic Minorities*. Any government action that intentionally discriminates on the basis of race or ethnicity is presumed invalid. For example, in *Palmore v. Sidoti*,[28] the state had refused to give child custody to a mother because her new spouse was racially different from the child. The practice was declared unconstitutional. The state had made a racial classification, it was presumed invalid, and the government had no *compelling need* to make such a ruling.

- *Fundamental Rights*. A government action interfering with a fundamental right also receives strict scrutiny and will likely be declared void. For example, New York State gave an employment preference to any veteran who had been a state resident when he entered the military. Newcomers who were veterans were less likely to get jobs, and therefore this statute interfered with the right to travel, a fundamental right. The Supreme Court declared the law invalid.[29]

INDIVIDUAL RIGHTS AND STATE ACTION

All of the rights discussed thus far offer protection only from government action, not from the conduct of private citizens or corporations. Suppose it is Sunday morning. You are happily reading the newspaper, sipping coffee, while your nine-year-old niece, visiting for the weekend, plays hopscotch on your front walk. There is a knock at the front door. The Neighborhood Association has arrived with a stern message: "Get the kid out of the neighborhood; she's not allowed." Astonished and enraged, you call your lawyer. But her answer leaves you dazed: You may not have children in your house. "But this is America!" you shout. "The Constitution," she replies, "does not apply."

Like 50 million other Americans, you live in a *common interest development (CID)*. Yours happens to be a gated community of single family homes, all of

---

[27] *United States v. Virginia*, 518 U.S. 515, 116 S. Ct. 2264, 1996 U.S. LEXIS 4259 (1996).

[28] 466 U.S. 429, 104 S. Ct. 1879, 1984 U.S. LEXIS 69 (1984).

[29] *Attorney General of New York v. Soto-Lopez*, 476 U.S. 898, 106 S. Ct. 2317, 1986 U.S. LEXIS 59 (1986).

which were built by a developer. When you bought the house, you automatically joined the Neighborhood Association. Other CIDs take different forms: condominiums, co-ops, or retirement or vacation communities. They are increasingly common, and some observers predict that, soon, about 25 percent of all Americans will live in one.

Some CIDs ban children from living in the development or even visiting. Some prohibit signs on the lawns or windows; others outlaw pets, certain flowers, laundry drying in the sun, day-care centers, or pickup trucks. But various features make CIDs attractive to prospective residents. CIDs are often gated or locked in other ways, so they may be safer than surrounding neighborhoods. The community collects its own fees and operates many services, such as water and sewer, road maintenance, garbage collection, and other work traditionally done by towns and cities. Because they are privately managed by boards elected by the residents, CIDs often do this work more promptly and efficiently than public agencies.

Towns or cities also find CIDs desirable since the CID does much of the municipal work itself, using fees collected from residents. While costing a local political unit no extra money, the CID offers an expanded tax base—a happy combination for local governments chronically short of revenue.

However, the price residents pay is more than cash: they do indeed forfeit constitutional rights. The Constitution protects citizens from government action, and the local CID is not a government. As the law currently stands, you are probably giving up constitutional protections when you enter a CID. If the Neighborhood Association demands that your niece leave, you will probably have to drive her home. Suppose the nasty Neighborhood Association official also notices that your cat looks heavy. "No cats over 20 pounds," he snarls. "Read the rules." The pet-weight rule is also probably enforceable: get that cat off the sofa and onto a treadmill, fast.

State Action

In some cases, the Supreme Court has found that a private organization has taken on all the characteristics of a government and thus should be treated as such for constitutional purposes. In *Marsh v. Alabama*,[30] a private company owned an entire town, where its employees lived and worked. The company brought a trespass case against someone distributing religious literature. However, since the company property had "all the characteristics of any other American town," the Supreme Court ruled that it must be *treated* as a town, meaning that constitutional protections must apply. The First Amendment protected the right to distribute religious material. This is the **state action doctrine.** But there are limits. In 1976 the Court ruled that the state action doctrine does *not* apply to shopping centers because they do not possess all of the attributes of a town.

Before too long the Court will probably have to decide whether a CID is free to make unlimited rules or is subject to the state action doctrine. Like the town in *Marsh*, many CIDs look and act like towns. But in *Marsh* the company owned the town; a CID is a group of owners banding together by agreement. The Court will have to decide whether that agreement can nullify constitutional rights.

---

30 326 U.S. 501, 66 S. Ct. 276, 1946 U.S. LEXIS 3097 (1946).

CHAPTER CONCLUSION

The legal battle over power never stops. The obligation of a state to provide equal educational opportunity for both genders relates to whether Tigard, Oregon, may demand some of Ms. Dolan's store lot for public use. Both issues are governed by one amazing document. That same Constitution determines what tax preferences are permissible, and even whether a state may require you to wear clothing. As social mores change in step with broad cultural developments, as the membership of the Supreme Court changes, the balance of power between federal government, state government, and citizens will continue to evolve. There are no easy answers to these constitutional questions because there has never been a democracy so large, so diverse, or so powerful.

CHAPTER REVIEW

1. The Constitution is a series of compromises about power.
2. Article I of the Constitution creates the Congress and grants all legislative power to it. Article II establishes the office of president and defines executive powers. Article III creates the Supreme Court and permits lower federal courts; the article also outlines the powers of the federal judiciary.
3. Under the Commerce Clause, Congress may regulate any activity that has a substantial effect on interstate commerce.
4. A state may not regulate commerce in any way that will interfere with interstate commerce.
5. Under the Supremacy Clause, if there is a conflict between federal and state statutes, the federal law preempts the field. Even without a conflict, federal law preempts if Congress intended to exercise exclusive control.
6. The president's key powers include making agency appointments, proposing legislation, conducting foreign policy, and acting as commander in chief of the armed forces.
7. The federal courts adjudicate cases and also exercise judicial review, which is the right to declare a statute or governmental action unconstitutional and void.
8. Freedom of speech includes symbolic acts. Political speech is protected unless it is intended and likely to create imminent lawless action.
9. The government may regulate the time, place, and manner of speech.
10. Obscene speech is not protected.
11. Commercial speech that is false or misleading may be outlawed; otherwise, regulations on this speech must be reasonable and directed to a legitimate goal.
12. Procedural due process is required whenever the government attempts to take liberty or property. The amount of process that is due depends upon the importance of the liberty or property threatened. (Due process issues involving *life* are discussed in Chapter 7, on crime.)
13. The Takings Clause prohibits a state from taking private property for public use without just compensation.

14. A substantive due process analysis presumes that any economic or social regulation is valid, and presumes invalid any law that infringes upon a fundamental right.

15. The Equal Protection Clause generally requires the government to treat people equally. Courts apply strict scrutiny in any equal protection case involving race, ethnicity, or fundamental rights; intermediate scrutiny to any case involving gender; and minimal scrutiny to an economic or social regulation.

16. Generally, constitutional rights protect citizens only from the action of the government, although under the state action doctrine, a private organization *may* be treated like the government if it has *all* the characteristics of one.

PRACTICE TEST

1. Michigan's Solid Waste Management Act (SWMA) generally prohibited Michigan counties from accepting for disposal solid waste that had been generated outside that county. Fort Gratiot operated a sanitary landfill in St. Clair County, Michigan. The county denied Fort Gratiot permission to bring in solid waste from out of state, and Fort Gratiot sued. This case involves the negative, or dormant, aspect of the Commerce Clause. What is the difference between that aspect and the positive aspect? What is the evil that the dormant aspect is designed to avoid? How would you rule in this case?

2. **YOU BE THE JUDGE WRITING PROBLEM** Scott Fane was a CPA licensed to practice in New Jersey and Florida. He built his New Jersey practice by making unsolicited phone calls to executives. When he moved to Florida, the Board of Accountancy there prohibited him (and all CPAs) from personally soliciting new business. Fane sued. Does the First Amendment force Florida to forgo foreclosing Fane's phoning? **Argument for Fane:** The Florida regulation violates the First Amendment, which protects commercial speech. Fane was not saying anything false or misleading, but was just trying to secure business. This is an unreasonable regulation, designed to keep newcomers out of the marketplace and maintain steady business and high prices for established CPAs. **Argument for the Florida Board of Accountancy:** Commercial speech deserves—and gets—a lower level of protection than other speech. This regulation is a reasonable method of ensuring that the level of CPA work in our state remains high. CPAs who personally solicit clients are obviously in need of business. They are more likely to bend legal and ethical rules to obtain clients and keep them happy, and will lower the standards throughout the state.

3. Dairy farming in Massachusetts became more expensive than in other states. In order to help its dairy farmers, the state began taxing all milk sales in the state, whether the milk was produced in state or out of state. The money went into a fund that was then distributed among Massachusetts milk producers as a subsidy for their milk. Discuss.

4. President Bush insisted that he had the power to send American troops into combat in the Middle East, without congressional assent. Yet before authorizing force in Operation Desert Storm, he secured congressional authorization. President Clinton stated that he was prepared to invade Haiti without a congressional vote. Yet he bargained hard to avoid an invasion, and ultimately American troops entered without the use of force. Why the seeming double talk by both presidents?

5. In the early 1970s, President Nixon became embroiled in the Watergate dispute. He was accused of covering up a criminal break-in at the national headquarters of the Democratic Party. Nixon denied any wrongdoing. A United States District Court judge ordered the president to produce tapes of conversations held in his office. Nixon knew that complying with the order would produce damaging evidence, probably destroying his presidency. He refused, claiming executive privilege. The case went to the Supreme Court. Nixon strongly implied that even if the Supreme Court ordered him to produce the tapes, he would refuse. What major constitutional issue did this raise?

6. **RIGHT & WRONG** In the landmark 1965 case of *Griswold v. Connecticut*, the Supreme Court examined a Connecticut statute that made it a crime for any person to use contraception. The majority declared the law an

unconstitutional violation of the right of privacy. Justice Black dissented, saying, "I do not to any extent whatever base my view that this Connecticut law is constitutional on a belief that the law is wise or that its policy is a good one. [It] is every bit as offensive to me as it is to the majority. [There is no criticism by the majority of this law] to which I cannot subscribe—except their conclusion that the evil qualities they see in the law make it unconstitutional." What legal doctrines are involved here? Why did Justice Black distinguish between his personal views on the statute and the power of the Court to overturn it? Should a federal court act as a "superlegislature," nullifying statutes with which it disagrees? If a court aggressively takes on social issues, what dangers—and what advantages—does that present to society?

7. You begin work at Everhappy Corp. at the beginning of November. On your second day at work, you wear a political button on your overcoat, supporting your choice for governor in the upcoming election. Your boss glances at it and says, "Get that stupid thing out of this office or you're history, chump." You protest that his statement (a) violates your constitutional rights and (b) uses a boring cliché. Are you right?

8. Gilleo opposed American participation in the war in the Persian Gulf. She displayed a large sign on her front lawn that read, "Say No to War in the Persian Gulf, Call Congress Now." The city of Ladue prohibited signs on front lawns and Gilleo sued. The city claimed that it was regulating "time, place, and manner." Explain that statement, and decide who should win.

9. A federal statute prohibits the broadcasting of lottery advertisements, except by stations that broadcast in states permitting lotteries. The purpose of the statute is to support efforts of states that outlaw lotteries. Edge Broadcasting operated a radio station in North Carolina (a nonlottery state) but broadcast primarily in Virginia (a lottery state). Edge wanted to advertise Virginia's lottery but was barred by the statute. Did the federal statute violate Edge's constitutional rights?

10. Fox's Fine Furs claims that Ermine owes $68,000 for a mink coat on which she has stopped making payments. Fox goes to court, files a complaint, and also asks the clerk to *garnish* Ermine's wages. A garnishment is a court order to an employer to hold an employee's wages, or a portion of them, and pay the money into court so that there will be money for the plaintiff, if she wins. What constitutional issue does Fox's request for garnishment raise?

11. David Lucas paid $975,000 for two residential lots on the Isle of Palms near Charleston, South Carolina. He intended to build houses on them. Two years later the South Carolina legislature passed a statute that prohibited building seaward of a certain line, and Lucas's property fell in the prohibited zone. Lucas claimed that his land was now useless and that South Carolina owed him its value. Explain his claim. Should he win?

12. This case concerns unequal taxes on property. In Pennsylvania, a county tax commissioner appraises land, meaning that he sets a value for the land, and the owner then pays real estate taxes based on that value. A commissioner valued land at its sales price, whenever it was sold. If land did not sell for many years, he made little or no adjustment in its appraised value. As a result, some property was assessed at 35 times as much as neighboring land. A corporate landowner sued. What constitutional issue is raised? What should the outcome be?

INTERNET RESEARCH PROBLEM

Visit **http://www.cs.cmu.edu/people/spok/banned-books.html**. Find a book that was formerly censored. Find another volume that is currently banned, either in the United States or elsewhere. How have changing mores affected censorship? Will the book that is currently outlawed someday be legal?

You can find further practice problems in the Online Quiz at http://beatty.westbuslaw.com or in the Study Guide that accompanies this text.

CHAPTER 5

INTENTIONAL TORTS AND BUSINESS TORTS

In a small Louisiana town, Don Mashburn ran a restaurant called Maison de Mashburn. The *New Orleans States-Item* newspaper reviewed his eatery, and here is what the article said:

"'Tain't Creole, 'tain't Cajun, 'tain't French, 'tain't country American, 'tain't good. I don't know how much real talent in cooking is hidden under the mélange of hideous sauces which make this food and the menu a travesty of pretentious amateurism but I find it all quite depressing. Put a yellow flour sauce on top of the duck, flame it for drama and serve it with some horrible multi-flavored rice in hollowed-out fruit and what have you got? A well-cooked duck with an ugly sauce that tastes too sweet and thick and makes you want to scrape off the glop to eat the plain duck. [The stuffed eggplant was prepared by emptying] a shaker full (more or less) of paprika on top of it. [One sauce created] trout à la green plague [while another should have been called] yellow death on duck."

Mashburn sued, claiming that the newspaper had committed libel, damaging his reputation and hurting his business.[1] Trout à la green plague will be the first course on our menu of tort law. Mashburn learned, as you will, why filing such a lawsuit is easier than winning it.

---

[1] *Mashburn v. Collin,* 355 So. 2d 879 (La. 1977).

This odd word "tort" is borrowed from the French, meaning "wrong." And that is what it means in law: a tort is a wrong. More precisely, **a tort is a violation of a duty imposed by the civil law.** When a person breaks one of those duties and injures another, it is a tort. The injury could be to a person or her property. Libel is one example of a tort where, for example, a newspaper columnist falsely accuses someone of being an alcoholic. A surgeon who removes the wrong kidney from a patient commits a different kind of tort, called negligence. A business executive who deliberately steals a client away from a competitor, interfering with a valid contract, commits a tort called interference with a contract. A con artist who tricks money out of you with a phony offer to sell you a boat commits fraud, yet another tort.

Because tort law is so broad, it takes a while—and two chapters—to understand its boundaries. To start with, we must distinguish torts from two other areas of law: criminal law and contract law.

It is a crime to steal a car, to embezzle money from a bank, to sell cocaine. As discussed in Chapter 1, society considers such behavior so threatening that the government itself will prosecute the wrongdoer, whether or not the car owner or bank president wants the case to go forward. A district attorney, who is paid by the government, will bring the case to court, seeking to send the defendant to prison and/or to fine him. If there is a fine, the money goes to the state, not to the victim.

In a tort case, it is up to the injured party, the plaintiff, to seek compensation. She must hire her own lawyer, who will file a lawsuit. Her lawyer must convince the court that the defendant breached some legal duty and ought to pay money damages to the plaintiff. The plaintiff has no power to send the defendant to jail. Bear in mind that a defendant's action might be both a crime *and* a tort. The con artist who tricks money out of you with a fake offer to sell you a boat has committed the tort of fraud. You may file a civil suit against him and will collect money damages if you can prove your case. The con artist has also committed the crime of fraud. The state will prosecute, seeking to imprison and fine him.

A tort is also different from a contract dispute. A contract case is based on an agreement two people have already made. One person then claims that the other one broke the agreement. For example, Deirdre claims that Raul promised to sell her 10,000 pairs of sneakers at a good price but has failed to deliver them. She files a contract lawsuit. In a tort case, there is usually no "deal" between the parties. Don Mashburn had never met the restaurant critic who attacked his restaurant and obviously had never made any kind of contract. The plaintiff in a tort case claims that *the law* itself creates obligations that the defendant has breached.

Tort law itself is divided into categories. In this chapter we consider **intentional torts**, that is, harm caused by a deliberate action. The newspaper columnist who wrongly accuses someone of being a drunk has committed the intentional tort of libel. The con artist who tricks money from you has committed the intentional tort of fraud. In the next chapter we examine **negligence and strict liability**, which are injuries caused by neglect and oversight rather than by deliberate conduct.

When we speak of intentional torts, we do not mean that the defendant intended to *harm* the plaintiff. The intentional part of these torts is simply the physical act. If the defendant does something deliberately and it ends up injuring somebody, she is probably liable even if she meant no harm. Intentionally throwing a snowball at a friend is a deliberate act; if the snowball permanently damages his eye, the harm is unintended, but the defendant is liable for the intentional tort of battery. We look first at the most important intentional torts and then at the most important business torts.

Differences between Contract, Tort, and Criminal Law

Type of Obligation	Contract	Tort	Criminal Law
How the obligation is created	The parties agree on a contract, which creates duties for both.	The civil law imposes duties of conduct on all persons.	The criminal law prohibits certain conduct.
How the obligation is enforced	Suit by plaintiff.	Suit by plaintiff.	Prosecution by government.
Possible result	Money damages for plaintiff.	Money damages for plaintiff.	Punishment for defendant, including prison and/or fine.
Example	Raul contracts to sell Deirdre 5,000 pairs of sneakers at $50 per pair, but fails to deliver them. Deirdre buys the sneakers elsewhere for $60 per pair and receives $50,000, her extra expense.	A newspaper falsely accuses a private citizen of being an alcoholic. The plaintiff sues and wins money damages to compensate for her injured reputation.	Leo steals Kelly's car. The government prosecutes Leo for grand theft, and the judge sentences him to two years in prison. Kelly gets nothing.

INTENTIONAL TORTS

DEFAMATION

The First Amendment guarantees the right to free speech, a vital freedom that enables us to protect other rights. But that freedom is not absolute. Courts have long recognized that we cannot permit irresponsible speech to harm another's reputation. Free speech should not include the right to falsely accuse your neighbor of selling drugs. That sounds sensible enough, yet once we say that free speech and personal reputation both deserve protection, we have guaranteed perpetual conflict.

The law of defamation concerns false statements that harm someone's reputation. Defamatory statements can be written or spoken. Written defamation is *libel*. Suppose a newspaper accuses a local retail store of programming its cash registers to overcharge customers, when the store has never done so. That is libel. Oral defamation is *slander*. If Professor Wisdom, in class, refers to Sally Student as a drug dealer, and Sally has never sold anything stronger than Arm & Hammer, he has slandered her.

There are four elements to a defamation case. **An element is a fact that a plaintiff must prove to win a lawsuit.** The plaintiff in *any* kind of lawsuit must prove *all* of the elements to prevail. The elements in a defamation case are:

- *Defamatory Statement.* This is a statement likely to harm another person's reputation. When Professor Wisdom accuses Sally of dealing drugs, that will clearly harm her reputation.

- *Falseness.* The statement must be false to be defamatory. If Sally Student actually sold marijuana to a classmate, then Professor Wisdom has a defense to slander.
- *Communicated.* The statement must be communicated to at least one person other than the plaintiff. If Wisdom speaks only to Sally and accuses her of dealing drugs, there is no slander. But there is if he shouts the accusation in a crowded hall.
- *Injury.* In slander cases, the plaintiff generally must show some injury. Sally's injury would be lower reputation in the school, embarrassment, and humiliation. But in libel cases, the law is willing to assume injury. Since libel is written, and more permanent, courts award damages even without proof of injury.[2]

Slander Per Se

Society has considered some statements to be so harsh that the plaintiff is not required to prove injury. These four kinds of slander are called *slander per se:* accusing the plaintiff of committing a serious crime, having a sexually transmitted disease, incompetence in her profession, or being an unchaste woman. (The sexual bias of the law caused it historically to assume that a reputation for promiscuity would hurt a woman's reputation but not a man's.) A plaintiff who proves slander per se will win, even if she cannot prove damages.

Opinion

Thus far, what we have seen is uncontroversial. If a television commentator refers to Frank Landlord as a "vicious slumlord who rents uninhabitable units," and Frank actually maintains his buildings perfectly, Frank will be compensated for the harm. But what if the television commentator states a harsh *opinion* about Frank? Remember that the plaintiff must demonstrate a "false" statement. **Opinion is generally a valid defense in a defamation suit because it cannot be proven true or false.**

Suppose that the television commentator says, "Frank Landlord certainly does less than many rich people do for our community." Is that defamation? Probably not. Who are the "rich people"? How much do they do? How do we define "does less"? These vague assertions indicate the statement is one of opinion. Even if Frank works hard feeding homeless families, he will probably lose a defamation case. The Internet, of course, permits worldwide dissemination of facts *and* opinion. The Web site **http://www.otap.com/angry/** is devoted to *angry comments* aimed at a variety of organizations. Are any of the posted statements defamatory?

A related defense involves cases where a supposed statement of fact should not be taken literally. "Reverend Wilson's sermons go on so long, many parishioners suffer brain death before receiving communion." Brain death is a tragic fact of medical science, but this speaker obviously exaggerates to express his opinion. No defamation.

Mr. Mashburn, who opened the chapter suing over his restaurant review, lost his case. The court held that a reasonable reader would have understood the statements to be opinion only. "A shaker full of paprika" and "yellow death on duck" were not to be taken literally but were merely the author's expression of his personal dislike.

What about a crude description of a college official, appearing in the school's newspaper? You be the judge.

---

2 In this century, when defamation by radio and television became possible, the courts chose to consider it libel, analogizing it to newspapers because of the vast audience. This means that in broadcasting cases, a plaintiff generally does not have to prove damages.

YEAGLE v. COLLEGIATE TIMES
255 Va. 293, 497 S.E.2d 136, 1998 Va. LEXIS 32
Virginia Supreme Court, 1998

Facts: Sharon Yeagle was assistant to the Vice President of Student Affairs at the Virginia Polytechnic Institute and State University. The state had an academic honors program called the Governor's Fellows Program, and one of Yeagle's duties was to help students apply. The school newspaper, the *Collegiate Times*, published an article describing the university's success at placing students in the Fellows Program. The article included a block quotation in larger print, attributed to Yeagle. Underneath Yeagle's name was the phrase, "Director of Butt Licking."

Yeagle sued the *Collegiate Times*, alleging that the vulgar phrase defamed her. The trial court dismissed the case, ruling that no reasonable person would take the words literally, and that the phrase conveyed no factual information. Yeagle appealed to the Virginia Supreme Court.

You Be the Judge: Was the phrase defamatory, or was it deliberate exaggeration that no reasonable person would take literally?

Argument for Yeagle: The disgusting phrase that the *Collegiate Times* used to describe Ms. Yeagle is defamatory for several reasons. The conduct described by the words happens to be a crime in Virginia, a violation of the state sodomy statute. Thus the paper is accusing her of criminal offenses that she has never committed. That is defamation per se, and in itself entitles Ms. Yeagle to damages.

If, however, defendants argue that the phrase must be interpreted figuratively, then the newspaper has accused Ms. Yeagle of currying favor, or directing others to do so, in a uniquely degrading fashion. The *Collegiate Times* is informing its readers that she performs her job in a sleazy, unprofessional manner evidently because she cannot succeed by merit. The paper is suggesting that she is devoid of integrity and capable of achieving goals only by devious, deviant methods.

Finally, the *Collegiate Times* is holding Ms. Yeagle up to ridicule and scorn, for no legitimate reason, and with the sole purpose of harming her reputation. The student editors may find it amusing to damage someone's career for their own idle purposes, but hardworking adults will not share the laughter. Ms. Yeagle should have had a chance to present her case in court and let a jury decide just how funny the article was.

Argument for Collegiate Times: Statements are only defamatory if a reasonable reader would understand them as asserting facts that can be proven true or false. There is no such statement in this case, and no defamation. No reasonable reader, after finishing an article about the Fellows Program, would believe that Ms. Yeagle was actually the director as described, or even that there is such a job. From the bluntness of the phrase, it is obvious that the words are hyperbole and have no meaning that can be proven true or false.

The paper chose to inject humor into its coverage of a mundane issue, for the entertainment of its readers. What Ms. Yeagle really objects to is the vulgarity of the phrase, and to that claim the paper pleads guilty. The *Collegiate Times* acknowledges that the phrase is off-color and might offend a few readers. There are two responses. First, the great majority of the paper's readers appreciate lively language that is at times irreverent. Second, vulgarity is not defamation. Freedom of speech is more important than the hurt feelings of an overly sensitive reader. Courts have long held that all citizens have the right to use language that may offend others, to choose words that are crude and even disgusting. For any reader who is quick to take offense, the proper recourse is not to file suit, but to put down the paper.

Public Personalities

The rules of the game change for those who play in public. Public officials and public figures receive less protection from defamation. An example of a **public official** is a police chief. A **public figure** is a movie star, for example, or a multimillionaire playboy constantly in the news. In the landmark case *New York Times Co. v. Sullivan*,[3] the Supreme Court ruled that the free exchange of information is vital in a democracy and is protected by the First Amendment to the Constitution. If the information wounds public people, that may just be tough luck.

The rule from the *New York Times* case is that a public official or public figure can win a defamation case only by proving actual malice by the defendant.

[3] 376 U.S. 254, 84 S. Ct. 710, 1964 U.S. LEXIS 1655 (1964).

Actual malice means that the defendant knew the statement was false or acted with reckless disregard of the truth. If the plaintiff merely shows that the defendant newspaper printed incorrect statements, even very damaging ones, that will not suffice to win the suit. In the *New York Times* case, the police chief of Birmingham, Alabama, claimed that the *Times* falsely accused him of racial violence in his job. He lost because he could not prove that the *Times* had acted with actual malice. If he could have shown that the *Times* knew the accusation was false, he would have won.

Like so many areas of tort law, defamation is in flux. New Jersey seems to be expanding the protection given to papers by enlarging the definition of "public personality." A newspaper article harshly criticized a lawn mower repair company, and the company sued for libel. The court of appeals ruled that, in New Jersey, any person or business that opens itself to the general public and subjects itself to public scrutiny is subject to the actual malice standard.[4] This is a potentially dramatic expansion of the media's protection. A newspaper or television station could run an investigative piece that seriously and unfairly harms a business, yet never have to compensate. Opponents of such changes argue that the law is encouraging inaccuracy and sloppy journalism. Proponents say that public activity in a free society may yield some bruises.

Can a hamburger sue for defamation? No, but the beef industry can—and did. About a dozen states have product-defamation statutes, which prohibit disparaging remarks about food produced or sold in the state. One of those statutes became prime-time news.

On Oprah Winfrey's television show, an anti-meat activist mentioned that some American cattle were fed ground-up meal made from dead livestock. He stated that such feeding might have contributed to the mad cow disease in Britain and added that the Food and Drug Administration had since banned the practice in the United States. His statements prompted Ms. Winfrey to blurt out, "It has just stopped me cold from eating another burger! I'm stopped!" The day after the program's broadcast, cattle futures dropped more than 10 percent and took weeks to recover (although other commodities also dropped sharply the same day).

Texas cattlemen sued Winfrey under the state's False Disparagement of Perishable Food Products Act, a statute that puts the burden on the defendant to demonstrate that any inaccurate statements about food had a basis in "reasonable and reliable scientific inquiry, facts or data." The food industry regards such laws as crucial, claiming that careless remarks can cause devastating losses to innocent producers. But consumer activists argue that the industry has sponsored product-defamation laws in an effort to stifle public-interest groups that criticize unsafe food practices. The trial judge dismissed the product-defamation claims against Ms. Winfrey, ruling that the statute did not cover beef. The case went to the jury on common law defamation charges. The cattlemen's lawyer told the jury that the industry was entitled "not to have our business damaged by a bunch of falsehoods shot out of Chicago." But the jury found in Ms. Winfrey's favor. According to one juror, the group concluded that the right of free speech was paramount.

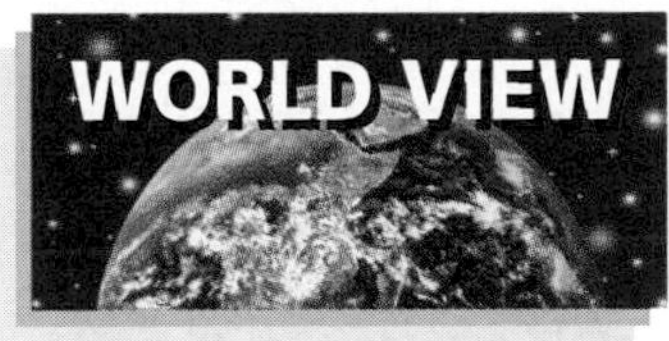

The First Amendment guarantees that the American press will be rough and tumble. Not so in other countries. Look at the profound effect of British libel laws.

Robert Maxwell was a multimillionaire entrepreneur who owned newspapers, magazines, and other enterprises around the world. His corporate empire was centered in London. When he died in 1991, he left a calamitous amount of debt and evidence of enormous financial fraud. Several corporations failed because of

---

[4] *Turf Lawnmower Repair, Inc. v. Bergen Record Corp.*, 269 N.J. Super. 370, 635 A.2d 575, 1994 N.J. Super. LEXIS 5 (1994).

his debt, causing massive layoffs, hardship to employees, and huge losses to shareholders. How had such fraud remained hidden? Was no one suspicious?

In fact, a great many people had serious suspicions. But British libel laws prevented them from speaking up. According to the *Wall Street Journal*,[5] Maxwell used the strict laws to intimidate the press and employees, preventing the kind of accusations and disclosures that would certainly have occurred in the United States. When employees raised questions about Maxwell's unauthorized loans or transfers of pension fund money to his private interests, Maxwell silenced them with threats of libel suits.

There is no "actual malice" standard in Britain for public figures. Further, once a plaintiff demonstrates that the defendant used defamatory language, the burden is on the defendant to prove the truth of what he said. This can be extremely difficult for a newspaper because the plaintiff will often have most of the relevant evidence. By contrast, in the United States, the newspaper need only show that the plaintiff is a public figure and that the newspaper used reasonable research methods, that is, that there was no malice. Only if the plaintiff could demonstrate malice would the newspaper have to show the truth of its allegations.

Privilege

Defendants receive additional protection from defamation cases when it is important for them to speak freely. **Absolute privilege** exists in courtrooms and legislative hearings. Anyone speaking there, such as a witness in court, can say anything at all and never be sued for defamation. If Walter testifies that Ernestine had insider knowledge when she traded stock, he cannot be sued for slander even if he is wrong. (If the testimony is false and Walter knows it, that would be perjury, but still not slander.) Courts extend an absolute privilege in those few instances when candor is essential to a functioning democracy.

Qualified privilege exists when two people have a legitimate need to exchange information. Suppose Trisha Tenant lives in a housing project. She honestly believes that her neighbor is selling guns illegally. She reports this to the manager of the project, who investigates and discovers the guns were toys, being sold legally. The report was false but Trisha is not liable for slander. She had a good faith reason to report this, and the manager needed to hear it.

As long as Trisha acts in good faith and talks only to someone who ought to know about the activity, she is protected by qualified privilege. In this way our society encourages behavior that is socially helpful. If the neighbor *had* been dealing in guns, Trisha's report might have saved lives. But Trisha will lose the privilege if she acts maliciously. If she telephones a friend in another town and accuses

Defamation cases show a tension between the public's need for information and a citizen's right to protect his reputation.

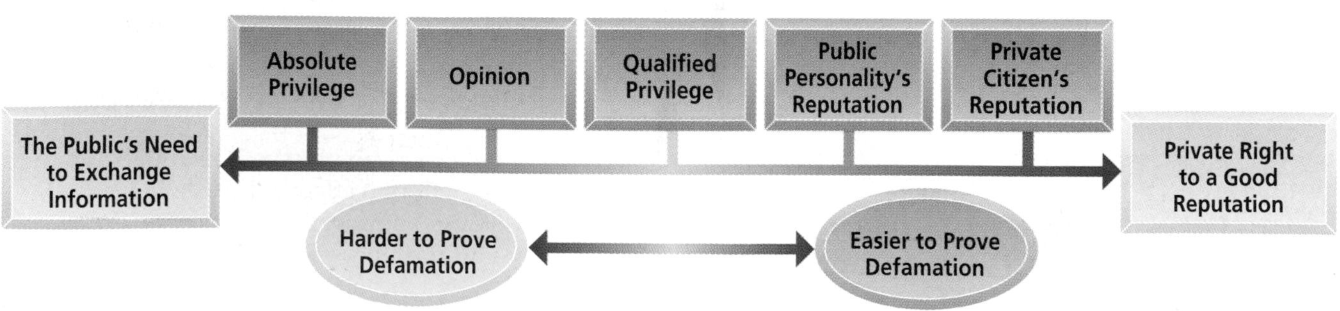

[5] Arthur S. Hayes, "Britain's Libel Laws Helped Maxwell Keep Charges from Public," *Wall Street Journal*, Dec. 9, 1991, p. B6.

the neighbor of dealing guns, she is committing slander because the friend has no need to know this.

FALSE IMPRISONMENT

False imprisonment is the intentional restraint of another person without reasonable cause and without consent. Suppose a bank teller becomes seriously ill and wants to go to the doctor, but the bank will not permit her to leave until she makes a final tally of her accounts. Against her wishes, company officials physically bar her from leaving the bank. That is false imprisonment. The restraint was unreasonable because her accounts could have been verified later.[6]

False imprisonment cases most commonly arise in retail stores, which sometimes detain employees or customers for suspected theft. Most states now have statutes governing the detention of suspected shoplifters. **Generally, a store may detain a customer or worker for alleged shoplifting provided there is a reasonable basis for the suspicion and the detention is done reasonably.** To detain a customer in the manager's office for 20 minutes and question him about where he got an item is lawful. To chain that customer to a display counter for three hours and humiliate him in front of other customers is unreasonable, and false imprisonment.

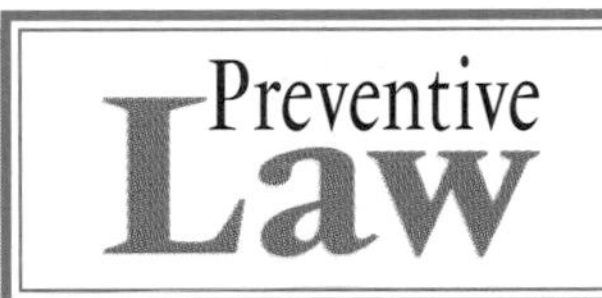

Assume that you are a junior vice president of a chain of 15 retail clothing stores, all located in your state. The president has asked you to outline a sensible plan, to be given to all employees, for dealing with suspected shoplifters. Here are some ideas to consider:

- There are competing social values. Shoplifting is very costly to our society, causing businesses to lose anywhere from $5 billion to $25 billion annually. On the other hand, no one wants to shop in a "police state" environment.
- What is a "reasonable" suspicion of shoplifting? What if a clerk sees a customer hurry out, wearing a sweater identical to those on display? Must the clerk have seen the customer pick up the sweater? Put it on?
- What is "reasonable" detention? Can you tackle someone running through the parking lot? Can you shoot him?
- How private should the detention be? If you make your accusation publicly, in the store, you will deter many others from committing theft. But if you are wrong, what tort have you committed?
- How much questioning do you want to do, and how much would you prefer to leave to police?
- Some people in our society are biased against others, based on race or gender, while others are entirely free of such biases. How do you take that into account?
- Some states have passed "civil fine" statutes, which allow stores to demand, in writing, a fine from the shoplifter of up to three times the value of the goods taken. Often the shoplifter pays up immediately to avoid criminal prosecution. Should you lobby the state legislature to pass such a statute?

How much discretion do we permit?

There are no perfect answers to these questions, but a manager clearly needs to consider them and to craft an approach that meets the legal standard: reasonable suspicion of shoplifting and reasonable detention.

[6] *Kanner v. First National Bank of South Miami*, 287 So. 2d 715, 1974 Fla. App. LEXIS 8989 (Fla. Dist. Ct. App. 1974).

INTENTIONAL INFLICTION OF EMOTIONAL DISTRESS

What should happen when a defendant's conduct hurts a plaintiff emotionally but not physically? Historically, not much did happen. Courts once refused to allow recovery, assuming that if they awarded damages for mere emotional injury, they would be inviting a floodgate of dubious claims. But gradually judges reexamined their thinking and reversed this tendency. The law of emotional distress has been upsetting people ever since. Today, most courts allow a plaintiff to recover for emotional injury that a defendant intentionally caused. As we see in the next chapter, some courts will also permit recovery when a defendant's *negligent* conduct caused the emotional injury.

The intentional infliction of emotional distress results from extreme and outrageous conduct that causes serious emotional harm. A credit officer was struggling vainly to locate Sheehan, who owed money on his car. The officer phoned Sheehan's mother, falsely identified herself as a hospital employee, and said she needed to find Sheehan because his children had been in a serious auto accident. The mother provided Sheehan's whereabouts, which enabled the company to seize his car. But Sheehan spent seven hours frantically trying to locate his supposedly injured children, who in fact were fine. The credit company was liable for the intentional infliction of emotional distress.[7]

By contrast, a muffler shop, trying to collect a debt from a customer, made six phone calls over three months, using abusive language. The customer testified that this caused her to be upset, to cry, and to have difficulty sleeping. The court ruled that the muffler shop's conduct was neither extreme nor outrageous and sent the customer home for another sleepless night.[8] The following case arose in a setting that guarantees controversy—an abortion clinic.

JANE DOE AND NANCY ROE v. LYNN MILLS
212 Mich. App. 73, 536 N.W.2d 824, 1995 Mich. App. LEXIS 313
Michigan Court of Appeals, 1995

Facts: Late one night, an anti-abortion protestor named Robert Thomas climbed into a dumpster located behind the Women's Advisory Center, an abortion clinic. He found documents indicating that the plaintiffs were soon to have abortions at the clinic. Thomas gave the information to Lynn Mills. The next day, Mills and Sister Lois Mitoraj created signs, using the women's names, indicating that they were about to undergo abortions, and urging them not to "kill their babies."

Doe and Roe (not their real names) sued, claiming intentional infliction of emotional distress (as well as breach of privacy, discussed later in this chapter). The trial court dismissed the lawsuit, ruling that the defendants' conduct was not extreme and outrageous. The plaintiffs appealed.

Issue: Have the plaintiffs made a valid claim of intentional infliction of emotional distress?

Excerpts from the Court's Per Curiam Decision: Liability for the intentional infliction of emotional distress has been found only where the conduct complained of has been so outrageous in character, and so extreme in degree, as to go beyond all possible bounds of decency, and to be regarded as atrocious and utterly

---

7 *Ford Motor Credit Co. v. Sheehan*, 373 So. 2d 956, 1979 Fla. App. LEXIS 15416 (Fla. Dist. Ct. App. 1979).

8 *Midas Muffler Shop v. Ellison*, 133 Ariz. 194, 650 P.2d 496, 1982 Ariz. App. LEXIS 488 (Ariz. Ct. App. 1982).

intolerable in a civilized community. Liability does not extend to mere insults, indignities, threats, annoyances, petty oppressions, or other trivialities. It has been said that the case is generally one in which the recitation of the facts to an average member of the community would arouse his resentment against the actor, and lead him to exclaim, "Outrageous!"

The conduct in this case involved defendants identifying plaintiffs by name and publicizing the fact of their abortions by displaying such information on large signs that were held up for public view. In ruling that defendants' conduct was not sufficiently extreme and outrageous so as to permit recovery, the trial court was influenced in part by its conclusion that the information disclosed did not concern a private matter, inasmuch as it was obtained from a document that had been discarded into the trash. [But the plaintiffs themselves never placed their names on the discarded papers, and even if they had, such an act would not have indicated consent to such publicity.] The trial court also observed that defendants have a constitutional right to "protest peaceably against abortion." However, the objectionable aspect of defendants' conduct does not relate to their views on abortion or their right to express those views, but, rather, to the fact that defendants gave unreasonable or unnecessary publicity to purely private matters involving plaintiffs. Finally, the trial court observed that there is no statute prohibiting the kind of activity engaged in by defendants. It is not necessary, however, that a defendant's conduct constitute a statutory violation in order for it to be found extreme and outrageous.

We are of the opinion that the trial court erred in granting the defendants' motion for summary disposition of plaintiffs' claim of intentional infliction of emotional distress. Defendants' conduct involved more than mere insults, indignities, threats, annoyances, or petty oppressions. We believe this is the type of case that might cause an average member of the community, upon learning of defendants' conduct, to exclaim, "Outrageous!" Because reasonable men may differ with regard to whether defendants' conduct may be considered sufficiently outrageous and extreme so as to subject them to liability for intentional infliction of emotional distress, this matter should be determined by the trier of fact.

[Summary judgment for the defendants is reversed, and the case is remanded for trial.]

BATTERY AND ASSAULT

These two torts are related, but not identical. **Battery is an intentional touching of another person in a way that is unwanted or offensive.** As mentioned earlier, there need be no intention to *hurt* the plaintiff. If the defendant intended to do the physical act, and a reasonable plaintiff would be offended by it, battery has occurred.

Suppose an irate parent throws a chair at a referee during his daughter's basketball game, breaking the man's jaw. It is irrelevant that the father did not intend to injure the referee. But a parent who cheerfully slaps the winning coach on the back has not committed battery, because a reasonable coach would not be offended. An executive who gives an unwanted sexual caress to a secretary also commits this tort, even if he assumed that any normal female would be ecstatic over his attentions. (This is also sexual harassment, discussed in Chapter 30, on employment law.)

Assault occurs when a defendant does some act that makes a plaintiff fear an imminent battery. It is assault even though the battery never occurs. Suppose Ms. Wilson shouts "Think fast!" at her husband and hurls a toaster at him. He turns and sees it flying at him. His fear of being struck is enough to win a case of assault, even if the toaster misses. If the toaster happens to strike him, Ms. Wilson has also committed battery.

Recall the shoplifting problem. Assume that a store guard pulls an unloaded pistol on Sandra Shopper, suspecting her of theft. Sandra faints and strikes her head on a counter. When sued for assault, the store defends by claiming the guard never touched her and the gun was unloaded. Obviously, the store did not have the benefit of this law course. A reasonable shopper would have feared imminent battery, and the store is liable for assault.

TRESPASS, CONVERSION, AND FRAUD

Trespass

Trespass is intentionally entering land that belongs to someone else or remaining on the land after being asked to leave. It is also trespass if you have some object, let's say a car, on someone else's property and refuse to remove it. "Intentionally" means that you deliberately walk onto the land. If you walk through a meadow, believing it to be a public park, and it belongs to a private owner, you have trespassed.

This shows that the law strongly values the rights of private property owners. How strongly? Heather installs a springloaded rifle in her house, aimed at the front door and tripped by a wire connected to the door. Bruno breaks in at night, planning to steal, and is shot. Bruno, now serving time for breaking and entering, sues. Is Heather liable? In most states, no, she is not. Most courts hold that a homeowner may use a springloaded rifle to prevent a major felony, like entering a dwelling at night.[9]

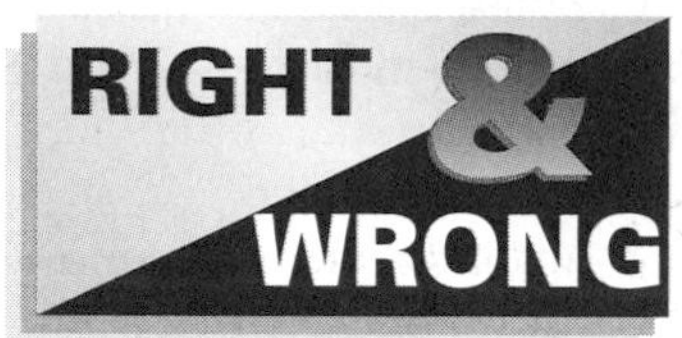

A few states disagree. Saying that we should not place a higher value on property than on human life, they make it unlawful to install a springloaded rifle. Do the reasonable fear and anger of a homeowner justify a springloaded weapon, even if it costs a human life? Should it matter whether the home is occupied? That is, should a homeowner be entitled to set up such a weapon in her vacation home, even when she is hundreds of miles away? What if someone entered the home for an innocent reason, seeking shelter from a storm or intending to repair a gas leak?

Conversion

Conversion is taking or using someone's personal property without consent. Personal property is any possession other than land. Priceless jewels, ratty sneakers, and a sailboat are all personal property. If Stormy sails away in Jib's sailboat and keeps it all summer, that is conversion. Stormy owes Jib the full value of the boat. This, of course, is similar to the crime of theft. The tort of conversion enables a plaintiff to pursue the case herself, without awaiting a criminal prosecution, and to obtain compensation.

Fraud

Fraud is injuring another person by deliberate deception. It is fraud to sell real estate knowing that there is a large toxic waste deposit underground of which the buyer is ignorant. Fraud is a tort, but it typically occurs during the negotiation or performance of a contract, and it is discussed in detail in Unit 2, on contracts.

---

[9] See, e.g., Restatement (Second) of Torts §85, permitting springloaded weapons wherever an actor himself could have used deadly force were he present, which, according to §143, includes defending a home from a breaking and entering during the nighttime. Compare the opposite result in *Katko v. Briney*, 183 N.W.2d 657, 1971 Iowa Sup. LEXIS 717 (Iowa 1971).

DAMAGES

Mitchel Bien, a deaf mute, enters the George Grubbs Nissan dealership, where folks sell cars aggressively. *Very* aggressively. Maturelli, a salesman, and Bien communicate by writing messages back and forth. Maturelli takes Bien's own car keys, and the two then test drive a 300ZX. Bien says he does not want the car, but Maturelli escorts him back inside and fills out a sales sheet. Bien repeatedly asks for his keys, but Maturelli only laughs, pressuring him to buy the new car. Minutes pass. Hours pass. Bien becomes frantic, writing a dozen notes, begging to leave, threatening to call the police. Maturelli mocks Bien and his physical disabilities. Finally, after four hours, the customer escapes.

Bien sues for the intentional infliction of emotional distress. Two former salesmen from Grubbs testify they have witnessed customers cry, yell, and curse as a result of the aggressive tactics. Doctors state that the incident has traumatized Bien, dramatically reducing his confidence and self-esteem and preventing his return to work even three years later.

The jury awards Bien damages. But how does a jury calculate the money? For that matter, why should a jury even try? Money can never erase pain or undo a permanent injury. The answer is simple: money, however inexact and ineffective, is the only thing a court has to give. Here is how damages are figured.

First, a plaintiff receives money for medical expenses that he has proven by producing bills from doctors, hospitals, physical therapists, and psychotherapists. Bien receives all the money he has paid. If a doctor testifies that he needs future treatment, Bien will offer evidence of how much that will cost. The **single recovery principle** requires a court to settle the matter once and for all, by awarding a lump sum for past and future expenses. A plaintiff may not return in a year and say, "Oh, by the way, there are some new bills."

Second, the defendants are liable for lost wages. The court takes the number of days or months that Bien missed work and multiplies that times his salary. If Bien is currently unable to work, a doctor estimates how many more months he will miss work, and the court adds that to his damages.

Third, a plaintiff is paid for pain and suffering. Bien testifies about how traumatic the four hours were and how the experience has affected his life. He may state that he now fears shopping, suffers nightmares, and seldom socializes. To bolster the case, a plaintiff uses expert testimony, such as the psychiatrists who testified for Bien. Awards for pain and suffering vary enormously, from a few dollars to many millions, depending on the injury and depending on the jury. In some lawsuits, physical and psychological pain are momentary and insignificant; in other cases, the pain is the biggest part of the verdict. In this case, the jury awarded Bien $573,815, calculated as in the table on the next page.[10]

PUNITIVE DAMAGES

Here we look at a different kind of award, one that is more controversial and potentially more powerful: punitive damages. The purpose is not to compensate the plaintiff for harm, because compensatory damages will have done that. **Punitive damages are intended to punish the defendant for conduct that is**

[10] The compensatory damages are described in *George Grubbs Enterprises v. Bien*, 881 S.W.2d 843, 1994 Tex. App. LEXIS 1870 (Tex. Ct. App. 1994). In addition to the compensatory damages described, the jury awarded $5 million in punitive damages. The Texas Supreme Court reversed the award of punitive damages, but not the compensatory. *Id.*, 900 S.W.2d 337, 1995 Tex. LEXIS 91 (Tex. 1995). The high court did not dispute the appropriateness of punitive damages, but reversed because the trial court failed to instruct the jury properly as to how it should determine the assets actually under the defendants' control, an issue essential to punitive damages but not compensatory.

Past medical	$ 70.00
Future medical	6,000.00
Past rehabilitation	3,205.00
Past lost earning capacity	112,910.00
Future lost earning capacity	34,650.00
Past physical symptoms and discomfort	50,000.00
Future physical symptoms and discomfort	50,000.00
Past emotional injury and mental anguish	101,980.00
Future emotional injury and mental anguish	200,000.00
Past loss of society and reduced ability to socially interact with family, former fiancee, and friends, and hearing (i.e., nondeaf) people in general	10,000.00
Future loss of society and reduced ability to socially interact with family, former fiancee, and friends, and hearing people	5,000.00
TOTAL	$573,815.00

extreme and outrageous. Courts award these damages in relatively few cases. When an award of punitive damages is made, it is generally in a case of intentional tort, although they occasionally appear in negligence suits.

The idea behind punitive damages is that certain behavior is so unacceptable that society must make an example of it. A large award of money should deter not only the defendant from repeating the mistake but others from ever making it. This is social engineering in an extreme form. Predictably, some believe punitive damages represent the law at its most avaricious while others attribute to them great social benefit.

One criticism of punitive damages has been that juries have too much discretion in making the award. A recent Supreme Court case illustrates this point and the current rules. Ira Gore purchased a new BMW automobile from an Alabama dealer and then discovered that the car had been repainted. He sued. At trial, BMW acknowledged a nationwide policy of not informing customers of predelivery repairs when the cost was less than 3 percent of the retail price. The company had sold about 1,000 repainted cars nationwide. The jury concluded that BMW had engaged in gross, malicious fraud and awarded Gore $4,000 in compensatory damages and $4 million in punitive damages. The Alabama Supreme Court reduced the award to $2 million, but the United States Supreme Court ruled that even that amount was grossly excessive. The Court held that in awarding punitive damages, a court must consider three "guideposts":

- The reprehensibility of the defendant's conduct
- The ratio between the harm suffered and the award; and
- The difference between the punitive award and any civil penalties used in similar cases.

The Court concluded that BMW had shown no evil intent and that Gore's harm had been purely economic (as opposed to physical). Further, the Court found the ratio of 500 to 1, between punitive and compensatory damages, to be excessive, although it offered no definitive rule about a proper ratio. On remand, the Alabama Supreme Court reduced the punitive damages award to $50,000.[11]

Studies indicate that punitive damages are rare and generally modest. Courts award them in about 6 percent of those cases that plaintiffs win. When compensatory damages are $10,000, punitive damages (when given) average $10,000; when the compensatory award is $100,000, the punitive award, if any, averages $66,000. But occasionally punitive awards are huge and generate tremendous publicity.

When the *Exxon Valdez* ran aground, it dumped 11 million gallons of oil into the sea; the oil eventually spread 470 miles along the Alaskan coast. Exxon spent over $2 billion cleaning up the spill and paid an additional $1.3 billion in civil and criminal penalties and settlements. A jury found Exxon liable to Alaskan fishermen and awarded $286 million in compensatory damages. Two months later that same jury came back with its award of punitive damages: an even $5 billion, the second largest verdict ever in a civil suit.[12] Not surprisingly, Exxon has appealed, claiming that the punitive award is excessive. To walk through a gallery of photographs devoted to the *Exxon Valdez* and other oil spills, visit **http://response.restoration.noaa.gov/photos/gallery.html.**

Do punitive damages present the revolting specter of money-grubbing lawyers convincing gullible juries to award preposterous verdicts to avaricious clients? Or do they demonstrate that idealistic lawyers, working with no guarantee of a payday,[13] can use the humane instincts of a jury to force callous corporations to consider something other than the fabled bottom line?

WALSTON v. MONUMENTAL LIFE INSURANCE CO.

129 Idaho 211, 923 P.2d 456, 1996 Ida. LEXIS 120

Idaho Supreme Court, 1996

Facts: Monumental Life Insurance sent James Walston a brochure advertising health insurance. The brochure included the endorsement of a Masonic organization that Walston trusted. In large letters the brochure advertised "lifetime benefits of up to $250,000." Walston applied, for himself and his wife. He filled out the necessary form, which included a statement that no person to be insured had been "treated for any type of cancer for the past five years." Walston's wife had undergone a mastectomy for breast cancer five years and fifteen days before he filled in the form. She had made two follow-up visits, for check-ups, within the five-year period.

One month after Walston applied for insurance, his wife was diagnosed with lung cancer, unrelated to her previous illness. She ultimately died from the lung cancer. Under the policy, Walston was entitled to $3,800 for his wife's unsuccessful treatments. But when Monumental investigated and learned of her previous illness, it accused Walston of lying on the application, and refused to pay.

Walston sued, and a jury awarded him $3,800 for breach of contract; $120,000 for the company's bad faith denial of benefits; and $10 million in punitive damages. The trial judge reduced the punitive damages to $3.2 million, and Monumental appealed.

Issue: Was the punitive damage award excessive?

---

11 *BMW of North America, Inc. v. Gore*, 517 U.S. 559, 116 S. Ct. 1589, 1996 U.S. LEXIS 3390 (1996).

12 The largest verdict came in 1985, in *Pennzoil v. Texaco*. See the section on interference with contract, later in the chapter.

13 Lawyers normally take personal injury cases on a contingency basis, meaning that they receive no money up-front from their client. Their fee will be a percentage of the plaintiff's judgment *if* she wins. Lawyers often take about one-third of the award. But if the defendant wins, the plaintiff's lawyer will have worked several years for no pay.

Excerpts from Judge Schroeder's Decision: James L. Wadhams, a former Nevada insurance official, was permitted to testify that the mailing sent to Walston violated Idaho insurance department advertising regulations and was designed to deceive. Wadhams testified that advertising the policy as a "high-limit" policy and referencing the $250,000 aggregate limit was misleading because of the internal limits on individual benefits contained within the policy which in fact made it a low-limits policy. It was virtually impossible to reach the overall limit advertised in the policy.

Wadhams testified that the denial of benefits on the basis that Mrs. Walston had undergone treatment within five years was improper, because Monumental imposed an unusual and strained interpretation on the term treatment. He described the way the policy was advertised and adjusted as an extreme deviation of reasonable standards of conduct. Evidence at trial indicated that Monumental's practices in this case were consistent with its usual way of doing business. The denial of benefits was approved by upper management. Management of Monumental did not see any problem with its conduct and intended to continue doing business in the same manner.

The facts of this case establish deceptive marketing practices by Monumental which are likely to continue if not deterred. The facts also establish bad faith denial of benefits practices which will continue if not deterred. The district court determined that a $3.2 million punitive damage award would deter Monumental and other companies. The district court arrived at this amount by calculating 5% of Monumental's annual profit. This is a reasonable method of determining an appropriate amount for deterrent purposes.

In analyzing whether [a punitive damages award] was grossly excessive in *BMW v. Gore*, the U.S. Supreme Court commented as follows: "Perhaps the most important indicium of the reasonableness of a punitive damages award is the degree of reprehensibility of the defendant's conduct. As the Court stated nearly 150 years ago, exemplary damages imposed on a defendant should reflect 'the enormity of his offense.'"

Repainting BMWs prior to sale does not rise high on the level of reprehensibility. Misrepresenting insurance coverage and refusal to pay a claim that any reasonable person would say was due does rise high on the reprehensibility scale. Monumental bought its way into Walston's door as a business endorsed by a Masonic organization that he felt he could trust. Monumental utilized deceptive practices in promoting its policy, including the representation that it was providing high limits coverage when the limits were quite low. Monumental refused to pay a claim on an unreasonable definition of treatment and steadfastly held to its position.

The punitive damage award in this case does not offend any constitutional standards. The decision of the district court is affirmed.

As long as juries get angry, punitive damage awards, though rarely granted, will occasionally be high. Sixty-nine-year-old Reba Gregory lived in a nursing home owned by Beverly Enterprises, Inc., the nation's largest operator of these facilities. She broke her shoulder and hip in a fall and sued, claiming that the operator chronically understaffed the facility and repeatedly used fraud to conceal problems from state regulators. The jury agreed, awarding Ms. Gregory $365,580 in compensatory damages—and $94.7 million in punitive damages. The company has appealed. The battle over a just verdict continues—worldwide.

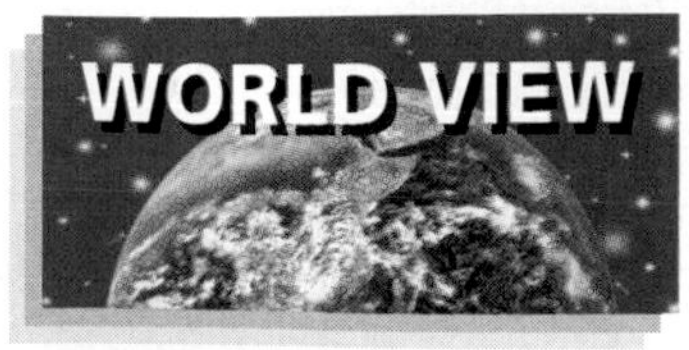

Huge damage awards can create controversy but so can small ones. Sesto Gherri is a laborer in central Italy. His 12-year-old son, Luigi, was killed in a road accident, and an Italian court awarded the family compensatory damages—of $780. The court indicated that because Luigi was the son of a laborer, he would never have been able to earn much money. Sesto attacked the ruling as "classist."

BUSINESS TORTS

In this section we look at four intentional torts that occur almost exclusively in a commercial setting: interference with a contract, interference with a prospective advantage, the rights to privacy and publicity, and Lanham Act violations. Note that several business torts are discussed elsewhere in the book:

- Patents, copyrights, and trademarks are discussed in Chapter 44, on intellectual property.
- False advertising, discussed in part under the Lanham Act section below, is considered more broadly in Chapter 42, on consumer law.
- Consumer issues are also covered in Chapter 42. The material in the present chapter focuses not on consumer claims but on disputes between businesses.

TORTIOUS INTERFERENCE WITH BUSINESS RELATIONS

Competition is the essence of business. Successful corporations compete aggressively, and the law permits and expects them to. But there are times when healthy competition becomes illegal interference. This is called tortious interference with business relations. It can take one of two closely related forms—interference with a contract or interference with a prospective advantage.

Tortious Interference with a Contract

Tortious interference with a contract exists only if the plaintiff can establish the following four elements:

- There was a contract between the plaintiff and a third party
- The defendant knew of the contract
- The defendant improperly induced the third party to breach the contract or made performance of the contract impossible; and
- There was injury to the plaintiff.

Because businesses routinely compete for customers, employees, and market share, it is not always easy to identify tortious interference. There is nothing wrong with two companies bidding against each other to buy a parcel of land, and nothing wrong with one corporation doing everything possible to convince the seller to ignore all competitors. But once a company has signed a contract to buy the land, it is improper to induce the seller to break the deal. The most commonly disputed issues in these cases concern elements one and three: Was there a contract between the plaintiff and another party? Did the defendant *improperly* induce a party to breach it? Defendants will try to show that the plaintiff had no contract.

A defendant may also rely on the defense of **justification**, that is, a claim that special circumstances made its conduct fair. To establish justification, a defendant must show that:

- It was acting to protect *an existing economic interest*, such as its own contract with the third party
- It was acting in the *public interest*, for example, by reporting to a government agency that a corporation was overbilling for government services; or

- The existing contract could be *terminated* at will by either party, meaning that although the plaintiff had a contract, the plaintiff had no long-term assurances because the other side could end it at any time.

Texaco v. Pennzoil

The largest verdict in the history of American law came in a case of contract interference. *Texaco, Inc. v. Pennzoil Co.* illustrates the two key issues: Did a contract exist, and was the defendant's behavior improper? In December 1983, Pennzoil made an unsolicited bid to buy 20 percent of Getty Oil at $100 per share. This offer was too low to satisfy the Getty board of directors, but it got the parties talking. The price increased to $110 per share, and the two sides began to put together pieces of a complicated deal: Gordon Getty would control four-sevenths of the Getty Oil stock, and Pennzoil would control three-sevenths. The J. Paul Getty Museum, which owned 11.8 percent of Getty stock, agreed to sell its shares *provided it was paid immediately*. Talks continued, the price moved up to $112.50 a share, and finally the Getty board voted to approve the deal. A press release announced an agreement in principle between Pennzoil and Getty.

Before the lawyers for both sides could complete the paperwork for the deal, Texaco appeared and offered Getty stockholders $125 per share for the entire company and later upped that offer to $128. Getty turned its attention to Texaco, leaving Pennzoil the jilted lover. This lover, though, decided to sue. In Texas state court, Pennzoil claimed that Texaco had interfered with a Pennzoil-Getty contract, costing Pennzoil vast amounts of money.

Pennzoil's strategy at trial was to vilify Texaco, depicting every move of the defendant as part of a strategy to wreck the Pennzoil-Getty deal. Texaco argued that there was no malice on its part because in fact there was no binding contract between the other two. All they had was an understanding in principle.

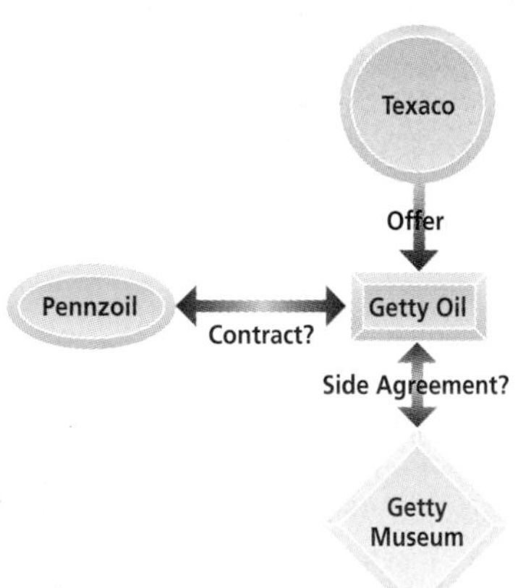

The $10 *billion* question. Texaco offered to pay $125 per share for Getty stock. The key issue was this: When Texaco made the offer, did a contract exist between Pennzoil and Getty? If, as the jury decided, there was a binding agreement, then Texaco committed tortious interference with a contract. If, however, Getty Corp. had a side agreement with the Getty Museum (one of its owners), then arguably there could be no contract between Getty and Pennzoil, and Texaco would have committed no tort at all.

But the jury bought Pennzoil's argument, and they bought it big: $7.53 billion in actual damages, plus $3 billion more in punitive damages. The total of $10.53 billion is the highest verdict in any law case anywhere, ever. Texaco did not happen to have $10 billion it could spare, and the verdict threatened to destroy the oil company. Texaco appealed, but Texas appeals courts require a bond, in this case a $10 billion bond, meaning that the money must be paid into court while the appeal goes forward. Instead, Texaco filed for bankruptcy. While Texaco pursued its appeal, the two sides discussed a possible settlement but appeared far apart.

In the state appeals court, Texaco continued to claim that Pennzoil and Getty never had a valid contract. It based its argument on an obscure rule of the Securities and Exchange Commission (SEC), Rule 10B-13. This rule prevents the parties in a takeover negotiation from arranging a "side deal" while an offer is pending. Texaco's argument thus became: Pennzoil's original $100 per share offer was still pending when the two sides came up with their $112.50 per share, "three-sevenths/four-sevenths" deal. That deal involved a side arrangement with the Getty Museum, which would get its money faster than any other shareholders would. Because it would get about $1 billion, early receipt was a major financial advantage. The deal violated Rule 10B-13 and was therefore invalid. There was no contract and Texaco could not legally have interfered.

Pennzoil responded by saying that it had planned all along to equalize any benefits that the Getty Museum got by paying additional money to the other shareholders. Further, said Pennzoil, even if a technical violation of Rule 10B-13 had occurred, Pennzoil would have applied to the SEC and obtained an exemption from the rule. The Court of Appeals in Texas was unpersuaded by most of Texaco's arguments. The court did lower the punitive damages by $2 billion, but it otherwise affirmed. The court did not accept the argument that Rule 10B-13 destroyed the contract.

Texaco appealed to the Texas Supreme Court, all the while continuing to negotiate with Pennzoil over a possible settlement. Texaco decided to concentrate its final appeal on the Rule 10B-13 argument. In other words, a $10 billion case would be decided on the classic "interference" issue of whether a contract existed. Texaco spent months trying to convince the SEC to enter the case and explain to the Texas Supreme Court precisely what the little known rule meant. Texaco received a huge boost when the SEC announced that it would in fact file a brief in the case. The brief it wrote seemed strongly to advance Texaco's argument. Pennzoil could sense that the tide was turning. And so, in December 1987, Pennzoil announced that the two parties had reached an agreement: Texaco would pay Pennzoil $3 billion as settlement for having wrongfully interfered with Pennzoil's agreement to buy Getty.

Tortious Interference with a Prospective Advantage

"Interference with a prospective advantage" is an awkward name for a tort that is simply a variation on interference with a contract. The difference is that, for this tort, there need be no contract; the plaintiff is claiming outside interference with an expected economic relationship. Obviously, the plaintiff must show more than just the hope of a profit. **A plaintiff who has a definite and reasonable expectation of obtaining an economic advantage may sue a corporation that maliciously interferes and prevents the relationship from developing.**

The defense of justification, discussed above, applies here as well. A typical example of justification is that the defendant is simply competing for the same business that the plaintiff seeks. There is nothing wrong with that. It becomes a tort when the defendant sets out to hurt the plaintiff by blocking some advantage from developing.

The following case, involving the Chicago Bulls basketball team, illustrates the difference between interference with a contract and interference with a prospective advantage.

FISHMAN v. ESTATE OF WIRTZ
807 F.2d 520, 1986 U.S. App. LEXIS 34177
United States Court of Appeals for the Seventh Circuit, 1986

Facts: In 1971 the Chicago Professional Basketball Corp. ("Chicago Basketball") decided to sell the Chicago Bulls, a professional basketball team that belonged to the National Basketball Association (NBA). Rich was president of Chicago Basketball. Plaintiff Fishman formed an investors' group to buy the team, and by January 1972 his group had reached an agreement in principle with Chicago Basketball for the sale. Fishman's group then attempted to lease the Chicago Stadium, which was controlled by Arthur Wirtz. But Wirtz declined to give Fishman a favorable lease.

Fishman then formed a new investors' group, "IBI," which resumed negotiations with Rich. By April 1972, he had competition: a group composed largely of the other members of the first Fishman group, with the addition of Arthur Wirtz, that had incorporated as "CPSC." Between March and May 1972, IBI and CPSC both offered to purchase the Bulls. Chicago Basketball formally accepted and executed IBI's contract. But the board of governors of the NBA would not give its approval because IBI lacked a stadium. The board told IBI it could reapply if it obtained a lease.

Fishman again tried to negotiate a lease with Wirtz, but Wirtz refused even to meet with him. He did, however, meet with Rich, and asked Rich to sell the Bulls to *his* group. Rich refused, saying that Chicago Basketball had a contract with IBI. Wirtz then made it clear to Fishman, Rich, and members of the NBA that he would never give IBI a lease at the Chicago Stadium, and that only his own group would have such a lease. Six days before the next NBA meeting, IBI executed a lease at the International Amphitheatre, a smaller stadium in Chicago.

The NBA board of governors met in New York City on July 11, 1972, and again voted to disapprove the sale to IBI, giving two reasons: (1) the Chicago Stadium, which was withheld from IBI but available to CPSC, was vastly superior to any other arena in Chicago and was in their opinion the only adequate facility in Chicago for NBA basketball; and (2) CPSC was the preferable group to acquire the Bulls. Chicago Basketball renewed negotiations with CPSC and made a deal in July 1972, which the NBA approved the next month.

IBI sued, claiming that the defendants had violated the Sherman Antitrust Act and Illinois law by interfering with plaintiffs' contract rights and prospective advantage. The United States District Court ruled for IBI on virtually all claims, and CPSC appealed.

Issue: Did CPSC interfere with IBI's contractual rights and/or its prospective advantage?

Excerpts from Circuit Judge Cudahy's Decision: The plaintiffs [charged] all defendants with tortious interference with contractual relations and tortious interference with prospective advantage. The district court ruled that the plaintiffs had proven both of these claims. We think that the district court erred in concluding that defendants had tortiously interfered with IBI's contract because IBI had no unconditional right under the contract to become the owner of the Bulls.

IBI executed a valid contract with Chicago Basketball, and there is no indication that Rich did not perform his obligations under the contract (using his best efforts to win the NBA's approval and transferring ownership of the Bulls in the event of NBA approval) as expected. IBI had an enforceable right in the performance of these obligations, but prior to NBA approval it had no more than an expectancy, however reasonable, in owning the Bulls. Thus, there could be no claim for tortious interference with the IBI-Chicago Basketball contract because that contract had not been breached.

Wirtz refused to lease the stadium to IBI and then submitted a competing bid for the Chicago Bulls. Was that a business tort?

The tort of unlawful interference with prospective advantage, on the other hand, does not depend on the existence of a contract. The essential elements are

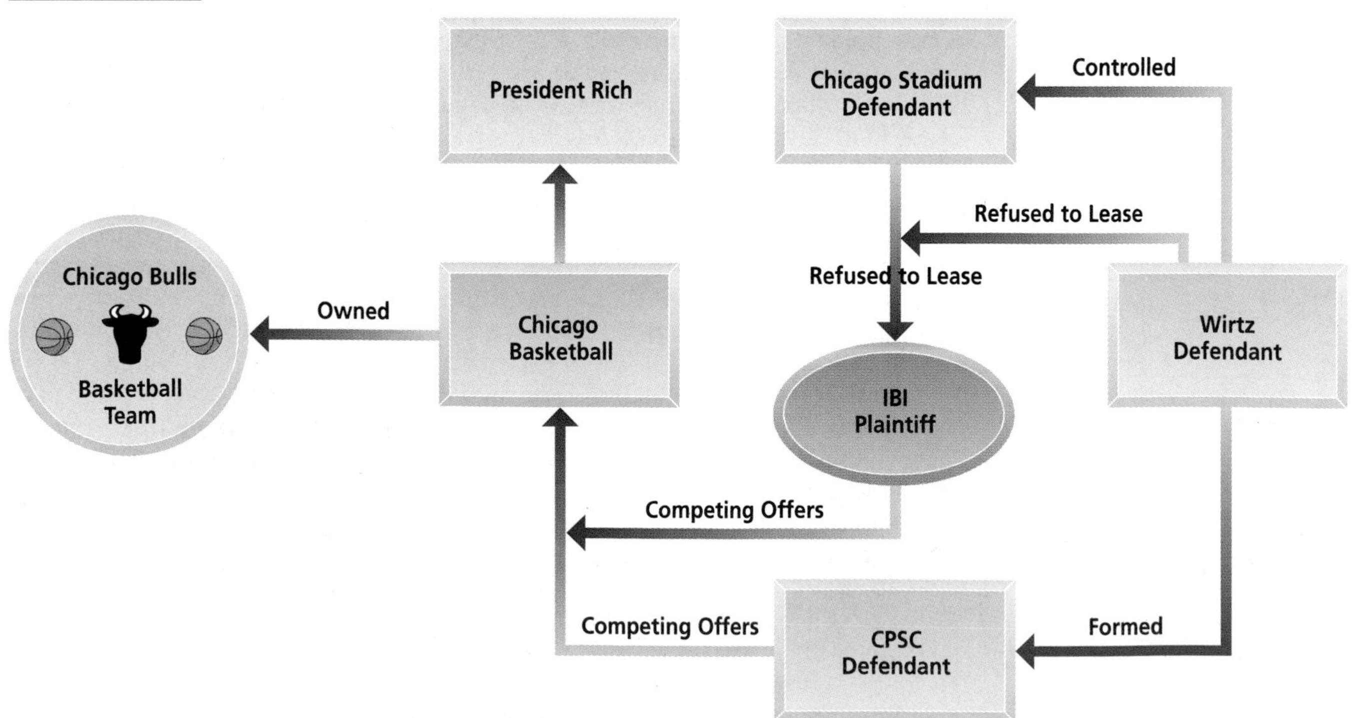

(1) plaintiff's reasonable expectation of entering a business relationship; (2) defendant's knowledge of that expectation; and (3) intentional interference by defendant that prevents plaintiff from realizing that expectation. [But a plaintiff will not succeed if the defendant had a "competitor's privilege or justification," i.e., if the defendant was competing fairly.]

The district court ruled that the competitor's privilege was not available to defendants because no competition was possible after the contract was signed. We have explained why we think this is clearly erroneous. Lawful competition before the NBA was a distinct possibility in this case. However, as we have noted, defendants competed unlawfully when they withheld the Chicago Stadium from IBI, and the district court also found that CPSC's competition was not privileged because the acts by which it interfered with IBI's expectancy were independently violations of federal antitrust law.

We conclude that under Illinois law the defendants' actions were not privileged as those of a competitor. IBI had a reasonable expectation of entering a valid business relationship with Rich. Defendants knew of this expectancy. Defendants intentionally interfered with this expectancy, through an unfair and anticompetitive act—the concerted refusal to lease the Stadium—that lost them their competitors' privilege. Thus, we approve the finding of liability on state law grounds, insofar as it is premised upon tortious interference with prospective advantage.

Privacy and Publicity

We live in a world of dazzling technology, and it is easier than ever—and more profitable—to spy on someone. For example, the Web page **http://www.thesmokinggun.com** specializes in publishing revealing data about celebrities. Does the law protect us? What power do we have to limit the intrusion of others into our lives and to prohibit them from commercially exploiting information about us? Privacy and publicity law involves four main issues: intrusion, disclosure, false information, and commercial exploitation.

Intrusion

Intrusion into someone's private life is a tort if a reasonable person would find it offensive. Peeping through someone's windows or wiretapping his telephone are obvious examples of intrusion. In a famous case involving a "paparazzo" photographer and Jacqueline Kennedy Onassis, the court found that the photographer had invaded her privacy by making a career out of photographing her. He had bribed doormen to gain access to hotels and restaurants she visited, had jumped out of bushes to photograph her young children, and had driven power boats dangerously close to her. The court ordered him to stop.[14] Nine years later the paparazzo was found in contempt of court for again taking photographs too close to Ms. Onassis. He agreed to stop once and for all—in exchange for a suspended contempt sentence.

"Hi, Bob," says the friendly voice on the phone. "Listen, I know you're coming to Happy City this week. We've got a great band playing at Pinky, our club. We're only a block from your hotel."

"Who is this?" Bob demands. "How on earth did you know I am going to Happy City?" The friendly caller laughs and mentions that Pinky features performers dressed only in flamingo feathers, dancing to the beat of Palestrina, a composer who died in 1594. "I know you love feathers and Palestrina," chuckles

---

[14] *Galella v. Onassis*, 487 F.2d 986, 1973 U.S. App. LEXIS 7901 (2d Cir. 1973).

the caller, "and this is the only place you can get them both." Bob slams the phone down, angry, embarrassed—and astonished.

How does the caller know so much? A month ago, when Bob booked a flight to Happy City, the airline sold his name to Gotcha!, a company that collects and sells information. Gotcha! also purchased data from Fluffy, a Web site about bars. Bob had once clicked onto the site, and while he viewed the page, Fluffy wrote a "cookie" onto Bob's hard drive. The cookie enabled Fluffy to track each visit Bob made to its site and other linked sites. Fluffy learned that Bob visited a site about bars with feather-dancers. When Gotcha! obtained Bob's name from Fluffy, it cross-checked its other databases and discovered Bob was headed for Happy City. Gotcha! had already purchased the names of all guests staying in the five best hotels at Happy City, so it was easy to learn Bob's address. Palestrina? Simple: Three years ago, Bob used his credit card to pay for tickets to a classical concert in Sioux City, Iowa, where he heard two Palestrina pieces. Having discovered Bob's entertainment tastes, Gotcha! was able to make the perfect match with Pinky, to which it sold all the data for a handsome profit.

Is all of this legal? *Any* of it? Is it ethical? There are no solid legal answers, because courts have yet to rule, but there is one easy prediction: the issues will be litigated, and courts will have to determine what protection common law intrusion rights afford us from the all-seeing eye of the computer. (*Did* Bob go to Pinky? Give him a call and find out. His phone number is on the Internet—as is yours—and Bob would be amazed to hear from you.)

Disclosure of Embarrassing Private Facts

A defendant (such as a media organization) is liable if it discloses to the public facts that a reasonable person would consider very embarrassing, and in which the public has no legitimate interest. Suppose a local newspaper reports that a particular high school student had a baby out of wedlock. The public has no need of that information, and the paper has committed a tort. Similarly, recall the case *Doe v. Mills*, earlier in this chapter, concerning the abortion demonstrators who publicized the names of women arriving at the clinic. The plaintiffs sued not only for the intentional infliction of emotional distress, but also for disclosure of embarrassing facts. By contrast, consider the case of a most unusual body surfer. He agreed to an interview with *Sports Illustrated* but then sued when the magazine divulged odd personal facts, including that he put out cigarettes in his mouth, dove off stairs to impress women, hurt himself so he could collect unemployment, and ate insects.[15] *Sports Illustrated* won. The court held that, bizarre as these revelations were, they were not sensationally embarrassing. Further, they were a legitimate part of a news story about an eccentric and daring body surfer.

False Light

Like defamation, this tort involves false information about the plaintiff. Unlike defamation, this tort can arise without harm to a plaintiff's reputation. **If false information portrays the plaintiff in a way that most people would find offensive, it is "false light."** A model named Robyn Douglass posed nude for a photographer and authorized him to publish the photos in *Playboy Magazine*. The photographer sold some to *Playboy* but later sold other photographs to *Hustler Magazine*. The court agreed with Douglass that this placed her in a false light by making her seem to be the sort of person who would pose for *Hustler*. A reasonable person might find that while *Playboy* is mildly erotic, *Hustler* concentrates on sex in ways that are crude and degrading. Douglass won $600,000.[16]

---

15 *Virgil v. Sports Illustrated*, 424 F. Supp. 1286, 1976 U.S. Dist. LEXIS 11779 (S.D. Cal. 1976).

16 *Douglass v. Hustler Magazine, Inc.*, 769 F.2d 1128, 1985 U.S. App. LEXIS 19980 (7th Cir. 1985).

Commercial Exploitation

This right prohibits the use of someone's likeness or voice for commercial purposes. This business tort is the flip side of privacy and covers the right to make money from publicity. For example, it would be illegal to run a magazine ad showing actress Sharon Stone holding a can of soda, without her permission. The ad would imply that she endorses the product. Someone's identity is her own, and it cannot be exploited unless she permits it. Ford Motor Co. hired a singer to imitate Bette Midler's version of a popular song. The imitation was so good that most listeners were fooled into believing that Ms. Midler was endorsing the product. That, ruled a court, violated her right to commercial exploitation.[17]

The cyberlaw hypothetical above, about Bob and the feather-dancers, also raises issues of commercial exploitation. When do operators of a Web site have the right to use information about users? Do they need your permission to sell your name and address? To make a profit from books you buy, places you go, entertainment you attend? Again, the law lags behind technology, and no court has yet answered the question.

THE LANHAM ACT

The Lanham Act, a federal statute, was passed in 1946 and amended in 1988. Section 43(a) of the statute provides broad protection against false statements intended to hurt another business. In order to win a case under this section, a plaintiff must prove three things:

- That the defendants made *false or misleading fact statements* about the plaintiff's business. This could be a false comparative ad, showing the plaintiff's product to be worse than it is, or it could be a misleading ad, which, though literally accurate, is misleading about the defendant's own product.
- That the defendants used the statements *in commercial advertising or promotion*. In order to protect First Amendment rights of free speech, particularly political and social commentary, this Act covers only commercial speech. A radio ad for beer could violate the Lanham Act; but a radio ad urging that smoking be abolished in public places is not a commercial statement and cannot violate the Act.
- That statements created the *likelihood of harm* to the plaintiff.

"Knock It Off brand food supplement will help you lose weight and gain muscle faster than any competing supplement," says the excited television commercial. A sculpted muscle-man flexes his pecs as the voice continues, "In tests with five leading competitors, Knock It Off users lost more pounds and added more strength than users of any other food supplement." A graph then shows that Knock It Off users did at least 30 percent better than users of the named competitors. Executives at CrunchTime supplement are unhappy when Knock It Off knocks CrunchTime out of the market lead. CrunchTime also believes the tests are fraudulent, and it sues.

At trial, the evidence indicates that Knock It Off did test its product against all others. An independent testing company established five groups of 100 supplement eaters, then weighed them all and measured them for strength, before and after the testing period. But during the test, Knock It Off offered all 100 of its users certain benefits: free use of a health club with a personal trainer, and three low-fat gourmet meals per day for the entire family. None of the other groups received

---

[17] *Midler v. Ford Motor Co.*, 849 F.2d 460, 1988 U.S. App. LEXIS 8424 (9th Cir. 1988).

such benefits. At the end of the trial period, the Knock It Off group was healthier. But at the end of the *trial,* CrunchTime is healthier—period.

Knock It Off has violated the Lanham Act. The television commercial was literally true because Knock It Off users did better than those who took the competing products. But the ads were misleading because viewers were never told about the extra benefits that one group received. The court issues an injunction, prohibiting Knock It Off from showing the commercial, and also awards damages, based on the profits CrunchTime lost.

CHAPTER CONCLUSION

This chapter has been a potpourri of sin, a bubbling cauldron of conduct best avoided. Although tortious acts and their consequences are diverse, two generalities apply. First, the boundaries of intentional torts are imprecise, the outcome of a particular case depending to a considerable extent upon the factfinder who analyzes it. Second, the thoughtful executive and the careful citizen, aware of the shifting standards and potentially vast liability, will strive to ensure that his or her conduct never provides that factfinder an opportunity to give judgment.

CHAPTER REVIEW

1. A tort is a violation of a duty imposed by the civil law.
2. Defamation involves a defamatory statement that is false, uttered to a third person, and causes an injury. Opinion and privilege are valid defenses.
3. Public personalities can win a defamation suit only by proving actual malice.
4. False imprisonment is the intentional restraint of another person without reasonable cause and without consent.
5. The intentional infliction of emotional distress involves extreme and outrageous conduct that causes serious emotional harm.
6. Battery is an intentional touching of another person in a way that is unwanted or offensive. Assault involves an act that makes the plaintiff fear an imminent battery.
7. Compensatory damages are the normal remedy in a tort case. In unusual cases, the court may award punitive damages, not to compensate the plaintiff but to punish the defendant.
8. Tortious interference with business relations involves the defendant harming an existing contract or a prospective relationship that has a definite expectation of success.
9. The related torts of privacy and publicity involve unreasonable intrusion into someone's private life, disclosure of embarrassing private facts in which the public has no legitimate interest, placing the plaintiff in a false light, or unfair commercial exploitation by using someone's name, likeness, or voice without permission.
10. The Lanham Act prohibits false statements in commercial advertising or promotion.

PRACTICE TEST

1. Benzaquin had a radio talk show in Boston. On the program, he complained about an incident earlier in the day, in which state trooper Fleming had stopped his car, apparently for lack of a proper license plate and safety sticker. Even though Benzaquin explained that the license plate had been stolen and the sticker had fallen onto the dashboard, Fleming refused to let him drive the car away, and Benzaquin and his daughter and two young grandsons had to find other transportation. On the show, Benzaquin angrily recounted the incident, then made the following statements about Fleming and troopers generally: "arrogants wearing trooper's uniforms like tights"; "little monkey, you wind him up and he does his thing"; "we're not paying them to be dictators and Nazis"; "this man is an absolute barbarian, a lunkhead, a meathead." Fleming sued Benzaquin for defamation. Comment.

2. You are a vice-president in charge of personnel at a large manufacturing company. In-house detectives inform you that Gates, an employee, was seen stealing valuable computer equipment. Gates denies the theft, but you believe the detectives and fire him. The detectives suggest that you post notices around the company, informing all employees what happened to Gates and why. This will discourage others from stealing. While you think that over, a phone call from another company's personnel officer asks for a recommendation for Gates. Should you post the notices? What should you say to the other officer?

3. Caldwell was shopping in a K-Mart store, carrying a large purse. A security guard observed her look at various small items such as stain, hinges, and antenna wire. On occasion she bent down out of sight of the guard. The guard thought he saw Caldwell put something in her purse. Caldwell removed her glasses from her purse and returned them a few times. After she left, the guard approached her in the parking lot and said that he believed she had store merchandise in her pocketbook but was unable to say what he thought was put there. Caldwell opened the purse, and the guard testified he saw no K-Mart merchandise in it. The guard then told Caldwell to return to the store with him. They walked around the store for approximately 15 minutes, while the guard said six or seven times that he saw her put something in her purse. Caldwell left the store after another store employee indicated she could go. Caldwell sued. What kind of suit did she file, and what should the outcome be?

4. Fifteen-year-old Terri Stubblefield was riding in the back seat of a Ford Mustang II when the car was hit from behind. The Mustang was engulfed in a ball of fire, and Terri was severely burned. She died. Terri's family sued Ford, alleging that the car was badly designed—and that Ford knew it. At trial, Terri's family introduced evidence that Ford knew the fuel tank was dangerous and that it could have taken measures to make the tank safe. There was evidence that Ford consciously decided not to remedy the fuel tanks in order to save money. The family sought two different kinds of damages from Ford. What were they?

5. **RIGHT & WRONG** In the *Stubblefield* case in Question 4, the jury awarded $8 million in punitive damages to the family. Ford appealed. Should the punitive damages be affirmed? What are the obligations of a corporation when it knows one of its products may be dangerous? Is an automobile company ethically obligated to make a *totally safe* car? Should we require a manufacturer to improve the safety of its cars if doing so will make them too expensive for many drivers? What would you do if you were a mid-level executive and saw evidence that your company was endangering the lives of consumers to save money? What would you do if you were on a *jury* and saw such evidence?

6. Tata Consultancy of Bombay, India, is an international computer consulting firm. It spends considerable time and effort recruiting the best personnel from India's leading technical schools. Tata employees sign an initial three-year employment commitment, often work overseas, and agree to work for a specified additional time when they return to India. Desai worked for Tata, but then quit and formed a competing company, which he called Syntel. His new company contacted Tata employees by phone, offering more money to come work for Syntel, bonuses, and assistance in obtaining permanent resident visas in the United States. At least 16 former Tata employees left their work without completing their contractual obligations and went to work for Syntel. Tata sued. What did it claim, and what should be the result?

7. Pacific Express began operating as an airline in 1982. It had routes connecting western cities with Los Angeles and San Francisco and by the summer of 1983 was beginning to show a profit. In 1983, United Airlines tried to enter into a cooperative arrangement with Pacific in which United would provide Pacific with passengers for some routes so that United could concentrate on its longer routes. Negotiations failed. Later that year, United expanded its routes to include cities that only Pacific had served. United also increased its service to cities in which the two airlines were already competing. By early 1984, Pacific Express was unable to compete and sought protection under bankruptcy laws. It also sued United, claiming interference with a prospective advantage. United moved for summary judgment. Comment.

8. **YOU BE THE JUDGE WRITING PROBLEM** Johnny Carson was for many years the star of a well-known television show, *The Tonight Show*. For about 20 years, he was introduced nightly on the show with the phrase, "Here's Johnny!" A large segment of the television watching public associated the phrase with Carson. A Michigan corporation was in the business of renting and selling portable toilets. The company chose the name "Here's Johnny Portable Toilets," and coupled the company name with the marketing phrase, "The World's Foremost Commodian." Carson sued, claiming that the company's name and slogan violated his right to commercial exploitation. **Argument for Carson:** The toilet company is deliberately taking advantage of Johnny Carson's good name. He worked hard for decades to build a brilliant career and earn a reputation as a creative, funny, likable performer. No company has the right to use his name, his picture, or anything else closely identified with him, such as the phrase "Here's Johnny." The pun is personally offensive and commercially unfair. **Argument for Here's Johnny Portable Toilets:** Johnny Carson doesn't own his first name. It is available for anyone to use for any purpose. Further, the popular term "john," meaning toilet, has been around much longer than Carson or even television. We are entitled to make any use of it we want. Our corporate name is amusing to customers who have never heard of Carson, and we are entitled to profit from our brand recognition.

9. A Quaker State motor oil television commercial stated: "Warning: Up to half of all engine wear can happen when you start your car. At this critical time, tests prove Quaker State 10W-30 flowed faster to all vital parts. In all size engines tested, Quaker State protected faster, so it protected better." In fact, Quaker State's tests showed that its oil did flow much faster. Contrary to expectations, however, this did not translate into reduced engine wear. Castrol, a competing motor oil, sued, seeking an injunction. What law is the suit based on? What does "seeking an injunction" mean in this context? What result?

10. Caudle worked at Betts Lincoln-Mercury dealer. During an office party, many of the employees, including president Betts, were playing with an electric auto condenser, which gave a slight electric shock when touched. Some employees played catch with the condenser. Betts shocked Caudle on the back of his neck and then chased him around, holding the condenser. The shock later caused Caudle to suffer headaches, to pass out, and eventually to require surgery on a nerve in his neck. Even after surgery, Caudle had a slight numbness on one side of his head. He sued Betts for battery. Betts defended by saying that it was all horseplay and that he had intended no injury. Please rule.

INTERNET RESEARCH PROBLEM

Take a look at **http://response.restoration.noaa.gov/index.html**. What are some of the long-term problems associated with oil spills? View some of the photos in the "gallery." Are punitive damages for oil spills appropriate or excessive?

You can find further practice problems in the Online Quiz at http://beatty.westbuslaw.com or in the Study Guide that accompanies this text.

CHAPTER 6

NEGLIGENCE AND STRICT LIABILITY

Party time! A fraternity at the University of Arizona welcomed new members, and the alcohol flowed freely. Several hundred people danced and shrieked and drank, and no one checked for proof of age. A common occurrence—but one that ended tragically. A minor student drove away, intoxicated, and slammed into another car. The other driver, utterly innocent of wrongdoing, was gravely injured.

The drunken student was obviously liable, but his insurance did not cover the huge medical bills. The injured man also sued the fraternity. Should that organization be legally responsible? The question leads to other, similar issues. Should a restaurant that serves a minor be liable for harm that the youth might cause? Should the restaurant be responsible for serving an intoxicated adult who causes damage? If *you* give a party, should you be responsible for any damage caused by your guests?

These are all practical questions—worth considering before you entertain—and moral ones as well. They are typical issues of negligence law. In this contentious area, courts continually face one question: *When someone is injured, how far should responsibility extend?*

NEGLIGENCE

We might call negligence the "unintentional" tort because it concerns harm that arises by accident. A person, or perhaps an organization, does some act, neither intending nor expecting to hurt anyone, yet someone is harmed. Should a court impose liability? The fraternity members who gave the party never wanted—or thought—that an innocent man would suffer terrible damage. But he did. Is it in society's interest to hold the fraternity responsible?

Before we can answer this question, we need some background knowledge. Things go wrong all the time, and people are hurt in large ways and small. Society needs a means of analyzing negligence cases consistently and fairly. We cannot have each court that hears such a lawsuit extend or limit liability based on an emotional response to the facts. One of America's greatest judges, Benjamin Cardozo, offered such an analysis more than 70 years ago. His decision still dominates negligence thinking today (though it did not convince all of the judges on his court), so we will let him introduce us to Helen Palsgraf.

PALSGRAF v. LONG ISLAND RAILROAD CO.
248 N.Y. 339, 162 N.E. 99, 1928
N.Y. LEXIS 1269
New York Court of Appeals, 1928

Facts: Ms. Palsgraf was waiting on a railroad platform. As a train began to leave the station, a man carrying a package ran to catch it. He jumped aboard but looked unsteady, so a guard on the car reached out to help him as another guard, on the platform, pushed from behind. The man dropped the package, which struck the tracks and exploded—since it was packed with fireworks. The shock knocked over some heavy scales at the far end of the platform, and one of them struck Palsgraf. She sued the railroad.

The jury found that the guards had acted negligently, and held the railroad liable. The company appealed.

Issue: **Assuming the guards did a bad job assisting the passenger, was the railroad liable for the injuries to Ms. Palsgraf?**

Excerpts from Judge Cardozo's Decision: The conduct of the defendant's guard, if a wrong in its relation to the holder of the package, was not a wrong in its relation to the plaintiff, standing far away. Relatively to her it was not negligence at all. Nothing in the situation gave notice that the falling package had in it the potency of peril to persons thus removed. Negligence is not actionable unless it involves the invasion of a legally protected interest, the violation of a right. Proof of negligence in the air, so to speak, will not do.

In every instance, before negligence can be predicated of a given act, back of the act must be sought and found a duty to the individual complaining, the observance of which would have averted or avoided the injury. What the plaintiff must show is a "a wrong" to herself; i.e., a violation of her own right, and not merely a wrong to someone else, nor conduct "wrongful" because unsocial.

There was nothing in the situation to suggest to the most cautious mind that the parcel wrapped in newspaper would spread wreckage through the station. If the guard had thrown it down knowingly and willfully, he would not have threatened the plaintiff's safety, so far as appearances could warn him. Liability can be no greater where the act is inadvertent.

Excerpts from Judge Andrews's Dissenting Opinion: We are told that there is no negligence unless there is in the particular case a legal duty to take care, and this duty must be one which is owed to the plaintiff himself and not merely to others. This I think too narrow a conception. Where there is the unreasonable act, and some right that may be affected there is negligence whether damage does or does not result. That is immaterial. Should we drive down Broadway at a reckless speed, we are negligent whether we strike an approaching car or miss it by an inch. The act itself is wrongful.

Due care is a duty imposed on each one of us to protect society from unnecessary danger, not to protect A, B or C alone. The proposition is this: Every one owes to the world at large the duty of refraining from those acts that may unreasonably threaten the safety of others.

Judge Cardozo prevailed. **To win a negligence case, the plaintiff must prove five elements:**

- **Duty of Due Care.** The defendant had a duty of due care *to this plaintiff.* This is Judge Cardozo's point.
- **Breach.** The defendant breached her duty.
- **Factual Cause.** The defendant's conduct actually caused the injury.
- **Foreseeable Harm.** It was foreseeable that conduct like the defendant's might cause *this type of harm.*
- **Injury.** The plaintiff has actually been hurt.

DUTY OF DUE CARE

The first issue may be the most difficult in all of tort law: Did the defendant have a duty of due care to the injured person? As the *Palsgraf* decision demonstrates, there is no unanimous answer, but most courts accept Cardozo's viewpoint. Today, judges draw an imaginary line around the defendant and say that she owes a duty to the people within this circle, but not to those outside it. The test is generally "foreseeability." **If the defendant could have foreseen injury to a particular person, she has a duty to him.** If she could not have foreseen the harm, there is usually no duty.

Some cases are easy. Suppose Glorious University operates a cafeteria. Does the school have a duty of due care to its diners? Absolutely. Management knows that a grimy kitchen can cause serious illness, so the university has a duty to each of its patrons. On the other hand, assume the school bookstore sells a road map of Greece to a student. During spring break, the student drives recklessly along a narrow country lane in Greece, injuring a farmer. The university could never have foreseen harm to a Greek farmer merely from selling a map, so it never had a duty to the man.

Let us apply these principles to the fraternity case.

HERNANDEZ v. ARIZONA BOARD OF REGENTS
177 Ariz. 244, 866 P.2d 1330, 1994 Ariz. LEXIS 6
Arizona Supreme Court, 1994

Facts: At the University of Arizona, the Epsilon Epsilon chapter of Delta Tau Delta fraternity gave a welcoming party for new members. The fraternity's officers knew that the majority of its members were under the legal drinking age, but permitted everyone to consume alcohol. John Rayner, who was under 21 years of age, left the party. He drove negligently and caused a collision with an auto driven by Ruben Hernandez. At the time of the accident, Rayner's blood alcohol level was .15, exceeding the legal limit. The crash left Hernandez blind, severely brain damaged and quadriplegic.

Hernandez sued Rayner, who settled the case, based on the amount of his insurance coverage. The victim also sued the fraternity, its officers and national organization, all fraternity members who contributed money to buy alcohol, the university, and others. The trial court granted summary judgment for all defendants and the court of appeals affirmed. Hernandez appealed to the Arizona Supreme Court.

Issue: **Did the fraternity and the other defendants have a duty of due care to Hernandez?**

Excerpts from Judge Feldman's Decision: Before 1983, this court arguably recognized the common-law rule of non-liability for tavern owners and, presumably, for social hosts. Traditional authority held that when "an able-bodied man" caused harm because of his intoxication, the act from which liability arose was the consuming not the furnishing of alcohol.

However, the common law also provides that:

> One who supplies [a thing] for the use of another whom the supplier knows or has reason to know to be likely because of his youth, inexperience, or otherwise to use it in a manner involving unreasonable risk of physical harm to himself and others is subject to liability for physical harm resulting to them.

We perceive little difference in principle between liability for giving a car to an intoxicated youth and liability for giving drinks to a youth with a car. A growing number of cases have recognized that one of the very hazards that makes it negligent to furnish liquor to a minor is the foreseeable prospect that the [youthful] patron will become drunk and injure himself or others. Accordingly, modern authority has increasingly recognized that one who furnishes liquor to a minor breaches a common law duty owed to innocent third parties who may be injured.

Furnishing alcohol to underaged drinkers violates numerous statutes. The conduct in question violates well-established common-law principles that recognize a duty to avoid furnishing dangerous items to those known to have diminished capacity to use them safely. We join the majority of other states and conclude that as to Plaintiffs and the public in general, Defendants had a duty of care to avoid furnishing alcohol to underage consumers.

Arizona courts, therefore, will entertain an action for damages against [one] who negligently furnishes alcohol to those under the legal drinking age when that act is a cause of injury to a third person. [Reversed and remanded.]

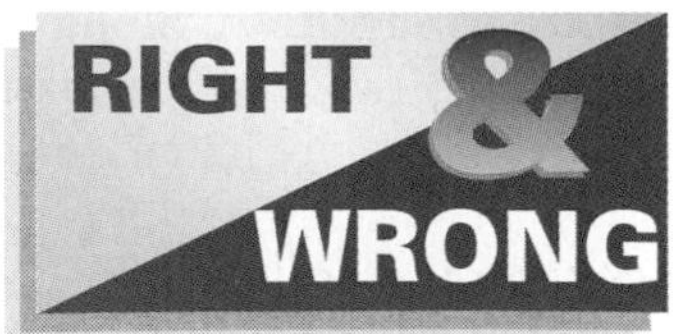

As the Arizona court notes, its decision agrees with the majority of courts that have considered the issue. In most (but not all) states, anyone serving alcohol to a minor is liable for injuries that result to a third party. The case raises other important issues:

- Should a social host who serves alcohol to an *adult* be liable for resulting harm? New Jersey has answered this question, "yes." In the Garden State, if a social host pours drinks for a friend, aware that he is becoming drunk, and the friend injures a third party, the host is fully liable. The great majority of states to consider this issue have reached the opposite conclusion, holding that a social host is *not* liable for harm caused by an adult drinker. Why do most states distinguish between adult and underage guests, holding a social host liable only for serving minors? Is the distinction persuasive?

- Many states now have some type of **dram act**, making liquor stores, bars, and restaurants liable for serving drinks to intoxicated customers who later cause harm. Why might a state create such responsibility while refusing to hold social hosts liable?

- There are many signs that society is fed up with drunk drivers. Who should make the decision about social host liability, a court or a legislature?

- Alcohol is the number one drug problem among young people. About 10 million drinkers are underage; 25 percent of them do not know that an alcohol overdose can be fatal. About eight minors die every day in alcohol-related crashes. For more gruesome statistics, see the impassioned and informative Web page of Mothers Against Drunk Drivers at **http://www.madd.org/**. The National Commission Against Drunk Driving offers additional material at **http://www.ncadd.com/**.

Affirmative Duty to Act

In general, the common law does not require a bystander to come to the assistance of a person in danger, assuming that the bystander did not create the danger. Henrietta, sitting in a café, watches as a piano, wrapped in a rope harness, rises majestically above the sidewalk. She notices that the frayed rope is about to snap, just as kindly Mr. Good approaches. Henrietta is not legally obligated to call out to him and incurs no liability if the piano crashes down with a lethal cacophony. This rule is discussed in detail in Chapter 3.

Landowner's Duty

The common law applies special rules to a landowner for injuries occurring on her property. In most states, the owner's duty depends on the status of the person injured.

Lowest Liability: Trespasser. A **trespasser** is anyone on the property without consent. A landowner is only liable to a trespasser for intentionally injuring him or for some other gross misconduct. The landowner has no liability to a trespasser for mere negligence. Jake is not liable if a vagrant wanders onto his land and is burned by defective electrical wires.

Occasional Liability: Children. The law makes exceptions when the trespassers are **children**. If there is some man-made thing on the land that may attract children, the landowner is probably liable for any harm. Daphne lives next door to a day-care center and builds a goldfish pond on her property. She is probably liable if a child wanders onto her property and drowns, unless she has fenced off the dangerous area.

Higher Liability: Licensee. A **licensee** is anyone on the land for her own purposes but with the owner's permission. A social guest is a typical licensee. A licensee is entitled to a warning of hidden dangers that the owner knows about. If Juliet invites Romeo for a late supper on the balcony and fails to mention that the wooden railing is rotted, she is liable when her hero plunges to the courtyard.

Highest Liability: Invitee. An **invitee** is someone on the property as of right because it is a public place or a business open to the public. The owner has a duty of reasonable care to an invitee. Perry is an invitee when he goes to the town beach. If riptides have existed for years and the town fails to post a warning, it is liable if Perry drowns. Perry is also an invitee when he shops at Daphne's Boutique. Daphne is liable if she ignores spilled coffee that causes Perry to slip.

The courts of some states have modified these distinctions, and a few have eliminated them altogether. California, for example, requires "reasonable care" as

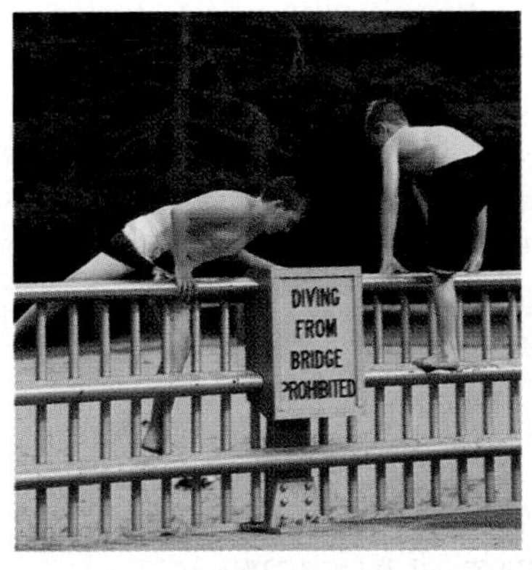

Does this sign protect the owner?

to all people on the owner's property, regardless of how or why they got there. But most states still use the classifications outlined above.

Crime and Tort: Landowner's Liability

Law shows us trends in social issues. Regrettably, a major concern of tort law today is how to respond to injury caused by criminals. If a criminal assaults and robs a pedestrian in a shopping mall, that act is a crime and may be prosecuted by the state. But prosecution leaves the victim uncompensated. The assault is also an intentional tort (discussed in Chapter 5), and the victim could file a civil lawsuit against the criminal. But most violent criminals have no assets. Given this economic frustration and the flexibility of the common law, it is inevitable that victims of violence look elsewhere for compensation.

As crimes now occur in offices, shopping malls, and parking lots, plaintiffs increasingly seek compensation from the owners of these facilities. Here we look at a landowner's liability for crime; later we consider an employer's liability.

ANN M. v. PACIFIC PLAZA SHOPPING CENTER
6 Cal. 4th 666, 863 P.2d 207, 1993 Cal. LEXIS 6127
Supreme Court of California, 1994

Facts: Ann M. worked at the Original 60 Minute Photo Co. in the Pacific Plaza Shopping Center, a strip mall in San Diego. About 25 commercial tenants occupied the center. She was the only employee on duty one day when a man walked in "just like a customer," pulled a knife, went behind the counter, and raped her. He robbed the store, fled, and was never caught.

Ann M. sued Pacific Plaza, claiming that it negligently failed to provide security patrols in the common areas of the shopping center. Under the terms of the lease, Pacific Plaza had exclusive control of these areas, and the right to police them if it chose.

Issue: **Did Pacific Plaza have a duty to Ann M. to provide security patrols?**

Excerpts from Judge Panelli's Decision: While the record includes some evidence of criminal activity on the shopping center's premises prior to Ann M.'s rape—bank robberies, purse snatchings, and a man pulling down women's pants—there is no evidence that Pacific Plaza had knowledge of these alleged criminal acts. In fact, Pacific Plaza offers uncontroverted evidence that it is the standard practice of [Pacific Plaza] to note or record instances of violent crime, and that [their] records contain no reference to violent criminal acts in the shopping center prior to Ann M.'s rape.

Ann M. presented evidence that the employees and tenants were concerned about their safety prior to her rape. These concerns centered around the presence of persons described as transients, who loitered in the common areas. One of the employees of the photo store called the police on two different occasions prior to the incident involved herein to complain that she felt threatened by persons loitering outside her employer's store. The photo store ultimately granted this employee permission to bring her dog to work for protection. This employee worked a late night shift, while Ann M. worked during the day. During periodic meetings of the merchants' association, an organization to which all tenants belonged, the tenants voiced complaints about a lack of security in the shopping center and the presence of transients.

The scope of [a landlord's] duty is determined in part by balancing the foreseeability of the harm against the burden of the duty to be imposed.

While there may be circumstances where the hiring of security guards will be required to satisfy a landowner's duty of care, such action will rarely, if ever, be found to be a "minimal burden." The monetary cost of security guards is not insignificant. No one really knows why people commit crime, hence no one really knows what is "adequate" deterrence in any given situation. Finally, the social costs of imposing a duty on landowners to hire private police forces are also not insignificant. For these reasons, we conclude that a high degree of foreseeability is required in order to find that the scope of a landlord's duty of care includes the hiring of security guards. We further conclude that the requisite degree of foreseeability rarely, if ever, can be proven in the absence of prior similar incidents of violent crime on the landowner's premises. To hold otherwise would be to impose an unfair burden upon landlords and, in effect, would force landlords to become the insurers of public safety, contrary to well-established policy in this state.

Turning to the facts of the case before us, we conclude that violent criminal assaults were not sufficiently foreseeable to impose a duty upon Pacific Plaza to provide security guards in the common areas. We, therefore, conclude that Pacific Plaza was entitled to summary judgment on the ground that it owed no duty to Ann M. to provide security guards in the common areas.

Tort liability (or lack of liability) for criminal acts is a major policy issue because someone will pay for the harm done. It may be the victim, the property owner, the employer, or society generally. If the law denies all liability, as in *Ann M.*, it is the victim who "pays" by remaining uncompensated. If a court holds a property owner or employer liable, the victim will feel better, but the defendant will probably pass on the expense to others. Society itself could reimburse crime victims directly, through state government, but only a few legislatures have voted such compensation.

BREACH OF DUTY

The second element of a plaintiff's negligence case is **breach of duty**. Courts apply the *reasonable person* standard: **a defendant breaches his duty of due care by failing to behave the way a reasonable person would under similar circumstances.** Reasonable "person" means someone of the defendant's occupation. A taxi driver must drive as a reasonable taxi driver would. A heart surgeon must perform bypass surgery with the care of a trained specialist in that field.

Two medical cases from Texas indicate how one court applies the reasonable person standard. In *Gooden v. Tips*,[1] the plaintiff, Gooden, was struck by an automobile driven by Dr. Tips's patient, who was under the influence of prescription Quaaludes at the time of the accident. Gooden claimed that the doctor breached his duty of due care by failing to warn his patient not to drive while taking the drug. The court held Dr. Tips liable for breaching his duty.

In *Casarez v. NME Hospitals, Inc.*,[2] Dr. Vasquez admitted to a hospital a patient who was terminally ill with acquired immune deficiency syndrome (AIDS). In his admission instruction, the doctor stated that the patient was HIV positive; he also told the nurses of the patient's condition. Dr. Vasquez did not, however, instruct anyone on the procedures to use with the patient. Casarez, a certified nursing assistant, was caring for the patient when he involuntarily spewed blood on Casarez's mouth, eyes, and arm. The patient died the next day. Casarez tested HIV positive.

Casarez sued Dr. Vasquez (among others), claiming that the doctor negligently failed to instruct him how to handle an AIDS patient. The Texas Court of Appeals was unpersuaded. Vasquez was indeed obligated to take precautions

[1] 651 S.W.2d 364, 1983 Tex. App. LEXIS 4388 (Tex. Ct. App. 1983).

[2] 883 S.W.2d 360, 1994 Tex. App. LEXIS 2091 (Tex. Ct. App. 1994).

with an AIDS patient, but he did everything reasonably required by ensuring that the staff knew of the patient's illness. He had no obligation to instruct staff in special procedures for such a patient because all hospital staff were already trained. Casarez and all others knew precisely what precautions to take, and Vasquez was not liable.

Crime and Tort Revisited: Negligent Hiring and Retention

In a recent one-year period, more than 1,000 homicides and 2 million attacks occurred in the workplace. Companies must beware because they can be liable for hiring or retaining violent employees. A mailroom clerk with a previous rape and robbery conviction followed a secretary home after work and fatally assaulted her. Even though the murder took place off the company premises, the court held that the defendant would be liable if it knew or should have known of the mail clerk's criminal history.[3] In other cases, companies have been found liable for failing to check an applicant's driving record, to contact personal references, and to search criminal records.

Courts have also found companies negligent for *retaining* dangerous employees. Randy Landin worked at Honeywell for two years, until he was imprisoned for strangling a co-worker. When he was released, Honeywell rehired him as a custodian. Workplace confrontations twice forced the company to transfer him to different facilities. Then he began to harass Kathleen Nesser, at work and at her home, until she asked to transfer to another office. Later, Nesser found death threats scratched in her locker door. Days later, Landin shot and killed the woman. When Nesser's family sued Honeywell, the court ruled that a jury could hold Honeywell responsible for negligently retaining a violent worker.[4]

What can an employer do to diminish the likelihood of workplace violence? Many things.

- Make workplace safety a priority. Many employers still do not believe that violence can occur in their company. They are seriously mistaken.
- Seek the assistance of security experts and mental health personnel in planning a company-wide safety program.
- Evaluate the workplace for unsafe physical features. Install adequate lighting in parking lots and common areas, hire security guards if necessary, and use closed-circuit television and identification cards. The judicial trend is toward greater liability. A decade ago, the victim of a parking lot assault could rarely recover from the store; today, such lawsuits are common and frequently successful.
- Ensure that the company uses thorough pre-hire screening, contacts all former employers, and checks all references and criminal records. Nursing homes have been among the most delinquent at this, too often hiring convicted assailants who have later attacked elderly residents. The financial liability for such cruel assaults can be enormous.
- Respond quickly to dangerous behavior. In many cases of workplace violence, the perpetrator had demonstrated repeated bizarre, threatening, or obsessive behavior on the job, but his supervisors had not taken it seriously.
- Offer counseling where appropriate and fire employees when necessary.

---

[3] *Gaines v. Monsanto,* 655 S.W.2d 568, 1983 Mo. LEXIS 3439 (Mo. Ct. App. 1983).

[4] *Yunker v. Honeywell,* 496 N.W.2d 419, 1993 Minn. App. LEXIS 230 (Minn. Ct. App. 1993).

Negligence Per Se

In certain areas of life, courts are not free to decide what a "reasonable" person would have done, because the state legislature has made the decision for them. **When a legislature sets a minimum standard of care for a particular activity, in order to protect a certain group of people, and a violation of the statute injures a member of that group, the defendant has committed negligence per se.** A plaintiff who can show negligence per se need not prove breach of duty.

In Minnesota, the state legislature became alarmed about children sniffing glue, which they could easily purchase in local stores. The legislature passed a statute prohibiting the sale to a minor of any glue containing toluene or benzene. About one month later, 14-year-old Steven Zerby purchased Weldwood Contact Cement from the Coast-to-Coast Store in his hometown. The glue contained toluene. Steven inhaled the glue and died from injury to his central nervous system.

The store clerk had not realized that the glue was dangerous. Irrelevant: he violated the statute. Perhaps a reasonable person would have made the same error. Irrelevant. The legislature had passed the statute to protect children; the sale of the glue violated the statute; and a child was injured. The store was liable.[5]

FACTUAL CAUSE AND FORESEEABLE HARM

A plaintiff must also show that the defendant's breach of duty caused the plaintiff's harm. Courts look at two issues to settle causation: Was the defendant's behavior the *factual cause* of the harm? Was *this type of harm foreseeable?*[6]

Factual Cause

Nothing mysterious here. **If the defendant's breach physically led to the ultimate harm, it is the factual cause**. Suppose that Dom's Brake Shop tells Customer his brakes are now working fine, even though Dom knows that is false. Customer drives out of the shop, cannot stop at a red light, and hits Bicyclist crossing at the intersection. Dom is liable to Bicyclist. Dom's unreasonable behavior was the factual cause of the harm. Think of it as a row of dominoes. The first domino (Dom's behavior) knocked over the next one (failing brakes), which toppled the last one (the cyclist's injury).

Suppose, alternatively, that just as Customer is exiting the repair shop, Bicyclist hits a pothole and tumbles off her cycle, avoiding Customer's auto. Bicyclist's injuries stem from her fall, not from the auto. Customer's brakes still fail, and Dom has breached his duty to Customer, but Dom is not liable to Bicyclist. She would have been hurt anyway. This is a row of dominoes that veers off to the side, leaving the last domino (cyclist's injury) untouched. No factual causation.

Foreseeable Type of Harm

For the defendant to be liable, the *type of harm* must have been reasonably foreseeable. In the case above, Dom could easily foresee that bad brakes would cause an automobile accident. He need not have foreseen exactly what happened. He did not know there would be a cyclist nearby. What he could foresee was this

---

[5] *Zerby v. Warren*, 297 Minn. 134, 210 N.W.2d 58 (1973).

[6] Courts often refer to these two elements, grouped together, as *proximate cause* or *legal cause*. But, as many courts acknowledge, those terms have created legal confusion, so we use *factual cause* and *foreseeable type of harm*, the issues on which most decisions ultimately focus.

general type of harm involving defective brakes. Because the accident that occurred was of the type he could foresee, he is liable.

By contrast, assume the collision of car and bicycle produces a loud crash. Two blocks away, a pet pig, asleep on the window ledge of a twelfth-story apartment, is startled by the noise, awakens with a start, and plunges to the sidewalk, killing a veterinarian who was making a house call. If the vet's family sues Dom, should it win? Dom's negligence was the factual cause: it led to the collision, which startled the pig, which flattened the vet. Most courts would rule, though, that Dom is not liable. The type of harm is too bizarre. Dom could not reasonably foresee such an extraordinary chain of events, and it would be unfair to make him pay for it. See Exhibit 6.1.

Another way of stating that Dom is not liable to the vet's family is by calling the falling pig a *superseding cause.* When one of the "dominoes" in the row is entirely unforeseeable, courts will call that event a superseding cause, letting the defendant off the hook. Negligence cases often revolve around whether the chain of events leading from the defendant's conduct to the injury was broken by a superseding cause.

In *Kowkabany v. The Home Depot, Inc.,*[7] Mr. and Ms. Remseyer bought four eight-foot landscape timbers at a Home Depot store. Mr. Remseyer and a Home Depot employee loaded the timbers into the back seat of his car, leaving them protruding about three feet out the front passenger window. After 20 minutes of driving, Remseyer approached Eva Kowkabany and another girl, both on bicycles. A car was coming from the other direction. Remseyer thought he could pass the girls safely, but the approaching car "squeezed him" and the timber struck Eva Kowkabany, severely injuring her. Kowkabany sued the Home Depot.

The Home Depot defended by saying that Remseyer's negligent driving caused the accident. Remseyer had indeed been negligent. Was his negligence a "superseding cause?" No, held the court.

Exhibit 6.1

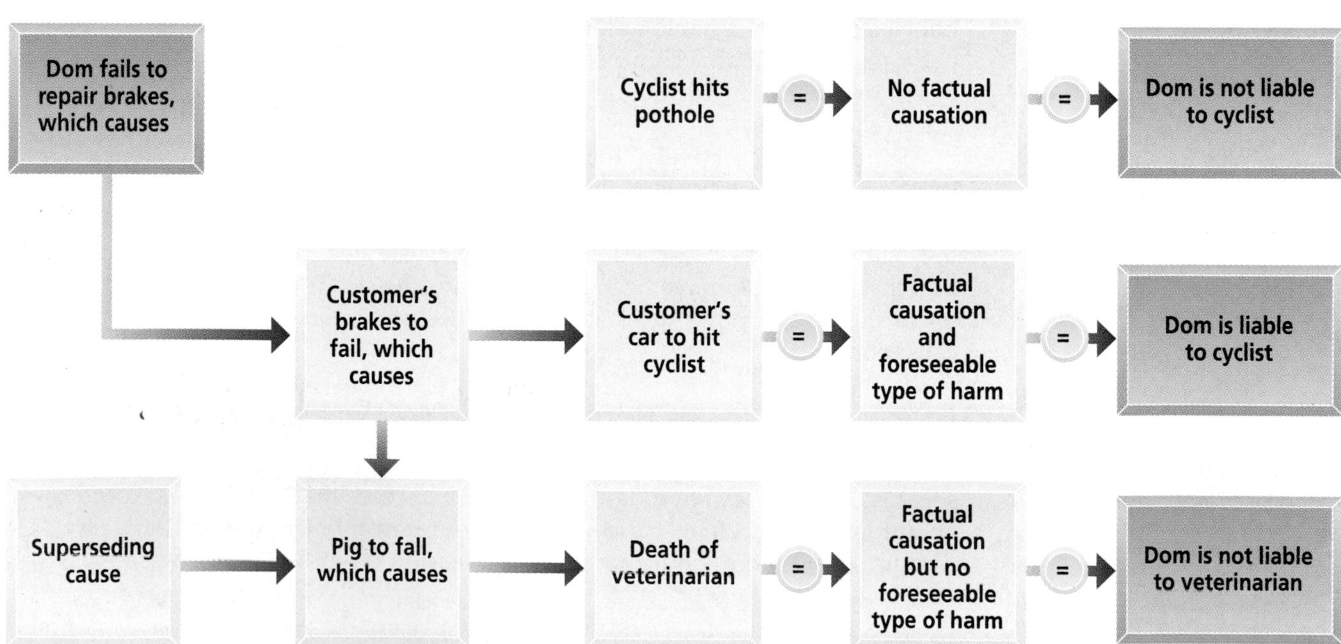

[7] 606 So. 2d 716, 1992 Fla. App. LEXIS 10835 (Fla. Dist. Ct. App. 1992).

> A [superseding] cause should only be found where the circumstances are highly unusual, extraordinary, bizarre or, stated differently, seem beyond the scope of any fair assessment of a danger created by the defendant's negligence. Applying the "highly unusual, extraordinary, bizarre" circumstances standard to the facts of this case, a jury could very reasonably find that Remseyer's poor judgment in driving his automobile, which resulted in the timber striking Ms. Kowkabany, was not so unusual or bizarre that it could not have reasonably been foreseen.

Res Ipsa Loquitur

Normally, a plaintiff must prove factual cause and foreseeable type of harm in order to establish negligence. But in a few cases, a court may be willing to *infer* that the defendant caused the harm, under the doctrine of ***res ipsa loquitur*** ("the thing speaks for itself"). Suppose a pedestrian is walking along a sidewalk when an air conditioning unit falls on his head from a third-story window. The defendant, who owns the third-story apartment, denies any wrongdoing, and it may be difficult or impossible for the plaintiff to prove why the air conditioner fell. In such cases, many courts will apply *res ipsa loquitur* and declare that **the facts imply that the defendant's negligence caused the accident.** If a court uses this doctrine, then the defendant must come forward with evidence establishing that it did *not* cause the harm.

Because *res ipsa loquitur* dramatically shifts the burden of proof from plaintiff to defendant, it applies only when (1) the defendant had exclusive control of the thing that caused the harm, (2) the harm normally would not have occurred without negligence, and (3) the plaintiff had no role in causing the harm. In the air conditioner example, most states would apply the doctrine and force the defendant to prove she did nothing wrong.

The following case illustrates several of the elements of negligence that we have examined so far.

GRIFFITH v. VALLEY OF SUN RECOVERY, INC.
126 Ariz. 227, 613 P.2d 1283
Arizona Court of Appeals, 1980

Facts: Don Gorney was a "repo man." A repossession person is someone authorized to find and take cars whose owners are behind on payments. A repossessor is allowed to drive away in such a car, provided he can do it peacefully. Gorney worked for Valley of Sun Recovery. He sought a car belonging to Linda Marsalek and Bob Williams. Gorney knew that there had been other, failed efforts to repossess the Marsalek car, including a violent confrontation involving attack dogs. He thought he could do better.

Gorney went to the car at 4:00 in the morning. He unscrewed the bulb in an overhead street lamp. He unlocked the car, setting off its alarm, and quickly hid. The alarm aroused the neighborhood. Williams and a neighbor, Griffith, investigated and concluded it was an attempted theft. They called the police. Gorney watched all of this from his hiding place. When everyone had gone, Gorney entered the car, again setting off the alarm and arousing the neighborhood. Williams and Griffith again emerged, as did another neighbor, dressed in his underwear and carrying a shotgun. They all believed they had caught a thief. Williams shouted for the gun and the neighbor passed it to him, but it went off accidentally and severely injured Griffith.

Griffith sued Valley of Sun. The trial court granted summary judgment for Valley of Sun, and Griffith appealed.

You Be the Judge:

- Did Valley of Sun have a *duty* to Griffith?
- If so, did the company *breach* its duty?
- If so, was the breach the *factual cause* of the injury?
- If so, was *this type of injury foreseeable*?

Argument for Griffith: Your honors, Mr. Griffith should be allowed to make his case to a jury and let it decide whether Valley of Sun's repossession led to his injury. Mr. Griffith has demonstrated every element of negligence. Valley of Sun had a duty to everyone in the area when it attempted to repossess a car. It could easily have foreseen injury. Car repossessions always involve antagonism between the car owner and the repo company.

Obviously, Gorney breached his duty. He was caught up in some fantasy, dreaming that he was Harrison Ford in an adventure film. He knew from previous repossession attempts that trouble was certain. But rather than minimizing the danger, he exacerbated it. He unscrewed a lightbulb, guaranteeing poor visibility and confusion. He set off the car alarm *twice,* making the whole neighborhood jittery.

Factual causation is indisputable. Had it not been for his preposterous game playing, no neighbors would have been outside, no guns present—and no accidental shooting. And this type of harm is easily foreseeable. We should have a chance to take our case to a jury.

Argument for Valley of Sun Recovery: Your honors, there are three good reasons to end this case today: no duty, no breach, no causation.

It is preposterous to suggest that Valley of Sun has a legal duty to an entire neighborhood. Car owners behind on their payments live in all parts of all communities. Is a repossession company to become an insurer of the entire city?

Yes, some danger is involved because delinquent owners are irresponsible and sometimes dangerous. Should we therefore allow them to keep their cars? Of course not. We must act, and that is what Valley of Sun does.

They do it safely, your honors. Even if there had been a duty, there was no breach. Mr. Gorney attempted to repossess when it was least likely anyone would see him. What should Mr. Gorney have done, asked for permission to take the car? *That* is a recipe for violence. If the owner were reasonable, there would be no repossession in the first place.

Factual causation? Valley of Sun did not create this situation. The car owner did. He bought the car and failed to pay for it. Even if there were factual causation, Valley of Sun is not liable because there is a superseding cause: the negligent use of a firearm by one of Mr. Griffith's neighbors. No jury should hear this case, your honors, because there is no case.

INJURY

Finally, a plaintiff must prove that he has been injured. In some cases injury is obvious. For example, Ruben Hernandez suffered grievous harm when struck by a drunk driver. But in other cases, injury is unclear. **The plaintiff must persuade the court that he has suffered a harm that is genuine, not speculative.**

A federal judge awarded $4 million to a California man who suffered severe brain damage after merchandise fell on him at a Wal-Mart store. Todd Caranto, a former Air Force medical corpsman, was Christmas shopping when more than a dozen heavy boxes of toys tumbled off high shelves and knocked him to the floor. The accident resulted in permanent brain damage and left the 26-year-old father of two unable to take care of himself. Caranto will require total care, 24 hours a day, for the rest of his life. He can walk but is unable to speak or communicate with anyone around him.

Other cases raise tougher questions. Among the most vexing are suits involving *future* harm. Exposure to toxins or trauma may lead to serious medical problems down the road—or it may not. A woman's knee is damaged in an auto accident, causing severe pain for two years. She is clearly entitled to compensation for her suffering. After two years, all pain may cease for a decade—or forever. Yet there is also a chance that in 15 or 20 years the trauma will lead to painful arthritis. A court must decide today the full extent of present *and future* damages; the single recovery principle, discussed in Chapter 5, prevents a plaintiff from returning to court years later and demanding compensation for newly arisen ailments. The challenge to our courts is to weigh the possibilities and percentages of future suffering and decide whether to compensate a plaintiff for something that might never happen.

The following lawsuit concerns a woman's fear of developing AIDS. This worry can be overwhelming. See the online mental health dictionary found at http://www.thebody.com/mental.html. A court must still decide, however, whether the cause of the unhappiness is genuine injury or speculation.

REYNOLDS v. HIGHLAND MANOR, INC.

24 Kan. App. 2d 859, 954 P.2d 11, 1998 Kan. App. LEXIS 20
Kansas Court of Appeals, 1998

Facts: Angelina Reynolds and her family checked into a Holiday Inn, but since the air conditioner did not work they requested a room change. As they were repacking their luggage, Reynolds felt for items left under the bed, and picked up what she thought was a candy wrapper. Reynolds felt a "gush" as she retrieved the item, which unfortunately turned out to be a wet condom. She screamed and quickly washed her hands. There was a second condom under the bed. Reynolds and her husband rushed to an emergency room, taking the condoms with them. Hospital staff said that they were unable to test the contents of the condoms. A doctor examined Reynolds's hand, which had a burn on the middle finger and bloody cuticles, but told her that there was nothing he could do if she had been exposed to infectious diseases.

The condom never was tested. Reynolds sued the motel, claiming among other things that she feared she would die of AIDS. The trial court dismissed the case, ruling that there was no showing of injury. Reynolds appealed.

Issue: Has Reynolds demonstrated injury?

Excerpts from Judge Penland's Decision: Plaintiff testified that after the incident, she feared she would die from AIDS. As a result of this anxiety, she claimed to have suffered headaches, diarrhea, and nausea. She could not say that she ever vomited and conceded that one type of medication she took caused her digestive problems. Plaintiff also testified to crying and shaking, and feeling overwhelmed with stress. Dr. Elias Chediak, the psychiatrist who treated plaintiff following the incident, testified that most of the time he saw her, "she was feeling pretty anxious, crying, feeling distressed," and she reported headaches and tense muscles. Dr. Chediak stated plaintiff had seen a neurologist who performed tests that turned out negative. According to Dr. Chediak, the neurologist concluded that any problems plaintiff had experienced were due to stress. Plaintiff also testified that because of her mental state, her sexual relations with her husband had decreased, but they continued to have unprotected sex after the incident, despite her purported fear she might have HIV.

[In an earlier case,] our Supreme Court held that a plaintiff may recover for anxiety based on reasonable fear that an existing injury will lead to the occurrence of a disease or condition in the future. For the fear to be reasonable, the court held the plaintiff must show that a substantial probability exists that such condition or disease will occur. Anxiety about a disease or condition developing from a physical injury is not recoverable as an element of mental distress where the medical evidence indicates the chance of such occurring is slight.

The uncontroverted evidence established that plaintiff took an HIV test four times following the incident, the last occurring more than 1 year after the incident. When an individual tests negative for HIV more than 1 year after exposure, a greater than 99% probability exists that HIV will not appear. Plaintiff has failed to establish even a minimal possibility, much less a substantial or even significant probability, that she will contract AIDS due to her contact with the condom in the motel. Because her fear of contracting the disease is unreasonable as a matter of law, she may not recover damages.

Affirmed.

Bystander Cases

What if a defendant injures one person but someone *else* sues for emotional suffering? In a landmark California case,[8] a driver negligently caused the death of a child. The child's mother was nearby and witnessed the accident, though the mother was never in danger from the car. The driver was clearly liable for the wrongful death. Was he additionally liable to the mother for her purely emotional suffering? Yes, said the California court. A bystander is entitled to damages for negligent infliction of emotional distress if (1) she was near the scene of the accident *and* (2) seeing the accident caused an immediate shock to her *and* (3) she is a close relative of the victim. Many but not all states now follow that rule.

DAMAGES

The plaintiff's damages in a negligence case are generally **compensatory damages**, meaning an amount of money that the court believes will restore him to the position he was in before the defendant's conduct caused an injury. In unusual cases, a court may award **punitive damages**, that is, money intended not to compensate the plaintiff but to punish the defendant. We discussed both forms of damages in Chapter 5.

CONTRIBUTORY AND COMPARATIVE NEGLIGENCE

Joe is a mental patient in a hospital. The hospital knows he is dangerous to himself and others, but it permits him to wander around unattended. Joe leaves the hospital and steals a gun. Shawn drives by Joe, and Joe waves the gun at him. Shawn notices a policeman a block away. But instead of informing the cop, Shawn leans out his window and shouts, "Hey, knucklehead, what are you doing pointing guns at people?" Joe shoots and kills Shawn.

Shawn's widow sues the hospital for negligently permitting Joe to leave. But the hospital, in defense, claims that Shawn's foolishness got him killed. Who wins? It depends on whether the state in which the suit is heard uses a legal theory called **contributory negligence**. This used to be the law throughout the nation, but it remains in effect in only a few states. It means that, even assuming the defendant is negligent, **if the plaintiff is even *slightly* negligent himself, he recovers nothing.** So if Shawn's homicide occurs in a contributory negligence state, the hospital is not liable regardless of how negligent it was.

Critics attacked the rule as unreasonable. A plaintiff who was 1 percent negligent could not recover from a defendant who was 99 percent negligent. So most states threw out the contributory negligence rule, replacing it with comparative negligence. **In a comparative negligence state, a plaintiff may generally recover even if she is partially negligent.** A jury will be asked to assess the relative negligence of plaintiff and defendant.

Suppose we are in a comparative negligence state, and the jury believes the hospital was 80 percent responsible for Shawn's death, and Shawn himself was 20 percent responsible. It might conclude that the total damages for Shawn's widow are $2 million, based on Shawn's pain in dying and the widow's loss of his income. If so, the hospital would owe $1.6 million, or 80 percent of the damages. See Exhibit 6.2.

Today, most but not all states have adopted some form of comparative negligence. Critics of comparative negligence claim that it rewards a plaintiff for being

[8] *Dillon v. Legg*, 68 Cal. 2d 728, 441 P.2d 912, 1968 Cal. LEXIS 201 (1968).

Exhibit 6.2
Defendant's negligence injures plaintiff, who suffers $2 million in damages.

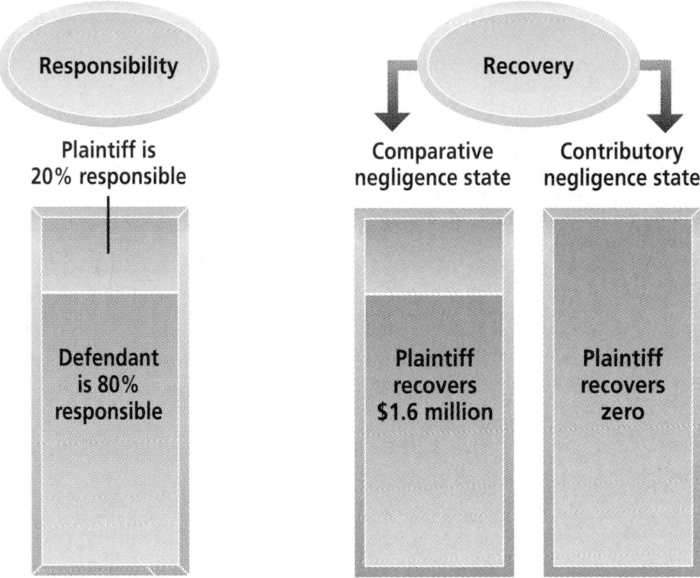

careless. Suppose, they say, a driver speeds to beat an approaching train, and the railroad's mechanical arm fails to operate. Why should we reward the driver for his foolishness? In response to this complaint, some comparative negligence states do *not* permit a plaintiff to recover anything if he was more than 50 percent responsible for his injury.

COMPARATIVE NEGLIGENCE AND ACCOUNTANTS

During the past decade, an ever greater number of accountants have been found liable for negligence. In some cases the negligent act is an inadequate corporate audit that a third party relies on when making an investment in the corporation. In other cases, an accountant fails to discover a crime, such as embezzlement, within a corporation.

Halla Nursery sued its accountant, Baumann-Furrie & Co., claiming that the firm had negligently failed to detect $135,000 worth of embezzlement by Halla's bookkeeper. The accounting firm responded that the nursery itself was responsible because it had failed to establish adequate internal financial controls. The jury found that 20 percent of the fault lay with the accountants and 80 percent rested with Halla. Because Minnesota denies recovery to a plaintiff that is more than 50 percent responsible, the nursery won nothing.[9]

STRICT LIABILITY

Some activities are so naturally dangerous that the law places an especially high burden on anyone who engages in them. A corporation that produces toxic waste can foresee dire consequences from its business that a stationery store cannot. This higher burden is **strict liability**. There are two main areas of business that incur strict liability: *ultrahazardous activity* and *defective products.* Defective products are discussed in Chapter 21, on products liability.

---

[9] *Halla Nursery v. Baumann-Furrie & Co.*, 454 N.W.2d 905, 1990 Minn. LEXIS 129 (Minn. 1990).

ULTRAHAZARDOUS ACTIVITY

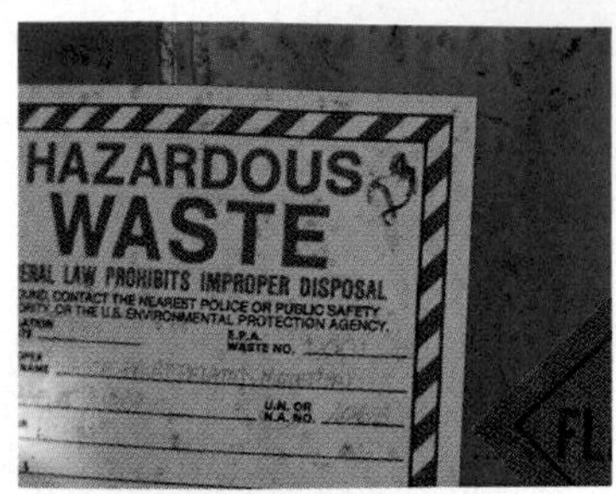

An ultrahazardous activity exposes a company to strict liability if anything goes wrong.

Ultrahazardous activities include using harmful chemicals, operating explosives, keeping wild animals, bringing dangerous substances onto property, and a few similar activities where the danger to the general public is especially great. **A defendant engaging in an ultrahazardous activity is virtually always liable for any harm that results.** Plaintiffs do not have to prove duty or breach or foreseeable harm. Recall the deliberately bizarre case we posed earlier of the pig falling from a window ledge and killing a veterinarian. Dom, the mechanic whose negligence caused the car crash, could not be liable for the veterinarian's death because the plunging pig was a superseding cause. But if the pig was jolted off the window ledge by Sam's Blasting Co., which was doing perfectly lawful blasting for a new building down the street, Sam is liable. Even if Sam took extraordinary care, it will do him no good at trial. The "reasonable person" rule is irrelevant in a strict liability case.

OLD ISLAND FUMIGATION, INC. v. BARBEE
604 So. 2d 1246, 1992 Fla. App. LEXIS 9297
Florida Court of Appeals, 1992

Excerpts from the Court's Decision: Old Island Fumigation, Inc., appeals from an order of summary judgment holding it strictly liable for damages to occupants of a building adjacent to the building fumigated. We affirm.

Old Island fumigated buildings A and B of a condominium complex. Buildings A and B, together with building C, form a U-shape; buildings B and C have between them an atrium and were thought to be separated by an impenetrable fire wall. Although Old Island evacuated occupants of buildings A and B before the fumigation, the company advised the occupants of building C that they could remain in their dwellings while the other buildings were treated.

Several residents of building C became ill shortly after the Vikane gas was released into the adjacent buildings. The hospital admission forms indicate that the cause of their illnesses was sulfuryl fluoride poisoning. Sulfuryl fluoride is the active chemical ingredient of Vikane. Several months after this incident, an architect hired by the fumigation company discovered that the fire wall between buildings B and C was defective and contained a four-foot-by-eighteen-inch open space through which the gas had entered building C. The defect was only visible from a vantage point within the crawl space and had been missed by various building inspectors and by the fumigation company itself during an earlier inspection.

The occupants of building C who had been felled by the Vikane fumes sued the fumigator for damages, alleging that they had suffered damages that resulted from the fumigator's acts. The fumigator defended on the ground that third parties—the architect and contractors—had actually caused plaintiffs' injuries by failing to construct properly the fire wall between buildings B and C. The plaintiffs moved for summary judgment arguing, inter alia, that the fumigator was strictly liable for damages caused by its performance of an ultrahazardous activity. The trial court granted the motion; the fumigator appeals.

Old Island Fumigation, Inc., is strictly liable for damages caused to the plaintiffs by its fumigation of the condominium complex. Fumigation is an ultrahazardous activity as it "necessarily involves a risk of serious harm to the person, land, or chattels of others which cannot be eliminated by the exercise of the utmost care, and is not a matter of common usage." Factors to be considered in determining whether activity is ultrahazardous activity are: whether activity involves high degree of risk of harm to property of others; whether potential harm is likely to be great; whether risk can be eliminated by exercise of reasonable care; whether activity is matter of common usage; whether activity is appropriate to place where conducted; whether activity has substantial value to community.

Old Island Fumigation is thus liable regardless of the level of care exercised in carrying out this activity. Any alleged negligence by a third party does not free the fumigation company from liability. The reason for imposing strict liability upon those who carry on abnormally dangerous activities is that they have for their own purposes created a risk that is not a usual incident of the ordinary life of a community. If the risk ripens into injury, it is immaterial that the harm occurs through the unexpectable action of a human being. This is true irrespective of whether the action of the human being which makes the abnormally dangerous activity harmful is innocent, negligent or even reckless. In sum, the trial court properly entered summary judgment against Old Island Fumigation on the issue of liability.

Affirmed.

As mentioned, maintaining a wild animal is also an ultrahazardous activity. If you own an elephant, beware. In one English case, a peaceable circus elephant was pestered by a small dog. It finally lunged for the dog and accidentally squashed a performing midget. The circus had to pay tall damages.[10] Interestingly, the same case in India would yield the opposite result, since in its native land an elephant is regarded as a domestic animal, imposing no strict liability.

Because "strict liability" translates into "defendant is liable," parties in tort cases often fight over whether the defendant was engaged in an ultrahazardous activity. If the court rules that the activity was ultrahazardous, the plaintiff is assured of winning. If the court rules that it was not ultrahazardous, the plaintiff must prove all elements of negligence.

Marshall Pontiac-Nissan hired 22-year-old Richard Hughes to remove debris stored near a dumpster, including bumpers, rims, and other pieces of scrap metal. Hughes used an oxyacetylene torch to do the work. A 55-gallon steel drum was in the vicinity, containing a small amount of flammable liquid, probably paint thinner. The torch ignited vapors from the drum, which exploded and struck Hughes. Hughes sustained a skull fracture, brain and eye damage, scarring, and disfigurement. He sued Marshall Pontiac-Nissan.

Hughes moved for summary judgment, claiming that Marshall was strictly liable. Hughes argued that Marshall had engaged in ultrahazardous activity by improperly disposing of flammable liquids and that there was thus no defense. But the trial court ruled that mere improper storage of flammable liquids was not an ultrahazardous activity and that Hughes must prove negligence. At trial, Marshall's expert witness testified that Hughes caused the explosion by failing to follow proper welding procedures and by working near a drum with unknown contents.

The jury found that Marshall had been negligent and that Hughes had suffered $1.8 million in damages. But it also found that Hughes had been comparatively negligent and that the damages should be reduced by 35 percent. Had the trial court found the storage to be an ultrahazardous activity, Marshall would have been strictly liable, and Hughes's comparative negligence would have been irrelevant.[11]

The battle over the meaning of "ultrahazardous" will go on. Connecticut courts have recently held that cutting timber is not an ultrahazardous activity, nor is burying an electrical power line. Other states have held that keeping even a domestic animal *does* create strict liability, if the owner knows that the animal has vicious tendencies. Plaintiffs and defendants will continue to fight over strict liability like cats and dogs.

---

[10] *Behrens v. Bertram Mills Circus, Ltd.*, 2 Q.B. 1, 14–15 (1957).

[11] *Hughes v. Marshall Pontiac-Nissan, Inc.*, Mass. Lawyers Weekly, Nov. 8, 1993, p. 3 (Mass. Superior Court, 1993).

CHAPTER CONCLUSION

Tort issues necessarily remain in flux, based on changing social values and concerns. There is no final word on what is an ultrahazardous activity, or how much security a shop owner must provide, or whether a social host can be liable for the destruction caused by a guest. What is clear is that a working knowledge of these issues and pitfalls can help everyone—business executive and ordinary citizen alike.

CHAPTER REVIEW

1. The five elements of negligence are duty of due care, breach, factual causation, foreseeable type of harm, and injury.
2. If the defendant could foresee that misconduct would injure a particular person, he probably has a duty to her.
3. In most states, a landowner's duty of due care is lowest to trespassers; often higher to children; higher still to a licensee (anyone on the land for her own purposes but with the owner's permission); and highest of all to an invitee (someone on the property as of right).
4. A defendant breaches his duty of due care by failing to behave the way a reasonable person would under similar circumstances.
5. Employers may be liable for negligent hiring or negligent retention of employees.
6. If a legislature sets a minimum standard of care for a particular activity in order to protect a certain group of people, and a violation of the statute injures a member of that group, the defendant has committed negligence per se.
7. If one event physically led to the ultimate harm, it is the factual cause.
8. For the defendant to be liable, the type of harm must have been reasonably foreseeable.
9. The plaintiff must persuade the court that he has suffered a harm that is genuine, not speculative.
10. In a contributory negligence state, a plaintiff who is even slightly responsible for his own injury recovers nothing; in a comparative negligence state, the jury may apportion liability between plaintiff and defendant.
11. A defendant is strictly liable for harm caused by an ultrahazardous activity or a defective product. Ultrahazardous activities include using harmful chemicals, blasting, and keeping wild animals. Strict liability means that if the defendant's conduct led to the harm, the defendant is liable, even if she exercises extraordinary care.

PRACTICE TEST

1. Irving was a notary public who prepared income tax returns for Maroevich. Irving agreed to draft a will for Maroevich, leaving all of the property to Maroevich's sister, Biakanja. When Maroevich died, the probate court refused to accept the will because Irving had failed to have the signatures properly witnessed. As a result, Biakanja inherited only one-eighth of the estate. She sued Irving. Irving defended by saying that he had no duty of due care to Biakanja because all of his dealings were with Maroevich and none were with her. Discuss.

2. Jason Jacque was riding as a passenger in a car driven by his sister, who was drunk and driving 19 mph over the speed limit. She failed to negotiate a curve, skidded off the road, and collided with a wooden utility pole erected by the Public Service Company of Colorado (PSC). Jacque suffered severe brain injury. He sued PSC for negligently installing the pole too close to the highway at a dangerous curve where an accident was likely to happen. The trial court gave summary judgment for PSC, ruling that PSC owed no duty to Jacque. He appealed. Please rule.

3. At approximately 7:50 P.M. bells at the train station rang and red lights flashed, signaling an express train's approach. David Harris walked onto the tracks, ignoring a yellow line painted on the platform instructing people to stand back. Two men shouted to Harris, warning him to get off the tracks. The train's engineer saw him too late to stop the train, which was traveling at approximately 99 mph. The train struck and killed Harris as it passed through the station. Harris's widow sued the railroad, arguing that the railroad's negligence caused her husband's death. Evaluate her argument.

4. A supervisor reprimanded an employee for eating in a restaurant when he should have been at work. Later, the employee showed up at the supervisor's office and shot him. Although the employee previously had been violent, management withheld this information from supervisory personnel. Discuss.

5. Ryder leased a truck to Florida Food Service; Powers, an employee, drove it to make deliveries. He noticed that the door strap used to close the rear door was frayed, and he asked Ryder to fix it. Ryder failed to do so in spite of numerous requests. The strap broke, and Powers replaced it with a nylon rope. Later, when Powers was attempting to close the rear door, the nylon rope broke and he fell, sustaining severe injuries to his neck and back. He sued Ryder. The trial court found that Powers's attachment of the replacement rope was a superseding cause, relieving Ryder of any liability, and granted summary judgment for Ryder. Powers appealed. How should the appellate court rule?

6. A new truck, manufactured by General Motors Corp., stalled in rush hour traffic on a busy interstate highway because of a defective alternator, which caused a complete failure of the truck's electrical system. The driver stood nearby and waved traffic around his stalled truck. A panel truck approached the GMC truck, and immediately behind the panel truck, Davis was driving a Volkswagen fastback. Because of the panel truck, Davis was unable to see the stalled GMC truck. The panel truck swerved out of the way of the GMC truck, and Davis drove straight into it. The accident killed him. Davis's widow sued GMC. GMC moved for summary judgment, alleging (1) no duty to Davis, (2) no factual causation, and (3) no foreseeable harm. Comment.

7. A prison inmate bit a hospital employee. The employee sued the state for negligence and lack of supervision, claiming a fear of AIDS. The plaintiff had tested negative for the AIDS virus three times, and there was no proof that the inmate had the virus. Comment on the probable outcome.

8. RIGHT & WRONG Swimming pools in private homes often have diving boards, but those in public parks, hotels, and clubs rarely do. Why is that? Is it good or bad?

9. There is a collision between cars driven by Candy and Zeke, and both drivers are partly at fault. The evidence is that Candy is about 25 percent responsible, for failing to stop quickly enough, and Zeke about 75 percent responsible, for making a dangerous turn. Candy is most likely to win:

(a) A lawsuit for battery

(b) A lawsuit for negligence, in a comparative negligence state

(c) A lawsuit for negligence, in a contributory negligence state

(d) A lawsuit for strict liability; or

(e) A lawsuit for assault.

10. YOU BE THE JUDGE WRITING PROBLEM When Thomas and Susan Tamplin were shopping at Star Lumber with their six-year-old daughter Ann Marie, a 150-pound roll of vinyl flooring fell on the girl, seriously injuring her head and pituitary gland. Ann was clearly entitled to recover for the physical harm, such as her fractured skull. The plaintiffs also sought recovery for potential future harm. Their medical expert was prepared to testify that, although Ann would probably develop normally, he could not rule out the slight possibility that her pituitary injury might prevent her from sexually maturing. Is Ann entitled to damages for future harm? **Argument for Ann:** This was a major trauma, and it is impossible to know the full extent of the future harm. Sexual maturation is a fundamental part of life; if there is a possibility that Ann will not develop normally, she is entitled to present her case to a jury and receive damages. **Argument for Star Lumber:** A plaintiff may not recover for speculative harm. The "slight possibility" that Ann could fail to develop is not enough for her to take her case to the jury.

11. Van Houten owned a cat and allowed it to roam freely outside. In the three years he had owned it, it had never bitten anyone. The cat entered Pritchard's garage. Pritchard attempted to move it outside his garage, and the cat bit him. As a direct result of the bite, Pritchard underwent four surgeries, was fitted with a plastic finger joint, and spent more than $39,000 in medical bills. He sued Van Houten, claiming both strict liability and ordinary negligence. Please evaluate his claims.

INTERNET RESEARCH PROBLEM

Everyone knows that drunk driving is bad, but many people still do it. Proceed to http://www.madd.org/. Find something that you did not know about drunk driving. What role should the law play in this problem, and what role should parents, students, and schools play?

You can find further practice problems in the Online Quiz at http://beatty.westbuslaw.com or in the Study Guide that accompanies this text.

CHAPTER 7

CRIME

Crime can take us by surprise. Stacey tucks her nine-year-old daughter, Beth, into bed. Promising her husband, Mark, that she will be home by 11:00 P.M., she jumps into her car and heads back to Be Patient, Inc. She puts a compact disc in the player of her $55,000 sedan and tries to relax. Be Patient is a health care organization that owns five geriatric hospitals. Most of its patients use Medicare, and Stacey supervises all billing to their largest client, the federal government.

She parks in a well-lighted spot on the street and walks to her building, failing to notice two men, collars turned up, watching from a parked truck. Once in her office she goes straight to her computer and works on billing issues. Tonight's work goes more quickly than she expected, thanks to new software she helped develop. At 10:30 she emerges from the building with a quick step and a light heart, walks to her car—and finds it missing.

A major crime has occurred during the 90 minutes Stacey was at her desk, but she will never report it to the police. It is a crime that costs Americans countless dollars each year, yet Stacey will not even mention it to friends or family. Stacey is the one who committed it.

When we think of criminals, we imagine the drug dealers and bank robbers endlessly portrayed on television. We do not picture corporate executives sitting at polished desks. "Street crimes" are indeed serious threats to our security and happiness. They deservedly receive the attention of the public and the law. (For a look at the FBI's 10 most wanted list, see **http://www.fbi.gov/mostwanted.htm**.) But when measured only in dollars, street crime takes second place to white-collar crime, which costs society *tens of billions* of dollars annually.

The hypothetical about Stacey is based on many real cases and is used to illustrate that crime does not always dress the way we expect. Her car was never stolen; it was simply towed. Two parking bureau employees, watching from their truck, saw Stacey park illegally and did their job. Stacey is the criminal. She committed Medicare fraud. Stacey has learned the simple but useful lesson that company profits rise when she charges the government for work Be Patient has never done. For months she billed the government for imaginary patients. Then she hired a computer hacker to worm into the Medicare computer system and plant a "Trojan horse," a program that seemed useful to Medicare employees but actually contained a series of codes opening the computer to Stacey. Stacey simply entered the Medicare system and altered the calculations for payments owed to Be Patient. Every month, the government paid Be Patient about $10 million for imaginary work. Stacey's scheme was quick and profitable—and a distressingly common crime.

What do we do about cases like these? What *should* we do? These questions involve multifarious fact issues and important philosophical values. In this chapter, we look first at the big picture of criminal law and then focus on that part of it that most affects business—white-collar crime. We examine four major issues:

- *Crime, Society, and Law*. What makes conduct criminal? We enumerate the basic elements that the prosecution must establish to prove that a crime has been committed, and also some of the most common defenses.
- *Crimes That Harm Business*. We look at specific crimes, such as fraud and embezzlement, that cost businesses enormous sums every year.
- *Crimes Committed by Business*. We analyze "white-collar crimes," which are generally committed by employees of corporations or partnerships and may be directed at consumers, other businesses, or the government.
- *Criminal Process and Constitutional Protections*. We examine how the Bill of Rights protects citizens subjected to search, interrogation, and trial. And we pay a final visit to Stacey.

CRIME, SOCIETY, AND LAW

CIVIL LAW/CRIMINAL LAW

Most of this book concerns the civil law—the rights and liabilities that exist between private parties. As we have seen, if one person claims that another has caused her a civil injury, she must file a lawsuit and convince a court of her damages.

The criminal law is different. Conduct is **criminal** when society outlaws it. When a state legislature or Congress concludes that certain behavior threatens the population generally, it passes a statute forbidding that behavior, in other words, declaring it criminal. Medicare fraud, which Stacey committed, is a crime because

Congress has outlawed it. Money laundering is a crime because Congress concluded it was a fundamental part of the drug trade and prohibited it.

Prosecution

Suppose the police arrest Roger and accuse him of breaking into a video store and stealing 25 video cameras, videos, and other equipment. **The owner of the video store is the one harmed, but it is the government that prosecutes crimes.** The local prosecutor will decide whether or not to charge Roger and bring him to trial.

Jury Right

The facts of the case will be decided by a judge or jury. A criminal defendant has a right to a trial by jury for any charge that could result in a sentence of six months or longer. The defendant may demand a jury trial or may waive that right, in which case the judge will be the factfinder.

Punishment

In a civil lawsuit, the plaintiff seeks a verdict that the defendant is liable for harm caused to her. But in a criminal case, the government asks the court to find the defendant **guilty** of the crime. The government wants the court to **punish** the defendant. If the judge or jury finds the defendant guilty, the court will punish him with a fine and/or a prison sentence. The fine is paid to the government, not to the injured person (although the court will sometimes order **restitution**, meaning that the defendant must reimburse the victim for harm suffered). It is almost always the judge who imposes the sentence. If the jury is not persuaded of the defendant's guilt, it will **acquit** him, that is, find him not guilty.

Felony/Misdemeanor

A **felony** is a serious crime, for which a defendant can be sentenced to one year or more in prison. Murder, robbery, rape, drug dealing, money laundering, wire fraud, and embezzlement are felonies. A **misdemeanor** is a less serious crime, often punishable by a year or less in a county jail. Public drunkenness, driving without a license, and simple possession of one marijuana cigarette are considered misdemeanors in most states.

PUNISHMENT

Why punish a defendant? Sometimes the answer is obvious. If a defendant has committed armed robbery, we want that person locked up. Other cases are not so apparent.

You are the judge in charge of sentencing Jason. He is a 61-year-old minister who has devoted 40 years to serving his community, leading his church, and helping to rehabilitate schools. Fifteen years ago he founded a children's hospital and has raised enormous sums to maintain it. He has labored with local government to rebuild abandoned housing and established a center for battered women. Jason suffers from a terminal illness and will die in three to four years. But the jury has just found that in his zeal to get housing built, Jason took kickbacks from construction firms run by gangsters. The construction companies padded their bills, some of which were paid with state and city money. They kicked back a small amount of this illegal profit to Jason, who gave the money to his charities. Jason thought of himself as Robin Hood, but the law regards him as a felon. You can fine Jason and/or sentence him to prison for a maximum of five years.

A flood of letters urges you to allow Jason to continue raising money and helping others. You need to understand the rationale of punishment. Over the past several centuries, philosophers in many countries—and judges in this country—have proposed various reasons for punishing the guilty.

Restraint

A violent criminal who appears likely to commit more crimes must be physically restrained. Here there is no pretense of prison being anything but a cage to protect the rest of society. (An online group that sees little good and much evil in our system of incarceration gives examples of perceived abuses at **http://www.prisonactivist.org/news/**.) In Jason's case, there is clearly no reason to restrain him.

Deterrence

Imprisonment may deter future crimes in two ways. **Specific deterrence** is intended to teach *this defendant* that crime carries a heavy price tag, in the hope that he will never do it again. **General deterrence** is the goal of demonstrating to *society generally* that crime must be shunned. Notice that both ideas of deterrence are utilitarian; that is, they are *means to an end*. Specific and general deterrence both assume that by imprisoning someone, the law achieves a greater good for everyone. Jason almost certainly requires no specific deterrence. Is general deterrence a reason to imprison him?

Retribution

The German philosopher Immanuel Kant (1724–1804) rejected the idea of deterrence. He argued that human beings were supremely important and as a result must always be treated as ends in themselves, *never as a means to an end*. Kant would argue that, if deterrence were legitimate, then it would be all right to torture prisoners—even innocent prisoners—if this deterred massive amounts of crime.

For Kant, there is only one valid reason to punish: the prisoner deserves it. This is the idea of **retribution**—giving back to the criminal precisely what she deserves. A moral world, said Kant, requires that the government administer to all prisoners a punishment exactly equal to the crime they committed. A murderer must be put to death (even if he is dying from an illness and would live only a few days); an executive who bribes a government official must suffer a punishment equal to the harm she caused. To Kant, all of Jason's good deeds would be irrelevant, as would his terminal illness. If three years is the appropriate imprisonment for the crime of fraud, then he must serve three years, even if he dies in prison, even if it stops him from raising $10 million for charity.

Related to the idea of retribution is **vengeance.** When a serious crime has occurred, society wants the perpetrator to suffer. If we punish no one, people lose faith in the power and effectiveness of government and may take the law into their own hands.

Inside a prison. Which rationale for punishment do you find most persuasive?

Rehabilitation

To rehabilitate someone is to provide training so that he may return to a normal life. Most criminal justice experts believe that little or no rehabilitation occurs in a prison, though other forms of punishment may achieve this worthy goal.

Jason's Case. What is your decision? Restraint and specific deterrence are unnecessary. You may imprison him for general deterrence or for retribution. Should you let him go free so that he can raise more money for good causes? In a similar case, a federal court judge decided that general deterrence was essential. To allow someone to go free, he said, would be to send a message that certain people can get away with crime. The judge sentenced the defendant to a prison term, though he shortened the sentence based on the defendant's age and ill health.[1]

The Prosecution's Case

In all criminal cases, the prosecution faces several basic issues.

Conduct Outlawed

Virtually all crimes are created by statute. The prosecution must demonstrate to the court that the defendant's alleged conduct is indeed outlawed by a statute. Returning to Roger, the alleged video thief, the state charges that he stole video cameras from a store, a crime clearly defined by statute as burglary.

Burden of Proof

In a civil case, the plaintiff must prove her case by a preponderance of the evidence.[2] But in a criminal case, the government must prove its case **beyond a reasonable doubt.** This is because the potential harm to a criminal defendant is far greater. Roger, the video thief, can be fined and/or sent to prison. The stigma of a criminal conviction will stay with him, making it more difficult to obtain work and housing. Therefore, in all criminal cases, if the jury has any significant doubt at all that Roger stole the video cameras, it *must* acquit him. This high standard of proof in a criminal case reflects a very old belief, inherited from English law, that it is better to set 10 guilty people free than to convict a single innocent one. We will see that our law offers many protections for the accused.

Actus Reus

Actus reus means the "guilty act." **The prosecution must prove that the defendant voluntarily committed a prohibited act.** Suppose Mary Jo files an insurance claim for a stolen car, knowing that her car was not stolen. That is insurance fraud. Filing the claim is the *actus reus:* Mary Jo voluntarily filled out the insurance claim and mailed it. At a bar, Mary Jo describes the claim to her friend, Chi Ling, who laughs and replies, "That's great. It'll serve the company right." Has Chi Ling committed a crime? No. There is no *actus reus,* because Chi Ling has done nothing illegal. Her cynical attitude may contribute to higher premiums for all of us, but criminal law punishes acts, not thoughts or omissions.

Mens Rea

The prosecution must also show ***mens rea*, a "guilty state of mind,"** on the defendant's part. This is harder to prove than *actus reus*—it requires convincing evidence about something that is essentially psychological. Precisely what "state of mind" the prosecution must prove varies, depending on the crime. We will discuss the exact *mens rea* requirement for various crimes later in the chapter. In general, however, there are four mental states that a prosecutor may be required to prove, depending on the crime:

General Intent. Most crimes require a showing of general intent, meaning that the defendant intended to do the prohibited physical action (the *actus reus*).

---

[1] *United States v. Bergman,* 416 F. Supp. 496, 1976 U.S. Dist. LEXIS 14577 (S.D.N.Y. 1976).

[2] See the earlier discussion in Chapter 2, on dispute resolution.

Suppose Miller, a customer in a bar, picks up a bottle and smashes it over the head of Bud. In a trial for criminal assault, the *mens rea* would simply be the intention to hit Bud. The prosecution need not show that Miller intended serious harm, only that he intended the blow.

How will a prosecutor prove what was in Miller's mind? By circumstantial evidence: a witness will describe how Miller picked up the bottle and what he did with it. A jury is free to conclude that Miller intended physical contact since there would be no other reason for his action.

Specific Intent. Some crimes require the prosecution to prove that the defendant willfully intended to do something beyond the physical act. For example, burglary requires proof that the defendant entered a building at night and intended to commit a felony inside, such as stealing property.

Reckless or Negligent Conduct. For a few crimes, the prosecution is concerned more with the defendant's irresponsible conduct than with what the defendant was thinking. **Criminal recklessness** means consciously disregarding a substantial risk of injury. One pedestrian who jokingly points a gun at another commits criminal recklessness. The danger of the gun going off is obvious, and the defendant is guilty even if no shot is fired. A slightly lesser crime, **criminal negligence,** refers to gross deviations from reasonable conduct. A hunter who sees movement and shoots at it, without bothering to determine whether the target is a turkey or a professor, commits criminal negligence.

Strict Liability. In strict liability cases, the prosecution must only prove *actus reus*. If the defendant committed the act, they are guilty, regardless of mental state or irresponsibility. For example, in an effort to improve the environment, many states now hold corporate defendants strictly liable for discharging certain pollutants into the air. If an oil refinery discharges toxic fumes, it is strictly liable, regardless of what efforts it may have taken to control emissions. Thus, strict liability crimes are the easiest for a prosecutor to prove and potentially the most dangerous to corporations.

DEFENSES

A criminal defendant will frequently dispute the facts that link her to the crime. For example, she might claim mistaken identity (that she merely resembles the real criminal) or offer an alibi (that she can prove she was elsewhere when the crime was committed). In addition, a defendant may offer **legal defenses.** Many of these are controversial, as we will see.

Insanity

A defendant who can prove that he was **insane** at the time of the criminal act will be declared not guilty. This reflects the moral basis of our criminal law. Insane people, though capable of great harm, historically have not been considered responsible for their acts. A defendant found to be insane will generally be committed to a mental institution. If and when that hospital determines he is no longer a danger to society, he will, in theory, be released. Some people applaud this as deeply humane, while others see it as muddled thinking that allows guilty people to walk free.

Two basic tests determine whether a defendant is insane. Some states recognize just one; others allow both.

M'Naghten Rule. The defendant must show (1) that he suffered a serious, identifiable mental disease and that because of it (2) he did not understand the nature of his act or did not know that it was wrong. Suppose Jerry, a homeless man, stabs

Phil. At trial, a psychiatrist testifies that Jerry suffers from chronic schizophrenia, that he does not know where he is or what he is doing, and that when he stabbed Phil he believed he was sponging down his pet giraffe. If the jury believes the psychiatrist, it may find Jerry not guilty by reason of insanity.

"Irresistible Impulse." Under this test, the defendant must convince a jury that a mental defect left him unable to control his behavior. Jerry testifies that when he stabbed Phil he knew it was wrong but he could not stop himself. His psychiatrist asserts that Jerry's chronic dementia leaves him physically unable to repress violent impulses. If the jury believes the testimony, it may find Jerry not guilty.

What if the alleged mental defect is a result of the defendant's own behavior? You be the judge.

BIEBER v. PEOPLE
856 P.2d 811, 1993 Colo. LEXIS 630
Supreme Court of Colorado, 1993

Facts: Donald Bieber walked up to a truck in which William Ellis was sitting and shot Ellis, whom he did not know, in the back of his head. He threw Ellis's body from the truck and drove away. Shortly before and after the killing, Bieber encountered various people in different places. He sang "God Bless America" and the "Marine Hymn" to them and told them he was a prisoner of war and was being followed by communists. He fired shots at some people, without injuring them, and aimed his gun at others. After the homicide he told people he had killed a communist on "War Memorial Highway." The police arrested him.

Bieber had a long history of drug abuse. As a teenager, he began using drugs, including amphetamines. As an adult, he continued his heavy drug use, while making money selling drugs. Several years before the homicide, Bieber voluntarily sought treatment for mental impairment, entering a hospital and saying he thought he was going to hurt someone. He was later released into a long-term drug program.

Bieber was charged with first degree murder. He pleaded not guilty by reason of insanity. An expert witness testified that he was insane, suffering from "amphetamine delusional disorder" (ADD), a recognized psychiatric illness resulting from long-term use of amphetamines and characterized by delusions. At trial, Bieber's attorney argued that he was not intoxicated at the time of the crime but that he was insane due to ADD. The trial court refused to instruct that Bieber could be legally insane due to ADD, and the jury found Bieber guilty of first degree murder. He appealed.

You Be the Judge: May a jury find that a defendant with ADD is legally insane?

Argument for Bieber: Your honors, Mr. Bieber acknowledges the rule that someone who becomes voluntarily intoxicated and commits an offense is liable for the crime. That rule is irrelevant here, since Mr. Bieber was not intoxicated at the time of this homicide. He was insane.

The state of Colorado has long held that insanity is a valid defense to a criminal charge. It is morally and legally proper to distinguish between people who commit a crime out of viciousness and those who suffer serious mental illness. Mr. Bieber suffered from amphetamine delusional disorder, a serious psychotic illness recognized by the American Psychiatric Association. There was overwhelming evidence that he was out of control and did not know what he was doing at the time of the homicide.

The fact that ADD is brought about by years of amphetamine use should make no difference in an insanity case. This man's reason was destroyed by a serious illness. He should not be treated the same as a cold-blooded killer who carries out a vicious killing for reasons of hatred or personal gain. Mr. Bieber had no motive to injure the victim, and a jury should have been allowed to consider his mental illness.

Argument for the State: Your honors, there is no qualitative difference between a person who drinks or takes drugs knowing that he or she will be momentarily "mentally defective" as an immediate result and one who drinks or takes drugs knowing that he or she may be "mentally defective" as an eventual, long-term result. In both cases, the person is aware of the possible consequences of his or her actions. We do not believe that in the latter case, such knowledge should be excused simply because the resulting affliction is more severe.

It is a matter of common knowledge that the excessive use of liquor or drugs impairs the perceptual, judgmental, and volitional faculties of the user. Also, because the intoxication must be "self-induced," the defendant necessarily must have had the conscious ability to prevent this temporary incapacity from coming into being at all. Self-induced intoxication by its very nature involves culpability. The moral blameworthiness lies in the voluntary impairment of one's mental faculties with knowledge that the resulting condition is a source of potential danger to others.

As a matter of public policy, therefore, we must not excuse a defendant's actions, which endanger others, based upon a mental disturbance or illness that he or she actively and voluntarily contracted. There is no principled basis to distinguish between the short-term and long-term effects of voluntary intoxication by punishing the first and excusing the second. If anything, the moral blameworthiness would seem to be even greater with respect to the long-term effects of many, repeated instances of voluntary intoxication occurring over an extended period of time. We ask that you affirm.

Jury Role. The insanity defense creates fear and confusion in the public, but most experts believe the concern is unwarranted. A Connecticut study showed that the defense was invoked in only one-tenth of 1 percent of criminal prosecutions in that state, and that in over 90 percent of *those* cases it still failed. Juries are reluctant to acquit based on insanity, probably fearing that the defendant will soon be back on the streets. But just the opposite is true. Most defendants acquitted by reason of insanity spend more time in a mental hospital than convicts spend in prison for the same act.

Entrapment

You go to a fraternity party where you meet a friendly new frat member, Joey. After a drink or two, Joey asks if you can get him some marijuana. You tell him you never use drugs. A week later you accidentally meet Joey in the cafeteria and he repeats the question, promising a very large profit if you will supply him with an ounce. You again say "no thanks." About once a week Joey bumps into you, in the school hallways, in the bookstore, at parties. He continues to ask you to "get him some stuff," and his offers grow more lucrative. Finally, after six requests, you speak to someone who is reputed to deal in drugs. You buy an ounce, then offer it to Joey at a large markup. Joey gratefully hands over the money, takes your package—and flashes his badge in your face, identifying himself as an undercover agent of the State Police. You are speechless, which is fine, since Joey informs you that you have the right to remain silent.

Drugs are a deadly serious problem in our society, involved directly or indirectly in more than half of all street crime. We need creative police efforts. Has this one gone too far? The issue is **entrapment. When the government induces the defendant to break the law, the prosecution must prove beyond a reasonable doubt that the defendant was predisposed to commit the crime.**

If the government cannot prove predisposition, the defendant is not guilty. In other words, the goal is to separate the cases where the defendant was innocent before the government tempted him from those where the defendant was only too eager to break the law.

JACOBSON v. UNITED STATES
503 U.S. 540, 112 S. Ct. 1535, 1992 U.S. LEXIS 2117
United States Supreme Court, 1992

Facts: In 1984 Keith Jacobson, a 56-year-old Nebraska farmer, ordered two magazines from a California adult bookstore: *Bare Boys I* and *Bare Boys II*. The magazines showed photos of nude preteen and teenage boys. At that time, the magazines were legal. The pictures startled Jacobson, who had expected pictures of young men 18 and over. Later, federal law changed, making it illegal to receive through the mail any sexual pictures of children.

Postal inspectors found Jacobson's name on the customer list of the California bookstore and began a two and one-half year campaign to entice him into ordering material that had become illegal. A postal inspector sent him a letter from the

"American Hedonist Society," a fictitious organization, urging that members had the right to "read what we desire." Jacobson joined, and answered a questionnaire about his sexual preferences. Two more fictitious organizations, both the creation of the postal service, began mailing him information and questionnaires. Jacobson responded, saying that he liked "good looking young guys (in their late teens and early 20's) doing their thing together," and that he was opposed to pedophilia. After 26 months of periodic contacts, a third fictitious agency began to solicit Jacobson. Finally, Jacobson ordered some sexual material, which depicted young boys engaged in sexual activities. He was arrested and convicted of violating federal law.

Issue: Did the government entrap Jacobson?

Excerpts from Justice White's Decision: By the time petitioner finally placed his order, he had already been the target of 26 months of repeated mailings and communications from Government agents and fictitious organizations.

The sole piece of preinvestigation evidence is petitioner's order and receipt of the Bare Boys magazines. But this is scant if any proof of petitioner's predisposition to commit an illegal act, the criminal character of which a defendant is presumed to know. It may indicate a predisposition to view sexually-oriented photographs that are responsive to his sexual tastes; but evidence that merely indicates a generic inclination to act within a broad range, not all of which is criminal, is of little probative value in establishing predisposition. Furthermore, petitioner was acting within the law at the time he received these magazines.

Law enforcement officials go too far when they implant in the mind of an innocent person the disposition to commit the alleged offense and induce its commission in order that they may prosecute. When the Government's quest for convictions leads to the apprehension of an otherwise law-abiding citizen who, if left to his own devices, likely would have never run afoul of the law, the courts should intervene.

We *reverse* the Court of Appeals' judgment affirming the conviction of Keith Jacobson.

Excerpts from Justice O'Connor's Dissenting Opinon: Keith Jacobson was offered only two opportunities to buy child pornography through the mail. Both times, he ordered. Both times, he asked for opportunities to buy more.

The first time the Government sent Mr. Jacobson a catalog of illegal materials, he ordered a set of photographs advertised as picturing "young boys in sex action fun." He enclosed the following note with his order: "I received your brochure and decided to place an order. If I like your product, I will order more later." The second time the Government sent a catalog of illegal materials, Mr. Jacobson ordered a magazine called "Boys Who Love Boys," described as: "11 year old and 14 year old boys get it on in every way possible. Oral, anal sex and heavy masturbation. If you love boys, you will be delighted with this."

It was the jury's task, as the conscience of the community, to decide whether or not Mr. Jacobson was a willing participant in the criminal activity here or an innocent dupe. The jury is the traditional "defense against arbitrary law enforcement." There is no dispute that the jury in this case was fully and accurately instructed on the law of entrapment, and nonetheless found Mr. Jacobson guilty. Because I believe there was sufficient evidence to uphold the jury's verdict, I respectfully *dissent*.

Final Note on Entrapment. In the hypothetical on the fraternity undercover agent buying marijuana from a reluctant seller, most courts would agree that this was entrapment. The seller said "no" five times. Unless the government has other evidence that the defendant was involved in dealing drugs, there appears to be no predisposition, and the entrapment defense is valid.

Justification

A defendant may plead justification where he committed a criminal act in order to avoid a greater harm. The harm being avoided must be greater than the harm caused by the criminal act, it must be imminent, and there must be no other alternative course of action. This rarely successful defense works only when the facts are compelling.

Suppose Roger, the video thief, admits breaking into the store but denies stealing anything. He claims that earlier in the day he had accidentally left in the store newly purchased medicine for his seriously ill son. The son needed his nighttime dosage and no pharmacy would refill Roger's prescription. He either had to break into the store or see his son suffer a potentially fatal seizure. If that is true, it is justification.

Duress

A defendant may plead duress if she can show that a threat by a third person caused her fear of imminent serious physical harm. The threatened harm must be physical. If Roger, the video thief, could show that a drug addict threatened to kill him if he did not steal the videos, he would have a valid duress defense.

By contrast, assume that Roger, a former accountant, stole the videos because he had been out of work for 14 months. A bank foreclosed his suburban home, and he had exhausted his savings during his job search. He and his two children were subsisting in an abandoned station wagon as his wife lay in a sanitorium, weak with tuberculosis. Roger was desperate for money to make a deposit on an apartment. His claim—and all claims—of *economic* duress will fail because there is no imminent physical harm.

CRIMES THAT HARM BUSINESS

Three major crimes involve taking money from businesses: larceny, fraud, and embezzlement. In each case the criminal ends up with money or property that belongs to someone else.

LARCENY

It is holiday season at the mall, the period of greatest profits—and the most crime. At the Foot Forum, a teenager limps in wearing ragged sneakers and sneaks out wearing Super Rags, valued at $145. Down the aisle at a home furnishing store, a man is so taken by a $375 power saw that he takes it. Sweethearts swipe sweaters, pensioners pocket produce. All are committing larceny.

Larceny is the trespassory taking of personal property with the intent to steal it. "Trespassory taking" means that someone else originally has the property. The Super Rags are personal property (not real estate), they were in the possession of the Foot Forum, and the teenager deliberately left without paying, intending never to return the goods. That is larceny. By contrast, suppose Fast Eddie leaves Bloomingdale's in New York, descends to the subway system, and jumps over a turnstile without paying. Larceny? No. He has "taken" a service—the train ride—but not personal property.

Every day in the United States, over $25 million in merchandise is stolen from retail stores. Economists estimate that *12 cents out of every dollar* spent in retail stores covers the cost of shoplifting. Some criminal experts believe that drug addicts commit over half of all shoplifting to support their habits. Stores have added electronic surveillance, security patrols, and magnetic antitheft devices, but the problem will not disappear.

FRAUD

Robert Dorsey owned Bob's Highland Chrysler in Highland, Illinois. To finance his purchases, Dorsey had a "floor-plan" loan from the First National Bank of Highland. Dorsey would order cars from Chrysler, and First National would pay Chrysler for them. In theory, Dorsey would sell the cars and repay First National.

Dorsey began to suffer money problems. Business at the dealership declined, and he was unable to support his extravagant lifestyle. In the spring of 1989, First National found evidence that Dorsey might have sold cars without paying off the loan. The bank contacted a state investigator who, in June 1990, notified Dorsey that he planned to review all dealership records. One week later a fire engulfed Bob's Highland Chrysler.

Larry Gilbert, a fire investigator, discovered that an electric iron had been connected to a timer, plugged into an electrical outlet, and placed over a pile of papers and files concerning the dealership's financing. The files and the iron had been doused with an accelerant. Two weeks later there was a second fire at the dealership, and this time investigators found the dealership sales records doused with gasoline.

The saddest part of this true story is that it is only too common. Some experts suggest that 1 percent of corporate revenues are wasted on fraud alone. Dorsey was convicted and imprisoned for committing two crimes that cost business billions of dollars annually—fraud and arson.[3]

Fraud refers to various crimes, all of which have a common element: **the deception of another person for the purpose of obtaining money or property from him.** Robert Dorsey's precise violation was bank fraud, a federal crime. It is **bank fraud** to use deceit to obtain money, assets, securities, or other property under the control of any financial institution. The maximum penalty is a fine of $1 million and/or a prison term of 30 years.[4]

Wire fraud and **mail fraud** are additional federal crimes, involving the use of interstate mail, telegram, telephone, radio, or television to obtain property by deceit.[5] For example, if Marsha makes an interstate phone call to sell land that she does not own, that is wire fraud.

Insurance fraud is another common crime. A Ford suddenly swerves in front of a Toyota, causing it to brake hard. A Mercedes, unable to stop, slams into the Toyota, as the Ford races away. Regrettable accident? No: a "swoop and squat" fraud scheme. The Ford and Toyota drivers were working together, hoping for an accident. The "injured" Toyota driver now goes to a third member of the fraud team—a dishonest doctor—who diagnoses serious back and neck injuries and predicts long-term pain and disability. The driver files a claim against the Mercedes's driver, whose insurer may be forced to pay tens or even hundreds of thousands of dollars for an accident that was no accident. Insurance companies investigate countless cases like this each year, trying to distinguish the honest victim from the criminal.

---

[3] *United States v. Dorsey*, 27 F.3d 285, 1994 U.S. App. LEXIS 15010 (7th Cir. 1994).

[4] 18 U.S.C. §1344.

[5] 18 U.S.C. §§1341–1346.

Imprisonment

The corporation itself cannot, of course, be imprisoned—or can it? Federal Judge Doumar found the Allegheny Bottling Co. guilty of price-fixing.[11] Allegheny, a Pepsi distributor, had agreed with a Coca-Cola distributor to fix an artificially high price for both drinks, earning an illegal profit of at least $10 million. Judge Doumar fined the company $1 million and *sentenced the corporation to three years in prison*. He threatened to lock Allegheny's doors and bar the employees from entering for that period. Ultimately, he suspended the sentence, meaning that he would not carry it out provided that Allegheny obeyed the law. His creative approach to sentencing may influence future corporate punishments.

Compliance Programs

The **Federal Sentencing Guidelines** are the detailed rules that judges must follow when sentencing defendants convicted of crimes in federal court. The guidelines instruct judges to determine whether, at the time of the crime, the corporation had in place a serious **compliance program**, that is, a plan to prevent and detect criminal conduct at all levels of the company. A company that can point to a detailed, functioning compliance program may benefit from a dramatic reduction in the fine or other punishment meted out. Indeed, a tough compliance program may even convince federal investigators to curtail an investigation and to limit any prosecution to those directly involved, rather than attempting to get a conviction against high-ranking officers or the company itself.

To persuade prosecutors or judges that it seriously intended to follow the law, a company must demonstrate a thorough and effective compliance plan:

- The program must be reasonably capable of reducing the prospect of criminal conduct.
- Specific, high-level officers must be responsible for overseeing the program.
- The company must not place in charge any officers it knows or should have known, from past experience, that are likely to engage in illegal conduct.
- The company must effectively communicate the program to all employees and agents.
- The company must ensure compliance by monitoring employees in a position to cheat and by promptly disciplining any who break the law.

SELECTED CRIMES COMMITTED BY BUSINESS

Workplace Crimes

The workplace can be dangerous. Working on an assembly line exposes factory employees to fast-moving machinery. For a roofer, the first slip may be the last. The invisible radiation in a nuclear power plant can be deadlier than a bullet. The most important statute regulating the workplace is the federal **Occupational Safety and Health Act of 1970 (OSHA),**[12] which sets safety standards for many

[11] *United States v. Allegheny Bottling Co.*, 695 F. Supp. 856, 1988 U.S. Dist. LEXIS 10693 (E.D. Va. 1988).

[12] 29 U.S.C. §§651 et seq. (1982).

industries.[13] May a state government go beyond standards set by OSHA and use the criminal law to punish dangerous conditions? In *People v. O'Neill,*[14] the courts of Illinois answered that question with a potent "yes," permitting a *murder prosecution* against corporate executives. Notice that whereas Wisconsin prosecuted RKI *Corporation* for vehicular homicide, Illinois brought this case against the corporate executives themselves.

Film Recovery Systems was an Illinois corporation in business to extract silver from used X-ray film and then resell it. Steven O'Neill was president of Film Recovery, Charles Kirschbaum was its plant manager, and Daniel Rodriguez the foreman. To extract the silver, workers at Film Recovery soaked the X-ray film in large, open, bubbling vats that contained sodium cyanide.

A worker named Stefan Golab became faint. He left the production area and walked to the lunchroom, where workers found him trembling and foaming at the mouth. He lost consciousness. Paramedics were unable to revive him. They rushed him to a hospital where he was pronounced dead on arrival. The Cook County medical examiner determined that Golab died from acute cyanide poisoning caused by inhalation of cyanide fumes in the plant.

Illinois indicted Film Recovery and several of its managers for murder. The indictment charged that O'Neill and Kirschbaum committed murder by failing to disclose to Golab that he was working with cyanide and other potentially lethal substances and by failing to provide him with appropriate and necessary safety equipment.

The case was tried to a judge without a jury. Workers testified that O'Neill, Kirschbaum, and other managers never told them they were using cyanide or that the fumes they inhaled could be harmful; that management made no effort to ventilate the factory; that Film Recovery gave the workers no goggles or protective clothing; that the chemicals they worked with burned their skin; that breathing was difficult in the plant because of strong, foul orders; and that workers suffered frequent dizziness, nausea, and vomiting.

The trial judge found O'Neill, Kirschbaum, and others guilty of murder. Illinois defines murder as performing an act that the defendant *knows will create a strong probability of death* in the victim, and the judge found they had done that. He found Film Recovery guilty of involuntary manslaughter. Involuntary manslaughter is *recklessly* performing an act that causes death. He sentenced O'Neill, Kirschbaum, and Rodriguez to 25 years in prison.

The defendants appealed, contending that the verdicts were inconsistent. They argued, and the Illinois Court of Appeals agreed, that the judge had made contradictory findings. Murder required the specific intent of *knowing there was a strong probability of death*, whereas the manslaughter conviction required *reckless* conduct. The appeals court reversed the convictions and remanded for a new trial.

Moments before the new trial was to start, O'Neill, Kirschbaum, and Rodriguez all pleaded guilty to involuntary manslaughter. They received sentences of three years, two years, and four months, respectively.

Money Laundering

Money laundering consists of taking the profits of criminal acts and either (1) using the money to promote crime or (2) attempting to conceal the source of the money.[15]

---

13 See Chapter 30, on employment law.

14 194 Ill. App. 3d 79, 550 N.E.2d 1090, 1990 Ill. App. LEXIS 65 (Ill. App. Ct. 1990).

15 18 U.S.C. §§1956 et seq.

Money laundering is an essential part of the corrosive traffic in drugs. Profits, all in cash, mount so swiftly that the most difficult step for a successful dealer is to use the money without alerting the government. The *Hurley* case, which appears in the following section on RICO, details the intricate steps taken by one group of money launderers to make drug money look legitimate. Their profits were extraordinary—and their punishment fitting.

RICO

The **Racketeer Influenced and Corrupt Organizations Act (RICO)**[16] is one of the most powerful and controversial statutes ever written. Congress passed the law primarily to prevent gangsters from taking money they earned illegally and investing it in legitimate businesses. But RICO has expanded far beyond the original intentions of Congress and is now used more often against ordinary businesses than against organized criminals. Some regard this wide application as a tremendous advance in law enforcement, but others view it as an oppressive weapon used to club ethical companies into settlements they should never have to make.

RICO creates both criminal and civil law liabilities. The government may prosecute both individuals and organizations for violating RICO. For example, the government may prosecute a mobster, claiming that he has run a heroin ring for years. It may also prosecute an accounting firm, claiming that it lied about corporate assets in a stock sale, to make the shares appear more valuable than they really were. If the government proves its case, the defendant can be hit with large fines and a prison sentence of up to 20 years. RICO also permits the government to seek forfeiture of the defendant's property. A court may order a convicted defendant to hand over any property or money used in the criminal acts or derived from them. Forfeiture sums can be huge, as the *Hurley* case, below, indicates.

RICO creates civil liability as well. The government, organizations, and individuals all have the right to file civil lawsuits, seeking damages and, if necessary, injunctions. For example, shareholders claiming that they were harmed by the accounting firm's lies could sue the firm for money lost in buying and selling the stock. RICO is powerful (and for defendants, frightening) in part because a civil plaintiff can recover **treble damages,** that is, a judgment for three times the harm actually suffered, and can also recover attorney's fees.

What is a violation of RICO? **RICO prohibits using two or more racketeering acts to accomplish any of these goals: (1) investing in or acquiring legitimate businesses with criminal money; (2) maintaining or acquiring businesses through criminal activity; or (3) operating businesses through criminal activity.**

What does that mean in English? It is a two-step process to prove that a person or an organization has violated RICO. We will assume that this is a criminal prosecution, though the steps are similar in a civil lawsuit.

- The prosecutor must show that the defendant committed two or more **racketeering acts,** which are any of a long list of specified crimes: embezzlement, arson, mail fraud, wire fraud, and so forth. Thus, if a gangster ordered a building torched in January and then burned a second building in October, that would be two racketeering acts. If a stockbroker told two customers that Bronx Gold Mines was a promising stock, when she knew that it was worthless, that would be two racketeering acts.
- The prosecutor must show that the defendant used these racketeering acts to accomplish one of the three *purposes* listed above. If the gangster committed two arsons and then used the insurance payments to buy a dry cleaning

[16] 18 U.S.C. §§1961–1968.

would violate RICO. If the stockbroker gave fraudulent advice
commissions to buy advertising for her firm, that would violate
le pu
ce—was to
, which are re involved money laundering and RICO violations.
ore.
would be deposited
account at Citizens B
Rhode Island went to Sac ned several precious metals companies, including
umentation; the gold was th nd; Trend Precious Metals in New York City; and
ecks recorded as payments International Metal Marketing and Clinton
ordinary operations of the Sa nment used RICO to prosecute Saccoccia and
ers. The government claimed that the defen-
through this laundering opera ng acts by laundering money, and then used
onna Saccoccia wired over $136 n e precious metals businesses. A jury con-
lombia; more than $97 million of th d them to prison and ordered them to for-
n Citizens Bank jointly controlled by the dispositions, demonstrating that this
llion, substantial sums were retained
pensation.
nt. Affirmed.

UNITED S
3 F.3d 1,
9318
nited
r the

	Forfeiture
d release	$ 37,456,100.79
release	$ 37,456,100.79
release	$136,344,231.86
elease	$136,344,231.86

elsewhere in the text. An increasing gned to punish those who harm the nental law.) Antitrust violations, in , can lead to criminal prosecutions. pter, in which the judge threatened to sed on price-fixing. (See Chapters 40 aud is a crime and can lead to severe es regulation.)

was insufficient evidence of had occurred, of each defen-

undering, and of each

rmed robbery and rape. They claim l the money from the cash register, aped her. Jake refuses to talk, but the community is outraged and wants a uestion Jake for hours without stop-? Beat him? After five hours of inter-nd a severe beating, Jake confesses. nd the clerk's watch. Does his guilt

We are no longer looking at the ele-far, but at the *process of investigating,* t. The first 10 amendments to the of Rights, control the behavior of all ook at some of the protections these

of the protections as written apply only to the process of **incorporation,** almost all to apply to federal, state, and local govern-

ndering operation took sev-iving large amounts of cash , Saccoccia would send one Richard Gizzarelli, to a pre-stomer's courier. Gizzarelli apartment in New York to

Some of the cash would be some of the remaining cash Angeles. Much of the rest of Trend and Saccoccia Coin in r in the car of a Saccoccia

ted by Saccoccia employees her greater than or less than anston. Saccoccia employees then drove to local banks where they purchamounts less than $10,000 payable to Trend, or cashier's cthan $10,000 payable to companies nominally owned by hese maneuvers—called "smurfing" in law enforcementor minimize the filing of accurate currency transaction rd by federal law for cash deposits in amounts of $10,000 o

Ultimately the local Rhode Island check, and money from the Hurley accounts wired to, the Trennk in Rhode Island. A smaller portion of the cash sent to occia Coin. That cash was used to buy gold without doc en resold to legitimate companies in exchange for ch for gold sales. Some of the cash was also used in the ccoccia Coin Shop, a heavily cash-based enterprise.

A staggering amount of money moved tion. [During one 18 month period,] Stephen or D il- lion to foreign bank accounts primarily in Co is amount was wired from the Trend account i Donna and Stephen. Apart from the $136 mi by the Saccoccias and their employees as com

A rational jury could convict each appella

Other Crimes

Additional crimes that affect business appea number of federal and state statutes are desi environment. (See Chapter 43, on environn which a corporation establishes a monopoly The *Allegheny Bottling* case, earlier in the chap lock up the company, was an antitrust case ba and 41, on antitrust law.) Finally, securities fr prison sentences. (See Chapter 38, on securiti

CONSTITUTIONAL PROTECTIONS

The police arrest Jake and charge him with a that he entered a convenience store, took al robbed the clerk of her wristwatch, and then r police are absolutely certain he is guilty. The conviction. Should the police be allowed to q ping? May they lock him in a walk-in freezer rogation, followed by 10 hours in a freezer a He tells the police where to find the money a render the police conduct acceptable?

These are issues of **criminal procedure.** ments of particular crimes, as we have thus *interrogating, and trying* a criminal defendar United States Constitution, known as the Bill law enforcement officers.[17] In this section we amendments offer.

---

[17] As discussed in Chapter 4, on constitutional law, most state government or the federal government. But through important criminal procedure rights have been expanded ments.

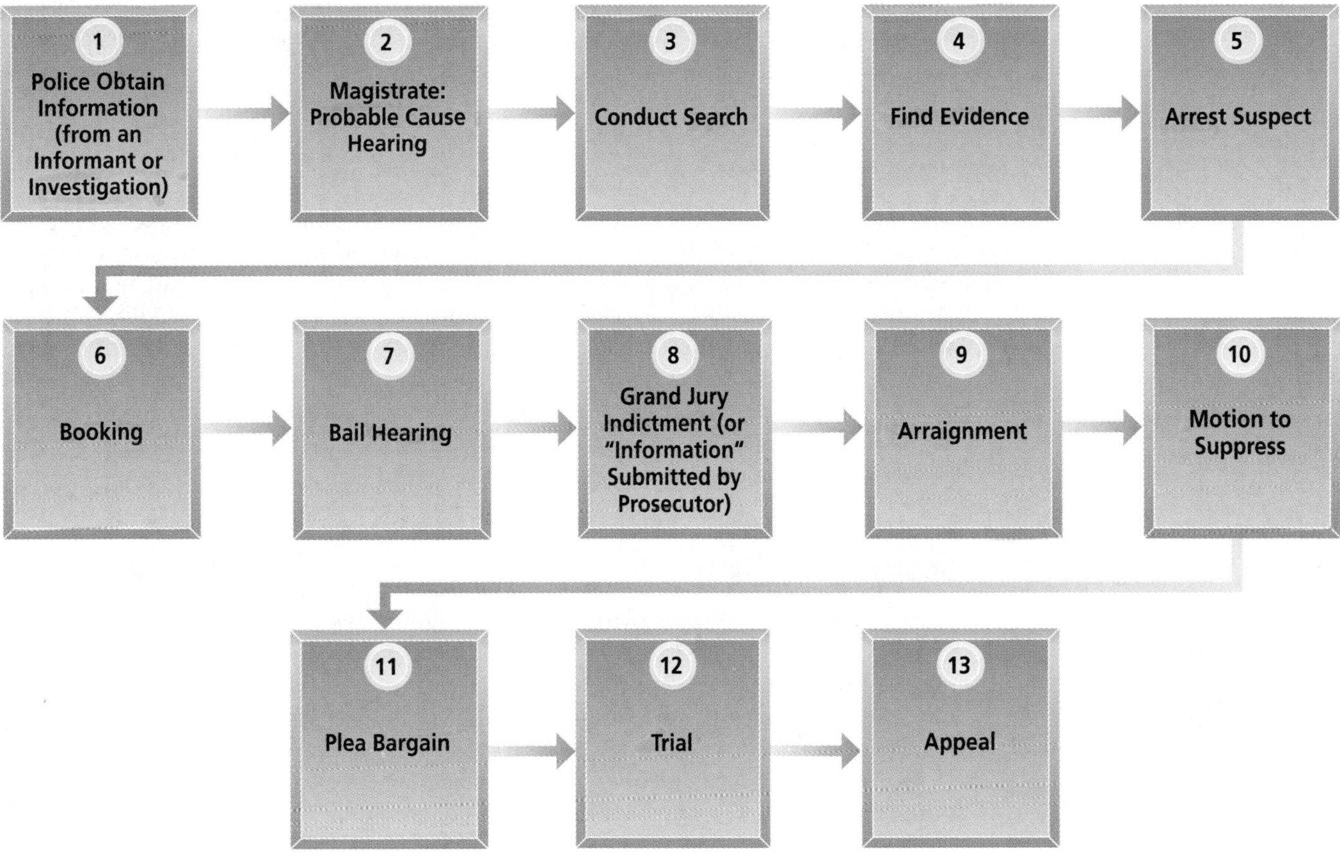

Exhibit 7.1

THE CRIMINAL PROCESS

In order to understand constitutional safeguards, we need to know how the police do their work. The exact steps will vary from case to case, but the summary in Exhibit 7.1 highlights the important steps.

Informant

Yasmin is a secretary to Stacey, the Be Patient executive who opened this chapter. On her lunch break, Yasmin gets up the courage to telephone an FBI office and speaks to Moe, an agent. She reports that Stacey routinely charges the government for patients who do not exist. Moe arranges to interview Yasmin at her apartment that evening. He tape-records everything she says, including her own job history, her duties at Be Patient, and how she knows about the fraud. Yasmin has not only seen the false bills, she has entered some of them on computers. The next day, Moe prepares an affidavit for Yasmin to sign, detailing everything she told him. An **affidavit** is simply a written statement signed under oath.

Warrant

Moe takes Yasmin's affidavit to a United States magistrate, an employee of the federal courts who is similar to a judge. Moe asks the magistrate to issue search warrants for Be Patient's patient records. A **search warrant** is written permission from a neutral official, such as the magistrate, to conduct a search. **A warrant must specify with reasonable certainty the place to be searched and the items to be seized.** This warrant application names all five of Be Patient's hospitals and asks to look through their admission notes, surgery notes, doctor's reports, and discharge data. It states that the records will be copied so that they can be compared with the bills the government has received.

Probable Cause

The magistrate will issue a warrant only if there is probable cause. **Probable cause** means that based on all of the information presented **it is likely that evidence of crime will be found in the place mentioned.** The magistrate will look at Yasmin's affidavit to determine (1) whether the informant (Yasmin) is reliable and (2) whether she has a sound basis for the information. If Yasmin is a five-time drug offender whose information has proven wrong in the past, the warrant should not issue. Here, Yasmin's career record is good, she has no apparent motive to lie, and she is in an excellent position to know what she is talking about. The magistrate issues the warrant, specifying exactly what records may be examined.

Search and Seizure

Armed with the warrants, Moe and other agents arrive at the various hospitals, show the warrants, and take away the appropriate records. The **search** may not exceed what is described in the warrant. Even if Moe suspects that Dr. Narkem is illegally drugging certain patients, he may not seize test tube samples from the lab. He may take only the records described in the warrant.

The agents cart the records back to headquarters and enter the data on a computer. The computer compares the records of actual patients with the bills submitted to the government and indicates that 10 percent of all bills are for fictional patients. Moe summarizes the new data on additional affidavits and presents the affidavits to the magistrate, who issues **arrest warrants,** authorizing the FBI to arrest Stacey and others involved in the overbilling.

Arrest

Moe arrives at Be Patient and informs Stacey that she is under arrest. He reads her the *Miranda* warnings, discussed below. He drives Stacey to FBI headquarters where she is **booked;** that is, her name, photograph, and fingerprints are entered in a log, along with the charges. She is entitled to a prompt **bail hearing.** A judge or magistrate will set an amount of bail that she must pay in order to go free pending the trial. The purpose of bail is to ensure that Stacey will appear for all future court hearings.

Indictment

Moe turns all of his evidence over to Larry, the local prosecutor for the United States. Larry presents the evidence to a **grand jury,** which is a group of ordinary citizens, like a trial jury. But the grand jury holds hearings for several weeks at a time, on many different cases. It is the grand jury's job to determine whether there is probable cause that this defendant committed the crime with which she is charged. Larry shows the computer comparison of the bills with the actual patient lists, and the grand jury votes to indict Stacey. An **indictment** is the government's formal charge that the defendant has committed a crime and must stand trial. The grand jury is persuaded that there is probable cause that Stacey billed for 1,550 nonexistent patients, charging the government for $290 million worth of services that were never performed. The grand jury indicts her for (1) Medicare fraud, (2) mail fraud, (3) computer crimes, and (4) RICO violations.[18] It also indicts Be Patient, Inc. and other employees.

Arraignment

Stacey is ordered back to court. A clerk reads her the formal charges of the indictment. The judge asks whether Stacey has a lawyer, and of course she does. If she did not, the judge would urge her to get one quickly. If a defendant cannot afford a lawyer, the court will appoint one to represent her free of charge. The judge now asks the lawyer how Stacey pleads to the charges. Her lawyer answers that she pleads not guilty to all charges.

Discovery

During the months before trial, both prosecution and defense will prepare the most effective case possible. There is less formal discovery than in civil trials. The prosecution is obligated to hand over any evidence favorable to the defense that the defense attorney requests. The defense has a more limited obligation to inform the prosecution. In most states, for example, if the defense will be based on an alibi, counsel must explain the alibi to the government before trial. In Stacey's case most of the evidence is data that both sides already possess.

Motion to Suppress

If the defense claims that the prosecution obtained evidence illegally, it will move to suppress it. A **motion to suppress** is a request that the court exclude certain evidence because it was obtained in violation of the Constitution. We look at those violations later.

Plea Bargaining

Sometime before trial the two attorneys will meet to consider a plea bargain. A **plea bargain** is an agreement between prosecution and defense that the defendant will plead guilty to a reduced charge, and the prosecution will recommend to the judge a relatively lenient sentence. Based on the RICO violations alone, Stacey faces a possible 20-year prison sentence, along with a large fine and a devastating forfeiture order. The government makes this offer: Stacey will plead guilty to 100 counts of mail fraud; Be Patient will repay all $290 million and an additional $150 million in fines; the government will drop the RICO and computer crime charges and recommend to the judge that Stacey be fined only $1 million and sentenced to three years in prison. In the federal court system, about 75 percent of all prosecutions end in a plea bargain. In state court systems the number is often higher.

Stacey agrees to the government's offer. The judge accepts the plea, and Stacey is fined and sentenced accordingly. A judge need not accept the bargain, but usually does.

---

[18] In federal court, when the defendant is charged with a felony, formal charges may be made only by indictment. In many state court cases, the prosecutor is not required to seek an indictment. Instead, she may file an **information,** which is simply a formal written accusation. In state courts, most cases now begin by information.

Trial and Appeal

When there is no plea bargain, the case must go to trial. The mechanics of a criminal trial are similar to those for a civil trial, described in Chapter 2, on dispute resolution. It is the prosecution's job to convince the jury beyond a reasonable doubt that the defendant committed every element of the crime charged. The defense counsel will do everything possible to win an acquittal. In federal courts, prosecutors obtain a conviction in about 80 percent of cases; in state courts, the percentage is slightly lower. Convicted defendants have a right to appeal, and again, the appellate process is similar to that described in Chapter 2.

THE FOURTH AMENDMENT

The Fourth Amendment prohibits the government from making illegal searches and seizures. This amendment protects individuals, corporations, partnerships, and other organizations.

In general, the police must obtain a warrant before conducting a search. There are six exceptions to this rule, in which the police **may search without a warrant:**

- *Plain View*. Police may search if they see a machine gun, for example, sticking out from under the front seat of a parked car.
- *Stop and Frisk*. If police have an articulable reason for suspecting that someone may be armed and dangerous, they may pat him down.
- *Emergencies*. If police pursue a store robber and catch him, they may search.
- *Automobiles*. If police have lawfully stopped a car and observe evidence of other crimes in the car, such as burglary tools, they may search.
- *Lawful Arrest*. Police may always search a suspect they have arrested.
- *Consent*. If someone in lawful occupancy of a home gives consent to a search, the police may do so.

Apart from those six cases, a warrant is required. If the police search without one, they have violated the Fourth Amendment. Even a search conducted with a warrant can violate the amendment. **A search with a warrant violates the Fourth Amendment if:**

- There was no probable cause to issue the warrant
- The warrant does not specify the place to be searched and the things sought; or
- The search extends beyond what is specified in the warrant.

Exclusionary Rule

Under the exclusionary rule, evidence obtained illegally may not be used at trial against the victim of the search. If the police conduct a warrantless search that is not one of the six exceptions, any evidence they find will be excluded from the trial.

Suppose when Yasmin called the FBI, Moe simply drove straight to one of Be Patient's hospitals and grabbed patient records. Moe lacked a warrant, and his search would be illegal. Stacey's lawyer would file a **motion to suppress** the evidence. Before the trial starts, the judge would hold a hearing. If he agreed that the search was illegal, he would **exclude** the evidence, that is, refuse to allow it in trial. The government could go forward with the prosecution only if it had other evidence.[19]

Is the exclusionary rule a good idea? The Supreme Court created the exclusionary rule to ensure that police conduct legal searches. The theory is simple: if police know in advance that illegally obtained evidence cannot be used in court, they will not be tempted to make improper searches.

Opponents of the rule argue that a guilty person may go free because one police officer bungled. They are outraged by cases like *Coolidge v. New Hampshire.*[20] Pamela Mason, a 14-year-old babysitter, was brutally murdered. Citizens of New Hampshire were furious, and the state's Attorney General personally led the investigation. Police found strong evidence that Edward Coolidge had done it. They took the evidence to the Attorney General who personally issued a search warrant. The search of Coolidge's car uncovered incriminating evidence, and he was found guilty of murder and sentenced to life in prison. But the United States Supreme Court reversed the conviction. The warrant had not been issued by a neutral magistrate. A law officer may not lead an investigation and simultaneously decide what searches are permissible.

After the Supreme Court reversed Coolidge's conviction, New Hampshire scheduled a new trial, attempting to convict him with evidence lawfully obtained. Before the trial began, Coolidge pleaded guilty to second degree murder. He was sentenced and remained in prison until his release in 1991, 27 years after his arrest.

In fact, very few people do go free because of the exclusionary rule. For example, a study by the General Accounting Office showed that suppression motions were filed in 10.5 percent of all federal prosecutions. But in 80 to 90 percent of those motions, the judge declared that the search was legal. Evidence was actually excluded in only 1.3 percent of all prosecutions. And in about one-half of *those* cases, the court convicted the defendant on other evidence. Only in 0.7 percent of all prosecutions did the defendant go free after the evidence was suppressed. Other studies reveal similar results.[21]

THE FIFTH AMENDMENT

The Fifth Amendment includes three important protections for criminal defendants: due process, double jeopardy, and self-incrimination.

Due Process

Due process requires fundamental fairness at all stages of the case. The basic elements of due process are discussed in Chapter 4, on constitutional law. In the context of criminal law, due process sets additional limits. The requirement that the

---

[19] There are two important exceptions to the exclusionary rule:

Inevitable Discovery Exception. Suppose that Moe's search of Be Patient is declared illegal. But then officials in the Medicare office testify that they were already aware of Be Patient's fraud, had already obtained some proof, and were about to seek a search warrant for the same records that Moe took. If the court believes the testimony, it will allow the evidence to be used. The inevitable discovery exception permits the use of evidence that would inevitably have been discovered even without the illegal search.

Good Faith Exception. Suppose the police use a search warrant believing it to be proper, but it later proves to have been defective. Is the search therefore illegal? No, said the Supreme Court in *United States v. Leon*, 468 U.S. 897, 104 S. Ct. 3405, 1984 U.S. LEXIS 153 (1984). As long as the police reasonably believed the warrant was valid, the search is legal. It would violate the Fourth Amendment if, for example, it was later shown that the police knew the affidavit used to obtain the warrant was filled with lies. In such a case, the search would be illegal and the evidence obtained would be excluded.

[20] 403 U.S. 443, 91 S. Ct. 2022, 1971 U.S. LEXIS 25 (1971).

[21] See the discussion in *United States v. Leon* (Justice Brennan, dissenting), cited at footnote 19.

prosecution disclose evidence favorable to the defendant is a due process rule. Similarly, if a witness says that a tall white male robbed the liquor store, it would violate due process for the police to place the male suspect in a lineup with four short women and two rabbits.

Double Jeopardy

The prohibition against **double jeopardy** means that a criminal defendant may be prosecuted only once for a particular criminal offense. The purpose is to guarantee that the government may not destroy the lives of innocent citizens with repetitive prosecutions. Assume that Roger, the video thief, goes to trial. But the police officer cannot remember what the suspect looked like, and the jury acquits. Later, the prosecutor learns that a second witness actually *videotaped* Roger hauling VCRs from the store. Too late. The Double Jeopardy Clause prohibits the state from retrying Roger for the same offense.

Self-Incrimination

The Fifth Amendment bars the government from forcing any person to testify against himself. In other words, the police may not use mental or physical coercion to force a confession out of someone. (This clause applies only to people; corporations and other organizations are not protected.) Society does not want a government that engages in torture. Such abuse might occasionally catch a criminal, but it would grievously injure innocent people and make all citizens fearful of the government that is supposed to represent them. Also, confessions that are forced out of someone are inherently unreliable. The defendant may confess simply to end the torture. So Jake, the rape-robbery suspect who confessed at the beginning of this section, will never hear his confession used against him in court. Unless the police have other evidence, he will walk free.

When the FBI arrests Stacey for Medicare fraud, she may refuse to answer any questions. The privilege against self-incrimination covers any statement that might help to prosecute her. So, if the FBI agent asks Stacey, "Did you commit Medicare fraud?" she will refuse to answer. If the agent asks, "What are your duties here?" she will also remain silent.

Miranda

In *Miranda v. Arizona*,[22] the Supreme Court ruled that a confession obtained from a custodial interrogation may not be used against a defendant unless he was first warned of his Fifth Amendment rights. A "custodial interrogation" means that the police have prevented the defendant from leaving (usually by arresting him) and are asking him questions. If they do that, and obtain a confession from the defendant, they may use that confession in court only if they first warned him of his Fifth Amendment rights. He must be told that:

- He has the right to remain silent
- Anything he says can be used against him at trial
- He has the right to a lawyer; and
- If he cannot afford a lawyer, the court will appoint one for him.

[22] 384 U.S. 436, 86 S. Ct. 1602, 1966 U.S. LEXIS 2817 (1966).

Exclusionary Rule (Again). If the police fail to give these warnings before interrogating a defendant, the exclusionary rule prohibits the prosecution from using any confession. The rationale is the same as for Fourth Amendment searches: suppressing the evidence means that the police will not attempt to get it illegally. But remember that the confession is void only if it results from custodial questioning. Suppose a policeman, investigating a bank robbery, asks a pedestrian if he noticed anything peculiar. The pedestrian says, "You mean after I robbed the bank?" Result? No custodial questioning, and the confession *may* be used against him.

THE SIXTH AMENDMENT

The Sixth Amendment guarantees the **right to a lawyer** at all important stages of the criminal process. Stacey, the hospital administrator, is entitled to have her lawyer present during custodial questioning and all court hearings. Because of this right, the government must **appoint a lawyer** to represent, free of charge, any defendant who cannot afford one.

THE EIGHTH AMENDMENT

The Eighth Amendment prohibits cruel and unusual punishment. The most frequently litigated issue under this clause has been capital punishment. In 1972, the United States Supreme Court ruled that Georgia had violated the Eighth Amendment by unfairly enforcing the death penalty, often penalizing African Americans and poor people more harshly than others. In response to the ruling, all states that allowed capital punishment revised their death penalty statutes. In 1976, in *Gregg v. Georgia*,[23] the Court upheld the revised Georgia statute. A state may execute a convicted criminal, provided its procedures guarantee basic fairness.

The Eighth Amendment also outlaws excessive fines. Forfeiture is the most controversial topic under this clause. **Forfeiture** is a *civil* law proceeding that is permitted by many different *criminal* statutes. Once a court has convicted a defendant under certain criminal statutes—such as RICO or a controlled substance law—the government may seek forfeiture of property associated with the criminal act. This can mean forfeiture of cash illegally earned from crime, or forfeiture of real estate where a drug sale took place. Edward Levin twice sold cocaine, with a total value of $250, at his own condominium, in which he had equity of about $68,000. After Levin was convicted of the cocaine sales, the court approved forfeiture of his condominium, finding that the difference between the crime and the penalty was not great enough to violate the Eighth Amendment.[24] The Supreme Court has ruled that the Eighth Amendment does govern forfeiture, but it has not specified when forfeiture becomes excessive.

---

[23] 428 U.S. 153, 96 S. Ct. 2909, 1976 U.S. LEXIS 82 (1976).

[24] *United States v. 38 Whalers Cove Drive*, 954 F.2d. 29, 1991 U.S. App. LEXIS 26900 (2d Cir. 1991).

CHAPTER CONCLUSION

Business crime appears in unexpected places, with surprising suspects. A corporate executive aware of its protean nature is in the best position to prevent it. Classic fraud and embezzlement schemes are often foiled with commonsense preventive measures. Federal Sentencing Guidelines make it eminently worthwhile for corporations to establish aggressive compliance programs. Sophisticated computer and money laundering crimes can be thwarted only with determination and the cooperation of citizens and police agencies. We can defeat business crime if we have the knowledge and the will.

CHAPTER REVIEW

1. The rationales for punishment include restraint, deterrence, retribution, and rehabilitation.
2. In all prosecutions, the government must establish that the defendant's conduct was outlawed, that the defendant committed the *actus reus,* and that he had the necessary *mens rea.*
3. In addition to factual defenses, such as mistaken identity or alibi, a defendant may offer various legal defenses, including insanity, entrapment, justification, and duress.
4. Larceny is the trespassory taking of personal property with the intent to steal.
5. Fraud refers to a variety of crimes, all of which involve the deception of another person for the purpose of obtaining money or property.
6. Arson is the malicious use of fire or explosives to damage or destroy real estate or personal property.
7. Embezzlement is the fraudulent conversion of property already in the defendant's possession.
8. Computer crimes include unauthorized access to any government computers or to a computer by means of an interstate line.
9. If a company's agent commits a criminal act within the scope of her employment and with the intent to benefit the corporation, the company is liable.
10. Money laundering consists of taking profits from a criminal act and either using them to promote crime or attempting to conceal their source.
11. RICO prohibits using two or more racketeering acts to invest in legitimate business or carry on certain other criminal acts. RICO permits civil lawsuits as well as criminal prosecutions.
12. The Fourth Amendment prohibits the government from making illegal searches and seizures.
13. The Fifth Amendment requires due process in all criminal procedures and prohibits double jeopardy and self-incrimination.
14. The Sixth Amendment guarantees criminal defendants the right to a lawyer.
15. Information obtained in violation of the Fourth, Fifth, or Sixth Amendment is generally excluded from trial.

16. The Eighth Amendment prohibits excessive fines and cruel and unusual punishments.

PRACTICE TEST

1. Arnie owns a two-family house in a poor section of the city. A fire breaks out, destroying the building and causing $150,000 damage to an adjacent store. The state charges Arnie with arson. Simultaneously, Vickie, the store owner, sues Arnie for the damage to her property. Both cases are tried to juries, and the two juries hear identical evidence of Arnie's actions. But the criminal jury acquits Arnie, while the civil jury awards Vickie $150,000. How did that happen?

2. **YOU BE THE JUDGE WRITING PROBLEM** An undercover drug informant learned from a mutual friend that Philip Friedman "knew where to get marijuana." The informant asked Friedman three times to get him some marijuana, and Friedman agreed after the third request. Shortly thereafter Friedman sold the informant a small amount of the drug. The informant later offered to sell Friedman three pounds of marijuana. They negotiated the price and then made the sale. Friedman was tried for trafficking in drugs. He argued entrapment. Was Friedman entrapped? **Argument for Friedman:** The undercover agent had to ask three times before Friedman sold him a small amount of drugs. A real drug dealer, predisposed to commit the crime, leaps at an opportunity to sell. If the government spends time and money luring innocent people into the commission of crimes, all of us are the losers. **Argument for the Government:** Government officials suspected Friedman of being a sophisticated drug dealer, and they were right. When he had a chance to buy three pounds, a quantity only a dealer would purchase, he not only did so, but bargained with skill, showing a working knowledge of the business. Friedman was not entrapped—he was caught.

3. **RIGHT & WRONG** Nineteen-year-old David Lee Nagel viciously murdered his grandparents, stabbing them repeatedly and slitting their throats, all because they denied him use of the family car. He was tried for murder and found not guilty by reason of insanity. He has lived ever since in mental hospitals. In 1994 he applied for release. The two psychiatrists who examined him stated that he was no longer mentally ill and was a danger neither to society nor to himself. Yet the Georgia Supreme Court refused to release him, seemingly because of the brutality of the killings. Comment on the court's ruling. What is the rationale for treating an insane defendant differently from others? Do you find the theory persuasive? If you do, what result must logically follow when psychiatrists testify that the defendant is no longer a danger? Should the brutality of the crime be a factor in deciding whether to prolong the detention? If you do not accept the rationale for treating such defendants differently, explain why not.

4. National Medical Enterprises (NME) is a large for-profit hospital and health corporation. One of its hospitals, Los Altos Hospital, in Long Beach, California, paid one doctor $219,275, allegedly for consulting work. In fact, the government claimed, the payment was in exchange for the doctor's referring to the hospital a large number of Medicare patients. Other NME hospitals engaged in similar practices, said the government. What crime is the government accusing NME of committing?

5. Kathy Hathcoat was a teller at a Pendleton, Indiana bank. In 1990 she began taking home money that belonged in her cash drawer. Her branch manager, Mary Jane Cooper, caught her. But rather than reporting Hathcoat, Cooper joined in. The two helped cover for each other by verifying that their cash drawers were in balance. They took nearly $200,000 before bank officials found them out. What criminal charge did the government bring against Hathcoat?

6. Federal law requires that all banks file reports with the IRS any time a customer engages in a cash transaction in an amount over $10,000. It is a crime for a bank to "structure" a cash transaction, that is, to break up a single transaction of more than $10,000 into two or more smaller transactions (and thus avoid the filing requirement). In *Ratzlaf v. United States*, 510 U.S. 135, 114 S. Ct. 655, 1994 U.S. LEXIS 936 (1994), the Supreme Court held that in order to find a defendant guilty of structuring, the government must prove that he specifically intended to break the law, that is, that he knew what he was doing was a crime and meant to commit it. Congress promptly passed a law "undoing" *Ratzlaf*. A bank official can now be convicted on evidence that he structured a payment, even with no evidence that he knew it was a crime. The penalties are harsh. (1) Why is structuring so serious? (2) Why did Congress change the law about the defendant's intent?

7. Conley owned video poker machines. They are outlawed in Pennsylvania, but he placed them in bars and clubs. He used profits from the machines to buy more machines. Is he guilty of money laundering?

8. Northwest Telco Corp. (Telco) provides long-distance telephone service. Customers dial a general access number, then enter a six-digit access code and then the phone number they want to call. A computer places the call and charges the account. On January 10, 1990, Cal Edwards, a Telco engineer, noticed that Telco's general access number was being dialed exactly every 40 seconds. After each dialing, a different six-digit number was entered, followed by a particular long-distance number. This continued from 10 P.M. to 6 A.M. Why was Edwards concerned?

9. Under a new British law, a police officer must now say the following to a suspect placed under arrest: "You do not have to say anything. But if you do not mention now something which you later use in your defense, the court may decide that your failure to mention it now strengthens the case against you. A record will be made of anything you say and it may be given in evidence if you are brought to trial." What does a police officer in the United States have to say, and what difference does it make at the time of an arrest?

10. After graduating from college, you work hard for 15 years, saving money to buy your dream property. Finally, you spend all your savings to buy a 300-acre farm with a splendid house and pool. Happy, an old college friend, stops by. She is saving *her* money to make a down payment on a coffee shop in town. You let her have a nice room in your big house for a few months, until she has the funds to make her down payment. But odd acquaintances stop by almost daily for short visits, and you realize that Happy is saving money from marijuana sales. You are unhappy with this, but out of loyalty you permit it to go on for a month. Why is that a big mistake?

INTERNET RESEARCH PROBLEM

A Web site devoted to scams is **http://www.digitalcentury.com/encyclo/update/crime.html**. Find a current con game that might victimize you. What steps should you take to avoid harm?

You can find further practice problems in the Online Quiz at http://beatty.westbuslaw.com or in the Study Guide that accompanies this text.

CHAPTER 8

INTERNATIONAL LAW

The day after Anfernee graduates from business school, he opens a shop specializing in sports caps and funky hats. Sales are brisk, but Anfernee is making little profit because his American-made caps are expensive. Then an Asian company offers to sell him identical merchandise for 45 percent less than the American suppliers charge. Anfernee is elated, but quickly begins to wonder. Why is the new price so low? Are the foreign workers paid a living wage? Could the Asian company be using child labor? The sales representative expects Anfernee to sell no caps except his. Is that legal? He also requests a $50,000 cash "commission" to smooth the export process in his country. That sounds suspicious. The questions multiply without end. Will the contract be written in English or a foreign language? Must Anfernee pay in dollars or some other currency? The foreign company wants a letter of credit. What does that mean? What law will govern the agreement? If the caps are defective, how will disputes be resolved—and where?

Anfernee should put this lesson under his cap: the world is now one vast economy, and negotiations quickly cross borders. Transnational business grows with breathtaking speed. In 1992, the United States exported $448 billion worth of goods and services; by 1997 that figure had swelled to more than $930 billion—a 110 percent increase in five years. Leading exports include industrial machinery, computers,

aircraft and other transportation equipment, electronic equipment, and chemicals. Before long, the value of *services* sold internationally may surpass that of goods.

Here are the leading trading partners of the United States:

Leading Purchasers from the United States	**Amount** *(in Billions of Dollars)*	**Rank** *(by Dollar Volume of Trade in 1996)*	**Leading Sellers to the United States**	**Amount** *(in Billions of Dollars)*
Canada	$133.7	1	Canada	$156.5
Japan	67.5	2	Japan	115.2
Mexico	56.0	3	Mexico	73.8
Britain	30.9	4	China	51.5
South Korea	26.6	5	Germany	38.9
Germany	23.5	6	Taiwan	29.9
Taiwan	18.4	7	Britain	28.9
Singapore	16.7	8	South Korea	22.7
Netherlands	16.6	9	Singapore	20.3
France	14.4	10	France	18.6
Total trade with the 10 nations	**404.3**			**556.3**

The end is nowhere in sight. By the year 2010, a dozen developing countries with a total population 10 times that of the United States will account for 40 percent of all export opportunities. In China alone roughly 300 million people are on the brink of joining the economic middle class—and the rank of potential consumers.

Who are the people who do all of this trading? Anfernee's modest sports cap concern is at one end of the spectrum. At the other are **multinational enterprises (MNEs)**, that is, companies doing business in several countries simultaneously.

MNEs and Power

An MNE can take various forms. It may be an Italian corporation with a wholly owned American subsidiary that manufactures electrical components in Alabama and sells them in Brazil. Or it could be a Japanese company that licenses a software company in India to manufacture computer programs for sale throughout Europe. One thing is constant: the power of these huge enterprises. Each of the top 10 MNEs earns annual revenue greater than the gross domestic product of *two-thirds of the world's nations*. Over 200 MNEs have annual sales exceeding $1 billion and more cash available at any one time than the majority of countries do. Money means power. This corporate might can be used to create jobs, train workers, and build life-saving medical equipment. Such power can also be used to corrupt government officials, rip up the environment, and exploit already impoverished workers. International law is vital.

TRADE REGULATION

Nations regulate international trade in many ways. In this section we look at export and import controls that affect trade out of and into the United States. **Exporting** is shipping goods or services out of a country. The United States, with its huge farms, is the world's largest exporter of agricultural products. **Importing** is shipping goods and services into a country. The United States suffers trade deficits every year because the value of its imports exceeds that of its exports, as the chart above indicates.

EXPORT CONTROLS

You and a friend open an electronics business, intending to purchase goods in this country for sale abroad. A representative of TaiLectron stops in to see you. TaiLectron is a Taiwanese electronics company, and the firm wants you to obtain for it a certain kind of infra-red dome. The representative explains that this electronic miracle helps helicopters identify nearby aircraft. You find a Pennsylvania company that manufactures the domes, and you realize that you can buy and sell them to TaiLectron for a handsome profit. Any reason not to? As a matter of fact, there is.

All nations limit what may be exported. In the United States, several statutes do this. The **Export Administration Act of 1985**[1] is one. This statute balances the need for free trade, which is essential in a capitalist society, with important requirements of national security. The statute permits the federal government to restrict exports if they endanger national security, harm foreign policy goals, or drain scarce materials.

The Secretary of Commerce makes a **Controlled Commodities List** of those items that meet any of these criteria. No one may export any commodity on the list without a license, and the license may well be denied. A second major limitation comes from the **Arms Export Control Act.**[2] This statute permits the president to create a second list of controlled goods, all related to military weaponry. Again, no person may export any listed item without a license.

The Arms Export Control Act will prohibit you from exporting the infra-red domes to the Taiwan company. They are used in the guidance system of 9-M Sidewinder air-to-air missiles, one of the most sophisticated weapons in the American defense arsenal. The Taiwanese government has attempted to obtain the equipment through official channels, but the American government has placed the domes on the list of restricted military items. When a U.S. citizen did send such goods to Taiwan, he was convicted and imprisoned.[3]

For national security reasons, the government clearly has the power to prohibit the export of military weaponry. But does that same rationale allow the government to halt the export of encryption technology over the Internet?

---

1 50 U.S.C. §2402 (1994).

2 22 U.S.C. §2778 (1994).

3 *United States v. Tsai*, 954 F.2d 155, 1992 U.S. App. LEXIS 601 (3d Cir. 1992).

Encryption is the process of using a computer program to ensure secrecy. Ordinary text is run through the encryption program, which uses a mathematical formula to transform the information into ciphertext. The ciphertext is unreadable except by those possessing the program. When the encrypted message arrives at another computer, an appropriate *de*cryption program transforms the message back into ordinary text. Scientists and programmers use encryption to protect everything from e-mail to bank ATM transactions to military intelligence.

Using its power under the Arms Export Control Act, the federal government passed regulations that prohibit anyone from posting an encryption program on the Internet without first obtaining a license. Since the World Wide Web is exactly that—worldwide—placing such information on the Web effectively exports it. The government insisted it had the right to ensure that an encryption program could not harm the country's foreign policy or national security.

A graduate student, Daniel Bernstein developed an encryption program he called "Snuffle." He wanted to place his program on the Web so that he could discuss it with other scientists, but was required to obtain permission first. Instead of filing for a license, he filed suit, claiming that the government's regulation violated his First Amendment right to free speech.

The United States District Court ruled that the licensing regulations did violate the First Amendment and that Bernstein was free to post his program on the Internet. The court explained that the government was engaging in *prior restraint*, that is, barring certain speech before it is uttered, which is almost always illegal. Simply claiming national security was not sufficient grounds for the government to impose this restraint. This is only the beginning of the battle over export control of that most precious commodity of all, information.[4]

IMPORT CONTROLS

Tariffs

Tariffs are the most widespread method of limiting what may be imported into a nation. **A tariff is a duty (a tax) imposed on goods when they enter a country.** Nations use tariffs primarily to protect their domestic industries. Because the company importing the goods must pay this duty, the importer's costs increase, making the merchandise more expensive for consumers. This renders domestic products more attractive. High tariffs unquestionably help local industry, but they proportionately harm local buyers. Consumers benefit from zero tariffs, because the unfettered competition drives down prices.

Tariffs change frequently. In 1997, the average duty on goods entering the United States was between 3 and 4 percent. But averages can be misleading. Mexican and Canadian companies send most of their products into the United States duty-free. Vietnam has a less favorable trade status, and tariffs on its goods average between 30 and 40 percent. Tariffs also vary widely from one product to another. Duties on textiles entering the United States are over 10 percent, but some other goods enter duty-free. Other nations also have uneven tariffs. Most goods enter Hong Kong duty-free, and Singapore's tariffs average only 0.3 percent. But duties average 30 percent in Angola and about 50 percent in Bangladesh. As we enter a new century, tariffs in most nations will decrease because of the General Agreement on Tariffs and Trade (GATT), discussed later in this chapter.

Classification. The U.S. Customs Service imposes tariffs at the point of entry into the United States. A customs official inspects the merchandise as it arrives

[4] Bernstein's court papers and related documents are—fittingly—available on the Web: http://www.eff.org/bernstein/Legal. The government's export regulations appear at http://www.eff.org/pub/Privacy/.

and **classifies** it, in other words, decides precisely what the goods are. This decision is critical because the tariff will vary depending on the classification, as Nissan's recent experience demonstrates.

MARUBENI AMERICA CORP. v. UNITED STATES
35 F.3d 530, 1994 U.S. App. LEXIS 24288
United States Court of Appeals for the Federal Circuit, 1994

Facts: One of Japan's major auto manufacturers, Nissan, found itself in the late 1980s behind the competition in the market for four-wheel drive "sport utility" vehicles. In order to catch up quickly, Nissan used its "Hardbody" truck line as the basis for designing and building its "Pathfinder" sport utility vehicle. The Pathfinder incorporated the Hardbody's frame side rails, front cab, and front suspension.

When the 1989 models arrived in the United States, the Customs Service had to classify them. The Service uses a **tariff schedule** to do this, which is a long list of goods, carefully described, with each type of good assigned a particular duty. The tariff schedule gave the Customs Service two possible classifications:

> Section 8704.31.00: Motor vehicle for the transport of goods.
> Section 8703.23.00: Motor cars and other motor vehicles principally designed for the transport of persons, including stations wagons and racing cars.

The "transport of persons" tariff was 2.5 percent but the "transport of goods" duty was exactly *10 times higher*. The Customs Service concluded that the Pathfinder was similar to a pick-up truck, declared it a "transport of goods" vehicle, and imposed the 25 percent duty, ruining Nissan's hope for profits. The company appealed. Customs appeals go first to the **Court of International Trade (CIT)** in Washington. The CIT trial included test drives of the Pathfinder and comparison vehicles (including the Hardbody), as well as videotapes of competing vehicles and expert testimony about engineering, design, and marketing. (Indeed, the court's work was so thorough, the next time your car needs servicing you might ask the CIT to take a look at it.) The CIT reversed the Customs Service, declaring the Pathfinder a passenger car. The Service appealed to the federal court of appeals.

Issue: Is the Pathfinder a vehicle for passengers or for the transport of goods?

Excerpts from Judge Rich's Decision: The CIT recognized that the Pathfinder was basically derived from Nissan's Hardbody truck line yet the Pathfinder was based upon totally different design concepts than a truck. The CIT correctly pointed out these differences and more importantly, the reasons behind the design decisions, including the need for speed and economy in manufacturing to capture the changing market, a market into which Nissan was a late entrant. The fact that a vehicle is derived in part from a truck or from a sedan is not, without more, determinative of its intended principal design objectives which were passenger transport and off-road capability.

Substantial structural changes were necessary to meet the design criterion of transporting passengers. The addition of the rear passenger seat required that the gas tank be moved to the rear and the spare tire relocated. This effectively reduces the cargo carrying capacity. Of particular importance was the design of a new rear suspension that was developed specifically to provide a smooth ride for passengers. New and different cross beams, not present on the Hardbody frame, were added to the Pathfinder's frame to accommodate the above changes.

Other design aspects that point to a principal design for passengers include: the spare tire and the rear seat when folded down intrude upon the cargo space; the cargo area is carpeted; a separate window opening in the pop-up tailgate accommodates passengers loading and unloading small packages without having to lower the tailgate. In contrast, the Hardbody truck bed can accommodate loading with a fork lift, clearly a design feature for cargo.

We hold that the court applied the correct legal standards, and that the evidence of record supports the CIT's decision that the Pathfinder is principally designed for the transport of persons.

Valuation. After classifying the imported goods, customs officials impose the appropriate duty ***ad valorem***, meaning "according to the value of the goods." In other words, the Service must determine the value of the merchandise before it can tax a percentage of that value. This step can be equally contentious, since goods will have different prices at each stage of manufacturing and delivery. The question is supposed to be settled by the **transaction value** of the goods, meaning the price actually paid for the merchandise when sold for export to the United States (plus shipping and other minor costs). But there is often room for debate, so importers use customs agents to help negotiate the most favorable valuation.

Duties for Dumping and Subsidizing

Dumping means selling merchandise at one price in the domestic market and at a cheaper, unfair price in an international market. Suppose a Singapore company, CelMaker, makes cellular telephones for $20 per unit and sells them in the United States for $12 each, vastly undercutting domestic American competitors. CelMaker may be willing to suffer short-term losses in order to drive out competitors for the American market. Once it has gained control of that market, it will raise its prices, more than compensating for its initial losses. And CelMaker may get help from its home government. Suppose the Singapore government prohibits foreign cellular phones from entering Singapore. CelMaker may sell its phones for $75 at home, earning such high profits that it can afford the temporary losses in America.

In the United States, the Commerce Department investigates suspected dumping. If the Department concludes that the foreign company is selling items at **less than fair value**, and that this harms an American industry, it will impose a **dumping duty** sufficiently high to put the foreign goods back on fair footing with domestic products.

Subsidized goods are also unfair. Suppose the Singapore government permits CelMaker to pay no taxes for 10 years. This enormous benefit will enable the company to produce cheap phones and undersell competitors. Again, the United States imposes a tariff on subsidized goods, called **countervailing duties**. If CelMaker sells phones for $15 that would cost an unsubsidized competitor $21 to make, it will pay a $6 countervailing duty on every phone entering the United States.

Nontariff Barriers

All countries use additional methods to limit imports. A **quota** is a limit on the quantity of a particular good that may enter a nation. For example, the United States, like most importing nations, has agreements with many developing nations, placing a quota on imported textiles. In some cases, textile imports from a particular country may grow by only a small percentage each year. Without such a limit, textile imports from the developing world would increase explosively because costs are so much lower there. As part of the GATT treaty (discussed below), the wealthier nations pledged to increase textile imports from the developing countries, but whether that has occurred is open to dispute.

An **import ban** means that particular goods are flatly prohibited. Some nations prohibit alcohol imports for religious reasons. The United States bars the importation of narcotic drugs. Virtually all countries from time to time halt certain goods for political purposes, for example, to protest the behavior of the exporting country. The United States has increasingly used economic sanctions in an effort to advance its foreign policy goals. During one three-year period, it threatened or imposed sanctions 60 times, against 35 nations. Sanctions were aimed at Colombia for permitting drug trafficking; the Netherlands, Switzerland, and other European nations for trading with Cuba; and Taiwan for environmental violations. Proponents of such sanctions consider them essential components of an ethical foreign policy. Opponents regard them as hypocritical efforts to feel morally superior.

Import bans illustrate another aspect of international trade: commerce can be lucrative, but it is also inherently risky, as the following merchants learned.

B-WEST IMPORTS, INC. v. UNITED STATES
75 F.3d 633, 1996 U.S. App. LEXIS 915
United States Court of Appeals for the Federal Circuit, 1996

this treaty only applies to Arms.

Facts: In May 1994, President Clinton announced that human rights abuses were continuing in China, and that the United States would respond with limited trade sanctions. The Arms Export Control Act (AECA), discussed earlier in the chapter, also permits the president to "control" arms imports. Based on that power, the president banned munitions from China. B-West Imports was in the business of importing arms from China. B-West and other companies filed suit, claiming that, while the president had the power to regulate arms trading, he had no authority to halt it altogether. The Court of International Trade ruled for the government, holding that the statutory power to "control" included the right to stop such importing altogether. B-West appealed.

Issue: Does the Arms Export Control Act authorize the president to ban arms from China?

Excerpts from Judge Bryson's Decision: Although [the AECA] grants the President the authority to "control" arms imports, the appellants argue that the term "control" limits the President to creating and operating a licensing system for arms importation, and does not allow the President to ban the importation of arms for which import permits have been granted. The appellants' statutory argument is unconvincing.

In the external sector of the national life, Congress does not ordinarily bind the President's hands so tightly that he cannot respond promptly to changing conditions or the fluctuating demands of foreign policy. Accordingly, when Congress uses far-reaching words in delegating authority to the President in the area of foreign relations, courts must assume, unless there is a specific contrary showing elsewhere in the statute or in the legislative history, that the legislators contemplate that the President may and will make full use of that power in any manner not inconsistent with the provisions or purposes of the Act. In a statute dealing with foreign affairs, a grant to the President which is expansive to the reader's eye should not be hemmed in or "cabined, cribbed, confined" by anxious judicial blinders.

As the court noted in [an earlier case] Presidents acting under broad statutory grants of authority have "imposed and lifted embargoes, prohibited and allowed exports, suspended and resumed commercial intercourse with foreign countries." Thus, the broad statutory delegation in the AECA incorporates "the historical authority of the President in the fields of foreign commerce and of importation into the country." We therefore agree with the Court of International Trade that the AECA authorizes the President not only to regulate arms importation through a licensing system, but also to prohibit particular importations altogether when the circumstances warrant.

Affirmed.

Money and politics are a volatile mix, as demonstrated by all recorded history from 3000 B.C. to the present. As long as nations have existed, they have engaged in disputes about quotas and import bans. And that is why more than 100 countries negotiated and signed the GATT treaty, the subject of the next section.

GENERAL AGREEMENT ON TARIFFS AND TRADE (GATT)

What is GATT? The greatest boon to American commerce in a century. The worst assault on the American economy in 200 years. It depends on whom you ask. Let's start where everyone agrees.

GATT is the General Agreement on Tariffs and Trade. This massive international treaty has been negotiated on and off since the 1940s to eliminate trade barriers and bolster commerce. GATT has already had considerable effect. In 1947 the worldwide average tariff on industrial goods was about 40 percent. By 1994 it had fallen to an average of 5 percent. The world's economies have exploded over that half century. Proponents of GATT applaud the agreement. Opponents scoff that both lower duties and higher trade would have arrived without GATT.

The most recent round of bargaining took seven hard years. Finally, in 1994, the United States and 125 other countries signed the treaty. A **signatory**, that is, a nation that signs a treaty, is still not bound by the agreement until it is **ratified**, that is, until the nation's legislature votes to honor it. In the United States, Congress voted to ratify GATT in December 1994. If the latest round of cuts is fully implemented, average duties in all signatories should drop to about 3.7 percent. Further, nearly half of all trade in industrial goods will be duty-free, at least in developed countries. That must be good—or is it?

Trade

Leading supporters of GATT suggest that its lower tariffs will increase world trade by $500 billion by the year 2005. The U.S. economy alone should grow by $122 billion. But opponents argue that $500 billion is small potatoes when you realize that five years into the new century the total world trade will be about $30 *trillion*.

The United States should be one of the biggest beneficiaries of lower tariffs because for decades this country has imposed lower duties than most other nations. American companies will for once compete on equal footing. A typical American family's annual income should increase by about $1,700 due to the more vigorous domestic economy.

But opponents claim that the United States will be facing nations with unlimited pools of exploited labor. These countries will dominate labor-intensive merchandise such as textiles, eliminating millions of American jobs. It is not fair for U.S. companies to struggle against companies from countries that have no labor standards and dirt cheap pay. This country will lose millions of jobs. And because the job losses will come in low-end employment, those put out of work will be precisely the ones least able to find a new job. The chasm between rich and poor will widen, and we will all be the losers.

World Trade Organization and the Environment

GATT created the **World Trade Organization (WTO)** to resolve trade disputes. The WTO is empowered to hear arguments from any signatory nation about tariff violations or nontariff barriers. This international "court" may order compliance from any nation violating GATT and may penalize countries by imposing trade sanctions. Proponents say that it is high time to have one international body to resolve complex issues impartially and create an international body of trade law that corporations can rely on when planning business.

Opponents fear the WTO. GATT generally prohibits nontariff barriers, and the WTO may well rule that some American economic sanctions, discussed above, violate the treaty.

In response, when Congress approved GATT, it passed a second law, nicknamed "Three strikes and *we're* out." Under the law, a group of American judges will review WTO decisions. If the panel concludes that there are three unprincipled rulings against the United States during any five-year period, it may recommend to Congress a vote to withdraw from the WTO. (The official Web site of the WTO, **http://www.wto.org/**, includes libraries on all sorts of international trade topics, from goods and services to dispute settlement and legal texts.)

Opponents of the new agreement argue that GATT may exacerbate environmental problems. Developing nations will be hard-pressed to pay for newly available goods. To bankroll the new expenses, these nations will sell off natural resources, eviscerating their future for short-term gains. Some statistics substantiate this argument. For example, the Costa Rican government decided to export more beef to the United States. To increase grazing land, the government has permitted over 80 percent of all Costa Rican rain forests to be leveled in just 20 years. The Philippines, in order to increase breeding areas for shrimp, has nearly destroyed its vast supply of mangrove swamps, which are essential spawning grounds for many species of ocean fish. But GATT supporters respond that such ecological damage has gone on independently of GATT and must be controlled accordingly.

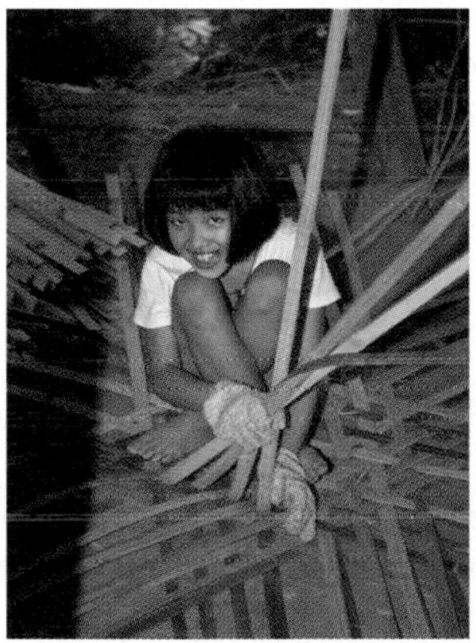

Is this right? Who should decide?

Child labor is an even more wrenching issue. The practice exists to some degree in all countries and is common throughout the developing world. The International Labor Organization, an affiliate of the United Nations, estimates that 120 million children between the ages of 5 and 14 work full-time, and 130 million more labor part-time. As the world generally becomes more prosperous, this ugly problem has actually increased. Children in developing countries typically work in agriculture and domestic work, but many toil in mines and others in factories, making rugs, glass, clothing, and other goods.

The rug industry illustrates the international nature of this tragedy. In the 1970s, the Shah of Iran banned child labor in rug factories, but many manufacturers simply packed up and moved to southern Asia. Today, in India and Pakistan, tens of millions of children, some as young as four, toil in rug workrooms, seven days a week, 12 hours a day. Many, shackled to the looms they operate, are essentially slaves, working for pennies a day or, in some cases, for no money at all.

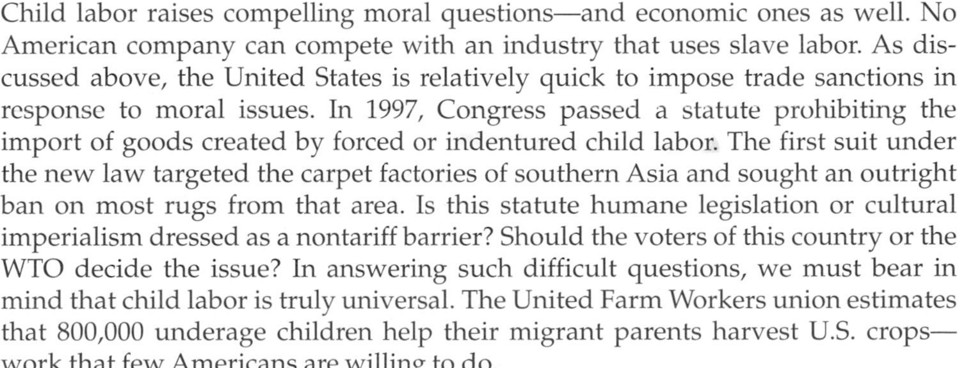

Child labor raises compelling moral questions—and economic ones as well. No American company can compete with an industry that uses slave labor. As discussed above, the United States is relatively quick to impose trade sanctions in response to moral issues. In 1997, Congress passed a statute prohibiting the import of goods created by forced or indentured child labor. The first suit under the new law targeted the carpet factories of southern Asia and sought an outright ban on most rugs from that area. Is this statute humane legislation or cultural imperialism dressed as a nontariff barrier? Should the voters of this country or the WTO decide the issue? In answering such difficult questions, we must bear in mind that child labor is truly universal. The United Farm Workers union estimates that 800,000 underage children help their migrant parents harvest U.S. crops—work that few Americans are willing to do.

Our response to such a troubling moral issue need not take the form of a statute or lawsuit. Duke University is one of the most popular names in sports apparel, and the school sells about $20 million worth of T-shirts, sweatshirts, jackets, caps, and other sportswear bearing its logo. To produce its clothing, the university licenses about 700 companies in the United States and 10 foreign countries. In response to the troubling issue of child labor, Duke adopted a code of conduct that prohibits its manufacturers from using forced or child labor and requires all of the firms to pay a minimum wage, permit union organizing, and maintain a safe workplace. The university plans to monitor the companies producing its apparel and terminate the contract for any firm that violates its rules.

Intellectual Property

Some foreign countries, particularly developing nations, have long ignored U.S. copyrights and patents. GATT changes things. It allows this country to halt duty-free imports from, and assess tariffs against, a nation that refuses to honor American copyrights or patents.

In addition, GATT creates certain new types of intellectual property. Rock bands and many performing artists have long complained of "bootlegging." When someone attending a concert makes an unauthorized recording or videotape and then sells it, that is a bootlegged version. Bootlegging is a common practice, earning millions of dollars for people who have contributed nothing to the performance. Under GATT, bootlegging is, for the first time, clearly outlawed in all signatory countries.

GATT Summary

The WTO has already enjoyed some important successes. Under the agency's supervision, 68 of the leading economic powers negotiated a new telecommunications treaty, opening a $600 billion industry to international competition for the first time. And the WTO has resolved many trade disputes that would otherwise have led to bitter tariff wars. The United States has brought over two dozen cases to the agency in its early years, winning some and losing others.

The first major loss concerned film. Eastman Kodak had long complained that the Japanese government, though never prohibiting imports of foreign film, had worked closely with Fuji and other Japanese film manufacturers to make it nearly impossible for American companies to compete. The WTO shocked U.S. officials when it ruled in favor of Fuji, declaring that there were no barriers to American competition. But even that "loss" may have promoted international trade, as the Japanese government guaranteed open markets, and U.S. officials asserted they would monitor implementation of the promises. Other countries have settled claims to avoid a fight in the WTO: Turkey eliminated discriminatory taxes on box office receipts for American films, and Portugal began protecting patents on U.S. pharmaceuticals.

It will be many years before we can fairly evaluate this enormous new treaty. In all likelihood, some of the most extreme claims will prove false, and the agreement's effects will evolve somewhere in the middle. Unquestionably, some industries will suffer, forcing workers into unemployment. Others will discover and exploit lucrative opportunities. Certainly, the environment must be guarded far more carefully than it currently is, whether GATT survives a decade or a century. Perhaps the final cost/benefit analysis of GATT will be decided not by the letter of its voluminous pages but by the spirit and good will of those who implement it.

Regional Agreements

Many regional agreements also regulate international trade. We will briefly describe some that affect the United States.

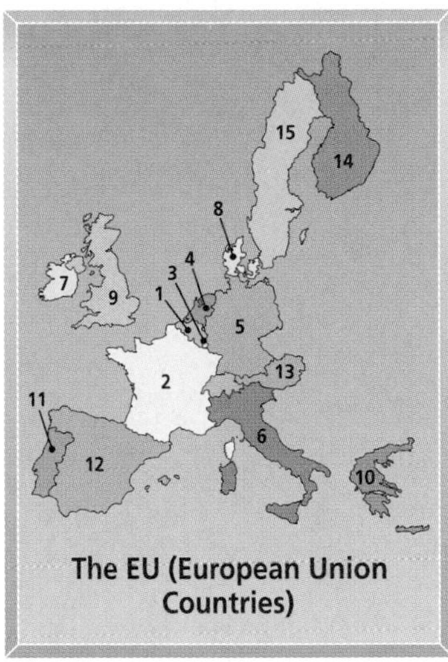

The EU (European Union Countries)

1 Belgium
2 France
3 Luxembourg
4 The Netherlands
5 Germany
6 Italy
7 Ireland
8 Denmark
9 The United Kingdom
10 Greece
11 Portugal
12 Spain
13 Austria
14 Finland
15 Sweden

The European Union

The European Union (EU) used to be known as the Common Market. The original six members—Belgium, France, Luxembourg, the Netherlands, West Germany, and Italy—have been joined by Ireland, Denmark, the United Kingdom, Greece, Portugal, Spain, Austria, Finland, and Sweden.

The EU is one of the world's most powerful associations, with a prosperous population of over 300 million. Its sophisticated legal system sets Union-wide standards for tariffs, dumping, subsidies, antitrust, transportation, and many other issues. The first goals of the EU were to eliminate trade barriers between member nations, establish common tariffs with respect to external countries, permit the free movement of citizens across its borders, and coordinate its agricultural and fishing policies for the collective good. The EU has largely achieved these goals and is now focusing on the euro, a common currency to be introduced between 1999 and 2002. Most of the EU nations have pledged to adopt the currency, expecting it to unify member economies. Skeptics suggest that EU countries are too diverse in culture and wealth to permit real economic unity.

NAFTA

In 1993, the United States, Canada, and Mexico signed the **North American Free Trade Agreement (NAFTA)**. The principal goal was to eliminate almost all trade barriers, tariff and nontariff, between the three nations. Like GATT, this trilateral (three-nation) compact has been controversial. It is similarly too early to know its overall effects, and there will probably never be agreement on NAFTA's value because the treaty has enriched some while impoverishing others. Unquestionably, trade between the three nations has increased enormously. Mexico now sells more to the United States than do Germany and the United Kingdom combined. The balance of trade between Mexico and the United States has changed dramatically, from a $5.4 billion American surplus in 1992 to an $18 billion deficit in 1996.

Opponents of the treaty argue that NAFTA costs the United States jobs and lowers the living standards of American workers by forcing them to compete with low-paid labor. For example, Swingline Staplers closed a factory in Queens, New York, after 75 years of operation and moved to Mexico. Instead of paying its American workers $11.58 per hour, Swingline will pay Mexican workers 50 cents an hour to do the same job. Proponents contend that although some jobs are lost, many others are gained, especially in fields with a future, such as high technology. They claim that as new jobs invigorate the Mexican economy, consumers there will be able to afford American goods for the first time, providing an enormous new market. Both Canadian and Mexican law are available online at http://www.lawsource.com/also/.

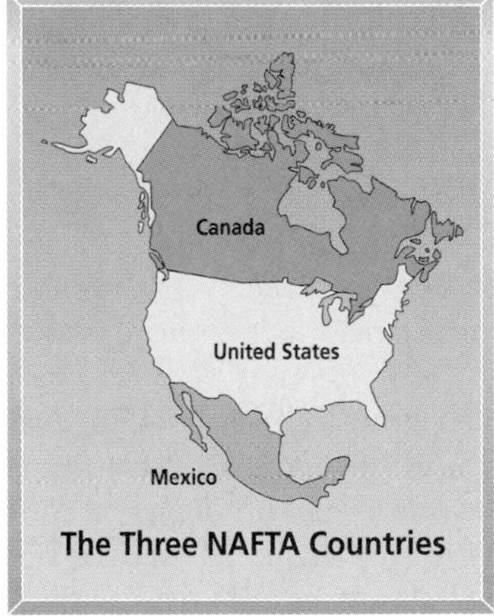

The Three NAFTA Countries

ASEAN

The Association of South-East Asian Nations (ASEAN) consists of nine countries: Brunei, Indonesia, Laos, Malaysia, Myanmar, the Philippines, Singapore, Thailand, and Vietnam. The group has negotiated for several years to reduce tariffs and aims to eliminate all duties between its members by 2003.

Mercosur

Brazil, Argentina, Uruguay, and Paraguay formed Mercosur to improve commerce among the four South American nations. Trade has in fact increased between Latin America's powerhouse economy, Brazil, and the three other countries. The group is currently considering the creation of a common currency, similar to the euro.

INTERNATIONAL SALES AGREEMENTS

Cowboy boots are hot in France. Actually, they can be uncomfortable no matter where you walk, but the point is they are selling fast in the land of Monet and Debussy. Big Heel, Inc., your small company in Tucson, Arizona, makes superb boots with exquisite detailing, and you realize that France could be a bonanza. Your first decision is how to produce and sell the boots in France. For our purposes, Big Heel has three choices:

- **Direct Sales**. You can continue to manufacture the boots in Tucson and sell them directly to French retailers.
- **Indirect Sales**. You can manufacture the boots in Tucson and use a French distributor to wholesale them to French stores.
- **Licensing**. You can license a French manufacturer to make Big Heel boots in France and wholesale them.

Each method presents advantages and difficulties. Doing business effectively in a foreign country *also* requires an understanding of that nation's personal customs and business practices. For a useful discussion of how human interactions affect commerce in Mexico, see **http://www.cs.unb.ca/~alopez-o/busfaq.html**.

DIRECT SALES

You decide to sell the boots directly. Le Pied D'Or, a new, fast-growing French chain of shoe stores, is interested in buying 10,000 pairs of your boots, at about $300 per pair. You must focus on two principal issues: the sales contract and letters of credit. You are wise enough to know that you must have a written contract—$3 million is a lot of money for Big Heel.

This is a contract for the sale of goods. **Goods** are things that can be moved, such as boots, airplanes, pencils, and computers. A sale of goods is governed by different law than the sale of real estate (e.g., a house) or securities (e.g., a share of stock) or services (e.g., accounting).

What Law Governs the Sale of Goods?

Potentially, three conflicting laws could govern your boot contract: Arizona law, French law, and an international treaty. Each is different, and it is therefore essential to negotiate which law will control.

Because this contract is for the sale of goods, Arizona law is its **Uniform Commercial Code (UCC)**. The UCC is discussed throughout Unit 3, on commercial transactions. It is a statute that has taken the common law principles of contract and modified them to meet the needs of contemporary business. Article 2 of the UCC governs the sale of goods. American business lawyers are familiar with the UCC and will generally prefer that it govern. French law is based on **Roman law** and the **Napoleonic Code** and is obviously different. French lawyers and business executives are naturally partial to it. How to compromise? Perhaps by using a neutral law.

The **United Nations Convention On Contracts For The International Sale Of Goods (CISG)** is the result of 50 years of work by various international groups, all seeking to create a uniform, international law on this important subject. Finally, in 1980, a United Nations conference adopted the CISG, though it became the law in individual nations only if and when they adopted it. The United States adopted the CISG in 1988. As of 1996, 46 countries had joined, including most of the principal trading partners of the United States.

The CISG applies automatically to any contract for the sale of goods between two parties, from different countries, each of which is a signatory. France and the United States have both signed. Thus the CISG automatically applies to the Big Heel–Pied D'Or deal unless the parties *specifically opt out*. If the parties want to be governed by other law, they must state very clearly that they exclude the CISG and elect, for example, the UCC.

Preventive Law

Should the parties allow the CISG to govern? They can make an intelligent choice by first understanding how the CISG differs from other law. Here are a few key differences between the CISG and the UCC:

- *Must the contract be written?* Under the UCC, a contract for the sale of goods valued at over $500 generally must be written to be enforceable. But the CISG does not require a writing for any contract. Be advised that discussions you consider informal or preliminary might create a contract under the CISG.
- *When is an offer irrevocable?* The UCC declares that an offer is irrevocable only if it is in writing and states that it will be held open for a fixed period. But the CISG makes some offers irrevocable even if unwritten.
- *What if an acceptance includes new terms?* Under the UCC, an acceptance generally creates a contract, even if it uses new terms. But the CISG insists on an acceptance that is a "mirror image" of the offer. Almost anything else constitutes a rejection.
- *What remedies are available?* The UCC entitles a plaintiff only to money damages for breach of a sales contract. But the CISG permits many plaintiffs to seek specific performance of the contract, that is, to force the other party to perform the contract.

Choice of Forum

The parties must decide not only what law governs, but where disagreements will be resolved. The French and American legal systems are dramatically different. In a French civil lawsuit, generally neither side is entitled to depose the other or to obtain interrogatories or even documents, in sharp contrast to the American system where such discovery methods dominate litigation. American lawyers, accustomed to discovery to prepare a case and advance settlement talks, are unnerved by the French system. Similarly, French lawyers are dismayed at the idea of spending two years taking depositions, exchanging paper, and arguing motions, all at great expense. At trial, the contrasts grow. In a French civil trial, there is generally no right to a jury. The rules of evidence are more flexible (and unpredictable), neither side employs its own expert witnesses, and the parties themselves never appear as witnesses.

Choice of Language and Currency

The parties must select a language for the contract and a currency for payment. Language counts because legal terms seldom translate literally. Currency is vital because the exchange rate may alter between the signing and payment. When the Indonesian rupiah plummeted at the end of 1997, an Indonesian company that had contracted in 1997 to buy U.S. computer hardware with dollars found itself paying 85 percent more than expected in March 1998. To avoid such calamities, companies engaged in international commerce often purchase from currency dealers a guarantee to obtain the needed currency at a future date for a guaranteed price. Assuming that Big Heel insists on being paid in U.S. dollars, Pied D'Or could obtain a quote from a currency dealer as to the present cost of obtaining $3 million at the time the boots are to be delivered. Pied D'Or might pay a 5 percent premium for this guarantee, but it will have insured itself against disastrous currency changes. (For up-to-the-minute conversion rates between virtually any two currencies, travel no further than **http://www.oanda.com/cgi-bin/ncc**.)

Choices Made. The parties agree that the contract price will be paid in U.S. dollars. Pied D'Or is unfamiliar with the UCC and absolutely refuses to make a deal unless either French law or the CISG governs. Your lawyer, Susan Fisher, recommends accepting the CISG, provided that the contract is written in English and that any disputes will be resolved in Arizona courts. Pied D'Or balks at this, but Fisher presses hard, and ultimately those are the terms agreed upon. Fisher is delighted with the arrangement, pointing out that the CISG provisions can all be taken into account as the contract is written, and that by using Arizona courts to settle any dispute, Big Heel has an advantage in terms of familiarity and location.

Letter of Credit

Because Pied D'Or is new and fast growing, you are not sure it will be able to foot the bill. Pied D'Or provides a letter of reference from its bank, La Banque Bouffon, but this is a small bank in Pleasanterie, France, unfamiliar to you. You need greater assurance of payment, and Fisher recommends that payment be made by **letter of credit**. Here is how the letter will work.

Big Heel demands that the contract include a provision requiring payment by confirmed, irrevocable letter of credit. Le Pied D'Or agrees. The French company now contacts its bank, La Banque Bouffon, and instructs Bouffon to issue a letter of credit to Big Heel. The letter of credit is a promise *by the bank itself* to pay Big Heel, if Big Heel presents certain documents. Banque Bouffon, of course, expects to be repaid by Pied D'Or. The bank is in a good position to assess Pied D'Or's creditworthiness, since it is local and can do any investigating it wants before issuing the credit. It may also insist that Pied D'Or give Bouffon a mortgage on property, or that Pied D'Or deposit money in a separate Bouffon account. Pied D'Or is the **account party** on the letter of credit, and Big Heel is the **beneficiary**.

But at Big Heel you are still not entirely satisfied about getting paid because you don't know anything about Bouffon. That is why you have required a *confirmed* letter of credit. Bouffon will forward its letter of credit to Big Heel's own bank, the Bandito Trust Company of Tucson. Bandito examines the letter and then *confirms* the letter. This is *Bandito's own guarantee* that it will pay Big Heel. Bandito will do this only if it knows, through international banking contacts, that Bouffon is a sound bank. The risk has now been spread to two banks, and at Big Heel you are confident of payment.

You get busy, make excellent boots, and pack them. When they are ready, you truck them to Galveston, where they are taken alongside a ship, *Le Fond de la Mer*. Your agent presents the goods to the ship's officials, along with customs documents that describe the goods. *Le Fond de la Mer*'s officer in turn issues your agent a **negotiable bill of lading**. This document describes *exactly* the goods received—their quantity, color, quality, and anything else important.

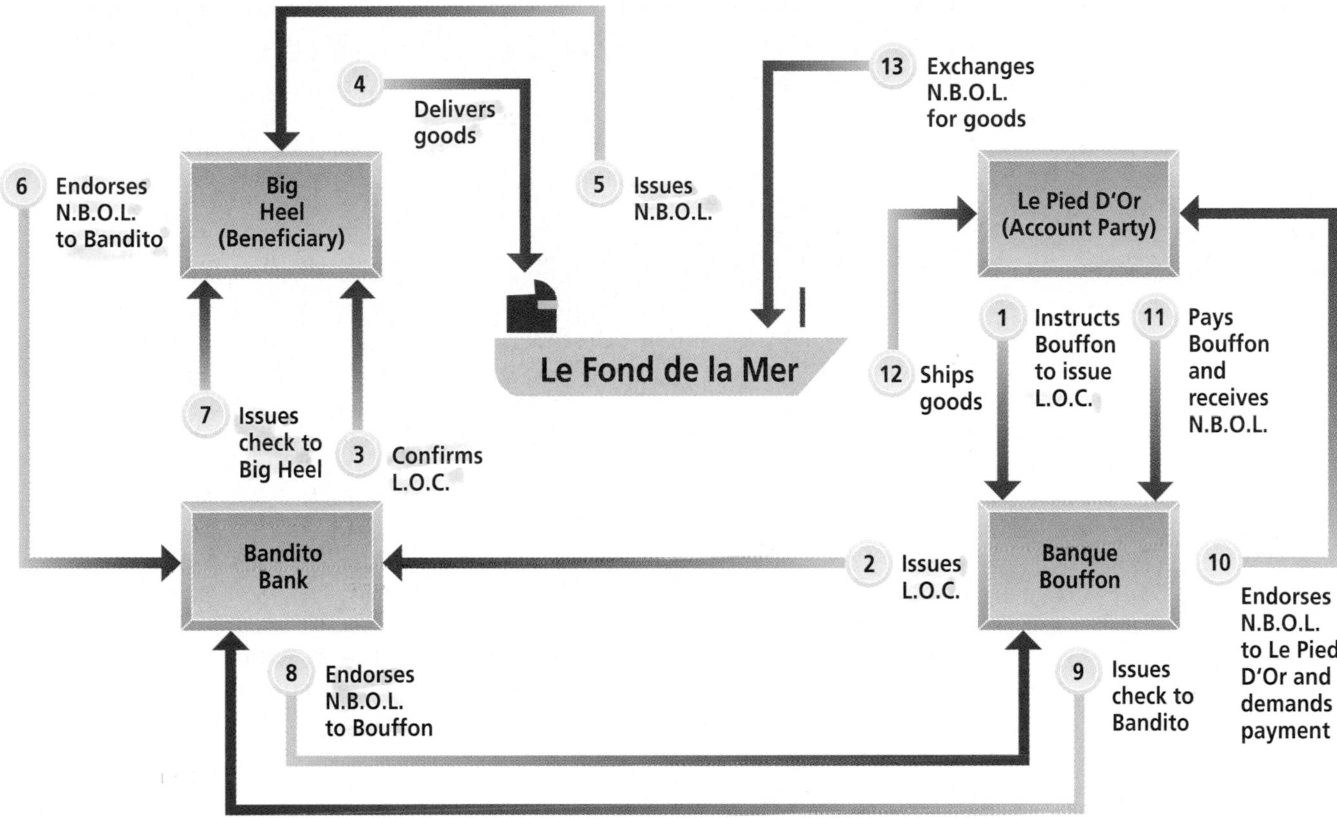

Exhibit 8.1

You now take the negotiable bill of lading to Bandito Trust. You also present to Bandito a **draft**, which is simply a formal order to Bandito to pay, based on the letter of credit. Bandito will look closely at the bill of lading, which must specify *precisely* the goods described in the letter of credit. Why so nitpicky? Because the bank is dealing only in paper. It never sees the boots. It is exchanging $3 million of its own money based on instructions in the letter of credit. It should pay only if the bill of lading indicates that *Le Fond de la Mer* received exactly what is described in the letter of credit. Bandito will decide whether the bill of lading is *conforming* or *nonconforming*. If the terms of both documents are identical, the bill of lading is conforming and Bandito must pay. If the terms vary, the bill of lading is nonconforming and Bandito will deny payment. Thus, if the bill of lading indicated 9,000 pairs of boots and 1,000 pairs of sneakers, it is nonconforming and Big Heel would get no money.

Bandito concludes that the documents are conforming, so it issues a check to Big Heel for $3 million. In return, you endorse the bill of lading and other documents over to the Bandito Bank, which endorses the same documents and sends them to Banque Bouffon. Bouffon makes the same minute inspection and then writes a check to Bandito. Bouffon then demands payment from Le Pied D'Or. Pied D'Or pays its bank, receiving in exchange the bill of lading and customs documents. Note that payment in all stages is now complete, though the boots are still rolling on the high seas. Finally, when the boots arrive in Le Havre, Pied D'Or trucks roll up to the wharf and, using the bill of lading and customs documents, collect the boots. See Exhibit 8.1.

Good news: They fit! Not all customers walk away in such comfort, as the following case indicates.

CENTRIFUGAL CASTING MACHINE CO., INC. v. AMERICAN BANK & TRUST CO.

966 F.2d 1348, 1992 U.S. App. LEXIS 13089
United States Court of Appeals for the Tenth Circuit, 1992

Facts: Centrifugal Casting Machine Co. (CCM) entered into a contract with the State Machinery Trading Co. (SMTC), an agency of the Iraqi government. CCM agreed to manufacture cast iron pipe plant equipment for a total price of $27 million. The contract specified payment of the full amount by confirmed irrevocable letter of credit. The Central Bank of Iraq then issued the letter, on behalf of SMTC (the "account party") to be paid to CCM (the "beneficiary"). The Banca Nazionale del Lavorov (BNL) confirmed the letter.

Following Iraq's invasion of Kuwait on August 2, 1990, President Bush issued two executive orders blocking the transfer of property in the United States in which Iraq held any interest. In other words, no one could use, buy, or sell any Iraqi property or cash. When CCM attempted to draw upon the letter of credit, the United States government intervened. The government claimed that like all Iraqi money in the United States, this money was frozen by the executive order. The United States District Court rejected the government's claim, and the government appealed.

Issue: **Is CCM entitled to be paid pursuant to the letter of credit?**

Excerpts from Judge Sentelle's Decision: The United States contends on appeal that the freeze of Iraq's assets furthers national policy to punish Iraq by preventing it from obtaining economic benefits from transactions with American citizens, and by preserving such assets both for use as a bargaining chip in resolving this country's differences with Iraq and as a source of compensation for claims Americans may have against Iraq. We agree that these policy considerations are compelling and that we are therefore required to construe Iraqi property interests broadly. However, we are not persuaded these policies would be furthered by [creating] a property interest on behalf of Iraq that would not otherwise be cognizable under governing legal principles.

Two interrelated features of the letter of credit provide it with its unique value in the marketplace and are of critical importance in our consideration of the United States's claim here. First, the simple result [of a letter of credit] is that the issuer [i.e., the bank] substitutes its credit, preferred by the beneficiary, for that of the account party. Second, the issuer's obligation to pay on a letter of credit is completely independent from the underlying commercial transaction between the beneficiary and the account party. Significantly, the issuer must honor a proper demand even though the beneficiary has breached the underlying contract; even though the insolvency of the account party renders reimbursement impossible; and notwithstanding supervening illegality, impossibility, war or insurrection. This principle of independence is universally viewed as essential to the proper functioning of a letter of credit and to its particular value, i.e., its certainty of payment.

This assurance of payment gives letters of credit a central role in commercial dealings, and gives them a particular value in international transactions, in which sophisticated investors knowingly undertake such risks as political upheaval or contractual breach in return for the benefits to be reaped from international trade. Law affecting such an essential instrument of the economy must be shaped with sensitivity to its special characteristics. Accordingly, courts have concluded that the whole purpose of a letter of credit would be defeated by examining the merits of the underlying contract dispute to determine whether the letter should be paid.

Because of the nature of a letter of credit, we conclude that Iraq does not have a property interest in the money CCM received under the letter. The United States contends in essence that Iraq has a property interest in this money because it was allegedly a contract payment made by Iraq, which Iraq should recover because CCM breached the contract. In so arguing, the United States makes a breach of contract claim on behalf of Iraq that Iraq has never made, creates a remedy for the contracting parties in derogation of the remedy they themselves provided and, most importantly, disregards the controlling legal principles with respect to letters of credit.

Affirmed.

INDIRECT SALES THROUGH A DISTRIBUTOR

You might also have decided that Big Heel would be better off doing business through a French shoe distributor, on the theory that the local company would have superior market knowledge and easier access to valuable retailers. The questions you face regarding choice of law, forum, and method of payment are identical to those you face in direct sales; they must be worked out in advance. But there is one additional problem that deserves close attention.

Suppose you choose Voleurs Freres, a French fashion distributor, to do all of Big Heel's work in France. Voleurs Freres will be an **exclusive dealer**, meaning that it will take on no other accounts of cowboy boots. In return you will give it an **exclusive distributorship**, indicating that no other French distributors will get a chance at Big Heel boots. This is a common method of working. Voleurs Freres benefits because no one else in France may distribute the valuable boots. Big Heel in turn need not worry that Voleurs Freres will devote more energy to a competing boot. It is a tidy relationship, but does it violate antitrust laws?

Antitrust laws make it illegal to destroy competition and capture an entire market. The United States and the EU both have strong antitrust laws that can potentially be applied domestically and in foreign countries.

EU Antitrust Law

The European Union law is found in Articles 85 and 86 of the Treaty of Rome. From the American point of view, the former is more important. **Article 85 outlaws any agreement, contract, or discussion that distorts competition within EU countries.** In other words, any attempt to gain a market edge by *avoiding* competition is going to be suspect. Suppose three Italian cosmetic firms agree to act in unison to increase earnings. They set common prices for makeup and agree that none will undersell the others. This greatly reduces competition, leaving the consumer with fewer options and more expensive products. Their deal violates Article 85.

Will Big Heel's contract with Voleurs Freres violate Article 85? There is no quick answer. You will need to do a careful market analysis and consult with French lawyers, who undoubtedly will have many questions. How popular are Big Heel boots in Europe? How many competitors would like to distribute them? How many other boot companies want Voleurs Freres to sell *their* products? Does the exclusive arrangement between Big Heel and Voleurs Freres diminish competition? Will consumers pay more because of the contract? These questions are a nuisance and an expense, but it is easier and cheaper to make the inquiry now than to face years of antitrust litigation.

American Antitrust Law

In the United States, the primary antitrust law is the **Sherman Act**.[5] This statute controls anticompetitive conduct that harms the American market. It will probably not affect the Big Heel–Voleurs Freres contract, since that deal is likely to have

[5] See Chapters 40–41, on antitrust law.

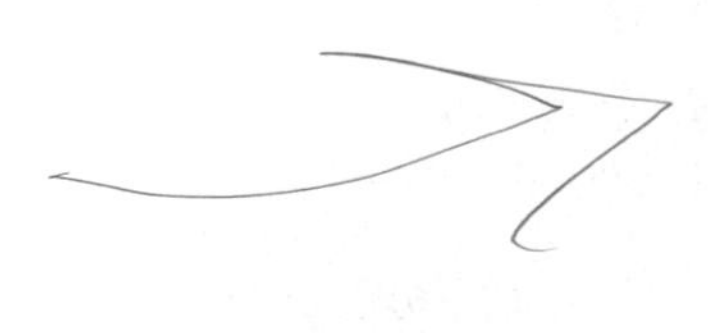

consequences only in Europe. But it is important to understand the Sherman Act when facing foreign competition. In effect, this statute is the American counterpart to Article 85. Any conduct that eliminates competition in the United States and enables one company, or group of companies, to control a market probably violates this law. And "any conduct" means that anticompetitive acts taking place in a foreign country may still violate the Sherman Act. A company doing business in the United States **may sue a competitor based on its conduct in a foreign country,** provided the local firm can show (1) that the foreign competitor *intends* to affect the U.S. market, and (2) that the foreign conduct has a *direct and substantial effect* on the U.S. market.

Let's look again at the Italian cosmetics makers. Suppose they decide to act in unison in the United States. They set common prices and agree not to compete with each other. That agreement is illegal. It violates the Sherman Act *even if all arrangements were made in Milan*. The companies intend to affect the U.S. market. When an American cosmetics firm demonstrates that the agreement caused it direct and substantial harm, the company may file suit in the United States against all three Italian corporations and expect to recover large damages.

International Comity

But what if the foreign corporation is doing business in a way that is entirely legal in its native country? May U.S. antitrust law still penalize the company's conduct if it harms American business? That was the question presented in the following case, which raises the issue of **international comity**. The word "comity" in this context means "concomitant jurisdiction," meaning that two courts have the right to hear a particular case. When those two courts are in different nations, the laws of the two countries may conflict. **In the event of a conflict, international comity requires one court to respect the other legal system and decline to hear a suit if it would more logically be resolved in the foreign country.** Does that principle govern the following case? The plaintiffs wanted the case heard in the United States under the Sherman Act, while the defendants wanted any dispute settled in Britain, where they believed British law would find them innocent of any wrongdoing.

HARTFORD FIRE INSURANCE CO. v. CALIFORNIA

509 U.S. 764, 113 S. Ct. 2891, 1993 U.S. LEXIS 4404
United States Supreme Court, 1993

Facts: Nineteen states and many private plaintiffs filed 36 separate lawsuits against various insurance companies, alleging several conspiracies to violate the Sherman Act. The conspiracies related to commercial general liability (CGL) insurance. CGL insurance covers the insured against accident and damage claims by customers, other companies, or the general public. The defendants were "reinsurance" companies. When a primary insurer issues a CGL policy to a corporation, it usually obtains for itself insurance to cover at least a portion of the risk it is assuming. The availability of reinsurance strongly affects the ability of primary insurers to provide coverage to customers. A primary insurer unable to obtain reinsurance will seldom issue coverage.

Lloyd's of London is a major reinsurance center. Various English syndicates, working through Lloyd's, provide reinsurance for companies throughout the world. The plaintiffs alleged that during the 1980s, reinsurers at Lloyd's forced American primary insurers to change the terms of their standard CGL insurance. These changes shortened the time during which a customer could file a claim under its policy, and eliminated certain claims altogether. These changes made CGL less valuable to the insured and more profitable to the reinsurers. The reinsurers were able to impose these changes because (1) there are only a few reinsurers worldwide and (2) all of the reinsurers worked in collusion to limit the coverage. They thus behaved in a monopolistic fashion, controlling the market and reducing customers' insurance coverage.

The United States District Court concluded that since the reinsurers' conduct was legal in Britain, international comity prevented an American court from hearing claims against the London defendants. The court dismissed the case against them. The United

States Court of Appeals reversed, holding that the case should go forward in this country. The London reinsurers appealed to the United States Supreme Court.

You Be the Judge: Does the principle of international comity prevent an American court from hearing these antitrust claims against London reinsurers?

Argument for the London Reinsurers: Your honors, for several reasons we urge American courts not to hear these antitrust claims against any London reinsurer. Lloyd's of London has been one of the world's most respected insurance organizations since 1688. Beginning in 1879, Parliament has directly regulated Lloyd's, and continues to control it today, pursuant to the Insurance Companies Act of 1982 and appropriate regulations. Under British law, insurance companies and reinsurance companies are *expressly exempt* from antitrust regulation. Everything that the defendants are alleged to have done in this case is *entirely legal* in Britain. It is an extraordinarily dangerous idea to permit the courts of one nation to subject foreign nationals to phenomenally expensive litigation for alleged conduct that was absolutely legal and proper where it was done.

Further, even though plaintiffs allege that the defendants' conduct technically violated American laws, there can be no suggestion that any of the reinsurers intended to harm any American corporation or citizen. This is not some shady conspiracy forged on a foggy night in an abandoned shack. The London reinsurers simply attempted to limit their own liability. They chose a lawful means to do it. They were doing, in other words, precisely what the plaintiffs in this case do when they buy insurance!

As this Court well knows, British courts have repeatedly expressed hostility to the extraterritorial application of American antitrust laws. So strong is the antagonism from earlier cases that English law now prohibits companies from supplying evidence and documents for use in antitrust proceedings in the United States. Even if this Court were to permit the suit to go forward, it would be nearly impossible for the plaintiffs to obtain documentary evidence to support their case from the only place from which it can come, England.

For all of these reasons, we urge the Court to rely on international comity and dismiss the case.

Argument for the Plaintiffs: Your honors, the defendants all engaged in conduct that they knew violated American antitrust laws. They did it for one reason: to increase their profits. That, of course, is why any corporation attempts to control a market. Here, by fixing deals with other major reinsurers, the Lloyd's syndicates were able to dictate the terms of American primary insurance and reduce coverage to the plaintiffs.

The defendants argue that they have obeyed British law, and that a so-called conflict in the laws requires American courts to stay away. But there is in fact no conflict between American and British law. It may be true that the reinsurers' monopolistic practices do not *violate* British law. But that does not mean that British law *requires* them to behave this way. It is black letter law that American antitrust laws may be applied against conduct that is lawful in a foreign nation. There would be a conflict only if British insurance law *required* Lloyd's firms to act collusively and attempt to control the American market. Obviously, it does not. The Lloyd's reinsurers are free to obey American law and British law, and that is what they ought to have done. They didn't, and we ask a chance to prove that in court.

These reinsurers are some of the most sophisticated business people in the world. They entered the American insurance market to make a profit and have stayed here many decades because they *are* earning money. But the profits were not vast enough, so they engaged in monopolistic, collusive practices to cut back the customer's ability to make a claim. And now, in dominating the American market, they claim they should not be governed by American law. Not fair, your honors. They can't have it both ways. If they enter this market, they must be governed by its laws the same as anyone else.

International claims of monopolization will increase as multinational enterprises, already powerful, merge with one another. Boeing Corp., the largest American manufacturer of aircraft, announced its plans to merge with McDonnell-Douglas, its largest American competitor. Federal antitrust regulators examined the deal and approved it, potentially creating the world's largest aerospace company. But the European Union intervened. EU regulators asserted that the new company would have enough clout to subdue competition in Europe and unfairly dominate its aerospace industry. American observers contended that the EU was interfering with an American merger simply to gain market share for the largest European aircraft maker, Airbus Industrie. After seven months of intense EU investigation of the merger and round-the-clock negotiations, Boeing agreed to certain changes.

The company gave up its position as exclusive supplier of planes to American, Delta, and Continental Airlines, thus allowing Airbus to bid for those jobs. Boeing also agreed to license certain patents to Airbus and to run McDonnell-Douglas as a separate entity. With those concessions, the EU agreed to Boeing's takeover, and the company acquired McDonnell-Douglas.

LICENSING A FOREIGN MANUFACTURER

Big Heel has a third option when selling abroad, which is to license a French manufacturer to produce Big Heel boots. It should do this only if it is convinced the manufacturer will maintain sufficiently high standards. Even so, there are two major issues.

First, Big Heel must ensure that all of its patents and trademarks are protected. In fact, France will honor both forms of American intellectual property, and there should be no problems. But some nations may ignore American intellectual property rights, and no company should establish a licensing arrangement without investigating. As mentioned above, the GATT should increase respect worldwide for the intellectual property rights created by all nations.

Second, if Big Heel grants an exclusive license to any French manufacturer, it could encounter exactly the same antitrust problems as those discussed above. It must analyze both EU and American antitrust law before taking the risk.

INVESTING ABROAD

Foreign investment is another major source of international commerce. Assume that Ambux is an American communications corporation that decides to invest in a growing overseas market. The president of Ambux is particularly interested in building telephone systems in the former republics of the Soviet Union, reasoning that these economies offer great opportunity for growth. She wants you to report to her on the most important issues concerning possible investment in Uzbekistan and other former Soviet republics. You quickly realize that such an investment presents several related issues:

- Repatriation of profits
- Expropriation
- Sovereign immunity
- Act of State doctrine
- Foreign corrupt practices

REPATRIATION OF PROFITS

Repatriation of profits occurs when an investing company pulls its earnings out of a foreign country and takes them back home. If Ambux builds a telephone system in Uzbekistan, it will plan to make money and then repatriate the profit to its headquarters in the United States. But Ambux must not assume an automatic right to do so. Many countries impose a much higher tax on repatriated profits than on normal income in order to keep the money in domestic commerce. Others bar repatriation altogether. Developing countries in particular want the money for further growth, and they tend to regard repatriation of rapidly earned profit as a close relative of exploitation. Thus, before Ambux invests anywhere, it must ensure that it can repatriate profits or be prepared to live with any limitations the foreign country might impose.

Fortunately, investing in Uzbekistan became more secure in 1994. The Uzbekistan parliament passed a new foreign investment law guaranteeing repatriation of profits without limit. Uzbekistan and the United States then signed a trade treaty guaranteeing unlimited repatriation for American investors. This treaty should suffice. But Ambux might still feel cautious. Uzbekistan is a new nation, and the mechanisms for actually getting the money out of Uzbekistan banks may be slow or faulty. The solution is to get a written agreement from the Minister of Commerce explicitly permitting Ambux to repatriate all profits and providing a clear mechanism to do it through the local banks.

EXPROPRIATION

Many nations, both developed and developing, **nationalize** property, meaning that they declare the national government to be the new owner. For example, during the 1940s and 1950s, Great Britain nationalized its coal, steel, and other heavy industries. The state assumed ownership and paid compensation to the previous owners. In the United States, nationalization is rare, but local governments often take land by eminent domain, to be used for roads or other public works. The United States Constitution requires that the owners be fairly compensated.

When a government takes property owned by foreign investors, it is called **expropriation**. Again, this practice is common and legal, provided there is adequate compensation. The U.S. government historically has acknowledged that the expropriation of American interests is legal, provided the host government pays the owners *promptly and fully, in dollars*. But if compensation is inadequate or long delayed, or made in a local currency that is hard to exchange, the taking is **confiscation**.

The courts of almost all nations concede that confiscation is illegal. But it can be difficult or impossible to prevent because courts of the host country may be partial to their own government. And any attempt to obtain compensation in an American court will encounter two separate problems: sovereign immunity and the Act of State doctrine.

Sovereign Immunity

Sovereign immunity holds that the courts of one nation lack the jurisdiction (power) to hear suits against foreign governments. Most nations respect this principle. In the United States, the **Foreign Sovereign Immunities Act (FSIA)** states that American courts generally cannot entertain suits against foreign governments. This is a difficult hurdle for a company to overcome when seeking compensation for foreign expropriation. There are three exceptions.

Waiver. A lawsuit is permitted against a foreign country that waives its immunity, that is, voluntarily gives up this protection. Suppose the Czech government wishes to buy fighter planes from an American manufacturer. The manufacturer might insist on a waiver in the sales contract, and the Czech Republic might be willing to grant one to get the weapons it desires. If the planes land safely but the checks bounce, the manufacturer may sue.

Commercial Activity. A plaintiff in the United States can sue a foreign country engaged in commercial activity, as opposed to political. Suppose the government of Iceland hires an American ecology-consulting firm to help its fishermen replenish depleted fishing grounds. Since fishing is a for-profit activity, the contract is commercial, and if Iceland refuses to pay, the company may sue in American courts.

Violation of International Law. A plaintiff in this country may sue a foreign government that has confiscated property in violation of international law, provided that the property either ends up in the United States or is involved in commercial activity that affects someone in the United States. Suppose a foreign government confiscates a visiting American ship, with no claim of right, and begins to use it for shipping goods for profit. Later, the ship carries some American produce. The taking was illegal, and it now affects American commerce. The original owner may sue.

Act of State Doctrine

He still has the sugar.

A second doctrine, annoyingly similar to sovereign immunity, could also affect Ambux or any company whose property is confiscated. The **Act of State doctrine** requires an American court to **abstain from any case in which a court order would interfere with the ability of the president or Congress to conduct foreign affairs.**

In the 1960s, Cuba expropriated American sugar interests, providing little or no compensation to the previous owners. The American owners sued, but in *Banco Nacional de Cuba v. Sabbatino*,[6] the United States Supreme Court refused to permit such suits in American courts. The Court ruled that even where there was strong evidence that the expropriation was illegal, American courts should not be involved because the executive and legislative branches must be free to conduct our foreign policy.

Investment Insurance

Companies eager to do business abroad but anxious about expropriation should consider publicly funded insurance. In 1971, Congress established the **Overseas Private Investment Corporation (OPIC)** to insure U.S. investors against overseas losses due to political violence and expropriation. OPIC insurance is available to investors at relatively low rates for investment in almost any country. The agency has had remarkable success at no cost to the U.S. government. Every year, OPIC participates in overseas ventures worth many billions of dollars, earning insurance fees that have paid the agency's entire budget and left a substantial surplus.

Should Ambux investigate OPIC insurance before investing in Uzbekistan? Absolutely. While the Uzbekistan government has the best of intentions with respect to foreign investment, the nation is young and the government has no track record. A government can change course as quickly as a gnat, and often with less planning. Why take unnecessary risks?

FOREIGN CORRUPT PRACTICES ACT

Suppose that while you are investigating Uzbekistan, an official from a nearby country contacts you. This official, Dr. "J.," says that Ambux is the perfect company to install a new, nationwide telephone system for his young republic. You are delighted with his enthusiasm. Over lunch, Dr. J. tells you that he can obtain an exclusive contract for Ambux to do the work, but you will have to pay him a commission of $750,000. Such a deal would be worth millions of dollars for Ambux, and a commission of $750,000 is economically sensible. Should you pay it?

The Foreign Corrupt Practices Act (FCPA)[7] makes it illegal for an American business person to give "anything of value" to any foreign official in order to

---

[6] 376 U.S. 398, 84 S. Ct. 923, 1964 U.S. LEXIS 2252 (1964).

[7] 15 U.S.C. §78 et seq.

influence an official decision. The classic example of an FCPA violation is bribing a foreign official to obtain a government contract. You must find out exactly why Dr. J. needs so much money, what he plans to do with it, and how he will obtain the contract.

You ask these questions, and Dr. J. responds, "I am a close personal friend of the Minister of the Interior. In my country, you must know people to make things happen. The minister respects my judgment, and some of my fee will find its way to him. Do not trouble yourself with details."

Bad advice. A prison sentence is not a detail. The FCPA permits fines of $100,000 for individuals and $1 million for corporations, as well as prison sentences of up to five years. If you pay money that "finds its way to the minister," you have violated the act.

It is sad but true that in many countries bribery is routine and widely accepted. When Congress investigated foreign bribes to see how common they were, more than 300 U.S. companies admitted paying hundreds of millions of dollars in bribes to foreign officials. Legislators concluded that such massive payments distorted competition between American companies for foreign contracts, interfered with the free market system, and undermined confidence everywhere in our way of doing business. The statutory response was simple: foreign bribery is illegal, plain and simple. The FCPA has two principal requirements:

- *Bribes.* The statute makes it illegal for U.S. companies and citizens to bribe foreign officials to influence a governmental decision. The statute prohibits giving anything of value and also bars using third parties as a conduit for such payments.

- *Record Keeping.* All publicly traded companies—whether they engage in international trade or not—must keep detailed records that prevent hiding or disguising bribes. These records must be available for U.S. government officials to inspect.

Lockheed Corp. secured a $79 million contract to sell C-130 Hercules transport aircraft to Egypt, anticipating a $12 million profit. One expense of obtaining the contract was a $1 million payment, made to a Swiss bank account, for the benefit of a former Lockheed consultant who had since become a member of the Egyptian parliament. Big mistake. In federal court, Lockheed later pleaded guilty to violating the FCPA, acknowledging that it had falsified records to cover up the bribe. The company paid a $24.8 million fine—double its profit. The Lockheed executive directly involved in the bribe, Suleiman Nassar, vice-president of international marketing, received a fine of $125,000 and an 18-month prison sentence.

Not all payments violate the FCPA. A **grease or facilitating payment is legal,** provided the company is paying a foreign official only to expedite performance of a routine function. Grease payments are common in many foreign countries to obtain a permit, process governmental papers, or obtain utility service. For example, the cost of a permit to occupy an office building might be $100, but the government clerk suggests that you will receive the permit faster (within this lifetime) if you pay $150, one-third of which he will pocket. Such small payments are legal. Further, a payment **does not violate the FCPA if it was legal under the written laws** of the country in which it was made. Since few countries establish written codes *permitting* officials to receive bribes, this defense is unlikely to help many Americans who hand out gifts.

Some illegal bribes are blatant. A suitcase full of cash is a ticket to jail. But some payments are subtler. Your company is bidding for the right to build a power station in rural Mexico, and an Italian company is your primary competitor. The Italian company offers to fly all of the relevant Mexican officials and their families to Venice for an all-expenses-paid holiday. Should you match the offer? Such a gift, clearly made to obtain an important contract, would only be lawful if *written* Mexican law permitted it. It is unlikely there is such a law. Never give any gift without checking with a lawyer to assure that local *written* law permits the payment.

Transparency International, an international nonprofit agency based in Germany, publishes a "corruption perception index," gauging how much dishonesty business people encounter in different nations. The 10 countries perceived to be the most corrupt in 1997 were Nigeria, Bolivia, Colombia, Russia, Pakistan, Mexico, Indonesia, India, Venezuela, and Vietnam. Among the nations listed as the least corrupt were Sweden, Finland, Singapore, the Netherlands, New Zealand, Denmark, Canada, Norway, Switzerland, and Australia. The full "corruption perception index" is available from Transparency International's homepage at http://www.transparency.de/. The agency listed the United States as the 16th least corrupt nation.

But corruption is a two-sided coin. Of the roughly 200 nations in the world, only Sweden and the United States prohibit their nationals from bribing foreign officials. Further, in many countries, a bribe paid to a foreign official may be deducted for tax purposes! Thus, if you attempted to bribe a government official in Denmark, you would probably fail and might be arrested. Yet a Danish company may use cash to corrupt an official in Nigeria and then deduct the payment as a business expense.

American executives have long complained that the FCPA puts their companies at a competitive disadvantage, and political leaders have lobbied for an international agreement. Finally, the efforts are reaching fruition. In December 1997, the Organization for Economic Cooperation and Development (OECD) produced a "Convention of Combatting Bribery of Foreign Public Officials in International Business Transactions." The 29 nations of the OECD include most of the world's economic powers. Five nonmembers of the OECD also signed. The Convention requires signatories to enact criminal penalties for offering or giving bribes to foreign officials. The Convention also compels signatories to enact record-keeping laws that will prevent companies from disguising bribes.

The Convention has various weaknesses, and it remains to be seen whether signatories will implement it aggressively. But the Convention is long overdue. The collapse of several Southeast Asian economies during 1997 and 1998 clearly demonstrated the destructive effects of corruption. Many of the nations that suffered most were considered rife with dishonest officials.

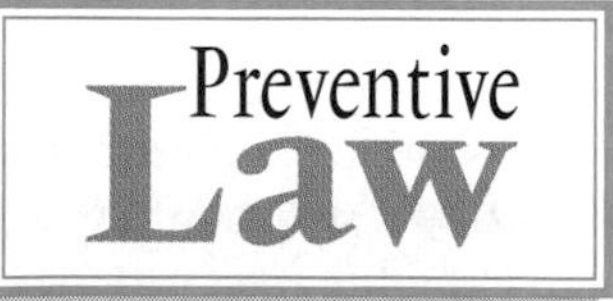

The best way for a company to avoid liability under the FCPA is to hire a compliance officer. This employee should conduct background checks on foreign agents and consultants to ensure that they are not making secret payments to obtain business. The compliance officer should insist on internal company auditing designed to deter and detect illicit payments. She must train all employees in the nuances of the law and create a system for reporting and investigating suspected breaches of the law.

CHAPTER CONCLUSION

Overseas investment, like sales abroad, offers potentially great rewards but significant pitfalls. A working knowledge of international law is essential to any entrepreneur or executive seriously considering foreign commerce. Issues such as choice of law, currency protection, antitrust statutes, and expropriation can mean the difference between profit and loss. As GATT and other treaties lower barriers, international trade will increase, and your awareness of these principles will grow still more valuable.

Chapter Review

1. Several statutes restrict exports from the United States that would harm national security, foreign policy, or certain other goals.
2. A tariff is a duty (tax) imposed on goods when they enter a country. The U.S. Customs Service classifies goods when they enter the United States and imposes appropriate tariffs.
3. Most countries, including the United States, impose duties for goods that have been dumped (sold at an unfairly low price in the international market) and for subsidized goods (those benefiting from government financial assistance in the country of origin).
4. The General Agreement on Tariffs and Trade (GATT), ratified by Congress in 1994, is lowering the average duties worldwide. Proponents see it as a boon to trade; opponents see it as a threat to American workers.
5. GATT created the World Trade Organization (WTO), which resolves disputes between signatories to the treaty.
6. A sales agreement between an American company and a foreign company may be governed by the UCC, by the law of the foreign country, or by the United Nations Convention On Contracts For The International Sale Of Goods (CISG). The CISG differs from the UCC in several important respects.
7. A confirmed, irrevocable letter of credit is an important means of facilitating international sales contracts, because the seller is assured of payment by a local bank as long as it delivers the specified goods.
8. Antitrust laws exist in the United States, the European Union (EU), and other countries. International merchants must be careful not to make agreements that would distort competition.
9. International comity requires a local court to respect the legal system of a foreign country and dismiss a lawsuit if the dispute would more logically be resolved in the other nation.
10. A foreign government may restrict repatriation of profits.
11. Expropriation refers to a government taking property owned by foreign investors. U.S. courts regard this as lawful, provided the country pays the American owner promptly and fully, in dollars.
12. Sovereign immunity means that, in general, American courts lack jurisdiction to hear suits against foreign governments, unless the foreign nation has waived immunity, is engaging in commercial activity, or has violated international law.

13. The Act of State doctrine requires an American court to abstain from any case in which a court order would interfere with the ability of the president or Congress to conduct foreign affairs.

14. The Foreign Corrupt Practices Act (FCPA) makes it illegal for an American business person to bribe foreign officials.

PRACTICE TEST

1. Arnold Mandel exported certain high-technology electronic equipment. Later, he was in court arguing that the equipment he shipped should not have been on the Department of Commerce's Commodity Control List. What items may be on that list, and why does Mandel care?

2. Sports Graphics, Inc. imports consumer goods, including "Chill" brand coolers, which come from Taiwan. Chill coolers have an outer shell of vinyl, with handles and pockets, and an inner layer of insulation. In a recent federal lawsuit, the issue was whether "Chill" coolers were technically "luggage" or "articles used for preparing, serving or storing food or beverages." Who were the parties to this dispute likely to be, and why did they care about such a technical description of these coolers?

3. **RIGHT & WRONG** Hector works in Zoey's importing firm. Zoey overhears Hector on the phone say, "O.K., 30,000 ski parkas at $80 per parka. You've got yourself a deal. Thanks a lot." When Hector hangs up, Zoey is furious, yelling, "I told you not to make a deal on those Italian ski parkas without my permission! I think I can get a better price elsewhere." "Relax, Zoey," replies Hector. "I wanted to lock them in, to be sure we had some in case your deal fell through. It's just an oral contract, so we can always back out if we need to." Is that ethical? How far can a company go to protect its interests? Does it matter that another business might make serious financial plans based on the discussion? Apart from the ethics, is Hector's idea smart?

4. **YOU BE THE JUDGE WRITING PROBLEM** Continental Illinois National Bank issued an irrevocable letter of credit on behalf of Bill's Coal Co. for $805,000, with the Allied Fidelity Insurance Co. as beneficiary. Bill's Coal Co. then went bankrupt. Allied then presented to Continental documents that were complete and conformed to the letter of credit. Continental refused to pay. Since Bill's Coal was bankrupt, there was no way Continental would collect once it had paid on the letter. Allied filed suit. Who should win? **Argument for Allied Fidelity:** An irrevocable letter of credit serves one purpose: to assure the seller that it will be paid if it performs the contract. Allied has met its obligation. The company furnished documents demonstrating compliance with the agreement. Continental *must* pay. Continental's duty to pay is an independent obligation, unrelated to the status of Bill's Coal. The bank issued this letter knowing the rules of the game and expecting to make a profit. It is time for Continental to honor its word. **Argument for Continental Bank:** In this transaction, the bank was merely a middleman, helping to facilitate payment of a contract. Allied has fulfilled its obligations under the contract, and we understand the company's desire to be paid. Regrettably, Bill's Coal is bankrupt. No one is going to be paid on this deal. Allied should have researched Bill's financial status more thoroughly before entering into the agreement. While we sympathize with Allied's dilemma, it has only itself to blame and cannot expect the bank to act as some sort of insurance company for a deal gone awry.

5. Jean-François, a French wine exporter, sues Bob Joe, a Texas importer, claiming that Bob Joe owes him $2 million for wine. Jean-François takes the witness stand to describe how the contract was created. Where is the trial taking place?

6. Zenith and other American manufacturers of television sets sued Matsushita and 20 other Japanese competitors, claiming that the Japanese companies had conspired to drive Zenith and the Americans out of the American market. Supposedly, the Japanese companies agreed to maintain artificially high prices in Japan and artificially low prices in the United States. The goal of the low prices in the United States was to destroy American competition, and the goal of the high prices in Japan was to earn sufficient profits at home so that the companies could tolerate the temporary losses in the United States. Is the conduct of Matsushita in Japan subject to the Sherman Act?

7. The Kyrgyz Republic is another of the new nations that broke away from the old Soviet Union. In September 1994, the government of Kyrgyzstan made two independent announcements: (1) it was abolishing all taxes on repatriation; (2) the government was resign-

ing and would shortly be replaced. Explain the significance of these announcements for an American company considering a major investment in Kyrgyzstan.

8. The Instituto de Auxilios y Viviendas is a government agency of the Dominican Republic. Dr. Marion Fernandez, the general administrator of the Instituto and Secretary of the Republic, sought a loan for the Instituto. She requested that Charles Meadows, an American citizen, secure the Instituto a bank loan of $12 million. If he obtained a loan on favorable terms, he would receive a fee of $240,000. Meadows secured a loan on satisfactory terms, which the Instituto accepted. He then sought his fee, but the Instituto and the Dominican government refused to pay. He sued the government in United States District Court. The Dominican government claimed immunity. Comment.

9. Environmental Tectonics Corp. and W. S. Kirkpatrick & Co. were both competing for a valuable contract with the Nigerian government. Kirkpatrick got it. Tectonics then sued Kirkpatrick in the United States, claiming that Kirkpatrick got the contract only because it bribed Nigerian officials. Kirkpatrick acknowledged that the district court had jurisdiction but argued that it should abstain from hearing the case. What doctrine does Kirkpatrick rely on, and what should the trial court do?

10. Blondek and Tull were two employees of an American company called Eagle Bus. They hoped that the Saskatchewan provincial government would award Eagle a contract for buses. To bolster their chances, they went to Saskatchewan and paid $50,000 to two government employees. Back in the United States, they were arrested and charged with a crime. Suppose they argue that even if they did something illegal, it occurred in Canada, and that is the only nation that can prosecute them. Comment on the defense.

11. Richard Johnson, an American citizen, was a highly trained electrical engineer who had worked for Hughes Aircraft and Norcroft Corp. He strongly believed in the cause of the Provisional Irish Republican Army (PIRA), which at the time was attacking British civilian and military targets in Northern Ireland and England. Johnson researched and developed explosives to be exported to Ireland and used by the PIRA. Christina Reid, an electrical engineer, worked with Johnson on IRA projects. She served as a courier of electronic components for remote-control bombs that the two sent to Northern Ireland. What legal problems did they risk by engaging in these transactions?

INTERNET RESEARCH PROBLEM

At http://www.sweatshops.org/, read about the worldwide problem of sweatshops. Is this a serious problem? If so, what role should the law play in its resolution? What can one student do about it?

You can find further practice problems in the Online Quiz at http://beatty.westbuslaw.com or in the Study Guide that accompanies this text.

CHAPTER 9

BUSINESS ETHICS AND SOCIAL RESPONSIBILITY

Under the direction of CEO Robert Mahoney, Diebold, Inc. is now the nation's leading manufacturer of automated teller machines, posting record sales for six consecutive years. The company has also been a cash machine for shareholders, as dividends have increased during each of the past 43 years. For all this, Mr. Mahoney has been rewarded handsomely. His annual compensation—salary, bonuses, and stock—has increased nearly fivefold in the past five years, from $464,250 to $2.37 million.

But Diebold's unionized factory workers have not been so fortunate. Under Mahoney's leadership, the company has shifted work to outside contractors and moved production from Ohio to lower-paying, nonunion plants in the South. Today, unionized workers in Ohio make less than they did a decade ago. Then Jim Ramey, an assembler at the Ohio plant, earned $11.83 an hour, $24,596 a year. Now he makes $9.93 an hour, $20,654 a year. Then Diebold employed 800 union workers in Ohio; today it has 58.

Donald Eagon, Diebold's vice-president for communications, says market forces dictate company salaries. Diebold has had to reduce factory workers' pay and cut costs to stay competitive in a global market where competitors look to places like

Southeast Asia for cheap labor. And Diebold has had to raise executives' salaries so that they will not be hired away by competitors.[1]

Business is an enormously powerful tool that corporate managers can use to accomplish many goals. They may wish to earn a good living, even to become wealthy, but they can also use their business skills to cure the ill, feed the hungry, entertain the bored, and in many other ways affect their community, their country, and their world.

This book is primarily about the impact of law on business. But law is only one set of rules that governs business; ethics is another. **Ethics is the study of how people ought to act**. Law and ethics are often in harmony. Most reasonable people agree that murder should be prohibited. But law and ethics are not always compatible. In some cases, it might be *ethical* to commit an *illegal* act; in others, it might be *unethical* to be *legal*. Here are two examples in which law and ethics might conflict:

> George Hart, a 75-year-old man confined to a wheelchair, robbed a bank in San Diego of $70 so that he could buy heart medicine. He entered a branch of the HomeFed Bank, where he had $4 in his account, and apologized while demanding $70 from a teller, threatening to blow up the bank if she did not comply. Mr. Hart was arrested minutes later when he tried to buy a $69 bottle of heart medicine at a nearby drugstore. Mr. Hart said he "hated to have to go to this extreme," but insisted he had tried every other way to find money to buy the medicine.[2]

In 1963, Martin Luther King, Jr., was arrested in Birmingham, Alabama, for leading illegal sit-ins and marches to protest laws that discriminated against African Americans. When eight local clergymen criticized his activities, King offered this defense:

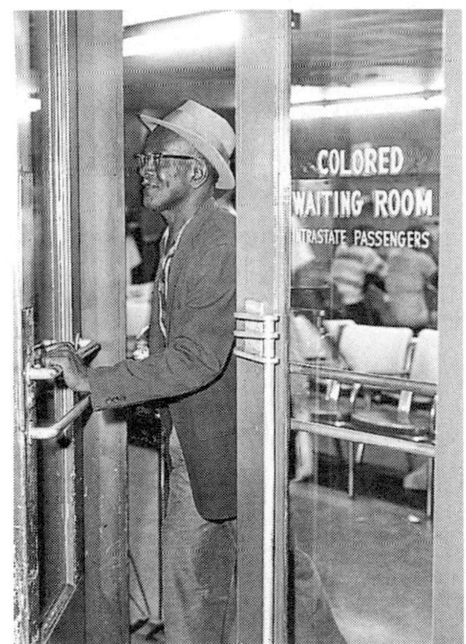

Is this law ethical?

> We know through painful experience that freedom is never voluntarily given by the oppressor; it must be demanded by the oppressed. . . . Perhaps it is easy for those who have never felt the stinging darts of segregation to say "Wait." . . . [W]hen you see the vast majority of your 20 million Negro brothers smothering in an air-tight cage of poverty in the midst of an affluent society; when you suddenly find your tongue twisted as you seek to explain to your six-year-old daughter why she can't go to the public amusement park that has just been advertised on television, and see tears welling up when she is told that Funtown is closed to colored children. . . . [W]hen you take a cross-country drive and find it necessary to sleep night after night in the uncomfortable corners of your automobile because no motel will accept you. . . . How can [we] advocate breaking some laws and obeying others? The answer lies in the fact that there are two types of laws: just and unjust. I agree with St. Augustine that "an unjust law is not law at all."[3]

Could one argue in the case of the bank robber that his actions, while illegal, were ethical? Would the argument be stronger if he had been stealing the money to help someone else? In the case of Martin Luther King, Jr., would it be reasonable to conclude not only that breaking the law was ethical, but also that *obeying* the

---

[1] Michael Winerip, "Canton's Economic Seesaw: Managers' Fortunes Rise as Workers Get Bumpy Ride," *New York Times*, July 7, 1996, p. 10. Copyright © 1996 by The New York Times Co. Reprinted by permission.

[2] "Bank Robber in Wheelchair Has an Alibi: His Medicine," *New York Times*, Jan. 18, 1991, p. A16.

[3] Martin Luther King, Jr., "Letter from Birmingham Jail," *The Christian Century*, June 12, 1963.

law would have been *unethical*? Were the eight clergymen who criticized King behaving unethically by upholding these odious laws?

The other chapters of this book focus on legal issues, but this chapter concentrates on ethics. In all of the examples in this chapter, the activities are *legal*, but are they *ethical*?

WHY BOTHER WITH ETHICS?

Business schools teach students how to maximize the profitability of an enterprise, large or small. Does ethical behavior maximize profitability? Some people argue that, in the *long run*, ethical behavior does indeed pay. But they must mean the *very* long run, because to date there is little evidence that ethical behavior necessarily pays, either in the short or the long run. For example, some companies that began by emphasizing ethical behavior have found this approach more difficult to maintain as they have grown.

Ben & Jerry's Homemade, Inc., an ice cream company, limited the salaries of its top managers to no more than seven times the pay of its lowliest worker. But when the original founders stepped down, they found that they had to pay more to hire their replacements. Typically, mutual funds that specialize in "socially responsible" companies—those with, say, strong environmental or equal-employment records—have performed worse than their ethics-neutral competitors.

Unethical companies may perform well financially. The Morgan Fun Shares fund purchases stock in tobacco, alcohol, and gambling companies on the theory that money can be made from vices, particularly if other investors shun the companies. Even for individuals, unethical behavior is no bar to financial success. The first antitrust laws in America were designed, at least in part, to restrain John D. Rockefeller's unethical activities. Yet, four generations later, his name is still synonymous with wealth and his numerous heirs can live comfortably on their inheritance from him.[4]

Some commentators have even argued that the ethical standards governing individuals do not apply to business. They contend that business is a *game*, with different rules. If insurance companies keep outdated actuarial tables that result in unfairly high premiums or use ingenious devices to discriminate against minorities, they are just playing the game particularly well. If you do not like it, get the law changed. Given these arguments, perhaps it is not surprising that half of the workers in a recent survey admitted that they had committed an illegal or unethical act in the prior year. They blamed the pressures of the workplace, such as difficulty balancing work and family or coping with a demanding boss.

If ethical behavior does not necessarily pay and unethical behavior sometimes does, why bother with ethics?

SOCIETY AS A WHOLE BENEFITS FROM ETHICAL BEHAVIOR

John Akers, the former chairman of IBM, argues that, without ethical behavior, a society cannot be economically competitive. He puts it this way:

> Ethics and competitiveness are inseparable. We compete as a society. No society anywhere will compete very long or successfully with people stabbing each other in the back; with people trying to steal from each other; with everything requiring notarized confirmation because you can't trust the other fellow; with every little squabble ending

[4] Chapter 40, on antitrust, discusses Rockefeller's career at greater length.

> in litigation; and with government writing reams of regulatory legislation, tying business hand and foot to keep it honest. That is a recipe not only for headaches in running a company, it is a recipe for a nation to become wasteful, inefficient, and noncompetitive. There is no escaping this fact: the greater the measure of mutual trust and confidence in the ethics of a society, the greater its economic strength.[5]

PEOPLE FEEL BETTER WHEN THEY BEHAVE ETHICALLY

Every business person has many opportunities to be dishonest. Consider how one person felt when he *resisted* temptation:

> Occasionally a customer forgot to send a bill for materials shipped to us for processing. . . . It would have been so easy to rationalize remaining silent. After all, didn't they deserve to lose because of their inefficiency? However, upon instructing our staff to inform the parties of their errors, I found them eager to do so. They were actually bursting with pride. . . . Our honesty was beneficial in subtle ways. The "inefficient" customer remained loyal for years. . . . [O]ur highly moral policy had a marvelously beneficial effect on our employees. Through the years, many an employee visited my office to let me know that they liked working for a "straight" company.[6]

Profitability is generally not what motivates managers to care about ethics. Managers want to feel good about themselves and the decisions they have made; they want to sleep at night. Their decisions—to lay off employees, install safety devices in cars, burn a cleaner fuel—affect peoples' lives. When two researchers asked business people why they cared about ethics, the answers had little to do with the profitability:

> The businesspeople we interviewed set great store on the regard of their family, friends, and the community at large. They valued their reputations, not for some nebulous financial gain but because they took pride in their good names.[7]

UNETHICAL BEHAVIOR CAN BE VERY COSTLY

Unethical behavior is a risky business strategy—it may lead to disaster. An engaged couple made a reservation, and put down a $1,500 deposit, to hold their wedding reception at a New Hampshire restaurant. Tragically, the bride died of asthma four months before the wedding. Invoking the terms of the contract, the restaurant owner refused to return the couple's deposit. In a letter to the groom, he admitted, "Morally, I would of course agree that the deposit should be returned." When newspapers reported this story, customers deserted the restaurant and it was forced into bankruptcy—over a $1,500 disagreement.[8] Unethical behavior does not always damage a business, but it certainly has the potential of destroying a company overnight. So why take the risk?

Even if unethical behavior does not devastate a business, it can cause other, subtler damage. In one survey, a majority of those questioned said that they had witnessed unethical behavior in their workplace and that this behavior had

---

[5] David Grier, "Confronting Ethical Dilemmas," unpublished manuscript of remarks at the Royal Bank of Canada, Sept. 19, 1989.

[6] Hugh Aaron, "Doing the Right Thing in Business," *Wall Street Journal*, June 21, 1993, p. A10. Republished with permission of The Wall Street Journal; permission conveyed through the Copyright Clearance Center, Inc.

[7] Amar Bhide and Howard H. Stevenson, "Why Be Honest if Honesty Doesn't Pay?" *Harvard Business Review*, Sept.–Oct. 1990, pp. 121–129, at 127.

[8] John Milne, "N.H. Restaurant Goes Bankrupt in Wake of Wedding Refund Flap," *Boston Globe*, Sept. 9, 1994, p. 25.

reduced productivity, job stability, and profits. Unethical behavior in an organization creates a cynical, resentful, and unproductive workforce.

For these reasons, many of America's major corporations actively encourage ethical behavior in their organizations. More than 500 companies have an ethics officer. These guardians of morality serve two purposes: they act as a sounding board for employees with ethical dilemmas, and they also enforce ethical standards within the company. If your co-worker is stealing office supplies, or you suspect a supervisor of having an affair with a subordinate, call the ethics officer to turn in the thief or to obtain advice on handling the sticky romance.

General Electric uses an illustration like the one below to demonstrate its approach to ethics. The company will not tolerate unethical managers, no matter how good their financial results, but it is willing to support employees who have the right values, whatever their results.

	High Performance	**Low Performance**
Ethical Values	THE SUPERSTARS: Bound for key leadership roles	THE SECOND-CHANCERS: Given more time or different roles
Unethical Values	? Increasing likelihood of quick removal—"the numbers" no longer protect or prolong you	THE FAILURES: Removed with no apology

So why bother with ethics? Because society benefits when managers behave ethically. Because ethical managers have happier, more satisfying lives. And because unethical behavior can destroy a business faster than a snake can bite.

WHAT IS ETHICAL BEHAVIOR?

It is one thing to decide, in theory, that being ethical is good; in practice, it can be much more difficult to make the right decisions. Supreme Court Justice Potter Stewart once said that he could not define pornography, but he knew it when he saw it. Many people feel the same way about ethics—that somehow, instinctively, they know what is right and wrong. In real life, however, ethical dilemmas are often not black and white, but many shades of gray. The purpose of this section is to analyze the following ethics checklist as an aid to managers in making tough decisions:

- What are the facts?
- What are the critical issues?
- Who are the stakeholders?
- What are the alternatives?
- What are the ethical implications of each alternative?
  - Is it legal?
  - How would it look in the light of day?
  - What are the consequences?

  - Does it violate important values?
  - Does it violate the Golden Rule?
  - Is it just?
  - Has the process been fair?
- Is more than one alternative right?
  - Which values are in conflict?
  - Which of these values are most important?
  - Can you find an alternative that is consistent with your values?

Analyzing the Ethics Checklist

What Are the Facts?

Although this question seems obvious, people often forget in the heat of battle to listen to (and, more importantly, to *hear*) all the different viewpoints. Instead of relying on hearsay and rumor, it is crucial to discover the facts, firsthand, from the people involved. It may be easy to condemn a bank robber, until learning the money was needed to buy medicine.

What Are the Critical Issues?

In analyzing ethical dilemmas, expand your thinking to include *all* the important issues. Avoid a narrow focus that encompasses only one or two aspects. In the case of the New Hampshire restaurant that refused to refund a deposit, the owner focused on the narrow legal issue. His interpretation of the *contract* was correct. But if the owner had expanded his thinking to include consideration for his customers, he might have reached a different decision.

Who Are the Stakeholders?

Stakeholders are all the people potentially affected by the decision. That list might include subordinates, bosses, shareholders, suppliers, customers, members of the community in which the business operates, society as a whole, or even more remote stakeholders, such as future generations. The interests of these stakeholders often conflict. Current shareholders may benefit from a company's decision to manufacture a product that contributes to global warming, while future generations are left to contend with a potential environmental nightmare.

What Are the Alternatives?

The next step is to list the reasonable alternatives. A creative manager may find a clever solution that is a winner for everyone. As Rebecca Jewett indicates in her interview later in this chapter, her aim is to find a solution that is "win-win" for all the stakeholders.

What Are the Ethical Implications of Each Alternative?

Is the Alternative Legal? Illegal may not always be synonymous with unethical, but, as a general rule, you need to think long and hard about the ethics of any illegal activities.

How Would the Alternative Look in the Light of Day? If your activities were reported on the evening news, how would you feel? Proud? Embarrassed?

Horrified? Undoubtedly, sexual harassment would be virtually eliminated if people thought that their parents, spouse, or partner would shortly see a video replay of the offending behavior.

What Are the Consequences of This Alternative? Ask yourself: Am I hurting anyone by this decision? Which alternative will cause the greatest good (or the least harm) to the most people? For example, you would like to fire an incompetent employee. That decision will clearly have adverse consequences for him. But the other employees in your division will benefit and so will the shareholders of your company. Over all, your decision will cause more good than harm.

You should look with a particularly critical eye if an alternative benefits you while harming others. Suppose that you become CEO of a company whose headquarters are located in a distant suburb. You would like to move the headquarters closer to your home to cut your commuting time. Of course, such a decision would be expensive for shareholders and inconvenient for other employees. Do you simply impose your will on the company or consider the consequences for everyone?

This approach to decision making was first developed by two nineteenth-century English philosophers, Jeremy Bentham and John Stuart Mill. It is called **utilitarianism** because Bentham and Mill argued that all decisions should be evaluated according to how much **utility** they create. Some commentators have criticized this approach on practical grounds—benefit and harm are difficult to measure. Others also argue that not all utility is equal. A band of robbers may receive more benefit from stealing money than the victim suffers harm, but most people would nonetheless argue that the decision to steal is wrong. Despite these criticisms, it is wise at least to consider the costs and benefits of a decision.

Does the Alternative Violate Important Values? In addition to consequences, consider fundamental values. It is possible to commit an act that does not harm anyone else, but is still the wrong thing to do. Suppose, for instance, that you are away from home and have the opportunity to engage in a temporary sexual liaison. You are absolutely certain that your spouse will never find out and your partner for the night will have no regrets or guilt. There would be no negative consequences, but you believe that infidelity is wrong, *regardless of the consequences*, so you resist temptation.

Some people question whether, as a diverse, heterogeneous society (not to mention, world), we have common values. But throughout history, and across many different cultures, common values do appear. The following values are almost universal:

- *Consideration* means being aware of and concerned about other people's feelings, desires, and needs. The considerate person is able to imagine how he would feel in someone else's place.
- *Courage* is the strength to act in the face of fear and danger. Courage can require dramatic action (saving a buddy on a battlefield) or quiet strength (doing what you think is right, despite opposition from your boss).
- *Integrity* means being sincere, honest, reliable, and loyal. If you have integrity, you do not criticize others behind their back or take credit for their ideas and efforts.
- *Self-control* is the ability to resist temptation. The person with self-control does not drink or eat too much, party too hard, watch too much television, or spend too much money.

Although reasonable people may disagree about a precise list of important values, most would agree that values matter. Try compiling your own list of values and then check it periodically to see if you are living up to it in your business and personal life.

Does the Alternative Violate the Golden Rule? We all know the Golden Rule: do unto others as you would have them do unto you. If one of the alternatives you are considering would be particularly unpleasant when done to you, reconsider.

Immanuel Kant, an eighteenth-century German philosopher, took the Golden Rule one step further with a concept he called the **categorical imperative**. According to Kant, you should not do something unless you would be willing for everyone else to do it, too (and not just to you). Imagine that you could cheat on an exam without getting caught. You might gain some short-term benefit—a higher grade. But what would happen if everyone cheated? The professor would have to make the exams harder or curve everyone's grade down. If your school developed a reputation for cheating, you might not be able to find a job after graduation. Cheating works only if most people are honest. To take advantage of everyone else's honesty is contemptible.

Is the Alternative Just? Are you respecting individual rights such as liberty (privacy, free speech, and religious freedom), welfare (employment, housing, food, education), and equality? Is it right to read an employee's e-mail or would that violate her right to privacy?

Has the Process Been Fair? Unequal outcomes are acceptable, provided they are the result of a fair process. At the end of a poker game, some players have won and others lost, but no one can complain that the result was unfair, unless players cheated. In a business context, a fair process means applying the same set of rules to everyone. If three of your subordinates are vying for the same promotion, it would be unfair to let one state her case to you but not the others.

Is More than One Alternative Right?

Thus far, the ethics checklist has served two purposes. It helps to clarify the issues at stake. It also filters out decisions that are downright wrong. Have you considered lying to a customer about product specifications? For a start, such an action violates principles of integrity, not to mention the Golden Rule. Nor would you want your activity to be revealed on the front page of the local newspaper.

Oftentimes, however, the most difficult decisions arise not in cases of right versus wrong but in situations of right versus right.[9] President Harry Truman's decision to drop atomic bombs on two Japanese cities is a classic example of right versus right. He argued that if he had not ended the war by using nuclear weapons, more Americans and Japanese would have died during a land invasion. Looking simply at the consequences, he concluded that the terrible suffering by the Japanese people was justified because, ultimately, fewer people died overall. At the same time, Truman's decision violated the Golden Rule and Kant's categorical imperative. Indeed, since the end of World War II, the United States has worked hard to ensure that no one else ever deploys nuclear weapons. The ethics checklist presents no clear-cut answer. In the end, Truman decided that the most right (or least wrong) choice was to end the war quickly.

Nuclear weapons make a dramatic example, but what about a more typical business decision? AT&T adopted a policy of cutting costs to maximize its stock price. To implement this policy, the company laid off 40,000 people, despite record profits. Even as workers suffered, shareholders benefited because the company's stock price rose in response to the layoff announcement. But is stock price the only issue? Does the company have an obligation to protect employee jobs? Is one right more important than another?

---

[9] For a thoughtful discussion of right versus right, see Joseph L. Badaracco, Jr., *Defining Moments: When Managers Must Choose between Right and Right* (Boston: Harvard Business School Press, 1997).

Which Values Are in Conflict? There are many ways to justify a decision to lay off workers, even 40,000 of them. If managers avoid layoffs, profits suffer, stock prices fall, companies merge, and executives lose their own jobs. In business school and on the job, managers learn how to analyze, compete, and win. Competing—and winning—are important. But what about other values, such as compassion and caring? Do the individual people affected by this decision matter, too?

Which of These Values Are Most Important? Suppose that, growing up, you had seen family members or neighbors suffering through bouts of unemployment. That experience might have taught you that compassion is a high priority. Managers must determine which values are important in their own lives.

Can You Find an Alternative That Is Consistent with Your Values? The decision you make not only determines the kind of person you are now, but also sets your course for the future. Can you reach a decision that is consistent with the kind of person you are or want to be? Instead of announcing massive layoffs, some companies offer generous severance packages, retraining programs, and other voluntary methods of reducing the workforce. Shareholders may receive less benefit, but employees suffer less harm.

APPLYING THE ETHICS CHECKLIST: MAKING DECISIONS

An organization has responsibilities to customers, employees, shareholders, and society generally, both here and overseas. Employees also have responsibilities to their organizations. The purpose of this section is to apply the ethics checklist to actual business dilemmas. The checklist does not lead to one particular solution; rather it is a method to use in thinking through ethics problems. The goal is for you to reach a decision that satisfies you. For other examples of ethical dilemmas and suggestions for resolving them, go to **http://www.mapnp.org/library/ethics/ethxgde.htm**.

ORGANIZATION'S RESPONSIBILITY TO SOCIETY

Ethics of Advertising

Facts. In the United States, teenagers routinely list alcohol commercials among their favorite advertisements. Adolescents who frequently see ads for alcohol are more likely to believe that drinkers are attractive, athletic, and successful. They are also more likely to drink, drink excessively, and drink in hazardous situations such as driving a car.

While Secretary of Health and Human Services, Louis W. Sullivan publicly denounced the test marketing of Uptown, a high-tar cigarette targeted at African Americans. He called it "contemptible that the tobacco industry has sought to increase their market" among minorities because this population was "already bearing more than its fair share of smoking-related illness and mortality." More pointed was comedian Jay Leno's jest that R. J. Reynolds named the cigarette Uptown "because the word 'Genocide' was already taken."[10]

A promotion for Request Jeans shows a man pinning a naked woman against a shower wall. In Canada, an advertisement features childlike model Kate Moss lying naked on a couch. Above the couch is a picture of the product being promoted—Calvin Klein's Obsession for Men. In England, an ad for a stereo shows a

[10] Richard W. Pollay, Jung S. Lee, and David Carter-Whitney, "Separate, but Not Equal: Racial Segmentation in Cigarette Advertising," *Journal of Advertising*, Mar. 1992, vol. 21, no. 1, p. 45.

picture of a woman with these words, "She's terrific in bed, she's witty and intelligent, but she didn't have a Linn hi-fi. Her sister did and I married her sister."

In Peru, a television commercial features Africans who are ready to devour white tourists until diverted by the offer of Nabisco pudding. In another Latin American ad, a man compares the thickness of Goodyear tires to the lips of his black partner.

Critical Issues. What are the obligations of advertising executives and marketing managers to those who see their ads? Is it ethical to sell jeans by glorifying rape? Are men more likely to commit rape as a result of seeing one of these advertisements? Is it ethical to entice teenagers into drinking or African Americans into smoking? An advertising executive asserts that Latin American audiences find racial stereotypes amusing. Does that justify racist ads?

Stakeholders. Ad designers are primarily responsible to their firms and the firms' clients. After all, designers are paid to sell product, not to make the world a better place. But what about the people who see the advertisements? Do the designers have any responsibility to them? Or to society as a whole?

Alternatives. Firms have at least four alternatives in dealing with issues of ethics in advertising. They can:

- Ignore ethics and simply strive to create promotions that sell the most product, whatever the underlying message
- Try, in a general way, to minimize racism, sexism, and other exploitation
- Include, as part of the development process, a systematic, focused review of the underlying messages contained in their advertisements; or
- Refuse to create any ads that are potentially demeaning, insensitive, or dangerous, recognizing that such a stand may lead to a loss of clients.

Ethical Implications. All of these alternatives are perfectly legal. And, far from the ad executives being embarrassed if the ads see the light of day, the whole purpose of ads is to be seen. As for the consequences, the ads may help clients sell their products. But the ads may also harm those who see them by encouraging, among other things, drinking, smoking, sexual assault, racism, and promiscuity. A manager might question whether these ads violate fundamental values. Are they showing consideration for others? Do they encourage self-control? As for the Golden Rule, how would an advertising executive feel about an ad in which he was being sexually assaulted? Or a promotion in which he was assumed to be less valuable than a stereo system? Are these ads just? Do they violate principles of equality? Is the process by which they have been created fair? Have those who may be adversely affected by them had an opportunity to be heard?

Would using this model for an ad be ethical?

Right versus Right. Most people using an ethics checklist would agree that an advertisement making fun of a black man's thick lips is offensive and wrong. But what about subtler issues? In a country with rampant anorexia among teenage girls, is it ethical to run ads with emaciated girls as role models? What about ads for lottery tickets? These tickets are largely purchased by those who can least afford to gamble. If you worked in an advertising agency or marketing department, you might feel a strong sense of loyalty to your company. But what about consideration for those who could be harmed by your ads? You must decide which values are important to you and look for solutions that enable you to live by these values.

Some of the ads described in this section appear stunningly tasteless. They could have been worse, however. The Ad Graveyard (**http://zeldman.com/ad.html**) offers examples of proposed ads that never saw the light of day, for very obvious reasons.

Gangsta Rap

Rap artist Ice-T and his band, Body Count, recorded a song called *Cop Killer* in which the singer gleefully anticipates slitting a policeman's throat. (The lyrics to this song are available at **http://www.cleat.org/remember/TimeWarner/lyrics.html**.

Time Warner, Inc. produced this song and other gangsta rap recordings with violent and sexually degrading lyrics. Recorded music is an important source of profits for the company, which is struggling with a $15 billion debt and a depressed stock price. If Time Warner renounces rap albums, its reputation in the music business—and future profits—might suffer. This damage could spill over into the multimedia market, which is crucial to Time Warner's future.

Although Gerald M. Levin, the company chairman, tried to lead an industry-wide effort to label provocative lyrics, other recording studios refused to cooperate. The companies could not agree on a definition of unacceptable language. Meanwhile, William J. Bennett, who directs a conservative research center, and C. Delores Tucker, the chairwoman of the National Political Congress of Black Women, sent letters to Time Warner board members protesting the company's support of gangsta rap. "I'm sure they've all given little commencement speeches at their prep schools where they deplore violence in society," Mr. Bennett said. "Where do they think violence comes from?"[11] At Time Warner's annual meeting, Ms. Tucker attacked the board of directors for distributing gangsta rap. She accused the company of contributing to the moral corruption of African American men and women. "Shame on our family, Time Warner, for producing this filth," she said.[12] Mr. Levin responded that the company had to balance its commitment to freedom of expression against the music's potential harm. Some Time Warner albums carry a sticker warning parents. Is that enough?

What would you do if you were the chairman of Time Warner? He is concerned about several important stakeholders—shareholders, consumers, suppliers (rap musicians). Which decision would be best for him? For society? For Time Warner shareholders? How would he justify this decision? Even if Time Warner was not ashamed of *Cop Killer,* Ice-T apparently was. The original draft of this chapter included a sample of the lyrics, but Ice-T would not give permission for their use. His lawyer said that Ice-T was so embarrassed by the public's outraged response to the song that he now refuses all requests for permission, in the hope that the lyrics will be forgotten. Which items on the ethics checklist should Ice-T have considered before recording this song? (Ice-T is not the first artist accused of corrupting morals. For a history of controversial music over the last 50 years, tune in to **http://ericnuzum.com/banned/index.html**.)

ORGANIZATION'S RESPONSIBILITY TO ITS CUSTOMERS

When buying a product, customers often provide more than just money—they reveal personal information, such as their name, address, and credit card number. When surfing the Internet, customers may provide even more intimate information—such as their telephone number, e-mail address, Social Security number, medical history, or sexual preference. Under federal law, Internet operators cannot collect information from children under 13 without parental permission, but

[11] Mark Landler, "Time Warner Seeks a Delicate Balance in Rap Music Furor," *New York Times*, June 5, 1995, p. A1.

[12] Mark Landler, "Time Warner Is Again Criticized for Distributing 'Gangsta' Rap," *New York Times*, May 16, 1997, p. D5.

adults are fair game.[13] Do Web site operators have an ethical obligation to their adult customers?

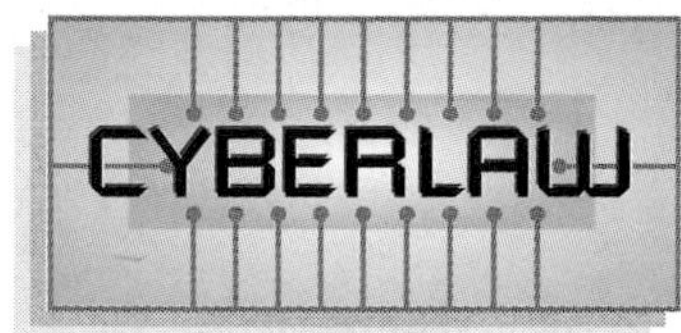

Looking for a new car, Dan Gillmor logged on to Autobytel.com. He gave his phone number so that dealers could call him with car prices. Having decided not to buy a car, he forgot all about his online search until several weeks later when he received a phone call at work offering him a new credit card. Without his knowledge, Autobytel had given his telephone number to the credit card company. No wonder that he refused when AT&T demanded his Social Security number before signing him up for cheap long-distance telephone rates over the Internet. To protect his privacy, he ultimately had to select another long-distance carrier.

This invasion of his Internet privacy caused Gillmor some inconvenience. The cost was higher for Naval Petty Officer Timothy McVeigh (who is no relation to the Oklahoma City bomber). When McVeigh filled out a user profile for America Online (AOL), he identified his marital status as "gay." In the midst of a Navy investigation into his sexual preference, a paralegal called AOL's toll-free number and simply asked the identity of the user who had filled out that profile. AOL told all and the Navy ordered McVeigh's dismissal.

Sitting in the privacy of your own home or office, typing into your computer, the Internet *feels* anonymous. It is anything but. E-commerce is booming and thousands of Web sites sell all sorts of stuff. Others give it away, in return for just a little data. You may not even be aware that you have supplied information. Suppose you send a blank e-mail to obtain a password. That e-mail may contain your name and the name of your employer. Or suppose you use your company e-mail account to log on to a pornographic Web site or a support group for victims of breast cancer. The name of your employer and your Internet Protocol address (which can be used to trace you) are available to the Web site operator.

Do companies have an ethical obligation to keep all this personal information confidential? In a survey of the 100 most frequented Web sites, only about half had any privacy policy at all. When policies do exist, they range from sturdy to anemic. *Wired* magazine's Web site states categorically that it "will not release your personal data to anyone else without your consent—period." Amazon.com "does not sell, trade, or rent your personal information to others. We may choose to do so in the future with trustworthy third parties, but you can tell us not to by sending a blank e-mail message to never@amazon.com." This interesting information is not displayed on the opening Web page, however, and is not easy to find. A Federal Trade Commission (FTC) study found that 92 percent of commercial Web sites collect personal information, but only 14 percent disclose their privacy policies. No surprise that only 61 percent of online users have ever seen a privacy notice when surfing the Web.

Ironically, Web site operators have an incentive *not* to disclose their privacy policies. Federal law does not require a policy, but if a Web site posts a policy and then violates it, the FTC will intervene because that constitutes an illegal, deceptive practice. Easier, and safer, then to have no policy at all. In response, a number of nonprofit organizations, such as TRUSTe (http://truste.org), now offer a seal of approval to companies that comply with their privacy standards. So far, however, only a few hundred Web sites have logged on to the TRUSTe plan.

The Electronic Privacy Information Center (http://www.epic.org) reveals the latest on Web privacy issues. For more about ethics on the Web, check in at

[13] Children's On-Line Privacy Protection Act of 1998.

http://www.netcheck.com. Visitors to this site can post complaints about and praise for Internet businesses. The site's philosophy is that "public pressure is the only real deterrent in this new frontier." Evidently, once posted, many complaints are resolved quickly. Which item on the ethics checklist does that recall?

ORGANIZATION'S RESPONSIBILITY TO ITS EMPLOYEES

Employee Safety

The following article gives a father's view on ethics in his daughter's workplace.

Early Saturday morning, my daughter Christian was robbed at knife-point. She was working the graveyard shift—alone—at a convenience store near her apartment. When Chrissie got this job, I was appalled. I told her she was crazy. But she is 19. She thinks she's invincible. She figured she could earn money and study during the quiet hours. Instead, she cleaned the storeroom and priced the Pop Tarts because that's what the late shift is supposed to do. With the store's lights ablaze, Chrissie strolled up and down the aisles with her pricing stamp; she was a kind of human guard dog, protecting the place against vandalism. She sold a couple of bucks worth of beer and gasoline and milk and cigarettes. And she listened to how quiet it can get in a darkened neighborhood in the middle of the night.

Then Saturday at about 3 A.M., some idiot high on drugs or wired with fear slipped into the store. He had wrapped his T-shirt around his face as a mask. He showed a knife and told Chrissie if she didn't open the cash register he would stab her or cut her face. She emptied the register. He told her to open the second register. She said it was empty. He got angry. He thought she was lying. He bounced on his toes and barked at her to open the second register. Just then, a customer drove up. The man with the knife grabbed the store money and fled.

I am so relieved she is alive, unhurt. At the same time, I am so angry with managers who hire people too young to know how vulnerable they are, and who put them, alone, in isolated, dangerous posts. I am so angry with the kind of corporate thinking that risks human life for clean floors and soup cans with price stickers. Those stores aren't open at 3 A.M. to sell cereal. They're open because the owners would have to pay someone to clean and stock anyway and you can't clean and stock when the aisles are filled with customers. So you might as well do it during the night. And you might as well keep the doors open, so you can pick up a buck or two from people who can't sleep or don't own beds. The "convenience" isn't the customer's; it's the owner's.

An executive at a convenience store chain (who wished to remain anonymous) responded this way:

> Look, this father has obviously been through a tough time and I don't blame him for being upset. But his allegations are absurd. First of all, convenience stores are called *convenience* stores because they're in busy locations and they're open all the time. That's our market niche. For many people who don't have cars, convenience stores are the only place they have to shop. We're a lifeline for them.
>
> In every store, we do a sales analysis for different time periods during the day. Believe me, we wouldn't be open at night if we weren't making money. As for cleaning and stocking—we can do that anytime. Heck, you see them cleaning and stocking in grocery stores during the day, don't you? As for marking goods, we don't even do that anymore. With all the automated technology, our cash registers read the little stripes on the can and that's all there is to it.
>
> Robberies do happen, but they are relatively rare, and we do everything we can to insure the safety of our employees and the security of our stores. You know, it costs us

a lot of money if one of our employees is harmed. In the case of a death, we typically settle for about $1 million, but some people have won jury verdicts of over $8 million dollars. Even when we have insurance, our premiums go sky high if we lose an employee. We try to keep our employees as secure as possible. We hire our own police to visit stores. We install "drop" safes into which employees can put money, but not get it out. We've added items like security cameras and panic buttons. We train our clerks to keep only $30 or $40 in the registers. That's why convenience store robberies have declined two percent over the last four years, while robberies in fast-food chains are way up, doubling in some cities.

One last point. You know, we're human. We hate it when our employees are hurt. And we'll do whatever we can to keep them safe—short of inconveniencing our customers.[14]

What ethical obligations do managers of convenience stores owe their employees? Their customers?

Third Shift Workers

To find out about other ethical dilemmas, we spoke with Rebecca Jewett about some of the issues she faced as president of Chadwick's of Boston. Chadwick's is a catalog company specializing in discount clothes. The company employs 2,000 people and has sales of nearly $300 million. Jewett is a graduate of Wellesley College and Harvard Business School.

QUESTION: What ethical dilemmas have you faced in dealing with your employees?

JEWETT: Let me give you one example. We used to run a third shift, from 11 P.M. to 7 A.M., that packed orders. It's a tough shift to run. There's a lot of very poor productivity. It's a shift where people do things like write graffiti on bathroom doors. It makes it very, very difficult to keep the building clean, which is important for everybody else. There's also less management on the third shift. The results just weren't worth the amount we were having to spend. So we decided to close down that shift.

QUESTION: One could argue that you had no special obligation to these employees. After all, they had been disruptive and destructive. What did you do?

JEWETT: We could have just laid them off, that's true. Our other choice was to offer them jobs on the first or second shift. We didn't really need them there. It wouldn't have created a financial crisis, but it would have put us in an awkward position. We also had to decide how much advance notice to give them. We could have waited until the last day if we wanted to.

QUESTION: What did you do?

JEWETT: In the end, we offered all of the associates jobs on the first or second shift. We also gave them one month's notice so they would have plenty of time to think things through and make arrangements. There were one or two women who had child care problems during the day, so we let them switch to answering the phones because that department still had a third shift.

QUESTION: How did this decision affect your stakeholders?

JEWETT: It may have hurt financial results, and therefore shareholders, in the short run. But it was nonetheless a good decision for the company because we'll get known as an employer who cares about its associates. What you want to do is to treat people fairly and openly. I try to understand the needs of the associates and our needs as a company and then find the common ground. I always believe that there is a win-win situation for us both.

---

[14] "Convenience Store Victimizes," Collin Conner writing in the *St. Petersburg Times*, June 7, 1989, p. 2. Reprinted by permission. *St. Petersburg Times*. Copyright 1989.

Did Jewett make the best decision? How do her actions fit into the ethics checklist?

ORGANIZATION'S RESPONSIBILITY TO ITS SHAREHOLDERS

In Japan, a CEO makes 20 to 25 times the pay of an average worker, compared with 30 to 35 times in Germany and 40 times in England. As we saw at the beginning of the chapter, the CEO of Diebold earns $2.37 million a year, while a factory worker receives only $20,654. The executive's salary is 115 times that of the worker. By international standards the Diebold CEO is overpaid, but his salary looks more modest in comparison with other American companies. The nation's top CEOs average $8.6 million annually, plus perks. This salary is 209 times the pay of the typical worker. American executives also have a lower tax rate than their overseas counterparts, so they take home an even larger share of their pay.

CEO salaries are generally set by a subcommittee of the board of directors. In theory, the subcommittee's goal should be to pay the minimum necessary to attract competent executives. In reality, however, most members of compensation committees are executives from other companies. Their real incentive may be to bid up the "going rate" for executive jobs. Evidence seems to suggest that executive pay has only a tenuous relationship to company performance. When 3M's shares declined 1 percent in value (during a year in which the stock market roared up 33 percent), CEO Livio DeSimone received a 40 percent pay increase to $6 million. Eastman Kodak also had a difficult year as it lost market share, laid off 19,000 workers, earned lower profits, and saw its stock price lag. CEO George Fisher fared better. The board of directors forgave him $1.82 million in interest on loans and granted him stock options worth $57 million.

Even salary plans that base compensation on performance do not always work as shareholders might wish. Under the typical performance plan, executives start with a large base salary that is unrelated to performance. This generous base may encourage them to take undue risks with the company. If the risk pays off, they will make a fortune; if not, they still pocket their large base salary, and shareholders bear the brunt of any disaster. Moreover, there is no obvious best method for evaluating performance. Should pay be based on profits? Stock prices? The overall economy may have as much impact on the company's results as the CEO's performance does. In a booming market, all stock prices tend to rise regardless of the CEO's efforts.

Graef Crystal, a leading authority on executive compensation, has this to say: "If you already have your foot to the floor, if I put any more gas in the tank, I can't go any faster. The only person who benefits from paying a CEO $20 million is his broker."[15]

According to Crystal, there is a relationship between pay and performance for CEOs with less than 10 years of tenure, but not for those who have been at the helm longer. "My theory is that if you've been a CEO for more than ten years, that you have personally appointed virtually every member of the board of directors," he said. "They're your creatures. They're the people you go golfing with, the people who thank you for putting them on the board, so whether or not you play the game fairly is up to what's inside you."[16] For more on executive compensation, pay attention to the Crystal Report Online at **http://www.crystalreport.com**.

Is there a solution to this problem? What are a CEO's ethical obligations when it comes to pay?

---

[15] Sean Keeler, "CEOs Earn Bigger Bucks in U.S. than in Japan, Germany, U.K.," *Montreal Gazette*, Oct. 4, 1994, p. D8.

[16] Ibid.

ORGANIZATION'S RESPONSIBILITY OVERSEAS

An American company's ethical obligations do not end at the border. What ethical duties does an American manager owe to stakeholders in countries where the culture and economic circumstances are very different?

Here is a typical story from Guatemala:

> My father left home a long time ago. My mother supported me and my five brothers and sisters by selling tortillas and corn. Our house was a tin shack on the side of the road. We were crowded with all of us in one room, especially when it rained and the roof and sides leaked. There were hundreds of squatters in the neighborhood, but one day the police came and cleared us all out. The owners of the land said we couldn't come back unless we paid rent. How could we afford that? I was 12 and my mother said it was time for me to work. But most people won't hire children. Lots of other kids shine shoes or beg, but I heard that the maquila [clothing factory] was willing to hire children if we would work as hard as older people.
>
> I can keep up with the grown-ups. We work from 6:00 in the morning to 6:30 at night, with half an hour break at noon. We have no other breaks the whole rest of the day. If I don't work fast enough, they hit me, not too hard, and threaten to fire me. Sometimes, if there is too much work to do, they'll lock the doors and not let us out until everything is finished.
>
> I'm always really tired at the end of the day and in the morning, too. But I earn $30 a week and without that money, we would not have enough to eat. My mother hopes all of my brothers and sisters can get jobs in the factory, too.
>
> Of course, I'd rather be in school where I could wear a uniform and have friends. Then I could get a job as a clerk at the medical clinic. I would find people's files and tell them how long before the doctor could see them.

American companies have invested more than $56 billion in developing countries. This sum has more than tripled in the last 15 years. Government officials and company executives alike assert that commerce with developing countries is crucial to U.S. prosperity. And the benefit is not one-sided: economists argue that low-wage plants are an essential first step in the modernization of developing countries. Industrialization in Indonesia has meant that only one-third of the children are malnourished, down from one-half. In response to international complaints about working conditions, textile firms in Bangladesh fired 30,000 young workers. Many of these children turned to prostitution or other industries like welding, where conditions are far more dangerous. Jeffrey Sachs, a leading economist and adviser to developing nations, says, "My concern is not that there are too many sweatshops but that there are too few. Those are precisely the jobs that were the steppingstone for Singapore and Hong Kong and those are the jobs that have to come to Africa to get them out of their backbreaking rural poverty."[17]

What are the ethical obligations of a company that uses foreign workers?

Many American companies, including such well-known names as Nike, Wal-Mart, Sears, Reebok, The Gap, Liz Claiborne, and Eddie Bauer, have been under attack for making goods in overseas sweatshops. Nike was particularly criticized for giving multimillion dollar endorsement contracts to stars such as Tiger Woods even as it pays its workers in China and Vietnam less than $2 a day and those in Indonesia less than $1 a day. Critics argue that workers in these countries need $3 a day to cover basic food, shelter, and clothing. Nike's chairman, Philip Knight, admitted, "The Nike product has become synonymous with slave wages, forced overtime and arbitrary abuse."[18] In response, Nike has agreed to increase the

---

[17] Allen R. Meyerson, "In Principle, a Case for More 'Sweatshops,'" *New York Times*, June 22, 1997, p. E5.

[18] Bob Herbert, "Nike Blinks," *New York Times*, May 21, 1998, p. A37.

minimum age for new workers to 18, raise air-quality controls and safety rules to U.S. levels, and allow independent monitoring groups into Nike factories. It has made no promise, however, to raise wages.

What ethical obligations do U.S. companies have to overseas workers? What decisions would you make if you were Philip Knight?

EMPLOYEES' RESPONSIBILITY TO THEIR ORGANIZATION

Joya is the head of the personal insurance division of a large insurance company. She is one of the few women in her industry to reach such a high level. Six months before, she was almost promoted to vice-president, but she lost out to Bill. He is now her boss, and she is determined to make the best of it. She and other department heads have an annual meeting with Bill to award raises and bonuses to all the mid-level managers in their departments. At this year's meeting, they will also discuss who should be promoted to head the marine insurance division. This decision is important to the firm because the marine division is large and profitable. The decision is also important to other department heads because they all work closely together. One difficult person can make everyone's life miserable. The promotion will mean a substantial raise to the person chosen.

In Joya's opinion, Ichiro is the most qualified person for this position. However, she knows that Bill will not support him. In Bill's view, Ichiro has two strikes against him: he is Japanese and a relatively recent immigrant to the United States. The CEO of the company has taken Ichiro with him several times on trips to Japan to explore the possibility of entering the Japanese market. Bill resents what he perceives as special treatment for Ichiro.

Although Joya is well aware of Bill's biases, she is nonetheless astonished by his behavior at the meeting. When Ichiro's name comes up as a potential candidate for promotion, Bill announces that the middle managers in the marine insurance division strongly object to Ichiro because of his drinking problem. Joya knows that this is all nonsense—Ichiro does not have a drinking problem and the mid-managers in his department think he would be a terrific choice. In her view, Bill is outright lying.

Based on Bill's false information, the other department heads agree that the promotion should go to Jim, who happens to be a friend of Bill's. Joya knows that Jim is unpopular in his division because of his harsh, demanding style. She thinks that his appointment as department head will be disastrous. At the end of the meeting, a satisfied Bill says that he will report the sense of the meeting to the CEO. He is confident that Jim will get the job.

Joya knows the CEO (they exchange pleasantries when passing in the hallways), but they have no regularly scheduled meetings. Nor is Joya likely to have the opportunity to mention Bill's behavior in a casual way. She is concerned that if she reports Bill is lying, the CEO will think she is causing trouble out of jealousy that Bill got the job she wanted.

What should Joya do?

CHAPTER CONCLUSION

Even employees who are ethical in their personal lives may find it difficult to uphold their standards at work if those around them behave differently. Managers wonder what they can do to create an ethical environment in their companies. To help foster a sense of ethics within their organizations, 90 percent of Fortune 500 companies and almost half of all other U.S. companies have developed their own formal ethics codes. For instance, Johnson & Johnson's corporate credo states that managers must make "just and ethical decisions" and all employees must be "good citizens." Many companies have instituted formal ethics training programs for their employees.

In the end, however, the surest way to infuse ethics throughout an organization is for top executives to behave ethically themselves. Few employees will bother to "do the right thing" unless they observe that their bosses value and support such behavior. To ensure a more ethical world, managers must be an example for others, both within and outside their organizations.

For further discussion and updates on ethical issues, check in at http://ethics.acusd.edu/index.html.

CHAPTER REVIEW

1. There are at least three reasons to be concerned about ethics in a business environment:
   - Society as a whole benefits from ethical behavior.
   - People feel better when they behave ethically.
   - Unethical behavior can be very costly.
2. The ethics checklist:
   - What are the facts?
   - What are the critical issues?
   - Who are the stakeholders?
   - What are the alternatives?
   - What are the ethical implications of each alternative?
     - Is it legal?
     - How would it look in the light of day?
     - What are the consequences?
     - Does it violate important values?
     - Does it violate the Golden Rule?
     - Is it just?
     - Has the process been fair?
   - Is more than one alternative right?
     - Which values are in conflict?
     - Which of these values are most important?
     - Can you find an alternative that is consistent with your values?

PRACTICE TEST

1. Interview subject Rebecca Jewett told this story of her life as an MBA student 15 years ago:

> During the spring of my first year, I took a Business Policy class. One of the young men in the class hung a bigger than life-size poster in the back of the room. It was a naked woman chained to a tree next to a Paul Bunyan-type man, fully-clothed in a flannel jacket, with a chain saw. He was starting to de-limb her. The class broke up. The professor was standing there doubled over in laughter. There were 85 men guffawing away as if it were the funniest thing they'd ever seen. The women just sat there with their mouths open.

Did this professor and these students behave ethically? What would you consider to be ethical behavior in this circumstance for the men, the women, and the professor?

2. An executive gave this account of the dilemma he faced in hiring undocumented workers:

> We have a big temporary workforce. At a time when the labor market was very tight, a guy came to us who runs a temporary agency for Vietnamese workers. He told us he could supply 40 Vietnamese any time. We hired them and, in fact, they were fabulous employees, they had twice the productivity of our best workers. We loved them. But when we asked him if every one of them was legally able to work here, he couldn't produce green cards.

It was then legal to hire workers without green cards. Would it have been ethical?

3. Executives were considering the possibility of moving their company to a different state. They wanted to determine if employees would be willing to relocate, but they did not want the employees to know the company was contemplating a move because the final decision had not yet been made. Instead of asking the employees directly, the company hired a firm to carry out a telephone survey. When calling the employees, these "pollsters" pretended to be conducting a public opinion poll and identified themselves as working for the new state's Chamber of Commerce. Has this company behaved in an ethical manner? Would there have been a better way to obtain this information?

4. Mark is an executive for a multinational office equipment company that would like to enter the potentially vast Chinese market. However, the official tariffs on office equipment imported into China are so high that these goods are uncompetitive in the local market. Mark discovers, however, that many companies sell their goods to importers off-shore (typically in Hong Kong). These importers then negotiate "special" tariff rates with Chinese officials. Because these custom officials are under pressure to meet revenue targets, sometimes they are willing to negotiate lower, unofficial rates. What would you do if you were Mark?

5. Professor Milton Friedman, a Nobel laureate in economics, has said: "The one and only social responsibility of business is to increase its profits." Dayton Hudson, a department store chain, says in its corporate constitution, "The business of business is serving society, not just making money." Which is it?

6. H. B. Fuller Co. of St. Paul is a leading manufacturer of industrial glues. Its mission statement says the company "will conduct business legally and ethically." It has endowed a university chair in Business Ethics and donates 5 percent of its profits to charity. But now it is under attack for selling its shoemakers' glue, Resistol, in Central America. Many homeless children in these countries have become addicted to Resistol's fumes. So widespread is the problem that glue-sniffers in Central America are called "resistoleros." Glue manufacturers in Europe have added a foul-smelling oil to their glue that discourages abusers. Fuller fears that the smell may also discourage legitimate users. What should Fuller do?

7. According to the Electronic Industries Association, questionable returns have become the toughest problem plaguing the consumer electronics industry. Some consumers purchase electronic equipment to use once or twice for a special occasion and then return it—a radar detector for a weekend getaway or a camcorder to videotape a wedding. Or a customer might return a cordless telephone because he cannot figure out how it works. The retailer's staff lacks the expertise to help, so they refund the customer's money and ship the phone back to the manufacturer labeled as defective. Excessive and unwarranted returns force manufacturers to repackage and reship perfectly good products, imposing extra costs that squeeze their profits and raise prices to consumers. One retailer returned a cordless telephone that was two years old and had been chewed up by a dog. What ethical obligations do consumers and retailers have in these circumstances?

8. Consider this complaint from an ethics professor:

> I make my living teaching and writing about ethics. . . . But in our own world—in our departments of philosophy and religious studies and medical humanities and ethics institutes—what happens?

- Job openings [for instructors] are announced for positions that are already earmarked for specific persons. . . . [O]ver half the positions announced in the official employment newsletter for the American Academy of Religion were not "real."
- It is extremely common for letters of application, even those responding to announced openings, to go without acknowledgment.
- There are numerous instances of candidates who are brought to campus for interviews and who wait in vain to hear anything from their prospective employers. When the candidates finally call, embarrassed but desperate, they are told, "Oh, that position has been filled."

Do recruiters have any ethical obligations to job candidates?

9. Six months ago, Todd, David, and Stacey joined a large, prestigious accounting firm in Houston. On paper, these three novices look similar and each graduated from a top MBA program. All three were assigned to work for the same client, a national restaurant chain. They quickly became fast friends and often lunched together. One day, a senior manager in the firm stopped by the conference room where Todd and David were working to ask if they would like to join him for lunch at the posh Hunter Club nearby. David said, "Thanks, that'd be great, but we usually eat lunch with Stacey. Could she come, too?" The manager hemmed and hawed for a minute, shifted his weight from one foot to the other, and finally said, "The Hunter Club doesn't allow women at lunch." What should Todd and David do?

10. Genentech, Inc. manufactures Protropin, a genetically engineered version of the human growth hormone. This drug's purpose is to enhance the growth of short children. Protropin is an important product for Genentech, accounting for more than one-third of the company's total revenue of $217 million. Although the drug is approved for the treatment of children whose bodies make inadequate quantities of growth hormone, many doctors prescribe it for children with normal amounts of growth hormone who simply happen to be short. There is no firm evidence that the drug actually increases growth for short children with normal growth hormone. Moreover, many people question whether it is appropriate to prescribe such a powerful drug for cosmetic reasons, especially when the drug may not work. Nor is there proof that it is safe over the long term. Is Genentech behaving ethically? Should it discourage doctors from prescribing the drug to normal, short children?

INTERNET RESEARCH PROBLEM

Go to **http://www.mapnp.org/library/ethics/ethxgde.htm** and click on *Ethics Tools: Resolving Ethical Dilemmas (with Real-to-Life Examples)*. Outline the steps you would take to resolve one of these dilemmas. Use the ethics checklist in this chapter to guide you.

You can find further practice problems in the Online Quiz at http://beatty.westbuslaw.com or in the Study Guide that accompanies this text.

UNIT 2

CONTRACTS

CHAPTER 10

INTRODUCTION TO CONTRACTS

In Marina del Rey, California, Cassandra sits on the sunny deck of her waterside condominium, sipping a *mocha latte* while watching spinnakers fill with the warm Pacific wind. She has just received an offer of $1.7 million to buy her condominium. Cassandra has decided to counteroffer for $1.9 million. She is in high spirits because she assumes that at the very worst she has $1.7 million guaranteed, and that represents a huge profit to her. Cassandra plans to buy a cheaper house in North Carolina and invest her profits so that she can retire early. She opens the newspaper, notices a headline "Hard Body Threatens Suit," and turns the page, thinking that a corporate lawsuit in Ohio is of no concern to her. She is mistaken and may learn some hard lessons about contract law.

A year earlier, Jerusalem Steel had signed a contract with Hard Body, a manufacturer of truck and bus bodies. Jerusalem was to deliver 20,000 tons of steel to Hard Body's plant in Joy, Ohio. Hard Body relied on the contract, hiring 300 additional workers even before the steel was delivered, so that the plant would be geared up and ready to produce buses when the metal arrived. To help deal with the new workers, Hard Body offered a mid-level personnel job to Nicole. Hard Body told Nicole, "Don't worry, we expect your job to last forever." Nicole, in turn, relied on that statement to quit her old job in Minneapolis, move to Joy, and sign an

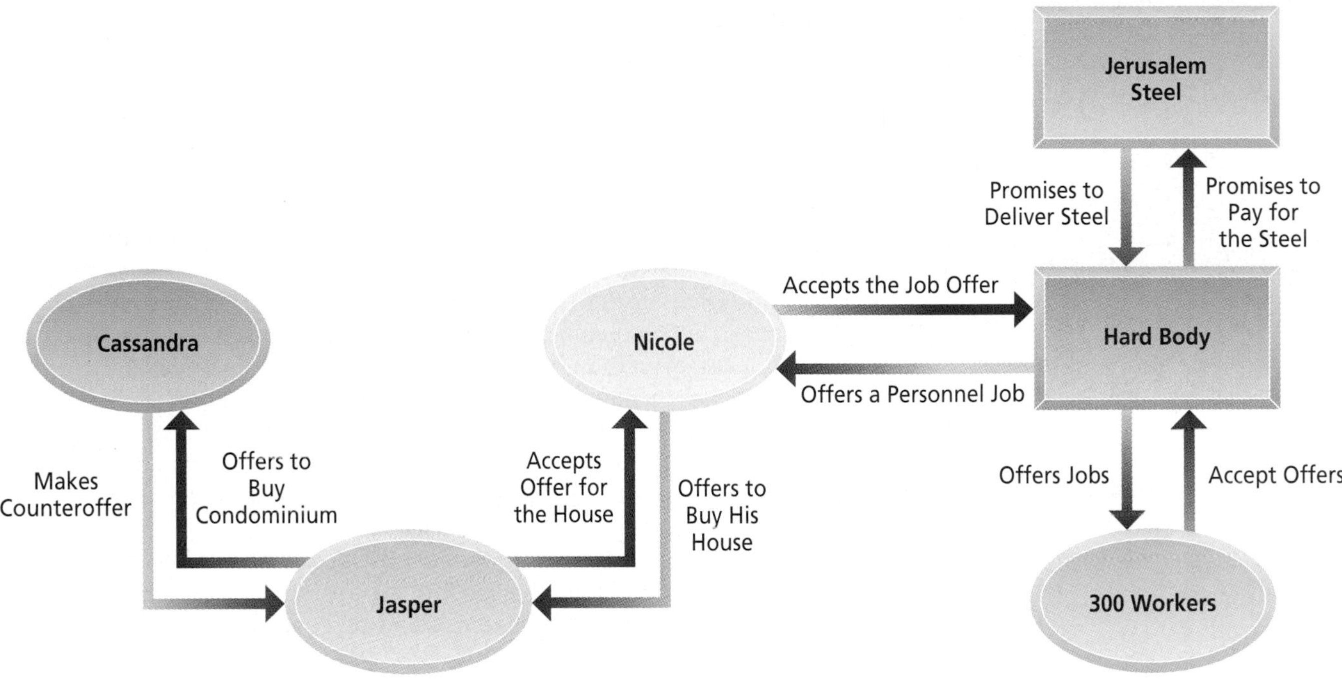

Exhibit 10.1
Contracts are intended to make business matters more predictable. Frequently, a series of contracts becomes mutually dependent.

agreement with Jasper to purchase his house for $450,000. Based on that sales contract, Jasper phoned his offer to Cassandra's real estate agent for $1.7 million. See Exhibit 10.1.

But in the year since Jerusalem signed its contract, the price of the specified steel has gone up 60 percent. Jerusalem now refuses to deliver the steel unless the price is renegotiated. Hard Body has insisted on the original contract price. Hard Body cannot afford to buy steel at the current price, which would make its deal to produce buses unprofitable. If Hard Body receives no steel, does it have a valid lawsuit against Jerusalem? May it force Jerusalem to deliver the steel? If it cannot get steel, may it lay off the newly hired workers? May it fire Nicole, or does she have a job for life? If Nicole loses her paycheck, will the law force her to buy a house she no longer wants? Jasper will never get such a good price from anyone else, because with no work at Hard Body property prices in Joy will plummet. May Jasper refuse to buy Cassandra's condo, or is he committed for $1.7 million?

CONTRACTS

THE PURPOSE OF A CONTRACT

Throughout this unit on contracts, we will consider issues like those raised in the Cassandra–Hard Body story. This long chain of mutually dependent people and companies exemplifies not only the law of contracts but the *purpose* of contracts. Parties enter into contracts attempting to control their future. **Contracts exist to make business matters more predictable.** Most contracts work out precisely as the parties intended because the parties fulfill their obligations. Most—but not all. In this unit we will study contracts that have gone wrong. We look at these errant deals to learn how to avoid the problems they manifest.

JUDICIAL ACTIVISM VERSUS JUDICIAL RESTRAINT

We will see that *the courts will not always do what we expect*. In most contract cases, it is true, judges do their best simply to enforce whatever terms the parties have agreed to. Even if the contract results in serious harm to one party, a court will generally enforce it. This is **judicial restraint**—a court taking a relatively passive role and requiring the parties to fulfill whatever obligations they agreed to, whether the deal was wise or foolish. Judges often say that it is not their job to rewrite a deal that the parties crafted. For example, if a real estate developer contracts with a builder to erect 10 expensive homes, but the housing market collapses before construction begins, the developer is still obligated to pay the builder for the houses, even though the expense will cause him devastating losses. Judicial restraint makes the law **less flexible but more predictable.**

On the other hand, some courts practice **judicial activism**. In contract law, this means that a court will ignore certain provisions of a contract, or an entire contract, if the judge believes that enforcing the deal would be unjust. Further, a court may be willing to artificially create a contract where none really existed, if the judge believes that is the only way to avoid injustice. Since judicial activism is always phrased in terms of "doing justice," it has an initial appeal. For example, when one party deceives the other with a misleading contract, it may be appropriate for a court to rewrite the agreement. But when a court practices judicial activism, it may diminish our ability to control our own future—which is the whole point of creating a contract. Judicial activism makes the law **more flexible but less predictable.** In this unit on contracts we look at many examples of both judicial activism and restraint.

ISSUES (AND ANSWERS)

The chain of contracts connecting Jerusalem Steel and Cassandra illustrates various contract problems. We consider each problem in detail in this unit, but here we briefly identify the issues and summarize the answers. **A contract has four elements:**

- **Agreement**. One party must make a valid offer, and the other party must accept it.
- **Consideration**. There has to be bargaining that leads to an exchange between the parties.
- **Legality**. The contract must be for a lawful purpose.
- **Capacity**. The parties must be adults of sound mind.

The chapters that follow cover each of the elements in sequence. Contract cases often raise several other important issues, which we examine in later chapters:

- **Consent**. Neither party may trick or force the other into the agreement.
- **Written Contracts**. Some contracts must be in writing to be enforceable.
- **Third Party Interests**. Some contracts affect people other than the parties themselves.
- **Performance and Discharge**. If a party fully accomplishes what the contract requires, his duties are discharged.
- **Remedies**. A court will award money or other relief to a party injured by a breach of contract.

When we apply these principles to the problem at this chapter's beginning, we see that Jerusalem Steel is almost certainly bound by its agreement. A rise in price is generally no excuse to walk away from a contract. Hard Body has made the bargain precisely to protect itself in case of a price rise. These are issues of offer and acceptance, consideration, and discharge. Can Hard Body force Jerusalem to deliver the steel? Probably not, as we learn in Chapter 18, on remedies. But Hard Body might be able to block Jerusalem from delivering the steel anywhere else. And Hard Body almost certainly is entitled to money damages if it is forced to buy steel at higher prices. If Hard Body is unable to obtain steel in the rising market, may it lay off its workers? Very likely, as Chapter 11, on agreement, indicates. Can it fire Nicole? The statement about expecting her job to last forever almost certainly creates no lifetime employment. In fact, even if Nicole has begun her job, the company can probably terminate her. What about the fact that she quit her job in reliance on this one? That raises an issue called promissory estoppel, which we discuss later in this chapter; it may or may not help Nicole, depending on the facts.

Must Nicole go through with her purchase of Jasper's house? Probably, as Chapters 15 and 18, on written contracts and remedies, will demonstrate. Do Jasper and Cassandra have a contract? No, because the agreement must be in writing to be enforceable. Even if there is no settled price, is Cassandra safe in assuming she has $1.7 million guaranteed? Not at all, as Chapter 11, on agreement, shows. If Cassandra had read this unit, she would be faxing a written contract to Jasper rather than waiting for her *latte* to cool.

ALL SHAPES AND SIZES

Some contracts are small. If you agree to sell your bicycle to your roommate for $75 at the end of the academic year, that is an enforceable agreement. But contracts can also be large. US Airways agreed to buy 400 narrow-body jets from Airbus Industrie, the European aircraft manufacturer. The value of the agreement? About $14 *billion*. Airbus was ecstatic, but not Boeing Aircraft Corp., its American competitor, which filed suit, claiming that US Airways had already signed a contract to purchase Boeing jets.

Many contracts involve public issues. When the owner of the Pittsburgh Pirates announced that he might sell the baseball team to out-of-town buyers, a group of local businesses banded together to buy the team and keep it in their city. The mayor publicly promised $25 million in city aid to enable the local businesses to make the purchase. But after the purchase, the city refused to honor the mayor's commitment. A court later ruled that the mayor's promise was unenforceable because he lacked the authority to make it. (The U.S. government contracts for more goods and services than any other organization in the world. To examine a few of the countless opportunities to sell things to Uncle Sam, browse through **http://www.fedmarket.com/**.)

Other contracts concern intensely private matters. Mary Beth Whitehead signed a contract with William and Elizabeth Stern, of New Jersey. For a fee of $10,000, Whitehead agreed to be impregnated with Mr. Stern's sperm, carry the baby to term, and then deliver it to the Sterns for adoption. But when little Melissa was born, Whitehead changed her mind and fled to Florida with the baby. The Sterns sued for breach of contract. Surrogacy contracts now lead to over 500 births per year. Are the contracts immoral? Should they be illegal? Are there limits to what one person may pay another to do? The New Jersey Supreme Court, the first to rule on the issue, declared the contract illegal and void. The court nonetheless awarded Melissa to the Sterns, saying that it was in the child's best interest to live with them. There will be many more rulings, in other states, before the legal status of surrogacy contracts is resolved.

makers are urging that Pennsylvania simply stop construction of the new system. Is Pennsylvania allowed to get out of the contract because its legislators now believe the whole system is unwise?

3. Central Maine Power Co. made a promotional offer in which it promised to pay a substantial sum to any homeowner or builder who constructed new housing heated with electricity. Motel Services, Inc., which was building a small housing project for the city of Waterville, Maine, decided to install electrical heat in the units in order to qualify for the offer. It built the units and requested payment for the full amount of the promotional offer. Is Central Maine obligated to pay? Why or why not?

4. Interactive Data Corp. hired Daniel Foley as an assistant product manager at a starting salary of $18,500. Over the next six years Interactive steadily promoted Foley until he became Los Angeles branch manager at a salary of $56,116. Interactive's officers repeatedly told Foley that he would have his job as long as his performance was adequate. In addition, Interactive distributed an employee handbook that specified "termination guidelines," including a mandatory seven-step pre-termination procedure. Two years later Foley learned that his recently hired supervisor, Robert Kuhne, was under investigation by the FBI for embezzlement at his previous job. Foley reported this to Interactive officers. Shortly thereafter, Interactive fired Foley. He sued, claiming that Interactive could only fire him for good cause, after the seven-step procedure. What kind of a claim is he making? Should he succeed?

5. The Hoffmans owned and operated a successful small bakery and grocery store. They spoke with Lukowitz, an agent of Red Owl Stores, who told them that for $18,000 Red Owl would build a store and fully stock it for them. The Hoffmans sold their bakery and grocery store and purchased a lot on which Red Owl was to build the store. Lukowitz then told Hoffman that the price had gone up to $26,000. The Hoffmans borrowed the extra money from relatives, but then Lukowitz informed them that the cost would be $34,000. Negotiations broke off and the Hoffmans sued. The court determined that there was no contract because too many details had not been worked out—the size of the store, its design, and the cost of constructing it. Can the Hoffmans recover any money?

6. **RIGHT & WRONG** You want to lease your automobile to a friend for the summer but do not want to pay a lawyer to draw up the lease. Joanna, a neighbor, is in law school. She is not licensed to practice law. She offers to draft a lease for you for $100, and you unwisely accept. Later, you refuse to pay her fee and she sues to collect. Who will win the lawsuit, and why? Apart from the law, was it morally right for the law student to try to help out by drafting the lease? Was she acting helpfully, or foolishly, or fraudulently? Is it just for you to agree to her fee and then refuse to pay it? What is society's interest in this dispute? Should a court be more concerned with the ethical issue raised by the conduct of the two parties or with the social consequences of this agreement?

7. Describe the role each of the following plays in contract law: the common law, the UCC, and the Restatement (Second) of Contracts.

8. **YOU BE THE JUDGE WRITING PROBLEM** John Stevens owned a dilapidated apartment that he rented to James and Cora Chesney for a low rent. The Chesneys began to remodel and rehabilitate the unit. Over a four-year period, they installed two new bathrooms, carpeted the floors, installed new septic and heating systems, and rewired, replumbed, and painted. Stevens periodically stopped by and saw the work in progress. The Chesneys transformed the unit into a respectable apartment. Three years after their work was done, Stevens served the Chesneys with an eviction notice. The Chesneys counterclaimed, seeking the value of the work they had done. Are they entitled to it? **Argument for Stevens:** Mr. Stevens is willing to pay the Chesneys exactly the amount he *agreed* to pay: nothing. The parties never contracted for the Chesneys to fix up the apartment. In fact, they never even *discussed* such an agreement. The Chesneys are making the absurd argument that anyone who chooses to perform certain work, without *ever discussing it* with another party, can finish the job and then charge it to the other person. If the Chesneys expected to get paid, obviously they should have said so. If the court were to allow this claim, it would be inviting other tenants to make improvements and then bill the landlord. The law has never been so foolish. **Argument for the Chesneys:** The law of quasi-contract was crafted for cases exactly like this. The Chesneys have given an enormous benefit to Stevens by transforming the apartment and enabling him to rent it at greater profit for many years to come. Stevens saw the work being done and understood that the Chesneys expected some compensation for these major renovations. If Stevens never intended to pay the fair value of the work, he should have stopped the couple from doing the work or notified them that there would be no compensation. It would be unjust to allow the landlord to seize the value of the work, evict the tenants who did it, and pay nothing.

9. Honeywell, Inc. and Minolta Camera Co. had a contract providing that Honeywell would give to Minolta various technical information on the design of a specialized camera lens. Minolta would have the right to use the information in its cameras provided that Minolta also used certain Honeywell parts in its cameras. Honeywell delivered to Minolta numerous technical documents, computer software, and test equipment, and Honeywell engineers met with Minolta engineers at least 20 times to discuss the equipment. Several years later, Honeywell sued, claiming that Minolta had taken the design information but failed to use Honeywell parts in its cameras. Minolta moved to dismiss, claiming that the UCC required lawsuits concerning the sale of goods to be filed within four years of the breach and that this lawsuit was too late. Honeywell answered that the UCC did not apply and that therefore Minnesota's six-year statute of limitations governed. Who is right?

10. Explain the difference between judicial restraint and judicial activism in contract law.

INTERNET RESEARCH PROBLEM

Visit http://www.law.cornell.edu/states/listing.html. Select a state. Then click on *judicial opinions.* Search for a case concerning "quasi-contract." What are the details of the quasi-contract dispute? Who won and why?

You can find further practice problems in the Online Quiz at http://beatty.westbuslaw.com or in the Study Guide that accompanies this text.

CHAPTER 11

AGREEMENT

Interior. A glitzy café, New York. Evening. Bob, a famous director, and Katrina, a glamorous actress, sit at a table, near a wall of glass looking onto a New York sidewalk that is filled with life and motion. Bob sips a margarita while carefully eyeing Katrina. Katrina stares at her wine glass.

BOB (smiling confidently): *Body Work* is going to be huge—for the right actress. I know a film that's gonna gross a hundred million when I'm holding one. I'm holding one.

KATRINA (perking up at the mention of money): It *is* quirky. It's fun. And she's very strong, very real.

BOB: She's you. That's why we're sitting here. We start shooting in seven months.

KATRINA (edging away from the table): I have a few questions. That nude scene.

BOB: The one on the toboggan run?

KATRINA: *That* one was O.K. But the one in the poultry factory—very explicit. I don't work nude.

BOB: It's not really nude. Think of all those feathers fluttering around.

KATRINA: It's nude.

BOB: We'll work it out. This is a romantic comedy, not tawdry exploitation. Katrina, we're talking $2.5 million. A little accommodation, please. $600,000 up front, and the rest deferred, the usual percentages.

KATRINA: Bob, my fee is $3 million. As you know. That hasn't changed.

Katrina picks up her drink, doesn't sip it, places it on the coaster, using both hands to center it perfectly. He waits, as she stares at it in silence.

BOB: We're shooting in Santa Fe, the weather will be perfect. You have a suite at the Excelsior plus a trailer on location.

KATRINA: I should talk with my agent. I'd need something in writing about the nude scene, the fee, percentages—all the business stuff. I never sign without talking to her.

Bob shrugs and sits back.

KATRINA (made anxious by the silence): I love the character, I really do.

BOB: You and several others love her. (That jolts her.) Agents can wait. I have to put this together fast. We can get you the details you want in writing. *Body Work* is going to be bigger than *Sleepless*.

That one hooks her. She looks at Bob. He nods reassuringly. Bob sticks out his hand, smiling. Katrina hesitates, lets go of her drink, and SHAKES HANDS, looking unsure. Bob signals for the check.

Do Bob and Katrina have a deal? *They* seem to think so. But is her fee $2.5 million or $3 million? What if Katrina demands that all nude scenes be taken out, and Bob refuses? Must she still act in the film? Or suppose her agent convinces her that *Body Work* is no good even with changes. Has Katrina committed herself? What if Bob auditions another actress the next day, likes her, and signs her? Does he owe Katrina her fee? Or suppose Bob learns that the funding has fallen apart and there will be no film. Is Katrina entitled to her money?

Bob and Katrina have acted out a classic problem in *agreement*, one of the basic issues in contract law. Their lack of clarity means that disputes are likely and lawsuits possible. Similar bargaining goes on every day around the country and around the world, and the problems created are too frequently resolved in court. Some of the negotiating is done in person; more is done over the phone, by fax, by business form—or all of them combined. This chapter highlights the most common sources of misunderstanding and litigation so that you can avoid making deals you never intended—or "deals" that you cannot enforce.

There almost certainly is no contract between Bob and Katrina. Bob's offer was unclear. Even if it was valid, Katrina counteroffered. When they shook hands, it is impossible to know what terms each had in mind.

MEETING OF THE MINDS

As courts dissect a negotiation that has gone awry, they examine the intent of the parties. **The parties can form a contract only if they had a meeting of the minds.** This requires that they (1) understood each other and (2) intended to reach an agreement.

Keep in mind that judges must make *objective assessments* of the respective intent of each party. A court will not try to get inside Katrina's head and decide what she was thinking as she shook hands. It will look at the handshake *objectively*, deciding how a reasonable person would interpret the words and conduct. Katrina may honestly have meant to conclude a deal for $3 million with no nude scenes, while Bob might in good faith have believed he was committing himself to

$2.5 million and absolute control of the script. Neither belief will control the outcome. A reasonable person observing their discussion would not have known what terms they agreed to, and hence there is no agreement.

OFFER

Bargaining begins with an offer. An offer is a serious matter because it permits the other party to create a contract by accepting. **An offer is an act or statement that proposes definite terms and permits the other party to create a contract by accepting those terms.**

The person who makes an offer is the **offeror**. The person to whom he makes that offer is the **offeree**. The terms are annoying but inescapable because, like handcuffs, all courts use them. In most contract negotiations, two parties bargain back and forth, maybe for minutes, perhaps for months. Each may make several offers, revoke some proposals, suggest counteroffers, and so forth. For our purposes, the offeror remains the one who made the first offer, and the offeree is the one who received the first offer. They keep those names regardless of how many counter-proposals each side makes.

Two questions determine whether a statement is an offer:

- Did the offeror *intend* to make a bargain?
- Are the terms of the offer definite?

PROBLEMS WITH INTENT

Zachary says to Sharon, "Come work in my English language center as a teacher. I'll pay you $500 per week for a 35-hour week, for six months starting Monday." This is a valid offer. Zachary intends to make a bargain and his offer is definite. If Sharon accepts, the parties have a contract that either one can enforce. By contrast, we will consider several categories of statements that are *generally not* valid offers. Effective negotiating requires legal knowledge and factual preparation. For an excellent discussion of how to research and negotiate a home improvement contract, see http://www.bbb.org/library/home-imp.html.

Invitations to Bargain

An invitation to bargain is not an offer. Suppose Martha telephones Joe and leaves a message on his answering machine, asking if Joe would consider selling his vacation condo on Lake Michigan. Joe faxes a signed letter to Martha saying, "There is no way I could sell the condo for less than $150,000." Martha promptly sends Joe a cashier's check for that amount. Does she own the condo? No. Joe's fax was not an offer. It is merely an invitation to bargain. Joe is indicating that he would be happy to receive an offer from Martha. He is not promising to sell the condo for $150,000 or for any amount.

Price Quotes

A price quote is generally not an offer. If Imperial Textile sends a list of fabric prices for the new year to its regular customers, the list is not an offer. Once again, the law regards it merely as a solicitation of offers. Suppose Ralph orders 1,000 yards of fabric, quoted in the list at $40 per yard. Ralph is making the offer, and Imperial may decline to sell at $40, or at any price, for that matter.

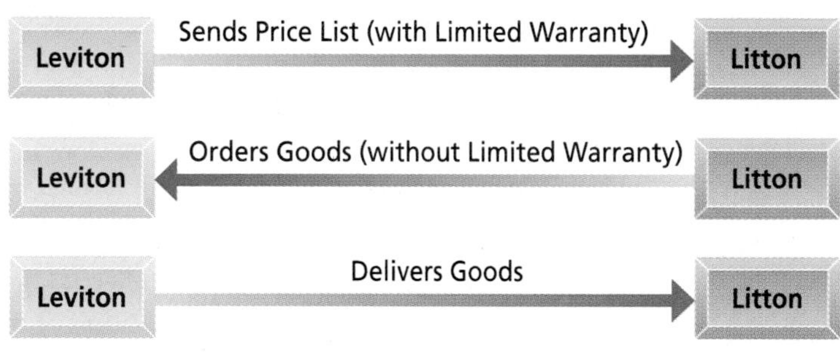

Exhibit 11.1

The *Litton* case demonstrates why it is important to distinguish a valid offer from a contract that is not an offer. Leviton was the first party to make a communication. But its price list (including a limited warranty) was *not* an offer. When Litton ordered goods (with no limit to the warranty), it was making an offer, which Leviton accepted by delivering the goods. The resulting contract did not contain the limited warranty that Leviton wanted, costing that company a $4 million judgment.

This can be an expensive point to learn. Leviton Manufacturing makes electrical fixtures and switches. Litton Microwave manufactures ovens. Leviton sent a price list to Litton, stating what it would charge for specially modified switches for use in Litton's microwaves. The price letter included a statement greatly limiting Leviton' s liability in the event of any problem with the switches. Litton purchased thousands of the switches and used them in manufacturing its microwaves. But consumers reported fires due to defects in the switches. Leviton claimed that under the contract it had no liability. But the court held that the price letter was not an offer. It was a request to receive an offer. Thus the contract ultimately formed did not include Leviton's liability exclusion. Litton won over $4 million.[1] See Exhibit 11.1.

Letters of Intent

In complex business negotiations, the parties may spend months bargaining over dozens of interrelated issues. Because each party wants to protect itself during the discussions, ensuring that the other side is serious without binding itself to premature commitments, it *may* make sense during the negotiations to draft a **letter of intent**. The letter can help distinguish a serious party from one with a casual interest, summarize the progress made thus far, and assist the parties in securing necessary financing. But a letter of intent contains a built-in danger: one party may regard it as less than a binding contract. Yet if it is not binding, what is it? As the following case illustrates, an ambiguous letter of intent is often an invitation to court.

QUAKE CONSTRUCTION v. AMERICAN AIRLINES
141 Ill. 2d 281, 565 N.E.2d 990, 1990 Ill. LEXIS 151
Supreme Court of Illinois, 1990

Facts: Jones Brothers Construction was the general contractor on a job to expand American Airlines' facilities at O'Hare International Airport. Jones Brothers invited Quake Construction to bid on the employee facilities and automotive maintenance shop ("the project"). Quake did bid, and Jones Brothers orally informed Quake that it was awarding Quake the project and would soon forward a contract. Jones Brothers wanted the license numbers of the subcontractors that Quake would be using, but Quake could not furnish those numbers until it had assured its subcontractors that they had the job. Quake did not want to give that

[1] *Litton Microwave Cooking Products v. Leviton Manufacturing Co., Inc.*, 15 F.3d 790, 1994 U.S. App. LEXIS 1876 (8th Cir. 1994).

assurance until *it* was certain of its own work. So Jones Brothers sent a letter of intent that stated, among other things:

> We have elected to award the contract for the subject project to your firm as we discussed on April 15, 1985. A contract agreement outlining the detailed terms and conditions is being prepared and will be available for your signature shortly.
>
> Your scope of work includes the complete installation of expanded lunchroom, restroom and locker facilities for American Airlines employees as well as an expansion of American Airlines existing Automotive Maintenance Shop. A sixty (60) calendar day period shall be allowed for the construction of the locker room, lunchroom and restroom area beginning the week of April 22, 1985. The entire project shall be complete by August 15, 1985.
>
> Subject to negotiated modifications for exterior hollow metal doors and interior ceramic floor tile material as discussed, this notice of award authorizes the work set forth in the [attached] documents at a lump sum price of $1,060,568.00.
>
> Jones Brothers Construction Corporation reserves the right to cancel this letter of intent if the parties cannot agree on a fully executed subcontract agreement.

The parties never signed the fully written contract, and ultimately Jones Brothers hired another company. Quake sued, seeking to recover the money it spent in preparation and its loss of anticipated profit.

Issue: **Was Jones Brothers' letter of intent a valid offer?**

Excerpts from Justice Calvo's Decision: If the parties intended that the document be contractually binding, that intention would not be defeated by the mere recitation in the writing that a more formal agreement was yet to be drawn. However, parties may specifically provide that negotiations are not binding until a formal agreement is in fact executed. Thus, although letters of intent may be enforceable, such letters are not necessarily enforceable unless the parties intend them to be.

In determining whether the parties intended to reduce their agreement to writing, the following factors may be considered: whether the type of agreement involved is one usually put into writing, whether the agreement contains many or few details, whether the agreement involves a large or small amount of money, whether the agreement requires a formal writing for the full expression of the covenants, and whether the negotiations indicated that a formal written document was contemplated at the completion of the negotiations.

[We conclude that] the letter was ambiguous. The letter of intent included detailed terms of the parties' agreement. The letter stated that Jones awarded the contract for the project to Quake. The letter stated further "this notice of award authorizes the work." Moreover, the letter indicated the work was to commence approximately 4 to 11 days after the letter was written. This short period of time reveals the parties' intent to be bound by the letter so the work could begin on schedule. We also agree that the cancellation clause exhibited the parties' intent to be bound by the letter because no need would exist to provide for the cancellation of the letter unless the letter had some binding effect. The cancellation clause also implied the parties' intention to be bound by the letter at least until they entered into the formal contract. These factors evinced the parties' intent to be bound by the letter.

On the other hand, the letter referred several times to the execution of a formal contract by the parties, thus indicating the parties' intent not to be bound by the letter. The cancellation clause could be interpreted to mean that the parties did not intend to be bound until they entered into a formal agreement. Therefore, the appellate court correctly concluded that the letter was ambiguous regarding the parties' intent to be bound by it.

Thus, we hold that the letter of intent in the case at bar is ambiguous regarding the parties' intent to be bound by it. Therefore, on remand, the circuit court should allow the parties to present parol evidence regarding their intent. The trier of fact must then determine, based on the parties' intent, whether the letter of intent is a binding contract.

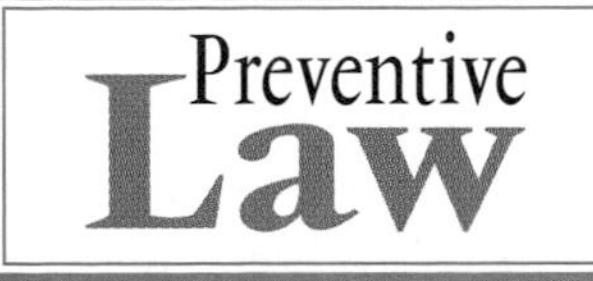

So after several years of litigation, Jones Brothers and Quake had to go *back* to court to try to prove whether they intended the letter to be binding. Every year there are countless cases just like *Quake*. The problem is that both sides permit ambiguity and vagueness to enter their negotiations. Sometimes parties do this accidentally, by paying too little attention to what they are saying. The solution is simple: think carefully before offering or responding.

At other times, with sophisticated business people, ambiguity may not be so accidental, as one party is trying to get a commitment from the other side without obligating itself. A party may feel *almost* ready to commit, yet still have reservations. It wants the *other* party to make a commitment, so that planning can go forward. This is understandable, but dangerous.

If you were negotiating for Jones Brothers and wanted to clarify negotiations without committing your company, how could you do it? State in the letter that it is *not a contract*, and that *neither side is bound by it*. State that it is a memorandum summarizing negotiations thus far, but that neither party will be bound until a full written contract is signed.

But what if Quake cannot get a commitment from its subcontractors until Quake is certain that it has the job? Quake should take the initiative and present Jones Brothers with its own letter of intent, stating that the parties *do* have a binding agreement for $1 million worth of work. Insist that Jones Brothers sign it. Jones Brothers would then be forced to decide whether it is willing to make a binding commitment. If Jones Brothers is not willing to commit, let it openly say so. At least both parties will know where they stand.

Advertisements

Mary Mesaros received a notice from the United States Bureau of the Mint, announcing a new $5 gold coin to commemorate the Statue of Liberty. The notice contained an order form stating:

> VERY IMPORTANT—PLEASE READ: YES, Please accept my order for the U.S. Liberty Coins I have indicated. I understand that all sales are final and not subject to refund. Verification of my order will be made by the Department of the Treasury, U.S. Mint. If my order is received by December 31, 1985, I will be entitled to purchase the coins at the Pre-Issue Discount price shown.

Mesaros ordered almost $2,000 worth of the coins. But the Mint was inundated with so many requests for the coin that the supply was soon exhausted. Mesaros and thousands of others never got their coins. This was particularly disappointing because the market value of the coins doubled shortly after their issue. Mesaros sued on behalf of the entire class of disappointed purchasers. Like most who sue based on an advertisement, she lost.[2]

An advertisement is generally not an offer. An advertisement is merely a request for offers. The consumer makes the offer, whether by mail, as above, or by arriving at a merchant's store ready to buy. The seller is free to reject the offer.

Note that while the common law regards advertisements as mere solicitations, consumers do have protection from those shopkeepers intent upon deceit. Almost every state has some form of **consumer protection statute.** These statutes outlaw false advertising. For example, an automobile dealer who advertises a remarkably low price but then has only one automobile at that price has probably violated a consumer protection statute because the ad was published in bad faith,

---

[2] *Mesaros v. United States*, 845 F.2d 1576, 1988 U.S. App. LEXIS 6055 (Fed. Cir. 1988).

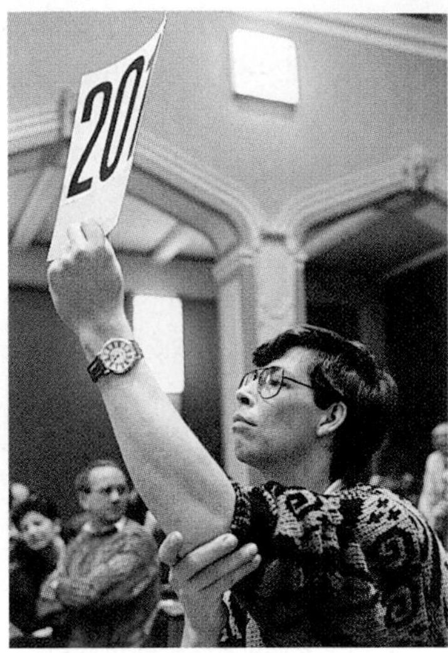

You have the high bid—but you may not have the property.

to trick consumers into coming to the dealership. The United States Mint did not violate any consumer protection statute because it acted in good faith and simply ran out of coins.

Auctions

It is the property you have always dreamed of owning—and it is up for auction! You arrive bright and early, stand in front, bid early, bid often, bid higher, bid highest of all—it's yours! For five seconds. Then, to your horror, the auctioneer announces that none of the bids were juicy enough and he is withdrawing the property. Robbery! Surely he cannot do that? But he can. Auctions are exciting and useful, but you must understand the rules.

Every day auctions are used to sell exquisite works of art, real estate, property confiscated from drug dealers, and many other things. Auctions for the sale of goods are governed by UCC §2-328; auctions for real estate are governed by the common law. The rules are similar and straightforward. **Placing an item up for auction is *not* an offer, it is merely a request for an offer.** The *bids* are the offers. If and when the hammer falls, the auctioneer has accepted the offer.

The important thing to know about a particular auction is whether it is conducted with or without reserve. Most auctions are *with reserve,* meaning that the items for sale have a minimum price. The law assumes that an auction is with reserve unless the auctioneer clearly states otherwise. The auctioneer will not sell anything for less than its reserve (minimum price). So when the bidding for your property failed to reach the reserve, the auctioneer was free to withdraw it.

The rules are different in an auction *without reserve.* Here there is no minimum. Once the first bid is received, the auctioneer must sell the merchandise to the highest bidder.

Welcome to our Web auction. We've got a brand new marmalite ring in *your size* that is *absolutely gorgeous! Click here* to place your bid on this demi-semi-precious beauty. Actually, you cannot click on this textbook (yet), but you can bid over the Internet. Web sites auction everything from rings to computers to cars. At some Web locations, consumers are purchasing from a large company, while at other sites individuals are putting their own goods (new or used) up for bid. The basic rules of contract still apply,[3] but there are certain dangers unique to electronic auctions. The Internet makes it easy for a seller to use a shill, that is, someone who helps the seller by bidding the price up, with no intention of actually buying the item. It is generally easy to spot a shill at a live auction—but not on the Internet. Other dangers arise because the buyer never sees the merchandise. Devious sellers can market inferior goods; crooks can take your money and deliver nothing at all. Protect yourself: before you bid, use the Internet to investigate the quality of the seller. Reputable auction companies permit complaints (and compliments) to be posted on the Web. If you can learn nothing about a seller, don't click.

PROBLEMS WITH DEFINITENESS

It is not enough that the offeror intends to enter into an agreement. **The terms of the offer must be definite.** If they are vague, then even if the offeree "accepts" the deal, a court does not have enough information to enforce it and there is no contract.

---

[3] Although common law and UCC provisions currently govern agreements made electronically, over the next few years, the UCC drafters will propose some significant changes in the law.

You want a friend to work in your store for the holiday season. This is a definite offer: "I offer you a job as a sales clerk in the store from November 1 through December 29, 40 hours per week at $10 per hour." But suppose, by contrast, you say: "I offer you a job as a sales clerk in the store from November 1 through December 29, 40 hours per week. We will work out a fair wage once we see how busy things get." Your friend replies, "That's fine with me." This offer is indefinite and there is no contract. What is a fair wage? $5 per hour? $15 per hour? How will the determination be made? There is no binding agreement.

The following case presents a problem with definiteness. You be the judge.

LEMMING v. MORGAN
228 Ga. App. 763, 492 S.E.2d 742,
1997 Ga. App. LEXIS 1264
Georgia Court of Appeals, 1997

Facts: Larry Lemming and Jackson Morgan were good friends who became business associates—and then ex-friends. According to Lemming, he and Morgan orally agreed to form a partnership. Lemming would use his business connections and influence to locate real estate that was ripe for development. He would help Morgan obtain financing and then assist in developing and reselling the property. Morgan would temporarily hold the property in his name alone because Lemming was going through a divorce and also had tax problems. The two men agreed that, "if and when Lemming's divorce and tax problems subsided," Morgan would transfer to Lemming one-half of all property and one-half of all profits.

Lemming claims that over a five-year period, he located five properties, which he helped Morgan develop and resell. Then Morgan refused to give Lemming his one-half stake. Lemming leaped into court. Morgan denied that the parties had ever formed a partnership. The trial court granted summary judgment for Morgan, ruling that even if the parties had made the agreement Lemming described, it was too indefinite to enforce. Lemming appealed.

You Be the Judge: Assuming the parties reached the agreement Lemming described, was it sufficiently definite to create a contract?

Argument for Lemming: Both parties understood exactly what the deal was. Mr. Lemming was temporarily unable to hold property in his name. But he was willing to help run the business, and Morgan eagerly exploited his friend's expertise. For five years Mr. Lemming did everything he could to make the business a success, and that is what has caused the problem: the business *succeeded*. With Mr. Lemming's guidance, the partners were able to buy intelligently, secure reasonable financing, and profitably develop the land. Now Morgan wants to keep 100 percent of the profits, and the trial court, astonishingly, has ruled that he may—without a trial! In other words, even if both parties intended to split the money, and Mr. Lemming did his share to create the profit, he earns nothing because of some technical rule of contract. Surely, the law was never intended to help a deceitful partner double his profit, nor to leave a hardworking, honest friend uncompensated for five years of labor.

Argument for Morgan: The rule requiring definite terms in an agreement is more than a minor technicality. To be enforceable, a promise must be sufficiently definite that a court can determine who was supposed to do what. Even if Mr. Morgan made the agreement Lemming describes, it is so vague that no court could possibly enforce it. Exactly *when* was Mr. Morgan supposed to transfer the property to Lemming? How was the division to be made: Would one person receive certain properties? Which ones? If there were profits, how were they to be calculated, and when paid? Mr. Morgan was the only one who borrowed money, bought the land, paid all interest and taxes, and assumed full liability. Why should Lemming be entitled to half, when Mr. Morgan bore all the risk? If the business had failed, would Lemming simply have watched while Mr. Morgan went bankrupt? An agreement missing one or two details may still create a valid contract, but here none of the key terms was settled and there is nothing for a court to enforce.

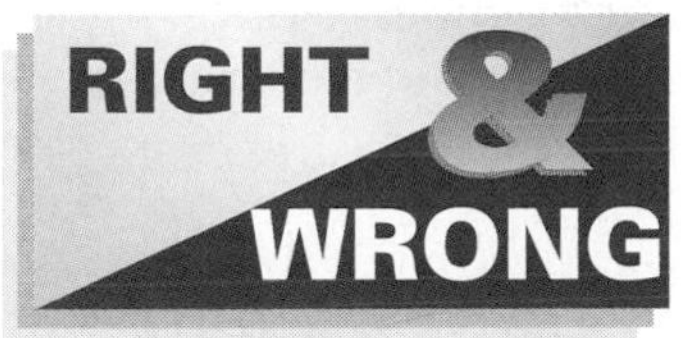

Why did Lemming want all property listed in Morgan's name? What ethical issues does this raise? If Lemming had proposed the partnership to you, how would you have responded?

An agreement with indefinite terms is generally unenforceable. But there is another reason to insist on clarity when negotiating a contract. If your deal is vague, you may find yourself living with unpleasant consequences, as the following article indicates.

NEWSWORTHY

Although New Orleans's garbage collection company brought extra trucks to the city over the weekend to try to catch up with a backlog of uncollected garbage, city officials said Monday that the company is still far behind its pickup schedule and it's likely more fines will be imposed.

The city fined Waste Management of New Orleans $100,000 last week for missing 8,800 residential garbage pickups, particularly in the Lower 9th Ward, and for leaving 60 piles of trash citywide. An additional fine of $180,000 will be levied if the company fails to develop an action plan to solve its collection lapses by the beginning of next week, said Nannette Jolivette, director of the Sanitation Department.

"They missed a lot of pickups Friday and then missed some Saturday," she said. "The $100,000 still stands and it doesn't look too good for them on the other fine."

Jolivette blamed vague contract language for many of the city's problems with Waste Management, whose 10-year collection contract is up for renewal December 31. For example, the contract does not require the company to use full-time workers on collection runs, so it saves money but loses effectiveness by using temporary workers, she said.

"They make their millions by putting out as little as they can, and they've been allowed to skim this way for 10 years," Jolivette said. "But I'm not going to back off of this, and we mean business when this is put out to bid."

Waste Management officials could not be reached for comment Monday, but they said last week they would do all they could to get caught up on their collection routes. A spokeswoman blamed the problems on the 4th of July holiday and subsequent hard rains.[4]

Preventive Law

What should the City of New Orleans do to improve sanitation collection?

UCC AND OPEN TERMS

Throughout this unit, we witness how the Uniform Commercial Code makes the law of sales more flexible. There are several areas of contract law where imperfect negotiations may still create a binding agreement under the Code, even though the same negotiations under the common law would have yielded no contract. "Open terms" is one such area.

Yuma County Corp. produced natural gas. Yuma wanted a long-term contract to sell its gas so that it could be certain of recouping the expenses of exploration and drilling. Northwest Central Pipeline, which operated an interstate pipeline, also wanted a deal for 10 or more years so it could make its own distribution contracts, knowing it would have a steady supply of natural gas in a competitive market. But neither Yuma nor Northwest wanted to make a long-term *price* commitment, because over a period of years the price of natural gas could double—or crash. Each party wanted a binding agreement without a definitive price. If their negotiations had been governed by the common law, they would have run smack

[4] James Varney, "More Garbage Fines Expected," *New Orleans Times-Picayune*, July 16, 1996, p. B1. Permission granted by The Times-Picayune Publishing Corporation. All rights reserved. Reprinted with permission.

into the requirement of definiteness—no price, no contract. But because this was a sale of goods, it was governed by the UCC.

> **UCC §2-204(3).** Even though one or more terms are left open, a contract for sale does not fail for indefiniteness if the parties have intended to make a contract and there is a reasonably certain basis for giving an appropriate remedy.

Thus a contract for the sale of goods may be enforced when a key term is missing. Business executives may have many reasons to leave open a delivery date, a price, or some other term. But note that the parties must still have *intended* to create a contract. The UCC will not create a contract where the parties never intended one.

In some cases the contract will state how the missing term is to be determined. Yuma County and Northwest drafted a contract with alternative methods of determining the price. In the event that the price of natural gas was regulated by the Federal Energy Regulatory Commission (FERC), the price would be the highest allowed by the FERC. If the FERC deregulated the price (as it ultimately did), the contract price would be the average of the two highest prices paid by different gas producers in a specified geographic area.

If the contract lacks a method for determining missing terms, the Code itself contains **gap-filler provisions**, which are rules for supplying missing terms. Some of the most important gap-filler provisions of the Code follow.

Open Price

In general, if the parties do not settle on a price, the Code establishes a *reasonable price*. This will usually be the market value or a price established by a neutral expert or agency. (UCC §2-305.)

Output and Requirements Provisions

An **output contract** obligates the seller to sell all of his output to the buyer, who agrees to accept it. For example, a cotton grower might agree to sell all of his next crop to a textile firm. A **requirements contract** obligates a buyer to obtain all of his needed goods from the seller. A vineyard might agree to buy all of its wine bottles from one supplier. Output and requirements contracts are by definition incomplete, since the exact quantity of the goods is unspecified. The Code requires that in carrying out such contracts, both parties act in good faith. Neither party may suddenly demand a quantity of goods (or offer a quantity of goods) that is disproportionate to their past dealings or their reasonable estimates. (UCC §2-306.)

Delivery, Time, and Payment

The Code provides terms for each of these issues. In general, the place of delivery is the seller's business. The time for shipping goods is usually a reasonable time, based on the normal trade practice. And payment is normally due when and where the buyer receives the goods. For each of these issues, the Code offers alternative provisions for cases with unusual facts. (UCC §§2-308 through 2-310.)

Warranties

Warranties are a source of frequent conflict between the parties because when something goes wrong, the costs can be enormous. Parties frequently enter a contract without agreeing on the warranty provisions, so the Code often supplies the terms. We consider warranty in detail in Chapter 21, on warranties and products liability. To summarize here, we can mention two important warranties that the Code implies. One is an **implied warranty of merchantability,** which means that the goods must be of at least average, passable quality in the trade. Ten thousand pairs of sneakers must be such that a typical shoe store would accept them. The other is an **implied warranty of fitness for a particular purpose.** If the seller knows that the buyer plans to use the goods for a particular purpose, the seller generally is held to warrant that the goods are in fact fit for that purpose. If an engine manufacturer knows that the buyer is going to use 10,000 engines in outboard motors, the Code normally considers that the manufacturer is warranting the engines for that purpose. (UCC §§2-312 through 2-317.)

Termination of Offers

As we have seen, the great power that an offeree has is to form a contract by accepting an offer. But this power is lost when the offer is terminated, which can happen in four ways: revocation, rejection, expiration, or operation of law.

Termination by Revocation

In general, the offeror may revoke the offer any time before it has been accepted. **Revocation is effective when the offeree receives it**. Douglas County, Oregon, sought bids on a construction job involving large quantities of rock. The Taggart Co. discovered a local source of supply with cheap rock and put in a bid. Shortly thereafter, Taggart discovered that the local rock was no longer for sale. Taggart hand delivered a written revocation of its bid. Later, the county opened all bids and accepted Taggart's low offer—but lost the case. By delivering its revocation, Taggart terminated the county's power to accept.[5]

Firm Offers and Revocability

Some offers cannot be revoked. A **firm offer** is one that by its own terms will be held open for a given period. Bonnie writes Clyde on January 2 and says, "I offer to sell you X for $1 million. This offer will be valid until February 2." Suppose Bonnie changes her mind on January 5 and wants to revoke. May she? It depends on "X."

Common Law Rule. **Under the common law, revocation of a firm offer is effective if the offeree receives it before he accepts.** Suppose Bonnie was offering to sell her ranch for that sum. Real estate is governed by the common law. On January 5 she faxed Clyde a revocation. On January 10 he mailed her an acceptance. Result? No contract—the revocation was effective.

Option Contract. With an option contract, an interested purchaser buys the right to have the offer held open. **The offeror may not revoke an offer during the option period.** Suppose Clyde is interested in Bonnie's ranch, but needs three weeks to learn whether he can finance the purchase. They agree that Clyde will pay $25,000 for Bonnie to hold open her offer until February 2. Clyde arranges financing on January 20, but later that day Bonnie notifies him she is selling to someone else. Result? Clyde can enforce *his* contract. Bonnie had no power to revoke because Clyde had purchased an option.

Sale of Goods. Once again, the UCC has changed the law on the sale of goods. A writing, signed by a *merchant*, offering to hold open an offer for a stated period, may not be revoked. The open period may not exceed three months. Thus, if Bonnie is a merchant, and the "X" she is offering to sell Clyde is 10,000 theatrical costumes, she may not revoke any time before February 2. (UCC §2-205.)

---

[5] *R. J. Taggart, Inc. v. Douglas County*, 31 Or. App. 1137, 572 P.2d 1050, 1977 Ore. App. LEXIS 2868 (Or. Ct. App. 1977).

Termination by Rejection

If an offeree rejects an offer, the rejection immediately terminates the offer. Suppose a major accounting firm telephones you and offers a job, starting at $80,000. You respond, "Nah. I'm gonna work on my surfing for a year or two." The next day you come to your senses and write the firm, accepting its offer. No contract. Your rejection terminated the offer and ended your power to accept.

Counteroffer. Frederick faxes Kim, offering to sell a 50 percent interest in the Fab Hotel in New York for only $135 million. Kim faxes back, offering to pay $115 million. Moments later, Kim's business partner convinces her that Frederick's offer was a bargain, and she faxes an acceptance of his $135 million offer. Does Kim have a binding deal? No. **A counteroffer is a rejection.** When Kim offered $115 million, she rejected Frederick's offer. Her fax became a new offer, for $115 million, which Frederick never accepted. The parties have no contract at any price.

Termination by Expiration

Quentin calls you and offers you a job as best boy on his next motion picture. He tells you, "I've got to know by tomorrow night." If you call him in three days to accept, you are out of the picture. **When an offer specifies a time limit for acceptance, that period is binding.**

If the offer specifies no time limit, the offeree has a reasonable period in which to accept. A reasonable period varies, depending upon the type of offer, previous dealings between the parties, and any normal trade usage. "Trade usage" means the customary practices in a particular industry. When the parties are bargaining face to face, any offer made will normally be valid only during that discussion. Neither party may call the next day to accept. Similarly, if the offer concerns a speculative item, such as commodities futures, the offer will be open very briefly. On the other hand, if a used car wholesaler faxes an offer to sell 50 used cars for $2,000 each, and the local custom is to respond within three days, an acceptance faxed within two days creates a contract.

Termination by Operation of Law

In some circumstances, the law itself terminates an offer. **Death or mental incapacity of the offeror terminates an offer, whether the offeree knows of the change or not.** Arnie offers you a job as an assistant in his hot-air balloon business. Before you can even accept, Arnie tumbles out of a balloon at 3,000 feet. The offer terminates along with Arnie.

Destruction of the subject matter terminates the offer. A used car dealer offers to sell you a rare 1938 Bugatti for $75,000 if you bring cash the next day. You arrive, suitcase stuffed with century notes, just in time to see Arnie drop 3,000 feet through the air and crush the Bugatti. The dealer's offer terminated.

ACCEPTANCE

As we have seen, when there is a valid offer outstanding, the offeree can create a contract by accepting. **The offeree must say or do something to accept.** Silence, though golden, is not acceptance. Marge telephones Vick and leaves a message on his answering machine: "I'll pay $75 for your law textbook from last semester. I'm desperate to get a copy, so I will assume you agree unless I hear from you by 6:00 tonight." Marge hears nothing by the deadline and assumes she has a deal. She is mistaken. Vick neither said nor did anything to indicate that he accepted.

If it arrives at your front door, consider your offer accepted.

When the offer is for a bilateral contract, the offeree generally must accept by making a promise. An employer calls you and says, "If you're able to start work two weeks from today, we can pay you $5,000 per month. Can you do it?" That is an offer for a bilateral contract. You must accept by promising to start in two weeks. If you make the promise, both sides are contractually bound from the moment you agree. You do not, however, have the option to think it over for two weeks and then show up.

When the offer is for a unilateral contract, the offeree must accept by performing. A newspaper telephones you: "If you write us a 5,000-word article on iguanas that can play bridge, and get it to us by Friday at noon, we'll pay you $750." The newspaper does not want a promise, it wants the article. If your work is ready on time, you get paid. If you never write a word, neither party owes the other anything.

With some offers it is unclear whether the offeror wants acceptance by promise or performance. **If the offer is ambiguous, the offeree may accept by either a promise or performance.** A contractor offered to lease a Link-Belt construction crane from a dealer for two months for $6,500 per month. The contractor signed and mailed a written lease that required him to insure the crane. The dealer read the lease, did not sign it, but delivered the crane. The crane was promptly destroyed. Was the contractor liable? Yes. The written lease invited acceptance by promise or by performance. The dealer accepted by delivering the crane, and the liability clause (requiring the contractor to obtain insurance) was part of their contract.[6] The rule is the same in cases involving the sale of goods. (UCC §2-206.)

MIRROR IMAGE RULE

If only he had known! A splendid university, an excellent position as department chair—gone. And all because of the mirror image rule.

Ohio State University wrote to Philip Foster offering him an appointment as a professor and chair of the art history department. His position was to begin July 1, and he had until June 2 to accept the job. On June 2, Foster telephoned the Dean and left a message accepting the position, *effective July 15*. Later, Foster thought better of it and wrote the university, accepting the school's starting date of July 1. Too late! Professor Foster never did occupy that chair at Ohio State. The court held that since his acceptance varied the starting date, it was a counteroffer. And a counteroffer, as we know, is a rejection.[7]

Was it sensible to deny the professor a job over a mere 14-day difference? Sensible or not, that is the law. **The common law mirror image rule requires that acceptance be on precisely the same terms as the offer.** If the acceptance contains terms that add or contradict the offer, even in minor ways, courts generally consider it a counteroffer. The rule worked reasonably well in the nineteenth century, when parties would write an original contract and exchange it, penciling in any changes. But now that businesses use standardized forms to purchase most goods and services, the rule creates enormous difficulties. Sellers use forms they have prepared, with all conditions stated to their advantage, and buyers employ their own forms, with terms they prefer. The forms are exchanged in the mail, with neither side clearly agreeing to the other party's terms.

The problem is known as the "battle of forms." Once again, the UCC has entered the fray, attempting to provide flexibility and common sense for those contracts involving the sale of goods. But for contracts governed by the common law, such as Professor Foster's, the mirror image rule is still the law.

---

6 *Anderson Excavating v. Certified Welding*, 769 P.2d 887, 1988 Wyo. LEXIS 185 (Wyo. 1988).

7 *Foster v. Ohio State University*, 41 Ohio App. 3d 86, 534 N.E.2d 1220, 1987 Ohio App. LEXIS 10761 (Ohio Ct. App. 1987).

UCC and the Battle of Forms

UCC §2-207 dramatically modifies the mirror image rule for the sale of goods. Under this provision, an acceptance that adds additional or different terms will often create a contract. The rule is intricate, but it is important to understand its basic features because most goods are bought and sold with standardized forms. Exhibit 11.2 illustrates UCC §2-207.

Additional or Different Terms

One basic principle of the common law of contracts remains unchanged: The key to creation of a contract is a valid offer that the offeree *intends* to accept. If there is no intent to accept, there is no contract. The big change brought about by UCC §2-207 is this: **an offeree who accepts may include in the acceptance terms that are additional to or different from those in the offer**. Thus, even with additional or different terms, the acceptance may well create a contract.

Example A. Wholesaler writes to Manufacturer, offering to buy "10,000 wheelbarrows at $50 per unit. Payable on delivery, 30 days from today's date." Manufacturer writes back, "We accept your offer of 10,000 wheelbarrows at $50 per unit, payable on delivery. Interest at normal trade rates for unpaid balances." Manufacturer clearly intends to form a contract. The company has added a new term, but there is still a valid contract.

However, if the offeree states that her acceptance is *conditioned on the offeror's assent* to the new terms, there is no contract.

Exhibit 11.2
UCC §2-207

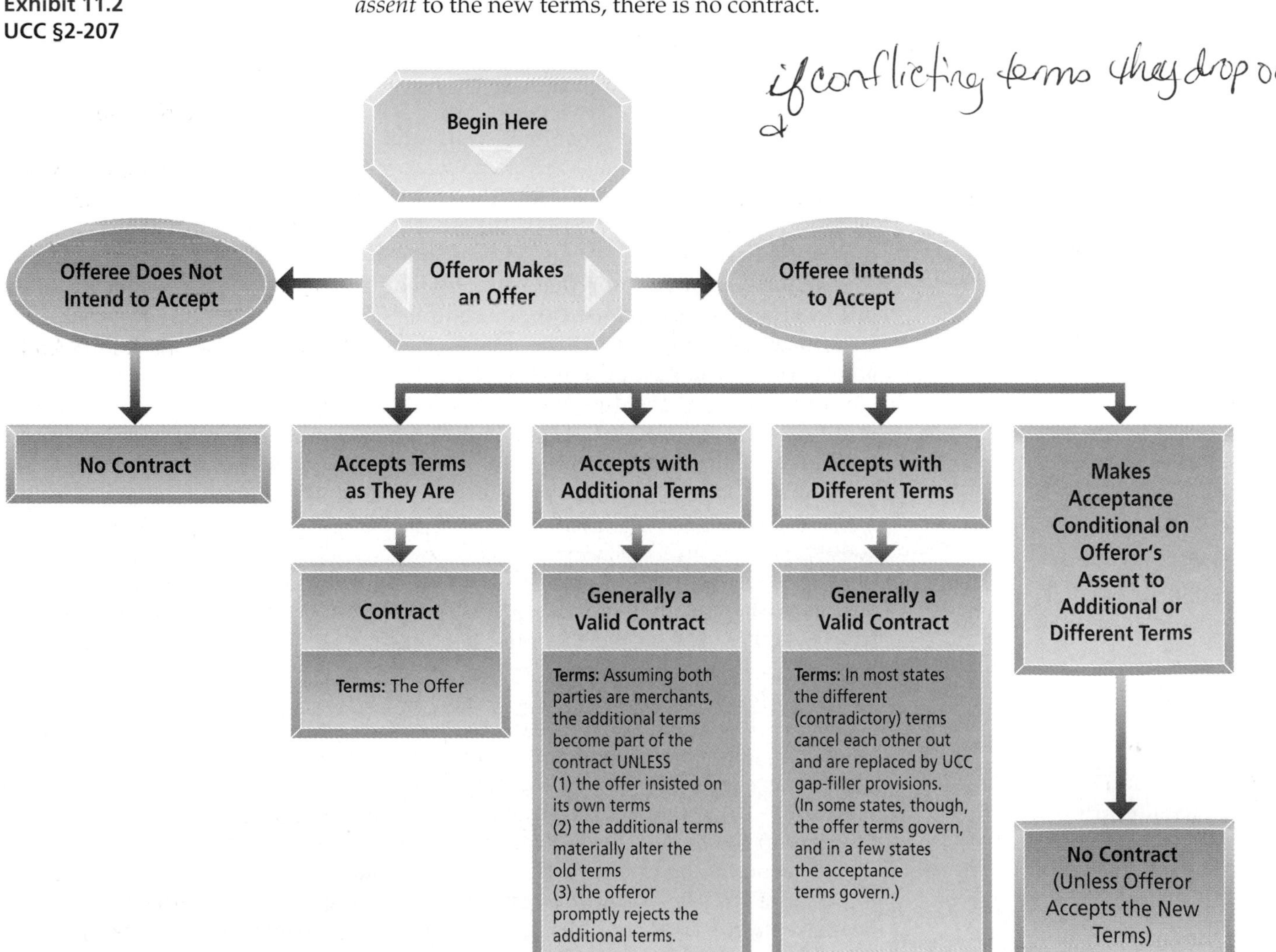

Example B. Same offer as above. Manufacturer adds the interest rate clause and states, "Our acceptance is conditional upon your agreement to this interest rate." Manufacturer has made a counteroffer. There is no contract, yet. If Wholesaler accepts the counteroffer, there is a contract; if Wholesaler does not accept it, there is no contract.

Additional terms are those that bring up new issues, such as interest rates, not contained in the original offer. Additional terms in the acceptance are considered proposals to add to the contract. Assuming that both parties are merchants, **the additional terms will generally become part of the contract**. Thus, in Example A, above, the interest rate will become a part of the binding deal. If Wholesaler is late in paying, it must pay whatever interest rate is current.

In three circumstances, the additional terms in the acceptance *do not* become part of the contract:

- If the original offer *insisted on its own terms*. In other words, if Wholesaler wrote, "I offer to buy them on the following terms and *no other terms*," then the Manufacturer is not free to make additions.
- If the additional terms *materially alter* the original offer. Suppose Manufacturer wrote back, "We accept your offer for 10,000 wheelbarrows. Delivery will be made within 180 days, unless we notify you of late delivery." Manufacturer has changed the time from 30 days to 180 days, with a possible extension beyond that. That is a material alteration, and it will not become part of the contract. By contrast, Manufacturer's new language concerning "interest at normal trade rates" was not a material alteration, and therefore that interest rate becomes part of the contract.
- If the offeror receives the additional terms and *promptly objects* to them.

Different terms are those that contradict terms in the offer. For example, if the seller's form states that it offers no warranty at all and the buyer's form says the seller warrants all goods for three years, the acceptance contains different terms. An acceptance may contain different terms and still create a contract. But in these cases, courts have struggled to decide what the terms of the contract are. **The majority of states hold that different (contradictory) terms cancel each other out.** Neither term is included in the contract. Instead, the neutral terms from the Code itself are "read into" the contract. These are the gap-filler terms discussed above. If, for example, the forms had contradictory warranty clauses (as they almost always do), the different terms would cancel each other out, and the warranty clauses from the UCC would be substituted.

Not all states follow this rule, however. Some courts have held that when the acceptance contains terms that contradict those in the offer, the language in the offer should be final. A few courts have ruled that the terms in the acceptance should control.

Here is a typical UCC §2-207 case in which the court must decide whether additional language "materially alters" the contract. The result is very different from what it would have been under the common law.

LEADERTEX v. MORGANTON DYEING & FINISHING CORP.

1994 U.S. Dist. LEXIS 11512
United States District Court, Southern District of New York, 1994

Facts: Leadertex is a New York corporation that manufactures fabrics and textiles. Morganton is a North Carolina corporation that dyes and finishes such products. The companies agreed that Leadertex would deliver fabric to Morganton for dyeing and finishing. When Leadertex then followed up with a written order, Morganton would dye the fabric and deliver it to a specified clothing manufacturer. When Morganton received a dye order, it would send Leadertex a confirmation. Morganton labeled these confirmations "contracts" or "supplemental contracts." Over six years, Leadertex sent over 100 orders to

Morganton, and Morganton sent back over 100 of these confirmations. Each confirmation stated on its face:

> This Quotation is given subject to all the terms and conditions on the reverse hereof, including the provisions for arbitration and exclusion of warranties.

The arbitration provision on the reverse stated:

> Any controversy or claim arising under or in relation to this order or contract, or any modification thereof, shall be settled by arbitration.

Leadertex filed suit against Morganton, claiming that Morganton was illegally holding 89,000 yards of its fabric. Morganton responded by moving to compel arbitration; that is, it sought a court order that any dispute between the parties must be settled by an arbitrator, not a federal court.

Issue: Does the arbitration clause on Morganton's confirmation slip obligate Leadertex to arbitrate its claims?

Excerpts from Judge Duffy's Decision: The relevant state law regarding this dispute is section 2-207 of New York's Uniform Commercial Code. Section 2-207 governs disputes involving the addition of terms in [contracts]. Specifically, section 2-207 provides that, as between merchants, additional terms included in a written confirmation will not become part of the contract if: (1) the offer expressly limits the acceptance to the terms of the offer; (2) they materially alter it; or (3) notification of objection to them has been or is given within a reasonable time.

In this case, the offer did not expressly limit its acceptance to the terms of its offer, and no notification of objection to the additional terms was made. Thus, an arbitration agreement exists unless the additional terms, i.e., the arbitration provision, materially alter the original offer. An arbitration clause is not a per se material alteration. Rather, a term is considered material if its inclusion in the contract "would result in surprise or hardship if incorporated without express awareness by the other party." Therefore, the issue is whether Leadertex was surprised or would endure hardship by the inclusion of the arbitration clause in the terms of the contract.

Clearly, Leadertex was not surprised by the inclusion of the term. Leadertex received without objection 100 separate "contracts" which contained a provision for arbitration of all disputes. Moreover, Leadertex, as a merchant in the textile industry, cannot be surprised by the inclusion of an arbitration clause. Indeed, the "widespread use of arbitration clauses in the textile industry puts a contracting party...on notice that its agreement probably contains such a clause," [citing an earlier case which also said:] "From our own experience we can almost take judicial notice that arbitration clauses are commonly used in the textile industry." Therefore, Leadertex was not "surprised" by Morganton's arbitration clause. In addition, Leadertex has not shown in any way that including the arbitration clause in the contract would impose a "hardship" for Leadertex. Therefore, the arbitration provision is not a material alteration of the contract. Accordingly, I find that an agreement to arbitrate exists.

COMMUNICATION OF ACCEPTANCE

The offeree must communicate his acceptance for it to be effective. The questions that typically arise concern the medium, the manner, and the time of acceptance.

Medium and Manner of Acceptance

The "medium" refers to whether acceptance is done in person or by mail, telephone, e-mail, or fax. The "manner" refers to whether the offeree accepts by promising, by making a down payment, by performing, and so forth. **If an offer**

demands acceptance in a particular medium or manner, the offeree must follow those requirements. Suppose a newly incorporated town offers a power company the right to provide electrical service to the residents. The offer states that the power company must accept in writing, and the writing must be delivered to the town's offices by a given date. If the power company orally notifies the town of its acceptance and begins its preparations for delivering electrical service, it has no contract.

If the offer does not specify a type of acceptance, the offeree may accept in any reasonable manner and medium. We have already seen that an offer generally may be accepted by performance or by a promise, unless it specifies a particular method. The same freedom applies to the medium. If Masako faxes Eric an offer to sell 1,000 acres in Montana for $800,000, Eric may accept by mail or fax. Both are routinely used in real estate transactions, and either is reasonable. The same rule applies for the sale of goods.[8] If Masako faxes Eric an offer to sell 20,000 pairs of jeans for $20 each, he may write or fax his reply.

Time of Acceptance: The Mailbox Rule

An acceptance is generally effective upon dispatch, meaning the moment it is out of the offeree's control. When Masako faxes her offer to sell land to Eric, and he mails his acceptance, the contract is binding the moment he puts the letter into the mail. In most cases, this **mailbox rule** is just a detail. But it becomes important when the offeror revokes her offer at about the same time the offeree accepts. Who wins? Suppose Masako's offer has one twist:

- On Monday morning, Masako faxes her offer to Eric.
- On Monday afternoon, Eric writes "I accept" on the fax.
- On Tuesday morning, Eric mails his acceptance.
- On Tuesday afternoon, Masako faxes Eric a revocation of her offer.
- On Thursday morning, Eric's acceptance arrives at Masako's office.

Outcome? Eric has an enforceable contract. Masako's offer was effective when it reached Eric. His acceptance was effective on Tuesday morning, when he mailed it. Nothing that happens later, such as Masako's attempt to revoke, can "undo" the contract.

SOLDAU v. ORGANON, INC.
860 F.2d 355, 1988 U.S. App. LEXIS 14757
United States Court of Appeals for the Ninth Circuit, 1988

Facts: Organon fired John Soldau. Then the company sent to him a letter offering to pay him double the normal severance pay, provided Soldau would sign a full release, that is, a document giving up any and all claims he might have against Organon. The release was included with the letter. Soldau signed it, dated it, and took it to the nearest post office, where he deposited it in the mailbox. When he returned home, Soldau discovered in the mail a check from Organon for the double severance pay. He hustled back to the post office, where he persuaded a postal clerk to open the mailbox and retrieve the release he had posted. He then cashed Organon's check and finally filed a suit against the company, alleging that his firing was age discrimination.

---

[8] UCC §2-206(1)(a).

The federal district court gave summary judgment for Organon, ruling that Soldau's acceptance of the proposed release was effective when he mailed it, creating a contract. He appealed.

Issue: Did Soldau create a contract by mailing the release?

Excerpts from the *Per Curiam* Decision:[9] The district court was clearly correct under California law. Soldau does not argue to the contrary. Instead, he contends that the formation and validity of the release are governed by federal law, and would not have been effective unless and until it had been received by Organon. We need not decide which body of law controls. Under federal as well as California law, Soldau's acceptance was effective when it was mailed.

The so-called "mailbox" or "effective when mailed" rule was adopted and followed as federal common law by the Supreme Court [at the beginning of this century]. We could not change the rule, and there is no reason to believe the Supreme Court would be inclined to do so. It is almost universally accepted in the common law world. It is enshrined in the Restatement (Second) of Contracts and endorsed by the major contract treatises.

Commentators are also virtually unanimous in [supporting the "effective upon dispatch" rule,] pointing to the long history of the rule; its importance in creating certainty for contracting parties; its essential soundness, on balance, as a means of allocating the risk during the period between the making of the offer and the communication of the acceptance or rejection to the offeror; and the inadequacy of the rationale offered by the Court of Claims for the change.

Since Soldau's contractual obligation to release Organon in return for Organon's obligation to make the enhanced severance payment arose when Soldau deposited his acceptance in the post office mailbox, his subsequent withdrawal of the acceptance was ineffectual.

Affirmed.

International business is booming, propelling many companies and nations to unprecedented prosperity. But those who enter the international marketplace must understand that their negotiations may be governed by neither the UCC nor American common law. The Convention On Contracts For The International Sale of Goods (CISG) controls a contract for the sale of goods between parties from two countries, if both nations have signed the relevant treaty. Most of the largest trading nations have signed the treaty. If the parties want a different law, such as the UCC, to govern their agreement, they must explicitly agree on that point.[10]

From time to time we will point out differences between the CISG and our own domestic contract law. The CISG rejects the mailbox rule. Under the CISG, an acceptance is not effective until the offeror receives it. Suppose that, from your manufacturing office in Cleveland, you mail offer sheets to a retailer in Paris and one in Los Angeles. If the store in Los Angeles signs the form and drops it back in the mail, there is a binding deal at that moment. Even if you do not receive the form for several days, the contract exists. If the retailer in Paris does the same thing, however, the CISG holds that there is no contract unless and until you receive the document.

The CISG generally requires acceptance to be a mirror image of the offer, thus rejecting the UCC's more liberal policy, which permits additional and even

---

[9] A *per curiam* opinion is made by the court as a whole, without identifying a particular judge as the author.

[10] For a detailed look at international trade generally, and the CISG in particular, see Chapter 8, on international law.

contradictory terms in an acceptance. The CISG allows only very minor changes in the acceptance. If you are doing business overseas and the CISG governs, beware that a battle of the forms may leave you with no enforceable deal.

PROMISSORY ESTOPPEL

Donald Moore and Clifford Garrett were interested in purchasing a small Michigan business called Winamac Plastics. They approached Max Brandt, a senior vice-president and loan officer at the First National Bank of Logansport, Indiana. Brandt already knew that Winamac had high debt and poor management, but he believed the company had valuable products and could be turned around. After several meetings, Brandt agreed that the bank would finance the purchase if Garrett and Moore moved Winamac to Logansport. Brandt also told the two that his personal lending authority was limited to $100,000. They expected to spend over $500,000 in restarting the company, and a loan for the remaining money would require committee approval.

Brandt approved a personal loan to Garrett and Moore of $100,000, most of which they used to acquire a two-thirds interest in Winamac. Later, Brandt prepared a loan application on behalf of Winamac itself, for $540,000. But the bank's committee turned down the loan because Winamac had such high debt.

Brandt assured the two entrepreneurs that the bank would approve a revised application, which he himself made. Garrett and Moore spent their remaining money setting up the company in Logansport. Months later, the bank turned down the second loan application. Garrett and Moore sued. Did they have any rights?

The trial court thought so, declaring that the various conversations created an oral contract to finance Winamac. The court awarded the plaintiffs $726,532, which included over $500,000 in lost profits. The appeals court affirmed. Were the two courts correct? No, ruled the Indiana Supreme Court. Here are the basic principles.

Did the parties intend to create a contract? Almost certainly. Clearly, the two entrepreneurs wanted a deal and thought they had one. Brandt was equally determined to finance the purchase.

Can we identify the terms of the contract? No. The "agreement" was fatally indefinite. Exactly how much money was to be loaned? What was the rate of interest? The loan's duration? The terms of repayment? The security for the loan? The parties never agreed on a single term. Perhaps if one item had been missing, the court might have supplied it. But since all key terms were absent, there could be no contract.

But Garrett and Moore had another possibility. **Under the doctrine of promissory estoppel, even if there is no contract, a promise may be enforceable if:**

- The offeror makes a promise knowing the offeree is likely to rely
- The offeree does in fact rely; and
- The only way to avoid injustice is to enforce the promise.

Here is how the court applied the doctrine to this case. Brandt did promise that the bank would lend whatever money was necessary to get Winamac back on its feet, although the amount was too indefinite to create a contract. Brandt knew the two men would rely on his promise, sinking their money into Winamac and moving it to Logansport. The Indiana Supreme Court concluded that the only way to avoid injustice was to enforce the promise, to a limited extent. Because there was no contract, the court refused to award lost profits. Instead, the plaintiffs received $73,000 in compensation for the money they spent relying on Brandt's promise. That was better than nothing, but far less than they would have obtained had there been a contract.[11]

Promissory estoppel is often a plaintiff's last-ditch argument. Frequently, judges reject such claims, ruling that no contract means no money. At other times, as Garrett and Moore discovered, a court enforces a promise but grants much less compensation than it would have if the parties had reached a clear agreement.

How could Garrett and Moore have protected themselves?

CHAPTER CONCLUSION

The law of offer and acceptance can be complex and even baffling. Yet for all its fault, the law is not the principal source of dispute between parties unhappy with negotiations. Most litigation concerning offer and acceptance comes from *lack of clarity* on the part of the people negotiating. Letters of intent are often an effort to "have it both ways," that is, to ensure the other side's commitment without accepting a corresponding obligation. Similarly, the "battle of the forms" is caused by corporate officers seeking to make a deal and hurry things forward without settling details. These, and the many other examples discussed, are all understandable given the speed and fluidity of the real world of business. But the executive who insists on clarity is likelier in the long run to spend more time doing business and less time in court.

CHAPTER REVIEW

1. The parties can form a contract only if they have a meeting of the minds, which requires that they understand each other and intend to reach an agreement.
2. An offer is an act or statement that proposes definite terms and permits the other party to create a contract by accepting those terms.
3. Invitations to bargain, price quotes, and advertisements are generally not offers. A letter of intent may or may not be an offer, depending upon the exact language and whether it indicates that the parties have reached an agreement.
4. The terms of the offer must be definite, although under the UCC the parties may create a contract that has open terms.
5. An offer may be terminated by revocation, rejection, expiration, or operation of law.
6. The offeree must say or do something to accept. Silence is not acceptance.
7. The common law mirror image rule requires acceptance on precisely the same terms as the offer. Under the UCC, an offeree may often create a contract even when the acceptance includes terms that are additional to or different from those in the offer.

[11] *Garrett v. First National Bank of Logansport*, 577 N.E.2d 949, 1991 Ind. LEXIS 130 (Ind. 1991).

8. If an offer demands acceptance in a particular medium or manner, the offeree must follow those requirements. If the offer does not specify a type of acceptance, the offeree may accept in any reasonable manner and medium.

9. An acceptance is generally effective upon dispatch, meaning from the moment it is out of the offeree's control.

10. Under the doctrine of promissory estoppel, even without a contract a promise may be enforceable if the offeror knows the offeree is likely to rely, the offeree does rely, and the only way to avoid injustice is to enforce the promise.

PRACTICE TEST

1. Arnold owned a Pontiac dealership and wanted to expand by obtaining a Buick outlet. He spoke with Patricia Roberts and other Buick executives on several occasions. He now claims that those discussions resulted in an oral contract that requires Buick to grant him a franchise, but the company disagrees. His strongest evidence of a contract is the fact that Roberts gave him forms on which to order Buicks. Roberts answered that it was her standard practice to give such forms to prospective dealers, so that if the franchise were approved, car orders could be processed quickly. Is there a contract?

2. The town of Sanford, Maine, decided to auction off a lot it owned. The town advertised that it would accept bids through the mail, up to a specified date. Arthur and Arline Chevalier mailed in a bid that turned out to be the highest. When the town refused to sell them the lot, they sued. Result?

3. Arturo hires Kate to work in his new sporting goods store. "Look," he explains, "I can only pay you $6.00 an hour. But if business is good a year from now, and you're still here, I'm sure I can pay you a healthy bonus." Four months later Arturo terminates Kate. She sues.

(a) Kate will win her job back, plus the year's pay and the bonus.

(b) Kate will win the year's pay and the bonus.

(c) Kate will win only the bonus.

(d) Kate will win only her job back.

(e) Kate will win nothing.

4. The Tufte family leased a 260-acre farm from the Travelers Insurance Co. Toward the end of the lease, Travelers mailed the Tuftes an option to renew the lease. The option arrived at the Tuftes' house on March 30, and gave them until April 14 to accept. On April 13, the Tuftes signed and mailed their acceptance, which Travelers received on April 19. Travelers claimed there was no lease and attempted to evict the Tuftes from the farm. May they stay?

5. Northrop is a huge defense firm, and Litronic manufactures electronic components such as printed wire boards. Northrop requested Litronic to submit an offer on certain printed boards. Litronic sent its offer form, stating a price and including its pre-printed warranty clause, which limited its liability to 90 days. Northrop orally accepted the offer, then sent its own purchase order form, which contained a warranty clause holding the seller liable with no time limit. Six months after the goods were delivered Northrop discovered they were defective. Northrop sued, but Litronic claimed it had no liability. Was there a contract? If not, why not? If there was a contract, what were its warranty terms?

6. "Huge selection of Guernsey sweaters," reads a newspaper ad from Stuffed Shirt, a clothing retailer. "Regularly $135, today only $65." Waldo arrives at Stuffed Shirt at 4:00 that afternoon, but the shop clerk says there are no more sweaters. He shows Waldo a newly arrived Shetland sweater that sells for $145. Waldo sues, claiming breach of contract and violation of a consumer protection statute. Who will prevail?

(a) Waldo will win the breach of contract suit and the consumer protection suit.

(b) Waldo will lose the breach of contract suit but might win the consumer protection suit.

(c) Waldo will lose the consumer protection suit but should win the breach of contract suit.

(d) Waldo will win the consumer protection suit only if he wins the contract case.

(e) Waldo will lose both the breach of contract suit and the consumer protection suit.

7. Consolidated Edison Co. of New York (Con Ed) sought bids from General Electric Co. (GE) and others to supply it with two huge transformers. Con Ed required that the bids be held open for 90 days. GE submitted a written bid and included a clause holding the bid open for 90 days. During that period, Con Ed accepted GE's bid, but GE refused to honor it. Is there a contract?

8. The Dukes leased land from Lillian Whatley. Toward the end of their lease, they sent Ms. Whatley a new contract, renewing the lease for three years and giving themselves the option to buy the land at any time during the lease for $50,000. Ms. Whatley crossed out the clause giving them an option to buy. She added a sentence at the bottom, saying, "Should I, Lillian Whatley, decide to sell at end [sic] of three years, I will give the Dukes the first chance to buy." Then she signed the lease, which the Dukes accepted in the changed form. They continued to pay the rent until Ms. Whatley sold the land to another couple for $35,000. The Dukes sued. Are the Dukes entitled to the land at $50,000? At $35,000?

9. RIGHT & WRONG Bill Brown Trucking specializes in hauling oversize loads, those that cannot fit on ordinary tractor-trailers. Brown met with James Wofford, an agent for Glens Falls Insurance, and asked Wofford for a "full coverage" policy. Brown showed Wofford photos of the kinds of loads his trucks hauled. Wofford issued Brown a policy, telling him, "You've got full coverage." One of Brown's trucks was hauling a large "asphalt dryer" on a tractor-trailer. The dryer itself struck a bridge overpass, but the truck was unhurt. Glens Falls refused coverage, pointing out that the policy was limited to accidents involving the "conveyance," meaning the truck. Brown sued. Assume that the policy clearly limited coverage to the "conveyance." Did Brown have a case? Regardless of the legal issues, does the insurance company have an ethical obligation to help one of its insured, or is it free to dispute any claim if the company believes it has a chance to win? Insurance contracts are drafted by the company, not the insured. Does that affect ethical considerations?

10. YOU BE THE JUDGE WRITING PROBLEM Academy Chicago Publishers (Academy) approached the widow of author John Cheever about printing some of his unpublished stories. She signed a contract, which stated:

> 2. The Author will deliver to the Publisher on a mutually agreeable date one copy of the manuscript of the Work as finally arranged by the editor and satisfactory to the Publisher in form and content. . . .
>
> 5. Within a reasonable time and a mutually agreeable date after delivery of the final revised manuscript, the Publisher will publish the Work at its own expense, in such style and manner and at such price as it deems best, and will keep the Work in print as long as it deems it expedient.

Within a year, Academy had located and delivered to Mrs. Cheever more than 60 unpublished stories. But she refused to go ahead with the project. Academy sued for the right to publish the book. The trial court ruled that the agreement was valid; the appeals court affirmed; and the case went to the Illinois Supreme Court. Was Academy's offer valid, and was the contract enforceable? **Argument for Mrs. Cheever:** The agreement is too vague to be enforceable. None of the essential terms are specified: the number of stories, their length, who selects them, the date of publication, the size or cost of the book, or anything else. There is no contract. **Argument for Academy:** Mrs. Cheever wanted to publish this book and agreed in writing to help Academy do so. Both parties understood the essential nature of the book and were willing to permit some flexibility, to ensure a good edition. She has no right to back out now.

11. Rebecca, in Honolulu, faxes a job offer to Spike, in Pittsburgh, saying, "We can pay you $55,000 per year, starting June 1." Spike faxes a reply, saying, "Thank you! I accept your generous offer, though I will also need $3,000 in relocation money. See you June 1. Can't wait!" On June 1 Spike arrives, to find that his position is filled by Gus. He sues Rebecca.

(a) Spike wins $55,000.

(b) Spike wins $58,000.

(c) Spike wins $3,000.

(d) Spike wins restitution.

(e) Spike wins nothing.

INTERNET RESEARCH PROBLEM

Search the Internet for an auction with a ring selling for over $500. Is the site reliable? Who is actually selling the item? If you were to pay for the ring, would you receive it? If you were unhappy with your purchase, what remedies would you have? How can you ascertain the Web site's reliability?

You can find further practice problems in the Online Quiz at http://beatty.westbuslaw.com or in the Study Guide that accompanies this text.

CHAPTER 12

CONSIDERATION

We have all made promises that we soon regretted. Mercifully, the law does not hold us accountable for everything we say. Yet some promises *must* be enforced. Which ones? The doctrine of consideration exists for one purpose: to distinguish promises that are binding from those that are not. Which of these four promises should a court enforce?

Promise One. In a delirious burst of affection, Professor Parsley says to a class of 50 students, "You've been a great class all semester. Next week I'm going to mail each of you a check for $1,000." But that night, the professor reconsiders and decides that her class is actually a patch full of cabbage heads whose idea of work is getting out of bed before noon. The following day, in class, Parsley announces that she has changed her mind. Mike, a student, sues for his $1,000. Should a court enforce the professor's promise?

Promise Two. After class, Parsley promises a student, Daisy, a part-time job as a researcher for the rest of the semester. "You can start on Monday," she says, "and we'll work out pay and all the details then." "You mean I can give up my job at Burger Bucket?" asks an elated Daisy. "Sure thing," chirps the prof. But on Monday, Parsley informs Daisy that she has lost the funding for her research and can offer no job. Daisy is unable to get back her position at Burger Bucket and sues Parsley.

Promise Three. Professor Parsley announces in class that she will be selling her skis at the end of the semester for $450. After class, Arabella says she would like to buy the skis but can only afford to pay $250. Parsley frowns and mutters, "They're worth a lot more than that." But Arabella looks so heartbroken that Parsley adds, "OK, what the heck. You can have them May 15." On that date Arabella shows up with the cash, but Parsley explains that another student offered her the full $450 for the skis and she sold them. Arabella purchases a nearly identical pair for $475 and sues Parsley.

Promise Four. The professor makes no promise at all. In fact, she announces in class that she will be unable to attend the next session because her favorite racehorse, Preexisting Duty, is running in the third race at the local track and she wants to be there. The students are crushed at the idea of missing a class. Sam wails, "Don't do this to us, Professor! I'll pay you twenty bucks if you'll be here to teach us." Other students chime in, and in a groundswell of tears and emotion, the students promise a total of $1,000 if Parsley will do her job. She agrees. When she arrives to teach the next class, 50 suddenly sullen students refuse to pay, and *she* sues.

Society could enforce *all* promises in the interests of simple morality. Or should it enforce only those where the two sides engaged in some bargaining? Does it matter whether someone relied on a promise? Should the outcome be different if someone is promising to do what she is already obligated to do? These are important policy questions, affecting promises for a hundred dollars and deals for a billion; their answers lie in the law of consideration.

A Bargain and an Exchange

Consideration is a required element of any contract. **Consideration means that there must be bargaining that leads to an exchange between the parties.** "Bargaining" indicates that each side is obligating itself in some way *to induce the other side to agree.* Generally, a court will enforce one party's promise only if the other party did something or promised something in exchange. Without an exchange of mutual obligations, there is usually no deal.

How would the four Parsley examples in the introduction work out? In the first case, Mike loses. There is no consideration because the students neither bargained for Parsley's promise nor gave anything in exchange for it. In the second case, there is also no contract because none of the terms were definite. What were Daisy's hours, her salary, her duties? But although she cannot sue on a contract, Daisy has a decent claim of promissory estoppel, the one major exception to the rule of consideration. Because Daisy relied on Parsley's promise, a court may give her some compensation. In case three, Arabella should win. A bargain and an exchange occurred. The professor promised to sell the skis at a given price, then broke her promise. Arabella will probably recover $225, the difference between the contract price and what she was forced to pay for substitute skis. Finally, in the fourth case, the professor loses. Clearly, bargaining and an exchange took place, but the professor only promised to do something that she was already obligated to do. The law does not respect such a promise.

We will look more deeply into these issues. First, a case to demonstrate the basic rule: there must be bargaining and an exchange.

KELSOE v. INTERNATIONAL WOOD PRODUCTS, INC.

588 So. 2d 877, 1991 Ala. LEXIS 1014
Supreme Court of Alabama, 1991

Facts: Carol Kelsoe worked at International Wood Products. One day her supervisor, Rene Hernandez, promised Kelsoe 5 percent of the company's stock. But he never gave her the shares, and she sued. The trial court gave a directed verdict for International Wood, and Kelsoe appealed.

Issue: **Is Hernandez's promise binding?**

Excerpts from Justice Houston's Decision: Kelsoe's employer, International Wood, through Rene Hernandez, Sr., one of the corporation's directors and its major stockholder, promised Kelsoe that it would issue 5 percent of the corporation's stock to her. Kelsoe's undisputed trial testimony reflects the nature of that promise:

Q. [by the lawyer for International Wood:] Ms. Kelsoe, you were compensated for your work at International Wood, weren't you?[1]

A. Yes, sir, I received a check.

Q. Were you pleased with your compensation?

A. Yes, sir.

Q. Did you think you were compensated well enough for the work you did?

A. I worked long hours, long hours.

Q. My question was did you think that you were adequately compensated for the work you did?

A. Yes, sir.

Q. Ms. Kelsoe, you never entered an agreement with Mr. Hernandez; "Mr. Hernandez, if I work long and hard and do this" and then he said, "I'll give you five percent of the corporation," did you?

A. No, sir.

Q. You never had that kind of a bargain, did you?

A. No, sir.

Q. And all the time, all the work you did was part of your normal job?

A. Yes, sir.

Q. And then [on] March 8th, you were getting a little reward that you didn't really expect, weren't you?

A. Yes, sir.

Q. You didn't expect to get that five percent, but it was nice, wasn't it?

A. Yes, sir.

Q. And you didn't expect it, though, did you?

A. No, sir.

Q. And you had no reason to expect it?

A. No, sir.

---

[1] International Wood's lawyer is cross-examining Ms. Kelsoe, so he is permitted to ask leading questions.

Q. And you just kept right on from March 8th doing your work, didn't you?

A. That's correct.

Q. And you didn't stay on [at] International Wood Products, you didn't commit yourself to Mr. Hernandez, "I'll stay on forever," did you? Or, "I'll stay on for five years in return for this?" You left yourself free to quit at any time, didn't you?

A. Yes, sir, that's correct.

Q. He just up one day and surprised you and said here is five percent of this corporation?

A. Yes, sir.

The trial court directed a verdict for International Wood on the ground that there was no consideration for International Wood's promise to issue the stock to Kelsoe. It is a well-settled general rule that consideration is an essential element of a contract. It is generally stated that in order to constitute consideration for a promise, there must have been an act, a forbearance, a detriment, or a return promise, bargained for and given in exchange for the promise. The undisputed evidence here shows that International Wood's promise to issue the stock to Kelsoe was gratuitous in nature and was prompted only by Kelsoe's past favorable job performance. As such, International Wood's promise was without consideration and created no legally enforceable contract right. The directed verdict for International Wood was proper.

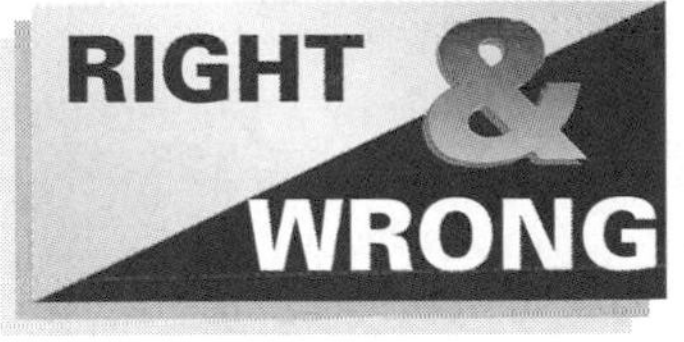

Because Kelsoe had given no consideration, International Wood was legally permitted to escape from its promise. But was that ethical? Should a corporation honor all commitments to employees? What policy would create the best workforce? What harm might befall a company that fulfilled all promises? What decision would you have made if you were Hernandez's boss and had the power to award the stock to Kelsoe or deny it?

When trying to enforce a defendant's promise, the plaintiff must show that she did something or promised something in exchange for that promise. What sort of action or promise is good enough? It need not be much. **Consideration can be anything that someone might want to bargain for.** As we explore this idea, we need to use two more legal terms: **promisor**, meaning the person who makes the promise, and **promisee**, the person to whom the promise is made. In consideration cases, a court is typically trying to determine whether the promisee should be able to enforce the promise, and the decision will depend upon whether the promisee gave consideration.

The thing bargained for can be another promise or action. Usually, the thing bargained for is another promise. In the *Kelsoe* case, suppose Hernandez had said, "I will give you 5 percent of our stock if you'll promise not to quit for three years," and Kelsoe had agreed to stay. Her promise would be consideration, making Hernandez's promise enforceable. They would have had a typical bilateral contract. See Exhibit 12.1.

The thing bargained for can be an action, rather than a promise. Suppose Professor Parsley says to Wade, "If you plow my driveway by tonight, I'll pay you $150." Her offer seeks an action, not a promise. If Wade plows the driveway, his work is consideration and the parties have a binding contract.

The thing bargained for can be a benefit to the promisor or a detriment to the promisee. If Hernandez had asked Kelsoe to stay on at International Wood, her promise to do so would have been a benefit to the company. That is consideration.

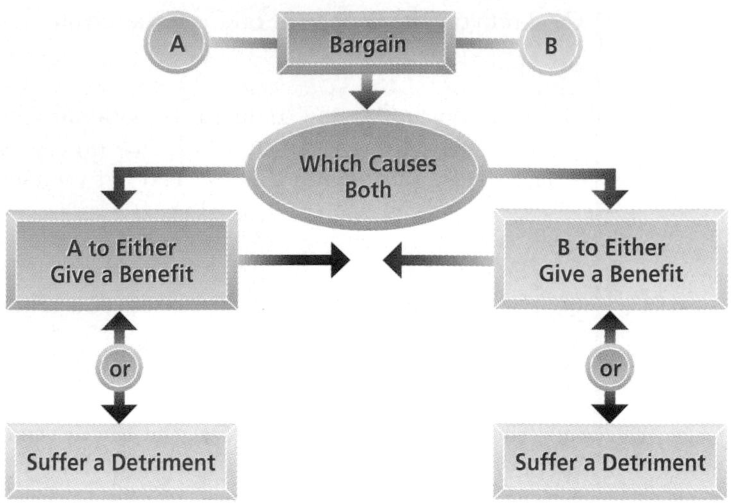

Exhibit 12.1
There is consideration to support a contract when A and B bargain, and their bargaining causes both A and B either to give a benefit to the other or to suffer a detriment.

Suppose Professor Parsley says to the class, "You're all in terrible shape. I offer $25 to anyone who enters next week's marathon and finishes the race." "No way," shouts Joanne. "But I'll do it for $100." Parsley agrees and Joanne completes the entire race. Her running was of no particular benefit to Parsley, but it was clearly a detriment to Joanne, so Parsley owes her $100.

The thing bargained for can be a promise to do something or a promise to refrain from doing something. Megan promises *to deliver* 1,000 canoes in two months if Casey agrees to pay $300 per canoe. Megan's promise is consideration. Leroy, who runs a beauty parlor, offers Chloe $75,000 not to open a beauty parlor within 30 miles. Chloe's promise *not to* compete is consideration.

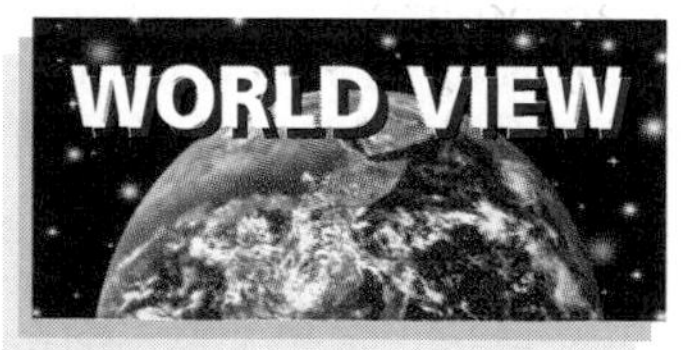

The concept of consideration is widespread, but not universal. In Singapore, consideration is required to make a binding agreement, and the doctrine means exactly what it does in the United States. Both nations trace their contract principles to a common source: England. For an interesting overview of Singapore's contract law, see **http://www.np.ac.sg/~rbj/con2.htm**. In Japan, by contrast, consideration is not essential, and an agreement made without it can be binding. An American executive negotiating a business deal with a Japanese counterpart should realize that a promise he views as casual could be legally enforceable in Japan. For a useful comparison of Japanese contract principles, see **http://www.japanlaw.com**.

The most famous of all consideration lawsuits began in 1869, when a well-meaning uncle made a promise to his nephew. Ever since *Hamer v. Sidway* appeared, generations of American law students have dutifully inhaled the facts and sworn by its wisdom; now you, too, may drink it in.

HAMER v. SIDWAY
124 N.Y. 538, 27 N.E. 256, 1891
N.Y. LEXIS 1396
New York Court of Appeals, 1891

Facts: This is a story with two Stories. William Story wanted his nephew to grow up healthy and prosperous. In 1869, he promised the 15-year-old boy (*also* William Story) $5,000 if the lad would refrain from drinking liquor, using tobacco, swearing, and playing cards or billiards for money until his twenty-first birthday. (In that wild era—can you believe it?—the nephew had a legal right to do all those things.) The nephew agreed and, what is more, he kept his word. When he reached his twenty-first birthday, the nephew notified his uncle that he had honored the agreement. The uncle congratulated the young man and promised to give him the money, but said he would wait a few more years before handing over the cash, until the nephew was mature enough to handle such a large sum. The uncle died in 1887 without having paid, and his estate refused to honor the promise. Because the nephew had transferred his rights in the money, it was a man named Hamer who eventually sought to collect from the uncle's estate. The estate argued that since the nephew had given no consideration for the uncle's promise, there was no enforceable contract. The trial court found for the plaintiff, and the uncle's estate appealed.

Issue: **Did the nephew give consideration for the uncle's promise?**

Excerpts from Justice Parker's Decision: The defendant contends that the contract was without consideration to support it, and therefore invalid. He asserts that the promisee, by refraining from the use of liquor and tobacco, was not harmed, but benefited; that that which he did was best for him to do, independently of his uncle's promise,—and insists that it follows that, unless the promisor was benefited, the contract was without consideration,— a contention which, if well founded, would seem to leave open for controversy in many cases whether that which the promisee did or omitted to do was in fact of such benefit to him as to leave no consideration to support the enforcement of the promisor's agreement. Such a rule could not be tolerated, and is without foundation in the law. Courts will not ask whether the thing which forms the consideration does in fact benefit the promisee or a third party, or is of any substantial value to any one. It is enough that something is promised, done, forborne, or suffered by the party to whom the promise is made as consideration for the promise made to him.

Now applying this rule to the facts before us, the promisee used tobacco, occasionally drank liquor, and he had a legal right to do so. That right he abandoned for a period of years upon the strength of the promise of the testator [that is, the uncle] that for such forbearance he would give him $5,000. We need not speculate on the effort which may have been required to give up the use of those stimulants. It is sufficient that he restricted his lawful freedom of action within certain prescribed limits upon the faith of his uncle's agreement, and now, having fully performed the conditions imposed, it is of no moment whether such performance actually proved a benefit to the promisor, and the court will not inquire into it.

ADEQUACY OF CONSIDERATION

Gold can make people crazy. At the turn of the 20th century, John Tuppela joined the gold rush to Alaska. He bought a mine and worked it hard, a disciplined man in an unforgiving enterprise. Sadly, his prospecting proved futile and mental problems overwhelmed him. In 1914, a court declared him insane and locked him in an institution in Portland, Oregon. Four years later, Tuppela emerged and learned to his ecstasy that gold had been discovered in his mine, now valued at over half a million dollars. But then the bad news hit: a court-appointed guardian had sold the mine for pennies while Tuppela was institutionalized. Destitute and forlorn, Tuppela begged relatives for a small amount of money to get him back to Alaska to launch a legal fight for the mine. Everyone regarded his cause as hopeless and refused him aid. Finally, he turned to his lifelong friend, Embola, saying, "If you will give me $50 so I can go to Alaska and get my property back, I will pay you $10,000 when I win my property." Embola accepted the offer, advancing the $50.

After a long and bitter fight, Tuppela won back his mine, though a guardian would still supervise his assets. Tuppela asked the guardian to pay the full $10,000 to Embola, but the guardian refused. Embola sued, and the issue was whether his

$50 was *adequate consideration* to support Tuppela's promise of $10,000. A happy ending: Embola won and recovered his money.

Courts seldom inquire into the *adequacy* of consideration. Although the difference between Embola's $50 and Tuppela's $10,000 was huge, it was not for a court to decide whether the parties had made an intelligent bargain. Embola undertook a risk and his $50 *was valid consideration*. The question of adequacy is for the parties as they bargain, not for the courts.

MUTUALITY OF OBLIGATIONS

Generally, both sides must be committed to the agreement to make it enforceable. Though courts will not inquire into the adequacy of consideration, they will insist that it be genuine. In some cases a party appears to make a commitment but actually does not. The result: no contract. Here we examine the major issues concerning mutuality.

ILLUSORY PROMISE

Annabel calls Jim and says, "I'll sell you my bicycle for 325 bucks. Interested?" Jim says, "I'll look at it tonight in the bike rack. If I like what I see, I'll pay you three and a quarter in the morning." At sunrise, Jim shows up with the $325 but Annabel refuses to sell. Can Jim enforce their deal? No. He said he would buy the bicycle *if he liked it*, keeping for himself the power to get out of the agreement for any reason at all. He is not committing himself to do anything, and the law considers his promise illusory, that is, not really a promise at all. **An illusory promise is not consideration.** Because he has given no consideration, there is no contract and *neither party* can enforce the deal. Is the promise in the following case illusory?

CULBERTSON v. BRODSKY
788 S.W.2d 156, 1990 Tex. App. LEXIS 1008
Texas Court of Appeals, 1990

Facts: Sam Culbertson had some Texas real estate to sell. He and Frederick Brodsky signed an option contract. Brodsky was to deliver a check for $5,000, representing "earnest money," to a bank. The bank would hold the check in escrow for 60 days. During that period, the bank would not cash it. Brodsky could inspect the property and perform engineering studies to determine whether the real estate could be used for his purposes. If he decided that the land was of no use to him, he could terminate the agreement and demand return of his earnest money. Ultimately, Brodsky decided that he did want to buy the land, but Culbertson refused to sell, claiming that Brodsky gave no consideration to support their contract. The trial court gave judgment for Brodsky, ordering Culbertson to convey the land. Culbertson appealed.

You Be the Judge: Did Brodsky give valid consideration that makes Culbertson's promise enforceable?

Argument for Culbertson: Your honors, Mr. Brodsky made a very sly promise, since it was in fact no promise at all. Brodsky insisted on keeping the right to terminate this phony agreement at any time, for any reason. Mr. Culbertson was expected to leave the property off the market for 60 valuable days while Brodsky took his own sweet time to inspect the land, perform engineering tests, make feasibility calculations, reconsider his position, and ultimately decide whether he had any interest in the property. If he decided *for any reason* that he no longer wanted the land, Brodsky could simply walk away from the deal. Please note that he didn't even lose the use of the $5,000. The bank was not permitted to cash the check until Brodsky made up his mind. No money ever left Brodsky's account—indeed, no money even had to be in his account, unless and until he decided to exercise his option.

A true option contract provides something for each party. The landowner is obligated to hold the property open for the buyer, but the buyer pays a fee for this privilege. Here, Brodsky was obligated to pay nothing and do nothing. He made no promise at all, and we urge that no contract resulted.

Argument for Mr. Brodsky: Your honors, it is rather disingenuous of Mr. Culbertson to pose as an injured party here. He is, in fact, a sophisticated property owner. He voluntarily entered into a contract with Mr. Brodsky for one reason: it was in his own interest. He concluded that the best way to "land" Mr. Brodsky was first to "hook" him with an option contract. He wanted Mr. Brodsky to show serious interest, and demanded earnest money. He got it. He insisted that Mr. Brodsky's check be held in escrow. He got it. Culbertson hoped that by getting this degree of commitment, Mr. Brodsky would perform the necessary tests on the land and conclude that he wanted to buy it. And that is *precisely what happened*. Mr. Brodsky, in total good faith, performed his tests, decided the land was what he had wanted, and exercised the option that Culbertson had sold him. But Culbertson decided to back out of the deal—presumably to sell elsewhere.

Now Culbertson comes into court and relies on a technical rule of contract law to try to weasel out of a good faith deal. The law of consideration was never intended to permit such chicanery.

SALES LAW: REQUIREMENTS AND OUTPUT CONTRACTS

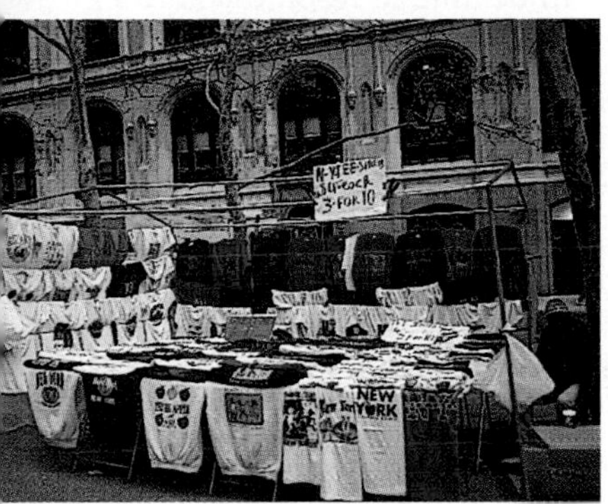

What are your obligations under a requirements contract?

You decide to open a "novelty T-shirt" business. You will buy plain white T-shirts from a wholesaler and then arrange for them to be printed with funny pictures and quotes. You will sell them to the public from a small booth you rent in a popular shopping mall. Your single biggest expense will be the wholesale cost of the T-shirts. How many will you need? You *think* that sales will soar, and you will need hundreds each week. But what if business lags? You do not want to overstock. Your solution may be a requirements contract.

In a requirements contract, the buyer agrees to purchase 100 percent of her goods from one seller. The seller agrees to sell the buyer whatever quantity she reasonably needs. The quantity is not stated in the contract, though it may be estimated, based on previous years or best calculations.

The common law regarded requirements contracts as void because the buyer held all the power. She could purchase a vast quantity or none at all. She was making no commitment, and hence was giving no consideration. Common law courts refused to enforce requirements contracts, as well as their counterpart, output contracts. **In an output contract, the seller guarantees to sell 100 percent of its output to one buyer, and the buyer agrees to accept the entire quantity.** For example, a timber company might agree to sell all of its wood products to a lumber wholesaler. The common law frowned because now it was the seller who was making no real commitment.

The problem with the common law rule was that many merchants valued these contracts. Consider the utility of requirements contracts. From the buyer's viewpoint, a requirements contract provides flexibility. The buyer can adjust purchases based on consumer demands. The agreement also guarantees her a source of goods in a competitive market. For a seller, the requirements agreement will ensure him at least this one outlet and will prevent competitors from selling to this buyer. The contract should enable the seller to spend less on marketing, and may enable him to predict sales more accurately. Output contracts have similar value.

The UCC responded in a forthright fashion: **Section 2-306 expressly allows output and requirements contracts in the sale of goods.**[2] However, the Code

[2] UCC §2-306(2) permits a related type of contract, the exclusive dealing agreement. Here, either a buyer or a seller of goods agrees to deal exclusively with the other party. The results are similar to an output or requirements agreement. Once again, one party is receiving a guarantee in exchange for a promise that the common law would have considered illusory. Under the Code, such a deal is enforceable.

places one limitation on how much the buyer may demand (or the seller may offer):

> A term which measures the quantity by the output of the seller or the requirements of the buyer means such actual output or requirements as may occur *in good faith*, . . .

The "good faith" phrase is critical. In requirements contracts, courts have ruled that it is the "good faith" that a buyer brings to the deal that represents her consideration.[3] In other words, by agreeing to act in good faith, she actually *is* limiting her options. Since she is obligating herself, the deal becomes binding. Beware that this is not just word play. A buyer *must make its requirement demands in good faith*, based on the expectations the parties had when they signed the deal.

Suppose, in your T-shirt business, you and the wholesaler agree on a two-year requirements contract with a fixed price of three dollars per T-shirt and an estimate of 150 T-shirts per week. If business is slow the first two months, you *are* permitted to purchase only 25 T-shirts per week in the event that is all you are selling. Should sales suddenly boom and you need 200 per week, you may also require that many. Both of those demands are made in good faith. But suppose the price of cotton skyrockets and the wholesale cost of T-shirts everywhere suddenly doubles. You have a two-year guaranteed price of three dollars per T-shirt. Could you demand 2,000 T-shirts per week, knowing that you will be able to resell the shirts to other retailers for a big profit? No. That is not acting in good faith based on the original expectations of the parties. The wholesaler is free to ignore your exorbitant demand. The legal requirement has come full circle: your good faith is valid consideration and makes the deal enforceable—but it is binding on you, too.

Requirements contracts provide security—at a cost. A price that seems attractive when the deal is made may be repugnant when the market changes. A savvy executive can protect his company by combining a requirements contract with flexible price arrangements.

John Stokes is the president of Electric Lite, a new, privately owned company that supplies power in Portland, Oregon. Like many such companies around the nation, Electric Lite got plugged in because federal and state regulators have opened to competition an industry once dominated by monopolies.

Stokes needed a guaranteed source of power to supply his customers, so he agreed to a requirements contract with a local power supplier. Stokes promised to purchase all the electricity he required from the company, which guaranteed to supply all the power Electric Lite needed. But at what price? On the one hand, with a fixed rate, a sudden drop in the wholesale cost of electricity could leave Electric Lite with a long-term obligation to pay exorbitantly for its supplies. On the other hand, a price tied to a floating index, such as the local wholesale electric rate, could become ruinous if those prices were to skyrocket. A final, critical variable was that Stokes did not know how many customers he would have over the next few years. He decided to hedge his bets.

Stokes agreed with his power source to establish a minimum/maximum range of expected power demand. As long as Electric Lite's needs fell within that band, it would pay its supplier a fixed rate. If the company required more electricity, it would pay for the additional power at a floating rate, tied to the local electricity index. If Stokes needed less power than he anticipated, he would be free to sell his unused power to third parties at the index price. Neither this formula nor any other guarantees a profit, but Stokes has creatively used a requirements contract and flexible pricing to give his company a strong chance in a competitive industry.

[3] *Famous Brands, Inc. v. David Sherman Corp.*, 814 F.2d 517, 1987 U.S. App. LEXIS 3634 (8th Cir. 1987).

PAST CONSIDERATION

In *Kelsoe v. International Wood Products, Inc.* (discussed earlier in this chapter), International Wood's manager, Hernandez, promised employee Carol Kelsoe some shares of the company stock, but never delivered them. She sued and lost, because there had been no bargaining and no exchange. Yet Hernandez must have had some reason for making the promise. Presumably, it was because of Kelsoe's good work for the company in years past. Could she claim the previous work as consideration? No.

Past consideration is generally no consideration. It all goes back to our basic definition of consideration, which requires bargaining and an exchange of obligations. If one party makes a promise based on what the other party has already done, there is no exchange, and there will usually be no enforceable contract.

DEMENTAS v. ESTATE OF TALLAS
95 Utah Adv. Rep. 28, 764 P.2d 628, 1988 Utah App. LEXIS 174
Utah Court of Appeals, 1988

Facts: Jack Tallas came to the United States from Greece in 1914. He lived in Salt Lake City for nearly 70 years, achieving great success in insurance and real estate. When he died, he left a large estate. During the last 14 years of his life, Tallas was a close friend of Peter Dementas, who helped him with numerous personal and business chores. Two months before his death, Tallas met with Dementas and dictated a memorandum to him, in Greek, stating:

> PETER K. DEMENTAS, is my best friend I have in this country and since he came to the United States he treats me like a father and I think of him as my own son. He takes me in his car grocery shopping. He drives me to the doctor and also takes me every week to Bingham to pick up my mail, collect the rents and manage my properties. For all the services Peter has given me all these years, I owe to him the amount of $50,000 (Fifty Thousand Dollars.) I will shortly change my will to include him as my heir.

Tallas signed the memorandum, but he did not in fact alter his will to include Dementas. The estate refused to pay, and Dementas sued. The trial was entertaining, thanks to Judge Dee, whose remarks included: "It's hearsay, I agree, but its damn good hearsay, and I want to hear it." Urging a lawyer to hurry up, the judge snapped, "Go on to your next question. This witness—who is supposed to be one witness for 15 minutes—is now into the second day, and we've still got the same witness. . . . At the rate we're going, I will have long retired and been happily fishing in Wyoming." Finally hearing something worthwhile from the witness, he interrupted, "Wait a minute. Wait. Wait. Wait. Now, the factfinder has finally got a fact. He said, 'I did it a lot of times.' I've identified a fact in a day and a half. Let's go to the next witness and see if we can find another one in this case."

Unfortunately for Dementas, when the testimony ground to a halt, Judge Dee ruled that there was no consideration to support Tallas's promise. Dementas appealed.

Issue: Was there consideration to make Tallas's promise enforceable?

Excerpts from Judge Orme's Decision: A generally accepted definition of consideration is that a legal detriment has been bargained for and exchanged for a promise. The mere fact that one man promises something to another creates no legal duty and makes no legal remedy available in case of non-performance. A performance or a returned promise must be bargained for.

In determining whether consideration to support a personal service contract exists, the focus is not whether the amount promised represents the fair market value for the services rendered. On the contrary, as a general rule it is settled that any detriment no matter how economically inadequate will support a promise. In this regard, the court correctly stated: "If Tallas thought it was worth 50,000 bucks to get one ride to Bingham, that's Tallas' decision.... The only thing you can't do is take it with you."

Even though the testimony showed that Dementas rendered at least some services for Tallas, the subsequent promise by Tallas to pay $50,000 for services already performed by Dementas is not a promise supported by legal consideration. Events which occur prior to the making of the promise and not with the purpose of inducing the promise in exchange are viewed as past consideration and are the legal equivalent of no consideration. This is so because the promisor is making his promise because those events occurred, but he is not making his promise in order to get them. There is no "bargaining"; no saying that if you will do this for me I will do that for you.

This rule can surely work unfair results and has accordingly been criticized and the object of legislation. Some courts have sought to enforce promises supported only by past consideration by invoking a "moral obligation" notion to make at least some of these promises enforceable. Although the "moral obligation" exception has not been embraced in Utah, other courts apply the exception in cases where services rendered in the past were rendered with the expectation of payment rather than gratuitously.

Even if the "moral obligation" doctrine applied in Utah, Dementas would not prevail. The trial court found that the services rendered by Dementas to Tallas were not rendered with the expectation of being compensated, but were performed gratuitously. That finding has not been shown to be erroneous.

[Judgment for the estate is *affirmed*.]

Exception: Economic Benefit

As the *Dementas* court mentions, there is a modest trend in the law in favor of enforcing promises based on past consideration *if that consideration was an economic benefit that was rendered with the expectation of payment*. The Restatement (Second) of Contracts §86 suggests that promises based on past consideration may be enforceable "to the extent necessary to avoid injustice." But as we can see from the *Kelsoe* and *Dementas* cases, the courts are loathe to carve exceptions into this venerable rule.

PROMISSORY ESTOPPEL

In the two preceding chapters we have seen that a plaintiff who cannot prove a binding contract *may* be able to recover under the doctrine of promissory estoppel. This doctrine is a result of judicial activism and requires a plaintiff to prove that:

- The offeror made a promise knowing the offeree was likely to rely
- The offeree did in fact rely; and
- The only way to avoid injustice is to enforce the promise.

We have seen, for example, that promissory estoppel may help a borrower when a bank loan is too indefinite to create a binding contract.[4] Promissory estoppel can also save a plaintiff who is unable to demonstrate consideration. If a promisor makes a promise but receives no consideration in return, there is no contract. But if the promisee reasonably relied on the promise, a court *may* enforce it.

---

[4] See the case of *First National Bank of Logansport v. Logan Manufacturing Co.*, 577 N.E.2d 949, 1991 Ind. LEXIS 130 (Ind. 1991), discussed in Chapter 11, on agreement.

John Grouse graduated from the University of Minnesota School of Pharmacy and began working at Richter Drug, a retail store in Minneapolis. But he wanted more interesting work in a clinical setting, so he applied for various jobs, including one at Group Health Plan. After several interviews, Group Health telephoned Grouse and offered him a job at one of its clinics. Grouse accepted, telling Group Health that he would need to give two weeks' notice to the retail pharmacy. Grouse promptly notified Richter Drug that he was leaving in two weeks. That same afternoon, Grouse received a job offer from a Veterans' Administration hospital in Virginia, but turned it down because of the Group Health offer. Group Health, meanwhile, was unable to obtain references for Grouse. The company hired someone else to take the position. Grouse was left with no job at all, and sued.

The trial court dismissed Grouse's case, ruling that there was no agreement. The Minnesota Supreme Court agreed that there was no valid contract, evidently because Group Health's offer was indefinite. But the court declared that Grouse had reasonably relied on Group Health's promise of a job and had been injured:

> A promise which the promisor should reasonably expect to induce action or forbearance on the part of the promisee and which does induce such action or forbearance is binding if injustice can be avoided only by enforcement of the promise. Group Health knew that to accept its offer Grouse would have to resign his employment at Richter Drug. Grouse promptly gave notice to Richter Drug and informed Group Health that he had done so when specifically asked by Elliott. Under these circumstances it would be unjust not to hold Group Health to its promise.[5]

But while promissory estoppel was invaluable to John Grouse, remember that it is very much the exception. Most courts think in traditional terms, and claims of promissory estoppel, though often made, are generally denied.

General Motors hoped to remodel its automobile plants at Ypsilanti, Michigan, but did not want to pay additional taxes on the improved building. The company sought a tax abatement (reduction) from Ypsilanti. Such an abatement is serious business, since a town is dependent on these taxes for its survival. In public hearings, General Motors stated that it intended to produce a new model Chevrolet Caprice in Ypsilanti, provided it could get the abatement. The company employed over 13,000 workers, so Ypsilanti was desperate to keep it happy. The town granted GM a 12-year abatement of 50 percent of all taxes due on the improvements, a tremendous savings for the company. But three years later, General Motors decided to move its Caprice production to a Texas factory, costing Ypsilanti thousands of jobs. The town sued and demonstrated that it had lost $2 million in revenue by granting the abatement.

The trial judge found promissory estoppel. He declared that GM had made a clear promise to remain in Ypsilanti, that the town had relied on the promise by giving the abatement, and had suffered enormous harm. The judge's anger rang out in unusually strong language:

> Each judge who dons this robe assumes the awesome, and lonely, responsibility to make decisions about justice, and injustice, which will dramatically affect the way people are forced to live their lives. Every such decision must be the judge's own and it must be made honestly and in good conscience. There would be gross inequity and patent unfairness if General Motors, having lulled the people of the Ypsilanti area into giving up millions of tax dollars which they so desperately need to educate their children and provide basic governmental services, is allowed to simply decide that it will desert 4,500 workers and their families because it thinks it can make these same cars a little cheaper somewhere else. Perhaps another judge in another court would not feel moved by that injustice and would labor to find a legal rationalization to allow such conduct. But in this court it is my responsibility to make that decision. My conscience will not allow this injustice to happen.

---

[5] *Grouse v. Group Health Plan, Inc.*, 306 N.W.2d 114, 1981 Minn. LEXIS 1319 (Minn. 1981).

The appeals court appreciated this extravagant language—and promptly reversed. It ruled that GM's statements about remaining in Ypsilanti were *not promises*. They were puffery, said the court, the kind of statements that any company seeking a tax advantage would make. Without a promise, there can be no promissory estoppel. Ypsilanti lost—as do most plaintiffs claiming promissory estoppel.[6]

The Michigan legislature responded to the Ypsilanti case by changing statutory law. Cities in Michigan must now obtain a written commitment from a company before granting an abatement.

PREEXISTING DUTY

You are building your dream house, a shingle and glass paragon of supernal originality, nestled on a hillside overlooking 300 acres of postcard-perfect wilderness. The builder has agreed to finish the project by September 1, and you have already sold your current house, scheduled the moving company, and committed yourself at a new job. But in July, the builder announces he cannot finish the job. You're furious. He replies that transporting material has proven more expensive than he anticipated, and also that his carpenters and electricians have raised their rates. He can complete the work only if you agree to pay an extra $60,000, on top of the $350,000 you have already promised. You cannot afford the extra money and bitterly resent paying. But you desperately need the house finished, so you agree. On September 1 you move in, and the builder arrives to collect the final $60,000. Must you pay?

No. The builder gave no consideration to support your promise to pay the extra $60,000. It is true that the builder promised to finish by September 1, and true that a promise to do something is normally valid consideration. But the builder was already obligated to finish on September 1. He has not taken on any increased burden. **A promise to do something the promisor is already obligated to do is not valid consideration.**

Of course, exceptions are the spice of law, and the preexisting obligation rule provides us with a rack full. Courts have created these exceptions because a rigid application of the rule may interfere with legitimate business goals.

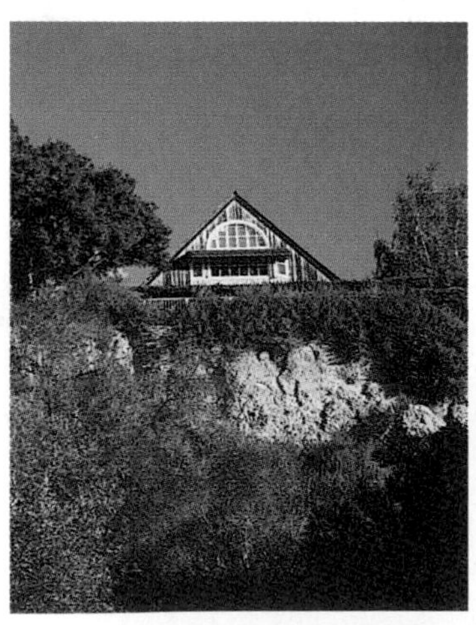
Can a builder enforce your promise to pay extra?

Exception: Additional Work

When a promisor agrees to do something above and beyond what he is obligated to do, his promise is valid consideration. Thus, if the builder asked for $60,000 extra but agreed that he would landscape the two acres surrounding the house, his promise is consideration. If you agree to pay the extra $60,000, you have created a binding contract.

Exception: Unforeseen Circumstances

Hugo has a deal to repair major highways. Hugo hires Hal's Hauling to cart soil and debris. Hal's trucks begin work, but after crossing the work site several times they sink to their axles in sinister, sucking slime. Hal demands an additional 35

[6] The appellate case is *Ypsilanti Township v. General Motors Corp.*, 201 Mich. App. 128, 506 N.W.2d 556, 1993 Mich. App. LEXIS 300 (Mich. Ct. App. 1993). The trial court's opinion is unpublished but quoted in the appellate decision and in Comment, 43 Case W. Res. L. Rev. 1475 (1993).

percent payment from Hugo to complete the job, pointing out that the surface was dry and cracked and that neither Hal nor Hugo was aware of the subsurface water. Hal howls that he must use different trucks with different tires and work more slowly to permit the soil to dry. Hugo hems and haws and finally agrees. But when the hauling is finished, Hugo refuses to pay the extra money. Is Hugo liable?

Yes. **When unforeseen circumstances cause a party to make a promise regarding an unfinished project, that promise is generally valid consideration.** Even though Hal is only promising to finish what he was already obligated to do, his promise is valid consideration because neither party knew of the subsoil mud. Hal was facing a situation quite different from what the parties anticipated. It is almost as though he were undertaking a new project. Hal has given consideration and Hugo is bound by his promise to pay extra money.

Unexpected problems such as subsoil water often arise in construction cases. A well-drafted contract will reduce the chances of a dispute. The parties should state in their agreement what conditions they expect to find, how they anticipate the work to proceed, and how they will compensate a party that encounters unexpected problems. For example, in the hauling contract, Hugo and Hal should have agreed on the following:

- A description of the surface and subsurface conditions that they anticipated
- The type of equipment necessary to haul it and the approximate time needed to transport a given quantity, such as "two hours per hundred cubic yards"
- A provision for periodic review of the conditions actually encountered; and
- A summary of how they will adjust the price—if at all—in the event the hauler encounters unexpected hardship.

Although drafting such a contract requires additional hours of work and some legal expense, it can easily save years of litigation and huge sums of money. To anticipate a problem is often to avoid it.

Exception: Mutual Rescission

If both parties agree that a modification is necessary, the surest way to accomplish that is to rescind the original contract and draft a new one. **To rescind means to cancel.** Thus, if neither party has completed its obligations, the agreement to rescind will terminate each party's rights and obligations under the old contract. This should be done in writing. Then the parties sign the new agreement. Most courts will enforce a mutual rescission unless it appears that one party unfairly coerced the other into the rescission.

Exception: Sale of Goods

Once again the UCC has changed the common law, making it easier for merchants to modify agreements for the sale of goods. UCC §2-209 provides:

- An agreement modifying a contract within this Article needs no consideration to be binding.
- A signed agreement which excludes modification or rescission except by a signed writing cannot be otherwise modified or rescinded.

Here is how these two provisions work together. Green Construction had a contract with the state of New Jersey to build highways. The company contracted with E.S.C. Stone Products to deliver 25,000 tons of crushed stone, which would be the underbase for the new roads. The contract stated that delivery of the stone would begin in September, be half finished by November, and entirely complete by April of the following year. But by New Year's Day, E.S.C. had delivered nary a pebble, and Green sued. E.S.C. contended that executives of the two companies had orally modified the agreement, allowing E.S.C. to deliver all the gravel in April and May.

Even if Green had orally made such an agreement, was it valid? Under the common law, the modification would be invalid. E.S.C. gave no consideration, since it was already obligated to deliver half the stone by November. But that is precisely the rule that the UCC has changed. Since this was a sale of goods, under §2-209(1), the modification could be valid even without consideration on the part of E.S.C.

Section (2), however, permits the parties to sign an agreement that forbids oral modifications. In their original contract, Green had included a clause stating that no modifications would be valid unless put in writing. There was no such written modification and Green won its lawsuit.[7]

SETTLEMENT OF DEBTS

You claim that your friend Felicity owes you $90,000, but she refuses to pay. Finally, when you are desperate, Felicity offers you a cashier's check for $60,000—provided you accept it as full settlement. To get your hands on some money, you agree and cash the check. The next day you sue Felicity for $30,000. Who wins? First, a related question.

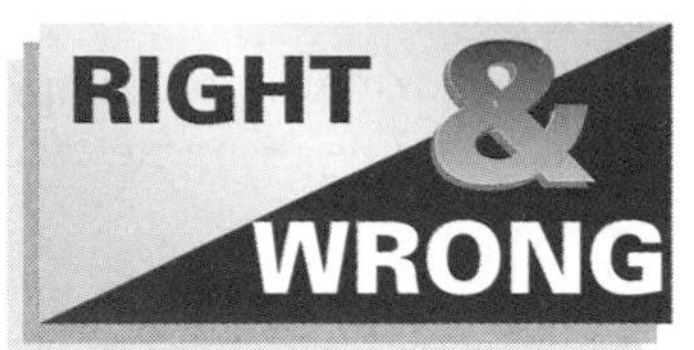

Even if you think you have a chance of winning, is it right to accept the money as full settlement and then sue for the balance? Under what circumstances would you feel ethically correct in doing that? When would you consider it wrong?

As to the legal outcome, it will depend principally upon one major issue: Was Felicity's debt liquidated or unliquidated?

LIQUIDATED DEBT

A **liquidated debt** is one in which there is no dispute about the amount owed. A loan is a typical example. If a bank lends you $10,000, and the note obligates you to repay that amount on June 1 of the following year, you clearly owe that sum. The debt is liquidated.

In cases of liquidated debt, if the creditor agrees to take less than the full amount as full payment, her agreement is not binding. The debtor has given no consideration to support the creditor's promise to accept a reduced payment, and therefore the creditor is not bound by her word. The reasoning is simply that the debtor is already obligated to pay the full amount, so no bargaining could reasonably cause the creditor to accept less. If Felicity's debt to you is liquidated, your agreement to accept $60,000 is not binding, and you will successfully sue for the balance.

---

[7] *Green Construction v. First Indemnity of America Insurance*, 735 F. Supp. 1254, 1990 U.S. Dist. LEXIS 12117 (D.N.J. 1990).

Exception: Different Performance

There is one important exception to this rule. If the debtor offers a *different performance* to settle the liquidated debt, and the creditor agrees to take it as full settlement, the agreement is binding. Suppose that Felicity, instead of paying $60,000, offers you five acres in Alaska and you accept. When you accept the deed to the land, you have given up your entire claim, regardless of the land's precise value.

UNLIQUIDATED DEBT

A debt is **unliquidated** for either of two reasons: (1) the parties dispute whether *any* money is owed, or (2) the parties agree that some money is owed but dispute *how much*. When a debt is unliquidated, for either reason, the parties may enter into a binding agreement to settle for less than what the creditor demands.

Such a compromise will be enforced if:

- The debt is unliquidated and
- The parties agree that the creditor will accept as full payment a sum less than she has claimed; and
- The debtor pays the amount agreed upon.

This agreement is called an **accord and satisfaction.** The accord is the agreement to settle for less than the creditor claims. The satisfaction is the actual payment of that compromised sum. An accord and satisfaction is valid consideration to support the creditor's agreement to drop all claims. Each party is giving up something: the creditor gives up her full claim, and the debtor gives up his assertion that he owed little or nothing.

Of course, parties who disagree over a debt are more than capable of later disagreeing about whether they reached an accord and satisfaction.

PIEROLA v. MOSCHONAS
687 A.2d 942, 1997 D.C. App. LEXIS 3
District of Columbia Court of Appeals, 1997

Facts: Pierola and Moschonas were both contractors. The men agreed to work together and obtained contracts to scrape and paint several water towers and bridges. They decided to split the profits 60/40 in Pierola's favor. Their joint effort lasted only a few weeks, though, because soon after they began work on a bridge, the men argued violently about how to do the scraping. Moschonas walked off the job, demanding his share of the profits. Pierola wrote Moschonas several checks. On the last check, written on Christmas Eve, Pierola allegedly wrote "paid in full" just below the dollar amount.

Moschonas filed suit. He claimed that Pierola had not in fact written "paid in full" on the check, and that he, Moschonas, was entitled to more money. Pierola argued that when Moschonas cashed the $5,000 check, the parties had reached an accord and satisfaction, extinguishing any other claims by Moschonas.

The trial court was not impressed with either party, finding that both lied under oath. The trial judge threatened to dismiss the case, but ultimately held that Pierola owed Moschonas more money. The judge ruled that there had been no accord and satisfaction because Pierola had not disputed the debt *in good faith*.

Issue: **Did the parties make an accord and satisfaction?**

Excerpts from Judge Steadman's Decision: Often, accord and satisfaction arises as a defense when one party tenders a check to the other that contains the phrase "payment in full" or other words to that effect. In cases like this, the debtor's act of cashing the check constitutes both the acceptance of the accord and its satisfaction.

The trial court found that on December 24, 1985 Pierola wrote Moschonas a check for $5,000. On the front of the check Pierola wrote "paid in full." Moschonas immediately cashed the check. These findings are supported by the record. Therefore, the existence of accord and satisfaction in this case must turn on whether Moschonas' claim was "legitimately disputed or unliquidated."

[The] debtor's mere refusal to pay the claim does not make it an unliquidated claim, if his refusal is arbitrary and known by him to have no just basis. In such a case his payment of less than the amount claimed does not operate as accord and satisfaction, even though it is so tendered and received. The reason for this is that he has acted in bad faith and that social policy is better served by denying full satisfaction. It is generally said that his payment, under these circumstances, is not a sufficient consideration for the creditor's agreement.

Here, Moschonas asserts that Pierola acted in bad faith because he merely "feigned disagreement" in order to assert an otherwise baseless accord and satisfaction defense. During the period from August to November Moschonas had received over a dozen checks totalling over $16,000 drawn on both payroll and non-payroll accounts, despite the fact that a profit-splitting contract was entered into in early September. The parties had had a heated disagreement regarding whether to sandblast or scrape the South Capitol Street Bridge, and as a result of that disagreement Moschonas had walked off the job before it was completed and not returned. These facts gave Pierola a legitimate basis to dispute Moschonas' claim to a flat 40% of the profits on both the bridge and tower contracts. Moreover, Moschonas himself admitted that when Pierola gave him the check on December 24, 1985 "[I was] trying to negotiate with him to show me how much money I had coming to me." That Pierola may have later lied about the contract is not controlling. There was at the time of the alleged accord and satisfaction a legitimate basis for the dispute. Accordingly, at the time of the Christmas Eve check the extent of Pierola's obligation to Moschonas was legitimately disputed, and Moschonas' act of cashing the $5,000 check marked "paid in full" constituted a valid accord and satisfaction.

Reversed.

PAYMENT BY CHECK

As the *Pierola* court notes, debtors commonly write "paid in full" on checks made out for less than the creditor claims. The common law rule was that cashing such a check *did* create accord and satisfaction. But several states disagreed, and the law has been muddled for decades.

UCC §3-311

A new UCC provision, §3-311, attempts to resolve the dispute. This section, currently the law in over 30 states, affirms the common law rule, but creates two exceptions. In general, placing a "full settlement" notation on a check *will* create an accord and satisfaction. So if Felicity's debt is unliquidated, and she gives you a check with "full payment of all debts" written on it, you lose any claim to more money when you cash the check.

The first exception concerns "organizations," which typically are businesses. The general rule of §3-311 is potentially calamitous to them, since a company that receives thousands of checks every day is unlikely to inspect all notations. A consumer who owes $12,000 on a credit card might write "full settlement" on a $200 check, potentially extinguishing the entire debt through accord and satisfaction.

Under the exception, if an organization notifies a debtor that any offers to settle for less than the debt claimed must be made to a particular official, and the check is sent to anyone else in the organization, depositing the check generally does *not* create an accord and satisfaction. Thus a clerk who deposits 900 checks daily for payment of MasterCard debts will not have inadvertently entered into dozens of accord and satisfaction agreements.

The second exception allows a way out to most creditors who have inadvertently created an accord and satisfaction. If, within 90 days of cashing a "full payment" check, the creditor offers repayment of the same amount to the debtor, there is no accord and satisfaction. Homer claims that Virgil owes him $7 million, but foolishly cashes Virgil's check for $3 million, without understanding that "paid in full" means just what it says. Homer has created an accord and satisfaction. But if he promptly sends Virgil a check for $3 million, he has undone the agreement and may sue for the full amount.

CHAPTER CONCLUSION

This ancient doctrine of consideration is simple to state but subtle to apply. The parties must bargain and enter into an exchange of promises or actions. If they do not, there is no consideration and the courts are unlikely to enforce any promise made. A variety of exceptions modify the law, but a party wishing to render its future more predictable—the purpose of a contract—will rely on a solid bargain and exchange.

CHAPTER REVIEW

1. (Consideration—Points 1-3) A promise is normally binding only if it is supported by consideration, which requires a bargaining and exchange between the parties.
2. The "thing" bargained for can be another promise or an action—virtually anything that a party might seek. It can create a benefit to the promisor or a detriment to the promisee.
3. The courts will seldom inquire into the adequacy of consideration.
4. (Mutuality of Obligation—Points 4-8) An illusory promise is not consideration.
5. Under sales law, requirement and output contracts are valid. Although one side controls the quantity, its agreement to make demands *in good faith* is consideration.
6. Past consideration is generally no consideration.
7. Under the doctrine of promissory estoppel, reliance may permit a party to enforce a promise even when there is no consideration; but this is an exception and courts are reluctant to grant it.
8. Under the doctrine of preexisting duty, a promise to do something that the promisor is already legally obligated to perform is generally not consideration.
9. (Settlement of Debts—Points 9-12) A liquidated debt is one in which there is no dispute about the amount owed.
10. For a liquidated debt, a creditor's promise to accept less than the full amount is not binding.

11. For an unliquidated debt, if the parties agree that the creditor will accept less than the full amount claimed and the debtor performs, there is an accord and satisfaction and the creditor may not claim any balance.

12. In most states payment by a check that has a "full payment" notation will create an accord and satisfaction unless the creditor is an organization that has notified the debtor that full payment offers must go to a certain officer.

PRACTICE TEST

1. An aunt saw her eight-year-old nephew enter the room, remarked what a nice boy he was, and said, "I would like to take care of him now." She promptly wrote a note, promising to pay the boy $3,000 upon her death. Her estate refused to pay. Is it obligated to do so?

2. **YOU BE THE JUDGE WRITING PROBLEM** Elio Pino took out a health insurance policy with the Union Bankers Insurance Co. Eighteen months later he became ill, suffered medical expenses, and filed a claim for benefits. Union Bankers wrote Pino this letter:

> Dear Mr. Pino:
>
> While servicing your claim, we learned that the medical facts on the application for this policy were not complete. If we had known the complete health history, we couldn't have issued this insurance. We must place you and ourselves back where we were when you applied for the policy and consider that the insurance was never in effect. (We are refunding the premiums you've paid us.)

Pino deposited the refund check, which was much less than his claim, and then sued for the full claim. Bankers Insurance argued that Pino had entered into an accord and satisfaction. The trial court gave summary judgment for the insurer, and Pino appealed. Did Pino enter into an accord and satisfaction by cashing the insurance company check? **Argument for Pino:** The insurance company has its contract law wrong. The company attempted to *rescind* the contract. Then it termed its unilateral act an accord and satisfaction. The company's attempts fail: a rescission requires the agreement of both parties; an accord and satisfaction needs a clear statement that the creditor is accepting the check as full payment. Neither occurred. **Argument for Union Bankers Insurance Co.:** This is classic accord and satisfaction. The company informed Mr. Pino that it regarded his application as false and offered him a partial payment as full settlement. He deposited the check, creating an accord and satisfaction, and has no claim for any more money.

3. **CPA QUESTION** For there to be consideration, there must be:

(a) A bargained-for detriment to the promisor(ee) or a benefit to the promisee(or)

(b) A manifestation of mutual assent

(c) Genuineness of assent

(d) Substantially equal economic benefits to both parties

4. Eagle ran convenience stores. He entered into an agreement with Commercial Movie in which Commercial would provide Eagle with videotape cassettes for rental. Eagle would pay Commercial 50 percent of the rental revenues. If Eagle stopped using Commercial's service, Eagle could not use a competitor's services for 18 months. The agreement also provided: "Commercial shall not be liable for compensation or damages of any kind, whether on account of the loss by Eagle of profits, sales or expenditures, or on account of any other event or cause whatsoever." Eagle complied with the agreement for two years but then began using a competitor's service, and Commercial sued. Eagle claimed that the agreement was unenforceable for lack of consideration. Did Eagle's argument fly?

5. American Bakeries had a fleet of over 3,000 delivery trucks. Because of the increasing cost of gasoline, the company was interested in converting the trucks to propane fuel. It signed a requirements contract with Empire Gas, in which Empire would convert "approximately 3,000" trucks to propane fuel, as American Bakeries requested, and would then sell all required propane fuel to run the trucks. But American Bakeries changed its mind and never requested a single conversion. Empire sued for lost profits. Who won?

6. **CPA QUESTION** Which of the following requires consideration in order to be binding on the parties?

(a) Modification of a contract involving the sale of real estate

(b) Ratification of a contract by a person after reaching the age of majority

(c) A written promise signed by a merchant to keep an offer to sell goods open for 10 days

(d) Modification of a sale of goods contract under the UCC

7. Tindall operated a general contracting business in Montana. He and Konitz entered into negotiations for Konitz to buy the business. The parties realized that Konitz could succeed with the business only if Tindall gave support and assistance for a year or so after the purchase, especially by helping with the process of bidding for jobs and obtaining bonds to guarantee performance. Konitz bought the business and Tindall helped with the bidding and bonding. Two years later, Tindall presented Konitz with a contract for his services up to that point. Konitz did not want to sign but Tindall insisted. Konitz signed the agreement, which said: "Whereas Tindall sold his contracting business to Konitz and thereafter assisted Konitz in bidding and bonding without which Konitz would have been unable to operate, NOW THEREFORE Konitz agrees to pay Tindall $138,629." Konitz later refused to pay. Comment.

8. Ripples was a catering business that rented commercial space from Le Havre. Under their agreement, Ripples was responsible for routine maintenance and for any improvements. Ripples did maintain the premises and made periodic improvements in order to attract customers. During one conversation between the parties, Ripples understood Le Havre to be guaranteeing 18 months' notice before Ripples could be evicted. Ripples continued to maintain and improve the premises as before. Later, Le Havre sought the eviction of Ripples on 30 days' notice. Ripples argues that promissory estoppel bars the eviction. Is it right?

9. RIGHT & WRONG Melnick built a house for Gintzler, but the foundation was defective. Gintzler agreed to accept the foundation if Melnick guaranteed to make future repairs caused by the defects. Melnick agreed but later refused to make any repairs. Melnick argued that his promise to make future repairs was unsupported by consideration. Who will win the suit? Is either party acting unethically? Which one, and why?

10. When White's wife died he filed a claim with Boston Mutual for $10,000 death benefits under her policy. The insurance company rejected the claim, saying that his wife had misrepresented her medical condition in the application form. The company sent White a check for $478.75, which it said represented "a full refund of all applicable premiums paid" for the coverage. Plaintiff deposited the check. Accord and satisfaction?

INTERNET RESEARCH PROBLEM

At **http://www.law.cornell.edu/ucc/ucc.table.html** click on *Article 2*. Find your way to §2-209, concerning contract modification. Write a clear one- or two-paragraph explanation of subsections (1) and (2). Explain what these subsections mean (in English) and how they work together.

You can find further practice problems in the Online Quiz at http://beatty.westbuslaw.com or in the Study Guide that accompanies this text.

CHAPTER 13

LEGALITY

Soheil Sadri, a California resident, did some serious gambling at Caesar's Tahoe casino in Nevada. And lost. To keep gambling, he wrote checks to Caesar's and then signed two memoranda pledging to repay money advanced. After two days, with his losses totaling more than $22,000, he went home. Back in California, Sadri stopped payment on the checks and refused to pay any of the money he owed Caesar's. The casino sued. In defense, Sadri claimed that California law considered his agreements illegal and unenforceable. He was unquestionably correct about one thing: **a contract that is illegal is void and unenforceable.**

In this chapter we examine a variety of contracts that may be void. Illegal agreements fall into two groups: those that violate a statute, and those that violate public policy.

CONTRACTS THAT VIOLATE A STATUTE

WAGERS

Gambling is one of America's fastest growing businesses. About one-half of the states now permit casinos, which generate annual revenue of more than $20 billion. State-sponsored lotteries, keno, and numbers games are also common. Almost 70 percent of Americans purchase at least one lottery ticket each year. Proponents urge that casinos create jobs and steady income, boosting state revenues and diminishing the influence of organized crime. Opponents of gambling argue that innocent citizens wager away money they can ill afford to lose, and that addicted gamblers destroy families. While the number of casinos grew explosively from the 1980s through the mid-1990s, the growth has now leveled off. Some states, such as New York, have refused to legalize casinos. Others, such as Iowa, permit wagering but have curtailed its growth. With states and citizens divided over the ethics of gambling, conflicts, such as the dispute between Sadri and Caesar's, are inevitable. The basic rule, however, is clear: **a gambling contract is illegal unless it is specifically authorized by state statute.**

In California, as in many states, gambling on credit is not allowed. In other words, it is illegal to lend money to help someone wager. A contract based on a gambling debt is unenforceable. But in Nevada, gambling on credit is legal, and debt memoranda such as Sadri's are enforceable contracts. Caesar's sued Sadri in California (where he lived). The result? The court admitted that California's attitude toward gambling had changed, and that bingo, poker clubs, and lotteries were common. Nonetheless, the court denied that the new tolerance extended to wagering on credit:

> There is a special reason for treating gambling on credit differently from gambling itself. Gambling debts are characteristic of pathological gambling, a mental disorder which is recognized by the American Psychiatric Association and whose prevalence is estimated at 2 to 3 percent of the adult population. Characteristic problems include extensive indebtedness and consequent default on debts and other financial responsibilities, . . . and financially motivated illegal activities to pay for gambling. Having lost his or her cash, the pathological gambler will continue to play on credit, if extended, in an attempt to win back the losses. In our view, this is why enforcement of gambling debts has always been against public policy in California and should remain so, regardless of shifting public attitudes about gambling itself. If Californians want to play, so be it. But the law should not invite them to play themselves into debt. The judiciary cannot protect pathological gamblers from themselves, but we can refuse to participate in their financial ruin.[1]

Caesar's lost and Sadri kept his money. The dispute is a useful starting place from which to examine contract legality because it illustrates two important themes. First, morality is a significant part of contract legality. In refusing to enforce an obligation that Sadri undeniably had made, the California court relied on the human and social consequences of gambling and on the ethics of judicial enforcement of gambling debts. Second, "void" really means just that: a court will not intercede to assist either party to an illegal agreement, even if its refusal leaves one party obviously shortchanged.

---

1 *Metropolitan Creditors Service of Sacramento v. Sadri*, 15 Cal. App. 4th 1821, 1993 Cal. App. LEXIS 559, 19 Cal. Rptr. 2d 646 (Cal. Ct. App. 1993).

Where there is money, there is the Net. Perhaps 100 Web sites now offer lotto, bingo, lucky 21, and countless other lotteries and games. Native American tribes run some of the Internet gambling; private companies operate other Web sites from the Caribbean and Europe. The sites are accessible to citizens of all states, including those that outlaw wagering. Should companies be able to earn profits from states where gambling is illegal? Who should determine what is morally and legally right? Early attempts at federal regulation have failed in Congress, but national legislation is probably inevitable. In the meantime, we offer some of the most popular Web gambling sites for your perusal.[2]

INVESTMENTS

Gambling need not involve roulette wheels or blackjack tables. Historically, many investments have come perilously close to being wagers. Look, for example, at commodities trading. In the nineteenth century, grain used to arrive in Chicago in massive quantities at harvest time, and prices would plummet. But prices soared during the winter, when the grain was used up. Farmers suffered in the autumn and consumers during the spring. To even things out, dealers began to sell "forward contracts," in which the grain would actually be sold, at a stated price, before it was delivered. The farmer was guaranteed that his price would not sink below a certain level, and consumers were assured that in lean times they would never pay more than the fixed sum. But then dealers began to buy and sell these contracts, essentially wagering on whether the market price would rise above or fall below the price guaranteed in the contract they purchased. If the market price of winter wheat, for example, rose to 75 cents a bushel, an investor holding a contract that entitled him to buy winter wheat at 50 cents a bushel had placed a winning bet. He could make his purchase at 50 cents and promptly sell at a profit, or simply sell the option, without ever touching the wheat. Other forms of gambling in investments began to appear. An "investor" could place a bet on the price of a share of stock, for example, Southern Pacific Railroad, without ever buying the share itself. The bet was a winner if the price rose, a loser if it fell, and the gambler never invested in the company.

Over the decades, courts and legislatures have outlawed most gambling on commodities and shares. In general, betting on share prices is illegal. (Buying a share is of course legal because the investor actually owns a percentage of the corporation.) Commodity trading is legal because the Supreme Court has ruled that the contracts are not merely speculative. An investor in 10,000 pork bellies has an enforceable contract and will either sell the investment or actually receive those 10,000 bellies.[3]

But the issue will not go away. Some of the hottest investment trading during the past 10 years has been in "derivatives." A derivative is any instrument or contract whose value depends upon the price of some *underlying reference*, which could be an interest rate or any other referral number. For example, an investor might purchase from a bank 1,000 home mortgages, all of whose interest rates are linked to the cost of living. Here, the underlying reference is the cost of living. The investor is in effect betting that the cost of living will rise, and that the mortgages will therefore become more valuable as their interest rates go up. Derivatives can be linked to a currency rate, an interest rate, the profitability of a particular corporation, the price of a share of stock, or almost anything else. Derivatives, like the commodities futures described above, can help level fluctuations in an important market. Airlines, for example, concerned about the volatile price of fuel, can pur-

[2] Did you honestly think we would help you squander your money over the Internet? No way.

[3] *Board of Trade of Chicago v. Christie Grain & Stock Co.*, 198 U.S. 236, 25 S. Ct. 637, 1905 U.S. LEXIS 1124 (1905).

chase derivatives linked to fuel prices, guaranteeing that their operating costs will stay within a predictable range. But the success or failure of the investment will depend upon something—an interest rate, the cost of fuel, and so forth—that the investor never owns.

This is not to say that derivatives *are* wagers, nor to suggest that they are bad. But many observers worry about the extent of derivative trading, especially given the fact that most of it is unregulated. For example, derivatives in the largely unregulated over-the-counter market are currently traded to the tune of $28 *trillion* per year. To add to the problem, many purchasers of derivatives, even large institutional investors, have no idea what they are buying or the risks involved. Orange County, California, was forced into the largest governmental bankruptcy in American history when its derivative investments lost over $1 billion in value in one year. The derivatives were far riskier than county executives realized. In the first important federal case to rule on the legality of derivatives, a major currency investor who lost millions in exchange-rate derivatives argued that his investments were illegal wagers. He lost the argument (and his money) when the court ruled that the investments were not wagers but legitimate currency exchanges.[4] But as the derivative market grows and losses increase, courts will undoubtedly look again at these investments. Clearly, derivatives have a useful role to play in the economy. But some may pose unacceptable risks because of their speculative nature.

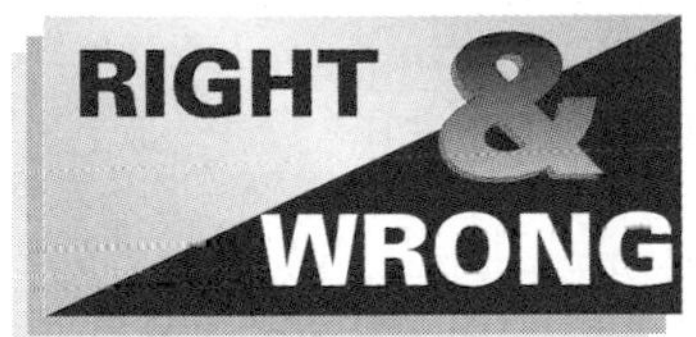

In what way are derivative investments like roulette wheels? Do derivatives have a social value that casino gambling lacks? Should society regulate derivatives more closely? If so, who should do the regulating?

INSURANCE

Yet another market in which "wagering" unexpectedly pops up is that of insurance. You may certainly insure your own life for any sum you choose. But may you insure someone *else's* life? **Someone taking out a policy on the life of another must have an insurable interest in that person.** A common reason for insuring someone else is that the other person owes you money. You want to be sure you are paid if something happens to her. But even when the insured person is a debtor, there are limits to what a court will permit, as the following case illustrates.

JIMENEZ v. PROTECTIVE LIFE INSURANCE CO.
8 Cal. App. 4th 528, 1992 Cal. App. LEXIS 947, 10 Cal. Rptr. 2d 326
California Court of Appeal, 1992

Facts: Kevin Breton was a laborer who worked for Manuel Jimenez and lived with Jimenez's family. Jimenez sold Breton a used motorcycle for $5,500, payable in weekly installments of $100, with 10 percent interest. Jimenez was worried about how he would be paid if Breton were injured or killed, so the two went to an insurance agent who represented Protective Life Insurance Co. (Protective). Jimenez purchased a policy on Breton's life, with death benefits of $160,000, plus a double indemnity provision if Breton were killed accidentally.

One month after Breton bought the motorcycle, he was killed in a collision with a car. Jimenez sought to collect $320,000 from Protective, but the insurance company offered only $5,764.58. This represented the motorcycle debt of $5,500, the insurance premium of $101.34, and interest at 7 percent. Jimenez sued, and the trial court granted him summary judgment in the amount of $320,000. Protective appealed.

[4] *Salomon Forex, Inc. v. Tauber*, 8 F.3d 966, 1993 U.S. App. LEXIS 27049 (4th Cir. 1993).

Issue: Is Jimenez entitled to the face value of the policy ($320,000) or only the amount of Breton's debt ($5,500)?

Excerpts from Judge Dabney's Decision: The central issue on appeal is the measure, under California law, of a creditor's insurable interest in the life of his debtor. Protective contends such interest is limited to the amount of the debt plus premiums paid, plus interest. The law is clear that a person taking out a policy of insurance upon the life of another must have an insurable interest in the life of the other person. Otherwise, the policy is a mere wager on the life of the person insured, and the policy is void as against public policy. In California, this principle has been codified. However, the code does not define the measure of an insurable interest in the life of another person based on a debtor-creditor relationship.

Our survey of the law of other jurisdictions has revealed two lines of authority on the issue. The courts of several jurisdictions have held that the amount of the creditor's insurable interest may be no greater than the amount of the debt, plus insurance premiums and interest. [In one federal case the court] held that a $3,000 policy on the life of a debtor to cover a debt of $70 was a wagering policy, and the debtor's assignment of the policy to the creditor was valid only to the extent of the debt.

In the second line of cases, the courts have held that a creditor's insurable interest may exceed the amount of the debt secured so long as there is not a gross disproportion between the two amounts. [The Pennsylvania Supreme Court] held that a policy of $3,000 was valid to secure a debt of $100. The court explained: "It needs no argument to show that, if my debtor owes me $1,000, a policy for $1,000 would be inadequate; for, if my debtor dies within 24 hours after the policy is taken out, I am a loser by the amount of the premium paid, and it would be but a few years before the interest on the debt and the premiums would exceed the debt. Every future payment then would be a loss; with the only alternative of adding to this loss year by year, or abandoning the policy altogether, and sinking the whole amount paid. It seems clear, upon reason, that the creditor may take out a policy in excess of his debt."

We conclude that the first line of cases provides the better rule. A "bright line" test is more practicable than an amorphous "proportionality" test. Thus, we determine that the extent of Jimenez's insurable interest in Breton's life was the amount Protective paid on the policy: the amount of the debt, plus the refund of the initial premium, plus interest on those two amounts. The trial court erred as a matter of law in granting summary adjudication on the contract cause of action. The judgment must therefore be reversed.

LICENSING STATUTES

You sue your next-door neighbor in small claims court, charging that he keeps a kangaroo in his backyard and that the beast has disrupted your family barbecues by leaping over the fence, demanding salad, and even punching your cousin in the ear. Your friend Foster, a graduate student from Melbourne, offers to help you prepare the case, and you agree to pay him 10 percent of anything you recover. Foster proves surprisingly adept at organizing documents and arguments. You win $1,200 and Foster demands $120. Must you pay? The answer is determined by the law of *licensing*.

States require licenses for anyone who practices a profession, such as law or medicine, works as a contractor or plumber, and for many other kinds of work. These licenses are required in order to protect the public. States demand that an electrician be licensed because the work is potentially dangerous to a homeowner: the person doing the work must know an amp from a watt. **When a licensing**

requirement is designed to protect the public, any contract made by an unlicensed worker is unenforceable. Your friend Foster is unlicensed to practice law. Even though Foster did a fine job with your small claims case, he cannot enforce his contract for $120.

States use other licenses simply to raise money. For example, most states require a license to open certain kinds of retail stores. This requirement does not protect the public, because the state will not investigate the store owner the way it will examine a prospective lawyer or electrician. The state is simply raising revenue. **When a licensing requirement is designed merely to raise revenue, a contract made by an unlicensed person is generally enforceable.** Thus, if you open a stationery store and forget to pay the state's licensing fee, you can still enforce a contract to buy 10,000 envelopes from a wholesaler at a bargain price.

Should the courts take licensing issues so seriously? Ask the homeowners who hired Lee Poole to exterminate bugs.

Lee Poole told residents of Houma, Louisiana, that he was a professional pest control expert, but he had never obtained a license to do the work. To eliminate roaches and other bugs common in the humid South, he used methyl parathion. The chemical did the job, all right. But methyl parathion is intended to eradicate boll weevils in cotton fields. In humans, the chemical causes nausea, blurred vision, convulsions, and even death. Farmers who use the product must stay out of their fields for 48 hours. Indoors, the toxic substance may remain for years. The Environmental Protection Agency's Emergency Response Branch evacuated dozens of homes in Houma until the poison could be removed. Poole was sentenced to two years in federal prison and ordered to pay $2.19 million to cover the cost of the cleanup (good luck getting the money). Meanwhile, in suburban Chicago, more than 90 homes were evacuated after another unlicensed worker used the same chemical. Who is the real pest here?

Many cases, such as the following one, involve contractors seeking to recover money for work they did without a license.

CEVERN, INC. v. FERBISH
666 A.2d 17, 1995 D.C. App. LEXIS 183
District of Columbia Court of Appeals, 1995

Facts: Cevern, Inc. was a small contractor. The company was bonded and insured, as local law required, but it did not have a license to do home improvement work. Cevern applied for such a license, and this is what then happened:

- August 24: The District of Columbia regulatory agency certified that Cevern met all of the requirements for a license (but it did not yet grant the license).
- August 27: Cevern's agents met with Robert Ferbish and Viola Stanton, and the parties signed a contract for Cevern to do extensive work on the Ferbish-Stanton home (to re-Ferbish it).
- August 31: The owners made an advance payment of $7,000 for the work. Cevern immediately began work on the project, digging a ditch and perhaps erecting a wall.
- September 5: Cevern paid its licensing fee and received the home improvement license.

Ferbish and Stanton later paid an additional $7,000 for Cevern's work but claimed that it was defective. When the owners refused to make a final payment of $10,295, the company sued. Ferbish counterclaimed for the $14,000 already paid, alleging that he and Stanton had spent an additional $43,000 to repair poor-quality work.

The trial court gave summary judgment for Ferbish and Stanton, ruling that Cevern's contract was void and unenforceable because the company had been unlicensed when the parties made the agreement. The judge ordered restitution (repayment) of the $14,000 the owners had paid. Cevern appealed.

Issue: Was the contract void because Cevern was unlicensed when the parties reached agreement?

Argument for Cevern: We concede that unlicensed contractors generally may not enforce contracts. That rule makes sense, to discourage unqualified companies from doing work that might endanger the public. This is no such case. The District's regulatory agency had already declared that Cevern met all licensing requirements. Cevern had only to pay the fee and collect its license. The company promptly did this and had the license in hand when it performed the bulk of the work. We are not dealing here with some fly-by-night con artist intent upon cheating innocent homeowners. Instead, we have a fully qualified contractor who had met every substantive requirement the law provides, and was merely a few days late in picking up its license. It is the homeowners who seek to pull a fast one: they wish to take advantage of a technical licensing rule to obtain first-rate work for free. Unfair!

Even if the court refuses to enforce the contract, we urge alternatively that it permit Cevern to collect quasi-contract damages. The owners have benefited and know that Cevern expected payment. Cevern should have a chance at trial to prove the extent of the benefit and to collect *quantum meruit* damages.

Argument for the Owners: Courts in this jurisdiction and around the country have long held that an unlicensed contractor may never enforce contracts. This old rule is designed to protect the public from shoddy work, and it should be enforced for two reasons. First, a contractor may easily comply. All the company needs to do is demonstrate its competence, fill out certain forms, and pay a fee. A contractor unable to do that is a dubious bet. Second, to permit this builder to recover for unlicensed work would encourage other unqualified contractors to try the same ruse: begin the work with glib assurances of a pending license, then hope for the best. If the license application is rejected, the homeowner might never know it, or might feel obligated to let the company finish, creating exactly the peril the rule is designed to avoid. The court should deny quasi-contract damages for the same reason: a void contract deserves no reward.

USURY

Henry Paper and Anthony Pugliese were real estate developers. They bought a \$1.7 million property in West Palm Beach, Florida, intending to erect an office building. They needed \$1 million to start construction but were able to raise only \$800,000. Walter Gross, another developer, agreed to lend them the final \$200,000 for 18 months at 15 percent interest. Gross knew the partners were desperate for the money, so at the loan closing, he demanded 15 percent equity (ownership) in the partnership, in addition to the interest. Paper and Pugliese had no choice but to sign the agreement. The two partners never repaid the loan, and when Gross sued, the court ruled they need never pay a cent. It pays to understand usury.

Usury laws prohibit charging excess interest on loans. A lender who charges a usurious rate of interest may forfeit the illegal interest, or all interest, or, in some states, the entire loan. Florida permits interest rates of up to 18 percent on loans such as Gross's. A lender who charges more than 18 percent loses the right to collect any interest. A lender who exceeds 25 percent interest forfeits the entire debt. Where was the usury? Just here: when Gross insisted on a 15 percent share of the partnership, he was simply extracting additional interest and disguising it as partnership equity. The Paper-Pugliese partnership had equity assets of \$600,000. A 15 percent equity, plus interest payments of 15 percent over 18 months, was the equivalent of a per annum interest rate of 45 percent. Gross probably thought he had made a deal that was too good to be true. And in the state of Florida, it was. He lost the entire debt.[5]

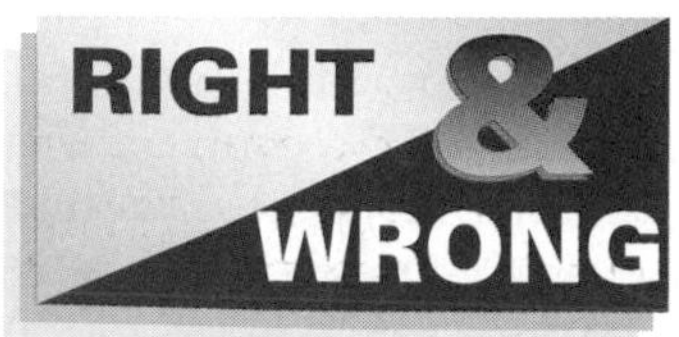

Is it fair for Paper and Pugliese to sign a deal and not keep it? Didn't they understand what they were agreeing to? In fact, there is a reason that a state may want to nullify a contract such as theirs. What is that reason? In thinking about the ethics of usury, consider the following news report.

[5] *Jersey Palm-Gross, Inc. v. Paper*, 639 So. 2d 664, 1994 Fla. App. LEXIS 6597 (Fla. Ct. App. 1994).

The highest loan rates go to those least able to pay, the roughly 35 million people who have no bank account. These workers live from paycheck to (small) paycheck. Frequently, they need cash before the next payday. The solution? A check cashing company. These businesses are legal in most but not all states and are typically unregulated, meaning they are free to charge whatever the market bears. It bears a lot.

Joanne, a fast-food worker, has a $200 check coming in two weeks, but she needs money today. She visits Poundaflesh Check Cashers, Inc. and arranges an "advance " on her pay. The stated interest rate is a tolerable 20 percent. But when her paycheck arrives, Joanne needs all of the money to pay the rent. Instead of repaying the loan, she "rolls it over," that is, extends it for another two weeks. Two weeks later, she repeats the process one last time, then finally pays off the loan. Here is what a six-week "advance" ultimately costs her:

Application fee	$ 15
Interest	40 (20% of $200)
First rollover fee (two additional weeks)	50
Second rollover fee (two additional weeks)	50
Total cost of borrowing $200	**$155**

Joanne paid 77 percent interest for a six-week loan—an annual percentage rate of more than *600 percent!*

Why do people take out loans with such diabolically high interest rates? They need the money. What *should* consumers do when they find themselves falling ever deeper into debt? One possibility is to contact American Consumer Credit Counseling, a nonprofit organization that helps people reduce debt while avoiding bankruptcy. The agency's phone number is (781) 893-7649; its Web site, http://www.consumercredit.com, provides a useful overview of potential remedies for a distraught debtor.

CONTRACTS THAT VIOLATE PUBLIC POLICY

In the preceding section, we saw that courts refuse to enforce contracts that violate a statute. In this section we examine cases in which no statute applies but where a *public policy* prohibits certain contracts. In other words, we focus primarily on the common law.

RESTRAINT OF TRADE

Free trade is the basis of the American economy, and any bargain that restricts it is suspect. Most restraint of free trade is barred by antitrust law. But it is the common law that still regulates one restriction on trade: agreements to refrain from competition. Some of these agreements are legal, some are void.

To be valid, an agreement not to compete must be ancillary to a legitimate bargain. "Ancillary" means that the noncompetition agreement must be part of a larger agreement. Suppose Cliff sells his gasoline station to Mina and the two agree that Cliff will not open a competing gas station within five miles anytime during the next two years. Cliff's agreement not to compete is ancillary to the sale of his service station. His noncompetition promise is enforceable. But suppose that Cliff and Mina already had the only two gas stations within 35 miles. They agree between themselves not to hire each other's workers. Their agreement might be profitable to them, because each could now keep wages artificially low. But their deal is ancillary to no legitimate bargain, and it is therefore void. Mina is free to hire Cliff's mechanic despite her agreement with Cliff.

The two most common settings for legitimate noncompetition agreements are the sale of a business and an employment relationship.

Sale of a Business

Kory has operated a real estate office, Hearth Attack, in a small city for 35 years, building an excellent reputation and many ties with the community. She offers to sell you the business and its goodwill for $300,000. But you need assurance that Kory will not take your money and promptly open a competing office across the street. With her reputation and connections, she would ruin your chances of success. You insist on a noncompete clause in the sale contract. In this clause, Kory promises that for one year she will not open a new real estate office or go to work for a competing company within a 10-mile radius of Hearth Attack. Suppose, six months after selling you the business, Kory goes to work for a competing relator, two blocks away. You seek an injunction to prevent her from working. Who wins?

When a noncompete agreement is ancillary to the sale of a business, it is enforceable if reasonable in time, geographic area, and scope of activity. In other words, a court will not enforce a noncompete agreement that lasts an unreasonably long time, covers an unfairly large area, or prohibits the seller of the business from doing a type of work that she never had done before. Measured by this test, Kory is almost certainly bound by her agreement. One year is a reasonable time to allow you to get your new business started. A 10-mile radius is probably about the area that Hearth Attack covers, and realty is obviously a fair business from which to prohibit Kory. A court will probably grant the injunction, barring Kory from her new job.

If, on the other hand, the noncompetition agreement had prevented Kory from working anywhere within 200 miles of Hearth Attack, and she started working 50 miles away, a court would refuse to enforce the contract. The geographic restriction is unreasonable, since Kory never previously did business 50 miles away, and Hearth Attack is unlikely to be affected if she works there now. There are always an enormous number of businesses available for purchase. For a sample listing, see **http://www.business-broker.com**.

Employment

When you sign an employment contract, the document may well contain a noncompete clause. Employers have legitimate worries that employees might go to a competitor and take with them trade secrets or other proprietary information. Some employers, though, attempt to place harsh restrictions on their employees, perhaps demanding a blanket agreement that the employee will never go to work for a competitor. Once again, courts look at the reasonableness of restrictions placed on an employee's future work. Because the agreement now involves the very livelihood of the worker, a court scrutinizes the agreement more closely.

A noncompete clause in an employment contract is generally reasonable—and enforceable—only to the extent necessary to protect (1) trade secrets, (2) confidential information, or (3) customer lists developed over an extended

period. In general, other restrictions on future employment are unenforceable.[6] Suppose that Gina, an engineer, goes to work for Fission Chips, a silicon chip manufacturer that specializes in defense work. She signs a noncompete agreement promising never to work for a competitor. Over a period of three years, Gina learns some of Fission's proprietary methods of etching information onto the chips. She acquires a great deal of new expertise about chips generally. And she periodically deals with Fission Chip's customers, all of whom are well-known software and hardware manufacturers. Gina accepts an offer from WriteSmall, a competitor. Fission Chips races into court, seeking an injunction that would prevent Gina from (1) working for WriteSmall; (2) working for any other competitor; (3) revealing any of Fission's trade secrets; (4) using any of the general expertise she acquired at Fission Chips; and (5) contacting any of Fission's customers.

This injunction threatens Gina's career. If she cannot work for a competitor, or use her general engineering skills, what *will* she do? And for exactly that reason, no court will grant such a broad order. The court will allow Gina to work for competitors, including WriteSmall. It will order her not to use or reveal any trade secrets belonging to Fission. She will, however, be permitted to use the general expertise she has acquired, and she may contact former customers since anyone could get their names from the yellow pages.

Back with more law in a minute, but first a check on rush hour traffic.

METRO TRAFFIC CONTROL, INC. v. SHADOW TRAFFIC NETWORK

22 Cal. App. 4th 853, 27 Cal. Rptr. 2d 573, 1994 Cal. App. LEXIS 137
California Court of Appeal, 1994

Facts: Metro Traffic Control contracted with Los Angeles radio stations to gather and broadcast local traffic information. Jeff Baugh and Robin Johnson worked for Metro as air traffic reporters, and Tommy Grskovich worked for Metro as a managing producer. All three had written employment at will contracts, meaning that either party could end the agreement at any time. Each contract contained a noncompete clause that prohibited the employee from working for a competitor for one year after leaving Metro.

One of Metro's customers was radio station KFWB in Los Angeles. Baugh, Johnson, and Grskovich all worked on broadcasts for KFWB. But KFWB did not renew its contract with Metro. Instead, the station gave its business to Metro's competitor, Shadow Traffic. Metro assured Baugh, Johnson, and Grskovich that they would have jobs at Metro, but the three employees left and began working for Shadow, on the KFWB job. Metro sued, seeking an injunction to bar their employment, based on the noncompete clauses. The trial court denied the injunction and Metro appealed.

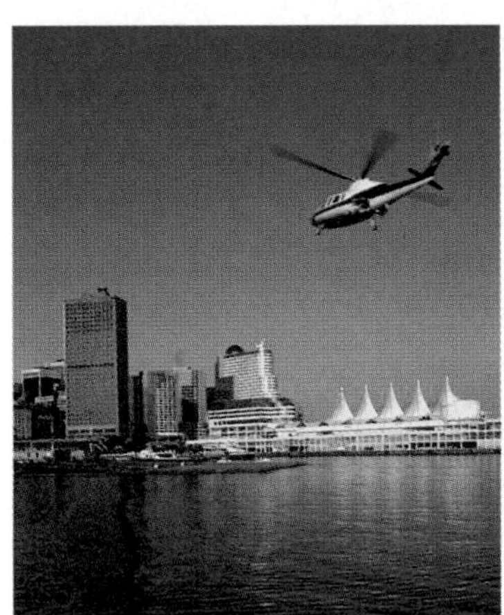

How much can an employer restrict an employee's future?

Issue: Is Metro entitled to an injunction prohibiting its former employees from working for Shadow?

Excerpts from Judge Vogel's Decision: The interests of the employee in his own mobility and betterment are deemed paramount to the competitive business interests of the employers, where neither the employee nor his new employer has committed any illegal act accompanying the employment change. Here, Metro complains that "every employee induced to leave Metro by Shadow has violated his or her restrictive covenant not to provide traffic reporting services to KFWB for a period of one year after the termination of their respective employment relation with Metro." This restriction standing by itself is unenforceable because it severely restricts Metro's employees' mobility and betterment.

---

[6] If the agreement restricts the employee from *starting a new business*, a court may apply the more lenient standard used for the sale of a business; the noncompete will be enforced if reasonable in time, geography, and scope of activity.

Metro argues that it has protectible trade secrets developed in the course of serving as KFWB's traffic reporter. It describes the trade secrets as information it has about the peculiar requirements imposed by KFWB on Metro's traffic reporting services during the term of their contract relationship. Metro delineates its alleged trade secrets in very general terms. William Gaines, the regional director of Metro, describes the trade secrets as KFWB's "very strict and particular requirements regarding the quality, sound and personality of the anchors reporting over its airways [and] KFWB hand-picks each of its anchors." Jennifer York is another of Metro's airborne reporters. She characterizes the trade secrets as the "significant knowledge regarding the special needs and requirements of KFWB.... KFWB has a particular style, sound and personality which it requires its anchors to use, a particular preference regarding the 'proper' format for reporting traffic, and particular requirements regarding the choice of words used by the anchors reporting traffic over its airwaves."

It appears that Metro's battery of radio announcers had the "quality, sound and personality" required by KFWB. These are subjective dimensions of the employees who were found acceptable to and approved by KFWB and not part of an informational base belonging to Metro. No doubt Metro conveyed to its employees KFWB's preferences and requirements regarding word choice and factual reporting but that does not amount to the compilation of an intangible personal property right owned by the employer. Actors, musicians, athletes, and others are frequently trained, tutored, and coached to satisfy the requirements of their sponsors and audiences, but their talents belong to them to contract away as they please. Simply hiring personnel who possess the requirements specified by a customer does not convert the employee into a "trade secret."

In summary, Metro has not demonstrated that it possesses any trade secret, and the trial court could rationally conclude that it is unlikely Metro will prevail on the merits. We hold the trial court did not abuse its discretion in denying the preliminary injunction.

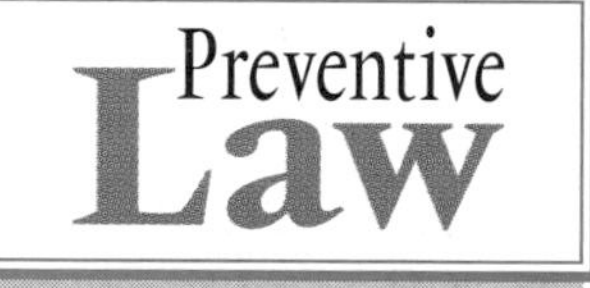

Noncompete clauses are litigated every day throughout the United States. This is often because the two parties failed to be *candid and realistic* about their requirements. An employee who is nervous about signing a noncompete should be free to discuss it without incurring the employer's anger. The employer should be able to explain what the noncompete means and why it is reasonable in terms of its coverage.

The Legality of Noncompetition Clauses

Type of Noncompetition Agreement	When Enforceable
Not ancillary to a legitimate bargain (such as sale of business or employment)	Never
Ancillary to a sale of business	To the extent reasonable in time, geography, and scope of activity
Employment	If reasonable, which generally means necessary to protect • Trade secrets • Confidential information • Customer lists developed over an extended period

Metro should have forced itself to look more realistically at what it gave its employees and what it needed in return. It might well be that working for Metro enabled the employee to tailor his voice to the requirements of a radio station. But, as the court pointed out, that is not really *training*. How could Metro have retained valued employees without using a noncompete?

Exculpatory Clauses

You decide to capitalize on your expert ability as a skier and open a ski school in Colorado, "Pike's Pique." But you realize that skiing sometimes causes injuries, so you require anyone signing up for lessons to sign this form:

> I agree to hold Pike's Pique and its employees entirely harmless in the event that I am injured in any way or for any reason or cause, including but not limited to any acts, whether negligent or otherwise, of Pike's Pique or any employee or agent thereof.

The day your school opens, Sara Beth, an instructor, deliberately pushes Toby over a cliff because Toby criticized her color combinations. Eddie, a beginning student, "blows out" his knee attempting an advanced racing turn. And Maureen, another student, reaches the bottom of a steep run and slams into a snowmobile that Sara Beth parked there. Maureen, Eddie, and Toby's family all sue Pike's Pique. You defend based on the form you had them sign. Does it save the day?

The form on which you are relying is an **exculpatory clause**, that is, one that attempts to release you from liability in the event of injury to another party. Exculpatory clauses are common. Ski schools use them and so do parking lots, landlords, warehouses, and day-care centers. All manner of businesses hope to avoid large tort judgements by requiring their customers to give up any right to recover. Is such a clause valid? Sometimes. Courts frequently—but not always—ignore exculpatory clauses, finding that one party was forcing the other party to give up legal rights that no one should be forced to surrender.

An exculpatory clause is generally unenforceable when it attempts to exclude an intentional tort or gross negligence. When Sara Beth pushes Toby over a cliff, that is the intentional tort of battery. A court will not enforce the exculpatory clause. Sara Beth is clearly liable.[7] As to the snowmobile at the bottom of the run, if a court determines that was gross negligence (carelessness far greater than ordinary negligence), then the exculpatory clause will again be ignored. If, however, it was ordinary negligence, then we must continue the analysis.

Exculpatory clauses are important to the operators of ski resorts.

An exculpatory clause is generally unenforceable when the affected activity is in the public interest, such as medical care, public transportation, or some essential service. Suppose Eddie goes to a doctor for surgery on his damaged knee, and the doctor requires him to sign an exculpatory clause. The doctor negligently performs the surgery, accidentally leaving his cuff links in Eddie's left knee. The exculpatory clause will not protect the doctor. Medical care is an essential service, and the public cannot give up its right to demand reasonable work.

But what about Eddie's suit against Pike's Pique? Eddie claims that he should never have been allowed to attempt an advanced maneuver. His suit is for ordinary negligence, and the exculpatory clause probably *does* bar him from recovery. Skiing is a recreational activity. No one is obligated to do it, and there is no strong public interest in ensuring that we have access to ski slopes.

An exculpatory clause is generally unenforceable when the parties have greatly unequal bargaining power. When Maureen flies to Colorado, suppose that the airline requires her to sign a form contract with an exculpatory clause. Because

[7] Note that Pike's Pique is probably not liable, under agency law principles that preclude an employer's liability for an employee's intentional tort.

the airline almost certainly has much greater bargaining power, it can afford to offer a "take it or leave it" contract. But because the bargaining power is so unequal, the clause is probably unenforceable. Does Pike's Pique have a similar advantage? Probably not. Ski schools are not essential and are much smaller enterprises. A dissatisfied customer might refuse to sign such an agreement and take her business elsewhere. A court probably will not see the parties as grossly unequal.

An exculpatory clause is generally unenforceable unless the clause is clearly written and readily visible. Thus, if Pike's Pique gave all ski students an eight-page contract, and the exculpatory clause was at the bottom of page seven in small print, the average customer would never notice it. The clause would be void.

In the following case, the court examined the issues of public interest and unequal bargaining power.

STANLEY v. CREIGHTON CO.

911 P.2d 705, 1996 Colo. App. LEXIS 19

Court of Appeals of Colorado, 1996

Facts: Charlene and Larry Stanley rented one of the Cottonwood Terrace Apartments from the Creighton Co. As Charlene Stanley was leaving the apartment, she slipped on a spot of clear ice that had formed on the landing. She fell down the stairs and was seriously injured. She and her husband filed suit, claiming that the ice had formed because Creighton had negligently repaired a leak in the roof. In Colorado, a statute holds a landlord liable for injuries caused by its failure to exercise reasonable care. But the Stanleys' lease contained an exculpatory clause that stated: "Lessor shall not be responsible for any damage or injury said Lessee may sustain from any cause whatsoever unless injury is a direct result of the Lessor's *gross* negligence."

The trial court granted summary judgment for Creighton, ruling that there was no evidence of gross negligence. The Stanleys appealed, arguing that the exculpatory clause was void.

Issue: **Was the exculpatory clause valid?**

Excerpts from Judge Davidson's Decision: The issue of the validity of an exculpatory clause implicates competing principles: freedom of contract and responsibility for damages caused by one's own negligent acts. In order to balance these principles fairly, the determination of the validity of a particular clause requires (1) consideration of the public policy implications of the subject matter involved (whether it concerns a duty to the public and whether the type of services performed affects the public interest) and (2) the circumstances of the specific contract (whether the contract was fairly entered into and whether the parties' intentions were expressed in clear and unambiguous language).

[1.]

We conclude that the subject matter involved here—waiver of claims of lessor negligence through an exculpatory clause in a form residential lease—is a matter of public interest. The statute, which includes, inter alia, the duty of a landlord to its tenant, explicitly sets forth that its purpose is to:

> Promote a state policy of responsibility by both landowners and those upon the land as well as to assure that the ability of an injured party to recover is correlated with his status as a trespasser, licensee, or invitee.

Furthermore, it is undisputed that a landlord's services are generally held out to the public and that housing rental is a matter of practical necessity to the public. Consequently, a public policy that protects tenants from a waiver clause is more compelling here, under a form residential lease, than it would be under a commercial lease. Finally, when a common area is involved, a major justification for upholding a private contract clause is eliminated—the tenant has neither any prospect of controlling the landlord's invocation of the lease waiver clause nor an ability to correct hazardous conditions.

In addition, permitting abrogation of responsibility to use reasonable care in common areas also is likely to have an adverse effect on non-parties to the agreement.

[2.]

Consideration of the bargaining power of the parties also indicates that the exculpatory clause is invalid. Exculpatory agreements are not necessarily void as long as one party is not at such obvious disadvantage in bargaining power that the effect of the contract is to put him at the mercy of the other's negligence. Here, it is undisputed that the clause was part of a standardized rental agreement, signed with no opportunity for negotiation or option for protection against negligence upon payment of an increased rental rate or special fee.

Consequently, in consideration of all the relevant factors, we hold that the exculpatory clause in the parties' residential rental agreement is void. The summary judgment is reversed and the cause remanded for further proceedings consistent with this opinion.

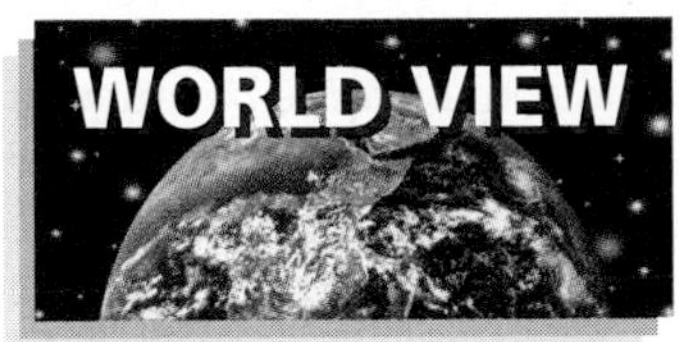

European countries also outlaw contracts that violate public policy. For an informal comparison of basic European contract principles with those of the United States, see http://www.kclc.or.jp/EUDialog/spiel.htm.

Bailment Cases

Exculpatory clauses are very common in bailment cases. **Bailment means giving possession and control of personal property to another person.** The person giving up possession is the **bailor**, and the one accepting possession is the **bailee**. When you leave your laptop computer with a dealer to be repaired, you create a bailment. The same is true when you check your coat at a restaurant or lend your Matisse to a museum. Bailees often try to limit their liability for damage to property by using an exculpatory clause.

Judges are slightly more apt to enforce an exculpatory clause in a bailment case, because the harm is to property and not person. But courts will still look at many of the same criteria we have just examined to decide whether a bailment contract is enforceable. In particular, when the bailee is engaged in an important public service, a court is once again likely to ignore the exculpatory clause. The following contrasting cases illustrate this.

In *Weiss v. Freeman,*[8] Weiss stored personal goods in Freeman's self-storage facility. Freeman's contract included an exculpatory clause relieving it of any and all liability. Weiss's goods were damaged by mildew and she sued. The court held the exculpatory clause valid. The court considered self-storage to be a significant business, but not as vital as medical care or housing. It pointed out that a storage facility would not know what each customer stored and therefore could not anticipate the harm that might occur. Freedom of contract should prevail, the clause was enforceable, and Weiss got no money.

In *Gardner v. Downtown Porsche Audi,*[9] Gardner left his Porsche 911 at Downtown for repairs. He signed an exculpatory clause saying that Downtown was "Not Responsible for Loss or Damage to Cars or Articles Left in Cars in Case

[8] 1994 Tenn. App. LEXIS 393 (Tenn. Ct. App. 1993).

[9] 180 Cal. App. 3d 713, 225 Cal. Rptr. 757, 1986 Cal. App. LEXIS 1542 (Cal. Ct. App. 1986).

of Fire, Theft, or Any Other Cause Beyond Our Control." Due to Downtown's negligence, Gardner's Porsche was stolen. The court held the exculpatory clause void. It ruled that contemporary society is utterly dependent upon automobile transportation and Downtown was therefore in a business of great public importance. No repair shop should be able to contract away liability, and Gardner won. (This case also illustrates that using 17 uppercase letters in one sentence does not guarantee legal victory.)

UNCONSCIONABLE CONTRACTS

Gail Waters was young, naive, and insecure. A serious injury when she was 12 years old left her with an annuity, that is, a guaranteed annual payment for many years. When Gail was 21, she became involved with Thomas Beauchemin, an ex-convict, who introduced her to drugs. Beauchemin suggested that Gail sell her annuity to some friends of his, and she agreed. Beauchemin arranged for a lawyer to draw up a contract, and Gail signed it. She received $50,000 for her annuity, which at that time had a cash value of $189,000 and was worth, over its remaining 25 years, $694,000. Gail later decided this was not an excellent bargain. Was the contract enforceable? That depends on the law of unconscionability.

An unconscionable contract is one that a court refuses to enforce because of fundamental unfairness. Historically, a contract was considered unconscionable if it was "such as no man in his senses and not under delusion would make on the one hand, and as no honest and fair man would accept on the other."[10] The two factors that most often led a court to find unconscionability were (1) **oppression**, meaning that one party used its superior power to force a contract on the weaker party, and (2) **surprise**, meaning that the weaker party did not fully understand the consequences of its agreement.

These cases have always been controversial because it is not easy to define oppression and unfair surprise. Further, anytime a court rejects a contract as unconscionable, it diminishes freedom of contract. If one party can escape a deal based on something as hard to define as unconscionability, then no one can rely as confidently on any agreement. This is another of the public policy issues we have seen throughout the law of contracts. As an English jurist said in 1824, "public policy is a very unruly horse, and when once you get astride it you never know where it will carry you."[11] With the creation of the Uniform Commercial Code (UCC), the law of unconscionability got a boost. The Code explicitly adopts unconscionability as a reason to reject a contract.[12] Although officially the Code applies only to the sale of goods, its unconscionability section has proven influential in other cases as well, and courts today are more receptive than they were 100 years ago to a contract defense of fundamental unfairness.

Gail Waters won her case. The Massachusetts high court ruled:

> Beauchemin introduced the plaintiff to drugs, exhausted her credit card accounts to the sum of $6,000, unduly influenced her, suggested that the plaintiff sell her annuity contract, initiated the contract negotiations, was the agent of the defendants, and benefited from the contract between the plaintiff and the defendants. The defendants were represented by legal counsel; the plaintiff was not. The cash value of the annuity policy at the time the contract was executed was approximately four times greater than the

---

[10] *Hume v. United States*, 132 U.S. 406, 411, 10 S. Ct. 134, 1889 U.S. LEXIS 1888 (1889), quoting *Earl of Chesterfield v. Janssen*, 38 Eng. Rep. 82, 100 (Ch. 1750).

[11] *Richardson v. Mellish*, 2 Bing. 229, 103 Eng. Rep. 294, 303 (1824).

[12] UCC §2-302.

> price to be paid by the defendants. For payment of not more than $50,000 the defendants were to receive an asset that could be immediately exchanged for $189,000, or they could elect to hold it for its guaranteed term and receive $694,000.
>
> The defendants assumed no risk and the plaintiff gained no advantage. We are satisfied that the disparity of interests in this contract is so gross that the court cannot resist the inference that it was improperly obtained and is unconscionable.[13]

At first blush, it sounds like a standard contingency fee agreement—even generous to the client by trial lawyers' standards. The lawyers who took the case fronted the initial costs, agreed not to take a penny if the client did not collect, and asked for only 15 percent if there was a settlement.

But when the client is the state of Texas, and the state's settlement with the tobacco industry is $15.3 billion, the result is not cheerful payment of the lawyers' bill, which comes to $2.3 billion (plus expenses, some lawyers argue). It is a Texas-size war.

Calling the proposed fees "outrageous," Governor George W. Bush has gone to federal court to block the payment to the roughly 150 lawyers who assisted Texas in the tobacco lawsuit. In return, the state's Attorney General, Dan Morales, the chief architect of the settlement, who believes that Governor Bush's move could undermine the accord, accused him of having "chosen to wrap himself in a tobacco leaf" and said the governor was pandering for campaign contributions from big tobacco in a future run for the White House.

The fight here mirrors one in Florida, where some lawyers are trying to collect up to 25 percent of that state's $11.3 billion settlement with the tobacco industry for health-related damages caused by smoking. That battle has the added twist of lawyers fighting among themselves over the share of any proceeds, but for now, a state judge has blocked some lawyers' attempts to collect fees by filing liens on the tobacco companies' payments to the state.

The Florida judge, Harold J. Cohen, of the Circuit Court in West Palm Beach, ruled that the lawyers may well be entitled to hundreds of millions of dollars for their work. But in a ruling that basically tore up the stipulated 25 percent, he wrote: "2.87 billion dollars simply shocks the conscience of the court. It is per se unreasonable."[14]

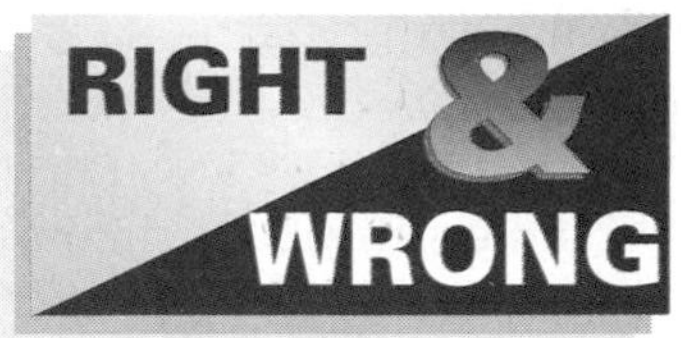

What are the strongest arguments for enforcing contingency fee agreements in tobacco litigation? For opposing them? Which do you find more persuasive? In a typical contingency agreement, for example, concerning product liability or negligence, the plaintiff's lawyer would receive about one-third of a settlement or judgment—if there is one.

Adhesion Contracts

A related issue concerns **adhesion contracts, which are standard form contracts prepared by one party and given to the other on a "take it or leave it" basis.** We have all encountered them many times when purchasing goods or services. When a form contract is vigorously negotiated between equally powerful corporations, the resulting bargain is generally enforced. But when the contract is simply presented to a consumer, who has no ability to bargain, it is an adhesion contract and subject to an unconscionability challenge.

13 *Waters v. Min Ltd.*, 412 Mass. 64, 587 N.E.2d 231, 1992 Mass. LEXIS 66 (1992).

14 Sam Verhovek, "Fat Fees in Tobacco Deals Signal New Foe for States: The Lawyers," *New York Times*, Feb. 9, 1998, p. A1. Copyright © 1998 by The New York Times Co. Reprinted by permission.

WORLDWIDE INSURANCE v. KLOPP
603 A.2d 788, 1992 Del. LEXIS 13
Supreme Court of Delaware, 1992

Facts: Ruth Klopp had auto insurance with Worldwide. She was injured in a serious accident that left her with permanent neck and back injuries. The other driver was uninsured, so Klopp filed a claim with Worldwide under her "uninsured motorist" coverage. Her policy required arbitration of such a claim, and the arbitrators awarded Klopp $90,000. But the policy also stated that if the arbitrators awarded more than the statutory minimum amount of insurance ($15,000), either side could appeal the award and request a full trial. Worldwide appealed and demanded a trial.

In the trial court, Klopp claimed that the appeal provision was unconscionable and void. The trial court agreed and entered judgment for the full $90,000. Worldwide appealed.

Issue: Is the provision that requires arbitration and then permits appeal by either party void as unconscionable?

Excerpts from Justice Walsh's Decision: The parties' views of the arbitration provision are polar opposites. Worldwide contends that the provision is a clear and unambiguous contractual undertaking granting both the insured and the insurer the right to appeal any award in excess of financial responsibility limits. Klopp argues that this provision is unconscionable and void as against public policy because it affords an advantage to one of the parties under a contract of adhesion.

The public policy of this State favors the resolution of disputes through arbitration. An insurance policy which provides for arbitration as its primary mechanism for dispute resolution is thus enforceable against the wishes of either contractual party. [But] our approval of the arbitration concept does not extend to any feature of a contract of adhesion, which, in whole or in part, is unconscionable.

Under the present policy language both parties are bound by a low award which an insurance company is unlikely to appeal. While high awards may be appealed by either party, common experience suggests that it is unlikely that an insured would appeal such an award. It is the insurer who, generally, would be dissatisfied with a high award. The policy provision thus presents an "escape hatch" to the insurer for avoidance of high arbitration awards, whether or not the award was fair and reasonable. However, the insured, who would tend to be dissatisfied with a low award, is barred from appealing such an award, i.e., an award under [$15,000].

In our view, the policy provision at issue here promotes litigation, circumvents the arbitration process and provides an arbitration escape device in favor of an insurance company. So viewed, the provision is contrary to the public policy of this State. Accordingly, we hold that a provision in an insurance policy which allows either party to demand a trial de novo, if the amount of an arbitrators' award exceeds a stated minimum amount but denies review for lesser awards, is void as against public policy and unenforceable. The Chancery Court was correct in striking this unconscionable clause.

The judgment of the Court of Chancery is *affirmed*.

Unconscionability and Sales Law

As mentioned above, the drafters of the UCC reinforced the principle of unconscionability by including it in the Code.

Section 2-302 provides:

> If the court as a matter of law finds the contract or any clause of the contract to have been unconscionable at the time it was made the court may refuse to enforce the contract, or it may enforce the remainder of the contract without the unconscionable

> clause, or it may so limit the application of any unconscionable clause as to avoid any unconscionable result.

In Code cases, the issue of unconscionability most often arises when a company attempts to limit the normal contract law remedies. Yet the Code itself allows such limitations, provided they are reasonable.

Section 2-719 provides in part:

> [A contract] may provide for remedies in addition to or in substitution for those provided [by the Code itself] *and may limit or alter the measure of damages recoverable*...as by limiting the buyer's remedies to return of the goods and repayment of the price. ...

In other words the Code includes two potentially competing sections. Section 2-719 permits a seller to insist that the buyer's only remedy for defective goods is return of the purchase price. But §2-302 says that *any unconscionable* provision is unenforceable. In lawsuits concerning defective goods, the seller often argues that the buyer's only remedies are those stated in the agreement, and the buyer responds that the contract limitation is unconscionable.

Electronic Data Systems (EDS) agreed to create complex software for Chubb Life America at a cost of $21 million. Chubb agreed to make staggered payments over many months, as work proceeded. The contract included a limitation on remedies, stating that if EDS became liable to Chubb, its maximum liability would be equal to two monthly payments.

EDS's work was woefully late and completely unusable, forcing Chubb to obtain its software elsewhere. Chubb sued, claiming $40 million in damages, based on money paid to EDS and funds spent purchasing alternative goods. EDS argued that the contract limited its liability to two monthly payments, a fraction of Chubb's damage. Chubb of course responded that the limitation was unconscionable.

The court noted that both parties were large, sophisticated corporations. As they negotiated the agreement, the companies both used experienced attorneys and independent consultants. This was no contract of adhesion presented to a meek consumer, but an allocation of risk resulting from hard bargaining. The court declared that the clause was valid and EDS owed no more than two monthly payments.[15]

CHAPTER CONCLUSION

It is not enough to bargain effectively and obtain a contract that gives you exactly what you want. You must also be sure that the contract is legal. A seemingly benign insurance contract might legally be an invalid wager. Unintentionally forgetting to obtain a state license to perform a certain job could mean you will never be paid for it. Bargaining a contract with a noncompete or exculpatory clause that is too one-sided may lead a court to ignore it. Legality is many faceted, sometimes subtle, and always important.

CHAPTER REVIEW

Illegal contracts are void and unenforceable. Illegality most often arises in these settings:

---

[15] *Colonial Life Insurance Co. v. Electronic Data Systems Corp.*, 817 F. Supp. 235, 1993 U.S. Dist. LEXIS 4123 (D.N.H. 1993).

1. *Wagering*. A purely speculative contract—whether for gambling, insurance, or investment—is likely to be unenforceable.

2. *Licensing*. When the licensing statute is designed to protect the public, a contract by an unlicensed plaintiff is generally unenforceable. When such a statute is designed merely to raise revenue, a contract by an unlicensed plaintiff is generally enforceable.

3. *Usury*. Excessive interest is generally unenforceable and may be fatal to the entire debt.

4. *Noncompete*. A noncompete clause in the sale of a business must be limited to a reasonable time, geographic area, and scope of activity. In an employment contract, such a clause is considered reasonable—and enforceable—only to protect trade secrets, confidential information, and customer lists.

5. *Exculpatory Clauses*. These clauses are generally void if the activity involved is in the public interest, the parties are greatly unequal in bargaining power, or the clause is unclear. In other cases they are generally enforced.

6. *Unconscionability*. Oppression and surprise may create an unconscionable bargain. An adhesion contract is especially suspect when it is imposed by a corporation on a consumer or small company. Under the UCC, a limitation of liability is less likely to be unconscionable when both parties are sophisticated corporations.

PRACTICE TEST

1. At a fraternity party, George mentions that he is going to learn to hang glide during spring break. Vicki, a casual friend, overhears him, and the next day she purchases a $100,000 life insurance policy on George's life. George has a happy week of hang gliding, but on the way home he is bitten by a parrot and dies of a rare tropical illness. Vicki files a claim for $100,000, but the insurance company refuses to pay.

(a) Vicki will win $100,000 but only if she mentioned animal bites to the insurance agent.

(b) Vicki will win $100,000 regardless of whether she mentioned animal bites to the insurance agent.

(c) Vicki will win $50,000.

(d) Vicki will win nothing.

2. For 20 years, Art's Flower Shop relied almost exclusively on advertising in the yellow pages to bring business to its shop in a small West Virginia town. One year the yellow pages printer accidentally omitted to print Art's ad, and Art's suffered an enormous drop in business. Art's sued for negligence and won a judgment of $50,000 from the jury, but the printing company appealed, claiming that under an exculpatory clause in the contract, the company could not be liable to Art's for more than the cost of the ad, about $910. Art's claimed that the exculpatory clause was unconscionable. Please rule.

3. James Wagner agreed to build a house for Nancy Graham. Wagner was not licensed as a contractor and Graham knew it. When the house was finished, Graham refused to pay the final $23,000, and Wagner sued. Who will prevail?

4. Brockwell left his boat to be repaired at Lake Gaston Sales. The boat contained electronic equipment and other personal items. Brockwell signed a form stating that Lake Gaston had no responsibility for any loss to any property in or on the boat. Brockwell's electronic equipment was stolen and other personal items were damaged, and he sued. Is the exculpatory clause enforceable?

5. McElroy owned 104 acres worth about $230,000. He got into financial difficulties and approached Grisham, asking to borrow $100,000. Grisham refused, but ultimately the two reached this agreement: McElroy would sell Grisham his property for $80,000, and the contract would include a clause allowing McElroy to repurchase the land within two years for

$120,000. McElroy later claimed the contract was void. Is he right?

6. **RIGHT & WRONG** Richard and Michelle Kommit traveled to New Jersey to have fun in the casinos. While in Atlantic City, they used their MasterCard to withdraw cash from an ATM conveniently located in the "pit," which is the gambling area of a casino. They ran up debts of $5,500 on the credit card and did not pay. The Connecticut National Bank sued for the money. What argument should the Kommits make? Which party, if any, has the moral high ground here? Should a casino offer ATM services in the gambling pit? If a credit card company allows customers to withdraw cash in a casino, is it encouraging them to lose money? Do the Kommits have any ethical right to use the ATM, attempt to win money by gambling, and then seek to avoid liability?

7. Guyan Machinery, a West Virginia manufacturing corporation, hired Albert Voorhees as a salesman and required him to sign a contract stating that if he left Guyan he would not work for a competing corporation anywhere within 250 miles of West Virginia for a two-year period. Later, Voorhees left Guyan and began working at Polydeck Corp., another West Virginia manufacturer. The only product Polydeck made was urethane screens, which comprised half of 1 percent of Guyan's business. Is Guyan entitled to enforce its non-compete clause?

8. KwikFix, a Fortune 500 company, contracts with Allied Rocket, another huge company, to provide the software for Allied's new Jupiter Probe rocket for $14 million. The software is negligently designed, and when the rocket blasts off from Cape Kennedy, it travels only as far as Fort Lauderdale. Allied Rocket sues for $200 million and proves that as a result of the disaster it lost a huge government contract, worth at least that much, which KwikFix was aware of. KwikFix responds that its contract with Allied included a clause limiting its liability to the value of the contract. Is the contract clause valid?

(a) The clause is unenforceable because it is unconscionable.

(b) The clause is unenforceable because it is exculpatory.

(c) The clause is enforceable because both parties are sophisticated corporations.

(d) The clause is enforceable because $200 million is an unconscionable claim.

9. 810 Associates owned a 42-story skyscraper in midtown Manhattan. The building had a central station fire alarm system, which was monitored by Holmes Protection. A fire broke out and Holmes received the signal. But Holmes's inexperienced dispatcher misunderstood the signal and failed to summon the fire department for about nine minutes, permitting tremendous damage. 810 sued Holmes, which defended based on an exculpatory clause that relieved Holmes of any liability caused in any way. Holmes's dispatcher was negligent. Does it matter *how* negligent he was?

10. **YOU BE THE JUDGE WRITING PROBLEM** Oasis Waterpark, located in Palm Springs, California, sought out Hydrotech Systems, Inc., a New York corporation, to design and construct a surfing pool. Hydrotech replied that it could design the pool and sell all the necessary equipment to Oasis, but could not build the pool because it was not licensed in California. Oasis insisted that Hydrotech do the construction work because Hydrotech had unique expertise in these pools. Oasis promised to arrange for a licensed California contractor to "work with" Hydrotech on the construction; Oasis also assured Hydrotech that it would pay the full contract price of $850,000, regardless of any licensing issues. Hydrotech designed and installed the pool as ordered. But Oasis failed to make the final payment of $110,000. Hydrotech sued. Can Hydrotech sue for either breach of contract or fraud (trickery)? **Argument for Oasis:** The licensing law protects the public from incompetence and dishonesty. The legislature made the section strict: no license, no payment. If the court were to start picking and choosing which unlicensed contractors could win a suit, it would be inviting incompetent workers to endanger the public and then come into court and try their luck. That is precisely the danger the legislature seeks to avoid. **Argument for Hydrotech:** This is not the kind of case the legislature was worried about. Hydrotech has never solicited work in California. Hydrotech went out of its way to avoid doing any contracting work, informing Oasis that it was unlicensed in the state. Oasis insisted on bringing Hydrotech into the state to do work. If Oasis has its way, word will go out that any owner can get free work done by hiring an *unlicensed* builder. Make any promises you want, get the work done to your satisfaction, and then stiff the contractor—you'll never have to pay.

11. The purchaser of a business insisted on putting this clause in the sales contract: The seller would not compete, for five years, "anywhere in the United

States, the continent of North America, or anywhere else on earth." What danger does that contract represent *to the purchaser?*

INTERNET RESEARCH PROBLEM

Go to http://www.law.cornell.edu/topics/state_statutes.html#criminal_code. Choose any state, and then search for that state's law on Internet gambling. Is it legal in that state? Has the state attempted to regulate this subject in any way? Do you believe the state will succeed? Conduct the same search in a second state and compare the results of the two searches.

You can find further practice problems in the Online Quiz at http://beatty.westbuslaw.com or in the Study Guide that accompanies this text.

CHAPTER 14

CAPACITY AND CONSENT

For Kevin Green, it was love at first sight. She was sleek, as quick as a cat, and a beautiful deep blue. He paid $4,600 cash for the used Camaro. The car soon blew a gasket, and Kevin demanded his money back. But the Camaro came with no guarantee, and the dealer refused. Kevin repaired the car himself. Next, some unpleasantness on the highway left the car a worthless wreck. Kevin received the full value of the car from his insurance company. Then he sued the dealer, seeking a refund of his purchase price. The dealer pointed out that it was not responsible for the accident, and that the car had no warranty of any kind. Yet *the trial court awarded Kevin the full $4,600*. How can this be? Should Kevin receive the full purchase price for a demolished car?

An 18-year-old college student has the legal capacity to create a binding contract, for example, to buy a car. She is obviously old enough to drive. Is she mature enough to *rent* a car? Many rental companies refuse to do business with drivers under 25, and even more reject those under 21. New York became the first state to outlaw age discrimination in automobile rentals. The state's highest court ruled that these businesses must make their cars available to drivers 18 and older. The judges did acknowledge that 18- to 25-year-olds cause a disproportionate number of serious accidents, and allowed rental agencies to charge them higher fees.

Exception (in Some States): Fully Executed Contracts

A minority of courts and legislatures have concluded that permitting minors to disaffirm and get back all of their money does injustice to honest retailers. These states distinguish between executory and executed contracts. For an **executory contract** (those that are not fully performed), *all* states apply the usual rule: the minor may disaffirm. But for a **fully executed contract** (one where both parties have fully performed), some states will permit the minor to get his money back only to the extent he can give restitution. Two examples should clarify.

Suppose 17-year-old Betsy goes to SoundBlast, a stereo dealer, and signs a contract to buy a $3,000 stereo. The system will be ready next week, when Betsy is obligated to pay for it in full. This is an executory contract. If Betsy returns to SoundBlast and tells them the deal is off, she has disaffirmed her contract. In *all* states, the store is entitled to no money.

Now assume that Betsy does buy the stereo system, paying $3,000 cash. Six months later she demands her money back. She returns the stereo in such bad shape that it is now worth only $800. A minority of states will require the store to refund only the $800. These states hold that it would be unfair for Betsy to get all of her money back, having enjoyed and ruined an expensive sound system. But note that in most states, such as Mississippi, the minor receives all of her money back, regardless of whether she can make full restitution.

Timing of Disaffirmance/Ratification

A minor may disaffirm a contract anytime before she reaches age 18. She also may disaffirm within a reasonable time *after* turning 18. Suppose that Betsy is 17 when she buys her stereo. Four months later she turns 18, and two months after that she disaffirms the contract. Her disaffirmance is effective. In most states, she gets 100 percent of her money back. In some cases minors have been entitled to disaffirm a contract several *years* after turning 18. But the minor's right to disaffirm ends if she later ratifies the contract.

If a minor enters into a contract and then, after turning 18, ratifies the deal, she loses her right to disaffirm and the agreement becomes fully enforceable. **Ratification** is made by any words or action indicating an intention to be bound by the contract. Suppose Betsy, age 17, buys her stereo on credit, promising to pay $150 per month. She has made only four payments by the time she turns 18, but after reaching her majority she continues to pay every month for six more months. Then she attempts to disaffirm. Too late. Her payment of the monthly bill for six months, as an adult, ratified the contract she entered into as a minor. She is now fully obligated to pay the entire $3,000, on the agreed-upon schedule.

Exception: Necessaries

There is one exception on which all states agree, and that is a contract for necessaries. A **necessary** is something essential to the minor's life and welfare. **On a contract for necessaries, a minor must pay for the value of the benefit received.**

In other words, the minor may still disaffirm the contract and return whatever is unused. But he is liable to pay for whatever benefit he obtained from the goods while he had them. Food, clothing, housing, and medical care are necessaries. Thus a 16-year-old who seeks emergency medical care and signs an agreement to pay for it is probably liable for the full bill. She has received the benefit of the services and must pay. A car, in most states, is *not* considered to be a necessary. Star Chevrolet argued that Kevin's Camaro ought to be considered a necessary, but the Mississippi court followed the general rule and held that it was not.

Exception: Misrepresentation of Age

The rules change somewhat if a minor lies about his age. Sixteen-year-old Dan is delighted to learn from his friend Betsy that a minor can buy a fancy stereo system, use it for a year or so, and then get his money back. Dan drops into SoundBlast and asks to buy a $9,000 surround-sound system. The store clerk, burned by Betsy, says that the store no longer sells expensive systems to punks. Dan produces a fake driver's license indicating that he is 19, and the clerk sells him the system. Two years later, Dan drives up to SoundBlast and unloads the system, now in shambles. He asks for his $9,000 back. Is he still permitted to disaffirm?

States have been troubled by this problem, and there is no clear rule. A few states will still permit Dan to disaffirm the contract entirely. The theory is that a minor must be saved from his own poor judgment, including his foolish lie. Many states, though, will prohibit Dan from disaffirming the contract. They take the reasonable position that the law was intended to protect childhood innocence, not calculated deceit. Some states take a middle position, permitting disaffirmance only if the other party (the retailer) will not be harmed. In such a state, Dan would receive only the present value of the stereo. Teenagers frequently lie about their age to purchase tobacco and alcohol, and, again, the law attempts to protect them. For compelling material on the effects of underage smoking, see these two Web sites: **http://www.paramountstations.com/common/teenfiles/smoking/index.html** and **http://www.tobaccofreekids.org/**. For similar information concerning alcohol, see **http://www.shorecrest.org/ClubTxt/sadd.html**.

The right of a minor to disaffirm a contract creates many unknowns for retail merchants. Could eight-year-old Ramona return a paperback book, stuck shut with peanut butter, and get her $7 back? Could friendly Bob return the used Corvette for which he paid $28,000, and demand his money back, though the smashed-up car is now worthless? There is no rule that guarantees a risk-free transaction, but any merchant should realize that he contracts with a minor at his peril. *If the dollar amount of a given contract creates a significant financial risk, the merchant should not enter into the deal if he doubts the customer's age*. The odds are that little Ramona will not return her book. If she does, she is probably entitled to her money, but $7 will not bankrupt the bookstore. It makes business sense to take this small risk, because the income from many sales will prove profitable regardless of what Ramona does. The Corvette is another matter. The $28,000 would be a serious loss for many dealerships. A prudent dealer should demand that someone co-sign the contract with Bob. The adult co-signer would be equally liable, and the dealership protected.

MENTALLY IMPAIRED PERSONS

You are a trial court judge. Don wants you to rule that his father, Cedric, is mentally incompetent and, on behalf of Cedric, to void a contract he signed. Here is the evidence:

Cedric is a 75-year-old millionaire who keeps $300,000 stuffed in pillow cases in the attic. He lives in a filthy house with a parrot, whom he calls the Bishop, an iguana named Orlando, and a tortoise known as Mrs. Sedgely. All of the pets have small beds in Cedric's grungy bedroom, and each one eats at the food-encrusted dining table with its master. Cedric pays college students $50 an hour to read poetry to the animals, but forbids reading any sonnets, which he regards as "the devil's handiwork." Don has been worried about Cedric's bizarre behavior for several years and has urged his father to enter a nursing home. Last week, when Don stopped in to visit, Cedric became angry at him, accusing his son of "dissing" the Bishop and Mrs. Sedgely, who were, according to Cedric, enjoying a fifteenth-century Castilian poem that Jane, a college student, was reading. Don then blurted out that Cedric was no longer able to take care of himself. Cedric snapped back, "I'll show you how capable I am." On the back of a 40-year-old menu he scratched out a contract, promising to give Jane "$100,000 today and $200,000 one year from today if she agrees to feed, house, and care for the Bishop, Orlando, and Mrs. Sedgely for the rest of their long lives." Jane promptly signed the agreement. Don urges that the court, on Cedric's behalf, declare the contract void. How will you rule? Courts often struggle when deciding cases of mental competence.

A person suffers from a mental impairment if by reason of mental illness or defect he is unable to understand the nature and consequences of the transaction.[2] The mental impairment can be insanity that has been formally declared by a court or mental illness that has never been ruled on but is now evident. The impairment may also be due to some other mental illness, such as schizophrenia, or to mental retardation, brain injury, senility, or any other cause that renders the person unable to understand the nature and consequences of the contract.

A party suffering a mental impairment generally creates only a voidable contract. The impaired person has the right to disaffirm the contract just as a minor does. But again, the contract is voidable, not void. The mentally impaired party generally has the right to full performance if she wishes.[3]

The law presumes that an adult is mentally competent. As always, courts respect the freedom to contract. Anyone seeking to avoid a contract because of mental impairment has the burden of proving the infirmity, since "mental incompetence" could be a very handy way out of a deal gone sour.

How will a court evaluate Cedric's mental status? Of course, if there had already been a judicial determination that he was insane, any contract he signed would be voidable. In fact, in some states his agreements would be *void*. Since no judge has issued such a ruling about Cedric, the court will listen to doctors or therapists who have evaluated him and to anyone else who can testify about Cedric's recent conduct. Finally, the court may choose to look at the contract itself, to see if it is so lopsided that no competent person would agree to it.

How will Don fare in seeking to preserve Cedric's wealth? Poorly. Unless Don has more evidence than we have heard thus far, he is destined to eat canned tuna while Jane and the Bishop dine on caviar. Cedric is unclean, decidedly eccentric, and possibly unwise. But none of those characteristics proves mental impairment. Neither does leaving a fortune to a poetry reader. If Don could produce evidence from a psychiatrist that Cedric, for example, was generally delusional or could not distinguish a parrot from a religious leader, that would persuade a court of mental impairment. But on the evidence presented thus far, Mrs. Sedgely and friends will be living well.[4]

---

2 Restatement (Second) of Contracts §15.

3 As mentioned below, in many states it is the law that if a court has actually judged someone legally insane, a contract he enters into is entirely void, not just voidable.

4 For a similar case, see *Harwell v. Garrett*, 239 Ark. 551, 393 S.W.2d 256, 1965 Ark. LEXIS 1033 (1965).

Intoxication

Similar rules apply in cases of drug or alcohol intoxication. When one party is so intoxicated that he cannot understand the nature and consequences of the transaction, the contract is voidable. Toby's father gives him a new Jaguar sports car for his birthday, and foolish Toby celebrates by getting drunk. Amy, realizing how intoxicated he is, induces Toby to promise in writing that he will sell his car to her the next day for $1,000. Toby may void the contract and keep his auto.

Restitution

A mentally infirm party who seeks to void a contract must make restitution. If a party succeeds with a claim of mental impairment, the court will normally void the contract but will require the impaired party to give back whatever she got. Suppose Danielle buys a Rolls Royce and promises in writing to pay $3,000 per month for five years. Three weeks later she seeks to void the contract on the grounds of mental impairment. She must return the Rolls. If the car has depreciated, Danielle normally will have to pay for the decrease in value. What happens if restitution is impossible? Generally, courts require a mentally infirm person to make full restitution if the contract is to be rescinded. If restitution is impossible, the court will not rescind the agreement unless the infirm party can show bad faith by the other. This is because, unlike minority, which is generally easy to establish, mental competence may not be so apparent to the other person negotiating. The Wisconsin court explains the difference.

HAUER v. UNION STATE BANK OF WAUTOMA
192 Wis. 2d 576, 532 N.W.2d 456, 1995 Wis. App. LEXIS 367
Wisconsin Court of Appeals, 1995

Facts: Kathy Hauer suffered a brain injury in a motorcycle accident. A court found that she was mentally incompetent and appointed a legal guardian. But a year later, her physician stated that Hauer had recovered to the point where she had ongoing memory, showed good judgment, and could manage her own affairs. The court ended her guardianship. Hauer had a monthly income of $900 from Social Security disability and interest from a mutual fund worth $80,000.

Shortly afterward, Hauer met Ben Eilbes, a young man who was trying to start a small business. The Union State Bank had already loaned Eilbes $7,600 to start his business, but he had defaulted. Eilbes convinced Kathy Hauer to invest in his business. He urged her to take out a short-term loan, using the mutual fund as collateral, and lend him the money.

Eilbes contacted Richard Schroeder, an assistant vice-president of Union State. The two agreed that Union State would give Hauer a short-term $30,000 loan, using her shares as collateral. Hauer signed the application, and Union State loaned her the money, which was due in a single payment in six months. Hauer gave the $30,000 to Eilbes, who put all of the money into his business and promptly went bankrupt. On the day her loan was due, Hauer sued Union State, seeking to void the contract.

At trial, the jury found that Hauer lacked mental capacity to enter into the loan, voided the loan, and ordered Union State to return her collateral.

Issue: **May Hauer void the contract based on mental impairment?**

Excerpts from Judge Snyder's Decision: Our review of the record reveals that there is credible evidence which the jury could have relied on in reaching its verdict. First, it is undisputed that Hauer was under court-appointed guardianship approximately one year before the loan transaction. Second, Hauer's testimony indicates a complete lack of understanding of the nature and consequences of the transaction. Third, Hauer's psychological expert, Charles Barnes, testified that Hauer was "very deficient in her cognitive abilities, her abilities to remember and to read, write and spell. . . . [S]he was very malleable, gullible, people could convince her of almost anything. . . ."

We [next] decide the legal question of whether Hauer may recover her collateral without liability for the loan proceeds.

If the contract is made on fair terms and the other party has no reason to know of the incompetency, the contract ceases to be voidable [if] the parties cannot be restored to their previous positions. If, on the other hand, the other party knew of the incompetency or took unfair advantage of the incompetent, consideration dissipated without benefit to the incompetent, need not be restored.

The Bank knew that Eilbes was in default of his loan at the Bank. Eilbes approached the Bank and laid all the groundwork for a loan to be given to a third-party investor, Hauer, whom the Bank did not know. Eilbes told Schroeder that he would get his defaulted loan current or pay it off entirely with Hauer's investment. Schroeder testified that upon investigating the matter initially, Hauer's stockbroker told him not to use Hauer's fund as collateral because she needed the fund to live on and Hauer could not afford to lose the fund. He further testified that it was possible that the stockbroker told him that Hauer suffered a brain injury. In addition, Hauer's banking expert opined that the Bank should not have made the loan.

We conclude that the evidence and reasonable inferences that can be drawn from the evidence support the jury's conclusion that the Bank failed to act in good faith.

Judgment *affirmed*.

REALITY OF CONSENT

Smiley offers to sell you his house for $300,000, and you agree in writing to buy. After you move in, you discover that the house is sinking into the earth at the rate of six inches per week. In 12 months, your only access to the house will be through the chimney. You sue, asking to rescind. You argue that when you signed the contract you did not truly consent because you lacked essential information. In this section we look at four claims that parties make in an effort to rescind a contract based on lack of valid consent: (1) misrepresentation or fraud, (2) mistake, (3) duress, and (4) undue influence.

MISREPRESENTATION AND FRAUD

Misrepresentation occurs when a party to a contract says something that is factually wrong. "This house has no termites," says a homeowner to a prospective buyer. If the house is swarming with the nasty pests, the statement is a misrepresentation. The misrepresentation might be innocent or fraudulent. If the owner believes the statement to be true and has a good reason for that belief, he has made an **innocent misrepresentation**. If the owner knows that it is false, the statement is **fraudulent misrepresentation**. To explain these concepts, we will assume that two people are discussing a possible deal. One is the "maker," that is, the person who makes the statement that is later disputed. The other is the "injured person," the one who eventually claims to have been injured by the statement. In order to rescind the contract, the injured person must show that the maker's statement was *either* fraudulent *or* a material misrepresentation. She does not have to show both. Innocent misrepresentation and fraud each make a contract voidable and permit the injured party to rescind. **To rescind a contract based on misrepresentation or fraud, a party must show three things: (1) there was a false statement of fact; (2) the statement was fraudulent or material; and (3) the injured person justifiably relied on the statement.**

Element One: False Statement of Fact

The injured party must show a false statement of fact. Notice that this does not mean the statement was a lie. If a homeowner says that the famous architect Stanford White designed his house, but Bozo Loco actually did the work, it is a false statement. The owner might have a good reason for the error. Perhaps a local history book identifies the house as a Stanford White. Or his words might be an intentional lie. In either case, it is a false statement of fact.

An **opinion**, though, is not a statement of fact. A realtor says, "I think land values around here will be going up 20 or 30 percent for the foreseeable future." That statement is pretty enticing to a buyer, but it is not a false statement of fact. The maker is clearly stating her own opinion, and the buyer who relies on it does so at his peril. Although there are exceptions, most opinions are no basis to rescind a contract. A close relative of opinion is something called "puffery."

Puffery. Get ready for one of the most astonishing experiences you've *ever had!* This section on puffery is going to be the *finest section of any textbook you have ever read!* You're going to find the issue intriguing, the writing dazzling, and the legal summary succinct and *literally unforgettable!!* "But what happens," you might wonder, "if this section fails to astonish? What if I find the issue dull, the writing mediocre, and the legal summary incomprehensible? Can I sue for misrepresentation?" No. The promises we made were mere puffery. A statement is **puffery** when a reasonable person would realize that it is a sales pitch, representing the exaggerated opinion of the seller. **Puffery is not a statement of fact.** Because puffery is not factual, it is never a basis for rescission.

Marie Rodio purchased auto insurance from Allstate and then, after she was involved in a serious accident, received from the company less money than she thought fair. She sued, arguing that the company had committed fraud by advertising that customers would be in "good hands." She lost when the state supreme court ruled that, even if she could prove the company did not treat her well, the ad was mere puffery and not fraud.[5] "The finest automobile you will ever drive" is another example of puffery, as is "The smoothest taste in the world" or "The Sale of the Century." In none of those cases will a disappointed party be allowed to rescind.

By contrast, when a freight company called Mason & Dixon Lines (M & D) hired Warren Byrd as a sales agent, it promised him "100 percent" support, including all necessary trucking equipment, so that he could effectively solicit business. The company failed to support Byrd and his income plummeted. Byrd sued, claiming that M & D had fraudulently induced him to contract. The company responded that any promises of assistance had been mere puffery. The Alabama Supreme Court disagreed, pointing out that the company's previous agents had suffered because of inadequate assistance and Byrd knew it. He had accepted the job only after the company explicitly promised him specific types of support. M & D's statements were material, and Byrd won damages for breach of contract and fraud.[6]

That brings us to the end of the section on puffery. The writing was pretty poor, but you still may not sue. Now for some *absolutely breathtaking* disputes

---

[5] *Rodio v. Smith*, 123 N.J. 345, 587 A.2d 621, 1991 N.J. LEXIS 21 (1991).

[6] *Mason & Dixon Lines, Inc. v. Byrd*, 601 So. 2d 68, 1992 Ala. LEXIS 598 (Ala. 1992).

have no calves. As a barren cow she was worth much less, so Walker contracted to sell her to T. C. Sherwood for $80. But when Sherwood came to collect Rose, the parties realized she was pregnant. Walker refused to part with the happy mother, and Sherwood sued. Walker defended, claiming that both parties had made a mistake and that the contract was voidable.

Mistake can occur in many ways. It may be a basic error about the quality of the thing being sold, as in Rose's case. It could be an erroneous prediction about future prices, such as an expectation that oil prices will rise. It might be a mechanical error, such as a builder offering to build a new home for $300 when he clearly meant to bid $300,000. Some mistakes lead to voidable contracts, others create enforceable deals. The first distinction is between bilateral and unilateral mistakes.

Bilateral Mistake

A **bilateral mistake** occurs when both parties negotiate based on the same factual error. Sherwood and Walker both thought Rose was barren, both negotiated accordingly, and both were wrong. The Michigan Supreme Court gave judgment for Walker, the seller, permitting him to rescind the contract because the parties were both wrong about the essence of what they were bargaining for.

If the parties contract based on an important factual error, the contract is voidable by the injured party. Sherwood and Walker were both wrong about Rose's reproductive ability, and the error was basic enough to cause a tenfold difference in price. Walker, the injured party, was entitled to rescind the contract. Note that the error must be *factual*. Suppose Walker sold Rose thinking that the price of beef was going to drop, when in fact the price rose 60 percent in five months. He made a mistake, but it was simply a business prediction that proved wrong. Walker would have no right to rescind.

Conscious Uncertainty. No rescission is permitted where one of the parties knows he is taking on a risk, that is, he realizes there is uncertainty about the quality of the thing being exchanged. Rufus offers 10 acres of mountainous land to Priscilla. "I can't promise you anything about this land," he says, "but they've found gold on every adjoining parcel." Priscilla, panting with gold lust, buys the land, digs long and hard, and discovers—mud. She may not rescind the contract. She understood the risk she was assuming, and there was no mutual mistake.

REILLEY v. RICHARDS
69 Ohio St. 3d 352, 632 N.E. 2d 507, 1994 Ohio LEXIS 1062
Ohio Supreme Court, 1994

Facts: Richards contracted to buy a lot from Reilley, intending to build a house on it. After closing, Richards discovered that much of the property was unbuildable, because it lay in a flood hazard area, a fact neither party knew when they agreed to the sale. Richards sued to rescind the contract. The trial court found mutual mistake and rescinded but the appeal court reversed. Richards sought review in the state's highest court.

Issue: **Is Richards entitled to rescind the contract based on mutual mistake?**

Excerpts from Judge Sweeney's Decision: [In an earlier case] we held that a buyer is entitled to rescission of a real estate purchase contract where there is a mutual mistake as to a material part of the contract and where the complaining party is not negligent in failing to discover the mistake. The intention of the parties must have been frustrated by the mutual mistake.

Both parties testified that, at the time of contracting, they were unaware that the property was in a floodplain. The Dublin City Engineer testified that it is illegal to build or place any fill in the floodway or within twenty feet of the boundaries of the floodway. David Norman, a professional engineer, testified that more than half of the property is in the flood hazard zone.

Further, Michael Kennedy, the builder who was to build appellant's residence, testified that, having seen the drawings showing where the floodplain and flood hazard zone are on the lot, he would not want to build on the lot because he could not warrant the property for one year, as is standard building practice.

Based upon the above, we find that the lack of knowledge that a significant portion of the lot is located in a floodway is a mistake of fact of both parties that goes to the character of the property such that it severely frustrates the appellant's ability to build a home on the property. Thus, it is a mutual mistake that is material to the subject matter of the contract.

Additionally, while appellant did have an escape clause in his first contract with appellee allowing him "sixty days from acceptance of this contract to satisfy himself that all soil, engineering, utility and other site related considerations are acceptable," this inspection provision does not mean that appellant assumed a duty to discover the floodplain. Appellant was a lawyer but he had no experience in real estate law and, thus, was an unsophisticated party at the time of the transaction. Appellant did have his builder inspect the property but he did not discover, and could not have discovered, the floodplain by looking at the property. The court of appeals wrongly concluded that appellant's failure to hire engineers to discover the floodplain within the sixty days constituted negligence. We agree with the trial court that appellant, an unsophisticated buyer, was not negligent in failing to discover that the lot was in a designated floodplain.

Judgment reversed.

Excerpts from Judge Bryant's Dissenting Opinion: Appellant independently came to the conclusion that he could not build a particular house on the lot. Appellant testified that he had not applied for a building or development permit because he did not want to pay the administrative costs of doing so. The majority even recognizes that a building might be permitted elsewhere on the subject lot. Since there has been no showing that a building could not be constructed on the lot, I do not believe there has been any mutual mistake as to a material fact. I agree with the court of appeals that the only mistake here is one of law, not fact.

I am also troubled by the majority's holding that appellant, a lawyer, has no obligation to use all his knowledge if the matter at issue is not within his area of practice. This holding does nothing to enhance the professional reputation of lawyers.

I also disagree with the majority's conclusion, as I believe the appellant assumed the risk of the property being situated in the floodplain since he drafted a contract containing [the escape clause]. Having voiced no objection within the sixty-day time period, appellant has waived any such objection.

Unilateral Mistake

Sometimes only one party enters a contract under a mistaken assumption, a situation called **unilateral mistake**. In these cases it is more difficult for the injured party to rescind a contract. This makes sense, since in a bilateral error neither side really knew what it was getting into, and rescission seems a natural remedy. But with unilateral mistake, one side may simply have made a better bargain than the other. As we have seen throughout this unit on contracts, courts are unwilling to undo an agreement merely because someone made a foolish deal. Nonetheless, if her proof is strong enough, the injured party in a case of unilateral mistakes still may rescind the contract.

To rescind for unilateral mistake, a party must demonstrate that she entered the contract because of a basic factual error and that either (1) enforcing the contract would be unconscionable *or* (2) the nonmistaken party knew of the error.[12]

---

[12] Restatement (Second) of Contracts §153.

Cosmo inherits his parents' house, along with 50 years of accumulated rubbish. He holds a yard sale and offers a dusty painting of a hummingbird for $25, "because it has a nice frame." Lucy recognizes the picture as the work of Martin Johnson Heade, a distinguished American artist. Knowing the picture to be worth at least half a million dollars, she buys it for $25, then promptly sells it for $800,000. When Cosmo sues for rescission, he will win. Cosmo's basic factual error was his ignorance that a famous artist created the work. Lucy knew of Cosmo's error, since otherwise he would never sell the picture so cheap. Cosmo has proven both elements and gets his picture back. Notice that Cosmo could also argue that it would be unconscionable to let Lucy benefit so hugely at his expense. The injured party needs to prove only unconscionability *or* knowledge of the error, but typically the two go together: when one party knows of the other's basic factual error, it will usually be unconscionable to enforce the bargain.

By contrast, suppose that Cosmo does realize he has inherited a Martin Johnson Heade. He asks a dealer what it is worth, and the dealer tells him "about $600,000." Cosmo sells it to Vince for $550,000, and Vince promptly resells it for $850,000. Can Cosmo rescind? No. If he underestimates the value, that is his tough luck. He has made an error in judgment about the fine art market, but not a basic factual mistake about the nature of the object he inherited.

DURESS

True consent is also lacking when one party agrees to a contract under **duress**. If kindly Uncle Hugo signs over the deed to the ranch because Niece Nelly is holding a Colt .45 to his head, Hugo has not consented in any real sense, and he will have the right to rescind the contract. **If one party makes an improper threat that causes the victim to enter into a contract, and the victim had no reasonable alternative, the contract is voidable.**[13] The key issues are thus whether there was an improper threat and whether the victim had a reasonable alternative.

On a Sunday morning, Bancroft Hall drove to pick up his daughter Sandra, who had slept at a friend's house. The Halls are black and the neighborhood was white. A suspicious neighbor called the police, who arrived, aggressively prevented the Halls from getting into their own car, and arrested the father. The officers took Hall to the police station for booking but eventually realized there might be some problems with the arrest, since neither of the Halls had violated any law or done anything wrong whatsoever. An officer told Hall that he could leave immediately if he signed a full release (stating that he had no claims of any kind against the police), but that if he refused to sign it he would be detained for a bail hearing. Hall signed the release, but later filed suit for false arrest, false imprisonment, battery, and civil rights violations. The police defended based on the release.

The court held that the release was voidable because Hall had signed it under duress. The threat to detain Hall for a bail hearing was clearly improper because he had committed no crime. He also had no reasonable alternative to signing. The Halls' suit went to trial, where the jury awarded them compensatory and punitive damages, plus attorney's fees, totaling over $525,000.[14]

By contrast, suppose Ferdinand takes his prize bull into Sybil's China Shoppe. The bull slips and falls on some spilled soup, breaking his spine. Ferdinand is furious and threatens to sue unless Sybil agrees to pay $10,000. Sybil signs an agreement admitting liability and promising to pay the money. Is the contract enforceable? Yes. Ferdinand's lawsuit would have been legitimate, and there is nothing improper about his threat. **A threat to file a lawsuit is only improper where there is no basis for the suit and its only purpose would be to harass.**

---

13 Restatement (Second) of Contracts § 175(1).

14 *Hall v. Ochs*, 817 F.2d 920, U.S. App. LEXIS 5822 (1st Cir. 1987).

ECONOMIC DURESS

If improper threats can permit one party to rescind a contract, then why not *economic* intimidation? Many plaintiffs have posed that question over the last half century, and courts have grudgingly yielded. Today, in most but not all states, economic duress can also be used to void a contract. But economic duress sounds perilously close to hard competition, in other words—business. The free market system is expected to produce tough competition. A smart, aggressive executive may bargain fiercely. How do we distinguish economic duress from successful business tactics? Courts have created no single rule to answer the question, but they do focus on certain issues.

In **analyzing a claim of economic duress**, courts look at these factors:

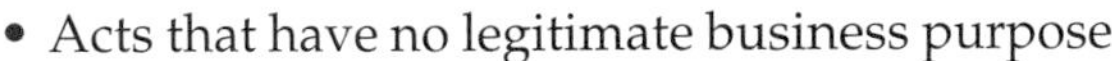

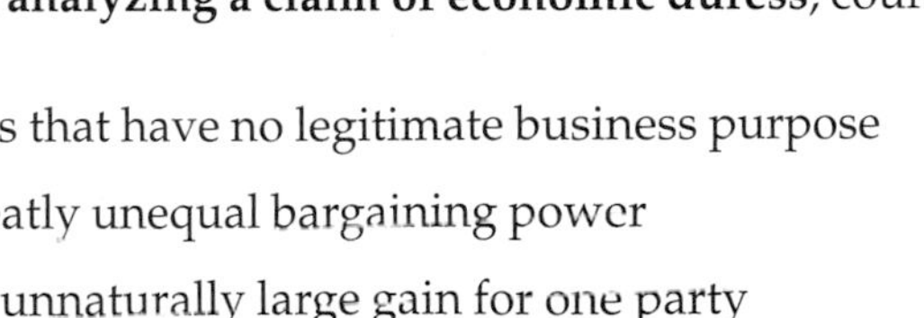

- Acts that have no legitimate business purpose
- Greatly unequal bargaining power
- An unnaturally large gain for one party
- Financial distress to one party

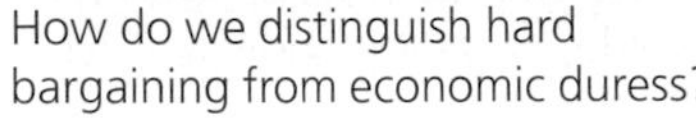

How do we distinguish hard bargaining from economic duress?

Mr. and Mrs. Loftins owned hundreds of acres of forest. International Paper Company (IPC) contracted with them to cut specially marked trees. The company then hired Bill Whilden, a logger, to cut and haul the trees under its supervision. When the job was done, Whilden sought his final $7,000 payment from IPC. But the Loftins claimed he had cut some unmarked trees. IPC refused to pay Whilden until he reluctantly signed an agreement to compensate the Loftins for any harm.

The Loftins sued IPC for $40,000, and the company responded that Whilden had assumed responsibility. But the state supreme court permitted the logger to void the agreement, based on economic duress. To induce Whilden to sign the contract, IPC had lied, telling him that about 30 trees were in dispute when it knew the Loftins claimed 650 had been wrongly cut. Further, the company had enjoyed greatly superior bargaining power, since Whilden desperately needed his paycheck.[15] For the British perspective on the distinction between hard bargaining and duress, see **http://uniserve.edu.au/law/pub/edinst/anu/contract/THEMODERNLAWOFDURESS2.html**.

Injured parties often claim economic duress, and the facts often present a closer call than in the *International Paper* case. Is the following case one of duress or hard bargaining?

PONDER v. LINCOLN NATIONAL SALES CORP.

612 So. 2d 1169, 1992 Ala. LEXIS 1363
Supreme Court of Alabama, 1992

Facts: Lincoln National Sales Corp. leased an office complex from Jack Ponder for three years, at $5.50 per square foot per year. The agreement gave Lincoln National an option to renew for a second three-year period at $7.70 per foot, and for a third at $8.25. Lincoln National did renew its lease for the second period, paying the agreed price. But the company told Ponder it would not renew for the third period at $8.25 per foot. Instead Lincoln National offered to enter into a five-year lease at only $5.23 per foot, saying that if Ponder would not agree to the reduced price, the company would build its own complex.

The rental market was poor, so Ponder concluded that he had no choice. He signed the five-year lease at $5.23 per foot. Ponder then sued, claiming that the company's economic duress had cost him $114,000 in lost rent. The trial court dismissed the case, and Ponder appealed.

[15] *International Paper Co. v. Whilden*, 469 So. 2d 560, 1985 Ala. LEXIS 3585 (Ala. 1985).

You Be the Judge: Did Ponder sign the modified lease under economic duress?

Argument for Ponder: Your honors, Lincoln National might just as well have held a pistol to Jack Ponder's head. He had absolutely no choice but to sign this trumped-up lease, and that was precisely what Lincoln National intended.

Six years ago, the parties made a fair and equitable bargain. They both knew that rental rates fluctuate, and they wanted to plan with some certainty. The contact they signed gave both parties something. Lincoln National got a reasonable rental rate, and the right to renew for additional three-year periods at very modest increases. If market prices had increased dramatically, Lincoln National would have been holding a real bargain, and everyone understood that. Jack Ponder also got some certainty, knowing that if Lincoln National exercised its renewal option, he would get a rent he could live with.

The parties understood that Lincoln National had two choices: to renew at the specified rates, which each considered a fair compromise, or to vacate the premises. What neither side foresaw was Lincoln National coming to Jack Ponder and saying, "We want to stay but at cheaper rents. We think we can squeeze a better deal out of you. Give us the price we demand or else." That isn't fair bargaining, your honors. The bargaining was done six years ago. This is economic duress, and the contract that Mr. Ponder was forced to sign should be voided.

Argument for Lincoln National: Your honors, Mr. Ponder confuses economic duress with intelligent business practices. The contract that the parties signed six years ago is an option contract. Lincoln National had the option to renew its lease at specified rents. But the company was under no *obligation* to renew. The option is just that: a right to renew if and only if Lincoln National wishes. Lincoln National might have asked, six years back, for a 10-year contract. Or Mr. Ponder might have insisted on a 10-year lease if he wished. What Lincoln National bargained for, and got, was the right to make a renewal decision a few years down the road.

Lincoln National decided not to renew. Yes, the company did ask for a new lease at lower rates. Mr. Ponder didn't have to agree but he chose to do so—a wise choice, given the weak market. This is not economic duress because Lincoln National has done nothing wrong. Indeed, given the soft rental market, Lincoln National would have been negligent *not* to bargain for a lower rate. Mr. Ponder agreed to a new lease at a given rental, and he must live with his bargain.

UNDUE INFLUENCE

She was single and pregnant. A shy young woman in a large city with no family nearby, she needed help and support. She went to the Methodist Mission Home of Texas where she found room and board, support—and a lot of counseling. Her discussions with a minister and a private counselor stressed one point: that she should give up her baby for adoption. She signed the adoption papers, but days later she decided she wanted the baby after all. Was there any ground to rescind? She claimed *undue influence*, in other words, that the Mission Home so dominated her thinking that she never truly consented. Where one party has used undue influence, the contract is voidable at the option of the injured party. There are two elements to the plaintiff's case. **To prove undue influence, the injured party must demonstrate:**

- **A relationship between the two parties either of trust or of domination,** ***and***
- **Improper persuasion by the stronger party.**[16]

In other words, a party seeking to rescind based on undue influence must first show that the parties had some close bond, either because one would normally have trusted and relied on the other or because one was able to dominate the other. Suppose that an 85-year-old woman owns an undeveloped island in the Caribbean but has no other assets or income. She lives in her daughter's house in

[16] Restatement (Second) of Contracts §177.

Minnesota, and the daughter uses financial superiority and greater strength to control every aspect of her mother's life. The daughter probably has a position of dominance. Second, the party seeking to rescind must show improper persuasion, which is an effort by the stronger party to coerce the weaker one into a decision that she otherwise would not have made. If the daughter berates her mother daily until the mother signs a will, leaving her the Caribbean island, that may well be undue influence.

Keeping those two factors in mind, what should be the outcome of the Methodist Mission case? The court held that the plaintiff had been young and extremely vulnerable during the emotional days following the birth of her child. The mission's counselor, to whom she turned for support, had spent day after day forcefully insisting that the young woman had no moral or legal right to keep her child. The harangue amounted to undue influence. The court voided the adoption agreement.[17]

Remember that the party claiming undue influence must show *both* a special relationship *and* improper persuasion. Janet Pagano was involved in a bitter divorce dispute with her husband. Ms. Pagano's lawyer was Richard Rinella. After a year and a half of litigation, with many months of fighting still ahead, Rinella had received only $2,500 in fees from Pagano. Shortly before a custody hearing, Rinella and Pagano met in the courthouse cafeteria. Rinella presented Pagano with a handwritten contract in which Pagano agreed to pay $30,000 for the services thus far rendered and gave Rinella a lien on her house. Pagano signed the agreement, but later claimed undue influence.

Clearly, Rinella occupied a position of trust, but Pagano still lost her case. The court ruled that Rinella used no improper persuasion. He explained all aspects of the contract clearly, and Pagano understood what she was agreeing to. The bill, though high, was reasonable and Pagano was not permitted to rescind.[18]

CHAPTER CONCLUSION

An agreement between two parties may not be enough to make a contract enforceable. A minor or a mentally impaired person may generally disaffirm contracts. Even if both parties are adults of sound mind, courts will insist that consent be genuine. Misrepresentation, mistake, duress, and undue influence all indicate that at least one party did not truly consent. As the law evolves, it imposes an increasingly greater burden of *good faith negotiating* on the party in the stronger position. Do not bargain for a contract that is too good to be true.

CHAPTER REVIEW

1. Capacity and consent are different contract issues that can lead to the same result: a voidable contract. A voidable agreement is one that can be canceled by a party who lacks legal capacity or who did not give true consent.

2. A minor (someone under the age of 18) generally may disaffirm any contract while she is still a minor or within a reasonable time after reaching age 18.

---

17 *Methodist Mission Home of Texas v. N A B*, 451 S.W.2d 539, 1970 Tex. App. LEXIS 2055 (Tex. Civ. App. 1970).

18 *In re Pagano*, 154 Ill. 2d 174, 607 N.E. 2d 1242, 1992 Ill. LEXIS 195 (1992).

3. A minor who disaffirms must make restitution; that is, she must return to the other party whatever consideration she received, such as goods that she purchased. If she cannot make restitution because the goods are damaged or destroyed, in most (but not all) states the minor is still entitled to disaffirm and receive her money.

4. A mentally impaired person may generally disaffirm a contract. In this case, though, he generally *must* make restitution.

5. *Fraud and Misrepresentation*. Both fraud and material misrepresentation are grounds for disaffirming a contract. The injured party must prove:
   (a) A false statement of fact and
   (b) Fraud or materiality; and
   (c) Justifiable reliance.

6. Silence amounts to misrepresentation only in four instances:
   (a) Where disclosure is necessary to *correct a previous assertion*
   (b) Where disclosure would correct a *basic mistaken assumption* on which the other party is relying
   (c) Where disclosure would correct the other party's *mistaken understanding about a writing*; or
   (d) Where there is a *relationship of trust* between the two parties.

7. *Mistake*. In a case of bilateral mistake, either party may rescind the contract. In a case of unilateral mistake, the injured party may rescind only upon a showing that enforcement would be unconscionable or that the other party knew of her mistake.

8. *Duress*. If one party makes an improper threat that causes the victim to enter into a contract, and the victim had no reasonable alternative, the contract is voidable.

9. Cases of economic duress are more common but harder to win. Courts will look at the parties' motives, their respective bargaining power, any unnaturally large gains, and resulting financial distress.

10. *Undue Influence*. Once again the injured party may rescind a contract, but only upon a showing of a special relationship *and* improper persuasion.

PRACTICE TEST

1. Raymond Barrows owned a 17-acre parcel of undeveloped land in Seaford, Delaware. For most of his life Mr. Barrows had been an astute and successful businessman, but by the time he was 85 years old, he had been diagnosed as "very senile and confused 90 percent of the time." Glenn Bowen offered to buy the land. Barrows had no idea of its value, so Bowen had it appraised by a friend, who said it was worth $50,000. Bowen drew up a contract, which Barrows signed. In the contract, Barrows agreed to sell the land for $45,000, of which Bowen would pay $100 at the time of closing; the remaining $44,900 was due whenever Bowen developed the land and sold it. There was no time limit on Bowen's right to develop the land nor any interest due on the second payment. Comment.

2. Ron buys from Karen 1,000 "Smudgy Dolls" for his toy store. Karen knows the dolls' heads are not properly attached but says nothing. Ron sells all of the dolls quickly and then has 1,000 unhappy customers

with headless dolls. Ron sues to rescind the contract with Karen and also seeks punitive damages. What is the likely outcome?

(a) Ron will be able to rescind, based on fraudulent nondisclosure, but he may not get punitive damages as well.

(b) Ron will be able to rescind, based on fraudulent nondisclosure, and may also obtain punitive damages.

(c) Ron will lose unless he can show that Karen intended to harm Ron's business.

(d) Ron will win only if he can show that both parties were mistaken about a basic assumption.

3. Andreini suffered from a nerve problem that was causing him to lose the use of his hands. Dr. Beck operated on Andreini's hands but the problem grew worse. A nurse told Andreini that Beck might have committed a serious error in the operation, causing Andreini's neuropathy to grow worse. Andreini returned to Beck for a second operation, which Beck assured him was certain to correct the problem. But after Andreini had been placed in a surgical gown, shaved, and prepared for surgery, Dr. Beck insisted that he sign a release relieving Beck of any liability for the first operation. Andreini did not want to sign it, but Beck refused to operate until he did. Later, Andreini sued Beck for malpractice. A trial court dismissed Andreini's suit based on the release. You are on the appeals court. Will you affirm the dismissal or reverse?

4. On television and in magazines, Maurine and Mamie Mason saw numerous advertisements for Chrysler Fifth Avenue automobiles. The ads described the car as "luxurious," "quality-engineered," and "reliable." When they went to inspect the car, the salesman told them the warranty was "the best ... comparable to Cadillacs and Lincolns." After the Masons bought a Fifth Avenue, they began to have many problems with it. Even after numerous repairs, the car was unsatisfactory and required more work. The Masons sued, seeking to rescind the contract based on the ads and the dealer's statement. Will they win?

5. John Marshall and Kirsten Fletcher decided to live together. They leased an apartment, each agreeing to pay one-half of the rent. When he signed the lease, Marshall was 17. Shortly after signing the lease, Marshall turned 18, and two weeks later he moved into the apartment. He paid his half of the rent for two months and then moved out because he and Fletcher were not getting along. Fletcher sued Marshall for one-half of the monthly rent for the remainder of the lease. Who wins?

6. Kerry finds a big green ring in the street. She shows it to Leroy, who says, "Wow. That could be valuable." Neither Kerry nor Leroy knows what the ring is made of or whether it is valuable. Kerry sells the ring to Leroy for $100, saying, "Don't come griping if it turns out to be worth two dollars." Leroy takes the ring to a jeweler who tells him it is an unusually perfect emerald, worth at least $75,000. Kerry sues to rescind.

(a) Kerry will win based on fraud.

(b) Kerry will win based on mutual mistake.

(c) Kerry will win based on unilateral mistake.

(d) Kerry will lose.

7. The McAllisters had several serious problems with their house, including leaks in the ceiling, a buckling wall, and dampness throughout. They repaired the buckling wall by installing I-beams to support it. They never resolved the leaks and the dampness. When they decided to sell the house, they said nothing to prospective buyers about the problems. They stated that the I-beam had been added for reinforcement. The Silvas bought the house for $60,000. Soon afterwards, they began to have problems with leaks, mildew, and dampness. Are the Silvas entitled to any money damages? Why or why not?

8. **RIGHT & WRONG** Sixteen-year-old Travis Mitchell brought his 19-year-old Pontiac GTO into M&M Precision Body and Paint for body work and a paint job. M&M did the work and charged $1,900, which Travis paid. Travis later complained about the quality of the work and M&M did some touching up, but Travis was still dissatisfied. Travis demanded his $1,900 back, but M&M refused to give it back since all of the work was "in" the car and Travis could not return it to the shop. The state of Nebraska, where this occurred, follows the majority rule on this issue. Does Travis get his money? What is the common law rule? Who *ought* to win? Is the common law rule fair? What is the rationale for the rule?

9. Roy Newburn borrowed money and bought a $49,000 truck from Treadwell Ford. A few months later the truck developed transmission problems. Newburn learned that the truck had 170,000 more miles on it than the odometer indicated. The company admitted the mileage and promised to install a new transmission free. Treadwell did install the new transmission, but when Newburn came to pick up the truck, Treadwell demanded that he sign a general release absolving the dealership of any claims based on the inaccurate mileage. Treadwell refused to turn over the truck until Newburn finally signed. The truck broke down again, and delays cost Newburn so much income that he fell behind on his loan payments and lost the truck. He sued Treadwell, which defended based on the release. Is the release valid?

10. YOU BE THE JUDGE WRITING PROBLEM Susan Gould was appointed to a three-year probationary position as a teacher at Sewanhaka High School. Normally, after three years, the school board either grants tenure or dismisses the teacher. The Sewanhaka school board notified Gould she would not be rehired. To keep the termination out of her file, Gould agreed to resign. In fact, because Gould had previously taught at a different New York school, state law required that she be given a tenure decision after only two years. If the board failed to do that, the teacher was automatically tenured. When she learned this, Gould sued to rescind her agreement to resign. Is Gould entitled to rescind the contract (i.e., her agreement to resign)? **Argument for Gould:** Both parties assumed that Gould was on probation and could be dismissed after three years. Neither party understood that after three years, Gould actually *had* tenure under New York State law. Gould would never have resigned had she understood she was entitled to tenure. The misunderstanding goes to the essence of the resignation agreement, and she should be permitted to rescind. **Argument for the School Board:** The school board has done nothing wrong here. It is unfair to penalize the school system for an honest mistake. If Gould is serious about her career, she should understand the tenure process and should take the trouble to inform the board about unusual rules that pertain to her case. She failed to do that, causing both parties to negotiate under a misperception, and she must bear the loss.

11. Morell bought a security guard business from Conley, including the property on which the business was located. Neither party knew that underground storage tanks were leaking and contaminating the property. After the sale, Morell discovered the tanks and sought to rescind the contract. Should he be allowed to do so?

INTERNET RESEARCH PROBLEM

Visit http://www.tobaccofreekids.org. Click on *Tobacco Marketing & Kids*. Use the ethics checklist from Chapter 9 to analyze the conduct described. Should society limit tobacco marketing? If not, why not? If so, should it be done by legislation, regulation, litigation, or some other means?

You can find further practice problems in the Online Quiz at http://beatty.westbuslaw.com or in the Study Guide that accompanies this text.

WRITTEN CONTRACTS

Oliver and Perry were college roommates, two sophomores with contrasting personalities. They were sitting in the cafeteria with some friends, Oliver chatting away, Perry slumped on a plastic bench. Oliver suggested that they buy a lottery ticket, as the prize for that week's drawing was $3 million. Perry muttered, "Nah. You never win if you buy just one ticket." Oliver bubbled up, "O.K., we'll buy a ticket every week. We'll keep buying them from now until we graduate. Come on, it'll be fun. This month, I'll buy the tickets. Next month, you will, and so on." Other students urged Perry to do it and, finally, grudgingly, he agreed. The two friends carefully reviewed their deal. Each party was providing consideration, namely, the responsibility for purchasing tickets during his month. The amount of each purchase was clearly defined at one dollar. They would start that week and continue until graduation day, two and a half years down the road. Finally, they would share equally any money won. As three witnesses looked on, they shook hands on the bargain. That month, Oliver bought a ticket every week, randomly choosing numbers, and won nothing. The next month, Perry bought a ticket with equally random numbers—and won $52 million. Perry moved out of their dorm room into a suite at the Ritz and refused to give Oliver one red cent. Oliver sued, seeking $26 million, and the return of

WIOR v. ANCHOR INDUSTRIES, INC.
669 N.E.2d 172, 1996 Ind. LEXIS 114
Indiana Supreme Court, 1996

Facts: Glenn Wior spent his adult life in the "needle trades," working for companies that sewed clothing and other textiles. Anchor Industries manufactured custom canvas and synthetic products for the outdoor recreation industry. Anchor offered Wior a job as plant supervisor at its factory in Evansville, Indiana. Wior did not want to leave his home and job in Indianapolis unless he had a long-term commitment. Allegedly, Anchor executives orally agreed to employ Wior for "20 plus years, until he retired." Wior accepted the offer, though the parties never put the agreement in writing.

Wior moved his family to Evansville, where he bought a home and began working for Anchor. Three months later, Anchor fired him, claiming that Wior did not "fit in." Wior filed suit, but the trial court granted summary judgment for the company because there was no writing to support the agreement. The appellate court reversed, holding that the contract *could* have been completed in one year. Anchor appealed to the state supreme court.

You Be the Judge: Does the statute of frauds bar enforcement of the oral agreement?

Argument for Anchor: Your honors, this is a very simple case. Wior claims that Anchor offered him a job that would last for at least 20 years. The statute of frauds is crystal clear that such an agreement, even if there had been one, must be in writing. This so-called deal was oral and unenforceable. We concede that if a company offered an employee a job "for life," with no time period specified, the agreement might be outside the statute of frauds. An employee could theoretically die within the first year, and thus the statute should not control. That isn't the case here. By Wior's own allegations, the supposed offer was for *at least* 20 years, until retirement. Neither the 20 years nor the retirement could theoretically occur within one year, and Wior, by his own allegations, has no case.

Argument for Wior: Your honors, this ancient rule was designed to prevent fraud, not to encourage it. Courts have interpreted the statute of frauds narrowly because of the injustice it might otherwise cause. Mr. Wior is hardworking, dedicated, and experienced in the industry, and Anchor wanted him. Wior was reluctant to leave Indianapolis for a smaller town, and a new job, unless he received a long-term commitment. Anchor gave it! The company knew it would never land a man of Wior's caliber unless it promised secure employment, so it offered a job until Mr. Wior retired. Wior accepted, sold his old home, bought a new one, and began work. For reasons we do not know, Anchor changed its mind and now wants to hide behind a technical rule of law. The court of appeals held that one technicality deserved another: the statute of frauds should not bar enforcement because the contract *could* have been performed within one year, had Mr. Wior died. This case should go to a jury, and a hardworking employee should have his chance to prove his damages.

PROMISE TO PAY THE DEBT OF ANOTHER

When one person agrees to pay the debt of another as a favor to that debtor, it is called a collateral promise, and it must be in writing to be enforceable. D. R. Kemp was a young entrepreneur who wanted to build housing in Tuscaloosa, Alabama. He needed $25,000 to complete a project he was working on, so he went to his old college professor, Jim Hanks, for help. The professor said he would see what he could do about getting Kemp a loan. Professor Hanks spoke with his good friend Travis Chandler, telling him that Kemp was highly responsible and would be certain to repay any money loaned. Chandler trusted Professor Hanks but wanted to be sure of his money. Professor Hanks assured Chandler that if for any reason Kemp did not repay the loan, he, Hanks, would pay Chandler in full. With that assurance, Chandler wrote out a check for $25,000, payable to Kemp, never having met the young man.

Kemp, of course, never repaid the loan. (Thank goodness he did not; this textbook has no use for people who do what they are supposed to.) Kemp exhausted the cash trying to sustain his business, which failed anyway, so he had nothing to give his creditor. Chandler approached Professor Hanks, who refused to pay (some professor!), and Chandler sued. The outcome was only too predictable.

When one party promises to pay the debt of another, the enforceability of that promise may depend upon whom the promisor intended to benefit.

Professor Hanks agreed to repay Kemp's debt *as a favor to Kemp*, making it a collateral promise. Chandler had nothing in writing, and that is exactly what he got from his lawsuit—nothing.

Exception: The Leading Object Rule

There is one major exception to the collateral promise rule. When the promisor guarantees to pay the debt of another and *the leading object of the promise is some benefit to the promisor himself,* then the contract will be enforceable even if unwritten. In other words, if the promisor makes the guarantee not as a favor to the debtor, but out of self-interest, the statute of frauds does not apply.

Robert Perry was a hog farmer in Ohio. He owed $26,000 to Sunrise Cooperative, a supplier of feed. Because Perry was in debt, Sunrise stopped giving him feed on credit and began selling him feed on a cash-only basis. Perry also owed money to Farm Credit Services, a loan agency. Perry promised Farm Credit he would repay his loans as soon as his hogs were big enough to sell. But Perry couldn't raise hogs without feed, which he lacked the money to purchase. Farm Credit was determined to bring home the bacon, so it asked Sunrise Cooperative to give Perry the feed on credit. Farm Credit orally promised to pay any debt that Perry did not take care of. When Perry defaulted on his payments to Sunrise, the feed supplier sued Farm Credit based on its oral guarantee. Farm Credit claimed the promise was unenforceable, based on the statute of frauds. But the court found in favor of Sunrise. The *leading object* of Farm Credit's promise to Sunrise was self-interest, and the oral promise was fully enforceable.[7]

PROMISE MADE BY AN EXECUTOR OF AN ESTATE

This rule is merely a special application of the previous one, concerning the debt of another person. An executor is the person who is in charge of an estate after someone dies. The executor's job is to pay debts of the deceased, obtain money owed to him, and disburse the assets according to the will. In most cases, the executor will use only the estate's assets to pay those debts. The statute of frauds comes into play only when an executor promises to pay an estate's debts with her *own* funds. **An executor's promise to use her own funds to pay a debt of the deceased must be in writing to be enforceable.** Suppose Esmeralda dies penniless, owing Tina $35,000. Emeralda's daughter, Sapphire, is the executor of her estate. Tina comes to Sapphire and demands her $35,000. Sapphire responds, "There is no money in mamma's estate, but don't worry, I'll make it up to you with my own money." Sapphire's oral promise is unenforceable. Tina should get it in writing while Sapphire is feeling generous.

PROMISE MADE IN CONSIDERATION OF MARRIAGE

Barney is a multimillionaire with the integrity of a gangster and the charm of a tax collector. He proposes to Li-Tsing, who promptly rejects him. Barney then pleads that if Li-Tsing will be his bride, he will give her an island he owns off the coast of California. Li-Tsing begins to see his good qualities and accepts. After they are married, Barney refuses to deliver the deed. Li-Tsing will get nothing from a court either, since **a promise made in consideration of marriage must be in writing to be enforceable.**

---

7 *Sunrise Cooperative v. Robert Perry*, 1992 Ohio App. LEXIS 3913 (Ohio Ct. App., 1992).

WHAT THE WRITING MUST CONTAIN

Each of the five types of contract described above must be in writing in order to be enforceable. What must the writing contain? It may be a carefully typed contract, using precise legal terminology, or an informal memorandum scrawled on the back of a paper napkin at a business lunch. The writing may consist of more than one document, written at different times, with each document making a piece of the puzzle. But there are some general requirements: **the contract or memorandum**:

- **Must be signed by the defendant, and**
- **Must state with reasonable certainty the name of each party, the subject matter of the agreement, and all of the essential terms and promises.**[8]

SIGNATURE

A statute of frauds typically states that the writing must be "signed by the party to be charged therewith," that is, the party who is resisting enforcement of the contract. Throughout this chapter we refer to that person as the defendant, since when these cases go to court, it is the defendant who is disputing the existence of a contract.

Judges define "signature" very broadly. Using a pen to write one's name, though sufficient, is not required. A secretary who stamps an executive's signature on a letter fulfills this requirement. Any other mark or logo placed on a document to indicate acceptance, even an "X," will likely satisfy the statute of frauds. Electronic commerce creates new methods of signing—and new controversies, discussed in the Cyberlaw feature later in the chapter.

REASONABLE CERTAINTY

Suppose Garfield and Hayes are having lunch, discussing the sale of Garfield's vacation condominium. They agree on a price and want to make some notation of the agreement even before their lawyers work out a detailed purchase and sales agreement. A perfectly adequate memorandum might say, "Garfield agrees to sell Hayes his condominium at 234 Baron Boulevard, apartment 18, for $350,000 cash, payable on June 18, 2003, and Hayes promises to pay the sum on that day." They should make two copies of their agreement and sign both. By doing that, they will avoid the problem that Drysdale and Hershon encountered when trying to purchase Tulip Hill, described above in *Hershon v. Cannon*. Notice that although Garfield's memo is short, it is *certain* and *complete*. This is critical because problems of vagueness and incompleteness often doom informal memoranda.

Vagueness

Ella Hayden owned valuable commercial property on a highway called Route 9. She wrote a series of letters to her stepson Mark, promising that several of the children, including Mark, would share the property. One letter said: "We four shall fairly divide on the Route 9 property. [sic]" Other letters said: "When the Route 9

---

[8] Restatement (Second) of Contracts §131.

Plaza is sold you can take a long vacation," and "The property will be sold. You and Dennis shall receive the same amount." Ella Hayden died, without leaving Mark anything. He sued, but got nothing. The court ruled:

> The above passages written by Ms. Hayden do not recite the essential elements of the alleged contract with reasonable certainty. The writings do not state unequivocally or with sufficient particularity the subject matter to which the writings relate, nor do they provide the terms and conditions of alleged promises made which constitute a contract. The alleged oral contract between Ms. Hayden and Mr. Hayden cannot be identified from the passages from Ms. Hayden's letters quoted above when applied to existing facts. In sum, Mr. Hayden's cause of action seeking an interest in the Route 9 property is foreclosed by the statute of frauds.[9]

Incompleteness

During Ronald McCoy's second interview with Spelman Memorial Hospital, the board of directors orally offered him a three-year job as assistant hospital administrator. McCoy accepted. Spelman's CEO, Gene Meyer, sent a letter confirming the offer, which said:

> To reconfirm the offer, it is as follows: 1. We will pay for your moving expenses. 2. I would like you to pursue your Master's Degree at an area program. We will pay 100% tuition reimbursement. 3. Effective September 26 you will be eligible for all benefits. 4. A starting salary of $48,000 annually with reviews and eligibility for increases at 6 months, 12 months and annually thereafter. 5. We will pay for the expenses of 3 trips, if necessary, in order for you to find housing. 6. Vacation will be for 3 weeks a year after one year, however, we do allow for this to be taken earlier. [Signed] Gene Meyer.

Spelman Hospital fired McCoy less than a year after he started work, and McCoy sued. The hospital's letter seems clear, and it is signed by an authorized official. The problem is, it is incomplete. Can you spot the fatal omission? The court did.

> To satisfy the statute of frauds, an employment contract—[or] its memorandum or note—must contain all essential terms, including duration of the employment relationship. Without a statement of duration, an employment at will is created which is terminable at any time by either party with no liability for breach of contract. McCoy's argument that the letter constituted a memorandum of an oral contract fails because the letter does not state an essential element, duration. The letter did not state that Spelman was granting McCoy employment for any term—only that his salary would be reviewed at six months, twelve months and "annually thereafter."[10]

These two lawsuits demonstrate the continuing force of the statute of frauds. In either case, if the promisor had truly wanted to make a binding commitment, he or she could have written the appropriate contract or memorandum in a matter of minutes. Great formality and expense are unnecessary. But the document *must be clear and complete,* or it will fail.

Because some merchants make dozens or even hundreds of oral contracts every year, the drafters of the UCC wanted to make the writing requirement less onerous for the sale of goods, to which we now turn.

---

9 *Hayden v. Hayden,* Mass. Lawyers Weekly No. 12-299-93 (Middlesex Sup. Ct. 1994).

10 *McCoy v. Spelman Memorial Hospital,* 845 S.W.2d 727, 1993 Mo. App. LEXIS 105 (Mo. Ct. App. 1993).

SALE OF GOODS

The UCC requires a writing for the sale of goods worth more than $500. This is the sixth and final contract that must be written, although the Code's requirements are easier to meet than those of the common law. **UCC §2-201**, the statute of frauds section, has three important elements: (1) the basic rule, (2) the merchants' exception, and (3) special circumstances. (To read the UCC online go to **http://www.law.cornell.edu/ucc/ucc.table.html**.)

UCC §2-201(1)—THE BASIC RULE

A contract for the sale of goods worth more than $500 is not enforceable unless there is some writing, signed by the defendant, indicating that the parties reached an agreement. The key difference between the common law rule and the UCC rule is that the Code does not require all of the terms of the agreement to be in writing. The Code looks for something simpler: an *indication that the parties reached an agreement*. The two things that *are* essential are the signature of the defendant and the quantity of goods being sold. The quantity of goods is required because this is the one term for which there will be no objective evidence. Suppose a short memorandum between textile dealers indicates that Seller will sell to Buyer "grade AA 100% cotton, white athletic socks." If the writing does not state the price, the parties can testify at court about what the market price was at the time of the deal. If the writing says nothing about the delivery date, the court will assume a reasonable delivery date, say, 60 days. But how many socks were to be delivered? 100 pairs or 100,000? The court will have no objective evidence. The quantity must be written. (A basic sale of goods contract appears at **http://www.lectlaw.com/forms/f124.txt**.)

Writing	Result
"Confirming phone conversation today, I will send you 1,000 reams of paper for laser printing, usual quality & price. [Signed,] Seller."	This memorandum satisfies UCC §2-201(1), and the contract may be enforced against the seller. The buyer may testify as to the "usual" quality and price between the two parties, and both sides may rely on normal trade usage.
"Confirming phone conversation today, I will send you best quality paper for laser printing, $3.25 per ream, delivery date next Thursday. [Signed,] Seller."	This memorandum is not enforceable because it states no quantity.

UCC §2-201(2)—THE MERCHANTS' EXCEPTION

When both parties are "merchants," that is, business people who routinely deal in the goods being sold, the Code will accept an even more informal writing. **Within a reasonable time of making an oral contract, if one merchant sends a written confirmation to the other, and the confirmation is definite enough to bind the *sender herself*, then the merchant who receives the confirmation will *also* be bound by it unless he objects in writing within 10 days.** This exception dramatically changes the rules from the common law. It only applies between two merchants, since the drafters of the Code assumed that experienced merchants are

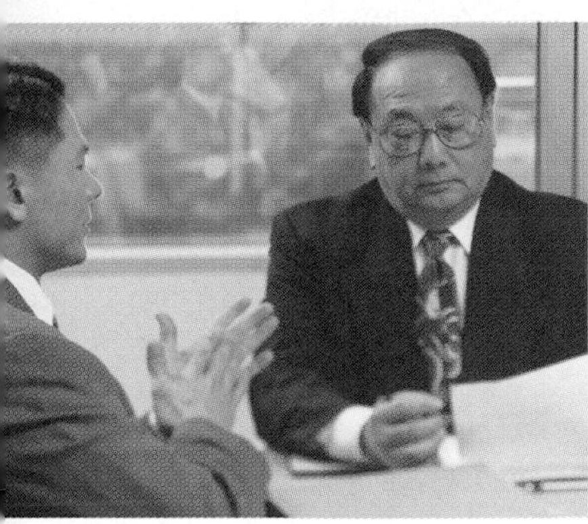
The UCC gives merchants special leeway—and important responsibilities.

able to take care of themselves in fast-moving negotiations. The critical difference is this: a writing may create a binding contract even when it is not signed by the defendant.

Madge manufactures "beanies," that is, silly caps with plastic propellers on top. Rachel, a retailer, telephones her and they discuss the price of the beanies, shipping time, and other details. Madge then faxes Rachel a memo: "This confirms your order for 2,500 beanies at $12.25 per beanie. Colors: blue, green, black, orange, red. Delivery date: 10 days. [Signed] Madge." Rachel receives the fax, reads it while negotiating with another manufacturer, and throws it in the wastebasket. Rachel buys her beanies elsewhere and Madge sues. Rachel defends, claiming there is no written contract because she, Rachel, never signed anything. Madge wins, under UCC §2-201(2). Both parties were merchants, because they routinely dealt in these goods. Madge signed and sent a confirming memo that could have been used to hold her, Madge, to the deal. When Rachel read it, she was not free to disregard it. Obviously, the intelligent business practice would have been to promptly fax a reply saying, "I disagree. We do not have any deal for beanies." Since Rachel failed to respond within 10 days, Madge has an enforceable contract. In the following case, the merchant's confirmation contained a troubling ambiguity.

GPL TREAMENT, LTD. v. LOUISIANA-PACIFIC CORP.
323 Or. 116, 914 P.2d 682, 1996 Ore. LEXIS 34
Oregon Supreme Court, 1996

Facts: GPL manufactures and sells cedar shakes, which are wooden shingles that many homeowners use for their roofs. Louisiana-Pacific (L-P) often purchased shakes from GPL. Executives of the two companies negotiated over the telephone and allegedly agreed that L-P would buy 88 truckloads of shakes. GPL sent an "Order Confirmation" form that included this language:

> "CONDITIONS OF SALES: GPL LTD.
> "All orders accepted subject to strikes, labor troubles, car shortages or other contingencies beyond our power to control. Any freight rate increases, sales, or use taxes is for buyers account.
> "SIGN CONFIRMATION COPY AND RETURN BY: _______ THANK YOU"

L-P neither signed nor rejected the form. The company accepted 13 truckloads of shakes but about that time the market price of shakes dropped, and L-P refused to accept any more. GPL sued. A jury awarded the company its lost profits, and the court of appeals affirmed. L-P appealed, arguing that, because GPL's form required the buyer to sign, no acceptance was valid without a signature.

Issue: Was GPL's form sufficient to satisfy the merchants' exception to the statute of frauds?

Excerpts from Judge Van Hoomissen's Decision: GPL's order confirmation forms unambiguously identify the parties to the alleged oral contract and the prices and quantities of the goods being sold. Each form was signed by GPL and sent to L-P, which did not object within 10 days of receipt. GPL's forms would have been "sufficient" against GPL, the sender, if GPL had attempted to rescind the contract because, for example, the price of cedar shakes had gone up substantially. We are unpersuaded by L-P's argument that inclusion of the words "sign confirmation copy and return" on GPL's order confirmation forms indicate any intention on GPL's part that it was not bound until L-P signed and returned copies of the forms indicating its approval. We do not read GPL's order confirmation forms to require L-P to signal its acceptance of the terms and conditions of the parties' alleged oral agreement. Rather, we read the forms to be nothing more than a request for an acknowledgment of the receipt of GPL's forms. Thus read, GPL's "sign and return" clause and its "order accepted by" signature line were merely record keeping devices of GPL. We hold, therefore, that GPL's forms were sufficient to satisfy the merchant's exception of [UCC 2-201(2)].

The decision of the Court of Appeals and the judgment of the [trial] court are affirmed.

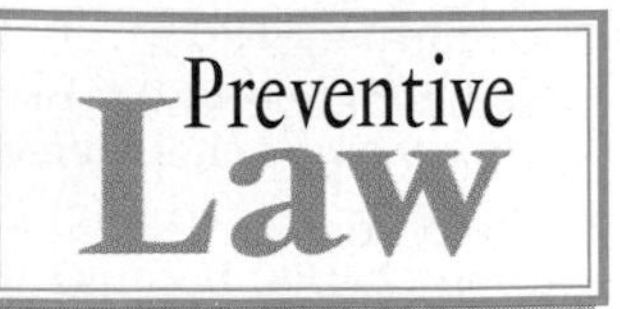

Assume that you work for GPL. What change in the form should you make?

UCC §2-201(3)—SPECIAL CIRCUMSTANCES

An oral contract *may* be enforceable, even without a written memorandum, if:

- **The seller is specially manufacturing the goods for the buyer,** *or*
- **The defendant admits in court proceedings that there was a contract,** *or*
- **The goods have been delivered or they have been paid for.**

In these three special circumstances, a court may enforce an oral contract even without a memorandum.

Specially Manufactured Goods

If a seller, specially manufacturing goods for the buyer, begins work on them before the buyer cancels, and the goods cannot be sold elsewhere, the oral contract is binding. Bernice manufactures solar heating systems. She phones Jason and orders 75 special electrical converter units designed for her heating system, at $150 per unit. Jason begins manufacturing the units, but then Bernice phones again and says she no longer needs them. Bernice is bound by the contract. The goods are being manufactured for her and cannot be sold elsewhere. Jason had already begun work when she attempted to cancel. If the case goes to court, Jason will win.

Admissions in Court

When the defendant admits in court proceedings that the parties made an oral contract, the agreement is binding. The Nebraska Builders Co. claimed that it had entered into a binding contract to buy construction cranes from Industrial Erectors for $450,000. There had been extensive negotiations between Hawkins (Nebraska Builders) and Brennan (Industrial Erectors), and many letters back and forth, but the documents were unclear about what the parties had agreed to. At trial, Brennan first denied that he had agreed to anything. But then came cross-examination:

> Q. At the meeting on October 14th in Chicago you specifically told Mr. Hawkins, did you not, that Industrial Erectors would not perform or supply any cranes on this project unless it received compensation somewhere in the neighborhood of $150,000 more than that set forth in its bid, isn't that correct?
>
> A. I believe it was stated, if the order was to be as per specified with the electrical circuitry and everything else, that there would be an increase to the contract.

Fatal slip. After all, if the purpose of the statute of frauds is to obtain the clearest evidence of what the parties intended, nothing can speak louder than the defendant's admission that they had a contract.[11]

Goods Delivered or Paid For

If the seller has delivered the goods, or the buyer has paid for them, the contract may be enforced even with nothing in writing. Malik orally agrees to sell 500 plastic chairs to University for use in its cafeteria. Malik delivers 300 of the chairs, but then University notifies him that it will not honor the deal. Malik is entitled to payment for the 300 chairs, though not for the other 200. Conversely, if University had sent a check for one-half of the chairs, it would be entitled to 250 chairs.

Cheap Cheep sends an e-mail to Pet Chain, offering to sell 1,000 canaries for $25 each. Pet Chain responds electronically, accepting the offer. But when the birds fly up to the door, Pet Chain refuses delivery, and Cheap Cheep sues. The statute of frauds requires this contract to be in writing. Is it? The defendant must have signed the contract or memorandum. Did Pet Chain do so?

The dazzling growth of the Internet has created countless opportunities for electronic commerce, and businesses are taking advantage. Observers estimate that by the turn of the century, U.S. enterprises alone will do tens of billions of dollars worth of buying and selling over the Internet. But what happens to the writing requirement when there is nothing on paper? And without a traditional signature, how can the parties—or a court—be certain that the defendant agreed to the deal? Because electronic commerce is so new, there are no definitive answers to these questions, but we can highlight some of the basic issues and make a few cautious predictions.

First, electronic commerce is efficient and profitable, meaning it is here to stay. Legislatures and courts will adapt. Recall that the UCC itself sprang to life because twentieth-century commercial practices had rendered some common law contract principles obsolete. Business leads, and the law follows.

Second, in disputes over electronic contracts, courts will continue to focus on the questions that have always been at the heart of business litigation: Did the parties intend to make a deal? If so, what were the terms? What evidence is there that the defendant agreed to the deal? The present statute of frauds requires some sort of "signing" to ensure that the defendant committed to the deal. But even at common law, this requirement does not mandate a traditional pen-and-ink signature. As mentioned above, corporate stamps, seals, or other marks indicating an assent to the bargain are sufficient. Today, an "electronic signature" could theoretically mean any of the following: a name typed at the bottom of an e-mail message; a retinal or vocal scan; a name signed by electronic pen on a writing tablet; a magnetic card using a personal identification number; or a public-key digital signature, created by complex encryption software. Legislatures and courts will have some picking and choosing to do, as they decide which of these "signatures" are necessary and which are sufficient.

A new UCC article 2B will appear soon, attempting to resolve many issues raised by new technology. As with all UCC provisions, however, article 2B will be the law nowhere until state legislatures adopt it. The new article will probably include these provisions:

---

[11] *Nebraska Builders Products Co. v. Industrial Erectors*, 239 Neb. 744, 478 N.W.2d 257, 1992 Neb. LEXIS 4 (1992).

- The basic idea of a "writing" will be replaced with that of a "record," a term that includes most electronic messages or transmittals. The concept of "signing" will give way to that of "authenticating," which means placing almost any electronic identifier on the record. Thus an e-mail message (record) that contains some type of electronic identifier (authentication) will probably satisfy the statute of frauds.

- The drafters of the article will probably recommend limiting the UCC statute of frauds to contracts valued at over $20,000. Most Internet purchases are below that level, meaning that in a few years there may be no "record" or "signature" requirement for many contracts.

Congress is also considering national legislation for electronic transactions. And the United Nations Commission on International Trade Law (UNCITRAL) has published a Model Law for consideration by countries throughout the world. With so much legal uncertainty, what should an executive do who wants to take advantage *now* of the Internet's commercial opportunities? Several things.

First, business leaders must learn the basic advantages and risks of electronic commerce. The greatest advantages are speed and convenience: parties 8,000 miles apart can record an agreement in seconds. Risks include lost or intercepted communications, fraudulently altered documents, and difficulties in authenticating the source of an offer or acceptance. Executives would be wise to understand public-key digital signatures. This encryption-based software provides the greatest security in sending and authenticating documents.

Second, a company that engages in a high volume of electronic agreements with a limited number of companies should consider a "master agreement," that is, a paper contract that describes the nature of the electronic transactions and allocates risk. The master agreement can specify what authentication the parties accept, who bears the loss if electronic documents are altered or lost, how the parties decide disputes (for example, with mediation or arbitration), and what limits are placed on liability.

Third, a firm that makes a pricey agreement should *put it in an old-fashioned written, signed contract*. If the deal is big enough to cause serious financial harm, a company should be cautious. Let other firms have the honor of creating electronic contract law through years of costly litigation.

PAROL EVIDENCE

Tyrone agrees to buy Martha's house for $800,000. The contract obligates Tyrone to make a 10 percent down payment immediately and pay the remaining $720,000 in 45 days. As the two parties sign the deal, Tyrone discusses his need for financing. Unfortunately, at the end of 45 days, he has been unable to get a mortgage for the full amount. He claims that the parties orally agreed that he would get his deposit back if he could not obtain financing. But the written agreement says no such thing, and Martha disputes the claim. Who will win? Probably Martha, because of the parol evidence rule. To understand this rule, you need to know two terms. **Parol evidence refers to anything (apart from the written contract itself) that was said, done, or written before the parties signed the agreement or as they signed it.** Martha's conversation with Tyrone about financing the house was parol evidence because it occurred as they were signing the contract. The other important term is **integrated contract**, which means a writing that the parties intend as the final, complete expression of their agreement. Now for the rule.

The parol evidence rule: When two parties make an integrated contract, neither one may use parol evidence to contradict, vary, or add to its terms. Negotiations may last for hours, weeks, or even months. Almost no contract includes everything that the parties said. When parties consider their agreement integrated, any statements they made before or while signing are irrelevant. If a court determines that Martha and Tyrone intended their agreement to be integrated, it will prohibit testimony about Martha's oral promises.

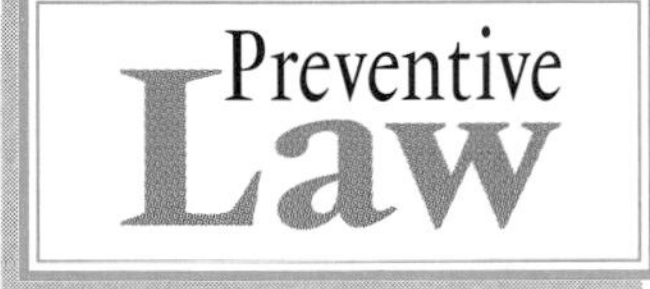

One way to avoid parol evidence disputes is to include an *integration clause*. That is a statement clearly proclaiming that this writing is the full and final expression of the parties' agreement, and that anything said before signing or while signing is irrelevant. For example, an art dealer may say to a prospective buyer, "Watteau's paintings have increased in value 10 percent every year for the last decade. They're going to continue to climb, I know it." Perhaps the dealer shows the customer an article on Watteau that claims that his paintings are still undervalued. When it is time to sign the contract, the dealer will not want these statements included, since they were meaningless puffery, and he has no intention of being bound by them. The dealer will include an integration clause, stating that the buyer is not relying on any promises, statements, or documents of any kind made or examined during negotiations, and that the written agreement is the complete expression of their contract.

EXCEPTION: AN INCOMPLETE OR AMBIGUOUS CONTRACT

If a court determines that a written contract is incomplete or ambiguous, it will permit parol evidence. As a result, in parol evidence cases, the primary argument is often about whether or not the written contract is clear and complete. Consider the following case:

CHEYENNE MOUNTAIN SCHOOL DISTRICT NO. 12 v. THOMPSON

861 P.2d 711, 1993 Colo. LEXIS 889
Supreme Court of Colorado, 1993

Facts: Dr. Loren Thompson was Superintendent of Schools for the Cheyenne Mountain School District in Colorado. His contract provided for salary of $62,500 and 20 vacation days annually, of which he had to use at least 10 per year. He could accumulate the remaining days to a maximum of 60. The contract said nothing about whether Thompson was entitled to compensation for unused vacation days if he quit. When Thompson resigned from his job, he had accumulated 33 unused vacation days, worth a substantial amount of money. When the school district refused to pay him for the unused time, he sued. The trial court prohibited parol evidence about vacation compensation, stating that the contract was complete and unambiguous. Since the agreement was silent about vacation compensation, Thompson was entitled to none. Thompson appealed and the case reached the Colorado Supreme Court.

Issue: May Thompson introduce parol evidence about vacation compensation?

Excerpts from Judge Vollack's Decision: Based on the pleadings and the four corners of the employment contract, the trial court concluded that the contract was not ambiguous and construed it to deny Thompson compensation for his unused vacation. The court relied on the parties' failure to provide explicitly for the additional compensation in the contract; the paragraph fixing Thompson's compensation at $62,500 annually; and paragraph 17, which would have denied fringe benefits to Thompson if he had been terminated without cause by the school board.

We first address whether Thompson's employment contract is ambiguous on the issue of compensation for unused vacation time. To ascertain whether certain provisions of a contract are ambiguous, the language used therein must be examined and construed in harmony with the plain and generally accepted meaning of the words employed and by reference to all the parts and provisions of the agreement and the nature of the transaction which forms its subject matter. A document is ambiguous when it is reasonably susceptible to more than one meaning. Parol evidence is admissible to explain or supplement the terms of an agreement, but not to vary or contradict them. A court should use parol evidence only when the agreement is so ambiguous that the intent of the parties is not clear.

The contract is silent on the specific question of whether Thompson is entitled to compensation for unused vacation at the expiration of his contract. Silence does not by itself necessarily create ambiguity as a matter of law. Silence does create ambiguity, however, when it involves a matter naturally within the scope of the contract. Compensation for unused accrued vacation on expiration of Thompson's contract is a matter naturally within the scope of the contract.

Because Thompson's employment contract is ambiguous on the issue of compensation for unused vacation time, the parties will be free to introduce at trial evidence extrinsic to the four corners of the document. Parol evidence will be admissible to assist the trier of fact in determining whether the parties intended that Thompson be compensated for the unused vacation time.

The employer normally drafts the employment contract. Was it ethical for the school district, having created the ambiguity, to litigate Thompson's claim all the way to the state's high court? How else might the parties have settled the dispute? Besides the money potentially owed to Thompson, what was the district worried about? What changes should the district make in future contracts?

EXCEPTION: MISREPRESENTATION OR DURESS

A court will permit parol evidence of misrepresentation or duress. A. O. Smith manufactured and sold grain storage systems for farmers. Alfred and Martha Keller, farmers, bought two systems, which included specially constructed silos and unloading equipment, all designed to keep oxygen away from the stored grain so it would stay fresh. The sales contract included several integration clauses, stating that the Kellers agreed that "any advertisements, brochures, and other written statements which he may have read are not guarantees and he has not relied upon them as such," and that the Kellers "relied on no other promises or conditions" except statements in the contract itself. The systems failed. The grain went bad, cattle developed sores, watery eyes, and other ailments, and some died. The Kellers sued, claiming that A. O. Smith had misrepresented its product. Smith moved to dismiss the case, claiming that the parol evidence rule barred the Kellers from relying on the advertising brochures. The state supreme court found in favor of the Kellers. A claim of misrepresentation is an exception to the parol evidence rule. Such a claim is not really based on the contract itself, but on the discussions of the parties leading up to the contract. The Kellers were permitted to introduce evidence that A. O. Smith misrepresented its storage systems.[12]

Remember, however, that ambiguity and misrepresentation are both exceptions. The basic rule favors the written contract as the full expression of the parties' intentions. More often than not, the written contract is all that a court considers in determining the parties' intentions.

---

12 The dispositive ruling came from the Colorado Supreme Court, in a case certified to it: *Keller v. A. O. Smith Harvestore Products, Inc.*, 819 P.2d 69, 1991 Colo. LEXIS 703 (Colo. 1991). The case was later remanded on the unrelated issue of prejudgment interest, 1991 U.S. App. LEXIS 31142 (10th Cir. 1991).

CHAPTER CONCLUSION

Some contracts must be in writing to be enforceable, and the writing must be clear and unambiguous. Drafting the contract need not be arduous. The disputes illustrated in this chapter could all have been prevented with a few carefully crafted sentences. It is worth the time and effort to write them.

CHAPTER REVIEW

1. Contracts that must be in writing to be enforceable concern:
   - The sale of any interest in land
   - Agreements that cannot be performed within one year
   - Promises to pay the debt of another
   - Promises made by an executor of an estate
   - Promises made in consideration of marriage; and
   - The sale of goods over $500
2. The writing must be signed by the defendant and must state the name of all parties, the subject matter of the agreement, and all essential terms and promises.
3. A contract or memorandum for the sale of goods may be less complete than those required by the common law.
   - The basic UCC rule requires only a memorandum signed by the defendant, indicating that the parties reached an agreement and specifying the quantity of goods.
   - Between merchants even less is required. If one merchant sends written confirmation of a contract, the merchant who receives the document must object within 10 days or be bound by the writing.
   - In the following special circumstances, no writing may be required: the goods are specially manufactured; one party admits in litigation that there was a contract; or one party pays for part of the goods or delivers some of the goods.
4. When an integrated contract exists, neither party may generally use parol evidence to contradict, vary, or add to its terms. Parol evidence refers to anything (apart from the written contract itself) that was said, done, or written before the parties signed the agreement or as they signed it.

PRACTICE TEST

1. **CPA QUESTION** Able hired Carr to restore Able's antique car for $800. The terms of their oral agreement provided that Carr was to complete the work within 18 months. Actually, the work could be completed within one year. The agreement is:

(a) Unenforceable because it covers services with a value in excess of $500

(b) Unenforceable because it covers a time period in excess of one year

(c) Enforceable because personal service contracts are exempt from the statute of frauds

(d) Enforceable because the work could be completed within one year

2. Richard Griffin and three other men owned a grain company called Bearhouse, Inc., which needed to borrow money. First National Bank was willing to loan $490,000, but insisted that the four men sign personal guaranties on the loan, committing themselves to repaying up to 25 percent of the loan each if Bearhouse defaulted. Bearhouse went bankrupt. The bank was able to collect some of its money from Bearhouse's assets, but it sued Griffin for the balance.

At trial, Griffin wanted to testify that before he signed his guaranty, a bank officer assured him that he would only owe 25 percent of *whatever balance was unpaid,* not 25 percent of the total loan. How will the court decide whether Griffin is entitled to testify about the conversation?

3. Donald Waide had a contracting business. He bought most of his supplies from Paul Bingham's supply center. Waide fell behind on his bills, and Bingham told Waide that he would extend no more credit to him. That same day, Donald's father, Elmer Waide, came to Bingham's store, and said to Bingham that he would "stand good" for any sales to Donald made on credit. Based on Elmer's statement, Bingham again gave Donald credit, and Donald ran up $10,000 in goods before Bingham sued Donald and Elmer. What defense did Elmer make and what was the outcome?

4. James River-Norwalk, Inc. was a paper and textile company that needed a constant supply of wood. James River orally contracted with Gary Futch to procure wood for the company, and Futch did so for several years. Futch actually purchased the wood for his own account and then resold it to James River. Do the parties have an agreement for services or for sale of goods? Why does it matter?

5. When Deana Byers married Steven Byers, she was pregnant with another man's child. Shortly after the marriage Deana gave birth. The marriage lasted only two months, and the couple separated. In divorce proceedings, Deana sought child support. She claimed that Steven had orally promised to support the child if Deana would marry him. Steven claims he never made the promise. Comment on the outcome.

6. **CPA QUESTION** Two individuals signed a contract that was intended to be their entire agreement. The parol evidence rule will prevent the admission of evidence offered to:

(a) Explain the meaning of an ambiguity in the written contract

(b) Establish that fraud had been committed in the formation of the contract

(c) Prove the existence of a contemporaneous oral agreement modifying the contract

(d) Prove the existence of a subsequent oral agreement modifying the contract

7. Lonnie Hippen moved to Long Island, Kansas, to work in an insurance company owned by Griffiths. After he moved there, Griffiths offered to sell Hippen a house he owned, and Hippen agreed in writing to buy it. He did buy the house and moved in, but two years later Hippen left the insurance company. He then claimed that at the time of the sale, Griffiths had orally promised to buy back his house at the selling price if Hippen should happen to leave the company. Griffiths defended based on the statute of frauds. Hippen argued that the statute of frauds did not apply because the repurchase of the house was essentially part of his employment with Griffiths. Comment.

8. **RIGHT & WRONG** Jacob Deutsch owned commercial property. He orally agreed to rent it for six years to Budget Rent-A-Car. Budget took possession, began paying monthly rent, and over a period of several months expended about $6,000 in upgrading the property. Deutsch was aware of the repairs. After a year, Deutsch attempted to evict Budget. Budget claimed it had a six-year oral lease, but Deutsch claimed that such a lease was worthless. Please rule. Is it ethical for Deutsch to use the statute of frauds in attempting to defeat the lease? Assume that, as landlord, you had orally agreed to rent premises to a tenant, but then for business reasons preferred not to carry out the deal. Would you evict a tenant if you thought the statute of frauds would enable you to do so? How should you analyze the problem? What values are most important to you?

9. Landlord owned a clothing store and agreed in writing to lease the store's basement to another retailer. The written lease, which both parties signed, (1) described the premises exactly, (2) identified the parties, and (3) stated the monthly rent clearly. But an appeals court held that the lease did not satisfy the statute of frauds. Why not?

10. **YOU BE THE JUDGE WRITING PROBLEM** Harrison Epperly operated United Brake Systems in Indianapolis, Indiana, and wanted to open a similar store in Nashville. He offered Kenneth Jarrett a job as manager, promising six months severance pay if the store was not profitable in six months, and 49 percent ownership if he managed the new store for 10 years. Jarrett agreed, but the two men never put the deal in writing. Under Jarrett's management, the Nashville branch grew dramatically. After four years of renting space, the company purchased the land and buildings it used. Epperly periodically acknowledged his promise to make Jarrett 49 percent owner of the Nashville branch, and from time to time he mentioned the arrangement to other workers. But after 10 years, Epperly sold United Brake, which had grown to 23

branches, to another company for $11 million. Jarrett sued Epperly for 49 percent of the Nashville branch. The trial court awarded Jarrett $812,000. Epperly appealed. Is Jarrett's contract with Epperly barred by the statute of frauds? **Argument for Epperly:** This alleged contract is unenforceable for two reasons. First, the agreement includes real estate, namely, the valuable land and buildings the company uses. A contract for the sale of any interest in land is unenforceable unless written. Second, the contract could not have been performed within one year. If there was a deal, then by Jarrett's own words the parties intended it to last 10 years. Ten years' work cannot be performed in one year. **Argument for Jarrett:** The agreement had nothing to do with land. Jarrett and Epperly agreed that Mr. Jarrett would obtain a 49 percent ownership of the *Nashville branch*. At the time they made that agreement, the Nashville branch had no real estate. There is no rule saying that a valid contract becomes invalid because a corporation acquires some land. The "not in one year" argument also misses the point. The primary obligation was to open the branch and manage it for six months. If it was not profitable, Mr. Jarrett would immediately receive six months' severance pay, and the contract would be fully performed by both parties in less than a year. Finally, Epperly made a binding commitment and Mr. Jarrett relied. Promissory estoppel prohibits Mr. Epperly from using deceit to profit.

11. Mast Industries and Bazak International were two textile firms. Mast orally offered to sell certain textiles to Bazak for $103,000. Mast promised to send documents confirming the agreement, but never did. Finally, Bazak sent a memorandum to Mast confirming the agreement, describing the goods, and specifying their quantity and the price. Bazak's officer signed the memo. Mast received the memo but never agreed to it in writing. When Mast failed to deliver the goods, Bazak sued. Who won?

INTERNET RESEARCH PROBLEM

Examine the lease at **http://www.kinseylaw.com/freestuff/leaseten/ResLease.html**. Is it important for a lease to be in writing? Who probably drafted the lease, a landlord or a tenant? How can you tell? Should any other provisions be included?

You can find further practice problems in the Online Quiz at http://beatty.westbuslaw.com or in the Study Guide that accompanies this text.

CHAPTER 16

THIRD PARTIES

"I am so glad you are here," your Aunt Serena whispers to you from her hospital bed. "Unlike my three worthless children, you have always cared about me." She gives your hand a squeeze. In strolls Earnest Meanwell, a friend of the family and recent law school graduate. Serena instructs him to draw up a will. Earnest protests that he lacks experience, but Serena snaps, "I have no time to waste. I'll pay you $2,000 to draft the document *now*." Meanwell agrees and writes the will by hand, leaving to you all of Serena's $11 million in assets, except for her "second best bed," which the three children are to share. Serena signs the will, and, under Earnest's anxious direction, you and a nurse add your names as witnesses.

A week later, Serena is dead—yet you are no richer. A probate judge blandly informs you that in your state, no one may inherit through a will that he himself witnessed. Meanwell's ignorance of the law means that Serena's three children take everything. You fume, contemplating a lawsuit against foolish Earnest. But you realize that you had no direct dealings with Earnest. Have you any other legal options? Yes: a third party claim.

The basic pattern in third party law is quite simple. Two parties make a contract, and their rights and obligations are subject to the rules that we have already studied: offer and acceptance, consideration, legality, and so forth. However, their contract affects a *third party*, one who had no role in forming the agreement itself. Sometimes the two contracting parties intend to benefit a third person. Those are cases of *third party beneficiary*. In other cases, one of the contracting parties may actually transfer his rights or responsibilities to a third party, raising issues of *assignment or delegation*. We consider the issues one at a time.

THIRD PARTY BENEFICIARY

The two parties who make a contract always intend to benefit themselves. Oftentimes their bargain will also benefit someone else. **A third party beneficiary is someone who was not a party to the contract but stands to benefit from it.** Many contracts create third party beneficiaries. In the chapter's introduction, Serena contracted with Meanwell to draw up a will that would leave you her estate. You stand to benefit not only from the will but from the contract that Serena and Meanwell made. As another example, suppose a city contracts to purchase from Seller 20 acres of an abandoned industrial site in a rundown neighborhood for a new domed stadium. The owner of a pizza parlor on the edge of Seller's land might benefit enormously. A once marginal operation could become a gold mine of cheese and pepperoni.

When the two contracting parties fulfill their obligations and the third party receives her benefit, there is no dispute to analyze. If Meanwell had drawn up the will properly, and if the city were to go ahead with the stadium, there would be no unhappy third parties. Problems arise when one of the parties fails to perform the contract as expected. The issue is this: *May the third party beneficiary enforce the contract?* Meanwell had a contract with Serena but he had no agreement with you. Should you be permitted to recover damages from him because he breached his deal with Serena? The pizza parlor owner was not a party to the contract for the sale of the stadium land. If the city breaks its agreement to buy the land, should the owner recover lost profits?

The outcome in cases like these depends upon the intentions of the two contracting parties. If they intended to benefit the third party, she will probably be permitted to enforce their contract. If they did not intend to benefit her, she probably has no power to enforce the agreement. The Restatement uses a bit more detail to analyze these cases. We must first recall the terms "promisor" and "promisee." The **promisor** is the one who makes the promise that the third party beneficiary is seeking to enforce. Parts of the contract may not interest her, so the Restatement looks only at the relevant promise, not at the entire contract. The **promisee** is the other party to the contract.

According to the **Restatement (Second) of Contracts §302: A beneficiary of a promise is an intended beneficiary and may enforce a contract if the parties intended her to benefit *and if either*** (a) enforcing the promise will satisfy a duty of the promisee to the beneficiary, or (b) the promisee intended to make a gift to the beneficiary.

Any beneficiary who is not an intended beneficiary is an **incidental beneficiary**, and may not enforce the contract. In other words, a third party beneficiary must show two things in order to enforce a contract that two other people created. First, she must show that the two contracting parties were aware of her situation and knew that she would receive something of value from their deal. Second, she must show that the promisee wanted to benefit her for one of two reasons: either to satisfy some duty owed or to make her a gift.

If the promisee is fulfilling some duty, the third party beneficiary is called a **creditor beneficiary**. Most often, the "duty" that a promisee will be fulfilling is a debt already owed to the beneficiary. If the promisee is making a gift, the third party is a **donee beneficiary**.[1] As long as the third party is either a creditor or a donee beneficiary, she may enforce the contract. If she is only an incidental beneficiary, she may not.

We will apply this rule to your claim against Meanwell. Like most contracts, the deal between Meanwell and Serena had two promises: Earnest's promise to draft a will and Serena's promise to pay $2,000. The promise that interests us here is the one Meanwell made. He agreed to draft a valid will, leaving all of her property to those she designated. He was the promisor and Serena was the promisee.

Did the two parties intend that the promise benefit you? Yes, they did. Serena wanted to leave you her money out of affection. Meanwell intended to do whatever his client requested. You have proven the first element of your case. Now you must show why the promisee, Serena, wanted to benefit you. Did she owe you money? No. Did she want to make a gift to you? Yes. *You win!* You are an intended third party beneficiary and may enforce the contract between Serena and her lawyer. Meanwell owes you $11 million, the value of what you would have received had he fulfilled his obligations under the contract.[2] See Exhibit 16.1.

By contrast, the pizza parlor owner will surely lose. A stadium is a multimillion dollar investment, and it is most unlikely that the city and the seller of the

Exhibit 16.1

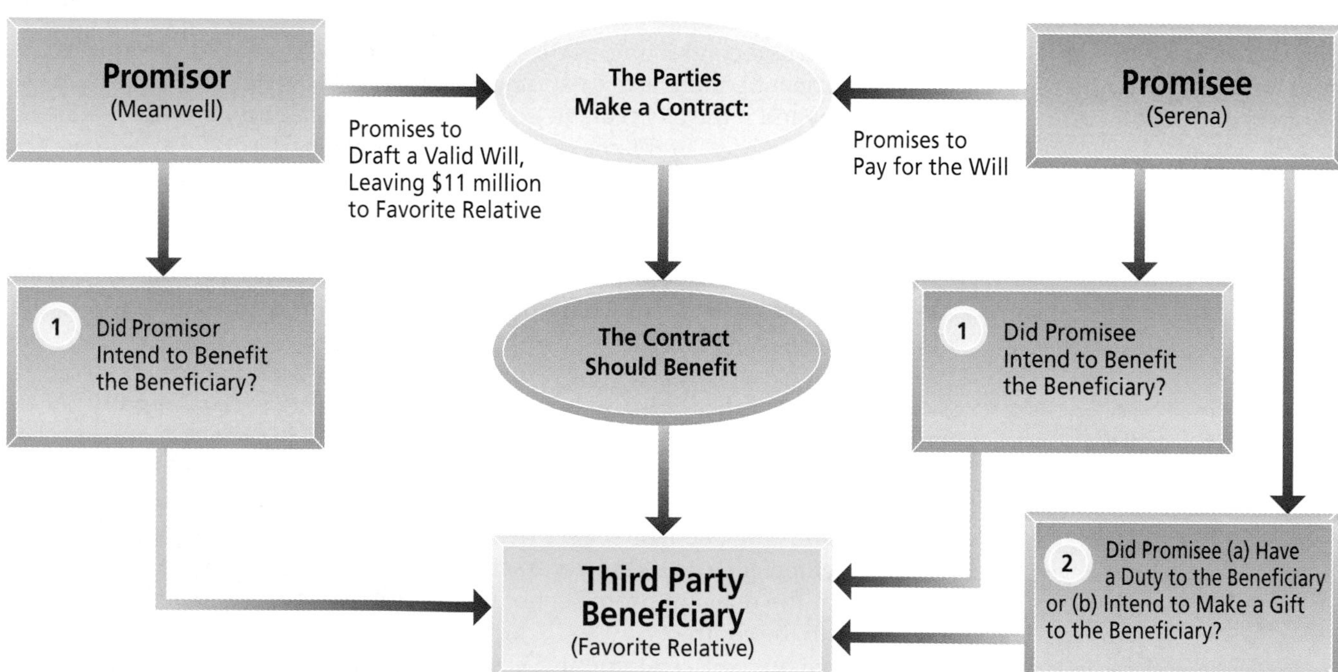

The issue: **May the third party beneficiary *enforce* the contract to which he was not a party?**

The answer: **A third party beneficiary may enforce a contract if (1) the parties intended to benefit him *and either* (2)(a) enforcing the promise will satisfy a duty of the promisee to the beneficiary or (2)(b) the promisee intended to make a gift to the beneficiary.**

In this case, **the parties intended to benefit the Favorite Relative, and the promisee (Serena) intended to make a gift to the Favorite Relative. Therefore, Favorite Relative *may* enforce the contract and wins $11 million from Meanwell.**

1 "Donee" comes from the word "donate," meaning "to give."

2 Based on *Guy v. Liederbach*, 501 Pa. 47, 459 A.2d 744, 1983 Pa. LEXIS 590 (1983).

land were even aware of the owner's existence, let alone that they intended to benefit him. He probably cannot prove either the first element or the second element, and certainly not both.

When negotiating an agreement, it is important to anticipate third party claims. Real Estate Support Services (RESS) performed house inspections for potential buyers. RESS contracted with a realtor, Coldwell Banker Relocation Services, Inc., to inspect houses and furnish reports to Coldwell. The agreement stated that the purpose of the reports was:

> To provide the client [Coldwell] with a report of a relocating employee's home, consisting of a series of visual inspection of items contained in pages 1 through 5 of this form, which the client may, at its discretion, disclose to other interested parties.

RESS inspected a house in Greencastle, Indiana, and gave its report to Coldwell, which passed the document on to Paul and Norma Nauman. The Naumans relied on the report and bought the house, but later discovered defects RESS had not mentioned. They sued RESS, claiming to be third party beneficiaries of the company's contract with Coldwell. The court ruled for the Naumans. Coldwell obviously intended to use the reports as a sales tool, and RESS knew it, making buyers such as the Naumans intended beneficiaries.[3]

Coldwell presented RESS with a contract that invited claims from third party beneficiaries. *That* was the time for RESS to decide, "Can we tolerate liability to all buyers who might see the report?" If the company was unwilling to assume such extensive liability, it should have proposed appropriate contract language, such as:

> RESS is preparing these reports exclusively for Coldwell's use. Coldwell will not disclose any report to a house purchaser or any other person without first obtaining written permission from RESS.

If Coldwell had accepted the language, there would have been no lawsuit. Perhaps Coldwell would have insisted on its right to disclose the reports to purchasers. Then RESS would have had two options: sign the contract, acknowledging the company's exposure to third parties, or walk away from the negotiations. To summarize:

- *Anticipate* problems. Examine the deal you are making from the perspective of others—in this case, third party beneficiaries.
- Force yourself to *decide now* what risks you can tolerate.
- *Negotiate* a contract that reflects your decisions. If you are unable to get a deal you can live with, do not sign.

The following case provides another example of unrealistic negotiations.

STARRETT v. COMMERCIAL BANK OF GEORGIA
226 Ga. App. 598, 486 S.E.2d 923, 1997 Ga. App. LEXIS 708
Georgia Court of Appeals, 1997

Facts: Robert Starrett borrowed money from the Commercial Bank of Georgia, using as security a house that he and his wife Jerry owned. Several years later the couple divorced. They amicably divided their assets in a "settlement agreement," which the court approved. The parties agreed to sell the house and disburse the proceeds in this order: first, to pay taxes and costs of the sale; second, to pay off in

[3] *Real Estate Support Services v. Nauman*, 644 N.E.2d 907, 1994 Ind. App. LEXIS 1796 (Ind. Ct. App. 1994).

full Robert Starrett's loan from Commercial; and third, to divide the remaining money, 65 percent to Jerry and 35 percent to Robert. The couple never did sell the property, and Robert Starrett died two years later. Robert's estate gave his 50 percent interest in the house to Commercial, but the bank could make no use of it as long as Jerry was half owner. Commercial filed suit, seeking full title. The trial court ruled that the bank was a third party beneficiary of the settlement agreement, and awarded it the house. Jerry Starrett appealed.

Issue: **Was the bank a third party beneficiary of the Starretts' agreement?**

Excerpts from Judge Ruffin's Decision: Starrett argues that the Bank is only an incidental, rather than intended, beneficiary to the divorce decree. We disagree. The divorce decree does not simply provide for sale of the property. It specifically requires "payment in full of [Robert Starrett's] outstanding loan with Commercial Bank which has a present balance of approximately $63,000.00." Through the agreement, the Starretts agreed to render performance to a named third party, the Bank. It is clear on the face of the contract that the [Starretts] intended [the Bank] to be the beneficiary of [the sale of the property] by their inclusion of [this payment provision] as a condition of the contract.

Starrett also argues that we should not uphold a decision that would allow any creditor provided for in a divorce decree to sue in the capacity of a third party beneficiary. [The Alabama Supreme Court, in a case called *Costanza*, held that a divorce settlement was intended only to finalize the property between the couple, not to benefit a bank mentioned in the agreement.]

Despite the similarity between this case and Costanza, we do not agree that the Bank's third-party beneficiary argument fails simply because the overall purpose of the Starretts' divorce decree was to effectuate the divorce and finalize the property agreement, rather than to benefit the bank. Notwithstanding the ultimate purpose of the agreement, individual contract provisions may be intended to benefit a stranger to the contract, thus creating a third-party beneficiary. In this case, the sale provision in the divorce decree was clearly intended to benefit the Bank by satisfying an outstanding loan balance. The trial court properly found that, as a matter of law, the Bank is a third-party beneficiary to the divorce agreement.

Affirmed.

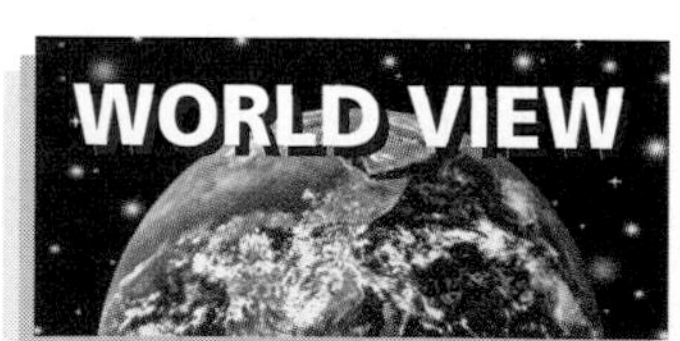

You are an executive with KeepTrak, a high-tech company whose new software helps distributors and retailers keep track of stock. Convinced that your programs are superior to the competition, you hurry into the international market, signing a deal with Mexware, a Mexican distributor of software. Mexware agrees to (1) translate your software into Spanish and (2) distribute the product throughout Latin America and Spain. Mexware hires TransLite, another Mexican company, to do the translation, providing the company with source code and other confidential information that belongs to your company. You insist that the contract between Mexware and TransLite state that both companies will protect the confidentiality of all KeepTrak information.

Suppose that TransLite breaches the confidentiality agreement, improperly selling some of your source code to competitors. Can KeepTrak sue TransLite directly? More importantly, will the threat of liability prevent TransLite from doing anything improper?

The confidentiality agreement between Mexware and TransLite clearly establishes KeepTrak as a third party beneficiary. Spain, Mexico, and most Latin American countries do recognize third party beneficiaries, but with a significant limitation. Most of these nations permit the obligor to revoke its commitment to a third party unless and until the third party gives notice that it "accepts" the benefits of the agreement. Under Mexican law, TransLite could back out of its agreement to maintain confidentiality unless KeepTrak gave written notice that it was relying on the agreement. As is so often the case, a few simple sentences make a world of difference. KeepTrak should deliver no source code until it has signed the contract between Mexware and TransLite, indicating its acceptance of the terms and its reliance on absolute confidentiality by all parties.

CONCLUDING NOTE ON THIRD PARTY BENEFICIARIES

In our networked society, information is exchanged faster and more widely than ever, making companies and consumers more interdependent. For example, an accounting firm might prepare an audit for a corporation and then later discover that other parties obtained the audit and relied on it by extending credit to the audited company. Those who create and process information must be certain not to create contract rights in third parties whom they do not wish to benefit. The most effective way to do that is with clear language in a written contract.

ASSIGNMENT AND DELEGATION

A contracting party may transfer his rights under the contract, which is called an **assignment of rights**. Or a contracting party may transfer her duties pursuant to the contract, which is a **delegation of duties**. Frequently, a party will make an assignment and delegation simultaneously, transferring both rights and duties to a third party.

Statutory and common law, the Restatement (Second) of Contracts, and the UCC all govern various aspects of assignments. For our purposes, the Restatement serves as a good summary of common law provisions. The UCC rules are generally similar, although we note some differences later on. Our first example is a sale of goods case, governed by the UCC, but the outcome would be the same under the Restatement.

Lydia needs 500 bottles of champagne. Bruno agrees to sell them to her for $10,000, payable 30 days after delivery. He transports the wine to her. Bruno happens to owe Doug $8,000 from a previous deal, so he says to Doug, "I don't have the money, but I'll give you my claim to Lydia's $10,000." Doug agrees. Bruno then *assigns* to Doug *his rights* to Lydia's money, and in exchange Doug gives up his claim for $8,000. Bruno is the **assignor, the one making an assignment,** and Doug is the **assignee, the one receiving an assignment.**

Why would Bruno offer $10,000 when he owed Doug only $8,000? Because all he has is a *claim* to Lydia's money. Cash in hand is often more valuable. Doug, however, is willing to assume some risk for a potential $2,000 gain.

Bruno notifies Lydia of the assignment. Lydia, who owes the money, is called the **obligor,** that is, the one obligated to do something. At the end of 30 days, Doug arrives at Lydia's doorstep, asks for his money, and gets it, since Lydia is obligated to him. Bruno has no claim to any payment. See Exhibit 16.2.

Lydia bought the champagne because she knew she could sell it at a profit. She promptly agrees to sell and deliver the 500 bottles to Coretta, at a mountaintop wilderness camp. Lydia has no four-wheel drive cars, so she finds Keith, who is willing to deliver the bottles for $1,000. Lydia *delegates her duty* to Keith to deliver the bottles to Coretta. Keith is now obligated to deliver the bottles to Coretta, the **obligee,** that is, the one who has the obligation coming to her. As we

Exhibit 16.2

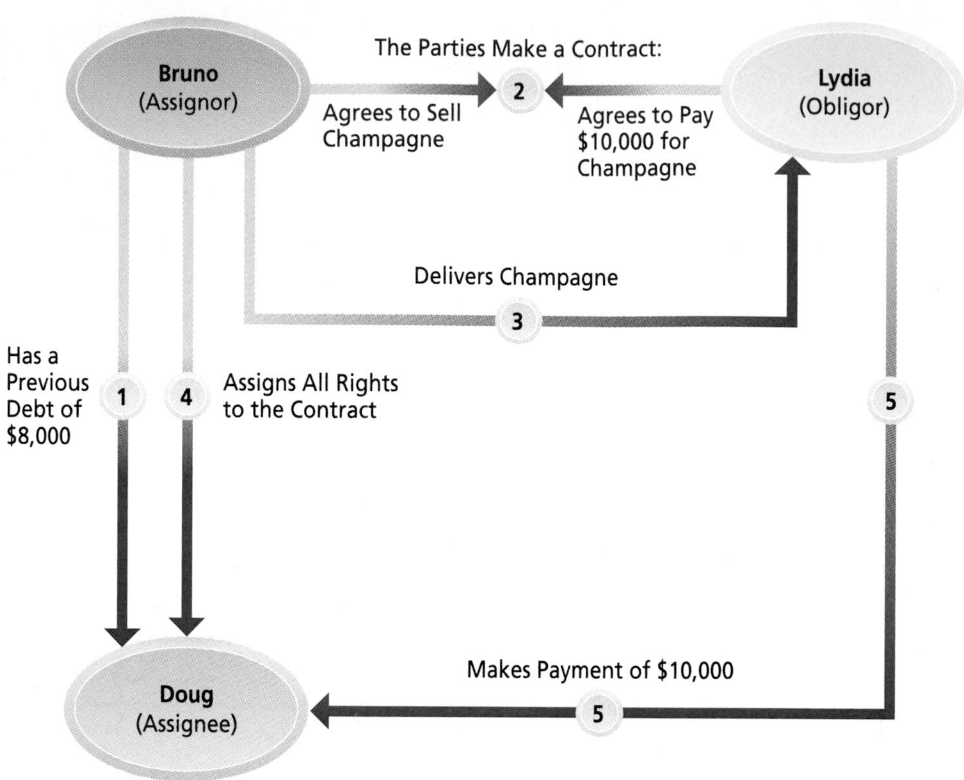

see later, Lydia also remains obligated to Coretta, the obligee, to ensure that the bottles are delivered. See Exhibit 16.3.

Assignment and delegation can each create problems. We will examine the most common ones.

ASSIGNMENT

What Rights Are Assignable?

Most contract rights are assignable, but not all. Disputes sometimes arise between the two contracting parties about whether one of the parties could legally assign her rights to a third party. The Restatement (Second) of Contracts §317(2) sums up the assignability of rights this way:

> **Any contractual right may be assigned unless assignment**
> **(a)** would substantially change the obligor's rights or duties under the contract; or
> **(b)** is forbidden by law or public policy; or
> **(c)** is validly precluded by the contract itself.[4]

Substantial Change. Subsection (a) prohibits an assignment if it would substantially change the obligor's situation. For example, Bruno is permitted to assign to Doug his rights to payment from Lydia because it makes no difference to Lydia whether she writes a check to one or the other. But suppose Erica, who lives on a one-quarter acre lot in Hardscrabble, hires Keith to mow her lawn once per week for the summer, for a total fee of $700. Erica pays up front, before she leaves for the summer. May she assign her right to weekly lawn care to Lloyd, who enjoys a

[4] Restatement (Second) of Contracts §317(2). And note that UCC §2-210(2) is, for our purposes, nearly identical.

Exhibit 16.3

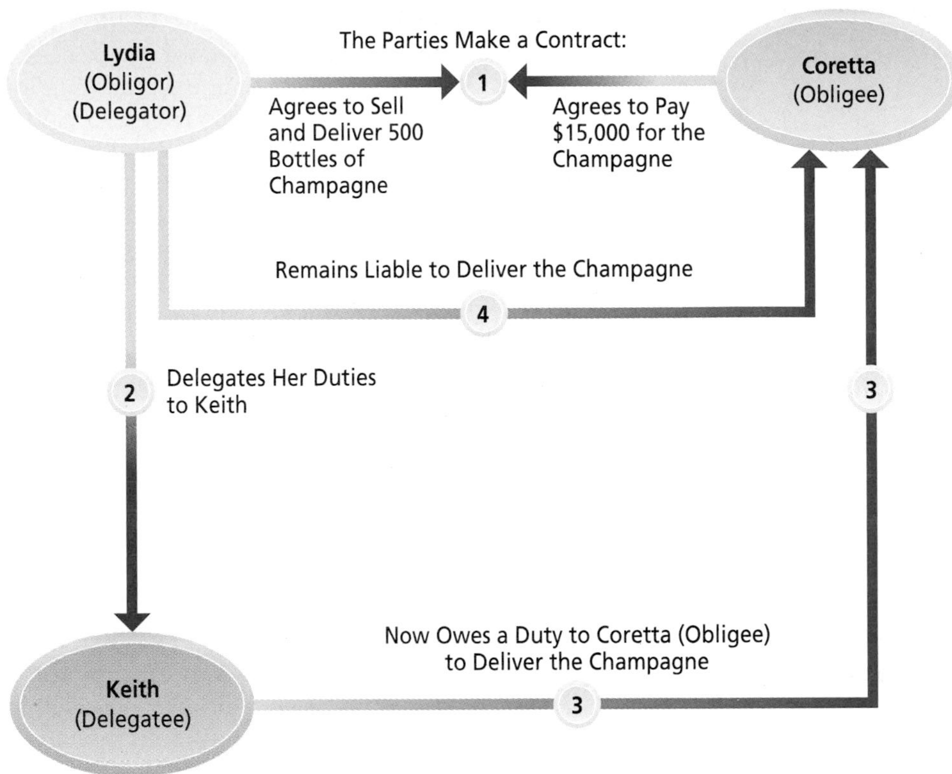

three-acre estate in Halcyon, 60 miles distant? No. The extra travel and far larger yard would dramatically change Keith's obligations, and Erica has no right to make the assignment.

Assignment is also prohibited when the obligor is agreeing to perform **personal services.** The close working relationship in such agreements makes it unfair to expect the obligor to work with a stranger. Warner, a feature film director, hires Mayer to be his assistant on a film to be shot over the next 10 weeks. Warner may not assign to Brothers his right to Mayer's work.

Public Policy. Some assignments are prohibited by public policy. For example, someone who has suffered a personal injury may not assign her claim to a third person. Vladimir is playing the piano on his roof deck when the instrument rolls over the balustrade and drops 35 stories, striking Wanda and bruising her elbow. Wanda has a valid tort claim against Vladimir, but she may not assign the claim to her father, Arturo. As a matter of public policy, all states have decided that the sale of personal injury claims would create an unseemly and unethical bazaar.

Contract Prohibition. Finally, one of the contracting parties may try to prohibit assignment in the agreement itself. For example, most landlords include in the written lease a clause prohibiting the tenant from assigning the tenancy without the landlord's written permission. Such clauses are generally, but not always, enforced by a court.

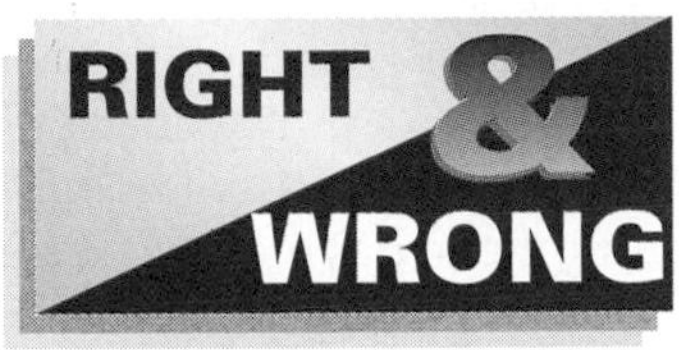

Suppose a commercial tenant informs its landlord that it wishes to assign its lease. The landlord investigates the assignee, that is, the new tenant, and discovers that it is highly reputable and financially sound. But the landlord also realizes that rental rates have risen. May the landlord deny permission to the tenant to assign its lease, hoping to write a new lease at a higher rent? Most states hold that a landlord may do just that, whether or not it is morally right.

Two tenants leased the property where they operated a successful deli. The long-term lease prohibited the tenants from assigning the lease without the landlord's permission. The tenants decided to sell their deli, and a buyer offered a good price. But the landlord refused assignment, meaning that the sale could not go through. The tenants sued, claiming that a landlord must permit assignment unless he has a *good faith* reason to deny it. Not so, said the Washington court. A party to a contract must perform an action in good faith only *if the contract requires that action*. This lease imposed no obligation on the landord to consent to assignment, so neither good faith nor bad faith was relevant. The court noted that, when the parties bargain a lease, the tenants could insist on a clause stating that a landlord may not unreasonably withhold permission to assign. These tenants failed to do that.[5]

Exactly the same issue landed before the California Supreme Court, which reached the opposite conclusion:

> Denying consent solely on the basis of personal taste, convenience or sensibility is not commercially reasonable. Nor is it reasonable to deny consent in order that the landlord may charge a higher rent than originally contracted for. [When] the lessee executed the lease he acquired the contractual right for the exclusive use of the premises, and all of the benefits and detriment attendant to possession, for the term of the contract. He took the downside risk that he would be paying too much rent if there should be a depression in the rental market. Why should he be deprived of the contractual benefits of the lease because of the fortuitous inflation in the marketplace?[6]

So the court permitted the tenant to assign its rights, even though the lease itself had prohibited assignment without the landlord's permission. Was this ruling a bold step forward for legal ethics? Or was it a fiat by a court imposing its morality on two parties who had, after all, freely entered into a lease? For an example of a residential lease with a no-assignment clause, see **http://www.kinseylaw.com/freestuff/leaseten/ResLease.html**. When you rent an apartment, the lease will probably contain a similar clause.

The following case begins with everyone's dream come true: a winning lottery ticket.

PETERSON v. DISTRICT OF COLUMBIA LOTTERY AND CHARITABLE GAMES CONTROL BOARD
673 A.2d 664, 1996 D.C. App. LEXIS 54
District of Columbia Court of Appeals, 1996

Facts: In 1986, Eugene Peterson won $1,050,000 in the District of Columbia Lucky Lotto Game, payable in 20 installments. In 1993, he assigned his future payments to Stone Street Capital, Inc., in exchange for a present-value lump sum. The District's Lottery and Charitable Games Control Board (the Board) refused to honor the assignment, based on its regulations. Peterson and Stone Street sued, but the trial court ruled that the assignment was illegal. Peterson and Stone Street appealed.

Issue: Was Peterson entitled to assign his lottery winnings?

Excerpts from Judge Farrell's Decision: Unless a contract contains "clear, unambiguous language" prohibiting an assignment, courts generally do not honor attempts to restrict the right to assign freely. The District concedes that the regulations contained no express prohibition on voluntary assignment of winnings. The District relies nonetheless on the language in the regulations discharging the Board of all liability "upon payment of a prize to the owner as described in section 603" in turn defined as "the person whose name appears [on the back of the ticket]." But while this language may be read to express an intent to bar assignments, it may also express no more than "a direction on how payment is to be

---

[5] *Johnson v. Yousoofian*, 84 Wash. App. 755, 930 P.2d 921, 1996 Wash. App. LEXIS 788 (Wash. Ct. App. 1996).

[6] *Kendall v. Ernest Pestana, Inc.*, 40 Cal. 3d 488, 709 P.2d 837, 1985 Cal. LEXIS 419 (Cal. 1985).

made," conveying the lesser intent that only a single winner (or successor in interest) may claim a prize. As a putative ban on voluntary assignments, the language is too ambiguous to overcome the presumption in our decisions favoring the free assignment of contracts.

Contending that this is not an ordinary contracts case because of the presence of a government agency, the District further points to evidence at trial of what it terms the Board's "unfailing interpretation of its regulations not to require it to pay a prize or installment to anyone other than the person who signed the winning ticket." It urges us to give this interpretation the deference normally accorded an agency's long-standing interpretation of its regulations. The difficulty with this position is two-fold. First, we deal here with the Board as a contracting party. When the government enters into contracts with private individuals, its rights and duties therein are governed generally by the law applicable to contracts between private individuals.

Moreover, the "unfailing" or uniform interpretation the District cites is less than apparent in the record. The trial court found this to consist largely of "some undisclosed, undated conversations with vendors and other such people over the phone about whether or not they could accept lottery payments." The court noted the absence of any documentary or tape-recorded evidence of the Board's policy, including the lack of written guidelines.

We hold that the regulations did not prohibit the assignment of Peterson's winnings.

How Rights Are Assigned

Writing. In general, an assignment may be written or oral, and no particular formalities are required. However, when someone wants to assign rights governed by the statute of frauds, she must do it in writing. Suppose City contracts with Seller to buy Seller's land for a domed stadium and then brings in Investor to complete the project. If City wants to assign to Investor its rights to the land, it must do so in writing.

Consideration. An assignment can be valid with or without consideration, but the lack of consideration may have consequences. Two examples should clarify this. Recall Bruno, who sells champagne to Lydia and then assigns to Doug his right to payment. In that case there *is* consideration for the assignment. Bruno assigns his rights only because Doug cancels the old debt, and his agreement to do that is valid consideration. **An assignment for consideration is irrevocable.** Once the two men agree, Bruno may not telephone Doug and say, "I've changed my mind, I want Lydia to pay me after all." Lydia's $10,000 now belongs to Doug.

But suppose that Bruno assigns his contract rights to his sister Brunhilde as a birthday present. This is a **gratuitous assignment**, that is, one made as a gift, for no consideration. **A gratuitous assignment is generally revocable if it is oral and generally irrevocable if it is written.** If Bruno orally assigns his rights to Brunhilde, but then changes his mind, telephones Lydia, and says, "I want you to pay me, after all," that revocation is effective and Brunhilde gets nothing. But if Bruno puts his assignment in writing and Brunhilde receives it, Bruno has given up his right to the money.

If you assign your rights under a contract, inform the obligor immediately—or live with the consequences.

Notice to Obligor. The assignment is valid from the moment it is made, regardless of whether the assignor notifies the obligor. But an assignor with common sense will immediately inform the obligor of the assignment. Suppose Maude has a contract with Nelson, who is obligated to deliver 700 live frogs to her shop. If Maude (assignor) assigns her rights to Obie (assignee), Maude should notify Nelson (obligor) the same day. If she fails to inform Nelson, he may deliver the frogs to Maude. Nelson will have no further obligations under the contract, and Maude will owe Obie 700 frogs. For a simple assignment, see http://www.lectlaw.com/forms/f013.txt.

Rights of the Parties after Assignment

Once the assignment is made and the obligor notified, the assignee may enforce her contractual rights against the obligor. If Lydia fails to pay Doug for the champagne she gets from Bruno, Doug may sue to enforce the agreement. The law will treat Doug as though he had entered into the contract with Lydia.

But the reverse is also true. **The obligor may generally raise all defenses against the assignee that she could have raised against the assignor.** Suppose Lydia opens the first bottle of champagne—silently. "Where's the pop?" she wonders. There is no pop because all 500 bottles have gone flat. Bruno has failed to perform his part of the contract, and Lydia may use Bruno's nonperformance as a defense against Doug. If the champagne was indeed worthless, Lydia owes Doug nothing.

Assignor's Warranty. The law implies certain warranties (assurances) on the part of the assignor. Unless the parties expressly agree to exclude them, the assignor warrants that (1) the rights he is assigning actually do exist, and (2) there are no defenses to the rights other than those that would be obvious, like nonperformance. But the assignor *does not* warrant that the obligor is solvent. Bruno is impliedly warranting to Doug that Lydia has no defenses to the contract, but he is not guaranteeing Doug that she has the money to pay, or that she will pay.

Differences under the UCC

As we mentioned, the Code's provisions regarding assignment, found in §2-210, are very similar to the Restatement section quoted above. Assignments are common in sales contracts. The UCC favors them and tends to limit contractual clauses that prohibit assignment. Thus, if a contract states in general terms that assignment is prohibited, the Code will limit that language to mean only that a party may not delegate his *duties*; assignment of the party's *rights* will still be allowed. If a contracting party wants to prohibit assignment of rights, it must specifically say so.[7]

Article 9 of the UCC does make significant changes in the common law concerning assignment of security interests. We discuss this in some detail in Chapter 26, on secured transactions; only one aspect concerns us here. **Security interest** means a legal right in personal property that assures payment. When an automobile dealer sells you a new car on credit, the dealer will keep a security interest in your car. If you do not make your monthly payments, the dealer retains a right to drive your car away, and that authority is called a security interest.

Companies that sell goods often prefer to assign their security interests to some other firm, such as a bank or finance company. The bank is the assignee. Just as we saw with the common law, the assignee of a security interest generally has all of the rights that the assignor had. And the obligor (the buyer) may also raise all of the defenses against the assignee that she could have raised against the assignor.

According to UCC §9-318, in general, the obligor on a sales contract may assert any defenses against the assignee that arise from the contract, and any other defenses that arose before notice of assignment. The Code's reference to any defenses that arise from the contract means that if the assignor breached his part of the deal, the obligor may raise that as a defense. Suppose a dealer sells you a new Porsche on credit, retaining a security interest. He assigns the security interest to the bank. The car is great for the first few weeks, but then the roof slides onto the street, both doors fall off, and the engine implodes. You refuse to make any more monthly payments. When the bank sues you, you may raise as a defense the

---

[7] UCC §2-210(3).

automobile's defects, just as you could have raised them against the dealer itself. Where the Code talks about other defenses that arose before notice of assignment, it refers, for example, to fraud. Suppose the dealer knew that before you bought the Porsche, it had been smashed up and rebuilt. If the dealer told you it was brand new, that was fraud, and you could raise the defense against the bank.

A contract may prohibit an obligor from raising certain defenses against an assignee. Sometimes a seller of goods will require the buyer to sign a contract that permits the seller to assign *and* prohibits the buyer from raising defenses against the assignee that he could have raised against the seller. University wants to buy a computer system on credit from Leland for $85,000. Leland agrees to the deal but insists that the contract permit him to assign his rights to anyone he chooses. He also wants this clause: "University agrees that it will not raise against an assignee any defenses that it may have had against Leland." This clause is sometimes called a *waiver clause*, because the obligor is waiving (giving up) rights. Courts may also refer to it as an *exclusion clause*, since the parties are excluding potential defenses. Leland wants a waiver clause because it makes his contract more valuable. As soon as University signs the agreement, Leland can take his contract to Krushem Collections, a finance company. Krushem might offer Leland $70,000 cash for the contract. Leland can argue, "You have to pay $80,000 for this. You are guaranteed payment by University, since they cannot raise any defenses against you, even if the computer system collapses in the first half-hour." Leland gets cash and need not worry about collecting payments. Krushem receives the full value of the contract, with interest, spread out over several years.

Under UCC §9-206, an agreement by a buyer (or lessee) that he will not assert against an assignee any claim or defense that he may have against the seller (or lessor) is generally enforceable by the assignee if he took the assignment in good faith, for value, without notice of the potential defenses. In other words, Leland's waiver clause with University is enforceable. If Leland assigns the contract to Krushem Collections and the system proves worthless, Krushem is still entitled to its monthly payments from University. The school must seek its damages against Leland—a far more arduous step than simply withholding payment.

These waiver clauses are generally *not* valid in consumer contracts. If Leland sold a computer system to a consumer (an individual purchasing it for her personal use), the waiver would generally be unenforceable. See Exhibit 16.4. The following case involves a waiver clause in an equipment lease. Who should win?

CHASE MANHATTAN BANK v. LAKE TIRE CO., INC.

496 N.E.2d 129, 1986 Ind. App. LEXIS 2851
Indiana Court of Appeals, 1986

Facts: Lake Tire Co. of Indiana signed an agreement with Scotti Commercial Co. to lease a machine designed to bend exhaust pipes so that mufflers could be fitted into different makes of cars. The lease contained the following waiver clause:

> ASSIGNMENT. This lease may be transferred by Scotti without notice, and in such event Scotti's assignee shall have all rights and remedies of Scotti. Lake Tire agrees that its obligations shall not be subject, as against any such assignee, to any defense or counterclaim available to Lake Tire against Scotti.

Scotti assigned its rights to Chase Manhattan Bank and notified Lake Tire of the assignment. Lake Tire made 11 payments to Chase but then informed Scotti and Chase that it would make no more payments because the machine failed to work. Scotti filed for bankruptcy. Chase sued Lake Tire, demanding the rest of the money. Lake Tire counterclaimed against Chase, alleging breach of contract.

The trial court gave judgment for Lake Tire. It concluded that Chase stood in the same position as Scotti had, that the machine was worthless, and that Chase should take nothing. It awarded Lake Tire $24,000 for various losses and expenses. Chase appealed.

You Be the Judge: Should Chase be able to enforce the waiver clause, prohibiting Lake Tire from raising defenses against an assignee?

Exhibit 16.4

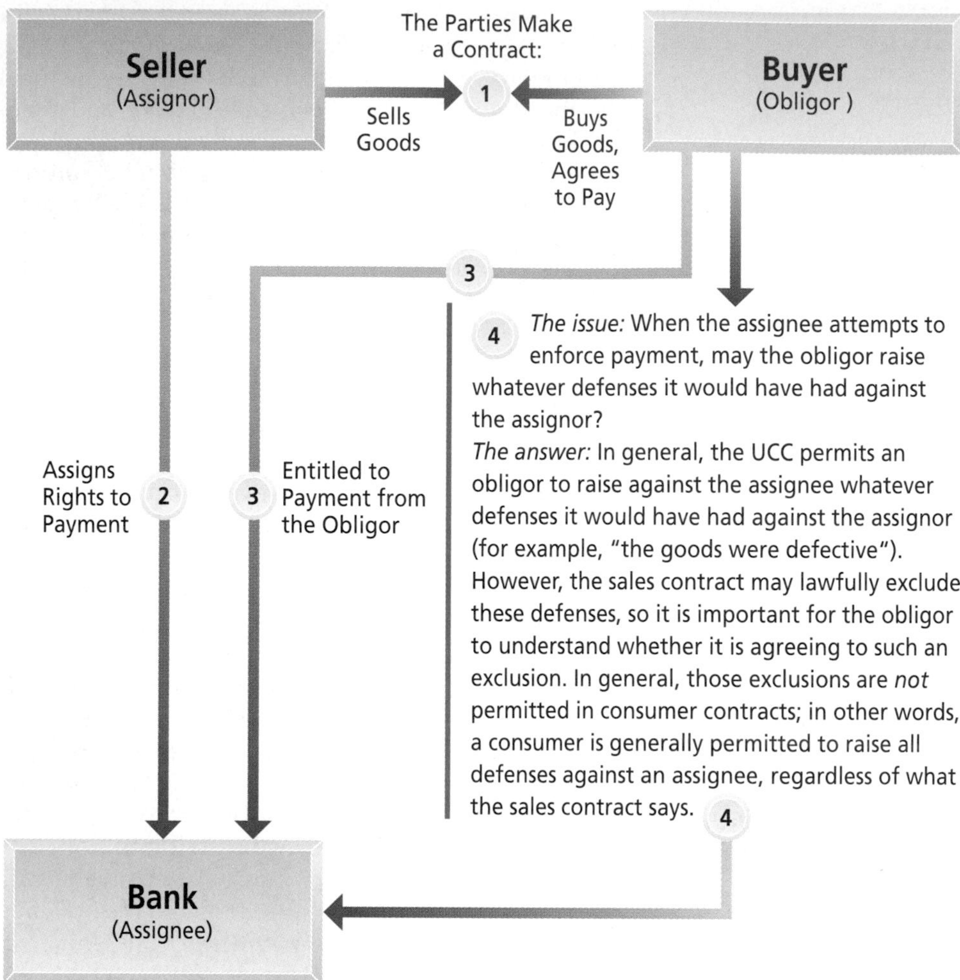

Argument for Chase: Your honors, the contract permitted Scotti to assign its rights, and prohibited Lake Tire from asserting against the assignee any defenses that it might have against Scotti. In other words, if the machine proved defective, Lake Tire agreed to raise that claim only against Scotti.

The waiver clause is valid and enforceable, according to UCC §9-206. Chase took the assignment in good faith, assuming that the contract was valid and relying on the waiver clause. The bank had no notice from either Scotti or Lake Tire that there was anything wrong with the pipe machine, and obviously there *was* nothing wrong with it then, since Lake Tire made 11 payments to the bank. Chase gave good value for this assignment, paying to Scotti the fair price for the contractual rights. The trial court treated Chase as "standing in the shoes" of Scotti, but that is exactly what the contract prohibits.

If Lake Tire did not want to abide by a waiver clause, it should not have signed one. In all likelihood, it received a better price from Scotti based on its willingness to accept the clause. It is all part of the give and take of bargaining, and this court should not now step in and rewrite the agreement. UCC §9-206 should be respected and this contract enforced.

Argument for Lake Tire: Your honors, what Chase is asking Lake Tire to do is this: continue making monthly payments for a worthless machine, without asserting any claims based on the product's defects. Lake Tire *cannot* make its claim against Scotti, since the company is bankrupt. And Chase argues that we should be *barred* from raising defenses against the bank.

Scotti drafted the contract, filled with small print, one clause of which is at issue here. Scotti attempted to sneak this one by Lake Tire, and it succeeded. It was unlikely that any officer of Lake Tire would spot this language, and inconceivable that he or she would understand its horrendous implications. Do we really want to impose upon small-business people an obligation to think through this scenario: that the lessor will assign its lease to a bank; that the leased equipment will prove useless; that the lessor will go bankrupt and be unable to repair the equipment or refund any money; that the bank will come knocking for its full payment; and that when the bank sues, the small business will be *legally unable to mention that the equipment was junk?* At the very least, your honors, if we are going to expect a business person to understand that sequence, we should require the party drafting the contract to put it in bold print and plain English.

Chase is a sophisticated international bank that understands the subtleties of waiver agreements. Chase knew that Lake Tire, like any small business, would expect to raise legitimate defenses. Chase was the party that could foresee everything that has happened, and it decided to take a flyer, hoping to enforce an unfair deal. The bank should not be able to profit from a combination of experience and cynicism.

DELEGATION OF DUTIES

Garret has always dreamed of racing stock cars. He borrows $250,000 from his sister, Maybelle, in order to buy a car and begin racing. He signs a promissory note in that amount, in other words, a document guaranteeing that he will repay Maybelle the full amount, plus interest, on a monthly basis over 10 years. Regrettably, during his first race, on a Saturday night, Garret discovers that he has a speed phobia. He finishes the race at noon on Sunday and quits the business. Garret transfers the car and all of his equipment to Brady, who agrees in writing to pay all money owed to Maybelle. For a few months Brady sends a check, but he is killed while watching bumper cars at a local carnival. Maybelle sues Garret, who defends based on the transfer to Brady. Will his defense work?

Garret has assigned his rights in the car and business to Brady and that is entirely legal. But more important, he has *delegated his duties* to Brady. Garret was the **delegator** and Brady was the **delegatee**. In other words, the promissory note he signed was a contract, and the agreement imposed certain *duties* on Garret, primarily the obligation to pay Maybelle $250,000 plus interest. Garret had a right to delegate his duties to Brady, but delegating those duties did not relieve Garret of his own obligation to perform them. When Maybelle sues, she will win. Garret, like many debtors, would have preferred to wash his hands of his debt, but the law is not so obliging.

One may delegate and one may not.

Most duties are delegable. But delegation does not by itself relieve the delegator of his own liability to perform the contract.

Garret's delegation to Brady was typical in that it included an assignment at the same time. If he had merely transferred ownership, that would have been only an assignment. If he had convinced Brady to pay off the loan without getting the car, that would have been merely a delegation. He did both at once. See Exhibit 16.5.

What Duties Are Delegable

The rules concerning what duties may be delegated mirror those about the assignment of rights. And once again, the common law, as summarized by the Restatement, agrees with the UCC.

An obligor may delegate his duties unless

(1) delegation would violate public policy, or

(2) the contract prohibits delegation, or

(3) the obligee has a substantial interest in personal performance by the obligor.[8]

[8] Restatement (Second) of Contracts §318. And see UCC §2-210, establishing similar limits.

Exhibit 16.5

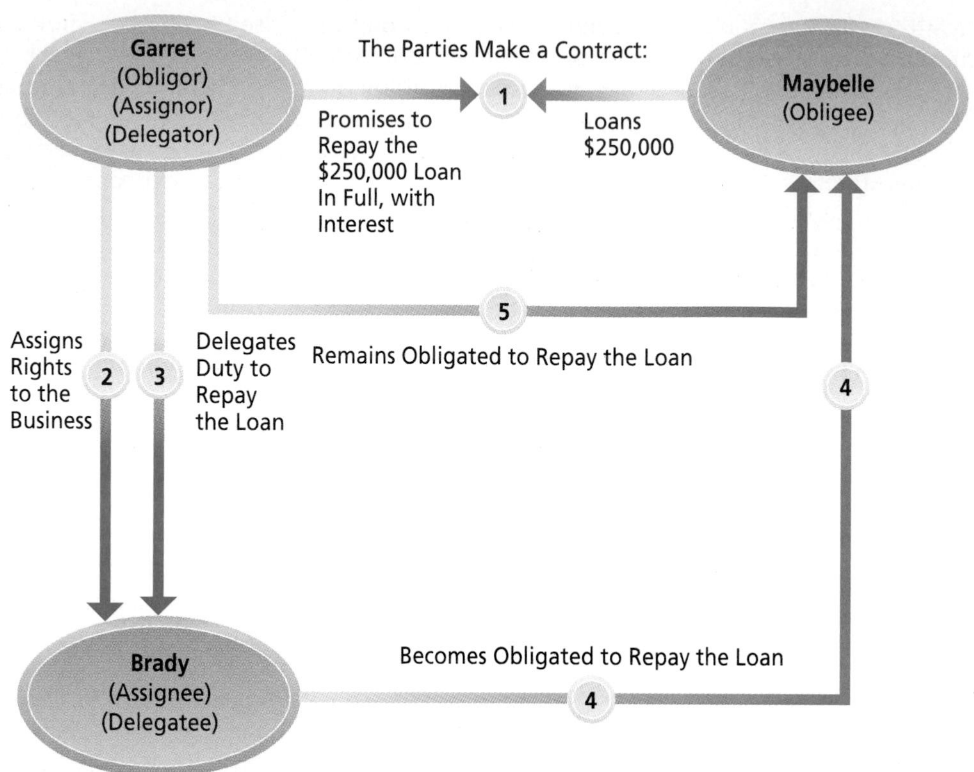

Public Policy. Delegation may violate public policy, for example, in a public works contract. If City hires Builder to construct a subway system, state law may prohibit Builder from delegating his duties to Beginner. The theory is that a public agency should not have to work with parties that it never agreed to hire.

Contract Prohibition. It is very common for a contract to prohibit delegation. We saw in the assignment section that courts may refuse to enforce a clause that limits one party's ability to assign its contract rights. That does *not* hold true with delegation. The parties may forbid almost any delegation, and the courts will enforce the agreement. Hammer, a contractor, is building a house and hires Spot as his painter, including in his contract a clause prohibiting delegation. Just before the house is ready for painting, Spot gets a better job elsewhere and wants to delegate his duties to Brush. Hammer may refuse the delegation even if Brush is equally qualified.

Substantial Interest in Personal Performance. Suppose Hammer had omitted the "nondelegation" clause from his contract with Spot. Could Hammer still refuse the delegation on the grounds that he has a substantial interest in having Spot do the work? No. Most duties are delegable. There is nothing so special about painting a house that one particular painter is required to do it. But some kinds of work do require personal performance, and obligors may not delegate these tasks. The services of lawyers, doctors, dentists, artists, and performers are considered too personal to be delegated. There is no single test that will perfectly define this group, but generally when the work will test *the character, skill, discretion, and good faith* of the obligor, she *may not* delegate her job.[9]

[9] An athlete who hires a sports agency depends upon its judgment and skill, meaning that the firm may not delegate its duties. For an online pitch from one such agency, see **http://www.teleport.com**.

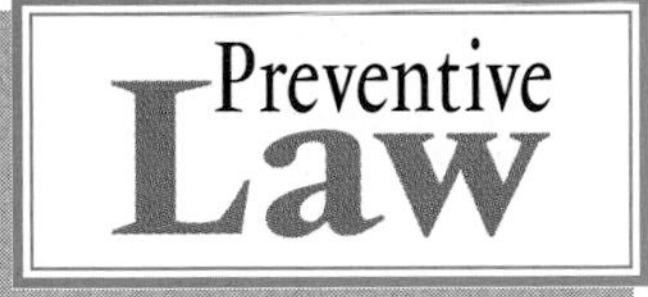

The law can be annoyingly vague, as it is with the test of "personal performance" contracts. But avoiding problems is not difficult. Before entering into a contract, briefly discuss delegation with the other party and decide what duties, if any, may be delegated. Then include an appropriate clause in the contract. As always, if there are differences over delegation, it is better to be aware of them early.

Improper Delegation and Repudiation. Sometimes parties delegate duties they should not. Suppose Spot, having agreed not to delegate his painting job, is so tempted by the higher offer from another contractor that he delegates the work anyway. Hammer informs Spot he will not allow Brush on the job site. If Spot still refuses to work, he has **repudiated** the agreement; in other words, he has formally notified the other side he will not perform his side of the contract. Hammer will probably sue him. On the other hand, if Hammer allows Brush up the ladder and Brush completes the job, Hammer has no claim against anybody.

Novation

As we have seen, a delegator does not get rid of his duties merely by delegating them. But there is one way a delegator can do so. **A novation is a three-way agreement in which the obligor delegates all duties to the delegatee and the obligee agrees to look only to the delegatee for performance. The obligee releases the obligor from all liability.**

Recall Garret, the forlorn race car driver. When he wanted to get out of his obligations to Maybelle, he should have proposed a novation. He would assign all rights and delegate all duties to Brady, and Maybelle would agree that *only Brady* was obligated by the promissory note, releasing Garret from his responsibility to repay. Why would Maybelle do this? She might conclude that Brady was a financially better bet than Garret and that this was the best way to get her money. Maybelle would prefer to have both people liable. But Garret might refuse to bring Brady into the deal until Maybelle permits a novation. In the example given, Garret failed to obtain a novation, and hence he and Brady (or Brady's estate) were *both* liable on the promissory note.

Since a novation has the critical effect of releasing the obligor from liability, you will not be surprised to learn that two parties to a contract sometimes fight over whether some event was a simple delegation of duties or a novation. Here is one such contest.

ROSENBERG v. SON, INC.
491 N.W.2d 71, 1992 N.D. LEXIS 202
Supreme Court of North Dakota, 1992

Facts: The Rosenbergs owned a Dairy Queen in Grand Forks, North Dakota. They agreed in writing to sell the Dairy Queen to Mary Pratt. The contract required her to pay $10,000 down and $52,000 over 15 years, at 10 percent interest. Two years later, Pratt assigned her rights and delegated her duties under the sales contract to Son, Inc. The agreement between Pratt and Son contained a "Consent to Assignment" clause that the Rosenbergs signed. Pratt then moved to Arizona and had nothing further to do with the Dairy Queen. The Rosenbergs never received full payment for the Dairy Queen. They sued Mary Pratt.

The trial court gave summary judgment for Pratt, finding that she was no longer obligated on the original contract. The Rosenbergs appealed.

Issue: Did Pratt obtain a novation relieving her of her duties under the original sales contract?

Excerpts from Chief Justice Erickstad's Decision: It is a well-established principle in the law of contracts that a contracting party cannot escape its liability on the contract by merely assigning its duties and rights under the contract to a third party.

It is evident from the express language of the assignment agreement between Pratt and Son, Inc., that only an assignment was intended, not a novation. The agreement made no mention of discharging Pratt from any further liability on the contract.

Furthermore, the agreement was between Pratt and Son, Inc.; they were the parties signing the agreement, not the Rosenbergs. An agreement between Pratt and Son, Inc., cannot unilaterally affect the Rosenbergs' rights under the contract. As mentioned earlier, the Rosenbergs did sign a consent to the assignment at the bottom of the agreement. However, by merely consenting to the assignment, the Rosenbergs did not consent to a discharge of the principal obligor—Pratt. Nothing in the language of the consent clause supports such an allegation. A creditor is free to consent to an assignment without releasing the original obligor.

We *reverse* the summary judgment and *remand* for further proceedings.

It appears that Mary Pratt, moving to Arizona, honestly thought she was not only out of the ice cream business but relieved of any debt to the Rosenbergs. This lawsuit undoubtedly came as a cold shock. What should she have done to avoid the dispute?

CHAPTER CONCLUSION

A **moment's caution!** That is what enables contracting parties to anticipate and realistically appraise any rights and responsibilities of third parties.

CHAPTER REVIEW

1. A third party beneficiary is an intended beneficiary and may enforce a contract if the parties intended her to benefit from the agreement and if either (1) enforcing the promise will satisfy a debt of the promisee to the beneficiary, or (2) the promisee intended to make a gift to the beneficiary. The intended beneficiary described in (1) is a *creditor beneficiary,* while (2) describes a *donee beneficiary*. Any beneficiary who meets neither description is an *incidental beneficiary* and has no right to enforce the contract.
2. An *assignment* transfers the assignor's contract rights to the assignee. A *delegation* transfers the delegator's duties to the delegatee.
3. A party generally may assign contract rights unless doing so would substantially change the obligor's rights or duties; is forbidden by law; or is validly precluded by the contract.
4. Once the assignment is made and the obligor notified, the assignee may enforce her contractual rights against the obligor. The obligor, in turn, may generally raise all defenses against the assignee that she could have raised against the assignor.

5. Under the UCC, the assignee may generally enforce a waiver that prohibits the obligor from raising defenses. This is not true, however, in most consumer contracts.

6. Duties are delegable unless delegation would violate public policy; the contract prohibits delegation; or the obligee has a substantial interest in personal performance by the obligor.

7. Unless the obligee agrees otherwise, delegation does not discharge the delegator's duty to perform.

8. A *novation* is a three-way agreement in which the obligor delegates all duties to the delegatee and the obligee agrees to hold only the delegatee responsible.

PRACTICE TEST

1. Intercontinental Metals Corp. (IMC) contracted with the accounting firm of Cherry, Bekaert & Holland to perform an audit. Cherry issued its opinion about IMC, giving all copies of its report directly to the company. IMC later permitted Dun & Bradstreet to examine the statements, and Raritan River Steel Co. saw a report published by Dun & Bradstreet. Relying on the audit, Raritan sold IMC $2.2 million worth of steel on credit, but IMC promptly went bankrupt. Raritan sued Cherry, claiming that IMC was not as sound as Cherry had reported, and that the accounting firm had breached its contract with IMC. Comment on Raritan's suit.

2. Angelo Zavarella and Yvette Rodrigues were injured in an automobile accident allegedly caused by a vehicle belonging to Truck Equipment of Boston. Travelers Insurance Co. paid insurance benefits to Zavarella and Rodrigues, who then assigned to Travelers their claims against Truck Equipment. Travelers sued Truck Equipment, which moved to dismiss. What is Truck Equipment's claim that the case should be dismissed, and how would you rule?

3. **CPA QUESTION** Yost contracted with Egan for Yost to buy certain real property. If the contract is otherwise silent, Yost's rights under the contract are:

(a) Assignable only with Egan's consent

(b) Nonassignable because they are personal to Yost

(c) Nonassignable as a matter of law

(d) Generally assignable

4. Woodson Walker and Associates leased computer equipment from Park Ryan Leasing. The lease said nothing about assignment. Park Ryan then assigned the lease to TCB as security for a loan. Park Ryan defaulted on its loan, and Walker failed to make several payments on the lease. TCB sued Walker for the lease payments. Please rule on two issues:

(a) Was the assignment valid, given the fact that the original lease made no mention of it?

(b) If the assignment was valid, may Walker raise defenses against TCB that it could have raised against Park Ryan?

5. Nationwide Discount Furniture hired Rampart Security to install an alarm in its warehouse. A fire would set off an alarm in Rampart's office, and the security company was then supposed to notify Nationwide immediately. A fire did break out, but Rampart allegedly failed to notify Nationwide, causing the fire to spread next door and damage a building owned by Gasket Materials Corp. Gasket sued Rampart for breach of contract, and Rampart moved for summary judgment. Comment.

6. C. Gaston Whiddon owned Gaston's LP Gas Co., Inc. Curtis Dufour purchased the company. Since Whiddon had personally operated the company for many years, Dufour was worried about competition from him and insisted on a noncompetition clause in the sales contract. The clause stated that Whiddon would not "compete with Gaston's LP Gas Co. anywhere south of Interstate Highway 20 for nine years." Three years later, the Herring Gas Co. offered to buy all of Dufour's gas business, assuming that Whiddon would not be a competitor for six more years. Dufour sold all of the assets to Herring, keeping the actual corporation "Gaston's LP Gas Co." for himself. What mistake in drafting have Dufour and Herring made?

7. **CPA QUESTION** One of the criteria for a valid assignment of a sales contract to a third party is that the assignment must:

(a) Not materially increase the other party's risk or duty

(b) Not be revocable by the assignor

(c) Be supported by adequate consideration from the assignee

(d) Be in writing and signed by the assignor

8. **RIGHT & WRONG** A century and a half ago an English judge stated: "All painters do not paint portraits like Sir Joshua Reynolds, nor landscapes like Claude Lorraine, nor do all writers write dramas like Shakespeare or fiction like Dickens. Rare genius and extraordinary skill are not transferable." What legal doctrine is the judge describing? What is the ethical basis of this rule?

9. Pizza of Gaithersburg, Maryland, owned five pizza shops. Pizza arranged with Virginia Coffee Service to install soft drink machines in each of its stores and maintain them. The contract made no mention of the rights of either party to delegate. Virginia Coffee delegated its duties to the Macke Co., leading to litigation between Pizza and Macke. Pizza claimed that Virginia Coffee was barred from delegating because Pizza had a close working relationship with the president of Virginia Coffee, who personally kept the machines in working order. Was the delegation legal?

10. **YOU BE THE JUDGE WRITING PROBLEM** David Ricupero suspected his wife Polly of having an affair, so he taped her phone conversations and, based on what he heard, sued for divorce. David's lawyer, William Wuliger, had the recorded conversations transcribed for use at trial. The parties settled the divorce out of court and signed an agreement that included this clause:

> Except as herein otherwise provided, each party hereto completely and forever releases the other and his attorneys from any and all rights each has or may have . . . to any property, privileges, or benefits accruing to either by virtue of their marriage, or conferred by the Statutory or Common Law of Ohio or the United States of America.

After the divorce was final, Polly sued William Wuliger for invasion of privacy and violation of federal wiretapping law. Wuliger moved to dismiss the case based on the clause quoted. Polly argued that Wuliger was not a party to the divorce settlement and had no right to enforce it. May Wuliger enforce the waiver clause from the Ricuperos' divorce settlement? **Argument for Wuliger:** The contract language demonstrates that the parties intended to release one another and their attorneys from any claims. That makes Wuliger an intended third party beneficiary, and he is entitled to enforce the agreement. If Polly did not want to release Wuliger from such claims, she was free not to sign the agreement. **Argument for Polly Ricupero**: A divorce agreement settles the affairs between the couple. That is all it is ever intended to do, and the parties here never intended to benefit a lawyer. Wuliger is only an incidental beneficiary and cannot use this contract to paper over his violation of federal wiretapping law.

11. Judith and John Brooks hired Wayne Hayes to build a house. The contract required Hayes to "provide all necessary labor and materials and perform all work of every nature whatsoever to be done in the erection of the residence." Hayes hired subcontractors to do all of the work. One of Hayes's employees checked on the work site daily, but neither Hayes nor any of his employees actively supervised the building. The Brookses were aware of this working arrangement and consented to it. The mason negligently installed the fireplace, ultimately leading to a serious fire. The Brookses sued Hayes for breach of contract. Hayes contended that when the Brookses approved of his hiring of subcontractors to do all work, that created a novation, relieving him of any liability. Discuss.

INTERNET RESEARCH PROBLEM

Go to http://www.kinseylaw.com/freestuff/leaseten/ResLease.html. Read clause 5(b) of the lease. What does the clause mean, in English? Do leases commonly include such clauses? Suppose you intend to rent an apartment next year, live there during the school year, and then sublet over the summer. What legal issue will probably arise concerning a sublet?

You can find further practice problems in the Online Quiz at http://beatty.westbuslaw.com or in the Study Guide that accompanies this text.

CHAPTER 17

PERFORMANCE AND DISCHARGE

Polly was elated. It was the grand opening of her new restaurant, Polly's Folly, and everything was bubbling. The wait staff hustled and Caesar, the chef, churned out succulent dishes. Polly had signed a contract promising him $1,000 per week for one year, "provided Polly is personally satisfied with his cooking." Polly was determined that her Folly would be a glorious one. Her three-year lease would cost $6,000 per month, and she had signed an advertising deal with Billboard Bonanza for the same period. Polly had also promised Eddie, a publicity agent, a substantial monthly fee, to begin as soon as the restaurant was 80 percent booked for one month. Tonight, with candles flickering at packed tables, Polly beamed.

After a week, Polly's smiles were a bit forced. Some of Caesar's new dishes had been failures, including a grilled swordfish that was hard to pierce and shrimp jambalaya that was too spicy for the owner. The restaurant was only 60 percent full, and the publicity agent yelled at Caesar for costing him money, though the chef pointed out that most of his dishes were very popular. Later that month, Polly disliked a veal dish and gagged on one of Caesar's soups. She fired her chef.

Then troubles gushed forth—literally. A water main burst in front of Polly's restaurant, flooding the street. The city embarked on a two-month repair job that ultimately took four times that long. The street

was closed to traffic, and no one could park within blocks of the Folly. For several months Polly bravely served food, but patronage dropped steadily, as hungry customers refused to deal with the bad parking and construction noise. Finally, behind on the rent and in debt to everyone, Polly closed her doors for good.

DISCHARGE

Grimly, the court doors swung open, offering a full menu of litigation. Polly's landlord sued for three years' rent, and Billboard Bonanza demanded its money for the same period. Caesar claimed his year's pay. Eddie, the agent, insisted on some money for his hard work.

Polly defended vigorously, seeking to be *discharged* from her various contracts. **A party is discharged when she has no more duties under a contract**. In each lawsuit, Polly asked a court to declare that her obligations were terminated and that she owed no money.

Most contracts are discharged by full performance. In other words, the parties generally do what they promise. Suppose, before the restaurant opened, Walter had promised to deliver 100 sets of cutlery to Polly and she had promised to pay $20 per set. Walter delivered the goods on time, and Polly paid on delivery. The parties got what they expected, and that contract was fully discharged.

Sometimes the parties discharge a contract by agreement. For example, the parties may agree to **rescind** their contract, meaning that they terminate it by mutual agreement.[1] If Polly's landlord believed he could get more rent from a new tenant, he might agree to rescind her lease. But he was dubious about the rental market and refused to rescind.

DEFENSES THAT DISCHARGE

At times a court may discharge a party who has not performed. When things have gone amiss, a judge must interpret the contract and issues of public policy to determine who in fairness should suffer the loss. In the lawsuits brought by the landlord and Billboard Bonanza, Polly argued a defense called "commercial impracticability," claiming that she should not be forced to rent space that was useless to her or buy advertising for a restaurant that had closed. From Polly's point of view, the claim was understandable. But we can also respect the arguments made by the landlord and the advertiser, that they did not cause the burst water main. Claims of commercial impracticability are difficult to win, and Polly lost against both of these opponents. Though she was making no money at all from the restaurant, the court found her liable in full for the lease and the advertising contract.[2]

Polly's argument against Caesar raised another issue of discharge. Caesar claimed that his cooking was good professional work and that all chefs have occasional snafus, especially in a new restaurant. But Polly responded that they had a "personal satisfaction" contract. Under such contracts, "good" work may not suf-

---

[1] The parties could also decide that one party's duties will be performed by someone else, a modification called a **novation**. Or they could create an **accord and satisfaction**, in which they agree that one party will substitute a new kind of performance in place of his contract obligations. See Chapter 16, on third parties, and Chapter 12, on consideration.

[2] Based on *Luminous Neon v. Parscale*, 17 Kan. App. 2d 241, 836 P.2d 1201, 1992 Kan. App. LEXIS 572 (Kan. Ct. App. 1992).

fice if it fails to please the promisee. Polly won this argument, and Caesar recovered nothing.

As to Eddie's suit, Polly raised a defense called "condition precedent," meaning that some event had to occur before she was obligated to pay. Polly claimed that she owed Eddie money only if and when the restaurant was 80 percent full, and that had never happened. The court agreed and discharged Polly on Eddie's claim.

We will analyze each of these issues, and begin with a look at conditions.

CONDITIONS

Parties often put conditions in a contract. **A condition is an event that must occur before a party becomes obligated under a contract.** Polly agreed to pay Eddie, the agent, a percentage of her profits, but with an important condition: 80 percent of the tables had to be booked for a month. Unless and until those tables were occupied, Polly owed Eddie nothing. That never happened, or, in contract language, the *condition failed*, and so Polly was discharged.

Conditions can take many forms. Alex would like to buy Kevin's empty lot and build a movie theater on it, but the city's zoning law will not permit such a business in that location. Alex signs a contract to buy Kevin's empty lot in 120 days, *provided that* within 100 days the city re-zones the area to permit a movie theater. If the city fails to re-zone the area by day 100, Alex is discharged and need not complete the deal. As another example, Friendly Insurance issues a policy covering Vivian's house, promising to pay for any loss due to fire, but only if Vivian furnishes proof of her damages within 60 days of the damage. If the house burns down, Friendly becomes liable to pay. But if Vivian arrives with the proof 70 days after the fire, she collects nothing. Friendly, though it briefly had a duty to pay, was discharged when Vivian failed to furnish the necessary information on time. For an example of a common conditional clause, see **http://www.hud.org/jkhud/jklbp2.htm**. The clause is designed to protect a purchaser of property who is concerned that the real estate may be contaminated with lead paint.

HOW CONDITIONS ARE CREATED

Express Conditions

The parties may expressly state a condition. Alex's contract with Kevin expressly discharged all obligations if the city failed to re-zone within the stated period. Notice that **no special language is necessary to create the condition**. Phrases such as "provided that" frequently indicate a condition, but neither those nor any other words are essential. As long as the parties *intended* to create a condition, a court will enforce it.

Because informal language can create a condition, the parties may dispute whether they intended one or not. Sand Creek Country Club, in Indiana, was eager to expand its clubhouse facilities and awarded the design work to CSO Architects. The club wanted the work done quickly but had not secured financing. The architects sent a letter confirming their agreement:

> It was our intent to allow Mr. Dan Moriarty of our office to start work on your project as early as possible in order to allow you to meet the goals that you have set for next fall. Also, it was the intent of CSO to begin work on your project and delay any billings to you until your financing is in place. As I explained to you earlier, we will continue on this course until we reach a point where we can no longer continue without receiving some payment.

The club gave CSO the go-ahead to begin design work, and the architects did their work and billed Sand Creek for $33,000. But the club, unable to obtain financing, refused to pay. Sand Creek claimed that CSO's letter created a *condition* in their agreement, namely, that the club would have to pay only if and when it obtained financing. The court was unpersuaded and ruled that the parties had never intended to create an express condition. The architects were merely delaying their billing as a convenience to the club. It would be absurd, said the court, to assume that CSO intended to perform $33,000 worth of work for free.[3]

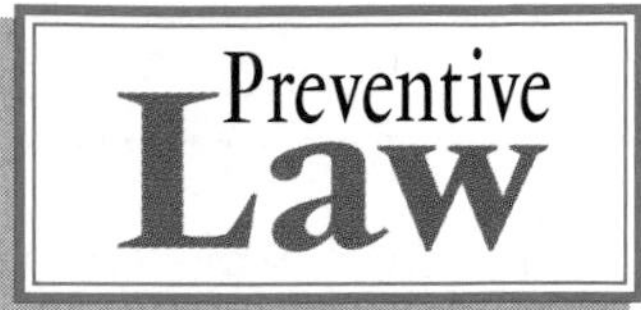

The Sand Creek case demonstrates the need for clarity in business dealings. The architect's letter should have emphasized that Sand Creek was obligated to pay the full amount, for example by saying: "CSO agrees to delay billing for a reasonable period but the Club remains liable for the full amount of the contract, whether or not it obtains financing." A one-sentence ambiguity meant that the firm could not obtain its money without a lawsuit and an appeal.

Implied Conditions

At other times, the parties say nothing about a condition, but it is clear from their agreement that they have implied one. Charlotte orally rents an apartment to Hakan for one year and promises to fix any problems in the unit. It is an implied condition that Hakan will promptly notify Charlotte of anything needing repair. Although the parties have not said anything about notice, it is only common sense that Hakan must inform his landlord of defects since she will have no other way to learn of them.

Conditions in the Outfield. Boston's baseball team, the Red Sox, signed Darren Lewis to play center field, a key position. The club considered him a fine defensive player but a dubious offensive performer, and the many conditional clauses in his contract reflected hard bargaining over a questionable athlete. The Red Sox guaranteed Lewis $500,000, a modest salary by today's standards. If the speedy outfielder appeared in 110 games (out of 162 total), his pay would increase to $900,000, and if he played in 120 games, he would earn $1 million. Further conditions related to a "Gold Glove" award, which coaches and managers throughout the league award annually to the top defensive performers at each position. If Lewis received even one vote for a Gold Glove, he would earn an extra $100,000, and an additional $100,000 if he won the award. Need more? The Red Sox had an option to re-sign Lewis for the following season for $800,000 (he had no say in the matter), but if the center-fielder played in 100 games, the team would lose that right, leaving Lewis free to negotiate for higher pay with other teams.

TYPES OF CONDITIONS

Courts divide conditional clauses into three categories: (1) condition precedent, (2) condition subsequent, and (3) concurrent conditions.[4] But what they have in common is more important than any of their differences. The key to all conditional

[3] *Sand Creek Country Club, Ltd. v. CSO Architects, Inc.*, 582 N.E.2d 872, 1991 Ind. App. LEXIS 2151 (Ind. Ct. App. 1991).

[4] The Restatement (Second) of Contracts has officially abandoned the terms "condition precedent" and "condition subsequent." See Restatement §§224 et seq. But courts routinely use the terms, so it is difficult to avoid the old distinctions.

clauses is this: **if the condition does not occur, one party will probably be discharged without performing.**

Condition Precedent

In this kind of condition, an event *must occur before* a duty arises. Polly's contract with Eddie concerned a condition precedent. Polly had no obligation to pay Eddie anything *unless and until* the restaurant was 80 percent full for a month. Since that never happened, she was discharged.

Condition Subsequent

The only difference here is that the condition must occur *after* the particular duty arises. If the condition does not occur, the duty is discharged. Vivian's policy with Friendly Insurance contains a condition subsequent. As soon as the fire broke out, Friendly became obligated to pay for the damage. But if Vivian failed to produce her proof of loss on time, Friendly's obligation was discharged.

Precedent/Subsequent Distinction—Who Cares?

The difference between condition precedent and condition subsequent is important for one reason: it tells us *who must prove* whether the condition occurred. If the parties agreed to a condition precedent, the plaintiff has the burden to prove that the condition happened, and hence that the defendant was obligated to perform. But with a condition subsequent, it is normally the defendant who must prove

Condition Precedent and Condition Subsequent Compared

	Condition Created	Does Condition Occur?	Duty Is Determined	Result
Condition Precedent	"Fee to be paid when restaurant is filled to 80% capacity for one month."	Condition DOES occur: restaurant is packed.	Duty arises: Polly owes Eddie his fee.	Polly pays the fee.
		Condition DOES NOT occur: restaurant is empty.	Duty never arises: Polly is discharged.	Polly pays nothing.

	Condition Created	Duty Is Determined	Does Condition Occur?	Result
Condition Subsequent	"Vivian must give proof of loss within 60 days."	Fire damages property, and Friendly Insurance becomes obligated to pay Vivian.	Condition DOES occur: Vivian proves her losses within 60 days.	Friendly pays Vivian for her losses.
			Condition DOES NOT occur: Vivian fails to prove her losses within 60 days.	Friendly is discharged and owes nothing.

that the condition occurred, relieving him of any obligation. Invariably, the distinction arises in insurance cases. Whether the insured customer or the insurance company must prove the condition often determines who wins the case.

ARKANSAS FARM BUREAU INS. FEDERATION v. RYMAN
309 Ark. 283, 831 S.W.2d 133, 1992 Ark. LEXIS 300
Supreme Court of Arkansas, 1992

So unfair so not enforced

Facts: Granville Ryman was killed in an auto accident. His insurance policy with Farm Bureau Mutual stated:

> The Company will pay for accidental death of a person insured under this policy. However, at the time of the accident, the person insured must be wearing a factory installed seat belt or lap and shoulder restraint, verifiable by the investigating officer.

When the investigating police officer arrived at the scene of Ryman's accident, paramedics were already transferring him to an ambulance. The officer could not determine whether Ryman had been wearing a seat belt, and the paramedics did not recall.

Farm Bureau refused to pay, claiming that the seat belt requirement was a condition precedent to its coverage and that Ms. Ryman had the burden of proving her husband *had been wearing a belt* when killed, a burden she failed to meet. Ms. Ryman argued that the clause was a condition subsequent. She claimed that when Granville Ryman died, Farm Bureau became obligated to pay benefits unless *the insurance company* could prove he was *not* wearing a belt.

Issue: Was the seat belt requirement a condition precedent, which Ms. Ryman must prove, or a condition subsequent, which the insurance company must demonstrate?

Excerpts from Judge Holt's Decision: The parties are correct in their respective arguments that the existence of a condition precedent places the burden of proof on the insured, while the insurer has the burden of proving an exclusion [in other words, a condition subsequent]. We agree with Mrs. Ryman, however, that the provision here involved an exclusion [and that the burden is on the company to prove he was *not* wearing a seat belt].

A similarly worded provision was involved in *Life and Casualty Ins. Co. of Tennessee v. Barefield*. There, the insured lost an eye when a stick was thrown toward the insured's car by another passing vehicle. The parties were bound by an insurance policy which covered bodily injuries caused by accidents from motor vehicles "provided that…there shall be some external or visible evidence on said vehicle of the collision or accident." This court construed the provision to be in the nature of an exclusion, thereby placing the burden on the insurer to show [no] such external damage to the insured's car. Likewise, the limiting language under the general coverage provision in this case could be construed as an exclusion.

We thus hold the requirement that the insured be wearing a seat belt at the time of the accident, such fact to be verified by the investigating officer, to constitute an exclusion under the policy, rather than a condition precedent, thereby placing the burden on the insurer to prove Mr. Ryman fell within such an exclusion. Since the insurer was unable to do so, we uphold the trial court's granting of summary judgment in Mrs. Ryman's favor.

Affirmed.

Concurrent Conditions

Here, both parties have a duty to perform *simultaneously*. Renee agrees to sell her condominium to Tim on July 5. Renee agrees to furnish a valid deed and clear title to the property on that date, and Tim promises to present a cashier's check for

$600,000. The parties have agreed to concurrent conditions. Each performance is the condition for the other's performance. If Renee arrives at the Registry of Deeds and can only say, "I'm pretty darn sure I own that property," Tim need not present his check; similarly, if Tim arrives only with an "IOU" scribbled on the back of a candy wrapper, Renee has no duty to hand over a valid deed.

Public Policy

At times a court will refuse to enforce an express condition on the grounds that it is unfair and harmful to the general public. In other words, a court might agree that the parties created a conditional clause but conclude that permitting its enforcement would hurt society. Did the insurance contract in the following case harm society? You be the judge.

ANDERSON v. COUNTRY LIFE INS. CO.

180 Ariz. 625, 886 P.2d 1381, 1994 Ariz. App. LEXIS 240
Arizona Court of Appeals, 1994

Facts: On November 26, a Country Life Insurance agent went to the house of Donald and Anna Mae Anderson. He persuaded the Andersons to buy a life insurance policy and accepted a check for $1,600. He gave the Andersons a "conditional receipt for medical policy," dated that day. The form stated that the Andersons would have a valid life insurance policy with Country Life, effective November 26, but only when all conditions were met. The most important of these conditions was that the Country Life home office accept the Andersons as medical risks. The Andersons were pleased with the new policy and glad that it was effective that same day.

It was not. Donald Anderson died of a heart attack a few weeks later. Country Life declined the Andersons as medical risks and refused to issue a policy. Anna Mae Anderson sued. Country Life pointed out that medical approval was a condition precedent. In other words, the company argued that the policy *would* be effective as of November 26, but only if it *later decided* to make the policy effective. Based on this argument, the trial court gave summary judgment for Country Life. Ms. Anderson appealed, claiming that the conditional clause was a violation of public policy.

You Be the Judge: Did the conditional clause violate public policy?

Argument for Ms. Anderson: Your honors, this policy is a scam. This so called "conditional receipt for medical policy" is designed to trick customers and then steal their money. The company leads people to believe they are covered as of the day they write the check. But they aren't covered until *much later,* when the insurer gets around to deciding the applicant's medical status.

The company gets the customer's money right away and gives nothing in exchange. If the company, after taking its time, decides the applicant is not medically fit, it returns the money, having used it for weeks or even months to earn interest. If, on the other hand, the insurance company decides the applicant is a good bet, it then issues the policy effective for weeks or months *in the past, when coverage is of no use.* No one can die retroactively, your honors. The company is being paid for a period during which it had no risk.

This is a fraud and a disgrace, and the company should pay the benefits it owes.

Argument for Country Life: Your honors, is Country Life supposed to issue life insurance policies without doing a medical check? That is the road to bankruptcy and would mean that no one could obtain this valuable coverage. Of course we do a medical inquiry, as quickly as possible. It's in our interest to get the policy decided one way or the other.

The policy clearly stated that coverage was effective *only when approved by the home office,* after all inquiries were made. The Andersons knew that as well as the agent. If they were covered immediately, why would the company do a medical check? Country Life resents suggestions that this policy is a scam, when in reality it is Ms. Anderson who is trying to profit from a tragedy that the company had nothing to do with.

The facts of this case are unusual. Obviously, most insureds do not die between application and acceptance. It would be disastrous for society to rewrite every insurance policy in this state based on one very sad fact pattern. The contract was clear and it should be enforced as written.

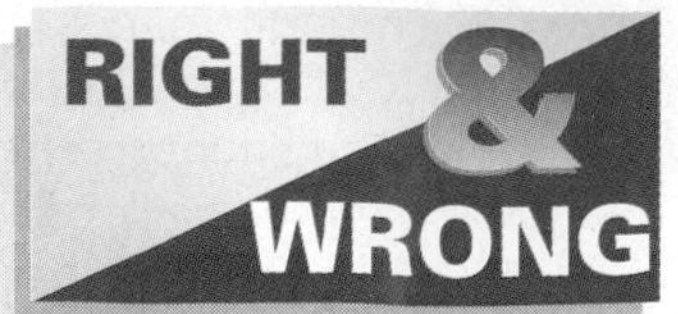

Imagine that you are a young insurance agent, eager to do a good job and advance your career. Your company urges you to sell insurance with "conditional receipts" such as the one used by Country Life. Would you do it?

PERFORMANCE

Caitlin has an architect draw up plans for a monumental new house, and Daniel agrees to build it by September 1. Caitlin promises to pay $900,000 on that date. The house is ready on time but Caitlin has some complaints. The living room was supposed to be 18 feet high but it is only 17 feet; the pool was to be azure yet it is aquamarine; the maid's room was not supposed to be wired for cable television but it is. Caitlin refuses to pay anything for the house. Is she justified? Of course not, it would be absurd to give her a magnificent house for free when it has only tiny defects. And that is how a court would decide the case. But in this easy answer lurks a danger. Technically, Daniel did breach the contract, and yet the law allows him to recover the full contract price, or virtually all of it. Once that principle is established, how far will a court stretch it? Suppose the living room is only 14 feet high, or 12 feet, or 5 feet? What if the foundation has a small crack? A vast and dangerous split? What if Daniel finishes the house a month late? Six months late? Three years late? At some point a court will conclude that Daniel has so thoroughly botched the job that he deserves little or no money. But where is that point? That is a question that businesses—and judges—face everyday.

The more complex a contract, the more certain that at least one party will perform imperfectly. Every house ever built has some defects. A delivery of a thousand bushels of apples is sure to include a few rotten ones. A custom-designed computer system for a huge airline is likely to have some glitches. The cases raise several related doctrines, all concerning how well a party *performed* its contract obligations.

STRICT PERFORMANCE AND SUBSTANTIAL PERFORMANCE

Strict Performance

When Daniel built Caitlin's house with three minor defects, she refused to pay, arguing that he had not *strictly performed* his obligations. She was right, yet she lost anyway. Courts dislike strict performance because it enables one party to benefit without paying, and sends the other one home empty-handed. **A party is generally not required to render strict performance unless the contract expressly demands it *and* such a demand is reasonable**. Caitlin's contract never suggested that Daniel would forfeit all payment if there were minor problems. Even if Caitlin had insisted on such a clause, few courts would have enforced it because the requirement would be unreasonable.

There are cases where strict performance does make sense. Marshall agrees to deliver 500 sweaters to Leo's store, and Leo promises to pay $20,000 cash on delivery. If Leo has only $19,000 cash and a promissory note for $1,000, he has failed to perform, and Marshall need not give him the sweaters. Leo's payment represents 95 percent of what he promised, but there is a big difference between cash and a promissory note.

Substantial Performance

Daniel, the house builder, won his case against Caitlin because he fulfilled most of his obligations, even though he did an imperfect job. Courts often rely on the substantial performance doctrine, especially in cases involving services as opposed to those concerning the sale of goods or land. **In a contract for services, a party that substantially performs its obligations will receive the full contract price, minus the value of any defects.** Daniel receives $900,000, the contract price, minus the value of a ceiling that is one foot too low, a pool the wrong color, and so forth. It will be for the trial court to decide how much those defects are worth. If the court decides the low ceiling is a $10,000 damage, the pool color worth $5,000 and the cable television worth $500, then Daniel receives $884,500.

On the other hand, a party that fails to give substantial performance may get nothing. **A party that fails to perform substantially receives nothing on the contract itself and will only recover the value of the work, if any.** If the foundation cracks in Caitlin's house and the walls collapse, Daniel will not receive his $900,000. In such a case he collects only the market value of the work he has done, which is probably zero.

When is performance substantial? There is no perfect test, but courts look at these issues:

- How much benefit has the promisee received?
- If it is a construction contract, can the owner use the thing for its intended purpose?
- Can the promisee be compensated with money damages for any defects?
- Did the promisor act in good faith?

The following case deals with the first three of these issues.

FOLK v. CENTRAL NATIONAL BANK & TRUST CO.
210 Ill. App. 3d 43, 1991 Ill. App. LEXIS 308
Illinois Court of Appeals, 1991

Facts: Byron Dragway, a dragstrip located in Byron, Illinois, needed work. Byron's insurance company insisted that the dragstrip be equipped with concrete retaining walls. Ronald Leek, Byron's president, decided to use the occasion to make other repairs, including resurfacing the 25-year-old surface. The dragstrip's starting area (the "starting pads") had a concrete surface, while the remainder of the track was asphalt. Leek hired Randy Folk to do all of the work. When Folk finished, Leek refused to pay, claiming that the work was shabby and would need to be entirely redone. Folk sued. The trial court gave judgment for Folk in the amount of $140,000, finding that, although there were problems, he had substantially performed. Byron Dragway appealed.

Issue: **Did Folk substantially perform?**

Excerpts from Justice Woodward's Decision: A contractor is not required to perform perfectly, but rather is held only to the duty of substantial performance in a workmanlike manner. Whether substantial performance has been given will depend upon the relevant facts of each case. However, the burden is on the contractor to prove the elements of substantial performance.

Duane Nichols, president of the UDRA, testified that the association is the largest owners and drivers association in the nation. It sponsors racing events throughout the country, featuring pro stock cars, super-charged funny cars,

If you cannot use the thing for its intended purpose, there is no substantial performance.

dragsters, and exhibition cars, which travel between 180 and 260 miles per hour. Inspecting the new track in fall 1987, Nichols observed that the new concrete [starting] pads were extremely smooth, plus there were significant dips in the concrete surface. Nichols particularly noted a dip where the concrete met the asphalt, an imperfection which would cause cars' tires to spin sideways. He observed several puddles in both asphalt lanes, where the surface dipped. Also, in fall 1987, Nichols attended a local meet held at Byron. Cars were having problems getting down the track, and several of them lost control, with one crashing. Nichols stated that no future UDRA events should be held at the track until the surface was repaired.

As to plaintiff's workmanship, the evidence points convincingly to its poor quality. [One expert] stated the defects of both the concrete starting pads and the asphalt surface were so severe that the total replacement of both was necessary. John Berg of Rockford Blacktop thought that the new asphalt surface would have to be ground off prior to the installation of a new surface.

[Folk did not substantially perform. Judgment *reversed*, in favor of Byron Dragway.]

The one aspect of substantial performance that the *Folk* case did not deal with is the **good faith** of the promisor. We consider this issue in a section soon to follow. Here, just note that even relatively minor defects may prevent a contractor from recovering his money *if he caused the defects in bad faith*. Keith builds a new dance studio for University. The floor is supposed to be cushioned with springs underneath. Keith omits the springs, saving himself money. Even though the new studio is usable, Keith acted in bad faith, since his failure was intentional. He will not receive the contract price and will have to prove what value his work has to University, making his recovery far more dubious.

PERSONAL SATISFACTION CONTRACTS

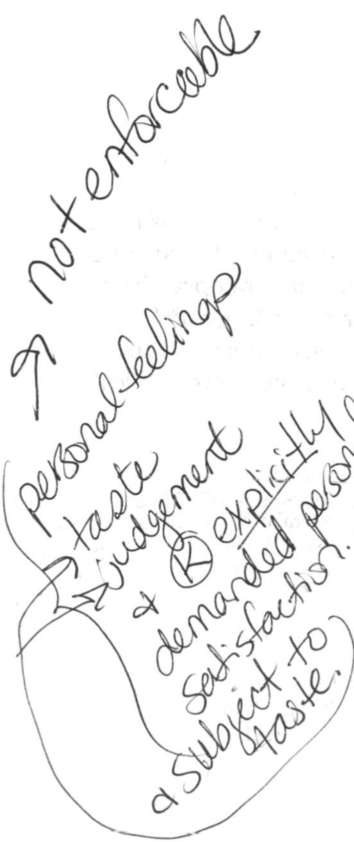

Sujata, president of a public relations firm, hires Ben to design a huge multimedia project for her company, involving computer software, music, and live actors, all designed to sell frozen bologna sandwiches to supermarkets. His contract guarantees him two years' employment, provided all of his work "is acceptable in the sole judgment of Sujata." Ben's immediate supervisor is delighted with his work and his colleagues are impressed—all but Sujata. Three months later she fires him, claiming that his work is "uninspired." Does she have the right to do that?

This is a **personal satisfaction contract, in which the promisee makes a personal, subjective evaluation of the promisor's performance**. Employment contracts may require personal satisfaction of the employer; agreements for the sale of goods may demand that the buyer be personally satisfied with the product; and deals involving a credit analysis of one party may insist that his finances be satisfactory to the other party. In resolving disputes like Ben and Sujata's, judges must decide: When is it fair for the promisee to claim that she is *not* satisfied? May she make that decision for any reason at all, even on a whim?

A court applies a subjective standard only if assessing the work involves personal feelings, taste, or judgment *and* the contract explicitly demanded personal satisfaction. A "subjective standard" means that the promisee's personal views will greatly influence her judgment, even if her decision is foolish and unfair. Artistic or creative work, or highly specialized tasks designed for a particular employer, may involve subtle issues of quality and personal preference. Ben's work combines several media and revolves around his judgment. Accordingly, the law applies a subjective standard to Sujata's decision. Since she concludes that his work is uninspired, she may legally fire him, even if her decision is irrational.

Note that the promisee, Sujata, has to show two things: that assessing Ben's work involves her personal judgment *and* that their contract explicitly demands personal satisfaction. If the contract were vague on this point, Sujata would lose. Had the agreement merely said, "Ben will at all times make his best efforts," Sujata could not fire him.

In all other cases, a court applies an objective standard to the promisee's decision. In other words, the objective standard will be used if assessing the work does not involve personal judgment *or if* the contract failed to explicitly demand personal satisfaction. An objective standard means that the promisee's judgment of the work must be reasonable. Suppose Sujata hires Leila to install an alarm system for her company, and the contract requires that Sujata be "personally satisfied." Leila's system passes all tests but Sujata claims, "It just doesn't make me feel secure. I know that some day it's going to break down." May Sujata refuse to pay? No. Even though the contract used the phrase "personally satisfied," a mechanical alarm system does not involve personal judgment and taste. Either the system works or it does not. A reasonable person would find that Leila's system is just fine and therefore, under the objective standard, Sujata must pay. The law strongly favors the objective standard because the subjective standard gives unlimited power to the promisee.

GOOD FAITH

The parties to a contract must carry out their obligations in good faith. The Restatement (Second) of Contracts §205 states: **"Every contract imposes upon each party a duty of good faith and fair dealing in its performance and its enforcement."** For its part, the UCC establishes a similar requirement for all contracts governed by the Code.[5] The difficulty, of course, is applying this general rule to the infinite problems that may arise when two people, or companies, do business. How far must one side go to meet its good faith burden? The Restatement emphasizes that the parties must remain faithful to the "agreed common purpose and justified expectations of the other party." Two examples should illustrate.

Marvin Shuster was a physician in Florida. Three patients sued him for alleged malpractice. Shuster denied any wrongdoing and asked his insurer to defend the claims. But the insurance company settled all three claims without defending and with a minimum of investigation. Shuster had to pay nothing, but he sued the insurance company claiming that it acted in bad faith. The doctor argued that the company's failure to defend him caused emotional suffering and meant that it would be impossible for him to obtain new malpractice insurance. The Florida Supreme Court found that the insurer acted in good faith. The contract clearly gave all control of malpractice cases to the company. It could settle or defend as it saw fit. Here, the company considered it more economical to settle

[5] UCC §1-203 states: "Every contract or duty within this Act imposes an obligation of good faith in its performance or enforcement." Unfortunately, the Code includes several other references to good faith, and not all are consistent. This has caused confusion and disagreement among the courts. See, e.g., §1-208, dealing with good faith in an acceleration clause, and §2-103(1)(b), defining good faith, as it applies to a merchant dealing in goods, to require not only honesty in fact but also commercial reasonableness. Does this latter definition extend to other Code situations, such as secured transactions? No, some courts have answered, including the Oregon Supreme Court in *United States National Bank of Oregon v. Boge*, 311 Or. 550, 814 P.2d 1082, 1991 Ore. LEXIS 52 (1991), holding that good faith in such cases requires only honesty in fact and nothing more. Because of the variations within the UCC itself, we look at these issues in detail in Chapters 19 and 26, on sales and secured transactions.

quickly, and Shuster should have known, from the contract language, that the insurer might choose to do so.[6]

In the following case, however, the court found bad faith on the part of an insurer.

THOMAS v. PRINCIPAL FINANCIAL GROUP
566 So. 2d 735, 1990 Ala. LEXIS 614
Supreme Court of Alabama, 1990

Facts: Barbara Thomas worked at the University of South Alabama Medical Center, which had a group life insurance policy with Principal Mutual. The policy covered all employees and their dependents, and defined "dependents" to include an unmarried child between 19 and 25 "provided he is attending school on a full-time basis and is dependent upon the [insured parent] for his principal support and maintenance."

Barbara Thomas had a 21-year-old daughter, Melinda Warren. In July 1984, Warren enrolled as a cosmetology student at the Mobile Academy of Hair Design. She paid full tuition and attended full-time until August 1985, when tragically she became disabled by ovarian cancer. The cancer prevented her from attending class and eventually left her entirely bedridden. She died of the disease in March 1987 at the age of 24.

Barbara Thomas filed a life insurance claim with Principal Mutual. But on the advice of its claims official, Ms. Robbins, the insurer refused to pay. Principal Mutual claimed that Warren was not a dependent at the time of her death, since she was not in school. Barbara Thomas sued, claiming not only benefits under the policy but additional damages for the alleged bad faith of Principal Mutual in denying the claim. The jury awarded her $1,000 on the contract claim, and $750,000 for the bad faith claim. The trial judge permitted the $1,000 contract claim to stand. But on the bad faith claim he gave judgment notwithstanding the verdict for the insurance company. Thomas appealed, and Principal Mutual appealed on the award of the $1,000.

Issue: Is Thomas entitled to damages on her contract claim and/or her bad faith claim?

Excerpts from Judge Houston's Decision: The record reveals that at the time she made her initial recommendation to deny Ms. Thomas's claim, Ms. Robbins was aware that the only reason Ms. Warren had stopped attending the Mobile Academy was "because she was sick." Ms. Robbins's notation in the claim file indicates that she knew that Ms. Warren had undergone extensive chemotherapy treatments, had been in the hospital on numerous occasions, and had been completely bedridden for approximately six months immediately preceding her death. However, portions of Ms. Robbins's deposition testimony were admitted at trial. The following is an excerpt from that testimony:

Q. Okay. When did [Principal Mutual] consider that she no longer qualified as being an insured, a dependent? Just give me a date and I will move on to something else.

(No reply)

Q. You can't give me a date?

A. No.

[6] *Shuster v. South Broward Hospital Dist. Physicians' Prof. Liability Ins. Trust*, 591 So. 2d 174, 1992 Fla. LEXIS 20 (Fla. 1992).

Q. But you know that as of the date of her death there was no coverage?

A. Correct.

Q. What's the basis of that opinion?

A. She was not attending school on a full time basis.

Q. If, instead of contracting cancer, she had been involved in an automobile accident through this entire period of time and had been bedridden in a coma, would you have paid the benefits under those circumstances for Melinda Warren?

A. I would have recommended they consider paying the claim.

Q. So, you make a distinction between an automobile accident and an illness?

A. She was—You are saying she was in a coma?

Q. Yes. Bedridden in a coma. You would have recommended—

A. I would have recommended that we consider paying the claim.

Q. Your recommendation would have been just the opposite of what it was?

A. Yes.

Q. Okay. Why do you make a distinction between an illness and an accident?

A. I am not making a distinction between an illness and an accident. She was in a coma.

Q. Which made her physically incapable of attending classes?

A. It would have made her—

Q. All right. Do you think Melinda Warren was physically capable of attending classes?

A. I don't know.

Q. Would that have influenced your decision?

A. If she had been physically capable?

Q. Yes. Physically capable.

A. Yes, it would have had an effect on my decision.

The evidence in this case was such that the jury could have reasonably found: that at least two of the examiners who reviewed Ms. Thomas's claim, Ms. Robbins and [her supervisor] exhibited confusion as to exactly what circumstances would warrant payment within the context of this case; and that throughout the claims review process, Principal Mutual's examiners either intentionally or recklessly failed to subject the results of the investigation to a cognitive evaluation and review.

For the foregoing reasons, we hold that the trial court erred in entering a judgment notwithstanding the verdict for Principal Mutual on the bad faith claim.

[The court affirmed the judgment for the $1,000 contract claim and reversed the trial court on the bad faith claim, thus reinstating the jury's verdict of $750,000. However, the judges also sent the case back to the trial court to consider the company's argument that $750,000 was excessive. On remand, the trial court determined that the punitive damage award was not excessive, and on appeal of *that* issue the Alabama Supreme Court affirmed. Ms. Thomas finally received $751,000.]

The 1996 Olympic Games in Atlanta were the most widely attended of the century, but many merchants wished they had stayed home. The city rented spaces on public property for street vendors to sell T-shirts, ice cream, and similar goods. A letter from the city proclaimed that Atlanta would "showcase exclusive vendors" to a "captive global audience." Eager merchants paid $10,000 and up for a space. But many arrived in Atlanta to find other vendors in their spaces. No one enjoyed much "exclusivity," as thousands of competing sellers set up stands on *private* property for a fraction of the fee that Atlanta charged for its public space.

Linda Dial hoped to sell water-absorbent headbands to hot sports fans. She spent $30,000 on two spaces, and $100,000 on inventory, only to discover that her spaces were on deserted streets, which the police had barricaded for safety reasons. After days of desperate calls to City Hall, she finally received new space—directly in front of other vendors, who responded furiously by tossing her goods into the gutter. Dial ultimately sold $750 worth of headbands. Collins Phillips, having lost his job as a Louisiana firefighter because of a back injury, journeyed to Atlanta to restore his family finances. Phillips paid $10,000 for an "exclusive" space where he could sell "New Orleans Jazzy Sno-Balls, " and another $15,000 for a vending wagon and merchandise. During 17 sweltering August days, Phillips sold 30 Sno-Balls in a nearly vacant area. Dozens of angry merchants have filed two class action lawsuits against the city, seeking $20 million for breach of contract, bad faith, and fraud. The city has denied wrongdoing, saying that police were obligated to re-route traffic due to the extraordinary crowds, and that it had no legal power to stop private vendors from competing with those it had licensed.

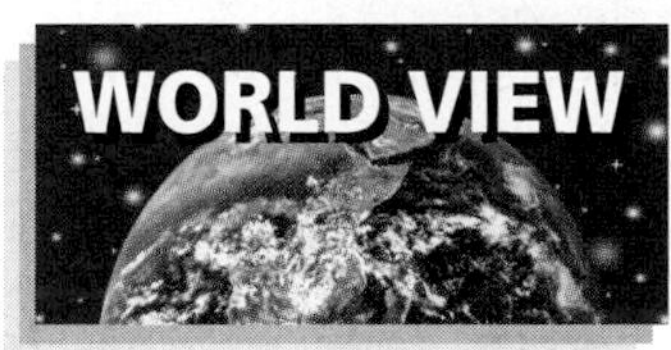

Under recent changes in Italian law, a party may be liable for bad faith in *negotiating* an agreement, as well as in performing. Suppose your business enters into contract talks with an Italian firm and then abruptly ends the discussions. If an Italian court concludes that you showed bad faith in terminating the negotiations, it can assess damages. The Italian company may recover for its lost opportunity, if it can show that the futile discussions prevented it from profiting elsewhere. This Italian version of bad faith is similar to the American concept of tortious interference with a prospective advantage, discussed in Chapter 5. For an analysis of the Italian contract principles, see **http://www.gelso.unitn.it/card-adm/Review/Business/Newsletter/Precontr.html.**

TIME OF THE ESSENCE CLAUSES

> Go, sir, gallop, and don't forget that the world was made in six days. You can ask me for anything you like, except time.
>
> *Napoleon*, to an aide, 1803

Generals are not the only ones who place a premium on time. Ask Gene LaSalle. The Seabreeze Restaurant agreed to sell him all of its assets. The parties signed a contract stating the price and closing date. Seabreeze insisted on a clause saying, "Seabreeze considers that time is of the essence in consummating the proposed transaction." Such clauses are common in real estate transactions and in any other agreement where a delay would cause serious damage to one party. LaSalle was unable to close on the date specified and asked for an extension. Seabreeze refused and sold its assets elsewhere. A Florida court affirmed that Seabreeze acted legally.

A time of the essence clause will generally make contract dates strictly enforceable. Seabreeze regarded a timely sale as important, and LaSalle agreed to the provision. There was nothing unreasonable about the clause, and LaSalle suffered the consequences of his delay.[7]

Suppose the contract had named a closing date but included no time of the essence clause. If LaSalle offered to close three days late, could Seabreeze sell elsewhere? No. **Merely including a date for performance does not make time of the essence**. Courts dislike time of the essence arguments because even a short delay may mean that one party forfeits everything it expected to gain from the bargain. If the parties do not clearly state that prompt performance is essential, then both are entitled to reasonable delays.

BREACH

When one party breaches a contract, the other party is discharged. The discharged party has no obligation to perform and may sue for damages. Edwin promises that on July 1 he will deliver 20 tuxedos, tailored to fit male chimpanzees, to Bubba's circus for $300 per suit. After weeks of delay Edwin concedes he hasn't a cummerbund to his name. Bubba is discharged and obviously owes nothing. In addition, he may sue Edwin for damages. If Bubba is forced to pay $350 elsewhere to obtain similar tuxedos, he will recover the difference in cost. Twenty tuxedos, at $50 extra per suit, means that Bubba will get $1,000 from Edwin.

MATERIAL BREACH

As we know, parties frequently perform their contract duties imperfectly, which is why courts accept substantial performance rather than strict performance, particularly in contracts involving services. In a more general sense, **courts will only discharge a contract if a party committed a *material* breach**. A material breach is one that substantially harms the innocent party and for which it would be hard to compensate without discharging the contract. Suppose Edwin fails to show up with the tuxedos on June 1, but calls to say they will arrive under the big top the next day. He has breached the agreement. Is his breach material? No. This is a trivial breach, and Bubba is not discharged. When the tuxedos arrive, he must pay.

ANTICIPATORY BREACH

Sally will receive her bachelor's degree in May and already has a job lined up for September, a two-year contract as window display designer for Surebet Department Store. The morning of graduation she reads in the paper that Surebet is going out of business that very day. Surebet has told Sally nothing about her status. Sally need not wait until September to learn her fate. Surebet has committed an **anticipatory breach by making it unmistakably clear that it will not honor the contract**. Sometimes a promisor will actually inform the promisee that it will not perform its duties. At other times, as here, the promisor takes some step that makes the breach evident. Sally is discharged and may immediately seek other work. She is also entitled to file suit for breach of contract. The court will treat Surebet's anticipatory breach just as though the store had actually refused to perform on September 1.

---

[7] *Seabreeze Restaurant, Inc. v. Paumgardhen*, 639 So. 2d 69, 1994 Fla. App. LEXIS 4546 (Fla. Dist. Ct. App. 1994).

STATUTE OF LIMITATIONS

A party injured by a breach of contract should act promptly. **A statute of limitations begins to run at the time of injury and will limit the time within which the injured party may file suit.** Statutes of limitation vary from state to state and even from issue to issue within a state. In some states, for example, an injured party must sue on oral contracts within three years, on a sale of goods contract within four years, and on some written contracts within five years. Failure to file suit within the time-limits discharges the party who breached the contract. Always consult a lawyer *promptly* in the case of a legal injury. We have seen the overlap of tort and contract in cases such as fraud, and statutes of limitations for tort are generally shorter than for contract. Further, some related areas of law, such as employment discrimination, have statutes of limitation that are numbered in days, not years. Do not wait, mate. For the British view of time of the essence clauses, material and anticipatory breach, and other issues of contract performance, see **http://online.anu.edu.au/law/pub/edinst/anu/contract/Seriousbreachitsvariousmeanings.html**.

IMPOSSIBILITY

"Your honor, my client *wanted* to honor the contract. He just couldn't. *Honest*." This plea often echoes around courtrooms, as one party seeks discharge without fulfilling his contract obligations. Does the argument work? It depends. If performing a contract was truly impossible, a court will discharge the agreement. But if honoring the deal merely imposed a financial burden, the law will generally enforce the contract.

TRUE IMPOSSIBILITY

These cases are easy—and rare. **True impossibility means that something has happened making it utterly impossible to do what the promisor said he would do**. Francoise owns a vineyard that produces Beaujolais Nouveau wine. She agrees to ship 1,000 cases of her wine to Tyrone, a New York importer, as soon as this year's vintage is ready. Tyrone will pay $50 per case. But a fungus wipes out her entire vineyard. Francoise is discharged. It is theoretically impossible for Francoise to deliver wine from her vineyard, and she owes Tyrone nothing.

Meanwhile, though, Tyrone has a contract with Jackson, a retailer, to sell 1,000 cases of any Beaujolais Nouveau wine at $70 per case. Tyrone has no wine from Francoise, and the only other Beaujolais Nouveau available will cost him $85 per case. Instead of making $20 per case, Tyrone will lose $15. Does this discharge Tyrone's contract with Jackson? No. It is possible for him to perform, just undesirable. He must fulfill his agreement.

True impossibility is generally limited to these three causes:

- *Destruction of the Subject Matter*, as happened with Francoise's vineyard.
- *Death of the Promisor in a Personal Services Contract*. When the promisor agrees personally to render a service that cannot be transferred to someone else, her death discharges the contract. Producer hires Josephine to write the lyrics for a new Broadway musical, but Josephine dies after writing only two words: "Act One." The contract was personal to Josephine and is now discharged. Neither Josephine's estate nor Producer has any obligation to the other. But notice that most contracts are *not* for personal services. Suppose that Tyrone, the wine importer, drowns in a bathtub filled with cheap gin. His contract to

sell wine to Jackson is *not* discharged, because anyone can deliver the required wine. Tyrone's estate remains liable on the deal with Jackson.

- *Illegality.* If the purpose of a contract becomes illegal, that change discharges the contract. Kitty hires Kato to work in her new Keno Klub (a club with electronic gambling games), but a month later the state legislature KO's keno, declaring that "Keno Korrupts." Kitty's contract is discharged.

COMMERCIAL IMPRACTICABILITY AND FRUSTRATION OF PURPOSE

It is rare for contract performance to be truly impossible, but common for it to become a financial burden to one party. Suppose Bradshaw Steel in Pittsburgh agrees to deliver 1,000 tons of steel beams to Rice Construction in Saudi Arabia at a given price, but a week later the cost of raw ore increases 30 percent. A contract once lucrative to the manufacturer is suddenly a major liability. Does that change discharge Bradshaw? Absolutely not. Rice signed the deal *precisely to protect itself against price increases*. As we have seen, the primary purpose of contracts is to enable the parties to control their future.

Yet there may be times when a change in circumstances is so extreme that it would be unfair to enforce a deal. What if a strike made it impossible for Bradshaw to ship the steel to Saudi Arabia, and the only way to deliver would be by air, at five times the sea cost? Must Bradshaw fulfill its deal? What if war in the Middle East meant that any ships or planes delivering the goods might be fired upon? Other changes could make the contract undesirable for *Rice*. Suppose the builder wanted steel for a major public building in Riyadh, but the Saudi government decided not to go forward with the construction. The steel would then be worthless to Rice. Must the company still accept it?

None of these hypotheticals involves true impossibility. It is physically possible for Bradshaw to deliver the goods and for Rice to receive. But in some cases it may be so dangerous or costly or pointless to enforce a bargain that a court will discharge it instead. Courts use the related doctrines of commercial impracticability and frustration of purpose to decide when a change in circumstances should permit one side to escape its duties.

Commercial impracticability means some event has occurred that neither party anticipated and *fulfilling the contract would now be extraordinarily difficult and unfair to one party*. If a shipping strike forces Bradshaw to ship by air, the company will argue that neither side expected the strike and that Bradshaw should not suffer a fivefold increase in shipping cost. Bradshaw will probably win the argument.

Frustration of purpose means some event has occurred that neither party anticipated and *the contract now has no value for one party*. If Rice's building project is canceled, Rice will argue that the steel now is useless to the company. Frustration cases are hard to predict. Some states would agree with Rice, but others would hold that it was Rice's obligation to protect itself with a government guarantee that the project would be completed. Courts consider the following factors in deciding impracticability and frustration claims:

- *Mere financial difficulties will never suffice to discharge a contract.* Barbara and Michael Luber divorced, and Michael agreed to pay alimony. He stopped making payments and claimed that it was impracticable for him to do so, because he had hit hard times and simply did not have the money. The court dismissed his argument, noting that commercial impracticability requires some *objective event* that neither party anticipated, not merely the financial deterioration of one party.[8]

[8] *Luber v. Luber*, 418 Pa. Super. 542, 614 A.2d 771, 1992 Pa. Super. LEXIS 3338 (Pa. Super. Ct. 1992).

- *The event must have been truly unexpected.* Wayne Carpenter bought land from the state of Alaska, intending to farm it and agreeing to make monthly payments. The sales contract stated that Alaska did not guarantee the land for agriculture or any other purpose. Carpenter struggled to farm the land but failed; as soon as the ground thawed, the water table rose too high for crops. Carpenter abandoned the land and stopped making payments. Alaska sued and won. The high court rejected Carpenter's claim of impracticability since the "event"—bad soil—was not unexpected. Alaska had warned that the land might prove unworkable, and Carpenter had no claim for commercial impracticability.[9]
- *If the promisor must use a different means to accomplish her task, at a greatly increased cost, she probably* does *have a valid claim of impracticability.* If a shipping strike forces Bradshaw to use a different means of delivery—say, air—and this multiplies its costs several times, the company is probably discharged. But a mere increase in the cost of raw materials, such as a 30 percent rise in the price of ore, will almost never discharge the promisor.
- *A* force majeure *clause is significant but not necessarily dispositive.* To protect themselves from unexpected events, companies sometimes include a *force majeure* clause, allowing cancellation of the agreement in case of extraordinary and unexpected events. A typical clause might permit the seller of goods to delay or cancel delivery in the event of "acts of God, fire, labor disputes, accidents or transportation difficulties." A court will always consider a *force majeure* clause, but may not enforce it if one party is trying to escape from routine financial problems.
- *The UCC permits discharge only for major, unforeseen disruptions.* **UCC§2-615** endorses commercial impracticability as a ground for discharge, but emphasizes that mere cost increases will not justify discharge, nor will simple inconvenience or financial loss.

IANNUCCILLO v. MATERIAL SAND AND STONE CO.
713 A.2d 1234, 1998 R.I. LEXIS 168
Rhode Island Supreme Court, 1998

Facts: Louis Iannuccillo wanted to erect a building on a lot he owned. He signed a contract with Leonard Pezza, who agreed to excavate and remove 50,000 to 60,000 cubic yards of gravel "and existing rock now exposed." The agreement permitted Pezza to haul away and sell the gravel, for which he expected to make a profit of about $40,000 to $50,000. The parties agreed to share the cost of blasting "at a price of $5,000 each," which would be the only money to change hands.

After Pezza brought in a blasting contractor to break up the large boulders, as contemplated, he discovered 10,000 cubic yards of ledge, that is, solid rock. Pezza could only complete excavation if the ledge were first blasted and removed, at a cost of about $60,000. Iannuccillo demanded that Pezza finish the excavation, and when he refused, the owner sued. The trial court awarded some money to Iannuccillo and both parties appealed.

Issue: Did commercial impracticability discharge Pezza's obligation to excavate?

Excerpts from Judge Weisberger's Decision: A party's performance under a contract is rendered impracticable upon the occurrence of an event or a manifestation of a circumstance the nonoccurrence of which was a basic assumption on which the contract was made.

We have said that a contract's performance will not be set aside merely because the performance under the contract becomes more difficult or expensive than originally anticipated. In [an earlier case] we explained that the "ultimate inquiry for the

[9] *State v. Carpenter*, 869 P.2d 1181, 1994 Alaska LEXIS 23 (Alaska 1994).

May one party demand additional money, beyond the contract price, if unforeseen circumstances cause additional expense?

purposes of accepting or rejecting a defense of impossibility is whether the intervening changes in circumstances were so unforeseeable that the risk of increased difficulty or expense should not be properly borne by [the party who declined to complete performance]." Arguably both parties to this contract were possessed of considerable knowledge, experience and sophistication regarding excavation and building-site preparation. Consequently the existence of ledge in an excavation of this size was not completely beyond the realm of foreseeable occurrences. In the case before us, however, the parties inserted an express term into the contract limiting Pezza's obligation to the removal of "existing rock now exposed."

Applying these principles to the facts before us compels a finding in favor of Pezza. Clearly the ledge was neither exposed at the time the parties entered into the contract nor anticipated. Its discovery altered substantially the complexity, difficulty and expense necessary to achieve the desired result. Accordingly we hold that the discovery of the ledge so increased the burden upon defendant Pezza that further performance pursuant to the terms of the contract was rendered impracticable.

[Commercial impracticability discharged Pezza's contract obligations.]

CHAPTER CONCLUSION

Negotiate carefully. A casually written letter may imply a condition precedent that the author never intended. The term "personal satisfaction" should be defined so that both parties know whether one party may fire the other on a whim. Never assume that mere inconvenience or financial loss will discharge contractual duties.

CHAPTER REVIEW

1. A condition is an event that must occur before a party becomes obligated. It may be stated expressly or implied, and no formal language is necessary to create one.
2. Strict performance, which requires one party to fulfill its duties perfectly, is unusual. In construction and service contracts, substantial performance is generally sufficient to entitle the promisor to the contract price, minus the cost of defects in the work.
3. Personal satisfaction contracts are interpreted under an objective standard, requiring reasonable ground for dissatisfaction, unless the work involves personal judgment *and* the parties intended a subjective standard.
4. Good faith performance is required in all contracts.
5. Time of the essence clauses result in strict enforcement of contract deadlines.
6. A material breach is the only kind that will discharge a contract; a trivial breach will not.
7. True impossibility means that some event has made it impossible to perform an agreement. It is typically caused by destruction of the subject matter, the death of an essential promisor, or intervening illegality.
8. Commercial impracticability means that some unexpected event has made it extraordinarily difficult and unfair for one party to perform its obligations.
9. Frustration of purpose may occur when an unexpected event renders a contract completely useless to one party.

PRACTICE TEST

1. Stephen Krogness was a real estate broker. He signed an agreement to act as an agent for Best Buy Co., which was interested in selling several of its stores. The contract provided that Best Buy would pay Krogness a commission of 2 percent for a sale to "any prospect submitted directly to Best Buy by Krogness." Krogness introduced Corporate Realty Capital (CRC) to Best Buy, and the parties negotiated a possible sale but could not reach agreement. CRC then introduced Best Buy to BB Properties (BB). Best Buy sold several properties to BB for a total of $46 million. CRC acted as the broker on the deal. After the sale, Krogness sought a commission of $528,000. Is he entitled to it?

2. RIGHT & WRONG Commercial Union Insurance Co. (CU) insured Redux, Ltd. The contract made CU liable for fire damage, but stated that the insurer would not pay for harm caused by criminal acts of any Redux employees. Fire destroyed Redux's property. CU claimed that the "criminal acts" clause was a condition precedent, but Redux asserted it was a condition subsequent. What difference does it make, and who is legally right? Does the insurance company's position raise any ethical issues? Who drafted the contract? How clear were its terms?

3. Evans built a house for Sandra Dyer, but the house had some problems. The garage ceiling was too low. Load-bearing beams in the "great room" cracked and appeared to be steadily weakening. The patio did not drain properly. Pipes froze. Evans wanted the money promised for the job, but Dyer refused to pay. Comment.

4. Stephen Muka owned U.S. Robotics. He hired his brother Chris to work in the company. His letter promised Chris $1 million worth of Robotics stock at the end of one year, "provided you work reasonably hard & smart at things in the next year." (We should all have such brothers.) Chris arrived at Robotics and worked the full year, but toward the end of the year Stephen died. His estate refused to give Chris the stock, claiming their agreement was a personal satisfaction contract and only Stephen could decide whether Chris had earned the reward. Comment.

5. Ken Ward was an Illinois farmer who worked land owned by his father-in-law, Frank Ruda. To finance his operation, he frequently borrowed money from Watseka First National Bank, paying back the loans with farming profits. But Ward fell deeper and deeper into debt and Watseka became concerned. When Ward sought additional loans, Watseka insisted that Ruda become a guarantor on all of the outstanding debt, and the father-in-law agreed. The new loans had an acceleration clause, permitting the bank to demand payment of the entire debt if it believed itself "insecure," that is, at risk of a default. Unfortunately, just as Ward's debts reached more than $120,000, Illinois suffered a severe drought, and Ward's crops failed. Watseka asked Ruda to sell some of the land he owned to pay back part of the indebtedness. Ruda reluctantly agreed but never did so. Meanwhile, Ward decreased his payments to the bank because of the terrible crop. Watseka then "accelerated" the loan, demanding that Ruda pay off the entire debt. Ruda defended by claiming that Watseka's acceleration at such a difficult time was bad faith. Who won?

6. In August 1985, Colony Park Associates signed a contract to buy 44 acres of residential land from John Gall. The contract stated that "closing will take place August 20, 1986." The year's delay was to enable Colony Park to obtain building permits to develop condominiums. Colony Park worked diligently to obtain all permits and kept Gall abreast of its efforts. But delays in sewer permits forced Colony Park to notify Gall it could not close on the agreed date. Colony Park suggested a date exactly one month later. Gall refused the new date and declined to convey the property to Colony Park. Colony Park sued. Gall argued that since the parties specified a date, time was of the essence and Colony Park's failure to buy on time discharged Gall. Please rule.

7. Loehmann's clothing stores, a nationwide chain with headquarters in New York, was the anchor tenant in the Lincoln View Plaza Shopping Center in Phoenix, Arizona, with a 20-year lease from the landlord, Foundation Development, beginning in 1978. Loehmann's was obligated to pay rent the first of every month and to pay common area charges four times a year. The lease stated that if Loehmann's failed to pay on time, Foundation could send a notice of default, and that if the store failed to pay all money due within 10 days, Foundation could evict. On February 23, 1987, Foundation sent to Loehmann's the common area charges for the quarter ending January 31, 1987. The balance due was $3,500. Loehmann's believed the bill was in error and sent an inquiry on March 18, 1987. On April 10, 1987, Foundation insisted on payment of the full amount within 10 days. Foundation sent the letter to the Loehmann's store in Phoenix. On April 13, 1987, the Loehmann's store received the bill and, since it was not responsible for payments, forwarded it to the New York office. Because the company had moved offices in New York, a Loehmann's officer did not see the bill until April 20. Loehmann's issued a check for the full amount on April 24 and mailed it the following day. On April 28 Foundation sued to evict; on April 29 the company received Loehmann's check. Please rule.

8. Omega Concrete had a gravel pit and factory. Access was difficult, so Omega contracted with Union Pacific Railroad (UP) for the right to use a private road that crossed UP property and tracks. The contract stated that use of the road was solely for Omega employees and that Omega would be responsible for closing a gate that UP planned to build where the private road joined a public highway. In fact, UP never constructed the gate; Omega had no authority to construct the gate. Mathew Rogers, an Omega employee, was killed by a train while using the private road to reach Omega. Rogers's family sued Omega, claiming, among other things, that Omega failed to keep the gate closed as the contract required. Is Omega liable based on that failure?

9. CPA QUESTION Nagel and Fields entered into a contract in which Nagel was obligated to deliver certain goods by September 10. On September 3, Nagel told Fields that he had no intention of delivering the goods. Prior to September 10, Fields may successfully sue Nagel under the doctrine of:

(a) Promissory estoppel

(b) Accord and satisfaction

(c) Anticipatory breach

(d) Substantial performance

10. YOU BE THE JUDGE WRITING PROBLEM Kuhn Farm Machinery, a European company, signed an agreement with Scottsdale Plaza Resort, of Arizona, to use the resort for its North American dealers' convention during March 1991. Kuhn agreed to rent 190 guest rooms and spend several thousand dollars on food and beverages. Kuhn invited its top 200 independent dealers from the United States and Canada and about 25 of its own employees from the United States, Europe, and Australia, although it never mentioned those plans to Scottsdale.

On August 2, 1990, Iraq invaded Kuwait and on January 16, 1991, the United States and allied forces were at war with Iraq. Saddam Hussein and other Iraqi leaders threatened terrorist acts against the United States and its allies. Kuhn became concerned about the safety of those traveling to Arizona, especially its European employees. By mid-February, 11 of the top 50 dealers with expense-paid trips had either canceled their plans to attend or failed to sign up. Kuhn postponed the convention. The resort sued. The trial court discharged the contract under the doctrines of commercial impracticability and frustration of purpose. The resort appealed. Did commercial impracticability or frustration of purpose discharge the contract? **Argument for Scottsdale Plaza Resort:** The resort had no way of knowing that Kuhn anticipated bringing executives from Europe, and even less reason to expect that if anything interfered with their travel, the entire convention would become pointless. Most of the dealers could have attended the convention, and the resort stood ready to serve them. **Argument for Kuhn:** The parties never anticipated the threat of terrorism. Kuhn wanted this convention so that its European executives, among others, could meet top North American dealers. That is now impossible. No company would risk employee lives for a meeting. As a result, the contract has no value at all to Kuhn, and its obligations should be discharged by law.

11. Krug International, an Ohio corporation, had a contract with Iraqi Airways to build aeromedical equipment for training pilots. Krug then contracted for Power Engineering, an Iowa corporation, to build the specialized gearbox to be used in the training equipment, for $150,000. Power did not know that Krug planned to resell the gearbox to Iraqi Airways. When Power had almost completed the gearbox, the Gulf War broke out and the United Nations declared an embargo on all shipments to Iraq. Krug notified Power that it no longer wanted the gearbox. Power sued. Please rule.

INTERNET RESEARCH PROBLEM

Notice how a conditional clause is written at http://www.hud.org/jkhud/jklbp2.htm. Assume you are selling a used car. You have agreed with the buyer on the sales price, to be paid in 10 days, and have told the buyer he may have the car inspected by a mechanic in the next 5 days. How would you write a conditional clause to protect yourself?

You can find further practice problems in the Online Quiz at http://beatty.westbuslaw.com or in the Study Guide that accompanies this text.

CHAPTER 18

REMEDIES

Anybody can wrestle an alligator. But Freddie could wrestle an alligator and a python *simultaneously*. Kira watched Freddie clamp the snake on the gator's back and pin them both to the hard red soil; and when the small roadside crowd screamed approval, she knew she was looking at profit. She immediately signed Freddie to a two-year contract, promising him $500 per week plus room and board. They agreed that Rasslin' Reptiles would start its tour in a month, as soon as Kira had everything ready. Kira then spent $20,000 on a used mobile home and paid $8,000 for two more alligators and another python. Next, she hustled out on the road, drumming up business. Country bars and suburban malls were intrigued by her promotional pitch, though slow with guarantees.

Some suggested they would pay her $500 to put on a show, if and when she arrived. Others promised to rent space to her, allowing her to charge admission. Everything was looking great, and Kira went back to collect her star performer. But Freddie had met the girl of his dreams.

BREACHING THE CONTRACT

The young woman had read Freddie one of her original sonnets, and the wrestler had fallen in love with poetry. He planned to enroll in State University's creative writing program. Kira hissed and thrashed to no avail, and finally sued. Freddie had certainly breached his contract. **Someone breaches a contract when he fails to perform a duty, without a valid excuse.** When the case gets to trial, a court will declare that Freddie is in breach of the agreement. But what will Kira's *remedy* be? **A remedy is the method a court uses to compensate an injured party.** How will a court help Kira? Should the court force Freddie to return to rasslin'? **An order forcing someone to do something, or refrain from doing something, is an injunction.** Courts seldom grant injunctions to compel a party to perform a job, since that would force two antagonistic people to work together. The court could prohibit Freddie from working elsewhere, and perhaps from going to school. Is that sensible?

The most common remedy, used in the great majority of lawsuits, is money damages. If the court decides to award Kira damages, how much money should she get? Kira may claim that she could have performed 8 to 10 shows a week, at $500 per show, for a total of $4,000 to $5,000 per week. Lost profits are considered ***expectation* damages**. Freddie will respond that all of the "shows" were hypothetical, since not one penny of income had been guaranteed. If Kira is not entitled to lost profits, should she receive the money spent on tour preparations? Such a remedy is called ***reliance* damages.**

How to help an injured party, without unfairly harming the other person, is the focus of remedies. Courts have struggled with remedies for centuries, but we will master them in one chapter. Kira will not obtain an injunction forcing Freddie to wrestle. An order barring him from college is also unlikely. And she will be hard-pressed to prove lost profits, since she had no guarantee of earnings. She should win something for her reliance on Freddie's deal since she spent $28,000 on major purchases. But she may not get that full amount because in losing Freddie's services she also shed the expense of an unproven road tour. The questions and issues created by Kira's broken road tour are typical remedy problems.

Though a court may have several alternative remedies available, it is important to note that almost all of them have one thing in common: the focus is on *compensating the injured party, rather than punishing the party in breach.* A court must decide whether to give Kira her lost profits or her expenses, but it will not consider sending Freddie to jail or assessing damages to punish him.

Critics argue that someone who willfully breaches a contract should pay a penalty. In Kira and Freddie's case, the stakes are modest. But what if a retail company deliberately breaches a $50 million deal with a manufacturer. That could cost the manufacturer hundreds or thousands of jobs; it might require closing a plant, and that in turn could damage an entire community. Should a remedy reflect morality? In this chapter we will see very few instances in which a court punishes unethical conduct. In most disputes, judges focus on compensating the injured person, not on punishing the party in breach.

IDENTIFYING THE "INTEREST" TO BE PROTECTED

The first step that a court takes in choosing a remedy is to decide what interest it is trying to protect. An **interest** is a legal right in something. Someone can have an interest in property, for example, by owning it, or renting it to a tenant, or lending money to buy it. He can have an interest in a *contract* if the agreement gives him some benefit. There are four principal contract interests that a court may seek to protect:

- *Expectation Interest*. This refers to what the injured party reasonably thought she would get from the contract. The goal is to put her in the position she would have been in if both parties had fully performed their obligations.
- *Reliance Interest*. The injured party may be unable to demonstrate expectation damages, perhaps because it is unclear he would have profited. But he may still prove that he *expended money* in reliance on the agreement and that in fairness he should receive compensation for the expenses.
- *Restitution Interest*. The injured party may be unable to show an expectation interest or reliance. But perhaps she has conferred a *benefit* on the other party. Here, the objective is to restore to the injured party the benefit she has provided.
- *Equitable Interest*. In some cases, money damages will not suffice to help the injured party. Something more is needed, such as an order to transfer property to the injured party (specific performance) or an order forcing one party to stop doing something (an injunction).

In this chapter, we look at all four interests.

EXPECTATION INTEREST

This is the most common remedy that the law provides for a party injured by a breach of contract. **The expectation interest is designed to put the injured party in the position she would have been in had both sides fully performed their obligations.** A court tries to give the injured party the money she would have made from the contract. If accurately computed, this should take into account all the gains she reasonably expected and all the expenses and losses she would have incurred. The injured party should not end up better off than she would have been under the agreement, nor should she suffer serious loss.

William Colby was a former director of the CIA. He wanted to write a book about his 15 years of experiences in Vietnam. He paid James McCarger $5,000 for help in writing an early draft and promised McCarger another $5,000 if the book was published. Then he hired Alexander Burnham to co-write the book. Colby's agent secured a contract with Contemporary Books, which included a $100,000 advance. But Burnham was hopelessly late with the manuscript and Colby missed his publication date. Colby fired Burnham and finished the book without him. Contemporary published *Lost Victory* several years late, and the book flopped, earning no significant revenue. Because the book was so late, Contemporary paid Colby a total of only $17,000. Colby sued Burnham for his lost expectation interest. The court awarded him $23,000, calculated as follows:

$100,000	advance, the only money Colby was promised
− 10,000	agent's fee
= 90,000	fee for the two authors, combined
divided by 2 = 45,000	Colby's fee
− 5,000	owed to McCarger under the earlier agreement
= 40,000	Colby's expectation interest
− 17,000	fee Colby received from Contemporary
= 23,000	Colby's expectation damages, that is, the amount he would have received had Burnham finished on time[1]

[1] *Colby v. Burnham*, 31 Conn. App. 707, 627 A.2d 457, 1993 Conn. App LEXIS 299 (Conn. App. Ct. 1993).

The *Colby* case presented an easy calculation of damages. Other contracts are complex. Courts typically divide the expectation damages into three parts: (1) compensatory (or "direct") damages, which represent harm that flowed directly from the contract's breach; (2) consequential (or "special") damages, which represent harm caused by the injured party's unique situation; and (3) incidental damages, which are minor costs such as storing or returning defective goods, advertising for alternative goods, and so forth. The first two, compensatory and consequential, are the important ones. We look at them one at a time.

COMPENSATORY DAMAGES

If a star walks off, who pays for the damage?

Compensatory damages are the most common monetary awards for the expectation interest. Courts also refer to these as "direct damages." **Compensatory damages are those that flow directly from the contract.** In other words, these are the damages that inevitably result from the breach. Suppose Ace Productions hires Reina to star in its new movie, *Inside Straight*. Ace promises Reina $3 million, providing she shows up June 1 and works until the film is finished. But in late May, Joker Entertainment offers Reina $6 million to star in its new feature, and on June 1 Reina informs Ace that she will not appear. Reina has breached her contract, and Ace should recover compensatory damages.

What are the damages that flow directly from the contract? Ace obviously has to replace Reina. If Ace hires Kween as its star and pays her a fee of $4 million, Ace is entitled to the difference between what it expected to pay ($3 million) and what the breach forced it to pay ($4 million), or $1 million in compensatory damages. Suppose the rest of the cast and crew are idle for two weeks because of the delay in hiring a substitute, and the lost time costs the producers an extra $2.5 million. Reina is also liable for those expenses. Both the new actress and the delay are inevitable.

Reasonable Certainty

The injured party must prove the breach of contract caused damages that can be quantified with reasonable certainty. What if *Inside Straight*, now starring Kween, bombs at the box office. Ace proves that each of Reina's last three movies grossed over $60 million, but *Inside Straight* grossed only $28 million. Is Reina liable for the lost profits? No. Ace cannot prove that it was Reina's absence that caused the film to fare poorly. The script may have been mediocre, or Kween's co-stars dull, or the publicity efforts inadequate. Ace *hoped* to gross over $60 million, but mere hopes create "speculative damages," worth zero. Because Ace cannot demonstrate a quantifiable box office loss directly attributable to Reina, it will get nothing for the disappointing ticket sales.

CONSEQUENTIAL DAMAGES

In addition to compensatory damages, the injured party may seek consequential damages or, as they are also known, "special damages." **Consequential damages are those resulting from the unique circumstances of *this injured party*.** The rule concerning this remedy comes from a famous 1854 case, *Hadley v. Baxendale*, which all American law students read. Now it is your turn.

HADLEY v. BAXENDALE
9 Ex. 341, 156 Eng. Rep. 145
Court of Exchequer, 1854

Facts: The Hadleys operated a flour mill in Gloucester. The crankshaft broke, causing the mill to grind to a halt. The Hadleys employed Baxendale to cart the damaged part to a foundry in Greenwich, where a new one could be manufactured. Baxendale promised to make the delivery in one day, but he was late transporting the shaft, and as a result the Hadleys' mill was shut for five extra days. They sued, and the jury awarded damages based in part on their lost profits. Baxendale appealed.

Issue: Should the defendant be liable for profits lost because of his delay in delivering the shaft?

Excerpts from Judge Alderson's Decision: Where two parties have made a contract which one of them has broken, the damages which the other party ought to receive in respect of such breach of contract should be such as may fairly and reasonably be considered either arising naturally, i.e. according to the usual course of things, from such breach of contract itself, or such as may reasonably be supposed to have been in the contemplation of both parties, at the time they made the contract, as the probable result of the breach of it. Now, if the special circumstances under which the contract was actually made were communicated by the plaintiffs to the defendants, and thus known to both parties, the damages resulting from the breach of such a contract, which they would reasonably contemplate, would be the amount of injury which would ordinarily follow from a breach of contract under these special circumstances so known and communicated. But, on the other hand, if these special circumstances were wholly unknown to the party breaking the contract, he, at the most, could only be supposed to have had in his contemplation the amount of injury which would arise generally, and in the great multitude of cases not affected by any special circumstances, from such a breach of contract.

Now, in the present case, if we are to apply the principles above laid down, we find that the only circumstances here communicated by the plaintiffs to the defendants at the time the contract was made, were, that the article to be carried was the broken shaft of a mill, and that the plaintiffs were the millers of that mill. But how do these circumstances shew [sic] reasonably that the profits of the mill must be stopped by an unreasonable delay in the delivery of the broken shaft by the carrier to the third person? Suppose the plaintiffs had another shaft in their possession put up or putting up at the time, and that they only wished to send back the broken shaft to the engineer who made it; it is clear that this would be quite consistent with the above circumstances, and yet the unreasonable delay in the delivery would have no effect upon the intermediate profits of the mill. It follows, therefore, that the loss of profits here cannot reasonably be considered such a consequence of the breach of contract as could have been fairly and reasonably contemplated by both the parties when they made this contract.

[The court ordered a new trial, in which the jury would *not* be allowed to consider the plaintiffs' lost profits.]

The rule from *Hadley v. Baxendale* has been unchanged ever since: **the injured party may recover consequential damages only if the breaching party should have foreseen them.**

Let us return briefly to *Inside Straight*. Suppose that, long before shooting began, Ace had sold the film's soundtrack rights to Spinem Sound for $2 million. Spinem believed it would make a profit only if Reina appeared in the film, so it demanded the right to discharge the agreement if Reina dropped out. When Reina quit, Spinem terminated the contract. Now, when Ace sues Reina, it will also seek $2 million in consequential damages for the lost music revenue. If Reina knew about Ace's contract with Spinem when she signed to do the film, she is liable for $2 million. If she never realized she was an essential part of the music contract, she owes nothing for the lost profits. (Because damage calculation can be complex, there are companies that specialize in doing the work on behalf of litigants or other interested parties. One such firm explains its services at **http://www.ei.com/concentrations/damages.htm**.)

Does the plaintiff in the following case deserve consequential damages?

LAWRENCE v. WILL DARRAH & ASSOCIATES, INC.
445 Mich. 1, 516 N.W.2d 43, 1994
Mich. LEXIS 890
Supreme Court of Michigan, 1994

Facts: Benjamin Lawrence purchased a tractor-trailer for long-distance hauling. He obtained an insurance policy covering theft from the Will Darrah agency. The policy noted that Lawrence would use the vehicle to haul freight. Two months after Lawrence bought the truck it was stolen, and he reported its theft to Will Darrah. The tractor-trailer was worth about $19,500.

The insurer delayed paying the claim. After several months, the agency agreed to pay $19,500, but by then Lawrence requested money covering profits he had lost as a result of the insurer's delay. The company refused to pay for lost profits, noting that the policy did not cover them.

Lawrence sued. The adjusters who worked for Will Darrah and handled the claim acknowledged that the company knew that Lawrence, like many of its customers, was a one-truck enterprise, with the vehicle his only source of income. The jury awarded Lawrence $70,800, representing the value of his truck and lost profits. The insurer appealed, claiming that Lawrence was entitled only to the truck's value. The appeals court reversed, stating that lost profits were not a foreseeable consequential damage. Lawrence appealed to the Michigan Supreme Court.

You Be the Judge: Under the insurance contract, were lost profits a foreseeable harm, entitling Lawrence to consequential damages?

Argument for Lawrence: Your honors, Will Darrah knew perfectly well that Mr. Lawrence operated a small trucking outfit with only one truck. The agency knew that without the truck he could make no money. The company understood that the longer it delayed payment, the more money its customer would lose.

Under the rule of *Hadley v. Baxendale*, foreseeability is the key. The insurer here could easily foresee everything that happened after the truck was stolen. The whole purpose of theft insurance is to enable the owner to buy a replacement vehicle quickly and get back on the road. It is true that the contract did not provide for lost profits but that was because the parties assumed the insurance benefits would be paid promptly. There is no rule that says consequential damages must be stated in the contract. The damages must simply be foreseeable, and these were. It's time for Will Darrah to pay.

Argument for Will Darrah: Your honors, we agree that foreseeability is the key to this case. We also think that it is easy to determine what the parties foresaw as Mr. Lawrence's potential losses. *They foresaw the things they listed in the contract.* The contract covered theft, fire, accident, and a few other losses. It did not cover lost profits. Why not? Because Mr. Lawrence chose not to insure lost profits, that's why. He might have insisted on covering lost profits, or numerous other potential problems. He didn't cover them, he didn't pay premiums based on them, he didn't mention them. The parties did not foresee them, and the insurer owes nothing but the value of the truck.

In *Hadley v. Baxendale* the court held that Baxendale could reasonably have assumed that the Hadleys had another shaft. Here, the insurers could reasonably have believed that Lawrence had other means to finance a new truck, and that some delay in paying the benefits would cause no particular harm. If a delay would prove critical, the burden was on Lawrence to inform the insurers of that when they drafted the contract, not after the loss occurred. The Hadleys' failure to notify Baxendale of their special circumstances cost them any claim of consequential damages, and Lawrence's failure should have the same result. We ask you to affirm the judgment of the appeals court.

INCIDENTAL DAMAGES

Incidental damages are the relatively minor costs that the injured party suffers when responding to the breach. When Reina, the actress, breaches the film contract, the producers may have to leave the set and fly back to Los Angeles to hire a new actress. The travel cost is an incidental damage. In another setting, suppose Maud, a manufacturer, has produced 5,000 pairs of running shoes for Foot The Bill, a retail chain, but Foot The Bill breaches the agreement and refuses to accept the goods. Maud will have to store the shoes and advertise for alternate buyers. The storage and advertising costs are incidental expenses, and Maud will recover them.

SALE OF GOODS

Under the Uniform Commercial Code (UCC), remedies for breach of contract in the sale of goods are similar to the general rules discussed throughout this chapter. UCC §§2-703 through 2-715 govern the remedies available to buyers and sellers.[2]

Seller's Remedies

If a buyer breaches a sale of goods contract, the seller generally has at least two remedies. She may resell the goods elsewhere. If she acts in good faith, she will be awarded **the difference between the original contract price and the price she was able to obtain in the open market.** Assume that Maud, the manufacturer, had a contract to sell her shoes to Foot The Bill for $35 per pair and Foot The Bill's breach forces her to sell them on the open market, where she gets only $28 per pair. Maud will win $7 per pair times 5,000 pairs, or $35,000, from Foot The Bill.

Alternatively, the buyer may choose not to resell and settle for the difference between the contract price and the market value of the goods. Maud, in other words, may choose to keep the shoes. If she can prove that their market value is $28 per pair, for example, by showing what other retailers would have paid her for them, she will still get her $7 each, representing the difference between what the contract promised her and what the market would support. In either case, the money represents compensatory damages. Maud is also entitled to incidental damages, such as the storage and advertising expenses described above. But there is one significant difference under the UCC: **Most courts hold that the seller of goods is *not* entitled to consequential damages.** Suppose Maud hired two extra workers to inspect, pack, and ship the shoes for Foot The Bill. Those are consequential damages, but Maud will not recover them because she is the seller and the contract is for the sale of goods.

Buyer's Remedies

The buyer's remedies under the Code are similar to those we have already considered. She typically has two options. First, the buyer can "cover" by purchasing substitute goods. To **cover** means to make a good faith purchase of goods similar to those in the contract. The buyer may then obtain **the difference between the original contract price and her cover price.** Alternatively, if the buyer chooses not to cover, she is entitled to the difference between the original contract price and the market value of the goods.

---

[2] We discuss these remedies in greater detail in Unit 3, on commercial transactions.

Suppose Mary has contracted to buy 1,000 six-foot Christmas trees at $25 per tree from Elmo. The market suddenly rises, and in the spirit of the season Elmo breaches his deal and sells the trees elsewhere. If Mary makes a good faith effort to cover but is forced to pay $40 per tree, she may recover the difference from Elmo, meaning $15 per tree times 1,000 trees, or $15,000. Similarly, if she chooses not to cover but can prove that $40 is now the market value of the trees, she is entitled to her $15 per tree.

Under the UCC, **the buyer *is* entitled to consequential damages provided that the seller could reasonably have foreseen them.** If Mary tells Elmo, when they sign their deal, that she has a dozen contracts to resell the trees, for an average price of $50 per tree, she may recover $25 per tree, representing the difference between her contract price with Elmo and the value of the tree *to her*, based on her other contracts.[3] If she failed to inform Elmo of the other contracts, she would not receive any money based on them. The buyer is also entitled to whatever incidental damages may have accrued.

We turn now to cases where the injured party cannot prove expectation damages.

RELIANCE INTEREST

George plans to manufacture and sell silk scarves during the holiday season. In the summer, he contracts with Cecily, the owner of a shopping mall, to rent a high-visibility stall for $100 per day. George then buys hundreds of yards of costly silk and gets to work cutting and sewing. But in September, Cecily refuses to honor the contract. George sues and easily proves Cecily breached a valid contract. But what is his remedy?

George cannot establish an expectation interest in his scarf business. He *hoped* to sell each scarf for a $40 gross profit. He *planned* on making $2,000 per day. But how much would he actually have earned? Enough to retire on? Enough to buy a salami sandwich for lunch? He has no way of proving his profits, and a court cannot give him his expectation interest. Instead, George will ask for *reliance damages*. **The reliance interest is designed to put the injured party in the position he would have been in had the parties never entered into a contract.** This remedy focuses on the time and money the injured party spent performing his part of the agreement.

George should be able to recover reliance damages from Cecily. Assuming he is unable to sell the scarves to a retail store, which is probable since retailers will have made purchases long ago, George should be able to recover the cost of the silk fabric he bought and perhaps something for the hours of labor he spent cutting and sewing. But reliance damages can be difficult to win because *they are harder to quantify*. Courts prefer to compute damages using the numbers provided in a contract. If a contract states a price of $25 per Christmas tree and one party breaches, the arithmetic is easy. Judges become uncomfortable when asked to base damages on vague calculations. How much was George's time worth in making the scarves? How good was his work? How likely were the scarves to sell? If George has a track record in the industry, he will be able to show a market price for his services. Without such a record, his reliance claim becomes a tough battle, as the following case demonstrates.

---

[3] As we discuss in the section on mitigation, later in the chapter, Mary will get only her consequential damages if she attempts to cover.

SULLIVAN v. OREGON LANDMARK-ONE, LTD.
122 Or. App. 1, 856 P.2d 1043, 1993 Or. App. LEXIS 1193
Oregon Court of Appeals, 1993

Facts: Russell and Jean Sullivan wanted to start a restaurant-bookstore. They had no experience running either kind of business. They spoke with an agent for Oregon Landmark-One about renting space. The Sullivans explained that they were new to these businesses and would be doing a great deal of preparatory work. The parties reached an agreement for the Sullivans to rent space. Landmark-One agreed to make specified improvements to the building at its own expense and then lease the space.

The Sullivans spent countless hours preparing to run their new business. They studied books on operating a restaurant, tested recipes, obtained financing, and purchased equipment. Since they were partly responsible for remodeling, they spoke with designers, reviewed building codes, and negotiated with contractors. Their expenses included equipment and supplies, interest on loans, license and legal fees, and office expenses.

Eight months after the parties signed their lease, Landmark-One told the Sullivans that it would not perform the renovations because the work would cost twice what it had calculated. The Sullivans sadly abandoned their project, sold much of their equipment, paid off their loans—and filed suit.

The Sullivans sought reliance damages. The jury awarded $2,502 for out-of-pocket expenses and $17,230 for the hours of work the Sullivans expended. The trial judge reduced the "hours" damages to $5,998 and awarded a total of $8,500. Landmark-One appealed, claiming that there was no evidence to support the money for the Sullivans' services.

Issue: Are the Sullivans entitled to reliance damages for the hours of work they performed?

Excerpts from Judge Landau's Decision: Reliance interest damages put the injured party in the position he or she would have been in had the contract not been entered. They may include out-of-pocket expenses incurred in reliance on the agreement, particularly those expenses that were necessary to prepare for performance of the contract.

The only evidence of [the plaintiffs'] loss, however, was their own opinion testimony concerning the value of their services. That evidence, by itself, is insufficient to establish that plaintiffs suffered any losses in reliance on the lease agreement. There is no evidence that plaintiffs quit their jobs to spend time preparing to operate the new restaurant. Plaintiffs were, in fact, unemployed when they entered into the agreement. There is, likewise, no evidence concerning the amount of money plaintiffs would have made elsewhere, had they not invested their time in preparing to operate the restaurant. Plaintiffs' opinion testimony concerning the value of their time is just that, and nothing more. It does nothing to establish that they actually would have been paid anything for their time had they not relied on their lease agreement with defendant. They have, in short, failed to produce any evidence of damages that would place them in the position they would have been in had the lease agreement never been executed.

We agree with defendant that the trial court erred in permitting any recovery of hours expended damages. We do not agree, however, that the trial court erred in allowing recovery of the out-of-pocket expenses. There was testimony that plaintiffs informed defendant's property manager that they intended to do substantial work in preparation for performance and that he knew of plaintiffs' efforts. There also was evidence of the amount of expenses plaintiffs actually incurred. That evidence is sufficient to support the award of the out-of-pocket expenses.

[The court affirmed the award of $2,502 in out-of-pocket expenses but denied all other damages.]

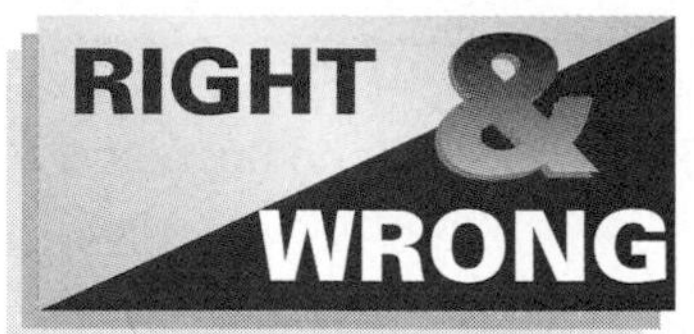

The Sullivans acted entirely in good faith, and Landmark-One willfully broke the agreement. Was the court right to adjudicate this case without considering those facts? Notice that the court allows the Sullivans nothing for the hours they spent on preparations. This illustrates how reluctant courts are to award damages that are hard to quantify. Is the result fair? How would you have ruled?

RELIANCE DAMAGES AND PROMISSORY ESTOPPEL

In several earlier chapters of this unit, we have seen that a plaintiff may sometimes recover damages based on promissory estoppel even when there is no valid contract. The plaintiff must show that the defendant made a promise knowing that the plaintiff would likely rely on it, that the plaintiff did rely, and that the only way to avoid injustice is to enforce the promise. **In promissory estoppel cases, a court will generally award only *reliance damages*.** It would be unfair to give expectation damages for the full benefit of the bargain when, legally, there has been no bargain.

Costas works as a chef in Philadelphia, making $40,000 per year. Lou greatly enjoys Costas's curried shrimp and wanders back into the kitchen. "Fabulous food," Lou gushes. "You ought to come out to Los Angeles. I'm part owner of a terrific restaurant, with several friends. I'll double your salary, if not more—guaranteed." Costas takes Lou at his word, quits his job, and travels out west—where no job awaits him. Costas cannot sue Lou based on a contract because none exists. Costas gave no consideration, since there was no exchange of bargaining or promises, and in any event, the terms of the offer were too vague to be enforceable. But Lou should have expected Costas to rely on his promise, and the only way to avoid injustice is to give Costas something. He will *probably* receive the value of his reliance on Lou's promise. If Costas is out of work six months, he may get $20,000 (six months of his *former* salary), plus his travel expenses and any additional living costs. But he will not receive any expectation interest, which would have been an annual salary of $80,000 or more.

Costa's predicament and the losing battle fought by the Sullivans demonstrate one fact of contract life: an injured party is much better off if he can prove an expectation interest in a valid contract. Reliance damages will generally be less and may be impossible to recover at all.

LAW AND EQUITY

Expectation and reliance interests are considered **legal remedies.** The other interests we will examine are equitable remedies. The difference is largely historical but still may affect a plaintiff's ability to obtain help from a court. As we saw in the textbook's introductory chapter, the common law developed in England, very gradually, over many centuries. English *law* courts gave money damages to the plaintiff, so money damages became known as "legal remedies."

In some cases, an English law court might refuse to hear a case, claiming that it lacked jurisdiction. Or the injured plaintiff might want more than mere money damages. For example, a plaintiff who had a contract to buy land might want the property itself, not money damages. When a law court would not or could not help, a plaintiff often took his case to the Chancellor in London. There was no jury in a Chancery case, but the Chancellor did have broader, more flexible powers than the law judges. The Chancellor's powers came to be known as **equitable remedies**. In the United States today, trial courts of general jurisdiction have the power to grant legal *and* equitable remedies. We now turn to an equitable remedy called restitution.

RESTITUTION INTEREST

Lillian and Harold Toews signed a contract to sell 1,500 acres of Idaho farmland to Elmer Funk. He was to take possession immediately, but would not receive the deed until he finished paying for the property, in 10 years. This arrangement enabled him to enroll in a government program that would pay him "set-asides" for *not* farming. Funk kept most aspects of his agreement. He did move onto the land and did receive $76,000 from the government for a year's worth of inactivity. (Nice work if you can get it.) The only part of the bargain Funk did not keep was his promise to pay. The Toewses sued. Funk had clearly breached the deal. But what remedy?

The Toewses still owned the land, so they did not need it reconveyed. Funk had no money to pay for the farm, so the Toewses would never get their expectation interest. And the Toewses had expended almost no money based on the deal, so they had no reliance interest. What they had done, though, was to *confer a benefit* on Funk. They had enabled him to obtain $76,000 in government money. The Toewses wanted a return of the benefit they had conferred on Funk, a remedy called restitution. **The restitution interest is designed to return to the injured party a benefit that he has conferred on the other party, which it would be unjust to leave with that person.** The Toewses argued that they had bestowed a $76,000 benefit on Funk and that it made absolutely no sense for him to keep it. The Idaho Court of Appeals agreed. It ruled that the Toewses had a restitutionary interest in the government set-aside money and ordered Funk to pay the money to the Toewses.[4]

Restitution is awarded in two types of cases. First, the law allows restitution when the parties have reached a contract and one of them breaches, as Funk did. In such cases, a court may choose restitution because no other remedy is available or because no other remedy would be as fair. Second, courts may award restitution in cases of quasi-contract, which we examined in earlier chapters. In quasi-contract cases, the parties never made a contract but one side did benefit the other. We consider each kind of restitution interest in turn.

RESTITUTION IN CASES OF A VALID CONTRACT

Restitution is a common remedy in contracts involving fraud, misrepresentation, mistake, and duress. In these cases, restitution often goes hand-in-hand with **rescission**, which means to "undo" a contract and put the parties where they were before they made the agreement. Courtney sells her favorite sculpture to Adam for $95,000, both parties believing the work to be a valuable original by Barbara Hepworth. Two months later, Adam learns that the sculpture is a mere copy, worth very little. A court will permit Adam to rescind the contract on the ground of mutual mistake. At the same time, Adam is entitled to restitution of the purchase price. Courtney gets the worthless carving and Adam receives his money back.

The following case involved fraud in the sale of a valuable property.

PUTNAM CONSTRUCTION & REALTY CO. v. BYRD
632 So. 2d 961, 1992 Ala. LEXIS 1289
Supreme Court of Alabama, 1992

Facts: Putnam Construction & Realty Co. owned the University Square Business Center (USBC), an office complex with several major tenants, including McDonnell-Douglas, TRW, and the Army Corps of Engineers. William Byrd and some partners (the "buyers") entered into a contract to buy USBC for slightly over $17 million. They financed the purchase with a $16.2 million loan from

[4] *Toews v. Funk*, 129 Idaho 316, 924 P.2d 217, 1994 Idaho App. LEXIS 75 (Idaho Ct. App. 1994).

Northwestern Mutual Life. Northwestern's loan was secured with a mortgage on the USBC, meaning that if the borrowers failed to repay the loan, Northwestern would own the property. Shortly after the sale closed, Byrd learned that several of the major tenants were leaving. The buyers sued Putnam, seeking rescission of the contract and restitution of their money. The trial court found that Putnam (the "sellers") had committed fraud. It rescinded the sales contract, returning the property to the sellers. It ordered the sellers to assume full liability for the mortgage. The trial court did not, however, order restitution of the buyers' expenses, such as the closing costs. The sellers appealed—which proved to be a big mistake.

Issue: Were the buyers entitled to rescission and/or restitution?

Excerpts from Justice Steagall's Decision: As early as December 1988, the sellers were aware that the Corps of Engineers was planning to build its own facility and eventually move into it. In spite of this knowledge, the sellers repeatedly told the buyers that the Corps of Engineers had no intention of leaving USBC and that it would probably agree to lease even more space. In May or June 1989, the sellers learned that McDonnell-Douglas was definitely going to move some of its personnel to new facilities, but did not report this information to the buyers. [The court concluded that the sellers had committed fraud.]

With the departure of its major tenants, the USBC does not have the profit potential the buyers bargained for and is, in fact, a liability to them. While the buyers could receive money damages to approximate the value of the lost leases, such an award would be speculative at best and would not abrogate the fact that the buyers now have a property that operates at an increasing loss. The equitable remedy of rescission, while difficult to execute, would more completely provide the buyers with the compensation they seek. The jury was, therefore, correct in determining that rescission is the proper remedy to be applied in this case.

We agree with the trial court that a reconveyance of USBC to the sellers, subject to the mortgage, "constitutes the most equitable result which can be achieved." Accordingly, we affirm those portions of the court's order relating to the reconveyance of USBC subject to the mortgage. We must also recognize, however, that the buyers incurred other substantial out-of-pocket costs to finance a transaction that was born out of the sellers' fraud. After carefully considering the evidence in this case, we conclude that repayment of the following costs is necessary to more equitably restore the buyers to the position they occupied before the sale: $483,006.75 in closing costs on the purchase of USBC; $121,000 in interest payments they paid to the sellers on the $1.5 million note; and the $500,000 in nonrefundable fees the buyers paid to Northwestern to obtain the loan. We remand this case for the trial court to enter a judgment ordering repayment of these costs.

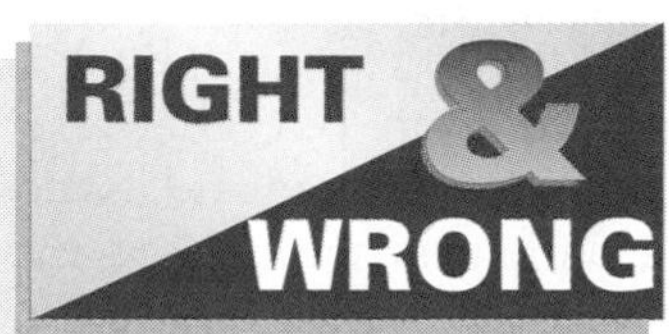

Imagine that you are the officer from Putnam in charge of negotiating the sale of USBC to the buyers. You learn that several major tenants are soon to depart and realize that if the buyers learn this they will lower their offer or reject the deal altogether. Your boss insists you tell the buyers that all tenants will be staying. What will you do?

RESTITUTION IN CASES OF A QUASI-CONTRACT

George Anderson owned a valuable 1936 Plymouth. He took it to Ronald Schwegel's repair shop, and the two orally agreed that Schwegel would restore the car for $6,000. Unfortunately, they never agreed on the word "restore." Anderson thought the term meant complete restoration, including body work and engine repairs, whereas Schwegel intended body work but no engine repairs. After doing some of the work, Schwegel told Anderson that the car needed substantial engine work, and asked for Anderson's permission to allow an engine shop to do it. Anderson agreed, believing the cost was included in the original estimate. When the car was finished and running smoothly, Schwegel demanded $9,800. Anderson refused to pay more than the $6,000 agreed price, and Schwegel sued.

The court held that there was no valid contract between the parties. A contract requires a meeting of the minds. Here, said the court, there was no meeting of the minds on what "restore" included, and hence Schwegel could not recover either his expectation or his reliance interest, since both require an enforceable agreement. Schwegel therefore argued "quasi-contract." In other words, he claimed that even if there had been no valid agreement, he had performed a service for Anderson and that it would be unjust for Anderson to keep it without paying. **A court may award restitution, even in the absence of a contract, where one party has conferred a benefit on another and it would be unjust for the other party to retain the benefit.** The court ruled that Schwegel was entitled to the full $3,800 above and beyond the agreed price because that was the fair market value of the additional work. Anderson had asked for the repairs and now had an auto that was substantially improved. It would be unjust, ruled the court, to permit him to keep that benefit for free.[5]

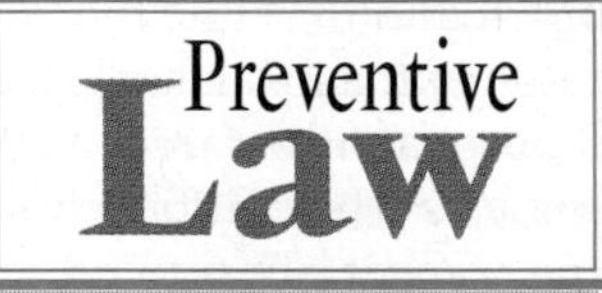

Of all the disputes in this unit, the one between Anderson and Schwegel was the easiest to prevent. The parties needed only a few lines on an estimate sheet, listing exactly which repairs would be included for $6,000 and which would not. Indeed, it is remarkable that the parties were able to discuss the matter on several occasions *without* specifying whether Schwegel would repair the engine. Which party is in the better position to ensure a clear agreement? If there was no meeting of the minds, whose fault was it?

OTHER EQUITABLE INTERESTS

In addition to restitution, the other three equitable powers that concern us are specific performance, injunction, and reformation.

SPECIFIC PERFORMANCE

Leona Claussen owned Iowa farmland. She sold some of it to her sister-in-law, Evelyn Claussen, and, along with the land, granted Evelyn an option to buy additional property at $800 per acre. Evelyn could exercise her option anytime during Leona's lifetime or within six months of Leona's death. When Leona died, Evelyn informed the estate's executor that she was exercising her option. But other relatives wanted the property and the executor refused to sell. Evelyn sued and asked for *specific performance*. She did not want an award of damages; she wanted the land itself. The remedy of specific performance forces the two parties to perform their contract.

A court will award specific performance, ordering the parties to perform the contract, only in cases involving the sale of land or some other asset that is unique. Courts use this equitable remedy when money damages would be inadequate to compensate the injured party. If the subject is unique and irreplaceable,

---

5 *Anderson v. Schwegel*, 118 Idaho 362, 796 P.2d 1035, 1990 Idaho App. LEXIS 150 (Idaho Ct. App. 1990).

money damages will not put the injured party in the same position she would have been in had the agreement been kept. So a court will order the seller to convey the rare object and the buyer to pay for it.

Historically, every parcel of land has been regarded as unique, and therefore specific performance is always available in real estate contracts. Evelyn Claussen won specific performance. The Iowa Supreme Court ordered Leona's estate to convey the land to Evelyn, for $800 per acre.[6] Generally speaking, either the seller or the buyer may be granted specific performance. One limitation in land sales is that a buyer may obtain specific performance only if she was ready, willing, and able to purchase the property on time. If Evelyn had lacked the money to buy Leona's property for $800 per acre within the six months' time limit, the court would have declined to order the sale. The following article illustrates a very human mistake that will invoke specific performance.

Dear Attorney:

We foolishly listed our home for sale last April. Our realty agent did a fine job and found a buyer by mid-May. The closing was supposed to be June 30. My husband and I bought a Florida condo in February and thought we wanted to move there to live year-round. But in May, after we agreed to sell our home, we went to visit our new condo for a week and encountered terrible heat and humidity. We instantly decided we only want to live in Florida in the winter.

The first week of June we notified our real-estate agent and the buyer that we changed our minds and wanted to cancel the sale. We immediately refunded the buyer's $5,000 deposit. But the buyers refused to take the money. A few weeks later we were served with legal papers for a lawsuit involving something called "specific performance." The buyers really want our house. What can we do to get out of this sale?

Answer: Unless there is a loophole in the sales contract, your home buyers will probably win their specific performance lawsuit to force you to honor the agreement and deliver the deed as you promised to do. Disliking the summer heat and humidity in Florida is not a legal reason for breaching your real estate sales contract.[7]

Other unique items, for which a court will order specific performance, include such things as rare works of art, secret formulas, patents, and shares in a closely held corporation. Money damages would be inadequate for all these things since the injured party, even if she got the cash, could not go out and buy a substitute item. By contrast, a contract for a new Jeep Cherokee Laredo is not enforceable by specific performance. If the seller breaches, the buyer is entitled to the difference between the contract price and the market value of the car. The buyer can take his money elsewhere and purchase a virtually identical auto.

INJUNCTION

You move into your new suburban house on two acres of land, and the fresh air is exhilarating. But the wind shifts to the west, and you find yourself thinking of farm animals, especially pigs. It turns out that your next-door neighbor just started an organic bacon ranch, and the first 15 porkers have checked in. You check out the town's zoning code, discover that it is illegal to raise livestock in the neighborhood, and sue. But money damages will not suffice, because you want

[6] *In re Estate of Claussen*, 482 N.W.2d 381, 1992 Iowa Sup. LEXIS 52 (Iowa 1992).

[7] Robert Bruss, "Compound Mistakes," *Chicago Tribune*, Nov. 5, 1995, p. 7P. © Tribune Media Services, Inc. All Rights Reserved. Reprinted with permission.

the bouquet to disappear. You seek the equitable remedy of injunction. **An injunction is a court order that requires someone to do something or refrain from doing something.**

The court will order your neighbor immediately to cease and desist raising any pigs or other farm animals on his land. "Cease" means to stop, and "desist" means to refrain from doing it in the future. The injunction will not get you any money, but it will move the pigs out of town, and that was your goal.

Injunctions are usually stated in the negative. Look, for example, at noncompetition agreements, where the seller of a business might promise the buyer that he will not open a competing activity in a specified area. If the seller breaches the agreement by opening an identical enterprise across the street, the court will order him *not* to compete within the specified area. In a copyright violation, a court will order a television producer *not* to make a movie-of-the-week based on a copyrighted script owned by someone else.

In the increasingly litigious world of professional sports, injunctions are commonplace. In the following basketball case, the trial court issued a **preliminary injunction,** that is, an order issued early in a lawsuit prohibiting a party from doing something *during the course of the lawsuit*. The court attempts to protect the interests of the plaintiff immediately. If, after trial, it appears that the plaintiff has been injured and is entitled to an injunction, the trial court will make its order a **permanent injunction**. If it appears that the preliminary injunction should never have been issued, the court will terminate the order. The Web site **http://www.kinseylaw.com/ATTY%20SERV/civil/complaints/injunction.html** provides a sample complaint requesting an injunction.

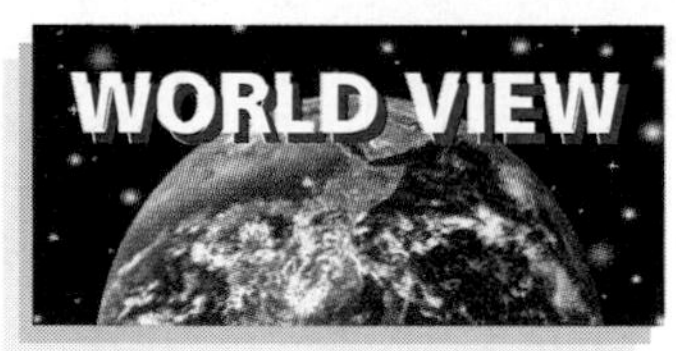

For several years, political activists in the United Kingdom have campaigned against British Aerospace, Europe's largest defense contractor, seeking to deter the company from manufacturing military weaponry. In response, British Aerospace has obtained injunctions prohibiting demonstrators from its property. The protesters vividly present their view of the political issues and resulting injunctions at **http://dialspace.dial.pipex.com/town/terrace/gdn22/BAe/index.html**. Not surprisingly, the company sees things differently, as it explains on its homepage, **http://www.bae.co.uk/html/if.html**.

BOSTON CELTICS LIMITED PARTNERSHIP v. SHAW
908 F.2d 1041, 1990 U.S. App. LEXIS 12117
United States Court of Appeals for the First Circuit, 1990

Facts: In 1989, Brian Shaw, an American basketball player, signed a two-year contract to play with the Italian team Il Messaggero Roma. The team agreed to pay him $800,000 per year and permitted Shaw to cancel the second year if he returned to the United States to play in the National Basketball Association (NBA).

In January 1990, Shaw signed a five-year contract to play for the Boston Celtics of the NBA. The Celtics agreed to pay him a $450,000 signing bonus and more than $1 million per year. In turn, Shaw agreed to cancel the second year of his contract with Il Messaggero.

In June 1990, Shaw told the Celtics that he had changed his mind and would play for Il Messaggero after all. The Celtics sought immediate arbitration, and the arbitrator ordered Shaw to play for the Boston club. He refused, and the Celtics filed suit. The trial court granted a preliminary injunction, ordering Shaw to rescind the contract with Il Messaggero and ordering him not to play for any team but the Celtics. In other words, like most injunctions, this one was stated in the negative. The court would not order Shaw to play for the Celtics, because that would force two antagonists to work together. But it prohibited him from playing elsewhere. Shaw appealed.

Issue: Did the trial court improperly issue a preliminary injunction?

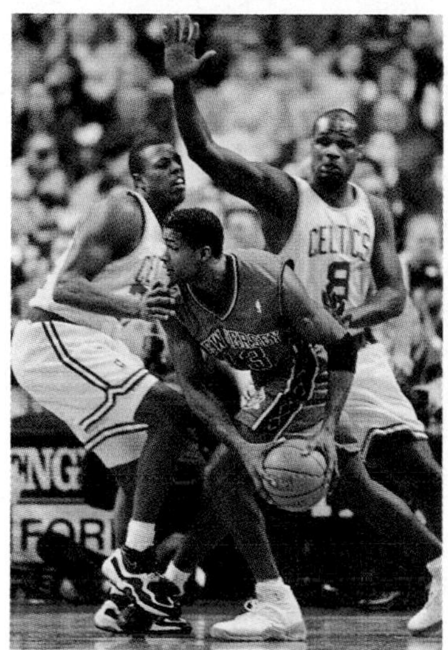

An injunction can halt play as quickly as a referee's whistle.

Excerpts from Chief Judge Breyer's Decision:[8] The only legal question before us is whether the district court acted outside its broad equitable powers when it issued the preliminary injunction. That is to say, did the court improperly answer the four questions judges in this Circuit must ask when deciding whether to issue a preliminary injunction. They are: (1) have the Celtics shown a likelihood of success on the merits? (2) have they shown that failure to issue the injunction would cause the Celtics "irreparable harm?" (3) does the "balance of harms" favor Shaw or the Celtics? and (4) will granting the injunction harm the "public interest?" Our examination of the record has convinced us that the court acted well within the scope of its lawful powers.

To begin with, the Celtics have shown a clear likelihood of success on the merits. The arbitration award is lawful, and courts have authority to enforce lawful arbitration awards. The Celtics also have demonstrated irreparable harm. Without speedy relief, they will likely lose the services of a star athlete next year, and, unless they know fairly soon whether Shaw will, or will not play for them, they will find it difficult to plan intelligently for next season.

Further, the court could reasonably find that the "balance of harms" favors the Celtics. Of course, a preliminary injunction, if ultimately shown wrong on the merits, could cause Shaw harm. He might lose the chance to play in the country, and for the team, that he prefers. [But that harm is offset by his $5 million contract with the Celtics.]

Finally, the court could properly find that issuing a preliminary injunction would not harm the public interest. Indeed, as we have pointed out, the public interest favors court action that effectuates the parties' intent to resolve their disputes informally through arbitration.

Shaw makes an additional argument. He notes that courts will not provide equitable relief such as an injunction to a party with "unclean hands," and he argues that the Celtics' hands are not clean. To support this argument, he has submitted an affidavit saying, in effect, that he signed the contract in a weak moment. His trip to Italy had made him "homesick"; he was "depressed" by what he viewed as undeserved and "negative criticism" in the Italian press; [and] he was not represented by an agent.

Other evidence in the record, however, which Shaw does not deny, shows that he is a college graduate; that he has played under contract with the Celtics before; that the contract is a standard form contract except for a few, fairly simple, rather clear, additions; that he had bargained with the Celtics for an offer that increased from $3.4 million (in December) to $5.4 million (less than one month later); that he looked over the contract before signing it; [and] that he told the American consul in Rome (as he signed it) that he had read and understood it.

Given this state of the record, the district court could easily, and properly, conclude that the Celtics' hands were not "unclean."

Affirmed.

REFORMATION

The final remedy, and perhaps the least common, is **reformation**, a process in which a court will partially "re-write" a contract. Courts seldom do this, because the whole point of a contract is to enable the parties to control their own futures. But a court may reform a contract if it believes a written agreement includes a simple mistake. Suppose that Roger orally agrees to sell 35 acres to Hannah for $600,000. The parties then draw up a written agreement, accidentally describing

[8] Chief Judge Breyer has since become a Justice of the United States Supreme Court.

the land as including 50 additional acres that neither party considered part of the deal. Roger refuses to sell. Hannah sues for specific performance, but asks the court to *reform* the written contract to reflect the true agreement. Most but not all courts would reform the agreement and enforce it.

A court may also reform a contract to save it. If Natasha sells her advertising business to Joseph and agrees not to open a competing agency in the same city anytime in the next 10 years, a court may decide that it is unfair to force her to wait a decade. It could reform the agreement and permit Natasha to compete, say, three years after the sale. But some courts are reluctant to reform contracts and would throw out the entire noncompetition agreement rather than reform it. Parties should never settle for a contract that is sloppy or overbroad, assuming that a court will later reform errors. They may find themselves stuck with a bargain they dislike or with no contract at all.

SPECIAL ISSUES OF DAMAGES

Finally, we consider some special issues of damages, beginning with a party's obligation to minimize its losses.

MITIGATION OF DAMAGES

A party injured by a breach of contract may not recover for damages that he could have avoided with reasonable efforts. In other words, when one party perceives that the other has breached or will breach the contract, the injured party must try to prevent unnecessary loss. A party is expected to **mitigate** his damages, that is, to keep damages as low as he reasonably can.

Malcolm agrees to rent space in his mall to Zena, for a major department store. As part of the lease, Malcolm agrees to redesign the interior to meet her specifications. After Malcolm has spent $20,000 in architect and design fees, Zena informs Malcolm that she is renting other space and will not occupy his mall. Malcolm nonetheless continues the renovation work, spending an additional $50,000 on materials and labor. Malcolm will recover the lost rental payments and the $20,000 expended in reliance on the deal. He will *not* recover the extra $50,000. He should have stopped work when he learned of Zena's breach.

Mitigation and the Sale of Goods

The UCC emphasizes the importance of mitigation. As mentioned earlier in the chapter, when a seller breaches, a buyer has the option of obtaining cover. If the buyer fails to cover, she will generally be *denied* consequential damages. Mary has a contract to buy 1,000 Christmas trees from Elmo for $25 each. The market value is $40 per tree, but Mary has arranged various contracts to resell the tress at $50 each. If Elmo breaches, Mary should try to cover. If she makes no effort to cover, the court will award her $15 per tree, representing the difference between the contract price and market value, but will not award her the consequential damages based on her own expectation of $50 per tree.

NOMINAL DAMAGES

Nominal damages are a token sum, such as one dollar, given to a plaintiff who demonstrates that the defendant breached the contract but cannot prove damages. A school board unfairly fires Gemma, a teacher. If she obtains a teaching job at a better school for identical pay the very next day, she probably can show no damages at all. Nonetheless, the school wrongfully terminated her, and a court may award nominal damages.

LIQUIDATED DAMAGES

It can be difficult or even impossible to prove how much damage the injured party has suffered. So lawyers and executives negotiating a deal may include in the contract a **liquidated damages clause, a provision stating in advance how much a party must pay if it breaches.** Assume that Laurie has hired Bruce to build a five-unit apartment building for $800,000. Bruce promises to complete construction by May 15. Laurie insists on a liquidated damages clause providing that if Bruce finishes late, Laurie's final price is reduced by $3,000 for each week of delay. Bruce finishes the apartment building June 30, and Laurie reduces her payment by $18,000. Is that fair? The answer depends on two factors: **A court will generally enforce a liquidated damages clause if (1) at the time of creating the contract it was very difficult to estimate actual damages, *and* (2) the liquidated amount is reasonable.** In any other case, the liquidated damage will be considered a **penalty** and will prove unenforceable.

We will apply the two factors to Laurie's case. When the parties made their agreement, would it have been difficult to estimate actual damages caused by delay? Yes. Laurie could not prove that all five units would have been occupied or how much rent the tenants would have agreed to pay. Was the $3,000 per week reasonable? Probably. To finance an $800,000 building, Laurie will have to pay at least $6,000 interest per month. She must also pay taxes on the land and may have other expenses. Laurie does not have to prove that every penny of the liquidated damages clause is justified, but only that the figure is reasonable. A court will probably enforce her liquidated damages clause.

On the other hand, suppose Laurie's clause demanded $3,000 per day. There is no basis for such a figure, and a court will declare it a *penalty clause,* and refuse to enforce it. Laurie will be back to square one, forced to prove in court any damages she claims to have suffered from Bruce's delay.

Note that merely using the phrase "liquidated damages clause" does not make the provision enforceable. As the following case illustrates, when there is a dispute, a court will decide whether the clause is a valid liquidated damages clause or an unenforceable penalty clause.

LAKE RIDGE ACADEMY v. CARNEY
66 Ohio St. 3d 376, 613 N.E.2d 183, 1993 Ohio LEXIS 1210
Supreme Court of Ohio, 1993

Facts: In March, Mr. Carney reserved a spot in the fourth grade class at Lake Ridge Academy for his son, Michael. He paid a $630 deposit and agreed in writing to pay the balance of the tuition, $5,610, later that year. The contract permitted Carney to cancel the agreement and withdraw his son with no further obligation provided he did so before August 1. If he failed to notify the school before that date, he became liable for the full tuition.

Carney wrote a letter notifying Lake Ridge that Michael would not attend. He dated the letter August 1, mailed it August 7, and the school received it August 14. Lake Ridge demanded its full tuition, Carney refused, and the school sued. One of the disputed issues was whether the liquidated damages clause was a penalty. The trial court found for Carney, but the court of appeals reversed, finding that the clause was valid. Carney appealed to the state's highest court.

Issue: Was the liquidated damages clause enforceable?

Excerpts from Judge Wright's Descision: Contracting parties may provide in advance for damages to be paid in the event of a breach as long as the provision does not disregard the principle of compensation. Determining whether stipulated damages are punitive or liquidated is not always easy. It is necessary to look to the whole instrument, its subject-matter, the ease or difficulty of measuring the breach in damages, and the amount of the stipulated sum, not only as compared with the value of the subject of the contract, but in proportion to the probable consequences of the breach.

We conclude that the damages in this case are liquidated damages [and thus enforceable].

When Carney and Lake Ridge entered into their contract the damages that Lake Ridge might suffer as a result of a breach by Carney were "uncertain as to amount and difficult of proof." Lake Ridge goes through a long budgeting process which begins each year in January and ends in the fall. The tuition money paid by students is pooled and goes towards staff salaries and benefits, department budgets, student materials, maintenance, improvements, and utilities. Trial testimony reveals that the school budget process is often an uncertain science; it is quite clear that Lake Ridge would be unable to calculate and prove the precise damages caused by the loss of one student's tuition.

Nor is the contract as a whole unreasonable. The headmaster testified that August 1 was chosen as the day before which notice of cancellation had to be given simply because the school had to know in order to meet its financial commitments. Carney had almost five months after he signed the contract to decide whether to cancel it. Because Lake Ridge's financial commitments became more firm as the school year approached, it is reasonable to assume that by August 1 the school was relying on Carney's full tuition payment.

For the latest in liquidated damage developments, watch cable television news—or simply your cable television *bill*. To obtain this service, consumers sign an agreement that often includes an automatic fee of $5 or more for any bills paid late. Cable companies claim that the charges are reasonable liquidated damages, but consumer advocates—and now some courts—consider the fees to be illegal penalties, out of all proportion to the minor damage caused when a customer fails to pay on time. In a class action in Baltimore, the judge declared that, in setting its $5 late fee, the cable company had been "haphazard, cavalier, careless and presumptuous." He ordered the cable provider to repay customers $5.4 million for the exorbitant charges and to reduce future late fees to a maximum of 50 cents. Consumers won similar sums in a class action in Washington, D.C., and lawsuits aimed at the late fees are pending in many other states.

PUNITIVE DAMAGES

We have seen that courts devote little time to morality when granting remedies for breach of contract. In most cases, a party who deliberately breaks its promise is treated the same as one who attempts but fails to honor its bargain. Occasionally, though, a court *will* take into account the question of what is morally right and order a breaching party to pay extra money damages because his conduct was socially intolerable.

Punitive damages are designed not to compensate the injured party but to punish the breaching party. The courts grant punitive damages *in addition* to the usual expectation, reliance, or restitution monies. The goal is to prevent the unethical party from repeating its offense and to deter others in society from similar behavior. Bear in mind that these are exceptional cases. In a contract case, courts will consider a punitive damages claim only when the breach of contract involves conduct such as fraud or bad faith.

How much money may a jury award to penalize a defendant? That question has produced a series of hotly contested cases, but no definitive answer. The United States Supreme Court has given some guidance on the issue in a case arising from Alabama, a state that has historically allowed relatively high punitive awards. After Ira Gore purchased a new BMW automobile, he discovered that the car had been repainted. When he sued, BMW admitted that it never told customers about minor predelivery repairs. The company had sold about 1,000 repainted cars nationwide. The jury concluded that BMW had engaged in gross, malicious fraud and awarded Gore compensatory damages of $4,000 and punitive damages of $4 million. The Alabama Supreme Court reduced the award to $2 million, but the United States Supreme Court said that sum was still too high. The justices declared that **in awarding punitive damages, a court must consider three "guideposts":**

- The reprehensibility of the defendant's conduct
- The ratio between the harm suffered and the award; and
- The difference between the punitive award and any civil or criminal penalties used in similar cases.

The Supreme Court concluded that BMW had shown no evil intent and that Gore's harm had been merely economic, not physical. The Court also found that the ratio between punitive and compensatory damages—500 to 1—was excessive, although it declined to set a proper ratio. On remand, the Alabama Supreme Court reduced the punitive damages award to $50,000.[9]

In the following case, the same two courts again wrangled over a large punitive award.

LIFE INSURANCE COMPANY OF GEORGIA v. DAISEY L. JOHNSON
701 So.2d 524, 1997 Ala. LEXIS 368
Alabama Supreme Court, 1997

Facts: Daisey L. Johnson, an 84-year-old woman with a third grade education, had spent her life as a domestic worker. Over a 25-year period, she purchased various insurance policies from Life Insurance Company of Georgia. The company's agent, Barbara Holt, came to Johnson's house monthly to collect premiums. On one visit, she recommended that Johnson purchase a "Medicare supplement policy," explaining that if Ms. Johnson were hospitalized, the policy would pay for bills not covered by Medicare. What Holt did not explain was that Ms. Johnson was already fully protected since she was enrolled in *Medicaid*, a separate government program for poor people. Before long, Ms. Johnson was paying about $103 per month for the new policy, almost one-third of her small fixed income.

Johnson sued Life of Georgia, alleging that the company had fraudulently sold her a worthless policy. The jury awarded her $250,000 in compensatory damages and $15 million in punitive damages. The Alabama Supreme Court lowered the punitive award to $5 million. The United States Supreme Court ordered the Alabama Supreme Court to reconsider whether the $5 million was reasonable in light of the three newly established "guideposts" from *BMW v. Gore*.

---

[9] *BMW of North America, Inc. v. Gore*, 517 U.S. 559, 116 S. Ct. 1589, 1996 U.S. LEXIS 3390 (1996).

Issue: Was the award of $5 million punitive damages reasonable?

Excerpts from Justice Shores's Decision: [A] former Life of Georgia agent, James Russell Clark, testified that his training could be summed up in three words: "Get the money." Life of Georgia's corporate officers testified during the plaintiff's presentation of her case that Life of Georgia had done nothing to try to prevent the sale of Medicare supplement policies to unqualified persons even though in 1992 Life of Georgia had been faced with trial in Mobile County and had experienced an adverse verdict of $1 million. The company continued its history of noncompliance, giving rise to the conclusion that even a million-dollar sanction against the company was not sufficient to deter its misconduct.

Applying the first guidepost, the reprehensibility of the defendant's conduct, we conclude that the evidence was sufficient to permit the jury to conclude that Life of Georgia's egregiously improper conduct was sufficiently reprehensible to give rise to tort liability and was sufficient to establish the high degree of culpability that warrants a substantial punitive damages award. Life of Georgia was aware that its actions or omissions were causing harm, but it did not change its policy. It consciously disregarded the rights of old, indigent, and uneducated citizens of Alabama.

[The court then focused on the second guidepost.] Unlike Dr. Gore and other BMW purchasers, who the United States Supreme Court concluded were not threatened with any additional potential harm by BMW's nondisclosure policy, the plaintiff here proved that there was a sizable group of Alabama citizens who were put at risk by the defendant's wrongful conduct. She proved that over 116,000 Alabamians have both Medicare and Medicaid; given the Medicare and Medicaid eligibility standards, we can conclude that these Alabamians are both old and poor.

Applying the Supreme Court's second guidepost, we conclude that following the remittitur of punitive damages to $3 million, as we order today, the ratio of exemplary damages to the compensatory damages of $250,000 will bear a reasonable relationship, given the facts in this case.

[As to the third guidepost, the court concluded that Alabama law provided no civil or criminal penalties to compare to this award. The court lowered the punitive award to $3 million, and affirmed.]

CHAPTER CONCLUSION

The powers of a court are broad and flexible and may suffice to give an injured party what it deserves. But problems of proof and the uncertainty of remedies demonstrate that the best solution is a carefully drafted contract and socially responsible behavior.

CHAPTER REVIEW

1. Someone breaches a contract when he fails to perform a duty, without a valid excuse.
2. A remedy is the method a court uses to compensate an injured party.
3. An interest is a legal right in something, such as a contract. The first step that a court takes in choosing a remedy is to decide what interest it is protecting.

4. The expectation interest puts the injured party in the position she would have been in had both sides fully performed. It has three components:
   (a) Compensatory damages, which flow directly from the contract.
   (b) Consequential damages, which result from the unique circumstances of the particular injured party. The injured party may recover consequential damages only if the breaching party should have foreseen them.
   (c) Incidental damages, which are the minor costs an injured party incurs responding to a breach.
5. The reliance interest puts the injured party in the position he would have been in had the parties never entered into a contract. It focuses on the time and money that the injured party spent performing his part of the agreement. If there was no valid contract, a court might still award reliance damages under a theory of promissory estoppel.
6. The restitution interest returns to the injured party a benefit that she has conferred on the other party, which it would be unjust to leave with that person. Restitution can be awarded in the case of a contract created, for example, by fraud, or in a case of quasi-contract, where the parties never created a binding agreement.
7. Specific performance, ordered only in cases of land or a unique asset, requires both parties to perform the contract.
8. An injunction is a court order that requires someone to do something or refrain from doing something.
9. Reformation is the process by which a court will—occasionally— rewrite a contract to ensure that it accurately reflects the parties' agreement and/or to maintain the contract's viability.
10. The duty to mitigate means that a party injured by a breach of contract may not recover for damages that he could have avoided with reasonable efforts.
11. Nominal damages are a token sum, such as one dollar, given to an injured plaintiff who cannot prove damages.
12. A liquidated damages clause will be enforced if and only if, at the time of creating the contract, it was very difficult to estimate actual damages *and* the liquidated amount is reasonable.
13. Punitive damages are designed not to compensate the injured party but to punish the breaching party.

PRACTICE TEST

1. Mr. and Ms. Beard contracted for S/E Joint Venture to build a house on property it owned, and then sell the completed house to the Beards for $785,000. S/E was late with construction and ultimately never finished the house or conveyed anything to the Beards, who sued. Evidence at trial demonstrated that S/E had clearly breached the contract and that the Beards had spent about $32,000 in rent because of the delay. There was testimony that the market value of the house as promised would have been about $100,000 more than the contract price, but this point was not clearly established because the trial judge considered it irrelevant. The judge awarded only the rental payments. Both sides appealed. Is the market value of the house, as it should have been built, relevant? How much money are the Beards entitled to?

2. Lewis signed a contract for the rights to all timber located on Nine Mile Mine. He agreed to pay $70 per thousand board feet ($70/mbf). As he began work, Nine Mile became convinced that Lewis lacked sufficient equipment to do the job well and forbade him to enter the land. Lewis sued. Nine Mile moved for summary judgment. The mine offered proof that the market value of the timber was exactly $70/mbf, and Lewis had no evidence to contradict Nine Mile. The evidence about market value proved decisive. Why? Please rule on the summary judgment motion.

3. Twin Creeks Entertainment signed a deal with U.S. JVC Corp. in which JVC would buy 60,000 feature film videocassettes from Twin Creeks over a three-year period. JVC intended to distribute the cassettes nationwide. Relying on its deal with JVC, Twin Creeks signed an agreement with Paramount Pictures, agreeing to purchase a minimum of $600,000 worth of Paramount cassettes over a two-year period. JVC breached its deal with Twin Creeks and refused to accept the cassettes it had agreed upon. Twin Creeks sued and claimed, among other damages, the money it owed to Paramount. JVC moved to dismiss the claim based on the Paramount contract, on the ground that Twin Creeks, the seller of goods, was not entitled to such damages. What kind of damages is Twin Creeks seeking? Please rule on the motion to dismiss.

4. Bingo is emerging as a rock star. His last five concerts have all sold out. Lucia signs a deal with Bingo to perform two concerts in one evening in Big City, for a fee of $50,000 for both shows. Lucia then rents the Auditorium for that evening, guaranteeing to pay $50,000. Bingo promptly breaks the deal before any tickets are sold. Lucia sues, pointing out that the Auditorium seats 3,000 and she anticipated selling all tickets for an average of $40 each, for a total gross of $120,000. How much will Lucia recover, if anything?

5. Racicky was in the process of buying 320 acres of ranch land. While that sale was being negotiated, Racicky signed a contract to sell the land to Simon. Simon paid $144,000, the full price of the land. But Racicky then went bankrupt, before he could complete the *purchase* of the land, let alone its sale. Which of these remedies should Simon seek: expectation, restitution, specific performance, or reformation?

6. Ambrose hires Bierce for $25,000 to supervise the production of Ambrose's crop, but then breaks the contract by firing Bierce at the beginning of the season. A nearby grower offers Bierce $23,000 for the same growing season, but Bierce refuses to take such a pay cut. He stays home and sues Ambrose. How much money, if any, will Bierce recover from Ambrose, and why?

7. Parkinson was injured in an auto accident by a driver who had no insurance. Parkinson filed a claim with her insurer, Liberty Mutual, for $2,000 under her "uninsured motorist" coverage. Liberty Mutual told her that if she sought that money, her premiums would go "sky high," so Parkinson dropped the claim. Later, after she had spoken with an attorney, Parkinson sued. What additional claim was her attorney likely to make?

8. **CPA QUESTION** Master Mfg., Inc. contracted with Accur Computer Repair Corp. to maintain Master's computer system. Master's manufacturing process depends on its computer system operating properly at all times. A liquidated damages clause in the contract provided that Accur would pay $1,000 to Master for each day that Accur was late responding to a service request. On January 12, Accur was notified that Master's computer system had failed. Accur did not respond to Master's service request until January 15. If Master sues Accur under the liquidated damage provision of the contract, Master will:

(a) Win, unless the liquidated damages provision is determined to be a penalty

(b) Win, because under all circumstances liquidated damage provisions are enforceable

(c) Lose, because Accur's breach was not material

(d) Lose, because liquidated damage provisions violate public policy

9. **CPA QUESTION** Kaye contracted to sell Hodges a building for $310,000. The contract required Hodges to pay the entire amount at closing. Kaye refused to close the sale of the building. Hodges sued Kaye. To what relief is Hodges entitled?

(a) Punitive damages and compensatory damages

(b) Specific performance and compensatory damages

(c) Consequential damages or punitive damages

(d) Compensatory damages or specific performance

10. **YOU BE THE JUDGE WRITING PROBLEM** John and Susan Verba sold a Vermont lakeshore lot to Shane and Deborah Rancourt for $115,000. The Rancourts intended to build a house on the property, but after preparing the land for construction, they learned that a wetland protection law prevented building near the

lake. They sued, seeking rescission of the contract. The trial court concluded that the parties had reached their agreement under a "mutual, but innocent, misunderstanding." The trial judge gave the Verbas a choice: they could rescind the contract and refund the purchase price, or they could give the Rancourts $55,000, the difference between the sales price and the actual market value of the land. The Rancourts appealed. Were the Rancourts entitled to rescission of the contract? **Argument for the Rancourts:** When the parties have made a mutual mistake about an important factual issue, either party is entitled to rescind the contract. The land is of no use to us and we want our money back. **Argument for the Verbas:** Both sides were acting in good faith and both sides made an honest mistake. We are willing to acknowledge that the land is worth somewhat less than we all thought, and we are willing to refund $55,000. The buyers shouldn't complain—they are getting the property at about half the original price, and the error was as much their fault as ours.

11. **RIGHT & WRONG** The National Football League owns the copyright to the broadcasts of its games. It licenses local television stations to telecast certain games and maintains a "blackout rule," which prohibits stations from broadcasting home games that are not sold out 72 hours before the game starts. Certain home games of the Cleveland Browns team were not sold out, and the NFL blocked local broadcast. But several bars in the Cleveland area were able to pick up the game's signal by using special antennas. The NFL wanted the bars to stop showing the games. What did it do? Was it unethical of the bars to broadcast the games that they were able to pick up? Apart from the NFL's legal rights, do you think it had the moral right to stop the bars from broadcasting the games?

INTERNET RESEARCH PROBLEM

You represent a group of neighborhood residents in a large city who are protesting construction of a skyscraper that will violate building height limitations. Draft a complaint, requesting an appropriate injunction. You may use the sample injunction complaint found at **http://www.kinseylaw.com/ATTY%20SERV/civil/complaints/injunction.html**.

You can find further practice problems in the Online Quiz at http://beatty.westbuslaw.com or in the Study Guide that accompanies this text.

UNIT 3

COMMERCIAL TRANSACTIONS

CHAPTER 19

INTRODUCTION TO SALES

He Sued, She Sued. Harold and Maude made a great couple because both were compulsive entrepreneurs. One evening they sat on their penthouse roofdeck, overlooking the twinkling Chicago skyline. Harold sipped a decaf coffee while negotiating, over the phone, with a real estate developer in San Antonio. Maude puffed a cigar as she bargained on a different line with a toy manufacturer in Cleveland. They hung up at the same time. "I did it!" shrieked Maude, "I made an incredible deal for the robots—five bucks each!" "No, *I* did it!" triumphed Harold, "I sold the 50 acres in Texas for $300,000 more than it's worth." They dashed indoors.

Maude quickly scrawled a handwritten memo, which said, "Confirming our deal—100,000 Psychopath Robots—you deliver Chicago—end of summer." She didn't mention a price, or an exact delivery date, or when payment would be made. She signed her memo and faxed it to the toy manufacturer. Harold took more time. He typed a thorough contract, describing precisely the land he was selling, the $2.3 million price, how and when each payment would be made and the deed conveyed. He signed the contract and faxed it, along with a plot plan showing the surveyed land. Then the happy couple grabbed a bottle of champagne, returned to the deck—and placed a side bet on whose contract would prove more profitable. The loser would have to cook and serve dinner for six months.

Neither Harold nor Maude ever heard again from the other parties. The toy manufacturer sold the Psychopath Robots to another retailer at a higher price. Maude was forced to buy comparable toys elsewhere for $9 each. She sued. And the Texas property buyer changed his mind, deciding to develop a Club Med in Greenland and refusing to pay Harold for his land. He sued. Only one of the two plaintiffs succeeded. Which one?

The adventures of Harold and Maude illustrate the Uniform Commercial Code (UCC) in action. The Code is the single most important source of law for people engaged in commerce and controls the vast majority of contracts made every day in every state. The Code is ancient in origin, contemporary in usage, admirable in purpose, and flawed in application. "Yeah, yeah, that's fascinating," snaps Harold, "but who wins the bet?" Relax, Harold, we'll tell you in a minute.

DEVELOPMENT OF COMMERCIAL LAW

During the fifteenth and sixteenth centuries, merchants in England and throughout Europe found the law of their respective nations cumbersome and inadequate for the settlement of commercial disputes. For example, in England, property had historically been the most important asset, and civil law revolved around the rights to land. Decisions in property disputes came slowly, and courts seldom thought in terms of a "contract." Even by the seventeenth century, English judges were only beginning to acknowledge that an exchange of mere promises, with no money or property changing hands, might lead to an enforceable agreement. But merchants dealt in the sale of goods, not real estate. Their livelihood depended upon promises, on the rapid movement of their wares, and on their ability to enforce bargains. Dissatisfied with the few remedies that courts offered, businessmen throughout England and the Continent began to treat their own customs as law and to settle disputes in trade organizations rather than civil courts. The body of rules they relied on became known as the *lex mercatoria*, or **law merchant**. The law merchant was thus a "custom made" law, created by the merchants who used it. The new doctrine focused on promises, the sale and exchange of goods, and payment.

Lord Mansfield (1705–1793), a justly famous English judge, began to use some of these commercial rules in his influential decisions, beginning the slow process of incorporating these new rules into the common law of contract. Over the next two centuries, common law judges employed more and more of the law merchant and at the same time began to develop specialized areas within commercial law. Courts began to distinguish the law for the sale of goods from the law governing, for example, payments by check or other negotiable instruments. Similar changes took place in the United States.

Throughout the first half of the twentieth century, commercial transactions changed dramatically in this country, as advances in transportation and communication revolutionized negotiation and trade. But the law lagged behind, evolving more slowly than commercial practices, hampered by common law differences between the states. The nation needed a modernized business law to give nationwide uniformity and predictability in a new and faster world. In 1942, two groups

Article 1: *General Provisions*	The purpose of the code, general guidance in applying it, and definitions.
Article 2: *Sale of Goods*	The sale of *goods*, such as a new car, 20,000 pairs of gloves, or 101 Dalmatians. This article is the heart of the UCC.
Article 2A: *Leases*	A temporary exchange of goods for money, such as renting a car.
Article 2B: *Software and Licenses*	Electronic contracts and the software that powers them.
Article 3: *Negotiable Instruments*	The use of checks, promissory notes, and other negotiable instruments.
Article 4: *Bank Deposits and Collections*	The rights and obligations of banks and their customers.
Article 4A: *Funds Transfers*	An instruction, given by a bank customer, to credit a sum of money to another's account.
Article 5: *Letters of Credit*	The use of credit, extended by two or more banks, to facilitate a contract between two parties who do not know each other and require guarantees by banks they trust.
Article 6: *Bulk Transfers*	The sale of a major part of a company's inventory or equipment.
Article 7: *Warehouse Receipts, Bills of Lading, and Other Documents of Title*	Documents proving ownership of goods that are being transported or stored.
Article 8: *Investment Securities*	Rights and liabilities concerning shares of stock or other ownership of an enterprise.
Article 9: *Secured Transactions*	A sale of goods in which the seller keeps a financial stake in the goods he has sold, such as a car dealer who may repossess the car if the buyer fails to make payments.

of scholars, the American Law Institute (ALI) and the National Conference of Commissioners on Uniform State Laws (NCCUSL), began the effort to draft a modern, national law of commerce. Led by Professor Karl N. Llewellyn, the scholars debated and formulated for nearly a decade. Finally, in 1952, Llewellyn and colleagues published their work—the Uniform Commercial Code. The entire Code is available online at http://www.law.cornell.edu/ucc/ucc.table.html.

THE CODE TODAY

The ALI and the NCCUSL revised the Code in 1957 and once again during the 1970s. Then, beginning in the mid-1980s, the two groups began their most ambitious overhaul, seeking to make substantial changes to almost all of the articles and to add new ones as well. The goals were to acknowledge lessons learned from the Code's first half-century; to accommodate new technology, such as sales made over the Internet; and to serve a business world that had shifted much of its focus from traditional manufacturing to services and information.

Remember, though, that, in a sense, the UCC is artificial because it is the creation of scholars, not legislators. No section of the Code, new or old, has any legal effect until a state legislature adopts it. In fact, all 50 states and the District of Columbia have adopted the UCC, but some have adopted the early versions from the 1950s and partially revised them, while other states have adopted more recent texts. Louisiana, with its French law heritage, has not adopted Articles 2, 2A, or 6 in any form. The drafters have not achieved nationwide uniformity, but they have brought commercial law much closer to that goal.

This book reflects recent Code revisions that states have actually adopted, including Article 4A, on funds transfers, and the suggested repeal of Article 6, on bulk transfers. The drafters have given substantial—and controversial—rewrites to the Code's core articles, 2 and 9, but as this book goes to press, no states have enacted them into law. Those revisions, therefore, will not be allowed an appearance in our book yet and must hover in the wings, hoping for a role in a few years. The legal scholars have also recommended significant alterations to Article 1, concerning definitions, and Article 2A, on leases, but again, they are only suggestions at this point. Finally, the Code's sponsors have drafted a new Article 2B, governing software contracts and licenses. We discuss some of its key recommendations in Chapter 15. (For online commentary about the proposed article, from a group of management information specialists, see http://www.simnet.org/public/ucc.html.) Although Article 2B is intended to govern most elements of electronic commerce, some state legislatures decided not to wait for its arrival. After concluding that business people urgently needed some predictability about agreements made electronically, they drafted their own statutes. The Web site http://www.mbc.com/ecommerce.html provides a useful state-by-state directory of current legislation concerning electronic commerce.

Throughout the revision process, the ALI and NCCUSL have been open to suggestions and comments from all interested parties—including business law students! All of the proposed changes to the UCC—revisions and new sections alike—are available online at http://www.law.upenn.edu/library/ulc/ulc.htm, and that Web site provides an opportunity for your input.

HAROLD AND MAUDE, REVISITED

Harold and Maude each negotiated what they believed was an enforceable agreement, and both filed suit: Harold for the sale of his land, Maude for the purchase of toy robots. Only one prevailed. The difference in outcome demonstrates one of the changes that the UCC has wrought in the law of commercial contracts and illustrates why everyone in business needs a working knowledge of the Code. As we revisit the happy couple, Harold is clearing the dinner dishes. Maude sits back in her chair, lights a cigar, and compliments her husband on the apple tart. Harold, scowling and spilling coffee, wonders what went wrong.

Harold's contract was for the sale of land and was governed by the common law of contracts. The common law statute of frauds requires any agreement for the sale of land to be in writing and *signed by the defendant*, in this case the buyer in Texas. Harold signed it, but the buyer never did, so Harold's meticulously detailed document was worth less than a five-cent cigar.

Maude's quickly scribbled memorandum, concerning psychotic robot toys, was for the sale of goods and was governed by Article 2 of the UCC. The Code requires less detail and formality in a writing. Because Maude and the seller were both merchants, the document she scribbled could be enforced *even against the defendant*, who had never signed anything. The fact that Maude left out the price and other significant terms was not fatal to a contract under the UCC, though under the common law such omissions would have made the bargain unenforceable. We will look in greater detail at these UCC changes. For now it is enough to see that the Code has carved major changes into the common law of contracts, alterations that Harold is beginning to appreciate.

THIS UNIT OF THE TEXT

This unit covers three principal subjects, all relating to commercial transactions that the Code governs. The first chapters concern the sale of goods and focus primarily on Article 2. In the present chapter we emphasize how Code provisions work together to change the common law. In the following chapters we examine title to goods (Chapter 20), then warranties and product liability (Chapter 21), and, finally, performance (Chapter 22).

The next group of three chapters (Chapters 23–25) surveys the law of negotiable instruments. Checks are the most common kind of negotiable instrument, but we will see that there are many other varieties and that each creates different rights and obligations. We conclude the unit with a chapter devoted to secured transactions (Chapter 26), that is, a sale of goods in which the seller keeps a financial stake in the goods he has sold, and a chapter that analyzes bankruptcy law (Chapter 27).

UCC BASICS

CODE'S PURPOSE

The Uniform Commercial Code proclaims its purposes clearly:

> UCC §1-102(2): Underlying purposes and policies of this Act are
> **(a)** to simplify, clarify and modernize the law governing commercial transactions;
> **(b)** to permit the continued expansion of commercial practices through custom, usage and agreement of the parties;
> **(c)** to make uniform the law among the various jurisdictions.

This is not mere boilerplate. To "modernize," in (a), requires a focus on the needs of contemporary business people, not on rules developed when judges rode horseback. Suppose a court must decide whether a writing is detailed enough to satisfy the Code's statute of frauds. The judge may rely on §1-102 to decide that because modern commerce is so fast, even the skimpiest of writings is good enough to demonstrate that the parties had reached a bargain. In doing so, the judge would deliberately be turning away from legal history to accommodate business practices in an electronic age.

Look at (c), which urges uniformity. Assume that a state supreme court must decide whether a merchant acted in good faith when trying to modify an unprofitable contract. The court may look to the high courts of other states for guidance, not because they are binding (which they are not) or even persuasive (which they may not be) but because uniformity is a valuable goal in itself.

Section 1-102 also states that "[t]his Act shall be liberally construed and applied to promote its underlying purposes," meaning that when in doubt, courts should focus on the goals described. The Code emphasizes *getting the right results*, rather than following rigid rules of contract law.

SCOPE OF ARTICLE 2

Because the UCC changes the common law, it is essential to know whether the Code applies in a given case. Negotiations may lead to an enforceable agreement when the UCC applies, even though the same bargaining would create no contract under the common law.

UCC §2-102: Article 2 applies to the sale of goods.[1] **Goods are things that are movable, other than money and investment securities.** Hats are goods, and so are railroad cars, lumber, books, and bottles of wine. Land is not a good, nor is a house. So an agreement for the delivery of 10,000 board feet of white pine is a contract for the sale of goods, and Article 2 governs it. But the article does not apply to a contract for the sale of an office building. A skyscraper is not movable (although an entire city *may* be[2]).

Article 2 regulates **sales**, which means that one party transfers title to the other in exchange for money. If you sell your motorcycle to a friend, that is a sale of goods. If you lend the bike to your friend for the weekend, that is not a sale and Article 2 does not apply. Article 2 also does not apply to the **leasing** of goods, for example, when you rent a car. A sale involves a permanent change in ownership whereas a lease concerns a temporary change in possession.

Leasing goods is an enormous part of business these days. Virtually every kind of commercial and industrial equipment, from computers to tractors to coffee pots, is leased every day around the country. For example, when you fly home, the aircraft you sit in is quite likely leased to the airline from which you bought your ticket. Over 20 percent of all capital investment in the United States is directly related to equipment leasing. Because leasing is so important, the drafters of the Code added a new article to cover the subject.

Article 2A governs the leasing of goods. About 40 states have adopted Article 2A, though unfortunately not all have adopted the same version. The law of leasing is therefore less uniform than that of sales. How does Article 2A compare to Article 2? Overall, it is similar, and many sections are almost identical. But there are some important differences, and anyone engaging in a significant amount of commercial leasing must become familiar with Article 2A. For our purposes, leasing law is a variation on the theme of Article 2, and we will concentrate on the principal melody of sales.

Mixed Contracts

Sophocles University hires ClickOn Computer to design software for the university's computerized grading system, which must be capable of recording and storing all grades, making the grades available to the students by telephone, computing averages, and printing transcripts. ClickOn agrees to design the software, install it, and train the staff in its use. But things go badly from day one. Sophocles gives ClickOn an "F" for effort and refuses to pay a nickel. Did the parties have an enforceable contract? Most of the bargaining was oral, and the only writings were a few short letters. If the common law governs the deal, it will be difficult or impossible to show an offer and acceptance with definite terms. But if the UCC controls, the writings may suffice to show a binding agreement.

To determine whether the UCC governs, we need to know what kind of an agreement the parties made. Was it one for the sale of goods (UCC) or one for

---

1 Officially, Article 2 tells us that it applies to *transactions* in goods, which is a slightly broader category than sale of goods. But most sections of Article 2, and most court decisions, focus exclusively on sales, and so shall we.

2 "If you are lucky enough to have lived in Paris as a young man, then wherever you go for the rest of your life, it stays with you, for Paris is a moveable feast." Ernest Hemingway, 1950.

services (common law)? In fact the agreement combined both goods and services and was therefore a *mixed contract*. **In a mixed contract involving sales and services, the UCC will govern if the *predominant purpose* is the sale of goods, but the common law will control if the predominant purpose is services.**

If ClickOn sues, the court must determine whether the predominant purpose was the design of the software and the training of staff, which are service work, or the sale of the software, which is a transaction in goods. In this case, the sale of the software predominated. ClickOn did its design work in order to sell an expensive software package to a customer. It was the software that generated the contract, not ClickOn's work in preparing it. So the UCC does govern, and ClickOn may have a valid contract. We return to this issue of mixed contracts later in the chapter, as we see how §2-102 interacts with other Code provisions.

MERCHANTS

The UCC gives merchants greater freedom to contract—and greater responsibility.

The UCC, we know, evolved indirectly from the law merchant, the commercial law developed by business people themselves. And the Code still attempts to meet the unique needs of the business world. But while the UCC offers a contract law that is more flexible than the common law, it also requires a higher level of responsibility from the merchants it serves. Those who make a living by crafting agreements are expected to understand the legal consequences of their words and deeds. Thus many sections of the Code offer two rules: one for "merchants" and one for everybody else.

UCC §2-104: A merchant is someone who routinely deals in the particular goods involved, *or* who appears to have special knowledge or skill in those goods, *or* who uses agents with special knowledge or skill in those goods. A used car dealer is a "merchant" when it comes to selling autos, because he routinely deals in them. He is not a merchant when he goes to a furniture store and purchases a new sofa. The salesman who sells new sofas is a merchant for that purpose.

The UCC frequently holds a merchant to a higher standard of conduct than a non-merchant. For example, a merchant may be held to an oral contract if she received written confirmation of it, even though the merchant herself never signed the confirmation. That same confirmation memo, arriving at the house of a non-merchant, would *not* create a binding deal. We will see many instances of this dual level of responsibility, one for a merchant and the other for a non-merchant. More often than not, it is apparent whether the parties are merchants. If a manufacturer of toy balloons agrees to sell 10,000 boxes of toy balloons to a toy retailer, both parties obviously are merchants. Other cases are less clear. Is a farmer a merchant? Farmers work long, hard hours in the field, yet today they may also be sophisticated commodities traders. Some courts have concluded they are merchants, but almost as many have decided they are not. The case of *Colorado-Kansas Grain Co. v. Reifschneider*, reported later in this chapter, illustrates this issue. First, we must plant a few more basic doctrines.

GOOD FAITH AND UNCONSCIONABILITY

Good Faith

The UCC imposes a duty of good faith in the performance of all contracts. Here is a $900,000 example.

The Kansas Municipal Gas Agency (KMGA) purchased natural gas for cities and towns in Kansas. KMGA requested proposals for a long-term gas contract from suppliers, stressing its need for a guaranteed supply. Vesta Energy Co.

responded, and the two sides agreed on essential terms, including price. Vesta began supplying natural gas while they worked out the last details of a long-term contract.

Suddenly, Vesta asked for a *force majeure* clause, which permits either party to cancel a contract in the event of specified disasters, such as tornadoes or other acts of God. Such clauses are common in the gas industry. But Vesta asked that the clause also permit it to end the arrangement in case of "failure of supply," meaning that Vesta could cancel the deal if it was unable to find affordable supplies. KMGA rejected the proposal, and Vesta stopped supplying gas. KMGA sued, claiming that Vesta had made its *force majeure* proposal in bad faith.

For *non-merchants*, good faith means honesty in fact. For a *merchant*, good faith means honesty in fact *plus* the exercise of reasonable commercial standards of fair dealing.[3] Thus, when parties perform a contract, or in certain cases when they negotiate, neither side may lie or mislead. Further, a party who is a merchant must act as fairly as the business community routinely expects.

The court found that Vesta had acted in bad faith. The parties already had a working agreement, and Vesta had sabotaged it because the price of natural gas had unexpectedly shot up 75 percent. In order to escape the unprofitable deal, Vesta proposed an outrageous *force majeure* clause, knowing that KMGA would reject it. Based on Vesta's bad faith negotiating, the court awarded KMGA $904,000, the amount the company lost by purchasing gas elsewhere.[4]

Unconscionability

The UCC employs a second principle to encourage fair play and just results: the doctrine of unconscionability. **UCC §2-302: A contract may be unconscionable if it is shockingly one-sided and fundamentally unfair.** If a court concludes that some part of a contract is unconscionable, it will refuse to enforce that provision. Courts seldom find a contract unconscionable if the two parties are businesses, but they are quicker to apply the doctrine when one party is a consumer.

Suppose Bill's Builderia sells building equipment. For every sales contract Bill uses a pre-printed form that says, among other things, that the buyer takes the item "as is" and that Bill is not liable for repairs or for compensatory or consequential damages. If Bill sells a $3,000 power mower to a landscape contractor and the machine falls to pieces, a court will probably enforce the limitation on liability. The law assumes that a professional contractor will have the sophistication to read and understand the contract and can bargain for different terms if he is unhappy. But if the buyer is a consumer, such as a homeowner intent on mowing his own lawn, a court will probably declare the clause *unconscionable*. Bill is in the business of selling the equipment and knows the risks. He has drafted the pre-printed contract. The homeowner is unlikely even to read the entire agreement, let alone understand phrases like "consequential damages." It would be unfair to enforce the clause against the consumer. We will look at this issue in more detail in Chapter 21, on warranties and products liability.

Good Faith and Unconscionability Distinguished. The doctrine of good faith focuses on a party's behavior as it performs an agreement: Was it attempting to carry out its obligations in a reasonable manner and do what both sides expected when they made the deal? Unconscionability looks primarily at the contract itself. Are any terms so grossly unfair that a court should reform or ignore them?

Next we examine how the basic ideas of scope, merchant status, and good faith interact with other UCC provisions in the creation of a contract.

---

[3] UCC §§1-201(19), 1-203, and 2-103.

[4] *Kansas Municipal Gas Agency v. Vesta Energy Co.*, 843 F. Supp. 1401, 1994 U.S. Dist. LEXIS 2240 (D. Kan. 1994).

CONTRACT FORMATION

The common law expected the parties to form a contract in a fairly predictable and traditional way: the offeror made a clear offer that included all important terms, and the offeree agreed to all terms. Nothing was left open. The drafters of the UCC recognized that business people frequently do not think or work that way and that the law should reflect business reality.

FORMATION BASICS: SECTION 2-204

UCC §2-204 provides three important rules that enable parties to make a contract quickly and informally:

1. *Any Manner That Shows Agreement*. The parties may make a contract in any manner sufficient to show that they reached an agreement. They may show the agreement with words, writings, or even their conduct. Lisa negotiates with Ed to buy 300 barbecue grills. The parties agree on a price, but other business prevents them from finishing the deal. Then six months later Lisa writes, "Remember our deal for 300 grills? I still want to do it if you do." Ed doesn't respond, but a week later a truck shows up at Lisa's store with the 300 grills, and Lisa accepts them. The combination of their original discussion, Lisa's subsequent letter, Ed's delivery, and her acceptance all adds up to show that they reached an agreement. The court will enforce their deal, and Lisa must pay the agreed-upon price.
2. *Moment of Making Is Not Critical*. The UCC will enforce a deal even though it is difficult, in common law terms, to say exactly when it was formed. Was Lisa's deal formed when they orally agreed? When he delivered? She accepted? The Code's answer: it doesn't matter. The contract is enforceable.
3. *One or More Terms May Be Left Open*. The common law insisted that the parties clearly agree on all important terms. If they did not, there was no meeting of minds and no enforceable deal. The Code changes that. **Under the UCC, a court may enforce a bargain even though one or more terms were left open.** Lisa's letter never said when she required delivery of the barbecues or when she would pay. Under the UCC, the omission is not fatal. As long as there is some certain basis for giving damages to the injured party, the court will do just that. Suppose Lisa refused to pay, claiming that the agreement included no date for her payment. A court would rule that the parties assumed she would pay within a commercially reasonable time, such as 30 days.

In the following case, the trial court based its ruling on the common law of contracts. The Georgia Appeals Court used two sections of the Code to reverse the outcome. Since the cases in this chapter all involve more than one Code section, we will outline the relevant provisions at the outset.

Code Provisions Discussed in This Case

Issue	Relevant Code Section
1. What law governs?	UCC §2-102: Article 2 applies to the sale of goods.
2. Did the parties form a contract?	UCC §2-204: The parties may make a contract in any manner sufficient to show agreement.

J. LEE GREGORY, INC. v. SCANDINAVIAN HOUSE, L.P.

209 Ga. App. 285, 433 S.E.2d 687, 1993 Ga. App. LEXIS 857
Georgia Court of Appeals, 1993

Facts: Scandinavian House owned an apartment building that needed new windows. J. Lee Gregory, doing business as Perma Sash, sent a proposal to Scandinavian offering to remove all old windows and install new ones for $453,000. About two-thirds of the price reflected material costs, and one-third labor.

Scandinavian sent back a letter stating: "Please consider this letter an indication of our intent to purchase the windows contained in your proposal. This is your authorization to begin the measuring and the preparation of shop and installation drawings. We reserve the option to negotiate terms and conditions of the proposal which may impact or affect the operation of the building and the installation of the windows."

Perma Sash then spent three weeks measuring windows and preparing shop drawings, which it sent to Scandinavian House. The drawings were fine, but the parties, which had agreed on the price, could not agree on the method of payment. Perma Sash wanted certain guarantees of payment that Scandinavian House refused to make. Scandinavian notified Perma Sash that the deal was off and bought its windows elsewhere.

Perma Sash sued. The trial court gave summary judgment for Scandinavian, finding that the UCC did not govern and that the parties had never finalized an enforceable contract. Perma Sash appealed.

Issues: What law governs the case? Did the parties form a contract?

Excerpts from Judge Murray's Decision: What was the dominant purpose of the transaction in [this] case? Was it the sale of goods or the rendition of services? It can hardly be said that the sale of the windows was "incidental" to the transaction. Rather it would appear that the rendition of services was the incidental factor. After all, approximately two-thirds of the cost of the transaction was allocated to the windows. Besides, the contract did not segregate the total price of the windows from the total price of the services to be rendered. Thus, we think the predominant character of the transaction was the sale of goods, even though a substantial amount of service was involved in installing the goods.

The mere fact that Scandinavian House would not have purchased the windows unless plaintiff installed them is of no consequence. When presented with two elements of a contract, each absolutely necessary if the subject matter is to be of any significant value to the purchaser, it is a futile task to attempt to determine which component is "more necessary." Thus, we must look to the predominant purpose, the thrust of the contract as it would exist in the minds of reasonable parties. There is no surer way to provide for predictable results in the face of a highly artificial classification system. Inasmuch as the predominant purpose of the transaction involved the sale of goods, the UCC applies. The trial court erred in ruling otherwise.

Having determined that the UCC applies to this hybrid transaction, we look to the UCC to determine if plaintiff and Scandinavian House entered into a contract for the sale and installation of the windows.

The UCC expands our conception of contract. It makes contracts easier to form, and it imposes a wider range of obligations than before. Parties may form a contract through conduct rather than merely through the exchange of communications constituting "offer and acceptance."

Assuming arguendo that the letter of intent was equivocal, we would find, nevertheless, that Scandinavian House intended to contract with plaintiff. Why? Because the conduct of the parties demonstrates an intention to contract. Lon Meyers gave a letter of intent to Gregory and informed him that Scandinavian

House had awarded the windows contract to plaintiff. The letter of intent authorized plaintiff to take measurements and prepare shop drawings. Pursuant to the letter, plaintiff took measurements in the apartment house. That was no small undertaking and it could not have been done without the cooperation of Scandinavian House. Ultimately, plaintiff completed and delivered the shop drawings to Scandinavian House.

The conduct of the parties is inconsistent with the theory that they only agreed to agree. The mere fact that plaintiff subsequently met with defendants to resolve the guarantee of payment issue does not negate the fact that the parties entered into a contract previously.

Judgment *reversed*.

Based on the UCC, J. Lee Gregory won a case that it would have lost under the common law. Next we look at changes the Code has made in the centuries-old requirement of a writing.

STATUTE OF FRAUDS

UCC §2-201 requires a writing for any sale of goods worth more than $500. However, under the UCC, the writing need not completely summarize the agreement, and it need not even be entirely accurate. Once again, the Code is modifying the common law rule, permitting parties to enforce deals with less formality. In some cases, the court grants an exception and enforces an agreement with no writing at all. Here are the rules.

Contracts for Goods over $500

Section 2-201 demands a writing for any contract of goods over this limit, meaning that virtually every significant sale of goods has some writing requirement. Remember that a contract for goods costing less than $500 is still covered by the UCC, but it may be oral.

Writing Sufficient to Indicate a Contract

The Code only requires a writing *sufficient to indicate* that the parties made a contract. In other words, the writing need not *be* a contract. A simple memo, or a letter or informal note, mentioning that the two sides reached an agreement, is enough. **In general, the writing must be signed by the defendant,** that is, whichever party is claiming there was no deal. Dick signs and sends to Shirley a letter saying, "This is to acknowledge your agreement to buy all 650 books in my rare book collection for $188,000." Shirley signs nothing. A day later, Louis offers Dick $250,000. Is Dick free to sell? No. He signed the memo, it indicates a contract, and Shirley can enforce it against him.

Now reverse the problem. Suppose that after Shirley receives Dick's letter, she decides against rare books in favor of original scripts from the *South Park* television show. Dick sues. Shirley wins because *she* signed nothing.

Incorrect or Omitted Terms

If the writing demonstrates the two sides reached an agreement, it satisfies §2-201 even if it omits important terms or states them incorrectly. Suppose Dick writes "$1888,000," indicating almost $2 million, when he meant to write "$188,000." The letter still shows that the parties made a deal, and the court will enforce it, relying on oral testimony to determine the correct price.

Enforceable Only to Quantity Stated

Since the writing only has to indicate that the parties agreed, it need not state every term of their deal. But one term is essential: quantity. **The Code will enforce the contract only up to the quantity of goods stated in the writing.** This is logical, since a court can surmise other terms, such as price, based on market conditions. Buyer agrees to purchase pencils from Seller. The market value of the pencils is easy to determine, but a court would have no way of knowing whether Buyer meant to purchase 1,000 pencils or 100,000; the quantity must be stated.

Merchant Exception

This is a major change from the common law. **When two merchants make an oral contract, and one sends a confirming memo to the other within a reasonable time, and the memo is sufficiently definite that it could be enforced against the sender herself, then the memo is also valid against the merchant who receives it, unless he objects within 10 days.** Laura, a tire wholesaler, signs and sends a memo to Scott, a retailer, saying, "Confm yr order today—500 tires cat #886—cat price." Scott realizes he can get the tires cheaper elsewhere and ignores the memo. Big mistake. Both parties are merchants, and Laura's memo is sufficient to bind her. So it also satisfies the statute of frauds *against Scott*, unless he objects within 10 days.

The following case illustrates the merchant exception.

Code Provisions Discussed in This Case

Issue	Relevant Code Section
1. Was this farmer a "merchant"?	UCC §2-104: A merchant is anyone who routinely deals in the goods involved (or has special knowledge or an agent with such knowledge).
2. Did the memo satisfy the statute of frauds?	UCC §2-201(2), the "merchant exception": When two merchants make an oral contract, and one sends a confirming memo to the other within a reasonable time, and the memo is sufficiently definite that it could be enforced against the sender herself, then the memo is also valid against the merchant who receives it, unless he objects within ten days.

COLORADO-KANSAS GRAIN CO. v. REIFSCHNEIDER

817 P.2d 637, 1991 Colo. App. LEXIS 259
Colorado Court of Appeals, 1991

Facts: Albert Reifschneider had been a farmer for 30 years. He owned and operated a 160-acre farm in Colorado. The Colorado-Kansas Grain Co. (CKG) bought and sold agricultural commodities, such as grain. CKG negotiated with Reifschneider to buy corn from him. The parties agreed that CKG would buy 12,500 bushels of corn at a market price of $2.25 per bushel, but Reifschneider told CKG that the deal would have to be approved by the First National Bank, which had loaned him money to grow the crop.

The parties talked with the First National, which approved the sale at the agreed-upon price. Reifschneider told CKG to draw up a contract reflecting the agreement. CKG prepared a written confirmation of the oral agreement, signed it, and mailed it to Reifschneider with instructions to sign it and return the original. Two months later, after Reifschneider had several more conversations with CKG, the farmer informed the company that he would not sign the agreement and believed that they did not have a deal.

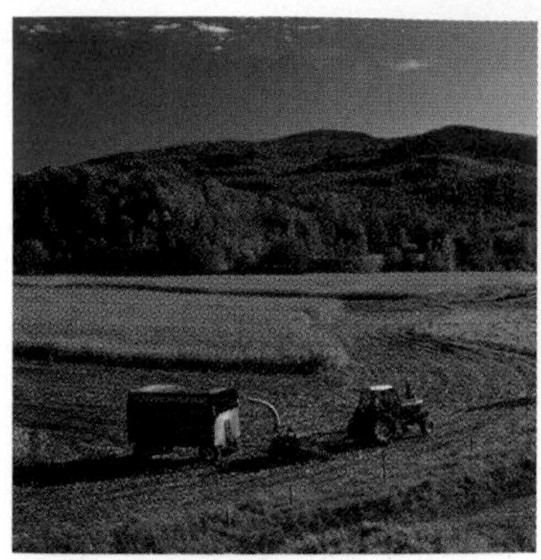
Merchant?

CKG purchased 12,500 bushels elsewhere at a higher cost and filed suit. The trial court gave judgment for CKG, concluding that Reifschneider was a merchant and that therefore CKG's memo was binding against him. Reifschneider appealed.

Issues: Was Reifschneider a "merchant"? Did the memo satisfy the statute of frauds?

Excerpts from Judge Jones's Decision: Defendant next contends that the trial court erred in its conclusion that he was a merchant under the UCC. He argues that, for purposes of contract formation regarding the statute of frauds, he is not a merchant and that, therefore, any contract between him and plaintiff cannot be enforced because it was not in writing. We perceive no error.

The question of whether a farmer is or can be a merchant for purposes of this UCC provision has not been addressed in Colorado. The courts among those states which have dealt with this issue are almost evenly split on whether a farmer can be a merchant.

We note that the cases which hold that farmers may be merchants reflect on the fact that today's farmer is involved in far more than simply planting and harvesting crops. Indeed, many farmers possess an extensive knowledge and sophistication regarding the purchase and sale of crops on the various agricultural markets. Often, they are more aptly described as agri-businessmen. Thus, we conclude that, for purposes of [2-201(2)] a farmer may be a merchant.

Here, the record reflects that defendant had dealt in corn or other agricultural commodities for at least twenty years. Moreover, defendant had served as president of a corporation involved in the purchase and sale of hay under futures contracts. And, defendant also had sold his own hay crops to third parties under futures contracts.

Furthermore, given defendant's level of experience and sophistication in the selling of corn and in futures contracts generally, we are unpersuaded that his lack of experience in corn futures precludes the determination of his status as a merchant. Thus, we conclude that under the circumstances of this case, the trial court did not err in concluding that defendant was a merchant. Accordingly, because the contract at issue here was between merchants and because defendant received a written confirmation and failed to object in writing within ten days of such receipt, a contract was formed under [§2-201(2)].

The judgment is *affirmed*.

Special Circumstances

Finally, an oral contract *may* be enforceable, even without a written memorandum, if (1) the seller is specially manufacturing the goods for the buyer, or (2) the defendant admits in court proceedings that there was a contract, or (3) the goods have been delivered or they have been paid for. We discuss these exceptions in detail in Chapter 15, on written contracts.

ADDED TERMS: SECTION 2-207

Under the common law's mirror image rule, when one party makes an offer, the offeree must accept those exact terms. If the offeree adds or alters any terms, the acceptance is ineffective and the offeree's response becomes a counteroffer. In one of its most significant modifications of contract law, the UCC changes that result. **Under §2-207, an acceptance that adds or alters terms will often create a contract.** The Code has made this change in response to the *battles of the form*. Every day, corporations buy and sell millions of dollars of goods using pre-printed forms. The vast majority of all contracts involve such documents. Typically, the buyer places an order using a pre-printed form, and the seller acknowledges with its own pre-printed acceptance form. Because each form contains language favorable to the party sending it, the two documents rarely agree. The Code's drafters concluded that the law must cope with real practices.

We discuss §2-207 in detail in Chapter 11 and summarize it here only to emphasize how it works with other UCC provisions. The section is confusing, and a diagram helps. **For a schematic look at UCC §2-207, see the illustration on page 263.**

Intention

The parties must still *intend* to create a contract. Section 2-207 is full of exceptions, but there is no change in this basic requirement of contract law. If the differing forms indicate that the parties never reached agreement, there is no contract.

Additional or Different Terms

An offeree may include a new term in his acceptance and still create a binding deal. Suppose Breeder writes to Pet Shop, offering to sell 100 guinea pigs at $2 each. Pet Shop faxes a memo saying, "We agree to buy 100 g.p. We get credit for any unhealthy pig." Pet Shop has added a new term, concerning unhealthy pigs, but the parties *have* created a binding contract because the writings show they intended an agreement. Now the court must decide what the terms of the contract are, since there is some discrepancy. The first step is to decide whether the new language is an *additional term* or a *different term*.

Additional Terms. **Additional terms are those that raise issues not covered in the offer.** The "unhealthy pig" issue is an additional term because the offer said nothing about it. **When both parties are *merchants*, additional terms generally become part of the bargain.** Pet Shop's insistence on credit for sick guinea pigs is binding on Breeder. In three circumstances, however, additional terms *do not* bind the parties:

- If the original offer *insisted on its own terms*. If Breeder offered the pets for sale "on these and no other terms," Pet Shop's additional language would not become part of their deal.
- If the additional terms *materially alter* the offer. Pet Shop's new language about credit for unhealthy animals is fairly uncontroversial. But suppose Pet Shop wrote back, "Breeder is liable for any illness of any animal in Pet Shop within 90 days of shipment of guinea pigs." Breeder would potentially have to pay for a $500 iguana with pneumonia or a $6,000 parrot with gout. This is a material alteration of the bargain and is *not* part of the contract.
- If the offeror *promptly objects* to the new terms. If Breeder received Pet Shop's fax and immediately called up to say, "no credit for unhealthy pigs," then Pet Shop's additional term is not part of their deal.

In all other circumstances, additional terms do become part of an agreement between merchants.

Different Terms. **These are terms that contradict those in the offer.** Suppose Brilliant Corp. orders 1,500 cellular phones from Makem Co., for use by Brilliant's sales force. Brilliant places the order using a pre-printed form stating that the product is fully warranted for normal use and that seller is liable for compensatory *and consequential* damages. This means, for example, that Makem would be liable for lost profits if a salesman's phone fails during a lucrative sales pitch. Makem responds with its own memo stating that in the event of defective phones, Makem is liable only to repair or replace, and *is not liable for consequential damages, lost profits, or any other damages.*

Makem's acceptance has included a *different* term because its language contradicts the offer. Almost all courts would agree that the parties intended to reach an agreement and therefore the contract is enforceable. The question is, what are its terms? Is the full warranty of the offer included, or the very limited warranty of the acceptance? The majority of states hold that **different terms cancel each other out.** Neither party's language goes into the contract. But what then *are* the terms of the deal?

If the evidence indicates that the parties had orally agreed on the issue disputed in the forms, then the courts will ignore the contradictory writings and enforce the oral contract. **If there is no clear oral agreement, the Code supplies its own terms, called gap-fillers,** which cover prices, delivery dates and places, warranties, and other subjects. In the cellular phone case, the contradicting warranty provisions cancel each other out. The parties had not orally agreed on a warranty, so a court would enforce the Code's gap-filler warranty, which *does* permit recovery of compensatory and consequential damages. Therefore, Makem *would* be liable for lost profits. We outline most of the gap-filler terms in Chapter 11. Warranty provisions are analyzed in greater detail in Chapter 21.

In the following case, the Rhode Island Supreme Court seeks the fairest method of sorting out conflicting terms.

Code Provisions Discussed in This Case

Issue	Relevant Code Section
1. Which are the terms of this agreement?	UCC §2-207: *Additional* terms generally but not always become part of the bargain. *Different* terms generally cancel each other out.
2. What is the Code's gap-filler provision concerning delivery?	UCC §2-309: The time for shipment or delivery if not agreed upon is a reasonable time.
3. What is a "reasonable"delivery time?	UCC §1-204: A "reasonable" time depends on the nature, purpose, and circumstances of the action.

SUPERIOR BOILER WORKS, INC. v. R. J. SANDERS, INC.
1998 R.I. LEXIS 153
Supreme Court of Rhode Island, 1998

Facts: R. J. Sanders, Inc. had a contract with the federal government to install the heating system at a federal prison camp. The company negotiated with Superior Boiler Works to purchase three large commercial units. On March 27, Superior sent a proposal to Sanders, offering to sell three boilers for a total of $156,000 and estimating time of delivery at four weeks. The parties exchanged further documents and held various discussions. Finally, on July 20, Sanders sent a "purchase order" for three boilers, agreeing to pay $145,827 and stating "Date required: 4 Weeks," that is, August 20. On August 6, Superior sent a "sales order," agreeing to sell the three boilers at that price, but providing a shipping date of October 1. This later delivery date forced Sanders to rent temporary boilers at a cost of $45,315. On October 1, Superior shipped the boilers, which arrived on October 5. Sanders sent a check in the amount of $100,000, claiming that Superior had delivered the boilers late and deducting the cost of its rental equipment. Superior sued for the additional $45,000 and moved for summary judgment, which the trial court granted. Sanders appealed, claiming that the contract had required Superior to deliver the boilers within four weeks.

Issue: Did Superior's October delivery breach the contract?

Excerpts from Judge Flanders's Decision: Sanders' amended purchase order of July 20 and Superior's August 6 response agree exactly on the specifications and on the price of the boilers. The fact that these two documents disagree on one important term—the time for delivery—does not prevent the formation of a contract under the UCC because it is apparent from their subsequent conduct that both parties intended to be bound contractually. What becomes of the parties' conflicting positions on the shipment period (Sanders' specified four-week delivery versus Superior's stated October 1 shipping date) is a question that must be considered in light of section 2-207(2).

[The court mentioned that other states had responded in various ways to "different" terms, that is, those that conflict. Judge Flanders declared that Rhode Island would side with the majority and adopt the "knock-out" rule, meaning that conflicting terms knock each other out, leaving a hole in the contract that is filled by one of the Code's gap-filler provisions.] Here, the void relating to delivery time would be filled by Section 2-309, which reads, "The time for shipment or delivery . . . if . . . not agreed upon shall be a reasonable time."

Because of the UCC's gap-filling provisions, we recognize that this approach might result in the enforcement of a contract term that neither party agreed to and, in fact, in regard to which each party expressed an entirely different preference. We note in response to this concern that the offeror and the offeree both have the power to protect any term they deem critical by expressly making acceptance conditional on assent to that term. And as merchants, both parties should have been well aware that their dealings were subject to the UCC and to its various gap-filling provisions. In this case, because the two variant shipping-date terms cancel each other out, the amended purchase order and the August 6 sales order formed a contract that required the three boilers to be delivered within a reasonable period after August 6.

In the usual case the question of what constitutes a reasonable time under the UCC is one for the finder of fact to determine from the nature, the purpose, and the circumstances surrounding the transaction, including the parties' course of dealing, usages of trade in the pertinent industry, or the parties' course of performance. See [UCC §1-204(2). In this case, however, the only available evidence indicated that Superior's performance was reasonable, by industry standards.]

For the foregoing reasons the appeal is denied, and the Superior Court's judgment is affirmed.

Section 2-207 is a noble but imperfect attempt to cope with battles of form. The section unfortunately does not resolve all doubt. If a buyer sends your company a purchase order form, with pre-printed terms, and you accept the offer using your own document, what are the terms of the agreement? Are your new terms "additional"? Do they "materially alter" the bargain? Or are your terms "different"? If you understand this section, you can make an educated guess, but you are unlikely to know for sure. How can you avoid a disastrous surprise?

First, *read all terms on both contracts.* Know everybody's terms, and figure out the important differences. This may sound obvious, but many merchants never read the fine print on *either* form. Second, if some of the terms on your contract are essential, *bargain for them.* Do not *assume* that your terms are the final ones; *make* them so by pushing the other party to accept them in writing. Notice, for example, that in the above case, Sanders specified delivery in four weeks, but never insisted on that date. The executives doing the bargaining might have included a phrase such as "these terms and no others." Their failure to do so cost the company

$45,000. Third, if the other side refuses to accept terms that you consider essential, *calculate your potential loss*. If your potential liability is more than you consider acceptable, your choices are to terminate the negotiations or to obtain insurance. It takes more time and effort this way, but you stay out of court.

OPEN TERMS: SECTIONS 2-305 AND 2-306

Open Prices

Under §2-305, the parties may conclude a contract even though they have not settled the price. Again, this is a change from the common law, which required certainty of such an important contract term. Under the Code, if the parties have not stated one, **the price is a reasonable price at the time of delivery.** A court will use market value and other comparable sales to determine what a reasonable price would have been. If the contract permits the buyer or seller to *determine* the price during contract performance, §2-305 requires that she do so in good faith.

Output and Requirements Contracts

Under §2-306, an output contract obligates the seller to sell all of his output to the buyer, who agrees to accept it. Suppose Joel has a small plant in which he manufactures large plants, that is, handcrafted artificial flowers and trees, made of silk and other expensive materials. Joel isn't sure how many he can produce in a year, but wants a guaranteed market. He makes an output contract with Yolanda, in which he promises to sell the entire output of his plant and she agrees to buy it all.

A requirements contract is the reverse, obligating a buyer to purchase all of his needed goods from the seller. Joel might sign a requirements contract with Worm Express, agreeing to buy from Worm all of the silk he needs. Both output and requirements contracts are valid under the Code, although they create certain problems. By definition, the exact quantity of goods is not specified. But then how much may one party demand? Is there any upper or lower limit?

The UCC requires that the parties in an output or requirements contract make their demands in good faith. For example, in a requirements contract, a buyer may not suddenly increase her demand far beyond what the parties expected merely because there has been a market change. Suppose the price of silk skyrockets. Joel's requirements contract obligates Worm Express to sell him all the silk he needs. Could Joel demand 10 times the silk he had anticipated, knowing he could re-sell it at a big profit to other manufacturers? No. That would be bad faith. Come on, Joel, play by the rules.

May the buyer *reduce* his demand far below what the parties anticipated? Yes, as long as he makes the reduction in good faith.

MODIFICATION

Terry, a business consultant, agrees to work for Awkward Co. to create a corporate reorganization plan and oversee its implementation. He promises to finish the job by October 15. By September, Terry is far behind schedule and asks Awkward for an extra three months and for 30 percent extra pay. Terry hints broadly that if the company refuses, he will walk off the job. Awkward agrees in writing to the extra time and money, and Terry finally finishes. Awkward then sues, based on Terry's late completion and overcharge. Who wins? Awkward. This was a services contract. Under the common law, a modification is invalid unless supported by additional consideration, which Terry never gave. Had the contract been one for the sale of goods, however, the outcome would have been different.

UCC §2-209: An agreement modifying a contract needs no consideration to be binding. Suppose Jeanette makes a deal to buy a used Mercedes "in good running order" from her sister, Valerie, for $19,000. Valerie writes to Jeanette confirming the agreement and promising to bring the car the following week. But before Valerie can deliver the car, a major transmission problem makes it inoperable. Valerie pays $1,200 to repair it. She telephones Jeanette and explains the extra cost. Jeanette faxes a note, promising to split the cost of the repair. Is Jeanette's promise enforceable? Valerie was already obligated to deliver a car in good running order. But under the UCC, contract modifications need no additional consideration to be valid. The UCC also permits the parties to modify some contracts orally. Regrettably, the Code is not crystal clear about which changes may be oral and which must be written. The wise executive will insist that all parties sign any proposed modifications. For better or worse, though, §2-209 clearly implies that some alterations may be enforceable even with nothing in writing, so never orally agree to a contract change unless you are prepared to live with it.[5]

The rules that permit informal modification of contracts are consistent with the Code's goal of simplifying business procedure and aligning the law with actual practice. You may not encounter that attitude when buying and selling overseas. A Russian company contracted in writing to buy goods from a foreign seller, who agreed to ship by sea and to insure. The seller never obtained insurance and the goods were damaged in transit. The Russian company sued for the damage. The seller replied that the parties had orally modified the agreement, with the buyer obtaining a lower price in exchange for its agreement to insure. The Russian High Arbitrazh Court ruled that any contract or modification *between a Russian company and a foreign one* must be in writing. The alleged modification was void and the seller was liable for the damaged goods.

Parties make a contract attempting to control their futures. But one party's certainty can be undercut by the ease with which the other party may obtain a modification. Section 2-209 acknowledges this tension by enabling the parties to limit modifications. **The parties may agree to prohibit oral modifications and insist that all modifications be in writing and signed. Between merchants, such a clause is valid. But if either party is *not* a merchant, such a clause is valid only if the non-merchant *separately signs it.***

Once again the Code gives greater protection to non-merchants than to merchants. Two merchants may agree, as part of their bargain, that any future modifications will be valid only if written and signed. But this limitation on modifications is not valid against a non-merchant unless she separately signs the limiting clause itself. Suppose a furniture retailer orders 200 beds from a manufacturer. The retailer's order form requires any modifications to be in writing. The manufacturer initials the retailer's form at the bottom. The parties have a valid agreement and no oral modifications will be enforced. But suppose the retailer sells a bed to a customer. The sales form also bars oral modifications. That prohibition is void unless the customer separately signs it.

The following case looks at an oral modification and once again requires a decision as to whether a party is a merchant. You decide.

[5] The confusion stems from the ambiguous language of §2-209(3), which requires a writing if "the contract as modified" is covered by §2-201, the statute of frauds provision. Some courts have interpreted this to mean that once a contract is covered by §2-201 and needs a writing to be enforceable, any modifications must also be in writing. But others have suggested that a writing is obligatory only if the modification brings the contract within §2-201 *for the first time*, or if the *modification itself* falls within §2-201, or if the modification *changes the quantity* terms of the original contract. There is no definitive answer to this problem, as the court noted in *Flowers Ginning Co. v. Arma, Inc.*, 1997 U.S. App. LEXIS 1054 (4th Cir. 1997). Actually there is: Get it write.

Code Provisions Discussed in This Case

Issue	Relevant Code Section
1. Was the tennis club a merchant?	UCC §2-104: A merchant is anyone who routinely deals in the goods involved (or has special knowledge or an agent with special knowledge).
2. Did the parties orally modify the contract?	UCC §2-209: The parties may prohibit oral modifications. Between merchants, such a clause is valid. If either party is *not* a merchant, such a clause is valid only if the non-merchant separately signed it.

YOU Be The Judge

CHESTNUT FORKS TENNIS CLUB v. T.J. INTERNATIONAL, INC.

1995 U.S. App. LEXIS 13279
United States Court of Appeals for the Fourth Circuit, 1995

Facts: Chestnut Forks Tennis Club is an indoor tennis complex in Warrenton, Virginia. The club constructed a new indoor tennis arena and hired Trus Joist to build and install the roof truss system. The contract price was $62,000. Trus Joist's contract contained express warranties guaranteeing that the trusses would be free of defects for a limited number of years. It also stated that no modifications of the contract were valid unless made in writing and signed by Trus Joist.

As Trus Joist was installing the roof, the partially completed system collapsed, damaging walls that had already been constructed and greatly delaying the opening of the new facility. The Chestnut Forks owners were furious. John Maloney, a general partner in the tennis club, spoke with William Walters, Trus Joist's national marketing manager, and threatened to terminate the agreement, saying he had great doubts about the joists' strength and durability. Walters promised to give Chestnut Forks a $26,000 credit for the damage done, roughly 40 percent of the contract price. And Walters also flatly guaranteed Maloney that the truss system would last from 80 to 100 years. Based on Walters's assurances, Maloney permitted Trus Joist to finish the job, which it did without additional problems.

There were no problems with the roof until *18 years later*, when engineers discovered that it was dangerously weakened. Chestnut Forks was forced to replace it at a cost of over $400,000. All of the express warranties in the Trus Joist contract had long since expired, and Trus Joist refused to pay for the work. Chestnut Forks sued. The district court gave summary judgment for Trus Joist, and Chestnut Forks appealed, claiming that the conversation between Walters and Maloney, 18 years earlier, had modified the contract.

You Be the Judge: Did Walters's statements modify the contract?

Argument for Chestnut Forks: Mr. Walters explicitly guaranteed Chestnut Forks that the system would last 80 to 100 years. This was no casual conversation. Trus Joist's original installation was a disaster. Chestnut Forks had grave doubts about the trusses and the company. The tennis club was prepared to terminate the deal, hire a competent company, and, if necessary, sue Trus Joist for an obvious breach of contract. Walters knew that and was determined to retain the job, so he reduced the price by 40 percent and guaranteed the product for 80 to 100 years. Without *both* of those promises, Chestnut Forks would have fired the defendants. Walters's words were a valid oral modification of the contract. The contract language supposedly prohibiting oral modifications is irrelevant. Chestnut Forks is not a merchant because it does not routinely deal in the kind of goods at issue here, roof trusses. A "no-modifications" clause is only binding on a non-merchant if that party separately signs it, and the club never did. Common sense and the UCC both require that Trus Joist live up to its oral promises.

Argument for Trus Joist: Your honors, we have here two experienced business enterprises directed by sophisticated executives. The parties bargained hard and hammered out a binding written agreement. Warranties are one of the most important parts of any agreement, and the parties carefully considered the warranties that Trus Joist was providing. Chestnut Forks was entirely satisfied with the warranty section. The club also agreed that no oral modifications would be binding on either side. And that, your honors, is it. The warranties have expired, and the plaintiffs have no case. Even if Mr. Walters made these alleged oral statements, they are irrelevant because no oral statements can modify this contract. Chestnut Forks desperately tries to save its case by claiming not to be a merchant, but it is obvious that the club is a business enterprise with experience and savvy. The "separate signing" provision in the Code is for the protection of the typical consumer buying something from a hardware store. The trial court correctly granted summary judgment for Trus Joist, and we ask you to affirm.

The following table concludes this chapter with an illustration of the Code's impact on the common law.

Selected Code Provisions That Change the Common Law

Issue	Common Law Rule	UCC Section	UCC Rule	Example
Contract formation	Offer must be followed by acceptance that shows meeting of the minds on all important terms.	§2-204 and §2-305	Contract can be made in any manner sufficient to show agreement; moment of making not critical; one or more terms, including the price, may be left open.	Tilly writes Meg, "I need a new van for my delivery company." Meg delivers a van and Tilly starts to use it. Under the common law, there is no contract, because no price was ever mentioned; under the UCC, the writing plus the conduct show an intention to contract (2-204). The price is a *reasonable* one (2-305).
Writing requirement	All essential terms must be in writing	§2-201	Any writing is sufficient if it indicates a contract; terms may be omitted or misstated; "merchant" exception can create a contract enforceable against a party who *receives* the writing and does nothing within 10 days.	Douglas, a car dealer, signs and sends to Michael, another dealer, a memo saying, "Confirming our deal for your blue Rolls." Michael reads it but ignores it; 10 days later Douglas has satisfied the statute of frauds under the UCC's merchant exception.
Added terms in acceptance	An acceptance that adds or changes any term is a counteroffer.	§2-207	Additional or different terms are not necessarily counteroffers; their presence does not prevent a contract from being formed, and in some cases the new terms will become a part of the bargain.	Shields sends a pre-printed form to Brooke, offering to buy 25 computers and stating a price; Brooke responds with her own pre-printed form, accepting the offer but adding a term that balances unpaid after 30 days incur a finance charge. The additional term is *not* a counteroffer; there *is* a valid contract; and the finance charge is part of the bargain.
Modification	A modification is valid only if supported by new consideration.	§2-209	A modification needs no consideration to be binding.	Martin, a computer manufacturer, agrees to sell Steve, a retailer, 500 computers at a specified price, including delivery. The next day Martin learns that his delivery costs have gone up 20%; he calls Steve, who faxes a note agreeing to pay 15% extra. Under the common law, the modification would be void; under the Code, it is enforceable.

CHAPTER CONCLUSION

The Uniform Commercial Code enables parties to create a contract quickly. While this can be helpful in a fast-paced business world, it also places responsibility on executives. Informal conversations may cause at least one party to conclude that it has a binding agreement—and the law may agree.

CHAPTER REVIEW

1. The Code is designed to modernize commercial law and make it uniform throughout the country.
2. Article 2 applies to the sale of goods, which are movable things other than money and investment securities.
3. Article 2A governs the leasing of goods.
4. In a mixed contract involving goods and services, the UCC applies if the *predominant purpose* is the sale of goods.
5. A merchant is someone who routinely deals in the particular goods involved, or who appears to have special knowledge or skill in those goods, or who uses agents with special knowledge or skill. The UCC frequently holds a merchant to a higher standard of conduct than a non-merchant.
6. The UCC imposes a duty of good faith in the performance of all contracts.
7. A contract is unconscionable if it is shockingly one-sided and fundamentally unfair. A court is much likelier to use unconscionability to protect a consumer than a corporation.
8. UCC §2-204 permits the parties to form a contract in any manner that shows agreement.
9. For the sale of goods over $500, UCC §2-201 requires some writing that indicates an agreement. Terms may be omitted or misstated, but the contract will be enforced only to the extent of the quantity stated.
10. When two merchants make an oral contract, and one sends a confirming memo to the other within a reasonable time, and the memo is sufficiently definite that it could be enforced against the sender herself, then the merchant who receives it will *also* be bound unless he objects within 10 days.
11. UCC §2-207 governs an acceptance that does not "mirror" the offer. *Additional terms* usually, but not always, become part of the contract. *Different terms* contradict a term in the offer. When that happens, most courts reject both parties' proposals and rely on gap-filler terms.
12. Under UCC §2-305 a contract is enforceable even if the price is not stated. In such cases the price must be reasonable.
13. UCC §2-306 requires both parties to perform output and requirements contracts in good faith.
14. UCC §2-209 permits contracts to be modified even if there is no consideration. The parties may prohibit oral modifications, but such a clause is ineffective against a non-merchant unless she signed it.

PRACTICE TEST

1. **CPA QUESTION** Cookie Co. offered to sell Distrib Markets 20,000 pounds of cookies at $1.00 per pound, subject to certain specified terms for delivery. Distrib replied in writing as follows: "We accept your offer for 20,000 pounds of cookies at $1.00 per pound, weighing scale to have valid city certificate." Under the UCC:

(a) A contract was formed between the parties

(b) A contract will be formed only if Cookie agrees to the weighing scale requirement

(c) No contract was formed because Distrib included the weighing scale requirement in its reply

(d) No contract was formed because Distrib's reply was a counteroffer

2. **CPA QUESTION** With regard to a contract governed by the UCC sales article, which one of the following statements is correct?

(a) Merchants and non-merchants are treated alike.

(b) The contract may involve the sale of any type of personal property.

(c) The obligations of the parties to the contract must be performed in good faith.

(d) The contract must involve the sale of goods for a price of more than $500.

3. Jim Dan, Inc. owned a golf course that had trouble with crab grass. Jim Dan bought 20 bags of Scotts Pro Turf Goosegrass/Crabgrass Control for $835 and applied it to the greens. The Pro Turf harmed the greens, causing over $36,000 in damage. Jim Dan sued Scotts. Scotts defended by claiming that it sold the Pro Turf with a clearly written, easy-to-read disclaimer that stated that in the event of damage, the buyer's only remedy would be a refund of the purchase price. Jim Dan, Inc. argued that the clause was unconscionable. Please rule.

4. **RIGHT & WRONG** Systems Design designed and installed a software system for the savings accounts of the Kansas City Post Office Employees Credit Union. The software caused many problems and, ultimately, a lawsuit. The court had to decide whether the UCC governed. In similar cases, courts from other states had found that such a contract was *predominantly for the sale of goods*. Based on that, and on the doctrine of *uniformity*, the court ruled that the UCC governed. What does "predominantly for the sale of goods" have to do with the decision? Why is "uniformity" a factor? A word about the ethics of uniformity. From the perspective of two parties in a business dispute, what is potentially *threatening* about the idea of uniformity? Why is the doctrine potentially *attractive* to two business executives attempting to negotiate a contract?

5. Mail Code, Inc. manufactured bar code machines for reading addresses on envelopes. Its offices were in Indiana. John Grauberger, who lived in Kansas, applied to become a dealer for the Mail Code machine in the Kansas area. He signed a dealer application form, agreeing to abide by the terms printed on it. Mail Code informed Grauberger that it accepted him as a dealer and showed him a dealer agreement outlining his duties. The agreement contained a "forum selection" clause, stating that any disputes would be settled in a court in Indiana. Grauberger made no objection. He purchased a bar code machine for $31,000, but it did not work. Grauberger sued in Kansas, but Mail Code attempted to have the case dismissed because it had not been brought in Indiana. Did the parties have a valid agreement? Was the forum selection clause part of the agreement?

6. The Massachusetts Bay Transit Authority (MBTA) awarded the Perini Corp. a large contract to rehabilitate a section of railroad tracks. The work involved undercutting the existing track, removing the ballast and foundation, rebuilding the track, and disposing of the old material. Perini solicited an offer from Atlantic Track & Turnout Co. for Atlantic to buy whatever salvageable material Perini removed. Perini estimated the quantity of salvageable material that would be available. Atlantic offered to purchase "all available" material over the course of Perini's deal with the MBTA, and Perini accepted. But three months into the project, the MBTA ran short of money and told Perini to stop the undercutting part of the project. That was the work that made Perini its profit, so Perini requested that the MBTA terminate the agreement, which the agency did. By that point Perini had delivered to Atlantic only about 15 percent of the salvageable material that it had estimated. Atlantic sued. What kind of contract do the parties have? Who should win and why?

7. Nina owns a used car lot. She signs and sends a fax to Seth, a used car wholesaler who has a huge lot of cars in the same city. The fax says, "Confirming our agrmt—I pick any 15 cars fr yr lot—30% below blue

book." Seth reads the fax, laughs, and throws it away. Two weeks later, Nina arrives and demands to purchase 15 of Seth's cars. Is he obligated to sell?

8. The Brugger Corp. owned a farm, operated by Jason Weimer, who acted as the company's business agent. Tri-Circle, Inc. was a farm equipment company. On behalf of Brugger, Weimer offered to buy from Tri-Circle certain equipment for use on the farm. Tri-Circle accepted the offer, using a pre-printed form. The form included a finance charge for late payment. Weimer's offer had said nothing about finance charges, but he made no objection to the new term. Tri-Circle supplied the farm equipment but later alleged that Brugger had refused to pay for $12,000 worth of the supplies. Tri-Circle sued. In deciding whether Tri-Circle was entitled to finance charges, the court first inquired whether Brugger, Weimer, and Tri-Circle were merchants. Why did it look into that issue? *Were* they merchants?

9. Which one of the following transactions is not governed by Article 2 of the UCC?

(a) Purchasing an automobile for $35,000

(b) Leasing an automobile worth $35,000

(c) Purchasing a radio worth $449

10. To satisfy the UCC statute of frauds regarding the sale of goods, which of the following must generally be in writing?

(a) Designation of the parties as buyer and seller

(b) Delivery terms

(c) Quantity of the goods

(d) Warranties to be made

11. Are you the typical student who just cannot get enough questions and quizzes about the UCC? Type your way to http://www.fullertonlaw.com/chapt12.htm. The Web site has a long discussion of the UCC, interspersed with contract hypotheticals and questions.

12. **YOU BE THE JUDGE WRITING PROBLEM** Brewster manufactured plastic bottles. Dial made personal care products at many plants around the country, including one in Salem, Virginia. The companies agreed that Dial would purchase from Brewster all of the plastic bottles it needed for its Salem factory. Dial estimated its requirements for one year at 7,850,000 bottles, but added a clause stating that "quantities are estimated only and do not bind Dial to purchase any minimum quantity." A few months later, Dial concluded that its Salem plant was unprofitable. The company closed the factory and notified Brewster that it would buy no bottles at all. Brewster sued. Did Dial have the right to reduce its orders to zero? **Argument for Brewster:** The parties had a clear contract for a massive number of bottles. Dial knew that this contract was extremely important to Brewster. Although Dial had some right to adjust its orders, it had no right to reduce them to zero. **Argument for Dial:** The issue is whether Dial acted in good faith. It did. The company had a legitimate reason for closing the factory—it was losing money—and with no factory it certainly did not need any bottles.

INTERNET RESEARCH PROBLEM

To find the latest legislation in your state regarding electronic contracts, go to http://www.mbc.com/ecommerce.html. Click on your state. Are electronic signatures valid in your state? Is there any pending legislation about these contracts?

You can find further practice problems in the Online Quiz at http://beatty.westbuslaw.com or in the Study Guide that accompanies this text.

CHAPTER 20

OWNERSHIP AND RISK

He drove his truck fast along the rough country road, hurrying through the shadows of the Cascade Mountains, passing close to the Rogue River. The door panel, freshly painted, read "Ernest Jenkins, Cattle Buyer." Spinning the wheel hard left he drove through an impressive gate, under a wooden sign proclaiming "Double Q Ranch." He knew the ranch by reputation and quickly saw that it was prosperous—a good place for a man like him to do business.

He introduced himself to Kate Vandermeer, the Double Q's business manager, and expressed an interest in buying 300 head of cattle. Vandermeer and the man mounted horses and rode out to inspect the herd. Vandermeer noticed that his boots were brand new and that he rode awkwardly.

He was satisfied with the cattle, so the two bargained, sitting on horseback and looking into the sunset. Vandermeer started at $310,000 and was surprised at how quickly they reached an agreement, at $285,000, a price she considered excellent. They agreed that Vandermeer would deliver the cattle by truck, in one week, in a nearby town. He would pay with a cashier's check and take possession of the cattle and all ownership documents, such as brand inspection certificates and veterinarian's certificates. Back at the ranch, Vandermeer offered him a drink, but he had to hurry to another appointment.

The next week, right on schedule, he arrived on Thursday and presented his cashier's check for the full amount. When they had transferred the livestock, Vandermeer suggested they talk over some future business, but he was again in a rush. They shook hands and parted, the man heading due east, fast.

The Double Q's bank sent the cashier's check for collection, but learned early the following week that it was forged. Vandermeer called the State Police, who traced the man's movements to the state line. Three weeks later and 1,600 miles east, the FBI located the cattle, with the prominent "QQ" brand, in stockyards in Omaha. Ned Munson had purchased the cattle from the man for $225,000, which he considered a bargain. He had paid with a cashier's check. Ernest Jenkins, of course, had disappeared—literally. The truck's freshly painted door now read, "Ted J. Pringle, Grain Merchant," and it was parked a long, long way from Omaha.

LEGAL INTEREST

Who owns the cows? The Double Q wanted its cattle back or $285,000. If Munson was dumb enough to pay money to a thief, that wasn't the ranch's problem. But Ned Munson claimed the cows were his. He had paid a fair price to a man who appeared to own them. If Vandermeer was so foolish as to give up the cattle to a con artist, let the ranch suffer the consequences. The Double Q sued. Both parties to this lawsuit are unhappy, but happily they have illustrated the theme for our chapter: When two parties claim a conflicting legal interest in particular goods, *who loses*? Who obtains the law's protection? These are disputes over *conflicting interests in goods*.

An interest is a legal right in something. More than one party can have an interest in particular goods. Suppose you lease a new car from a dealer, agreeing to pay $300 per month for three years. Several parties will have legal interests in the car. The dealer still *owns* the car—interest number one. At the end of three years, the dealer gets it back. For three years, you have the *use* of the car—interest number two. You may use the car for all normal purposes but are obligated to make monthly payments. Your payments go to a finance agency, which has made an arrangement with the dealer, to obtain the right to your $300 monthly payment. The finance agency has a *security interest* in the car—interest number three. If you fail to pay on time, the finance company has the right to repossess your car. If you take the car to a garage for maintenance, the garage has *temporary possession* of the car—interest number four. The garage has the right to keep the car locked up over night, to work on it, and to test drive it. Sometimes legal interests can clash, and it is those conflicts we look at here.

Often the parties will claim ownership, each arguing that his interest is stronger than the other's. But in this chapter we also consider cases where each party argues that the *other* one owns the goods. Suppose a seller manufactures products for a buyer, but while the goods are being shipped, they are destroyed in a fire. Seller may argue that it no longer owned the goods, but buyer will claim it had not yet acquired them. In other cases, a *third party* will be involved. You pay $30,000 cash to buy a new car and expect to pick it up in three days. But the day before you arrive, the dealer's bank seizes all of the cars on the lot, claiming the dealer has defaulted on loans. Now the fight over legal interest is between you and the bank, with the dealer a relatively passive observer.

In the cattle case, three parties had a legal interest in the goods. The Double Q ranch originally had valid **title** to the cattle, **meaning the normal rights of ownership**. Ernest Jenkins, the scam artist, acquired a lesser interest. His contract with

Double Q was fraudulent because Jenkins intended to cheat the ranch. Nonetheless, he did have an agreement. He obtained **voidable title**, meaning limited rights in the goods, inferior to those of the owner.[1] Finally, Ned Munson makes a claim to the cattle based on his payment and his possession of the cows and all documents.

The court will use various sections of the UCC to determine who keeps the cows and who bears the loss. Ned Munson should win the cattle. He was probably acting in good faith and a commercially reasonable manner when he bought the cows from a man who appeared to be a lawful cattle buyer. The Double Q must bear the loss. If, however, the Double Q can convince a court that Munson acted irresponsibly, because he had grounds for suspecting Jenkins, the court might order Munson to pay for the cattle.[2]

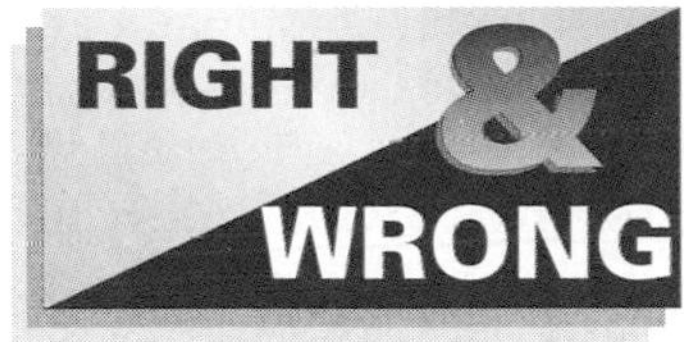

As we look at this issue and others like it, ask yourself whether the UCC rules and the court decisions accomplish two sensible goals: (1) to be fair to innocent parties and (2) to encourage reasonable business practices nationwide. Both Munson and the Double Q were innocent parties. Jenkins was the bad guy. Why let Munson keep the livestock? Because he probably did all that a reasonable business person should do in buying cattle. He paid a fair (though low) price to a man who had all the normal ownership documents. The Code *could* place a greater burden on Munson and require, for example, that he investigate Jenkins's background. The law *could* force Munson to check the history of the cattle and find out how Jenkins acquired them. But such rules would hogtie the cattle industry. Most sales are legitimate; cattle ranchers and buyers must be able to buy and sell quickly, responding to market conditions and opportunities for profit.

Notice that in this case and most others, the Code focuses on basic fairness and sensible business practices. Munson wins because he acted reasonably and in good faith, *not* because he happens to hold certain certificates to the animals. The Code's authors have labored to get away from legal formalities and give results that make sense, as we see in the next section.

IDENTIFICATION, TITLE, AND INSURABLE INTEREST

Historically, courts settled disputes about legal interest by looking at one thing: title. The drafters of the UCC concluded that "title" was too abstract an answer for the assorted practical questions that arose. It could be hard to prove exactly who did have title, and it made no sense to settle a wide variety of business problems with one legal idea. Today, title is only one of several issues that a court will use to resolve conflicting interests in goods. *Identification* and *insurable interest* have become more important as title has diminished in significance. We can begin to understand all three doctrines if we examine how title passes from seller to buyer.

EXISTENCE AND IDENTIFICATION

Title in goods can pass from one person to another only if the goods exist and have been identified to the contract.

---

[1] We discuss voidability in detail in Chapter 14, on capacity and consent.

[2] For a cattle case that raises these and other issues, see *Rudiger Charolais Ranches v. Van De Graaf Ranches*, 994 F.2d 670, 1993 U.S. App. LEXIS 12412 (9th Cir. 1993).

Existence

Goods must exist before title can pass.[3] Although most goods do exist when people buy and sell them, some have not yet come into being, such as crops to be grown later. A farmer may contract to sell corn even before it is planted, but title to the corn cannot pass until the corn exists.

Identification

Goods must be identified to the contract before title can pass.[4] This means that the parties must have designated the specific goods being sold. Identification is an important concept that applies in other areas besides the passing of title. Often identification is obvious. If Dealer agrees to sell to Buyer a 60-foot motor yacht with identification number AKX472, the parties have identified the goods. But suppose Paintco agrees to sell Brushworks 1,000 gallons of white base paint at a specified price. Paintco has 25,000 gallons in its warehouse. Title cannot pass until Paintco identifies the specific gallons that will go to Brushworks.

The parties may agree in their contract how and when they will identify the goods.[5] They are free to identify them to the contract any way they want. Paintco and Brushworks might agree, for example, that within one week of signing the sales agreement, Paintco will mark appropriate gallons. If the gallons are stored 50 to a crate, then Paintco will have a worker stick a "Brushworks" label on 20 crates. Once the label is on, the goods are identified to the contract.

If the parties do not specify, identification will occur according to these rules:[6]

- Identification occurs when the parties enter into a contract if the agreement describes specific goods that already exist. If the Dealer agrees to sell a yacht and the parties include the ID number in their contract, the goods are identified (even though the parties never use the term "identify").
- For unborn animals, identification generally takes place when they are conceived; for crops, identification normally happens when they are planted.
- For other goods, identification occurs when the seller marks, ships, or in some other way indicates the exact goods that are going to the buyer.

PASSING OF TITLE

Once goods exist and are identified to the contract, title can pass from one person to another. **Title may pass in any manner on which the parties agree (UCC §2-401).** Once again, the Code allows the parties to control their affairs with commonsense decisions. The parties can agree, for example, that title passes when the goods leave the manufacturer's factory, or when they reach the shipper who will transport them, or at any other time and place. If the parties do not agree on passing title, §2-401 decides. There are two possibilities:

- *When the goods are being moved,* title passes to the buyer when the seller completes whatever transportation it is obligated to do. Suppose the Seller is in

---

3 UCC §2-105(2).

4 UCC §2-401(1).

5 UCC §2-501(1).

6 UCC §2-501.

Milwaukee and the Buyer is in Honolulu. The contract requires the Seller to deliver the goods to a ship in San Francisco. Title passes when the goods reach the ship.

- *When the goods are not being moved*, title passes when the seller delivers ownership documents to the buyer. Suppose Seller, located in Louisville, has already manufactured 5,000 baseball bats, which are stored in a warehouse in San Diego. Under the terms of their contract, Buyer will take possession of the bats at the warehouse. When Seller gives Buyer ownership documents, title passes. If the contract does not require Seller to give such documents, title passes when the parties form the contract. For example, if the Buyer owns the warehouse where the bats are stored, Buyer needs no documents to take possession; title passes when the parties reach agreement.

INSURABLE INTEREST

Closely related to identification and title is the idea of insurable interest. Anyone buying or selling expensive goods should make certain that the goods are insured. There are some limits, though, on who may insure goods, and when. As we saw in Chapter 13, a party may insure something—property, a human life—only when she has a legitimate interest in it. If the person buying the policy lacks a real interest in the thing insured, the law regards the policy as a gambling contract and considers it void.

When does someone have an insurable interest in goods? The Code gives one answer for buyers and one for sellers. **A buyer obtains an insurable interest when the goods are identified to the contract (UCC §2-501).** Suppose, in January, Grain Broker contracts with Farmer to buy his entire wheat crop. Neither party mentions "identification." In January, the crop is not identified, and Broker has no insurable interest. In May, after weeks of breaking the soil, Farmer plants his wheat crop. Once he has planted it, the goods are identified. The Broker, who now has an insurable interest, purchases insurance. In July, a drought destroys the crop, and the Broker never gets one grain of wheat. The Broker need not worry: he is insured.

The seller's insurable interest is different. **The seller retains an insurable interest in goods as long as she has either title to the goods or a security interest in them (UCC §2-501).** "Security interest" refers to cases in which the buyer still owes the seller some money for the goods. Suppose Flyola Manufacturing sells a small aircraft to WingIt, a dealer, for $300,000. WingIt pays $30,000 cash and agrees to pay interest on the balance until it sells the plane. Flyola has an insurable interest even while the aircraft is in WingIt's showroom and may purchase insurance anytime until WingIt pays off the last dime.

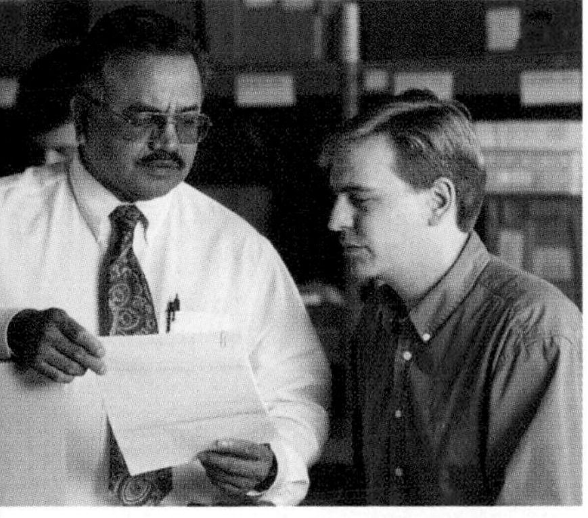

Seller and Buyer may both have an insurable interest in these goods.

What this means is that a seller and buyer can have an insurable interest in the same goods simultaneously. Suppose the heavy metal band Gentle Bunnies hires Inkem Corp., in Minneapolis, to make 25,000 T-shirts with the Gentle Bunnies logo, for sale at rock concerts. The parties agree that the T-shirts are identified as soon as the logo is printed, and that title will pass when Inkem delivers the T-shirts to the office of the Bunnies' manager in Kansas City. Inkem obviously has an insurable interest while the company is making the T-shirts and continues to have an interest until it delivers the T-shirts in Kansas City. But the Gentle Bunnies' insurable interest arises the moment their logo is stamped on each shirt, so the Bunnies could insure the goods while they are still stored in Inkem's factory. Why would the Bunnies spend hard earned cash to insure goods they do not have? They may be uncertain that Inkem has obtained proper insurance.

In the following case, a car accident leads several insurance companies to dispute who owned the damaged auto. Each company wants to claim that the car belonged to—someone *else*.

Code Provisions Discussed in This Case

Issue	Relevant Code Section
1. Which party had title to the car?	UCC §2-401: Title to goods may pass in any manner on which the parties agree.
2. Did the seller have an insurable interest in the car?	UCC §2-501: The seller retains an insurable interest in the goods as long as it holds title to or a security interest in them.

VALLEY FORGE INSURANCE CO. v. GREAT AMERICAN INSURANCE CO.
1995 Ohio App. LEXIS 3939
Ohio Court of Appeals, 1995

Facts: On a Friday afternoon, Karl and Linda Kennedy went to John Nolan Ford to buy a new Ford Mustang. The parties signed all necessary documents, including a New Vehicle Buyer's Order, an Agreement to Provide Insurance, and credit applications. The Kennedys made a down payment, but could not arrange financing before the dealership closed. John Nolan Ford determined that the Kennedys were creditworthy and allowed them to take the car home for the weekend. That evening, Karl Kennedy permitted his brother-in-law, Cella, to take the car for a drive, along with a passenger named Campbell. Cella wrecked the car, injuring his passenger. Campbell sued, and the question was which insurance company was liable for all of the harm: John Nolan Ford's insurer (Milwaukee Mutual), Cella's insurer (Valley Forge), or Kennedy's insurer (Great American). The trial court ruled that title had never passed to Kennedy and found Milwaukee Mutual liable. The company appealed.

Issue: Had title passed to Kennedy at the time of the accident?

Excerpts from the Per Curiam Decision: Milwaukee argues that the risk of loss and insurable interest had passed because the car had been delivered. Further, Milwaukee states that the Kennedys explicitly agreed to provide insurance. Great American counters that the parties had "otherwise explicitly agreed" in the New Vehicle Buyer's Order that any interest in the car would not pass until "either the full purchase price is paid in cash or a satisfactory deferred payment agreement is executed by the parties[.]" No financing had been arranged at the time of the accident.

Two terms of the New Vehicle Buyer's Order apply to the situation at bar. Under the "Agreement" provision, the contract states that "it is expressly agreed that the purchaser acquires no right, title or interest in or to the property which he agrees to purchase hereunder until such property is delivered to him and either the full purchase price is paid in cash or a satisfactory deferred payment agreement is executed by the parties hereto[.]"

Milwaukee also argues that the Kennedys explicitly agreed to provide insurance by signing the "Agreement to Provide Insurance." While the agreement does state that the Kennedys agreed to provide insurance, it is not clear when the Kennedys were to obtain the insurance. In fact, because the agreement refers to an "instalment [sic] contract," it is possible that the Kennedys were to provide insurance once a financing agreement was reached. In light of the fact that the agreement is ambiguous, we construe the contract strictly against the drafter and hold that any agreement to provide insurance was to take effect after financing was obtained.

We hold that because the parties had otherwise agreed that interest in the car, including insurable interest, would not pass until the financing was complete, John Nolan Ford still had the risk of loss and the insurable interest when the accident occurred. [Affirmed.]

WHEN THE SELLER HAS IMPERFECT TITLE

BONA FIDE PURCHASER

Some people are sleazy, and sales law must accommodate that reality. In the chapter opener we saw a scam artist purchase cattle from a respectable ranch and sell them to an honest dealer. The bad guy skipped town, leaving a dispute between two innocent companies. Either the original owner (the ranch) or the buyer (the cattle dealer) must bear the loss. Who loses?

The Question: Who must suffer the loss?

Owner →	**Bad Guy** →	**Buyer**
(has valid title)	(obtains goods from Owner and sells)	(buys goods from Bad Guy)

First we need to know what kind of title Bad Guy obtains: Is it void or voidable? If Bad Guy *steals* the goods from Owner, Bad Guy obtains **void title, which is no title at all**. When Bad Guy sells the goods to Buyer, she also gets *no title at all*. Abe steals Marvin's BMW and promptly sells it to Elaine for $35,000 cash. Two weeks later the police locate the car. When Abe stole it, he obtained void title. He had no title to convey to Elaine and that is what she received—none. Elaine must return the car to Marvin and suffer the $35,000 loss for Abe's theft. This policy makes sense because Marvin has done nothing wrong. If the law permitted Elaine to get valid title, it would encourage theft.

If Bad Guy *purchases* the goods from Owner, using fraud or deception, he obtains **voidable title, meaning limited rights in the goods, inferior to those of the Owner**. The owner should be able to recover the goods from the Bad Guy, but not from anyone else who ends up with them. Suppose Emily agrees to buy Marvin's *other* car, a Jeep. She gives him a check for $20,000 and he signs the vehicle over to her. Emily knows her check will bounce; she has used fraud to obtain the car. As a result, Emily obtains only voidable title. If Marvin learns of the deception before Emily sells the car to someone else, he will get his Jeep back.

Unfortunately, Emily is slippery, not stupid. She quickly sells the Jeep to Seth for cash. By the time the check bounces, Emily is gone and Seth has the car. Who keeps the Jeep? Seth wins the car if he is a bona fide purchaser. **A person with voidable title has power to transfer valid title for value to a good faith purchaser, generally called a *bona fide purchaser* or *BFP*.**[7]

[7] UCC §2-403(1).

Seth can prove that he is a bona fide purchaser by showing two things:

- That he gave value for the goods, *and*
- That he acted in good faith.

It is generally easy for purchasers to show that they gave value. The buyer could give cash or a check or could agree to extinguish a debt, that is, to forgive some money that Bad Guy owed. The real issue becomes whether the buyer acted in good faith. If Seth paid a reasonable purchase price and Emily showed him convincing identification and signed over to him all purchase documents, Seth acted in good faith. He keeps the Jeep and Marvin loses.

On the other hand, suppose Seth knows the brand new Jeep is worth more than $28,000. Emily seems in a frantic hurry to sell the car. She cannot produce the car's registration but promises to send it within three days. Emily's conduct together with the $8,000 discount would make a reasonable person suspicious. Seth is not acting in good faith and therefore is not a bona fide purchaser. Marvin receives the car back, and Seth pays dearly for his automotive lust.

The Answer: Who loses?

Owner ⟶	**Bad Guy** ⟶	**Buyer**
The Owner has good title.	(1) Bad Guy STEALS the goods, obtaining *void* title (no title) and sells to the Buyer.	Buyer receives no title.
	(2) Bad Guy PURCHASES the goods, obtaining *voidable* title, and sells to the Buyer.	(a) If the Buyer gives value for the goods and acts in good faith, he is a BFP and receives good title. (b) If the Buyer is not a BFP, he receives no title.

Works of art are often beautiful, but some have an ugly past. During the Holocaust years of 1933–1945, Nazis stole from European Jews more than 200,000 paintings and sculptures, worth billions of dollars. After World War II, the German government returned many of the works to the original owners, their survivors, or the country from which the art had been looted. Nonetheless, hundreds of people have come forward claiming ownership of paintings that hang in public museums or private homes. Critics have also claimed that European governments made desultory efforts to locate missing heirs because they wanted to keep valuable works for their national collections. The French government has long denied this charge, but recently it made an effort to encourage rightful claimants to come forward by holding a major exhibition of paintings acknowledged to have been stolen.

It is often difficult to determine whether a work was actually stolen or simply sold privately because the market for artistic goods is fluid and informal, with many sellers, buyers, and brokers insisting on secrecy. Legal differences also cloud matters. As we have seen, in the United States, *a thief conveys no title.* If a Rembrandt drawing stolen by the Nazis winds up in an American collection, a court will generally order it returned to the owner's heirs. Under the statutes of most European countries, however, a purchaser who has no reason to suspect that she is buying stolen goods *generally obtains good title.* An art collector in Milan who makes a bona fide purchase of a Degas painting from a dealer in Zurich can typically keep the work, even if it later turns out to have been stolen. Fortunately, most European museums have not used this legal loophole to retain works when presented with valid evidence of theft. Yet when the fall of the Soviet government revealed that Russian art museums had deliberately hidden thousands of looted works, the Russian parliament passed a statute prohibiting their return. Private collectors also may be tempted to use European civil law to hang on to their goods.

ENTRUSTMENT

Your old Steinway grand piano needs a complete rebuilding. You hire Fred Showpan, Inc., a company that repairs and sells instruments. Showpan hauls your piano away and promises to return it in perfect shape. Two months later, you are horrified to spot Showpan's showroom boarded up and pasted with bankruptcy notices. Worse still, you learn that Fred sold your beloved instrument to a customer, Frankie List. When you track down List, he gives you nothing but a sonatina, claiming he paid $18,000 for the piano and likes it just fine. Is he entitled to keep it?

Quite likely he is. Section 2-403(1), the BFP provision we just discussed, would not apply because Showpan did not *purchase* the piano from you. But §2-403(2) does apply. This is the "entrustment" section, and it covers cases in which the owner of goods voluntarily leaves them with a merchant, who then sells the goods without permission. According to **UCC §2-403(2), any entrusting to a merchant who deals in goods of that kind gives him power to transfer all rights of the entruster to a buyer in the ordinary course of business.** There are several important ideas in this section:

Entrusting means delivering goods to a merchant or permitting the merchant to retain them.[8] In the piano example, you clearly entrusted goods to a merchant. If you buy a used car from Fast Eddie's Fast Wheels and then leave it there for a week, while you obtain insurance, you have entrusted it to Eddie.

Deals in Goods of That Kind

The purpose of the section is to protect innocent buyers who enter a store, see the goods they expect to find, and purchase something, having no idea that the storekeeper is illegally selling the property of others. Buyers should not have to demand proof of title to everything in the store. Further, if someone has to bear the risk, let it be the person who has entrusted her goods; she is in the best position to investigate the merchant's integrity. But this protection does not extend to a buyer who arrives at a vacuum cleaner store and buys an $80,000 mobile home parked in the lot.

In the Ordinary Course of Business

This means that the buyer must act in good faith, without knowing that the sale violates the owner's rights. If Frank List buys your piano assuming that Showpan owns it, he has acted in good faith. If Frank was your neighbor and recognized your instrument, he is not buying in the ordinary course of business and must hand over the piano.

Of course, a merchant who violates the owner's rights is liable to that owner. If Showpan were still in business when you discovered your loss, you could sue and recover the value of the piano. The problems arise when the merchant is unable to reimburse the owner. The following case explores these concepts. You make the call.

---

[8] For a discussion of who is and who is not a merchant, see Chapter 19.

Code Provisions Discussed in This Case

Issue	Relevant Code Section
1. Did the buyer obtain the goods from a "merchant"?	UCC §2-104: A merchant is anyone who routinely deals in the goods involved (or has special knowledge or an agent with special knowledge).
2. Did the buyer obtain good title?	UCC §2-403(2): Any entrusting of goods to a merchant who deals in goods of that kind gives him power to transfer all rights of the entruster to a buyer in the ordinary course of business.

YOU Be The Judge

PEREZ-MEDINA v. FIRST TEAM AUCTION, INC.

206 Ga. App. 719, 426 S.E.2d 397, 1992 Ga. App. LEXIS 1755
Georgia Court of Appeals, 1992

Facts: At a farm auction, Juan Perez-Medina and Julio Lara bid against each other on a tractor, and Perez-Medina bought it for $66,500. At a second auction the same day, Perez-Medina bought some equipment that he wanted to add to his tractor. At this auction he again encountered Lara, and the two agreed that Lara would install the new equipment. With Perez-Medina's consent, Lara took the tractor to his place of business to work on it.

Weeks later, Perez-Medina came to the shop and paid $10,000 for Lara to do the work they had agreed on. Lara in fact was a dealer in farm machinery. He regularly bought such equipment at auctions, then repaired and sold it. Perez-Medina testified, though, that Lara's shop appeared to him to be a repair shop rather than a heavy equipment sales shop.

First Team Auction had done business with Lara on a regular basis. Lara executed a standard pre-auction document declaring that he owned the tractor. Georgia law does not require a bill of sale or other ownership papers for a tractor. First Team then bought the tractor from Lara for $54,000. When Perez-Medina learned of this, he demanded the tractor back, but First Team refused. The trial court gave summary judgment in favor of First Team, and Perez-Medina appealed.

You Be the Judge: Did First Team acquire good title to the tractor based on UCC §2-403(2)?

Argument for Perez-Medina: Your honors, UCC §2-403(2) does not apply, for several reasons. First, the section only protects a buyer who purchases *from a merchant*. Julio Lara was not and is not a merchant. When Mr. Perez-Medina visited, it was clear to him that Lara operated a repair shop. He had no idea that Lara bought and sold such goods. This extraordinary provision of the Code permits an owner to lose his valuable property through no fault of his own. A court should apply it only when the owner realized he was entrusting goods to someone who might be tempted to sell them.

Second, Mr. Perez-Medina never *entrusted* the tractor to Lara. He simply asked Lara to repair the machine. First Team is arguing that a perfectly honest farmer should lose his hard earned property simply because he took it to a repair shop for work. That means every time we take our car to a garage for an oil change, the garage is free to sell it and the owner gets nothing.

Third, the auction company did not buy the tractor *in the ordinary course of business* because it lacked good faith. This is a $65,000 piece of equipment, not a pack of chewing gum. First Team should have inquired where Lara got the equipment and why he wanted to sell it so cheap. We ask you to order First Team to deliver the tractor to its rightful owner, Mr. Perez-Medina.

Argument for First Team: Your honors, we agree that the three issues mentioned resolve this case. But the law requires you to affirm summary judgment for First Team Auction. First, Mr. Lara was and is a merchant. Perez-Medina met Lara *at two farm auctions in one day*. What did he think Lara was doing there, painting landscapes? Lara *had* to be a merchant: first he tried to buy the same tractor; then he offered to rebuild it for Perez-Medina. If he had been a farmer, he wouldn't have offered to make repairs; had he merely owned a repair shop, he wouldn't have attempted to buy the tractor himself.

Second, Perez-Medina did indeed entrust the machine to Lara. Perez-Medina argues that he never intended Lara to sell it. We know that. The whole point of §2-403(2) is that buyers obtain good title even when the owner never authorized the sale.

Third, First Team acted entirely in good faith by buying in the ordinary course of business. It had done business with Lara before, and had no reason to suspect any wrongdoing here. First Team in good faith purchased goods entrusted to a merchant, and Mr. Perez-Medina must suffer the consequences.

CREDITOR'S RIGHTS

In the entrustment section, we considered the rights of the *owner* of goods and how her interests might conflict with those of a merchant and a buyer. A related issue concerns a *creditor*, that is, someone with a financial stake in the goods that the merchant is selling. Suppose a merchant borrows money from a finance company to buy fish tanks with built-in televisions, to entertain bored guppies. The finance company is now the merchant's creditor. The merchant agrees that when she sells any of the TV Tanks, she will pay a percentage of the proceeds to the finance company. But if she sells tanks to a buyer without giving one cent to her creditor, does the buyer get to keep the fish tanks? To determine an answer, we need to know whether the sale was made in the ordinary course of business or in bulk, and also whether the merchant was selling "returnable" goods.

ORDINARY SALES

Article 9 of the Code controls the rights of secured parties. We look closely at it in Chapter 26. Briefly, UCC §9-307 governs the rights of a creditor, a merchant, and a buyer in the ordinary course of business. Suppose the Nickel & Dime Bank loans Yoyo's Yacht Sales $100,000 to purchase two yachts wholesale. The yachts arrive at Yoyo's and remain in the showroom, but Nickel & Dime retains a security interest in both. If Yoyo fails to repay its loan, the bank is entitled to seize the yachts. Further, Yoyo is obligated to notify the bank immediately of a sale and hold the money until the bank gets its share. Unaware of Nickel & Dime's security interest, Liz pays $80,000 for one of the yachts. Yoyo grabs the money and sails into the horizon, leaving the bank in his wake. May Nickel & Dime take Liz's new yacht? No. **UCC §9-307 generally permits a buyer in the ordinary course of business to take the goods free and clear of the security interest.**

Naturally, there are exceptions, and you will *not* want to miss the full story in the secured transactions chapter. But for present purposes, the ordinary customer who purchases goods from a store will keep them regardless of any problems the store has with its creditors. The policy behind the law is obvious: to enable consumers to buy and merchants to sell. If you had to trace the chain of title before you bought a pair of socks at Discount City, commerce would grind to a halt. Section 9-307 keeps things flowing along.

BULK SALES

Suppose Nickel & Dime Bank also has a security interest in the exotic cars on display at Pearl's High Performance Cars. Beryl, a rich college student, wants to impress her boyfriend Sylvester, so she takes him to Pearl's. "Pick out a car you like," she whispers to Sylvester, and he chooses a silver Jaguar. Beryl promptly buys the car for Sylvester, who is delighted. Pearl senses that Beryl is not your typical undergraduate and gently takes her aside. After a cheery chat, Beryl also buys Sylvester one Lamborghini, two Ferraris, an Aston Martin, four Porsches, and Pearl's desks, chairs, water cooler, and filing cabinets—everything in the store. Pearl takes her profits and flies to the remote isle of Encantada, never to be heard from again. Sylvester is ecstatic, but not Nickel & Dime. The bank had a security interest in the cars, and now it wants its money or the cars. Who wins?

Pearl has made a bulk sale to Beryl. **A bulk sale is one that includes most or all of the inventory in a store**. It hardly seems fair that a buyer such as Beryl should receive the same protection from a creditor that the law gives to a purchaser in the ordinary course of business. It is one thing to buy a yacht, or a pair of socks, knowing nothing about any creditors. It is quite different to buy the entire inventory of a store. A bulk buyer could anticipate that the seller has creditors, who may have invested heavily, helping to make the business a success.

To avoid such unfairness, the drafters of the UCC wrote Article 6 to govern the rights of the bulk seller, the bulk buyer, and their creditors. The article forces both the seller and his buyer to ensure that all creditors receive notice of a bulk sale before it happens and payment of money owed once the sale goes through.

Article 6 requires that:

- **The seller supply the buyer with a complete list of his creditors**, including even those claims that the seller disputes, and
- **The buyer notify all creditors of the bulk sale before it takes place**, so that the creditors may protect their security interests.

If the buyer fails to notify a creditor before the sale occurs, that creditor retains his security rights in the property for six months after the sale. So a creditor who learned of the sale after it happened could seize the goods from the *buyer*.

Article 6 has been a mixed blessing. Many states have found that it places a great burden on the buyer of a business, who is probably acting entirely in good faith. The article requires a buyer to make an exhaustive investigation of the seller's credit obligations and notify all creditors, or face the possibility that he will purchase a huge inventory and lose it. Because of widespread unhappiness with the article, the UCC drafters recommended in 1989 that all states repeal it. The drafters realized that some states would not want to take so drastic a step, so they also offered a revised Article 6. The new Article 6 makes it easier for a buyer to meet his obligations. For example, the buyer need do nothing if the secured assets are *less* than $10,000 or *greater* than $25 million. Finally, if the seller has over 200 creditors, the buyer may notify them by publication rather than individually.

At least 35 states have repealed Article 6, and about five have adopted the new, revised version. The remaining states retain the old Article 6, but many are considering repeal.

RETURNABLE GOODS

Sometimes the seller will allow the buyer to return goods even when he has no complaints about their quality. This, too, can create a problem for creditors. A bank may extend a loan to a business based on the inventory. The bank is willing to lend money since it can seize the goods if the merchant fails to pay on time. But what if the merchant *does not own* some of the goods, because he intends to return them to the original owner? If the merchant fails to pay his loan, who gets the goods—the creditor (bank) or the owner of the goods? The Code considers two types of contract that permit a buyer to return goods.

Sale on Approval

If a buyer takes goods intending to *use* them herself, but has the right to return the goods to the seller, it is a "sale on approval." Max manufactures bar code readers, the machines that scan magnetic bar codes on merchandise. He wants to sell half a dozen to Pinky's Superette, but Pinky isn't sure the machines are worth the price. To encourage Pinky, Max allows her to take the machines and try them out. At the end of 60 days she may return them or pay full price. There really is no *sale* until Pinky has formally accepted the goods.

Under UCC §2-326(2), in a sale on approval, the goods *are not* subject to the buyer's creditors until the buyer accepts them. Suppose Pinky has borrowed $200,000 from the bank and has given a security interest "in all goods in the store now or in the future." The bar code machines are "goods in the store," and if Pinky fails to pay her loans, the bank will try to seize the equipment. But this is a sale on approval, and the bank has no right to Max's machines.

Preventive Law

A finance company will often extend credit based on a merchant's inventory. A creditor considering such a loan must determine what goods, if any, are "sale on approval," since those goods give the creditor no security.

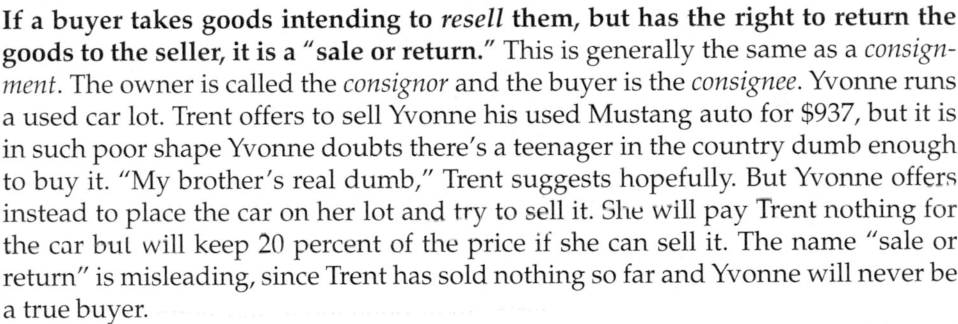

Sale or Return

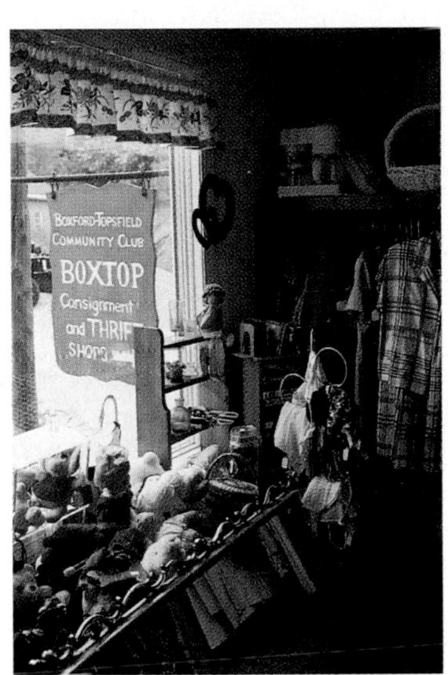

If you are thinking of consigning an expensive clock to this shop, what risk do you run?

If a buyer takes goods intending to *resell* them, but has the right to return the goods to the seller, it is a "sale or return." This is generally the same as a *consignment*. The owner is called the *consignor* and the buyer is the *consignee*. Yvonne runs a used car lot. Trent offers to sell Yvonne his used Mustang auto for $937, but it is in such poor shape Yvonne doubts there's a teenager in the country dumb enough to buy it. "My brother's real dumb," Trent suggests hopefully. But Yvonne offers instead to place the car on her lot and try to sell it. She will pay Trent nothing for the car but will keep 20 percent of the price if she can sell it. The name "sale or return" is misleading, since Trent has sold nothing so far and Yvonne will never be a true buyer.

Under **UCC §2-326, in a sale or return, the goods *are* subject to the claims of the buyer's creditors**. Suppose Yvonne fails to pay back some loans. Her creditors will instantly round up the Mustang, and Trent will never get a dime for his car.

At times it will be unclear just what the parties intended when the buyer took the goods. Where the buyer's purpose is to resell the goods, the law will presume that it is a sale or return and will enable creditors to take the merchandise. The Code demands this result to protect innocent creditors. A seller who leaves goods with a buyer for resale is protected from potential creditors only if (1) the seller attaches to the goods a sign indicating that she has consigned it with the buyer, or (2) the buyer is generally known to creditors to be in the resale business, or (3) the seller files in the appropriate state office a formal statement of her ownership interest in the goods, pursuant to Article 9 of the Code.

Trent's Mustang *would have been* safe from creditors if Trent had placed a large sign indicating his ownership, or if the bank had realized that Yvonne routinely resold cars for other people, or if Trent had filed the kind of formal papers that we discuss in Chapter 26, on secured transactions. But without such protection, Trent loses his car. (Of course, as is true with most commerce, goods can be consigned and sold over the Internet. One example of an Internet consignor is **http://www.secondhand.com**.) In the following case, the creditor is the Internal Revenue Service, which is trying to snare a woman's gold bracelet. The nerve!

KNIGHT v. UNITED STATES
838 F. Supp. 1243, 1993 U.S. Dist. LEXIS 13634
United States District Court, Middle District of Tennessee, 1993

Facts: Linda Knight had purchased a gold bracelet 22 years earlier. It meant a great deal to her, but now she was desperate for cash. A friend arranged to place the bracelet on consignment with a shop called The Alamo, which specialized in western clothing and accessories. Regrettably, The Alamo and its owners, Tony and Susan Alamo, had fallen slightly behind in their federal income taxes. When Linda Knight dropped off her bracelet, the Alamos owed just over $7.25 million to the government, and the IRS was tired of waiting. It seized everything in the store, including Linda's bracelet. She sued. Since the facts were undisputed, both Knight and the IRS moved for summary judgment.

Issue: Was the IRS entitled to Knight's gold bracelet?

Excerpts from Judge Echols's Decision: Tennessee's Commercial Code specifically defines the relative rights of a consignor and consignee when a creditor of the consignee claims an interest in the consigned goods. Tennessee law requires the consignor to take certain affirmative steps in order to protect their interest in the consigned goods against claims by the consignee's creditors while the goods are in the consignee's possession. The parties' intent is no longer determinative of the nature of the transaction.

It is undisputed that neither Knight nor The Alamo marked the bracelet with any type of sign which would have indicated to customers or any other third party that the bracelet was on consignment from Knight. It is likewise undisputed that Knight did not make the required filings with the state in order to protect and perfect her security interest in the bracelet. Finally, the affidavits of employees of The Alamo indicate that it was not "substantially engaged" in the consignment business. Indeed, the employees' affidavits confirm that The Alamo only rarely accepted goods on consignment, and would only do so on those rare occasions when the consignor was a person with whom the employees were personally acquainted. Based upon these undisputed facts, this court is of the opinion that Knight has failed to satisfy her burden of proving that The Alamo was "substantially engaged" in the consignment business.

In this case, the undisputed facts indicate that Knight took none of the three precautionary steps to protect her property interest in the bracelet. Therefore, the IRS, as a rightful creditor of the consignee, was legally entitled to seize the consigned goods in satisfaction of the consignee's debt.

For the foregoing reasons, [Knight's] motion for summary judgment is hereby *denied*, the [government's] motion for summary judgment is hereby *granted*, and this action is accordingly *dismissed*.

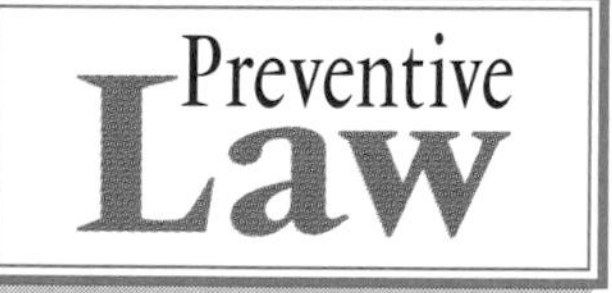

You have a used computer that is still worth several hundred dollars, and you want to sell it so you can purchase a more powerful model. A friend who works in a used computer store offers to sell it for you on consignment. But you also know of a shop that deals exclusively in consigned goods. Where are you better off placing your computer?

The issues we have looked at thus far involve someone doing something wrong, often a scoundrel selling goods that he never owned. Now we turn to cases where there may be no wrongdoer.

RISK OF LOSS

Accidents hurt businesses. When goods are damaged, the law may again need to decide whether it is the seller or buyer who must suffer the loss. In the cases we have seen thus far, the parties were arguing, "It's mine!"—"Like heck, it's *mine!*" In risk of loss cases, the parties are generally shouting, "It was yours!"— "No way, chump, it was *yours!*"

Athena, a seafood wholesaler, is gearing up for the Super Bowl, which will bring 110,000 hungry visitors to her city for a week of eating and gabbing. Athena orders 25,000 lobsters from Poseidon's Fishfoods, 500 miles distant, and simultaneously contracts with a dozen local restaurants to re-sell them. Poseidon loads the lobsters, still kicking, into refrigerated railcars owned by Demeter Trucking. But halfway to the city, the train collides with a prison van. None of the convicts escape but the lobsters do, hurtling into the swamps from which they are never recaptured. Athena loses all of her profits and sues. As luck would have it, Demeter Trucking had foolishly economized by letting its insurance lapse. Poseidon claims the goods were out of its hands. Who loses?

The common law answered this problem by looking at which party had title to the goods at the time of loss. But the Code again rejects this abstract concept, striving once more for a practical solution. The UCC permits the parties to agree on who bears the risk of loss. **UCC §2-509(4) states that the parties may allocate the risk of loss any way they wish**.

Often the parties will do just that, avoiding arguments and litigation in the event of an accident. As part of her agreement with Poseidon, Athena should have included a one-sentence clause, such as "Seller bears all risk of loss until the lobsters are delivered to Athena's warehouse." As long as the parties make their risk allocation clear, the Code will enforce it.

SHIPPING TERMS

The parties can quickly and easily allocate the risk of loss by using common shipping terms that the Code defines. FOB means free on board; FAS indicates free alongside a ship; and CIF stands for cost, insurance, and freight. By combining these designations with other terms, the parties can specify risk in a few words:

- *FOB place of shipment*. The seller is obligated to put the goods into the possession of the carrier at the place named. The seller bears the expense *and risk* until they are in the carrier's possession. From that moment onward, the buyer bears the risk.
- *FOB place of destination*. The seller must deliver the goods at the place named and bears the expense *and risk* of shipping.
- *FAS a named vessel*. The seller at his expense *and risk* must deliver the goods alongside the named vessel and obtain proper receipts.
- *CIF*. The price includes in a lump sum the cost of the goods and the insurance and freight to the named destination.
- *C & F*. The price includes in a lump sum the cost of the goods and freight, but *not* insurance.

Thus, if Athena had put a clause in her contract saying, "FOB Athena's warehouse," Poseidon would have born the risk of any loss up to the time the lobsters were unloaded in Athena's possession. Poseidon would then have known that it must insure the lobsters during transit. For an example of all shipping terms, as they actually appear in the statutes of one state (Maine), see **http://janus.state.me.us/legis/statutes**.

WHEN THE PARTIES FAIL TO ALLOCATE THE RISK

If the parties fail to specify when the risk passes from seller to buyer, the Code provides the answer. When neither party breached the contract, §2-509 determines the risk; when a party has breached the contract, §2-510 governs. The full analysis

Most sales contracts are *shipment contracts*. What risk does the buyer assume in such a deal?

of risk is somewhat intricate, so we first supply you with a short version: **When neither party has breached, the risk of loss generally passes from seller to buyer when the seller has transported the goods as far as he is obligated to. When a party has breached, the risk of loss generally lies with that party**.

And now, for the courageous, the full version of how the Code allocates the risk of loss when the parties failed to specify it.

When Neither Party Breaches

In the example of Athena and Poseidon, both parties did what they were supposed to do, so there was no breach of contract. To settle these cases, we need to know whether the contract obligated the seller to ship the goods or whether the goods were handled in some other way. There are three possibilities: (1) the contract required the seller to ship the goods, or (2) the contract involved a bailment, or (3) other cases.

If the Seller Must Ship the Goods. Most contracts require the seller to arrange shipment of the goods. In a *shipment contract*, the seller must deliver the goods *to a carrier*, which will then transport the goods to the buyer. The carrier might be a trucking company, railroad, airline, or ship, and is generally located near the seller's place of business. **In a shipment contract, the risk passes to the buyer when the seller delivers the goods to the carrier**. Suppose Old Wood, in North Carolina, agrees to sell $100,000 worth of furniture to Pioneer Company, in Anchorage. The contract requires Old Wood to deliver the goods to Great Northern Railroad lines in Chicago. From North Carolina to Chicago, Old Wood bears the risk of loss. Once the furniture is on board the train in Chicago, the risk of loss passes to Pioneer. If the train derails in Montana and every desk and chair is squashed, Pioneer owes the full $100,000 to Old Wood.

In a *destination contract*, the seller is responsible for delivering the goods *to the buyer*. In a destination contract, risk passes to the buyer when the goods reach the destination. If the contract required Old Wood to deliver the furniture to Pioneer's warehouse in Anchorage, then Old Wood bears the loss for the entire trip. If the train travels 3,000 miles and then plunges off a bridge in Alaska, 45 feet from its destination, Old Wood picks up the tab.

If There Is a Bailment. Freezem Corp. produces 500 room air conditioners and stores them in Every-Ware's Warehouse. This is a **bailment, meaning that one person or company is legally holding goods for the benefit of another**. Freezem is the **bailor**, the one who owns the goods, and Every-Ware is the **bailee**, the one with temporary possession. (For a sample bailment contract, see **http://www.gate.net/~legalsvc/autobail.html**.) Suppose Freezem agrees to sell 300 of its air conditioners to KeepKool Appliances. KeepKool does not need the machines in its store for six months, so it plans to keep them at Every-Ware's until then. But two weeks after Freezem and KeepKool make their deal, Every-Ware burns to the ground. Who bears the loss of the 300 air conditioners? **If the contract requires a bailee to hold the goods for the buyer, the risk passes when the buyer obtains documents entitling her to possession, or when the bailee acknowledges her right to the goods.** If fire broke out in Every-Ware's before KeepKool received any documents enabling it to take the air conditioners away, then the loss would fall on Freezem.

Other Cases. The great majority of contracts involve either shipment by the seller or a bailment. In the remaining cases, if the seller is a *merchant*, risk passes to the buyer on receipt. This means that a merchant is only off the hook if the buyer actually accepts the goods. If the seller is *not a merchant*, risk passes when the seller tenders the goods, meaning that she makes them available to the buyer. The Code is giving more protection to buyers when they deal with a merchant. But if the buyer is purchasing from a non-merchant, the Code assumes they are on equal footing, and the seller is relieved of liability when she merely tenders the goods.

When One Party Breaches

Still there? Excellent. We now look at how the Code allocates risk when one of the parties does breach. Again there are three possibilities: (1) seller breaches and buyer rejects; (2) seller breaches, buyer accepts, but then revokes; or (3) buyer breaches.

Seller Breaches and Buyer Rejects. PlayStore, a sporting goods store, orders 75 canoes from Floataway. PlayStore specifies that the canoes must be 12 feet long, lightweight metal, dark green. Floataway delivers 75 canoes to Truckit, a trucking company. When Truckit's trucks arrive, PlayStore finds that the canoes are the right material and color, but 18 feet long. PlayStore rejects the craft, and Truckit heads back to Floataway. But one of the trucks is hijacked and the 25 canoes it carries are never recovered. Floataway demands its money for the 25 lost canoes. Who loses?

Floataway had delivered **nonconforming goods**, that is, merchandise that is different from what the contract specified. A buyer has a right to reject nonconforming goods. **When the buyer rejects nonconforming goods, the risk of loss remains with the seller until he cures the defect or the buyer decides to accept the goods**. In our example, Floataway must suffer the loss for the stolen canoes. If PlayStore had decided to accept the canoes, even though they were the wrong size, then the risk would have passed to the sports store.

Seller Breaches, Buyer Accepts, but Then Revokes. PlayStore orders 200 tennis rackets from High Strung. When the rackets arrive, they seem fine, so the store accepts them. But then a salesperson notices that the grips are loose. Every racket has the same problem. PlayStore returns the rackets to High Strung, but they are destroyed when a blimp crashes into the delivery truck. **When a buyer accepts goods but then rightfully revokes acceptance, the risk remains with the seller to the extent the buyer's insurance will not cover the loss**. If PlayStore's insurance covers the damaged rackets, there is no problem. If PlayStore's insurance does not cover the loss of goods in transit, High Strung must pay.

Buyer Breaches. One last time. PlayStore orders 60 tents from ExploreMore. About the time the tents leave the factory, PlayStore decides to drop its line of camping goods and specialize in team sports. PlayStore notifies ExploreMore it wants to explore less, and will not pay. The tents are destroyed in a collision involving a prison van and a train carrying lobsters. This time, PlayStore is liable. **When a buyer breaches the contract before taking possession, it assumes the risk of loss to the extent the seller's insurance is deficient**.

Exhibit 20.1 on page 465 should clarify.

In the following case, neither party breached, so §2-509 governs.

Code Provisions Discussed in This Case

Issue	Relevant Code Section
1. Did the parties create a bailment?	In a bailment, one person legally holds goods for the benefit of another.
2. Which party bore the risk of the horse's death?	UCC §2-509(2): If the contract requires a bailee to hold the goods for the buyer, the risk passes when the buyer obtains documents entitling her to possession, or when the bailee acknowledges her right to the goods.

HARMON v. DUNN
1997 Tenn. App. LEXIS 217
Tennessee Court of Appeals, 1997

Facts: Bess Harmon owned a two-year-old Tennessee Walking Horse named Phantom Recall. Harmon, who lived in Tennessee, boarded her horse with Steve Dunn, at his stables in Florence, Alabama. Dunn cared for Phantom Recall and showed him at equestrian events. Harmon instructed Dunn to sell the horse for $25,000, and Dunn arranged for his friend Scarbrough to buy the colt. On June 30, Dunn delivered Scarbrough's $25,000 check to Harmon, who handed over the horse's certificate of registration and a "transfer of ownership" document. That night at a horse show Dunn told Scarbrough that he had delivered the check and had the ownership papers in his car. Dunn did not actually give the documents to his friend. Scarbrough knew that Phantom Recall was at Dunn's stable, where Scarbrough had boarded other horses. Sadly, the colt developed colitis and died suddenly, on July 4. Scarbrough stopped payment on his check, and Harmon sued for her money. The trial court found for Harmon and Scarbrough appealed.

Issue: **Which party bore the risk of Phantom Recall's death?**

Excerpts from Judge Farmer's Decision: [UCC §2-509 states:] Risk of loss in the absence of breach. . . .

> **(2)** Where the goods are held by a bailee to be delivered without being moved, the risk of loss passes to the buyer:
> **(a)** on his receipt of a negotiable document of title covering the goods, or
> **(b)** on acknowledgment by the bailee of the buyer's right to possession of the goods, or
> **(c)** after his receipt of a non-negotiable document of title or other written direction to deliver . . .

We conclude that the facts before us clearly establish a bailor-bailee relationship between Harmon and Dunn. It is not disputed that the latter was the agent of the former. Here, it was agreed that Dunn would train and care for Phantom Recall at the Dunn Stables in Florence, Alabama. He was also responsible for transporting the horse to various shows. The record establishes that prior to the horse's death, he had been entered and shown by Dunn himself in three separate events.

Having established Dunn a bailee for purposes of [§2-509(2)] and in the absence of any prior arrangement with Dunn or Harmon that the horse be delivered elsewhere upon purchase from the latter, we find that the risk of loss passed to Scarbrough if and when the applicable provisions under subsection (2) occurred. Subsection (2)(a) and (b) provide that the risk of loss passes to the buyer "on his receipt of a negotiable document of title covering the goods; or on acknowledgment by the bailee of the buyer's right to possession of the goods."

We find that Scarbrough received the ability to control possession of the horse no later than July 1 irrespective of the fact that he did not actually receive physical possession of the ownership documents at that time. The documents which were necessary for transfer of ownership and taking possession of the horse were already in the hands of the bailee. We find an actual physical back and forth exchange between the two unnecessary under these facts where the bailee and the seller's agent are one and the same. Certainly Scarbrough had the ability to control possession of the horse no later than July 1 when he was made aware that Dunn had the transfer papers.

[Affirmed.]

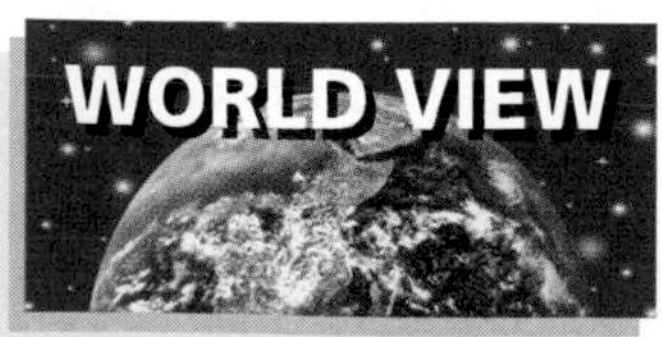

Repeat viewers of the film *Titanic* will be relieved to learn that maritime disasters are relatively rare. Eighty thousand large ships cruise the high seas, but only 150 to 200 suffer major accidents in a typical year, and few of these involve loss of life. Nonetheless, business people *should* be wary because a heavily laden ship can sink a small business. As the holiday season approached, the MSC *Carla*, a giant freight

Exhibit 20.1

Did the Parties Allocate the Risk in Their Contract?

If the parties have allocated the risk in their contract, that agreement will control and everything on this chart is gloriously irrelevant.

If the parties have *not* allocated the risk of loss, then §2-509 and §2-510 will determine who suffers the loss.

In using the two Code sections to determine the risk, the first question is whether either party has breached the contract.

No Breach (§2-509)

If neither party breaches, there are three possibilities:

1. Contract requires Seller to ship goods by carrier.
   - a. *Shipment Contract* requires Seller to deliver the goods to a carrier. → **Risk** passes to Buyer when Seller delivers goods to carrier.
   - b. *Destination Contract* requires Seller to deliver goods to a specified destination. → **Risk** passes to Buyer when carrier tenders goods at the destination.
2. Contract requires a bailee to hold goods for Buyer. → **Risk** passes to Buyer when she obtains documents entitling her to possession, or when Bailee acknowledges she is entitled to possession.
3. Other cases.
   - a. If Seller *is* a merchant → **Risk** passes to Buyer on receipt of goods.
   - b. If Seller *is not* a merchant → **Risk** passes to Buyer on tender of delivery.

Breach (§2-510)

If a party breaches, there are three possibilities:

1. Seller breaches. The goods are nonconforming and the Buyer rightfully rejects them. → **Risk** remains with the Seller until he cures the defects or the Buyer decides to accept the goods.
2. Seller breaches. The buyer accepts but then revokes his acceptance. → **Risk** remains with the Seller to the extent that the Buyer's own insurance is deficient.
3. Buyer breaches. Buyer repudiates conforming goods or in some other way breaches the contract before he takes possession of the goods. → **Risk** passes to the Buyer to the extent that the Seller's insurance is deficient, for a commercially reasonable time.

ship en route to Boston from Le Havre, ran into a violent storm off the Azores. Thirty-foot waves pounded the vessel until it split in two. Helicopters rescued the desperate crew. Half of the freighter sank, carrying its cargo to the bottom, and the other half was towed to shore, with some goods intact. *Which* goods? An executive from Rockport shoes paced the wharves in Boston, wondering if the company would get its 18,000 pairs of shoes; Swiss merchants feared they might have suffered the largest loss of wine in maritime history; buyers from Filene's Basement worried about how they would replace 600 Fendi handbags, if necessary; and exporters and importers around the world hurried to the phones—or the courtroom—seeking to protect themselves from the loss of furniture, beer, electronic goods, and countless other items. Accidents happen, and it is vital that merchants anticipate what might go wrong, allocate risk in all contracts, and calculate how to survive any mishaps.

CHAPTER CONCLUSION

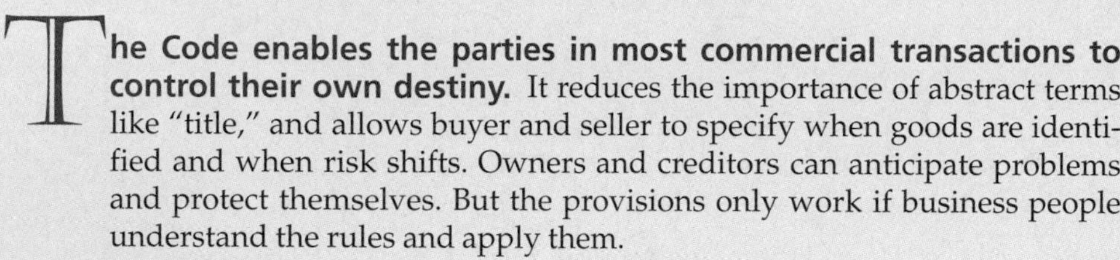

The Code enables the parties in most commercial transactions to control their own destiny. It reduces the importance of abstract terms like "title," and allows buyer and seller to specify when goods are identified and when risk shifts. Owners and creditors can anticipate problems and protect themselves. But the provisions only work if business people understand the rules and apply them.

CHAPTER REVIEW

1. An *interest* is a legal right in something. *Title* means the normal rights of ownership.
2. Goods must *exist* and be *identified* to the contract before title can pass. The parties may agree in their contract how and when they will identify goods; if they do not specify, the Code stipulates when it happens. The parties may also state when title passes, and once again, if they do not, the Code provides rules.
3. A buyer obtains an *insurable interest* when the goods are identified to the contract. A seller retains an insurable interest in goods as long as she has either title or a security interest in them.
4. *Void title* is no title at all. *Voidable title* means limited rights in the goods, inferior to those of the owner. A person with voidable title has power to transfer good title to a *bona fide purchaser (BFP)*, that is, someone who purchases in good faith, for value.
5. Any *entrusting* of goods to a merchant who deals in goods of that kind gives him the power to transfer all rights of the entruster to a buyer in the ordinary course of business.
6. A buyer in the ordinary course of business generally takes goods free and clear of any security interest. But that will not be true in a *bulk sale*, unless the seller and buyer ensure that all creditors receive notice of the sale before it takes place. And there are different rules if the goods are returnable. In a sale on approval, the goods *are not* subject to the buyer's creditors until the buyer accepts them; in a sale or return, the goods *are* subject to the buyer's creditors.
7. In their contract, the parties may allocate the *risk of loss* anyway they wish. If they fail to do so, the Code provides several steps to determine who pays for

any damage. When neither party has breached, the risk of loss generally passes from seller to buyer when the seller has transported the goods as far as he is obligated to. When a party has breached, the risk of loss generally lies with the party that has breached.

PRACTICE TEST

1. **CPA QUESTION** On Monday, Wolfe paid Aston Co., a furniture retailer, $500 for a table. On Thursday, Aston notified Wolfe that the table was ready to be picked up. On Saturday, while Aston was still in possession of the table, it was destroyed in a fire. Who bears the loss of the table?

(a) Wolfe, because Wolfe had title to the table at the time of loss

(b) Aston, unless Wolfe is a merchant

(c) Wolfe, unless Aston breached the contract

(d) Aston, because Wolfe had not yet taken possession of the table

2. **CPA QUESTION** Under UCC Article 9 on secured transactions, which of the following statements is correct concerning the disposition of goods by a secured creditor after a debtor defaults on a loan?

(a) A good faith purchaser of the goods for value and without knowledge of any defects in the sale takes free of any security interest.

(b) The debtor may not redeem the goods after the default.

(c) Secured creditors retain the right to redeem the goods after they are sold to a third party.

(d) The goods may be disposed of only at a public sale.

3. Franklin Miller operated Miller Seed Co. in Pea Ridge, Arkansas. He bought, processed, and sold fescue seed, which is used for growing pasture and fodder grass. Farmers brought seed to Miller who would normally clean, bag, and store it. In some cases the farmers authorized Miller to sell the seed, in some cases not. Miller mixed together the seed that was for sale with the seed in storage so that a customer could not see any difference between them. Miller defaulted on a $380,000 loan from the First State Bank of Purdy. First State attempted to seize all of the seed in the store. Tony Havelka, a farmer, protested that his 490,000 pounds of seed was merely in storage and not subject to First State's claim. Who is entitled to the seed?

4. **RIGHT & WRONG** Myrna and James Brown ordered a $35,000 motor home from R.V.Kingdom, Inc. The manufacturer delivered the vehicle to R.V.-Kingdom, with title in the dealer's name. The Browns agreed to accept the motor home, but soon regretted spending the money and asked R.V.Kingdom to resell it. The motor home stayed on R.V.Kingdom's lot for quite a few months, but when the Browns decided to come get it, they learned that R.V.Kingdom had illegally used the vehicle as collateral for a loan and that a bank had repossessed it. The Browns filed a claim with their insurance company, State Farm. The insurer agreed that the vehicle had been stolen and agreed that the Browns' policy covered newly acquired vehicles. But the company refused to pay, claiming that the Browns had not taken title or possession to the goods and therefore had no insurable interest. The Browns sued. Please rule on their case. Let us also look at the ethics of the case by creating a contrasting hypothetical. Suppose that among the insurance company's thousands of customers was Arvee, a recreational vehicle dealership similar to the one in the real case. Imagine that Arvee had taken in an automobile for resale from a customer named Parker, and kept the vehicle on its lot. If Parker's auto were stolen, what argument would the insurance company be making? How would the company define insurable interest in *that* case?

5. Article 6 of the Code requires that before a merchant makes a bulk sale, she must give a list of her creditors to the buyer, who must notify all of them. Is a landlord, who rents space to the merchant, a creditor entitled to such notice? The states are split on this question. Make a policy argument that a landlord *is* entitled to Article 6 protection, and a second argument that a landlord is *not* entitled.

6. Fay Witcher owned a Ford Bronco. Steve Risher operated a used car lot. (We know where this one's heading.) Witcher delivered his automobile to Risher, asking him to resell it if he could. Witcher specified that he wanted all cash for his car, not part cash plus a trade-in. Risher sold the car to Richard Parker for $12,800, but took a trade-in as part payment. Risher promised to deliver the Bronco's certificate of title to Parker within a few days, but never did. He was also obligated to

deliver most of the proceeds of the sale to Witcher, the owner, but also failed to do that. Parker claimed that the car was rightfully his. Witcher argued that Parker owned nothing because he never got the title and because Witcher never got his money. Who loses?

7. Universal Consolidated Cos. contracted with China Metallurgical Import and Export Corp. (CMIEC) to provide CMIEC with new and used equipment for a cold rolling steel mill. Universal then contracted with Pittsburgh Industrial Furnace Co. (Pifcom) to engineer and build much of the equipment. The contract required Pifcom to deliver the finished equipment to a trucking company, which would then transport it to Universal. Pifcom delivered the goods to the trucking company as scheduled. But before all of the goods reached Universal, CMIEC notified Universal it was canceling the deal. Universal, in turn, notified Pifcom to stop work, but all goods had been delivered to the shipper and ultimately reached Universal. Pifcom claimed that it retained title to the goods, but Universal claimed that title had passed to it. Who is right?

8. Bradkeyne International, Ltd., an English company, bought a large quantity of batteries from Duracell, Inc. The contract specified delivery "FOB Jacksonville, Florida." Duracell supervised the loading of the batteries onto a ship in Jacksonville in early July, and they arrived in England in August. When loaded onto the ship, the batteries were conforming goods that could be used for normal purposes. But on board the ship, excessive heat damaged them. By the time they reached England, they were worth only a fraction of the original price. Bradkeyne sued Duracell. Who loses?

9. CPA QUESTION On September 10, Bell Corp. entered into a contract to purchase 50 lamps from Glow Manufacturing. Bell prepaid 40 percent of the purchase price. Glow became insolvent on September 19 before segregating, in its inventory, the lamps to be delivered to Bell. Bell will *not* be able to recover the lamps because:

(a) Bell is regarded as a merchant

(b) The lamps were not identified to the contract

(c) Glow became insolvent fewer than 10 days after receipt of Bell's prepayment

(d) Bell did not pay the full price at the time of purchase

10. YOU BE THE JUDGE WRITING PROBLEM Construction Helicopters paid Heli-Dyne Systems $315,000 for three helicopters that were in Argentina. Two were ready to fly and one was disassembled for routine maintenance. The contract said nothing about risk of loss (the parties could have saved a lot of money by reading this chapter). Heli-Dyne arranged for an Argentine company to oversee their loading on board the freight ship *Lynx*. The two helicopters and 25 crates containing the disassembled craft were properly loaded, but when the ship arrived in Miami, only 7 of the crates appeared. Heli-Dyne refused to supply more parts and Construction sued. Who bears the loss? **Argument for Construction:** Construction had no control over the goods until they reached Miami. Although we do not know exactly what happened to the crates, we know the one party that had *nothing* to do with the loss: Construction. The company should not pay for damage it never caused. **Argument for Heli-Dyne:** Because the contract failed to specify risk of loss, it is a shipment contract. In such an agreement, risk of loss passes to the buyer when the seller delivers the goods to a carrier. Heli-Dyne delivered the goods and has no further responsibility.

11. CPA QUESTION Quick Corp. agreed to purchase 200 typewriters from Union Suppliers, Inc. Union is a wholesaler of appliances and Quick is an appliance retailer. The contract required Union to ship the typewriters to Quick by common carrier, "FOB Union Suppliers, Inc. Loading Dock." Which of the parties bears the risk of loss during shipment?

(a) Union, because the risk of loss passes only when Quick receives the typewriters

(b) Union, because both parties are merchants

(c) Quick, because title to the typewriters passed to Quick at the time of shipment

(d) Quick, because the risk of loss passes when the typewriters are delivered to the carrier

INTERNET RESEARCH PROBLEM

You own two powerful Clydesdale draft horses. A friend asks to borrow the horses for three months to give hayrides. You agree, provided your friend takes proper care of these valuable animals, providing good feed, adequate rest, and veterinary treatment. Examine the bailment contract at **http://www.gate.net/~legalsvc/autobail.html**; then draft a bailment agreement.

You can find further practice problems in the Online Quiz at http://beatty.westbuslaw.com or in the Study Guide that accompanies this text.

CHAPTER 21

WARRANTIES AND PRODUCT LIABILITY

You are sitting in a fast-food restaurant in Washington, D.C. Your friend Ben, who works for a congressman, is eating with one hand and gesturing with the other. "We want product liability reform and we want it now," he proclaims, stabbing the air with his free hand. "It's absurd, these multimillion dollar verdicts, just because something has a *slight defect.*" He waves angrily at the absurdity, takes a ferocious bite from his burger—and with a loud CRACK breaks a tooth. Ben howls in pain and throws down the bun, revealing a large piece of bone in the meat. As he tips back in misery, his defective chair collapses, and Ben slams into the tile, knocking himself unconscious. Hours later, when he revives in the hospital, he refuses to speak to you until he puts in a call to his lawyer.

PRODUCT LIABILITY

Ben and his lawyer will be chatting about **product liability**, which refers to goods that have caused an injury. The harm may be physical, as it was in Ben's case. Or it can be purely economic, as when a corporation buys a computer so defective it must be replaced, costing the buyer lost time and profits. The injured party may have a choice of possible remedies, including:

- *Warranty*, which is an assurance provided in a sales contract
- *Negligence*, which refers to unreasonable conduct by the defendant, and
- *Strict liability*, which prohibits defective products whether the defendant acted reasonably or not.

We discuss each of these remedies in this chapter. What all product liability cases have in common is that a person or business has been hurt by goods. We focus primarily on cases where the *sale* of goods leads to the injury, but we also examine product liability issues where there has been no sale. We begin with warranties.

A warranty is a contractual assurance that goods will meet certain standards. It is normally a manufacturer or a seller who gives a warranty, and a buyer who relies on it. A warranty might be explicit and written: "The manufacturer warrants that the light bulbs in this package will provide 100 watts of power for 2,000 hours." Or a warranty could be oral: "Don't worry, this machine can harvest any size of wheat crop ever planted in the state." The manufacturer may offer a warranty as a means of attracting buyers: "We provide the finest, bumper-to-bumper warranty in the automobile industry." Or *the law itself* may impose a warranty on goods, requiring the manufacturer to meet certain standards whether it intends to or not. Here we consider two broad categories: express warranties and implied warranties.

EXPRESS WARRANTIES

An express warranty is one that the seller creates with his words or actions.[1] Whenever a seller *clearly indicates* to a buyer that the goods being sold will meet certain standards, she has created an express warranty. For example, if the sales clerk for a paint store tells a professional house painter that "this exterior paint will not fade for three years, even in direct sunlight," that is an express warranty and the store is bound by it. Or, if the clerk gives the painter a brochure that makes the same promise, the store is again bound by its express warranty. On the other hand, if the sales person merely says, "I know you're going to be happy with this product," there is no warranty, because the promise is too vague. The UCC establishes that the seller may create an express warranty in three ways: (1) with an affirmation of fact or a promise; (2) with a description of the goods; or (3) with a sample or model. In addition, the buyer must demonstrate that what the seller said or did was the *basis of the bargain*.

AFFIRMATION OF FACT OR PROMISE

Any affirmation of fact—or any promise—can create an express warranty.[2] An affirmation of fact is simply a statement about the nature or quality of the goods, such as "This scaffolding is made from the highest grade of steel available at any

[1] UCC §2-313.

[2] UCC §2-313(1)(a).

price," or "This car will accelerate from 0 to 60 in 8.3 seconds." A promise includes phrases such as "We guarantee you that this air conditioning system will cool your building to 72 degrees, regardless of the outdoor temperature."

A common problem in cases of express warranty is to separate true affirmations of fact from mere sales puffery or seller's opinion, which creates no express warranty. "You meet the nicest people on a Honda" is mere puffery. If you purchase a Honda and meet only deadbeats, the manufacturer owes you nothing.

A statement is more likely to be an affirmation of fact if:

- *It is specific and can be proven true or false.* Suppose the brochures of a home builder promise to meet "the strictest building codes." Since there is a code on file, the builder's work can be compared to it, and his promise is binding.

- *It is written.* An oral promise *can* create an express warranty. But promises in brochures are more likely to be taken seriously. Statements in a *written contract* are the likeliest of all to create a binding warranty.

- *Defects are not obvious.* If a used car salesman tells you that a car is rust free, when the driver's door is pockmarked with rust, you should not take the statement seriously—since a court will not, either.

- *Seller has greater expertise.* If the seller knows more than the buyer, his statements will be more influential with buyer and court alike. If your architect assures you that the new porch will be warm in winter, the law recognizes that you will naturally rely on her expertise.

DESCRIPTION OF GOODS

Any description of the goods can create an express warranty.[3] The phrase could be oral or written. A description might be a label on a bag of seed, referring to the seed as a particular variety of tomato; it could be a tag on airplane parts, assuring the buyer that the goods have met safety tests. Wherever the words appear, if they describe the goods as having particular characteristics or qualities, the seller has probably created an express warranty.

SAMPLE OR MODEL

Any sample or model can create an express warranty.[4] A sample can be a very effective way of demonstrating the quality of goods to a customer. However, a seller who uses a sample is generally warranting that the merchandise sold will be just as good. Glyptal, Inc. had a contract to paint railway cars and needed to create paint to the railroad's specifications. Glyptal asked Engelhard Corp. for sample pigments, specifying the viscosity (thickness) of the paint. Engelhard furnished samples of Cadmium 20 paint, which Glyptal tested in its paint sprayers and found satisfactory. But when Glyptal ordered a full shipment, the paint was too thick and could not be used in the sprayers. Engelhard had breached an express warranty.[5]

BASIS OF BARGAIN

The seller's conduct must have been part of the basis of the bargain. To prove an express warranty, a buyer must demonstrate that the two parties *included the statements or acts in their bargain.* Some courts have interpreted this to mean that the

---

[3] UCC §2-313(1)(b).

[4] UCC §2-313(1)(c).

[5] *Glyptal Inc. v. Engelhard Corp.*, 801 F. Supp. 887, 1992 U.S. Dist. LEXIS 14225 (D. Mass. 1992).

buyer must have *relied* on the seller's statements. There is logic to this position. For example, suppose a sales brochure makes certain assurances about the quality of goods, but the buyer never sees the brochure until she files suit. Should the seller be held to an express warranty? Some courts would rule that the seller is not liable for breach of warranty.

Other courts, however, have ruled that a seller's statement can be part of the basis of the bargain even when the buyer has not clearly relied on it. These courts are declaring that a seller who chooses to make statements about his goods will be held to them, *unless the seller can convince a court that he should not be liable*. This is a policy decision, taken by many courts, to give the buyer the benefit of the doubt, since the seller is in the best position to control what he says.

The following case involves a diamond bracelet and raises two issues of express warranty. First, were the seller's words an affirmation of fact or mere sales puffery? Second, were the seller's words part of the basis of the bargain?

DAUGHTREY v. ASHE
243 Va. 73, 413 S.E.2d 336, 1992 Va. LEXIS 152
Virginia Supreme Court, 1992

Facts: Hayes Daughtrey went to Sidney Ashe's jewelry shop to buy a diamond bracelet for his wife. Ashe showed Daughtrey a $15,000 bracelet and described the stones as "nice diamonds." Ashe then prepared an insurance estimate form that said:

> The following represents our estimate for insurance purposes only, of the present retail replacement cost of identical items, and not necessarily the amounts that might be obtained if the articles were offered for sale: bracelet, set with 28 brilliant full ct of diamonds weighing a total of 10 carats. H color and v.v.s. quality. Appraised value: $25,000.

The term "v.v.s. quality," used by gemologists and jewelers, is one of the highest ratings for a diamond. Daughtrey bought the bracelet for $15,000. Four years later, another jeweler inspected the bracelet and told him that the diamonds were not v.v.s. quality, but a substantially lower grade. Daughtrey demanded that Ashe replace the bracelet with one mounted with v.v.s. diamonds. Ashe offered to refund the purchase price, but Daughtrey refused because diamond values had risen. He sued. The trial court ruled for Ashe, declaring that he had never expressly warranted the diamonds. Daughtrey appealed.

Issues: Were Ashe's statements an express warranty? Were Ashe's statements part of the basis of the bargain?

Excerpts from Judge Whiting's Decision: The Ashes argue that the statement in the appraisal form is not an express warranty for two reasons. First, they say the appraisal on its face stated that it was "for insurance purposes only." However, we think that the balance of the language in the appraisal form demonstrates that the limiting language relates only to the statement of the appraised value. Therefore, Ashe's description of the grade of the diamonds should be treated as any other statement he may have made about them.

Second, the Ashes contend that Ashe's statement of the grade of the diamonds is a mere opinion and, thus, cannot qualify as an express warranty under the Code.

Clearly, Ashe intended to sell Daughtrey v.v.s. diamonds. He testified that he used only the term "nice" diamonds but "[n]ever mentioned vvs because [Daughtrey] didn't know anything about vvs." Later, Ashe testified that "I know when I sold the bracelet and I classified it as vvs, I knew it was vvs." Given these considerations, we conclude that Ashe's description of the goods was more than his opinion; rather, he intended it to be a statement of a fact. Therefore, the court erred in holding that the description was not an express warranty.

Next, the Ashes maintain that because the description of the diamonds as v.v.s. quality was not discussed, Daughtrey could not have relied upon Ashe's warranty and, thus, it cannot be treated as "a part of the basis of the bargain."

In our opinion, the "part of the basis of the bargain" language does not establish a buyer's reliance requirement. Instead, this language makes a seller's description of the goods that is not his mere opinion a representation that defines his obligation.

Ashe introduced no evidence of any factor that would take his affirmation of the quality of the diamonds out of the agreement. Therefore, his affirmation was "a part of the basis of the bargain." Accordingly, we hold that the Daughtreys are entitled to recover for their loss of bargain, and that the court erred in ruling to the contrary.

Reversed and *remanded*.

The Virginia Supreme Court put the burden on Ashe to prove that his statement was *not* the basis of the bargain, rather than requiring Daughtrey to demonstrate that he had relied on it. Is that sensible? Is it fair?

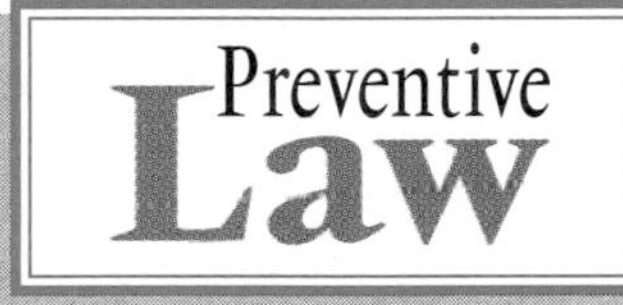

Warranties are boring, so many consumers ignore them. The next time you are about to commit that error, think of Peru. The South American nation bought a dozen Soviet-built MIG-29s, fighter planes that would make its air force the best equipped in Latin America. Peru, a poor country that could barely afford the $350 million price tag, purchased the jets from Belarus, which had obtained them after the fall of the Soviet Union. Fighter aircraft need constant, highly sophisticated maintenance every few hours. These planes were useless without a superior, long-term warranty, and sadly, they came with none at all. Belarus had neither the technicians nor the equipment to service the aircraft. Russia had earned no profit from the sale, so it refused to maintain them. Peruvian generals were left on the ground, pointing fingers at each other for an ill-considered purchase. Check that warranty! (For a Web site that evaluates software warranties and lauds those it finds superior, fly to **http://www.zdnet.com/anchordesk/hallofame/**.

IMPLIED WARRANTIES

Sean decides to plow driveways during the winter. Emily sells him a snowplow and installs it on his truck, but makes no promises about its performance. When winter arrives, Sean has plenty of business, but finds that the plow cannot be raised or lowered whenever the temperature falls below 40 degrees. He demands a refund from Emily, but she declines, saying, "I never said that thing would work in the winter. No express warranties, no luck." Scandalous! Is she off the hook? No. It is true she made no express warranties. But many sales are covered by implied warranties.

Implied warranties are those created by the Code itself, not by any act or statement of the seller. The Code's drafters concluded that goods should generally meet certain standards of quality, regardless of what the seller did or did not say. So the Code creates an implied warranty of merchantability and an implied warranty of fitness.

Implied Warranty of Merchantability

This is the most important warranty in the Code. Buyers, whether individual consumers or billion dollar corporations, are likelier to rely on this than any other section, and sellers must understand it thoroughly when they market goods. **Unless excluded or modified, a warranty that the goods shall be merchantable is implied in a contract for their sale, if the seller is a merchant with respect to goods of that kind.** *Merchantable* means that the goods are fit for the ordinary purposes for which they are used.[6] This rule contains several important principles:

- *Unless excluded or modified* means that the seller does have a chance to escape this warranty. We later discuss what steps a seller may take if she wants to sell goods that are *not* merchantable.
- *Merchantability* requires that goods be fit for their normal purposes. A ladder, to be merchantable, must be able to rest securely against a building and support someone who is climbing it. The ladder need not be serviceable as a boat ramp.
- *Implied* means that the law itself imposes this liability on the seller.
- *A merchant with respect to goods of that kind* means that the seller is someone who routinely deals in these goods or holds himself out as having special knowledge about these goods.

Dacor Corp. manufactured and sold scuba diving equipment. Dacor ordered air hoses from Sierra Precision, specifying the exact size and couplings so that the hose would fit tightly and safely into Dacor's oxygen units. Within about one year, customers returned a dozen Dacor units, complaining that the hose connections had cracked or sheared and were unusable. Dacor recalled 16,000 units and refit them with safe hoses, at a cost of more than $136,000. Dacor sued Sierra, claiming a breach of the implied warranty of merchantability. The Illinois court first ruled that Sierra was a merchant with respect to scuba hoses, because it routinely manufactured and sold them. The court then ruled:

> There is no evidence suggesting that these hose assemblies were subjected to anything other than normal use. Since the kind of failure experienced in connection with the returned hose assemblies would be life-threatening if it occurred under water, the hose assemblies were not fit for the purpose for which they were used within the meaning of section 2-314.

The court ordered Sierra to pay $136,721.[7]

The scuba equipment was not merchantable, because a properly made scuba hose should *never* crack under normal use. But what if the product being sold is food, and the food contains something that is harmful—yet quite normal?

GOODMAN v. WENCO FOODS, INC.

333 N.C. 1, 423 S.E.2d 444, 1992 N.C.LEXIS 671
Supreme Court of North Carolina, 1992

Facts: Fred Goodman and a friend stopped for lunch at a Wendy's restaurant in Hillsborough, North Carolina. Goodman had eaten about half of his double hamburger when he bit down and felt immediate pain in his lower jaw. He took from his mouth a triangular piece of cow bone, about one-sixteenth to one-quarter inch thick and one-half inch long, along with several pieces of his teeth. Goodman's pain was intense and his dental repairs took months.

---

6 UCC §2-314(1).

7 *Dacor Corp. v. Sierra Precision*, 1993 U.S. Dist. LEXIS 8009 (N.D. Ill. 1993).

The restaurant purchased all of its meat from Greensboro Meat Supply Company (GMSC). Wendy's required its meat to be chopped and "free from bone or cartilage in excess of 1/8 inch in any dimension." GMSC beef was inspected continuously by state regulators and was certified by the United States Department of Agriculture (USDA). The USDA considered any bone fragment less than three-quarters of an inch long to be "insignificant."

Goodman sued, claiming a breach of the implied warranty of merchantability. The trial court dismissed the claim, ruling that the bone was natural to the food and that the hamburger was therefore fit for its ordinary purpose. The appeals court reversed this, holding that a hamburger could be unfit even if the bone occurred naturally. Wendy's appealed to the state's highest court.

Issue: **Was the hamburger unfit for its ordinary purpose because it contained a harmful but natural bone?**

Excerpts from Judge Exum's Decision: We hold that when a substance in food causes injury to a consumer of the food, it is not a bar to recovery against the seller that the substance was "natural" to the food, provided the substance is of such a size, quality or quantity, or the food has been so processed, or both, that the substance's presence should not reasonably have been anticipated by the consumer.

A triangular, one-half-inch, inflexible bone shaving is indubitably "inherent" in or "natural" to a cut of beef, but whether it is so "natural" to hamburger as to put a consumer on his guard—whether it "is to be reasonably expected by the consumer"—is, in most cases, a question for the jury. We are not requiring that the respondent's hamburgers be perfect, only that they be fit for their intended purpose. It is difficult to conceive of how a consumer might guard against the type of injury present here, short of removing the hamburger from its bun, breaking it apart and inspecting its small components.

Wendy's argues that the evidence supported its contention that its hamburger complied with [federal and state] standards. Wendy's reasons that [state and federal regulators permit] some bone fragments in meat and that its hamburgers are therefore merchantable as a matter of law. The court of appeals rejected this argument, noting that compliance "with all state and federal regulations is only some evidence which the jury may consider in determining whether the product was merchantable." We agree.

We thus conclude, as did the court of appeals majority, that a jury could reasonably determine the meat to be of such a nature, i.e., hamburger, and the bone in the meat of such a size that a consumer of the meat should not reasonably have anticipated the bone's presence. The court of appeals therefore properly reversed the directed verdict for Wendy's on plaintiff's implied warranty of merchantability claim.

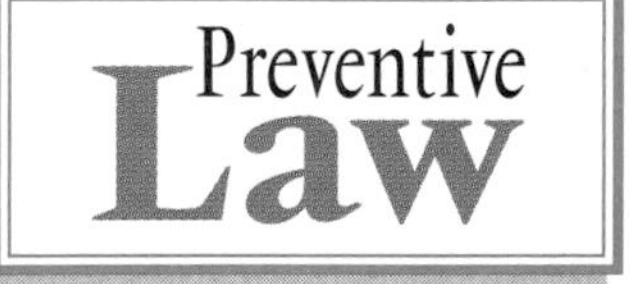

Notice some important implications of the *Goodman* ruling. The court says that a hamburger need not be perfect, but it must be fit for its ordinary purpose, that is, being eaten by someone who has not brought an X-ray machine with him to the restaurant. Whether this hamburger, or any other, *is* fit for its ordinary purpose will be a question for the jury. How will a jury tend to vote in a defective food case? To rephrase the question, did you wince just a bit reading about broken teeth? Will a jury? If that is so, how should a restaurant protect itself?

Wendy's had relied in part on the certification of the state and federal inspectors, but the court found that a consumer's expectations were more important. What other options does Wendy's have?

IMPLIED WARRANTY OF FITNESS FOR A PARTICULAR PURPOSE

The other warranty that the law imposes on sellers is the implied warranty of fitness for a particular purpose. This cumbersome name is often shortened to the *warranty of fitness*. **Where the seller at the time of contracting knows about a particular purpose for which the buyer wants the goods, and knows that the buyer is relying on the seller's skill or judgement, there is (unless excluded or modified) an implied warranty that the goods shall be fit for such purpose.**[8] Here are the key points:

- *Particular Purpose*. The seller must know about some special use that the buyer plans for the goods. For example, if a lumber salesman knows that a builder is purchasing lumber to construct houses in swampland, the Code implies a warranty that the lumber will withstand water. But notice that the seller must realize this at the time the bargain is struck. If the lumber company learns of the particular use when it delivers the goods, there is no implied warranty.
- *Seller's Skill*. The buyer must be depending upon the seller's skill or judgement in selecting the product, and the seller must know it. Suppose the builder says to the lumber salesman, "I need four-by-eights that I will be using to build a house in the swamp. What do you have that will do the job?" The builder's reliance is obvious and the warranty is established. By contrast, suppose that an experienced Alaskan sled-driver offers to buy your three huskies, telling you she plans to use them to pull sleds. She has the experience and you do not, and if the dogs refuse to pull more than a one-pound can of dog food, you have probably breached no implied warranty.
- *Exclusion or Modification*. Once again, the seller is allowed to modify or exclude any warranty of fitness, as we see below.

Warranties Compared

Express Warranty	Implied Warranty of Merchantability	Implied Warranty of Fitness for a Particular Purpose
The Rule: Seller can create an express warranty with any affirmation or promise, with any description of the goods, or with any sample or model, *provided the words or sample are part of the basis of the bargain*. *Example:* Manufacturer sends Retailer a brochure describing its brand of children's bicycle. The brochure states that "these bikes will last for a minimum of eight years of normal use." If the handlebars snap off after six months, Manufacturer has breached its express warranty.	*The Rule:* With certain exceptions, the Code *implies a warranty* that the goods will be fit for their ordinary purpose. *Example:* Manufacturer sells Retailer 300 "children's bicycles." There is no brochure and no promise made by Manufacturer about the bikes' quality. The UCC implies a warranty that the bikes will be fit for ordinary riding by children. But the cycles might not be strong enough to withstand mountain racing, and there is no warranty to that effect.	*The Rule:* With some exceptions, the Code *implies* a warranty that the goods are fit for the buyer's special purpose, provided that the seller knows of that purpose when the contract is made and knows of the buyer's reliance. *Example:* Retailer orders from Manufacturer "300 mountain bikes, for racing," and Manufacturer agrees. The UCC implies a warranty that the bikes will withstand the added stress of mountain racing.

[8] UCC §2-315.

Two Last Warranties: Title and Infringement

Strapped for cash, Maggie steals her boyfriend's rusty Chevy and sells it to Paul for $2,500. As we saw in Chapter 20, Maggie gets no valid title by her theft, and therefore Paul receives no title either. When the boyfriend finds his car parked at a nightclub, he notifies the police and gets his wheels back. Poor Paul is out of pocket $2,500 and has no car to show for it. That clearly is unjust, and the UCC provides Paul with a remedy: **the seller of goods warrants that her title is valid and that the goods are free of any security interest that the buyer knows nothing about, unless the seller has clearly excluded or modified this warranty.**[9] Once again, the Code is imposing a warranty on any seller except those who explicitly exclude or modify it. When Maggie sells the car to Paul, she warrants her valid title to the car and simultaneously breaches that warranty, since she obviously has no title. Paul will win a lawsuit against Maggie for $2,500.

Notice that the warranty concerning a security interest applies only if the buyer is ignorant of it. Suppose that Doug borrows money from the bank to buy a fishing boat, with the bank retaining a security interest in the boat.[10] Becky knows of the security interest, but nonetheless buys the boat from Doug. Doug has *not* breached any implied warranty, because Becky knew what she was getting into.

The same Code section imposes a warranty against claims of infringement by third parties. **Unless otherwise agreed, a seller who is a merchant warrants that the goods are free of any rightful claim of copyright, patent, or trademark infringement.**[11] Wesley sells to Komputer Corp. a device that automatically blasts purple smoke out of a computer screen anytime a student's paper is really dreadful. Unless Komputer Corp. agrees otherwise, Wesley is automatically giving the buyer a warranty that no one else invented the device or has any copyright, patent, or trademark in it.

Disclaimers and Defenses

There are several limitations on warranties. A seller may disclaim *warranties*, meaning that he eliminates express or implied warranties covering the goods. Or the seller may limit the buyer's *remedy*, which means that even if there is a breach of warranty, the buyer still may have only a very limited chance to recover against the seller.

Disclaimers

A disclaimer is a statement that a particular warranty *does not* apply. The Code permits the seller to disclaim most warranties.

Oral Express Warranties

Under the Code, a seller may disclaim an oral express warranty. Suppose Traffic Co. wants to buy a helicopter from HeliCorp for use in reporting commuter traffic. HeliCorp's salesman tells Traffic Co., "Don't worry, you can fly this bird day and night for six months with nothing more than a fuel stop." HeliCorp's contract

[9] UCC §2-312(1).

[10] A security interest is described in Chapter 20, on ownership and risk.

[11] UCC §2-313(3).

may disclaim the oral warranty. The contract could say, "HeliCorp's entire warranty is printed below. Any statements made by any agent or salesperson are disclaimed and form no part of this contract." That disclaimer is valid. If the helicopter requires routine servicing between flights, HeliCorp has not breached an oral warranty.

Written Express Warranties

This is the one type of warranty that is difficult or impossible to disclaim. If a seller includes an express warranty in the *sales contract*, any disclaimer is invalid. Suppose HeliCorp sells an industrial helicopter for use in hauling building equipment. The sales contract describes the aircraft as "operable to 14,000 feet." Later, in the contract, a limited warranty disclaims "any other warranties or statements that appear in this document or in any other document." That disclaimer is invalid. The Code will not permit a seller to take contradictory positions in one document. The goal is simply to be fair, and the Code assumes that it is confusing and unjust for the seller to say one thing to help close a deal and the opposite to limit its losses.[12]

What if the express written statement is in a different document, such as a sales brochure? The disclaimer is void if it would *unfairly surprise* the buyer. Assume, again, that HeliCorp promises a helicopter that requires no routine maintenance for six months, but this time the promise appears in a sales brochure that Traffic Co. reads and relies on. If HeliCorp attempts to disclaim the written warranty, it will probably fail. Most people take written information seriously. If Traffic signed its contract assuming it would get the kind of quality promised in the brochure, that promise is probably binding. HeliCorp's effort to disclaim a written express warranty would be valid only if the company *negotiated* the disclaimer with Traffic and expressed it so clearly that Traffic realized the brochure's promises were no longer part of the bargain.[13]

Implied Warranties

A seller may disclaim the implied warranty of merchantability provided he *actually mentions the word "merchantability"* and makes the disclaimer conspicuous. Courts demand to see the word "merchantability" in the disclaimer to be sure the buyer realized she was giving up this fundamental protection. If the word is there and the disclaimer is conspicuous enough that the buyer should have seen it, she has forfeited the warranty. A seller may disclaim the implied warranty of fitness with any language that is clear and conspicuous.

General Disclaimers

To make life easier, the Code permits a seller to disclaim all implied warranties by conspicuously stating that the goods are sold "as is" or "with all faults." Notice the tension between this provision and the discussion about disclaiming a war-

---

[12] UCC §2-316(1).

[13] Two cases illustrate differing court reactions to a disclaimer. In *Western Recreational Vehicles v. Swift Adhesives*, 23 F.3d 1547, 1994 U.S. App. LEXIS 10363 (9th Cir. 1994), the court stated that it does not favor disclaimers of warranty, and that a disclaimer is ineffective unless it was explicitly negotiated and sets forth with particularity the qualities not warranted. By contrast, in *Effanzee Assoc. v. Thermo Electron Corp.*, 1994 U.S. Dist. LEXIS 773 (E.D. Pa. 1994), the court considered promotional literature that assured the product would perform reliably for "thousands of hours," though the written warranty limited the guarantee to 500 hours. The court enforced the limited warranty, concluding that the parties intended the limited warranty to control because the terms were reasonable and conspicuous and presumably the result of bargaining.

ranty of merchantability. A seller who wants to disclaim *only* the warranty of merchantability must explicitly mention that term; but a seller wishing to exclude *all* implied warranties may do so with a short expression, such as "sold as is."

Consumer Sales

As we have seen many times in the Code, protection is often stronger for consumers than for businesses. *Many states prohibit a seller from disclaiming implied warranties in the sale of consumer goods.* In these states, if a home furnishings store sells a bunk bed to a consumer, and the top bunk tips out the window on the first night, the seller is liable. If the sales contract clearly stated "no warranties of merchantability or fitness," the court would reject the clause and find that the seller breached the implied warranty of merchantability.

Some courts dislike disclaimers. Other courts respect the right of a seller to disclaim but insist on strict compliance with disclaimer rules, such as mentioning the word "merchantability." An astute seller will take no chances. Disclaimers must be conspicuous, so the seller should print them in boldface with large capital letters that are, ideally, a different color from the rest of the contract.

REMEDY LIMITATIONS

Simon Aerials, Inc. manufactured boomlifts, the huge cranes used to construct multistoried buildings. Simon agreed to design and build eight unusually large machines for Logan Equipment Corp. Simon delivered the boomlifts late, and they functioned poorly. Logan requested dozens of repairs and modifications, which Simon attempted to accomplish over many months, but the equipment never worked well. Logan gave up and sued for $7.5 million, representing the profits it expected to make from renting the machines and the damage to its reputation. Logan clearly had suffered major losses, and it recovered—nothing. How could that be?

Simon had negotiated **a limitation of remedy** clause, by which **the parties may limit or exclude the normal remedies permitted under the Code.**[14] These important rights are entirely distinct from disclaimers. A disclaimer limits the seller's warranties and thus affects whether the seller has breached her contract. A remedy limitation, by contrast, states that if a party does breach its warranty, the injured party will not get all of the damages the Code normally allows.

In its contract, Simon had agreed to repair or replace any defective boomlifts, but that was all. The agreement said that if a boomlift was defective, and Logan lost business, profits, and reputation, Simon was not liable. The court upheld the remedy limitation. Since Simon had repeatedly attempted to repair and redesign the defective machines, it had done everything it promised to do. Logan got nothing.[15]

We compare disclaimers and remedy limitations in the table on the next page.

Consequential Damages

Simon's contract clause was a typical one. Sellers frequently use a remedy limitation to avoid liability for consequential damages, which can be vast. Recall that a party injured by breach of contract normally gets *compensatory* damages.[16] In the

---

[14] UCC §2-719. A few states prohibit remedy limitations, but most permit them.

[15] *Logan Equipment Corp. v. Simon Aerials, Inc.*, 736 F. Supp. 1188, 1990 U.S. Dist. LEXIS 5720 (D. Mass. 1990).

[16] Compensatory, consequential, and incidental damages are discussed in Chapter 18, on remedies.

sale of goods that means the difference between the value of the goods promised and those actually delivered. A seller can anticipate and probably tolerate such damages, since the seller understands exactly how much it costs to repair or replace the goods it has sold. **Consequential damages**, however, are different. They are losses stemming from the particular requirements of the buyer. The buyer might have entered into dozens of contracts in reliance on the goods it expects from the seller. The seller will have no way of knowing how great the consequential damages could be. Logan Equipment claimed that it would have earned profits in the millions, and it was just such a claim that Simon had determined to avoid.

Notice that there is one major limitation on these clauses: **an exclusion of consequential damages is void if it is unconscionable.** "Unconscionable" means that a remedy restriction is shockingly one-sided and fundamentally unfair.[17] If the buyer is a consumer, a court will be likelier to consider such an exclusion unfair, since the typical consumer will not understand the terms and may never even notice them. If the buyer is a consumer who suffers a *personal injury*, a court is nearly certain to reject the exclusion. It is unfair for a corporation to market defec-

Code Section	**Purpose**	**Setting**	**Contract Language**	**Result**
Disclaimers: UCC §2-316	Limits warranties, whether express or implied. This section will determine *whether there has been a breach.*	Seller sells Buyer a used "tire shredding machine." UCC §2-314 implies a warranty of merchantability, meaning that the machine will be good for its ordinary purpose, which is shredding tires in a commercial recycling business.	Seller includes in the contract a clause stating that the tire shredder is sold "as is." Under §2-316, this phrase excludes all implied warranties, meaning that the implied warranty of merchantability will NOT apply here.	One tire goes through the machine, the tire emerges completely intact, and the machine falls to pieces. *Result:* Seller has NOT breached the contract, and Buyer gets no damages.
Remedy limitations: UCC §2-719	Limits the remedies available *when one party has breached* the contract.	Seller sells Buyer 10,000 computer circuit boards at $200 each, which Buyer uses in its laptops.	Seller requires a clause limiting Buyer's remedies to "replace or repair." If the boards fail, Seller will replace or repair them for free. But Buyer is permitted NO OTHER REMEDY. Buyer may not seek consequential damages, which would include lost profits and injured reputation.	All of the boards malfunction, and Buyer's customers are angry *at Buyer*. Buyer must take the computers back, losing all of its expected profits and also suffering a serious loss of reputation in the high-tech world. Seller IS in breach of the contract and must repair or replace all circuit boards at its expense. But Seller owes NOTHING for Buyer's lost profits or injured reputation.

[17] UCC §2-719. We discuss unconscionability under the Code in Chapter 19.

tive goods and escape liability because an unsuspecting consumer failed to understand contract language. Suppose Byron buys a hot-air popper that comes with a label excluding consequential damages. Byron is seriously burned when the popper ignites. Virtually all courts will ignore the consequential damages exclusion and apply a warranty of merchantability to the popper, permitting Byron to recover his full damages. His compensatory damages are insignificant: the cost of a new popper. His consequential damages are enormous: medical expenses, pain and suffering, and lost income.

However, when the buyer is a corporation, courts assume it had adequate legal advice and an opportunity to reject unacceptable terms. When two companies agree to a remedy limitation, they are allocating the risk of loss as one part of their bargain. A court will seldom substitute its judgment for that of the contracting companies. In the *Logan Equipment* case, both parties were corporations, and sophisticated executives negotiated the boomlift sale. The court found nothing unconscionable in the bargain and enforced the limitation that the parties had agreed to.[18]

Rich and Enza Hill bought a computer from Gateway 2000, using a credit card to make the purchase over the phone. The Hills complained that their computer was defective and eventually filed suit. The court, however, dismissed their case. Why? The box that arrived at their doorstep contained not only their chosen hardware but a contract from Gateway. The contract stated that the buyer agreed to all of its terms unless she returned the computer within 30 days. One of the terms obligated the buyer to arbitrate any disputes, rather than litigate. The arbitration had to take place in Chicago and be conducted according to the rules of French-based International Chamber of Commerce (ICC). Among other things, the ICC rules require any complaining party (such as the Hills) to pay a large fee—as high as $5,000 in some cases. The rules also require the losing party to pay the *other* side's attorney's fees. The court declared:

> Practical considerations support allowing vendors to enclose the full legal terms with their products. Cashiers cannot be expected to read legal documents to customers before ringing up sales. If the staff at the other end of the phone for direct-sales operations such as Gateway's had to read the four-page statement of terms before taking the buyer's credit card number, the droning voice would anesthetize rather than enlighten many potential buyers.[19]

This controversial ruling is not the final word on the subject. Critics complained that the decision enables merchants to draft arbitration clauses so onerous that consumers will have no recourse for defective goods. Supporters respond that companies are entitled to protect themselves from frivolous lawsuits designed to extort, rather than compensate. The UCC authors have addressed issues of hardware and software liability in the new Article 2B, but it is too early to determine what rules the various states will adopt.

PRIVITY

When two parties contract, they are *in privity*. If Lance buys a chain saw from the local hardware store, he is in privity with the store. But Lance has no privity with Kwiksaw, the manufacturer of the chain saw. Under traditional contract law,

---

[18] *Logan Equipment*, 736 F. Supp. at 1195.

[19] *Hill v. Gateway 2000, Inc.*, 105 F.3d 1147, 1997 U.S. App. LEXIS 176 (7th Cir. 1997).

a plaintiff injured by a breach of contract could only sue a defendant with whom he had privity. So, a hundred years ago, if Lance's chain saw had been seriously defective, he could have sued only the store. Kwiksaw would have defended successfully, claiming "lack of privity". This hurt consumers because the local retailer might have lacked assets to compensate for serious injuries. Today, privity is gradually disappearing as a defense. The various states are approaching the issue in different ways, so there is no one rule. We can, however, highlight the trends.

Personal Injury

Where a product causes a personal injury, most states permit a warranty suit even without privity. If the chain on Lance's power saw flies off and slashes his arm, he has suffered a personal injury. Of course, he may sue the store, with which he has privity. But he wants to sue the manufacturer, which has more money. In the majority of states, he will be able to sue the manufacturer for breach of warranty even though he had no privity with it.[20] (Note that Lance is sure to make other claims against the manufacturer, including *negligence* and *strict liability*, both discussed below.)

Economic Loss

If the buyer suffers only economic loss, privity *may* still be required to bring a suit for breach of warranty. If the buyer is a business, the majority of states require privity. Fab-Rik makes fabric for furniture and drapes, which it sells to various wholesalers. Siddown makes sofas. Siddown buys Fab-Rik fabric from a wholesaler and, after installing it on 200 sofas, finds the material defective. Siddown may sue the wholesaler but, in most states, will be unable to sue Fab-Rik for breach of any warranties. There was no privity.

By contrast, when the buyer is a consumer, more states will permit a suit against the manufacturer, even without privity. Lance, the consumer, buys his power saw to landscape his property. This time the saw malfunctions without injuring him, but Lance must buy a replacement saw for considerably more money. Many states—but not all—will permit him to recover his losses from Kwiksaw, the manufacturer, on the theory that Kwiksaw intends its product to reach consumers and is in the best position to control losses.

---

[20] The Code offers three alternative versions of its rule concerning privity: UCC §2-318, Alternatives A, B, and C, with each state free to adopt whichever version the legislature prefers. Alternative A, the most restrictive, extends a warranty in the cases of personal injury to the buyer and members of his family and household. But the comments to this section indicate that this extension to household members does not *preclude* claims brought by non-household members. The drafters have left it up to the states to decide whether additional injured parties could sue. Several states that have adopted this version of the privity rule have permitted warranty claims by injured parties who were not household members. Dahlia buys a weed cutter manufactured by Thorn and sold by Hardware, and loans it to Rose, who is cut when it malfunctions. Many, but not all, states that have adopted Alternative A would allow Rose to sue Thorn.

Alternative B is more expansive, explicitly permitting a warranty suit by any injured natural person (non-corporation) who could reasonably be affected by the product. In states that have adopted this section, Rose would certainly be permitted to sue Thorn. Alternative C, the most expansive, permits recovery by natural persons and corporations and allows suits for *economic* loss as well as personal injury. What does all this mean? The privity requirement is disappearing in personal injury cases and diminishing in cases of economic loss.

Buyer's Misconduct

Lord & Taylor warranted that its false eyelashes would function well and cause no harm. But when Ms. Caldwell applied them, they severely irritated one eye. She sued but the store prevailed. Why? Caldwell applied the eyelashes improperly, getting the glue into one eye. On her other eye she used the product correctly and suffered no harm. Her misuse proved painful to her eye—and fatal to her lawsuit.[21]

Misuse by the buyer will generally preclude a warranty claim.[22] Common sense tells us that the seller only warrants its goods if they are properly used. For example, Joy and Bailey Gillespie bought a new car but immediately noticed that noxious fumes entered the passenger compartment. The car came with a warranty, but the Gillespies lost their suit for the simple reason that before going to court, they drove the car *62,000 miles*. Joy Gillespie's doctor told her the fumes were harming her health, but the couple did nothing for three years. This was a breach, not of warranty, but of common sense, and the Gillespies coughed their way into court and lost.[23]

Statute of Limitations and Notice of Breach

It is right that a seller be responsible for the goods it places in the market. On the other hand, a seller should not face potential liability *forever*. A company cannot be a perpetual insurer for goods that it sold decades earlier. And so the UCC imposes two important time limits on a buyer's claim of breach.

The Code prescribes a four-year statute of limitations.[24] This means that the buyer must bring any lawsuit for breach of a warranty no later than four years after the goods were delivered. When the parties contract, they may shorten that period to no less than one year, but they may not extend it. Suppose PlaneJane, an airline, buys 10 new aircraft from Flyem, a manufacturer, taking delivery on June 1, 2001. In the fall of 2003, PlaneJane begins to discover structural weaknesses in the wings, which Flyem repeatedly repairs over the next few months. PlaneJane must decide whether to file a lawsuit. If the airline believes all problems are corrected, fine. But if it has any doubts about the aircraft fitness, PlaneJane must sue promptly. On June 2, 2004, any lawsuit for breach of warranty is barred by the statute of limitations.

The Code puts an additional burden on a buyer asserting a breach of warranty. **The UCC requires that a buyer notify the seller of defects within a reasonable time.**[25] The purpose here is to enable the seller to cure, by repairing or replacing, any problems with the goods. Ideally, a seller that receives notice of a potential breach will fix the problem and there will *be* no lawsuit.

---

21 *Caldwell v. Lord & Taylor, Inc.*, 142 Ga. App. 137, 235 S.E.2d 546 (Ga. Ct. App. 1977).

22 Some courts characterize the misuse as "comparative negligence" or "contributory negligence" or "failure of proximate cause." These tort terms are discussed in Chapter 6, dealing with negligence and strict liability. For our purposes here, it is enough to understand that misuse generally precludes a warranty claim.

23 *Gillespie v. American Motors Corp.*, 69 N.C. App. 531, 317 S.E.2d 32, 1984 N.C. App. LEXIS 3470 (N.C. Ct. App. 1984).

24 UCC §2-725.

25 UCC §2-607.

What is a reasonable amount of time depends upon the circumstances. An inexperienced consumer could reasonably take many months to figure out that a new laptop computer had a serious operating defect. Further, a delay of six or eight months would not harm a large computer manufacturer. On the other hand, a corporate buyer of perishable food products must act very fast if it claims the goods are defective.

NEGLIGENCE

A buyer of goods may have remedies other than warranty claims. One is negligence, which we discuss in detail in Chapter 6. Here we focus on how this law applies to the sale of goods. Negligence, as you will recall, is notably different from contract law. In a contract case, the two parties have reached an agreement, and the terms of their bargain will usually determine how to settle any dispute. If the parties agreed that the seller disclaimed all warranties, then the buyer may be out of luck. But in a negligence case, there has been no bargaining between the parties, who may never have met. A consumer injured by an exploding cola bottle is unlikely to have bargained for her beverage with the CEO of the cola company. Instead, the law *imposes* a standard of conduct on everyone in society, corporation and individual alike. The two key elements of this standard, for present purposes, are *duty* and *breach*. A plaintiff injured by goods she bought must show that the defendant, usually a manufacturer or seller of a product, had a duty to her and breached that duty.[26] A defendant has a duty of due care to anyone who could foreseeably be injured by its misconduct. Generally, it is the duty to act as *a reasonable person* would in like circumstances; a defendant who acts unreasonably has breached its duty.

In negligence cases concerning the sale of goods, plaintiffs most often raise one or more of these claims:

- *Negligent Design*. The buyer claims that the product injured her because the manufacturer designed it poorly. Negligence law requires a manufacturer to design a product free of *unreasonable* risks. The product does not have to be absolutely safe. An automobile that guaranteed a driver's safety could be made but would be prohibitively expensive. Reasonable safety features must be built in, if they can be included at a tolerable cost.

- *Negligent Manufacture*. The buyer claims that the design was adequate but that failure to inspect or some other sloppy conduct caused a dangerous product to leave the plant.

- *Failure to Warn*. A manufacturer is liable for failing to warn the purchaser or users about the dangers of normal use and also foreseeable misuse. However, there is no duty to warn about obvious dangers, a point evidently lost on some manufacturers. A Batman costume came with this statement: "For play only: Mask and chest plate are not protective; cape does not enable user to fly."

In the following case, the plaintiffs raise issues of negligent design and failure to warn, concerning a disposable lighter. You decide.

---

[26] A plaintiff in a negligence case must also prove three other elements: factual causation, foreseeable type of harm, and injury. For a discussion of those elements, see Chapter 6. We focus in this chapter on duty and breach because those two elements take on special importance in product liability cases.

BOUMELHEM v. BIC CORP.
211 Mich. App. 175, 535 N.W.2d 574, 1995 Mich. App. LEXIS 228
Michigan Court of Appeals, 1995

Facts: Ibrahim Boumelhem, aged four, began playing with a Bic disposable lighter that his parents had bought. He started a fire that burned his legs and severely burned his six-month-old brother over 85 percent of his body. Ibrahim's father sued Bic, claiming that the lighter was negligently designed because it could have been child-proof. He also claimed failure to warn, because the lighter did not clearly warn of the danger to children.

The *Boumelhem* court considered evidence and analyses from several other cases against Bic. The court noted that consumers use over 500 million disposable lighters annually in the United States. Each lighter provides 1,000 to 2,000 lights. During one three-year period, children playing with disposable lighters started 8,100 fires annually, causing an average of 180 people to die every year, of whom 140 were children under five. Another 990 people were injured. The average annual cost of deaths, injuries, and property damage from child-play fires was estimated at $310 to $375 million, or 60 to 75 cents per lighter sold. Bic had acknowledged in earlier litigation that it was foreseeable lighters would get into children's hands and injure them. Bic had also agreed that it was feasible to make a more child-resistant lighter.

The trial court relied on a recently decided Michigan case. In *Adams v. Perry Furniture Co.*,[27] four minor children had died in a fire started when one of them was playing with a Bic lighter. The *Adams* court had found no negligent design and no failure to warn, and dismissed all claims. The trial court in the present case followed *Adams* and dismissed Boumelhem's claims. He appealed.

You Be the Judge: Did Bic negligently design its disposable lighter? Did Bic negligently fail to warn of the lighter's dangers?

Argument for Boumelhem: Your honors, the *Adams* court decided the issues wrongly. There is a reason that new plaintiffs are back in this court, the year after *Adams*, raising related issues against Bic: the company is killing hundreds of children every year. In its efforts to maximize corporate profits, it is literally burning these children to death and injuring hundreds more. That's wrong.

Bic has acknowledged that its disposable lighters can and will get into the hands of children. Bic knows full well that its product will injure or kill a certain percentage of these children—very young children. Bic has admitted that it could design a child-proof lighter, and it knows perfectly well how to include effective warnings on its lighters. But rather than improve product design and give effective warnings, Bic prefers to do business as usual and litigate liability for injured and murdered children.

We ask this court to rule that Bic breached its duty to design and manufacture a lighter that will keep our kids safe, and breached its duty to warn.

Argument for Bic: Your honors, the Bic Corp. is as horrified as anyone over the injuries to these children and the deaths of other kids. But Bic is not responsible. The children's parents are responsible. We sympathize with their grief but not with their attempt to pass parental responsibility onto the shoulders of a corporation. There are several reasons Bic is not liable in this case.

First, the *Adams* court decided the matter, and that precedent is binding. Precedent is important because it enables all members of society to understand their duties and liability. The issues here are identical to *Adams*, and the outcome should be also.

Second, Bic has no duty to design a different lighter. The test in design defect cases is whether the risks are unreasonable in light of the foreseeable injuries. Young children can hurt themselves in countless ways, from falls to poisonings to automobile injuries. There is one answer to these dangers, and it is called good parenting. The parents who bought this lighter purchased it because it could start a fire. The moment they purchased it, they assumed the obligation to keep it away from their children. These are useful products, which is why Bic sells hundreds of millions per year. Other consumers should not be forced to pay an outrageously high price for a simple tool, just because some parents fail to do their job.

The failure to warn argument is even weaker. The law imposes no failure to warn when the danger is obvious. Every adult knows that lighters are *potentially* dangerous, if misused, or if passed on to children. Does the court really think anyone would be helped by a warning that said, "This lighter starts fires. Don't give it to children."

Your honors, a tragic accident that the parents could have prevented should not move this court to rewrite basic negligence law. Bic did all it reasonably should have and is not liable.

---

[27] 198 Mich. App. 1, 497 N.W.2d 514, 1993 Mich. App. LEXIS 33 (Mich. Ct. App. 1993).

STRICT LIABILITY

The other tort claim that an injured person can bring against the manufacturer or seller of a product is strict liability. Like negligence, strict liability is a burden created by the law rather than by the parties. And, as with all torts, strict liability concerns claims of physical harm. But there is a key distinction between negligence and strict liability: in a negligence case, the injured buyer must demonstrate that the seller's conduct was unreasonable. Not so in strict liability.

In strict liability, the injured person need not prove that the defendant's conduct was unreasonable. The injured person must show only that the defendant manufactured or sold a product that was defective and that the defect caused harm. Almost all states permit such lawsuits, and most of them have adopted the summary of strict liability provided by the Restatement (Second) of Torts **§402A.** (The American Law Institute has voted to revise strict liability law,[28] but its proposed changes have not yet been adopted in any states, so we focus on existing law.) Because §402A is the most frequently cited section in all of tort law, we quote it in full:

> **(1)** One who sells any product in a defective condition unreasonably dangerous to the user or consumer or to his property is subject to liability for physical harm thereby caused to the ultimate user or consumer, or to his property, if
> **(a)** the seller is engaged in the business of selling such a product, and
> **(b)** it is expected to and does reach the user or consumer without substantial change in the condition in which it is sold.
>
> **(2)** The rule stated in Subsection (1) applies although
> **(a)** the seller has exercised all possible care in the preparation and sale of his product, and
> **(b)** the user or consumer has not bought the product from or entered into any contractual relation with the seller.

These are the key terms in subsection (1):

- *Defective condition unreasonably dangerous to the user*. The defendant is liable only if the product is defective when it leaves his hands. There must be something wrong with the goods. If they are reasonably safe and the buyer's mishandling of the goods causes the harm, there is no strict liability. If you attempt to open a soda bottle by knocking the cap against a counter, and the glass shatters and cuts you, the manufacturer owes nothing.

  The article sold must be *more dangerous* than the ordinary consumer would expect. A carving knife can produce a lethal wound, but everyone knows that, and a sharp knife is not unreasonably dangerous. On the other hand, prescription drugs may harm in ways that neither a lay person nor a doctor would anticipate. The manufacturer *must provide adequate warnings* of any dangers that are not apparent.

- *In the business of selling*. The seller is liable only if she normally sells this kind of product. Suppose your roommate makes you a peanut butter sandwich and, while eating it, you cut your mouth on a sliver of glass that was in the jar. The

---

28 The American Law Institute has voted to replace §402A with the Restatement (Third) of Torts: Product Liability. By way of preview, we note that the Restatement (Third) makes some controversial proposals. Section 2 of the new draft creates different tests for manufacturing, design, and warning defects. *Strict liability applies only to manufacturing defects*, and that is a big change. As to defective design cases, §2 (b) requires a plaintiff to prove that a safer design existed and that the defendant's failure to use it made the product dangerous. This is a significantly tougher standard for an injured party to meet. It is too early to know whether these changes will prove popular with state legislatures.

peanut butter manufacturer faces strict liability as does the grocery store where your roommate bought the goods. But your roommate is not strictly liable because he does not serve sandwiches as a business.

- *Reaches the user without substantial change.* Obviously, if your roommate put the glass in the peanut butter thinking it was funny, neither the manufacturer nor the store is liable.

And here are the important phrases in subsection (2).

- *Has exercised all possible care.* This is the heart of strict liability, which makes it a potent claim for consumers. *It is no defense that the seller used reasonable care.* If the product is dangerously defective and injures the user, the seller is liable even if it took every precaution to design and manufacture the product safely. Suppose the peanut butter jar did in fact contain a glass sliver when it left the factory. The manufacturer proves that it uses extraordinary care in keeping foreign particles out of the jars and thoroughly inspects each container before it is shipped. The evidence is irrelevant. The manufacturer has shown that it was not *negligent* in packaging the food, but reasonable care is irrelevant in strict liability.

- *No contractual relation.* Remember "privity,"from the warranty discussion? Privity only exists between the user and the person from whom she actually bought the goods. This sentence in §402A means that *privity is not required.* Suppose the manufacturer that made the peanut butter sold it to a distributor, which sold it to a wholesaler, which sold it to a grocery store, which sold it to your roommate. You may sue the manufacturer, distributor, wholesaler, and store, even though you had no privity with any of them.

Plaintiffs injured in a car accident sometimes allege that a manufacturing or design defect caused their injury. In rare cases, verdicts include punitive damages. In a few cases, where evidence indicated that an automaker refused to fix known defects because of the cost, juries have awarded over $100 million to a single victim. Consumers interested in researching the safety of individual automobiles will find crash test reports on the Web page of the Insurance Institute for Highway Safety: **http://www.insure.com/auto/models/crashmv.html**.

The following case finds §402A poised at the cutting edge of another major tort issue.

AMERICAN TOBACCO CO., INC. v. GRINNELL
951 S.W.2d 420, 1997 Tex. LEXIS 56
Texas Supreme Court, 1997

Facts: In 1952, 19-year-old Wiley Grinnell began smoking Lucky Strikes cigarettes, which the American Tobacco Co. manufactured. He smoked until 1985, when his doctors told him he had lung cancer. Soon afterward, he filed suit against American Tobacco, alleging strict liability and other claims. Tragically, he died within a year, but his family continued the litigation. The trial court dismissed the case but the appeals court reversed. American Tobacco appealed.

Issue: **Have the Grinnells made valid strict liability claims?**

Excerpts from Judge Cornyn's Decision: A product may be unreasonably dangerous because of a defect in marketing, design, or manufacturing. The Grinnells allege that the cigarettes sold by American were unreasonably dangerous due to each of the three types of defect.

Two decades ago, was it "common knowledge in the community" that tobacco was addictive? For that matter, is it common knowledge *now*?

Marketing Defect: A defendant's failure to warn of a product's potential dangers when warnings are required is a type of marketing defect. [However, under §402A, if the "ordinary consumer with knowledge common to the community" is aware of the danger, there is generally no duty to warn.] Regarding the general health risks associated with smoking, the Tennessee Supreme Court held as early as 1898 that these risks were "generally known." On certiorari, the United States Supreme Court observed:

> We should be shutting our eyes to what is constantly passing before them were we to affect an ignorance of the fact that a belief in [cigarettes'] deleterious effects, particularly upon young people, has become very general, and that communications are constantly finding their way into the public press denouncing their use as fraught with great danger. . . .

We conclude that the general health dangers attributable to cigarettes were commonly known as a matter of law by the community when Grinnell began smoking. We cannot conclude, however, that the specific danger of nicotine addiction was common knowledge when Grinnell began smoking. Addiction is a danger apart from the direct physical dangers of smoking because the addictive nature of cigarettes multiplies the likelihood of and contributes to the smoker's ultimate injury, in Grinnell's case, lung cancer. This Court has also recognized the seriousness of addiction and the need for manufacturers to warn of this danger in the context of prescription drugs.

The Surgeon General spoke to the addictive nature of tobacco in [a 1988 report]. In that report, the Surgeon General concluded that: (1) cigarettes and other forms of tobacco are addicting, (2) nicotine is the drug in tobacco that causes addiction, and (3) the pharmacologic and behavioral processes that determine tobacco addiction are similar to those that determine addiction to drugs such as heroin and cocaine.

Because we conclude that American did not conclusively establish that the danger of addiction to nicotine was common knowledge, the Grinnells may maintain their strict liability marketing defect claims to the extent they are based on the addictive qualities of cigarettes, if no other defenses defeat those claims.

Design Defect: The duty to design a safe product is an obligation imposed by law. [In an earlier case, the court held that in evaluating design defects, a jury should consider: the utility of the product to the user and the general public; the availability of a safer design; the ability of the manufacturer to eliminate the unsafe characteristics of the design; and the knowledge and expectations of the ordinary users.]

Ultimately, the Grinnells essentially concede that no reasonably safer alternatives exist, but argue that all cigarettes are defective and unreasonably dangerous nonetheless. Because American conclusively proved that no reasonably safer alternative design exists for its cigarettes, we hold that summary judgment was proper on all of the Grinnells' design defect claims, including those based on the addictive quality of cigarettes.

Manufacturing Defect: [The Grinnells offered evidence that the cigarettes contained pesticide residue.] Under Texas law, a plaintiff has a manufacturing defect claim when a finished product deviates, in terms of its construction or quality, from the specifications or planned output in a manner that renders it unreasonably dangerous. American, conceding that its cigarettes contain pesticide residue, argues that summary judgment was proper because all cigarette manufacturers fumigate their tobacco with some type of pesticide, and residue inevitably remains after fumigation. Simply because certain precautions or improvements in manufacturing technology, which could eliminate pesticide residue from cigarettes, are universally disregarded by an entire industry does not excuse their omission. Although pesticide residue may be found in many if not all cigarettes, it is not an ingredient American intended to incorporate into its cigarettes. Analyzed in this light, the presence of pesticide residue could be a manufacturing defect, not a design defect. Therefore, American did not conclusively negate the existence of a defect in its cigarettes.

[The court permitted the Grinnells' case to go forward on the failure to warn and defective manufacturing claims, as they related to nicotine addiction. The court granted summary judgment for American Tobacco as to almost all of the Grinnells' other claims, including negligence, breach of warranty, fraud, and misrepresentation.]

Tobacco use is more common in almost all other countries than it is in the United States. Tobacco *litigation*, however, is less common—or was. Plaintiffs in other nations are beginning to follow the American lead. In Canada, plaintiffs have brought individual and class action claims similar to those made by the Grinnells. French antismoking groups have won lawsuits claiming that the tobacco companies made insufficient warnings on cigarette packs. In Brazil, the family of a deceased smoker won damages for his death. Japanese plaintiffs are attempting to block the import of American tobacco products. Meanwhile, in the United States, more than half of the state governments have filed class action suits seeking to recoup the health care costs created by tobacco-related illnesses. The first four states to settle their cases were Florida, Minnesota, Mississippi, and Texas, which agreed to accept a total of $36 *billion* from the tobacco companies to end the litigation. During discovery in these cases, the states uncovered thousands of tobacco company documents demonstrating the industry's awareness of nicotine's addictive power. These papers now circulate among overseas plaintiffs, enhancing their ability to seek compensation.

TIME LIMITS: TORT VERSUS CONTRACT

Statutes of Limitations in Tort

We have seen that for *warranty* cases, the UCC imposes a four-year statute of limitation. By contrast, most states have a different statute of limitations for tort claims. Many states set a three-year limit, though some are shorter and others longer. But the key element is this: in a tort case, the statute of limitations runs *from the time the defect was discovered*. Even though the three-year period is shorter, the time for filing a suit may be much longer because a defect may not appear for many years.

Many product liability cases involve both warranty and tort claims. Should a court apply the statute of limitations from the Code or from tort law? The analysis begins with the **economic loss doctrine: when an injury is purely economic, and arises from a contract made by two businesses, the injured party may only sue under the UCC.** This rule is primarily for contracts between two businesses; if the buyer is a consumer, most courts will not apply it. The economic loss doctrine has two important consequences for corporate buyers.

First, **the four-year statute of limitations will apply in all cases of economic loss.** Suppose a corporation discovers that a product it purchased five years ago is defective and has caused major losses. The company probably has *no* remedy. Neibarger purchased an automated milking system for his dairy from Universal Cooperatives. Over the next few years, many of his cows became sick with mastitis; some died, and others had to be sold for beef. Seven years after he bought the equipment, Neibarger learned that Universal had improperly designed and installed the vaccum system that is an essential part of the machine. He sued, claiming massive damage to his farming operation, but the Michigan Supreme Court applied the economic loss doctrine. Neibarger's loss was commercial, resulting from a contract that two corporations had negotiated. His only possible remedy was under the UCC, but the Code's statute of limitations had expired. In the end he had no remedy.[29]

Second, **where the sales contract includes proper disclaimers or remedy limitations, a buyer barred from a negligence case may have no remedy at all.** The economic loss doctrine prohibits a corporation from suing in negligence when its loss is purely commercial. That leaves a lawsuit under the UCC. But if the seller has disclaimed all warranties and/or prohibited certain remedies (such as consequential damages), the buyer may be left with no basis for a lawsuit.

A Final Issue: Statutes of Repose

In tort cases, the passage of time provides a seller with two possible defenses. We have seen that the statute of limitations requires that a lawsuit be brought within a specified period, such as three years, beginning when the defect is discovered or should have been discovered. **A statute of repose places an absolute limit on when a lawsuit may be filed, regardless of when the defect is discovered.** Jeffrey Oats was riding in the back seat of a Nissan 280Z sports car when it was involved in an accident. Tragically, Oats suffered spinal cord injuries that left him a quadriplegic. Oats sued Nissan, based on defective design, claiming that the rear seat lacked adequate head and leg room and that the car's body panels lacked sufficient strength. He argued that these defects only became apparent in an accident. But the Idaho Supreme Court dismissed his claims because the car was 11 years old at the time of the accident. The Idaho statute of repose prohibits most product liability suits filed more than 10 years after the goods were sold, regardless of when the defects were discoverable.[30]

OTHER LEGISLATION

Congress and state legislatures frequently pass statutes affecting product liability. A summary of all the legislation would create an overwhelming and uninformative list, so we mention only a few statutes to indicate that sellers must consider other laws when designing and marketing goods, and that buyers who believe they have been injured may have remedies beyond those discussed in the chapter.

LEMON LAWS

It is intensely frustrating—and expensive—for consumers when a new car is defective and spends more time in the repair shop than on the road. So, many states have passed lemon laws, which entitle the buyer to receive a refund if the car has defects that substantially impair its value and safety. This right may prove more valuable than a limited warranty, which might only entitle the buyer to repeated attempts at servicing. To test-drive one state's lemon law, stop in anytime at **http://www.boylanbrown.com/**. Click on "Legal Talk," then "Featured Articles," and then "New York State Lemon Law." The public has clamored for more laws to protect it against unscrupulous sellers. Some states have added lemon laws for used cars. California, among others, has responded with a *puppy* lemon law, enabling buyers to obtain refunds for cats and dogs that were sick when purchased. You may view the law—but please do not feed it—at **http://www.dogplay.com/lemonlaw.html**.

---

[29] *Neibarger v. Universal Cooperatives, Inc.*, 439 Mich. 512, 486 N.W.2d 612, 1992 Mich. LEXIS 1502 (1992).

[30] *Oats v. Nissan Motor Corp.*, 126 Idaho 162, 879 P.2d 1095, 1994 Ida. LEXIS 116 (1994).

CONSUMER PROTECTION LAWS

Virtually all states also have consumer protection laws, which focus on a merchant's bad faith or deceit. Consumers can use these statutes, which are discussed in Chapter 42, to recover for defective goods or inadequate service.

MAGNUSON-MOSS WARRANTY ACT

This statute protects consumers who purchase household goods by ensuring basic fairness in the seller's warranty. The statute does not *require* any warranties at all, but covers cases in which a seller chooses to give one. Most sellers of consumer goods do provide some form of express warranty to attract buyers. Magnuson-Moss requires the seller to indicate whether a warranty is full or limited, and to describe clearly what is and is not warranted. The Act also sets certain minimum standards for an express warranty, requiring, for example, that at the very least a seller agree to repair or replace a defective item. Finally, the Act generally forbids a seller who has chosen to give an express warranty to disclaim implied warranties such as the Code's warranties of merchantability and fitness. For a detailed look at Magnuson-Moss, visit http://www.ftc.gov/bcp/conline/pubs/buspubs/warranty/undermag.htm.

Suppose Flybynite Corp. wants to unload 10,000 snowmobiles that it knows do not work in the snow. To attract customers, it prominently features "EXPRESS WARRANTY" in its ads. But the warranty only promises that "the snowmobile is guaranteed to start within 10 seconds, every time, for 60 days." The warranty then goes on to say, "Seller disclaims all other warranties, express or implied, whether of merchantability, fitness, or any other kind." Buyers discover that their snowmobiles start up quickly but cannot be operated in the snow because the treads are defective. Under Magnuson-Moss, Flybynite cannot disclaim the warranties of merchantability and fitness. Since the snowmobiles are not merchantable, any consumer will get his money back. The company has also violated the consumer protection laws of most states, and an angry buyer might even get treble damages and attorney's fees.

CHAPTER CONCLUSION

Both sellers and buyers of goods must understand the basic principles of product liability law. A seller must understand warranty, negligence, and strict liability law and consider all of those principles when designing, manufacturing, and marketing goods. A buyer, on the other hand, should be aware that each theory provides a possible basis for compensation and that consumers receive particularly strong protection.

CHAPTER REVIEW

Products can injure. The harm may be economic or physical. The plaintiff might have a remedy in *warranty*, which is found in the UCC, or one in *tort*, either for negligence or strict liability. The economic loss doctrine states that, when the injured party is a corporation and the harm is purely economic, the only remedies available are the warranty provisions of the Code. If a corporation suffers physical injury, it will probably be able to sue in tort. A consumer who suffers a physical injury can definitely sue in both tort and warranty, and a consumer who suffers an economic injury can generally, but not always, sue in both.

The Code prescribes a four-year statute of limitations for breaches of warranty. In tort cases, the statute of limitations runs from whenever the plaintiff should have discovered the defect. For ease of review, the following chart summarizes the different warranty and tort remedies.

	Contract or Tort	Source of Law	Summary of the Rule	Example	Potential Issue
Express Warranty	Contract	UCC §2-313	May be created by an affirmation of fact, a promise, a description of goods, or a sample, but it must have been the basis of the bargain.	Salesman says, "This helicopter will operate perfectly at 16,000 feet."	Written contract may disclaim any and all *oral* warranties.
Implied Warranty of Merchantability	Contract	UCC §2-314	The Code implies that the goods are fit for their ordinary use.	Buyer purchases a deep freezer. The Code implies a warranty that it will keep food frozen.	Seller may disclaim this warranty only if a conspicuous disclaimer includes the word "merchantability."
Implied Warranty of Fitness	Contract	UCC §2-315	The Code implies that the goods are fit for buyer's special purpose that seller knows about.	Where seller knows (1) buyer wants pine trees to plant in sandy soil, and (2) buyer is relying on seller's judgment, the trees carry an implied warranty that they will grow in that soil.	Seller may disclaim this warranty with conspicuous writing, but note that some states will disregard a disclaimer of *any* implied warranty in a consumer sale.
Implied Warranty of Title	Contract	UCC §2-312	The Code implies that seller has good title, free of any security interests and claims of patent, copyright, or trademark.	Seller sells a stolen car to buyer, who must later return it to the rightful owner. Seller has breached his warranty of good title and owes buyer her full damages.	Buyer is not protected against any security interests that she knows about.
Negligence	Tort	Common law	Seller is liable if she fails to show level of conduct that a *reasonable person* would use.	Manufacturer sells bathing suit made of miracle fabric; buyer swims in ocean where saltwater makes garment transparent; seller's failure to test the suit in saltwater was unreasonable and leaves seller liable. If seller had thoroughly tested and this was a freak occurrence, there would probably be no negligence.	No duty to warn if the danger is obvious. (In the bathing suit example, the danger is *not* obvious and there was a duty to warn.)

	Contract or Tort	Source of Law	Summary of the Rule	Example	Potential Issue
Strict Liability	Tort	Restatement §402A (subject to new revisions) and common law	Seller liable if the product leaves in a dangerously defective condition.	Can of barbecue lighter fluid explodes in user's hand because the can's metal was defective; manufacturer took every reasonable precaution to test and inspect every can leaving factory; that reasonable care is *irrelevant* and seller is liable.	Injured buyer need not prove negligence but must prove that the product was defective.

PRACTICE TEST

1. **CPA QUESTION** Vick bought a used boat from Ocean Marina that disclaimed "any and all warranties." Ocean was unaware the boat had been stolen from Kidd. Vick surrendered it to Kidd when confronted with proof of the theft. Vick sued Ocean. Who prevails?

(a) Vick, because the implied warranty of title has been breached

(b) Vick, because a merchant cannot disclaim implied warranties

(c) Ocean, because of the disclaimer of warranties

(d) Ocean, because Vick surrendered the boat to Kidd

2. **CPA QUESTION** To establish a cause of action based on strict liability in tort for personal injuries resulting from using a defective product, one of the elements the plaintiff must prove is that the seller (defendant):

(a) Failed to exercise due care

(b) Was in privity of contract with the plaintiff

(c) Defectively designed the product

(d) Was engaged in the business of selling the product

3. Leighton Industries needed steel pipe to build furnaces for a customer. Leighton sent Callier Steel an order for a certain quantity of "A 106 Grade B"steel. Callier confirmed the order and created a contract by sending an invoice to Leighton, stating that it would send "A 106 Grade B"steel, as ordered. Callier delivered the steel and Leighton built the furnaces, but they leaked badly and required rebuilding. Tests demonstrated that the steel was not, in fact, "A 106 Grade B,"but an inferior steel. Leighton sued. Who wins?

4. **YOU BE THE JUDGE WRITING PROBLEM** United Technologies advertised a used Beechcraft Baron airplane for sale in an aviation journal. Attorney Thompson Comerford was interested and spoke with a United agent who described the plane as "excellently maintained"and said it had been operated "under §135 flight regulations," meaning the plane had been subject to airworthiness inspections every 100 hours. Comerford arrived at a Dallas airport to pick up the plane, where he paid $80,000 for it. He signed a sales agreement stating that the plane was sold "as is" and that there were "no representations or warranties, express or implied, including the condition of the aircraft, its merchantability or its fitness for any particular purpose." Comerford attempted to fly the plane home, but immediately experienced problems with its brakes, steering, ability to climb, and performance while cruising. (Otherwise it was fine.) He sued, claiming breach of express and implied warranties. Did United Technologies breach express or implied warranties? **Argument for Comerford:** United described the airplane as "excellently maintained," knowing that

Mr. Comerford would rely. United bragged about §135 servicing, when that was obviously a lie. The company should not be allowed to say one thing and put the opposite in writing. **Argument for United Technologies:** Comerford is a lawyer, and we assume he can read. The contract could not have been clearer. The plane was sold as is. There were no warranties. If Comerford disliked the terms, he should have bargained for a different contract—or walked away. He knew he was buying a risky plane, and it is his to keep.

5. Round Tire Co. sells 1,000 tires to Green Rent-a-Car for use on Green's fleet. The same day it sells one new tire to Betty Blue for use on her car. For both sales, Round uses a sales agreement that includes: "LIMITATION OF REMEDIES. Round agrees to repair or replace any tire which Round determines was defective, within 12 months or 25,000, whichever comes first. Buyer agrees that this is Buyer's SOLE REMEDY; Buyer is not entitled to consequential or incidental damages or any other remedy of any kind." All of Round's tires prove defective. Green is so disgusted it immediately purchases substitute tires from another manufacturer. Green loses $12,000 in extra tire costs and $75,000 in lost rental payments because many of its cars must be off the road waiting for tires. Betty Blue's new tire blows out as she is driving to church, and Betty suffers broken bones. Green and Blue both sue. Predict the outcomes.

6. RIGHT & WRONG Texaco, Inc. and other oil companies sold mineral spirits in bulk to distributors, which then resold to retailers. Mineral spirits are used for cleaning. Texaco allegedly knew that the retailers, such as hardware stores, frequently packaged the mineral spirits (illegally) in used half-gallon milk containers and sold them to consumers, often with no warnings on the packages. Mineral spirits are harmful or fatal if swallowed. David Hunnings, aged 21 months, found a milk container in his home, swallowed the mineral spirits, and died. The Hunnings sued Texaco in negligence. The trial court dismissed the complaint and the Hunnings appealed. What is the legal standard in a negligence case? Have the plaintiffs made out a valid case of negligence? Remember that at this stage a court is not deciding who wins, but what standard a plaintiff must meet in order to take its case to a jury. Assume that Texaco knew about the repackaging and the grave risk, but continued to sell in bulk because doing so was profitable. (If the plaintiffs cannot prove those facts, they will lose even if they *do* get to a jury.) Would that make you angry? Does that mean such a case should go to a jury? Or would you conclude that the fault still lies with the retailer and/or the parents? In that case, the court should dismiss the suit against Texaco.

7. Boboli Co. wanted to promote its "California style" pizza, which it sold in supermarkets. The company contracted with Highland Group, Inc. to produce two million recipe brochures, which would be inserted in the carton when the freshly baked pizza was still very hot. Highland contracted with Comark Merchandising to print the brochures. But when Comark asked for details concerning the pizza, the carton, and so forth, Highland refused to supply the information. Comark printed the first lot of 72,000 brochures, which Highland delivered to Boboli. Unfortunately, the hot bread caused the ink to run, and customers opening the carton often found red or blue splotches on their pizzas. Highland refused to accept additional brochures, and Comark sued for breach of contract. Highland defended by claiming that Comark had breached its warranty of merchantability. Please comment.

8. CPA QUESTION Which of the following conditions must be met for an implied warranty of fitness for a particular purpose to arise? I. The warranty must be in writing. II. The seller must know that the buyer was relying on the seller in selecting the goods.

(a) I only

(b) II only

(c) Both I and II

(d) Neither I nor II

9. CPA QUESTION Under the UCC sales article, an action for breach of the implied warranty of merchantability by a party who sustains personal injuries may be successful against the seller of the product only when:

(a) The seller is a merchant of the product involved

(b) An action based on negligence can also be successfully maintained

(c) The injured party is in privity of contract with the seller

(d) An action based on strict liability in tort can also be successfully maintained

10. **CPA QUESTION** Which of the following factors is least important in determining whether a manufacturer is strictly liable in tort for a defective product?

(a) The negligence of the manufacturer
(b) The contributory negligence of the plaintiff
(c) Modifications to the product by the wholesaler
(d) Whether the product caused injuries

INTERNET RESEARCH PROBLEM

Look at **http://www.insure.com/auto/models/index.html**. Which cars are safer than average? Less safe? How important is auto safety to you? Are you willing to pay more for a safe car? Who should be the final judge of auto safety: auto companies, insurance companies, juries, government regulators, or consumers?

You can find further practice problems in the Online Quiz at http://beatty.westbuslaw.com or in the Study Guide that accompanies this text.

CHAPTER 22

PERFORMANCE AND REMEDIES

Patrick runs his own business, making hand-printed silk neckties, each depicting a famous work of art. Sales are booming and he has hired Hannah as a helper. Alden, who runs a chain of upmarket clothing stores, contracts to buy 1,000 of Patrick's ties for $30 each, to be delivered by September 1. In mid-July, Hannah leaves—to open her own business. Patrick manages to finish the ties and delivers them August 15. But Alden claims that the colors are not as subtle as the samples he had seen. Patrick admits that Alden might be right, and promises to deliver 1,000 *new* ties on time. Alden snaps, "Thanks, pal, not interested. I need a supplier I can depend on. I'll get my merchandise elsewhere." In September, Alden's shops are filled with ties made by *Hannah*, which Alden bought at $24 per item. Is that just? No.

Alden has violated at least one and possibly two provisions of the Uniform Commercial Code (UCC). The Code requires that Patrick have a chance to *cure*, meaning to deliver a new shipment of satisfactory goods. It also looks as though Alden acted in bad faith, weaseling out of his contract with Patrick so that he could purchase cheaper goods. These are typical issues of *contract performance* under the Code, which we look at in this chapter along with principles of *remedy*. By all means, let us begin in good faith.

GOOD FAITH

The R. G. Ray Corp. needed T-bolts to use in certain automobile parts it was manufacturing for the Garrett Co. Ray contracted for Maynard Manufacturing to deliver 57,000 T-bolts and provided Maynard with detailed specifications. The contract stated that Ray would be the "final judge" of whether the T-bolts conformed to its specifications and that Ray had the right to return any or all nonconforming bolts. **Conforming goods satisfy the contract terms. Non-conforming goods do not.**[1] Unfortunately, Ray rejected the 57,000 bolts and sued, demanding every penny it had paid as well as additional damages for its lost business with Garrett. Ray moved for summary judgment, pointing out that the contract explicitly allowed it to judge the bolts, to reject any it found unsatisfactory, and to cancel the contract. The court acknowledged that the contract did give Ray these one-sided powers, yet it denied summary judgment. There was still an issue of *good faith*.

The Code requires *good faith* in the performance and enforcement of every contract. Good faith means honesty in fact. Between merchants, it also means the use of reasonable commercial standards of fair dealing.[2] So Ray's right to reject the T-bolts was not absolute. There was some evidence that Ray had lost its contract with Garrett for reasons having nothing to do with Maynard's T-bolts. If that was true, and Ray had rejected the T-bolts simply because it no longer needed them, then Ray acted in bad faith and would be fully liable on the contract. The court ruled that Maynard should have its day in court to prove bad faith.[3]

With this good faith requirement in mind, we look first at the seller's obligations, and then at those of the buyer.

SELLER'S OBLIGATIONS (AND A FEW RIGHTS)

The seller's primary obligation is to deliver conforming goods to the buyer.[4] But because a buyer might not be willing or able to accept delivery, the UCC demands only that the seller make a reasonable *attempt* at delivery. **The seller must *tender* the goods, which means to make conforming goods available to the buyer.**[5] Normally, the contract will state where and when the seller is obligated to tender delivery. For example, the parties may agree that Manufacturer is to tender 1,000 computer printers at a certain warehouse on July 3. If Manufacturer makes the

---

1 UCC §2-106(2).

2 UCC §§1-203, 2-103(1)(b).

3 *R. G. Ray Corp. v. Maynard Manufacturing Co.*, 1993 U.S. Dist. LEXIS 15754 (N.D. Ill. 1993).

4 UCC §2-301.

5 UCC §2-503.

printers available on that date, Buyer is obligated to pick them up then and there, and is in breach if it fails to do so.

Although a seller must always tender delivery, that does not mean a seller always transports the goods. Sometimes the contract will require the buyer to collect the goods. Regardless of where delivery is being made, however, the seller must (1) make the goods available at a reasonable time, (2) keep the goods available for a reasonable period, and (3) deliver to the buyer any documents that it needs to take possession. And as we have said, the seller is expected to deliver *conforming* goods, which brings us to the next rule.

PERFECT TENDER RULE

Under the perfect tender rule, the buyer may reject the goods if they fail *in any respect* to conform to the contract.[6] Under the common law, before the Code was drafted, the perfect tender rule required that the seller deliver goods that conformed absolutely to the contract specifications. The buyer had the right to reject goods with even minor deviations. Although commentators had criticized the rule for decades and courts had carved many exceptions into the rule, the drafters of the UCC retained it.

Stanley and Joan Jakowski agreed to buy a new Camaro automobile from Carole Chevrolet. The contract stated that Carole would apply a polymer undercoating. The Jakowskis paid in full for the car but the next day informed Carole that the car lacked the undercoating. Carole acknowledged the defect and promised to apply the undercoating, but before it could do so, a thief stole the car. The Jakowskis demanded their money back, but Carole refused, saying that the risk of loss had passed to the Jakowskis when Carole tendered delivery. The Jakowskis sued, claiming that they had rejected the Camaro as non-conforming. Carole responded that this was absurd: the car was perfect in every respect except for the very minor undercoating, which Carole had promised to fix promptly. Carole Chevrolet was correct in its description of the car, but lost the case because of the perfect tender rule.

The New Jersey court found that the defect was minor, but said that, "despite seller's assertion to the contrary, the degree of their nonconformity is irrelevant in assessing the buyer's concomitant right to reject them. . . . [N]o particular quantum of nonconformity is required." The Jakowskis had lawfully rejected nonconforming goods, and Carole Chevrolet was forced to pay them the full value of the missing car.[7]

RESTRICTIONS ON THE PERFECT TENDER RULE

The Code includes sections that limit the perfect tender rule's effect. Indeed, courts often apply the limitations more enthusiastically than the rule itself, and so while perfect tender is the law, it must be understood in the context of other provisions. We will look at the most common ways that the law—or the parties themselves—undercut the perfect tender rule. In doing so, we will see the typically flexible approach that the Code takes to a business transaction, in contrast to the inflexible and potentially harsh results of the perfect tender rule.

---

[6] UCC §2-601.

[7] *Jakowski v. Carole Chevrolet, Inc.*, 180 N.J. Super. 122, 433 A.2d 841, 1981 N.J. Super. LEXIS 635 (N.J. Super. Ct. 1981).

Usage of Trade, Course of Dealing, and Course of Performance

The Code takes the commonsense view that a contract for the sale of goods does not exist in a vacuum. **"Usage of trade" means any practice that members of an industry *expect* to be part of their dealings.**[8] The Code requires that courts consider trade usage when they interpret contracts, which means that the perfect tender rule may not permit a buyer to reject goods with minor flaws. For example, the textile industry interprets the phrase "first quality fabric" to permit a limited number of flaws in most materials. If a seller delivers 1,000 bolts of fabric and 5 of them have minor defects, the seller *has not* violated the perfect tender rule; in the textile industry, such a minor nonconformity *is* perfect tender.

The course of dealing between the two parties may also limit the rule. **"Course of dealing" refers to previous commercial transactions between the same parties.**[9] The Code requires that the current contract be interpreted in the light of any past dealings that have created reasonable expectations. Suppose a buyer orders 20,000 board feet of "highest grade pine" from a lumber company, just as it has in each of the three previous years. In the earlier deliveries, the buyer accepted the lumber even though 1 or 2 percent was not the highest grade. That course of dealing will probably control the present contract, and the buyer will not be permitted suddenly to reject an entire shipment because 1 percent is a lower grade of pine.

The course of performance has the same effect on contract interpretation. **"Course of performance" refers to the history of dealings between the parties *in this one contract*, and thus assumes that it is the kind of contract demanding an ongoing relationship.**[10] Suppose a newspaper company signs a deal to purchase five tons of newsprint from a paper company every week for a year, and the contract also specifies the grade of paper to be delivered. If, during the first three months, the newspaper company routinely accepts paper containing a small number of flaws, that course of performance will control the contract. During the final month, the newspaper may not suddenly reject the type of paper it had earlier accepted.

Parties' Agreement

The parties may limit the effect of the perfect tender rule by drafting a contract that permits imperfection in the goods. In some industries this is routine practice. For example, contracts requiring the seller to design or engineer goods specially for the buyer will generally state a level of performance that the equipment must meet. If the goods meet the level described, the buyer has no right to reject, even if the product has some flaws.

Computer software plays an ever growing role in all business, and corporations routinely purchase software designed especially for them. But software almost always has at least minor flaws, and a software manufacturer might fail the perfect tender rule on every sale. A wise software seller will insist that the contract establish tolerances for expected levels of failure and permit adequate opportunities to correct any defects.

[8] UCC §1-205(2).

[9] UCC §1-205(1).

[10] UCC §2-208(1).

A seller who delivers nonconforming goods is generally entitled to a reasonable opportunity to cure.

Cure

A basic goal of the UCC is a fully performed contract that leaves both parties satisfied. The seller's right to *cure* helps achieve this goal. **When the buyer rejects nonconforming goods, the seller has the right to cure, by delivering conforming goods before the contract deadline.**[11] LightCo is obligated to deliver 10,000 specially manufactured bulbs to Burnout Corp. by September 15. LightCo delivers the bulbs on August 20, and on August 25 Burnout notifies the seller that the bulbs do not meet contract specifications. If LightCo promptly notifies Burnout that it intends to cure and then delivers conforming light bulbs on September 15, it has fulfilled its contract obligations, and Burnout must accept the goods. A contract should not fail when a seller shows every willingness to cure the problem.

The seller may even cure *after the contract deadline* if the seller (1) reasonably believed the original goods were acceptable and (2) promptly notified the buyer of his intent to cure within a reasonable time. This gives the seller a second chance to replace defective goods. Suppose Chip Co. delivers 25,000 computer chips to Assembler one day before the contract deadline, and two days later Assembler notifies Chip that the goods are defective. If Chip had thoroughly tested the chips before they left its factory and reasonably believed they met contract specifications, then Chip may cure by promptly notifying Assembler that it will supply conforming goods within a reasonable period. Thus, even if the conforming chips arrive two weeks after the contract deadline, Chip will have cured unless Assembler can show that the delay caused it serious harm.

In the following case, an irate homeowner kindly helps us demonstrate why sellers get a chance to cure.

FERJUTZ v. HABITAT WALLPAPER & BLINDS, INC.

1996 Ohio App. LEXIS 2868
Ohio Court of Appeals, 1996

Facts: Nancy Ferjutz went to a Habitat Wallpaper & Blinds store, where she ordered 43 custom-made blinds for her new house. She made a deposit, which included a fee for a "perfect fit agreement." An installer measured her windows and returned a month later for installation. A few of the blinds were one eighth of an inch too wide, so the installer placed temporary shades over the affected windows and took away the defective products. Habitat repaired them at its expense. The company then notified Ferjutz that a worker would install the repaired blinds, but she refused the company access to her house. Ferjutz purchased replacement blinds for all the windows in her house and filed suit against Habitat. The company filed a counter-claim, demanding payment for its goods. The trial court found that Ferjutz had breached the contract, and awarded Habitat $4,380.58. Ferjutz appealed.

Issues: **Did Ferjutz breach the contract? Did Habitat?**

Excerpts from Judge Harper's Decision: Ms. Ferjutz had a perfect fit agreement with Habitat for custom-made blinds. The fit agreement included a provision that any correction of fit would be made at Habitat's expense, within a reasonable time after the discovery of a defect(s). Herein, Ms. Ferjutz's window orders were processed in a timely fashion. Once Habitat discovered the fitting problems, it immediately proceeded to correct them. Under [UCC §2-508], Habitat had reasonable time to cure the nonconforming blinds and expeditiously proceeded to cure the defects. Habitat provided Ms. Ferjutz with replacement blinds while her blinds were being repaired. Ms. Ferjutz's attempted revocation was ineffective in light of her unwillingness to give Habitat reasonable time to cure the

[11] UCC §2-508.

non-conforming blinds. The trial court found that Habitat corrected the non-conforming blinds within a "reasonable" time period.

Given the foregoing evidence, the trial court correctly determined that Habitat was entitled to $4,380.58 in damages because Ms. Ferjutz breached her agreement with Habitat, and her revocation was ineffective. Judgement affirmed.

Substantial Impairment

In two cases the Code permits a buyer to refuse goods only if their non-conformity *substantially impairs* their value. This is a higher standard for the buyer to meet. **A buyer who claims goods are non-conforming must show that the defects *substantially impair* their value (1) if the buyer is revoking acceptance of goods or (2) if the buyer is rejecting an installment.** So a buyer who accepts a dozen cement mixers, but later discovers problems with their engines, may revoke his acceptance only by showing that the defects have caused him serious problems. Similarly, if a contract requires a buyer to accept one shipment of diesel fuel each month for two years, the buyer may reject one monthly installment only if the problem with the fuel substantially lowers its value. We consider this issue from the buyer's perspective later in the chapter.

Basic Obligation: The seller's basic obligation is to deliver conforming goods. **The perfect tender rule permits the buyer to reject the goods if they are in any way non-conforming.** But many Code provisions limit the harshness of the perfect tender rule.

Limitation on Seller's Obligation	Code Provision	Effect on Seller's Obligations
Good faith	§1-201(19) and §2-103(1)(b)	Prohibits the buyer from using the perfect tender rule as a way out of a contract that has become unprofitable.
Course of dealing, usage of trade, and course of performance	§1-205(1), §1-205(2), and §2-208	If applicable, will limit the buyer's right to reject for relatively routine defects.
The parties' agreement	§2-601	May describe tolerances for imperfections in the goods.
Cure	§2-508	Allows the seller to replace defective goods with conforming goods, if time permits.
Revocation of acceptance	§2-608	A buyer who has accepted goods may later revoke them only if she can show that the defects *substantially impair* its value.
Installment contracts	§2-612	A buyer may reject an installment only if the defects *substantially impair* its value.
Destruction of goods	§2-613	If goods identified to the contract are destroyed, the contract is void.
Commercial impracticability	§2-615	A supervening event excuses performance of a contract, if the event was not within the parties' contemplation when they made the agreement.

Destruction of the Goods

A farmer contracts to sell 250,000 pounds of sunflowers to a broker. The contract describes the 250 acres that the farmer will plant to grow the flowers. He plants his crop on time but a drought destroys most of the plants, and he is able to deliver only 75,000 pounds. Is the farmer liable for the flowers he could not deliver? No. Is the broker required to accept the smaller crop? No. **If identified goods are totally destroyed before risk passes to the buyer, the contract is void. If identified goods are partially destroyed, the buyer may choose whether to accept the goods at a reduced price or void the contract.**[12]

The crop of sunflowers was identified to the contract when the farmer planted it.[13] When a drought destroyed most of the crop, the contract became voidable. The buyer had the right to accept the smaller crop, at a reduced price, or to reject the crop entirely. The farmer is not liable for the shortfall, because the destruction was not his fault.[14]

Commercial Impracticability

Commercial impracticability means that a supervening event excuses performance of a contract, if the event was not within the parties' contemplation when they made the agreement.[15] An event is "supervening" if it interrupts the normal course of business and dominates performance of the contract. But a supervening event will excuse performance only if neither party had thought there was any serious chance it would happen.

Harris RF Systems was an American company that manufactured radio equipment. Svenska, a Swedish corporation, bought Harris radio systems and sold them in many countries, including Iran. One contract required Harris to ship a large quantity of spare radio parts, which Svenska would pay $600,000 for and then resell in Iran. Harris attempted to ship the parts to Svenska but U.S. Customs seized the goods, and the U.S. Department of Defense then notified Harris that it feared the parts would be of military value to Iran. Harris executives met several times with Defense Department officials and officers of Svenska, attempting to work out a compromise.

The Defense Department acknowledged that technically Harris was licensed to ship the goods but made two things clear: first, that it would litigate rather than permit the goods to reach Iran, and second, that if Harris attempted to complete the sale in Iran, the department would place all of Harris's future radio shipments on a Munitions List, making it difficult to ship them anywhere in the world. Svenska, on the other hand, pointed out that it had binding contracts to deliver the radio parts to various customers in Iran. If the parts were not forthcoming, Svenska would hold Harris liable for all of its losses. Harris attempted to reach a satisfactory compromise with all parties but failed and eventually agreed not to ship the parts overseas.

Svenska sued. Harris defended, relying on commercial impracticability. Harris persuaded the court that neither party had foreseen the government's intervention and that both parties realized it would be virtually impossible to export goods the Defense Department was determined to block. The court dismissed Svenska's suit.[16]

---

12 UCC §2-613.

13 Identification of goods is discussed in Chapter 20, on ownership and risk.

14 Based on *Red River Commodities, Inc. v. Eidsness*, 459 N.W.2d 805, 1990 N.D. LEXIS 159 (N.D. 1990).

15 UCC §2-615.

16 *Harriscom Svenska AB v. Harris Corp.*, 1990 U.S. Dist. LEXIS 20006 (W.D.N.Y. 1990).

Sellers offer many excuses to avoid contracts. A merchant may plead that her own supply of goods failed. Courts generally assume that the parties *did* contemplate failure of supply, and therefore reject the excuse, holding the seller liable. On the other hand, natural disasters, such as hurricanes or tornadoes, may relieve a party from performing. (The Federal Emergency Management Agency provides valuable online advice about avoiding some disasters and preparing for others. The Web site discusses everything from tsunamis to winter driving and appears at **http://www.fema.gov**.)

LAMBERT v. CITY OF COLUMBUS
242 Neb. 778, 496 N.W.2d 540, 1993 Neb. LEXIS 102
Supreme Court of Nebraska, 1993

Facts: The city of Columbus, Nebraska, agreed to pay Mr. and Mrs. Lambert $25,000 for 12 acres of land, on which it planned to build a flood control channel. The Army Corps of Engineers, which was managing the project, estimated that excavation would produce 336,000 cubic yards of excess earth. The city agreed to give the Lamberts 61,000 cubic yards and sell them 25,000 additional cubic yards at only $.15 per yard. But as construction went forward, the flood control plans changed, and the Corps of Engineers used most of the excavated dirt to strengthen the channel. The city could deliver only a fraction of the earth it had promised the Lamberts, and the couple sued.

The city claimed that it had become commercially impracticable to perform its part of the contract, but the trial court found for the Lamberts, awarding $144,613. The city appealed.

You Be the Judge: Did commercial impracticability excuse the city's failure to perform?

Argument for the City: Your honors, the City cannot deliver what it does not possess. When the parties created this bargain, both sides relied on estimates made by the Army Corp of Engineers. Had those predictions proven accurate, the City would have had more than sufficient soil to fulfill its obligations. The building of this important project took unexpected turns, and the Corps was forced to use most of the earth. It isn't there to sell, and the City cannot sell it. This contract is commercially impracticable.

Argument for the Lamberts: Your honors, there is a lot of dirt in this world. If the City did not obtain the quantity it expected from the excavation, it must buy it elsewhere and deliver it to the Lamberts. Just because the City was genuinely surprised by the lack of available earth does not mean it is relieved of its contract obligations. Parties sign contracts precisely to ensure that both sides will do what they have promised, whether convenient or not. The failure of supply does not relieve the seller of its obligations, in this case or any other.

The table earlier in this section outlines the seller's obligations.

BUYER'S OBLIGATIONS (AND A FEW RIGHTS)

The buyer's primary obligation is to accept conforming goods and pay for them.[17] The buyer must also **provide adequate facilities to receive the goods.**[18] For example, if the contract requires the seller to deliver to the buyer's warehouse, and the parties anticipate that delivery will be by rail, then the buyer must have facilities for unloading railcars at its warehouse.

[17] UCC §2-301.

[18] UCC §2-503(1)(b).

INSPECTION AND ACCEPTANCE

The buyer generally has the right to inspect the goods before paying or accepting.[19] If the contract is silent on this issue, the buyer may inspect. Typically, a buyer will insist on this right. An exception is contracts in which the parties agree there is *no* right to inspect—for example, a contract allowing shipment *C.O.D.*, which means "cash on delivery." In that case, the buyer must pay upon receipt and do her inspecting later.

Along with the right of inspection comes the obligation to do it within a reasonable time and to notify the seller promptly if the buyer intends to reject the goods. **The buyer accepts goods** if (1) after a reasonable opportunity to inspect, she indicates to the seller that the goods are conforming or that she will accept them in spite of non-conformity; or (2) she has had a reasonable opportunity to inspect the goods and has *not rejected them*; or (3) she performs some act indicating that she now owns the goods, such as altering or reselling them.[20]

Partial Acceptance

A buyer has the right to accept some goods while rejecting others if the goods can be divided into *commercial units*. Such a unit is any grouping of goods that the industry normally treats as a whole. For example, one truckload of gravel would be a commercial unit. If the contract called for 100 truckloads of gravel, a buyer could accept the 10 that conformed to contract specifications while rejecting the 90 that did not.

Revocation

As we mentioned earlier, a buyer has a limited right to revoke acceptance of goods. **A buyer may revoke acceptance but only if the nonconformity *substantially impairs* the value of the goods and only if she had a legitimate reason for the initial acceptance.**[21] This means the perfect tender rule does *not* apply: a buyer in this situation may not revoke because of minor defects. Further, the buyer must show that she had a good reason for accepting the goods originally. Acceptable reasons would include defects that were not visible on inspection or defects that the seller promised but failed to cure.

In the following case, the court had to decide whether an inspection amounted to an acceptance.

FELTNER v. D & H IMPACT MARKETING, INC.
1995 U.S. Dist. LEXIS 11363
United States District Court, Southern District of New York, 1995

Facts: C. Elvin Feltner operated Broadcast Promotions, Inc., which owned several television stations. To increase revenue, Feltner decided to offer new advertisers books of valuable discount coupons to use at local stores. Feltner contracted to buy 90,000 coupon books from D & H Impact Marketing for $360,000. Feltner specified that the coupons be redeemable at local merchants and be valid for at least several months.

D & H printed and delivered the coupon books, but they did not help Feltner sell advertising time. He never paid for the books but sued instead, claiming that the books were not for local merchants and had early expiration dates. D & H counter-claimed, seeking the full contract price. D & H then moved for summary

---

[19] UCC §2-513.

[20] UCC §2-606.

[21] UCC §§2-607, 608.

judgment, claiming that Feltner's inspection of the booklets amounted to acceptance.

Issue: Did Feltner accept the goods by inspecting them?

Excerpts from Judge Cote's Decision: Before accepting the coupon books, plaintiffs had the right to inspect them. It is undisputed that Feltner inspected the books. It is similarly undisputed that plaintiffs made no attempt to return the books at that time, nor have they done so to date. [Not only did plaintiffs not return the books, they made substantial efforts to sell them as part of their marketing plan.] Plaintiffs do not effectively dispute their failure to reject the books, and this failure, after a reasonable opportunity to inspect, resulted in acceptance of the books by plaintiffs. Once a buyer of goods has accepted the goods, the buyer must pay at the contract rate. Furthermore, acceptance of the goods shifts the burden to the buyer "to establish any breach with respect to the goods accepted."

Assuming, as we must for purposes of this motion, that the coupon books were non-conforming, and that their non-conformity "substantially impaired" their value, plaintiffs still do not assert adequate grounds under [UCC] §2-608 for revocation of their acceptance. All of the defects asserted by plaintiffs in their Complaint, i.e., the short period before expiry and the fact that the majority of the coupons were not for local merchants, were readily discoverable upon inspection. Plaintiffs proffer no explanation for their failure to discover these defects in an inspection they do not dispute took place. Plaintiffs arguably assert that D & H made various "assurances" as to the characteristics of the coupon books in November 1991 in an effort to induce plaintiffs to enter into the contracts. Plaintiffs do not assert, however, that D & H made any further assurances that the coupon books shipped had these characteristics and that it was therefore unnecessary for plaintiffs to inspect them. Accordingly, plaintiffs cannot now revoke their acceptance.

Accordingly, D & H is entitled to summary judgment.

Rejection

The buyer may reject non-conforming goods by notifying the seller within a reasonable time.[22] Huntsville Hospital purchased electrocardiogram equipment from Mortara Instrument for $155,000. The equipment failed to work properly and caused continual problems for the hospital, which notified Mortara within a reasonable time that it was rejecting. The hospital asked Mortara to pick up the equipment and refund the full purchase price, but Mortara did neither. When the hospital sued, Mortara claimed that the hospital should have returned the equipment to Mortara and that its failure left it liable for the full cost. The court of appeals was unpersuaded and gave judgment for the hospital, declaring that the hospital's only obligation was to notify the seller of a rejection and hold the goods for the seller to collect.[23]

Installment Contracts

An **installment contract** is one that requires goods to be delivered in separate lots. If Bus Co. contracts for Oil Co. to deliver 5,000 gallons of gasoline every week for one year, that is an installment contract. **A buyer may reject a non-conforming installment but only if it *substantially impairs* the value of that installment and**

---

22 UCC §§2-601, 602.

23 *Huntsville Hospital v. Mortara Instrument*, 57 F.3d 1043, 1995 U.S. App. LEXIS 16925 (11th Cir. 1995).

cannot be cured.[24] The perfect tender rule does not apply. Bus Co. has no right to reject an installment containing 4,900 gallons of gasoline, because the minor shortfall does not impair the shipment's substantial value. On the other hand, if Oil Co. delivered gasoline with lead in it, Bus Co. could reject it, since Bus Co. is legally prohibited from using the gas. (Remember, though, that Oil Co., like all sellers, has the right to cure.)

Remedies: Assurance and Repudiation

We have looked at the rights and obligations of the two parties. Now we turn our attention to the remedies they may employ. The first, assurance and repudiation, is available to both buyer and seller.

Assurance

One party to a contract may begin to fear that the other is not going to perform its obligations. **When there are reasonable grounds for insecurity, a party may demand written assurance of performance from the other party, and until he receives it, generally may suspend his own performance.**[25] Suppose Auto Co. plans to give away 50,000 videos as a promotion for its new car, to be introduced October 1. VidKids has promised to copy, package, and deliver the tapes no later than September 20. On September 1, Auto learns that VidKids has not yet begun to package the video. Auto may demand written assurance that VidKids will meet the deadline. VidKids is obligated to respond promptly and assure Auto that it will perform.

Repudiation

A party repudiates a contract by indicating that it will not perform. A party may repudiate by notifying the other party that it will not perform, by making it clear from its conduct, or by failing to answer a demand for assurance. Suppose VidKids' president calls Auto and admits, "We're having a lot of staff problems. The earliest we're going to get you that video is mid- or late October." VidKids has repudiated the contract. Similarly, if VidKids fails to respond to Auto's demand for assurance, Auto may consider that a repudiation.

When either party repudiates the contract, the other party may (1) for a reasonable time await performance or (2) resort to any remedy for breach of contract. In *either* case it may suspend its own performance.[26] In the VidKids case, it would be unreasonable for Auto to wait, because time is of the essence. So once VidKids has repudiated, Auto should protect itself by pursuing a remedy for breach, such as arranging for another company to produce the goods. (We discuss the buyer's remedies for breach later in this chapter.)

We turn now to remedies intended exclusively for the seller.

---

24 UCC §2-612.

25 UCC §2-609.

26 UCC §2-610.

SELLER'S REMEDIES

When a buyer breaches a contract, the Code provides the seller with a variety of potential remedies. Exactly which ones are available depends upon who has the goods (buyer or seller) and what steps the seller took after the buyer breached. The seller can always **cancel the contract**. She may also be able to:

- Stop delivery of the goods
- Identify goods to the contract
- Resell and recover damages
- Obtain damages for non-acceptance, or
- Obtain the contract price.

STOP DELIVERY

Sometimes a buyer breaches before the seller has delivered the goods, for example, by failing to make a payment due under the contract or perhaps by repudiating the contract. If that happens, **the seller may refuse to deliver the goods.**[27] If, when the buyer breaches, the seller has already placed the goods in the hands of a carrier, the seller may instruct the carrier not to deliver the goods provided the shipment is at least a carload or larger.

IDENTIFY GOODS TO THE CONTRACT

If the seller has not yet identified goods to the contract when the buyer breaches, he may do so as soon as he learns of the breach.[28] Suppose an electronics manufacturer, with 5,000 compact disc players in its warehouse, learns that a retailer refuses to pay for the 800 units it contracted to buy. The manufacturer may now attach a label to 800 units in its warehouse, identifying them to the contract. This will help it recover damages when it resells the identified goods or uses one of the other remedies described below.

RESALE

A seller may resell goods that the buyer has refused to accept, provided she does it reasonably. **If the resale is commercially reasonable, the seller may recover the difference between the resale price and contract price, plus incidental damages, minus expenses saved.**[29] Incidental damages are expenses the seller incurs in holding the goods and reselling them, costs such as storage, shipping, and advertising for resale. The seller must deduct expenses saved by the breach. For example, if the contract required the seller to ship heavy machinery from Detroit to San Diego, and the buyer's breach enables the seller to sell its goods in Detroit, the seller must deduct from its claimed losses the transportation costs that it saved.

---

27 UCC §2-705.

28 UCC §2-704.

29 UCC §2-706.

A seller who acts in a commercially reasonable manner is entitled to the following damages:

Contract price (the price Seller expected from the original contract)
– the resale price (the money Seller got at resale)
+ incidental damages (storage, advertising, etc.)
– expenses saved

= Seller's damages

The issue that most often arises is whether the resale was commercially reasonable. Consider the following case.

DEUTZ-ALLIS CREDIT CORP. v. BAKIE LOGGING
121 Idaho 247, 824 P.2d 178, 1992 Ida. App. LEXIS 12
Idaho Court of Appeals, 1992

Facts: Bakie Logging Co. bought a tractor for $70,000 to use in its Idaho logging operations but soon fell behind in its payments. Deutz-Allis repossessed the tractor and attempted to sell it through one of its dealers, but after three months had received no offers, so the company decided to auction it. The tractor sold at auction for $22,783, leaving an unpaid balance of $47,965, for which Deutz-Allis sued Bakie. The trial court gave judgment for Deutz-Allis in the full amount, and Bakie appealed, claiming that the auction had been commercially unreasonable.

Issue: Did Deutz-Allis resell the tractor in a commercially reasonable manner?

Excerpts from Judge Silak's Decision: At trial, Bakie presented evidence to show that the auctioneering company that conducted the auction in question was primarily in the business of auctioning farm equipment, with the auctioning of logging equipment constituting less than 5 percent of the company's business. The record also shows that the dozer was the only piece of non-farming equipment present at the auction in question; the remainder of the merchandise all being farming equipment. Mr. Bakie, who attended the auction but did not register as a bidder, testified that he thought only two persons bid on the dozer at the auction. Bakie also introduced evidence that the dozer was worth $40,000, however, this estimate of the dozer's value could not be fixed to any particular point in time.

To establish that the dozer's resale had been conducted in a commercially reasonable manner, Deutz-Allis presented evidence to show the following: that after repossession of the dozer, Deutz-Allis placed the dozer for sale on the lot of Moscow Implement, a Deutz-Allis dealer in Moscow, Idaho, and advertised its resale to other Deutz-Allis dealers throughout the country; that Deutz-Allis also advertised the dozer in the *Seattle Times;* that when no private sale of the dozer had been realized after three months, Deutz-Allis decided to place the dozer for sale at public auction; that Mr. Bakie received notice of the time and place of the public auction; that the auction was advertised by handbills and in newspapers in Washington, Oregon, Idaho, and Montana; that handbills were also sent directly to numerous individuals and implement dealers; that prior to the auction, the dozer was appraised by Deutz-Allis to be worth between $15,000 and $30,000; that over 500 people attended the auction, with 194 of them registered as potential buyers; that the bidding on the dozer was competitive; that the auction took place in an area where a great deal of logging was performed and was conducted by Urban J. "Shorty" Arnzen, a professional auctioneer.

We hold that there was substantial, although conflicting, evidence to support the trial court's finding that the dozer's resale had been conducted in a commercially reasonable manner.

[*Affirmed.*]

A seller is also permitted to resell goods privately, that is, by simply negotiating a deal with another party. But if the seller does so, she must first give the buyer reasonable notice of the private resale.

DAMAGES FOR NON-ACCEPTANCE

A seller who does not resell, or who resells unreasonably, may recover the difference between the original contract price and the market value of the goods at the time of delivery.[30] Oilko agrees to sell Retailer 100,000 barrels of a certain grade of gasoline for $60 per barrel, to be delivered in Long Beach, California, on November 1. Oilko tenders the gasoline on November 1, but Retailer refuses to accept it. On February 20, Oilko resells the gasoline to another purchaser for $52 per barrel and sues Retailer for $800,000 (the difference between its contract price and what it finally obtained), plus the cost of storage. Will Oilko win? No. Oilko's resale was unreasonable. Because there is a ready market for gasoline, Oilko should have resold immediately. Because Oilko acted unreasonably, it will not obtain damages under the Code's resale provision. Oilko will be forced to base its damages on market value.

Often this remedy will be less valuable to the seller than resale damages. Suppose that on November 1 the market value of Oilko's gasoline was $59 per barrel. Oilko's contract with Retailer was actually worth only one dollar per barrel to Oilko, the amount by which its contract price exceeded the market value. That is all that Oilko will get in court.[31] A seller with a chance to resell should be certain to do it reasonably. If Oilko had resold promptly and for some reason obtained only $52 per barrel, it probably would have recovered its entire $800,000 loss. The following chart compares resale and non-acceptance damages:

Resale Damages §2-706		Non-Acceptance Damages §2-708	
Contract price	$6,000,000	Contract price	$6,000,000
Resale price	–5,200,000	Market value of goods	–5,900,000
	$ 800,000		$ 100,000

ACTION FOR THE PRICE

The seller may recover the contract price if (1) the buyer has accepted the goods *or* (2) the seller's goods are conforming and the seller is unable to resell after a reasonable effort.[32] Royal Jones was a company that constructed rendering plants, that is, factories that use sophisticated equipment to extract valuable minerals from otherwise useless material. Royal Jones contracted for First Thermal to construct three rendering tanks, at a cost of $64,350. First Thermal built the tanks to Royal Jones's specifications but Royal Jones never accepted or paid for them, and First Thermal sued. Royal Jones argued that First Thermal deserved no money because it had not attempted to resell the goods, but the court awarded the full contract price, stating:

> First Thermal proved that any effort at resale would have been unavailing because these were the only rendering tanks First Thermal ever made, the tanks were manufac-

[30] UCC §2-708.

[31] Based on *Baii Banking Corp. v. Atlantic Richfield Co.*, 1993 U.S. Dist. LEXIS 14107 (S.D.N.Y. 1993).

[32] UCC §2-709.

tured according to Royal Jones's specifications, First Thermal had no other customers to which it could resell the tanks, and it was unaware how the tanks could have been marketed for resale.[33]

Resale is normally the safest route for an injured seller to recover the maximum amount, but when it is unrealistic, as in the *First Thermal* case, a lawsuit for the full price is appropriate. All of the seller's remedies are summarized in the chapter review at the end of the chapter. We now move on to the buyer's remedies.

BUYER'S REMEDIES

The buyer, too, has a variety of potential remedies. If a seller fails to deliver goods or if the buyer rightfully rejects the goods, the buyer is entitled to **cancel the contract**. She may also **recover money paid** to the seller, assuming she has not received the goods. In addition, she may be able to:

- Cover
- Obtain damages for non-delivery
- Obtain incidental *and consequential* damages
- Recover the goods themselves by an order for specific performance, or
- Recover liquidated damages.

COVER

If the seller breaches, the buyer may "cover" by reasonably obtaining substitute goods; it may then obtain the difference between the contract price and its cover price, plus incidental and consequential damages, minus expenses saved.[34] Casein, a protein derived from milk, is used to make cheese and to process many other foods. Erie Casein Co. contracted with Anric Corp. to supply several hundred thousand pounds of casein for about $1 per pound. Half was to be delivered in March of the first year and the other half in March of the second year. By May of the first year, Anric had not finished its first delivery because it was having difficulty obtaining the casein, but Erie told Anric to keep trying. Anric delivered some of the casein later the same year, but by March of the second year was forced to admit it could not meet the second delivery. Anric suggested that it might be able to obtain more casein in the autumn of that second year.

Erie waited until August of the second year, but finally obtained its casein elsewhere at a price of $1.45 per pound. Erie sued Anric for the extra money it had paid, about $66,000. Anric argued that Erie had no right to the difference, because Erie had waited until the price of casein was sky-high before obtaining substitute goods.

The court found for Erie. Even though the company might have covered a year earlier, when the price was much lower, it was reasonable for the buyer to wait because Anric indicated it might be able to supply the goods later. Erie had acted in good faith, and when it ultimately covered, it did so at the best price it

---

[33] *Royal Jones & Associates, Inc. v. First Thermal Systems, Inc.*, 566 So. 2d 853, 1990 Fla. App. LEXIS 6596 (Fla. Ct. App. 1990).

[34] UCC §2-712.

could find. An injured buyer does not have to do a perfect job of covering, only a reasonable job, and Erie got its full $66,000.[35]

Note that an injured buyer may also be awarded consequential damages, which we discuss below. Finally, if covering saves expense, the savings are deducted from any damages.

NON-DELIVERY

In some cases the buyer does not cover, or fails to cover *reasonably*, leaving it with damages for non-delivery. **The measure of damages for non-delivery is the difference between the market price at the time the buyer learns of the breach and the contract price, plus incidental and consequential damages, minus expenses saved.**[36] Suppose that, in the case described above, Erie had not covered but simply filed suit against Anric. Instead of its $66,000, Erie would have obtained the difference between its contract price with Anric and the market value on the date of breach. That market price was probably only a few pennies higher than the contract price, and Erie would have obtained less than $10,000.

ACCEPTANCE OF NON-CONFORMING GOODS

A buyer will sometimes accept non-conforming goods from the seller, either because no alternative is available or because the buyer expects to obtain some compensation for the defects. **Where the buyer has accepted goods but notified the seller that they are non-conforming, he may recover damages for the difference between the goods as promised and as delivered, plus incidental and consequential damages.**[37]

INCIDENTAL AND CONSEQUENTIAL DAMAGES

An injured buyer is generally entitled to incidental and consequential damages. Incidental damages cover such costs as advertising for replacements, sending buyers to obtain new goods, and shipping the replacement goods. Consequential damages can be much more extensive and may include lost profits. A buyer expecting to resell goods may obtain the loss of profit caused by the seller's failure to deliver.

A buyer, however, only gets consequential damages for harm that was unavoidable. Suppose Wholesaler has a contract to sell 10,000 rosebushes at $10 per bush to FloraMora. Wholesaler contracts to buy 10,000 rosebushes from Growem at $6 per bush, but Growem fails to deliver. Wholesaler in fact could obtain comparable roses at $8 per bush, but fails to do so and loses the chance to sell to FloraMora. Wholesaler sues Growem, seeking the $4 per bush profit it would have made on the FloraMora deal. The company will receive only $2 per bush, representing the difference between its contract price and the market value of the plants. Wholesaler will be denied the additional $2 per bush because it failed to cover.

In the following case, the court decides whether *future* profits may be too speculative to award as consequential damages.

---

[35] *Erie Casein Co. v. Anric Corp.*, 217 Ill. App. 3d 602, 577 N.E.2d 892, 1991 Ill. App. LEXIS 1429 (Ill. App. Ct. 1991).

[36] UCC §2-713.

[37] UCC §2-714.

SMITH v. PENBRIDGE ASSOCIATES, INC.
440 Pa. Super. 410, 655 A.2d 1015, 1995 Pa. Super. LEXIS 574
Superior Court of Pennsylvania, 1995

Facts: Donna and Alan Smith wanted to raise emus, which are flightless Australian birds that look like ostriches. The creatures produce rapidly in almost any terrain and are sold for their meat, which is high in protein and low in fat, and for their oil, leather, and feathers. The Smiths paid Tomie Clark, the manager of Penbridge Farms, $4,000 as a down payment for "Andrew" and "Rachel," which the farm called a "proven breeder pair." Since it is impossible to discern an emu's gender by looking, the Smiths asked Clark several times if the two birds were male and female, and he assured them that the pair had successfully produced chicks the previous breeding season.

The Smiths placed the prospective lovebirds in the same pen, but the breeding season passed without a hint of romance. Donna Smith noticed that both birds were grunting, something that only male emus do. She phoned Penbridge Farms, which advised her to "vent sex" the animals, a manual procedure used to determine gender. Donna performed this agreeable task and learned that Andrew and Rachel were both gentlemen. The would-be breeders asked for their money back but Penbridge refused, so the Smiths flew into court. The trial judge awarded the couple $105,215, representing lost profits from their anticipated chicks. Penbridge appealed, arguing that a buyer cannot count her chicks before they have hatched.

Issue: Did the trial court err by awarding lost profits?

Excerpts from Judge Popovich's Decision: [Penbridge claimed that the] evidence was speculative and insufficient to support an award of consequential damages, including damages for lost profits. [Penbridge argued that, since] the breeding of emus is a relatively new business, and there is no reliable data to project the ultimate success in breeding emus, the [Smiths'] claims for loss of chick production are entirely speculative and do not meet the "reasonable certainty" requirement of the law of damages.

The Uniform Commercial Code provides the following circumstances for the recovery of consequential damages resulting from the breach of the seller: any loss resulting from general or particular requirements and needs of which the seller at the time of contracting had reason to know and which could not reasonably be prevented by "cover" or otherwise. [UCC §2-715(2).]

The "proven breeder pair" had produced sixteen (16) chicks in the previous breeding season. [The Smiths] presented testimony revealing that it was reasonable to expect a doubling of chick production from a proven breeder pair in the following year.

The determination of damages lies with the fact finder, who weighs the evidence and assesses the credibility of the witnesses. Although the court recognized that emu breeding was a relatively new commercial business, it determined that the award of consequential damages could be calculated with a reasonable degree of certainty from the evidence adduced at trial. The court below initially found that the value of a three-month old chick produced from the [previous] season was $5,000.00. The lower court then concluded that [the Smiths] suffered incidental and consequential damages in the amount of $90,000.00. In arriving at that figure, the court below was conservative in its finding of the expected chick production from the [previous] breeding season absent appellant's breach. From our thorough evaluation of the record, we conclude that the evidence was sufficient for the lower court to measure [the Smith's] lost profits with a reasonable degree of certainty. The basis for this rule is that the breaching party should not be allowed to shift the loss to the injured party when damages, even if uncertain in amount, were certainly the responsibility of the party in breach.

Order affirmed.

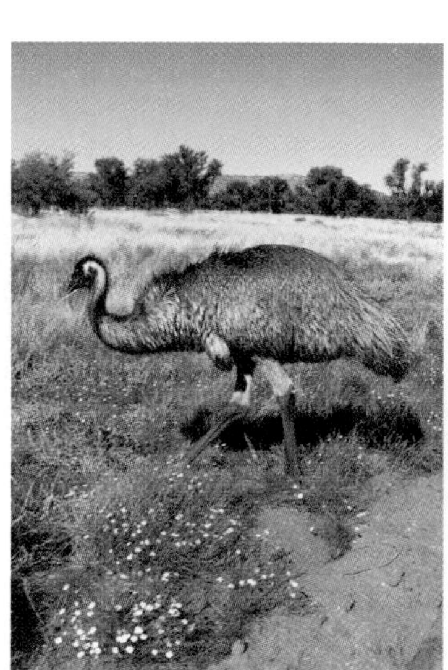

The birds cannot fly. Will the claims?

SPECIFIC PERFORMANCE

If the contract goods are unique, or the buyer is unable to obtain cover, the buyer may be allowed ***specific performance***, which means a court order requiring the seller to deliver those particular goods.[38] This remedy is most common when the goods are one-of-a-kind. Suppose Gallery agreed to sell to Trisha an original Corot painting for $120,000, but then refused to perform (because another buyer offered more money). Trisha can obtain specific performance because the painting cannot be replaced: the court will order Gallery to deliver the work. By contrast, a car rental company stymied by a dealer's refusal to sell 500 new Ford Mustangs will not obtain specific performance, since the rental company can simply buy the same cars from another dealer (cover) and sue for the difference.

LIQUIDATED DAMAGES

Liquidated damages are those that the parties agree, at the time of contracting, will compensate the injured party. **They are enforceable, but only in an amount that is reasonable in light of the harm, the difficulties of proving actual loss, and the absence of other remedies.**[39] A clause that establishes unreasonably large or unreasonably small liquidated damages is void. Courts only enforce a liquidated damages clause if it would have been difficult to estimate actual damages when the parties reached the agreement.

Cessna Aircraft agreed to build a "Citation V" business jet and sell it to Aero Consulting for $3,995,000. Cessna's contract required Aero to pay an initial deposit of $125,000, a second deposit of $300,000 six months prior to delivery, and the balance upon delivery. The contract also stated that if Aero failed to pay the balance due, Cessna would keep all deposited monies by way of liquidated damages.

Aero made both deposits and Cessna built the plane and tendered it to Aero, but Aero refused to pay the full balance due. Cessna notified Aero that it would keep the $425,000 deposited. When Aero sued, seeking a return of the deposits, the issue was whether this liquidated damage was fair. The court concluded that it was. At the time Cessna entered into the deal, it was difficult to estimate actual damages in the event of Aero's breach. The long period required to build a jet aircraft and the uncertainties about supply and demand in the marketplace meant that neither party could say for sure how much Cessna would lose should Aero breach. Further, the liquidated damage here was about 10 percent of the total cost, not an unreasonably high figure. Cessna kept the money (and the plane).[40]

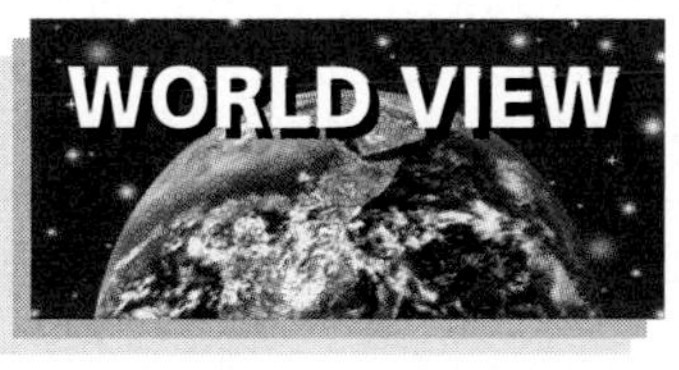

Liquidated damages can be a powerful tool to ensure fair play in the international market. Consider the problem of gray-market goods. These are products that a manufacturer intends for sale in foreign countries but which wind up in the hands of an unauthorized local retailer. You own a vineyard that has strong domestic sales, and you wish to expand into Europe. To penetrate the Italian market, you offer your product at steep discounts to an Italian importer; your intent is that the company will sell your wine cheap to retailers, and the low prices will entice consumers to try it. The importer, however, sells every available bottle to a local Italian merchant, who ships all the wine back to the United States and undersells

[38] UCC §2-716.

[39] UCC §2-718.

[40] *Aero Consulting Corp. v. Cessna Aircraft Co.*, 867 F. Supp. 1480, 1994 U.S. Dist. LEXIS 16668 (D. Kan. 1994).

your own product, taking advantage of your advertising and infuriating established dealers. Indeed, such a resale could occur before your wine ever left the country. What to do? Include a liquidated damages clause in the sales contract with the Italian importer, requiring a substantial penalty if any of your exported wine finds its way back home.

Are liquidated damages clauses legal overseas? It depends on the country, and you must be certain the language will work before you rely on it. In Italy, such clauses are common and valid. Generally speaking, there is no restriction on the size of the penalties, making these clauses potentially more forceful than they are in the United States.[41]

DAMAGE LIMITATIONS AND EXCLUSIONS

The Code allows parties to draft a contract that limits or excludes the normal remedies discussed in this chapter. For example, parties can agree that if the seller delivers non-conforming goods, the buyer's only remedy is to demand repair or replacement. We discussed these limits in the preceding chapter and will not repeat the information here. By way of a quick summary, we can say that while the parties may exclude most remedies, there are two important restrictions:

- **A court generally will not enforce a limitation that leaves the injured party with no remedy at all.** Suppose a remedy limitation states that a buyer of software is only entitled to repair, but the software is so badly designed that no amount of repairing solves the problem. A court will ignore the limitation, and the buyer will be entitled to the full range of remedies we have discussed.
- **A court will not enforce an unconscionable exclusion of consequential damages.** If the buyer is a consumer, a court is likely to ignore any exclusion of consequential damages. So, if a consumer purchases a used car from a dealer who excludes such damages, and the consumer is injured when the radiator explodes, the contract limitation will do the seller no good.

CHAPTER CONCLUSION

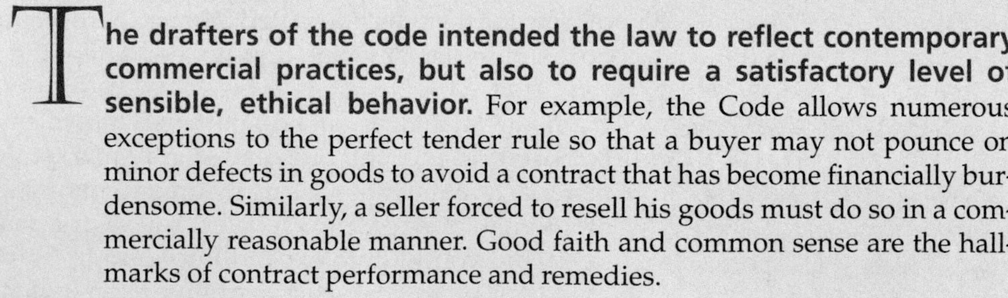

The drafters of the code intended the law to reflect contemporary commercial practices, but also to require a satisfactory level of sensible, ethical behavior. For example, the Code allows numerous exceptions to the perfect tender rule so that a buyer may not pounce on minor defects in goods to avoid a contract that has become financially burdensome. Similarly, a seller forced to resell his goods must do so in a commercially reasonable manner. Good faith and common sense are the hallmarks of contract performance and remedies.

CHAPTER REVIEW

1. Conforming goods are those that satisfy the contract terms; non-conforming goods fail to do so.
2. The Code requires good faith in the performance and enforcement of every contract.

---

41 Italian courts often order full payment of the liquidated amount even if the actual loss appears to be substantially less. However, under Article 1384 of the Civil Code, the courts do have the power to reduce damages if there has been part performance, or if the liquidated amount is clearly excessive.

3. The seller must tender the goods, which means make conforming goods available to the buyer. The perfect tender rule permits a buyer to reject goods that are non-conforming in any respect, although there are numerous exceptions.
4. Usage of trade, course of dealing, and course of performance may enable a seller to satisfy the perfect tender rule even though there are some defects in the goods.
5. When the buyer rejects non-conforming goods, the seller has the right to cure by delivering conforming goods before the contract deadline.
6. If identified goods are destroyed before risk passes to the buyer, the contract is void.
7. Under commercial impracticability, a supervening event excuses performance if it was not within the parties' contemplation when they made the contract.
8. The buyer generally has the right to inspect goods before paying or accepting. If the buyer does not reject goods within a reasonable time after inspecting them, she may be deemed to have accepted them.
9. A buyer may revoke his acceptance of non-conforming goods, but only if the defects substantially impair the value of the goods.
10. A buyer may reject non-conforming goods by notifying the seller within a reasonable time.

The following chart summarizes the contrasting remedies available to the two parties.

Seller's Remedies	**Issue**	**Buyer's Remedies**
§2-705: The seller generally may stop delivery, whether it was to be done by the seller herself or a carrier.	DELIVERY	§2-716: Specific performance: buyer may obtain specific performance only if the goods are unique.
§2-706: Resale: If the resale is made in good faith and a commercially reasonable manner, the seller may recover the difference between the resale price and the contract price, plus incidental costs, minus savings.	WHEN THE INJURED PARTY MAKES AN ALTERNATE CONTRACT	§2-712: Cover: The buyer may purchase alternate goods and obtain the difference in price, plus incidental and consequential damages, minus expenses saved.
§2-708: Non-acceptance: The measure of damages for non-acceptance is the difference between the market price at the time and place of tender and the contract price (plus incidental damages minus expenses saved).	WHEN THE GOODS HAVE NOT CHANGED HANDS	§2-713: Non-delivery: If the seller fails to deliver, the buyer's damages are the difference between the market price at the time he learned of the breach and the contract price (plus incidental and consequential damages, minus expenses saved).

Seller's Remedies	Issue	Buyer's Remedies
§2-709: The seller may sue for the price.	WHEN THE BUYER HAS ACCEPTED THE GOODS	§2-714: A buyer who has accepted non-conforming goods and notified the seller may recover damages for resulting losses.
§§2-706, 2-708, 2-709, 2-710: The seller is entitled to incidental damages but *not* consequential damages.	INCIDENTAL AND CONSEQUENTIAL DAMAGES	§2-715: The buyer is entitled to incidental and consequential damages.
LIQUIDATED DAMAGES §2-718: Either party may obtain liquidated damages but only in an amount that is reasonable at the time of the contract.		
REMEDY LIMITATION §2-719: The parties may add or exclude remedies, but no remedy limitation will be allowed if it results in the injured party obtaining no relief at all; consequential damages may not be limited in cases where doing so would be unconscionable.		

PRACTICE TEST

1. CPA QUESTION Smith contracted in writing to sell Peters a used personal computer for $600. The contract did not specifically address the time for payment, place of delivery, or Peters's right to inspect the computer. Which of the following statements is correct?

(a) Smith is obligated to deliver the computer to Peters's home.

(b) Peters is entitled to inspect the computer before paying for it.

(c) Peters may not pay for the computer using a personal check unless Smith agrees.

(d) Smith is not entitled to payment until 30 days after Peters receives the computer.

2. CPA QUESTION Cara Fabricating Co. and Taso Corp. agreed orally that Taso would custom manufacture a compressor for Cara at a price of $120,000. After Taso completed the work at a cost of $90,000, Cara notified Taso that the compressor was no longer needed. Taso is holding the compressor and has requested payment from Cara. Taso has been unable to resell the compressor for any price. Taso incurred storage fees of $2,000. If Cara refuses to pay Taso and Taso sues Cara, the most Taso will be entitled to recover is:

(a) $92,000

(b) $105,000

(c) $120,000

(d) $122,000

3. Jewell-Rung was a Canadian corporation that imported and sold men's clothing at wholesale. Haddad was a New York corporation that manufactured and sold men's clothing under the "Lakeland" label. The companies agreed that Haddad would sell 2,325 Lakeland garments to Jewell-Rung, for $250,000. Jewell-Rung began to take orders for the garments from its Canadian customers. Jewell-Rung had orders for about 372 garments when it learned that Haddad planned to allow another company, Olympic, the exclusive Canadian right to manufacture and sell Lakeland garments. Jewell-Rung sued Haddad for its lost profits. Haddad moved for summary judgment, claiming that Jewell-Rung could not recover lost profits because it had not "covered." Is Haddad right? Why might Jewell-Rung not have covered?

4. RIGHT & WRONG Laura and Bruce Trethewey hired Basement Waterproofing Nationwide, Inc. to waterproof the walls in their basement for a fee of $2,500. BWNI's contract stated: "BWNI will service any seepage in the areas waterproofed at no additional cost to the customer. All labor and materials will be at the company's expense. Liability for any damage shall be limited to the total price paid for this contract." The material that BWNI used to waterproof the Tretheweys' walls swelled and caused large cracks to open in the walls. Water poured into the basement, and the Tretheweys ultimately spent $38,000 to repair the damage. They sued, claiming negligence and breach of warranty, but BWNI claimed its liability was limited to $2,500. Please rule. Apart from the legal ruling, comment on ethics. BWNI wanted to protect itself against unlimited damage claims. Is this a legitimate way to do it? Is this how BWNI would wish to be treated itself? If you think BWNI *did* behave ethically, what advice would you have for consumers who hire home improvement companies? If you believe the company did *not* behave ethically, imagine that you are a BWNI executive, charged with drafting a standard contract for customers. How would you protect your company's interests while still acting in a way you consider moral?

5. Cargill, Inc. sold cottonseed, which is used in feed for dairy cattle. Bill Storms, a dairy farmer, agreed to buy 17 truckloads of cottonseed from Cargill for $176 per ton, to be delivered at Storms's farm. Storms had the option of accepting the seed at any time during the next nine months. Over the first two months, Storms ordered three truckloads of seed and paid Cargill, but Storms then informed Cargill that he would accept no more cottonseed. What rights does Cargill have?

6. Mastercraft Boat manufactured boats and often used instrument panels and electrical systems assembled and/or manufactured by Ace Industries. Typically, Ace would order electrical instruments and other parts and assemble them to specifications that Mastercraft provided. Mastercraft decided to work with a different assembler, M & G Electronics, so it terminated its relationship with Ace. Mastercraft then requested that Ace deliver all of the remaining instruments and other parts that it had purchased for use in Mastercraft boats. Ace delivered the inventory to Mastercraft, which inspected it and kept some of the items, but returned others to Ace, stating that the shipment had been unauthorized. Later, Mastercraft requested that Ace deliver the remaining parts (which Mastercraft had sent back to Ace) to M & G, which Ace did. Mastercraft then refused to pay for these parts, claiming that they were non-conforming. Is Ace entitled to its money for the parts?

7. Allied Semi-Conductors International agreed to buy 50,000 computer chips from Pulsar, for a total price of $365,750. Pulsar delivered the chips, which Allied then sold to Apple Computer. But at least 35,000 of the chips proved defective so Apple returned them to Allied, which sent them back to Pulsar. Pulsar agreed to replace any defective chips, but only after Allied, at its expense, tested each chip and established the defect. Allied rejected this procedure and sued. Who wins?

8. Lewis River Golf, Inc. grew and sold sod. It bought seed from defendant, O. M. Scott & Sons, under an express warranty. But the sod grown from the Scott seeds developed weeds, a breach of Scott's warranty. Several of Lewis River's customers sued, unhappy with the weeds in their grass. Lewis River lost most of its customers, cut back its production from 275 acres to 45 acres, and destroyed all remaining sod grown from Scott's seeds. Eventually, Lewis River sold its business at a large loss. A jury awarded Lewis River $1,026,800, largely for lost profits and loss of goodwill. Scott appealed, claiming that a plaintiff may not recover for lost profits and goodwill. Comment.

9. CPA QUESTION On February 15, Mazur Corp. contracted to sell 1,000 bushels of wheat to Good Bread, Inc. at $6 per bushel with delivery to be made on June 23. On June 1, Good advised Mazur that it would not accept or pay for the wheat. On June 2, Mazur sold the wheat to another customer at the market price of $5 per bushel. Mazur had advised Good that it intended to resell the wheat. Which of the following statements is correct?

(a) Mazur can successfully sue Good for the difference between the resale price and the contract price.

(b) Mazur can resell the wheat only after June 23.

(c) Good can retract its anticipatory breach at any time before June 23.

(d) Good can successfully sue Mazur for specific performance.

10. CPA QUESTION Under a contract governed by the UCC sales article, which of the following statements is correct?

(a) Unless both the seller and the buyer are merchants, neither party is obligated to perform the contract in good faith.

(b) The contract will not be enforceable if it fails to expressly specify a time and a place for delivery of the goods.

(c) The seller may be excused from performance if the goods are accidentally destroyed before the risk of loss passes to the buyer.

(d) If the price of the goods is less than $500, the goods need not be identified to the contract for title to pass to the buyer.

11. The AM/PM Franchise association was a group of 150 owners of ARCO Mini-Market franchises in Pennsylvania and New York. Each owner had an agreement to operate a gas station and mini-market, obtaining all gasoline, food, and other products, from ARCO. The Association sued, claiming that ARCO had experimented with its formula for unleaded gasoline, using oxinol, and that the poor-quality gas had caused serious engine problems and a steep drop in customers. The Association demanded (1) lost profits for gasoline sales, (2) lost profits for food and other items, and (3) loss of goodwill. The trial court dismissed the case, ruling that the plaintiff's claims were too speculative, and the Association appealed. Please rule.

12. YOU BE THE JUDGE WRITING PROBLEM Clark Oil agreed to sell Amerada Hess several hundred thousand barrels of oil at $24 each by January 31, with the sulfur content not to exceed 1 percent. On January 26, Clark tendered oil from various ships. Most of the oil met specifications, but a small amount contained excess sulfur. Hess rejected all of the oil. Clark recirculated the oil, meaning that it blended the high-sulfur oil with the rest, and notified Amerada that it could deliver 100 percent of the oil, as specified, by January 31. Hess did not respond. On January 30, Clark offered to replace the oil with an entirely new shipment, due to arrive February 1. Hess rejected the offer. On February 6, Clark retendered the original oil, all of which met contract terms, and Hess rejected it. Clark sold the oil elsewhere for $17.75 per barrel and filed suit. Is Clark entitled to damages? **Argument for Clark:** A seller is entitled to cure any defects. Clark did so in good faith and offered all of the oil by the contract deadline. Clark went even further, offering an entirely new shipment of oil. Hess acted in bad faith, seeking to obtain cheaper oil. Clark is entitled to the difference between the contract price and its resale price. **Argument for Hess:** Hess was entitled to conforming goods, and Clark failed to deliver. Under the perfect tender rule, that is the end of the discussion. Hess had the right to reject non-conforming goods, and it promptly did so. Hess chose not to deal further with Clark because it had lost confidence in Clark's ability to perform.

INTERNET RESEARCH PROBLEM

At http://www.law.cornell.edu/ucc/ucc.table.html, click on *Article 2*, and find your way to §2-615. You represent a buyer of goods who insists that the goods be delivered on time, regardless of any natural disasters. Read the opening sentence, as well as subsection (a). Draft a provision that requires the seller to deliver on time, period.

You can find further practice problems in the Online Quiz at http://beatty.westbuslaw.com or in the Study Guide that accompanies this text.

CHAPTER 23

CREATING A NEGOTIABLE INSTRUMENT

The figure lay on the couch by the fireplace. No signs of violence were visible, and a casual observer would have thought the man was napping. But Detective Waterston's trained eye immediately recognized the unnatural stiffness and pallor of a corpse. Walking behind the body, she saw matted blood against black hair and a heavy brass fireplace iron on the floor. She also noticed the crumpled document clutched in the victim's hand.

As the coroner was removing the body, Waterston slipped the crumpled paper out of the corpse's grasp. Sergeant Malloy asked whether she was ready to interview witnesses. "No," she said thoughtfully, looking at the document, "I believe I have everything I need right here." An hour later, the police arrested Tony Jenkins, the dead man's business partner. Jenkins immediately confessed.

"How did you know?" Malloy demanded.

"Simple," Waterston responded, "The answer is right here on this promissory note." She spread the crumpled page on the table. "On the front, it's a straightforward note for $1 million, payable by Tony Jenkins, the accused, to Letitia Lamour on August 1. You remember—she was recently arrested for selling fraudulent securities. Jenkins must have invested in one of her enterprises. It gets even more interesting on the back, though," she said, turning the paper over. "Lamour held on to the note for some time.

But you see, on August 15th, she wrote on the back 'Pay to the order of Sebastian Haverstock.' "

"The dead man," Malloy whistled through his teeth.

"Precisely. Haverstock and Jenkins were planning to take their computer software company public in a month or two. The sale would have made them both wealthy men. But Haverstock called Jenkins to demand payment on the note. Jenkins did not have a million dollars; he had lost everything in a series of unfortunate investments. Haverstock demanded that Jenkins turn over his shares in the company as payment for the note. In his rage and frustration, Jenkins picked up the first thing that came to hand and struck Haverstock with the brass iron. An antique instrument and very heavy.

"It's a shame, really," Detective Waterston continued. "If Jenkins had understood Article 3 of the Uniform Commercial Code, he would not have been tempted to murder. In fact, he owed Haverstock nothing. You see, the note was overdue—it should have been paid on August 1st, but today is the 31st. You can't be a holder in due course on an overdue note. Since Haverstock was not a holder in due course, Jenkins could have used the fraud claim he had against Lamour as a defense to Haverstock's demand for payment. In any event, Haverstock was well aware that Lamour had committed fraud—he was the one who set her up in business in the first place. Jenkins could have used Haverstock's knowledge of the fraud as another weapon against any demands for payment. That legal weapon would have been a better choice than a fireplace iron," Waterston concluded wryly.

COMMERCIAL PAPER

Commercial paper plays an important role in your life if you write checks or borrow money. Historically speaking, however, commercial paper is a relatively new development. In early human history, people lived on whatever they could hunt, grow, or make for themselves. Imagine what your life would be like if you had to subsist only on what you could make yourself. Certainly, many law professors would starve—their torts are inedible. Over time, people improved their standard of living by bartering for goods and services they could not make themselves. But traders needed a method for keeping account of who owed how much to whom. The first currencies—gold and silver, whether in bullion or coins—had two disadvantages: they were easy to steal and heavy to carry. Paper currency solved the weight problem, but was even easier to filch than gold. As a result, money had to be kept in a safe place, and banks developed to meet that need. However, money in a vault is not very useful unless it can be readily spent. Society needed a system for transferring paper funds easily. Commercial paper is that system. (For more on the history of money, see **http://www.ex.ac.uk/~RDavies/arian/llyfr.html** and **http://www.treas.gov/kids/money/kymintro.html**.)

Commercial paper is a contract to pay money. It is used as:

- **A Substitute for Money.** When Darla stops at the Drive-In-Convenience Store to buy food for dinner, she has only 32¢ in her wallet. Not a problem, she can pay by check. Darla's check is a promise that she has money in the bank. It is also an order to the bank to transfer funds to Drive-In-Convenience. Darla is going to eat immediately (in the car on the way home), and the store would also like to be paid expeditiously. For commercial paper to be a substitute for money, it must be payable on demand.

- **A Loan of Money.** This type of commercial paper is a contract to pay what is owed sometime in the future. Darla buys a beautiful concert grand piano that costs more than her parents paid for their first house. She does not have enough money in the bank to write a check for the full amount, so she signs a **promissory note,** that is, an assurance that she will pay for the piano in five years. The manager at the Angel House of Music does not expect to take the note to Darla's bank and be paid right away; he understands that he will have to wait.

The four previous chapters covered the Uniform Commercial Code (UCC) and the sale of goods. This chapter and the following two focus on Articles 3 and 4 of the UCC as they regulate commercial paper. Originally, commercial paper was governed by the Uniform Negotiable Instruments Act but in 1951, this statute was absorbed into the UCC. Most states first adopted Articles 3 and 4 in the early 1960s. In 1990, these articles were modernized to resolve problems that had arisen under the old version, to update archaic language, and to respond to technological changes. All states except two have now adopted this new version.[1]

The purpose of the UCC articles on negotiable instruments is to facilitate commerce. When the United States Treasury issues money, it is consistent—all dollar bills look alike. But when practically the entire population of the United States issues commercial paper, creativity takes over and consistency disappears. The purpose of Articles 3 and 4 is to transform these pieces of paper into something almost as easily transferable and reliable as money. As the following news report indicates, commercial paper is important the world over.

To play a major role in international trade, developing countries find that they must develop a reliable system of commercial paper. China recently passed its first law on commercial paper. Before the law was enacted, Chinese legislators researched the use of commercial paper within the country and also studied laws overseas. Their goal was to ensure that Chinese law was consistent with, and would enhance China's role in, international trade and investment. Similarly, the government of Vietnam is currently developing a law on negotiable instruments to facilitate foreign investment and foster economic growth.

The fundamental "rule" of commercial paper can be stated this way: **The possessor of a piece of commercial paper has an unconditional right to be paid, as long as (1) the paper is *negotiable*; (2) it has been *negotiated* to the possessor; (3) the possessor is a *holder in due course*; and (4) the issuer cannot claim any of a limited number of "real" *defenses*.** This rule is the backbone of the chapter, and in the following sections we define and explain its terms: "negotiable," "negotiated," "holder in due course," and "defenses." You will want to keep this rule in mind throughout the chapter.

Types of Negotiable Instruments

There are two kinds of commercial paper: negotiable and non-negotiable instruments. Article 3 of the Code covers only negotiable instruments; non-negotiable instruments are governed by ordinary contract law. There are also two categories of negotiable instruments: notes and drafts. The essential difference between the

[1] The legislatures of New York and South Carolina expect to consider the new versions of Articles 3 and 4 soon. They have already passed revisions to Article 4A.

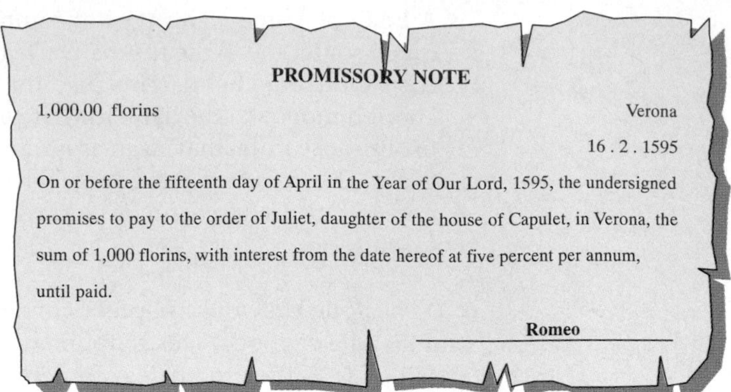
PROMISSORY NOTE

1,000.00 florins Verona

16 . 2 . 1595

On or before the fifteenth day of April in the Year of Our Lord, 1595, the undersigned promises to pay to the order of Juliet, daughter of the house of Capulet, in Verona, the sum of 1,000 florins, with interest from the date hereof at five percent per annum, until paid.

Romeo

In this note, Romeo is the maker and Juliet is the payee.

two is that a note is a *promise* to do something while a draft is an *order* to someone else to do it. This is an overview; now for the details.

A **note** (also called a **promissory note**) is your promise that you will pay money. A promissory note is used in virtually every loan transaction, whether the borrower is buying a multimillion dollar company, a house, or a TV set. For example, the National Basketball Association permits players to borrow money from their team. If Kobe Bryant borrows $5 million from the Los Angeles Lakers, he must sign a note promising to repay the money. Bryant is the **maker** because he is the one who has made the promise. His team is called the **payee** because it expects to be paid. Remember that only *two* parties are involved in a note: the maker and the payee. Some notes are due at a definite date in the future. Others are **payable on demand,** which means that the maker must pay whenever he is asked. Thus, Bryant's note could be payable, say, in three years when his contract expires, or it could be payable on demand (which means that, if his team is ever annoyed at him, it could insist on immediate payment). The Web site **http://www.legaldocs.com/** provides a sample promissory note with fill-in blanks.

If the note is made by a bank, it is called a **certificate of deposit** (also known as a CD). When investors loan money to a bank, the bank gives them a note promising to repay the loan at a specific date in the future. The bank is the maker and the investor is the payee. The bank pays a higher rate of interest on CDs than it does on regular savings accounts because the investor cannot demand payment on the CD until its due date. In return for the lower rate on a savings account, the depositor can withdraw that money anytime. To compare CD and savings account rates, see **http://www.bankrate.com/brm/default.asp?web=brm**.

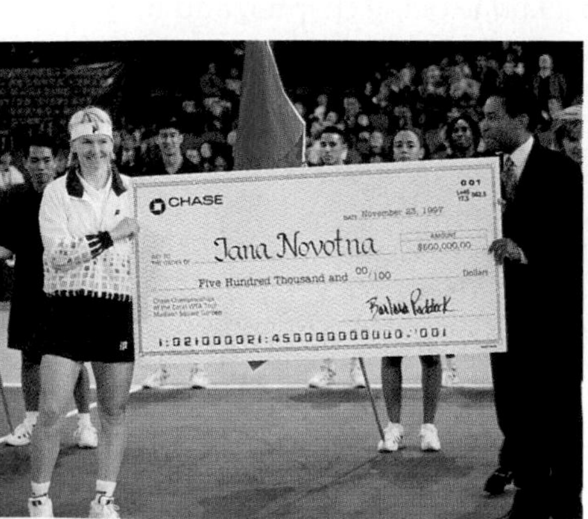

In this check, Corel WTA Tour is the drawer, Novotna is the payee, and Chase is the drawee.

A **draft** is an order directing someone else to pay money for you. A **check** is the most common form of a draft—it is an order telling a bank to pay money. In a draft three people are involved: the **drawer** orders the **drawee** to pay money to the **payee**. Now before you slam the book shut in despair, let us sort out the players. Suppose that Jana Novotna wins the Corel WTA Tour in New York. The WTA writes her a check for $500,000. This check is simply an order by the WTA (the drawer) to its bank (the drawee) to pay money to Novotna (the payee). The terms make sense if you remember that, when you take money out of your account, you *draw* it out. Therefore, when you write a check, you are the draw*er* and the bank is the draw*ee*. The person to whom you make out the check is being paid, so he is called the pay*ee*.

The following table illustrates the difference between notes and drafts. Even courts sometimes confuse the terms *drawer* (the person who signs a check) and *maker* (someone who signs a promissory note). But the UCC is a very precise set of rules, so it is important to get the details right. **Issuer** is an all-purpose term that means both maker and drawer.

	Who Pays	Who Plays
Note	You make a promise that you will pay.	Two people are involved: maker and payee.
Draft	You order someone else to pay.	Three people are involved: drawer, drawee, and payee.

Jana Novotna presumably feels confident that the WTA has enough money in its account to cover the check. When Stewart Student goes to the MegaLoud store to buy a $3,000 sound system, MegaLoud has no way of knowing if his check is good. Even if MegaLoud calls the bank to confirm Stewart's balance, he could withdraw it all by the time the check is deposited that evening. To protect itself, MegaLoud insists upon a cashier's check. A **cashier's check** is drawn by a bank on itself. When Stewart asks for a cashier's check, the bank takes the money out of his account on the spot and then issues a check itself, payable out of its own funds. When MegaLoud gets the cashier's check from Stewart, it knows that the check is good as long as the bank itself is solvent.

All checks are drafts, but not all drafts are checks. A draft is a check only if it is drawn on a bank. Sometimes drafts are drawn on individuals or companies. Suppose that in September, Sasha's Saddlery sells 16 saddles to the Circle S Stable. The stable expects that, in December, it will receive its first deposits from tourists making reservations for the following summer. The stable promises to pay Sasha $8,000 in January. Sasha is happy to make the sale, but she needs the funds now. So she prepares a draft ordering Circle S to pay $8,000 to Citizen's Bank in January. After Circle S signs (**accepts**) the draft, Sasha takes it to Citizen's, which investigates Circle S's credit reputation. Satisfied, it agrees to buy the draft for $7,000. (It pays less than the full amount because it has to wait for the money and because there is always a chance Circle S will not pay.) Sasha is the drawer, Circle S the drawee, and Citizen's Bank the payee. So Sasha's Saddlery receives $7,000 from Citizen's in September. In January, Circle S pays Citizen's the full $8,000.

The draft on Circle S is a **trade acceptance,** which is a draft drawn by a seller of goods on the buyer and payable to the seller or some third party. In our case, Sasha is the seller, Circle S the buyer, and Citizen's the third party that will be paid. To be valid, the draft must be accepted (that is, signed) by the buyer. A **sight draft** is payable on demand; a **time draft** is payable in the future. Circle S's draft is a time draft because it is not payable until January.

Sasha books a trip to England to find a new supplier of saddles. Concerned about carrying too much cash, she decides to buy $1,000 of **traveler's checks**. To purchase the checks, Sasha goes to a bank (such as Citizen's) or a company (such as American Express) and pays $1,000 plus a handling fee of about 1 percent. Before she leaves the building, she signs the front of the checks. When she needs to make a purchase in England, she signs the front of the check again. The payee then compares the two signatures to make sure they are the same and that the checks are valid. Once the payee has accepted the checks, only Citizen's is liable. The payee's bank presents the checks to Citizen's for payment. Note that Citizen's is both the drawer and the drawee because it issues the checks in its own name (as drawer) and it pays the checks when presented (as drawee). If the checks are drawn on American Express, they are technically drafts, but not checks, because American Express is not a bank. Traveler's checks have two advantages: (1) the English merchant accepts a check from Sasha, whom he does not know, because he trusts Citizen's (or American Express); and (2) if Sasha loses the checks, Citizen's (or American Express) will replace them for free.

NEGOTIABILITY

To work as a substitute for money, commercial paper must be freely transferable in the marketplace. In other words, it must be *negotiable*. Suppose that Krystal buys a used car from the Trustie Car Lot for her business, Krystal Rocks. She cannot afford to pay the full $15,000 right now, but she is willing to sign a note promising to pay later. Trustie is happy to sell a car to Krystal, but he needs the cash *now* so that he can buy more cars to sell to other customers. Reggie's Finance Co. is happy to buy Krystal's promissory note from Trustie, but the price Reggie is willing to pay depends upon whether her note is negotiable.

The possessor of *non*-negotiable commercial paper has the same rights—no more, no less—as the person who made the original contract. With non-negotiable commercial paper the transferee's rights are *conditional* because they depend upon the rights of the original party to the contract. If, for some reason, the original party loses his right to be paid, so does the transferee. The value of non-negotiable commercial paper is greatly reduced because the transferee cannot be absolutely sure what his rights are or whether he will be paid at all.

If Krystal's promissory note is non-negotiable, Reggie gets exactly the same rights that Trustie had. As the saying goes, he steps into Trustie's shoes. Other people's shoes may not be a good fit. Suppose that Trustie tampered with the odometer and, as a result, Krystal's car is worth only $12,000 instead of the $15,000 she paid for it. If, under contract law, she owes Trustie only $12,000, then that is all she has to pay Reggie, even though the note *says* $15,000.

The possessor of *negotiable* commercial paper has *more* rights than the person who made the original contract. With negotiable commercial paper, the transferee's rights are *unconditional* and generally do not depend upon the rights of the original party to the contract. As long as the transferee is a *holder in due course* (discussed later in this chapter), he is entitled to be paid the full amount of the note, regardless of the relationship between the original parties (with a few limited exceptions). If Krystal's promissory note is a negotiable instrument, she must pay the full amount to whoever has possession of it, no matter what complaints she might have against Trustie. Even if the car explodes within the month, Krystal must still pay Reggie the full $15,000.

Exhibit 23.1 illustrates the difference between negotiable and non-negotiable commercial paper.

REQUIREMENTS FOR NEGOTIABILITY

Because negotiable instruments are more valuable than non-negotiable ones, it is important for buyers and sellers to be able to tell, easily and accurately, if an instrument is indeed negotiable. An instrument is negotiable if it meets the six standards set out in UCC §3-104(a).[2]

1. **The Instrument Must Be in *Writing*.** Trustie cannot negotiate Krystal's *oral* promise to pay $15,000. However, the writing need not be on any official form or even on paper. To protest a speeding ticket, Barry Lee Brown of Missoula, Montana, wrote a check for the $35 fine on a pair of old (but clean!) underpants. The bank cashed it.

2. **The Instrument Must Be *Signed* By the Maker or Drawer.** Any signature counts—initials, an "X," a stamp—as long as the issuer intends to indicate her

[2] Section 3-104(a) sets out all the requirements of negotiability. Sections 3-105 to 3-119 then describe the requirements in more detail.

Exhibit 23.1

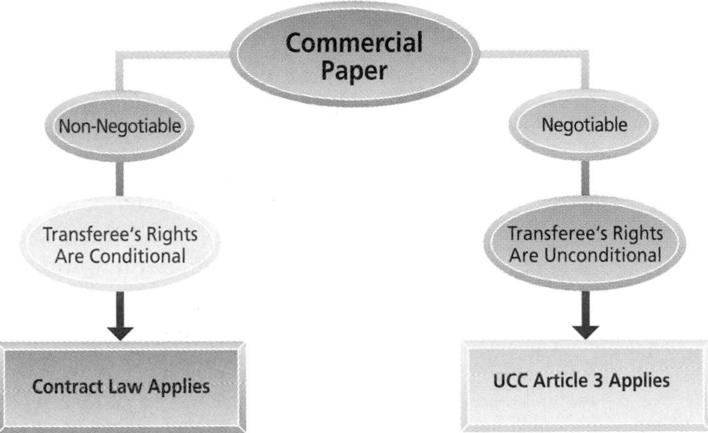

signature. If Krystal normally signs her documents with an interlocking heart logo, that symbol counts as a signature. Since Krystal is buying the car for her business, Krystal Rocks, she can simply sign the document using this trade name, and that is a valid signature.

3. **The Instrument Must Contain an *Unconditional Promise* or *Order* to Pay.** The whole point of a negotiable instrument is that the holder can sleep soundly at night confident that he will be paid *without conditions*. If Krystal's promissory note says, "I will pay $15,000 as long as the car is still in working order," it is not negotiable. If, however, the note says, "I will pay $15,000 for the yellow car," it is negotiable because this statement is not a *condition*, it is simply describing the transaction.

   The instrument must also contain a promise or order to pay. It is not enough simply to say, "Krystal owes Trustie $15,000." She has to indicate that she owes the money and also that she intends to pay it. "Krystal promises to pay Trustie $15,000," would work.

4. **The Instrument Must State a *Definite Amount* of Money.** It is not easy to sell an instrument if the buyer cannot tell how much it is worth; to be negotiable, therefore, the document must clearly state how much money is owed. If the document is a note, with interest due, matters become more complicated. The holder may not be able to tell how much interest is owing simply by looking at the note. If Krystal's note says, "$15,000 with annual interest of 10 percent," Reggie can easily calculate the interest. If, on the other hand, the note says, "with interest at 1 percent above prime rate," Reggie cannot tell the total amount owed unless he checks the prime rate in his newspaper. No matter: under §3-112, an instrument with a variable interest rate is considered to be negotiable, even though the holder must look elsewhere to calculate the amount owing. Suppose that Krystal's note says, "I promise to pay $15,000 worth of diamonds." This note is not negotiable because it does not state a definite amount of *money*.

5. **The Instrument Must Be Payable on *Demand* or at a *Definite Time*.** To determine what an instrument is worth, the holder must know when he will be paid. Ten thousand dollars today is worth more than $10,000 the day the earth stands still.

   A demand instrument must be paid whenever the holder requests payment. If an instrument is undated, it is treated as a demand instrument and is negotiable. There is one exception to this rule. If an undated promissory note says, "payable in 90 days," the instrument is not payable on demand and is non-negotiable. The maker of the note clearly did not intend to pay it on demand, but there is no way of knowing when she did intend to pay it.

An instrument can be negotiable even if it will not be paid until some time in the future, provided that the payment date can be determined when the document is made. A graduate of a well-known prep school has written a generous check to his alma mater each year, but for payment date he puts, "The day the headmaster is fired." These checks are not negotiable because they are neither payable on demand nor at a definite time. When he writes the checks, no one knows when (or whether) the headmaster will be fired. If the headmaster is finally fired, the checks do not suddenly become negotiable.

Suppose that Krystal simply signs her note without specifying the due date. Reggie can demand payment anytime. By contrast, if the due date on the note is Easter 2004, Reggie may have to check his calendar to figure out when that is (since the date of Easter changes every year), but the note is nonetheless negotiable. If, however, the due date on the note is "three months after Krystal receives her MBA degree," the note is non-negotiable because the date of Krystal's graduation is uncertain.

6. **The Instrument Must Be Payable to *Order* or to *Bearer*.** To be negotiable, an instrument must be either order paper or bearer paper. **Order paper** must include the words "Pay to the order of" someone (or an equivalent, such as "Pay to someone, or order"). If the note simply says "Pay to Trustie," it is not negotiable. By including the word "order," the maker is indicating that the instrument is not limited to only one person. "Pay to the order of Trustie Car Lot" means that the money will be paid to Trustie *or to anyone Trustie designates*.

   If the note is made out "To bearer," it is **bearer paper** and can be redeemed by any holder in due course. The good news is that bearer paper is easily and freely transferable, but the bad news is that it may be too easily redeemed. Suppose that Krystal's note is payable to bearer and Reggie mails it to his sweetheart Sue as a birthday present. If dastardly Dan steals the note from Sue's mailbox and sells it to unknowing Neal, Krystal will have to pay Neal when he presents the note.

   A note is bearer paper if it is made out to "bearer" or it is *not* made out to any specific person. If Krystal's note says, "Pay to the order of cash," or "Pay to the order of a Happy Birthday," it is bearer paper. If Krystal signs a note but leaves blank the space after "Pay to the order of," that note is bearer paper, and any holder in due course can redeem it.

The rules for checks are different from other negotiable instruments. All checks are, by definition, negotiable. Most checks are pre-printed with the words, "Pay to the order of," but sometimes people inadvertently cross out "order of." Even so, the check is still negotiable. Checks are frequently received by consumers who, sadly, have not completed a course on business law. The drafters of the UCC did not think it fair to penalize them when the drawer of the check was the one who made the mistake. If a check is made out to "Reggie *and* Sue," both payees must sign it before it can be transferred. If the check is made out to "Reggie *or* Sue," the signature of either is sufficient.

An instrument must be *signed* by the maker or drawer. This sounds straightforward, but what does it mean to sign a note or draft? Many people, for example, use computer programs that permit them to pay bills online. How do they sign an online check? How does their bank know the signature is valid? The answer is a "digital signature." This computer signature does not look like handwriting;

instead, it is a unique series of letters and numbers in code. A digital signature can actually be safer than the traditional signature on paper (called a "wet" signature). If the digital document is dishonestly altered, the sender and recipient can tell.

Utah was the first state to pass a statute providing that digital signatures have the same legal status as wet versions. Now, virtually every state has either passed a digital statute or is considering such legislation.

Some states are also considering statutes that would permit "biometric" signatures. As in a spy movie, people could identify themselves by fingerprint, retina scan, or voiceprint. To speed up transactions at teller windows, Chase Manhattan Bank now uses voiceprints to identify customers. This identification process is not the same as a legal signature, but Chase soon expects to use voiceprints to authenticate telephone transactions.

INTERPRETATION OF AMBIGUITIES

Perhaps you have noticed that people sometimes make mistakes. Although the UCC establishes simple and precise rules for creating negotiable instruments, people do not always follow these rules to the letter. It might be tempting simply to invalidate defective documents (after all, money is at stake here). But instead, the UCC favors negotiability and has rules to resolve uncertainty and supply missing terms.

Notice anything odd about the check pictured below? Is it for $1,500 or $15,000? When the terms in a negotiable instrument contradict each other, three rules apply:

- Words take precedence over numbers.
- Handwritten terms prevail over typed and printed terms.
- Typed terms win over printed terms.

According to these rules, Krystal's check is for $15,000 because, in a conflict between words and numbers, words win.

What is wrong with the promissory note on the next page? The interest rate is left blank. When this happens, UCC §3-112 directs that the judgment rate applies. The **judgment rate** is simply the rate that courts use on court-ordered judgments. Remember also that when the date is missing, an instrument is payable on demand.

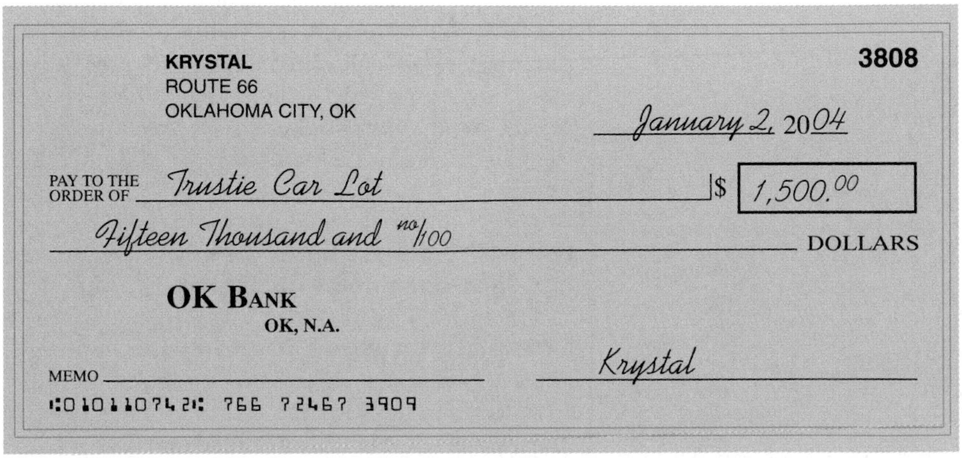

KRYSTAL
ROUTE 66
OKLAHOMA CITY, OK

3808

January 2, 2004

PAY TO THE ORDER OF Trustie Car Lot $ 1,500.00

Fifteen Thousand and no/100 DOLLARS

OK BANK
OK, N.A.

MEMO

Krystal

⑆010110742⑆ 766 72467 3909

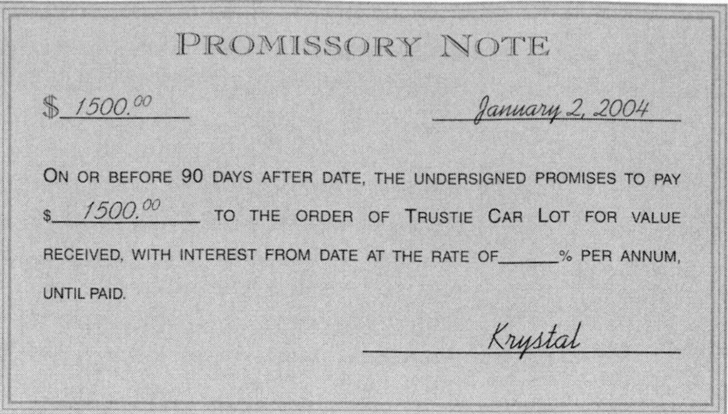
PROMISSORY NOTE

$ 1500.00 January 2, 2004

ON OR BEFORE 90 DAYS AFTER DATE, THE UNDERSIGNED PROMISES TO PAY $ 1500.00 TO THE ORDER OF TRUSTIE CAR LOT FOR VALUE RECEIVED, WITH INTEREST FROM DATE AT THE RATE OF ____% PER ANNUM, UNTIL PAID.

Krystal

Careful proofreading will avoid many of these problems with negotiable instruments. Always read an instrument before signing it and never sign an instrument that has contradictory or blank terms.

In the following case, a set of notes deviated slightly from the requirements of the UCC. Are the notes negotiable despite the errors?

***IN RE* BOARDWALK MARKETPLACE SECURITIES LITIGATION**
688 F. Supp. 115, 1987 U.S. Dist. LEXIS 15122
United States District Court, District of Connecticut, 1987

Facts: Investors purchased interests in limited partnerships that were organized to redevelop property in Atlantic City, New Jersey. To finance their purchases, the investors executed promissory notes payable to American Funding Limited. The notes stated, in part:

> I will pay__monthly installments of principal and interest, each in the amount of $__, commencing on the__day of__19__ (estimated first payment date). Lender will notify me in writing of the first payment due date, the amount of the first payment, the date of the first payment, the date of the final payment and the amount of the final payment.

In the blanks, someone had handwritten figures representing the number of monthly payments, the amount of each payment, and an estimated date on which the payments were to begin.

American Funding Limited sold these notes to various banks. When the redevelopment plan collapsed, many of the investors ceased making payments on their notes. The investors asserted that the notes were non-negotiable because the payment date was not definite. The banks argued that, whether or not the payment date was definite, equity demanded that the notes be treated as if they were negotiable so that the banks, which were innocent of all wrongdoing, could collect the money owed them. If the notes were non-negotiable, the banks' right to collect might be defeated by claims the investors had against American Funding.

Issues: Did these notes comply with UCC requirements for negotiability? If not, should the notes be treated as if they were negotiable?

Excerpts from Judge Eginton's Decision: The investors pose a narrow challenge to the notes' claimed negotiability, alleging that in contravention of §3-104(1)(c) they are neither payable on demand nor at a definite time. The initial question is whether these notes are payable at a "definite time."

The notes do not satisfy the requirements of definite time. Subsection (a) [of the UCC] reads "on or before a stated date or at a fixed period after a stated date." Logically, a note containing an estimated first payment date and a provision which states that the lender will notify the maker of the actual first payment date does not fall within the confines of this subsection.

The overarching concern of the Code and thereby Article Three is to promote the free flow of commerce. The decision was made that a set of formal requisites which the terms of commercial paper must meet would best serve these purposes. One requisite is that the paper be negotiable. The formalities of negotiability arose in history out of the law merchant. Today, they are codified in Article Three. There is no particular magic to them; the drafters could have chosen other formalities, although some are obvious.

Because the prerequisites to negotiability are formal, it is both simple and necessary to comply with them. To hold that these notes are negotiable would certainly preserve the integrity of these notes and in that limited sense serve the interests of commerce; however, it would reward shoddy drafting and introduce unnecessary doubt into the formalities of negotiability. The reason for employing formalities in legal rules is to preclude the kinds of arguments that the banks offer to circumvent them here. It will not do to argue that the goal of promoting the expansion of commerce with predictably negotiable paper is served by artful reconstruction of the formalities set up initially to serve that same goal.

[The court concluded that the notes were not negotiable.]

Was the result in this case fair? These investors were using a technicality of Article 3 to avoid paying legitimate debt. Why should the banks (and their shareholders or depositors) suffer when they had absolutely no involvement in the investment scheme?

NEGOTIATION

Remember the fundamental rule that underlies this chapter: the possessor of a piece of commercial paper has an unconditional right to be paid, as long as (1) the paper is negotiable, (2) it has been negotiated to the possessor, (3) the possessor is a holder in due course, and (4) the issuer cannot claim any of a limited number of "real" defenses. To be negotiable, an instrument must be order paper (payable to the order of someone) or bearer paper (payable to anyone in possession). These two types of instrument have different rules for negotiation: **to be negotiated, order paper must first be *indorsed* and then *delivered* to the transferee. Bearer paper must simply be *delivered* to the transferee; no indorsement is required**.[3]

In its simplest form, **an indorsement is the signature of the payee**. Tess writes a rent check for $475 to her landlord, Larnell. He would like to use this money to pay Patty for painting the building. If Larnell signs the back of the check and delivers it to Patty, he has met the two requirements for negotiating order paper: indorsement and delivery. If Larnell delivers the check to Patty but forgets to sign it, the check has not been indorsed and therefore cannot be negotiated—it has no value to Patty. Similarly, the check is of no use to Patty if Larnell signs it but never gives it to her. If someone forges Larnell's name, the indorsement is invalid and no subsequent transfer counts as a negotiation.

---

[3] §3-201. The UCC spells the word "indorsed." Outside the UCC, the word is more commonly spelled "endorsed."

Suppose that Tess misspells Larnell's name as "Larnelle." Larnell's indorsement is valid whether he signs the check "Larnell" or "Larnelle." However, when he gives the check to Patty, she may insist that he indorse it *both* ways, just to be safe.

There are three different types of indorsements:

- **Blank Indorsement**. A blank indorsement occurs when Larnell simply signs the check on the back without designating any particular payee. A blank indorsement turns the check into bearer paper. Larnell can give the check to Patty the painter or Ellen the electrician. In either case, he has properly negotiated the check.

- **Special Indorsement**. A special indorsement limits an instrument to one particular person. If Larnell writes on the back of the check, "Pay Ellen Wilson" or "Pay to the order of Ellen Wilson," then only Ellen can cash the check.

- **Restrictive Indorsement**. A restrictive indorsement limits the check to one particular use. When Ellen receives the check from Larnell, she writes on the back, "For deposit only," and then signs her name. The check can only be deposited in Ellen's account. If Conrad finds the check, he cannot cash it or deposit it in his own account. This type of indorsement is the safest.

Note that indorsements can be used to change an instrument from order paper to bearer paper or vice versa. If Tess makes a check out to cash, it is bearer paper. When Larnell writes on the back, "Pay to the order of Patty," it becomes order paper. If Patty simply signs her name, the check becomes bearer paper again. And so on it could go forever.[4] If the check is bearer paper, Larnell can negotiate it simply by giving it to Patty. His indorsement is not required.

HOLDER IN DUE COURSE

A holder in due course has an automatic right to receive payment for a negotiable instrument (unless the issuer can claim a limited number of "real" defenses). If the possessor of an instrument is not a holder in due course, then his right to payment depends upon the relationship between the issuer and payee. He inherits whatever claims and defenses arise out of that contract. Clearly, then, holder in due course status dramatically increases the value of an instrument because it enhances the probability of being paid.

REQUIREMENTS FOR BEING A HOLDER IN DUE COURSE

Under §3-302 of the UCC, a holder in due course is a *holder* who has given *value* for the instrument, in *good faith, without notice* of outstanding claims or other defects.

---

[4] Even when all the space on the back of the check is filled, the holder can attach a separate paper for indorsements, called an **allonge**.

Holder

A holder in due course must, first of all, be a holder. A **holder** is someone who has possession of a negotiable instrument that she has received through a valid negotiation. When Felix borrows money from his mother, she insists that he sign a promissory note for the loan. He promptly writes, "I hereby promise to pay to the order of Imogene $5,000." He signs his name and gives the note to her. She is a holder because she has received the note through a valid negotiation. She would like to give the note to her lawyer, Lance, to pay the legal bill she incurred when Felix smashed up a nightclub. If she simply hands the note to Lance, he is not a holder because the note is not payable to him. If she writes on the back of the note, "Pay to the order of Lance," but does not give it to him, he is not a holder either.

Value

A holder in due course must give value for an instrument. **Value** means that the holder has *already* done something in exchange for the instrument. Lance has already represented Felix, so he has given value. Once Imogene indorses and delivers the note to Lance, he is a holder in due course. Although a promise to do something in the future is *consideration* under contract law, such a promise does not count as *value* under Article 3. If the holder receives an instrument in return for a promise, he does not deserve to be paid unless he performs the promise. But if he were a holder in due course, he would be entitled to payment whether he performed or not. For example, suppose that Imogene gave Lance the promissory note in exchange for his promise to represent Felix in an upcoming arson trial. Lance would not be a holder in due course because he has not yet performed the service. It would be unfair for him to be a holder in due course, with an unconditional right to be paid, if he, in fact, does not represent Felix.

Someone who receives a negotiable instrument as a gift is not a holder in due course because he has not given value. If Imogene gives Felix's note to her daughter, Joy, as a birthday present, Joy is not a holder in due course.

Good Faith

There are two tests to determine if a holder acquired an instrument in good faith. The holder must meet both of these tests:

- **Subjective Test.** Did the holder *believe* the transaction was honest in fact?
- **Objective Test.** Did the transaction *appear* to be commercially reasonable?

Felix persuades his elderly neighbor, Serena, that he has invented a fabulous beauty cream guaranteed to remove wrinkles. She gives him a $10,000 promissory note, payable in 90 days, in return for exclusive sales rights in Pittsburgh. Felix sells the note to his old friend Dick for $2,000. Felix never delivers the sales samples to Serena. When Dick presents the note to Serena, she refuses to pay on the grounds that Dick is not a holder in due course. She contends that he did not buy the note in good faith.

Dick fails both tests. Any friend of Felix knows he is not trustworthy, especially when presenting a promissory note signed by an elderly neighbor. Dick did not believe the transaction was honest in fact. Also, $10,000 notes are not usually discounted to $2,000; $9,000 would be more normal. This transaction is not commercially reasonable, and Dick should have realized immediately that Felix was up to no good.

In the following case, the plaintiff also failed two tests: he neither gave value nor acted in good faith.

ROSENBAUM v. BULOW
1997 Bankr. LEXIS 555
United States Bankruptcy Court for the Eastern District of North Carolina, 1997

Facts: Maude Knox Rosenbaum was convicted of "obtaining property by false pretenses" (more commonly referred to as "fraud"). Pending the outcome of her appeal, she was sent to Women's Prison in Raleigh, North Carolina. Prison was not to her liking, but she could not raise bail of $50,000. Nor could she find a bondsman willing to post bail for her.[5]

Rosenbaum turned to her sister, Louise Knox, for help. Knox asked for money from a number of friends and acquaintances, who evidently felt Rosenbaum was just fine where she was. Finally, Harvey Bowen, a local used car dealer, agreed to post the $7,500 bond in exchange for a $7,500 promissory note secured by Rosenbaum's house. In other words, Bowen asked to be paid $7,500 even though he was entitled to a refund of his entire bond if Rosenbaum returned to prison as required. There was only one problem with this arrangement: Bowen was not a licensed bondsman. Thus, under state law, Rosenbaum had no obligation to pay him for posting bail. Shortly after obtaining the note from Rosenbaum, Bowen attempted to solve this problem by asking her to sign a second note that was identical to the first, except this time W. F. Bulow was the payee. (Bulow was married to Bowen's niece, but he was not a licensed bondsman either.) When Bulow tried to collect on the note, Rosenbaum argued that he was not entitled to be paid because he neither gave value nor acted in good faith.

Issues: Did Bulow give value for the promissory note? Did he act in good faith?

Excerpts from Judge Leonard's Decision: Bulow gave no value to Rosenbaum in exchange for her execution of the note. It is true that Bowen gave something of value to Rosenbaum, and that Bowen then arranged for Bulow to be named the beneficiary of these instruments. However, there is no credible evidence that Bulow gave value to Bowen in exchange for this benefit. To the contrary, the evidence establishes that Bowen simply used Bulow's name to mask his own illegal activity. At most, these facts support the inference that Bulow was the gratuitous beneficiary of Bowen's illegally obtained profit. This inference does not satisfy the "for value" requirement of §3-302.

Nor can Bulow show that he took these instruments in good faith as required by §3-302. Bulow has presented no credible explanation for his acquisition of Rosenbaum's note. He concedes that he gave nothing of value to Rosenbaum in exchange for these documents, and in particular, that he did not give the $7,500 consideration recited in the note. It is also clear that he and Rosenbaum had no acquaintance prior to her execution of these documents. On these facts, it strains credulity to think that Bulow was unaware of the true arrangement between Bowen and Rosenbaum. However, even if Bulow knew nothing of Bowen's unsavory activity, his failure to acquaint himself with the circumstances of this transaction would amount to bad faith. When a perfect stranger makes an unsolicited promise to pay $7,500 and secures this promise with a lien on her house, good

---

[5] Typically, a prisoner will be released if a licensed bail bondsman is willing to post a cash bond equal to 15 percent of bail (in this case $7,500). The prisoner pays the bondsman a fee equal to 10 percent of the bond (here it would be $750). If the prisoner fails to return to prison when ordered by the court, the bondsman must pay the balance owing (that is, $42,500). Naturally, a licensed bondsman will post bail only if he is quite sure the defendant will return as promised. When the defendant does return, the bondsman gets back the bond of $7,500 and keeps the $750 fee as well.

faith and common sense impose a minimal duty of inquiry on the recipient. Bulow's acceptance of these documents without some investigation into their origin precludes a finding that he took them in good faith.

Based on the foregoing, the court holds that the promissory note granted by Maude Lee Knox Rosenbaum to W. F. Bulow [is] void and unenforceable.

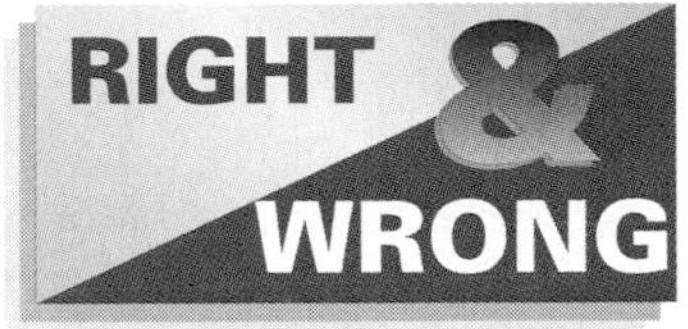

In Chapter 9, we talked about Right v. Right. This case is, in some sense, about Wrong v. Wrong. Harvey Bowen serves as a bondsman, although he is not licensed. Maude Rosenbaum refuses to pay $7,500, although she has signed a promissory note. Why did the court view her act as less wrong than his?

Notice of Outstanding Claims or Other Defects

In certain circumstances, a holder is on notice that an instrument has an outstanding claim or other defect.

1. **The Instrument is Overdue.** An instrument is overdue the day after its due date. At that point, the recipient is on notice that it may have a defect. He ought to wonder why no one has bothered to collect the money owed. However, an instrument is not overdue simply because the interest is unpaid. If, on July 25, Dick buys Harriet's note that was due on July 24, Dick is not a holder in due course because the note is overdue. But if he buys the note on July 23, knowing that Harriet has not paid all the interest owing, he can still be a holder in due course.

   A check is overdue 90 days after its date. Any other *demand* instrument is overdue (1) the day after a request for payment is made or (2) a reasonable time after the instrument was issued. Suppose that Felix tries to sell Tom a demand note from Serena. If Felix happens to mention, "I asked the old lady for the money yesterday, but so far, no luck," then Tom is not a holder in due course because he knows the note is overdue.

2. **The Instrument Is Dishonored.** To dishonor an instrument is to refuse to pay it. If Tom knows that Serena has refused to pay her note, then Tom cannot be a holder in due course. Likewise, once a check has been stamped, "Insufficient Funds" by the bank, it has been dishonored, and no one who obtains it afterward can be a holder in due course.

The holder of this note should realize that there may be a problem.

PROMISSORY NOTE

$500.00 September 5, 1950

On or before 60 days after date, I promise to pay $500 to the order of Soames for value received.

Irene

3. **The Instrument is Altered, Forged, or Incomplete.** Anyone who knows that an instrument has been altered or forged cannot be a holder in due course. Suppose Joe wrote a check to Tony for $200. While showing the check to Liza, Tony cackles to himself and says, "Can you believe what that goof did? Look, he left the line blank after the words 'two hundred.'" Taking his pen out with a flourish, Tony changes the zeroes to nines and adds the words, "ninety-nine." He then indorses the check over to Liza, who is definitely not a holder in due course. However, if, instead of giving the check to Liza, Tony sells it to Kate, she is a holder in due course because she had no idea the check had been altered.

   Likewise, if Joe filled out the check, but failed to sign it, Liza cannot be a holder in due course after she watches Tony fill in Joe's signature. And even if Liza did not see the forgery, she might be on notice if Tony has misspelled Joe's name as "Jo."

   Sometimes people (foolishly) sign blank promissory notes or checks. These makers are liable for any amount subsequently filled in. However, anyone who is aware that a material term was added later is not a holder in due course. Suppose that Joe gives Tony a signed, blank check. If Tony fills in the amount in front of Liza, then naturally she is not a holder in due course. But if Tony fills in the check *before* he gives it to Liza, she is a holder in due course.

4. **The Holder Has Notice of Certain Claims or Disputes.** No one can qualify as a holder in due course if she is on notice that (1) someone else has a claim to the instrument or (2) there is a dispute between the original parties to the instrument. Matt hires Sheila to put aluminum siding on his house. In payment, he gives her a $15,000 promissory note with the due date left blank. They agree that the note will not be due until 60 days after completion of the work. Despite the agreement, Sheila fills in the date immediately and sells the note to Rupert at American Finance Corp., who has bought many similar notes from Sheila. Rupert knows that the note is not supposed to be due until after the work is finished. Usually, before he buys a note from her, he demands a signed document from the homeowner certifying that the work is complete. Also, he lives near Matt and can see that Matt's house is only half finished. Rupert is not a holder in due course because he has reason to suspect there is a dispute between Sheila and Matt.

   Holder in due course status is determined *when the holder receives the instrument*. If, at the very moment when he takes possession, the holder has no notice of outstanding claims or other defects, then he is a holder in due course, no matter what else happens afterward. If Rupert knows nothing of Sheila's sneaky ways when he buys Matt's note, then he is a holder in due course even if Matt calls him 10 minutes later to report that Sheila has violated their contract.

In the following case, Avon thought that American Express should have realized something fishy was going on.

HARTFORD ACCIDENT & INDEMNITY CO. v. AMERICAN EXPRESS, CO.
74 N.Y.2d 153, 542 N.E.2d 1090, 1989 N.Y. LEXIS 881
New York Court of Appeals, 1989

Facts: As manager of the import/export department at Avon Products, Stratford Skalkos had authority to requisition checks up to $25,000 on his signature alone. For nearly three years, Skalkos used that authority to steal $162,538.65 from Avon. Skalkos followed a simple pattern: he altered the names of the payees so that, although they still sounded like company suppliers, the checks could be cashed by businesses to which he owed money personally. He used these checks to pay for personal expenses such as credit card charges, an opera subscription, car maintenance bills, and apartment furnishings. For example, he sent American Express 15 Avon checks that were payable to "Amerex Corp." Similarly, he sent three Avon checks to the Metropolitan Opera Association, Inc., payable to "Metropolitan Opng. Co.," "Metropolitan Opptg. Inc." and "Metropolitan Oprtg. Co." By the movement of one letter, E.J. Audi, Inc. (a furniture store) became "E. Jaudi, Inc."

Avon sued the recipients of the checks, demanding that the funds be returned. The trial court ruled against Avon and granted defendants' motion for summary judgment, concluding that defendants were holders in due course and thus took the checks free of any claims or defenses. The appellate division affirmed. Avon appealed.

Issue: **Were the defendants holders in due course?**

Excerpts from Judge Kaye's Decision: To be a holder in due course a party must take the instrument "without notice that it is overdue or has been dishonored or of any defense against or claim to it on the part of any person." Plaintiff contends that defendants took the checks from Skalkos with notice of Avon's claim—in particular, that they took with notice that Avon had not authorized defendants to apply its funds to Skalkos' personal indebtedness.

[P]laintiff asserts that defendants were on notice of Avon's claims by virtue of UCC §3-304(1)(a): "The purchaser has notice of a claim or defense if …the instrument is so incomplete, bears such visible evidence of forgery or alteration, or is otherwise so irregular as to call into question its validity, terms or ownership or to create an ambiguity as to the party to pay." Plaintiff argues that the misnomers [misspelled names] were so irregular as to call the validity of the checks into question.

[It] will be rare that an instrument will be so irregular as to call into question its validity, terms or ownership. Indeed, as explained in the Official Comment, the irregularity contemplated by §3-304(1)(a) is "notice to the purchaser of something wrong." By any measure, the misnomers—correctly portrayed by [the trial court] as minor errors or misspellings—were not irregularities of such magnitude as to put a holder on notice that something was "wrong."

As [the trial court] observed, the use of corporate checks to pay employees' debts "is an every day occurrence in the business world. Employers often help an employee to maintain a residence as an inducement to continued employment in an area where living expenses are high. Employers often pay for the entertainment of customers by an employee. Employers often pay for travel and transportation expenses of an employee." Defendants themselves in their summary judgment submissions have indicated that they regularly receive payment through corporate accounts for goods or services furnished to individuals.

Parties who take commercial paper for value "'[are] not bound at [their] peril to be upon the alert for circumstances which might possibly excite the suspicions of wary vigilance.'" Thus we conclude as a matter of law that defendants did not have notice of Avon's claim under UCC §3-304.

Finally, the result we reach promotes the policy favoring ready negotiability of commercial paper, assuring that good faith purchasers need not stand as insurers of the honesty of a drawer corporation's employees. And it assigns losses by the relative responsibility of the parties, allocating liability to the party best able to prevent them. As among the eight parties to this dispute Avon—whose misplaced trust or inattention enabled its employee to misappropriate funds, undetected, for several years—was plainly the party best able to prevent the losses and to protect itself by insurance. The losses were therefore properly allocated to Avon, not defendants.

Accordingly, the order of the appellate division dismissing the complaint should be *affirmed*, with costs.

SHELTER RULE

Under the shelter rule, the transferor of an instrument passes on all of his rights. When a holder in due course transfers an instrument, the recipient acquires all the same rights ***even if she is not a holder in due course herself.*** [6]

One Saturday, you and your dad are working in the family grocery store when Mike, an old family friend, comes in. Mike was recently laid off from his job, and since then he has run up a good-sized tab at the store. Although your dad feels sorry for Mike, there is a limit to how much free food he can hand out and still stay in business. After filling up a basket, Mike comes over and shows you both a demand promissory note for $500 from Chuck, Mike's former boss. "I think this ought to cover most of my tab," Mike says with some pride. Mike indorses it over to your dad and everyone is happy—until, that is, your father takes the note to Chuck for payment. Chuck is furious because he had given Mike the note in payment for commissions on sales that, as it turns out, Mike had never actually completed. Mike had simply lied to get the note. Your dad goes pale until you remind him that, as a holder in due course, he is entitled to be paid by Chuck. After all, your dad did not know about the dispute between Mike and Chuck when he accepted the note.

What if, instead of taking the note to Chuck, your dad tries to sell it to Molly? She looks at it and says, "I hear Mike's in some trouble over this note, lied to Chuck or something." Even so, Molly buys it. Since she knows that Chuck has a defense, she is not a holder in due course. Why then would she buy the note? The shelter rule permits Molly to be paid *as if she were* a holder in due course herself. The purpose of this rule is to protect not Molly, but your father. Suppose that everyone in town now knows of Mike's little fraud. It does not do your father much good to be a holder in due course if he cannot transfer the instrument to someone else. A holder in due course can always demand payment himself and so can anyone who buys the instrument from him. That is reassuring news for your father and other holders in due course.

There is one small exception. If a holder in due course transfers the instrument back to a prior holder who was a party to fraud involving the instrument, that prior holder does not acquire the rights of a holder in due course. So, if your father transfers the note back to Mike, then Mike does not acquire the rights of a holder in due course because he was a party to the original fraud.

DEFENSES AGAINST A HOLDER IN DUE COURSE

Negotiable instruments are meant to be a close substitute for money, and, as a general rule, holders expect to be paid. However, an issuer may legitimately refuse to pay an instrument under certain circumstances. Section 3-305 of the UCC lists so-called *real* defenses that an issuer may legitimately use even against a holder in due course. If the holder is not in due course but is simply a plain ordinary holder, the issuer may use both real defenses and *personal* defenses. **Real and personal defenses are valid against an ordinary holder; only real defenses can be used against a holder in due course.**

Real Defenses

The following real defenses are valid against both a holder and a holder in due course:

Forgery. If Sharon forges Jared's name to a promissory note and sells it to Jennifer, Jared does not have to pay Jennifer, even if she is a holder in due course.

---

[6] §3-203(b).

Bankruptcy. If Jared's debts are discharged in a bankruptcy proceeding after he has signed a promissory note, he does not have to pay the note, even to a holder in due course.

Minority. If a minor has the right to void a contract under state law, then he also has the right not to pay a negotiable instrument, even to a holder in due course.

Alteration. If the amount of an instrument is wrongfully changed, the holder in due course can collect only the original (correct) amount. If the instrument was incomplete, the holder in due course can collect the full face amount, even if the instrument was incorrectly filled in. Suppose that Jared gives a $2,000 promissory note to Rose. As soon as he leaves, she whips out her pen and adds a zero to the note. She then takes it to the auto showroom to pay for her new car. If the showroom is a holder in due course, it is entitled to be paid the original amount of the note ($2,000), not the altered amount ($20,000). But, if Jared had accidentally forgotten to fill out the amount of the note, and Rose wrote in $20,000, the showroom could recover the full $20,000. Although the two notes *look* the same, they have a different result. In the case where Rose changed the amount, Jared was not to blame; but he *was* at fault for signing a blank note.

Duress, Mental Incapacity, or Illegality. These are customary contract defenses that you remember well from your study of contracts. They are a defense against a holder in due course if they are severe enough to make the underlying transaction void (not simply voidable) under state law. An instrument is not valid even in the hands of a holder in due course if, for example, Rose holds a gun to Jared's head to force him to sign it; or Jared has been declared mentally incompetent at the time he signs it; or Jared is using the instrument is to pay for something illegal (cocaine, say).

Fraud in the Execution. A holder in due course cannot recover on an instrument that resulted from fraud in the execution, that is, if the issuer has been tricked into signing without knowing what the instrument is and without any reasonable way to find out. Jared cannot read English. Helen, his boss, tells him that he must sign a document required by the company's health insurance plan. In fact, the document is a promissory note, payable to Helen. Jared does not have to pay the note, even to a holder in due course, because of fraud in the execution.

In the following case, a farmer says he is not liable on a note because there was fraud in the execution. You be the judge.

FDIC v. CULVER
640 F. Supp. 725, 1986 U.S. Dist. LEXIS 23201
United States District Court, District of Kansas, 1986

Facts: Gary Culver, a farmer in Missouri, was having financial problems. He agreed that Nasib Ed Kalliel would assume financial control of the farm, while Culver managed the farming operation. Culver would receive both a salary and a share of the profits. After a few months, Culver informed Kalliel that he urgently needed money to stave off foreclosure. One week later, the Rexford State Bank in Rexford, Kansas, wire-transferred $30,000 to Culver's bank in King City, Missouri. Culver thought that Kalliel would be responsible for repaying the money.

About one week later, Jerry Gilbert, who worked for Kalliel, approached Culver and told him that "Rexford State Bank wanted to know where the $30,000 went, for their records." Gilbert presented Culver with a document and asked him to sign it. According to Gilbert, the document was merely a receipt for the $30,000 Culver had received. Culver signed the document without intending to commit himself to its repayment.

The document Culver signed was a pre-printed promissory note form, payable to the Rexford State Bank. It contained no execution date, maturity date, principal amount, or interest rate. Although Culver assumed that the figure $30,000 would eventually be written on the document, some unknown individual filled in $50,000 instead and also filled in all other blanks. Although Culver received only $30,000, the Rexford State Bank had deposited the full $50,000 in an account controlled by Kalliel.

The Federal Deposit Insurance Corporation (FDIC), representing the Rexford State Bank, sued

Culver to enforce the note. Culver acknowledged that the FDIC was a holder in due course, but asserted the defense of fraud, relying on a provision of the UCC stating:

> [A] holder in due course . . . takes the instrument free from . . . (2) all defenses of any party to the instrument with whom the holder has not dealt except . . . (c) such misrepresentation as has induced the party to sign the instrument with neither knowledge nor reasonable opportunity to obtain knowledge of its character or its essential terms.

You Be the Judge: Can Culver use the defense of fraud to avoid paying the $50,000 note?

Argument for the FDIC (representing the Rexford Bank): Under the statute, Culver is liable on the note unless, when he signed it, he had "neither knowledge nor *reasonable opportunity* to obtain knowledge of its character or essential terms." Culver had every opportunity to obtain knowledge of the note—all he had to do was read it before he signed it. That's hardly too much to ask. He knows how to read; he simply could not be bothered to take the effort. It is bad luck for Culver, but he could easily have prevented this misfortune if he had been careful and prudent. The Rexford Bank, on the other hand, is completely without fault.

Culver also alleges he is not responsible because the note was blank when he signed it. But the UCC provides that "when an incomplete instrument has been completed, [a holder in due course] may enforce it as completed." Culver in effect signed a blank check and now he is responsible for whatever amount someone else fills in.

Culver has a valid claim against Gilbert or Kalliel or whoever filled in the note. But neither of those men is before the court today. As between the careless Culver and the innocent Rexford Bank, Culver must pay.

Argument for Culver: The UCC clearly provides that someone who is induced by misrepresentation to sign a note "without knowledge of its character" is not liable on the instrument. Culver had no idea that the "receipt" was really a promissory note. These two types of instruments are totally different in character. Obviously, he would never have signed the document if he had known it was a note, especially since it was blank. All of the important terms on the note were missing: execution date, maturity date, principal amount, and interest rate. He had no way to learn of those terms. He clearly did not know the "character" of the document. This is a classic case of fraud in the execution.

The FDIC says that Culver was negligent. Look, this is Missouri, where people trust each other. Culver was crossing the street one day, preoccupied with his farm, when someone he knows well asked him to sign a receipt. Any reasonable person in Missouri would have done precisely as Culver did. Now the FDIC is trying to collect $50,000 from him, when all he ever received was $30,000. What if the note had been for $50 million, would the FDIC want that too?

Personal Defenses

Personal defenses are valid against a holder, but *not* against a holder in due course. Typically, personal defenses have some connection to the initial transaction in which the instrument was issued.

Breach of Contract. Ross signs a contract to sell a new airplane to Paige in return for a $1 million promissory note. If Paige discovers that the plane is defective and that Ross has breached the contract, she can refuse to pay him because he is a mere holder. If, however, Ross sells the note to Helga, a holder in due course, Paige must pay her.

Lack of Consideration. Ross gives his mother, Gertrude, a $1,000 check for her birthday. Then they have a disagreement over where to spend Thanksgiving, so Ross stops payment on Gertrude's check. Gertrude has no right to the $1,000 because she is a mere holder who did not give value for the check. But if Gertrude has already cashed the check at her bank, Ross must pay the bank because it is a holder in due course. Even though the check was a gift, and therefore lacking in value, the bank is a holder in due course because it has given value for the check, even if Gertrude has not.

Prior Payment. Two years before, Gertrude had loaned Ross money to start his airplane business. When he paid off the note to Gertrude, he forgot to retrieve the original from her. Angry at him over the check, she sells the note to Carla. Of course, Ross would not have to pay Gertrude *again*, but he cannot refuse to pay Carla, who is a holder in due course. The moral is: when you pay off a note, be sure to retrieve it or mark it canceled.

Unauthorized Completion. Ross writes a check to Carla to pay the note. He forgets to fill in the amount of the check, but Carla very helpfully does, for $5,000 more than he actually owes. If she uses that check to pay her debt at the bank, the bank is a holder in due course, and Ross must honor the check. Remember, however, that if the bank knew Carla had filled in the amount, it would not be a holder in due course and could not recover on the check.

Fraud in the Inducement. Suppose that Carla gives Sean a promissory note to buy stock in his company. It turns out that the company is a fraud. Carla would not have to pay Sean (a holder), but, if Sean transfers the note to Peter, a holder in due course, Carla must pay Peter even though the underlying contract was fraudulent. Note that *fraud in the execution* (real defense) has a different result from *fraud in the inducement* (personal defense).

Non-Delivery. The note that Carla issued to Sean was bearer paper. When Oliver steals it and sells it to a holder in due course, Carla must pay the note even though neither she nor Sean had ever delivered it to the holder. Carla would not have to pay Oliver because he is a mere holder and she did not deliver it to him.

The following table lists, for quick reference, real and personal defenses.

Real Defenses	Personal Defenses
Forgery	Breach of contract
Bankruptcy	Lack of consideration
Minority	Prior payment
Alteration	Unauthorized completion
Duress	Fraud in the inducement
Mental incapacity	Non-delivery
Illegality	
Fraud in the execution	

Claims in Recoupment

A **claim in recoupment** is not the same as a defense, but it has a similar impact. It means that the issuer subtracts (i.e. "sets off") any other claims he has against the initial payee from the amount he owes on the instrument. The distinction is subtle, but a *claim in recoupment* means, "I'm not going to pay the full amount of the instrument because she owes me money for something else" whereas a *defense* means, "I owe her less money on the instrument than I promised."

A claim in recoupment is valid against a holder but not against a holder in due course. Carla gives Sean a promissory note to pay for stock that turns out to be fraudulent. Therefore, Carla has a defense against Sean when he requests that she pay her note. Suppose, however, that the stock is perfectly legitimate, but Sean has never paid Carla $18,000 for the used car he bought from her. When Sean presents the note on the stock deal for payment, Carla makes a claim for recoupment and subtracts $18,000 from the amount owing on the note. If, however, Sean had already sold the note to Olaf, a holder in due course, Carla would have to pay the full amount of the note and then sue Sean for the $18,000.

CONSUMER EXCEPTION

In the eighteenth and nineteenth centuries, negotiable instruments often circulated through several hands. The business community treated them as money. The concept of holder in due course was essential because the instruments had little use if they could not be transferred for value. In the modern banking system, however, instruments are much less likely to circulate. Currently, the most common use for negotiable instruments is in consumer transactions. A consumer pays for a refrigerator by giving the store a promissory note. The store promptly sells the note to a finance company. Even if the refrigerator is defective, under Article 3 the consumer must pay full value on the note because the finance company is a holder in due course. Some commentators have argued that the concept of holder in due course no longer serves a useful purpose and that it should be eliminated once and for all (and with it Article 3 of the UCC).

No state has yet taken such a dramatic step. Instead, some states have forbidden sellers from taking any negotiable instruments, other than a check, as payment for consumer goods or services. Other states require promissory notes given by a consumer to carry the words "consumer paper." Notes with this legend are non-negotiable.

Meanwhile, the Federal Trade Commission (FTC) has special rules for consumer sales. A **consumer sale** is one in which a consumer borrows money from a lender to purchase goods and services from a seller who is affiliated with the lender. If Sears loans money to Gerald to buy a big-screen TV at Sears, that is a consumer sale. It is not a consumer sale if Gerald borrows money from his cousin Vinnie to buy the TV from Sears. The FTC requires all promissory notes in consumer sales to contain the following language:

> NOTICE
>
> ANY HOLDER OF THIS CONSUMER CREDIT CONTRACT IS SUBJECT TO ALL CLAIMS AND DEFENSES WHICH THE DEBTOR COULD ASSERT AGAINST THE SELLER OF GOODS OR SERVICES OBTAINED PURSUANT HERETO OR WITH THE PROCEEDS HEREOF. RECOVERY HEREUNDER BY THE DEBTOR SHALL NOT EXCEED AMOUNTS PAID BY THE DEBTOR HEREUNDER.

Under §3-106(d) of the UCC, no one can be a holder in due course of an instrument with this language. If the language is omitted from a consumer note, it is possible to be a holder in due course, but the seller can be punished by a fine of up to $10,000.

Sometime in your life, you may well sign a promissory note for a consumer loan. Before signing, make sure that the note contains this FTC language.

CHAPTER CONCLUSION

Whenever someone acquires commercial paper, the first question he ought to ask is, "How certain is it that I will be paid the face value of this document?" Article 3 of the UCC contains the answer to this question: if a negotiable instrument is negotiated to a holder in due course, then that holder knows he has an unconditional right (subject only to a few real defenses) to be paid the value of the note. In some ways, Article 3 is like a marine drill instructor: rigid, but, as long as you follow the rules, you know exactly where you stand.

CHAPTER REVIEW

1. Commercial paper is a contract to pay money. It can be used either as a substitute for money or as a loan of money.
2. The possessor of a piece of commercial paper has an unconditional right to be paid, as long as:
   - The paper is negotiable
   - It has been negotiated to the possessor
   - The possessor is a holder in due course, and
   - The issuer cannot claim any of the few "real" defenses.
3. The possessor of non-negotiable commercial paper has the same rights—no more, no less—as the person who made the original contract. The possessor of negotiable commercial paper has more rights than the person who made the original contract.
4. To be negotiable, an instrument must:
   - Be in writing
   - Be signed by the maker or drawer
   - Contain an unconditional promise or order to pay
   - State a definite amount of money
   - Be payable on demand or at a definite time, and
   - Be payable to order or to bearer.
5. When the terms in a negotiable instrument contradict each other, three rules apply:
   - Words take precedence over numbers.
   - Handwritten terms prevail over typed and printed terms.
   - Typed terms win over printed terms.
6. To be negotiated, order paper must first be indorsed and then delivered to the transferee. Bearer paper must simply be delivered to the transferee; no indorsement is required.
7. A holder in due course is a holder who has given value for the instrument, in good faith, without notice of outstanding claims or other defects.
8. These real defenses are valid against both a holder and a holder in due course:
   - Forgery
   - Bankruptcy

- Minority
- Alteration
- Duress, mental incapacity, or illegality
- Fraud in the execution

9. These personal defenses are valid against any holder except a holder in due course:
   - Breach of contract
   - Lack of consideration
   - Prior payment
   - Unauthorized completion
   - Fraud in the inducement
   - Non-delivery
10. A claim in recoupment cannot be used against a holder in due course.
11. The Federal Trade Commission requires all promissory notes in consumer sales to contain language preventing any subsequent holder from being a holder in due course.

PRACTICE TEST

1. George Robinson purchased a certificate of deposit from the West Greeley National Bank in Colorado and directed that the proceeds be paid to his stepdaughter, Loretta Wygant, upon his death. One year later, however, he orally requested the bank to change the beneficiary to his new wife, Hope Robinson. Six months later he died. Both the widow and stepdaughter claimed the proceeds of the certificate. The stepdaughter argued that the certificate of deposit was a negotiable instrument and, therefore, required her indorsement to change the beneficiary. Do you agree?

2. **CPA QUESTION** In order to negotiate bearer paper, one must:

(a) Indorse the paper

(b) Indorse and deliver the paper with consideration

(c) Deliver the paper

(d) Deliver and indorse the paper

3. **CPA QUESTION** Bond fraudulently induced Teal to make a note payable to Wilk, to whom Bond was indebted. Bond delivered the note to Wilk. Wilk negotiated the instrument to Monk, who purchased it with knowledge of the fraud and after it was overdue. If Wilk qualifies as a holder in due course, which of the following statements is correct?

(a) Monk has the standing of a holder in due course through Wilk.

(b) Teal can successfully assert the defense of fraud in the inducement against Monk.

(c) Monk personally qualifies as a holder in due course.

(d) Teal can successfully assert the defense of fraud in the inducement against Wilk.

4. Shelby wrote the following check to Dana. When is it payable and for how much?

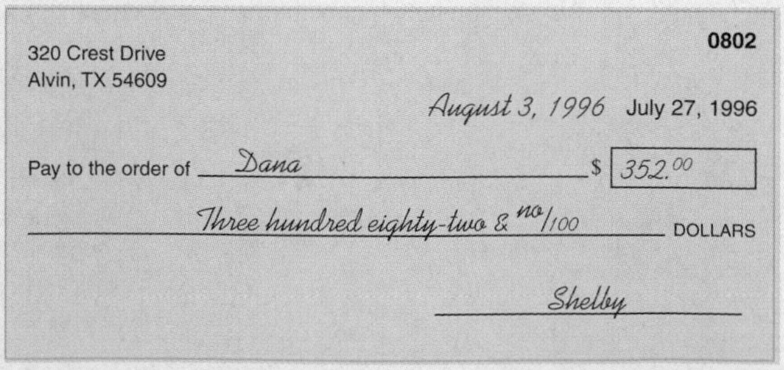

320 Crest Drive
Alvin, TX 54609

0802

August 3, 1996 July 27, 1996

Pay to the order of *Dana* $ *352.00*

Three hundred eighty-two & no/100 DOLLARS

Shelby

5. After Irene Nusor fell behind on her mortgage payments, she answered an advertisement from Best Financial Consultants offering attractive refinancing opportunities. During a meeting at a McDonald's restaurant, a Best representative told her that the com-

pany would arrange for a complete refinancing of her home, pay off two of her creditors, and give her an additional $5,000 in spending money. Nusor would only have to pay Best $4,000. Nusor signed a blank promissory note that was filled in later by Best representatives for $14,986.61 payable in 60 days at an annual interest rate of 18 percent. Within two weeks, Best sold the note to Parkhill for just under $14,000. Best paid $5,997.25 to one of Nusor's creditors but never fulfilled its other promises. Nusor refused to pay the note, alleging that Parkhill was not a holder in due course. Is Nusor liable to Parkhill?

6. On June 30, John N. Willis signed a demand promissory note for $1,620 to the Camelot Country Club in Carrollton, Texas. The note stated that it was being given in payment for a membership in the Country Club, but, in fact, the club was insolvent, its memberships had no value, and Willis was already a member. He was also the club's golf pro. Willis signed the note at the request of the club's manager to enable the club to borrow money from the Commonwealth National Bank to meet its payroll. The Bank of Dallas purchased the note on July 14 and immediately made demand. Willis alleged the note was overdue and therefore the bank could not be a holder in due course. Do you agree?

7. Sam Kay signed a promissory note for $220,000 that was payable to Investments, S.A., Inc., a company of which he was the principal stockholder. The company then indorsed the note over to its lawyers, Arthur B. Cunningham and Philip T. Weinstein, to pay past and future legal fees. Kay claimed the company owed $3,557.53 in fees; the lawyers testified they had performed "more than $20,000" worth of work on the date they received the note. Were the lawyers holders in due course?

8. YOU BE THE JUDGE WRITING PROBLEM A columnist for the *Arizona Republic/Phoenix Gazette* received the following problem from a reader. How would you answer it?

> A check cashing company was suing a local businessman. The check cashing company said they accepted a check this businessman had given an ex-employee and later found out he had stopped payment. "We cannot locate the ex-employee so we opted to sue the issuing company," they said. The businessman said that he found out after he had given this ex-employee a check that he had made a mistake. He had the bank issue a stop payment. "I have a right to tell our bank not to pay a check. The check is null and void," the businessman said. "It is a worthless piece of paper. Go after the person who gave you the check." The check company argued that a check is a negotiable instrument. Placed in interstate commerce, the check is a promise to pay the holder in due course. The stop payment only stopped the bank from paying the check. The company that issued the check placed it in interstate commerce and is legally bound to pay the face amount of the check, the check company argued. "We are the holder and have a right to be paid." Who is right?[7]

9. How would you advise this troubled newspaper reader?

> *Q:* I have paid off a loan and have a receipt from the lender for payment, but the lender will not give me the original promissory note. Do I need the original promissory note?

10. Gina and Douglas Felde purchased a Dodge Daytona with a 70,000-mile warranty. They signed a loan contract with the dealer to pay for the car in 48 monthly installments of $250. The dealer sold the contract to the Chrysler Credit Corp. Soon, the Feldes complained that the car had developed a tendency to accelerate abruptly and without warning. Neither of two Dodge dealers was able to correct the problem. The Feldes filed suit against Chrysler Credit Corp., but the company refused to rescind the loan contract. The company argued that, as a holder in due course on the note, it was entitled to be paid regardless of any defects in the car. How would you decide this case if you were the judge?

11. RIGHT & WRONG S. J. Littlegreen owned the Lookout Mountain Hotel. In financial trouble, he put the hotel on the market at a price of $850,000. C. Abbott Gardner was his real estate agent. To obtain more time to sell, Littlegreen decided to refinance his debt. Mr. Rupe agreed to lend Littlegreen $300,000. When this loan was ready for closing, Gardner informed Littlegreen that he expected a commission of 5 percent of the amount of the loan, or $15,000. Gardner threatened to block the loan if his demands were not met.

---

[7] Quentin V. Tolby, "Stopping Payment Not Always Enough," *Arizona Republic/Phoenix Gazette*, July 5, 1995, p. 3. Reprinted with permission of the author.

Littlegreen needed the proceeds of the loan badly, so he agreed to give Gardner $4,000 in cash and a promissory note for $11,000. On what grounds might Littlegreen claim that the note is invalid? Would this be a valid defense? Even if Gardner was in the right legally, was he in the right ethically? Would he like everyone in town to know that he had squeezed Littlegreen in this way? How would he have felt if he had been in Littlegreen's position? Does might make right?

12. Catherine Wagner suffered serious physical injuries in an automobile accident and became acutely depressed as a result. One morning, she received a check for $17,400 in settlement of her claims arising out of the accident. She indorsed the check and placed it on the kitchen table. She then called Robert Scherer, her long-time roommate, to tell him the check had arrived. That afternoon, she jumped from the roof of her apartment building, killing herself. The police found the check and a note from her, stating that she was giving it to Scherer. Had Wagner negotiated the check to Scherer?

INTERNET RESEARCH PROBLEM

Go to **http://www.legaldocs.com** and fill in the blanks of a promissory note. Who is the maker, and who is the payee of your note? Did you create a demand note?

You can find further practice problems in the Online Quiz at http://beatty.westbuslaw.com or in the Study Guide that accompanies this text.

CHAPTER 24

LIABILITY FOR NEGOTIABLE INSTRUMENTS

Willie groaned under his breath. How had he ever gotten into this mess? Producing a rock video for the Hot Tamales had seemed a golden opportunity. He loved the music, and he didn't even mind living in a trailer on location, but the business end was driving him to despair. That morning, he had glanced out his trailer window and seen Vidalia slinking across the set. How could he have been so stupid as to let her finance the video? "Willie, darling," she had purred, as a circle of smoke from her cigarette caught in his throat, "I know that your promissory note for $50,000 isn't due 'til next month, but I simply do *not* like the music in this video, and I *cannot* support what I do not like. It would be so bad for my karma. But, take your time, dearest one, my driver will be back this afternoon to collect what you owe me."

Sitting in his trailer holding his head in his hands, Willie heard a timid knock. Opening the door, he saw a teenage girl smiling at him. "Hi, Mister Willie," she beamed. "I'm Vera Brown. My mom sent me over to collect the rent check for the trailer. And could I please, please have your autograph? Your work is so awesome."

Willie smiled. "Sure, kiddo, here's my autograph and here's the rent check."

Seeing a helpful, enthusiastic kid like Vera helped brighten an otherwise dark day. But his

spirits took a blow later that afternoon when the landlady came by for her check and Willie discovered she had no daughter. He immediately called his bank to stop payment on the check, only to discover that his balance was zero dollars and zero cents. Vera had used her computer to create a second check drawn on Willie's account. She had then forged his signature and cashed both checks before skipping town.

To understand the full impact of the day's catastrophes, Willie needs a crash course on liability for negotiable instruments:

- *The Promissory Note to Vidalia*. When Willie gave a promissory note in payment for the debt, the debt was *suspended* until the note comes due. *Verdict:* Vidalia cannot collect her money until next month when the note is due.
- *The Rent Check to the Landlady*. Vera was not Mrs. Brown's lovely daughter; she was an impostor. Banks are not liable on checks that the issuer voluntarily gives to an impostor.[1] *Verdict:* The bank will not reimburse Willie for the rent check. Of course, Willie must still pay the landlady.
- *The Check That Vera Forged*. A bank is liable if it pays a check on which the issuer's name is forged. *Verdict:* The bank must reimburse Willie for the second check.

INTRODUCTION

In Chapter 23, you learned that the issuer of a negotiable instrument is liable to a holder in due course, unless the issuer can assert one of a limited number of real defenses. Against a mere holder, an issuer can assert both personal and real defenses. The life of a negotiable instrument, however, is more complicated than these simple statements indicate. Not everyone who signs a negotiable instrument is an issuer, and not everyone who presents an instrument for payment is a holder in due course or even a holder. This chapter focuses on the liability of these extra players: non-issuers who sign an instrument and non-holders who receive payment. The liability of someone who has signed an instrument is called **signature liability**. The liability of someone who receives payment is called **warranty liability**.

WARNING: The material in this chapter is complex. Please do not proceed further unless you understand the prior paragraph.

THE CONTRACT VERSUS THE INSTRUMENT

People generally do not hand out promissory notes or checks to strangers. Negotiable instruments are issued to fulfill a contract. The instruments create a *second* contract to pay the debt created by the *first* agreement. When Beverly agrees to buy a house from John, that is Contract No. 1. When she gives him a promissory note in payment, that is Contract No. 2. When Jodie buys lunch with a Visa card, her promise to repay Visa by check at the end of the month is Contract No. 1. The check she mails to Visa is Contract No. 2.

Once an instrument has been accepted in payment for a debt, the debt is *suspended* until the instrument is paid or dishonored. When Beverly buys a house

[1] You remember from Chapter 23 that *issuer* means the *drawer* of a check or the *maker* of a note.

from John, she pays with a promissory note that is not due for five years. Until she defaults on the note, he cannot sue her for payment even if, after a year, he decides he wants all the money right away. When Visa receives Jodie's check, her debt is suspended until the company tries to cash the check. If the check is returned for insufficient funds, the obligation is revived and Visa can pursue Jodie until she pays it for real.

ENFORCING AN INSTRUMENT

The signature liability rules determine who is liable on an instrument. But *to whom* are they liable? Who has the right to demand payment? Uniform Commercial Code (UCC) §3-301 provides this list:

- A holder of the instrument
- Anyone to whom the **shelter rule** applies (that is, any non-holder with the rights of a holder; review the shelter rule discussion in Chapter 23 if this explanation makes no sense to you)
- A holder who has lost the instrument[2]

Recall that a holder is someone in possession of an instrument that has been validly negotiated.[3] Keep in mind, however, that the real and personal defenses discussed in Chapter 23 can be used against a holder. Therefore, in practice, the answer to the question "Who has the right to demand payment on an instrument?" is "A holder against whom no defenses can be used." Exhibit 24.1 illustrates this concept.

PRIMARY VERSUS SECONDARY LIABILITY

A number of different people may be liable on the same negotiable instrument, but some are *primarily* liable, others are only *secondarily* liable. Someone with **primary liability** is unconditionally liable—he must pay unless he has a valid defense. Those with **secondary liability** only pay if the person with primary liability does not. The holder of an instrument must first ask for payment from those

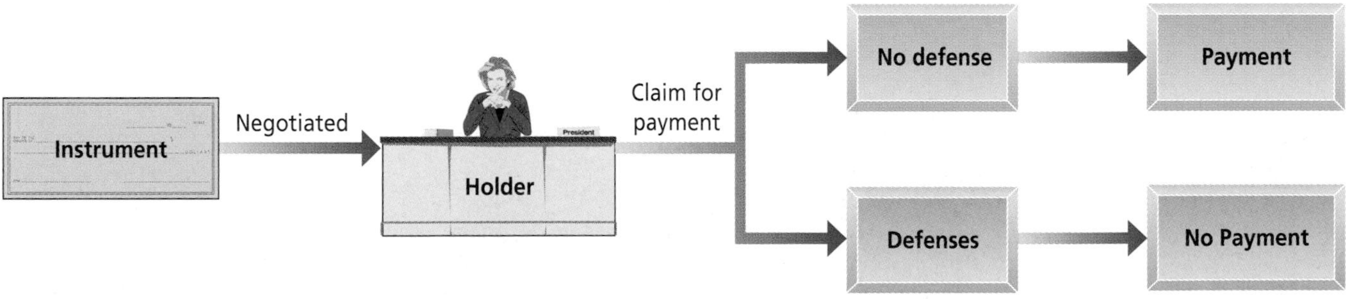

Exhibit 24.1

[2] Although technically some non-holders (such as a holder who has lost the instrument) can demand payment, in this chapter we use "holder" as shorthand to include anyone entitled to enforce an instrument.

[3] Negotiation is discussed in Chapter 23.

who are primarily liable before making demand against anyone who is only secondarily liable.

THE PAYMENT PROCESS

The payment process comprises as many as three steps:

- **Presentment**. Presentment means that the holder of the instrument demands payment from someone who is obligated to pay it (such as the maker or drawee).[4] To present, the holder must (1) exhibit the instrument, (2) show identification, and (3) surrender the instrument (if paid in full) or give a receipt (if only partially paid).
- **Dishonor**. The instrument is due, but the maker (of a note) or the drawee (of a draft) refuses to pay.[5]
- **Notice of Dishonor**. The holder of the instrument notifies those who are secondarily liable that the instrument has been dishonored.[6] This notice can be given by any reasonable means, including oral, written, or electronic communication. It must, however, be given within 30 days of the dishonor (except in the case of banks, which must give notice by midnight of the next banking day). The notice must simply identify the instrument and indicate that it has been dishonored. Anyone who has ever bounced a check has received a notice of dishonor—a check stamped, "Insufficient Funds."

SIGNATURE LIABILITY

Virtually everyone who signs an instrument is potentially liable for it, but the liability depends upon the capacity in which it was signed. The maker of a note, for example, has different liability from an indorser. Capacity can sometimes be difficult to determine if the signature is not labeled—"maker," "indorser," "guarantor," "acceptor," etc. (All of these terms will be defined below.) In the absence of a

This check has been dishonored.

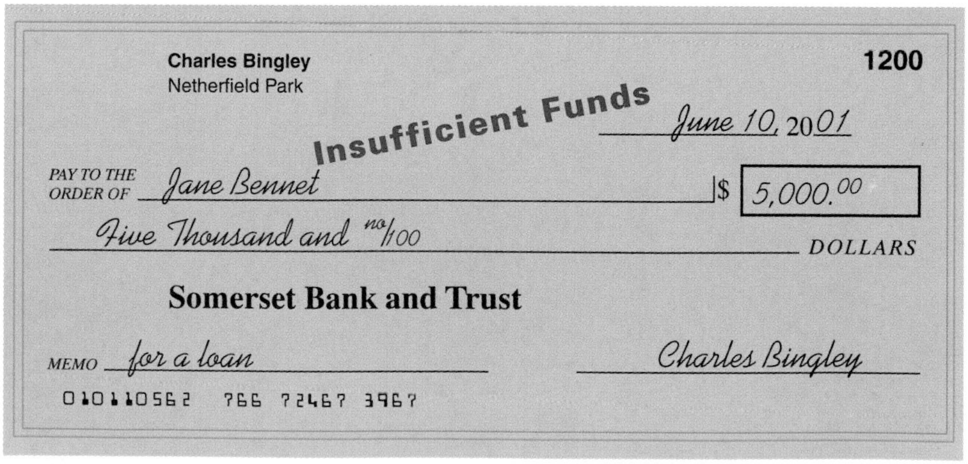

Charles Bingley
Netherfield Park
1200
Insufficient Funds
June 10, 2001
PAY TO THE ORDER OF Jane Bennet $ 5,000.00
Five Thousand and no/100 DOLLARS
Somerset Bank and Trust
MEMO for a loan
Charles Bingley
010110562 766 72467 3967

---

4 UCC §3-501.

5 UCC §3-502.

6 UCC §3-503.

label, courts generally look at the location of the signature. Someone who signs a check or a note in the lower right-hand corner is presumed to be an issuer. If a drawee bank signs on the face of a check, it is an acceptor. Someone who signs on the back of an instrument is considered to be an indorser.

MAKER

As you remember from Chapter 23, the issuer of a note is called the **maker**. **The maker is *primarily* liable.**[7] He has promised to pay, and pay he must, unless he has a valid defense.[8] If two makers sign a note, they are both **jointly and severally** liable. The holder can demand full payment from either or partial payment from both. Suppose that Shane offers to buy Marilyn's bookstore in return for a $20,000 promissory note. Because Shane has no assets, Marilyn insists that his supplier, Alexis, also sign the note as co-maker. Once Alexis signs the note, Marilyn has the right to demand full payment from either her or Shane. Of course, if Alexis pays the note, she can demand that Shane reimburse her. If Shane refuses, it is Alexis's problem, not Marilyn's.

DRAWER

A check is the most common form of a draft—it is an order telling a bank to pay money. Throughout this chapter, we will use checks as an example because they are the most familiar form of draft, but these same rules apply to all drafts. The **drawer** is the person who writes the check.

The drawer of a check has *secondary* liability. He is not liable until he has received notice that the bank has dishonored the check.[9] Although the bank pays the check with the drawer's funds, the drawer is secondarily liable in the sense that he does not have to write a new check or give cash to the holder unless the bank dishonors the original check. Suppose that Shane writes a $10,000 check to pay Casey for new inventory. Casey is nervous and, before he can get to the bank to deposit the check, he calls Shane seven times to ask whether the check is good. He even asks Shane for payment in cash instead of by check. Shane finally snarls

Molly Megabucks is only secondarily liable, but no one is primarily liable until the bank accepts the check.

Molly Megabucks
New York, N.Y.

0912

August 27, 2001

PAY TO THE ORDER OF John Penny $ 15,000.00

Fifteen Thousand and no/100 DOLLARS

TSN Savings Bank

MEMO real estate

Molly Megabucks

010110562 766 72467 3967

---

[7] UCC §3-412.

[8] For example, if the maker goes bankrupt, he does not have to pay the note because bankruptcy is a defense even against a holder in due course.

[9] UCC §3-414.

at Casey, "Just go cash the check and get off my back, will you?" At this point, Casey has no recourse against Shane because Shane is only secondarily liable.

Sadly, however, Casey's fears are realized. When he presents the check to the bank teller, she informs him that Shane's account is overdrawn. Casey snatches the check off the counter and hurries over to Shane's shop. It makes no difference that Casey forgot to let the teller stamp "Insufficient Funds" on the check—notice of dishonor can be made orally. Once the bank has refused to pay, the check has been dishonored. Casey has informed Shane, who must now pay the $10,000.

DRAWEE

The **drawee** is the bank on which a check is drawn. Since the draw*er* of a check is only secondarily liable, logically you might expect the drawee bank to be primarily liable. That is not the case, however. When a drawer signs a check, the instrument enters a kind of limbo. **The bank is not liable to the holder and owes no damages to the holder for refusing to pay the check.**[10] The bank may be liable to the drawer for violating their checking account agreement, but this contract does not extend to the holder of the check.

When a holder presents a check, the bank can do one of the following:

- Pay the check. In this case, the holder has no complaints.
- Dishonor the check. In this case, the holder must pursue remedies against the drawer.

What if Casey is afraid to take a check from Shane? After all, even if Shane has enough money in his account at the moment, it may be gone by the time Casey deposits the check and his bank presents it for payment. To protect himself, Casey can insist that Shane give him a certified check. A **certified** or **accepted** check is one that the drawee bank has signed. This signature is a promise that the bank will pay the check out of its own funds. The bank then becomes *primarily* liable, and Casey is sure to be paid as long as the bank stays solvent. To protect itself once it certifies the check, Shane's bank will immediately remove that money from his account. The cost of certifying a check is typically about $10.

In the following case, a bank refused to pay three checks even though the drawer had sufficient funds in his account. Should the bank be liable to the holder of these checks?

FOUR CIRCLE CO-OP v. KANSAS STATE BANK & TRUST
771 F. Supp. 1144, 1991 U.S. Dist. LEXIS 10648
United States District Court, District of Kansas, 1991

Facts: John Fleming was a grain dealer who maintained a checking account at Kansas State Bank and Trust Co. (KSBT). He also borrowed money from KSBT. On July 25, Fleming informed the bank that he had lost over $1 million speculating in the commodity futures market and would be unable to pay his loan. On July 26, KSBT seized the funds in Fleming's checking account to pay part of his debt to the bank. The plaintiffs are farmers who sold grain to Fleming before July 25. He had issued checks to them at a time when he had sufficient funds in his account to cover the checks. By the time these checks were presented for payment, however, his account no longer had funds to pay the checks because the bank had seized all his money. Accordingly, the checks were dishonored. In their suit, plaintiffs allege that KSBT wrongfully dishonored the checks.

---

[10] UCC §3-408.

Issue: Does a bank have an obligation to honor a check if the account has sufficient funds?

Excerpts from Judge Crow's Decision: [The plaintiffs'] argument simply ignores K.S.A. 84-3-409, which provides in pertinent part:

> (1) A check or other draft does not of itself operate as an assignment of any funds in the hands of the drawee available for its payment, and the drawee is not liable on the instrument until he accepts it.

[I]f a seller sells goods to a buyer and the buyer's bank dishonors the buyer's check payable to the seller in spite of sufficient funds and the absence of a stop order, the seller has no direct recourse against the buyer's bank. The best that the seller can do is to move against the buyer on the check or on the underlying obligation; the buyer can then move against his bank for wrongfully dishonoring an item that was "properly payable."

In short, this section continues prior law in recognizing not one ounce of privity between the holder of a check and the drawee bank. Nor can the holder sue the drawee bank for wrongful dishonor of an insolvent depositor's check just because the bank dishonored the item in order to protect its own interests. In such a case, the holder's recourse is against the drawer and any indorsers. The position urged by the plaintiffs is simply irreconcilable with the law of Kansas.

KSBT's motion for summary judgment is granted.

INDORSER

An **indorser** is anyone, other than an issuer or acceptor, who signs an instrument. Shane gives Hannah a check to pay her for installing new shelves in his bookstore. On the back of Shane's check, Hannah writes, "Pay to Christian," signs her name, and then gives the check to Christian in payment for back rent. Underneath Hannah's name, Christian signs his own name and gives the check to Trustie Car Lot as a deposit on his new Volkswagen bug. Hannah and Christian are both indorsers. This is the chain of ownership:

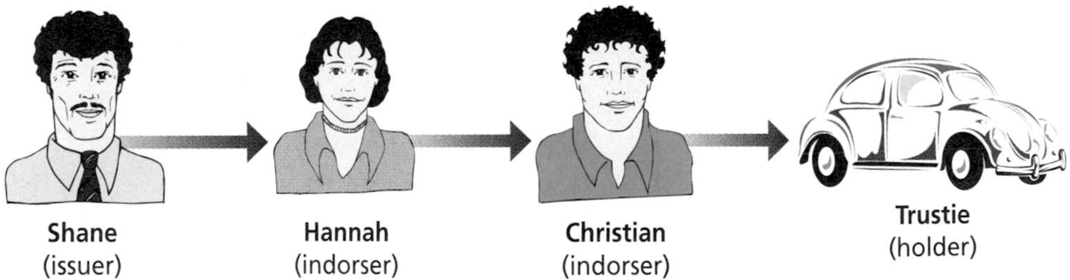

Indorsers are *secondarily* liable; they must pay if the issuer or drawee does not. But indorsers are only liable to those who come *after* them in the chain of ownership, not to those who held the instrument beforehand.[11] If Shane refuses to pay Trustie, the auto dealership can demand payment from Christian or Hannah. If Christian pays Trustie, Christian can then demand payment from Hannah. If, however, Hannah pays Trustie, she has no right to go after Christian because he is not liable to a previous indorser.

[11] UCC §3-415.

There are some exceptions to this rule. **Indorsers are not liable if (1) they write the words "without recourse" next to their signature on the instrument, (2) a bank certifies the check, (3) the check is presented for payment more than 30 days after the indorsement, or (4) the check is dishonored and the indorser is not notified within 30 days.** Christian has doubts about the creditworthiness of Hannah and Shane, so he writes the words "without recourse" when he indorses the check to Trustie. This sounds like a good idea and perhaps every indorser should try it. However, if the manager of Trustie Car Lot is familiar with the UCC, he will not accept an instrument that has been indorsed without recourse because he wants to make sure that Christian is also liable, not just Shane and Hannah. After all, Christian is the person he knows.

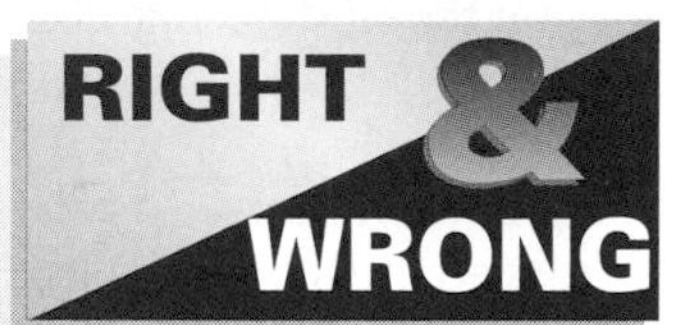

Christian can limit his liability as an indorser by signing "without recourse." Most people, not having had the benefit of a business law class, would not know the significance of these words. Is it ethical for Christian to indorse the check without recourse, thereby shifting the risk of Shane or Hannah's default onto the trusting Trustie?

ACCOMMODATION PARTY

An **accommodation party** is someone—other than an issuer, acceptor, or indorser—who adds her signature to an instrument for the purpose of being liable on it.[12] The accommodation party typically receives no direct benefit from the instrument but is acting for the benefit of the **accommodated party**. Shane wants to buy a truck from the Trustie Car Lot. Trustie, however, will not accept a promissory note from Shane unless his father, Walter, also signs it. Shane has no assets, but Walter is wealthy. When Walter signs, he becomes an accommodation party to Shane, who is the accommodated party. The accommodation party can sign for an issuer, acceptor, or indorser. Anyone who signs an instrument is deemed to be an accommodation party unless it is clear that he is an issuer, acceptor, or indorser.

An accommodation party has the same liability to the holder as the person for whom she signed. The holder can make a claim directly against the accommodation party without first demanding payment from the accommodated party. Walter is liable to Trustie, whether or not Trustie first demands payment from Shane. If forced to pay Trustie, Walter can try to recover from Shane.

An accommodation party sounds like what non-lawyers would call a "guarantor," but under the UCC these terms sometimes have a different meaning. Someone who writes, "I guarantee this *instrument*," is an accommodation party. But someone who writes, "I guarantee *collection*," is not liable until the accommodated party fails to pay. If Walter had written "to guarantee collection" before signing his name, Trustie could not have collected from him until Shane refused to pay the note.

In an earlier example, Shane's supplier, Alexis, had signed a note as co-maker. What is the difference between a co-maker and an accommodation party? The co-maker is liable both to the holder and to the other co-maker. The accommodation party is liable only to the holder, not to the other maker. If Shane pays the note on which Alexis is co-maker, then Alexis is liable to him for half the payment. But if

---

[12] UCC §3-419.

Shane pays the note on which Walter is the accommodation party, Walter has no liability to Shane.

People sign for the debts of their friends and relatives with such abandon that one can only assume they do not fully understand the situation. As the saying goes, nothing is more dangerous than a fool with a pen. Certainly, Yeung Sau-lin hurt herself with her pen. The 53-year-old mother of four was jailed for two years when her decision to guarantee a friend's $300,000 loan went horribly wrong. The friend defaulted and disappeared, leaving Yeung to face loan sharks who pressured her into taking part in a bad check scheme. Yeung pleaded guilty to charges that she had written $4.1 million in bad checks.[13]

Because of cases like this, the Federal Trade Commission now requires consumer debts to carry the following notice for guarantors:

> **Notice to Co-Signer**
> You are being asked to guarantee this debt. Think carefully before you do. If the borrower doesn't pay the debt, you will have to. Be sure you can afford to pay if you have to, and that you want to accept this responsibility. You may have to pay up to the full amount of the debt if the borrower does not pay. . . . The creditor can collect this debt from you without first trying to collect from the borrower . . .[14]

In the following case, an accommodation party argued that she was not liable because she did not receive the proceeds from the loan. Was she correct in her interpretation of the UCC?

IN RE **COUCHOT**
169 B.R. 40, 1994 Bankr. LEXIS 899
United States Bankruptcy Court, Southern District of Ohio, 1994

Facts: Kathy J. Couchot and her mother-in-law, Jean Couchot, borrowed $6,317.48 from Star Bank to pay the funeral expenses of Kathy's husband. Jean executed a note to the bank, and Kathy signed as an accommodation party. To disburse the proceeds of the loan, Star Bank issued a check payable to "Kathy *and* Jean Couchot." Somehow this check was altered to read "Kathy *or* Jean Couchot." Jean cashed the check and used the loan proceeds to pay her son's funeral expenses and some of Kathy's back taxes and insurance premiums. Jean did not repay the loan to the bank; Kathy made six payments before defaulting.

Issues: Is an accommodation party liable for the full amount of a note when she received only a small portion of the proceeds? Is an accommodation party liable even though the check was altered?

Excerpts from Judge Clark's Decision: [Kathy Couchot]'s contention that she is only liable to Star Bank for the consideration she directly received from the loan is incorrect and misconstrues the nature of an accommodation party. It is basic hornbook law that consideration does not have to be received by an accommodation party to support her obligation. Time and again sureties respond to a holder's suit by arguing, "I am a surety and I did not receive consideration for my contract." This is a losing argument. Regardless whether the surety signs gratuitously or receives compensation, his obligation is supported by the consideration which moves from the creditor to the principal debtor.

---

13 "Loan Decision Leads to Prison," *South China Morning Post*, Aug. 6, 1994, p. 5.

14 F.T.C. Trade Regulation Rule Concerning Credit Practices, 16 C.F.R. 444.3.

Also unavailing is [Kathy Couchot]'s argument that the check issued by Star Bank relieves her from the terms of the [note]. [Kathy Couchot] relies on U.C.C. 3-407 which provides that: "(A) Any alteration of an instrument is material which changes the contract of any party thereto in any respect. . . ." While it is clear that the check was materially altered, there is absolutely no evidence that the check was fraudulently altered. [Kathy Couchot]'s own testimony established that the loan proceeds were used precisely as envisioned by the parties. In any event, finding no fraud in this case, it is unnecessary to further examine the effects of the altered check. The court finds that [Kathy Couchot] cosigned the promissory note to Star Bank, . . . and that the loan proceeds were used as anticipated by [her].

[Kathy Couchot was ordered to pay the note.]

AGENT

Many business transactions are conducted by agents acting on behalf of a principal. A corporation, for example, cannot sign an instrument itself; all of its transactions must be conducted by company employees. When signing for a principal, the agent must be careful to ensure that only the principal is liable.

To avoid personal liability when signing an instrument, an agent must (1) indicate that she is signing as an agent and (2) give the name of the principal.[15] An agent who fails to follow these two simple steps will be *personally* liable on the instrument to any holder in due course who did not know that the agent was acting for someone else. The agent will not be liable to holders who are not in due course if she can prove that the original parties did not intend for her to be liable. An agent who signs her name, "Harley Calhoun, as agent for Slippery Corp." is safe; she is not liable on the instrument. But if Harley simply signs the note, "Harley Calhoun, Agent," then she will be personally liable to Ralph, a holder in due course, unless she can prove that Ralph knew she was acting for someone else when he acquired the note. (That is a great deal of trouble easily avoided by simply including the name of the principal.) Even if Ralph is not a holder in due course, Harley will be liable unless she can prove that the original parties never intended her to be.

The principal is liable if the agent signs correctly, the agent signs just her own name, or the agent signs only the name of the principal. Thus, if Harley signs the note, "Harley Calhoun" *or* "Slippery Corp.," the corporation is liable to Ralph (and so is Harley). He can sue either. If Ralph recovers from Harley, she can try to recover from Slippery; but if the company goes out of business, Harley will find herself in a sticky situation. Exhibit 24.2 illustrates the liability of agents and principals.

This rule establishing an agent's liability on negotiable instruments is, in some ways, the perfect kind of law: it is a simple, straightforward guideline that guarantees protection to those who follow it. Never sign an instrument (or any contract for that matter) as an agent without giving the name of the principal and indicating that you are an agent.

Checks are an exception to this general rule on agent liability. If an agent is authorized to sign a check on the principal's bank account, the agent is not personally liable even if she forgets to indicate that she is simply an agent. Because the check is probably printed with the principal's name anyway, no one is likely to think that the check is coming out of the agent's personal funds.

15 UCC §3-402.

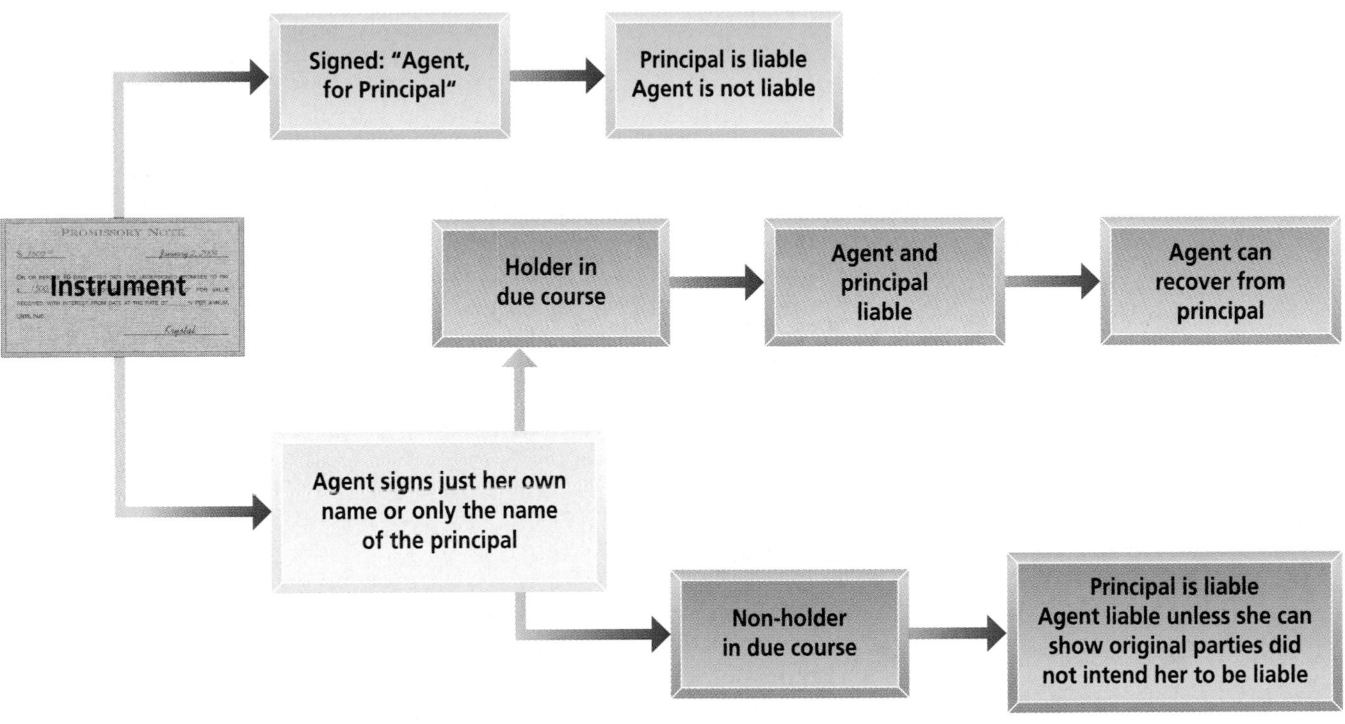

Exhibit 24.2

WARRANTY LIABILITY

Warranty liability rules apply when someone receives payment on an instrument that is invalid because it has been forged, altered, or stolen.

BASIC RULES OF WARRANTY LIABILITY

1. **The culprit is always liable.** If a forger signs someone else's name to an instrument, that signature counts as the *forger's*, not as that of the person whose name she signed. The forger is liable for the value of the instrument plus any other expenses or lost interest that subsequent parties may experience because of the forgery. If Hope signs David's name on one of his checks, Hope is liable, but not David. Although this is a sensible rule, the problem is that forgers are difficult to catch and, even when found, often do not have the money to pay what they owe.

2. **The drawee bank is liable if it pays a check on which the *drawer's* name is forged. The bank can recover from the payee only if the payee had reason to suspect the forgery.**[16] If a bank cashes David's forged check, it must reimburse him whether or not it ever recovers from Hope. Suppose that Hope forged the check to pay for a new tattoo. If Gus, the owner of the tattoo parlor, deposits the check and the bank pays it, the bank cannot recover from Gus unless he had reason to suspect the forgery. Perhaps Gus did suspect because the mystery customer asked to have "Hope" tattooed on her biceps, not "David." She did not look much like a "David" either.

[16] UCC §3-418.

Why hold the bank liable for something that is not its fault? In theory, the bank has David's signature on file and can determine that Hope's version does not match. As the saying goes, the drawee must know the drawer's signature as a mother knows her own child. Such a rule may have been appropriate in an era when people went to their neighborhood bank to cash checks and a teller would indeed recognize dear Miss Plotkin's signature. In this day and age, most checks—especially those for small amounts—are handled by machine, so perhaps this rule makes less sense. Nonetheless, the rule stands, for good reason or bad. Banks have two choices: (1) examine the signature on each presented check or (2) purchase forgery insurance.

3. **In any other case of wrongdoing, a person who first acquires an instrument from a culprit is ultimately liable to anyone else who pays value for it.** This rule is based on the provisions in Article 3 of the UCC that establish transfer and presentment warranties.

TRANSFER WARRANTIES

When someone transfers an instrument, she warrants that:

- She is a holder of the instrument
- All signatures are authentic and authorized
- The instrument has not been altered
- No defense can be asserted against her, and
- As far as she knows the issuer is solvent.[17]

When someone transfers an instrument, she promises that it is valid. The culprit—the person who created the defective instrument in the first place— is always liable, but if he does not pay what he owes, the person who took it from him is liable in his place. She may not be that much at fault, but she is more at fault than any of the other innocent people who paid good value for the instrument.

Suppose that Annie writes a check for $100 to pay for a fancy dinner at Barbara's Bistro. Cecelia steals the check from Barbara's cash register, indorses Barbara's name, and uses the check to buy a leather jacket from Deirdre. In her turn, Deirdre takes the check home and indorses it over to her condominium association to pay her monthly service fee. Barbara notices the check is gone and asks Annie to stop payment on it. Once payment is stopped, the condominium association cannot cash the check. Who is liable to whom? The chain of ownership looks like this:

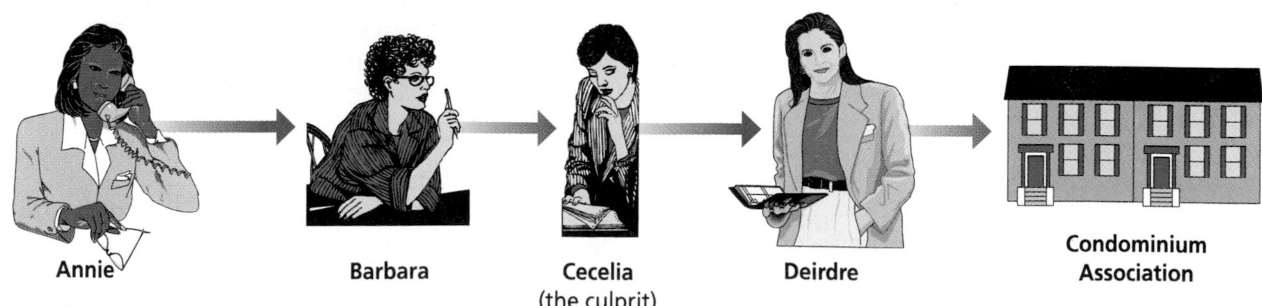

[17] UCC §3-416.

Cecelia is the culprit and, of course, she is liable. Unfortunately, she is currently studying at the University of the Azores and refuses to return to the United States. The condominium association makes a claim against Deirdre. When she transferred the check, she warranted that all the signatures were authentic and authorized, but that was not true because Barbara's signature was forged. (Deirdre should have asked Cecelia for identification.) Deirdre cannot make a claim against Annie or Barbara because neither of them violated their transfer warranties—they were both holders, and all the signatures at that point were authentic and authorized.

There are a few additional wrinkles to the transfer warranty rules:

- When someone violates the transfer warranties, she is liable for the value of the instrument, plus expenses and interest. If the condominium association is charged a fee by the bank for the returned check, Deirdre must pay it.
- Transfer warranties flow to all subsequent holders in good faith who have indorsed the instrument. If the condominium association indorses the check over to its maintenance company, Deirdre is liable to the condo association when the maintenance company makes a claim against it.
- If the instrument is *bearer* paper, the transfer warranties extend only to the first transferee. If Annie had made her check out to cash, it would have been bearer paper, and her transfer warranties would have extended only to Barbara. However, if Barbara transfers the check to Claudia, Barbara's transfer warranties extend to Claudia; Annie's do not.
- If a warranty claim is not made within 30 days of discovering the breach, damages are reduced by the amount of harm that the delay caused. Suppose that the condominium association waits two months to tell Deirdre the check is invalid. Cecelia has been into Deirdre's store several times to try on matching leather pants. By the time Deirdre finds out the check is bad, Cecelia has again left town. Deirdre may not be liable on the check at all because the delay has prevented her from making a claim against Cecelia.
- Transfer warranties apply only if the instrument has been transferred for consideration. Suppose Deirdre gives the check to an employee, Emily, as a birthday present. When the check turns out to be worthless, Emily has no claim against Deirdre.

COMPARISON OF SIGNATURE LIABILITY AND TRANSFER WARRANTIES

Transfer warranties fill in holes left by the signature liability rules:

- A forged signature is invalid and therefore creates no signature liability on the part of the person whose name was signed. However, someone who receives a forged instrument may recover under transfer warranty rules, which provide that anyone who transfers a forged instrument is liable for it.
- The signature liability rules do not apply to the transfer of bearer paper. Bearer paper can be negotiated simply by delivery; no indorsement is required. No signature means no signature liability (for anyone other than the issuer—who is the only person actually signing the instrument). Transfer warranties apply to each transfer of bearer paper (although the transferor of bearer paper is liable only to the person to whom he gives the instrument, not to any transferees further down the line).
- Under the signature liability rules, the holder of an instrument cannot make a claim until the issuer has been notified that the instrument was presented and

dishonored. Under the transfer warranty rules, the holder need not wait for presentment or dishonor before making a claim against the transferor.

PRESENTMENT WARRANTIES

Transfer warranties impose liability on anyone who sells a negotiable instrument, such as Deirdre. **Presentment warranties** apply to someone who demands payment for an instrument from the maker, drawee, or anyone else liable on it. Thus, if the condominium association cashes Annie's check, it is subject to presentment warranties because it is demanding payment from her bank, the drawee. In a sense, transfer warranties apply to all transfers *away* from the issuer; presentment warranties apply when the instrument *returns* to the maker or drawee for payment. As a general rule, payment on an instrument is final, and the payer has no right to a refund, unless the presentment warranties are violated.

Anyone who presents a *check* for payment warrants that:

- She is a holder
- The check has not been altered, and
- She has no reason to believe the drawer's signature is forged.[18]

If any of these promises is untrue, the bank has a right to demand a refund from the presenter. Suppose that Adam writes a $500 check to pay Bruce for repairing his motorcycle. Bruce changes the amount of the check to $1,500 and indorses it over to Chip as payment for an oil bill. When Chip deposits the check, the bank credits his account for $1,500 and deducts the same amount from Adam's account. When Adam discovers the alteration, the bank is forced (for reasons discussed in Chapter 25) to credit his account for $1,000. Chip violated his *presentment* warranties when he deposited an altered check (even though he did not *know* it was altered). Although Chip was not at fault, he must still reimburse the bank for $1,000. But Chip is not without recourse—Bruce violated his *transfer* warranties to Chip (by transferring an altered check). Bruce must repay the $1,000. Chip loses out only if he cannot make Bruce pay.

Anyone who presents a *promissory note* for payment makes only one warranty—that he is a holder of the instrument. Someone presenting a note does not need to warrant that the note is unaltered or the maker's signature is authentic because a note is presented for payment to the issuer himself. The issuer presumably remembers the amount of the note and whether he signed it. Suppose Adam gives a promissory note to Bruce to pay for a new motorcycle. If Bruce increases the note from $5,000 to $10,000 before he presents it for payment in six months' time, Adam will almost certainly realize the note has been changed and refuse to pay it.

The presenter of a note warrants that he is a holder. A forged signature prevents subsequent owners from being a holder, so anyone who presents a note with a forged signature is violating the presentment warranties. Suppose that Bruce is totally honest and does not alter the note, but Chip steals it and forges Bruce's indorsement before passing the note on to Donald, who presents it to Adam for payment. Donald has violated his *presentment* warranties because he is not a holder. Adam can refuse to pay him. For his part, Donald can claim repayment from Chip who violated his *transfer* warranties by passing on a note with a forged signature.

[18] UCC §3-417.

In the following case, the payee on a check made only a minor alteration. Did he violate his presentment warranties?

IN RE **YAGOW**
61 B.R. 109, 1986 Bankr. LEXIS 6136
United States Bankruptcy Court, District of North Dakota, 1986

Facts: Merlyn Yagow borrowed money from Production Credit Association (P.C.A.) to finance farming expenses. P.C.A. began to fear that Yagow would not be able to pay his debt, so it required him to accept payment for his crops with checks that named him and P.C.A. as co-payees. This way, Yagow could not cash the checks without P.C.A.'s indorsement. Yagow sold corn to Merlin Claus who paid $897.82 by check made out to "D & M Trust [Delores and Merlyn Yagow] + P.C.A." When Yagow deposited this check, the "+" had been changed to "or." Yagow also sold corn to Farmer's Co-op Elevator Co., which paid $5,698.71 by check made out to "Merlyn Yagow, Alvin Yagow, P.C.A." When Yagow deposited this check, the comma between Alvin Yagow and P.C.A. appeared as "or." Each of these checks was indorsed by Merlin Yagow alone, not by P.C.A.

P.C.A. sued the bank for having paid these three checks. In its turn, the bank filed suit against Yagow demanding indemnification for the P.C.A. claims.

Issue: Did Yagow violate his presentment warranties when he altered and deposited these three checks?

Excerpts from Judge Hill's Decision: Each of the checks were originally drawn naming P.C.A. as joint payee and thereby requiring P.C.A.'s endorsement for negotiation. At the time of receiving payment on the three checks, Merlyn Yagow under applicable commercial law made two warranties. He first warranted he had good title to the checks and/or was authorized to receive payment on behalf of P.C.A. In addition, he warranted that the checks had not been materially altered. The evidence is clear that the checks were altered between the time they were given to [Yagow] by the drawer and the time [Yagow] presented them to the Bank to be cashed. The checks from the Elevator and the Claus' had been changed from joint payee checks requiring all payee endorsements to alternative payee checks requiring the endorsement of only one payee.

Merlyn Yagow is the only person who had custody of the checks and the only one who had the motive and means to make the alterations. The Court believes that the changes in the Elevator and the Claus' checks were made by [Yagow] with the knowledge that they would have the effect of requiring only his endorsement and thereby avoid endorsement by P.C.A. and probably turnover of the proceeds to P.C.A., as P.C.A. had previously requested. These alterations constituted material alterations because they changed the checks as originally drawn and changed the relationship of the payees from joint to several. Being a material alteration, Merlyn Yagow by causing the same to be done breached his presentment warranty to the Bank.

For the reasons stated, it is ordered that Judgment be entered in favor of Sargent County Bank against [Yagow] for indemnification in such amounts as the Bank may be found liable to P.C.A.

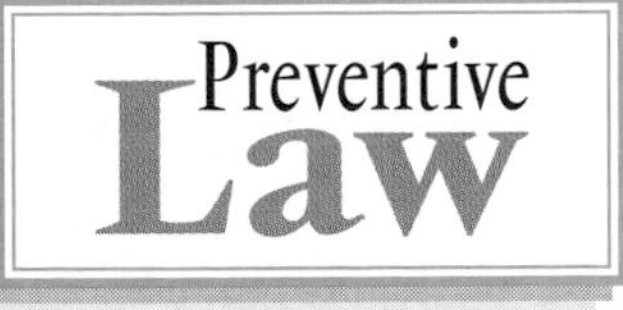

The person who first takes a forged or altered instrument from the culprit is liable to everyone thereafter who gives value for the instrument. Therefore, before accepting an instrument, it is absolutely essential to obtain foolproof identification and to examine the instrument carefully for any signs of alteration. For advice on how to avoid check fraud, see http://www.loderdrew.com/html/how_to_avoid_check_fraud.html and also http://www.occ.treas.gov/chckfrd/contents.htm.

OTHER LIABILITY RULES

This section contains other UCC rules that establish liability for wrongdoing on instruments.

CONVERSION LIABILITY

Conversion means that (1) someone has stolen an instrument or (2) a bank has paid a check that has a forged indorsement.[19] The rightful owner of the instrument can recover from either the thief or the bank.

For example, Glenn Altman was a lawyer representing Barbara Kirchoff. He settled her case for $12,000, but when he received the check, he forged her indorsement and deposited the check in his own account without telling her. He gave her the money four months later, but by then she had discovered his dishonesty. What claims do the various parties have?

Kirchoff has a claim against the bank because it paid a check with a forged indorsement. If the bank pays Kirchoff, then it can recover from Altman because he violated his presentment warranties. Note, however, that Kirchoff could not sue Altman for violating presentment warranties because he had not presented the check to her for payment. Nor could she sue him for violating transfer warranties because he had not transferred the check *to* her. To the contrary, he had transferred the check *away* from her.

Can Kirchoff sue Altman for conversion because he stole the check from her? A payee (i.e., Kirchoff) can bring a conversion action only if she, or her agent, actually takes delivery of the check. Until Kirchoff (or her agent) receives the check, it does not belong to her. In this case, Kirchoff could bring a conversion suit because Altman *was* her agent and he received the check for her. If Altman had simply been a stranger who stole the check from the mail, Kirchoff could not sue him. Her only claim would be against the issuer of the check for non-payment of the debt. The issuer is liable on the debt until the check arrives.

Can the issuer of the check sue Altman for conversion? No, an action for conversion cannot be brought by an issuer because the check technically belongs to the payee (Kirchoff). The issuer can bring a claim only against the bank that pays the forged check.

IMPOSTOR RULE

If someone issues an instrument to an impostor, then any indorsement in the name of the payee is valid as long as the person (a bank, say) who pays the instrument does not know of the fraud.[20] A teenager knocks on your door one afternoon. He tells you he is selling magazine subscriptions to pay for a school trip to Washington, D.C. After signing up for *Career* and *Popular Accounting*, you make out a check to "Family Magazine Subscriptions." Unfortunately, the boy does not represent Family Magazine at all. He does cash the check, however, by forging an indorsement for the magazine company. Is the bank liable for cashing the fraudulent check?

No. The teenager was an impostor—he said he represented the magazine company, but he did not. If anyone indorses the check in the name of the payee (Family Magazine Subscriptions), you must pay the check and the bank is not

[19] UCC §3-420.

[20] UCC §3-404(a).

liable. Does this rule seem harsh? Maybe, but you were in the best position to determine if the teenager really worked for the magazine company. You were more at fault than the bank, and you must pay. Of course, the teenager would be liable to you, if you could ever find him.

FICTITIOUS PAYEE RULE

If someone issues an instrument to a person who does not exist, then any indorsement in the name of the payee is valid as long as the person (a bank, say) who pays the instrument does not know of the fraud.[21] The impostor rule applies if you give a check with a real name to the wrong person. The fictitious payee rule applies if you write a check to someone who does not exist. The following article illustrates this rule.

Shari Lee Neiman pleaded guilty to stealing more than $8,000 from Columbia Association, a nonprofit group that manages recreational facilities in Columbia, Maryland. Neiman was charged with issuing paychecks to a fictitious employee, Elizabeth W. Nehring. The association discovered the theft through an internal audit of the Supreme Sports Club, whose expenses were over budget. The audit traced the creation of the fictitious employee to the computer operated by Neiman, whose responsibilities included issuing paychecks to association employees. Neiman has a sister, Wendy Elizabeth Neiman, who applied to the Maryland Motor Vehicle Administration for a new driver's license using the surname Nehring. A search of both sisters' homes produced two ATM cards and printed checks with the surname Nehring.[22]

Should the bank be liable for checks payable to someone who did not exist? Shari Neiman's employer was in a better position than the bank to prevent this fraud. Unfortunately, it has only itself to blame.

EMPLOYEE INDORSEMENT RULE

If an employee with responsibility for issuing instruments forges a check or other instrument, then any indorsement in the name of the payee, or a similar name, is valid as long as the person (a bank, say) who pays the instrument does not know of the fraud.[23] A dishonest employee, especially one with the authority to issue checks, has the opportunity to steal a great deal of money. The employer cannot shift blame (and liability) onto the bank that unknowingly cashes the forged checks because the employer was more to blame—it not only hired the thief, it failed to supervise him carefully.

Dennis M. Hartotunian had a major gambling problem—he owed nearly $10 million. Unfortunately, he was also the controller and accountant for the Aesar Group, a precious metals company. Over the course of three years, he wrote himself 154 checks worth $9.24 million. Any check for more than $500 required the signature of Aesar's general manager, but Hartotunian forged it. After an internal audit revealed that millions were missing, company officers asked to talk

---

[21] UCC §3-404(b).

[22] Adam Sachs, "Former Employee Pleads Guilty to Stealing $8,450 from CA," *Baltimore Sun*, Sep. 20, 1994, p. 3B. Reprinted with permission.

[23] UCC §3-405.

with Hartotunian. When he heard they were coming, he walked out and never came back.

It is always a bad sign when the company controller disappears. If an employee is generally authorized to prepare or sign checks, then the bank is not liable on checks that the employee forges. Hartotunian was clearly covered by this rule because he was the company controller. If he had been a mailroom employee without authority to sign checks, the bank would have been liable. The employee indorsement rule applies to both single and double forgeries. In a ***single forgery,*** the employee writes a check to himself, signs his employer's name, and cashes the check. In a ***double forgery,*** the employee writes a check to someone else, forges his employer's name, and also forges the name of the payee.

NEGLIGENCE

Regardless of the impostor rule, the fictitious payee rule, and the employee indorsement rule (the "three rules"), **anyone who behaves negligently in creating or paying an unauthorized instrument is liable to an innocent third party.** If two people are negligent, they share the loss according to their negligence. Here are two examples:

- **Anyone who is careless in paying an unauthorized instrument is liable, despite the three rules.**[24] Suppose that the boy selling bogus magazine subscriptions goes into the bank and indorses the check: "Family Magazine Subscriptions, by Butch McGraw." The teller peers over her counter and sees a 13-year-old boy standing there with torn jeans and a baseball cap on backwards. She may be negligent if she cashes the check without asking for further identification. Or suppose that a local bank teller knew that no one by the name of Elizabeth W. Nehring worked at Columbia Association. Then the bank could be liable for having paid the checks that were deposited into this fictitious person's account.
- **Anyone who is careless in allowing a forged or altered instrument to be created is also liable, whether or not he has violated one of the three rules.** The classic case establishing this rule was *Young v. Grote*, an 1827 English case. A businessman who was going abroad signed five checks and gave them to his wife with instructions that they were to be used for business expenses. A clerk in the company helpfully showed the missus how to fill out the checks, carefully instructing her to leave a blank space in front of the number. The clerk used this space to add a "3" in front of a "50" and then cashed the £350 check. The court held that the drawee bank was not liable because, "If Young, instead of leaving the check with a female, had left it with a man of business, he would have guarded against fraud in the mode of filling it up."[25] Today, we hiss at the sexist sentiment, but it illustrates the point. Anyone who carelessly creates a situation that facilitates the forgery or alteration of an instrument cannot recover against a party who pays the instrument in good faith.

In the following case, the Professional Golf Association had a bad lie. Who must take penalty strokes—the PGA or its bank?

---

[24] UCC §§3-404(d), 3-405(b).

[25] *Young v. Grote*, 4 Bing. 253 (Common Pleas), *quoted in* Douglas J. Whaley, *Problems and Materials on Payment Law* (Boston: Little, Brown & Co., 1995), at 253.

GULF STATES SECTION, PGA, INC. v. WHITNEY NATIONAL BANK OF NEW ORLEANS

689 So. 2d 638, 1997 La. App. LEXIS 167
Court of Appeal of Louisiana, Fourth Circuit, 1997

Facts: Robert Brown was the executive director of the Gulf States Section of the Professional Golf Association (PGA). He was responsible for paying bills and handling the bank account. Brown used Quicken, a computer program, to write checks. These checks were kept in a box beneath the printer stand in his office.

Adrenetti Collins was a secretary who worked in the PGA office with Brown. During a four-month period, she forged 18 PGA checks totaling $22,699.81. To avoid detection, she intercepted two of the bank statements sent by Whitney National Bank and replaced them with forged statements that left out the numbers of the checks she had stolen. The usual Whitney statement was printed on vanilla-colored paper measuring a non-standard 6¾ × 11 inches. The forged statements were on standard 8½ × 11 inch white paper. They were not dated but they did contain the Whitney logo. Brown received two forged statements and then no statements at all for two months. Shortly thereafter, Collins asked for a leave of absence.

Whitney's policy was to verify signatures on checks equal to or greater than $5,000. One of the forged checks was in the amount of $5,000, but Whitney did not verify Brown's signature before paying it. Brown's signature was a semilegible letter or two and a long loop. The forged signature on the check looked very similar to the real one.

Issue: Is Whitney liable to the PGA for the forged checks it paid?

Argument for the PGA: The general rule is that a person is not liable on an instrument unless his signature appears on it. Brown's signature did not appear on these checks, so only the bank is liable on them.

As for the PGA's alleged negligence, Brown traveled extensively and was not available to supervise the office staff carefully. Is this negligence? If so, half the companies in America are negligent, too. Don't forget that Brown stored the checks in his private office. Whitney admits that it did not verify the signatures on any of the checks, even the one for $5,000. This is in direct violation of its own policies. If Whitney had simply followed its policies, the forgeries would have been detected months earlier.

Argument for Whitney: Generally, a bank is liable for forged checks unless it can show that (1) the customer was negligent; (2) the negligence substantially contributed to the forgery; and (3) the bank paid the forged instruments in accordance with reasonable commercial banking industry standards.

The PGA was clearly negligent in this case. The checks should have been locked up, not sitting under the printer in an open box. Brown should have realized that checks were missing, and he should have noticed that the bank statements were forged. Without his negligence, Collins could never have committed the forgeries. In any event, she would have been caught much earlier—when the first bank statement was received, not four months later.

As for the bank's failure to verify Brown's signature, the forgery was close enough to his sloppy writing that no one could have realized the signature was a fake.

CRIMES

It is beyond the scope of this chapter to catalogue all of the crimes that can be committed with negotiable instruments, but students should be aware of these.

Bouncing a Check

It is illegal to write a check on an account that has insufficient funds. Generally, no serious penalties are imposed if sufficient funds are immediately deposited. (This is a good thing, considering that 600 *million* checks bounce each year.) However, both banks and merchants impose substantial fees for their trouble. People who make a career of bouncing checks may find they have plenty of time to bone up on UCC Article 3 in the prison library.

Check Kiting

It is illegal to kite checks. E. F. Hutton was a thriving brokerage firm until ambitious branch managers began boosting profits with a check-kiting scheme. A Hutton manager would overdraw an account in Bank A and deposit that check in Bank B. Bank B would begin paying interest on the funds before the check had cleared. The manager would then write a check on Bank B to cover the deficit in Bank A, in the process overdrawing Bank B. One Hutton account in a Virginia bank was overdrawn by an average of $9 million a day. Interest earned on these overdrafts accounted for as much as 70 percent of the Washington office's gross income. In 20 months, Hutton made at least $8 million, but the resulting scandal drove the firm out of business.

Forgery

It is illegal to forge an instrument or to pass on (**utter**) an instrument that one knows to be forged.

Fraudulent checks cost banks 10 times more money each year than robbers do — $815 million versus $65 million. To protect themselves, some banks are now requiring customers to provide a fingerprint as an ID for cashing checks. This requirement reduces check fraud by up to 80 percent. But some consumers are refusing to give banks their finger, protesting that the law on negotiable instruments does not require payees on checks to provide fingerprints. Fingerprints may ultimately be the least of consumer worries, however. Some companies are now developing identification systems using voice or eye retinal patterns.[26]

DISCHARGE

DISCHARGE OF THE OBLIGOR

Discharge means that liability on an instrument terminates. Article 3 establishes five different ways to discharge an instrument:[27]

- **By Payment.** Payment discharges an instrument, as long as the payment is *from* someone obliged to pay and goes *to* the holder. If you mail a check to the wrong bank when paying off a promissory note, you obviously have not discharged the note. Or if you ask an employee to take money to the bank to pay off the note, but she goes to Hawaii instead, no discharge has occurred. Similarly, payment does not discharge an instrument if the payor knows that the instrument is stolen. Suppose you have given a promissory note to Lou. He complains to you that his employee Stephanie stole it. If you pay Stephanie when she presents the note, you have not discharged it.
- **By Agreement.** The parties to the instrument can agree to a discharge, even if the instrument is not paid. The discharge, however, must be in writing; it cannot be oral. You give a promissory note to your company to pay for company stock. The company president tells you that the company will forgive the loan and discharge the note as a reward for your fabulous performance. A few

---

[26] Peter Sinton, "Banks Use Fingerprint as an ID for Checks," *San Francisco Chronicle*, Mar. 21, 1997, p. D1. © *San Francisco Chronical*. Reprinted by permission.

[27] UCC Article 3, Part 6.

months later the president is ousted. Your agreement was not in writing and you are liable on the note. (You may have a contract claim against the company, but the note itself is still valid.)

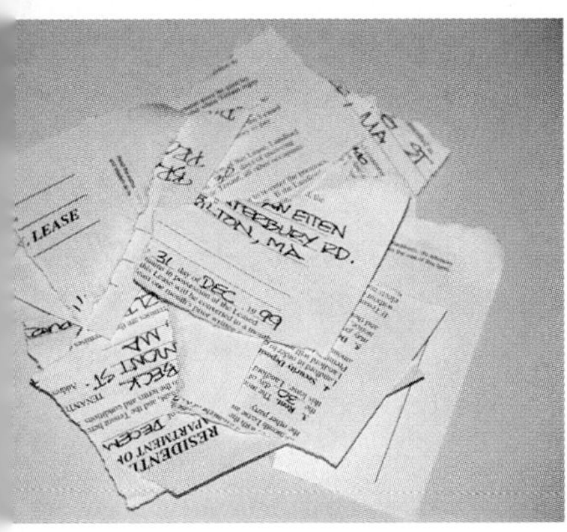
One way to cancel an instrument.

- **By Cancellation.** Cancellation means the intentional, voluntary surrender, destruction, or disfigurement of an instrument. If Ted accidentally forgets to take a check out of his pocket before throwing his shirt in the wash, he has not canceled the check (even though it was destroyed) because the destruction was unintentional. If, while arguing with his business partner, he takes her promissory note and tears it into a thousand pieces while screaming, "This is what I think of you and your business skills," he has canceled the note. He could achieve the same result less dramatically by simply writing "canceled" on it or by giving it back to her.
- **By Certification.** When a bank certifies or accepts a check, the drawer and all indorsers of the check are discharged, and only the bank is liable.
- **By Alteration.** An instrument is discharged if its terms are intentionally changed. Laura gives Todd a promissory note. Thinking he is being very clever, Todd changes the amount of her note from $200 to $2,000. He has actually done Laura a favor because he has discharged the note.

Keep in mind, however, that no discharge is effective against a holder in due course who acquires the instrument without knowledge of the discharge. If Todd sells Laura's note to Max, who does not know of the discharge, Max can enforce the instrument against Laura, but only for the original amount of $200.

DISCHARGE OF AN INDORSER OR ACCOMMODATION PARTY

Article 3 provides that virtually any change in an instrument that harms an indorser or accommodation party also discharges them unless they consent to the change. These fatal changes include an extension of the due date on the instrument, a material modification of the instrument, or any impairment of the collateral that secures the instrument. When Chelsea borrows money from Jordan, she signs a promissory note due on December 24. Helena guarantees the note. Chelsea cannot pay, but Jordan does not have the stomach for declaring Chelsea in default on Christmas Eve. He generously extends the due date for another week. Helena is no longer liable, even secondarily, because Jordan has granted an extension of the due date.

CHAPTER CONCLUSION

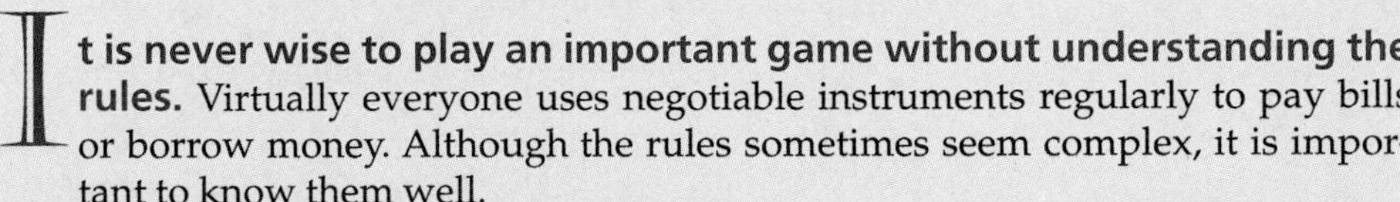
It is never wise to play an important game without understanding the rules. Virtually everyone uses negotiable instruments regularly to pay bills or borrow money. Although the rules sometimes seem complex, it is important to know them well.

CHAPTER REVIEW

1. Someone who is primarily liable on a negotiable instrument must pay unless he has a valid defense. Those with secondary liability only pay if the person with primary liability does not.

2. The payment process for a negotiable instrument comprises as many as three steps:
   - *Presentment*. The holder makes a demand for payment to the issuer.
   - *Dishonor*. The instrument is due, but the issuer does not pay.
   - *Notice of Dishonor*. The holder of the instrument notifies those who are secondarily liable that the instrument has been dishonored.
3. The maker of a note is primarily liable.
4. The drawer of a check has secondary liability: he is not liable until he has received notice that the bank has dishonored the check.
5. Indorsers are secondarily liable; they must pay if the issuer does not. But an indorser is only liable to those who come after him in the chain of ownership, not to those who held the instrument before he did.
6. The accommodation party signs an instrument to benefit the accommodated party. By signing the instrument, an accommodation party agrees to be liable on it, whether or not she directly benefits from it.
7. To avoid personal liability when signing an instrument, an agent must indicate that he is signing as an agent and must give the name of the principal.
8. The basic rules of warranty liability are as follows:
   - The culprit is always liable.
   - The drawee bank is responsible if it pays a check on which the drawer's name is forged.
   - In any other case of wrongdoing, a person who initially acquires an instrument from a culprit is ultimately liable to anyone else who pays value for it.
9. When someone transfers an instrument, she warrants that:
   - She is a holder of the instrument
   - All signatures are authentic and authorized
   - The instrument has not been altered
   - No defense can be asserted against her, and
   - As far as she knows the issuer is solvent.
10. Anyone who presents a check for payment warrants that:
    - She is a holder
    - The check has not been altered, and
    - She has no reason to believe the drawer's signature is forged.
11. The presenter of a note only warrants that he is a holder.
12. Conversion means that (1) someone has stolen an instrument or (2) a bank has paid a check that has a forged indorsement.
13. *Impostor Rule*. If someone issues an instrument to an impostor, then any indorsement in the name of the payee is valid as long as the person who pays the instrument is ignorant of the fraud.
14. *Fictitious Payee Rule*. If someone issues an instrument to a person who does not exist, then any indorsement in the name of the payee is valid as long as the person who pays the instrument does not know of the fraud.

15. *Employee Indorsement Rule.* If an employee with responsibility for issuing instruments forges a check or other instrument, then any indorsement in the name of the payee is valid as long as the person who pays the instrument is ignorant of the fraud.

16. Anyone who behaves negligently in creating or paying an unauthorized instrument is liable to an innocent third party.

17. Discharge means that liability on an instrument terminates. An instrument may be discharged by payment, agreement, cancellation, certification, or alteration.

PRACTICE TEST

1. Marie Kless hired an attorney, James R. Gunderman, to collect money owed her on a mortgage. Gunderman was successful in his attempt to recover the money, but when he received the check payable to Kless for $26,676.16, he forged her indorsement and deposited the check in his own account at Manufacturers Hanover Trust Co. He later withdrew the entire amount. Is the bank liable to Kless?

2. CPA QUESTION Vex Corp. executed a negotiable promissory note payable to Tamp, Inc. The note was collaterized by some of Vex's business assets. Tamp negotiated the note to Miller for value. Miller indorsed the note in blank and negotiated it to Bilco for value. Before the note became due, Bilco agreed to release Vex's collateral. Vex refused to pay Bilco when the note became due. Bilco promptly notified Miller and Tamp of Vex's default. Which of the following statements is correct?

(a) Bilco will be unable to collect from Miller because Miller's indorsement was in blank.

(b) Bilco will be able to collect from either Tamp or Miller because Bilco was a holder in due course.

(c) Bilco will be unable to collect from either Tamp or Miller because of Bilco's release of the collateral.

(d) Bilco will be able to collect from Tamp because Tamp was the original payee.

3. CPA QUESTION A check has the following indorsements on the back:

Paul Frank
without recourse
George Hopkins
payment guaranteed
Ann Quarry
Collection guaranteed
Rachel Ott

Which of the following conditions occurring subsequent to the indorsements would discharge all of the indorsers?

(a) Lack of notice of dishonor

(b) Late presentment

(c) Insolvency of maker

(d) Certification of check

4. CPA QUESTION Which of the following actions does not discharge a prior party to a commercial instrument?

(a) Good faith payment or satisfaction of the instrument

(b) Cancellation of that prior party's indorsement

(c) The holder's oral renunciation of that prior party's liability

(d) The holder's intentional destruction of the instrument

5. Phariss operated a business known as Railroad Salvage Co. He filed a claim in bankruptcy court against the Chicago, Rock Island and Pacific Railroad. Phariss then left Iowa and closed his bank account with the Security State Bank in Independence. Somehow, Carl Eddy obtained possession of the check that the railroad issued in payment of Phariss's claim. Eddy indorsed the check "Railroad Salvage Co. Carl Eddy" and deposited it in his own account at Security State Bank. After Eddy filed for bankruptcy, Phariss sued the bank, alleging that it was liable to him for having paid the check over an unauthorized indorsement. Is Security State Bank liable to Phariss? On what theory?

6. YOU BE THE JUDGE WRITING PROBLEM Melco, Inc. issued a promissory note for $12,000, payable to the order of Marjorie Irene Floor. On the back of the note, Charles Melvin had signed the following statement: "For and in consideration of funds advanced herein to Melco, Inc., we irrevocably guarantee Marjorie Irene Floor against loss by reason of non-payment of this note." Floor sued Melvin to enforce the note before demanding payment from the issuer. Is Melvin liable on the note before demand is made on the issuer? **Argument for Floor:** Melvin was an accommodation party and, as such, was liable on the instrument even if no demand had been made on the issuer. **Argument for Melvin:** If the accommodation party writes, "I guarantee collection," he is not liable until the issuer fails to pay. In this case, the words Melvin wrote are the equivalent of "I guarantee collection." **Floor's response**: To avoid liability in this case, Melvin had to comply with the exact requirements of the statute. How was she to know that he thought he was writing the equivalent of "I guarantee collection"?

7. Sidney Knopf entered into a contract for $35,000 with MacDonald Roofing Co., Inc. to reroof Knopf's building. Knopf made his initial payment by writing a check for $17,500 payable to "MacDonald Roofing Company, Inc., and D-FW Supply Company." MacDonald took the check to D-FW and requested an indorsement. MacDonald Roofing was a customer of D-FW, so D-FW indorsed the check. When MacDonald failed to complete the roofing work, Knopf filed suit for damages against D-FW. Knopf argues that D-FW was liable as an indorser. Do you agree?

8. **RIGHT & WRONG** Steven was killed in an automobile accident. His wife, Debra, was the beneficiary of a life insurance policy for $60,000. She decided to move from Bunkie to Sulphur, Louisiana. Before she could leave, however, arrangements had to be made to settle outstanding debts. Debra executed a document authorizing her mother-in-law, Helen, to sign checks on Debra's account at the bank. Debra also signed several blank checks and gave them to Helen with instructions to use them to pay off the remaining debt on Debra's trailer. When Helen received the life insurance checks, she deposited them in Debra's account. So far so good. But then she immediately withdrew $50,000 from the account by using one of the blank checks Debra had left her. She did not use these funds to pay off the trailer debt. When Debra discovered the theft, she sued the bank for having paid an unauthorized check. How would you rule in this case? Debra has suffered a grievous loss—her husband died tragically in an automobile accident. She trusted her mother-in-law and counted on her help. Should the bank show compassion? If the bank made good on the forged checks, how great would be the injury to the bank's shareholders compared with the harm to Debra if she loses this entire sum?

9. James A. Arnold and Marvin D. Smith signed two promissory notes for a total of $25,000 payable to the Bostwick Banking Co. The defendants argued that they were not liable on the notes because they had signed as agents for Sunshine Sales Corp. The notes made no reference to Sunshine, but the defendants alleged that an officer at Bostwick had promised to type "Sunshine Sales Corporation" above their signatures on the notes. Are the defendants liable on the notes?

10. Fire damaged a building. Six different payees were entitled to part of the proceeds from the $32,534 insurance check: Pioneer Bank & Trust Co.; First Federal Savings and Loan; Donald Hayner; Andrew Van Styn; Theresa Fox; and Lash, Warner & Associates. Fox (who, as it turns out, was aptly named) asked Lash, Warner to indorse the check. At that point, the check already had signatures of every payee except Fox. Fox deposited the check at the Bank of Ravenswood (Ravenswood), which forwarded the check to Connecticut National Bank (Connecticut) for final payment. It turned out that the indorsements of Hayner and Van Styn had been forged. In a separate suit, they recovered the full amount of the check from Ravenswood and Connecticut. These two banks then sued Lash, Warner for violating its transfer warranties under the UCC. Is Lash, Warner liable to the banks?

11. Using the company's check-signing machine, Doris Britton forged $148,171.30 of checks on the account of her employer, Winkie, Inc. One of Britton's jobs at the company was to prepare checks for the company president, W. J. Winkie, Jr., to sign. He did not (1) look at the sequence of check numbers; (2) examine the monthly account statements; or (3) reconcile company records with bank statements. Winkie's bank, as a matter of policy, did not check indorsements on checks with a face value of less than $1,000. By accident, it paid a forged check that had not even been indorsed. Is the bank liable to Winkie, Inc. for the forged checks?

INTERNET RESEARCH PROBLEM

At http://www.occ.treas.gov/chckfrd/contents.htm, the United States Treasury offers advice on how to avoid check fraud. Click on *Altered Checks* and *Telemarketing Fraud*. Have you ever violated this advice and left yourself vulnerable to fraud?

You can find further practice problems in the Online Quiz at http://beatty.westbuslaw.com or in the Study Guide that accompanies this text.

CHAPTER 25

LIABILITY FOR NEGOTIABLE INSTRUMENTS: BANKS AND THEIR CUSTOMERS

For Jeffrey, it was the best of times and it was the worst of times—he had started his own computer business. There were days when he could not believe the utter bliss of being on his own. Then there were days when absolutely everything went wrong and he looked longingly out his window at the McDonald's across the street, wondering if he could get a job there.

At the moment, Jeffrey was pretty miserable. He and his chief financial officer, Marnie, were meeting with their banker to sort out the company account. Although he thought he had thousands of dollars in the bank, a supplier had called the day before to complain about a bounced check. Jeffrey was very good at numbers that had "CPU" or "megabyte" after them, but he never had time for finances.

"Hmmm, now let's see," said Leena, the banker, as she peered at her computer screen. "Your account is deep into the red."

"What an old clunker," Jeffrey thought, looking at Leena's computer. "Must be five years old." He was imagining what one of his sleek new machines would look like on Leena's desk when her shocking statement forced him to pull his attention back to finances. "I couldn't possibly be overdrawn," he insisted, "I haven't written a check in weeks."

Leena countered, "Maybe not, but you have been withdrawing $500 a day from the automatic teller machine."

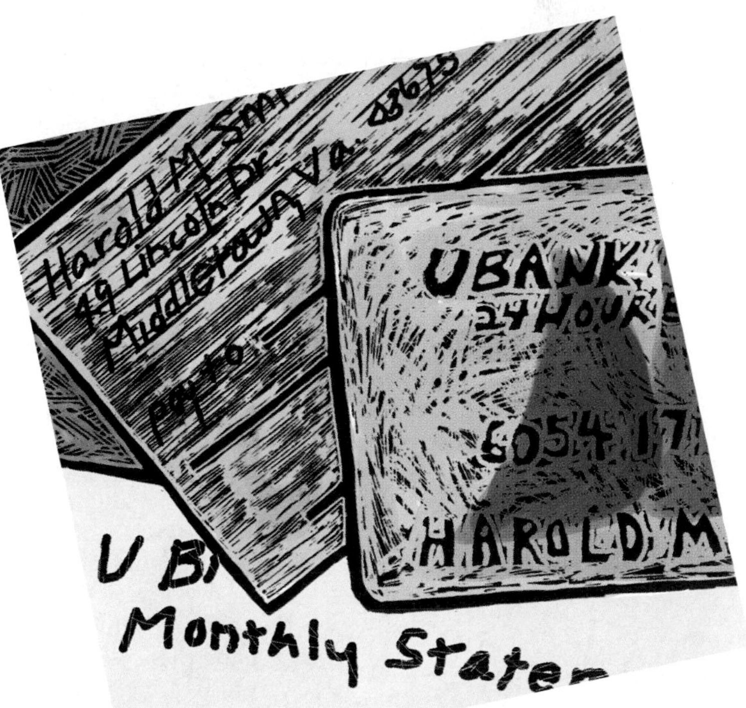

"Not a chance," said Jeffrey, "I don't have an ATM card."

"Indeed you do," Leena insisted, "We sent them to all our customers last fall."

"Hold on," Marnie interrupted. "Jeffrey never asked the bank to validate his ATM card, so the bank is liable for all unauthorized withdrawals."

Leena smiled grimly. "How nice to be an authority on the UCC. But, Jeffrey, I see that last month you wrote a check to your landlord for $18,000."

Jeffrey turned pale. "That was for 18 *hundred* dollars, not 18 *thousand*."

"I have a copy of your canceled checks right here on the screen. Let's take a look. Yes, this check is definitely for $18,000. Here, you can see." She swiveled her monitor so Jeffrey could look at the screen.

He tugged at his hair. "Someone added extra zeros and the word 'thousand.' If you look carefully, you can see that the writing is slightly different."

"That's too bad," said Leena, with insincere sympathy. "But perhaps you can recover from the landlord."

"No way," Marnie interrupted again. "When a check is altered, the customer is only required to pay the *original* amount. Jeffrey is liable for $1,800, the *bank* is liable for the rest."

"One last matter," said Leena, gnawing on her pencil stub. "We received word this morning that the $4,000 check you deposited three months ago has bounced. The customer who gave you that check has closed his account and disappeared. We have taken the $4,000 out of your checking account."

"Wait," Marnie protested indignantly. "You can't do that. A bank can't wait three months to dishonor a check. Jeffrey gets to keep that money!"

For Jeffrey, it was the spring of hope, not the winter of despair.

INTRODUCTION

Americans write over 60 billion checks each year. They also execute 11 billion transactions at the more than 165,000 automatic teller machines (ATMs) located every place from banks to grocery stores, gas stations, and airports. This chapter is about the laws that govern the relationship between banks and their customers, both for traditional activities such as check writing and newer activities like electronic fund transfers at ATMs. Parts of this chapter will seem familiar to you from reading Chapter 24. Because checks are a form of draft, they are covered by Article 3 of the Uniform Commercial Code (UCC). Article 4 governs bank deposits and collections. Some of the provisions in Article 4 are very similar to those in Article 3. When the two conflict, Article 4 controls.

WHO'S WHO

UCC §4-105 defines the different roles of banks:

- **Depositary Bank.** The first bank to *take* a check is called the depositary bank. (A bank that *cashes* a check is not a depositary bank.) Suppose that Chicago White Sox, Inc. writes a check on its account at the LaSalle Bank to pay star player Frank Thomas. If he deposits the check in his account at Harris Bank, then Harris is the depositary bank.

Exhibit 25.1

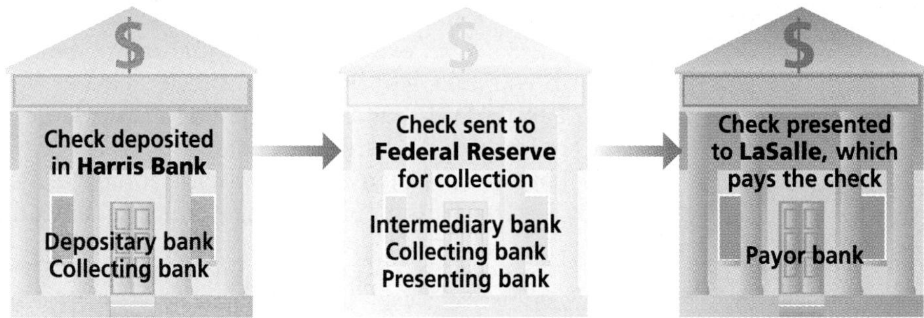

- **Payor Bank.** A bank that is called a *drawee* bank in Article 3 is termed a *payor* bank in Article 4 because it pays the issuer's check. The Chicago White Sox, Inc. is the issuer of the check, and the LaSalle Bank is the payor bank.
- **Intermediary Bank.** An intermediary bank is any bank that handles a check during the collection process, *except* the depositary or payor bank. Instead of presenting the check directly to LaSalle for payment, Harris Bank may send it to the Federal Reserve bank, which serves as a central clearinghouse for checks. The Federal Reserve then sends the check to LaSalle for payment. The Federal Reserve is an intermediary bank.
- **Collecting Bank.** A collecting bank is any bank that handles a check during the collection process, except the payor bank. Both Harris and the Federal Reserve are collecting banks.
- **Presenting Bank.** A presenting bank is a bank that submits a check to the payor bank. The Federal Reserve is the presenting bank.

As you can see, the same bank may carry several different labels. Exhibit 25.1 sets out the roles that the various banks play in the transaction between the White Sox and Frank Thomas.

CHECKING ACCOUNTS

When a customer deposits money in a checking account, the bank becomes a debtor to the customer—the bank owes the customer money. At the same time, the bank serves as an agent for the customer. The legal relationship between the customer and the bank is based on both the checking account agreement and Article 4. The checking account agreement is simply a contract between the bank and the customer. Article 4 is, in essence, a default option; it applies unless the bank and customer agree to different terms. No matter what the agreement says, however, a bank cannot avoid liability for careless or bad faith actions. To pursue a complaint against a bank, see http://www.occ.treas.gov/.

THE BANK'S DUTY TO PROVIDE INFORMATION

The UCC does not require banks to provide customers with a monthly statement that lists transactions. Virtually every bank does so, however, because customers expect it. If a bank provides a statement, it must either include canceled checks or a list of check numbers, amounts, and dates of payment.[1] Returning canceled checks is an expensive habit that many banks would like to break.[2] Nonetheless, most banks still do return canceled checks because customers like to have them. People find that a photocopy of a canceled check is the best proof that a bill has been paid. If a bank does not return canceled checks, it must keep legible copies on hand for seven years and provide copies to customers within a reasonable time.

The Truth in Savings Act[3] requires banks that send statements to include:

- The interest rate paid on the account
- The amount of interest the account has earned
- Any fees imposed by the bank
- The number of days covered by the statement

Before customers open an account (and in advertisements), a bank must disclose to them:

- The interest rate paid on the account
- How long this interest rate will be in effect
- Any requirements (such as minimum account balance or initial deposit) that the customer must meet to earn the advertised rate
- Any fees or penalties imposed by the bank

THE BANK'S DUTY TO PAY

A bank must pay a check if the check is authorized by the customer and complies with the terms of the checking account agreement.[4] A bank may, however, choose the order in which it pays authorized checks. Suppose that Elizabeth writes a check to each of her four sisters: Jane ($100), Mary ($50), Lydia ($40), and Kitty ($10). When the sisters appear at the bank the next morning to cash the checks, they discover Elizabeth has only $100 in her account. The bank is free to choose which sisters it pays. It is not forced to pay the sister who appears first nor must it pay Mary, Lydia, and Kitty together, instead of Jane by herself.

The bank can, if it chooses, pay all the sisters' checks, even though payment would cause an overdraft in Elizabeth's account. (Usually, customers have the opposite problem—their bank refuses to pay an overdraft.) If an account has an overdraft, the bank may either repay itself out of the customer's next deposit or try to collect the amount directly from the customer. For example, a bookie demanded that a gambler repay his debts *immediately*. The gambler did not want to pay, but he also did not want his legs broken. It was midnight and no banks were open. He wrote a check, knowing that his account was virtually on empty. It is not clear what he thought the bookie would do when the check bounced, but at that particular midnight, he was more concerned with the present than the future.

---

[1] UCC §4-406.

[2] Originally, banks returned checks because they did not want the expense of storing all that paper. With advances in technology and increases in postal rates, it is now cheaper simply to store micro-copies.

[3] 12 U.S.C. §§4301-4313.

[4] §§4-401(a), 4-402(a).

His plan was upset, however, when the bank honored his check, despite the overdraft, and then demanded payment from him. Though highly indignant, he nonetheless had to pay. There is a moral to this story about both overdrafts and gambling.

WRONGFUL DISHONOR

If a bank violates its duty and wrongfully dishonors an authorized check, it is liable to the customer for all *actual* and *consequential* damages. Bouncing a check is not only embarrassing, it can cost real money—a retailer may charge for a returned check, the customer's credit rating may suffer, or the customer may even be arrested. When it has wrongfully dishonored a check, the bank is liable for these damages. What should the bank's liability be in the following case?

CITY NATIONAL BANK OF FORT SMITH v. GOODWIN

301 Ark. 182, 783 S.W.2d 335, 1990 Ark. LEXIS 49
Supreme Court of Arkansas, 1990

Facts: City National Bank of Fort Smith (CNB) had two customers with similar names: Larry J. Goodwin and Larry K. Goodwin. Larry K. defaulted on two loans from CNB. Jim Geels, a collection officer at the bank, sought to take money from Larry K.'s checking account and credit it to the loan (which he had the right to do). On November 26, he pulled Larry K.'s loan file to check his Social Security number, but the file had Larry J.'s number instead. Geels took $3,229.07 from the checking account of Larry J. and his wife, Sandra.

On November 30, Sandra Goodwin received written notice from CNB that four checks she had written between November 21 and 26 had been returned for insufficient funds and that the Goodwins' joint checking account had a zero balance. Ms. Goodwin knew the bank was in error and requested that CNB both call and send certified letters of apology to the merchants involved. On Monday, December 2, she called three of the businesses to which she had written the checks. None of them had received a call or letter. Later in the day, Geels promised Ms. Goodwin that letters would be sent to the merchants stating that the bank was at fault. On the next day, December 3, he did mail the letters.

Subsequently, CNB learned in a letter from the Goodwins' attorney that other checks written to merchants on November 12 and 21 had also bounced. CNB wrote a letter to one merchant and called the other, stating that it was the bank's fault that the checks were returned. On February 6, the Goodwins filed suit against CNB alleging that CNB wrongfully dishonored seven checks. The jury found for the Goodwins and awarded compensatory damages of $10,000 and punitive damages of $30,000. The bank appealed.

Issue: Is a bank liable for punitive damages when it wrongfully dishonors a customer's check?

Excerpts from Judge Holt's Decision: This court has indicated that punitive damages may be recoverable where a payor bank wrongfully dishonors a check written by its customer. However, only actual damages are recoverable where the dishonor occurs through a mistake. This court has not defined the parameters of the concept, "mistaken dishonor." Other courts, interpreting provisions identical to Ark. Code Ann. §4-4-402, have defined "mistaken dishonor" as wrongful dishonor done erroneously or unintentionally. The word "mistake" is to be construed as limited to wrongful dishonor made in good faith.

There was simply no evidence presented that CNB acted in bad faith or that it deliberately or willfully dishonored the Goodwins' checks. It simply confused the identities of Larry K. and Larry J. Goodwin and, as a result, setoff the checking account of Larry J. Goodwin and Sandra Goodwin instead of the accounts of Larry K. Goodwin. In sum, the dishonor of the Goodwins' checks occurred through a mistake. Accordingly, punitive damages were not recoverable.

In law cases, the issues of punitive and compensatory damages may be so interwoven that an error with respect to one requires a retrial of the whole case. This court has held that where the issue of punitive damages is erroneously submitted to the jury, together with the defendant's financial condition, an award of compensatory damages cannot stand. Accordingly, we *reverse* and *remand* the entire case for further proceedings consistent with this opinion.

Banks are in a difficult position. If they refuse to pay an *authorized* check, they are liable for damages. On the other hand, if they pay an *unauthorized* check, they must bear the liability and recredit the customer's account. Following are the most common problems banks face in determining which checks to pay and which to dishonor.

The Death of a Customer

If a customer dies, the bank may continue to pay checks *for 10 days* after it learns of the death, unless it receives a stop payment order from someone claiming an interest in the account.[5] After all, the customer was alive when he wrote the checks. Refusing to pay may cause hardship for innocent merchants who accepted checks in return for goods. A refusal to pay may also complicate matters for his family when they sort out his financial affairs. Certainly, the last thing his widow wants is for all his checks to bounce.

In reality, however, banks typically do freeze an account after the holder dies. First, a bank must stop payment on checks if someone else makes a claim to the funds in the account, no matter how weak that claim is. If Mildred, a seventh cousin twice removed, makes a claim, the bank must stop payment. Second, although Article 4 permits banks to pay checks even after the customer has died, most states require banks to freeze enough money to cover the decedent's taxes. Since the bank does not know what the decedent will ultimately owe, it typically freezes the entire account.

Incompetent Customers

Once a bank is notified that a court has found a customer to be incompetent, it is liable if it pays the customer's checks. The bank is under no obligation to determine competence itself. It may continue to pay checks until it has received notice that a court has determined the customer is incompetent.

Forgery

If a bank pays a check on which the issuer's name is forged, it must recredit the issuer's account. When a bank pays a forged check, either the bank or the customer will lose money, except in the unlikely event that the forger repays what he has stolen. As a matter of policy, the drafters of the UCC decided that the payor bank should bear the risk of forgery, rather than the customer. Most banks take two steps to guard against losses: they examine the signatures on all checks above a certain dollar amount, and they carry forgery insurance.

---

[5] UCC §4-405.

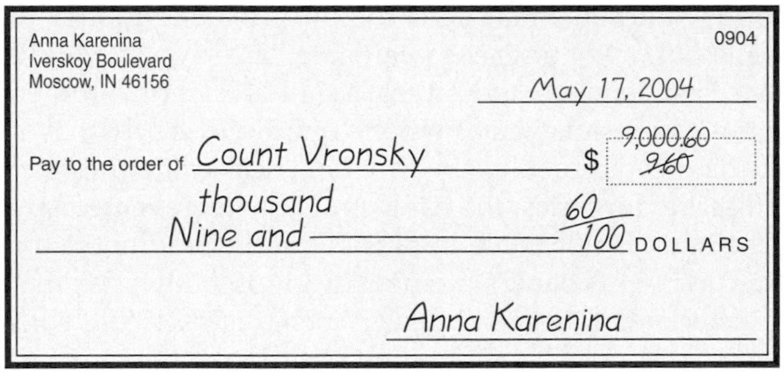

Anna Karenina
Iverskoy Boulevard
Moscow, IN 46156
0904
May 17, 2004
Pay to the order of Count Vronsky $ 9,000.60 ~~9.60~~
Nine thousand and 60/100 DOLLARS
Anna Karenina

If the bank pays this check, it is liable for the full amount because the check has obviously been altered.

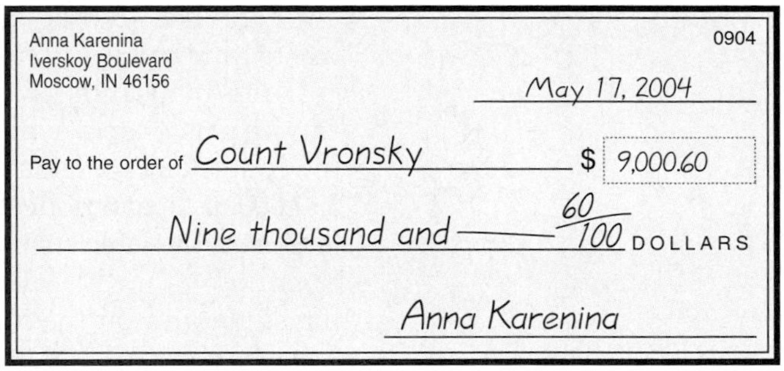

Anna Karenina
Iverskoy Boulevard
Moscow, IN 46156
0904
May 17, 2004
Pay to the order of Count Vronsky $ 9,000.60
Nine thousand and 60/100 DOLLARS
Anna Karenina

Anna Karenina originally wrote this check for $9.60. Because the check looks unaltered, she is liable for $9.60, and the bank is liable for the balance.

Exhibit 25.2

Alteration

If a bank pays a check that has been altered, the customer is liable only for the original terms of the check, and the bank is liable for the balance.[6] There is one exception to this rule: if the alteration is obvious, the bank is liable for the full amount of the check because it should have known better than to pay it in the first place. Exhibit 25.2 illustrates this rule.

Completion

If an incomplete check is later filled in by someone other than the original issuer, the bank is not liable unless it was on notice that the completion was improper.[7] Joey and Lisa want to buy, renovate, and resell a two-family house. They think they have located the perfect choice, but negotiations are still incomplete when Joey leaves town on business for a few days. He signs a blank check and leaves it with Lisa to pay his half of the deposit, if their offer is accepted. Lisa absentmindedly uses the check as a bookmark and forgets to remove it before she returns the book to the library. Marian the librarian finds the check and, glorying in the thought of hundreds of new books, fills in the library's name and the amount of $10,000. If Lisa realizes the check is missing and notifies the bank, then the bank is liable to Joey if it later pays the check. Otherwise, the bank owes Joey nothing.

Comparative Negligence and Bank Statements

Customers must use reasonable care in examining their bank statements to look for forged or altered checks. If a customer is careless, the bank is not liable for the faulty checks. Moreover, if a customer fails to notify the bank of a forgery or alteration within 30 days of receiving a statement, then the bank is not liable for any subsequent bad checks by the same wrongdoer. However, if both the customer and the bank are careless, a comparative negligence standard is used, and the bank's liability is reduced by the amount of the customer's negligence.[8] In any case, a customer cannot recover for a forgery or alteration if it is reported more than one year after receiving the statement that first revealed the problem.

6 UCC §4-401(d).

7 UCC §4-401(d).

8 UCC §4-406.

Tom likes to brag at family gatherings that he is too busy making money to waste time balancing his checkbook. "My time is so valuable," he says, "it would cost me thousands of dollars just to open the envelope." His careful brother, David, gets a certain amount of secret satisfaction when Tom discovers that, over the course of a year, his name has been forged to six different checks amounting to $30,000. If he had noticed the earlier forgeries, the bank could have prevented any losses on the later checks. The bank is not liable because Tom did not report the forgeries within 30 days of receiving his bank statement. Suppose, however, that the signatures on the forged checks had been written in a childish scribble with crayon. The bank would then be negligent in not having noticed the obvious forgery. If the bank was two-thirds to blame and Tom one-third, the bank would owe Tom $20,000, not the full $30,000.

Stale Checks

A bank is not *required* to pay checks that are presented more than six months after their date, but it is not liable if it does pay.[9] In 1962, John Glenn became the first person to orbit the earth. Many people were so eager to have his autograph that they did not cash checks he gave them. In 1974, Glenn was elected senator from Ohio. Suppose that one of his admirers became so disgusted with his political views that she no longer treasured his autograph and tried, in 1974, to cash a check from 1962. Would she be successful? Although Glenn's bank, as a matter of policy, would probably reject the 12-year-old check, it would not be liable to Glenn if it paid. Exhibit 25.3 shows a check that a bank refused to pay.

Post-dated Checks

A post-dated check is one that is presented for payment before its date. **A bank is not liable for paying a post-dated check unless the customer has notified the bank in advance that a post-dated check is coming.**[10] Under the old version of Article 4, banks were not supposed to cash checks until their due date. So, for example, customers could mail off a set of post-dated checks to pay all their bills while on vacation, knowing that the bank would not pay the checks until their due dates. When Article 4 was revised, however, banks argued that this rule was impractical at a time when most banks use machines to process checks. The extra expense of manually reviewing each check is not worth the limited benefit to a few customers.

Stop Payment Orders

Even if a check is authorized when issued, the customer has the right to stop payment later. **As a general rule, if a bank pays a check over a stop payment order, it is liable to the customer for any loss he suffers.**[11] However, a bank customer must be aware of these additional rules:

- Any account holder has the right to stop payment, even someone who did not sign the check.
- A stop payment order is valid only if it describes the check with reasonable certainty and the bank receives the order before paying, or certifying, the check.

---

9 UCC §4-404.

10 UCC §4-401(c).

11 UCC §4-403.

- An oral stop payment order is valid for only 14 days; a written order expires in six months. This is an important point. Many people think that, once they have stopped payment on a check, they can relax and forget about it. Not true. One woman, for example, wrote a $1,000 check to a contractor. When he told her he had lost the check, she stopped payment and gave him a new one, which he promptly cashed. Ten months later, he cashed the old check, too. The customer could have continued to renew the stop payment order every six months (at a cost of about $20 each time), but that would have been a hassle. The only surefire method for stopping a check permanently is to close the old account and open a new one.

Typically, a customer issues a stop payment order because she is having a disagreement over a contract. The customer may or may not be in the right. If a bank accidentally pays a check in violation of a stop payment order, it retains the right to recover from whichever party to the contract was wrong. The "bank is **subrogated to**" the rights of the parties, which means that the bank can substitute for, or take the place of, either party. Section 4-407 provides: **If a bank pays a check despite a valid stop payment order, it inherits the rights of the customer against the payee and of the payee against the customer.**

Exhibit 25.3
Wells Fargo Bank refused to pay this stale check 11 months after it was issued.

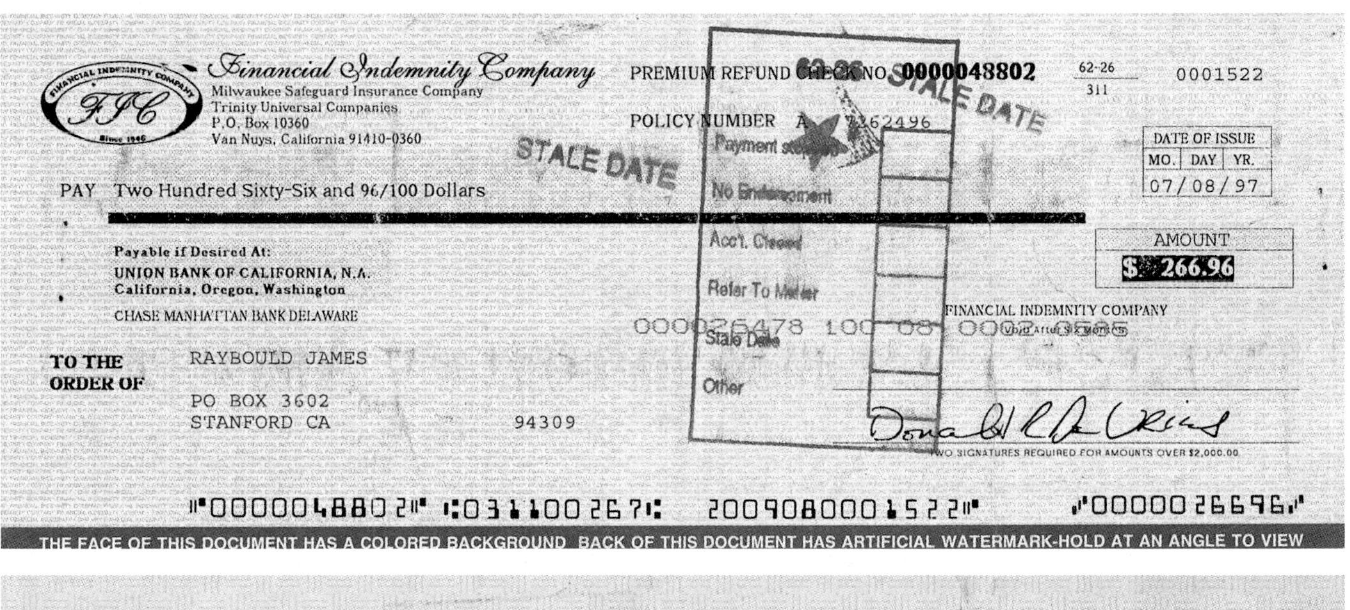

Financial Indemnity Company
Milwaukee Safeguard Insurance Company
Trinity Universal Companies
P.O. Box 10360
Van Nuys, California 91410-0360

PREMIUM REFUND CHECK NO. 0000048802 62-26/311 0001522

POLICY NUMBER A 362496

STALE DATE

DATE OF ISSUE MO. DAY YR. 07/08/97

PAY Two Hundred Sixty-Six and 96/100 Dollars

AMOUNT $ 266.96

Payable if Desired At:
UNION BANK OF CALIFORNIA, N.A.
California, Oregon, Washington
CHASE MANHATTAN BANK DELAWARE

Payment stopped
No Endorsement
Acc't. Closed
Refer To Maker
Stale Date
Other

FINANCIAL INDEMNITY COMPANY
Void After Six Months

TO THE ORDER OF RAYBOULD JAMES
PO BOX 3602
STANFORD CA 94309

TWO SIGNATURES REQUIRED FOR AMOUNTS OVER $2,000.00

⑈0000048802⑈ ⑆031100267⑆ 2009080001522⑈ ⑈0000026696⑈

THE FACE OF THIS DOCUMENT HAS A COLORED BACKGROUND BACK OF THIS DOCUMENT HAS ARTIFICIAL WATERMARK-HOLD AT AN ANGLE TO VIEW

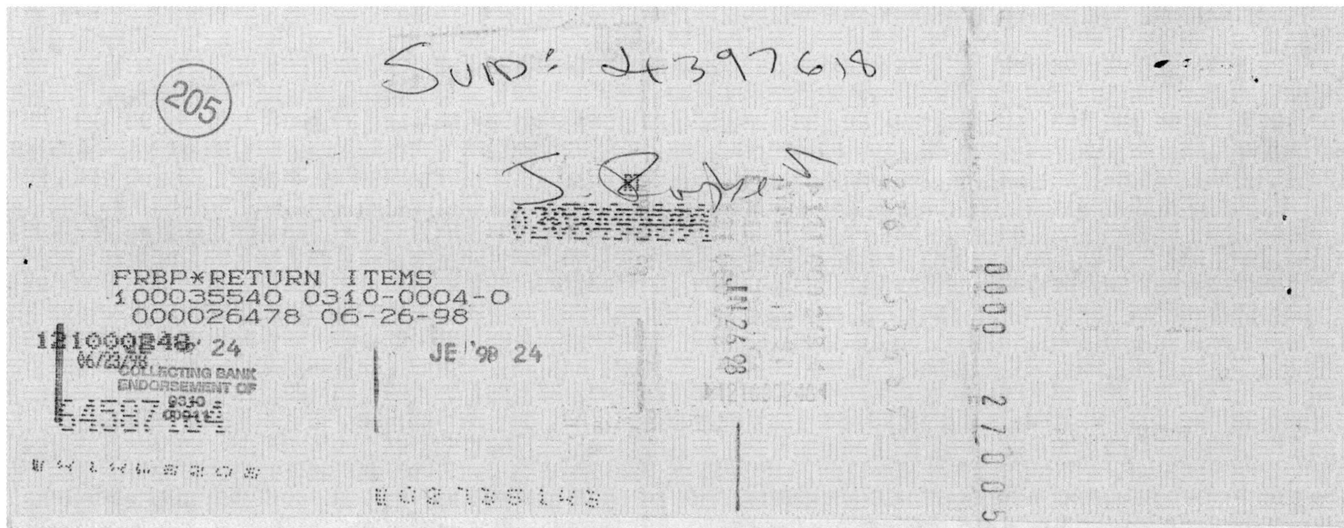

205

FRBP*RETURN ITEMS
100035540 0310-0004-0
000026478 06-26-98

121000248 24
06/23/98
COLLECTING BANK
ENDORSEMENT OF

JE '98 24

Suppose that Jonathan crashes his car into a tree. AutoWrecks does a super job of fixing the car, but on the way home from the shop, Jonathan is so busy changing radio stations, fastening his seat belt, and eating lunch that he crashes into a telephone pole. In the ambulance, he uses his cellular phone to call the bank and stop payment on his check to AutoWrecks. If the bank stops payment, AutoWrecks will sue Jonathan because it was not to blame for the new accident and deserves to be paid for the work it has done. Suppose, however, that the bank makes a mistake and pays the check. Jonathan will demand that the bank recredit his account. At this point, the bank *is subrogated to* the rights of AutoWrecks. The bank will try to prove that Jonathan ought to have paid the check anyway and, therefore, he was not harmed by the bank's error. This is not an ideal situation for the bank; it would rather not be involved in the disputes of its customers. But a right of subrogation is better than nothing, especially if the check is for a substantial sum.

In this instance, the bank inherited the rights of the payee (AutoWrecks) against the issuer (Jonathan). The right of subrogation also works the other way: the bank may inherit the issuer's right to sue the payee. Suppose that Henry (the payee) is an art dealer who sells a sculpture to Wyoming Foundry Studios for $11,500. Wyoming stops payment on the check because the sculpture is not as Henry had advertised it. The bank mistakenly pays the check anyway. It must recredit Wyoming's account, but it is then subrogated to Wyoming's rights against Henry. In a similar case, the court required Henry to repay the bank the money he received from Wyoming.

In the following case, the bank did not stop payment because the customer slightly misidentified the check. Who should be liable—the customer or the bank? You be the judge.

PARR v. SECURITY NATIONAL BANK

680 P.2d 648, 1984 OK CIV APP 16,
1984 Okla. Civ. App. LEXIS 99
Court of Appeals of Oklahoma, 1984

Facts: Joan Parr sent Champlin Oil a check for $972.96. The next day, she called Security National Bank (Bank) to stop payment. She gave the Bank her account number, the check number, the date, the payee, and the amount of the check. Unfortunately, she told the Bank that the check had been for $972.46, instead of $972.96. The next day, the Bank paid the check.

Parr brought suit against the Bank. In its defense, the Bank explained that its computers were programmed to stop payment only if the reported amount of the check was correct. It argued that Parr's 50-cent error relieved the Bank of liability. Section 4-403(1) of the Oklahoma UCC provides:

> A customer may by order to his bank stop payment of any item payable for his account but the order must be received at such time and in such manner as to afford the bank a reasonable opportunity to act on it. . . .

You Be the Judge: Did the Bank have a reasonable opportunity to stop payment on a check when the description received was exact in all respects except for a single digit error in the check amount?

Argument for Parr: Under §4-403, banks are required to obey stop payment orders, notwithstanding the difficulty, inconvenience, and expense. This is not an optional service provided at the Bank's convenience, it is required by law. The Bank argues that it is not at fault because its computer failed to find this check. The Bank made two choices: (1) it used a computer to sort checks, and (2) it programmed the computer to search for stopped checks by amount alone. The Bank evidently found benefits to this system that outweighed the risk that an item might be inaccurately described in a stop order. The bank made a decision to accept that risk; it cannot now shirk its responsibility.

Furthermore, the Bank could have avoided this whole problem if it had simply informed Ms. Parr that the amount listed in the stop order had to be exact. It would never occur to a reasonable person that, having given the date, number, and payee of this check, the amount also had to be accurate to the last penny. The Bank argues that, if it refunds money to Parr, she will be unfairly enriched because her debt to Champlin Oil will be paid, and she will recover from the Bank. There is an easy answer to this argument: the Bank is subrogated to her rights and can pursue Champlin Oil to recover the wrongful payment. Why should Ms. Parr be forced to sue the oil company when the bank made the mistake?

Argument for the Bank: The law generally provides that whoever makes a mistake pays for it. Who made the mistakes here? Parr did. First, she wrote a check that, in fact, she did not want paid. Under the UCC her bank must stop payment on a check that has been received "in such manner as to afford the bank a reasonable opportunity to act." But then Parr made a second mistake—she gave the Bank the wrong amount for the check. Parr argues that, if the Bank uses check processing machines, it must bear the risk of loss. *Every* bank uses check processing machines. It is standard in the industry. We do it to keep our expenses low. And who benefits from lower expenses? Customers, of course. Parr cannot have it both ways. She cannot take the benefit of lower fees and then complain that her bank uses machines to process checks.

Parr also argues that, if she had known that the Bank's machines look for the amount of a check, she would have taken more care to provide the right number. In short, Parr admits she was careless, but she expects the Bank to pay the price for her carelessness. If the Bank is liable for the check, Parr will have her cake and eat it, too: Champlin will be paid and she will have her money. She suggests that the Bank can sue Champlin. Once again, she is trying to foist her mistakes off on an innocent party. The Bank did not have a disagreement with Champlin, so why should it have to fight Parr's battle?

Consumer advocates suggest that bank customers should follow these safeguards:

- *Read bank statements.* Many financial advisers now say that it is not crucial to balance a checkbook, but it is important to look at bank statements (and canceled checks, if there are any) to detect anything out of the ordinary.
- *Keep bank statements and canceled checks.* Without this documentation, it is difficult to prove the bank has made an error.
- *Look at receipts from ATMs.* Richard Kessel, the executive director of the New York State Consumer Protection Board, says, "I wouldn't walk away without a record of the transaction, and I would always make sure it's correct."
- *Write immediately to the bank if there is an error in a statement or ATM receipt.* Mail the information to a specific person who handles consumer complaints; then keep a record of when you contacted the bank, the names of any people you spoke to, and what they said. Be persistent. If you do not hear from the bank, or the answer is unsatisfactory, take your complaint to a higher level in the bank.
- *If you cannot resolve your dispute directly with the bank, write to the agency that regulates it.* Ask someone at your bank for the name of its primary regulator, or call your state banking department and ask for help.[12]

CUSTOMER'S RIGHT TO WITHDRAW FUNDS

One August 7, a Los Angeles woman deposited a $7,500 check drawn on a bank in suburban New York. She was told that she could not withdraw these funds for 10 working days, that is, until August 21. On August 19, when the bank still would not let her withdraw the money, she called the issuer of the check and discovered that the funds had been paid out on August 9. "So my bank," she says, "learned that the check was good right away, and just held my money all that time! Isn't that unfair?"[13]

Banks and their customers have a debtor/creditor relationship. Customers loan banks money that the banks must repay when the customers write a check. No one likes to give money back, banks included. For years, consumer groups

[12] Christine Dugas, "Fighting the Bank," *Newsday*, Nov. 13, 1994, p. 3. Copyright 1994 Newsday, Inc.

[13] S. J. Diamond, "Odyssey of a Check," *Los Angeles Times*, Feb. 15, 1986, p. 1.

complained about delays like the one this Los Angeles woman suffered. They estimated that almost 3 percent of all bounced checks had been written against funds that had already been paid but were not yet available. The law now sets strict guidelines establishing when banks must make funds available.

To understand why banks are frequently slow in making funds available to their customers, consider the payment process for a typical check. Suppose that Heathcliff is a rescue ranger on Mt. Rainier in Washington. At the height of summer, he spends most of his days on the cold, stormy mountain rescuing lost and injured hikers. No surprise then when he decides to go to hot, humid Miami, as far from Mt. Rainier as possible, for his two-week August vacation. He sends a check for $3,000 to the Wuthering Heights hotel. The check is drawn on the Seattle Payor Bank. (If the labels of the various banks—Payor, Depositary—confuse you, refer back to the first section of the chapter.) Here is what happens to Heathcliff's check:

1. Cathy, the owner of Wuthering Heights, deposits Heathcliff's check in the Miami Depositary Bank. When Heathcliff originally ordered his checks from the Seattle Payor bank, they arrived already encoded with symbols that a computer can read. The fractional number in the upper right-hand corner is the routing symbol, Seattle Payor's address, if you will. The number on the bottom left-hand side of the check is Heathcliff's account number. When Cathy deposits the check Heathcliff wrote, the Miami Depositary Bank encodes the amount of the check on the bottom right-hand side so that computers can read that, too. Miami Depositary also issues a *provisional credit* to Cathy's account. It may permit her to draw against this credit, but it is not required to do so.

2. If Miami Depositary and Seattle Payor were in the same geographic region, Miami Depositary would send the check directly to Seattle Payor, or the two banks would exchange checks through a central clearinghouse nearby.

3. Since Miami Depositary and Seattle Payor are not near each other, Miami Depositary sends the check to the Federal Reserve Bank of Atlanta, which is the regional Federal Reserve bank for Florida.[14] Like a game of hot potato, each bank in the collection process must pass a check along before midnight of the next banking day after it receives the check (the so-called **midnight deadline**).

4. The Federal Reserve Bank of Atlanta issues the Miami Depositary bank a *provisional credit* and sends the check to the Federal Reserve Bank in San Francisco, which covers the western part of the United States.

5. The San Francisco Federal Reserve issues a *provisional credit* to the Atlanta Federal Reserve and then presents the check for payment to the Seattle Payor Bank.

6. Seattle Payor examines Heathcliff's account to determine whether the check is good. If Seattle Payor wants to dishonor the check, it must do so before the midnight deadline; otherwise it is *accountable* for the check and must pay it even if Heathcliff cannot. If the check is good, Seattle Payor does not send a formal notice; it simply lets the midnight deadline expire. If the midnight deadline passes without dishonor, all of the *provisional credits* become final, and Cathy can use the funds in her account. Heathcliff is then ready to spend two lovely weeks at sea level, far from the perils of Mt. Rainier.

---

[14] To learn more about the Federal Reserve system, see **http://www.bog.frb.fed.us/** and **http://www.bog.frb.fed.us/otherfrb.htm**.

7. If Seattle Payor dishonors a check of less than $2,500, it can return the check along the same route that it originally traveled, and the provisional credits are canceled at each step of the way as the check bounces back. Again, the banks must pass the check along before their midnight deadline expires. Nonetheless, if a number of banks are involved (as in this example), the return of a dishonored check can take some time. That delay may create a problem for Miami Depositary because, under current law, it is required to make the funds available to Cathy within five business days. If Cathy withdraws the money and skips town, Miami Depositary is left holding the bad check. Small checks create small problems, but large bounced checks can be painful indeed. For this reason, if Seattle Payor dishonors a check of $2,500 or more, it must return the check *directly* to Miami Depositary. If notice does not reach Miami Depositary within two days after Seattle Payor receives the check, Seattle Payor must indemnify Miami Depositary for any losses caused by the delay. Seattle Payor *must* follow this protocol for any check of $2,500 or more, but it is *permitted* to do the same for all checks, even those below the threshold amount of $2,500.

8. Once Miami Depositary receives the notice of dishonor, it will charge back Cathy's account for the amount of the check (and typically a handling fee).

Exhibit 25.4 illustrates the payment process for a check.

Traditionally, the check collection process was controlled by Article 4 and the Federal Reserve Board Regulation J. In 1988, Congress reacted to consumer complaints by passing the Expedited Funds Availability Act (EFAA), which superseded many of the provisions in the UCC and Regulation J. This statute specifies the maximum time a bank may hold funds before allowing a customer to withdraw them. A bank can always pay *earlier* if it wants. The table at the top of the next page lists rules that establish how quickly you can *write a check* against funds in your account. A different set of rules applies if you want to withdraw *cash* out of your account. These hold periods do *not* apply to new accounts, accounts with repeated overdrafts, and any other situation in which a bank has reasonable cause to believe the check is uncollectible.

Banks are at greater risk when customers withdraw cash than when they write a check: the bank still has a number of days before a check must be paid; the

Exhibit 25.4

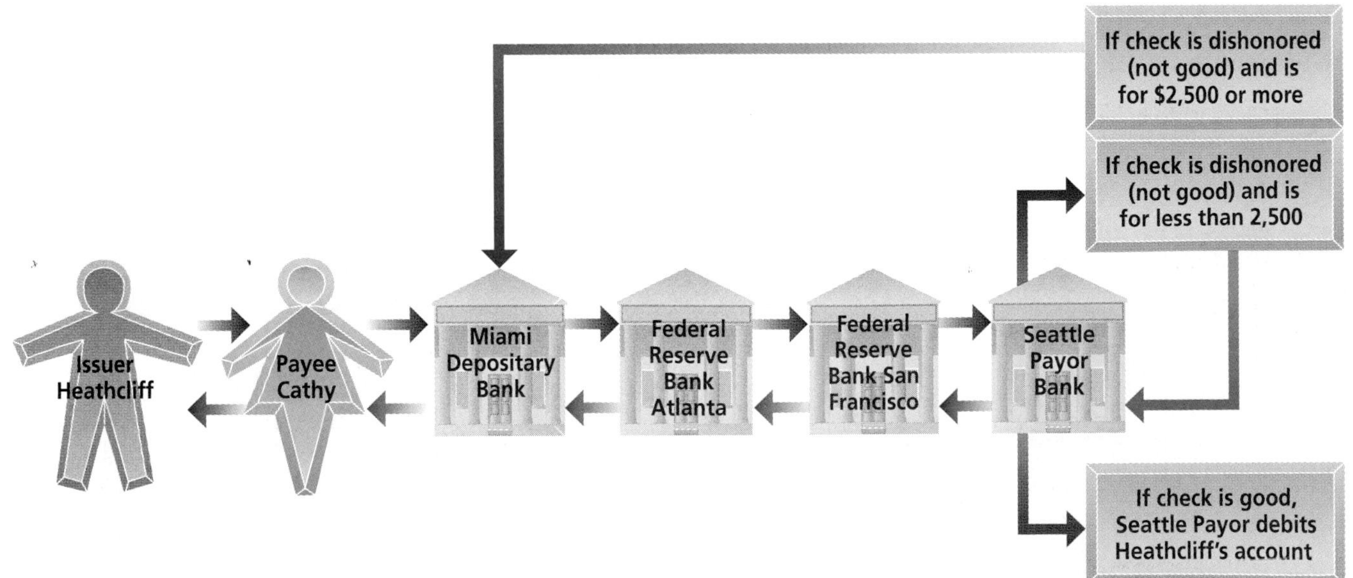

Item Deposited	When Funds May Be Withdrawn by Check:
Cash Cashier's check Certified check Government check Check drawn on same bank Wire transfer	• Next business day, if deposited with a teller • Second business day, if deposited in an ATM
Local check (both the depositary bank and the payor bank are in the same region)	• Next business day, for the first $100 • Second business day, for the balance up to $5,000 • Ninth business day, for the balance over $5,000
Nonlocal check	• Next business day, for the first $100 • Fifth business day, for the balance up to $5,000 • Ninth business day, for the balance over $5,000

cash is gone immediately. Therefore, **customers must wait longer to withdraw cash than they do to write a check.** On the next business day after depositing a check, a customer can withdraw the first $100 in cash. He can withdraw $400 more in cash by 5:00 P.M. on the same day that the funds are available for check writing. The rest of the deposit can be withdrawn the day after funds are available for check writing. Exhibit 25.5 illustrates these rules on funds availability.

Exhibit 25.5[15]

Monday (Day 0)	Tuesday (Day 1)	Wednesday (Day 2)	Thursday (Day 3)	Friday (Day 4)	Monday (Day 5)	Tuesday (Day 6)
Local Check $1,000	$100 check or $100 cash	$900 check or $400 cash	$500 cash			
Nonlocal Check $1,000	$100 check or $100 cash				$900 check or $400 cash	$500 cash

[15] Adapted from a chart prepared by the Federal Reserve Board. *Reprinted in* Douglas J. Whaley, *Problems and Materials on Payment Law* (Boston: Little, Brown & Co., 1995), at 218.

Electronic Banking

Back to the Future

In 1968, a bank in Philadelphia installed the first automated teller machine (ATM) in the United States. Until that time, anyone who needed money for the weekend had two choices: cash a check at the bank before it closed (at 3:00 P.M. on Friday, 1:00 P.M. on Saturday) or find a local merchant who would cash a small check after hours. The same person had two options for paying a bill: cash or check. Today, thanks to advances in electronic fund transfers, we have options that were barely imagined a generation ago:

- ATMs that dispense cash around the clock, accept deposits, and make transfers between accounts
- Point of sale (POS) terminals that deduct funds directly from a bank account with a debit card instead of a check
- Automatic deposit systems that allow employers to deposit salaries directly into employees' accounts, instead of sending checks
- Services that permit consumers to pay their bills over telephone lines

These new services offer added convenience and efficiency to consumers who can now obtain cash day or night and pay their bills with a few clicks of the mouse. They also reduce costs for banks—shipping billions of checks around the globe is expensive. But the advances in technology are so new that this area of the law is changing rapidly and will undoubtedly continue to do so for some time.

A few years ago hardly anyone even knew what debit cards were. But banks began to promote them heavily, even mailing out unsolicited cards to their customers. (Each time a consumer uses a card, the bank collects a fee from the merchant. Currently, most banks do not charge consumers, but reserve the right to do so in the future, once the cards catch on.) Now, more than one in four Americans carries a debit card. But many are still confused about all those pieces of plastic in their wallets:

- *Debit Cards versus ATM Cards.* The very same piece of plastic can be both an ATM card and a debit card, depending on where you use it. If you want to buy dinner, you can put your card in an ATM, punch in your personal identification number (PIN), and withdraw cash on the spot. Or you can take your card to a restaurant that has a point of sale terminal. At the end of the meal, you present the card and your meal is paid for. What is the difference? Everyone accepts cash; not all restaurants have point of sale terminals. Your money from the ATM disappears from your account immediately; the debit card transaction takes a day or two to register (especially on the weekend). If you lose your wallet on the way to the restaurant, the cash is gone for good, but your losses on the debit card are limited. (These limits are discussed in the next section.)
- *Debit Cards versus Credit Cards.* At the restaurant, you might have a choice between using your debit card or a credit card (although more restaurants accept credit cards). What is the difference here? If you pay with a credit card, the money stays firmly in your account until you pay your credit card bill. With a debit card, the funds disappear from your account much sooner. If you do not keep track, your checks may bounce. Also, many credit cards now offer perks such as frequent flyer mileage.

- *Debit Cards versus Checks.* Many restaurants accept checks reluctantly or not at all. They inevitably make a great production of copying all the details from your two pieces of identification. Debit cards are easier, and in both cases, your funds disappear from your account within days. At the end of the month, however, most banks will send you canceled checks. With debit cards you get only a bank statement. Debit cards work best if you are organized about record keeping.

ELECTRONIC FUND TRANSFER ACT

In the beginning, electronic fund transfers were governed by contract between a bank and its customers, not by state or national statutes. Some banks treated their customers better than others. For example, roughly one-third of banks refused to recredit a customer for unauthorized transfers. Thus, if Biff stole Marty's ATM card and emptied his account, Marty was simply out of luck. Gradually, states began to regulate electronic transfers. This was better than nothing, but it did not solve the problem of interstate transfers. In 1978, Congress passed the Electronic Fund Transfer Act (EFTA) to protect **consumers.** The statute defines a consumer as "any natural person," that is, not a corporation or business. Following are the major provisions of the EFTA.

Required Electronic Fund Transfers

Employers may not require their employees to receive paychecks via an electronic fund transfer at *a particular bank*. Suppose the CEO of MegaCorp. has decided that the company must cut costs to stay competitive in its industry. Her chief financial officer tells her the company can save thousands of dollars in administrative expenses if it pays employees via electronic fund transfers instead of by check. (On average, it costs about 42 cents to issue and mail a paper check but only 2 cents to process an electronic payment.) In addition, the Dawes Bank will agree to give MegaCorp. favorable financing on a major loan if the company pays all employees by electronic fund transfer to Dawes. Under the EFTA, MegaCorp. can require all employees to receive their pay via an electronic fund transfer, but the company cannot require employees to be paid at Dawes.

Cards

If a bank sends an electronic fund transfer card (for example, an ATM card) to a consumer who has not requested it, the card must be invalid until the consumer requests validation. Otherwise, if banks sent valid ATM cards to consumers who were not expecting them, the cards could be stolen and used without the consumer ever knowing. To validate a card, the bank typically assigns the consumer a PIN. The card does not work unless the PIN is entered with each transaction.

Documentation

A bank must provide consumers with (1) a transaction statement each time an electronic fund transfer is made at an ATM and (2) a monthly (or, in the case of infrequent transactions, quarterly) statement reporting all electronic fund transfers for the period.

Preauthorized Transfers

Consumers sometimes ask banks to wire funds on a regular basis—to pay the monthly mortgage, say. A bank may not make preauthorized transfers without written instructions from the consumer. The consumer can stop payment of the transfer by oral or written notice up to three business days before the scheduled date.

Errors

If, within 60 days of receiving a bank statement, a consumer tells the bank (either orally or in writing) that the account is in error, the bank must investigate and report the result of its investigation to the consumer within 10 *business* days. If the bank discovers an error, it must recredit the consumer's account (including interest) within one *business* day. If the bank cannot complete its investigation within 10 business days, it must provisionally recredit the consumer's account (including interest) pending the termination of its investigation, which must be completed within 45 *calendar* days. If the bank finds there was no error, it must give the consumer a full explanation in writing within three *business* days of so finding. When a bank violates this provision, it must pay the consumer treble damages (three times the amount in dispute). Exhibit 25.6 illustrates these rules.

The EFTA was promulgated to address the following kinds of errors:

- *Unauthorized Transfer*. Someone withdraws money from an account without permission.
- *Disbursement Error*. The consumer receives $80 from the ATM, but $100 is deducted from her account.
- *Omitted Transfer*. A transfer is never applied to an account. (For some reason, omitted deposits are reported more often than omitted withdrawals.)
- *Computational Error*. The bank makes a mathematical miscalculation.

Exhibit 25.6

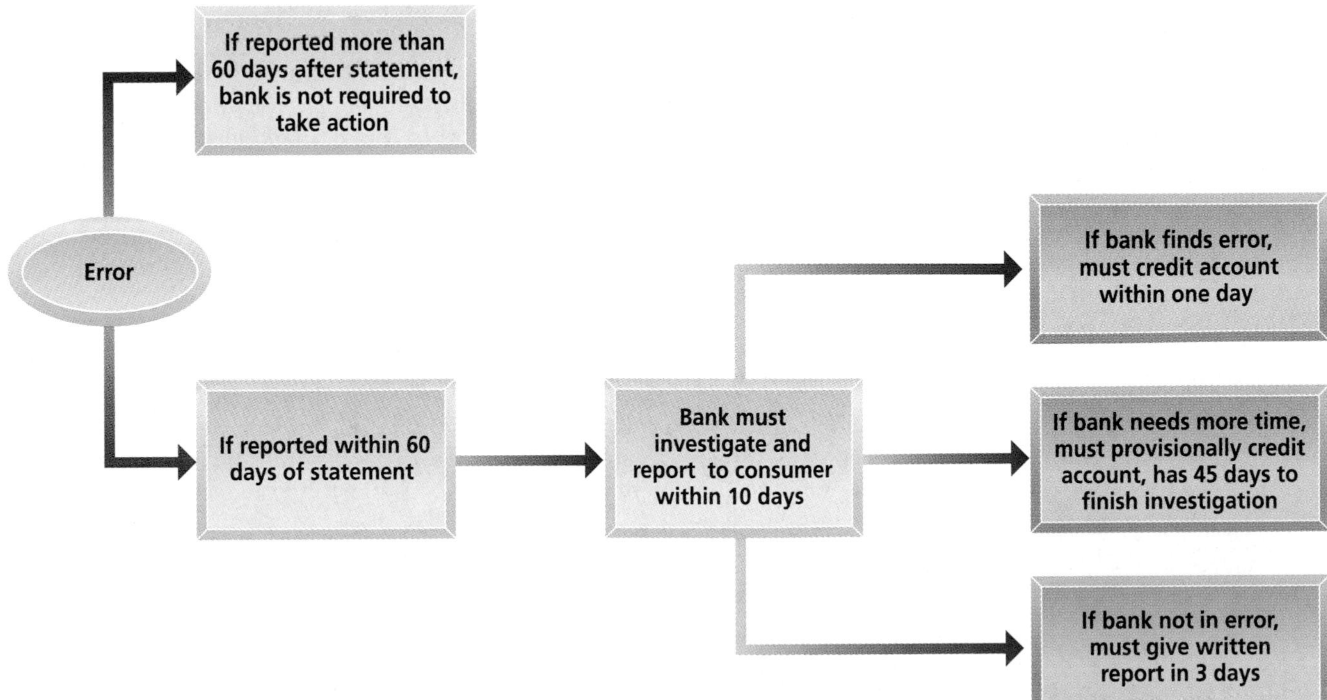

Consumer Liability for Unauthorized Transactions

When a thief steals an ATM card, it is important for the consumer to report the theft to the bank as quickly as possible.[16] If she reports the loss within two days of discovering it, she is liable only for the first $50 stolen. If she reports the loss after two days, but within 60 days of receiving her bank statement that shows the unauthorized withdrawal, she is liable for a maximum of $500. After 60 days, she is liable for the full amount.

If an unauthorized transfer takes place without the use of a stolen card, the consumer is liable only for $50, provided that she tells the bank within 60 days of receiving her bank statement. (Clever thieves can, for example, make cards that will work in someone else's account.[17]) If the bank fails to give a consumer either a PIN or some other device to make unauthorized withdrawals difficult, the consumer is not liable for any amount. You remember that, if a customer's negligence contributes to a check forgery, the bank may not be liable. That is not true for electronic funds: the bank is liable even if the customer was negligent. Suppose Marty writes his PIN on his ATM card and then accidentally leaves the card at the ATM. When Biff uses the card to withdraw funds, the bank is still liable for any withdrawal in excess of $50 (which is why many banks limit daily withdrawals to, say, $500). Who is liable in the following incident?

As a young couple sat one night in the empty bleachers of a ballpark near San Francisco, two men accosted them and demanded their wallets. When the robbers discovered an ATM card, they ordered the victims to walk to a nearby shopping center, about a half-mile away, and withdraw $200 from a bank machine. The suspects then fled on foot.[18]

Crimes at ATMs have become increasingly common. Who is responsible for the $200 that this young couple lost? Robbery is an "unauthorized electronic fund transfer," so the couple will be liable only for $50, provided they tell the bank within 60 days. The bank must pick up the tab for the remaining $150.

When a consumer is robbed at an ATM, the bank is liable for any losses over $50 if reported to the bank within 60 days.

Bank's Liability

As we have seen, the bank's liability for *unauthorized* transfers depends upon how soon the consumer reports the loss. In addition, a bank is liable to a consumer for any damages caused by the bank's failure to make an *authorized* electronic fund transfer. Bert asks the Tomes Bank to transfer funds every month to pay his mortgage. He goes off hiking in Alaska for the summer, secure in the knowledge that his mortgage will be paid while he is gone. When he returns to find his house in foreclosure proceedings because the bank did not make the payments, he can recover damages from the bank.

System Malfunction

If a system malfunction prevents an electronic fund transfer, the consumer's obligation to make the payment is suspended until the malfunction is repaired or until the intended recipient has, in writing, requested nonelectronic payment. If

---

16 The Web site **http://www.ftc.gov/bcp/menu-credit.htm** tells you what to do if you lose a credit card.

17 See Question 7 of the Practice Test at the end of the chapter for an example.

18 "Police Searching for ATM Robbery Suspects," *San Francisco Chronicle*, July 17, 1995, p. C12. The Web site **http://www.calbankers.com/legal/atmsurv.html** gives advice about avoiding crime at ATMs.

Bert's mortgage payment is not made because of a system malfunction, the mortgage company cannot charge him a penalty or foreclose on his house during the time the system is down. In fact, he has no obligation to make the payment until the system is working again or until the mortgage company, in writing, requests payment by check.

Disclosure

All of these rules must be disclosed to the consumer (in readily understandable language!) before she opens an account that has electronic fund transfer capability. In addition, banks are required to post all ATM fees on the machine itself.

The goal of the EFTA is to protect consumers. As the following case illustrates, however, that protection goes only so far. It is important for consumers to pay careful attention to the EFTA time limits.

KRUSER v. BANK OF AMERICA

230 Cal. App. 3d 741, 1991 Cal. App. LEXIS 523, 281 Cal. Rptr. 463

Court of Appeal of California, 1991

Facts: Mr. and Mrs. Kruser each had an ATM card for their joint account at the Bank of America (Bank). The Bank referred to this as a "Versatel" card. Mr. Kruser believed his card was destroyed in September 1986. It turned out, however, that someone used it to make an unauthorized withdrawal of $20 from the account in December 1986. That same month, Mrs. Kruser underwent surgery and was hospitalized for 11 days. She then spent six or seven months recuperating at home. Her recovery underwent a nasty setback, however, when she discovered in September 1987 that someone had illegally withdrawn $9,020 from the account during July and August 1987. The Bank refused to refund the money. The Krusers sued, but the trial court granted the Bank's motion for summary judgment. The Krusers appealed.

Issue: Did the Krusers' failure to report the unauthorized withdrawal in December prevent them from recovering the much larger amount stolen in July and August?

Excerpts from Judge Stone's Decision: Appellants [that is, Mr. and Mrs. Kruser] contend the December withdrawal of $20 was so isolated in time and minimal in amount that it cannot be considered in connection with the July and August withdrawals. They assert the [lower] court's interpretation would have absurd results which would be inconsistent with the primary objective of the EFTA—to protect the consumer. They argue that if a consumer receives a bank statement which reflects an unauthorized minimal electronic transfer and fails to report the transaction to the bank within 60 days of transmission of the bank statement, unauthorized transfers many years later, perhaps totaling thousands of dollars, would remain the responsibility of the consumer.

The result appellants fear is avoided by the requirement that the bank establish the subsequent unauthorized transfers could have been prevented had the consumer notified the bank of the first unauthorized transfer. Here, although the unauthorized transfer of $20 occurred approximately seven months before the unauthorized transfers totaling $9,020, it is undisputed that all transfers were made by someone using Mr. Kruser's card which the Krusers believed had been destroyed prior to December 1986. According to the declaration of Yvonne Maloon, the Bank's Versatel risk manager, the Bank could have and would have canceled Mr. Kruser's card had it been timely notified of the December unauthorized transfer. In that event Mr. Kruser's card could not have been used to accomplish the unauthorized transactions in July and August.

Appellants contend the facts establish that Mrs. Kruser, who was solely responsible for reconciling the bank statements, was severely ill when the December withdrawal occurred. Therefore, they claim they were entitled to an extension of time within which to notify the Bank. The evidence appellants rely upon indicates Mrs. Kruser left her house infrequently during the first six or seven months of 1987 while she was recuperating. Mrs. Kruser admits, however, she received and reviewed bank statements during her recuperation. Therefore, we need not consider whether Mrs. Kruser's illness created circumstances which might have excused her failure to notice the unauthorized withdrawal pursuant to the applicable sections. She in fact did review the statements in question.

Moreover, nothing in the record reflects any extenuating circumstances which would have prevented Mr. Kruser from reviewing the bank statements. The understanding he had with Mrs. Kruser that she would review the bank statements did not excuse him from his obligation to notify the bank of any unauthorized electronic transfers.

We affirm the judgment and award costs on appeal to respondent.

Someone uses Mr. Kruser's ATM card to withdraw $20. Mrs. Kruser undergoes major surgery and fails to notice the unauthorized withdrawal. (How many *healthy* people would notice one unauthorized $20 withdrawal?) Six months later, someone steals more than $9,000 from the Krusers' account and the Bank refuses to pay. It litigates the case to the appeals court, undoubtedly incurring well more than $9,000 in legal fees. Why did the Bank do this? Was it the right thing to do?

Wire Transfers

Electronic fund transfers are important to consumers, but the amount of money they transfer pales in comparison with wholesale wire transfers among banks and their commercial customers. Within the United States, the Federal Reserve system maintains a wire transfer system called "Fedwire." More than $989 billion is sent each day via Fedwire; the average amount per transaction is $3 million. International wire transfers are handled by Clearinghouse Interbank Payments System (CHIPS), based in New York. About $1.3 trillion is sent through CHIPS each day; the average wire is nearly $7 million. As the following newspaper article indicates, new technology creates new opportunities—and new problems.

A $10 million computer fraud against Citibank appears to be the first successful penetration by a hacker into the systems that transfer trillions of dollars a day around the world's banks. A 34-year-old Russian and his accomplices were accused of tapping into Citibank's computer system and transferring $10 million to various bank accounts in this country and overseas. Citibank noticed the activity after several of its customers complained about unauthorized transfers from their accounts. Banking experts said similar break-ins were bound to occur as more banking business is done electronically and more powerful personal computers become available.[19]

UCC Article 4A regulates *nonconsumer* wire transfers. A wire transfer is a type of **payment order.** Article 4A governs payment orders while Article 3 deals with

---

[19] Saul Hansell, "Citibank Fraud Case Raises Computer Security Questions," *New York Times*, Aug. 19, 1995, p. 31. Copyright © 1995 by The New York Times Co. Reprinted by permission.

checks. The difference between a check and a payment order has sometimes been described as push-pull. A check permits the payee to *pull* money out of the issuer's account while a payment order *pushes* money out of the issuer's account into the payee's.

Suppose that Cooper, Inc. plans to buy Maxine, Inc.'s water ride park in Columbia, South Carolina. Cooper could write a check for $1 million to Maxine on Cooper's CoopBank. When Maxine presents that check for payment, CoopBank will pull $1 million out of Cooper's account. If, however, Cooper sends a wire to Maxine for the same amount, CoopBank takes the money out of the account and then uses a wire to push that money to the local Federal Reserve bank. The Federal Reserve bank debits CoopBank's account there and pushes the funds to Maxine's bank, MaxBank. The Federal Reserve notifies MaxBank that it has received $1 million for Maxine. MaxBank pushes the money into Maxine's account. Exhibit 25.7 illustrates the difference between checks and payment orders.

Article 4A uses the following terminology to describe the various participants in a wire transfer:

- **Originator.** The person who sends the first payment order in a transaction (Cooper)
- **Originator's Bank.** The bank that issues the originator's payment order (CoopBank)
- **Sender.** Anyone who gives instructions to a receiving bank (Cooper, CoopBank, and Federal Reserve bank)
- **Beneficiary.** The person who receives the payment order (Maxine)
- **Receiving Bank.** Any bank to which the sender's instructions are sent (CoopBank, Federal Reserve bank, and MaxBank)
- **Intermediary Bank.** Any receiving bank other than the originator's bank or the beneficiary's bank (Federal Reserve bank)
- **Beneficiary's Bank.** The bank identified in the payment order, which has an account in the beneficiary's name (MaxBank)

Exhibit 25.7

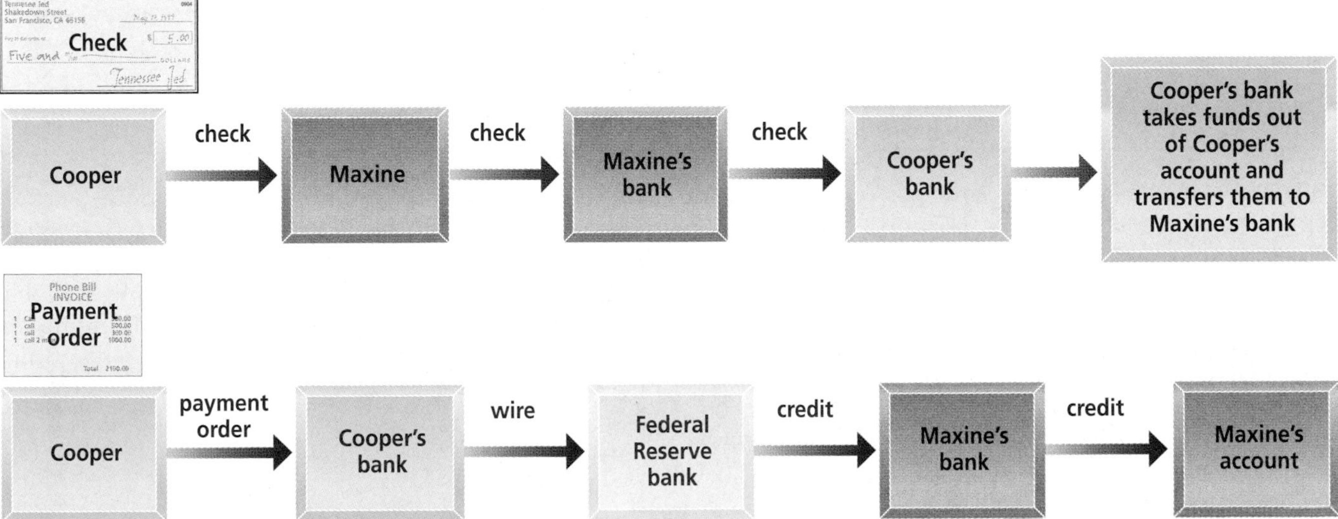

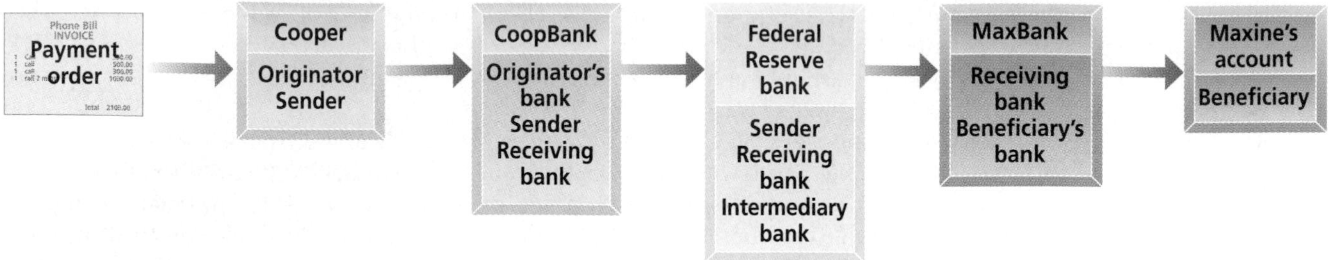

Exhibit 25.8

Exhibit 25.8 illustrates the terminology used to describe the participants in Cooper's wire transfer to Maxine.

Wire transfers often involve very large sums of money. What happens when mistakes occur, as mistakes inevitably will?

Bank Sends the Wrong Amount of Money

If a bank sends more money than the payment order specified, it is liable for the extra amount. Its recourse is to recover the excess from the beneficiary. If the bank sends too little money, the originator must pay only the amount sent, not the amount of the order.[20]

Bank Sends Money to the Wrong Person

If any bank issues a payment order to the wrong person, the bank is liable for the full amount of the payment. It can try to recover from the unintended recipient. The originator and any prior bank are not liable.[21]

Sometimes, a beneficiary's bank receives a payment order with an account name and number that do not match. If the bank notices the mismatch, it should not pay any account. If the bank does not notice and pays the account specified by the number, it is not liable even if that turns out to be the wrong account. The originator is liable. If the beneficiary's bank relies on the name instead of the number, it is liable and must reimburse the originator. As you can imagine, banks have a tendency to look only at the account number, not at the name. There is, however, one major exception to this rule. If a nonbank originator gives the wrong number and the right name, he is not liable when the payment is made to the wrong person unless *his* bank warned him that the beneficiary's bank would make payment based on the number, not the name.[22]

In the following case, Marine Midland Bank in New York sent a sizable sum to the wrong bank in the wrong country.

IRWIN FASHION IMPORTS INC. v. MARINE MIDLAND BANK
New York Law Journal, Sept. 8, 1994, p. 21
Supreme Court of New York, 1994

Facts: Irwin Fashion Imports, Inc. (Irwin) imported fabrics from Eastern Europe. Irwin paid for these purchases with electronic wire transfers through Marine Midland Bank (Midland). On five different dates, Irwin's employee, Judith Gill, gave instructions to Marie Castellanos, head of Midland's Global Funds Department, to wire payments to Mosilana, a fabric supplier. These funds, in the amount of $1,345,819.60, were to be wired to Mosilana's bank, Banka Brno-

20 UCC §4A-303(a), (b).

21 UCC §4A-303(c).

22 UCC §4A-207.

Mesto in Brno-Mesto, Czechoslovakia. Instead, Castellanos wired the funds to Intersped, at Panonska Bank in Novi Sad, Yugoslavia. Intersped was a courier that had provided services in the past to Irwin.

When Mosilana told Irwin it had not received the funds, Irwin paid Mosilana again and then sued Midland for the misplaced money. It turned out that one of the wire transfers, in the amount of $177,819, had not been paid by an intermediary bank after the United States imposed sanctions against Yugoslavia. The intermediary bank refunded that payment to Irwin with interest. Castellanos admitted she had made an error in sending that wire transfer but denied that she or Midland had any responsibility for the four other missing payments.

Issue: Is Midland liable for sending wire transfers to the wrong party?

Excerpts from Justice Wright's Decision: The instructions issued by plaintiff appear to be specific and quite clear and unmistakable and the errors of Ms. Castellanos appear to be equally so, mistaken, that is, by her. Ms. Castellanos, instead of relying upon instructions from plaintiff as to routing, appears to have relied on one concerning Intersped. Contributing to her errors was the fact that she admitted that some documents related to transfers and instructions were not read completely. As a consequence, a transfer of the sum of $462,189.23 found its way to Yugoslavia, as did $72,352.43; $520,301.55; $113,156.95; and the previously mentioned $177,819.67 (that has now been refunded to plaintiff, with interest.)

Ms. Castellanos sought to show in her testimony that her routing instructions [from the plaintiff] were in error and that she was not, except for her earlier mentioned concession of error as to the item for $177,819.67. There was extended testimony about confusion said to have existed concerning Banka Brno-Mesto, with a belief expressed that no such bank existed. Interestingly, defendant appears to have sent five wire transfers to a bank it said it could not find and that it believed did not exist. One transfer of $113,156.95 was "formatted incorrectly" by the defendant.

Despite the conceded errors of Ms. Castellanos, she sought desperately to cast blame upon plaintiff's Judith Gill, an accusation that Ms. Gill contested and denied. The defensive attitude of Ms. Castellanos did not come across as either candid or truthful and impressed the court as [an] invention of desperate convenience uttered in the tradition of the morality of self-interest and anxiety to focus blame from her employer to the plaintiff. It was an incredible performance, but not a persuasive one. Except for the one admission pro confesso of a mistake, Ms. Castellanos was wholly unsuccessful in mustering credibility. Often, her claims were rebutted by documentary evidence that made her out to be either simply wrong, or a liar.

On the basis of the credible evidence, because of defendant's failed execution properly of the wire transfers, defendant is liable not only for interest, but for plaintiff's "expenses in the funds transfer and for incidental expenses" resulting from "improper execution." Such expenses include "reasonable attorney's fees."

Settle judgment in accordance with the foregoing.

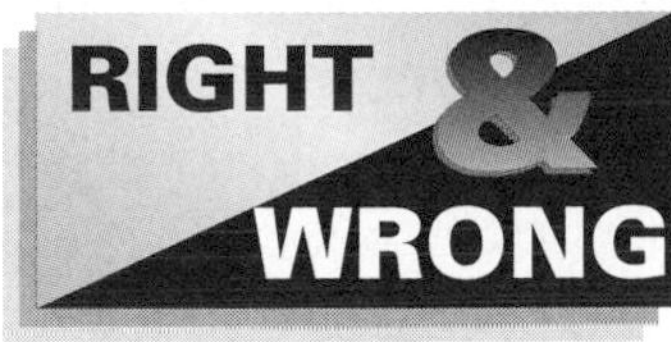

The bank in this case made a mistake—it wired a customer's money to the wrong account at the wrong bank in the wrong country. Having made a mistake, the bank then forced the hapless customer to suffer the delay and expense of litigation. Was that the right thing to do? What should the bank have done?

CHAPTER CONCLUSION

This area of law merits careful study for two reasons. First, it is important to everyone who has ever written a check or used an ATM, which is to say, virtually everyone. Second, the law is changing rapidly. A generation ago, no one would have asked "How much do I owe if my ATM card is stolen?" because ATMs did not exist. In many cases, the questions are still the same—"When can a bank pay a post-dated check?"—but now the answer is different.

CHAPTER REVIEW

1. If a bank wrongfully dishonors an authorized check, it is liable to the customer for all actual and consequential damages.
2. A bank is not liable for paying the checks of an incompetent customer until it knows that the customer has been adjudicated incompetent. If a customer dies, the bank may continue to pay checks for 10 days after it learns of the death, unless it receives a stop payment order from someone claiming an interest in the account.
3. If a bank pays a check on which the issuer's name is forged, it must recredit the issuer's account.
4. If a bank pays a check that has been altered, the customer is liable only for the original terms of the check, and the bank is liable for the balance.
5. If a bank pays an incomplete check that was filled in by someone other than the original issuer, the bank is not liable unless it was on notice that the completion was improper.
6. A bank is not required to pay checks that are presented more than six months after their date, but it is not liable if it does pay.
7. A bank has no liability for paying a check before its date unless the customer notifies the bank in advance that the check is coming.
8. If a bank pays a check over a stop payment order, it is liable to the customer for any loss he suffers as a result. The bank is subrogated to the rights of both the customer and the payee.
9. If a bank sends an electronic fund transfer card (for example, an ATM card) to a consumer who has not requested it, the card must be invalid until the consumer requests validation.
10. If, within 60 days of receiving a bank statement, a consumer tells the bank (either orally or in writing) that the account is in error, the bank must investigate and report the result of its investigation to the consumer within 10 business days.
11. When a thief uses a stolen card to withdraw money, the consumer is not liable for more than $50, provided she notifies the bank within two business days that the card has been stolen.
12. If a bank issues a payment order to the wrong person, the bank is liable for the full amount of the payment.

PRACTICE TEST

1. On May 1, Lucile Fischer indorsed a $2,000 check. That same day, Nevada State Bank cashed the check and initiated collection through Valley Bank. Ninety days later, on July 28, Valley Bank notified State Bank that the check had been dishonored, stating "original lost in transit—account closed." On July 29, State Bank debited Fischer's account for $2,000. Fischer sued State Bank for a refund, alleging that the notice of dishonor had not been made in a timely fashion. State Bank initiated collection within one day of Fischer's indorsement and gave notice of dishonor within one day of receiving such notice. Must State Bank refund the $2,000?

2. Hassan Qassemzadeh had an account at the IBM Poughkeepsie Employees Federal Credit Union. On December 1, he wrote a check for $9.60, which was altered and subsequently cashed for $9,000.60. In January, the Credit Union mailed his statement to his niece, as he had directed. This statement indicated that the check had been paid on January 6 for $9,000.60. Qassemzadeh notified the Credit Union of the alteration the following January. Is the Credit Union liable to Qassemzadeh for the amount of the altered check?

3. Begg & Daigle, Inc. wrote a check for $31,989.80 to Newwall Interior Partitions, Inc. Begg then asked Chemical Bank to stop payment on the check. In November, the bank accidentally paid the check. This payment was reflected in Begg's November statement, but Begg did not discover the mistaken payment until the following February. In the meantime, Begg sent a second check to Newwall in payment of the full amount. Begg demanded that the bank recredit its account for the amount of the stopped check. Is the bank liable for paying this check over the stop payment order?

4. This question appeared in the (Minneapolis) *Star Tribune* in 1993. How would you answer it?

> Q.—I have a payroll check issued to me that was misplaced and recently found. The check is from 1974 but nothing on the check says it must be cashed within a certain amount of time. Will a bank accept this check?

5. Woodhaven Knitting Mills wrote a check to Ava Industries for $19,500, drawn on Manufacturers Hanover Trust Co. Woodhaven asked Manufacturers Hanover to stop payment on the check, but the bank paid the check accidentally. The bank was subrogated to Woodhaven's interest against Ava, and Ava paid the bank $5,000. As a result, the bank's loss was reduced from $19,500 to $14,500. The bank filed suit against Woodhaven for $14,500, alleging that Woodhaven owed that sum to Ava. Does the bank have a valid claim against Woodhaven?

6. The following article appeared in the *Los Angeles Times*. Is there anything Elowsky could have done to reduce Prudential Bache's losses?

> A former Prudential Bache Finance vice president testified Friday that she accepted a $2-million postdated check from ZZZZ Best carpet cleaning kingpin Barry Minkow after he flew her to Los Angeles, showered her with flowers and took her out for an intimate seaside dinner in Malibu. Sheri Elowsky, 31, said she was surprised by the attentions from Minkow, who "complimented me on my looks, my intelligence, [and] ... told me that I was intimidating because I was so bright." After a "lark" of a weekend in Los Angeles, she said, she called Minkow to tell him she had approved a $225,000 extension on the young entrepreneur's $5 million credit line with Prudential Bache. "He ended the conversation by saying, 'I love you,'" said Elowsky. . . . Two days later, ZZZZ Best's stock dropped by nearly 25 percent in trading of more than 2 million shares. Minkow failed to return [Elowsky's] frantic phone calls to ZZZZ Best headquarters. . . . A day later, she reached two members of ZZZZ Best's board of directors, who told her that Minkow had resigned the night before "for health reasons" and that the $2 million postdated check "would not be honored."[23]

7. Rev. Janet Hooper Ritchie knew that the shoe store at Buckland Hills mall in Manchester, Connecticut, would not accept a Discover credit card, so she stopped at the ATM for a $100 cash advance. Ritchie, a Congregational minister, inserted her card only to have it returned with a slip that said her withdrawal had been rejected. As the ATM screen flashed a similar message, Ritchie thought that it was odd the slip did not bear the name of a bank. A few days later, she learned she was one of more than 100 customers bilked of confidential code information through the

[23] Kim Murphy, "Minkow Wooed and Swindled Her, Loan Officer Says," *Los Angeles Times*, Oct. 22, 1988, Part 2, p. 1. Copyright 1988, *Los Angeles Times*. Reprinted by permission.

phony ATM. The crooks made off with a total of $100,000 after using the code information to make counterfeit bank cards. They hit ATMs up and down the East Coast to pillage customer accounts. Who is liable for these losses—the banks or the customers whose accounts were looted?

8. **CPA QUESTION** In general, which of the following statements is correct concerning the priority among checks drawn on a particular account and presented to the drawee bank on a particular day?

(a) The checks may be charged to the account in any order convenient to the bank.

(b) The checks may be charged to the account in any order provided no charge creates an overdraft.

(c) The checks must be charged to the account in the order in which the checks were dated.

(d) The checks must be charged to the account in the order of lowest amount to highest amount to minimize the number of dishonored checks.

9. Harriet goes to the teller window and deposits a $1,000 tax refund check from the United States Treasury into her checking account. Two business days later, she sees the apartment of her dreams and wants to withdraw the entire $1,000 in cash to put down a security deposit and first month's rent on the apartment before anyone else sees it. She:

(a) Can withdraw only $100

(b) Can withdraw only $400

(c) Can withdraw the whole amount

(d) Cannot withdraw anything

10. **RIGHT & WRONG** Sandra Bisbey authorized her bank to make monthly electronic fund transfers to her life insurance company. In September, Bisbey's account did not have enough funds to cover this payment so no transfer was made. In October, Bisbey's account still lacked sufficient funds, but the bank made payments for both months anyway and sent two overdraft notices to her (but did not charge an overdraft fee). Bisbey, having forgotten her nonpayment in September, believed that the bank had erroneously made two payments in October. She called the bank to report this alleged error. Ten days later, an official of the bank telephoned her and explained that both payments had been proper. Bisbey filed suit under the EFTA, alleging that the bank unlawfully failed to inform her of the result of its investigation. Did the bank violate the EFTA? Is it liable even if its violation caused no harm to the plaintiff? The bank's actions actually benefited Bisbey: she received insurance coverage without paying an overdraft fee. Was it right for her to file suit under these circumstances?

11. Shawmut Bank in Massachusetts transferred $10,000 from the account of American Optical Corp. via Fedwire to the account of Fernando Degan at the First American Bank in West Palm Beach, Florida. Although the money was intended for Degan and the payment order had his name alone, Shawmut listed an account number at First American that was jointly held by Degan and Joseph Merle, rather than the account that was held solely by Degan. Once the money was transferred into the joint account, Merle withdrew it. Shawmut sued First American, alleging that First American was liable for the mistaken transfer because it had placed the funds in a joint account, not in Degan's sole account as the payment order had indicated. Is First American liable to Shawmut?

12. **YOU BE THE JUDGE WRITING PROBLEM** Roger Duchow (owner of Duchow's Marine, Inc.) borrowed money from General Electric Capital Corp. (GECC) to buy boats for his business. He agreed that when he sold a boat, he would deposit the funds in a blocked account at Central Bank. Funds could be withdrawn from this blocked account only with GECC's signature. Duchow also had a separate, unrestricted account at Central. Duchow sold a yacht and, in an effort to defraud GECC, told the buyer to wire the $215,000 purchase price to the *unrestricted* account. The buyer's bank sent the wire transfer to an intermediary bank, Banker's Bank. But Banker's instructions to Central included only Duchow's name, omitting his account number. As luck would have it, the money was put in the blocked account. Duchow immediately ordered Central to transfer the funds to his unrestricted account, which Central did. Duchow quickly spent the money and had no other assets. Is Central liable to GECC? **Argument for Central**: The Bank simply followed instructions that Banker's had originally issued and that had been accidentally left off the payment order. Central was not to blame for Duchow's fraud. **Argument for GECC**: Central had an obligation to follow the wire instructions. But once the funds landed in the blocked account, Central had to make a nonclerical decision—to move or not to move. No law required it to transfer the funds, especially since the account clearly had GECC's name on it.

Internet Research Problem

Visit the Federal Reserve Board's Web site at http://www.bog.frb.fed.us to find out where the Federal Reserve bank for your region is located. Where did you send the last check you mailed? Was it in the same region? What difference does it make if you sent a check out of the region?

You can find further practice problems in the Online Quiz at http://beatty.westbuslaw.com or in the Study Guide that accompanies this text.

CHAPTER 26

SECURED TRANSACTIONS

Dear Diane:

My boyfriend has a problem with the bank that doesn't make sense. He had a car loan, and after he had made payments for two years and two months, he got laid off from his job. When he missed three payments, the bank repossessed the car and sold it at an auction. Now the bank's lawyer says that my boyfriend still owes money to the bank. He has to pay for something he doesn't have?

Signed,

Unfair

Dear Unfair: When the bank lent your boyfriend money, he signed a note promising to pay back the full amount of the loan—whether the car existed three years later or not. The bank kept what is called a security interest in the car. That means that if your boyfriend stopped making payments, the bank could repossess the car, sell it, and use the proceeds to pay off all or part of the debt.

The trouble is that cars depreciate. Though he may have bought the car for $6,000, two and a half years later it may be worth only $2,000—although he still owes $3,000 to the bank. Cars bring less money at auction than they do when sold by an individual or on a car lot. Instead of going for $2,000, the car may have been auctioned to a wholesaler for $1,200. That scenario would leave your boyfriend having no car but still owing the bank about $1,800. You may want a lawyer of your own to look over the fine print, but it's likely that your boyfriend is legally obligated to ante up.

Signed,
Diane[1]

BASIC TERMS DEFINED

Diane is right. We can sympathize with "Unfair," but the bank is probably entitled to its money. The boyfriend and the bank had entered into a *secured transaction*, meaning that one party gave credit to another, demanding assurance of repayment. When a used car lot sells a car on credit for $6,000, or a bank takes collateral for a $600 million corporate loan, the parties have created a secured transaction.

Article 9 of the Uniform Commercial Code (UCC) governs secured transactions in personal property. It is essential to understand the basics of this law because we live and work in a world economy based solidly—or shakily—on credit. Gravity may cause the earth to spin, but secured transactions keep the commercial world going 'round. The quantity of disputes tells us how important this law is: about *one-half of all UCC lawsuits* involve Article 9. This part of the Code employs terms not used elsewhere, so we must lead off with some definitions:

- **Fixtures** are goods that have become attached to real estate. For example, heating ducts are *goods* when a company manufactures them and also when it sells them to a retailer. But when a contractor installs the ducts in a new house, they become *fixtures*.
- **Security interest** means an interest in personal property or fixtures that secures the performance of some *obligation*. If an automobile dealer sells you a new car on credit and retains a security interest in the car, it means she is keeping legal rights *in your car*, including the right to drive it away if you fall behind in your payments. Usually, the obligation is to pay money, such as the money due on the new car. Occasionally, the obligation is to perform some other action, but in this chapter we concentrate on the payment of money because that is what security interests are generally designed to ensure.
- **Secured party** is the person or company that holds the security interest. The automobile dealer who sells you a car on credit is the secured party.
- **Collateral** is the property subject to a security interest. When a dealer sells you a new car and keeps a security interest, the vehicle is the collateral.
- **Debtor** is the person who owes money or some other obligation to the secured party. If you buy a car on credit, you are the debtor.
- **Security agreement** is the contract in which the debtor gives a security interest to the secured party. This agreement protects the secured party's rights in the collateral.
- **Default** occurs when the debtor fails to pay money that is due, for example, on a loan or for a purchase made on credit. Default also includes other failures by the debtor, such as failing to keep the collateral insured.

---

1 Diane Crowley, "Bank Seizes Car, So Why Must Her Beau Pay Up?" *Chicago Sun Times*, May 18, 1993, §2, p. 36. Reprinted with special permission from the Chicago Sun-Times, Inc. © 1999.

- **Repossession** occurs when the secured party takes back collateral because the debtor has defaulted. Typically, the secured party will demand that the debtor deliver the collateral; if the debtor fails to do so, the secured party may find the collateral and take it.
- **Perfection** is a series of steps the secured party must take to protect its rights in the collateral against people other than the debtor. This is important because if the debtor cannot pay his debts, several creditors may attempt to seize the collateral. To perfect its rights in the collateral, the secured party will typically file certain papers with a state agency.
- **Financing statement** is a document that the secured party files to give the general public notice that it has a secured interest in the collateral.

Here is an example using the terms just discussed. A medical equipment company manufactures a CAT scan machine and sells it to a clinic for $2 million, taking $500,000 cash and the clinic's promise to pay the rest over five years. The clinic simultaneously signs a security agreement, giving the manufacturer a security interest in the CAT scan. If the clinic fails to make its payments, the manufacturer can repossess the machine. The manufacturer then promptly files a financing statement in an appropriate state agency. This *perfects* the manufacturer's rights, meaning that its security interest in the CAT scan is now valid against all the world. Exhibit 26.1 illustrates this transaction.

If the clinic goes bankrupt and many creditors try to seize its assets, the manufacturer has first claim to the CAT scan machine. The clinic's bankruptcy is of great importance. When a debtor has money to pay all of its debts, there are no concerns about security interests. A creditor insists on a security interest to protect itself in the event the debtor *cannot* pay all of its debts. The secured party intends

Exhibit 26.1

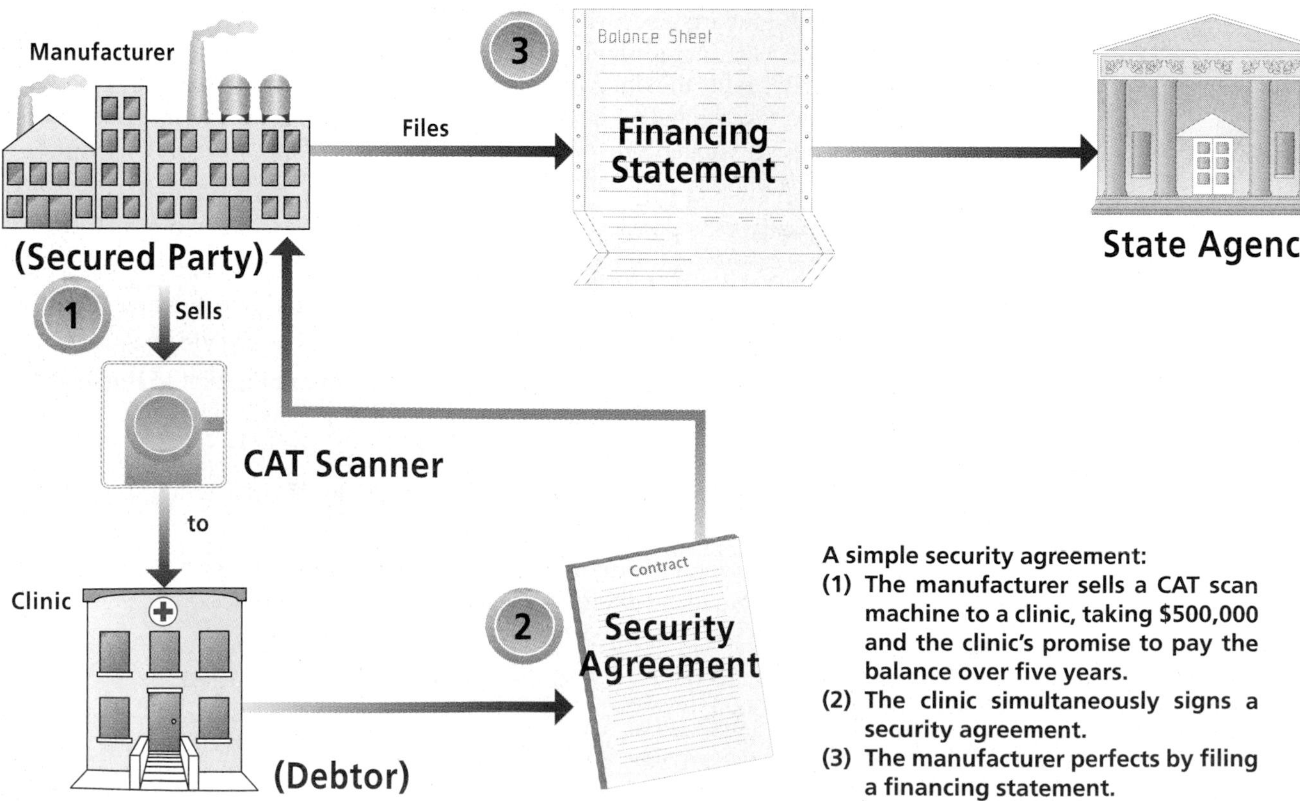

A simple security agreement:

(1) The manufacturer sells a CAT scan machine to a clinic, taking $500,000 and the clinic's promise to pay the balance over five years.

(2) The clinic simultaneously signs a security agreement.

(3) The manufacturer perfects by filing a financing statement.

(1) to give itself a legal interest in specific property of the debtor and (2) to establish a priority claim in that property, ahead of other creditors. In this chapter we look at a variety of issues that arise in secured transactions.

NEW ARTICLE 9

The drafters of the UCC have issued important revisions to Article 9. Since no states have adopted the proposed changes yet, we describe existing law throughout this chapter. We will mention a few of the suggested revisions but not until the end of the chapter, to minimize confusion.

With basic terms defined, we now need to analyze *when* Article 9 applies.

SCOPE OF ARTICLE 9

Article 9 applies to any transaction intended to create a security interest in personal property or fixtures. The personal property used as collateral may be goods, such as cars or hats, but it may also be a variety of other things:

- **Instruments.** Drafts, checks, certificates of deposit, and notes may all be used as collateral, as may stocks, bonds, and other securities.
- **Documents of Title.** These are papers used by an owner of goods who ships or stores them. The documents are the owner's proof that he owns goods no longer in his possession. For example, an owner sending goods by truck will obtain a *bill of lading*, a receipt indicating where the goods will be shipped and who gets them when they arrive. Similarly, a *warehouse receipt* is the owner's receipt for goods stored at a warehouse. The owner may use these and other similar documents of title as collateral.
- **Accounts.** Accounts include any right to receive payment for goods sold or leased, other than rights covered by chattel paper or instruments. This category includes, for example, accounts receivable, indicating that various buyers owe a merchant money for goods they have already received.
- **General Intangibles.** These include copyrights, patents, trademarks, goodwill, and related rights to payment.
- **Chattel Paper.** Chattel paper is any writing that indicates two things: (1) a debtor owes money and (2) a secured party has a security interest in specific goods. Chattel paper most commonly occurs in a consumer sale on credit. If a dealer sells an air conditioner to a customer, who agrees in writing to make monthly payments and also agrees that the dealer has a security interest in the air conditioner, that agreement is chattel paper. The confusing point is that the same chattel paper may be collateral for a second security interest. The dealer who sells the air conditioner could *use* the chattel paper to obtain a loan. If the dealer gives the chattel paper to a bank as collateral for the loan, the bank has a security interest *in the chattel paper*, while the dealer continues to have a security interest *in the air conditioner*.
- **Goods**. For purposes of secured transactions, the Code divides goods into four categories. In some cases, the rights of the parties will depend upon what category the goods fall into. The categories are as follows:
    - *Consumer goods* are those used primarily for personal, family, or household purposes.

- *Equipment* means goods used primarily in business, whether a commercial enterprise, farm, or profession.
- *Farm products* are crops, livestock, or supplies used directly in farming operations (as opposed to the business aspects of farming).
- *Inventory* consists of goods held by someone for sale or lease, such as all of the beds and chairs in a furniture store.

So Article 9 applies anytime the parties intended to create a security interest in any of the things listed above.

ATTACHMENT OF A SECURITY INTEREST

Attachment is a vital step in a secured transaction. This means that the secured party has taken three steps to create an enforceable security interest:

- The two parties made a security agreement, *and either* (1) the security agreement is in writing, describes the collateral, and is signed by the debtor, *or* (2) the secured party has possession of the collateral.
- The secured party gave value in order to get the security agreement.
- The debtor has rights in the collateral.[2]

AGREEMENT

Without an agreement, there can be no security interest. Generally, the agreement will be in writing and signed by the debtor. A written agreement must reasonably identify the collateral, and a secured party should make that description as precise as possible. For example, a written security agreement at a minimum might:

- State that Happy Homes, Inc. and Martha agree that Martha is buying an Arctic Co. refrigerator, and identify the exact unit by its serial number
- Give the price, the down payment, the monthly payments, and interest rate
- State that because Happy Homes is selling Martha the refrigerator on credit, it has a security interest in the refrigerator; and
- Provide that if Martha defaults on her payments, Happy Homes is entitled to repossess the refrigerator.

An actual security agreement will add many details, such as Martha's obligation to keep the refrigerator in good condition and to deliver it to the store if she defaults; a precise definition of "default"; and how Happy Homes may go about repossessing the goods if Martha defaults.

Possession

The security agreement need not be in writing *if* the parties have an oral agreement *and* the secured party has possession of the collateral. If you loan your neighbor $75,000 and he gives you a Winslow Homer watercolor as collateral, you have an attached security interest in the painting once it is in your possession. It would still be wise to put the agreement in writing, to be certain both parties

2 UCC §9-203.

understand all terms and can prove them if necessary; but the writing is not legally required.

The following case is typical of Article 9 disputes, in that it was fought out in bankruptcy court. A debtor claimed to have a security interest in property owned by a bankrupt company. Had the parties made a security agreement?

IN RE **CFLC, INC.**
209 B.R. 508, 1997 Bankr. LEXIS 821
United States Bankruptcy Appellate Panel of the Ninth Circuit, 1997

Facts: Expeditors was a freight company that supervised importing and exporting for Everex Systems, Inc. Expeditors negotiated rates and services for its client and frequently had possession of Everex's goods. During a 17-month period, Expeditors sent over 300 invoices to Everex. Each invoice stated that the customer either had to accept all of the invoice's terms or to pay cash, receiving no work on credit. One of those terms gave Expeditors a general lien on all of the customer's property in its possession. In other words, if the customer failed to pay a bill, Expeditors claimed the right to retain the goods, auction them, and keep enough of the proceeds to pay its overdue bills.

Everex filed for bankruptcy. Expeditors expedited its way into the court proceedings, claiming the right to sell Everex's goods, worth about $81,000. The trial judge rejected the claim, ruling that Expeditors lacked a valid security interest. Expeditors appealed.

Issue: **Did Expeditors have a security interest in Everex's goods?**

Excerpts from Judge Ollason's Decision: Under the common law, silence in the face of an offer is not an acceptance, unless there is a relationship between the parties or a previous course of dealing pursuant to which silence would be understood as acceptance.

In this case, Expeditors and Everex had been doing business for about one and one-half years. They had never discussed the terms of the invoice nor negotiated for a security interest. Everex had never expressly acknowledged the invoice terms by accepting or objecting to them, nor did it take actions which acknowledged Expeditors' alleged general lien on the goods. Its only pertinent acts were its payment of the invoices and silence as to the added terms.

The evidence consisting of Everex's receipt and payment of invoices containing terms for a general lien in the goods in favor of Expeditors did not amount to an agreement for such a security interest, pursuant to [UCC §9-105]. As a matter of law, the repetitive sending by Expeditors to Everex of terms which Expeditors wished to be made part of the oral contract was not evidence of course of dealing because an agreement did not exist as to the security interest which could be supplemented by such evidence.

Affirmed.

Expeditors thought—or hoped—that it had a security interest, but the invoices failed to achieve that goal, so the company failed to obtain the money it was owed. How *should* Expeditors have protected itself?

VALUE

For the security interest to attach, the secured party must give value. Usually, the value will be apparent. If a bank loans $400 million to an airline, that money is the value, and the bank may therefore obtain a security interest in the planes that the airline is buying. If a store sells a living room set to a customer for a small down payment and two years of monthly payments, the value given is the furniture.

Future Value

The parties may also agree that some of the value will be given in the future. For example, a finance company might extend a $5 million line of credit to a retail store even though the store initially takes only $1 million of the money. The remaining credit is available whenever the store needs it to purchase inventory. The Code considers the entire $5 million line of credit to be value.[3]

DEBTOR RIGHTS IN THE COLLATERAL

The debtor can only grant a security interest in goods if he has some legal right to those goods himself. Typically, the debtor owns the goods. But a debtor may also give a security interest if he is leasing the goods or even if he is a bailee, meaning that he is lawfully holding them for someone else. The legal interest need not be very great, but there must be *some* right. Suppose Importer receives a shipment of scallops on behalf of Seafood Wholesaler. Wholesaler asks Importer to hold the scallops for three days as a favor, and to keep a customer happy, Importer agrees. Importer then arranges a $150,000 loan from a bank, using the scallops as collateral. Although Importer has acted unethically, it does have *some right* in the collateral—the right to hold them for three days. That is enough to satisfy this rule.

By contrast, suppose Railroad is transporting 10 carloads of cattle on behalf of Walter, the owner. A devious Meat Dealer uses forged documents to trick Railroad into believing that Meat Dealer is entitled to the animals. Meat Dealer trucks the cattle away and uses them to obtain a bank loan, giving the bank a security interest in the animals. That "security interest" has never attached and is invalid, because Dealer had *no* legal interest in the cattle. When Walter, the rightful owner, locates his cattle, he may take them back. The bank can only hope to find the deceitful Dealer, who in fact has probably disappeared.

Result

Once the security interest has attached to the collateral, the secured party is protected against the debtor. If the debtor fails to pay, the secured party may repossess the collateral.

ATTACHMENT TO FUTURE PROPERTY

The security agreement may specify that the security interest attaches to personal property that the debtor does not yet possess but might obtain in the future.

After-Acquired Property

After-acquired property refers to items that the debtor obtains after the parties have made their security agreement. **The parties may agree that the security interest attaches to after-acquired property**.[4] Basil is starting a catering business, but owns only a beat-up car. He borrows $55,000 from the Pesto Bank, which takes a security interest in the car. But Pesto also insists on an after-acquired clause. When Basil purchases a commercial stove, cooking equipment, and freezer, Pesto's security interest attaches to each item as Basil acquires it.

---

[3] UCC § 9-204(3).

[4] UCC §9-204(1).

Proceeds

Proceeds are whatever is obtained by a debtor who sells the collateral or otherwise disposes of it. **The secured party *automatically* obtains a security interest in the proceeds of the collateral, unless the security agreement states otherwise.**[5] Suppose the Pesto Bank obtains a security interest in Basil's $800 freezer. Basil then decides he needs a larger model and sells the original freezer to his neighbor for $600. The $600 cash is proceeds, in which Pesto automatically obtains a security interest. If for some reason the parties do not want the security interest to extend to proceeds (which would be very unusual), they must make that clear in the security agreement.

PERFECTION

NOTHING LESS THAN PERFECTION

Once the security interest has attached to the collateral, the secured party is protected *against the debtor*. Pesto Bank loaned money to Basil and has a security interest in all of his property. If Basil defaults on his loan, Pesto may insist he deliver the goods to the bank. If he fails to do that, the bank can seize the collateral. But Pesto's security interest is valid only against Basil; if a third person claims some interest in the goods, the bank may never get them. For example, Basil might have taken out *another* loan, from his friend Olive, and used the same property as collateral. Olive knew nothing about the bank's original loan. To protect itself against Olive, and all other parties, the bank must *perfect* its interest.

There are several kinds of perfection:

- Perfection by filing
- Perfection by possession
- Perfection of consumer goods
- Perfection of movable collateral and fixtures

In some cases the secured party will have a choice of which method to use; in other cases only one method works.

PERFECTION BY FILING

The most common way to perfect is by filing a financing statement with one or more state agencies. A **financing statement** gives the names of all parties, describes the collateral, and outlines the security interest. Filing enables any interested person to learn about the security interest. Suppose the Pesto Bank obtains a security interest in Basil's catering equipment and then perfects by filing with the Secretary of State in the state capital. When Basil asks his friend Olive for a loan, she will check the records in the Secretary of State's office to see if any other creditor has a security interest in his catering equipment. Olive's search uncovers Basil's previous security agreement, and she realizes it would be unwise to make the loan. If Basil were to default, the collateral would go straight to Pesto Bank, leaving Olive empty-handed. See Exhibit 26.2. For a sample financing statement, see **http://www.ibitexas.com/legaldocs/uccfinst.htm**.

---

[5] UCC §9-203(3).

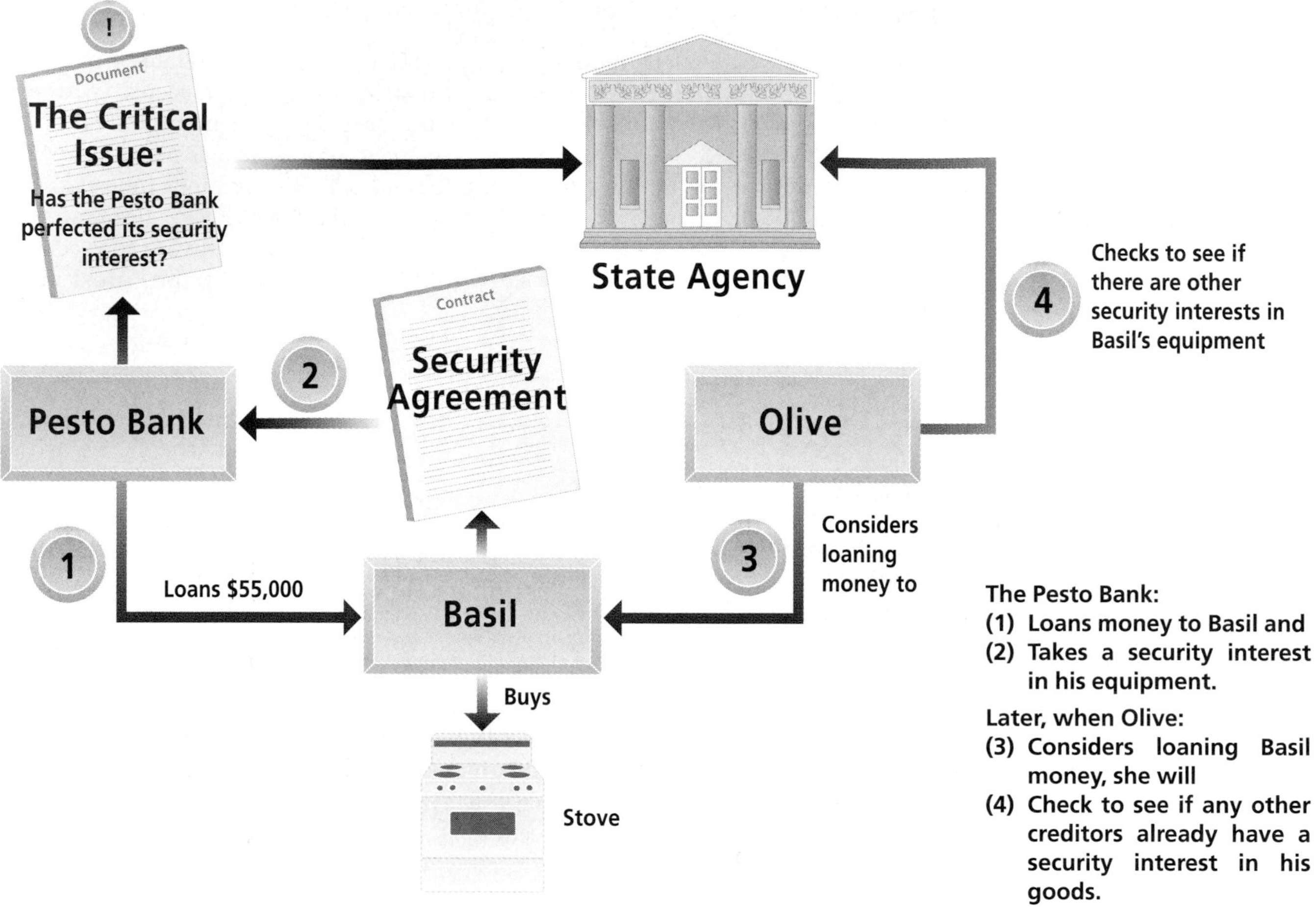

Exhibit 26.2

If the collateral is either *accounts* or *general intangibles*, filing is the only way to perfect. Suppose Nester uses his copyright in a screenplay as collateral for a loan. The bank that gives him the loan may perfect *only* by filing.

The most common problems that arise in filing cases are (1) whether the financing statement contained enough information to put other people on notice of the security interest, and (2) whether the secured party filed the papers in the right place.

Contents of the Financing Statement

A financing statement is sufficient if it provides the name and address of the debtor and the secured party, the signature of the debtor, and a description of the collateral.[6] The address of the secured party is important so that anyone searching the records may contact that creditor and obtain more information. The collateral must be described accurately so that another party contemplating a loan to the debtor will understand which property is already secured.

Finally, the name of the debtor is critical because that is what an interested person will search for among the thousands of other financing statements on file. If the debtor is an individual, the secured party must use the individual name, not a trade name. Billy and Brenda Nowling operated a lawnmower shop under the name "B & B Equipment." Roberts Supply Co. sold much of the inventory to the Nowlings on credit and took a security interest in the merchandise. Roberts duly filed its financing statement under the name "B & B Equipment." When, sadly, the Now-

[6] UCC §9-402.

lings went bankrupt, other creditors sought their goods, but Roberts claimed a perfected security interest. Who won? The other creditors. Roberts should have filed the financing statement under the names "Billy and Brenda Nowling." To be on the safe side, Roberts could *also* have filed under the trade name. But by filing only under "B & B," Roberts failed to notify companies that might extend credit to the Nowlings personally, and as a result, Roberts's security interest gained it nothing.[7]

A similar issue arose in the following case. Did the filing give fair notice to others?

THE FIRST NATIONAL BANK OF LACON v. STRONG
278 Ill. App. 3d 762, 633 N.E.2d 432, 1996 Ill. App. LEXIS 169
Illinois Court of Appeal, 1996

Facts: Elmer and Pam Strong leased and operated service stations. They were incorporated as "E. Strong Oil Co.," although they used "Strong Oil Co." as their trade name. The First National Bank of Lacon loaned the couple $75,000. The promissory note named "Strong Oil Co." as the borrower. Both Elmer and Pam signed the note, along with an agreement that gave the bank a security interest in the company's inventory, equipment, accounts, and other assets. The bank filed a financing statement, listing the debtor as "Strong Oil Co."

The Illinois Department of Revenue seized all of the company's assets, claiming $229,000 in unpaid motor fuel taxes. The bank sued, claiming that it was entitled to all of the property, based on its security interest. The issue was whether the bank had perfected its interest. If the bank *had* perfected, it was entitled to the property. If the bank had failed to do so, because it filed under the name Strong rather than "E. Strong," the Department could take everything. The trial court found that the bank had validly perfected its interest, and the Department appealed.

You Be the Judge: Did the bank have a perfected security interest in the property?

Argument for the Department of Revenue: Financing statements are designed to permit interested parties to search an index and determine quickly if a debtor has other creditors. Accuracy is essential because the statements are indexed alphabetically by debtor. There are millions of secured transactions annually, and many companies and organizations have similar names. A creditor looking under "E. Strong" would be far from "Strong Oil," where the bank chose to file. Must a searcher also look under "Elmer Strong," "E & P Strong," "Strong Oil," "Strong Gasoline," "Strong Service Stations," and a hundred other permutations? Because the bank could not be bothered to verify the name of its debtor, it failed to perfect and must suffer the loss.

Argument for the Bank: The Department's greed exceeds its common sense. The purpose of filing is to give a reasonably prudent creditor the chance to check on the credit of its prospective debtor. The company was much better known by its trade name, Strong Oil Co., than by its corporate name, E. Strong. Any prudent company that considered extending credit to the Strongs would have looked under Strong Oil—exactly where the bank filed. The Code was never intended to elevate nit-picking to the status of policy.

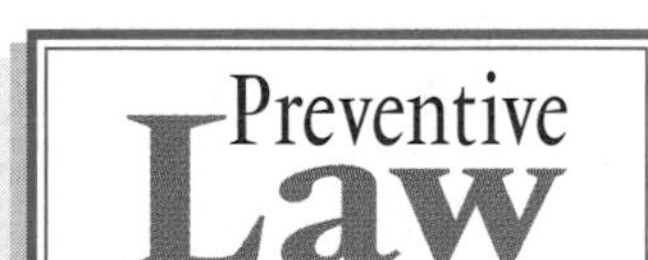

Regardless of who wins this case, litigating it to the appellate level cost all parties a great deal of time and money. How could the bank have avoided the problem in the first place?

Place of Filing

Exactly *where* a secured party should file its financing statement varies from state to state, and also depends upon the type of collateral. **In general, state statutes require filing with the Secretary of State (normally in the state capital) and/or in**

[7] *In re Nowling*, 124 B.R. 858, 1991 U.S. Dist. LEXIS 3445 (N.D. Fla. 1991).

the "local county."[8] The local county is generally where the debtor lives or keeps the goods or has its principal place of business. If the collateral is timber, minerals, fixtures, or something else closely connected with real estate, the local county will generally be where a mortgage for the property would be filed. It is of the utmost importance that a secured party follow local state rules *to the letter*. Ask Wilfred Sherman.

The Shetland Co. imported lamps. Sherman loaned the company $500,000 and obtained a security interest in its accounts and inventory. He filed a financing statement with the Secretary of State. But when (naturally) Shetland went bankrupt, Sherman was unable to recover the accounts or the inventory. Why? Under the Code version used in many states, it is sufficient for a secured party to file merely with the Secretary of State *provided* that the debtor has more than one place of business. (If the debtor has 15 places of business in the state, it would be absurd to require the secured party to file in each.) But if the debtor has *only one* place of business, the Code requires the secured party to file both with the Secretary of State *and* in the county where the debtor is located. Shetland had two offices, but it had only *one* place of business, and Sherman therefore should have filed in the local county *and with* the Secretary of State. He had filed only with the Secretary of State. His mistake was understandable and highly technical—but expensive. He never recovered his $500,000.[9]

Duration of Filing

Once a financing statement has been filed, it is effective for five years. After five years it will expire and leave the secured party unprotected, unless she files a **continuation statement** within six months prior to expiration. The continuation statement is valid for an additional five years. The secured party may continue to do this indefinitely, every five years.[10]

PERFECTION BY POSSESSION

As we have seen, if the collateral is accounts or general intangibles, the creditor may perfect his interest *only* by filing. But for all other forms of property, the secured party may perfect by filing *or* by taking possession of the collateral. So if the collateral is a diamond brooch or 1,000 shares of stock, a bank may perfect its security interest by holding the items until the loan is paid off. When the debtor gives collateral to the secured party, it is often called a **pledge**: the debtor pledges her goods to secure her performance, and the secured party (sometimes called the **pledgee**) takes the goods to perfect its interest.

Perfection by possession has some advantages. First, notice to other parties is very effective. No reasonable finance company assumes that it can obtain a security interest in a Super Bowl championship ring when *another creditor* already holds the ring. Second, possession enables the creditor to ensure that the collateral will not be damaged during the life of the security interest. A bank that loans money based on a rare painting may worry about the painting's condition, but it knows the painting is safe if it is locked up in the bank's vault. Third, if the debtor defaults, a secured party obviously has no difficulties repossessing goods that it already holds.

Of course, for some collateral, possession is impractical. If a consumer buys a new yacht on credit, the seller can hardly expect to perfect its security interest by

---

[8] UCC §9-401.

[9] *In re Shetland Co.*, 1992 U.S. Dist. LEXIS 17028 (D. Mass. 1992).

[10] UCC §9-403(3).

possession. The buyer would become edgy sailing the boat around the dealer's parking lot. In such a case, the secured party must perfect by filing.

Mandatory Possession

For two types of collateral, possession is the *only* way the Code permits a party to perfect. **Generally, a party must perfect a security interest in *money* or *instruments* by taking possession.**[11] Instruments and money are easy to transfer and may be impossible to distinguish from *other* instruments or money. So a party with a security interest in either one must take possession to perfect. Suppose Ed's Real Estate claims that Jennifer, a former employee, has opened her own realty business in violation of their agreement. Jennifer promises to move her business to another city within 90 days, and Ed agrees not to sue. To secure Jennifer's promise to move, Ed takes a security interest in $50,000 cash. If she fails to move on time, he is entitled to the money. To perfect that interest, Ed must take possession of the money and hold it until Jennifer is out of town.

Care of the Collateral

Possession gives several advantages to the secured party, but also one important duty: **a secured party must use reasonable care in the custody and preservation of collateral in her possession.**[12] If the collateral is something tangible, such as a painting, the secured party must take reasonable steps to ensure that it is safe from harm. What if shares of stock are the collateral?

HUTHER v. MARINE MIDLAND BANK, N.A.
143 Misc. 2d 697, 541 N.Y.S.2d 902, 1989 N.Y. Misc. LEXIS 649
City Court of New York, 1989

Facts: In 1985, William Huther borrowed $31,000 from Marine Midland Bank and secured repayment with shares of stock in Eastman Kodak and Mobil Corp. In 1986, Congress enacted a tax reform bill, effective January 1, 1987, that affected capital gains, which are profits earned from the purchase and sale of something, such as shares of stock. Under the new tax law anyone who realized a capital gain during 1986 would save a considerable amount in taxes, compared to someone making that same sale in 1987.

Huther decided to sell his stock before the end of the year and use his capital gains savings to help repay the loan. On December 18, 1986, he telephoned Jack Broomfield, the lending officer at Midland, and arranged for the sale of his stock. Broomfield told Huther that it was "bank policy" to use the bank's own brokerage service to handle the sale of stock when the shares were held as collateral. Huther had his own broker, but since Broomfield insisted, he consented to using the bank's broker for this sale.

On December 24, 1986, Broomfield went to Huther's office to open an account with Marine's brokerage service. Huther signed the application and authorized the sale of his shares. Broomfield then personally took the stock from the bank's vault and sent it by courier to New York City. But the bank's broker failed to sell the stock until January 5, 1987, forcing Huther to pay a significantly increased tax bill. Huther sued Midland.

Issue: Did Marine violate its duty to use reasonable care concerning the collateral?

---

[11] UCC §9-304(1).

[12] UCC §9-207.

Excerpts from Judge Regan's Decision: A secured lender must use reasonable care in the custody and preservation of the collateral he possesses. And a secured party is liable for "any loss" caused by his failure to meet that obligation.

Under the facts as found, the defendants had four business days left in 1986 to perform the sales contract, and they had reasonable notice that a sale in 1986 was necessary to preserve Mr. Huther's tax advantages. This finding is buttressed by the fact that during December 1986, it was common knowledge throughout the securities industry that stock-owning taxpayers were selling off securities in record-setting volume in order to reap the benefits of the soon-to-expire capital gains income tax treatment.

Accepting these criteria for professional competence, the court holds that it was incumbent upon these defendants to inform Mr. Huther of the choices he had as to the manner in which the stock sale could be accomplished. And it was also incumbent upon them to follow his instructions diligently and correctly. On the brokerage services agreement, Huther indicated that he wanted a "cash" account for this transaction, and that meant delivery on the day of the contract, or on the next business day thereafter. A stockbroker of ordinary acumen would have performed the conditions of this stock sale as "cash" within one or two business days. Yet, the defendants took six days. Because these defendants failed to meet that standard, they are guilty of negligence, and have violated the statutory command of UCC §9-207.

Plaintiff is entitled to judgment.

PERFECTION OF CONSUMER GOODS

The Code gives special treatment to security interests in most consumer goods. Merchants sell a vast amount of consumer goods on credit. They cannot file a financing statement for every bed, television, and stereo for which a consumer owes money. Yet perfecting by possession is also impossible, since the consumer will take the goods home. To understand the UCC's treatment of these transactions, we need to know two terms. The first is *consumer goods*, which as we saw earlier means goods used primarily for personal, family, or household purposes. The second term is *purchase money security interest*.

A purchase money security interest (PMSI) is one taken by the person who sells the collateral or by the person who advances money so the debtor can buy the collateral.[13] Assume the Gobroke Home Center sells Marion a $5,000 stereo system. The sales document requires a payment of $500 down and $50 per month for the next 300 years, and gives Gobroke a security interest in the system. Because the security interest was "taken by the seller," the document is a PMSI. It would also be a PMSI if a bank had loaned Marion the money to buy the system and the document gave the bank a security interest. See Exhibit 26.3

But aren't all security interests PMSIs? No, many are not. Assume a finance company loans an airline $50 million to design, build, and install a new computer reservation system. The finance company wants its loan secured *now*, not with something that will be built over a few years. So it takes a security interest in five of the airline's planes. That is not a PMSI because the debtor did not use the borrowed money to buy the collateral. Or suppose a bank loans a retail company $800,000 and takes a security interest in the store's present inventory. That is not a PMSI since the store did not use the money to purchase the collateral.

What must Gobroke Home Center do to perfect its security interest? Nothing. **A PMSI in consumer goods perfects automatically, without filing.**[14] Marion's

---

13 UCC §9-107.

14 UCC §9-302(1)(d).

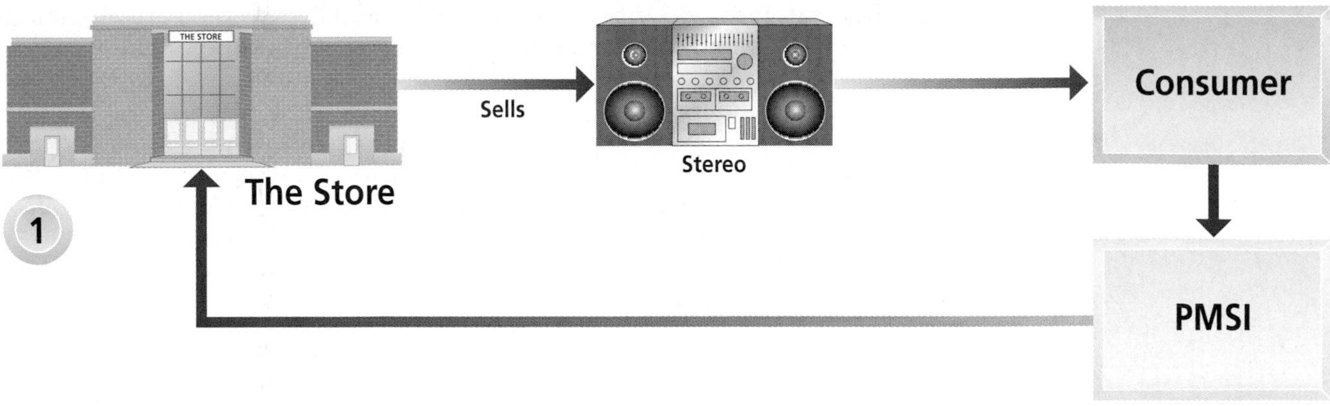

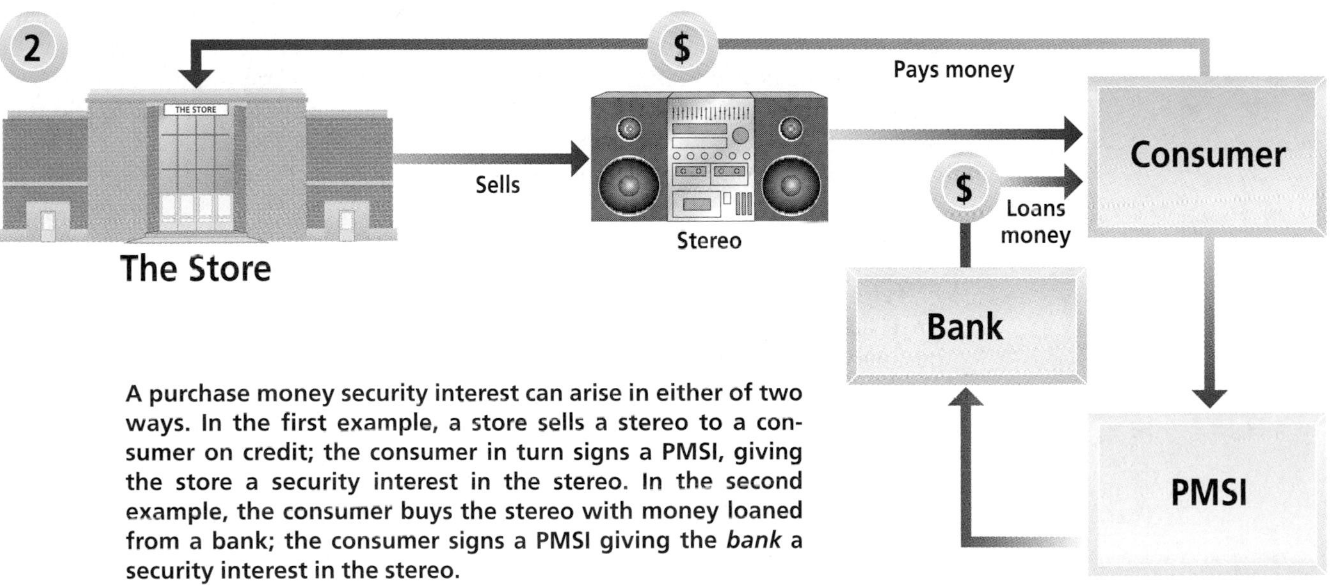

A purchase money security interest can arise in either of two ways. In the first example, a store sells a stereo to a consumer on credit; the consumer in turn signs a PMSI, giving the store a security interest in the stereo. In the second example, the consumer buys the stereo with money loaned from a bank; the consumer signs a PMSI giving the *bank* a security interest in the stereo.

Exhibit 26.3

new stereo is clearly consumer goods, because she will use it only in her home. Gobroke's security interest is a PMSI, so the interest has perfected automatically.

PERFECTION OF MOVABLE COLLATERAL AND FIXTURES

The rules for perfection are slightly different for security interests in movable goods, such as cars and boats, and in fixtures. We look briefly at each.

Movable Goods Generally

Goods that are easily moved create problems for creditors. Suppose a bank in Colorado loans Dorothy money, takes a security interest in her Degas sculpture, and perfects its interest in the proper state offices in Colorado. But then Dorothy moves to Ohio and uses the same collateral for another loan. A lender in Ohio will never discover the security interest perfected in Colorado. If Dorothy defaults, who gets the sculpture?

For most collateral, a security interest perfected in one state is valid in a second state for four months after the property is brought into that new state. This rule applies to goods, documents, and instruments. If the secured party re-perfects in the new state within four months of entering it, the security interest remains valid. If the secured party fails to re-perfect in the new state, the security interest lapses after four months. Suppose Dorothy takes her Degas into Ohio on February 10, and on March 5 uses it as collateral for a new loan. The original Colorado bank still has a valid security interest in the sculpture and may seize the art if Dorothy defaults. But if Dorothy applies for her new loan on October 10, and the Colorado bank has failed to re-perfect, the Colorado bank has lost its protection.[15]

Motor Vehicles and Boats

The Code provisions about perfecting generally do not apply to motor vehicles. Cars are not only numerous and expensive, they are easily moved. Filing may well be ineffective, and possession is impossible. As a result, almost all states have created special laws to deal with this problem.

State title laws generally require that a security interest in an automobile be noted directly on the vehicle's certificate of title. A driver needs a certificate of title to obtain registration plates, so the law presumes that the certificate will stay with the car. By requiring that the security interest be noted on the certificate, the law gives the best possible notice to anyone thinking of buying the car or accepting it as collateral. Generally, if a buyer or lender examines the certificate and finds no security interest, he may accept the vehicle for sale, or as collateral, and take it free of any interest. In most states, the same requirement applies to boats.

Fixtures

Fixtures, you recall, are goods that have become attached to real estate. The Code's provisions for perfecting security interests in fixtures are among its most complex because fixtures involve so many variables. Typically, the contest is between a creditor holding a security interest in a fixture, such as a furnace, and another creditor with rights in the real estate, such as a bank holding a mortgage on the house. We cannot undertake here a thorough explanation of the rules governing perfection of fixtures, but we can highlight the issues that arise so that you realize the difficulties that fixtures present. Common disputes concern:

- The status of the personal property when the security interest was created (were they goods? were they already fixtures?)
- The status of the real estate when the security interest was created (did a creditor already have an interest in the real estate?)
- The timing of perfection (which was recorded first, the security interest in the fixtures or the real estate?); and
- The physical status of the fixtures (can they be easily removed, without harming the real estate?).[16]

Any creditor who considers accepting collateral that might become a fixture must anticipate these problems and clarify with the debtor exactly what she plans to do with the goods. Armed with that information, the creditor should consult local law on fixtures and make an appropriate security agreement (or refuse to accept the fixture as collateral).

---

[15] Note that this general rule does not apply to accounts, general intangibles, chattel paper, or minerals. For each of those types of property the Code provides special, fairly complex rules, beyond the scope of this textbook. A secured party faced with such an issue must consult local law.

[16] UCC §9-313.

PROTECTION OF BUYERS

Generally, once a security interest is perfected, it remains effective regardless of whether the collateral is sold, exchanged, or transferred in some other way. Bubba's Bus Co. needs money to meet its payroll, so it borrows $150,000 from Francine's Finance Co., which takes a security interest in Bubba's 180 buses and perfects its interest. Bubba, still short of cash, sells 30 of his buses to Antelope Transit. But even that money is not enough to keep Bubba solvent: he defaults on his loan to Francine and goes into bankruptcy. Francine pounces on Bubba's buses. May she repossess the 30 that Antelope now operates? Yes. The security interest continued in the buses even after Antelope purchased them, and Francine can whisk them away. (Antelope has a valid claim against Bubba for the value of the buses, but the claim may prove fruitless, since Bubba is bankrupt.)

There are some exceptions to this rule. The Code gives a few buyers special protection.

BUYERS IN ORDINARY COURSE OF BUSINESS

A buyer in ordinary course of business (BIOC) is someone who buys goods in good faith from a seller who routinely deals in such goods.[17] For example, Plato's Garden Supply purchases 500 hemlocks from Socrates' Farm, a grower. Plato is a BIOC: he is buying in good faith and Socrates routinely deals in hemlocks. This is an important status, because a BIOC is generally not affected by security interests in the goods.

A buyer in ordinary course of business takes the goods free of a security interest created by his seller even though the security interest is perfected.[18] Suppose that, a month before Plato made his purchase, Socrates borrowed $200,000 from the Athenian Bank. Athenian took a security interest in all of Socrates' trees and perfected by filing. Then Plato purchased his 500 hemlocks. If Socrates defaults on the loan, Athenian will have *no right* to repossess the 500 trees that are now at the Garden Supply. Plato took them free and clear. (Of course, Athenian can still attempt to repossess other trees from Socrates.)

The BIOC exception is designed to encourage ordinary commerce. A buyer making routine purchases should not be forced to perform a financing check before buying. But the rule creates its own problems. A creditor may extend a large sum of money to a merchant based on collateral, such as inventory, only to discover that by the time the merchant defaults the collateral has been sold. Because the BIOC exception undercuts the basic protection given to a secured party, the courts interpret it narrowly. BIOC status is available only if the *seller created the security interest*. Oftentimes a buyer will purchase goods that have a security interest created by someone *other than* the seller. If that happens, the buyer is not a BIOC. The following case illustrates the problem. Both the debtor and the secured party transferred their interests to others, so there are ultimately four parties. Such complexity is part of the real world of business.

---

17 UCC §1-201(9). You may feel as the authors do that the phrase should be "a buyer in *the* ordinary course of business." For some reason the drafters of the Code eschewed the definite article. The Code is not universally acclaimed for the euphony of its prose.

18 UCC §9-307(1). In fact, the buyer takes free of the security interest *even if the buyer knew of it*. Yet a BIOC, by definition, must be acting in good faith. Is this a contradiction? No. Plato might know that a third party has a security interest in Socrates' crops, yet not realize that his purchase violates the third party's rights. Generally, for example, a security interest will permit a retailer to sell consumer goods, the presumption being that part of the proceeds will go to the secured party. A BIOC cannot be expected to determine what a retailer plans to do with the money he is paid.

DEUTSCHE CREDIT CORP. v. CASE POWER & EQUIPMENT CO.

179 Ariz. 155, 876 P.2d 1190, 1994 Ariz. App. LEXIS 127
Arizona Court of Appeals, 1994

Facts: Richard and Marsha Steensland owned and operated two companies, RSS, Inc. and All Quip, Inc., both of which bought and sold heavy equipment. RSS purchased an industrial excavator from Takeuchi Manufacturing under an installment contract, agreeing to make monthly payments. Takeuchi took a security interest in the machine and then assigned its interest to Deutsche Credit Corp. In other words, Deutsche paid Takeuchi for the right to the payments RSS was obligated to make, and in return Takeuchi transferred the security interest to Deutsche. Takeuchi then perfected the security interest by filing, with Deutsche's name on the financing statement.

Two years later, without notifying Deutsche, RSS conveyed the excavator to All Quip, which, shortly afterwards, sold it to Case Power. See Exhibit 26.4. Case had purchased many items of heavy machinery from All Quip over a period of several years.

RSS then (did you guess it?) defaulted on its payment obligations to Deutsche. Deutsche attempted to repossess the excavator, but Case argued that it was a buyer in ordinary course from All Quip, and thus owned the machine free of any interest that Deutsche claimed. The trial court gave summary judgment for Deutsche, and Case appealed.

Issue: Was Case a buyer in ordinary course?

Excerpts from Judge Voss's Decision: [To qualify as a BIOC,] the buyer must establish: (1) he bought the collateral from a person in the business of selling goods of that kind; (2) he bought in good faith and without knowledge that the sale would violate the ownership rights or a security interest of a third party; and (3) the security interest to which the collateral was subject was created by his seller.

Here, in response to Deutsche's motion for summary judgment, Case offered evidence sufficient to establish that All Quip was in the business of selling heavy equipment of the kind that Case bought from it; that Case bought the Tiger excavator in good faith and paid substantial value for it; and that Case lacked any knowledge of the existence of Deutsche's security interest, much less that the sale was in violation of it. Accordingly, had Case also tendered sufficient evidence to raise a triable fact issue on whether Deutsche's security interest was "created by [Case's] seller," Case was potentially entitled to prevail under UCC section 9-307(1), and the trial court would have erred in granting summary judgment against it. Case, however, failed to show how the creation of the security interest could arguably be attributed to All Quip.

Here there is no dispute that RSS created the security interest under which Deutsche claims, while All Quip actually sold the collateral to Case. Accordingly, Case is ineligible for the protection of section 9-307(1) absent a showing that the corporate existence of both RSS and All Quip may legitimately be disregarded and the Steenslands themselves viewed as both the creators of Deutsche's security interest and the sellers of the collateral to Case.

The mere fact that corporations have the same officers does not make one liable for the acts of the other.

As filed, Case's response to Deutsche's motion for summary judgment demonstrated only that Case could prove the Steenslands were the sole shareholders, directors, and officers of both RSS and All Quip. That showing was plainly insufficient to justify treating the two corporations and the Steenslands as a single entity that was Case's "seller" under UCC section 9-307(1).

While we admit some discomfort at the harshness of the result in this case, the language of section 9-307(1) clearly dictates that a buyer is only protected from security interests "created by his seller." Thus, the trial court did not err in granting summary judgment for Deutsche.

Affirmed.

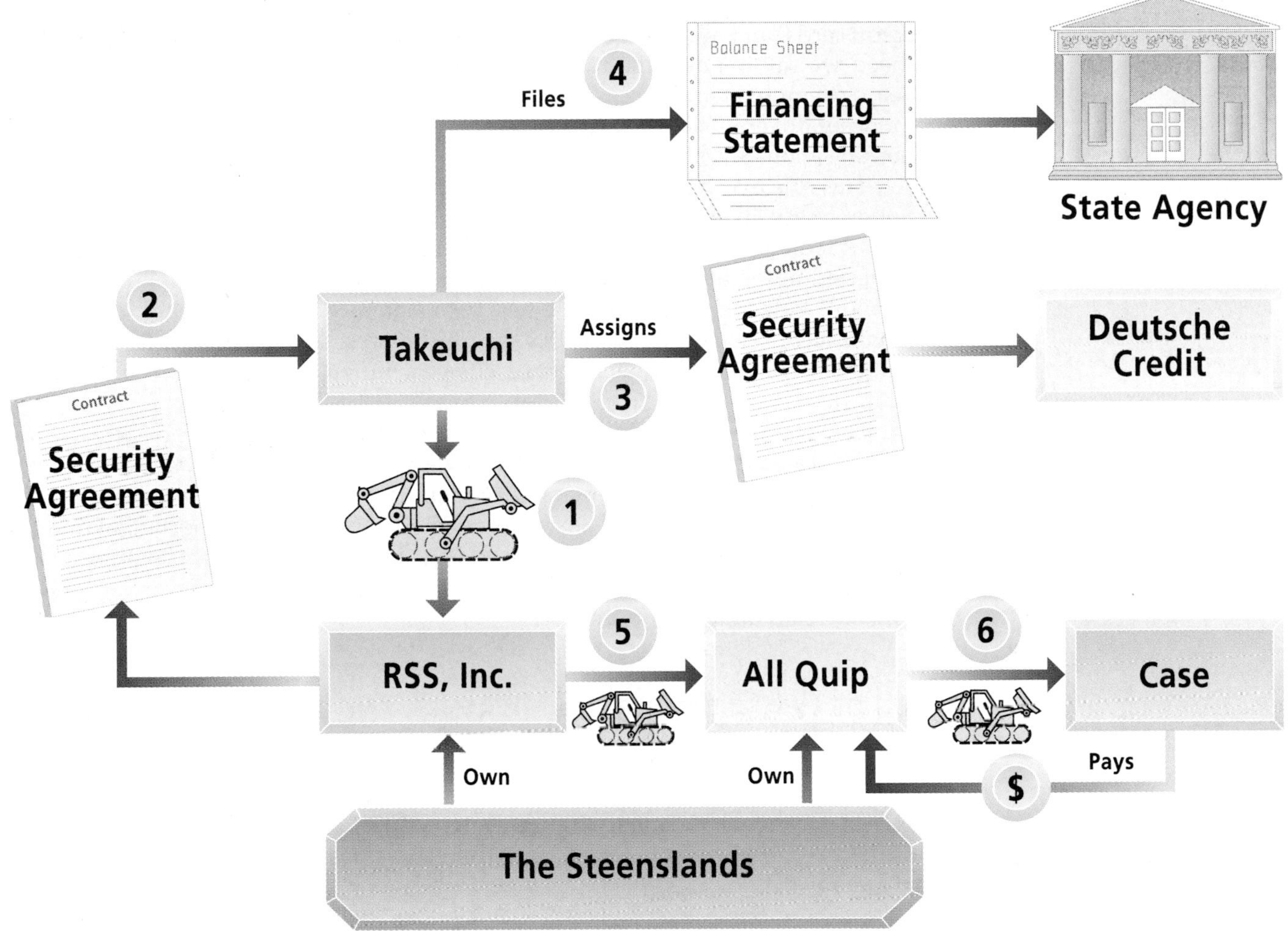

(1) RSS, Inc. bought an excavator from Takeuchi, which (2) took a security interest in the machine. Takeuchi (3) assigned its interest to Deutsche and also (4) perfected. RSS (5) conveyed the machine to All Quip, which later (6) sold it to Case. Deutsche's security interest will prevail unless Case is a BIOC.

Exhibit 26.4

Buyers of Consumer Goods

Another exception exists to protect buyers of consumer goods who do not realize that the item they are buying has a security interest in it. This exception tends to apply to relatively casual purchases, such as those between friends. It does not concern buyers in ordinary course of business, since that issue is handled by the exception discussed above.

In the case of consumer goods, a buyer takes free of a security interest if he is not aware of the security interest, he pays value for the goods, he is buying for his own family or household use, and the secured party has not yet filed a financing statement.[19]

Here is how this exception works. Charles Lau used a Sears credit card to buy a 45-inch TV, a sleeper sofa, love seat, entertainment center, diamond ring, gold chain, and microwave. He had the items delivered to the house of his girlfriend,

19 UCC §9-307.

Teresa Rierman, because he did not want his father to know he had been using the credit card (can't imagine why). Lau later sold the items to Teresa's family and then (need we say it?) defaulted on his payments to Sears and declared bankruptcy. Sears attempted to repossess its merchandise, but the Riermans claimed they were innocent buyers. The court ruled that if the Riermans could show that they knew nothing about Sears's security interest in the goods, they could keep the goods.[20]

This rule may be confusing because earlier we discussed the automatic perfection of a security interest in consumer goods. When Sears sold the merchandise to Lau, it took a purchase money security interest in consumer goods. That interest perfected automatically (without filing) and was valid against *almost* everyone. Suppose Lau had used the furniture as collateral to obtain a bank loan. Sears would have retained its perfected security interest in the goods, and when Lau defaulted, Sears could have repossessed everything, leaving the bank with no collateral and no money.

The one person that Sears's perfected security interest could not defeat, however, was a buyer purchasing for *personal use without knowledge of the security interest*, in other words, the Riermans. Assuming the Riermans knew nothing of the security interest, they win. If Sears considers this type of loss important, it must, in the future, protect itself by filing a financing statement. Taking this extra step will leave Sears protected against *everyone*. Then, if a buyer defaults, Sears can pull the sofa out from under any purchaser.

BUYERS OF CHATTEL PAPER, INSTRUMENTS, AND DOCUMENTS

We have seen that debtors often use chattel paper, instruments, or documents as collateral. Because each of these is so easily transferred, the Code gives buyers special protection. **A buyer who purchases chattel paper or an instrument in the ordinary course of her business, and then takes possession, generally takes free of any security interest.**[21]

Suppose Tele-Maker sells 500 televisions to Retailer on credit, keeping a security interest in the televisions and the proceeds. The proceeds are any money or paper that Retailer earns from selling the sets. Retailer sells 300 of the sets to customers, most of whom pay on credit. The customers sign chattel paper, promising to pay for the sets over time (and giving Retailer a security interest in the sets). All of this chattel paper is proceeds, so Tele-Maker has a perfected security interest in it. The chattel paper is worth about $150,000 if all of the customers pay in full. But Retailer wants money now, so Retailer sells its chattel paper to Financer, who pays $120,000 cash for it. Next, Retailer defaults on its obligation to pay Tele-Maker for the sets. Tele-Maker cannot repossess the televisions, because each customer was a BIOC (buyer in ordinary course of business) and took the goods free of any security interest. So Tele-Maker attempts to repossess the *chattel paper*. Will it succeed? No. The buyer of chattel paper takes it free of a perfected security interest. See Exhibit 26.5.

What could Tele-Maker have done to prevent this disaster?

---

[20] *In re Lau*, 140 B.R. 172, 1992 Bankr. LEXIS 671 (N.D. Ohio 1992).

[21] UCC §9-308.

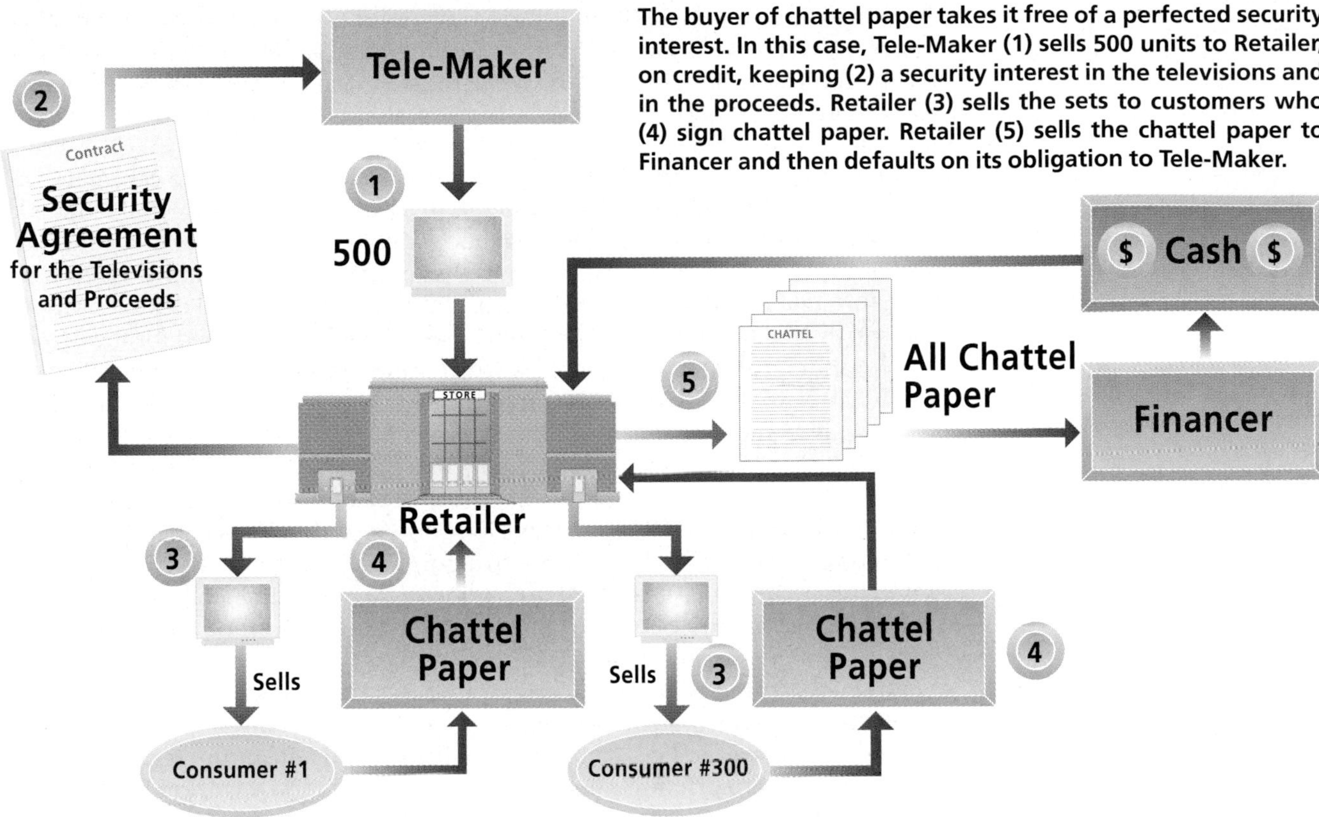

The buyer of chattel paper takes it free of a perfected security interest. In this case, Tele-Maker (1) sells 500 units to Retailer, on credit, keeping (2) a security interest in the televisions and in the proceeds. Retailer (3) sells the sets to customers who (4) sign chattel paper. Retailer (5) sells the chattel paper to Financer and then defaults on its obligation to Tele-Maker.

Exhibit 26.5

Other Paper

Similar rules apply for holders in due course of instruments (discussed in Chapters 23 and 24, on negotiable instruments) and for purchasers of securities and documents of title. The details of those rules are beyond the scope of this chapter, but once again the lesson for any lender is simple: a security interest is safest when the collateral is in your vault. If you do not take possession of the paper, you may lose it to an innocent buyer.[22]

LIENS

Law student Paul King got a costly lesson when his $28.09 check for an oil change bounced and the repo man snatched his prized Corvette. The bill for the car's return: $644. King was a third-year law student, working part-time in a private firm in Houston. He had just walked in from lunch when co-workers told him his car was being towed.

"I thought they were joking," King said. They weren't. King saw a tow truck backing up to his car and hurried out to speak with the workers. They advised him that Texas law authorized them to pick up his car to satisfy a lien, for work done to the car. King hurried inside to telephone the company that had performed the oil change. Unable to make a deal on the phone, he ran back outside and found—no car.

[22] UCC §9-309.

King phoned Harris County Repossession to see about getting his car back. That's easy, they told him. But you owe some fees: $28.09 for the oil change, $20 for the returned check, $25 for the legal notice in the newspapers, $21.24 per day for storage—plus, of course, the $550 repossession fee.[23]

Is that legal? Probably. The service station had a lien on the car. **A lien is a security interest created by law (rather than by agreement).** State and federal law both allow parties to assert a lien against a debtor under prescribed conditions. For example, a state may claim a lien based on unpaid taxes, as we see in a later case; the state is giving notice to the world that it may seize the debtor's property and sell it. A company may claim a lien based on work performed for the debtor.

To understand the difference between a lien and a security interest, assume that when Paul King bought his Corvette, he made a down payment and signed a security agreement to ensure future payments. *His agreement* gave the dealer a security interest in the sports car. Later, when he paid for an oil change, his check bounced. *State law* gave the service station a lien on the auto, meaning the right to hold the car if it is in the garage and to seize the auto if it is elsewhere. Because automobile repossessions provide such a graphic view of secured transactions, we will return to the subject later in the chapter. In the meantime, the commercial Web site **http://www.pimall.com/nais/n.repo.html** offers a blunt, grimly intriguing look at car repossession from the perspective of those who earn a living at it.

In this case, the oil company had an **artisan's lien, meaning a security interest in *personal property*** created when a worker makes some improvement to the property. A car mechanic, a computer repairman, and a furniture restorer all create artisan's liens. A **mechanic's lien** is similar, **created when a worker improves *real property.*** A carpenter who puts an addition on a kitchen and a painter who paints the kitchen's interior both have a mechanic's lien on the house. The owner of an apartment may obtain a **landlord's lien** in a tenant's personal property if the tenant fails to pay the rent. These security interests vary from state to state, so an affected person must consult local law. For an example of a mechanic's lien, go to **http://nvlaw.com/** and click on "mechanic's lien."

Because liens are the creation of statutes, rather than agreements, Article 9 generally does not apply. The one aspect of liens that Article 9 does govern is priority between lienholders and other secured parties, which we examine below. In Paul King's case, the repair shop certainly had a valid lien on his car, even though the amount in question was small. The company's method of *collecting* on its lien is more debatable. King admitted that the company had telephoned him and given him a chance to pay for the bounced check. Some courts would hold that the repair shop had done all it was required to do, but others might rule that it should have shown more patience and avoided running up the bill.

PRIORITIES AMONG CREDITORS

What happens when two creditors have a security interest in the same collateral? The party who has **priority** in the collateral gets it. Typically, the debtor lacks assets to pay everyone, so all creditors struggle to be the first in line. After the first creditor has repossessed the collateral, sold it, and taken enough of the proceeds to pay off his debt, there may be nothing left for anyone else. (There may not even

[23] Rad Sallee and James T. Campbell, "Repo Men Hitch Up Big Fee to Car," *Houston Chronicle,* Oct. 15, 1991, §A, p. 21. Copyright 1991 Houston Chronicle Publishing Company. Reprinted with permission. All rights reserved.

March 1:	April 2:	May 3:	The Winner:
First Bank loans money and perfects its security interest by filing a financing statement.	Second Bank loans money and perfects its security interest by filing a financing statement.	Diminishing goes bankrupt, and both banks attempt to take the rolling stock.	First Bank, because it perfected first.

be enough to pay the first creditor all that he is due, in which case that creditor will sue for the deficiency.) Who gets priority? There are three principal rules.

The first rule is easy: **a party with a perfected security interest takes priority over a party with an unperfected interest.**[24] This, of course, is the whole point of perfecting: to ensure that your security interest gets priority over everyone else's. On August 15, Meredith's Market, an antique store, borrows $100,000 from the Happy Bank, which takes a security interest in all of Meredith's inventory. Happy Bank does not perfect. On September 15, Meredith uses the same collateral to borrow $50,000 from the Suspicion Bank, which files a financing statement the same day. On October 15, as if on cue, Meredith files for bankruptcy and stops paying both creditors. Suspicion wins because it holds a perfected interest, whereas the Happy Bank holds merely an unperfected interest.

The second rule: **if neither secured party has perfected, the first interest to attach gets priority.**[25] Suppose that Suspicion Bank and Happy Bank had both failed to perfect. In that case, Happy Bank would have the first claim to Meredith's inventory, since Happy's interest *attached* first.

And the third rule follows logically: **between perfected security interests, the first to file or perfect wins.**[26] Diminishing Perspective, a railroad, borrows $75 million from the First Bank, which takes a security interest in Diminishing's rolling stock (railroad cars) and immediately perfects by filing. Two months later, Diminishing borrows $100 million from Second Bank, which takes a security interest in the same collateral and also files. When Diminishing arrives, on schedule, in bankruptcy court, both banks will race to seize the rolling stock. First Bank gets the railcars because it perfected first.

PRIORITY INVOLVING A PURCHASE MONEY SECURITY INTEREST

You may recall that a purchase money security interest (PMSI) is a security interest taken by the seller of the collateral or by a lender whose loan enables the debtor to buy the collateral. On November 1, Manufacturer sells a specially built lathe to Tool Shop for $80,000 and takes a security interest in the lathe. The parties have created a PMSI. Parties holding a PMSI often take priority over other perfected security interests in the same goods, even if the other security interest was perfected first. How can the conflict arise? Suppose that on February 1, Tool Shop had borrowed $100,000 from the Gargoyle Bank, giving Gargoyle a security interest in after-acquired property. When the lathe arrives at the Tool Shop on November 1, Gargoyle's security interest attaches to it. But Manufacturer has a PMSI in the lathe, and hence the conflict.

---

24 UCC §9-301(1)(a).

25 UCC §9-312(5)(b).

26 UCC §9-312(5)(a).

We need to examine PMSIs involving inventory and those involving noninventory. **Inventory means goods that the seller is holding for sale or lease in the ordinary course of its business.** The furniture in a furniture store is inventory; the store's computer, telephones, and filing cabinets are not.

PMSI in Inventory

A PMSI in inventory takes priority over a conflicting perfected security interest (even one perfected earlier), if two conditions are met:

- Before filing its PMSI, the secured party must check for earlier security interests and, if there are any, must notify the holder of that interest concerning the new PMSI.
- The secured party must then perfect its PMSI (normally by filing) *before* the debtor receives the inventory.

If the holder of the PMSI has met both of these conditions, its PMSI takes priority over any security interests filed earlier, as illustrated in the chart below.

PMSI in Non-Inventory Collateral

PMSIs are often given for non-inventory goods. For example, Computer Co. sells a $300,000 computer system to Hotel, for use in reservations and billing. The computer is not inventory because it is not for sale. But if Computer Co. sells the computer on credit, it will be certain to take a PMSI. Suppose Hotel had already borrowed money from a bank and had given the bank a security interest in all of its after-acquired property. When the hotel defaults on its loan and its computer payments, who gets the goods?

A PMSI in collateral other than inventory takes priority over a conflicting security interest if the PMSI is perfected at the time the debtor receives the collateral or within 10 days after he receives it.[27] As long as Computer Co. perfects (by filing) within 10 days of delivering the computer, its PMSI takes priority over the bank's earlier security interest. Computer Co. may repossess the machine, and the bank may never get a dime back.

A PMSI in Inventory May Obtain Priority

1. February 1: Coltrane Bank loans Monk's Jazz Store $90,000, taking a security interest in all after-acquired property, including inventory.	**2. March 2:** Monk offers to buy 10 saxophones from Webster's Supply for $3,000 each.	**3. March 3:** Webster checks the financing records and learns that Coltrane Bank has a security interest in all of Monk's after-acquired property.	**4. March 4:** Webster notifies Coltrane Bank that he is selling 10 saxophones to Monk for $30,000 and is taking a PMSI in the instruments, which Webster carefully describes.
5. March 4: Webster files a financing statement indicating a PMSI in the 10 saxophones.	**6. March 5:** Webster sells the 10 saxophones to Monk.	**7. September:** Monk goes bankrupt.	**8. The Winner:** Webster. His PMSI in inventory takes priority over Coltrane's earlier interest.

---

27 UCC §9-312(4).

Again we must note that the PMSI exception undercuts the ability of a creditor to rely on its perfected security interest. As a result, courts insist that a party asserting the PMSI exception demonstrate that it has complied with every requirement. However, when the PMSI holder does so, the results are dramatic.

WHAYNE SUPPLY CO., INC. v. COMMONWEALTH OF KENTUCKY REVENUE CABINET
925 S.W.2d 185, 1996 Ky. LEXIS 64
Kentucky Supreme Court, 1996

Facts: In December, the Kentucky state tax authority, which happens to be called the Revenue Cabinet, filed a tax lien against Panbowl Energy. (We explained tax liens earlier in the chapter.) The following June, Panbowl bought a powerful drill from Whayne Supply, making a down payment of $11,500, promising to pay the balance of $220,000, and signing a security agreement with Whayne as creditor. The next day, Whayne filed a financing statement in the proper county clerk's office.

Panbowl, of course, defaulted on its payments and surrendered the drill to Whayne, which sold the equipment for $58,500, leaving a deficiency of just over $100,000. The Cabinet filed suit, seeking the $58,500 in proceeds. The trial court gave summary judgment to the Cabinet; the appeals court affirmed; and Whayne appealed.

Issue: **Did the Cabinet's tax lien have priority?**

Excerpts from Judge Graves's Decision: Whayne has a perfected PMSI in the equipment. [UCC §9-312(4)] gives Whayne superiority over all other security interests in the equipment, including prior filed security interests. [Section 9-312(4)] is an exception to the general priority rule of [UCC §9-312(5)] which provides priority to the first security interest to file or perfect.

Without the credit extended by Whayne or some lender, there would have been no transfer of property and thus no property upon which the Cabinet could assert a lien. Said differently, Whayne provided the equipment in exchange for a promissory note and a PMSI from Panbowl. Since Whayne furnished the asset upon credit, its lien is superior to all others. It would be absurd to believe that without a superior status, Whayne would furnish the equipment on credit. Surely no rational vendor would sell goods on credit and immediately be relegated to an inferior lien status. Unless priority is granted to a PMSI, whether it be a vendor or lender, credit based on sales transactions will virtually cease.

[Reversed.]

DEFAULT AND TERMINATION

We have reached the end of the line. Either the debtor has defaulted, or it has performed its obligations and may terminate the security agreement.

DEFAULT

The parties define "default" in their security agreement. **Generally, a debtor defaults when he fails to make payments due or enters bankruptcy proceedings.** The parties can agree that other acts will constitute default, such as the debtor's failure to maintain insurance on the collateral. When a debtor defaults, the secured party has two principal options: (1) it may take possession of the collateral, or (2) it may file suit against the debtor for the money owed. The secured party does not have to choose between these two remedies; it may try one remedy, such as repossession, and if that fails, attempt the other.[28]

Taking Possession of the Collateral

When the debtor defaults, the secured party may take possession of the collateral.[29] How does the secured party accomplish this? In either of two ways. The secured party may act on its own, without any court order, and simply take the collateral, provided this can be done *without a breach of the peace.* Otherwise, the secured party must file suit against the debtor and request that the court *order* the debtor to deliver the collateral.[30]

Suppose a consumer bought a refrigerator on credit and defaulted. The security agreement may require the consumer to make the collateral available in a reasonable time and manner, such as by emptying the refrigerator of all food and having it ready for a carrier to take away. When the refrigerator is ready, the retailer can haul it away. What if the consumer refuses to cooperate? May the retailer break into the consumer's house to take the collateral? No. Breaking into a house is a clear breach of the peace and violates Article 9.

Secured parties often repossess automobiles without the debtor's cooperation. Typically, the security agreement will state that, in the event of default, the secured party has a right to take possession of the car and drive it away. As we saw earlier, the secured party could be the seller, or it could be a mechanic with an artisan's lien on the car.

Help Wanted. Sophisticated financial company, with extensive client list and rapidly changing investment portfolio, seeks aggressive self-starter who understands complex Chapter 9 transactions, enjoys working long hours, and does not mind getting shot at. Must think quickly under pressure and successfully negotiate in diverse settings, such as on street corners with stark naked people who are wielding machetes. No experience necessary but driver's licence and good night vision essential.

We are, in short, seeking a "repo person," someone who will help us recover cars from purchasers who have failed to make monthly payments. Automobile dealers hire us to repossess a vehicle, and we assign the jobs to our agents. If hired, you will be expected to do your job as quietly as possible, stealing unseen onto the debtor's property, often at night, attempting to drive away unnoticed. You should repossess 100 to 125 cars a year. That allows for a day or so to locate particularly troublesome owners, and additional time to gain safe access.

You should be aware that modest problems may occur when an owner *does* spot one of our agents. Unpleasantness in the past included:

- Angry owners who have howled at, bitten, and attacked repo agents.
- An enraged debtor who leapt out of bed and ran screaming down the street, naked, in pursuit of his former car.
- Various deadbeats who forced their children to lie in the street, blocking the vehicle's departure.
- A doctor who leaned out of the window of a distinguished teaching hospital and fired four shots at our agent, who was attempting to repossess the doctor's BMW.

---

[28] UCC §9-501.

[29] UCC §9-503.

[30] UCC §9-503.

Every year, one or two repo agents are killed somewhere in the United States. This is a lively job, with good pay and benefits, including life insurance.

Disposition of the Collateral

Once the secured party has obtained possession of the collateral, it has two choices. The secured party may (1) dispose of the collateral or (2) retain the collateral as full satisfaction of the debt.

Why is the secured party required to notify the debtor before selling the collateral?

Disposal of the Collateral. **A secured party may sell, lease, or otherwise dispose of the collateral in any commercially reasonable manner.**[31] Typically, the secured party will sell the collateral in either a private or a public sale. First, however, the debtor must receive *reasonable notice* of the time and place of the sale, so that she may bid on the collateral. The higher the price that the secured party gets for the collateral, the lower the balance still owed by the debtor. Giving the debtor notice of the sale, and a chance to bid, ensures that the collateral will not be sold for an unreasonably low price.

Suppose Bank loans $65,000 to Farmer to purchase a tractor. While still owing $40,000, Farmer defaults. Bank takes possession of the tractor and then notifies Farmer that it intends to sell the tractor at an auction. Farmer has the right to attend and bid on the tractor.

When the secured party has sold the collateral, it applies the proceeds of the sale: first, to its expenses in repossessing and selling the collateral, and second, to the debt. Assume Bank sold the tractor for $35,000, and that the process of repossessing and selling the tractor cost $5,000. Bank applies the remaining $30,000 to the debt.

Deficiency or Surplus. The sale of the tractor yielded $30,000 to be applied to the debt, which was $40,000. The disposition has left a **deficiency**, that is, insufficient funds to pay off the debt. **The debtor is liable for any deficiency**. So the bank will sue the farmer for the remaining $10,000. On the other hand, sometimes the sale of the collateral yields a **surplus**, that is, a sum greater than the debt. In that case, the secured party must pay the surplus to the debtor.[32]

Retention of Collateral. The secured party may, if it prefers, notify the debtor that it intends to retain the collateral. The debtor has 21 days to object. **If the debtor does not object within 21 days, the secured party automatically forecloses on the collateral, that is, obtains valid title**.[33] But in accepting the collateral, the secured party gives up any claim to the debt, or to any deficiency. If the secured party discovers that the collateral is worth less than the debt, it is out of luck. Suppose the buyer of a $500,000 computer system has defaulted, and the manufacturer has repossessed the collateral. The manufacturer may decide it can modify the computer system and sell it elsewhere at a profit greater than the buyer's debt. The manufacturer will then notify the buyer that it plans to retain the system. If the buyer does not object, the manufacturer automatically owns the system after 21 days.

If the debtor objects to retention of the collateral, the secured party must then dispose of the collateral as described above, typically by sale, and apply the proceeds accordingly. Why would a debtor object? Because it believes the collateral is worth more than the debt. The debtor anticipates that a sale will create a surplus.

Right of Redemption. Up to the time the secured party disposes of the collateral, the debtor has the right to **redeem** it, that is, to pay the full value of the debt. If the debtor redeems, she obtains the collateral back. Sylvia borrows $25,000 from

31 UCC §9-504.

32 UCC §9-504(2).

33 UCC §9-505.

the bank and pledges a ruby necklace as collateral. She defaults, still owing $9,000, and the bank notifies her that it will sell the necklace. If Sylvia pays the full $9,000 before the sale occurs, plus any expenses the bank has incurred in arranging the sale, she receives her necklace back.

Proceeding to Judgment

Occasionally, the secured party will prefer to ignore its rights in the collateral and simply sue the debtor. **A secured party may sue the debtor for the full debt.**[34] Why would a creditor, having gone to so much effort to perfect its security interest, ignore that interest and simply file a lawsuit? The collateral may have decreased in value and be insufficient to cover the debt. Suppose a bank loaned $300,000 to a debtor to buy a yacht. The debtor defaults, owing $190,000. The bank discovers that the yacht is now worth only $110,000. It is true that the bank could sell the yacht and sue for the deficiency. But the sale will take time and the outcome is uncertain. Suppose the bank knows that the debtor has recently paid cash for a $2 million house. The bank may promptly file suit for the full $190,000. The bank will ask the court to freeze the debtor's bank account and legally hold the house until the suit is resolved. The bank expects to prove the debt quickly—the loan documents are clear and the amount of debt is easily calculated. It will obtain its $190,000 without ever touching the yacht.

TERMINATION

Finally, we need to look at what happens when a debtor *does not* default, but pays the full debt. Once that happens, the secured party must complete a **termination statement**, a document indicating that it no longer claims a security interest in the collateral.

For a consumer debt, the secured party must file the termination statement in every place that it filed a financing statement. The secured party must do this within one month from the date the debt is fully paid, or within 10 days of a demand from the consumer, whichever comes first. So if the consumer pays her final installment on May 5, and on May 6 she demands that the secured party file termination statements, the creditor must do it by May 16. For other secured transactions, the secured party must send the termination statement to the debtor himself, so that the debtor can file it. In both cases, the goal is the same: to notify all interested parties that the debt is extinguished.

ARTICLE 9 REVISIONS

We conclude with a glimpse of the future. The American Law Institute and the National Conference of Commissioners on Uniform State Laws have recommended significant revisions of Article 9. Commentators and various state legislatures are beginning to consider the proposals, which include:

- *Expanded Scope.* The revisions would permit Article 9 secured transactions in deposit accounts, health care accounts, tort claims, and *payment intangibles,* which include such things as the right to receive license royalties.
- *Creation and Perfection.* The changes would permit the creditor to use a supergeneric phrase such as "all personal property" or "all assets" in the financing

[34] UCC §9-501.

statement (though not in the security agreement). For instruments, a party could perfect not only by possession, as is now allowed, but also by filing.

- *Filing*. To make filing more efficient, the revisions eliminate all local (county) filings except for fixtures. The new version would also require the filer to use the debtor's registered name and not a trade name, the very issue in *First National Bank of Lacon v. Strong* earlier in this chapter. Many other changes, large and small, have been proposed, but further discussion should await legislative action.

CHAPTER CONCLUSION

Secured transactions are essential to modern commerce. Billions of dollars worth of goods are sold on credit annually, and creditors normally demand an assurance of payment. A secured party that understands Article 9 and follows its provisions to the letter should be well protected. A company that operates in ignorance of Article 9 invites disaster, because others may obtain superior rights in the goods, leaving the "secured" party with no money, no security—and no sympathy from the courts.

CHAPTER REVIEW

1. Article 9 applies to any transaction intended to create a security interest in personal property or fixtures.
2. Attachment means that (1) the two parties made a security agreement, *and either* (a) the security agreement is in writing, describes the collateral, and is signed by the debtor, *or* (b) the secured party has possession of the collateral; and (2) the secured party gave value in order to get the security agreement; and (3) the debtor has rights in the collateral.
3. A security interest may attach to after-acquired property.
4. Attachment protects against the debtor. Perfection of a security interest protects the secured party against parties other than the debtor.
5. Filing is the most common way to perfect. It is essential to file in all required offices and to include sufficient information in the financing statement so that other people are on notice that there is a security interest in the debtor's property.
6. For most but not all forms of collateral, the secured party may perfect by taking possession of it. A secured party holding collateral must use reasonable care to maintain it.
7. A purchase money security interest (PMSI) is one taken by the person who sells the collateral or by the person who advances money so the debtor can buy the collateral.
8. A PMSI in consumer goods perfects automatically, without filing.
9. A buyer in ordinary course of business (BIOC) takes the goods free of a security interest created by his seller even though the security interest is perfected.
10. A buyer of consumer goods takes free of a security interest if she is not aware of the interest, pays value for the goods, and is buying for family or household use, *and if* the secured party has not yet filed a financing statement.

11. A buyer who purchases chattel paper or an instrument in the ordinary course of his business, and then takes possession, generally takes free of any security interest.
12. Priority among secured parties is as follows:
    (a) A party with a perfected security interest takes priority over a party with an unperfected interest.
    (b) If neither secured party has perfected, the first interest to attach gets priority.
    (c) Between perfected security interests, the first to file or perfect wins.
13. A PMSI may take priority over a conflicting perfected security interest (even one perfected earlier) if the holder of the PMSI meets certain conditions.
14. When the debtor defaults, the secured party may take possession of the collateral on its own, without a court order, if it can do so without a breach of the peace.
15. A secured party may sell, lease, or otherwise dispose of the collateral in any commercially reasonable way, or, if it prefers, it may retain the collateral as full payment of the obligation, unless the debtor objects.
16. A secured party may ignore the collateral and sue the debtor for the full debt.
17. When the debtor pays the full debt, the secured party must complete a termination statement, notifying the public that it no longer claims a security interest in the collateral.

PRACTICE TEST

1. CPA QUESTION Under the UCC Secured Transactions Article, which of the following actions will best perfect a security interest in a negotiable instrument against any other party?

(a) Filing a security agreement

(b) Taking possession of the instrument

(c) Perfecting by attachment

(d) Obtaining a duly executed financing statement

2. CPA QUESTION Under the UCC Secured Transactions Article, perfection of a security interest by a creditor provides added protection against other parties in the event the debtor does not pay its debts. Which of the following parties is **not** affected by perfection of a security interest?

(a) Other prospective creditors of the debtor

(b) The trustee in a bankruptcy case

(c) A buyer in ordinary course of business

(d) A subsequent personal injury judgment creditor

3. Eugene Ables ran an excavation company. He borrowed $500,000 from the Highland Park State Bank. Ables signed a note promising to repay the money and an agreement giving Highland a security interest in all of his equipment, including after-acquired equipment. Several years later, Ables agreed with Patricia Myers to purchase a Bantam Backhoe from her for $16,000, which he would repay at the rate of $100 per month, while he used the machine. Ables later defaulted on his note to Highland, and the bank attempted to take the backhoe. Myers and Ables contended that the bank had no right to take the backhoe. Was the backhoe covered by Highland's security interest? Did Ables have sufficient rights in the backhoe for the bank's security interest to attach?

4. Jerry Payne owed the First State Bank of Pflugerville $342,000. The loan was secured by a 9.25-carat diamond ring. The bank claimed a default on the loan and, without notifying Payne, sold the ring. But the proceeds did not pay off the full debt, and the bank sued Payne for the deficiency. Is Payne liable for the deficiency?

5. John and Clara Lockovich bought a 22-foot Chaparrel Villian II boat from Greene County Yacht

Club for $32,500. They paid $6,000 cash and borrowed the rest of the purchase money from Gallatin National Bank, which took a security interest in the boat. Gallatin filed a financing statement in Greene County, Pennsylvania, where the bank was located. But Pennsylvania law requires financing statements to be filed in the county of the debtor's residence, and the Lockoviches lived in Allegheny County. The Lockoviches soon washed up in Bankruptcy Court. Other creditors demanded that the boat be sold, claiming that Gallatin's security interest had been filed in the wrong place. Who wins? (Please be advised: this is a trick question.)

6. The Copper King Inn, Inc. had money problems. It borrowed $62,500 from two of its officers, Noonan and Patterson, but that did not suffice to keep the inn going. So Noonan, on behalf of Copper King, arranged for the inn to borrow $100,000 from Northwest Capital, an investment company that worked closely with Noonan in other ventures. Copper King signed an agreement giving Patterson, Noonan, and Northwest a security interest in the inn's furniture and equipment. But the financing statement that the parties filed made no mention of Northwest. Copper King went bankrupt. Northwest attempted to seize assets, but other creditors objected. Is Northwest entitled to Copper King's furniture and equipment?

7. McMann Golf Ball Co. manufactured, as you might suppose, golf balls. Barwell, Inc. sold McMann a "preformer," a machine that makes golf balls, for $55,000. Barwell delivered the machine on February 20. McMann paid $3,000 down, the remainder to be paid over several years, and signed an agreement giving Barwell a security interest in the preformer. Barwell did not perfect its interest. On March 1, McMann borrowed $350,000 from First of America Bank, giving the bank a security interest in McMann's present and after-acquired property. First of America perfected by filing on March 2. McMann, of course, became insolvent, and both Barwell and the bank attempted to repossess the preformer. Who gets it?

8. Sears sold a lawn tractor to Cosmo Fiscante for $1,481. Fiscante paid with his personal credit card. Sears kept a valid security interest in the lawnmower, but did not perfect. Fiscante had the machine delivered to his business, Trackers Raceway Park, the only place he ever used the machine. When Fiscante was unable to meet his obligations, various creditors attempted to seize the lawnmower. Sears argued that because it had a purchase money security interest (PMSI) in the lawnmower, its interest had perfected automatically. Is Sears correct?

9. CPA QUESTION On March 1, Green went to Easy Car Sales to buy a car. Green spoke to a salesperson and agreed to buy a car that Easy had in its showroom. On March 5, Green made a $500 down payment and signed a security agreement to secure the payment of the balance of the purchase price. On March 10, Green picked up the car. On March 15, Easy filed the security agreement. On what date did Easy's security interest attach?

(a) March 1

(b) March 5

(c) March 10

(d) March 15

10. CPA QUESTION Mars, Inc. manufactures and sells VCRs on credit directly to wholesalers, retailers, and consumers. Mars can perfect its security interest in the VCRs it sells without having to file a financing statement or take possession of the VCRs if the sale is made to:

(a) Retailers

(b) Wholesalers that sell to distributors for resale

(c) Consumers

(d) Wholesalers that sell to buyers in ordinary course of business

11. RIGHT & WRONG The Dannemans bought a Kodak copier worth over $40,000. Kodak arranged financing by GECC and assigned its rights to that company. Although the Dannemans thought they had purchased the copier on credit, the papers described the deal as a lease. The Dannemans had constant problems with the machine and stopped making payments. GECC repossessed the machine and, without notifying the Dannemans, sold it back to Kodak for $12,500, leaving a deficiency of $39,927. GECC sued the Dannemans for that amount. The Dannemans argued that the deal was not a lease but a sale on credit. Why does it matter whether the parties had a sale or a lease? Is GECC entitled to its money? Finally, comment on the ethics. Why did the Dannemans not understand the papers they had signed? Who is responsible for that? Are you satisfied with the ethical conduct of the Dannemans? Kodak? GECC?

12. YOU BE THE JUDGE WRITING PROBLEM Dupont Feed bought and sold agricultural products. Dupont borrowed $300,000 from Wells Fargo Bank and gave Wells Fargo a security interest in all inventory, including after-acquired inventory. Wells Fargo perfected its interest by filing on June 17, 1982. Later, Dupont borrowed $150,000 from the Rushville National Bank and used the money to buy fertilizer. Dupont gave a PMSI to Rushville in the amount of $150,000. Rushville filed its financing statement in February 1984 at the County Recorder's office—the wrong place to file a financing statement for inventory. Then Dupont took possession of the fertilizer, and finally, in December 1984 Rushville filed correctly, with the Indiana Secretary of State. Dupont defaulted on both loans. Rushville seized the fertilizer and Wells Fargo sued, claiming that it had perfected first. Rushville asserted that it had a PMSI, which took priority over an earlier-filed security interest. Does Rushville's PMSI take priority over Wells Fargo? (Go slowly, the rules are very technical.) **Argument for Rushville:** It is black letter law that PMSIs take priority over virtually everything, including interests perfected earlier. We are not fools at Rushville: we would not loan $150,000 to buy inventory if our security interest in that inventory was instantly inferior to someone else's. **Argument for Wells Fargo:** A PMSI in inventory gets priority only if the secured party perfects before the debtor receives the collateral. When Dupont obtained the fertilizer, Rushville had not perfected, because it had filed in the wrong office. It only perfected long after Dupont bought the inventory, and thus Rushville's PMSI does not get priority.

INTERNET RESEARCH PROBLEM

At **http://www.law.cornell.edu/ucc/ucc.table.html**, click on *Article 9* and make your way to §9-402. Notice that subsection (3) provides a simple, clear form for a financing statement. Using that form as a guide, draft a financing statement that you would rely on to loan $12,000 to a friend, using his 2001 Jeep Cherokee as collateral.

You can find further practice problems in the Online Quiz at http://beatty.westbuslaw.com or in the Study Guide that accompanies this text.

CHAPTER 27

BANKRUPTCY

George Bryan Brummell, known as Beau Brummell, was a celebrity in nineteenth-century England. Known for his impeccable sense of style, he was the leading arbiter of taste and fashion for more than 20 years. This role was demanding—he routinely spent five hours a day simply getting dressed. After bathing in eau de cologne and water, he would spend an hour with his hairdresser and another two hours tying his cravat. Although he had inherited modest wealth, his extravagant lifestyle brought him to ruin. He fled to France to escape his creditors, taking his lavish tastes with him. After 14 years in France, he was thrown in debtors' prison. Brummell ultimately died in a mental institution there.

For actress Kim Basinger, a modern celebrity, bankruptcy had a different outcome. A Los Angeles jury ordered her to pay $8.1 million to Main Line Pictures, Inc. because she broke her promise to appear in *Boxing Helena*, a film about a doctor who cuts off his lover's arms and legs. Five days after the verdict, she filed for bankruptcy protection, claiming $5 million in assets and $11 million in liabilities.

Despite filing for bankruptcy, Basinger spent $43,000 per month, including $6,100 for clothes; $4,000 for recreation, clubs, and entertainment; $7,000 for pet care and other personal expenses; as well as $9,000 in alimony to her ex-husband. She

also reported owning $592,000 in furniture and clothing and $192,000 in jewelry. In the meantime, she made no payments to creditors—those who had arranged her travel, repaired her home, or cut her grass.[1]

Traditionally, the goal of English bankruptcy law was to protect creditors and punish debtors. Creditors had the right to seize a bankrupt's assets and have him incarcerated in a squalid debtors' prison. Once in jail, the debtor had no way to earn money to pay his debts. His only hope was the kindness of family and friends. Many of America's first settlers fled England to escape debtors' prison. As if to compensate for England's harsh regime, American bankruptcy laws have always been relatively lenient toward debtors.

The drafters of the United States Constitution thought bankruptcy was so important it should be regulated by Congress, not the states. For the first 100 years, however, Congress failed to develop a successful bankruptcy system. Time and again, Congress passed bankruptcy statutes, only to repeal them a few years later. In this vacuum, regulation fell more or less to the states. Finally, in 1898, Congress passed a statute that remained in effect until it was overhauled in 1978. Since then, Congress has passed three major amendments—in 1984, 1986, and 1994. Still not satisfied, Congress established a commission to recommend changes in the bankruptcy laws. The National Bankruptcy Review Commission's report created great controversy: creditor groups (particularly issuers of credit cards) protested that the recommendations were not tough enough on debtors; consumer organizations complained about their harshness. All parties began to lobby Congress, which has yet to find a suitable compromise. The commission's report is available at **http://www.nbrc.gov/**.

OVERVIEW OF THE BANKRUPTCY CODE

The federal Bankruptcy Code (Code) is divided into eight chapters. All chapters except one have odd numbers. Chapters 1, 3, and 5 are administrative rules that generally apply to all types of bankruptcy proceedings. These chapters, for example, define terms and establish the rules of the bankruptcy court. Chapters 7, 9, 11, 12, and 13 are substantive rules for different types of bankruptcies. All of these substantive chapters have one of two objectives—rehabilitation or liquidation. (The text of the Bankruptcy Code is available at **http://www4.law.cornell.edu/uscode/11/**.)

REHABILITATION

The objective of Chapters 11 and 13 is to rehabilitate the debtor. Many debtors can return to financial health provided they have the time and breathing space to work out their problems. These chapters hold creditors at bay while the debtor develops a payment plan. In return for retaining some of their assets, debtors typically promise to pay creditors a portion of their future earnings.

---

[1] Carol Marie Cropper, "The Basinger Bankruptcy Bomb," *New York Times*, Jan. 1, 1995, §3, p. 1. Copyright © 1995 by The New York Times Co. Reprinted by permission. A California appeals court overturned the judgment against Basinger in the Main Line suit and ordered a new trial. On the eve of retrial, Basinger settled for $3.8 million. By this time, however, she had only $1.75 million in assets available for distribution to creditors, so her bankruptcy case continued.

LIQUIDATION

When debtors are unable to develop a feasible plan for rehabilitation under Chapter 11 or 13, Chapter 7 provides for liquidation (also known as a **straight bankruptcy**). Most of the debtor's assets are distributed to creditors, but the debtor has no obligation to share future earnings.

CHAPTER DESCRIPTION

The following options are available under the Bankruptcy Code:

Number	Topic	Description
Chapter 7	Liquidation	The bankrupt's assets are sold to pay creditors. If the debtor owns a business, it terminates. The creditors have no right to the debtor's future earnings.
Chapter 9	Municipal bankruptcies	This chapter is not covered in this book.
Chapter 11	Reorganization	This chapter is designed for businesses and wealthy individuals. Businesses continue in operation, and creditors receive a portion of both current assets and future earnings.
Chapter 12	Family farmers	This chapter is not covered in this book.
Chapter 13	Consumer reorganizations	Chapter 13 offers reorganizations for the typical consumer. Creditors usually receive a portion of the individual's current assets and future earnings.

Debtors are often eligible to file under more than one chapter. No choice is irrevocable because both debtors and creditors have the right to ask the court to convert a case from one chapter to another at any time during the proceedings. For example, if creditors have asked for liquidation under Chapter 7, a consumer debtor may request rehabilitation under Chapter 13. Kim Basinger originally filed under Chapter 11 but, unable to reach agreement with her creditors, converted to liquidation under Chapter 7.

GOALS

The Bankruptcy Code has three primary goals:

- *To preserve as much of the debtor's property as possible.* In keeping with this goal, the Code requires debtors to disclose all of their assets and prohibits them from transferring assets immediately before a bankruptcy filing.
- *To divide the debtor's assets fairly between the debtor and creditors.* On the one hand, creditors are entitled to payment. On the other hand, debtors are often so deeply in debt that full payment is virtually impossible in any reasonable period of time. The Code tries to balance the creditors' desire to be paid with the debtors' right to get on with their lives unburdened by prior debts.
- *To divide the debtor's assets fairly among creditors.* Creditors rarely receive all they are owed, but at least they are treated fairly, according to established rules. Creditors do not benefit from simply being the first to file or from any other gamesmanship.

CHAPTER 7 LIQUIDATION

All bankruptcy cases proceed in a roughly similar pattern, regardless of chapter. We use Chapter 7 as a template to illustrate common features of all bankruptcy cases. Later on, the discussions of the other chapters will indicate how they differ from Chapter 7.

FILING A PETITION

Any individual, partnership, corporation, or other business organization that lives, conducts business, or owns property in the United States can file under the Code. (Chapter 13, however, is available only to individuals.) The traditional term for someone who could not pay his debts was "**bankrupt**," but the Code uses the term "**debtor**" instead. We use both terms interchangeably.

A case begins with the filing of a bankruptcy petition in federal district court. The district court typically refers bankruptcy cases to a specialized bankruptcy judge. Either party can appeal the decision of the bankruptcy judge back to the district court and, from there, to the federal appeals court.

Debtors may go willingly into the bankruptcy process by filing a **voluntary petition** or they may be dragged into court by creditors who file an **involuntary petition**. Originally, when the goal of bankruptcy laws was to protect creditors, voluntary petitions did not exist; all petitions were involuntary. Because the bankruptcy process is now viewed as being favorable to debtors, the vast majority of bankruptcy filings in this country are voluntary petitions.

Voluntary Petition

Any debtor may file for bankruptcy. It is not necessary that the debtor's liabilities exceed assets. Debtors sometimes file a bankruptcy petition because cash flow is so tight they cannot pay their debts, even though they are not technically insolvent. The voluntary petition must include the following documents:

Document	Description
Petition	Begins the case. Easy to fill out, it requires checking a few boxes and typing in little more than name, address, and Social Security number.
List of Creditors	The names and addresses of all creditors.
Schedule of Assets and Liabilities	A list of the debtor's assets and debts.
Claim of Exemptions	A list of all assets that the debtor is entitled to keep.
Schedule of Income and Expenditures	The debtor's job, income, and expenses.
Statement of Financial Affairs	A summary of the debtor's financial history and current financial condition. In particular, the debtor must list any recent payments to creditors and any other property held by someone else for the debtor.

Involuntary Petition

Creditors may force a debtor into bankruptcy by filing an involuntary petition. The creditors' goal is to preserve as much of the debtor's assets as possible and to ensure that all creditors receive a fair share. Naturally, the Code sets strict limits—debtors cannot be forced into bankruptcy every time they miss a credit card payment. **An involuntary petition must meet all of the following requirements:**

- The debtor must owe at least $10,000 in unsecured claims to the creditors who file.[2]
- If the debtor has at least 12 creditors, three or more must sign the petition. If the debtor has fewer than 12 creditors, any one of them can file a petition.
- The creditors must allege either that a custodian for the debtor's property has been appointed in the prior 120 days or that the debtor has generally not been paying debts that are due.

What does "a custodian for the debtor's property" mean? *State* laws sometimes permit the appointment of a custodian to protect a debtor's assets. The Code allows creditors to pull a case out from under state law and into federal bankruptcy court by filing an involuntary petition. Creditors also have the right to file an involuntary petition if they can show that the debtor is not paying debts. In the event that a debtor objects to an involuntary petition, the bankruptcy court must hold a trial to determine whether the creditors have met the Code's requirements.

Once a voluntary petition is filed or an involuntary petition approved, the bankruptcy court issues an **order for relief**. This order is an official acknowledgment that the debtor is under the jurisdiction of the court, and it is, in a sense, the start of the whole bankruptcy process. An involuntary debtor must now make all the filings that accompany a voluntary petition.

TRUSTEE

The trustee is responsible for gathering the bankrupt's assets and dividing them among creditors. This is a critical role in a bankruptcy case. Trustees are typically lawyers or CPAs, but any generally competent person can serve. Creditors have the right to elect the trustee, but often they do not bother. It used to be that the judge would then appoint a trustee. But both debtors and creditors complained that judges could not be impartial when resolving subsequent disputes that involved the very trustees they had appointed. To solve this problem, the U.S. Attorney General now appoints a **U.S. Trustee** for each region of the country. This U.S. Trustee is responsible for appointing trustees when necessary and also overseeing the administration of bankruptcy law in the region.

---

[2] In Chapter 26, on secured transactions, we discuss the difference between secured and unsecured claims at some length. A secured claim is one in which the creditor has the right to foreclose on a specific piece of the debtor's property (known as **collateral**) if the debtor fails to pay the debt when due. For example, if Lee borrows money from GMAC Finance to buy a car, the company has the right to repossess the car if Lee fails to repay the loan. GMAC's loan is **secured**. An **unsecured** loan has no collateral. If the debtor fails to repay, the creditor can make a general claim against the debtor but has no right to foreclose on a particular item of the debtor's property.

CREDITORS

The U.S. Trustee calls a meeting of creditors sometime within 20 to 40 days after the order for relief. At the meeting, the bankrupt must answer (under oath) any question the creditors pose about his financial situation. If the creditors want to elect a trustee, they do so at this meeting.

Unsecured creditors must submit a *proof of claim* within 90 days after the meeting of creditors. The proof of claim is a simple form stating the name of the creditor and the amount of the claim. The trustee and the debtor also have the right to file on behalf of a creditor. But if a claim is not filed, the creditor loses any right to be paid. The trustee, debtor, or any creditor can object to a claim on the grounds that the debtor does not really owe that money. The court then holds a hearing to determine the validity of the claim.

Secured creditors do not file proofs of claim unless the claim exceeds the value of their collateral. In this case, they are unsecured creditors for the excess amount and must file a proof of claim for it. Suppose that Deborah borrows $750,000 from Morton in return for a mortgage on her house. If she does not repay the debt, he can foreclose. Unfortunately, property values plummet, and by the time Deborah files a voluntary petition in bankruptcy, the house is worth only $500,000. Morton is a secured creditor for $500,000 and need file no proof of claim for that amount. But he is an unsecured creditor for $250,000 and will lose his right to this excess amount unless he files a proof of claim for it.

AUTOMATIC STAY

A fox chased by hounds has no time to make rational long-term decisions. What that fox needs is a safe burrow. Similarly, it is difficult for debtors to make sound financial decisions when hounded night and day by creditors shouting, "Pay me! Pay me!" The Code is designed to give debtors enough breathing space to sort out their affairs sensibly. An automatic stay is a safe burrow for the bankrupt. It goes into effect as soon as the petition is filed. **An automatic stay prohibits creditors from collecting debts that the bankrupt incurred before the petition was filed.** Creditors may not sue a bankrupt to obtain payment nor may they take other steps, outside of court, to pressure the debtor for payment. In the following case, the landlord ate crow instead of Chinese food.

IN RE **SECHUAN CITY INC.**
96 B.R. 37, 1989 Bankr. LEXIS 103
United States Bankruptcy Court, Eastern District of Pennsylvania, 1989

Facts: The Sechuan Garden restaurant leased space from North American Motor Inns, Inc. (Hotel). The entrance to the restaurant was in the Hotel lobby. The restaurant did not have a liquor license, but the Hotel bar would deliver drinks to restaurant guests at their tables. Sechuan Garden filed a voluntary petition in bankruptcy. Although the Hotel manager, Jose Garcia, knew that the bankruptcy court had entered an automatic stay, he posted the signs shown on the next page at all Hotel entrances, in the Hotel lobby, and immediately outside the restaurant doors located in the lobby.

The restaurant's revenues dropped $1,000 a week for three weeks until Garcia finally removed the signs. Garcia testified that he had posted the signs to "shame" and "embarrass" the restaurant's owners into paying their bills.

Issue: **Did the Hotel violate Sechuan Garden's automatic stay?**

At least debtors are entitled to an automatic stay.

NOTICE
PLEASE DON'T PATRONIZE THE SECHUAN GARDEN
THIS RESTAURANT UNFAIR TO MANAGEMENT
IT DOES NOT PAY IT'S (sic) BILLS
THANK YOU

THE TENANT HAS DISHONORED ITS
OBLIGATION FOR PAYMENT
TO THE LANDLORD

NOTICE
NO ALCOHOLIC BEVERAGES ARE ALLOWED
TO BE CONSUMED IN THE RESTAURANT AREA
UNDER PENALTY OF LAW
THANKS
N.A.M.I. MGMT

Excerpts from Judge Fox's Decision:[3] The automatic stay is one of the fundamental debtor protections provided by the bankruptcy laws. It gives the debtor a breathing spell from his creditors. It stops all collection efforts, all harassment, and all foreclosure actions. It permits the debtor to attempt a repayment or reorganization plan or simply to be relieved of the financial pressures that drove him into bankruptcy.

The automatic stay also provides creditor protection. Without it, certain creditors would be able to pursue their own remedies against the debtor's property. Those who acted first would obtain payment of the claims in preference to and to the detriment of other creditors. [The Code] specifically enjoins: "any act to collect, assess, or recover a claim against the debtor that arose before the commencement of the case under this title." The language of this subsection is very broad, and is designed to prevent creditor coercion and harassment of the debtor. The conduct prohibited ranges from that of an informal nature, such as by telephone contact or by dunning letters to more formal judicial and administrative proceedings.

Here, I conclude that the Hotel undertook a studied effort to coerce payment of the [restaurant's] prepetition claim. Defendants' contention that they simply sought to inform the public of the debtor's bankruptcy filing and not to harm the debtor is belied by the striking appearance of the signs, the signs' content (requesting the debtor's restaurant not be patronized), by the testimony which conceded that the defendants' conduct was intended to shame and embarrass, and by the defendants' attempt to discourage customers by refusing the service of alcoholic drinks. While the lessor did not bring suit against the debtor, its actions were designed to place the debtor in a position of either paying the lessor's prepetition claim or losing business due to defendants' actions. These actions were prohibited by the automatic stay and resulted in clear harm to the debtor.

[The court ordered the hotel to pay the bankruptcy trustee $3,000 in damages and $600 in attorney's fees.]

[3] No surprise that Judge Fox appreciates the importance of an automatic stay.

lifestyle while his investment bank flourished. But when the bank failed, Lawrence was faced with debts of $6 million. On the eve of the bankruptcy filing, Diana suddenly announced that she wanted a divorce. In what had to be the most amicable breakup ever, Lawrence willingly transferred all of his assets to her. The unhappy couple went on to obtain their divorce in only two months, a speed that the bankruptcy court referred to as "astonishing." The court indignantly found that the transfer had been fraudulent.[5]

Not all payments by a debtor prior to filing are considered voidable preferences or fraudulent transfers. **A trustee cannot void prepetition payments made *in the ordinary course*.** In a business context, that means a trustee cannot void payments from, say, a grocery store to its regular cookie supplier. For consumers, the trustee cannot void payments below $600 or other routine payments, say, to the electric or water company. In these situations, the bankrupt is clearly not trying to cheat creditors. Even the insolvent are allowed to shower with the light on.

PAYMENT OF CLAIMS

Imagine a crowded delicatessen on Saturday evening. People are pushing and shoving because they know there is not enough food for everyone; some customers will go home hungry. The delicatessen could simply serve whoever pushes to the front of the line, or it could establish a number system to ensure that the most deserving customers are served first—long-time patrons or those who called ahead. The Code has, in essence, adopted a number system to prevent a free-for-all fight over the bankrupt's assets. Indeed, one of the Code's primary goals is to ensure that creditors are paid in the proper order, not according to who pushes to the front of the line.

All claims are placed in one of three classes: (1) secured claims, (2) priority claims, and (3) unsecured claims. The second class—priority claims—has seven subcategories; the third class—unsecured claims—has three. **The trustee pays the bankruptcy estate to the various classes of claims in order of rank.** A higher class is paid in full before the next class receives any payment at all. In the case of *priority* claims, each *subcategory* is paid in order, with the higher subcategory receiving full payment before the next subcategory receives anything. If there are not enough funds to pay an entire subcategory, all claimants in that group receive a pro rata share. The rule is different for unsecured claims. All categories of *unsecured* claims are treated the same, and if there are not enough funds to pay the *entire* class, everyone in the class shares pro rata. If, for example, there is only enough money to pay 10 percent of the claims owing to unsecured creditors, then each creditor receives 10 percent of her claim. In bankruptcy parlance, this is referred to as "getting 10 cents on the dollar." The debtor is entitled to any funds remaining after all claims have been paid. The payment order is shown in Exhibit 27.1.

Exhibit 27.1

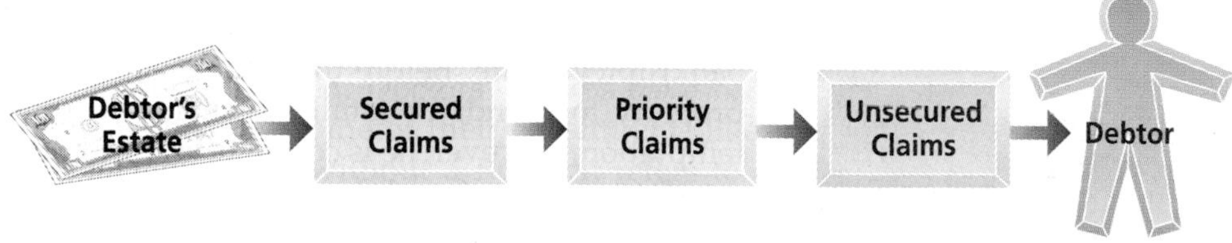

[5] *In re Williams*, 159 B.R. 648, 1993 Bankr. LEXIS 1482 (Bankr. D.R.I. 1993), *remanded*, 190 B.R. 728, 1996 U.S. Dist. LEXIS 539.

Secured Claims

Creditors whose loans are secured by specific collateral are paid first. Secured claims are fundamentally different from all other claims because they are paid by selling a specific asset, not out of the general funds of the estate. Sometimes, however, collateral is not valuable enough to pay off the entire secured debt. In this case, the creditor must wait in line with the unsecured creditors for the balance. Deborah (whom we met earlier in the section entitled "Creditors") borrowed $750,000 from Morton, secured by a mortgage on her house. By the time she files a voluntary petition, the house is worth only $500,000. Morton is a secured creditor for $500,000 and is paid that amount as soon as the trustee sells the house. But Morton is an unsecured creditor for $250,000 and will only receive this amount if the estate has enough funds to pay the unsecured creditors.

Priority Claims

There are seven subcategories of priority claims. Each category is paid in order, with the first group receiving full payment before the next group receives anything.

- *Administrative Expenses.* These include fees to the trustee, lawyers, and accountants.
- *Gap Expenses.* If creditors file an involuntary petition, the debtor will continue to operate her business until the order for relief. Any expenses she incurs in the ordinary course of her business during this so-called **gap period** are paid now.
- *Payments to Employees.* The trustee now pays back wages to the debtor's employees for work performed during the 90 days prior to the date of the petition. The trustee, however, can pay no more than $4,000 to each employee. Any other wages become unsecured claims.
- *Employee Benefit Plans.* The trustee pays what the debtor owes to employee pension, health, or life insurance plans for work performed during the 180 days prior to the date of the petition. The total payment for wages and benefits under this and the prior paragraph cannot exceed $4,000 times the number of employees.
- *Consumer Deposits.* Any individual who has put down a deposit with the bankrupt for consumer goods is entitled to a refund of up to $1,800. If Stewart Student puts down a $2,000 deposit on a Miata sports car that he intends to buy in a month when he begins work, he is entitled to a refund of $1,800 when the Trustie Car Lot goes bankrupt.
- *Alimony and Child Support.* The trustee pays any outstanding court orders for alimony and child support.
- *Taxes.* The trustee pays the debtor's income taxes for the three years prior to filing and property taxes for one prior year.

Unsecured Claims

Last, and frequently very much least, the trustee pays unsecured claims. All three of these unsecured subcategories have an equal claim and must be paid together.

- *Secured Claims That Exceed the Value of the Available Collateral.* If funds permit, the trustee pays Morton the $250,000 that his collateral did not cover.

- *Priority Claims That Exceed the Priority Limits.* The trustee now pays employees, Stewart Student, and the tax authorities who were not paid in full the first time around because their claims exceeded the priority limits.
- *All Other Unsecured Claims.* Unsecured creditors have now reached the delicatessen counter. They can only hope that some food remains.

DISCHARGE

Filing a bankruptcy petition is embarrassing, time-consuming, and disruptive. It can affect the debtor's credit rating for years, making the simplest car loan a challenge. To encourage debtors to file for bankruptcy despite the pain involved, the Code offers a powerful incentive: the **fresh start**. Once a bankruptcy estate has been distributed to creditors, they cannot make a claim against the debtor for money owed before the filling, *whether or not they actually received any payment.* These pre-petition debts are **discharged**. All is forgiven, if not forgotten.

Discharge is an essential part of bankruptcy law. Without it, debtors would have little incentive to take part. To avoid abuses, however, the Code limits both the type of debts that can be discharged and the circumstances under which discharge can take place.

Debts That Cannot Be Discharged

The following debts are *never* discharged, and the debtor remains liable in full until they are paid:

- Income taxes for the three years prior to filing and property taxes for the prior year.
- Money obtained fraudulently. Kenneth Smith ran a home repair business that fleeced senior citizens by making unnecessary repairs. Three months after he was found liable for fraud, he filed a voluntary petition in bankruptcy. The court held that his liability on the fraud claim could not be discharged.[6]
- Any loan of more than $1,000 that a consumer uses to purchase luxury goods within 60 days before the order for relief is granted.
- Cash advances on a credit card totaling more than $1,000 that an individual debtor takes out within 60 days before the order of relief.
- Debts omitted from the Schedule of Assets and Liabilities that the debtor filed with the petition, if the creditor did not know about the bankruptcy and therefore did not file a proof of claim.
- Money that the debtor stole or obtained through a violation of fiduciary duty.
- Money owed for alimony, maintenance, or child support.
- Debts stemming from intentional and malicious injury.
- Fines and penalties owed to the government.
- Liability for injuries caused by the debtor while operating an automobile under the influence of drugs or alcohol. Yet another reason why friends don't let friends drive drunk.
- Liability for breach of duty to a bank. During the 1980s, a record number of savings and loans failed because their officers had made too many risky loans

---

[6] *In re Smith,* 848 F.2d 813, 1988 U.S. App. LEXIS 8037 (7th Cir. 1988).

(in some cases to friends and family). This provision, added to the Code in 1990, was designed to prevent these officers from declaring bankruptcy to avoid their liability to bank shareholders.

- Student loans guaranteed by the government cannot be discharged for seven years after the due date. The bankruptcy court may discharge these loans only if the student has acted in good faith and payment of the loans would cause undue hardship.

In the following case, a landlord asked the bankruptcy court to discharge a debt to his tenants. You be the judge.

COHEN v. DE LA CRUZ
523 U.S. 213, 118 S. Ct. 1212, 1998 U.S. LEXIS 2119
United States Supreme Court, 1998

Facts: Edward Cohen was a landlord in Hoboken, New Jersey. The rents that he charged his tenants violated the local rent control ordinance. The Hoboken Rent Control Administrator ordered him to refund $31,382.50 in overcharges. Instead of paying the tenants, Cohen filed a petition for bankruptcy under Chapter 7 and asked the court to discharge his debts.

The Bankruptcy Code prohibits the discharge of "any debt . . . for money, property, [or] services, to the extent obtained by . . . actual fraud." The tenants filed a proceeding in the Bankruptcy Court, arguing that the debt owed to them arose from rent payments obtained by "actual fraud" and, therefore, was not dischargeable. The tenants also argued that they were entitled to punitive damages (under the local consumer protection statute). Ruling in the tenants' favor, the Bankruptcy Court decided that the debt was not dischargeable. It also awarded the tenants punitive damages and attorney's fees totaling $94,147.50. Cohen appealed, arguing that the debt itself might not be dischargeable, but the punitive damages were. The Court of Appeals for the Third Circuit upheld the verdict. However, its decision on the punitive damages issue conflicted with the opinion of the Ninth Circuit in a similar case. Cohen appealed and the Supreme Court granted certiorari.

You Be the Judge: Are punitive damages for fraud dischargeable under Chapter 7 of the Bankruptcy Code?

Argument for Cohen: The Bankruptcy Code clearly prohibits the discharge of any debt "obtained by . . . actual fraud." In this case, the amount of money obtained by actual fraud was $31,382.50. The additional $94,147.50 was awarded as punishment for committing fraud, but not for the "actual fraud" itself. The Court must enforce the statute as written. If Congress had wanted to include punitive damages on the list of nondischargeable items, it could have done so.

Argument for the Tenants: It has long been a basic policy of the Bankruptcy Code to afford relief only to honest but unfortunate debtors. Cohen deliberately violated rent control ordinances and then filed for bankruptcy in a clear effort to avoid his legitimate financial obligations. He is anything but an honest debtor.

The Bankruptcy Code involves a trade-off between the creditors' right to be paid and the debtor's right to a fresh start. Typically, there is some justice on both sides. But not in this case. To permit this debtor a fresh start would simply aid and abet his effort to flout the rent control laws. Congress could not have thought Cohen was more entitled to protection than his unfortunate tenants.

Circumstances That Prevent Debts from Being Discharged

Apart from identifying the *kinds* of debts that cannot be discharged, the Code also prohibits the discharge of debts under the following *circumstances*:

- *Business Organizations*. Under Chapter 7 (but *not* the other chapters), the debts of partnerships and corporations cannot be discharged. Once its assets have been distributed, the organization must cease operation. If it continues in business, it is responsible for all pre-petition debts. Shortly after E. G. Sprinkler Corp. entered into an agreement with its union employees, it filed for bankruptcy under Chapter 7. Its debts were discharged, and the company began operation again. A court ordered it to pay its obligations to the employees because, once the company resumed business, it was responsible for all of its pre-filing debts.[7]

- *Repeated Filings for Bankruptcy*. Congress feared that some debtors, attracted by the lure of a fresh start, would make a habit of bankruptcy. Therefore, a debtor who has received a discharge under Chapter 7 or 11 cannot receive another discharge under Chapter 7 for at least six years after the prior filing.
- *Revocation*. A court can revoke a discharge within one year if it discovers the debtor engaged in fraud or concealment.
- *Dishonesty or Bad Faith Behavior*. The court may deny discharge altogether if the debtor has, for example, made fraudulent transfers, hidden assets, falsified records, disobeyed court orders, refused to testify, or otherwise acted in bad faith.

Reaffirmation

Sometimes debtors are willing to **reaffirm** a debt, meaning they promise to pay even after discharge. They may want to reaffirm a secured debt to avoid losing the collateral. For example, a debtor who has taken out a loan secured by a car may reaffirm that debt so that the finance company will agree not to repossess it. Sometimes debtors reaffirm because they feel guilty, or they want to maintain a good relationship with the creditor. They may have borrowed from a family member or an important supplier. Because discharge is a fundamental pillar of the bankruptcy process, courts look closely at each reaffirmation to ensure that the creditor has not unfairly pressured the bankrupt. To be valid, the reaffirmation must meet the following requirements:

- It must not violate common law standards for fraud, duress, or unconscionability. If creditors force a bankrupt into reaffirming a debt, the reaffirmation is invalid.
- It must have been filed in court before the discharge is granted.
- It must clearly disclose that the debtor has the right to rescind at any time up to the date of the discharge or 60 days after the agreement is filed in court, whichever is later.
- Either the court must determine that the agreement is in the debtor's best interest and does not impose undue hardship, or the attorney representing the debtor must file an affidavit in court stating that the debtor's consent was informed and voluntary and the agreement does not create a hardship.
- In the case of an individual debtor, the court must explain both the terms of the agreement and the fact that it is not required by law.

As the following article illustrates, bankruptcy courts take the reaffirmation rules very seriously.

NEWSWORTHY

Because a disabled, financially strapped Massachusetts father was desperate to keep a television set to entertain his children, Sears, Roebuck & Company has been tarnished by a national credit card scandal.

The father, Francis M. Latanowich, overwhelmed by his monthly bills from Sears, turned for help to Carol Kenner, chief judge of the United States Bankruptcy Court in Boston. Mr. Latanowich, who was living on a monthly Social Security check, complained to Judge Kenner in a hand-scrawled note that his payments to

[7] *In re Goodman*, 873 F.2d 598, 1989 U.S. App. LEXIS 5472 (2d Cir. 1989).

Sears to keep his television and car battery were making it impossible for him to feed his children. Judge Kenner wondered why Sears was in contact with Mr. Latanowich, who had gone through bankruptcy proceedings that should have wiped clean his debts to the company.

Her astonishing conclusion: Sears had talked Mr. Latanowich into signing a new debt-collection contract that used threatening wording, that it had been told in court was illegal, and then, to avoid having the contract thrown out, had ignored its obligation to file it with the bankruptcy court for review. Further inquiries revealed that Sears had been doing much the same with other debtors. It had routinely skipped filing such contracts and had collected up to $160 million without judicial oversight.

The subsequent debt-collection scandal at Sears, the nation's largest retail credit card issuer, immediately focused attention on the credit practices of other retailers. Two, May Department Stores and Montgomery Ward, were hit with class action lawsuits over their reaffirmation practices. Federated Department Stores (the parent of Macy's and Bloomingdale's), realizing that it, too, had a problem, mounted a preemptive strike. Upon investigation, it discovered that 17 percent of the 17,000 reaffirmations collected in the prior decade had not been filed with courts. It devised a plan to send refunds totaling $4.3 million to the 3,000 people affected.[8]

In this case, crime definitely did not pay. Sears subsequently pleaded guilty to criminal fraud charges and paid a $60 million fine. The company also paid $185 million in reimbursements and penalties to cardholders and $40 million in state fines. Sears wrote off an additional $120 million owed by cardholders under the reaffirmation agreements and spent about $56 million in legal fees.

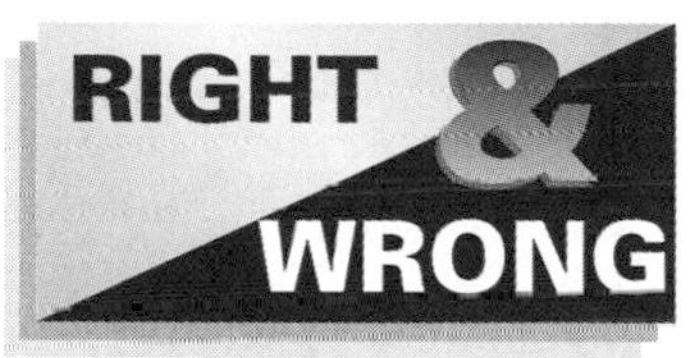

At some point in your life, you will borrow money. What *moral* obligation do you have to repay legitimate debts? Should you take the view that, if bankruptcy laws permit you to default on debts, then why not do so? Alternatively, if you get over your head in debt, should you struggle to pay even though you legitimately qualify for bankruptcy protection? Do the laws determine for you what is right and wrong, or should you have your own standard?

CHAPTER 11 REORGANIZATION

For a business, the goal of a Chapter 7 bankruptcy is euthanasia—putting it out of its misery by shutting it down and distributing its assets to creditors. Chapter 11 has a much more complicated and ambitious goal—resuscitating a business so that it can ultimately emerge as a viable economic concern. Keeping a business in operation benefits virtually all company stakeholders: employees, customers, creditors, shareholders, and the community.

Both individuals and businesses can use Chapter 11. Businesses usually prefer Chapter 11 over Chapter 7 because Chapter 11 does not require them to dissolve at the end as Chapter 7 does. The threat of death creates a powerful incentive to try rehabilitation under Chapter 11. Individuals, however, tend to prefer Chapter 13 because it is specifically designed for them.

A Chapter 11 proceeding follows many of the same steps as Chapter 7: a petition (either voluntary or involuntary), order for relief, meeting of creditors, proofs of claim, and an automatic stay. There are, however, some significant differences.

[8] Barnaby J. Feder, "The Harder Side of Sears," *New York Times*, July 20, 1997, p. C1. Copyright © 1997 by The New York Times Co. Reprinted by permission.

DEBTOR IN POSSESSION

Chapter 11 does not require a trustee. The bankrupt is called the **debtor in possession** and, in essence, serves as trustee. The debtor in possession has two jobs: to operate the business and to develop a plan of reorganization. A trustee is chosen only if the debtor is incompetent or uncooperative. In that case, the creditors can elect the trustee, but if they do not choose to do so, the U.S. Trustee appoints one.

CREDITORS' COMMITTEE

In a Chapter 11 case, the creditors' committee plays a particularly important role because there is no neutral trustee to watch over their interests. The committee has the right to help develop the plan of reorganization and to participate in any other way necessary to protect the interests of its constituency. The U.S. Trustee typically appoints the seven largest *un*secured creditors to the committee. Secured creditors do not serve because their interests require less protection. If the debtor is a corporation, the U.S. Trustee may also appoint a committee of **equity security holders** to represent shareholder interests. The Code refers to the **claims** of creditors and the **interests** of shareholders.

PLAN OF REORGANIZATION

Once the bankruptcy petition is filed, an automatic stay goes into effect to provide the debtor with temporary relief from creditors. The next stage is to develop a plan of reorganization that provides for the payment of debts and the continuation of the business. For the first 120 days after the order for relief, the debtor has the exclusive right to propose a plan. If the plan is accepted by the shareholders and creditors within 180 days of the order for relief, then the bankruptcy case terminates and the debtor implements the plan. Generally, the creditors and shareholders will accept a plan only if they expect to be better off with a reorganization than they would be with a liquidation. If they reject the debtor's plan, the creditors or shareholders may file alternative plans. The debtor has a strong incentive to develop a fair plan the first time because the creditors' proposals are likely to be less favorable.

The following article illustrates the important role the creditors' committee can play in developing a plan of reorganization.

Integrated Resources, a nationwide real estate syndication firm, went through one of the ugliest bankruptcy cases ever. Most observers agree that the haggling would probably still be going on but for a tenacious money manager from San Francisco named Meridee Moore, who was head of a creditors' committee. Moore brought a spirit of compromise into a case that many thought was hopelessly paralyzed by mistrust and suspicion. Some creditors cited her self-effacing sense of humor. Others pointed to her almost superhuman stamina—she made a telephone call about the case on the day her third daughter was born. And she clearly had a firm grasp of financial details. But her biggest contribution seems to have been in devising a businesslike strategy that fostered both speed and trust. For example, Moore put a persuasive price tag on each moment of delay. She calculated that it cost $7 million a month to stay in bankruptcy. Repeatedly, she argued that any battle that would slow the settlement by a month had better produce more than $7 million in fresh money for creditors. If it didn't, then peaceful settlements made more sense.

The lesson from the Integrated Resources case? No system can resolve disputes without the cooperation of the people involved. That is where persuasive negotiators like Moore come in.[9]

CONFIRMATION OF THE PLAN

Anyone who proposes a plan of reorganization must also prepare a **disclosure statement** to be mailed out with the plan. This statement provides creditors and shareholders enough information to make an informed judgment. The statement describes the company's business, explains the plan, calculates the company's liquidation value, and assesses the likelihood that the debtor can be rehabilitated. The court must approve a disclosure statement before it is sent to creditors and shareholders.

All the creditors and shareholders have the right to vote on the plan of organization. In preparation for the vote, each creditor and shareholder is assigned to a class. Everyone in a class has similar claims or interests. Chapter 11 classifies claims in the same way as Chapter 7: (1) secured claims, (2) priority claims, and (3) unsecured claims. Each secured claim is usually in its own class because each one is secured by different collateral. Shareholders are also divided into classes, depending upon their interests. For example, holders of preferred stock are in a different class from common shareholders.

Creditors and shareholders receive a ballot with their disclosure statement to vote for or against the plan of reorganization. After the vote, the bankruptcy court holds a **confirmation hearing** to determine whether it should accept the plan. **The court will approve a plan if a majority *of each class* votes in favor of it.** Even if some classes vote against the plan, the court can still confirm it under what is called a **cramdown** (as in "the plan is crammed down the creditors' throats"). The court will not impose a cramdown unless, in its view, the plan is fair. If the court rejects the plan of reorganization, the creditors must develop a new one. In the following case, some creditors objected to the cramdown.

IN RE RIVERS END APARTMENTS, LTD.

167 B.R. 470, 1994 Bankr. LEXIS 688
United States Bankruptcy Court, Southern District of Ohio, 1994

Facts: Rivers End Apartments, Ltd. (Rivers End) owned an apartment complex in Jacksonville, Florida. It owed $1,325,000 to Peoples Southwest Real Estate Limited Partnership (Peoples). Rivers End filed a voluntary petition for relief under Chapter 11 and prepared a plan of reorganization. Peoples voted against the plan, arguing that Rivers End would never be able to implement it successfully. Rivers End asked the bankruptcy court to approve the plan over Peoples' objection.

Issue: Should the court impose a cramdown?

Excerpts from Judge Sellers's Decision: To establish feasibility under [the Code], a proponent must demonstrate that its plan offers "a reasonable prospect of success" and is workable. Specifically, a plan proponent must show that its projections of future earnings and expenses are derived from realistic and reasonable assumptions and that it has the ability to make the proposed payments.

[9] Diana B. Henriques, "Tenacity Solves an Ugly Bankruptcy," *New York Times*, Nov. 15, 1994, p. D1. Copyright © 1994 by The New York Times Co. Reprinted by permission.

Without serious dispute from Peoples, Rivers End has established the feasibility of its Plan.

David E. Williams, Vice-President of Cardinal [the Rivers End general partner], testified regarding the Plan's projections and assumptions. From his testimony, it is clear that Mr. Williams has spent much time reviewing and analyzing the economic projections which drive the Plan economics. The methodology for deriving the Property's future economic projections assumes a growth in income and expenses each year. Mr. Williams concluded that this anticipated growth is "reasonable and achievable." To support this conclusion, Mr. Williams testified about the anticipated growth in the Jacksonville area generally. Peoples' evidence failed to contradict Mr. Williams's conclusions regarding the economic projections for Rivers End. Based upon the evidence, the court finds those projections realistic and reasonable.

Robert E. Pausch, also a Vice-President for Cardinal, testified regarding the ability of Rivers End to make the proposed payments under the Plan. Generally, his testimony established that Rivers End will be adequately capitalized as the plan is proposed and that the Plan is structured in a manner to support all liabilities of the partnership. He also discussed in detail the payments to be made under the Plan and adequately demonstrated that, based on the economic projections supported by Mr. Williams's testimony, Rivers End could produce sufficient cash flow to meet those payments.

The court finds from the evidence that the Plan is based upon reasonable and realistic projections and offers a reasonable likelihood of success. The court may confirm a Chapter 11 plan over the objection of a dissenting class if that plan meets the requirements of [the Code]. Accordingly, Peoples' objection to confirmation is *overruled*.

DISCHARGE

A confirmed plan of reorganization is binding on the debtor, creditors, and shareholders. **The debtor now owns the assets in the bankrupt estate, free of all obligations except those listed in the plan.** Under a typical plan of reorganization, the debtor gives some current assets to creditors and also promises to pay them a portion of future earnings. In contrast, the Chapter 7 debtor typically relinquishes all assets (except exempt property) to creditors but then has no obligation to turn over future income. Exhibit 27.2 illustrates the steps in a Chapter 11 bankruptcy.

In recent years, Chapter 11 has been controversial. The statute's goal is to help companies revive and reorganize, but many commentators argue that it has not achieved this objective. Of the companies that file for bankruptcy protection, only 1 in 27 files under Chapter 11. More than 80 percent of the companies that begin in Chapter 11 ultimately liquidate rather than reorganize. Even the firms that do reorganize often suffer financial trouble again. Some end up in Chapter 11 several times.

Moreover, Chapter 11 proceedings are expensive and time-consuming. On average, they take 18 months, and companies typically spend between 3 and 8 percent of their assets on legal and accounting fees. Commentators also argue that Chapter 11 gives shareholders so much power that they walk away with more than their fair share of the company's assets. Judges are reluctant to confirm a reorganization plan without the consent of the shareholders. While shareholders delay, creditors lose the interest they are owed on their money. Creditors often find it cost-effective to agree that shareholders should receive more than they deserve, simply to end the proceedings.

In the United States, most financially troubled companies liquidate under Chapter 7 rather than reorganizing under Chapter 11. As the following article explains, the opposite is true in Asia.

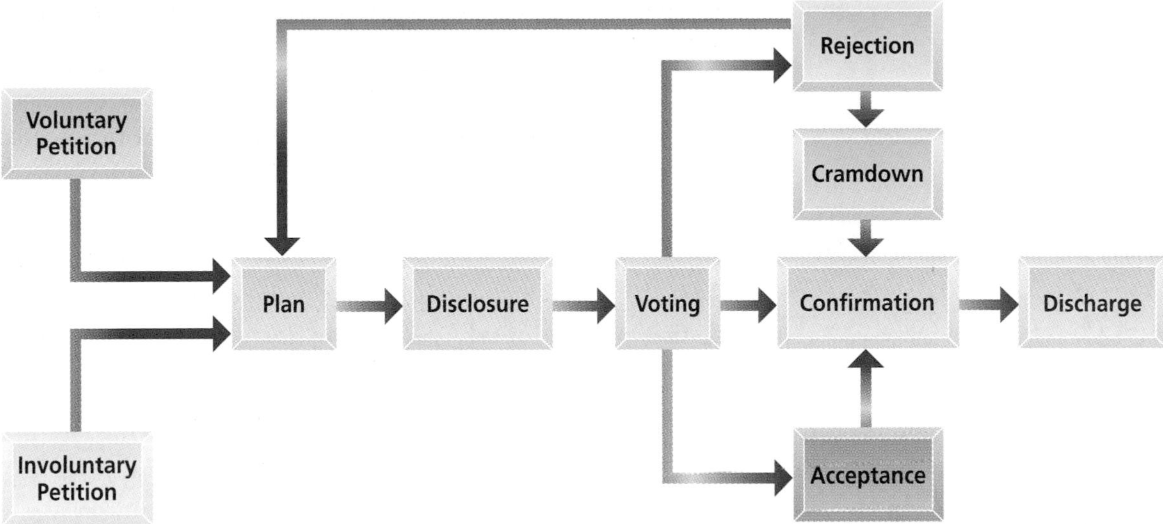

Exhibit 27.2

No business failure in Japan has been more traumatic than that of Hokkaido Takushoku Bank, one of the nation's biggest financial institutions. Its collapse sent the entire financial system into a tailspin and set off alarm bells that are still ringing in markets worldwide.

But now, take a walk inside the marble-pillared, wood-paneled halls of the bank's headquarters here on the northern island of Hokkaido. On a recent morning, more than 120 customers bustled about, making deposits and withdrawals. It is not that the bank rose like a phoenix from the ashes. It just never burned up. After announcing that the bank had failed, the government plugged it into a life-support system, and nothing really changed. It will be acquired soon by another institution, but many of its money-losing operations could continue indefinitely under another name.

Something similar is happening throughout Asia: corporations are "failing" in record numbers, but many keep on going anyway. As a result, the feeble are not eliminated, the fat is not trimmed, and the region's long-term prospects suffer. In Asia, big companies often hang on until they simply expire in a cloud of debt, rather than liquidate themselves or file for bankruptcy protection to restructure. In most countries here, the legal framework for bankruptcy is vague and loosely formed, management is given little protection against creditors, and there is rarely any thoroughgoing change. This sets the stage, not for a Darwinian struggle but for survival of the flimsiest.[10]

CHAPTER 13 CONSUMER REORGANIZATIONS

The purpose of Chapter 13 is to rehabilitate an individual debtor. It is not available at all to businesses or to individuals with more than $250,000 in unsecured debts or $750,000 in secured debts. Under Chapter 13, the bankrupt consumer typically keeps most of her assets in exchange for a promise to repay some of her debts using future income. Therefore, to be eligible, the debtor must have a regular source of income. Individuals usually choose this chapter because it is easier

[10] Sheryl WuDunn, "Bankruptcy the Asian Way," *New York Times*, Sept. 8, 1998, p. C1. Copyright © 1998 by The New York Times Co. Reprinted by permission.

and cheaper than Chapters 7 and 11. Consequently, more money is retained for both creditors and debtor.

A bankruptcy under Chapter 13 generally follows the same course as Chapter 11: the debtor files a petition, creditors submit proofs of claim, the court imposes an automatic stay, the debtor files a plan and the court confirms the plan. But there are some differences.

BEGINNING A CHAPTER 13 CASE

To initiate a Chapter 13 case, the debtor must file a voluntary petition. **Creditors cannot use an involuntary petition to force a debtor into Chapter 13.** In all Chapter 13 cases, the U.S. Trustee appoints a trustee to supervise the debtor, who remains in possession of the bankruptcy estate. The trustee also serves as a central clearinghouse for the debtor's payments to creditors. The debtor pays the trustee who, in turn, transmits these funds to creditors. For this service, the trustee is allowed to keep 10 percent of the payments.

PLAN OF PAYMENT

The debtor must file a plan of payment within 15 days after filing the voluntary petition. Only the debtor can file a plan; the creditors have no right to file their own version. Under the plan, the debtor must (1) commit some future earnings to pay off debts, (2) promise to pay all secured and priority claims in full, and (3) treat all remaining classes equally.

Within 30 days after filing the plan of payment, the debtor must begin making payments to the trustee under the plan. The trustee holds these payments until the plan is confirmed and then transmits them to creditors. The debtor continues to make payments to the trustee until the plan has been fully implemented. If the plan is rejected, the trustee returns the payments to the debtor.

Only the bankruptcy court has the authority to confirm or reject a plan of payment. Creditors have no right to vote on it. However, to confirm a plan, the court must ensure that:

- The creditors have the opportunity to voice their objections at a hearing
- All of the unsecured creditors receive at least as much as they would have under Chapter 7
- The plan is feasible and the bankrupt will be able to make the promised payments
- The plan does not extend beyond three years without good reason and in no event lasts longer than five years; and
- The debtor is acting in good faith, making a reasonable effort to pay obligations.

In the following case, a creditor argued that the debtor's plan was not made in good faith.

***IN RE* LEMAIRE**
898 F.2d 1346, 1990 U.S. App. LEXIS 4374
United States Court of Appeals for the Eighth Circuit, 1990

Facts: As Paul Handeen got out of his car one Sunday morning, Gregory LeMaire shot at him nine times with a bolt action rifle. The first two shots missed Handeen, but the third struck him on the left side of the neck. As Handeen sought shelter behind his car, LeMaire circled after him. The next two shots missed; then one hit Handeen inside his left knee. Another bullet went through Handeen's right nostril, shattered the roof of his mouth, and pierced his tongue. LeMaire's next shot went through Handeen's arm and lodged in his spine, while a final bullet struck Handeen's ankle. LeMaire pleaded guilty to a charge of aggravated assault and served 27 months in prison. After his release, he returned to graduate school at the University of Minnesota and earned his doctorate in experimental behavioral pharmacology.

Handeen received a judgment of $50,000 against LeMaire. To avoid paying this judgment, LeMaire filed a bankruptcy petition under Chapter 13. He proposed a plan under which he would pay his creditors 42 percent of their claims. The bankruptcy court confirmed the plan over Handeen's objection. Handeen appealed to the district court, arguing that LeMaire had not filed his plan in good faith. The district court affirmed and, upon appeal, the appeals court also affirmed. Handeen then asked for a rehearing. This time, the appeals court granted a rehearing *en banc*. (Usually, only three judges hear an appeal. "*En banc*" means that all the judges on the court hear it.)

Issues: Is a judgment awarded to the victim of an intentional shooting dischargeable under Chapter 13? Did LeMaire file his plan in good faith?

Excerpts from Judge Gibson's Decision: Handeen argues that the bankruptcy court should not have confirmed LeMaire's Chapter 13 plan because LeMaire did not propose it in good faith. In evaluating LeMaire's motivation and sincerity, the bankruptcy court balanced Handeen's desire to be compensated for his injuries against LeMaire's desire to have a fresh start and found the latter to outweigh the former in importance. The court noted that, while LeMaire had been unable to pay his debt to his victim, he had paid his debt to society by serving a prison sentence and had attempted to reorder his life and make a fresh start. The court found that forcing LeMaire to be burdened the rest of his life with a judgment which would continue to accrue interest, result in endless garnishments, and prevent him from accumulating property would be inimical to such a fresh start. The court concluded that LeMaire had made a wholehearted attempt to pay Handeen as much as possible, and that LeMaire's motivation was proper and his sincerity real.

We are convinced that the court's analysis here fails to properly consider the strong public policy factors, inherent in the Bankruptcy Code, which are implicated in discharging this debt. We do not believe that LeMaire has fulfilled the good faith requirement of Chapter 13. The record here very clearly indicates that LeMaire intended to kill Handeen, he shot at him nine times, he hit him with five of the bullets, and he nearly succeeded in his intention. While pre-filing conduct is not determinative of the good faith issue, it is nevertheless relevant. When we consider the pre-filing conduct here, including the maliciousness of the injury which LeMaire inflicted upon Handeen, in light of the lack of other factors sufficient to establish good faith, we are persuaded that the bankruptcy court clearly erred in finding that LeMaire proposed his plan in good faith.

We remand this case to the district court with instructions to remand, in turn, to the bankruptcy court for further proceedings consistent with this opinion.

DISCHARGE

Once confirmed, a plan is binding on all creditors, whether they like it or not. **The debtor is washed clean of all pre-petition debts except those provided for in the plan, but, unlike under Chapter 7, the debts are not *permanently* discharged.** If the debtor violates the plan, all of the debts are revived, and the creditors have a right to recover them under Chapter 7. The debts become permanently discharged only when the bankrupt fully complies with the plan.

If the debtor's circumstances change, the debtor, the trustee, or unsecured creditors can ask the court to modify the plan. Under prior law, only the debtor could request a modification, and, even now, most such requests come from debtors whose income has declined. However, if the debtor's income rises, the creditors or the trustee can, in theory, ask that payments increase, too.

FAIRNESS UNDER THE CODE

For hundreds of years, scores of countries have struggled to devise a bankruptcy system that is fair to all participants. Congress has amended the federal Bankruptcy Code repeatedly over the last 20 years. Why all the dissatisfaction? Here are three particularly controversial issues in bankruptcy law.

DOES THE CODE UNFAIRLY FAVOR DEBTORS?

What do celebrities Shannen Doherty, Burt Reynolds, M. C. Hammer, Dorothy Hamill and Ricki Lake have in common? Like Kim Basinger, they are all erstwhile millionaires who filed for bankruptcy. A surge in bankruptcy filings has led some commentators to argue that bankruptcy laws need to be tightened. The following article, however, suggests that the problem lies, not with bankruptcy laws, but rather with credit card companies that issue too many cards to too many people.

The Founding Fathers—not a few of whom had personal financial difficulties—perceived that allowing people to persist in financial servitude due to unpayable debts would create social disruption. Yet what if Americans abuse their bankruptcy privilege to skip out on debts they could very well pay? The consumer credit industry maintains that we are doing just this on a burgeoning scale. Industry representatives point to the fact that personal bankruptcy filings have hit an all-time annual high of 1.4 million, during a period of low unemployment when consumers are in their best financial shape in many years. Credit industry analysts hold that the stigma of bankruptcy has traditionally kept people honest about their ability to pay debts. Earlier generations of debtors lashed themselves to austerity budgets, sold off possessions, and worked extra shifts to avoid the shame of defaulting. But today, says the industry, many debtors have come to see bankruptcy as a convenient loophole against collections.

Harvard Law professor Elizabeth Warren rejects the "brazen bankrupt" hypothesis. "If stigma had declined," says Warren, "you would expect to see people declare earlier rather than later in their economic collapse. Instead, people who file for bankruptcy today are in worse condition than their counterparts who filed 15 years ago." Then, the average filer went before a judge with debts that equaled 60 percent of a year's income. Today, the average filer holds off until owing 80 percent of a year's income.

The fundamental reason for the epidemic of financial failures, Warren concludes, is that Americans simply owe more and more money. "Many people are wound too tight," Warren says. "After they pay their basic expenses and the minimum on their credit cards, there's very little left. They've put themselves in a position where they can keep going as long as everything runs smoothly but they are extremely vulnerable if anything goes wrong. As soon as they hit one of life's bumps in the road, they're into the ditch. The bankruptcy rate was steady for two decades and then jumped when most states deregulated interest rates on credit cards." Because credit card issuers' costs have fallen, their profits have continued to rise even as bankruptcies have proliferated. This has made them extremely eager to sell Americans more debt.[11]

---

[11] David Anderson, "A Tale of Two Stigmas," *Harvard Magazine*, Jan.–Feb. 1999, p. 19. Reprinted by permission from the author.

The National Foundation for Consumer Credit offers advice to debtors about bankruptcy—and the alternatives. Click on http://www.nfcc.org/ to take the Debt Test.

IS THE CODE UNFAIR TO PRODUCT LIABILITY PLAINTIFFS?

The focus of bankruptcy law has changed. Originally, the goal was to protect creditors by ensuring that the bankrupt's assets were safe until they could be distributed. Increasingly, however, bankruptcies are designed less to protect creditors than to give companies breathing space to sort out a whole raft of problems having little to do with traditional bankruptcy—such as liability for pollution, faulty products, and burdensome labor contracts.

Johns-Manville was once the world's largest manufacturer of asbestos. Company management had long suspected that exposure to asbestos caused lung cancer, and indeed, it carefully screened employees to document this damage. But the company deceived workers, assuring them that asbestos was safe. In the end, Manville was hit with 52,400 asbestos-related tort suits. The company responded by filing for bankruptcy. A few years later, Dow Corning Corp. also sought bankruptcy protection in the face of thousands of claims from women alleging they were injured by the company's silicone breast implants.

Critics argue that bankruptcy court is not the appropriate place to deal with these massive liability claims. They should be weighed by a jury after extensive expert testimony—not decided by a judge whose primary agenda is to keep the company in business. Critics also argue that companies like Manville and Dow Corning are simply using bankruptcy law to avoid legitimate debts. At the time of filing, both companies had assets that were much greater than their liabilities. Under Manville's reorganization plan, the company placed $1.104 billion in a trust and promised to contribute 20 percent of its yearly profits for as long as claims remained outstanding. Within two years of the plan's approval, however, the trust began to run out of money. It seems likely that a substantial number of claimants will not be paid.

The companies respond, however, that a bankruptcy filing ensures all claimants will be treated equally and, in any event, creditors will receive more under reorganization than they would under liquidation. Until Congress comes up with a better option, they say, the bankruptcy courts will have to do.

BANKRUPTCY LAW OVERSEAS

This chapter has focused on American bankruptcy law. What happens if a debtor owns assets in several countries? Most scholars agree on what the rules ought to be: the country where the debtor has the most assets ought to serve as a home country for an international reorganization or liquidation of all the debtor's assets, wherever located. However, international bankruptcy law is like the weather—everyone talks about it, but no one does anything. Instead, the existing international approach can best be described as a grab rule—creditors in each country grab whatever assets they can find within their own borders. Any remaining assets are then, in theory, distributed to creditors in other countries. In practice, of course, assets are rarely available for international distribution. The Web site http://www.legalresource.com/ provides links to other sites with information about bankruptcy law overseas.

CHAPTER CONCLUSION

Whenever an individual or organization incurs more debts than it can pay in a timely fashion, everyone loses. The debtor loses control of his assets and the creditors lose money. Bankruptcy laws cannot create assets where there are none (or not enough), but they can ensure that the debtor's assets, however limited, are fairly divided between the debtor and creditors. Any bankruptcy system that accomplishes this goal must be deemed a success.

CHAPTER REVIEW

This chart sets out the important elements of each bankruptcy chapter.

	Chapter 7	Chapter 11	Chapter 13
Objective	Liquidation	Reorganization	Consumer reorganization
Who May Use It	Individual or organization	Individual or organization	Individual
Type of Petition	Voluntary or involuntary	Voluntary or involuntary	Only voluntary
Administration of Bankruptcy Estate	Trustee	Debtor in possession (trustee selected only if debtor is unable to serve)	Trustee
Selection of Trustee	Creditors have right to elect trustee; otherwise, U.S. Trustee makes appointment.	Usually no trustee	Appointed by U.S. Trustee
Participation in Formulation of Plan	No plan is filed.	Both creditors and debtor can propose plans.	Only debtor can propose a plan.
Creditor Approval of Plan	Creditors do not vote.	Creditors vote on plan, but court may approve plan without the creditors' support.	Creditors do not vote on plan.
Impact on Debtor's Post-petition Income	Not affected; debtor keeps all future earnings.	Must contribute toward payment of pre-petition debts	Must contribute toward payment of pre-petition debts

PRACTICE TEST

1. Mark Milbank built custom furniture in Port Chester, New York. His business was unsuccessful, and he repeatedly borrowed money from his wife and her father. He promised that the loans would enable him to spend more time with his family. Instead, he spent more time in bed with his next-door neighbor. After the divorce, his ex-wife and her father demanded repayment of the loans. When Milbank filed under Chapter 13, his ex-wife and her father asked the court not to discharge Milbank's debts on the grounds that he had acted in bad faith toward them. Should the bankruptcy court discharge Milbank's loans?

2. CPA QUESTION Decal Corp. incurred substantial operating losses for the past three years. Unable to meet its current obligations, Decal filed a petition of reorganization under Chapter 11 of the federal Bankruptcy Code. Which of the following statements is correct?

(a) A creditors' committee, if appointed, will consist of unsecured creditors.

(b) The court must appoint a trustee to manage Decal's affairs.

(c) Decal may continue in business only with the approval of a trustee.

(d) The creditors' committee must select a trustee to manage Decal's affairs.

3. James Hartley, the owner of an auto parts store, told an employee, Rickey D. Jones, to clean and paint some tires in the basement. Highly flammable gasoline fumes accumulated in the poorly ventilated space. Hartley threw a firecracker into the basement, as a joke, intending only to startle Jones. Sparks from the firecracker caused an explosion and fire that severely burned Jones. He filed a personal injury suit against Hartley for $1 million. Is this debt dischargeable under Chapter 7?

4. **CPA QUESTION** A voluntary petition filed under the liquidation provisions of Chapter 7 of the federal Bankruptcy Code:

(a) Is **not** available to a corporation unless it has previously filed a petition under the reorganization provisions of Chapter 11 of the Code

(b) Automatically stays collection actions against the debtor **except** by secured creditors

(c) Will be dismissed unless the debtor has 12 or more unsecured creditors whose claims total at least $5,000

(d) Does **not** require the debtor to show that the debtor's liabilities exceed the fair market value of assets

5. After filing for bankruptcy, Yvonne Brown sought permission of the court to reaffirm a $6,000 debt to her credit union. The debt was unsecured and she was under no obligation to pay it. The credit union had published the following notice in its newsletter:

> If you are thinking about filing bankruptcy THINK about the long-term implications. This action, filing bankruptcy, closes the door on TOMORROW. Having no credit means no ability to purchase cars, houses, credit cards. Look into the future—no loans for the education of your children.

Should the court approve Brown's reaffirmation?

6. **RIGHT & WRONG** On November 5, The Fred Hawes Organization, Inc., a small subcontractor, opened an account with Basic Distribution Corp., a supplier of construction materials. Hawes promised to pay its bills within 30 days of purchase. Although Hawes purchased a substantial quantity of goods on credit from Basic, it made few payments on the accounts until the following March when it paid Basic over $21,000. On May 14, Hawes filed a voluntary petition under Chapter 7. Does the bankruptcy trustee have a right to recover this payment? Is it fair to Hawes's other creditors if Basic is allowed to keep the $21,000 payment?

7. Robert Britton was an office manager at the Academy of Cosmetic Surgery Medical Group. Mary Price made an appointment for a consultation about a lipectomy (removal of abdominal fat). Britton wore a name tag that identified him as a doctor, and was addressed as "doctor" by the nurse. Britton and the nurse then examined Price. Britton touched the area of her stomach where there was excess fat and showed her where the incision would be made. A doctor who worked for the Academy actually performed the surgical procedure on Price at the Academy's offices, with Britton present. After the procedure, Price went to a hospital suffering from severe pain. The hospital staff found that a tube had been left in her body at the site of the incision. The area of the incision became infected, and Price ultimately required corrective surgery. The jury awarded her $275,000 in damages in a fraud suit against Britton. He subsequently filed a Chapter 7 bankruptcy petition. Is this judgment dischargeable in bankruptcy court?

8. Why did Kim Basinger (see the chapter introduction) file under Chapter 11 rather than Chapter 13?

9. **CPA QUESTION** Unger owes a total of $50,000 to eight unsecured creditors and one fully secured creditor. Quincy is one of the unsecured creditors and is owed $6,000. Quincy has filed a petition against Unger under the liquidation provisions of Chapter 7 of the federal Bankruptcy Code. Unger has been unable to pay debts as they become due. Unger's liabilities exceed Unger's assets. Unger has filed papers opposing the bankruptcy petition. Which of the following statements regarding Quincy's petition is correct?

(a) It will be dismissed because the secured creditor failed to join in the filing of the petition.

(b) It will be dismissed because three unsecured creditors must join in the filing of the petition.

(c) It will be granted because Unger's liabilities exceed Unger's assets.

(d) It will be granted because Unger is unable to pay Unger's debts as they become due.

10. YOU BE THE JUDGE WRITING PROBLEM Lydia D'Ettore received a degree in computer programming at Devry Institute of Technology, with a grade-point average of 2.51. To finance her education, she borrowed $20,516.52 from a federal student loan program. After graduation, she could not find a job in her field, so she went to work as a clerk at a salary of $12,500. D'Ettore and her daughter lived with her parents free of charge. After setting aside $50 a month in savings and paying bills that included $233 for a new car (a Suzuki Samurai) and $50 for jewelry from Zales, her disposable income was $125 per month. D'Ettore asked the bankruptcy court to discharge the debts she owed Devry. Under the Code, these student loans cannot be discharged unless they impose an "undue hardship" on the debtor. Did the debts to Devry Institute impose an undue hardship on D'Ettore?**Argument for D'Ettore**: Lydia D'Ettore lives at home with her parents. Even so, her disposable income is a meager $125 a month. She would have to spend every single penny of her disposable income for nearly 15 years to pay back her $20,000 debt to Devry. That would be an undue hardship. **Argument for the Creditors**: The U.S. government guaranteed D'Ettore's loan. Therefore, if the court discharges it, the American taxpayer will have to pay the bill. Why should taxpayers subsidize an irresponsible student? D'Ettore must also stop buying new cars and jewelry. And why should the government pay her debts while she saves money every month?

11. Dr. Ibrahim Khan caused an automobile accident in which a fellow physician, Dolly Yusufji, became a quadriplegic. Dr. Khan signed a contract for the lifetime support of Dr. Yusufji. When he refused to make payments under the contract, she sued him and obtained a judgment for $1,205,400. Dr. Khan filed a Chapter 11 petition. At the time of the bankruptcy hearing, five years after the accident, Dr. Khan had not paid Dr. Yusufji anything. She was dependent on a motorized wheelchair; he drove a Rolls-Royce. Is Dr. Khan's debt dischargeable under Chapter 11?

INTERNET RESEARCH PROBLEM

An up-to-date description of new bankruptcy statutes that Congress is currently considering is at **http://www.abiworld.org/**. The e-mail addresses of the congressional sponsors are included. Send one of these sponsors a brief e-mail arguing for or against a proposed statute. Bring your message and any response you receive to class.

You can find further practice problems in the Online Quiz at http://beatty.westbuslaw.com or in the Study Guide that accompanies this text.

UNIT 4

AGENCY AND EMPLOYMENT LAW

CHAPTER 28

AGENCY: THE INSIDE RELATIONSHIP

It was a perfect spring day in Ashland, Ohio. Roger was having a great game as his Ohio State lacrosse team played a close match against Ashland University. Carefully gauging an Ashland pass, Roger stuck his stick out, intercepted the ball, whipped around, and launched a shot on goal. Score! His hands went up in the air. He never saw the Ashland player jump him from behind and knock him to the ground. But he did see the player stand over him, yelling obscenities. He also saw his teammate Brian grab the opponent in a bear hug. And he saw the Ashland player twist violently, throwing Brian to the ground, where he lay motionless. Brian never walked again—the blow to his head as he hit the ground left him a paraplegic. Brian sued Ashland, alleging that the university was responsible for his injury.[1]

Brian's parents hired a real estate broker to find a new house that was handicap accessible. They were so delighted with the one-story bungalow she located that they did not begrudge paying her an $18,000 commission. But after the sale they discovered that the seller of the house had also paid her a commission. They sued for the return of their $18,000.

[1] Based on *Hanson v. Kynast*, 24 Ohio St. 3d 171, 494 N.E.2d 1091, 1986 Ohio LEXIS 667 (Ohio 1986).

Nonetheless, the house was perfect for their needs, and they stocked it with all the custom-made items that Brian required. Because these medical devices were so expensive, they asked their insurance agent to increase their house coverage from $400,000 to $800,000. Brian and his parents suffered a terrible blow a few months later when they returned home from an exhausting visit to the hospital to find their new house burned to the ground. They were even more distressed when they discovered that the insurance agent had misread his notes and only increased their policy to $480,000. They sued him for $320,000.

This example raises several questions of agency law. Thus far, this book has primarily dealt with issues of individual responsibility: What happens if *you* knock someone down or *you* sign an agreement? Agency law, on the other hand, is concerned with your responsibility for the actions of others. What happens if your agent assaults someone or enters into an agreement? Agency law presents a significant trade-off: if you do everything yourself, you have control over the result. But the size and scope of your business (and your life) will be severely limited. Once you hire other people, you can accomplish a great deal more, but your risk of legal liability increases immensely. Though it might be safer to do everything yourself, that is not a practical decision for most business owners (or most people). The alternative is to hire carefully and to limit the risks as much as possible by understanding the law of agency.

Was Ashland University liable for Brian's injuries? It would have been if the Ashland player had been an agent of the university. But, on a similar set of facts, the Ohio Supreme Court held that the Ashland player was not an agent because Ashland had no *control* over him and he was not playing for the school's *benefit*. However, the real estate broker was an agent for Brian's parents. She violated her *duty of loyalty* to them when she acted for both buyer and seller in the same transaction, without disclosing her dual role to both parties. An agent who violates this important duty must forfeit her commission. And the insurance agent violated his *duty of care* when he bought a policy in the wrong amount for Brian's parents. An agent who violates this duty is liable for the harm his carelessness has caused—in this case $320,000.

CREATING AN AGENCY RELATIONSHIP

Principals have substantial liability for the actions of their agents.[2] Therefore, disputes about whether an agency relationship exists are not mere legal quibbles but important issues with potentially profound financial consequences. According to the Restatement of Agency:

> **Agency is the fiduciary relation which results from the manifestation of consent by one person to another that the other shall act on his behalf and subject to his control, and consent by the other so to act.**[3]

[2] The word "principal" is always used when referring to a person. It is not to be confused with the word "principle," which refers to a fundamental idea.

[3] Section 1 of the Restatement (Second) of Agency (1958), prepared by the American Law Institute.

In other words, in an agency relationship, someone (the agent) agrees to perform a task for, and under the control of, someone else (the principal). To create an agency relationship, there must be:

- A **principal** and
- An **agent**
- Who mutually **consent** that the agent will act on behalf of the principal and
- Be subject to the principal's **control**
- Thereby creating a **fiduciary** relationship.

CONSENT

To establish consent, the principal must ask the agent to do something and the agent must agree. In the most straightforward example, Brian's parents asked their insurance agent to buy a policy on their house, and he agreed. Matters were more complicated, however, when David Hudson went drinking at a tavern in Little Compton, Rhode Island. The beer he drank was brewed by Anheuser-Busch and sold to a distributor who sold it to the tavern who hired a bartender who served Hudson—all too many glasses. After leaving the tavern, Hudson crashed into Christopher Lawrence's car, killing the young man. Lawrence's parents sued Anheuser-Busch and the distributor alleging that the companies had an agency relationship with the tavern. The court, however, found that no agency relationship existed:

> The brewer and the distributor submitted affidavits stating that they had never entered into an agreement either written or oral with the tavern, either for the sale of their products or for any other reason; that they never authorized the tavern to take any action on their behalf or as a representative of their companies; that they had no beneficial interest in the tavern; and that they had no knowledge of the tavern ever purporting to act on their behalf, and that if it had done so, such occurrence would have been without their consent.[4]

In other words, the brewer and the distributor had not *consented* to any agency relationship with the tavern, and therefore they were not liable for what the tavern had done.

CONTROL

Principals are liable for the acts of their agents because they exercise control over the agents. If principals direct their agents to commit an act, it seems fair to hold the principal liable when that act causes harm. In the following example, did Northwest Airlines exercise control over Kuwait Air?

The horse-drawn caisson wound slowly through Arlington National Cemetery and stopped in front of lot number 59, the section reserved for victims of terrorist acts. The flag-draped casket of William L. Stanford, one of the two Agency for International Development auditors killed by plane hijackers in Iran, was carried to the gravesite amid full military honors. Three volleys of rifle fire pierced the unusually warm December air as scores of family, friends and colleagues lowered their heads and wept. Stanford, 52, was killed as he was traveling to join his wife

[4] *Lawrence v. Anheuser-Busch, Inc.*, 523 A.2d 864, 1987 R.I. LEXIS 451 (R.I. 1987).

and 13-year-old daughter in Karachi, Pakistan, where he intended to spend the holidays.[5]

The hijacked plane—with William Stanford aboard—was a Kuwait Airways (KA) flight from Kuwait to Pakistan. Stanford had originally purchased a ticket on Northwest Airlines but had traded in his Northwest ticket for a seat on the KA flight. Stanford's widow sued Northwest on the theory that KA was Northwest's agent. The airlines had an agreement permitting passengers to exchange tickets from one to another. In this case, however, the court found that no agency relationship existed because Northwest had no *control* over KA.[6] Northwest did not tell KA how to fly planes or handle terrorists; therefore it should not be liable when KA made fatal errors. An agent and principal must not only *consent* to an agency relationship, but the principal must also have *control* over the agent.

FIDUCIARY RELATIONSHIP

A fiduciary relationship is a special relationship, with high standards. The beneficiary places special confidence in the fiduciary who, in turn, is obligated to act in good faith and candor, putting his own needs second. The purpose of a fiduciary relationship is for one person to benefit another. **Agents have a fiduciary duty to their principals.** When, in the chapter introduction, Brian's parents hired a real estate broker to find a house for them, she was a fiduciary, obligated to act in their best interest alone. She violated this duty when she also acted for the seller of the house, without telling Brian's parents.

All three elements—consent, control, and a fiduciary duty—are necessary to create an agency relationship. In some relationships, for example, there might be a *fiduciary duty* but no *control*. A trustee of a trust must act for the benefit of the beneficiaries, but the beneficiaries have no right to control the trustee. Therefore, a trustee is not an agent of the beneficiaries. *Consent* is present in every contractual relationship, but that does not necessarily mean that the two parties are agent and principal. If Horace sells his car to Lily, they both expect to benefit under the contract, but neither has a *fiduciary duty* to the other and neither *controls* the other, so there is no agency relationship.

ELEMENTS NOT REQUIRED FOR AN AGENCY RELATIONSHIP

Consent, control, and a fiduciary relationship are necessary to establish an agency relationship. The following elements are **not** required:

- *A Written Agreement*. In most cases, an agency agreement does not have to be in writing. An oral understanding is valid, except in one circumstance—the **equal dignities rule**. According to this rule, if an agent is empowered to enter into a contract that must be in writing, then the appointment of the agent must also be written. For example, under the statute of frauds a contract for the sale of land is unenforceable unless in writing, so the agency agreement to sell land must also be in writing. Suppose that Albert hires Hannah to find a buyer for his house. If Albert wants Hannah to sign the sales contract for him, he must grant her that authority *in writing*.

---

[5] Mary Jordan, "Terrorists' Victim Is Buried," *Washington Post*, Dec. 18, 1984, p. A14. © 1984, The Washington Post. Reprinted with permission.

[6] *Stanford v. Kuwait Airways Corp.*, 648 F. Supp. 1158, 1986 U.S. Dist. LEXIS 18880 (S.D.N.Y. 1986).

- *A Formal Agreement*. The principal and agent need not agree formally that they have an agency relationship. They do not even have to think the word "agent." As long as they act like an agent and principal, the law will treat them as such.
- *Consideration*. An agency relationship need not meet all the standards of contract law. For example, a contract is not valid without consideration, but an agency agreement is valid *even if the agent is not paid*. If Hannah is Albert's friend and agrees to find a buyer for his house without charging a commission, she is nonetheless his agent.

EMPLOYEES AS AGENTS

Sometimes the process of determining whether an agency relationship exists can be complex. There is, however, one helpful shortcut: **all employees are agents**. Thus reasonable people might disagree over whether Kuwait Airways was an agent for Northwest or whether a tavern was an agent for Anheuser-Busch, but clearly William Stanford, as an employee of the Agency for International Development, was AID's agent. Likewise, the bartender who sold the drinks to David Hudson was an agent for the tavern because he was a tavern employee.

In the next chapter, the distinction between different types of agents will become important. For now, it is necessary only to be aware that employees are agents.[7]

DUTIES OF AGENTS TO PRINCIPALS

Agents owe a fiduciary duty to their principals. In the following example, these employees of International Creative Management (ICM) were agents—they had agreed to act on behalf of ICM and be subject to its control. Did they violate their duty?

At 11:30 one night, Jeff Berg, the chairman of ICM in Hollywood, received an emergency phone call from a company assistant. Unexpectedly returning to the office, the assistant had come upon several employees hauling boxes of files out to station wagons and cars. The culprits were four top employees leaving to start their own creative management firm. "This was an act of trespass," Mr. Berg said. "We have been advised by counsel that this conduct is actionable." Mr. Berg added that the material taken involved documents about clients and the firm's business matters. ICM represents stars such as Mel Gibson, Julia Roberts, Arnold Schwarzenegger, Michelle Pfeiffer, Jodie Foster, and other artists listed at **http://www.hollywoodu.com/stars.htm**. Under pressure from Mr. Berg, the employees returned all the files by dawn.[8]

DUTY OF LOYALTY

The agent must act solely for the benefit of the principal in all matters connected with the agency.[9] The agent has an obligation to put the principal first, to strive to accomplish the principal's goals. By removing files that belonged to ICM,

[7] The fact that employees are agents does not mean that they have unlimited authority to act for their principals. Thus a production line employee is an agent for his company, and if he injures someone within the scope of his employment, his company is liable. It is unlikely, however, that he has authority to sign a contract on behalf of his employer.

[8] Bernard Weinraub, "After Dark, 4 Agents Light Out," *New York Times*, Mar. 30, 1995, p. C13. Copyright © 1995 by The New York Times Co. Reprinted by permission.

[9] Restatement (Second) of Agency §387.

these employees were violating their duty of loyalty to their principal because they were acting in their own interest, not that of their principal. It is not surprising that, once caught, they returned the property immediately. The various components of the duty of loyalty follow.

Hope could keep this Humvee only with ICM's permission.

Outside Benefits

An agent may not receive profits unless the principal knows and approves. Suppose that Hope, an employee of ICM, has been representing Arnold Schwarzenegger in his latest movie negotiations.[10] He often drives her to meetings in his new Humvee military vehicle. He is so thrilled that she has arranged for him to star in the new movie, *Little Men*, that he buys her a Humvee. Can Hope keep this generous gift? Only with ICM's permission. She must tell ICM about the Humvee; the company may then take the vehicle itself or allow her to keep it.

Confidential Information

The ability to keep secrets is important in any relationship, but especially a fiduciary relationship. **Agents can neither disclose nor use for their own benefit any confidential information they acquire during their agency.** As the following case shows, this duty continues even after the agency relationship ends.

ABKCO MUSIC, INC. v. HARRISONGS MUSIC, LTD.
722 F.2d 988, 1983 U.S. App. LEXIS 15562
United States Court of Appeals for the Second Circuit, 1983

Facts: Bright Tunes Music Corp. (Bright Tunes) owned the copyright to the song "He's So Fine." The company sued George Harrison, a Beatle, alleging that the Harrison composition "My Sweet Lord" copied "He's So Fine." At the time the suit was filed, Allen B. Klein handled the business affairs of the Beatles.

Klein (representing Harrison) met with the president of Bright Tunes to discuss possible settlement of the copyright lawsuit. Klein suggested that Harrison might be interested in purchasing the copyright to "He's So Fine." Shortly thereafter, Klein's management contract with the Beatles expired. Without telling Harrison, Klein began negotiating with Bright Tunes to purchase the copyright to "He's So Fine" for himself. To advance these negotiations, Klein gave Bright Tunes information about royalty income for "My Sweet Lord"—information that he had gained as Harrison's agent.

The trial judge in the copyright case ultimately found that Harrison had infringed the copyright on "He's So Fine" and assessed damages of $1,599,987. After the trial, Klein purchased the "He's So Fine" copyright from Bright Tunes and with it, the right to recover from Harrison for the breach of copyright.

Issue: Did Klein violate his fiduciary duty to Harrison by using confidential information after the agency relationship terminated?

Excerpts from Judge Pierce's Decision: There is no doubt that the relationship between Harrison and [Klein] prior to the termination of the management agreement was that of principal and agent, and that the relationship was fiduciary in nature. [A]n agent has a duty not to use confidential knowledge acquired in his employment in competition with his principal. This duty exists as well after the employment is terminated as during its continuance. On the other hand, use of

---

[10] Do not be confused by the fact that these ICM employees work as agents for movie stars. As employees of ICM, their duty is to the company. The employees are agents of ICM, and ICM works for the celebrities.

information based on general business knowledge or gleaned from general business experience is not covered by the rule, and the former agent is permitted to compete with his former principal in reliance on such general publicly available information.

The evidence presented herein is not at all convincing that the information imparted to Bright Tunes by Klein was publicly available. Under the circumstances of this case, where there was sufficient evidence to support the district judge's finding that confidential information passed hands, or, at least was utilized in a manner inconsistent with the duty of a former fiduciary at a time when litigation was still pending, we conclude that the district judge did not err in holding that [Klein] had breached [his] duty to Harrison.

While the initial attempt to purchase [the copyright to "He's So Fine"] was several years removed from the eventual purchase on [Klein]'s own account, we are not of the view that such a fact rendered [Klein] unfettered in the later negotiations. Taking all of these circumstances together, we agree that [Klein's] conduct did not meet the standard required of him as a former fiduciary.

To listen to the two songs involved in this case tune in to **http://www.benedict.com**.

Klein was angry that the Beatles had failed to renew his management contract. Was it reasonable for him to think that he owed no duty to the principal who had fired him? Should his sense of ethics have told him that his behavior was wrong? Would the ethics checklist in Chapter 9 have helped Klein to make a better decision?

Competition with the Principal

Agents are not allowed to compete with their principal in any matter within the scope of the agency business. If Allen Klein had purchased the "He's So Fine" copyright while he was George Harrison's agent, he would have committed an additional sin against the agency relationship. Owning song rights was clearly part of the agency business, so Klein could not make such purchases without Harrison's consent. Once the agency relationship ends, however, so does the rule against competition. Klein was entitled to buy the *"He's So Fine"* copyright after the agency relationship ended (as long as he did not use confidential information).

Conflict of Interest between Two Principals

Unless otherwise agreed, an agent may not act for two principals whose interests conflict. Suppose Travis represents both director Steven Spielberg and actress Julia Roberts. Spielberg is casting the title role in his new movie, *Nancy Drew: Girl Detective,* a role that Roberts covets. Travis cannot represent these two clients when they are negotiating with each other, unless they both know about the conflict and agree to ignore it. Similarly, a real estate agent cannot represent both the buyer and the seller of a piece of land. The following article illustrates the dangers of acting for two principals at once.

Faced with growing health care and retirement costs, the Sisters of Charity decided to sell a 207-acre property that they owned in New Jersey. The order of nuns soon found, however, that the world is not always a charitable place. They agreed to sell the land to Linpro for nearly $10 million. But before the deal closed, Linpro signed a contract to resell the property to Sammis for $34 million. So, you say, the sisters made a bad deal. There is no law against that. But it turned out that the nuns' lawyer, Peter Berkley, also represented Sammis. He knew about the deal between Sammis and Linpro, but never told the sisters. Was that the charitable—

or legal—thing to do? For ideas on how Berkley should have handled this delicate situation, look at the discussion on dual agency at http://www.royallepage.ca/halifax/agency.htm.

Secretly Dealing with the Principal

If a principal hires an agent to arrange a transaction, the agent may not become a party to the transaction without the principal's permission. Matt Damon became an overnight sensation after starring in the movie *Good Will Hunting*. Suppose that he hired Trang to read scripts for him. Unbeknownst to Damon, Trang had written her own script, which she thought would be ideal for him. She may not sell it to him without revealing that she wrote it herself. Damon may be perfectly happy to buy Trang's script, but he has the right, as her principal, to know that she is the person selling it.

Appropriate Behavior

An agent may not engage in inappropriate behavior that reflects badly on the principal. This rule applies even to *off-duty* conduct. In the following article, police officers were off-duty and in a different city, but their conduct caused bystanders to lose respect for their principal—the New York City Police Department. Afterwards, many of the officers who could be identified were dismissed from the force.

Donna Smith, a letter carrier from Soddy Daisy, Tennessee, was awakened at 3:15 A.M. in her Washington, D.C. hotel room by a fire alarm. Opening her door to a thick fog of what appeared to be smoke, she clamped a wet towel to her face and followed a stream of coughing guests in a stumbling flight down the stairs and into the street. Fear slowly gave way to puzzlement as it became apparent that the hotel was not on fire. Spent fire extinguishers lying on the floor were the source of the apparent smoke.

Only later did the hotel guests find that they had been the victims of New York police officers on a drunken rampage. Near the end of National Police Week, during two nights of debauchery at four Washington hotels, New York officers sprayed fire extinguishers, set off fire alarms and slid naked down escalator railings they had lubricated with beer. "It was a total irritant," said Jim Fox, a hotel guest. "How can you have respect for law enforcement after this?"[11]

One of the most common, and difficult, issues facing employees is their duty to their principal after they have decided to seek employment elsewhere. How do they comply with their *duty of loyalty* when they know they are going to quit their job? In the following case, you be the judge.

CHERNOW v. REYES
239 N.J. Super. 201, 570 A.2d 1282, 1990 N.J. Super. LEXIS 67
Superior Court of New Jersey, Appellate Division, 1990

Facts: Ronald Chernow was in the business of auditing telephone bills to make sure customers were not overcharged. Chernow hired Angelo Reyes as an auditor. Reyes did not perform any sales work for Chernow, who already had a sales force. Chernow did not ask Reyes to sign a noncompete contract (a promise not to compete after leaving Chernow's employ).

The two men had a falling out. Chernow refused to give Reyes a raise or listen to his suggestions for expanding the business. Reyes quit but, before leaving, formed another corporation to compete against Chernow. He made copies of Chernow's standard

[11] Adam Nossiter and Julia Campbell, "Police Frenzy: Guests at Hotel Offer Accounts," *New York Times*, June 4, 1995, p. 1. Copyright © 1995 by The New York Times Co. Reprinted by permission.

forms and obtained three audit customers. Reyes also solicited a fourth account, but performed no work for this customer until after he had quit working for Chernow. He did all of this without Chernow's knowledge. Reyes never solicited any of Chernow's customers or any customers Chernow had considered soliciting, nor did he slacken his work efforts for Chernow during the regular 9-to-5 workday. Reyes did his own soliciting and auditing activities at night and on weekends, lunch hours, and vacation days.

You Be the Judge: Has Reyes violated his duty of loyalty to his employer Chernow?

Argument for Chernow: Reyes is the epitome of a disloyal employee. Chernow took him in and taught him the business. In return, Reyes sneaked around behind Chernow's back, stealing potential customers. Simply because Chernow had never solicited these customers did not mean that he never intended to approach them. If Reyes felt his behavior was acceptable, why didn't he tell Chernow what he was doing? Because he knew his conduct was disloyal.

An employee must not act contrary to the employer's interest. If Reyes wished to leave his job, fine. But he was legally obligated to quit before starting his own business. Until then, any telephone auditing work he did should have been for Chernow. Reyes should not be sitting at his desk in Chernow's office, auditing his own clients during lunch hour. That is not the action of a loyal employee.

Argument for Reyes: Slavery is dead. Chernow did not own Reyes body and soul, 24 hours a day. Reyes was entitled to weekends and evenings off. It was during this *time off* that he started his own business. Even during these off hours, he never solicited Chernow's clients. Reyes and Chernow had argued about expanding the business. When Chernow said no, Reyes decided to pursue these opportunities himself. Of course, he did not tell Chernow what he was doing. Chernow was a volatile person who would have been angry. But that does not make his anger reasonable. He might not like the color of Reyes's car or the restaurants he frequented, but it was none of his business, because it all happened off duty. Remember, too, that Reyes never acted as a salesperson for Chernow. Therefore, when Reyes went out to solicit customers for his own business, he was not doing something he had been hired to do for Chernow.

Reyes has to earn a living. He could not afford to leave his job with Chernow until he was sure he could support himself. As long as he was completely loyal to Chernow during business hours, what more could anyone expect? Reyes had only four customers, and the trial court determined that his conduct did not hinder Chernow's business in any way. Chernow has brought suit for the sole purpose of punishing Reyes.

An agent is bound by the duty of loyalty, *whether or not the agent and principal have consciously agreed to it*. It is irrelevant that George Harrison never expressly prohibited his agent from revealing the royalty income on "My Sweet Lord." The agent should have known his obligations. However, a principal and agent can change the rules by agreement. If the agent had gone to Harrison and asked permission to reveal confidential information, it would have been up to Harrison to grant permission or not, as he chose. If he had agreed, the agent would not have been liable. **The duty of loyalty applies unless the principal and agent expressly agree to change it.**

OTHER DUTIES OF AN AGENT

In June, Mr. and Mrs. Harding left for a five-week trip to England. Before leaving, they hired Angie to sell or rent their vacation house in Grantham, New Hampshire. The regional "Multiple Listing Service" was the best way to publicize a house for sale. But Angie was busy with one thing or another and never got around to listing the Harding's house. However, at the end of June, Angie was contacted by the Fords, who happened to be friends of friends. They told her that their son was a contractor who would like to build a house for them in Grantham, but they needed to rent a place to live in the meantime. Angie showed them the Hardings' house as a rental. Although it was not quite right for the Fords (too many stairs, no separate apartment for Mrs. Ford's mother), it was the best they had seen, so they offered to rent it for a year at $750 per month, beginning the first of September.

Angie called Mrs. Harding in England and told her that the Fords "were a nice couple who might very well be interested in buying the house after a year's rental." Mrs. Harding responded that $750 was too low, especially over the summer months when the house often rented out for as much as $1,000 per *week*. She proposed a contract from September 1 to June 1 at a rent of $800. Angie indicated that the Fords would probably be willing to make a deal on that basis because they loved the house. Mrs. Harding told Angie to call back if there was any problem, but otherwise she would sign the lease when she returned home. The following week, the Fords told Angie that they would agree to $800 a month, but insisted on being able to stay from September to September so that they would have time to complete construction on their new house.

Angie had a list of the Hardings' phone numbers in England, but she made no further effort to contact them there. Instead, she left a message on their home answering machine. When the Fords pressed her three or four times for a definite answer, she said she could not get in touch with the Hardings and suggested the Fords look for another house. When Mrs. Harding returned home, she called Angie and was told that "the Fords are coming up next week to confirm everything." Mrs. Harding called the Fords herself. She then learned the truth about what had happened and also that the Fords were going to Grantham to look at another house, which they ultimately rented.

Although Angie had not violated her *duty of loyalty* to the Hardings, they were still angry at her. Had she violated any of the other duties that agents owe to their principals?

Duty to Obey Instructions

An agent must obey her principal's instructions, unless the principal directs her to behave illegally or unethically. Mrs. Harding instructed Angie to call her if the Fords rejected the offer. Angie violated her duty to obey instructions when she neglected to call Mrs. Harding back. If, however, the Hardings had asked her to say that the house's basement was dry, when in fact it looked like a rice paddy every spring, Angie would be under no obligation to follow those illegal instructions.

Duty of Care

An agent has a duty to act with reasonable care. In other words, an agent must act as a reasonable person would, under the circumstances. A reasonable person would not have left a message on the Hardings' home answering machine when she knew they were in Europe.

Under some circumstances, an agent is held to a higher—or lower—standard than usual. **An agent with special skills is held to a higher standard because she is expected to use those skills.** A trained real estate agent should know enough to use the "Multiple Listing Service."

But suppose the Hardings had asked their neighbor, Jed, to help them sell their house. Jed is not a trained real estate agent, and he is not being paid, which makes him a *gratuitous agent*. A gratuitous agent is held to a lower standard because he is doing his principal a favor and, as the old saying goes, you get what you pay for—up to a point. **Gratuitous agents are liable if they commit *gross* negligence, but not *ordinary* negligence.** If Jed, as a gratuitous agent, left the Hardings an important message on their answering machine because he forgot they were in England, he would not be liable to them for that ordinary negligence. But if the answering machine had a message that *warned* him the Hardings were away and would not be picking up messages, he would be liable for gross negligence and a violation of his duty.

Duty to Provide Information

An agent has a duty to provide the principal with all information in her possession that she has reason to believe the principal wants to know. She also has a duty to provide accurate information. Angie's most egregious error as an agent was her failure to tell the Hardings about the Fords' final offer. She also told the Hardings information that was not true—that the Fords might want to buy the house. In the following case, the agent violated both its duty of care and its duty to provide information.

GRIGSBY v. O.K. TRAVEL

118 Ohio App. 3d 671, 693 N.E.2d 1142, 1997 Ohio App. LEXIS 875
Court of Appeals of Ohio, 1997

Facts: In the window of O.K. Travel, Oma Grigsby saw an advertisement for a tour of Israel that was organized by Trinity Tours. Grigsby signed up for the tour and paid O.K. About a week before Grigsby was to leave for the tour, O.K discovered that Trinity was out of business. O.K. contacted the American Society of Travel Agents, which notified O.K. that Trinity did not carry the financial bond required by the state of Ohio. Grigsby filed suit against O.K., alleging that it had violated its duty of care and its duty to provide information.

Issue: Did O.K. violate the duties it owed Grigsby?

Excerpts from Judge Painter's Decision: Customers come to travel agents because these agents hold themselves out as having knowledge about how to travel to places "foreign" to the traveler. For this reason, travel agents are the special agents of the traveler for securing a trip. A travel agent is more than a ticket supplier. Travel agents have become a professional segment of today's complex travel world.

When assisting in planning a vacation, a travel agent has a duty to act with the care, skill, and diligence that a fiduciary rendering that kind of service would reasonably be expected to use. The agent must make reasonable inquiries into the current financial stability of the person or entity with whom she recommended her principal do business. The duty, then, is to discover and disclose material information that is reasonably obtainable. If a tour operator or promoter defaults due to discoverable circumstances, the travel agent earning a commission from selling the tours should bear the loss if the agent fails to disclose the relevant risks.

Trinity, as a tour promoter, was required to register with the Secretary of State before commencing business in this state. A tour promoter must also provide a bond ($50,000 for interstate or international travel) in favor of the state before commencing operations. Upon registration, a tour promoter shall use the statement "registered Ohio tour promoter" and its registration number in any and all advertisements in Ohio. The advertisement for the Israel tour from Trinity was devoid of this statement and Trinity's registration number. Trinity could not have even provided a registration number because it was not registered in Ohio and never provided a bond, as statutorily required.

O.K. breached its duty to Grigsby by failing to disclose to Grigsby that Trinity was not registered in Ohio and had no bond posted which could have provided security in case it defaulted. This information was reasonably obtainable, and in fact should have been clear to O.K. (at least O.K. was put on notice), because Trinity's advertisement did not have the statutorily required language and registration number.

The judgment of the trial court in favor of Grigsby is affirmed.

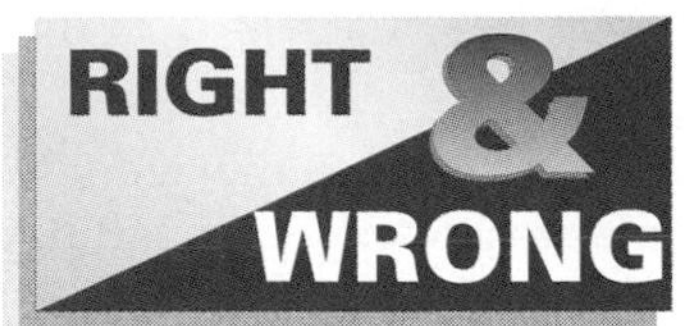

As we have seen in this section, agents have certain *legal* obligations to their principals. Would you, as an agent, also feel *ethical* duties to your principal? The Code of Ethics for the National Association of Realtors is available at **http://www.nnerealestate.com/MOV_CODE.htm**. Are these ethical standards different from the legal rules?

PRINCIPAL'S REMEDIES WHEN THE AGENT BREACHES A DUTY

A principal has three potential remedies when an agent breaches her duty:

- The principal can recover from the agent any **damages** the breach has caused. Thus, if the Hardings can only rent their house for $600 a month instead of the $800 the Fords offered, Angie would be liable for $2,400—$200 a month for one year.
- If an agent breaches the duty of loyalty, he must turn over to the principal any **profits** he has earned as a result of his wrongdoing. Thus, after Klein violated his duty of loyalty to Harrison, he forfeited profits he would have earned from the copyright of "He's So Fine."
- If the agent has violated her duty of loyalty, the principal may **rescind** the transaction. When Trang sold a script to her principal, Matt Damon, without telling him that she was the author, she violated her duty of loyalty. Damon could rescind the contract to buy the script.[12]

DUTIES OF PRINCIPALS TO AGENTS

In a typical agency relationship, the agent agrees to perform tasks for the principal, and the principal agrees to pay the agent. The range of tasks undertaken by an agent is limited only by the imagination of the principal. Because the agent's job can be so varied, the law has needed to define an agent's duties carefully. The role of the principal, on the other hand, is typically less complicated—often little more than writing a check to pay the agent. Thus the law enumerates fewer duties for the principal. Primarily, the principal must reimburse the agent for reasonable expenses and cooperate with the agent in performing agency tasks. The respective duties of agents and principals can be summarized as follows:

Duties of Agents to Principals	Duty of Principals to Agents
Duty of loyalty	Duty to reimburse
Duty to obey instructions	Duty to cooperate
Duty of care	
Duty to provide information	

[12] A principal can rescind his contract with an agent who has violated her duty, but, as we shall see in the next chapter, the principal might *not* be able to rescind a contract with a third party when the agent misbehaves.

DUTY TO REIMBURSE THE AGENT

As a general rule, the principal must **indemnify** (that is, reimburse) the agent for any expenses she has reasonably incurred. These reimbursable expenses fall into three categories.

Payments Made by the Agent While Carrying out His Duties

Peace Baptist Church of Birmingham, Alabama, asked its pastor, W. L. Lauderdale, to borrow money and buy land for a new church. Lauderdale repaid some of the borrowed money out of his own pocket. After his death, his heirs sued the church, asking for repayment. In finding in favor of the heirs, the court held that **a principal must indemnify an agent for any expenses or damages reasonably incurred in carrying out his agency responsibilities.**[13]

In this case, the church had specifically authorized Reverend Lauderdale to borrow the money and purchase the land. **A principal must also indemnify an agent for an *unauthorized* purchase if the agent *reasonably* believed he was authorized and the principal received a *benefit*.** Even if Reverend Lauderdale was not authorized, if he believed he was and the church obtained the land it needed at a favorable price, it would have to reimburse him for his expenses.

Torts Committed by the Agent

A principal must indemnify an agent for tort claims brought by a third party if the principal authorized the agent's behavior and the agent did not realize he was committing a tort. Marisa owns all the apartment buildings on Elm Street, except one. She hires Rajiv to manage the units and tells him that, under the terms of the leases, she has the right to ask guests to leave if a party becomes too rowdy. But she forgets to tell Rajiv that she does not own one of the buildings, which happens to house a college sorority. One night, when the sorority is having a rambunctious party, Rajiv hustles over and starts ejecting the noisy guests. The sorority is furious and sues Rajiv for trespass. If the sorority wins its suit against Rajiv, Marisa would have to pay the judgment, plus Rajiv's attorney's fees, because she had told him to quell noisy parties, and he did not realize he was trespassing.

Contracts Entered into by the Agent

The principal must indemnify the agent for any liability she incurs from third parties as a result of entering into a contract on the principal's behalf, including attorney's fees and reasonable settlements. An agent signed a contract to buy cucumbers for Vlasic Food Products Co. to use in making pickles. When the first shipment of cucumbers arrived, Vlasic inspectors found them unsuitable and directed the agent to refuse the shipment. The agent found himself in a pickle when the cucumber farmer sued. The agent notified Vlasic, but the company refused to defend him. He settled the claim himself for $29,000 and, in turn, sued Vlasic. The court ordered Vlasic to reimburse the agent because he had notified them of the suit and had acted reasonably and in good faith.[14]

---

13 *Lauderdale v. Peace Baptist Church of Birmingham*, 246 Ala. 178, 19 So. 2d 538, 1944 Ala. LEXIS 508 (1944).

14 *Long v. Vlasic Food Products Co.*, 439 F.2d 229, 1971 U.S. App. LEXIS 11455 (4th Cir. 1971).

DUTY TO COOPERATE

Principals have a duty to cooperate with their agent; they cannot impede the agent's efforts.

The principal must furnish the agent with the opportunity to work. If Lewis agrees to serve as Ida's real estate agent, Ida must allow Lewis access to the house. It is unlikely that Lewis will be able to sell the house without taking anyone inside.

The principal cannot unreasonably interfere with the agent's ability to accomplish his task. Suppose that Ida allows Lewis to show the house, but she refuses to clean it and then makes disparaging comments to prospective purchasers. "I really get tired of living in such a dank, dreary house," she says. "And the neighborhood children are vicious juvenile delinquents." This behavior would constitute unreasonable interference with an agent.

Note, however, that **unless the agency contract provides otherwise, the principal is allowed to compete with her agent.** Unless Ida has promised Lewis the exclusive right to sell the house, Ida can hire other real estate agents or even sell the house herself.

The principal must perform her part of the contract. Once the agent has successfully completed the task, the principal must pay him, even if the principal has changed her mind and no longer wants the agent to perform. Ida is a 78-year-old widow who has lived alone for many years in a house that she loves. Her asking price is outrageously high—$550,000. But, lo and behold, Lewis finds a couple who are happy to pay Ida's asking price. There is only one problem. Ida does not really want to sell. She put her house on the market because she enjoys showing it to all the folks who move to town. She rejects the offer. Now there is a second problem. The contract provided that Lewis would find a willing buyer at the asking price. Since he has done so, Ida must pay his real estate commission, even if she does not want to sell her house.

TERMINATING AN AGENCY RELATIONSHIP

Either the agent or the principal can terminate the agency relationship at any time. In addition, the relationship terminates automatically if the principal or agent can no longer perform their required duties or a change in circumstances renders the agency relationship pointless.

TERMINATION BY AGENT OR PRINCIPAL

The two parties—principal and agent—have five choices in terminating their relationship:

- *Term Agreement.* The principal and agent can agree in advance how long their relationship will last. Alexandra hires Boris to help her purchase exquisite enameled Easter eggs made for the Russian czars by Fabergé. If they agree that the relationship will last five years, they have a term agreement.
- *Achieving a Purpose.* The principal and agent can agree that the agency relationship will terminate when the principal's goals have been achieved. Alexandra and Boris might agree that their relationship will end when Alexandra has purchased 10 eggs.
- *Mutual Agreement.* No matter what the principal and agent agree at the start, they can always change their minds later on, as long as the change is mutual. If

This is one of the Fabergé eggs that Alexandra is seeking.

Boris and Alexandra originally agree to a five-year term, but after only three years Boris decides he wants to go back to business school and Alexandra runs out of money, they can decide together to terminate the agency.

- *Agency at Will.* If they make no agreement in advance about the term of the agreement, either principal or agent can terminate at any time.
- *Wrongful Termination.* An agency relationship is a *personal* relationship. Hiring an agent is not like buying a book. You might not care which copy of the book you buy, but you do care which agent you hire. If an agency relationship is not working out, the courts will not force the agent and principal to stay together. **Either party always has the *power* to walk out. They may not, however, have the *right*.** If one party's departure from the agency relationship violates the agreement and causes harm to the other party, the wrongful party must pay damages. He will nonetheless be permitted to leave. If Boris has agreed to work for Alexandra for five years but he wants to leave after three, he can leave, provided he pays Alexandra the cost of hiring and training a replacement.

If the agent is a *gratuitous* agent (i.e., is not being paid), he has both the power and the right to quit any time he wants, regardless of the agency agreement. If Boris is doing this job for Alexandra as a favor, he will not owe her damages when he stops work.

Principal or Agent Can No Longer Perform Required Duties

If the principal or the agent is unable to perform the duties required under the agency agreement, the agreement terminates.

Loss of Qualification

The agent or the principal may need a license to perform duties under the agency agreement. If either one of them is unable to obtain—or keep—the necessary license, the agency agreement ends. Caleb hires Allegra to represent him in a lawsuit. If she is disbarred, their agency agreement terminates because the agent is no longer allowed in court. Alternatively, suppose that Emil hires Bess to work in his gun shop. If he loses his license to sell firearms, their agency relationship terminates.

Bankruptcy

The bankruptcy of the agent or the principal terminates an agency relationship only if it affects their ability to perform. Bankruptcy rarely interferes with an agent's responsibilities. After all, there is generally no reason why an agent cannot continue to act for the principal whether the agent is rich or poor. Suppose that Lewis, the real estate agent, gets in over his head buying real estate for his own account. During a downturn in the market, he is unable to meet his mortgage payments, so he seeks the protection of the bankruptcy courts. He can continue to represent Ida or anyone else who wants to sell a house.

If the agent's bankruptcy does interfere with his ability to perform, then the agency relationship terminates. Chung works for Blue Chip Investments as a financial adviser, helping individuals organize their finances. If he were to go bankrupt, he would not exactly be a good advertisement for his employer, and his agency relationship would terminate.

The bankruptcy of a principal is different, however, because after filing for bankruptcy, the principal loses control of his assets. A bankrupt principal may be unable to pay the agent or honor contracts that the agent enters into on his behalf. Therefore, the bankruptcy of a principal is more likely to terminate an agency relationship.

Death or Incapacity of the Principal or Agent

An agency relationship terminates upon the death or incapacity of either the principal or the agent. Agency is a personal relationship, and when the principal dies, the agent cannot act on behalf of a nonexistent person.[15] Of course, a nonexistent person cannot act either, so the relationship also terminates when the agent dies. Incapacity has the same legal effect because either the principal or the agent is, at least temporarily, unable to act. Incapacity includes physical or mental disability.

Disloyalty of Agent

If the agent violates her duty of loyalty, the agency agreement automatically terminates. Agents are appointed to represent the principal's interest; if they fail to do so, there is no point to the relationship. Sam is negotiating a military procurement contract on behalf of his employer, Missiles R Us, Inc. In the midst of these negotiations, he becomes very friendly with Louisa, the government negotiator. One night over drinks, he tells Louisa what Missiles' real costs are on the project and the lowest bid it could possibly make. By passing on this confidential information, Sam has violated his duty of loyalty, and his agency relationship terminates.

CHANGE IN CIRCUMSTANCES

After the agency agreement is negotiated, circumstances may change. If these changes are significant enough to undermine the purpose of the agreement, then the relationship ends automatically. Andrew hires Melissa to sell his country farm for $100,000. Shortly thereafter, the largest oil reserve in North America is discovered nearby. The farm is now worth 10 times Andrew's asking price. Melissa's authority terminates automatically.

Loss or Destruction of Subject Matter

Andrew is fortunate that his farm is now worth so much, because his financial affairs are in grave disorder. Earlier in the year, he hired Damian to sell his Palm Beach condominium, but before Damian could even measure the living room, Andrew's creditors attached the condo. Damian is no longer authorized to sell the real estate because Andrew does not own it free and clear. He has "lost" the subject matter of his agency agreement with Damian.

Change of Law

If the agent's responsibilities become illegal, the agency agreement terminates. Oscar has hired Marta to ship him succulent avocados from California's Imperial Valley. Before she sends the shipment, Mediterranean fruit flies are discovered, and all fruits and vegetables in California are quarantined. The agency agreement terminates because it is now illegal to ship the California avocados.

EFFECT OF TERMINATION

Once an agency relationship ends, the agent no longer has the authority to act for the principal. If she continues to act, she is liable to the principal for any damages he incurs as a result. The Mediterranean fruit fly quarantine ended Marta's agency. If she sends Oscar the avocados anyway and he is fined for possession of a fruit fly, Marta must pay the fine.

---

[15] Restatement (Second) of Agency §120, Comment *a*.

The agent loses her authority to act, but some of the duties of both the principal and agent continue even after the relationship ends.

Principal's Duty to Indemnify Agent

Oscar must reimburse Marta for expenses she incurred before the agency ended. If Marta accumulated mileage on her car during her search for the perfect avocado, Oscar must pay her for gasoline and depreciation. But he owes her nothing for her expenses after the agency relationship ends.

Confidential Information

Remember the "He's So Fine" case earlier in the chapter. George Harrison's agent used confidential information to negotiate, on his own behalf, the purchase of the "He's So Fine" copyright. An agent is not entitled to use confidential information, even after the agency relationship terminates.

In the following case, the agent and principal quarreled over two issues: Did a change in circumstances terminate the agency relationship? What duties did the former agent owe his ex-principal?

FEDERAL PANTS, INC. v. STOCKING
762 F.2d 561, 1985 U.S. App. LEXIS 27419
United States Court of Appeals for the Seventh Circuit, 1985

Facts: Federal Pants, Inc. and D-S Enterprises were both in the "diversion business." They acquired well-known, name-brand products from a manufacturer and then resold the merchandise to discount stores that were not authorized dealers. Sometimes manufacturers will not sell to "diverters" because they do not want their merchandise in discount stores. Nike was willing to sell to D-S, but not to Federal Pants. So D-S and Federal Pants made a deal that D-S would purchase merchandise from Nike and resell it to Federal Pants. In return, Federal Pants guaranteed a bank loan for D-S.

For a period of two months, D-S purchased over $1 million in Nike merchandise and resold it to Federal Pants. When Nike discovered what D-S was doing, it immediately stopped deliveries. D-S threatened to sue Nike. In settlement, Nike offered D-S one last shipment but demanded payment in advance. D-S offered part of the shipment to Federal Pants, but Federal Pants did not have enough cash to pay in advance, so D-S sold the merchandise to one of Federal Pants' customers.

Federal Pants filed a lawsuit, alleging that D-S had breached its agency agreement with Federal Pants by refusing to sell it the last Nike shipment. It also alleged that D-S had violated its duty of loyalty by using Federal Pants' confidential information (i.e., its customer lists) to sell the Nike merchandise to a Federal Pants customer.

Issues: Was Nike's refusal to sell to D-S a change in circumstances that terminated the agency agreement between D-S and Federal Pants? After the agreement ended, what duties did D-S owe Federal Pants?

Excerpts from Judge Flaum's Decision: [T]he authority of an agent terminates when he receives notice of the happening of an event or of a change in circumstances from which he should reasonably infer that the principal does not consent to the further exercise of authority or would not consent if he knew the facts. [A]ny agency relationship that may have existed between Federal Pants and D-S came to an end when Nike terminated D-S as an authorized Nike dealer. Thus, any Nike merchandise received by D-S pursuant to the settlement negotiations with Nike was obtained for its own rather than for Federal Pants' benefit.

Federal Pants claimed that D-S Enterprises misused confidential information in selling the Nike settlement goods to Federal Pants' principal customers and engaged in unauthorized competition in sell[ing] directly to Federal Pants' customers. [A]n agent is subject to a duty not to compete with his principal concerning the subject matter of his agency. This duty not to compete, however, ceases upon the termination of the agency relationship. Although prohibited from using trade secrets or other confidential information given to him only for the principal's use, an agent is permitted to use general information concerning the principal's method of business and the names of customers retained in the agent's memory, if not acquired in violation of his duty as an agent.

In this case, the agency or contractual relationship between D-S and Federal Pants terminated before D-S and Nike had reached their settlement agreement and before D-S had attempted to find buyers for the Nike settlement goods. Since the relationship between D-S and Federal Pants had already terminated, D-S was free to solicit Federal Pants' former customers.

IRREVOCABLE AGENCY RELATIONSHIP

Michele borrows money from Gustav. As collateral, she grants him a mortgage on her land. If she does not pay her debt to Gustav, he has the right to sell her land and recover what she owes him. In theory, when Gustav sells Michele's land, he looks a lot like her agent. However, their relationship is different from a true agency. You remember that a typical agency relationship is established to benefit the principal. But here, Gustav has the right to sell Michele's land to benefit himself. He has what is called a **power coupled with an interest.** In other words, he has the right to sell Michele's land because she owes him something. He has benefited her by loaning her the money; now she must benefit him by allowing him to sell the land if she does not pay the debt.

In the case of a power coupled with an interest, only the agent can terminate the relationship. The principal has neither the *power* nor the *right* to terminate. Michele would like to terminate if she could, because then her land would not be at risk, but it would be unfair to Gustav if she did. This special kind of agency relationship (a power coupled with an interest) does not terminate upon the death or incapacity of either the principal or agent. If Gustav were to die, Michele would owe the money to his heirs, and they would have the right to sell her land if she did not pay her debt. If Michele died, her estate would be obligated to pay the debt to Gustav before it could distribute any assets to her heirs.

CHAPTER CONCLUSION

When students enroll in a business law course, they fully expect to learn about torts and contracts, corporations and partnerships. They probably do not think much about agency law; many of them have not even heard the term before. Yet it is an area of the law that affects us all because each of us has been and will continue to be both an agent and a principal many times in our lives.

CHAPTER REVIEW

1. In an agency relationship, a principal and an agent mutually consent that the agent will act on behalf of the principal and be subject to the principal's control, thereby creating a fiduciary relationship.

2. An agency relationship can exist without either a written agreement, a formal agreement, or consideration.
3. An agent owes these duties to the principal: duty of loyalty, duty to obey instructions, duty of care, and duty to provide information.
4. The principal has three potential remedies when the agent breaches her duty: recovery of damages the breach has caused, recovery of any profits earned by the agent from the breach, and rescission of any transaction with the agent.
5. The principal has two duties to the agent: to reimburse legitimate expenses, and to cooperate with the agent.
6. Both the agent and the principal have the power to terminate an agency relationship, but they may not have the right. If the termination violates the agency agreement and causes harm to the other party, the wrongful party must pay damages.
7. An agency relationship automatically terminates if the principal or agent can no longer perform the required duties or if a change in circumstances renders the agency relationship pointless.
8. Once an agency relationship ends, the agent no longer has the authority to act for the principal. If she continues to act, she is liable to the principal for any damages he incurs as a result.
9. In the case of a power coupled with an interest, only the agent has the right to terminate the relationship.

PRACTICE TEST

1. This is a tale of marital woe. At the urging of her husband, Phyllis Thropp placed $40,000 in a brokerage account with her husband's friend Richard Gregory, a broker at Bache Halsey. Mrs. Thropp opened the account in her name alone and did not authorize Gregory to discuss the account with Mr. Thropp, nor did she authorize Mr. Thropp to act for her. Undeterred by this technicality, Mr. Thropp forged his wife's name to a power of attorney that authorized him to make decisions for her. He gave this document to Gregory. In the course of the next year, Mr. Thropp ordered Gregory to sell his wife's securities. He then asked Gregory to issue checks to his wife. After forging her name to the checks, he cashed them and used the money to pay his gambling debts. Gregory did not process the power of attorney form according to standard Bache procedures. When the Thropps saw Gregory socially, Mrs. Thropp frequently asked him how her account was doing. Gregory somehow neglected to mention that it was not doing very well at all. He never told her about the numerous sales. Can this marriage be saved? No, the Thropps were divorced. Did Richard Gregory violate his fiduciary duty to Mrs. Thropp?

2. Herbert Chew worked for Bethlehem Steel Co. The company required all employees who missed work to produce a written explanation within 15 days. A medical excuse required a note from a doctor. Dr. Paul Meyer operated on Chew. The day after the surgery, Chew asked Meyer to sign a form for the company. He told the doctor that failure to send in the form could "cost me my job." Meyer refused to sign the form at that moment, but promised to have his secretary send it within the week. Chew asked the doctor several times in the next week whether the form had been sent. Meyer did finally send the form—one day late. Chew was fired. A rational question is: Who would want to work for this employer anyway? But the legal issue is: As a gratuitous agent, did Dr. Meyer have any obligation to Mr. Chew? Meyer was a gratuitous agent because he had been hired to operate on Chew, not to fill out forms. Once he agreed to notify the company, he became a gratuitous agent for that purpose.

3. The German-American Vocational League was formed in New York during World War II to serve as a propaganda agency for the German Reich. Under U.S. law, all foreign agents were required to register. Neither the Vocational League nor its officers registered. When they were charged with violating U.S. law, they argued that they were not agents of the German government because they had no formal agency agreement. Their one written agreement with the German Reich said nothing about being a propaganda agency. Is a formal contract necessary to establish an agency relationship?

4. CPA QUESTION Pell is the principal and Astor is the agent in an agency coupled with an interest. Who has the right to terminate the agency before the interest has expired?

	Pell	**Astor**
(a)	Yes	Yes
(b)	No	Yes
(c)	No	No
(d)	Yes	No

5. CPA QUESTION A principal and agent relationship requires a:

(a) Written agreement

(b) Power of attorney

(c) Meeting of the minds and consent to act

(d) Specified consideration

6. YOU BE THE JUDGE WRITING PROBLEM Frank Secan sought to buy land in Arizona that was owned by David Egelston. Secan gave a written offer on the land to a real estate agent, Becky Gogle, and asked her to transmit it to Egelston. Gogle told Secan that she was working with two other men who were interested in buying the land, but she would transmit the offer. She duly did so. She failed, however, to tell Secan that Egelston made a counteroffer to the two other men, who then bought the property. Did Gogle violate her duty to Secan? **Argument for Secan:** As Secan's agent, Gogle had a duty to provide information. Her failure to tell him about the counteroffer caused him harm. **Argument for Gogle:** Gogle had only one duty—to transmit the offer. Once she did that, her agency relationship with Secan ended, and she had no further obligation.

7. RIGHT & WRONG Radio TV Reports (RTV) was in the business of recording, transcribing, and monitoring radio and video programming for its clients. The Department of Defense (DOD) in Washington was one of RTV's major clients. Paul Ingersoll worked for RTV until August 31. In July, the DOD solicited bids for a new contract for the following year. During this same month, Ingersoll formed his own media monitoring business, Transmedia. RTV and Transmedia were the only two bidders on the DOD contract, which was awarded to Transmedia. Did Ingersoll violate his fiduciary duty to RTV? Aside from his legal obligations, did Ingersoll behave ethically? How does his behavior look in the light of day? Was it right?

8. Barbara Gelfand and her husband asked Action Travel Center, Inc. to book a cruise for them. They told the agency that they had to travel on a new cruise ship because of Mrs. Gelfand's medical condition. Older ships had chemicals that made her ill. The Travel Center sent Mrs. Gelfand a brochure for the *Costa Riviera,* described as a new ship making its maiden voyage. During the course of the cruise, Mrs. Gelfand became very ill and was forced to fly to Fort Lauderdale for hospitalization. It turned out that the *Costa Riviera* was an old ship that had merely been refurbished. Has the Travel Center violated its duty of care?

9. The Fellowship is a not-for-profit corporation whose primary purpose is promoting fellowship among Baptists. Its annual meeting was held at the Indianapolis Baptist Temple. Dr. Greg Dixon, the head of the Temple, invited various missions and vendors to attend the meeting and set up display booths. Rodger Keener wanted to buy a bus for his church. One of the Temple employees suggested he talk with Robert Crist, who had a booth at the annual meeting. Crist and Keener flew to Crist's business in Perryville, Indiana. The plane crashed and Keener was killed. Was Crist an agent of the Fellowship?

10. David and Fiona Rookard purchased tickets for a trip through Mexico from a Mexicoach office in San Diego. Mexicoach told them that the trip would be safe. It did not tell them, however, that their tickets had disclaimers written in Spanish warning that, under Mexican law, a bus company is not liable for any harm that befalls its passengers. The Rookards did not read Spanish. They were injured in a bus accident caused by gross negligence on the part of the driver. Did Mexicoach violate its duty to provide information?

11. Penny Wilson went to Arlington Chrysler-Plymouth-Dodge to buy an automobile. Penny told

Arlington that, as a minor, she could not buy the car unless she obtained credit life insurance that would pay the balance of any loan owing if her mother died. She also disclosed that her mother had cancer. Arlington was an agent for Western Pioneer Life Insurance Co. Western Pioneer reported that a credit insurance policy would be valid unless Mrs. Wilson died within six months. In fact, the policy was invalid if Mrs. Wilson died of cancer within *one year.* Seven months later, Mrs. Wilson died and Western Pioneer refused to pay. Penny Wilson sued Western Pioneer and Arlington. The trial court found Western Pioneer liable, but not Arlington. Was Western Pioneer liable for Arlington's legal expenses?

Internet Research Problem

The Code of Ethics for the National Association of Realtors is available at http://www.nnerealestate.com/MOV_CODE.htm. Do these rules require realtors to treat clients better—or worse—than agency law demands? In what ways?

You can find further practice problems in the Online Quiz at http://beatty.westbuslaw.com or in the Study Guide that accompanies this text.

CHAPTER 29

AGENCY: THE OUTSIDE RELATIONSHIP

Some people simply do not know their own best interest. Sarah's boss was like that. Jamie was an awfully nice guy, but his business would have been more successful if he had listened to Sarah once in a while. His company supplied product demonstrators to grocery stores. He hired and trained the people who stand in the aisles offering samples of salsa-flavored taco chips or chewy marshmallow chip cookies.

A manager from the Lone Star grocery store chain called to offer a contract for the Fort Worth area. It was a tempting offer, but Jamie told Sarah to refuse. At the price the chain was proposing, Jamie would barely be able to pay his workers the minimum wage. He doubted that he could find qualified staff at that price. Sarah disagreed. She believed you could always find good workers if you looked hard enough. Besides, Lone Star had thousands of stores nationwide, and this was a great opportunity to get a foot inside its very large door.

Against orders, but thinking only about what was best for Jamie, Sarah called back to *accept* the offer. She knew that he would be terribly grateful—someday. Unfortunately, on the day when Jamie did find out, he was furious. He was even angrier when he called his lawyer to rescind the contract and found out that he was legally committed to the deal

Sarah had made. He then ordered Sarah to take personal responsibility for the contract and make sure there were no problems.

Sarah trained new workers and sent them off to demonstrate flavored popcorn. Eager to make a good impression, Hugo rushed to cook his first batch of popcorn without carefully reading the instructions. Instead of adding *1/3* cup of peppermint popcorn, he put in *3* cups. Attracted by the wonderful smell, Tori stood by Hugo's stand, waiting for the popcorn to finish. With a flourish, Hugo raised the lid of the pan, and the popcorn exploded in Tori's face, causing severe burns.

It is virtually impossible to run a modern business without agents. However, hiring an agent dramatically increases the risk of legal liability. A principal may be liable in contract for agreements that the agent signs and also liable in tort for any harm the agent causes. Indeed, once a principal hires an agent, he may be liable to third parties for her acts, even if she *disobeys* instructions. Although Jamie specifically told Sarah not to accept the Lone Star contract, Jamie is bound by the contract because Sarah *appeared* to act with authority. Jamie is also liable in tort to Tori because his subagent (an agent hired by his agent) caused harm. This risk of liability means that it is important to understand agency law.

PRINCIPAL'S LIABILITY FOR CONTRACTS

Many agents are hired for the primary purpose of entering into contracts on behalf of their principals. Salespeople, for example, may do little other than sign on the dotted line. Most of the time, the principal is delighted to be bound by these contracts. But that is not always the case, as we saw with Jamie and Sarah. Sometimes the agent disobeys orders. As a general rule, however, the principal has no right to rescind a contract entered into by his agent. After all, if someone is going to be penalized, it should be the principal who hired the disobedient agent, not the innocent third party.

The principal is bound by the acts of an agent if (1) the agent has *authority*, or (2) the principal, for reasons of fairness, is *estopped* from denying that the agent had authority, or (3) the principal *ratifies* the acts of the agent.

To say that the principal is "bound by the acts" of the agent means that the principal is as liable as if he had performed the acts himself. It also means that the principal is liable for statements the agent makes to a third party. In addition, the principal is deemed to know any information that the agent knows or should know. Suppose that the grocery store tells Sarah that it cannot pay for the demonstrators unless she submits Social Security numbers for them by the end of the month. If Jamie fails to give the numbers to the store because Sarah forgets to tell him, he has no right to payment.

AUTHORITY

A principal is bound by the acts of an agent if the agent has authority. **There are three types of authority: express, implied, and apparent.** Express and implied authority are categories of **actual** authority because the agent *is* truly authorized to act for the principal. In apparent authority, the principal is liable for the agent's actions even though the agent was *not* authorized.

Express Authority

The principal grants **express authority** by words or conduct that, reasonably interpreted, cause the agent to believe the principal desires her to act on the principal's account.[1] In other words, the principal asks the agent to do something and the agent does it. Craig calls his stockbroker, Alice, and asks her to buy 100 shares of Superior Corp. for his account. She has *express authority* to carry out this transaction.

Sometimes reasonable people might disagree about what the principal actually asked the agent to do. **In cases of ambiguity about the principal's intent, the courts look at the principal's *objective* manifestation, not his *subjective* intent.** Craig stops by the brokerage house and leaves a signed note on Betsy's desk that says, "Please buy 100 shares of Superior Corp. stock." Craig thought he was leaving the note on Alice's desk. Betsy has the right to purchase the stock (and Alice loses out on the commission) because Craig's actions count, not his thoughts.

Likewise, it does not matter how the principal's wishes are communicated. As long as the agent receives them, she is authorized to act. If, instead of leaving a note to Alice, Craig had told Betsy what he wanted Alice to do and Betsy had, in turn, passed the word to Alice, then Alice would be authorized to act.

Implied Authority

Unless otherwise agreed, authority to conduct a transaction includes authority to do acts that are reasonably necessary to accomplish it.[2] David has recently inherited a house from his grandmother in Wichita Falls, Kansas. He hires Nell, one of his grandmother's neighbors, to auction off the house and its contents. As David well knows, only a licensed auctioneer is permitted to conduct an auction. Nell hires an auctioneer, advertises the event, rents a tent, and generally does everything necessary to conduct a successful auction. She withholds the amounts she has spent and sends the tidy balance to David, along with receipts for her expenses. Totally outraged, he calls her on the phone, "How dare you hire an auctioneer and rent a tent? I never gave you permission! Who said you could run advertisements? I absolutely *refuse* to pay these expenses!"

David is wrong. A principal almost never gives an agent absolutely complete instructions. Unless some authority were implied, David would have had to say, "Open the car door, get in, put the key in the ignition, drive to the store, buy stickers, mark an auction number on each sticker" . . . and so forth. To solve this problem, the law assumes that the agent has authority to do anything that is *reasonably* necessary to accomplish her task.

Apparent Authority

A principal can be liable for the acts of an agent who is not, in fact, acting with authority if the principal's conduct causes a third party reasonably to believe that the agent is authorized. In the case of *express* and *implied* authority, the principal has authorized the agent to act. Apparent authority is different: the principal has *not* authorized the agent, but has done something to make an innocent third party *believe* the agent is authorized. As a result, the principal is every bit as liable to the third party as if the agent did have authority. Mary works for Dinners Delite, a company that sells tasty, low-fat frozen foods door-to-door. She enjoys calling on people, but often ends up spending the dinner hour with only

---

[1] Restatement (Second) of Agency §26.

[2] Restatement (Second) of Agency §35.

one customer, talking away and eating samples. Finally, her boss fires her. When he asks her to return her samples and order forms, she lies and tells him that everything was stolen. She then calls on all her customers, takes many large orders, and keeps the payments herself. The orders go in the trash. When last sighted, Mary was sunning herself at a Cuban resort.

Someone is going to be out a good deal of money. Although it should be Mary, the customers will not be able to reach her in Cuba. Either her customers will go hungry, or the company will have to reimburse them. What is the fair result? The law takes the view that the principal is liable, not the third party, because the principal, by word or deed, allowed the third party to believe that the agent was acting on the principal's behalf. The principal could have prevented the third party from losing money. When Mary stole the customers' money, she was *not* an agent for Dinners Delite, *but the customers believed she was* because the company had never told them that she had been dismissed. Nor did the company retrieve her samples and order forms. Dinners Delite must reimburse the customers for the money Mary took. Thus, in apparent authority, the agent *appears* to have authority, even though she does not. Of course, Dinners Delite has the right to recover from Mary, if it can track her down.

Remember that the issue in apparent authority is always what the *principal* has done to make the *third party* believe that the *agent* actually has authority. Suppose that Mary had never worked for Dinners Delite but, on her own, printed order forms and prepared phony samples. The company would not be liable for the orders she took, because it had never done or said anything that would *reasonably* make a third party believe Mary was its agent.

In this example, the issue was whether Mary was Dinners Delite's agent at all. Issues of apparent authority also arise in cases like the following where the agent is, in fact, an agent, but has exceeded his *actual* authority.

BADGER v. PAULSON INVESTMENT CO.

311 Or. 14, 803 P.2d 1178, 1991 Ore. LEXIS 7
Supreme Court of Oregon, 1991

Facts: Zbigniew Lambo and Scott Kennedy worked as brokers for Paulson Investment Co., a stock brokerage firm in Oregon. Lambo and Kennedy violated securities laws by selling unregistered stock to Paulson's customers. This stock proved to be worthless. Although the customers acknowledged that Lambo and Kennedy did not have actual or implied authority to sell the stock, they nonetheless sued Paulson on the grounds that the brokers had apparent authority at the time the sale took place. A jury found for the customers, but the trial court overturned the jury verdict (by entering a judgment notwithstanding the verdict).

Issues: Did the two brokers have apparent authority to sell the unregistered stock? If the brokers had apparent authority, is Paulson liable for their actions?

Excerpts from Judge Peterson's Decision: Apparent authority is created only by some conduct of the principal which, when reasonably interpreted, causes a third party to believe that the principal consents to have the apparent agent act for him on that matter. The third party must also rely on that belief. There is sufficient evidence to support a finding that Kennedy and Lambo were acting within the apparent authority of Paulson. When Kennedy went to work for Paulson, it sent its customers letters announcing Kennedy's association with Paulson. With these announcements, Paulson, who did not inform its customers of any limitations on Kennedy's authority to act for Paulson, conferred on Kennedy the authority to represent Paulson in securities sales and investment transactions.

Following the announcements, conduct evincing a grant of authority continued. Kennedy's written communications with the plaintiffs concerning the securities were on Paulson's stationery, signed by Kennedy, and mailed by Lambo. Sales presentations touting the securities involved in this case were made by Kennedy and Lambo. The sales presentations occurred on Paulson's premises, and on at least one occasion, during normal business hours. Furthermore, both Kennedy and Lambo received calls regarding the securities at Paulson's place of business.

At no time were any of the plaintiffs notified that the sale of the securities had not been approved by Paulson or that Kennedy and Lambo were acting solely on their own behalf. Although Paulson may have forbade its sales representatives to present or sell nonapproved securities, liability based on the agency principle of apparent authority may be imposed even though the principal expressly forbade the conduct in question.

There is also evidence that from the information provided to them by Paulson, the plaintiffs reasonably believed that Kennedy and Lambo were authorized to act for Paulson concerning the securities sold by Kennedy and Lambo to the plaintiffs.

The evidence is sufficient to support the jury's verdict that Kennedy and Lambo conducted the illegal sales with the apparent authority of Paulson. Paulson, therefore, is liable as a principal for the plaintiffs' damages. The trial court erred in granting judgment notwithstanding the verdict to Paulson.

Paulson was liable to customers although its agents had exceeded their authority. A principal may also be liable to its *own* employees when a supervisor acts without authority. For example, when Betty Trail became pregnant, her supervisor granted her a lengthy leave of absence. The supervisor was authorized to grant only short-term leaves. When the appropriate form arrived on the president's desk, he denied Trail's request. The court held that the supervisor did not have express or implied authority to grant the leave, but she did have apparent authority. The employer was bound by her conduct and Trail was entitled to a lengthy leave.[3]

As the *Trail* case illustrates, employees who act without authority may still bind their principal if their actions reasonably appear to be related to their job. To avoid problems, an employer must clearly communicate the limits of a supervisor's authority. For example, the company should have explicitly stated in its employee manual that the supervisor's authority to grant leaves was limited to, say, absences of one month or less.

ESTOPPEL

No one may claim that a person was *not* his agent, if he knew that others thought the person *was* acting on his behalf, and he failed to correct their belief. He is *estopped* from denying an agency relationship. Paul Murphy approached the Sperry Rand Corp. with a promising idea for marketing Remington shavers. A dermatologist had recently conducted a pilot study indicating that the Remington product was better for the skin than ordinary razors and other electric shavers. Murphy proposed hiring a dermatologist to do a more thorough study that could be used as the basis for a national marketing campaign. Sperry Rand agreed to Murphy's plan. Murphy later produced a report from Dr. William Hill, Jr., indicating that Remington was indeed superior. Sperry Rand publicized this report in full-page advertisements in newspapers and magazines. There was only one problem—Hill had not written the report and had not agreed

[3] *Trail v. Industrial Commn. of Missouri*, 540 S.W.2d 179, 1976 Mo. App. LEXIS 2174 (Mo. Ct. App. 1976).

to allow his name to be used in the ad campaign. Murphy had *said* he was Hill's agent and had negotiated on Hill's behalf, but neither statement was true. Murphy did *not* have *apparent authority* because Hill had done nothing to lead Sperry Rand to believe Murphy was his agent.

The court, however, found Sperry Rand not liable on a theory of estoppel. Hill discovered the ad campaign in March but did not complain to Sperry Rand until November. By the simple act of making a prompt phone call, the doctor could have prevented most of the harm the advertisements caused him. Because Hill did not tell Sperry Rand of its error, he lost his right to recover damages from the corporation.[4]

Estoppel is, in a sense, a first cousin to *apparent authority*. In cases of apparent authority the principal has done something to lead a reasonable person to believe that the person pretending to be an agent really is an agent. In the case of estoppel, the principal has never done anything affirmatively to imply that the person pretending to be an agent really is one, but when he finds out people think he has an agent, he does not tell them otherwise.

RATIFICATION

If a person accepts the benefit of an unauthorized transaction or fails to repudiate it, then he is as bound by the act as if he had originally authorized it. He has *ratified* the act.[5] Many of the cases in agency law involve instances in which one person acts *without* authority for another. To avoid liability, the alleged principal shows that he had not authorized the task at issue. But sometimes, after the fact, the principal decides that he approves of what the agent has done even though it was not authorized at the time. The law would be perverse if it did not permit the principal, under those circumstances, to agree to the deal the agent has made. The law is not perverse, but it is careful. Even if an agent acts without authority, the principal can decide later to be bound by her actions as long as these requirements are met:

- The "agent" indicates to the third party that she is acting for a principal.
- The "principal" knows all the material facts of the transaction.
- The "principal" accepts the benefit of the whole transaction, not just part.
- The third party does not withdraw from the contract before ratification.

A night clerk at the St. Regis Hotel in Detroit, Michigan, was brutally murdered in the course of a robbery. A few days later, the *Detroit News* reported that the St. Regis management had offered a $1,000 reward for any information leading to the arrest and conviction of the killer. Two days after the article appeared, Robert Jackson turned in the man who was subsequently convicted of the crime. But then it was Jackson's turn to be robbed—the hotel refused to pay the reward on the grounds that the manager who had made the offer had no authority. Jackson still had one weapon left: he convinced the court that the hotel had ratified the offer. One of the hotel's owners admitted he read the *Detroit News*. The court concluded that if someone reads a newspaper, he is sure to read any articles about a business he owns; therefore, the owner must have been aware of the offer.

---

4 *Sperry Rand Corp. v. Hill*, 356 F.2d 181, 1966 U.S. App. LEXIS 7491 (1st Cir. 1966).

5 Restatement (Second) of Agency § 82.

He accepted the benefit of the reward by failing to revoke it publicly. This failure to revoke constituted a ratification and the hotel was liable.[6]

Estoppel and ratification are easy to confuse. *Ratification* applies when the principal accepts the benefit of the contract. The hotel owner benefited from the reward because he wanted the murderer to be caught. *Estoppel* applies when the alleged principal does *not* want the benefit of the contract, but delays in telling the innocent third party of the mistake. The doctor did not want his name tied to a nonexistent research report in a national ad campaign. If the doctor had accepted the benefit of the contract, by receiving payment, for instance, then he would have *ratified* the contract. As it was, he accepted no benefit, but he waited so long to contact Sperry Rand that he was *estopped* from recovering damages.

Lucy owns a movie theater in Boise, Idaho. Her friend Rick sometimes disagrees with Lucy's choice of films. She likes action flicks starring Jean-Claude Van Damme; Rick prefers foreign movies with subtitles. One day, Rick is waiting for Lucy in her office when the phone rings; it is a film distributor asking for the theater's movie order. Rick pretends he is the owner and quickly orders *Il Postino*, a romantic Italian movie, and *L'Affreux*, a French film. To obtain these two fabulous flicks, Rick agrees to pay double Lucy's usual price.

When Lucy returns, Rick tells her about the two films but not about the higher price. Although Lucy is annoyed, she signs and returns the confirmation slip when it comes from the distributor. But first she crosses out *L'Affreux* because the reviews are horrible. Lucy has not ratified the contract, for several reasons:

- Rick did not indicate to the salesperson that he was working for someone else.
- Lucy did not know all the material facts—that Rick had agreed to pay double her price.
- Lucy did not ratify the whole transaction because she crossed out one film.

SUBAGENTS

Many of the examples offered thus far in this chapter involve a single agent acting for a principal. Real life is often more complex. Daniel, the owner of a restaurant, hires Michaela to manage it. She in turn hires chefs, waiters, and dishwashers. Daniel has never even met the restaurant help, yet they are also his agents, albeit a special category called **subagent**. Michaela is called an **intermediary agent**—someone who hires subagents for the principal.

As a general rule, an agent has no authority to delegate her tasks to another unless the principal authorizes her to. But when an agent is authorized to hire a subagent, the principal is as liable for the acts of the subagent as he is for the acts of a regular agent. Daniel authorizes Michaela to hire a restaurant staff. She hires Lydia to serve as produce buyer. When Lydia buys food for the restaurant, Daniel must pay the bill.

The intermediary agent is not liable to the principal for the misdeeds of the subagent, unless she was negligent in hiring. Lydia is supposed to buy premium lettuces like arugula and radicchio. But iceberg is much cheaper so she orders a carload of these plebeian greens. Daniel is furious because he must pay for all the lettuce, even though he cannot possibly use it in his exotic salads. He blames Michaela for hiring Lydia in the first place. But Michaela is not liable unless she had some reason to know that Lydia was trouble.

---

[6] *Jackson v. Goodman*, 69 Mich. App. 225, 244 N.W.2d 423, 1976 Mich. App. LEXIS 741 (Mich. Ct. App. 1976).

AGENT'S LIABILITY FOR CONTRACTS

The agent's liability on a contract depends upon how much the third party knows about the principal. Disclosure is the agent's best protection against liability.

FULLY DISCLOSED PRINCIPAL

An agent is not liable for any contracts she makes on behalf of a *fully* disclosed principal. A principal is fully disclosed if the third party knows of his *existence* and his *identity*. Augusta acts as agent for Parker when he buys Tracey's prize-winning show horse. Augusta and Tracey both grew up in posh Grosse Pointe, Michigan, where they attended the same elite schools. Tracey does not know Parker, but she figures any friend of Augusta's must be okay. She figures wrong—Parker is a charming deadbeat. He injures Tracey's horse, fails to pay the full contract price, and promptly disappears from the face of the earth. Tracey angrily demands that Augusta make good on Parker's debt. Unfortunately for Tracey, Parker was a fully disclosed principal—Tracey knew of his *existence* and his *identity*. Although Tracey partly relied on Augusta's good character when contracting with Parker, Augusta is not liable because Tracey knew who the principal was and could have (should have) investigated him. Augusta did not promise anything herself, and Tracey's only recourse is against the principal, Parker (wherever he may be).

To avoid liability when signing a contract on behalf of a principal, an agent must clearly state that she is an agent and must also identify the principal. Augusta should sign a contract on behalf of her principal, Parker, as follows: "Augusta, as agent for Parker" or "Parker, by Augusta, Agent."

PARTIALLY DISCLOSED PRINCIPAL

In the case of a *partially* disclosed principal, the third party can recover from either the agent or the principal. A principal is partially disclosed if the third party knew of his *existence* but not his *identity*. Suppose that, when approaching Tracey about the horse, Augusta simply says, "I have a friend who is interested in buying your champion." Any friend of Augusta's is a friend of Tracey's—or so Tracey thinks. Parker is a partially disclosed principal because Tracey knows only that he exists, not who he is. She cannot investigate his credit because she does not know his name. Tracey relies solely on what she is able to learn from the agent, Augusta. Of course, the principal, Parker, is also liable because the contract was made on his behalf.

UNDISCLOSED PRINCIPAL

In the case of an *undisclosed* principal, the third party can recover from either the agent or the principal. A principal is undisclosed if the third party did not know of his existence. Suppose that Augusta simply asks to buy the horse herself, without mentioning that she is purchasing it for Parker. In this case, Parker is an undisclosed principal because Tracey does not know that Augusta is acting for someone else. Both Parker and Augusta are liable. As Exhibit 29.1 illustrates, the principal is *always* liable, but the agent is not unless the principal's identity is a mystery.

In some ways, the concept of an undisclosed principal violates principles of contract law. If Tracey does not even know that Parker exists, how can they have an agreement or a meeting of the minds? Is such an arrangement fair to Tracey? As Supreme Court Justice Oliver Wendell Holmes put it, "common sense is opposed

Exhibit 29.1

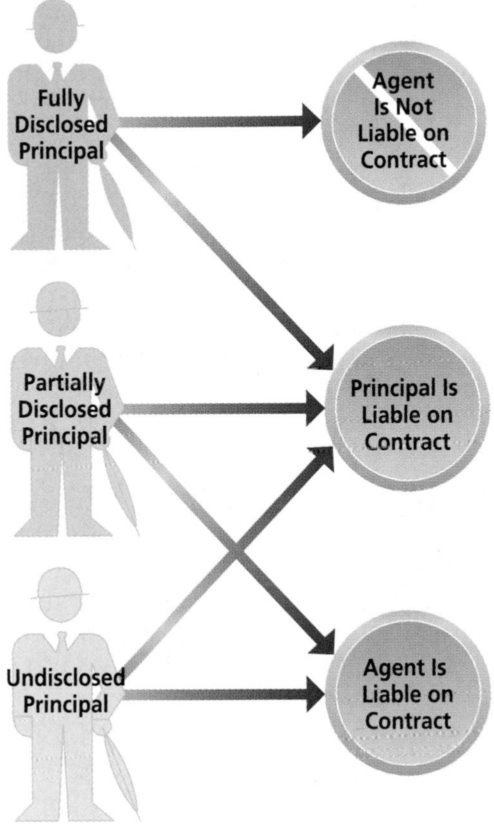

to allowing a stranger to my overt acts and to my intentions, a man of whom I have never heard, to set up a contract against me which I had supposed I was making with my personal friend."[7] Nonetheless, a contract with an undisclosed principal is binding. The following incident illustrates why.

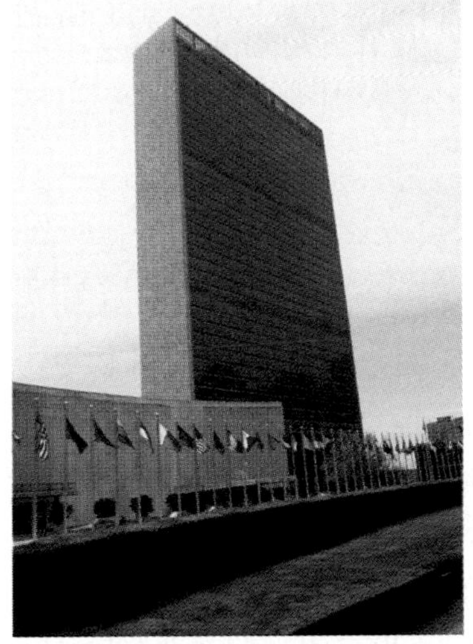
If it were not for William Zeckendorf and his agents, UN headquarters might be in Boston.

William Zeckendorf was a man with a plan. For years he had been eyeing a six-block tract of land along New York's East River. It was a wasteland of slums and slaughterhouses, but he could see its potential. The meat packers had refused to sell to him, however, because they knew they would never be permitted to build slaughterhouses in Manhattan again. Finally, in 1946, he got the phone call he had been waiting for. The companies were willing to sell—at $17 a square foot, when surrounding land cost less than $5. Undeterred, Zeckendorf immediately put down a $1 million deposit. But to make his investment worthwhile, he needed to buy the neighboring property—once the slaughterhouses were gone, this other land would be much more valuable. Zeckendorf was well-known as a wealthy real estate developer; he had begun his business career managing the Astor family's real estate holdings. If he personally tried to negotiate the purchase of the surrounding land, word would soon get out that he was trying to put together a large parcel. Prices would skyrocket and the project would become too costly. So he hired agents to purchase the land for him. To further conceal his involvement, he went to South America for a month. When he returned, his agents had completed 75 different purchases, and he owned 18 acres of land.

Shortly afterwards, the United Nations began seeking a site for its headquarters. President Truman favored Boston, Philadelphia, or a location in the Midwest.

[7] Holmes, "The History of Agency," *in* Association of American Law Schools, *Select Essays in Anglo-American Legal History* (Boston: Little, Brown & Co., 1909), vol. 3, p. 368.

The UN committee suggested Greenwich or Stamford, Connecticut. But John D. Rockefeller settled the question once and for all. He purchased Zeckendorf's land for $8.5 million and donated it to the UN (netting Zeckendorf a profit of $2 million). Without the cooperation of agency law, the UN headquarters would not be in New York today.

The law permits the concept of an undisclosed principal out of commercial necessity. There are times when the right of the third party to know the identity of the principal is outweighed by the law's interest in ensuring the smooth operation of commerce. Also, if contracts with an undisclosed principal were not enforceable, the agent would complete the transaction herself and immediately turn around and contract with the principal directly. Permitting contracts with an undisclosed principal eliminates the need for this additional step. The following article suggests that Harvard behaved unethically when it purchased land secretly. Do you agree?

Harvard University has bought 52 acres during the past nine years in a secret buying spree that increases the school's land in Allston (across the river from its Cambridge headquarters) by more than a third. Working through the Beal Cos., a prominent real estate development company, Harvard spent $88 million to buy 14 separate parcels. Harvard officials said the university made the purchases without revealing its identity to the sellers, residents, local politicians, or city officials because property owners would have drastically inflated the prices if they knew Harvard was the buyer. "We were really driven by the need to get these properties at fair market value" and avoid "overly inflated acquisition costs," said James H. Rowe, vice-president for public affairs at Harvard. But those who were left in the dark—including Mayor Thomas M. Menino—weren't buying it. "That's absurd," Menino scoffed. "Without informing anyone or telling anybody? That's total arrogance." Menino was so incensed that he adopted a mocking singsong tone to express his view of Harvard's attitude, saying: "We're from Harvard, and we're going to do what we want."

"As far as I'm concerned, they practiced a deception," said Ray Mellone, chairman of a neighborhood task force. "There are a lot of people who are going to say we can't trust them. We have to make the process work, and that means making the neighborhood involved, not having deals made in a back room and then coming to us and saying: 'Take it or leave it.'"[8]

Because of concerns about fair play, there are some exceptions to the rule on undisclosed principals. **A third party is not bound to the contract with an undisclosed principal if (1) the contract specifically provides that the third party is not bound to anyone other than the agent, or (2) the agent lies about the principal because she knows the third party would refuse to contract with him.** A cagey property owner, when approached by one of Harvard's agents, could have asked for a clause in the contract providing that the agent was not representing someone else. If the agent told the truth, the owner could have demanded a higher price. If the agent lied, then the owner could have rescinded the contract when the truth emerged. Suppose that a property owner said to one of the agents, "I don't mind selling this land to you, but I certainly wouldn't want Harvard to get it." The agent responded, "You can be sure this land will never end up in Harvard's

[8] Tina Cassidy and Dan Aucoin, "Harvard Reveals Secret Purchases of 52 Acres Worth $88M in Allston," *Boston Globe*, June 10, 1997, p. A1. Republished with permission of The Boston Globe; permission conveyed through the Copyright Clearance Center, Inc.

hands." When the irate owner later discovers the agent lied, he can rescind the contract. If, on the other hand, the agent merely *suspects* that the owner does not want to sell his land to Harvard, but the owner never specifically *says so*, there is no right to rescind.

As the following case illustrates, the rules on undisclosed principals place auctioneers in a perilous position.

POWERS v. COFFEYVILLE LIVESTOCK SALES CO.
665 F.2d 311, 1981 U.S. App. LEXIS 15671
United States Court of Appeals for the Tenth Circuit, 1981

Facts: Jack and Rita Powers purchased 312 head of cattle at a weekly auction conducted by Coffeyville Livestock Sales Co. They did not know who had consigned the cattle to Coffeyville for auction. The Powers, in turn, sold 159 of this lot to Leonard Hoefling. He sued the Powers, alleging the cattle were diseased and dying in large numbers, and recovered $38,360. The Powers then sought reimbursement from Coffeyville, alleging that it was liable as an agent acting for an undisclosed principal.

Issue: Is Coffeyville liable to the Powers for defects in the cattle it auctioned?

Excerpts from Judge Logan's Decision: Under traditional agency law, an agent is liable as if it were the principal when the agent acts for an undisclosed principal. This rule applies whether the agent holds itself out as principal or only as agent but does not disclose the identity of its principal. Applying this common law rule to auctioneers, an auctioneer is liable as a seller if the auctioneer fails to disclose to the buyer the identity of the principal. It appears Coffeyville did not usually disclose the identity of the owners of the cattle to purchasers at its auctions. At its livestock ring, Coffeyville commonly commingled cattle of several owners. The auctioneer sold the cattle by size or description rather than by owner or point of origin. Apparently buyers often purchased cattle of numerous owners and without knowing the owners' identities. [M]ore than 130 different persons were the owners of the 312 head of cattle the Powers purchased in this particular sale. The record, then, suggests that Coffeyville did not disclose the owners' identities to the Powers.

[We therefore find for the Powers. Coffeyville is liable to the Powers for defects in the cattle.]

Having lost this case, Coffeyville could, presumably, recover from the principals for whom it sold the cattle.

UNAUTHORIZED AGENT

Thus far in this section, we have been discussing an agent's liability to a third party for a transaction that was authorized by the principal. Sometimes, however, agents act without the authority of a principal. **If the agent has no authority (express, implied, or apparent), the principal is not liable and the agent is. An alleged agent acting without any principal (or principle!) at all is also liable to the third party.** Suppose that Augusta agrees to sell Parker's horse to Tracey. Unfortunately, Parker has never met Augusta and has certainly not authorized this transaction. Augusta is hoping that she can persuade him to sell, but Parker refuses. Augusta, but not Parker, is liable to Tracey for breach of contract.

PRINCIPAL'S LIABILITY FOR TORTS

A master is liable for physical harm caused by the negligent conduct of servants within the scope of employment.[9] This principle of liability is called ***respondeat superior,*** which is a Latin phrase that means, "let the master answer." Under the theory of *respondeat superior*, the principal is liable for the agent's misbehavior whether or not the principal was at fault. Indeed, the principal is liable even if he forbade or tried to prevent the agent from misbehaving. This sounds like a harsh rule. The logic is that, since the principal controls the agent, he should be able to *prevent* misbehavior. If he cannot prevent it, at least he can *insure* against the risks. Furthermore, the principal may have deeper pockets than the agent or the injured third party and thus be better able to *afford* the cost of the agent's misbehavior. What is the principal's liability in the following situation?

James is the resident manager of the apartment building where Linda lives. Linda notices James staring at her while she lies by the apartment swimming pool. Later, James makes off-color, flirtatious, and unwelcome remarks. When he goes to Linda's apartment to repair a leak in her shower, he puts his arm around Linda, tells her she is an attractive woman, and refers to her breasts as "headlights." She pushes James away. He grabs her breast and, after being pushed away again, grabs her buttock as she walks away from him.[10]

James would clearly be liable to Linda, but that is small consolation since his assets are as minuscule as his self-control. Is the landlord, Chris, liable for James's behavior? Yes, under *respondeat superior*. Although Chris did not authorize James's behavior, he could have prevented the harassment by hiring more carefully or firing at the first sign of trouble. He also could have raised his rents slightly to cover any judgments entered against him. In any event, he is better able to compensate Linda than James is.

To apply the principle of *respondeat superior*, it is important to understand each of the following terms: *master and servant, scope of employment, negligent and intentional torts*, and *physical harm*.

MASTER AND SERVANT

There are two kinds of agents: (1) *servants* and (2) *independent contractors*. **A principal *may be* liable for the torts of a servant but generally is *not* liable for the torts of an independent contractor.** Because of this rule, the distinction between a servant and an independent contractor is important. Employees are always servants. When determining if other agents are servants, courts consider whether:

- The principal controls details of the work.
- The principal supplies the tools and place of work.
- The agents work full-time for the principal.
- The agents are paid by time, not by the job.

---

[9] Restatement (Second) of Agency §243.

[10] Robert Bruss, "Landmark Case; Landlord May be Sued for Manager's Sex Harassment," *Chicago Tribune*, May 14, 1995, p. C8. Based on *Beliveau v. Caras*, 873 F. Supp. 1393, 1995 U.S. Dist. LEXIS 4923 (C.D. Cal. 1995).

- The work is part of the regular business of the principal.
- The principal and agents believe they have an employer-employee relationship.
- The principal is in business.[11]

Do not be misled by the term *servant*. A servant does not mean Jeeves, the butler, or Maisie, the maid. In fact, if Mrs. Dillworth hires Jeeves and Maisie for the evening from a catering firm, they are *not* her servants, they are independent contractors. On the other hand, the president of General Motors is a servant of that corporation.

Liza works for the Ace Accounting firm. The firm sends her to audit the Base Co. Ace supervises her work carefully and supplies her with the computer and books she needs to perform an audit. Liza works full-time for Ace and is paid by the month. Her work is part of Ace's regular business, and she thinks of herself as Ace's employee. Liza is indeed Ace's servant. As for Base, it may want to control her work, but it cannot. It does not supply her tools, but only a temporary place to work. She does not work full-time for, nor is she paid directly by, Base. Being audited is not Base's regular business. Liza and Base do not think of themselves as employer and employee. Liza may be the Ace who works for Base, but she is Base's independent contractor, not its servant. If Liza spills a cup of hot coffee and severely burns someone at Base, Ace is liable because she is an Ace servant. Base is not liable because, for it, she is only an independent contractor.

Principals prefer agents to be considered independent contractors not servants because, as a general rule, principals are not liable for the torts of an independent contractor. There is, however, one exception to this rule: **The principal is liable for the physical torts of an independent contractor *only if* the principal has been negligent in hiring or supervising her.** Remember that, under *respondeat superior*, the principal is liable *without fault* for the physical torts of servants. The case of independent contractors is different: the principal is liable only if he was *at fault* by being careless in his hiring or supervising. Was the supermarket at fault in the following case?

DURAN v. FURR'S SUPERMARKETS, INC.
921 S.W.2d 778, 1996 Tex. App. LEXIS 1345
Court of Appeals of Texas, 1996

Facts: Steve Romero was an off-duty police officer working as a security guard for Furr's Supermarkets. He approached a car parked in the supermarket's fire lane and began yelling at a passenger to move it. The passenger, Graciela Duran, asked Romero for his name. He opened the car door and tried to pull her out, all the while threatening to arrest her. Duran ultimately required surgery to repair the injury that his tugs and twists caused to her left arm.

Duran filed suit against Furr's. The supermarket filed a motion for summary judgment on the grounds that it was not responsible for Romero's conduct because he was an independent contractor. Duran argued that Furr's had been negligent in hiring Romero. The trial court granted the motion for summary judgment.

Issues: Was Furr's negligent in hiring Romero? Is it liable for Romero's conduct?

Excerpts from Judge McClure's Decision: The basis of responsibility under the doctrine of negligent hiring is the master's own negligence in hiring or retaining in his employ an incompetent servant whom the master knows or by the

---

[11] Restatement (Second) of Agency §220(2).

exercise of reasonable care should have known was incompetent or unfit and thereby creating an unreasonable risk of harm to others. The evidence showed that Furr's did not require Romero to complete a job application and otherwise made no inquiry into his background as a police officer. Furr's never interviewed Romero or spoke with him before he began working at the store. If Furr's had conducted an investigation of Romero's performance as a police officer, it would have learned that Romero had a prior complaint for using vulgar and abusive language towards a member of the public while on duty as a police officer.

Duran argues that this complaint demonstrates Romero's propensity for aggressive behavior so that Furr's could have reasonably anticipated that Romero might verbally and physically abuse a patron of the store. On the other hand, Furr's argues that even if it had discovered the prior complaint, the information would not have caused Furr's to reasonably anticipate his physical assault upon Duran. In attempting to distinguish between the prior verbal abuse complaint and the physical assault upon Duran, Furr's ignores the evidence showing that Romero first verbally abused Duran during this incident. According to Duran, the verbal abuse escalated into the physical assault. We find that a fact question is raised whether knowledge of this abusive language complaint would put a reasonable person on notice that Romero might verbally abuse a store patron, and that such conduct might escalate into a physical assault. Because of the existence of this fact issue, summary judgment on this ground is improper.

SCOPE OF EMPLOYMENT

Principals are only liable for torts that a servant commits within the *scope of employment*. If an employee leaves a pool of water on the floor of a store and a customer slips and falls, the employer is liable. But if the same employee leaves water on his own kitchen floor and a friend falls, the employer is not liable because the employee is not acting within the scope of employment. A servant is acting within the scope of employment if the act:

- Is one that servants are generally responsible for
- Takes place during hours that the servant is generally employed
- Is part of the principal's business
- Is similar to the one the principal authorized
- Is one for which the principal supplied the tools; and
- Is not seriously criminal.

Scope of employment cases raise two major issues: *authorization* and *abandonment*.

Authorization

In authorization cases, the agent is clearly working for the principal but commits an act that the principal has not authorized. Although Jane has often told the driver of her delivery van not to speed, Hank ignores her instructions and plows into Bernadette. At the time of the accident, he is working for Jane, delivering flowers for her shop, but his act is not authorized. **An act is within the scope of employment, even if expressly forbidden, if it is of the same general nature as that authorized or if it is incidental to the conduct authorized.**[12] Hank was authorized to drive the van, but not to speed. However, his speeding was of the same general nature as the authorized act, so Jane is liable to Bernadette. In the following case,

[12] Restatement (Second) of Agency §229(1).

an employee was engaged in unauthorized behavior while on company business. Did his actions fall within the scope of his employment? You be the judge.

CONNER v. MAGIC CITY TRUCKING SERVICE, INC.
592 So. 2d 1048, 1992 Ala. LEXIS 26
Supreme Court of Alabama, 1992

Facts: Sarah Conner worked for A-Pac, which was building a roadway. A-Pac had hired Magic City to supply dirt. Conner was responsible for punching holes in a ticket to tally the amount of dirt each Magic City truck brought in. When a driver was ready to dump the dirt from the truck, Conner would often release the truck's latch as a courtesy to the driver, who would otherwise have to climb out of the truck to release it.

Magic City employee David King drove up wearing a Halloween mask. Conner punched King's load ticket but ignored the mask. King asked, "You're not going to say anything?" Conner did not comment or respond to this question, and King left. He later returned to Conner's post with a second load of dirt, this time without the mask. Conner punched his load ticket, and King told her to release the latch on his truck quickly or else he would "put [his] friend" on her. Conner attempted to release the latch but could not budge it. Conner told King, who had a tool for forcing the release of the latch, to release it himself. King again threatened to "put [his] friend" on her if Conner did not quickly release the latch. King began chasing Conner with a very large snake. King's Magic City supervisor laughed as Conner ran from King. Eventually, King gave up the chase and threw the snake at Conner. She collapsed with severe medical problems.

You Be the Judge: Under *respondeat superior*, is Magic City liable for the actions of its employee, King? Was King acting within the scope of his employment?

Argument for Conner: An employee is acting within the scope of his employment if the conduct is of the same general nature as that authorized or incidental to that authorized. Sarah Conner would never have met David King if he had not been working for Magic City. He was angry at her because she did not release the latch on his truck. What could be more incidental to his job than that?

Respondeat superior is based on the concept of control. The principal is able to control the agent to prevent him from misbehaving. While David King was tormenting Sarah Conner, King's supervisor stood and *laughed*. He did not even tell King to stop. Sarah Conner has suffered serious injuries as a result of King's behavior on the job. In all fairness, Magic City should bear liability for the harm caused by its employee.

Argument for Magic City: When King brought in the Halloween mask and snake, he was not acting in furtherance of his employer's goals or business. His employer did not approve of or condone his behavior. Snakes have nothing to do with King's job, and his actions were not within the scope of his employment.

Conner blames Magic City because King's supervisor stood by and laughed. Consciously or not, people often react to bizarre antics with laughter even when they disapprove of the behavior. Magic City is sorry King behaved so badly. But the company did *not* authorize his actions and should not be liable for them.

Abandonment

The second major issue in a *scope of employment* case involves abandonment. **The master is liable for the actions of the servant that occur while the servant is at work, but not for actions that occur after the servant has abandoned the master's business.** Although the rule sounds straightforward, the difficulty lies in determining whether the employee has in fact abandoned the master's business. The employer is liable if the employee is simply on a *detour* from company business, but the employer is not liable if the employee is off on a *frolic of his own*. Suppose that Hank, the delivery van driver, speeds during his afternoon commute home. A servant is generally not acting within the scope of his employment when he commutes to and from work, so his master, Jane, is not liable. Or suppose that, while on the way to a delivery, he stops to see his favorite movie classic, *Dead on Arrival*. Unable to see in the darkened theater, he knocks Anna down, causing grave harm.

Jane is not liable because Hank's visit to the movies is outside the scope of his employment. On the other hand, if Hank stops at the Burger King drive-in window en route to making a delivery, Jane is liable when he crashes into Anna on the way out of the parking lot, because this time he is simply making a detour. The distinction between a *frolic* and a *detour* can sometimes seem obscure. The following case clarifies the distinction.

O'CONNOR v. MCDONALD'S RESTAURANTS OF CALIFORNIA, INC.

220 Cal. App. 3d 25, 1990 Cal. App. LEXIS 448
California Court of Appeals, 1990

Facts: One August evening from about 8 P.M. until 2 A.M. Evans and several co-workers scoured the children's playground at McDonald's San Ysidro restaurant. This special cleaning prepared the restaurant for inspection as part of McDonald's "spring-blitz" competition. Evans—who aspired to a managerial position—worked without pay in the cleanup party. His voluntary contribution of work and time was the type of extra effort necessary for advancement in the McDonald's organization.

After completing the cleanup, Evans and four fellow employees went to the house of Joe Duffer, who had also participated in the evening's work. Evans and the others talked shop and socialized for several hours. On his way home at 6:30 A.M., Evans collided with a motorcycle driven by Martin O'Connor. The motorcyclist was seriously injured, and his left leg had to be amputated below the knee.

O'Connor filed a lawsuit for negligence against Evans and McDonald's. The trial court found that Evans was acting outside the scope of his employment at the time of the accident, and granted summary judgment for McDonald's. O'Connor appealed.

Issue: Was Evans acting within the scope of his employment at the time of the accident?

Excerpts from Judge Kremer's Decision: The record contains evidence McDonald's encourages its employees and aspiring managers to show greater dedication than simply working a shift and going home. O'Connor presented McDonald's operations and training manual and employee handbook to demonstrate how McDonald's fosters employee initiative and involvement in problem solving. Such evidence could reasonably support a finding of a direct and specific connection between McDonald's business and the gathering at Duffer's because the gathering was consistent with the "family" spirit and teamwork emphasized by McDonald's in its communications with employees. Such evidence could also reasonably support a finding McDonald's emphasis on teamwork made a group discussion of McDonald's business at Duffer's house a foreseeable continuation of Evan's special errand. Much of the conversation during the gathering centered on McDonald's business or concerned employee-manager relations. The group discussed the cleaning activities of the spring blitz to determine whether they might return to the restaurant to correct any deficiencies.

McDonald's contends the asserted managerial discussions at Duffer's house went beyond the scope of work Evans was hired to do. Evans's direct supervisor Cardenas asserted Evans "was under no instruction from me, or any other authorized employee of McDonald's, with respect to his activities after he left the restaurant. I had no knowledge that other co-employees would go to Joe Duffer's house after the final clean-up." McDonald's also presented evidence it required official employee conferences be attended by a salaried manager and no such salaried manager attended the Duffer gathering. However, these facts do not compel a finding as a matter of law contrary to O'Connor's claim McDonald's implicitly encouraged Evans to continue his special errand by conferring with co-employees on what they might do to win the spring blitz competition.

Such evidence raises a triable factual issue about the combination of personal entertainment and company business at Duffer's house. Where the employee may be deemed to be pursuing a business errand and a personal objective simultaneously, he will still be acting within the scope of his employment.

The summary judgement is *reversed*.

NEGLIGENT AND INTENTIONAL TORTS

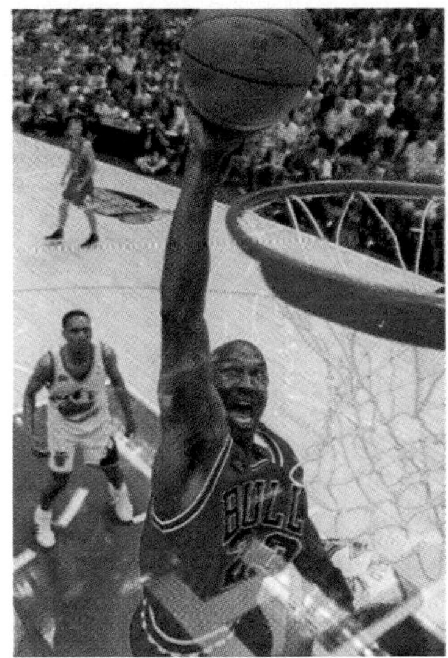

Is the team liable for the harm these players cause?

The master is liable if the servant commits a *negligent* tort that causes physical harm to a person or property. When Evans crashed into O'Connor, he committed a negligent tort, and McDonald's is liable if all the other requirements for *respondeat superior* are met.

A master is *not* liable for the *intentional* torts of the servant *unless* the servant was motivated, at least in part, by a desire to serve the master, or the conduct was reasonably foreseeable. During an NBA basketball game, Hakeem pushes Alonzo into some chairs under the basket to prevent him from scoring a breakaway layup. Hakeem's team is liable for his actions because he was motivated, at least in part, by a desire to help his team. But if Hakeem hits Alonzo in the parking lot after the playoffs are over, Hakeem's team is *not* liable because he is no longer motivated by a desire to help the team. His motivation now is personal revenge or frustration.

The courts (of law, not basketball) are generally expansive in their definition of behavior that is intended to serve the master. In one case, a police trainee shot a fellow officer while practicing his quick draw technique. In another, a drunken sailor knocked a shipmate out of bed with the admonition, "Get up, you big son of a bitch, and turn to," after which the two men fought. The courts ruled that both the police trainee and the sailor were motivated by a desire to serve their master and, therefore, the master was liable for their intentional torts.[13]

Even if the servant was not motivated by a desire to serve his master, the master is liable if the conduct was reasonably foreseeable. Barbara Marston went to see a psychiatrist, Dr. E. Philip Nuernberger, for biofeedback therapy to cure her chronic headaches and back pain. After two sessions Dr. Nuernberger began kissing and fondling her. Marston became increasingly depressed. Under a theory of *respondeat superior*, she sued the clinic where Dr. Nuernberger worked. At trial, experts testified that any sexual contact with a patient is totally unethical, has no therapeutic purpose, is purely personal, and could not be motivated by any desire to serve the clinic. But the court held for the patient on the grounds that "[s]exual relations between a psychologist and a patient is a well-known hazard and thus, to a degree, foreseeable and a risk of employment."[14]

PHYSICAL HARM

In the case of *physical* torts, a master is liable for the negligent conduct of a servant that occurs within the scope of employment. The rule for *nonphysical* torts (that is, torts that harm only reputation, feelings, or wallet) is different. Nonphysical torts are treated more like a contract claim, and the principal is liable only if the servant acted with actual, implied, or apparent authority. For example, the Small Business Administration (SBA) granted Midwest Knitting Mills, Inc. more than $2 million

---

13 *Nelson v. American-West African Line, Inc.*, 86 F.2d 730, 1936 U.S. App. LEXIS 3841 (2d Cir. 1936), and *Thompson v. United States*, 504 F. Supp. 1087, 1980 U.S. Dist. LEXIS 15834 (D.S.D. 1980).

14 *Marston v. Minneapolis Clinic of Psychiatry & Neurology, Ltd.*, 329 N.W.2d 306, 1982 Minn. LEXIS 1891 (Minn. 1982).

in loans, but the SBA employee in charge of the case never told Midwest. (He was allegedly a drug addict.) The company sued the SBA for the negligence of its employee. Although the conduct had occurred within the scope of employment, it was a nonphysical tort. Since the employee had not acted with actual, implied, or apparent authority, the SBA was not liable.[15]

Misrepresentation and defamation are, however, treated differently from other nonphysical torts.

Misrepresentation

A principal is liable if:

- The agent makes a misrepresentation
- The agent has express, implied, or apparent authority
- The third party relies on the misrepresentation; and
- The third party suffers harm.

This rule applies to any agent, not just a servant. If the agent is authorized to make a *truthful* statement, the principal is liable for any related *false* statement.

Althea hires Morris, a real estate agent, to sell a piece of land. Morris knows that part of the land floods every spring, but when Helen inquires about flooding, Morris lies. He is not authorized to make the *false* statement, but he is authorized to make statements about the land. Althea is liable to Helen for any harm caused by Morris's misrepresentation, even though Morris is an independent contractor.

Defamation

A principal is liable if:

- The agent makes a defamatory statement
- The agent has express, implied, or apparent authority; and
- The third party is harmed by the statement.

Again, this rule applies to all agents, not simply to servants. If the agent is authorized to make a *truthful* statement, the principal is liable for any related *defamatory* statements.

A newspaper reporter writes an untrue story alleging that the mayor has been taking kickbacks from contractors who work for the city. The reporter has defamed the mayor, and the newspaper is liable because the reporter is an agent authorized to write the article, even though he is not authorized to write false statements.

Electronic communication has created new risks for employers. They fear that their employees may commit libel by sending flaming e-mails or violate intellectual property laws by downloading copyrighted software from the Internet. Is the company liable in these circumstances? What if an employee posts defamatory information on an Internet newsgroup? Even if the employee is not authorized, she may have *apparent* authority—especially if the posting appears with a company e-mail address. For this reason, companies increasingly monitor their

---

[15] *Midwest Knitting Mills, Inc. v. United States*, 741 F. Supp. 1345, 1990 U.S. Dist. LEXIS 8663 (E.D. Wis. 1990).

employees' e-mail content and Internet usage. Some companies also require employees, when posting on a newsgroup, to include a disclaimer that they do not speak for their company.

AGENT'S LIABILITY FOR TORTS

The focus of this chapter has been on the *principal's* liability for the agent's torts. But it is important to remember that **agents are always liable for their own torts.** Agents who commit torts are personally responsible, whether or not their principal is also liable. In the *McDonald's* case, the plaintiff filed suit against *both* Evans (the agent) and McDonald's (the principal). Even if the tort was committed to benefit the principal, the agent is still liable. So the sailor who got into a fistfight while rousting a shipmate from bed is liable even though he thought he was acting for the benefit of his principal.

This rule makes obvious sense. If the agent were not liable, he would have little incentive to be careful. Imagine Hank driving his delivery van for Jane. If he were not personally liable for his own torts, he might think, "If I drive fast enough, I can make it through that light even though it just turned red. And if I don't, what the heck, it'll be Jane's problem, not mine." Agents, as a rule, may have fewer assets than their principal, but it is important that their personal assets be at risk in the event of their negligent behavior.

If the agent and principal are *both* liable, which does the injured third party sue? The principal and the agent are *jointly and severally* liable, which means that the injured third party can sue either one or both, as she chooses. Of course, she cannot recover twice. If she collects the full amount from the principal, she cannot sue the agent, and vice versa. If she recovers from the principal, he can sue the agent.

CHAPTER CONCLUSION

Most people will, at some point in their lives, serve as a principal and as an agent. This is particularly true for those in business—few businesses operate without agents. Though essential, the agent-principal relationship is nonetheless a potential landmine of liability. In some sense, this entire chapter is a lesson in preventive law. By understanding agency law, principals and agents can both avoid liability.

CHAPTER REVIEW

1. A principal is bound by the contracts of the agent if the agent has express, implied, or apparent authority. The principal is also bound by the contracts of the agent if the principal is estopped from denying the agent had authority, or if the principal ratifies the acts of the agent.

2. The principal grants express authority by words or conduct that, reasonably interpreted, cause the agent to believe that the principal desires her to act on the principal's account.

3. Implied authority includes authority to do acts that are incidental to a transaction, usually accompany it, or are reasonably necessary to accomplish it.

4. Apparent authority means that a principal is liable for the acts of an agent who is not, in fact, acting with authority if the principal's conduct causes a third party reasonably to believe that the agent is authorized.

5. Under the theory of estoppel, no one may claim that a person was *not* his agent, if he knew that others thought the person *was* acting on his behalf, and he failed to correct their belief.

6. Ratification means that someone agrees to an act that he had not originally unauthorized. A ratified transaction is treated as if it had been authorized from the beginning.

7. An agent is not liable for any contract she makes on behalf of a fully disclosed principal. In the case of a partially disclosed or undisclosed principal, both the agent and the principal are liable on the contract.

8. Under *respondeat superior*, a master is liable when a servant acting within the scope of employment commits a negligent tort that causes physical harm to a person or property. Under some circumstances, a master is also liable for a servant's intentional torts.

9. The principal is only liable for the torts of an independent contractor if the principal has been negligent in hiring or supervising him.

10. A principal is liable for nonphysical torts only if the servant acts with actual, implied, or apparent authority.

11. Agents are always liable for their own torts.

PRACTICE TEST

1. It was Christmas time in the city, and Mrs. Pommert decided to surprise her husband by buying holiday decorations for his hardware store. Singing along with the carols on the car radio, Mrs. Pommert ran a stop sign and crashed into Mr. Bryan's car. Called to the scene by the police, Mr. Pommert took the decorations out of his wife's car and placed them in his own. Mr. Bryan alleged that Mr. Pommert was liable as Mrs. Pommert's principal because he had ratified her purchase of the Christmas decorations when he placed them in his car. Do you agree?

2. **CPA QUESTION** Cox engaged Datz as her agent. It was mutually agreed that Datz would **not** disclose that he was acting as Cox's agent. Instead he was to deal with prospective customers as if he were a principal acting on his own behalf. This he did and made several contracts for Cox. Assuming Cox, Datz, or the customer seeks to avoid liability on one of the contracts involved, which of the following statements is correct?

(a) Cox must ratify the Datz contracts in order to be held liable.

(b) Datz has **no** liability once he discloses that Cox was the real principal.

(c) The third party can avoid liability because he believed he was dealing with Datz as a principal.

(d) The third party may choose to hold either Datz or Cox liable.

3. This article appeared in *Newsday:*

> As the first legal claim was filed in the wake of yesterday's deadly subway crash at Union Square, personal injury attorneys said the city Transit Authority was certain to be held responsible for the loss of life and injuries in the wreck. Even if the motorman were found to have been under the influence of drugs or alcohol, the Transit Authority bears responsibility for the negligence of its employees.[16]

Is this story accurate? Under what legal theory would the Transit Authority be liable?

[16] Anthony M. DeStefano, "Wreck's 1st Legal Claim Seeks $10M for Injuries," *Newsday*, Aug. 29, 1991, p. 10. Copyright 1991 Newsday, Inc. Reprinted with permission.

4. **RIGHT & WRONG** Dr. James Leonard wrote Dr. Edward Jacobson and offered him the position of Chief of Audiology at Jefferson Medical College in Philadelphia. In the letter, Leonard stated that this appointment would have to be approved by the promotion and appointment committee. Jacobson believed that the appointment committee acted only as a "rubber stamp" affirming whatever recommendation Leonard made. Jacobson accepted Leonard's offer and proceeded to sell his house and quit his job in Colorado. You can guess what happened next. Two weeks later, Leonard sent Jacobson another letter, rescinding his offer because of opposition from the appointment committee. Jacobson conceded that Leonard did not have express or implied authority to enter into binding employment contracts on behalf of the medical college. On what grounds could Jacobson bring a lawsuit? Would he prevail? Regardless of the medical school's legal obligation, does the appointment committee have an ethical obligation to Dr. Jacobson? Would any of the questions on the ethical checklist in Chapter 9 make the committee members think twice about what they have done?

5. One Friday afternoon, a custodian at the Lazear Elementary School in Oakland, California, raped an 11-year-old student in his office on the school premises. The student sued the school district on a theory of *respondeat superior*. Is the school district liable for this intentional tort by its employee?

6. One night, someone stole a disassembled 1970 Ford Boss engine from Richard Marrotta's porch. Shortly thereafter, Richard Pears told state troopers that Harry Schikora, a fellow high school student, had offered to sell the engine to him. On the troopers' instructions, Pears met Schikora at the King Trucking Co. yard to view the engine. Trooper Ellis tried to call Ed King, owner of the trucking yard, to obtain consent to search the yard. Ed King was out of town but had left his brother Dean in charge. Ed had never specifically authorized Dean to admit troopers to the premises, but Dean executed a written consent to search. The troopers found the engine, and Schikora was convicted of theft. Schikora appealed on the grounds that the search warrant was illegal because Dean was not authorized to consent to the search of Ed's business. If the search was illegal, the police would not be allowed to present any evidence they found at the trucking yard. Did Dean King have the authority to consent to the search?

7. This article appeared in the *New York Times*:

> A week after criminal charges were announced in the death of tennis star Vitas Gerulaitis, his mother filed suit yesterday against eight defendants, including the owner of the Long Island estate where Mr. Gerulaitis died of carbon monoxide poisoning last fall. Prosecutors have charged that a new swimming pool heater, installed at a cost of $8,000, was improperly vented and sent deadly fumes into a pool house where Mr. Gerulaitis was taking a nap. The lawsuit accuses the companies that manufactured, installed and maintained the pool heater, and the mechanic who installed it, with negligence and reckless disregard for human life. It makes similar charges against the owners of the oceanfront estate, Beatrice Raynes and her son Martin, a real-estate executive.[17]

Why would the owners of the estate be liable?

8. **CPA QUESTION** A principal will **not** be liable to a third party for a tort committed by an agent:

(a) Unless the principal instructed the agent to commit the tort

(b) Unless the tort was committed within the scope of the agency relationship

(c) If the agency agreement limits the principal's liability for the agent's tort

(d) If the tort is also regarded as a criminal act

9. As a child, Clive Thomas became a permanent resident of the United States. Three decades later, still not a citizen, he pleaded guilty to conspiracy to possess cocaine for sale and was sentenced to seven years' imprisonment. He was released from prison after two years because of his cooperation in a major narcotics investigation. Thomas and an Assistant United States Attorney signed a formal "letter of agreement" in which Thomas promised to work as a cooperating witness for two years. In return, the United States government agreed not to deport him. Shortly thereafter, the United States Immigration and Naturalization Service (INS) ordered him deported. Thomas argued that the Assistant United States Attorney had implied authority to bind the United States government and therefore the INS could not deport him. Do you agree?

10. A. B. Rains worked as a broker for the Joseph Denunzio Fruit Co. Raymond Crane offered to sell

[17] Vivian S. Toy, "Gerulaitis's Mother Files Suit in Son's Carbon Monoxide Death," *New York Times*, June 1, 1995, p. B5. Copyright © 1995 by The New York Times Co. Reprinted by permission.

Rains nine carloads of Emperor grapes. Rains accepted the offer on behalf of Denunzio. Later, Rains and Denunzio discovered that Crane was an agent for John Kazanjian. Who is liable on this contract?

11. Roy Watson bought vacuum cleaners from T & F Distributing Co. and then resold them door-to-door. He was an independent contractor. Before hiring Watson, the president of T & F checked with two former employers but could not remember if he called Watson's two references. Watson had an extensive criminal record, primarily under the alias Leroy Turner, but he was listed in FBI records under both Leroy Turner and Roy Watson. T & F granted Watson sales territory that included Neptune City, New Jersey. This city required that all "peddlers" such as Watson be licensed. Applicants for this license were routinely fingerprinted. T & F never insisted that Watson apply for such a license. Watson attacked Miriam Bennett after selling a vacuum cleaner to her at her home in Neptune City. Is T & F liable to Bennett?

12. YOU BE THE JUDGE WRITING PROBLEM Sara Kearns went to an auction at Christie's to bid on a tapestry for her employer, Nardin Fine Arts Gallery. The good news is that she purchased a Dufy tapestry for $77,000. The bad news is that it was not the one her employer had told her to buy. In the excitement of the auction, she forgot her instructions. Nardin refused to pay and Christie's filed suit. Is Nardin liable for the unauthorized act of its agent? **Argument for Christie's:** Kearns executed a bidder form as agent for Nardin. This is a common practice for many purchasers. Christie's cannot possibly ascertain in each case the exact nature of the bidder's authority. Whether or not Kearns had actual authority, she certainly had apparent authority and Nardin is liable. **Argument for Nardin:** Kearns was not authorized to purchase the Dufy tapestry, and therefore Christie's must recover from her, not us.

INTERNET RESEARCH PROBLEM

Acting as an undisclosed principal, William Zeckendorf employed agents to purchase the land in New York on which the United Nations headquarters was ultimately built. Can you find any other examples on the Internet of business dealings in which agents made purchases for an undisclosed principal? Were these business arrangements ethical? What risks did the agents face?

You can find further practice problems in the Online Quiz at http://beatty.westbuslaw.com or in the Study Guide that accompanies this text.

CHAPTER 30

EMPLOYMENT LAW

"On the killing beds you were apt to be covered with blood, and it would freeze solid; if you leaned against a pillar, you would freeze to that, and if you put your hand upon the blade of your knife, you would run a chance of leaving your skin on it. The men would tie up their feet in newspapers and old sacks, and these would be soaked in blood and frozen, and then soaked again, and so on, until by nighttime a man would be walking on great lumps the size of the feet of an elephant. Now and then, when the bosses were not looking, you would see them plunging their feet and ankles into the steaming hot carcass of the steer. . . . The cruelest thing of all was that nearly all of them—all of those who used knives—were unable to wear gloves, and their arms would be white with frost and their hands would grow numb, and then of course there would be accidents."[1]

[1] From Upton Sinclair, *The Jungle* (New York: Bantam Books, 1981), p. 80, a 1906 novel about the meat-packing industry.

INTRODUCTION

For most of history, the concept of career planning was unknown. By and large, people were born into their jobs. Whatever their parents had been—landowner, soldier, farmer, servant, merchant, or beggar—they became, too. People not only knew their place, they also understood the rights and obligations inherent in each position. The landowner had the right to receive labor from his tenants, but he also cared for them if they fell ill. Certainly, there were abuses, but at a time when people held religious convictions about their position in life and workers had few expectations that their lives would be better than their parents', the role of law was limited. The primary English law of employment simply established that, in the absence of a contract, an employee was hired for a year at a time. This rule was designed to prevent injustice in an agrarian society. If an employee worked through harvest time, the landowner could not fire him in the unproductive winter. Conversely, a worker could not stay the winter and then leave for greener pastures in the spring.

In the eighteenth and nineteenth centuries, the Industrial Revolution profoundly altered the employment relationship. Many workers left the farms and villages for large factories in the city. Bosses no longer knew their workers personally, so they felt little responsibility toward them. The old laws that had suited an agrarian economy with stable relationships did not fit the new employment conditions. Instead of duties and responsibilities, courts emphasized the freedom to contract. Since employees could quit their factory jobs whenever they wanted, it was only fair for employers to have the same freedom to fire a worker. That was indeed the rule adopted by the courts: unless workers had an explicit employment contract, they were employees at will. **An *employee at will* could be fired for a good reason, a bad reason, or no reason at all.** For nearly a century, this was the basic common law rule of employment. A court explained the rule this way:

> Precisely as may the employee cease labor at his whim or pleasure, and, whatever be his reason, good, bad, or indifferent, leave no one a legal right to complain; so, upon the other hand, may the employer discharge, and, whatever be his reason, good, bad, or indifferent, no one has suffered a legal wrong.[2]

However evenhanded this common law rule of employment may have sounded in theory, in practice it could lead to harsh results. The lives of factory workers were grim. It was not as if they could simply pack up and leave; conditions were no better elsewhere. For the worker, freedom to contract often meant little more than freedom to starve to death. Courts and legislatures gradually began to recognize that individual workers were generally unable to negotiate fair contracts with powerful employers. Over the course of the twentieth century, employment law changed dramatically. Now, the employment relationship is more strictly regulated by statutes and by the common law. No longer can a boss discharge an employee for any reason whatsoever.

Note that many of the statutes discussed in this chapter were passed by Congress and therefore apply nationally. The common law, however, comes from state courts and only applies locally. We will look at a sampling of cases that illustrate national trends, even though the law may not be the same in every state.

This chapter covers four topics in employment law: (1) employment security, (2) safety and privacy in the workplace, (3) financial protection, and (4) employment discrimination.

---

[2] *Union Labor Hospital Assn. v. Vance Redwood Lumber Co.*, 112 P.886, 888, 1910 Cal. LEXIS 417 (Cal. 1910).

EMPLOYMENT SECURITY

NATIONAL LABOR RELATIONS ACT

Without unions to represent employee interests, employers could simply fire any troublemaking workers who complained about conditions in factories or mines. By joining together, workers could bargain with their employers on more equal terms. Naturally, the owners fought against the unions, firing organizers and even hiring goons to beat them up. Distressed by anti-union violence, Congress passed the **National Labor Relations Act** in 1935. Known as the **NLRA** or the **Wagner Act**, this statute:

- Created the National Labor Relations Board to enforce labor laws
- Prohibits employers from penalizing workers who engage in union activity (for example, joining a preexisting union or forming a new one); and
- Requires employers to "bargain in good faith" with unions.

Labor law is covered at greater length in Chapter 31.

FAMILY AND MEDICAL LEAVE ACT

In 1993, Congress passed the Family and Medical Leave Act (FMLA), which guarantees both men and women up to 12 weeks of *unpaid* leave each year for childbirth, adoption, or medical emergencies for themselves or a family member. An employee who takes a leave must be allowed to return to the same or an equivalent job with the same pay and benefits. The FMLA applies only to companies with at least 50 workers and to employees who have been with the company full-time for at least a year. About 44 percent of women and 50 percent of men in the workforce are covered.

When Randy Seale's wife went into premature labor with triplets, he stayed home from his job as a truck driver with Associated Milk Producers, Inc. in Roswell, New Mexico. However, the milk of human kindness did not flow in this company's veins: it promptly fired the expectant father. Since Seale was an employee at will, the company's action would have been perfectly legal without the FMLA. But after the U.S. Department of Labor filed suit, the company agreed to pay Seale $10,000.

Concerned that the FMLA would impose too heavy a burden on business, Congress appointed a bipartisan commission to study its impact. The commission reported that, because leaves are unpaid, only about 4 percent of eligible workers actually ask for time off. More than three-quarters of the companies surveyed said that the cost of compliance was small. The commission generally found "an overall picture of enhanced employee productivity, good will and willingness 'to go the extra mile.'" The commission's report is available at **http://www.ilr.cornell.edu/lib/bookshelf/e_archive/FamilyMedical/**.

WRONGFUL DISCHARGE

Olga Monge was a schoolteacher in her native Costa Rica. After moving to New Hampshire, she attended college in the evenings to earn U.S. teaching credentials. At night, she worked at the Beebe Rubber Co. During the day, she cared for her husband and three children. When she applied for a better job at her plant, the foreman offered to promote her if she would be "nice" and go out on a date with him. When she refused, he assigned her to a lower wage job, took away her overtime, made her clean the washrooms, and generally ridiculed her. Finally, she collapsed at work and he fired her.[3]

Imagine that you are one of the judges who decided this case. Olga Monge has been treated abominably, but she was an employee at will and, as you well know, could be fired for any reason. But how can you let the foreman get away with this despicable behavior? The New Hampshire Supreme Court decided that even an employee at will has rights:

> We hold that a termination by the employer of a contract of employment at will which is motivated by bad faith or malice or based on retaliation is not in the best interest of the economic system or the public good and constitutes a breach of the employment contract.[4]

The employment at will doctrine was created by the courts. Because that rule has sometimes led to absurdly unfair results, the courts have now created a major exception to the rule—**wrongful discharge**. The *Monge* case illustrates this concept. ***Wrongful discharge* prohibits an employer from firing a worker for a *bad reason*.** There are three categories of wrongful discharge claims: public policy, contract law, and tort law.

Public Policy

The *Monge* case is an example of the **public policy rule**. Unfortunately, naming the rule is easier than defining it, because its definition and application vary from state to state. **In essence, the public policy rule prohibits an employer from firing a worker for a reason that violates basic social rights, duties, or responsibilities.** Virtually every employee who has ever been fired feels that a horrible injustice has been done. The difficulty, from the courts' perspective, is to distinguish those cases of dismissal that are offensive enough to arouse the community at large from those that outrage only the employee. The courts have primarily applied the public policy rule when an employee refuses to violate the law or insists upon exercising a legal right or performing a legal duty.

Refusing to Violate the Law. Larry Downs went to Duke Hospital for surgery on his cleft palate. When he came out of the operating room, the doctor instructed a nurse, Marie Sides, to give Downs enough anesthetic to immobilize him. Sides refused because she thought the anesthetic was wrong for this patient. The doctor angrily administered the anesthetic himself. Shortly thereafter, Downs stopped breathing. Before the doctors could resuscitate him, he suffered permanent brain damage. When Downs's family sued the hospital, Sides was called to testify. A number of Duke doctors told her that she would be "in trouble" if she testified. She did testify and, after three months of harassment, was fired. When she sued Duke University, the court held:

> It would be obnoxious to the interests of the state and contrary to public policy and sound morality to allow an employer to discharge any employee, whether the employment be for a designated or unspecified duration, on the ground that the employee declined to commit perjury, an act specifically enjoined by statute. To hold otherwise would be without reason and contrary to the spirit of the law.[5]

---

[3] *Monge v. Beebe*, 114 N.H. 130, 316 A.2d 549, 1974 N.H. LEXIS 223 (1974).

[4] Id. at 133.

[5] *Sides v. Duke University*, 74 N.C. App. 331, 328 S.E.2d 818, 1985 N.C. App. LEXIS 3501 (N.C. Ct. App. 1985).

As a general rule, employees may not be discharged for refusing to break the law. For example, courts have protected employees who refused to participate in an illegal price-fixing scheme, falsify pollution control records required by state law, pollute navigable waters in violation of federal law, or assist a supervisor in stealing from customers.[6] In the following case, an employee refused to commit a misdemeanor—indecent exposure.

WAGENSELLER v. SCOTTSDALE MEMORIAL HOSPITAL
147 Ariz. 370, 710 P.2d 1025, 1985 Ariz. LEXIS 250
Supreme Court of Arizona, 1985

Facts: Kay Smith was Catherine Wagenseller's supervisor at Scottsdale Memorial Hospital. Together with nurses from other hospitals, the two women went on an eight-day rafting trip down the Colorado River. As the trip progressed, Wagenseller became increasingly offended by Smith's behavior: heavy drinking, and public urination, defecation, and bathing. At the end of the trip, Wagenseller refused to join in a parody of the song "Moon River," which concluded with members of the group "mooning" the audience. After returning from the trip, Smith and others performed the "Moon River" skit twice at the hospital. Again, Wagenseller refused to participate. Smith began harassing Wagenseller, using abusive language and embarrassing her in front of other staff. Before the trip, Wagenseller had received consistently favorable job performance evaluations. Six months after the outing, she was fired. Wagenseller contended she was fired for reasons that contravene public policy.

The trial court dismissed her claims on a motion for summary judgment. The appeals court affirmed this dismissal. Wagenseller appealed.

Issue: Does the public policy doctrine prohibit the hospital from firing Wagenseller?

Excerpts from Judge Feldman's Decision: The Hospital argues that an "at-will" employee may be fired for cause, without cause, or for "bad" cause. In recent years there has been apparent dissatisfaction with the absolutist formulation of the common law at-will rule. With the rise of large corporations conducting specialized operations and employing relatively immobile workers who often have no other place to market their skills, recognition that the employer and employee do not stand on equal footing is realistic. In addition, unchecked employer power, like unchecked employee power, has been seen to present a distinct threat to the public policy carefully considered and adopted by society as a whole. As a result, it is now recognized that a proper balance must be maintained among the employer's interest in operating a business efficiently and profitably, the employee's interest in earning a livelihood, and society's interest in seeing its public policies carried out.

The trend has been to modify the at-will rule by creating exceptions to its operation. The most widely accepted approach is the "public policy" exception, which permits recovery upon a finding that the employer's conduct undermined some important public policy. In general, it can be said that public policy concerns what is right and just and what affects the citizens of the State collectively. It is to be found in the State's constitution and statutes and, when they are silent, in its judicial decisions.

---

[6] *Tameny v. Atlantic Richfield Co.*, 27 Cal. 3d 167, 610 P.2d 1330, 1980 Cal. LEXIS 171 (1980); *Trombetta v. Detroit, T. & I. R. R.*, 81 Mich. App. 489, 265 N.W.2d 385, 1978 Mich. App. LEXIS 2153 (Mich. Ct. App. 1978); *Sabine Pilot Service, Inc. v. Hauck*, 28 Tex. Sup. J. 339, 687 S.W.2d 733, 1985 Tex. LEXIS 755 (1985); *Vermillion v. AAA Pro Moving & Storage*, 146 Ariz. 215, 704 P.2d 1360, 1985 Ariz. App. LEXIS 592 (Ariz. Ct. App. 1985).

[T]he interests of the economic system will be fully served if employers may fire for good cause or without cause. The interests of society as a whole will be promoted if employers are forbidden to fire for cause which is "morally wrong." We therefore adopt the public policy exception to the at-will termination rule. We hold that an employer may fire for good cause or for no cause. He may not fire for bad cause—that which violates public policy.

[Not all unfair terminations are violations of public policy.] For example the Oregon Supreme Court refused to recognize a cause of action for the discharge of an employee who claimed he was wrongfully terminated for exercising his statutory right as a stockholder to examine the books of his corporate employer. The court based its determination on its finding that the right claimed was "not one of public policy, but the private and proprietary interest of stockholders, as owners of the corporation."

In the case before us, Wagenseller refused to participate in activities which arguably would have violated our indecent exposure statute. [T]his statute was enacted to preserve and protect the commonly recognized sense of privacy and decency. The statute does, therefore, recognize bodily privacy as a "citizen's social right." We are compelled to conclude that termination of employment for refusal to participate in public exposure of one's buttocks is a termination contrary to the policy of this state. [The Arizona Supreme Court overturned the lower court's grant of summary judgment and remanded the case for trial.]

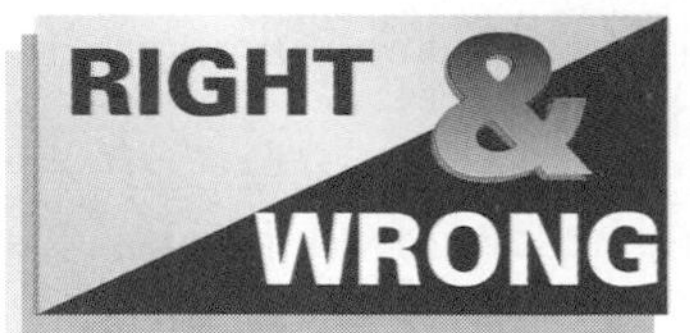

Does an employer ever have the right to require workers to participate in an illegal scheme? Suppose that compliance with state pollution control regulations would force a company out of business. When the life of the company is at stake, does the boss have a right to expect a worker to cooperate by fudging records?

Exercising a Legal Right. As a general rule, an employer may not discharge a worker for exercising a legal right if that right supports public policy. Dorothy Frampton injured her arm while working at the Central Indiana Gas Co. Her employer (and its insurance company) paid her medical expenses and her salary during the four months she was unable to work. When she discovered that she also qualified for benefits under the state's workers' compensation plan, she filed a claim and received payment. One month later, the company fired her without giving a reason. In her suit against the gas company, the court held:

> The [Workers' Compensation] Act creates a duty in the employer to compensate employees for work-related injuries and a right in the employee to receive such compensation. If employers are permitted to penalize employees for filing workmen's compensation claims, a most important public policy will be undermined. Employees will not file claims for justly deserved compensation—opting, instead, to continue their employment without incident. The end result, of course, is that the employer is effectively relieved of his obligation.[7]

Performing a Legal Duty. Courts have consistently held that an employee may not be fired for serving on a jury. Employers sometimes have difficulty replacing employees who are called up for jury duty and, therefore, prefer that their workers find some excuse for not serving. But jury duty is an important civic duty that employers are not permitted to undermine.

What about an employee who performs a good deed that is not legally required? Kevin Gardner had just parked his armored truck in front of a bank in Spokane, Washington, when he saw a man with a knife chase the manager out of the bank. While running past the truck, the manager looked directly at Gardner

---

[7] *Frampton v. Central Indiana Gas Co.*, 260 Ind. 249, 297 N.E.2d 425, 1973 Ind. LEXIS 522 (1973).

and yelled, "Help me, help me." Gardner got out of his truck and locked the door. By then, the suspect had grabbed another woman, put his knife to her throat, and dragged her into the bank. Gardner followed them in, tackled the suspect, and disarmed him. The rescued woman hailed Gardner as a hero, but his employer fired him for violating a "fundamental" company rule that forbade drivers to leave their armored trucks unattended. However, the court held for Gardner on the grounds that, although there is no affirmative legal duty to intervene in such a situation, society values and encourages voluntary rescuers when a life is in danger.[8]

Unlike Kevin Gardner's heroics, which did not injure his employer, whistleblowers do harm their employers (at least in the short-run). **Whistleblowers** are employees who disclose illegal behavior on the part of their employer. Here is the story of Henry Boisvert.

FMC Corp. sold 9,000 Bradley Fighting Vehicles to the U.S. Army for as much as $1.5 million each. But the Bradley was controversial from the moment it began rolling off FMC's manufacturing lines. Designed to carry soldiers around battlefields in Eastern Europe, its ability to "swim" across rivers and lakes was an important part of its job description. But Henry Boisvert, a testing supervisor for FMC, charged that the Bradley swam like a rock. Boisvert said he first encountered problems with the Bradley in the early days of the Army procurement process. He had one driven into a test pond and watched it quickly fill with water. FMC welders who worked on Bradleys claimed they weren't given enough time to do their work properly and so would simply fill gaps with putty. FMC quashed Boisvert's report on the Bradley and fired him when he refused to sign a falsified version. FMC disputes his account, but a jury ultimately agreed with him.[9]

The law on whistleblowers varies across the country. Federal statutes protect certain kinds of employee conduct in specific industries. Some states provide broad protection and others offer none at all. As a general rule, however, whistleblowers are protected in the following situations:

- *Wrongdoing by Government Contractors.* Henry Boisvert refused to sign his name to a report he thought was inaccurate. As a result, he may soon be signing a check from FMC for $100 million. Boisvert recovered from FMC under the False Claims Act, a statute Congress amended in 1986 to prevent retaliation against employees who report wrongdoing by government contractors. The Act permits individuals to sue these contractors on behalf of the federal government and to receive between 15 and 30 percent of any damage awards. In the first 10 years of the statute, the government recovered $3.3 billion, with $195 million going to those who blew the whistle. The Act also prohibits employers from firing workers who bring suit under the statute. In 1997, a federal district court in Houston held that the False Claims Act is unconstitutional.[10] This decision has been criticized by other courts, and ultimately the United States Supreme Court may have to decide the fate of the Act.

- *Constitutional Protection for Government Employees.* Employees of federal, state, and local governments have a right to free speech under the United States Constitution. Therefore, the government cannot retaliate against public employees who blow the whistle, as long as the employee is speaking out on a

---

[8] *Gardner v. Loomis Armored, Inc.*, 913 P.2d 377, 1996 Wash. LEXIS 109 (1996).

[9] Lee Gomes, "A Whistle-Blower Finds Jackpot at the End of His Quest," *Wall Street Journal*, April 27, 1998, p. B1. Republished with permission of The Wall Street Journal; permission conveyed through the Copyright Clearance Center, Inc.

[10] *United States v. St. Luke's Episcopal Hospital*, 982 F. Supp. 1261, 1997 U.S. Dist. LEXIS 16954 (S.D. Tex. 1997).

matter of public concern. For example, a New York City child welfare agency received numerous reports that six-year-old Elisa Izquierdo was being abused. After Elisa was beaten to death by her mother, ABC News broadcast an interview with a social worker from the agency. She stated on air that "The workers who are considered the best workers are the ones who seem to be able to move cases out quickly. . . . There are lots of fatalities the press doesn't know anything about." By giving this interview, the social worker violated New York City rules prohibiting employees from disclosing information about families supervised by city agencies. The city suspended the social worker from her job, and she sued. The court acknowledged that the government has the right to prohibit some employee speech. However, if the employee speaks on matters of public concern, the government bears the burden of justifying any retaliation. In this case, the court held for the social worker. The city reinstated her and gave her back pay.[11]

- *Statutory Protection for Federal Employees*. Congress passed the Civil Service Reform Act in 1978 and the Whistleblower Protection Act in 1989. These two statutes prevent retaliation against federal employees who report wrongdoing. They also permit the award of back pay and attorney's fees to the whistleblower. This statute was used to prevent the National Park Service from disciplining two managers who wrote a report expressing concern over development in Yellowstone National Park.
- *When an Employee Is Involved in the Illegal Activity*. As we have seen, courts protect employees from retaliation for refusing to commit an illegal act. As a variation on the same theme, most courts will protect employees who report illegal activity out of fear that otherwise they will be implicated. For example, Emart Sheets was quality control director for Teddy's Frosted Foods, Inc., a frozen food producer. The company fired him after he reported to his boss that some of the company's vegetables were substandard and some meat products were underweight. The court held that his discharge was wrongful because, as director of quality control, he might have been prosecuted for violating Connecticut food labeling laws.[12]
- *When an Employee Is Not Involved in Illegal Activity*. The courts in some states will protect employees who disclose illegal activities even if they are not personally involved. An Illinois court held that International Harvester Co. could not fire an employee for telling law enforcement officials about a co-worker's criminal activities.[13] The outcome was different for Donald Smith, however. He had been employed by Calgon Carbon Corp. for his entire adult life, working his way up from floor sweeper to Supervisor of Warehouse and Inventory Control. He discovered that 73,000 pounds of caustic soda had spilled into the river next to the warehouse. His boss told him to ignore the spill, but Smith instead reported it to corporate headquarters. He was fired. The court held that, since Smith had no responsibility for reporting spills, the public's interest "in harmony and productivity in the workplace must prevail over the public's interest in encouraging an employee in Smith's position to express his 'informed view.'"[14]

For more information about the legal rights of whistleblowers, see **http://www.whistleblowers.org/**. The Web site at **http://www.whistleblower.org/**

[11] *Harman v. City of New York*, 140 F.3d 111, 1998 U.S. App. LEXIS 5567 (2d Cir. 1998).

[12] *Sheets v. Teddy's Frosted Foods, Inc.*, 179 Conn. 471, 427 A.2d 385, 1980 Conn. LEXIS 690 (1980).

[13] *Palmateer v. International Harvester Co.*, 85 Ill. 2d 124, 421 N.E.2d 876, 1981 Ill. LEXIS 282 (1981).

[14] *Smith v. Calgon Carbon Corp.*, 917 F.2d 1338, 1990 U.S. App. LEXIS 19193 (3rd Cir. 1990).

www/checklist.htm offers advice to those who are thinking about blowing the whistle.

Contract Law

Traditionally, many employers (and employees) thought that only a formal, signed document qualified as an employment contract. Increasingly, however, courts have been willing to enforce an employer's more casual promises, whether written or oral. Sometimes courts have also been willing to *imply* contract terms in the absence of an *express* agreement.

Truth in Hiring. **Oral promises made during the hiring process can be enforceable, even if not approved by the company's top executives.** When the Tanana Valley Medical-Surgical Group, Inc. hired James Eales as a physician's assistant, it promised him that as long as he did his job, he could stay there until retirement age. Six years later the company fired him without cause. The Alaska Supreme Court held that the clinic's promise was enforceable.[15]

When the Automobile Club of Michigan hired William J. Bullock as a salesman, his supervisor promised him lifetime employment as long as he did not steal company funds. Fourteen years later, Bullock was fired when he failed to meet new company sales quotas. He sued the club, alleging that it had breached the supervisor's 14-year-old promise. The auto club argued that the suit should be dismissed because policy statements in subsequent employee handbooks made clear that no employee jobs were guaranteed. The Michigan Supreme Court held that an employer's oral promise is enforceable even if contradicted by later written policies.[16]

In the cases of both Eales and Bullock, the employer could have kept its promise but chose not to. **Courts have also held employers liable when they make promises that they *cannot* keep.** An engineer recovered $160,000 after a defense contractor laid him off. When the firm had hired him, it did not tell him that its work on the B-2 bomber was being scaled back. The firm also had lied about how much of the company's work was defense related. Therefore the contractor was liable even though it had no work for the engineer to do. Victoria Stewart joined the New York law firm, Jackson & Nash, because it promised her a major environmental law client. The client never materialized, and the firm's efforts to obtain new clients failed. A court decided that she had a valid claim.[17]

Employee Handbooks. The employee handbook at Blue Cross & Blue Shield stated that employees could be fired only for just cause and then only after warnings, notice, a hearing, and other procedures. Charles Toussaint was fired summarily five years after he joined the insurance company. Although this decision was ultimately reviewed by the personnel department, company president, and chairman of the board of trustees, Toussaint was not given the benefit of all of the procedures in the handbook. The court held that **an employee handbook creates a contract.**[18]

Employers concerned about their potential liability for implied contracts are now taking steps to protect themselves. Some employers require new hires to sign a document acknowledging that (1) they are employees at will, (2) they can be terminated at any time for any reason, and (3) no one at the company has made any oral representations concerning the terms of employment. These employers caution

[15] *Eales v. Tanana Valley Medical-Surgical Group, Inc.*, 663 P.2d 958, 1983 Alas. LEXIS 430 (Alaska 1983).

[16] *Bullock v. Automobile Club of Michigan*, 432 Mich. 472, 444 N.W.2d 114, 1989 Mich. LEXIS 1411 (1989).

[17] *Stewart v. Jackson & Nash*, 976 F.2d 86, 1992 U.S. App. LEXIS 23373 (2d Cir. 1992).

[18] *Toussaint v. Blue Cross & Blue Shield*, 408 Mich. 579, 292 N.W.2d 880, 1980 Mich. LEXIS 227 (1980).

interviewers not to make promises. Their employee handbooks now feature stern legal warnings, rather than friendly welcomes.

Alternatively, some employers establish a "peer review" process to ensure workers are not fired for bad reasons. Ruth Hatton, who had worked for 19 years as a waitress at the Red Lobster chain, was fired for stealing a guest comment card. Within three weeks after she asked for a peer review, the company convened a panel consisting of two managers and three hourly workers to review the case. Hatton had pocketed the guest comment card of a couple after they complained that she was uncooperative and their prime rib was too rare. She testified that she had taken the meat back to the kitchen several times and had even offered the couple a free dessert. She also said that she had intended to show the card to her boss, but forgot. Although initially the panelists split by rank, with the hourly employees supporting Hatton, they eventually agreed unanimously to restore her job, but did not give her the three weeks' pay she had missed. Both sides were content with the outcome and avoided protracted litigation. Many companies mandate that, if the internal review process fails, the case must go to binding arbitration, not to court.

DaimlerChrysler instituted such a program of internal review and external arbitration for all nonunion salaried employees, including the chief executive officer. Nationally, more than half of all executive contracts require that disputes go to arbitration, not litigation.

Covenant of Good Faith and Fair Dealing. A covenant of good faith and fair dealing prohibits one party to a contract from interfering with the other's right to benefit under the contract. **In some cases, courts will imply a covenant of good faith and fair dealing in an at-will employment relationship.**

When Forrest Fleming went to work for Parametric Technology Corp., the company promised him valuable stock options if he met his sales goals. He would not be able to *exercise* the options (that is, purchase the stock), however, until several years after they were granted and then only if he was still employed by the company. During his four years with Parametric, Fleming received options to purchase about 18,000 shares for as little as 25 cents each. The shares ultimately traded in the market for as much as $50. Although Fleming exercised some options, the company fired him three months before he became eligible to purchase an additional 1,000 shares. The jury awarded him $1.6 million in damages. Although Parametric had not violated the explicit terms of the option agreement, the jury believed it had violated the covenant of good faith and fair dealing by firing Fleming to prevent him from exercising his remaining options.

Tort Law

Workers have successfully sued their employers under the following tort theories.

Defamation. **Employers may be liable for defamation when they give false and unfavorable references about a former employee.** John R. Glennon, Jr., was the branch manager of Dean Witter's Nashville office. Dean Witter fired him and filed a termination notice with the National Association of Securities Dealers saying that Glennon "was under internal review for violating investment-related statutes." This statement was untrue, and Witter had to pay $1.5 million in damages for defamation.

More than half of the states, however, recognize a qualified privilege for employers who give references about former employees. A **qualified privilege** means that employers are liable only for false statements that they know to be false or that are primarily motivated by ill will. After Becky Chambers left her job at American Trans Air, Inc., she discovered that her former boss was telling anyone who called for a reference that Chambers "does not work good with other people," is a "troublemaker," and "would not be a good person to rehire." Chambers was unable, however, to present compelling evidence that her boss had been primarily motivated by ill will. Neither Trans Air nor the boss was held liable for these statements because they were protected by the qualified privilege.[19]

Even if the employer wins, a trial is an expensive and time-consuming undertaking. Not surprisingly, companies are leery about offering any references for former employees. The company gains little benefit from giving an honest evaluation and may suffer substantial liability. As a matter of policy, many companies instruct their managers to reveal only a person's salary and dates of employment and not to offer an opinion on job performance. According to one survey, only 55 percent of former employers are totally honest when they give references.

Employers are afraid of liability if they give a negative reference, but are they liable if they tell less than the whole truth? Generally, courts have held that employers do not have a legal obligation to disclose information about former employees. For example, while Jeffrey St. Clair worked at the St. Joseph Nursing Home, he was disciplined 24 times for actions ranging from extreme violence to drug and alcohol use. When he applied for a job with Maintenance Management Corp. (MMC), St. Joseph refused to give any information other than St. Clair's dates of employment. When he savagely murdered a security guard at his new job, the guard's family sued, but the court dismissed the case.[20] In some recent cases, however, courts have held that, when a former worker is potentially dangerous, employers do have an obligation to disclose this information. For example, officials from two junior high schools gave Robert Gadams glowing letters of recommendation without mentioning that he had been fired for inappropriate sexual conduct with students. While an assistant principal at a new school, he molested a 13-year-old. Her parents sued the former employers. The court held that the writer of a letter of recommendation owes to third parties (in this case, the student) "a duty not to misrepresent the facts in describing the qualifications and character of a former employee, if making these misrepresentations would present a substantial, foreseeable risk of physical injury to the third persons."[21] As a result of cases such as this, it makes sense to disclose past violent behavior.

To assist employers who are asked for references, Lehigh economist Robert Thornton has written "The Lexicon of Intentional Ambiguous Recommendations" (LIAR). For a candidate with interpersonal problems, he suggests saying, "I am pleased to say that this person is a former colleague of mine." For the lazy worker, "In my opinion, you will be very fortunate to get this person to work for you." For the criminal, he suggests, "He's a man of many convictions" and "I'm sorry we let her get away." For the untrustworthy candidate, "Her true ability is deceiving."[22]

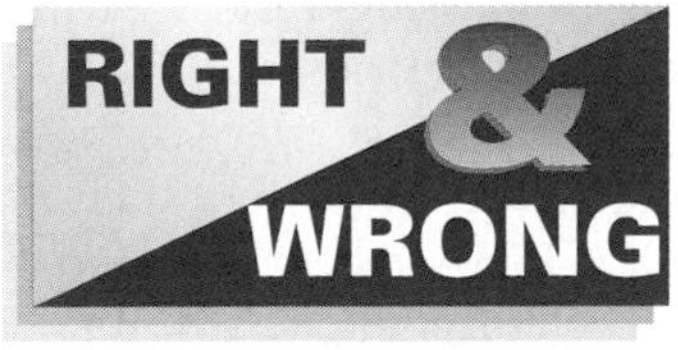

All joking aside, what if someone calls you to check references on a former employee who had a drinking problem? The job is driving a van for junior high school sports teams. What is the manager's ethical obligation in this situation? Many managers say that, in the case of a serious problem such as alcoholism, sexual harassment, or drug use, they will find a way to communicate that an employee is unsuitable. What if the ex-employee says she is reformed? Aren't people entitled to a second chance? Is it right to risk a defamation suit against your company to protect others from harm?

---

19 *Chambers v. American Trans Air, Inc.*, 577 N.E.2d 612, 1991 Ind. App. LEXIS 1413 (Ind. Ct. App. 1991).

20 *Moore v. St. Joseph Nursing Home, Inc.*, 184 Mich. App. 766, 459 N.W.2d 100, 1990 Mich. App. LEXIS 285 (Mich. Ct. App. 1990).

21 *Randi W. v. Muroc Joint Unified School District*, 14 Cal. 4th 1066, 929 P.2d 582, 1997 Cal. LEXIS 10 (1997), *modified*, 14 Cal. 4th 1282c, 97 Cal. Daily Op. Service 1439.

22 *Wall Street Journal*, Mar. 22, 1994, p. 1.

Intentional Infliction of Emotional Distress. Employers who condone cruel treatment of their workers face liability under the tort of intentional infliction of emotional distress. For example:

- When a 57-year-old social-work manager at Yale–New Haven Hospital was fired, she was forced to place her personal belongings in a plastic bag and was escorted out the door by security guards in full view of gaping co-workers. A supervisor told her that she would be arrested for trespassing if she returned. A jury awarded her $105,000.
- An employee swore at a co-worker and threatened her with a knife because she rejected his sexual advances. Her superiors fired her for complaining about the incident. A court held that the employer had inflicted emotional distress.[23]
- On the other hand, another court held that an employee who was fired for dating a co-worker did not have a valid claim for infliction of emotional distress.[24]

SAFETY AND PRIVACY IN THE WORKPLACE

WORKPLACE SAFETY

In 1970, Congress passed the Occupational Safety and Health Act (OSHA) to ensure safe working conditions. Under OSHA:

- Employers must comply with specific health and safety standards. For example, health care personnel who work with blood are not permitted to eat or drink in areas where the blood is kept and must not put their mouths on any instruments used to store blood. Protective clothing—gloves, gowns, and laboratory coats—must be impermeable to blood.
- Employers are under a general obligation to keep their workplace "free from recognized hazards that are causing or are likely to cause death or serious physical harm" to employees.
- Employers must keep records of all workplace injuries and accidents.
- The Occupational Safety and Health Administration (also known as OSHA) may inspect workplaces to ensure that they are safe. OSHA may assess fines for violations and order employers to correct unsafe conditions.

For most of its history, OSHA concentrated on manufacturing and construction businesses because 70 percent of reported workplace injuries occurred in these industries. But now only 40 percent of workplace injuries take place in these traditional industries, so OSHA has turned its focus to newer concerns, such as workplace violence and repetitive stress injuries (RSI). OSHA recently issued a report on workplace violence in late-night businesses (e.g., convenience stores and gas stations). The agency recommended that employers improve lighting, remove obstructive signs from windows, install video cameras, and hire two workers instead of one. As for RSI, OSHA now receives more than 322,000 case reports each year. In 1995, the agency issued a draft set of ergonomic standards aimed at preventing RSI, but the draft met so much resistance from employers that OSHA

---

[23] *Hogan v. Forsyth Country Club Co.*, 79 N.C. App. 483, 340 S.E.2d 116, 1986 N.C. App. LEXIS 2098 (N.C. Ct. App. 1986).

[24] *Patton v. J. C. Penney Co.*, 301 Or. 117, 719 P.2d 854, 1986 Ore. LEXIS 1144 (1986).

withdrew it. The agency recently announced new efforts to prepare ergonomic standards. When ready, these standards will be available on the OSHA ergonomic Web site (**http://www.osh.net/ergo.htm**).

EMPLOYEE PRIVACY

Upon opening the country's first moving assembly line 80 years ago, Henry Ford issued a booklet, "Helpful Hints and Advice to Employees," that warned against drinking, gambling, borrowing money, taking in boarders, and practicing poor hygiene. Ford also created a department of 100 investigators for door-to-door checks on his employees. The right to hire, fire, and make an honest profit is enshrined in American tradition. But so is the right to privacy. Justice Louis D. Brandeis called it the "right to be let alone—the most comprehensive of rights and the right most valued by civilized men."

Employers have a legitimate interest in increasing productivity and profits. With this goal in mind, some companies ban workplace romances for fear that they will upset other employees. Wal-Mart fired two employees for living together because one of them was married to someone else. The court upheld Wal-Mart's right to do so.[25]

In an era of rapidly expanding health care costs, employers are also concerned about the health of their workers. Some companies have banned *off-duty* smoking and have even fired employees who show traces of nicotine in their blood. But health—and privacy concerns—do not end with smoking. Some employers would prefer not to hire gay workers because AIDS treatments are so expensive. What protection do workers have against intrusive employers?

Off-Duty Conduct

At least 29 jurisdictions have passed laws that protect the right of employees to smoke cigarettes while off-duty. Some of these statutes permit *any* lawful activity when off-duty, including drinking socially, having high cholesterol, being overweight, or engaging in dangerous hobbies—bungee jumping or roller blading, for instance. Whether these statutes also protect extramarital sexual activity is unclear because in many states such behavior is illegal.

Alcohol and Drug Testing

Government employees can be tested for drug and alcohol use only if they show signs of use or if they are in a job where this type of abuse endangers the public. Most states permit private employers to administer alcohol and drug tests. According to one survey, more than 80 percent of large firms test employees for drugs.

Lie Detector Tests

Under the Employee Polygraph Protection Act of 1988, employers may not require, or even *suggest*, that an employee or job candidate submit to a lie detector test, except as part of an "on-going investigation" into crimes that have occurred.

Electronic Monitoring of the Workplace

Technological advances in communications have raised a host of new privacy issues.

---

[25] *State of New York v. Wal-Mart Stores, Inc.*, 621 N.Y.S. 2d 158, 1995 N.Y. App. Div. LEXIS 17 (N.Y. App. Div. 1995).

More than one-third of American companies monitor employee use of electronic equipment in the workplace: telephone calls, voice mail, e-mail, and Internet usage. **The Electronic Communications Privacy Act of 1986 (ECPA) permits employers to monitor workers' telephone calls and e-mail messages if (1) the employee consents, (2) the monitoring occurs in the ordinary course of business, or (3) in the case of e-mail, the employer provides the e-mail system.** However, bosses may not disclose any private information revealed by the monitoring.

About 15 percent of companies monitor their employees' e-mail (as compared with the 40 percent that listen to telephone conversations). Although workers may feel that their e-mail should be private, employers argue that this monitoring improves employee productivity and protects the company from lawsuits. For example, a West Coast company fired a woman "because of a tough economy." When she sued, her attorneys demanded access to the company's e-mail system as part of the discovery process. They found a message from the woman's supervisor saying, "Get that bitch out of here as fast as you can. I don't care what it takes. Just do it." The supervisor had long since erased the message from his computer, but it had remained buried in the system. A few hours after the message was revealed in court, the company settled for $250,000. If the employee had known that his e-mail would be read by others, perhaps he would not have sent such an inflammatory statement.

Many companies also monitor employee use of the Internet. They are concerned not only about lawsuits but also that workers may be wasting time. During one month, employees at IBM, Apple Computer, and AT&T logged on to *Penthouse* magazine's Web site 12,823 times, using the equivalent of more than 347 workdays. One company discovered that some of its employees were using their company computers to buy and sell child pornography. Companies fear that even legal logging on to sexually explicit sites may give rise to sexual harassment claims.

In the following case, two employees used company e-mail to trash talk. Could they be fired for their indiscretion?

MICHAEL A. SMYTH v. THE PILLSBURY CO.

914 F. Supp. 97, 1996 U.S. Dist. LEXIS 776
United States District Court for the Eastern District of Pennsylvania, 1996

Facts: The Pillsbury Co. repeatedly assured its employees that all company e-mail was confidential. The company promised not to intercept e-mail or use it against employees as grounds for reprimand or termination. One evening at home, Michael Smyth and his supervisor engaged in a series of e-mail exchanges that threatened to "kill the backstabbing bastards" (that is, company sales managers) and referred to the planned holiday party as the "Jim Jones Koolaid affair." The company found out about these e-mails and fired both men. Smyth sued, alleging that the company had violated his right to privacy.

You Be the Judge: Is company e-mail private?

Argument for Smyth: The public policy doctrine prohibits an employer from firing a worker for a reason that violates basic social rights, duties, or responsibilities. Privacy is a fundamental social right that tort law protects. There are two issues under tort law:

- Did Pillsbury intrude into Smyth's life in a manner that any reasonable person would find offensive?
- Did Smyth have a reasonable expectation of privacy?

The answer to both of these questions is a resounding, "Yes." Today, people use e-mail almost as often as the telephone. They correspond not only with co-workers but also with friends and family members. Sitting in the privacy of their office or home, they do not expect their employer to be reading their e-mail.

Particularly in this case, Smyth had a reasonable expectation of privacy. The company had told him repeatedly that it would not read his e-mail. How could the company make such a promise and then fire him because he believed it?

Argument for Pillsbury: Smyth behaved in an unprofessional and unacceptable manner. The company had no choice but to fire him after he made death threats against other employees. What if the company had done nothing and he had carried out those threats?

Furthermore, Smyth could not have a reasonable expectation of privacy with an e-mail system that the company established and maintained for the use of its employees. Nor would a reasonable person find this intrusion offensive. No one forced Smyth to share his feelings about the company; he wrote and sent those e-mail messages *voluntarily*. This juvenile and inappropriate behavior demonstrated that he is totally unsuited for employment at Pillsbury. He has no one to blame but himself.

FINANCIAL PROTECTION

Congress and the states have enacted laws that provide employees with a measure of financial security. All of the laws in this section were created by statute, not by the courts.

FAIR LABOR STANDARDS ACT

Passed in 1938, the Fair Labor Standards Act (FLSA) regulates wages and limits child labor. The wage provisions do not apply to managerial, administrative, or professional staff, which means that accounting, consulting, and law firms (among others) are free to require as many hours a week as their employees can humanly perform without having to pay overtime or the minimum wage.

Minimum Wage

The current federal minimum wage is $5.15 per hour, although some states have set a higher minimum. Employers can pay students and apprentices under age 20 a training wage of $4.25 per hour.

Overtime Pay

The FLSA does not limit the number of hours a week that an employee can work (or a student can study!), but it does specify that workers must be paid time and a half for any hours over 40 in one week.

Child Labor

The FLSA prohibits "oppressive child labor," which means that children under 14 may work only in agriculture and entertainment. Fourteen- and 15-year-olds are permitted to work *limited* hours after school in nonhazardous jobs. Sixteen- and 17-year-olds may work *unlimited* hours in nonhazardous jobs.

WORKERS' COMPENSATION

Workers' compensation statutes ensure that employees receive payment for injuries incurred at work. Before workers' comp, injured employees could recover damages only if they sued their employer. It is the brave (or carefree) worker who is willing to risk a suit against his own boss. Lawsuits poison the atmosphere at work. Moreover, employers frequently won these suits by claiming that (1) the injured worker was contributorily negligent, (2) a fellow employee had caused the accident, or (3) the injured worker had assumed the risk of injury. As a result, seriously injured workers (or their families) often had no recourse against the employer.

Workers' comp statutes provide a fixed, certain recovery to the injured employee, no matter who was at fault for the accident. In return, employees are not permitted to sue their employers for negligence. The amounts allowed (for medical expenses and lost wages) under workers' comp statutes are often less than a worker might recover in court, but the injured employee trades the certainty of some recovery for the higher risk of rolling the dice at trial. Payments are approved by an administrative board that conducts an informal hearing into each claim. These payments are funded either through the purchase of private insurance or by a tax on employers—a tax that is based on how many injuries their employees have suffered. Thus employers have an incentive to maintain a safe working environment.

As the following article indicates, however, employees who suffer particularly egregious injuries may prefer to sue in court rather than accept the relatively small payments available under workers' comp.

A 27-year-old assistant manager at Saks Fifth Avenue, who was raped twice by a security guard, filed a $50 million negligence suit against the swanky retailer. In its background check, the store had failed to discover that the guard had previously been convicted of sexual assault. Despite its apparent negligence, Saks asked to have the case dismissed on the grounds that the attack was covered by workers' comp. Such a ruling would limit damages to lost wages and medical expenses—far less than the $50 million the manager sought.

Saks little imagined the furor its defense would create. A New York congresswoman and a state senator drafted federal and state laws that would prohibit employers from using workers' comp statutes in sex crimes. The National Organization of Women threatened to boycott the store and asked top fashion designers to stop doing business with Saks. In the end, the retailer agreed to give the manager a "substantial cash payment" and to drop the workers' comp defense in any further sexual assault cases. Said Rep. Carolyn Maloney, "Employers have to stop using workers' comp as a shield when negligence in the workplace results in rape. It's a terribly sad day in America when rape is considered all in a day's work."

SOCIAL SECURITY

The federal Social Security system began in 1935, during the depths of the Great Depression, to provide a basic safety net for the elderly, ill, and unemployed. **Currently, the Social Security system pays benefits to workers who are retired, disabled, or temporarily unemployed and to the spouses and children of disabled or deceased workers.** It also provides medical insurance to the retired and disabled.

Before Social Security, breadlines were often the only safety net available to the unemployed.

The Social Security program is financed through a tax on wages that is paid by employers, employees, and the self-employed. Currently, employees pay a tax of 6.2 percent on their first $76,200 of income, and employers must match the employee's contribution. Since the self-employed have no boss to pay half the Social Security tax, they must pay both halves themselves.

Although the Social Security system has done much to reduce poverty among the elderly, many worry that it cannot survive in its current form. When workers pay taxes, the proceeds do not go into a savings account for their retirement, but instead are used to pay benefits to current retirees. In 1940, there were 40 workers for each retiree; currently, there are 3.3. By 2030, when the last baby boomers retire, there will be only 2 workers to support each retiree—a prohibitive burden. No wonder baby boomers are often cautioned not to count on Social Security when making their retirement plans.

The Federal Unemployment Tax Act (FUTA) is the part of the Social Security system that provides support to the unemployed. FUTA establishes some national standards, but states are free to set their own benefit levels and payment schedules. These payments are funded by a tax on employers. A worker who quits voluntarily or is fired for just cause is ineligible for benefits. While receiving payments, she must make a good faith effort to look for other employment.

PENSION BENEFITS

In 1974, Congress passed the Employee Retirement Income Security Act (ERISA) to protect workers covered by private pension plans. Under ERISA, employers are not required to establish pension plans, but if they do, they must follow these federal rules. The law was aimed, in particular, at protecting benefits of retired workers if their companies subsequently go bankrupt. The statute also prohibits risky investments by pension plans. In addition, the statute sets rules on the vesting of benefits. (An employer cannot cancel *vested* benefits; *nonvested* benefits are forfeited when the employee leaves.) Before ERISA, retirement benefits at some companies did not vest until the employee retired—if he quit or was fired before retirement, even after years of service, he lost his pension. Under current law, employee benefits vest after five years of employment.

EMPLOYMENT DISCRIMINATION

In the last four decades, Congress has enacted important legislation to prevent discrimination in the workplace.

EQUAL PAY ACT OF 1963

Under the Equal Pay Act, an employee may not be paid at a lesser rate than employees of the opposite sex for equal work. "Equal work" means tasks that require equal skill, effort, and responsibility under similar working conditions. If the employee proves that she is not being paid equally, the employer will be found liable unless the pay difference is based on merit, productivity, seniority, or some factor other than sex. A "factor other than sex" includes prior wages, training, profitability, performance in an interview, and value to the company. For example, female agents sued Allstate Insurance Co. because its salary for new agents was based, in part, on prior salary. The women argued that this system was unfair because it perpetuated the historic wage differences between men and women. The court, however, held for Allstate.[26]

Some employees have argued that equal pay for equal work is not enough to remedy the effects of past discrimination. They point to examples such as (female) librarians in Virginia who, with 10 years of experience and a master's degree, earn the same salary as (male) maintenance supervisors with a high school diploma. The solution, they argue, is **comparable worth**—equal pay for work of comparable value. Two people should be paid the same if their jobs, however different, require the same level of skill, education, and responsibility.

Supporters of comparable worth argue that traditional female occupations, such as nurse, teacher, waitress, and secretary, pay less than equivalent male jobs because of bias left over from the days of open discrimination against women. For instance, Westinghouse Corp. formerly had separate male and female job categories with corresponding wage rates. After the Equal Pay Act, the company kept female grades 1–5 in place and made the male jobs into grades 6–10, with higher wages. As a general rule, the more a job category is dominated by women, the less it pays.

---

[26] *Kouba v. Allstate Insurance Co.*, 691 F.2d 873, 1982 U.S. App. LEXIS 24479 (9th Cir. 1982).

Opponents of comparable worth argue that it would be a disastrous intrusion into the marketplace and would create economic chaos as courts, consultants, and managers struggled to assess the value of jobs. Only the market can set wages at an equilibrium between supply and demand. If librarians feel that janitors are overpaid, there is a simple solution—they should become janitors, too. Although some employers have agreed to undertake comparable worth studies to settle litigation, the courts have generally not been receptive to this concept. The Equal Pay Act does not require equal pay for work of comparable worth.

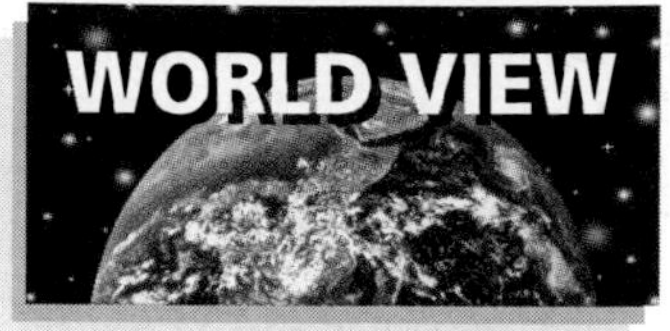

In the absence of overt discrimination, U.S. courts have by and large let market forces set wages. The European Union (EU) has taken a different approach. To reduce the wage disparities between men and women, it requires member countries to adopt comparable worth regulations. To implement a comparable worth pay plan, a company must determine the relative value of its jobs by conducting detailed evaluation studies that consider the skill, level of responsibility, physical and mental effort, and working conditions of each job.

TITLE VII

Title VII of the Civil Rights Act of 1964 prohibits employers from discriminating on the basis of race, color, religion, sex, or national origin. (The text of Title VII is available at http://www.eeoc.gov/laws/vii.html.) Originally, "sex" was not included in the statute, but two days before passage, Rep. Howard Smith of Virginia added this word. His intention was not to promote equal opportunity for women, but rather to scuttle the bill. He figured that nobody—but nobody—would vote for a statute that prohibited discrimination against women. He thought wrong, and the most important piece of antidiscrimination legislation in the United States passed.

Title VII prohibits (1) discrimination in the workplace, (2) sexual harassment, and (3) discrimination because of pregnancy. It also permits employers to develop affirmative action plans.

Proof of Discrimination

Discrimination under Title VII means firing, refusing to hire, failing to promote, or otherwise reducing a person's employment opportunities because of race, color, religion, sex, or national origin. This protection applies to every stage of the employment process from job ads to postemployment references and includes placement, wages, benefits, and working conditions.

Plaintiffs in Title VII cases can prove discrimination two different ways: disparate treatment and disparate impact.

Disparate Treatment. To prove a disparate treatment case, the plaintiff must show that she was *treated* differently because of her sex, race, color, religion, or national origin. The required steps in a disparate treatment case are:

Step 1. The plaintiff presents evidence that the defendant has discriminated against her because of a protected trait. This is called a *prima facie* case. The plaintiff is not required to prove discrimination; she need only create a *presumption* that discrimination occurred.

Step 2. The defendant must present evidence that its decision was based on *legitimate, nondiscriminatory* reasons.

Step 3. To win, the plaintiff must now prove that the employer discriminated. She may do so by showing that the reasons offered were simply a *pretext*.

Proving a case of disparate treatment is like a tennis match. Here is how the match goes:

1. The plaintiff serves the ball by making a ***prima facie*** case. That means she presents evidence that an employer has discriminated against her. At this point, she does not have to *prove* discrimination; she must simply produce evidence that could *indicate* discrimination. She does not have to ace the defendant at this stage; she simply has to put the ball in play. Suppose that Louisa applies for a job coaching a boys' high school ice hockey team. She was an All-American hockey star in college and made the U.S. National team. Although Louisa is obviously qualified for the job, Harry, the school principal, rejects her and continues to interview other people. This is not *proof* of discrimination, because Harry may have a perfectly good, nondiscriminatory explanation. However, his behavior could have been motivated by discrimination.
2. The ball is now in Harry's court. He must show a legitimate, nondiscriminatory reason for rejecting Louisa. He might say, for example, that he wanted someone with prior coaching experience. Although Louisa is clearly a great player whom he admires immensely, she has never coached before. This is a great return shot, and the ball is back in Louisa's court.
3. Louisa must now prove, by a preponderance of the evidence, that Harry's reason was simply a *pretext* for not hiring her. She might show that he had recently hired a male tennis coach who had no prior coaching experience. Or Harry's assistant might testify that Harry said, "No way I'm going to put a woman on the ice with those guys." If she can present evidence such as this, Louisa wins the point and match.

Disparate Impact. Disparate impact becomes an issue if the employer has a rule that, *on its face,* is not discriminatory, but *in practice* excludes too many people in a protected group. The steps in a disparate impact case are:

Step 1.	The plaintiff must present a *prima facie* case. The plaintiff is not required to prove discrimination; he need only show a disparate impact—that the employment practice in question excludes a disproportionate number of people in a protected group (women and minorities, for instance).
Step 2.	The defendant must show that the employment practice was job-related.
Step 3.	To win, the plaintiff must now prove either that the employer's reason is a pretext or that other, less discriminatory rules would achieve the same results.

Suppose that Harry will only hire teachers who are at least 5 feet 10 inches tall and weigh 170 pounds. He says he is afraid that students will literally push around anyone smaller. When Chou Ping, an Asian male, applies for a job, he cannot meet Harry's physical requirements. Here is what might happen in their legal contest:

1. Chou Ping must show that Harry's rule, *in fact,* eliminates more women or minorities than white males. He might offer evidence that 50 percent of all white males can meet Harry's standard, but only 20 percent of white women and Asian males qualify.
2. Harry must demonstrate that his rule is *job-related*. He might produce evidence, for example, that teachers are regularly expected to wrestle students

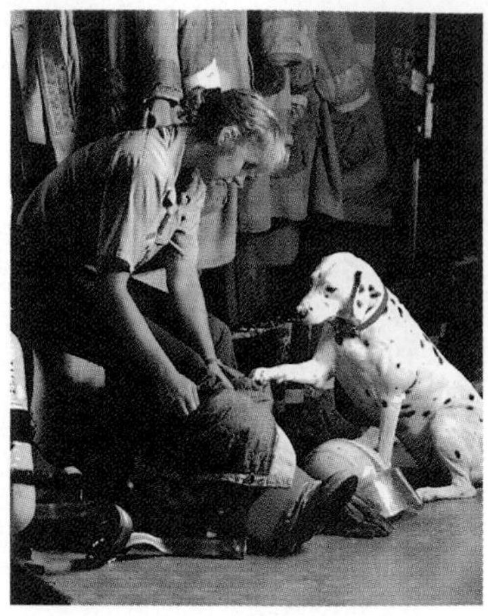

Does it matter if she is not as strong?

into their classroom seats. Further, he cites studies showing his standards are essential for this task.

3. Chou Ping will still win if he shows either that Harry's reason is a pretext or that other, less discriminatory rules would achieve the same results. Perhaps all teachers could take a self-defense course or engage in martial arts training.

Is Harry's reason valid? Compare his situation with a case involving firefighters. The city of Columbus, Ohio, required all applicants for firefighting jobs to take a written examination and a physical test. Nine percent of male applicants passed the physical test, compared with 2 percent of women. This evidence established a *prima facie* case. Columbus responded that physical skill was important for firefighters and the test was job-related. However, the city's own consultant had told it that four physical attributes are important for firefighters: strength, endurance, agility, and good health. The city's exam was a poor test of endurance and did not test agility at all. The court ordered the city to prepare a new physical exam that was job-related. The court explicitly stated that the city was not required to hire a quota of women; it was simply obligated to use a selection method that reasonably measured job performance.[27]

Religion

Employers must make *reasonable accommodation* for a worker's religious beliefs unless the request would cause *undue hardship* for the business. Scott Hamby told his manager at Wal-Mart that he could never work on Sunday because that was his Sabbath. It also happened to be one of the store's busiest days. When the manager forced Hamby to quit, he promptly sued on the grounds of religious discrimination. Lawsuits such as his are on the rise as more businesses remain open on Sundays. Wal-Mart denied wrongdoing but settled the case with a cash payment of undisclosed amount. It also established a company-wide training program on religious accommodation.

Defenses to Charges of Discrimination

Under Title VII, the defendant has three possible defenses.

Merit. A defendant is not liable if he shows that the person he favored was the most qualified. Test results, education, or productivity can all be used to demonstrate merit, provided they relate to the job in question. Harry can show that he hired Bruce instead of Louisa because Bruce has a master's degree in physical education and seven years of coaching experience. On the other hand, the fact that Bruce scored higher on the National Latin Exam in the eighth grade is not a good reason to hire him over Louisa.

Seniority. A legitimate seniority system is legal, even if it perpetuates past discrimination. Suppose that Harry has always chosen the most senior assistant coach to take over as head coach when a vacancy occurs. Since the majority of the senior assistant coaches are male, most of the head coaches are, too. Such a system does not violate Title VII.

Bona Fide Occupational Qualification. An employer is permitted to establish discriminatory job requirements if they are *essential* to the position in question. Such a requirement is called a **bona fide occupational qualification (BFOQ)**. Catholic schools may, if they choose, refuse to hire non-Catholic teachers; mail order companies may refuse to hire men to model women's clothing. Generally, however, courts are not sympathetic to claims of BFOQ. They have, for example, almost always rejected BFOQ claims that are based on customer preference. Thus airlines could not refuse to hire male flight attendants even though travelers pre-

---

[27] *Brunet v. City of Columbus*, 642 F. Supp. 1214, 1986 U.S. Dist. LEXIS 25574 (S.D. Ohio 1986).

fer female attendants.[28] The major exception to this customer preference rule is sexual privacy: an employer may refuse to hire women to work in a men's bathroom and vice versa.

The Hooters restaurant chain refused to hire male waiters, arguing that its customers preferred attractive, buxom young women in revealing uniforms. Hooters asserted that it hired only women because the primary function of a Hooters Girl was to "provide vicarious sexual recreation." The Equal Employment Opportunity Commission (EEOC) countered, however, that "no physical trait unique to women is required to serve food and drink to customers in a restaurant." It ordered Hooters to pay $10 million to the men who were denied jobs as waiters.[29] After a public outcry ensued, the EEOC withdrew its order. It stated that, since a group of men had filed a private lawsuit already, the commission would devote its resources to other cases. Hooters settled the private lawsuit for $3.75 million and a promise that it would create a few support jobs, such as bartender and host, that could be filled by men or women. The settlement allows Hooters to continue to hire a female staff of Hooters Girls.

Affirmative Action

Affirmative action has become a hot political issue: white males protest that such programs are reverse discrimination against them; political candidates campaign on anti-affirmative action platforms.

Affirmative action is not required by Title VII, nor is it prohibited. Affirmative action programs have three different sources:

- *Litigation*. Courts have the power under Title VII to order affirmative action to remedy the effects of past discrimination.
- *Voluntary Action*. Employers can voluntarily introduce an affirmative action plan to remedy the effects of past practices or to achieve equitable representation of minorities and women.
- *Government Contracts*. In 1965, President Johnson signed Executive Order 11246, which prohibits discrimination by federal contractors. This order had a profound impact on the American workplace because one-third of all workers are employed by companies that do business with the federal government. If an employer found that women or minorities were underrepresented in its workplace, it was required to establish goals and timetables to correct the deficiency. In 1995, however, the Supreme Court dramatically limited the extent to which the government can require contractors to establish affirmative action programs. The Court ruled that these programs are permissible only if they serve a "compelling national interest" and are "narrowly tailored" so that they minimize the harm to white males. The government must be able to show that (1) the programs are needed to overcome specific past discrimination, (2) they have time limits, and (3) nondiscriminatory alternatives are not available.[30] Vowing to "mend, not end" affirmative action, President Clinton directed administration officials to review all federal programs. As a result of this review, the administration eliminated or altered 17 affirmative action programs, leading to a sharp decrease in the number of federal contracts awarded to companies owned by women and minorities.

Despite concerns about affirmative action, a federal panel set up to study the progress made by women and minorities in American industry found that white

---

[28] *Diaz v. Pan American World Airways, Inc.*, 442 F.2d 385, 1971 U.S. App. LEXIS 10920 (5th Cir. 1971).

[29] As discussed below, under Title VII the EEOC has the right to file suit on behalf of a plaintiff.

[30] *Adarand Constructors, Inc. v. Pena*, 515 U.S. 200, 115 S. Ct. 2097, 1995 U.S. LEXIS 4037 (1995).

males constitute 29 percent of the workforce, but hold 95 percent of senior management positions.

Sexual Harassment

When Professor Anita Hill accused Supreme Court nominee Clarence Thomas of sexually harassing her, people across the country were glued to their televisions, watching the Senate hearings on her charges. Thomas was ultimately confirmed to the Supreme Court, but "sexual harassment" became a household phrase. The number of cases—and the size of the damage awards—sky-rocketed. In 1997, more than 15,000 sexual harassment charges were filed.

Everyone has heard of sexual harassment, but few people know exactly what it is. Men fear that a casual comment or glance will be met with career-ruining charges; women claim that men "just don't get it." So what is sexual harassment anyway? **Sexual harassment involves unwelcome sexual advances, requests for sexual favors, and other verbal or physical conduct of a sexual nature.** There are two major categories of sexual harassment: (1) *quid pro quo* and (2) hostile work environment.

Quid Pro Quo. From a Latin phrase that means "this for that," *quid pro quo* harassment occurs if any aspect of a job is made contingent upon sexual activity. In other words, when a banker says to a secretary, "You can be promoted to teller if you sleep with me," that is *quid pro quo* sexual harassment.

Hostile Work Environment. This is a more subtle claim and the one that managers worry about most. An employee has a valid claim of sexual harassment if sexual talk and innuendo are so pervasive that they interfere with her (or his) ability to work. Courts have found that offensive jokes, comments about clothes or body parts, and public displays of pornographic pictures create a hostile environment. In the following case, the company president repeatedly insulted and demeaned his female employees.

TERESA HARRIS v. FORKLIFT SYSTEMS, INC.
510 U.S. 17, 114 S. Ct. 367, 1993 U.S. LEXIS 7155
United States Supreme Court, 1993

Facts: Teresa Harris was a manager at Forklift Systems; Charles Hardy was its president. Hardy frequently made inappropriate sexual comments to Harris and other women at the company. For example, he said to Harris, in the presence of others, "You're a woman, what do you know?" and "We need a man as the rental manager." He called her "a dumb ass woman" and suggested that the two of them "go to the Holiday Inn to negotiate her raise." He also asked Harris and other female employees to get coins from his front pants pocket. He insisted that Harris and other women pick up objects he had thrown on the ground. When Harris complained to Hardy, he apologized and claimed he was only joking. A month later, while Harris was arranging a deal with one of Forklift's customers, he asked her, in front of other employees, "What did you do, promise the guy some sex Saturday night?"

Harris sued Forklift, claiming that Hardy had created an abusive work environment. The federal trial court ruled against Harris on the grounds that Hardy's comments might offend a reasonable woman, but they were not severe enough to have a serious impact on Harris's psychological well-being. The appeals court confirmed, and the Supreme Court granted certiorari.

Issue: To be a violation of Title VII, must sexual harassment seriously affect the employee's psychological well-being?

Excerpts from Justice O'Connor's Decision: Title VII of the Civil Rights Act of 1964 makes it "an unlawful employment practice for an employer to discriminate against any individual with respect to his compensation, terms, conditions, or privileges of employment, because of such individual's race, color, religion, sex, or national origin." As we made clear in [a prior case] this language "is not limited to 'economic' or 'tangible' discrimination. The phrase 'terms, conditions, or privileges of employment' evinces a congressional intent 'to strike at the entire spectrum of disparate treatment of men and women in employment'," which includes requiring people to work in a discriminatorily hostile or abusive environment. When the workplace is permeated with "discriminatory intimidation, ridicule, and insult," that is "sufficiently severe or pervasive to alter the conditions of the victim's employment and create an abusive working environment," Title VII is violated.

This standard, which we reaffirm today, takes a middle path between making actionable any conduct that is merely offensive and requiring the conduct to cause a tangible psychological injury. As we pointed out in [the prior case], "mere utterance of an epithet which engenders offensive feelings in an employee," does not sufficiently affect the conditions of employment to implicate Title VII. Conduct that is not severe or pervasive enough to create an objectively hostile or abusive work environment—an environment that a reasonable person would find hostile or abusive—is beyond Title VII's purview. Likewise, if the victim does not subjectively perceive the environment to be abusive, the conduct has not actually altered the conditions of the victim's employment, and there is no Title VII violation.

But Title VII comes into play before the harassing conduct leads to a nervous breakdown. A discriminatorily abusive work environment, even one that does not seriously affect employees' psychological well-being, can and often will detract from employees' job performance, discourage employees from remaining on the job, or keep them from advancing in their careers. Moreover, even without regard to these tangible effects, the very fact that the discriminatory conduct was so severe or pervasive that it created a work environment abusive to employees because of their race, gender, religion, or national origin offends Title VII's broad rule of workplace equality.

We therefore believe the [trial court] erred in relying on whether the conduct "seriously affected plaintiff's psychological well-being" or led her to "suffer injury." Certainly Title VII bars conduct that would seriously affect a reasonable person's psychological well-being, but the statute is not limited to such conduct. So long as the environment would reasonably be perceived, and is perceived, as hostile or abusive . . . there is no need for it also to be psychologically injurious.

Employees who commit sexual harassment are liable for their own misdeeds. But is their company also liable? The Supreme Court has held that:

- If the victimized employee has suffered a "tangible employment action" such as firing, demotion, or reassignment, the company is liable to her for sexual harassment by a supervisor.

- If the victimized employee has not suffered a tangible employment action, the company is not liable if it can prove that (1) it used reasonable care to prevent and correct sexually harassing behavior, and (2) the employee unreasonably failed to take advantage of the complaint procedure or other preventive opportunities provided by the company.[31]

---

[31] *Burlington Industries, Inc. v. Ellerth*, 524 U.S. 742, 118 S. Ct. 2257, 1998 U.S. LEXIS 4217 (1998); *Faragher v. Boca Raton*, 524 U.S. 775, 118 S. Ct. 2275, 1998 U.S. LEXIS 4216 (1998).

Corning Consumer Products Co. asks its employees to apply four tests in determining whether their behavior constitutes sexual harassment:

- Would you say or do this in front of your spouse or parents?
- What about in front of a colleague of the opposite sex?
- Would you like your behavior reported in your local newspaper?
- Does it need to be said or done at all?

Procedures and Remedies

Before a plaintiff in a Title VII case brings suit, she must first file a complaint with a federal agency, the Equal Employment Opportunity Commission (EEOC). (The EEOC's Web site is **http://www.eeoc.gov/**.) The EEOC then has the right to sue on behalf of the plaintiff. This is a favorable arrangement for the plaintiff because the government pays the legal bill. If the EEOC decides *not* to bring the case, or does not make a decision within six months, it issues a **right to sue letter**, and the plaintiff may proceed on her own in court. The number of employment discrimination cases more than doubled between 1992 and 1996 (from 10,000 to 23,000). At the same time, the EEOC dramatically decreased the number of lawsuits that it filed—from 322 in 1995 to 161 in 1996. Many states also have their own version of the EEOC, but these state commissions are often understaffed.

Remedies available to the successful plaintiff include hiring, reinstatement, retroactive seniority, back pay, reasonable attorney's fees, and punitive damages of up to $300,000.

Pregnancy

Under the Pregnancy Discrimination Act of 1978, an employer may not fire or refuse to hire a woman because she is pregnant. An employer must also treat pregnancy as any other temporary disability. If, for example, employees are allowed time off from work for other medical disabilities, women must also be allowed a maternity leave. The United States, Australia, and New Zealand are the only industrialized nations that do not require employers to provide paid maternity leave.

AGE DISCRIMINATION

The Age Discrimination in Employment Act (ADEA) of 1967 prohibits age discrimination against employees or job applicants who are at least 40 years old. An employer may not fire, refuse to hire, fail to promote, or otherwise reduce a person's employment opportunities because he is 40 or older. Under this statute, an employer may not require a worker to retire at any age. Police and top-level corporate executives are exempted from the retirement rules, so they may indeed be forced to retire at a certain age.

The procedure for an age-bias claim is similar to that under Title VII—plaintiffs must first file a charge with the EEOC. If the EEOC does not take action, they can file suit themselves.

In the following case, Sears did not actually *fire* the employees; it simply made work so unpleasant for them that they quit. In the eyes of the law, that is as bad as terminating them.

JAMES v. SEARS, ROEBUCK & CO.

21 F.3d 989, 1994 U.S. App. LEXIS 7073
United States Court of Appeals for the Tenth Circuit, 1994

Facts: Sears offered the employees in its Ogden, Utah retail store and service center a buy-out. Employees who agreed to quit would receive a week of severance pay for each year they had worked at Sears, up to 26 weeks. At the same time, Sears also offered early retirement to employees 50 years of age or older. Employees accepting early retirement *lost* 35 percent of their accrued pension.

Sears made it clear to the plaintiffs, all of whom were over 50, that if they did not accept the offer, a pretext would be found for firing them. Although the plaintiffs were top sellers, their supervisors threatened, pressured, and systematically "wrote them up" for failing to meet sales quotas that other salespeople almost never met. An internal Sears' document showed that the company expected 13 older employees, but no employees under 40, to leave under the retirement/buy-out plan. A jury found that the company had discriminated against the plaintiffs on the basis of age. The company appealed.

Issue: **Did Sears discriminate against its employees because of their age?**

Excerpts from Judge Brorby's Decision: The facts before the jury presented either an ill-conceived and poorly executed corporate efficiency move or a deliberate corporate attempt to reduce payroll costs by replacing experienced and well-paid workers 40 years of age or older with lesser experienced and lower paid, younger workers.

A perceived demotion or reassignment to a job with lower status or lower pay may, depending upon the individual facts of the case, constitute aggravating factors that would justify a finding of constructive discharge. ["Constructive discharge" means forcing someone to quit. It is the legal equivalent of firing someone.] An offer of early retirement may constitute constructive discharge if the employee demonstrates each choice facing the employee makes him worse off, and if he refuses the offer and decides to stay, his employer will treat him less favorably than other employees because of age. Therefore, the record fully supports the jury's finding of constructive discharge of the retail store Plaintiffs.

Sears told some nontargeted employees they could retain their assignments when they were offered the buy-out. Sears cut only the jobs of the two oldest, full-time clerical employees of the center, while it hired part-time, predominantly younger clerical employees shortly afterwards.

The jury heard sufficient evidence to infer Sears' reasons were pretextual and the real reason for Sears' actions was the Plaintiffs' ages. Accordingly, we affirm its findings of age discrimination and constructive discharge.

Oliver Wendell Holmes, Jr., one of the greatest Supreme Court Justices of the twentieth century, was 61 when appointed to the high court. He served with distinction for over 30 years.

During a recession in the early 1990s, companies felt great pressure to lower costs. They were sometimes tempted to replace older, higher paid workers with younger, less expensive employees. Courts traditionally held that replacing expensive, older workers with cheaper, younger ones was illegal discrimination under the ADEA. Indeed, in the *Sears* case above, the court castigated the company for its "deliberate corporate attempt to reduce payroll costs by replacing experienced and well-paid workers 40 years of age or older with lesser experienced and lower paid, younger workers." In some recent cases, however, courts have held that an employer is entitled to prefer *lower paid* workers even if that preference results in the company also choosing *younger* workers. As the court put it in one case, "An action based on price differentials represents the very quintessence of a legitimate business decision."[32] The Supreme Court has not ruled on

[32] *Marks v. Loral Corp.*, 57 Cal. App. 4th 30, 1997 Cal. App. LEXIS 611 (Cal. Ct. App. 1997).

this issue directly, but it has suggested that the primary goal of the ADEA is to prevent employment decisions based on stereotypes about the productivity and competence of older workers. Policies that have the effect of treating older people more harshly do not violate the law as long as the employer is wholly motivated by factors other than age.[33]

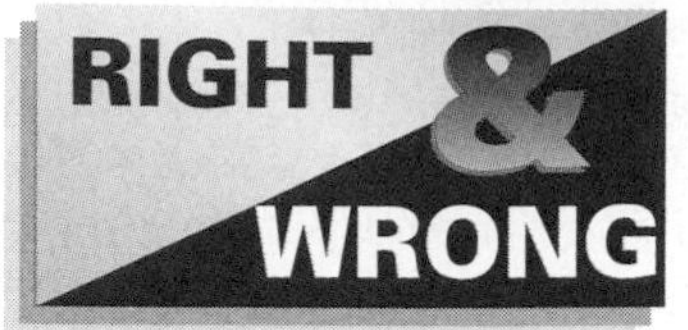

A court summed up the age discrimination dilemma thus:

> We are not unmindful of the pain attendant with the loss of any job, particularly when the loss is sustained by an older worker for whom retraining may be more difficult. [W]e are [also] not unmindful that the image of some newly minted whippersnapper MBA who tries to increase corporate profits—and his or her own compensation—by across-the-board layoffs is not a pretty one. Even so, [Congress never] intended the age discrimination laws to inhibit the very process by which a free market economy—decision making on the basis of cost—is conducted and by which, ultimately, real jobs and wealth are created.[34]

Apart from legal issues, does a "newly minted whippersnapper MBA" (or any other manager) have an ethical obligation to older employees for whom opportunities may be limited? How would you want to be treated when you are old?

AMERICANS WITH DISABILITIES ACT

Passed in 1990, the Americans with Disabilities Act (ADA) prohibits employers from discriminating on the basis of disability. (The text of the ADA is available at **http://www.eeoc.gov/laws/ada.html**. The Justice Department's ADA home page is **http://www.usdoj.gov/crt/ada/adahom1.htm**.) As with Title VII, a plaintiff under the ADA must first file a charge with the EEOC. If the EEOC decides not to file suit, the individual may do so himself.

A disabled person is someone with a physical or mental impairment that substantially limits a major life activity, or someone who is regarded as having such an impairment. This definition includes the mentally ill, the blind, epileptics, dyslexics, AIDS patients, and *recovered* drug addicts and alcoholics. It does not cover people with sexual disorders, pyromania, exhibitionism, homosexuality, or compulsive gambling.

An employer may not disqualify an employee or job applicant because of disability as long as she can, with *reasonable accommodation*, perform the *essential functions* of the job. An accommodation is not reasonable if it would create *undue hardship* for the employer. In one case, a court held that a welder who could perform 88 percent of a job was doing the essential functions. Reasonable accommodation includes buying necessary equipment, providing readers or interpreters, or permitting a part-time schedule. In determining undue hardship, *relative* cost, not *absolute* cost, is the issue. Even an expensive accommodation—such as hiring a full-time reader—is not considered an undue hardship unless it imposes a significant burden on the overall finances of the company.

An employer may not ask about disabilities before making a job offer. The interviewer may ask only whether an applicant can perform the work. Nor can an employer require applicants to take a medical exam unless the exam is (1) job-related and (2) required of all applicants for similar jobs. However, drug testing is permitted. After a job offer has been made, an employer may require a medical test, but it must be related to the *essential functions* of the job. For example, an

---

[33] *Hazen Paper Co. v. Biggins*, 507 U.S. 604, 113 S. Ct. 1701, 1993 U.S. LEXIS 2978 (1993).

[34] *Marks, supra*, note 32.

employer could not test the cholesterol of someone applying for an accounting job because high cholesterol is no impediment to good accounting.

An employer may not discriminate against someone because of his *relationship* with a disabled person. For example, an employer cannot refuse to hire an applicant because he has a child with Down's syndrome or a spouse with cancer.

In 1997, the EEOC issued rules on the treatment of mental disabilities. These rules were based on an assumption of parity—that physical and mental disabilities should be treated the same. The difficulty is that physical ailments such as diabetes and deafness may be easy to diagnose, but what does a supervisor do when an employee is chronically late, rude, or impulsive? Does this mean the worker is mentally disabled or just a lazy, irresponsible jerk? Among other accommodations, the EEOC rules indicated that employers should be willing to put up barriers to isolate people who have difficulty concentrating, provide detailed day-to-day feedback to those who need greater structure in performing their jobs, or allow workers on antidepressants to come to work later if they are groggy in the morning.

Although these rules are still new, early signs indicate that the courts are not as accommodating of mental illness as the EEOC. In one case, for example, an engineer had been criticized for his "negative attitude." Later his supervisor warned him that he might be terminated if his behavior did not improve. He then told the company that the warning had caused him to be depressed, which, in turn, affected his ability to interact with other people. He asked, as a special accommodation, that he be assigned to clerical work that did not require him to run meetings. The company fired him. Although EEOC guidelines state that interacting with others is a major life activity, the court held that it is not. Therefore the engineer was not disabled for purposes of the ADA.[35]

While lauding the ADA's objectives, many managers have been apprehensive about its impact on the workplace. On the plus side, they acknowledge that society is clearly better off if every member has the opportunity to work. And as advocates for the disabled point out, we are all, at best, only temporarily able-bodied.

It also turns out that the costs of complying with the ADA have been far less than managers originally feared. One survey found that the median cost per disabled employee is $233. Sears, Roebuck & Co. is committed to employing the disabled, and its workforce includes people with a wide range of disabilities. Yet most of the company's accommodations have cost little or nothing. Sears allowed an employee recovering from foot surgery to wear sneakers on the sales floor. The company purchased a $250 ergonomic chair for a worker with a sore back. In contrast, Sears must spend roughly $2,000 to terminate and replace an employee.

When cases go to litigation, employers win about 90 percent of the time. Workers are caught in something of a legal Catch-22: they must prove that they can perform the essential functions of the job, but they must also show that their disability limits a major life activity. Employees have filed tens of thousands of complaints, however, so many legal question marks remain. In the end, the courts must do a sensitive job of balancing the needs of the disabled with the rights of managers to run a profitable business.

Every applicant feels slightly apprehensive before a job interview, but now the interviewer may be even more nervous—fearing that every question is a potential land mine of liability. Most interviewers (and students who have read this chapter) would know better than Delta Airlines interviewers who allegedly asked applicants about their sexual preference, birth control methods, and abortion history.

[35] *Soileau v. Guildford of Maine*, 105 F.3d 12, 1997 U.S. App. LEXIS 1171 (1st Cir. 1997).

Don't Even Consider Asking	Go Ahead and Ask
Can you perform this function with or without reasonable accommodation?	Would you need reasonable accommodation in this job?
How many days were you sick last year?	How many days were you absent from work last year?
What medications are you currently taking?	Are you currently using drugs illegally?
Where were you born?	Are you authorized to work in the United States?
How old are you?	What work experience have you had?
When did you graduate from college?	Where did you go to college?
How did you learn this language?	What languages do you speak and write fluently?
Have you ever been arrested?	Have you ever been convicted?
Do you plan to have children? How old are your children? What method of birth control do you use?	Can you work weekends? Travel extensively?
What is your corrected vision?	Do you have 20/20 corrected vision?
Are you a man or a woman? Are you single or married? What does your spouse do? What will happen if your spouse is transferred? What clubs, societies, or lodges do you belong to?	Leave well enough alone!

The most common gaffe on the part of interviewers? Asking women about their child-care arrangements. That question assumes the woman is responsible for child care. The list above provides guidelines for interviewers.

CHAPTER CONCLUSION

Although managers sometimes feel overwhelmed by the long list of laws that protect workers, the United States guarantees its workers fewer rights than virtually any other industrialized nation. For instance, Japan, Britain, France, Germany, and Canada all require employers to show just cause before terminating workers. Although American employers are no longer insulated from minimum standards of fairness, reasonable behavior, and compliance with important policies, they still have great freedom to manage their employees.

Chapter Review

1. The traditional common law rule of employment provided that an employee at will could be fired for a good reason, a bad reason, or no reason at all.
2. The National Labor Relations Act prohibits employers from penalizing workers for union activity.
3. The Family and Medical Leave Act guarantees workers up to 12 weeks of unpaid leave each year for childbirth, adoption, or medical emergencies for themselves or a family member.
4. An employer who fires a worker for a *bad* reason is liable under a theory of wrongful discharge.
5. Oral promises made during the hiring process may be enforceable, even if not approved by the company's top executives. An employee handbook may create a contract.
6. The goal of the Occupational Safety and Health Act is to ensure safe conditions in the workplace.
7. The Fair Labor Standards Act regulates minimum and overtime wages. It also limits child labor.
8. Workers' compensation statutes ensure that employees receive payment for injuries incurred at work.
9. The Social Security system pays benefits to workers who are retired, disabled, or temporarily unemployed and to the spouses and children of disabled or deceased workers.
10. The Employee Retirement Income Security Act regulates private pension plans.
11. The Equal Pay Act prohibits an employer from considering the gender of a worker when setting compensation.
12. Title VII of the Civil Rights Act of 1964 prohibits employers from discriminating on the basis of race, color, religion, sex, or national origin.
13. The Age Discrimination in Employment Act prohibits age discrimination against employees or job applicants who are age 40 or older.
14. The Americans with Disabilities Act prohibits employers from discriminating on the basis of disability.

Practice Test

1. When Theodore Staats went to his company's "Council of Honor Convention," he was accompanied by a woman who was not his wife although he told everyone she was. The company fired him. Staats alleged that his termination violated public policy because it infringed upon his freedom of association. He also alleged that he had been fired because he was too successful—his commissions were so high, he outearned even the highest paid officer of the company. Has Staat's employer violated public policy?

2. This article appeared in the *Wall Street Journal*:

> When Michelle Lawrence discovered she was pregnant, she avoided telling Ron Rogers, the owner of the Los Angeles public relations agency where she worked as manager of media relations. "I had heard he wasn't

> crazy about pregnant women," she says. Instead, she asked her immediate supervisor to pass along the news. Mr. Rogers didn't speak to her for a week. His first comment was, "Congratulations on your pregnancy. My sister vomited for months." A few weeks later, Ms. Lawrence was fired. Mr. Rogers told her the business was shifting away from her area of expertise.[36]

Does Lawrence have a valid claim against Rogers? Under what law?

3. Reginald Delaney managed a Taco Time restaurant in Portland, Oregon. Some of his customers told Mr. Ledbetter, the district manager, that they would not be eating there so often because there were too many black employees. Ledbetter told Delaney to fire Ms. White, who was black. Delaney did as he was told. Ledbetter's report on the incident said: "My notes show that Delaney told me that White asked him to sleep with her and that when he would not that she started causing dissension within the crew. She asked him to come over to her house and that he declined." Delaney refused to sign the report because it was untrue, so Ledbetter fired him. What claim might Delaney make against his former employer?

4. When Walton Weiner interviewed for a job with McGraw-Hill, Inc., he was assured that the company would not terminate an employee without "just cause." Weiner also signed a contract specifying that his employment would be subject to the provisions of McGraw-Hill's handbook. The handbook said, "[The] company will resort to dismissal for just and sufficient cause only, and only after all practical steps toward rehabilitation or salvage of the employee have been taken and failed. However, if the welfare of the company indicates that dismissal is neccessary, then that decision is arrived at and is carried out forthrightly." After eight years, Weiner was fired suddenly for "lack of application." Does Weiner have a valid claim against McGraw-Hill?

5. RIGHT & WRONG John Mundorf hired three women to work for Gus Construction Co. as traffic controllers at road construction sites in Iowa. Male members of the construction crew incessantly referred to the women as "f—king flag girls." They repeatedly asked the women if they "wanted to f—k" or engage in oral sex. One crew member held a woman up to the cab window so other men could touch her. Another male employee exposed himself to the women. Male employees also urinated in a woman's water bottle and the gas tank of her car. Mundorf, the supervisor, was present during some of these incidents. He talked to crew members about their conduct, but the abuse soon resumed and continued until the women quit. What claim might the women make against their co-workers? Is Gus Construction Co. liable for the acts of its employees? What procedure must the women follow to pursue their claim? Why do you think these men behaved this way? Why did they want to humiliate their co-workers? What should the supervisor have done when he observed these incidents? What would you have done if you were the supervisor? A fellow employee?

6. CPA QUESTION An unemployed CPA generally would receive unemployment compensation benefits if the CPA:

(a) Was fired as a result of the employer's business reversals

(b) Refused to accept a job as an accountant while receiving extended benefits

(c) Was fired for embezzling from a client

(d) Left work voluntarily without good cause

7. Debra Agis worked in a Ground Round restaurant. The manager, Roger Dionne, informed the waitresses that "there was some stealing going on." Until he found out who was doing it, he intended to fire all the waitresses in alphabetical order, starting with the letter "A." Dionne then fired Agis. Does she have a valid claim against her employer?

8. The Duke Power Co. refused to transfer any employees at its generating plant to better jobs unless they had a high school diploma or could pass an intelligence test. The company was willing to pay two-thirds of the tuition for an employee's high school training. Neither a high school education nor the intelligence test was significantly related to successful job performance. Both requirements disqualified African Americans at a substantially higher rate than white applicants. Is the company in violation of Title VII?

9. The Lillie Rubin boutique in Phoenix would not permit Dick Kovacic to apply for a job as a salesperson. It only hired women to work in sales because fit-

---

[36] Sue Shellenbarger, "As More Pregnant Women Work, Bias Complaints Rise," *Wall Street Journal*, Dec. 6, 1993, p. B1. Republished with permission of The Wall Street Journal; permission conveyed through the Copyright Clearance Center, Inc.

tings and alterations took place in the dressing room or immediately outside. The customers were buying expensive clothes and demanded a male-free dressing area. Has the Lillie Rubin store violated Title VII? What would its defense be?

10. **YOU BE THE JUDGE WRITING PROBLEM** Nationwide Insurance Co. circulated a memorandum asking all employees to lobby in favor of a bill that had been introduced in the Pennsylvania House of Representatives. By limiting the damages that an injured motorist could recover from a person who caused an accident, this bill would have saved Nationwide significant money. Not only did John Novosel refuse to lobby, but he privately criticized the bill for harming consumers. Nationwide was definitely not on his side—it fired him. Novosel filed suit, alleging that his discharge had violated public policy by infringing his right to free speech. Did Nationwide violate public policy by firing Novosel? **Argument for Novosel:** The United States Constitution and the Pennsylvania Constitution both guarantee the right to free speech. Nationwide has violated an important public policy by firing Novosel for expressing his opinions. **Argument for Nationwide:** For all the high-flown talk about the Constitution, what we have here is an employee who refused to carry out company policy. If the employee prevails in this case, where will it all end? What if an employee for a tobacco company refuses to market cigarettes because he does not approve of smoking? How can businesses operate without loyalty from their employees?

11. When Thomas Lussier filled out a Postal Service employment application, he did not admit that he had twice pleaded guilty to charges of disorderly conduct. Lussier suffered from Post Traumatic Stress Disorder (PTSD) acquired during military service in Vietnam. Because of this disorder, he sometimes had panic attacks that required him to leave meetings. He was also a recovered alcoholic and drug user. During his stint with the Postal Service, he had some personality conflicts with other employees. Once another employee hit him. He also had one episode of "erratic emotional behavior and verbal outburst." In the meantime, a postal employee in Ridgewood, New Jersey, killed four colleagues. The Postmaster General encouraged all supervisors to identify workers who had dangerous propensities. Lussier's boss discovered that he had lied on his employment application about the disorderly conduct charges and fired him. Is the Postal Service in violation of the law?

Internet Research Problem

At **http://www.disgruntled.com/dishome.html**, employees tell how and why they were fired. If these employees filed a lawsuit, would they win? Under what legal theory?

You can find further practice problems in the Online Quiz at http://beatty.westbuslaw.com or in the Study Guide that accompanies this text.

CHAPTER 31

LABOR LAW

A strike! For five weeks the union workers have been walking picket lines at JMJ, a manufacturer of small electrical engines. An entire town of 70,000 citizens, most of them blue-collar workers, is sharply divided, right down to the McNally kitchen table. Buddy, age 48, has worked on the assembly lines at JMJ for more than 25 years. Now he's sipping coffee in the house where he grew up. His sister Kristina, age 46, is a vice-president for personnel at JMJ. The two have always been close. In high school, Kristina idolized her older brother, the football and track star. Buddy was immensely proud of his kid sister's academic triumphs, boasting to the world that she would "be the first lady president." Today, though, conversation is halting.

"It's time to get back together, Buddy," Kristina murmurs. "The strike is hurting the whole company—and the town."

"Not the *whole* town, Kristina," he tries to quip lightly. "Your management pals still have fat incomes and nice houses."

"Oh yeah?" she attempts to joke, "you haven't seen our porch lately."

"Go talk to Tony Falcione," Buddy replies. "He can't pay his rent."

"Talk to the Ericksons," Kristina snaps back, "they don't even work for JMJ. Their sandwich shop is going under because none of you guys stop in for lunch. Come back to work."

"Never. Not with that clause on the table."

That clause is management's proposal for the new union contract—one that Kristina helped draft. The company officers want the right to subcontract work, that is, to send it out for other companies to perform.

"Buddy, we need the flexibility. K-Ball is underselling us by 35 percent. If we can't compete, there won't be *any* jobs or *any* contract!"

"The way to save money is not by sending our jobs overseas, where a bunch of foreigners will work for 50 bucks a month."

"O.K., fine. Tell me how we *should* save money."

"Kristina, I really do not know how you can sit at this table and say these things—in this household. You never would have got a fancy college degree if Dad hadn't made union wages."

"If we can't sell motors to Latin America, we're out of business. *Then* what's your union going to do for you? All we're asking is the right to subcontract some of the smallest components. Everything else gets built here."

"This is just the start. Next it'll be the wiring, then the batteries, then you'll assemble the whole thing over there—and that'll be it for me. You take that clause off the table, we'll be back in 15 minutes."

"Never."

Buddy stands up. They stare silently, sadly, at each other, and then Kristina says, in a barely audible voice, "I have to tell you this. My boss is starting to talk about hiring replacement workers." Buddy walks out.

Some Americans revere unions, believing that organized labor has pulled the working class up from poverty and shielded it from exploitative management. Others loathe organized labor, convinced that unions foment mindless conflicts, decrease productivity, increase costs, and harm corporations and the economy generally. Why do unions exist?

UNIONS DEVELOP . . . AND THE LAW RESPONDS

During the nineteenth century, as industrialization spread across America, workers found employment conditions increasingly unbearable and wages inadequate. Here is a contemporary account of mining in the American West:

> View their work! Descending from the surface in the shaft-cages, they enter narrow galleries where the air is scarce respirable. By the dim light of their lanterns a dingy rock surface, braced by rotting props, is visible. The stenches of decaying vegetable matter, hot foul water, and human excretions intensify the effects of the heat. The men throw off their clothes at once. Only a light breech-cloth covers their hips, and thick-soled shoes protect their feet from the scorching rocks and steaming rills of water that trickle over the floor. Except for these coverings they toil naked, with heavy drops of sweat starting from every pore.[1]

Temperatures in the mines were well over 100 degrees. Miners drank more than three gallons of water every day. Some suddenly collapsed, with swollen veins,

---

[1] Eliot Lord, *Comstock Mining and Miners* (Washington: G.P.O., 1883), p. 386, *quoted in* Richard E. Lingenfelter, *The Hardrock Miners* (Berkeley: University of California Press, 1974), p. 13.

purple faces, and glazed eyes. Within minutes they were dead, but even before they died, their places in the mine were taken by other workers desperate for pay.

Conditions were equally oppressive in the new factories back east. Workers, often women and sometimes children, worked 60 to 70 hours per week and sometimes more, standing at assembly lines in suffocating, dimly lit factories, performing monotonous yet dangerous work with heavy machinery. A visitor to a factory in Lowell, Massachusetts, in 1855 was shocked by the degrading conditions and the exhausting hours required of all workers.

> I inquired of the agent of a principal factory whether it was the custom of the manufacturers to do anything for the physical, intellectual, and moral welfare of their work-people. "We never do," he said. "As for myself, I regard my work-people just as I regard my machinery. So long as they can do my work for what I choose to pay them, I keep them, getting out of them all I can. What they do or how they fare outside my walls I don't know, nor do I consider it my business to know. When my machines get old and useless, I reject them and get new, and these people are part of my machinery."[2]

Because of the intolerable conditions and impoverishing wages, workers began to band together into unions. But early in the nineteenth century, American courts regarded any coordinated effort by workers as a criminal conspiracy. Courts convicted workers merely for the *act of joining together*, even if no strike took place. In 1842 the Massachusetts high court became the first to reject this use of the criminal law. The court ruled that workers could join together for legitimate economic goals; their efforts would become criminal only if the workers used illegal means to achieve them.[3] Other courts came to agree, and so management resorted to the civil law to curtail unions.

In 1890 Congress passed the Sherman Act to outlaw monopolies.[4] For the next 40 years, courts relied on this statute to issue anti-strike injunctions, declaring that strikes illegally restrained trade. A company could usually obtain an immediate injunction merely by alleging that a strike *might* cause harm. Courts were so quick to issue injunctions that most companies became immune to union efforts. But with the economic collapse of 1929 and the vast suffering of the Great Depression, public sympathy shifted to the workers. Congress responded with the first of several landmark statutes.

In 1932 Congress passed the **Norris-LaGuardia Act**, which prohibited federal court injunctions in nonviolent labor disputes. No longer could management obtain an injunction merely by mentioning the word "strike." By taking away the injunction remedy, Congress was declaring that workers should be permitted to organize unions and to use their collective power to achieve legitimate economic ends. The statute led to explosive growth in union membership.

In 1935 Congress passed the Wagner Act, generally known as the **National Labor Relations Act (NLRA)**. This is the most important of all labor laws. A fundamental aim of the NLRA is the establishment and maintenance of industrial peace, to preserve the flow of commerce. The NLRA ensures the right of workers to form unions and encourages management and unions to bargain collectively and productively. For our purposes, §§7 and 8 of the NLRA are the most important.

Section 7 guarantees employees the right to organize and join unions, bargain collectively through representatives of their own choosing, and engage in

---

[2] Massachusetts Senate Dock. no. 21, 1868, p. 23, *quoted in* Norman Ware, *The Industrial Worker* (Chicago: Quadrangle Books, 1964), p. 77.

[3] *Commonwealth v. Hunt*, 45 Mass. 111, 4 Met. 111 (1842).

[4] See Chapters 40 and 41, on antitrust law.

other concerted activities. This is the cornerstone of union power. With the enactment of the NLRA, Congress put an end to any notion that unions were criminal or inherently illegal by explicitly recognizing that workers could join together and bargain as a group, using their collective power to seek better conditions. Section 8 reinforces these rights by outlawing *unfair labor practices.*

Section 8(a) makes it an unfair labor practice (ULP) for an employer:

- To interfere with union organizing efforts
- To dominate or interfere with any union
- To discriminate against a union member, or
- To refuse to bargain collectively with a union.

The NLRA also established the **National Labor Relations Board (NLRB)** to administer and interpret the statute and to adjudicate labor cases. For example, when a union charges that an employer has committed an unfair labor practice—say, by refusing to bargain—the ULP charge goes first to the NLRB.

The NLRB has two primary tasks:

- *Representation.* The Board decides whether a particular union is entitled to represent a group of employees.
- *Unfair Labor Practices.* The Board adjudicates claims by either the employer or workers that the other side has committed a ULP.

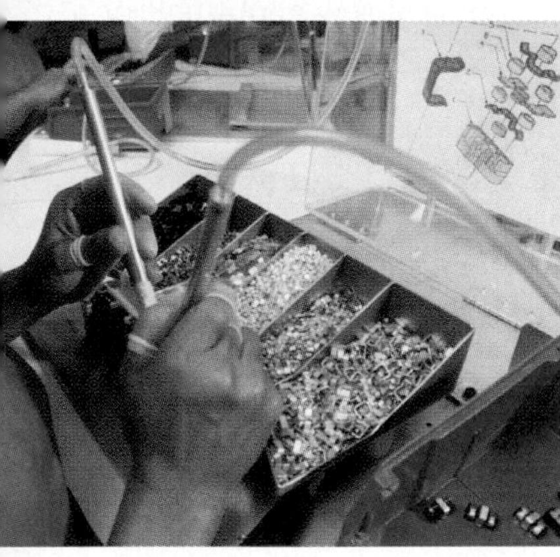

As industry changes, labor changes with it. Do these changes spell the end of unionization, or are the unions merely undergoing a transition as labor catches up with the modern economy?

To accomplish these tasks, the NLRB has several divisions. Although the agency is headquartered in Washington, it performs the greatest volume of its work in local offices. **Regional offices**, each headed by a regional director, are located throughout the country. These local offices handle most ULP claims. The General Counsel, a staff of lawyers, investigates such claims. If the General Counsel's office believes that a party has committed a ULP, it prosecutes the case before an administrative law judge (ALJ).

The **Board** itself, which sits in Washington, has five members, all appointed by the president. The Board makes final agency decisions about representation and ULP cases. But note that the Board has no power to *enforce* its orders. If it is evident that the losing party will not comply, the Board must petition a federal appeals court to enforce the order. Typically, the steps resulting in an appeal follow this pattern: the Board issues a decision, for example, finding that a company has unfairly refused to bargain with a union. The Board orders the company to bargain. The Board then appeals to the United States Court of Appeals to enforce its order, and the company *cross-appeals,* requesting the court *not* to enforce the Board's order. (The NLRB describes its mission and methods at **http://www.nlrb.gov/**.)

Throughout the 1930s and 1940s, unions grew in size and power. As strikes became more common, employers complained loudly of union abuse. Unions coerced unwilling workers to join and engaged in *secondary boycotts,* picketing an innocent company to stop it from doing business with an employer the union was fighting. In 1947 Congress responded with the Taft-Hartley Act, also known as the **Labor-Management Relations Act**, designed to curb union abuses. The statute amended §8 of the NLRA to outlaw certain unfair labor practices *by unions.*

Section 8(b) makes it an unfair labor practice for a union:

- To interfere with employees who are exercising their labor rights under §7
- To encourage an employer to discriminate against a particular employee because of a union dispute

- To refuse to bargain collectively, or
- To engage in an illegal strike or boycott, particularly secondary boycotts.

Finally, in the 1950s the public became aware that certain labor leaders were corrupt. Some officers stole money from large union treasuries, rigged union elections, and stifled opposition within the organization. In response, in 1959 Congress passed the Landrum-Griffin Act, generally called the **Labor-Management Reporting and Disclosure Act (LMRDA)**. The LMRDA requires union leadership to make certain financial disclosures and guarantees free speech and fair elections within a union.

These landmark federal labor laws are outlined below:

Four Key Labor Statutes

Norris-LaGuardia Act (1932)	Prohibits federal court injunctions in peaceful strikes.
National Labor Relations Act (1935)	Guarantees workers' right to organize unions and bargain collectively. Prohibits an employer from interfering with union organizing or discriminating against union members. Requires an employer to bargain collectively.
Labor-Management Relations Act (1947)	Prohibits union abuses such as coercing employees to join. Outlaws secondary boycotts.
Labor-Management Reporting and Disclosure Act (1959)	Requires financial disclosures by union leadership. Guarantees union members free speech and fair elections.

Today, labor abuses are less visible—but as ugly as ever. From New York City to Los Angeles, desperately poor, frightened immigrants cut and sew about half of all the garments this country produces, often working in appalling sweatshops where conditions are little better than in nineteenth-century factories. Frequently, the employees are undocumented immigrants who speak no English, know nothing of their rights, and fear that any complaints they make will lead to deportation. Exploitative owners force the workers to toil 50 to 60 hours a week with few breaks in cramped rooms with weak lighting, no ventilation, and inadequate sanitation. Pay is below the minimum wage—and vicious bosses often steal the small amounts they promised. For a report on sweatshops in the United States, see **http://www.uniteunion.org/sweatshops/sweatshop.html**.

STATE LABOR LAW

All states have labor statutes. Some are comprehensive, while others focus on narrow issues. For example, certain states prohibit particular kinds of picketing, while many states outlaw strikes by public employees. A court enforces a state statute when no federal law applies. In general, when a federal law such as the NLRA does apply, it controls the outcome. This is the doctrine of *preemption*, discussed in Chapter 4, on constitutional law. **Preemption: states have no jurisdiction to regulate any labor issue that is governed by federal law.**

In this chapter, we look principally at federal law because it is uniform and because it controls the most fundamental issues of labor policy.

LABOR UNIONS TODAY

Organized labor is shrinking in the United States. In the 1950s about 25 percent of the workforce belonged to a union. Today, only about 15 percent of all workers are union members. Employers point to this figure with satisfaction and claim that it shows that unions have failed their memberships. In an increasingly high-tech, service-oriented economy, employers argue, there is no place for organized labor. Union supporters respond that although the country has shed many old factories, workers have not benefited. Throughout the 1980s and 1990s, they assert, compensation for executives has soared into the stratosphere, with many CEOs earning several *million* dollars per year, while wages for the average worker, in real dollars, have fallen for two decades and are now 22 percent below their levels of the 1970s.

Whether organized labor is disappearing from the United States or is only retreating temporarily, labor law still affects many. About 17 million workers are union members. The largest unions are national in scope, with hundreds of affiliated **locals** throughout the country. A local is the regional union, which represents workers at a particular company. For example, over 2.2 million teachers belong to the National Education Association, with thousands of locals spread throughout the nation.

For the first time in U.S. history, a significant number of doctors are joining unions. Most are doing this in response to managed health care. Many physicians complain that health maintenance organizations require them to spend less time with patients, do more paperwork to justify their medical choices, and offer fewer services and medications to deserving patients. To reverse that trend, both doctors and nurses are forming their own labor organizations. (For the most recent union statistics, work your way to the Web page of the Bureau of Labor Statistics, at **http://stats.bls.gov/blshome.htm**.)

ORGANIZING A UNION

EXCLUSIVITY

It is difficult to organize a union. When a worker starts to talk about collective action, or when an organizer appears from a national union, many employees are suspicious or fearful; some may be hostile. Management will generally be opposed—sometimes fiercely opposed—to any union organizing effort. The fight can become ugly, and all because of one principle: *exclusivity*.

Under §9 of the NLRA, a validly recognized union is the *exclusive* representative of the employees. This means that the union will represent all of the designated employees, regardless of whether a particular worker *wants* to be represented. The company may not bargain directly with any employee in the group, nor with any other organization representing the designated employees.

A collective bargaining unit is the precisely defined group of employees who will be represented by a particular union. Suppose a hotel workers' union attempts to organize the Excelsior Hotel. The union will seek to represent some of

Excelsior's employees, but not all. The union may represent, for example, all maids, busboys, and bellhops. Those employees are in the collective bargaining unit. Many other people who work for the hotel will *not* be in the collective bargaining unit. Managers who run the hotel, reservation agents who work in other cities, launderers who work in separate facilities for a different employer—all of these people are *outside* the collective bargaining unit and will be unaffected by the union's bargaining.

It is the union's *exclusive* right to bargain for the unit that gives the organization its power. But some employees may be unhappy with the way a union exercises this power. In the following case, workers believed the union was failing to represent them on a vital issue. Should they be allowed to bargain on their own behalf? You be the judge.

EMPORIUM CAPWELL CO. v. WESTERN ADDITIONAL COMMUNITY ORGANIZATION
420 U.S. 50, 95 S. Ct. 977, 1975 U.S. LEXIS 134
United States Supreme Court, 1975

Facts: Emporium Capwell operated a department store in San Francisco. The Department Store Employees Union represented all stock workers. Several black union members complained to the union about racial discrimination in promotions, asserting that highly qualified black workers were routinely passed over in favor of less qualified whites. The union promised to pursue the issue with management, but the black employees were not satisfied with the union's effort. The unhappy workers demanded to speak with top management of the store and then, without the union's permission, picketed the store and handed out leaflets accusing the company of discrimination. Emporium Capwell fired the picketing employees. The resulting case went all the way to the Supreme Court.

In most labor cases, the union is on one side and management is on the other. In this case, the black employees were on one side, with the union on the other. The union argued that exclusivity prohibited any group of workers from demanding to meet separately with management. It claimed that the disgruntled workers violated the NLRA by insisting on separate bargaining, and that it was proper for the company to fire the workers. In other words, the union placed a higher value on exclusivity than on maintaining the jobs of those employees. The black workers, on the other hand, argued that eliminating discrimination was more important than union exclusivity. They insisted that management had no right to fire them and that they were entitled to get their jobs back and to bargain independently.

You Be the Judge: Did the picketing employees violate the NLRA by demanding to bargain directly with management?

Argument for the Union: Your honors, exclusivity is the core of a union's strength. If management is free to talk with employees individually—or if it can be *compelled* to talk with them—the union has no leverage. An astute manager will quickly use worker conflicts as a tool to divide the union and destroy it. By cutting deals with favored employees, management could demonstrate to all workers that affiliation with the union is a losing tactic, and that the smart worker bargains for himself—and then does what management tells him to do.

Racial discrimination is a terrible evil. It must be eradicated from the workplace. This union is committed to fighting prejudice. But the union must do it *collectively*. If an exception to the principle of exclusivity can be carved out for one important issue, such as race discrimination, then an exception can be carved out for other important issues, such as gender bias, age discrimination, language differences, retirement pay, health benefits . . . and on and on. To allow this group of picketers to pursue a worthy goal with separate bargaining would be to destroy the union—and ensure that *no* valuable goals are obtained.

Argument for the Picketing Workers: Congress granted employees the right to organize *for their mutual benefit*, not to advance the cause of unions. A labor organization is a means to an end, not an end in itself. When a union fails to support its members on a vital issue, employees must be free to fend for themselves. Race discrimination is not a simple bargaining issue like retirement benefits; it is a vital matter of human dignity. This union failed to act promptly and vigorously to protect its black members and end discrimination. Why should those employees now be shackled to an organization that has failed them?

It makes no difference *why* the union failed to protect its members. Weak-kneed, docile union leadership can be just as devastating to the cause of racial equality as bad faith. We are not asking that union members be free to pursue every petty complaint directly with management. To equate racial justice with retirement benefits is to ignore the singular evil of discrimination. We merely ask that, when a union fails to protect its members concerning a profound issue such as this, the injured employees be allowed to speak for themselves.

ORGANIZING

A union organizing effort generally involves the following pattern.

Campaign

Union organizers talk with employees—or attempt to talk—and interest them in forming a union. The organizers may be employees of the company, who simply chat with fellow workers about unsatisfactory conditions. Or a union may send nonemployees of the company to hand out union leaflets to workers as they arrive and depart from the factory.

Authorization Cards

Union organizers ask workers to sign authorization cards, which state that the particular worker requests the specified union to act as her sole bargaining representative.

Recognition

If a union obtains authorization cards from a sizable percentage of workers, it seeks **recognition** as the exclusive representative for the bargaining unit. The union may ask the employer to recognize it as the bargaining representative, but most of the time employers refuse to recognize the union voluntarily. The NLRA permits an employer to refuse recognition.

Petition

Assuming that the employer does not voluntarily recognize a union, the union generally petitions the NLRB for an election. It must submit to the NLRB regional office authorization cards signed by at least 30 percent of the workers. The regional office verifies whether there are enough valid cards to warrant an election and looks closely at the proposed bargaining unit to make sure that it is appropriate. If the regional director determines that the union has identified an appropriate bargaining unit and has enough valid cards, it orders an election.

Election

The NLRB closely supervises the election to ensure fairness. All members of the proposed bargaining unit vote on whether they want the union to represent them. If more than 50 percent of the workers vote for the union, the NLRB designates that union as the exclusive representative of all members of the bargaining unit. When unions hold representation elections in private corporations, they win about half the time. Labor organizations claim that management typically uses paid company time to campaign against the union. Employers respond that labor loses elections because workers fear that a union will hurt them, not help. Among public employers, unions generally do much better, winning about 85 percent of representation campaigns. Public employers often do not campaign against the union.

These are some of the issues that most commonly arise during an organizing effort: (1) What may a union do during its organizing campaign? (2) What may the employer do to defeat the campaign? (3) What is an appropriate bargaining unit?

WHAT WORKERS MAY DO

The NLRA guarantees employees the right to talk among themselves about forming a union, to hand out literature, and ultimately to join a union.[5] Workers may urge other employees to sign authorization cards and may vigorously push their cause. When employees hand out leaflets, the employer generally may not limit the content. In one case a union distributed leaflets urging workers to vote against political candidates who opposed minimum wage laws. The employer objected to the union using company property to distribute the information, but the Supreme Court upheld the union's right. Even though the content of the writing was not directly related to the union, the connection was close enough that the NLRA protected the union's activity.[6]

There are, of course, limits to what union organizers may do. The statute permits an employer to restrict organizing discussions if they interfere with discipline or production. A worker on a moving assembly line has no right to walk away from his task to talk with other employees about organizing a union; the employer may insist that the worker stay at his job and leave discussions until lunch or some other break.[7]

WHAT EMPLOYERS MAY DO

As mentioned above, an employer may prohibit employees from organizing if the efforts interfere with the company's work. In a retail store, for example, management may prohibit union discussions in the presence of customers, because the discussions could harm business.

May the employer speak out against a union organizing drive? Yes. Management is entitled to communicate to the employees why it believes a union will be harmful to the company. But the employer's efforts must be limited to explanation and advocacy. **The employer may vigorously present anti-union views to its employees, but may not use either threats or promises of benefits to defeat a union drive.**[8] Notice that the employer is prohibited not only from threatening reprisals, such as firing a worker who favors the union, but also from offering benefits designed to defeat the union. A company that has vigorously rejected employee demands for higher wages may not suddenly grant a 10 percent pay increase in the midst of a union campaign.

It is an unfair labor practice for an employer to interfere with a union organizing effort. Normally, a union claiming such interference will file a ULP charge. If the Board upholds the union's claim, it will order the employer to stop its interference and permit a fair election. In some cases, though, management's interference is so pervasive and intrusive that the Board may conclude an election would be pointless. **When an employer outrageously interferes with a union organizing campaign, the NLRB may forgo the normal election, certify the union as the exclusive representative, and order the company to bargain.** This *bargaining order* is an extreme measure, and the Board uses it only when an employer has shown

---

[5] NLRA §7.

[6] *Eastex, Inc. v. NLRB*, 434 U.S. 1045, 98 S. Ct. 888, 1978 U.S. LEXIS 547 (1978).

[7] *NLRB v. Babcock & Wilcox Co.*, 351 U.S. 105, 76 S. Ct. 679, 1956 U.S. LEXIS 1721 (1956).

[8] *NLRB v. Gissel Packing Co.*, 395 U.S. 575, 89 S. Ct. 1918, 1969 U.S. LEXIS 3172 (1969).

extreme anti-union animus. In the following case, the union contended that the employer had done just that.

NLRB AND UNION OF NEEDLETRADES INDUSTRIAL AND TEXTILE EMPLOYEES, LOCAL 76 v. INTERSWEET, INC.
125 F.3d 1064, 1997 U.S. App. LEXIS 25240
United States Court of Appeals for the Seventh Circuit, 1997

Facts: Intersweet, Inc. manufactured sugar wafers, but conditions in the plant had gone sour. The Needletrades Union conducted three organizational meetings, and 19 of the company's 31 employees signed union representation cards. Later that same month, Intersweet's owner, Julius Meerbaum, suddenly fired all employees. The next day, he recalled 10 of the 31 workers. Eight of the 10 had not signed union cards and the others *claimed* they had not. Meerbaum required the rehired employees to work 50 to 60 hours per week, instead of the normal 40. Workers overheard company supervisors say that no one active in the union would ever be rehired.

An administrative law judge ruled that the company had committed outrageous unfair labor practices, and ordered the company to bargain with the union, without an election. The NLRB petitioned the court of appeals to enforce its order.

Issue: Was the NLRB's order to bargain justified?

Excerpts from Judge Rovner's Decision: Between the time of the mass terminations and the imposition of the [bargaining] order, Julius Meerbaum, who had been responsible for the shutdown of the plant in 1993, passed away. Intersweet argues that Julius' death obviated the need for the bargaining order by removing any lingering impact of the unfair practices for which he was responsible. Although Julius Meerbaum had passed away, three members of Intersweet's previous management staff, John Meerbaum, Jose Diaz and David Sabin were still running the company. Thus, aside from the fact that Julius was gone, Intersweet's management had not meaningfully changed, and the company was still controlled by the Meerbaum family. In fact, because the individuals that were still present had been responsible for implementing Julius' directive to shut down the plant, the Board found that they may be more closely associated with the terminations than Julius himself, whose involvement was remote and perhaps even unknown to the workers.

The Board did not abuse its discretion in determining that the change in circumstances did not alleviate the need for a bargaining order. Intersweet discharged its entire workforce, rehired only those employees that it believed had not signed union cards, and then openly disclosed to returning employees that the terminations were related to union affiliation. It is difficult to imagine a more egregious attempt to defeat unionization. The management team responsible for these practices remained essentially intact, and there is no reason to believe that the workforce, although expanded, would not continue to be chilled by the earlier actions. The Board considered each of Intersweet's arguments and rejected them in a well-reasoned opinion. We find no abuse of discretion, and the Board's petition for enforcement of its order is GRANTED.

APPROPRIATE BARGAINING UNIT

When a union petitions the NLRB for an election, the Board determines whether the proposed bargaining unit is appropriate. **The Board generally certifies a proposed bargaining unit if and only if the employees share a community of interest.** Employers frequently assert that the bargaining unit is inappropriate. If the Board agrees with the employer and rejects the proposed bargaining unit, it dismisses the union's request for an election. The Board pays particular attention to two kinds of employees: managerial and confidential.

Managerial employees must be excluded from the bargaining unit.[9] An employee is managerial if she is so closely aligned with management that her membership in the bargaining unit would create a conflict of interest between her union membership and her actual work. Courts generally find such a conflict only if *the employee is substantially involved in the employer's labor policy*.

For example, a factory worker who spends one-third of his time performing assembly work but two-thirds of his time supervising a dozen other workers is so closely aligned with management that he could not fairly be part of the bargaining unit. There would be constant tension between his supervisory work and his advocacy on behalf of the union. By contrast, an engineer who analyzes production methods and merely reports her findings to management may not be closely aligned with the employer. Unless the engineer has actual control over personnel decisions, she can probably be included in a bargaining unit of other engineers.[10]

Confidential employees are generally excluded from the bargaining unit.[11] A confidential employee is one who works so closely with executives or other management employees that there would be a conflict of interest if the employee were in the bargaining unit. An executive secretary may be so intimately acquainted with her boss's ideas, plans, and other confidential information that it would be unfair to allow her to join a bargaining unit of other secretaries.

Once the Board has excluded managerial and confidential employees, it looks at various criteria to decide whether the remaining employees should logically be grouped in one bargaining unit, that is, whether they share a **community of interest**. The Board looks for:

- Rough equality of pay and benefits, and methods of computing both
- Similar total hours per week and type of work
- Similar skills and training, and
- Previous bargaining history and the number of authorization cards from any different groups within the unit.

Having applied these criteria to all members of the proposed unit, the Board either certifies the bargaining unit or rejects the unit and dismisses the union's petition. Suppose the employees in a public high school decide to organize. The Board will probably find that an appropriate bargaining unit includes all academic teachers and physical education teachers because they do roughly similar work and are paid similarly. The principal and vice-principal will not be included in the unit because their work is supervisory and administrative and they are paid on a separate scale.

COLLECTIVE BARGAINING

The goal of bargaining is a contract, which is called a **collective bargaining agreement (CBA)**. As mentioned, Congress passed the NLRA to foster industrial peace, and a CBA is designed to do that. But problems arise as union and employer advocate their respective positions. Three of the most common conflicts are (1) whether an issue is a mandatory subject of bargaining, (2) whether the parties are bargaining in good faith, and (3) how to enforce the agreement. For a Web page devoted to articles and reports on collective bargaining, see **http://www.ilr.cornell.edu/depts/ICB/briefing/**.

---

[9] *NLRB v. Bell Aerospace Co., Div. of Textron, Inc.*, 416 U.S. 267, 94 S. Ct. 1757, 1974 U.S. LEXIS 35 (1974).

[10] See, e.g., *NLRB v. Case Corp.*, 995 F.2d 700, 1993 U.S. App. LEXIS 13246 (7th Cir. 1993).

[11] Ibid.

SUBJECTS OF BARGAINING

Can American labor compete with lower paid foreign workers? Should management have the unfettered right to transfer jobs overseas?

The NLRA *permits* the parties to bargain almost any subject they wish, but *requires* them to bargain certain issues. **Mandatory subjects include wages, hours, and other terms and conditions of employment.** Either side may propose to bargain *other* subjects, but neither side may insist upon bargaining them.

Management and unions often disagree as to whether a particular topic is mandatory or not. Typically, unions attempt to expand the number of mandatory subjects, seeking more input into a greater number of issues, while the company argues that subjects are not mandatory and are none of the union's business. In general, a court is likely to find a given issue mandatory when it *directly relates* to individual workers; when a subject only indirectly affects employees, it is likely to be found not mandatory. In passing the NLRA, Congress never intended a union negotiator to become an equal partner in running the business.

Courts generally find these subjects to be mandatory: pay, benefits, order of layoffs and recalls, production quotas, work rules (such as safety practices), retirement benefits, and in-plant food service and prices (e.g., cafeteria food). Courts usually consider these subjects to be nonmandatory: product type and design, advertising, sales, financing, corporate organization, and location of plants.

Today, some of the angriest disputes between management and labor arise from a company's desire to subcontract work and/or to move plants to areas with cheaper costs. **Subcontracting** means that a manufacturer, rather than producing all parts of a product and then assembling them, contracts for other companies, frequently overseas, to make some of the parts. Is a business free to subcontract work? That depends on management's motive. **A company that subcontracts in order to maintain its economic viability is probably *not* required to bargain first; however, bargaining *is* mandatory if the subcontracting is designed to replace union workers with cheaper labor.**

Dorsey Trailers manufactured dump trucks. During a period of heavy sales, Dorsey subcontracted some of its production work to Bankhead Enterprises, which agreed to manufacture two trucks per week and split the profits. The union filed a ULP charge, claiming that subcontracting was a mandatory subject of bargaining, and that Dorsey had no right to make the deal before negotiating with the union.

The court noted that Dorsey was losing business because it could not fill orders fast enough. The dump truck industry was cyclical, and in a period of strong demand, the company had to be able to manufacture its goods quickly. Dorsey had been unable to hire enough welders and other skilled workers to keep up with demand. The court stated that Dorsey could not survive without the subcontracting. Further, the company had not reduced union jobs; it had simply failed to add more union workers—through no fault of its own. Dorsey was free to subcontract without bargaining the issue.[12]

Ford and the United Auto Workers (UAW) signed a contract aimed at resolving the subcontracting issue. Ford employs roughly 100,000 UAW workers. The CBA requires the company to maintain UAW jobs at no less than 95 percent of the current number. If Ford begins to manufacture auto parts that it previously subcontracted, the company is permitted to pay dramatically lower wages to all those hired to do the new work. Thus each side gets something: the union obtains additional jobs, while Ford pays less to the new workers.

[12] *Dorsey Trailers, Inc. Northumberland PA Plant v. NLRB*, 134 F.3d 125, 1998 U.S. App. LEXIS 764 (3rd. Cir. 1998).

Plant closings, which can result in hundreds or thousands of lost jobs, are also a volatile issue. Although the job losses are potentially greater than those that result from subcontracting, management is not obligated to bargain such a decision. **An employer is not required to bargain over the closing of a plant, only the *effects* of the closing.**[13]

The reasoning behind this rule is basic: the company that opened a plant ought to be able to close it. The competing interest of the employees—the need for work—is obviously strong but not strong enough to mandate bargaining. Further, having concluded that the employer has the right to shut down a facility, courts also allow the employer to do so fairly quickly. Management may need speed and flexibility in effecting such major business changes. In contrast, the union will want to slow down or prevent the closing. The two sides will have few things to discuss, and mandated bargaining will gain little for employees while potentially costing the company time and money. When a plant closing will cost jobs, management must bargain such things as the order of layoffs, but it need not bargain the closing itself.

Employer and Union Security

Both the employer and the union will seek clauses making their positions more secure. Management, above all, wants to be sure that there will be no strikes during the course of the agreement. For its part, the union tries to ensure that its members cannot be turned away from work during the CBA's term, and that all newly hired workers will affiliate with the union. We look at several union security issues.

No Strike/No Lockout. Most agreements include some form of no-strike clause, meaning that the union promises not to strike during the term of the contract. In turn, unions insist on a no-lockout clause, meaning that in the event of a labor dispute, management will not prevent union members from working. **No-strike and no-lockout clauses are both legal.**

Closed Shop. A closed shop means the employer must hire only union members. Though obviously very attractive to a union, effectively giving it veto power over new hires, a closed shop is not possible. **A closed shop is illegal.** Indeed, for a union to bargain for a closed shop violates the NLRA .

Union and Agency Shops. In a union shop, membership in the union becomes compulsory *after* the employee has been hired. Thus management retains an unfettered right to hire whom it pleases, but all new employees who fit into the bargaining unit must affiliate with the union. **A union shop is generally legal.** There are two limitations, however. First, new members need not join the union for 30 days. Second, the new members, after joining the union, can only be required to pay initiation fees and union dues. If the new hire decides he does not want to participate in the union, the union may not compel him to do so, and management may not terminate him (pursuant to a CBA) for his refusal. This is a compromise, designed to protect workers from having to play an active role in a union, while ensuring that the union receives normal dues from all employees, whether they participate in union affairs or not. If employees could avoid dues, they would be "free riders," benefiting from the union's bargaining without paying for it.

An **agency shop** is similar to a union shop. Here, the new hire must pay union fees but need not actually join the organization. In both a union shop and an agency shop, the worker may insist on paying only the percentage of dues that is devoted to collective bargaining, contract administration, and grievances. An

[13] *First National Maintenance Corp. v. NLRB*, 452 U.S. 666, 101 S. Ct. 2573, 1981 U.S. LEXIS 117 (1981).

employee could refuse to pay, for example, the percentage of union dues devoted to organizing other companies.[14]

Some states have passed so-called **right to work** laws, which restrict or even outlaw union shop and agency shop agreements. These statutes typically prohibit a labor organization from demanding that all employees join the union or pay dues. Right to work laws prompt an intense response from both supporters and opponents of organized labor, and the Internet offers plenty of evidence. At http://www.nrtw.org/, the National Right to Work Legal Defense Foundation explains these statutes and counsels employees about their rights to reject union membership and avoid paying dues. The organization also discusses what it considers to be union abuses. Meanwhile the AFL-CIO, the nation's largest labor organization, offers statistics demonstrating that union workers earn higher pay than their nonunion counterparts in virtually all jobs and professions, and that wages are lower in right to work states than elsewhere in the country. See its Web page at http://www.aflcio.org/.

Hot Cargo Clause. A hot cargo clause would prohibit an employer from doing business with a specified company. A union might like such a clause to put pressure on the *other* company, where the union already has a dispute. But the effort must fail: **hot cargo clauses are illegal.**

DUTY TO BARGAIN

Both the union and the employer must bargain in good faith with an open mind. However, they are *not* obligated to reach an agreement. This means that the two sides must meet and make a reasonable effort to reach a contract. The goal is good faith bargaining, with the hope that it will lead to a contract and labor peace. Each side must listen to the other's proposals and consider possible compromises. But the NLRA does not require agreement. Suppose a union proposes a 15 percent pay increase, and management offers a 1 percent raise. Each side is required to attend bargaining sessions, listen to the other side's proposal, and consider its supporting argument. But neither side has to agree. Management need not raise its offer to 2 percent, nor must the union drop its demand. However, **if an employer states that it is financially unable to meet the union's demands, the union is entitled to see records that support the claim.** It is an unfair labor practice for an employer to say, "We can't afford a pay raise now," and then refuse to supply its financial data. An employer could easily destroy good faith bargaining if it were allowed to claim financial impossibility without demonstrating it. Similarly, if an employer argues that it must subcontract work to save money, it must furnish the documents it is relying on in making its proposal.

Sometimes an employer will attempt to make changes without bargaining the issues at all. However, **management may not unilaterally change wages, hours, or terms and conditions of employment without bargaining the issues to impasse.** "Bargaining to impasse" means that both parties must continue to meet and bargain in good faith until it is clear that they cannot reach an agreement. The goal in requiring collective bargaining is to bring the parties together, to reach an agreement that brings labor peace. In one case, the union won an election, but before bargaining could begin, management changed the schedule from five 8-hour days to four 10-hour days a week. The company also changed its layoff policy from one of strict seniority to one based on ability and began laying off employees based on alleged poor performance. The court held that each of these acts violated the company's duty to bargain. The employer ultimately might be

[14] *Communications Workers of America v. Beck*, 487 U.S. 735, 108 S. Ct. 2641, 1988 U.S. LEXIS 3030 (1988).

allowed to make every one of these changes, but first it had to bargain the issues to impasse.[15]

For the same reasons, though the employer may implement new policies after impasse, it may *implement only what it has proposed at the table.* Again, it would defeat the purpose of the NLRA if a company were free to implement a business decision that it had never proposed; the two sides *could not* have discussed plans that were never offered at the table. Exhibit 31.1 outlines the respective bargaining rights and responsibilities between employers and unions.

Illegal implementation put major league baseball players back on the field after the longest strike in sports history. The CBA had expired, and the players' union bargained with team owners throughout the spring and summer. The two sides could not agree, primarily because the owners demanded a salary cap, which would give all teams equal payrolls. In August the players struck, ending the season without a World Series for the first time in more than 100 years. The two sides continued talking until December, when the owners announced they were implementing their salary cap proposal and changing various aspects of "free agency," the policy that allows a player to seek the highest salary from any team. A federal district court judge ruled that the owners had violated the NLRA by unilaterally imposing new rules concerning a mandatory subject (free agency)

Exhibit 31.1

The NLRA requires that the employer and the union meet. They *must* bargain mandatory subjects and *may* bargain permissive subjects. The employer may not make any unilateral change concerning a mandatory subject until bargaining has reached an impasse.

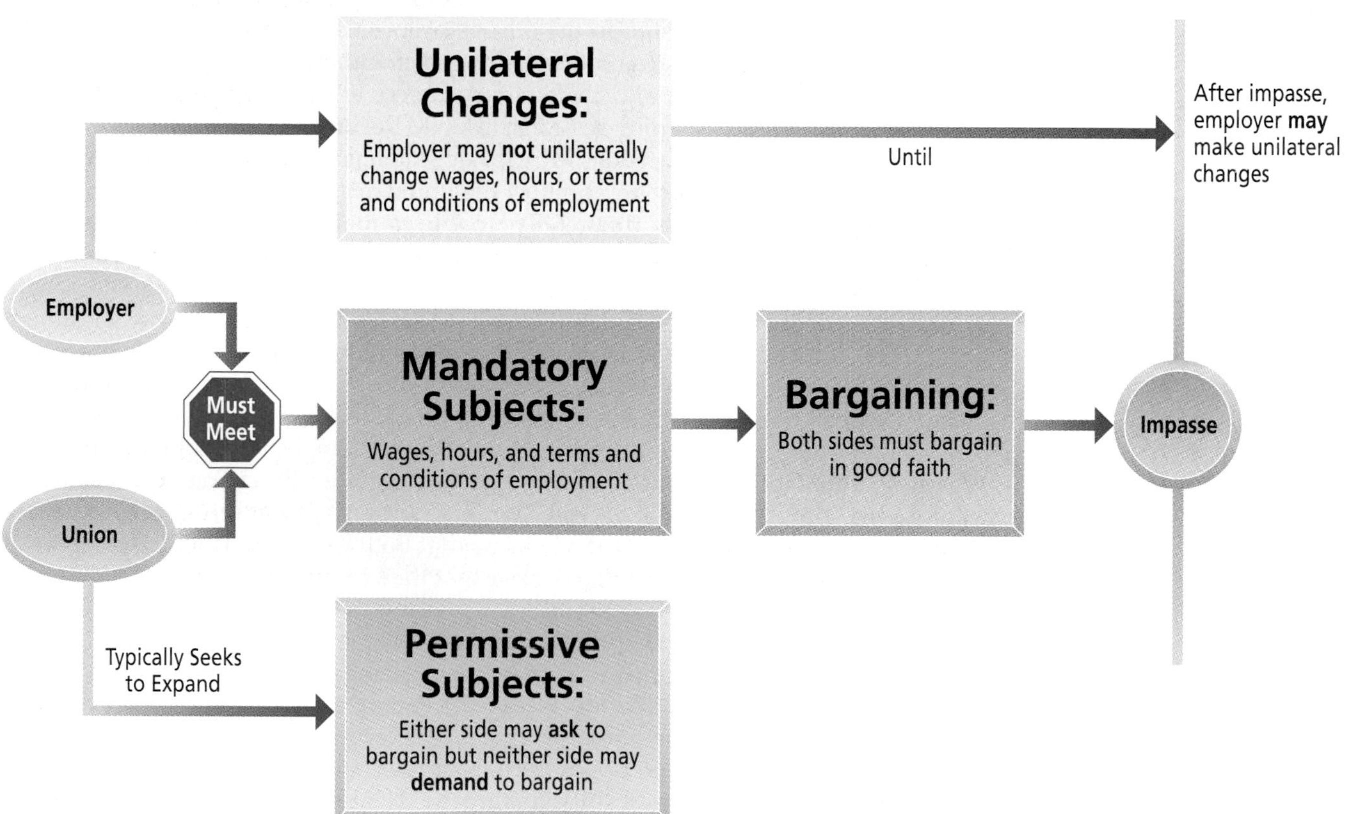

[15] *Adair Standish Corp. v. NLRB*, 912 F.2d 854, 1990 U.S. App. LEXIS 14670 (6th Cir. 1990).

that they had never bargained. The judge ordered the owners back to the table, and the parties finally agreed to a new CBA.

ENFORCEMENT

Virtually all collective bargaining agreements provide for their own enforcement, typically through **grievance-arbitration**. Suppose a company transfers an employee from the day shift to the night shift, and the worker believes the contract prohibits such a transfer for any employee with her seniority. The employee complains to the union, which files a **grievance**, that is, a formal complaint with the company, notifying management that the union claims a contract violation. Generally, the CBA establishes some kind of informal hearing, usually conducted by a member of management, at which the employee, represented by the union, may state her case and respond to the company's assertions. The manager has a limited time period—say, seven days—to decide the grievance.

If, after the manager's decision, the employee is still dissatisfied, the union normally has the right to appeal to some kind of formal hearing, perhaps before a top company executive or committee. This appeal hearing is slightly more formal. If this hearing still fails to satisfy the employee, the union typically may file for **arbitration**, that is, a formal hearing before a neutral arbitrator. In the arbitration hearing, each side is represented by its lawyer. The arbitrator is required to decide the case based on the CBA. An arbitrator finds either for the employee, and orders the company to take certain corrective action, or for the employer, and dismisses the grievance. (The American Arbitration Association offers its rules, procedures, and forms at **http://www.adr.org/**.)

A CBA also permits the company to file a grievance. Its complaint normally goes directly to arbitration. In the vast majority of grievances, the arbitrator's decision is final. In a limited number of cases, however, the losing party attempts to convince a federal court that the arbitration award is unjust. Usually, such an appeal is futile. **Courts generally do not examine the merits of an arbitrator's decision.** The idea of all contracts, including CBAs, is to give the parties a chance to control their own destiny. When a CBA states that grievances should be settled by arbitration, courts seldom undercut the contract by reviewing the arbitrator's award. Of course, a rule would hardly be a rule without an exception. **A court may refuse to enforce an arbitrator's award that is contrary to public policy.** So if an arbitrator's decision encourages either party to violate the law or engage in clearly immoral conduct, a court will probably nullify the award. But like most exceptions, this one is very narrowly interpreted, as the following case illustrates.

UNITED PAPERWORKERS INTERNATIONAL UNION v. MISCO, INC.

484 U.S. 29, 108 S. Ct. 364, 1987 U.S. LEXIS 5028
United States Supreme Court, 1987

Facts: Misco, Inc. operated a paper plant in Louisiana. The company had a collective bargaining agreement with the United Paperworkers (the Union), which permitted either side to file grievances and take them to final, binding arbitration. The CBA also permitted the company to post work rules. Rule II.1 notified employees that they could be dismissed for bringing alcohol or drugs onto company premises or arriving for work under the influence of such substances.

Isiah Cooper, an employee covered by the CBA, operated a slitter-rewinder machine, which used sharp blades to cut rolling coils of paper. The machine was hazardous and had caused numerous injuries over the years. Cooper had twice been reprimanded for deficient performance. Two days after the second reprimand, police searched Cooper's house, pursuant to a search warrant, and discovered a large amount of marijuana. Later that day, police apprehended Cooper in the backseat of another worker's car, a white Cutlass, parked in the company lot.

There was marijuana smoke in the air and a lighted marijuana cigarette in the ashtray in the front seat. Police arrested Cooper and then searched *his* car, where they found a plastic scales case and some marijuana.

When the Company learned of Cooper's presence in the white Cutlass, it discharged him for having drugs on the premises. He filed a grievance. Eight months later, shortly before the arbitration hearing began, the Company learned that the police had found marijuana in Cooper's own car. The arbitrator found in Cooper's favor, stating that because he was in the backseat of the Cutlass and the marijuana was in the front, the Company had no evidence he had used or possessed an illegal substance on the premises. The arbitrator refused to consider the marijuana found in Cooper's own car because the Company had not known about it when it fired him.

The Company filed suit in United States District Court, which vacated the arbitrator's decision, holding that public policy prohibits the use of marijuana. The court of appeals affirmed the district court, and the union sought review by the Supreme Court.

Issue: Was the district court correct in overruling the arbitrator on public policy grounds?

Excerpts from Justice White's Decision: The Court made clear almost 30 years ago that the courts play only a limited role when asked to review the decision of an arbitrator. The courts are not authorized to reconsider the merits of an award even though the parties may allege that the award rests on errors of fact or on misinterpretation of the contract. The federal policy of settling labor disputes by arbitration would be undermined if courts had the final say on the merits of the awards.

The Company's position, simply put, is that the arbitrator committed grievous error in finding that the evidence was insufficient to prove that Cooper had possessed or used marijuana on company property. But the court of appeals, although it took a distinctly jaundiced view of the arbitrator's decision in this regard, was not free to refuse enforcement because it considered Cooper's presence in the white Cutlass, in the circumstances, to be ample proof that Rule II.1 was violated. No dishonesty [on the arbitrator's part] is alleged; only improvident, even silly, factfinding is claimed.

Nor was it open to the court of appeals to refuse to enforce the award because the arbitrator, in deciding whether there was just cause to discharge, refused to consider evidence unknown to the Company at the time Cooper was fired. The parties bargained for arbitration to settle disputes and were free to set the procedural rules for arbitrators to follow if they chose. Article VI of the agreement, entitled "Arbitration Procedure," did set some ground rules for the arbitration process. It forbade the arbitrator to consider hearsay evidence, for example, but evidentiary matters were otherwise left to the arbitrator. Here the arbitrator ruled that in determining whether Cooper had violated Rule II.1, he should not consider evidence not relied on by the employer in ordering the discharge, particularly in a case like this where there was no notice to the employee or the Union prior to the hearing that the Company would attempt to rely on after-discovered evidence. This, in effect, was a construction of what the contract required when deciding discharge cases: an arbitrator was to look only at the evidence before the employer at the time of discharge.

The parties did not bargain for the facts to be found by a court, but by an arbitrator chosen by them who had more opportunity to observe Cooper and to be familiar with the plant and its problems. Nor does the fact that it is inquiring into a possible violation of public policy excuse a court for doing the arbitrator's task.

The judgment of the court of appeals is *reversed*.

CONCERTED ACTION

Concerted action refers to any tactics union members take in unison to gain some bargaining advantage. It is this power that gives a union strength. **The NLRA guarantees the right of employees to engage in concerted action for mutual aid or protection.**[16] The most common forms of concerted action are strikes and picketing.

STRIKES

The NLRA guarantees employees the right to strike, but with some limitations.[17] A union has a guaranteed right to call a strike if the parties are unable to reach a collective bargaining agreement. A union may call a strike to exert economic pressure on management, to protest an unfair labor practice, or to preserve work that the employer is considering sending elsewhere. (For a listing of unions currently on strike, see **http://www.igc.org/strike/**.) Note that the right to strike can be waived. Management will generally insist that the CBA include a **no-strike clause**, which prohibits the union from striking while the CBA is in force. A strike is illegal in several other situations as well; here we mention the most important.

Cooling Off Period

Once the union agrees to a CBA, it may not strike to terminate the agreement, or modify it, without giving management 60 days' notice. Suppose a union contract expires July 1. The two sides attempt to bargain a new contract, but progress is slow. The union may strike as an economic weapon, but must notify management of its intention to do so *and then must wait 60 days*. This cooling off period is designed to give both sides a chance to reassess negotiations and to decide whether some additional compromise would be wiser than enduring a strike.

Statutory Prohibition

Many states have outlawed strikes by public employees. In some states, the prohibition applies to selected employees, such as firefighters or teachers. In other states, *all* public employees are barred from striking, whether or not they have a contract. The purpose of these statutes is to ensure that unions do not use the public health or welfare as a weapon to secure an unfair bargaining advantage. However, even employees subject to such a rule may find other tactics to press their cause.

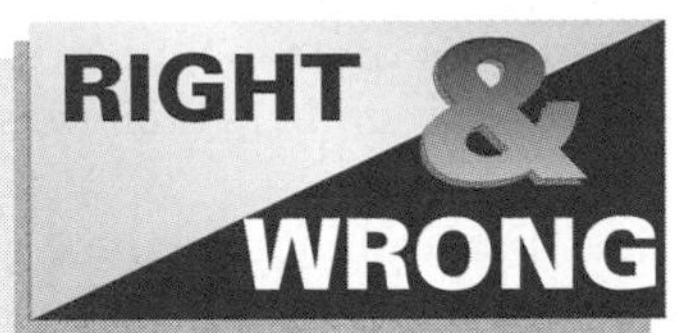

Jen has worked hard throughout high school, achieving a 3.8 GPA and high test scores, and now she is ready to apply to some of the best colleges in the country. All of her teachers think she is an extraordinary student—yet no one will write her a letter of recommendation.

The teacher's union has been bargaining a new contract for a year and a half. The teachers seek a 4 percent raise; the school board has offered 1 percent. The struggle has grown increasingly bitter. There will be no strike—state law prohibits that—but the teachers have decided they will "work to rule," meaning that they will do only what their (expired) contract requires: teach classes, issue grades, and so forth. No teacher will write a letter of recommendation, coach a team, supervise detention, or offer extra help to a student.

---

[16] NLRA §7.

[17] NLRA §13.

"This stinks," wails Jen. "I've never asked for extra assistance. I've tried to be helpful in class, and a lot of times, I've tutored other kids. This is the one time in my life I really need my teachers to be there for me, and they're turning their backs."

"My heart goes out to Jen," responds her American history teacher, "but our problem is simple: as long as we quietly ask for decent pay, no one listens. Students and parents notice us only when they suffer inconvenience."

"This is a moral outrage!" shouts Jen's father. "These so-called teachers have no right to hurt my child over their pay disputes. If they were serious about their profession, they would do everything they could to help the children who are entrusted to them. Our high school normally sends 95 percent of its students to good colleges, and now the teachers are sabotaging everything."

"If the parents were serious about education," the history teacher retorts, "or truly concerned about their children's welfare, they would demand that the town pay respectable salaries. They prefer lower taxes so they can spend more on fancy cars."

Who is right?

Violent Strikes

The NLRA prohibits violent strikes. Violence does sometimes occur on the picket line, when union members attempt to prevent other workers from entering the job site. Or a union may stage a **sit-down strike**, in which members stop working but remain at their job posts, physically blocking replacement workers from taking their places. Any such violence is illegal.

Partial Strikes

A partial strike occurs when employees stop working temporarily, then resume, then stop again, and so forth. This tactic is particularly disruptive because management cannot bring in replacement workers. A union may either walk off the job or stay on it, but it may not alternate.

REPLACEMENT WORKERS

When employees go on strike, management generally wants to replace them to keep the company operating. When replacement workers begin to cross a union picket line, tempers are certain to explode, and entire communities may feel the repercussions. Are replacement workers legal? Yes. **Management has the right to hire replacement workers during a strike.** May the employer offer the replacement workers *permanent* jobs, or must the company give union members their jobs back when the strike is over? It depends on the type of strike.

After an *economic strike*, an employer may not discriminate against a striker, but the employer is *not* obligated to lay off a replacement worker to give a striker his job back. An economic strike is one intended to gain wages or benefits. When a union bargains for a pay raise but fails to get it and walks off the job, that is an economic strike. During such a strike, an employer may hire permanent replacement workers. When the strike is over, the company has no obligation to lay off the replacement workers to make room for the strikers. However, if the company does hire more workers, it may not discriminate against the strikers.

After a *ULP strike*, a union member is entitled to her job back, even if that means the employer must lay off a replacement worker. Suppose management refuses to bargain in good faith, by claiming poverty without producing records to substantiate its claim. The union strikes. Management's refusal to bargain was an unfair labor practice, and the strike is a ULP strike. When it ends, the striking workers must get their jobs back.

GENERAL INDUSTRIAL EMPLOYEES UNION, LOCAL 42 v. NLRB
951 F.2d 1308, 1991 U.S. App. LEXIS 30086
Court of Appeals for the District of Columbia, 1991

Facts: Mohawk Liqueur Corp.'s collective bargaining agreement with Local 42 (the union) was about to expire, and the parties were negotiating a new contract. Mohawk submitted its final offer, including a statement that it would not pay the last cost of living adjustment (COLA) due under the *old* contract for work already performed. The union declared this an unfair labor practice and struck. Mohawk unilaterally implemented its final offer and refused to pay the COLA. Negotiations resumed, and about two months later Mohawk agreed to make the old COLA payment. The company then warned the workers that they would be permanently replaced if they failed to return by August 4.

On August 3, the union met. The workers agreed that the COLA payment was no longer an issue, but voted to continue the strike. The employees hoped to force Mohawk to divulge the names of certain workers the company planned to discharge; they also wanted the company to offer a general amnesty to all strikers and grant certain financial benefits. Mohawk replaced all striking workers. On August 11 the union voted to return to work. Mohawk reinstated some but not all of the strikers, and five months later the parties reached a new contract.

The Board determined that what had begun as a ULP strike had changed into an economic one, and that Mohawk had lawfully replaced some workers permanently. The union appealed.

Issue: Was Mohawk entitled to replace workers permanently?

Excerpts from Judge Silberman's Decision: Employees who take part in [an economic strike] run the risk of permanent replacement by new hires. But unfair labor practice strikers are entitled to reinstatement if they wish to return to work and, if denied reemployment, are also entitled to back pay from the date of denial.

The causes of a strike can, of course, change over time. Sometimes a strike that starts for economic reasons is prolonged by the employer's subsequent unlawful conduct and is thereby "converted" from an economic to an unfair labor practice strike. Similarly (although there are fewer examples), an unfair labor practice strike can be converted to an economic strike if the illegal acts that originally caused the dispute fade in significance and the employees continue the strike solely to enforce their economic demands on the employer.

The [August 3 union] meeting's avowed purpose was to decide whether to prolong the strike. The minutes of the meeting, the motion by which the strikers decided not to return to work, and the testimony before the ALJ all demonstrate that the reasons for continuing the strike had nothing whatsoever to do with Mohawk's prior violations of the NLRA. Rather, the record indicates that the strikers wished to obtain information on discharges, amnesty for strike misconduct, and COLAs in the new contract. The May 31 COLA came into the deliberations only when the Union negotiator and attorney explained why it was no longer a reason to strike. The evidence relating to both the August 11 negotiating session (such as testimony that the parties agreed the COLA issue had been "settled" and the Union's announcement that it was withdrawing its COLA grievance) and the August 12 Union meeting also supports the Board's conclusion that the strike was prolonged for reasons entirely unrelated to Mohawk's unfair labor practices.

[The Board's order, declaring the permanent replacements lawful, is *affirmed*.]

PICKETING

Picketing the employer's workplace in support of a strike is generally lawful. Striking workers are permitted to establish picket lines at the employer's job site and to urge all others—employees, replacement workers, and customers—not to cross the line. But the picketers are not permitted to use physical force to *prevent* anyone from crossing the line. The NLRA does not authorize or protect violence on the picket line. The company may terminate violent picketers and permanently replace them, regardless of the nature of the strike.

Secondary boycotts are generally illegal. A secondary boycott is a picket line established not at the employer's premises but at the workplace of a *different* company that does business with the union's employer. Such a boycott is designed to put pressure on the union's employer by forcing other companies to stop doing business with it. Suppose Union is on strike against Truck Co. Union is free to picket Truck Co.'s office or terminal. If Truck Co. hires replacement workers, the trucks will be back on the road, making deliveries. Now Union wants to put additional pressure on Truck Co., so it sets up picket lines at a *supermarket* where Truck Co. delivers. Union attempts to persuade customers not to shop at the store and other workers, including delivery drivers, not to enter the premises. If allowed, the picketing might result in the supermarket demanding that Truck Co. compromise with Union. But this is a secondary boycott, so it is illegal. Truck Co. and the supermarket will obtain an injunction, prohibiting the secondary boycott. See Exhibit 31.2.

LOCKOUTS

The workers have bargained with management for weeks, and discussions have turned belligerent. It is 6:00 A.M., the start of another day at the factory. But as 150 employees arrive for work, they are amazed to find the company's gate locked and armed guards standing on the other side. What is this? A lockout.

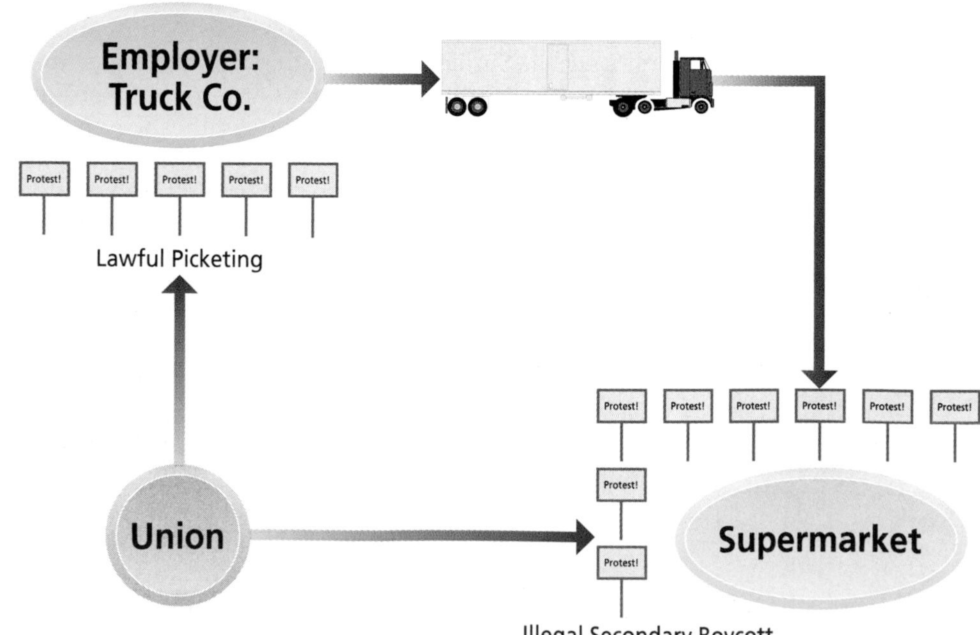

Exhibit 31.2
A union striking against Truck Co. may lawfully picket the employer, using peaceful means to urge all others to stay away. But if the union attempts to put indirect pressure on Truck Co. by picketing one of the company's customers, it is engaging in an illegal secondary boycott.

The power of a union comes ultimately from its potential to strike. But management, too, has weapons. In a lockout, management prohibits workers from entering the premises, denying the employees work and a chance to earn a paycheck. Most, but not all, lockouts are legal.

A defensive lockout is almost always legal. It is one way management can respond to union pressure such as a sit-down strike or a **whipsaw strike**, which may occur when a union is simultaneously bargaining with various employers. Suppose a machinists' union is simultaneously bargaining a contract with three engine manufacturers, attempting to obtain an identical contract from all of the companies. To pressure the companies, the union might choose to strike against only *one* of the manufacturers. This is a whipsaw strike, and it can be very effective because the struck company, losing money while the others profit, will push strongly for a compromise. But management of all three companies may respond by locking out the workers from *all* factories, even those where no strike is under way. That is a defensive lockout, and it is legal.

An offensive lockout is legal if the parties have reached a bargaining impasse. Management, bargaining a new CBA with a union, may wish to use a lockout to advance its position. It is allowed to do so *provided the parties have reached an impasse*. If there is no impasse, a lockout will *probably* be illegal. Most courts consider that a lockout before impasse indicates hostility to the union. That kind of general antagonism to a union is illegal because the NLRA guarantees employees the right to organize. In addition, management usually *must notify the union before locking it out*. Again, the purpose of the NLRA is to bring the parties together through bargaining. A lockout is a legitimate method to pressure a union into compromise, but it can have that effect only if the union is warned and given a chance to bargain.

MULTI-EMPLOYER BARGAINING AND ANTITRUST LAW

Unions often bargain simultaneously with several—or even hundreds—of employers in a particular industry. Multi-employer bargaining can benefit both sides. For the union, it is a way to obtain a contract for employees in many plants, or even nationwide, all at once. For management, it is a way of avoiding costly whipsaw strikes, in which a union closes one employer at a time, achieving maximum leverage in the process.

Does multi-employer bargaining violate antitrust law? The Sherman Act prohibits companies from banding together to fix costs, destroy competition, or dominate a market.[18] Individual workers unhappy with a multi-employer contract have periodically filed suit, claiming that multi-employer bargaining violates the Sherman Act by allowing companies to agree on uniform wages. These lawsuits invariably fail, however. **The Supreme Court has consistently held that multi-employer bargaining does not violate antitrust laws.** Congress passed the NLRA in order to achieve labor peace, and multi-employer bargaining helps accomplish that goal. Employers *do* diminish competition when they bargain together, but strikes pose a greater threat to the economy than employer collusion. Today, more than 40 percent of major collective bargaining agreements involve groups of employers in such diverse industries as construction, transportation, retail trade, clothing manufacture, real estate, and professional sports.

The Supreme Court has gone even further, permitting a group of employers to *implement* a proposal together, once the parties have bargained to impasse. The

[18] See Chapters 40 and 41, on antitrust law.

CBA between the National Football League (NFL) and the football players' union expired. During negotiations for a new contract, the NFL proposed a plan that would allow each club in the league a "developmental squad" of six players, who would practice with the team but play in games only as substitutes for injured players. The parties negotiated but could not agree on the pay or benefits for these players. The NFL unilaterally implemented a salary of $1,000 per week by sending each of its member clubs a uniform contract for use with developmental squad players. Claiming that the NFL clubs had violated the Sherman Act, 235 of the players filed suit. They lost. The Supreme Court held that the NLRA took precedence over the antitrust laws and affirmed the owners' right to implement.[19]

REGULATING UNION AFFAIRS

Along with a union's exclusive bargaining power goes a duty of fairness to all of its members. Known as the union's *duty of fair representation,* it was created by the NLRA and the Labor-Management Reporting and Disclosure Act. **The duty of fair representation requires that a union represent all members fairly, impartially, and in good faith.** A union is not entitled to favor some members over others. No union may discriminate against a member based on impermissible characteristics such as race or sex. A union is allowed to discipline a member for certain acts, such as engaging in an illegal strike or working for wages below union scale. But the union may *not* discipline a member for criticizing union leadership or attempting to replace the leadership through a proper election.

Unions must make reasonable decisions about whether to pursue an employee's grievance. A member may sue his union, claiming that the organization violated its duty of fair representation by deciding not to pursue a grievance on his behalf. But courts generally allow unions a *wide range of latitude* in deciding whether to pursue a grievance. **A union's decision not to file a grievance is illegal only if it was arbitrary, discriminatory, or in bad faith**.

Most employees fail when claiming that a union violated its duty of fair representation. Ramon Hayes worked at the Peoples Gas, Light and Coke Co. Peoples Gas fired him for theft, and the union filed a grievance. Before the grievance could be arbitrated, Hayes was convicted on drug charges. The union, mistakenly believing Hayes had been convicted on the *theft* accusation, withdrew its grievance. Later, the union learned of its error, but refused to pursue the grievance because Peoples Gas had added the drug charge as a reason for the dismissal. A court ruled that the union had probably been inept and negligent in dismissing the original grievance, but had shown no *bad faith* in its belief that the grievance was futile. The union had not violated its duty of fair representation.[20]

---

[19] *Brown v. Pro Football, Inc.*, 518 U.S. 231, 116 S. Ct. 2116, 1996 U.S. LEXIS 4047 (1996).

[20] *Hayes v. People's Gas, Light and Coke Co.*, 1992 U.S. App. LEXIS 30592 (7th Cir. 1992).

CHAPTER CONCLUSION

Workers first attempted to organize unions in this country about 200 years ago in response to appalling working conditions. These conditions are *generally* better today, and contemporary clashes between union and management are less likely to stem from sweltering temperatures in a mine than from a management decision to subcontract work or from a teacher's refusal to write college recommendations. But although the flash points have changed, labor law is still dominated by issues of organizing, collective bargaining, and concerted action.

CHAPTER REVIEW

1. Section 7 of the National Labor Relations Act (NLRA) guarantees employees the right to organize and join unions, bargain collectively, and engage in other concerted activities.
2. Section 8(a) of the NLRA makes it an unfair labor practice for an employer to interfere with union organizing, discriminate against a union member, or refuse to bargain collectively.
3. Section 8(b) of the NLRA makes it an unfair labor practice for a union to interfere with employees who are exercising their rights under §7, to encourage an employer to discriminate against an employee because of a labor dispute, to refuse to bargain collectively, or to engage in an illegal strike or boycott.
4. Section 9 of the NLRA makes a validly recognized union the *exclusive* representative of the employees.
5. During a union organizing campaign, an employer may vigorously present anti-union views to its employees, but it may not use threats or promises of benefits to defeat the union effort.
6. The National Labor Relations Board (NLRB) will certify a proposed bargaining unit only if the employees share a community of interest.
7. The employer and the union *must* bargain over wages, hours, and other terms and conditions of employment. They *may* bargain other subjects, but neither side may insist on doing so.
8. The union and the employer must bargain in good faith, but they are not obligated to reach an agreement. Management may not unilaterally change wages, hours, or terms and conditions of employment without bargaining to impasse.
9. The NLRA guarantees employees the right to strike, with some limitations.
10. After an *economic* strike, an employer is not obligated to lay off replacement workers to give a striker her job back, but it may not discriminate against a striker. After a *ULP* strike, the striking worker must get her job back.
11. Picketing the employer's workplace in support of a strike is generally lawful; a secondary boycott is generally illegal.
12. An employer may lock out workers, but only after giving them notice.
13. Multi-employer bargaining and implementation do not violate antitrust laws.
14. The duty of fair representation requires that a union represent all members fairly, impartially, and in good faith.

PRACTICE TEST

1. Power, Inc. operated a surface coal mine in central Pennsylvania. Financial losses led it to lay off a number of employees. After that, several employees contacted the United Mine Workers of America (UMWA), which began an organizing drive at the company. Power's general manager and foreman both warned the miners that if the company was unionized, it would be shut down. An office manager told one of the miners that the company would get rid of union supporters. Shortly before the election was to take place, Power laid off 13 employees, all of whom had signed union cards. One employee, who had not signed a union card, had low seniority but was not laid off. Later, one of Power's lawyers told several miners that anyone caught helping the 13 laid-off workers by contributing to a union hardship fund would "be out there looking for help from somebody else." Comment.

2. Triec, Inc. is a small electrical contracting company in Springfield, Ohio, owned by its executives Yeazell, Jones, and Heaton. Employees contacted the International Brotherhood of Electrical Workers, which began an organizing drive. Six of the 11 employees in the bargaining unit signed authorization cards. The company declined to recognize the union, which petitioned the NLRB to schedule an election. The company then granted several new benefits for all workers, including higher wages, paid vacations, and other measures. When the election was held, only 2 of the 11 bargaining unit members voted for the union. Did the company violate the NLRA?

3. Q-1 Motor Express was an interstate trucking company. When a union attempted to organize Q-1's drivers, it met heavy resistance. A supervisor told one driver that if he knew what was good for him, he would stay away from the union organizer. The company president told another employee that he had the right to fire everybody, close the company, and then rehire new drivers after 72 hours. He made numerous other threats to workers and their families. Based on the extreme nature of the company's opposition, what exceptional remedy did the union seek before the NLRB?

4. Douglas Kuroda worked for the Hertz Corp. He and his supervisor had a heated argument in which Kuroda told his boss, "You may have a master's degree but you don't know shit." The supervisor instructed Kuroda to punch out for the day, but Kuroda refused to leave until security officers escorted him off the premises. Hertz fired him, and Kuroda filed a grievance. The union represented Kuroda at an arbitration hearing. During the hearing, the union made no objection to certain evidence that the company offered to demonstrate why it fired Kuroda. The arbitrator ruled in favor of the company. Kuroda sued his union (and also Hertz). What kind of claim is he making against the union? Is he likely to win his claim?

5. Gibson Greetings, Inc. had a plant in Berea, Kentucky, where the workers belonged to the International Brotherhood of Firemen & Oilers. The old CBA expired, and the parties negotiated a new one, but were unable to reach an agreement on economic issues. The union struck. At the next bargaining session, the company claimed that the strike violated the *old* CBA, which had a no-strike clause and which stated that the terms of the old CBA would continue in force as long as the parties were bargaining a *new* CBA. The company refused to bargain until the union at least agreed that by bargaining, the company was not giving up its claim of an illegal strike. The two sides returned to bargaining, but meanwhile the company hired replacement workers. Eventually, the striking workers offered to return to work, but Gibson refused to rehire many of them. In court, the union claimed that the company had committed a ULP by (1) insisting the strike was illegal and (2) refusing to bargain until the union acknowledged the company's position. Why is it very important to the union to establish the company's act as a ULP? *Was* it a ULP?

6. YOU BE THE JUDGE WRITING PROBLEM Plainville Ready Mix Concrete Co. was bargaining a CBA with the drivers' union. Negotiations went forward, on and off, over many months, with wages the major source of disagreement. Plainville made its final offer of $9.50 per hour, with step increases of $.25 per hour in a year and another $.25 per hour the following year. The plan also included certain incentive pay. The union refused to accept the offer, and the two sides reached an impasse. Plainville then announced it was implementing its plans. It established a wage rate of $9.50 per hour but eliminated the step increases and incentive pay. Was the company's implementation of the wage increase legal? **Argument for Plainville:** The NLRA only requires the company to bargain in good faith, which we did. The law does not obligate us to agree to anything. Once the parties reached an impasse, Plainville could implement any plan it wanted. **Argument for the Union:** When the parties reach an impasse, the employer is permitted to implement whatever it proposed at the bargaining table. It would defeat the purpose of collective bargaining if a company could implement plans it had never proposed.

7. Eads Transfer, Inc. was a moving and storage company with a small workforce represented by the General Teamsters, Chauffeurs and Helpers Union. When the CBA expired, the parties failed to reach agreement on a new one, and the union struck. As negotiations continued, Eads hired temporary replacement workers. After 10 months of the strike, some union workers offered to return to work, but Eads made no response to the offer. Two months later, more workers offered to return to work, but Eads would not accept any of the offers. Eventually, Eads notified all workers that they would not be allowed back to work until a new CBA had been signed. The union filed ULP claims against the company. Please rule.

8. Olivetti Office U.S.A., Inc. was located in Newington, Connecticut, and its workers were represented by the United Automobile, Aerospace and Agriculture Implement Workers of America. The company's president reported to the union that Olivetti was losing money. He insisted that unless the union renegotiated certain wage increases in the current CBA, Olivetti would subcontract work to cheaper parts of the country to save money. The union requested to bargain over the proposed subcontracting, and Olivetti agreed. But when the sides met, the company would not permit the union to see the financial data that supported its arguments. After several meetings, the company declared an impasse, implemented its subcontracting proposal, and laid off workers in Connecticut. The union claimed this was a ULP. Was it?

9. Fred Schipul taught English at the Thomaston (Connecticut) High School for 18 years. When the position of English Department chairperson became vacant, Schipul applied, but the Board of Education appointed a less senior teacher. Schipul filed a grievance, based on a CBA provision that required the Board to promote the most senior teacher where two or more applicants were equal in qualification. Before the arbitrator ruled on the grievance, the Board eliminated all department chairpersons. The arbitrator ruled in Schipul's favor. The Board then reinstated all department chairs—all but the English Department. Comment.

10. Labor Day is a national holiday originally intended to celebrate the contributions of working men and women. But for most people today it simply means a day off from work—or the day before school begins. What are some reasons that unions have declined in membership and power? Are there are any reasons to think that organized labor may rebound and increase its strength?

11. **RIGHT & WRONG** The chapter refers in several places to the contentious issue of subcontracting. Make an argument for management in favor of a company's ethical right to subcontract, and one for unions in opposition.

INTERNET RESEARCH PROBLEM

Take a look at **http://www.uniteunion.org/sweatshops/sweatshop.html**. What are sweatshops? Do they exist in the United States? Click on *students against sweatshops*. Describe a current student campaign about this issue. Do you agree or disagree with what the students are doing? Why?

You can find further practice problems in the Online Quiz at http://beatty.westbuslaw.com or in the Study Guide that accompanies this text.

UNIT 5

BUSINESS ORGANIZATIONS

CHAPTER 32

STARTING A BUSINESS

At long last, Rachel was in love. For years, she had yearned to start her own business, but the perfect concept always eluded her. Then, surfing the Internet one day, she found the idea she had been searching for: movie theaters that show only classic films. Sure, you can rent *Star Wars* or *Gone with the Wind* anytime, but the little box at home cannot compete with a large screen and digital sound. At home, Atlanta simply does not burn as hot. According to the Internet, these theaters were already a rave success in Paris. Why not in Des Moines?

Rachel began looking for investors. Finally, at her nineteenth lunch meeting, she found Ross, who was as enthusiastic as she. Two days later, they signed a lease on a suitable property. Prospects for the business looked great. Then, while riding his bike on company business, Ross crashed into a pedestrian. Only when Rachel was served with a complaint did she learn that their business was a partnership, which meant that she and Ross were both personally liable for his accident.

In a panic, Rachel resumed surfing the Net, this time looking for legal information. She downloaded a sample corporate charter and formed a corporation, BigScreen, Inc. Now she and Ross enjoyed limited liability and could sell stock to outside investors. Their college friend from Hong

Kong, Liang, was the first to buy shares. But other prospective purchasers insisted that BigScreen be organized as an S corporation for tax reasons. Back to the Internet, where Rachel learned that non-resident aliens could not hold stock in S corps. Liang's participation disqualified BigScreen.

By this time, Rachel was surfing in desperation. At last she found an answer: BigScreen could become a limited liability company. This form of business provided all the advantages of an S corp with none of the disadvantages. She and Ross immediately formed an LLC, transferred BigScreen's assets, and sighed in relief—until tax day. The IRS considered their transfer of assets to be a sale. Suddenly, they faced a huge tax bill, with no way to pay it. Ross announced he was withdrawing from the business.

"You promised to stay five years," Rachel insisted.

"Yeah," Ross agreed, "but I never signed the operating agreement, so tough luck for you."

"Ross, I trusted you," Rachel protested.

"Frankly, my dear, I don't give a damn," replied Ross, slamming the door as he left.

Many people dream of starting their own business. They look for exactly the right idea to power a company to success. Creativity is an important ingredient for any successful start-up. So are hard work and finely honed business skills. And so is the law. Time and again in these next chapters we will see that legal issues can have as profound an impact on the success of a company as any business decision. The law affects virtually every aspect of business. Wise (and successful) entrepreneurs know how to use the law to their advantage.

To begin, entrepreneurs must select a form of organization. The correct choice can reduce taxes, liability, and conflict while facilitating outside investment. If entrepreneurs do not make a choice for themselves, the law will automatically select a (potentially undesirable) default option. Numerous alternatives are available: sole proprietorship, general partnership, limited partnership, corporation, limited liability company, limited liability partnership, joint venture, business trust, or cooperative. The Web site http://www.inreach.com/sbdc/book/ offers links to a book on how to start a business. It includes an "Entrepreneur Test" to assess whether you have the right personality characteristics.

SOLE PROPRIETORSHIPS

A sole proprietorship is an unincorporated business owned by a single person. It is the most common form of business organization. For example, 15-year-old Andre Ware sells safety products—reflectors, fire extinguishers, smoke detectors—door-to-door in Plano, Texas. In Cleveland, Linda Brazdil runs ExSciTe (which stands for Excellence in Science Teaching), a company that helps teachers prepare hands-on science experiments in the classroom using such basic items as vinegar, lemon juice, and red cabbage. (Students do *not* have to eat their mistakes.)

Sole proprietorships are easy and inexpensive to create and operate. There is no need to hire a lawyer or register with the government. The company is not even required to file a separate tax return—all profits and losses are reported on the owner's personal return. A very few states, such as California, require sole proprietors to obtain a business license. Some cities and towns also require a business license. And states generally require sole proprietors to register their business name if it is different from their own. Linda Brazdil, for example, would file a "d/b/a" or "doing business as" certificate for "ExSciTe."

Sole proprietorships also have some serious disadvantages. First, the owner of the business is responsible for all of the business's debts. If ExSciTe cannot pay its suppliers or if a student is injured by an exploding cabbage, Linda Brazdil is *personally* liable. She may have to sell her house and car to pay the debt. Second, the owner of a sole proprietorship has limited options for financing her business. Debt is generally her only source of working capital because she has no stock to sell. If someone else brings in capital and helps with the management of the business, then it is a partnership, not a sole proprietorship. For this reason, sole proprietorships work best for small businesses without large capital needs. Go to **http://www.ezaccounting.com/previewcal1a.html** for help in preparing a sole proprietorship balance sheet and income statement.

No form of organization is right—or wrong—for everyone. Consider these very different experiences of two small-business owners.

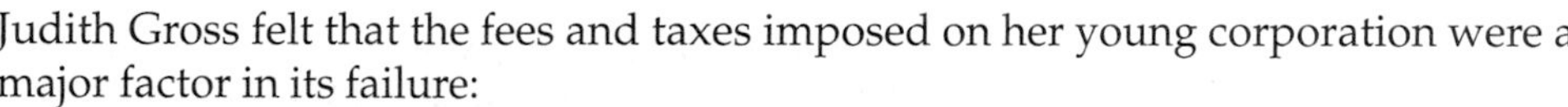

Judith Gross felt that the fees and taxes imposed on her young corporation were a major factor in its failure:

> It seemed like a dream come true. I always thought I had the right instincts to publish a newsletter. When 500 people packed a seminar on a controversial new technology sweeping my industry, dollar signs danced in my head. I was on my way. Now, two and a half years later, I realize that what I was on my way to was becoming one of those small-business owners who list failure on their resumes.
>
> Incorporating my business was a major mistake because the expenses were more than I could afford. I did not find out until later that 76 percent of all small businesses operate as sole proprietorships. Although being a corporation protected me in case of a lawsuit, I got a shock when my accountant pointed out the disadvantages of incorporation in the heavily taxed, heavily regulated nation's capital. Now I realize that incorporating is good for a company when raising capital is an essential part of the ongoing business. Real estate and construction are two examples that come to mind. But a service business, which relies mostly on money put up by the people involved, would be better operated as a sole proprietorship or partnership.[1]

For Beth and Drexel Wright, however, a sole proprietorship was disastrous. Mr. Wright was the founder and sole proprietor of Quaker Siding Co., a construction and remodeling business in Millville, Pennsylvania. Within a year of their marriage, the Wrights went into bankruptcy proceedings. Because the company was a sole proprietorship, the court liquidated many of their personal assets—farm equipment, cattle, vehicles, rental properties—to pay creditors. For a time, they were afraid they might even lose their home. Four years later, the Wrights reached an agreement with their creditors and were allowed out of bankruptcy. They immediately incorporated their business as Quaker Construction Services, Inc.

GENERAL PARTNERSHIPS

A partnership is an unincorporated association of two or more co-owners who carry on a business for profit.[2] Each co-owner is called a *general partner*. Each partner is personally liable for the debts of the enterprise whether or not she caused them. Thus a partner is liable for any injury that another partner or an employee causes while on partnership business as well as for any contract signed

[1] Judith Gross, "Autopsy of a Business," *Home Office Computing*, Oct. 1993, vol. 11, no. 10, p. 52. Reprinted with permission.

[2] Uniform Partnership Act §6(1).

on behalf of the partnership. This form of organization can be particularly risky if the group of owners is large and the partners do not know each other.

Daniel Matter knows firsthand about the risks of a partnership. A former partner in the accounting firm Pannell Kerr Foster, he thought he had heard the last of the firm when he resigned his partnership. He was wrong. *Seven* years later, he and 260 other former partners of the California firm were served with a 78-page lawsuit seeking $24 million in damages. The lawsuit alleged that Pannell Kerr had been negligent in preparing financial reports for a bankrupt Tennessee savings and loan. Although Daniel Matter had never worked for that particular client, he was potentially liable because he had been a partner when the audit was done. At age 53, Matter feared losing everything he owned.

As many law, accounting, and consulting firms have grown larger, they have discovered another disadvantage to partnerships: management can be difficult. In theory, all partners in a firm are equal and have an equal right to share in management. When two sisters-in-law form a small accounting firm, they can easily discuss business issues—from hiring a new associate to choosing a brand of telephone. But when the partnership has 1,000 accountants speaking four different languages on three continents, consultation becomes difficult. Although most large firms authorize a small management committee to make day-to-day decisions, other partners may still expect to be consulted. One partner in a law firm complained bitterly when all 163 partners were assembled to vote on the style of ceiling tile for the conference room. Yet, to be fair, the managing partner had called for the vote because everyone had complained when he changed the typeface on the firm's stationery without consulting them.

Partnerships have other disadvantages. Financing a partnership may be difficult because the firm cannot sell shares as a corporation does. The capital needs of the partnership must be met by contributions from partners or by borrowing. Likewise, a partner only has the right to transfer the *value* of her partnership interest, not the interest itself. She cannot, for example, transfer the right to participate in firm management. Take the case of Evan and his mother. She is a partner in the immensely profitable McBain Consulting firm. She dies, leaving him an orphan with no siblings. He overcomes his grief as best he can and goes to her office on the next Monday to take over her job and her partnership. Imagine his surprise when her partners tell him that, as her sole heir, he can inherit the *value* of her partnership, but not the partnership itself. He is out on the sidewalk within the hour. The partners have promised him a check in the mail.

If a partner decides to leave a partnership, he is typically entitled to his share of the value of the partnership. But how does the partnership determine that value? Often with great difficulty. The departing person is in the odd position of arguing that, although he no longer cares to be a partner, the business is nonetheless immensely valuable. Naturally, the partnership asserts the opposite. It is wise, therefore, for partners to agree in advance how a partnership interest will be valued when a partner leaves (or dies). A typical agreement might specify a formula for calculating the value as well as a mechanism for resolving disputes.

Given these disadvantages, why does anyone do business as a partnership? Like sole proprietorships, partnerships are easy to form. Although a partnership should have a written agreement, it is perfectly legal without one (a sample agreement is available at **http://www.legaldocs.com/**). In fact, nothing is required in the way of forms or filings or agreements. The partnership simply needs at least two people who share in the management and profits. Forming a partnership is so easy that sometimes people do so without knowing it, but that is a story for the next two chapters.

A partnership is not a taxable entity, which means it does not pay taxes itself. All income and losses are passed through to the partners and reported on their personal income tax returns. Corporations, by contrast, are taxable entities and pay income tax on their profits. Shareholders must then pay tax on dividends from the corporation. Thus a dollar is taxed only once before it ends up in a partner's bank account, but twice before it is deposited by a shareholder.

Exhibit 32.1 compares the single taxation of partnerships with the double taxation of corporations. Suppose, as shown in the exhibit, that a corporation and a partnership each receive $10,000 in additional income. The corporation pays tax at a top rate of 35 percent.[3] Thus the corporation pays $3,500 of the $10,000 in tax. The corporation pays out the remaining $6,500 as a dividend of $2,167 to each of its three shareholders. Then the shareholders are taxed at the top individual rate of 39.6 percent, which means they each pay a tax of $858. They are each left with $1,309. Of the initial $10,000, more than 60 percent ($6,074) has gone to the Internal Revenue Service (IRS).

Compare the corporation to a partnership. The partnership itself pays no taxes, so it can pass on $3,333 to each of its partners. At the 39.6 percent rate, they will each pay an individual income tax of $1,320. As partners, they pocket $2,013, which is $704 more than they could keep as shareholders. Of the partnership's initial $10,000, about 40 percent ($3,960) has gone to the IRS—compared with the corporation's 60 percent.

Reduced taxation is a partnership's major advantage over a corporation. A partnership also has an important advantage over a sole proprietorship—partners. Sole proprietors are on their own; partners have colleagues to help them and, equally important, to supply capital for the business. Sole proprietorships often turn into partnerships for exactly this reason.

Finally, partnerships have substantial law and tradition behind them. Historically, many states would not allow professionals such as accountants, engineers, lawyers, and health care professionals (e.g., doctors, dentists, pharmacists)

Exhibit 32.1

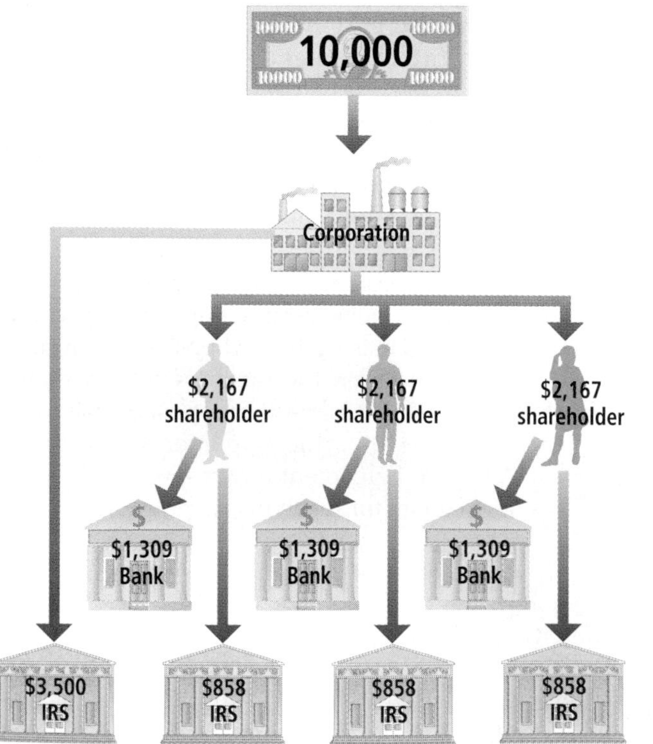

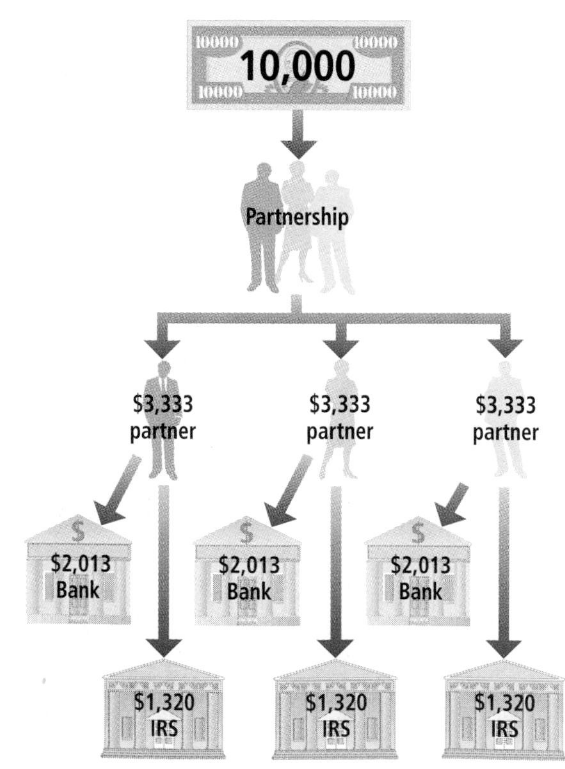

[3] This is the federal tax rate; most states also levy a corporate tax.

to limit their liability by incorporating. The idea was that their work is so important and potentially so harmful that they should be encouraged to practice carefully and competently. Nothing focuses a person's mind like the thought of paying from his own pocket for any mistakes. Consequently, professionals had no choice but to be partners. But even today, although most states have changed their laws to permit professionals to limit their liability by organizing as professional corporations and limited liability companies (discussed later in this chapter), some businesses have resolutely remained partnerships.

PROFESSIONAL CORPORATIONS

Most states now allow professionals to incorporate, but in a special way. These organizations are called "professional corporations" or "PCs." **In many states, PCs provide more liability protection than a partnership.** If a member of a PC commits malpractice, the corporation's assets are at risk, but not the personal assets of the innocent members. If Drs. Sharp, Payne, and Graves form a *partnership*, all the partners will be personally liable when Dr. Payne accidentally leaves her scalpel inside a patient. If the three doctors have formed a *PC* instead, Dr. Payne's Aspen condo and the assets of the PC will be at risk, but not the personal assets of the two other doctors.

Generally, the shareholders of a PC are not personally liable for the contract debts of the organization, such as leases or bank loans. Thus, if Sharp, Payne & Graves, P.C. is unable to pay its rent, the landlord cannot recover from the personal assets of any of the doctors. As partners, the doctors would be personally liable.

PCs have some limitations. First, all shareholders of the corporation must be members of the same profession. For Sharp, Payne & Graves, P.C., that means all shareholders must be licensed physicians. Other valued employees cannot own stock. Second, like other corporations, the required legal technicalities for forming and maintaining a PC are expensive and time-consuming. Third, tax issues can be complicated. A PC is a separate taxable entity, like any other corporation. It must pay tax on its profits, and then its shareholders pay tax on any dividends they receive. *Salaries*, however, are deductible from firm profits. Thus the PC can avoid taxes on its profits by paying out all profits as salary. But any profits remaining in firm coffers *at the end of the year* are taxable. To avoid tax, PCs must be careful to calculate their profits accurately and pay them out before year's end. This chore can be time-consuming, and any error may cause unnecessary tax liability.

LIMITED PARTNERSHIPS

The Montreal Expos are owned by a limited partnership.

The owners of the Montreal Expos asked investment banker Jacques Menard to find a buyer for the baseball team. Instead, he found 11 other people to help him buy the team. They formed a limited partnership, and each purchaser invested between $1 million and $7 million. During their first year of ownership, the Expos lost nearly $5 million and their final 14 home games, finishing in the cellar of their division. Given this dismal showing, management had no choice but to fire popular team manager, Buck Rodgers. Then a concrete beam in the team's stadium collapsed.

Fortunately, the owners had formed a *limited* partnership. Limited partnerships and general partnerships have similar names but, like many siblings, they operate very differently. Here are the major differences between these two types of organizations.

STRUCTURE

General partnerships have only *general* partners. Limited partnerships have two types of partners—*limited* partners and *general* partners. A limited partnership must have at least one of each.

LIABILITY

All the partners in a general partnership are *personally* liable for the debts of the partnership. **In a limited partnership, only the general partners are *personally* liable.** As a rule, the limited partners are like corporate shareholders—they risk only their investment in the partnership (which is called their "capital contribution"). No matter how much money the Expos lose, creditors cannot take the personal property of the limited partners. Once the assets of the limited partnership are exhausted, the creditors can go after the personal wealth of the general partners.

One potential pitfall does lurk for limited partners: a limited partner will be treated as a general partner (and therefore be *personally* liable to a third party) if (1) the limited partner helps control the business and (2) the third party reasonably believes that the limited partner is a general partner. Many disputes have arisen over this rule. However, the most recent version of the Revised Uniform Limited Partnership Act has reduced litigation on this issue by listing these specific circumstances under which a limited partner will *not* be considered a general partner:

- Being an agent or employee of the partnership
- Being a consultant to the partnership
- Guaranteeing partnership debt
- Attending a partnership meeting
- Voting on various partnership activities[4]

For example, as a limited partner in a real estate partnership, Cassidy is not personally liable for the partnership's debts even if she goes to work for it as a project manager. But if, in dealing with potential customers, she implies that she is a general partner, she becomes as liable as one.

Again, the general partners of a limited partnership are personally liable for all the debts of the partnership. Back in Montreal, that might be of some concern to Claude Brochu, the Expos' general partner. If creditors are unable to collect from the team, they will claim Brochu's house and other personal assets. To avoid this problem, Brochu could have formed a corporation—Brochu, Inc.—to serve as general partner. Then, only the assets of the corporation, not Brochu's personal assets, would have been at risk. This is precisely what most entrepreneurs do when they form limited partnerships. The major disadvantage is simply the effort of forming two entities—the corporate general partner and the limited partnership.

Some states now permit limited liability limited partnerships. **In a *limited liability limited partnership*, the general partner is not personally liable for the debts of the partnership**. These statutes effectively remove the major disadvantage of limited partnerships.

---

[4] The National Conference of Commissioners of Uniform State Laws prepared the original Limited Partnership Act in 1916. Since then, the Act has been amended twice—in 1976 and 1985. Most states have passed some version of the revised Act.

FORMATION

General partnerships can be formed very casually, sometimes without the partners even being aware of it. Not so for limited partnerships: the general partners must file a **certificate of limited partnership** with their Secretary of State. Although most limited partnerships do have a partnership agreement, it is not required. (A sample limited partnership agreement is available at **http://www.legaldocs.com/** or **http://www.tannedfeet.com/html/legal_forms.html**.) Failure to comply with the necessary formalities can cause serious problems, as the following case illustrates.

CELLWAVE TELEPHONE SERVICES L.P. v. FCC

30 F.3d 1533, 1994 U.S. App. LEXIS 21834
United States Court of Appeals for the D.C. Circuit, 1994

Facts: Cellwave Telephone Services Limited Partnership applied to the Federal Communications Commission (FCC) for a license to operate and construct cellular telephone systems in two rural areas. The FCC awards these licenses by lottery. Cellwave won the lottery, but upon investigation, the FCC discovered that Cellwave had never filed its limited partnership certificate with the Secretary of State in Delaware although all the limited partners had signed the limited partnership agreement. The FCC dismissed Cellwave's application on the grounds that the partnership did not exist when the application was filed.

You Be the Judge: Did the FCC have the right to dismiss Cellwave's application?

Argument for Cellwave: Of all the petty, bureaucratic decisions! The limited partnership was effectively in existence as soon as the limited partners signed the agreement. It is not as if the Secretary of State had to *approve* the certificate in any way. He could not refuse to accept it for filing. The filing simply provides an official record that the partnership exists. But the FCC did not need official notice; it had the original agreement, which is better than a certificate from the Secretary of State.

Argument for the FCC: The number one priority of the FCC is to ensure adequate service for everyone in America. For many people in rural areas, a cellular phone is the most reliable means of communication. When it awards a license, the FCC has to be sure that the licensee will be able to develop a telephone system. Without these strict rules, people would sign up for the lottery and then, once they had won, try to put together a company. The FCC cannot take that chance with rural citizens. If Cellwave cannot manage a simple legal task like organizing a limited partnership, how can it run a telephone system?

Cellwave argues that all the limited partners had signed the limited partnership agreement and that is sufficient. The FCC did not make up the rules; it is simply following Delaware law, which says very precisely, "a limited partnership is formed at the time of the filing of the initial certificate of limited partnership in the Office of the Secretary of State." What could be clearer than that? If Cellwave has a problem with the law, it should talk with its legislators.

MANAGEMENT

General partners have the right to manage a limited partnership. That is only fair, considering they also bear the risk of personal liability. Limited partners are essentially passive investors with few management rights beyond the right to be informed about the partnership business. Exhibit 32.2 illustrates the roles of the partners in a limited partnership. Limited partnership agreements can, however, expand the rights of limited partners. These agreements, for example, often permit a substantial majority (i.e., two-thirds) of the limited partners to remove a general partner. In any event, when *general* partnerships grow large, management becomes difficult. But because *limited* partners are not allowed to manage, a limited partnership can handle a very large number of partners.

Exhibit 32.2

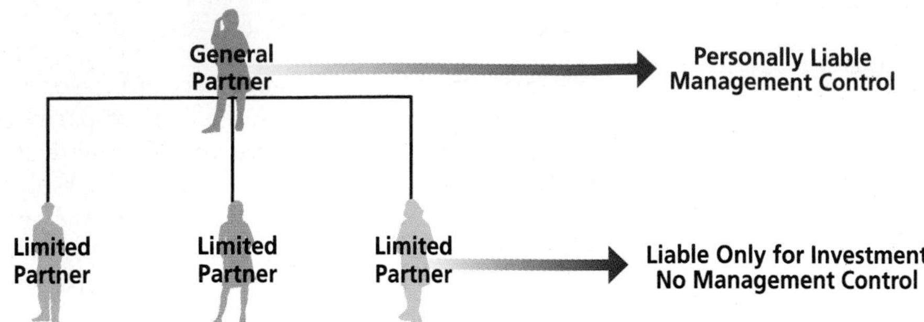

TRANSFER OF OWNERSHIP

Limited partners do not have an automatic right to sell their interests in the partnership to a new limited partner; they can generally do so only if the partnership agreement or the other partners permit. However, unless the partnership agreement provides otherwise, limited partners do have the right to withdraw, and the partnership must compensate them for their interest. A general partner in a limited partnership has the right to withdraw at any time. The limited partnership can continue as long as at least one general partner remains and is willing to carry on the business.

Limited partnerships and general partnerships have one crucial attribute in common: neither is a taxable entity. Income is taxed only once before landing in a partner's pocket, and partners can deduct losses against their other income. Tax issues become even more important if the business is sold. When a corporation sells its assets, the corporation pays tax first. Then when it distributes the profits to the shareholders, they pay tax, too. If a limited partnership sells its assets, the profits go straight to the partners because the partnership itself pays no taxes. For this reason, business lawyers often advise entrepreneurs to consider a limited partnership instead of a corporation. Nevertheless, clients sometimes resist because they are simply not as familiar with the limited partnership form.

CORPORATIONS

Although the concept of a corporation is very old—it began with the Greeks and spread from them through the Romans into English law—corporations were traditionally viewed with deep suspicion. What were shareholders doing to need limited liability? Why did they have to cower behind a corporate shield? For this reason, shareholders originally needed special permission to form a corporation. In England, corporations could be created only by special charter from the king or, later, from Parliament. But with the advent of the Industrial Revolution, large-scale manufacturing enterprises needed huge amounts of capital from investors who were not involved in management and did not want to be personally liable for the debts of an organization that they were not managing. In 1811, New York became the first jurisdiction in the United States to permit routine incorporation.[5]

State laws regulate corporations, but federal statutes determine their tax status. Many states treat small corporations differently and even give them a different name: close corporations. The federal tax code also provides more favorable

[5] An Act Relative to Incorporation for Manufacturing Purpose, 1811 N.Y. Laws ch. 67, §111.

Exhibit 32.3
Both a regular and a close corporation can be either a C or an S corporation.

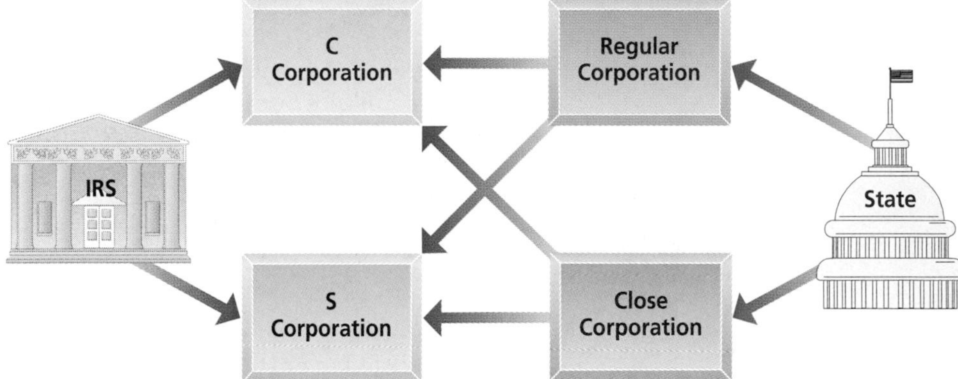

tax treatment to some small corporations and calls them S corporations. But the two sets of statutes are completely independent. Thus a close corporation or a regular (nonclose) corporation may or may not be an S corporation. Exhibit 32.3 illustrates the difference between state and IRS regulation of corporations.

Corporations in General

When Judy George was a young child, her parents started a plating business using a process her father had invented. Like many entrepreneurs, her parents devoted so much time and energy to this new project that they were rarely at home. Feeling abandoned by her parents, George became obsessed with her surroundings. If she could make her room just the way she wanted it, she would feel safe. As she put it, "Design was a way of fulfilling my own personal fantasy." She also vowed that one day she would start her own business to make money and create beautiful designs. George realized her dream when she started Domain, an upscale, European-style chain of furniture stores.

George's lawyer suggested that she incorporate Domain. He explained that a corporation would offer the protection of limited liability. If Domain flopped, and could not pay its bills, George and her backers would lose their investment in the company, but not their other assets.

He also explained that limited liability does not protect against all debts. Individuals are always responsible for their *own* acts. If a Domain employee was in an accident with a company van, Domain would be liable for any harm to the other driver, but its investors would not be personally liable. If George herself crashed the van, Domain would be liable, and *so would George*. If Domain did not pay the judgment, George would have to, from her personal assets if necessary. A corporation protects managers and investors from personal liability for the debts of the corporation and the actions of others, but not against personal negligence (or other torts and crimes).

Corporations have other advantages besides limited liability. They provide flexibility for enterprises small (with one owner) and large (thousands of shareholders). For example, partnership interests are not transferable without the permission of the other partners, whereas corporate stock can be easily bought and sold. Further, when a sole proprietor dies, legally so does the business. But corporations have perpetual existence: they can continue without their founders.

The major disadvantage of a corporation is simply the expense and effort required to create and operate it. Because corporations are taxable entities, they must pay taxes and file returns. The cost of establishing a corporation may exceed $1,000 in legal and filing fees, not to mention the cost of the annual filings that states require. Corporations must also hold annual meetings for both shareholders and directors. Minutes of these meetings must be kept indefinitely in the company minute book.

Judy George knew that she needed at least $3 million to get Domain up and running. She could not borrow that much money, so she needed to sell stock. She chose the corporate form of organization primarily because it would be the most convenient for raising funds.

CLOSE CORPORATIONS

Reynoldo has always been a fabulous cook. He, his son Juan, and Juan's friend Marta have decided to open a restaurant featuring "cucina nueva"—modern, light Latin American food. Reynoldo will do the cooking in the back, while Juan and Marta run the front operation, everything from maitre d' to accountant. They will finance the start-up costs of *Abogado Verde* by borrowing from the local bank; the loan will be secured by a mortgage on their houses. One of the first questions they face is, What form of organization? A sole proprietorship will not work, because there are three of them. They are concerned about the liability of a partnership. A corporation may be the best option, except it seems like an expensive bother. Who would be on their board of directors? Why do they even need a board? They have no plans to sell shares to the public. They want to act like a partnership, with all decisions made equally, but they need the legal protection of a corporation.

Their lawyer suggests that a close corporation might be the best choice. Originally, the terms **"close corporation"** and **"closely held corporation"** referred simply to a company whose stock was not publicly traded on a stock exchange (in other words, a "privately held" company). Most close corporations are small, although some privately held corporations, such as Hallmark Cards, Inc. and Mars, Inc. (maker of Mars candy bars) are huge. Beginning in New York in 1948, states began to amend their corporation statutes to make special provisions for entrepreneurs such as the *Abogado Verde* team. By now, roughly half the states have made some special accommodation for close corporations. In some states, a corporation must affirmatively elect to be treated as a close corporation; in others, any corporation can take advantage of these special provisions. Now when lawyers refer to close corporations, they usually mean not merely a privately held company, but one that has taken advantage of the close corporation provisions of its state code.

Although the provisions of close corporation statutes vary from state to state, they tend to have certain common themes:

- **Protection of Minority Shareholders.** Marta is concerned that Reynoldo and Juan may form an alliance and vote against her. Close corporations are permitted great leeway to prevent such problems. For example, *Abogado Verde, Inc.* could require a unanimous vote of all shareholders to choose officers, set salaries, or pay dividends. It could grant each shareholder veto power over all important corporate decisions. With provisions such as these, Marta can ensure that she has input into all important decisions.
- **Transfer Restrictions.** What would happen if Reynoldo sold some of his shares to his other (irresponsible) children? Or if Marta and Juan broke up, and Juan sold shares to his new girlfriend? Close corporation statutes often limit a shareholder's ability to sell shares without first offering them to the other owners. Similarly, if Reynoldo died, Juan and Marta would have the first option to buy his stock.
- **Flexibility.** Close corporations can typically operate without a board of directors, a formal set of bylaws, or annual shareholder meetings.

- **Dispute Resolution.** The three shareholders are allowed to agree in advance that any one of them can dissolve the corporation if some particular event occurs or, if they choose, for any reason at all. Marta could, for example, insist on the right to dissolve the corporation herself at any time, or if revenues for a month fall below a certain level. Even without such an agreement, a shareholder can ask a court to dissolve a close corporation if the other owners behave "oppressively" or "unfairly." The mere threat of such an action will be some check on Reynoldo and Juan.

The following case illustrates that, no matter how badly a shareholder behaves, her rights in a close corporation are still protected.

MICHAEL L. RETZER v. NANCY B. RETZER

578 So. 2d 580, 1990 Miss. LEXIS 858

Supreme Court of Mississippi, 1990

Facts: Shortly after Mr. and Mrs. Retzer were married, they moved to Greenville, Mississippi, and opened a McDonald's restaurant. Mr. Retzer managed the restaurant, working 18 hours a day. Mrs. Retzer made little contribution to the business. Mr. Retzer subsequently purchased four additional McDonald's restaurants, transferring ownership of them to Retzer and Retzer, Inc., a Mississippi close corporation. Mr. and Mrs. Retzer each owned 1,600 shares of the corporation.

Mr. Retzer discovered that his wife was having an affair with their attorney. As a condition for salvaging their marriage, Mrs. Retzer agreed to end the affair. She also permitted the corporation to issue 10 additional shares to Mr. Retzer to give him corporate control.

Mrs. Retzer was a profligate spender, often paying more than $3,000 for a dress. When she overdrew her checking account, an officer at the bank would notify Mr. Retzer so that he could replenish her account. Once, when he let her checks bounce, Mrs. Retzer came to his office and began throwing pieces of valuable porcelain. Mr. Retzer called the pastor to calm her down.

Despite the agreement with her husband, Mrs. Retzer continued her affair. The Retzers subsequently divorced on the grounds of Mrs. Retzer's adultery. Their joint net worth was $4 million.

Issue: What are Mr. Retzer's obligations to Mrs. Retzer as a minority shareholder in Retzer and Retzer, Inc.?

Excerpts from Justice Hawkins's Decision: Where divorce has been granted to the husband on the ground of the wife's adultery, this court has consistently denied any alimony, period. Mr. Retzer does have substantial financial obligations to Mrs. Retzer, however, arising from her ownership of almost half of the shares of Retzer and Retzer, Inc.

Courts look quite differently upon the respective duties existing between majority and minority shareholders in publicly held and close corporations. Retzer and Retzer, Inc., is a very close corporation, which has existed solely for the financial benefit of two people, the Retzers. For almost two decades, and through Mr. Retzer's management, the corporation has indeed furnished them both with large incomes. Now, through ownership of ten more shares than she, Mr. Retzer has control of the management of Retzer and Retzer. As such, under well-settled principles he has a fiduciary obligation to Mrs. Retzer in the management of her property. He has a trustee's duty to preserve, protect and produce income from her corporate shares.

He must manage the corporation prudently, and after paying necessary and reasonable expenses, and setting aside whatever is reasonably necessary for corporate reserves and equipment and facilities, pay her 49.8 percent of the net remaining. He will not be acting at arm's length, but as trustee over her shares. He must keep her currently, fully and accurately informed and abreast of his management, and under regular periodic accounting. While their interest as husband and wife was essentially identical, now they are adverse to each other. This will make his conduct as trustee that much more subject to close scrutiny by a chancery court.

With the hostility existing between them, it would no doubt be preferable if somehow the property of Mr. and Mrs. Retzer were entirely separate, with neither depending on the other. The fact remains that at present they are Siamese twins in Retzer and Retzer. If the burden becomes unduly oppressive for either, the chancery court is not without power to give relief, even to appointing a receivership for the corporation or dissolving it.

This case also alludes to the major disadvantage of a close corporation. Because minority shareholders are given such a strong voice, it is easy for stalemates to develop. In such a case, shareholders may ask a court to dissolve the enterprise. Is your relationship ready for entrepreneurship? The Web site **http://www.ltbn.com/index.html/** offers advice to entrepreneurial couples.

S Corporations

Although entrepreneurs are often optimistic about the likely success of their new enterprise, in truth, the majority of new businesses lose money in their early years. Only about half of all start-ups *survive* as long as eight years. Congress created S corporations (aka "S corps") to encourage entrepreneurship through tax breaks. The name "S corporation" comes from the provision of the Internal Revenue Code that created this form of organization. **Shareholders of S corps have the best of all worlds: the limited liability of a corporation and the tax status of a partnership.** Like a partnership, an S corp is not a taxable entity—all of the company's profits and losses pass through to the shareholders, who pay tax at their individual rates. It avoids the double taxation of a regular corporation (called a "C corporation"). If, as is often the case, the start-up loses money, investors can deduct these losses against their other income.

When a group of wealthy investors decided to start a magazine called *Living Alternatives*, their lawyer suggested they organize as an S corp. The investors knew that magazines are risky and that most start-ups fail. But successful magazines are very profitable, and these investors believed in the magazine's mission—teaching consumers how to protect the environment. Typical articles covered solar power and compost toilets. The magazine failed after a year, in part, the owners speculated, because the name did not sound like an environmental journal. At least, the investors could deduct these losses against their other (ample) income. Without this incentive, many of them would never have made the initial investment.

If *Living Alternatives* had been profitable, the investors might have decided to continue as an S corporation to avoid the double taxation on dividends. Eventually, however, most companies terminate their S election because of the limitations on this form of organization:

- There can be only one class of stock (although voting rights can vary within the class).
- There can be only 75 shareholders.
- Shareholders must be individuals, estates, charities, pension funds, or trusts, not partnerships or corporations.
- Shareholders must be citizens or residents of the United States, not non-resident aliens.

• All shareholders must agree that the company should be an S corporation.

Although *most* states follow the federal lead on S corporations, a small number treat an S corp like a regular C corporation. In these states, the companies must pay state corporate tax.

LIMITED LIABILITY COMPANIES

You may be thinking that there are already as many different forms of organization as any entrepreneur could possibly need, but, as you have seen, none of them is perfect. In a continuing search for earthly perfection, states recently began to permit limited liability companies (LLCs). **An LLC offers the limited liability of a corporation and the tax status of a partnership, without the disadvantages of an S corporation.**

To organize an LLC, you generally need two documents: a charter and an operating agreement. The charter is short, containing basic information such as name and address. It must be filed with the Secretary of State in your jurisdiction. (A sample charter is available at **http://www.lectlaw.com/formb.htm**.)

An operating agreement sets out the rights and obligations of the owners, called *members*. Although some states do not require an operating agreement, lawyers recommend them as a way to avoid disputes. A sample is shown at **http://www.tannedfeet.com/assets/images/Operating_Agreement_for_a_Limited_Liability_Company.pdf**. The following case illustrates the perils of not having an operating agreement.

ZAUGG & ZAUGG ARCHITECTS v. WAGNER
1997 Ohio App. LEXIS 3987
Court of Appeals of Ohio, 1997

Facts: John and Marion Zaugg were partners in Zaugg & Zaugg Architects. They agreed with four other men—Edmonds, Schenk, Siegenthaler, and Wagner—to build a residential golf course. The Zauggs were to furnish architectural services in return for partial payment and part ownership in the project. One year after the Zauggs began working on the venture, the group set up a limited liability company called "Glenleigh Falls Development Co., Ltd." They filed Articles of Organization with the Secretary of State in Ohio and began work on the operating agreement.

Three months after the Articles were filed, the Zauggs billed Glenleigh $108,178.54 for the hundreds of hours they had worked on the project. Shortly thereafter, the group met to sign the operating agreement. Schenk refused to sign and announced he was withdrawing from the venture. Siegenthaler said he would not sign until the agreement had been reviewed by his attorney. The remaining members (including the two Zauggs) did sign. Shortly thereafter, the Zauggs agreed to accept payment of only $58,288.54. When even this amount was not forthcoming, they withdrew from the LLC and filed suit, seeking payment for their architectural services. Wagner and Glenleigh (the LLC) counter-claimed, alleging that the Zauggs had wrongfully withdrawn.

Issue: Did the Zauggs wrongfully withdraw from the limited liability company?

Excerpts from Judge Milligan's Decision: The draft operating agreement provided that no member shall have the right to voluntarily withdraw from the company. [Appellants (Glenleigh and Wagner)] argue that the Zauggs are bound by the withdrawal provision, as they signed the agreement. Appellant ignores the requirement that the agreement be a valid agreement of the members. The agreement was not the agreement of the members, but only the agreement of some of the members. The agreement could not bind several of the members, while the remainder of the members would be governed by a separate inconsistent set of rules, all in governance of the same legal entity.

It is apparent from both the document itself and the evidence concerning the discussions surrounding its drafting that the members had not reached agreement on the provisions in this operating agreement. Because this agreement is not a valid agreement of the members of the company, the Zauggs were permitted to withdraw from the company in accordance with [state statute] and were not bound by the withdrawal provision of the incomplete, proposed agreement.

LLCs have become a popular form of organization. Here are some of the reasons:

- **Limited Liability.** As in a corporation, members are not personally liable for debts of the company. They risk only their investment.
- **Tax Status.** As in a partnership, income flows through the company to the individual members, avoiding the double taxation of a corporation.
- **Duration.** As we will see in the next chapter, a partnership terminates upon the death, withdrawal, or bankruptcy of a partner. In many states, an LLC survives the departure of a member.
- **Management.** LLCs are permitted to have managers, who may or may not be members. Managers of an LLC are not personally liable, in contrast with the general partners of a limited partnership, who are. Unlike corporations, LLCs are not required to hold annual meetings or maintain a minute book.
- **Flexibility.** Unlike S corporations, LLCs can have members that are corporations, partnerships, or non-resident aliens. LLCs can also have different classes of stock.

But this is an imperfect world, and even LLCs have flaws:

- **Legal Uncertainties.** LLCs are a new form of organization. Although Wyoming passed the first LLC statute in 1978, most states did not follow suit until after 1991. This means three things. First, state laws vary widely. This inconsistency can be confusing if you form an LLC in one state, but do business in several others. Second, there are few court decisions interpreting the LLC statutes. These few cases sometimes disagree.[6] Third, some entrepreneurs are reluctant to try the unfamiliar. Said Diane Nelson, co-owner of Diane Nelson Fine Art in Laguna Beach, California, "We were really considering it. We felt insecure; we didn't know enough. We formed an S corporation instead, because we were familiar with it."
- **The IRS versus the States.** Individual states regulate the formation of an LLC, but the IRS determines its tax status. Coordination among these various jurisdictions is not always smooth. The original IRS regulations had strict require-

[6] For example, a federal court in Michigan held that an LLC is a partnership for purposes of diversity jurisdiction, which means that if any member lives in the same state as the opposing party, the case cannot be heard in federal court. However, an Illinois court held the opposite—that an LLC is a corporation for purposes of jurisdiction, which means that it is treated as a resident only of the state in which it was formed.

ments for LLCs, and states had no choice but to reflect these requirements in their laws. But then, in 1996, the IRS eliminated most of its requirements. Some states have followed the IRS lead, but others have not. California, for one, has announced that it will not. To take one example, the IRS has eliminated its original rule that LLCs have at least two members. Many states, however, still prohibit one-member LLCs.

- **Expenses.** Some states, such as California, charge higher fees for LLCs than for corporations.
- **Transferability of Interests.** In some states, a member must have permission from the other owners to transfer all his ownership rights. Without this approval, the new owner may not, for example, be able to vote.
- **Going Public.** LLCs must be privately held; they cannot sell stock publicly (on an exchange or otherwise). However, it is relatively easy to switch from an LLC to a corporation if the members decide to go public.
- **Changing to an LLC.** Despite these flaws, you are convinced that an LLC is right for you. You are going to switch your corporation to an LLC first thing Monday morning. Hold on for one second. The IRS considers this change to be a sale of the corporate assets, so you would have to pay taxes on their value. For this reason, few corporations have made the change. However, switching from a partnership to an LLC is not considered a sale and does not have the same adverse tax impact.

LIMITED LIABILITY PARTNERSHIPS

Some states will not permit *professionals* to organize as an LLC but instead offer the option of a limited liability partnership (LLP). Traditionally, a member of an LLP was protected from liability for the misconduct of other members or employees, but was still personally responsible for her own malpractice and the contract debts of the partnership (such as bank loans and leases). However, the modern trend is to permit professionals to form LLCs or to provide partners in LLPs with the same liability protection as members of LLCs.

The Revised Uniform Partnership Act (RUPA), which has now been passed by more than half of the states, provides that **partners in an LLP are not *personally* liable for debts of the partnership (whether arising from contract or tort).**[7] However, partners are always liable for their own misconduct. Suppose that Oliver, Ed, and Jessie, three newly minted CPAs, form an LLP. Jessie has inherited $100 million, but Ed and Oliver's combined net worth will barely buy a ticket to the movies. Flush with optimism, the three partners rent fancy downtown space. Unfortunately, Oliver forgets on which side of the ledger to put the debits and credits so he botches an annual audit for the firm's major client. Embroiled in malpractice litigation, the firm is unable to pay its rent. The jury in the malpractice case returns a verdict for $5 million. Who is liable for what? Only the LLP is liable for the overdue rent. Only Oliver and the LLP are liable for the malpractice verdict. Ed and Jessie just lose their investment in the LLP. Neither the landlord nor the client has any right to Jessie's personal fortune.

Does this result seem unfair? Some states that permit professionals to limit their liability through LLPs or LLCs also require that they maintain a certain amount of malpractice insurance.

[7] RUPA §306(c).

JOINT VENTURES

Dutch entertainment giant PolyGram, which has been steadily muscling into the mainstream movie business, announced a key partnership with longtime Hollywood players Tom Pollock and Ivan Reitman. The five-year deal calls for PolyGram, the world's largest recorded-music company, to set up a joint venture in Santa Barbara that will generate three to five films a year. PolyGram, which scored a major hit with *Bean*, will own a third of the yet-to-be-named production company. Pollock, head of Universal Studios' movie operations for a decade, and Reitman, who directed *Animal House, Ghostbusters, Twins*, and *Dave*, will own the rest.

PolyGram did not disclose how much it will invest in the joint venture, which will handle Reitman's movies and seek projects from other directors and producers. The company has made similar joint venture deals with director Tony Scott and actress Jodie Foster. "PolyGram is taking a reasonably conservative approach in these joint ventures with pretty professional names," said Harold Vogel, an analyst at Cowen & Co. in New York.[8]

Pollock and Reitman are not liable on a contract between PolyGram and Sheryl Crow, because it is not related to the limited purpose of their joint venture.

This newspaper article refers to this business arrangement as both a "partnership" and a "joint venture." What is the difference in meaning? **A joint venture is a partnership for a limited purpose.** PolyGram, Pollock, and Reitman do not intend to work together on all their movies. They have joined together for the limited purpose of making three to five films a year. If they had joined in a full-scale partnership, all three parties would be bound by contracts that any one of them signed. In a joint venture, only contracts relating to the limited purpose are binding on all three. If PolyGram signs a music contract with Sheryl Crow, Pollock and Reitman are not liable on that contract. But if the PolyGram/Pollock/Reitman joint venture enters into a contract with Jennifer Aniston to star in a movie, Pollock and Reitman are liable, too. Nonprofit enterprises do not qualify as joint ventures—the purpose, however limited, must include making a profit.

OTHER FORMS OF ORGANIZATION

When starting a business, most entrepreneurs choose one of the forms of organization that we have discussed. There are, however, an assortment of other, less common forms that we must briefly cover—not so much because you are likely to use one of them yourself, but so that you will know what they are if you come across them in your business life or in reading the newspaper.

BUSINESS TRUSTS

A business trust is an unincorporated association run by trustees for the benefit of investors (who are called "beneficiaries"). This arrangement sounds like an unfavorable one for investors. They buy certificates in the trust, just as shareholders buy stock in a corporation, but they have fewer rights than shareholders. They do not elect the trustees; if a trustee resigns or dies, the other trustees choose a replacement. The trustees can take almost any action without approval of the investors and can issue an unlimited number of shares. The beneficiaries are not

[8] Dave McNary, "PolyGram Sets Up Key Joint Venture," *The Daily News of Los Angeles*, Feb. 14, 1998, p. B2. Reprinted with permission.

liable for the debts of the trust. Theoretically, the trustees are liable, but the trust agreement usually protects them from liability.

Ordinary businesses usually do not consider this form of organization, but it does make sense for mutual funds and other management investment companies. Investors buy shares or certificates in the trust. The trustees, who are investment experts, invest the funds, paying out any returns to the investors, minus management fees. If investors are unhappy with a fund's performance, they do not have the right to vote out the trustees, but they can sell their shares and take their money elsewhere. It would be difficult to run an investment company if the beneficiaries were always changing trustees and investment style. A mutual fund is the one type of investment where it makes sense that investors *cannot* replace trustees.

COOPERATIVES

Cooperatives are groups of individuals or businesses that join together to gain the advantages of volume purchases or sales. Profits are distributed to members using whatever formula they choose. Unincorporated cooperatives are generally subject to partnership law; incorporated cooperatives are governed by corporation law. The following article illustrates a common form of cooperative.

By the winter of 1882, the price of textbooks and firewood had risen to intolerable levels, and a group of Harvard undergraduates decided to do something about it. Suspecting price gouging on the part of Harvard Square merchants, they persuaded classmates to pay $2 a year to join a student-run retailing venture. They then set up shop on a five-foot-long shelf in a Cambridge tobacco store. Today, the Harvard Cooperative Society, known affectionately as the "Coop" (as in hens), is the oldest, largest, and most successful retail cooperative in the nation, with annual sales of more than $50 million. The members—students, alumni and employees of Harvard, MIT, and a handful of smaller schools in the area—own the Coop. These owners spend more than $30 million a year in the store.[9]

FRANCHISES

This chapter has presented an overview of the various forms of organization. Franchises are not, strictly speaking, a separate form of organization. They are included here because they represent an important option for entrepreneurs. In the United States, 1 in 12 small businesses is a franchise. Franchises generate sales of close to $1 trillion each year and provide jobs for more than eight million people. Well-known franchises include Dunkin' Donuts, Midas Muffler, and McDonald's. Most franchisors and franchisees are corporations, although they could legally choose to be any of the forms discussed in this chapter.

Buying a franchise is a compromise between starting one's own business as an entrepreneur and working for someone else as an employee. Franchisees are free to choose which franchise to buy, where to locate it, and how to staff it. But they are not completely on their own. They are buying an established business with all the kinks worked out. In case the owner has never boiled water before, the McDonald's operations manual explains everything from how to set the temperature controls on the stove, to the number of seconds that fries must cook, to the

[9] "The Expanding Harvard Coop," *New York Times*, Nov. 11, 1980, p. D1. The data on sales were obtained from the Coop's "Annual Report to Members" in 1994.

length of time they can be held in the rack before being discarded. And a well-known name like McDonald's or Mrs. Fields ought, by itself, to bring customers through the door.

There is, however, a fine line between being helpful and being oppressive. Franchisees sometimes complain that franchisor control is too tight—tips on cooking fries might be appreciated, but rules on how often to sweep the floor are not. Sometimes franchisors, in their zeal to maintain standards, prohibit innovation that appeals to regional tastes. Just because spicy biscuits are unpopular in New England does not mean they should be banned in the South.

Franchises can be very costly to acquire, anywhere from several thousand dollars to $1.2 million. That fee is usually payable up front, whether or not a cookie or burger is ever sold. On top of the up-front fee, franchisees also pay an annual fee that is a percentage of *gross sales revenues*, not *profit*. Sometimes the fee seems to eat up all the profits. Franchisees also complain when they are forced to buy supplies from headquarters. In theory, the franchisors can purchase hamburger meat and paper plates more cheaply in bulk. On the other hand, the franchisees are a captive audience, and they allege that headquarters has little incentive to keep prices low. Franchisees also grumble when they are forced to contribute to expensive "co-op advertising" that benefits all the outlets in the region. As the following article illustrates, franchisees can have very different experiences.

For James Hamilton, a franchise was the greatest thing since, well, sliced bread. His first Subway sandwich shop, opened six years ago in the Lemon Grove area of San Diego, was such a success that he has since acquired five other shops.

But Robert Rosinski's three Little Caesar's Pizza Restaurants landed Rosinski in the soup. The parent company allowed other Little Caesar's stores to open nearby and then began running national ads that offered two pizzas for $5.99, $1.26 less than they cost Rosinski to make. Driven to the brink of bankruptcy, he sold his stores back to the franchisor for pennies on the dollar.[10]

Although franchises were once relatively unregulated, the states and the federal government have dramatically increased their supervision and regulation of these businesses. The Federal Trade Commission (FTC) requires that, at least 10 days prior to the sale, franchisors must give prospective franchisees an **offering circular** that reveals, among other interesting facts:

- Any litigation against the company
- Whether it has ever gone through bankruptcy proceedings
- All fees
- Estimates of the required initial investment
- What goods must be purchased from the franchisor
- The number of franchisees in operation
- How many franchisees have gone out of business in the prior year

The offering circular must also contain audited financial statements and a sample set of the contracts that a franchisee is expected to sign. For more information about FTC rules on offering circulars, see **http://www.ftc.gov/**.

---

10 Frank Green, "Franchise Is a Ticket to Freedom, or Failure," *San-Diego Union-Tribune*, May 31, 1994, p. C-3.

The purpose of the offering circular is to ensure that the franchisor discloses all relevant facts. It is not a guarantee of quality. Under FTC rules, the following notice must appear in bold on the cover page of the offering circular: **"To protect you, we've required your franchisor to give you this information. We haven't checked it, and don't know if it's correct."**

Suppose you obtain an offering circular for "Shrinking Cats," a franchise that offers psychiatric services for neurotic felines. The company has lost money on all the outlets it operates itself; it has sold only three franchises, two of which have gone out of business; and all the required contracts are ridiculously favorable to the franchisor. Nevertheless, the FTC will still permit sales as long as the franchisor discloses all the information required in the offering circular. Nor will the FTC investigate to make sure that the information is accurate. After the fact, if the FTC discovers the franchisor has violated the rules, it may sue on your behalf. (You also would have the right to bring suit.) But that is cold comfort amidst the devastation of a failed business.

Some states also regulate the sale of franchises. They often require franchisors to register and to provide offering circulars, but the franchisor can use the same circular to meet the requirements of both the state and the FTC. The states that do regulate franchisors are often stricter than the FTC. California, for instance, requires franchisors to file all advertisements ahead of time. Some states will not permit a franchisor to register unless it can meet minimum capital requirements. State laws may also prohibit unfair terms in the franchising contract.

Despite efforts on the part of the federal and state governments to regulate this important area of commerce, many franchisees feel that the playing field is not yet level. However, the following case has helped even the score.

VYLENE ENTERPRISES, INC. v. NAUGLES, INC.
90 F.3d 1472, 1996 U.S. App. LEXIS 24005
United States Court of Appeals for the Ninth Circuit, 1996

Facts: Vylene Enterprises, Inc. bought a restaurant franchise in Long Beach, California, from Naugles, Inc. The franchise agreement did not grant Vylene an exclusive territory. Ten years later, Naugles opened a new restaurant that offered smaller portions at a lower price. It was 1.4 miles from Vylene's location. Vylene had already been struggling financially, and this new restaurant caused a further decline in sales. Vylene sued Naugles.

Issue: **Did Naugles have the right to open a new restaurant near an existing franchise?**

Excerpts from Judge Nelson's Decision: Vylene did not have any rights to exclusive territory under the terms of the franchise agreement, and we do not impliedly read any such rights into the contract. [Notwithstanding, under California law, all contracts have an implied covenant of good faith and fair dealing.] Naugles' construction of a competing restaurant within a mile and a half of Vylene's restaurant was a breach of the covenant of good faith and fair dealing. The bad faith character of the move becomes clear when one considers that building the competing restaurant had the potential to not only hurt Vylene, but also to reduce Naugles' royalties from Vylene's operations.

In a recent survey of U.S. franchisors, 63 percent said they are currently selling franchises overseas; 83 percent said they would like to. The top five foreign markets are Western Europe, the Pacific Rim, South America, Central Europe, and Southeast Asia. In Japan, a businessman named Kyiochi Yamaguchi already owns six American franchises: Bathtub Doctor, Sparkle Wash, Metal Maintenance, Ceiling Magic, Blind Magic, and NonSlide. He would like to acquire a seventh franchise—his possible choices range from pizza restaurants to sign makers to Internet advertisers. For more information about franchising overseas, browse the International Franchise Association's Web site at http://www.franchise.org.[11]

CHAPTER CONCLUSION

The process of starting a business is immensely time-consuming. Eighteen-hour days are the norm. Not surprisingly, entrepreneurs are sometimes reluctant to spend their valuable time on legal issues that, after all, do not contribute directly to the bottom line. No customer buys more biscuits because the franchise is a limited liability company instead of a corporation. Wise entrepreneurs know, however, that careful attention to legal issues is an essential component of success. The form of organization affects everything from taxes to liability to management control. The idea for the business may come first, but legal considerations occupy a close second place.

CHAPTER REVIEW

	Separate Taxable Entity	Personal Liability for Owners	Ease of Formation	Transferable Interests (Easily Bought and Sold)	Perpetual Existence	Other Features
Sole Proprietorship	No	Yes	Very easy	No, can only sell entire business	No	
General Partnership	No	Yes	Easy	No	No	Supported by law and tradition Management can be difficult.
Professional Corporation	Yes	Yes, for own malpractice, not for malpractice of others or contract debts of organization	Difficult	Shareholders must all be members of same profession.	Yes, as long as it has shareholders	Complex tax issues
Limited Partnership	No	Yes, for general partner No, for limited partners	Difficult	Yes (for limited partners), unless partnership agreement provides otherwise	No	
Limited Liability Limited Partnership	No	No	Difficult	Yes (for limited partners), unless partnership agreement provides otherwise	No	
Corporation	Yes	No	Difficult	Yes	Yes	

[11] Jan Norman, "A World of Franchises," *The Orange County Register*, Sept. 16, 1997, p. CO1. Reprinted by permission of The Orange County Register, Copyright 1997.

	Separate Taxable Entity	Personal Liability for Owners	Ease of Formation	Transferable Interests (Easily Bought and Sold)	Perpetual Existence	Other Features
Close Corporation	Yes, for C corporation No, for S corporation	No	Difficult	Transfer restrictions	Yes	Protection of minority shareholders No board of directors required Stalemates may develop.
S Corporation	No	No	Difficult	Transfer restrictions	Yes	Only 75 shareholders Only one class of stock Shareholders must be individuals, estates, trusts, charities, or pension funds and be citizens or residents of the United States. All shareholders must agree to S status.
Limited Liability Company	No	No	Difficult	Varies by state	Varies by state	No limit on the number of shareholders, the number of classes of stock, or the type of shareholder
Limited Liability Partnership	No	Varies by state, but generally no	Difficult	No	No	
Joint Venture	No	Yes	Easy	No	No	Partnership for a limited purpose
Business Trust	Yes	No	Difficult	Yes	Yes	Most commonly used by mutual funds and other investment companies
Cooperative	All these issues depend on the form of organization chosen by participants.					Groups of individuals or businesses that join together to gain the advantages of volume purchases or sales
Franchise	All these issues depend on the form of organization chosen by participants.					Established business Name recognition Management assistance Loss of control Fees may be high.

PRACTICE TEST

1. **RIGHT & WRONG** Lee McNeely told Hardee's officials that he was interested in purchasing multiple restaurants in Arkansas. A Hardee's officer told him that any of the company-owned stores in Arkansas would be available for purchase. However, the company urged him to open a new store in Maumelle and sent him a letter estimating first-year sales at around $800,000. McNeely built the Maumelle restaurant, but gross sales the first year were only $508,000. When McNeely asked to buy an existing restaurant, a Hardee's officer refused, informing him that Hardee's rarely sold company-owned restaurants. The offering circular contained no misstatements, but McNeely brought suit alleging fraud in the sale of the Maumelle franchise. Does McNeely have a valid claim against Hardee's? Apart from the legal issues, did Hardee's officers behave ethically? Would they want their behavior to be publicized? Would they like to be treated this way themselves? Is all fair in love, war, and franchising?

2. **CPA QUESTION** Assuming all other requirements are met, a corporation may elect to be treated as an S corporation under the Internal Revenue Code if it has:

(a) Both common and preferred stockholders

(b) A partnership as a stockholder

(c) Seventy-five or fewer stockholders

(d) The consent of a majority of the stockholders

3. Under Delaware law, a corporation cannot appear in court without a lawyer, but a partnership can. Fox Hollow Ventures, Ltd. was a limited liability company. One of its employees, who was not a lawyer, appeared in court to represent the company. Does an LLC more closely resemble a partnership, which may represent itself in court, or a corporation, which requires representation by a lawyer?

4. **CPA QUESTION** Which of the following statements is correct concerning the similarities between a limited partnership and a corporation?

(a) Each is created under a statute and must file a copy of its certificate with the proper state authorities.

(b) All corporate stockholders and all partners in a limited partnership have limited liability.

(c) Both are recognized for federal income tax purposes as taxable entities.

(d) Both are allowed statutorily to have perpetual existence.

5. Alan Dershowitz, a law professor famous for his wealthy clients (O. J. Simpson, Claus von Bulow, Leona Helmsley), joined with other lawyers to open a kosher delicatessen, Maven's Court. Dershowitz met with greater success at the bar than in the kitchen—the deli failed after barely a year in business. One supplier sued for overdue bills. What form of organization would have been the best choice for Maven's Court?

6. **CPA QUESTION** A joint venture is a(an):

(a) Association limited to no more than two persons in business for profit

(b) Enterprise of numerous co-owners in a nonprofit undertaking

(c) Corporate enterprise for a single undertaking of limited duration

(d) Association of persons engaged as co-owners in a single undertaking for profit

7. Mrs. Meadows opened a biscuit shop called The Biscuit Bakery. The business was not incorporated. Whenever she ordered supplies, she was careful to sign the contract in the name of the business, not personally: The Biscuit Bakery by Daisy Meadows. Unfortunately, she had no money to pay her flour bill. When the vendor threatened to sue her, Mrs. Meadows told him that he could only sue the business, because all the contracts were in the business's name. Will Mrs. Meadows lose her dough?

8. **YOU BE THE JUDGE WRITING PROBLEM** Heinz Wartski invented a data collector device to analyze fuel consumption and acceleration in automobiles. He and Terence Bedford formed Fleet Tech, Inc., a close corporation, to develop and market the device. When the venture did not succeed as anticipated, Bedford induced the board of directors to fire Wartski. With Fleet Tech's money all but gone and its debts mounting, the directors voted to authorize Bedford either to sell the company or to file for bankruptcy. Bedford offered to buy the shares for $1. The sale took place, over Wartski's objection. Shortly after buying all the stock, Bedford sold the company to Allied Corp. for $890,267 and a promise of future royalty payments totaling at least $1.2 million. Do Wartski or any of the other shareholders have a right to share in these payments? **Argument for Wartski:** Shareholders in a close corporation owe each other a fiduciary duty. Bedford should not be allowed to profit at the expense of the other shareholders. **Argument for Bedford:** The direc-

tors fired Wartski because he ruined the company. They then authorized Bedford to sell what was left. Everything Bedford did was legal.

9. Arnold and Judith Germain bought two franchises from My Pie International, Inc. They did not receive the franchise disclosure statement from My Pie until two years after the purchase. Did My Pie violate FTC rules?

10. The Logan Wright Foundation (LWF), an Oklahoma nonprofit corporation, was a partner in a partnership formed to operate two Sonic Drive-In restaurants. LWF asked the court to require the IRS to return taxes that LWF had paid on behalf of Sonic. LWF argued that it was not responsible for Sonic's taxes because LWF was merely a limited partner, with limited liability to the partnership's creditors, including the IRS. The partnership had never filed a certificate of limited partnership with the Secretary of State. Is it a valid limited partnership?

INTERNET RESEARCH PROBLEM

At http://www.ftc.gov, the Federal Trade Commission provides information on enforcement cases it has brought against franchisors who violate FTC rules. Do you see a pattern? Are some violations more common than others? How can you avoid falling prey to an unsuitable franchise offering?

You can find further practice problems in the Online Quiz at http://beatty.westbuslaw.com or in the Study Guide that accompanies this text.

CHAPTER 33

LIFE AND DEATH OF A PARTNERSHIP

Chase stood at the edge of a meadow near the top of the Porcupine Mountains in the Upper Peninsula of Michigan. The sun glistened off apple blossoms, birds called to each other, and the Lake of the Clouds stretched out to the horizon below. Chase had never been happier. As an architect, he believed in designing houses that blended with nature. Sharing his vision, Danielle had hired him to create a house for this perfect location. The large budget would allow Chase to realize many of his architectural beliefs. But he needed help—a landscape designer and a decorator who could work with the spectacular setting and his splendid design.

Bailey was Chase's choice for the interior design; she could create the sleek, warm look he sought. With Zack's landscape plan, the house would appear to be a natural part of the site. At their first meeting, all three designers committed to the project and rapidly agreed to a deal: Chase would receive 50 percent of the profits, Bailey and Zack 25 percent each. All three would have veto rights over the work of the other two. As the meeting ended, Chase poured glasses of sparkling water. "Here's to our new partnership. We'll build the most beautiful house in America," he said, rising to his feet. The three raised a toast to their success.

The honeymoon lasted only a few weeks. Chase and Bailey immediately fell out over the width of the hallways. Chase designed them unusually narrow to create a dramatic entrance into each room. But none of Bailey's antique Persian carpets would fit. When Bailey suggested consulting the owner, Chase blew up. "What do owners know?" he demanded. Zack sided with Bailey on that issue. But then both Chase and Bailey disagreed with Zack, who wanted to relocate the house to save some specimen trees. "Lose the view to save a few ratty old trees?" Bailey asked incredulously. Outvoted, Zack quit in disgust. Bailey and Chase began to suspect they were in trouble.

The plight of this threesome illustrates common partnership problems. Although Chase, Bailey, and Zack never signed an agreement or filed a form, they nonetheless had formed a partnership. Not only did they refer to themselves as partners, but they intended to share profits and co-manage the business. The partnership was for a specific undertaking—building a house. When Zack left before finishing the project, he *wrongfully* dissociated from the partnership. The law would permit him to leave, but it would also require him to pay damages for any harm caused by his early departure.

INTRODUCTION

Partnerships have two important advantages: they do not pay taxes and they are easy to form.[1] Many professionals, such as accountants and lawyers, have traditionally favored this form of organization. Some of the rules can be complex, however, and, like any relationship, a partnership requires careful tending.

Partnerships have an ancient history. They existed as long ago as ancient Babylon, and the modern law of partnerships originated with the Italian merchants of the late Middle Ages. Traditionally, in this country, partnerships were regulated by common law, but a lack of consistency among the states became troublesome as interstate commerce grew. To solve this problem, the National Conference of Commissioners on Uniform State Laws proposed the Uniform Partnership Act (UPA) in 1914. Ultimately, 49 states passed the UPA in some form or other, Louisiana being the exception, as usual, because of its legal foundation in the French Napoleonic Code. Hardly anything turns out perfect the first try, so in 1992 the Commissioners on Uniform State Laws proposed a Revised Uniform Partnership Act (RUPA). A majority of states have now passed the RUPA, so we use it as the basis for our discussion of partnership law. To make matters confusing, however, the National Conference of Commissioners has changed the official name of the RUPA to the UPA. To avoid confusion, we continue to use the term RUPA, as courts do.

Partnerships existed in ancient Babylon.

Although the UPA and the RUPA have made life easier, common law still plays an important role in regulating partnerships. To some degree, that is always true with statutes. No matter how well written they are, the courts are called upon to interpret some provisions. In addition, the UPA and the RUPA direct courts to apply common law to resolve any issue that they do not cover. Finally, many of the rules in the UPA and the RUPA are so-called **default rules**, meaning that they apply unless the partners reach a different agreement. When partners write their own rules, they must sometimes ask the courts to interpret ambiguous provisions.

[1] These issues are discussed at greater length in Chapter 32, on starting a business. Although the partnership itself does not pay taxes, each partner must pay taxes on his share of the partnership's profits.

CREATING A PARTNERSHIP

Some legal relationships are carefully delineated. By and large, people know whether they are married or not. Did they obtain a license and say "I do"? Similarly, people usually know if they have formed a corporation. Did they file the requisite form? Partnerships are trickier, more like living together than getting married. It can be difficult to tell if a live-in relationship—or a partnership—really exists. Sometimes people *think* they have a partnership—they may even have signed an agreement—but the law refuses to recognize it. Other times, they do not think of themselves as partners, but the law does. The RUPA does not require partnerships to prepare a written agreement or make a formal filing. However, it does *permit* a partnership to file a statement with the local Secretary of State that contains basic information about the partnership.[2] (For examples of a partnership agreement, go to **http://www.lectlaw.com/formb.htm** or **http://www.legaldocs.com**.)

How can you tell if you have a partnership? According to the RUPA:

> **The association of two or more persons to carry on as co-owners a business for profit forms a partnership, whether or not the persons intend to form a partnership.**[3]

Note that a partnership is an association of two or more people. If only one person is involved in the business, it is a sole proprietorship, not a partnership. It is also important to understand the terms "association" and "co-owners [of] a business for profit."

ASSOCIATION

An "association" means a voluntary relationship. To be a partnership, the members must indicate their willingness to be considered partners. However, many roads lead to this destination. Unlike a corporation, where the incorporator must follow a specific set of requirements, in a partnership no prescribed steps are required. The law does not require a formal agreement, either written or oral. Nor is a formal agreement enough on its own to create a partnership. In a partnership, actions speak louder than words. If the people *act* like partners, then the law will treat them as such. If they *do not* act like partners, then nothing they say or write will make them a partnership.

The following two cases illustrate this point. In the first case, the court determined that two people who had no express agreement to be partners were in fact a partnership. In the second case, two people with a written partnership agreement turned out not to be partners at all.

***IN RE* MARRIAGE OF CYNTHIA HASSIEPEN**
269 Ill. App. 3d 559, 646 N.E.2d 1348, 1995 Ill. App. LEXIS 101
Appellate Court of Illinois, 1995

Facts: Cynthia and Kevin Von Behren were divorced. Shortly after the divorce, Kevin began living with Brenda. Kevin and Brenda began an electrical contracting business, called Von Behren Electric. Kevin contributed an old pickup truck and a drill; he also performed the actual contracting work. Brenda used her credit cards to purchase other business supplies and managed the office. She continued to work at her job as a court reporter for two years after starting the business. Brenda and Kevin did not pay themselves a salary, but instead withdrew money from a joint account for both personal and business expenditures. Later on, Brenda and Kevin married.

---

[2] RUPA §105.

[3] RUPA §202.

When the annual income from Von Behren Electric exceeded $100,000, Cynthia asked the court to increase Kevin's child support payments. Kevin argued that, since he and Brenda were partners, he was entitled to only half of the business's profits and, therefore, his child support should not be increased.

Cynthia pointed to the following facts to support a conclusion that Kevin and Brenda were *not* partners in Von Behren Electric:

- Prior to their marriage, Kevin and Brenda filed separate tax returns, in which Kevin reported all of the business income and Brenda reported only her court reporting income.
- Kevin put "sole proprietorship" in bold letters on the top of his tax return.
- No written partnership agreement existed.
- Kevin and Brenda never informed their accountant that they were a partnership.
- No business signs indicated that the business was a partnership.
- Business cards for Von Behren Electric, Inc. stated "Kevin Von Behren/Owner."
- When Kevin answered interrogatories for this case, he stated that he was sole owner and that Brenda worked for him.

Issue: **Were Kevin and Brenda partners?**

Excerpts from Judge Steigmann's Decision: The existence of a partnership is a question of the parties' intent and is based upon all the facts and circumstances surrounding the formation of the relationship at issue. The trial court found that Brenda was "substantially and integrally involved in the Von Behren electrical business and shared in the economic results of the business," and concluded that their business relationship was a partnership.

Obviously, Kevin and Brenda are not sophisticated business people. While the trial court should consider the absence of written formalities, that is only one factor to weigh when determining if a partnership exists. In this case, both Kevin and Brenda provided services for the business, Brenda provided credit for the initial operations of the business, and Kevin contributed assets to the business. Also, all the money earned by the business was put into their joint account and used for reinvestment in the business or for their personal needs. The receipt of a share of the business profits is *prima facie* evidence that a person is a partner in the business.

Accordingly, we conclude that the trial court did not err by finding that Kevin and Brenda were partners. Kevin's child support payments should be based on half of the income produced by Von Behren Electric.

Compare the result in *Hassiepen* with the following case.

GREEN v. SCHAGRIN
1989 Del. Super. LEXIS 295
Superior Court of Delaware, 1989

Facts: Joseph DiFebo was married when he met Nancy Green one winter. By summer, they became romantically involved, and he moved into her home. In the fall, Green borrowed money from DiFebo to make a down payment on the purchase of four houses. She bought all four properties in her name alone. Shortly before Thanksgiving, DiFebo moved out of Green's house. The following winter, he moved back in. He remained until summer, when he moved out for good. During their last winter together, the two parties signed this document:

> Nancy R. Green and Joseph A. DiFebo are equal partners in the following Wilmington, Delaware properties: 807 Pine Street, 427 East 3rd St., 611 East 7th Street, 613 East 7th Street.

On the death of Nancy R. Green, her half interest is left to her daughters, Kelly R. Green and Stacy R. Green. On the death of Joseph A. DiFebo, his half interest is left to his daughters, Amy DiFebo and Beth Durham.

If Nancy R. Green survives Joseph A. DiFebo she makes all decisions on the above properties.

DiFebo did some repair work on the buildings, but never asked Green for a share of the rentals. When the city condemned one of the properties, Green refused to give DiFebo half the proceeds. DiFebo testified that, in his mind, the money he transferred to Green established a partnership between them. Green testified that at no time did she consider their arrangement to be a partnership.

Issue: **Were these buildings owned by Nancy Green individually or by a partnership between Green and Joseph DiFebo?**

Excerpts from Judge Herlihy's Decision: The mere existence of an agreement does not conclusively prove the existence of a partnership. Here we have a document not titled partnership agreement and not signed by the parties as partners. While the opening paragraph refers to the parties as "equal partners," that is the only reference to a partnership relationship. It is the intention of the parties, as expressed by the agreement, which is paramount. There is little intention expressed in this document except for a testamentary disposition upon the death of each party. That can hardly be classified as sufficient to prove a partnership existed between these parties. Further, the circumstances under which this document was drafted do not evidence an intention to establish a partnership.

There are additional and significant elements of a partnership on which [DiFebo] has not met his burden. The intent to divide the profits is an indispensable element of a partnership. The document is totally silent on sharing profits. While [DiFebo] testified at trial that he viewed the arrangement he had with plaintiff as a partnership involving shared profits, he has never shared any and up until the sale he never asked for any sharing. He allowed Green to assume the security and loan obligations alone and to pay alone whatever tax obligations flowed from the rental income. It is not a defense or sufficient explanation to his course of conduct that he chose to hide the existence of this arrangement from his wife. Therefore, not only is the document totally silent on profit sharing, defendant's conduct for several years demonstrated no interest in profit sharing.

[DiFebo's] claim for one-half of the net proceeds from the sale is *Denied*.

Are these courts simply being contrary? One finds that a partnership existed, even though the parties had *not* signed an agreement, while the other court said there was no partnership although the parties *had* signed an agreement. Clearly, a written agreement is neither necessary nor sufficient for creating a partnership. What factors did the courts consider crucial in determining whether a partnership exists?

CO-OWNERS OF A BUSINESS FOR PROFIT

To be a partnership, the participants must share profits. Nancy Green and Joseph DiFebo may have signed a document declaring themselves to be partners, but they did not share profits, so they did not have a partnership.

Profits count, not revenues. Revenues mean gross income. Profits equal gross income less expenses. When Ashley leases space in the mall for her roller blade business, her rent is $400 per month, plus 25 percent of her revenues. Ashley and her landlord are not partners and their incentives are very different. If Ashley buys the skates for $55, it is a better deal for her to sell 50 pair at $110 each (generating $5,500 in revenue and $2,750 in profit) than 100 pair at $65 (generating $6,500 in revenue and $1,000 in profit). Not true for the landlord, who would prefer the higher revenue and lower profit.

Participants in an enterprise cannot be partners unless they share profits, but not all profit-sharers are partners. To determine whether profit-sharers are partners, courts follow these rules:

- *Profit-sharing is a requirement for a partnership, but it is not enough, by itself, to create one.* To motivate her employees, Carrie institutes a profit-sharing plan that distributes 10 percent of the business's profits to employees at the end of the year. Carrie still runs the business herself, and her employees are not partners.

- *Partners share in the management of the business.* If participants are not involved in management, the courts will generally not consider them to be partners.

- *Not all managers are partners.* The courts have generally held that a creditor who is simply trying to preserve his equity is not a partner. Warren lends $1 billion to an investment banking partnership shortly before the federal government discovers that the partnership had violated federal rules on bond trading. This scandal sends the partnership into a tailspin. To rescue his investment, Warren steps in to manage the firm. Is Warren a partner? Probably not. Similarly, employees who manage a business are not necessarily considered partners. An accounting firm hires Dominic to serve as its chief executive officer, managing the day-to-day functions of the partnership. He has been hired to carry out the partners' responsibilities, but he is not a partner himself.

- *An agreement to share in losses is strong evidence of a partnership.* Although landlords, employees, and even creditors may share in business profits, usually no one other than a partner is willing to sign on for a share of the losses.

- *If the participants receive other income, they are less likely to be considered partners.* Anthony and Jackie are twins who work as office managers for competing real estate partnerships. They each share in their firm's profits—Anthony receives 2 percent, Jackie 10 percent. But Anthony also receives a monthly salary of $2,000. A court would be more likely to find that Jackie is a partner because her share of the profits is her only income from her full-time job. For Anthony, the profit-sharing looks more like a bonus than a return on ownership.

- *Transferring property to a business is strong evidence of a partnership,* but failure to do so does not necessarily mean that there is no partnership.

- *Referring to yourselves as partners is not enough to create a partnership, but in a close case, it may help sway a court.* In the *Green* case, the two litigants said in writing that they were partners, but that was not enough to persuade the court because other more important factors, such as profit-sharing, were missing.

- *Charitable businesses are not partnerships.* When Aaron and Elijah agree to run the annual jamboree at their children's school, they expect to clear a profit of $35,000 after expenses, but they are not partners because their fund-raising has a charitable purpose.

Exhibit 33.1 illustrates the process of determining whether a partnership exists.

This is a good time to go back and look at *Hassiepen* and *Green*. Why did the courts decide that Kevin and Brenda were partners but not Nancy and Joe? Which

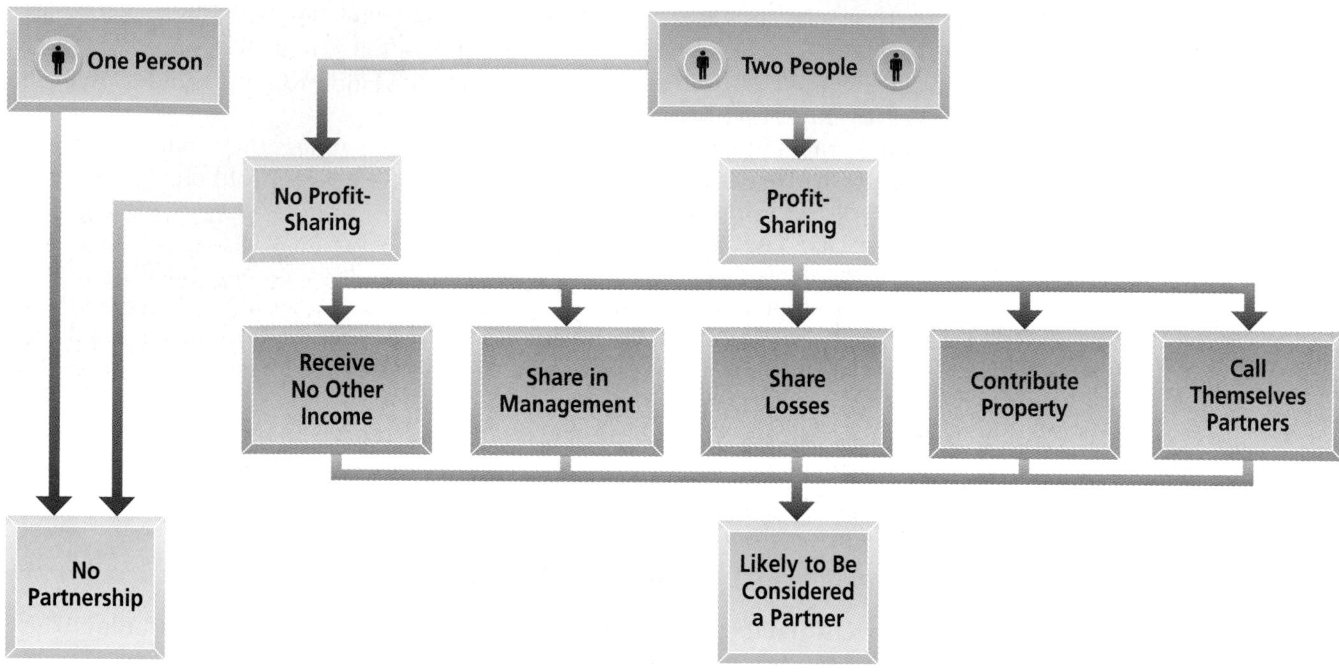

Exhibit 33.1

of the issues outlined in Exhibit 33.1 were important? Even lawyers struggle with these issues, as the following article illustrates. William Kunstler was famous for representing clients such as Martin Luther King, Jr., the Chicago Seven political revolutionaries, the Black Panthers, and some of the suspects in the World Trade Center bombing.

For 20 years, William Moses Kunstler, the shaman and showman lawyer of the radical left, started his mornings by climbing upstairs to the second floor of his Greenwich Village brownstone, taking coffee to the bedside of his wife, Margaret Ratner. After breakfast, Mr. Kunstler would commute to work simply by tromping downstairs to the brownstone's ground-floor office. There, for the last 11 years of his life, he fought the government in hundreds of cases with his acolyte and sidekick, Ronald L. Kuby, the voluble, pony-tailed man whom he held out to the public as his partner.

Both Ms. Ratner and Mr. Kuby were unabashedly devoted to Mr. Kunstler. But his partner in life and his partner in law did not much care for each other. Within three months of Mr. Kunstler's death, the two were caught in a vicious battle over who had the rights to Mr. Kunstler's name, his files, his legacy. Perhaps reluctant to hurt either his wife or his surrogate son, Mr. Kunstler neglected to leave clear instructions about the future of his practice after his death. Mr. Kuby insisted that he was entitled to the status of Mr. Kunstler's full partner. Ms. Ratner maintained that he was merely an employee. Their feud grew so vitriolic that Ms. Ratner padlocked the storage area beneath the office. Mr. Kuby filed a complaint against her with the attorney disciplinary committee, accusing her of potentially violating the confidentiality of Mr. Kunstler's case files. Ms. Ratner ordered him to move out. When Mr. Kuby did, he locked Mr. Kunstler's computer with a secret password.

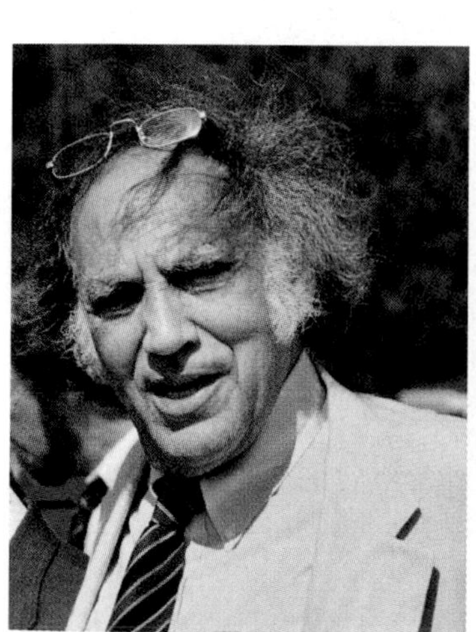

Was Kunstler's law firm a partnership?

Mr. Kunstler had permitted the practice's letterhead to read "Kunstler and Kuby." In his autobiography, Mr. Kunstler described Mr. Kuby as his "partner and alter ego." But Mr. Kunstler had never formalized the partnership with a contract or tax filings. Despite the letterhead, Mr. Kuby was paid as an employee and had never shared in the firm's meager profits and losses.

Ms. Ratner has sued Mr. Kuby. The issue before the State Supreme Court in Manhattan is whether Mr. Kuby had indeed been Mr. Kunstler's legal partner and had a claim on the firm's case files, accounts, and name.[4]

PARTNERSHIP BY ESTOPPEL

In the *Green* case, DiFebo wanted to be considered a partner so that he could share in the profits of the enterprise. *Partnership by estoppel* is concerned with the opposite situation—a person does not want to be considered a partner because he wishes to avoid the *liability* of the partnership. The twist is that partnership by estoppel applies in situations where the participants are *not*, in fact, partners but are held to be liable as if they were.

Partnership by estoppel applies if:

- **Participants tell other people that they are partners (even though they are not), or they allow other people to say, without contradiction, that they are partners**
- **A third party relies on this assertion; and**
- **The third party suffers harm.**

Delores Haught chose Dr. William C. Martin to be her obstetrician. After seeing her for three months, Dr. Martin told her that he had brought in a partner, Dr. John Maceluch, and suggested that she make some appointments with him as well. Martin and Maceluch were not, in fact, partners, but Haught did not know this. She began to alternate appointments between the two doctors.

When Haught went into labor, Dr. Martin was out of the country. All night long, the nurses at the hospital repeatedly called Dr. Maceluch to tell him that they feared Haught's baby was not receiving enough oxygen. When Maceluch arrived at the hospital in the morning, he observed that Haught's baby was in distress, but, instead of performing a cesarean section immediately, he undertook an elective hysterectomy on another patient. In the middle of that procedure, a nurse interrupted him to tell him that Haught's baby was in serious trouble. He finished the hysterectomy before performing Mrs. Haught's cesarean section. Her baby was born alive, but with serious and permanent brain damage.[5] Is Dr. *Martin* liable for Dr. *Maceluch's* negligence?

Dr. Martin would have been liable if he had been Dr. Maceluch's partner. The court determined, however, that the doctors were not, in fact, real partners. But Dr. Martin was liable for Dr. Maceluch's negligence as a *partner by estoppel* because:

- Dr. Martin told Mrs. Haught that he and Dr. Maceluch were partners
- Mrs. Haught relied on this statement—she made an appointment to see Dr. Maceluch only because Dr. Martin said they were partners—and
- Mrs. Haught was harmed by Dr. Maceluch's malpractice.

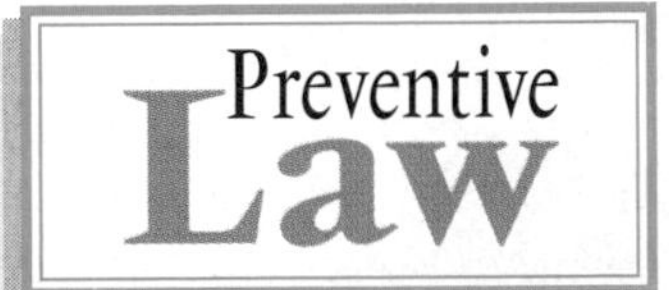

Dr. Martin could have avoided this problem by being very careful *not* to refer to Dr. Maceluch as his partner. Presumably, he used the word "partner" to reassure Mrs. Haught. Instead of "partner," he could have said "colleague," "associate," or "assistant." Dr. Martin should also have been careful to correct anyone who referred to Dr. Maceluch as his partner.

[4] Jan Hoffman, "Kunstler's Partner in Life Battles His Partner in Law," *New York Times*, Dec. 15, 1996, §1, p. 49. Copyright © 1996 by The New York Times Co. Reprinted by permission.

[5] *Haught v. Maceluch*, 681 F.2d 290, 1982 U.S. App. LEXIS 17123 (5th Cir. 1982).

TERMINATING A PARTNERSHIP

Students often find the rules governing partnership formation to be murky. In fitting symmetry, the same used to be true of the termination process. However, the drafters of the RUPA made a heroic effort to clarify the process. You can decide if they succeeded.

PARTNERSHIP AT WILL VERSUS TERM PARTNERSHIP

The rules on dissociation depend, in part, on the type of partnership. If the partners have not agreed how long their partnership will last, they have a **partnership at will**, and any of them can leave at any time, for any reason. If Taylor, Jay, and Gabriela buy Speedy Donut, a racehorse that they manage together, splitting all profits, they are partners. (We will call them the Donut Partnership.) Without a thought for the future, they make no agreement about the duration of the partnership. They see their business as a lark, to last as long as they are having fun. When Taylor splits after only two months, leaving Jay and Gabriela to bear all the expenses, they have no legal right to complain.

With a **term partnership**, the partners have agreed in advance how long it will last. At the end of the specified term, the partnership automatically ends. If Taylor, Jay, and Gabriela agree to sell Speedy Donut and end their business relationship in five years, or if they agree the partnership will end when Speedy runs in the Kentucky Derby, they have a term partnership.

DISSOCIATION

A partnership begins with an association of two or more people. Appropriately, the end of a partnership begins with a *dissociation*. **A dissociation occurs when a partner quits.** However, a dissociation does not inevitably lead to the termination of the partnership business. A dissociation is a fork in the road: **when one or more partners dissociate, the partnership can either buy out the departing partner(s) and continue in business or wind up the business and terminate the partnership.** Exhibit 33.2 illustrates the dissociation process under the RUPA.

Exhibit 33.2

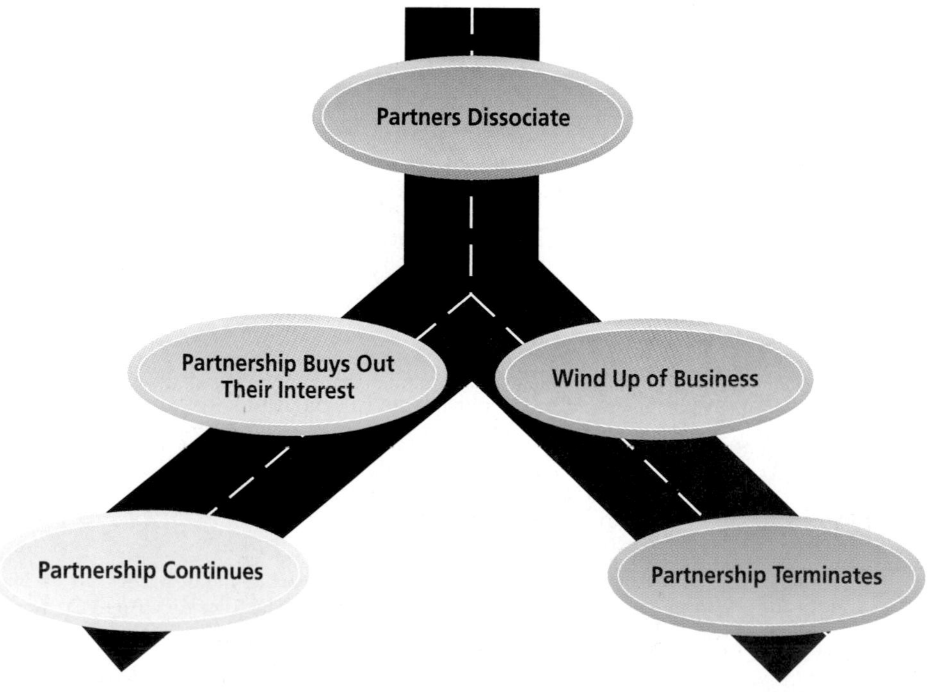

Rightful versus Wrongful Dissociation

A partnership is a personal relationship built on trust. As Chapter 34 underscores, all partners are agents for the partnership, and each partner is *personally* liable for its debts. The actions of one partner can profoundly affect the financial health of every other partner. Under these circumstances, courts will not force someone to remain in a partnership, no matter what the partnership agreement says, any more than they will force a couple to stay married because of their vows at the altar. Partners can always leave a partnership, but, like any divorcing spouse, they may have to pay a financial penalty for doing so. As courts are wont to say: **a partner always has the *power* to leave a partnership but may not have the *right*.** In other words, a partner can always dissociate, but she may have to pay damages for any harm that her departure causes.

Rightful Dissociation. A rightful dissociation occurs if:

- *A partner in a partnership at will serves notice that he intends to withdraw.* The moment Taylor notifies the partnership that he is leaving, he is dissociated, even if he does not plan to leave until later.
- *The partners agree in advance on an event that causes dissociation.* Jay plans to attend business school in three years, so the partnership agreement provides that he will be automatically dissociated from the partnership at that point.
- *The partner dies or becomes incompetent.*
- *The partner is expelled by the other partners.* Partnership agreements can establish a process for expelling a partner. Often, under such agreements, the partnership does not even have to give a reason for expulsion. If a certain percentage of the partners (say, 75 percent) vote against someone, she is out. Even without an agreement, the RUPA permits the expulsion of a partner if (1) it is illegal to carry on the business with her or (2) she has transferred her partnership interest. Thus, if the Donut Partnership agreement permits expulsion by a vote of two-thirds of the partners, Jay and Gabriela can expel Taylor, even if he is the hardest working member of the group. Suppose, however, that the Donut Partnership has no agreement. To appease a loan shark named Mad Mike, Gabriela transfers to him her right to partnership earnings. The Donut Partnership has the automatic right to expel her.

Did Butler & Binion have the right to expel Colette Bohatch?

The following case raises two issues: Did a law firm violate its partnership agreement? Does a partnership have a duty to be fair when expelling a partner? You be the judge.

BOHATCH v. BUTLER & BINION
977 S.W.2d 543, 41 Tex. Sup. J. 308, 1998 Tex. LEXIS 13
Supreme Court of Texas, 1998

Facts: After four years as an associate in the Washington office of the Texas law firm Butler & Binion, Colette Bohatch became a partner. John McDonald, the managing partner of the office, and Richard Powers, a partner, were the only other attorneys in this office. All three worked almost exclusively for Pennzoil.

Once Bohatch became a partner, she began receiving internal firm reports showing the number of hours each attorney billed. She became concerned that McDonald was overbilling Pennzoil. She and Powers reviewed portions of McDonald's time diary. She then met with Louis Paine, the firm's managing partner, to discuss her concerns. The following day, McDonald informed her that Pennzoil was not satisfied with her work. This was the first time she had ever received such criticism.

Over the next month, two senior partners investigated Bohatch's complaint. They reviewed the Pennzoil bills and supporting computer printouts.

They then discussed the allegations with Pennzoil's in-house counsel, who felt that the bills were reasonable.

Paine met with Bohatch and told her that the firm's investigation revealed no basis for her contentions. He added that she should begin looking for other employment, but that the firm would continue to provide her a small monthly income, insurance coverage, office space, and a secretary. After this meeting, Bohatch received no further work assignments from the firm. Five months later, without notice, the firm refused to pay Bohatch her standard year-end bonus. According to the partnership agreement, a bonus could not be reduced without notice. Six months later the firm stopped paying her a monthly income and told her to vacate her office. Bohatch found a new job and then filed suit. Three days later, the firm voted formally to expel her from the partnership in accordance with the partnership agreement.

At trial, the jury awarded Bohatch $57,000 for lost wages, $250,000 for mental anguish, and $4 million in punitive damages. The trial court reduced the punitive damages to around $237,000 and both sides appealed.

You Be the Judge: Did Butler & Binion violate its partnership agreement? Did it wrongfully expel Colette Bohatch from the partnership?

Argument for Bohatch: The partnership agreement stated that the firm could not reduce a partner's year-end bonus without notice. But that is exactly what Butler & Binion did.

In addition, the firm has a fundamental duty to be fair in its treatment of partners. Bohatch blew the whistle on a partner who had systematically overbilled a major client. The firm should have been grateful. No matter what the partnership agreement says, if the court permits Butler & Binion to retaliate against a partner who in good faith reports suspected overbilling, partners everywhere will be afraid to report wrongdoing. If lawyers are discouraged from reporting violations of professional conduct, clients will suffer and so will the reputation of the legal profession.

Argument for Butler & Binion: No one denies that the firm has the right to reduce a partner's compensation. Although technically the partnership did not give the required notice, it had told her she was fired. Did she really expect to receive a bonus that year?

Under its partnership agreement, the firm had the right to expel Bohatch for good reason or no reason. She claims that is unfair. But partnerships are based on the fundamental concept that partners may choose with whom they wish to associate. A partnership exists because partners place confidence and trust in one another. Once Bohatch accused McDonald of cheating a client, there was no way they could continue to work together. Someone had to go, and, since no evidence supported her claims, she was the obvious choice.

Wrongful Dissociation. A *wrongful* dissociation occurs if:

- *A partner violates the partnership agreement.* The Donut Partnership agreement prohibits racetrack betting. When Taylor wins the Pick Six, he is automatically dissociated.
- *A partner in a term partnership withdraws before the end of the term.* The Donut Partnership is supposed to last five years, but Jay withdraws after five months.
- *A court expels a partner in a term partnership because her behavior is harmful.* A court has the right to expel a partner who engages in wrongful conduct that harms the partnership or violates the partnership agreement in a serious way. Gabriela drugs the favored Speedy Donut so that she can win a bet on a long shot in the race. A court could expel her and that would constitute a wrongful dissociation.
- *A partner in a term partnership becomes bankrupt.*

Once a partner is dissociated, the remaining partners must decide how to proceed; they can either continue the partnership as an ongoing business or terminate it.

CONTINUATION OF THE PARTNERSHIP BUSINESS

If a partner is dissociated from the partnership, the other partners can, by unanimous vote, continue the business, but they must buy out the ex-partner.[6] Most large firms simply provide in their partnership agreement that, upon dissociation, the business continues.

Financial Settlement

If the partnership decides to continue, it must pay the ex-partner the value of her share of the business. This value is equal to her share of the proceeds if (1) the partnership was sold as an ongoing business or (2) the partnership's assets were liquidated, whichever calculation is greater. For example, if Gabriela is adjudged incompetent by a court, she is automatically dissociated from the Donut Partnership. At that point, Speedy is worth $500,000 and the partnership has debts of $50,000, for a total value of $450,000. Gabriela is entitled to at least a one-third share—$150,000. If, however, the partnership is worth $600,000 as an ongoing business, Gabriela is entitled to $200,000.

Now the plot thickens. If Gabriela's dissociation was *wrongful*, the partnership can subtract any damages she caused from the amount it owes her. A court expels Gabriela from the partnership because she drugged Speedy. His recovery is slow and he is unable to race for months, costing the partnership $100,000. Taylor and Jay could subtract that $100,000 from the $200,000 they owe her, so she ultimately receives a check for only $100,000. If her bad acts caused more than $200,000 in damage, she owes them money.

Liability of the Dissociated Partner to Outsiders for Debts Incurred *before* Dissociation

A dissociated partner is liable to outsiders for debts incurred during her term as a partner, but the partnership must indemnify her for these debts. After Gabriela departs, a bank sues the partnership for failure to pay its loan. Although Gabriela is no longer a partner, she was one when the partnership borrowed the money. As we will see in the next chapter, the bank may be able to recover from her. If it does, however, the partnership must *indemnify* her; that is, the partnership must reimburse her for any amounts she pays the bank. This is only fair because, when the partnership bought out her share, it reduced the payment to reflect liabilities such as this.

Liability of the Dissociated Partner to Outsiders for Debts Incurred *after* Dissociation

A dissociated partner is liable to outsiders for the debts of the partnership incurred within two years after she leaves, but only if the creditor reasonably believes she is still a partner. The partnership must indemnify her for these debts. If Taylor and Jay buy an expensive saddle on credit from their regular supplier, Gabriela is also liable unless the saddler knows she is dissociated. The partnership would have to reimburse her (if it has enough funds). To protect herself, however, Gabriela can file a *statement of dissociation* with the Secretary of State. Although the saddler rarely spends his free afternoons perusing the public records, he is deemed to have notice of this filing 90 days after Gabriela makes it.

---

[6] If the ex-partner's dissociation was rightful, she can vote in this decision. If her dissociation was wrongful, she has no right to vote.

Liability of the Dissociated Partner to the Partnership

If the ex-partner harms the partnership after she leaves, she is liable for the damage she causes. If Gabriela lets a feed supplier believe that she is still a partner and then buys feed on credit, the partnership may be liable for her charges. If so, she must reimburse the partnership.

TERMINATION OF THE PARTNERSHIP BUSINESS

When a partner is dissociated, the partnership may choose to terminate the business rather than continue it. **Ending a partnership business involves three steps: dissolution, winding up, and termination.**

Dissolution

The RUPA lists circumstances under which a partnership automatically dissolves. This provision is a *default* rule, meaning that the partners can agree otherwise if they want. **Partners can always decide (by unanimous vote) to continue a partnership.** Indeed, even after the winding up process begins, the partners can change their minds and continue the business.

Unless the partners agree otherwise, a partnership dissolves under the following circumstances:

- *In a partnership at will, when a partner notifies the partnership that he intends to withdraw.*
- *In a term partnership when:*
  - *A partner is dissociated and half of the remaining partners vote to wind up the partnership business.* When Jay dies, he is dissociated from the partnership. If Gabriela votes to wind up the business, the partnership is dissolved.
  - *All the partners agree to dissolve.* Although the Donut Partnership is supposed to last five years, Taylor, Jay, and Gabriela can agree among themselves to wind up the business whenever they want. If Speedy Donut is a cream puff on the racetrack, they can decide to dissolve their partnership and sell the pastry.
  - *The term expires or the partnership achieves its goal.* If Speedy Donut runs in the Derby, the Donut Partnership automatically dissolves.
- *In any partnership when:*
  - *An event occurs which the partners had agreed would cause dissolution.* The Donut Partnership agreement provided that the partnership would dissolve if Speedy failed to win a race in any 12-month period. When Speedy goes winless, the partnership dissolves.
  - *The partnership business becomes illegal.* If horse racing is banned, the Donut Partnership automatically dissolves.
  - *A court determines that the partnership is unlikely to succeed.* If the partners simply cannot get along or they cannot make a profit, any partner has the right to ask a court to dissolve the partnership. In the following case, the court decided that the partners simply could not work together.

NEMAZEE CAPITAL CORP. v. ANGULO CAPITAL CORP.
1996 U.S. Dist. LEXIS 10750
United States District Court for the Southern District of New York, 1996

Facts: Nemazee Capital, owned by Hassan Nemazee, signed a partnership agreement (the Agreement) with Angulo Capital, owned by Gerard Angulo. The partnership bought The San Juan Star (The Star), Puerto Rico's English-language newspaper and the partnership's principal asset. Angulo relocated to Puerto Rico and assumed the day-to-day responsibilities of running The Star as its chief executive officer. The partners quarreled so bitterly that they ultimately ended up in court, each accusing the other of violating the partnership agreement.

Issues: **Does the court have the authority to dissolve a partnership? How should this dissolution be effected?**

Excerpts from Judge Owen's Decision: [Two years after acquiring The Star], the partners' relationship began to deteriorate. At trial, Nemazee and Angulo sought to lay blame for this deterioration on each other's actions and alleged breaches of the Agreement. Their hostility and animosity, the substantial depths of which were revealed at trial, appear to flow from some never-to-be-discovered source but, once unleashed, have sadly, yet understandably, resulted in a barrage of acrimonious charges and countercharges across the courtroom. These thrusts and parries, flowing from mutual antagonism, which under some circumstances might be taken as breaches of obligations that one partner owes another, I see as little more than evidence of that antagonism, not rising to the level of independent breaches of the Agreement, such that one partner should be labeled "innocent" and the other "guilty."

It is well within the court's broad, equitable powers to direct dissolution of a partnership where the partners are unable to cooperate, such that the original goals of the partnership agreement are frustrated. And this result follows not only when such want of confidence is occasioned by the misconduct or gross mismanagement of the partner against whom dissolution is sought, but when such want of confidence and distrust has arisen from other circumstances, provided it has become such as cannot probably be overcome.

Because I find that dissolution is warranted on the basis of the irreconcilable differences between Nemazee and Angulo, I do not reach, even if I could answer, the question of assigning blame for the claimed wrongful acts and breaches of the Agreement that the parties charge each other with, for so enshrouded in now-impenetrable murk of the past is the well-spring of what is today a river of acted-out animosity.

Accordingly, making no findings as to any fault of either partner, I decline to order a liquidation of assets, and instead direct that Angulo, who desires to make a career out of running The Star, is to be permitted to continue to manage the newspaper if he agrees to buy out Nemazee, or if Nemazee's partnership interest can be otherwise disposed of. Failing this, the interests of justice may require a public sale with a distribution of the proceeds to the partners. The parties may apply to the Court at any time during the effectuation of the foregoing to deal with any legitimately perceived problem or concern.

The foregoing is so ordered.

Winding Up

During the winding up process, all debts of the partnership are paid, and the remaining proceeds are distributed to the partners.

Who Does It? Unless the partnership agreement provides otherwise, any partner who has not wrongfully dissociated has the right to oversee the winding up.

Are They Paid? Partners are entitled to reasonable compensation for their work in winding up the partnership.

What Do They Do? The winding up process can be complex and take as long as several years to complete. The partners in charge can either sell the entire business as a whole, sell the individual assets of the business, distribute specific assets to the partners, or some combination of these options. They have the right to complete unfinished transactions and do whatever is necessary to wind up the business, but they do *not* have the right to take on new business.

If Taylor is winding up the Donut Partnership, he can sell Speedy Donut outright, buy feed for him until the sale, sue to recover any winnings that have not been paid, and settle partnership debts. But can he enter the horse in additional races? In a similar case, a court permitted the partner in charge of winding up a racing business to pay entrance fees for races, even though the horses would, in all likelihood, be sold before the races. The court assumed that buyers would pay more for horses that were eligible to race in upcoming events.[7]

The partnership is bound by the acts of the partners in charge of winding up. As the following case illustrates, this rule can sometimes lead to unhappy results.

JEFFERSON INSURANCE CO. v. CURLE

771 S.W.2d 424, 1989 Tenn. App. LEXIS 30

Tennessee Court of Appeals, 1989

Facts: Michael Curle and Steven Shelley were partners doing business under the name C & S Roofing. When the partnership dissolved, Curle agreed to complete one unfinished project (the Bishop house) and left Shelley to wind up the other partnership business. Shelley canceled the partnership's general liability insurance policy without telling Curle. While painting the Bishop house, Dennis Whitsett fell through a hole in the roof that the partnership had left covered only with tar paper. When Whitsett sought to recover from the partnership for his serious injuries, Curle and Shelley asked the insurance company to pay the claim.

The trial court found the policy canceled as to Steven Shelley, individually, but in full force and effect as to the partnership and Michael Curle, individually. The insurance company appealed.

Issue: **Was the partnership bound by Shelley's decision during the winding up process to cancel the policy, even though he had not told Curle?**

Excerpts from Judge McLemore's Decision: [The Tennessee Partnership Act] clearly states: "After dissolution a partner can bind the partnership. . .by any act appropriate for winding up partnership affairs or completing transactions unfinished at dissolution." The liquidating partner owes a continuing fiduciary duty to the other partners and has an obligation to act equitably toward them. However, these obligations run between partners and do not absolve any partner from being bound by the liquidating partner's actions in winding up partnership affairs. In the present case, we hold Shelley's cancellation of the partnership insurance policy and collection of unused premiums to be within his authority in winding up the partnership's affairs.

For the foregoing reasons, the judgment of the trial court holding the policy canceled as to Steven Shelley, individually, is *affirmed*, but that portion of the judgment holding that the policy is in full force and effect as to C & S Roofing, a partnership, and Michael Curle, individually, is *reversed*; and we hold that the policy is canceled as to all insureds and, thus, provides no coverage to any of the defendants for the accident alleged by Dennis Whitsett.

---

[7] *Central Trust & S. Deposit Co. v. Respass*, 112 Ky. 606, 66 S.W. 421 (1902).

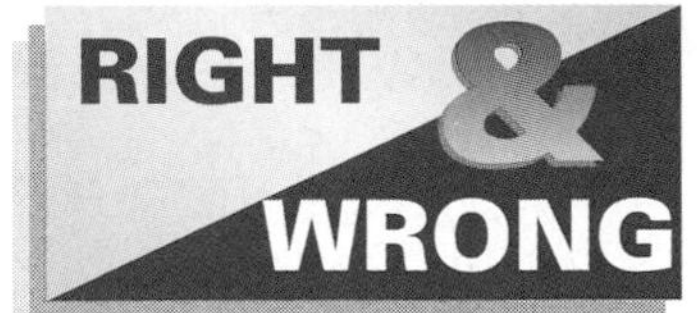

Was the result in this case fair? What is the public policy behind this rule?

Who Is Liable if a Partner Takes on New Business? During the winding up process, the partners continue to be liable for the debts of the partnership that were incurred before dissolution. But what if a partner oversteps her bounds during the winding up process and takes on new business? All the other partners are liable unless they have filed a *statement of dissolution* with the Secretary of State. This statement is effective 90 days after it is filed. A sample notice of dissolution is available at http://sddt.com/files/notices/dissolution/pn96060550203.html.

How Are Partnership Proceeds Distributed? During the winding up process, the assets of the partnership are paid out in the following order:

- First, to creditors of the partnership, including creditors who are partners. Suppose that the Donut Partnership has assets of $30,000. It owes $20,000 each to the feed supplier, the stabler, and Jay, for a total of $60,000. It will pay $10,000 to each of the three creditors—Jay is treated exactly like the outsiders.
- Second, any leftover funds (or obligations) are distributed to the partners. Unless the partnership agreement provides otherwise, partners share equally in profits—and losses. In this example, the Donut Partnership had only enough assets to pay half its $60,000 debt. Each partner would then contribute $10,000 to pay the amount still owing. Jay's payment would be a wash—he owes $10,000, but he is also entitled to be paid $10,000.

Termination

After the sometimes lengthy and complex winding up, the actual termination of a partnership is anticlimactic. Termination happens automatically once the winding up is finished. The partnership is not required to do anything official; it can go out of the world even more quietly and simply than it came in.

CHAPTER CONCLUSION

Partnerships are a deceptively simple form of organization. They are easy to form, sometimes so easy that the participants do not even know they have created one. Yet partnerships are governed by a complex and overlapping set of rules: the UPA or RUPA, the common law, and the partnership agreement (if one exists). There are two lessons to be learned from this chapter: (1) Do not form a partnership by accident; do it deliberately or not at all. (2) Do not form a partnership without understanding the rules that regulate them.

CHAPTER REVIEW

1. In determining whether a partnership exists, a court will consider whether the parties:
   - Intend to have a partnership
   - Share the profits of the business

- Receive other income
- Exercise control over the business
- Share in the losses of the business
- Contributed property to the business, and
- Refer to themselves as partners.

2. If someone is not a member of a partnership, she will nonetheless be considered a partner by estoppel if she (1) tells other people she is a partner or allows other people to say, without contradiction, that she is a partner; (2) a third party relies on this assertion; and (3) the third party suffers harm.
3. A dissociation occurs when a partner leaves the partnership.
4. When one or more partners dissociate, the partnership can either buy out the departing partner(s) and continue in business or wind up the business and terminate the partnership.
5. A partner always has the *power* to leave a partnership but may not have the *right*.
6. If partners do not have an agreement about the duration of their partnership, it is called a partnership at will, and any of them can leave at any time for any reason.
7. With a term partnership, the partners have agreed in advance how long it will last.
8. A dissociated partner is liable to outsiders for debts incurred during her term as a partner, but the partnership must indemnify her for these debts.
9. A dissociated partner is liable for the debts of the partnership incurred within two years after she leaves, but only if the creditor reasonably believes she is still a partner. The partnership must indemnify her for these debts.
10. If the partners decide to end the partnership business, they must take three steps: dissolution, winding up, and termination.
11. During the winding up process, the partners have the right to complete unfinished transactions and do whatever is necessary to terminate the business. They do not have the right to take on new business.
12. During the winding up process, the assets of the partnership are paid out:
    (a) First, to creditors of the partnership, including creditors who are partners.
    (b) Second, to partners.

PRACTICE TEST

1. Mrs. Perry parked her new Chevrolet in the parking lot at the airport in Springfield, Ohio. Bryan Little was giving flying lessons to Edward Selders. Little told Selders to taxi a plane off the runway. Selders, standing on the ground next to the plane, cranked up the engine. The throttle was set too far open, so the plane began to move. Selders chased the plane on foot, grabbed its left wing, and swung the airplane in a semicircle, crashing it into Perry's car. Little operated his flying business under the name "Little-Greiner Air Service." Bryan Little and Carl Greiner were not partners, but Perry sued them both on a theory of partnership by estoppel. She argued that they had used a name for their business that sounded like a partnership. She had never heard of their business until the collision. Is Greiner liable to Perry as a partner by estoppel?

2. Suppose that in the chapter's opening vignette Chase, Bailey, and Zack signed a document stating, "The undersigned expressly agree that they are not partners." If they continued to work together on the house, sharing the profits and the management, would they have been partners?

3. A bulldozer burned to ashes in Arkansas. For Lawrence Nolen, the good news was that the bulldozer was insured. The bad news was that Dennis Burnett claimed half the proceeds as Nolen's partner. Nolen and Burnett had not signed a partnership agreement. This is how Nolen testified at trial:

> Burnett talked of buying a dozer. I told him I could borrow the money and set up payments on it. Later I told him if he'd come up with his $5,000 that half the dozer was his. That was the deal. I bought the dozer, borrowed the money from the bank. The note was in my name. I bought the insurance on the dozer. I had a bank account in my name and it was used only for the dozer business. In the meantime I paid him for his time. I may have opened an account at the store for N&B Dozer just to keep my purchases at the store separate from my personal purchases.

Others testified that the parties had agreed they would divide any and all profits on an equal basis, one-half to each, once the bank loan had been paid in full. Had Nolen and Burnett formed a partnership to own and operate the bulldozer?

4. **CPA QUESTION** Which of the following is **not** necessary to create a partnership?

(a) Execution of a written partnership agreement

(b) Agreement to share ownership of the partnership

(c) Intention of conducting a business for profit

(d) Intention of creating a relationship recognized as a partnership

5. Marilyn Baker and Reuben Waters lived in the Franklin Hotel, a run-down boarding house in Monroe, North Carolina. At various times, their residence lacked hot water, heat, and windows, but did come equipped with leaking ceilings, defective locks, faulty plumbing, trash in the hallways, roaches, and rats. A partnership consisting of Claude Mosley and Jacob Blackwood owned the hotel for two years. It then transferred the hotel to two corporations and dissolved. Three years later, before winding up was complete, Baker and Waters sued the partnership for violations of landlord-tenant law that occurred prior to its dissolution. Is the partnership liable, after its dissolution, for events that occurred beforehand?

6. **RIGHT & WRONG** Arthur Engelbrecht, John McCullough, and George Gilling formed a partnership to drill and maintain cesspools for two years. After less than two months, McCullough and Gilling sent a letter to Engelbrecht informing him that they were dissolving the partnership. Engelbrecht sued McCullough and Gilling, asking the court to declare that the partnership still existed and he had the right to continue in the business. Do McCullough and Gilling have the power to dissolve a term partnership before the end of the term? Aside from the legal issue, is it fair to Engelbrecht to allow his two partners to walk away from their partnership? He had counted on a two-year commitment; they gave only two months.

7. Jerome Gull, Ruth Van Epps, and David Werth practiced law together in an at-will partnership until Gull withdrew to practice on his own. The partnership was thereby dissolved, and Van Epps and Werth began the winding up process. It dragged on for three years because the three lawyers could not agree on Gull's fair share of partnership assets. He claimed that he was entitled to a percentage of the profits that Van Epps and Werth earned from new business that they undertook during the winding up period. Do you agree?

8. Megan, Lauren, and Kristen formed a partnership called Hot Wheels to deliver take-out food from restaurants to customers' homes. Megan loaned the partnership $20,000 to purchase delivery vans and fund cash needs for the first few months. In addition, the partnership borrowed $30,000 from their former business law teacher, Professor Lawless. They agreed to share equally in the profits of the enterprise. After a year and a half, they sold the business for $74,000. How will these funds be distributed?

9. Suppose that, in the prior example, the partnership sold the business for $26,000. What are the financial obligations of each partner?

10. **YOU BE THE JUDGE WRITING PROBLEM** Hubert Shuptrine, an artist, entered into an agreement with R. L. Brown for the reproduction and distribution of his paintings. Shuptrine was to receive 50 percent of the gross sales revenues. Brown was responsible for all losses and for management of the business. Before leaving on a trip to Israel, where he feared he might be in some danger, Brown signed a partnership agree-

ment with Shuptrine stating that they jointly owned the business. Shortly after Brown returned from the trip, the two men terminated their business relationship, and Shuptrine revoked his authorization for the sale of prints. When Brown continued selling the prints, Shuptrine filed suit. Brown argued that the two had formed a partnership and that he was authorized to sell assets of the partnership. Were Shuptrine and Brown partners? **Argument for Shuptrine:** A partnership agreement does not create a partnership. Brown alone managed the business. Shuptrine shared only revenues, not profits. **Argument for Brown:** Shuptrine and Brown both provided services to the business: Brown paid for the printing, and Shuptrine did the artwork. These two men signed a partnership agreement, and they obviously intended to be partners.

11. If a partner dissociates, he is entitled to:

(a) Force the termination of the partnership

(b) Receive indemnification from liability for present partnership debt

(c) Receive indemnification from damages he caused the partnership

(d) Receive only his share of the value of the partnership assets upon liquidation

INTERNET RESEARCH PROBLEM

The Web site http://www.lectlaw.com/form/f068.tst has posted the partnership agreement for a real partnership. Can you foresee any problems that might arise under this agreement? Are there any obvious omissions or problematic provisions? The same Web site also offers guidelines for drafting a partnership agreement. Does the real agreement follow these guidelines?

You can find further practice problems in the Online Quiz at http://beatty.westbuslaw.com or in the Study Guide that accompanies this text.

CHAPTER 34

PARTNERSHIP IN OPERATION

When Dr. John N. Sheagren, an internist on the faculty of George Washington University Medical Center, wrote his book, *Financial Advice for Physicians*, he emphasized investment in insurance and stocks. Investing in real estate, he warned, requires "specialized skill and advice." "I would have to say I did not follow my own advice," Dr. Sheagren observed after he invested $12,000 in a general partnership that failed. "It was my own stupidity." To date, Dr. Sheagren has lost "dramatically more" than his original $12,000 investment.

Dr. Michael Corrado made the same mistake. He lost more than $100,000 on his $20,000 investment in a partnership that bought a downtown Washington building. He could lose even more—as a general partner, he is personally liable for mortgages totaling about $1.5 million.

Despite a lack of business knowledge, many doctors invest in partnerships. "We go to medical school, spend years learning a specialty, then suddenly find ourselves making a lot of money and we just don't know how to handle it," one doctor said. "The medical schools don't teach anything about it; it takes a lot of time to learn to be a wise investor, and with all our professional obligations we just don't take the time."

One psychiatrist, speaking of the salesperson who talked him into investing in a partnership, said,

"I remember one time I asked, in particular, 'Do I have to read this and can I understand it if I read it?' And he said, 'This is just some sort of contract . . . just go ahead and sign it.' So I did."[1]

After studying this chapter, you will know how to avoid the pitfalls into which these doctors jumped. This chapter focuses on two important issues of partnership law: (1) the liability of partners to outsiders and (2) the duties that partners owe each other. Before beginning, it is important to understand one crucial difference between partners' liability to outsiders and to each other. Under the Revised Uniform Partnership Act (RUPA), **the rules governing the liability of partners to outsiders are *mandatory*.** Partners may *not* change them. **The rules governing the relationship among partners are *default* provisions.** With a few exceptions, partners can change these rules by oral or written agreement.[2] (Use the search engine at **http://www.toolkit.cch.com/** to find information about partnership agreements and many other partnership issues.)

RELATIONSHIP BETWEEN PARTNERS AND OUTSIDERS

In the relationship between partners and outsiders, two questions arise: When is the partnership liable to outsiders? If the partnership is liable, who must pay the debt?

LIABILITY OF THE PARTNERSHIP TO OUTSIDERS

Under the RUPA, **every partner is an agent of the partnership for the purpose of its business.**

Authority

Partnership liability is based on the rules of agency law, discussed in Chapters 28 and 29. As an agent, a partner has three types of authority:

- **Actual Authority.** A partnership is liable for any act of a partner that it authorized.
- **Implied Authority.** A partnership is liable for any act of a partner that is reasonably necessary to carry out an authorized transaction.
- **Apparent Authority.** A partnership is liable for an *unauthorized* act of a partner if the partner appears to be carrying on the business of the partnership or even business of the same type. Suppose Tamika and Martin buy and sell used books. Without Martin's knowledge, Tamika promises to pay a large sum for Jane's record collection. Jane is a regular customer of the TM Partnership and simply assumes that Tamika has authority to act. The TM Partnership is liable because buying used records is the same kind of business as buying used books. Martin was in the dark, but now he is in the red.

A partnership's liability for the acts of its partners is one of the most important concepts in partnership law. See if you can identify the three types of authority in this example. Sam and Julia agree to develop SuperMall. Sam funds the operation while Julia supervises construction and leasing. Later, Julia is also responsible for

---

[1] Douglas Feaver, "Doctor's 'Own Stupidity,'" *Washington Post*, Feb. 8, 1977, p. A1. © 1977, The Washington Post. Reprinted with permission.

[2] The exceptions are listed in RUPA §103.

collecting rent checks. Sam opens an account in his own name at the bank and executes a power of attorney authorizing Julia to make deposits and withdrawals from that account. Julia forges Sam's name on the signature card for a second account at the bank that is in both their names. Over the next 18 months, Julia deposits more than $100,000 worth of checks in the joint account rather than in Sam's individual account. While searching for papers in Julia's desk, Sam stumbles on the statement for the joint account and realizes that she has been cheating him.

Sam recovers what he can from Julia and then sues the bank for having allowed Julia to set up the joint account and deposit Sam's checks into it. Is the bank liable? In a similar case, the court concluded:[3]

- Although Julia and Sam did not think of themselves as partners, they were, in fact, partners in SuperMall. (If you are wondering why, review the first half of Chapter 33.)
- When Sam signed the power of attorney, he gave Julia *actual* authority to deposit checks into Sam's *individual* account. The bank had no liability for any acts committed by Julia with actual authority.
- Although Julia was a partner, she did not have *implied* authority to deposit checks into the *joint* account because Sam had not authorized that account.
- The bank was not liable because, as a partner, Julia had *apparent* authority to deposit checks into the *joint* account. These deposited checks *appeared* to be carrying on the business of the partnership, and the bank did not know that Julia was acting without authority.
- The bank would have been liable if Sam had specifically told its officers that Julia was *not* authorized to open a separate account because then Julia would not have had apparent authority.

Ratification

As with every agency relationship, partners can *ratify* unauthorized acts. **If the partnership accepts the benefit of the unauthorized transaction or fails to repudiate it, the partnership has ratified it.** Once ratified, these actions are as valid as if they had been authorized from the beginning.

In the following case, 20 Price Waterhouse partners learned about authority and ratification the hard way.

CASCADE PARTNERSHIP v. COMMISSIONER OF INTERNAL REVENUE
T.C. Memo 1996-299, 1996 Tax Ct. Memo LEXIS 316
United States Tax Court, 1996

Facts: John R. Walsh, Jr. organized Cascade Partnership as a tax shelter for 20 of his fellow partners at Price Waterhouse (PW). However, Walsh himself was not a partner in Cascade. The partnership agreement stated: "All decisions and management of the partnership shall be made by the majority of the shares held by the partners."

Some years after its formation, Cascade received an audit notice from the Internal Revenue Service (IRS). Owing to the complexity of the issues involved, the IRS was unable to complete its investigation in the time allowed by statute. Therefore, the IRS asked Walsh to sign a form granting an extension. The form was supposed to be signed by the so-called tax matters partner (TMP). Since Walsh was not a partner in Cascade, he asked James M. Costello to sign. Although Costello was a Cascade partner, he was not the TMP. Costello signed the form

[3] *Grosberg v. Michigan National Bank—Oakland*, 420 Mich. 707, 362 N.W.2d 715, 1984 Mich. LEXIS 1302 (1985).

without investigating whether he was authorized to sign as TMP or generally on behalf of Cascade.

Two years later, the IRS notified Cascade that it owed more than $1 million in taxes. Cascade argued that the IRS's assessment was invalid because Costello had not been authorized to sign the extension.

Issues: **Did Costello have authority to sign the extension? Did the partnership ratify Costello's action?**

Excerpts from Judge Gerber's Decision: A partner who deals with third persons without notice of any lack of authority, binds the other partners if the transaction be such as the public may reasonably conclude is directly and necessarily embraced within the partnership business as being incident or appropriate to such business according to the course and usage of conducting it.

[Cascade] argues that the partnership agreement modified the normal provisions of the [partnership] statute. [Cascade] refers to paragraph 11 of the partnership agreement that provides: "All decisions and management of the partnership shall be made by the majority of the shares held by the partners." [Cascade] contends that the quoted provision generally limits any partner from acting on behalf of the partnership.

The facts in this case show that the partnership was aware of the circumstances. Walsh, the promoter and manager of the partnership, specifically requested Costello to execute the consent. Costello was requested by [the IRS's] agents to notify the other partners of action taken by [the IRS]. There is no question that Costello, Walsh, and the other partners were aware that the [IRS] was acting on Costello's execution of documents, including the consent and correspondence with [the IRS]. We also note that Walsh, Costello, and the other 19 partners of Cascade were all partners in a nationally known firm of certified public accountants that, among other matters, specializes in Federal taxation.

Finally, it is clear that [the IRS] did not know that Costello was not the appointed or qualified TMP and that Costello's representations were reasonably relied on to [the IRS's] substantial detriment. Under these circumstances, we hold that Cascade is estopped to deny Costello's authority to execute a consent binding the partnership to an extension of the period for assessment.

The underlying concept of the implied ratification principle is to reach the same result where the person(s) with control over the authority allow others to exercise it without repudiation.

Information

As agent, a partner has a duty to pass on all relevant information to the partnership. Whether or not a partner actually fulfills this obligation, the partnership is treated as if it had been notified. Under the RUPA, **whatever one partner knows, the partnership is deemed to know.** The leases at the SuperMall require tenants to notify the landlord if they will not be renewing. One of the tenants gives notice to Sam, who forgets to pass that information on to Julia. As a result, she does not look for a replacement tenant. If someone is going to lose money because of Sam's mistake, in all fairness it should be the partnership, which had the bad judgment to take on an unreliable partner.

Tort Liability

A partnership is responsible for the *intentional* and *negligent* torts of a partner that occur *in the ordinary course* of the partnership's business or with the *actual* authority of the partners. When a potential tenant asks Julia how many customers enter the mall each day, she purposely tells him a number that is 50 percent higher than the truth. The partnership is liable for this intentional misrepresentation because it occurred in the ordinary course of the partnership's business. In the following case, a partner in a law firm took money from a friend. Was the partnership liable? You be the judge.

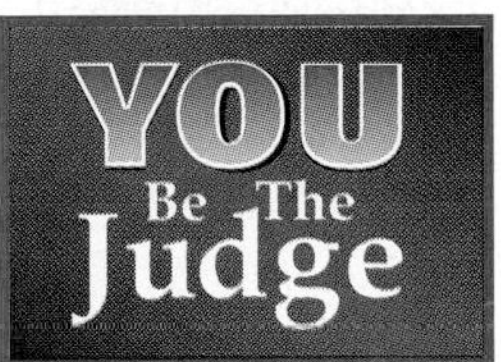

PHILLIPS v. CARSON
240 Kan. 462, 731 P.2d 820, 1987 Kan. LEXIS 252
Supreme Court of Kansas, 1987

Facts: The Phillips and the Carsons had been friends for several years before Mr. Phillips died. Mrs. Phillips paid Mr. Carson, as partner in a law firm, $80,000 to handle her husband's estate. For no extra charge, the firm handled a number of other legal matters for her.

One evening at a party, Carson told Phillips that he was having financial problems. Fearful that he might be suicidal, she loaned him and his wife $270,000. To secure the loan, Carson gave her a mortgage on property in Arizona. Later, Carson asked Phillips to release her mortgage so that he could sell the land. He offered her a mortgage on land in Kansas and told her that this would put her in a better position. Carson prepared a mortgage on the Kansas property but failed to file it with the Register of Deeds. Carson's correspondence with Phillips, whether relating to her husband's estate or the loans, was typed on firm letterhead by his secretary at the firm. Phillips knew that the secretary did both firm and personal work for Carson.

Carson filed for bankruptcy protection. Because Phillips's mortgage had never been filed, she had little chance of receiving repayment on her loan. She filed suit against Carson and his law firm. The lower court found that Carson had been negligent for not filing the mortgage.

You Be the Judge: Is the law firm liable for Carson's negligence? Must it repay the money that Phillips loaned Carson?

Argument for Phillips: The firm argues that it is not responsible for what Carson did because he was not acting in the ordinary course of the partnership's business. But advising a client on loans, security, and the method of recording a mortgage is part of a law firm's business. If Carson had given Phillips this advice on a loan that she was making to someone else, the firm would certainly have been liable for his malpractice. And if Carson had not performed legal work for her, he would never have known how wealthy she was and he would never have been able to steal from her.

Phillips signed the loan documents at the firm, and Carson's correspondence about the loans was on firm letterhead. A number of firm attorneys, besides Carson, worked for her, and she paid the firm a generous fee. The law firm was perfectly willing to accept Phillips's money, and now it should accept responsibility for her injury.

Argument for the Law Firm: Phillips and Carson were friends long before she became a client of the firm. They were at a party when she agreed to make the loan to both him *and his wife*. That loan had nothing to do with ordinary law firm business; it was about friendship. Carson did not learn about Phillips's financial situation through work he had done at the firm. They had been friends for years, and he knew all along that she was wealthy.

The fee that Phillips paid the firm was for probating her husband's estate, not for advising her on the loans. She knew that Carson's secretary did personal work for him at the office, and the loans did not become law firm business simply because Carson's secretary typed the documents. Phillips could not have believed that the partnership authorized Carson to borrow money from clients. Certainly, no one at the firm ever told her so. Phillips was unlucky in her choice of friends, and now she wants the law firm to pay.

PAYING THE DEBTS OF THE PARTNERSHIP

The basic rule of partnership liability is simply stated: **all partners are personally liable for all debts of the partnership.** This rule applies whether or not the individual partner was in any way responsible for the debts. All of a partner's assets are at risk. The following article discusses the bankruptcy of an accounting partnership. Some of the partners lost their pensions; others forfeited their houses.

When the accounting firm Laventhol & Horwath asked Jay Brandzel to join the partnership, he accepted with delight. Not so Arthur Adler. He turned down the partners at L & H when they knocked on his door. Bruce Joans was indecisive. He accepted a partnership but then backed out immediately. Small comfort—when the firm filed for bankruptcy, it asked him to contribute thousands of dollars toward a settlement of the partnership's debts. No wonder that an associate at one firm said, "My biggest nightmare is not making partner, and my second biggest nightmare is making partner."[4]

Joint and Several Liability

Partners have *joint and several* liability for partnership obligations. Joint and several liability means that a creditor can sue the partnership and the partners together or in separate lawsuits or in any combination. The partnership and the partners are all individually liable for the full amount of the debt, but, obviously, the creditor cannot keep collecting after he has already received the total amount owed. **Also note that, even if creditors have a judgment against an individual partner, they cannot go after that partner's assets until all the partnership's assets are exhausted.**

Letitia, one of the world's wealthiest people, enters into a partnership with penniless Harry to drill for oil on her estate. While driving on partnership business, Harry crashes into Gus, seriously injuring him. Gus can sue any combination of the partnership, Letitia, and Harry for the full amount, even though Letitia was 2,000 miles away on her Caribbean island when the accident occurred and she had many times cautioned Harry to drive carefully. Even if Gus obtains a judgment against Letitia, however, he cannot recover against her while the partnership still has assets. So, for all practical purposes, he must try to collect first against the partnership. If the partnership is bankrupt and he manages to collect the full amount from Letitia, he cannot then try to recover against Harry. (As we will see in a minute, Letitia may be able to recover from Harry some portion of what she paid Gus.)

Letitia is not wild about Harry's behavior, so she insists that he agree in writing to share all liabilities of the partnership 50/50. Unfortunately for Letitia, the liability rule is *mandatory*, not a default provision, so her agreement with Harry has absolutely no impact on the rights of Gus or any other creditor. He can still recover from Letitia for all debts of the partnership. She can always try to recover from Harry, but he is penniless, so good luck.

Liability of Incoming Partners

The RUPA provides that a partner is *personally* liable only for obligations the partnership incurred *while* he was a partner. His liability for debts incurred *before* he became a partner is limited to his investment in the partnership. Does this rule make sense? Why should an incoming partner be liable in any way for debts the partnership incurred before he became a partner? Consider these questions in light of the following article about Englishman Robert Maxwell. Long known as an international wheeler-dealer, Maxwell stole money from his companies' pension plans to pay for the purchase of newspapers and publishing houses around the world. He drowned after falling—or jumping—over the side of his yacht late one evening. After his death, investigators discovered that more than $1 *billion* was missing from his various enterprises.

[4] Alison Leigh Cowan, "The New Letdown: Making Partner," *New York Times*, Apr. 1, 1992, p. D1. Copyright © 1992 by The New York Times Co. Reprinted by permission.

Though British publisher Robert Maxwell drowned at sea several years ago, his ghost still haunts his investment bank, Goldman, Sachs. A tussle is brewing among Goldman partners over how they should divide $250 million in costs from a settlement that the securities firm reached with pension funds looted by the late publisher. Goldman allegedly sold pension assets without returning the proceeds to the pension funds.

Now Goldman management is grappling with the nettlesome issue of which partners will pay the settlement. Senior partners have proposed allocating the cost to those who were Goldman partners when the Maxwell transactions occurred. But some ex-partners are balking because they would end up paying nearly half of the settlement—as much as $4 million apiece. These alumni argue that all of Goldman's current partners will benefit from the settlement and so the partnership should pay a share of the costs, too. The ex-partners also complain that they had no say over the amount of the settlement, so why should they be asked to write a check for it?[5]

In a sense, the RUPA supports both of these positions. Goldman's ex-partners are *personally* liable for debts incurred while they were members of the firm. However, current partners are also liable, up to the amount of their investment in the partnership, for debts incurred even before they joined. Of course, Goldman's current assets are substantial, so it is up to the management committee to decide how much should be paid personally by the former *partners* and how much by the current *partnership*. In any event, former partners generally are not liable for debts of the partnership incurred after they have left.

Although the RUPA rules seem straightforward, life often is not. In the following case, it is not clear when the debt arose.

CITIZENS BANK OF MASSACHUSETTS v. PARHAM-WOODMAN MEDICAL ASSOCIATES
874 F. Supp. 705, 1995 U.S. Dist. LEXIS 697
United States District Court, District of Virginia, 1995

Facts: On April 30, Citizens Bank and Parham-Woodman Medical Associates signed a loan agreement for $2 million to fund construction of a medical office building. Between April 30 and June 3 of the following year, the bank advanced the partnership a total of $1,457,123. Drs. Richard L. Hunley, Nada Tas, and Joseph Tas became partners in Parham-Woodman three weeks later, on June 25. After June 25, the bank advanced an additional $542,876. When the partnership defaulted on the loan, the bank demanded that Hunley and the two Tases repay the loan out of their personal assets.

Issue: **Are Drs. Hunley and Tas personally liable for a loan that the bank authorized before they became partners but paid out afterwards?**

Excerpts from Judge Payne's Decision: The partnership entitlement to receive the loan proceeds, and its correlative obligation to repay all proceeds received, were established by the documents executed on April 30. The bank was not thereafter free to impose additional conditions precedent to the making of any advance. Nor was the bank free to refuse the advances so long as the contractually specified conditions were satisfied and so long as there were no contractual defaults.

[The Virginia Partnership Act] makes an incoming partner liable for "all the obligations of the partnership arising before his admission," but provides that "this liability shall be satisfied only out of partnership property." Where a

---

[5] Anita Raghavan, "Goldman's Partners Contend with Maxwell Legacy," *Wall Street Journal*, Apr. 12, 1995, p. C1. Republished with permission of The Wall Street Journal; permission conveyed through the Copyright Clearance Center, Inc.

partnership undertakes a debt before a new partner is made, "the credit of [the] new member . . . does not enter into the consideration of the creditors of the old firm, and it would be manifestly unjust to hold the new partner liable." These decisions and the longstanding principle which they confirm support the view that a partnership obligation arises when the creditor extends the credit to the partnership. In this instance, that occurred on April 30 and not on the occasion when the bank disbursed each advance. This rule enables potential creditors of the partnership to know that what they see of a partnership is what they can reach and it permits potential incoming partners to avoid surprise liabilities.

The court finds that all of the partners are liable for the debt owed the bank, but that the liability of Richard L. Hunley, Joseph Tas, and Nada Tas may be satisfied only out of partnership assets.

Relationship among Partners

The rules governing the relationship between partners and outsiders are mandatory; the partners cannot change them. In contrast, the rules regulating the relationship among partners are more flexible—the partners can alter many of them by agreement. If these rules can be changed, why are they in the RUPA at all? As discussed in Chapter 33, partnerships are often formed casually. Sometimes the partners themselves do not even realize they have a partnership. In situations such as these, the default rules apply. Also, some partnerships may not want to undertake the effort and expense of preparing their own agreement. For them, the off-the-rack rules work well enough, and they do not need a custom-tailored version.

Financial Rights

Sharing Profits

Partners share profits equally, unless they agree otherwise. This basic rule applies no matter how much money, time, or effort an individual partner contributes to the partnership. After graduation, Dawn convinces her friends, Niels and Sonya, to return with her to Jackson, Mississippi, to open a coffee bar. Niels and Sonya each contribute the $15,000 they won as prizes during their last year in business school. Since their school awarded no prizes for giving the best parties, Dawn has nothing to contribute financially. But she does know Jackson. When Dawn's Coffee Bar opens for business, she attracts sell-out crowds. Meanwhile, Niels and Sonya are working 20-hour days, first renovating the building and then serving customers. Dawn rarely sees the dawn, or even noon. Niels and Sonya have contributed more time and money and may have done more for the bar's success, but they must share profits equally with Dawn, unless the three agreed otherwise.

Sharing Losses

Partners share losses according to their share of profits, unless they agree otherwise. If Dawn's Coffee Bar fizzles after the first few months of success, then Dawn is responsible for one-third of the losses because she received one-third of the profits. Too late for her to argue that it was not *her* fault the business failed.

Any agreement among partners to share losses is binding only on them, not on outsiders. No one in Jackson wants to sue Dawn who is, after all, a friend. What if the creditors decide to ignore Dawn and pursue Niels and Sonya?

Remember the rules about liability discussed earlier in the chapter. Partners are jointly and severally liable for the debts of the partnership. If the partnership has insufficient assets, creditors have no obligation to pursue the three partners equally. They can ignore Dawn and collect against Niels and Sonya. But Dawn is not home free; Niels and Sonya can demand that she pay them for her share of the partnership debts.

Payment for Work Done

Partners are not entitled to any payment beyond their share of profits, unless they agree otherwise. Niels and Sonya are not entitled to a greater share of the profits in return for their extra work. What if they ask to be paid standard wages for the time they spend waitering? According to the RUPA, they are entitled to *nothing* more than their share of the profits. It is simply too difficult for the courts to evaluate each partner's contributions. ("Sonya didn't get to work until 9:15." "That's not true, I was there at 8:45 but you didn't see me because I was out back washing your dirty dishes . . . .") The RUPA rule may seem arbitrary, but at least it is easy to enforce. We saw the only exception to this rule in Chapter 33. Partners are entitled to remuneration for services performed in winding up the partnership.

Although Niels and Sonya do not receive payment for their labor, they are entitled to reimbursement for out-of-pocket expenses incurred on behalf of the partnership. If, for example, they run out of clean dish towels one day and Niels dashes across the street to the Five & Dime to buy new ones, the partnership must reimburse him.

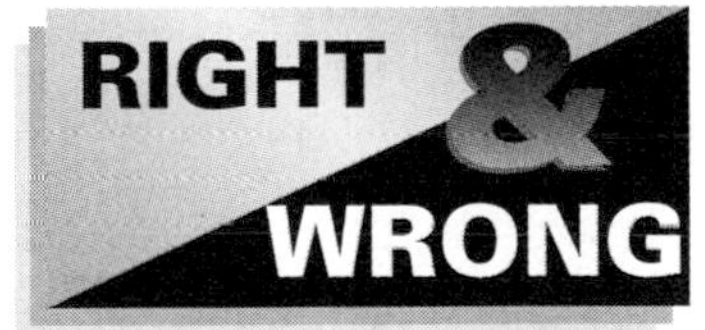

Courts cannot sort out which partner has put in the most hours. But Dawn knows that Sonya and Niels have worked harder. She does not have a *legal* obligation to pay them more; what about an *ethical* obligation?

Did the plaintiff in the following case deserve payment for the work he performed for the partnership? Did the court make the right decision legally? Ethically?

BOUSHEHRY v. ISHAK
550 N.E.2d 784, 1990 Ind. App. LEXIS 230
Court of Appeals of Indiana, 1990

Facts: Fred Boushehry and Jerry Ishak formed a partnership to buy land and develop a housing subdivision. They put down a deposit on property owned by Thomas Clouse and began work to obtain a zoning permit. Because the two partners were quarreling over what type of zoning permit to obtain, they failed to purchase the land on the required date. The next day, Clouse sent them a letter notifying them that they had forfeited their deposit. Boushehry asked Ishak to see Clouse and try to salvage the deal. Clouse refused to talk with Ishak, but called Boushehry and told him that Ishak was trying to close the deal without him. This was not true, but Boushehry did not tell Clouse the real reason for Ishak's visit. Boushehry then purchased the land himself.

Ishak filed suit against Boushehry demanding *quantum meruit*, that is, payment for the services he had rendered the partnership in developing the land. He argued that he was entitled to compensation because he earned no profit from the partnership. The trial court decided that Ishak's efforts had indeed enriched Boushehry, and ordered him to pay Ishak $20,000.

Issue: Is Ishak entitled to payment for the services he rendered the partnership?

Excerpts from Judge Buchanan's Decision: Indiana partnership law provides:

> The rights and duties of the partners in relation to the partnership shall be determined, subject to any agreement between them, by the following rules: . . . No partner is entitled to remuneration for acting in the partnership business. . . .

Thus it has been held that a partner is not entitled to compensation for his services rendered to the partnership unless there is an agreement to the contrary. As a partner's rights are determined by the partnership agreement and by statute, Ishak was not entitled to recover the value of his services on the basis of *quantum meruit*. His services were rendered to the partnership in return for a share of the partnership's profit and he is entitled to no other compensation, absent an agreement to the contrary.

Judgment *reversed* and *remanded* for further proceedings consistent herewith.[6]

Partnership Property

All partnership property belongs to the partnership as a whole, not to the individual partners. A partner has no right to use or sell property, except for the benefit of the partnership. Suppose that the partnership owns the building that houses their coffee bar. Upstairs, above the bar, are three apartments. "Wow! This is great," says Niels, "I get the front unit." Does Niels have the right to live in one of the three apartments? After all, Dawn and Sonya can have the other two. Although the arrangement *sounds* fair, in fact, Niels has no right to live there, unless the other partners agree. Partnership property is owned by the partnership, not by each partner individually. If the partnership owns a car, Niels can drive it on partnership business, but he would have no right to use it for a date Saturday night.

Right to Transfer a Partnership Interest

A partnership is a personal relationship built on trust. Therefore, a partner can no more sell his partnership share to a stranger than a spouse can come home one night and announce, "I'm leaving the marriage but, don't worry, I've found a substitute." **Without the approval of the other partners, a partner cannot sell her share; she can only transfer her right to receive profits and losses. A new partner can only be admitted to a partnership by unanimous consent of the other partners.** It would be unfair to force partners to work with, or face unlimited liability for, someone they do not consider trustworthy. Sonya gets in serious debt to a fellow gambler, Nathan Detroit. Fearful that Nathan will ruin her manicure if she does not pay her debt, she agrees to give him her share of the partnership, which is her only asset. He knows a lot about coffee, and she is sure he will do fine as a partner. Although Niels and Dawn feel sorry for Sonya's predicament, they refuse to admit Nathan as a partner. Without their permission, Sonya has no right to transfer ownership rights or management authority to Nathan. Niels and Dawn cannot be forced to work with someone they do not want to touch with a 10-foot pole. However, Sonya can transfer to Nathan the right to receive her share of the partnership's profits.

What if Sonya refuses to assign to Nathan her right to receive profits from the partnership? **Creditors can attach partnership profits through a *charging order*. A charging order** is simply a court order granting a third party the right to receive a share of partnership profits. In the case of a partnership at will, once Nathan has a charging order, he can ask the court to dissolve the partnership and order the

[6] On rehearing, the court of appeals ordered a new trial on a different issue. 560 N.E.2d 116, 1990 Ind. App. LEXIS 1293 (Ind. Ct. App. 1990).

partners to wind up the business. With a term partnership, Nathan must wait until the end of the term.

Similar rules apply when a partner dies. A partner's heirs have no right to specific partnership property; they do not become partners themselves, nor do they have any say in partnership management. They do have a right to receive the value of a partnership share. In large, sophisticated partnerships, the partnership agreement will usually short-circuit arguments by establishing in advance how to calculate the value of a share.

MANAGEMENT RIGHTS

Right to Manage

Each and every partner has equal rights in the management and conduct of the business, unless the partners agree otherwise. In a large partnership, with hundreds of partners, too many cooks can definitely spoil the firm's profitability. That is why large partnerships are almost always run by one or a few partners who are designated as **managing partners** or **members of the executive committee.** Some firms are run almost dictatorially by the partner who brings in the most business (called a "rainmaker"). Nonetheless, even in relatively autocratic firms, the atmosphere tends to be less hierarchical than in a corporation, where employees are accustomed to the concept of having a boss. Whatever the reality, partners by and large like to think of themselves as being the equal of every other partner. The following article illustrates how English law firms have dealt with these management issues.

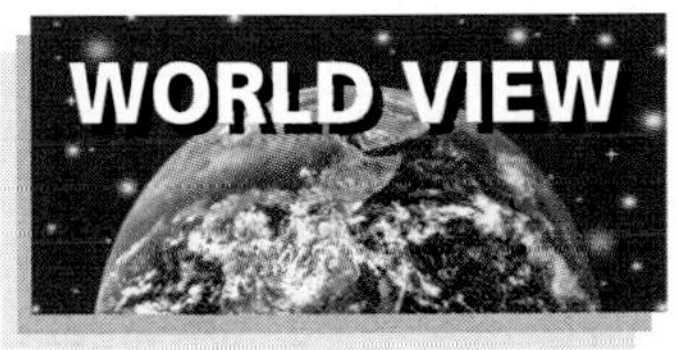

It is still fashionable in legal circles to talk about City of London law firms as being unmanageable and to blame the partnership structure. "It's a bit like trying to run a [publicly traded corporation] with all the shareholders standing in your office," says Geoffrey Howe, managing partner of Clifford Chance, the UK's largest law partnership.

While the continuing commitment of the leading firms to the partnership ideal contradicts such statements, they are not made entirely in jest. As law firms began to grow dramatically in the 1970s and 1980s and competition increased, the weaknesses of partnership—conservatism, slowness of response and decision taking—forced them to adopt corporate management systems within the partnership structure. "It became necessary to effectively disenfranchise partners on management decisions," says Bill Tudor John, senior partner of Allen & Overy. "Management by committee had become unworkable."

Most firms agree that there is no right or wrong way of managing law firms. But a pattern has emerged. The partnership as a whole remains the supreme decision-taking body, but the issues on which all partners must vote have been substantially reduced. Partnership votes tend to be confined to the election of new partners, profit share, and changes to the partnership agreement, although some firms still require a full vote on significant capital expenditure such as new premises or the opening of overseas offices.

Below the partners is the partnership board or council usually chaired by the senior partner, with the managing partner taking the chief executive role. Other members of the board are elected from the partnership to represent different areas of the practice. Partner boards concentrate on strategy, finances, and the big picture. Executive management has devolved to the managing partner assisted by outsiders brought in to perform specific tasks.[7] (For information about British partnership law, see **http://www.gordonbancks.co.uk/compco01.htm.**)

---

[7] "The pitfalls of partnership," *Financial Times*, Feb. 23, 1996, p. 18. Reprinted with permission of the Financial Times.

Right to Bind the Partnership

As discussed in the first section of this chapter, partners are agents of the partnership and have the *power* to bind the partnership through actual, implied, or apparent authority. The partnership is liable to third parties for a partner's actions. If these actions are not authorized by the partnership, the partner still has the *power* to bind the partnership, but not the *right*. In this case, the partnership is liable to the third party, and the partner is liable to the partnership. If the partner has both the *power* and the *right*, he is not personally liable to the partnership no matter how harmful his actions.

A partner is authorized to bind the partnership for any transaction within the ordinary course of its business, *unless* the partner knows that the other partners would disapprove. Dawn decides she would rather buy coffee from Hadley than from the regular supplier in New York. She has the authority to switch suppliers, unless she *knows* that Sonya and Niels think Hadley's coffee tastes too much like the Mississippi River. If Dawn signs a contract with Hadley, knowing that her partners disapprove, the partnership is liable to Hadley, but she is liable to the partnership.

Right to Vote

Unless the partners agree otherwise, all partners have an equal vote, regardless of their contributions to the partnership. For ordinary partnership affairs, the majority has the right to make a decision. To amend the partnership agreement or to make decisions outside the ordinary course of business, the vote must be unanimous. What happens when Dawn wants to introduce herbal teas, over Niels's dead body? The partners vote. Since this is an ordinary partnership matter, the majority rules. If Dawn can get Sonya on her side, she will win approval for the healthy teas. It makes no difference that Dawn never contributed any cash to the partnership; she has the right to vote.

This is the default rule, but many partnerships change it by agreement. Accounting or law firms, for instance, often award partners a certain number of points each year, based on how much business they bring in or how hard they work. The more points, the higher their compensation and the more their votes count. Some firms, run by a particularly powerful partner, may effectively have only one vote—his. The managing partner of a large law firm once said, "This partnership has a one man, one vote rule, and I'm the one man."

Right to Know

It is difficult to manage an enterprise without adequate information. Therefore, the RUPA grants each partner the right to inspect and copy the partnership's books and records. This right is unconditional and does not depend upon the partner's purpose or motive. However, books and records are not enough, by themselves, to keep a partner fully informed. Therefore, the RUPA requires all partners and the partnership to *volunteer* any information that might reasonably be necessary for other partners to exercise their rights. All partners and the partnership also have a duty to supply any other information that a partner reasonably requests. These rules are *mandatory*; the partners may not change them by agreement among themselves.

Suppose that Dawn decides to leave the partnership. When she approaches Niels and Sonya about selling her interest to them, they must volunteer all relevant information about the value of the partnership. For instance, if Niels knows of a buyer who is interested in purchasing their building at a handsome price, he must tell Dawn (even if she never asks) to ensure that she negotiates the buyout price with full information.

MANAGEMENT DUTIES

Partners have the *right* to manage the partnership. In addition, they also have *duties* to the partnership and the other partners. These duties are mandatory; the partners may not waive them.

Duty of Care

Partners have a duty to avoid gross negligence and willful misconduct. **Partners are liable to the partnership for gross negligence, reckless conduct, intentional misconduct, or a knowing violation of the law. Partners are *not* liable for *ordinary* negligence.** Suppose that Max, Cara, and Brooke are partners in a law firm in Beverly Hills. While representing a client, Max makes a careless error—he files a securities form one day late. The client is fined $10,000, which the partnership pays. Cara is furious at Max and insists that he pay the amount himself. Brooke, however, had been paying attention during her law school course on partnership law, so she can point out to Cara that Max is *not* personally liable for the $10,000 and the partnership cannot recover from him because his error is ordinary negligence, not gross negligence or a knowing violation of the law. Yet another reason to choose one's partners carefully. If, however, Max assaults a client, the partnership can recover from him because that is intentional misconduct.

Duty of Loyalty

Partners have a fiduciary duty to their partnership.

Competing with the Partnership. Each partner must turn over to the partnership all earnings from any activity that is related to the partnership's business. While Cara is vacationing near Santa Fe, a guest in the next-door hacienda is arrested in the middle of the night for drunk driving. Cara goes down to the police station and persuades the police officer to release the guest. Her new client gratefully insists on paying her $5,000 for her efforts. Cara figures the fee will go a long way toward paying the cost of her vacation. Cara figures wrong. She must turn the fee over to the partnership because she earned it doing the kind of work that the partnership does. It is irrelevant that she was on vacation.

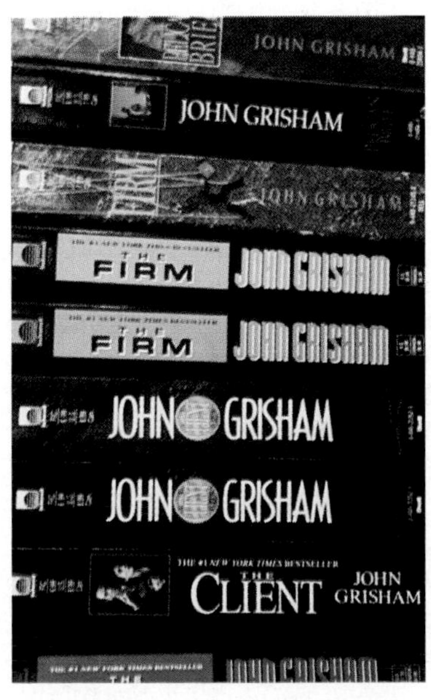

Must John Grisham share his royalties with his partners?

Suppose that Brooke teaches business law part-time at California University. When she decides to write her own business law text, numerous publishers enter a bidding war for her manuscript, and she ultimately accepts a six-figure offer. Must she share the proceeds with her partners? Maybe. Many law firms take the view that, if their partners write about law, the fees belong to the firm. In at least one situation like Brooke's, a partner left his firm to avoid sharing royalties with the partnership. What if Brooke writes a *novel* about a woman partner in a three-person law firm in Beverly Hills? Or what if she serves as a reserve officer in the National Guard? Clearly, her military salary is not connected with the partnership's business. Presumably, neither are her fictional efforts.

Taking a Business Opportunity. A partner may not take an opportunity away from the partnership unless the other partners consent. The partnership wants to enhance its law library. Max notices an advertisement in the paper for a complete set of law books. If he buys them himself for his home use without telling his partners, he is violating his fiduciary duty by taking an *opportunity* away from the partnership. The partnership is entitled either to the books themselves or to the value of the opportunity Max took.

Using Partnership Property. A partner must turn over to the partnership any profit he earns from use of partnership property without the consent of the partners. The partnership's office is in an old, beautifully restored historic building. Max runs a party-planning service on the side—MAXimum Fun. He occasionally holds parties on the weekends in the partnership's elegant foyer without telling Brooke and Cara. When they find out, they are maximum angry, and for good reason—Max has violated his fiduciary duty to the partnership. Of course, if Brooke and Cara *consent* to Max's use of the office, he is not required to turn the profits over to the partnership. Remember that in *Phillips v. Carson*, earlier in this chapter, Carson conducted personal business at his law firm office. The law firm was not entitled to any profits he earned from these extracurricular activities because it knew about them and consented.

Conflict of Interest. A partner has a conflict of interest whenever the partnership does business with him, a member of his family, or a business partly or fully owned by him. Suppose that Max hires MAXimum Fun to put on the firm's tenth anniversary celebration. Unless the other partners consent in advance, Max must turn over to the partnership any profits he earns from the party. In the following case, one partner bought partnership property at a public auction. Is that a conflict of interest?

MARSH v. GENTRY

642 S.W.2d 574, 1982 Ky. LEXIS 315
Supreme Court of Kentucky, 1982

Facts: Tom Gentry and John Marsh were partners in a business that bought and sold racehorses. The partnership paid $155,000 for *Champagne Woman*, who subsequently had a foal named *Excitable Lady*. The partners decided to sell *Champagne Woman* at the annual Keeneland auction, the world's premier thoroughbred horse auction. On the day of the auction, Gentry decided to bid on the horse personally, without telling Marsh. Gentry bought *Champagne Woman* for $135,000. Later, he told Marsh that someone from California had approached him about buying *Excitable Lady*. Marsh agreed to the sale. Although he repeatedly asked Gentry the name of the purchaser, Gentry refused to tell him. Not until 11 months later, when *Excitable Lady* won a race at Churchill Downs, did Marsh learn that Gentry had been the purchaser. Marsh became the Excitable Man.

Issue: **Did Gentry violate his fiduciary duty when he bought partnership property without telling his partner?**

Excerpts from Justice O'Hara's Decision: Admittedly, at an auction sale, the specific identity of a purchaser cannot be ascertained before the sale, but [Kentucky partnership law] required a full disclosure by Gentry to Marsh that he would be a prospective purchaser. As to the private sale of *Excitable Lady*, Marsh consented to a sale from the partnership, at a specified price, to the prospective purchaser in California. Even though Marsh obtained the stipulated purchase price, a partner has an absolute right to know when his partner is the purchaser. Partners scrutinize buy-outs by their partners in an entirely different light than an ordinary third party sale. This distinction is vividly made without contradiction when Marsh later indicated that he would not have consented to either sale had he known that Gentry was the purchaser. Under these facts, it is obvious that Gentry failed to disclose all that he knew concerning the sales, including his desire to purchase partnership property.

[P]artners, in their relations with other partners, [must] maintain a higher degree of good faith due to the partnership agreement. The requirement of full disclosure among partners as to partnership business cannot be escaped. Had

Gentry made a full disclosure to his partner of his intentions to purchase the partnership property, Marsh would not later be heard to complain of the transaction.

Finally, Gentry maintains that it is an accepted practice at auction sales of thoroughbreds for one partner to secretly bid on partnership stock to accomplish a buy-out. We would emphatically state, however, for the benefit of those engaged in such practices, that where an "accepted business practice" conflicts with existing law, the law whether statutory or court ordered, is controlling. To hold otherwise would be chaotic.

Good Faith and Fair Dealing

Partners have an obligation of good faith and fair dealing to each other and to the partnership. They must deal with each other *fairly* and *noncoercively*. Behavior that would be acceptable in an arm's-length transaction may be unacceptable between partners. Hartz Mountain Industries, Inc. was the managing partner of a real estate business in northern New Jersey. Eugene Heller was Hartz's partner. According to the partnership agreement, when Heller left the partnership, Hartz would have the properties appraised and buy Heller's share. Hartz had the right to choose the appraiser. Over Heller's objection, Hartz chose Robert DiFalco. Hartz's own internal appraisals valued the properties at more than $214 million, but DiFalco produced an appraisal of $133 million, a slight discrepancy of more than $80 million.

The court found that, while Hartz had technically complied with the partnership agreement, it had breached its obligation of good faith and fair dealing. Courts generally give a great deal of credence to appraisals, especially when both parties have agreed in advance to the appraisal process. The purpose of doing an appraisal is to *prevent* litigation. If parties litigate the appraisal, the whole process is undermined. But the court did not accept the appraisal in this case because Hartz had violated its fiduciary duty to Heller by choosing such an unreliable appraiser. The court quoted the famous opinion of Justice Cardozo in *Meinhard v. Salmon*:

> [Partners] owe to one another, while the enterprise continues, the duty of the finest loyalty. Many forms of conduct permissible in a workaday world for those acting at arm's length, are forbidden to those bound by fiduciary ties. A trustee is held to something stricter than the morals of the market place. Not honesty alone, but the punctilio of an honor the most sensitive, is then the standard of behavior. As to this there has developed a tradition that is unbending and inveterate. Uncompromising rigidity has been the attitude of courts of equity when petitioned to undermine the rule of undivided loyalty by the "disintegrating erosion" of particular exceptions. Only thus has the level of conduct for fiduciaries been kept at a level higher than that trodden by the crowd.[8]

Modest Exceptions

Despite Justice Cardozo's resounding sentiments, the RUPA has provided partners with a small amount of wiggle room when dealing with their partnership. According to the RUPA, a partner does not violate his duty, "merely because the partner's conduct furthers the partner's own interest."[9] Likewise, the RUPA provides that, if partners lend money to the partnership or otherwise transact business with it, they have the same rights as any nonpartner would.[10] These provisions should make for some interesting cases.

---

[8] *Meinhard v. Salmon*, 249 N.Y. 458, 164 N.E. 545, 546, 1928 N.Y. LEXIS 830 (1928), *quoted in Heller v. Hartz Mountain Industries, Inc.*, 270 N.J. Super. 143, 636 A.2d 599, 1993 N.J. Super. LEXIS 903 (N.J. Super. Ct. Law Div. 1993).

[9] RUPA §404(e).

[10] RUPA §404(f).

Chapter Conclusion

Justice Cardozo used old-fashioned language like "the punctilio of an honor the most sensitive." In some ways, a partnership is an old-fashioned form of organization. From the late 1770s until the mid-nineteenth century, virtually all businesses were partnerships. Then corporations gained in popularity, and now new forms have arisen such as limited liability companies and limited liability partnerships (both discussed in Chapter 32). These new forms of organization have many of the advantages of a partnership without the unlimited liability.

It is no surprise that many accounting firms changed their form of organization away from partnerships—they faced $30 *billion* in liability claims in the United States alone, arising primarily out of the savings and loan crisis in the late 1980s. When savings and loan institutions failed, their accounting firms were frequently held responsible. (Chapter 39 provides a lengthier discussion of accountants' liability.) Many law firms also question whether a partnership is still the best option available. Most investment banks, brokerage firms, and advertising agencies have long since switched to a more corporate form of organization.

On the other hand, many organizations continue to *act* like partnerships even though they have changed their official form of organization. And, before the partnership baby gets thrown out with the liability bath water, it is worth noting that many organizations—law, accounting, and investment banking firms to name a few—have been highly successful as partnerships. The lack of hierarchy in partnerships encourages collaboration and teamwork while the lure of ownership motivates and inspires employees.

In the end, the future of partnerships may lie in the hands of juries. Large verdicts against accounting and law firms cannot help but frighten partners everywhere.

Chapter Review

1. The rules governing the liability of partners to outsiders are *mandatory*. Generally, the rules governing the relationship among partners are *default* provisions.
2. Every partner is an agent of the partnership for the purpose of its business. A partnership is responsible for the intentional and negligent torts of a partner that occur in the ordinary course of the partnership's business or with the actual authority of the other partners.
3. All partners are personally liable for all debts of the partnership. Partners have joint and several liability for partnership obligations.
4. A partner is personally liable only for obligations the partnership incurred while she was a partner. Her liability for debts incurred before she became a partner is limited to her investment in the partnership.
5. Unless they agree otherwise, partners:
   - Share profits equally
   - Share losses according to their share of profits
   - Are not entitled to any payment beyond their share of profits
   - Have no right to use or sell specific partnership property, except for the benefit of the partnership, and

- Each have an equal vote, regardless of their contributions to the partnership.

6. Without the approval of the other partners, a partner cannot sell her share. She can only transfer the right to receive profits and losses. A new partner can be admitted to a partnership only by unanimous consent of the other partners.
7. Creditors can attach partnership profits through a charging order.
8. Each partner has equal rights in the management and conduct of the business, unless the partners agree otherwise. For ordinary partnership affairs, a majority of the partners can make a decision. To amend the partnership agreement or to make decisions outside the ordinary course of business, the vote must be unanimous.
9. Partners are liable to the partnership for any damages resulting from their gross negligence, reckless conduct, intentional misconduct, or a knowing violation of the law. Partners are *not* liable to the partnership for *ordinary* negligence.
10. Each partner must turn over to the partnership all earnings from any activity that is related to the partnership's business.
11. A partner may not take an opportunity away from the partnership unless the other partners consent.
12. A partner has a conflict of interest whenever the partnership does business with him, a member of his family, or a business partly or fully owned by him.
13. Partners have an obligation of good faith and fair dealing to each other and to the partnership.

PRACTICE TEST

1. While Warren Lyon was representing Betty Cook in divorce proceedings, she inherited $60,000. Lyon suggested Cook invest her money in a corporation of which he was president. Although he promised her a substantial return, the company went bankrupt shortly thereafter. Lyon was a partner in the law firm Brundidge, Fountain, Elliott & Churchill. The firm was not in the business of giving investment advice, it did not know that Lyon was giving such advice, and it did not receive any fee from Cook for the "investment service." Is the law firm liable for Cook's loss?

2. **YOU BE THE JUDGE WRITING PROBLEM** Karen Stanton and T. O. King entered into a 50/50 partnership to buy a house in Montecito, California, known as *Tara*, which they intended to sell at a profit. Stanton was to make all payments on the loan they had taken out to buy the property. If she failed to make a payment by a specified deadline, King had the right to pay it. For each $1,000 he paid, his share of the partnership would increase by 1.4 percent. When it came time for the first two mortgage payments, Stanton told King that she intended to make them, but she would be late. He offered to make the payments instead. Each month thereafter, King made all the payments without telling Stanton, until her interest in *Tara* was gone with the wind. Has King violated his duty to Stanton? **Argument for Stanton:** Partners have an obligation of good faith and fair dealing to each other. King should have notified Stanton that he was making the payments. Instead, he took advantage of her to gain ownership of the property. **Argument for King:** Stanton had agreed that, if King made payments, her ownership share would be reduced accordingly. Although King did not tell her he was making the payments, she must have known that either he was or the partnership was in default. In either case, she would lose ownership. Did she think the tooth fairy was paying off the mortgage?

3. **RIGHT & WRONG** While Gerald Lawlis was a partner in the Indiana law firm Kightlinger & Gray, he

developed a drinking problem. The partnership arranged for him to receive counseling, and, after one relapse, he appeared to have solved his problem. Two years after he took his last drink, the partnership expelled him. Under the terms of the partnership agreement, any partner could be expelled for any reason by a two-thirds vote of the remaining partners. The firm wanted to reduce the number of partners, and it selected Lawlis because his alcoholism had made him the least productive partner. Have the partners violated their fiduciary duty to him? Aside from the partners' legal obligation to Lawlis, do they have an *ethical* responsibility to him? Is the decision right? Does it exhibit consideration and courage?

4. Longview Estates was a partnership formed to purchase property from Conklin Farm and develop it for residential condominiums. The partnership executed a $9 million promissory note to Conklin Farm. Joel Leibowitz transferred his 30 percent share of the partnership to his wife, Doris. Five months later, she transferred it back to him. During that period, over $1 million in interest accrued on the note and was not paid. Conklin Farm sued Doris for 30 percent of the $1 million accrued interest. Is a new partner personally liable for the interest on a preexisting partnership debt when that interest accrues after the new partner was admitted into the partnership?

5. David Schoenborn and his brother, Jerome, entered into a farming partnership, but every time they went into the fields together, they seemed to get into an argument. When Jerome went to a bank to take out a personal loan, the banker asked him for a list of the equipment he used for farming, "whether it was in the partnership or solely owned." Jerome gave the banker a list of all property, including partnership property, indicating which was his and which belonged to the partnership. Later, he learned that the bank had used all the property, including what belonged to the partnership, as collateral for the loan. Jerome paid off the loan shortly thereafter. When David learned that the partnership property was listed as collateral for Jerome's personal loan, he was furious. He sued, demanding compensation for Jerome's use of the partnership property as collateral. Is David entitled to this compensation?

6. CPA QUESTION Cobb, Inc., a partner in TLC Partnership, assigns its partnership interest to Bean, who is not made a partner. After the assignment, Bean asserts the right to (1) participate in the management of TLC and (2) Cobb's share of TLC's partnership profits. Bean is correct as to which of these rights?

(a) 1 only

(b) 2 only

(c) 1 and 2

(d) Neither 1 nor 2

7. Seventy-Three Land, Inc. sued Maxlar Partners for the balance due on a note made by the partnership. Max Odlen, a partner, asked the court to dismiss the claim against him personally because the plaintiff had not first tried to collect against the partnership. Must a creditor attempt to collect against the partnership first, before it sues an individual partner?

8. CPA QUESTION Ted Fein, a partner in the ABC Partnership, wishes to withdraw from the partnership and sell his interest to Gold. All of the other partners in ABC have agreed to admit Gold as a partner and to hold Fein harmless for the past, present, and future liabilities of ABC. A provision in the original partnership agreement states that the partnership will continue upon the death or withdrawal of one or more of the partners. As a result of Fein's withdrawal and Gold's admission to the partnership, Gold:

(a) Is personally liable for partnership liabilities arising before and after his admission as a partner

(b) Has the right to participate in the management of ABC

(c) Acquired only the right to receive Fein's share of the profits of ABC

(d) Must contribute cash or property to ABC in order to be admitted with the same rights as the other partners

9. Dutch, Bill, and Heidi were equal partners in a lawn care business. Bill and Heidi wanted to borrow money from the bank to buy more trucks and expand the business. Dutch was dead set against the idea. When the matter came to a vote, Bill and Heidi voted in favor, Dutch against. Dutch was so annoyed that he told the bank not to lend the money and, further, that he would not be responsible for repaying the loan. The bank loaned the money, the business failed, and the bank sued all three partners. Is Dutch liable on the loan?

10. Brothers Sydney and Ashley Altman were partners in a real estate partnership in southeastern Pennsylvania. They received identical salaries. Sydney moved to Florida to establish residency so that he could obtain a divorce there. His lawyer told him not to return to Pennsylvania until he had resolved his marital problems. After Sydney had been gone almost a year, Ashley decided to increase his own salary to compensate for the additional work he was doing. Does Ashley have the right to pay himself more if he is doing more work?

11. Columbia Mortgage Co. loaned $1.5 million to the Pacific Rim Partnership. When the partnership defaulted on its first payment (always a bad sign), Columbia asked for more collateral. Nathan Hsieh, who was a partner in Pacific Rim, gave Columbia a mortgage on another piece of property called the "Y" property. Hsieh did not own the "Y" property—the Sunland Partnership did. Hsieh was a partner in Sunland. Did Hsieh have the right, as a partner in Sunland, to give a mortgage on the Sunland property? If Hsieh did not have this right, can Columbia still enforce the mortgage that Hsieh granted?

INTERNET RESEARCH PROBLEM

The Web site at http://www.gordonbancks.co.uk/compco01.htm provides an overview of British partnership law. Are there any obvious differences between American and British law? What might be the reasons for these differences?

You can find further practice problems in the Online Quiz at http://beatty.westbuslaw.com or in the Study Guide that accompanies this text.

CHAPTER 35

LIFE AND DEATH OF A CORPORATION

Many people dream of starting their own business. For Judy George, the moment had come. She was ready to open Domain—a chain of upscale stores selling European-style furnishings and accessories. Her business plan was in place and her investors were ready; all she needed was to take care of legal matters. But she knew that legal issues were no small detail and that the choices she made would have a major impact on the success of her business.

In this chapter you will learn how to form a corporation and also how to avoid traps that await the unwary entrepreneur, before and after a business is formed. Finally, you will learn how to dissolve a corporation.

BEFORE THE CORPORATION IS FORMED

To get Domain up and running, Judy George had more to do than seemed humanly possible. She had to find store locations, buy inventory, hire employees—it all seemed overwhelming. Her lawyer cautioned her not to do *too* much, *too* quickly. The corporation had not been formed, and she needed to be careful to avoid liability as a promoter.

PROMOTER'S LIABILITY

The promoter is the person who creates the corporation. It is her idea; she raises the capital, hires the lawyers, calls the shots. Judy George was Domain's promoter. Sometimes, promoters are so eager to get their business going that they sign contracts on behalf of the corporation before it is legally formed. Suppose that George finds the perfect location for her flagship store. She is desperate to sign the lease before someone else snatches the opportunity away, but Domain does not yet legally exist—it is not incorporated. What would happen if she signed the lease anyway? The rules are straightforward:

- **The promoter is personally liable on any contract signed before the corporation is formed.** If George signs the lease before Domain, Inc. legally exists, she is personally liable for the rent due.
- **The corporation is not liable on any contracts signed *before* incorporation unless it *adopts* the contract *after* incorporation.** What does **adoption** mean? Either the board of directors takes a formal vote saying, "We hereby adopt this contract," or they act as if they had adopted it. If Domain uses the space George rented, it has adopted the contract. But George is still not off the hook.
- **Even if the corporation adopts the contract, the promoter is still liable until the third party (in this case, the landlord) agrees to a *novation*.** A **novation** creates a *new* contract with different parties. Even if Domain adopts the contract, George is still personally liable to the landlord until the landlord signs a new contract with George and Domain explicitly stating that only the corporation is liable, not George.

Like most sets of rules, this one has an exception:

- **If the contract clearly indicates that the other party is relying *only* on the corporation, although he knows the corporation does not yet exist, the promoter is released from liability once the corporation adopts the contract.** If the lease states that Domain is not yet formed but will be liable when it is formed, then George is not personally liable for rental payments once Domain adopts the contract.

In the following case, two entrepreneurs argue that it is not fair for *both* the individuals and the corporation to be liable. Do you agree?

WOLFE v. WARFIELD
266 Md. 621, 296 A.2d 158, 1972
Md. LEXIS 768
Maryland Court of Appeals, 1972

Facts: Arnold Wolfe was a young carpenter trying to break into the contracting business. Elkan Groll, a local architect, asked Wolfe to bid on a house that Groll had designed for Dr. Warfield. Wolfe's bid came in 25 percent less than Groll's cost estimate for the house. Wolfe was hired and began work in mid-July. A week or so later, he and his partner, Ginsburg, filed the articles of incorporation for Wolfe-Ginsburg Construction, Inc.

Both Wolfe and Ginsburg worked on the house. Dr. Warfield made payments to the corporation. By early August, the project was in trouble; Groll had noticed more than 60 deficiencies. He discovered that 30 brick columns had been omitted from the basement walls. Wood beams had been used instead of the specified steel beams. The lumber was a lower grade than the architect had specified. Groll said he did not know whether to blow up the house or try and salvage what was there.

Dr. Warfield terminated the contract and sued Wolfe, Ginsburg, and Wolfe-Ginsburg Construction, Inc. for damages. Wolfe and Ginsburg argued that if they were liable as promoters, then the corporation must be absolved and that, conversely, if the corporation was held liable, they, as individuals, must not be.

Issue: **Are Wolfe, Ginsburg, and Wolfe-Ginsburg Construction, Inc. all liable to Dr. Warfield?**

Excerpts from Judge McWilliams's Decision: While Dr. Warfield made payments to the corporation, at the request of Wolfe or Ginsburg, it does not appear that he ever indicated an intention to look to the corporation for performance to the exclusion of Wolfe or Wolfe and Ginsburg. Acceptance of the benefits under a contract justifies the inference that the corporation has accepted or adopted it. Although the corporation becomes liable, the promoter also remains individually liable in the absence of an agreement that he is to be relieved of such responsibility.

DEFECTIVE INCORPORATION

A promoter is liable on contracts signed before the corporation exists. But what if the promoter signs a contract *thinking* the corporation has been formed only to discover later that the incorporation is somehow defective? In these situations, the law is reasonably tolerant. Consider the following examples.

De Jure Corporation

"*De jure*" is Latin for "by law." **A *de jure* corporation means that the promoter has substantially complied with the requirements for incorporation, but has made some minor error.** She has perhaps misspelled the name of the corporation's registered agent (more about the registered agent later). In this case, no one, not even the state, can challenge the validity of the corporation.

De Facto Corporation

"*De facto*" is Latin for "in fact." **A *de facto* corporation means that the promoter has made a good faith effort to incorporate and has actually used the corporation to conduct business.** In this case, the state can challenge the validity of the corporation, but a third party cannot. Suppose that Judy George fills out the incorporation form and files it, but the Secretary of State does not stamp it for weeks. In the meantime, George signs a lease for Domain. In many states, no stamp means no corporation. Nonetheless, George has a *de facto* corporation because she made a reasonable effort to incorporate and has used the corporation to conduct business. The landlord cannot challenge the validity of the corporation and claim that George is personally liable on the lease. Only the corporation is liable.

Corporation by Estoppel

A corporation by estoppel means that, if a party enters into a contract *believing* the corporation exists, he cannot later take advantage of the fact that it does not. Suppose that George's attorney tells her that Domain, Inc. has been formed but, in fact, he never even attempted to incorporate it. In the meantime, George orders truckloads of furniture in Domain's name. Under the theory of corporation by estoppel, George is *not* personally liable even though the corporation does not exist. Both she and the furniture dealer thought she was buying on behalf of the corporation. Why should the dealer receive a windfall, and why should George be penalized, simply because her lawyer made a mistake? This rule works both ways: if a bank loans money to Domain, Inc., George cannot refuse to pay it back simply because Domain does not yet exist.

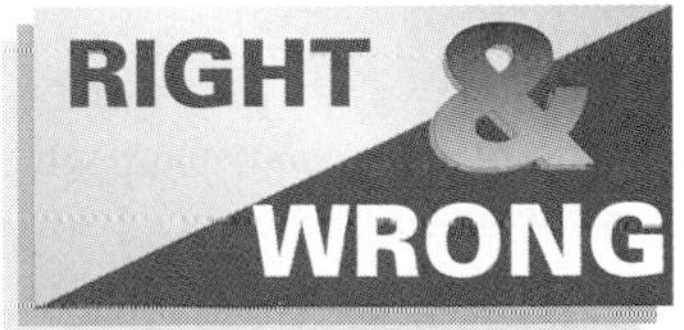

Whenever courts use the term "estoppel," it means that they are basing a decision on fairness rather than strict legal rules. Is corporation by estoppel a fair concept? What about *de facto* corporation? What is fair in the following case?

HILL v. COUNTRY CONCRETE CO., INC.
108 Md. App. 527, 672 A.2d 667, 1996 Md. App. LEXIS 35
Court of Special Appeals of Maryland, 1996

Facts: When Cecil Hill, Sr. and Michael Newman started a construction business, they asked an attorney to form a corporation named "C&M Builders, Inc." The attorney told them this name was available and that they could proceed with their business preparations. In November, Hill and Newman ordered checks and stationery, opened a bank account, and painted their trucks, all with the name "C&M Builders, Inc." For reasons unknown, their attorney did not attempt to file the articles of incorporation until the following February. In the meantime, someone else formed a corporation using that name, so Hill and Newman had to choose another. The articles of incorporation for H&N Construction, Inc. were filed in May.

Using the name "C&M Builders, Inc.," Hill and Newman then placed an order with County Concrete. No one at County had ever heard of C&M Builders, so an employee went to investigate a job site. There he learned that Hill and Newman were involved with the corporation, and because he knew Hill by reputation, he agreed to establish an account in the name of "C&M Builders, Inc." Over the next two years, H&N sent letters and checks to County that bore the C&M name. When H&N failed to pay the remaining $55,000 it owed, County filed suit against Hill personally. County did not learn the corporation's real name until Hill was deposed during the course of this lawsuit.

You Be the Judge: Is Hill liable to County for the debts of H&N under a theory of *de facto* corporation or corporation by estoppel?

Arguments for County: To qualify as a *de facto* corporation, the shareholders must believe in *good faith* that they have done everything necessary to incorporate. Hill was acting in good faith—at the beginning. When he first ordered signs, checks, and stationery, he thought he had the right to use the C&M name. But he continued using the name for years after he had learned that it was not available. That was not good faith. It is illegal to use a corporate name that is misleadingly similar to another corporation. Imagine the surprise of the real C&M when it received a complaint from County, a company with which it had never dealt. County did not find out H&N's real name until this litigation had been going on for more than two years.

Good faith is also required in a defense based on corporation by estoppel. The term "estoppel" implies that it would be unfair for the shareholders to be found liable. Hill has forfeited his right to any defense based on fairness or equity.

Arguments for Hill: County thought it was dealing with a corporation, and it was—only the corporation had a different name. So what? The corporation could have been named XYZ, Inc. or even DUH Corp., and County would have extended credit. Hill was operating a *de facto* corporation: he made a reasonable effort to incorporate, and he used the corporation to conduct business.

Corporation by estoppel also applies in this case. County believed it was doing business with a corporation. The name of the corporation had no impact on the outcome of this business relationship. No matter what the corporation was called, it still would not have been able to pay its debts. Hill is guilty of only one offense—stinginess. He did not want to buy new stationery. Is that so wrong? Why should County be able to take advantage of a mere technicality?

INCORPORATION PROCESS

The mechanics of incorporation are easy: simply fill out the form and mail it (with a check) to the Secretary of State. Nonetheless, this document needs to be completed with some care. The corporate charter defines the corporation, including everything from the company's name to the number of shares it will issue and the liability of its directors. States use different terms to refer to a charter; some call it the "articles of incorporation," others use "articles of organization," and still others say "certificate" instead of "articles." All of these terms mean the same thing. Similarly, some states use the term "shareholders," and others use "stockholders"; they are both the same.

There is no federal corporation code, which means that a company can incorporate only under state law, not federal law. No matter where a company actually does business, it may incorporate in any state. This decision is important because the organization must live by the laws of whichever state it chooses for incorporation. Like snowflakes, no two state laws are identical, but many have similar features. To encourage even more similarity, the American Bar Association drafted the Revised Model Business Corporation Act as a guide for states. Many states use the Act as a model, although some of the largest or most commercially important states, such as California, New York, and Delaware, do not. In discussing corporate law in this and the following chapters, we will give examples from both the Model Act and specific states, especially Delaware. Why Delaware? Despite its small size, it has a disproportionate influence on corporate law. More than 280,000 corporations are incorporated there, including 60 percent of Fortune 500 companies.

WHERE TO INCORPORATE?

Companies generally incorporate either in their home state or in Delaware. They typically must pay filing fees and franchise taxes in their state of incorporation as well as in any state in which they do business. To avoid this double set of fees, a business that will be operating primarily in one state would probably select that state for incorporation rather than Delaware. But if a company is going to do business in several states, it might consider choosing Delaware (or, perhaps, Ohio, Pennsylvania, or Nevada). More information about Delaware corporate law is available at **http://www.state.de.us/corp/**. Or browse **http://www.findlaw.com/11stategov/indexcorp.html** for links to all state corporation Web sites.

Delaware has not always been a popular choice for corporations. In the early 1900s, New Jersey held the position that Delaware does today. When Woodrow Wilson became governor (on his way to the White House), he toughened New Jersey's laws. Looking for a state with a more hospitable environment, companies found one across the Delaware River. What is good for business is good for Delaware, too. Each year it collects more than $300 million—about 20 percent of its total revenues—in filing fees and taxes from companies that, for the most part, conduct little business in the state.

Delaware offers corporations several advantages:

- *Laws That Favor Management.* Delaware laws offer flexibility. For example, if the shareholders want to take a vote in writing instead of holding a meeting, many other states require the vote to be unanimous; Delaware requires only a majority to agree. The Delaware legislature also tries to keep up-to-date by changing its code to reflect new developments in corporate law. For example, it was one of the first states to eliminate a rigid format for corporate charters.
- *An Efficient Court System.* Delaware has a special court (called "Chancery Court") that hears nothing but business cases and has judges who are experts

in corporate law. In other states, judges who practiced in fields such as criminal law or divorce also hear corporate cases.[1] In an emergency involving, say, a hostile takeover, Delaware judges will hear cases and reach decisions on short notice. This preferential treatment is typically not available in other states.

- *An Established Body of Precedent*. Because so many businesses incorporate in the state, its courts hear a vast number of corporate cases, creating a large body of precedent. Thus lawyers feel they can more easily predict the outcome of a case in Delaware than in a state where few corporate disputes are tried each year.

The financial bonanza that Delaware realizes from its incorporation business has not gone unnoticed by other states. New York, Ohio, Pennsylvania, and, ironically, New Jersey have all modified their corporate laws to attract incorporation business. Large companies in the western part of the country often choose Nevada as their home state because of its attractive laws. Of course, management—not shareholders—chooses the state of incorporation and pays the state fees. Some commentators argue that states are so eager to attract corporate revenue that their laws unfairly favor management over shareholders. They refer to this competition as the "race to the bottom." However, some recent studies indicate that, when a company reincorporates in Delaware, its stock price does not go down. Evidently, financial markets do not perceive shareholders to be at a disadvantage in Delaware.

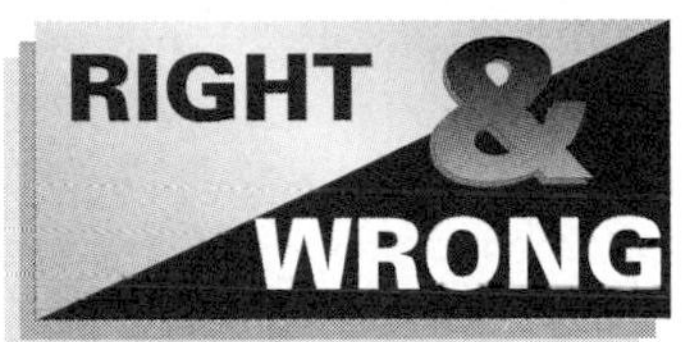

Is it ethical for promoters deliberately to choose a state of incorporation that offers less protection to shareholders than, say, the state in which they do most of their business? What rules do you think a promoter should follow in selecting a state of incorporation?

Once a company has decided *where* to incorporate, the next step is to prepare and file the charter. The charter must always be filed with the Secretary of State; some jurisdictions also require that it be filed in a county office. Some states supply a form to be completed. Delaware and the Model Act require that certain information be included, but the incorporators can list it any way they want. The incorporators may also include some optional provisions. Sample articles of incorporation are available at **http://www.tannedfeet.com/assets/images/articles_of_incorp.PDF** and **http://www.state.de.us/corp/**.

CHARTER'S REQUIRED PROVISIONS

Name

The Model Act imposes two requirements in selecting a name. First, all corporations must use one of the following words in their name: "corporation," "incorporated," "company," or "limited." Delaware also accepts some additional terms, such as, "association" or "institute." Both the Model Act and Delaware permit abbreviations (such as "inc." or "corp.") or equivalent terms in another language (such as "S.A.," which is French for corporation—it literally means "Société Anonyme").

[1] When Pennzoil sued Texaco in Texas over a breach of contract, the judge who tried the case was experienced in hearing divorce cases. Many lawyers felt that his ignorance of corporate matters contributed to the jury's Texas-sized verdict—$11 *billion*.

Second, under both the Model Act and Delaware law, a new corporate name must be different from that of any corporation, limited liability company, or limited partnership that already exists *in that state*. If your name is Freddy Dupont, you cannot name your corporation "Freddy Dupont, Inc." because Delaware already has a company named E. I. Dupont de Nemours & Co. It does not matter that Freddy Dupont is your real name or that the existing company is a large chemical business while you want to open a video arcade. The names are too similar.

What if you wake from a deep sleep late one night with the perfect corporate name in your head, but the charter is not quite ready for filing? You can reserve a name in Delaware for 30 days by calling (900) 420-8042. A fee of $10 will be charged to your telephone. That takes care of Delaware, but you know your corporation will soon be going national. How can you protect your name in other states? Under the Model Act, you can register a name for 120 days by paying a fee. However, many states are more like Delaware than the Model Act on this issue. If they let you reserve a name at all, it is often for a short period of time. Alternatively, you can form a "nameholder" organization: a separate corporation that incurs minimum annual fees because it is inactive.

All this bother and expense discourage most start-ups from reserving their names nationwide. If they later expand into another state where someone else is already using their name, they either buy the name back or use a different name in that jurisdiction. The problem multiplies if they want to register their name overseas as well. When Steven Spielberg, Jeffrey Katzenberg, and David Geffen launched their Hollywood studio, DreamWorks SKG, they spent nearly $500,000 to clear rights to the name in 108 countries around the world. (Of course, that was a small drop in the $2 billion bucket they raised from investors.) The following article illustrates the perils of choosing a name first and checking later.

Citigroup, Inc., the colossus that Travelers Group and Citicorp propose creating, may have hit a bump in the race to the financial future: Renata McGriff. Ms. McGriff started a computer business that distributes gift certificates over the Internet. It just happens to bear the name Citigroup, Inc. Ms. McGriff turned on her TV set and saw Travelers Chairman Sanford I. Weill and Citicorp Chairman John S. Reed announcing their merger. "A reporter asks Sandy, 'What is the name of your new company?' and he says, 'Citigroup,'" she recalled. "And my whole stomach fell out. I said, 'Oh my God, how can this be?'"

Neither Citicorp nor Travelers executives returned her calls in the first days after the merger. She did get through to an acquaintance at Citicorp and explained the problem, she said. Soon afterward, a man came to the lobby of the apartment building where she lives and quizzed the concierge about the existence of a "Citigroup" in the building. When the concierge demanded a name, the man left a name and a phone number that later turned out to be a nonworking exchange, she said.

Richard Howe, a Citicorp spokesman, said that the company sent a "representative" to investigate Ms. McGriff. "It's a standard procedure to determine whether the company is legitimate." "What we want is them to come to us with respect and with courtesy even though I'm small," Ms. McGriff responded. "What we want is not to be investigated. Who are we to them? I think this is despicable."

Mr. Howe confirmed that a Citicorp attorney did finally phone Ms. McGriff. "We have been in touch with her and we're sure we can resolve this in a positive way," he said. Mr. Howe also said that Messrs. Weill and Reed hadn't researched names when they picked one for their $70 billion merger. The transaction "came together very late," he said.[2]

[2] Matt Murray, "Citigroup Inc. Merger May Break New Ground, but Name Doesn't," *Wall Street Journal*, Apr. 13, 1998, p. C1. Republished with permission of The Wall Street Journal; permission conveyed through the Copyright Clearance Center, Inc.

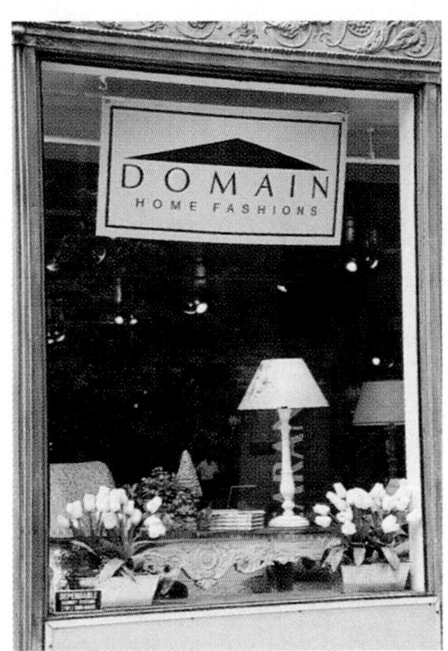

Judy George felt that Domain was the perfect name for her chain of stores.

As this article indicates, choosing the right corporate name can be difficult. When Judy George started her company, she considered other names such as Intimacy and Sanctuary before settling on Ciao Italia, Inc. Afterwards, her advertising agency suggested a change to Domain. "It was probably the most emotional part of the process of putting this deal together," George explained. "When I heard 'Domain' I couldn't even talk. I couldn't work. All the heartfelt stuff about the concept just exploded. I just *knew*."

Address and Registered Agent

A company must have an official address in the state in which it is incorporated so that the Secretary of State knows where to contact it. The company must also have an official address so that anyone who sues the corporation can serve the complaint in-state. Since most companies incorporated in Delaware do not actually have an office there, they hire a registered agent to serve as their official presence in the state. Agents typically charge about $100 annually for this service.

Incorporators

The incorporator signs the charter and delivers it to the Secretary of State for filing. The incorporator is not required to buy stock nor does he necessarily have any future relationship with the company. Domain's incorporator was William B. Simmons, Jr., the young lawyer who prepared the charter. If no lawyer is involved, the promoter typically serves as incorporator. The incorporator can incur liability only if he knows that something in the charter is not true when he signs it.

Purpose

The corporation is required to give its purpose for existence. In the nineteenth century, when corporations were a new concept, states thought it important to keep tight control over them. Under the ***ultra vires*** **doctrine**, a corporation cannot undertake any transaction unless its charter specifically permits it. For example, if the purpose clause in Domain's charter said "To operate a retail home furnishings business," then the company might not be allowed to sell clothing or open restaurants.

Corporate officers understandably chafed at this restriction. To avoid problems of *ultra vires*, most companies now use a very broad purpose clause such as Domain's:

> The nature of the business or purposes to be conducted or promoted is to engage in any lawful act or activity for which corporations may be organized under the General Corporation Law of Delaware.

Essentially, the only way to violate this purpose clause is to commit an illegal act. Shareholders, the corporation, or the state government can sue to prevent an employee of a corporation from engaging in *ultra vires* activity.

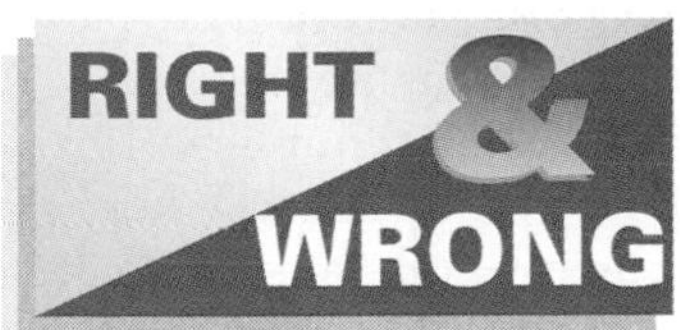

The purpose of the *ultra vires* doctrine was to protect shareholders. A corporation could not change its business without consulting them. Now promoters have found a way to avoid this constraint. Is that an ethical choice? Should shareholders be consulted before a corporation makes a major change in its business?

Stock

The charter must provide three items of information about the company's stock.

Number of Shares. Before stock can be sold, it must first be authorized in the charter. The corporation can authorize as many shares as the incorporators choose, but the more shares, the higher the filing fee. In Delaware, the price is $.01 per share for the first 20,000 shares (a total of $200); $.005 apiece for up to 2 million shares; and $.004 each for all shares over 2 million. If a company wants more shares after incorporation, it simply amends its charter and pays the additional fee. The Domain charter initially authorized 10,000 shares; it now has 11,372,716.

Stock that has been authorized but not yet sold is called **authorized and unissued.** Stock that has been sold is termed **authorized and issued** or **outstanding.** Stock that the company has sold but later bought back is **treasury stock.**

Par Value. The concept of par value was designed to protect investors. Originally, par value was supposed to be close to market price. A company could not issue stock at a price less than par, which meant that it could not sell to insiders at a sweetheart price well below market value. (Once the stock was *issued*, it could be *traded* at any price.) In modern times, par value does not relate to market value; it is usually some nominal figure such as 1¢ or $1 per share. Companies can even dispense with the concept altogether and issue stock that has no par value. When making this decision, it is important to check the state's filing fees because they may be based on the par value of the company's stock. Domain stock has a par value of 1¢ per share. The Model Act does not even refer to "par value" and permits stock to be issued at any price set by the board of directors.

In Delaware, shareholders may pay for stock in cash, by note (a promise to pay), or by prior service to the organization. Under the Model Act, payment may also be made by a promise for future services, but in many states (including Delaware) future promises are considered too ephemeral to count as payment.

Classes and Series. Different shareholders often make different contributions to a company. Some may be involved in management, while others may simply contribute financially. Early investors may feel that they are entitled to more control than those who come along later (and who perhaps take less risk). Corporate structure can be infinitely flexible in defining the rights of these various shareholders. Stock can be divided into categories called **classes**, and these classes can be further divided into subcategories called **series**. All stock in a series has the same rights, and all series in a class are fundamentally the same, except for minor distinctions. For example, in a class of preferred stock, all shareholders may be entitled to a dividend, but the amount of the dividend may vary by series. Different classes of stock, however, may have very different rights—a class of preferred stock is different from a class of common stock. Exhibit 35.1 illustrates the concept of class and series. Defining the rights of a class or series of stock is like baking a cake—the stock can contain virtually any combination of the following ingredients (although the result may not be to everyone's taste):

- *Dividend Rights*. The charter establishes whether the shareholder is entitled to dividends and, if so, in what amount. No matter what the charter says, the corporation may not pay dividends unless it is solvent, that is, unless it has enough assets to pay its debts.

- *Voting Rights*. Shareholders are usually entitled to elect directors and vote on charter amendments, among other issues, but these rights can vary between different series and classes of stock. When Ford Motor Co. went public in 1956, it issued Class B common stock to members of the Ford family. This class of stock holds 40 percent of the voting power of the company and, thus, can elect

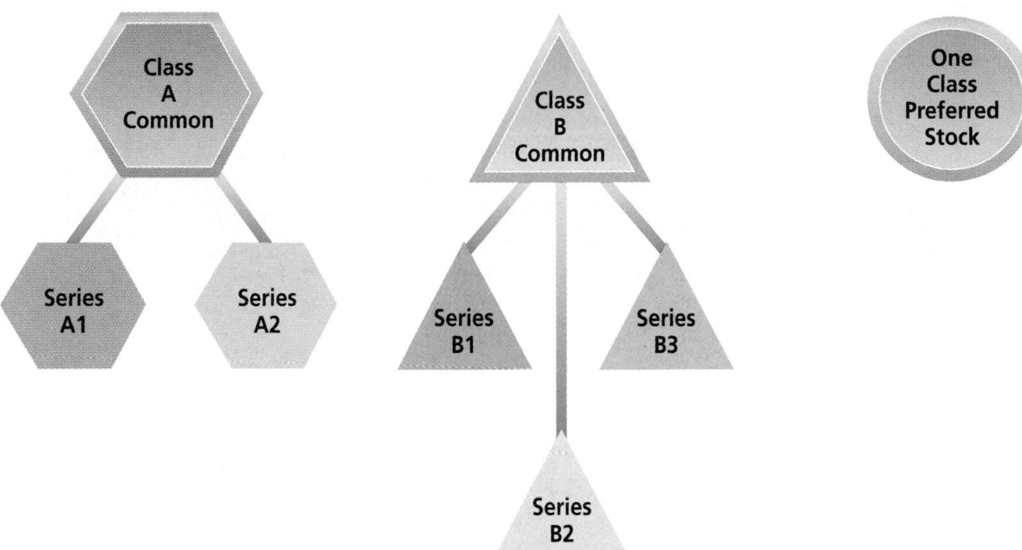

Exhibit 35.1

40 percent of the directors. These rights give the Ford family effective control over the company. Not surprisingly, the chairman of the company is often named "Ford."

- *Liquidation Rights*. The charter specifies the order in which classes of stockholders will be paid upon dissolution of the company. This provision is important if there are not enough assets to pay everyone.
- *Preemptive Rights*. If a corporation later issues additional shares of its stock, the original shareholders will own a smaller percentage of the company. For example, if a company has 10 shareholders, each owning one share, and it later issues another 10 shares to others, each of the old shareholders will then own 5 percent of the company instead of 10 percent. To prevent this **dilution**, some companies grant preemptive rights: the old shareholders have the right to acquire enough new stock to prevent their share of the company from being diminished. In our example, each old shareholder would be entitled to buy one new share. Of course, they are not required to buy this stock.
- *Conversion Rights*. Some classes of stock may have the right to convert into shares of a different class. For example, if a company does not meet its financial projections, nonvoting stock may have the right to convert into voting stock.
- *Redemption Rights*. Similarly, the shareholders of some classes of stock may have the right to force a company to buy their stock back if, for example, the company does not meet its financial goals.

These are the ingredients for any class or series of stock. Some stock comes prepackaged like a cake mix. "Preferred" and "common" stock are two classic types. The Model Act does not use these terms, but many states still do.

Owners of *preferred stock* have preference on dividends and liquidation. If a class of preferred stock is entitled to dividends, then it must receive its dividends before common stockholders are paid theirs. If holders of **cumulative preferred** stock miss their dividend one year, common shareholders cannot ever be paid until this missing dividend is distributed to the cumulative preferred shareholders, no matter how long that takes. Alternatively, holders of **non-cumulative preferred** stock lose an annual dividend for good if the company cannot afford it in the year it is due. When a company dissolves, preferred stockholders have the

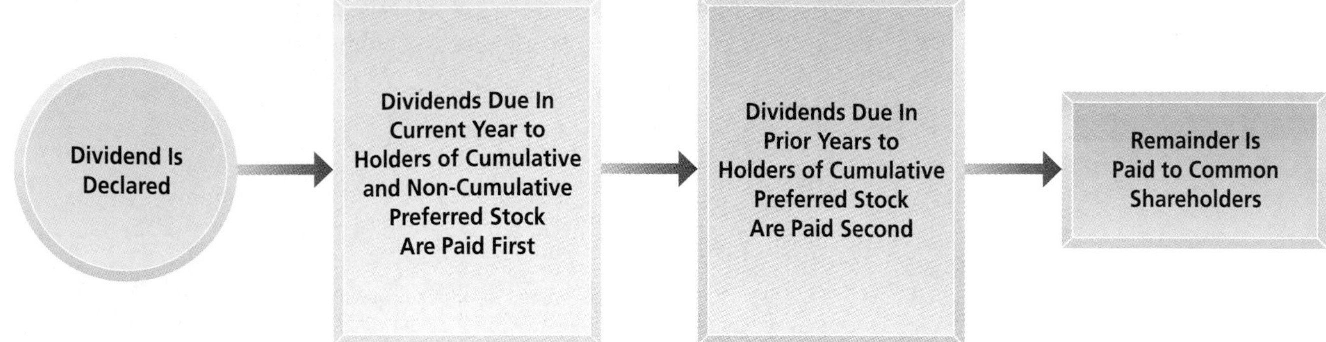

Exhibit 35.2

right to receive their share of corporate assets before common shareholders. Exhibit 35.2 illustrates the order of payment for dividends.

Preferred stock can have any combination of other ingredients, such as preemptive rights or conversion rights. Sometimes preferred shareholders have voting rights, but usually they do not. Venture capitalists (professional investors who are in the business of financing companies) often choose preferred stock because it enables them to share the increased equity value if the company does well and also to be ahead of the other stockholders (such as the founders) when it comes to dividends and liquidation.

***Common stock* is last in line for any corporate payouts, including dividends and liquidation payments.** If the company is liquidated, creditors of the company and preferred shareholders are paid before common shareholders. But being a common shareholder is not all bad news—common shareholders typically have most of the voting rights. They also have greater profit potential; preferred stock typically has a limit on the size of dividends, common does not. If the business does well, common stock will increase in value faster than preferred stock.

The Domain charter demonstrates how flexible stock classes and series can be. The company began with common stock only. Now it has two classes of stock—common and cumulative preferred. The preferred is divided into 11 series, one for each group of investors. Both classes have one vote for each share of stock, and the preferred shareholders may convert their stock into common shares, but the conversion rate is different for each series.

This ends our discussion of Domain. Like virtually all businesses, the company has seen some lean times, but it has survived and flourished. There are now 23 Domain stores, and George plans to open 65 more.

Charter's Optional Provisions

Many corporations add optional provisions to their charters. Bear in mind, however, that once a provision is in the charter, it can be changed only by a vote of the shareholders and the filing of an amendment with the Secretary of State. This process can be cumbersome and expensive. Therefore, when in doubt, it is usually a good idea *not* to include extra provisions in the charter. Nonetheless, some provisions are so important that they belong there, despite the effort and expense.

Indemnification of Officers and Directors

Although incorporation protects shareholders against personal liability for the debts of the company, anyone involved in the management of the business can be personally liable for his own wrongdoing. For example, shareholders may sue officers and directors for making an unprofitable decision. The potential liability in such a lawsuit is enormous. Even if the director or officer is found not liable, the legal fees can be devastating. Not surprisingly, many people refuse to serve as an officer or director unless the company **indemnifies** them, that is, pays any liability (including legal fees) they incur from doing their job. Consider the following example.

Leonard Shoen not only founded U-Haul, the truck rental company, he also raised 12 children. His family may have been big, but it was not happy. Son Joe forced Leonard into retirement and took over management. Joe then assaulted brother Sam at one board meeting and brother Mike at another. Two years later, Leonard joined forces with six of his children to regain his place on the board. Their goal was to sell the company.

When Joe resisted, Leonard and his allies filed suit, charging that the board of directors had violated its duty to shareholders. A jury agreed—it ordered Joe and the other directors to pay the plaintiffs $1.47 *billion*. The judge ultimately reduced the verdict to $461 million. Because U-Haul had promised to indemnify its directors "to the full extent of the law," the company was forced to sell new shares of stock to raise the money owed.

Jury verdicts against management can be enormous. Raising half a billion dollars is difficult for a company and virtually impossible for individuals. However, even if the charter requires the company to indemnify directors and officers, state laws may not permit it to do so. The Model Act:

- *Requires* a company to indemnify managers who win a lawsuit brought against them because of their role as director or officer
- *Permits* a company to indemnify managers who believed their actions were not opposed to the best interests of the company; and
- *Prohibits* a company from indemnifying managers who intentionally harmed the company or its shareholders, or violated criminal law, or improperly received some financial benefit.

Other members of the board determine if the managers have met these standards, unless the other members were also involved in the lawsuit. In that event, either the shareholders determine whether the managers are entitled to indemnification, or the board appoints an outside lawyer to make the decision. In the U-Haul case, other members of the board were involved in the lawsuit, so the company appointed an outside lawyer.

Is this legal standard also ethical? Is it fair to shareholders for a company to indemnify directors who have acted in a manner that is "not opposed to the best interests" of their company? Do shareholders have a right to expect more?

An indemnification agreement does not have to be included in a company's charter to be effective. It can be a separate agreement. A cumulative voting provision, on the other hand, is effective only if placed in the charter.

Cumulative Voting

For sheer drama, few corporate battles have exceeded the fight between the elephant, Gulf Oil, and the flea, Mesa Petroleum. When T. Boone Pickens, the CEO of Mesa, announced that Gulf Oil was badly managed, he was picking on the sixth largest oil company in America. Pickens nominated himself to be Gulf's savior. His plan was to buy enough of the company's shares so that he could elect himself to the board of directors. Pickens's goal was possible only because Gulf was incorporated in Pennsylvania, a state with cumulative voting.

At the time, Gulf Oil had 15 directors, all elected annually. Under a *regular* voting system, the 15 people who receive the most votes are awarded the seats. If Pickens owned one share, he could vote for as many as 15 *different* candidates, but he could not pool his votes; that is, he could not cast multiple votes for any one candidate. Thus he could only vote for himself once. To be sure of getting elected to the board, he would have to buy half of Gulf's shares, plus one. Gulf had 165 million shares outstanding, so Pickens would have to buy 82,500,001 shares. Once he had bought that many shares, he could elect *all* the directors, because he would own a majority of the company's stock. As Gulf's stock was trading at around $40 per share, Pickens would have had to invest more than $3 billion ($3,300,000,040) to achieve his goal.

Under a cumulative voting system, however, Pickens is allowed to pool his shares and vote them all for the same person (namely, himself). How many shares would Pickens have to own to elect himself to the board? This is the formula:

$$\text{Number of shares needed to elect one director} = \frac{\text{Number of shares outstanding}}{\text{Number of directors being elected} + 1} + 1$$

This is how the formula worked in Pickens's case, where x stands for the number of shares he needed to elect one director:

$$x = \frac{165{,}000{,}000}{15 + 1} + 1$$

$$x = 10{,}312{,}501$$

This 10 million shares is a lot less than the 82 million he needed under a regular voting system. At a price per share of $40, Pickens would have to invest roughly $400 million ($412,500,040) under a cumulative voting system, compared with $3 billion under a regular system.

In a desperate effort to prevent Pickens from being elected to its board of directors, Gulf called a special meeting of shareholders to change its state of incorporation from Pennsylvania to Delaware and eliminate cumulative voting. For months, both sides ran full-page advertisements in newspapers across the country to persuade shareholders. Gulf spent $9 million and Mesa $8 million on the fight alone, not counting money spent buying Gulf shares. In the end, Gulf won the battle but lost the war. It won the shareholder vote by a small margin, but the company was so weakened by this fight that it sold out to Chevron Oil shortly thereafter. The fight so frightened other companies that many changed their state of organization to Delaware to avoid cumulative voting. Pennsylvania changed its statute so that it is now in agreement with the Model Act: any company can choose to have cumulative voting; none is required to.

A dissident shareholder battling company management is more likely to be elected to the board of directors in a company with cumulative voting. Thus few companies permit cumulative voting because it decreases management control over the board. Managers argue that directors should represent the interests of all stockholders, but cumulative voting creates special loyalty to particular groups. Managers also assert that a board needs to work as a team and that cumulative voting can create contentious factions. For their part, shareholders argue that cumulative voting is fundamentally fair, that shareholders with a large stake in the company ought to be represented on the board.

AFTER INCORPORATION

Once the charter has been filed (and the filing fee paid), the corporation legally exists, but work is not done yet. The shareholders must still complete a few additional tasks.

DIRECTORS AND OFFICERS

Once the corporation is organized, shareholders elect directors. Under the Model Act, a corporation is required to have at least one director, unless *all* the shareholders sign an agreement that eliminates the board. To elect directors, the shareholders may hold a meeting, or, in the more typical case for a small company, they elect directors by **written consent**. (In most states, all the shareholders must sign, but in Delaware a majority is sufficient.) A typical written consent looks like this:

Classic American Novels, Inc.
Written Consent

The undersigned shareholders of Classic American Novels, Inc., a corporation organized and existing under the General Corporation Law of the State of Wherever, hereby agree that the following action shall be taken with full force and effect as if voted at a validly called and held meeting of the shareholders of the corporation:

Agreed: That the following people are elected to serve as directors for one year, or until their successors have been duly elected and qualified:

Herman Melville

Louisa May Alcott

Mark Twain

Dated: ________ Signed: ____________________
Willa Cather

Dated ________ Signed: ____________________
Nathaniel Hawthorne

Dated ________ Signed: ____________________
Harriet Beecher Stowe

Once shareholders have chosen the directors, the directors must elect the officers of the corporation. They can use a consent form, if they wish. The Model Act is flexible. It simply requires a corporation to have whatever officers are described in the bylaws. The same person can hold more than one office.

The written consents and any records of actual meetings are kept in a **minute book,** which is the official record of the corporation. Entrepreneurs sometimes feel they are too busy to bother with all these details, but, if a corporation is ever sold, the lawyers for the buyers will *insist* on a well-organized and complete minute book. In one case, a company that was seeking a $100,000 bank loan could not find all of its minutes. Many of its early shareholders and directors were not available to re-authorize prior deeds. In the end, the company had to merge itself into a newly created corporation so it could start fresh with a new set of corporate records. The company spent $10,000 on this task, a large chunk out of the $100,000 loan.

BYLAWS

The **bylaws** list all the "housekeeping" details for the corporation. For example, bylaws set the date of the annual shareholders' meeting, define what a quorum is (i.e., what percentage of stock must be represented for a meeting to count), indicate how many directors there will be, give titles to officers, fix the procedure for calling a special meeting of the shareholders or directors, and establish the fiscal (i.e., tax) year of the corporation. When there is a choice, it is usually better to place provisions in the bylaws rather than the charter, because the bylaws are easier to change. Under the Model Act, directors can amend the bylaws without calling a meeting of the shareholders or paying a filing fee. The shareholders can always override the directors if they want, but they rarely do. A sample set of bylaws is available at **http://www.lectlaw.com/forms/f151.txt** and **http://www.tannedfeet.com/html/legal_forms.htm**.

SHAREHOLDER AGREEMENTS

Sometimes shareholders want to agree in advance how they will vote their stock. For example, Craig O. McGaw was willing to sell a majority interest in Cellular One to Affiliated Publications, but he was not willing to give up control of the company. After all, he had single-handedly built it into the largest cellular telephone company in the United States. His solution? McGaw and Affiliated entered into a shareholder agreement requiring Affiliated to vote its stock as McGaw directed. Affiliated trusted McGaw's business acumen enough to want him to continue running the company although he was only a minority shareholder.

Sometimes, shareholders use a voting trust instead of a shareholder agreement to accomplish the same goal. The shareholders transfer their stock to a trust, granting the trustee power to vote it. While a shareholder agreement may be limited to votes on specific issues (such as electing directors), the trustee has control over the trust shares for every vote. Under the Model Act, a voting trust is limited to 10 years, while a shareholder agreement can last forever. For a sample shareholder agreement, browse **http://www.tannedfeet.com/html/legal_forms.htm**.

The shareholders of a start-up company often work together intensively. If a shareholder sells her stock to someone who does not share the same vision, conflict is inevitable. To avoid this situation, shareholders of start-ups typically sign a shareholder agreement, granting a right of first refusal on the company's stock. In a typical agreement, if a shareholder wants to sell, she must first offer the stock to the company at the same price that the outsider has offered. If, after 30 days, the company has not agreed to buy the stock, she must then offer it to the other shareholders. Only if they also refuse to buy it within 30 days, can she then sell it to an outsider at the same price that she offered to the company and shareholders. Similarly, if a shareholder dies, his estate may be required to offer the stock to the company or other shareholders. In these circumstances, it is more difficult to determine the market value of the stock, so the shareholder agreement often provides a formula for making this determination.

ISSUING DEBT

To get rockin' and rollin' initially, the House of Jazz in Fort Pierce, Florida, needed $150,000. It followed the beat of many new companies and borrowed these funds. Most start-ups pay the debt out of corporate profits, but the House of Jazz is trying a different rhythm. The club introduced Business Networking Wednesday as a forum for local area business people. The highlight of the evening, though, is not business chitchat, but a weekly drawing for Florida lottery tickets. Anyone who actually wins the lottery with these tickets keeps the proceeds, *minus* the club's $150,000 debt.

Most start-up companies begin with some combination of equity and debt. Equity (i.e., stock) is described in the charter; debt is not. Authorizing debt is often one of the first steps a new company takes. The House of Jazz had several options:

- **Bonds** are long-term debt secured by some of the company's assets. If the company is unable to pay the debt, creditors have a right to specific assets, such as accounts receivable or inventory. (If the House of Jazz's creditors took over its inventory, at least they could drown their sorrows.)
- **Debentures** are long-term *unsecured* debt. If the company cannot meet its obligations, the debenture holders are paid after bondholders, but before stockholders.
- **Notes** are short-term debt, typically payable within five years. They may be either secured or unsecured.

FOREIGN CORPORATIONS

A company is called a *domestic* corporation in the state where it incorporates and a *foreign* corporation everywhere else. States have only limited control over foreign corporations.

Qualifying to Do Business

Ned has sworn that he will never again suffer through a bitter Chicago winter. No, he is not relocating; he has invented a new fabric that looks like fur. It is better than the original, though, because it breathes, repels water, and is washable. He knows that his business will soon be a national success.

Ned, like many entrepreneurs before him, incorporates Fabulous Fake Furs, Inc. (FFF) in Delaware. He is still, however, living in Chicago (where he now *adores* the winter). Company headquarters are down the street from his condominium. The main manufacturing facility is in Texas, with warehouses in Minnesota and New York. A sales staff calls on all the major department stores and catalogue companies across the country.

Ned has obligations to the state of Delaware—he must pay taxes and annual fees. But what about the other states where he is doing business? Someone had to pay to build the roads and educate the workforce in these states. Must he contribute, too? The states certainly think so. They require a foreign corporation that is doing business within their borders to register with them and obtain a "certificate of authority." This registration process is called **qualifying to do business.**

What constitutes "doing business"? **Opening an office or establishing any other ongoing presence counts as doing business.** Clearly, FFF must register in Illinois, Texas, Minnesota, and New York because it has a permanent presence in these states. Typically, the following activities do *not* count as doing business: holding meetings, opening a bank account, owning property, soliciting sales orders, or any isolated transaction. If FFF's directors hold a meeting in Alaska, Ned attends a trade show in Wisconsin, or a sales rep takes an order at a store in California, these activities do not constitute doing business, and FFF does not have to register in these states.

To qualify, a company must file corporate documents with the state, list a registered agent, and pay annual fees and taxes on income generated in that jurisdiction. As a general rule, of course, companies would prefer not to register. Some states fine companies that are doing business without registering. Under the Model Act, a company that is doing business without qualifying cannot bring a lawsuit in that state until it registers (and pays back fees and taxes). But note that, if the company is *not* actually doing business, then it may file suit without qualifying first.

Defending a Lawsuit

We have talked about where FFF can sue. But what about the flip side to this question: Where can FFF *be* sued? It has the *right* to defend against a lawsuit anyplace, but would it be *fair* to require FFF to defend in an inconvenient state where it has never done business? What if Carmel files a patent infringement suit against FFF in Idaho, where she happens to live? FFF has not registered in Idaho because it is not doing business there. Can Ned be forced to defend a suit in a state that he has never visited?

Defending against a lawsuit in another state is tiresome and expensive. Ned might have to live in a hotel room for weeks before and during trial. He would certainly need to hire local lawyers. A jury might favor the local resident. All things considered, he would rather fight the battle elsewhere, preferably Chicago. **A corporation can be sued in a state only if the firm has sufficient contact so that a suit would not violate "traditional notions of fair play and substantial justice."** FFF can be sued in Idaho only if the company has had sufficient contact with the state that it would be fair to have a trial there. A company does not have to qualify in order to be sued—"sufficient contact" is less than "doing business." In this case, FFF has had no contact with Idaho, and Carmel could not bring her suit there.

The following table illustrates the circumstances under which a foreign corporation may sue and be sued:

	May File Suit	Must Defend a Suit
Qualifies to do business	Yes	Yes
Should qualify to do business, but fails to	No	Yes
Has "sufficient minimum contacts," but is not required to qualify	Yes	Yes
Has less than "sufficient minimum contacts"	Yes	No

DEATH OF THE CORPORATION

Sometimes, business ideas are not successful and the corporation fails. This death can be voluntary (the shareholders elect to terminate the corporation) or forced (by court order). Sometimes, a court takes a step that is much more damaging to shareholders than simply dissolving the corporation—it removes the shareholders' limited liability.

PIERCING THE CORPORATE VEIL

One of the major purposes of a corporation is to protect its owners—the shareholders—from personal liability for the debts of the organization. Sometimes, however, a court will **pierce the corporate veil**; that is, the court will hold shareholders personally liable for the debts of the corporation. Courts generally pierce a corporate veil in four circumstances:

- *Failure to Observe Formalities*. If an organization does not act like a corporation, it will not be treated like one. It must, for example, hold required shareholders' and directors' meetings (or sign consents), keep a minute book as a record of these meetings, and make all the required state filings. Even a corporation with only one shareholder must comply with these formalities. Sole shareholders usually just sign a written consent in lieu of a meeting. In addition, officers must be careful to sign all corporate documents with a corporate title, not as an individual. Otherwise, creditors may well be in doubt about whether they were dealing with an individual or a corporation. An officer should sign like this:

  Classic American Novels, Inc.

  By: ______________________________

  Stephen Crane, President

  If he signs simply, "Stephen Crane," creditors may successfully claim that he is personally liable.

- *Commingling of Assets*. Nothing makes a court more willing to pierce a corporate veil than evidence that shareholders have mixed their assets with those of the corporation. Sometimes, for example, shareholders use corporate assets to pay their personal debts or even mix corporate and personal funds in one bank account. If shareholders commingle assets, it is genuinely difficult for creditors to determine which assets belong to whom. This confusion is generally resolved in favor of the creditors—*all* assets are deemed to belong to the corporation.

- *Inadequate Capitalization*. If the founders of a corporation do not raise enough capital (either through debt or equity) to give the business a fighting chance of paying its debts, courts may require shareholders to pay corporate obligations. If the shareholders do not have sufficient capital for their corporation, they need to buy adequate insurance, particularly to protect against tort liability. Judges are likelier to hold shareholders liable if the alternative is to send an injured tort victim away empty-handed.

- *Fraud*. Corporations cannot be used to shelter fraud. Imagine that a con artist forms a corporation entitled Brooklyn Bridge, Inc. He then sells shares in the organization by convincing "investors," aka "pigeons," that the company really does own the famous New York landmark. If he is caught, the pigeons can go after his personal assets, even though the fraud was committed in the name of a corporation.

Although it is difficult to feel sorry for shareholders who commit intentional wrongdoing such as fraud, some of these corporate sins involve carelessness more than anything else. What about the following case—was the wrongdoing careless or intentional? Should the corporate shareholders be liable?

RICE v. ORIENTAL FIREWORKS CO.
75 Or. App. 627, 707 P.2d 1250, 1985 Ore. App. LEXIS 3928
Oregon Court of Appeals, 1985

Facts: J. C. Oriental Fireworks, Inc. was a broker and distributor of professional display fireworks. Gregory Rice filed this claim against Oriental and J. C. Chou for injuries Rice suffered while setting off fireworks. Although Rice bought the fireworks from the corporation, he sought to pierce the corporate veil and obtain a judgment against Chou personally. The trial court, however, granted Chou's motion to be removed from the case as a defendant. Chou then dismissed Oriental's Oregon lawyer and allowed an uncontested judgment to be entered against the company for $432,000 because the corporation had virtually no assets to pay the judgment.

Fireworks cause injuries. If a corporation that sells fireworks fails to purchase adequate insurance, its shareholders may be personally liable.

Chou and his wife owned all the stock of the six-year-old company. Chou was president, treasurer, and chairman of the board; his wife was vice-president. The Chous kept no records or minutes of any meetings of the shareholders or directors, except for a signed unanimous consent in lieu of the directors' first meeting. The corporation grossed from $230,000 to $400,000 annually, but its assets never exceeded $13,182. It had never obtained liability insurance, although, as Chou stated, accidents do occur, and lawsuits arise "as a general rule, right after July 4th." Chou also indicated that the lack of liability insurance motivated injured customers to bring actions against other defendants.

Issue: **Can the plaintiff pierce the corporate veil and hold Chou personally liable?**

Excerpts from Judge Warren's Decision: There are three criteria for imposing liability on a shareholder: (1) The shareholder must have controlled the corporation; (2) the shareholder must have engaged in improper conduct in his exercise of control over the corporation; and (3) the shareholder's improper conduct must have caused plaintiff's inability to obtain an adequate remedy from the corporation.

We conclude that plaintiff has demonstrated a *prima facie* case for disregarding the corporate form of Oriental. Chou had complete control over officer and director decisions and, with his wife, has control over shareholder decisions. Chou engaged in improper conduct in the exercise of control over Oriental in two respects. First, he disregarded corporate roles and formalities which serve to protect the rights and define the responsibilities of owners, directors, officers, employees, creditors, government entities and the public at large. Second, Chou failed adequately to capitalize the corporation. A corporation is inadequately capitalized when its assets are insufficient to cover its potential liabilities, which are reasonably foreseeable from the nature of the corporation's business. Finally, there can be no doubt that Chou's failure adequately to capitalize or obtain insurance coverage for Oriental has caused plaintiff to have an inadequate remedy against the corporation.

Reversed and *remanded*.

TERMINATION

Terminating a corporation is a three-step process:

- *Vote*. The directors recommend to the shareholders that the corporation be dissolved, and a majority of the shareholders agree.
- *Filing*. The corporation files "Articles of Dissolution" with the Secretary of State.
- *Winding Up*. The officers of the corporation pay its debts and distribute the remaining property to shareholders. When the winding up is completed, the corporation ceases to exist.

The Secretary of State may dissolve a corporation that violates state law by, for example, refusing to pay the required annual fees. Similarly, a court may dissolve a corporation if it is insolvent or if its directors and shareholders cannot resolve conflict over how the corporation should be managed. The court will then appoint a receiver to oversee the winding up.

CHAPTER CONCLUSION

**lthough entrepreneurs may ultimately select a different form of organization, almost all of them at least consider organizing their business as a corporation.** Most of the country's largest businesses are corporations. Although corporations are an exceedingly useful form of organization, they are also exceedingly formal. State corporation codes contain precise rules that must be followed to the letter. To do otherwise is to court disaster.

CHAPTER REVIEW

1. Promoters are personally liable for contracts they sign before the corporation is formed unless the corporation and the third party agree to a novation.
2. Companies generally incorporate in the state in which they will be doing business. However, if they intend to operate in several states, they may choose to incorporate in a jurisdiction known for its favorable corporate laws, such as Delaware or Nevada.
3. A corporate charter must generally include the company's name, address, registered agent, purpose, and a description of its stock. The charter must be signed by at least one incorporator.
4. A company's charter may include a number of optional provisions such as cumulative voting and indemnification for officers and directors.
5. A corporation must register in every state in which it is doing business.
6. A court may, under certain circumstances, pierce the corporate veil and hold shareholders personally liable for the debts of the corporation.
7. Termination of a corporation is a three-step process requiring a shareholder vote, the filing of "Articles of Dissolution," and the winding up of the enterprise's business.

PRACTICE TEST

1. Michael Ferns incorporated Erin Homes, Inc. to manufacture mobile homes. He issued himself a stock certificate for 100 shares for which he made no payment. He and his wife served as officers and directors of the organization, but, during the eight years of its existence, the corporation held only one meeting. Erin always had its own checking account, and all proceeds from the sales of mobile homes were deposited there. It filed federal income tax returns each year, using its own federal identification number. John and Thelma Laya paid $17,500 to purchase a mobile home from Erin, but the company never delivered it to them. The Layas sued Erin Homes and Michael Ferns, individually. Should the court "pierce the corporate veil" and hold Ferns personally liable?

2. CPA QUESTION Destiny Manufacturing, Inc. is incorporated under the laws of Nevada. Its principal place of business is in California, and it has permanent sales offices in several other states. Under the circumstances, which of the following is correct?

(a) California may validly demand that Destiny incorporate under the laws of the state of California.

(b) Destiny must obtain a certificate of authority to transact business in California and the other states in which it does business.

(c) Destiny is a foreign corporation in California, but **not** in the other states.

(d) California may prevent Destiny from operating as a corporation if the laws of California differ regarding organization and conduct of the corporation's internal affairs.

3. Davis Ajouelo signed an employment contract with William Wilkerson. The contract stated: "Whatever company, partnership, or corporation that Wilkerson may form for the purpose of manufacturing shall succeed Wilkerson and exercise the rights and assume all of Wilkerson's obligations as fixed by this contract." Two months later, Wilkerson formed Auto-Soler Co. Ajouelo entered into a new contract with Auto-Soler providing that the company was liable for Wilkerson's obligations under the old contract. Neither Wilkerson nor the company ever paid Ajouelo. He sued Wilkerson personally. Does Wilkerson have any obligations to Ajouelo?

4. **CPA QUESTION** Generally, a corporation's articles of incorporation must include all of the following **except** the:

(a) Name of the corporation's registered agent

(b) Name of each incorporator

(c) Number of authorized shares

(d) Quorum requirements

5. **RIGHT & WRONG** This case arises out of an unpaid hotel bill. An organization called the 21st Century Commission on African American Males made arrangements for a conference at the Omni Shoreham Hotel in Washington. J. D. Andrews signed the contract on behalf of the commission. Although the commission made some payments, $88,044.07 was still outstanding on the bill. The commission was not incorporated at the time of the conference, but it did subsequently incorporate. The Carnegie Corp. of New York, Xerox Corp., former Virginia Governor L. Douglas Wilder, and former United States Senator Terry Sanford were active participants in and organizers of the commission. Their employees served on a planning committee for the commission. This planning committee entered into the agreement with the Shoreham Hotel. Were Carnegie, Xerox, Wilder, and Sanford liable for the hotel bill as promoters of the commission? Whether or not the defendants were *legally* responsible for the debt, did they have an *ethical* obligation to pay? Did their wealth and fame lure the hotel into a contract with the commission? What would the ethics checklist in Chapter 9 suggest as a possible answer?

6. **CPA QUESTION** A corporate stockholder is entitled to which of the following rights?

(a) Elect officers

(b) Receive annual dividends

(c) Approve dissolution

(d) Prevent corporate borrowing

7. The Resolution Trust Corp. (RTC) sued the directors of the Commonwealth Savings Association seeking to recover from them personally $200 million that the bank lost in bad real estate loans. The directors approved the loans after state and federal regulatory agencies had issued reports criticizing the bank's loan practices. The directors failed to implement policies and procedures to prevent problems with the loan portfolio and failed to monitor loan officers adequately. There was no evidence that the directors knowingly committed illegal acts or acts outside their authority. Under Texas law, the RTC could recover for the directors' negligence only if their acts were *ultra vires*. Were these acts *ultra vires*?

8. Waste Management, Inc., the country's largest waste hauler, changed its name to WMX Technologies, Inc. Similarly, U.S. Steel changed its moniker to USX Corp. and American Airlines became AMR Corp. What legal steps would be necessary for WMX to protect its new corporate name?

9. Norton Waltuch was an officer of Conticommodity Services. The Commodities Futures Trading Corp. (CFTC) and certain individuals sued him for violating the rules on commodities trading. Conticommodity, not Waltuch, made settlement payments to all of the individual plaintiffs. Waltuch individually settled the CFTC charges against him. Waltuch then asked Conticommodity to indemnify him for the $2 million in legal expenses he had incurred defending himself against these suits. Under Delaware law, an officer can be indemnified if he shows that he "has been successful on the merits or otherwise" in defense of the actions against him. Waltuch argued that he was entitled to indemnification because the suits brought by individuals had been settled without any payment from him. Should Conticommodity indemnify Waltuch?

10. **YOU BE THE JUDGE WRITING PROBLEM** For Donald Sondergard, Alka-Seltzer brought disaster, not relief. He took Alka-Seltzer Plus to cure a cold, but it reacted with a prescription drug he was also taking and caused his blood pressure to shoot up. He suffered a stroke. On the day he took the Alka-Seltzer, Sondergard was living in Utah, but he later moved to South Dakota. Alka-Seltzer is manufactured by Miles, Inc., an Indiana corporation. Miles sells Alka-Seltzer in all 50 states. Miles did not qualify to do business in South Dakota until two years after Sondergard's injury. Sondergard then filed suit in South Dakota. Is Miles required to defend a lawsuit in South Dakota? **Argument for Sondergard:** Whether or when Miles

qualified to do business in South Dakota is irrelevant. The important issue is whether it is fair for Miles to be sued in South Dakota. Selling products in the state is enough to justify a suit here. **Argument for Miles:** How can it be fair to haul Miles into court in South Dakota for something that happened in a *different* state and *before* Miles qualified here? This case has absolutely nothing to do with South Dakota.

11. Angelica is planning to start a home security business in McGehee, Arkansas. She plans to start modestly but hopes to expand her business within 5 years to neighboring towns and, perhaps, within 10 years to neighboring states. Her inclination is to incorporate her business in Delaware? Is her inclination correct?

INTERNET RESEARCH PROBLEM

Think of an idea for a new company and prepare a corporate charter for your business. You can find a sample Delaware charter at http://www.state.de.us/corp/. For extra credit, find a sample charter for your own state.

You can find further practice problems in the Online Quiz at http://beatty.westbuslaw.com or in the Study Guide that accompanies this text.

CHAPTER 36

CORPORATE MANAGEMENT

Suppose that you are a shareholder of Wallace Computer Services, Inc. The company's stock is trading between $35 and $40 when, out of the blue, Moore Corp. offers to buy all the stock for $56 a share. A few days later, Moore raises its offer to $60. Wow! You quickly tender your stock to Moore and sit back to wait for the check, while visions of luxury dance in your head. You are in good company: the owners of nearly three-quarters of Wallace stock also tender. But the check never comes because Wallace's board of directors turns down the offer. How is that? The board says that the company is worth more. How much more? Well, a year after the board rejected Moore's $60 offer, Wallace stock is trading at $56. During the same period, the stock market has risen 20 percent. If you had sold your Wallace stock and invested the proceeds in the market, your $60 would now be worth $72. Wallace shareholders have lost out on $74 million in that year alone. But the worst is not over. During the next few years, while the stock market continues to rise, Wallace stock hits a low of $15.44.

You had hoped that your profits from Wallace would enable you to quit your day job at Chase Manhattan Bank and start a business of your own. Bitter that your dream has been deferred, you often complain to your co-workers about this grave injustice, "How totally unfair, how outrageous for a board to ignore the best interests of its own shareholders!" Then one day over lunch the conversation turns to Michael Price, a prominent mutual fund manager, who has purchased 6.1 percent of Chase's stock. He reportedly is pushing the bank's board to start an auction for its stock and then sell out to the highest bidder. Your co-workers are nervous because they know the new owner will try to increase profits by firing as many workers as possible. Rumors are flying that that board will soon start to fire employees itself to preempt Price. You and your fellow workers fear pink slips in the next paycheck. How could the board turn its back on loyal, long-term employees? And how will you survive with no savings and no job?[1]

Before the Industrial Revolution in the eighteenth and nineteenth centuries, a business owner typically supplied both capital and management. However, the capital needs of the great manufacturing enterprises spawned by the Industrial Revolution were larger than any small group of individuals could supply. To find capital, firms sought outside investors, who often had neither the knowledge nor the desire to manage the enterprise. Investors without management skills complemented managers without capital. (Throughout this chapter, "manager" includes both directors and officers.)

Modern businesses still have the same vast need for capital and the same division between managers and investors. Since shareholders are too numerous and too uninformed to manage the enterprises they own, they elect directors to manage for them. The directors set policy and then appoint officers to implement corporate goals. The Revised Model Business Corporation Act describes the directors' role thus: "All corporate powers shall be exercised by or under the authority of, and the business and affairs of the corporation managed under the direction of, its board of directors. . . ."

Directors have the authority to manage the corporate business, but they also have important responsibilities to shareholders and perhaps also to other **stakeholders**—employees, customers, creditors, suppliers, and neighbors—who are affected by corporate decisions. As the opening vignette illustrates, the interests of these various stakeholders often conflict. This chapter is about the rights—and the responsibilities—of directors and officers to manage these conflicts.

MANAGERS VERSUS SHAREHOLDERS: THE INHERENT CONFLICT

After years of intermittent shortages, aggressive exploration had increased the world's oil supply to the point that it exceeded demand by about half a million barrels a day. Excess supply caused prices to fall. That might be good news for consumers, but it was bad news for oil companies. With prices low and exploration costs high, oil companies in the United States were spending more to find a new barrel of oil than the oil was worth. Mobil Oil found only 68 cents worth of oil for every dollar it spent on exploration. While Mobil continued to look for oil, other companies drastically reduced their exploration budgets. Exxon Corp. decided it was cheaper to buy reserves on Wall Street by purchasing its own stock than to

[1] If you are interested in following the stock price of a particular company, click on **http://stockmaster.com**. If you want to pretend to play the market for Hollywood movies, try **http://www.hsx.com**.

explore for new reserves. Instead of drilling, Exxon used much of its cash flow to buy back 28 percent of its outstanding stock. That simple financial maneuver increased the company's reserves per share and caused its stock price to rise.[2]

This episode illustrates the ongoing debate over corporate governance in America. Managers serve at least three masters: themselves, shareholders, and stakeholders. These masters have conflicting goals:

- **Managers** want, first, to keep their jobs and, second, to build an institution that will survive them. For managers of oil companies, this means that they must continue to explore for oil because, without reserves, their companies cannot survive.
- **Shareholders** want a high stock price, *right now*, not five years from now. Oil company shareholders prefer the Exxon strategy because it potentially increases the company's stock price. The alternative—exploration that returns 68 cents on the dollar—will not help stock prices, at least in the short run.
- **Stakeholders**, those who work for Exxon, use oil products, manufacture drilling equipment, or own a grocery store in a town where Exxon is the major employer, want exploration to continue. Oil may be in surplus now, but energy demand is certain to rise dramatically as emerging nations industrialize. Without oil exploration, American consumers may again suffer through bouts of high prices and rationed gasoline. Moreover, without continued exploration some of those who work directly or indirectly for Exxon will lose their jobs.

Which managers did a better job—Exxon's or Mobil's? The answer depends on whom you ask. Only one thing is clear: managers cannot please all the stakeholders all the time.[3] At **http://www.corporateinformation.com/**, you can find updates on all the companies that are mentioned in this book.

The courts have generally held that **managers have a fiduciary duty to act in the best interests of the corporation's shareholders**. Since shareholders are primarily concerned about their return on investment, managers must *maximize shareholder value*, which means providing shareholders with the highest possible financial return from dividends and stock price. However, reality is more complicated than this simple rule indicates. It is often difficult to determine which strategy will best maximize shareholder value. And what about *stake*holders? Must managers totally ignore their interests? In the following case, the court explicitly permits the board to consider the interests of stakeholders over those of some shareholders.

UNOCAL CORP. v. MESA PETROLEUM CO.

493 A.2d 946, 1985 Del. LEXIS 482
Supreme Court of Delaware, 1985

Facts: Mesa Petroleum Co. offered to purchase 64 million shares of Unocal's stock at a cash price of $54 per share. Upon merger of the two companies, Mesa planned to exchange the remaining Unocal shares for "junk bonds" that Mesa (but no one else, including the court) valued at $54 per share. Unocal's investment bankers advised the board of directors that the Mesa proposal was wholly inade-

[2] Toni Mack et al., "History Is Full of Giants That Failed To Adapt," *Forbes*, Feb. 28, 1994, p. 73. Reprinted by permission of Forbes Magazine © Forbes 1999 Forbes 1994.

[3] In any event, we can never know which managers were right because Exxon and Mobil subsequently decided to merge (to create Exxon-Mobil).

quate and that an offer of over $60 per share would have been reasonable. The board rejected the Mesa offer and then made its own competing offer of $72 per share to all shareholders except Mesa. (This type of offer is called a "selective exchange offer.") The board's offer effectively preempted Mesa, because no shareholder would accept the $54 Mesa offer when the $72 Unocal offer was also available. The Delaware court issued a temporary restraining order against Unocal's offer unless it included Mesa.

Issues: Could Unocal make an offer to buy stock from all shareholders except Mesa? In making this offer, did Unocal have the right to consider the interests of other stakeholders?

Excerpts from Justice Moore's Decision: In the board's exercise of corporate power to forestall a takeover bid our analysis begins with the basic principle that corporate directors have a fiduciary duty to act in the best interests of the corporation's stockholders. The restriction placed upon a selective stock repurchase is that the directors may not have acted solely or primarily out of a desire to perpetuate themselves in office. This entails an analysis by the directors of the nature of the takeover bid and its effect on the corporate enterprise. Examples of such concerns may include: inadequacy of the price offered, nature and timing of the offer, questions of illegality, the impact on "constituencies" other than shareholders (i.e., creditors, customers, employees, and perhaps even the community generally), the risk of nonconsummation, and the quality of securities being offered in the exchange. While not a controlling factor, it also seems to us that a board may reasonably consider the basic stockholder interests at stake, including those of short term speculators, whose actions may have fueled the coercive aspect of the offer at the expense of the long-term investor.

In adopting the selective exchange offer, the board stated that its objective was either to defeat the inadequate Mesa offer or, should the offer still succeed, provide its stockholders with $72 a share. We find that both purposes are valid. However, such efforts would have been thwarted by Mesa's participation in the exchange offer. First, if Mesa could tender its shares, Unocal would effectively be subsidizing the former's continuing effort to buy Unocal stock at $54 per share. Second, Mesa could not, by definition, fit within the class of shareholders being protected from its own coercive and inadequate tender offer. Thus, we are satisfied that the selective exchange offer is reasonably related to the threats posed.

The decision of the Court of Chancery is therefore *reversed*, and the preliminary injunction is *vacated*.

This case illustrates the inherent conflicts of interest facing every board. The court suggests that the interests of the directors themselves and of short-term speculators are secondary to those of long-term investors and other stakeholders. The next section looks more closely at directors' responsibilities to their various constituencies.

RESOLVING THE CONFLICT: THE BUSINESS JUDGMENT RULE

Officers and directors have a fiduciary duty to act in the best interests of their stockholders, but under the **business judgment rule** the courts allow managers great leeway in carrying out this responsibility. The business judgment rule is not a statute, but a common law concept that virtually every court in the country recognizes. To be protected by the business judgment rule, managers must act in good faith:

Duty of Loyalty	**1.** Without a conflict of interest
Duty of Care	**2.** With the care that an ordinarily prudent person would take in a similar situation, and
	3. In a manner they reasonably believe to be in the best interests of the corporation.

The business judgment rule is two shields in one: it protects both the manager and her decision. If a manager has complied with the rule, a court will not hold her personally liable for any harm her decision has caused the company, nor will the court rescind her decision. If the manager violates the business judgment rule, then she has the burden of proving that her decision was fair to the shareholders. If it was not fair, she may be held personally liable, and the decision can be rescinded.

The business judgment rule accomplishes three goals:

- *It permits directors to do their job.* Business is risky. No one can guarantee perfect decision making all the time. If directors were afraid they would be liable for every decision that led to a loss, they would never make a decision, or at least not a risky one.

- *It keeps judges out of corporate management.* Shareholders would generally prefer that their investments be overseen by experienced corporate managers, not judges. Without the business judgment rule, judges would be tempted, if not required, to second-guess managers' decisions.

- *It encourages directors to serve.* No one in his right mind would serve as a director if he knew that every decision was open to attack in the courtroom. Even if the company pays the legal bills, who wants to spend years in litigation?

Analysis of the business judgment rule is typically divided into two parts. The obligation of a manager to act without a conflict of interest is called the **duty of loyalty**. The requirements that a manager act with care and in the best interests of the corporation are referred to as the **duty of care**.

Duty of Loyalty

The duty of loyalty prohibits managers from making a decision that benefits them at the expense of the corporation.

Self-Dealing

Consider whether the manager in the following article has violated his duty of loyalty to Vie de France:

To its Washington, D.C. customers, the name Vie de France conjures up the tastes and smells of freshly baked croissants or crusty baguettes. But according to Lloyd J. Faul, a fired executive, not all of the smells emanating from the company were pleasant. Grands Moulins de Paris International, France's largest flour miller, bought 26 percent of Vie de France and then dispatched Jean-Paul Vilgrain to serve as Vie's CEO. Vilgrain's family was one of Grand Moulins' largest shareholders. Faul alleges that, once installed, Vilgrain sold a license to a Japanese company to sell products in Japan under the name "Vie de France" in exchange for royalties to be paid to Grands Moulins (not to Vie de France). He refused to approve a sale of Vie de France to Pillsbury unless Pillsbury would purchase flour mixes sold by Grands Moulins. Vilgrain also locked Faul out of Vie's headquarters when Faul refused to falsify an affidavit that would allow Vilgrain's son to renew his American working papers.[4]

Self-dealing is a violation of the duty of loyalty. There are two kinds of self-dealing:

- **Business Self-Dealing.** The manager makes decisions that benefit other companies with which he has a relationship. If Vilgrain licensed Vie's name, but arranged for the proceeds to go to Moulins, or if he refused to sell Vie unless Pillsbury agreed to a contract with Moulins, then Vilgrain has engaged in business self-dealing.

- **Personal Self-Dealing.** The manager benefits personally. If Vilgrain demanded the falsification of his son's working papers, he would be benefiting personally.

Once a manager engages in self-dealing, the business judgment rule no longer applies. This does not mean the manager is automatically liable to the corporation or that his decision is automatically void. All it means is that the court will no longer presume that the transaction was acceptable. Instead, the court will scrutinize the deal more carefully. A self-dealing transaction is valid in any one of the following situations:

- **The disinterested members of the board of directors approve the transaction.** Disinterested directors are those who do not themselves benefit from the transaction.

- **The disinterested shareholders approve it.** The transaction is valid if the shareholders who do not benefit from it are willing to approve it.

- **The transaction was fair to the corporation**. In determining fairness, the courts will consider whether the price was reasonable and how important the transaction was to the corporation.

Exhibit 36.1 illustrates the rules on self-dealing.

What about the Vie de France transactions? They had not been approved by the disinterested members of the board of directors or the disinterested shareholders. Were they fair to the corporation? If the deals were not fair, the corporation could rescind them and hold Vilgrain personally liable. In the end, however, none

---

[4] B. H. Lawrence, "En Garde; the Battle at Vie de France," *Washington Post*, Apr. 24, 1989, p. F1.

Exhibit 36.1

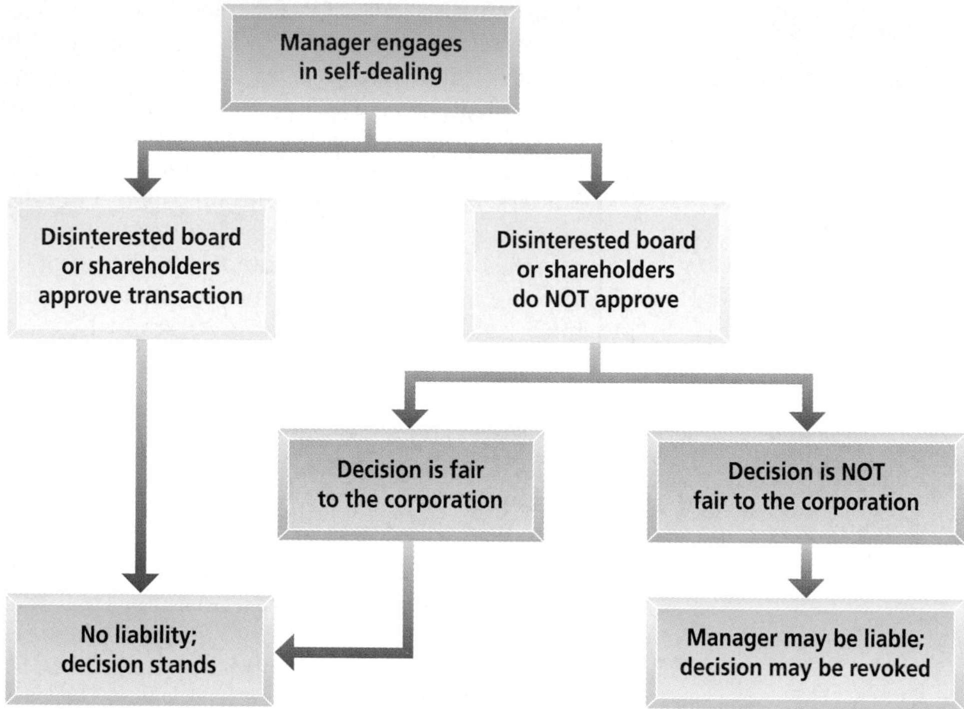

of the Vie de France shareholders filed suit against the company or Vilgrain. A few months after Faul left the company, Vilgrain was named president and CEO. Two years later, the company sold its bakery business, keeping only its restaurant and frozen food divisions.

Corporate Opportunity

The self-dealing rules prevent managers from *forcing* their companies into unfair deals. The corporate opportunity doctrine is the reverse—it prohibits managers from *excluding* their company from favorable deals. **Managers are in violation of the corporate opportunity doctrine if they compete against the corporation without its consent.**

Charles Guth was president of Loft, Inc., which operated a chain of candy stores. These stores sold Coca-Cola. Guth purchased the Pepsi-Cola Co. personally, without offering the opportunity to Loft. The Delaware court found that Guth had violated the corporate opportunity doctrine and ordered him to transfer all his shares in Pepsi to Loft.[5] That was in 1939 and Pepsi-Cola was bankrupt; today, PepsiCo, Inc. is worth $53 billion.

If a manager first offers an opportunity to disinterested directors or shareholders, and they turn it down, the manager then has the right to take advantage of the opportunity himself. (Remember that "disinterested directors or shareholders" are those who do not personally benefit from the transaction.) Sometimes, however, either through oversight or ignorance, managers do not seek permission in advance. To avoid violating the corporate opportunity doctrine, the manager must show after the fact that the company would have been unable to benefit from the opportunity. In the following case, a director took an opportunity without formally offering it to the company first. But all was not lost.

[5] *Guth v. Loft*, 5 A.2d 503, 23 Del. Ch. 255, 1939 Del. LEXIS 13 (Del. 1939).

BROZ v. CELLULAR INFORMATION SYSTEMS, INC.
673 A.2d 148, 1996 Del. LEXIS 105
Supreme Court of Delaware, 1996

Facts: Robert F. Broz was a director of Cellular Information Systems, Inc. (CIS), which had recently emerged from lengthy and contentious bankruptcy proceedings. Broz learned that a cellular telephone service license covering part of Michigan was for sale. The chief executive of CIS assured Broz that the company was not interested in the license. Broz then purchased the license himself. When new owners acquired CIS, they sued Broz, claiming that he had violated the corporate opportunity doctrine. The Delaware trial court found in favor of the new owners of CIS.

Issue: **Did Broz violate the corporate opportunity doctrine?**

Excerpts from Judge Veasey's Decision: CIS was not financially capable of exploiting the Michigan-2 opportunity. The record shows that CIS was in a precarious financial position at the time [the seller] presented the Michigan opportunity to Broz. Despite the fact that the nature of the Michigan opportunity was historically close to the core operations of CIS, changes were in process. At the time the opportunity was presented, CIS was actively engaged in the process of divesting its cellular license holdings. CIS' articulated business plan did not involve any new acquisitions.

In concluding that Broz had usurped a corporate opportunity, the [trial court] placed great emphasis on the fact that Broz had not formally presented the matter to the CIS board. In so holding, the trial court erroneously grafted a new requirement onto the law of corporate opportunity, viz., the requirement of formal presentation under circumstances where the corporation does not have an interest, or financial ability.

Of course, presenting the opportunity to the board creates a kind of "safe harbor" for the director, which removes the specter of a post hoc judicial determination that the director or officer has improperly usurped a corporate opportunity. Thus, presentation avoids the possibility that an error in the fiduciary's assessment of the situation will create future liability for breach of fiduciary duty. It is not the law of Delaware that presentation to the board is a necessary prerequisite to a finding that a corporate opportunity has not been usurped.

Therefore, we hold that Broz did not breach his fiduciary duties to CIS. Accordingly, we REVERSE the judgment of the [trial court].

A manager will often find it difficult to prove that the company could not have used an opportunity itself. However, these disputes are easy to avoid—the manager must simply ask permission first. If the company finds out after the fact that a manager has taken a corporate opportunity, it may not choose to litigate the issue, but the manager's career at that company will effectively be over. Certainly, if a manager suspects that company officers would be displeased to learn about his new sideline, that is an indication that he is skating on thin ice.

DUTY OF CARE

In addition to the *duty of loyalty*, managers also owe a *duty of care*. **The duty of care requires officers and directors to act in the best interests of the corporation and to use the same care that an ordinarily prudent person would in the management of her own assets**. In managing her own property, an ordinarily prudent person would have a rational business purpose, avoid illegal behavior, and make informed decisions. Officers and directors of corporations must do no less.

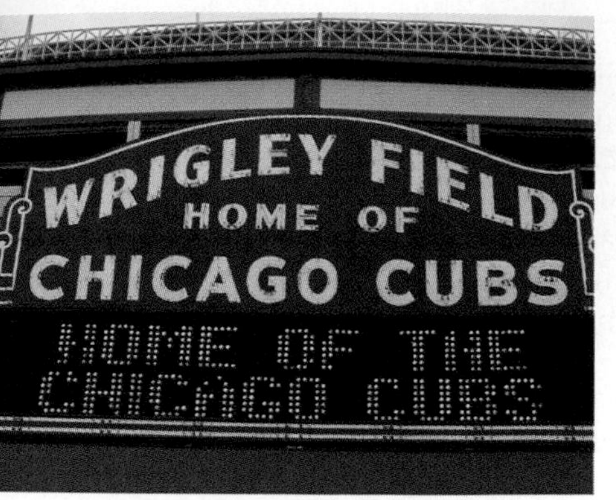

The Chicago Cubs ultimately decided to light Wrigley Field, but it was management's decision, not the shareholders'.

Rational Business Purpose

Courts generally agree in principle that directors and officers are liable to shareholders for decisions that have no rational business purpose. In practice, however, these same courts have been extremely supportive of managerial decisions, looking hard to find some justification. For decades, the Chicago Cubs baseball team refused to install lights in Wrigley Field. Cubs' fans could only take themselves out to the ball game during the day. A shareholder sued on the grounds that the Cubs' revenues were peanuts and crackerjack compared with those generated by other teams that played at night. The Cubs defended their decision on the grounds that a large night crowd would cause the neighborhood to deteriorate, depressing the value of Wrigley Field (which was not owned by the Cubs). The court rooted for the home team and found that the Cubs' excuse was a "rational purpose" and a legitimate exercise of the business judgment rule.[6]

If a decision does not have a rational business purpose, the managers are liable and the decision can be rescinded. If a court decides that there is a rational business purpose, both the manager and the decision are protected.

Legality

Courts are generally unsympathetic to managers who engage in illegal behavior, even if their goal is to help the company. For example, the managing director of an amusement park in New York used corporate funds to purchase the silence of people who threatened to complain that the park was illegally operating on Sunday. The court ordered the director to repay the money he had spent on bribes, even though the company had earned large profits on Sundays.[7]

Informed Decision

Generally, courts will protect managers who make an *informed* decision, even if the decision ultimately harms the company. Making an informed decision means carefully investigating the facts. However, even if the decision is uninformed, the directors will not be held liable if the decision was entirely fair to the shareholders. The board of Technicolor, Inc. agreed to sell the film processing company, knowing little about the terms of the deal and without seeking other bidders. The directors simply knew that the sales price was higher than the appraised value of the company. Five years later, the buyer sold the company for a $750 million profit. The former shareholders sued, alleging that the directors had made an uninformed decision. The appeals court held that, because the directors had been so careless, they had to prove that the price, and the process by which it had been determined, were both fair.[8]

Exhibit 36.2 provides an overview of the duty of care.

---

[6] *Shlensky v. Wrigley*, 95 Ill. App. 2d 173, 237 N.E.2d 776, 1968 Ill. App. LEXIS 1107 (Ill. App. Ct. 1968).

[7] *Roth v. Robertson*, 64 Misc. 343, 118 N.Y.S. 351, 1909 N.Y. Misc. LEXIS 279 (N.Y. 1909).

[8] The appeals court sent the case back to the lower court to determine whether the deal had been fair to the shareholders. *Cede & Co., Inc. v. Technicolor, Inc.*, 634 A.2d 345, 1993 Del. LEXIS 398 (Del. 1993). The lower court ultimately decided that the transaction had indeed been fair. *Cinerama, Inc. v. Technicolor, Inc.*, 663 A.2d 1134, 1994 Del. Ch. LEXIS 178 (Del. Ch. 1994). The appeals court, however, disagreeing with the valuation method used by the trial court, reversed that decision and remanded it once again to the trial court for further proceedings. *Cede & Co. v. Technicolor*, 684 A.2d 289, 1996 Del. LEXIS 386 (Del. 1996).

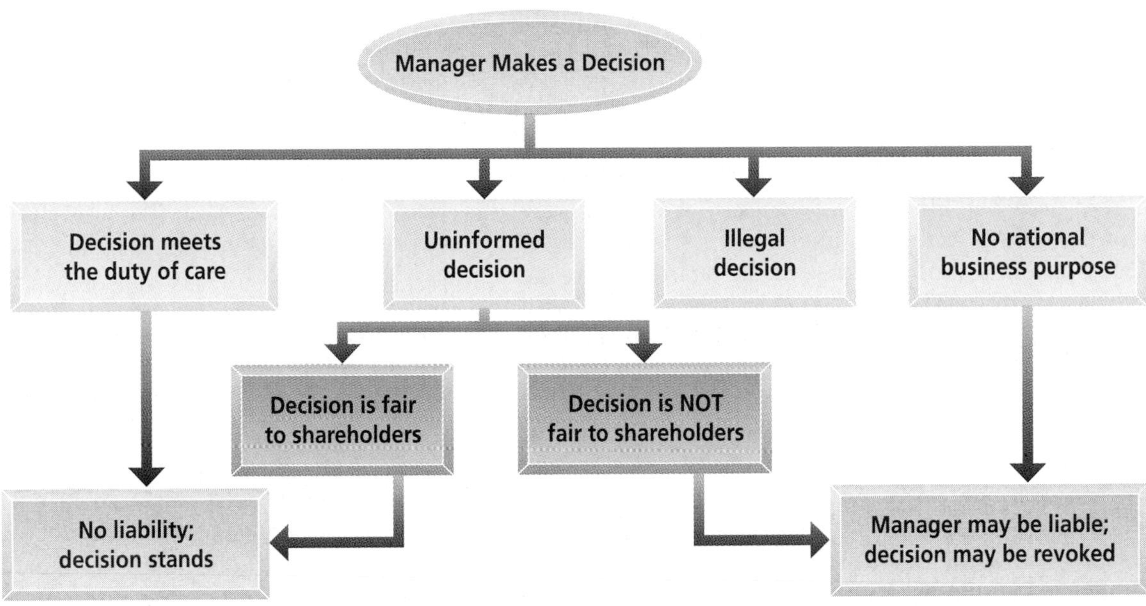

Exhibit 36.2

In the following case, shareholders sued the board of directors for accepting a purchase price that they felt was too low. Did the directors violate their duty of care? You be the judge. It is a long and complex case but an important one.

SMITH v. VAN GORKOM

488 A.2d 858, 1985 Del. LEXIS 590
Supreme Court of Delaware, 1985

Facts: Trans Union was a publicly traded company in the railcar leasing business. Jerome Van Gorkom had been its chief executive officer for more than 17 years. He was nearing the mandatory retirement age of 65 and was concerned about maximizing the value of his 75,000 shares of Trans Union stock. In the preceding five years, Trans Union's stock had traded at a high of $39.50 and a low of $24.25 per share. The price was now about $37.

Although Trans Union had hundreds of millions of dollars in annual cash flow, it did not have enough income to take advantage of large investment tax credits (ITCs). Van Gorkom fretted that competitors who could efficiently use their ITCs would be able to cut their lease prices and take business away from Trans Union. He believed that Trans Union would be more profitable if it were bought by a company that could use the credits.

On September 13, Van Gorkom met with Jay Pritzker, a well-known corporate takeover specialist, to discuss the potential market for Trans Union. Van Gorkom suggested to Pritzker that a leveraged buyout (LBO) could be done at $55 per share. (In an LBO the acquiring company buys the target company's stock using a loan secured by the target's assets.) On Thursday, September 18, Pritzker offered to buy all of Trans Union's stock for $55 per share. The offer expired three days later, on Sunday evening.

On Saturday, Van Gorkom met separately with senior managers and later with the board of directors. Salomon Brothers, the company's investment banker, was not invited to attend. At both meetings, Van Gorkom disclosed the offer and described its terms, but furnished no copies of the proposed agreement. At the first meeting with senior management, the managers' reaction to the Pritzker proposal was completely negative—they feared losing their jobs, they did not like Pritzker, and they thought the price was too low. Nevertheless, Van Gorkom proceeded to the board meeting.

The board was composed of five inside and five outside directors. Of the outside directors, four were corporate CEOs and one was the former Dean of the University of Chicago Business School. None was an investment banker or trained financial analyst. All members of the board were familiar with the company's financial condition and the ITC problem. They had all recently reviewed the company's five-year forecast as well as a comprehensive 18-month study by a well-known consulting firm.

Van Gorkom explained that the issue was not whether $55 per share was the highest price the company could obtain, but whether it was a fair price that the stockholders should be given the opportunity to accept or reject. He also explained that the company had the right to accept a higher offer, if one were made. Van Gorkom did not disclose to the board that he had proposed the $55 price in his negotiations with Pritzker. The company's attorney advised the directors that they might be sued if they failed to accept the offer. The company's chief financial officer said that $55 was "in the range of a fair price" for an LBO, but "at the beginning of the range." The board approved the sale.

Van Gorkom executed the agreement at a formal social event that he hosted for the opening of the Chicago Lyric Opera. Neither he nor any other director read the agreement before signing it. The company issued a press release announcing that Trans Union had entered into a "definitive" agreement with Pritzker. At the same time, it hired Salomon Brothers to solicit other offers. No one else made a firm offer, perhaps because other bidders believed the company was already committed to Pritzker. On February 10, 69 percent of the stockholders of Trans Union voted in favor of the Pritzker proposal.

The plaintiff, Alden Smith, objected to the sale because he did not want to pay tax on the huge profits he realized.

You Be the Judge: Did the directors of Trans Union violate their duty of care to the corporation by making an uninformed decision? Did the shareholders consent to the board's decision?

Argument for the Shareholders: The whole procedure for this sale was shockingly casual. Van Gorkom signed the final agreement at a social function. When the directors voted to sell the company, they had not (1) tried to negotiate a higher price with Pritzker, (2) read the agreement, (3) consulted their investment bankers, or (4) determined the intrinsic value of the company. The stock price simply represents the value of a minority stake (one share); a controlling share is worth more, but the board did not know how much more.

The board did not know this important information and neither did the shareholders when they approved the sale. For that reason, the shareholder consent is invalid.

Argument for the Board of Directors: Pritzker paid a fair price for the Trans Union stock. It represented a premium of (1) 62 percent over the average of the high and low price in the prior year, (2) 48 percent over the last closing price, and (3) 39 percent over the highest price at which the stock had *ever* traded. The plaintiffs suggest that the "intrinsic value" of the company was higher. The board hired Salomon Brothers to look for better offers and agreed to pay them a fee equal to three-eighths of 1 percent of any increase over $55 that the company received. Salomon would have earned millions of dollars if it had found a buyer willing to pay more than Pritzker.

Jerome Van Gorkom served the company for 24 years, and he knew $55 was a favorable price. He also had an enormous incentive to obtain the highest price available because he personally owned 75,000 shares. The five inside directors had collectively worked for the company for 116 years. The outside directors knew the company well, and they were experienced business people; four of them were CEOs of their own large companies. The board was forced to make a decision quickly because Pritzker's offer expired in three days. What could an expert have discovered in three days that the board did not already know? The Trans Union lawyer warned the directors that if they refused the offer, they would be sued.

Alden Smith's tax problems are not a legitimate reason to hold the board liable. The business judgment rule is meant to protect a board that makes a good faith decision. This board did what it thought best for all of the company's shareholders, not for Alden Smith alone. ■

Remember that managers are only liable if they make an uninformed decision *and* the transaction is unfair to the shareholders. If the appeals court in the *Trans Union* case determined that the directors had violated their duty of care, it would remand the case to the lower court to determine if $55 was a fair price.

Recently, some states have modified their business judgment rule to increase protection for directors. These states either limit liability by statute or permit corporations to include charter provisions that shield directors from personal liability.

MORE CONFLICT: TAKEOVERS

The business judgment rule is an important guideline for officers and directors in the routine management of corporations. Beginning in the 1980s, however, the business judgment rule also played a crucial role in the merger mania that swept corporate America. But the business judgment rule was not, by itself, sufficient for resolving all the new issues that arose in these battles. In response, both Congress and many state legislatures passed statutes that defined the roles of the various combatants in hostile takeovers. Thus the law of takeovers is rooted in both common and statutory law. Articles on all the latest corporate law issues are available at http://www.ljx.com/practice/corporate/index.html.

There are three ways to acquire control of a company:

- **Buy the company's assets.** Such a sale must be approved by both the shareholders and the board of directors of the acquired company.
- **Merge with the company.** In a merger, one company absorbs another. The acquired company ceases to exist. A merger must also be approved by the shareholders and the board of directors of the target. Even if the current directors object, an acquiring company could buy enough stock to replace the board, but these battles are difficult and often end in defeat for the acquirer (for reasons discussed in Chapter 37, on shareholders).
- **Buy stock from the shareholders.** This method is called a **tender offer** because the acquirer asks shareholders to "tender," or offer their stock for sale. Unlike the other methods of obtaining control, approval from the board of directors of the target company is not strictly necessary. As long as shareholders tender enough stock, the acquirer gains control. Typically, the bidder makes an offer (at a price above market value) by placing large advertisements in newspapers across the country. The offer is usually contingent—if a certain percentage of the shareholders do not tender, the offer terminates automatically. A tender offer is called a **hostile takeover** if the board of the target resists.

Two scenarios are common in hostile takeovers:

- The target has assets that the bidder genuinely wants.
- A speculator plans to acquire control and then resell all or part of the company at a profit. Speculators, sometimes called **corporate raiders**, often say that they are acquiring stock in a company because it is undervalued; their ostensible goal is to improve management and raise stock prices. In practice, however, they rarely manage the companies they acquire. Either another bidder comes along who buys their stock at a higher price; the raiders dismember the company and sell its parts; or the company buys its own stock back at a higher-than-market price. (Management is willing to pay a premium price to keep the company intact and their jobs safe.)

The number of tender offers reached an all-time high in the mid-1980s, declined in popularity during the recession of 1989–1990, and revived again in the 1990s. In the beginning, state and federal governments barely regulated tender offers at all. Over time, targets began to ask Congress and their state legislatures to umpire these increasingly rancorous battles. Both states and the federal government have stepped into the ring as referees, generally more on the side of the target than of the bidder.

FEDERAL REGULATION OF TENDER OFFERS: THE WILLIAMS ACT

Congress passed the first major takeover legislation in 1968. The Williams Act applies only if the target company's stock is publicly traded. Under the Williams Act:

- Any individual or group who together acquire more than 5 percent of a company's stock must file a public disclosure document (called a "Schedule 13D") with the Securities and Exchange Commission (SEC)
- On the day a tender offer begins, a bidder must file a disclosure statement with the SEC
- A bidder must keep a tender offer open for at least 20 days initially and for at least 10 days after any change in the terms of the offer
- Any shareholder may withdraw acceptance of the tender offer at any time while the offer is still open
- If the bidder raises the price offered, all selling shareholders must be paid the higher price, regardless of when they tendered; and
- If the stockholders tender more shares than the bidder wants to buy, it must purchase shares pro rata (in other words, it must buy the same proportion from everyone, *not* first come, first served).

Observe that the Williams Act regulates only the behavior of the *bidder*, not that of the *target* company. After Congress passed the Act, the number of tender offers declined and the average premium over market price increased. But target companies did not rely merely on the Williams Act to protect against the threat of takeovers. They were busy formulating other defenses.

STATE REGULATION OF TAKEOVERS

A company's response to a takeover attempt is largely governed by state law, both common and statutory.

Common Law of Takeovers

Potential targets were not content to sit watching nervously as aggressive bidders, also called **sharks**, swallowed up other companies. Instead, they adopted defensive measures known as **antitakeover devices** or **shark repellents**. Common shark repellents include the following:

- **Asset Lockup**. Suppose that Ingrid is the CEO of Casablanca, Inc., a successful film production company that owns a vast and valuable library of old films. Turner has indicated that he may want to acquire Casablanca because he covets its library. Ingrid tries to pass the bait to someone else either by selling the film library or by giving someone else the option to buy it.
- **Greenmail**. Ingrid suspects that Turner is not really interested in owning Casablanca stock; he simply wants to turn a quick profit. Ingrid offers to buy back Turner's stock at a price 30 percent higher than he paid for it.
- **Poison Pills**. Now Ingrid gets truly creative. She asks the shareholders to amend the company charter so that Casablanca can issue a share of preferred stock to each shareholder. The charter amendment provides that, if a shark purchases more than 20 percent of Casablanca's stock and subsequently merges with Casablanca, the preferred stock can be converted into a share of the acquiring company. Thus, for each share of Casablanca that Turner buys, he

Companies have been creative in fighting off sharks.

also has to give away one of his own shares, making the takeover much more expensive for Turner. No wonder these, and other similar tactics, are called "poison pills"; they could certainly prove fatal to a shark.

- **Chewable Poison Pills**. In the face of complaints by institutional shareholders that poison pills are nothing more than protection for incompetent managers, some companies have adopted chewable poison pills instead. These pills are exactly like a poison pill except that they expire automatically if a cash tender offer is made for 100 percent of the company's stock, at a price at least 25 percent above market value. This provision gives Ingrid plenty of clout when negotiating with outsiders, but limits her ability to turn down an offer that is clearly in the shareholders' best interest.
- **Dead-Hand Poison Pills**. Turner might try to elect some of his supporters to the board of Casablanca so that they could eliminate the poison pill. But a dead-hand poison pill can be removed only by vote of the directors who installed the bill, or by their handpicked successors. In this way, the decision is in the "dead hands" of the prior board. Dead-hand poison pills are not valid in all states, but, if Casablanca is incorporated in a state that does permit this defense, Turner's supporters would not be able to remove Casablanca's poison pill.
- **Staggered Board of Directors**. Although in many companies directors must run for reelection each year, Casablanca has a staggered board. Each director serves a three-year term, and only 4 of the 12 directors are elected each year. If Turner takes over the company, he will not gain control of the board for two years, and it will be three before he can replace all the directors.
- **Supermajority Voting**. Ordinarily, shareholders can approve charter amendments by a majority vote. If Ingrid wants to make a takeover more difficult, she can ask shareholders to amend Casablanca's charter to require a *supermajority* vote of, say, 80 percent to approve a merger. Thus Turner will not be able to merge his company with Casablanca unless he buys 80 percent of Casablanca.
- **White Knight**. Because Turner has publicly criticized Ingrid's management of Casablanca, she despises him and would prefer to sell to *anyone* else. She locates another buyer who she hopes will retain her management team.

Management typically cannot use poison pills, staggered boards of directors, supermajority voting, and white knights without shareholder approval. However, shareholders often vote in favor of management proposals without asking many questions. Shareholder approval is not required to implement the other shark repellents.

Antitakeover devices are a mixed blessing—they are beneficial if used to ensure that shareholders receive the highest possible price for their stock in the event of a sale. But they can be harmful to shareholders if used only to protect management from being fired. The legal rules on antitakeover devices are complex and sometimes seem to depend on the idiosyncrasies of a particular case. But these are the general guidelines:

- **When establishing takeover defenses, shareholder welfare must be the board's primary concern**. The directors may institute shark repellents, but they must do so to ensure that bids are high, not to protect their own jobs. A poison pill is acceptable if it gives management enough bargaining power to negotiate a high price for shareholders, but not if it makes a takeover impossible.
- **If it is clear that the company will ultimately be sold, the board must auction the company to the highest bidder; it cannot give preferential treatment to a lower bidder**. The board cannot sell the company to a white knight at a lower

price than someone else has offered, no matter how much management might personally dislike the shark.

In the chapter's opening vignette, Wallace Computer Services fought off a takeover attempt. Read on to find out how.

MOORE CORP. LTD. v. WALLACE COMPUTER SERVICES, INC.
907 F. Supp. 1545, 1995 U.S. Dist. LEXIS 18882
United States District Court for the District of Delaware, 1995

Facts: Under the terms of a poison pill adopted by Wallace Computer Services, Inc., each existing shareholder had the right to purchase Wallace stock at half price, in the event that 20 percent of Wallace's stock was acquired in a hostile takeover. Five years later, Moore Corp. offered to buy all Wallace's stock for $56 a share, which was 27 percent over the current market price. However, the offer was contingent upon the Wallace board eliminating the poison pill.

Wallace consulted with Goldman, Sachs, its investment banker, which advised the company that the offer was inadequate, but did not indicate what the shares were really worth. Moore then raised its offer price to $60 per share, and again the bankers opined that the offer was inadequate. Both the board and Goldman believed that Wallace's recently adopted corporate strategy would lead to an increased stock price. Indeed, the company's recent financial results had been better than expected.

Despite these improved results, more than 73 percent of Wallace shareholders offered their shares to Moore. When Wallace refused to remove the poison pill, Moore filed suit.

Issue: Was the board's refusal to remove the poison pill a violation of the business judgment rule?

Excerpts from Judge Schwartz's Decision: When a board is confronted with a hostile tender offer, it has the obligation to determine whether the offer is in the best interests of the corporation and its shareholders. Collectively, the Board considered Wallace's current business plans and strategies, its financial projections, its current financial results and future projections, and the opinion of Goldman in arriving at its decision that the $56 offer was inadequate. Further, several individual members of the Board took the position that, based on their knowledge and experience, the offer seemed to be a "low ball" offer. The same investigative procedure was followed when Moore raised its offer price to $60. The Wallace Board's decision reflected the belief that the fourth quarter of [the fiscal year] promised to be a good one. That belief became a reality: sales had increased 32% to 33% over the prior year, and profits had increased 32%. These data suggested to the Board that Wallace could achieve returns greater than Moore's offer, while allowing the shareholders to retain their ownership interest. Accordingly, the Court cannot conclude that the Wallace Board lacked good faith or acted unreasonably in its investigation of the Moore offer.

Moore's tender offer poses a threat that shareholders might tender their shares without appreciating the fact that after substantial capital investment, Wallace is actually witnessing the beginning of the pay-off of its business strategy. The Court therefore finds that Moore's tender offer poses a threat to Wallace that shareholders, because they are uninformed, will cash out before realizing the fruits of the substantial technological innovations achieved by Wallace.

[F]ailing to redeem a poison pill can be justified by considerations other than maximizing current share value. In [a prior case], the Supreme Court of Delaware noted, "[A] board of directors, while always required to act in an informed manner, is not under any per se duty to maximize shareholder value in the short term, even in the context of a takeover."

In light of the foregoing, the Court concludes the Wallace Board has demonstrated that its retention of the poison pill falls within the range of reasonableness.

As we saw at the beginning of the chapter, Wallace's favorable financial results turned out to be unsustainable. Neither the board of directors nor the court could see into the future. Did the court make the right decision with the information it had at the time? Does the business judgment rule adequately balance the rights of shareholders against those of company managers?

State Antitakeover Statutes

In fighting takeover battles, companies have also found support in state governments, as the following article demonstrates.

Until this October, the world of corporate raiders and hostile takeovers seemed a million miles from the small Nashua (New Hampshire) factory where Louis C. Chagnon carries on the work of his great-grandfather running a company that builds what many see as the Cadillac of machines that fold and seal cardboard boxes. But all that changed when an unsolicited merger agreement landed on Mr. Chagnon's desk at the International Paper Box Machine Co.

Mr. Chagnon quickly persuaded state officials to grant him a multimillion dollar loan guarantee designed to fend off what he described as a hostile offer that jeopardized the jobs of 150 employees at the 93-year-old, closely held company. State governments have long offered tax breaks and other favors to corporations that threaten to leave or promise to bring new jobs. And several have enacted broad antitakeover legislation to protect local companies. But never, before, experts say, has a state gone so far as to side with management in a corporate battle for control.

New Hampshire's action infuriated dissident shareholders. The dissidents want to sell the company to outsiders, rather than allow Mr. Chagnon to buy them out. The dissidents protest that Chagnon's buyout would leave the company hobbled with debt. For his part, Mr. Chagnon argues that the $8 million offer severely undervalues a company with $20 million in annual sales, even though it only makes a modest profit. "These corporate raiders are interlopers," said a state official who approved the loan to International. "They want to make a quick buck at the expense of 150 people who have good jobs in this community."[9]

As this article indicates, legislators may not care if a group of directors is thrown into the unemployment line, but they do fear the impact on the local economy if a major employer leaves. When the Belzberg family threatened a hostile takeover of auto parts manufacturer Arvin Industries, the Indiana legislature quickly passed a tough antitakeover bill that had been drafted by Arvin's own lawyers. Shortly thereafter, Arvin and the Belzbergs settled. Arvin was not only the second largest employer in Columbus, Indiana, it was an all-purpose fairy godmother. Among its charitable activities, it built two new schools, subsidized the salary of the school superintendent, and opened a summer camp. Columbus residents were delighted that Arvin survived the takeover attempt, but company shareholders might have preferred a bidding war for their stock. After all, shareholders do not necessarily care if the children of Columbus spend their summers at leafy Camp Grenada or sleazy Mall City. Once again, the interests of these two corporate constituencies clash. In the following case, a bidder challenged the constitutionality of the Indiana antitakeover statute.

---

[9] Charles V. Bagli, "A State Steps into a Takeover Battle," *New York Times*, Dec. 13, 1996, p. D2.

CTS CORP. v. DYNAMICS CORPORATION OF AMERICA
481 U.S. 69, 107 S. Ct. 1637, 1987 U.S. LEXIS 1811
United States Supreme Court, 1987

Facts: Dynamics Corporation of America announced a tender offer for the shares of CTS Corp., an Indiana corporation. Under Indiana law, anyone who acquired a controlling interest in the stock of a company could not vote the stock until permitted by the other shareholders of the acquired company. The shareholder vote was not held until the next annual meeting unless the bidder was willing to pay all the expenses of holding a special meeting promptly. Dynamics filed suit alleging that the federal Williams Act preempted the Indiana statute (the Statute), that is, that the Williams Act governed takeovers and thus the conflicting state statute was void.

Issue: **Is the Statute preempted by the Williams Act?**

Excerpts from Justice Powell's Decision: Absent an explicit indication by Congress of an intent to preempt state law, a state statute is preempted only where compliance with both federal and state regulations is a physical impossibility, or where the state law stands as an obstacle to the accomplishment and execution of the full purposes and objectives of Congress. Because it is entirely possible for entities to comply with both the Williams Act and the Statute, the Statute can be preempted only if it frustrates the purposes of the federal law. The Indiana statute must not, for instance, operate to favor management against offerors, to the detriment of shareholders.

Although Dynamics finds evidence of an intent to favor management in several features of the Statute, this Court does not agree. The Statute does impose some added expenses on the offeror, requiring it, inter alia, to pay the costs of special shareholder meetings to vote on the transfer of voting rights. In our view, the expenses of such a meeting fairly are charged to the offeror. A corporation pays the costs of annual meetings that it holds to discuss its affairs. If an offeror—who has no official position with the corporation—desires a special meeting solely to discuss the voting rights of the offeror, it is not unreasonable to have the offeror pay for the meeting.

The Statute operates on the assumption, implicit in the Williams Act, that independent shareholders faced with tender offers often are at a disadvantage. By allowing such shareholders to vote as a group, the Statute protects them from the coercive aspects of some tender offers. Because the Indiana Statute protects the independent shareholder against the contending parties, it furthers a basic purpose of the Williams Act, placing investors on an equal footing with the takeover bidder. Accordingly, we hold that the Williams Act does not preempt the Indiana Act.

Most states have now passed laws to deter hostile takeovers. Among the common varieties are the following:

- **Statutes That Automatically Impede Hostile Takeovers.** These statutes, for instance, might ban hostile mergers for five years after the acquirer buys 10 percent of a company. Or investors who acquire as much as 20 percent of a company lose their voting rights unless the other shareholders move to reinstate them (not likely!). These provisions do not apply to bids that have been approved by the board of directors. In many states, such as Delaware, the board can opt out of the statute altogether.
- **Statutes That Authorize Companies to Fight Off Hostile Takeovers.** These statutes typically permit management, when responding to a hostile takeover, to consider the welfare of company stakeholders, such as the community, customers, suppliers, and employees. Some even go so far as to allow management to consider the regional or national economy. Since takeovers are almost

always harmful to these other constituencies, company management has a ready excuse for fighting the takeover.

Most of these statutes do not totally eliminate hostile takeovers. A determined, well-financed bidder can still be successful. After all, about one-third of hostile bidders win their fight. But these state statutes do tip the playing field in favor of management. In the process, they prevent some takeovers that shareholders might want, but they also ensure that shareholders receive a high price in those takeovers that are successful.

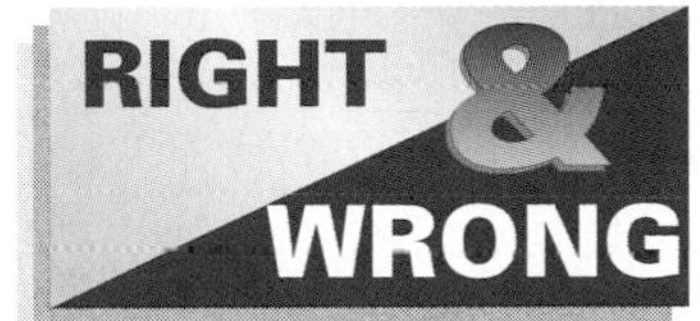

Supporters of these state statutes argue that large, publicly traded corporations owe a duty to all of their constituencies. The loss of a large corporate presence can be immensely disruptive to a community. Perhaps a state should have the right to prevent economic upheaval within its borders.

Opponents contend that shareholders own the company and their interests ought to be paramount. Antitakeover legislation entrenches management and prevents shareholders from obtaining the premium that accompanies a takeover. Opponents also argue that, if other *stake*holders are so concerned with the well-being of the company, let them put their money where their mouths are and buy stock. And if current managers cannot offer shareholders as high a stock price as an outside raider, they ought to be replaced.

Delaware companies can opt out of the antitakeover statute. Is that the ethical choice for directors?

This chapter has presented the arguments for and against hostile takeovers. Both sides would agree, however, that there is nothing like a spate of hostile takeovers to shake up the status quo. At least that seems to be the view of the International Monetary Fund (IMF). For a long time, South Korea seemed poised to become an economic superpower. But the country had always resisted foreign investment. Most of its large enterprises were part of tightly knit family-owned conglomerates called "chaebols." Then financial crisis hit and the country was forced to seek aid from the IMF. The IMF's record $58 billion bailout came with strings attached: South Korea had to allow hostile takeovers by foreign investors. President Kim Dae Jung told the Korean parliament that the country needed foreign capital to pay back its debts and make its economy more competitive. For information on 87 stock exchanges the world over (including South Korea), travel to **http://www.gsionline.com/exchange.htm.**

CHAPTER CONCLUSION

Managers of corporations have a fiduciary duty to shareholders and are charged with running the organization for their benefit. The law, whether federal or state, common or statutory, grants managers great freedom in deciding how to promote the shareholders' interest. Particularly in the takeover arena, lawmakers have given managers considerable leeway in defending their organizations from outside attack.

CHAPTER REVIEW

1. Officers and directors have a fiduciary duty to act in the best interests of the shareholders of the corporation.

2. The business judgment rule protects managers from liability for their decisions as long as the managers observe the duty of care and the duty of loyalty.
3. Under the duty of loyalty, managers may not take advantage of an opportunity that rightfully belongs to the corporation.
4. Managers may not enter into an agreement on behalf of their corporation that benefits them personally, unless the board of directors or the shareholders have first approved it. If the manager does not seek the necessary approval, the business judgment rule no longer applies, and the manager will be liable unless the transaction was fair to the corporation.
5. Under the duty of care, managers must make honest, informed decisions that have a rational business purpose.
6. The Williams Act regulates the activities of a bidder in a tender offer for stock in a publicly traded corporation.
7. Under common law, shareholder welfare must be the board's primary concern when establishing takeover defenses. If it is clear that the company will ultimately be sold, the board must auction the company to the highest bidder; it cannot give preferential treatment to a lower bidder.
8. Many states have passed antitakeover statutes that render hostile takeovers more difficult for the bidder.

PRACTICE TEST

1. **RIGHT & WRONG** Ronald O. Perelman, chairman of the board and CEO of Pantry Pride, met with his counterpart at Revlon, Michel C. Bergerac, to discuss a friendly acquisition of Revlon by Pantry Pride. Revlon rebuffed Pantry Pride's overtures, perhaps in part because Bergerac did not like Perelman. The Revlon board of directors agreed to sell the company to Forstmann Little & Co. at a price of $56 per share. Pantry Pride announced that it would engage in fractional bidding to top any Forstmann offer by a slightly higher one. To discourage Pantry Pride, the Revlon board granted Forstmann the right to purchase Revlon's Vision Care and National Health Laboratories divisions at a price some $100–$175 million below their value. Was the board within its rights in selling off these two divisions? Do the shareholders of Revlon have the right to prevent a sale of the company to Forstmann at a price lower than Pantry Pride offered? Is it ethical for a board to base a takeover decision on personal animosity? What are a board's ethical obligations to shareholders?

2. **YOU BE THE JUDGE WRITING PROBLEM** Asher Hyman and Stephen Stahl formed a corporation named "Ampersand" to produce plays. Both men were employed by the corporation. After producing one play, Stahl decided to write *Philly's Beat*, focusing on the history of rock and roll in Philadelphia. As the play went into production, however, the two men quarreled over Hyman's repeated absences from work and the company's serious financial difficulties. Stahl resigned from Ampersand and formed another corporation to produce the play. Did the opportunity to produce *Philly's Beat* belong to Ampersand? **Argument for Stahl:** Ampersand was formed for the purpose of producing plays, not writing them. When Stahl wrote *Philly's Beat*, he was not competing against Ampersand. Furthermore, Ampersand could not afford to produce the play even if it had had the opportunity. **Argument for Hyman:** Ampersand was in the business of producing plays, and it wanted *Philly's Beat*. Ampersand was perfectly able to afford the cost of production—until Stahl resigned.

3. Some companies adopt a staggered board of directors as an antitakeover defense. How does a staggered board affect cumulative voting?

4. Vern Hayes owned 32 percent of Coast Oyster Co. and served as president and director. The company owned several large oyster beds, including two located in Washington State. Coast was struggling to pay its debts, so Hayes suggested that the company sell the Washington beds to Keypoint Co. After the

sale, other officers at Coast discovered that Hayes owned 50 percent of Keypoint. They demanded that he give the Keypoint stock to Coast. Did Hayes violate his duty to Coast?

5. An appraiser valued a subsidiary of Signal Co. at between $230 million and $260 million. Six months later, Burmah Oil offered to buy the subsidiary at $480 million, giving Signal only three days to respond. The board of directors accepted the offer, without obtaining an updated evaluation of the subsidiary or determining if other companies would offer a higher price. Members of the board were sophisticated, with a great deal of experience in the oil industry. A Signal Co. shareholder sued to prevent the sale. Is the Signal board protected by the business judgment rule?

6. Employees of Exxon Corp. paid some $59 million in corporate funds as bribes or political payments to Italian political parties to secure special political favors and other illegal commitments. Several Exxon directors were aware of these illegal payments. The board of directors decided not to sue the employees and directors who had committed the illegal acts. Was this decision protected by the business judgment rule?

7. Four employees of Allis-Chalmers Manufacturing Co. were indicted for violations of U.S. antitrust laws. The directors had no knowledge of the violations until the indictments were announced. Plaintiffs alleged that the directors had violated their duty of care by not establishing an antitrust prevention program at the company. Are these directors protected by the business judgment rule?

8. The board of Harmony, Inc. is concerned that the company may be the target of a hostile takeover. It has decided to adopt antitakeover devices. Which one of the following statements is **not** true?

(a) Harmony may divest one of its divisions, as long as it does so at fair market value.

(b) Harmony may adopt a poison pill, as long as the purpose is to give management enough bargaining power to negotiate a high price for shareholders.

(c) If it becomes clear that Harmony is going to be sold, the directors have an obligation to auction the company off to the highest bidder, no matter how loathsome the directors find the bidder to be.

(d) If Harmony offers to buy back any of its stock, it must treat its shareholders equally.

9. **CPA QUESTION** Davis, a director of Active Corp., is entitled to:

(a) Serve on the board of a competing business

(b) Take sole advantage of a business opportunity that would benefit Active

(c) Rely on information provided by a corporate officer

(d) Unilaterally grant a corporate loan to one of Active's shareholders

10. Klinicki and Lundgren started an air taxi service in Berlin, Germany, under the name Berlinair, Inc. Lundgren was approached by a group of travel agents who were interested in hiring an air charter business to take German tourists on vacation to warmer climes. Lundgren formed Air Berlin Charter Co. (ABC) and was its sole owner. On behalf of ABC, he entered into an air charter contract with the Berlin travel agents. Lundgren concealed his negotiations from Klinicki, even though he used Berlinair working time, staff, money, and facilities. Lundgren defended his behavior on the grounds that Berlinair could not afford to enter into a contract with the travel agents. Has Lundgren violated the corporate opportunity doctrine?

11. Both Viacom and Paramount owned a diverse group of entertainment businesses. QVC was a televised shopping channel. The Paramount board of directors accepted a merger offer from Viacom at a price of $69 per share. QVC and Viacom then entered a bidding war for Paramount. QVC ultimately made the highest offer at $90 per share. The Paramount board rejected QVC's bid on the grounds that a Viacom merger would be more in keeping with Paramount's business strategy. Does a board of directors have the right to reject a high bidder on the belief that the low bidder would be better for the company?

INTERNET RESEARCH PROBLEM

Look at http://www.ljx.com/practice/corporate/ to find an interesting article on the relationship between corporate managers and shareholders. In particular, can you find an article about takeovers? Are there any recent developments in takeover law?

You can find further practice problems in the Online Quiz at http://beatty.westbuslaw.com or in the Study Guide that accompanies this text.

CHAPTER 37

SHAREHOLDERS

Morrison Knudsen Corp. is a construction company famous for having built such landmarks as the Hoover Dam, the San Francisco Bay Bridge, and the U.S. Embassy in Saigon. But when William Agee returned to his hometown of Boise, Idaho, to run the company, trouble began almost at once. He committed the company to a series of high-profile projects that resulted in losses of more than $300 million. Senior executives resigned or were fired; during Agee's tenure, the company averaged both a new chief financial officer and a new president every 18 months. Morale sank amidst allegations that Agee had ordered employees' telephones tapped. Even as the company struggled, Agee's compensation more than doubled in five years, from just under $900,000 to more than $2.4 million. Unpopular in Boise, Agee moved to an estate in Pebble Beach, California, forcing company executives to travel regularly from Idaho. Employees were ordered to perform personal chores for Agee: once the bid on an important project had to wait until the graphics department finished making life-sized unicorns for an Agee family birthday party. A corporate jet, free legal services when he changed his middle name (from Reynolds to Joseph)—what Agee wanted, he got from Morrison Knudsen.

The party finally ended when the company suffered a $350 million loss. With banks refusing to renew loans unless Agee left, the board had little choice but to ask for his resignation and file for bankruptcy protection.

INTRODUCTION

Corporate shareholders own $13 trillion in assets worldwide. At one time, corporate stock was primarily owned by individuals, but now institutional investors—pension plans, mutual funds, insurance companies, banks, foundations, and university endowments—own more than 50 percent of all shares publicly traded in the United States.[1]

Shareholders may technically own the companies in which they invest, but their power over these enterprises is very limited. As Chapter 36 revealed, ***directors, not shareholders,* have the right to manage the corporate business.** However, not all directors are created equal. **Inside directors**, who are also officers in the corporation, have typically controlled their company's board. **Outside directors** (also called **independent directors**) do not work for the company and have traditionally played a lesser role.[2] They have been described derisively as "ornaments on a corporate Christmas tree" or "parsley on the fish." Nominated by their friend, the chief executive (CEO), and elected by shareholders without question, these directors could collect handsome paychecks while simply rubber-stamping the CEO's decisions. Without a watchdog board, CEOs have great latitude in running their companies. As the Morrison Knudsen episode illustrates, they sometimes abuse this power. The results are predictable: studies show that a weak board means higher pay for the boss and lower stock prices for the shareholders. But investors are no longer content to be ignored; they are now demanding that boards remember who the real owners are.

So what can shareholders do to protect their investment? Institutional investors, with enormous sums to invest, have little choice but to buy the stock of large companies. If they are unhappy with management, it is difficult for them to do the "Wall Street walk"—that is, sell their shares—because a sale of their stock would depress the market price. And where would they invest the proceeds? Institutional investors cannot all profit simply by trading shares among themselves. For better or worse, the fate of fund managers hangs on the success of these large companies.

Shareholders have discovered that one of their most effective weapons is "management by embarrassment." Simply publicizing management abuses often shames companies into making changes. The California Public Employees Retirement System (CalPERS) is famous (or notorious, depending on your perspective) for using its clout to change management policies. Each year, it reviews its portfolio to identify the 10 worst performers. It then meets with the management of these companies to suggest changes. Companies fear that, if they do not

---

[1] Shareholders play a very different role in privately held companies than in publicly traded corporations. Not only do privately held corporations have fewer shareholders, but these owners take a more active role in management, often serving as a director, officer, or employee. A public corporation is one that (1) has completed a public offering under the Securities Act of 1933, or (2) has securities traded on a national exchange, or (3) has at least 500 shareholders and total assets that exceed $10 million. For a discussion of public corporations, see Chapter 38, on securities law.

[2] Although the terms *outside* and *independent* are often used interchangeably, an outside director is not *always* independent. In the *Disney* case later in the chapter, for example, shareholders alleged that outside directors were not independent because they were under Michael Eisner's influence.

toe the CalPERS line, this major shareholder will lead a noisy, public campaign for change. On average, firm performance improves after intervention by CalPERS.

Similarly, investors have worked hard to establish accepted guidelines for corporate governance. For example, a blue ribbon commission of the National Association of Corporate Directors published guidelines for boards of directors. The commission's most important recommendations were that:

- Independent directors should fill a majority of board seats. They should also meet regularly on their own without the inside directors.
- Key board committees (such as the compensation committee) should consist solely of independent directors.
- Directors should own substantial stock in the company.
- The board should regularly evaluate and review the CEO.

Corporate governance is of such interest to investors that many Web sites contain discussions of these issues. Take a look, for example, at http://www.ljx.com/practice/corporate/. As the following article illustrates, even shareholders of the Magic Kingdom have rebelled.

Michael Eisner's ears are ringing these days with other people's theories about management and corporate governance. The chairman and chief executive of Walt Disney Co. isn't impressed. "I don't know whether pension funds and law professors really know how these companies are run," he says. "I didn't go to business school, so I didn't have the benefit of two years of intensive training in this area," he adds facetiously. "But what I read about what is expected I find quite counterintuitive—for me and for this company."

Mr. Eisner's intuition has consistently won big returns for investors during his 12½ years at the helm. But his way of doing things is getting him something much less appealing: shareholder pressure to reform a handpicked board that some corporate-governance experts say isn't independent enough. Disney counts 12 of its 16 directors as independent, but most of them have some close personal or professional ties to Mr. Eisner or the company. They include his personal lawyer, his children's former elementary school principal, an architect who has done work for Disney, and three former Disney executives.

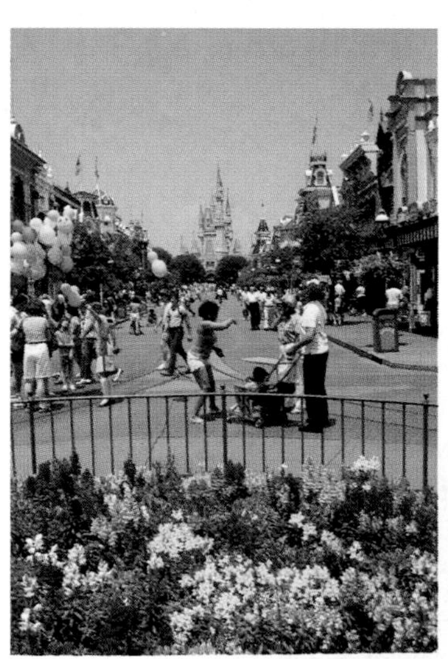
Even in the Magic Kingdom, shareholders have revolted.

Some shareholders are also upset about two cases of executive pay: the contract the board recently gave Mr. Eisner to stay another 10 years that included eight million stock options, and a multimillion dollar payout the board made to terminate Michael Ovitz's failed 14-month stint as company president. Executive Compensation Reports, a newsletter, estimates that Mr. Eisner's package is the largest options grant ever to a sitting chief executive.

While a number of major corporations have felt heat from shareholder activists in recent years, Disney has until now been protected from such critics by its strong returns. As Mr. Eisner likes to point out, Disney's market capitalization has soared to $53 billion from $2 billion under his leadership. Critics acknowledge Disney's impressive track record, but counter that the company's snowballing success has left it dangerously dependent on just one man who, despite a talented team of division heads, has a propensity to micromanage, a history of heart trouble, and no heir apparent. The current flare-up raises a key question: Is success a substitute for strong corporate-governance standards that check a company's management in good times as well as bad?[3]

---

[3] Bruce Orwall and Joann S. Lublin, "The Plutocracy: If a Company Prospers, Should Its Directors Behave by the Book?" *Wall Street Journal*, Feb. 2, 1997, p. 1. Republished with permission of The Wall Street Journal; permission conveyed through the Copyright Clearance Center, Inc.

What control do shareholders have over Michael Eisner at Disney or William Agee at Morrison Knudsen? The first section of this chapter explores the rights of shareholders. The second section looks at how shareholders enforce these rights.

RIGHTS OF SHAREHOLDERS

If you own a car, you expect to be able to drive it whenever you want. If you own it with four of your friends, you may not be able to use it every Saturday night, but you will get to drive it *sometimes*, even if only on Sunday mornings. Of course, you will also be responsible for changing the oil sometimes, too. Owning stock in a corporation is different. As an owner, you have no right to use any *specific* asset of the corporation. If you own stock in Starbucks Corp., your share of stock plus $1.50 entitles you to a cup of coffee, the same as everyone else. By the same token, if the pipes freeze and the local Starbucks store floods, the manager has no right to call you, as a shareholder, to help clean up the mess. **As a shareholder you have neither the *right* nor the *obligation* to manage the day-to-day business of the enterprise.** What rights do you have?

RIGHT TO INFORMATION

A company's obligation to provide shareholders with financial information depends on whether it is publicly or privately held. States, which regulate private corporations, generally do not require automatic disclosure of financial information to shareholders. Although the Revised Model Business Corporation Act (Model Act) does require some disclosure, most states do not follow its recommendation. In contrast, the Securities and Exchange Commission (SEC) carefully regulates publicly held corporations and requires them to provide shareholders with extensive financial data.

Even if a corporation is not required to volunteer information, shareholders have the right to obtain certain data upon request. **Under the Model Act, shareholders with a proper purpose have the right to inspect and copy the corporation's minute book, accounting records, and shareholder lists.** A **proper purpose** is one that aids the shareholder in managing and protecting her investment. If Celeste receives an offer to sell her shares in a bakery, Devil Desserts, Inc., she may want to look carefully at the company's accounting records to determine the value of her stock. Or, if she is convinced the directors are mismanaging the company, she might demand a list of shareholders so that she can ask them to join her in a lawsuit. The company may not *like* this purpose, but it is *proper* and the company is required to give her the list. If, however, Celeste wants to use the shareholder list as a potential source for her new mail-order catalogue featuring exercise equipment, the company could legitimately turn her down.

In the following case, an employee, who also happened to be a shareholder, was fired from his company for sexual harassment. He asked for information that would support a lawsuit against the company. Did he have a proper purpose?

BERGMANN v. LEE DATA CORP.
467 N.W.2d 636, 1991 Minn. App. LEXIS 302
Court of Appeals of Minnesota, 1991

Facts: Daryl J. Bergmann was both an employee and a shareholder of Lee Data Corp. After being fired for sexual harassment, he filed suit against the company. In his role as company shareholder, Bergmann requested a list of directors and shareholders, information regarding sexual harassment and discrimination complaints against Lee, the number of female and minority employees, and records relating to remedial actions taken to eliminate discrimination and sexual harassment. The stated purpose for the request was to identify and evaluate misconduct by Lee's officers. Lee sent Bergmann some of the items he requested, such as the list of directors and shareholders, but refused to provide the other material. Bergmann then sought an injunction to force the company to comply. The trial court denied Bergmann's request.

Issue: Did Bergmann have a proper purpose for requesting these records?

Excerpts from Judge Huspeni's Decision: A "proper purpose" is one reasonably related to the person's interest as a shareholder. Examples of a "proper purpose" are: valuation of shares; determination of management competence; and communication with other shareholders for a number of purposes. A shareholder who has gained access to any corporate record including the share register may not use or furnish to another for use the corporate record or a portion of the contents for any purpose other than a proper purpose.

This court is mindful that hostility between the parties, a threatened lawsuit, or an attempt to gain control of a corporation are not sufficient in and of themselves to prevent the showing of a "proper purpose." Nonetheless, the interests Bergmann is pursuing are not those created by reason of his being a shareholder of the company. Given the context in which the injunction is sought, Bergmann's requests serve no useful purpose other than the personal interests of Bergmann. In this case, Bergmann's assertion that he sought inspection to investigate alleged officer misconduct and to communicate with stockholders created a prima facie showing of proper purpose, but was rebutted by Lee's evidence that the actual purpose was to improve Bergmann's position in the pending suit against Lee. Specifically, Lee noted that Bergmann sought documents concerning sexual harassment and discrimination, including those concerning Bergmann's termination from employment. This purely personal purpose is improper as not reasonably related to Bergmann's interest as a shareholder.

The decision of the trial court is *affirmed*.

RIGHT TO VOTE

A corporation must have at least one class of stock with voting rights. Typically, common shareholders have the right to vote and preferred shareholders do not, but there are many exceptions to this rule.

Proxies

Under common law, shareholders could not cast a vote unless they attended the shareholders' meeting. Such a rule in a publicly traded corporation would effectively disfranchise many shareholders who have neither the time nor the interest to travel around the country attending meetings. Modern statutory law permits shareholders to appoint someone else to vote for them. Confusingly, both this person and the document the shareholder signs to appoint the substitute voter are called a **proxy**.

Under the Model Act, a proxy is valid for only 11 months, unless the form provides for a longer period. For public corporations, however, SEC rules specify that a proxy is valid only for the next meeting. After that, it automatically expires. Under both state and federal law, the shareholder can revoke a proxy at any time, unless the proxy is **coupled with an interest**, which means that (1) the designated voter has paid for the proxy, by, for example, buying the shareholder's stock or loaning him money, with the stock as security; or (2) the shareholder has signed a voting agreement or trust that specifies how she will vote her stock (voting agreements are discussed in Chapter 35).

Under SEC rules, companies are not required to solicit proxies. However, a meeting is invalid unless a certain percentage of shareholders attend, either in person or by proxy. This attendance requirement is referred to as a **quorum**. As a practical matter, if a public company with thousands of investors does not solicit proxies, it will not obtain a quorum. Therefore, virtually all public companies do solicit proxies. Along with the proxy, the company must also give shareholders a **proxy statement** and an **annual report**. The proxy statement provides information on everything from management compensation to a list of directors who miss too many meetings. The annual report contains detailed financial data.

Even if a company decides not to solicit proxies for a shareholder meeting, it cannot avoid its obligation to communicate with its shareholders. The SEC requires public companies, whether or not they solicit proxies, to give shareholders all the information required in a proxy statement and an annual report.

Under SEC rules, companies can offer (but not require) electronic delivery of proxy statements and annual reports. Intel Corp. was one of the first companies to make its proxy statements and annual reports available on a Web site. The company first sent investors a request for consent to receive the documents electronically. About 10 percent of shareholders returned the consent. The company then sent them notice of the Web site address. Proxy cards (for voting) could not be downloaded, however; each shareholder was sent a hard copy. Read about Intel's policies on corporate governance at **http://www.intc.com/intel/finance/corp_gov.htm**.

Typically, only the company itself solicits proxies for a shareholder meeting, but sometimes shareholders who disapprove of company policies try to convince other shareholders to appoint them as proxy instead of management. These dissident shareholders must also prepare a proxy statement that discloses, among other information, who they are, how they are financing their opposition, and how many other proxy contests they have participated in. If enough shareholders give their proxies to the dissidents, then the dissidents can elect themselves or their representatives to replace the board of directors.

Recently, groups of dissident shareholders have begun to use the Internet to coordinate their efforts and maximize their impact. They post proxy materials, press releases, and letters on a Web site and then take out ads in newspapers to publicize the address. Sometimes, investors have used Web sites to encourage opposition to management initiatives without having to incur the expense of soliciting proxies.

The first proxy contest was held in 1915, when the shareholders of General Motors removed the founder from office (although they later voted him back in). It was not until 1998, however, that an institutional investor actually dismissed an entire board from office. TIAA-CREF, one of the nation's largest pension and insurance funds, led a proxy contest to replace the directors of Furr's/Bishop's, Inc. TIAA-CREF was spurred to action when the price of the cafeteria company plummeted from $33.75 to $1.25. Circumstances were particularly favorable for a shareholder revolt—not only had Furr's stock price fallen precipitously, but eight investors owned 84 percent of the stock. TIAA-CREF could stage the coup with a few phone calls and without the expense or effort of having to persuade thousands of shareholders. Nonetheless, this victory has been referred to, dramatically if not originally, as "the shot heard round the world."

Shareholder Proposals

Some shareholders who oppose a company policy may not aspire to a board seat or perhaps cannot afford to send material individually to other investors. Such shareholders may use an alternative method, provided by the SEC, for communicating with fellow shareholders. **Under SEC rules, any shareholder who owns at least 1 percent of the company or $2,000 of stock can require that one proposal be placed in the company's proxy statement to be voted on at the shareholder meeting.** In practice, many of these resolutions have a political agenda: save the environment, withdraw from Myanmar, protect gay and lesbian workers. Others relate to corporate-governance issues: eliminate pensions for directors, permit secret ballots, adopt cumulative voting. Each year, public companies vote on about 450 shareholder proposals. Prior to 1985, only *two* proposals had been approved—ever. Currently, about 10 to 20 receive a majority vote each year, a definite improvement (or deterioration, depending on your perspective).

Shareholder resolutions have had a larger impact than their success rate would indicate. The mere threat of a shareholder proposal sometimes causes directors to act. Even if a proposal fails, the target company may quietly implement it afterwards, especially if it received a substantial vote in favor. The pressure of shareholder proposals is credited with inducing many American companies to withdraw from South Africa in protest against its apartheid regime. That these resolutions did not receive a majority vote was almost irrelevant.

As the following article illustrates, companies generally view shareholder proposals as a nuisance.

At the General Electric shareholder meeting last month, there were several items of business likely to irritate even the most mild-mannered CEO. First, there was a proposal to limit GE's spending on political contributions, which the resolution's sponsor labeled "nothing more than a thinly disguised bribe." Then there was a proposal to cap the chief executive officer's salary, linking it to the pay of the lowliest janitor in the company. And finally there was Sister Patricia Daly.

Sister Pat stood up to advocate a shareholder resolution on GE's pollution of the Hudson River. She called on the company to publicize the danger of eating fish from the river and to stop fostering misleading studies. And she compared the company's claims that PCBs are harmless with claims made by tobacco industry executives about the harmlessness of smoking.

That is when John F. Welch, Jr., GE's chairman and chief executive, blew up. "That's an outrageous comparison," he shouted at the nun. "You owe it to God to be on the side of truth." As Sister Pat, a Dominican nun from Newton, New Jersey, recalled afterwards, "He totally lost it."

In the end, the resolution was backed by 7.6 percent of the shares voted at the meeting, a figure GE characterized as a resounding defeat but which was sufficient to get it on the proxy ballot again next year. Although Sister Pat's resolution failed, it clearly rattled the company.[4]

In the past, companies generally opposed shareholder resolutions and battled to keep them out of proxy materials. Now, however, companies often feel they have little choice but to negotiate, particularly when institutional investors raise issues of corporate governance. Nearly half of all shareholder proposals are now withdrawn before a vote because the company capitulates. For instance, institutional investors asked Colgate-Palmolive Co. to permit secret ballots at share-

---

[4] Elizabeth Kolbert, "It's the Nun Vs. the C.E.O," *New York Times,* May 25, 1998, p. B1.

holder meetings. This issue is a favorite of activists, who fear that without secret ballots a company may pressure shareholders to toe the party line. Colgate-Palmolive agreed to the proposal without ever submitting it to a shareholder vote. TIAA-CREF, the large pension and insurance company, typically reaches private agreements with three-quarters of the companies it approaches. The Walt Disney Co., however, is not among the accommodating. As we saw earlier in this chapter, chief executive Michael Eisner refused shareholder requests for a more independent board. When put to a vote, the proposal received 35 percent of the votes.

If a company refuses to include a shareholder proposal in its proxy material, shareholders can appeal to the SEC. These are the major SEC regulations on shareholder resolutions:

- *The proposals are generally not binding on the company.* The SEC recommends that proposals be in the form of a request or recommendation because state laws sometimes prohibit resolutions that are binding on the company. A winning shareholder vote is, at least from a legal perspective, often largely a moral victory, although the directors will certainly feel pressure to follow such a recommendation.
- *If dissident shareholders are running for director, they must prepare their own proxy statement; they cannot piggyback on the company's.* If shareholders could run for director simply by placing their name in the proxy statement, the result might be hundreds of candidates and thousands of confused shareholders.
- *The proposal cannot relate to the ordinary business operations of the corporation.* Shareholders of Excalibur Technologies, Inc. proposed that the company post its SEC filings on the company Web site. You might think that a "Technologies" company would willingly agree. You might also think that the SEC would favor the widest possible disclosure. You would be wrong. The SEC ruled the proposal out of bounds because it related to ordinary business operations.
- *The proposal must relate to operations accounting for at least 5 percent of total assets, gross sales, or net earnings.* AT&T refused to include in its proxy statement an anti-Israel proposal from a white supremacy group on the grounds that the company's business with Israel accounted for less than 1 percent of sales.
- *The proposal cannot interfere with the company's proxy solicitation.* Management can exclude more than one proposal on the same topic and proposals that were voted down decisively in the past.
- *The proposal cannot require the company to violate a federal or state law.* Bell & Howell excluded a shareholder proposal that called for the company to hire qualified women because the proposal might require the company to violate federal and state antidiscrimination laws.
- *The shareholder cannot use a proposal to seek satisfaction of a personal grievance against the company.* In the *Lee* case above, the company excluded a proposal requested by an employee/shareholder who had been fired for sexual harassment.

If you would like to sponsor your own shareholder proposal, **http://www.iraa.com** offers step-by-step instructions.

Let there be no doubt, the American brand of shareholder activism is spreading abroad. In the past, European companies could largely ignore shareholder views, but now they are forced to pay more attention if they wish to attract capital in an increasingly global market.

In Germany, shareholder activists have fought bitterly against companies, such as Borg-Warner, that have engaged in a series of takeovers. The shareholders of the target companies claim that Borg-Warner has undervalued their shares. In Italy, investors are suing over the recent government bailout of Banco di Napoli, which wiped out the ownership of minority investors. In Switzerland, the maverick investor Martin Egner harasses corporations and banks to provide greater shareholder value.

Some of the most bitter battles have been fought in France, where government traditions and corporate cronyism create a particularly tangled web. When a French utilities conglomerate proposed taking over the country's largest media group, it did not reckon with Colette Neuville. Mrs. Neuville, a soft-spoken woman in her 60s, filed a suit contending that shareholders in the target company were getting a raw deal. As a result, the conglomerate sweetened its bid by $10 a share.[5]

Shareholder Meetings

A company must hold an **annual meeting** of shareholders, if for no other reason than to elect directors. Under the Model Act, the board of directors and shareholders owning at least 10 percent of the company's stock each have the right to call a **special meeting** to vote on an emergency issue that cannot wait until the next annual meeting—for example, to conclude a merger or sell off substantial assets. Everyone who owns stock on the **record date** must be sent notice of a meeting, whether it is an annual or special meeting. The record date can be any day that is no more than 70 days before the meeting. The votes taken at a shareholder meeting are not valid unless a **quorum** is present, meaning that shareholders representing a certain percentage of the shares entitled to vote either attend or send in their proxy cards.

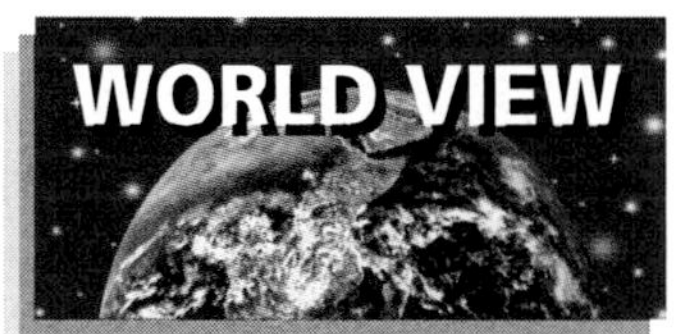

Managers the world over have at least one attribute in common: they like their annual meetings short and sweet. And generally they used to get exactly that. In the United States, often the larger the company, the fewer the shareholders in attendance. Annual meetings were dull affairs, with droning presentations by management. Japanese companies went even further, stacking their meetings with employees who regularly broke into enthusiastic applause. The typical annual meeting in Japan lasted barely half an hour.

But with the rise of shareholder activism in both countries, annual meetings have become more contentious. To reduce attendance, some U.S. companies have relocated their meetings. Florida Progress, a utility with many elderly investors who lived in Florida, moved its annual meeting to Texas. Only 25 shareholders attended, down from the usual 300. Faced with financial difficulties, Morrison Knudsen decided to hold its annual meeting in Boston, far from its headquarters in Boise, Idaho.

Japanese companies worry not only about dissident shareholders, but also about **sokaiya**—gangsters who threaten to disrupt an annual meeting unless the company buys peace. To solve these twin problems, 95 percent of the companies traded on the Tokyo Stock Exchange now hold their annual meetings on the same day. This solution not only spreads both shareholders and gangsters thin, but also limits press coverage.

Perhaps Bell & Howell has the most effective solution. It was the first American company to supplement its traditional annual meeting with a "cyber-

[5] John Tagliabue, "Compliments of U.S. Investors: New Activism Shakes Europe's Markets," *New York Times*, Apr. 25, 1998, p. D1. Copyright © 1998 by The New York Times Co. Reprinted by permission.

cast" online. Internet attendees could ask questions via e-mail. Questions lose some of their sting when zapped via e-mail.

Election and Removal of Directors

Shareholders have the right to elect directors and also to remove them from office. Under the Model Act, shareholders can remove directors at any time for any reason. As the following article illustrates, however, boards sometimes wish they had the power to remove directors.

It has been more than seven weeks since Albert J. "Chain-Saw Al" Dunlap was summarily tossed out as chairman and chief executive of Sunbeam Corp. by his board of directors. But that indignity hasn't stopped the tenacious Mr. Dunlap from faithfully attending board meetings for the Delray Beach, Florida consumer-products concern. The reason: until last night, Mr. Dunlap, who was blamed for failing to deliver the turnaround he promised, was still a member of Sunbeam's board. Now a spokesman for Mr. Dunlap says he has cut a deal to leave his director's chair.

Since Sunbeam's charter, common for Delaware corporations, calls for shareholders to remove directors, Sunbeam would need to accept Mr. Dunlap's plan or hold a special shareholder meeting, wait until the annual meeting expected next spring, or solicit written consents from holders in lieu of a meeting. Did Mr. Dunlap's presence make the board feel awkward? "I can't comment," says another board member.[6]

In theory, shareholders elect directors and directors then appoint officers. Typically, however, the *real* relationship between directors and shareholders in public companies is very different from this formula. Yes, shareholders elect the directors, but the shareholders almost always vote for nominees chosen by the board itself. The CEO is often the chairman of the board and may even serve on the committee that nominates new directors. Whether the CEO is a member or not, nominating committees rarely choose candidates that the CEO opposes. The *officers* are really choosing the *directors*, not the other way around.

William Agee handpicked 9 of the 10 Morrison Knudsen board members, most of whom were personal friends. Moreover, the wives of many of the directors served on the board of a charity that Mrs. Agee ran. Although some of Agee's selections, such as superinvestor Peter Lynch and former baseball commissioner Peter Ueberroth, looked great on paper, perhaps their judgment was clouded by their friendship with him.

Shareholders have begun to complain about such cozy arrangements. The blue ribbon commission of the National Association of Corporate Directors recommended that companies bar employees from serving on the committee that nominates new directors. A substantial number of public companies have followed this advice.

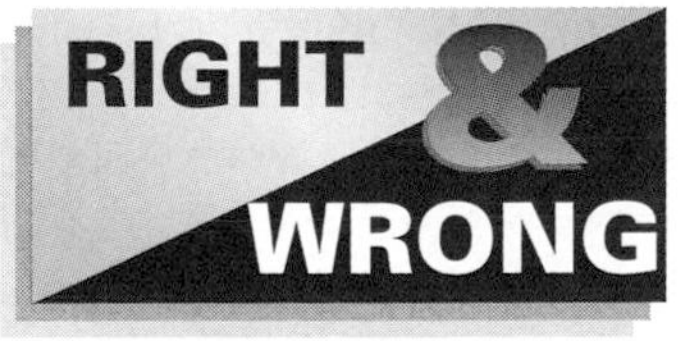

Is it a good idea for CEOs to be involved in selecting directors? What characteristics should a nominating committee look for in potential candidates? Should companies allow shareholders to have input into the selection process? How might such a system work?

---

[6] Martha Brannigan, "If 'Chain-Saw Al' Is Listening In, Can't Sunbeam's Board Hang Up?" *Wall Street Journal*, Oct. 5, 1998, p. B1. Republished with permission of The Wall Street Journal; permission conveyed through the Copyright Clearance Center, Inc.

Compensation for Officers and Directors

For many children, *Pat the Bunny* is their first book. It contains few words but much interaction. "Readers" can pat the bunny, sniff the flowers, and play peekaboo with the blanket. After *Pat the Bunny*, many children graduate to *The Poky Little Puppy*, *Richard Scarry's Busy, Busy Town*, and *Disney's Mulan*, all published by Golden Books Family Entertainment, Inc.

Despite its portfolio of classics, Golden Books was having financial difficulties. The company hired Richard Snyder, an experienced publishing executive, to solve its distribution and sales problems. Such experience does not come cheap. At Golden Books, he was the third highest paid executive in the publishing industry. But an executive does not live by pay alone. Snyder relocated the company to posh new quarters, hired a private chef, and used the corporate jet for vacations. He also hired other executives (including his wife) at salaries two to three times the industry average. In return, investors expected the stock price to zoom. They just did not expect it to zoom *down*. Not only did the stock price plummet 80 percent, but the company was put up for sale. In the midst of this turmoil, the board doubled Snyder's salary and paid him a $500,000 signing bonus for extending his contract two years.

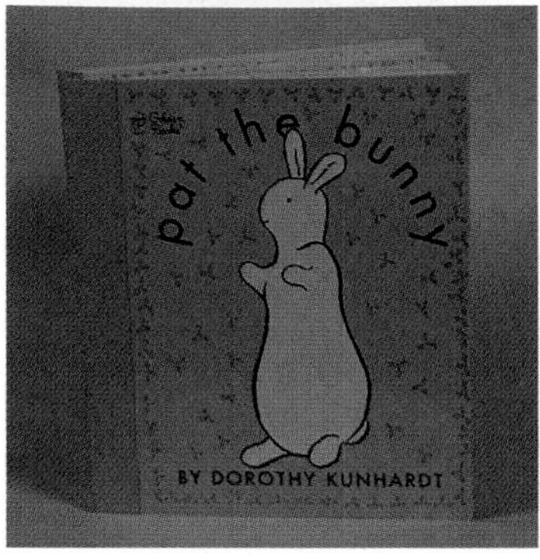

While readers patted the bunny, Golden Books padded its executive payroll.

To many investors, sky-high executive salaries have become the symbol of all that is wrong with corporate governance. And in many companies, salaries are the least of the compensation. Executives also receive lavish perks, retirement plans, and stock options. Executives have long received such perks as country club memberships, cars, and use of company aircraft, but signing bonuses and new houses have now become common. And stock options have soared to unimagined heights.[7] Software giant Borland International offered a new hire a $3.86 million signing bonus, $3.85 million toward the purchase of a new house, and $9.6 million in stock options. But that was peanuts compared with the oats that Quaker Oats gave its new executive. Robert Morrison earned $200,000 at his former job, but to lure him away, Quaker offered him a $3.2 million signing bonus and $82 million in stock options. As we saw with Golden Books, even failure is well rewarded. When AT&T fired John Walter after less than one year, the board of directors offered him $26 million in severance pay. No wonder that executive compensation has become the hottest topic for shareholder proposals. And no surprise that, so far, these shareholder efforts have had little impact.

Why has executive pay become so lavish?

- *Directors, not shareholders, set executive compensation.* Unless directors are major shareholders of the company (which is seldom the case), generous executive compensation has little impact on directors' income. It is easy to be generous with other people's money

- *The busier the directors, the higher the executive pay.* Generally, executives are more likely to be overpaid if directors serve on many boards. These directors may be too busy to pay attention to such details. Such trophy directors may also be afraid that if they offend a chief executive at one company, word will get around, jeopardizing their position on other boards. For example, when Joseph

[7] A stock option gives the holder the right to buy shares at a certain price, called the *exercise price*. Usually, the exercise price equals the market price at the time the option is granted. Sometimes, however, the exercise price is lower than market price, guaranteeing an immediate profit because the holder can exercise the option at the low price and then sell the stock at the higher market value. Other times the exercise price is higher than market value as an incentive to the executive to create profits that will push the market price up.

A. Califano, Jr. was Secretary of Health, Education and Welfare, he was responsible for the welfare of the nation's poor. Now, as director of nine companies, he affects the welfare of the wealthy. According to compensation expert Graef Crystal, the executives at Califano's companies are overpaid by 281 percent. Because of examples such as this, the blue ribbon commission of the National Association of Corporate Directors recommended that directors serve on no more than three or four boards.

- *Most executives are above average.* Of course, not everyone can be above average, but most directors believe that their executives are. No one wants to admit to hiring incompetents. Suppose that you are on a company's compensation committee and have data about industry averages. If your executives are above average, you should pay them above-average salaries. If they are not above average, you should fire them, which few boards want to do, except in the face of disaster. If you raise salaries, the industry average also rises. The next company that sets compensation has an even higher bar to jump. For example, Colgate-Palmolive awarded two million stock options to its CEO on the understanding that he would receive no further grants for five years. Three years later, however, when consultants found that the CEO's compensation had fallen below the median, the company immediately awarded him an additional 2.6 million options.

- *Pay-for-performance plans have backfired.* Concerned about escalating executive salaries, shareholder activists began advocating "pay-for-performance" plans. The theory is that, if executives receive stock options instead of cash salaries, their incentives will be more closely aligned with those of shareholders. It is a good theory, but in practice, it has tended to become a "heads I win, tails you lose" game. When stock prices soared in a bull market, options became unexpectedly valuable. In some cases, managers were richly rewarded even when their company had underperformed the (rising) market. Boards of directors did not counteract this unexpected windfall by *raising* the price of the options. However, when stock prices fell, boards feared that, if they held managers to the bad bargain, many of them would leave. So the boards *lowered* the price of the options. For example, during one three-month period, the stock price of (the inaccurately named) Ascend Communications fell from $86 to $36. Many stock options were then *underwater*; that is, the exercise price (at which employees could buy stock) was higher than the market price. No problem: the board simply repriced the options so that the exercise price was lower than market value. When the Ascend stock continued its descent to $23, the board again lowered the option price. These actions transferred $1 billion from shareholders to employees.

For more information about executive compensation, pay attention to **http://www.paywatch.org**. Run by the AFL-CIO labor union, this Web site has an understandably jaundiced view of lavish paychecks. Wondering about your own current or future salary? Check in at **http://wageweb.com/** to find compensation data for over 150 different types of jobs.

As the following case demonstrates, shareholders' efforts to challenge executive compensation have met with little success. An officer's salary is presumed to be reasonable unless she voted for it as a director of the company. (Officers should excuse themselves from all such votes.) To be successful in challenging an executive's compensation, shareholders must prove that the board was grossly uninformed or that the amount was so high that it had *no relation* to the value of the services performed and was really a gift. The courts tend to be unsympathetic to this line of argument.

IN RE **THE WALT DISNEY COMPANY DERIVATIVE LITIGATION**
1998 Del. Ch. LEXIS 186
Court of Chancery of Delaware, New Castle, 1998

Facts: As head of Creative Artists Agency (CAA), a major talent agency, Michael Ovitz was often called the "Most Powerful Man in Hollywood." Disney hired Ovitz to be its president. After 14 months, all parties agreed that the experiment had failed, so Ovitz left Disney—but not empty-handed. Under his employment contract, he was entitled to $140 million in severance pay. The court described this severance payment as "larger than almost anyone anywhere will receive in the lifetime of any of the parties, and perhaps larger than any ever paid."[8] Shareholders of Disney sued to prevent payment. Disney filed a motion to dismiss the lawsuit.

Issue: Did the Disney directors have the right to pay $140 million to an employee who had worked at the company unsuccessfully and for only 14 months?

Excerpts from Judge Chandler's Decision: Just as the 85,000-ton cruise ships Disney Magic and Disney Wonder are forced by science to obey the same laws of buoyancy as Disneyland's significantly smaller Jungle Cruise ships, so is a corporate board's extraordinary decision to award a $140 million severance package governed by the same corporate law principles as its everyday decision to authorize a loan. When the laws of buoyancy are followed, the Disney Magic can stay afloat as well as the Jungle Cruise vessels. When the Delaware General Corporation Law is followed, a large severance package is just as valid as an authorization to borrow. Nature does not sink a ship merely because of its size, and neither do courts overrule a board's decision to approve and later honor a severance package, merely because of its size. Unless Plaintiffs can plead with specificity facts that the Board was corrupted and could not make a decision fairly and independently, in the best interests of the Corporation, then the Board's decision will stand.

Plaintiffs claim that the directors were not properly informed before they adopted the Employment Agreement because they did not know the value of the compensation package offered to Ovitz. To that end, Plaintiffs offer several statements made by Graef Crystal, the financial expert who advised the Board on the Employment Agreement, including his admission that "nobody quantified [the total cost of the severance package] and I wish we had."

Disney's expert did not consider an inquiry into the potential cost of Ovitz's severance benefits to be critical or relevant to the Board's consideration of the Employment Agreement. Merely because Crystal now regrets not having calculated the package is not reason enough to overturn the judgment of the Board then. It is the essence of the business judgment rule that a court will not apply 20/20 hindsight to second guess a board's decision, except "in rare cases [where] a transaction may be so egregious on its face that board approval cannot meet the test of business judgment."[9] I think it a correct statement of law that the duty of care is still fulfilled even if a Board does not know the exact amount of a severance payout but nonetheless is fully informed about the manner in which such a payout would be calculated. A board is not required to be informed of every fact, but rather is required to be reasonably informed.

Plaintiffs also allege that the Board's approval of the Employment Agreement constitutes waste. Under well-settled Delaware law, directors are only liable for waste when they "authorize an exchange that is so one sided that no business person of ordinary, sound judgment could conclude that the corporation has received adequate consideration." Here, the Board determined that in order to attract Ovitz

[8] As Ira Gershwin so lyrically put it, "Nice work if you can get it, and if you get it—won't you tell me how?"

[9] Chapter 36 contains an in-depth discussion of the business judgment rule.

to Disney, Disney would have to offer him a highly attractive compensation package. This they did.

[T]he Plaintiffs have failed to create a reasonable doubt that the Board's decision to approve the Employment Agreement was a product of the Board's business judgment. As such, Plaintiffs claims of breach of fiduciary duty and Waste must be dismissed.

When German automotive giant Daimler Benz AG agreed to merge with Chrysler Corp., observers wondered how well the different cultures would fit together. To take one instance, the Daimler chief executive earned a paltry $2 million, while his counterpart at Chrysler received $16 million. Together, the top *10* Daimler executives earned $11 million, while Chrysler's top *5* received $50 million.

Daimler's salaries are more in keeping with those in the rest of the world. Median compensation for the CEOs of large American companies is more than four times greater than the pay in equivalent British companies. This difference is largely owing to stock options. American companies award lavish stock options, but salaries overseas are primarily cash. British companies began to grant options in the 1980s, but are not yet on the level of American firms. Other countries have begun to follow America's lead: Japan recently revised its statutes to permit stock options, and companies in Australia, France, Germany, and the Netherlands have begun to grant options.

The political climate in many countries makes executives reluctant to accept exorbitant pay packages. They worry that extravagant compensation could cause social unrest. Moreover, other cultures often reward collective efforts instead of singling out a few for special treatment. Whatever the political environment, however, globalization of the world's economy has created unparalleled mobility across borders. Executives overseas fear that, if they do not match American salaries, they may lose their best and brightest to American companies.

As we have seen, directors set the salaries of company officers. **Typically, directors also set their own compensation (unless the charter or bylaws provide otherwise).** Directors of Fortune 200 companies earn on average $114,000 annually, consisting of $53,000 in cash, $59,000 in stock, and $2,000 in pension benefits. Over a recent four year period, compensation for directors at Fortune 200 companies has risen 45 percent. Directors of small companies earn much less, about $12,000 annually in cash, but they are often granted substantial stock options, which could, in theory, increase dramatically in value.

Investors worry that well-paid directors may feel more loyalty to the board that nominated them than to the shareholders who ostensibly elected them. To ease this concern, many companies now grant directors stock in addition to or instead of their cash salaries, on the theory that directors who also own stock will think more like shareholders. At one time less than half of Fortune 200 firms granted stock to directors; four years later 95 percent did. All of the increase in director compensation over the four year period was a result of stock grants.

Fundamental Corporate Changes

A corporation must seek shareholder approval before undergoing any of the following fundamental changes:

- **Mergers**. As a general rule, one corporation cannot merge with another unless a majority of both sets of shareholders approve. This rule is always true for shareholders of the *acquired* company, because they are always affected by the merger. But when an elephant acquires a peanut, it makes little sense for the elephant to vote. So shareholders of the *acquiring* company vote only if the merger will have a major impact on their company. There is one exception to these rules: a parent that owns 90 percent or more of a subsidiary can merge with the subsidiary in a **short-form merger** without seeking the approval of either set of shareholders. After all, the merger will certainly be approved, so why waste time and money taking a vote?

- **Sale of Assets**. Generally, shareholders are not asked to approve the sale of corporate assets. After all, one could hardly ask shareholders of Philip Morris to approve the sale of every pack of cigarettes at every convenience store in the country. But what if Philip Morris management decided that the company should sell its cigarette business and enter the health club field? Any sale not "in the regular course of business" needs shareholder approval.
- **Dissolution**. A corporation cannot *voluntarily* dissolve without shareholder approval. However, as discussed in Chapter 35, on the life and death of a corporation, the state or a court can *involuntarily* dissolve a corporation regardless of shareholder views.
- **Amendments to the Charter**. Directors propose amendments to the charter, but these amendments are not valid unless approved by shareholders.
- **Amendments to the Bylaws**. Both directors and shareholders have the right to amend the bylaws. There is one restriction, however: the amendment cannot grant authority that exceeds the limits set by state law. For example, shareholders cannot adopt an amendment that allows them to manage the ordinary business of the company. Philip Morris shareholders could not pass an amendment setting the price of a pack of cigarettes, but they could change the date or location of the annual meeting.

  Bylaw amendments have become a favorite tool of shareholder activists because, unlike the typical shareholder proposal, an amendment is *binding* on the company. CalPERS proposed a bylaw amendment at Advanced Micro Devices, Inc. to separate the jobs of chairman and CEO. Shareholders at Exxon Corp. proposed that the company amend its bylaws to establish a shareholder advisory committee for the board. Activists must be careful, however, not to step on the board's right to manage the company. Thus the Exxon proposal would have been invalid if it had granted the shareholder advisory committee the right to approve executive appointments.

RIGHT TO DISSENT

If a corporation decides to undertake a fundamental change, the Model Act and many state laws require the company to buy back the stock of any shareholders who object to this decision. This process is referred to as **dissenters' rights**, and the company must pay "fair value" for the stock. Fundamental changes include a merger, an exchange of the company's stock for that of another firm, a sale of most of the company's assets, or an amendment to the charter that would adversely affect a shareholder's rights (to vote, for instance). Devil Desserts, Inc. manufactures sinfully rich chocolate delights. The board of directors is now considering a merger with Angel Treats Ltd., a company that sells low-fat, low-calorie (and in shareholder Celeste's opinion, low-taste) desserts. Celeste fully expects the value of the company to plummet after the merger, but her fellow shareholders support the board's decision. In a public company, Celeste could simply sell her stock, but Devil is a close corporation and there is no market for its stock. To dissent, Celeste must notify the company before the meeting at which the shareholders will vote, and then either vote against the transaction or abstain. She has the right to dissent because a merger is a fundamental change, but she would not have this right if Devil Desserts simply introduced a new product or opened a new store.

RIGHT TO PROTECTION FROM OTHER SHAREHOLDERS

Minority shareholders are those who do not own enough stock to control the corporation. In a close corporation, 51 percent is considered to be a controlling share. Since a public corporation has a more diffuse group of shareholders, as little as 20 percent may be enough for control.

The courts have long recognized that minority shareholders are entitled to extra protection because it is easy (perhaps even natural) for controlling shareholders to take advantage of them. The right to dissent provides valuable protection, but it is not in itself enough. **In addition, controlling shareholders have a fiduciary duty to the minority.** As fiduciaries, they may not use their power to benefit themselves alone or to harm the minority.

Ordinary Business Transactions

Minority shareholders have the right to overturn an ordinary business transaction between the corporation and a controlling shareholder, unless the corporation can show that the transaction is *fair* to the minority shareholders. The Sinclair Oil Co. owned 97 percent of Sinclair Venezuelan Oil Co. (Sinven). Sinven's minority shareholders complained that Sinclair

- Forced Sinven to pay dividends so large that the subsidiary faced bankruptcy
- Hired other, wholly owned, subsidiaries but not Sinven, and
- Refused to force its other subsidiaries to abide by their contracts with Sinven; for instance, a Sinclair subsidiary signed a contract with Sinven to buy crude oil but failed to purchase the required amount.[10]

Were these transactions fair to Sinven's minority shareholders?

Excluding Minority Shareholders

Controlling shareholders must include minority shareholders in any favorable arrangements that they make for their own stock. A successful savings and loan (S&L) had stock that traded at $2,400 a share. Despite the S&L's success, its stock seldom traded because of the high price. The controlling shareholder could have split the stock so that shareholders received 100 shares worth $24 each. Instead, he concocted a shrewd plan whereby he and his friends (who together owned 85 percent of the stock) exchanged their S&L stock for shares in a new corporation. Stock of the new company sold well, but there was still virtually no market for the remaining S&L shares. The court held that the controlling shareholders could not exclude the minority without a compelling business purpose, which did not exist in this case.[11]

Expelling Shareholders

There is an old saying that you can choose your friends but not your family. Can you choose your fellow shareholders? Sometimes, relations between shareholders become so bitter that the majority attempts to expel a minority owner. **Many states prohibit a company from expelling shareholders unless the firm pays a fair price for the minority stock and the expulsion has a legitimate business purpose.** Delaware has an even higher standard—the transaction must be "entirely fair." This standard requires that both the price and the process of

---

10 *Sinclair Oil Corp. v. Levien*, 280 A.2d 717, 1971 Del. LEXIS 225 (Del. 1971).

11 *Jones v. H. F. Ahmanson & Co.*, 1 Cal. 3d 93, 460 P.2d 464, 1969 Cal. LEXIS 195 (1969).

approval be fair. Of course, when the shareholders are also family, relations can become really hostile. You be the judge.

LERNER v. LERNER
306 Md. 771, 511 A.2d 501, 1986 Md. LEXIS 264
Maryland Court of Appeals, 1986

Facts: The Lerner Corp. developed and managed real estate in the Washington, D.C. area. Theodore Lerner owned 70 shares of the company; his brother, Lawrence, owned 25. Lawrence's health was failing so, on doctor's orders, he began spending six months of the year in Florida. When he returned from Florida each spring, he was often critical of decisions that Theodore had made. One year, he returned to discover that Theodore had used company funds to develop projects from which Lawrence was excluded. Lawrence also objected to hefty pay increases the company had granted to members of Theodore's family.

Fed up with these complaints, Theodore fired Lawrence from his position as officer and director. When Lawrence sued Theodore, reports of their quarrel appeared in the local press. Enraged by these news stories, Theodore called a special shareholder meeting to approve charter amendments that would reclassify each existing share of stock into 1/35th of a share. A reverse split at that ratio meant that Theodore would own two shares while Lawrence would hold 5/7ths of a share. The proposed amendment provided for the company to buy out any fractional shares. In this case, Lawrence would own no stock.

You Be the Judge: Does a controlling shareholder have the right to expel a minority shareholder?

Argument for Theodore: Lawrence's attorneys cannot cite a single provision of state law that prohibits a company from revising its charter, reducing its capital, and buying out fractional shares. The company has the right to do it, and a good reason to do it. Five years ago, Lawrence began spending six months of each year in Florida, leaving Theodore to manage the company. Lawrence caused great disruption when he complained about every decision Theodore made. If he cared so much, he should have been working on the business, not his tan.

Lawrence's lawsuit was the final straw. The publicity has already dissuaded at least two prospective customers from hiring the company. Some top employees have considered leaving. The business will not survive if Lawrence continues to be a shareholder. Theodore has a legitimate business purpose for expelling Lawrence and has offered a fair price. What more can Lawrence expect?

Argument for Lawrence: As majority shareholder, Theodore owes a fiduciary duty to Lawrence. That means he has an obligation to behave in a trustworthy and honorable fashion, to put Lawrence's interests ahead of his own. Instead, he is trying to expel Lawrence from the company. The price the company offered for Lawrence's stock may be fair, but Lawrence does not want cash. He wants to be part of the ongoing business that has supported him and his family for most of his adult life.

What would ownership mean if a controlling shareholder could buy in stock anytime and for any reason? Theodore has to have a good reason—a legitimate business purpose. He has none. Lawrence has a right to offer advice on company management, and that does not constitute a legitimate reason for expulsion. Nor does the lawsuit. Lawrence would not have needed to file suit if Theodore had been acting as a fiduciary should. As for the customers who refused to hire the company, one of the witnesses who testified in court is the father-in-law of Theodore's son. He is hardly credible.

RIGHT TO MONITOR

As owners of an enterprise, shareholders play a relatively passive role. Primarily, they have the right to *monitor*, meaning the right to receive information and the right to vote on proposals put to them by the board. Shareholders do not, by and large, have the right to *initiate* corporate changes.

What could the Morrison Knudsen shareholders have done to stop William Agee? Not much. They could not have prevented the company from entering into unprofitable contracts; nor could they have fired Agee, cut his compensation, or taken his jet away. Nor could they have set dividends or initiated a merger, a sale, a dissolution, or even a charter amendment. The shareholders could have made recommendations; but they could not have forced the board to follow any of them.

Their only chance of reining in Agee would have been to elect a new board with the *hope* that different directors would be more sensitive to shareholder views. In the end, Morrison Knudsen shareholders, like shareholders in large corporations everywhere, had few options other than the "Wall Street walk."

What would a perfect system of corporate governance look like? One commentator proposes this description:

> An ideal system of corporate governance would do several things. It would, first, give a boss enough freedom to manage well. It would ensure that he used that freedom to manage the firm in the interests of shareholders. And, if somebody else could do a better job, it would let her. In such a system, the boss would know what shareholders expected; and shareholders would have enough information to judge whether their expectations were being met—and the power to act decisively if they weren't.[12]

Do you agree with this description of an ideal system of corporate governance? What are the problems with the American system? What could be done to improve it? How would these improvements be implemented?

ENFORCING SHAREHOLDER RIGHTS

After William Agee left Morrison Knudsen, the directors discovered that the company was, if anything, in worse condition than they thought. They expected a $175 million annual loss, but the actual deficit was closer to $310 million. The day this additional loss was announced, the acting chairman resigned. Bankers were stunned. The company's stock, which had been trading at nearly $30 per share a year earlier, fell to $6. For investors, even worse was yet to come. After the company filed for bankruptcy protection, shareholders were forced to accept a plan of reorganization that made their shares worthless. The company then issued new stock to its creditors. Eighteen different groups of shareholders filed suit against the company.

Shareholders in serious conflict with management have three different mechanisms for enforcing their rights: a derivative lawsuit, a direct lawsuit, or a class action.

DERIVATIVE LAWSUITS

A derivative lawsuit is brought by *shareholders* to remedy a wrong to the *corporation*. The suit is brought in the name of the corporation, and all proceeds of the litigation go to the corporation. The shareholders of Morrison Knudsen were understandably angry at William Agee and the board of directors that appointed him and supported him for so long. The shareholders, however, could not sue either the directors or Agee directly because, technically, they were not injured—the corporation was. Of course, the shareholders felt as if they had been injured when their stock became worthless. Nonetheless, the corporation, *not the shareholders*, has the right to sue. And who would authorize a suit against the directors on behalf of the corporation? The directors, of course. Because the directors are unlikely to sue themselves, the law permits derivative actions by which shareholders can sue managers who have violated their duty to the corporation. Because damages go *to the corporation*, the individual shareholders benefit only to the extent that the settlement causes their stock to rise in value.

The same rule applies if an outsider harms the corporation. If Morrison Knudsen decides not to sue a customer that has refused to pay its bill, the shareholders can do so, but only in a derivative action, that is, only in the name of the corporation. Once again, any recovery goes to the corporation.

---

12 "Survey of Corporate Governance," *The Economist*, Jan. 29, 1994.

Litigation is tremendously expensive. How can shareholders afford to sue if they are not entitled to damages? A corporation that loses a derivative suit must pay the legal fees of the victorious shareholders. Most derivative lawsuits are litigated by lawyers eager to earn these fees. (Losing shareholders are not required to pay the corporation's legal fees.[13]) It is likely for instance, that the cases against Morrison Knudsen were initiated by lawyers who sought out shareholders and persuaded them to sue. Without this incentive, few shareholders would bring derivative suits, and much corporate wrongdoing would go unpunished. As we have seen, shareholders have limited power; derivative lawsuits are a means of protecting their rights.

There is some concern, however, that lawyers who bring derivative suits have an incentive to settle quickly to ensure that they receive *some* compensation. Even if the shareholders' claim is strong, their lawyers might prefer a small, but guaranteed, payment rather than an uncertain chance at a larger amount after trial. If the case goes to trial and their clients lose, the lawyers receive nothing.

In some cases, these settlement payments are little more than bribes to ignore wrongdoing. On the other hand, lawyers sometimes bring so-called **strike suits**—claims without merit that corporations settle simply to avoid the nuisance of litigation. Many states and the federal government have established rules that are meant to curb abuses while fairly balancing the rights of the various parties. Most derivative suits are brought in Delaware, so this discussion is based on Delaware law. In many cases, however, federal law and other state statutes are similar to those of Delaware.

Approval of Settlements

To ensure that lawyers consider the welfare of their clients when settling a derivative action, all settlements must be approved by the court.

Making Demand

Before bringing suit, shareholders must first "make demand" on the board of directors. In other words, they must notify the board that the corporation has been wronged and ask the board to bring suit in the name of the corporation directly. There is one crucial exception to this rule: shareholders are not required to make demand if it would *clearly be futile* because a majority of the directors either have a conflict of interest or were careless when making the decision.

If Demand Is Required

If shareholders are required to make demand, the board has three choices:

1. It can agree with the shareholders and file suit on behalf of the corporation. In this case, the shareholders cannot bring their own derivative action. Although, technically, the board is required to put the interests of the corporation first, boards almost never decide to file suit themselves.
2. The board can reject the demand (or fail to respond). To proceed with their suit in this case, the plaintiffs must convince the court that the board has violated the business judgment rule because it had a conflict of interest or was careless in rejecting the demand.
3. The board can appoint a Special Litigation Committee (SLC). The SLC is typically comprised of at least two independent directors (usually those elected

[13] Under the Private Securities Litigation Reform Act, class action plaintiffs in suits brought under the securities laws must pay the corporation's legal expenses if the court determines that the suit was frivolous or abusive. 104 Pub. L. No. 67, 109 Stat. 737.

after the disputed activity occurred). If the SLC determines that the lawsuit is without merit, then the court must generally dismiss the case unless the shareholders can show the rejection was uninformed or not in good faith. There does not appear to be a single case in which an SLC recommended that litigation continue or a court overturned the decision of an SLC.

Exhibit 37.1 illustrates the course of derivative litigation. The most important issue is whether a court will require demand. Shareholders know that, if they make demand, the directors will appoint an SLC, which will then kill the suit. Therefore, shareholders typically file suit without making demand and wait for the company to go to court to ask that the suit be dismissed unless demand is

Exhibit 37.1

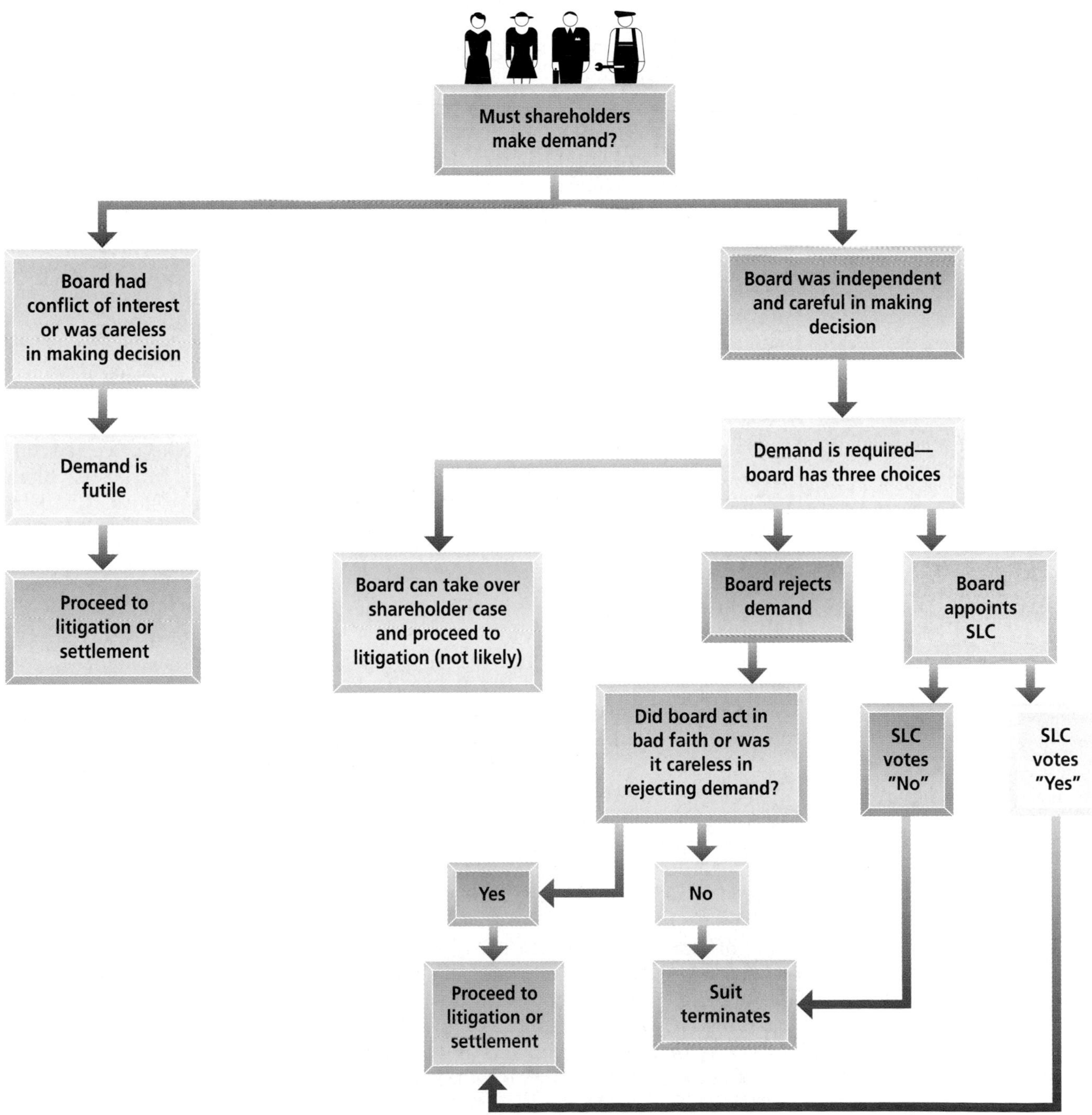

made. If the court indeed requires demand, the shareholders know they have lost and typically withdraw the case. If, however, the shareholders can convince the court that demand is *not* required, the shareholders have won and the parties settle. For example, recall that in the *Disney* case earlier in this chapter, shareholders objected to the large severance payment the company made to Michael Ovitz. As you can see from the name of the case, it was a derivative action brought by shareholders. In the following excerpt, the court addresses the issue of making demand.

_IN RE_ THE WALT DISNEY COMPANY DERIVATIVE LITIGATION
1998 Del. Ch. LEXIS 186
Court of Chancery of Delaware, New Castle, 1998

Facts: Walt Disney Co. hired Michael Ovitz to be its president. Ovitz resigned after 14 months, taking with him $140 million in severance payment. Without making demand, shareholders filed a derivative action. Disney filed a motion to dismiss the lawsuit until the shareholders made demand.

Issue: Are the Disney shareholders required to make demand before filing a derivative action?

Excerpts from Judge Chandler's Decision: The mere presence of a majority of board members [with a conflict of interest] is sufficient to excuse demand. [A] board member is considered to be disinterested when he or she neither stands to benefit financially nor suffer materially from the decision whether to pursue the claim sought in the derivative plaintiff's demand.

Plaintiffs offer several reasons for their assertion that the Board is not independent. Chief among them is Plaintiffs' assertion that Eisner dominates and controls the Board. In order to prove domination and control by Eisner, Plaintiffs must demonstrate that a majority of the Board could not exercise business judgment independent of Eisner in deciding whether to approve the Employment Agreement.

I begin my analysis with [Roy E.] Disney, who earns a substantial salary and receives numerous, valuable options on Disney stock. As a top executive, his compensation is set by the Board, not solely by Eisner. Furthermore, Mr. Disney, along with his family, owns approximately 8.4 million shares of Disney stock. At today's prices these shares are worth $2.1 billion. The only reasonable inference that I can draw about Mr. Disney is that he is an economically rational individual whose priority is to protect the value of his Disney shares, not someone who would intentionally risk his own and his family's interests in order to placate Eisner.

Plaintiffs allege that director Robert A.M. Stern's financial dealings with Disney were sufficiently large to cast a reasonable doubt upon his ability to consider a demand disinterestedly. Plaintiffs point out that Stern, an architect, had been commissioned to design several buildings for the Company and one for Eisner, for which his firm had collected millions of dollars in fees from Disney and Eisner. I agree with Plaintiffs: The fact that Stern's architectural firm has received, and perhaps continues to receive, payments from Disney over a period of years raises a reasonable doubt as to Stern's independent judgment with respect to the Employment Agreement.

Plaintiffs also allege that Father Leo J. O'Donovan is incapable of rendering independent business judgment. O'Donovan is the president of Georgetown University, the alma mater of one of Eisner's sons and the recipient of over $1 million of donations from Eisner. Plaintiffs do not allege any personal benefit received by O'Donovan—in fact, they admit that O'Donovan is forbidden, as a Jesuit priest, from collecting any director's fee. I do not believe that Plaintiffs have presented a reasonable doubt as to the independence of O'Donovan.

Director Reveta F. Bowers is the principal of the elementary school that Eisner's children once attended. Plaintiffs suggest that because Bowers' salary as a teacher is low compared to her director's fees and stock options, "only the most rigidly formalistic or myopic analysis" would view Bowers as not beholden to Eisner. To follow Plaintiffs' urging would be to discourage the membership on corporate boards of people of less-than extraordinary means. Such "regular folks" would face allegations of being dominated by other board members, merely because of the relatively substantial compensation provided by the board membership compared to their outside salaries. I am especially unwilling to facilitate such a result.

As for director Sidney Poitier, Plaintiffs do not allege that he is dominated by Eisner. Plaintiffs do allege, however, that Poitier is a longtime client of Creative Artists Agency—the talent agency that Ovitz founded—and through his relationship with CAA, he has earned millions of dollars. Although Poitier had enjoyed a successful relationship with Ovitz and CAA, (a) Ovitz is no longer the head of CAA, and (b) it does not follow that Poitier is incapable of considering Ovitz's compensation package without bias. My judgment might be otherwise if Poitier continued to receive material benefits from CAA and Ovitz was concurrently involved with that firm.

Plaintiffs come up short; [a majority of the] directors who approved the Agreement were independent in deciding the issues of Ovitz's compensation and free of domination from Eisner. Accordingly, demand is not excused.

More Fortune 500 companies are incorporated in Delaware than in any other state, making its corporate law the most influential in the nation. However, the American Law Institute Corporate Governance Project and the Model Act have both deviated from Delaware law by proposing that demand be required in *all* derivative cases. They essentially ignore the possibility that demand might be futile. Recently, the Supreme Court of Pennsylvania adopted this approach.[14] Although Pennsylvania law is not as important as Delaware's, it is nonetheless growing in influence and could well represent the future of derivative actions.

DIRECT LAWSUITS

Shareholders are permitted to sue the corporation directly only if their own rights have been harmed. If, for example, the corporation denies shareholders the right to inspect its books and records or to hold a shareholder meeting, they may sue in their own name and keep any damages awarded. The corporation is not required to pay the shareholders' legal fees; winning shareholders can use part of any damage award for this purpose. With a direct action, shareholders are more likely to get their day in court because they are not required to make demand first.

CLASS ACTION LAWSUITS

If a group of shareholders all have the same claim, they can join together and file suit as a class action, rather than suing separately. By joining forces, they can share the expense and effort of litigation. It is also far more efficient for the judicial system for one court to try one case than for tens or hundreds of courts all over the country to try the same issue. For obvious reasons, companies tend to resist class actions. In such suits, management is assailed by many small shareholders who otherwise could not afford to (or would not bother to) sue individually.

---

[14] *Peco Energy Co. v. Mikalauskas*, 547 Pa. 600, 692 A.2d 1042, 1997 Pa. LEXIS 789 (Pa. 1997).

Most jurisdictions have strict requirements governing class actions, such as the following:

- The case cannot proceed unless a judge **certifies** the class. To be certified, all the members of the class must have a similar case without any conflicts of interest.
- A judge will not certify a class unless it is so large that individual suits are impractical. A class comprised of all Morrison Knudsen shareholders would be large enough.
- Any settlement must be approved by a judge. This requirement is meant to ensure fairness to all class members and to protect the class from their lawyers who may prefer to settle early on terms favorable to themselves (that is, with a large award of attorney's fees) rather than going to trial or insisting on a settlement that is best for shareholders.

Note that a class action can be either a derivative suit or a direct action. If a Morrison Knudsen shareholder sued the board for breaching its fiduciary duty to the company, that would be a derivative action in the name of the corporation. It could also be a class action on behalf of all the shareholders. If the company refused to pay a dividend that it owed, the shareholders could sue the corporation, either individually or in a class action representing all shareholders.

The following table displays some of the important distinguishing features of derivative suits, direct actions, and class actions:

Features	Derivative Action	Direct Action	Class Action
Enforces the Rights of:	The corporation	The shareholder(s)	Either the shareholder(s) or the corporation depending on whether the suit is a derivative or direct action
Damages Are Paid to:	The corporation	The shareholder(s)	Either the corporation or the shareholder(s) depending on whether the suit is a derivative or direct action
Number of Plaintiffs	One or more	One or more	Many
Procedural Requirements	• Plaintiffs make demand on the board unless clearly futile. • If demand is futile, plaintiffs proceed with the case. • If demand is made, the board appoints an SLC, which can terminate the case. • Settlements must be approved by the court.	The same as regular litigation	• Class must be certified by the court. • Settlement must be approved by the court.

CHAPTER CONCLUSION

Shareholders own their corporation, but they have few of the rights typically associated with ownership. They have no right to use any specific asset of the corporation; they have no voice in managing the company's day-to-day affairs; they cannot hire or fire employees or set compensation. If management harms the value of their investment, shareholders cannot sue in their own name, but only on behalf of the company. Despite these severe restrictions, shareholders are increasingly flexing their muscles and calling directors and officers to account. This trend is sure to continue over the next decade.

CHAPTER REVIEW

1. The Securities and Exchange Commission (SEC) regulates the relationship between publicly held corporations and their shareholders. The SEC plays a less active role in privately held corporations.
2. More than 50 percent of the stock of public corporations is owned by institutional investors. Although historically content to be passive owners, these institutions have recently become much more active in the management of the companies in which they own stock.
3. Shareholders have the right to:
   - Receive annual financial statements
   - Inspect and copy the corporation's records (for a proper purpose)
   - Elect and remove directors; and
   - Approve fundamental corporate changes, such as a merger or a major sale of assets.
4. Virtually all publicly held companies solicit proxies from their shareholders. A proxy authorizes someone else to vote in place of the shareholder.
5. Under certain circumstances, public companies must include shareholder proposals in the proxy statement.
6. The SEC requires public corporations to disclose detailed information about executive compensation in the proxy statement. However, shareholders do not have the right to interfere with board decisions on this issue.
7. A shareholder who objects to a fundamental change in the corporation can insist that her shares be bought out at fair value. This protection is referred to as "dissenters' rights."
8. Controlling shareholders:
   - May not enter into unfair business transactions with the corporation
   - Have a fiduciary duty to minority shareholders
   - May not exclude minority shareholders from beneficial arrangements involving stock; and
   - Are prohibited from expelling minority shareholders, unless the expulsion is done for a legitimate business purpose
9. A derivative lawsuit is brought by shareholders to remedy a wrong to the corporation. The suit is brought in the name of the corporation, and all proceeds of the litigation go to the corporation.

10. If a group of shareholders all have the same claim against the corporation, they can join together and file a class action, rather than suing separately.

PRACTICE TEST

1. The New York State Common Retirement Fund wanted A&P (the grocery store chain) to permit large shareholders to place comments about the company's financial performance in its proxy statement. Would a shareholder proposal or an amendment to the company's bylaws be a better strategy for achieving this goal?

2. Shareholders lost their gamble when they bought stock of Jackpot Enterprises, Inc. Fed up with management, a shareholder asked the company to include a proposal in the proxy statement that would require the board of directors to sell or merge the company. Must Jackpot include this proposal in its proxy statement?

3. William H. Sullivan, Jr. purchased all the voting shares of the New England Patriots Football Club, Inc. (the Old Patriots). He organized a new corporation called the New Patriots Football Club, Inc. The boards of directors of the two companies agreed to merge. After the merger, the nonvoting stock in the Old Patriots was to be exchanged for cash. Do minority shareholders of the Old Patriots have the right to prevent the merger? If so, under what theory?

4. Daniel Cowin was a minority shareholder of Bresler & Reiner, Inc., a public company that developed real estate in Washington, D.C. He alleged numerous instances of corporate mismanagement, fraud, self-dealing, and breach of fiduciary duty by the board of directors. He sought damages for the diminished value of his stock. Could Cowin bring this suit as a direct action, or must it be a derivative suit?

5. The board of directors of Finalco Group, Inc. decided to sell most of the company's assets to Western Savings and Loan Association. Shortly after the proposed sale was announced, Finalco's largest shareholder said he opposed the transaction. Does Finalco need his approval for the sale?

6. **RIGHT & WRONG** Edgar Bronfman, Jr. dropped out of high school to go to Hollywood and write songs and produce movies. Eventually, he left Hollywood to work in the family business—the Bronfmans own 36 percent of Seagram Co., a liquor and beverage conglomerate. Promoted to president of the company at the age of 32, Bronfman seized a second chance to live his dream. Seagram received 70 percent of its earnings from its 24 percent ownership of DuPont Co. Bronfman sold this stock *at less than market value* to purchase (at an inflated price) 80 percent of MCA, a movie and music company that had been a financial disaster for its prior owners. Some observers thought Bronfman had gone Hollywood, others that he had gone crazy. After the deal was announced, the price of Seagram shares fell 18 percent. Was there anything Seagram shareholders could do to prevent what to them was not a dream but a nightmare? Apart from legal issues, was Bronfman's decision ethical? What ethical obligations does he owe Seagram's shareholders?

7. When Classic Corp. went public at $12 a share, its waterbed business was floating along nicely—the company had annual sales of $23 million and turned a hefty profit. The company then sprang a leak and suffered through many years of losses. Isaac Fogel, who owned 64 percent of the stock, decided to take the company private again (by buying shareholders' stock) at a price of 20 *cents* a share. Classic hired two financial advisers who opined that the buyout price was fair. The board of directors voted in favor of the sale and then sent shareholders a voluminous document announcing a special shareholder meeting to vote on the buyout. Do the minority shareholders have any rights?

8. The president of R. Hoe & Co., Inc. refused to call a special meeting of the shareholders although 55 percent of the shareholders requested it. One purpose of the meeting was to demand that the former president be reinstated. Are these two requests within the power of the shareholders?

9. Prior to the DuPont Co.'s annual shareholder meeting, Friends of the Earth Oceanic Society submitted a proposal requiring the company to (1) accelerate its phaseout of the production of chlorofluorocarbons and halons, (2) present to shareholders a report detailing research and development efforts to find environmentally sound substitutes, and (3) report to shareholders on marketing plans to sell those substitutes. Must DuPont include this proposal in its proxy material for the annual meeting?

10. **YOU BE THE JUDGE WRITING PROBLEM** Two shareholders of Bruce Co., Harry and Yolan Gilbert,

were fighting management for control of the company. They asked for permission to inspect Bruce's stockholder list so that they could either solicit support for their slate of directors at the upcoming stockholder meeting, or attempt to buy additional stock from other stockholders, or both. Bruce's board refused to allow the Gilberts to see the shareholder list on the grounds that the Gilberts owned another corporation that competed with Bruce. Do the Gilberts have the right to see Bruce's shareholder list? **Argument for the Gilberts:** If shareholders of a company have a proper purpose, they are entitled to inspect shareholder lists. Soliciting votes and buying stock are both proper purposes. **Argument for Bruce:** The Gilberts are simply offering a pretext. They could use this information to compete against the company. No shareholder has the right to cause harm.

INTERNET RESEARCH PROBLEM

Starting at http://www.corporateinformation.com/, find information on a company's shareholder proposals. (Type in a company name, then click on *FreeEdgar Filings*; choose *View Filings* and *Proxy Statement*.) What were these proposals about? What was the outcome of the shareholder vote? Can you find a proposal that shareholders supported?

You can find further practice problems in the Online Quiz at http://beatty.westbuslaw.com or in the Study Guide that accompanies this text.

CHAPTER 38

SECURITIES REGULATION

In 1926, America was gripped by a fever of stock market speculation. "Playing the market" became a national mania. The most engrossing news on any day's front page was the market. Up and up it soared. The cause of this psychological virus is uncertain, but the focus of the infection was the New York Stock Exchange. Between 1926 and 1929, annual volume leaped from 451 million to over 1.1 billion shares. In one year alone, the price of AT&T went from $179.50 to $335.62.

Much of this feverish trading was done on margin. Customers put down only 10 or 20 percent of a stock's purchase price and then borrowed the rest from their broker. This easy-payment plan excited the gambling instinct of unwary amateurs and professional speculators alike. By September 1929, the volume of these margin loans was equal to about half the entire public debt of the United States.

On September 4, 1929, stock prices began to soften, and for the next month they slid gently. Over the weekend of October 19, brokers sent out thousands of margin calls, asking customers to pay down loans that now exceeded the value of their stock. If customers failed to pay, brokers dumped their stock on the market, causing prices to fall further and brokers to make more margin calls. Soon there was a mad scramble of selling as prices plunged in wild disorder. Tens of thousands of

The effect of the 1929 stock market crash was immediate and devastating.

investors across the country were wiped out. On Tuesday, October 29, 1929, the speculative boom completely collapsed. That day, 4 million shares were traded, a record that stood for 30 years. From the peak of the bull market in September to the debacle of October 29, over $32 billion of equity value simply vanished from the earth.

The stock market crash spawned the Great Depression—the most pervasive, persistent, and destructive economic crisis the nation has ever faced. Retail trade fell by one-half, automobile production by two-thirds, steel by three-quarters. In 1933, more businesses failed than in any other year in history. Surviving businesses responded to the crisis by cutting dividends, reducing inventories, laying off workers, slashing wages, and canceling capital investments.

Unemployment statistics were the most poignant of all. In 1932, one in every five people in the labor force was out of a job. Million of others were underemployed, working only two or three days a week for wages that could not support a family. Distress cut indiscriminately across all economic and social classes. Bankers, insurance agents, architects, and lawyers joined the throng of unemployed. Articles such as the following were common in newspapers across the land:

> *New York, Jan. 6, 1933 (AP)*—After vainly trying to get a stay of dispossession until Jan. 15 from his apartment in Brooklyn, yesterday, Peter J. Cornell, 48 years old, a former roofing contractor out of work and penniless, fell dead in the arms of his wife. A doctor gave the cause of his death as heart disease, and the police said it had at least partly been caused by the bitter disappointment of a long day's fruitless attempt to prevent himself and his family being put out on the streets.[1]

INTRODUCTION

At the time of the great stock market crash, there was no federal securities law, only state law. Congress recognized that the country needed a national securities system if it was to avoid another such catastrophe. In 1933, Congress passed the Securities Act of 1933 (1933 Act) to regulate the issuance of new securities. The next year, it passed the Securities Exchange Act of 1934 (1934 Act) to regulate companies with publicly traded securities. The 1934 Act also established the Securities and Exchange Commission (SEC), the regulatory agency that oversees the securities industry.

THE SECURITIES AND EXCHANGE COMMISSION

The SEC is generally well regarded by those it regulates and has a reputation for hiring lawyers who are both intelligent and practical. The SEC creates law in three different ways:

- **Rules**. The securities statutes are often little more than general guides. Through its rules, the SEC fills in the crucial details.

[1] The material in this section is adapted from Cabell Phillips, *From the Crash to the Blitz* (Toronto: Macmillan, 1969).

- **Releases**. These are informal pronouncements from the SEC on current issues. Releases often operate as two-way communication. When the SEC issues a release to announce a proposed change in the rules, it also asks for comments on the proposal.
- **No-Action Letters**. Anyone who is in doubt about whether a particular transaction complies with the securities laws can ask the SEC directly. The response is called a no-action letter because it states that "the staff will recommend that the Commission take no action" if the transaction is done in a specified manner.

In addition to creating laws, the SEC has the power to enforce them. It can bring **cease and desist orders** against those who violate the securities laws, and it can also levy fines or confiscate profits from illegal transactions. Those accused of wrongdoing can appeal these sanctions to the courts. The SEC does not have the authority to bring a criminal action; it refers criminal cases to the Justice Department.

What Is a Security?

Both the 1933 and the 1934 Acts regulate securities. The official definition of a security includes a note, stock, treasury stock, bond, debenture, evidence of indebtedness, certificate of interest or participation in any profit-sharing agreement, collateral-trust certificate, preorganization certificate or subscription, and 15 other equivalents. Courts have interpreted this definition to mean that **a security is any transaction in which the buyer (1) invests money in a common enterprise and (2) expects to earn a profit predominantly from the efforts of others**.

This definition covers investments that are not necessarily called *securities*. For example, they may be called orange trees. W. J. Howey Co. owned large citrus groves in Florida. It sold these trees to investors, most of whom were from out of state and knew nothing about farming. Purchasers were expected to hire someone to take care of their trees. Someone like Howey-in-the-Hills, Inc., a related company that just happened to be in the service business. Customers were free to hire any service company, but 85 percent of the acreage was covered by service contracts with Howey-in-the-Hills. The court held that Howey was selling a security (no matter how orange or tart), because the purchaser was investing in a common enterprise (the orange grove) expecting to earn a profit from Howey's farmwork.

Other courts have interpreted the term "security" to include animal breeding arrangements (chinchillas, silver foxes, or beavers, take your pick); condominium purchases in which the developer promises the owner a certain level of income from rentals; and even investments in whiskey. Life Partners was a company that aimed to help AIDS patients. Was it selling a security?

SEC v. LIFE PARTNERS, INC.
87 F.3d 536, 1996 U.S. App. LEXIS 16117
United States Court of Appeals for the District of Columbia Circuit, 1996

Facts: Life Partners, Inc. (LPI) bought life insurance policies from AIDS victims at a discount from face value. It then repackaged these policies and sold them to investors who recovered the full face value of the policy after the patient died. LPI evaluated the patient's medical condition, reviewed his insurance policy, negotiated the purchase price, and prepared the legal documents. Investors could pay as little as $650 and buy as little as 3 percent of the benefits of a policy. Once an investor acquired an interest in a policy, she could avail herself of LPI's ongoing administrative services, which included monitoring the patient's health, assuring that the policy did not lapse, and arranging for resale of the investor's interest if requested.

Although the investment might sound macabre, it offered a valuable benefit to the terminally ill patient who was able to secure much needed income in the final years of life when employment was unlikely and medical bills were overwhelming. This arrangement was known as a "viatical settlement" after the ecclesiastical term "viaticum" (communion given to the dying). The viatical settlement industry emerged during the late 1980s as a result of the AIDS crisis and grew rapidly, from $5 million in life insurance policies in 1989 to roughly $200 million in 1995. LPI was the largest viatical settlement organizer in the country, accounting for approximately one-half of the total settlement volume in 1994. The SEC sued LPI, alleging that it was selling a security without registration.

You Be the Judge: Was Life Partners selling a security?

Argument for the SEC: LPI purchases policies from dying patients. The company then pools these policies, sells fractional interests to investors, and pays off investors when the patients die. The investors play no role, other than writing a check. These viatical settlements are clearly a common enterprise in which investors rely completely on the efforts of LPI.

Argument for LPI: The securities laws do not apply to LPI's efforts, which take place *before* the investors make their purchase. At that point, the investors can evaluate LPI for themselves. After the purchase, profitability is determined by the timing of the patient's death, which is outside LPI's control (we hope). After the investment, LPI plays only a clerical role; thus the investors are not earning a profit predominantly from its efforts.

SECURITIES ACT OF 1933

The 1933 Act requires that, before offering or selling securities, the issuer must register the securities with the SEC, unless the securities qualify for an exemption. An **issuer** is the company that issues the stock. Registering securities with the SEC in a public offering is a major undertaking, but the 1933 Act exempts some securities and also some particular types of transactions from the full-blown registration requirements of a public offering.

It is also important to remember that **when an issuer registers securities, the SEC does not investigate the quality of the offering.** Permission from the SEC to sell securities does not mean that the company has a good product or will be successful. SEC approval simply means that, on the surface, the company has answered all relevant questions about itself and its major products. The guiding principle of the federal securities laws is that investors can make a reasoned decision on whether to buy or sell securities if they have full and accurate information about a company and the security it is selling. For example, the Green Bay Packers football team sold an offering of stock to finance stadium improvements. The prospectus admitted:

> IT IS VIRTUALLY IMPOSSIBLE that any investor will ever make a profit on the stock purchase. The company will pay no dividends, and the shares cannot be sold.

This does not sound like a stock you want in your children's college fund; on the other hand, the SEC will not prevent Green Bay from selling it, or you from buying it, as long as you understand what the risks are.

One last point: **the 1933 Act prohibits fraud in *any* securities transaction.** Anyone who issues fraudulent securities is in violation of the 1933 Act, whether or not the securities are registered. Both the SEC and any purchasers of the stock can sue the issuer.

Companies must deliver certain documents to investors and also file them with the SEC. Most companies now make their required SEC filings electronically, using the EDGAR (Electronic Data Gathering, Analysis, and Retrieval) system. Once filed with the SEC, this information is available online (at http://www.sec.gov). Each day, Web surfers "hit" EDGAR half a million times and download 2.5 million pages.

Companies can fulfill their SEC filing requirements online with EDGAR, but delivering documents to investors electronically is more difficult because computer literacy and availability among investors vary widely. The SEC does permit issuers to communicate electronically with investors, provided that the following standards are met:

- *Consent.* Although many investors have computers, an issuer cannot assume that all do, or that all want to receive data this way. Therefore, an electronic document is only valid if the investor agrees to receive information in this form.
- *Notice.* A company cannot simply post information on its Internet Web site, because investors will not necessarily know it is there. The issuer must notify investors, via e-mail or snail mail, that information is available.
- *Access.* The recipients must have access to the information for a reasonable period of time and be able to download or print it. The investor can always request the paper version of a document, even after consenting to electronic delivery.

Companies communicate with investors via the Internet, and so does the SEC. Omnigene Diagnostics, Inc. was touted on various online investment bulletin boards, so when the SEC halted trading in this dubious stock, it announced the action on America Online. SEC enforcement officials also regularly surf the Net, looking for illegal activity.

General Exemption

Before offering securities for sale, the issuer must determine whether they are exempt from registration under the 1933 Act. Typically, exemptions are based on two factors: the type of security and the type of transaction. However, the National Securities Markets Improvement Act of 1996 gave the SEC new authority under both the 1933 and the 1934 Acts to grant exemptions that are "in the public interest" and "consistent with the protection of investors." The SEC has not yet determined how it will use this new authority.

Exempt Securities

The 1933 Act exempts some types of securities from registration because they (1) are inherently low risk, (2) are regulated by other statutes, or (3) are not really investments. The following securities are exempt from registration:

- **Government securities**, which include any security issued or guaranteed by federal or state government
- **Bank securities**, which include any security issued or guaranteed by a bank
- **Short-term notes**, which are high-quality negotiable notes or drafts that are due within nine months of issuance and are not sold to the general public

- **Nonprofit issues**, which include any security issued by a nonprofit religious, educational, or charitable organization
- **Insurance policies and annuity contracts**, which are governed by insurance regulations[2]

EXEMPT TRANSACTIONS

Section 4(2) of the 1933 Act exempts from registration "transactions by an issuer not involving any public offering." These are simple words to define a complex problem. In effect, the 1933 Act says that an issuer is not required to register securities that are sold in a private offering, that is, an offering with only a few investors or a relatively small amount of money involved. In private offerings, the full-blown disclosure of a public offering is neither necessary nor appropriate. For instance, a group of sophisticated investors who know an industry well do not need full disclosure. If the amount at stake is less than $10 million or $15 million, it would not make economic sense for the issuer to incur the heavy expense of a public offering.

There is an important distinction between exempt *securities* and exempt *transactions*. Exempt *securities* are always exempt, throughout their lives, no matter how many times they are sold. Stock sold in an exempt *transaction* is exempt only that one time, not necessarily in any subsequent sale. Suppose that Country Bank sells stock to the public. Under the 1933 Act, the bank is never required to register these securities, no matter how many times they are sold. On the other hand, suppose that Tumbleweed, Inc., a quilt maker, sells $5 million worth of stock in a private offering that is exempt from registration. Shamika buys 100 shares of this stock. Seven years later, the company decides to sell stock in a public offering that must be registered. As part of this public offering, Shamika sells her 100 shares. This time, the shares must be registered because they are being sold in a *public offering*.

Most small companies use private, not public, offerings to raise capital. There are three different types of private offerings—intrastate, Regulation D, and Regulation A—each with its own set of rules.

Intrastate Offering Exemption

Under SEC Rule 147, an issuer is not required to register securities that are *offered* and *sold* only to residents of the state in which the issuer is incorporated and does business. This exemption was designed to provide local financing for local businesses. To qualify under Rule 147, 80 percent of the issuer's revenues and assets must be in-state, and it must also intend to spend 80 percent of the offering's proceeds in-state. Neither the issuer nor any purchaser can sell the securities outside the state for nine months after the offering.

Rule 147 is a **safe harbor**—if an issuer totally complies with it, the offering definitely qualifies as intrastate. But even if the issuer does not comply absolutely with the rule, the SEC or the courts may still consider the offering to be intrastate; however, the issuer cannot be sure in advance how the decision will come out. Sonic was a Utah corporation that sold stock to Utah residents. *Seven* months later, the company sold stock to an Illinois company. Although Sonic violated Rule 147 by making the second sale too early, the court held that the company had nonetheless qualified for an intrastate offering because it had not intended, at the time of

[2] Life Partners was selling the rights to already existing policies, not the policies themselves. The insurance companies that issued the policies initially were not required to register them.

the original offering, to sell stock outside Utah.[3] Although Sonic had not totally complied with Rule 147, it had come close enough to avoid liability. A safe harbor is safer, but a voyage outside its boundaries does not necessarily end in disaster.

Regulation D

Three different types of private offerings can be made under Regulation D (often referred to as Reg D) under Rules 504, 505, and 506.

Rule 504. Under this rule, a company:

- May sell up to $1 million in securities during each 12-month period
- May advertise and sell the stock to an unlimited number of investors, and
- Is not required to register with the SEC.

Furthermore, the stock is not restricted, which means that the purchaser can resell it without registration. Essentially, the SEC does not want to get involved in such small offerings (except in the case of fraud, in which it is always interested). Some observers question the SEC's hands-off approach to these small offerings—$1 million may not be much to a company, but it can mean a great deal to individual investors.

Rule 505. This rule permits a company to sell up to $5 million of stock during each 12-month period, subject to the following restrictions:

- The company may not advertise the stock publicly. Therefore, a company generally cannot place offering materials on its Web site, although the SEC has been working with companies to develop Web sites with password protection that enable qualified investors to view offering documents online.
- The issuer can sell to as many *accredited investors* as it wants, but is limited to only 35 *unaccredited investors*. **Accredited investors** are institutions (such as banks and insurance companies) or wealthy individuals (with a net worth of more than $1 million or an annual income of more than $200,000).
- The company need not provide information to accredited investors but must make some disclosure to unaccredited investors. This requirement provides issuers with a serious incentive to avoid unaccredited investors because the disclosure requirements, although less demanding than for a public offering, are nonetheless burdensome.
- Stock purchased under this rule is restricted, which means it must be purchased for investment purposes. As a general rule, the buyer cannot resell the security, either publicly or privately, for one year.

Rule 506. This rule is similar to Rule 505. The differences are that:

- There is no limit on the amount of stock a company can sell.
- If an unaccredited purchaser is unsophisticated, he must have a **purchaser representative** to help him evaluate the investment. Is an *unsophisticated* investor someone who does not care for opera? No, it is someone who is unable to assess the risks of the offering himself.

The following table sets out the menu of choices under Reg D:

---

[3] *Busch v. Carpenter*, 827 F.2d 653, 1987 U.S. App. LEXIS 11034 (10th Cir. 1987).

	Maximum Value of Securities Sold in a 12-Month Period	Maximum Number of Investors	Is Disclosure Required?	Is Public Advertising Permitted?	Are Securities Restricted?
Rule 504	$1 million	No limit	No	Yes	No
Rule 505	$5 million	No limit on accredited investors; no more than 35 unaccredited investors	Only for unaccredited investors	No	Yes
Rule 506	No limit	No limit on accredited investors; no more than 35 unaccredited investors, who must either be sophisticated or have a purchaser representative	Only for unaccredited investors	No	Yes

Regulation A

Although an offering under Regulation A is *called* a private offering, it really is a small public offering. **Reg A permits an issuer to sell $5 million of securities *publicly* in any 12-month period**. The issuer must give each purchaser an offering circular that provides the same disclosure required for unaccredited investors under Reg D. The following table compares a public offering, Reg A, and Reg D:

	Public Offering	Regulation A	Regulation D
Maximum Value of Securities Sold	No limit	$5 million	$1 million, $5 million, or no limit, depending on the rule
Public Solicitation of Purchasers	Permitted	Permitted	Permitted only under Rule 504
Suitability Requirements for Purchasers	No requirements	No requirements	Must determine if investors are accredited or sophisticated (no requirement for Rule 504)
Disclosure Requirements	Elaborate registration statement, audited financials	Offering circular that is less detailed than a registration statement	Rule 504: none Rules 505 and 506: none for accredited investors, the same requirements as Reg A for unaccredited investors
Resale of Securities	Permitted	Permitted	Permitted under Rule 504, otherwise not permitted for one year
Number of Offerings in 1997	5,890	111	2,528

Direct Public Offerings

Traditionally, a small company either sold stock to people it knew or hired an investment banker to place the securities. But now, as many as one-third of the companies trying to raise capital in the United States for the first time do a direct public offering (DPO) instead of going through Wall Street. The catch is that the companies have to sell the stock themselves. They make these offerings under Reg A or Rule 504 because both permit public offerings of stock without registration under the 1933 Act. Here is how some companies do it:

In 1995, Spring Street Brewery, a New York microbrewery, became the first company to conduct an offering on the Internet. It established a home page that allowed potential investors to examine and download its offering documents. In the end, it raised $1.6 million.

Thanksgiving Coffee Co. of Fort Bragg, California, used both cybertechnology and the old-fashioned face-to-face approach. It had originally planned simply to sell to its loyal customer base. "You think that everybody who knows about you will line up around the block to buy stock, but you have to put the offering in front of potential investors' faces seven times to get them to take action," says Thanksgiving general manager Rick Moon. He did just that. He put offering notices on coffee-bean bags; he hung announcements on bean dispensers. Vendors got the advertisements, as did mail-order customers. Information about the stock sale appeared on the company's World Wide Web site, in its catalog, and in advertisements in targeted magazines. Anyone who called about the stock got regular updates on the offering. In the end, the huge effort paid off. By the time the offering closed, Thanksgiving Coffee had sold 20 percent of its stock for $1.25 million.[4]

PUBLIC OFFERINGS

When a company wishes to raise significant amounts of capital from a large number of people, it is time for a public offering. A company's first public sale of securities is called an **initial public offering** or an **IPO**. Here is one company's experience with an IPO.

Shortly after graduating from the Massachusetts Institute of Technology, Daniel Schwinn and Frank Slaughter founded Shiva Corp. (pronounced SHE-va) in Burlington, Massachusetts. (Information about the company is available at http://www.Shiva.com.) The company makes hardware and software that allow personal computers to tie directly into a corporate network from outside the office. Although within a decade sales had reached $42 million and net income was $2.7 million, the company was constantly strapped for cash to fund expansion. Its two founders began thinking about a public offering.

Underwriting

As we have seen, companies can sell stock directly to the public, but they primarily do so if the amounts involved are small. Shiva sought to raise more than $20 million, so it decided to hire an investment bank to serve as underwriter. In a **firm commitment** underwriting, the underwriter buys the stock from the issuer and resells it to the public. The underwriter bears the risk that the stock may sell at a lower price than expected. In a **best efforts** underwriting, the underwriter does

---

[4] Stephanie Gruner, "When Mom & Pop Go Public," *INC.*, Dec. 1996, p. 66. Republished with permission of INC Magazine; permission conveyed through the Copyright Clearance Center, Inc.

not buy the stock but instead acts as the company's agent in selling it. If the stock sells at a low price, the company, not the underwriter, is the loser.

In underwriting, as in life, timing is everything. As it happened, just when Shiva hoped to complete its offering, Wall Street's interest in the high-tech sector suddenly cooled. Investment bankers offered the company only $6 a share for its stock. Shiva decided to wait. Within three months, the market in high-tech stocks picked up again. The company's president, Frank Ingari, and its chief financial officer, Cynthia Deysher, went to New York to sign on with the investment bank Goldman Sachs. Shiva agreed to sell Goldman 2.4 million shares at a tentative price of $12 per share.

Registration Statement

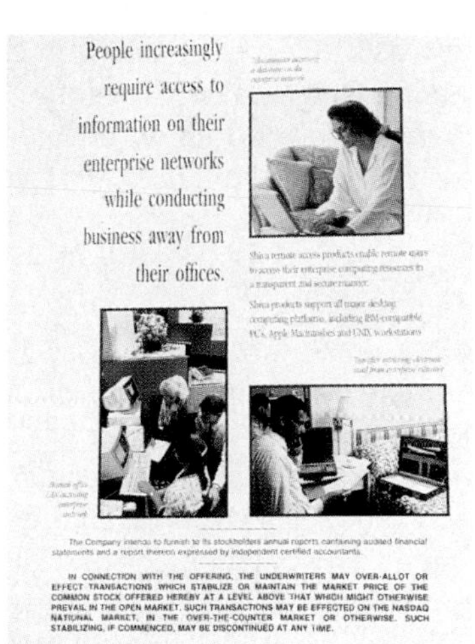
People increasingly require access to information on their enterprise networks while conducting business away from their offices.

Shiva remote access products enable remote users to access their enterprise computing resources in a transparent and secure manner.

Shiva products support all major desktop computing platforms, including IBM-compatible PCs, Apple Macintoshes and UNIX workstations

The Company intends to furnish to its stockholders annual reports containing audited financial statements and a report thereon expressed by independent certified accountants.

IN CONNECTION WITH THE OFFERING, THE UNDERWRITERS MAY OVER-ALLOT OR EFFECT TRANSACTIONS WHICH STABILIZE OR MAINTAIN THE MARKET PRICE OF THE COMMON STOCK OFFERED HEREBY AT A LEVEL ABOVE THAT WHICH MIGHT OTHERWISE PREVAIL IN THE OPEN MARKET. SUCH TRANSACTIONS MAY BE EFFECTED ON THE NASDAQ NATIONAL MARKET, IN THE OVER-THE-COUNTER MARKET OR OTHERWISE. SUCH STABILIZING, IF COMMENCED, MAY BE DISCONTINUED AT ANY TIME.

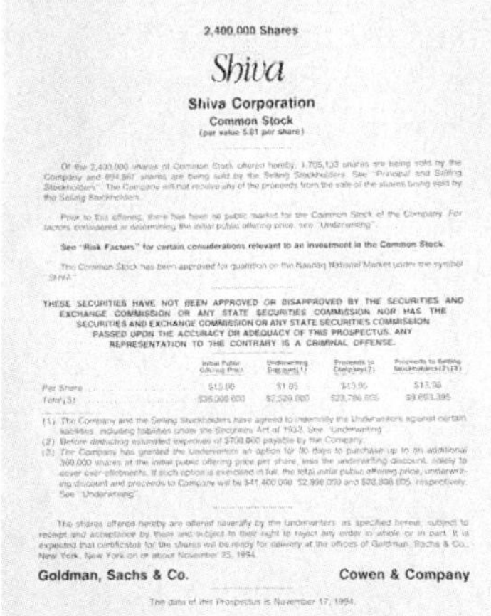
2,400,000 Shares

Shiva

Shiva Corporation

Common Stock

(par value $.01 per share)

See "Risk Factors" for certain considerations relevant to an investment in the Common Stock.

THESE SECURITIES HAVE NOT BEEN APPROVED OR DISAPPROVED BY THE SECURITIES AND EXCHANGE COMMISSION OR ANY STATE SECURITIES COMMISSION NOR HAS THE SECURITIES AND EXCHANGE COMMISSION OR ANY STATE SECURITIES COMMISSION PASSED UPON THE ACCURACY OR ADEQUACY OF THIS PROSPECTUS. ANY REPRESENTATION TO THE CONTRARY IS A CRIMINAL OFFENSE.

	Initial Public Offering Price	Underwriting Discount(1)	Proceeds to Company(2)	Proceeds to Selling Stockholders(2)(3)
Per Share	$15.00	$1.05	$13.95	$13.95
Total(3)	$36,000,000	$2,520,000	$23,786,605	$9,693,395

Goldman, Sachs & Co. Cowen & Company

The date of this Prospectus is November 17, 1994.

Each investor who purchased stock in Shiva Corp.'s initial public offering received this prospectus. Shiva also filed it with the SEC as part of the company's registration statement. The inside cover illustrates the dual nature of a prospectus—both disclosure document and sales pitch.

The **registration statement** has two purposes: to notify the SEC that a sale of securities is pending and to disclose information to prospective purchasers. The registration statement must include detailed information about the issuer and its business, a description of the stock, the proposed use of the proceeds from the offering, audited balance sheets for two years, and audited income statements for the three years before that. Preparing a registration statement is neither quick—it typically takes two to three months—nor inexpensive. Shiva spent $900,000 on audits and other expenses.

Within a month of hiring an investment bank, Shiva filed its *preliminary* draft of the registration statement with the SEC. This preliminary draft is called a **red herring** because it contains a notice in red ink warning that the securities cannot yet be sold.[5] The SEC typically spends between 30 and 100 days reviewing this preliminary draft of the registration statement. Remember that the Commission does not assess the value of the stock or the merit of the investment. Its role is to ensure that the company has disclosed enough to enable investors to make an informed decision.

Prospectus

Typically, buyers never see the registration statement; they are given the **prospectus** instead. In the SEC filing, the prospectus is a pull-out section in the middle of the registration statement. The prospectus includes all of the important disclosures about the company, while the registration statement includes additional information that is of interest to the SEC but not to the typical investor, such as the names and addresses of the lawyers for the issuer and underwriter. All investors must receive a copy of the prospectus before purchasing the stock.

Sales Effort

The SEC closely regulates an issuer's sales effort. Its goal is to prevent a company from hyping a stock before the prospectus is available to investors.

Pre-Filing Period. This is the time before the registration statement is filed. It is also known as the **quiet period**. The SEC permits only the merest of sales effort—an announcement that the offering will be made, but no mention of the price or the underwriter. Even a speech by a company officer, press releases, or postings on the company's Web site praising the company can be considered an illegal sales effort during this period.

Waiting Period. This is the time after the registration statement has been filed but before the SEC has approved it. The underwriter can publish a **tombstone ad**,

[5] The term "red herring" is a bit of a joke because, outside securities offerings, it means a false clue.

that is, a simple, unadorned announcement of the offering that includes the amount and type of security, the name of the underwriter, and the price of stock. You can see many of these ads in the *Wall Street Journal* and also on company Web sites. During the waiting period, the underwriter may distribute the preliminary prospectus. It can also solicit offers, but cannot make sales. The underwriter uses this period to estimate market demand for the stock. It **makes book**, meaning that it talks with traders to determine how many shares it can sell and at what price. It also takes **indications of interest** from traders but makes no sales.

During the waiting period, Goldman and Shiva began the **road show**—the cross-country road trip to convince traders that Shiva was a stock their clients should buy. Ingari and Schwinn spent a grueling two weeks visiting 16 cities. At each stop, they made the same impassioned pitch to such influential traders as Fidelity Investments, Wellington Management, Janus, and Alliance Capital. "We felt like door-to-door salesmen," Ingari said. So strong was the response that in the second week of the road show, Goldman suggested raising the price to $15 a share, from $12, and selling an additional 360,000 shares. When the road show ended, orders for the stock exceeded the number of shares by a factor of 30. That the IPO would be hot was certain. But how hot?

Going Effective

Once its review of the preliminary registration statement is complete, the SEC sends the issuer a **comment letter,** listing changes that must be made to the registration statement. An issuer almost always amends the registration statement at least once, and sometimes more than once. After the SEC has approved a final registration statement (which includes, of course, the final prospectus), the issuer then decides on a date to **go effective,** that is, to begin selling the stock. One last step remained: Goldman and Shiva had to agree on an opening price. They decided to raise the price from $12 to $15 per share. Shiva would sell to Goldman at $13.95 per share, and Goldman, in turn, would sell it on the market at $15.

The night before the sale, Shiva executives and the underwriters met for dinner and made bets about the next day's closing price and trading volume. No one guessed nearly high enough. As soon as Goldman sold at $15, the price zoomed to $30.50. The stock closed that day at $31.50 per share. At Goldman, there were hugs, tears of joy, and champagne toasts. But founders Schwinn and Slaughter, with their stock suddenly worth $30 million each, suffered chest pains. And Ingari, the president and chief executive, felt even worse. As the value of his stake in Shiva soared past $14 million, he fled to the men's room. "I was ready to throw up, I was sweating badly, and I could barely stand up. When I looked in the mirror, I had blood coming out of my nose."

In the end, Shiva raised $28 million that day, and its founders and other insiders, who sold about 700,000 shares, took home another $10 million. Goldman earned almost $3 million, or 7 percent of the proceeds. Did Goldman price the offering too low? Pricing an IPO is more art than science. Everyone would like the price to rise gently. At all cost, however, the underwriter wishes to avoid a disaster in which the stock price collapses, leaving it with a large loss. Of course, the underwriter looks bad if the company sells stock for a lot less than it is worth. Shares that Goldman sold in the morning for $15 were trading for twice that amount later in the day. Half of the initial worth of Shiva's stock, or about $43 million, went into the pockets of early buyers who "flipped" the stock, selling it immediately to other investors. Since that opening day, the stock price has climbed as high as $85 per share. In hindsight, Goldman should have priced the stock higher, but it is not clear that it or anyone else could reasonably have predicted the market's reaction.

Frank Slaughter went home after the IPO and spent a day "scrubbing toilets—to retain some humility." He had come through one of the most unnerving, and quintessential, rites of passage of the American capitalist system. The company obtained money to develop new products and build factories. The public got a chance to buy in. And the company's founders, and other key insiders, found a way to cash out.[6]

In its transition to a market economy, Russia is developing a securities market. To date, this market has tended to be underregulated and overhyped. The Russian government began by issuing privatization vouchers to all its citizens. These vouchers could be used to invest in newly privatized companies. Investment options varied widely. At a "privatization festival" in a Moscow exhibition hall, young men and women with neat business suits and alarmingly friendly smiles waved photocopies of their factories' business plans. Shares in these enterprises have since turned out to be worthless.

Because investing in legitimate enterprises proved so difficult, millions of Russians were attracted to the MMM Joint Stock Co. Its shareholders paid with cash instead of vouchers, but they could double their investment in a month. MMM's massive advertising campaign (evidently where most of its investors' money went) worked wonders, too. After *Newsweek* ran a story describing MMM as a "fast-growing" company, TV ads claimed that "according to analysts of the American magazine *Newsweek* MMM Invest is the most promising company in Russia."

Shortly thereafter, Russian authorities called MMM a scam and arrested Sergei Mavrodi, its president. Angry shareholders carried banners reading "Hands Off Mavrodi." Meanwhile, MMM devalued its shares by more than 99 percent in a single day. The Russian government indicated that it did not intend to bail shareholders out. That left Russian investors on their own with MMM, a company that once said it could not turn in its first-quarter balance sheets because the only copy was stolen off a bus on the way to the Finance Ministry.[7]

SALES OF RESTRICTED SECURITIES

After the public offering, Shiva insiders still owned a substantial block of stock. Between them, Schwinn, Slaughter, and Ingari held stock or options for 2.8 million shares. With the stock trading as high as $85 per share, on paper they were worth $238 million, but they could not actually sell their stock, at least not right away. **Rule 144 limits the resale of two types of securities: *control securities* and *restricted securities*.**

A **control security** is stock held by any shareholder who owns more than 10 percent of a class of stock or by any officer or director. In any three-month period, such an insider can sell only an amount of stock equal to the average weekly trading volume for the prior four weeks or 1 percent of the number of shares outstanding, whichever is greater. Shiva had 9,589,000 shares outstanding and an (unusually high) average weekly trading volume of roughly 938,000. A Shiva insider could sell at most 938,000 shares during each three-month period. In a company with a more typical trading volume, the number might be a tenth of that. The purpose of this rule is to protect other investors from precipitous declines in stock price. If company insiders sold all of their stock in one day, the price would plunge, causing losses to the other shareholders.

---

[6] The information about Shiva Corp. is from Glenn Rifkin, "Anatomy of a Highflying IPO, Nosebleeds and All," *New York Times*, Feb. 19, 1995, p. F7. Copyright © 1995 by The New York Times Co. Reprinted by permission.

[7] Carrol Bogert, Betsy McKay, and Dorinda Elliott, "Our Life as Ivan Investor," *Newsweek*, Aug. 15, 1994, p. 61. © 1994 Newsweek, Inc. All rights reserved. Reprinted by permission.

Exhibit 38.1
The Sale of Restricted Securities under Rule 144

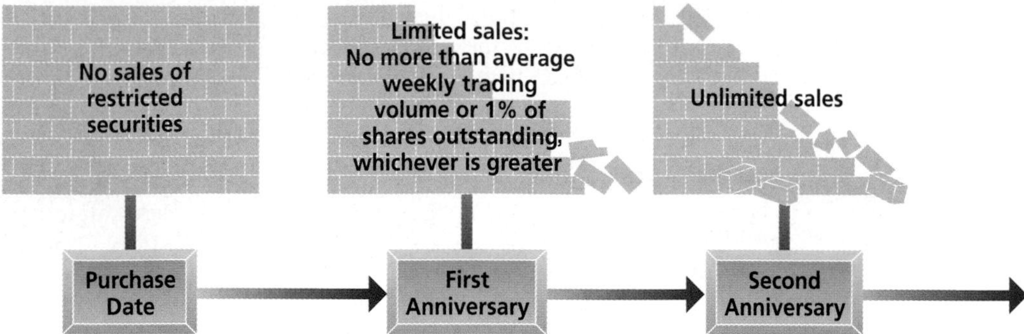

For owners of restricted securities, the rules are more complex. A **restricted security** is any stock purchased in a private offering (such as Regulation D). These securities may not be sold within one year of the offering. After the first year, restricted securities can be sold as long as the sale does not exceed the limitations that apply to control stock: the greater of the average weekly trading volume for the prior four weeks or 1 percent of the number of shares outstanding. After two years, restricted securities can be sold freely, unless they are also control securities, in which case those restrictions still apply. Exhibit 38.1 illustrates the sale of restricted securities under Rule 144:

LIABILITY

Liability for Unregistered Securities

Section 12(a)(1) of the 1933 Act imposes liability on anyone who sells a security that is not registered and not exempt. The purchaser of the security can demand rescission—a return of his money in exchange for the stock—or, if he no longer owns the stock, he can ask for damages.

Fraud

Under §12(a)(2) of the 1933 Act, the seller of a security is liable for making any material misstatement or omission, either oral or written, in connection with the offer or sale of a security. This provision applies to both *public* and *private* offerings if there is some use of interstate commerce, such as the mails, telephone (even for an *intra*state call), or check (which clears). It is difficult to imagine a securities transaction that does not involve interstate commerce. The SEC provides information on how to invest wisely and avoid securities fraud at http://www.sec.gov/invkhome.htm. The North American Securities Association also offers advice on "how to spot a con artist" and popular securities scams (http://www/nasaa.org/investoredu). You can obtain disciplinary reports on securities firms or individual brokers at http://www.nasdr.com. To report fraud, contact the SEC at its Complaint Center (http://www.sec.gov/enforce/comctr.htm) or via e-mail at enforcement@sec.gov.

Criminal Liability

Under §24 of the 1933 Act, the Justice Department can prosecute anyone who willfully violates the Act. The maximum penalty is five years' imprisonment and a $10,000 fine.

Liability for the Registration Statement

Section 11 of the 1933 Act establishes the penalties for any errors in a registration statement. **If a final registration statement contains a material misstatement or omission, the purchaser of the security can recover from everyone who signed the registration statement.** This list of signatories includes the issuer, its directors, and chief officers; experts (such as auditors, engineers, or lawyers); and the underwriters. Everyone who signed the registration statement is jointly and severally liable for any error, except the experts, who are liable only for misstatements in the part of the registration statement for which they were responsible.[8] Thus an auditor is liable for misstatements in the financials but not, say, for omissions about the CEO's criminal past.

To prevail under §11, the plaintiff need only prove that there was a material misstatement or omission and that she lost money. **Material** means important enough to affect an investor's decision. The plaintiff does not have to prove that she relied on (or even *read*) the registration statement, that she bought the stock from the issuer, or that the defendant was negligent. The plaintiff can recover the difference between what she paid for the stock and its value on the date of the lawsuit. Suppose that Pet Detective, Inc. does an IPO. A week later, Ace Investora buys 1,000 shares at $10 a share. He knows nothing about the company, but he likes the name. This stock turns out to be a dog—Pet Detective has only two agencies, not the 200 stated in the registration statement. When the stock falls to 10 cents, Investora can sue under §11 for $9,900.

All is not hopeless, however, for those who have signed the registration statement. If the statement contains a material misstatement or omission, the company is liable and has no defense. But everyone else who signed the registration statement can avoid liability by showing that he investigated the registration statement as thoroughly as a "prudent person in the management of his own property." This investigation is called **due diligence**. Its importance cannot be overstated. The SEC does not conduct its own investigation to ensure that the registration statement is accurate. It can only ensure that, on the surface, the issuer has supplied all relevant information. If an issuer chooses to lie, the SEC has no way of knowing. It is the job of the underwriters to check the accuracy of the filing. Thus underwriters typically spend two or three weeks visiting the company, reading all its corporate documents (including minutes back to the beginning), and calling its bankers, customers, suppliers, and competitors to ensure that the registration statement is accurate and no skeletons have been overlooked.

When §11 was first passed, investment bankers were outraged. Some predicted that this liability provision would cause capital in America to dry up, that grass would grow on Wall Street. In fact, the first case under §11 arose 35 years and 27,000 registration statements later. In this case—*Escott v. Barchris Construction Corp.*—the registration statement was seriously flawed.[9] The underwriter failed to read the minutes of the executive committee meetings that revealed the company to be in serious financial condition. Much of the company's alleged backlog of orders was to nonexistent corporations. Proceeds of the offering were earmarked to pay off debt, not to buy new plant and equipment, as the registration statement had indicated. The company's directors, underwriters, and underwriters' counsel were liable.

Although *Barchris* still strikes fear in the hearts of underwriters, some commentators now argue that underwriters do not take their due diligence obligations seriously enough. Was there adequate disclosure in the following case?

---

[8] Joint and several liability is discussed in Chapter 34.

[9] 283 F. Supp. 643, 1968 U.S. Dist. LEXIS 3853 (S.D.N.Y. 1968).

IN RE **DONALD J. TRUMP CASINO SECURITIES LITIGATION**

7 F.3d 357, 1993 U.S. App. LEXIS 26691

United States Court of Appeals for the Third Circuit, 1993

Facts: Donald J. Trump formed the Taj Mahal Associates Limited Partnership, which sold $675 million in bonds to the public. The partnership used the proceeds to purchase and complete construction on the Taj Mahal, a casino/hotel occupying 17 acres of land on the boardwalk in Atlantic City, New Jersey. The Taj Mahal was widely touted as Atlantic City's largest and most lavish casino resort. After the partnership filed for bankruptcy, the purchasers of the bonds filed suit, alleging that the bond prospectus contained material misstatements and omissions.

Issue: Did the Taj Mahal prospectus contain material omissions or misstatements?

Excerpts from Judge Becker's Decision: The plaintiffs allege that the prospectus contained material misrepresentations. Their principal claim is that the defendants had neither an honest belief in nor a reasonable basis for one statement in the prospectus: "The Partnership believes that funds generated from the operation of the Taj Mahal will be sufficient to cover all of its debt service (interest and principal)."

The prospectus at issue contained an abundance of warnings and cautionary language which bore directly on the prospective financial success of the Taj Mahal and on the Partnership's ability to repay the bonds. [N]o reasonable investor could believe anything but that the Taj Mahal bonds represented a rather risky, speculative investment which might yield a high rate of return, but which alternatively might result in no return or even a loss. For example, [the prospectus] stated:

> The Taj Mahal has not been completed and, accordingly, has no operating history. The Taj Mahal will be the largest casino/hotel complex in Atlantic City, with approximately twice the room capacity and casino space of many of the existing casino/hotels in Atlantic City. [No] other casino/hotel operator has had experience operating a complex the size of the Taj Mahal in Atlantic City. Consequently, no assurance can be given that, once opened, the Taj Mahal will be profitable or that it will generate cash flow sufficient to provide for the payment of the debt service.

The prospectus additionally reported that there were risks of delay in the construction of the Taj Mahal and a risk that the casino might not receive the numerous essential licenses and permits from the state regulatory authorities.

In this case the Partnership did not bury the warnings about risks amidst the bulk of the prospectus. Indeed, it was the allegedly misleading statement which was buried amidst the cautionary language. Moreover, an investor would have read the sentence immediately following the challenged statement, which cautioned: "no assurance can be given, however, that actual operating results will meet the Partnership's expectations."

Within this broad context the statement at issue was, at worst, harmless. In other words, cautionary language, if sufficient, renders the alleged omissions or misrepresentations immaterial as a matter of law. Of course, a vague or blanket (boilerplate) disclaimer which merely warns the reader that the investment has risks will ordinarily be inadequate to prevent misinformation. To suffice, the cautionary statements must be substantive and tailored to the specific future projections, estimates or opinions in the prospectus which the plaintiffs challenge.

[W]e think it clear that the accompanying warnings and cautionary language served to negate any potentially misleading effect that the prospectus' statement about the Partnership's belief in its ability to repay the bonds would have on a reasonable investor.

The investors in the Taj Mahal casino sued on the grounds that they had not been adequately warned of the risks. What information should they have known before making an investment decision?

Stuart Wechsler, a New York lawyer representing the bondholders, bemoaned this decision as "another nail in the coffin of prospectus disclosure. The prospectus is becoming a useless document."[10] Is Mr. Wechsler's interpretation of this case correct?

SECURITIES EXCHANGE ACT OF 1934

Most buyers do not purchase new securities from the issuer in an initial public offering. Rather they buy stock that is publicly traded in the open market. This stock is, in a sense, *secondhand* because others, perhaps many others, have already owned it. The purpose of the 1934 Act is to maintain the integrity of this secondary market.

GENERAL PROVISIONS OF THE 1934 ACT

Registration Requirements

As we have seen, the 1933 Act requires an issuer to register securities before selling them. That is a onetime effort for the company. The 1933 Act does not require the issuer to provide shareholders with any additional information in later years. Suppose that an automobile company registered and sold securities for the first time in 1946. Purchasers of those securities knew a lot about the firm—in 1946. But how can current investors assess the company? The 1934 Act plugs this hole. It requires issuers with publicly traded stock to continue to make information available to the public so that current—and potential—shareholders can evaluate the company. It is often said that the 1933 Act registers securities, and the 1934 Act registers companies.

Under the 1934 Act, an issuer must register with the SEC if (1) it completes a public offering under the 1933 Act, or (2) its securities are traded on a national exchange (such as the New York Stock Exchange), or (3) it has at least 500 shareholders and total assets that exceed $10 million. A company can *de*register if its number of shareholders falls below 300 or if it has fewer than 500 shareholders and assets of less than $10 million.

Disclosure Requirements—Section 13

Like the 1933 Act, the 1934 Act focuses on disclosure. The difference is that the 1933 Act requires onetime disclosure when a company sells stock to the public. The 1934 Act requires *ongoing*, regular disclosure for any company with a class of stock that is publicly traded. Companies that are required to register under the 1934 Act are called **reporting companies**. There are currently more than 15,000 reporting companies.

Section 13 requires reporting companies to file the following documents:

- An initial, detailed information statement when the company first registers (similar to the filing required under the 1933 Act)
- Annual reports on Form 10-K, containing audited financial statements, a detailed analysis of the company's performance, and information about officers and directors

[10] Edward Felsenthal, "Prospectus Liability," *Wall Street Journal*, Oct. 18, 1993, p. B8.

- Quarterly reports on Form 10-Q, which are less detailed than 10-Ks and contain unaudited financials

- Form 8-Ks to report any significant developments, such as bankruptcy, a change in control, a purchase or sale of significant assets, the resignation of a director as a result of a policy dispute, or a change in auditing firms

Recall that under the 1933 Act a prospectus must be given to investors. Under the 1934 Act, a reporting company is only required to send the annual report to shareholders. It files the other reports with the SEC; these documents are a matter of public record and are available to anyone, shareholder or not, who goes in person to an SEC public reading room or who accesses SEC records through EDGAR, its online system. Also, companies often place these reports on their Internet Web sites.

Proxy Requirements—Section 14

As discussed in Chapter 37, most shareholders of public corporations do not attend annual shareholder meetings. Instead, the company solicits their proxies, permitting them to vote by mail rather than in person. If a company solicits proxies, it is required to supply shareholders with a proxy statement that is intended to give them enough information to make informed decisions about the company. The proxy statement contains detailed information about officers and directors, including their experience, relationship with the company, and compensation. (The annual report provides financial information.) Proxy statements must also be filed with the SEC. Proxy contests and shareholder proposals are discussed in Chapter 37.

Under SEC rules, a company is not *required* to solicit proxies from shareholders, but if it does not, it is unlikely to obtain the quorum needed for the meeting to be held. In any event, a company cannot avoid its responsibility to inform shareholders. Whether or not it solicits proxies, it is still required to furnish shareholders with an information statement that contains essentially the same material as a proxy statement.

The following article discusses the benefits—and costs—of being a public company.

Businesses, large and small, go public for many reasons: the infusion of cash, publicity, prestige, and the fact that once a company's stock is publicly traded, it is easier to raise money in the future. Maryland-based RWD Technologies, Inc., which specializes in worker-productivity issues, raised about $38 million through its IPO. Even with big sales last year—$86 million—RWD is "more substantial as a public company," said chief financial officer Ron Holtz. The offering also helped the company to hire, retain, and motivate employees by offering them stock options.

The advantages of going public can be as simple as the publicity generated. For example, articles about RWD's initial public offering, such as one published by *Forbes* magazine after RWD's IPO, give the company more credibility with its Fortune 500 customers, Holtz said.

But making an IPO isn't all cash and free publicity. Nothing is private in a public company. Public companies have to disclose everything that happens—layoffs, debts, etc. If owners or management misrepresent actions at the company, they are targets for lawsuits from stockholders and can even be sent to jail.

A premature IPO can spell disaster for a company, said Dick Prins, senior vice-president at brokerage Ferris Baker Watts, Inc. If a company misses its projections in the first quarter as a public firm—even by 1 or 2 cents per share—stockholders may sell in droves. From then on, the company has to "super perform" to regain the trust of the market, Prins said. About 20 percent of public companies are currently in this situation. The underperforming companies will find it difficult to raise money in the future, can't invest as liberally for the future as they would like, and have to live quarter to quarter. "They have all the negatives of a public company, with none of the positives," Prins said.

Even with the infusion of cash, companies will find that going public is very expensive. RWD Technologies spent about $1 million to go public, Holtz said, and its brokerage firm took 7 percent of the proceeds. Brokerage fees can go as high as 18 percent of the money raised. RWD also now must pay about $300,000 to $400,000 in yearly expenses that it didn't pay before, including directors' and officers' insurance, SEC filing fees, investment staff salaries, mailings to investors, and higher attorney and accountants' fees.[11]

Short-Swing Trading—Section 16

During congressional hearings after the 1929 stock market crash, witnesses testified that insiders had manipulated the stock market. For example, insiders would buy a large block of stock, announce a substantial dividend, and then divest before the dividend was reduced. Section 16 was designed to prevent corporate insiders—officers, directors, and shareholders who own more than 10 percent of the company—from taking unfair advantage of privileged information to manipulate the market.

Section 16 takes a two-pronged approach:

- First, insiders must **report** their trades of company stock on Form 4 by the tenth day of the following month.
- Second, insiders must **turn over to the corporation** any profits they make from the purchase and sale or sale and purchase of company securities in a six-month period. Section 16 is a strict liability provision. It applies even if the insider did not actually take advantage of secret information or try to manipulate the market; if she bought and sold or sold and bought stock in a six-month period, she is liable.

Suppose that Manuela buys 20,000 shares of her company's stock in June at $10 a share. In September, her (uninsured) summer house in Florida is destroyed by a hurricane. To raise money for rebuilding, she sells the stock at $12 per share, making a profit of $40,000. Her house will have to remain in ruins because she has violated §16 and must turn over the profit to her company.

As some observers have commented, §16 is both too broad and too narrow: it penalizes innocent trading where there is no insider information and ignores guilty insider trading that has occurred only once in a six-month period. During the stock market mini-crash in 1987, many officers and directors bought stock of their own companies to take advantage of bargain prices. If they had sold stock any time in the previous six months, their subsequent purchase violated §16 because they had *sold and then purchased* stock. But, if an insider sells stock because he knows the company's profit figures are down, he has not violated §16 unless he had also bought stock in the prior six months. (As we will see, he may be in violation of Rule 10b-5.)

---

11 Suzanne E. Stipe, "In the Public Eye IPO Can Mean Cash, Publicity—or Disaster," *Baltimore Business Journal*, Mar. 27, 1998, p. 27. Reprinted with permission.

LIABILITY

Section 18

Under §18, anyone who makes a false or misleading statement in a filing under the 1934 Act is liable to buyers or sellers who (1) acted in reliance on the statement and (2) can prove that the price at which they bought or sold was affected by the false filing. Section 18 applies to all filings under the 1934 Act, including proxy statements and annual reports.

Section 10(b)

Section 18 applies only to *filings* under the 1934 Act. What happens if a company executive makes a false public *statement* about the company? Or writes an untrue statement somewhere other than in a filing? In one case, a corporate officer bought up shares of his company's stock even as he made pessimistic public statements about the company. That is the type of behavior that §10(b) is designed to prevent. **Section 10(b) prohibits fraud in connection with the purchase and sale of any security, whether or not the security is registered under the 1934 Act.**

The SEC adopted Rule 10b-5 to clarify §10(b), but the rule is still a relatively vague, catch-all provision designed to fill any holes left by other sections of the securities laws.[12] Interpretation has largely been left to the courts, which generally have interpreted Rule 10b-5 as follows:

- **A Misstatement or Omission of a Material Fact.** Anyone who fails to disclose material information, or makes incomplete or inaccurate disclosure, is liable. **Material** has the same meaning as under the 1933 Act: important enough to affect an investor's decision. For example, a company repeatedly and falsely denied that it was involved in merger negotiations. It was liable even though the negotiations had only been in a preliminary stage.[13]
- ***Scienter*.** This is a legal term meaning *willfully, knowingly, or recklessly*. To be liable under Rule 10b-5, the defendant must have (1) known (or been reckless in not knowing) that the statement was inaccurate and (2) intended for the plaintiff to rely on the statement. Negligence is not enough. A group of shareholders sued the accounting firm Ernst & Ernst because it had failed to discover, during the course of an audit, that a company's chief executive was stealing funds. According to the shareholders, the auditors should have discovered that the executive refused to allow anyone else to open his mail and, therefore, should have been suspicious of other wrongdoing. The court found Ernst & Ernst not liable. Although it may have been negligent, it had not *intentionally* or even *recklessly* facilitated fraud.[14]
- **Purchase or Sale.** Rule 10b-5 includes both buyers and sellers. It does not include, however, someone who *failed* to purchase stock because of a material misstatement. In the case of the company executive who spread negative rumors about his company while he bought stock, those who sold because of his false rumors could sue under Rule 10b-5, but not those who simply failed to buy.

---

[12] Rule 10b-5 prohibits any person, in connection with a purchase or sale of any security, from (1) employing any device, scheme, or artifice to defraud; (2) making any untrue statement of a material fact or omitting to state a material fact necessary in order to make the statements made, in light of the circumstances under which they were made, not misleading; or (3) engaging in any act, practice, or course of business that operates or would operate as a fraud or deceit upon any person.

[13] *Basic Inc. v. Levinson*, 485 U.S. 224, 108 S. Ct. 978, 1988 U.S. LEXIS 1197 (1988).

[14] *Ernst & Ernst v. Hochfelder*, 425 U.S. 185, 96 S. Ct. 1375, 1976 U.S. LEXIS 2 (1976).

- **Reliance**. To bring suit, a plaintiff must show that she relied on the misstatement or omission. In the case of open-market trades, reliance is difficult to prove, so the courts are willing to assume it.

During a recent nine-year period, 25 percent of the corporations in America, including each of the 10 biggest firms in Silicon Valley, were sued by shareholders. Some commentators call these suits "legalized extortion"; others say it is the only way to prevent fraud.[15] Consider these two case histories.

Kenwood and Helena Perkins lived in the upscale San Diego community of Rancho Bernardo and were looking forward to a comfortably secure retirement. That was before they invested in Technical Equities Corp. Its auditors and brokerage firms were well-known, but that did not prevent the company from collapsing in the largest financial scandal in California's history. The Perkinses were devastated. "I had fears of going on welfare," Mrs. Perkins said. Instead, Mr. Perkins went back to work at age 65. The couple sold their home and moved to a trailer park. Then they joined a lawsuit against the company, its bankers, investment bankers, and auditors. After legal fees, they recovered about 60 percent of their losses. "We're still living in the mobile home park," Mr. Perkins said, "but our future is reasonably secure, and it would not have been without that money."

John G. Adler came to the United States from his native Hungary, as a penniless 19-year-old escaping the Russians. After 20 years with IBM, he became president of Adaptec, a computer parts manufacturer in Milpitas, Calif. The company's revenues exceeded $100 million, but one year, Mr. Adler learned that various sales glitches would cause fourth-quarter revenues to be about 15 percent lower than Wall Street expected. The shortfall seemed minor, but Mr. Adler decided to hold a conference call to alert the handful of analysts who followed his company. When the market opened the next day, Adaptec's stock fell more than 30 percent. Within three days, the first of seven lawsuits had been filed against the company, alleging that it should have made a public announcement, not a private phone call. In the end, the company spent $2 million in legal fees and settled the cases for $4.3 million. Adler objected to the settlement because he felt he had done nothing wrong, but lawyers advised him that a trial would cost far more.[16]

The Private Securities Litigation Reform Act of 1995

In 1995, Congress passed an amendment to the 1934 Act intended to discourage fraud suits by shareholders. Under this amendment, companies are liable to shareholders for so-called forward-looking statements (that is, financial projections or statements about future plans) *only if* (1) the company fails to include a warning that the predictions may not come to pass, *and* (2) the shareholders can show that company executives knew the predictions were false. Suppose a pharmaceutical company predicts that a new drug will generate billions in sales, but two years later the drug is a total failure. Before 1995, shareholders would have had a strong case against the company, but now the company would not be liable as long as it had disclosed, at the time of making the prediction, reasons why the drug might not be a success. Even if the company failed to mention these reasons, it would be liable only if executives knew the prediction to be false when they made it.

Thus far this statute has not diminished the number of lawsuits filed under §10(b). (Shareholders even sued Shiva, the company discussed earlier in the

---

15 Jim Barlow, "Stock Suit Filings Wear Down Firms," *Houston Chronicle*, May 4, 1995, p. 1.

16 Diana B. Henriques, "Investing It; Making It Harder for Investors to Sue," *New York Times*, Sep. 10, 1995, p. 1.

chapter, when its stock price fell.) However, the nature of the allegations has changed. Now, the majority of these suits allege accounting fraud or insider trading; very few are based solely on claims of misleading predictions.[17] For more information about these lawsuits, browse at **http://securities.stanford.edu**. This site provides over 1,000 securities fraud complaints, as well as court orders and written testimony.

INSIDER TRADING

Insider trading is immensely tempting. Anyone with reliable secret information can earn millions of dollars overnight. Costandi Nasser bought shares of Santa Fe International, Inc. after learning that Kuwait Petroleum Co. was set to acquire the company. His profit? $4.6 million in three weeks. The down-side? Insider trading is a crime punishable by fines of up to $1.1 million and prison sentences of up to 10 years. The guilty party may also be forced to turn over to the SEC three times the profit made. Ivan Boesky paid $100 million and spent two years in prison. Dennis Levine suffered an $11.6 million penalty and three years in prison.

Why is insider trading a crime? Who is harmed? After all, if you buy or sell stock in a company, presumably you are reasonably content with the price or you would not have traded. There are three reasons why insider trading is illegal:

- It offends our fundamental sense of fairness. No one wants to be in a poker game with marked cards.
- Investors will lose confidence in the market if they feel that insiders have an unfair advantage.
- Investment banks typically "make a market" in stocks, meaning that they hold extra shares so that orders can be filled smoothly. If an insider buys stock because she knows the company is about to sign an important contract, she earns the profit on that information at the expense of the marketmaker who sold her the stock. These marketmakers expect to earn a certain profit. If they do not earn it from normal stock appreciation, they simply raise the commission they charge for being a marketmaker. As a result, everyone who buys and sells stock pays a slightly higher price because insider trading skims off some of the profits.

As noted, Rule 10b-5 is a vaguely worded rule that generally prohibits fraud. The language of the rule never explicitly mentions insider trading, but courts have interpreted it to prohibit this activity. Although the courts are nominally *interpreting* the rule, in fact, they are more or less fashioning this crime out of whole cloth. Insider trading has been described as "the judicial oak that has grown from little more than a legislative acorn." The current rules on insider trading are as follows:

- **Strangers**. The SEC has argued many times that anyone in possession of nonpublic material information must disclose it or refrain from trading. The courts, however, have definitively rejected this approach. The Supreme Court has held that **someone who trades on inside information is liable only if he has a fiduciary duty to the company whose stock he has traded.** Suppose that, while looking in a dumpster, Harry finds correspondence indicating that

[17] Some plaintiffs tried to do an end run around this statute by filing suit in a state court (under more favorable state law). Congress passed the Securities Litigation Uniform Standards Act of 1998 to force plaintiffs in certain types of securities cases to file suit in federal court (under federal law).

MediSearch, Inc. will shortly announce a major breakthrough in the treatment of AIDS. Harry buys the stock, which promptly quadruples in value. Harry will be dining at the Ritz, not in the dumpster nor in federal prison, because he has no fiduciary duty to MediSearch.

- **Fiduciaries**. Anyone who works for a company is a fiduciary. **A fiduciary violates Rule 10b-5 if she trades stock of her company while in possession of nonpublic material information.** If the Director of Research for MediSearch learns of the promising new treatment for AIDS and buys stock in the company before the information is public, she has violated Rule 10b-5. This rule applies not only to employees who work for the company, but also to **constructive insiders**—others who have an indirect employment relationship, such as employees of the company's auditors or law firm. Thus, if a lawyer who works at the firm that is patenting MediSearch's new discovery buys stock before the information is public, she has violated Rule 10b-5.

- **Tippers**. Now things become really complicated. **Insiders who pass on nonpublic, material information are liable under Rule 10b-5, even if they do not trade themselves, as long as (1) they know the information is confidential and (2) they expect some personal gain.** Personal gain is loosely defined. Essentially, any gift to a friend counts as personal gain. W. Paul Thayer was a corporate director, deputy defense secretary, and former fighter pilot ace who gave stock tips to his girlfriend in lieu of paying her rent. That counted as personal gain and he spent a year and a half in prison.

- **Tippees**. **Those who receive tips—tippees—are liable for trading on inside information, even if they do not have a fiduciary relationship to the company, as long as (1) they know the information is confidential, (2) they know it came from an insider who was violating his fiduciary duty, and (3) the insider expected some personal gain.** Barry Switzer, then head football coach at the University of Oklahoma, went to a track meet to see his son compete. While sunbathing on the bleachers, he overheard someone talking about a company that was going to be acquired. Switzer bought the stock but was acquitted of insider trading charges, because the insider had not breached his fiduciary duty. He had not tipped anyone on purpose—he had simply been careless. Also, Switzer did not know that the insider was breaching a fiduciary duty, and the insider expected no personal gain.[18]

- **Takeovers**. Frustrated by its lack of success under Rule 10b-5, the SEC adopted Rule 14e-3. **This rule prohibits trading on inside information during a tender offer if the trader knows the information was obtained from either the bidder or the target company.** The trader or tipper need not have violated a fiduciary duty. (Tender offers are discussed in detail in Chapter 37, on shareholders.)

- **Misappropriation**. In an effort to tighten the insider trading noose further, the SEC developed a new theory—misappropriation. Under this theory, **a person is liable if he trades in securities (1) for personal profit, (2) using confidential information, and (3) in breach of a fiduciary duty to the source of the information.** This theory applies even if that source was not the company whose stock was traded. Foster Winans wrote a column for the *Wall Street Journal* entitled, "Heard on the Street" in which he reported rumors he had heard about

[18] *SEC v. Switzer*, 590 F. Supp. 756, 1984 U.S. Dist. LEXIS 15303 (W.D. Okla. 1984). After this case, some wags joked, "When Barry Switzer listens, people talk."

companies. Frequently, the stock of these companies would rise or fall in response to his story. He began leaking information about his columns in advance to Peter Brant, a stockbroker at Kidder, Peabody & Co. Brant would trade the stock and split the profits with Winans. After the first episode, the SEC noticed the abnormally large trade. When it called the company to find out who was buying, the officers said they could think of no explanation except that the company had been the subject of a "Heard on the Street" column. It was all over for Winans, though the SEC let him pass on information a few more times, to make sure.

But had Winans and Brant violated Rule 10b-5? Not according to traditional insider trading rules. Neither of them had a fiduciary relationship to the company whose stock was traded. When the case went to the Supreme Court, it split 4–4 on the issue of misappropriation (there were only eight judges because one had resigned and his successor had not yet been appointed). However, the Court did find 8–0 that Winans was guilty of mail and wire fraud for having violated the *Wall Street Journal*'s rules about confidentiality.[19] Ten years later, the Supreme Court finally resolved the misappropriation issue.

UNITED STATES v. O'HAGAN
521 U.S. 642, 117 S. Ct. 2199, 1997 U.S. LEXIS 4033
United States Supreme Court, 1997

Facts: Grand Metropolitan PLC (Grand Met) hired the law firm of Dorsey & Whitney to represent it in a takeover of Pillsbury Co. James O'Hagan, a partner in Dorsey & Whitney, did not work for Grand Met, but he did purchase significant amounts of Pillsbury stock during this period. After Grand Met publicly announced its takeover attempt, the price of Pillsbury stock rose dramatically. O'Hagan sold his stock at a profit of more than $4.3 million. A jury convicted O'Hagan of misappropriation in violation of §10(b), and he was sentenced to prison.[20] The appeals court reversed, ruling that misappropriation is not a violation of §10(b). The Supreme Court granted *certiorari*.

Issue: Is misappropriation a violation of §10(b)?

Excerpts from Justice Ginsburg's Decision: Under the "traditional" or "classical theory" of insider trading liability, §10(b) and Rule 10b-5 are violated when a corporate insider trades in the securities of his corporation on the basis of material, nonpublic information. The classical theory applies not only to officers, directors, and other permanent insiders of a corporation, but also to attorneys, accountants, consultants, and others who temporarily become fiduciaries of a corporation.

The "misappropriation theory" holds that a person commits fraud "in connection with" a securities transaction, and thereby violates §10(b) and Rule 10b-5, when he misappropriates confidential information for securities trading purposes, in breach of a duty owed to the source of the information. Under this theory, a fiduciary's undisclosed, self-serving use of a principal's information to purchase or sell securities, in breach of a duty of loyalty and confidentiality, defrauds the principal of the exclusive use of that information.

The two theories are complementary, each addressing efforts to capitalize on nonpublic information through the purchase or sale of securities. The classical the-

---

[19] *Carpenter v. United States*, 484 U.S. 19, 108 S. Ct. 316, 1987 U.S. LEXIS 4815 (1987).

[20] This was not the sum total of O'Hagan's problems. He used the profits he gained through this trading to conceal his previous embezzlement of client funds. There is a moral here.

ory targets a corporate insider's breach of duty to shareholders with whom the insider transacts; the misappropriation theory outlaws trading on the basis of nonpublic information by a corporate "outsider" in breach of a duty owed not to a trading party, but to the source of the information. The misappropriation theory is thus designed to protect the integrity of the securities markets against abuses by "outsiders" to a corporation who have access to confidential information that will affect the corporation's security price when revealed, but who owe no fiduciary or other duty to that corporation's shareholders.

A company's confidential information qualifies as property to which the company has a right of exclusive use. The undisclosed misappropriation of such information, in violation of a fiduciary duty constitutes fraud akin to embezzlement.

The theory is also well-tuned to an animating purpose of the Exchange Act: to insure honest securities markets and thereby promote investor confidence. Although informational disparity is inevitable in the securities markets, investors likely would hesitate to venture their capital in a market where trading based on misappropriated nonpublic information is unchecked by law. An investor's informational disadvantage vis-à-vis a misappropriator with material, nonpublic information stems from contrivance, not luck; it is a disadvantage that cannot be overcome with research or skill.

It makes scant sense to hold a lawyer like O'Hagan a §10(b) violator if he works for a law firm representing the target of a tender offer, but not if he works for a law firm representing the bidder. The text of the statute requires no such result. The misappropriation at issue here was properly made the subject of a §10(b) charge because it meets the statutory requirement that there be "deceptive" conduct "in connection with" securities transactions.

If you learn confidential information about a company, what can you do? Of course, it is always safe *not* to trade. If you want to trade anyway, you should wait 24 to 48 hours after the information is disseminated through wire services or in the financial press.

FOREIGN CORRUPT PRACTICES ACT

In the 1970s, more than 450 major U.S. corporations paid millions of dollars in foreign bribes. The Japanese premier and the Italian president both resigned after it was revealed that Lockheed had paid them off. In the Netherlands, members of the royal family were implicated in the scandal. Many of these payments had been labeled "commissions" or other legitimate business expenses and then illegally deducted from the company's income tax. In response, Congress passed the Foreign Corrupt Practices Act as an amendment to the 1934 Act.

Under the Foreign Corrupt Practices Act, it is a crime for *any American company* (whether reporting under the 1934 Act or not) to make or promise to make payments or gifts to foreign officials, political candidates, or parties in order to influence a governmental decision, even if the payment is legal under local law. There is one exception: it is legal for a company to make payments to a foreign official to expedite a "routine governmental action." Anyone who violates the law is subject to fines of up to $100,000 and imprisonment for up to five years.

Congress believed that the ready availability of corporate "slush funds" had facilitated the payment of bribes. Therefore, it also tightened accounting standards for companies that report under the 1934 Act. It requires *reporting companies* to (1) keep books that accurately and fairly reflect the transactions of the issuer, and (2) maintain a system of internal controls that ensures transactions are executed only "in accordance with management's authorization."

For years, American companies complained that they were handicapped when competing against rivals who could bribe their way to success overseas. The U.S. government estimated that American companies lost contracts worth more than $15 billion a year to competitors who paid bribes. But in 1997, 34 developed countries signed a treaty in Paris outlawing bribery of foreign officials.

What's wrong with bribery anyway? Many business people think it is relatively harmless, just a cost of doing business, like New York's high taxes or Germany's high labor costs. Corruption is not a victimless crime. Poor people in poor countries are the losers when officials are on the take: corruption means that good projects are squeezed out by bad ones. And corruption can reduce a country's entire administration to a state of decay. Honest officials give up. Bribes grow ever bigger and more ubiquitous. The trough becomes less well stocked; the snouts plunge deeper.[21]

Which countries are most corrupt? Nigeria, Bolivia, Colombia, Russia, and Pakistan lead the list of shame. The most honest? Denmark, Finland, Sweden, New Zealand, and Canada. (The United States is fifteenth on the honest list.)

BLUE SKY LAWS

At the end of the nineteenth century, years before the great stock market crash, states had already begun to regulate the sale of securities. These statutes are called **blue sky laws** (because crooks were willing to sell naive investors a "piece of the great blue sky"). Currently, all states and the District of Columbia have blue sky laws. To sell securities, an issuer must comply with both state and federal securities laws. "Blue skying" a 50-state securities offering is no small feat, because there is little uniformity among the statutes. Although most states have adopted the Uniform Securities Act, they have so customized it that "uniform" is a misnomer. Often, securities approved by the SEC will be offered only in a limited number of states either because state securities commissioners have denied clearance or because the issuer will not make the effort to seek clearance in all jurisdictions.

Although the 1933 Act is primarily concerned with adequate disclosure, many state statutes focus on the quality of the investment and require a so-called **merit review**. In 1981, the Massachusetts securities commissioner refused to allow Apple Computer Co. to sell its initial public offering in Massachusetts because he believed the stock, selling at 92 times earnings, was too risky. He "protected" Massachusetts residents from this investment.

Most states now permit so-called SCORs (small company offering registrations). If a company issues less than $1 million in stock in a 12-month period, it is required to file only a relatively simple form (U-7) in any state in which it wishes to sell the securities. The company is then free to advertise and sell to anyone in these states. There is no limit on the number of investors. Each year, somewhere between 80 and 100 companies file a SCOR. (Such an offering is already exempt from registration with the SEC under Rule 504.)

To make life easier for issuers of stock, Congress also passed the National Securities Markets Improvement Act of 1996. Essentially, states may no longer regulate offerings of securities that are:

---

21 "Who Will Listen to Mr. Clean?" *The Economist*, Aug. 2, 1997, p. 52.

- Traded on a national exchange
- Exempt under Rule 506, or
- Sold to "qualified purchasers" (a term the SEC has not yet defined).

The states may still prosecute those who commit securities fraud. They may also require issuers to file notices and pay fees for all offerings except those involving nationally traded securities.

CHAPTER CONCLUSION

The 1929 stock market crash and the Great Depression that followed were an economic catastrophe for the United States. The Securities Act of 1933 and the Securities Exchange Act of 1934 were designed to prevent such disasters from ever occurring again. This country has enjoyed more than 70 years of prosperity that is based, at least in part, on a reliable and honest securities market. The securities laws deserve some of the credit for that stability.

CHAPTER REVIEW

1. A security is any transaction in which the buyer invests money in a common enterprise and expects to earn a profit predominantly from the efforts of others.
2. Before any offer or sale, an issuer must register securities with the SEC, unless the securities qualify for an exemption.
3. These securities are exempt from the registration requirement: government securities, bank securities, short-term notes, nonprofit issues, insurance policies, and annuity contracts.
4. The following table compares the different types of securities offerings:

	Public Offering	**Intrastate Offering**	**Regulation A**	**Regulation D: Rule 504**	**Regulation D: Rule 505**	**Regulation D: Rule 506**
Maximum Value of Securities Sold	Unlimited	Unlimited	$5 million	$1 million	$5 million	Unlimited
Public Solicitation of Purchasers	Permitted	Permitted	Permitted	Permitted	Not permitted	Not permitted
Suitability Requirements for Purchasers	No requirements	Must reside in issuer's state	No requirements	No requirements	No limit on accredited investors; no more than 35 unaccredited investors	No limit on accredited investors; no more than 35 unaccredited investors who, if unsophisticated, must have a purchaser representative

	Public Offering	Intrastate Offering	Regulation A	Regulation D: Rule 504	Regulation D: Rule 505	Regulation D: Rule 506
Disclosure Requirements	Elaborate registration statement; audited financials	None	Offering circular that is less detailed than a registration statement	None	Same requirements as Reg A for unaccredited investors; no disclosure to accredited investors	Same requirements as Reg A for unaccredited investors; no disclosure to accredited investors
Resale of Securities	Permitted	Permitted, but may not be made out of state for nine months	Permitted	Permitted	Not permitted for one year	Not permitted for one year

5. If a final registration statement contains a material misstatement or omission, the purchaser of a security offered under that statement can recover from everyone who signed it.
6. The 1934 Act requires public companies to make regular filings with the SEC.
7. Under §16, insiders who buy and sell or sell and buy company stock within a six-month period must turn over to the corporation any profits from the trades.
8. Section 10(b) prohibits fraud in connection with the purchase and sale of any security, whether or not the issuer is registered under the 1934 Act.
9. Section 10(b) also prohibits insider trading.
10. Under the Foreign Corrupt Practices Act, it is a crime for any U.S. company to make payments to foreign officials to influence a government decision. This statute also requires reporting companies to keep accurate records.

PRACTICE TEST

1. Christopher Stenger bought 12 Impressionist paintings from R. H. Love Galleries for $1.5 million. Love told Stenger that art investment would produce a safe profit. The two men agreed that Stenger could exchange any painting within five years for any one or two other paintings with the same or greater value. When Stenger's paintings did not increase in value, he sued Love, arguing that the right to trade paintings made them securities. Is Stenger correct?

2. CPA QUESTION When a common stock offering requires registration under the Securities Act of 1933:

(a) The registration statement is automatically effective when filed with the SEC

(b) The issuer would act unlawfully if it were to sell the common stock without providing the investor with a prospectus

(c) The SEC will determine the investment value of the common stock before approving the offering

(d) The issuer may make sales 10 days after filing the registration statement

3. Fluor, an engineering and construction company, was awarded a $1 billion project to build a coal gasification plant in South Africa. Fluor signed an agreement with a South African client that prohibited them both from announcing the agreement until March 10. Accordingly, Fluor denied all rumors that a major transaction was pending. Between March 3 and March 6, the State Teachers Retirement Board pension fund sold 288,257 shares of Fluor stock. After the contract was announced, the stock price went up. Did Fluor violate Rule 10b-5?

4. **CPA QUESTION** Hamilton Corp. makes a $4.5 million securities offering under Rule 505 of Regulation D of the Securities Act of 1933. Under this regulation, Hamilton is:

(a) Required to provide full financial information to accredited investors only

(b) Allowed to make the offering through a general solicitation

(c) Limited to selling to no more than 35 nonaccredited investors

(d) Allowed to sell to an unlimited number of investors both accredited and nonaccredited

5. Does this excerpt from the *Boston Globe* reveal any potential securities law problems?

> Berkshire Ice Cream's down-home investment strategy is paying off for more than 100 people who last year put up $800 to $1,000 to "own" a company cow. Last month, the company sent out about $32,000 to investors who bought a total of 110 cows a year ago, with the expectation of a 20 percent annual return on their money. [I]nitially, there were 63 investors who agreed to finance the purchase of a cow—which the company then cares for—in return for a piece of the company's profits.[22]

6. **RIGHT & WRONG** Ira Waldbaum was president and controlling shareholder of Waldbaum, Inc., a large supermarket chain. After deciding to accept A & P's offer to purchase the chain, he told his sister, Shirley Witkin, about the offer so that she would be ready to sell her shares. He admonished her not to tell anyone, but she told her daughter, Susan Loeb, who passed the word (and the warning) on to her husband, Keith Loeb. The next day, Keith told his broker, Robert Chestman, about the impending sale and ordered some Waldbaum stock. Chestman purchased 11,000 shares of the stock for himself and his clients, at a price of roughly $25 per share. The A&P offer was for $50 per share. Did Chestman violate Rule 10b-5? Whether or not Chestman's trades were legal, did they harm anyone? How do they look in the light of day? Were Loeb's actions right? How might they have affected his wife (and other stakeholders)?

7. **CPA QUESTION** Pace Corp. previously issued 300,000 shares of its common stock. The shares are now actively traded on a national securities exchange. The original offering was exempt from registration under the Securities Act of 1933. Pace has $2.5 million in assets and 425 shareholders. With regard to the Securities Exchange Act of 1934, Pace is:

(a) Required to file a registration statement because its assets exceed $2 million in value

(b) Required to file a registration statement even though it has fewer than 500 shareholders

(c) Not required to file a registration statement because the original offering of its stock was exempt from registration

(d) Not required to file a registration statement unless insiders own at least 5 percent of its outstanding shares of stock

8. **YOU BE THE JUDGE WRITING PROBLEM** World-Wide Coin Investments, Inc. sold rare coins, precious metals, camera equipment, and Coca-Cola collector items. Its stock was registered with the SEC under the 1934 Act. Joseph Hale was the controlling shareholder, chairman of the board, CEO, and president. World-Wide's independent auditor warned Hale that the company's faulty system of accounting procedures was causing problems with inventory control. Furthermore, the auditor could not document transactions, and it had found that the books and records of the company were inaccurate. Is World-Wide in violation of the Foreign Corrupt Practices Act? **Argument for the SEC:** Without exception, all reporting companies are required to maintain accurate books and records. **Argument for World-Wide**: This is a small company, and the cost of such an elaborate internal control system would bankrupt it.

9. Consider this scenario from the periodical *Investor's Business Daily, Inc.*:

> You're in line at the grocery store when you overhear a stranger say: "That new widget is going to make XYZ Co. a fortune. I can't wait until the product launches tomorrow."

---

[22] Ellen Labr, "Investors Milk Profits of Ice Cream Firm, "*Boston Globe*, July 30, 1995, p. 38. Republished with permission of The Boston Globe; permission conveyed through the Copyright Clearance Center, Inc.

What do you do? (a) Nothing? (b) Call your broker and buy as much XYZ Co. stock as you possibly can?

10. Malaga Arabian Limited Partnership sold investments in the Spanish Arabian horse industry under Rule 506. James E. Mark, who purchased one of the partnership interests, alleged that the partnership violated Rule 506 because it never gave him any disclosure about the risks of the investment. He was not an accredited investor. At trial, the partnership said that it had surveyed investors to ensure that they were either accredited or sophisticated but had not actually read the surveys and did not have them available for the trial court. Is this offering exempt from registration under the 1933 Act?

11. CoolCom, Inc. sends notice to all its shareholders that its annual report and proxy soliciting materials are on its Internet Web site. It provides investors with the Internet location and a telephone number that they may call to request a paper copy. Is CoolCom in compliance with SEC rules?

INTERNET RESEARCH PROBLEM

Choose a company, go to the EDGAR database at the SEC (http://www.sec.gov), and look at all filings this company has made during the last year. What filings has it made and why? Extra credit: search EDGAR for a prospectus for an initial public offering.

You can find further practice problems in the Online Quiz at http://beatty.westbuslaw.com or in the Study Guide that accompanies this text.

CHAPTER 39

ACCOUNTANTS: LIABILITY AND PROFESSIONAL RESPONSIBILITY

John Z. DeLorean flew high with his stainless steel gull-winged sports car. The British government was so impressed with his new American company that it spent $130 million to entice him to open a manufacturing plant in troubled Northern Ireland. DeLorean promised to create 2,000 jobs. In the end, DeLorean's company crashed and burned in spectacular fashion. It ended up in bankruptcy court, but that was the least of his—or anyone else's—problems.

DeLorean was accused of stealing $17.6 million from the Irish enterprise. He was arrested in the United States on drug trafficking charges after undercover agents videotaped him selling cocaine, allegedly in an effort to finance his business. He was also charged with racketeering amid allegations that he had defrauded investors through the use of dummy corporations around the world.

In the end, however, DeLorean walked away virtually scot-free. Despite the videotaped evidence, he was acquitted on the drug charges in Los Angeles. A Detroit jury acquitted him on the racketeering counts. He left bankruptcy court with $1 million in cash, the promise of $2 million more, a $6.5 million apartment on New York's Fifth Avenue, and the patents to his car.

Who paid for DeLorean's sins? The British government and Northern Ireland were losers—

1,500 jobs were lost when the Irish plant closed. Worse, the highly publicized disaster discouraged other companies from investing in Northern Ireland. In the end, however, the biggest loser may have been Arthur Andersen, DeLorean's accounting firm. Andersen paid the British government $35 million to settle a lawsuit. After years of litigation, a New York jury recently found that Andersen was negligent in auditing DeLorean's financial statements and ordered it to pay $46.2 million to the company's shareholders and creditors. With interest, this total may rise to $110 million. Andersen was held liable because it knew that DeLorean had shifted $17.6 million from the Irish subsidiary to a Panamanian corporation. The accountants thought the transfer was part of a complex effort to avoid British taxes; instead it was a simple attempt at theft. Despite this knowledge, Andersen issued a clean opinion. Andersen partners are bitter that they have been made a scapegoat for DeLorean's misdeeds.

INTRODUCTION

The accounting profession is at a crossroads. A field that, not too long ago, seemed a safe, secure place to spend a career has now become as risky as neurosurgery. The Big Five firms alone have more than $30 *billion* in claims outstanding against them.[1] Lawsuits closed Laventhol & Horwath, the country's seventh largest accounting firm. In a survey of partners who left Big Five accounting firms, roughly one-third said they had departed because of concerns about legal liability. Liability insurance is increasingly expensive and difficult to obtain. Some small firms elect to drop their insurance, hoping that if they "go bare," they will make a less enticing target.

Overseas, the picture is also bleak. Accounting firms are under fire throughout Europe, from England to Finland to Spain. PricewaterhouseCoopers and Ernst & Young were sued in London for $8 billion in connection with their audit of the failed Bank of Credit and Commerce International (BCCI). In Australia, a branch of KPMG paid $97 million to settle a claim.

The causes of this crisis in the accounting profession are numerous:

- **Savings and Loan Crisis**. A record number of savings and loan institutions failed when the real estate market turned soft. These banks had loaned too much money on too little collateral. The federal government, which paid back much of the depositors' money, sued accounting firms that, in some cases, had given clean bills of health only a few months before the thrifts went bankrupt.

- **Unrealistic Expectations**. When a company goes under, shareholders often blame accountants for not sounding an early warning of financial distress. Accountants argue that the public expects too much. No auditor can detect all fraud on the part of determined and clever management. Nor should auditors serve as guarantors of a firm's financial health. (To see some examples of creative accounting, check out http://www.imagen.net/howenow/.)

[1] The Big Five firms are Arthur Andersen, Deloitte Touche Tohmatsu, Ernst & Young, KPMG, and PricewaterhouseCoopers.

- **Competition**. Accountants prefer not to talk about this issue. Fierce competition has driven down the prices for audits. Some firms even use audits as loss leaders—conducting them virtually for free in return for consulting work on other issues. As the price for audits declines, firms tend to spend less time on them. Accountants may also fear that, if they raise too many red flags during audits, they will scare away clients. Competition also drives firms to be less choosy about their clients. Among Laventhol & Horwath's clients were a jailed swindler, a penny-stock company repeatedly charged with fraud, and imprisoned televangelist Jim Bakker. The accounting firm was hit with a $184 million fraud claim for its work with Bakker's "Praise the Lord" organization.

Combined litigation losses for the Big Five now exceed $1 billion annually, an amount equal to 12 percent of their annual audit and accounting revenue. Not surprisingly, accounting firms are trying to reverse this trend. The first step for many is to walk away from risky clients. Big Five accounting firms are now dropping about 100 large (that is, publicly traded) clients a year. Although dramatic, this step cannot entirely solve the problem—accounting firms cannot drop all their clients. This chapter looks at other methods for reducing legal liability.

AUDITS

Traditionally, accountants gave tax advice and performed audits. Now, many of the larger firms also provide general management consulting on issues far afield from their traditional expertise—everything from information systems to long-range planning. Nonetheless, audits are still the bread and butter of many accountants, and most of the cases in this chapter involve audits that went awry. It is important therefore to understand the audit process.

Even in the traditional field of auditing, the accountant's role has altered. Formerly, auditors were primarily a watchdog for management, charged with detecting and anticipating financial problems. As the public ownership of stocks increased, however, investors began to need reliable financial information for evaluating their investments. Whereas the accountant had traditionally been a watchdog *for* management, investors needed a watchdog to keep an eye *on* management. Now, one of the accountant's most important roles is to serve as an independent evaluator of the financial statements issued by management to investors and creditors. The audit report of a CPA firm, particularly one of the Big Five, is practically required as an admission ticket to the capital markets—investors will not put up their money without it. In a very real sense, accountants serve two masters—company management and the investing public.

When conducting an audit, accountants verify information provided by management. Since it is impossible to check each and every transaction, they verify a sample of various types of transactions. If these are accurate, they assume all are. To verify transactions, accountants use two mirror image processes—vouching and tracing. In **vouching**, they choose a transaction listed in the company's books and check backwards to make sure that there are original data to support it. They might, for example, find in accounts payable a bill for the purchase of 1,000 reams of photocopy paper. They would check to ensure that all the paper had actually arrived and that the receiving department had properly signed and dated the invoice. The auditors would also check the original purchase order to ensure the acquisition was properly authorized in the first place. In **tracing**, the accountant begins with an item of original data and traces it forward to ensure that it has been properly recorded throughout the bookkeeping process. For example, the sales ledger might report that 1,000 copies of a software program were sold to a distributor. The accountant checks the information in the sales ledger against the original invoice to ensure that the date, price, quantity, and customer's name all match. The auditor then verifies each step along the paper trail until the software leaves the warehouse.

Since accountants do not check every transaction, the process of selecting those items that will be verified requires skill and experience. Auditors must continually modify their original plan to reflect discoveries they make during the audit. If they find that one aspect of the company's accounting system seems weak, they need to check those results more carefully.

In performing their duties, accountants must follow two sets of rules: (1) generally accepted accounting principles (GAAP) and (2) generally accepted auditing standards (GAAS). **GAAP** are the rules for preparing financial statements, and **GAAS** are the rules for conducting audits. These two sets of standards include broadly phrased general principles as well as specific guidelines and illustrations. The application and interpretation of these rules require acute professional skill.

OPINIONS

After an audit is complete, the accountant issues an opinion on the financial statements that indicates how accurately those statements reflect the company's true financial condition. The auditor has four choices:

- **Unqualified Opinion**. Also known as a **clean** opinion, this is the most favorable report an auditor can give. It indicates that the company's financial statements fairly present its financial condition in accordance with GAAP. A less than clean opinion is a warning to potential investors and creditors that something may be wrong.

- **Qualified Opinion**. This opinion indicates that although the financial statements are generally accurate, there is nonetheless an outstanding, unresolved issue. This may be a violation of GAAP or perhaps some important issue whose ultimate impact is uncertain. For example, the company may face potential liability from environmental law violations, but the liability cannot yet be accurately estimated. Depending upon the reason for the qualification, this type of opinion does not necessarily prevent a company from borrowing money or selling stock.

- **Adverse Opinion**. This opinion is definitely bad news. In the auditor's view, the company's financial statements do not accurately reflect its financial position. In other words, the company is lying about its finances (or to put it more politely, is "materially misstating certain items on its financial statements"). A company with an adverse opinion is generally unable to sell stock or borrow money.

- **Disclaimer of Opinion**. Although not as damning as an adverse opinion, a disclaimer is still not good news. It is issued when the auditor does not have enough information to form an opinion. If the auditor knows that the statements are inaccurate, she cannot hide behind a disclaimer of opinion; she must issue an adverse opinion.

The following article illustrates the important role that audits play in the financial health of the world economy. The International Accounting Standards Committee discloses its own proposal for international standards at **http://www.iasc.org.uk**.

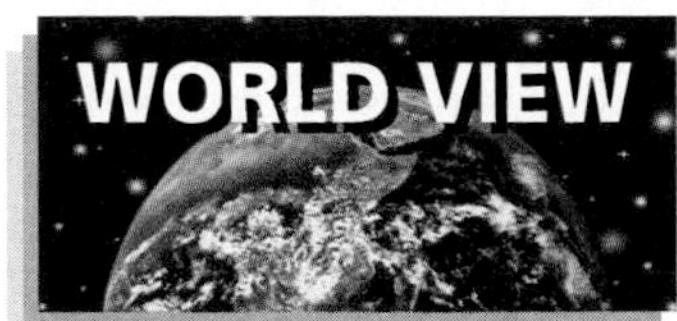

After putting their stamp of approval on the financial statements of Asian financial institutions that then collapsed, the world's five largest accounting firms are coming under increasing pressure to strengthen their audit procedures in Asian and other emerging markets. The Big Five, which audit almost all major corporations in the United States, also audited most of the big Asian banks that failed, according to a study by the United Nations. Investors and lenders had been given a false sense of assurance that the banks were strong when they saw the accounting firms' names on the audited financial statements. The study urged the Big Five firms to do the same strong auditing tests on financial statements in Asia that they do in the United States and Europe.

The United Nations study reviewed the financial statements of the largest companies and banks in South Korea, Thailand, Indonesia, Malaysia, and the Philippines. The study said that poor accounting did not directly cause the Asian financial crisis. But it said that the Asian financial difficulties would have been detected sooner, and the crisis would have been less severe, if the accounting methods used by the companies and their auditors had been stronger.[2]

LIABILITY TO CLIENTS

Clients file roughly 80 percent of all cases brought against accountants.[3] These suits are based on contract, negligence, fraud, or breach of trust.

CONTRACT

Contracts between accountants and their clients are either written or oral. A written contract is often called an **engagement letter**. The contract has both express and implied terms. The accountant *expressly* promises to perform a particular project by a given date. The accountant also *implies* that she will work as carefully as an ordinarily prudent accountant would under the circumstances. When an accountant enters into a contract to prepare, say, tax returns, she is making two promises—to complete the returns on time and to prepare them accurately. If she fails to do either, she has breached her contract and may be liable for any damages that result.

NEGLIGENCE

An accountant is liable for negligence to a client who can prove both of the following elements:

- **The accountant breached his duty to his client by failing to exercise the degree of skill and competence that an ordinarily prudent accountant would under the circumstances.** For example, if the accountant fails to follow GAAP or GAAS, he has almost certainly breached his duty. But the reverse is not true—compliance with GAAP and GAAS does not necessarily protect an accountant from liability.

---

[2] Melody Petersen, "U.N. Report Faults Big Accountants in Asia Crisis," *New York Times*, Oct. 24, 1998, p. C1. Copyright © 1998 by The New York Times Co. Reprinted by permission.

[3] Clients include "successors" such as trustees in bankruptcy. If a client files for bankruptcy protection, a trustee is sometimes appointed. This trustee has the right to pursue the bankrupt's claims. Chapter 27, on bankruptcy, discusses this issue in more detail.

- **The accountant's violation of duty caused harm to the client.** To recover damages, the client must be able to show that the accountant's misdeeds injured her.

In the following case, the accountant undoubtedly violated his duty to his client, but did he cause harm?

GREENSTEIN, LOGAN & CO. v. BURGESS MARKETING, INC.
744 S.W.2d 170, 1987 Tex. App. LEXIS 9279
Court of Appeals of Texas, 1987

Facts: Greenstein, Logan & Co. audited Burgess Marketing, Inc., a company that owned gasoline stations and convenience stores in central Texas. For three years, Greenstein failed to discover that Burgess's comptroller was underpaying the company's federal excise taxes. Because the company's financial statements reported a net profit and positive net worth, management did not know that Burgess was actually insolvent and operating at a substantial monthly deficit. The Internal Revenue Service levied a $2.7 million tax lien against the company.

After finding that Greenstein had negligently failed to perform the audits in accordance with GAAS, the jury awarded Burgess $3.5 million in damages. Greenstein argued on appeal that its negligence had not harmed Burgess because the company would have had to pay the federal excise tax in any event. Greenstein's negligence simply delayed a legitimate payment. The jury was effectively holding Greenstein liable for Burgess's tax liability.

Issue: Did Greenstein's negligence harm Burgess?

Excerpts from Judge Thomas's Decision: Certified public accountants are liable for the damages proximately caused by their negligence just like other skilled professions. Accordingly, they owe their clients a duty to exercise the degree of care, skill and competence that reasonably competent members of their profession would exercise under similar circumstances.

An accountant usually discharges the duty owed to his client by complying with recognized industry standards, such as the "Generally Accepted Auditing Standards," when performing an audit. [An accounting professor testified that Greenstein's] work on the two audits [was] such a "flagrant, violent violation of the generally accepted auditing standards" that he felt compelled to testify against them.

Burgess immediately resumed paying the correct federal excise tax each month as soon as the underpayment was discovered, and Burgess immediately increased prices on non-gasoline items sold at the company's convenience stores and imposed stringent cost controls. These management decisions resulted in the company's operations again becoming profitable within six months. If Greenstein had discovered the underpayment [earlier] Burgess could have then made the same management decisions which he later made. This would have enabled Burgess to discharge the tax liability, plus penalties and interest, out of its operating profits without jeopardizing the company's existence.

The jury could have reasonably concluded from this evidence that the negligent failure of Greenstein to perform the audits in accordance with generally accepted auditing standards was a substantial factor in bringing about Burgess's bankruptcy, and that the damage would not have occurred but for such negligence.

Billy Joel may have liked uptown girls, but he had a downtown accountant.

Burgess could have brought suit against Greenstein for breach of contract in addition to negligence. The contract had, after all, implied that Greenstein would comply with GAAS. Although most negligence claims also involve a breach of contract, the reverse is not always true—breach of contract claims do not necessarily involve negligence. As mentioned earlier in the chapter, Big Five firms have begun to drop risky clients for fear of liability claims. If such a dismissal violates the terms of the engagement letter, the accounting firm is in breach of contract, but is not negligent.

FRAUD

An accountant is liable for fraud if (1) she makes a false statement of fact, (2) she either knows it is not true or recklessly disregards the truth, and (3) the client justifiably relies on the statement.[4] For example, Greenstein would have committed fraud if it had known that the Burgess financial statements were inaccurate, and the company reasonably relied on those financials.

A fraud claim is an important weapon because it permits the client to ask for punitive damages. In negligence or contract cases, a client is typically entitled only to compensatory damages.[5] For example, an angry Billy Joel sued his business manager (and ex-wife's brother) for financial mismanagement. He claimed a mere $30 million on the negligence and breach of contract claims but asked for $60 million in punitive damages on a fraud claim.

BREACH OF TRUST

Accountants occupy a position of enormous trust because financial information is often sensitive and confidential. Clients may put as much trust in their accountant as they do in their lawyer, minister, or psychiatrist. **Accountants have a legal obligation to (1) keep all client information confidential, and (2) use client information only for the benefit of the client.** What happens when an accounting firm discovers that one of its clients may injure other clients? In the following case, the firm made the wrong choice.

WAGENHEIM v. ALEXANDER GRANT & CO.

19 Ohio App. 3d 7, 482 N.E.2d 955, 1983 Ohio App. LEXIS 11194
Court of Appeals of Ohio, 1983

Facts: Joel S. Wagenheim founded Consolidata Services, Inc. (CDS) to provide bookkeeping and payroll services to businesses. Each new payroll client was required to deposit money with CDS to ensure that there would always be sufficient funds to cover the payroll checks. The contracts placed no restrictions on the use of the deposits by CDS except that, upon termination of a contract, the deposit was to be returned within 30 days.

CDS hired Alexander Grant & Co. as its accounting firm. Many of the clients who used CDS's payroll services were also clients of Alexander Grant, and, in fact, many had chosen Alexander Grant upon the recommendation of CDS and vice versa. When accountants from Alexander Grant discovered that CDS was $150,000 short of cash in its payroll account, they insisted that CDS disclose its cash flow problems to its clients immediately before any further funds were received. Wagenheim asked for time to raise the missing money. If forced to notify clients, he wanted to do so himself. CDS had never failed to fulfill its payroll obligations or return its customers' deposits.

---

[4] Fraud is discussed at greater length in Chapter 14, on capacity and consent.

[5] Compensatory and punitive damages are discussed in Chapter 5, on intentional torts, and Chapter 18, on remedies.

The next day, without notifying Wagenheim, Alexander Grant began calling their mutual clients to advise them not to send additional payroll funds to CDS. Most of the clients canceled their contracts with CDS. Ten days later, CDS closed down operations. Wagenheim sued Alexander Grant for breach of trust. The jury returned an award of $1.32 million.

Issue: Did Alexander Grant breach its duty of trust to Wagenheim and CDS?

Excerpts from Judge Strausbaugh's Decision: A client should be entitled to freely disclose information concerning his financial status to his accountant without fear that such information will be exposed to the public. This is not to say that a client enjoys an absolute right, but rather that he possesses a limited right against such a disclosure, subject to exceptions prompted by the supervening interests of the public. Ohio recognizes no statutory or common-law privilege prohibiting an accountant from revealing in a court of justice information acquired during an accountant-client relationship.

As has been created in both the legal and medical professions, the State Accountancy Board has promulgated its own code of professional conduct. [The Code states:] "A certified public accountant or public accountant shall not disclose any confidential information obtained in the course of a professional engagement except with the consent of the client."

[A] mere breach of the ethical concepts established by the accountancy board does not provide a cause of action for misconduct; however, these standards do give credence to the proposition that it is within the expectations of both parties involved that these restrictions will not be violated. In essence, there is a reasonable expectation that Alexander Grant in providing accounting services to the public will conduct itself in a professional manner consistent with those standards established within the state. As a result, there is a legal obligation existing in every accountant-client relationship in which it participates, unless specifically excluded, that all information communicated to the defendant by its client in confidence should not be disclosed without the client's prior consent.

Judgment *affirmed.*

LIABILITY TO THIRD PARTIES

Suppose that a professional basketball team signs a star college player to a three-year contract. A leading cardiologist examines the player and pronounces him "in perfect health." You purchase stock in the team in reliance on this assertion. Unfortunately, the cardiologist is wrong, and the player collapses in his first pro game. His career is over and the team's future is bleak. The value of your stock plummets. Although you feel the doctor has singlehandedly wiped out your investment, you cannot recover from him because he owes you no duty.

Suppose, on the other hand, that you had purchased stock in the team because you were impressed with its financial prospects as revealed in its audited financial statements. Unfortunately, the team's auditors overstated the company's income. The value of the stock dives when the mistake comes to light. You may be able to recover from the auditors. Why are accountants different from doctors or other professionals?

No issue in the accounting field is more controversial than liability to third parties. Plaintiffs argue that auditors owe a duty to a trusting public that doctors (and other professionals) do not. The job of the auditor, they say, is to provide an independent, professional source of assurance that the audited company's financial statements are accurate. If the auditors do their job properly, they have nothing to fear. The accounting profession rebuts, however, that if everyone who has ever been harmed even remotely by a faulty audit can recover damages, there will soon be no auditors left.

One observation before beginning: accountants are generally not liable to third parties in *contract* because there is no in *privity of contract*.[6] Most third parties are incidental beneficiaries who are not entitled to enforce a contract. (We discuss third party beneficiaries in Chapter 16.)

NEGLIGENCE

Accountants' liability for negligence to third parties is determined by state law. Most states follow one of the following rules: the *Ultramares* doctrine, the foreseeable doctrine, or the Restatement doctrine.

Ultramares Doctrine

In 1931, while serving on the New York Court of Appeals, Judge Benjamin Cardozo decided the case of *Ultramares Corp. v. Touche*,[7] an influential decision that is still the law in a number of states. Fred Stern & Co. imported rubber. Stern asked the Ultramares Corp. for a loan to finance these purchases. As a condition of any loans, Ultramares insisted upon an audited balance sheet. The auditors, Touche, Niven & Co., never learned exactly who would see the financial statements, but knew a number of potential creditors might. On the basis of a balance sheet listing a net worth of $1 million, Ultramares loaned money to Stern. In reality, however, the company was insolvent; management had falsified the books. The auditors failed to follow paper trails leading to "off-the-books" transactions that, if properly analyzed, would have revealed the company's insolvency. When Stern failed to repay the loans, Ultramares sued Touche for negligence. The jury awarded Ultramares $187,576.32. (The case was decided in 1931, at the height of the Great Depression. That was real money.)

Cardozo overturned the jury's verdict. If third parties were able to recover for negligence against an accounting firm, then "[a] thoughtless slip or blunder, the failure to detect a theft or forgery beneath the cover of deceptive entries, may expose accountants to a liability in an indeterminate amount for an indeterminate time to an indeterminate class." Cardozo thought this hazard too extreme. **Under the *Ultramares* doctrine, accountants who fail to exercise due care are liable to a third party only if they know that the third party (1) will see their work product and (2) will rely on the work product for a particular, known purpose**. To be liable, the accountants must know the identity of the third party.

Consider an example of a later case in which a court found an accountant liable under the *Ultramares* doctrine: a limited partner sued an accountant who failed to disclose in an audit report that the general partners were withdrawing funds in violation of the partnership agreement. The limited partnership agreement contained an express provision requiring an annual audit by a CPA, and the auditor

---

[6] Two parties are in "privity of contract" if they have entered into a contract with each other. If two parties enter into a contract that affects a third party, that third party is not in privity.

[7] 255 N.Y. 170, 174 N.E. 441, 1931 N.Y. LEXIS 660 (1931).

had also prepared the partnership's tax returns on which the limited partners relied in preparing their personal returns. The accountant knew that his work product would be shown to the limited partners, and he knew their identity.[8]

Cardozo decided *Ultramares* in 1931, and since then, some of the country's notions about liability have changed. Although some states still follow the *Ultramares* doctrine, other jurisdictions have adopted different rules.

Foreseeable Doctrine

The courts in a limited number of states have held that an accountant is liable to any *foreseeable* users who suffer harm as a result of her carelessness. For example, Harry and Barry (we are not making this up) Rosenblum sold their business to Giant Stores Corp. in return for Giant common stock. In assessing the value of this stock, the two men relied on an audit by Touche Ross & Co. (which had the bad luck to be the accounting firm in the landmark cases that established both the *Ultramares* doctrine and the foreseeable doctrine). You will not be surprised to learn that Giant's financial statements turned out to be fraudulent and the stock worthless. Giant had manipulated its books by falsely recording assets that it did not own and omitting substantial amounts of accounts payable. **The court held that an accountant who fails to exercise due care is liable to a third party if (1) it was foreseeable that the third party would receive financial statements from the accountant's client, and (2) the third party relied on these statements.**[9] This standard creates greater liability for accountants than the *Ultramares* doctrine.

Restatement Doctrine

The majority of state courts have rejected the *Ultramares* doctrine as too narrow and the foreseeable doctrine as too broad. They prefer, instead, a middle ground that was adopted by the Restatement (Second) of Torts. **According to the Restatement, accountants who fail to exercise due care are liable to (1) anyone they knew would rely on the information and (2) anyone else in the same class.**

Suppose, for example, that Adrienne knows she is preparing financial statements for the BeachBall Corp. to use in obtaining a bank loan from the First National Bank of Tucson. If Adrienne is careless in preparing the statements and BeachBall bursts, she will be liable to First Bank *under all three tests:* the *Ultramares* doctrine, the foreseeable doctrine, and the Restatement doctrine.

Suppose, however, that the company takes its financial statements to the Last National Bank of Tucson instead. Under the *Ultramares* doctrine, Adrienne would not be liable because she did not prepare the documents for the Last Bank. She would be liable under the foreseeable doctrine because it was foreseeable that the Last Bank would receive the financial statements from the client and rely on them. She would also be liable under the Restatement doctrine because the Last Bank is in the *same class* as the First Bank. Once Adrienne knows that a bank will rely on the statements she has prepared, the identity of the particular bank should not make any difference to her when doing her work.

Suppose next that BeachBall uses the financial statements to persuade a landlord to rent a manufacturing facility. In this case, Adrienne would be liable under the foreseeable doctrine because this was a foreseeable use of the financial state-

---

[8] *White v. Guarente*, 43 N.Y.2d 356, 372 N.E.2d 315, 1977 N.Y. LEXIS 2470 (1977).

[9] *H. Rosenblum, Inc. v. Adler*, 93 N.J. 324, 461 A.2d 138, 1983 N.J. LEXIS 2717 (N.J. 1983).

ments. She would not be liable under the Restatement doctrine, however, because the landlord is not in the same class as the First Bank, for whom Adrienne knew she was preparing the documents. Finally, if a major shareholder of BeachBall uses the financial statements to convince her boyfriend to marry her, Adrienne is not liable under any doctrine. The following table summarizes the three doctrines:

Under this doctrine:	Accountants who fail to exercise due care are liable to a third party if:
Ultramares Doctrine	They know the identity of the third party who: • Will see their work product, and • Will rely on the work product for a particular, known purpose
Foreseeable Doctrine	• It is foreseeable that the third party will receive financial statements from the accountant's client, and • The third party relies on these statements
Restatement Doctrine	• The accountants knew the third party would rely on the information, or • The third party was in the same class as someone who the accountant knew would rely on the information

In the following case, the California Court of Appeal applied the foreseeable doctrine, but the California Supreme Court overturned the lower court's decision and adopted the Restatement doctrine instead. Do you agree with the court's logic?

BILY v. ARTHUR YOUNG & CO.

3 Cal. 4th 370, 834 P.2d 745, 1992 Cal. LEXIS 3971
Supreme Court of California, 1992

Facts: Osborne Computer Corp. was among the first companies to manufacture portable personal computers. Sales of the company's sole product, the Osborne I computer, quickly reached $10 million per month, making the company one of the fastest growing enterprises in the history of American business. Arthur Young audited Osborne's financial statements. Shortly after plaintiffs purchased stock in Osborne, the company's sales declined sharply because of manufacturing problems with the new "Executive" model. When the Executive appeared on the market, sales of the Osborne I naturally decreased, but the company could not produce Executive units fast enough to replace Osborne I sales. The emergence of the IBM personal computer and IBM-compatible software further damaged Osborne's sales because the Osborne computers were not IBM compatible. Osborne filed for bankruptcy.

Arthur Young did not perform its audit in accordance with GAAS. Moreover, one of Arthur Young's auditors discovered millions of dollars in unrecorded liabilities, such as customer rebates and product returns. He recommended that a letter be sent to the company's board of directors disclosing this material weakness in the company's internal accounting controls, but his superiors at Arthur Young disagreed, and no letter was sent. The jury found Arthur Young liable for negligence and awarded damages of $4.3 million. The court of appeal affirmed.

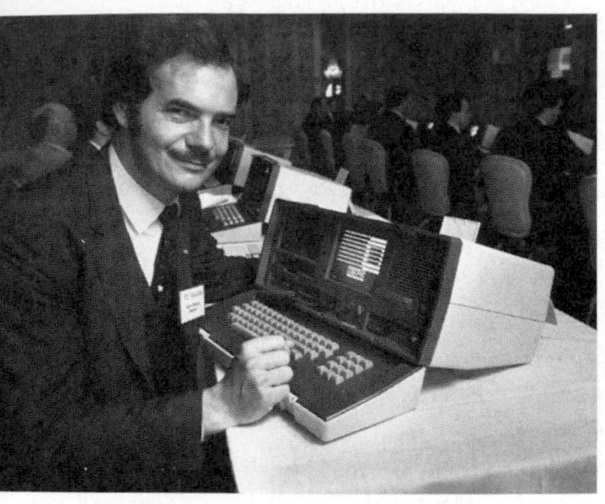

The investors in Osborne Computer Corp. expected this computer to set the world on fire. Instead, the company went up in smoke.

Issue: Under what circumstances is an auditor liable to third parties for negligence?

Excerpts from Chief Justice Lucas's Decision: A distinguishing mark of a profession is acceptance of its responsibility to the public. [But] an auditor is a watchdog, not a bloodhound. The client engages the auditor, pays for the audit, and communicates with audit personnel throughout the engagement. Because the auditor cannot in the time available become an expert in the client's business and record-keeping systems, the client necessarily furnishes the information base for the audit. Once the report reaches the client, the extent of its distribution and the communications that accompany it are within the exclusive province of client management. Thus, regardless of the efforts of the auditor, the client retains effective primary control of the financial reporting process.

Moreover, an audit report is not a simple statement of verifiable fact. Rather, an audit report is a professional opinion based on numerous and complex factors. [T]he report is based on the auditor's interpretation and application of hundreds of professional standards, many of which are broadly phrased and readily subject to different constructions. Using different initial assumptions, different sampling techniques, and the wisdom of 20–20 hindsight, few CPA audits would be immune from criticism.

As a group of corporate insiders and venture capitalists who were closely following the Cinderella-like transformation of the company, plaintiffs perceived an opportunity to make a large sum of money in a very short time by investing in a company they believed would (literally within months) become the dominant force in the personal computer market. Although hindsight suggests they misjudged a number of major factors (including, at a minimum, the product, the market, the competition, and the company's manufacturing capacity), plaintiffs' litigation-focused attention is now exclusively on the auditor and its report. Plaintiffs would have us believe that, had the Arthur Young report disclosed deficiencies in accounting controls and the $3 million loss (on income of over $68 million), they would have ignored all the other positive factors that triggered their interest (such as the company's rapid growth in sales, its dynamic management, and the intense interest of underwriters in a public offering) and flatly withheld all their funds.

[J]udicial endorsement of third party negligence suits against auditors limited only by the concept of forseeability raises the spectre of multi-billion-dollar professional liability that is distinctly out of proportion to: (1) the fault of the auditor (which is necessarily secondary and may be based on complex differences of professional opinion); and (2) the connection between the auditor's conduct and the third party's injury (which will often be attenuated by unrelated business factors that underlie investment and credit decisions). As a matter of economic and social policy, third parties should be encouraged to rely on their own prudence, diligence, and contracting power, as well as other informational tools. If, instead, third parties are simply permitted to recover from the auditor for mistakes in the client's financial statements, the auditor becomes, in effect, an insurer of not only the financial statements, but of bad loans and investments in general.

[This court adopts the Restatement doctrine and *reverses* the judgment of the court of appeal, which was based on the foreseeable doctrine.]

The opinion in *Bily* focused on fairness—to both auditors and third parties. Is one of these three doctrines—*Ultramares*, foreseeable, or the Restatement—fairer than the others? A few states have rejected all three doctrines and developed their own. Would a different doctrine be fairer than the standard three?

FRAUD

Under common law, courts consider fraud to be much worse than negligence because it is intentional. Therefore, the penalty is heavier. **An accountant who commits fraud is liable to any *foreseeable* user of the work product who justifiably relied on it**. This rule applies in all jurisdictions, even those that have adopted the *Ultramares* doctrine.

LIABILITY FOR QUALIFIED OPINIONS

Auditors can, under some circumstances, protect themselves from liability by issuing a less than clean opinion, that is, a qualified, adverse, or disclaimer of opinion. To avoid liability, the less than clean opinion must be issued for the right reasons. For example, if the auditor indicates that it has issued a qualified opinion because of uncertainty about environmental litigation, then it is not liable when the lawsuit bankrupts the company. But if the company runs into financial trouble because of some other problem that the auditors should have discovered, they are liable, despite their qualified opinion. For example, if the company survives its environmental lawsuit unscathed but runs into trouble because of inventory thefts that the auditors should have caught, the auditors would be liable.

SECURITIES ACT OF 1933

Third parties who have been injured by an accountant's error often file suit under the securities laws. Chapter 38, on securities regulation, provides a general overview of the liability provisions for both the Securities Act of 1933 (1933 Act) and the Securities Exchange Act of 1934 (1934 Act). This chapter offers a summary of these liability provisions as they affect accountants.

The 1933 Act requires an issuer to register securities before offering them for sale to the public. To do this, the issuer files a registration statement with the Securities and Exchange Commission (SEC). This registration statement must include audited financial statements. **Under §11 of the 1933 Act, auditors are liable for any material misstatement or omission in the financial statements that they prepare for a registration statement**.

To prevail under §11, the plaintiff must prove only that (1) the registration statement contained a material misstatement or omission and (2) she lost money. Ernst & Young served as the auditor for FP Investments, Inc., a company that sold interests in tax shelter partnerships. These partnerships were formed to cultivate tropical plants in Hawaii. The prospectus for this investment neglected to mention that the partnerships did not have enough cash on hand to grow the plants. A jury found that Ernst & Young violated §11 and awarded damages of $18.9 million to the investors.[10]

However, auditors can avoid liability under §11 by showing that they made a reasonable investigation of the financial statements and had reasonable grounds to believe the statements contained no material omissions or misstatements. This investigation is called **due diligence**. Typically, auditors will not be liable if they can show that they complied with GAAP and GAAS.

In the following case, the registration statement revealed some, but not all, of an investment's risks. The fund declined in value—for a reason that *was* disclosed. Should the accountant be liable for the *undisclosed* risks?

---

[10] *Hayes v. Haushalter*, 1994 U.S. App. LEXIS 23608 (9th Cir. 1994).

RODNEY v. KPMG PEAT MARWICK

143 F.3D 1140, 1998 U.S. App. LEXIS 9454

United States Court of Appeals for the Eighth Circuit, 1998

Facts: The plaintiffs invested in the Piper Funds Institutional Government Income Portfolio (the Fund). The Fund invested heavily in a type of security, called a "derivative," that is very sensitive to fluctuations in interest rates. If rates go up, the value of derivatives goes down, and vice versa. The Fund had disclosed this interesting fact in its registration statement. When the Federal Reserve Board tightened monetary policy, interest rates rose, and the price of Fund shares fell sharply. The investors filed suit against KPMG under §11 of the 1933 Act, alleging that its audit should have disclosed the following discrepancies:

- The Fund invested in a type of derivative that was not disclosed in the registration statement. This new type of investment was also sensitive to interest rate changes.
- The Fund's portfolio had a longer life expectancy than disclosed. For this type of investment, the longer the life expectancy, the higher the risk.
- The Fund's registration statement promised that it would not invest in illiquid securities (that is, securities that are not readily marketable). As much as 52 percent of the Fund's portfolio was illiquid.

You Be the Judge: Was KPMG's failure to disclose this information a material omission? Should the accounting firm be liable to investors?

Argument for KPMG: After reading the registration statement, no reasonable person could fail to understand that the Fund intended to purchase highly risky investments. In particular, investors were on full notice that, if interest rates went up, the value of their investment would go down. That is exactly what happened. The Fund's investments may not have complied *exactly* with the guidelines in the registration statement, but the risk was the same. When the information in a registration statement clearly discloses the precise risks that ultimately cause a decline in the stock's value, investors can hardly claim that they were misled.

Argument for the Investors: The registration statement was inaccurate. Although investors were warned about the danger of rising interest rates, they were not told about the other risks. If the truth about the Fund's investments had been disclosed, the plaintiffs might have avoided the Fund or at least bought at a cheaper price. Suppose an investment involves 10 risks, but purchasers are only told about three of them. If the investment declines in value because one of the disclosed risks comes to pass, a violation of the statute has still occurred because the other seven should have been disclosed, too. Under §11, plaintiffs need prove only that the registration statement contained a material misstatement and they lost money. Investors had the right to know not only that their purchase was risky, but how risky and why.

SECURITIES EXCHANGE ACT OF 1934

A company that is subject to the 1934 Act must file with the SEC an annual report containing audited financial statements and quarterly reports with unaudited financials.

Liability for Inaccurate Disclosure in a Required Filing

Under §18 of the 1934 Act, an auditor who makes a false or misleading statement in a required filing is liable to any buyer or seller of the stock who has acted in reliance on the statement. The auditors can avoid liability by showing that they acted in *good faith* and did not know the information was misleading.

Fraud

Primary Liability. Most securities litigation against accountants is brought under §10(b) and Rule 10b–5 of the 1934 Act. **Under §10(b), an auditor is liable for making (1) a misstatement or omission of a material fact (2) knowingly or recklessly (3) that the plaintiff relies on in purchasing or selling a security.** This is called **primary** liability because the accountants are liable for statements that they made themselves.

At the heart of §10(b) cases is this question: What can shareholders reasonably expect an accountant to uncover in the course of an audit? Consider the following news report. Did the auditors make a knowing or reckless misstatement?

Miniscribe appeared to be a wildly successful Colorado company that manufactured computer hard disk drives. Customers were buying disk drives faster than the company could make them—a lot faster. Company officers were afraid the stock price would plummet if investors found out about the shortage, so they developed a plan to solve the problem—temporarily. First, they created a computer program, subtly entitled "Cook Book," to inflate inventory numbers. Then they helped their sales numbers by shipping out bricks wrapped up to look like disk drives. The final step was to alter the company's financial statements to pretend that the bricks were computer parts.

The company's chief financial officer directed one of his employees, Warren Perry, to break into the auditors' locked trunks to alter the financial statements. During a tour in the U.S. Navy, Perry had seen a film on how to pick locks. After breaking into the trunks, he transposed numbers on the financial statements, figuring that if the discrepancies were detected, he could claim they were keypunch errors. (Wrong!)

When investors sued Arthur Young for violating §10(b), the accounting firm argued it should not be responsible for a company that was willing to break into locked trunks. For their part, the plaintiffs contended that the company's behavior was so egregious, the accounting firm certainly should have noticed there was a problem. The jury awarded the plaintiffs $550 million, although the parties subsequently settled the case for a lesser amount.

Aiding and Abetting. For a *primary* violation of §10(b), the defendant must have made a knowing or reckless omission or misstatement himself. That can be difficult to prove. Some plaintiffs successfully argued that even an accountant who had not made knowing or reckless misstatements himself could be liable for **aiding and abetting** others who made untrue statements. These cases created enormous potential liability for accountants. In 1994, however, the Supreme Court overruled this whole line of cases, holding that private plaintiffs cannot recover damages on claims of aiding and abetting.[11] What the Supreme Court giveth, Congress (at least partly) taketh away. Congress amended the 1934 Act to permit the *SEC* to prosecute those who aid and abet others in making untrue statements in connection with the purchase or sale of a security.[12]

Whistleblowing

Under §10A, a new provision added to the 1934 Act, auditors who suspect that a client has committed an illegal act must ensure that the client's board of directors is notified. If the board fails to take appropriate corrective action, the auditors must issue an official report to the board. If the board receives such a report from its auditors, it must notify the SEC within one business day (and send a copy of this notice to its accountant). If the auditors do not receive this copy, they must notify the SEC themselves.

The scope of §10A is broad, covering insider trading, price-fixing, and any other violations of state and federal law. While doing an audit of the Cronos Group, Arthur Andersen questioned a $1.5 million "disbursement." When the shipping company refused either to provide an explanation or to investigate this mysterious payment, the accounting firm filed an official report with the board of

---

11 *Central Bank v. First Interstate Bank*, 511 U.S. 164, 114 S. Ct. 1439, 1994 U.S. LEXIS 3120 (1994).

12 Private Securities Litigation Reform Act, 15 U.S.C.S. §78t(f).

directors and resigned as Cronos's auditor. Cronos then filed the Andersen report with the SEC, which investigated the incident. Not surprisingly, many auditors are unenthusiastic about this new statute. It is not a pretty choice—the wrath of the SEC if they fail to cooperate or the anger of their clients if they do comply.

Joint and Several Liability

Traditionally, liability under the 1934 Act was **joint and several**. When several different participants were potentially liable, a plaintiff could sue any one defendant or any group of defendants for the full amount of the damages. If a company committed fraud and then went bankrupt, its accounting firm might well be the only defendant with assets. Even if the accountants had caused only, say, 5 percent of the damages, they could be liable for the full amount.

Congress recently amended the 1934 Act to provide that accountants are liable jointly and severally only if they knowingly violate the law. Otherwise, the defendants are proportionately liable, meaning that they are liable only for the share of the damages that they themselves caused.

CRIMINAL LIABILITY

Thus far the discussion has focused on civil liability. The penalty for a civil offense is the payment of monetary damages. However, some offenses are criminal acts for which the punishment is a fine and imprisonment:

- The Justice Department has the right to prosecute willful violations under either the 1933 Act or the 1934 Act.
- The Internal Revenue Code imposes various criminal penalties on accountants for wrongdoing in the preparation of tax returns.
- Many states prosecute violations of their securities laws.

OTHER ACCOUNTANT-CLIENT ISSUES

THE ACCOUNTANT-CLIENT RELATIONSHIP

Suppose that your Big Five accounting firm audits Learn.com, Inc., a hot new Internet company that provides online training services. When a corporate customer buys Learn.com's software, it needs an army of consultants to install the software, fine-tune it, and train company employees to use it. Learn.com recommends to purchasers that they hire the consulting branch of your accounting firm for this purpose. Last year, consulting fees from Learn.com were 10 times your auditing fees.

While auditing Learn.com, you discover questionable accounting practices. In your opinion, the company should not only change these questionable practices, but also restate its earnings. If you insist, Learn.com may walk away from your firm altogether. If the company remains a client and restates its earnings, sales may suffer, jeopardizing your firm's business installing software.

The SEC has long been concerned about the relationship between accountants and the companies they audit. The SEC rules of practice specify that an accountant who engages in "unethical or improper professional conduct" may be banned from practice before the SEC.[13] Auditors who are banned or suspended cannot

[13] 17 C.F.R. §201.102(e)(1)(iv).

perform the audits required by the 1933 and 1934 Acts—quite a professional blow. Each year, the SEC charges about 25 accountants with unprofessional conduct.

As an example of unethical or unprofessional conduct, SEC rules prohibit accountants from owning stock in a company that their firm audits.[14] The SEC recently accused PricewaterhouseCoopers of violating this rule. The agency discovered 70 cases in which the firm's partners, employees, and pension fund owned stock of audit clients. PricewaterhouseCoopers accepted censure, agreed to stop the practice, and paid $2.5 million for programs to increase awareness of the SEC's rules on this issue.[15]

Buying stock in a company that your firm audits creates obvious conflicts. However, the SEC is now concerned about subtler behavior. The agency recently created the Independent Standards Board to decide whether its rules should be tightened. The SEC has asked the Standards Board to propose a rule requiring auditors to meet annually with the boards of any companies for which they perform both auditing and consulting services to explain why these potential conflicts do not, in fact, impair their judgment.

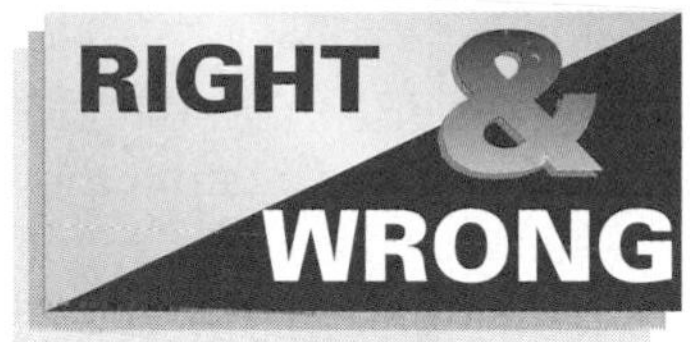

Your team arrives at a client's office to begin its audit. An eager young manager is introduced to you as your host for the week. After a warm welcome, he gives you an "audit-planning memo" that lists meals at fancy restaurants, trips to NBA basketball games, and shopping. Should you accept this hospitality? Could it interfere with your ability to audit carefully? Could it create the *appearance* of a conflict of interest? Would it fail any of the ethics tests in Chapter 9?

Why was the auditor so careless in the following case?

POTTS v. SECURITIES AND EXCHANGE COMMISSION
151 F.3d 810, 1998 U.S. App. LEXIS 17831
United States Court of Appeals for the Eighth Circuit, 1998

Facts: Robert D. Potts, a partner at the accounting firm Deloitte & Touche, served as the concurring partner for audits of Kahler Corp. A concurring partner reviews the work of, and acts as a sounding board for, the accountants who actually perform the audit.

This case involved Kahler's accounting treatment of the University Park hotel. For two years, Kahler accounted for the hotel as an asset held for sale. As a result, the first year Kahler showed a net gain instead of a $1 million loss; the second year its loss was $1.8 million instead of $2.8 million. Before a property can count as an asset held for sale, the company must commit to a formal plan to sell its entire interest in the property. Kahler did not have a formal plan, and it was seeking investors to buy only part of the hotel. Although Kahler's board of directors first authorized the partial sale of the hotel in April, the company backdated this approval to the beginning of the year.

Potts reviewed the file that showed Kahler's board had authorized the sale of only a partial interest in the hotel. On Potts's suggestion, Gregory Melsen, the lead auditor, met with Kahler's internal audit committee; afterwards Melsen assured Potts that Kahler was committed to a complete sale of the hotel. Potts took Melsen's word for it without further investigation. Melsen, however, had no evidence and was relying on nothing more than the audit committee's say-so. Nonetheless, Potts signed off on the Kahler audits. The SEC suspended Potts for improper professional conduct on the grounds that he had acted with reckless disregard of his duties as an independent auditor. Potts appealed.

Issue: Should Potts be suspended from practice before the SEC?

---

[14] Rule 2-01(b) of Regulation S-X.

[15] In the Matter of PricewaterhouseCoopers, Administrative Proceedings, File No. 3-9809, Release No. 1098, Jan. 14. 1999.

Excerpts from Judge Fagg's Decision: Potts contends the record fails to sustain the SEC's finding of recklessness. To be reckless, Potts's performance had to represent an extreme departure from the standards of ordinary care, which presented a danger of misleading buyers or sellers that [was] either known to [Potts or was] so obvious that [Potts] must have been aware of it. The question in this case is whether the record shows Potts's conduct amounted to an egregious refusal to see the obvious, or to investigate the doubtful.

Kahler's accounting treatment of the hotel mattered. It made all the difference between showing a profit instead of a loss. Despite this evident importance, and despite signals that Kahler's treatment of the hotel was suspect, Potts approved the audits based on Melsen's unprobed, untested representations. Most glaringly, Potts countenanced Kahler's backdating of the "asset held for sale" treatment to the start of [the year]. From all this, reasonable people could conclude Potts's conduct was reckless. We affirm the SEC's order.

ACCOUNTANT-CLIENT PRIVILEGE

Traditionally, an accountant-client privilege did not exist under federal law. Accountants were under no obligation to keep confidential any information they received from their clients. In one notorious case, the IRS suspected that the owner of a chain of pizza parlors was underreporting his income. The agency persuaded the owner's CPA, James Checksfield, to spy on him for eight years. (The IRS agreed to drop charges against Checksfield, who had not paid his own taxes for three years.) Thanks to the information that Checksfield passed to the IRS, his client was indicted on criminal charges of evading taxes by failing to report over $300,000 in income.

Congress recently passed the Internal Revenue Service Restructuring and Reform Act that was intended, in part, to reduce IRS abuse of taxpayers. This statute provides limited protection for confidential communications between accountants and clients. That is the good news. The bad news is the word "limited." This new privilege applies only in civil cases involving the IRS or the U.S. government. It does not apply to criminal cases, civil cases not involving the U.S. government, or cases with other federal agencies such as the SEC. Nor does it apply to the preparation of tax returns. Thus, for example, this new accountant-client privilege would not have protected Checksfield's client because he was charged with a criminal offense.

Some states do recognize an accountant-client privilege, but a state privilege applies only to issues of state law and provides no protection against federal charges. The Checksfield case took place in Missouri, which does have an accountant-client privilege. However, because the IRS filed suit, federal law applied and Checksfield's information could be used in court. In the end, however, the IRS dropped the tax evasion charges out of concern that a jury would not believe Checksfield's testimony. Indeed, Checksfield suffered worse punishment than his client—the Missouri state board of accountancy revoked his CPA license for violating state law.

Working Papers

When working for a client, accountants use the client's own documents and also prepare working papers of their own—notes, memoranda, research. In theory, each party owns whatever it has prepared itself. Thus accountants own the working papers they have created. In practice, however, the client controls even the accountant's working papers. The accountant (1) cannot show the working papers to anyone without the client's permission (or a valid court order) and (2) must allow the client access to the working papers.

PROFESSIONAL RESPONSIBILITY

Are accountants ethical? Business executives think so, at least compared with other professionals. In a poll, 24 percent of executives cited accountants as the most ethical professionals, behind engineers at 34 percent. Investment bankers were in last place with 1 percent of the vote.

What is ethical behavior in the accounting profession? The American Institute of Certified Public Accountants (AICPA) issues a Code of Professional Conduct that establishes ethical standards for AICPA members. (The AICPA Code is available at **http://www.aicpa.org/**.) This code affects more than just AICPA members, however, because courts have consistently held that all accountants, even those who are not members of AICPA, must follow it. (In the *Wagenheim* case, earlier in this chapter, Alexander Grant was held liable for violating the professional code of the Ohio accountancy board. That state code was based on the AICPA Code.)

Here are the six fundamental principles of professional conduct listed in the code and a sample of rulings that interpret them:

I. *Responsibilities*. In carrying out their responsibilities as professionals, members should exercise sensitive professional and moral judgments in all their activities.

II. *The Public Interest*. Members should accept the obligation to act in a way that will serve the public interest, honor the public trust, and demonstrate commitment to professionalism.

III. *Integrity*. To maintain and broaden public confidence, members should perform all professional responsibilities with the highest sense of integrity.

IV. *Objectivity and Independence*. A member should maintain objectivity and be free of conflicts of interest in discharging professional responsibilities. A member in public practice should be independent in fact and appearance when providing auditing and other attestation services.

V. *Due Care*. A member should observe the profession's technical and ethical standards, strive continually to improve competence and the quality of services, and discharge professional responsibility to the best of the member's ability.

VI. *Scope and Nature of Services*. A member in public practice should observe the Principles of the Code of Professional Conduct in determining the scope and nature of services to be provided.

Rulings:

- An auditor should not accept more than a token gift from a client.
- Auditors may provide advisory services for a client, attend board meetings, counsel on potential expansion plans, advise on banking relationships, and interpret financial statements, forecasts, and other analyses.
- An accountant should not perform an audit for a client who has not paid its fee, whether billed or unbilled, for more than one year prior to the date of the audit report. An auditor might not be objective if she suspects that payment is contingent upon the client receiving a clean opinion.
- If a client offers employment to an accountant participating in an engagement, the accountant must remove herself from the engagement until she has rejected the employment offer.
- An accountant should not audit a financial institution if his credit card loans and cash advances from that institution exceed $5,000. An accountant can establish independence by reducing the outstanding balance to $5,000 or less.

CHAPTER CONCLUSION

Accountants serve many masters and, therefore, face numerous potential conflicts. Clients, third parties, and the government all rely on their work. Privy to clients' most intimate financial secrets, accountants must decide which of these secrets to reveal and which to keep confidential. The wrong decision may destroy the client or, alternatively, subject the accountant to a multimillion judgment for harm caused to third parties. To avoid litigation, accountants must always use the most scrupulous legal and ethical judgment. And even that may not be enough.

CHAPTER REVIEW

1. Accountants are liable to their clients for negligence if:
- They breach their duty to their clients by failing to exercise the degree of skill and competence that an ordinarily prudent accountant would under the circumstances, and
- The violation of this duty causes harm to the client.

2. Accountants are liable for fraud if:
- They make a false statement of fact
- They know it is not true or recklessly disregard the truth, and
- The client justifiably relies on the statement.

3. Accountants have a legal obligation to:
- Keep all client information confidential, and
- Use client information only for the benefit of the client.

4. State law determines an accountant's liability for negligence to third parties. Most states follow one of the following three rules:

(a) *Ultramares* Doctrine. Accountants who fail to exercise due care are only liable to a third party if they know the identity of the third party who:
- Will see their work product, and
- Will rely on the work product for a particular, known purpose.

(b) Foreseeable Doctrine. Accountants who fail to exercise due care are liable to a third party if:
- It is foreseeable that the third party will receive financial statements from the client, and
- The third party relies on these statements.

(c) Restatement Doctrine. Accountants who fail to exercise due care are liable to:
- Anyone they knew would rely on the information, and
- Anyone else in the same class.

5. An accountant who commits fraud is liable to any foreseeable user of the work product who justifiably relies on it.

6. Under §11 of the 1933 Act, auditors are liable for any material misstatement or omission in the financial statements that they provide for a registration statement.

7. Under §10(b) of the 1934 Act, an auditor is liable for making (1) any misstatement or omission of a material fact in financial statements (2) knowingly or recklessly (3) that the plaintiff relies on in purchasing or selling a security.

8. The SEC can prosecute those who aid and abet others in making untrue statements in connection with the purchase or sale of a security.

9. Under §10A of the 1934 Act, auditors who suspect that a client has committed an illegal act must ensure that the client's board of directors is notified.

10. Under the 1934 Act, accountants are liable jointly and severally only if they knowingly violate the law. Otherwise, they are proportionately liable.

11. A limited accountant-client privilege exists under federal law. Some states also recognize this privilege and apply it in matters involving state law.

PRACTICE TEST

1. Krouse, Kern & Co., Inc. made errors in its audit of Summit Power. Toro Co. relied on Krouse's faulty financial statements when making loans to Summit. Krouse did not know that Toro would rely on these reports. Indiana adheres to the *Ultramares* doctrine. Is Krouse liable to Toro?

2. **RIGHT & WRONG** Wayne and Arlene Selden invested in Competition Aircraft, a company that had once sold airplanes. Sometime later, however, it became a fraud and simply pretended to sell airplanes. After the company went bankrupt, the Seldens sought to recover from accountant William Burnett. He had recommended the investment to several of his clients, who communicated his recommendation to the Seldens. The Seldens were not Burnett's clients. The court adopted the Restatement doctrine. Is Burnett liable? Whether or not Burnett faces legal liability, was it a good idea for him to recommend investments to his clients? Does it create any potential conflicts of interest?

3. Color-Dyne printed patterns on carpets. After reviewing the company's audited financial statements, the plaintiffs provided materials to Color-Dyne on credit. These financial statements showed that Color-Dyne owned $2 million in inventory. The audit failed to reveal, however, that various banks held secured interests in this inventory. The accountant did not know that the company intended to give the financial statements to plaintiffs or any other creditors. Color-Dyne went bankrupt. Is the accountant liable to plaintiffs under the Restatement doctrine?

4. **CPA QUESTION** To be successful in a civil action under §11 of the Securities Act of 1933 concerning liability for a misleading registration statement, the plaintiff must prove:

	Defendant's Intent to Deceive	Plaintiff's Reliance on the Registration Statement
(a)	No	Yes
(b)	No	No
(c)	Yes	No
(d)	Yes	Yes

5. James and Penelope Monroe purchased securities offered by Hughes Homes, Inc., a retailer of manufactured housing in Tacoma, Washington. During its audit, Deloitte & Touche found that Hughes Homes' internal controls had flaws. As a result, the accounting firm adjusted the scope of its audit to perform independent testing to verify the accuracy of the company's financial records. Satisfied that the internal controls were functional, Deloitte issued a clean opinion. After Hughes Homes became insolvent, the Monroes sued Deloitte for violating §11 of the 1933 Act. They alleged that Deloitte's failure to disclose that it had found flaws in Hughes's internal control system was a material omission. GAAS did not require disclosure. Is Deloitte liable?

6. **CPA QUESTION** One of the elements necessary to hold a CPA liable to a client for conducting an audit negligently is that the CPA:

(a) Acted with *scienter* or guilty knowledge

(b) Was a fiduciary of the client

(c) Failed to exercise due care

(d) Executed an engagement letter

7. When Jeff Hall told one of the general partners of the Edge Energies limited partnerships that he did not wish to invest in these ventures, the general partner suggested he call Ronald W. Jackson, the partnerships' accountant. Jackson told Hall that Edge Energies partnerships were a "good deal," that they were "good moneymakers," and "they were expecting something like a two-year payoff." In fact, Jackson knew that the operators were mismanaging these ventures, and that the partnerships were bad investments. Hall relied on Jackson's recommendation and invested in Edge Energies. He subsequently lost his entire investment. Is Jackson liable to Hall? Does it matter which negligence doctrine applies?

8. **CPA QUESTION** A CPA's duty of due care to a client most likely will be breached when a CPA:

(a) Gives a client an oral instead of a written report

(b) Gives a client incorrect advice based on an honest error judgment

(c) Fails to give tax advice that saves the client money

(d) Fails to follow generally accepted auditing standards

9. The British Broadcasting Corp. (BBC) broadcast a TV program alleging that Terry Venables, a former professional soccer coach, had fraudulently obtained a £1 million loan by misrepresenting the value of his company. Venables had been a sportscaster for the BBC but had switched to a competing network. The source of the BBC's story was "confidential working papers" from Venables's accountant. According to the accountant, the papers had been stolen. Who owns these working papers? Does the accountant have the right to disclose the content of working papers?

10. **YOU BE THE JUDGE WRITING PROBLEM** Medtrans, an ambulance company, was unable to pay its bills. In need of cash, it signed an engagement letter with Deloitte & Touche to perform an audit that could be used to attract investors. Unfortunately, the audit had the opposite effect. The unaudited statements showed earnings of $1.9 million, but the accountants calculated that the company had actually lost about $500,000. While in the process of negotiating adjustments to the financials, Deloitte resigned. Some time passed before Medtrans found another auditor, and, in that interim, a potential investor withdrew its $10 million offer. Is Deloitte liable for breach of contract? **Argument for Medtrans**: Once an accountant has undertaken to serve a client, he cannot resign in a manner that causes harm to the client. Deloitte should have been more persistent in resolving the dispute and should not have resigned until the company could find another auditor. **Argument for Deloitte**: An auditor's duty is not only to the client but also to the public trust. Thus an auditor is required to place the integrity of the financial reporting process above the client. Deloitte had no choice but to resign, and quickly, when the client was uncooperative.

11. A partnership of doctors in Billings, Montana, sought to build a larger office building. They decided to finance this project using industrial revenue bonds under a complex provision of the Internal Revenue Code. They hired Peat Marwick to do the required financial work. The deal was all set to close when it was discovered that the accountants had made an error in structuring the deal. As a result, the partnership was forced to pay a significantly higher rate of interest. When the partnership sued Peat for breach of contract, the accounting firm asked the court to dismiss the claim on the grounds that the client could only sue in tort. Peat argued that it had performed its duties under the contract. The statute of limitations had expired for a tort case but not for a contract case. Should the doctors' case be dismissed?

INTERNET RESEARCH PROBLEM

Go to the SEC Web site (**http://www.sec.gov**) and click on *Enforcement Division*. Find five examples of actions that the SEC has brought against accountants. (You might try typing the term "accounting violations" in the search box.) What does the SEC allege that the accountants have done? What provisions of the securities laws has the SEC accused them of violating?

You can find further practice problems in the Online Quiz at http://beatty.westbuslaw.com or in the Study Guide that accompanies this text.

UNIT 6

GOVERNMENT REGULATION

CHAPTER 40

ANTITRUST: LAW AND COMPETITIVE STRATEGY, PART I

Mike Elliott was not looking for trouble when he brought an order form for Girl Scout cookies to work. Mr. Elliott, an employee at DaimlerChrysler's factory in Dearborn, Michigan, started asking co-workers to buy a few boxes on behalf of his girlfriend's eight-year-old daughter. "I worked for four or five hours, and suddenly this lady came up to me and said that a guy who worked 50 feet down the line from me was selling them cheaper," Mr. Elliott says. "The first thing that everyone thinks is, 'You're trying to rip me off. '"

In an increasingly competitive marketplace, price wars are breaking out over Thin Mints and Peanut Butter Patties. The 36,500-member Michigan Metro Council, citing rising costs and the need to subsidize inner city troops, reluctantly raised its price to $3 a box this year. The neighboring—but much smaller—Macomb County Girl Scout Council stayed at $2.50 a box, setting the stage for a marketing battle. However, most of the troops in this skirmish are not Scouts: they are grown-ups who peddle the cookies at work. Such scenarios have been repeated in other parts of the country, as many of the nation's 330 Girl Scout councils go through their annual pricing debate. Why don't the councils simply agree on one national price? Because antitrust laws prohibit price-fixing.[1]

Competition is an essential element of the American economic system. This is the topic of Chapters 40 and 41. What are the laws governing competition? Why have they developed this way? How can business executives make the right decisions?

IN THE BEGINNING

Throughout much of the nineteenth century, competition in America was largely a local affair. The country was so big and transportation so poor that companies primarily competed in small local markets. It was too costly to transport goods great distances. State laws rather than national statutes regulated competition.

By the second half of the nineteenth century, four railroad lines crossed the continent from coast to coast. For the first time, national markets were a real possibility. John D. Rockefeller saw the potential. In 1859, Edwin L. Drake, a retired railroad conductor, drilled the first commercially successful oil well in the United States. Three years later, when the 23-year-old Rockefeller entered the scene, the oil industry was full of producers too small to benefit from economies of scale. Production was inefficient, and prices varied dramatically in different parts of the country.

Rockefeller set out to reorganize the industry. He began by buying refineries, first in Cleveland and then in other cities. He and his partners spread into all segments of the oil industry—buying oil fields, building pipelines, and establishing an efficient marketing system. To unify the management of these companies, they transferred their stock to the Standard Oil Trust. By 1870, Rockefeller had achieved his goal—the Standard Oil Trust controlled virtually all the oil in the country, from producer to consumer. Rockefeller was the wealthiest person in the world. Even now, his great-grandchildren can live comfortably on their inheritances.

Some of Rockefeller's tactics were controversial. When a competitor tried to build an oil pipeline, Rockefeller used every weapon short of violence to stop it. He planted stories in the press suggesting the pipes would leak and ruin nearby fields. He flooded local builders with orders for tank cars so no workers would be available to build the pipeline. When the pipeline was finished, he refused to allow his oil to flow through it. These tactics were frightening, especially in an industry as important as oil. What if Rockefeller decided to raise prices unfairly? Or cut off oil altogether? Newspapers began to attack him ferociously.

SHERMAN ACT

With the coming of the railroads, it became clear that large companies might be able to control other industries as well. To prevent extreme concentrations of economic power, Congress passed the **Sherman Act** in 1890. It was one of the first national laws designed to regulate competition. Because this statute was aimed at the Standard Oil Trust and other similar organizations, it was termed **antitrust** legislation. In 1892, the Ohio Supreme Court dissolved the Standard Oil Trust,

[1] Rebecca Blumenstein, "Cookie Price War Sends Adult Troops into Marketing Battle," *Wall Street Journal*, Mar. 8, 1996, p. A1. Republished with permission of The Wall Street Journal; permission conveyed through the Copyright Clearance Center. Inc.

which was replaced by the Standard Oil Co. But the government was not satisfied until a spring day in 1911, when Supreme Court Chief Justice Edward White quietly read aloud his dramatic 20,000-word opinion ordering the breakup of Standard Oil.[2] The 33 companies that made up Standard Oil were forced to compete as separate businesses. Today, descendants of Standard Oil include Amoco, Atlantic Richfield, Chevron, Exxon, Mobil, and Pennzoil. Imagine what kind of giant they would be if still united.

For the first 70 or so years after the passage of the Sherman Act, most scholars and judges took the view that large concentrations of economic power were suspect, even if they had no obvious impact on competition itself. Big was bad. Big meant too much economic and political power. As Senator John Sherman, sponsor of the Sherman Act, put it, a nation that "would not submit to an emperor should not submit to an autocrat of trade." Fragmented, competitive markets were desirable in and of themselves. Standard Oil should not control the oil markets, even if the company was very efficient and had gained control by completely acceptable methods.

CHICAGO SCHOOL

Beginning in the 1960s and 1970s, however, a group of influential economists and lawyers at the University of Chicago began to argue that the goal of antitrust enforcement should be *efficiency*. Let a company grow as large as it likes provided that this growth is based on a superior product or lower costs, not ruthless tactics. Insist on a clean fight, and do not handicap large successful companies to help the slower runners. Some companies will thrive, others will die, but in either case, the consumer will come out ahead. Adherents of the **Chicago School** argued further that the market should decide the most efficient size for each industry. In some cases, such as automobiles or long-distance telephone service, the most efficient size might be very large indeed. Under traditional antitrust analysis, courts often asked, "Has a *competitor* been harmed?" The Chicago School suggests that courts should ask instead, "Has *competition* been harmed?"

At the turn of the twentieth century, President Theodore Roosevelt personally plotted the breakup of Standard Oil. (As one of Rockefeller's compatriots said of Roosevelt, "We bought the son of a bitch, and then he didn't stay bought.") At the turn of the twenty-first century, two descendants of Standard Oil—Exxon and Mobil—announced their intention to merge. This time, not one politician so much as grabbed a microphone to object to the recombination. Where once size alone was cause for concern, now regulators believe that a certain bulk may be necessary if American companies are to compete in the intense global economy.

Antitrust policy, however, continues to evolve. Adherents of the so-called **Post Chicago School** are beginning to recognize that competition alone may not be enough to protect consumers. For example, an industry with a large number of competitors may foster collusion, not competition. Or, activities that appear consumer-friendly, such as giving a product away for free, may in the long run harm consumers. (See, for example, the discussion in Chapter 41 of Microsoft's decision to give away its Internet browser.) Now, when deciding whether to take action, federal trustbusters are beginning to focus directly on consumers, asking two questions: Will this action cause consumers to pay higher prices? Are the higher prices sustainable in the face of existing competition? As you read the cases throughout this chapter and the next, think about which factors the court considered important: size, competition, or the impact on consumers.

---

[2] *Standard Oil Company of New Jersey v. United States*, 221 U.S. 1, 31 S. Ct. 502, 1911 U.S. LEXIS 1725 (1911).

OVERVIEW OF ANTITRUST LAWS

The major provisions of the antitrust laws are:

- Section 1 of the Sherman Act prohibits all agreements "in restraint of trade."
- Section 2 of the Sherman Act bans "monopolization"—the wrongful acquisition of a monopoly.
- The Clayton Act prohibits anticompetitive mergers, tying arrangements, and exclusive dealing agreements.
- The Robinson-Patman Act bans price discrimination that reduces competition.

The full text of all the antitrust statutes is available at **http://www.ftc.gov/ogc/stat2.htm**.

In 1914, Congress passed the **Clayton Act** in part because the courts were not enforcing the Sherman Act as strictly as it had intended. The purpose of the Clayton Act was to clarify the earlier statute. As a result, the two laws overlap significantly. The **Robinson-Patman Act** (passed in 1936) is an amendment to the Clayton Act. Rather than systematically reviewing the terms of each statute in order, this chapter and the next focus instead on the *kinds of behavior* that the antitrust laws regulate.

Violations of the antitrust laws are divided into two categories: **per se** and **rule of reason**. As the name implies, *per se* violations are automatic. Defendants charged with this type of violation cannot defend themselves by saying, "But the impact wasn't so bad," or "No one was hurt." The court will not listen to excuses, and the defendants are subject to both *criminal* and *civil* penalties. Typically, the Justice Department has sought criminal sanctions only against *per se* violators.

Rule of reason violations, on the other hand, are illegal only if they have an anticompetitive impact. To determine if an activity is an unreasonable restraint of trade, the courts consider its circumstances, intent, and impact. For example, if competitors join together and agree that they will not deal with a particular supplier, their action is illegal only if it harms competition. Although rule of reason violators may be subject to civil penalties or private lawsuits, traditionally the Justice Department has not sought criminal penalties against them.

Both the Justice Department and the Federal Trade Commission (FTC) have authority to enforce the antitrust laws. However, only the Justice Department can bring criminal proceedings; the FTC is limited to civil injunctions and other administrative remedies. In addition to the government, anyone injured by an antitrust violation has the right to sue for damages. The United States is unusual in this regard—in most other countries, only the government is able to sue antitrust violators. A successful plaintiff can recover treble damages from the defendant. Nonetheless, many companies prefer to leave antitrust enforcement to the government and avoid burdensome legal fees.

COMPETITIVE STRATEGIES

In developing a competitive strategy, managers typically consider two different approaches:

- Cooperative strategies that allow companies to work together to their mutual advantage
- Aggressive strategies, designed to create an advantage over competitors

Chapter 41 focuses on aggressive strategies. In this chapter we consider three different types of cooperative strategies that are potentially illegal:

- **Horizontal agreements** among competitors. An agreement between Levi Strauss and Calvin Klein Jeans—both manufacturers of denim jeans—would be a horizontal agreement.
- **Vertical agreements** among participants at different stages of the production process. An agreement between Levi Strauss and the Limited—one company makes jeans, the other sells them—would be a vertical agreement.
- **Mergers and joint ventures** among competitors. Here, companies go beyond simple agreements to combine forces more permanently. (Joint ventures are defined and discussed in Chapter 32, on starting a business.)

The following table lists the cooperative strategies that will be discussed in this chapter:

Horizontal Strategies	Vertical Strategies	Mergers
Market division	Reciprocal dealing	Horizontal mergers
Price-fixing	Price discrimination	Vertical mergers
Bid-rigging		Joint ventures
Refusal to deal		

HORIZONTAL COOPERATIVE STRATEGIES

Although the term "cooperative strategies" *sounds* benign, these tactics are often harmful to competition. Many horizontal cooperative strategies are *per se* violations of the law and can lead to prison terms, heavy fines, and expensive lawsuits with customers and competitors.

MARKET DIVISION

Any effort by a group of competitors to divide its market is a *per se* violation of §1 of the Sherman Act. Illegal arrangements include agreements to allocate customers, territory, or products. For example, these business schools would be in violation if:

- Georgetown agreed to accept only men and, in return, George Washington would take only women[3]
- Stanford agreed to accept only students from west of the Mississippi, leaving the east to Yale, or
- Northwestern agreed not to provide courses in entrepreneurship, while the University of Chicago eliminated its international offerings.

Despite the severe penalties imposed on violators, market division is a tempting strategy in a highly competitive market. Here are two cases from opposite ends of the country:

[3] This, of course, does not mean that all single-sex schools are violating the antitrust laws. They are in violation only if their admissions policy results from an *agreement* with competitors.

Prosecutors in New York recently settled an antitrust case against Thomas Gambino, the alleged capo of the Gambino crime family. Gambino pleaded guilty, paid a $12 million fine, and agreed to sell the most profitable part of his trucking business. His crime? He made a deal with three other truckers that gave each the right to serve certain sewing shops. These shops depend on the truckers to move their clothes to Seventh Avenue showrooms. Although Gambino acknowledged he had made the agreement, he argued that the truckers provided the sewing shops with many benefits, even bringing them business. Far from *harming* the shops, in his view, the agreement had *helped* them. No matter, any agreement not to compete is a *per se* antitrust violation.

Across the country in Washington State, three companies that controlled 80 percent of the state yearbook market paid $520,000 to settle a lawsuit alleging that the companies had illegally divided the yearbook market. A school district purchasing manager became suspicious when the companies doubled their prices one year. He wondered how they could manage such increases if there were competition in the market.

PRICE-FIXING AND BID-RIGGING

When competitors agree on the prices at which they will buy or sell products or services, their price-fixing is a *per se* violation of §1 of the Sherman Act. Bid-rigging is also a *per se* violation. In bid-rigging, competitors eliminate price competition by agreeing on who will submit the lowest bid. In an early case, the defendants argued that price-fixing was only wrong if the prices were *unfair*. The Supreme Court disagreed. In its view, prices should be set by markets, not by competitors—or judges. Moreover, "the reasonable price fixed today may become the unreasonable price of tomorrow."[4]

To understand price-fixing, put yourself in Jake Stone's shoes. A recent business school graduate, his student loans are larger than the Pentagon's annual budget, and his new bride is still working on her degree. They would like to get on with their adult life—buy a house, have children—but first they must establish themselves financially. However, after a year selling milk for Borden in Florida, Jake's commissions are still so low that he can scarcely survive financially, and he has missed some payments on his student loans. Milk is a commodity product, so it is difficult to convince customers that Borden's is better. He asks his boss for permission to lower prices and undercut competitors. But as soon as he offers a lower price, customers call their regular suppliers, who match, or even undercut, Jake's bid. His regular customers hear about these offers and demand the same low prices. His boss is irate over the reduced profits.

One day, when Jake is having lunch at the local burger hut, a middle-aged fellow comes over and introduces himself. He is a salesperson for Pet, one of Borden's major competitors, and he invites Jake to breakfast the following day with a couple of other guys. "Give you a good chance to learn something about this business," he says with a smile. Desperate to learn how to sell in this tough market, Jake goes to the breakfast. He must be doing something wrong. At breakfast, he learns what it is. The two men from Pet offer Jake a deal: if he will deliberately bid too high on a contract for the school districts in Pinellas County, they will give Borden part of the milk business elsewhere in Florida. If Jake refuses, well, they just smile at that. This kind of arrangement has been going on for years in the milk business in Florida. Jake's boss used to be a salesperson; maybe she was in on it, too. What should Jake do?

---

[4] *United States v. Trenton Potteries Co.*, 273 U.S. 392, 47 S. Ct. 377, 1927 U.S. LEXIS 975 (1927).

For the better part of a century, price-fixing and bid-rigging have been illegal, yet they never seem to go away. Here are some examples:

- *Dairy Industry*. Jake Stone's story is based on a true pricing conspiracy. By some estimates, price-fixing raised milk prices in Florida by 14 percent. Violations were first discovered when the Florida Attorney General began using a computer to analyze milk bids. Forty-three companies were convicted or pleaded guilty; two dozen individuals went to prison. Companies paid fines in excess of $90 million.[5]
- *College Athletics*. Colleges began to complain about the cost of their athletic programs. In particular, the cost of the coaching staffs seemed out of control. After all, some *assistant* coaches were being paid as much as $70,000 a year. In response, NCAA schools (that is, members of the National Collegiate Athletic Association) agreed to cap the salaries of assistant coaches at (a very stingy) $12,000. But a court blew the whistle, finding that the NCAA had engaged in illegal price-fixing. A jury awarded the coaches $66 million.
- *Airlines*. The Justice Department accused eight major airlines of negotiating agreements to raise fares and end discounts by sending elaborate signals about planned price changes over their jointly owned computerized ticket information system. Alaska Airlines, American, Continental, Delta, Northwest, TWA, United, and USAir agreed to new rules designed to prevent price-fixing in their industry.

For information about new and interesting price-fixing cases, check out **http://www.antitrust.org/**.

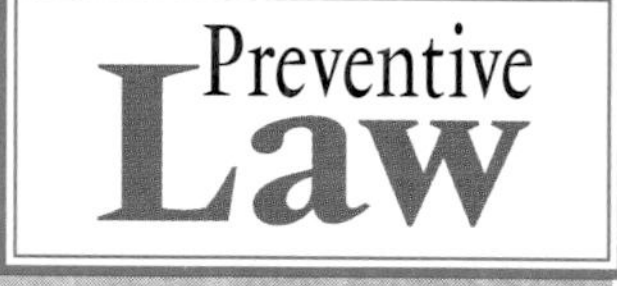

Price-fixing is a pervasive problem. It may be an exaggeration to say that "everyone is doing it," but it is no exaggeration to say "a lot of people are." What can managers do to prevent price-fixing violations?

- **Recognize the problem**. Certain industry conditions make price-fixing particularly tempting: a crowded and mature market, declining demand, difficulty in cutting costs, little product differentiation, or a threat to survival. Under these unfavorable market conditions, managers must learn to compete on dimensions other than price, such as special features or exceptional service.
- **Educate employees**. Employees often fall into antitrust trouble when they are uncertain about the line between legitimate market research and unlawful agreements with competitors. A sales rep who meets with a customer may bring back information about price changes a competitor plans to make next month. Some managers see it as a small next step to call their counterpart at the competing company and "confirm" the information obtained, but that conversation comes perilously close to an agreement between two competitors to coordinate their prices. Education can take many forms: presentations by company lawyers, constant reminders by management, and legal videos.
- **Set a good example**. The behavior of those in authority serves as an important role model to others. No company will escape the price-fixing virus unless the managers themselves have clean hands.
- **Adjust appraisal methods**. If salary, bonus, and advancement are based entirely on the volume of sales and profits, the pressure to fix prices will be that

[5] Jake Stone is not a real person, but this case is based on a true incident that occurred in Florida.

much greater. Better to compensate the sales forces on straight salary and evaluate on the basis of effort, not volume.

- **Centralize pricing decisions**. Salespeople who set their own prices are more susceptible to outside pressures. If price changes receive top management attention, violations of the law will decrease.
- **Avoid trade association meetings**. If an industry is particularly susceptible to price-fixing, it may be necessary to forgo trade association meetings altogether. As one executive put it, "Familarity breeds attempt."[6]

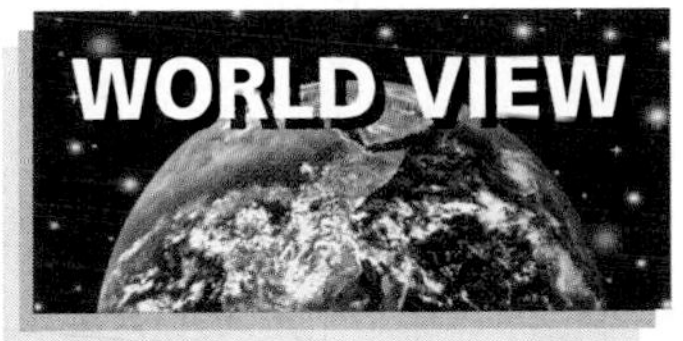

Antitrust laws in the United States are stricter—and more diligently enforced—than those in most other countries. How far offshore do our laws stretch? American companies that engage in anticompetitive behavior overseas are generally subject to U.S. antitrust laws only if their behavior has an impact on trade in the United States. When are foreign companies subject to U.S. antitrust laws? The following case addresses this issue.

UNITED STATES v. NIPPON PAPER INDUSTRIES CO., LTD.
109 F.3d 1, 1997 U.S. App. LEXIS 4939
United States Court of Appeals for the First Circuit, 1997

Facts: Nippon Paper Industries Co., Ltd. (NPI) was a Japanese company that manufactured fax paper. In a series of meetings held only in Japan, NPI agreed with a group of other companies to fix the price of thermal fax paper throughout North America. NPI subsequently sold $6 million worth of the paper in the United States at inflated prices. The U.S. Justice Department obtained a criminal indictment alleging that NPI had violated §1 of the Sherman Act.

NPI moved to dismiss the indictment on the grounds that the conduct in question, if it occurred at all, had taken place in Japan. The district court agreed with NPI and dismissed the case. The Justice Department appealed.

Issue: Does the Sherman Act apply to conduct that took place entirely overseas?

Excerpts from Judge Selya's Decision: Our law has long presumed that legislation of Congress, unless a contrary intent appears, is meant to apply only within the territorial jurisdiction of the United States. In *American Banana Co.*, the Court considered the application of the Sherman Act in a civil action concerning conduct which occurred entirely in Central America and which had no discernible effect on imports to the United States. The Court held that the defendant's actions abroad were not proscribed by the Sherman Act.

Our jurisprudence is precedent-based, but it is not static. In *Hartford Fire Ins. Co.*, the Justices [permitted] antitrust claims under Section One to go forward despite the fact that the actions which allegedly violated Section One occurred entirely on British soil. While noting *American Banana*'s initial disagreement with this proposition, the *Hartford Fire* Court deemed it "well established by now that the Sherman Act applies to foreign conduct that was meant to produce and did in fact produce some substantial effect in the United States."

To sum up, the case law now conclusively establishes that antitrust actions predicated on wholly foreign conduct which has an intended and substantial effect in the United States come within Section One's jurisdictional reach. We accept the government's cardinal argument, reverse the order of the district court, reinstate the indictment, and remand for further proceedings.

---

[6] Jeffrey Sonnenfeld and Paul R. Lawrence, "Why Do Companies Succumb to Price Fixing?" *Harvard Business Review*, July-Aug. 1978, pp. 145–157.

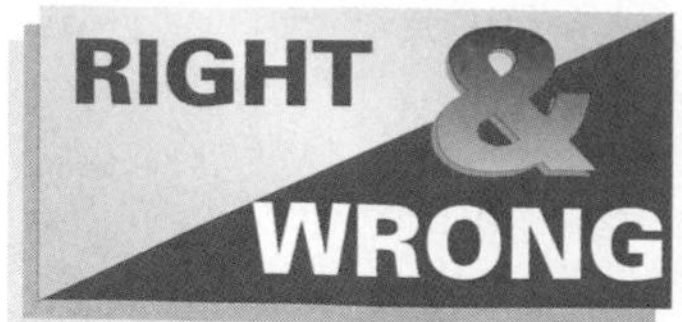

The ethics discussion in Chapter 9 considered the possibility that illegal behavior could sometimes be ethical. Price-fixing is a *per se* violation of the law. Are there times when it might nonetheless be ethical? For example, every year the Council of Fashion Designers of America puts on a major fashion show under tents in New York's Bryant Park. This show offers an opportunity for up-and-coming designers to mix with more established names—and to attract media attention. The newcomers complained, however, that they could not compete with famous designers and attract vital media attention without hiring top models. But the price of these superstar models was too high: upwards of $10,000 for a three-hour show. Sympathetic to the newcomers' plight, the Council capped modeling fees at $750 an hour for supermodels and $500 for rookies. Is this price-fixing illegal? Is it ethical to protect the inexperienced designers?

REFUSALS TO DEAL

Every company generally has the right to decide with whom it will or will not do business. **However, a refusal to deal violates the Sherman Act if it harms competition.** In a **refusal to deal**, a group of competitors boycotts a buyer, supplier, or even another competitor. This is a rule of reason violation, illegal only if it harms competition. For example, a group of clothing manufacturers agreed that they would not sell apparel to retailers who also bought from style pirates—companies that copied the manufacturers' designs. The Supreme Court held that this was an illegal refusal to deal because it was harming competition.[7] In the following case, an upstart law school claimed that the powerful American Bar Association (ABA) had engaged in an illegal refusal to deal. You weigh the arguments and provide a verdict.

MASSACHUSETTS SCHOOL OF LAW AT ANDOVER v. AMERICAN BAR ASSOCIATION

107 F.3d 1026, 1997 U.S. App. LEXIS 3602
United States Court of Appeals for the Third Circuit, 1997

Facts: In good entrepreneurial fashion, Massachusetts School of Law (MSL) identified a market niche and moved to fill it. The niche was low-cost legal education. While tuition at other law schools averaged nearly $20,000 a year, MSL charged only $9,000. But the school could not provide Ritz service at Motel 6 prices; it was unable to meet the ABA's strict accreditation standards. In particular, MSL could not meet the ABA's standards on student/faculty ratio, part-time faculty, teaching load, sabbaticals, limits on the number of hours students could be employed, and number of books in the library. The Massachusetts Board of Regents accredited MSL, but the ABA would not. As a result, MSL graduates could take the bar examination only in Massachusetts and four other states. MSL's enrollment and tuition revenues suffered. The school alleged that the ABA had engaged in an illegal boycott by refusing to accredit it.

You Be the Judge: Is the ABA's refusal to accredit MSL an illegal boycott?

Argument for MSL: The ABA's accreditation standards strike at the very heart of our mission, which is to provide affordable, high-quality legal education to people from less-than-privileged backgrounds. These include minority members, white ethnics, middle-aged people changing careers, and members of the working class. Of course, it would be wonderful if every student could afford to pay Ivy League tuition and attend law school full-time for three years. But are only the wealthy eligible to be lawyers?

The ABA's accreditation rules are designed to prevent low-cost competition. They have little bearing on the quality of a legal education. If we can find qualified instructors who are willing to work longer hours for lower pay, why should the ABA interfere? The

---

7 *Fashion Originators' Guild of America, Inc. v. Federal Trade Commission*, 312 U.S. 457, 61 S. Ct. 703, 1941 U.S. LEXIS 1318 (1941).

ABA standards might make sense at a school where faculty conduct research, but many able teachers (perhaps even the best teachers) are not interested in research. As for limiting student hours, medical residents often work 80 or 100 hours a week. Why shouldn't our full-time students be permitted to work more than 20 hours a week? Not everyone can afford to be unemployed. The ABA even wants to tell us how many books (and chairs!) we must have in our library. Those rules may have been sensible before computers, but if our students have access to LEXIS or WESTLAW, why do they need books?

The ABA has induced a boycott of MSL by state bar authorities who refuse to permit our students to *take* the bar exam. This boycott has an adverse impact on competition in the law school market—it reduces competition for law students by discouraging applications to MSL. With less competition, other schools can charge higher prices. Moreover, the ABA and state bar authorities want to restrict the number of lawyers and ensure higher pay for those who have already made it over the barrier.

Argument for the ABA: Lawyers fill a crucial role in our society. An incompetent lawyer is as dangerous as an ill-trained doctor. *Someone* has to set standards for law schools. Otherwise, unscrupulous diploma mills would unleash thousands of unqualified lawyers onto an unsuspecting public.

MSL has implied that we want to limit the supply of lawyers. Nothing could be further from the truth. More lawyers means more members for our organization. Rather, our goal is to prevent the profession as a whole from being discredited by a few incompetents.

We have set basic standards to ensure that new lawyers are adequately trained. If faculty teach too many hours, they have no time to stay abreast of new developments in their field or meet with students outside class. What kind of faculty can a school attract if it underpays them and forces them to teach a grueling schedule? As for student hours, "The law is a jealous mistress." Law students do more than memorize; they must *think* about the law. Concentration and thought are simply not possible for students who both work and attend school full-time. LEXIS and WESTLAW are valuable resources, but lawyers must know how to use law books. Besides, many research sources are not available by computer.

We have not organized a boycott. We have set standards that any state can embrace or reject. Massachusetts has accredited MSL and that is its prerogative. When a product fails to receive the "Good Housekeeping Seal of Approval," it does not mean that Good Housekeeping has organized a boycott. If MSL has difficulty attracting law students, it should look more carefully at its faculty, curriculum, and facilities.

Harvard University has a much grander law library than Massachusetts School of Law. Did the ABA violate the law when it refused to accredit MSL?

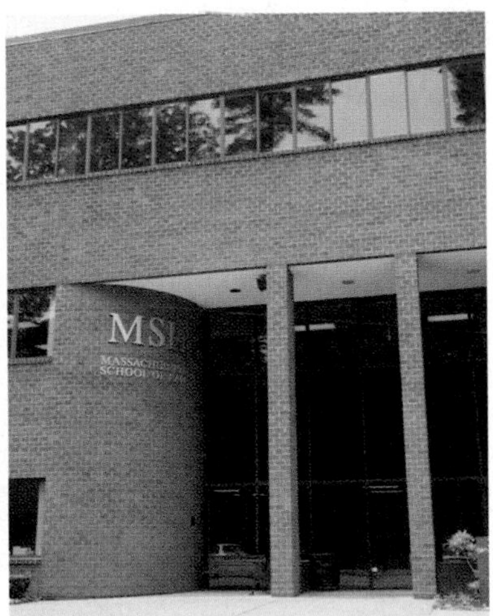

VERTICAL COOPERATIVE STRATEGIES

Vertical cooperative strategies are agreements among participants at different stages of the production process.

RECIPROCAL DEALING AGREEMENTS

Under a reciprocal dealing agreement, a buyer refuses to purchase goods from a supplier unless the supplier also purchases items from the buyer. Imagine that you are in the business of processing beets into sugar. During this process, it is easy to separate the seeds, which can then be used to grow more beets. Why not suggest to your beet suppliers that they buy their seeds from you? Why not further suggest that if *they* are not willing, you will find other suppliers who are?[8]

You are proposing a reciprocal dealing agreement. In the past, such arrangements were common. Many major corporations even kept computer records of purchases, sales, and "balance of trade" with other companies. Although these arrangements might have made *business* sense, the government took the view that they were also *rule of reason* violations of the Sherman Act; that is, they were illegal if they had an anticompetitive effect. The government brought suit against several companies, including a beet processor. It also halted a number of mergers that might have resulted in internal reciprocal arrangements. In recent years, however, the government has brought few of these cases. Reciprocal dealing agreements are likely to be a problem now only if they foreclose a *significant share* of the market and if the participants *agree* not to buy from others.

PRICE DISCRIMINATION

Under the Robinson-Patman Act, it is illegal to charge different prices to different purchasers if:

- The items are the same, and
- The price discrimination lessens competition.

However, it is legal to charge a lower price to a particular buyer if:

- The costs of serving this buyer are lower, or
- The seller is simply meeting competition.

Congress passed the Robinson-Patman Act (RPA) in 1936 to prevent large chains from driving small, local stores out of business. Owners of these "Ma and Pa stores" complained that the large chains could sell goods cheaper because suppliers charged them lower prices. As a result of the RPA, managers who would otherwise like to develop different pricing strategies for specific customers or regions may hesitate to do so for fear of violating this statute. In reality, however, they have little to fear.

Under the RPA, a plaintiff must prove that price discrimination occurred *and* that it lessened competition. It is now perfectly permissible, for example, for a supplier to sell at a different price to its Texas and California distributors, or to its health care and educational distributors, as long as the distributors are not in competition with each other.

The RPA also expressly permits price variations that are based on differences in cost. Thus Mattel would be perfectly within its legal rights to sell dolls to Toys "R" Us at a lower price than to the local Toy Shoppe if Mattel's costs are lower. Toys "R" Us often buys shipments the size of railroad containers that cost less to deliver than individual cartons. Toys "R" Us may also be willing to purchase in

---

[8] See *Betaseed, Inc. v. U & I, Inc.*, 681 F.2d 1203, 1982 U.S. App. LEXIS 17190 (9th Cir. 1982).

February—a month when toy demand is low. If it is cheaper to sell to Toys "R" Us, Mattel can legitimately charge lower prices.

Over the last decade, the federal government has virtually abandoned its enforcement of the RPA. Between 1937 and 1971, the FTC brought an average of 40 price discrimination cases each year; recently, it has averaged only one or two. Some federal officials have even urged that the RPA be repealed to prevent it from interfering with the smooth operation of the market. This fade-out of government action has left enforcement in the hands of individual plaintiffs, but these cases are receiving little encouragement from the courts. The following Supreme Court case indicates how difficult it is for plaintiffs to win under the RPA.

J. TRUETT PAYNE CO., INC. v. CHRYSLER MOTORS CORP.

451 U.S. 557, 101 S. Ct. 1923, 1981 U.S. LEXIS 49
United States Supreme Court, 1981

Facts: Truett Payne Co. went out of business after several decades as a Chrysler-Plymouth dealer in Birmingham, Alabama. The company alleged that Chrysler's various sales incentive programs violated the Robinson-Patman Act. Chrysler paid a bonus of several hundred dollars for each car sold that exceeded the dealer's sales objective. Payne received fewer bonuses than its competitors because Chrysler set Payne's objectives higher than other dealers'. Payne argued that it had effectively paid more for its automobiles than its competitors. Payne also contended that its damages should be based on (1) the price difference multiplied by the number of cars that it purchased and (2) the value of the company, which was now out of business. The jury returned a verdict against Chrysler and awarded Payne $111,247.48 in damages, which the district court trebled. After the court of appeals reversed, the Supreme Court granted *certiorari*.

Issue: **Did Chrysler's sales incentive programs violate the Robinson-Patman Act?**

Excerpts from Justice Rehnquist's Decision: Petitioner [that is, Payne] contends that once it has proved a price discrimination in violation of [the Robinson-Patman Act] it is entitled at a minimum to so-called "automatic damages" in the amount of the price discrimination. [In fact, it] must prove more than a violation of [the Act] since such proof establishes only that injury may result. [Petitioner must also prove actual damages.]

[The evidence for damages] consisted primarily of the testimony of petitioner's owner, Mr. Payne, and an expert witness, a professor of economics. Payne testified that the price discrimination was one of the causes of the dealership going out of business. In support of that contention, he testified that his salesmen told him that the dealership lost sales to its competitors, and that its market share of retail Chrysler-Plymouth sales in the Birmingham area [declined 4% in one year]. Payne contended that it was proper to infer that the 4% drop was a result of the incentive programs.

He also testified that the discrimination caused him to "force" business so that he could meet his assigned quotas. That is, his desire to make a sale induced him to "overallow" on trade-ins, thus reducing his profits on his used car operation. Payne adduced evidence showing that his average gross profit on used car sales was below that of his competitors, though that same evidence revealed that his average gross profit on new sales was higher.

Neither Payne nor petitioner's expert witness offered documentary evidence as to the effect of the discrimination on retail prices. Although Payne asserted that his salesmen and customers told him that the dealership was being undersold, he admitted he did not know if his competitors did in fact pass on their lower costs to their customers. Petitioner's expert witness testified that petitioner was harmed by the discrimination even if the favored purchasers did not lower their retail prices, since petitioner in that case would make less money per car.

We emphasize that even if there has been a violation of the Robinson-Patman Act, petitioner is not excused from its burden of proving antitrust injury and damages. For the foregoing reasons, the judgment of the Court of Appeals is vacated, and the case is remanded for proceedings consistent with this opinion.

It is so ordered.

In the past, the accepted formula for determining damages in a Robinson-Patman Act case was the difference between the two prices times the number of units purchased. These numbers are relatively easy to calculate. However, as the *Payne* case illustrates, now it is not enough to prove that competitors are able to buy at a lower cost. The plaintiff must also show that these competitors passed their savings on to customers and, as a result, plaintiff lost profits. These are difficult facts to prove. Antitrust lawyers often advise their clients not to worry too much about price discrimination suits because dissatisfied customers will usually not seek damages in court but will instead try to negotiate a better price.

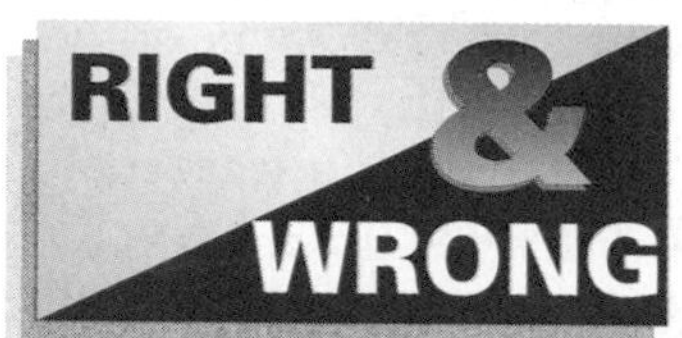

Although the *legal* environment is now more conducive to price discrimination, what about the ethical ramifications? Which stakeholders benefit and which suffer from such a practice?

MERGERS AND JOINT VENTURES

The Clayton Act prohibits mergers that are anticompetitive. Companies with substantial assets must notify the FTC *before* consummating a merger.[9] This notification gives the government an opportunity to prevent a merger ahead of time, rather than trying to untangle one after the fact.

Mergers have never been more popular. In one recent year, the U.S. government examined 4,728 proposed mergers, almost double the average of the prior five years. Among the mega-deals the government has recently reviewed are Exxon's $80 billion offer for Mobil Corp. and Bell Atlantic's $23 billion purchase of Nynex.

HORIZONTAL MERGERS

A horizontal merger involves companies that compete in the same market. Traditionally, the government has aggressively sought to prevent horizontal mergers that could lead to a monopoly or even a highly concentrated industry. In the *Von's Grocery* case, decided in 1966, the Supreme Court upheld the Justice Department in its suit to prevent the merger of two grocery chains that represented only 7.5 percent of the grocery market in Los Angeles.[10] Compare that decision with the following case, decided almost 20 years later.

---

[9] Notification is required if (1) one company has assets of at least $100 million and the other has assets of at least $10 million, and (2) the acquiring company is purchasing stock worth at least $15 million or 15 percent of the voting securities of the acquired company.

[10] *United States v. Von's Grocery Co.*, 384 U.S. 270, 86 S. Ct. 1478, 1966 U.S. LEXIS 2823 (1966).

UNITED STATES v. WASTE MANAGEMENT, INC.
743 F.2d 976, 1984 U.S. App. LEXIS 18843
United States Court of Appeals for the Second Circuit, 1984

Facts: Waste Management, Inc. (WMI) acquired Texas Industrial Disposal, Inc. (TIDI). Both companies were in the trash collection business. In Dallas, their combined market share was 48.8 percent. The trial court held that the merger was illegal and ordered WMI to divest itself of TIDI.

Issue: Did WMI violate the Clayton Act by acquiring TIDI?

Excerpts from Judge Winter's Decision: A post-merger market share of 48.8 percent is sufficient to establish *prima facie* illegality under *United States v. Philadelphia National Bank* and its progeny. That decision held that large market shares are a convenient proxy for appraising the danger of monopoly power resulting from a horizontal merger. Under its rationale, a merger resulting in a large market share is presumptively illegal, rebuttable only by a demonstration that the merger will not have anticompetitive effects.

[In the present case, the *Philadelphia National Bank*] presumption is rebutted by the fact that competitors can enter the Dallas waste hauling market with such ease. WMI argues that it is unable to raise prices over the competitive level because new firms would quickly enter the market and undercut them. A person wanting to start in the trash collection business can acquire a truck, a few containers, drive the truck himself, and operate out of his home. A great deal depends on the individual's personal initiative, and whether he has the desire and energy to perform a high quality of service. If he measures up well by these standards, he can compete successfully with any other company for a portion of the trade, even though a small portion. Over the last 10 years or so a number of companies have started in the commercial trash collection business.

We conclude that the 48.8 percent market share attributed to WMI does not accurately reflect future market power. Since that power is in fact insubstantial, the merger does not, therefore, substantially lessen competition in the relevant market and does not violate the [Clayton Act].

Traditionally, market share was the most important factor in evaluating mergers. In defining the relevant market, the U.S. government has become increasingly sensitive to issues of global competition. Thus the merger of the German Daimler-Benz with the American Chrysler Corp. caused little concern because their share of the world automobile market is small.

As *Waste Management* indicates, however, market share is no longer the sole issue in merger cases. The government and the courts now also consider how the merger will affect competition and consumers. Thus the government cleared a merger between aircraft giants Boeing and McDonnell Douglas, which together have a virtual monopoly on the American aircraft business. But the aircraft market is global, and American companies face severe competition from Europe's Airbus consortium. Therefore, the government believes that the merger will not harm competition.

Conversely, the FTC blocked the merger of office supply giants, Staples, Inc. and Office Depot. Nationally, these two retailers control only 4 percent of the market for office supplies. Is the FTC harking back to the days of *Von's Grocery*? Not exactly. The office superstores' national market share is relatively low because they have no stores at all in many areas of the country. Rather than national market share, the FTC focused instead on their ability to control prices locally. The agency found that, when both stores operate in the same market, prices are significantly lower than when only one store is present. Thus a box of file folders costs $1.72 in Orlando, Florida (where both stores compete) and $4.17 in nearby Leesburg (where Office Depot has a monopoly). In the FTC's view, if the two stores combined, they would have enough power in local markets to raise prices and harm consumers.

Ralph Nader, a longtime consumer advocate, runs a Web site that assesses potential mergers from the consumer point of view. You can find it at **http://www.essential.org/antitrust/mergers/**. Or, for a merger simulation game, play with **http://www.antitrust.org/**.

Making sense of American antitrust law can be difficult enough, but, as the following article illustrates, when a merger involves companies from different countries, the outcome can be even harder to predict.

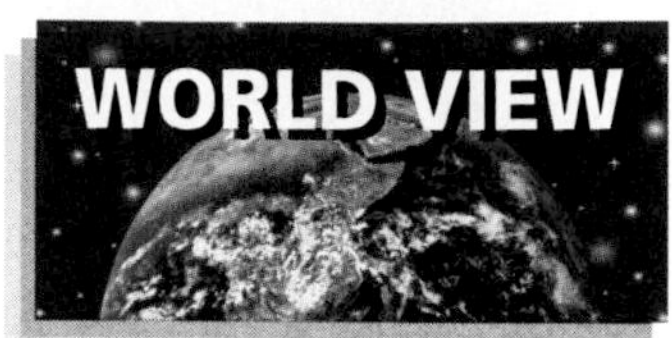

Somewhere between Washington and Brussels, the proposed alliance between American Airlines and British Airways is stuck in a holding pattern. Trustbusters in America and Europe are delaying the airline linkup because they fear it may harm competition. Unfortunately, they appear likely to disagree about what the airlines must do for their deal to past muster. A decade ago, such clashes were rarities. But as trade and foreign direct investment flourish, national competition policies have taken on global importance. A government's decision to block a merger, tolerate a cartel, or prohibit a business practice can have a significant impact on the flow of trade—and can potentially cause economic harm in countries half a world away.

When it comes to competition policy, there may be little common ground across the globe. Roughly half of the World Trade Organization's 132 members do not even have competition laws, and those that do have widely differing views. Some countries, for example, tolerate price-fixing, while others unreservedly condemn it. There are also disagreements on important issues such as the standards by which proposed mergers should be judged.[11] Information on antitrust policy around the world is available at **http://www.oecd.org/daf/clp/LINKS.HTM**.

VERTICAL MERGERS

A vertical merger involves companies at different stages of the production process—for example, when a producer of a final good acquires a supplier or vice versa. Vertical mergers can also be anticompetitive, especially if they reduce entry into a market by putting a lock on an important supplier or a top distributor. Consider the following example.

International Management Group (IMG) is a management conglomerate that dominates the tennis world. IMG operates tournaments, sets up exhibitions, holds broadcast rights, and manages the careers of more than 100 pros, including top-ranked player Pete Sampras. Recently, IMG acquired the Nick Bolletieri Tennis Academy, training ground for many of the sport's present and future stars. IMG's competitors question whether this acquisition violates the antitrust laws. Says the head coach of another tennis academy, "You name it, IMG owns it, owns tournaments, owns the players, owns the academy. It's impossible to compete at that level, so we don't even bother to try.[12]

IMG's acquisition of the Nick Bolletieri Tennis Academy was a vertical merger—IMG acquired a source of supply for its management group. The Justice

---

[11] "The Borders of Competition," *The Economist*, July 4, 1998, p. 69. © 1998 The Economist Newspaper Groups, Inc. Reprinted with permission. Further reproduction prohibited.

[12] Robin Finn, "Mixed Doubles: Players as Business," *New York Times*, Mar. 16, 1994, p. B17. Copyright © 1994 by The New York Times Co. Reprinted by permission.

Department has not been overly concerned about vertical mergers. The department's guidelines provide that it will challenge vertical mergers only if they are likely to increase entry barriers in a concentrated market. For many years, the Justice Department did not challenge *any* vertical mergers. Recently, however, the FTC forced the restructuring of four vertical mergers. In one case, a leading western utility bought a coal producer. The FTC required the merged company to sell some of the coal mines. These cases may augur a new "get-tough" stance by the government.

JOINT VENTURES

Sometimes companies may prefer a single-purpose joint venture rather than a merger. A number of joint ventures have been reported recently:

- In real estate, Donald Trump announced a joint venture with the Cheng family of Hong Kong to develop the Riverside South project in Manhattan.
- In advertising, Home Shopping Network entered into a joint venture to produce infomercials worldwide.
- In communications, Sprint has a joint venture with Electronic Data Systems (once owned by Ross Perot) to recruit small and medium-sized businesses to its long-distance service.

The government will usually permit a single-purpose joint venture, even between competitors with significant market power. The FTC approved, over strenuous objections from competitors, a joint venture between General Motors and Toyota to produce cars. The FTC challenged none of the joint ventures listed above.

CHAPTER CONCLUSION

Consumers may benefit when competitors cooperate. A joint venture could increase efficiency; a reciprocal dealing agreement might lower costs. For over 100 years, however, Congress and the courts have been concerned that *too* much cooperation among competitors is harmful to consumers. When competitors divide their market or fix prices, they benefit but consumers suffer. The purpose of the antitrust laws in the United States is to keep businesses on a narrow road. On the one hand, they may not swerve to one side and work too closely with competitors. Nor, as we see in the next chapter, may they swerve to the other side and attack competitors too aggressively.

CHAPTER REVIEW

1. Antitrust laws are serious business: violations can lead to prison sentences and hefty financial penalties, including treble damages.
2. There are two categories of antitrust violations: *per se* and rule of reason. *Per se* violations are automatic; courts do not consider mitigating circumstances. Rule of reason violations, on the other hand, are illegal only if they have an anticompetitive impact.

3. Any effort by a group of competitors to divide their market is a *per se* violation of the Sherman Act. Illegal arrangements include agreements to allocate customers, territory, or products.
4. Price-fixing and bid-rigging are *per se* violations of the Sherman Act.
5. Every company generally has the right to decide with whom it will do business. However, the Sherman Act prohibits competitors from joining together in an agreement to exclude a particular supplier, buyer, or even another competitor, if the agreement would hurt competition.
6. Reciprocal dealing agreements violate the Sherman Act if they foreclose competitors from a significant part of the market.
7. The Robinson-Patman Act prohibits companies from selling the same item at different prices if the sale lessens competition. However, a seller may charge different prices if these prices reflect different costs.
8. Under the Clayton Act, the federal government has the authority to prohibit anticompetitive mergers and joint ventures.

PRACTICE TEST

1. Harcourt Brace Jovanovich (HBJ) granted BRG an exclusive license to market HBJ's bar review materials in Georgia and to use HBJ's trade name. HBJ agreed not to compete with BRG in Georgia, and BRG agreed not to compete with HBJ outside the state. HBJ was entitled to receive $100 per student enrolled by BRG and 40 percent of revenues over $350 per student. Did this agreement violate the antitrust laws?

2. The National Football League does not permit its teams to draft players before their senior year. Could you argue that this policy violates the antitrust laws?

3. Traditionally, large Dallas law firms all paid their first-year associates almost exactly the same salary. Pay for summer associates also varied little from firm to firm. If you were a Justice Department lawyer, would this evidence strike you as suspicious? Is it likely that the firms have violated the antitrust laws?

4. Fifty bakeries in New York formed an association. They developed a system of distribution under which stores were only allowed to buy from a single baker. A store that wanted to shift to another baker had to consult the association and pay cash to the former baker. The association also decided to raise the retail price of bread from 75 to 85 cents. All the association's members printed the new price on their bread sleeves. Are the bakeries in violation of the antitrust laws?

5. Fifty restaurants in Boston threatened to stop accepting the American Express card if the company refused to reduce the commission it charged on each purchase. Visa International, one of American Express's rivals, offered to pay the group's legal expenses. American Express then lowered its commission. For restaurants that processed more than $10 million in annual volume, American Express reduced charges from 3.25 percent to 2.75 percent. Rates for restaurants processing less than $10 million but more than $1 million a year fell to 3 percent. The company did not lower rates for restaurants with volume lower than $1 million a year. Have either the restaurants, Visa, or American Express potentially violated the antitrust laws?

6. The Venice Hospital purchased a one-half interest in a company that rents and sells home medical equipment. Home health care nurses (who were not hospital employees), were "encouraged" to refer patients who needed home health equipment to the hospital's new company. The nurses understood that if they did not cooperate, the hospital would not refer home care patients to them. The hospital's share of the home medical equipment market rose from 9.2 percent to 61 percent. Is the hospital in violation of the antitrust laws?

7. Reserve Supply Corp., a cooperative of 379 lumber dealers, charged that Owens-Corning Fiberglass Corp. violated the Robinson-Patman Act by selling at lower prices to Reserve's competitors. Owens-Corning claimed that it had granted lower prices to a number of Reserve's competitors in order to meet, but not beat, the prices of other insulation manufacturers. Before lowering prices, Owens-Corning salespeople were required to seek approval from higher level officials in the company who checked that the discount prices were necessary to meet the competition. Is Owens-Corning in violation of the Robinson-Patman Act?

8. **YOU BE THE JUDGE WRITING PROBLEM** After acquiring the Schick brand name and electric shaver assets, North American Phillips controlled 55 percent of the electric shaver industry in the United States. Remington, a competitor, claimed that the acquisition of such a large market share was a violation of the Clayton Act because the increased competition from Phillips would decrease Remington's profits. Does Remington have a valid claim? **Argument for Remington:** A 55 percent market share is anticompetitive. It will give Phillips the power to control prices and harm consumers. **Argument for Phillips:** Remington fears for its own profits. Antitrust law protects competition, not competitors. The acquisition should not be halted without evidence of harm to consumers.

9. In recent years, the percentage of American gross domestic product spent on health care has grown rapidly, to about 14 percent. A major source of expenditure has been purchases of very expensive, high-tech medical equipment. To control health care expenses, hospitals now often join together to share the cost of this equipment. Could these joint purchases violate the antitrust laws?

10. BMW sold automobiles in Germany to Caribe BMW, which in turn sold the cars in Puerto Rico. BMW also sold cars to its wholly owned North American distributor, which then resold them to Caribe's competitors for less than Caribe paid BMW. Caribe filed suit against BMW, alleging a violation of the Robinson-Patman Act. In its defense, BMW argued that because it was a different company from its distributor, the case involved two companies selling to two competitors, and, therefore, there is no violation. What would you decide if you were the judge in this case?

11. **RIGHT & WRONG** MasterCard discovered that some of its cardholders were using their MasterCards in pornographic bookstores. MasterCard asked Maryland National Bank to cancel its MasterCard contract with these bookstores. The stores brought suit against the bank and MasterCard, alleging that their boycott was an illegal refusal to deal. Was this boycott illegal under the Sherman Act? Did MasterCard have an ethical obligation to prohibit the use of its cards in pornographic stores?

INTERNET RESEARCH PROBLEM

Choose one of the mergers featured at http://www.essential.org/antitrust/mergers or one of the price-fixing cases at http://www.antitrust.org/cases/pricefixing.html. If you were a judge, how would you decide this case? What are your reasons?

You can find further practice problems in the Online Quiz at http://beatty.westbuslaw.com or in the Study Guide that accompanies this text.

CHAPTER 41

ANTITRUST: LAW AND COMPETITIVE STRATEGY, PART II

"For a firm that has doubled in size every two years, Microsoft has demonstrated a remarkable fixation with one goal: to propagate its Windows operating system across the entire range of modern computing. Its secret is a culture in which such hackneyed labels as 'aggressive' and 'focused' actually mean something. Yet, as the firm's power grows, so do doubts about whether this combination of strategy and culture can be sustained. Squeezed between market dominance and antitrust authorities, is it possible for Microsoft's corporate culture to remain as uncompromising as it is today?

"The idea that Microsoft might curb its ultracompetitiveness, or the snarling aggression with which it meets any challenge to its Windows monopoly, is regarded as ridiculous by people who know Bill Gates. And, for all practical purposes, Microsoft is Bill Gates. In most companies, strategy is devised at the top and loses coherence as it passes down each tier of management. At Microsoft, strategy starts with Mr. Gates, but loses nothing as it is taken up by the people who run different parts of the business. If anything, it is burnished until it glistens, harder and more perfect than ever. As a result no company has a stronger sense of where it is going and how it intends to get there. That destination is 'Windows Everywhere.'

"When you are already as big as Microsoft, warp-speed growth means eating quite a lot of other people's lunches. But as Microsoft grows, its dominance unites competitors against it and inevitably it draws the unwelcome eye of the antitrust authorities. Yet if Microsoft were to adapt its culture to its market dominance, what then? Could it settle for a slower rate of growth and look benignly on the efforts of its competitors? You can imagine a company that might. But that company would not be Microsoft."[1]

Chapter 40 focused on competitors who violate the law by working too closely together. That has not been Microsoft's problem! This chapter considers strategies that are too aggressive or unfair.

MONOPOLIZATION

Aggressive competition is beneficial for consumers—up until the moment a company develops enough power to control a market. One purpose of the Sherman Act, enacted in 1890, is to prevent this type of control. **Under §2 of the Act, it is illegal to monopolize or attempt to monopolize a market.** To monopolize means to acquire a monopoly in the wrong way. *Having* a monopoly is legal unless it is *gained* or *maintained* by using wrongful tactics. (The full text of all the antitrust statutes is available at **http://www.ftc.gov/ogc/stat2.htm**.)

To determine if a defendant has illegally monopolized, we must ask three questions:

- **What is the market?** Without knowing the market, it is impossible to determine if someone is controlling it.
- **Does the company control the market?** Without control, there is no monopoly.
- **How did the company acquire or maintain its control?** Monopolization is illegal only if gained or kept in the wrong way.

WHAT IS THE MARKET?

This question is not as easy to answer as it sounds. Some people refer to the antitrust laws as the "Economists' Full-Employment Acts" because antitrust litigation requires testimony from economic experts.

Imagine that your company sells soft drinks with unusual food flavors—steak and cheese, among others. For some reason, you are the only company that sells food-flavored soft drinks so, by definition, you control 100 percent of the market. But is that the *relevant* market? Perhaps the relevant market is flavored drinks or soft drinks or all beverages. The question economists ask is: **How high can your prices rise before your buyers will switch to a different product?** If a price rise from $1.00 to $1.05 a bottle causes many of your customers to desert to Snapple or Coke, it is clear you are part of a larger market. Moreover, if changes in the prices

---

[1] "Microsoft's Contradiction," *The Economist*, Jan. 31, 1998, p. 65. © 1998 The Economist Newspaper Groups, Inc. Reprinted with permission. Further reproduction prohibited. www.economist.com

of other drinks affect *your* sales, your products and theirs are probably close competitors. However, if you could raise your price to $5.00 per bottle and still hold on to many of your customers, then you might well be in your own market.

DOES THE COMPANY CONTROL THE MARKET?

You have 100 percent of the food-flavored soft drink market (although only 1 percent of the overall soft drink market and an infinitesimal percentage of the total beverage market). Traditionally, courts considered a share anywhere between 70 and 90 percent to constitute a monopoly. However, in the following case, Judge Kozinski indicates that market share is not important if other competitors can enter the market anytime they want (or anytime you raise your prices or lower your quality). **No matter what your market share, you do not have a monopoly unless you can exclude competitors or control prices.** Judge Kozinski certainly has a sense of humor—his opinion is larded with movie titles. How many can you find?

UNITED STATES v. SYUFY ENTERPRISES
903 F.2d 659, 1990 U.S. App. LEXIS 7396
United States Court of Appeals for the Ninth Circuit, 1990

Facts: Raymond Syufy entered the Las Vegas cinema market with a splash by opening a six-screen theater. His theaters are among the finest built and best run in the nation, making him something of a local hero. Syufy's entry into the Las Vegas market caused a stir, precipitating a titanic bidding war. Soon, theaters in Las Vegas were paying some of the highest license fees in the nation, while distributors sat back and watched the easy money roll in. After a hard-fought battle among several contenders, Syufy gained the upper hand. Three of his rivals saw their future as rocky and decided to sell out to Syufy, leaving a small exhibitor of mostly second-run films as Syufy's only competitor in Las Vegas. The Justice Department brought this antitrust suit to force Syufy to disgorge the theaters he had purchased from his former competitors.

Issue: **Did Syufy have an illegal monopoly?**

Excerpts from Judge Kozinski's Decision: Monopoly power is the power to exclude competition or control prices. Time after time, we have recognized this basic fact of economic life: A high market share, though it may ordinarily raise an inference of monopoly power, will not do so in a market with low entry barriers or other evidence of a defendant's inability to control prices or exclude competitors.

When Syufy acquired his competitors' theaters he temporarily diminished the number of competitors in the Las Vegas first-run film market. But this does not necessarily indicate foul play; many legitimate market arrangements diminish the number of competitors. It would be odd if they did not, as the nature of competition is to make winners and losers. If there are no significant barriers to entry, however, eliminating competitors will not enable the survivors to reap a monopoly profit; any attempt to raise prices above the competitive level will lure into the market new competitors able and willing to offer their commercial goods or personal services for less.

Syufy was unable to maintain market share. [In one year,] Syufy raked in 93 percent of the gross box office from first-run films in Las Vegas. [Three years later,] that figure had fallen to 75 percent. The government insists that 75 percent is still a large number, and we are hard-pressed to disagree; but that's not the point. The antitrust laws do not require that rivals compete in a dead heat, only that neither is unfairly kept from doing his personal best.

It can't be said often enough that the antitrust laws protect competition, not competitors. The record here conclusively demonstrates that neither acquiring the screens of his competitors nor working hard at better serving the public gave Syufy deliverance from competition.

The Justice Department also alleges that Syufy, top gun in the Las Vegas movie market, had the power to push around Hollywood's biggest players, dictating to them what prices they could charge for their movies. The evidence does not support this view. Syufy has at all times paid license fees far in excess of the national average. While successful, Syufy is in no position to put the squeeze on distributors. It would have been risky business even to try.

By finding that Syufy did not possess the power to set prices or to exclude competition, the district court removed the firing pins from the government's litigation arsenal. Without these essential elements, its lawsuit collapses like a house of cards.

How Did the Company Acquire or Maintain Its Control?

Possessing **a monopoly is not necessarily illegal; using *"bad acts"* to acquire or maintain one is.** If the law prohibited the mere possession of a monopoly, it might discourage companies from producing excellent products or offering low prices. Anyone who can produce a better product cheaper than anyone else is entitled to a monopoly. In your case, you have very cleverly developed a secret method for adding flavors to carbonated water. You also have an efficient factory and highly trained workers, so you can sell your drinks for 5¢ a bottle less than your competitors. If, in fact, you do have a monopoly, it is for all the right reasons. You have demonstrated exactly the kind of innovative, efficient behavior that benefits consumers. If you were sued for a violation of the antitrust laws, you would win.

Some companies use ruthless tactics to acquire or maintain a monopoly. It is these "bad acts" that render a monopoly illegal. In the past, the definition of bad acts was broad, and any company with a monopoly could be in violation unless it showed that, despite its best efforts to duck, a monopoly had been *thrust upon* it. In 1945, a famous judge, with the appropriate name of Learned Hand, found that Alcoa's monopoly in the aluminum industry was illegal because the company had repeatedly expanded capacity to anticipate demand.[2] In his view, the company should have waited to expand until demand actually existed. Alcoa was in violation because it could have easily *avoided* a monopoly—the monopoly had not been thrust upon it.

Everyone makes mistakes. Although Learned Hand is generally considered one of the greatest judges of his era, most commentators now believe that *Alcoa* was wrongly decided. *Berkey Photo* is a more typical modern case.[3] Berkey accused Eastman Kodak Co. of repeatedly and unnecessarily changing the size of its cameras to confound competitors who manufactured film to fit them. Although Learned Hand most likely would have found such actions to be illegal, the *Berkey* court rejected the view that monopolies are acceptable only if *thrust upon* the defendant and instead held that aggressive competitive strategies are legal even if they have the effect of hindering competitors. In finding Kodak not liable, the court reasoned that the company would not have repeatedly changed camera and film specifications if consumers had objected. The success or failure of Kodak's

[2] *United States v. Aluminum Co. of America*, 148 F.2d 416, 1945 U.S. App. LEXIS 4091 (2d Cir. 1945). Judge Hand's parents did not necessarily foresee his illustrious career when naming him. "Learned" was his mother's maiden name, and it was the tradition in his family to give the mother's name to one of the children.

[3] *Berkey Photo, Inc. v. Eastman Kodak Co.*, 603 F.2d 263, 1979 U.S. App. LEXIS 13692 (2d Cir. 1979), *cert. denied*, 444 U.S. 1093, 100 S. Ct. 1061, 1980 U.S. LEXIS 923 (1980).

strategy ought to be determined in the market and not by the courts. The following news report details British Airway's aggressive tactics against a competitor. Would the *Berkey* court have considered this strategy acceptable?

Lord King, the chairman of British Airways (BA), apologized to Richard Branson, the head of Virgin Atlantic Airways, for BA's dirty tricks. Among other tactics, BA:

- Approached Virgin's customers to persuade them to switch to BA flights
- Refused to cooperate on maintenance and training
- Obtained customers' files by tapping into Virgin's computer
- Contacted customers and pretended to represent Virgin, and
- Spread untrue, harmful rumors about Mr. Branson.

London's High Court ordered BA to pay Branson $900,000 in libel damages. Shortly thereafter, Lord King lost his job.

Branson recently filed an antitrust suit against BA in the United States, seeking $325 million in damages. Were BA's actions legitimate competitive strategies? Or did the company go too far?

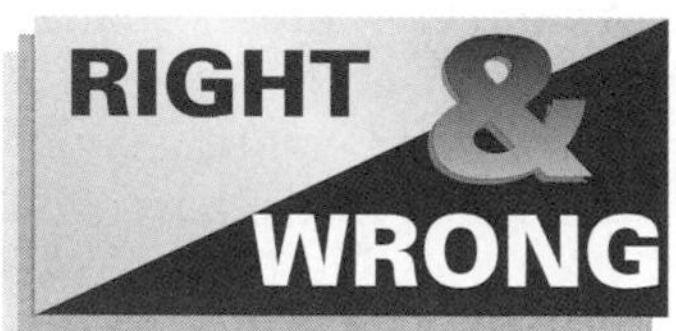

Whether or not these activities were *legal*, were they *ethical*? How do you think Lord King felt when these activities were reported in the newspaper? Would he have minded if Branson had used the same tactics against BA? Did BA's strategy pay in the short run? In the long run? If you were running BA, what guidelines would you give your employees?

MICROSOFT REVISITED

The article on the first page of this chapter says that Bill Gates and Microsoft are renowned for their "snarling aggression." Competitors complained bitterly to the U.S. Justice Department that Microsoft had violated the Sherman Act by pursuing its strategies too aggressively. For more than a decade, the Justice Department investigated, negotiated, and litigated with Microsoft. Not only is this case the most significant antitrust battle of the era, but it is also shaping an industry crucial to the world economy. Has Microsoft illegally created or maintained a monopoly? Time to analyze the facts.

What Is Microsoft's Market?

Microsoft produces two types of software: an operating system and applications.[4] What is the relevant market? Is it operating software for personal computers (PCs), all software, or perhaps the computer industry as a whole? If Microsoft shoots prices sky-high on its operating system, buyers will switch to some other *operating* software, but not to other *applications* software. Similarly, if Microsoft raises the price on Word (its word-processing program), users might switch to WordPerfect, but not to a different operating program. Applications and operating systems are presumably two different markets.

[4] Operating systems are the programs that tell electronic circuits how to work as a computer. They provide a platform to launch applications software, which are programs that perform specific tasks, such as word processing or financial analysis.

Does Microsoft Control a Market?

Ninety percent of the world's PCs use Windows, the Microsoft operating system. Microsoft also has 93 percent of the world market for office suites,[5] 45 percent of global software sales, and 1 percent of the computer industry. The company's market share suggests that it may have a monopoly in both operating systems and office suites. However, the *Syufy* case says that a large market share is not sufficient proof of a monopoly. There must also be evidence that the company can control prices or exclude competitors. During a five-year period, the average price Microsoft charged PC manufacturers for licensing Windows rose from $19.03 to $49.40. As the cost of Microsoft software was increasing, the total cost of PCs generally was falling, with the result that Microsoft's share of the total cost of a PC grew fivefold, to 2.5 percent. This sounds as if Microsoft could indeed control prices.

How Did Microsoft Acquire Its Control?

Microsoft's monopoly violates the law only if the company used "bad acts" to acquire it. Here are some of Microsoft's strategies that prompted its competitors to complain:

- As Windows rapidly became the industry standard, companies such as Lotus and WordPerfect, which make spreadsheet and word-processing software, were desperate to obtain advance copies of Windows so that they could start adapting their programs to it. They claim that Microsoft would not let them have Windows until it had first created its *own* applications software. Microsoft leveraged its strength in the operating system market to gain share in the applications market.
- The company offered substantial discounts (up to two-thirds off) to computer makers that agreed to buy Microsoft software for every computer they made, whether or not they actually *installed* the program on every machine. These "per processor" deals discouraged manufacturers from installing any other operating system because they had already paid for the Microsoft product. Competitors fumed when manufacturers would not even consider their products.
- Microsoft pressured computer manufacturers into signing long-term exclusive contracts for Windows.

If these claims were true, would they be bad enough to violate the law? What would Judge Learned Hand have said? If you worked for the Justice Department, is this a case you would want to bring? If you were a Microsoft executive, would you have recommended against some of these strategies? Exhibit 41.1 illustrates the Microsoft analysis.

After investigating these claims, the Justice Department entered into a consent decree (a settlement) with Microsoft. The company agreed not to tie products together; that is, it would not require a manufacturer that purchased Windows to buy applications (such as the office suite). It stopped its "per processor" deals that required manufacturers to pay license fees for every machine sold. The company also stopped issuing licenses that lasted more than one year. However, the consent decree specifically permitted Microsoft to develop integrated products. When asked the impact of this settlement, Bill Gates replied, "Nothing."

---

[5] Office suites are packages of programs that include a word-processor, a spreadsheet, presentation software, and personal information managers.

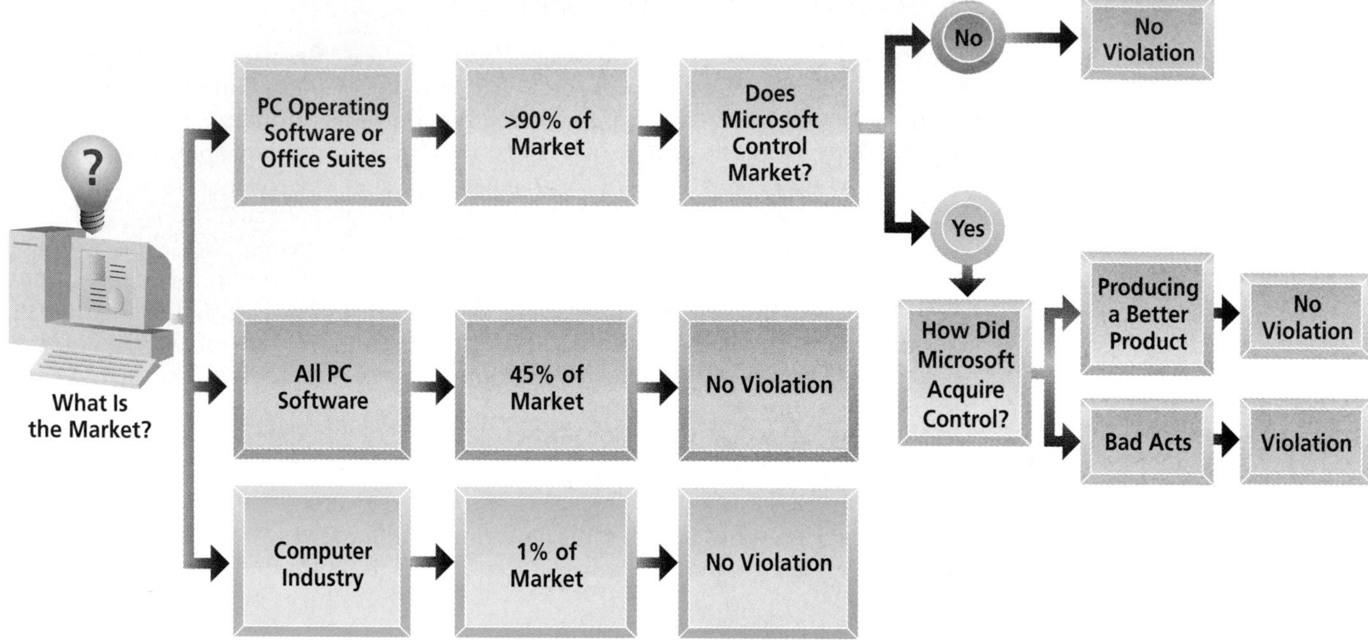

Exhibit 41.1

Apparently, the Justice Department did not share his view. When Microsoft announced plans to acquire Intuit, Inc., which makes the most popular personal finance software package, the Justice Department filed suit. Microsoft withdrew from the deal rather than face protracted litigation.

The consent decree and the Intuit dispute were, however, simply opening skirmishes in what turned out to be a major war between the government and Microsoft. Three years after the decree, the parties went to court, with Microsoft's very existence at stake. According to the government, Microsoft had violated the consent decree by allegedly committing yet more "bad acts":

- Microsoft officials allegedly met with Netscape and offered to divvy up the market for Internet browsers (programs that surf the Web). At that point, Netscape owned the leading browser. When Netscape refused the first offer, Microsoft tried to license Netscape software, threatening "to bury" Netscape if the company refused.
- When Netscape rejected that offer, too, Microsoft deployed hundreds of programmers to develop Internet Explorer, its own browser. Although the company spent more than $100 million on this project, it bundled the browser with Windows and gave the browser away free. Internal Microsoft documents presented at trial indicated that this plan was designed to "cut off the air supply" of Netscape.
- When Compaq, a major manufacturer of PCs, decided to sell its computers preloaded with Netscape, Microsoft threatened to withhold the Windows operating system from all future Compaq machines. Compaq promptly dropped Netscape.
- When America On-Line (AOL) considered using Netscape as its browser, Microsoft allegedly offered to allow the AOL icon on the Windows desktop (some of the most desirable real estate in computerland) if, in return, AOL would use Internet Explorer. Bill Gates reportedly said at a meeting, "How much do we need to pay you to damage Netscape? This is your lucky day."

Microsoft disputes the government's charges. According to Microsoft:

- Under the consent decree, the company had the right to develop integrated products. Microsoft argues that the Web browser is an integrated product allowing seamless travel between a hard drive and the Internet. Using two different products would be awkward and annoying for the consumer.
- Where is the harm when Microsoft provides a free browser that consumers can easily ignore or replace? Anyone who prefers Netscape can download it for free from the Netscape Web site.
- Microsoft is fighting for every corporation's right to innovate, free from the supervision of a "Federal Bureau of Operating Systems." Do we want the government determining the future of technology?

The company won an important battle against the Justice Department. Initially, the district court ordered Microsoft to stop bundling its browser with Windows, at least until the trial ended and a final judgment could be reached. However, the appeals court sided with Microsoft and overruled the trial court.[6] The appeals court reasoned that, because an integrated browser works better than the stand-alone variation, Microsoft had a legitimate business reason for bundling the products. Courts should generally defer to a company's judgment on these issues, in the absence of strong evidence to the contrary.

The case was then remanded back to the district court to proceed with the trial. This time, the government won a round. The trial judge found that Microsoft had used "bad acts" to create and maintain a monopoly that ultimately harmed consumers. In any event, as technology continues to evolve, appeals and new suits are certain between these adversaries for the foreseeable future. For more on the government's viewpoint, click on **http://www.usdoj.gov/atr/cases/ms_index.htm**. Microsoft presents its side at **http://www.microsoft.com/presspass/doj/background.htm**. Whoever wins the legal fight, Microsoft may be losing the public relations battle, at least judging by the cartoon below.

From Newsweek, Jan 5, 1998, p. 117 © Tribune Media Services, Inc. All Rights Reserved. Reprinted with permission.

---

[6] *United States v. Microsoft Corp.*, 147 F.3d 935, 331 U.S. App. D.C. 121, 1998 U.S. App. LEXIS 13242 (D.C. Cir. 1998).

What is wrong with monopolies anyway? South Africa offers a vivid illustration. Nearly 80 percent of private industry is controlled by five superconglomerates. In staples like beer and sugar, one or two producers dominate the market and set prices. Goods that Americans take for granted, from steaks to new cars to televisions, are so expensive that the average South African cannot afford them. Other evils also stem from concentrated ownership: price-fixing, excessive secrecy, stultifying bureaucracy, lackluster research and development, protectionist tariffs. Said one observer, "The effect of all this concentration is that South Africa has built bureaucrats in the private sector. You look at the streets—people go home at half past 4 o'clock. There's no competitiveness. There aren't any entrepreneurs."[7]

PREDATORY PRICING

Predatory pricing occurs when a company lowers its prices below cost to drive competitors out of business. Once the predator has the market to itself, it raises prices to make up lost profits—and more besides.

Recall that, under §2 of the Sherman Act, it is illegal "to monopolize" and also to "attempt to monopolize." Typically, the goal of a predatory pricing scheme is either to win control of a market or to maintain it. A ban on these schemes prevents monopolization and attempts to monopolize. To win a predatory pricing case, the plaintiff must prove three elements:

- The defendant is selling its products *below cost*.
- The defendant *intends* that the plaintiff go out of business.
- If the plaintiff does go out of business, the defendant will be able to earn sufficient profits to *recoup* its prior losses.

The classic example of predatory pricing is a large grocery store that comes into a small town offering exceptionally low prices subsidized by profits from its other branches. Once all the "Ma and Pa" corner groceries go out of business, MegaGrocery raises its prices to much higher levels.

Predatory pricing offers a good example of how attitudes toward antitrust laws have changed. Formerly, courts took predatory pricing very seriously. The term certainly *sounds* bad. But despite its name, courts generally are not as concerned about predatory pricing now as they used to be. For one thing, consumers benefit from price wars, at least in the short run. For another, the cases are hard to prove. Here is why:

- **The defendant is selling its products below cost.** This rule sounds sensible, but what does "cost" mean? As you know from your economics courses, there are many different kinds of costs—total, average variable, marginal, to name a few. Under current law, any price below *average variable cost* is generally presumed to be predatory.[8] The rule may be easy to state, but, in real life, average variable cost is difficult to calculate. First, plaintiffs must obtain most of the data from the defendant. Even if a defendant has a good idea of what its average variable costs are, it will not necessarily tell all in court. Moreover, many of the economic decisions about what items fit into which cost category are sub-

[7] Donald G. McNeil, Jr., "Keeping Corporate Score," *New York Times*, Mar. 2, 1996, p. A31. Copyright © 1996 by The New York Times Co. Reprinted by permission.

[8] To calculate average variable cost, add all the firm's costs except its fixed costs and then divide by the total quantity of output.

jective. It is difficult for the plaintiff to prove that its subjective view is closer to the truth than the defendant's.

- **The defendant intends that the plaintiff go out of business.** Even if Ma and Pa can calculate MegaGrocery's average variable cost to the satisfaction of a court, they will not necessarily win their case. They must prove that MegaGrocery *intended* to put them out of business. That is a pretty tall order, short of finding some smoking gun like a strategic plan that explicitly says MegaGrocery wants Ma and Pa gone.
- **If the plaintiff does go out of business, the defendant will be able to earn sufficient profits to recoup its prior losses.** Until Ma and Pa go out of business, MegaGrocery will lose money—after all, it is selling food below cost. To win their case, Ma and Pa must show that MegaGrocery will be able to make up all its lost profits once the corner grocery is out of the way. They need to prove, for example, that no other grocery chain will come to town. It is difficult to prove a negative proposition like that, especially in the grocery business where barriers to entry are low.

Recently, plaintiffs simply have not had much success with predatory pricing suits. For example, Liggett began selling generic cigarettes 30 percent below the price of branded cigarettes. Brown & Williamson retaliated by introducing its own generics at an even lower price. Liggett sued, claiming that Brown's prices were below cost. The Supreme Court agreed that Brown was not only selling below cost but also intended to harm Liggett. Brown still won the case, however, because there was no evidence that it would be able to recover its losses from the below-cost pricing. If Brown raised its prices, other competitors would come back into the market.[9]

You remember that Microsoft gave away its Internet browser for free, as part of a package with Windows. The company argued that it was causing no harm because a free browser benefits consumers. The Justice Department alleged that Microsoft was engaging in predatory pricing for the purpose of harming Netscape. Those facts alone are not enough to prove predatory pricing, however. The government would also have to show that, if Netscape went out of business, Microsoft could raise its prices without fear that other competitors would enter the market.

TYING ARRANGEMENTS

A tying arrangement is an agreement to sell a product on the condition that the buyer also purchases a different (or tied) product. A tying arrangement is illegal under §3 of the Clayton Act and §1 of the Sherman Act if:

- Two products are clearly separate
- The seller requires the buyer to purchase the two products together
- The seller has significant power in the market for the tying product, and
- The seller is shutting out a significant part of the market for the tied product.

Six movie distributors refused to sell individual films to television stations. Instead, they insisted that a station buy an entire package of movies. To obtain classics such as *Treasure of the Sierra Madre* and *Casablanca* (the **tying product**), the

[9] *Brooke Group Ltd. v. Brown & Williamson Tobacco Corp.*, 509 U.S. 209, 113 S. Ct. 2578, 1993 U.S. LEXIS 4245 (1993).

Should a movie distributor have to buy Tugboat Annie in order to get Ingrid Bergman?

station also had to purchase such forgettable films as *Nancy Drew Troubleshooter*, *Gorilla Man*, and *Tugboat Annie Sails Again* (the **tied product**).[10] Is this an illegal tying arrangement? These are the questions to ask:

- **Are the two products clearly separate?** A left and right shoe are *not* separate products, and a seller can legally require that they be purchased together. *Gorilla Man*, on the other hand, is a separate product from *Casablanca*.
- **Is the seller requiring the buyer to purchase the two products together?** Yes, that is the whole point of these "package deals."
- **Does the seller have significant power in the market for the tying product?** In this case, the tying products are the classic movies. Since they are copyrighted, no one else can show them without the distributor's permission. The six distributors controlled a great many classic movies. So, yes, they do have significant market power.
- **Is the seller shutting out a significant part of the market for the tied product?** In this case, the tied products are the undesirable films like *Tugboat Annie Sails Again*. Television stations forced to take the unwanted films did not buy "B" movies from other distributors. These other distributors were effectively foreclosed from a substantial part of the market.

The film distributors argued that their creditor had forced them to sell movies in blocks as a condition of the loan. The court was unimpressed by that argument, holding that a contract is no excuse for wrongful behavior and that the six distributors had indeed engaged in illegal tying. In the following case, Mercedes-Benz decided to include floor mats as standard equipment. Is that illegal tying?

LLOYD DESIGN CORP. v. MERCEDES-BENZ OF NORTH AMERICA, INC.

66 Cal. App. 4th 716, 1998 Cal. App. LEXIS 768
Court of Appeal of California, 1998

Facts: Mercedes-Benz sells less than 1 percent of all automobiles in this country, but among luxury cars, it holds about a 10 percent market share. Floor mats were originally optional accessories in Mercedes cars. Lloyd Design Corp. sold floor mats to some Mercedes dealerships, which, in turn, sold the mats to consumers. Mercedes then decided to make floor mats standard equipment. Dealers reported that luxury car customers expected floor mats, and a growing number of competitors provided them.

Lloyd had been selling some $250,000 in floor mats to Mercedes dealerships in California, but lost this entire business after the change in policy. Lloyd filed suit against Mercedes, claiming that the decision to deliver the cars with floor mats constituted an illegal tying arrangement.

You Be the Judge: Did Mercedes engage in illegal tying when it provided floor mats in its automobiles?

Argument for Lloyd: These two products—cars and floor mats—are clearly separate products. They have traditionally been sold separately. Mercedes is now requiring that they be purchased together. The company has significant power in the market for luxury cars and is forcing customers to buy a product that they may not want. This is a classic case of illegal tying and, like all tying arrangements, it serves no purpose beyond the suppression of competition.

Argument for Mercedes: Floor mats are not a separate product; they are a fundamental part of the car. Does Lloyd believe that Mercedes should sell just the engine and the body, and that everything else—including the mirrors, seats, and steering wheel—is a different product?

Moreover, Mercedes controls only 10 percent of the luxury car market; it cannot force consumers to buy a product they do not want. Nor is Mercedes attempting to control the floor mat market. This market is still highly competitive, but now manufacturers are competing to sell to Mercedes, rather than to dealers. There is no harm to competition and no illegal tying. Nor is there any harm to consumers—they are receiving a floor mat for free.

[10] *United States v. Loew's Inc.*, 371 U.S. 38, 83 S. Ct. 97, 1962 U.S. LEXIS 2332 (1962).

CONTROLLING DISTRIBUTORS AND RETAILERS

The goal of an aggressive strategy is to force competitors out of a market—by undercutting their prices or tying products together, for example. Controlling distributors and retailers is another method for excluding competitors. It is difficult to compete in a market if you are foreclosed from the best distribution channels.

ALLOCATING CUSTOMERS AND TERRITORY

As you saw in Chapter 40, a *horizontal* agreement by *competitors* to allocate customers and territories is a *per se* violation of §1 of the Sherman Act. At one time, courts held that a *vertical* allocation agreement between firms at different levels of the production process was also a *per se* violation. However, in the landmark *GTE Sylvania* case, **the Supreme Court ruled that a vertical allocation of customers or territory is illegal only if it adversely affects competition in the market as a whole.**[11] It is a rule of reason, not a *per se*, violation. (See Chapter 40 for a discussion of the difference between *per se* and rule of reason violations.)

Suppose that Hi-Fat Favorites, Inc. produces an expensive, rich, creamy ice cream. It grants its distributors the exclusive right to sell in a particular territory or the exclusive right over a particular type of customer (convenience stores, university dining halls, or large grocery chains). In return for these exclusive rights, Hi-Fat requires the distributors to stock a large range of flavors, hire highly trained (expensive) sales help, and advertise widely. Such requirements not only increase sales but also enhance distributor loyalty. The distributors have such a large investment in Hi-Fat's products that they are reluctant to switch to another manufacturer. A change would mean unloading a large inventory, developing new advertisements, and laying off some of the sales force.

Hi-Fat clearly has good business reasons for adopting such a plan. It is reducing **intrabrand** competition (among its *dealers*) but enhancing **inter-brand** competition (between *brands*). With its committed dealer network, Hi-Fat can compete more fiercely against other brands. Vertical allocation is a rule of reason violation, which means that the law will intervene only if Hi-Fat's activities have an anticompetitive impact on the market as a whole. But since Hi-Fat's plan increases interbrand competition, it is unlikely to have an anticompetitive impact.

EXCLUSIVE DEALING AGREEMENTS

An exclusive dealing contract is one in which a distributor or retailer agrees with a supplier not to carry the products of any other supplier. Under §1 of the Sherman Act and §3 of the Clayton Act, exclusive dealing contracts are subject to a rule of reason and are illegal only if they have an anticompetitive effect.

Consider the case of Ben & Jerry's. With over $100 million in sales, it was a major player in the ice cream market. And some of its competitors alleged that it was playing hardball. Just ask Amy Miller. She started Amy's Ice Creams in a small storefront in Austin, Texas. Her ice cream was so popular that she decided to begin producing pints for sale in grocery stores. But when she tried to enter the Houston market, Sunbelt, the dominant distributor in the area, refused to carry her desserts. She thinks Sunbelt turned her down because Ben & Jerry's had forbidden it to carry other premium brands.

Ironically, the ice cream was once in the other bowl, so to speak. When Ben and Jerry were the new boys on the block, they discovered that Pillsbury (owner

[11] *Continental T.V., Inc. v. GTE Sylvania Inc.*, 433 U.S. 36, 97 S. Ct. 2549, 1977 U.S. LEXIS 134 (1977).

of Häagen-Dazs) included provisions in its contracts that prohibited distributors from carrying Ben & Jerry's brand. When Ben & Jerry's produced written contracts containing these exclusory clauses, Pillsbury backed down immediately. Thereafter, no one in the industry used written distribution contracts.

Amy Miller threatened to sue Ben & Jerry's for violating the antitrust laws with exclusive dealing contracts. In determining if these agreements had an anticompetitive impact on the market, a court would consider the following factors:

- **The number of other distributors available.** Amy said that no one but Sunbelt would do because only the best distributors were able to preserve the ice cream's quality.
- **The portion of the market foreclosed by the exclusive dealing agreements.** Without Sunbelt, Amy's Ice Creams could not penetrate the Houston market, so it had to shut down its pint production line.
- **The ease with which new distributors could enter the market.** Sunbelt had few, if any, competitors. Presumably, the market was a difficult one to enter.
- **The possibility that Amy could distribute the products herself.** Not a chance. Amy could barely manage to *make* the ice cream.
- **The legitimate business reasons that might have led the distributor to accept an exclusive contract.** Here is what Sunbelt's vice-president had to say: "We already had our table full with super premium pints. We felt Amy's was an under-financed product and we would have had to replace a high-volume product to give it a shot. And we personally did not think the product was very good. We also did not know if the company had the finances to assure continuous production."[12]

Would an exclusive dealing agreement between Ben & Jerry's and Sunbelt be anticompetitive? If so, would their business reasons justify the contract?

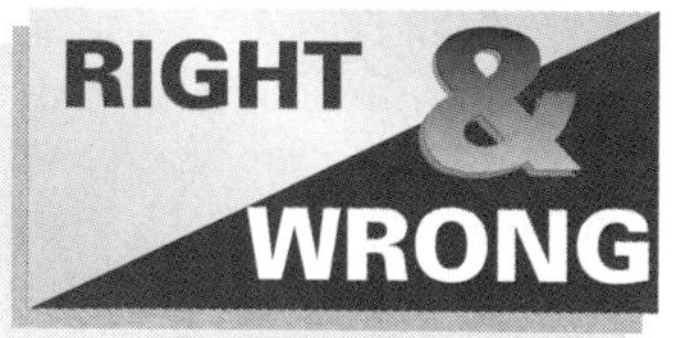

Ben & Jerry's always prided itself on its hippie culture and social consciousness. Among other activities, it sent a bus with solar-powered freezers around the country giving away free ice cream, and it underwrote the Newport Rock Festival. It also used executive titles such as "The Big Cheese" (read CEO) and "P.R. Info Queen" (read Director of Marketing). If you were to write a corporate credo for Ben & Jerry's, what would it say? Would the company's treatment of Amy Miller fit the credo?

RESALE PRICE MAINTENANCE

Peter Polites (pronounced po-LEE-tus), owner of a Nine West store in New Jersey, slashed the price of a popular, smart-looking women's shoe last winter, knowing he would attract many more customers—and still earn a smooth 60 percent on each pair. But Mr. Polites's sale irritated some managers at large department stores down the hall in the Mall at Short Hills. One Nordstrom manager, he said, walked into Mr. Polites's small store, picked some shoes off the shelf, looked at the prices, slammed them down, and left without a word.

Mr. Polites said the Nordstrom manager later explained that the flats Mr. Polites had reduced to $49.99 from $60 were included on a confidential list of

[12] Rickie Windle, "Ben & Jerry's Creams Amy's," *Austin Business Journal*, Oct. 4, 1993, vol. 13, no. 33, §1, p. 1.

Who should determine how much you will pay for these shoes?

styles—known as the "off-limits list"—whose prices Nine West Group, Inc. rarely, if ever, lets stores mark down. Mr. Polites's low prices also maddened executives at Nine West, the footwear giant that says it sells one out of every five pairs of shoes sold to women in the United States. Vincent Camuto, chief executive of Nine West, called Mr. Polites and demanded that he end his sale. When Mr. Polites refused, Mr. Camuto told him that in that case, "We can't ship you those shoes."[13]

Is it legal for Nine West to cut off a retailer who refuses to raise his prices? This question is at the heart of an important antitrust conundrum—the validity of **resale price maintenance (RPM)**. RPM means the manufacturer sets *minimum* prices that retailers may charge. In other words, it prevents retailers from discounting. Why does the manufacturer care? After all, once the retailer purchases the shoes, the manufacturer has made its profit. The only way the manufacturer makes more money is to raise its *wholesale* price, not the *retail* price. RPM guarantees a profit margin for the *retailer*. Although discounting may increase sales, some manufacturers prefer to guarantee their dealers' margins through RPM, for several reasons:

- RPM builds loyalty among retailers because they know they will make a profit on the line.
- Many manufacturers do not like discounting because they fear it conditions customers to buy only when items are marked down. When the retailer realizes at the end of the year that it is not making money, it demands new products, which might require expensive retooling by the manufacturer.
- A manufacturer may want to maintain an upscale brand image, which could be destroyed by discount prices.
- Extra service at the retail level may enhance brand image. If the shoes do not fit, Nine West customers will not wear them. To find a good fit, customers often need a large selection of sizes and the assistance of a trained salesperson. Discounters are less likely to keep an extensive inventory and an experienced sales staff.
- Discounters "free-ride" off high-quality stores. Small shop owners see red when customers ask for endless advice and try on countless shoes only to make the actual purchase from a discounter.

Of course, some customers prefer cheaper shoes even if that means less sales assistance. Why should they be required to buy shoes from an expensive store with a highly trained staff? Because, RPM advocates argue, it is only fair for manufacturers to decide how and at what price their products are sold. Consumer advocates contend, on the other hand, that Nine West is simply protecting dealers from competition. Discounting may or may not harm products, but, they insist, RPM certainly hurts consumers.

Whatever the pros and cons, RPM has been a *per se* violation of §1 of the Sherman Act since the Supreme Court decided the *Dr. Miles* case in 1911.[14] Despite the Court's ruling, the Justice Department has not always pursued RPM cases aggressively, believing that they should be rule of reason, not *per se*, violations. Indeed, during one 10-year period, the Justice Department did not bring a single RPM case. In this hands-off atmosphere, RPM flourished.

[13] Melody Petersen, "Treading a Contentious Line," *New York Times*, Jan. 13, 1999, p. C1. Copyright © 1999 by The New York Times Co. Reprinted by permission.

[14] *Dr. Miles Medical Co. v. John D. Park & Sons*, 220 U.S. 373, 31 S. Ct. 376, 1911 U.S. LEXIS 1685 (1911).

When the Supreme Court agreed to decide an RPM case (brought by an individual plaintiff), the Justice Department filed a brief recommending that the Court apply a rule of reason rather than a *per se* rule. However, many members of Congress opposed RPM because they were concerned about protecting their constituents. Congress passed a law prohibiting the Justice Department from making oral arguments in favor of RPM before the Court. Here is what the Supreme Court decided in that case:

MONSANTO CO. v. SPRAY-RITE SERVICE CORP.

465 U.S. 752, 104 S. Ct. 1464, 1984 U.S. LEXIS 39
United States Supreme Court, 1984

Facts: Monsanto refused to renew Spray-Rite as a herbicide dealer. Spray-Rite filed suit, alleging that Monsanto had terminated the distributorship because other dealers had complained about Spray-Rite's discount prices. According to Spray-Rite, this constituted illegal resale price maintenance. Monsanto asserted that Spray-Rite's distributorship had been terminated because of its failure to hire trained sales people and engage in adequate promotion. The jury found for Spray-Rite and awarded $3.5 million in damages, which were trebled to $10.5 million. Monsanto appealed and the Supreme Court granted *certiorari*.

Issue: Did Monsanto engage in illegal resale price maintenance?

Excerpts from Justice Powell's Decision: [T]here is a basic distinction between concerted and independent action—a distinction not always clearly drawn by parties and courts. A manufacturer of course generally has a right to deal, or refuse to deal, with whomever it likes, as long as it does so independently. [A] manufacturer can announce its resale prices in advance and refuse to deal with those who fail to comply. And a distributor is free to acquiesce in the manufacturer's demand in order to avoid termination.

On a claim of [resale price maintenance], the antitrust plaintiff must present evidence sufficient to carry its burden of proving that there was such agreement [between the manufacturer and distributors]. Permitting an agreement to be inferred merely from the existence of complaints, or even from the fact that termination came about "in response to" complaints, could deter or penalize perfectly legitimate conduct. Such complaints arise in the normal course of business and do not indicate illegal concerted action.

Thus, something more than evidence of complaints is needed. [T]he antitrust plaintiff should present direct or circumstantial evidence that reasonably tends to prove that the manufacturer and others had a conscious commitment to a common scheme designed to achieve an unlawful objective. Applying this standard to the facts of this case, we believe there was sufficient evidence for the jury reasonably to have concluded that Monsanto and some of its distributors were parties to an "agreement" or "conspiracy" to maintain resale prices and terminate price cutters.

[T]he remaining question is whether the termination of Spray-Rite was part of or pursuant to that agreement. It would be reasonable to find that it was. Following the termination, there was a meeting between Spray-Rite's president and a Monsanto official. There was testimony that the first thing the official mentioned was the many complaints Monsanto had received about Spray-Rite's prices. Spray-Rite's president testified, Monsanto officials made explicit threats to terminate Spray-Rite unless it raised its prices. In any event, we cannot say that the courts below erred in finding that Spray-Rite produced substantial evidence of the concerted action required by §1 of the Sherman Act.

The Court rejected the Justice Department's view and ruled unanimously that **RPM is a *per se* violation of the law. A manufacturer may not enter into an**

agreement with distributors to fix prices. However, the Court did create a potential loophole when it said that an agreement cannot be inferred simply because a manufacturer cuts off one distributor after receiving complaints from another. Unilateral action by a manufacturer is legal; an agreement with distributors is not.

RPM is illegal. How can a manager stay out of trouble?

- Never agree with a customer on the price it will charge for a product.
- Never promise a customer that you will terminate a competing retailer for selling at a discount.
- Be aware that any efforts to impose a pricing schedule on a retailer or distributor, whether by using incentives or threats, *may* be a violation of the law.

VERTICAL MAXIMUM PRICE-FIXING

In *Monsanto v. Spray-Rite*, the Supreme Court held that resale price maintenance is a *per se* violation of the Sherman Act. In that case, the manufacturer set the *minimum* prices its distributors could charge. In the following case, the Supreme Court dealt with a similar issue, but with one crucial difference—an oil company set the *maximum* price its distributors could charge. Is vertical maximum price-fixing also a *per se* violation of the Sherman Act?

STATE OIL CO. v. KHAN

522 U.S. 3, 118 S. Ct. 275, 1997 U.S. LEXIS 6705
United States Supreme Court, 1997

Facts: When State Oil Co. leased a gas station to Barkat Khan, it capped the maximum price that Khan could charge for gas. Khan sued State Oil, alleging that this agreement was illegal price-fixing under the Sherman Act. The district court dismissed Khan's claim. The appeals court reversed, holding that the State Oil agreement was a *per se* violation of the Sherman Act. The appeals court decision was based on *Albrecht v. Herald Co.*, a prior Supreme Court case. State Oil appealed and the Supreme Court granted *certiorari*.

Issue: Is vertical maximum price-fixing a *per se* violation of the Sherman Act?

Excerpts from Justice O'Connor's Decision: In *Albrecht v. Herald Co.*, this Court held that vertical maximum price fixing is a per se violation of [the Sherman Act]. We conclude that *Albrecht* should be overruled. Our analysis is guided by our general view that the primary purpose of the antitrust laws is to protect interbrand competition. "Low prices," we have explained, "benefit consumers regardless of how those prices are set, and so long as they are above predatory levels, they do not threaten competition." Our interpretation of the Sherman Act also incorporates the notion that condemnation of practices resulting in lower prices to consumers is "especially costly" because "cutting prices in order to increase business often is the very essence of competition." So informed, we find it difficult to maintain that vertically-imposed maximum prices could harm consumers or competition to the extent necessary to justify their per se invalidation.

The *Albrecht* Court also expressed the concern that maximum prices may be set too low for dealers to offer consumers essential or desired services. But such conduct, by driving away customers, would seem likely to harm manufacturers as well as dealers and consumers, making it unlikely that a supplier would set such a price as a matter of business judgment.

Finally, *Albrecht* reflected the Court's fear that maximum price fixing could be used to disguise arrangements to fix minimum prices, which remain illegal per se. Although we have acknowledged the possibility that maximum pricing might mask minimum pricing, we believe that such conduct can be appropriately recognized and punished under the rule of reason. In our view, rule-of-reason analysis will effectively identify those situations in which vertical maximum price fixing amounts to anticompetitive conduct.

Resale price maintenance—setting *minimum* prices—is a *per se* violation of the Sherman Act because it tends to lead to *higher* prices for consumers. Vertical *maximum* price-fixing tends to lead to *lower* prices for consumers, so it is a rule of reason violation, illegal only if it has an adverse impact on competition.

CHAPTER CONCLUSION

Lawmakers in both the courts and Congress are continually seeking the right balance between competition that is healthy and aggression that is destructive. They understand that managers must compete hard if their businesses are to grow and thrive, but not so aggressively that they harm competition in the process. Although managers sometimes resent the constraints imposed on them by antitrust laws, it is these laws that ensure the fair and open competition necessary for a healthy economy. In the end, the antitrust laws benefit us all. To learn more about antitrust law, see **http://www.webcounsel.com/**, which has a comprehensive list of antitrust Web sites.

CHAPTER REVIEW

1. To determine if a company is guilty of monopolization, ask three questions:
   - What is the market?
   - Does the company control the market?
   - How did the company acquire its control?
2. Possessing a monopoly need not be illegal; acquiring or maintaining it through "bad acts" is.
3. To win a predatory pricing case, a plaintiff must prove three elements:
   - The defendant is selling its products below cost.
   - The defendant intends that the plaintiff go out of business.
   - If the plaintiff does go out of business, the defendant will be able to earn sufficient profit to recoup its prior losses.
4. A tying arrangement is illegal if:
   - The two products are clearly separate
   - The seller requires that the buyer purchase the two products together
   - The seller has significant power in the market for the tying product, and
   - The seller is shutting out a significant part of the market for the tied product.

5. Efforts by a manufacturer to allocate customers or territory among its distributors are subject to a rule of reason. These allocations are illegal only if they adversely affect competition in the market.

6. An exclusive dealing contract is one in which a distributor or retailer agrees with a supplier not to carry the products of any other supplier. Exclusive dealing contracts are subject to a rule of reason and are prohibited only if they have an anticompetitive effect.

7. When a manufacturer enters into an agreement with distributors or retailers to fix minimum prices, this arrangement is called resale price maintenance. RPM is a *per se* violation of the law.

8. Vertical maximum price-fixing is a rule of reason violation of the Sherman Act. It is illegal only if it has an adverse impact on competition.

PRACTICE TEST

1. Electronic Payment Services, Inc. (EPS) operates an automatic teller network in five states. This network allows customers to withdraw money at banks other than their own. The network carries out 92 million transactions each month. EPS prohibits banks that are part of the network from using outside companies to process automatic teller transactions; all transactions must be processed either by the bank itself or by EPS. Is EPS in violation of the law?

2. BAR/BRI is a company that prepares law students for bar exams. With branches in 45 states, it has the largest share of the bar review market in the country. Barpassers is a much smaller company located only in Arizona and California. BAR/BRI distributed pamphlets on campuses falsely suggesting Barpassers was near bankruptcy. Enrollments in Barpassers' courses dropped, and the company was forced to postpone plans for expansion. Does Barpassers have an antitrust claim against BAR/BRI?

3. Pilkington P.L.C. is a British company owned 80 percent by the American glassmaker, Libby-Owens-Ford. Pilkington developed technology for producing the flat sheets of glass used in windowpanes and car windows. Virtually all of the world's glass factories operate under Pilkington licenses, including plants in Russia and China. The Justice Department brought suit against Pilkington, alleging that it monopolized glass-making technology. Does the U.S. Justice Department have any authority over this British company?

4. **YOU BE THE JUDGE WRITING PROBLEM** American Academic Suppliers (AAS) and Beckley-Cardy (B-C) both sold educational supplies to schools. B-C's sales began to plummet, and it was rapidly losing market share. The company responded by reducing its catalogue prices 5 to 12 percent. It also offered a discount of 25 to 40 percent in states in which AAS was making substantial gains. What claim might AAS make against B-C? Is it likely to prevail in court? **Argument for AAS:** B-C has committed predatory pricing. The company is selling below cost for the purpose of driving us out of business. **Argument for B-C:** Even if we were to drive AAS out of business, we do not have enough market power to recoup our losses.

5. Two medical supply companies in the San Francisco area provide oxygen to homes of patients. The companies are owned by the doctors who prescribe the oxygen. These doctors make up 60 percent of the lung specialists in the area. Does this arrangement create an antitrust problem?

6. The city of Montgomery, Alabama, awarded Montgomery Cablevision Enterprises, Inc. (MC) a franchise to provide cable television services. Ninety-two percent of the homes in the Montgomery area that subscribed to cable TV already used Storer Cable Communications. MC asked the Turner Network for a contract to carry its programming, but Turner refused. MC also unsuccessfully approached ESPN about carrying its football package. At the same time, Storer entered into exclusive contracts with ESPN and Turner. MC filed suit against ESPN, Turner, and Storer. What claims did MC make? How would you decide the case if you were the judge?

7. Japanese companies sell more products in the United States than American companies sell in Japan.

American business leaders and members of Congress have long been concerned about this imbalance. They suspect that the Japanese system of keiretsu tends to block efforts by U.S. companies to enter Japanese markets. Keiretsu are traditional groups of Japanese companies that tend to deal primarily with each other and are often affiliated by means of minority shareholdings, shared directors, memberships in common organizations, and dealings with the same banks. Could the U.S. Justice Department challenge these keiretsu arrangements under American antitrust law? What provisions of antitrust law might the system of keiretsu violate?

8. Videos of *Jurassic Park* and *Snow White and the Seven Dwarfs* were due in stores the same month. The stores ought to have been delighted at the prospect of having two blockbusters to sell, but instead they were worried—how to price the videos? Both Disney (*Snow White*) and MCA/Universal (*Jurassic Park*) were longtime proponents of MAP—minimum advertised pricing. In other words, if retailers sold the videos at prices below $14.95, the studios would not subsidize their advertising budgets. Many retailers would have *liked* to sell the videos at $14.95, but they were afraid competitors would undercut them. To make matters even more complicated, they had all heard rumors that Disney planned to take other steps against retailers who ignored MAP, such as delaying shipment of the next hit—*The Lion King*. Is MAP legal? What if the studios take "other steps"?

9. Whatever else might be said about professional football in the United States, it does seem to breed a hardy group of fans who do not fear litigation. Football aficionados from Dallas to New England have instituted no fewer than five lawsuits, claiming that a National Football League team violated the Sherman Act by requiring an individual who wished to purchase a season ticket for all regular season games to buy, in addition, tickets for one or more preseason games. Under what provision of the Sherman Act might this practice be a violation? How would a court decide this case?

10. **RIGHT & WRONG** A mildly retarded 18-year-old woman and her mother (the Nelsons) brought a malpractice suit against one of the doctors at the Monroe Regional Medical Center. As a result, the Monroe Clinic notified the Nelsons that it would no longer treat them on a nonemergency basis. The patients then went to another local clinic, which was later acquired by Monroe. The merged clinic refused to treat the Nelsons on a nonemergency basis, so the Nelsons were obliged to seek medical treatment in another town 40 miles away. Has Monroe violated the antitrust laws? Whether or not the Monroe clinic has violated the antitrust laws, is it ethical to deny treatment to a patient?

INTERNET RESEARCH PROBLEM

The Web site **http://www.webcounsel.com/** shows you how to research an antitrust case on the Internet, and **http://www.mlb.com/compete.htm** describes recent antitrust cases. Use these two sites to identify a new antitrust case and then learn more about the companies and issues involved. Write a brief description of the case and the arguments on both sides.

You can find further practice problems in the Online Quiz at http://beatty.westbuslaw.com or in the Study Guide that accompanies this text.

CHAPTER 42

CONSUMER LAW

Three women signed up for a lesson at the Arthur Murray dance studio in Washington, D.C. Expecting a session of decorous fun, they instead found themselves in a nightmare of humiliation and coercion:

- "First of all, I did not want the [additional] lesson, and I think it was unpleasant because I had three, maybe four, people, as I say, pressuring me to buy something by a certain time, and I do recall asking that I be let to think, let me think it over, and I was told that the contest would end at 6 o'clock or something to that effect and if I did not sign by a certain time it would be too late. I think we got under the deadline by maybe a minute or two. If I had been given time to think, I would not have signed that contract."
- "I tried to say no and get out of it and I got very, very upset because I got frightened at paying out all that money and having nothing to fall back on. I remember I started crying and couldn't stop crying. All I thought of was getting out of there. So finally after—I don't know how much time, Mr. Mara said, well, I could sign up for 250 hours, which was half the 500 Club, which would amount to $4,300. So I finally signed it. After that, I tried to raise the money from the bank and found I couldn't get a loan for that amount and I didn't have any savings and I had to get a bank

loan to pay for it. That was when I went back and asked him to cancel that contract. But Mr. Mara said that he couldn't cancel it."

- "I did not join the carnival. I did not wish to join the carnival, and while it was only an additional $55, I had no desire to join. [My instructor] asked everyone in the room to sit down in a circle around me and he stood me up in that circle, in the middle of the circle, and said, 'Everybody, I want you to look at this woman here who is too cheap to join the carnival. I just want you to look at a woman like that. Isn't it awful?'"

Because of abuses such as these, the Federal Trade Commission ordered the Arthur Murray dance studio to halt its high-pressure sales techniques, limit each contract to no more than $1,500 in dance lessons, and permit all contracts to be canceled within seven days.[1]

INTRODUCTION

Years ago consumers typically dealt with merchants they knew well. A dance instructor in a small town would not stay in business long if he tormented his elderly, vulnerable clients. As the population of this country grew and cities expanded, however, merchants became less and less subject to community pressure. The law has supplemented, if not replaced, these informal policing mechanisms. Both Congress and the states have passed statutes that protect consumers from the unscrupulous. But the legal system in America is generally too slow and expensive to handle small cases. The women who fell into the web of Arthur Murray lost a few thousand dollars and suffered some emotional distress, but they had neither the wealth nor the energy to sue the studio themselves. To aid consumers such as these, Congress empowered federal agencies to enforce consumer laws. The Federal Trade Commission (FTC) is the most important of these agencies.

FEDERAL TRADE COMMISSION

Congress created the FTC in 1915 to regulate business. Although its original focus was on antitrust law, it now regulates a wide range of business activities that affect consumers, everything from advertising to consumer loans to warranties to debt collection practices.[2] It is, if you will, the consumer's best friend in Washington. The FTC has several options for enforcing the law:

- *Voluntary Compliance.* When the FTC determines that a business has violated the law, it first asks the offender to sign a voluntary compliance affidavit promising to stop the prohibited activity.
- *Administrative Hearings and Appeals.* If the company refuses to stop voluntarily, the FTC takes the case to an administrative law judge (ALJ) within the agency. The violator may settle the case at this point by signing a **consent order**. If the case proceeds to a hearing, the ALJ has the right to issue a **cease and desist order**, commanding the violator to stop the offending activity. The FTC issued

[1] *In re Arthur Murray Studio of Washington, Inc.*, 78 F.T.C. 401, 1971 FTC LEXIS 75 (1971).

[2] Chapters 40 and 41 discuss the FTC's role in antitrust enforcement.

a cease and desist order against the Arthur Murray dance studio. A defendant can appeal such an order to the five Commissioners of the FTC, from there to a federal appeals court, and ultimately to the United States Supreme Court. Both the Commissioners and the Fifth Circuit Court of Appeals confirmed the cease and desist order against Arthur Murray. The case never reached the Supreme Court.

- *Penalties*. The penalty for each violation of a voluntary compliance affidavit, consent order, or cease and desist order is $11,000. The same penalty also applies to each knowing violation of (1) an FTC rule or (2) a cease and desist order issued against *someone else*. For example, the Arthur Murray studio could be liable for violating an FTC cease and desist order prohibiting high-pressure sales by the Fred Astaire studio. In addition, the FTC can file suit in federal court asking for damages on behalf of an injured consumer if (1) the defendant has violated FTC rules and (2) a reasonable person would have known under the circumstances that the conduct was dishonest or fraudulent.

SALES

Section 5 of the Federal Trade Commission Act (FTC Act) prohibits "unfair and deceptive acts or practices." You can report an unfair or deceptive practice to the FTC at its Web site (**http://www.ftc.gov**).

DECEPTIVE ACTS OR PRACTICES

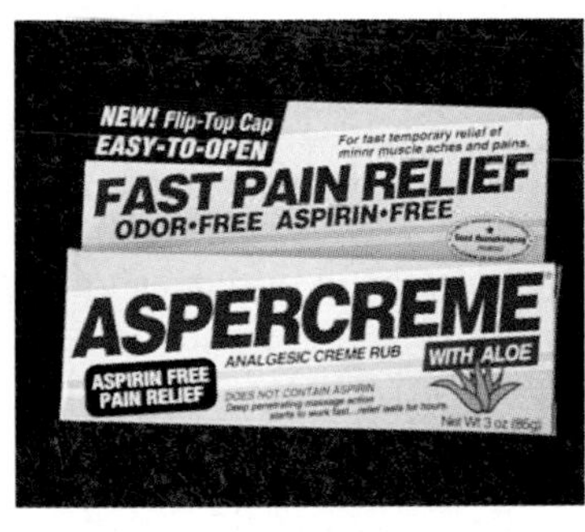

To avoid confusing consumers, the FTC required Aspercreme to disclose that it offers "Aspirin Free Pain Relief."

Many deceptive acts or practices involve advertisements. **Under the FTC Act, an advertisement is deceptive if it contains an important misrepresentation or omission that is likely to mislead a reasonable consumer.** A company advertised that a pain-relief ointment called "Aspercreme" provided "the strong relief of aspirin right where you hurt." From this ad and the name of the product, do you assume that the ointment contains aspirin? Are you a reasonable consumer? Consumers surveyed in a shopping mall believed the product contained aspirin. In fact, it does not. The FTC required the company to disclose that there is no aspirin in Aspercreme.[3] You may have noticed that television advertisements for this product still state, "Aspercreme does not contain aspirin."

Is there anything wrong with the following ads?

[3] *In re Thompson Medical Co., Inc.*, 104 F.T.C. 648, 1984 FTC LEXIS 6 (1984).

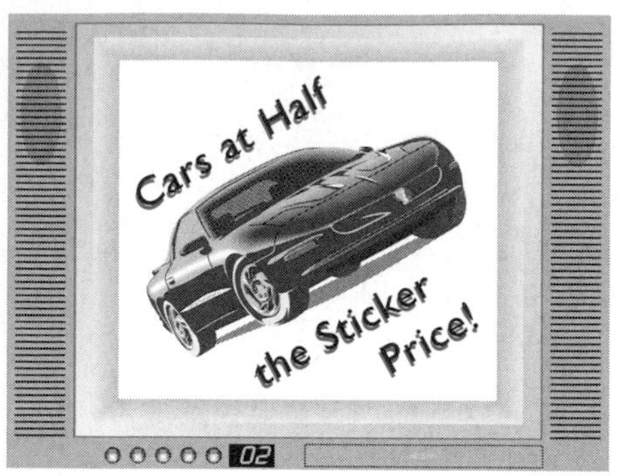

Do not believe a word of them, warns the FTC. It takes more than three minutes a day to get a washboard stomach, no matter what equipment you use. As for the #1 Doctor Recommended Ensure, the doctors in the survey were asked which liquid meal they would choose, if they were going to recommend one to a patient. In fact, most doctors would not recommend Ensure to the healthy adults pictured in the advertisements. The half-price cars were for lease, not sale. By the end of the lease, owners would have paid only half the value of the cars, but they would also have to return the cars to the dealer. Was the company in the following case deceptive about its cure for baldness?

FTC v. PANTRON I CORP.
33 F.3d 1088, 1994 U.S. App. LEXIS 22977
United States Court of Appeals for the Ninth Circuit, 1994

Facts: Pantron I Corp. marketed the Helsinki Formula, a conditioner and shampoo costing $49.95 for a three-month supply. Pantron's advertisements (including late-night infomercials hosted by the "Man from U.N.C.L.E.," Robert Vaughn) claimed scientific studies proved that the Formula promoted growth of new hair on bald men.

At trial, three doctors testified that there was "no reason to believe" from current scientific data that the Helsinki Formula would cure or prevent baldness and that the studies on which Pantron relied did not meet generally accepted scientific standards. Users of the Helsinki Formula (or any other baldness cure) may indeed experience hair regrowth because of the so-called *placebo effect*. Frequently, products with no medicinal value work for psychological reasons. A patient who takes sugar pills believing they are pain relievers may feel better, although the pills themselves are worthless in treating pain. Hair growth products have a particularly strong placebo effect.

Pantron introduced evidence from 18 men who experienced hair regrowth or a reduction in hair loss after using the Formula. It also introduced evidence of a "consumer satisfaction survey" that showed positive results in 70 percent of those who had used the product for six months or more. Over half of Pantron's orders came from repeat purchasers; it received very few written complaints; and fewer than 3 percent of its customers asked for their money back.

The trial court decided that Pantron could state, in its advertisements, that the Helsinki Formula was effective to some extent for some people in treating baldness. However, the ads must disclose that (1) the Formula was more likely to stop hair loss than grow new hair, and (2) the claims were not supported by scientific studies that met U.S. standards.

Issue: Are the advertisements for the Helsinki Formula deceptive?

Excerpts from Judge Reinhardt's Decision: Where, as here, a product's effectiveness arises solely as a result of the placebo effect, a representation that the product is effective constitutes a false advertisement even though some consumers may experience positive results. Under the evidence in the record before us, it appears that massaging vegetable oil on one's head would likely produce the same positive results as using the Helsinki Formula. All that might be required would be for Wesson Oil to remove Florence Henderson as its flack and substitute infomercials with Mr. Vaughn that promote its product as a baldness cure.

As the FTC has explained, "The Commission cannot accept as proof of a product's efficacy a psychological reaction stemming from a belief which, to a substantial degree, was caused by respondent's deceptions." Indeed, were we to hold otherwise, advertisers would be encouraged to foist unsubstantiated claims on an unsuspecting public in the hope that consumers would believe the ads and the claims would be self-fulfilling. Moreover, allowing advertisers to rely on the placebo effect would not only harm those individuals who were deceived; it would create a substantial economic cost as well, by allowing sellers to fleece large numbers of consumers who, unable to evaluate the efficacy of an inherently useless product, make repeat purchases of that product. [W]e conclude that the district court erred in deciding that the FTC had not shown that Pantron's effectiveness claims were false.

UNFAIR PRACTICES

The FTC Act also prohibits unfair acts or practices. **The Commission considers a practice to be *unfair* if it meets all of the following three tests:**

- *It causes a substantial consumer injury*. This can mean physical or financial injury. A furnace repair company that dismantled home furnaces for "inspection" and then refused to reassemble them until the consumers agreed to buy services or replacement parts had caused a substantial consumer injury.
- *The harm of the injury outweighs any countervailing benefit*. A pharmaceutical company sold a sunburn remedy without conducting adequate tests to ensure that it worked. The expense of these tests would have forced the company to raise the product's price. The company had demonstrated that the product was safe, and there was evidence in the medical literature that the ingredients when used in other products were effective. The FTC determined that, although the company was technically in violation of its rules, the benefit to consumers of a cheaper product more than outweighed the risk of injury to them.
- *The consumer could not reasonably avoid the injury*. The FTC is particularly vigilant in protecting susceptible consumers—such as the elderly or the ill—who are less able to avoid injury. For instance, the Commission looks especially carefully at those who offer a cure for cancer.

In addition, the FTC may decide that a practice is unfair simply because it violates public policy even if it does not meet these three tests. The Commission refused to allow a mail-order company to file collection suits in states far from where the defendants lived because the practice was unfair, whether or not it met the three tests.

What is the difference between *deceptive* and *unfair*? Consider this case: Audio Communications, Inc. (ACI) ran a telephone service for children. By dialing a 900 number, children could listen to recorded stories or games featuring characters such as Santa Claus and the Easter Bunny. ACI ran advertisements on children's TV shows and in children's magazines. The FTC held that the ads were *deceptive* because they did not reveal that the phone calls cost money. Moreover, the ads promised a free gift in return for one phone call. In reality, callers (who were, after all, young children) could not obtain a gift without following several complicated steps that were explained very rapidly. Often, more than one call was necessary to obtain the gift. This practice was also *unfair* because children often made the calls without parental permission. Parents (who paid the bill) had little control over children (who made the call). In its consent order, the FTC required ACI to include in all of its advertisements the following statement: "Kids, you must ask your mom or dad and get their permission before you call. This call costs money."[4]

The Internet opens the way to a brave new world of information. Whatever you want to know, you likely can find it on the Internet: The population of Tanzania? The weather in Beijing? The schedule of performances for the Spanish Riding School in Vienna? But information flows both ways. While you are downloading data from the Web, you may also be uploading all sorts of personal information. Some sites explicitly disclose that the price of admission is data about you. Other sites secretly place a cookie on your hard drive—not a chewy treat, but a file to store the information that you provide. When you revisit the site, it automatically enters your hard drive and opens the cookie file so that it knows who you are. Have you noticed that some Web sites greet you by name when you sign on? This feature can be a real convenience—no need to reenter your credit card number each time you place an order. But do you really want your credit card number—or your taste in music—floating in cyberspace?

Both private industry and the government are beginning to take small steps toward greater privacy protection. Some Web browsers have a feature that automatically notifies you whenever a Web site transmits a cookie to your hard drive. The Center for Democracy and Technology (**http://www.cdt.org**) filed a complaint with the FTC alleging that Intel, the microchip manufacturer, committed an unfair trade practice when it shipped the Pentium III chip. This chip came embedded with a serial number that could be used to identify the source of any Internet communications such as e-mail or online purchases. Intel thought the serial number would be helpful in controlling hackers and online fraud. When privacy advocates objected, Intel began shipping the chip with the serial number turned off. However, a clever hacker or webmaster might be able to activate the feature secretly. It turned out that Intel was not alone in using serial numbers to identify a source computer. The Windows operating system automatically embedded a unique identifying number in every document created by Word or Excel. Microsoft, creator of Windows, agreed to eliminate the identifying number in subsequent software releases. Even video games played over a network automatically generate an ID number that enables the server to verify the authenticity of the software. The moral? Do not expect to be anonymous on the Internet.

The FTC continues to investigate the need for more privacy regulations to protect consumers. Meanwhile, the agency's Web site offers tips for protecting your privacy: *A Consumer's Guide to Travel in Cyberspace* (**http://www.ftc.gov/bcp/conline/pubs/online/sitesee/index.html**).

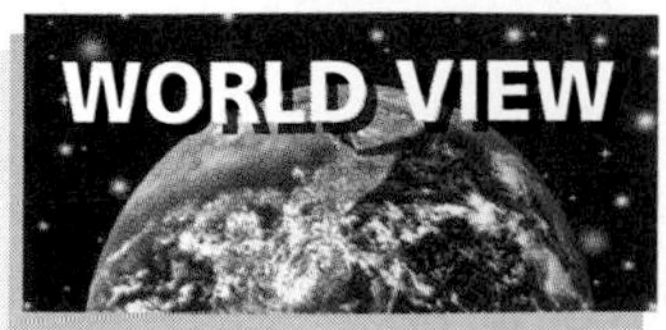

The European Union (EU) recently introduced a privacy law that is much tougher than U.S. regulations. Before a company in the EU can sell your personal data to another firm, it must ask your permission, tell you who will be receiving the information, and let you review the material so you can correct any errors.

Ordinarily, when the EU passes a law that is different from U.S. laws, both sides live and let live. That may not be possible in this case because the new statute prohibits companies in the EU from transmitting personal data to countries without adequate protection—such as the United States. This provision

[4] F.T.C., 56 C.F.R. 22432 (May 15, 1991).

could force a change in the way many American companies routinely do business and strain trade relations between the United States and the EU.

OTHER SALES PRACTICES

Bait and Switch

FTC rules prohibit bait and switch advertisements: a merchant may not advertise a product and then disparage it to consumers in an effort to sell a different item. In addition, merchants must have enough stock on hand to meet reasonable demand for any advertised product. Sears, Roebuck and Co. ran many advertisements like the following:

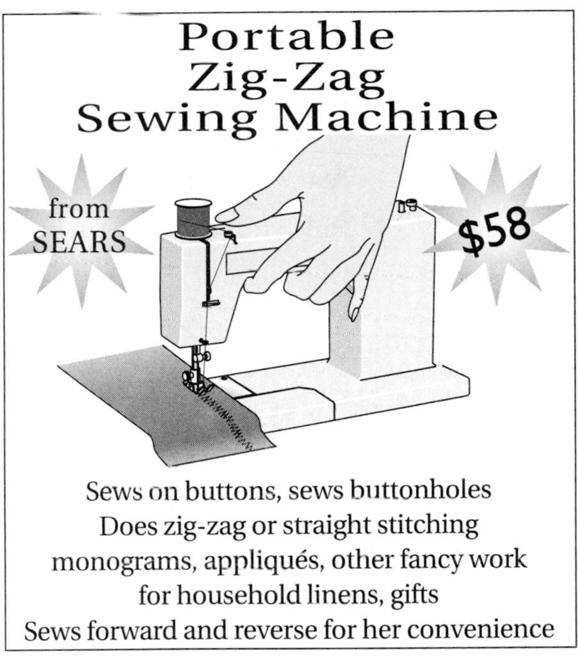

When eager customers went to buy this fabulous item, they were told that the machines were noisy, did not come with Sears' standard sewing machine guarantee, and could neither stitch in reverse nor do buttonholes. Also, the store was out of stock and would not be receiving any new machines for a long time.[5]

This is bait and switch advertising and it violates FTC rules. The **bait** is an alluring offer that sounds almost too good to be true. Of course, it is. The advertiser does not wish to sell the advertised merchandise; it wants to **switch** consumers to another, higher-priced product. The real purpose of the advertisement is simply to find customers who are interested in buying.

Mail or Telephone Order Merchandise

Roughly 50 percent of American adults order from a catalogue each year. Before the FTC issued rules, catalogue companies often failed to deliver orders when promised. Now, only 5 percent of orders fail to meet the following **FTC guidelines on mail and telephone order merchandise:**

---

5 *In re Sears, Roebuck and Co.*, 89 F.T.C. 229, 1977 FTC LEXIS 225 (1977).

- Mail-order companies must ship an item within the time stated or, if no time is given, within 30 days after receipt of the order.
- If a company cannot ship the product when promised, it must send the customer a notice with the new shipping date and an opportunity to cancel. If the new shipping date is within 30 days of the original one, and the customer does not cancel, the order is still on.
- If the company cannot ship within 30 days of the original date, it must send the customer another notice. This time, however, the company must cancel the order unless the customer returns the notice, indicating that he still wants the item.

For example, Dell Computer Corp. advertised that its Dimension computer came with the "Dell Software Suite." In fact, for several months the suite was not available. Instead of the software, Dell sent customers a coupon for the suite "when available." The FTC charged Dell with violations of the mail or telephone order rules because the company:

- Knew it could not ship the software within 30 days
- Failed to offer buyers the opportunity to cancel their orders, and
- Did not cancel the orders automatically as it should have under the rules.[6]

Unordered Merchandise

Under §5 of the FTC Act, anyone who receives unordered merchandise in the mail can treat it as a gift. She can use it, throw it away, or do whatever else she wants with it.

There you are, watching an infomercial for Anushka products, guaranteed to fight that scourge of modern life—cellulite! Rushing to your phone, you place an order. The Anushka cosmetics arrive, but for some odd reason, the cellulite remains. A month later another bottle arrives, like magic, in the mail. The magic spell is broken, however, when you get your credit card bill and see that, without your authorization, the company has charged you for the new supply of Anushka. Is this a hot new marketing technique? Not exactly. The FTC ordered the company to cease and desist this unfair and deceptive practice. The company improperly billed its customers, said the FTC, and should have notified them that they were free to treat the unauthorized products as a gift, to use or throw out as they wished.[7]

Door-to-Door Sales

Consumers at home need special protection from unscrupulous salespeople. In a store, customers can simply walk out, but at home they may feel trapped. Also, it is difficult at home to compare products or prices offered by competitors. Under the FTC door-to-door rules, **a salesperson is required to notify the buyer that she has the right to cancel the transaction prior to midnight of the third business day thereafter.** This notice must be given both orally and in writing; the actual cancellation must be in writing. The seller must return the buyer's money within

---

[6] *United States v. Dell Computer Corp.*, 1998 FTC LEXIS 30 (1998).

[7] *In the Matter of Synchronal Corp.*, 116 F.T.C. 1190, 1993 FTC LEXIS 280 (1993).

10 days. The following news report illustrates an illegal method of selling magazine subscriptions.

A federal judge assessed a $50,000 civil penalty against a door-to-door magazine sales company. Customers who purchased magazine subscriptions from Tork & Associates were given (partial) receipts that misrepresented their right to cancel. The receipt indicated that a customer wishing to cancel was required to submit a copy of the complete receipt, the canceled check, the salesperson's name, the magazine name, the date of the transaction, and the total cost. Since the salesperson never gave the customer the complete receipt, it was difficult to comply. In two years, Tork generated $2 million in revenues.[8]

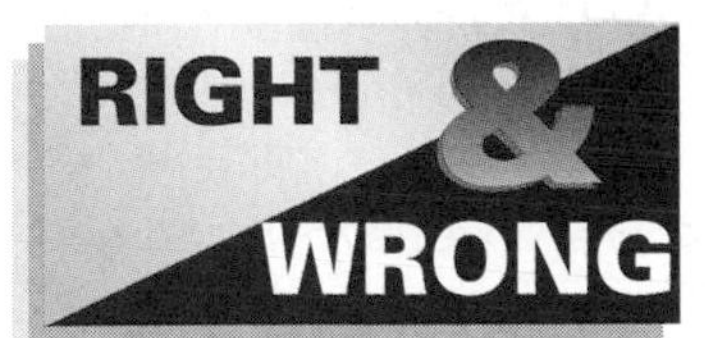

A vice-president of Grolier, the encyclopedia company, made the following statement:

> The proposition that a buyer should have the right to whimsically change his mind with respect to a transaction which has been formalized by an agreement containing all of the elements of a legally binding contract, is indeed, a revolutionary legal concept. This proposal represents an attack on the basic contractual concepts which are the foundation of the American economic system.[9]

Do you agree with this statement? Why is this executive so concerned about customers having three days to reconsider door-to-door sales?

CONSUMER CREDIT

Historically, the practice of charging interest on loans was banned by most countries and by three of the most prominent religions—Christianity, Islam, and Judaism. As the European economy developed, however, money lending became essential. To compromise, governments began to permit interest charges but limited the maximum rate to 6 percent. European settlers carried this concept to the United States, which soon adopted the 6 percent rule, too.

Even in modern times, most states limit the maximum interest rate a lender may charge. The New York usury statute permits rates as high as 25 percent, while the California limit is 12 percent. The penalty for violating usury statutes varies among the states. Depending upon the jurisdiction, the borrower may be allowed to keep (1) the interest above the usury limit, (2) all of the interest, or (3) all of the loan and the interest.

Before Congress passed the Truth in Lending Act (TILA), lenders found many creative methods to disguise the real interest rate and circumvent the law. For example, they would use a so-called add-on rate. That is, they would charge the permissible interest rate but would insist that the borrower begin to repay the loan in installments immediately. The borrower only had effective use of the money for half the term of the loan. Suppose that a car dealer loaned a customer $3,600 for three years, at 8 percent. The total interest would be .08 × $3,600 × 3 = $864. If the borrower was required to repay $100 of the principal each month, she would be repaying half the loan within 18 months, but would still pay the full $864 in interest. This customer's real interest rate was 16 percent, not 8 percent.

---

[8] Nancy Stancill, "Door-to-Door Firm Hit with $50,000 Penalty," *Houston Chronicle*, Jan. 28, 1993, p. A17.

[9] *Quoted in* Douglas Whaley, *Problems and Materials on Consumer Law* (Boston: Little, Brown & Co., 1991), at p. 135.

TRUTH IN LENDING ACT

The problem with add-ons and other such devices designed to hide the real rate of interest from the authorities is that they also hide it from the borrower. Before TILA, many consumers had no idea what interest rate they were really paying. Congress passed the statute to ensure that consumers were adequately informed about credit terms before entering into a loan and could compare the cost of credit. TILA does not regulate interest rates or the terms of a loan; these are still set by state law. It simply requires lenders to *disclose* the terms of a loan in an understandable and complete manner.

TILA applies to a transaction only if all of the following tests are met:

- *It is a consumer loan.* That means a loan to an individual for personal, family, or household purposes but not a loan to a business. For example, TILA does not apply to a loan on a truck used to sell produce.
- *The loan has a finance charge or will be repaid in more than four installments.* Sometimes finance charges masquerade as installment plans. Boris can pay for his big-screen TV in six monthly installments of $200 each, or he can pay $900 cash up front. If he chooses the installment plan, he is effectively paying a finance charge of $300. That is why TILA applies to loans with more than four installments.
- *The loan is for less than $25,000 or secured by a mortgage on real estate.* If Boris borrows money to buy a $1 million house, TILA applies, but not if he buys a $50,000 yacht.
- *The loan is made by someone in the business of offering credit.* If Boris borrows $5,000 from his friend Ludmilla to buy a riding mower, TILA does not apply. If he borrows the money from Friendly Neighborhood Loan Depot, Inc., TILA does apply.

Required Disclosure

In all loans regulated by TILA:

- *The disclosure must be clear and in meaningful sequence.* A finance company violated TILA when it loaned money to Dorothy Allen. The company made all the required disclosures but scattered them throughout the loan document and intermixed them with confusing terms that were not required by TILA.[10] A TILA disclosure statement should not be a game of *Where's Waldo.*
- *The lender must disclose the finance charge.* The finance charge is the amount, in dollars, the consumer will pay in interest and fees over the life of the loan. It is important for consumers to know this amount because otherwise they may not understand the real cost of the loan. Of course, the longer the loan, the higher the finance charge. Someone who borrows $5 for 10 years at 10 percent annual interest will pay $.50 each year for 10 years, for a total finance charge of $5—equal to the principal borrowed. In 25-year mortgages, the finance charge will almost always exceed the amount of the principal.
- *The creditor must also disclose the annual percentage rate (APR).* This number is the actual rate of interest the consumer pays on an annual basis. Without this disclosure, it would be easy in a short-term loan to disguise a very high APR because the finance charge is low. Boris borrows $5 for lunch from his

[10] *Allen v. Beneficial Fin. Co. of Gary*, 531 F.2d 797, 1976 U.S. App. LEXIS 12935 (7th Cir. 1976).

employer's credit union. Under the terms of the loan, he must repay $6 the following week. His finance charge is only $1, but his APR is astronomical—20 percent per week for a year.

All TILA loans must meet these three requirements. TILA requires additional disclosure for two types of loans—open-end credit and closed-end credit.

Open-End Credit. This is a credit transaction in which the lender makes a *series* of loans that the consumer can repay at once or in installments. The typical VISA or MasterCard account is open-end credit—the cardholder has a choice of paying his balance in full each month or making only the required minimum payment.[11] The lender must disclose credit terms in any advertisements. In addition, before beginning an open-end credit account, the lender must disclose to the consumer when a finance charge will be imposed and how the finance charge will be calculated (for example, whether it will be based on the account balance at the beginning of the billing cycle, the end, or somewhere in between). **In each statement, the lender must disclose the following:** the amount owed at the beginning of the billing cycle (the previous balance); amounts and dates of all purchases, credits and payments; finance charges; and the date by which a bill must be paid to avoid finance charges. The Federal Reserve Board offers advice on choosing a credit card at http://www.bog.frb.fed.us/pubs/shop/.

Closed-End Credit. In a closed-end transaction, there is only one loan, and the borrower knows the amount and the payment schedule in advance. Boris enters into a closed-end transaction when he buys a $20,000 car and agrees to make specified monthly payments over five years. Before a consumer enters into a closed-end transaction, the lender must disclose the cash price; the total down payment; the amount financed; an itemized list of all other charges; the number, amount, and due dates of payments; the total amount of payments; late payment charges; penalties for prepaying the loan; and the lender's security interest in the item purchased.[12]

Other TILA Provisions

Rescission. **Under TILA, consumers have the right to rescind a mortgage for up to three business days after the signing.** If the lender does not comply with the disclosure provisions of TILA, the consumer can rescind for up to three years from the date of the mortgage. Scam artists sometimes prey upon the elderly who are vulnerable to pressure and upon the poor who may not have access to conventional financing. These swindlers offer home equity loans, secured by a second mortgage, to finance fraudulent repairs. (There are, of course, many legitimate lenders in the home equity business.) The following news report shows scam artists at work.

Mack and Jacqueline Moon of East Baltimore hired a home improvement contractor to install a dropped ceiling, paneling, and cabinets in the unfinished basement of their rowhouse. The couple were determined not to put a second mortgage on their house, anticipating they would need backup money to pay medical expenses for their 10-year-old daughter who had lupus. They signed the contract a few days later after a second salesman assured them, "We were able to work it out, and you don't have to worry about a mortgage." The Moons were never given copies of the loan documents nor told of the 17 percent interest rate. A year later, when they

[11] Open-end credit rules apply to all consumer credit cards, even American Express, which requires the balance to be paid every month.

[12] See Chapter 26, on secured transactions, for a discussion of security interests.

tried to use their home's equity to pay medical bills for their daughter, who had since died, they discovered they had given a second mortgage to the lender without knowing it.[13]

The Moons were able to rescind the loan because the lender had not made adequate disclosure. This right of rescission does *not* apply to a *first* mortgage used to finance a house purchase or to any refinancing with the consumer's existing lender. The table below summarizes the major provisions of TILA.

Advertising. TILA is meant to enable consumers to shop around and compare available financing alternatives. With this goal in mind, the statute requires lenders to advertise their rates accurately. A lender cannot "bait and switch"; that is, it cannot advertise rates unless they are generally available to anyone who applies. Moreover, if the lender advertises any credit terms, it must tell the whole story. For example, if it advertises "Nothing down, 12 months to pay," it must also disclose the APR and other terms of repayment.

Enforcement. The FTC generally has the right to enforce TILA. In addition, consumers who have been injured by any violation (except for the advertising provisions) have the right to file suit.

Special Credit Card Rules. Your wallet is missing, and with it your cash, your driver's license, a photo of your dog, a coupon for a free video rental and—oh! no!—all your credit cards! It is a disaster, to be sure. But it could have been worse. There was a time when you would have been responsible for every charge the thief rang up. **Now, under TILA, you are liable only for the first $50 in charges the thief makes before you notify the credit card company.** If you call the company before any charges are made, you have no liability at all. But if, by the time you contact the company, the speedy robber has completely furnished her apartment on your card, you are still liable only for $50. Of course, if you carry a wallet full of cards, $50 for each one can add up to a sizable total.

Suppose that a credit card company mails a card to you that you did not order and someone steals it out of your mailbox. You know nothing about the card until

TILA applies to a transaction only if:	• It is a consumer loan • The loan has a finance charge or will be repaid in more than four installments • The loan is for less than $25,000 or to secure a mortgage on real estate, and • The loan is made by someone in the business of offering credit.
In all loans regulated by TILA:	• The disclosure must be clear and in meaningful sequence, and • The lender must disclose the finance charge and the annual percentage rate (APR).
Consumers have the right to rescind a mortgage:	• For up to three business days after the signing, or • For up to three years from the date of the mortgage if the lender does not comply with TILA disclosure provisions. • This provision does not apply if the mortgage is a first mortgage used to finance a house purchase or a refinancing with the consumer's existing lender.

[13] Lorraine Mirabella, "With Hopes of Improving Their Homes, Many Owners Fall Prey to Loan Scams," *Baltimore Sun*, Sep. 4, 1994, p. 1K. Reprinted with permission.

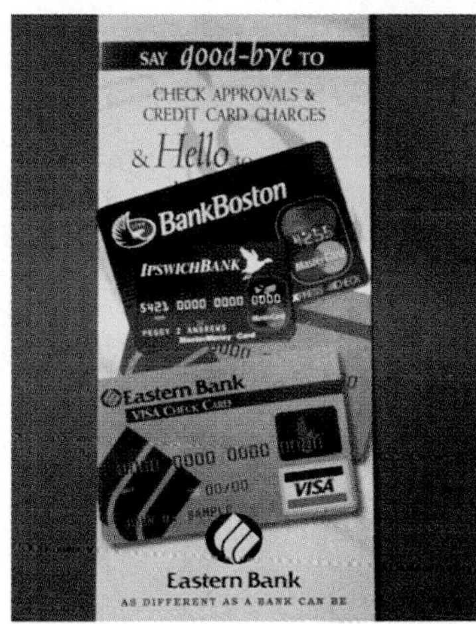

These two pieces of plastic look the same, but offer different legal protections.

the bills arrive. If you did not request the card, and it is not a renewal or substitute for a card you already have, you are not liable, even for the $50.

You use your credit card to buy a new computer at ShadyComputers. When you arrive home and start to load software, you discover the hard disk is only 1 gigabyte, not 20 gigabytes as advertised. The computer crashes six times the first day. In short, you have a major, $2,200 problem. But all is not lost. **In the event of a dispute between a customer and a merchant, the credit card company cannot bill the customer if** (1) she makes a good faith effort to resolve the dispute, (2) the dispute is for more than $50, and (3) the merchant is in the same state where she lives or is within 100 miles of her house.

What happens if the merchant and the consumer cannot resolve their dispute? Or if the merchant is not in the same state as the consumer? Clearly, credit card companies do not want to be caught in the middle between consumer and merchant. In practice, they now require all merchants to sign a contract specifying that, in the event of a dispute between the merchant and a customer, the credit card company has the right to charge back the merchant's account. If a customer seems to have a reasonable claim against a merchant, the credit card company will typically transfer the credit it has given the merchant back to the customer's account. Of course, the merchant can try to sue the customer for any money owed.

If the merchant agrees to provide a refund, it must send a credit notice to the credit card company within seven business days, and the credit card company must credit the customer's account within three business days.

Debit Cards. So your wallet is missing, and with it your debit card. No problem, right, it is just like a credit card? Wrong. Debit cards look and feel like credit cards, but legally they are a different plastic altogether. Debit cards work like checks (which is why they are also called **check cards**). When you use your debit card, the bank deducts money directly from your account, which means there is no bill to pay at the end of the month (and no interest charges on unpaid bills). That is the good news. The bad news is that your liability for a stolen debit card is much greater. If you report the theft within two days of discovering it, the bank will make good on all losses above $50. If you wait until after two days, your bank will only replace stolen funds above $500. After 60 days, all losses are yours: the bank will not repay any stolen funds.

FAIR CREDIT BILLING ACT

The Fair Credit Billing Act (FCBA) provides additional protection for credit card holders. Is there anyone in America who has not sometime or other discovered an error in a credit card bill? Before Congress passed the FCBA in 1975, a dispute with a credit card company often deteriorated into an avalanche of threatening form letters that ignored any response from the hapless cardholder. **Under the FCBA:**

- If, within 60 days of receipt of a bill, a consumer writes to a credit card company to complain about the bill, the company must acknowledge receipt of the complaint within 30 days.
- Within two billing cycles (but no more than 90 days) the credit card company must investigate the complaint and respond:
  - In the case of an error, by correcting the mistake and notifying the consumer
  - If there is no error, by writing to the consumer with an explanation.
- Whether or not there was a mistake, if the consumer requests it, the credit card company must supply documentary evidence to support its position—for example, copies of the bill signed by the consumer or evidence that the package actually arrived.

- The credit card company cannot try to collect the disputed debt or close or suspend the account until it has responded to the consumer complaint.

- The credit card company cannot report to credit agencies that the consumer has an unpaid bill until 10 days after the response. If the consumer still disputes the charge, the credit card company may report the amount to a credit agency but must disclose that it is disputed.

In the following case, American Express made a big mistake picking on a law professor. The court's opinion was written by Abner J. Mikva, a highly regarded judge on the federal appeals court. He was clearly exasperated by American Express's arguments and used strong language to reprimand the company—and the lower court. Since Judge Mikva had served in Congress, he could speak with some authority about Congress's approach to consumer legislation.

GRAY v. AMERICAN EXPRESS CO.

743 F.2d 10, 240 U.S. App. D.C. 10, 1984 U.S. App. LEXIS 19033
United States Court of Appeals for the District of Columbia Circuit, 1984

Facts: In December, Oscar Gray used his American Express credit card to buy airline tickets costing $9,312. American Express agreed that Gray could pay for the tickets in 12 monthly installments. In January, Gray paid $3,500 and then in February an additional $1,156. In March, American Express billed Gray by mistake for the entire remaining balance, which he did not pay. In April, Gray and his wife went out for dinner to celebrate their wedding anniversary. When he tried to pay with his American Express card, the restaurant told him that the credit card company had not only refused to accept the charges for the meal, but had instructed the restaurant to confiscate and destroy the card. While still at the restaurant, Gray spoke to an American Express employee on the telephone who informed him, "Your account is canceled as of now."

Gray wrote to American Express, pointing out the error. For more than a year, the company failed to respond to Gray or to investigate his claim. It then turned the bill over to a collection agency. Gray sued American Express for violating the Fair Credit Billing Act. The trial court granted summary judgment to American Express and dismissed the complaint on the grounds that Gray had waived his rights under the Act.

Issue: Is American Express liable to Gray for violating the Fair Credit Billing Act?

Excerpts from Judge Mikva's Decision: The contract between Gray and American Express provides: "We can revoke your right to use [the card] at any time. We can do this with or without cause and without giving you notice." American Express concludes from this language that the cancellation was not of the kind prohibited by the Act, even though the Act regulates other aspects of the relationship between the cardholder and the card issuer.

[T]he Act states that, during the pendency of a disputed billing, the card issuer shall not cause the cardholder's account to be restricted or closed because of the failure of the obligor to pay the amount in dispute. American Express seems to argue that, despite that provision, it can exercise its right to cancellation for cause unrelated to the disputed amount, or for no cause, thus bringing itself out from under the statute. At the very least, the argument is audacious. American Express would restrict the efficacy of the statute to those situations where the parties had not agreed to a "without cause, without notice" cancellation clause, or to those cases where the cardholder can prove that the sole reason for cancellation was the amount in dispute. We doubt that Congress painted with such a faint brush.

The effect of American Express's argument is to allow the equivalent of a "waiver" of coverage of the Act simply by allowing the parties to contract it away. Congress usually is not so tepid in its approach to consumer problems. The rationale of consumer protection legislation is to even out the inequalities that consumers normally bring to the bargain. To allow such protection to be waived by boiler plate language of the contract puts the legislative process to a foolish and unproductive task. A court ought not impute such nonsense to a Congress intent on correcting abuses in the market place.

The district court's order of summary judgment and dismissal is hereby *vacated*.

FAIR CREDIT REPORTING ACT

Gossip and rumor can cause great harm. Bad enough when whispered behind one's back, worse yet when placed in files and distributed to potential creditors. Most adults rely on credit—to acquire a house, credit cards, or overdraft privileges at the bank. A sullied credit report makes life immensely more difficult. The goal of the Fair Credit Reporting Act (FCRA) is to ensure that consumer credit reports are accurate.

The FCRA regulates **consumer reporting agencies**. These are businesses that supply consumer reports to third parties. If an insurance agency or bank conducts its own investigation to determine whether a consumer is creditworthy, the FCRA does not apply. A **consumer report** is any communication about a consumer's creditworthiness, character, general reputation, or lifestyle that is considered as a factor in establishing credit, obtaining insurance, securing a job, acquiring a government license, or for any other legitimate business need.

Under the FCRA:

- A consumer report can be used only for a legitimate business need, and a consumer reporting agency must be careful not to supply reports that will be used for any other purpose. A nosy neighbor does not have the right to order a report.
- A consumer reporting agency cannot report obsolete information. Ordinary credit information is obsolete after seven years, bankruptcies after 10 years. **Investigative reports** that discuss character, reputation, or lifestyle become obsolete in three *months*. Some commentators argue that the type of information contained in investigative reports is not relevant and should not be used at all. Although the FCRA does not limit the kinds of information that can be collected and reported, it does specify that an investigative report cannot be ordered without first informing the consumer.
- An employer cannot request a consumer report on any current or potential employee without the employee's permission. An employer cannot take action because of information in the consumer report without first giving the current or potential employee a copy of the report and a description of the employee's rights under this statute.
- Anyone who makes an adverse decision against a consumer because of a credit report must reveal the name and address of the reporting agency that supplied the information. An "adverse decision" includes denying credit or charging higher rates.
- Upon request from a consumer, a reporting agency must disclose all information in his file, the source of the information (except for investigative reports), the name of anyone to whom a report has been sent in the prior year (two years for employment purposes), and the name of anyone who has requested a report in the prior year.

- If a consumer tells an agency that some of the information is incorrect, the agency must investigate and delete data that it finds to be untrue. The consumer also has the right to give the agency a short report telling his side of the story. The agency must then include the consumer's statement with any credit reports it supplies and also, at the consumer's request, send the statement to anyone who has received a report within six months (or two years for employment purposes).

The following article illustrates the usefulness of the FCRA.

Kimberly Dorcik wanted a new job. An assistant manager at a Lechters housewares store, she applied for the manager's position at Ups 'N Downs, a women's clothing store a dozen doors away in Solano Mall, in Fairfield, California. But her hopes for the job, which paid a few thousand dollars more than the $22,000 she was earning, vanished, she said, when the staff member taking her application whispered: "We're not supposed to tell anybody, but we pull credit reports on people. Is that going to be a problem?"

Ms. Dorcik remembers mumbling a noncommittal response, but she knew that it was going to be a problem. Three years earlier, when she was 19, she had had emergency surgery resulting from complications from pregnancy. Because of what she calls a clerical error, $30,000 in medical bills were still unpaid and in dispute, tainting her credit history. Ms. Dorcik did not get the job, and she said she was almost certain that the deciding factor was her credit history. The FCRA now requires employers to tell applicants like Ms. Dorcik if credit histories are being used as part of hiring. Employers will also have to obtain written permission from applicants before even requesting a credit history. If someone is turned down for a job and a credit report was used in the decision, the applicant can presumably weed out wrong information in the report and reapply.[14]

A recent survey revealed that 70 percent of credit reports contain errors. About one-third of the reports contain serious mistakes. Consumer advocates recommend that every year you check your credit reports from each of the three major reporting agencies: Equifax (800-685-1111; **http://www.equifax.com**), Experian (800-682-7654; **http://www.experian.com/**), and Trans Union (800-916-8800; **http://www.transunion.com/consumer**). A report is free if you have been turned down for credit within 60 days; otherwise, it generally costs $8, although, in some states, it is free. If you find any errors, notify the agency in writing and warn it that failing to make corrections is a violation of the law. At **http://www.ftc.gov/bcp/conline/pubs/credit/crdtdis.htm**, the FTC offers advice on how to dispute credit report errors.

Also, under the Financial Services Modernization Act of 1999, banks must notify consumers before disclosing any personal information to a third party. The bank may not make the disclosure if the consumer objects. Moreover, it is illegal to use false pretenses to obtain information about a customer from a bank.

FAIR DEBT COLLECTION PRACTICES ACT

The introduction to the Fair Debt Collection Practices Act (FDCPA) states that "Abusive debt collection practices contribute to the number of personal bankruptcies, to marital instability, to the loss of jobs, and to invasions of individual pri-

---

[14] Anthony Ramirez, "Name, Resumé, References. And How's Your Credit," *New York Times*, Aug. 31, 1997, p. F8. Copyright © 1997 by The New York Times Co. Reprinted by permission.

vacy."[15] Congress did not mention it, but debt collection practices can also disrupt Super Bowl Sunday. Debt collectors want to catch their prey off guard, and what better time than when the entire nation is at home, glued to the television? If the phone rings, sports fans assume it is a friend calling to gab about the game.

Is that legal? It depends. The FDCPA provides that a collector must, within five days of contacting a debtor, send the debtor a written notice containing the amount of the debt, the name of the creditor to whom the debt is owed, and a statement that if the debtor disputes the debt (in writing), the collector will cease all collection efforts until it has sent evidence of the debt. **Also under the FDCPA, collectors may not:**

- Call or write a debtor who has notified the collector in writing that he wishes no further contact
- Call or write a debtor who is represented by an attorney
- Call a debtor before 8:00 A.M. or after 9:00 P.M.
- Threaten a debtor or use obscene or abusive language
- Call or visit the debtor at work if the consumer's employer prohibits such contact
- Imply that they are attorneys when they are not
- Threaten to arrest consumers who do not pay their debts
- Make other false or deceptive threats, that is, threats that would be illegal if carried out or which the collector has no intention of doing—such as suing the debtor or seizing property
- Contact acquaintances of the debtor for any reason other than to locate the debtor (and then only once), or
- Tell acquaintances that the consumer is in debt.

Of course, these rules do not prevent the collector from filing suit against the debtor. In the event of a violation of the FDCPA, the debtor is entitled to damages, court costs, and attorney's fees. The FTC also has authority to enforce the Act.

The following case illustrates the types of abuses that the FDCPA was designed to prevent.

PITTMAN v. J. J. MAC INTYRE CO. OF NEVADA
969 F. Supp. 609, 1997 U.S. Dist. LEXIS 15826
United States District Court for the District of Nevada, 1997

Facts: Marijo Pittman defaulted on a $1,500 loan from the Boulder Dam Credit Union. J. J. Mac Intyre Co. tried to collect the loan for Boulder. Pittman reached a settlement with Boulder and then filed suit against Mac Intyre for violating the FDCPA. Mac Intyre filed a motion to dismiss Pittman's lawsuit. The details of Mac Intyre's activities are set out in the opinion of the court.

Issue: Did Mac Intyre violate the FDCPA?

Excerpts from Judge George's Decision: The FDCPA provides that a debt collector, without prior consent of the consumer, may not communicate with a consumer in connection with the collection of any debt at any unusual time or place or a time or place known or which should be known to be inconvenient to the consumer. Pittman alleges that on January 31, the defendant called her at her

---

[15] 15 U.S.C. §1692(a).

place of employment, in [an] effort to collect on the debt. The defendant's own account summary states that Pittman told the defendant that she could not talk at work. Pittman alleges that she had told this to the defendant many times prior. Notwithstanding the warning on January 31 and the alleged warnings on prior occasions, the defendant called the plaintiff again on September 7 at her place of employment to collect on the debt. This court finds that under this set of facts, plaintiff could be entitled to relief for the defendant's alleged violation.

Plaintiff also alleges that the defendant violated [the section] of the FDCPA which prohibits a debt collector from engaging "in any conduct the natural consequence of which is to harass, oppress, or abuse any person in connection with the collection of a debt." Plaintiff alleges that any of the three communications at issue constitutes a violation of this provision. [P]laintiff also could show, given the facts presented, that the defendant's calls on January 31 and September 7 to Pittman's work place were abusive and made for the purpose of harassment.

On August 14, plaintiff satisfied her debt directly with Boulder. Plaintiff alleges that the defendant's phone calls on September 7 and September 25 in which the defendant made further attempts to collect on the fully satisfied debt, violated the FDCPA [which] specifically prohibits "the false representation of the character, amount, or legal status of any debt." The defendant's primary argument is that it cannot be held liable for violation of these sections because the defendant had no knowledge that the plaintiff had satisfied the debt with the original creditor. [T]he defendant's own account summary has multiple entries stating that the plaintiff was making payments directly to Boulder. [U]nder these circumstances, a trier of fact could conclude that the conduct of the defendant was "unfair or unconscionable."

IT IS HEREBY ORDERED that defendant J. J. Mac Intyre Co., Inc.'s motion to dismiss is DENIED.

If a debt collector calls you, what can you do? First of all, be sure to write down his name and the name of the agency for which he works. Tell the caller that you are recording the conversation and then do so. Send a letter to the agency, requesting that it not contact you. Report any violations to the FTC at **http://www.ftc.gov/bcp/conline/pubs/credit/fdc.htm**.

EQUAL CREDIT OPPORTUNITY ACT

The Equal Credit Opportunity Act (ECOA) prohibits any creditor from discriminating against a borrower because of race, color, religion, national origin, sex, marital status, age (as long as the borrower is old enough to enter into a legal contract), or because the borrower is receiving welfare. A lender must respond to a credit application within 30 days. If a lender rejects an application, it must either tell the applicant why or notify him that he has the right to a written explanation of the reasons for the rejection. The following news report illustrates the types of abuses that the ECOA is designed to prevent.

Florence and Joe made an offer to buy a new home at the Meadowood housing development near Tampa. The developer accepted their offer, contingent upon their obtaining a mortgage. When the couple filed an application with Rancho Mortgage and Investment Corp., they were surprised by the hostility of Rancho's loan processor. She requested information they had already supplied and repeatedly questioned them about whether they intended to occupy the house, which was about 80 miles from their jobs. Florence and Joe insisted they wanted to live near their son and daughter-in-law and escape city crime. Rancho turned down their mortgage, refusing to give either an oral or a written explanation. The house was sold to another buyer.

Joe and Florence didn't get mad, they got even. They sued under the ECOA. Rancho was ordered to pay the African American couple $35,000.[16]

In the following case, the lender asked a spouse to co-sign her husband's loan. Did this request violate the ECOA? You be the judge.

AMERICAN SECURITY BANK, N.A. v. YORK
1992 U.S. Dist. LEXIS 14309
United States District Court for the District of Columbia, 1992

Facts: John York and Michael Lipson borrowed money several times from American Security Bank (ASB) to finance their business deals. When the two men met with their loan officer to request an additional $13.5 million, he told them that their wives would have to sign any additional loan. ASB imposed this requirement before undertaking any study of the two men's creditworthiness. Under ASB's standards, York and Lipson were entitled to the loan on their own merits, without their wives' signatures. In granting the loan, ASB did not actually consider the wives' personal assets or the assets that each couple held jointly.

The two wives signed the loan, the two husbands defaulted, and ASB sued for payment. The two wives counter-claimed, alleging that ASB had violated the Equal Credit Opportunity Act and that, therefore, neither they nor their husbands were required to repay the loan. They also asked for damages. ASB filed a motion for summary judgment, asking the court to dismiss the counter-claim.

You Be the Judge: Did ASB violate the Equal Credit Opportunity Act when it insisted that a wife guarantee her husband's loan? What is the appropriate remedy for a violation?

Argument for ASB: There was a time when banks and other lenders would not give credit to a married woman without her husband's permission. The purpose of the ECOA is to permit married women to obtain credit on their own. In this case, the two women are arguing that ASB violated the law by *giving* them credit. This interpretation stands the law on its head. They are taking a statute designed to prevent the *denial* of credit and saying it applies to the *granting* of a loan. That is clearly not what Congress had in mind.

Even if ASB did violate the ECOA, the loan is still valid. The two women may be entitled to some damages, but this is a $13.5 million loan. Surely, they are not suggesting that their damages for this technical violation equal $13.5 million. If ASB has violated the Act, the court should enforce the loan and impose modest damages.

Argument for Ms. York and Ms. Lipson: ASB misreads the ECOA. This statute prevents discrimination because of marital status. These two women had no connection to the loan except that they were married to the men who wanted to borrow money. The two women had no ownership interest in the business and played no role in the loan negotiations. If they had not been married, the ASB would never have asked them to sign the note. The bank discriminated on the basis of marital status when it demanded of a married woman what it would not have asked of a single person.

ASB asked the wives to sign before even checking their husbands' credit status. ASB has admitted that the two husbands were creditworthy on their own. If the men had not been married, ASB would have given them the loan. ASB asked the wives to sign, simply because they were there.

As for the damage question, if ASB had not violated the ECOA, the two wives would not have signed the loan and they would not now be liable. If they have to pay the loan, their damages are indeed $13.5 million.

CONSUMER LEASING ACT

If you, like many other consumers, lease a car rather than buy it, you are protected under the Consumer Leasing Act (CLA) as long as your lessor regularly leases items to individuals for personal use and the total payments under the lease do not exceed $25,000. The CLA does not apply to the rental of real property—that is,

[16] Robert J. Bruss, "Home Buyers Sue Mortgage Lender for Racial Discrimination," *Tampa Tribune*, Nov. 5, 1994, p. 3.

to house or apartment leases. **Before a lease is signed, a lessor must disclose the following in writing:**

- All required payments, including deposits, down payments, taxes, and license fees
- The number and amount of each monthly payment
- Balloon payments (that is, payments due at the end of the lease)
- Required insurance payments
- Available warranties
- Maintenance requirements
- Penalties for late payments
- The consumer's right to purchase the leased property
- The consumer's right to terminate a lease early
- Any penalties for early termination

MAGNUSON-MOSS WARRANTY ACT

When Senator Frank E. Moss sponsored the Magnuson-Moss Warranty Act, this is how he explained the need for such a statute:

> [W]arranties have for many years confused, misled, and frequently angered American consumers. . . . Consumer anger is expected when purchasers of consumer products discover that their warranty may cover a 25-cent part but not the $100 labor charge or that there is full coverage on a piano so long as it is shipped at the purchaser's expense to the factory. . . . There is a growing need to generate consumer understanding by clearly and conspicuously disclosing the terms and conditions of the warranty and by telling the consumer what to do if his guaranteed product becomes defective or malfunctions.[17]

The Magnuson-Moss Warranty Act does not require manufacturers or sellers to provide a warranty on their products. **The Act does require any supplier that offers a written warranty on a consumer product that costs more than $15 to disclose the terms of the warranty in simple, understandable language *before the sale*.** Required disclosure includes the following:

- The name and address of the warrantor
- The parts that are covered and those that are not
- What services the warrantor will provide, at whose expense, and for what period of time
- A statement of what the consumer must do and what expenses he must pay

Although suppliers are not required to offer a warranty, if they do offer one they must indicate whether it is *full* or *limited*. Under a **full warranty**, the warrantor must promise to fix a defective product for a reasonable time without charge; if, after a reasonable number of efforts to fix the defective product, it still does not work, the consumer must have the right to a refund or a replacement without charge; but the warrantor is not required to cover damage caused by the consumer's unreasonable use.

---

[17] *Quoted in* David G. Epstein and Steve H. Nickles, *Consumer Law* (Eagan, Minn.: West, 1981).

CONSUMER PRODUCT SAFETY

In 1969, the federal government estimated that consumer products caused 30,000 deaths, 110,000 disabling injuries, and 20 million trips to the doctor. Toys were among the worst offenders, injuring 700,000 children a year. Children were cut by Etch-a-Sketch glass panels, choked by Zulu gun darts, and burned by Little Lady toy ovens. Although injured consumers had the right to seek damages under tort law, Congress passed the Consumer Product Safety Act (CPSA) in 1972 to prevent injuries from occurring in the first place. This Act created the Consumer Product Safety Commission to evaluate consumer products and develop safety standards. The Commission can impose civil and criminal penalties on those who violate its standards. Individuals have the right to sue under the CPSA for damages, including attorney's fees, from anyone who knowingly violates a consumer product safety rule. You can find out about product recalls or file a report on an unsafe product at the Commission's Web site (**http://www.cpsc.gov/**).

In the following news report, an investigator for the Consumer Product Safety Commission describes his job.

I gather information on accidents through the newspapers, hospitals, and call-in complaints, and then I go out to investigate the people involved. The agency has a database, covering close to 100 hospital emergency rooms, which constantly key in data to determine when, where, and how accidents occur. If that information causes us to have suspicions that a product is dangerous, then we review corporate records to determine whether the company is in compliance with whatever law may apply. If our suspicions remain, then we collect a sample of the suspect product and submit it to our Washington, D.C. laboratory for engineering analysis. If the product is proven to be defective, we ask the company to recall the product, and if it should refuse, we have the authority to take further legal action. However, most companies want to comply. We do not get involved with people being reimbursed for having been ripped off or mistreated in any way. We represent the consumer public as opposed to the individual.[18]

CHAPTER CONCLUSION

Virtually no one will go through life without reading an advertisement, ordering from a catalogue, borrowing money, needing a credit report, or using a consumer product. It is important to know your rights.

CHAPTER REVIEW

1. The Federal Trade Commission (FTC) prohibits "unfair and deceptive acts or practices." A practice is unfair if it meets the following three tests:
   - It causes a substantial consumer injury.
   - The harm of the injury outweighs any countervailing benefit.
   - The consumer could not reasonably avoid the injury.

[18] Beatrice Michaels Shapiro, "Product Safety Investigator," *Chicago Tribune*, Aug. 23, 1992, p. 33. Reprinted with permission.

2. The FTC considers an advertisement to be deceptive if it contains an important misrepresentation or omission that is likely to mislead a reasonable consumer.

3. FTC rules prohibit bait and switch advertisements. A merchant may not advertise a product and then disparage it to consumers in an effort to sell a different item.

4. Consumers may keep as a gift any unordered merchandise that they receive in the mail.

5. Under the FTC door-to-door rules, a salesperson is required to notify the buyer that she has the right to cancel the transaction prior to midnight of the third business day thereafter.

6. In all loans regulated by the Truth in Lending Act (TILA), the disclosure must be clear and in meaningful sequence. The lender must disclose the finance charge and the annual percentage rate.

7. Under TILA, consumers have the right to rescind a mortgage (other than a first mortgage) for three business days after the signing. If the lender does not comply with the disclosure provisions of TILA, the consumer may rescind for up to three years from the date of the mortgage.

8. Under TILA, a credit card holder is liable only for the first $50 in unauthorized charges made before the credit card company is notified that the card was stolen.

9. In the event of a dispute between a customer and a merchant, the credit card company cannot bill the customer if:
   - She makes a good faith effort to resolve the dispute
   - The dispute is for more than $50, and
   - The merchant is in the same state where she lives or is within 100 miles of her house.

10. Under the Fair Credit Billing Act, a credit card company must promptly investigate and respond to any consumer complaints about a credit card bill.

11. Under the Fair Credit Reporting Act:
    - A consumer report can be used only for a legitimate business need
    - A consumer reporting agency cannot report obsolete information
    - An employer cannot request a consumer report on any current or potential employee without the employee's permission, and
    - Anyone who makes an adverse decision against a consumer because of a credit report must reveal the name and address of the reporting agency that supplied the negative information.

12. Under the Fair Debt Collection Practices Act, a debt collector may not harass or abuse debtors.

13. The Equal Credit Opportunity Act prohibits any creditor from discriminating against a borrower on the basis of race, color, religion, national origin, sex, marital status, age, or because the borrower is receiving welfare.

14. The Magnuson-Moss Warranty Act requires any supplier that offers a written warranty on a consumer product costing more than $15 to disclose the terms of the warranty in simple and readily understandable language before the sale.

15. The Consumer Product Safety Commission evaluates consumer products and develops safety standards.

PRACTICE TEST

1. In August, Dorothy Jenkins went to First American Mortgage and Loan Association of Virginia (the Bank) to sign a second mortgage on her home. Her first mortgage was with a different bank. She left the closing without a copy of the required Truth in Lending Act disclosure forms. Jenkins defaulted on her loan payments, and, the following May, the Bank began foreclosure proceedings on her house. In June, she notified the Bank that she wished to rescind the loan. Does Jenkins have a right to rescind the loan 10 months after it was made?

2. **YOU BE THE JUDGE WRITING PROBLEM** Process cheese food slices must contain at least 51 percent natural cheese. Imitation cheese slices, by contrast, contain little or no natural cheese and consist primarily of water, vegetable oil, flavoring agents, and fortifying agents. Kraft, Inc. makes Kraft Singles, which are individually wrapped process cheese food slices. When Kraft began losing market share to imitation slices that were advertised as both less expensive and equally nutritious as Singles, Kraft responded with a series of advertisements designed to inform consumers that Kraft Singles cost more than imitation slices because they are made from five ounces of milk. Kraft does use five ounces of milk in making each Kraft Single, but 30 percent of the calcium contained in the milk is lost during processing. Imitation slices contain the same amount of calcium as Kraft Singles. Are the Kraft advertisements deceptive? **Argument for Kraft:** This statement is completely true—Kraft does use five ounces of milk in each Kraft Single. The FTC is assuming that the only value of milk is the calcium. In fact, people might prefer having milk rather than vegetable oil and flavoring agents, regardless of the calcium. **Argument for the FTC:** It is deceptive to advertise more milk if the calcium is the same after all the processing.

3. Joel Curtis was two and his brother, Joshua, was three years old when their father left both children asleep in the rear seat of his automobile while visiting a friend. His cigarette lighter was on the dashboard of the car. After awaking, Joshua began playing with the lighter and set fire to Joel's diaper. Do the parents have a claim against the manufacturer of the lighter under the Consumer Product Safety Act?

4. Josephine Rutyna was a 60-year-old widow who suffered from high blood pressure and epilepsy. A bill collector from Collections Accounts Terminal, Inc. called her and demanded that she pay $56 she owed to Cabrini Hospital Medical Group. She told him that Medicare was supposed to pay the bill. Shortly thereafter, Rutyna received a letter from Collections that stated:

> You have shown that you are unwilling to work out a friendly settlement with us to clear the above debt. Our field investigator has now been instructed to make an investigation in your neighborhood and to personally call on your employer. The immediate payment of the full amount, or a personal visit to this office, will spare you this embarrassment.

Has Collections violated the law?

5. Thomas Pinner worked at a Sherwin-Williams paint store that was managed by James Schmidt. Pinner and Schmidt had a falling out when, according to Pinner, "a relationship began to bloom between Pinner and one of the young female employees, the one Schmidt was obsessed with." Pinner quit. Schmidt claimed that Pinner owed the company $121.71 for paint he had taken but not paid for. Sherwin-Williams reported this information to Chilton, who ran a credit reporting agency. Pinner's attorney sent a letter to Chilton notifying him that Pinner disputed the accuracy of the Sherwin-Williams charges. Chilton contacted Schmidt who confirmed that Pinner's account remained delinquent. Chilton failed to note in Pinner's file that a dispute was pending. Thereafter, Pinner was denied credit cards at two

stores. Have Schmidt and Chilton violated the Fair Credit Reporting Act?

6. Kathleen Carroll, a single woman, applied for an Exxon credit card. Exxon rejected her application without giving any specific reason and without providing the name of the credit bureau it had used. When Carroll asked for a reason for the rejection, she was told that the credit bureau did not have enough information about her to establish creditworthiness. In fact, Exxon had denied her credit application because she did not have a major credit card or a savings account, she had been employed for only one year, and she had no dependents. Did Exxon violate the law?

7. In October, Renie Guimond discovered that her credit report at TransUnion Credit Information Co. incorrectly stated that she was married, used the name "Ruth Guimond," and had a credit card from Saks Fifth Avenue. After she reported the errors, TransUnion wrote her in November to say that it had removed this information. However, in March, TransUnion again published the erroneous information. The following October, TransUnion finally removed the incorrect information from her file. Guimond was never denied credit because of these mistakes. Is TransUnion liable for violating the Fair Credit Reporting Act?

8. The National Coalition for Consumer Education and MasterCard International created the following quiz to help consumers find out how smart they are about buying on credit:

(a) What's the best way to correct a mistake on your credit card bill?

- **(i)** Call your credit card issuer immediately and explain the mistake.
- **(ii)** Circle the mistake in red and return the bill to your card issuer.
- **(iii)** Immediately write a letter to your credit card issuer and clearly describe the problem.

(b) How should you handle an unauthorized charge (a purchase that you didn't make) if you see one on your credit card statement?

- **(i)** Write a letter to the company that accepted your card for payment to absolve yourself of any liability.
- **(ii)** Call your credit issuer immediately to alert them.
- **(iii)** Note the error on your credit card bill and refuse to pay it.[19]

9. Thomas Waldock purchased a 1983 BMW 320i from Universal Motors, Inc. It was warranted "to be free of defects in materials or workmanship for a period of three years or 36,000 miles, whichever occurs first." Within the warranty period, the car's engine failed and upon examination was found to be extensively damaged. Universal denied warranty coverage because it concluded that Waldock damaged the engine by over-revving it. Waldock vehemently disputed BMW's contention. He claimed that, while being driven at a low speed, the engine emitted a gear-crunching noise, ceased operation, and would not restart. Is Universal in violation of the law?

10.

GET ENOUGH BROADLOOM TO CARPET ANY
AREA OF YOUR HOME OR APARTMENT
UP TO 150 SQUARE FEET CUT, MEASURED, AND
READY FOR INSTALLATION FOR ONLY $77.
GET 100% DUPONT CONTINUOUS FILAMENT
NYLON PILE BROADLOOM.
CALL COLLECT

When customers called this number, New Rapids Carpet Center, Inc. sent salespeople to visit them at home to sell them carpet that was not as advertised—it was not continuous filament nylon pile broadloom, and the price was not $77. Has New Rapids violated a consumer law?

11. **RIGHT & WRONG** After TNT Motor Express hired Joseph Bruce Drury as a truck driver, it ordered a background check from Robert Arden & Associates. TNT provided Drury's Social Security number and date of birth, but not his middle name. Arden discovered that a Joseph *Thomas* Drury, who coincidentally had the same birth date as Joseph *Bruce* Drury, had served a prison sentence for drunk driving. Not knowing that it had the wrong Drury, Arden reported this information to TNT, which promptly fired Drury. When he asked why, the TNT executive merely stated,

[19] "Give Yourself Some Credit if You Pass This Quiz," *Times-Picayune*, Apr. 7, 1994, p. E5. Permission granted by the Times-Picayune Publishing Corporation. All rights reserved. Reprinted with permission.

"We do not discuss these matters." Did TNT violate the law? Whether or not TNT was in violation, did its executives behave ethically? Who would have been harmed or helped if TNT managers had informed Drury of the Arden report?

INTERNET RESEARCH PROBLEMS

1. The FTC provides *A Consumer's Guide to Travel in Cyberspace* at http://www.ftc.gov/bcp/conline/pubs/online/sitesee/index.html. Are you surprised by anything you read on this Web site? Have you ever violated the FTC's advice on how to protect yourself in cyberspace?

2. The Consumer Product Safety Commission (http://www.cpsc.gov) lists products that have been recalled and provides consumers with a telephone number for contacting the manufacturer. Choose a recalled product and telephone the manufacturer to find out how it is handling the problem. Also see if you can find the manufacturer's Web site to learn if it has disclosed the recall there. What do you think of the manner in which the manufacturer has handled the recall? Is the manufacturer providing adequate protection to consumers?

You can find further practice problems in the Online Quiz at http://beatty.westbuslaw.com or in the Study Guide that accompanies this text.

CHAPTER 43

ENVIRONMENTAL LAW

"When my mother was left a widow almost 50 years ago, she taught school to support her family. A few years after my father's death, she took her savings and bought a small commercial building on a downtown lot in our little town in Oregon. The building, she said, would offer what my father couldn't—a source of support in her old age. In one half of the building was a children's clothing store, in the other a dry cleaners. The two stores served Main Street shoppers for years.

"Now the building that once represented security has produced a menace with the potential to bankrupt my mother. The discovery of contamination in city park well water triggered groundwater tests in the area. Waste products discarded by dry cleaners were identified as a likely source of contamination. Although a dry cleaner hasn't operated for 20 years on my mother's property, chemicals remain in the soil. Mother knew nothing of this hazard until a letter came from the Oregon Department of Environmental Quality. It said she should decide if she would oversee further testing and cleanup herself or if she would let the government handle it. In either case, my mother would pay the costs.

"The building is worth just under $70,000. Cleanup costs will be at least $200,000. At 84, my mother has enough savings to preserve her independence. She does not have enough money to bear the enormous costs of new community standards. The dry cleaner that operated in my mother's building disposed of chemicals the same way other dry cleaners did. None of these businesses was operated in a negligent fashion. They followed standards accepted by the community at the time. Now we are learning that we must live more carefully if we are to survive in a world that is safe and clean. My question is: Who will pay? Who will be responsible for cleaning up environmental messes made before we knew better?"[1]

INTRODUCTION

The environmental movement in the United States began in 1962 with the publication of Rachel Carson's book, *Silent Spring*. She exposed the deadly—and lingering—impact of DDT and other pesticides. These chemicals spread a wide web, poisoning not only the targeted insects, but the entire food chain—fish, birds, and even humans. Since Carson first sounded the alarm, environmental issues have appeared regularly in the news—everything from acute disasters such as the *Exxon Valdez* oil spill in Alaska to chronic concerns over pesticide residues in food. For more about Rachel Carson (and links to other environmental Web sites), visit **http://www.rachelcarson.org/**.

The environmental movement began with the fervor of a moral crusade. How could anyone be against a clean environment? It has become clear, however, that the issue is more complex. It is not enough simply to say, "We are against pollution." As the opening vignette reveals, the question is: Who will pay? Who will pay for past damage inflicted before anyone understood the harm that pollutants cause? Who will pay for current changes necessary to prevent damage now and in the future? Are car owners willing to spend $100 or $1,000 more per car to prevent air pollution? Are easterners ready to ban oil drilling in the Arctic National Wildlife Refuge in Alaska if that means higher prices for heating oil? Will loggers in the West give up their jobs to protect endangered species? Are all consumers willing to pay more to insulate their homes? George Bush, a Republican president, said, "Beyond all the studies, the figures, and the debates, the environment is a moral issue." But Newt Gingrich, a Republican Speaker of the House of Representatives, called the Environmental Protection Agency "the biggest job-killing agency in inner-city America."[2]

The cost-benefit trade-off is particularly complex in environmental issues because those who pay the cost often do not receive the benefit. If a company dumps toxic wastes into a stream, its shareholders benefit by avoiding the expense of safe disposal. Those who fish or drink the waters pay the real costs without receiving any of the benefit. Economists use the term ***externality*** to describe the situation in which people do not bear the full cost of their decisions. Externalities prevent the market system from achieving a clean environment on its own. Only government involvement can realign costs and benefits.

ENVIRONMENTAL PROTECTION AGENCY

Thirty years ago, environmental abuses were (ineffectively) governed by tort law and a smattering of local ordinances. Now, environmental law is a mammoth structure of federal and state regulation. In 1970, Congress created the Environ-

---

1 Carolyn Scott Kortge, "Taken to the Cleaners," *Newsweek*, Oct. 23, 1995, p. 16. Reprinted with permission.

2 Both men are *quoted in* Robert V. Percival, Alan S. Miller, Christopher H. Schroeder, and James P. Leape, *Environmental Regulation* (Boston: Little, Brown & Co., 1992), p. 1, and 1995 supp. p. 2.

mental Protection Agency (EPA) to consolidate environmental regulation under one roof. Among government agencies, only the military is larger. When Congress passes a new environmental law, the EPA issues regulations to implement it. The agency can bring administrative enforcement action against those who violate its regulations. An administrative law judge (ALJ) within the agency hears these actions. Either party can appeal this decision to a United States Court of Appeals and, from there, to the Supreme Court. Those who violate environmental laws are liable for civil damages. In addition, some statutes, such as the Clean Water Act, the Resource Conservation and Recovery Act, and the Endangered Species Act, provide for *criminal* penalties, including imprisonment. The EPA is not shy about seeking criminal prosecutions of those who knowingly violate these statutes, and of those corporate officers who fail to prevent criminal negligence by their employees.

AIR POLLUTION

On October 26, 1948, almost half of the 10,000 people in Donora, Pennsylvania, fell ill from air pollution. A weather inversion trapped industrial pollutants in the air, creating a lethal smog. Twenty residents ultimately died. Although air pollution rarely causes this type of acute illness, it can cause or increase the severity of diseases that are annoying, chronic, or even fatal—such as pneumonia, bronchitis, emphysema, and cancer. Even apart from the health risks, air pollution can be irritating: it blocks visibility, damages car exteriors, and grimes windowsills.

There are three major sources of air pollution: coal-burning utility plants, factories, and motor vehicles. Residential furnaces, farm operations, forest fires, and dust from mines and construction sites also contribute. Local regulation is ineffective in controlling air pollution. For instance, when cities limited pollution from factory smokestacks, plants simply built taller stacks that sent the pollution hundreds, or even thousands, of miles away. Local governments had little incentive to prevent this long-distance migration. Recognizing the national nature of the problem, Congress passed three air pollution laws during the 1950s and 1960s. With little enforcement bite and no EPA to ensure implementation, these statutes had minimal impact.

CLEAN AIR ACT

Dissatisfied by this lack of progress, Congress passed the Clean Air Act of 1970. **The Clean Air Act has four major provisions:**

- **Primary Standards.** Congress directed the EPA to establish **national ambient air quality standards** (known as NAAQSs) for primary pollution, that is, pollution that harms the public health. The EPA's mandate was to set standards that protected public health and provided an adequate margin of safety *without regard to cost*. Pollution may not exceed these limits anyplace in the country. The EPA must regularly update the rules to reflect the latest scientific evidence.

- **Secondary Standards.** Congress also directed the EPA to establish NAAQSs for pollution that may not be a threat to health but has other unpleasant effects, such as obstructing visibility and harming plants or other materials.

- **State Implementation Plans (SIPs).** The Clean Air Act envisioned a partnership between the EPA and the states. After the EPA set primary and secondary standards, states would produce SIPs to meet the primary standards within three years and the secondary standards within a reasonable time. If a SIP was not acceptable, the EPA would produce its own plan for that state. In formulating their SIPs, states were required to identify the major sources of pollution. Each polluter would then be given a pollution limit to bring the area into compliance with national standards. The worse the pollution in a particular area, the tougher the regulations.

- **Citizen Suits.** The Clean Air Act (and many other environmental statutes) permits anyone to file suit against a polluter or against the EPA for failing to enforce the statute. Citizens have often been more assertive than the EPA in enforcing environmental statutes. For instance, the Arizona Center for Law in the Public Interest has sued the EPA more than a dozen times for failing to impose sufficiently strict air quality standards on Phoenix and Tucson.

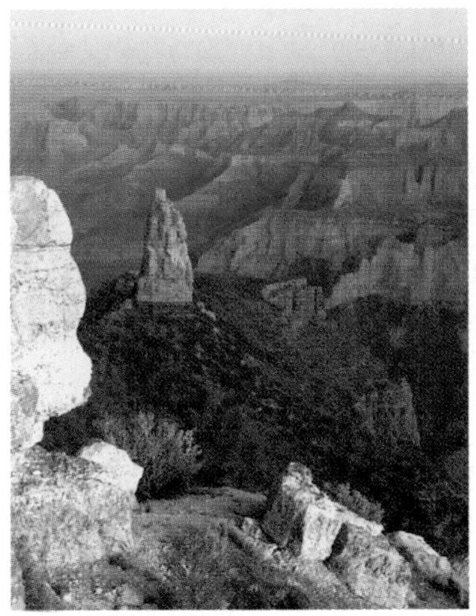

Is it worth half a billion dollars to improve winter visibility at the Grand Canyon by 7 percent?

Although air quality throughout the country has improved dramatically, a 1990 EPA study revealed that, 20 years after passage of the Clean Air Act, virtually every American was still breathing unsafe levels of some pollutants. In 1990, Congress amended the Act, setting more realistic goals but also higher penalties for failure. For instance, the deadline for Los Angeles was extended to 2010, but the penalty for noncompliance was increased—a cutoff of federal highway funds (a serious blow indeed in Los Angeles) and the threat of even stricter controls. Already, everything in California from lawn mowers to bakeries to barbecue grills is subject to increasingly strict standards. Recently, the city of Los Angeles asked the EPA for permission to weaken some of its anti-pollution regulations, such as required ride-share programs at shopping centers and sports arenas. The EPA rejected this request, however, and insisted on the tougher standards. Information about violations of the Clean Air Act is available online at **http://www.EPA.gov/oeca/sfi**.

In the following case, a power plant argued that the EPA had imposed a solution whose cost far outweighed its benefit. There is only one Grand Canyon. Should visibility there be preserved at any cost?

YOU Be The Judge

CENTRAL ARIZONA WATER CONSERVATION DISTRICT v. EPA

990 F.2d 1531, 1993 U.S. App. LEXIS 5881
United States Court of Appeals for the Ninth Circuit, 1993

Facts: In the Clean Air Act, Congress directed the EPA to issue regulations that would protect visibility at national landmarks. The Navaho Generating Station (NGS) is a power plant 12 miles from the Grand Canyon. In response to a citizen suit filed by the Environmental Defense Fund under the Clean Air Act, the EPA ordered NGS to reduce its sulfur dioxide emissions by 90 percent. To do so would cost NGS $430 million initially in capital expenditures and then $89.6 million annually. Average winter visibility in the Grand Canyon would be improved by at most 7 percent, but perhaps less. NGS sued to prevent implementation of the EPA's order. A court may nullify an EPA order if it determines that the agency action was arbitrary and capricious.

You Be the Judge: Did the EPA act arbitrarily and capriciously in requiring NGS to spend half a billion dollars to improve winter visibility at the Grand Canyon by at most 7 percent?

Argument for NGS: This case is a perfect example of environmentalism run amok. Half a billion dollars for the *chance* of increasing winter visibility at the Grand Canyon by 7 percent? No rational person would choose to spend his own money that way, but the EPA is happy to spend NGS's. Winter visitors to the Grand Canyon would undoubtedly prefer that NGS provide them with a free lunch rather than a 7 percent improvement in visibility. The EPA order is simply a waste of money.

Argument for the EPA: Under the Clean Air Act, Congress instructed the EPA to protect visibility at national landmarks such as the Grand Canyon. How can NGS, or anyone else, measure the benefit of protecting a national treasure like the Grand Canyon? Even people who never have and never will visit it during the winter sleep better at night knowing that the Canyon is protected. NGS has been causing harm to the Grand Canyon, and now it should remedy the damage.

Courts generally defer to federal agencies, whose experts deal with similar problems all the time. The EPA has greater expertise in these matters than either NGS or this court.

Although the Clean Air Act reduced concentrations of some of the most harmful chemicals—carbon monoxide, sulfur dioxide, ground-level ozone—new scientific evidence indicated that the EPA standards were not strict enough. Even lower levels of these chemicals can cause health problems. In response to this new evidence, the EPA tightened its standards, predicting that stricter rules could save 20,000 lives a year and eliminate 250,000 cases of asthma. However, critics argued that the benefits of these regulations was too low to justify the enormous costs. They pointed to a recent study calculating that EPA regulations during the last 10 years cost about $50 million for each year of life saved. (In other words, for each $50 million spent, one person lives one year longer.) In contrast, home smoke alarms cost about $200,000 for each additional year of life, and mammograms for women over 50 cost a mere $17,000 for each year saved. The Clean Air Act directs the EPA to set air quality standards without regard to cost. How much is a year of life worth? What if it is your life?[3]

New Sources of Pollution

Some states had air so clean that they could have allowed air quality to decline and still have met EPA standards. However, the Clean Air Act declared that one of its purposes was to "protect and enhance" air quality. Using this phrase, the Sierra Club sued the EPA to prevent it from approving any SIPs that met EPA standards but nonetheless permitted a decline in air quality. As a result of this suit, the EPA developed a **prevention of significant deterioration (PSD)** program. **No one may undertake a building project that will cause a major increase in pollution without first obtaining a permit from the EPA.** The agency will grant permits only if an applicant can demonstrate that (1) its emissions will not cause an overall decline in air quality and (2) it has installed the **best available control technology** for every pollutant.

The PSD program prohibits any deterioration in current air quality, *regardless of health impact*. In essence, national policy values a clean environment for its own sake, apart from any health benefits.

Acid Rain

In some places, rain is now 10 times more acidic than it would naturally be. The results of acid rain are visible in the eastern United States and Canada—damaged forests, crops, and lakes. Acid is primarily created by sulfur emissions from large coal-burning utility plants in the Midwest. Many of these plants were built before the Clean Air Act, when the easiest way to meet state and local standards (while keeping electricity prices low) was to build tall stacks that would send the sulfur dioxide far away. Terrific for Ohio, not so wonderful for Maine.

The Clean Air Act banned the tall-stack solution, leaving coal plants, in theory, with two choices: install (expensive) scrubbers or buy (cheaper) low-sulfur

[3] "Clean Air, Dirty Fight," *The Economist*, Mar. 15, 1997, p. 29.

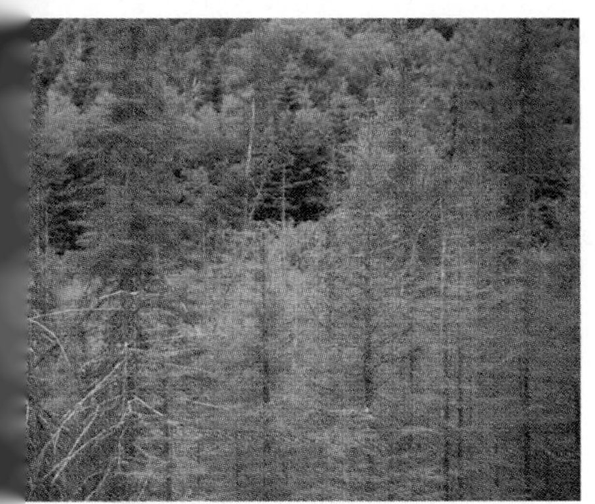

The acid rain that caused this damage probably came from a power plant hundreds, if not thousands, of miles away.

western coal. Under pressure from members who represented states with high-sulfur coal, Congress compromised and required all power plants to install scrubbers regardless of the coal they burned. In this way, western coal would have no advantage.

In 1990, Congress amended the Clean Air Act to require power plants to cut their sulfur dioxide emissions by half. This time, however, Congress did not specify how the goal should be achieved and instead offered new methods for minimizing costs and maximizing economic efficiency. **Power plants have four options for meeting emissions standards: (1) installing scrubbers, (2) using low-sulfur coal, (3) switching to alternative fuels (such as natural gas), or (4) trading emissions allowances.** This last alternative requires some explanation. Each year, every utility receives an emissions allowance, meaning that it is allowed to emit a certain number of tons of pollutants. If a company does not need its entire allowance, because it uses cleaner fuels or has installed pollution control devices, it can sell the leftover allowance to other companies or stockpile the allowance for future use. Plants with high levels of pollution either buy more allowances or reduce their own emissions, depending on which alternative is cheaper. In effect, the government establishes the maximum amount of pollution, and then the market sets the price for meeting the national standard.

The market for sulfur dioxide emissions has become remarkably efficient and effective. Power plants now have a financial incentive to reduce pollution through innovation. In some years, pollution from sulfur dioxide has declined by as much as 25 percent, at a cost one-tenth the original estimate. For more information on the emissions trading program, click on http://www.epa.gov/acidrain/. This Web site reveals who has bought allowances and at what cost. Note that sometimes the highest bidders are organizations such as the Maryland Environmental Law Society, which buy emissions allowances simply to keep polluters from using them.

Automobile Pollution

The Clean Air Act of 1970 directed the EPA to reduce automobile pollution levels by 90 percent within six years. Although the technology to achieve this goal did not then exist, Congress believed that the auto industry would, if forced, be able to develop the necessary innovations. This approach has been referred to as **technology forcing,** in the sense that the industry will be forced to develop the technology. Indeed, by 1975, General Motors developed a catalytic converter that not only reduced harmful emissions but improved fuel economy.

Although new cars are 97 percent cleaner than 1970 models, motor vehicles are still a major source of air pollution, releasing more than 50 percent of the hazardous pollutants in the air. Each car may be cleaner, but Americans are driving more—and bigger—cars more miles on more trips. During 1970, Americans traveled one trillion miles, but by 2000 the total had increased to four trillion miles. To counteract this increase, Congress has required oil companies to produce cleaner gasoline. It has also required automakers to build **low-emission vehicles**, such as cars powered by electricity or natural gas. The most polluted cities must also reduce auto use by encouraging car pools.

Air Toxics

Some pollutants are so potent that even tiny amounts cause harm. For instance, the EPA has never been able to establish a safe level of exposure to asbestos. Each year, 2.7 billion pounds of toxics spew into the air in the United States, causing an estimated annual increase of 3,000 cancer deaths. Because the Clean Air Act directed the EPA to set safety standards that provided an adequate margin of safety without regard to cost, the agency in theory has no choice except an outright ban on some pollutants. Such a ban would shut down the steel, chemical, and petroleum industries, among others. The EPA does not consider such a strategy to be politically viable.

The Environmental Defense Fund sued the EPA to force compliance with the law. Nevertheless, by 1990, the agency had proposed standards for only seven substances. Although these standards do not eliminate health risks, they are set at the lowest feasible level given existing technology. The courts have upheld these standards.

In 1990 amendments to the Clean Air Act, Congress directed the EPA to set standards for each of 189 specific pollutants and any other toxics the EPA wanted to include. The EPA may base these standards initially on the **maximum achievable control technology (MACT).** Within eight years of developing MACT rules, the EPA must raise the standards to a level at which the risk of cancer from these substances is no more than one in one million over a lifetime. This two-step process is meant to create an incentive for polluters to continue to develop better technology.

Under the Clean Air Act, the EPA is required to create a Web site showing what would happen if an accident occurred at any of the 66,000 locations around the United States where dangerous chemicals are stored. But the Federal Bureau of Investigation and the Central Intelligence Agency are concerned that this worst-case data would enable a terrorist group to identify the most dangerous industrial sites in the United States with a few clicks on a laptop. The EPA's security consultants estimate that putting this information on a Web site would double the probability of a terrorist attack.

GLOBAL WARMING

Over the last 100 years, the average temperature worldwide has increased between 0.5° and 1.1°F. If current trends continue, the world's average temperature over the next 100 years will rise another 2° to 6°, producing the warmest climate in the history of humankind. (By comparison, the planet is only 5° to 9° warmer than during the last ice age.) The impact of this climate change is potentially catastrophic: a rise in sea level that would engulf coastal areas, a devastating decline in fishing stocks, the death of major forests, and a loss of farmland worldwide.

Global warming is the most complex environmental problem of the new millennium because its cause is uncertain and any solution requires international political cooperation coupled with major lifestyle changes. Very little is known about global warming with scientific certainty; much of the evidence is circumstantial. Most scientists now believe that certain gases—chlorofluorocarbons, carbon dioxide, methane, and nitrous oxide—create a greenhouse effect by trapping heat in the earth's atmosphere. Since the great epoch of industrialization began in the eighteenth century, the amount of these gases released into the atmosphere has increased dramatically, and the earth has also become strikingly warmer.

Skeptics argue, however, that the world naturally goes through cycles of heat and cold and it is simply in a heat cycle now. Moreover, they insist that we should have much clearer proof of the connection between the greenhouse gases and global warming before undertaking the major changes that any reduction would require—such as driving smaller cars on fewer trips or paying higher prices for gas and oil. The Energy Department has estimated that, to fight global warming effectively, U.S. gasoline prices would have to rise by as much as $1.91 a gallon and electricity prices might have to increase by 86 percent. Despite these doubts, a number of major corporations such as British Petroleum and DuPont have voluntarily reduced their emissions, arguing that the scientific evidence of global warming is alarming enough to justify immediate action. To see a skeptical view of global warming, click on http://www.globalwarming.org/index.html. A more balanced view is available at http://www.law.pace.edu/env/energy/globalwarming.html.

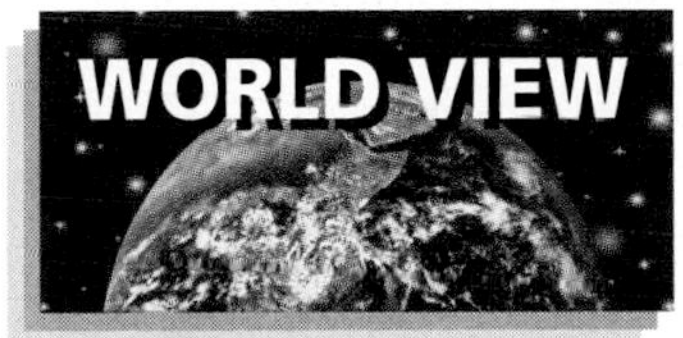

In 1997, representatives of more than 150 countries met in Kyoto, Japan to discuss reducing greenhouse gases. Many eyes turned toward the United States, which, with 5 percent of the world's population, consumes 25 percent of its energy—more than twice as much as the next industrial country. The United States ultimately signed the Kyoto Protocol, which requires the country to reduce emissions by the year 2012 to a level 7 percent below 1990 amounts.

Treaties are not binding in the United States until ratified by the Senate, however, and U.S. negotiators have said that they will not submit the treaty for ratification unless other countries develop a system of trading emissions like the one that has worked so well in the United States (see the discussion above under Acid Rain). Such a system would permit the United States to meet its goals by paying other nations to reduce their pollution to levels lower than the treaty requires. This plan makes economic sense because the cost of reducing pollution overseas, where few controls are in place, is four times cheaper than in the United States, where all the easy, inexpensive options have long since been implemented.

Opponents point out, however, that Ukraine and Russia are the only two countries that have met their Kyoto guidelines, and unfortunately, their success is the result of economic collapse not deliberate policy. Critics argue that the U.S. trading plan is simply a way to permit the United States to continue its polluting ways by paying off desperate Eastern European countries.

Developing countries such as India and China refused to make cuts in emissions or to commit to the trading plan. In their view, global warming has been caused by the excesses of rich countries, and any cure that involved poorer nations would unfairly hinder their economic growth.

WATER POLLUTION

One day, thousands of Milwaukeeans suddenly began to suffer nausea, cramps, and diarrhea. The suspected culprit? *Cryptosporidium,* a tiny protozoan that usually resides in the intestines of cattle and other animals. Ironically, the parasite may have entered Milwaukee's water supply at a purification plant on Lake Michigan. Officials suspect that infected runoff from dairy farms spilled into Lake Michigan near the plant's intake pipe. Doctors advised those with a damaged immune system (such as AIDS patients) to avoid drinking municipal water. Most Milwaukeeans were taking no chances—more than 800,000 switched to boiled or bottled water.

Polluted water can cause a number of loathsome diseases, such as typhus and dysentery. But by 1930, most American cities had dramatically reduced outbreaks of waterborne diseases by chlorinating their water. (The parasite that caused the Milwaukee outbreak is relatively immune to chlorine.) However, industrial discharges into the water supply have increased rapidly, with a visible impact on water quality. These industrial wastes may not induce acute illnesses like typhus, but they can cause serious diseases such as cancer. There is more at stake than health alone; clean water is valued for esthetics, recreation, and fishing.

CLEAN WATER ACT

In 1972, Congress passed a statute that is now called the Clean Water Act (CWA). This statute had two ambitious goals: (1) to make all navigable water suitable for swimming and fishing by 1983, and (2) to eliminate the discharge of pollutants into navigable water by 1985. Like the Clean Air Act, the CWA sets goals without regard to cost; leaves enforcement primarily to the states, with oversight by the EPA; and permits citizen suits. Also, like the Clean Air Act, the CWA's goals have not been met.

Industrial Discharges

The CWA prohibits any single producer from discharging pollution into water without a permit from the EPA. Before granting a permit, the EPA must set limits, by industry, on the amount of each type of pollution any single producer (called a **point source**) can discharge. These limits must be based on the **best available technology**. The EPA faces a gargantuan task in determining the best available technology that *each* industry can use to reduce pollution. Furthermore, standards become obsolete quickly as technology changes.

The CWA also requires the EPA to measure water quality broadly to determine if the permit system is working. Until clean water standards are met, every point source is held to the same standard, whether it is discharging into a clean ocean that can handle more pollution or a stagnant lake that cannot. Since determining the impact of a particular discharge may not be possible, especially when it is mingled with others, it is easier for the EPA to set the same standards for everyone. Easier and fairer—Congress did not want states to lure industry with promises of laxer pollution rules.

Water Quality Standards

The CWA requires states to set EPA-approved water quality standards and develop plans to achieve them. The first step in developing a plan is to determine how each body of water is used. Standards may vary depending upon the designated use—higher for recreational lakes than for a river used to irrigate farmland. No matter what the water's designated use, standards may not be set at a level lower than its current condition. Congress is not in the business of permitting *more* pollution.

States are supposed to pay special attention to so-called **non-point sources**, that is, pollutants with no single source, such as water runoff from agricultural land or city streets. This runoff may contain gasoline, pesticides, or bacteria. Congress left non-point source pollution to the states because it is so difficult to regulate. This regulation also involves complex issues such as land use planning that are, in theory, better handled at the local level than by national fiat. However optimistic Congress may have been, to date the states have not successfully implemented this section of the CWA. They appear to lack both the political will and the technological know-how, for which they are not totally to blame. Determining the impact of individual pollutants on the overall quality of a body of water used for many different purposes is a complex problem. Land use planning requires a delicate and volatile mix of consensus and control.

As the ambitious goals set by the CWA have not been met, Congress has granted numerous extensions. Evaluating progress under the statute depends upon one's perspective. The EPA, for instance, proudly announces on its Web site that whereas only a third of the nation's waters were safe for fishing and swimming in 1972, today two-thirds are safe (**http://www.EPA.gov/owow/CWA/history.htm**). Environmental advocates are less impressed. When the agency's own independent auditing branch examined environmental enforcement, it found widespread violations of the law. For instance, 75 percent of the streams in Missouri were not swimmable. Many environmental advocates have filed citizen suits to force the EPA to toughen its enforcement. In response to a suit by the Sierra Club, the federal court in Atlanta ordered the EPA to enforce the CWA more diligently.[4] In the following case, the American Canoe Association challenged the EPA for failing to enforce the CWA.

AMERICAN CANOE ASSOCIATION, INC. v. EPA
30 F. Supp. 2d 908, 1998 U.S. Dist. LEXIS 19785
United States District Court for the Eastern District of Virginia, 1998

Facts: The American Canoe Society sued the EPA for failing to require the state of Virginia to establish total maximum daily loads (TMDLs) for Virginia's waters. A TMDL is a plan assessing the reduction in pollution that is necessary to meet CWA standards. A TMDL also allocates responsibility among polluters for this reduction. The EPA contends that it is not required to take action until a state submits a TMDL, at which point it must approve or disapprove the plan. The EPA filed a motion to dismiss.

Issue: **Does the CWA require the EPA to take action against a state that has not submitted a required plan?**

Excerpts from Judge Ellis's Decision: Under EPA's reading of the statute, its duty to approve or disapprove TMDLs and promulgate its own lists in the event of disapproval is triggered only by the states' submission of TMDL lists. In EPA's view, inaction by states, for however long a period, imposes no duty on EPA. Plaintiffs respond that Virginia's failure to submit its TMDL lists by the 1979 deadline or in the nearly twenty years following constitutes a constructive submission that no TMDLs are required for the state's water, which the CWA compels EPA to disapprove as inadequate.

Under EPA's theory of the case, a statute creates a[n] enforceable duty only when it provides a date-certain deadline for agency action. Here, EPA alleges, no date-certain deadline exists. [T]he CWA appears to offer such a readily-ascertainable deadline. [It] provides that state TMDL lists must be submitted to the EPA no later than 180 days after EPA's publication of its first water pollutants list (June 26, 1979); that EPA must approve or disapprove the submissions within 30 days after that (July 26, 1979); and that if disapproved, the EPA must promulgate its own TMDL lists within 30 days (August 25, 1979). The deadline for EPA's approval or disapproval of state submissions would appear to be July 26, 1979.

EPA's alternative interpretation of the statute would allow recalcitrant states to short-circuit the Clean Water Act and render it a dead letter. It seems highly likely that Congress intended that EPA should be required to act not only when states promulgate lists that fail to meet the standards, but also when states completely ignore their mandatory statutory responsibilities and fail to promulgate any list at all. Here, the appropriate remedy for the plaintiffs' TMDL complaints would appear to be an order directing EPA to approve or disapprove Virginia's constructive submission within 30 days and, if the submission is disapproved, to proceed to promulgate its own lists.

---

[4] *Sierra Club v. Hankinson*, 939 F. Supp. 872, 1996 U.S. Dist. LEXIS 13853 (N.D. Ga. 1996).

Wetlands

Although wetlands may not look attractive, they fill an important ecological role.

Wetlands are the transition areas between land and open water. They may look like swamps, they may even be swamps, but their unattractive appearance should not disguise their vital role in the aquatic world. They are natural habitats for many fish and wildlife. They also serve as a filter for neighboring bodies of water, trapping chemicals and sediments. Moreover, they are an important aid in flood control because they can absorb a high level of water and then release it slowly after the emergency is past.

The CWA prohibits any discharge of dredge and fill material into wetlands without a permit. Although filling in wetlands requires a permit, many other activities that harm wetlands, such as draining them, do not. (However, many states require permits for draining wetlands.) Between 1975 and 1985, more than three million acres of wetlands were destroyed. In the following decade, only one million acres of wetlands disappeared. Although some people consider that to be good news, others view it as an ecological disaster. The government's official policy is no net loss of wetlands. Some scientists have recommended that the nation actually restore 10 million acres.

Sewage

Plumbing drains must be attached to either a septic system or a sewer line. A septic system is, in effect, a freestanding waste treatment plant. A sewer line, on the other hand, feeds into a publicly owned wastewater treatment plant, also known as a municipal sewage plant. **Under the CWA, a municipality must obtain a permit for any discharge from a wastewater treatment plant.** To obtain a permit, the municipality must first treat the waste to reduce its toxicity. However, taxpayers have stubbornly resisted the large increases in taxes or fees necessary to fund required treatments. Since the fines imposed by the EPA are almost always less than the cost of treatment, some cities have been slow to comply. The following news report illustrates the complex trade-offs between costs and benefits.

In the two years since Tom Cox took over as general manager of Constitution Marina, located in one of the sludgiest pockets of Boston's infamously sludgy Inner Harbor, he has seen an entire ecosystem reborn before his eyes. At the mouth of a now-sealed effluent pipe that once poured sewer waste directly into his anchorage, baby herring and krill shrimp feed. "This spring, for the first time in a decade, we even had porpoises in the Inner Harbor, and seals flopping onto my docks. Boston Harbor," Cox says, "is definitely back."[5]

Back? The Boston Harbor? The harbor that was gruesomely swamped with human waste during the disastrous crash of the old Deer Island treatment plant? The harbor that only a few years ago still reeked of 350 years of ill use?

The harbor has passed a vital milestone on its voyage from toilet bowl for 43 cities and towns to tourist attraction and recharging jobs engine. The new $183 million Deer Island sewage-treatment plant received a formal commission, and its predecessor, an obsolete and overburdened albatross that once channeled raw sewage directly in the bay, was bulldozed into dust.

This transformation has not come cheap. Sewer user charges for residents of the greater Boston area have risen more than 560 percent in the past decade, becoming among the highest in the country. These charges are expected to rise an additional 50 to 75 percent in the next few years. In protest, angry ratepayers dumped tea boxes full of sewer bills into the harbor.

[5] Tom Mashberg, "Harbor Cleans Up Its Act," *Boston Herald*, July 30, 1995, p. 1. Reprinted with permission of the Boston Herald.

OTHER WATER POLLUTION STATUTES

The Safe Drinking Water Act of 1974:

- Requires the EPA to set national standards for contaminants potentially harmful to human health that are found in drinking water
- Assigns enforcement responsibility to the states but permits the EPA to take enforcement action against states that do not adhere to the standards
- Prohibits the use of lead in any pipes through which drinking water flows, and
- Requires community water systems to send every customer an annual *consumer confidence report* disclosing the level of contaminants in the drinking water. (One can only hope that consumers will remain confident after receiving the report.) To find out more about your drinking water, turn on **http://www.epa.gov/ogwdw/dwinfo.htm**.

The **Ocean Dumping Act of 1972** prohibits the dumping of wastes in ocean water without a permit from the EPA.

Congress passed the **Oil Pollution Act of 1990** in response to the mammoth 1989 *Exxon Valdez* oil spill in Prince William Sound, Alaska. To prevent defective boats from leaking oil, this statute sets design standards for ships operating in U.S. waters. It also requires shipowners to pay for damage caused by oil discharged from their ships.

Although few would argue with the concept that those who spill ought to pay, there has been great controversy over how to measure damages. The U.S. government proposed that damages should be based on the subjective value that people assign to an injured area. Suppose that an oil spill prevents 1,000 people from using a beach. The government proposal would base the fine on the value that these people report (in a survey) that they place on a day of swimming or walking on the beach. If sea fowl are injured by the spill, nearby residents would be asked what they would be willing to pay to save a bird from death. Oil companies prefer to pay only the cost of fixing the damage. If 1,000 seagulls are killed by a spill, oil companies contend that the proper fine should equal the cost of cleaning up the area and increasing the number of seagulls. That might mean importing seagulls or augmenting their food supply.

WASTE DISPOSAL

The time is 1978. The place is 96th Street in Niagara Falls, New York. Six women are afflicted with breast cancer, one man has bladder cancer, another suffers from throat cancer. A seven-year-old boy suddenly goes into convulsions and dies of kidney failure. Other residents have chromosomal abnormalities, epilepsy, respiratory problems, and skin diseases. This street is three blocks away from Love Canal.

In 1945, Hooker Chemical Co. disposed of 21,800 tons of 82 different chemicals by dumping them into Love Canal or burying them nearby. An internal memorandum warned that this decision would lead to "potential future hazard" and be a "potential source of lawsuits." A year later, the company's lawyer wrote that "children in the neighborhood use portions of the water for swimming and, as a matter of fact, just before we left the site we saw several young children walking down the path with what appeared to be bathing costumes in hand." He suggested that Hooker build a fence around the canal, but the company never did. Instead, it sold the land to the local school board to build an elementary school.

When the company's executive vice-president recommended against the sale, the company inserted a clause in the deed to eliminate the company's liability.

Schoolchildren tripped over drums of chemicals that worked their way up to the surface. Some children were burned playing with hot balls of chemical residue—what they called "fire stones"—that popped up through the ground. Homeowners noticed foul odors in their basements after heavy rains. Finally, a national health emergency was declared at Love Canal, and a joint federal-state program relocated 800 families. In 1994, Occidental Chemical Corp. (which had since bought Hooker) agreed to pay the state of New York $98 million to settle a lawsuit over Love Canal.[6] Two years later, the EPA settled its lawsuit with Occidental for $129 million.

In its time, what Hooker did was not unusual. Companies historically dumped waste in waterways, landfills, or open dumps. Out of sight was out of mind. Waste disposal continues to be a major problem in the United States. It has been estimated that the cost of cleaning up existing waste products will exceed $1 *trillion*. At the same time, the country continues to produce more than six billion tons of agricultural, commercial, industrial, and domestic waste each year. Ironically, air and water pollution control devices have added to the problem because the pollutants they remove from the air and water become waste that must be discarded somewhere.

Two major statutes regulate wastes. The Resource Conservation and Recovery Act (RCRA) focuses on *preventing* future Love Canals by regulating the production and disposal of solid wastes, both toxic and otherwise. The Comprehensive Environmental Response, Compensation, and Liability Act (CERCLA), also referred to as **Superfund**, focuses on *cleaning up* existing hazardous waste sites.

RESOURCE CONSERVATION AND RECOVERY ACT

The RCRA establishes rules for treating both hazardous wastes and other forms of solid waste (such as ordinary garbage).

Solid Waste

Before 1895, the city of New York did not collect garbage. Residents simply piled it up in the streets, causing the streets to rise five feet in height over the century. At present, each American generates 4.4 pounds of solid waste a *day*, an increase of 60 percent since 1960.

But most Americans never gave much thought to their garbage until the infamous case of the garbage barge. The trouble arose in 1983 when the New York legislature banned new landfills (garbage dumps) on Long Island. Three years later, the landfill began to fill up in Islip, a bedroom community outside New York City. Lowell Herrelson, an Alabama businessman, offered to put the Islip garbage on a barge and ship it to another state. But once he filled the barge, no other state would take the garbage. Loaded with 3,186 tons of waste, the barge traveled over 6,000 miles in five months and was turned away by six states and three countries before returning to New York and anchoring near the Statue of Liberty. Its movements were reported daily in the newspapers and even became the subject of the *Tonight Show* monologue: "The only town to send its garbage on a 6,000 mile cruise." The garbage was ultimately burned in a Brooklyn incinerator, but not before Herrelson had lost $500,000 in the venture. Islip introduced recycling and built a $38 million garbage incinerator.

---

[6] William Glaberson, "Love Canal: Suit Focuses on Records from 1940s," *New York Times*, Oct. 22, 1990, p. B1. Copyright © 1990 by The New York Times Co. Reprinted by permission.

The disposal of nonhazardous solid waste has generally been left to the states, but they must follow guidelines set by the RCRA. **The RCRA:**

- Bans new open dumps
- Requires that garbage be sent to sanitary landfills
- Sets minimum standards for landfills
- Requires landfills to monitor nearby groundwater
- Requires states to develop a permit program for landfills; and
- Provides some financial assistance to aid states in waste management.

The federal Office of Management and Budget (OMB) objected to the solid waste regulations that the EPA intended to issue under the RCRA because, according to the OMB's calculations, complying with the proposed regulations would have cost more than $19 billion for every life saved. Not worth it, said the OMB. As a result, the EPA's revised regulations are more flexible than the original version.

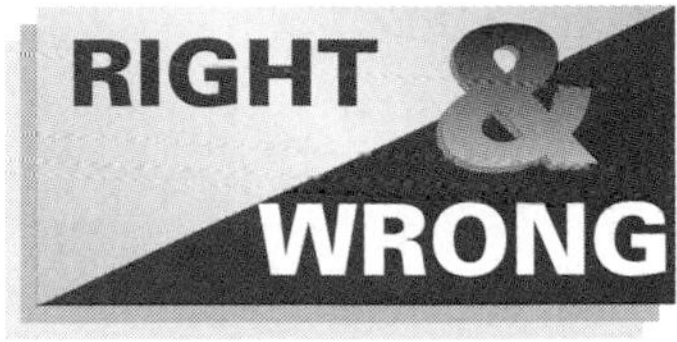

The dispute between the EPA and the OMB typifies the ongoing conflict in environmental law. On the one hand, the EPA argues that scientific data are uncertain and the health risks of pollutants may be much worse than we realize. The EPA's goal is to stop pollution virtually without regard to cost. The OMB, on the other hand, prefers to base decisions on a numerical cost-benefit analysis. The OMB believes that a clean-air-and-water-for-its-own-sake approach makes little economic sense. Is a human life worth $19 billion?

Underground Storage Tanks

Concerned that underground gasoline storage tanks were leaking into water supplies, Congress required the EPA to issue regulations for detecting and correcting leaks in existing tanks and establishing specifications for new receptacles. Anyone who owns property with an underground storage tank must notify the EPA and comply with regulations that require installation of leak detectors, periodic testing, and, in some cases, removal of old tanks.

Identifying Hazardous Wastes

The EPA must establish criteria for determining what is, and is not, hazardous waste. It must then prepare a list of wastes that qualify as hazardous.

Tracking Hazardous Wastes

Anyone who creates, transports, stores, treats, or disposes of more than a certain quantity of hazardous wastes must apply for an EPA permit. All hazardous wastes must be tracked from creation to final disposal. They must be disposed of at a certified facility. Any company that generates more than 100 kilograms of hazardous waste in any month (roughly 200,000 firms nationwide) must obtain an identification number for its wastes. When it ships this waste to a disposal facility, it must send along a multicopy manifest that identifies the waste, the transporter, and the destination. The company must notify the EPA if it does not receive a receipt from the disposal site indicating that the waste has been received.

The penalties for violating the RCRA are serious, as the following case illustrates.

UNITED STATES v. KELLY
167 F.3d 1176, 1999 U.S. App. LEXIS 2093
United States Court of Appeals for the Seventh Circuit, 1999

Facts: Leo Kelly owned and operated a business that removed underground storage tanks. In a surprise inspection, the Wisconsin Department of Natural Resources (WDNR) discovered 150 rusted barrels leaking hazardous wastes onto Kelly's land. He refused to remove the barrels until the WDNR obtained a court order.

Later, CCF, Inc. hired Kelly to remove six underground storage tanks from its property. Small amounts of hazardous waste—gasoline, heating oil, diesel fuel, and sludge—remained in the tanks. Although the WDNR told Kelly to take the tanks to a licensed facility, Kelly instead sent them to Winter Auto Salvage, which does not sound like, and in fact was not, a licensed hazardous waste facility. A jury convicted Kelly of violating the RCRA, and the court sentenced him to 41 months in prison. Kelly appealed.

Issue: Did Kelly violate the RCRA?

Excerpts from Judge Coffey's Decision: At trial, Kelly put forth a "mistake of fact" defense and he attempted to establish that in spite of the fact that he had been warned and instructed to deposit the barrels at a site licensed to accept hazardous materials, he somehow mistakenly believed that the substance in the barrels was nothing but gasoline, which he admits is hazardous but, he avers, is not "waste," and thus is not governed by RCRA.

Kelley apparently would have us establish a rule that mandates [jury] instructions be given in a RCRA case which divides the term "hazardous waste" into two separate components, each with its distinct definition. We do not agree that this proposed division is required. What is necessary is that the jury find Kelly knowingly transported "hazardous waste" as defined by RCRA. The jury heard conflicting testimony on the issue of whether Kelly had knowledge of what was inside the barrels, and agreed with the government's position. It was a question of credibility for the jurors to decide, and they simply did not believe Kelly.

[Affirmed.]

SUPERFUND

In the vignette that opened this chapter, an elderly woman faced financial ruin from the cost of cleaning up pollutants that her dry cleaner tenants had left. The RCRA was designed to ensure safe disposal of current hazardous wastes. In contrast, the goal of Superfund (also known as CERCLA) is to clean up hazardous wastes that have been improperly dumped in the past.

Under CERCLA, anyone who has ever owned or operated a site on which hazardous wastes are found, or who has transported wastes to the site, or who has arranged for the disposal of wastes that were released at the site, is liable for (1) the cost of cleaning up the site, (2) any damage done to natural resources, and (3) any required health assessments.

In a "shovels first, lawyers later" approach, Congress established a $15.2 billion revolving trust fund (the Superfund) for the EPA to use in cleaning up sites even before obtaining reimbursement from those responsible for the damage. Any reimbursements go into the trust fund to be used to repair other sites. The trust fund was initially financed by a tax on the oil and chemical industries, which produce the bulk of hazardous waste. Recently, however, the taxes expired, and Congress has thus far refused to renew them, thereby threatening the viability of the statute.

Since its creation in 1980, Superfund has been hugely controversial. President Carter signed the statute immediately before he left office, but the Reagan administration that followed largely ignored it. During its first five years, the EPA cleaned up only five sites. Congress then took action to strengthen enforcement. As a result, twice as many cleanups have been completed in the past 5 years as in the preceding 12. However, these cleanups cost more than $30 billion and have typically taken 11 years per site. Meanwhile, one in four Americans, including 10 million children below the age of 12, lives within four miles of a Superfund site.

Property owners have complained, and litigated, bitterly because:

- Current and former owners are liable, even though they did nothing illegal at the time, and indeed even if they did nothing more than own property where someone else dumped hazardous wastes. In addition, officers or controlling shareholders in closely held corporations can be personally liable for operations of the company.
- Polluters have joint and several liability—each polluter is responsible for the entire cost of cleaning up a site, even if it contributed only a portion of the pollution. A polluter can reduce its liability only by proving that it caused a smaller percentage of the damage, but that proof is often impossible.
- The expense of a Superfund cleanup can be devastating—higher than $100 million on some sites. Property owners have often viewed litigation as a better investment. More than 50 percent of total Superfund spending has gone to administrative and legal expenses.
- Congress requires that land be returned to pristine condition. Owners point to scientific evidence indicating that this goal is often impossible to achieve, given existing knowledge. Once again, cost-benefit analysis enters the picture as property owners argue that the cost of perfection is higher than the benefit. To encourage redevelopment of contaminated land, the EPA has implemented a "Brownsfield" program that bases the cleanup levels for some property on potential risk to human health. However, Superfund proponents counter that, to be safe, all hazardous wastes should be removed. They offer as Exhibit A the Forrest Glen real estate development in upstate New York. The developers knew they could buy the land cheap because it had been used as a hazardous waste dump. Instead of cleaning it up, they slapped on a bucolic name. Now chemicals ooze up on lawns.

Virtually any commercial real estate is at risk for Superfund liability. Before purchasing land, it is important to investigate whether it has ever been used to dispose of hazardous wastes. Consider testing the soil and groundwater. It might also be a good idea to ask the seller for indemnification against CERCLA liability or to purchase CERCLA insurance.

In the following case, the Supreme Court clarified an important issue of Superfund liability.

UNITED STATES v. BESTFOODS
524 U.S. 51, 118 S. Ct. 1876, 1998 U.S. LEXIS 3733
United States Supreme Court, 1998

Facts: Ott Chemical Co. was a wholly owned subsidiary of CPC International, Inc. Some of Ott's managers also worked directly for CPC. Ott littered the land around its chemical plant with thousands of leaking and exploding drums of hazardous waste, and the soil and water were saturated with noxious chemicals. The EPA estimated that the cost of cleaning up the site would be tens of millions of dollars. It filed suit under CERCLA against CPC. Ott was bankrupt.

The district court concluded that CPC was liable under CERCLA. The court of appeals reversed, holding that CPC was not liable for the actions of its subsidiary. The Supreme Court granted *certiorari.*

Issue: When is a parent liable under CERCLA for the actions of its subsidiary?

Excerpts from Justice Souter's Decision: It is a general principle of corporate law deeply ingrained in our economic and legal systems that a parent corporation is not liable for the acts of its subsidiaries. But there is an equally fundamental principle of corporate law, applicable to the parent-subsidiary relationship as well as generally, that the corporate veil may be pierced and the shareholder held liable for the corporation's conduct when the corporate form would otherwise be misused to accomplish certain wrongful purposes, on the shareholder's behalf. Nothing in CERCLA purports to rewrite this well-settled rule. The Court of Appeals was accordingly correct in holding that when (but only when) the corporate veil may be pierced, may a parent corporation be charged with CERCLA liability for its subsidiary's actions.

[However,] nothing in the statute's terms bars a parent corporation from direct liability for its own actions in operating a facility owned by its subsidiary. The question is not whether the parent operates the subsidiary, but rather whether it operates the facility, and that operation is evidenced by participation in the activities of the facility, not the subsidiary. The District Court emphasized the facts that CPC placed its own high-level officials on Ott's board of directors and in key management positions at Ott, and that those individuals made major policy decisions and conducted day-to-day operations at the facility. In imposing direct liability on these grounds, the District Court failed to recognize that it is entirely appropriate for directors of a parent corporation to serve as directors of its subsidiary, and that fact alone may not serve to expose the parent corporation to liability for its subsidiary's acts. The Government would have to show that, despite the general presumption to the contrary, the officers and directors were acting in their capacities as CPC officers and directors, and not as Ott officers and directors, when they committed those acts.

The District Court found that G.R.D. Williams, CPC's governmental and environmental affairs director, actively participated in and exerted control over a variety of Ott environmental matters. We think that these findings are enough to raise an issue of CPC's operation of the facility through Williams's actions. Prudence thus counsels us to remand for reevaluation of Williams's role, and of the role of any other CPC agent who might be said to have had a part in operating the facility.

It is so ordered.

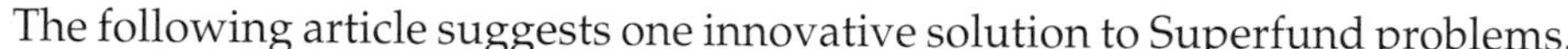

The following article suggests one innovative solution to Superfund problems.

Wells, Maine—Michael Salmon looks through a high chain-link fence at a hazardous waste dump with a gaze that a cat might give to a caged canary. Mr. Salmon is part of a radical experiment here to end litigation among the parties believed to have sent their used motor oil to this dump. For a fee, his company, TRC Cos., Windsor, Connecticut, will assume the liability burdens of 397 major players in the case. Then TRC will schedule a site cleanup. When the slight, crew-cut 43-year-old vice-president for TRC looks through the fence, he is thinking about how his work crews can make a kind of cement out of the seven-foot thick piles of oil sludge layered under this birdless, weed-filled field and then bury the cement in an underground vault. In two years, he says, it will be a baseball field.

Until now, nobody has figured out how to stop this type of litigation. TRC's solution? Trim the number of liable parties to one. TRC agreed to take on everyone's liability—for a price. And an insurance company agreed to issue TRC a new type of environmental-insurance policy called a "cleanup-cost cap," to protect TRC against higher than expected cleanup costs. Lawyers say the basic cleanup costs are between $10 million and $15 million, with the insurance policy roughly double that. This summer, again assuming the final details are resolved, the lawyers will walk away from this case, leaving Mr. Salmon and his TRC crews to start the cleanup.[7]

CHEMICALS

More than 70,000 chemicals are used in food, drugs, cosmetics, pesticides, and other products. Some of these chemicals are known to accumulate in human tissue and cause, among other harm, cancer, birth defects, and neurological damage. A man born in the 1940s is twice as likely to develop cancer as his grandfather was. Many scientists believe that chemicals are a likely culprit for this increased risk. However, only 2 percent of these 70,000 chemicals have been adequately tested to determine their total health impact. Almost 70 percent have not been tested at all. Scientists know virtually nothing about their impact on the health of wildlife.

Several federal agencies share responsibility for regulating chemicals. The Food and Drug Administration (FDA) has control over foods, drugs, and cosmetics. The Occupational Safety and Health Administration (OSHA) is responsible for protecting workers from exposure to toxic chemicals. The Nuclear Regulatory Commission (NRC) regulates radioactive substances. The EPA regulates pesticides and other toxic chemicals.

FEDERAL INSECTICIDE, FUNGICIDE, AND RODENTICIDE ACT

The Federal Insecticide, Fungicide, and Rodenticide Act (FIFRA) requires manufacturers to register all pesticides with the EPA. Before registering a pesticide, the EPA must ensure that its benefits exceed its (then-known) risks. However, many of the 50,000 pesticides currently registered with the EPA were approved at a time when little was known about their risks. In 1972, Congress directed the EPA to reevaluate all registered pesticides and cancel those whose risks exceed their benefits. This process has been very slow. Before the EPA cancels a registration, the manufacturer is entitled to a formal hearing, which may take several years. In the event of an emergency, the EPA may order an immediate suspension; otherwise the chemical stays on the market until the hearing. If a pesticide is banned, the EPA must reimburse end users of the chemicals for their useless inventory.

FEDERAL FOOD, DRUG, AND COSMETIC ACT

The Federal Food, Drug, and Cosmetic Act requires the EPA to set maximum levels for pesticide residue in raw or processed food. The Food and Drug Administration can confiscate food with pesticide levels that exceed the EPA standards.

FOOD QUALITY PROTECTION ACT OF 1996

The Food Quality Protection Act requires the EPA to set pesticide standards at levels that are safe for children. If the data for children are unclear, the EPA must reduce levels to one-tenth the amount now permitted in food. The EPA must also consider all sources of exposure. Thus, for example, in setting limits for

[7] John J. Fialka, "Maine Experiment May Point the Way to Ending Tangle of Litigation Around U.S. Superfund Law," *Wall Street Journal*, Apr. 29, 1998, p. A24. Republished with permission of The Wall Street Journal; permision conveyed through the Copyright Clearance Center, Inc.

pesticides on grapes, the EPA must factor in other sources of pesticides, such as drinking water.

This statute is highly controversial. The pesticide industry argues that the EPA could effectively ban many valuable chemicals for years while careful research into their impact on children is conducted. Environmental advocates, on the other hand, are dismayed that the EPA has not demanded more thorough research before setting standards for some pesticides.

TOXIC SUBSTANCES CONTROL ACT

The Toxic Substances Control Act (TSCA) regulates chemicals other than pesticides, foods, drugs, and cosmetics. For example, it regulates lead in gasoline and paints. **Before selling a new chemical (or an old chemical being used for a new purpose), the manufacturer must register it with the EPA.** As part of the registration process, the manufacturer must present evidence of the chemical's impact on health and the environment. The EPA may prohibit the manufacture, sale, or a particular use of any chemical that poses an unreasonable risk.

NATURAL RESOURCES

Thus far, this chapter has focused on the regulation of pollution. Congress has also passed statutes whose purpose is to preserve the country's natural resources.

NATIONAL ENVIRONMENTAL POLICY ACT

The National Environmental Policy Act of 1969 (NEPA) requires all *federal agencies* to prepare an *environmental impact statement* (EIS) for every major federal action significantly affecting the quality of the human environment. An EIS is a major undertaking—often hundreds, if not thousands, of pages long. It must discuss (1) environmental consequences of the proposed action, (2) available alternatives, (3) direct and indirect effects, (4) energy requirements, (5) impact on urban quality, historic, and cultural resources, and (6) means to mitigate adverse environmental impacts. Once a draft report is ready, the federal agency must hold a hearing to allow for outside comments.

The EIS requirement applies not only to actions *undertaken* by the federal government, but also to activities *regulated* or *approved* by the government. For instance, the following projects required an EIS:

- Expanding the Snowmass ski area in Aspen, Colorado—because approval was required by the Forest Service
- Adding a runway to the Sky Harbor airport in Tempe, Arizona
- Killing a herd of wild goats that was causing damage at the Olympic National Park (outside Seattle)
- Closing a road to create a beachside pavilion in Redondo Beach, California
- Creating a golf course outside Los Angeles—because the project required a government permit to build in wetlands.

The EIS process is controversial. If a project is likely to have an important impact, environmentalists almost always litigate the adequacy of the EIS. Industry advocates argue that environmentalists are simply using the EIS process to delay—or halt—any projects they oppose. In 1976, seven years after NEPA was passed, a dam on the Teton River in Idaho burst, killing 17 people and causing $1 billion in property damage. The Department of the Interior had built the dam in the face of allegations that its EIS was incomplete; it did not, for example, confirm that a large earth-filled dam resting on a riverbed was safe. To environmentalists, this tragedy graphically illustrated the need for a thorough EIS.

Researchers have found that the EIS process generally has a beneficial impact on the environment. The mere prospect of preparing an EIS tends to eliminate the worst projects. Litigation over the EIS eliminates the next weakest group. If an agency does a good faith EIS, honestly looking at the available alternatives, projects tend to be kinder to the environment, at little extra cost.

ENDANGERED SPECIES ACT

The Endangered Species Act (ESA):

- Requires the Secretary of Commerce or the Secretary of the Interior to prepare a list of species that are in danger of becoming extinct
- Requires the government to develop plans to revive these species
- Requires all federal agencies to ensure that their actions will not jeopardize an endangered species
- Prohibits any sale or transport of these species
- Makes any taking of an endangered animal species unlawful—taking is defined as harassing, harming, killing, or capturing any endangered species or modifying its habitat in such a way that its population is likely to decline—and
- Prohibits the taking of any endangered plant species on federal property.

No environmental statute has been more controversial than the ESA. In theory, everyone is in favor of saving endangered species. There are currently 632 endangered species (306 animals and 326 plants) on the U.S. list, and species are becoming extinct at 50 to 100 times the rate one would expect to occur naturally. To quote the House of Representatives Report on the ESA:

> As we homogenize the habitats in which these plants and animals evolved . . . we threaten their—and our own—genetic heritage. . . . Who knows, or can say, what potential cures for cancer or other scourges, present or future, may lie locked up in the structures of plants which may yet be undiscovered, much less analyzed?

In practice, however, the cost of saving a species can be astronomical. One of the earliest ESA battles involved the snail darter—a three-inch fish that lived in the Little Tennessee River. The Supreme Court upheld a decision under the ESA to halt work on a dam that would have blocked the river, flooding 16,500 acres of farmland and destroying the snail darter's habitat. To the dam's supporters, this decision was ludicrous: stopping a dam (on which $100 million in taxpayer money had already been spent) to save a little fish that no one had ever even thought of before the dam (or damn) controversy. The real agenda, they argued, was simply to halt development. Environmental advocates argued, however, that the wanton destruction of whole species will ultimately and inevitably lead to disaster for humankind. In the end, Congress overruled the Supreme Court and authorized completion of the dam. It turned out that the snail darter has survived in other rivers.

The snail darter was the first in a long line of ESA controversies that have included the spotted owl, the gnatcatcher, and the San Bruno Elfin butterfly, among others. Although the government pays out $227 million a year to enforce the ESA, and private citizens spend millions more, only about 55 species have revived enough to be delisted since 1973 when the statute was passed. Much time and money have been spent on litigation.

Recently, the government introduced the Habitat Conservation Plan (HCP) as a blueprint for compromise. In an HCP, developers agree to conserve some land in return for developing other property as they want. These deals contain a "no surprises" clause, meaning that the government has no right to retrieve land once it has been approved for development, even if scientists later determine that a particular species needs that habitat for survival. Unfortunately, the natural world is full of surprises, and environmentalists worry about the ultimate impact of these HCPs. In the short run, however, the success has been striking. For example, to save the gnatcatcher, a songbird found near San Diego, federal and local governments agreed to set aside 82,000 acres that they owned. They bought an additional 27,000 acres, at a cost of $300 million, and developers donated 63,000 acres more. In return, the developers earned the right to build on their remaining land without limitation. More than 16 million acres, including 10 percent of timberland in the Pacific Northwest, are now designated HCPs.

In the long run, the real issue is not how much land developers will give up, but how each of us will change our lifestyle. The government recently announced that nine wild salmon species in the Pacific Northwest are threatened. The Columbia River used to be home to 16 million salmon, but dozens of dams now block the river, interfering with the fish's annual migration. Fewer than a million salmon remain. The following article discusses some of the remedies that may be necessary to save the salmon.

With the salmon crisis, you step out the door and the rain that's running off your front lawn, awash in fertilizer, is a problem. You drive to work (alone) and you are adding to the oil and other chemicals that all eventually drain into the streams. You work for a company that wants to expand its offices into what is a salmon habitat, which describes just about every wetland within a day's drive of Seattle. At home, you turn on a light that is fed cheaply by the very dams that make it nearly impossible for salmon to swim upstream. For us to change this chain of events requires changing our lifestyles, which is something most Northwesterners have always seemed loath to do. We don't want anyone to tell us what to do with our lot size or with that instrument that is most integral to life here: the sport utility vehicle. All of a sudden being for the salmon means being against building a new home wherever you'd like, being for increased taxes, being prepared to change suburban life.

As this new debate begins, the phrase "putting salmon before people" will be heard over and over. Somehow the people need to line up behind the fish, that the fish are like the canary in the coal mine. Now, the salmon are making us look not just at what we can do with the rivers but at what we can do with the way we commute and choose our homes and shop and live. The question is, Will it be too much of a hassle for us to look at ourselves?[8]

[8] Robert Sullivan, "And Now, the Salmon War," *New York Times*, Mar. 20, 1999, p. A15. Copyright © 1999 by The New York Times Co. Reprinted by permission.

CHAPTER CONCLUSION

Environmental laws have a pervasive impact on our lives. The cost has been great—whether it is the higher price for cars with pollution control devices or the time spent filling out environmental impact statements. Some argue that cost is irrelevant, that a clean environment has incalculable value for its own sake. Others insist on a more pragmatic approach and want to know if the benefits outweigh the costs.

What benefits has the country gained from environmental regulation? Since 1970, when Congress created the EPA, the record on common air pollutants, such as lead, has been extraordinarily successful. Total emissions of lead nationwide have declined by 96 percent. Before 1970, emissions of sulfur dioxide had been increasing rapidly. Since then, in spite of strong economic growth and an increase in population, these emissions have dropped. Despite this progress, however, 107 million Americans live in areas that do not meet EPA quality standards.

As for water, wetland acreage continues to decline at a rapid rate. However, the number of Americans whose sewage goes to wastewater treatment facilities has increased from 85 million to 173 million. Two-thirds of the nation's waters are safe for fishing and swimming, up from only one-third when the Clean Water Act was passed.

Despite this progress, as a nation we still face many intractable problems. We have not developed a political consensus on global warming. The health effects of pesticides in our food supply are uncertain. Superfund and the Endangered Species Act are mired in a thornbush of litigation. One government agency concluded:

> Taken as a whole, environmental trends data suggest that over the past two decades the United States has been fairly successful in protecting and improving environmental quality when the existence of a problem has been widely recognized and the sources of the problem well defined. In cases where general recognition of a problem emerged slowly over time, or where the sources of a problem were diverse and widely dispersed, progress has been slow and painful, at best.[9]

If, after reading this chapter, you are concerned about the future of the environment, click on http://www.goldmanprize.org/ to read about people who have made a difference around the world. This Web site highlights winners of the Goldman Environmental Prize, an award that is given each year to six environmental heroes—one from each inhabited continent. The prizes are awarded for sustained and important efforts to preserve the environment.

CHAPTER REVIEW

1. The following table provides a list of environmental statutes:

Air Pollution	Water Pollution	Waste Disposal	Chemicals	Natural Resources
Clean Air Act	Clean Water Act	Resource Conservation and Recovery Act	Federal Insecticide, Fungicide, and Rodenticide Act	National Environmental Policy Act

[9] Council on Environmental Quality, Twentieth Annual Report (1990).

Air Pollution	Water Pollution	Waste Disposal	Chemicals	Natural Resources
	Safe Drinking Water Act Ocean Dumping Act Oil Pollution Act	Comprehensive Environmental Response, Compensation, and Liability Act (Superfund or CERCLA)	Federal Food, Drug, and Cosmetic Act Food Quality Protection Act Toxic Substances Control Act	Endangered Species Act

2. Under the Clean Air Act of 1970, the Environmental Protection Agency must establish national ambient air quality standards for both primary and secondary pollution. States must produce implementation plans to meet the EPA standards.
3. Under the Clean Air Act, power plants may trade emission allowances.
4. The Clean Water Act prohibits the discharge of pollution into water without a permit from the EPA. States must set EPA-approved water quality standards and develop plans to achieve them. The Clean Water Act also prohibits any discharge of dredge and fill material into a wetland without a permit.
5. The Safe Drinking Water Act requires the EPA to set national standards for every contaminant potentially harmful to human health that is found in drinking water.
6. The Ocean Dumping Act prohibits the dumping of wastes in ocean water without a permit from the EPA.
7. The Oil Pollution Act of 1990 sets design standards for ships operating in U.S. waters and requires shipowners to pay for damage caused by oil discharged from their ships.
8. The Resource Conservation and Recovery Act establishes rules for treating hazardous wastes and other forms of solid waste.
9. Under CERCLA, anyone who has ever owned or operated a site on which hazardous wastes are found, or who has transported wastes to the site, or who has arranged for the disposal of wastes that were released at the site, is liable for (1) the cost of cleaning up the site, (2) any damage done to natural resources, and (3) any required health assessments.
10. The Federal Insecticide, Fungicide, and Rodenticide Act requires manufacturers to register all pesticides with the EPA.
11. The Federal Food, Drug, and Cosmetic Act requires the EPA to set maximum levels for pesticide residue in raw or processed food. The Food Quality Protection Act requires the EPA to set pesticide standards at levels that are safe for children.
12. Under the Toxic Substances Control Act, manufacturers must register new chemicals with the EPA.

13. The National Environmental Policy Act requires all federal agencies to prepare an environmental impact statement for every major federal action significantly affecting the quality of the environment.

14. The Endangered Species Act prohibits activities that cause harm to endangered species.

PRACTICE TEST

1. Astro Circuit Corp. in Lowell, Massachusetts, manufactured printed circuit boards. David Boldt was in charge of the production line. In theory, the company pretreated its industrial waste to remove toxic metals, but, in practice, the factory was producing twice as much wastewater as the treatment facility could handle. The company often bypassed the treatment facility and dumped wastewater directly into the city sewer. Once, when caught by the city, Boldt wrote a letter implying that the violation was a temporary aberration. Boldt felt that he was caught "between the devil and the deep blue sea." It was his job to keep the production line moving, but he had no place to put the waste product. Has Boldt violated the law? What penalties might he face?

2. The U.S. Forest Service planned to build a road in the Nezperce National Forest in Idaho to provide access to loggers. Is the Forest Service governed by any environmental statutes? Must it seek permission before building the road?

3. In 1963, FMC Corp. purchased a manufacturing plant in Virginia from American Viscose Corp., the owner of the plant since 1937. During World War II, the government's War Production Board had commissioned American Viscose to make rayon for airplanes and truck tires. In 1982, inspections revealed carbon disulfide, a chemical used to manufacture this rayon, in groundwater near the plant. American Viscose was out of business. Who is responsible for cleaning up the carbon disulfide? Under what statute?

4. Tariq Ahmad owned Shankman Laboratories. He decided to dispose of some of the lab's hazardous chemicals by shipping them to his home in Pakistan. He sent the chemicals to Castelazo & Associates (in the United States) to prepare the materials for shipment. Ahmad did not tell the driver who picked up the chemicals that they were hazardous. Nor did he give the driver any written documentation. Ahmad had packed the chemicals hurriedly in flimsy containers that were unsafe for transporting hazardous materials. He also grossly misrepresented to Castelazo the amount and type of hazardous material that he was shipping to Pakistan. Has Ahmad violated U.S. law? What penalties might he face?

5. Lead is a poison that has no known beneficial function in the body but can cause anemia, kidney damage, severe brain damage, and death. The EPA set national ambient air quality standards for lead at a level that would prevent the occurrence of erythrocyte protoprophyrin (EP) elevation in children. Although EP elevation by itself has no known adverse health effects, it is one of the first measurable indicators of exposure to lead. The Lead Industries Association challenged this standard in court, arguing that (1) the EPA did not have authority to set a standard based on EP elevation when there was no evidence that EP elevation caused harm, and (2) the EPA should have considered the devastating economic impact of its decision on industrial sources of lead emissions. How would you decide this case if you were the judge?

6. Why has the United States been more successful in controlling air pollution than water pollution?

7. Suppose that you are the manager of the General Motors HumVee plant in Mishawaka, Indiana. HumVees are the successor to the U.S. Army jeep and have become popular recreational vehicles among the rich and famous. Arnold Schwarzenegger has several. The HumVee requires special protective paint that reacts with other chemicals during the application process to create ozone, a pollutant. You want to increase production of HumVees. Are there any legal requirements you must observe, or can you simply increase production?

8. Alcan Aluminum Corp. manufactures aluminum sheet in Oswego, New York. It hired the Mahler Cos. to dispose of an emulsion used during the manufacturing process. This emulsion contained a variety of hazardous substances. Without Alcan's knowledge, Mahler dumped the emulsion into a borehole that

connected to deep underground mines along the Susquehanna River in Pennsylvania. You can guess what happened next. Approximately 100,000 gallons of water contaminated with hazardous substances spilled from the borehole into the river. The EPA paid to clean up the river and then sued Alcan along with others who had hired Mahler for hazardous waste disposal. All other defendants settled. The court entered judgment against Alcan in the amount of $473,790.18, which was the difference between the full response costs the government had incurred in cleaning the river and the amount the government had recovered from the settling defendants. Is Alcan required to pay this amount?

9. In 1991, Illinois passed a statute requiring its four largest generating plants to install scrubbers so that they could continue using high-sulfur Illinois coal. What federal law was this Illinois statute designed to overcome? *Extra credit question*: On what grounds did a federal appeals court strike down the Illinois statute?

10. The marbled murrelet is a rare seabird that lives only in old-growth forests on the West Coast. Logging has destroyed so much of its habitat that its numbers in California have declined from 60,000 to between 2,000 and 5,000. Pacific Lumber Co. wanted to harvest trees from 137 acres of land it owned in the Owl Creek forest in California. It originally received approval to log, on the condition that it would cooperate with regulators to protect the murrelet. But the company sneaked in one weekend and cut down trees before it met the condition. Caught in the act, it promised no more logging until it had a plan to protect the birds. This time it waited until the long weekend over Thanksgiving to take down some more trees. Finally, a federal court ordered a permanent halt to any further logging. There was no evidence that the company had harmed the murrelet. Had it violated the law?

11. **RIGHT & WRONG** Geronimo Villegas owned a blood-testing lab in Brooklyn, New York. He threw vials of human blood from the lab into the Hudson River. A group of eighth graders on a field trip to Staten Island discovered 70 of these glass vials along the shore. Ten vials contained blood infected with the highly contagious hepatitis-B virus. Did Villegas violate the Clean Water Act? Why had Villegas disposed of the vials in this way? Whether or not he was in violation of the statute, was his behavior ethical? Did he violate any of the ethical tests from Chapter 9?

12. **YOU BE THE JUDGE WRITING PROBLEM** The Lordship Point Gun Club operated a trap and skeet shooting club in Stratford, Connecticut, for 70 years. During this time, customers deposited close to 5 million tons of lead shot and 11 million pounds of clay target fragments on land around the club and in Long Island Sound. Forty-five percent of sediment samples taken from the Sound exceeded the established limits for lead. Was the Gun Club in violation of the RCRA? **Argument for the Gun Club:** The Gun Club does not *dispose* of hazardous wastes, within the meaning of the RCRA. Congress meant the statute to apply only to companies in the business of manufacturing articles that produce hazardous waste. If the Gun Club happens to produce wastes, that is only *incidental* to the normal use of a product. **Argument for the plaintiff:** Under the RCRA, lead shot is hazardous waste. The law applies to anyone who produces hazardous waste, no matter how.

INTERNET RESEARCH PROBLEMS

1. Using the information provided at http://www.globalwarming.org/index.htm and http://www.law.pace.edu/env/energy/globalwarming.html, write an essay summarizing your views on global warming. What should our own government, and other governments, do? What should you do personally?

2. Choose a body of water located near you and look at http://www.EPA.gov/surf/locate/index.html to learn about its environmental health. Is the water more or less polluted than you expected?

You can find further practice problems in the Online Quiz at http://beatty.westbuslaw.com or in the Study Guide that accompanies this text.

UNIT 7

PROPERTY

CHAPTER 44

INTELLECTUAL PROPERTY

It is hard to imagine that a Goliath like the $12 billion American music industry could see a 19-year-old college sophomore as a threat to its long-term financial health. But when Brian Matiash, a computer engineering major, boots up the computer in his dorm room at Syracuse University on a typical evening, several hundred e-mail messages will await him, each a request for digital copies of recorded music. He will fire up his computer, which is equipped with a hard drive that holds copies of literally hundreds of songs and a CD burner, a device that allows him to copy those songs onto blank compact disks.

Mr. Matiash is part of a thriving underground network of digital music scavengers, mostly college students, who copy and trade music files globally over the Internet in violation of copyright laws. To the recording industry, Mr. Matiash's hobby is deeply disturbing. There are suddenly hundreds if not thousands of people around the globe creating vast electronic libraries of copy-protected music and posting it to the Internet in a format that allows for sound of near-CD quality. That means that potential consumers have a free alternative to buying music.

Mr. Matiash said, "I feel bad sometimes because I know I'm making a mess for the music companies. I know it's technically a crime." Last year, Polygram and 11 other record companies joined the Recording

Industry Association of America in lawsuits accusing three commercial Web sites of copyright infringement. That suit was settled last summer, but most music distribution is generated not by commercial sites but by hobbyists. The Recording Industry Association of America employs people to surf the Web looking for sites where copy-protected material is posted and is experimenting with software that automatically searches the Internet for such sites. When sites are found, officials usually notify the Internet service provider, often a university, which then typically asks the site's owner to remove the offending material. So far, that effort does not appear to have slowed the pirates. "I pretty much can guarantee everyone that I can find any song I want on the Internet if you give me a day or two," Mr. Matiash said.[1]

INTRODUCTION

For much of history, land was the most valuable form of property. It was the primary source of wealth and social status. Today, intellectual property is a major source of wealth. New ideas—for manufacturing processes, computer programs, medicines, books—bring both affluence and influence.

Although both can be valuable assets, land and intellectual property are fundamentally different. The value of land lies in the owner's right to exclude, to prevent others from entering it. Intellectual property, however, has little economic value unless others use it. This ability to share intellectual property is both good news and bad. On the one hand, the owner can produce and sell unlimited copies of, say, a software program, but, on the other hand, the owner has no easy way to determine if someone is using the program for free. The high cost of developing intellectual property, combined with the low cost of reproducing it, makes it particularly vulnerable to theft. As much as 35 percent of the software in use in America may be bootlegged (that is, copied and sold without permission).

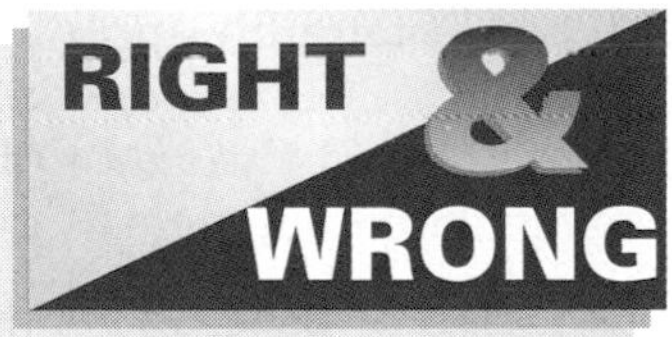

Because intellectual property is nonexclusive, many people see no problem in using it for free. For example, students often argue that it is okay to copy CDs for their friends. How can copying a few CDs hurt a big recording studio? But if record companies earn lower royalties, they will produce fewer songs and music lovers everywhere will suffer. Some commentators suggest that the United States has been a technological leader partly because its laws have always provided strong protection for intellectual property. The Constitution provided for patent protection early in the country's history. In contrast, one of the oldest civilizations in the world, China, has been relatively slow in developing new technology. It did not institute a patent system until 1985.

PATENTS

A patent is a grant by the government that permits the inventor exclusive use of an invention for 20 years (or 14 years in the case of design patents). During this period, no one may make, use, or sell the invention without permission. In return, the inventor publicly discloses information about the invention that anyone can use upon expiration of the patent.

[1] Jason Chervokas, "Internet CD Copying Tests Music Industry," *New York Times*, Apr. 6, 1998, p. D3.

TYPES OF PATENTS

There are three type of patents: utility patents, design patents, and plant patents.

Utility Patent

Whenever people use the word "patent" by itself, they are referring to a utility patent. This type of patent is available to those who invent (or significantly improve) any of the following:

Type of Invention	Example
Mechanical invention	A hydraulic jack used to elevate heavy aircraft
Electrical invention	A prewired, portable wall panel for use in large, open-plan offices
Chemical invention	The chemical 2-chloroethylphosphonic acid used as a plant growth regulator
Process	A method for applying a chemical compound to an established plant such as rice in order to inhibit the growth of weeds selectively; the application can be patented separately from the actual chemical
Machine	A device that enables a helicopter pilot to control all flight functions (pitch, roll, and heave) with one hand
Composition of matter	A sludge used as an explosive at construction sites; the patent specifies the water content, the density, and the types of solids contained in the mixture

A patent is not available solely for an idea, but only for its tangible application. Thus patents are *not* available for laws of nature, scientific principles, mathematical algorithms, or formulas such as $a^2 + b^2 = c^2$. In recent years, the status of computer software has been controversial: Is it an (unpatentable) mathematical formula or a (patentable) process or machine? The following case answers this question.

STATE STREET BANK & TRUST CO. v. SIGNATURE FINANCIAL GROUP, INC.
149 F.3d 1368, 1998 U.S. App. LEXIS 16869
United States Court of Appeals for the Federal Circuit,[2] 1998

Facts: Signature Financial Group, Inc. owns a patent on a computer software program that aids in the administration of mutual funds. The so-called Hub and Spoke System allows several mutual funds, or "Spokes," to pool their investment funds into a single portfolio, or "Hub." In this way, the funds can share administrative costs. Each Spoke sells shares to the public, and the cost of these shares depends upon the value of the assets pooled in the Hub. Therefore, each day within hours of the close of the stock market, each fund's administrator must know the value to the nearest penny of its pooled shares. The Signature software made this calculation.

State Street Bank and Trust Co. negotiated with Signature for a license to use its software. When negotiations broke down, State Street brought suit alleging that the patent was invalid. The trial court granted State Street's motion for summary judgment.

[2] Recall from Chapter 2 that the Court of Appeals for the Federal Circuit is the thirteenth United States Court of Appeals. It hears appeals from specialized trial courts.

Issue: Is data processing software patentable?

Excerpts from Judge Rich's Decision: [The Supreme] Court has held that mathematical algorithms are not patentable subject matter to the extent that they are merely abstract ideas. From a practical standpoint, this means that to be patentable an algorithm must be applied in a "useful" way.

Today, we hold that the transformation of data, representing discrete dollar amounts, by a machine through a series of mathematical calculations into a final share price, constitutes a practical application of a mathematical algorithm, formula, or calculation, because it produces "a useful, concrete and tangible result"—a final share price momentarily fixed for recording and reporting purposes.

The question of whether a claim encompasses statutory subject matter should focus on the essential characteristics of the subject matter, in particular, its practical utility. For purpose of our analysis, [this] claim is directed to a machine programmed with the Hub and Spoke software and admittedly produces a "useful, concrete, and tangible result." This renders it statutory subject matter, even if the useful result is expressed in numbers, such as price, profit, percentage, cost, or loss.

Reversed and remanded.

The *State Street* case could have a profound impact on e-commerce as companies rush to patent techniques for doing business over the Internet. For example, Priceline.com recently received a patent for the reverse auction system offered on its Web site (http://www.priceline.com). Customers list the price (backed up by a credit card) that they are willing to pay for an airline ticket, hotel room, car, or other item. Priceline then scours its database to find a seller willing to make a deal at that price.

Proponents of these patents argue that they permit innovators on the Internet to protect their ideas. Otherwise, it is easy for copycats to open a rival Web site overnight. Critics counter that these patents could stifle e-commerce by limiting the use of new ideas. For example, a company called E-Data has sued, claiming that it owns the patent for the idea of selling software over the Internet.

Braun patented the design, not the function, of this blender.

Design Patent

A design patent protects the appearance, not the function, of an item. It is granted to anyone who invents a new, original, and ornamental design for an article. For example, Braun, Inc. patented the look of its handheld electric blenders. Design patents last only 14 years, not 20.

Plant Patent

Anyone who creates a new type of plant can patent it, *provided that* the inventor is able to reproduce it asexually—through grafting, for instance, not by planting its seeds. For example, one company patented its unique heather plant.

Requirements for a Patent

To obtain a patent, the inventor must show that her invention meets all of the following tests:

- **Novel**. An invention is not patentable if it (1) is known or has already been used in this country, or (2) has been described in a publication here or overseas. For example, an inventor discovered a new use for existing chemical compounds but was not permitted to patent it because the chemicals had already been described in prior publications, though the new uses had not.[3]

- **Nonobvious**. An invention is not patentable if it is obvious to a person with ordinary skill in that particular area. An inventor was not allowed to patent a waterflush system designed to remove cow manure from the floor of a barn because it was obvious.[4]
- **Useful**. To be patented, an invention must be useful. It need not necessarily be commercially valuable, but it must have some current use. Being merely of scientific interest is not enough. Thus a company was denied a patent for a novel process for making steroids because they had no therapeutic value.[5]

A searchable database of all patents issued since 1976 is available at the Patent and Trademark Office's Web site: **http://www.uspto.gov/patft/index.html**. To find out just how creative inventors can be, check out the Wacky Patent of the Month at **http://colitz.com/site/wacky.htm**.

PATENT APPLICATION AND ISSUANCE

To obtain a patent, the inventor must file a complex application with the federal Patent and Trademark Office (PTO) in Washington, D.C. If a patent examiner determines that the application meets all legal requirements, the PTO will issue the patent. If the examiner denies the patent application, the inventor can appeal that decision to the PTO Board of Appeals and from there to the Court of Appeals for the Federal Circuit in Washington. Alternatively, upon denial of the application, the inventor can file suit against the PTO in the federal district court in Washington.

Priority between Two Inventors

When two people invent the same product, who is entitled to a patent—the first to invent or the first to file an application? Generally, the person who invents and *puts the invention into practice* has priority over the first filer. Having the idea is not enough—the inventor must actually use the product.

Prior Sale

However, an inventor must apply for a patent within one year of selling the product commercially. The purpose of this rule is to encourage prompt disclosure of inventions. It prevents someone from inventing a product, selling it for years, and then obtaining a 20-year monopoly with a patent.

Provisional Patent Application

Investors who are unable to assess the market value of their ideas sometimes hesitate to file a patent application because the process is expensive and cumbersome. To solve this problem, the PTO now permits inventors to file a **provisional patent application (PPA)**. The PPA is a simpler, shorter, cheaper application that gives

[3] *In re Schoenwald*, 964 F.2d 1122, 1992 U.S. App. LEXIS 10181 (Fed. Cir. 1992).

[4] *Sakraida v. Ag Pro, Inc.*, 425 U.S. 273, 96 S. Ct. 1532, 1976 U.S. LEXIS 146 (1976).

[5] *Brenner v. Manson*, 383 U.S. 519, 86 S. Ct. 1033, 1966 U.S. LEXIS 2907 (1966).

inventors the opportunity to show their ideas to potential investors without incurring the full expense of a patent application. PPA protection lasts only one year. To maintain protection after that time, the inventor must file a regular patent application. So far, about 10 percent of all patent applications have been for provisional patents.

Duration of a Patent

After 1861, patents in the United States were valid for 17 years from the date of *issuance*. However, in 1994, Congress ratified an international treaty called the General Agreement on Tariffs and Trade (GATT). One of GATT's provisions required patents in all signatory countries to be valid for 20 years from the date of *filing*. (This change does not apply to design patents, which are still valid for only 14 years.) The average patent in the United States is issued 19 months after filing, so this change is generally favorable to inventors who will, on average, have 18 years and five months of coverage instead of 17 years. Sometimes, however, the PTO takes considerably longer than 19 months to issue a patent. In some cases of delay, the patent may be extended for up to 5 years beyond the typical 20-year term.

Infringement

A patent holder has the exclusive right to use the invention during the term of the patent. The holder can bring suit to recover damages and to enjoin the future use of any product that is substantially the same as the patent. A court may award damages to compensate for (1) reasonable royalties, (2) lost profits, and (3) interest since the date of the infringement. In the case of intentional infringement or bad faith, a court may treble the damages and also award attorney's fees.

The PTO issued a patent to Compton's New Media for a technique that allowed computer users to retrieve information from multimedia databases. Compton's had developed this technique for its CD-ROM encyclopedia. After the PTO issued this patent, Compton's announced that it would begin to charge licensing fees to all other software companies that used the same technology—virtually everyone with multimedia CD-ROMs. Many in the computer industry protested to the PTO, claiming that the patented technology was neither new nor nonobvious because it had already been used many times. The PTO reversed itself and rejected Compton's application.

This example illustrates a troublesome problem with software patents. Before 1980, software could not be patented. Therefore, companies protected it by keeping it secret. Even though software can now be patented, many companies have not taken advantage of this change in the law. They have elected to continue keeping their software secret. As a result, the PTO cannot always determine what is novel and what is not because it does not know what is being used secretly.

Submarine patents present a similar problem. These are patent applications that lie submerged in the PTO for years, without anyone knowing they are there. The technology becomes widespread and competitors happily go about using it. Suddenly, the PTO issues a patent, and the new owner has the right to demand licensing fees from current users. For example, Microsoft recently obtained a patent for cascading style sheets. This widely used technology facilitates the design of Web pages. Much to everyone's relief, Microsoft offered to license the technology for free. Nevertheless, technology companies worry that other patent applications may be lurking in the PTO. In the wrong hands, they could threaten the structure of the online world.

COPYRIGHTS

The holder of a copyright owns the *particular tangible expression* of an idea, but not the underlying idea or method of operation. Abner Doubleday could copyright a book setting out his particular version of the rules of baseball, but he could not copyright the rules themselves nor could he require players to pay him a royalty. Similarly, the inventor of double-entry bookkeeping could copyright a pamphlet explaining his system but not the system itself.

Unlike patents, the ideas underlying copyrighted material need not be novel. Two movies that came out at the same time—*Armageddon* and *Deep Impact*—were both based on the idea of meteors destroying the earth. Neither violated the other's copyright because their *expressions* of the basic idea were different.

The Copyright Act lists nine protected categories: literature, music, drama, choreography, pictures, sculpture, movies, recordings and architectural works. A copyright is valid until 70 years after the death of the work's only or last living author. In the case of works owned by a corporation—Mickey Mouse, for instance—the copyright lasts 95 years from publication or 120 years from creation. Once the copyright expires, anyone may use the material. Mark Twain died in 1910, so anyone may now publish *Tom Sawyer* without permission and without paying a copyright fee.

A work is automatically copyrighted once it is in tangible form. For example, once a songwriter puts notes on paper, the work is copyrighted without further ado. But if she whistles a happy tune without writing it down, the song is not copyrighted, and anyone else could use it without permission. Registration with the Copyright Office of the Library of Congress is necessary only if the holder wishes to bring suit to enforce the copyright. Although authors still routinely place the copyright symbol (©) on their works, such a precaution is not necessary in the United States. However, some lawyers still recommend using the copyright symbol because other countries recognize it. Also, the penalties for intentional copyright infringement are heavier than for unintentional violations, and the presence of a copyright notice is evidence that the infringer's actions were intentional.

INFRINGEMENT

Anyone who uses copyrighted material without permission is violating the Copyright Act. **To prove a violation, the plaintiff must present evidence that the work was original** and that either:

- The infringer actually copied the work, or
- The infringer had access to the original and the two works are substantially similar.

A court may (1) prohibit the infringer from committing further violations, (2) order destruction of the infringing material, and (3) require the infringer to pay damages, profits earned, and attorney's fees. The story that opened this chapter illustrates how widespread copyright infringement has become.

FAIR USE

The purpose of copyright laws is to encourage creative work. A writer who can control, and profit from, artistic work will be inclined to produce more. If enforced oppressively, however, the copyright laws could stifle creativity by denying access to copyrighted work. **The doctrine of *fair use* permits limited use of copyrighted material without permission of the author for purposes such as criticism, com-**

ment, news reporting, scholarship, or research. A reviewer is permitted, for example, to quote from a book without the author's permission.

Also under the fair use doctrine, faculty members are permitted to photocopy and distribute copyrighted materials to students, as long as the materials are brief and the teacher's action is spontaneous. If, over his breakfast coffee one morning, Professor Learned spots a terrific article in *Mad Magazine* that perfectly illustrates a point he intends to make in class that day, the fair use doctrine permits him to photocopy the page and distribute it to his class. However, under a misinterpretation of the fair use doctrine, some faculty were in the habit of routinely preparing lengthy course packets of copyrighted material without permission of the authors. In *Basic Books, Inc. v. Kinko's Graphic Corp.*[6] a federal court held that this practice violated the copyright laws because the material was more than one short passage and because it was sold to students. Now, when professors put together course packets, they (or the copy shop) must obtain permission and pay a royalty for the use of copyrighted material.

After releasing the third Star Wars movie, *The Return of the Jedi*, Lucasfilm, Ltd. waited 16 years to produce the fourth film in the series, *Episode I—The Phantom Menace*. Many of *Episode I*'s most fervent fans were born after *Jedi* came out. The myth of Star Wars was kept alive by books, fanzines (magazines devoted to Star Wars), fan fiction (unauthorized stories about Star Wars characters), and Internet Web sites such as **www.theforce.net** and **www.flyingarmadillo.com**.

For all those years, Lucasfilm made no protest. Then, several months before *Episode I*'s release, the studio began to crack down on unauthorized use of its copyrighted characters. It even filed suit against Little, Brown & Co. for publishing *The Unauthorized Star Wars Compendium*. Little, Brown claims fair use, that it is simply commenting and reporting on an important cultural phenomenon. Meanwhile, Paramount Pictures has taken action against Star Trek Web sites, and 20th Century Fox is going after sites that feature its hit TV show, *The X-Files*.

PARODY

Parody has a long history in the United States—some of our most cherished songs have been the basis of parodies. Before Francis Scott Key wrote the words to the *Star-Spangled Banner*, other lyrics that mocked colonial governors had been set to the same music. (The tune was well known as a drinking song.) During the Civil War, this parody of the *Battle Hymn of the Republic* expressed anti-war sentiment:

> Tell Abe Lincoln of Antietam's bloody dell
> Tell Abe Lincoln where a thousand heroes fell
> Tell Abe Lincoln and his gang to go to hell
> And we'll go marching home.

The Capitol Steps, a singing group in Washington, wrote this version of Jerome Kern's song *Old Man River* to make fun of the scandals during President Clinton's administration:

> Ol' Man Zipper, that Ol' Man Zipper
> He must know somethin', but don't say nothin'
> He just keeps pollin', his polls keep rollin' along

(For more parodies by the Capitol Steps, dance over to their Web site: **http://www.capsteps.com/**.) Have the Capitol Steps violated Kern's copyright? After

[6] 758 F. Supp. 1522, 1991 U.S. Dist. LEXIS 3804 (S.D.N.Y. 1991). A federal appeals court reached the same result in *Princeton University Press v. Michigan Document Services, Inc.*, 99 F.3d 1381, 1996 U.S. App. LEXIS 29132 (6th Cir. 1996).

all, they did use his music. What if the words in a parody are in poor taste or express opinions with which the original creator disagrees? The Capitol Steps appear to be on safe ground. The United States has a long history of protecting the expression of unpopular ideas and the Supreme Court recently extended this protection to parodies. The rap group 2 Live Crew recorded a parody of the song *Oh, Pretty Woman*. The group had asked permission, but the holder of the copyright refused. Justice David Souter wrote, "We are called upon to decide whether 2 Live Crew's commercial parody of Roy Orbison's song, 'Oh, Pretty Woman,' may be a fair use within the meaning of the Copyright Act of 1976." The Court's decision included Appendix A and Appendix B, which incorporated the full lyrics of the songs. The following are excerpts from those appendices in the Court's decision.

Original:	**Parody:**
Pretty Woman, walking down the street,	Big hairy woman you need to shave that stuff
Pretty Woman, the kind I like to meet,	Big hairy woman you know I bet it's tough
Pretty Woman, I don't believe you, you're not the truth,	Big hairy woman all that hair it ain't legit
No one could look as good as you Mercy	'Cause you look like "Cousin It" Big hairy woman

The Court held that parody is a fair use of copyrighted material as long as the use of the original is not excessive. The parody may copy enough to remind the audience of the original work but not so much that the parody harms the market for the original. The Supreme Court remanded the case to the trial court to determine if the 2 Live Crew version had copied too much or harmed the market for a nonparody rap version of *Oh, Pretty Woman*.[7] The two sides ultimately settled with 2 Live Crew agreeing to pay royalties.

COMPUTERS

Computers have created their own unique copyright problems. The Copyright Act includes "computer data bases, and computer programs to the extent that they incorporate authorship in the programmer's expression of original ideas, as distinguished from the ideas themselves." However, courts have hundreds of years of experience with ordinary copyrights, whereas computer issues are new.

Software

A computer software program has three different parts:

- **Codes**. Both source and object codes can be copyrighted. Computer programmers write programs in source code, which is then translated into object code for the computer to read. The object code is a series of 0s and 1s that flip switches in the computer. Although object codes can be read only by machines, not humans, they are nonetheless copyrightable.[8]
- **Structure**. Two programs that accomplish the same result may have a very different structure. This structure is copyrightable. Rand Jaslow copied the pro-

[7] *Campbell v. Acuff-Rose Music, Inc.*, 510 U.S. 569, 114 S. Ct. 1164, 1994 U.S. LEXIS 2052 (1994).

[8] *Apple Computer, Inc. v. Franklin Computer Corp.*, 714 F.2d 1240, 1983 U.S, App. LEXIS 24388 (3rd Cir. 1983).

gram that Elaine Whelan designed to manage the finances of a dental lab. Although the programs were written in a different computer language, Jaslow had copied Whelan's structure and organization. The court held that Jaslow had violated Whelan's copyright.[9]

- **Look and Feel**. Two computer programs may accomplish the same tasks, but nonetheless look very different on screen. They may, for example, use different icons and different commands. One program may symbolize "delete" by using a trash can while another uses a red circle with a line through it. In the following case, Lotus Development Corp. argued that Borland International, Inc. had violated copyright law by copying the look and feel of Lotus's most popular program. You be the judge.

LOTUS DEVELOPMENT CORP. v. BORLAND INTERNATIONAL, INC.

516 U.S. 233, 116 S. Ct. 804, 1996 U.S. LEXIS 470
United States Supreme Court, 1996

Facts: Lotus 1–2–3 is a computer spreadsheet program that Lotus designed, copyrighted, and sold. Users manipulate and control the program via a series of menu commands, such as "Copy," "Print," and "Quit." In all, 1–2–3 has 469 commands arranged into more than 50 menus and submenus.

Borland has a spreadsheet program, entitled "Quattro Pro." Borland did not copy any of Lotus's underlying computer code, but, to make the program attractive to 1–2–3 users, Quattro Pro contained a "Lotus Emulation Interface." After activating this Interface, Borland users would see the Lotus menu commands on their screens and could interact with Quattro Pro as if using Lotus 1–2–3, albeit with a slightly different screen and with many Borland options not available in the Lotus program. Borland admits that it copied Lotus's program but argues that the "look and feel" of a program are not copyrightable.

You Be the Judge: Can Lotus copyright the look and feel of its computer program?

Argument for Borland: Under the Copyright Act, no one can copyright an idea or a method of operation. A method of operation means the process by which a machine works, whether it be a car, food processor, computer, or videocassette recorder (VCR). The Lotus menu is like the buttons on a VCR—Record, Play, Stop/Eject. How the buttons are arranged and labeled does not make them an expression of the abstract method of operating a VCR. Instead, the buttons are themselves the method of operation. Highlighting the "Print" command in Lotus 1–2–3, or typing the letter "P," is analogous to pressing a VCR button labeled "Play." Just as one could not operate a buttonless VCR, it would be impossible to operate Lotus 1–2–3 without using its menu.

Under Lotus's theory, every computer program would have different commands. The user might, for example, have to learn many different commands for Print. This is not only absurd, but an unreasonable burden on computer users. At some point, computer programs will have to duplicate each other because there are only so many ways to tell a computer to print.

Argument for Lotus: An author can copyright the expression of an idea, but not the idea itself. Lotus could not copyright the idea of a spreadsheet program, but it can copyright its unique expression of that idea—the types and arrangement of commands, for instance. In developing Quattro Pro, Borland could have constructed a perfectly satisfactory menu using its own commands, not Lotus's. Instead of "Quit," Borland could have said "Exit." Instead of "Copy," Borland could have said "Clone," "Ditto," or "Duplicate." We know that Borland could have constructed an alternate menu because, in fact, it did. Quattro Pro users have a choice between the Lotus or the Quattro Pro menu.

All computer software is nothing more than a method for operating a computer. If the court agrees with Borland, virtually no software would be copyrightable. Borland argues that the Lotus commands are the same as buttons on a VCR. There is one significant difference, however: VCRs are not copyrightable, whereas computer programs are.

Lotus worked for years to develop 1–2–3 and Borland simply stole it. Lotus had a dominant share of the spreadsheet market, and Borland knew its program could not compete unless it attracted 1–2–3 users. It is clear that Borland violated Lotus's copyright.

[9] *Whelan Assoc., Inc. v. Jaslow Dental Laboratory, Inc.*, 797 F.2d 1222, 1986 U.S. App. LEXIS 27796 (3rd Cir. 1986).

Internet

The good news is that Mary Schmich wrote an influential article in the *Chicago Tribune*. The bad news is that people deleted her name, attributed the article to Kurt Vonnegut, and sent it around the world via e-mail. Tom Tomorrow's cartoon was syndicated to 100 newspapers, but, by the time the last papers received it, the cartoon had already gone zapping around cyberspace. Since his name had been deleted, some editors thought *he* had plagiarized it.

In response to such incidents, Congress recently passed the **Digital Millennium Copyright Act**, which provides that:

- It is illegal to delete copyright information, such as the name of the author or the title of the article. It is also illegal to distribute false copyright information. Thus, anyone who e-mailed Schmich's article without her name on it, or who claimed it was his own work, would be violating the law.
- It is also illegal to circumvent encryption or scrambling devices that protect copyrighted works. For example, some software programs are designed so that they can only be copied once. Anyone who overrides this protective device to make another copy is violating the law. Also, if movies and songs are distributed in a scrambled form over the Internet to people who pay for the descrambler, anyone who unscrambles without paying is in violation. The statute does permit purchasers of copyrighted software to make one backup copy.

TRADEMARKS

A trademark is any combination of words and symbols that a business uses to identify its products or services and distinguish them from others. Trademarks are important to both consumers and businesses. Consumers use trademarks to distinguish between competing products. People who feel that Nike shoes fit their feet best can rely on the Nike trademark to know they are buying the shoe they want. A business with a high-quality product can use a trademark to develop a loyal base of customers who are able to distinguish its product from another.

TYPES OF MARKS

There are four different types of marks:

- **Trademarks** are affixed to *goods* in interstate commerce.
- **Service marks** are used to identify services, not products. Fitness First, Burger King, and Weight Watchers are service marks. For the remainder of this chapter, the terms "trademark" and "mark" are used to refer to both trademarks and service marks.
- **Certification marks** are words or symbols used by a person or organization to attest that products and services produced by others meet certain standards. The Good Housekeeping Seal of Approval means that the Good Housekeeping organization has determined that a product meets its standards.
- **Collective marks** are used to identify members of an organization. The Lions Club, the Girls Scouts of America, and the Masons are examples of collective marks.

OWNERSHIP AND REGISTRATION

Under common law, the first person to use a mark in trade owns it. Registration with the federal government is not necessary. However, under the federal Lanham Act, the owner of a mark may register it on the Lanham Act Principal Register. Once the mark is registered, the symbol ® may be placed next to it. Registration has several advantages:

- Even if a mark has been used in only one or two states, registration makes it valid nationally.
- Registration notifies the public that a mark is in use because anyone who applies for registration first searches the Public Register to ensure that no one else has rights to the mark.
- Five years after registration, a mark becomes virtually incontestable because most challenges are barred.
- The damages available under the Lanham Act are higher than under common law.
- The holder of a registered trademark has first option to use it as an Internet domain name.

Under the Lanham Act, the owner files an application with the PTO (Patent and Trademark Office) in Washington, D.C. The PTO will accept an application only if the owner has already used the mark attached to a product in interstate commerce or promises to use the mark within six months after the filing. (The PTO will also grant one six-month extension automatically and has the right to grant extensions for up to three years from filing.) In addition, the applicant must be the *first* to use the mark in interstate commerce. Initially, the trademark is valid for 10 years, but the owner can renew it for an unlimited number of 10-year terms as long as the mark is still in use. For the first five years after registration, the mark can be challenged by anyone who believes that it is not valid. Trademark searches are free on PTO's Web site: http://www.uspto.gov/tmdb/index.html.

VALID TRADEMARKS

Words (Reebok), symbols (Microsoft's flying window logo), phrases ("Just do it"), shapes (a Coca-Cola bottle), sounds (NBC's three chimes), and even scents (plumeria blossoms on sewing thread) can be trademarked. **To be valid, a trademark must be distinctive**—that is, the mark must clearly distinguish one product from another. There are five basic categories of distinctive marks:

- **Fanciful marks** are made-up words such as Converse or Saucony.
- **Arbitrary marks** use existing words that do *not* describe the product—Prince tennis racquets, for example. No one really thinks that these racquets are designed by or for royalty.
- **Suggestive marks** *indirectly* describe the product's function. Greyhound implies that the bus line is swift, and Coppertone suggests what customers will look like after applying the product.
- Marks with **secondary meaning** cannot, by themselves, be trademarked, unless they have been used so long that they are now associated with the product in the public's mind. When a film company released a movie called *Ape*, it

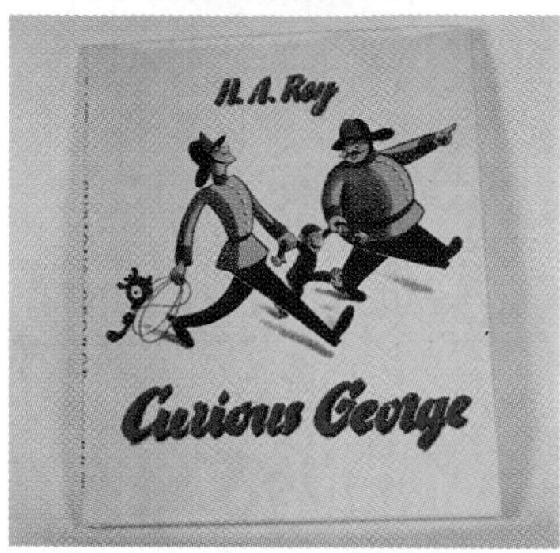

Is Furious George too similar to Curious George?

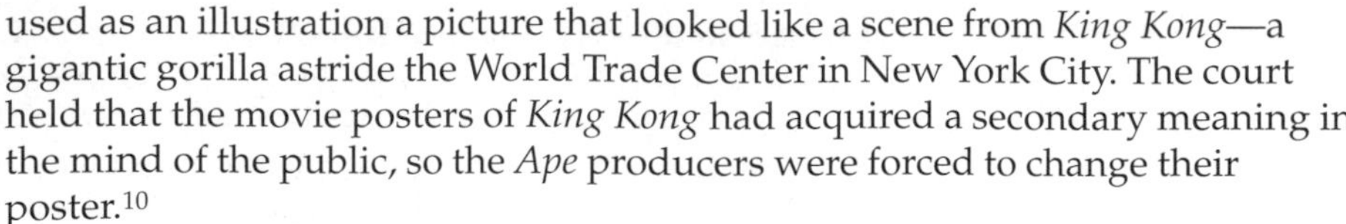

used as an illustration a picture that looked like a scene from *King Kong*—a gigantic gorilla astride the World Trade Center in New York City. The court held that the movie posters of *King Kong* had acquired a secondary meaning in the mind of the public, so the *Ape* producers were forced to change their poster.[10]

- **Trade dress** is the image and overall appearance of a business or product. It may include size, shape, color, or texture. The Supreme Court held that a Mexican restaurant was entitled to protection under the Lanham Act for the shape and general appearance of the exterior of its restaurant as well as the decor, menu, servers' uniforms, and other features reflecting the total image of the restaurant.[11]

The following categories are not distinctive and *cannot* be trademarked:

- **Similar to an Existing Mark**. To avoid confusion, the PTO will not grant a trademark that is similar to one already in existence on a similar product. Once the PTO had granted a trademark for "Pledge" furniture polish, it refused to trademark "Promise" for the same product. "Chat noir" and "black cat" were also too similar because one is simply a translation of the other. Houghton-Mifflin Co. sued to prevent a punk rock band from calling itself Furious George because the name is too similar to Curious George, the star of a series of children's books.
- **Generic Trademarks**. No one is permitted to trademark an item's ordinary name—"shoe" or "book," for example. Sometimes, however, a word begins as a trademark and later becomes a generic name. Zipper, escalator, aspirin, linoleum, thermos, yo-yo, and nylon all started out as trademarks, but became generic. Once a name is generic, the owner loses the trademark because the name can no longer be used to distinguish one product from another—all products are called the same thing. That is why, in advertisements for Sanka, people ask for "a cup of Sanka-brand decaffeinated coffee." And why Xerox Corp. encourages people to say, "I'll photocopy this document," rather than "I'll xerox it." Martini, jeep, and rollerblade are trademarks that seem destined for generic status.
- **Descriptive Marks**. Words cannot be trademarked if they simply describe the product—such as "low-fat," "green," or "crunchy." Descriptive words can, however, be trademarked if they do *not* describe that particular product because they then become distinctive rather than descriptive. "Blue Diamond" is an acceptable trademark for nuts as long as the nuts are neither blue nor diamond-shaped.

Microsoft introduced its Internet Explorer software to great fanfare. There was only one problem: SyNet, Inc. had trademarked the name a year before. What was Microsoft to do? First, it offered $75,000 to buy the rights to the name, but the owner of SyNet refused to sell. Then Microsoft claimed that Internet Explorer could not be trademarked at all because it was a descriptive mark. Microsoft argued that Internet Explorer simply described software for surfing the Net, just as chocolate fudge describes candy. However, a day after trial began in federal court in Chicago, SyNet accepted Microsoft's $5 million settlement offer.

---

10 *Paramount Pictures Corp. v. Worldwide Entertainment Corp.*, 2 Media L. Rep. 1311, 195 U.S.P.Q. (BNA) 536, 1977 U.S. Dist. LEXIS 17931 (S.D.N.Y. 1977).

11 *Two Pesos, Inc. v. Taco Cabana, Inc.*, 505 U.S. 763, 112 S. Ct. 2753, 1992 U.S. LEXIS 4533 (1992).

- **Names**. The PTO generally will not grant a trademark in a surname because other people are already using it and have the right to continue. No one could register "Jefferson" as a trademark. However, a surname can be used as part of a longer title—"Jefferson Home Tours," for instance. Similarly, no one can register a geographical name such as "Boston" unless it is also associated with another word, such as "Boston Ale."
- **Deceptive Marks**. The PTO will not register a mark that is deceptive. It refused to register a trademark with the words "National Collection and Credit Control" and an eagle superimposed on a map of the United States because this trademark gave the impression that the organization was an official government agency.
- **Scandalous or Immoral Trademarks**. The PTO refused to register a mark that featured a nude man and woman embracing. In upholding the PTO's decision, the court was unsympathetic to arguments that this was the perfect trademark for a newsletter on sex.[12]

In the following case, the Supreme Court decided whether a color could be trademarked.

QUALITEX & CO. v. JACOBSON PRODUCTS, INC.
514 U.S. 159, 115 S. Ct. 1300, 1995 U.S. LEXIS 2408
United States Supreme Court, 1995

Facts: Since the 1950s, Qualitex has used a special shade of green-gold color on the pads that it makes for dry cleaning presses. After Jacobson Products (a Qualitex rival) began to use a similar shade on its own press pads, Qualitex registered its color as a trademark and filed suit against Jacobson for trademark infringement.

Issue: Does the Lanham Act permit a color to be trademarked?

Excerpts from Justice Breyer's Decision: The language of the Lanham Act describes [trademarks] in the broadest of terms. It says that trademarks "include any word, name, symbol, or device, or any combination thereof." Since human beings might use as a "symbol" or "device" almost anything at all that is capable of carrying meaning, this language, read literally, is not restrictive. If a shape, a sound, and a fragrance can act as symbols why can a color not do the same?

We cannot find in the basic objectives of trademark law any obvious theoretical objection to the use of color alone as a trademark, where that color identifies and distinguishes a particular brand (and thus indicates its "source"). Indeed, the district court, in this case, entered findings that show Qualitex's green-gold press pad color has met these requirements. The green-gold color acts as a symbol. Having developed secondary meaning (for customers identified the green-gold color as Qualitex's), it identifies the press pad's source.

Jacobson says that, if the law permits the use of color as a trademark, it will produce uncertainty and unresolvable court disputes about what shades of a color a competitor may lawfully use. Because lighting (morning sun, twilight mist) will affect perceptions of protected color, competitors and courts will suffer from "shade confusion" as they try to decide whether use of a similar color on a similar product does, or does not, confuse customers and thereby infringe a trademark. We do not believe, however, that color, in this respect, is special. Courts traditionally decide quite difficult questions about whether two words or phrases or symbols are sufficiently similar, in context, to confuse buyers. They have had to compare,

---

[12] *In re McGinley*, 660 F.2d 481, 211 U.S.P.Q. (BNA) 668, 1981 CCPA LEXIS 177 (C.C.P.A. 1981).

for example, such words as "Bonamine" and "Dramamine" (motion-sickness remedies); "Huggies" and "Dougies" (diapers); "Cheracol" and "Syrocol" (cough syrup).

We conclude that the Ninth Circuit erred in barring Qualitex's use of color as a trademark.

INFRINGEMENT

To win an infringement suit, the trademark owner must show that the defendant's trademark is likely to deceive customers about who has made the goods or provided the services. The rightful owner is entitled to (1) an injunction prohibiting further violations, (2) destruction of the infringing material, (3) up to three times actual damages, (4) any profits the infringer earned on the product, and (5) attorney's fees.

Many Web sites give away free information and (try to) make money selling advertisements. To be successful, the sites must attract hordes of visitors. What can they do to lure cybersurfers? Some site operators embed words like "sex" and "nudity" in invisible coding, even if the sites have nothing to do with sex. Although visitors cannot see the words, search engines will still call up the site. Not content with these generic lures, Calvin Designer Label (no relation to Calvin Klein, the clothing designer) embedded the words "Playboy" and "Playmate" in machine-readable code on its Web site. A federal court entered a restraining order preventing Calvin Designer from infringing on Playboy's trademarks.[13]

FEDERAL TRADEMARK DILUTION ACT OF 1995

Before Congress passed the Federal Trademark Dilution Act of 1995, a trademark owner could win an infringement lawsuit only by proving that consumers would be deceived about who had really made the product. **The new statute prevents others from using a trademark in a way that dilutes its value**, even though consumers are not confused about the origin of the product. Thus, for example, Hasbro, Inc. trademarked "Candyland" for use on a children's board game. Internet Entertainment Group, Ltd. used the name Candyland to identify a sexually explicit Internet site (candyland.com). Although consumers were unlikely to think that Hasbro had developed the Candyland site, the court held that Internet Entertainment had diluted the value of the Candyland trademark.[14]

DOMAIN NAMES

Internet addresses, known as domain names, can be immensely valuable. Shopping.com paid $750,000 to acquire its domain name from the previous (lucky) owner. Compaq Computer Corp. purchased altavista.com for its Altavista search engine from (the unrelated) Altavista Technologies, Inc. The price was $3.3 million.

Who has rights to a domain name? The National Science Foundation, which traditionally maintained the Internet, granted Network Solutions, Inc. (NSI), a private company, the right to allocate domain names. In the beginning, NSI charged no fee for domain names and the rule was "first come, first served." Then so-called "cybersquatters" began to register domain names, not to use, but to sell to

13 *Playboy Enterprises, Inc. v. Calvin Designer Label*, 985 F. Supp. 1220, 1997 U.S. Dist. LEXIS 14345 (N.D. Cal. 1997).

14 *Hasbro, Inc. v. Internet Entertainment Group*, 1996 U.S. Dist LEXIS 11626 (N.D. Wash. 1996).

others. Some cybersquatters specialized in catchy words or phrases (food.com). Others focused on celebrity names—offering "Michael J. Fox" for $10,000 or "Bill Gates" for $1 million. A religious group, called the Friend to Friend Foundation, even financed its operations by registering hundreds of domain names for resale.

What if cybersquatters obtain a domain name that happens to be someone else's trademark—Coca-Cola.com, for example? In response to complaints, NSI began suspending any domain name that was challenged by the holder of a registered trademark. For instance, NSI would not allow Princeton Review to keep kaplan.com, which Princeton had acquired simply to inconvenience its arch-rival in the test preparation business. Congress then passed the Anticybersquatting Consumer Protection Act, which permits both trademark owners and famous people to sue anyone who registers their name as a domain name in "bad faith." The rightful owner of a trademark is entitled to damages of up to $100,000. Some fear, however, that this statute will become a heavy club in the hands of corporations who may use it to threaten innocent holders of domain names. Critics cite as examples the boy who registered his nickname, Pokey, only to be threatened by the maker of Pokey toys and a girl named Veronica whose domain name was challenged by Archie Comics. To discover if your name has been taken, explore **http://www.networksolutions.com/cgi-bin/whois/whois**.

Ironically, some of the companies that have complained most loudly about cybersquatters sometimes find the mouse is in the other hand—companies are buying up insulting domain names to prevent critics from acquiring them. To avoid Toys R Us's fate (**http://www.toysrussucks.com**), some companies now routinely acquire the domain name that combines their corporate name with "sucks." Still, critics can be creative. See, for example **http://www.untied.com**, which offers pages of complaints about United Airlines and includes advice on how to sue the airline in small claims court. Some companies have filed suit to prevent this negative use of their names, but the courts have generally been unsympathetic. A federal court in California ruled against Bally Total Fitness Holding Corp. when it sued the owner and operator of **http://www.compupix.com/ballysucks**.[15] The court held that no reasonable consumer would assume that the Web site was in any way sponsored by or affiliated with Bally.

Sometimes businesses want to trademark a domain name. The PTO will issue such a trademark only for services offered via the Internet. Thus it trademarked "eBay" for "on-line trading services in which seller posts items to be auctioned and bidding is done electronically." The PTO will not trademark a domain name that is merely an address and does not identify the service provided.

As both the value and the number of domain names have soared, the government decided to transfer all management of the Internet, including the allocation of names, to a private, nonprofit, international organization, the Internet Corporation for Assigned Names and Numbers (Icann). The United Nations World Intellectual Property Organization has begun drafting a proposed set of rules for the allocation of domain names.

HARMONIZING INTERNATIONAL LAWS

In a global economy, intellectual property is no longer limited to one country or region. Many American patents, copyrights, and trademarks are valuable overseas just as foreign intellectual property rights have value here—BMW, Beaujolais, and the Beatles are some obvious examples. A number of treaties protect intellectual property worldwide.

---

15 *Bally Total Fitness Holding Corp. v. Faber*, 29 F. Supp. 2d 1161, 1998 U.S. Dist. LEXIS 21459 (C.D. Cal. 1998).

system is the concomitant right to have the ingenuity and industry one invests in the success of the business or occupation protected from the gratuitous use of that "sweat-of-the-brow" by others.

[C]ourts are reluctant to protect customer lists to the extent they embody information which is "readily ascertainable" through public sources, such as business directories. On the other hand, where the employer has expended time and effort identifying customers with particular needs or characteristics, courts will prohibit former employees from using this information to capture a share of the market. As a general principle, the more difficult information is to obtain, and the more time and resources expended by an employer in gathering it, the more likely a court will find such information constitutes a trade secret.

In the case at bar, Morlife's president testified about the difficulty encountered by sales personnel in getting past the "gatekeepers" and identifying and gaining access to the actual decisionmakers with the authority to purchase roofing services. Morlife developed its customer base by investment in telemarketing, sales visits, mailings, advertising, membership in trade associations, referrals and research. Out of 100 persons contacted by the telemarketing department, only about 10 result in contacts. He estimated an initial visit by a Morlife salesperson costs the company $238.

The record amply supports that reasonable steps were taken by Morlife to protect the information from disclosure. [C]ustomer information was stored on computer with restricted access. Moreover, in its employment contract signed by Perry, Morlife included a confidentiality provision expressly referring to its customer names and telephone numbers. The Morlife employee handbook contained an express statement that employees shall not use or disclose Morlife secrets or confidential information subsequent to their employment including "lists of present and future customers."

The judgment is affirmed.

Morlife brought this case in state court under the Uniform Trade Secrets Act. Until recently, the sole federal law on trade secrets prohibited theft only from the federal government, not from private businesses. When the theft of trade secrets reached $24 billion a year, Congress began to fear that, without a national plan to protect economic information, the country could not maintain its industrial and economic edge or safeguard national security. Congress responded with **the Economic Espionage Act of 1996. This statute prohibits any attempt to steal trade secrets for the benefit of someone other than the owner, including for the benefit of any foreign government.** Thus Kai-Lo Hsu was charged under this statute for his alleged attempt to steal the formula for manufacturing Taxol, an anticancer drug produced by Bristol-Myers. Hsu's employer, Yuen Foong Paper Co. in Taiwan, wanted to diversify into biotechnology and obtain technology from advanced countries.[19]

Preventive Law

In formulating a policy on trade secrets, a company should:

- Identify specific information that is a trade secret.
- Set out the company's trade secret policy in writing (including what is secret) and require employees to sign this agreement. The company cannot simply identify everything as secret. Both employees and courts are less likely to treat a policy seriously if the company makes no effort to distinguish the important from the trivial.

[19] *United States v. Kai-Lo Hsu*, 155 F.3d 189, 1998 U.S. App. LEXIS 20810 (3rd Cir. 1998).

- Allow access only to those employees who need the information to perform their jobs.
- Remind employees who leave the firm that they are still bound by the trade secret agreement.

CHAPTER CONCLUSION

Intellectual property takes many different forms. It can be an Internet domain name, a software program, a cartoon character, a formula for motor oil, or a process for making anticancer drugs. Because of its great variety, intellectual property is difficult to protect. Yet, for many individuals and companies, intellectual property is the most valuable asset they will ever own. As its economic value increases, so does the need to understand the rules of intellectual property law.

CHAPTER REVIEW

	Patent	Copyright	Trademark	Trade Secrets
Protects:	Mechanical, electrical, chemical inventions; processes; machines; composition of matter; designs; plants	The tangible expression of an idea, but not the idea itself	Words and symbols that a business uses to identify its products or services	A formula, device, process, method, or compilation of information that, when used in business, gives the owner an advantage over competitors who do not know it
Requirements for Legal Protection:	Application approved by PTO	An item is automatically copyrighted once it is in tangible form.	Use is the only requirement; registration is not necessary but does offer some benefits.	Must be kept confidential
Duration:	20 years after the application is filed (14 years for a design patent)	70 years after the death of the work's only or last living author	Valid for 10 years but the owner can renew for an unlimited number of terms as long as the mark is still being used	As long as it is kept confidential

PRACTICE TEST

1. For many years, the jacket design for Webster's Ninth New Collegiate Dictionary featured a bright red background. The front was dominated by a "bull's eye" logo. The center of the bull's eye was white with the title of the book in blue. Merriam-Webster registered this logo as a trademark. Random House published a dictionary with a red dust jacket, the title in large black and white letters, and Random House's "house" logo—an angular drawing of a house—in white. What claim might Merriam-Webster make against Random House? Would it be successful?

2. "Hey, Paula," a pop hit that spent months on the music charts, was back on the radio 30 years later, but in a form the song's author never intended. Talk-show host Rush Limbaugh played a version with the same music as the original but with lyrics that poked fun at President Bill Clinton's alleged sexual misconduct with Paula Jones. Has Limbaugh violated the author's copyright?

3. From the following description of Jean-Pierre Foissey's activities one evening, can you guess what he is doing and why?

> Mr. Foissey waits until sundown. Then it is time to move. A friend whom he employs drops him off by car near the plum orchard, turning off the headlights as they approach. Mr. Foissey and another operative move quickly through adjacent cornfields and enter the orchard, careful not to leave footprints. Armed with a flashlight, his associate crawls through the orchard reading aloud the numbers on labels attached to the trees by the grower. Mr. Foissey picks leaves off the trees and marks the tree numbers on them. He takes those leaves back to an expert who will examine their size, shape, color, and texture, and also test their DNA.[20]

4. Rebecca Reyher wrote (and copyrighted) a children's book entitled *My Mother Is the Most Beautiful Woman in the World*. The story was based on a Russian folktale told to her by her own mother. Years later, the children's TV show *Sesame Street* televised a skit entitled "The Most Beautiful Woman in the World." The *Sesame Street* version took place in a different locale and had fewer frills, but the sequence of events in both stories was identical. The author of the *Sesame Street* script denied he had ever seen Reyher's book but said his skit was based on a story told to his sister some 20 years before. Has *Sesame Street* infringed Reyher's copyright?

5. Roger Schlafly applied for a patent for two prime numbers. (A prime number cannot be evenly divided by any number other than itself and 1—3, 7, 11, 13, for example.) Schlafly's numbers are a bit longer—one is 150 digits, the other is 300. His numbers, when used together, can help perform the type of mathematical operation necessary for exchanging coded messages by computer. Should the PTO issue this patent?

6. DatagraphiX manufactured and sold computer graphics equipment that allowed users to transfer large volumes of information directly from computers to microfilm. Customers were required to keep maintenance documentation on-site for the DatagraphiX service personnel. The service manual carried this legend: "No other use, direct or indirect, of this document or of any information derived therefrom is authorized. No copies of any part of this document shall be made without written approval by DatagraphiX." Additionally, on every page of the maintenance manual the company placed warnings that the information was proprietary and not to be duplicated. Frederick J. Lennen left DatagraphiX to start his own company that serviced DatagraphiX equipment. Can DatagraphiX prevent Lennen from using its manuals?

7. Richard Q. Yardley applied for a design patent on a watch with a caricatured figure on the dial. The character's arms served as the hour and minute hands of the watch. Because Yardley had copyrighted the design on the watch, the PTO rejected his application for a design patent. Should Yardley be permitted to obtain both a copyright and a patent on the same design?

8. Babe Ruth was one of the greatest baseball players of all time. After Ruth's death, his daughters registered the words "Babe Ruth" as a trademark. MacMillan, Inc. published a baseball calendar that contained three Babe Ruth photos. Ruth's daughters did not own the specific photographs, but they objected to the use of Ruth's likeness. As holders of the Babe Ruth trademark, do his daughters have the right to prevent others from publishing pictures of Ruth without their permission?

9. Harper & Row signed a contract with former President Gerald Ford to publish his memoirs. As part of the deal, the two agreed that *Time* magazine could print an excerpt from the memoirs shortly before the book was published. *Time* was to pay $25,000 for this right. Before *Time* published its version, *Nation* magazine published an *unauthorized* excerpt. *Time* canceled

---

[20] Thomas Kamm, "Patented Plums Give French Fruit Sleuth His Raison D'être," *Wall Street Journal*, Sep. 18, 1995, p. A1. Republished with permission of The Wall Street Journal; permission conveyed through the Copyright Clearance Center, Inc.

its article and refused to pay the $25,000. Harper sued *Nation* for copyright infringement. What was *Nation*'s defense? Was it successful?

10. Frank B. McMahon wrote one of the first psychology textbooks to feature a light and easily readable style. He also included many colloquialisms and examples that appealed to a youthful student market. Charles G. Morris wrote a psychology text book that copied McMahon's style. Has Morris infringed McMahon's copyright?

11. **RIGHT & WRONG** After Edward Miller left his job as a salesperson at the New England Insurance Agency, Inc., he took some of his New England customers to his new employer. At New England, the customer lists had been kept in file cabinets. Although the company did not restrict access to these files, it claimed there was a "you do not peruse my files and I do not peruse yours" understanding. The lists were not marked "confidential" or "not to be disclosed." Did Miller steal New England's trade secrets? Whether or not he violated the law, was it ethical for him to use this information at his new job?

12. **YOU BE THE JUDGE WRITING PROBLEM** Three inventors developed a software program that generated a particularly clear screen display on a computer. The PTO refused to issue a patent for this software. Do the inventors have a right to a patent? **Argument for the PTO:** This software is merely a series of mathematical formulas that cannot be patented. **Argument for the inventors:** The program is not merely a mathematical concept or an abstract idea, but rather a specific machine to produce a useful, concrete, and tangible result.

Internet Research Problem

Think of a name for an interesting new product. Look at http://www.uspto.gov/tmdb/index.html to see if this name is available as a trademark. Also look at http://www.networksolutions.com/cgi-bin/whois/whois to see if it is available as an Internet domain name.

You can find further practice problems in the Online Quiz at http://beatty.westbuslaw.com or in the Study Guide that accompanies this text.

CHAPTER 45

REAL PROPERTY

Some men have staked claims to land for its oil, others for its gold. But Paul Termarco and Gene Murdoch are staking their claim to an island using . . . hot dogs. Their quest to market frankfurters in the New Jersey wilderness has made their children blush with embarrassment, their wives shrug in bewilderment, and strangers burst into laughter. But for three years, the two friends from West Milford have sold chili dogs, cheese dogs, and the ever traditional, hold-everything-but-the-mustard hot dogs from a tiny island in Greenwood Lake. Now it seems as though everyone knows about "Hot Dog Island."

"People love it," said Termarco. "They say, 'Thank you for being here.' I always say, 'No. Thank *you*.' " The personalized service and the inexpensive prices (hot dogs cost $1.75, chili dogs, cheese dogs, and sauerkraut, $2.00) have cultivated a base of regulars. "I think it's great. It's better than going to a restaurant for two hours and spending a lot of money," said Joan Vaillant, who frequently jet skis to the island for hot dogs slathered in mustard.

At two-eighths of an acre, the island's pile of craggy rocks, scrubby bushes, and a few ash trees are difficult to spot. Termarco doesn't mind. "Not everyone can say they own an island," he boasted. Termarco and Murdoch decided to claim the slip of land after chatting with a local restaurateur a few years ago. Termarco had just finished suggesting that the man expand his lake-side business to the island when Murdoch kicked his friend under the table.

"We left thinking, 'We can do this ourselves,'" said Murdoch, who rushed to the township offices the following day to see who owned the island.

Property records showed that the state owned the lake and lake floor, but nobody owned the island. An attorney told them about the law of adverse possession written in the 1820's. If Murdoch and Termarco could show that they used the island for five years, it would be theirs. As crazy as the scheme sounded, Murdoch figured it was worth trying.[1]

Can two friends acquire an island simply by *pretending* they own it? Yes. It is quite possible that the men will eventually own their island. As we will see, the law of adverse possession permits people to obtain title to land by using it, if they meet certain stringent criteria. We examine the rules later in the chapter and decide how likely Murdoch and Termarco are to succeed. For now, the lesson is that real property law can provide surprises—and profit.

NATURE OF REAL PROPERTY

We need to define a few terms. A **grantor** is an owner who conveys his property, or some interest in it, to someone else, called the **grantee**. If you sell your house to Veronica, you are the grantor and she is the grantee. Real property may be any of the following:

- **Land**. Land is the most common and important form of real property. In England, land was historically the greatest source of wealth and social status, far more important than industrial or commercial enterprises. As a result, the law of real property has been of paramount importance for nearly 1,000 years, developing very gradually to reflect changing conditions. Some real property terms sound medieval for the simple reason that they *are* medieval. By contrast, the common law of torts and contracts is comparatively new. (For a fascinating look at the English and Roman roots of our property law, dig down to **http://www.snowcrest.net/siskfarm/tableoc.html**.)
- **Buildings**. Buildings are real property. Houses, office buildings, and factories all fall (or stand) in this category.
- **Subsurface Rights**. In most states, the owner of the land also owns anything under the surface, down to the center of the earth. In some cases the subsurface rights may be worth far more than the surface land, for example if there is oil or gold underfoot. Although the landowner generally owns these rights, she may sell them, while retaining ownership of the surface land. Suppose Terry buys land in the country to get away from the materialistic rat race and then discovers natural gas under the surface. She may choose to sell the natural gas rights to an energy company. Terry keeps the rights to use the surface for whatever she wishes, and may later sell these rights to anyone she pleases; but the

[1] Leslie Haggin, "Pair Stake Their Claim to Hot Dog Island," *Record (Bergen, N.J.)*, Sep. 5, 1994, p. A12. Excerpted with permission of The Record, Hackensack, NJ.

energy company owns the subsurface rights. It will have the right to enter Terry's land, drill for the gas, and conduct it away by pipe. The company could also sell the subsurface rights, if it wished.

- **Air Rights**. The owner of land owns the air space above the land. Suppose you own an urban parking lot. The owner of an adjacent office building wishes to build a walkway across your parking lot to join her building with a neighboring skyscraper. The office owner needs your permission to build across the air space and will expect to pay you a handsome fee for the privilege. Because cities are by definition crowded, air space is often very valuable. Some companies, such as railroads, own a great deal of air space and earn considerable coin selling thin air.

- **Plant Life.** Plant life growing on land is real property, whether the plants are naturally occurring, such as trees, or cultivated crops. When a landowner sells his property, plant life is automatically included in the sale, unless the parties agree otherwise. A landowner may also sell the plant life separately, if he wishes. A sale of the plant life alone, without the land, is a sale of goods. (Goods, as you may recall, are movable things.) If Douglas agrees to sell all of the fir trees on his property, this sale of goods will be governed by the Uniform Commercial Code (UCC), regardless of whether Douglas or the buyer is obligated to cut the trees.[2]

- **Fixtures.** Fixtures are goods that have become attached to real property. A house (which is real property) contains many fixtures. The furnace and heating ducts were goods when they were manufactured and when they were sold to the builder, because they were movable. But when the builder attached them to the house, the items became fixtures. By contrast, neither the refrigerator nor the grand piano is a fixture.

When an owner sells real property, the buyer normally takes the fixtures, unless the parties specify otherwise. Sometimes it is difficult to determine whether something is a fixture. The general rule is this: **an object is a fixture if a reasonable person would consider the item to be a permanent part of the property**, taking into account attachment, adaptation, and other objective manifestations of permanence:

- *Attachment*. If an object is attached to property in such a way that removing it would damage the property, it is probably a fixture. Heating ducts *could* be removed from a house, but only by ripping open walls and floors, so they are fixtures.

- *Adaptation*. Something that is made or adapted especially for attachment to the particular property is probably a fixture, such as custom-made bookshelves fitted in a library.

- *Other Manifestations of Permanence*. If the owner of the property clearly *intends* the item to remain permanently, it is probably a fixture. Suppose a homeowner constructs a large concrete platform in his backyard, then buys a heavy metal shed and puts it on the platform. His preparatory work indicates that he expects the shed to remain permanently, and a court would likely declare it a fixture.

In the following case, the court was faced with an item that is movable by its very design, yet may have become a fixture.

---

[2] UCC §2-107 (2).

DRONEY v. DRONEY
102 Md. App. 672, 651 A.2d 415, 1995 Md. App. LEXIS 1
Maryland Court of Special Appeals, 1995

Facts: Mary Ann Droney and her husband, John, bought land in Garrett County, Maryland. They then purchased a "double-wide" mobile home, which they transported to the property. The Droneys removed the mobile home's wheels and bolted it to concrete pilings. They hooked up water, electric, and septic systems and attached gutters, downspouts, new siding, and a 2,000-pound stone fireplace. The Droneys continued to register the mobile home as a vehicle with the Motor Vehicle Administration (MVA), listing both parties as owners and a bank as holder of a security interest.

Unfortunately, the Droneys divorced. They agreed that John would convey certain property to Mary Ann, which he did, and she in turn would deed to him "all Garrett County real estate." Mary Ann gave John the *land* in Garrett County but retained the mobile home, claiming it was not real estate.

The trial court ordered Ms. Droney to convey the mobile home to John. She refused, and the court found her in contempt, ordering her jailed for two years. To avoid the jail sentence, she signed over the mobile home and then appealed the court's order.

Issue: **Is the mobile home a fixture?**

Excerpts from Judge Hollander's Decision: Ms. Droney argues that the judgment did not order her to transfer the home, only the "real estate." She contends that the MVA records and security interest documents clearly establish that the home is a "vehicle," and not a part of the land. To this end, Ms. Droney cites several sections from [the Maryland Transportation Code defining mobile home, vehicle, and certificates of title for vehicles].

We do not agree that these statutory sections conclusively establish that the disputed property is a motor vehicle. Initially, we observe that the definitions cited by appellant are expressly limited in their applicability to [the transportation code itself]. Therefore, the statutory sections cited do not modify the common law of real property and fixtures. Also, Ms. Droney has not provided any legal authority for the proposition that an object is always a motor vehicle so long as MVA records say the object is a motor vehicle, even when the object otherwise has all the indicia of a home and is immobile.

In the instant case, the trial court's analysis of the facts supported its finding that the home had become a fixture; the court was not clearly erroneous. With respect to attachment to the land, the facts showed that the wheels had been removed and the home had been attached to the ground with bolts and utility lines. The parties also had installed a 2,000-pound fireplace and had covered the exterior of the house with siding. Regarding the adaptation of the land to the use of the home, the record also showed that the Droneys built a deck entirely surrounding the house and planted shrubs around the house. Mr. Droney testified that any attempt to remove the home would "wreck" it. In short, the home was not moving anywhere.

Affirmed.

ESTATES IN REAL PROPERTY

Use and ownership of real estate can take many different legal forms. A person may own property outright, having the unrestricted use of the land and an unlimited right to sell it. However, someone may also own a lesser interest in real property. For example, you could inherit the *use* of a parcel of land during your lifetime, but have no power to leave the land to your heirs. Or you could retain ownership and possession of some land yet allow a corporation to explore for oil and drill wells. The different rights that someone can hold in real property are known as **estates** or **interests**. Both terms simply indicate specified rights in property.

FREEHOLD ESTATES

The owner of a freehold estate has the present right to possess the property and to use it in any lawful way she wants. The three most important freehold estates are (1) fee simple absolute, (2) fee simple defeasible, and (3) life estate.

Fee Simple Absolute

A fee simple absolute provides the owner with the greatest possible control of the property. When we think of buying a house or owning land outright, we are usually referring to fee simple absolute, the most common form of land ownership. Suppose Cecily inherits a fee simple interest in a 30-acre vineyard. Cecily may use the land for any purpose that the law allows. She may continue to raise grapes, or, if she hates wine, she may rip up the vines and plant apple trees, build a condominium complex, or allow the land to go to waste. Although zoning laws may regulate her use, nothing in Cecily's estate itself limits her use of the land.

Cecily may pass on to her heirs her entire estate, that is, her full fee simple absolute. This makes a fee simple absolute potentially infinite in duration, with each generation leaving the same full ownership privileges to the next.

Fee Simple Defeasible

Other estates contain more limited rights than the fee simple absolute. Suppose that during his life, Wily establishes the Wily Church of Perfection. Upon his death, Wily leaves a 100-acre estate to the church for as long as it keeps the name "Wily Church of Perfection." Wily has included a significant limitation in the church's ownership. The church has a fee simple defeasible.

A fee simple defeasible may terminate upon the occurrence of some limiting event. If the congregation decides to rename itself the Happy Valley Church of Perfection, the church automatically loses its estate in the 100 acres. Ownership of the land then **reverts** to Wily's heirs, meaning title goes back to them. Because the heirs might someday inherit the land, they are said to have a *future interest* in the 100 acres. We look at future interests later.

A landowner who creates a fee simple defeasible generally does so to ensure that property is used in a particular way, perhaps as a school or church or playground. In some cases a landowner will create such a fee to guarantee that a particular activity, such as gambling or residential subdivision, does *not* take place. In the following case, a California city was surprised to learn that this ancient doctrine still has plenty of life.

WALTON v. CITY OF RED BLUFF
2 Cal. App. 4th 117, 3 Cal. Rptr. 2d 275, 1991 Cal. App. LEXIS 1474
California Court of Appeal, 1991

Facts: In 1908 and 1916, Mrs. Elizabeth Kraft and her son, Edward Kraft, granted to the city of Red Bluff two adjoining properties, with buildings, for use as a public library. The grants from the Krafts required continuous use as a public library and stated that the property would return to the Kraft family if the city ever used it for other purposes.

In 1986, Red Bluff decided that the buildings were too small for its needs and moved all of the books to a new building nearby. The city used the Kraft property for other civic purposes such as town meetings, social gatherings, and school tutoring. Herbert Kraft Walton, a descendant and heir, filed suit seeking to have the property reconveyed to him. The trial court found for Red Bluff, and Walton appealed.

Issue: Did Red Bluff violate the terms of the grants, so the property must now revert to Walton?

Excerpts from Judge Carr's Decision: The grants provide in part: "If the property herein conveyed shall at any time be abandoned by the said Town of Red Bluff, . . . or if the said property shall cease to be used, for library purposes, by said Town, . . . or shall be put to [any] use other [than] the uses and purposes herein specifically referred to, . . . then the grant and conveyance herein made shall cease and terminate, and the title to the said property and all the improvements thereon shall at once revert to [the Kraft family].

Red Bluff admits all the books were removed from the library as of September 1986. The trial court framed the issue as one of abandonment. But the grantors specified that "if the said property shall cease to be used, for library purposes" the grants terminate.

Whether Red Bluff intended to "abandon" the use purpose of the property or not, it removed the books and stopped using the premises for library purposes. The grants defined library purposes broadly to include various educational endeavors, but there is no evidence any of these other activities took place. It stopped using the grant for library purposes and the property must go back to the Kraft heir.

At oral argument Red Bluff focussed on the "changed conditions" doctrine. The power of termination expires when it becomes "obsolete." In a leading case involving a covenant restricting the use of lots to residential purposes it was said that "where there has been a change in the uses to which the property in the neighborhood is being put, so that such property is no longer residence property, it would be unjust, oppressive, and inequitable to give effect to the restrictions, if such change has resulted from causes other than their breach." In this case the alleged change in circumstance is that Red Bluff needs a bigger, modern library building, not that the present building cannot be used for the purposes of the grant or that the use of surrounding property makes operation of a library impracticable. In these circumstances there is nothing inequitable about enforcing the restriction in the grant.

The judgment is *reversed* with directions to the trial court to enter a judgment [granting title to] Walton.

Life Estate

A life estate is exactly what you would think: **an estate for the life of some named person**. For example, Aretha owns Respect Farm, and in her will she leaves it to Max, for his lifetime. Max is the **life tenant**. He is entitled to live on the property and work it as a normal farm during his lifetime. He may grow and harvest crops and retain all the profits. But the moment Max dies, the farm reverts to Aretha or her heirs.

The life tenant must keep the property in reasonable repair during his lifetime and may not damage the property. As we saw earlier, Cecily, the owner of a fee simple absolute in a vineyard, was entitled to mow down the vines and turn the property into a miniature-golf park if she wanted; Max, a life tenant, has no such rights. Aretha's heirs, who will obtain the property on Max's death, are entitled to enter upon the farm to ensure that he is not damaging the property and to take any other sensible steps to ensure that their future property is protected. For example, if a stream through the farm threatens to flood a valuable field, Aretha's heirs have the right to charge onto the property yelling "Dam it!" and then, if Max failed to do so, to dam it.

NON-FREEHOLD ESTATES

A non-freehold is entirely different from the freehold estates we have seen. It involves a **lease** in which the owner, the landlord, agrees to permit a tenant to use and possess the property. When you lease an apartment from a landlord you have a leasehold, or a non-freehold estate. We discuss these estates in detail in Chapter 46, on landlord-tenant law.

CONCURRENT ESTATES

When two or more people own real property at the same time, they have **concurrent estates**. The most common forms of concurrent estates are tenancy in common, joint tenancy, marital property, and condominiums and cooperatives.

Tenancy in Common

The most common form of concurrent estate is **tenancy in common**. Suppose Patricia owns a house or, in legal terms, owns a fee simple absolute estate in the house. Patricia agrees to sell her house to Quincy and Rebecca. When she **conveys** the deed, that is, transfers the deed, "to Quincy and Rebecca," those two now have a tenancy in common. This kind of estate can also be created in a will. If Patricia had died still owning the house, and left it in her will to "Sam and Tracy," then Sam and Tracy would have a tenancy in common.

A tenancy in common might have 2 owners or 22. Each owner is called a **tenant in common** or **co-tenant**. The tenants in common do not own a particular section of the property; they own an equal interest in the entire property. Quincy and Rebecca each own a 50 percent interest in the entire house.

Any co-tenant may convey her interest in the property to another person. Thus, if Rebecca moves 1,000 miles away, she may sell her 50 percent interest in the house to Sidney. Further, when a co-tenant dies, her interest in the property passes to her heirs, along with all of her other assets.

Partition. Since any tenant in common has the power to convey her interest, some people may find themselves sharing ownership with others they do not know or, worse, dislike. What to do? **Partition**, or division of the property among the co-tenants. Any co-tenant is entitled to demand partition of the property. If the various co-tenants cannot agree on a fair division, a co-tenant may request a court to do it. **All co-tenants have an absolute right to partition.**

A court will normally attempt a **partition by kind**, meaning that it actually divides the land equally among the co-tenants. If three co-tenants own a 300-acre farm, and the court can divide the land so that the three sections are of roughly equal value, it will perform a partition in kind, even if one or two of the co-tenants oppose partition. If partition by kind is impossible because there is no fair way to divide the property, the court will order the real estate sold and the proceeds divided equally.

Joint Tenancy

Joint tenancy is similar to tenancy in common but is used less frequently. The parties, called joint tenants, again own a percentage of the entire property and also have the absolute right of partition. The primary difference is that **a joint tenancy includes the right of survivorship**. This means that when one joint tenant dies, his interest in the property passes to *the surviving joint tenants*. Recall that a tenant in common, by contrast, has the power to leave his interest in the real estate to his

Tenancy in Common

Three tenants in common, each owning a 1/3 interest in the entire property.

Alice
dies
Kate
Kate inherits and becomes a tenant in common with Ben and Clem
Kate

Ben
Ben
sells
Larry
Larry buys and becomes a tenant in common with Kate and Clem

Clem
Clem
Clem

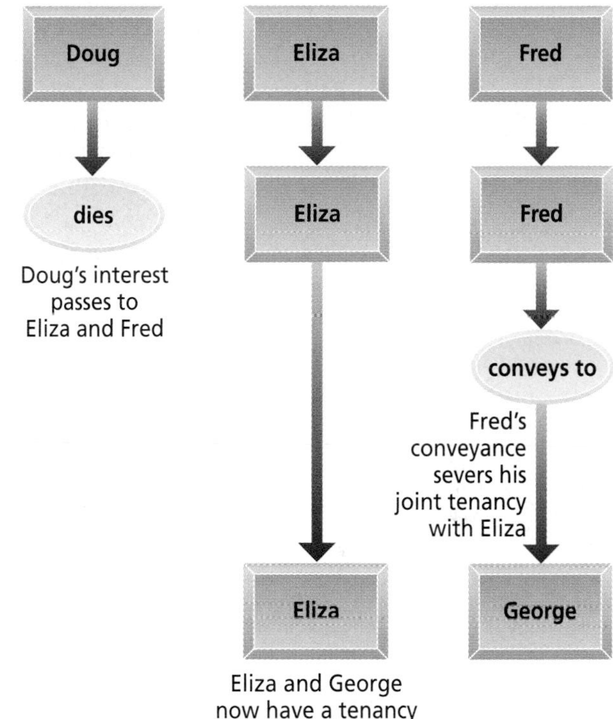

Exhibit 45.1

heirs. Because a joint tenant cannot leave the property to his heirs, courts do not favor this form of ownership. The law presumes that a concurrent estate is a tenancy in common; a court will interpret an estate as a joint tenancy only if the parties creating it clearly intended that result.

Joint tenancy has one other curious feature. Although joint tenants may not convey their interest by will, they may do so during their lifetime. If Frank and George own vacation property as joint tenants, Frank has the power to sell his interest to Harry. But as soon as he does so, the joint tenancy is **severed**, that is, broken. Harry and George are now tenants in common, and the right of survivorship is destroyed. Exhibit 45.1 illustrates tenancy in common and joint tenancy.

Marital Property

Two forms of concurrent ownership are available only to married couples: tenancy by the entirety and community property.

Tenancy by the Entirety. This form of ownership exists in slightly over half of the states. **The husband and wife each own the entire property, and they both have a right of survivorship.** So when the husband dies, his one-half interest in the property automatically passes to his wife. Neither party has a right to convey his or her interest. If the parties wish to sell their interests, they must do so together. An advantage of this is that no creditor may seize the property based on a debt incurred by only one spouse. If a husband goes bankrupt, creditors may not take his house if he and his wife own it as tenants by the entirety. Divorce terminates a tenancy by the entirety and leaves the two parties as tenants in common.

Community Property. French and Spanish settlers brought **community property** law to the South and West, and nine states still use this form of ownership for a married couple.[3] This system allows the husband and wife to maintain separate ownership of assets they bring to the marriage or inherit. Those assets are called **separate property**. They remain the private property of each spouse during the marriage. Either spouse may convey separate property to another person during the marriage and may leave the separate property to anyone he or she wishes. But income or assets that either party *earns* during the marriage are considered **community property, which must be equally shared** during the marriage, regardless of who earns it. Neither party may convey community property without the consent of the other. When a spouse dies, one-half of the community property goes to the surviving spouse, and the other half goes to the heirs of the deceased.

Suppose Margarita marries Jean Claude in Texas, a community property state. At the time of the marriage, Jean Claude owns a ranch but Margarita owns nothing. Jean Claude's ranch is separate property. He is free to convey it to someone else during his lifetime, and at his death he may leave it to anyone he wishes. During the marriage, Margarita inherits a Renoir painting worth $3 million; it is separate property, which she may freely dispose of. While married, Jean Claude earns $6,000 per year, translating children's poetry. Margarita earns $900,000 producing gory television shows. The income is community property, and each spouse is entitled to $453,000 per year. (A thorough and comprehensible discussion of one state's marital property laws can be found at **http://www.rbvdnr.com/te/1g.htm**.)

Condominiums and Cooperatives

There is a major difference between a condominium and a cooperative. How does that difference affect life inside the building?

Condominiums and cooperatives are forms of concurrent ownership that have enjoyed increasing popularity as the cost of home ownership has skyrocketed. Both forms of ownership are most common in apartment buildings with multiple units, though they can be used in other settings, such as a cluster of houses on a single parcel of land. Here we look at the typical setting, a multi-unit apartment building.

In a condominium, the owner of the apartment typically has a fee simple absolute in his particular unit. He is normally entitled to sell or lease the unit, must pay taxes on it, and may receive the normal tax deduction if he is carrying a mortgage. The apartment owner is also a tenant in common as to all common areas, such as hallways, parking areas, roofdeck, exterior grounds, and so forth. All unit owners belong to a condominium association, which manages the common areas. The association arranges exterior maintenance, such as snow plowing, lawn care, and painting. Each unit owner pays a set monthly fee for routine maintenance. The association may impose additional **assessments**, that is, special fees for unusual work, such as major roof repair.

In a cooperative, the residents generally do not own their particular unit. Instead, they are shareholders in a corporation that owns the building and leases specified units to the shareholders. Suppose Mandy buys unit 5F in an apartment building in New York City, where cooperatives are the norm. What Mandy is actually buying is a block of shares in the corporation that owns her building; she has no freehold estate in unit 5F. However, her shares entitle her to a perpetual lease on unit 5F.

The corporation not only owns the cooperative building, it *runs* the building, too. This means the corporation's board of directors have near dictatorial power over who buys shares in the cooperative and how owners live.

[3] The nine states are Arizona, California, Idaho, Louisiana, Nevada, New Mexico, Texas, Washington, and Wisconsin.

New York City has more cooperative apartments than anyplace else in the country and offers copious evidence of the unrestricted authority of co-op boards. Before permitting the sale of a unit, boards scrutinize prospective buyers, demanding exhaustive evidence of long-term financial stability. A board might reject an investment banker who earns $300,000 per year because she is a recent graduate, or because it disapproves of her social life—or without even giving a reason. Once in a co-op, a new owner may find the board even more intrusive. In some buildings, no dogs are allowed. Some boards require dogs to ride in freight elevators, while another went further, also restricting poorly dressed *guests* to service elevators. (Would the dogs resent this?) Various buildings ban pianos; some prohibit cooking in woks, because other residents complain about the smell; and at least one co-op board outlawed sitting in the lobby while wearing flippers. For more on the power of community associations generally, see **http://www.meislik.com/articles/art03.htm**.

FUTURE INTERESTS

A property owner may convey less than all of his rights to another person. For example, if Andrew has a fee simple absolute in Serenity Farm, he may convey a life estate to Claire, meaning that Claire gets the property only for her life. The remaining rights in the land are called future interests.

Future interests are presently existing nonpossessory rights that may or may not develop later. The rights are *presently existing* because they can be bought and sold immediately. They are *nonpossessory* because they do not permit the holder to take immediate possession of the land. Some future interests definitely create the right to possession later on, while other future interests create only the possibility of possession. We look at three future interests: a reversion, a remainder, and a possibility of reverter.

Reversion

If Andrew conveys Serenity Farm "to Claire for her life," Claire has a life estate in the property. Andrew has a **reversion**, meaning that upon Claire's death the property automatically returns to him or to his heirs. The significance of a future interest is this: even though Claire may live for 50 more years, Andrew may convey his reversion at any time. The right to own Serenity Farm upon Claire's death is a valuable right, and Andrew may sell the reversion to Xerxes for $1 million. Xerxes has to bide his time until Claire's death, but when she dies, the land is his.

Remainder

Suppose Andrew conveys Tranquility Farm "to Douglas for life, and then to Ernie." Douglas has a life estate and Ernie has a **remainder**. A remainder has exactly the same value as a reversion. The difference is that when the life tenant dies, the property goes to a named third person, not to the original owner.

Possibility of Reverter

This future interest applies when a property owner has granted a fee simple defeasible. Suppose Andrew conveys Utopia Farm "to Fredericka for as long as she continues to raise winter wheat." Fredericka has a fee simple defeasible and will keep the farm, and may leave it to her heirs, as long as the winter wheat grows. Andrew has the possibility of reverter because the farm will revert to him (or his heirs) if Fredericka (or her heirs) fails to grow winter wheat.

Future Interests

Example: Andrew owns a fee simple absolute in property and . . .	What was conveyed?	What future interest remains?
Conveys the property "to Betty."	Sale of the entire estate	None
Conveys the property "to Claire for her life."	Life estate	Andrew has a reversion. The property reverts to him or his heirs upon Claire's death.
Conveys the property "to Douglas for his life and then to Ernie."	Life estate	Ernie has a remainder and Andrew has nothing.
Conveys "to Fredericka as long as she grows winter wheat."	Fee simple defeasible	Andrew has a possibility of reverter. The property reverts to him or his heirs *if* Fredericka or any of her heirs cease to grow winter wheat.

NONPOSSESSORY INTERESTS

All of the estates and interests that we have examined thus far focused on one thing: possession of the land. Now we look at interests that *never* involve possession. These interests may be very valuable, even though the holder never lives on the land.

EASEMENTS

The Alabama Power Co. drove a flatbed truck over land owned by Thomas Burgess, damaging the property. The power company did this to reach its power lines and wooden transmission poles. Burgess had never given Alabama Power permission to enter his land, and he sued for the damage that the heavy trucks caused. He recovered—nothing. Alabama Power had an *easement* to use Burgess's land.

An easement gives one person the right to enter land belonging to another and make a limited use of it, without taking anything away. Burgess had bought his land from a man named Denton, who years earlier had sold an easement to Alabama Power. The easement gave the power company the right to construct several transmission poles on one section of Denton's land and to use reasonable means to reach the poles. Alabama Power owned that easement forever, and when Burgess bought the land, he took it subject to the easement. Alabama Power drove its trucks across a section of land where the power company had never gone before, and the easement did not explicitly give the company this right. But the court found that the company had no other way to reach its poles, and therefore the easement allowed this use. Burgess is stuck with his uninvited guest as long as he owns the land.[4]

There are two kinds of easements. The first, an **easement appurtenant**, benefits its owner in the use of *another parcel of land*. Suppose Madeline buys vacation land that is near a lake but without waterfront access. Wade owns lakefront land, and he sells Madeline an easement, allowing her to cross his property, on foot or in

[4] *Burgess v. Alabama Power Co.*, 658 So. 2d 435, 1995 Ala. LEXIS 119 (Ala. 1995).

a car, to reach the water. This is an easement appurtenant, since it benefits its owner (Madeline) in the use of her land. Madeline's land is the **dominant tenement**, that is, the property that benefits from the easement. Wade's parcel is the **servient tenement**, the land that is burdened by the easement. Typically, the dominant tenement is adjacent to the servient, but it need not be.

An easement appurtenant *runs with the land*, meaning that if the owner of the dominant tenement sells her land, the buyer acquires the easement as well. However, the owner may *not* sell an easement by itself to someone else. If Madeline sells her property to Jason, he acquires the right to waltz across Wade's land. But Madeline has no right to sell only the easement to Jason, while retaining her property.

The second kind of easement, an **easement in gross**, benefits its owner but *not in the use of other land*. The Alabama Power Co. had an easement in gross in Burgess's land. The company had the right to install power lines across the property and use reasonable means to reach them. However, this right did not benefit any other property owned by the company, so it was an easement in gross. Most easements in gross *may* be sold. If Alabama Power no longer needed its power lines on Burgess's land, it could sell its easement to another company, for example, a cable television company.[5]

Creation of Easements

Grant or Reservation. Property owners normally create easements in one of two ways. A **grant** occurs when a landowner expressly intends to convey an easement to someone else. This is how Alabama Power acquired its easement. The company offered to buy the right to use the land, and Denton agreed to sell. The parties signed an agreement and *recorded* the easement, meaning they placed it on file in the land registry, so that interested parties were on notice. When Burgess bought the land from Denton, he knew (or should have known) about the easement.

A **reservation** occurs when an owner sells land but keeps some right to enter the property. A farmer might sell 40 acres to a developer but reserve an easement giving him the right to drive his equipment across a specified strip of the land.

Implication or Necessity. Easements are less frequently created in these two ways. An **easement by implication** arises when an owner subdivides land in a way that *clearly implies* the creation of an easement in favor of the new parcels. Suppose Jason owns lakefront property with a boat ramp. He subdivides his land and sells several parcels that do not reach the lake, promising all purchasers use of the boat ramp. This subdivision clearly implies the right to cross Jason's land to use the boat ramp, since there is no other access. The new owners have an easement by implication.

An **easement by necessity** arises when the dominant tenement *absolutely must* make use of other property. Yolanda leases a ninth floor apartment to Darrin. Darrin has an easement by necessity to use the stairs and elevators, since he has no other method of reaching his apartment, short of skydiving.

Prescription. Joseph Leto bought undeveloped land in 1946 and used it on weekends for family gatherings, picnicking, and nature walks. He reached his property by using a jeep trail that crossed land he did not own, land eventually purchased by Digital Equipment Corp. (DEC). Leto continued to use the trail for nearly 30 years, until DEC sued to keep him off its property. Neither DEC nor the previous owner had ever given Leto permission to use the land. Did Leto have an

---

[5] A related nonpossessory estate—and one that can benefit society and posterity—is a **conservation easement**, in which a property owner agrees to forbid certain development on her property, forever. For an interesting discussion of how the Canadian province of Ontario uses these easements to preserve historic architecture and virgin wilderness, take a look at **http://www.heritagefdn.on.ca/Heritage/conservation2.htm**.

easement? Yes, he had an **easement by prescription**.[6] An easement by prescription may arise when someone makes use of property belonging to another, if his use is:

- Open and notorious
- Adverse to the owner, and
- Continuous and uninterrupted for the number of years required by local statute.

The theory of easement by prescription is that landowners must take some initiative to protect their property rights. If they fail to do so, they may lose certain rights in their land (or, as we will see in the section on adverse possession, they may lose the land altogether). But someone seeking an easement by prescription must satisfy each element. His use of the property must be open and notorious, so that a reasonable landowner would be aware of what is happening and have a chance to stop it. The use must be adverse to the owner, meaning without the owner's permission. A landowner who *permits* another to cross his land nullifies any possibility of easement by implication. Finally, the use must continue without interruption for as long as required by the state statute, which is often seven years but may be more or less in a particular state. Joseph Leto continued his use of the trail for nearly 30 years, much longer than the local statute required. Once he acquired the easement by prescription, it was potentially his forever, and when DEC acquired the land, it did so subject to Leto's easement.

During the nineteenth century, many railroads obtained easements to lay down rails, and, by 1900, trains ran on over 300,000 miles of track throughout the country. Today, railroads use less than half that much track. What happens to the thousands of miles of unused land? Some state laws, and some contracts, require property to revert to the owner when an easement is abandoned. Yet federal, state, and local governments have turned many miles of unused track into trails for hiking and biking. Environmentalists strongly support this "rails to trails" conversion. Some property owners believe that their reversionary rights are being violated and demand compensation. Local governments point out that they continue to shore up and maintain the original rail bank, for possible future train use, and that the easements are therefore not abandoned.

Easements, whether created by grant or otherwise, come in all sizes. Is the easement in the following case *too* big?

CARVIN v. ARKANSAS POWER AND LIGHT
14 F.3d 399, 1993 U.S. App. LEXIS 33986
United States Court of Appeals for the Eighth Circuit, 1993

Facts: Between 1923 and 1947, Arkansas Power & Light (AP&L) constructed several dams on two Arkansas lakes, Hamilton and Catherine. The company then obtained "flood easements" on property adjoining the lakes. AP&L obtained some of the easements by grant and others by reservation, selling lakeside property and keeping the easement. These flood easements permitted AP&L to "clear of trees, brush and other obstructions and to submerge by water" certain acreage, which was described exactly. AP&L prop-

[6] *Digital Equipment Corp. v. Leto*, Mass. Lawyers Weekly No. 14–008–94 (Mass. Land Court 1994).

erly recorded the easements, and when the current landowners bought lakeside property, they were aware of the documents.

During one 12-hour period in May 1990, extraordinarily heavy rains fell in the Ouachita River Basin, including both lakes. In some areas, over 10 inches of rain fell, causing the water to reach the highest levels ever recorded, even washing away the equipment designed to measure rainfall. To avoid flooding Lake Hamilton, AP&L opened the gates of a dam called Carpenter. This caused Lake Catherine to flood, with water in some places rising 25 feet. This flood caused massive damage to the plaintiffs' houses, with water in some cases rising to the roof level.

Several dozen landowners sued, claiming that AP&L was negligent in opening one dam without simultaneously opening another and also in failing to warn homeowners of the intended action. The federal district court granted summary judgment for AP&L, based on the flood easements, and the landowners appealed.

You Be the Judge: Did the easements relieve AP&L from liability for flooding?

Argument for the Landowners: Your honors, no sane homeowner would give a power company the right to do what this company has done. AP&L has destroyed land, demolished houses, and ruined lives. AP&L opened a dam knowing that this would flood the shores of Lake Catherine and inundate dozens of properties. Does the power company think the homeowners are simply crazy? That is the only reason someone would voluntarily permit such conduct.

These flood easements were many years old, created long before many of the present owners bought their property. None of them ever dreamed something like this could happen. Even if the easements were once valid, they should not be enforced any longer.

Further, even if the easements were still valid, and we maintain they were not, no easement authorizes negligence. At most the easements would permit some minimal flooding by a carefully controlled process, after adequate notice to everyone concerned. Here there was no notice, no care, no decency at all. AP&L should not be allowed to rely on ancient pieces of paper to wash away land and ruin lives.

Argument for AP&L: Your honors, the flooding was caused by an act of God—unprecedented rain—not by anything AP&L did. It is true that the company opened the dam without notice, for the simple reason that there was no time to give notice. AP&L not only had the right to act quickly, it had the *duty* to act quickly, to protect residents of a much wider area.

Your honors, a flood easement exists for one reason: to allow a company, when necessary, to flood land. The company knew it had the legal right to do this, based on the easements, and that there was no alternative.

The landowners argue that no sane person would grant such an easement, but in every instance here, that is just what has happened. It is true that many of these owners did not grant the easements, but their predecessors did. The value of the property would naturally decline somewhat with a flood easement attached, and as a result these owners paid less for their property. They were on notice of the easements, every one of which was recorded, and they had plenty of opportunity to decide whether to take on the risk. All of the owners made calculated decisions to accept the risk, and they must now live with their choices.

PROFIT

A *profit* gives one person the right to enter land belonging to another and take something away. You own 100 acres of vacation property, and suddenly a mining company informs you that the land contains valuable nickel deposits. You may choose to sell a profit to the mining company, allowing it to enter your land and take away the nickel. You receive cash up front, and the company earns money from the sale of the mineral. The rules about creating and transferring easements apply to profits, as well.

LICENSE

A license gives the holder temporary permission to enter upon another's property. Unlike an easement or profit, a license is a *temporary* right. When you attend a basketball game by buying a ticket, the basketball club that sells you the ticket is the licensor and you are the licensee. You are entitled to enter the licensor's premises, namely the basketball arena, and to remain during the game, though the club can revoke the license if you behave unacceptably.

MORTGAGE

Generally, in order to buy a house, a prospective owner must borrow money. The bank or other lender will require security before it hands over its money, and the most common form of security for a real estate loan is a mortgage. **A mortgage is a security interest in real property.** The homeowner who borrows money is the **mortgagor**, because she is *giving* the mortgage to the lender. The lender, in turn, is the **mortgagee**, the party acquiring a security interest. The mortgagee in most cases obtains a **lien** on the house, meaning the right to foreclose on the property if the mortgagor fails to pay back the money borrowed. A mortgagee forecloses by taking legal possession of the property, auctioning it to the highest bidder, and using the proceeds to pay off the loan. (For an excellent discussion of foreclosure sales, and the opportunities and dangers they present, see **http://users.aol.com/jpfalk/fcsales.htm**.)

SALE OF REAL PROPERTY

For most people, buying or selling a house is the biggest, most important financial transaction they will make. Here we consider several of the key issues that may arise.

SELLER'S OBLIGATIONS CONCERNING THE PROPERTY

Historically, the common law recognized the rule of *caveat emptor* in the sale of real property—that is, let the buyer beware. If a buyer walked into his new living room and fell through the floor into a lake of toxic waste, it was his tough luck. But the common law changes with the times, and today courts place an increasing burden of fairness on the sellers of real estate. Two of the most significant obligations are the implied warranty of habitability and the duty to disclose defects.

Implied Warranty of Habitability

Most states now impose an implied warranty of habitability on a builder who sells a new home. This means that, whether he wants to or not, the builder is guaranteeing that the new house contains **adequate materials and good workmanship**. The law implies this warranty because of the inherently unequal position of builder and buyer. Some defects might be obvious to a lay observer, such as a room with no roof or a front porch that sways whenever the neighbors sneeze. But only the builder will know if he made the frame with proper wood, if the heating system was second rate, the electrical work shabby, and so forth. Note that the law implies this warranty only to protect buyers of residential property. There is *no* such implied warranty for the sale of new *commercial* buildings, although over the next decade or two some courts could begin to impose one.

In most states, the warranty extends for a reasonable time, not only to the original purchaser but to subsequent buyers as well. How long is reasonable? Ask Rich Rosen.

HERSHEY v. RICH ROSEN CONSTRUCTION CO.
169 Ariz. 110, 817 P.2d 55, 1991 Ariz. App. LEXIS 205
Arizona Court of Appeals, 1991

Facts: In 1976, Rich Rosen Construction Co. built a stucco house in Phoenix, Arizona. The initial buyer lived in the home without problems until 1985, when he sold it to a second owner, who rented the house to Marjatta and James Hershey. After the Hersheys lived in the house for six months, they offered to buy it. They conducted a "walk-around inspection," saw no problems, and bought it in May 1986. After a heavy rainstorm in August 1987, the Hersheys noticed bulging in the stucco. The expert who examined the stucco reported that, "The stucco exterior on your home is one of the worst examples of material selection and application that I have encountered in the past 10–12 years. I would categorize the material selection and workmanship as below average to almost criminal."

The trial court awarded the Hersheys $16,500, the cost of repairing the stucco. Rosen appealed, claiming first that the Hershey's inspection of the house was inadequate, and second that even if there was an implied warranty of habitability, it was unreasonable to enforce it 12 years after he built the house.

Issues: Did the Hersheys adequately inspect the house? Was a warranty of habitability in effect 12 years after construction?

Excerpts from Judge Jacobson's Decision: Another of defendant's suggestions of a defense was that plaintiffs failed to reasonably inspect the home before purchasing. It claims that such an inspection would have revealed the potential of the disastrous defect of workmanship this house had. There is no evidence of such a claim. Plaintiffs bought the home in 1986. At that time, there were a few cracks in the stucco of a normal nature. Not until 1987 did separation of the stucco from the exterior sheathing begin to manifest itself in chunks falling off and bulging. Its rapid acceleration since indicates that only from 1987 would a reasonable purchaser have been put on any kind of notice that a disastrous problem lay hidden beneath the exterior stucco and paint.

We disagree with defendant's contention that a "reasonable inspection" must include, as one of its components, an inspection by an expert or professional home inspection service to scrutinize the house for internal defects prior to purchase. Rather, under the policies stated in [earlier cases], an implied warranty should be voided for lack of a "reasonable inspection" only if the defect could have been discovered during an inspection made by the average purchaser, not an expert.

Defendant also contends that the trial court's extension of an implied warranty more than 12 years after completion of construction is unreasonable, and fails to meet the limitations on the warranty set forth by the supreme court in [earlier cases]. The standard to be applied in determining whether or not there has been a breach of warranty is one of reasonableness in light of surrounding circumstances. The age of a home, its maintenance, the use to which it has been put, are but a few factors entering into this factual determination at trial.

In this case, the trial court heard expert testimony that a stucco exterior has a normal life expectancy in the Arizona desert of 30 to 50 years, and defendant conceded that the stucco process applied to plaintiff's house could be reasonably expected to last more than the 12 years that it did. The evidence also established that the damage from the defective stucco application was gradual and progressive, occurring over a period of at least ten years, and was not discoverable by reasonable inspection until it actually was discovered. Under these circumstances, we find no error in the trial court's conclusion that, based on the expected life of the defective component of the house, 12 years was not an unreasonable period for an implied warranty of habitability and workmanship to exist.

Based on the foregoing, we *affirm* the judgment of the trial court.

Duty to Disclose Defects

The seller of a home must disclose facts that a buyer does not know and cannot readily observe, if they materially affect the property's value. Roy and Charlyne Terrell owned a house in the Florida Keys, where zoning codes required all living areas to be 15 feet above sea level. They knew that their house violated the code because a bedroom and bathroom were on the ground floor. They offered to sell the house to Robert Revitz, assuring him that the property complied with all codes and that flood insurance would cost about $350 per year. Revitz bought the house, moved in, and later learned that because of the code violations, flood insurance would be slightly more expensive—costing just over *$36,000 per year*. He sued and won. The court declared that the Terrells had a duty to disclose the code violations; it ordered a rescission of the contract, meaning that Revitz got his money back. The court mentioned that the duty to disclose was wide-ranging and included leaking roofs, insect infestation, cracks in walls and foundations, and any other problems that a buyer might be unable to discern.[7] We discuss this rapidly evolving area of the law more fully in Chapter 14, on capacity and consent.

SALES CONTRACT AND TITLE EXAMINATION

The statute of frauds requires that an agreement to sell real property must be in writing to be enforceable. A contract for the sale of a house is often several pages of dense legal reading, in which the lawyers for the buyer and seller attempt to allocate risks for every problem that might go wrong. However, the contract *need* not be so thorough. A written contract for the sale of land is generally valid if it includes the names of all parties, a precise description of the property being sold, the price, and signatures.

Once the parties have agreed to the terms and signed a contract, the buyer's lawyer performs a **title examination**, which means that she, or someone she hires, searches through the local land registry for all documents that relate to the property. The purpose is to ensure that the seller actually has valid title to this land, since it is dispiriting to give someone half a million dollars for property and then discover that he never owned it and neither do you. Even if the seller owns the land, his title may be subject to other claims, such as an easement or profit. In some cases the buyer's lawyer will issue a certificate of title, describing precisely what title the seller has (such as fee simple absolute) and whether there are any limitations to it (such as a profit to remove all trees). Or the lawyer may hire a title company to perform the search and issue a report. A buyer may also choose to buy title insurance, a policy in which the insurance company, after making its own title examination, guarantees to pay the buyer for any losses if she later discovers the seller lacked good title.

CLOSING AND DEEDS

While the buyer is checking the seller's title, she also probably needs to arrange financing, as described above in the section on mortgages. When the title work is complete and the buyer has arranged financing, the parties arrange a **closing**, a

[7] *Revitz v. Terrell*, 572 So. 2d 996, 1990 Fla. App. LEXIS 9655 (Fla. Dist. Ct. App. 1990).

meeting at which the property is actually sold. The seller brings to the closing a **deed**, which is the document proving ownership of the land. The seller signs the deed over to the buyer in exchange for the purchase price. The buyer pays the price either with a certified check and/or by having her lender pay. If a lender pays part or all of the price, the buyer executes a mortgage to the lender as part of the closing.

Different types of deeds provide different assurances about what the seller is conveying to the buyer. **A general warranty deed normally contains the following five covenants (promises):**

- *Covenant of Seisin*. (Did we mention that some terms might sound medieval?) Here, the grantor warrants that he owns whatever estate he is conveying. If the deed describes a fee simple absolute, this covenant guarantees that is what the grantor is delivering.

- *Covenant of Right to Convey*. The grantor promises that he has the power to make this conveyance.

- *Covenant against Encumbrances*. Here the grantor is assuring that the land is free of any easement, profit, mortgage, and the like.

- *Covenant of Quiet Enjoyment*. The grantor assures that no other person can lawfully claim the land.

- *Covenant of Warranty*. The grantor promises to defend the grantee if any third party claims to own the land.

The general warranty deed normally makes all of these covenants against problems arising *before* the grantor took the land or *while* he owned it. That makes this the best deed from the buyer's point of view.

A **special warranty deed** is more limited. It typically includes the same five covenants listed above, but the covenants apply only against problems arising *while* the grantor owned the land, *not* those that might have arisen earlier.

A **quitclaim deed** warrants nothing. The grantor simply transfers whatever right, title, or interest he has, if any. Most buyers of property will refuse to accept a quitclaim deed. The real value of this deed lies in clearing up property disputes. Suppose there is a possible claim that Becky has an easement by prescription to drive across Nick's land, even though Becky never uses that route. To have clear title to his land, Nick may ask Becky to execute a quitclaim deed. If she does so, the parties never need to determine whether Becky had a valid claim, since she is conveying any rights she may have had to Nick. For a sample quitclaim deed, pack up and move to **http://www.gate.net/~legalsvc/quit.html**.

RECORDING

Recording the deed means filing it with the official state registry. The registry clerk places a photocopy of the deed in the agency's bound volumes and indexes the deed by the name of the grantor and the grantee. Recording is a critical step in the sale of land, because it puts all the world on notice that the grantor has sold the land. It has little effect between grantor and grantee: once the deed and money are exchanged, the sale is generally final between those two. But recording is vital to protect the general public.

Suppose Roger sells his farm to Alicia for $600,000. Alicia records her deed within minutes of the purchase. The public is now on notice that Alicia owns the property. A month later Roger offers to sell the land to Dana for $500,000. Dana must check the registry, where she will quickly learn that Roger does not own the land. Suppose that, without checking the registry of deeds, Dana pays the full amount and Roger gives her a fraudulent deed. Alicia's property is safe, and Dana gets nothing: she was obligated to search the registry before buying. Dana has a valid claim against Roger, but if he has skipped town, the claim may be useless.

By contrast, suppose that Alicia sells the land to Pete, who *fails* to record his deed. A week later, Alicia offers the same property to Reggie, who checks the registry and sees no mention of the sale to Pete. If Reggie pays for the land, he will probably get valid title to it because he is a **bona fide purchaser**, that is, someone who gives value (money) in good faith for property. Reggie believed in good faith that Alicia owned the farm, since his search of the registry indicated no defects in his title. He gave value by paying $500,000. A bona fide purchaser generally takes the land over a buyer (Pete) who failed to record.

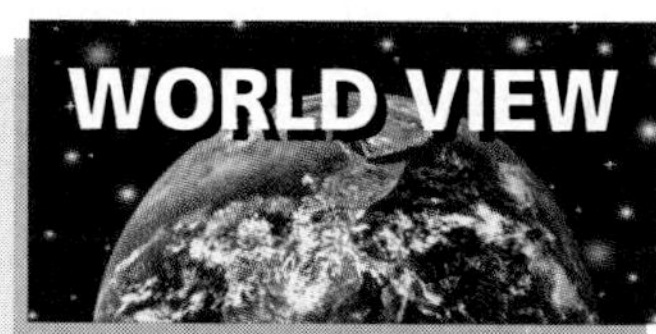

You have spotted your dream vacation property on a pristine beach in Baja California. The next-door neighbor, a retired U.S. citizen, offers to sell you the property at a fair price. You draw up a contract in English and take the plunge. Mistake! Buying land in any foreign country presents pitfalls that you must consider. You might construct a $700,000 beach house, only to discover that you do not own the sandy soil on which it stands. In Mexico, all land within 66 feet of the high-tide mark is federal property and cannot be sold to anyone. Further, as a foreigner, you have no right to buy Mexican real estate within 31 miles of the ocean. Thousands of innocent U.S. citizens have lost millions of dollars paying for Mexican property they never acquire. Your friendly neighbor may have known of the local law and intended to cheat you, or he may have been equally ignorant and be horrified to learn that his own house stands on slippery ground. Know and respect local laws and customs before you write a check. (And by the way, in Mexico, a contract is binding only if written in Spanish.)

ADVERSE POSSESSION

You may recall Paul Termarco and Gene Murdoch, who opened this chapter by trying to sell you—and all the world—a hot dog from an island in the middle of a New Jersey lake. As we mentioned then, Termarco and Murdoch have their sights set on more than mustard and relish: they hope that by using the island *as if* they own it, they *will* own it. They are relying on the doctrine of adverse possession. This old rule of law is analogous to easement by prescription, which we analyzed earlier. Under certain conditions, easement by prescription permits a person who makes use of land continuously to establish an easement for that use. Adverse possession goes even farther and allows someone to take title to land if she meets certain tests.

To gain ownership of land by adverse possession, the user must prove:

- Entry and exclusive possession
- Open and notorious possession
- A claim adverse to the owner, and
- Continuous possession for a statutory period.

ENTRY AND EXCLUSIVE POSSESSION

The user must take physical possession of the land and must be the only one to do so. If the owner is still occupying the land, or if other members of the public share its use, there can be no adverse possession.

OPEN AND NOTORIOUS POSSESSION

The user's presence must be visible and generally known in the area, so that the owner is on notice that his title is contested. This ensures that the owner can protect his property by ejecting the user. Someone making secret use of the land gives the owner no opportunity to do this, and hence acquires no rights in the land.

A CLAIM ADVERSE TO THE OWNER

The user must clearly assert that the land is his. He does not need to register a deed or take other legal steps, but he must act as though he is the sole owner. If the user occupies the land with the owner's permission, there is no adverse claim and the user acquires no rights in the property. To succeed, the user must protect his possession of the land against all others the way any normal landowner would. This may mean erecting a home if the area is residential, or fencing property that is used to graze cattle, or posting "no trespassing" signs in a wilderness area.

Must the user *believe* he has a title or only act as though he does? The states are divided on this question. Many states focus only on the adverse *acts* of the user: it is sufficient if his conduct indicates he is the sole owner, regardless of what he thinks. This is the modern trend. But other states require a mistaken *belief* that the user has title to the land. For example, some states require that the user demonstrate "color of title," meaning that he has some document that *he believed* gave him good title to the land, though in reality it never did.

CONTINUOUS POSSESSION FOR THE STATUTORY PERIOD

State statutes on adverse possession prescribe a period of years for continuous use of the land. Originally, most states required about 20 years to gain adverse possession, but the trend has been to shorten this period. Many states now demand 10 years, but a few require only 5 years' use. The reason for shortening the period is to reward those who *make use* of land. Even within a single state, statutes may prescribe various periods for different types of land. For example, adverse possession in a wilderness area may require more than 20 years' possession.

Regardless of the length required, the use must be continuous. In a residential area, the user would have to occupy the land year round for the prescribed period. In a wilderness area generally used only in the summer, a user could gain ownership by seasonal use.

A user may be able to meet the statutory period by **tacking**, which permits her to add onto her years of occupancy any years certain predecessors were in possession. The predecessors must have been in *privity* with the current user, meaning there was some legal relationship. Suppose that for 12 years, Martha adversely possesses land owned by Jake. Martha then moves, selling her interest in the land to Nancy, who occupies the land for 9 years. The total of 21 years is sufficient for adverse possession in any state, and Nancy now owns the land.

Sailing back to Hot Dog Island, how will Murdoch and Termarco fare? They are off to a good start. They have certainly entered on the land and established themselves as the exclusive occupants. Their use is open and notorious, allowing anyone who claims ownership to take steps to eject them from the property. Their actions are adverse to anyone else's claim. If the two hot dog entrepreneurs keep grilling those dogs for the full statutory period, they should take title to the island.

In the following case, the couple claiming adverse possession must do without friendly hot dog sellers because they have taken up residence in a ghost town.

RAY v. BEACON HUDSON MOUNTAIN CORP.

88 N.Y.2d 154, 666 N.E.2d 532, 1996 N.Y. LEXIS 676
Court of Appeals of New York, 1996

Facts: In 1931, Rose Ray purchased a cottage in a mountain-top resort town in the Adirondacks, at the same time agreeing to rent the land on which the structure stood. The long-term lease required her to pay the real estate taxes and provided that when the tenancy ended, the landlord would buy back the cottage at fair market value. In 1960, the landlord terminated the lease of everyone in the town, so Ray and all other residents packed up and left. She died in 1962, without ever getting a penny for the cottage. The next year, Mt. Beacon Incline Lands, Inc. bought all rights to the abandoned 156-acre resort.

Robert and Margaret Ray, the son and daughter-in-law of Rose Ray, reentered the cottage and began to use it one month per year, every summer from 1963 to 1988. They paid taxes, insured the property, installed utilities, and posted "no trespassing" signs.

In 1978, Beacon Hudson bought the resort in a tax foreclosure sale. Finally, in 1988, the Rays filed suit, claiming title to the cottage by adverse possession. Beacon Hudson counter-claimed, seeking to eject the Rays. The trial court ruled for the couple. The appellate court reversed, stating that the Rays had been absent too frequently to achieve adverse possession. The Rays appealed to New York's highest court.

Issue: **Did the Rays acquire title by adverse possession?**

Excerpts from Judge Titone's Decision: The element of continuity will be defeated where the adverse possessor interrupts the period of possession by abandoning the premises. However, the hostile claimant's actual possession of the property need not be constant to satisfy the "continuity" element of the claim. Rather, the requirement of continuous possession is satisfied when the adverse claimant's acts of possessing the property are consistent with acts of possession that ordinary owners of like properties would undertake.

Here, defendant claims that plaintiffs' possession of the property was not continuous because they were physically present there for only one month out of the summer season. However, this argument fails to take into consideration plaintiffs' other acts of dominion and control over the premises that are indicative of their actual possession of an estate in land. Here, plaintiffs' installation of utilities and over-all preservation of the cottage, a permanent and substantial structure, in a veritable ghost town, for the duration of the statutory period demonstrates continuous, actual occupation of land by improvement. Thus, plaintiffs' actual summertime use for a full month each season, coupled with their repeated acts of repelling trespassers, improving, posting, padlocking and securing of the property in their absences throughout the statutory period, demonstrated their continuous dominion and control over, and thus possession of, the property.

Such seasonal presence, coupled with plaintiffs' preservation of the premises for the statutory period of 10 years—which was made more obvious by the fact that all neighboring structures had collapsed due to vandalism and abandonment—was sufficient to place the record owner on notice of their hostile and exclusive claim of ownership.

[The appellate court is reversed and the Rays obtain title by adverse possession.]

LAND USE REGULATION

NUISANCE LAW

A nuisance is an unprivileged interference with a person's use and enjoyment of her property. Offensive noise, odors, or smoke often give rise to nuisance claims. Courts typically balance the utility of the act that is causing the problem against the harm done to neighboring property owners. If a suburban homeowner begins to raise pigs in her backyard, the neighbors may find the bouquet offensive; a court will probably issue an **abatement**, that is, an order requiring the homeowner to eliminate the nuisance. For some practical advice on how to quiet noisy neighbors, see http://lawcrawler.findlaw.com/NOLO/nn167.html.

Community members can use the old doctrine of nuisance for more serious problems than pigs. An apartment building in Berkeley, California, became widely known as a drug house, and the neighbors suffered. Here is how two of the neighbors described their lives:

> I have been confronted by the drug dealers, drug customers, and prostitutes that frequent and work around and from 1615–1617 Russell Street. Weekly I have lost many hours of sleep from the cars that burn rubber after each drug buy in the middle of the night.
>
> Because of this illegal activity my child is unable to use our front yard and I even have to check the back yard since it has been intruded upon from time to time by people running from the police. He is learning to count by how many gunshots he hears and can't understand why he can't even enjoy our rose garden.

These were but two of the affidavits written by neighbors of a 36-unit building owned by Albert Lew. Month after month neighbors complained to Lew that his tenants were destroying the neighborhood. But Lew refused to evict the drug dealers or take any serious steps to limit the crime. So the neighbors used the law of nuisance to restore their community.

Sixty-six neighbors of the drug house each filed a small claims case against Lew, claiming that he was permitting a nuisance to exist on his property. The neighbors won their small claims cases, but Lew appealed, as he had a right to, for a new trial in Superior Court. A sergeant testified that he had been to the building over 250 times during two years. Residents testified about how frightening life had become. The Superior Court awarded damages of $218,325 to the neighbors and the court of appeals affirmed the award, holding that neighbors injured by a nuisance may seek an abatement and damages. As Lew discovered, the law of nuisance can be a powerful weapon for a better neighborhood.[8]

ZONING

Zoning statutes are state laws that permit local communities to regulate building and land use. The local communities, whether cities, towns, or counties, then pass zoning ordinances that control many aspects of land development. For example, a town's zoning ordinance may divide the community into an industrial zone where factories may be built, a commercial zone in which stores of a certain size are allowed, and several residential zones in which only houses may be constructed. Within the residential zones there may be further divisions, for example,

[8] *Lew v. Superior Court*, 20 Cal. App. 4th 866, 1993 Cal. App. LEXIS 1198 (Cal. Ct. App. 1993).

permitting two-family houses in certain areas and requiring larger lots in others. For a look at the zoning code of one city—Portland, Oregon—go to **http://www.europa.com/pdxplan/zoning/zonetoc.html#10**.

An owner prohibited by an ordinance from erecting a certain kind of building, or adding on to his present building, may seek a **variance** from the zoning board, meaning an exception granted for special reasons unique to the property. Whether a board will grant a variance generally depends upon the type of the proposed building, the nature of the community, the reason the owner claims he is harmed by the ordinance, and the reaction of neighbors.

Many people abhor "adult" businesses, such as strip clubs and pornography shops. Urban experts agree that a large number of these concerns in a neighborhood often causes crime to increase and property values to drop. Nonetheless, many people patronize such businesses, which can earn a good profit. Should a city have the right to restrict adult businesses? New York City officials determined that the number of sex shops had grown steadily for two decades and that their presence harmed various neighborhoods. With the support of community groups, the city passed a zoning ordinance that prohibited adult businesses from all residential neighborhoods, from some commercial districts, *and* from being within 500 feet of schools, houses of worship, day-care centers, or other sex shops (to avoid clustering). Owners and patrons of these shops protested, claiming that the city was unfairly denying the public access to a form of entertainment that it obviously desired. Are such ordinances good? Are they fair? Why or why not?

EMINENT DOMAIN

Eminent domain is the power of the government to take private property for public use. A government may need land to construct a highway, airport, university, or public housing. All levels of government—federal, state, and local—have this power. But the Fifth Amendment of the United States Constitution states: ". . . nor shall private property be taken for public use, without just compensation." The Supreme Court has held that this clause, the Takings Clause, applies not only to the federal government but also to state and local governments. So, although all levels of government have the power to take property, they must pay the owner a fair price.

A "fair price" generally means the reasonable market value of the land. Generally, if the property owner refuses the government's offer, the government will file suit seeking **condemnation** of the land, that is, a court order specifying what compensation is just and awarding title to the government.

A related issue concerns local governments requiring property owners to *dedicate* some of their land to public use, in exchange for zoning permission to build or expand on their own property. For example, if a store owner wishes to expand his store, a town might grant zoning permission only if the owner dedicates a different part of his property for use as a public bike path. The Supreme Court has recently diminished the power of local governments to require such dedication.[9]

---

[9] The Supreme Court's ruling came in *Dolan v. City of Tigard*, 512 U.S. 374, 114 S. Ct. 2309, 1994 U.S. LEXIS 4836 (1994), which we discuss in more detail in Chapter 4, on constitutional law.

CHAPTER CONCLUSION

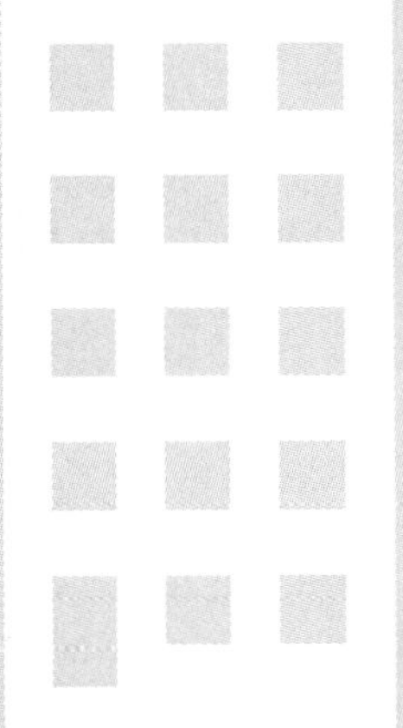

Real property law is ancient but forceful, as waterfront property owners discovered when a power company flooded their land and an old-fashioned *easement* deprived them of compensation. Had the owners truly understood nonpossessory interests when they bought their property, they would have realized the risk the investment represented. Similarly, a knowledge of the various freehold estates will enable a property owner to avoid the kind of error that cost the city of Red Bluff its library building. Real property may not be quite as important today as it was in medieval England, but it is still a source of wealth and power—and worth understanding.

CHAPTER REVIEW

1. Real property includes land, buildings, air and subsurface rights, plant life, and fixtures. A fixture is any good that has become attached to other real property, such as land.
2. A fee simple absolute provides the owner with the greatest possible control of the property, including the right to make any lawful use of it and to sell it.
3. A fee simple defeasible may terminate upon the occurrence of some limiting event.
4. A life estate permits the owner to possess the property during her life, but not to sell it or leave it to heirs.
5. When two or more people own real property at the same time, they have a concurrent estate. In both a tenancy in common and a joint tenancy, all owners have a share in the entire property. The primary difference is that joint tenants have the right of survivorship, meaning that when a joint tenant dies, his interest passes to the other joint tenants. A tenant in common has the power to leave her estate to her heirs.
6. Tenancy by the entirety and community property are both concurrent estates available only to married couples.
7. In a condominium, the owner of an apartment generally has a fee simple absolute in the particular unit, whereas in a cooperative, a resident owns shares in a corporation and then leases his unit from the corporation.
8. Future interests are presently existing nonpossessory rights that may or may not develop later.
9. An easement gives a person the right to enter land belonging to another and make a limited use of it, without taking anything away.
10. A profit gives one person the right to enter land belonging to another and take something away, such as timber or minerals.
11. The implied warranty of habitability means that a builder selling a new home guarantees the adequacy of materials and workmanship.
12. The seller of a home must disclose facts that a buyer does not know and cannot readily observe, if they materially affect the property's value.
13. A general warranty deed offers the greatest protection to a buyer, a special warranty deed less protection, and a quitclaim deed very little.

14. Adverse possession permits the user of land to gain title if he can prove entry and exclusive possession, open and notorious possession, a claim adverse to the owner, and continuous possession for the required statutory period.

15. Nuisance law, zoning ordinances, and eminent domain all permit a government to regulate property and in some cases to take it for public use.

PRACTICE TEST

1. Thayer owned a farm in Illinois. For over half a century, various farmers had cut across his land to reach a second farm that had no other access to the road. Thayer never granted permission to these other farmers, but neither had he ever stopped them. In 1989, Page bought the second farm, of about 120 acres. He, too, cut across Thayer's property to reach the town road. Shortly after buying his farm, Page began to improve his access across Thayer's property. Page brought in large road-building equipment to level and solidify the road and make it safe for his heavy farm equipment. Thayer attempted to stop this work by constructing a barricade across the entrance to the disputed area. Page sued. Was he entitled to use and improve the "road" across Thayer's property?

2. Paul and Shelly Higgins had two wood stoves in their home. Each rested on, but was not attached to, a built-in brick platform. The downstairs wood stove was connected to the chimney flue and was used as part of the main heating system for the house. The upstairs stove, in the master bedroom, was purely decorative. It had no stovepipe connecting it to the chimney. The Higginses sold their house to Jack Everitt, and neither party said anything about the two stoves. Is Everitt entitled to either stove? Both stoves?

3. In 1944, W. E. Collins conveyed land to the Church of God of Prophecy. The deed said: "This deed is made with the full understanding that should the property fail to be used for the Church of God, it is to be null and void and property to revert to W. E. Collins or heirs." In the late 1980s, the church wished to move to another property and sought a judicial ruling that it had the right to sell the land. The trial court ruled that the church owned a fee simple absolute and had the right to sell the property. Comment.

4. Howard Geib, Walker McKinney, and John D. McKinney owned two vacation properties as joint tenants with right of survivorship. The parties were not getting along well, and Geib petitioned the court to partition the properties. The trial court ruled that the fairest way to do this was to sell both properties and divide the proceeds. The two McKinneys appealed, claiming that a partition by sale was improper because it would destroy their right of survivorship. Comment.

5. Summey Building Systems built a condominium project in Myrtle Beach, South Carolina. The project included an adjacent parking deck. Shortly after Summey relinquished control to the condominium association, the deck began to experience problems. Water and caustic materials leaked through the upper deck and dripped onto cars parked underneath. Cracks appeared, and an expert concluded that the bond between the top deck and the structural supports was insufficient. Repairs would cost about $205,000. Summey had never warranted that the deck would be free of all problems. Is the company liable for the repairs?

6. Mark Wasser negotiated to purchase a 67-year-old apartment building from Michael and Anna Sasoni. The Sasonis told Wasser that the building was "a very good building" and "an excellent deal." The contract stated that the Wassers took the building "as is" and that there were no express or implied warranties or representations. After Wasser took over the building, he discovered that it needed major structural repairs. He sued the Sasonis, claiming that they had failed to disclose defects. Who wins? (Slow down before answering.)

7. Nome 2000, a partnership, owned a large tract of wilderness land in Alaska. The Fagerstrom family had used the property for camping and holidays since about 1944. In 1966, Charles and Peggy Fagerstrom marked off an area for a cabin and brought material to build the cabin, but never did so. In about 1970, they built a picnic area on the land, and in about 1974, they placed a camper trailer on the land, where it remained until the lawsuit. In 1987, Nome 2000 sued to eject the Fagerstroms from the land. The Fagerstroms had used the land only during the summer months. No one lived in the area during the winter months, when it was virtually uninhabitable. Who wins Nome's suit?

8. **YOU BE THE JUDGE WRITING PROBLEM** Frank Deluca and his son David owned the Sportsman's Pub on Fountain Street in Providence, Rhode Island. The Delucas applied to the city for a license to employ topless dancers in the pub. Did the city have the power to deny the Delucas' request? **Argument for the Delucas:** Our pub is perfectly legal. Further, no law in Rhode Island prohibits topless dancing. We are morally and legally entitled to present this entertainment. The city should not use some phony moralizing to deny customers what they want. **Argument for Providence:** This section of Providence is zoned to prohibit topless dancing, just as it is zoned to bar manufacturing. There are other parts of town where the Delucas can open one of their sleazy clubs if they want to, but we are entitled to deny a permit in this area.

9. **CPA QUESTION** On July 1, 1992, Quick, Onyx, and Nash were deeded a piece of land as tenants in common. The deed provided that Quick owned one-half the property and Onyx and Nash owned one-quarter each. If Nash dies, the property will be owned as follows:

(a) Quick ½, Onyx ½.

(b) Quick ⅝, Onyx ⅜.

(c) Quick ⅓, Onyx ⅓, Nash's heirs ⅓.

(d) Quick ½, Onyx ¼, Nash's heirs ¼.

10. **RIGHT & WRONG** In 1966, Arketex Ceramic Corp. sold land in rural Indiana to Malcolm Aukerman. The deed described the southern boundary as the section line between sections 11 and 14 of the land. Further south than this section line stood a dilapidated fence running east to west. Aukerman and Arketex both believed that this fence was the actual southern boundary of his new land, though in fact it lay on Arketex's property.

Aukerman installed a new electrified fence, cleared the land on "his" side of the new fence, and began to graze cattle there. In 1974, Harold Clark bought the land that bordered Aukerman's fence, assuming that the fence was the correct boundary. In 1989, Clark had his land surveyed and discovered that the true property line lay north of the electric fence. Aukerman filed suit, seeking a court order that he had acquired the disputed land by adverse possession. The statutory period in Indiana is 20 years. Who wins? Who *ought* to win? Does adverse possession make sense as a social policy? Why or why not?

11. **CPA QUESTION** Which of the following deeds will give a real property purchaser the greatest protection?

(a) Quitclaim

(b) Bargain and sale

(c) Special warranty

(d) General warranty

INTERNET RESEARCH PROBLEM

Your sister Samantha, owns a Montana ranch. For years, she and a neighbor have disputed ownership of 200 valuable acres. Samantha, exhausted, refuses to litigate, but you are willing to fight it out with her neighbor because the land is so valuable. How might a quitclaim deed be useful? Examine such a document at **http://www.gate.net/~legalsvc/quit.html**. Then draft an agreement between you and Samantha concerning the land.

You can find further practice problems in the Online Quiz at http://beatty.westbuslaw.com or in the Study Guide that accompanies this text.

CHAPTER 46

LANDLORD-TENANT

On a January morning in Studio City, California, Alpha Donchin took her small Shih Tzu dog for a walk. Suddenly, less than a block from her house, two large rottweilers attacked Donchin and her pet. The heavy animals mauled the 14-pound Shih Tzu, and when Donchin picked her dog up, the rottweilers knocked her down, breaking her hip and causing other serious injuries.

Ubaldo Guerrero, who lived in a rented house nearby, owned the two rottweilers, and Donchin sued him. But she also sued Guerrero's *landlord*, David Swift, who lived four blocks away from the rental property. Donchin claimed that the landlord was liable for her injuries, because he knew of the dogs' vicious nature and permitted them to escape from the property he rented to Guerrero. Should the landlord be liable for injuries caused by his tenant's dogs?

As is typical of many landlord-tenant issues, the law in this area is in flux. Under the common law, a landlord had no liability for injuries caused by animals belonging to a tenant, and many states adhere to that rule. But some states are expanding the landlord's liability for injuries caused on or near his property. The California court ruled that Donchin *could* maintain her suit against Swift. If Donchin could prove that Swift knew the dogs were dangerous and allowed them to escape through a defective fence, the landlord would be liable for her injuries.[1]

One reason for the erratic evolution of landlord-tenant law is that it is really a combination of three venerable areas of law: property, contract, and negligence. The confluence of these legal theories produces results that are unpredictable but interesting and important. (To read some articles on the latest issues in this rapidly evolving area, visit **http://little.nhlink.net/nhlink/housing/cto/**.) We begin our examination of landlord-tenant law with an analysis of the different types of tenancy.

A freehold estate is the right to possess real property and use it in any lawful manner. What we think of as "owning" land is in fact a freehold estate. **When an owner of a freehold estate allows another person temporary, exclusive possession of the property, the parties have created a landlord-tenant relationship.** The freehold owner is the **landlord**, and the person allowed to possess the property is the **tenant**. The landlord has conveyed a **leasehold** interest to the tenant, meaning the right to temporary possession. Courts also use the word "**tenancy**" to describe the tenant's right to possession.

A leasehold may be commercial or residential. In a commercial tenancy, the owner of a building may rent retail space to a merchant, offices to a business, or industrial space to a manufacturer. When someone rents an apartment or house, he has a residential leasehold.

Three Legal Areas Combined

Property law influences landlord-tenant cases because the landlord is conveying rights in real property to the tenant. She is also keeping a **reversionary interest** in the property, meaning the right to possess the property when the lease ends. Contract law plays a role because the basic agreement between the landlord and tenant is a contract. **A lease is a contract that creates a landlord-tenant relationship.** And negligence law increasingly determines the liability of landlord and tenant when there is an injury to a person or property. Many states have combined these three legal issues into landlord-tenant statutes; you can see a typical statute at **http://www.rilin.state.ri.us/Statutes/TITLE34/34-18/INDEX.HTM**.

Notice the difference between a leasehold and a **license**, which is discussed in Chapter 45, on real property. A licensor, such as the owner of a football stadium, licenses patrons to enter the premises (the stadium) for a limited period, such as for one football game. But the licensor retains possession and control of the property, and the licensee (the patron) shares his right with thousands of others. A landlord, by contrast, gives up possession of the premises to the tenant and may regain possession only when the lease has terminated. The tenant has exclusive possession during the tenancy.

Lease

The statute of frauds generally requires that a lease be in writing. Some states will enforce an oral lease if it is for a short term, such as one year or less, but even when an oral lease is permitted, it is wiser for the parties to put their agreement in writing, because a written lease avoids many misunderstandings. At a minimum, a lease must state the names of the parties, the premises being leased, the duration

---

[1] *Donchin v. Guerrero*, 34 Cal. App. 4th 1832, 1995 Cal. App. LEXIS 462 (Cal. Ct. App. 1995).

of the agreement, and the rent. But a well-drafted lease generally includes many provisions, called covenants. A **covenant** is simply a promise by either the landlord or the tenant to do something or refrain from doing something. For example, most leases include a covenant concerning the tenant's payment of a security deposit and the landlord's return of the deposit, a covenant describing how the tenant may use the premises, and several covenants about who must maintain and repair the property, who is liable for damage, and so forth. The parties should also agree about how the lease may be terminated and whether the parties have the right to renew it.

In a residential lease, the landlord generally presents the tenant with a form lease, and the tenant has little opportunity or power to negotiate the terms. This does not mean that the tenant is powerless. If the terms of a lease are too one-sided, a court may refuse to enforce them. We will look later, for example, at exculpatory clauses in leases and see that they are often void. In a commercial lease, both parties generally have the opportunity to negotiate terms that provide adequate protection. It is imperative that the lease clearly set forth the parties' respective rights and obligations. The following news report indicates what can happen when a lease is unclear about liability for property damage.

On Tuesday, a rumor that seemed too good to be true spread through a North Philadelphia neighborhood about a nearby warehouse that had been damaged by fire: new, boxed pieces of furniture and electronic equipment were up for grabs. The rumor also had it that the owner would not press charges against people who helped themselves. So residents wasted no time in doing just that, many pulling up to the six-story warehouse in pickup trucks. Others just carried the chairs, couches, tables, televisions, and videocassette recorders out, police officers said today.

And both halves of the rumor turned out to be correct: about 20 people detained by the police were released after the building's owner, involved in a liability dispute with the tenant, refused to press charges. The warehouse covers a city block. Most of the first floor was filled with furniture and electronic equipment stored there by a Philadelphia discount store.

The building has been damaged recently by two fires set by arsonists. After the first, which caused about $1 million in damage, the building was boarded up, a Philadelphia arson detective said. But firefighters were forced to unseal it to douse a second blaze last Thursday. The police have no suspects in either fire. The building was not immediately resealed because the discount store, Philadelphia Surplus, and the building's owner, H & L Trading, Ontario Associates of New York, are in a legal dispute, along with their insurance companies, over who should be liable for damages from the first fire. When police officers arrested looters early Tuesday, the tenant, the owner, and the insurance companies denied responsibility and refused to press charges because of their liability fight. The first batch of looters told neighbors about their luck and attracted a crowd to the site.[2]

TYPES OF TENANCY

There are four types of tenancy: a tenancy for years, a periodic tenancy, a tenancy at will, and a tenancy at sufferance. The most important feature distinguishing one from the other is how each tenancy terminates. In some cases, a tenancy terminates automatically, while in others, one party must take certain steps to end the agreement.

[2] "Warehouse Dispute Gives Looters a Free Pass," *New York Times*, Nov. 23, 1995, p. A22. Copyright © 1995 by The New York Times Co. Reprinted by permission.

TENANCY FOR YEARS

Any lease for a stated, fixed period is a tenancy for years. If a landlord rents a summer apartment for the months of June, July, and August of next year, that is a tenancy for years. A company that rents retail space in a mall beginning January 1, 2002, and ending December 31, 2007, also has a tenancy for years. A tenancy for years terminates automatically when the agreed period ends.

PERIODIC TENANCY

A periodic tenancy is created for a fixed period and then automatically continues for additional periods until either party notifies the other of termination. This is probably the most common variety of tenancy, and the parties may create one in either of two ways. Suppose a landlord agrees to rent you an apartment "from month to month, rent payable on the first." That is a periodic tenancy. The tenancy automatically renews itself every month, unless either party gives adequate notice to the other that she wishes to terminate. A periodic tenancy could also be for one-year periods—in which case it automatically renews for an additional year if neither party terminates—or for any other period.

The parties also create a periodic tenancy if, when a *tenancy for years* expires, the tenant continues to pay rent and the landlord accepts it. Ariadne agrees to rent property called Naxos for three years, with rent payable once per month. When the three years are up, the tenancy for years expires automatically. Ariadne continues to pay the monthly rent, however, and the landlord accepts her checks. The parties have created a periodic tenancy.

What is the period? If the tenant is renting *commercial property*, the new periodic tenancy is for the same period as the old tenancy for years, up to a maximum of one year. In other words, if Naxos is an office building, Ariadne's new periodic tenancy is for one year (since her original lease was for more than a year). Once the landlord accepts a single monthly rental check, both he and Ariadne are bound for the full year. In many states, if the property is *residential*, the new periodic tenancy is month-to-month. If Naxos is a vacation house, either party can end the lease with 30 days' notice. A landlord's notice terminating a tenancy is often called a **notice to quit**.

TENANCY AT WILL

A tenancy at will has no fixed duration and may be terminated by either party at any time. Tenancies at will are unusual tenancies.[3] Typically, the agreement is vague, with no specified rental period and with payment, perhaps, to be made in kind. The parties might agree, for example, that a tenant farmer could use a portion of his crop as rent. Since either party can end the agreement at any time, it provides no security for either landlord or tenant.

TENANCY AT SUFFERANCE

A tenancy at sufferance occurs when a tenant remains on the premises, against the wishes of the landlord, after the expiration of a true tenancy. Thus a tenancy at sufferance is not a true tenancy because the tenant is staying without the

---

[3] The courts of some states, annoyingly, use the term "tenancy at will" for what are, in reality, periodic tenancies. They do this to bewilder law students and even lawyers, a goal at which they are quite successful. This text uses tenancy at will in its more widely known sense, meaning a tenancy terminable at any time.

landlord's agreement. The landlord has the option of seeking to evict the tenant or of forcing the tenant to pay rent for a new rental period. The following case illustrates the relationship between the different kinds of tenancy.

KREUTTER v. MIDWEST MEDICAL HOMECARE, INC.
195 Wis. 2d 681, 538 N.W.2d 861, 1995 Wisc. App. LEXIS 759
Wisconsin Court of Appeals, 1995

Facts: Midwest Medical leased office space from Clyde Kreutter for one year, from August 1989 through July 1990. Midwest remained in the space beyond that date, continuing to pay monthly rent. In May 1991, Kreutter notified his tenant that he was increasing the rent beginning the following August, and Midwest paid the higher amount; the same thing happened in 1993. Then, in December 1993, Midwest notified its landlord that it intended to terminate the lease and vacate the premises on February 28, 1994. Kreutter filed suit for five months' rent, from March through July 1994. The trial court gave summary judgment for the landlord and Midwest appealed.

Issue: **Was Midwest liable for the additional rent?**

Excerpts from Judge Anderson's Decision: The Tenant argues that the "court erred in ruling that the relationship between the parties was a periodic yearly tenancy. The relationship was a periodic monthly tenancy which was lawfully terminated." In determining the type of tenancy involved in the present case, we must apply the facts to the applicable landlord/tenant statutes. [The relevant statute provides:]

> Creation of Periodic Tenancy by Holding Over. (a) Nonresidential leases for a year or longer. If premises are leased for a year or longer primarily for other than private residential purposes, and the tenant holds over after expiration of the lease, the landlord may elect to hold the tenant on a year-to-year basis. (b) All other leases. If premises are leased for less than a year for any use, or if leased for any period primarily for private residential purposes, and the tenant holds over after expiration of the lease, the landlord may elect to hold the tenant on a month-to-month basis; but if such lease provides for a weekly or daily rent, the landlord may hold the tenant only on the periodic basis on which rent is computed.

In the present case, the premises was leased for a year for nonresidential use, placing it under subsec. (a). The Tenant decided to pay the higher rate of rent and "hold over" after the expiration of the lease agreement. The Landlord elected to hold the Tenant on a year-to-year basis when it accepted rent after the expiration of the lease. There is no genuine issue as to any material fact and the Landlord is entitled to judgment as a matter of law.

Suppose you are a manager at Midwest Medical. When the lease comes up for renewal, the company wants to stay, but does not want to renew the lease for a full year. Having taken this law course, you realize that paying the August rent will have exactly that effect. What should you do?

LANDLORD'S DUTIES

DUTY TO DELIVER POSSESSION

The landlord's first important duty is to deliver possession of the premises at the beginning of the tenancy, that is, to make the rented space available to the tenant. In most cases this presents no problems and the new tenant moves in. But what happens if the previous tenant has refused to leave when the new tenancy begins?

The "English rule" obligates the landlord to remove the previous tenant in time for the new tenant to take possession. The majority of American states enforce this rule. If the old tenant is still in possession when the new tenant arrives, the landlord has breached the lease. The new tenant has two alternative remedies. She may terminate the lease and sue the landlord for costs she incurs obtaining other accommodations. Or she may affirm the lease, refuse to pay rent for the period in which she cannot take possession, sue for the cost of other accommodations, and then take possession when the old tenant is finally evicted.

The "American rule" is more favorable to the landlord. (Although called the American rule, this is in fact the minority rule in this country—anything to keep you off balance.) This rule holds that the landlord has no duty to deliver actual possession of the premises. If the previous tenant remains in possession, the landlord has not breached the lease. Under this rule, the new tenant generally has the power to act as a landlord toward the old tenant. The new tenant may evict the old tenant and recover damages caused by her delay in leaving. Alternatively, the new tenant may treat the holdover as a tenant at will for a new rental period and may charge the normal rent for that period.

QUIET ENJOYMENT

All tenants are entitled to quiet enjoyment of the premises, meaning the right to use the property without the interference of the landlord. Most leases expressly state this covenant of quiet enjoyment. And if a lease includes no such covenant, the law implies the right of quiet enjoyment anyway, so all tenants are protected. If a landlord interferes with the tenant's quiet enjoyment, he has breached the lease, entitling the tenant to damages.

The most common interference with quiet enjoyment is an **eviction**, meaning some act that forces the tenant to abandon the premises. Of course, some evictions are legal, as when a tenant fails to pay the rent. But some evictions are illegal. There are two types of eviction: actual and constructive.

Actual Eviction

If a landlord prevents the tenant from possessing the premises, he has *actually* evicted her. Suppose a landlord decides that a group of students are "troublemakers." Without going through lawful eviction procedures in court, the landlord simply waits until the students are out of the apartment and changes all the locks. By denying the students access to the premises, the landlord has actually evicted them and has breached their right of quiet enjoyment. He is liable for all expenses they suffer, such as retrieving their possessions, the cost of alternate housing, and moving expenses. In some states he may be liable for punitive damages for failing to go through proper eviction procedures.

Even a partial eviction is an interference with quiet enjoyment. Suppose Louise rents an apartment with a storage room. If the landlord places his own goods in the storage room, he has partially evicted Louise because a tenant is entitled to the *exclusive* possession of the premises. In all states Louise would be allowed to deduct from her rent the value of the storage space, and in many states she would not be obligated to pay *any* rent for the apartment as long as the landlord continued the partial eviction.

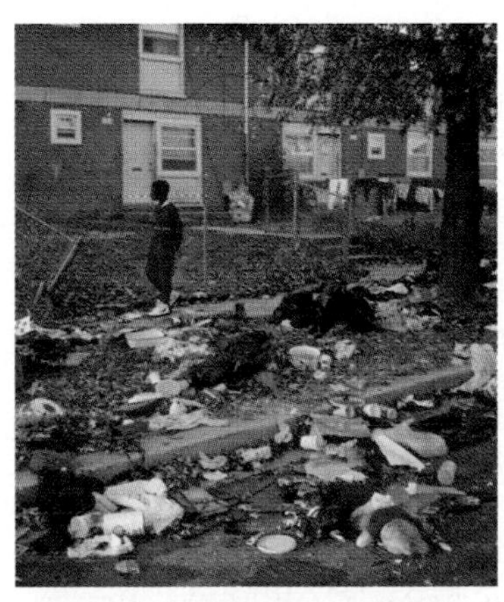

If conditions are intolerable, the landlord has constructively evicted the tenant.

Constructive Eviction

If a landlord substantially interferes with the tenant's use and enjoyment of the premises, he has constructively evicted her. Courts construe certain behavior as the equivalent of an eviction. In these cases, the landlord has not actually prevented the tenant from *possessing* the premises, but has instead interfered so greatly with her *use and enjoyment* that the law regards the landlord's actions as equivalent to an eviction. Suppose the heating system in an apartment house in Juneau, Alaska, fails during January. The landlord, an avid sled dog racer, tells the tenants he is too busy to fix the problem. If the tenants move out, the landlord has constructively evicted them and is liable for all expenses they suffer.

To claim a constructive eviction, the tenant must vacate the premises. The tenant must also prove that the interference was sufficiently serious and lasted long enough that she was forced to move out. A lack of hot water for two days is not fatal, but lack of any water for two weeks creates a constructive eviction.

In the following case a group of students alleged constructive eviction.

HOME RENTALS CORP v. CURTIS

236 Ill. App. 3d 994, 602 N.E.2d 859, 1992 Ill. App. LEXIS 1745
Illinois Court of Appeals, 1992

Facts: Home Rentals Corp. owned about 300 rental properties, including a single-family house located near Southern Illinois University (SIU). Henry Fisher was a rental agent for Home Rentals. In February, Fisher agreed to rent the house to a group of four SIU students. The house was then in good condition. The parties signed a written lease, for the rental period from August 17 to the following August 13 at a rent of $740 per month. The students paid $1,980, to cover a security deposit and the last two months' rent.

When the students arrived in August, they found the house in dreadful condition, as the court describes. They refused to live in it, and Home Rentals sued for $6,900, the value of the year's lease minus the money paid. The students counterclaimed, arguing constructive eviction. The trial court found for the students and awarded them $1,980. Home Rentals appealed.

Issue: **Did Home Rentals constructively evict the students?**

Excerpts from Judge Harrison's Decision: The first to reach the scene was Mike Fraser, who arrived in Carbondale on August 15. At that time the electricity had not yet been turned on, and he was not able to view the premises during daylight hours until Wednesday, August 16. What Fraser found then was a house that was not fit for human habitation.

Roaches had overrun the rooms. The kitchen was so filthy and so infested by bugs that food could not be stored there. The living room carpet smelled, and one could actually see outside through holes in the wall around the frame of the front door. The bathrooms were unsanitary, and when the water was turned on the following day, August 17, Fraser discovered that not one of the toilets in the building worked. He also discovered that one of the bathtubs did not drain at all, while another drained only slowly, and that bathroom waste water drained directly onto the floor of the basement. In attempting to explain this open drain at trial, Henry Fisher tried to assert that it was simply part of the washing machine hookup. As evidence that this was laundry-related, he pointed to white matter on the basement floor by the drain which he claimed was spilled laundry detergent. Other evidence indicated, however, that the white matter was, in fact, a mass of roach eggs.

Fraser testified that he spoke with Fisher at Home Rentals on the 16th and told him that the place was uninhabitable because of the filth and the roaches. Fisher's response was to suggest that the students buy roach bombs and cleaning supplies to take care of the problems themselves, although he did offer to reimburse them for those items and represented that he would arrange to have an exterminator spray.

Hopeful that the situation might somehow be salvaged, defendants spent several days attempting on their own to make the house liveable. Although an exterminator finally appeared on Friday, August 18, or Saturday, August 19, the problem of roach infestation continued, and Home Rentals did nothing about the dirt or plumbing problems. On Monday, August 21, defendants finally gave up. They packed up their property and sought housing elsewhere.

A constructive eviction occurs where a landlord has done "something of a grave and permanent character with the intention of depriving the tenant of enjoyment of the premises."

The record is clear that defendants had notified Home Rentals of all their complaints by August 17, when the lease term was scheduled to commence. This was four full days before they finally gave up and moved.

Considering the magnitude of the problems, four days were opportunity enough for Home Rentals to act. We note, moreover, that there is no indication that giving Home Rentals additional time would have made any difference.

Affirmed.

Other Interference

A landlord's conduct may interfere with quiet enjoyment even when it is not so harmful as to force a constructive eviction. Suppose a landlord, living in the ground floor unit, gives trumpet lessons in his apartment six nights a week until 1:00 A.M., producing such a cacophony that a group of students, living upstairs, can neither study nor sleep. If the students continue to live in the apartment, because they cannot afford a better place, there has been no constructive eviction. But the landlord's conduct interferes with the tenants' quiet enjoyment, and the students are entitled to damages.

DUTY TO MAINTAIN PREMISES

Historically, the common law placed no burden on the landlord to repair and maintain the premises. This made sense because rental property had traditionally been farmland. Buildings, such as a house or barn, were far less important than the land itself, and no one expected the landlord to fix a leaking roof. Today, the vast majority of rental property is used for housing or business purposes. Space in a building is frequently all that a tenant is renting, and the condition of the building is of paramount importance. Most states have changed the common law rule and placed various obligations on the landlord to maintain the property.

In most states, a landlord has a duty to deliver the premises in a habitable condition and a continuing duty to maintain the habitable condition. This duty overlaps with the quiet enjoyment obligation, but it is not identical. The tenant's right to quiet enjoyment focuses primarily on the tenant's *ability to use* the rented property. The landlord's duty to maintain the property focuses on whether the property *meets a particular legal standard*. The required standard may be stated in the lease, created by a state statute, or implied by law.

A landlord's duty to maintain the premises may be stated in the lease, created by statute, or implied by law.

Lease

The lease itself generally obligates the landlord to maintain the exterior of any buildings and the common areas. If a lease does not do so, state law may imply the obligation.

Building Codes

Many state and local governments have passed building codes, which mandate minimum standards for commercial and/or residential property. The codes are likely to be stricter for residential property and may demand such things as minimum room size, sufficient hot water, secure locks, proper working kitchens and bathrooms, absence of insects and rodents, and other basics of decent housing. Generally, all rental property must comply with the building code, whether the lease mentions the code or not.

Implied Warranty of Habitability

Students Maria Ivanow, Thomas Tecza, and Kenneth Gearin rented a house from Les and Martha Vanlandingham. The monthly rent was $900. But the roommates failed to pay any rent for the final five months of the tenancy. After they moved out, the Vanlandinghams sued. How much did the landlords recover? Nothing. The landlords had breached the implied warranty of habitability.

The implied warranty of habitability requires that a landlord meet all standards set by the local building code, or that the premises be fit for human habitation. Most states, though not all, *imply* this warranty of habitability, meaning that the landlord must meet this standard whether the lease includes it or not. In some states, the implied warranty means that the premises must at least satisfy the local building code. Other states require property that is "fit for human habitation," which means that a landlord might comply with the building code yet still fail the implied warranty of habitability, if the rental property is unfit to live in.

The Vanlandinghams breached the implied warranty. The students had complained repeatedly about a variety of problems. The washer and dryer, which were included in the lease, frequently failed. A severe roof leak caused water damage in one of the bedrooms. Defective pipes flooded the bathroom. The refrigerator frequently malfunctioned, and the roommates repaired it several times. The basement often flooded, and when it was dry, rats and opossums lived in it. The heat sometimes failed.

In warranty of habitability cases, a court normally considers the severity of the problems and their duration. If the defective conditions seriously interfere with the tenancy, the court declares the implied warranty breached and orders a **rent abatement**, that is, a reduction in the rent owed. The longer the defects continued and the greater their severity, the more the rent is abated. In the case of Maria Ivanow and friends, the court abated the rent 50 percent. The students had already paid more than the abated rent to the landlord, so they owed nothing for the last five months.[4]

Tenant Remedies for Defective Conditions

The students in the above case demonstrated one remedy often available to a tenant whose landlord has breached the warranty of habitability. Not all states permit rent abatement, but the majority do. Other states allow alternative, or additional, remedies for defective conditions. A tenant must check the law of his state before using any of the remedies discussed. For tenant rights in your state, see **http://www.tenantsunion.org/tulist.html**, which provides links to tenant organizations throughout the nation. For a useful series of form letters concerning defective conditions, problems with neighbors, interference with quiet enjoyment, and other common tenant concerns, see **http://little.nhlink.net/nhlink/housing/cto/letters/letrs.htm**.

Rent Withholding. Many states allow a tenant to withhold rent, representing the decreased value of the premises. The tenant must first notify the landlord of

---

[4] *Vanlandingham v. Ivanow*, 246 Ill. App. 3d 348, 615 N.E.2d 1361, 1993 Ill. App. LEXIS 985 (Ill. Ct. App. 1993).

the problems and allow her a reasonable period to make repairs. If she fails to remedy the problem, the tenant may then withhold a portion of the rent, while continuing to live in the premises. The tenant should withhold a portion of the rent that approximates the seriousness of the defective conditions. A wise tenant saves the withheld rent, in case a court later orders part or all of it paid to the landlord. In a *rent strike*, a group of tenants in the same building refuses to pay their landlord because of uniformly deplorable conditions. By acting collectively, the tenants may wield greater power against an abusive landlord than they could individually.

Repair and Deduct. In some states, if a tenant notifies the landlord of a serious defect and the landlord fails to remedy the problem, the tenant may deduct a reasonable amount of money from the rental payment and have the repair made himself. States that allow this remedy place a maximum figure on the amount of money a tenant may deduct, such as one or two months' rent.

Suit for Damages. A landlord who refuses to repair significant defects is breaching the lease and/or state law, and the tenant may simply sue for damages. Often, though, rent withholding is a more effective way to force repairs, since the landlord may respond more quickly when the money stops flowing.

DUTY TO RETURN SECURITY DEPOSIT

Most landlords require tenants to pay a security deposit, in case the tenant damages the premises. In many states, a landlord must either return the security deposit soon after the tenant has moved out or notify the tenant of the damage and the cost of the repairs. Failure to do one or the other may prove costly, as the landlord in the following case discovered.

BIRNEY v. BARRETTA
1993 Conn. Super. LEXIS 2005
Connecticut Superior Court,
1993

Facts: Mark Birney and his family rented a house from Richard Barretta for $1,200 per month and paid a security deposit of $2,400. After Birney moved out, he requested the return of his security deposit but never received it. Birney sued, seeking double damages under the Connecticut security deposit statute. Barretta claimed that he owed Birney nothing, because Birney had damaged the premises and Barretta had used the money for repairs.

Issue: Was Barretta entitled to retain the security deposit?

Excerpts from Judge Riddle's Decision: The security deposit act applies to all landlords. The person who is the landlord at the time that the tenant vacates is responsible for returning the deposit. The landlord must return the security deposit, plus interest, "within 30 days after the termination of a tenancy." In the context of the security deposit act, this refers to the date the tenant vacates. To trigger the time limits, however, the tenant must give the landlord a written notice of his forwarding address.

In this case, the plaintiff sent a registered mail letter and it was received by the landlord. That letter provided the plaintiff's forwarding address at Milford, Connecticut. The landlord's duty is to return the security deposit, plus interest, or to account in writing for his claims against the deposit and to return any portion of the deposit, plus interest, against which he has no claim.

If the landlord withholds any of the deposit, the act requires "a written statement itemizing the nature and amount" of the damages claimed as a result of the tenant's failure to comply with his obligations. The itemization must be specific, both as to the nature of the items of damage and as to their costs. The refund or the accounting must be delivered to the tenant within 30 days after the tenant vacates. The refund must include statutorily mandated interest on the deposit.

The plaintiff testified he never received a refund or an accounting. The defendant said his girlfriend mailed an accounting to the plaintiff. The defendant did not produce a copy of it or his girlfriend's testimony at trial. He did not specify the date it was prepared or mailed. The court, therefore, credits the testimony of the plaintiff and finds that the defendant violated [the statute] by failing to provide the refund or an accounting. The doubling of the security deposit is mandatory. Therefore, the plaintiff is entitled to $4800.00 in double damages.

Final Word on Security Deposits

The discussion and case both concerned residential leases, where security deposits are almost inevitable. Note that, in a commercial lease, the tenant may have less statutory protection than Mark Birney received, but more bargaining power. A financially sound company might negotiate a lease with no security deposit or perhaps offer a letter of credit for security, instead of cash. The interest saved over several years could be substantial. For a thoughtful article on this, see http://www.meislik.com/articles/art01.htm.

TENANT'S DUTIES

DUTY TO PAY RENT

> My landlord said he's gonna raise the rent. "Good," I said, " 'cause *I* can't raise it."
>
> *Slappy White,* comedian, 1921–1995

Rent is the compensation the tenant pays the landlord for use of the premises, and paying the rent, despite Mr. White's wistful hope, is the tenant's foremost obligation. The lease normally specifies the amount of rent and when it must be paid. Typically, the landlord requires that rent be paid at the beginning of each rental period, whether that is monthly, annually, or otherwise.

Both parties must be certain they understand whether the rent includes utilities such as heat and hot water. Some states mandate that the landlord pay certain utilities, such as water. Many leases include an **escalator clause**, permitting the landlord to raise the rent during the course of the lease if his expenses increase for specified reasons. For example, a tax escalator clause allows the landlord to raise the rent if his real estate taxes go up. Any escalator clause should state the percentage of the increase that the landlord may pass on to the tenant.

Landlord's Remedies for Nonpayment of Rent

If the tenant fails to pay rent on time, the landlord has several remedies. She is entitled to apply the security deposit to the unpaid rent. She may also sue the tenant for nonpayment of rent, demanding the unpaid sums, cost of collection, and interest. Finally, the landlord may evict a tenant who has failed to pay rent.

State statutes prescribe the steps a landlord must take to evict a tenant for nonpayment. Typically, the landlord must serve a termination notice on the tenant and wait for a court hearing. At the hearing the landlord must prove that the tenant has failed to pay rent on time. If the tenant has no excuse for the nonpayment, the court grants an order evicting him. The order authorizes a sheriff to remove the tenant's goods and place them in storage, at the tenant's expense. However, if the tenant was withholding rent because of unlivable conditions, the court may refuse to evict. The Web site **http://www.tiac.net/users/nhpoa/other.htm** contains invaluable information about a landlord's rights and remedies in every state in the country.

Duty to Mitigate

Pickwick & Perkins, Ltd. was a store in the Burlington Square Mall in Burlington, Vermont. Pickwick had a five-year lease, but abandoned the space almost two years early and ceased paying rent. The landlord waited approximately eight months before renting the space to a new tenant and then sued, seeking the unpaid rent. Pickwick defended on the grounds that Burlington had failed to **mitigate damages**, that is, to keep its losses to a minimum by promptly seeking another tenant. Burlington argued that it had no legal obligation to mitigate. Burlington's position accurately reflected the common law rule, which permitted the landlord to let the property lie vacant and allow the damages to add up. But the common law evolves over time, and this time the Vermont Supreme Court changed the rule. The judges pointed out that, historically, a lease was a conveyance of an estate, and property law had never required mitigation. However, the court asserted, a lease is now regarded as both a contract and a conveyance. Under contract law, the nonbreaching party must make a reasonable effort to minimize losses, and that same rule applies, said the court, to a landlord. Burlington lost. The Vermont ruling is typical of current decisions, although some courts still do not require mitigation.[5]

Duty to Use Premises for Proper Purpose

A lease normally lists what a tenant may do in the premises and prohibits other activities. For example, a residential lease allows the tenant to use the property for normal living purposes, but not for any retail, commercial, or industrial purpose. A commercial lease might allow a tenant to operate a retail clothing store, but not a restaurant. A landlord may evict a tenant who violates the lease by using the premises for prohibited purposes.

A tenant may not use the premises for any illegal activity, such as gambling or selling drugs. The law itself implies this condition in every lease, so a tenant who engages in illegal acts on the leased property is subject to eviction, regardless of whether the lease mentions such conduct.

Duty Not to Damage Premises

A tenant is liable to the landlord for any significant damage he causes to the property. The tenant is not liable for normal wear and tear. If, however, he knocks a hole in a wall or damages the plumbing, the landlord may collect the cost of repairs, either by using the security deposit or by suing, if necessary. A landlord may also seek to evict a tenant for serious damage to the property.

A tenant is permitted to make reasonable changes in the leased property so that he can use it as intended. Someone leasing an apartment is permitted to hang pictures on the wall. But a tenant leasing commercial space should make certain

---

[5] *O'Brien v. Black,* 162 Vt. 448, 648 A.2d 1374, 1994 Vt. LEXIS 89 (1994).

that the lease specifies the alterations he can make and whether he is obligated to return the premises to their original condition at the end of the lease.

Recall from Chapter 45 that a **fixture** is an item of personal property that is permanently attached to real estate. A furnace is a fixture, as are custom cabinets installed in a kitchen. The common law rule held that all fixtures belonged to the landlord. The contemporary trend, though, is the opposite. In commercial leases, it is common for tenants to install expensive equipment as part of their business, for example, commercial ovens in a restaurant. These are called **trade fixtures**. Most states permit commercial tenants to remove trade fixtures, provided the tenant restores the property to its original condition. In residential leases, some states still prohibit the tenant from removing a fixture, but courts today are likelier to permit removal, provided the tenant does not harm the premises in the process.

Duty Not to Disturb Other Tenants

Most leases, commercial and residential, include a covenant that the tenant will not disturb other tenants in the building. A landlord may evict a tenant who unreasonably disturbs others. The test is *reasonableness*. A landlord does not have the right to evict a residential tenant for giving one loud party but may evict a tenant who repeatedly plays loud music late at night and disturbs the quiet enjoyment of other tenants.

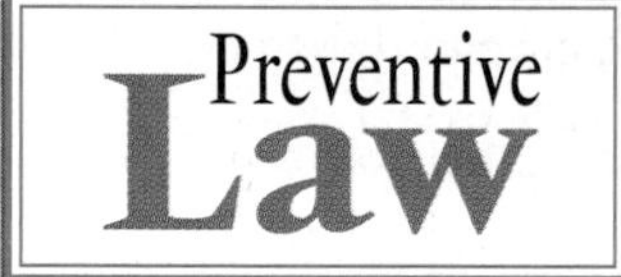

Landlords not only have the *right* to evict tenants who seriously disturb others, they may have the *duty* as well. Carmen Burgos lived in an apartment in the Queens borough of New York City, with her elderly mother and two teenage children. Ms. Burgos had no problems for over 10 years, until the landlord rented a neighboring unit to tenants who began to deal drugs from their apartment. Ms. Burgos repeatedly complained to the landlord, but he did nothing. The drug dealer began to terrorize Ms. Burgos and her family, smashing her car windows, throwing things at her door, and cursing at her family at all hours of the night. Still the landlord took no steps. Finally, Ms. Burgos abandoned her unit, leaving several months' rent unpaid. The landlord sued her for unpaid rent, but the court found he had failed to protect Ms. Burgos from other tenants and was entitled to no rent. This landlord lost rental income and watched his building deteriorate, all because he failed to enforce the terms of the tenancy against the troublemaker.[6]

Animal Attacks

Dogs bite, cats scratch, wolves maul. In most states, the owner of an animal is responsible for any harm it causes. A tenant is liable if her dog intimidates or attacks other tenants. The landlord has the right to evict a tenant whose animal abuses other tenants. In some states, a landlord may have a *duty* to evict, following the logic of the *Burgos* decision, above.

States do not agree, however, on whether the landlord is liable for harm caused by a tenant's animals. The common law rule holds a landlord free of any responsibility for harm caused by a tenant's animal. California and some other states disagree and declare a landlord potentially liable. We revisit this issue later in the chapter. Of course, if either the landlord *or* the tenant were to show common sense and respond quickly to a dangerous animal, there would be no injury and no need for a court to rule on liability.

---

[6] *Auburn Leasing Corp. v. Burgos*, 609 N.Y.S.2d 549, 1994 N.Y. Misc. LEXIS 68 (N.Y. Civ. Ct. 1994).

Change in the Parties

Sometimes the parties to a lease change. This can happen when the landlord sells the property or when a tenant wants to turn the leased property over to another tenant.

Sale of the Property

Generally, the sale of leased property does not affect the lease but merely substitutes one landlord, the purchaser, for another, the seller. The lease remains valid, and the tenant enjoys all rights and obligations until the end of the term. The new landlord may not raise the rent during the period of the existing lease or make any other changes in the tenant's rights.

There is one exception. If the tenant is not in possession when the property is sold *and* the tenant's lease was never recorded with the registry of deeds, then the buyer need not honor the lease. If the buyer has no way of knowing there *is* a tenant, she should not be required to respect the lease.

Assignment and Sublease

A tenant who wishes to turn the property over to another tenant will attempt to assign the lease or to sublet it. In an **assignment**, the tenant transfers all of his legal interest to the other party. The original tenant is the **assignor** and the new tenant is the **assignee**.[7] If a tenant validly assigns a lease, the assignee obtains all rights and liabilities under the lease. The assignee is permitted to use and enjoy the property and must pay the rent. The assignor remains liable to the landlord unless the landlord explicitly releases him, which the landlord is unlikely to do. This means that if the new tenant fails to pay the rent on time, the landlord can sue both parties, old and new, seeking to evict both and to recover the unpaid rent from both.

A landlord generally insists on a covenant in the lease prohibiting the tenant from assigning without the landlord's written permission. The landlord chose to do business with one person and should not be forced to accept a stranger as tenant. How much discretion does a landlord have in deciding whether to permit assignment? It depends on state law and the language of the lease.

Many leases include a covenant that the landlord will not "unreasonably withhold" permission to assign. That covenant is enforceable, and a landlord who arbitrarily refuses permission to assign is liable for all damage she has caused. If the lease contains no limit on the landlord's ability to refuse assignment, may she refuse for no valid reason? It depends on the state. **A dwindling majority of states allows a landlord to reject assignment for any reason or no reason.** An increasing number of courts require the landlord to make her decision *reasonably*. She may consider the assignee's financial stability and intended use of the premises, but may not reject an assignment simply because it is inconvenient.

In a **sublease**, the tenant remains a tenant of the landlord and turns over *some* of his rights to a new tenant. The original tenant is the **sublessor** and the new tenant is the **sublessee**. The sublessor remains fully liable to the landlord for all provisions of the lease, including payment of rent and proper care of the premises. The sublessee has no legal relationship with the landlord, but has a normal tenant's obligations to the sublessor. The sublessee must pay rent to the sublessor and must return the property in good condition at the end of the sublease.

---

[7] We discuss assignment of contracts in Chapter 16, on third parties.

Why would a tenant sublet property rather than assign it? Often because rental rates have risen during the course of the original tenancy, and the tenant believes he can make a profit by subletting the premises at a higher rent than he is paying the landlord.

Must a landlord agree to a sublease? The rules are essentially the same as for an assignment. The lease probably requires the tenant to obtain the landlord's permission before subletting. In a growing minority of states, the landlord may not unreasonably withhold that permission.

D. L. Development, Inc. was a tenant on five acres of commercial property owned by Bessie Nance. The lease was for 99 years, with 68 years remaining. Property values had increased dramatically, and the lease was no longer profitable to Nance. D. L. Development wished to sublease some of its space to McCaw Cellular Communications for installation of a cellular telephone antenna, and McCaw signed a sublease for 10 years. D. L. Development then asked Nance to approve the sublease, but she refused, stating that she would agree to it only if D. L. Development renegotiated the terms of the original lease. The court held that Nance was holding the sublease hostage in an effort to squeeze more rent out of D. L. Development, and that this was unreasonable. The court ordered Nance to pay her tenant all profits lost from the failed sublease.[8]

INJURIES

You invite a friend to dinner in your rented home, but after the meal she slips and falls, seriously injuring her back. Are you liable? Is the landlord?

TENANT'S LIABILITY

A tenant is generally liable for injuries occurring within the premises she is leasing, whether that is an apartment, a store, or otherwise. If a tenant permits grease to accumulate on a kitchen floor and a guest slips and falls, the tenant is liable. If a merchant negligently installs display shelving that tips onto a customer, the merchant pays for the harm. Generally, a tenant is not liable for injuries occurring in common areas over which she has no control, such as exterior walkways. If a tenant's dinner guest falls because the building's common stairway has loose steps, the landlord is probably liable.

LANDLORD'S LIABILITY

Common Law Rules

Historically, the common law held a landlord responsible for injuries on the premises only in a limited number of circumstances, which we will describe. In reading these common law rules, be aware that many states have changed them, dramatically increasing the landlord's liability.

Latent Defects. If the landlord knows of a dangerous condition on the property and realizes the tenant will not notice it, the landlord is liable for any injuries. For example, if a landlord knows that a porch railing is weak and fails to inform the

[8] *D. L. Development, Inc. v. Nance*, 894 S.W.2d 258, 1995 Mo. App. LEXIS 431 (Mo. Ct. App. 1995).

tenant, the landlord is responsible if the tenant plunges off the porch. But notice that, under the common law, if the landlord notifies the tenant of the latent defect, he is no longer liable.

Common Areas. The landlord is usually responsible for maintaining the common areas, and along with this obligation may go liability for torts. As we saw above, if your guest falls down stairs in a common hallway because the stairs were defective, the landlord is probably liable.

Negligent Repairs. Even in areas where the landlord has no duty to make repairs, if he volunteers to do so and does the work badly, he is responsible for resulting harm.

Public Use. If the premises are to be used for a public purpose, such as a store or office, the landlord is generally obligated to repair any dangerous defects, although the tenant is probably liable as well. The purpose of this stricter rule is to ensure that the general public can safely visit commercial establishments. If a landlord realizes that the plate glass in a store's door is loose, he must promptly repair it or suffer liability for any injuries.

Modern Trend

Increasingly, state legislatures and courts are discarding the common law classifications described above and holding landlords liable under the normal rules of negligence law. **In many states, a landlord must use reasonable care to maintain safe premises and is liable for foreseeable harm.** For example, the common law rule merely required a landlord to notify a tenant of a latent defect, such as a defective porch railing. Most states now have building codes that require a landlord to maintain structural elements such as railings in safe condition. States further imply a warranty of habitability, which mandates reasonably safe living conditions. So, in many states, a landlord is no longer saved from negligence suits merely by giving notice of defects—he has to fix them. Suppose that a bathroom faucet is loose, causing hot water to leak continuously, and the landlord has failed to repair it in spite of frequent requests by the tenant. If the faucet suddenly breaks open and hot water scalds the tenant's guest, the landlord is liable in many states. The landlord's responsibility, however, depends upon his receiving notice of the defect from the tenant.

As always, the common law advances in a disorderly fashion, and state courts disagree about what "reasonable care" requires. The following pair of cases illustrate the diversity of issues—and conflicting arguments—that a landlord must consider before renting units. You make the calls.

MCGUIRE v. K & G MANAGEMENT CO.

1998 Ohio App. LEXIS 4742
Ohio Court of Appeals, 1998

Facts: The McGuire family rented a second-story apartment from K & G Management, which managed a residential complex on behalf of Avant Co. Robin McGuire notified K & G that a window screen in her son's bedroom was loose and had fallen out once. Neighbors had also complained about loose-fitting screens. Five days after Robin reported the loose screen, her son, 26-month-old Devin, was playing in his bedroom with his eight-year-old cousin. Somehow, Devin fell or leaned into the window screen, which gave way. Devin fell to the ground and was seriously hurt.

The McGuires filed suit against K & G and Avant, claiming negligence. In Ohio (and most states), a landlord has a statutory duty to "make all repairs and do whatever is reasonably necessary to put and keep the premises in a fit and habitable condition." The trial court granted summary judgment for both defendants, ruling that the defendants had no duty to install screens strong enough to restrain a child. The McGuires appealed.

You Be the Judge: Are the McGuires entitled to a trial on their claim of negligence?

Argument for the McGuires: Both defendants have a statutory duty to keep the apartment fit and habitable, and both failed to do that. The screen was loose and they knew it, but failed to fix it. The danger of a child falling was entirely foreseeable, and the defendants are responsible. No parent can watch a child 24 hours a day. Young children climb and play anywhere they can reach. A landlord who makes a profit renting apartments to families should use reasonable care to protect all family members, young and old.

Argument for K & G and Avant: A window screen is not a child restraint. A screen is designed to keep insects and birds out, not to hold children in. A normal window screen, no matter how tightly installed, would not restrain a child. If all landlords throughout the state are suddenly obligated to install child-proof screens, let the legislature announce the new rule and provide time to comply. We do not think that the voters want to pay the additional rent required to cover such a huge expense.

MATTHEWS v. AMBERWOOD ASSOCIATES LIMITED PARTNERSHIP, INC.

351 Md. 544, 719 A.2d 199, 1998 Md. LEXIS 807
Maryland Court of Appeals, 1998

Facts: Shelly Morton leased an apartment owned by Amberwood and operated by Monocle Management. The lease permitted the landlord to evict any tenant who broke the "House Rules," one of which prohibited pets. Morton kept her boyfriend's pit bull, named Rampage (!), in her apartment. At times she kept Rampage chained outside the apartment house. When Morton was near the dog, he was not violent, but when she was absent, Rampage would attempt to attack anyone who came near him. Numerous maintenance workers had been unable to perform service work because Rampage barked and lunged at them. The workers reported each of these incidents to Monocle.

Shanita Matthews and her 16-month-old son, Tevin, visited Morton and her child, something they had done many times. As the adults worked on a puzzle in the dining room, the children played in the living room. Morton briefly left the apartment, and suddenly Rampage attacked Tevin. The dog grabbed the boy by the neck and shook him. Matthews was unable to free her son. She yelled for help and called 911. Morton reentered the apartment, could not free the boy, grabbed a knife, and repeatedly stabbed the animal, which finally released Tevin. An ambulance arrived, but an hour after reaching the hospital, Tevin died from his injuries.

Matthews sued Amberwood and Monocle. The jury awarded her $5,018,750 for the wrongful death of her son. The defendants appealed.

You Be the Judge: Does a landlord owe a duty to a social guest of a tenant for an attack within the tenant's apartment?

Argument for Matthews: The House Rules prohibited pets. Monocle knew that Morton was breaking the rule and keeping an especially dangerous animal. Monocle should have acted to protect the other residents and all guests to the complex. The companies' failure to enforce their own rules led directly to the death of a child.

Argument for the Defendants: Neither the owner nor the management company has control over the apartment or what goes on inside it. The companies could not have foreseen this attack, nor could they have done anything to stop it. Matthews knew the dog's nature. She had no business leaving her son alone with such a vicious beast.

Pit bulls and other so-called attack dogs have become such a menace in some French neighborhoods that the French Assembly voted unanimously to ban them from French soil. Owners of various breeds deemed dangerous must sterilize their pets immediately. The law prohibits breeding, importing, buying, or selling any of the animals. The French agricultural minister predicts that the affected breeds will disappear within the first decade of the new century.

Exculpatory Clauses

You have found an apartment you can afford, in the right neighborhood, and the landlord presents you with a lease to sign. You notice an **exculpatory clause**, which states that the landlord is *not* liable for any injuries that occur on the rented premises, whether to you or your guests, regardless of the cause. You feel uncomfortable about the clause because it seems to suggest that the landlord can ignore serious defects and still escape liability. Should you sign the lease?

Today, **exculpatory clauses are generally void in residential leases.** Courts dislike such clauses because the parties typically have unequal bargaining power, and the goal of the law is to encourage safe housing managed by responsible landlords. So courts in many states simply ignore exculpatory clauses and apply normal rules of negligence to determine whether or not a landlord is liable for an injury. However, this is not universally the case; in some states, a court may still enforce an exculpatory clause in a residential lease. A concerned tenant should learn the local law before signing such a lease.

Exculpatory clauses are much more likely to be enforced in commercial leases. A court assumes that a merchant is capable of effective bargaining. A business tenant might agree to an exculpatory clause because the landlord accommodated him in some way, such as with a lower rent.

CRIME

Landlords may be liable in negligence to tenants or their guests for criminal attacks that occur on the premises. Courts have struggled with this issue and have reached opposing results in similar cases. The very prevalence of crime sharpens the debate. What must a landlord do to protect a tenant? Courts typically answer the question by looking at four factors.

- *Nature of the Crime.* How did the crime occur? Could the landlord have prevented it?
- *Reasonable Person Standard.* What would a reasonable landlord have done to prevent this type of crime? What did the landlord actually do?
- *Foreseeability.* Was it reasonably foreseeable that such a crime might occur? Were there earlier incidents or warnings?
- *Prevalence of Crime in the Area.* If the general area, or the particular premises, has a high crime rate, courts are more likely to hold that the crime was foreseeable and the landlord responsible.

The following case highlights some of the issues facing courts as they apply changing mores to a tragic loss.

BROCK v. WATTS REALTY CO., INC.
582 So. 2d 438, 1991 Ala. LEXIS 71
Alabama Supreme Court, 1991

Facts: Beverly Jackson lived in an apartment owned by James Levie and managed by Watts Realty. She and Beverly Silliman were both involved romantically with Curtis Hawkins, and the two women periodically argued and exchanged threats. One morning, at 9:00 A.M., Jackson called the Birmingham police and reported that a prowler was at the "back part" of her apartment. Sergeant Roger Harrison arrived at the apartment about 9:07 and saw no one at the front door, which was locked. Immediately after Harrison knocked, he saw Silliman exit through the rear door of the apartment. When police entered the apartment, they found Jackson stabbed to death. Silliman pleaded guilty to murder.

Savana Brock, Beverly Jackson's mother, sued Levie and Watts, claiming that their failure to repair a defective lock on the apartment's rear door had enabled Silliman to enter the unit and kill her daughter. The trial court gave summary judgment for both defendants, ruling that they had not been negligent. Brock appealed.

Issue: Is Beverly Jackson's mother entitled to a trial on her negligence claim?

Excerpts from Justice Steagall's Decision: [Brock bases her lawsuit on the Birmingham Housing Code, which reads:]

> *Windows, exterior doors, etc.* Every window, exterior door and basement hatchway shall be reasonably weathertight, watertight and rodentproof and shall be kept in sound working condition and good repair. Locks shall be provided on all exterior doors and all exterior openable windows.

Although the issue before us is one of first impression, Florida recently held landlords to a statutory duty to protect their tenants from the criminal acts of third persons in *Paterson v. Deeb*.[9] In that case, a female tenant was sexually assaulted by an unknown assailant in her apartment building, which had a front door with a faulty lock and a rear door with no lock. The plaintiff, as here, had previously notified the landlord of the inadequate security and had expressed concerns for her safety.

The Florida court went on to discuss at length the foreseeability issue in the causation context and stated:

> In view of the obvious purpose of the statutory duty to provide locks and security to prevent potential [damage] caused by the acts of unwarranted trespassers on the leased premises, we expressly decline to require as the essential predicate to liability allegation and proof that the landlord had actual or constructive knowledge of prior similar criminal acts committed on the premises. We are not willing to give the landlord one free ride, as it were, and sacrifice the first victim's right to safety upon the altar of foreseeability by slavishly adhering to the now-discredited notion that at least one criminal assault must have occurred on the premises before the landlord can be held liable.

We agree with the Florida court's reasoning and hold that the two Birmingham Housing Code ordinances created a duty on the part of Levie and Watts Realty to maintain the locks on Jackson's doors "in satisfactory working condition" because the resulting crime (Jackson's murder) was one the general risk of which was foreseeable, regardless of whether there had been prior similar incidents in the area.

[Reversed and remanded.]

CHAPTER CONCLUSION

A century ago no plaintiff would even have argued that a landlord was responsible for bites inflicted by a tenant's dog, for children falling from windows, or for a tenant's death by murder. But living patterns alter, social mores reflect the change, and the law—in theory—responds to both. The current trend is clearly for expanded landlord liability, but how far that will continue is impossible to divine.

CHAPTER REVIEW

1. When an owner of a freehold estate allows another person temporary, exclusive possession of the property, the parties have created a landlord-tenant relationship.

---

[9] 472 So.2d 1210, 1985 Fla. App. LEXIS 15035 (Fla Dist. Ct. App. 1985).

2. Any lease for a stated, fixed period is a tenancy for years. A periodic tenancy is created for a fixed period and then automatically continues for additional periods until either party notifies the other of termination. A tenancy at will has no fixed duration and may be terminated by either party at any time. A tenancy at sufferance occurs when a tenant remains, against the wishes of the landlord, after the expiration of a true tenancy.

3. All tenants are entitled to the quiet enjoyment of the premises, without the interference of the landlord.

4. A landlord may be liable for constructive eviction if he substantially interferes with the tenant's use and enjoyment of the premises.

5. The implied warranty of habitability requires that a landlord meet all standards set by the local building code and/or that the premises be fit for human habitation.

6. The tenant is obligated to pay the rent, and the landlord may evict for nonpayment. The modern trend is to require a landlord to mitigate damages caused by a tenant who abandons the premises before the lease expires.

7. A tenant is liable to the landlord for any significant damage he causes to the property.

8. A tenant must not disturb other tenants.

9. A tenant typically may assign a lease or sublet the premises only with the landlord's permission, but the current trend is to prohibit a landlord from unreasonably withholding permission.

10. At common law, a landlord had very limited liability for injuries on the premises, but today many courts require a landlord to use reasonable care and hold her liable for foreseeable harm.

11. Landlords may be liable in negligence to tenants or their guests for criminal attacks on the premises. Courts determine liability by looking at factors such as the nature of the crime, what a reasonable landlord would have done to prevent it, and the foreseeability of the attack.

PRACTICE TEST

1. **CPA QUESTION** Which of the following forms of tenancy will be created if a tenant stays in possession of the leased premises without the landlord's consent, after the tenant's one-year written lease expires?

(a) Tenancy at will
(b) Tenancy for years
(c) Tenancy from period to period
(d) Tenancy at sufferance

2. **CPA QUESTION** A tenant's personal property will become a fixture and belong to the landlord if its removal would:

(a) Increase the value of the personal property
(b) Cause a material change to the personal property
(c) Result in substantial harm to the landlord's property
(d) Change the use of the landlord's property back to its prior use

3. Loren Andreo leased retail space in his shopping plaza to Tropical Isle Pet Shop for five years, at a monthly rent of $2,100. Tropical Isle vacated the premises 18 months early, turned in the key to Andreo, and acknowledged liability for the unpaid rent. Andreo placed a "for rent" sign in the store window and spoke to a commercial real estate broker about the space. But he did not enter into a formal listing agreement with the broker, or take any other steps to rent the space, for about nine months. With approximately nine months

remaining on the unused part of Tropical's lease, Andreo hired a commercial broker to rent the space. He also sued Tropical for 18 months' rent. Comment.

4. Philip Schwachman owned a commercial building and leased space to Davis Radio Corp. for use as a retail store. In the same building, Schwachman leased other retail space to Pampered Pet, a dog grooming shop. Davis Radio complained repeatedly to Schwachman that foul odors from Pampered Pet entered its store and drove away customers and workers. Davis abandoned the premises, leaving many months' rent unpaid. Schwachman sued for unpaid rent and moved for summary judgment. What ruling would you make on the summary judgment motion?

5. William Bryant was walking along the street in Conway, Arkansas, when a rottweiler (sound familiar?) and two pit bulls attacked and seriously injured him. Mona Jones owned the dogs, who had escaped from the house she rented from Karen and Ted Putnam. Bryant sued the Putnams for negligence, and they moved for summary judgment. Arkansas applies the traditional common law rule to this case. Who wins on the summary judgment motion?

6. YOU BE THE JUDGE WRITING PROBLEM Jane Doe (not her real name) worked as a secretary in a large commercial building in Washington D.C. Dominion Bank, which owned the building, decided to sell it. It stopped giving new leases for office space, in anticipation of the sale, and gradually 5 of the building's 13 floors became vacant. The bank did not close off the vacant floors, and as the vacancies increased, tenants in the building began to complain to the landlord about vagrants, "street persons," "strange people," and others entering the building and engaging in drug deals or prostitution in the uncontrolled spaces. Jane Doe left her office one morning about 9:20 A.M. to go to a nearby shop. She entered the elevator on the eleventh floor and rode down, but the elevator stopped at an abandoned floor, and a large male boarded. He grabbed Doe in a choke hold and dragged her down the hallway through unlocked doors to a vacant office, where he raped and robbed her. Doe sued the Dominion Bank in United States District Court. A security expert testified that all vacant offices and floors should have been sealed off. Is the bank liable for Doe's injuries? **Argument for Jane Doe:** The bank created a dangerous situation by gradually abandoning a commercial building. Tenants repeatedly told the bank about the vagrants, and it was entirely foreseeable that a violent crime would result. The bank should be held to a "reasonable person" standard, one that it clearly failed to meet. **Argument for Dominion Bank:** A landlord is not and should not be liable for violent crime. The bank is not a police force. The bank's obligation was to keep the rented premises, meaning Doe's office, in good working order, which it did. Do not try to hold a bank liable just because there has been a personal tragedy.

7. Doris Rowley rented space from the city of Mobile, Alabama, to run the Back Porch Restaurant. Her lease prohibited assignment or subletting without the landlord's permission. Rowley's business became unprofitable, and she asked the city's real estate officer for permission to assign her lease. She told the officer that she had "someone who would accept if the lease was assigned." Rowley provided no other information about the assignee. The city refused permission. Rowley repeated her requests several times without success, and finally she sued. Rowley alleged that the city had unreasonably withheld permission to assign and had caused her serious financial losses as a result. Comment.

8. Kenmart Realty sued to evict Mr. and Ms. Alghalabio for nonpayment of rent and sought the unpaid monies, totaling several thousand dollars. In defense, the Alghalabios claimed that their apartment was infested with rats. They testified that there were numerous rat holes in the walls of the living room, bedroom, and kitchen, that there were rat droppings all over the apartment, and that on one occasion they saw their toddler holding a live rat. They testified that the landlord had refused numerous requests to exterminate. Please rule on the landlord's suit.

9. CPA QUESTION To be enforceable, a residential real estate lease must:

(a) Require the tenant to obtain liability insurance

(b) Entitle the tenant to exclusive possession of the leased property

(c) Specify a due date for rent

(d) Be in writing

10. CPA QUESTION A tenant renting an apartment under a three-year written lease that does **not** contain any specific restrictions may be evicted for:

(a) Counterfeiting money in the apartment

(b) Keeping a dog in the apartment

(c) Failing to maintain a liability insurance policy on the apartment

(d) Making structural repairs to the apartment

11. **RIGHT & WRONG** Lisa Preece rented an apartment from Turman Realty, paying a $300 security deposit. Georgia law states: "Any landlord who fails to return any part of a security deposit which is required to be returned to a tenant pursuant to this article shall be liable to the tenant in the amount of three times the sum improperly withheld plus reasonable attorney's fees." When Preece moved out, Turman did not return her security deposit, and she sued for triple damages plus attorney's fees, totaling $1,800. Turman offered evidence that its failure to return the deposit was inadvertent and that it had procedures reasonably designed to avoid such errors. Is Preece entitled to triple damages? Attorney's fees? What is the rationale behind a statute that requires triple damages? Is it ethical to force a landlord to pay $1,800 for a $300 debt?

INTERNET RESEARCH PROBLEM

Go to http://www.tenantsunion.org/tulist.html, and search for the law of your state concerning a landlord's obligation to provide a habitable apartment. Now assume that you are living in a rental unit with serious defects. Draft a letter to the landlord asking for prompt repairs. You may use the form letters provided at http://little.nhlink.net/nhlink/housing/cto/letters/letrs.htm as a guide.

You can find further practice problems in the Online Quiz at http://beatty.westbuslaw.com or in the Study Guide that accompanies this text.

CHAPTER 47

PERSONAL PROPERTY

"My only child is a no-good thief," Riley murmurs sadly to his visitors. "He has always treated me contemptuously. Now he's been sentenced to five years for stealing from a children's charity. He is my only heir, but why should I leave him everything?" Riley continues talking to his three guests: a bishop, a rabbi, and Earnest, a Boy Scout leader. "I have $500,000 in stocks and bonds in my bank deposit box. Tomorrow morning I'm going down to the bank, take out all the papers, and hand them over to the Boy Scouts so that other kids won't turn out so bad." Everyone applauds his generosity, and they photograph Riley and Earnest shaking hands. But the following morning, on his way to the bank, Riley is struck by an ambulance and killed. A dispute arises over the money. The three witnesses assure the court that Riley was on his way to give the money to the Boy Scouts. From prison, the ne'er-do-well son demands the money as Riley's sole heir. Who wins? This is a typical issue of personal property law.

Personal property means all property other than real property. In Chapter 45 we saw that real property means land and things firmly attached to it, such as buildings, crops, and minerals. All other property is personal property—a bus, a toothbrush, a share of stock. Most personal property is goods, meaning something that can be moved. We have already examined the purchase and sale of goods, which are governed by the Uniform Commercial Code. In this chapter we look at several other ways in which personal property can be acquired, including gifts and found property. In the section on gifts we learn that Riley's no-good son gets the money. Riley intended to give the stocks and bonds to the Boy Scouts the following day, but he never completed a valid gift because he failed to *deliver* the papers. Then we turn to disputes over found property. And finally we examine bailments, which occur when the owner of personal property permits another to possess it.

GIFTS

A gift is a voluntary transfer of property from one person to another without any consideration. It is the lack of consideration that distinguishes a gift from a contract. Contracts usually consist of mutual promises to do something in the future. Each promise is consideration for the other one, and the mutual consideration makes each promise enforceable. But a gift is a one-way transaction, without consideration. The person who gives property away is the **donor** and the one who receives it is the **donee**.[1]

A gift involves three elements:

- The donor intends to transfer ownership of the property to the donee immediately.
- The donor delivers the property to the donee.
- The donee accepts the property.

INTENTION TO TRANSFER OWNERSHIP

The donor must intend to transfer ownership to the property right away, immediately giving up all control of the item. Notice the two important parts of this element. First, the donor's intention must be to *transfer ownership*, that is, to give title to the donee. Merely proving that the owner handed you property does not guarantee that you have received a gift; if the owner only intended that you use the item, there is no gift and she can demand it back.

Second, the donor must also intend the property to transfer *immediately*. A promise to make a gift in the future is unenforceable. Promises about future behavior are governed by contract law, and a contract is unenforceable without consideration. If Sarah hands Lenny the keys to a $600,000 yacht and says, "Lenny, it's yours," then it *is* his, since Sarah intends to transfer ownership right away. But if Sarah says to Max, "Next week I'm going to give you my used bicycle," Max has not received a gift of the bike because Sarah did not intend an immediate transfer. Nor does Max have an enforceable contract, since there is no consideration for Sarah's promise.

A *revocable gift* is a contradiction in terms, because it violates the rule just discussed. It is not a gift and the donee keeps nothing.[2] Suppose Harold tells his daughter Faith, "The mule is yours from now on, but if you start acting stupid

---

1 For a useful discussion of the tax consequences of gifts, see http://lawcrawler.findlaw.com/NOLO/nn203.html.

2 The only exception to this rule is a gift *causa mortis*, discussed later in the chapter.

again, I'm taking her back." Harold has retained some control over the animal, which means he has not intended to transfer ownership. There is no gift, and Harold still owns the mule.

When Dominic Tenaglia's automobile broke down, his brother Nick generously offered to give him a replacement car. Nick delivered a Chevrolet to Dominic, and both brothers understood that the car was a gift. Nick wrote "gift" on the car's certificate of title, but did not immediately give the certificate to Dominic. A week later, while Dominic was driving the Chevrolet, he was involved in an accident. Both brothers had insurance, through different insurers, for cars they owned. The two companies disputed which one was responsible for Dominic's accident. The court determined that Nick's company was still liable for any damage caused by the Chevrolet. Nick had presented the car to Dominic but had not relinquished all control over it. Ownership of a car requires possession of the certificate of title. Because Nick still had the certificate at the time of the accident, he had the power to take back the Chevrolet whenever he wanted, and he had not made a valid gift of the automobile. Dominic's insurer won the case.[3]

Delivery

Physical Delivery

The donor must deliver the property to the donee. Generally, this involves physical delivery. If Anna hands Eddie a Rembrandt drawing, saying "I want you to have this forever," she has satisfied the delivery requirement. In the chapter opening, Riley promised to give half a million dollars to the Boy Scouts the following day. But he never delivered the stocks and bonds, so there was no gift. The Boy Scouts get nothing, and all of the money becomes part of Riley's estate, which passes to his unworthy son.

Constructive Delivery

Physical delivery is the most common and the surest way to make a gift, but it is not always necessary. **A donor makes constructive delivery by transferring ownership without a physical delivery.** Most courts permit constructive delivery only when physical delivery is impossible or extremely inconvenient. Suppose Anna wants to give her niece Jen a blimp, which is parked in a hangar at the airport. The blimp will not fit through the doorway of Jen's dorm. Instead of flying the aircraft to the university, Anna may simply deliver to Jen the certificate of title and the keys to the blimp. When she has done that, Jen owns the aircraft.

A donor may accomplish constructive delivery in other ways. Suppose that Anna's shares are locked in a safe deposit box at the bank, and that only one key opens the box. If Anna gives that key to Jen and tells her she may have the shares in the box, then the gift is complete as of that moment. But the result is probably different if Anna has two keys to the box and parts with only one of them. Jen goes to empty out the safe deposit box only to discover it already *is* empty, because Anna has beaten her there. There probably has been no gift. Anna's retention of one key indicates she did *not* intend to give Jen the stocks, and Anna's withdrawal of the shares confirms that view.

Delivery to an Agent

A donor might deliver the property to an agent, either someone working for him or for the donee. If the donor delivers the property to his own agent, there is no

[3] *Motorists Mutual Insurance Co. v. State Farm Mutual Automobile Insurance Co.*, 1990 Ohio App. LEXIS 3027 (Ohio Ct. App. 1990).

gift. By definition the agent works for the donor, and thus the donor still has control and ownership of the property. But if the donor delivers the property to the donee's agent, the gift is made.

Property Already in Donee's Possession

Sometimes a donor decides to give property to a donee who already has possession of it. In that case, no delivery is required, and the donee need only demonstrate that the donor intended to transfer present *ownership*. Larry lends a grand piano to Leslie for the summer. At the end of the summer, Larry announces that she can keep the instrument. As long as Larry clearly intends that Leslie gets ownership of the piano, the gift is completed.

INTER VIVOS GIFTS AND GIFTS *CAUSA MORTIS*

A gift can be either *inter vivos* or *causa mortis*. An ***inter vivos* gift** means a gift made "during life," that is, when the donor is not under any fear of impending death. The vast majority of gifts are *inter vivos*, involving a healthy donor and donee. Shirley, age 30 and in good health, gives her husband Terry an eraser for his birthday. This is an *inter vivos* gift, which is absolute. The gift becomes final upon delivery, and the donor *may not* revoke it. If Shirley and Terry have a fight the next day, Shirley has no power to erase her eraser gift.

A **gift *causa mortis*** is one made in contemplation of approaching death. The gift is valid if the donor dies as expected, but is revoked if he recovers. Suppose Lance's doctors have told him he will probably die of a liver ailment within a month. Lance calls Jane to his bedside and hands her a fistful of emeralds, saying, "I'm dying, these are yours." Jane sheds a tear, then sprints to the bank. If Lance dies of the liver ailment within a few weeks, Jane gets to keep the emeralds. The law permits the gift *causa mortis* to act as a substitute for a will, since the donor's delivery of the property clearly indicates his intentions. But note that this kind of gift is revocable. Since a gift *causa mortis* is conditional (upon the donor's death), the donor has the right to revoke it at any time before he dies. If Lance telephones Jane the next day and says that he has changed his mind, he gets the jewels back. Further, if the donor recovers and does not die as expected, the gift is automatically revoked.

ACCEPTANCE

The donee must accept the gift. This rarely leads to disputes, but if a donee should refuse a gift and then change her mind, she is out of luck. Her repudiation of the donor's offer means there is no gift, and she has no rights in the property.

The following case offers neighbors, relatives, failing health, and plenty of money—always a volatile mix.

JAMISON v. ESTATE OF GOODLETT
56 Ark. App. 71, 938 S.W.2d 865, 1997
Ark. App. LEXIS 75
Arkansas Court of Appeals, 1997

Facts: Robert Goodlett, a bachelor, owned a 300-acre farm, a store, and other property in Arkansas. His cousin lived on an adjoining farm; the cousin's daughter, Sara Goodlett Jamison, and her husband, Val, often visited Robert. Goodlett became ill and asked Val Jamison to take him to the hospital. The next day, while hospitalized, Goodlett asked Jamison to help him pay some bills. Jamison arranged for bank officials to visit the hospital, where, with Goodlett's agreement, they empowered Jamison to use Goodlett's checking account.

According to Jamison, when Goodlett learned from his doctor that he must undergo life-threatening surgery, Goodlett said that he wanted to give all of his property and money to Jamison and his wife. There were no other witnesses. Jamison had a lawyer draw up a "power of attorney" form, which Goodlett signed, giving Jamison the right to dispose of Goodlett's property. Goodlett actually lived several more years. During that period, Jamison transferred the farm to his wife and all of Goodlett's cash, about $185,000, to himself. He continued to pay all of Goodlett's bills; paid taxes in Goodlett's name on the interest earned from the cash; leased the land to another farmer in Goodlett's name; and gave Goodlett periodic reports on the money and the farm. Jamison claimed that Goodlett never objected to the transfer of the money and property and that, if he had, Jamison would have given it back. After Goodlett died, a trial court ordered the Jamisons to return the property and cash (with interest) to the estate. They appealed, claiming an *inter vivos* gift.

You Be the Judge: Did Goodlett make an *inter vivos* gift?

Argument for the Jamisons: Your honors, the three elements of a valid gift are intent, delivery, and acceptance, and all three are undeniably present. Robert Goodlett had a long-term friendship with his relative Sara and her husband, Val, which is why he turned to them when he became ill. Goodlett asked bank officers to give Jamison the power to sign checks. Goodlett also signed a power of attorney, understanding that Jamison then had complete control of the property and money. Goodlett lived for several years without once objecting to the arrangement. He intended this transfer as a gift. Delivery occurred when the property changed hands. The Jamisons' acceptance is obvious because they operated the farm and controlled the money for several years. The gift is complete and the estate has no legitimate claim, only a greedy desire for money that Goodlett disposed of long ago.

Argument for the Estate: The Jamisons probably did help Robert Goodlett, and they should be thanked. But there was no gift and they may not keep his property. The element of intent requires that the donor give up ownership immediately and permanently. Yet the Jamisons' conduct indicated that Goodlett never gave up ownership. They paid taxes and leased the property in Goodlett's name, reported the farm's condition to him, and remained willing to return the property if he asked for it. A "revocable" gift is no gift at all. Goodlett never objected to the Jamisons' role as caretaker because it never occurred to him that they would claim ownership rights.

The following table distinguishes between a contract and a gift:

A Contract and a Gift Distinguished

A Contract:

Lou: I will pay you $2,000 to paint the house, if you promise to finish by July 3.	Abby: I agree to paint the house by July 3, for $2,000.

Lou and Abby have a contract. Each promise is consideration in support of the other promise. Lou and Abby can each enforce the other's promise.

A Gift:

Lou hands Phil two opera tickets, while saying:

Lou: I want you to have these two tickets to *Rigoletto*.	Phil: Hey, thanks.

This is a valid *inter vivos* gift. Lou intended to transfer ownership immediately and delivered the property to Phil, who now owns the tickets.

Neither Contract nor Gift:

Lou: You're a great guy. Next week, I'm going to give you two tickets to *Rigoletto*.	Jason: Hey, thanks.

There is no gift because Lou did not intend to transfer ownership immediately, and he did not deliver the tickets. There is no contract because Jason has given no consideration to support Lou's promise.

FOUND PROPERTY

Dejected and ashamed, you walk to the university with your head hung low, knowing that your failure to study means you will fare poorly on today's quiz concerning *found property*. Suddenly, there is a gleam of light, not in your mind (which is vacant), but right there on the sidewalk. You stoop to pick it up—a ring! You stop in at the local jewelry shop, where you learn this ruby marvel is worth just over $700,000. Dazzled and delighted, you walk into the classroom and take the test. Question 1 reads: "A student discovers a ruby ring while walking to class. May the student keep the ring?" You have no idea what the answer is and you cannot concentrate anyway. So you write the two safest words in the law: "It depends." That is a fine start, but to learn the full answer, read on.

The law of found property has bewitched the courts of this country for nearly two centuries. Judges have made valiant attempts to base their rulings on principles of sound public policy, but the results have been confusing and contradictory. **The primary goal of the common law has been to get found property back to its proper owner, if possible.** The finder must make a good faith effort to locate the owner of the property and return the goods to him. In some states, the finder is obligated to notify the police of what she has found and entrust the property to them until the owner can be located or until a stated period has passed. **A second policy has been to reward the finder if no owner can be located.** But courts are loath to encourage trespassing, so finders who discover personal property on someone else's land generally cannot keep it. Those basic policies yield various outcomes, depending on the nature of the property. There are four kinds of found property:

- **Abandoned property** is something that the owner has knowingly discarded because she no longer wants it. A vase thrown into a garbage can is abandoned. Generally, the finder is permitted to keep abandoned property. But because the owner loses all rights in abandoned property, a court never *presumes* abandonment. The finder must prove that the owner intended to relinquish all rights.

- **Lost property** is something accidentally given up. A ring that falls off a finger into the street is lost property. Usually, the finder of lost property has rights superior to all the world except the true owner. If the true owner comes forward, he gets his property back; otherwise, the finder may keep it. However, if the finder has discovered the item on land belonging to another, the landowner is probably entitled to keep it.

- **Mislaid property** is something the owner has intentionally placed somewhere and then forgotten. A book deliberately placed on a bus seat by an owner who forgets to take it with her is mislaid property. Generally, the finder gets no rights in property that has simply been mislaid. If the true owner cannot be located, the mislaid item belongs to the owner of the premises where the item was found.

- **Treasure trove** is coins or currency concealed by an owner so long ago that it is likely the owner has died. A sackful of 1850 gold coins, found under the roots of a 150-year-old tree, is treasure trove. The finder can generally keep treasure trove.

Many states have enacted laws, called **finding statutes** or **estray statutes,** governing found property. In some cases, the legislation incorporates the common law principles outlined above, but in other states the new law modifies the old rules. A New York statute, for example, has removed the distinction between lost and mislaid property and now generally permits the finder to keep what he has discovered, regardless of where he found it. The finder is, however, required to turn over the property either to the police or the owner of the premises where the item was found. If the true owner is not located during a stated period, the finder is then entitled to whatever he found.

Iowa's estray statute is different. Even with a statute, some cases are close calls.

BENJAMIN v. LINDNER AVIATION, INC.
534 N.W.2d 400, 1995 Iowa Sup. LEXIS 166
Iowa Supreme Court, 1995

Facts: State Central Bank repossessed an airplane when its owner defaulted on a loan. The bank, as the new owner, took the plane to Lindner Aviation for routine maintenance. Heath Benjamin, a mechanic, performed the work. When Benjamin removed panels from the underside of the left wing, he found two packets inside, wrapped in aluminum foil. Inside the packets were $18,000 in $20 bills. Benjamin showed the packets to his supervisor, offering to split the money with him. But the supervisor gave the money to Lindner's president, who delivered it to the police.

Pursuant to the Iowa finder's statute, Chapter 644, Benjamin filed papers claiming to be the finder. Lindner and the bank also claimed ownership. The police published notices of the discovery, but no owner came forward within the 12-month statutory period. Benjamin filed a complaint seeking to have a court declare the money his. The trial court ruled that the Iowa statute applied only to lost money and declared that this money was mislaid. It awarded the money to the bank, as owner of the aircraft, though it awarded Benjamin a 10 percent finder's fee. Benjamin appealed.

Issue: **Who owns the money?**

Excerpts from Justice Ternus's Decision: The place where Benjamin found the money and the manner in which it was hidden are important here. The bills were carefully tied and wrapped and then concealed in a location that was accessible only by removing screws and a panel. These circumstances support an inference that the money was placed there intentionally. This inference supports the conclusion that the money was mislaid.

The same facts that support the trial court's conclusion that the money was mislaid prevent us from ruling as a matter of law that the property was lost. Property is not considered lost unless considering the place where and the conditions under which the property is found, there is an inference that the property was left there unintentionally. Contrary to Benjamin's position the circumstances here do not support a conclusion that the money was placed in the wing of the airplane unintentionally.

We also reject Benjamin's assertion that as a matter of law this money was abandoned property. Both logic and common sense suggest that it is unlikely someone would voluntarily part with over $18,000 with the intention of terminating his ownership. The location where this money was found is much more consistent with the conclusion that the owner of the property was placing the money there for safekeeping. We will not presume that an owner has abandoned his property when his conduct is consistent with a continued claim to the property.

Because the money discovered by Benjamin was properly found to be mislaid property, it belongs to the owner of the premises where it was found. Mislaid property is entrusted to the owner of the premises where it is found rather than the finder of the property because it is assumed that the true owner may eventually recall where he has placed his property and return there to reclaim it.

We think that the premises where the money was found is the airplane, not Lindner Aviation's hangar where the airplane happened to be parked when the money was discovered. If the true owner of the money attempts to locate it, he would initially look for the plane; it is unlikely he would begin his search by contacting businesses where the airplane might have been inspected. Therefore, we affirm the trial court's judgment that the bank, as the owner of the plane, has the right to possession of the property as against all but the true owner.

Benjamin claims that if he is not entitled to the money, he should be paid a 10 percent finder's fee under Section 644. The problem with this claim is that only the finder of "lost goods, money, bank notes, and other things" is rewarded with a finder's fee under Chapter 644. Because the property found by Benjamin was mislaid property, not lost property, [Chapter] 644 does not apply here. The trial court erred in awarding Benjamin a finder's fee.

ACCESSION

Accession occurs when one person uses labor and/or materials to add value to personal property belonging to another. This generally occurs by agreement. Suppose Leasing Corp. agrees to lease a truck to Delivery Co., for use in its business. The contract may permit Delivery to modify the truck's storage space to meet its special needs. If so, the agreement should also state whether Delivery has to return the truck to its original condition at the end of the lease, and whether Delivery is entitled to any payment for improvements made.

But sometimes one party makes accessions without agreement. If the improvements can be "undone" without damage to the property, then the improver must do that. For example, if Delivery Co. simply bolts a few shelves into the truck, it should remove them before returning the truck. Problems arise when the improvements cannot be removed without damaging the property. Assuming the property has become more valuable, must the owner pay the improver for the work done? It normally depends upon whether the improver acted wrongfully or mistakenly.

WRONGFUL ACCESSIONS

If the improver knows he is making accessions without authority, the owner may generally take the improved property without compensating for the work done. Suppose the lease between Leasing Corp. and Delivery Co. states that Delivery may not modify the truck without written permission. Delivery goes ahead anyway and reconfigures the truck to meet its needs. Even if the work substantially increases the truck's value, Leasing Corp. probably owes nothing for the accessions.

MISTAKEN ACCESSIONS

If the improver mistakenly believes he is entitled to add accessions, the owner probably has to pay for the increased value. Suppose that, based on its previous leases with Leasing Corp., Delivery Co. believes it has the right to modify its new truck, though in fact it has no such permission. If the modifications increase the value of the vehicle, Leasing probably has to pay for the accessions.

BAILMENT

A bailment is the rightful possession of goods by one who is not the owner. The one who delivers the goods is the **bailor** and the one in possession is the **bailee.** Bailments are common. Suppose you are going out of town for the weekend and loan your motorcycle to Stan. You are the bailor and your friend is the bailee.

When you check your suitcase with the airline, you are again the bailor and the airline is the bailee. If you rent a car at your destination, you become the bailee while the rental agency is the bailor. In each case, someone other than the true owner has rightful, temporary possession of personal property.

The parties generally—but not always—create a bailment by agreement. In each of the examples, the parties agreed to the bailment. In two cases, the agreement included payment, which is common but not essential. When you buy your airline ticket, you pay for your ticket, and the price includes the airline's agreement, as bailee, to transport your suitcase. When you rent a car, you pay the bailor for the privilege of using it. By loaning your motorcycle, you engage in a bailment without either party paying compensation.

A bailment without any agreement is called a constructive, or involuntary, bailment. Suppose you find a wristwatch in your house that you know belongs to a friend. As we saw in the section above, you are obligated to return the watch to the true owner, and until you do so, you are the bailee, liable for harm to the property. This is called a constructive bailment because, with no agreement between the parties, the law is *construing* a bailment.

Because the bailor is the one who delivers the goods to another, the bailor is typically the owner, but he need not be. Suppose that Stan, who borrowed your motorcycle, allows his girlfriend Sheila to try out the bike, and she takes it to a mall where she jumps over a row of six parked cars. Stan, the bailee from you, has become a bailor, and Sheila is his bailee.

CONTROL

To create a bailment, the bailee must assume physical control with intent to possess. A bailee may be liable for loss or damage to the property. But it is not fair to hold him liable unless he has taken physical control of the goods, intending to possess them.

Disputes about whether someone has taken control often arise in parking lot cases. When a car is damaged or stolen, the lot's owner may try to avoid liability by claiming it lacked control of the parked auto and therefore was not a bailee. If the lot is a "park and lock" facility, where the car's owner retains the key and the lot owner exercises *no control at all,* then there may be no bailment, and no liability for damage. (For a sample automobile bailment form, see **http://www.gate.net/~legalsvc/autobail.html**.)

Jack Sonneveldt was a guest at the O'Hare Marriott Hotel outside Chicago. Sonneveldt arrived at the hotel in a 40-foot customized coach. He attempted to park in the hotel's valet parking area, but employees asked him to leave the vehicle in the hotel's general parking lot across the street. During the night, the $265,000 coach was stolen. If the hotel was a bailee, it would be liable. Sonneveldt's insurance company, Michigan Mutual, sued the hotel—and lost. The court ruled:

> The complaint indicates that the Sonneveldt driver drove the Prevost coach into the lot and parked the vehicle himself. Nowhere does it suggest that Marriott was left with a set of keys to the coach, or that the hotel otherwise accepted or obtained actual control over the vehicle. Without the keys, Marriott had neither partial nor complete control over the Prevost coach.[4]

By contrast, when a driver leaves her keys with a parking attendant, the lot clearly is exercising control of the auto, and the parties have created a bailment.

---

[4] *Michigan Mutual Insurance Co. v. Marriott Corp.,* 1992 U.S. Dist. LEXIS 5696 (N.D. Ill. 1992).

The lot is probably liable for loss or damage. What about cases in the middle, where the driver keeps her keys but the lot owner exercises *some other control?* The following lawsuit indicates the modern trend.

PARK 'N GO OF GEORGIA, INC. v. UNITED STATES FIDELITY & GUARANTY CO.
266 Ga. 787, 471 S.E.2d 500, 1996 Ga. LEXIS 357
Supreme Court of Georgia, 1996

Facts: Park 'N Go operated a parking/shuttle service near Atlanta's Hartsfield International Airport. A fence surrounded the 13-acre flat-surface lot, which had entrance and exit gates, a limited staff, and no security system. To enter, a patron would drive his vehicle to the entry gate, take from a machine a bar-coded ticket with a liability disclaimer on the back, park and lock his vehicle, and, taking the keys with him, wait for a shuttle bus to transport him to the airport. On returning to the lot, the customer would drive his car to the exit window, present his ticket, pay, and leave.

Torrential rains flooded the parking lot, damaging over 200 automobiles, whose owners filed suit for negligence. Park 'N Go had two kinds of insurance with United States Fidelity & Guaranty Co. (USF&G): a $250,000 policy covering goods bailed to the facility; and a $1 million policy for other injuries or damage, specifically *excluding goods involved in a bailment.* Park 'N Go claimed that no bailment existed for the autos and that the $1 million policy covered the damaged cars. USF&G argued that there was a bailment, leaving the insurance company liable for only $250,000 of the damage. The issue reached the Georgia Supreme Court.

Issue: **Was there a bailment?**

Excerpts from Judge Hines's Decision: A bailment relationship is created when one party is involved in an undertaking for a consideration to safeguard the personal property of another and exercises complete dominion at all times over the property. For all practical purposes, Park 'N Go, by virtue of its lot design and processing procedures, exercised complete dominion over the vehicles parked on its lot. The fact that in most instances the vehicle owner retained the keys did not alter the measure of control held by Park 'N Go so as to negate the existence of a bailment.

[A Georgia statute] unequivocally recognizes the bailment relationship between garage owners and their customers:

> The relationship of the owner of an automobile and the owner of the garage in which the automobile is stored is that of bailor and bailee. The bailee is bound to use ordinary care for the safekeeping and return of the automobile.

The fact the Park 'N Go facility was an open-air lot did not render it any less of a "garage" for the purposes of the statutory presumption. There is no basis in the law for a distinction. Nor is there any reason in fact here to distinguish Park 'N Go's situation. The lack of an enclosed storage structure did not diminish the degree of control exercised by Park 'N Go. It was unquestionably a bailee of the vehicles parked at its facility.

The purported disclaimer printed on the back of the parking tickets did not, in and of itself, alter the existence of the bailment relationship between Park 'N Go and its customers. The mere receipt of a printed notice of the bailee's attempt to disavow liability is insufficient to do so. In order to uphold such a disclaimer, at a minimum there must be affirmative evidence of the bailor's awareness of it. Park 'N Go employed no mechanism, either in its parking procedures or on the parking ticket itself for patron acknowledgment of the disclaimer. Therefore, it was not effective to remove the parked vehicles from Park 'N Go's "care, custody or control."

RIGHTS OF THE BAILEE

The bailee's primary right is possession of the property. **Anyone who interferes with the bailee's rightful possession is liable to her.** Suppose that, after you loan your motorcycle to Stan, Mel sees Stan park the bike, realizes Stan isn't the owner, rides the motorcycle away, and locks it up until you return. Mel is liable to Stan for any damages Stan suffered while deprived of transportation.

Even a bailor is liable if he wrongfully takes back property from a bailee. If a car agency rents Francine a car for a three-day weekend but then repossesses it to use elsewhere, it is liable to her for any damages, even though it owns the car. The bailor must abide by the agreement.

The bailee is typically, though not always, permitted to use the property. Obviously, a customer is permitted to drive a car rented from an agency. When a farmer loans his tractor to a neighbor, the bailee is entitled to use the machine for normal farm purposes. But some bailees have no authority to use the goods. If you store your furniture in a warehouse, the storage company is your bailee, but it has no right to curl up in your bed.

The bailee may be entitled to compensation. This depends upon the agreement. If Owner leaves a power boat at the boatyard for repairs, the boatyard, a bailee, is entitled to payment for the work it does. As with any contract, the exact compensation should be clearly agreed upon before any work begins. If there is no agreement, the boatyard will probably receive the reasonable value of its services.

DUTIES OF THE BAILEE

The bailee is strictly liable to redeliver the goods on time to the bailor or to whomever the bailor designates. Strict liability means there are virtually no exceptions. Rudy stores his $6,000 drum set with Melissa's Warehouse while he is on vacation. Blake arrives at the warehouse and shows a forged letter, supposedly from Rudy, granting Blake permission to remove the drums. If Melissa permits Blake to take the drums, she will owe Rudy $6,000, even if the forgery was a high-quality job.

Due Care

The bailee is obligated to exercise due care. **The level of care required depends upon who receives the benefit of the bailment.** There are three possibilities.

- *Sole Benefit of Bailee.* If the bailment is for the sole benefit of the bailee, the bailee is required to use **extraordinary care** with the property. Generally, in these cases, the bailor loans something for free to the bailee. Since the bailee is paying nothing for the use of the goods, most courts (though not all) consider her the only one to benefit from the bailment. If your neighbor loans you a power lawn mower, the bailment is probably for your sole benefit. You are liable if you are even slightly inattentive in handling the lawn mower and can expect to pay for virtually any harm done.
- *Mutual Benefit.* When the bailment is for the mutual benefit of bailor and bailee, the bailee must use **ordinary care** with the property. Ordinary care is what a reasonably prudent person would use under the circumstances. When you rent a car, you benefit from the use of the car, and the agency profits from the fee you pay. When the airline hauls your suitcase to your destination, both parties benefit. Most bailments benefit both parties, and courts decide the majority of bailment disputes under this standard.

- *Sole Benefit of Bailor*. When the bailment benefits only the bailor, the bailee must use **only slight care**. This kind of bailment is called a **gratuitous bailment**, and the bailee is liable only for **gross negligence**. Sheila enters a greased-pig contest and asks you to hold her $140,000 diamond engagement ring while she competes. You put the ring in your pocket. Sheila wins the $20 first prize but the ring has disappeared. This was a gratuitous bailment, and you are not liable to Sheila unless she can prove gross negligence on your part. If the ring dropped from your pocket or was stolen, you are not liable. If you used the ring to play catch with friends, you are liable.

Burden of Proof

In an ordinary negligence case, the plaintiff has the burden of proof to demonstrate that the defendant was negligent and caused the harm alleged. In bailment cases, the burden of proof is reversed. **Once the bailor has proven the existence of a bailment and loss or harm to the goods, a presumption of negligence arises, and the burden shifts to the bailee to prove adequate care.** This is a major change from ordinary negligence cases. Georgina's car is struck by another auto. If Georgina sues for negligence, it is her burden to prove that the defendant was driving unreasonably and caused the harm. By comparison, assume that Georgina rents Charley her sailboat for a month. At the end of the month, Charley announces that the boat is at the bottom of Lake Michigan. If Georgina sues Charley, she only needs to demonstrate that the parties had a bailment and that Charley failed to return the boat. The burden then shifts to Charley to prove that the boat was lost through no fault of his own. If Charley cannot meet that burden, Georgina recovers the full value of the boat.

In the following case, the court looks at the two principal issues we have examined: whether there was a bailment, and whether the bailee exercised adequate care.

GIN v. WACKENHUT CORP.
741 F. Supp. 1454, 1990 U.S. Dist. LEXIS 8718
United States District Court for the District of Hawaii, 1990

Facts: Max Gin and Johnnie Fong had a partnership specializing in wholesale jewelry. They often traveled to jewelry shows and conventions to display their wares. Max Gin left a jewelry show in Miami and went to the airport, where he intended to catch a flight to New Orleans, for another trade show. Gin checked his suitcases with a curbside skycap and proceeded to the departure gate. He held one carry-on bag, containing $140,000 in jewelry.

Wackenhut operated the security checkpoint at the entrance to the departure gate. Like most, this checkpoint had an X-ray machine for baggage and a magnetometer to detect metal carried by passengers. Gin waited at one side until the line of people waiting for the magnetometer had dwindled. He then placed his bag on the conveyor belt and stepped up to the magnetometer. Just at that moment a woman wearing a heavy coat abruptly cut in front of Gin and passed through the magnetometer. She activated the metal detection alarm. The Wackenhut employee who operated the magnetometer motioned for Gin to wait on the terminal side of the machine, while the woman emptied her pockets onto a tray. She passed through the machine again and once more the alarm sounded. She emptied more items from her pockets, but again set off the alarm. Only on the fourth attempt did she proceed through the magnetometer. Gin walked through the machine, went to pick up his jewelry bag—and found it gone. He dashed through the departure lounge searching for the bag and sought police help, but to no avail.

Gin sued, alleging negligent bailment. Wackenhut defended, claiming that no bailment had arisen and that, even if it had, the company used adequate care.

Some bailments endure for years, but others last only for moments. Ten seconds' possession may result in dramatic liability.

Issues: Was there a bailment? If so, had Wackenhut used adequate care?

Excerpts from Judge King's Decision: Although the law of bailments is well settled, the brevity of the alleged bailment makes this case somewhat novel.

This court is convinced that in the instant case a bailment was created. In proceeding through the security checkpoint, plaintiff placed his bag upon the X-ray conveyor belt. From the moment the bag entered the machine the plaintiff surrendered control to the defendant. The defendant could stop the bag in the machine for prolonged examination, could run it through the machine a second time, or could order it opened for an examination of its contents. Further, passengers such as the plaintiff have virtually no control over the length of time they will be separated from their bag. This time could vary from a few seconds to several minutes. It is also noteworthy that plaintiff could not retrieve his bag until the Wackenhut employee operating the magnetometer permitted plaintiff to pass into the concourse area. Due to the orientation of the X-ray machine and the magnetometer, it was impossible for a passenger waiting in line for the magnetometer to see his bag after it emerged from the X-ray machine. Although the period of separation might be brief, the plaintiff had surrendered possession and control of his belongings and a bailment was created.

Negligence: Under Florida law, once a plaintiff has proven the existence of a bailment, and demonstrated the failure of the bailee to return the bailed goods, a presumption of negligence on the part of the bailee arises. In order to avoid liability for the lost goods, the defendant has the burden of showing that he exercised the degree of care required by the nature of the bailment.

The court finds that Wackenhut failed to exercise the requisite degree of care in the instant case. Wackenhut knew passengers could not keep a visual watch over their bags throughout the inspection process. In addition, the defendant's own witness testified that carry-on bags had been lost, either through theft or inadvertence, an average of twice each week over the past several years. Despite this knowledge the defendant evidently made no effort either to more closely coordinate the screening of passengers with their baggage, to reorient the X-ray machine and magnetometer so that passengers could watch their bags during the security check, or to simply post a sign alerting passengers that thefts frequently occurred.

[The court awarded the plaintiffs $140,000.]

Exculpatory Clauses

Bailees often use exculpatory clauses in an effort to limit their liability. **An exculpatory clause is any part of a contract that attempts to relieve one of the parties of future liability.** Exculpatory clauses are commonly employed in parking garages, coat check locations (restaurants or museums), warehouses, suitcase lockers, and so forth. For example, an exculpatory clause at a coat check might state that the restaurant is not responsible for any loss or damage to the customer's coat. Are such clauses valid? Occasionally.

If the bailor is a corporation and it has bargaining power roughly equal to the bailee's, a court will probably enforce a bailment exculpatory clause. If Manufacturer agrees to park five of its aircraft in a hangar owned by Hannah Corp., and Hannah's storage contract states that it is not responsible for any losses caused by fire, flood, or hurricane, then Hannah is probably protected when fire destroys Manufacturer's planes. Both parties are corporations, and the law assumes they should live with whatever agreement they bargained. However, even if the parties have equal bargaining power, an exculpatory clause is generally unenforceable if it attempts to exclude an intentional tort or gross negligence.

When the bailor is a consumer, the exculpatory clause stands on shaky ground, because judges generally presume the parties have unequal bargaining power. Courts look to see whether the clause was clearly written and easily visible. More often than not, a court will reject an exculpatory clause against a bailor who is a consumer. We discuss exculpatory clauses in greater detail in Chapter 13, on contract legality.

RIGHTS AND DUTIES OF THE BAILOR

The bailor's rights and duties are the reverse of the bailee's. The bailor is entitled to the return of his property on the agreed-upon date. He is also entitled to receive the property in good condition and to recover damages for harm to the property, if the bailee failed to use adequate care.

LIABILITY FOR DEFECTS

Depending upon the type of bailment, the bailor is potentially liable for known or even unknown defects in the property. **If the bailment is for the sole benefit of the bailee, the bailor must notify the bailee of any known defects.** Suppose Megan lends her stepladder to Dave. The top rung is loose and Megan knows it, but forgets to tell Dave. The top rung crumbles and Dave falls onto his girlfriend's iguana. Megan is liable to Dave and the girlfriend unless the defect in the ladder was obvious. Notice that Megan's liability is not only to the bailee, but also to any others injured by the defects. Megan would not be liable if she had notified Dave of the defective rung.

In a mutual-benefit bailment, the bailor is liable not only for known defects but also for unknown defects that the bailor could have discovered with reasonable diligence. Suppose RentaLot rents a power sander to Dan. RentaLot does not realize that the sander has faulty wiring, but a reasonable inspection would have revealed the problem. When Dan suffers a serious shock from the defect, RentaLot is liable to him, even though it was unaware of the problem.

If the bailor is in the business of renting property, the bailment is probably subject to implied warranties. As we saw in Chapter 21, on product liability, Article 2A of the Uniform Commercial Code creates various implied warranties for goods leased by a merchant. A merchant is someone in the business of leasing that type of goods. A car rental company is a merchant with respect to its cars, so it rents the autos subject to implied warranties that they are fit for their normal purposes. Because these warranties are implied by law, they normally exist whether the parties say anything about them or not. Bailors may attempt to limit these implied warranties by provisions in the bailment agreement, but courts disfavor such limitations, especially when the bailee is a consumer. For a full discussion of implied warranties, see Chapter 21, on products liability.

COMMON CARRIERS AND CONTRACT CARRIERS

A carrier is a company that transports goods for others. It is a bailee of every shipment entrusted to it. There are two kinds of carriers: common carriers and contract carriers. The distinction is important because each type of company has a different level of liability.

A **common carrier** makes its services available on a regular basis to the general public. For example, a trucking company located in St. Louis that is willing to haul freight for anyone, to any destination in the country, is a common carrier. **Generally, a common carrier is strictly liable for harm to the bailor's goods.**

Common carriers are governed by a statute known as the Carmack Amendment.[5] Under this law, a bailor needs only to establish that it delivered property to the carrier in good condition and that the cargo arrived damaged. The carrier is then liable unless it can show that it was not negligent *and* that the loss was caused by an act of God (such as a hurricane), an act of a public enemy (a nation at war with the United States), an act of the bailor itself (for example, by packaging the goods improperly), an act of a public authority (for example, a state inspector forcing a delay), or the inherent nature of the goods (such as fruit that spoiled naturally). These are hard defenses to prove, and in most cases a common carrier is liable for harm to the property.

A common carrier is, however, allowed to limit its liability by contract. For example, a common carrier might offer the bailor the choice of two shipping rates: a low rate, with a maximum liability, say, of $10,000, or a higher shipping rate, with full liability for any harm to the goods. In that case, if the bailor chooses the lower rate, the limitation on liability is enforceable. Even if the bailor proves a loss of $300,000, the carrier owes merely $10,000.

A **contract carrier** does not make its services available to the general public, but engages in continuing agreements with particular customers. Assume that Steel Curtain Shipping is a trucking company in Pittsburgh that hauls cargo to California for two or three steel producers and carries manufactured goods from California to Pennsylvania and New York for a few West Coast companies. Steel Curtain is a contract carrier. **A contract carrier does not incur strict liability.** The normal bailment rules apply, and a contract carrier can escape liability by demonstrating that it exercised due care of the property.

INNKEEPERS

Hotels, motels, and inns frequently act as bailees of their guests' property. Most states have special innkeeper statutes that regulate liability.

Hotel patrons often assume that anything they bring to a hotel is safe. But some state innkeeper statutes impose an absolute limit on a hotel's liability. Other statutes require guests to leave valuables in the inn's safe deposit box. And even that may not be enough to protect them fully. For example, a state statute might require the guest to register the nature and value of the goods with the hotel. Wise guests realize that they should make no assumptions about safety. Do not leave valuables in a hotel unless you know the rules, as the following case indicates.

NUMISMATIC ENTERPRISES v. HYATT CORP.

797 F. Supp. 687, 1992 U.S. Dist. LEXIS 10199
United States District Court for the Southern District of Indiana, 1992

Facts: Mark Teller and Norman Applebaum were partners in M. Louis Teller Numismatic Enterprises, a partnership in the business of buying and selling rare coins. They traveled to Indianapolis, Indiana, to attend a coin convention. They brought with them a large black double combination lock briefcase containing virtually the entire partnership inventory of rare coins, valued at over $300,000.

When the partners arrived at the Hyatt Regency hotel, an employee named Ms. Atkinson took them to the safe deposit room and assigned them a box. Ms. Atkinson gave them one of the two keys required to open the box. The next morning, Teller opened the safe deposit box to retrieve the coins. The box was empty.

[5] 49 U.S.C. §11707.

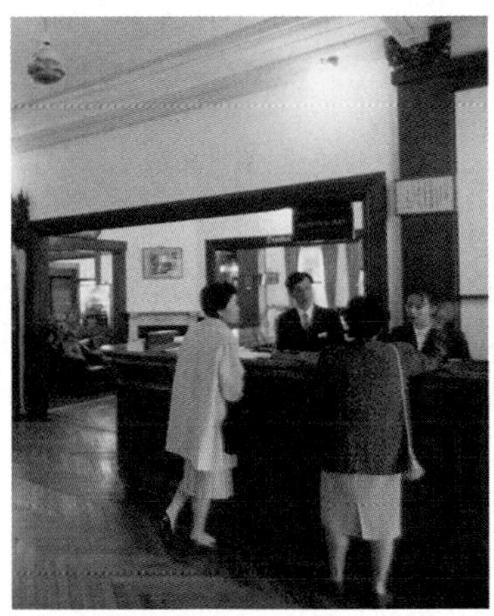

When checking into a hotel, it is best to make no assumptions about the safety of your valuables or the innkeeper's liability for their loss.

The partners sued, claiming that Hyatt had breached its duty as a bailee. Hyatt moved for summary judgment, contending that under the Indiana Innkeeper statute it had no liability.

Issue: Has Hyatt breached its duty as a bailee?

Excerpts from Judge Noland's Decision: The Indiana Innkeeper statute provides as follows:

> A hotel, apartment hotel, or inn, or the proprietor or manager thereof, shall not be liable for the loss of or damage to any merchandise samples or merchandise for sale, whether such loss or damage is occasioned by the negligence of such proprietor or manager or his agents or otherwise, unless the guest or other owner shall have given prior written notice of having brought such merchandise into the hotel and of the value thereof, the receipt of such notice shall have been acknowledged in writing by the proprietor, manager or other agent and in no event shall such liability exceed the sum of four hundred dollars ($400.00) unless the manager or proprietor of such hotel, apartment hotel, or inn shall have contracted in writing to assume a greater liability.

In the present case, there does not appear to be any dispute that the plaintiffs failed to comply with the statute's requirements. Although it might be argued that the Hotel had sufficient notice under the statute as a result of its employee's observation of the coins and her conversation with plaintiff Teller, this argument ignores the fact that sufficient notice under the Indiana Innkeepers' statute requires more than the mere statement that merchandise is being brought into a hotel or inn.

The court finds persuasive the defendant's argument that the Safe Deposit Record cannot be construed as sufficient notice under the Indiana Innkeepers' statute because it did not inform the Hyatt Regency of the fact that the plaintiffs were bringing their merchandise into the Hotel or the estimated value thereof. Although the Hyatt Regency's agent (Atkinson) signed the Safe Deposit Record, thereby witnessing plaintiff Teller's execution of the form (and, at least implicitly, the fact that Teller had read the "Rules and Regulations Governing Safe Deposit Boxes"), her signature hardly constitutes a written acknowledgement that the Hotel had received sufficient notice under the statute. Even if Ms. Atkinson's signature could somehow be interpreted as the equivalent of a written acknowledgement that plaintiff Teller was bringing merchandise into the Hotel (on the theory that Teller provided Atkinson and her employer with "notice" of that fact when he (1) told her he was with the Coin Show, and (2) proceeded to place the partnership inventory in the safe deposit box while in her presence), it would nevertheless fail as to constitute a valid acknowledgement. Under the statute, an innkeeper's agent must acknowledge notice which includes a declaration of the value of the guest's merchandise. As the Seventh Circuit observed [in an earlier case] such notice and acknowledgment are required in Indiana for a salutary reason—"to protect innkeepers from undisclosed excessive liability."

For the foregoing reasons, the court concludes that the defendant's motion for summary judgment should be *granted*. Judgment is hereby entered in favor of the defendant and against the plaintiffs. The plaintiffs shall accordingly take nothing by way of their amended complaint.

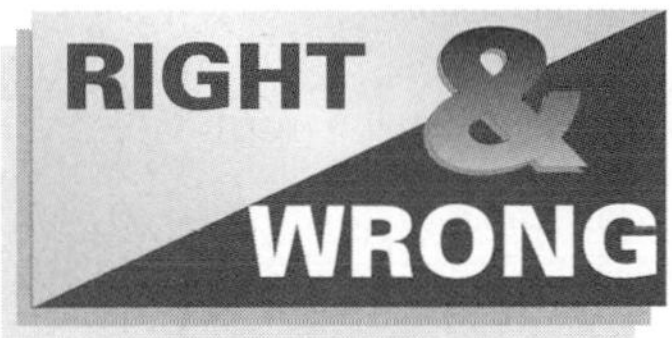

Was it right for the Hyatt hotel to accept the coins from a paying guest and then refuse liability when the coins were stolen? What steps could the hotel have taken to avoid disputes like this? Were the guests naive to assume that their coins were protected? How should they have protected themselves?

CHAPTER CONCLUSION

One deduction from this chapter is that carrying a suitcase filled with rare coins or jewelry is as risky as . . . one would think. A more general conclusion is that personal property law plays an almost daily role in all of our lives. The manager of a parking lot, the owner of a repair shop, and the operator of an airport security system must all realize that they may incur substantial liability for personal property, whether they intend to accept that obligation or not. Understanding personal property law can be worth a lot of money—but never carry all of it with you.

CHAPTER REVIEW

1. A gift is a voluntary transfer of property from one person to another without consideration. The elements of a gift are intention to transfer ownership immediately, delivery, and acceptance.

2. The finder of property must attempt to locate the true owner, unless the property was abandoned. State estray statutes have made some changes in the common law, but the following principles generally govern:
   - Abandoned property—the finder may keep it.
   - Lost property—the finder generally has rights superior to everyone but the true owner, except that if she found it on land belonging to another, the property owner generally is entitled to it.
   - Mislaid property—generally, the finder has no rights in the property.
   - Treasure trove—generally, the finder may keep it.

3. Accession occurs when one person uses labor and/or materials to add value to personal property belonging to another. If the improver knows he is making accessions without authority, the owner may generally take the improved property without compensating for the work done. If the improver mistakenly believes he is entitled to add accessions, the owner probably has to pay for the increased value.

4. A bailment is the rightful possession of goods by one who is not the owner. The one who delivers the goods is the bailor and the one in possession is the bailee. To create a bailment, the bailee must assume physical control with intent to possess.

5. The bailee is always entitled to possess the property, is frequently allowed to use it, and may be entitled to compensation.

6. The bailee is strictly liable to redeliver the goods to the bailor.

7. The bailee is obligated to exercise due care. The level of care required depends upon who receives the benefit of the bailment: if the bailee is the sole beneficiary, she must use extraordinary care; if the parties mutually benefit, the bailee must use ordinary care; and if the bailor is the sole beneficiary of the bailment, the bailee must use only slight care.

8. Once the bailor has proven the existence of a bailment and loss, a presumption of negligence arises, and the burden shifts to the bailee to prove adequate care.

9. Exculpatory clauses, seeking to relieve a bailee of liability for damage to the goods, may be enforced between two corporations of equal bargaining power but are seldom enforced against a consumer.

10. The bailor must keep the property in suitable repair, free of any hidden defects. If the bailor is in the business of renting property, the bailment is probably subject to implied warranties.

11. Generally, a common carrier is strictly liable for harm to the bailor's goods. A contract carrier incurs only normal bailment liability.

12. The liability of an innkeeper is regulated by state statute. A guest intending to store valuables with an innkeeper must follow the statute to the letter.

PRACTICE TEST

1. While in her second year at the Juilliard School of Music in New York City, Ann Rylands had a chance to borrow for one month a rare Guadagnini violin, made in 1768. She returned the violin to the owner in Philadelphia, but telephoned her father to ask if he would buy it for her. He borrowed money from his pension fund and paid the owner. Ann traveled to Philadelphia to pick up the violin. She had exclusive possession of the violin for the next 20 years, using it in her professional career. Unfortunately, she became an alcoholic, and during one period when she was in a treatment center, she entrusted the violin to her mother for safekeeping. At about that time, her father died. When Ann was released from the center, she requested return of the violin, but her mother refused. Who owns the violin?

2. **RIGHT & WRONG** Jane says to Cody, "If you will agree to work as my yard man, I'll pay you $1,000 per week for a normal work week. You can start on Monday, and I'll guarantee you eight months' work." Cody is elated at his good fortune and agrees to start work on Monday. Later that day, Cody, still rejoicing, says to Beth, his girlfriend, "You know those sapphire earrings in the jewelry store that you're wild about? At the end of next week I'm going to buy them for you." On Monday, Jane realizes what a foolish thing she said, and refuses to hire Cody. Cody, in turn, refuses to buy the earrings for Beth. Cody sues Jane and wins; Beth sues Cody and loses. Why the opposite outcomes? What basic ideas of fairness underlie the two results?

3. Ronald Armstead worked for First American Bank as a courier. His duties included making deliveries between the bank's branches in Washington, D.C. Armstead parked the bank's station wagon near the entrance of one branch in violation of a sign saying: "No Parking Rush Hour Zone." In the rear luggage section of the station wagon were four locked bank dispatch bags, containing checks and other valuable documents. Armstead had received tickets for illegal parking at this spot on five occasions. Shortly after Armstead entered the bank, a tow truck arrived and its operator prepared to tow the station wagon. Transportation Management, Inc. operated the towing service on behalf of the District of Columbia. Armstead ran out to the vehicle and told the tow truck operator that he was prepared to drive the vehicle away immediately. But the operator drove away with the station wagon in tow. One and one-half hours later, a bank employee paid for the car's release, but one dispatch bag, containing documents worth $107,000, was missing. First American sued Transportation Management and the District of Columbia. The defendants sought summary judgment, claiming they *could not* be liable. Were they correct?

4. During the Great Depression of the 1930s, the federal government's Works Progress Administration hired artists to create public works of art. The goal was to provide employment and beautify the nation. The artist James Daugherty painted six murals on the walls of the public high school in Stamford, Connecticut. During the 1970s, the city began to restore its high school. The architect and school officials agreed that the Daugherty murals should be preserved. They arranged for the construction workers to remove the murals to prevent harm. By accident, the workers rolled them up and placed them near the trash dumpsters for disposal. A student found the murals and took them home, and later notified the federal government's General Services Administration (GSA) of his find. The GSA arranged to transport the murals to an art restorer, named Hiram Hoelzer, for storage and eventual restoration, when funds could be arranged. Over *19 years* went by before anyone notified the Stamford School system where the murals were. In the meantime, neither the GSA nor anyone else paid Hoelzer for the storage or restoration. By 1989 the murals were valued at $1.25 million by Sotheby's, an art auction house. Hoelzer filed suit, seeking a declaration that the murals had been abandoned. Were they abandoned? What difference does it make?

5. **CPA QUESTION** Which of the following requirements must be met to create a bailment?

I. Delivery of personal property to the intended bailee

II. Possession by the intended bailee

III. An absolute duty on the intended bailee to return or dispose of the property according to the bailor's directions

(a) I and II only

(b) I and III only

(c) II and III only

(d) I, II, and III

6. Two cases in the text involved traveling salespeople carrying valuable samples: *Gin v. Wackenhut Corp.* and *Numismatic Enterprises v. Hyatt Corp.* Both owners sued, based on a claim of bailment. One plaintiff won, and one lost. Why the different outcomes?

7. Marjan International Corp. sells handmade oriental rugs. V. K. Putman, Inc. is a Montana trucking company. Marjan delivered valuable rugs to Putman for shipment from New York City to Tacoma, Washington. Unfortunately, there were several delays in transit. The truck driver encountered snow storms and closed roads. His truck also overheated and required repairs in a garage. Before the driver resumed the trip, he stopped to pick up and load other goods. When the truck finally arrived in Tacoma, two bales of rugs were missing. Marjan sued, on the grounds that Putman was a common carrier, but Putman claimed it was a contract carrier. What difference does it make whether Putman was a common carrier or a contract carrier, and how is that determined?

8. Lonny Joe owned two rare 1955 Ford Thunderbird automobiles, one red and one green, both in mint condition. He stored the cars in his garage. His friend Stephanie wanted to use the red car in a music video, so Lonny Joe rented it to her for two days, for $300 per day. When she returned the red car, Lonny Joe discovered a long scratch along one side. That same day, he noticed a long scratch along the side of the green car. He sued Stephanie for harm to the red car. Lonny Joe sued an electrician for damage to the green car, claiming that the scratch occurred while the electrician was fixing a heater in the garage. Explain the different burdens of proof in the two cases.

9. The government accused Carlo Francia and another of stealing a purse belonging to Frances Bainlardi. A policeman saw Francia sorting through the contents of the purse, which included a photo identification of Bainlardi. Francia kept some items, such as cash, while discarding others. At trial, Francia claimed that he had thought the purse was lost or abandoned. Besides the fact that Francia's accomplice was holding burglary tools, what is the weakness in Francia's defense?

10. **YOU BE THE JUDGE WRITING PROBLEM** Eileen Murphy often cared for her elderly neighbor, Thomas Kenney. He paid her $25 per day for her help and once gave her a bank certificate of deposit worth $25,000. She spent the money. Murphy alleged that shortly before his death, Kenney gave her a large block of shares in three corporations. He called his broker, intending to instruct him to transfer the shares to Murphy's name, but the broker was ill and unavailable. So Kenney told Murphy to write her name on the shares and keep them, which she did. Two weeks later Kenney died. When Murphy presented the shares to Kenney's broker to transfer ownership to her, the broker refused because Kenney had never endorsed the shares as the law requires, that is, signed them over to Murphy. Was Murphy entitled to the $25,000? To the shares? **Argument for Murphy:** The purpose of the law is to do what a donor intended, and it is obvious that Kenney intended Murphy to have the $25,000 and the shares. Why else would he have given them to her? A greedy estate should not be allowed to interfere with the deceased's intention. **Argument for the Estate:** Murphy is not entitled to the $25,000 because we have no way of knowing what Kenney's intentions were when he gave her the money. She is not entitled to the shares of stock because Kenney's failure to endorse them over to her meant he never *delivered* them, and that is an essential element of a gift.

11. You decide to open a rental store, renting everything from lawn mowers to power saws to complete dinner service for 150. What principles of bailment law should you be aware of?

INTERNET RESEARCH PROBLEM

You own a helicopter worth $250,000. A business associate wishes to use it for one week to show prospective clients around various islands in the Caribbean. You are willing to let him use it, for a fee of $15,000. Draft a bailment agreement. Use the form supplied at http://www.gate.net/~legalsvc/autobail.html as a model.

You can find further practice problems in the Online Quiz at http://beatty.westbuslaw.com or in the Study Guide that accompanies this text.

CHAPTER 48

ESTATE PLANNING

Pablo Picasso created hundreds of paintings and sculptures as well as thousands of drawings and sketches. (He was said to have settled restaurant bills by drawing sketches on napkins.) His personal life was unconventional, featuring a series of wives, mistresses, and children, both legitimate and illegitimate. Despite this large group of feuding heirs, he did not make a will before his death.

After four years of litigation, a French court decided that Picasso's estate would be shared by his widow, Jacqueline (who later committed suicide); two grandchildren by his legitimate child, Paulo (who died of cirrhosis of the liver); and his three illegitimate children, Maya, Claude, and Paloma. By the time the decision was reached, legal fees had swallowed up all the cash in the estate, but there was still an enormous stock of artworks. His daughter Paloma recalls: "There was a day finally when we all met, everyone with their lawyers, their assistants, their au pairs, all the most prestigious lawyers in France, and we drew lots for all the different categories of art and my nephew, who was the youngest person present, pulled numbers out of a hat. There were a few tensions, like in every family."[1]

[1] Lynn Barber, "A Perfectly Packaged Picasso," *Independent*, Dec. 9, 1990, p. 8. Reprinted by permission of The Independent (London).

INTRODUCTION

There is one immutable law of the universe: "You can't take it with you." As the Egyptian pharaohs discovered, regardless of your fame or wealth, eventually you and your material goods will part. But you can control where your assets go after your death, and you may even be able to determine how they are spent. Or you can decide, as Picasso did, not to bother with an estate plan and let your heirs litigate their hearts out.

DEFINITIONS

Like many areas of the law, estate planning uses its own terminology:

- **Estate Planning**. The process of giving away property after (or in anticipation of) death.
- **Estate**. The legal entity that holds title to assets after the owner dies and before the property is distributed.
- **Decedent**. The person who has died.
- **Testator** or **Testatrix**. Someone who has signed a valid will. **Testatrix** is the female version (from the Latin).
- **Intestate**. To die without a will.
- **Heir**. Technically, the term "heir" refers to someone who inherits from a decedent who died intestate. **Devisee** means someone who inherits under a will. However, common parlance and many courts use "heir" to refer to anyone who inherits property, and we follow that usage in this chapter.
- **Probate**. The process of carrying out the terms of a will.
- **Executor** or **Executrix**. A personal representative chosen by the decedent to carry out the terms of the will. An **executrix** is a female executor.
- **Administrator** or **Administratrix**. A personal representative appointed by the probate court to oversee the probate process for someone who has died intestate. As you can guess, an **administratrix** is a female administrator.
- **Grantor** or **Settlor**. Someone who creates a trust.
- **Donor**. Someone who makes a gift or creates a trust.

Throughout this chapter, we use the masculine and feminine versions of testator, executor, and administrator interchangeably. These are dated terms that reflect a sexist era when men and women had different legal rights. It would be more progressive to bury these words in the same graveyard as "authoress" and "poetess," but courts and lawyers still use them and so must we.

PURPOSE

Estate planning has two primary goals: to ensure that property is distributed as the owner desires and to minimize estate taxes. Although tax issues are beyond the scope of this chapter, they are an important element of estate planning, often affecting not only how people transfer their property but, in some cases, to whom. For instance, wealthy people may give money to charity, at least in part, to minimize the taxes on the rest of their estate. Under federal law, the first $675,000 of an estate generally passes tax-free. (The amount of this federal deduction will gradually rise to $1 million by 2006.) On assets above this level, the estate tax rate rises as high as 55 percent. Not surprisingly, people with estates significantly above the federal deduction often spend a great deal of time and effort trying to minimize their taxes. To learn more about rich folk and their estate planning, visit the U.S. Trust Survey of Affluent Americans at **http://www.ustrust.com/affluent.htm**.

PROBATE LAW

The federal government and many states levy estate taxes, although the tax rate imposed by states is typically much lower. Only the states, and not the federal government, have probate codes to regulate the creation and implementation of wills and trusts. These codes vary from state to state. This chapter, therefore, speaks only of general trends among the states. Certainly, anyone who is preparing a will must consult the laws of the relevant state. To make probate law more consistent, the National Conference of Commissioners on Uniform State Laws issued a Uniform Probate Code (UPC). At this writing, 18 states have adopted it.

Eventually, we will all be separated from our property. We have four options for disposing of it: gift, will, intestacy, or trust. These choices can be used alone or in combination.

GIFTS

Anyone who is of sound mind may give property away during his lifetime. Although Chapter 47 covers the legal issues involved in making a gift, it is also important to understand the role of gifts in estate planning. **Gifts offer these advantages:**

- *Gifts can be used to reduce estate taxes.* Under current law, a donor may give away $10,000 per year, per recipient, tax-free. A married couple with three married children and nine grandchildren can give away $300,000 each year tax-free (each spouse can give $10,000 to 3 children, 3 in-laws, and 9 grandchildren). That is money on which the couple will not have to pay estate taxes. Any individual who gives away more than $10,000 to one recipient must pay a gift tax.
- *Gifts are not taxable to the recipient.* The donor of a gift must pay taxes on any amount above $10,000, but the recipient does not pay tax on a gift.
- *Gifts create pleasure.* The donor has the satisfaction of seeing recipients (such as children or grandchildren) going to college, buying a house, visiting DisneyWorld.

Gifts also have disadvantages:

- *The donor loses control.* Grandparents have sometimes watched in sadness as their gifts are used to buy a yacht rather than a college education—or, even worse, admission into a cult.
- *Gifts are irrevocable.* Some parents are so eager to avoid estate taxes that they give away more than they can afford and find themselves, in old age, asking for "loans" from their children. In counseling clients, lawyers often quote the saying: "When parents give money to their children, they all laugh. When children give money to their parents, they all cry."

If people knew when they were going to die, they could simply give away all their assets ahead of time. But since few individuals are privy to this information, they must elect one of the other three choices: will, intestacy, or trust.

WILLS

A will is a legal document that disposes of the testator's property after death. It can, in most instances, be revoked or altered at any time until death. Virtually every adult, even those with only modest assets, should have a will:

- To ensure that their assets (modest though they may be) are distributed in accordance with their wishes.
- To select a personal representative to oversee the estate. If the decedent does not name an executor in a will, the court will appoint an administrator. Generally, people prefer to have a friend, rather than a court, in charge of their property.
- To avoid unnecessary fees. Those who die intestate often leave behind issues for lawyers to resolve. Recall that Picasso's estate spent its cash on legal fees to determine the rights of his illegitimate children. The artist could easily have resolved these issues in a will and ensured a greater inheritance for all of his heirs. A properly drafted will can also reduce the estate tax bill. In addition, estates are usually required to purchase an insurance policy to reimburse the heirs if the executor or administratrix steals assets. Theft is rare, and a will can eliminate this requirement.
- To provide guardians for minor children. If parents do not appoint a guardian before they die, a court will. Presumably, the parents are best able to make this choice. Of course, it is essential to discuss this assignment with the appointed guardians. No one likes to be surprised with the news that they now have two fewer friends and three additional children.

REQUIREMENTS FOR A VALID WILL

Generally speaking, a person may leave his assets to whomever he wants. There are, however, some important exceptions to this general rule.

Legal Age

The testatrix must be of legal age, which is typically 18. Minors do not have the right to manage valuable property (such as stocks or real estate) on their own; nor can they decide where it goes after their death. State intestacy laws make this choice for them. That is why gifts to minor children are often made in trust, with the trust instrument determining how the property will be distributed if the beneficiary dies while a minor.

Testamentary Capacity

The testator must be of sound mind. This does not mean that he has to be a chess grandmaster. To have testamentary capacity, he must simply be sane and competent, that is, able to understand what a will is, more or less what he owns, who his relatives are, and how he is disposing of his property. Sometimes there may be a fine line between eccentric and insane as, for example, when someone leaves his money to his cat. But without medical evidence of insanity, wills are difficult to overturn.

No Undue Influence

A will is invalid if someone has subjected the testatrix to undue influence. The law recognizes that even ordinary, run-of-the-mill love is an extraordinarily powerful force. Undue influence is more than that. It means that one person has enough power over another to force him to do something against his free will. Consider the following news report.

There was never any question that Basia Piasecka wielded extraordinary influence over J. Seward Johnson, the heir to the Johnson & Johnson fortune. From the moment she was hired as his cook, she captivated him. Within three years of meeting her, the 76-year-old heir had divorced his wife and married Basia. Together, they embarked on an epic spending spree characterized by his indulgence and her excess. She set records at art auctions, but that was small scale compared with her construction of a country home in New Jersey.

Ill with cancer, Seward spent his days chatting amiably with workers, at times seeming totally befuddled. Basia underwent a personality change, becoming the nouveau riche from hell. She spent hundreds of thousands of dollars moving newly installed walls, windows, doors, switches, and trees, sometimes feet, sometimes fractions of an inch. Her attitude toward her husband changed, too. She berated and humiliated him in front of others.

In the 12 years they were married, he changed his will 22 times. Each time, he increased Basia's share. In the end, she inherited virtually all of his $402 million estate. His six children, who already had sizable trusts, were left in the cold along with the Harbor Branch foundation, a charity that Seward had founded and supported for years.[2]

Did Basia Piasecka exercise undue influence over Seward Johnson?

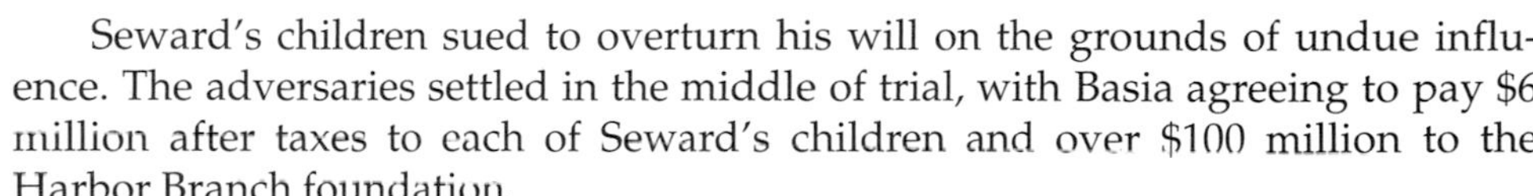

Seward's children sued to overturn his will on the grounds of undue influence. The adversaries settled in the middle of trial, with Basia agreeing to pay $6 million after taxes to each of Seward's children and over $100 million to the Harbor Branch foundation.

Disputed wills make for hard cases. The court must read the mind of someone who is now dead. The following case illustrates the difficulty of determining, after the fact, whether the decedent was of sound mind or had been subjected to undue influence.

***IN RE* ESTATE OF HAGUE**
894 S.W.2d 684, 1995 Mo. App. LEXIS 183
Court of Appeals of Missouri, 1995

Facts: Richard Hague, Sr. was 61 years old when Barbara, his wife of many years and the mother of his four children, died of cancer. Richard himself had recently been diagnosed with cancer. After Barbara's death, Richard became despondent. He and his wife had been in the flea market business, but he sold virtually all his possessions at auction, giving half the proceeds to his children. Richard had a good relationship with his children, playing cards and going on trips with them. A son who was released from prison moved in with his father.

[2] Joseph Mattin, "A Contest of Wills, a Picture of Greed," *Buffalo News*, June 27, 1993, p. 12.

Four months after Barbara died, Richard met Faith MacArthur. Re-energized, he began a new flea market business with her. She sold her house and moved in with him, refurnishing his house with her possessions. Richard's relationship with his children deteriorated. He asked his son to move out and demanded that the children return the money he had given them. He was irritated that they disliked Faith. Normally friendly and good-humored, Richard became increasingly argumentative.

As evidence of their father's mental incompetence, the children testified that during the auction of his household goods, he stood up and complained angrily that the prices were not high enough. The auctioneer was forced to stop the auction and resume it a week later. Richard was also confused about one of Barbara's hospital bills and refused to pay it, forcing the hospital to sue him. Before that, he had always been scrupulous about paying bills on time. He also became obsessed with sex. Four days after Barbara's death, he proposed a sexual liaison with his sister-in-law. He discussed intimate sexual matters with his children, apparently without inhibition. This was out of character for Richard.

One witness testified that Faith ordered Richard about in a peremptory manner. Richard lamented that he could do nothing to please Faith. When asked why he did not kick her out, Richard said she would have no place to go. One daughter said her father came to her house crying because Faith "was threatening to leave him all the time, and he said it was our fault."

In January, Richard made a will leaving Faith everything but his house. In April, he made a new will leaving her all his assets. In October, Richard died, and his children challenged the validity of his wills. The jury decided that Richard was not of sound mind and that Faith had unduly influenced him. Faith appealed.

Issues: Was Richard of sound mind when he made his will? Did Faith unduly influence him?

Excerpts from Judge Kennedy's Decision: We remind ourselves that neither judge nor jury may make a will for the decedent. If he had the mental capacity to make a will, and if he made it of his own volition, so that it may be said to be his will and not that of another, then it is not our place to pass judgment on his motives or his wisdom in making the will he made, nor to substitute our own judgment for his. One has the right to do as he pleases with what is his.

Undue influence is "such influence as amounts to force, coercion, or overpersuasion, which destroys the free agency and will power of the testator." Motive and opportunity alone are not enough to establish undue influence. The only testimony about the actual making of the wills is the testimony of Richard Hague, Sr.'s, attorney. She testified to the testator's resoluteness in both will changes, i.e., in the January will and the April will. Faith was not involved in the contacts with the attorney. We hold, therefore, there was no evidence of undue influence which would invalidate decedent's will.

We find the evidence falls far short of establishing testamentary incapacity on the part of Richard Hague, Sr. At the time of making the April will—until a few days before his death in October of 1992—decedent was attending to the ordinary affairs of life and was in full control of his faculties; there is no ground in the evidence for any notion that he did not have a good grasp on his property; there is no ground in the evidence for a belief he did not know and understand who were the "natural objects of his bounty," and no evidence that he did not evaluate the claims of his children and of Faith. Another person than he might have placed a different assessment on the relative claims of the children and Faith. But Richard made his judgment by his own lights, and it was his to make. [The evidence indicates that] Richard was intelligent, strong-minded and independent, until the time of his death, and that Faith had no role at all in the making of his April 29 will.

Judgment *reversed* and cause *remanded* with directions to enter judgment in favor of the defendant.

Legal Technicalities

The testator must comply with the legal requirements for executing a will: it must be in writing, and the testator must sign it or direct someone else to sign it for him, if he is too weak. Generally, two witnesses must also sign the will. No one named in a will should also serve as a witness because, in many states, a witness may not inherit under a will.

Holographic Will. Although it is always a good idea to comply with the legal technicalities, sometimes courts will accept a holographic will. **A *holographic will* is handwritten and signed by the testatrix, but not witnessed.** Suppose Rowena is on a plane that suffers engine trouble. For 15 minutes, the pilot struggles to control the plane. Despite his efforts, it crashes, killing everyone aboard. During those 15 minutes, Rowena writes on a Post-it note, "This is my last will and testament. I leave all my assets to the National Gallery of Art in Washington, D.C." She signs her name, but her fellow passengers are too frantic to witness it. This note is found in the wreckage of the plane. Her previous will, signed and witnessed in a lawyer's office, left everything to her beau, Ivan. Who will inherit, Ivan or the National Gallery?

Holographic wills are valid in approximately 30 states, and at least one court has accepted a handwritten Post-it note that had not been witnessed. Most of these 30 states will also accept a pre-printed will form as a holographic will (that is, unwitnessed), as long as the testator fills in all the blanks by hand and signs it. (In some states, however, one printed or typed word is enough to invalidate a holographic will.) The National Gallery would inherit Rowena's property if she wrote the will by hand. If, however, she typed it on a laptop, printed it, and signed it without witnesses, it would be invalid in most states, and Ivan would inherit under her prior will. States are less willing to accept typed forms for fear that the testatrix may have signed it without knowing what it was.

Nuncupative Will. Some states will also accept a **nuncupative will**. This is the formal term for an oral will. For a nuncupative will to be valid, the testatrix must know she is dying, there must be three witnesses, and these witnesses must know that they are listening to her will. Suppose that Rowena survives the airplane crash for a few hours. Instead of writing a will on the plane, she whispers to a nurse in the hospital, "I'd like all my property to go to the Angell Memorial Cat Hospital." This oral will is valid if there are two other witnesses and Rowena also says, "I'm dying. Please witness my oral will." The cat hospital, however, is only entitled to her personal property. Nuncupative wills cannot be used to dispose of real estate. Ivan would inherit her farm.

Spouse's Share

A spouse is entitled to a **forced share** of the decedent's estate. In community property states, a spouse can override the will and claim one-half of all marital property acquired during the marriage, except property that the testator inherited or received as a gift.[3] Although this rule sounds easy and fair, implementation can be troublesome. If a couple has been married for many years and has substantial assets, it can be very difficult to sort out what is and is not community property.

[3] Arizona, California, Idaho, Louisiana, Nevada, New Mexico, Texas, Washington, and Wisconsin are community property states.

Suppose that the testatrix inherited a million dollars 20 years before her death. She and her husband both earned sizable incomes during their careers. How can a court tell what money bought which asset? Anyone in a situation such as this should keep detailed records.

In most non-community property states, a spouse can override the will and claim some percentage (usually one-third to one-half) of the decedent's probate estate. This rule is subject to two criticisms. First, the decedent is able to keep substantial assets out of her estate. Jointly owned property, assets in trust, life insurance policies, and pension benefits are not part of the probate estate. Second, the forced share may be unfair in a marriage of short duration.

To avoid these injustices and to solve the bookkeeping problems created by community property laws, the Uniform Probate Code (UPC) adopted a compromise rule. Under the UPC, a surviving spouse is entitled to whichever is greater: $50,000, or a percentage of *all* the decedent's assets, including non-probate assets. The percentage depends upon how long the couple was married. At 5 years, a spouse is entitled to 15 percent; at 10 years, 30 percent; and at 15 years, 50 percent.[4] Suppose that, when Drew and Sandy marry, Drew has assets of $500,000 while Sandy has virtually nothing. If Drew dies anytime during the first five years of their marriage, Sandy is entitled to $50,000. At five years, the share automatically goes up to $75,000. After 15 years, it reaches the maximum of $250,000.

Children's Share

Parents are not required to leave assets to their children. They may disinherit their children for any reason.[5] In most states, this is true even if the children are minors whom the testator was obligated to support while alive.

However, the law presumes that a **pretermitted child** (that is, a child left nothing in the parent's will) was omitted by accident, unless the parent clearly indicates in the will that he has omitted the child on purpose. To do so, he must either leave her some nominal amount, such as $1, or specifically write in the will that the omission was intentional: "I am making no bequest to my daughter because she has chosen a religion of which I disapprove."

Under the common law, a pretermitted child is entitled to the same share she would have received if her parent had died intestate. Under the UPC, however, the rules are more complicated:

- The pretermitted child is entitled to an inheritance only if she was born after the will was executed.
- The pretermitted child has no right to inherit if the parent, before death, has already given her a reasonable share of assets or if the testator left most of his money to the child's other parent.
- If the testator had no living children when he made his will, the pretermitted child is entitled to the same share she would have received if the parent had died intestate.
- If the parent had other children when he made his will, the pretermitted child is entitled to share in whatever the other children received. For example, if the parent left half of his estate to the one child who was alive when he made his

---

[4] UPC §2-201.

[5] The only exception to this rule is Louisiana, whose laws are based on the French model.

will, the child born afterwards would be entitled to one-quarter of the estate (one-half of the other child's one-half).

Despite all these rules and presumptions, a parent can still disinherit his child.

In the United States and the United Kingdom, parents can cut their children off without a penny. Not so in virtually all other European countries. In France, both legitimate and illegitimate children are entitled to a share (although illegitimate children born in an adulterous relationship receive only half the normal share). Indeed, most European countries, except Russia, recognize the rights of illegitimate children to inherit automatically from a parent's estate.

In drafting a will, lawyers almost always use the term **issue** instead of children. Issue means all descendants such as children, grandchildren, great-grandchildren, and so on. If the will leaves property to "my children" and one child dies before the testator, the child's children would not inherit their parent's share.

The will must also indicate whether issue are to inherit per stirpes or per capita. **Per stirpes** means that each *branch* of the family receives an equal share. Each child receives the same amount, and, if a child has already died, her heirs inherit her share. **Per capita** means that each *heir* receives the same amount. If the children have died, then each grandchild inherits the same amount. Suppose that Gwendolyn has two children, Lance and Arthur. Lance has one child, Arthur has four. Both sons predecease their mother. If Gwendolyn's will says "per stirpes," Lance's child will inherit her father's entire share, which is half of Gwendolyn's estate. Arthur's four children will share their father's portion, so each will receive one-eighth (¼ × ½). If Gwendolyn's will says, "per capita," each of her grandchildren will inherit one-fifth of her estate. Although it might sound fairer to give all grandchildren the same inheritance, most people choose a per stirpes distribution, on the theory that they are treating their *children* equally. The following chart illustrates the difference between per stirpes and per capita.

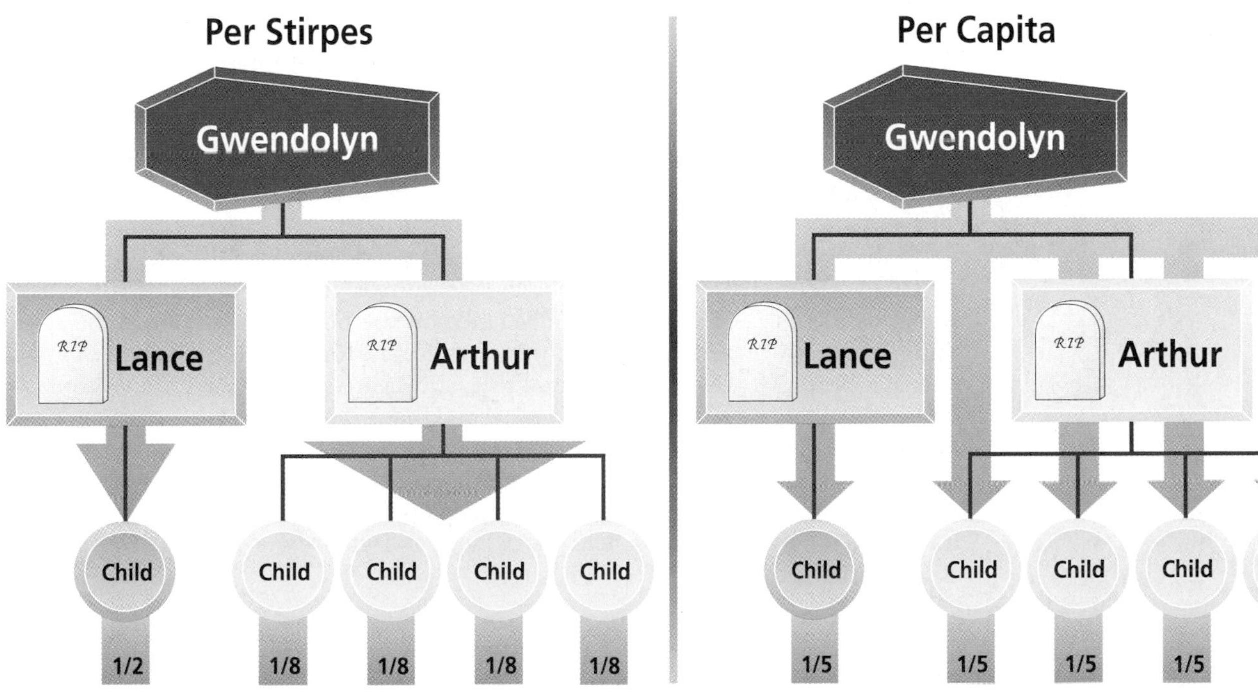

AMENDING A WILL

A testator can generally revoke or alter a will at any time prior to death. In most states, he can revoke a will by destroying it, putting an X through it, writing "revoked" (or some synonym) on it, or signing a new will. He can also execute an amendment—called a **codicil**—to change specific terms of the will, while keeping the rest of it intact. A codicil must meet all the requirements of a will, such as two witnesses. Suppose that Uncle Herman, who has a long and elaborate will, now wants his sterling silver Swiss Army knife to go to Cousin Larry rather than Niece Shannon. Instead of redoing his whole will, he can ask his lawyer to draw up a codicil changing only that one provision.

If a testator executes a new instrument but does not expressly revoke prior wills, his descendants are likely to fight over whether he intended a codicil or a new will. Generally, a subsequent instrument revokes a prior will if it is clear the testator intended to do so or if the new instrument is inconsistent with the prior will. Cecelia makes a will leaving her house to her daughter, Charlotte, and nothing to her son, Charles. If she later draws up a new instrument leaving the house to Charles, she has revoked her first will because her second will is inconsistent. But, if she wins the lottery and leaves that cash to Charles in a new instrument, she has not revoked the prior will, she has simply supplemented it.

A change in family situation may also revoke a will automatically. Under the UPC, divorce or annulment cancels a will. In many states, marriage, divorce, or the birth of a child revokes a will unless the instrument was clearly executed with that event in mind. A testatrix can state in the will, for instance, that she is making it in anticipation of her marriage.

CONTRACTUAL WILLS

A testator cannot revoke a *contractual* will, that is, a will that was signed as part of an agreement with another person. Ulf and Nicole meet and fall in love at the Shady Acres Retirement Community. They have much in common besides their mutual love of aerobics: each has one prior marriage, two children, and $3 million. After they marry, they agree to prepare new wills that leave all assets to the other spouse or, if the spouse is not alive, per stirpes to all six children equally. In this way, they can provide for each other during their lives, knowing that whatever is left over will go equally to their children. What could be fairer than that? But after Ulf goes to the great aerobics studio in the sky, Nicole promptly changes her will to leave all her money, and his, to her own three children. Can she do this dastardly deed?

It depends on whether they have created a valid contract. Ulf and Nicole have executed **reciprocal wills**—their wills are mirror images of each other. Presumably, they signed their wills in reliance on the other person doing the same thing. Clearly, it is not fair to Ulf (or his children) for Nicole to change her will after his death. However, as a general rule, courts are reluctant to enforce contractual wills unless the agreement is very clear. **Under the UPC, a reciprocal will can be revoked unless it specifically states that it cannot be, or unless the testator signs a separate contract promising not to revoke it.**[6]

In the following case, there was *circumstantial* evidence that a couple had contractual wills. But the court held that *clear and convincing evidence* is required to enforce such a contract.

---

[6] UPC §2-514.

TIERNEY v. LANTZ
505 N.W.2d 513, 1993 Iowa App. LEXIS 85
Court of Appeals of Iowa, 1993

Facts: Lyman Kentner, a widower with eight adult children, married Zella, a widow with three adult children. Nine years later, Lyman died intestate. His only asset was a house jointly owned with Zella, which passed to her automatically. A few years later, Zella died with a net worth of $233,000. Her will left her entire estate to her relatives.

Lyman's children alleged that Lyman and Zella had agreed when they married to divide their combined estates among their children equally. Lyman's and Zella's mutual wills were unsigned and made no reference to an agreement declaring them to be contractual or mutual. However, several of Lyman's children testified they had had conversations with their father and Zella during which Lyman stated that he and Zella had agreed to divide the assets equally among all their children. The district court dismissed the claim, and Lyman's children appealed.

Issue: **Did Lyman and Zella have contractual wills?**

Excerpts from Judge Donielson's Decision: In its order, the district court found there was credible circumstantial evidence that Lyman and Zella had a testamentary plan to dispose of their property, upon the death of the survivor, in equal shares among all eleven children. However, the court found there was no clear and convincing evidence that the parties agreed they would not revoke the wills or that they understood the testamentary plan was irrevocable.

To establish the contractual nature of mutual wills, the claimant must prove either the parties had agreed they would not revoke the wills once made or that the testamentary plan was irrevocable. Contractual or mutual wills which do not refer to a contract may be binding nevertheless if oral testimony at trial provides clear and convincing evidence the parties contracted with each other.

On our review, we find no clear and convincing evidence that the parties agreed they would not revoke their wills. The fact Lyman and Zella at one point had a testamentary plan to provide for all eleven children does not establish Zella had agreed to contractual wills. Neither of the unsigned wills made any reference to a mutual agreement. The only evidence indicating there was some agreement to establish contractual wills came from the self-serving testimony of Lyman's children.

It is not enough that Lyman believed an agreement to establish irrevocable, contractual wills had been reached. There must be clear and convincing evidence that both parties had reached such an agreement. As Lyman's children failed to establish by clear and convincing evidence either the existence of an agreement to create contractual wills or that the testamentary plan was irrevocable, we conclude the district court properly dismissed the claim of Lyman's children.

INTESTACY

Almost three-quarters of Americans die intestate—that is, without a will. In this event, the law steps in and determines how to distribute the decedent's property. Although, in theory, intestacy laws are supposed to be based on what most people would prefer, in practice, they are not. The vast majority of married people, for instance, leave all their assets to their surviving spouse. Most intestacy laws do not. In some states, if a married person dies intestate, some portion of her property (one-half or two-thirds) goes to her spouse, and the remainder to her issue (including grandchildren). Few people would actually want grandchildren to take a share of their estate in preference to their spouse. In other states, the decedent's estate is shared among her issue, her spouse, and her parents. If she has no issue, her spouse shares the estate with her parents.

These are the rules under the UPC:

If:	**Then:**
the decedent has issue, but no spouse,	the issue inherit the entire estate.
the decedent has a spouse, but no parents or issue,	the surviving spouse inherits the entire estate.
the decedent has a spouse and parents, but no issue,	the surviving spouse inherits $200,000 and 75 percent of the balance; the remainder goes to the parents.
the decedent has a spouse and issue, and all issue are by the surviving spouse,	the spouse inherits the entire estate.
the decedent has issue by someone other than the surviving spouse,	the spouse inherits the first $100,000 and 50 percent of the balance; the remainder goes to the issue.
the decedent has no spouse or issue,	his parents inherit equally.
the decedent has no spouse, issue, or parents, and:	his siblings inherit equally.
the decedent's siblings are dead,	their issue inherit.
the decedent has no siblings or issue of siblings,	his grandparents inherit.
his grandparents are dead,	his grandparents' issue inherit.
he runs out of relatives,	his property goes to the state.[7]

Most people have other wishes for their estate—it rarely makes sense to die without a will.

If intestacy is a bad idea, what about drafting your own will? Warren Burger did. Of course, he was the retired Chief Justice of the United States Supreme Court. Except for misspelling the word "executor," and omitting language that would have permitted his executor to sell real estate, he did fine. These errors were relatively harmless, and his property ended up going to his children, as he had planned. He was not an estate planner, but he was a lawyer and, presumably, a fairly competent one. Someone less competent runs the risk of making an error on some picky detail. For example, an heir might find that his inheritance has been voided because he witnessed the will. Advice on drafting a will is available on the Internet (for example, at **http://www.mtpalermo.com**). Computer software or form books in the library can also be helpful. Nonetheless, it is usually safer to hire an estate lawyer, especially if you have enough property to incur estate taxes. Still, a do-it-yourself will is often better than none.

[7] UPC §2-102.

SIMULTANEOUS DEATHS

Adam Janus died after taking a Tylenol capsule that some (still unidentified) person laced with cyanide. Stanley and Theresa Janus, Adam's brother and sister-in-law, returned from their honeymoon to join the mourners at Adam's house in Chicago. Not knowing the cause of Adam's death, they each took contaminated Tylenol. Stanley died immediately; Theresa survived for 48 hours on life support systems. Stanley's assets went first to Theresa and then to her father. If Theresa had not survived Stanley, his assets would have gone to his mother—clearly, a more equitable result.

To prevent injustices such as this, **the UPC (and many state laws) provide that, when two people who would inherit from each other die simultaneously, both are deemed to have been the last to die.** The UPC defines a simultaneous death as one in which both people die within 120 hours. If the UPC had been in effect in Illinois when Stanley and Theresa Janus died, Stanley's assets would have gone to his mother because the law would have presumed that he had been the last to die (and Theresa's assets would have gone to her father).

POWER OF ATTORNEY

A **durable power of attorney** is a document that permits the **attorney-in-fact** to act for the principal. (An attorney-in-fact need not be a lawyer.) The power of attorney is effective until the principal dies or revokes it. An **immediate power** becomes effective when signed; a **springing power** is effective at some time in the future, typically when the principal becomes incompetent and is no longer able to manage his affairs.

Lawyers generally recommend that their clients execute a durable power of attorney, particularly if they are elderly or in poor health. The power of attorney permits the client not only to choose an attorney-in-fact, but also to give advance instructions, such as "loan money to my son, Billy, if ever he needs it." If a client becomes incompetent and has no power of attorney, a court will appoint a guardian.

PROBATE

The testatrix is obviously not able to implement the terms of the will from beyond the grave, so she appoints an executor for this task. Typically, the executor is a family member, lawyer, or close friend. If the decedent does not select an executor, the probate court appoints an administrator to fulfill the same functions. The executor (or the administrator) has important responsibilities and, in a large estate, may spend a significant amount of time carrying out his functions. He has a fiduciary duty to the estate and is potentially liable to the heirs for any mistakes—from bad investment choices to errors in property valuation. Both the executor and the administrator are entitled to reasonable compensation—typically between 1 and 5 percent of the estate's value, although family members and friends often waive the fee.

Once the testator dies, the executor takes over. The executor must:

- **Admit the will to probate**. The executor must find the will and then file it in probate court. The testatrix should give her executor a copy of the will when she executes it.

- **Send notices**. The executor must notify the testatrix's creditors and all *potential* heirs, even those not mentioned in the will. Creditors typically have about five months to file their claims against the estate.
- **Gather assets**. The executor must compile a list of all assets—and their values. Real estate, stock in closely held businesses, artwork, jewelry, and other personal items must be appraised.
- **Manage assets**. During the probate process, the executor is responsible for everything from cutting the grass at the family home to managing the stock portfolio.
- **Pay debts and expenses**. The executor must pay all debts of the estate and reasonable expenses, such as the cost of the funeral.
- **Pay taxes and file estate tax returns**. The executor may have to file as many as four sets of tax returns: state and federal *income* tax returns for the last year of the decedent's life, and state and federal *estate* tax returns.
- **Distribute assets**. The entire probate process is lengthy, typically taking anywhere from 6 to 18 months. During this period, heirs often ask for advances against their share. The executor has the authority to give advances, but he is personally liable to the other heirs for any overpayments.

Once the creditors are paid, the tax returns filed, and the assets distributed, the probate process is over.

PROPERTY NOT TRANSFERRED BY WILL

A will does not control the distribution of joint property, retirement benefits, or life insurance. As explained in Chapter 47, property that is held in a joint tenancy automatically passes to the surviving owner, regardless of provisions in the decedent's will. This form of ownership is often used by family members—spouses or parents and children—as a simple method of transferring ownership without a will. Pension plans, other retirement benefits, and life insurance are also excluded from the decedent's estate and pass to whomever she has named as beneficiary.

ANATOMICAL GIFTS

As immunosuppressant drugs improve, doctors are increasingly successful at transplanting human organs. The demand for these organs—hearts, corneas, kidneys, pituitary glands, skin—is much greater than the supply. **The Uniform Anatomical Gift Act (UAGA) allows an individual to indicate her desire to be a donor either by putting a provision in her will or by signing an organ donation card in the presence of two witnesses.** A sample organ donation card is available at **http://www.delafe.com/form/frmdonor.htm**. If the donor makes the gift by will, this provision takes effect before probate—after a lengthy probate process, the organs would be less useful. The UAGA also provides that, unless a decedent has affirmatively indicated her desire not to be a donor, family members have the right to make a gift of her organs after death.

ADVANCE DIRECTIVES

Three times a day, a nurse snapped the flip tops on two small cans and poured the protein into a bag suspended from an IV-stand. A pump clicked on and the whitish liquid flowed through a pencil-thin plastic tube directly into the stomach of Nancy Cruzan, 32. An automobile accident had deprived her of oxygen for 14 minutes, destroying the part of her brain that controlled her thoughts, emotions, and actions. She spent seven years in a deep coma at the Missouri Rehabilitation Center, apparently perceiving neither herself nor her surroundings.

Cruzan's knees and arms were permanently curved into a fetal position. Her hands were twisted so tightly that the fingernails cut her wrists. She had primitive, involuntary functions, such as sleep and wake cycles. When her eyes opened, they moved randomly around the room. She responded to pain, and one nurse swore that Cruzan cried when a Valentine's Day card was read to her. Medical history has no record of anyone in her condition ever recovering. But experts said that if she continued to be fed, she could live for another 25 years.

Cruzan's parents found the thought of such a prolonged existence unbearable for their once-attractive, vibrant, and fun-loving daughter. Nancy would not have chosen to continue living that way, they said. They wanted her to die. The Cruzans' decision to stop feeding their daughter turned into a two-year legal battle that stretched from the small probate courtroom in Joplin, Missouri, to the marble chamber of the United States Supreme Court.[8]

Gary Rickman and Yvette Williams were among a group that petitioned two Missouri courts to resume the feeding of Cruzan. Rickman stated, "As for myself, I can't think of any case where euthanasia is OK. I want to live." Williams added, "They said Nancy wouldn't want to live like this. Well, nobody would like to live like that. But everybody goes through hard times in their lives. I'm not happy all the time either. Nancy was a very healthy disabled person. She didn't even have bedsores. Like, what is a good quality of life?"[9]

Nancy Cruzan's tragedy led to a national debate over the right to die. **The Supreme Court ruled that family members can choose to discontinue treatment for an incompetent person if there is evidence the patient would have made that choice herself.**[10] But, said the Court, to protect the rights of someone who cannot speak for herself, the state has the right to demand a high standard of proof in determining what she would have wanted. After the Supreme Court decision, the probate court in Missouri heard new witnesses testify that Cruzan had said she would not want to live "like a vegetable." The lower court considered this clear and convincing evidence about Cruzan's wishes and granted the family permission to withhold feeding.

Spurred by the *Cruzan* case, many people executed so-called **living wills** or **advance directives**. Living wills permit adults to refuse extreme medical treatment that would prolong their lives, such as artificial feeding, cardiac resuscitation, or mechanical respiration. In addition, a living will can be used to appoint a **health care proxy** to make decisions for a person who has become incompetent. A sample living will is available at the Choice in Dying Web site at **http://www.choices.org**. In addition, the Federal Patient Self-Determination Act requires hospitals to notify patients that they have the right to refuse life-saving measures if they are near death.

To date, living wills have not been particularly effective. A recent study found that 80 percent of doctors ignore the wishes of patients and their families. Large numbers of patients die alone and in pain in intensive care units. When patients request "Do Not Resuscitate" orders to ensure that they will not be revived in the event of a medical emergency, doctors take an average of 22 to 73 *days* to write the orders. As a result, half of these patients spend at least eight days in a coma or on a

[8] Rita Ciolli, "Is There a Right to Die?" *Newsday*, Dec. 3, 1989, p. 12.

[9] Pamela Warrick, "Protesters Plotted 'Rescue'—And Then It Was Too Late," *Los Angeles Times*, Jan. 10, 1991, p. E1. Copyright 1991 Los Angeles Times. Reprinted by permission.

[10] *Cruzan v. Director, Missouri Department of Health*, 497 U.S. 261, 110 S. Ct. 2841, 1990 U.S. LEXIS 3301 (1990).

mechanical respirator. Half of these patients are also in moderate to severe pain for their last three days of life. Results did not change, even when researchers made additional efforts to foster communication between doctors and their patients. The researchers concluded that the doctors knew their patients' wishes but chose to ignore them. What can a patient do? Dr. George J. Annas, a professor of medical ethics, suggests patients should go home to die, away from the technology of a hospital.

Doctors are permitted to shorten a patient's life by withholding medical treatment. Can they go the next step and prescribe medication to end the life of a terminal patient who is suffering intolerably? In the following case, the court considered the legality of a statute in the state of Washington that makes **assisted suicide** a felony. Other states have similar statutes. How much control should people have over the manner of their death? Should the terminally ill have the right to end their lives? You be the judge.

WASHINGTON v. GLUCKSBERG

521 U.S. 702, 117 S. Ct. 2258, 1997 U.S. LEXIS 4039
United States Supreme Court, 1997

Facts: The plaintiffs are five physicians who treat terminally ill patients, three patients in the terminal stage of excruciatingly painful illnesses, and Compassion in Dying (an organization that provides support to mentally competent, fatally ill adults considering suicide). The state of Washington passed a statute making assisted suicide a felony punishable by up to five years in prison and a $10,000 fine. Plaintiffs argued that this statute was unconstitutional. The trial court found for the plaintiffs, but the court of appeals reversed. The Supreme Court granted *certiorari*.

You Be the Judge: Does a state have the right to punish those who assist the terminally ill to commit suicide?

Argument for the Plaintiffs: The Fourteenth Amendment of the United States Constitution declares that the state may not "deprive any person of life, liberty, or property, without due process of law." The Supreme Court has, in the past, interpreted this provision to prevent the government from interfering in personal decisions relating to marriage, procreation, contraception, family relationships, child rearing, and education. For example, in *Roe v. Wade*, the Supreme Court held that a woman has the right to an abortion. If she has the right to terminate her pregnancy, surely she must have the right to terminate her own life. The choice to end one's life, to avoid unbearable pain, is among the most intimate and personal choices a person may make, a choice central to personal dignity and autonomy, central to the liberty protected by the Fourteenth Amendment.

In the *Cruzan* case, the Supreme Court suggested that an individual has the right to refuse life-saving treatment. No constitutional distinction can be drawn between the withdrawal of medical treatment that results in death and the hastening of death by taking prescribed drugs. The plaintiffs in this case suffered horribly from incurable diseases. Would any of us want to be in their place? If we were, wouldn't we want the right to control when and how we die?

Argument for the State of Washington: The plaintiffs argue that, since *Cruzan* permits doctors to withhold life support, it also permits them to aid in a suicide. There is an enormous difference between *withholding* aid and actively *killing* someone. This difference has long been recognized in tort law. You may not be liable for allowing someone to drown, but you will certainly be liable for pushing him into the pond.

The American Medical Association's Code of Medical Ethics declares, "Physician-assisted suicide is fundamentally incompatible with the physician's role as healer." The AMA also argues that the physician's constant search for weapons to combat disease would be impeded if killing were as acceptable an option for the physician as curing.

Without this anti-suicide statute, the elderly and the infirm will be pressured to consent to their own deaths. Minorities and the poor would also be susceptible to manipulation in a regime of assisted suicide. Pain is a significant factor in creating a desire for assisted suicide, and doctors are notoriously less aggressive in providing pain relief to the underprivileged.

For over 700 years, Anglo-American common law has punished those who help suicides. Most states that have considered this issue have decided that assisted suicide should be illegal. Given this history, it is difficult to argue that the Constitution somehow protects, as a fundamental liberty, the right to assisted suicide.

Between 60 and 70 percent of Americans think that assisted suicide should be legal. Roughly 20 percent of doctors who regularly care for terminally ill patients report that they have been asked to help a patient die. Yet, only about 5 percent of these doctors have actually provided assistance, largely because it is illegal. Oregon is the only state that allows doctors to prescribe a fatal dose of drugs to a dying patient.

TRUSTS

Trusts are an increasingly popular method for managing assets, both during life and after death. **A trust is an entity that separates legal and beneficial ownership.** It involves three people: the grantor (also called the settlor or donor), who creates and funds it; the trustee, who manages the assets; and the beneficiary, who receives the financial proceeds. The trustee technically owns the property, but she must use it for the good of the beneficiary. In other words, the trustee holds **legal** title, while the beneficiary holds **equitable** title. A grantor can create a trust during her lifetime or after her death through her will. **There are four requirements for establishing a trust:**

- **Legal Capacity**. As with any contract, the grantor must be of legal age and sound mind.
- **Trustee**. The grantor must appoint at least one trustee (who may be the grantor himself). The trust does not end if the appointed trustee dies or resigns. Either the trust instrument provides for successor trustees, or a court can appoint one.
- **Beneficiary**. A trust must have specific beneficiaries although it need not list them by name. It can instead list a class, such as "living children of the grantors."
- **Trust Property**. The grantor must transfer specific assets to the trust, although these assets can be nominal. A grantor might, for instance, establish a trust with $10 and then add other assets later.

ADVANTAGES AND DISADVANTAGES

Why do people use trusts? These are among the advantages:

- **Control**. The grantor can control her assets after her death. In the trust document, she can direct the trustees to follow a specific investment strategy, and she can determine how much income the beneficiaries receive. As an example, suppose the grantor has a husband and children. She wants to provide her husband with adequate income after her death, but she does not want him to spend so lavishly that nothing is left for the children. Nor does she want him to spend all her money on his second wife. The grantor could create a trust in her will that allows her husband to spend the income and, upon his death, gives the principal to their children.
- **Caring for Children**. Minor children cannot legally manage property on their own, so parents or grandparents often establish trusts to take care of these assets until the children grow up.
- **Tax Savings**. Although tax issues are beyond the scope of this chapter, it is worth noting that many married couples use a so-called **marital trust** to minimize their estate taxes.

- **Privacy**. A will is filed in probate court and becomes a matter of public record. Anyone can obtain a copy of it. Some companies are even in the business of providing copies to celebrity hounds. Jacqueline Kennedy Onassis's will is particularly popular. Trusts, however, are private documents and are not available to the public. To see summaries of celebrity wills, dig into http://www.willsofrichandfamous.com. (The summaries are free; copies of the entire will are available for a fee.)
- **Probate**. A will must go through the often lengthy probate process, so the heirs may not receive assets for some time. Assets that are put into a trust *before the grantor dies* do not go through probate; the beneficiaries have immediate access to them.

The major *disadvantage* of a trust is expense. Although it is always possible for the grantor to establish a trust himself with the aid of software or form books, trusts are complex instruments with many potential pitfalls. Do-it-yourself trusts are a recipe for disaster. In addition to the legal fees required to establish a trust, the trustees may have to be paid. Professional trustees typically charge an annual fee of about 1.5 percent of the trust's assets. Family members usually do not expect payment. Trusts can also save some money, however, because the grantor will have fewer assets to probate and therefore the executor's fees will be lower.

TYPES OF TRUSTS

Depending upon the goal in establishing a trust, a grantor has several different choices.

Living Trust

Also known as an *inter vivos* trust, a living trust is established while the grantor is still alive. In the typical living trust, the grantor serves as trustee during his lifetime. He maintains total control over the assets and avoids a trustee's fee. If the grantor becomes disabled or dies, the successor trustee, who is named in the trust instrument, takes over automatically. All of the assets stay in the trust and avoid probate. Typically, a grantor will also make a will to cover any assets omitted (accidentally or on purpose) from the trust. To put an asset in the trust, the grantor simply changes the ownership name. He could, for example, change the deed to his house from "Rudolf Nureyev" to "R. Nureyev Trust." Finally, most living trusts are **revocable**, meaning that the grantor can undo the trust or change it at anytime.

Testamentary Trust

A testamentary trust is created by a will. It goes into effect when the grantor dies. Naturally, it is **irrevocable** because the grantor is dead. The grantor's property must first go through probate, on its way to the trust. Older people tend to use a living trust because they want to ensure that their assets will be properly managed if they become disabled. Younger people typically opt for a testamentary trust because the probability they will become disabled any time soon is remote. Also they want to avoid the effort of transferring their assets to the trust.

Charitable Trust

A charitable trust is created to carry out a charitable purpose. It does not provide income for the grantor's family, or even for specific people, but rather it supports some general charitable purpose—caring for the poor of Philadelphia, promoting public education, or improving the environment.

A charitable trust can last forever, and sometimes this longevity presents a problem as society changes. However, under the doctrine of ***cy pres***—which means "as near as may be"—a court can change a trust's purpose if the original objective is no longer suitable, possible, or legal. The court will usually select a charitable purpose that is close to the grantor's original goal. For instance, in 1861 a man left $10,000 to help fight against slavery. After slavery ended, his heirs argued that the money was rightfully theirs because the trust had fulfilled its purpose. Applying the doctrine of *cy pres*, the court held that the funds should be used for the general assistance and education of African Americans.[11]

Spendthrift Trust

A spendthrift trust prevents creditors from attaching a beneficiary's interest in the trust. Creditors cannot force the trustees to pay the beneficiary's share of either income or principal to them. Of course, once the beneficiary receives money from the trust, his creditors can try to claim *those funds* from him. Spendthrift clauses do not protect against creditors if the beneficiary was also the grantor of the trust. Otherwise, it would be easy for people to incur debt and then establish a spendthrift trust to protect their assets. Spendthrift clauses also do not protect against claims for child support or alimony or against creditors who supplied necessaries. In the following case, the beneficiary of a spendthrift trust caused a horrible car accident. Should trust assets be protected from tort claims?

SLIGH v. FIRST NATIONAL BANK OF HOLMES COUNTY

704 So. 2d 1020, 1997 Miss. LEXIS 505
Supreme Court of Mississippi, 1997

Facts: Gene A. Lorance was an alcoholic who had been convicted numerous times of drunk driving and had also been involved in several automobile accidents. Aware that he was likely to be sued sooner or later, his mother set up two spendthrift trusts to protect her gifts to him from creditors.

While driving drunk, Lorance got into an accident that left William B. Sligh with a broken spine, paralysis, incontinence, and loss of all sexual function. Lorance was convicted of the crime of driving under the influence. Sligh also sued in tort and won a judgment of $5 million. Lorance had no assets other than his interest as beneficiary of the two spendthrift trusts. Sligh sued to reach those assets, alleging that spendthrift trusts should not be used as a shield against tort liability. The trial court dismissed his claim, and he appealed to the Mississippi Supreme Court.

Issue: Can tort creditors attach the assets of a spendthrift trust?

Excerpts from Justice Mills's Decision: [O]ne can identify three public policy considerations observed by this Court when enforcing spendthrift trust provisions: (1) the right of donors to dispose of their property as they wish; (2) the public interest in protecting spendthrift individuals from personal pauperism, so that they do not become public burdens; and (3) the responsibility of creditors to make themselves aware of their debtors' spendthrift trust protections.

[T]he courts have laid some stress on the fact that the creditors had only themselves to blame for extending credit to a person whose interest under [a spendthrift] trust had been put beyond their reach. Certainly, the situation of a tort creditor is quite different from that of a contract creditor. A man who is about to be

[11] *Jackson v. Phillips*, 96 Mass. (14 Allen) 539 (1867).

knocked down by an automobile has no opportunity to investigate the credit of the driver of the automobile and has no opportunity to avoid being injured no matter what the resources of the driver may be.

As for the public interest in protecting spendthrift individuals from personal pauperism, we believe that this interest is not as strong in the case of tort judgment creditors, where the inability to collect on their claims may well result in their own personal pauperism. If one must choose whom to reduce to personal pauperism in such a case, the spendthrift tortfeasor or the innocent tort judgment creditor, we are inclined to choose the party at fault, especially where that fault rises to the level of gross negligence or intentional conduct.

Clearly, the right of donors to place restrictions on the disposition of their property is not absolute. Rather, a donor may dispose of his property as he sees fit so long as such disposition does not violate the law or public policy. We find that it is indeed against public policy to dispose of property in such a way that the beneficiary may enjoy the income from such property without fear that his interest may be attached to satisfy the claims of his gross negligence or intentional torts. Accordingly, we reverse and render.

Totten Trust

A Totten Trust is a bank account held by the grantor "in trust" for someone else. If Lucy deposits money in a bank account that she opens in the name of "Lucy Diamond in trust for Schuyler," this account is a Totten Trust. There once was a great deal of controversy about whether these bank accounts were really trusts and whether they were revocable or irrevocable. Finally, in *In re Totten*, a New York court ruled that these accounts are revocable trusts.[12] The grantor (that is, the person who opened the bank account) has total control over the money during her lifetime. At her death, the beneficiary has the right to whatever is left in the account. What happens if the grantor leaves the money in the account to someone else in her will? Some states hold that the money goes to the person named in the will. Other states, and the UPC, hold that the person named on the bank account is entitled to the money.[13]

Resulting Trust

A resulting trust is created when a trust terminates before its assets are exhausted. The assets are returned to the grantor. Suppose Mary sets up a trust to pay her grandson William's college tuition. If William does not spend all the trust's assets on his education, it might seem fair for him to keep whatever is leftover. In fact, the law creates a resulting trust in favor of Mary, and the trustees must return the assets to her.

Constructive Trust

If someone wrongfully obtains ownership of property, he is deemed to be holding that property in constructive trust for the real owner. Suppose, for instance, that Fiona uses fraud, duress, or undue influence to force Trevor to give her a piece of land. Trevor can reclaim the property on the theory that Fiona is holding it in constructive trust for him. He will also be able to reclaim any rents Fiona collected on the property while she held it.

---

[12] 179 N.Y. 112, 71 N.E. 748, 1904 N.Y. LEXIS 1076 (N.Y. 1904).

[13] UPC §6-106.

TRUST ADMINISTRATION

The primary obligation of trustees is to carry out the terms of the trust. They may exercise any powers expressly granted to them in the trust instrument and any implied powers reasonably necessary to implement the terms of the trust, unless that power has been specifically prohibited. Suppose that a grantor establishes a trust for the benefit of his grandchildren. Trust assets include a valuable piece of land. If the trust instrument says nothing about buying and selling land, the trustee has the power to sell it. But, if the trust instrument specifically prohibits the sale of real estate, the trustee must turn down all offers, no matter how favorable.

In carrying out the terms of the trust, the trustees have a fiduciary duty to the beneficiary. This fiduciary duty includes:

- **A Duty of Loyalty**. In managing the trust, the trustees must put the interests of the beneficiaries first. They must disclose any relevant information to the beneficiaries. They may not commingle their own assets with those of the trust, do business with the trust (unless expressly permitted by the terms of the trust), or favor one beneficiary over another.

- **A Duty of Care**. The trustee must act as a reasonable person would when managing the assets of *another*. (This is a higher standard than requiring a trustee to act as a reasonable person would when managing his *own* affairs.) The trustee must make careful investments, keep accurate records, and collect debts owed the trust.

In their accountings, trustees must typically distinguish between principal and income. For example, a grantor will often provide that her spouse (the **income beneficiary**) receives the income of a trust during his lifetime while the principal goes to her children (the **remaindermen**). Especially if the husband and children are not on good terms, they will both watch the trustee carefully to see what he counts as income and principal. Fortunately, he can use the Uniform Principal and Income Act as a guide. Under the Act, principal includes (1) the trust's original assets, (2) proceeds from the sale of any assets, and (3) stock splits or dividends paid in stock. Income includes (1) cash dividends from stocks, (2) interest, and (3) rental income.

The trustee must also take care to pay trust expenses out of the correct account. He must use principal to pay capital improvements (such as building an office complex on trust land), and income to pay ordinary expenses such as property taxes, maintenance, and insurance premiums.

A trustee is liable to the beneficiaries of the trust if she breaches her duty. W. Averell Harriman was the scion of a wealthy New York family. When he died, he left half of his $65 million estate outright to his wife, Pamela Harriman, and half in trust for his two daughters from an earlier marriage (who were in their 70s). Pamela was a trustee and had the right to appoint the other trustees. She had been married twice before, to Winston Churchill's son and to Hollywood producer Leland Hayward. After Averell's death, she became ambassador to France, partly because of her generous contributions to the Democratic Party.

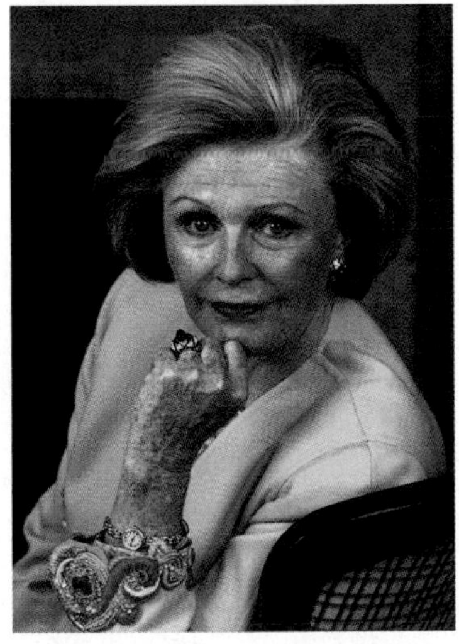

Ambassador to France and fund-raiser extraordinaire for the Democratic Party, Pamela Harriman had many skills. Managing trust funds does not appear to have been one of them.

Under Pamela's care, the trust assets were invested in a series of risky real estate deals, including a seedy conference center in New Jersey that had once been a Playboy Club. The beneficiaries filed suit against her when they discovered that trust assets had declined in value from $30 million to $3 million. She and the children ultimately settled their litigation for an undisclosed sum, and then both sides filed suit against the two other trustees. This litigation also was settled.

A trust itself cannot be sued. So, if someone has a claim against a trust, he must name the trustee as the defendant. The trustee has the right to reimbursement from the trust for any damages paid on behalf of the trust (that were not his fault). Suppose that a glass window falls out of a building owned by a trust and strikes a pedestrian. The injured person would sue the trustee. If found liable, the trustee could recover from the trust unless there was evidence that the window fell out because the trustee had been negligent in maintaining the building.

TERMINATION

A trust ends upon the occurrence of any of these events:

- On the date indicated by the grantor.
- If the trust is revocable, when revoked by the grantor. Even if the trust is irrevocable, the grantor and all the beneficiaries can agree to revoke it. If the grantor is dead, a court can terminate a trust if all the beneficiaries agree and termination would not frustrate the purpose of the trust.
- When the purpose of the trust has been fulfilled. If the grantor established the trust to pay college tuition for his grandchildren, the trust ends when the last grandchild graduates.

Even if one of these events does not occur, a noncharitable trust cannot last forever. The **Rule Against Perpetuities** provides that a trust must end within 21 years of the death of some named person who is alive when the trust is created. Thus, for instance, a grantor could legitimately establish a trust that ends 21 years after the death of whichever of his children was living when he made the trust. He could not, however, create a trust that ends upon the death of all of his grandchildren, because that might well be more than 21 years after the death of any person he could name who was living when he made the trust.

CHAPTER CONCLUSION

Attitudes toward inherited money vary greatly. Warren Buffett, whose holdings in Berkshire Hathaway, Inc. are worth about $40 billion, disapproves of inherited wealth. His children have occasionally borrowed money from him, but he insists that they sign formal loan documents and repay the loans. Other wealthy, and not so wealthy, people spend considerable time and effort minimizing their estate taxes and maximizing their children's inheritance. Neither view is right or wrong. People are perfectly entitled to dispose of their money as they see fit. The only mistake is not deciding.

CHAPTER REVIEW

1. For a will to be valid, the testatrix must be of legal age and sound mind. She must also comply with the necessary legal technicalities.
2. A holographic will is handwritten by the testator but not witnessed.
3. A spouse is entitled to a certain share of the decedent's estate, but children have no automatic right to share in a parent's estate.
4. A testator may generally revoke or alter a will at any time prior to death.

5. A testator cannot revoke a contractual will, that is, a will that was signed as part of an agreement with another person.

6. Almost three-quarters of Americans die intestate—that is, without a will. In this event, the law determines how the decedent's property will be distributed.

7. A will does not control the distribution of joint property, life insurance, or retirement benefits.

8. A living will permits an adult to refuse medical treatment that would prolong life.

9. A trust is an entity that separates legal and beneficial ownership.

10. A spendthrift trust prevents creditors from attaching a beneficiary's interest in the trust.

11. A Totten Trust is a bank account held by the grantor "in trust" for someone else.

12. In carrying out the terms of a trust, the trustees have a fiduciary duty to the beneficiary.

PRACTICE TEST

1. When Frank Gilbert died, he left behind an eight-page typed will, prepared by an attorney, and handwritten notes dated two years later. The notes were found folded together in a sealed envelope. On the back of a business card, Frank had written: "Jim and Margaret I have appro $50,000.00 in Safe. See Buzz if anything happens [signed] Frank Gilbert." On the back of a pay stub, Frank had written: "Jim & Margaret $20,000.00 the Rest divided Equally the other Living Survivors Bro. & Sisters [signed] Frank Gilbert." He had written on the envelope: "I gave to Jim and Margaret this card which I Stated what to do." Jim was one of Frank's brothers; Margaret was Jim's wife. The typed will granted Jim a share of Frank's other assets besides the $50,000 in the safe. Jim's siblings argued that the handwritten notes were a new will that revoked the typed document and that, therefore, Jim and Margaret were entitled to $20,000 and nothing more. Jim argued that the handwritten notes were a codicil, giving him $20,000 in addition to his share under the will. Who is correct?

2. Kevin Fitzgerald served in the Massachusetts House of Representatives. A priest alerted him that Mary Guzelian, a street person who roamed his district, had trash bags stuffed with money in her ghetto apartment. Fitzgerald visited the apartment with his top aide, Patricia McDermott. Two weeks later, Guzelian signed a will, drafted by one of Fitzgerald's acquaintances, that left Guzelian's $400,000 estate to Fitzgerald and McDermott. Fitzgerald claimed not to know about the will until Guzelian's death four years later. Guzelian, 64, suffered from chronic paranoid schizophrenia and severe health problems. Would her sister have a claim on Guzelian's estate?

3. **CPA QUESTION** A decedent's will provided that the estate was to be divided among the decedent's issue, per capita and not per stirpes. If there are two surviving children and three grandchildren who are children of a predeceased child at the time the will is probated, how will the estate be divided?

(a) ½ to each surviving child

(b) ⅓ to each surviving child and ⅑ to each grandchild

(c) ¼ to each surviving child and ⅙ to each grandchild

(d) ⅕ to each surviving child and grandchild

4. After nearly 40 years of marriage, Frank Honigman executed a new will that left his wife only the minimum required by law. The balance went to his brothers and sisters. For some time before his death, using obscene and abusive language, Honigman had repeatedly told both friends and strangers that his wife was unfaithful. Honigman was normal and rational in other respects but his suspicions were untrue. They were based on such evidence as the fact that, when he left the house, his wife would ask him when he planned to return. Also, whenever the telephone rang, Mrs. Honigman answered it. For the last two years of

his life he forbade her to answer the telephone. Is Mr. Honigman's will valid?

5. When Beryl H. Buck died, her will established a $260 million trust to provide for the needy in Marin County, California, and for other charitable purposes in that county. Four years later, the trustee asked the probate court to apply the doctrine of *cy pres* to permit the trust to spend a portion of its income outside the borders of Marin County. The trustee found it difficult to spend the trust's vast income in that affluent county. How would you decide this case if you were the judge?

6. CPA QUESTION A personal representative of an estate would breach her fiduciary duties if she:

(a) Combined personal funds with funds of the estate so that both could purchase treasury bills

(b) Represented the estate in a lawsuit brought against it by a disgruntled relative of the decedent

(c) Distributed property in satisfaction of the decedent's debts

(d) Engaged a non-CPA to prepare the records for the estate's final accounting

7. Rodney Sharp, a 56-year-old dairy farmer whose education did not go beyond the eighth grade, developed a close relationship with Jean Kosmalski, a schoolteacher 16 years his junior. Kosmalski performed domestic tasks for Sharp and was his frequent companion. Sharp asked her to marry him, but she refused. He gave her many expensive presents and permitted her to withdraw substantial amounts of money from his bank account. Together they renovated his farmhouse in furtherance of "domestic plans." While the renovations were still in progress, Sharp transferred the farm to Kosmalski. Five months later, she broke off their relationship and ordered Sharp to move out. Kosmalski took possession of the home, the farm, and all the equipment, leaving Sharp with assets of $300. What claim might Sharp bring against Kosmalski?

8. While Robert and Marie Blanchette were married, Robert bought shares of stock through a weekly payment program. To avoid the expense of probate, he had the stock issued to himself and Marie as joint tenants. Marie took no part in the purchase of the stock and did not know how many shares were acquired. When the couple divorced, Marie claimed that half of the shares belonged to her. The court said that the same rule applied to these shares as to a Totten Trust. In that case, who owned the stock?

9. This question appeared in the *Minneapolis Star Tribune*'s annual Consumer Quiz: What does intestate mean?

(a) A highway that crosses from one state to another

(b) A highway that remains within a state

(c) A male hormonal imbalance

(d) None of the above

10. YOU BE THE JUDGE WRITING PROBLEM John and Helena Lemp had three children. After their divorce, John married Mary. John and Mary prepared reciprocal wills, leaving their estates to each other, with the balance to the three children upon the death of the surviving spouse. After John's death, Mary signed a new will leaving everything to her relatives instead of her stepchildren. John and Mary did not sign a contract that prohibited them from revoking their wills, and the wills themselves contained no contractual language. Did Mary have the right to revoke her will? **Argument for the children:** John and Mary clearly had an agreement that they would leave all their property to each other and then to the children. John abided by his side of the agreement, and so should Mary. **Argument for Mary:** John and Mary did not sign a contract agreeing to reciprocal wills, and the wills themselves made no reference to a contract, so Mary was free to change her will at any time.

11. RIGHT & WRONG Alan Chang established a spendthrift trust for which he was both trustee and beneficiary. He gave the trust a piece of property. Could a bank, to which he owed money, attach the property in his trust? Regardless of the legal issues, are spendthrift trusts ethical? Why should anyone have the right to shield assets from creditors?

INTERNET RESEARCH PROBLEM

Fill out your own organ donor card (available at **http://www.delafe.com/form/frmdonor.htm**) or advance directive (see **http://www.choices.org**).

You can find further practice problems in the Online Quiz at http://beatty.westbuslaw.com or in the Study Guide that accompanies this text.

CHAPTER 49

INSURANCE

In his job at the National Institutes of Health, Dr. James A. Magner analyzes the molecular structure of a hormone that stimulates the thyroid gland. One evening at home, he was trying to figure out the life insurance policy he had purchased. Glancing at the rows of figures, he could not understand precisely what the coverage was or what benefits the policy gave him, nor could he recall how much he was supposed to pay each year. "I try to be an intelligent consumer," he said. "It was inscrutable." Before deciding which coverage to buy, Magner had asked a second agent for prices on an equivalent $100,000 policy. But when he got back a complicated set of numbers, he recalled, "I couldn't compare."

Like half the people who purchase life insurance in this country, Magner ended up buying a policy from someone he knew—in this case, his sister-in-law. He said he still does not know if he got the best buy. The physician is not alone. Even insurance company executives and other experts say there are so many variations in prices, benefits, and types of policies offered by life insurance companies that they cannot compare them accurately without a computer analysis.[1]

[1] Ronald Kessler, "Insurance: Costly Enigma," *Washington Post*, Mar. 20, 1983, p. A1. © 1983, The Washington Post. Reprinted with permission.

INTRODUCTION

No matter how careful our behavior, we are all subject to risk—from automobile accidents, injury, illness, fires, early death, and other catastrophes. No wonder that, from earliest times, people have sought insurance against these unpredictable and unpreventable dangers. Today, a typical family spends about 15 percent of its disposable income on insurance, more than on any other single category except food and housing. Yet few contracts are as complex and difficult to understand as insurance policies. In comparison, mortgage contracts read like a good novel. It is hardly surprising that in public opinion polls measuring reputation for honesty and ethical standards, insurance salespeople consistently rank near the bottom of the list of professionals, above only advertising practitioners and car sellers. The purpose of this chapter is to learn about the standard components of an insurance contract, the most common types of insurance, and your rights and duties as a purchaser of insurance. For general advice from the insurance industry on everything from what to do after a car accident to avoiding catastrophes at work, click on the Insurance Information Institute at **http://www.iii.org/**.

It is important to begin by defining these key terms:

- **Person**. An individual, corporation, partnership, or any other legal entity.
- **Insurance**. A contract in which one person, in return for a fee, agrees to guarantee another against loss caused by a specific type of danger.
- **Insurer**. The person who issues the insurance policy and serves as guarantor.
- **Insured**. The person whose loss is the subject of the insurance policy.
- **Owner**. The person who enters into the insurance contract and pays the premiums.
- **Premium**. The consideration that the owner pays under the policy.
- **Beneficiary**. The person who receives the proceeds from the insurance policy.

The beneficiary, the insured, and the owner can be, but are not necessarily, the same person. If a homeowner buys fire insurance for her house, she is the insured, the owner, and the beneficiary because she bought the policy and receives the proceeds if her house burns down. If a mother buys a life insurance policy on her son that is payable to his children in the event of his death, then the mother is the owner, the son is the insured, and the grandchildren are the beneficiaries.

Before beginning a study of insurance law, it is important to understand the economics of the insurance industry. Suppose that you have recently purchased a $500,000 house. The probability your house will burn down in the next year is 1 in 1,000. That is a low risk, but the consequences would be devastating, especially since you could not afford to rebuild. Instead of bearing that risk yourself, you take out a fire insurance policy. You pay an insurance company $1,200 in return for a promise that, if your house burns down in the next 12 months, the company will pay you $500,000. The insurance company sells the same policy to 1,000 similar homeowners, expecting that on average one of these houses will burn down. If all 1,000 policyholders pay $1,200, the insurance company takes in $1.2 million each year, but expects to pay out only $500,000. It will put some money aside in case two houses burn down, or even worse, a major forest fire guts a whole tract of houses. It must also pay overhead expenses such as marketing and administration. And, of course, shareholders expect profits.

INSURANCE CONTRACT

An insurance policy must meet all the common law requirements for a contract. There must be an offer, acceptance, and consideration. The owner must have legal capacity; that is, he must be an adult of sound mind. Fraud, duress, or undue influence invalidates a policy. In theory, insurance contracts need not be in writing because the statute of frauds does not apply to any contract that can be performed within one year and it is possible that the house may burn down or the car may crash within a year. Some states, however, specifically require insurance contracts to be in writing.[2]

OFFER AND ACCEPTANCE

The purchaser of a policy makes an offer by delivering an application and a premium to the insurer. The insurance company then has the option of either accepting or rejecting the offer. **It can accept by oral notice, by written notice, or by delivery of the policy. It also has a fourth option—a written binder.** A **binder** is a short document acknowledging receipt of the application and premium. It indicates that a policy is *temporarily* in effect but does not constitute *final* acceptance. The insurer still has the right to reject the offer once it has examined the application carefully. Kyle buys a house on April 1 and wants insurance right away. The insurance company issues a binder to him the same day. If Kyle's house burns down on May 1, the insurer must pay, even though it has not yet issued the final policy. If, however, there is no fire, but on May 1 the company decides Kyle is a bad risk, it has the right to reject his application at that time.

Sometimes, insurance companies accept a premium but delay making a decision on whether to accept or reject the contract. In theory, the policy is not in effect and the applicant has no coverage (unless the company has issued a binder). However, some courts have held that unreasonable delay constitutes acceptance. For instance, on November 6, a K-Mart employee applied for a $50,000 life insurance policy through a company-owned insurer. She paid weekly premiums through K-Mart. On January 25, the insurance company decided to issue a policy for $5,000. On February 6, the woman died. On February 9, the insurance company mailed the $5,000 policy to her. When her heirs sued, the court held that the insurance company was liable for the entire $50,000 because its delay had been excessive and unreasonable.[3]

LIMITING CLAIMS BY THE INSURED

Insurance policies can sometimes look like a quick way to make easy money. More than one person suffering from overwhelming financial pressure has insured a building to the hilt and then burned it down for the insurance money. Unbelievably, more than one parent has killed a child to collect the proceeds of a life insurance policy. Therefore, the law has created a number of rules to protect insurance companies from fraud and bad faith on the part of insureds. In addition, policies often have provisions designed to prevent insureds from making an undue profit.

---

[2] See Unit 2 for a general discussion of contracts. Chapter 15, on written contracts, covers the statute of frauds.

[3] *Carney v. Lone Star*, 540 So. 2d 415, 1989 La. App. LEXIS 320 (La. 1989).

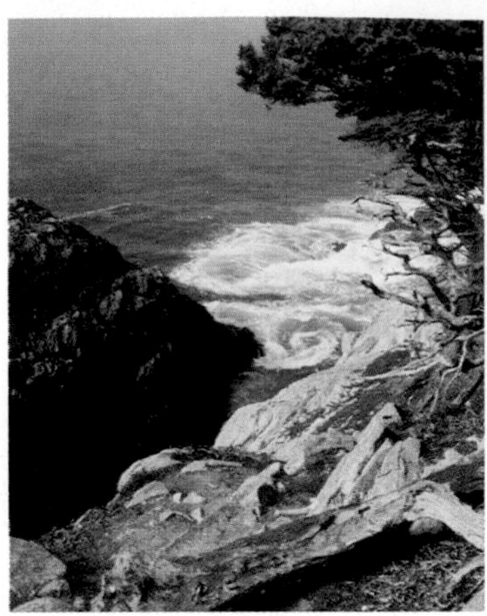

Virginia Rearden pushed Deana Wild to her death from a Big Sur cliff. If the insurance company had known that Rearden did not have an insurable interest in Wild, the company would have refused to issue the policy, and Wild might not have died.

Insurable Interest

An insurance contract is not valid unless the owner has an *insurable interest* in the subject matter of the policy. To understand why an insurable interest is important, read this tragic story. Twenty-year-old Deana Wild was thrilled when James Coates proposed to her. To celebrate their engagement, they took a sightseeing trip along the California coast with Coates's mother, Virginia Rearden. They seemed to be just one big happy family. Only one problem: Wild slipped while walking along the edge of a cliff at Big Sur and fell to her death. That would have been the end of the story except that, the day before, Wild had taken out a $35,000 life insurance policy, naming Coates and Rearden as beneficiaries. When the insurance company investigated, it learned that Coates was married to someone else. He could not be Wild's fiancé, and neither he nor Rearden had an insurable interest in Wild. It also turned out that Rearden had taken out the policy without Wild's knowledge. Rearden was convicted of first degree murder and sentenced to life in prison without parole.

These are the rules on insurable interest:

- **Definition**. A person has an **insurable interest** if she would be harmed by the danger that she has insured against. The goal is to eliminate any incentive to cause damage in order to collect from the insurance company. If Jessica takes out a fire insurance policy on her own house, she will presumably be reluctant to burn it down. However, if she buys a policy on Nathan's house, she will not mind, she may even be delighted, when fire sweeps through the house. It is a small step to saying that she might even burn the house down herself. Presumably, Virginia Rearden would have been less tempted to kill her son's real fiancée.

- **Time of Loss**. The insurable interest must exist at the time *the loss occurs*. If Jessica takes out a policy on her barn, but then sells the barn to Nathan, she cannot recover on the policy if the barn burns down while Nathan owns it because she no longer has an insurable interest. The insurable interest need not exist at the time the *policy was purchased*. Thus, if Nathan takes out a policy before he buys the barn, but the loss occurs while he owns it, he can recover on the policy.

- **Amount of Loss**. The insurable interest can be no greater than the actual amount of loss suffered. If the barn is worth $50,000, but Jessica insures it (and pays premiums) for $100,000, she will recover only $50,000 when it burns down. The goal is to make sure that Jessica does not profit from the policy.

- **Property Insurance**. Virtually any economic interest in property qualifies as an insurable interest. Anyone who owns, or has a security interest in, property has an insurable interest.[4] Thus both the mortgagee (that is, the person who loans money on the property) and the mortgagor (the person who borrows the money) have an insurable interest. Or, to take another example, National Filtering sold Ellis & Co. a license to use a patented oil filtering process. The license fees were based on the amount of oil Ellis filtered. The license was exclusive, which meant that if Ellis's plant was destroyed, National Filtering would receive no income. National took out property insurance on the plant. When it burned down, the insurance company claimed that National had no insurable interest. The court, however, sided with National, holding that an

[4] Security interests are covered in Chapter 26.

insurable interest existed because National suffered a loss when the plant was destroyed.[5]

- **Life Insurance**. A person always has an insurable interest in his own life and the life of his spouse or fiancée. Parents and *minor* children also have an insurable interest in each other. Typically, other relatives, including parents and *adult* children as well as siblings, aunts, uncles, nephews, nieces, and cousins, have an insurable interest only if they have some financial stake in each other. For example, sisters who live together have an insurable interest because, if one dies, the other might not be able to maintain the house on her own.

- **Work Relationships**. Business partners, employers, and employees have an insurable interest in each other if they would suffer some financial harm from the death of the insured. For example, a start-up company will often buy **key person life insurance** on its officers to compensate the company if an important person dies.

Misrepresentation

Insurers have the right to void a policy if, during the application process, the insured makes a material misstatement or conceals a material fact. The policy is voidable whether the misstatement was oral or in writing, intentional or unintentional. **Material** means that the misstatement or omission affected the insurer's willingness to issue the policy. For example, a father asserted in an application for automobile insurance that he owned the car when, in fact, his 20-year-old son did. When the son was involved in an accident, the insurer refused to pay. However, the court ruled that the misrepresentation had not been material because the insurance policy clearly disclosed that the principal driver would be a male under the age of 25. The premium and the policy would have been no different if the insurer had known that the son owned the car.[6] In the following case, the applicant lied about his health. Were his misstatements material?

GOLDEN RULE INSURANCE CO. v. HOPKINS
788 F. Supp. 295, 1991 U.S. Dist. LEXIS 19970
United States District Court for the Southern District of Mississippi, 1991

Facts: Brian Hopkins submitted an application to Golden Rule Insurance Co. for medical and life insurance. In filling out the application, he answered "no" to questions asking whether he had had any of the following conditions: heart murmur, growths, skin disorders, immune deficiencies, sexually transmitted diseases, or any disorders of the glands. In response to questions about past surgery, Hopkins reported that he had had tonsils and hemorrhoids removed.

A year later, Hopkins was hospitalized. While in the hospital, he was diagnosed with AIDS. In his discharge summary, Dr. William A. Causey stated that Hopkins had tested HIV positive three years before. (HIV is the virus that causes AIDS.) Shortly thereafter, Dr. Causey wrote to Golden Rule to say that he was mistaken and that Hopkins was not HIV positive. During the trial, however, Dr. Causey admitted that he was not eager to tell insurance companies information that would harm his patients. The following year, Hopkins died of AIDS. Golden Rule rescinded Hopkins's policies, contending that his application contained material misrepresentations.

---

[5] *National Filtering Oil Co. v. Citizens' Insurance Co.,* 106 N.Y. 535, 13 N.E. 337, 1887 N.Y. LEXIS 906 (1887).

[6] *Employers' Liability Assurance Co. v. Vella,* 366 Mass. 651, 321 N.E.2d 910, 1975 Mass. LEXIS 1127 (1975).

Issues: Did Hopkins materially misrepresent his health when applying for insurance? Does Golden Rule have the right to rescind his insurance policies?

Excerpts from Judge Wingate's Decision: The court finds that at the time of filling out the application the defendant misrepresented the following items about his health condition: (1) the history of skin disorders; (2) the diagnosis of mitral valve prolapse (and accompanying heart murmur); (3) the recurring problem of swollen lymph glands; (4) the presence of rectal warts (condylomata acuminata) which required surgical removal 17 months before submission of the application; and (5) an HIV positivity between one and three years prior to the issuance of the policy.

All of these undisclosed conditions affected Golden Rule's risk of loss under the disputed policy. In Mississippi, an insurer has a right to rescind an insurance policy when the insured's application contains a false statement, and "such false statement materially affected either the acceptance of the risk or the hazard assumed by the insurer."

Dr. Brobson Lutz, an expert in infectious diseases, opined that Hopkins, a practicing homosexual, was HIV positive before [he applied for insurance]. This court is persuaded by Dr. Lutz' testimony and is convinced that Hopkins' demonstrated symptoms show HIV positivity before [he applied for insurance].

In conclusion, for the reasons above discussed, the court finds that plaintiff is legally entitled to rescind the insurance policy and coverage thereafter. Thus, Golden Rule is released from the obligation to pay for any of the medical costs and expenses incurred by Hopkins' hospitalization and treatment. Defendant will receive back all premiums paid under the policy, plus interest.

The Web site **http://www.insurancefraud.org** offers "Fraud Case of the Week," which describes new and creative methods of committing insurance fraud.

Warranties

Insurers have the right to void a policy if the insured violates a warranty. A warranty is a condition contained in the policy. Suppose a movie theater's liability policy contains a condition requiring two ushers to be present at all times in each theater. If a fire starts in a theater in which there is no usher, the insurance company is not liable. In theory, the policy is void whether or not the violation actually contributes to the risk. Suppose, however, that the theater burns down because the electrical system short-circuits. Only one usher is present, but there is nothing she (or a hundred) ushers could have done to prevent this type of fire. It is a slow Wednesday afternoon, only five patrons are in the theater, and none of them is injured. Nonetheless, under a strict interpretation, the policy is voidable. Some states have modified the harshness of this rule by requiring that the policy be valid unless the violation is material. Typically, the **test of materiality** is whether the breach actually increased the risk. A jury would determine if the risk of harm was higher with one usher than with two.

Deductibles, Co-insurance, and Pro Rata Provisions

Deductibles. Insurance companies fear that policyholders have an incentive to behave carelessly or to make false claims. After all, the insured has already paid for the protection, so why not make a claim? Someone with automobile insurance may be tempted to drive carelessly or park her car in an unsafe area, figuring that if anything goes wrong, the insurer will pay. To discourage the insured from incurring losses, policies often have a **deductible provision that requires the insured to pay a certain amount of the claim herself.** Presumably, an insured will be less likely to park in the car theft capital of the country if she knows the insurer will not reimburse her for the first $500 of her claim. A deductible also decreases the insurer's administrative costs by preventing many small claims.

Co-insurance. Many insurance policies also have a co-insurance provision. **Co-insurance means that the insured must pay some percentage of the entire loss.** In contrast, a deductible only requires the insured to pay a fixed amount, however large the claim. The purpose of co-insurance is to encourage insureds to keep their losses as low as possible. Some policies, such as health insurance, may have both a deductible and co-insurance. When Tim goes to see a doctor for a sprained ankle, the bill is $150. If his policy has a deductible of $5, he will pay that amount for his visit, no matter how much the total bill is. If, instead, the policy has co-insurance, he might pay 20 percent of the total, or $30. If the policy has both a deductible and co-insurance, he will pay: $5 + (.20 × $145) = $34.

Co-insurance provisions are also common in property insurance policies—with a wrinkle. Here is the co-insurance rule for *property* insurance: **If a policy has a co-insurance provision and the owner insures for less than a specified percentage (typically 80 percent) of the value of the property, he is entitled to full payment of the *policy amount* only if the property is totally destroyed. If it is only partly destroyed, he recovers only a percentage of the policy amount.**

The logic behind the rule is this: if the owner insures for less than the required 80 percent (or whatever the policy specifies), he is assumed to be self-insuring some part of his losses. If his property is only partly damaged, he will receive reimbursement equal to only part of the policy. Suppose that Kendall owns a house that would cost $200,000 to rebuild. He insures it for $100,000, and his policy has an 80 percent co-insurance clause. If a storm strikes, causing $50,000 of damage, he might think that he is entitled to the full $50,000 because, after all, he has a $100,000 policy. But he is wrong. His insurer will use this formula to calculate its payment:

$$\text{Total recovery} = \text{Actual loss} \times \frac{\text{Amount of insurance}}{\text{Percent of co-insurance} \times \text{Value of property}}$$

In our example, the actual loss is $50,000, the amount of insurance is $100,000, the percent of co-insurance is 80 percent, and the value of the property is $200,000.

$$\text{Kendall's recovery} = \$50{,}000 \times \frac{\$100{,}000}{.80 \times \$200{,}000}$$

$$= \$31{,}250$$

Instead of a $50,000 reimbursement, Kendall will receive only $31,250. If his house was totally destroyed, the co-insurance clause would not apply, and he would be entitled to a full $100,000 payment.

Pro Rata Provisions. In a continuing effort to make sure that insureds do not profit unduly, most policies have a ***pro rata* clause that prevents an insured from collecting more than the actual damage suffered.** Suppose that Heloise purchases four fire insurance policies for $100,000 each on the same $200,000 warehouse. When it burns down, she can only collect a total of $200,000, not $400,000. Each insurance company pays this amount:

$$\text{Payment} = \text{Actual loss} \times \frac{\text{Amount of policy}}{\text{Total amount of all policies}}$$

$$= \$200{,}000 \times \frac{\$100{,}000}{\$400{,}000}$$

$$= \$50{,}000$$

SUBROGATION

Subrogation means the substitution of one person for another. **If an insurance company pays a claim, it is subrogated to the rights of the insured, meaning that the company acquires whatever rights the insured had against any third parties.** The following news report illustrates this concept.

After two teenagers burglarized, ransacked, and vandalized her home two years ago, Sandra Steers was thankful her homeowner's insurance reimbursed her for the immense damage and property loss. Steers says she was not interested in suing the burglars. She simply wanted to put the trauma behind her and get on with her life.

So it was unsettling for Steers to read in the newspapers that she had filed a lawsuit against the convicted burglars, seeking at least $15,000 in damages from them. "It's a lie because I'm not getting any money and I'm not suing anybody," she said. "I wouldn't dream of suing anybody after what I went through with this house. As far as I'm concerned, it's over with."

After reading about the lawsuit, Steers checked with the court and learned that a lawsuit had, indeed, been filed there in her name. She was dumbfounded, she says, because it was done completely without her knowledge. However, what happened to Steers was perfectly legal. It has to do with a legal maneuver called subrogation, which had apparently been included in her homeowner's policy.[7]

Once Steers's insurance company paid her claim, it acquired all her rights against the burglars. Steers's policy contained a subrogation clause, but the insurance company would have had a right of subrogation, as a matter of law, even without such a clause. Subrogation serves two purposes:

- It prevents the insured from recovering twice—once from the insurance company and once from the person who caused the damage. Without subrogation, Steers could have sued the burglars herself and recovered from them, too.
- It reduces the cost of insurance for everyone. If an insurance company receives reimbursement from a third party, it can offer lower premiums.

If the insured waives her claim against the third parties, then the insurance company also loses any rights it might have against them. Thus, if Steers had promised not to sue the burglars, the insurance company would have lost its right to sue, too. However, it would also have lost its obligation to pay Steers's claim.

The principle of subrogation applies to property and fire insurance, but not to life insurance. It is so difficult to put an economic value on someone's life that the concern over double recovery does not apply. If Steers had been killed by the burglars, her life insurance company would *not* have been subrogated to her family's right to recover against the murderers.

SURETYSHIP

Suretyship is the mirror image of subrogation. In subrogation, the insurance company succeeds to the *rights* of the insured. **In suretyship, the insurance company succeeds to the *obligations* of the insured.** A suretyship contract protects one

---

[7] Doreen Guarino, "Woman's Suit Against Burglars Surprise to Her," *Journal Inquirer*, Apr. 9, 1994, p. A4. Reprinted with permission.

party to a contract against default by another. For example, federal contractors are often required to post surety bonds to ensure completion of their job. If they fail to finish the contract, the surety pays the cost of hiring someone else. For large contracts, sureties are almost always insurance companies, but individuals and others can also serve as sureties. Suppose a landlord refuses to rent an apartment to a college student unless his parents agree to be liable for the rent if he defaults. The parents are sureties.

The following case demonstrates the difference between subrogation and suretyship. A man acted as a surety for his brother on a bank loan and then was subrogated to the claim of the bank. This case also illustrates the dangers of doing business with family or friends. The brother was not exactly grateful for the help he received.

HOOPES v. HOOPES
124 Idaho 518, 861 P.2d 88, 1993 Ida. App. LEXIS 155
Court of Appeals of Idaho, 1993

Facts: Zion's National Bank of Utah foreclosed on a farm owned by Lowell Hoopes. Under Idaho law, Lowell had the right to reclaim his farm if he repaid the loan within one year. Eleven months after the foreclosure, Lowell asked his brother, Melvin, to act as a surety on a loan from the First Bank of Afton that could be used to repay the Zion loan. Melvin agreed to co-sign the loan and also to assign four certificates of deposit (CDs) to the Afton bank as collateral.

Lowell was unable to pay the loan when due. In the meantime, the Federal Deposit Insurance Corporation had taken over the Afton bank. It seized the CDs and used them to pay the loan. Melvin filed suit against his brother to collect the amount of the CDs. At trial, the court ruled that Melvin was a surety for Lowell and that he had gained all rights of the Afton bank through subrogation. The district court ordered Lowell to pay Melvin the principal of the debt and all interest due. Lowell filed this appeal, claiming that Melvin was not subrogated to the rights of the bank.

Issue: **Did Melvin became subrogated to the rights of the bank when his CDs were used to pay off the loan?**

Excerpts from Judge Perry's Decision: Subrogation, in its broadest sense, is the substitution of one person for another. It is considered a creature of equity and is so administered as to secure real and essential justice without regard to form, and it will not be allowed where it would work an injustice to others. Lowell asserts that the district court erred in finding subrogation. Melvin did not come to the action with "clean hands," and, therefore, Melvin is barred from seeking an equitable remedy.

Lowell alleges that Melvin's true desire was to possess the farm and that the entire lawsuit was merely an attempt to gain title. The Idaho courts have long subscribed to the principle that "he who comes into equity must come with clean hands," and "a litigant may be denied relief by a court of equity on the ground that his conduct has been inequitable, unfair and dishonest, or fraudulent and deceitful as to the controversy in issue." We think that application of the clean hands doctrine must be based upon a litigant's conduct, not upon his other private motivations. In this case, regardless of Melvin's motivation for becoming a surety for Lowell, we can find nothing inequitable in his paying the loan, nor in his attempts to recover the money lost on the delinquent loan. We perceive no grounds for application of the clean hands doctrine against Melvin.

The judgment is *affirmed.*

BAD FAITH BY THE INSURER

Insurance policies often contain a *covenant of good faith and fair dealing*. Even if the policy itself does not *explicitly* include such a provision, an increasing number of courts (but not all) *imply* this covenant. An insurance company can violate the covenant of good faith and fair dealing by (1) fraudulently inducing someone to buy a policy, (2) refusing to pay a valid claim, or (3) refusing to accept a reasonable settlement offer that has been made to an insured. When an insurance company violates the covenant of good faith and fair dealing, it becomes liable for both compensatory and punitive damages.[8]

Fraud

In recent years, a number of insurance companies have paid serious damages to settle fraud charges involving the sale of life insurance. The companies would train their salespeople to tell elderly customers that a new policy was better when, in fact, it was much worse. State Farm Insurance agreed to pay its customers $200 million to settle such a suit. As the following article indicates, State Farm was not alone in this scam.

After a two-year investigation of the Prudential Insurance Company of America, the nation's largest insurer, officials in Florida concluded that the company deliberately set out to cheat its customers for more than a decade. Prudential has agreed to pay restitution that could run to as much as $2 billion.

The tactic used repeatedly by Prudential agents was to persuade customers to use the cash that had built up in their life insurance policies to buy new policies with greater coverage, with the promise that their premiums would not increase. The agents earned new commissions and the company's market share grew. But when the cash value of the original policies was depleted by the demands for premiums for the second policies, customers began receiving much higher bills. Many people could not make the payments and lost all their coverage. In those cases, the company had received years of premiums and now no longer faced the prospect of ever having to pay a death benefit.

In some of its training seminars, Prudential taught agents either to commit fraud or to use misleading techniques. Agents were also trained to target the elderly. One complaint received by the Florida Department of Insurance was from a 60-year-old woman who had told an agent that she could not afford more insurance. "The next thing I know," she said, "a nurse comes to my door to give me a physical" as required for a new policy. "It wasn't until then," the woman told investigators, "that I realized I had another policy that would drain my old policy."[9]

Refusing to Pay a Valid Claim

Perhaps because juries feel sympathy for those who must deal with an immovable bureaucracy, damage awards are often sizeable when an insurance company has refused to pay a legitimate claim. For example, a jury in Ohio entered a $13 million verdict against Buckeye Union Insurance Co. for its bad faith refusal to pay a

---

[8] Compensatory and punitive damages are covered in Chapter 18, on remedies.

[9] Joseph B. Treaster and Melody Petersen, "Florida Study Claims That Prudential Cheated Customers," *New York Times*, Dec. 22, 1997, p. A20. Copyright © 1997 by The New York Times Co. Reprinted by permission.

claim. An Ohio sheriff stopped the automobile of 19-year-old Eugene Leber. As the sheriff approached Leber's car, he slipped on ice and his gun discharged. By incredible bad luck, the bullet struck Leber, permanently paralyzing him from the rib cage down. The insurance company recognized that it was liable under the policy, but it nonetheless fought the case for *16* years.

Consumers complain that insurance companies often "low-ball"—that is, they make an unreasonably low offer to settle a claim. Some insurance companies even set claims quotas that limit how much their adjusters can pay out each year, regardless of the merits of each individual claim. If juries continue to award multimillion dollar verdicts, insurance companies may decide simply to pay the claims.

Refusing to Accept a Settlement Offer

An insurer also violates the covenant of good faith and fair dealing when it *wrongfully* refuses to settle a claim. Suppose that Dmitri has a $100,000 automobile insurance policy. After he injures Tanya in a car accident, she sues him for $5 million. As provided in the policy, Dmitri's insurance company defends him against Tanya's claim. She offers to settle for $100,000, but the insurance company refuses because it only has $100,000 at risk anyway. It may get lucky with the jury. Instead, a jury comes in with a $2 million verdict. The insurance company is only liable for $100,000, but Dmitri must pay $1.9 million. In the following case, the court found that an insurance company had acted in bad faith when it refused to accept a reasonable settlement offer.

BERGLUND v. STATE FARM MUTUAL AUTOMOBILE INSURANCE CO.
121 F.3d 1225, 1997 U.S. App. LEXIS 22609
United States Court of Appeals for the Eighth Circuit, 1997

Facts: At an intersection in rural Iowa, Thomas Berglund ran a stop sign and struck a van. Ronald Jalas and his wife were seriously injured, and their four-year-old daughter, Jazelle, was killed. Two of the Jalases' other children had previously died.

The Jalases sued the Berglunds, who had two insurance policies: a $500,000 automobile policy with State Farm and a $1 million excess liability insurance policy with Grinnell Mutual. The excess policy applied only after other insurance was exhausted. The Jalases offered to settle for $1.51 million. As required by the insurance contract, State Farm was defending the Berglunds. If State Farm had accepted this offer, the Berglunds would have had to contribute only $10,000. State Farm's claims committee officially valued the claim at $200,000. However, several committee members felt the claim was worth more, as did a consultant at corporate headquarters. This consultant recommended that the company offer the full $500,000. Instead, State Farm offered the Jalases $300,000, which they refused.

At trial, the jury awarded the Jalases $1,897,703.80. After the two insurance companies paid, the Berglunds owed about $400,000. The Berglunds brought this lawsuit asserting that State Farm acted in bad faith. A jury awarded damages of $530,831.42, including punitive damages. State Farm appealed.

Issue: Did State Farm act in bad faith in its representation of the Berglunds?

Excerpts from Judge Fagg's Decision: When an insurer recognizes the probability that an adverse verdict will exceed policy limits, the boundaries of "good faith" become compressed in favor of the insured. In assessing good faith, the test is whether the insurer has approached the matter of settlement as if policy limits do not exist. The jury could reasonably find State Farm did not ignore its policy limits during settlement negotiations.

State Farm also contends no reasonable jury could find State Farm's failure to offer its policy limits proximately caused the judgment over $1.5 million. State Farm blames Grinnell Mutual. A senior claims attorney for Grinnell Mutual testified he would not have contributed $1 million towards settlement, but [a] Grinnell supervisor testified she believed as early as a month before trial that a $800,000 verdict was a very real possibility, and the company would have contributed $300,000. Other experts testified the claim was worth more than the offered settlement of $1.51 million. Until State Farm offered its limits, however, Grinnell Mutual had no obligation to pay anything or to evaluate seriously the Jalases' claim.

Further, the Jalases' attorney testified that in his experience, both he and his clients become "weak-kneed" in the face of substantial offers, and Grinnell Mutual's supervisor testified that about half the plaintiffs demanding over $1 million accept lesser amounts. Under the circumstances, we believe a jury could reasonably find the case would have been settled, and State Farm's failure to offer its policy limits proximately caused the excess judgment.

We affirm the bad faith and punitive damage ruling.

TYPES OF INSURANCE

Insurance is available for virtually any risk. Bruce Springsteen, Michael Jackson, Billy Joel, and the Rolling Stones have insured their voices. When Kerry Wallace shaved her head in the Star Trek films, she bought insurance in case her hair failed to grow back. Food critic Egon Ronay insured his taste buds. Forty members of a Whiskers Club insured their beards against fire and theft. And an amateur dramatics group took out insurance to protect against the risk that a member of the audience might die laughing. Most people, however, get by with six different types of insurance: property, life, health, disability, liability, and automobile.

PROPERTY INSURANCE

Property insurance (also known as **casualty insurance**) covers physical damage to real estate, personal property (boats, furnishings), or inventory from causes such as fire, smoke, lightning, wind, riot, vandalism, or theft. Typically, these **policies do *not* cover**:

- **Earthquakes and Floods.** Earthquakes are generally not covered unless the policyholder pays for a special **rider** (attachment). Flood coverage also requires a special rider if the property is in a designated flood area.
- **Friendly Fire.** A friendly fire is in a place where fires belong—a boiler, a fireplace, a stove. In theory, fires in these locations are easily controlled and, therefore, their damage is not covered. Once the fire escapes, the damage is covered. For example, when a woman threw her denture into a trash fire, the insurance company did not pay to replace it because the fire had not escaped from its intended confines.[10] If the trash fire had burned down the woman's garage with her denture in it, the company would have paid to replace both the garage and the denture.

[10] *Owens v. Milwaukee Insurance Co.*, 125 Ind. App. 208, 123 N.E.2d 645, 1955 Ind. App. LEXIS 124 (Ind. Ct. App. 1955).

- **Employee Theft or Embezzlement.** Typically, these losses are covered only if the insured purchases a special rider.

- **Transportation Insurance.** A business must purchase special insurance to cover products that have been sold and are being transported to the new buyer.

LIFE INSURANCE

Life insurance is really death insurance—it provides for payments to a beneficiary upon the death of the insured. The purpose is to replace at least some of the insured's income so that her family will not be financially devastated.

Term Insurance

Term insurance is the simplest, cheapest life insurance option. It is purchased for a specific period, such as 1, 5, or 20 years. If the insured dies during the period of the policy, the insurance company pays the policy amount to the beneficiary. If the owner stops paying premiums, the policy terminates and the beneficiary receives nothing. As the probability of death rises with age, so do the premiums. A $100,000 policy on a 25-year-old nonsmoker costs about $135 annually; at age 60 the same policy costs $600. Term insurance is the best choice for a person who simply wants to protect his family by replacing his income if he dies. Typically, people buy insurance when they have a dependent spouse or children. If the spouse is self-supporting and the children have graduated from college, then there is little need for life insurance.

Whole Life Insurance

Whole life or **straight life** insurance is designed to cover the insured for his entire life. A portion of the premiums pays for insurance, and the remainder goes into savings. This savings portion is called the **cash value** of the policy. The savings accrue without being taxed until the policy is cashed in. The owner can borrow against the cash value, in many cases at a below-market rate. In addition, if the owner cancels the policy, the insurance company will pay her the policy's cash value. When the owner purchases the policy, the company sets a premium that stays constant over the life of the policy. The size of the premium depends upon the insured's age and health. A 25-year-old nonsmoker pays annual premiums of roughly $1,000 per year on a $100,000 policy.

The advantage of a whole life policy is that it forces people to save. It also has some significant disadvantages:

- The investment returns from the savings portion of whole life insurance have traditionally been mediocre. Today, mutual funds generally offer better investment opportunities.

- A significant portion of the premium goes to pay overhead and commissions. Agents have a great incentive to sell whole life policies, rather than term, because their commissions are much higher. In the first year of a whole life policy, the agent's commission is typically about 55 percent of the premium. In the case of the healthy 25-year-old, the agent earns $550 (.55 × $1,000). On a term policy, the agent typically earns only a 35 percent commission, or $47 (.35 × $135). After the first year, commissions on a whole life policy are much lower.

As a general rule, over the first 10 years of a policy, an agent earns a total commission equal to the first year's premium. After 10 years, he earns only 2 percent of the premium each year.

- Unless the customer holds a policy for about 20 years, it will typically generate little cash value. Half of all whole life policyholders drop their policies in the first seven or eight years. At that point, the policy has generated little more than commissions for the agent.
- Whole life insurance provides the same amount of insurance throughout the insured's life. In contrast, most people need more insurance when they have young children and less as they approach retirement age.
- It is difficult to compare whole life insurance policies. Recall the article that opened this chapter. Even a highly educated research physician could not understand his life insurance policy. This is a common problem. Although one policy can cost twice as much as another equivalent choice, the numbers are presented in such a complex way that consumers are usually unable to calculate the real price. Instead, they tend to rely on their agent's representations. The agent does not necessarily have an incentive to keep the customer's price low. Other countries have tried a different approach.

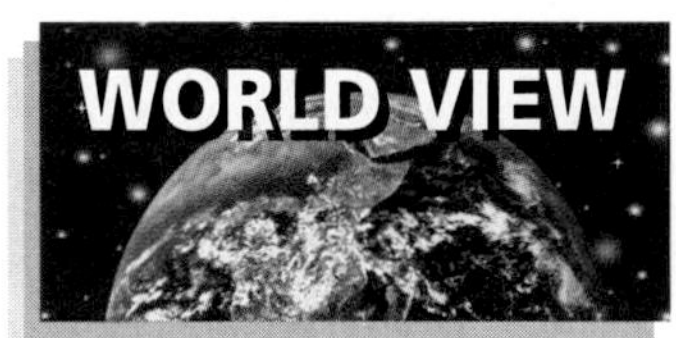

Overseas, in Australia, France, Norway, and the United Kingdom, insurance companies can charge whatever price they want, but they must disclose fees, commissions, and the investment yield on a policy. As a result, prices have fallen dramatically. Before these disclosure rules went into effect, commissions for the first year of a policy in Australia were 80 percent of the premium; now they are 45 percent. In France, commissions run from 3 percent to 30 percent. Agents in some countries, such as the U.K., now often work for a salary rather than a commission, which further reduces their incentive to sell the most expensive products. In the United States, insurance companies have managed to forestall any major efforts by the states to reform the industry.

Universal Life

Universal life insurance is a flexible combination of whole life and term. The owner can adjust the premiums over the life of the policy and also adjust the allocation of the premiums between insurance and savings. The options are complex and often difficult for the customer to understand.

Annuities

As life expectancy has increased, people have begun to worry as much about supporting themselves in their old age as they do about dying young. Sales of life insurance have stagnated while the number of annuities sold each year is growing rapidly. **Annuities are the reverse of life insurance—they make payments *until* death whereas life insurance pays *after* death.** In the basic annuity contract, the owner makes a lump-sum payment to an insurance company in return for a fixed annual income for the rest of her life, no matter how long she lives. If she dies tomorrow, the insurance company makes a huge profit. If she lives to be 95, the company loses money. But whatever happens, she knows she will have an income until the day she dies.

In a **deferred annuity contract**, the owner makes a lump-sum payment but receives no income until some later date, say, in 10 or 20 years when he retires. From that date forward, he will receive payments for the rest of his life.

Accidental Death

Many life insurance policies pay an additional sum if the insured dies in an accident rather than from an illness. Indeed, some policies double the payout in the case of an accidental death. This is called a **double indemnity clause**. In the following case, an insurance company argued that a cocaine overdose was not an accidental death.

WEIL v. FEDERAL KEMPER LIFE ASSURANCE CO.
7 Cal. 4th 125, 866 P.2d 774, 1994 Cal. LEXIS 11
Supreme Court of California, 1994

Facts: Federal Kemper Life Assurance Co. issued a $100,000 double indemnity life insurance policy to Michael P. Weil, then 22. In the event that Weil died by accidental means, the policy would pay an additional $100,000, for a total of $200,000.

Ten years later, Weil summoned a female prostitute to his hotel room in San Francisco. She saw him ingest cocaine from a dish in the bathroom. He then collapsed and died. The autopsy found cocaine in his system. There was no evidence of trauma.

Kemper paid Weil's mother and sister the base amount of $100,000. It refused, however, to pay the additional $100,000 on the grounds that his death had not been accidental. The superior court ruled that plaintiffs were entitled to the additional benefit. The court of appeal confirmed and Kemper appealed.

Issue: Are Michael Weil's beneficiaries entitled to the accidental death benefit under his life insurance policy?

Excerpts from Justice George's Decision: It is readily apparent that the risks attending the consumption of [an illegal substance] are so great that death must be considered a common, natural or substantially likely consequence. [B]ecause the user may not be certain of the purity or strength of a particular dosage of an illegal substance, the possibility of overdose is a closely related consequence of ingestion, inhalation, or injection, and the circumstance of the overdose itself does not operate as an independent or intervening means of death in the sequence of causation from the initial voluntary act to the death resulting from it. Therefore, the insured is not entitled to coverage for such a death under an "accidental means" policy.

For the foregoing reasons, we *reverse* the judgment of the court of appeal.

Excerpts from Justice Mosk's Dissent: If pressed to say what it is, the layperson might reply that an accidental death is generally a death caused by injury, giving as examples deaths from automobile collisions, airplane crashes, fires, drownings, falls, poisonings, firearm mishaps, criminal assaults, and the like. When the issue is dispassionately considered, it appears that the goal of the courts should be to distinguish between cases in which the insured's act would be commonly viewed as tantamount to suicide and those in which it would not. We have all seen or heard of acts so reckless—or so brave—that we exclaim, "it would be suicide to do that," even though we know the actor does not actually intend self-destruction. Those are the acts, I submit, that an insured cannot reasonably expect will trigger coverage for accident insurance: to do so would, as in the case of actual suicide, defeat the purpose of such insurance and amount to a fraud on its premium structure.

Conversely, in all cases in which the insured's act was more than negligent but not tantamount to suicide, the insured can reasonably expect to be covered. There is simply no principled way to deny ordinary accident insurance coverage for losses resulting from acts of this type. However understandable it may be for a court to disapprove of such acts, the disapproval is misplaced here. Here we deal

Death from illegal drugs is not accidental, at least under insurance law.

with the law of contracts, not the law of torts or crimes. The insurance company does not represent the public safety concerns of society but the commercial interests of its owners.

HEALTH INSURANCE

The United States spends 13 percent of its gross domestic product (GDP) on health care, a higher percentage than any other country in the world. The total spent on health care *premiums* exceeds $100 billion annually. Most people who have health insurance obtain it through their employer. This insurance is so expensive, however, that employers generally do not offer it to lower-paid workers. Most unemployed people are also uninsured. As a result, even though the United States pays more for health insurance than any other country, it also has the largest percentage of citizens without coverage—16 percent.

Traditional health care plans are **pay for service**. The insurer pays for virtually any treatment that any doctor orders. The good news under this system is that policyholders have the largest possible choice of doctor and treatment. The bad news is that doctors and patients have an incentive to overspend on health care because the insurance company picks up the tab. That is certainly one reason health care spending is so high in this country. It has been estimated that as many as one-third of the medical procedures performed in pay for service plans have little medical justification.

Now many insurers and employers are experimenting with **managed care plans**. There are many variations on this theme, but they all work to limit patient and doctor choice. In some plans, the patient has a primary care physician who must approve all visits to specialists. In **health maintenance organizations**, known as **HMOs**, the patient can be treated only by doctors in the organization, unless there is some extraordinary need for an outside specialist. In some HMOs, each primary care physician is given a per patient budget. If she exceeds the budget, she must pay the overage herself.

Neither type of plan is perfect. In pay for service plans, doctors have an incentive to overtreat. In managed care plans, they may have an incentive to undertreat. For example, a recent study revealed that managed care plans tend to treat mental illness primarily with drugs. A combination of drugs and therapy is more successful but also more expensive. Many managed care plans provide excellent care, but whatever their strengths and weaknesses, they seem destined to become the norm in American health care.

DISABILITY INSURANCE

Disability insurance replaces the insured's income if he becomes unable to work because of illness or injury. "Ah!" you think, "that will never happen to me." In fact, the average person is seven times more likely to be disabled for at least 90 days than she is to die before age 65. Half of all mortgage foreclosures are caused by an owner's disability. Everyone should have disability insurance to replace between 60 and 75 percent of their income. (There is no need for 100 percent replacement because expenses for the unemployed are lower.) Many employers provide disability protection.

LIABILITY INSURANCE

Most insurance—property, life, health, disability—is designed to reimburse the insured (or her family) for any harm she suffers. Liability insurance is different. **Its**

purpose is to reimburse the insured for any liability she incurs by (accidentally) harming someone else. This type of insurance covers tort claims by:

- Those injured on property owned by the insured—the mail carrier who slips and falls on the front sidewalk or the child who drowns in the pool
- Those injured by the insured away from home or business—the jogger crushed by an insured who loses control of his rollerblades, and
- Those whose property is damaged by the insured—the owner whose stone wall is pulverized by the insured's swerving car.

These are the types of claims covered in a *personal* liability policy. *Business* liability policies may also protect against other sorts of claims:

- Professional malpractice on the part of an accountant, architect, doctor, engineer, or lawyer. The premiums for this type of insurance have increased dramatically in recent years, and some professionals have opted to "go bare" in the hope that they will present a less appealing target to plaintiffs.
- Product liability for any injuries caused by the company's products.
- Employment practices liability insurance to protect employers against claims of sexual harassment, discrimination, and wrongful termination. A recent survey revealed that 56 percent of U.S. companies have been sued by an employee. Now, 50 percent of the Fortune 500 carry this type of insurance.

As you can imagine, liability policies do not protect the insured against *intentional* torts. Otherwise, someone contemplating a tort would simply purchase insurance first and then commit the tort with peace of mind, knowing that he would not suffer any financial liability.[11] In the following case, the court was asked to decide whether the tort was intentional. You be the judge.

SPENGLER v. STATE FARM FIRE AND CASUALTY CO.
568 So. 2d 1293, 1990 Fla. App. LEXIS 7581
Florida District Court of Appeal, 1990

Facts: Andreu Harvey and Faye Spengler had been dating for approximately five months. Harvey's house was in a neighborhood plagued with crime, and it had been burglarized twice. In one of these episodes, the burglar had climbed in through the bathroom window. Harvey kept a handgun in a holster hanging on the headboard of his bed.

One night, a noise from the bathroom awoke Harvey. He whispered to Spengler, "Did you hear that?" From the light of a street lamp that shone dimly through the hallway near the bathroom, he saw a shadowy figure coming through the bedroom door. Pulling out his gun, he fired three times. After the first shot, the figure screamed and fell to the floor. After the third shot, Harvey realized he had hit and wounded Spengler.

She sought to recover from Harvey's insurer, State Farm Fire and Casualty Co. The policy contained a provision excluding coverage for bodily injury that is either expected or intended by the insured. State Farm refused to pay.

You Be the Judge: Did Harvey shoot Spengler intentionally? Can Spengler recover under Harvey's policy?

Argument for Spengler: Harvey intended to shoot a burglar, not his girlfriend. His act was negligent, not

[11] Typically, employment practices liability insurance does not protect the person who actually commits the wrongdoing—the sexual harasser, for instance—but it does protect the innocent insureds, such as the company itself.

intentional. He should have checked to see if Spengler was still in bed next to him. He should have called her name. There are many things he could have done to avoid this accident, but he did not and that was negligent.

Harvey's policy excludes coverage for *intentional* torts. Here, the shooting was an accident, because Harvey did not intend the injury to Spengler. He intended to harm the burglar. Harvey's action was a classic negligent tort and Spengler should recover.

Argument for State Farm: Harvey clearly intended to commit bodily harm. After all, when you fire a gun at someone, you are usually intending to cause harm.

Even if Harvey did not intend to hurt Spengler, some behavior is so careless that it is the equivalent of intent. The whole purpose of the exclusion in Harvey's insurance policy is to prevent exactly this type of wanton and malicious behavior. If State Farm has to pay Spengler for her injuries, what kind of precedent does that create? No one has to be careful with a gun anymore. You can shoot first and ask questions later. It is difficult for us to understand why, when a man wakes up in the night and shoots his girlfriend, his insurance company should pay.

AUTOMOBILE INSURANCE

An automobile insurance policy is a combination of several different types of coverage that, depending on state law, are either mandatory or optional. The total premium is the sum of the premiums for each of these separate parts. These are the basic types of coverage:

- **Collision**. This provision covers the cost of repairing or replacing a car that is damaged in an accident. Creditors with a security interest in a car usually require this type of coverage.
- **Comprehensive**. This provision covers fire, theft, and vandalism—but not collision. Creditors also expect an owner to carry this type of coverage.
- **Liability**. This provision covers harm the owner causes to other people or their property—their body, car, or stone wall. Most states require drivers to carry liability insurance.
- **Uninsured Motorist**. This provision covers the owner and anyone else in the car who is injured by an uninsured motorist. Some states require this type of coverage.

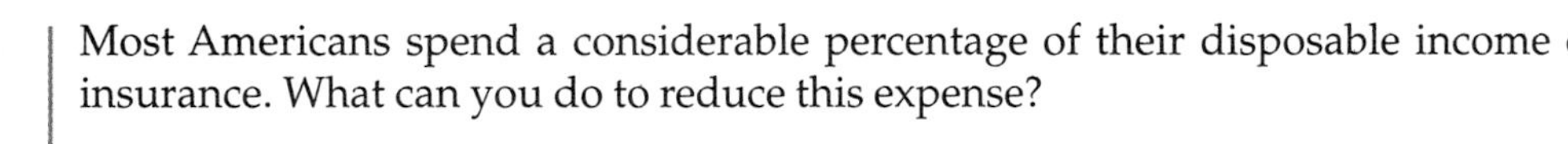

Most Americans spend a considerable percentage of their disposable income on insurance. What can you do to reduce this expense?

- **Do not insure against every risk.** If you can afford the loss yourself, it is better not to purchase insurance. About half of every dollar that consumers spend on insurance is paid back in claims; the other half goes to the company's profits and overhead. For example, salespeople often try very hard to sell extended warranties on consumer electronic devices and appliances such as televisions, VCRs, and refrigerators. These warranties are simply insurance plans that require the store to fix the item if something goes wrong. Stores often make a larger profit from the warranty than from the product itself—the markup on the warranty can be as high as 80 percent and may account for 24 percent of a sales clerk's income. Some consumer electronic stores earn 50 percent of their profit from these warranties. If you self-insure, odds are you will come out ahead in the long run.
- **Do not buy "special occasion" insurance.** After a major plane crash, sales of flight accident insurance jump. If you need life insurance, you should have it, no matter how you die. Your family does not need more money because you die in a plane crash rather than a car accident. The same rule holds true for

other special occasion policies such as cancer insurance. You need health insurance regardless of your illness. Indeed, to protect the elderly who buy most of these policies, some states have outlawed cancer insurance.

- **Select as high a deductible as you can afford.** The higher the deductible, the lower the premium. Over the lifetime of your house or car, you can save thousands of dollars by self-insuring the small losses and buying insurance to protect only against major catastrophes. Many companies have also begun to self-insure.
- **Shop for the best price.** The lowest cost company may charge as little as two-thirds as much as its highest price competitor. The Internet offers a great opportunity to compare prices for different types of insurance. Try http://www.answercenter.com, http://www.insuremarket.com, http://www.insweb.com/, http://itechusa.com, http://quickquote.com/, or http://www.quotesmith.com.
- **Shop for quality.** An insurance company can fail as easily as any other business. What a disaster to pay premiums, only to discover later that you are not in safe hands after all. Recently, the health insurance industry has seen more than its fair share of scams involving companies that take premiums and then promptly go out of business.
- **Do not buy the same coverage twice.** Many automobile insurance policies and credit cards provide coverage for rental cars. Before buying coverage when you rent a car, check to see if you are already covered.

CHAPTER CONCLUSION

There will always be insurance, at least until life is risk-free. This chapter has covered the most common types of insurance, but as new risks arise, insurance companies create new products. For example:

- Patent-infringement insurance for *defendants* in patent cases. Particularly popular in high-technology industries, these policies pay the liability and legal expenses for companies charged with infringing someone else's patent.
- Patent-infringement insurance for *plaintiffs* in patent cases. For the first time, insurance companies have begun to offer policies that pay the legal bills of plaintiffs who believe that their patents have been violated. A patent may be the most valuable asset a small company owns, and the ability to protect it in court could be critical to the company's future.
- Environmental liability insurance to protect against cleanup costs on newly acquired property that may turn out to be contaminated.
- Internet insurance to protect against dangers as varied as hackers, viruses, or libel committed on a company Web site.

CHAPTER REVIEW

1. An insurance policy must meet all the common law requirements for a contract—offer, acceptance, and consideration.

2. A person has an insurable interest if she would be harmed by the danger that she has insured against.
3. Insurers have the right to void a policy if the insured violates a warranty, makes a material misstatement, or conceals a material fact.
4. A deductible provision requires the insured to pay a certain amount of the claim herself.
5. Co-insurance means that the insured must pay some percentage of the entire loss.
6. A *pro rata* clause prevents an insured from collecting more than the actual damage suffered.
7. If an insurance company pays a claim, it is subrogated to the rights of the insured.
8. Many courts have held that insurance policies contain a covenant of good faith and fair dealing and have found insurance companies liable for punitive damages if they refuse to pay legitimate claims.
9. Property insurance covers physical damage to real estate, personal property (boats, furnishings), or inventory from causes such as fire, smoke, lightning, wind, riot, vandalism, or theft.
10. Life insurance is really death insurance—it provides payments to the beneficiary upon the death of the insured.
11. Annuities are the reverse of life insurance policies; they make payments *until* death.
12. Disability insurance replaces the insured's income if he becomes unable to work because of illness or injury.
13. Liability insurance reimburses the insured for any liability she incurs by accidentally harming someone else.
14. An automobile insurance policy is a combination of several different types of coverage that, depending on state law, are either mandatory or optional.

PRACTICE TEST

1. **CPA QUESTION** If a debtor defaults and the debtor's surety satisfies the obligation, the surety acquires the right of:

(a) Subrogation

(b) Primary lien

(c) Indemnification

(d) Satisfaction

2. **YOU BE THE JUDGE WRITING PROBLEM** Linda Richmond and Eddie Durham had two children before they were divorced. Under the terms of their divorce decree, Durham obtained title to their house. When he died suddenly of a heart attack, the children inherited the house. Richmond moved into the house with the children and began paying the mortgage that was in Durham's name. She also took out fire insurance. Ten months later, fire totally destroyed the house. The insurance company refused to pay a benefit under the policy because Richmond did not have an insurable interest in the property. Do you agree? **Argument for the insurance company:** Linda Richmond did not own the house; therefore, she had no insurable interest. **Argument for Richmond:** She was harmed when the house burned down because she and her children had no place to live. She was paying the mortgage, so she also had a financial interest.

3. Mark Zulcosky applied for life insurance with Farm Bureau Life Insurance Co. On the application he indicated that he had not received any traffic tickets in the preceding five years. In fact, he had received several such citations for driving while intoxicated. Two years later, Mark was shot to death. When Farm Bureau discovered the traffic tickets, it denied coverage to his beneficiary. Was Farm Bureau in the right?

4. **CPA QUESTION** Hart owned a building with a fair market value of $400,000. The building was covered by a $300,000 fire insurance policy containing an 80 percent co-insurance clause. What amount would Hart recover if a fire totally destroyed the building?

(a) 0

(b) $240,000

(c) $256,000

(d) $300,000

5. Dannie Harvey sued her employer, O. R. Whitaker, for sexual harassment, discrimination, and defamation. Whitaker counter-claimed for libel and slander, requesting $1 million in punitive damages. Both Whitaker and Harvey were insured by Allstate, under identical homeowner's policies. This policy explicitly promised to defend Harvey against the exact claim Whitaker had made against her. Harvey's Allstate agent, however, told her that she was not covered. Because the agent kept all copies of Harvey's insurance policies in his office, she took him at his word. She had no choice but to defend against the claim on her own. Whitaker mounted an exceedingly hostile litigation attack, taking 80 depositions. After a year, Allstate agreed to defend Harvey. However, instead of hiring the lawyer who had been representing her, it chose another lawyer who had no expertise in this type of case and was a close friend of Whitaker's attorney. Harvey's new lawyer refused to meet her or to attend any depositions. Harvey and Whitaker finally settled. Whitaker had spent $1 million in legal fees, Harvey $169,000, and Allstate $2,513. Does Harvey have a claim against Allstate?

6. A female employee accused lawyer Mark D. Greenman of sexual harassment. A jury found him liable for the intentional infliction of emotional distress and ordered him to pay her $11,100. He demanded that his insurance company pay this claim under a liability policy. Is the company liable?

7. Clyde Anderson received a letter from his automobile insurance company notifying him that it would not renew his policy that was set to expire on February 28. Anderson did not obtain another policy, and, on March 1, at 2:30 A.M., he struck another vehicle, killing two men. Later that day, Anderson applied for insurance coverage. As part of this application, he indicated that he had not been involved in any accident in the last three years. The new policy was effective as of 12:01 A.M. on March 1. Will the estates of the two dead men be able to recover under this policy?

8. Mrs. Nelson put a five-pound chicken in an aluminum pan on top of an electric stove that was turned up to "high." A family friend called to ask Mr. and Mrs. Nelson to come for a visit. Forgetting about the chicken, they left the house around 11:00 A.M. and returned in the late afternoon. The entire contents of the home were damaged by smoke and soot. When the Nelsons filed a claim, their insurance company argued that no fire had escaped the stove. The Nelsons, for their part, claimed that the fire had escaped from the range and burned holes in the floors, woodwork, and walls of the kitchen. Why do they care whether the fire had escaped?

9. On March 17, T.F. had unprotected sexual intercourse with a woman. Within a few days he noticed several genital sores, which later disappeared. On May 4 and May 18, R.W. and T.F. engaged in unprotected sexual intercourse. On May 23, R.W. noticed genital sores. Four days later, she was diagnosed with genital herpes. She filed suit against T.F. for negligently transmitting genital herpes to her. Was T.F.'s act intentional or negligent? Was it covered under his liability insurance policy?

10. **CPA QUESTION** To recover under a property insurance policy, an insurable interest must exist:

	When the Policy Is Purchased	At the Time of Loss
(a)	Yes	Yes
(b)	Yes	No
(c)	No	Yes
(d)	No	No

11. **RIGHT & WRONG** Donna and Carl Nichols each bought term life insurance from Prudential Insurance Company of America. These policies contained a rider providing that, if the insured became disabled, the premiums did not have to be paid and the policy would still stay in effect. This term is called a "waiver of premium." Carl became totally disabled and his premi-

ums were waived. Some years later, two Prudential sales managers convinced the Nicholses to convert their term life insurance policies into whole life insurance policies. They promised that, once Carl made the conversion, he would only have to pay premiums on the new policy for a six-month waiting period. They even wrote "WP to be included in this policy" on the application form. "WP" stood for waiver of premium benefit. Only after the new policy was issued did the Nicholses learn that Prudential would not waive the premium. The Nicholses had exchanged a policy on which they owed nothing further for a policy on which they now had to pay premiums that they could not afford. Do the Nicholses have a claim against Prudential? Regardless of the legal outcome, did Prudential have an ethical obligation to the Nicholses?

INTERNET RESEARCH PROBLEM

Go to http://www.insurancefraud.org and look up the latest insurance regulations and legislation in your state. What is the goal of these rules—to protect consumers or the insurance industry? While you are at this Web site, read about the "Fraud Case of the Week."

You can find further practice problems in the Online Quiz at http://beatty.westbuslaw.com or in the Study Guide that accompanies this text.

APPENDIX A

THE CONSTITUTION OF THE UNITED STATES

Preamble

We the People of the United States, in Order to form a more perfect Union, establish Justice, insure domestic Tranquility, provide for the common defense, promote the general Welfare, and secure the Blessings of Liberty to ourselves and our Posterity, do ordain and establish this Constitution for the United States of America.

ARTICLE I

Section 1.

All legislative Powers herein granted shall be vested in a Congress of the United States, which shall consist of a Senate and House of Representatives.

Section 2.

The House of Representatives shall be composed of Members chosen every second Year by the People of the several States, and the Electors in each State shall have the Qualifications requisite for Electors of the most numerous Branch of the State Legislature.

No Person shall be a Representative who shall not have attained to the Age of twenty five Years, and been seven Years a Citizen of the United States, and who shall not, when elected, be an Inhabitant of that State in which he shall be chosen.

Representatives and direct Taxes shall be apportioned among the several States which may be included within this Union, according to their respective Numbers, which shall be determined by adding to the whole Number of free Persons, including those bound to Service for a Term of Years, and excluding Indians not taxed, three fifths of all other Persons. The actual Enumeration shall be made within three Years after the first Meeting of the Congress of the United States, and within every subsequent Term of ten Years, in such Manner as they shall by Law direct. The number of Representatives shall not exceed one for every thirty Thousand, but each State shall have at Least one Representative; and until such enumeration shall be made, the State of New Hampshire shall be entitled to chuse three, Massachusetts eight, Rhode Island and Providence Plantations one, Connecticut five, New-York six, New Jersey four, Pennsylvania eight, Delaware one, Maryland six, Virginia ten, North Carolina five, South Carolina five, and Georgia three.

When vacancies happen in the Representation from any State, the Executive Authority thereof shall issue Writs of Election to fill such vacancies.

The House of Representatives shall chuse their Speaker and other Officers; and shall have the sole Power of Impeachment.

Section 3.

The Senate of the United States shall be composed of two Senators from each State, chosen by the Legislature thereof, for six Years; and each Senator shall have one Vote.

Immediately after they shall be assembled in Consequence of the first Election, they shall be divided as equally as may be into three Classes. The Seats of the Senators of the first Class shall be vacated at the Expiration of the second Year, of the second Class at the Expiration of the fourth Year, and of the third Class at the Expiration of the sixth Year, so that one third may be chosen every second Year; and if Vacancies happen by Resignation or otherwise, during the Recess of the Legislature of any State, the Executive thereof may make temporary Appointments until the next Meeting of the Legislature, which shall then fill such Vacancies.

No Person shall be a Senator who shall not have attained to the Age of thirty Years, and been nine Years a Citizen of the United States, and who shall not, when elected, be an Inhabitant of that State for which he shall be chosen.

The Vice President of the United States shall be President of the Senate, but shall have no Vote, unless they be equally divided.

The Senate shall chuse their other Officers, and also a President pro tempore, in the Absence of the Vice President, or when he shall exercise the Office of President of the United States.

The Senate shall have the sole power to try all Impeachments. When sitting for that Purpose, they shall be an Oath or Affirmation. When the President of the United States is tried, the Chief Justice shall preside: And no Person shall be convicted without the Concurrence of two thirds of the Members present.

Judgment in Cases of Impeachment shall not extend further than to removal from Office, and disqualification to hold and enjoy any Office of honor, Trust or Profit under the United States: but the Party convicted shall nevertheless be liable and subject to Indictment, Trial, Judgment and Punishment, according to Law.

Section 4.

The Times, Places and Manner of holding Elections for Senators and Representatives, shall be prescribed in each State by the Legislature thereof: but the Congress may at any time by Law make or alter such Regulations, except as to the Places of chusing Senators.

The Congress shall assemble at least once in every Year, and such Meeting shall be on the first Monday in December, unless they shall by Law appoint a different Day.

Section 5.

Each House shall be the Judge of the Elections, Returns and Qualifications of its own Members, and a Majority of each shall constitute a Quorum to do Business; but a smaller Number may adjourn from day to day, and may be authorized to compel the Attendance of absent Members, in such Manner, and under such Penalties as each House may provide.

Each House may determine the Rules of its Proceedings, punish its Members for disorderly Behaviour, and, with the Concurrence of two thirds, expel a Member.

Each House shall keep a Journal of its Proceedings, and from time to time publish the same, excepting such Parts as may in their Judgment require Secrecy; and the Yeas and Nays of the Members of either House on any question shall, at the Desire of one fifth of those Present, be entered on the Journal.

Neither House, during the Session of Congress, shall, without the Consent of the other, adjourn for more than three days, nor to any other Place than that in which the two Houses shall be sitting.

Section 6.

The Senators and Representatives shall receive a Compensation for their Services, to be ascertained by Law, and paid out of the Treasury of the United States. They shall in all Cases, except Treason, Felony and Breach of the Peace, be privileged from Arrest during their Attendance at the Session of their respective Houses, and in going to and returning from the same; and for any Speech or Debate in either House, they shall not be questioned in any other Place.

No Senator or Representative shall, during the Time for which he was elected, be appointed to any civil Office under the Authority of the United States, which shall have been created, or the Emoluments whereof shall have been encreased during such time; and no Person holding any Office under the United States, shall be a Member of either House during his Continuance in Office.

Section 7.

All Bills for raising Revenue shall originate in the House of Representatives; but the Senate may propose or concur with Amendments as on other Bills.

Every Bill which shall have passed the House of Representatives and the Senate, shall, before it become a Law, be presented to the President of the United States; If he approve he shall sign it, but if not he shall return it, with his Objections to that House in which it shall have originated, who shall enter the Objections at large on their Journal, and proceed to reconsider it. If after such Reconsideration two thirds of that House shall agree to pass the

Bill, it shall be sent, together with the Objections, to the other House, by which it shall likewise be reconsidered, and if approved by two thirds of that House, it shall become a Law. But in all such Cases the Votes of both Houses shall be determined by Yeas and Nays, and the Names of the Persons voting for and against the Bill shall be entered on the Journal of each House respectively. If any Bill shall not be returned by the President within ten Days (Sundays excepted) after it shall have been presented to him, the Same shall be a Law, in like Manner as if he had signed it, unless the Congress by their Adjournment prevent its Return, in which Case it shall not be a Law.

Every Order, Resolution, or Vote to which the Concurrence of the Senate and House of Representatives may be necessary (except on a question of Adjournment) shall be presented to the President of the United States; and before the Same shall take Effect, shall be approved by him, or being disapproved by him, shall be repassed by two thirds of the Senate and House of Representatives, according to the Rules and Limitations prescribed in the Case of a Bill.

Section 8.

The Congress shall have Power to lay and collect Taxes, Duties, Imposts and Excises, to pay the Debts and provide for the common Defence and general Welfare of the United States; but all Duties, Imposts and Excises shall be uniform throughout the United States;

To borrow Money on the credit of the United States;

To regulate Commerce with foreign Nations, and among the several States, and with the Indian Tribes;

To establish an uniform Rule of Naturalization, and uniform Laws on the subject of Bankruptcies throughout the United States;

To coin Money, regulate the Value thereof, and of foreign Coin, and fix the Standard of Weights and Measures;

To provide for the Punishment of counterfeiting the Securities and current Coin of the United States;

To establish Post Offices and post Roads;

To promote the Progress of Science and useful Arts, by securing for limited Times to Authors and Inventors the exclusive Right to their respective Writings and Discoveries;

To constitute Tribunals inferior to the supreme Court;

To define and punish Piracies and Felonies committed on the high Seas, and Offenses against the Law of Nations;

To declare War, grant Letters of Marque and Reprisal, and make Rules concerning Captures on Land and Water;

To raise and support Armies, but no Appropriation of Money to that Use shall be for a longer Term than two Years;

To provide and maintain a Navy;

To make Rules for the Government and Regulation of the land and naval Forces;

To provide for calling forth the Militia to execute the Laws of the Union, suppress Insurrections and repel Invasions;

To provide for organizing, arming, and disciplining, the Militia, and for governing such Part of them as may be employed in the Service of the United States, reserving to the States respectively, the Appointment of the Officers, and the Authority of training the Militia according to the discipline described by Congress;

To exercise exclusive Legislation in all Cases whatsoever, over such District (not exceeding ten Miles square) as may, by Cession of particular States, and the Acceptance of Congress, become the Seat of the Government of the United States, and to exercise like Authority over all Places purchased by the Consent of the Legislature of the State in which the Same shall be, for the Erection of Forts, Magazines, Arsenals, dock-Yards, and other needful Buildings;—And

To make all Laws which shall be necessary and proper for carrying into Execution the foregoing Powers, and all other Powers vested by this Constitution in the Government of the United States, or in any Department or Officer thereof.

Section 9.

The Migration or Importation of such Persons as any of the States now existing shall think proper to admit, shall not be prohibited by the Congress prior to the Year one thousand eight hundred and eight, but a Tax or Duty may be imposed on such Importation, not exceeding ten dollars for each Person.

The Privilege of the Writ of Habeas Corpus shall not be suspended, unless when in Cases of Rebellion or Invasion the public Safety may require it.

No Bill of Attainder or ex post facto Law shall be passed.

No Capitation, or other direct, Tax shall be laid, unless in Proportion to the Census or Enumeration herein before directed to be taken.

No Tax or Duty shall be laid on Articles exported from any State.

No Preference shall be given by any Regulation of Commerce or Revenue to the Ports of one State over those of another; nor shall Vessels bound to, or from, one State, be obliged to enter, clear, or pay Duties in another.

No Money shall be drawn from the Treasury, but in Consequence of Appropriations made by Laws; and a regular Statement and Account of the Receipts and Expenditures of all public Money shall be published from time to time.

No Title of Nobility shall be granted by the United States: And no Person holding any Office of Profit or Trust under them, shall, without the Consent of the Congress, accept of any present, Emolument, Office, or Title, of any kind whatever, from any King, Prince, or foreign State.

Section 10.

No State shall enter into any Treaty, Alliance, or Confederation; grant Letters of Marque and Reprisal; coin Money; emit Bills of Credit; make any Thing but gold and silver Coin a Tender in Payment of Debts; pass any Bill of Attainder, ex post facto Law, or Law impairing the Obligation of Contracts, or grant any Title of Nobility.

No State shall, without the Consent of the Congress, lay any Imposts or Duties on Imports or Exports, except what may be absolutely necessary for executing its inspection Laws: and the net Produce of all Duties and Imposts, laid by any State on Imports or Exports, shall be for the Use of the Treasury of the United States; and all such Laws shall be subject to the Revision and Controul of the Congress.

No State shall, without the Consent of Congress, lay any Duty of Tonnage, keep Troops, or Ships of War in time of Peace, enter into any Agreement or Compact with another State, or with a foreign Power, or engage in War, unless actually invaded, or in such imminent Danger as will not admit of delay.

ARTICLE II

executive

Section 1.

The executive Power shall be vested in a President of the United States of America. He shall hold his Office during the Term of four Years, and, together with the Vice President, chosen for the same Term, be elected, as follows:

Each State shall appoint, in such Manner as the Legislature thereof may direct, a Number of Electors, equal to the whole Number of Senators and Representatives to which the State may be entitled in the Congress: but no Senator or Representative, or Person holding an Office of Trust or Profit under the United States, shall be appointed an Elector.

The Electors shall meet in their respective States, and vote by Ballot for two Persons, of whom one at least shall not be an Inhabitant of the same State with themselves. And they shall make a list of all the Persons voted for, and of the Number of Votes for each; which List they shall sign and certify, and transmit sealed to the Seat of the Government of the United States, directed to the President of the Senate. The President of the Senate shall, in the presence of the Senate and House of Representatives, open all the Certificates, and the Votes shall be counted. The Person having the greatest Number of Votes shall be the President, if such Number be a Majority of the whole Number of Electors appointed; and if there be more than one who have such Majority, and have an equal Number of Votes, then the House of Representatives shall immediately chuse by Ballot one of them for President; and if no Person have a Majority, then from the five highest on the List the said House shall in like Manner chuse the President. But in chusing the President, the Votes shall be taken by States, the Representation from each State having one Vote; A quorum for this Purpose shall consist of a Member or Members from two thirds of the States, and a Majority of all the States shall be necessary to a Choice. In every Case, after the Choice of the President, the Person having the greatest Number of Votes of the Electors shall be the Vice President. But if there should remain two or more who have equal Votes, the Senate shall chuse from them by Ballot the Vice President.

The Congress may determine the Time of Chusing the Electors, and the Day on which they shall give their Votes; which Day shall be the same throughout the United States.

No Person except a natural born Citizen, or a Citizen of the United States, at the time of the Adoption of this Constitution, shall be eligible to the Office of President; neither shall any Person be eligible to that Office who shall not have attained to the Age of thirty five Years, and been fourteen Years a Resident within the United States.

In Case of the Removal of the President from Office, or of his Death, Resignation, or Inability to discharge the Powers and Duties of the said Office, the Same shall devolve on the Vice President, and the Congress may by Law provide for the Case of Removal, Death, Resignation or Inability, both of the President and Vice President, declaring what Officer shall then act as President, and such Officer shall act accordingly, until the Disability be removed, or a President shall be elected.

The President shall, at stated Times, receive for his Services, a Compensation, which shall neither be encreased nor diminished during the Period for which he shall have been elected, and he shall not receive within that Period any other Emolument from the United States, or any of them.

Before he enter on the Execution of his Office, he shall take the following Oath or Affirmation:—"I do solemnly swear (or affirm) that I will faithfully execute the Office of President of the United States, and will to the best of my Ability, preserve, protect and defend the Constitution of the United States."

Section 2.

The President shall be Commander in Chief of the Army and Navy of the United States, and of the Militia of the several States, when called into the actual Service of the United States; he may require the Opinion, in writing, of the principal Officer in each of the executive Departments, upon any Subject relating to the Duties of their respective Offices, and he shall have Power to grant Reprieves and Pardons for Offenses against the United States, except in Cases of Impeachment.

He shall have Power, by and with the Advice and Consent of the Senate, to make Treaties, providing two thirds of the Senators present concur; and he shall nominate, and by and with the Advice and Consent of the Senate, shall appoint Ambassadors, other public Ministers and Consuls, Judges of the supreme Court, and all other Officers of the United States, whose Appointments are not herein otherwise provided for, and which shall be established by Law: but the Congress may by Law vest the Appointment of such inferior Officers, as they think proper, in the President alone, in the Courts of Law, or in the Heads of Departments.

The President shall have Power to fill up all Vacancies that may happen during the Recess of the Senate, by granting Commissions which shall expire at the End of their next Session.

Section 3.

He shall from time to time give to the Congress Information of the State of the Union, and recommend to their Consideration such Measures as he shall judge necessary and expedient; he may, on extraordinary Occasions, convene both Houses, or either of them, and in Case of Disagreement between them, with Respect to the Time of Adjournment, he may adjourn them to such Time as he shall think proper, he shall receive Ambassadors and other public Ministers; he shall take Care that the Laws be faithfully executed, and shall Commission all the Offices of the United States.

Section 4.

The President, Vice President and all civil Officers of the United States, shall be removed from Office on Impeachment for, and Conviction of, Treason, Bribery, or other high Crimes and Misdemeanors.

ARTICLE III

Section 1.

The judicial Power of the United States, shall be vested in one supreme Court, and in such inferior Courts as the Congress may from time to time ordain and establish. The Judges, both of the supreme and inferior Courts, shall hold their Offices during good Behaviour, and shall, at Times, receive for their Services, a Compensation, which shall not be diminished during their Continuance in Office.

So can't hold $ against them

Section 2.

The judicial Power shall extend to all Cases, in Law and Equity, arising under this Constitution, the Laws of the United States, and Treaties made, or which shall be made, under their Authority;—to all Cases affecting Ambassadors, other public Ministers and Consuls;—to all Cases of admiralty and maritime Jurisdiction;—to Controversies to which the United States shall be a Party;—to controversies between two or more States;—between a State and Citizens of another State;—between Citizens of different States;—between Citizens of the same State claiming Lands under Grants of different States; and between a State, or the Citizens thereof, and foreign States, Citizens or Subjects.

In all Cases affecting Ambassadors, other public Ministers and Consuls, and those in which a State shall be Party, the supreme Court shall have original Jurisdiction. In all the other Cases before mentioned, the supreme Court shall have appellate Jurisdiction, both as to Law and Fact, with such Exceptions, and under such Regulations as the Congress shall make.

The Trial of all Crimes, except in Cases of Impeachment, shall be by Jury; and such Trial shall be held in the State where the said Crimes shall have been committed; but when not committed within any State, the Trial shall be at such Place or Places as the Congress may by Law have directed.

Section 3.

Treason against the United States, shall consist only in levying War against them, or in adhering to their Enemies, giving them Aid and Comfort. No Person shall be convicted of Treason unless on the Testimony of two Witnesses to the same overt Act, or on Confession in open Court.

The Congress shall have Power to declare the Punishment of Treason, but no Attainder of Treason shall work Corruption of Blood, or Forfeiture except during the Life of the Person attainted.

ARTICLE IV

Section 1.

Full Faith and Credit shall be given in each State to the public Acts, Records, and judicial Proceedings of every other State. And the Congress may by general Laws prescribe the Manner in which such Acts, Records and Proceedings shall be proved, and the Effect thereof.

Section 2.

The Citizens of each State shall be entitled to all Privileges and Immunities of Citizens in the several States.

A Person charged in any State with Treason, Felony, or other Crime, who shall flee from Justice, and be found in another State, shall on Demand of the executive Authority of the State from which he fled, be delivered up, to be removed to the State having Jurisdiction of the Crime.

No Person held to Service or Labour in one State, under the Laws thereof, escaping into another, shall, in Consequence of any Law or Regulation therein, be discharged from such Service or Labour, but shall be delivered up on Claim of the Party to whom such Service or Labour may be due.

Section 3.

New States may be admitted by the Congress into this Union; but no new State shall be formed or erected within the Jurisdiction of any other State; nor any State be formed by the Junction of two or more States, or Parts of States, without the Consent of the Legislatures of the States concerned as well as the Congress.

The Congress shall have Power to dispose of and make all needful Rules and Regulations respecting the Territory or other Property belonging to the United States; and nothing in this Constitution shall be so construed as to Prejudice any Claims of the United States, or of any particular State.

Section 4.

The United States shall guarantee to every State in this Union a Republican Form of Government, and shall protect each of them against Invasion; and on Application of the

Legislature, or of the Executive (when the Legislature cannot be convened) against domestic Violence.

ARTICLE V

The Congress, whenever two thirds of both Houses shall deem it necessary, shall propose Amendments to this Constitution, or, on the Application of the Legislatures of two thirds of the several States, shall call a Convention for proposing Amendments, which, in either Case, shall be valid to all Intents and Purposes, as Part of this Constitution, when ratified by the Legislatures of three fourths of the several States, or by Conventions in three fourths thereof, as the one or the other Mode of Ratification may be proposed by the Congress; Provided that no Amendment which may be made prior to the Year One thousand eight hundred and eight shall in any Manner affect the first and fourth Clauses in the Ninth Section of the first Article; and that no State, without its Consent, shall be deprived of its equal Suffrage in the Senate.

ARTICLE VI

All Debts contracted and Engagements entered into, before the Adoption of this Constitution, shall be as valid against the United States under this Constitution, as under the Confederation.

This Constitution, and the Laws of the United States which shall be made in Pursuance thereof; and all Treaties made, or which shall be made, under the Authority of the United States, shall be the supreme Law of the Land; and the Judges in every State shall be bound thereby, any Thing in the Constitution or Laws of any State to the Contrary notwithstanding.

The Senators and Representatives before mentioned, and the Members of the several State Legislatures, and all executive and judicial Officers, both of the United States and of the Several States, shall be bound by Oath or Affirmation, to support this Constitution; but no religious Test shall ever be required as a Qualification to any Office or public Trust under the United States.

ARTICLE VII

The Ratification of the Conventions of nine States, shall be sufficient for the Establishment of this Constitution between the States so ratifying the Same.

AMENDMENT I [1791].

Congress shall make no law respecting an establishment of religion, or prohibiting the free exercise thereof; or abridging the freedom of speech, or the press; or the right of the people peaceably to assemble, and to petition the Government for a redress of grievances.

AMENDMENT II [1791].

A well regulated Militia, being necessary to the security for a free State, the right of the people to keep and bear Arms, shall not be infringed.

AMENDMENT III [1791].

No Soldier shall, in time of peace be quartered in any house, without the consent of the Owner, nor in time of war, but in a manner to be prescribed by law.

AMENDMENT IV [1791].

The right of the people to be secure in their persons, houses, papers, and effects, against unreasonable searches and seizures, shall not be violated, and no Warrants shall issue, but upon probable cause, supported by Oath or Affirmation, and particularly describing the place to be searched, and the persons or things to be seized.

AMENDMENT V [1791].

No person shall be held to answer for a capital, or otherwise infamous crime, unless on a presentment or indictment of a Grand Jury, except in cases arising in the land or naval forces, or in the Militia, when in actual service in time of War or public danger; nor shall any person be subject for the same offense to be twice put in jeopardy of life or limb; nor shall be compelled in any criminal case to be a witness against himself, nor be deprived of life, liberty, or property, without due process of law; nor shall private property be taken for public use, without just compensation.

AMENDMENT VI [1791].

In all criminal prosecutions, the accused shall enjoy the right to a speedy and public trial, by an impartial jury of the State and district wherein the crime shall have been committed, which district shall have been previously ascertained by law, and to be informed of the nature and cause of the accusation; to be confronted with the Witnesses against him; to have compulsory process for obtaining witnesses in his favor, and to have the Assistance of counsel for his defence.

AMENDMENT VII [1791].

In suits at common law, where the value in controversy shall exceed twenty dollars, the right of trial by jury shall be preserved, and no fact tried by a jury, shall be otherwise re-examined in any Court of the United States, than according to the rules of the common law.

AMENDMENT VIII [1791].

Excessive bail shall not be required, no excessive fines imposed, nor cruel and unusual punishments inflicted.

AMENDMENT IX [1791].

The enumeration in the Constitution, of certain rights, shall not be construed to deny or disparage others retained by the people.

AMENDMENT X [1791].

The powers not delegated to the United States by the Constitution, nor prohibited by it to the States, are reserved to the States respectively, or to the people.

AMENDMENT XI [1798].

The judicial power of the United States shall not be construed to extend to any suit in law or equity, commenced or prosecuted against one of the United States by Citizens of another State, or by Citizens or Subjects of any Foreign State.

AMENDMENT XII [1804].

The Electors shall meet in their respective states and vote by ballot for President and Vice-President, one of whom, at least, shall not be an inhabitant of the same state with themselves; they shall name in their ballots the person voted for as President, and in distinct ballots the person voted for as Vice-President, and they shall make distinct lists of all persons voted for as President, and of all persons voted for as Vice-President, and of the number of votes for each, which lists they shall sign and certify, and transmit sealed to the seat of the government of the United States, directed to the President of the Senate;—The President of the Senate shall, in the presence of the Senate and House of Representatives, open all the certificates and the votes shall then be counted;—The person having the greatest number of votes for President, shall be the President, if such number be a majority of the whole number of Electors appointed; and if no person have such majority, then from the persons having the highest numbers not exceeding three on the list of those voted for as President, the House of Representatives shall choose immediately, by ballot, the President. But in choosing the President, the votes shall be taken by states, the representation from each state having one vote; a quorum for this purpose shall consist of a member or members from two-thirds of the states, and a majority of all the states shall be necessary to a choice. And if the House of Representatives shall not choose a President whenever the right of choice shall devolve upon them, before the fourth day of March next following, then the Vice-President shall act as President, as in the case of the death or other constitutional disability of the President. The person having the greatest number of votes as Vice-President, shall be the Vice-President, if such number be a majority of the whole number of Electors appointed, and if no person have a majority, then from the two highest numbers on the list, the Senate shall choose the Vice-President; a quorum for the purpose shall consist of two-thirds of the whole number of Senators, and a majority of the whole number shall be necessary to a choice. But no person constitutionally ineligible to the office of President shall be eligible to that of the Vice-President of the United States.

AMENDMENT XIII [1865].

Section 1. Neither slavery nor involuntary servitude, except as a punishment for crime whereof the party shall have been duly convicted, shall exist within the United States, or any place subject to their jurisdiction.

Section 2. Congress shall have power to enforce this article by appropriate legislation.

AMENDMENT XIV [1868].

Section 1. All persons born or naturalized in the United States, and subject to the jurisdiction thereof, are citizens of the United States and of the State wherein they reside. No State shall make or enforce any law which shall abridge the privileges or immunities of citizens of the United States; nor shall any State deprive any person of life, liberty, or property, without due process of law; nor deny to any person within its jurisdiction the equal protection of the laws.

Section 2. Representatives shall be appointed among the several States according to their respective numbers, counting the whole number of persons in each State, excluding Indians not taxed. But when the right to vote at any election for the choice of electors for President and Vice President of the United States, Representatives in Congress, the Executive and Judicial officers of a State, or the members of the Legislature thereof, is denied to any of the male inhabitants of such State, being twenty-one years of age, and citizens of the United States, or in any way abridged, except for participation in rebellion, or other crime, the basis of representation therein shall be reduced in the proportion which the number of such male citizens shall bear the whole number of male citizens twenty-one years of age in such State.

Section 3. No person shall be a Senator or Representative in Congress, or elector of President and Vice President, or hold any office, civil or military, under the United States, or under any State, who, having previously taken an oath, as a member of Congress, or as an officer of the United States, or as a member of any State legislature, or as an executive or judicial officer of any State, to support the Constitution of the United States, shall have engaged in insurrection or rebellion against the same, or given aid or comfort to the enemies thereof. But Congress may by a vote of two-thirds of each House, remove such disability.

Section 4. The validity of the public debt of the United States, authorized by law, including debts incurred for payment of pensions and bounties for services in suppressing insurrection or rebellion, shall not be questioned. But neither the United States nor any State shall assume or pay any debt or obligation incurred in aid of insurrection of rebellion against the United States, or any claim for the loss or emancipation of any slave; but all such debts, obligations and claims shall be held illegal and void.

Section 5. The Congress shall have power to enforce, by appropriate legislation, the provisions of this article.

AMENDMENT XV [1870].

Section 1. The right of citizens of the United States to vote shall not be denied or abridged by the United States or by any State on account of race, color, or previous condition of servitude.

Section 2. The Congress shall have power to enforce this article by appropriate legislation.

AMENDMENT XVI [1913].

The Congress shall have power to lay and collect taxes on incomes, from whatever source derived, without apportionment among the several States, and without regard to any census or enumeration.

AMENDMENT XVII [1913].

The Senate of the United States shall be composed of two Senators from each State, elected by the people thereof, for six years; and each Senator shall have one vote. The electors in each State shall have the qualifications requisite for electors of the most numerous branch of the State legislatures.

When vacancies happen in the representation of any State in the Senate, the executive authority of each State shall issue writs of election to fill such vacancies; *Provided,* That the legislature of any State may empower the executive thereof to make temporary appointments until the people fill the vacancies by election as the legislature may direct.

This amendment shall not be construed as to affect the election or term of any Senator chosen before it becomes valid as part of the Constitution.

AMENDMENT XVIII [1919].

Section 1. After one year from the ratification of this article the manufacture, sale, or transportation of intoxicating liquors within, the importation thereof into, or the exportation thereof from the United States and all territory subject to the jurisdiction thereof for beverage purposes is hereby prohibited.

Section 2. The Congress and the several States shall have concurrent power to enforce this article by appropriate legislation.

Section 3. This article shall be inoperative unless it shall have been ratified as an amendment to the Constitution by the legislatures of the several States, as provided in the Constitution, within seven years from the date of the submission hereof to the States by the Congress.

AMENDMENT XIX [1920].

The right of citizens of the United States to vote shall not be denied or abridged by the United States or by any State on account of sex.

Congress shall have power to enforce this article by appropriate legislation.

AMENDMENT XX [1933].

Section 1. The terms of the President and Vice President shall end at noon on the 20th day of January, and the terms of Senators and Representatives at noon on the 3d day of January, of the years in which such terms would have ended if this article had not been ratified; and the terms of their successors shall then begin.

Section 2. The Congress shall assemble at least once in every year, and such meeting shall begin at noon on the 3d day of January, unless they shall by law appoint a different day.

Section 3. If, at the time fixed for the beginning of the term of the President, the President elect shall have died, the Vice President elect shall become President. If a President shall not have been chosen before the time fixed for the beginning of his term, or if the President elect shall have failed to qualify, then the Vice President elect shall act as President until a President shall have qualified; and the Congress may by law provide for the case wherein neither a President elect nor a Vice President elect shall have qualified, declaring who shall then act as President, or the manner in which one who is to act shall be selected, and such person shall act accordingly until a President or Vice President shall have qualified.

Section 4. The Congress may by law provide for the case of the death of any of the persons from whom the House of Representatives may choose a President whenever the right of choice shall have devolved upon them, and for the case of the death of any of the persons from whom the Senate may choose a Vice President whenever the right of choice shall have devolved upon them.

Section 5. Sections 1 and 2 shall take effect on the 15th day of October following the ratification of this article.

Section 6. This article shall be inoperative unless it shall have been ratified as an amendment to the Constitution by the legislatures of three-fourths of the several States within seven years from the date of its submission.

AMENDMENT XXI [1933].

Section 1. The eighteenth article of amendment to the Constitution of the United States is hereby repealed.

Section 2. The transportation or importation into any State, Territory, or possession of the United States for delivery or use therein of intoxicating liquors, in violation of the laws thereof, is hereby prohibited.

Section 3. This article shall be inoperative unless it shall have been ratified as an amendment to the Constitution by conventions in the several States, as provided in the Constitution, within seven years from the date of the submission hereof to the States by the Congress.

AMENDMENT XXII [1951].

Section 1. No person shall be elected to the office of the President more than twice, and no person who has held the office of President, or acted as President, for more than two years of a term to which some other person was elected President shall be elected to the office of the President more than once. But this Article shall not apply to any person holding the office of President when this Article was proposed by the Congress, and shall not prevent any person who may be holding the office of President, or acting as President, during the term within which this Article becomes operative from holding the office of President, or acting as President during the remainder of such term.

Section 2. This article shall be inoperative unless it shall have been ratified as an amendment to the Constitution by the legislatures of three-fourths of the several States within seven years from the date of its submission to the States by the Congress.

AMENDMENT XXIII [1961].

Section 1. The District constituting the seat of Government of the United States shall appoint in such manner as the Congress may direct:

A number of electors of President and Vice President equal to the whole number of Senators and Representatives in Congress to which the District would be entitled if it were a State, but in no event more than the least populous State; they shall be in addition to those appointed by the States, but they shall be considered, for the purposes of the election of President and Vice President, to be electors appointed by a State; and they shall meet in the District and perform such duties as provided by the twelfth article of amendment.

Section 2. The Congress shall have power to enforce this article by appropriate legislation.

AMENDMENT XXIV [1964].

Section 1. The right of citizens of the United States to vote in any primary or other election for President or Vice President, for electors for President or Vice President, or for Senator or Representative in Congress, shall not be denied or abridged by the United States or any State by reason of failure to pay any poll tax or other tax.

Section 2. The Congress shall have power to enforce this article by appropriate legislation.

AMENDMENT XXV [1967].

Section 1. In case of the removal of the President from office or of his death or resignation, the Vice President shall become President.

Section 2. Whenever there is a vacancy in the office of the Vice President, the President shall nominate a Vice President who shall take office upon confirmation by a majority vote of both Houses of Congress.

Section 3. Whenever the President transmits to the President pro tempore of the Senate and the Speaker of the House of Representatives his written declaration that he is unable to discharge the powers and duties of his office, and until he transmits to them a written declaration to the contrary, such powers and duties shall be discharged by the Vice President as Acting President.

Section 4. Whenever the Vice President and a majority of either the principal officers of the executive departments or of such other body as Congress may by law provide, transmit to the President pro tempore of the Senate and the Speaker of the House of Representatives their written declaration that the President is unable to discharge the powers and duties of his office, the Vice President shall immediately assume the powers and duties of the office as Acting President.

Thereafter, when the President transmits to the President pro tempore of the Senate and the Speaker of the House of Representatives his written declaration that no inability exists, he shall resume the powers and duties of his office unless the Vice President and a majority of either the principal officers of the executive department or of such other body as Congress may by law provide, transmit within four days to the President pro tempore of the Senate and the Speaker of the House of Representatives their written declaration that the President is unable to discharge the powers and duties of his office. Thereupon Congress shall decide the issue, assembling within forty-eight hours for that purpose if not in session. If the Congress, within twenty-one days after receipt of the latter written declaration, or, if Congress is not in session, within twenty-one days after Congress is required to assemble, determines by two-thirds vote of both Houses that the President shall continue to discharge the same as Acting President; otherwise, the President shall resume the powers and duties of his office.

AMENDMENT XXVI [1971].

Section 1. The right of citizens of the United States, who are eighteen years of age or older, to vote shall not be denied or abridged by the United States or by any State on account of age.

Section 2. The Congress shall have power to enforce this article by appropriate legislation.

AMENDMENT XXVII [1992].

No law, varying the compensation for the services of the Senators and Representatives, shall take effect, until an election of Representatives shall have intervened.

APPENDIX B

UNIFORM COMMERCIAL CODE

ARTICLE I
GENERAL PROVISIONS

PART 1 Short Title, Construction, Application and Subject Matter of the Act

§ 1–101. Short Title.

This Act shall be known and may be cited as Uniform Commercial Code.

§ 1–102. Purposes; Rules of Construction; Variation by Agreement.

(1) This Act shall be liberally construed and applied to promote its underlying purposes and policies.

(2) Underlying purposes and policies of this Act are

(a) to simplify, clarify and modernize the law governing commercial transactions;

(b) to permit the continued expansion of commercial practices through custom, usage and agreement of the parties;

(c) to make uniform the law among the various jurisdictions.

(3) The effect of provisions of this Act may be varied by agreement, except as otherwise provided in this Act and except that the obligations of good faith, diligence, reasonableness and care prescribed by this Act may not be disclaimed by agreement but the parties may by agreement determine the standards by which the performance of such obligations is to be measured if such standards are not manifestly unreasonable.

(4) The presence in certain provisions of this Act of the words "unless otherwise agreed" or words of similar import does not imply that the effect of other provisions may not be varied by agreement under subsection (3).

(5) In this Act unless the context otherwise requires

(a) words in the singular number include the plural, and in the plural include the singular;

(b) words of the masculine gender include the feminine and the neuter, and when the sense so indicates words of the neuter gender may refer to any gender.

§ 1–103. Supplementary General Principles of Law Applicable.

Unless displaced by the particular provisions of this Act, the principles of law and equity, including the law merchant and the law relative to capacity to contract, principal and agent, estoppel, fraud, misrepresentation, duress, coercion, mistake, bankruptcy, or other validating or invalidating cause shall supplement its provisions.

§ 1–104. Construction Against Implicit Repeal.

This Act being a general act intended as a unified coverage of its subject matter, no part of it shall be deemed to be impliedly repealed by subsequent legislation if such construction can reasonably be avoided.

§ 1–105. Territorial Application of the Act; Parties' Power to Choose Applicable Law.

(1) Except as provided hereafter in this section, when a transaction bears a reasonable relation to this state and also to another state or nation the parties may agree that the law either of this state or of such other state or nation shall govern their rights and duties. Failing such agreement this Act applies to transactions bearing an appropriate relation to this state.

(2) Where one of the following provisions of this Act specifies the applicable law, that provision governs and a contrary agreement is effective only to the extent permitted by the law (including the conflict of laws rules) so specified:

Rights of creditors against sold goods. Section 2–402.

Applicability of the Article on Leases. Sections 2A–105 and 2A–106.

Applicability of the Article on Bank Deposits and Collections. Section 4–102.

Governing law in the Article on Funds Transfers. Section 4A–507.

[Publisher's Editorial Note: If a state adopts the repealer of Article 6—Bulk Transfers (Alternative A), there should not be any item relating to bulk transfers. If, however, a state adopts Revised Article 6—Bulk Sales (Alternative B), then the item relating to bulk sales should read as follows:]

Bulk sales subject to the Article on Bulk Sales. Section 6–103.

Applicability of the Article on Investment Securities. Section 8–110.

Perfection provisions of the Article on Secured Transactions. Section 9–103.

§ 1–106. Remedies to Be Liberally Administered.

(1) The remedies provided by this Act shall be liberally administered to the end that the aggrieved party may be put in as good a position as if the other party had fully performed but

neither consequential or special nor penal damages may be had except as specifically provided in this Act or by other rule of law.

(2) Any right or obligation declared by this Act is enforceable by action unless the provision declaring it specifies a different and limited effect.

§ 1–107. Waiver or Renunciation of Claim or Right After Breach.

Any claim or right arising out of an alleged breach can be discharged in whole or in part without consideration by a written waiver or renunciation signed and delivered by the aggrieved party.

§ 1–108. Severability.

If any provision or clause of this Act or application thereof to any person or circumstances is held invalid, such invalidity shall not affect other provisions or applications of the Act which can be given effect without the invalid provision or application, and to this end the provisions of this Act are declared to be severable.

§ 1–109. Section Captions.

Section captions are parts of this Act.

PART 2 General Definitions and Principles of Interpretation

§ 1–201. General Definitions.

Subject to additional definitions contained in the subsequent Articles of this Act which are applicable to specific Articles or Parts thereof, and unless the context otherwise requires, in this Act:

(1) "Action" in the sense of a judicial proceeding includes recoupment, counterclaim, set-off, suit in equity and any other proceedings in which rights are determined.

(2) "Aggrieved party" means a party entitled to resort to a remedy.

(3) "Agreement" means the bargain of the parties in fact as found in their language or by implication from other circumstances including course of dealing or usage of trade or course of performance as provided in this Act (Sections 1–205, 2–208, and 2A–207). Whether an agreement has legal consequences is determined by the provisions of this Act, if applicable; otherwise by the law of contracts (Section 1–103). (Compare "Contract".)

(4) "Bank" means any person engaged in the business of banking.

(5) "Bearer" means the person in possession of an instrument, document of title, or certificated security payable to bearer or indorsed in blank.

(6) "Bill of lading" means a document evidencing the receipt of goods for shipment issued by a person engaged in the business of transporting or forwarding goods, and includes an airbill. "Airbill" means a document serving for air transportation as a bill of lading does for marine or rail transportation, and includes an air consignment note or air waybill.

(7) "Branch" includes a separately incorporated foreign branch of a bank.

(8) "Burden of establishing" a fact means the burden of persuading the triers of fact that the existence of the fact is more probable than its non-existence.

(9) "Buyer in ordinary course of business" means a person who in good faith and without knowledge that the sale to him is in violation of the ownership rights or security interest of a third party in the goods buys in ordinary course from a person in the business of selling goods of that kind but does not include a pawnbroker. All persons who sell minerals or the like (including oil and gas) at wellhead or minehead shall be deemed to be persons in the business of selling goods of that kind. "Buying" may be for cash or by exchange of other property or on secured or unsecured credit and includes receiving goods or documents of title under a pre-existing contract for sale but does not include a transfer in bulk or as security for or in total or partial satisfaction of a money debt.

(10) "Conspicuous": A term or clause is conspicuous when it is so written that a reasonable person against whom it is to operate ought to have noticed it. A printed heading in capitals (as: NON-NEGOTIABLE BILL OF LADING) is conspicuous. Language in the body of a form is "conspicuous" if it is in larger or other contrasting type or color. But in a telegram any stated term is "conspicuous". Whether a term or clause is "conspicuous" or not is for decision by the court.

(11) "Contract" means the total legal obligation which results from the parties' agreement as affected by this Act and any other applicable rules of law. (Compare "Agreement".)

(12) "Creditor" includes a general creditor, a secured creditor, a lien creditor and any representative of creditors, including an assignee for the benefit of creditors, a trustee in bankruptcy, a receiver in equity and an executor or administrator of an insolvent debtor's or assignor's estate.

(13) "Defendant" includes a person in the position of defendant in a cross-action or counterclaim.

(14) "Delivery" with respect to instruments, documents of title, chattel paper, or certificated securities means voluntary transfer of possession.

(15) "Document of title" includes bill of lading, dock warrant, dock receipt, warehouse receipt or order for the delivery of goods, and also any other document which in the regular course of business or financing is treated as adequately evidencing that the person in possession of it is entitled to receive, hold and dispose of the document and the goods it covers. To be a document of title a document must purport to be issued by or addressed to a bailee and purport to cover goods in the bailee's possession which are either identified or are fungible portions of an identified mass.

(16) "Fault" means wrongful act, omission or breach.

(17) "Fungible" with respect to goods or securities means goods or securities of which any unit is, by nature or usage of trade, the equivalent of any other like unit. Goods which are not fungible shall be deemed fungible for the purposes of this Act to the extent that under a particular agreement or document unlike units are treated as equivalents.

(18) "Genuine" means free of forgery or counterfeiting.

(19) "Good faith" means honesty in fact in the conduct or transaction concerned.

(20) "Holder," with respect to a negotiable instrument, means the person in possession if the instrument is payable to bearer or, in the case of an instrument payable to an identified person, if the identified person is in possession. "Holder" with respect to a document of title means the person in possession if the goods are deliverable to bearer or to the order of the person in possession.

(21) To "honor" is to pay or to accept and pay, or where a credit so engages to purchase or discount a draft complying with the terms of the credit.

(22) "Insolvency proceedings" includes any assignment for the benefit of creditors or other proceedings intended to liquidate or rehabilitate the estate of the person involved.

(23) A person is "insolvent" who either has ceased to pay his debts in the ordinary course of business or cannot pay his debts as they become due or is insolvent within the meaning of the federal bankruptcy law.

(24) "Money" means a medium of exchange authorized or adopted by a domestic or foreign government and includes a monetary unit of account established by an intergovernmental organization or by agreement between two or more nations.

(25) A person has "notice" of a fact when

(a) he has actual knowledge of it; or

(b) he has received a notice or notification of it; or

(c) from all the facts and circumstances known to him at the time in question he has reason to know that it exists.

A person "knows" or has "knowledge" of a fact when he has actual knowledge of it. "Discover" or "learn" or a word or phrase of similar import refers to knowledge rather than to reason to know. The time and circumstances under which a notice or notification may cease to be effective are not determined by this Act.

(26) A person "notifies" or "gives" a notice or notification to another by taking such steps as may be reasonably required to inform the other in ordinary course whether or not such other actually comes to know of it. A person "receives" a notice or notification when

(a) it comes to his attention; or

(b) it is duly delivered at the place of business through which the contract was made or at any other place held out by him as the place for receipt of such communications.

(27) Notice, knowledge or a notice or notification received by an organization is effective for a particular transaction from the time when it is brought to the attention of the individual conducting that transaction, and in any event from the time when it would have been brought to his attention if the organization had exercised due diligence. An organization exercises due diligence if it maintains reasonable routines for communicating significant information to the person conducting the transaction and there is reasonable compliance with the routines. Due diligence does not require an individual acting for the organization to communicate information unless such communication is part of his regular duties or unless he has reason to know of the transaction and that the transaction would be materially affected by the information.

(28) "Organization" includes a corporation, government or governmental subdivision or agency, business trust, estate, trust, partnership or association, two or more persons having a joint or common interest, or any other legal or commercial entity.

(29) "Party", as distinct from "third party", means a person who has engaged in a transaction or made an agreement within this Act.

(30) "Person" includes an individual or an organization (See Section 1–102).

(31) "Presumption" or "presumed" means that the trier of fact must find the existence of the fact presumed unless and until evidence is introduced which would support a finding of its non-existence.

(32) "Purchase" includes taking by sale, discount, negotiation, mortgage, pledge, lien, issue or re-issue, gift or any other voluntary transaction creating an interest in property.

(33) "Purchaser" means a person who takes by purchase.

(34) "Remedy" means any remedial right to which an aggrieved party is entitled with or without resort to a tribunal.

(35) "Representative" includes an agent, an officer of a corporation or association, and a trustee, executor or administrator of an estate, or any other person empowered to act for another.

(36) "Rights" includes remedies.

(37) "Security interest" means an interest in personal property or fixtures which secures payment or performance of an obligation. The retention or reservation of title by a seller of goods notwithstanding shipment or delivery to the buyer (Section 2–401) is limited in effect to a reservation of a "security interest". The term also includes any interest of a buyer of accounts or chattel paper which is subject to Article 9. The special property interest of a buyer of goods on identification of those goods to a contract for sale under Section 2–401 is not a "security interest", but a buyer may also acquire a "security interest" by complying with Article 9. Unless a consignment is intended as security, reservation of title thereunder is not a "security interest", but a consignment in any event is subject to the provisions on consignment sales (Section 2–326).

Whether a transaction creates a lease or security interest is determined by the facts of each case; however, a transaction creates a security interest if the consideration the lessee is to pay the lessor for the right to possession and use of the goods is an obligation for the term of the lease not subject to termination by the lessee, and

(a) the original term of the lease is equal to or greater than the remaining economic life of the goods,

(b) the lessee is bound to renew the lease for the remaining economic life of the goods or is bound to become the owner of the goods,

(c) the lessee has an option to renew the lease for the remaining economic life of the goods for no additional consideration or nominal additional consideration upon compliance with the lease agreement, or

(d) the lessee has an option to become the owner of the goods for no additional consideration or nominal additional consideration upon compliance with the lease agreement.

A transaction does not create a security interest merely because it provides that

(a) the present value of the consideration the lessee is obligated to pay the lessor for the right to possession and use of the goods is substantially equal to or is greater than the fair market value of the goods at the time the lease is entered into,

(b) the lessee assumes risk of loss of the goods, or agrees to pay taxes, insurance, filing, recording, or registration fees, or service or maintenance costs with respect to the goods,

(c) the lessee has an option to renew the lease or to become the owner of the goods,

(d) the lessee has an option to renew the lease for a fixed rent that is equal to or greater than the reasonably predictable fair market rent for the use of the goods for the term of the renewal at the time the option is to be performed, or

(e) the lessee has an option to become the owner of the goods for a fixed price that is equal to or greater than the reasonably predictable fair market value of the goods at the time the option is to be performed.

For purposes of this subsection (37):

(x) Additional consideration is not nominal if (i) when the option to renew the lease is granted to the lessee the rent is stated to be the fair market rent for the use of the goods for the term of the renewal determined at the time the option is to be performed, or (ii) when the option to become the owner of the goods is granted to the lessee the price is stated to be the fair market value of the goods determined at the time the option is to be performed. Additional consideration is nominal if it is less than the lessee's reasonably predictable cost of performing under the lease agreement if the option is not exercised;

(y) "Reasonably predictable" and "remaining economic life of the goods" are to be determined with reference to the facts and circumstances at the time the transaction is entered into; and

(z) "Present value" means the amount as of a date certain of one or more sums payable in the future, discounted to the date certain. The discount is determined by the interest rate specified by the parties if the rate is not manifestly unreasonable at the time the transaction is entered into; otherwise, the discount is determined by a commercially reasonable rate that takes into account the facts and circumstances of each case at the time the transaction was entered into.

(38) "Send" in connection with any writing or notice means to deposit in the mail or deliver for transmission by any other usual means of communication with postage or cost of transmission provided for and properly addressed and in the case of an instrument to an address specified thereon or otherwise agreed, or if there be none to any address reasonable under the circumstances. The receipt of any writing or notice within the time at which it would have arrived if properly sent has the effect of a proper sending.

(39) "Signed" includes any symbol executed or adopted by a party with present intention to authenticate a writing.

(40) "Surety" includes guarantor.

(41) "Telegram" includes a message transmitted by radio, teletype, cable, any mechanical method of transmission, or the like.

(42) "Term" means that portion of an agreement which relates to a particular matter.

(43) "Unauthorized" signature means one made without actual, implied, or apparent authority and includes a forgery.

(44) "Value". Except as otherwise provided with respect to negotiable instruments and bank collections (Sections 3–303, 4–210 and 4–211) a person gives "value" for rights if he acquires them

(a) in return for a binding commitment to extend credit or for the extension of immediately available credit whether or not drawn upon and whether or not a charge-back is provided for in the event of difficulties in collection; or

(b) as security for or in total or partial satisfaction of a pre-existing claim; or

(c) by accepting delivery pursuant to a pre-existing contract for purchase; or

(d) generally, in return for any consideration sufficient to support a simple contract.

(45) "Warehouse receipt" means a receipt issued by a person engaged in the business of storing goods for hire.

(46) "Written" or "writing" includes printing, typewriting or any other intentional reduction to tangible form.

§ 1–202. Prima Facie Evidence by Third Party Documents.

A document in due form purporting to be a bill of lading, policy or certificate of insurance, official weigher's or inspector's certificate, consular invoice, or any other document authorized or required by the contract to be issued by a third party shall be prima facie evidence of its own authenticity and genuineness and of the facts stated in the document by the third party.

§ 1–203. Obligation of Good Faith.

Every contract or duty within this Act imposes an obligation of good faith in its performance or enforcement.

§ 1–204. Time; Reasonable Time; "Seasonably".

(1) Whenever this Act requires any action to be taken within a reasonable time, any time which is not manifestly unreasonable may be fixed by agreement.

(2) What is a reasonable time for taking any action depends on the nature, purpose and circumstances of such action.

(3) An action is taken "seasonably" when it is taken at or within the time agreed or if no time is agreed at or within a reasonable time.

§ 1–205. Course of Dealing and Usage of Trade.

(1) A course of dealing is a sequence of previous conduct between the parties to a particular transaction which is fairly to be regarded as establishing a common basis of understanding for interpreting their expressions and other conduct.

(2) A usage of trade is any practice or method of dealing having such regularity of observance in a place, vocation or trade as to justify an expectation that it will be observed with respect to the transaction in question. The existence and scope of such a usage are to be proved as facts. If it is established that such a usage is embodied in a written trade code or similar writing the interpretation of the writing is for the court.

(3) A course of dealing between parties and any usage of trade in the vocation or trade in which they are engaged or of which they are or should be aware give particular meaning to and supplement or qualify terms of an agreement.

(4) The express terms of an agreement and an applicable course of dealing or usage of trade shall be construed wherever reasonable as consistent with each other, but when such construction is unreasonable express terms control both course of dealing and usage of trade and course of dealing controls usage of trade.

(5) An applicable usage of trade in the place where any part of performance is to occur shall be used in interpreting the agreement as to that part of the performance.

(6) Evidence of a relevant usage of trade offered by one party is not admissible unless and until he has given the other party

such notice as the court finds sufficient to prevent unfair surprise to the latter.

§ 1–206. Statute of Frauds for Kinds of Personal Property Not Otherwise Covered.

(1) Except in the cases described in subsection (2) of this section a contract for the sale of personal property is not enforceable by way of action or defense beyond five thousand dollars in amount or value of remedy unless there is some writing which indicates that a contract for sale has been made between the parties at a defined or stated price, reasonably identifies the subject matter, and is signed by the party against whom enforcement is sought or by his authorized agent.

(2) Subsection (1) of this section does not apply to contracts for the sale of goods (Section 2–201) nor of securities (Section 8–113) nor to security agreements (Section 9–203).

§ 1–207. Performance or Acceptance Under Reservation of Rights.

A party who with explicit reservation of rights performs or promises performance or assents to performance in a manner demanded or offered by the other party does not thereby prejudice the rights reserved. Such words as "without prejudice", "under protest" or the like are sufficient.

§ 1–208. Option to Accelerate at Will.

A term providing that one party or his successor in interest may accelerate payment or performance or require collateral or additional collateral "at will" or "when he deems himself insecure" or in words of similar import shall be construed to mean that he shall have power to do so only if he in good faith believes that the prospect of payment or performance is impaired. The burden of establishing lack of good faith is on the party against whom the power has been exercised.

§ 1–209. Subordinated Obligations.

An obligation may be issued as subordinated to payment of another obligation of the person obligated, or a creditor may subordinate his right to payment of an obligation by agreement with either the person obligated or another creditor of the person obligated. Such a subordination does not create a security interest as against either the common debtor or a subordinated creditor. This section shall be construed as declaring the law as it existed prior to the enactment of this section and not as modifying it. Added 1966.

Note: This new section is proposed as an optional provision to make it clear that a subordination agreement does not create a security interest unless so intended.

ARTICLE 2

SALES

PART 1 Short Title, Construction and Subject Matter

§ 2–101. Short Title.

This Article shall be known and may be cited as Uniform Commercial Code—Sales.

§ 2–102. Scope; Certain Security and Other Transactions Excluded From This Article.

Unless the context otherwise requires, this Article applies to transactions in goods; it does not apply to any transaction which although in the form of an unconditional contract to sell or present sale is intended to operate only as a security transaction nor does this Article impair or repeal any statute regulating sales to consumers, farmers or other specified classes of buyers.

§ 2–103. Definitions and Index of Definitions.

(1) In this Article unless the context otherwise requires

(a) "Buyer" means a person who buys or contracts to buy goods.

(b) "Good faith" in the case of a merchant means honesty in fact and the observance of reasonable commercial standards of fair dealing in the trade.

(c) "Receipt" of goods means taking physical possession of them.

(d) "Seller" means a person who sells or contracts to sell goods.

(2) Other definitions applying to this Article or to specified Parts thereof, and the sections in which they appear are:

"Acceptance". Section 2–606.
"Banker's credit". Section 2–325.
"Between merchants". Section 2–104.
"Cancellation". Section 2–106(4).
"Commercial unit". Section 2–105.
"Confirmed credit". Section 2–325.
"Conforming to contract". Section 2–106.
"Contract for sale". Section 2–106.
"Cover". Section 2–712.
"Entrusting". Section 2–403.
"Financing agency". Section 2–104.
"Future goods". Section 2–105.
"Goods". Section 2–105.
"Identification". Section 2–501.
"Installment contract". Section 2–612.
"Letter of Credit". Section 2–325.
"Lot". Section 2–105.
"Merchant". Section 2–104.
"Overseas". Section 2–323.
"Person in position of seller". Section 2–707.
"Present sale". Section 2–106.
"Sale". Section 2–106.
"Sale on approval". Section 2–326.
"Sale or return". Section 2–326.
"Termination". Section 2–106.

(3) The following definitions in other Articles apply to this Article:

"Check". Section 3–104.
"Consignee". Section 7–102.
"Consignor". Section 7–102.
"Consumer goods". Section 9–109.
"Dishonor". Section 3–502.
"Draft". Section 3–104.

(4) In addition Article 1 contains general definitions and principles of construction and interpretation applicable throughout this Article.

§ 2–104. Definitions: "Merchant"; "Between Merchants"; "Financing Agency".

(1) "Merchant" means a person who deals in goods of the kind or otherwise by his occupation holds himself out as having

knowledge or skill peculiar to the practices or goods involved in the transaction or to whom such knowledge or skill may be attributed by his employment of an agent or broker or other intermediary who by his occupation holds himself out as having such knowledge or skill.

(2) "Financing agency" means a bank, finance company or other person who in the ordinary course of business makes advances against goods or documents of title or who by arrangement with either the seller or the buyer intervenes in ordinary course to make or collect payment due or claimed under the contract for sale, as by purchasing or paying the seller's draft or making advances against it or by merely taking it for collection whether or not documents of title accompany the draft. "Financing agency" includes also a bank or other person who similarly intervenes between persons who are in the position of seller and buyer in respect to the goods (Section 2–707).

(3) "Between merchants" means in any transaction with respect to which both parties are chargeable with the knowledge or skill of merchants.

§ 2–105. Definitions: Transferability; "Goods"; "Future" Goods; "Lot"; "Commercial Unit".

(1) "Goods" means all things (including specially manufactured goods) which are movable at the time of identification to the contract for sale other than the money in which the price is to be paid, investment securities (Article 8) and things in action. "Goods" also includes the unborn young of animals and growing crops and other identified things attached to realty as described in the section on goods to be severed from realty (Section 2–107).

(2) Goods must be both existing and identified before any interest in them can pass. Goods which are not both existing and identified are "future" goods. A purported present sale of future goods or of any interest therein operates as a contract to sell.

(3) There may be a sale of a part interest in existing identified goods.

(4) An undivided share in an identified bulk of fungible goods is sufficiently identified to be sold although the quantity of the bulk is not determined. Any agreed proportion of such a bulk or any quantity thereof agreed upon by number, weight or other measure may to the extent of the seller's interest in the bulk be sold to the buyer who then becomes an owner in common.

(5) "Lot" means a parcel or a single article which is the subject matter of a separate sale or delivery, whether or not it is sufficient to perform the contract.

(6) "Commercial unit" means such a unit of goods as by commercial usage is a single whole for purposes of sale and division of which materially impairs its character or value on the market or in use. A commercial unit may be a single article (as a machine) or a set of articles (as a suite of furniture or an assortment of sizes) or a quantity (as a bale, gross, or carload) or any other unit treated in use or in the relevant market as a single whole.

§ 2–106. Definitions: "Contract"; "Agreement"; "Contract for Sale"; "Sale"; "Present Sale"; "Conforming" to Contract; "Termination"; "Cancellation".

(1) In this Article unless the context otherwise requires "contract" and "agreement" are limited to those relating to the present or future sale of goods. "Contract for sale" includes both a present sale of goods and a contract to sell goods at a future time. A "sale" consists in the passing of title from the seller to the buyer for a price (Section 2–401). A "present sale" means a sale which is accomplished by the making of the contract.

(2) Goods or conduct including any part of a performance are "conforming" or conform to the contract when they are in accordance with the obligations under the contract.

(3) "Termination" occurs when either party pursuant to a power created by agreement or law puts an end to the contract otherwise than for its breach. On "termination" all obligations which are still executory on both sides are discharged but any right based on prior breach or performance survives.

(4) "Cancellation" occurs when either party puts an end to the contract for breach by the other and its effect is the same as that of "termination" except that the cancelling party also retains any remedy for breach of the whole contract or any unperformed balance.

§ 2–107. Goods to Be Severed From Realty: Recording.

(1) A contract for the sale of minerals or the like (including oil and gas) or a structure or its materials to be removed from realty is a contract for the sale of goods within this Article if they are to be severed by the seller but until severance a purported present sale thereof which is not effective as a transfer of an interest in land is effective only as a contract to sell.

(2) A contract for the sale apart from the land of growing crops or other things attached to realty and capable of severance without material harm thereto but not described in subsection (1) or of timber to be cut is a contract for the sale of goods within this Article whether the subject matter is to be severed by the buyer or by the seller even though it forms part of the realty at the time of contracting, and the parties can by identification effect a present sale before severance.

(3) The provisions of this section are subject to any third party rights provided by the law relating to realty records, and the contract for sale may be executed and recorded as a document transferring an interest in land and shall then constitute notice to third parties of the buyer's rights under the contract for sale.

PART 2 Form, Formation and Readjustment of Contract

§ 2–201. Formal Requirements; Statute of Frauds.

(1) Except as otherwise provided in this section a contract for the sale of goods for the price of $500 or more is not enforceable by way of action or defense unless there is some writing sufficient to indicate that a contract for sale has been made between the parties and signed by the party against whom enforcement is sought or by his authorized agent or broker. A writing is not insufficient because it omits or incorrectly states a term agreed upon but the contract is not enforceable under this paragraph beyond the quantity of goods shown in such writing.

(2) Between merchants if within a reasonable time a writing in confirmation of the contract and sufficient against the sender is received and the party receiving it has reason to know its contents, it satisfies the requirements of subsection (1) against such party unless written notice of objection to its contents is given within ten days after it is received.

(3) A contract which does not satisfy the requirements of subsection (1) but which is valid in other respects is enforceable

(a) if the goods are to be specially manufactured for the buyer and are not suitable for sale to others in the ordinary course of the seller's business and the seller, before notice of repudiation is received and under circumstances which reasonably indicate that the goods are for the buyer, has made either a substantial beginning of their manufacture or commitments for their procurement; or

(b) if the party against whom enforcement is sought admits in his pleading, testimony or otherwise in court that a contract for sale was made, but the contract is not enforceable under this provision beyond the quantity of goods admitted; or

(c) with respect to goods for which payment has been made and accepted or which have been received and accepted (Sec. 2–606).

§ 2–202. Final Written Expression: Parol or Extrinsic Evidence.

Terms with respect to which the confirmatory memoranda of the parties agree or which are otherwise set forth in a writing intended by the parties as a final expression of their agreement with respect to such terms as are included therein may not be contradicted by evidence of any prior agreement or of a contemporaneous oral agreement but may be explained or supplemented

(a) by course of dealing or usage of trade (Section 1–205) or by course of performance (Section 2–208); and

(b) by evidence of consistent additional terms unless the court finds the writing to have been intended also as a complete and exclusive statement of the terms of the agreement.

§ 2–203. Seals Inoperative.

The affixing of a seal to a writing evidencing a contract for sale or an offer to buy or sell goods does not constitute the writing a sealed instrument and the law with respect to sealed instruments does not apply to such a contract or offer.

§ 2–204. Formation in General.

(1) A contract for sale of goods may be made in any manner sufficient to show agreement, including conduct by both parties which recognizes the existence of such a contract.

(2) An agreement sufficient to constitute a contract for sale may be found even though the moment of its making is undetermined.

(3) Even though one or more terms are left open a contract for sale does not fail for indefiniteness if the parties have intended to make a contract and there is a reasonably certain basis for giving an appropriate remedy.

§ 2–205. Firm Offers.

An offer by a merchant to buy or sell goods in a signed writing which by its terms gives assurance that it will be held open is not revocable, for lack of consideration, during the time stated or if no time is stated for reasonable time, but in no event may such period of irrevocability exceed three months; but any such term of assurance on a form supplied by the offeree must be separately signed by the offeror.

§ 2–206. Offer and Acceptance in Formation of Contract.

(1) Unless other unambiguously indicated by the language or circumstances

(a) an offer to make a contract shall be construed as inviting acceptance in any manner and by any medium reasonable in the circumstances;

(b) an order or other offer to buy goods for prompt or current shipment shall be construed as inviting acceptance either by a prompt promise to ship or by the prompt or current shipment of conforming or nonconforming goods, but such a shipment of non-conforming goods does not constitute an acceptance if the seller seasonably notifies the buyer that the shipment is offered only as an accommodation to the buyer.

(2) Where the beginning of a requested performance is a reasonable mode of acceptance an offeror who is not notified of acceptance within a reasonable time may treat the offer as having lapsed before acceptance.

§ 2–207. Additional Terms in Acceptance or Confirmation.

(1) A definite and seasonable expression of acceptance or a written confirmation which is sent within a reasonable time operates as an acceptance even though it states terms additional to or different from those offered or agreed upon, unless acceptance is expressly made conditional on assent to the additional or different terms.

(2) The additional terms are to be construed as proposals for addition to the contract. Between merchants such terms become part of the contract unless:

(a) the offer expressly limits acceptance to the terms of the offer;

(b) they materially alter it; or

(c) notification of objection to them has already been given or is given within a reasonable time after notice of them is received.

(3) Conduct by both parties which recognizes the existence of a contract is sufficient to establish a contract for sale although the writings of the parties do not otherwise establish a contract. In such case the terms of the particular contract consist of those terms on which the writings of the parties agree, together with any supplementary terms incorporated under any other provisions of this Act.

§ 2–208. Course of Performance or Practical Construction.

(1) Where the contract for sale involves repeated occasions for performance by either party with knowledge of the nature of the performance and opportunity for objection to it by the other, any course of performance accepted or acquiesced in without objection shall be relevant to determine the meaning of the agreement.

(2) The express terms of the agreement and any such course of performance, as well as any course of dealing and usage of trade, shall be construed whenever reasonable as consistent with each other; but when such construction is unreasonable, express terms shall control course of performance and course of performance shall control both course of dealing and usage of trade (Section 1–205).

(3) Subject to the provisions of the next section on modification and waiver, such course of performance shall be relevant to show a waiver or modification of any term inconsistent with such course of performance.

§ 2–209. Modification, Rescission and Waiver.

(1) An agreement modifying a contract within this Article needs no consideration to be binding.

(2) A signed agreement which excludes modification or rescission except by a signed writing cannot be otherwise modified or

rescinded, but except as between merchants such a requirement on a form supplied by the merchant must be separately signed by the other party.

(3) The requirements of the statute of frauds section of this Article (Section 2–201) must be satisfied if the contract as modified is within its provisions.

(4) Although an attempt at modification or rescission does not satisfy the requirements of subsection (2) or (3) it can operate as a waiver.

(5) A party who has made a waiver affecting an executory portion of the contract may retract the waiver by reasonable notification received by the other party that strict performance will be required of any term waived, unless the retraction would be unjust in view of a material change of position in reliance on the waiver.

§ 2–210. Delegation of Performance; Assignment of Rights.

(1) A party may perform his duty through a delegate unless otherwise agreed or unless the other party has a substantial interest in having his original promisor perform or control the acts required by the contract. No delegation of performance relieves the party delegating of any duty to perform or any liability for breach.

(2) Unless otherwise agreed all rights of either seller or buyer can be assigned except where the assignment would materially change the duty of the other party, or increase materially the burden or risk imposed on him by his contract, or impair materially his chance of obtaining return performance. A right to damages for breach of the whole contract or a right arising out of the assignor's due performance of his entire obligation can be assigned despite agreement otherwise.

(3) Unless the circumstances indicate the contrary a prohibition of assignment of "the contract" is to be construed as barring only the delegation to the assignee of the assignor's performance.

(4) An assignment of "the contract" or of "all my rights under the contract" or an assignment in similar general terms is an assignment of rights and unless the language or the circumstances (as in an assignment for security) indicate the contrary, it is a delegation of performance of the duties of the assignor and its acceptance by the assignee constitutes a promise by him to perform those duties. This promise is enforceable by either the assignor or the other party to the original contract.

(5) The other party may treat any assignment which delegates performance as creating reasonable grounds for insecurity and may without prejudice to his rights against the assignor demand assurances from the assignee (Section 2–609).

PART 3 General Obligation and Construction of Contract

§ 2–301. General Obligations of Parties.

The obligation of the seller is to transfer and deliver and that of the buyer is to accept and pay in accordance with the contract.

§ 2–302. Unconscionable Contract or Clause.

(1) If the court as a matter of law finds the contract or any clause of the contract to have been unconscionable at the time it was made the court may refuse to enforce the contract, or it may enforce the remainder of the contract without the unconscionable clause, or it may so limit the application of any unconscionable clause as to avoid any unconscionable result.

(2) When it is claimed or appears to the court that the contract or any clause thereof may be unconscionable the parties shall be afforded a reasonable opportunity to present evidence as to its commercial setting, purpose and effect to aid the court in making the determination.

§ 2–303. Allocation or Division of Risks.

Where this Article allocates a risk or a burden as between the parties "unless otherwise agreed", the agreement may not only shift the allocation, but may also divide the risk or burden.

§ 2–304. Price Payable in Money, Goods, Realty, or Otherwise.

(1) The price can be made payable in money or otherwise. If it is payable in whole or in part in goods each party is a seller of the goods which he is to transfer.

(2) Even though all or part of the price is payable in an interest in realty the transfer of the goods and the seller's obligations with reference to them are subject to this Article, but not the transfer of the interest in realty or the transferor's obligations in connection therewith.

§ 2–305. Open Price Term.

(1) The parties if they so intend can conclude a contract for sale even though the price is not settled. In such a case the price is a reasonable price at the time for delivery if

(a) nothing is said as to price; or

(b) the price is left to be agreed by the parties and they fail to agree; or

(c) the price is to be fixed in terms of some agreed market or other standard as set or recorded by a third person or agency and it is not so set or recorded.

(2) A price to be fixed by the seller or by the buyer means a price for him to fix in good faith.

(3) When a price left to be fixed otherwise than by agreement of the parties fails to be fixed through fault of one party the other may at his option treat the contract as cancelled or himself fix a reasonable price.

(4) Where, however, the parties intend not to be bound unless the price be fixed or agreed and it is not fixed or agreed there is no contract. In such a case the buyer must return any goods already received or if unable so to do must pay their reasonable value at the time of delivery and the seller must return any portion of the price paid on account.

§ 2–306. Output, Requirements and Exclusive Dealings.

(1) A term which measures the quantity by the output of the seller or the requirements of the buyer means such actual output or requirements as may occur in good faith, except that no quantity unreasonably disproportionate to any stated estimate or in the absence of a stated estimate to any normal or otherwise comparable prior output or requirements may be tendered or demanded.

(2) A lawful agreement by either the seller or the buyer for exclusive dealing in the kind of goods concerned imposes unless otherwise agreed an obligation by the seller to use best efforts to supply the goods and by the buyer to use best efforts to promote their sale.

§ 2–307. Delivery in Single Lot or Several Lots.

Unless otherwise agreed all goods called for by a contract for sale must be tendered in a single delivery and payment is due only on such tender but where the circumstances give either party the right to make or demand delivery in lots the price if it can be apportioned may be demanded for each lot.

§ 2–308. Absence of Specified Place for Delivery.

Unless otherwise agreed

(a) the place for delivery of goods is the seller's place of business or if he has none his residence; but

(b) in a contract for sale of identified goods which to the knowledge of the parties at the time of contracting are in some other place, that place is the place for their delivery; and

(c) documents of title may be delivered through customary banking channels.

§ 2–309. Absence of Specific Time Provisions; Notice of Termination.

(1) The time for shipment or delivery or any other action under a contract if not provided in this Article or agreed upon shall be a reasonable time.

(2) Where the contract provides for successive performances but is indefinite in duration it is valid for a reasonable time but unless otherwise agreed may be terminated at any time by either party.

(3) Termination of a contract by one party except on the happening of an agreed event requires that reasonable notification be received by the other party and an agreement dispensing with notification is invalid if its operation would be unconscionable.

§ 2–310. Open Time for Payment or Running of Credit; Authority to Ship Under Reservation.

Unless otherwise agreed

(a) payment is due at the time and place at which the buyer is to receive the goods even though the place of shipment is the place of delivery; and

(b) if the seller is authorized to send the goods he may ship them under reservation, and may tender the documents of title, but the buyer may inspect the goods after their arrival before payment is due unless such inspection is inconsistent with the terms of the contract (Section 2–513); and

(c) if delivery is authorized and made by way of documents of title otherwise than by subsection (b) then payment is due at the time and place at which the buyer is to receive the documents regardless of where the goods are to be received; and

(d) where the seller is required or authorized to ship the goods on credit the credit period runs from the time of shipment but post-dating the invoice or delaying its dispatch will correspondingly delay the starting of the credit period.

§ 2–311. Options and Cooperation Respecting Performance.

(1) An agreement for sale which is otherwise sufficiently definite (subsection (3) of Section 2–204) to be a contract is not made invalid by the fact that it leaves particulars of performance to be specified by one of the parties. Any such specification must be made in good faith and within limits set by commercial reasonableness.

(2) Unless otherwise agreed specifications relating to assortment of the goods are at the buyer's option and except as otherwise provided in subsections (1)(c) and (3) of Section 2–319 specifications or arrangements relating to shipment are at the seller's option.

(3) Where such specification would materially affect the other party's performance but is not seasonably made or where one party's cooperation is necessary to the agreed performance of the other but is not seasonably forthcoming, the other party in addition to all other remedies

(a) is excused for any resulting delay in his own performance; and

(b) may also either proceed to perform in any reasonable manner or after the time for a material part of his own performance treat the failure to specify or to cooperate as a breach by failure to deliver or accept the goods.

§ 2–312. Warranty of Title and Against Infringement; Buyer's Obligation Against Infringement.

(1) Subject to subsection (2) there is in a contract for sale a warranty by the seller that

(a) the title conveyed shall be good, and its transfer rightful; and

(b) the goods shall be delivered free from any security interest or other lien or encumbrance of which the buyer at the time of contracting has no knowledge.

(2) A warranty under subsection (1) will be excluded or modified only by specific language or by circumstances which give the buyer reason to know that the person selling does not claim title in himself or that he is purporting to sell only such right or title as he or a third person may have.

(3) Unless otherwise agreed a seller who is a merchant regularly dealing in goods of the kind warrants that the goods shall be delivered free of the rightful claim of any third person by way of infringement or the like but a buyer who furnishes specifications to the seller must hold the seller harmless against any such claim which arises out of compliance with the specifications.

§ 2–313. Express Warranties by Affirmation, Promise, Description, Sample.

(1) Express warranties by the seller are created as follows:

(a) Any affirmation of fact or promise made by the seller to the buyer which relates to the goods and becomes part of the basis of the bargain creates an express warranty that the goods shall conform to the affirmation or promise.

(b) Any description of the goods which is made part of the basis of the bargain creates an express warranty that the goods shall conform to the description.

(c) Any sample or model which is made part of the basis of the bargain creates an express warranty that the whole of the goods shall conform to the sample or model.

(2) It is not necessary to the creation of an express warranty that the seller use formal words such as "warrant" or "guarantee" or that he have a specific intention to make a warranty, but an affirmation merely of the value of the goods or a statement purporting to be merely the seller's opinion or commendation of the goods does not create a warranty.

§ 2–314. Implied Warranty: Merchantability; Usage of Trade.

(1) Unless excluded or modified (Section 2–316), a warranty that the goods shall be merchantable is implied in a contract for their sale if the seller is a merchant with respect to goods of that kind. Under this section the serving for value of food or drink to be consumed either on the premises or elsewhere is a sale.

(2) Goods to be merchantable must be at least such as

(a) pass without objection in the trade under the contract description; and

(b) in the case of fungible goods, are of fair average quality within the description; and

(c) are fit for the ordinary purpose for which such goods are used; and

(d) run, within the variations permitted by the agreement, of even kind, quality and quantity within each unit and among all units involved; and

(e) are adequately contained, packaged, and labeled as the agreement may require; and

(f) conform to the promises or affirmations of fact made on the container or label if any.

(3) Unless excluded or modified (Section 2–316) other implied warranties may arise from course of dealing or usage of trade.

§ 2–315. Implied Warranty: Fitness for Particular Purpose.

Where the seller at the time of contracting has reason to know any particular purpose for which the goods are required and that the buyer is relying on the seller's skill or judgment to select or furnish suitable goods, there is unless excluded or modified under the next section an implied warranty that the goods shall be fit for such purpose.

§ 2–316. Exclusion or Modification of Warranties.

(1) Words or conduct relevant to the creation of an express warranty and words or conduct tending to negate or limit warranty shall be construed wherever reasonable as consistent with each other, but subject to the provisions of this Article on parol or extrinsic evidence (Section 2–202) negation or limitation is inoperative to the extent that such construction is unreasonable.

(2) Subject to subsection (3), to exclude or modify the implied warranty of merchantability or any part of it the language must mention merchantability and in case of a writing must be conspicuous, and to exclude or modify any implied warranty of fitness the exclusion must be by a writing and conspicuous. Language to exclude all implied warranties of fitness is sufficient if it states, for example, that "There are no warranties which extend beyond the description on the face hereof."

(3) Notwithstanding subsection (2)

(a) unless the circumstances indicate otherwise, all implied warranties are excluded by expressions like "as is", "with all faults" or other language which in common understanding calls the buyer's attention to the exclusion of warranties and makes plain that there is no implied warranty; and

(b) when the buyer before entering into the contract has examined the goods or the sample or model as fully as he desired or has refused to examine the goods there is no implied warranty with regard to defects which an examination ought in the circumstances to have revealed to him; and

(c) an implied warranty can also be excluded or modified by course of dealing or course of performance or usage of trade.

(4) Remedies for breach of warranty can be limited in accordance with the provisions of this Article on liquidation or limitation of damages and on contractual modification of remedy (Sections 2–718 and 2–719).

§ 2–317. Cumulation and Conflict of Warranties Express or Implied.

Warranties whether express or implied shall be construed as consistent with each other and as cumulative, but if such construction is unreasonable the intention of the parties shall determine which warranty is dominant. In ascertaining that intention the following rules apply:

(a) Exact or technical specifications displace an inconsistent sample or model or general language of description.

(b) A sample from an existing bulk displaces inconsistent general language of description.

(c) Express warranties displace inconsistent implied warranties other than an implied warranty of fitness for a particular purpose.

§ 2–318. Third Party Beneficiaries of Warranties Express or Implied.

Note: If this Act is introduced in the Congress of the United States this section should be omitted. (States to select one alternative.)

Alternative A A seller's warranty whether express or implied extends to any natural person who is in the family or household of his buyer or who is a guest in his home if it is reasonable to expect that such person may use, consume or be affected by the goods and who is injured in person by breach of the warranty. The seller may not exclude or limit the operation of this section.

Alternative B A seller's warranty whether express or implied extends to any natural person who may reasonably be expected to use, consume or be affected by the goods and who is injured in person by breach of the warranty. A seller may not exclude or limit the operation of this section.

Alternative C A seller's warranty whether express or implied extends to any person who may reasonably be expected to use, consume or be affected by the goods and who is injured by breach of the warranty. A seller may not exclude or limit the operation of this section with respect to injury to the person of an individual to whom the warranty extends. As amended 1966.

§ 2–319. F.O.B. and F.A.S. Terms.

(1) Unless otherwise agreed the term F.O.B. (which means "free on board") at a named place, even though used only in connection with the stated price, is a delivery term under which

(a) when the term is F.O.B. the place of shipment, the seller must at that place ship the goods in the manner provided in this Article (Section 2–504) and bear the expense and risk of putting them into the possession of the carrier; or

(b) when the term is F.O.B. the place of destination, the seller must at his own expense and risk transport the goods to that place and there tender delivery of them in the manner provided in this Article (Section 2–503);

(c) when under either (a) or (b) the term is also F.O.B. vessel, car or other vehicle, the seller must in addition at his own expense and risk load the goods on board. If the term is F.O.B. vessel the buyer must name the vessel and in an appropriate case the seller must comply with the provisions of this Article on the form of bill of lading (Section 2–323).

(2) Unless otherwise agreed the term F.A.S. vessel (which means "free alongside") at a named port, even though used only in connection with the stated price, is a delivery term under which the seller must

(a) at his own expense and risk deliver the goods alongside the vessel in the manner usual in that port or on a dock designated and provided by the buyer; and

(b) obtain and tender a receipt for the goods in exchange for which the carrier is under a duty to issue a bill of lading.

(3) Unless otherwise agreed in any case falling within subsection (1)(a) or (c) or subsection (2) the buyer must seasonably give any needed instructions for making delivery, including when the term is F.A.S. or F.O.B. the loading berth of the vessel and in an appropriate case its name and sailing date. The seller may

treat the failure of needed instructions as a failure of cooperation under this Article (Section 2–311). He may also at his option move the goods in any reasonable manner preparatory to delivery or shipment.

(4) Under the term F.O.B. vessel or F.A.S. unless otherwise agreed the buyer must make payment against tender of the required documents and the seller may not tender nor the buyer demand delivery of the goods in substitution for the documents.

§ 2–320. C.I.F. and C. & F. Terms.

(1) The term C.I.F. means that the price includes in a lump sum the cost of the goods and the insurance and freight to the named destination. The term C. & F. or C.F. means that the price so includes cost and freight to the named destination.

(2) Unless otherwise agreed and even though used only in connection with the stated price and destination, the term C.I.F. destination or its equivalent requires the seller at his own expense and risk to

(a) put the goods into the possession of a carrier at the port for shipment and obtain a negotiable bill or bills of lading covering the entire transportation to the named destination; and

(b) load the goods and obtain a receipt from the carrier (which may be contained in the bill of lading) showing that the freight has been paid or provided for; and

(c) obtain a policy or certificate of insurance, including any war risk insurance, of a kind and on terms then current at the port of shipment in the usual amount, in the currency of the contract, shown to cover the same goods covered by the bill of lading and providing for payment of loss to the order of the buyer or for the account of whom it may concern; but the seller may add to the price the amount of premium for any such war risk insurance; and

(d) prepare an invoice of the goods and procure any other documents required to effect shipment or to comply with the contract; and

(e) forward and tender with commercial promptness all the documents in due form and with any indorsement necessary to perfect the buyer's rights.

(3) Unless otherwise agreed the term C. & F. or its equivalent has the same effect and imposes upon the seller the same obligations and risks as a C.I.F. term except the obligation as to insurance.

(4) Under the term C.I.F. or C. & F. unless otherwise agreed the buyer must make payment against tender of the required documents and the seller may not tender nor the buyer demand delivery of the goods in substitution for the documents.

§ 2–321. C.I.F. or C. & F.: "Net Landed Weights"; "Payment on Arrival"; Warranty of Condition on Arrival.

Under a contract containing a term C.I.F. or C. & F.

(1) Where the price is based on or is to be adjusted according to "net landed weights", "delivered weights", "out turn" quantity or quality or the like, unless otherwise agreed the seller must reasonably estimate the price. The payment due on tender of the documents called for by the contract is the amount so estimated, but after final adjustment of the price a settlement must be made with commercial promptness.

(2) An agreement described in subsection (1) or any warranty of quality or condition of the goods on arrival places upon the seller the risk of ordinary deterioration, shrinkage and the like in transportation but has no effect on the place or time of identification to the contract for sale or delivery or on the passing of the risk of loss.

(3) Unless otherwise agreed where the contract provides for payment on or after arrival of the goods the seller must before payment allow such preliminary inspection as is feasible; but if the goods are lost delivery of the documents and payment are due when the goods should have arrived.

§ 2–322. Delivery "Ex-Ship".

(1) Unless otherwise agreed a term for delivery of goods "ex-ship" (which means from the carrying vessel) or in equivalent language is not restricted to a particular ship and requires delivery from a ship which has reached a place at the named port of destination where goods of the kind are usually discharged.

(2) Under such a term unless otherwise agreed

(a) the seller must discharge all liens arising out of the carriage and furnish the buyer with a direction which puts the carrier under a duty to deliver the goods; and

(b) the risk of loss does not pass to the buyer until the goods leave the ship's tackle or are otherwise properly unloaded.

§ 2–323. Form of Bill of Lading Required in Overseas Shipment; "Overseas".

(1) Where the contract contemplates overseas shipment and contains a term C.I.F. or C. & F. or F.O.B. vessel, the seller unless otherwise agreed must obtain a negotiable bill of lading stating that the goods have been loaded on board or, in the case of a term C.I.F. or C. & F., received for shipment.

(2) Where in a case within subsection (1) a bill of lading has been issued in a set of parts, unless otherwise agreed if the documents are not to be sent from abroad the buyer may demand tender of the full set; otherwise only one part of the bill of lading need be tendered. Even if the agreement expressly requires a full set

(a) due tender of a single part is acceptable within the provisions of this Article on cure of improper delivery (subsection (1) of Section 2–508); and

(b) even though the full set is demanded, if the documents are sent from abroad the person tendering an incomplete set may nevertheless require payment upon furnishing an indemnity which the buyer in good faith deems adequate.

(3) A shipment by water or by air or a contract contemplating such shipment is "overseas" insofar as by usage of trade or agreement it is subject to the commercial, financing or shipping practices characteristic of international deep water commerce.

§ 2–324. "No Arrival, No Sale" Term.

Under a term "no arrival, no sale" or terms of like meaning, unless otherwise agreed,

(a) the seller must properly ship conforming goods and if they arrive by any means he must tender them on arrival but he assumes no obligation that the goods will arrive unless he has caused the non-arrival; and

(b) where without fault of the seller the goods are in part lost or have so deteriorated as no longer to conform to the contract or arrive after the contract time, the buyer may proceed as if there had been casualty to identified goods (Section 2–613).

§ 2–325. "Letter of Credit" Term; "Confirmed Credit".

(1) Failure of the buyer seasonably to furnish an agreed letter of credit is a breach of the contract for sale.

(2) The delivery to seller of a proper letter of credit suspends the buyer's obligation to pay. If the letter of credit is dishonored, the seller may on seasonable notification to the buyer require payment directly from him.

(3) Unless otherwise agreed the term "letter of credit" or "banker's credit" in a contract for sale means an irrevocable credit issued by a financing agency of good repute and, where the shipment is overseas, of good international repute. The term "confirmed credit" means that the credit must also carry the direct obligation of such an agency which does business in the seller's financial market.

§ 2–326. Sale on Approval and Sale or Return; Consignment Sales and Rights of Creditors.

(1) Unless otherwise agreed, if delivered goods may be returned by the buyer even though they conform to the contract, the transaction is

(a) a "sale on approval" if the goods are delivered primarily for use, and

(b) a "sale or return" if the goods are delivered primarily for resale.

(2) Except as provided in subsection (3), goods held on approval are not subject to the claims of the buyer's creditors until acceptance; goods held on sale or return are subject to such claims while in the buyer's possession.

(3) Where goods are delivered to a person for sale and such person maintains a place of business at which he deals in goods of the kind involved, under a name other than the name of the person making delivery, then with respect to claims of creditors of the person conducting the business the goods are deemed to be on sale or return. The provisions of this subsection are applicable even though an agreement purports to reserve title to the person making delivery until payment or resale or uses such words as "on consignment" or "on memorandum". However, this subsection is not applicable if the person making delivery

(a) complies with an applicable law providing for a consignor's interest or the like to be evidenced by a sign, or

(b) establishes that the person conducting the business is generally known by his creditors to be substantially engaged in selling the goods of others, or

(c) complies with the filing provisions of the Article on Secured Transactions (Article 9).

(4) Any "or return" term of a contract for sale is to be treated as a separate contract for sale within the statute of frauds section of this Article (Section 2–201) and as contradicting the sale aspect of the contract within the provisions of this Article on parol or extrinsic evidence (Section 2–202).

§ 2–327. Special Incidents of Sale on Approval and Sale or Return.

(1) Under a sale on approval unless otherwise agreed

(a) although the goods are identified to the contract the risk of loss and the title do not pass to the buyer until acceptance; and

(b) use of the goods consistent with the purpose of trial is not acceptance but failure seasonably to notify the seller of election to return the goods is acceptance, and if the goods conform to the contract acceptance of any part is acceptance of the whole; and

(c) after due notification of election to return, the return is at the seller's risk and expense but a merchant buyer must follow any reasonable instructions.

(2) Under a sale or return unless otherwise agreed

(a) the option to return extends to the whole or any commercial unit of the goods while in substantially their original condition, but must be exercised seasonably; and

(b) the return is at the buyer's risk and expense.

§ 2–328. Sale by Auction.

(1) In a sale by auction if goods are put up in lots each lot is the subject of a separate sale.

(2) A sale by auction is complete when the auctioneer so announces by the fall of the hammer or in other customary manner. Where a bid is made while the hammer is falling in acceptance of a prior bid the auctioneer may in his discretion reopen the bidding or declare the goods sold under the bid on which the hammer was falling.

(3) Such a sale is with reserve unless the goods are in explicit terms put up without reserve. In an auction with reserve the auctioneer may withdraw the goods at any time until he announces completion of the sale. In an auction without reserve, after the auctioneer calls for bids on an article or lot, that article or lot cannot be withdrawn unless no bid is made within a reasonable time. In either case a bidder may retract his bid until the auctioneer's announcement of completion of the sale, but a bidder's retraction does not revive any previous bid.

(4) If the auctioneer knowingly receives a bid on the seller's behalf or the seller makes or procures such a bid, and notice has not been given that liberty for such bidding is reserved, the buyer may at his option avoid the sale or take the goods at the price of the last good faith bid prior to the completion of the sale. This subsection shall not apply to any bid at a forced sale.

PART 4 Title, Creditors and Good Faith Purchasers

§ 2–401. Passing of Title; Reservation for Security; Limited Application of This Section.

Each provision of this Article with regard to the rights, obligations and remedies of the seller, the buyer, purchasers or other third parties applies irrespective of title to the goods except where the provision refers to such title. Insofar as situations are not covered by the other provisions of this Article and matters concerning title became material the following rules apply:

(1) Title to goods cannot pass under a contract for sale prior to their identification to the contract (Section 2–501), and unless otherwise explicitly agreed the buyer acquires by their identification a special property as limited by this Act.

Any retention or reservation by the seller of the title (property) in goods shipped or delivered to the buyer is limited in effect to a reservation of a security interest. Subject to these provisions and to the provisions of the Article on Secured Transactions (Article 9), title to goods passes from the seller to the buyer in any manner and on any conditions explicitly agreed on by the parties.

(2) Unless otherwise explicitly agreed title passes to the buyer at the time and place at which the seller completes his performance with reference to the physical delivery of the goods, despite any reservation of a security interest and even though a document of title is to be delivered at a different time or place; and in particular and despite any reservation of a security interest by the bill of lading

(a) if the contract requires or authorizes the seller to send the goods to the buyer but does not require him to deliver them at destination, title passes to the buyer at the time and place of shipment; but

(b) if the contract requires delivery at destination, title passes on tender there.

(3) Unless otherwise explicitly agreed where delivery is to be made without moving the goods,

(a) if the seller is to deliver a document of title, title passes at the time when and the place where he delivers such documents; or

(b) if the goods are at the time of contracting already identified and no documents are to be delivered, title passes at the time and place of contracting.

(4) A rejection or other refusal by the buyer to receive or retain the goods, whether or not justified, or a justified revocation of acceptance revests title to the goods in the seller. Such revesting occurs by operation of law and is not a "sale".

§ 2–402. Rights of Seller's Creditors Against Sold Goods.

(1) Except as provided in subsections (2) and (3), rights of unsecured creditors of the seller with respect to goods which have been identified to a contract for sale are subject to the buyer's rights to recover the goods under this Article (Sections 2–502 and 2–716).

(2) A creditor of the seller may treat a sale or an identification of goods to a contract for sale as void if as against him a retention of possession by the seller is fraudulent under any rule of law of the state where the goods are situated, except that retention of possession in good faith and current course of trade by a merchant-seller for a commercially reasonable time after a sale or identification is not fraudulent.

(3) Nothing in this Article shall be deemed to impair the rights of creditors of the seller

(a) under the provisions of the Article on Secured Transactions (Article 9); or

(b) where identification to the contract or delivery is made not in current course of trade but in satisfaction of or as security for a pre-existing claim for money, security or the like and is made under circumstances which under any rule of law of the state where the goods are situated would apart from this Article constitute the transaction a fraudulent transfer or voidable preference.

§ 2–403. Power to Transfer; Good Faith Purchase of Goods; "Entrusting".

(1) A purchaser of goods acquires all title which his transferor had or had power to transfer except that a purchaser of a limited interest acquires rights only to the extent of the interest purchased. A person with voidable title has power to transfer a good title to a good faith purchaser for value. When goods have been delivered under a transaction of purchase the purchaser has such power even though

(a) the transferor was deceived as to the identity of the purchaser, or

(b) the delivery was in exchange for a check which is later dishonored, or

(c) it was agreed that the transaction was to be a "cash sale", or

(d) the delivery was procured through fraud punishable as larcenous under the criminal law.

(2) Any entrusting of possession of goods to a merchant who deals in goods of that kind gives him power to transfer all rights of the entruster to a buyer in ordinary course of business.

(3) "Entrusting" includes any delivery and any acquiescence in retention of possession regardless of any condition expressed between the parties to the delivery or acquiescence and regardless of whether the procurement of the entrusting or the possessor's disposition of the goods have been such as to be larcenous under the criminal law.

(4) The rights of other purchasers of goods and of lien creditors are governed by the Articles on Secured Transactions (Article 9), Bulk Transfers (Article 6) and Documents of Title (Article 7).

PART 5 Performance

§ 2–501. Insurable Interest in Goods; Manner of Identification of Goods.

(1) The buyer obtains a special property and an insurable interest in goods by identification of existing goods as goods to which the contract refers even though the goods so identified are nonconforming and he has an option to return or reject them. Such identification can be made at any time and in any manner explicitly agreed to by the parties. In the absence of explicit agreement identification occurs

(a) when the contract is made if it is for the sale of goods already existing and identified;

(b) if the contract is for the sale of future goods other than those described in paragraph (c), when goods are shipped, marked or otherwise designated by the seller as goods to which the contract refers;

(c) when the crops are planted or otherwise become growing crops or the young are conceived if the contract is for the sale of unborn young to be born within twelve months after contracting or for the sale of crops to be harvested within twelve months or the next normal harvest season after contracting whichever is longer.

(2) The seller retains an insurable interest in goods so long as title to or any security interest in the goods remains in him and where the identification is by the seller alone he may until default or insolvency or notification to the buyer that the identification is final substitute other goods for those identified.

(3) Nothing in this section impairs any insurable interest recognized under any other statute or rule of law.

§ 2–502. Buyer's Right to Goods on Seller's Insolvency.

(1) Subject to subsection (2) and even though the goods have not been shipped a buyer who has paid a part or all of the price of goods in which he has a special property under the provisions of the immediately preceding section may on making and keeping good a tender of any unpaid portion of their price recover them from the seller if the seller becomes insolvent within ten days after receipt of the first installment on their price.

(2) If the identification creating his special property has been made by the buyer he acquires the right to recover the goods only if they conform to the contract for sale.

§ 2–503. Manner of Seller's Tender of Delivery.

(1) Tender of delivery requires that the seller put and hold conforming goods at the buyer's disposition and give the buyer any notification reasonably necessary to enable him to take delivery. The manner, time and place for tender are determined by the agreement and this Article, and in particular

(a) tender must be at a reasonable hour, and if it is of goods they must be kept available for the period reasonably necessary to enable the buyer to take possession; but

(b) unless otherwise agreed the buyer must furnish facilities reasonably suited to the receipt of the goods.

(2) Where the case is within the next section respecting shipment tender requires that the seller comply with its provisions.

(3) Where the seller is required to deliver at a particular destination tender requires that he comply with subsection (1) and also in any appropriate case tender documents as described in subsections (4) and (5) of this section.

(4) Where goods are in the possession of a bailee and are to be delivered without being moved

(a) tender requires that the seller either tender a negotiable document of title covering such goods or procure acknowledgment by the bailee of the buyer's right to possession of the goods; but

(b) tender to the buyer of a non-negotiable document of title or of a written direction to the bailee to deliver is sufficient tender unless the buyer seasonably objects, and receipt by the bailee of notification of the buyer's rights fixes those rights as against the bailee and all third persons; but risk of loss of the goods and of any failure by the bailee to honor the non-negotiable document of title or to obey the direction remains on the seller until the buyer has had a reasonable time to present the document or direction, and a refusal by the bailee to honor the document or to obey the direction defeats the tender.

(5) Where the contract requires the seller to deliver documents

(a) he must tender all such documents in correct form, except as provided in this Article with respect to bills of lading in a set (subsection (2) of Section 2–323); and

(b) tender through customary banking channels is sufficient and dishonor of a draft accompanying the documents constitutes non-acceptance or rejection.

§ 2–504. Shipment by Seller.

Where the seller is required or authorized to send the goods to the buyer and the contract does not require him to deliver them at a particular destination, then unless otherwise agreed he must

(a) put the goods in the possession of such a carrier and make such a contract for their transportation as may be reasonable having regard to the nature of the goods and other circumstances of the case; and

(b) obtain and promptly deliver or tender in due form any document necessary to enable the buyer to obtain possession of the goods or otherwise required by the agreement or by usage of trade; and

(c) promptly notify the buyer of the shipment.

Failure to notify the buyer under paragraph (c) or to make a proper contract under paragraph (a) is a ground for rejection only if material delay or loss ensues.

§ 2–505. Seller's Shipment Under Reservation.

(1) Where the seller has identified goods to the contract by or before shipment:

(a) his procurement of a negotiable bill of lading to his own order or otherwise reserves in him a security interest in the goods. His procurement of the bill to the order of a financing agency or of the buyer indicates in addition only the seller's expectation of transferring that interest to the person named.

(b) a non-negotiable bill of lading to himself or his nominee reserves possession of the goods as security but except in a case of conditional delivery (subsection (2) of Section 2–507) a non-negotiable bill of lading naming the buyer as consignee reserves no security interest even though the seller retains possession of the bill of lading.

(2) When shipment by the seller with reservation of a security interest is in violation of the contract for sale it constitutes an improper contract for transportation within the preceding section but impairs neither the rights given to the buyer by shipment and identification of the goods to the contract nor the seller's powers as a holder of a negotiable document.

§ 2–506. Rights of Financing Agency.

(1) A financing agency by paying or purchasing for value a draft which relates to a shipment of goods acquires to the extent of the payment or purchase and in addition to its own rights under the draft and any document of title securing it any rights of the shipper in the goods including the right to stop delivery and the shipper's right to have the draft honored by the buyer.

(2) The right to reimbursement of a financing agency which has in good faith honored or purchased the draft under commitment to or authority from the buyer is not impaired by subsequent discovery of defects with reference to any relevant document which was apparently regular on its face.

§ 2–507. Effect of Seller's Tender; Delivery on Condition.

(1) Tender of delivery is a condition to the buyer's duty to accept the goods and, unless otherwise agreed, to his duty to pay for them. Tender entitles the seller to acceptance of the goods and to payment according to the contract.

(2) Where payment is due and demanded on the delivery to the buyer of goods or documents of title, his right as against the seller to retain or dispose of them is conditional upon his making the payment due.

§ 2–508. Cure by Seller of Improper Tender or Delivery; Replacement.

(1) Where any tender or delivery by the seller is rejected because non-conforming and the time for performance has not yet expired, the seller may seasonably notify the buyer of his intention to cure and may then within the contract time make a conforming delivery.

(2) Where the buyer rejects a non-conforming tender which the seller had reasonable grounds to believe would be acceptable with or without money allowance the seller may if he seasonably notifies the buyer have a further reasonable time to substitute a conforming tender.

§ 2–509. Risk of Loss in the Absence of Breach.

(1) Where the contract requires or authorizes the seller to ship the goods by carrier

(a) if it does not require him to deliver them at a particular destination, the risk of loss passes to the buyer when the goods are duly delivered to the carrier even though the shipment is under reservation (Section 2–505); but

(b) if it does require him to deliver them at a particular destination and the goods are there duly tendered while in the possession of the carrier, the risk of loss passes to the buyer when the goods are there duly so tendered as to enable the buyer to take delivery.

(2) Where the goods are held by a bailee to be delivered without being moved, the risk of loss passes to the buyer

(a) on his receipt of a negotiable document of title covering the goods; or

(b) on acknowledgment by the bailee of the buyer's right to possession of the goods; or

(c) after his receipt of a non-negotiable document of title or other written direction to deliver, as provided in subsection (4)(b) of Section 2–503.

(3) In any case not within subsection (1) or (2), the risk of loss passes to the buyer on his receipt of the goods if the seller is a merchant; otherwise, the risk passes to the buyer on tender of delivery.

(4) The provisions of this section are subject to contrary agreement of the parties and to the provisions of this Article on sale on approval (Section 2–327) and on effect of breach on risk of loss (Section 2–510).

§ 2–510. Effect of Breach on Risk of Loss.

(1) Where a tender or delivery of goods so fails to conform to the contract as to give a right of rejection the risk of their loss remains on the seller until cure or acceptance.

(2) Where the buyer rightfully revokes acceptance he may to the extent of any deficiency in his effective insurance coverage treat the risk of loss as having rested on the seller from the beginning.

(3) Where the buyer as to conforming goods already identified to the contract for sale repudiates or is otherwise in breach before risk of their loss has passed to him, the seller may to the extent of any deficiency in his effective insurance coverage treat the risk of loss as resting on the buyer for a commercially reasonable time.

§ 2–511. Tender of Payment by Buyer; Payment by Check.

(1) Unless otherwise agreed tender of payment is a condition to the seller's duty to tender and complete any delivery.

(2) Tender of payment is sufficient when made by any means or in any manner current in the ordinary course of business unless the seller demands payment in legal tender and gives any extension of time reasonably necessary to procure it.

(3) Subject to the provisions of this Act on the effect of an instrument on an obligation (Section 3–310), payment by check is conditional and is defeated as between the parties by dishonor of the check on due presentment.

§ 2–512. Payment by Buyer Before Inspection.

(1) Where the contract requires payment before inspection non-conformity of the goods does not excuse the buyer from so making payment unless

(a) the non-conformity appears without inspection; or

(b) despite tender of the required documents the circumstances would justify injunction against honor under the provisions of this Act (Section 5–114).

(2) Payment pursuant to subsection (1) does not constitute an acceptance of goods or impair the buyer's right to inspect or any of his remedies.

§ 2–513. Buyer's Right to Inspection of Goods.

(1) Unless otherwise agreed and subject to subsection (3), where goods are tendered or delivered or identified to the contract for sale, the buyer has a right before payment or acceptance to inspect them at any reasonable place and time and in any reasonable manner. When the seller is required or authorized to send the goods to the buyer, the inspection may be after their arrival.

(2) Expenses of inspection must be borne by the buyer but may be recovered from the seller if the goods do not conform and are rejected.

(3) Unless otherwise agreed and subject to the provisions of this Article on C.I.F. contracts (subsection (3) of Section 2–321), the buyer is not entitled to inspect the goods before payment of the price when the contract provides

(a) for delivery "C.O.D." or on other like terms; or

(b) for payment against documents of title, except where such payment is due only after the goods are to become available for inspection.

(4) A place or method of inspection fixed by the parties is presumed to be exclusive but unless otherwise expressly agreed it does not postpone identification or shift the place for delivery or for passing the risk of loss. If compliance becomes impossible, inspection shall be as provided in this section unless the place or method fixed was clearly intended as an indispensable condition failure of which avoids the contract.

§ 2–514. When Documents Deliverable on Acceptance; When on Payment.

Unless otherwise agreed documents against which a draft is drawn are to be delivered to the drawee on acceptance of the draft if it is payable more than three days after presentment; otherwise, only on payment.

§ 2–515. Preserving Evidence of Goods in Dispute.

In furtherance of the adjustment of any claim or dispute

(a) either party on reasonable notification to the other and for the purpose of ascertaining the facts and preserving evidence has the right to inspect, test and sample the goods including such of them as may be in the possession or control of the other; and

(b) the parties may agree to a third party inspection or survey to determine the conformity or condition of the goods and may agree that the findings shall be binding upon them in any subsequent litigation or adjustment.

PART 6 Breach, Repudiation and Excuse

§ 2–601. Buyer's Rights on Improper Delivery.

Subject to the provisions of this Article on breach in installment contracts (Section 2–612) and unless otherwise agreed under the sections on contractual limitations of remedy (Sections 2–718 and 2–719), if the goods or the tender of delivery fail in any respect to conform to the contract, the buyer may

(a) reject the whole; or

(b) accept the whole; or

(c) accept any commercial unit or units and reject the rest.

§ 2–602. Manner and Effect of Rightful Rejection.

(1) Rejection of goods must be within a reasonable time after their delivery or tender. It is ineffective unless the buyer seasonably notifies the seller.

(2) Subject to the provisions of the two following sections on rejected goods (Sections 2–603 and 2–604),

(a) after rejection any exercise of ownership by the buyer with respect to any commercial unit is wrongful as against the seller; and

(b) if the buyer has before rejection taken physical possession of goods in which he does not have a security interest under the provisions of this Article (subsection (3) of Section 2–711), he is under a duty after rejection to hold them with reasonable care at the seller's disposition for a time sufficient to permit the seller to remove them; but

(c) the buyer has no further obligations with regard to goods rightfully rejected.

(3) The seller's rights with respect to goods wrongfully rejected are governed by the provisions of this Article on seller's remedies in general (Section 2–703).

§ 2–603. Merchant Buyer's Duties as to Rightfully Rejected Goods.

(1) Subject to any security interest in the buyer (subsection (3) of Section 2–711), when the seller has no agent or place of business

at the market of rejection a merchant buyer is under a duty after rejection of goods in his possession or control to follow any reasonable instructions received from the seller with respect to the goods and in the absence of such instructions to make reasonable efforts to sell them for the seller's account if they are perishable or threaten to decline in value speedily. Instructions are not reasonable if on demand indemnity for expenses is not forthcoming.

(2) When the buyer sells goods under subsection (1), he is entitled to reimbursement from the seller or out of the proceeds for reasonable expenses of caring for and selling them, and if the expenses include no selling commission then to such commission as is usual in the trade or if there is none to a reasonable sum not exceeding ten per cent on the gross proceeds.

(3) In complying with this section the buyer is held only to good faith and good faith conduct hereunder is neither acceptance nor conversion nor the basis of an action for damages.

§ 2–604. Buyer's Options as to Salvage of Rightfully Rejected Goods.

Subject to the provisions of the immediately preceding section on perishables if the seller gives no instructions within a reasonable time after notification of rejection the buyer may store the rejected goods for the seller's account or reship them to him or resell them for the seller's account with reimbursement as provided in the preceding section. Such action is not acceptance or conversion.

§ 2–605. Waiver of Buyer's Objections by Failure to Particularize.

(1) The buyer's failure to state in connection with rejection a particular defect which is ascertainable by reasonable inspection precludes him from relying on the unstated defect to justify rejection or to establish breach

(a) where the seller could have cured it if stated seasonably; or

(b) between merchants when the seller has after rejection made a request in writing for a full and final written statement of all defects on which the buyer proposes to rely.

(2) Payment against documents made without reservation of rights precludes recovery of the payment for defects apparent on the face of the documents.

§ 2–606. What Constitutes Acceptance of Goods.

(1) Acceptance of goods occurs when the buyer

(a) after a reasonable opportunity to inspect the goods signifies to the seller that the goods are conforming or that he will take or retain them in spite of their nonconformity; or

(b) fails to make an effective rejection (subsection (1) of Section 2–602), but such acceptance does not occur until the buyer has had a reasonable opportunity to inspect them; or

(c) does any act inconsistent with the seller's ownership; but if such act is wrongful as against the seller it is an acceptance only if ratified by him.

(2) Acceptance of a part of any commercial unit is acceptance of that entire unit.

§ 2–607. Effect of Acceptance; Notice of Breach; Burden of Establishing Breach After Acceptance; Notice of Claim or Litigation to Person Answerable Over.

(1) The buyer must pay at the contract rate for any goods accepted.

(2) Acceptance of goods by the buyer precludes rejection of the goods accepted and if made with knowledge of a non-conformity cannot be revoked because of it unless the acceptance was on the reasonable assumption that the non-conformity would be seasonably cured but acceptance does not of itself impair any other remedy provided by this Article for non-conformity.

(3) Where a tender has been accepted

(a) the buyer must within a reasonable time after he discovers or should have discovered any breach notify the seller of breach or be barred from any remedy; and

(b) if the claim is one for infringement or the like (subsection (3) of Section 2–312) and the buyer is sued as a result of such a breach he must so notify the seller within a reasonable time after he receives notice of the litigation or be barred from any remedy over for liability established by the litigation.

(4) The burden is on the buyer to establish any breach with respect to the goods accepted.

(5) Where the buyer is sued for breach of a warranty or other obligation for which his seller is answerable over

(a) he may give his seller written notice of the litigation. If the notice states that the seller may come in and defend and that if the seller does not do so he will be bound in any action against him by his buyer by any determination of fact common to the two litigations, then unless the seller after seasonable receipt of the notice does come in and defend he is so bound.

(b) if the claim is one for infringement or the like (subsection (3) of Section 2–312) the original seller may demand in writing that his buyer turn over to him control of the litigation including settlement or else be barred from any remedy over and if he also agrees to bear all expense and to satisfy any adverse judgment, then unless the buyer after seasonable receipt of the demand does turn over control the buyer is so barred.

(6) The provisions of subsections (3), (4) and (5) apply to any obligation of a buyer to hold the seller harmless against infringement or the like (subsection (3) of Section 2–312).

§ 2–608. Revocation of Acceptance in Whole or in Part.

(1) The buyer may revoke his acceptance of a lot or commercial unit whose non-conformity substantially impairs its value to him if he has accepted it

(a) on the reasonable assumption that its non-conformity would be cured and it has not been seasonably cured; or

(b) without discovery of such non-conformity if his acceptance was reasonably induced either by the difficulty of discovery before acceptance or by the seller's assurances.

(2) Revocation of acceptance must occur within a reasonable time after the buyer discovers or should have discovered the ground for it and before any substantial change in condition of the goods which is not caused by their own defects. It is not effective until the buyer notifies the seller of it.

(3) A buyer who so revokes has the same rights and duties with regard to the goods involved as if he had rejected them.

§ 2–609. Right to Adequate Assurance of Performance.

(1) A contract for sale imposes an obligation on each party that the other's expectation of receiving due performance will not be impaired. When reasonable grounds for insecurity arise with respect to the performance of either party the other may in writing demand adequate assurance of due performance and until he receives such assurance may if commercially reasonable suspend any performance for which he has not already received the agreed return.

(2) Between merchants the reasonableness of grounds for insecurity and the adequacy of any assurance offered shall be determined according to commercial standards.

(3) Acceptance of any improper delivery or payment does not prejudice the aggrieved party's right to demand adequate assurance of future performance.

(4) After receipt of a justified demand failure to provide within a reasonable time not exceeding thirty days such assurance of due performance as is adequate under the circumstances of the particular case is a repudiation of the contract.

§ 2–610. Anticipatory Repudiation.

When either party repudiates the contract with respect to a performance not yet due the loss of which will substantially impair the value of the contract to the other, the aggrieved party may

(a) for a commercially reasonable time await performance by the repudiating party; or

(b) resort to any remedy for breach (Section 2–703 or Section 2–711), even though he has notified the repudiating party that he would await the latter's performance and has urged retraction; and

(c) in either case suspend his own performance or proceed in accordance with the provisions of this Article on the seller's right to identify goods to the contract notwithstanding breach or to salvage unfinished goods (Section 2–704).

§ 2–611. Retraction of Anticipatory Repudiation.

(1) Until the repudiating party's next performance is due he can retract his repudiation unless the aggrieved party has since the repudiation cancelled or materially changed his position or otherwise indicated that he considers the repudiation final.

(2) Retraction may be by any method which clearly indicates to the aggrieved party that the repudiating party intends to perform, but must include any assurance justifiably demanded under the provisions of this Article (Section 2–609).

(3) Retraction reinstates the repudiating party's rights under the contract with due excuse and allowance to the aggrieved party for any delay occasioned by the repudiation.

§ 2–612. "Installment Contract"; Breach.

(1) An "installment contract" is one which requires or authorizes the delivery of goods in separate lots to be separately accepted, even though the contract contains a clause "each delivery is a separate contract" or its equivalent.

(2) The buyer may reject any installment which is non-conforming if the non-conformity substantially impairs the value of that installment and cannot be cured or if the non-conformity is a defect in the required documents; but if the non-conformity does not fall within subsection (3) and the seller gives adequate assurance of its cure the buyer must accept that installment.

(3) Whenever non-conformity or default with respect to one or more installments substantially impairs the value of the whole contract there is a breach of the whole. But the aggrieved party reinstates the contract if he accepts a non-conforming installment without seasonably notifying of cancellation or if he brings an action with respect only to past installments or demands performance as to future installments.

§ 2–613. Casualty to Identified Goods.

Where the contract requires for its performance goods identified when the contract is made, and the goods suffer casualty without fault of either party before the risk of loss passes to the buyer, or in a proper case under a "no arrival, no sale" term (Section 2–324) then

(a) if the loss is total the contract is avoided; and

(b) if the loss is partial or the goods have so deteriorated as no longer to conform to the contract the buyer may nevertheless demand inspection and at his option either treat the contract as avoided or accept the goods with due allowance from the contract price for the deterioration or the deficiency in quantity but without further right against the seller.

§ 2–614. Substituted Performance.

(1) Where without fault of either party the agreed berthing, loading, or unloading facilities fail or an agreed type of carrier becomes unavailable or the agreed manner of delivery otherwise becomes commercially impracticable but a commercially reasonable substitute is available, such substitute performance must be tendered and accepted.

(2) If the agreed means or manner of payment fails because of domestic or foreign governmental regulation, the seller may withhold or stop delivery unless the buyer provides a means or manner of payment which is commercially a substantial equivalent. If delivery has already been taken, payment by the means or in the manner provided by the regulation discharges the buyer's obligation unless the regulation is discriminatory, oppressive or predatory.

§ 2–615. Excuse by Failure of Presupposed Conditions.

Except so far as a seller may have assumed a greater obligation and subject to the preceding section on substituted performance:

(a) Delay in delivery or non-delivery in whole or in part by a seller who complies with paragraphs (b) and (c) is not a breach of his duty under a contract for sale if performance as agreed has been made impracticable by the occurrence of a contingency the non-occurrence of which was a basic assumption on which the contract was made or by compliance in good faith with any applicable foreign or domestic governmental regulation or order whether or not it later proves to be invalid.

(b) Where the causes mentioned in paragraph (a) affect only a part of the seller's capacity to perform, he must allocate production and deliveries among his customers but may at his option include regular customers not then under contract as well as his own requirements for further manufacture. He may so allocate in any manner which is fair and reasonable.

(c) The seller must notify the buyer seasonably that there will be delay or non-delivery and, when allocation is required under paragraph (b), of the estimated quota thus made available for the buyer.

§ 2–616. Procedure on Notice Claiming Excuse.

(1) Where the buyer receives notification of a material or indefinite delay or an allocation justified under the preceding section he may by written notification to the seller as to any delivery concerned, and where the prospective deficiency substantially impairs the value of the whole contract under the provisions of this Article relating to breach of installment contracts (Section 2–612), then also as to the whole,

(a) terminate and thereby discharge any unexecuted portion of the contract; or

(b) modify the contract by agreeing to take his available quota in substitution.

(2) If after receipt of such notification from the seller the buyer fails so to modify the contract within a reasonable time not exceeding thirty days the contract lapses with respect to any deliveries affected.

(3) The provisions of this section may not be negated by agreement except in so far as the seller has assumed a greater obligation under the preceding section.

PART 7 Remedies

§ 2–701. Remedies for Breach of Collateral Contracts Not Impaired.

Remedies for breach of any obligation or promise collateral or ancillary to a contract for sale are not impaired by the provisions of this Article.

§ 2–702. Seller's Remedies on Discovery of Buyer's Insolvency.

(1) Where the seller discovers the buyer to be insolvent he may refuse delivery except for cash including payment for all goods theretofore delivered under the contract, and stop delivery under this Article (Section 2–705).

(2) Where the seller discovers that the buyer has received goods on credit while insolvent he may reclaim the goods upon demand made within ten days after the receipt, but if misrepresentation of solvency has been made to the particular seller in writing within three months before delivery the ten day limitation does not apply. Except as provided in this subsection the seller may not base a right to reclaim goods on the buyer's fraudulent or innocent misrepresentation of solvency or of intent to pay.

(3) The seller's right to reclaim under subsection (2) is subject to the rights of a buyer in ordinary course or other good faith purchaser under this Article (Section 2–403). Successful reclamation of goods excludes all other remedies with respect to them.

§ 2–703. Seller's Remedies in General.

Where the buyer wrongfully rejects or revokes acceptance of goods or fails to make a payment due on or before delivery or repudiates with respect to a part or the whole, then with respect to any goods directly affected and, if the breach is of the whole contract (Section 2–612), then also with respect to the whole undelivered balance, the aggrieved seller may

(a) withhold delivery of such goods;

(b) stop delivery by any bailee as hereafter provided (Section 2–705);

(c) proceed under the next section respecting goods still unidentified to the contract;

(d) resell and recover damages as hereafter provided (Section 2–706);

(e) recover damages for non-acceptance (Section 2–708) or in a proper case the price (Section 2–709);

(f) cancel.

§ 2–704. Seller's Right to Identify Goods to the Contract Notwithstanding Breach or to Salvage Unfinished Goods.

(1) An aggrieved seller under the preceding section may

(a) identify to the contract conforming goods not already identified if at the time he learned of the breach they are in his possession or control;

(b) treat as the subject of resale goods which have demonstrably been intended for the particular contract even though those goods are unfinished.

(2) Where the goods are unfinished an aggrieved seller may in the exercise of reasonable commercial judgment for the purposes of avoiding loss and of effective realization either complete the manufacture and wholly identify the goods to the contract or cease manufacture and resell for scrap or salvage value or proceed in any other reasonable manner.

§ 2–705. Seller's Stoppage of Delivery in Transit or Otherwise.

(1) The seller may stop delivery of goods in the possession of a carrier or other bailee when he discovers the buyer to be insolvent (Section 2–702) and may stop delivery of carload, truckload, planeload or larger shipments of express or freight when the buyer repudiates or fails to make a payment due before delivery or if for any other reason the seller has a right to withhold or reclaim the goods.

(2) As against such buyer the seller may stop delivery until

(a) receipt of the goods by the buyer; or

(b) acknowledgment to the buyer by any bailee of the goods except a carrier that the bailee holds the goods for the buyer; or

(c) such acknowledgment to the buyer by a carrier by reshipment or as warehouseman; or

(d) negotiation to the buyer of any negotiable document of title covering the goods.

(3)

(a) To stop delivery the seller must so notify as to enable the bailee by reasonable diligence to prevent delivery of the goods.

(b) After such notification the bailee must hold and deliver the goods according to the directions of the seller but the seller is liable to the bailee for any ensuing charges or damages.

(c) If a negotiable document of title has been issued for goods the bailee is not obliged to obey a notification to stop until surrender of the document.

(d) A carrier who has issued a non-negotiable bill of lading is not obliged to obey a notification to stop received from a person other than the consignor.

§ 2–706. Seller's Resale Including Contract for Resale.

(1) Under the conditions stated in Section 2–703 on seller's remedies, the seller may resell the goods concerned or the undelivered balance thereof. Where the resale is made in good faith and in a commercially reasonable manner the seller may recover the difference between the resale price and the contract price together with any incidental damages allowed under the provisions of this Article (Section 2–710), but less expenses saved in consequence of the buyer's breach.

(2) Except as otherwise provided in subsection (3) or unless otherwise agreed resale may be at public or private sale including sale by way of one or more contracts to sell or of identification to an existing contract of the seller. Sale may be as a unit or in parcels and at any time and place and on any terms but every aspect of the sale including the method, manner, time, place and terms must be commercially reasonable. The resale must be reasonably identified as referring to the broken contract, but it is not necessary that the goods be in existence or that any or all of them have been identified to the contract before the breach.

(3) Where the resale is at private sale the seller must give the buyer reasonable notification of his intention to resell.

(4) Where the resale is at public sale

(a) only identified goods can be sold except where there is a recognized market for a public sale of futures in goods of the kind; and

(b) it must be made at a usual place or market for public sale if one is reasonably available and except in the case of goods which are perishable or threaten to decline in value speedily the seller must give the buyer reasonable notice of the time and place of the resale; and

(c) if the goods are not to be within the view of those attending the sale the notification of sale must state the place where the goods are located and provide for their reasonable inspection by prospective bidders; and

(d) the seller may buy.

(5) A purchaser who buys in good faith at a resale takes the goods free of any rights of the original buyer even though the seller fails to comply with one or more of the requirements of this section.

(6) The seller is not accountable to the buyer for any profit made on any resale. A person in the position of a seller (Section 2–707) or a buyer who has rightfully rejected or justifiably revoked acceptance must account for any excess over the amount of his security interest, as hereinafter defined (subsection (3) of Section 2–711).

§ 2–707. "Person in the Position of a Seller".

(1) A "person in the position of a seller" includes as against a principal an agent who has paid or become responsible for the price of goods on behalf of his principal or anyone who otherwise holds a security interest or other right in goods similar to that of a seller.

(2) A person in the position of a seller may as provided in this Article withhold or stop delivery (Section 2–705) and resell (Section 2–706) and recover incidental damages (Section 2–710).

§ 2–708. Seller's Damages for Non-Acceptance or Repudiation.

(1) Subject to subsection (2) and to the provisions of this Article with respect to proof of market price (Section 2–723), the measure of damages for non-acceptance or repudiation by the buyer is the difference between the market price at the time and place for tender and the unpaid contract price together with any incidental damages provided in this Article (Section 2–710), but less expenses saved in consequence of the buyer's breach.

(2) If the measure of damages provided in subsection (1) is inadequate to put the seller in as good a position as performance would have done then the measure of damages is the profit (including reasonable overhead) which the seller would have made from full performance by the buyer, together with any incidental damages provided in this Article (Section 2–710), due allowance for costs reasonably incurred and due credit for payments or proceeds of resale.

§ 2–709. Action for the Price.

(1) When the buyer fails to pay the price as it becomes due the seller may recover, together with any incidental damages under the next section, the price

(a) of goods accepted or of conforming goods lost or damaged within a commercially reasonable time after risk of their loss has passed to the buyer; and

(b) of goods identified to the contract if the seller is unable after reasonable effort to resell them at a reasonable price or the circumstances reasonably indicate that such effort will be unavailing.

(2) Where the seller sues for the price he must hold for the buyer any goods which have been identified to the contract and are still in his control except that if resale becomes possible he may resell them at any time prior to the collection of the judgment. The net proceeds of any such resale must be credited to the buyer and payment of the judgment entitles him to any goods not resold.

(3) After the buyer has wrongfully rejected or revoked acceptance of the goods or has failed to make a payment due or has repudiated (Section 2–610), a seller who is held not entitled to the price under this section shall nevertheless be awarded damages for non-acceptance under the preceding section.

§ 2–710. Seller's Incidental Damages.

Incidental damages to an aggrieved seller include any commercially reasonable charges, expenses or commissions incurred in stopping delivery, in the transportation, care and custody of goods after the buyer's breach, in connection with return or resale of the goods or otherwise resulting from the breach.

§ 2–711. Buyer's Remedies in General; Buyer's Security Interest in Rejected Goods.

(1) Where the seller fails to make delivery or repudiates or the buyer rightfully rejects or justifiably revokes acceptance then with respect to any goods involved, and with respect to the whole if the breach goes to the whole contract (Section 2–612), the buyer may cancel and whether or not he has done so may in addition to recovering so much of the price as has been paid

(a) "cover" and have damages under the next section as to all the goods affected whether or not they have been identified to the contract; or

(b) recover damages for non-delivery as provided in this Article (Section 2–713).

(2) Where the seller fails to deliver or repudiates the buyer may also

(a) if the goods have been identified recover them as provided in this Article (Section 2–502); or

(b) in a proper case obtain specific performance or replevy the goods as provided in this Article (Section 2–716).

(3) On rightful rejection or justifiable revocation of acceptance a buyer has a security interest in goods in his possession or control for any payments made on their price and any expenses reasonably incurred in their inspection, receipt, transportation, care and custody and may hold such goods and resell them in like manner as an aggrieved seller (Section 2–706).

§ 2–712. "Cover"; Buyer's Procurement of Substitute Goods.

(1) After a breach within the preceding section the buyer may "cover" by making in good faith and without unreasonable delay any reasonable purchase of or contract to purchase goods in substitution for those due from the seller.

(2) The buyer may recover from the seller as damages the difference between the cost of cover and the contract price together with any incidental or consequential damages as hereinafter defined (Section 2–715), but less expenses saved in consequence of the seller's breach.

(3) Failure of the buyer to effect cover within this section does not bar him from any other remedy.

§ 2–713. Buyer's Damages for Non-Delivery or Repudiation.

(1) Subject to provisions of this Article with respect to the proof of market price (Section 2–723), the measure of damages for non-delivery or repudiation by the seller is the difference between the market price at the time when the buyer learned of the breach and the contract price together with any incidental and consequential damages provided in this Article (Section

2–715), but less expenses saved in consequence of the seller's breach.

(2) Market price is to be determined as of the place for tender or, in cases of rejection after arrival or revocation of acceptance, as of the place of arrival.

§ 2–714. Buyer's Damages for Breach in Regard to Accepted Goods.

(1) Where the buyer has accepted goods and given notification (subsection (3) of Section 2–607) he may recover as damages for any non-conformity of tender the loss resulting in the ordinary course of events from the seller's breach as determined in any manner which is reasonable.

(2) The measure of damages for breach of warranty is the difference at the time and place of acceptance between the value of the goods accepted and the value they would have had if they had been as warranted, unless special circumstances show proximate damages of a different amount.

(3) In a proper case any incidental and consequential damages under the next section may be recovered.

§ 2–715. Buyer's Incidental and Consequential Damages.

(1) Incidental damages resulting from the seller's breach include expenses reasonably incurred in inspection, receipt, transportation and care and custody of goods rightfully rejected, any commercially reasonable charges, expenses or commissions in connection with effecting cover and any other reasonable expense incident to the delay or other breach.

(2) Consequential damages resulting from the seller's breach include

(a) any loss resulting from general or particular requirements and needs of which the seller at the time of contracting had reason to know and which could not reasonably be prevented by cover or otherwise; and

(b) injury to person or property proximately resulting from any breach of warranty.

§ 2–716. Buyer's Right to Specific Performance or Replevin.

(1) Specific performance may be decreed where the goods are unique or in other proper circumstances.

(2) The decree for specific performance may include such terms and conditions as to payment of the price, damages, or other relief as the court may deem just.

(3) The buyer has a right of replevin for goods identified to the contract if after reasonable effort he is unable to effect cover for such goods or the circumstances reasonably indicate that such effort will be unavailing or if the goods have been shipped under reservation and satisfaction of the security interest in them has been made or tendered.

§ 2–717. Deduction of Damages From the Price.

The buyer on notifying the seller of his intention to do so may deduct all or any part of the damages resulting from any breach of the contract from any part of the price still due under the same contract.

§ 2–718. Liquidation or Limitation of Damages; Deposits

(1) Damages for breach by either party may be liquidated in the agreement but only at an amount which is reasonable in the light of the anticipated or actual harm caused by the breach, the difficulties of proof of loss, and the inconvenience or nonfeasibility of otherwise obtaining an adequate remedy. A term fixing unreasonably large liquidated damages is void as a penalty.

(2) Where the seller justifiably withholds delivery of goods because of the buyer's breach, the buyer is entitled to restitution of any amount by which the sum of his payments exceeds

(a) the amount to which the seller is entitled by virtue of terms liquidating the seller's damages in accordance with subsection (1), or

(b) in the absence of such terms, twenty per cent of the value of the total performance for which the buyer is obligated under the contract or $500, whichever is smaller.

(3) The buyer's right to restitution under subsection (2) is subject to offset to the extent that the seller establishes

(a) a right to recover damages under the provisions of this Article other than subsection (1), and

(b) the amount or value of any benefits received by the buyer directly or indirectly by reason of the contract.

(4) Where a seller has received payment in goods their reasonable value or the proceeds of their resale shall be treated as payments for the purposes of subsection (2); but if the seller has notice of the buyer's breach before reselling goods received in part performance, his resale is subject to the conditions laid down in this Article on resale by an aggrieved seller (Section 2–706).

§ 2–719. Contractual Modification or Limitation of Remedy.

(1) Subject to the provisions of subsection (2) and (3) of this section and of the preceding section on liquidation and limitation of damages,

(a) the agreement may provide for remedies in addition to or in substitution for those provided in this Article and may limit or alter the measure of damages recoverable under this Article, as by limiting the buyer's remedies to return of the goods and repayment of the price or to repair and replacement of non-conforming goods or parts; and

(b) resort to a remedy as provided is optional unless the remedy is expressly agreed to be exclusive, in which case it is the sole remedy.

(2) Where circumstances cause an exclusive or limited remedy to fail of its essential purpose, remedy may be had as provided in this Act.

(3) Consequential damages may be limited or excluded unless the limitation or exclusion is unconscionable. Limitation of consequential damages for injury to the person in the case of consumer goods is prima facie unconscionable but limitation of damages where the loss is commercial is not.

§ 2–720. Effect of "Cancellation" or "Rescission" on Claims for Antecedent Breach.

Unless the contrary intention clearly appears, expressions of "cancellation" or "rescission" of the contract or the like shall not be construed as a renunciation or discharge of any claim in damages for an antecedent breach.

§ 2–721. Remedies for Fraud.

Remedies for material misrepresentation or fraud include all remedies available under this Article for non-fraudulent breach. Neither rescission or a claim for rescission of the contract for sale nor rejection or return of the goods shall bar or be deemed inconsistent with a claim for damages or other remedy.

§ 2–722. Who Can Sue Third Parties for Injury to Goods.

Where a third party so deals with goods which have been identified to a contract for sale as to cause actionable injury to a party to that contract

(a) a right of action against the third party is in either party to the contract for sale who has title to or a security interest or a special property or an insurable interest in the goods; and if the goods have been destroyed or converted a right of action is also in the party who either bore the risk of loss under the contract for sale or has since the injury assumed that risk as against the other;

(b) if at the time of the injury the party plaintiff did not bear the risk of loss as against the other party to the contract for sale and there is no arrangement between them for disposition of the recovery, his suit or settlement is subject to his own interest, as a fiduciary for the other party to the contract;

(c) either party may with the consent of the other sue for the benefit of whom it may concern.

§ 2–723. Proof of Market Price: Time and Place.

(1) If an action based on anticipatory repudiation comes to trial before the time for performance with respect to some or all of the goods, any damages based on market price (Section 2–708 or Section 2–713) shall be determined according to the price of such goods prevailing at the time when the aggrieved party learned of the repudiation.

(2) If evidence of a price prevailing at the times or places described in this Article is not readily available the price prevailing within any reasonable time before or after the time described or at any other place which in commercial judgment or under usage of trade would serve as a reasonable substitute for the one described may be used, making any proper allowance for the cost of transporting the goods to or from such other place.

(3) Evidence of a relevant price prevailing at a time or place other than the one described in this Article offered by one party is not admissible unless and until he has given the other party such notice as the court finds sufficient to prevent unfair surprise.

§ 2–724. Admissibility of Market Quotations.

Whenever the prevailing price or value of any goods regularly bought and sold in any established commodity market is in issue, reports in official publications or trade journals or in newspapers or periodicals of general circulation published as the reports of such market shall be admissible in evidence. The circumstances of the preparation of such a report may be shown to affect its weight but not its admissibility.

§ 2–725. Statute of Limitations in Contracts for Sale.

(1) An action for breach of any contract for sale must be commenced within four years after the cause of action has accrued. By the original agreement the parties may reduce the period of limitation to not less than one year but may not extend it.

(2) A cause of action occurs when the breach occurs, regardless of the aggrieved party's lack of knowledge of the breach. A breach of warranty occurs when tender of delivery is made, except that where a warranty explicitly extends to future performance of the goods and discovery of the breach must await the time of such performance the cause of action accrues when the breach is or should have been discovered.

(3) Where an action commenced within the time limited by subsection (1) is so terminated as to leave available a remedy by another action for the same breach such other action may be commenced after the expiration of the time limited and within six months after the termination of the first action unless the termination resulted from voluntary discontinuance or from dismissal for failure or neglect to prosecute.

(4) This section does not alter the law on tolling of the statute of limitations nor does it apply to causes of action which have accrued before this Act becomes effective.

ARTICLE 2A

LEASES

PART 1 General Provisions

§ 2A–101. Short Title.

This Article shall be known and may be cited as the Uniform Commercial Code—Leases.

§ 2A–102. Scope.

This Article applies to any transaction, regardless of form, that creates a lease.

§ 2A–103. Definitions and Index of Definitions.

(1) In this Article unless the context otherwise requires:

(a) "Buyer in ordinary course of business" means a person who in good faith and without knowledge that the sale to him [or her] is in violation of the ownership rights or security interest or leasehold interest of a third party in the goods buys in ordinary course from a person in the business of selling goods of that kind but does not include a pawnbroker. "Buying" may be for cash or by exchange of other property or on secured or unsecured credit and includes receiving goods or documents of title under a pre-existing contract for sale but does not include a transfer in bulk or as security for or in total or partial satisfaction of a money debt.

(b) "Cancellation" occurs when either party puts an end to the lease contract for default by the other party.

(c) "Commercial unit" means such a unit of goods as by commercial usage is a single whole for purposes of lease and division of which materially impairs its character or value on the market or in use. A commercial unit may be a single article, as a machine, or a set of articles, as a suite of furniture or a line of machinery, or a quantity, as a gross or carload, or any other unit treated in use or in the relevant market as a single whole.

(d) "Conforming" goods or performance under a lease contract means goods or performance that are in accordance with the obligations under the lease contract.

(e) "Consumer lease" means a lease that a lessor regularly engaged in the business of leasing or selling makes to a lessee who is an individual and who takes under the lease primarily for a personal, family, or household purpose [, if the total payments to be made under the lease contract, excluding payments for options to renew or buy, do not exceed $].

(f) "Fault" means wrongful act, omission, breach, or default.

(g) "Finance lease" means a lease with respect to which:

(i) the lessor does not select, manufacture, or supply the goods;

(ii) the lessor acquires the goods or the right to possession and use of the goods in connection with the lease; and

(iii) one of the following occurs:

(A) the lessee receives a copy of the contract by which the lessor acquired the goods or the right to possession and use of the goods before signing the lease contract;

(B) the lessee's approval of the contract by which the lessor acquired the goods or the right to possession and use of the goods is a condition to effectiveness of the lease contract;

(C) the lessee, before signing the lease contract, receives an accurate and complete statement designating the promises and warranties, and any disclaimers of warranties, limitations or modifications of remedies, or liquidated damages, including those of a third party, such as the manufacturer of the goods, provided to the lessor by the person supplying the goods in connection with or as part of the contract by which the lessor acquired the goods or the right to possession and use of the goods; or

(D) if the lease is not a consumer lease, the lessor, before the lessee signs the lease contract, informs the lessee in writing (a) of the identity of the person supplying the goods to the lessor, unless the lessee has selected that person and directed the lessor to acquire the goods or the right to possession and use of the goods from that person, (b) that the lessee is entitled under this Article to the promises and warranties, including those of any third party, provided to the lessor by the person supplying the goods in connection with or as part of the contract by which the lessor acquired the goods or the right to possession and use of the goods, and (c) that the lessee may communicate with the person supplying the goods to the lessor and receive an accurate and complete statement of those promises and warranties, including any disclaimers and limitations of them or of remedies.

(h) "Goods" means all things that are movable at the time of identification to the lease contract, or are fixtures (Section 2A–309), but the term does not include money, documents, instruments, accounts, chattel paper, general intangibles, or minerals or the like, including oil and gas, before extraction. The term also includes the unborn young of animals.

(i) "Installment lease contract" means a lease contract that authorizes or requires the delivery of goods in separate lots to be separately accepted, even though the lease contract contains a clause "each delivery is a separate lease" or its equivalent.

(j) "Lease" means a transfer of the right to possession and use of goods for a term in return for consideration, but a sale, including a sale on approval or a sale or return, or retention or creation of a security interest is not a lease. Unless the context clearly indicates otherwise, the term includes a sublease.

(k) "Lease agreement" means the bargain, with respect to the lease, of the lessor and the lessee in fact as found in their language or by implication from other circumstances including course of dealing or usage of trade or course of performance as provided in this Article. Unless the context clearly indicates otherwise, the term includes a sublease agreement.

(l) "Lease contract" means the total legal obligation that results from the lease agreement as affected by this Article and any other applicable rules of law. Unless the context clearly indicates otherwise, the term includes a sublease contract.

(m) "Leasehold interest" means the interest of the lessor or the lessee under a lease contract.

(n) "Lessee" means a person who acquires the right to possession and use of goods under a lease. Unless the context clearly indicates otherwise, the term includes a sublessee.

(o) "Lessee in ordinary course of business" means a person who in good faith and without knowledge that the lease to him [or her] is in violation of the ownership rights or security interest or leasehold interest of a third party in the goods, leases in ordinary course from a person in the business of selling or leasing goods of that kind but does not include a pawnbroker. "Leasing" may be for cash or by exchange of other property or on secured or unsecured credit and includes receiving goods or documents of title under a pre-existing lease contract but does not include a transfer in bulk or as security for or in total or partial satisfaction of a money debt.

(p) "Lessor" means a person who transfers the right to possession and use of goods under a lease. Unless the context clearly indicates otherwise, the term includes a sublessor.

(q) "Lessor's residual interest" means the lessor's interest in the goods after expiration, termination, or cancellation of the lease contract.

(r) "Lien" means a charge against or interest in goods to secure payment of a debt or performance of an obligation, but the term does not include a security interest.

(s) "Lot" means a parcel or a single article that is the subject matter of a separate lease or delivery, whether or not it is sufficient to perform the lease contract.

(t) "Merchant lessee" means a lessee that is a merchant with respect to goods of the kind subject to the lease.

(u) "Present value" means the amount as of a date certain of one or more sums payable in the future, discounted to the date certain. The discount is determined by the interest rate specified by the parties if the rate was not manifestly unreasonable at the time the transaction was entered into; otherwise, the discount is determined by a commercially reasonable rate that takes into account the facts and circumstances of each case at the time the transaction was entered into.

(v) "Purchase" includes taking by sale, lease, mortgage, security interest, pledge, gift, or any other voluntary transaction creating an interest in goods.

(w) "Sublease" means a lease of goods the right to possession and use of which was acquired by the lessor as a lessee under an existing lease.

(x) "Supplier" means a person from whom a lessor buys or leases goods to be leased under a finance lease.

(y) "Supply contract" means a contract under which a lessor buys or leases goods to be leased.

(z) "Termination" occurs when either party pursuant to a power created by agreement or law puts an end to the lease contract otherwise than for default.

(2) Other definitions applying to this Article and the sections in which they appear are:

"Accessions". Section 2A–310(1).
"Construction mortgage". Section 2A–309(1)(d).
"Encumbrance". Section 2A–309(1)(e).
"Fixtures". Section 2A–309(1)(a).
"Fixture filing". Section 2A–309(1)(b).
"Purchase money lease". Section 2A–309(1)(c).

(3) The following definitions in other Articles apply to this Article:

"Account". Section 9–106.
"Between merchants". Section 2–104(3).
"Buyer". Section 2–103(1)(a).
"Chattel paper". Section 9–105(1)(b).
"Consumer goods". Section 9–109(1).
"Document". Section 9–105(1)(f).
"Entrusting". Section 2–403(3).
"General intangibles". Section 9–106.
"Good faith". Section 2–103(1)(b).
"Instrument". Section 9–105(1)(i).
"Merchant". Section 2–104(1).
"Mortgage". Sect 9–105(1)(j).
"Pursuant to commitment". Section 9–105(1)(k).
"Receipt". Section 2–103(1)(c).
"Sale". Section 2–106(1).

"Sale on approval". Section 2–326.
"Sale or return". Section 2–326.
"Seller". Section 2–103(1)(d).

(4) In addition Article 1 contains general definitions and principles of construction and interpretation applicable throughout this Article.

As amended in 1990.

§ 2A–104. Leases Subject to Other Law.

(1) A lease, although subject to this Article, is also subject to any applicable:

(a) certificate of title statute of this State: (list any certificate of title statutes covering automobiles, trailers, mobile homes, boats, farm tractors, and the like);

(b) certificate of title statute of another jurisdiction (Section 2A–105); or

(c) consumer protection statute of this State, or final consumer protection decision of a court of this State existing on the effective date of this Article.

(2) In case of conflict between this Article, other than Sections 2A–105, 2A–304(3), and 2A–305(3), and a statute or decision referred to in subsection (1), the statute or decision controls.

(3) Failure to comply with an applicable law has only the effect specified therein.

As amended in 1990.

§ 2A–105. Territorial Application of Article to Goods Covered by Certificate of Title.

Subject to the provisions of Sections 2A–304(3) and 2A–305(3), with respect to goods covered by a certificate of title issued under a statute of this State or of another jurisdiction, compliance and the effect of compliance or noncompliance with a certificate of title statute are governed by the law (including the conflict of laws rules) of the jurisdiction issuing the certificate until the earlier of (a) surrender of the certificate, or (b) four months after the goods are removed from that jurisdiction and thereafter until a new certificate of title is issued by another jurisdiction.

§ 2A–106. Limitation on Power of Parties to Consumer Lease to Choose Applicable Law and Judicial Forum.

(1) If the law chosen by the parties to a consumer lease is that of a jurisdiction other than a jurisdiction in which the lessee resides at the time the lease agreement becomes enforceable or within 30 days thereafter or in which the goods are to be used, the choice is not enforceable.

(2) If the judicial forum chosen by the parties to a consumer lease is a forum that would not otherwise have jurisdiction over the lessee, the choice is not enforceable.

§ 2A–107. Waiver or Renunciation of Claim or Right After Default.

Any claim or right arising out of an alleged default or breach of warranty may be discharged in whole or in part without consideration by a written waiver or renunciation signed and delivered by the aggrieved party.

§ 2A–108. Unconscionability.

(1) If the court as a matter of law finds a lease contract or any clause of a lease contract to have been unconscionable at the time it was made the court may refuse to enforce the lease contract, or it may enforce the remainder of the lease contract without the unconscionable clause, or it may so limit the application of any unconscionable clause as to avoid any unconscionable result.

(2) With respect to a consumer lease, if the court as a matter of law finds that a lease contract or any clause of a lease contract has been induced by unconscionable conduct or that unconscionable conduct has occurred in the collection of a claim arising from a lease contract, the court may grant appropriate relief.

(3) Before making a finding of unconscionability under subsection (1) or (2), the court, on its own motion or that of a party, shall afford the parties a reasonable opportunity to present evidence as to the setting, purpose, and effect of the lease contract or clause thereof, or of the conduct.

(4) In an action in which the lessee claims unconscionability with respect to a consumer lease:

(a) If the court finds unconscionability under subsection (1) or (2), the court shall award reasonable attorney's fees to the lessee.

(b) If the court does not find unconscionability and the lessee claiming unconscionability has brought or maintained an action he [or she] knew to be groundless, the court shall award reasonable attorney's fees to the party against whom the claim is made.

(c) In determining attorney's fees, the amount of the recovery on behalf of the claimant under subsections (1) and (2) is not controlling.

§ 2A–109. Option to Accelerate at Will.

(1) A term providing that one party or his [or her] successor in interest may accelerate payment or performance or require collateral or additional collateral "at will" or "when he [or she] deems himself [or herself] insecure" or in words of similar import must be construed to mean that he [or she] has power to do so only if he [or she] in good faith believes that the prospect of payment or performance is impaired.

(2) With respect to a consumer lease, the burden of establishing good faith under subsection (1) is on the party who exercised the power; otherwise the burden of establishing lack of good faith is on the party against whom the power has been exercised.

PART 2 Formation and Construction of Lease Contract

§ 2A–201. Statute of Frauds.

(1) A lease contract is not enforceable by way of action or defense unless:

(a) the total payments to be made under the lease contract, excluding payments for options to renew or buy, are less than $1,000; or

(b) there is a writing, signed by the party against whom enforcement is sought or by that party's authorized agent, sufficient to indicate that a lease contract has been made between the parties and to describe the goods leased and the lease term.

(2) Any description of leased goods or of the lease term is sufficient and satisfies subsection (1)(b), whether or not it is specific, if it reasonably identifies what is described.

(3) A writing is not insufficient because it omits or incorrectly states a term agreed upon, but the lease contract is not enforceable under subsection (1)(b) beyond the lease term and the quantity of goods shown in the writing.

(4) A lease contract that does not satisfy the requirements of subsection (1), but which is valid in other respects, is enforceable:

(a) if the goods are to be specially manufactured or obtained for the lessee and are not suitable for lease or sale to others in the ordinary course of the lessor's business, and the lessor, before notice of repudiation is received and under circumstances that reasonably indicate that the goods are for the lessee, has made either a substantial beginning of their manufacture or commitments for their procurement;

(b) if the party against whom enforcement is sought admits in that party's pleading, testimony or otherwise in court that a lease contract was made, but the lease contract is not enforceable under this provision beyond the quantity of goods admitted; or

(c) with respect to goods that have been received and accepted by the lessee.

(5) The lease term under a lease contract referred to in subsection (4) is:

(a) if there is a writing signed by the party against whom enforcement is sought or by that party's authorized agent specifying the lease term, the term so specified;

(b) if the party against whom enforcement is sought admits in that party's pleading, testimony, or otherwise in court a lease term, the term so admitted; or

(c) a reasonable lease term.

§ 2A–202. Final Written Expression: Parol or Extrinsic Evidence.

Terms with respect to which the confirmatory memoranda of the parties agree or which are otherwise set forth in a writing intended by the parties as a final expression of their agreement with respect to such terms as are included therein may not be contradicted by evidence of any prior agreement or of a contemporaneous oral agreement but may be explained or supplemented:

(a) by course of dealing or usage of trade or by course of performance; and

(b) by evidence of consistent additional terms unless the court finds the writing to have been intended also as a complete and exclusive statement of the terms of the agreement.

§ 2A–203. Seals Inoperative.

The affixing of a seal to a writing evidencing a lease contract or an offer to enter into a lease contract does not render the writing a sealed instrument and the law with respect to sealed instruments does not apply to the lease contract or offer.

§ 2A–204. Formation in General.

(1) A lease contract may be made in any manner sufficient to show agreement, including conduct by both parties which recognizes the existence of a lease contract.

(2) An agreement sufficient to constitute a lease contract may be found although the moment of its making is undetermined.

(3) Although one or more terms are left open, a lease contract does not fail for indefiniteness if the parties have intended to make a lease contract and there is a reasonably certain basis for giving an appropriate remedy.

§ 2A–205. Firm Offers.

An offer by a merchant to lease goods to or from another person in a signed writing that by its terms gives assurance it will be held open is not revocable, for lack of consideration, during the time stated or, if no time is stated, for a reasonable time, but in no event may the period of irrevocability exceed 3 months. Any such term of assurance on a form supplied by the offeree must be separately signed by the offeror.

§ 2A–206. Offer and Acceptance in Formation of Lease Contract.

(1) Unless otherwise unambiguously indicated by the language or circumstances, an offer to make a lease contract must be construed as inviting acceptance in any manner and by any medium reasonable in the circumstances.

(2) If the beginning of a requested performance is a reasonable mode of acceptance, an offeror who is not notified of acceptance within a reasonable time may treat the offer as having lapsed before acceptance.

§ 2A–207. Course of Performance or Practical Construction.

(1) If a lease contract involves repeated occasions for performance by either party with knowledge of the nature of the performance and opportunity for objection to it by the other, any course of performance accepted or acquiesced in without objection is relevant to determine the meaning of the lease agreement.

(2) The express terms of a lease agreement and any course of performance, as well as any course of dealing and usage of trade, must be construed whenever reasonable as consistent with each other; but if that construction is unreasonable, express terms control course of performance, course of performance controls both course of dealing and usage of trade, and course of dealing controls usage of trade.

(3) Subject to the provisions of Section 2A–208 on modification and waiver, course of performance is relevant to show a waiver or modification of any term inconsistent with the course of performance.

§ 2A–208. Modification, Rescission and Waiver.

(1) An agreement modifying a lease contract needs no consideration to be binding.

(2) A signed lease agreement that excludes modification or rescission except by a signed writing may not be otherwise modified or rescinded, but, except as between merchants, such a requirement on a form supplied by a merchant must be separately signed by the other party.

(3) Although an attempt at modification or rescission does not satisfy the requirements of subsection (2), it may operate as a waiver.

(4) A party who has made a waiver affecting an executory portion of a lease contract may retract the waiver by reasonable notification received by the other party that strict performance will be required of any term waived, unless the retraction would be unjust in view of a material change of position in reliance on the waiver.

§ 2A–209. Lessee Under Finance Lease as Beneficiary of Supply Contract.

(1) The benefit of a supplier's promises to the lessor under the supply contract and of all warranties, whether express or implied, including those of any third party provided in connection with or as part of the supply contract, extends to the lessee to the extent of the lessee's leasehold interest under a finance lease related to the supply contract, but is subject to the terms of the warranty and of the supply contract and all defenses or claims arising therefrom.

(2) The extension of the benefit of a supplier's promises and of warranties to the lessee (Section 2A–209(1)) does not: (i) modify the rights and obligations of the parties to the supply contract, whether arising therefrom or otherwise, or (ii) impose any duty or liability under the supply contract on the lessee.

(3) Any modification or rescission of the supply contract by the supplier and the lessor is effective between the supplier and the lessee unless, before the modification or rescission, the supplier has received notice that the lessee has entered into a finance lease related to the supply contract. If the modification or rescission is effective between the supplier and the lessee, the lessor is deemed to have assumed, in addition to the obligations of the lessor to the lessee under the lease contract, promises of the supplier to the lessor and warranties that were so modified or rescinded as they existed and were available to the lessee before modification or rescission.

(4) In addition to the extension of the benefit of the supplier's promises and of warranties to the lessee under subsection (1), the lessee retains all rights that the lessee may have against the supplier which arise from an agreement between the lessee and the supplier or under other law.

As amended in 1990.

§ 2A–210. Express Warranties.

(1) Express warranties by the lessor are created as follows:

(a) Any affirmation of fact or promise made by the lessor to the lessee which relates to the goods and becomes part of the basis of the bargain creates an express warranty that the goods will conform to the affirmation or promise.

(b) Any description of the goods which is made part of the basis of the bargain creates an express warranty that the goods will conform to the description.

(c) Any sample or model that is made part of the basis of the bargain creates an express warranty that the whole of the goods will conform to the sample or model.

(2) It is not necessary to the creation of an express warranty that the lessor use formal words, such as "warrant" or "guarantee," or that the lessor have a specific intention to make a warranty, but an affirmation merely of the value of the goods or a statement purporting to be merely the lessor's opinion or commendation of the goods does not create a warranty.

§ 2A–211. Warranties Against Interference and Against Infringement; Lessee's Obligation Against Infringement.

(1) There is in a lease contract a warranty that for the lease term no person holds a claim to or interest in the goods that arose from an act or omission of the lessor, other than a claim by way of infringement or the like, which will interfere with the lessee's enjoyment of its leasehold interest.

(2) Except in a finance lease there is in a lease contract by a lessor who is a merchant regularly dealing in goods of the kind a warranty that the goods are delivered free of the rightful claim of any person by way of infringement or the like.

(3) A lessee who furnishes specifications to a lessor or a supplier shall hold the lessor and the supplier harmless against any claim by way of infringement or the like that arises out of compliance with the specifications.

§ 2A–212. Implied Warranty of Merchantability.

(1) Except in a finance lease, a warranty that the goods will be merchantable is implied in a lease contract if the lessor is a merchant with respect to goods of that kind.

(2) Goods to be merchantable must be at least such as

(a) pass without objection in the trade under the description in the lease agreement;

(b) in the case of fungible goods, are of fair average quality within the description;

(c) are fit for the ordinary purposes for which goods of that type are used;

(d) run, within the variation permitted by the lease agreement, of even kind, quality, and quantity within each unit and among all units involved;

(e) are adequately contained, packaged, and labeled as the lease agreement may require; and

(f) conform to any promises or affirmations of fact made on the container or label.

(3) Other implied warranties may arise from course of dealing or usage of trade.

§ 2A–213. Implied Warranty of Fitness for Particular Purpose.

Except in a finance lease, if the lessor at the time the lease contract is made has reason to know of any particular purpose for which the goods are required and that the lessee is relying on the lessor's skill or judgment to select or furnish suitable goods, there is in the lease contract an implied warranty that the goods will be fit for that purpose.

§ 2A–214. Exclusion or Modification of Warranties.

(1) Words or conduct relevant to the creation of an express warranty and words or conduct tending to negate or limit a warranty must be construed wherever reasonable as consistent with each other; but, subject to the provisions of Section 2A–202 on parol or extrinsic evidence, negation or limitation is inoperative to the extent that the construction is unreasonable.

(2) Subject to subsection (3), to exclude or modify the implied warranty of merchantability or any part of it the language must mention "merchantability", be by a writing, and be conspicuous. Subject to subsection (3), to exclude or modify any implied warranty of fitness the exclusion must be by a writing and be conspicuous. Language to exclude all implied warranties of fitness is sufficient if it is in writing, is conspicuous and states, for example, "There is no warranty that the goods will be fit for a particular purpose".

(3) Notwithstanding subsection (2), but subject to subsection (4),

(a) unless the circumstances indicate otherwise, all implied warranties are excluded by expressions like "as is," or "with all faults," or by other language that in common understanding calls the lessee's attention to the exclusion of warranties and makes plain that there is no implied warranty, if in writing and conspicuous;

(b) if the lessee before entering into the lease contract has examined the goods or the sample or model as fully as desired or has refused to examine the goods, there is no implied warranty with regard to defects that an examination ought in the circumstances to have revealed; and

(c) an implied warranty may also be excluded or modified by course of dealing, course of performance, or usage of trade.

(4) To exclude or modify a warranty against interference or against infringement (Section 2A–211) or any part of it, the language must be specific, be by a writing, and be conspicuous, unless the circumstances, including course of performance, course of dealing, or usage of trade, give the lessee reason to know that the goods are being leased subject to a claim or interest of any person.

§ 2A–215. Cumulation and Conflict of Warranties Express or Implied.

Warranties, whether express or implied, must be construed as consistent with each other and as cumulative, but if that construction is unreasonable, the intention of the parties determines which warranty is dominant. In ascertaining that intention the following rules apply:

(a) Exact or technical specifications displace an inconsistent sample or model or general language of description.

(b) A sample from an existing bulk displaces inconsistent general language of description.

(c) Express warranties displace inconsistent implied warranties other than an implied warranty of fitness for a particular purpose.

§ 2A–216. Third-Party Beneficiaries of Express and Implied Warranties.

Alternative A A warranty to or for the benefit of a lessee under this Article, whether express or implied, extends to any natural person who is in the family or household of the lessee or who is a guest in the lessee's home if it is reasonable to expect that such person may use, consume, or be affected by the goods and who is injured in person by breach of the warranty. This section does not displace principles of law and equity that extend a warranty to or for the benefit of a lessee to other persons. The operation of this section may not be excluded, modified, or limited, but an exclusion, modification, or limitation of the warranty, including any with respect to rights and remedies, effective against the lessee is also effective against any beneficiary designated under this section.

Alternative B A warranty to or for the benefit of a lessee under this Article, whether express or implied, extends to any natural person who may reasonably be expected to use, consume, or be affected by the goods and who is injured in person by breach of the warranty. This section does not displace principles of law and equity that extend a warranty to or for the benefit of a lessee to other persons. The operation of this section may not be excluded, modified, or limited, but an exclusion, modification, or limitation of the warranty, including any with respect to rights and remedies, effective against the lessee is also effective against the beneficiary designated under this section.

Alternative C A warranty to or for the benefit of a lessee under this Article, whether express or implied, extends to any person who may reasonably be expected to use, consume, or be affected by the goods and who is injured by breach of the warranty. The operation of this section may not be excluded, modified, or limited with respect to injury to the person of an individual to whom the warranty extends, but an exclusion, modification, or limitation of the warranty, including any with respect to rights and remedies, effective against the lessee is also effective against the beneficiary designated under this section.

§ 2A–217. Identification.

Identification of goods as goods to which a lease contract refers may be made at any time and in any manner explicitly agreed to by the parties. In the absence of explicit agreement, identification occurs:

(a) when the lease contract is made if the lease contract is for a lease of goods that are existing and identified;

(b) when the goods are shipped, marked, or otherwise designated by the lessor as goods to which the lease contract refers, if the lease contract is for a lease of goods that are not existing and identified; or

(c) when the young are conceived, if the lease contract is for a lease of unborn young of animals.

§ 2A–218. Insurance and Proceeds.

(1) A lessee obtains an insurable interest when existing goods are identified to the lease contract even though the goods identified are nonconforming and the lessee has an option to reject them.

(2) If a lessee has an insurable interest only by reason of the lessor's identification of the goods, the lessor, until default or insolvency or notification to the lessee that identification is final, may substitute other goods for those identified.

(3) Notwithstanding a lessee's insurable interest under subsections (1) and (2), the lessor retains an insurable interest until an option to buy has been exercised by the lessee and risk of loss has passed to the lessee.

(4) Nothing in this section impairs any insurable interest recognized under any other statute or rule of law.

(5) The parties by agreement may determine that one or more parties have an obligation to obtain and pay for insurance covering the goods and by agreement may determine the beneficiary of the proceeds of the insurance.

§ 2A–219. Risk of Loss.

(1) Except in the case of a finance lease, risk of loss is retained by the lessor and does not pass to the lessee. In the case of a finance lease, risk of loss passes to the lessee.

(2) Subject to the provisions of this Article on the effect of default on risk of loss (Section 2A–220), if risk of loss is to pass to the lessee and the time of passage is not stated, the following rules apply:

(a) If the lease contract requires or authorizes the goods to be shipped by carrier

(i) and it does not require delivery at a particular destination, the risk of loss passes to the lessee when the goods are duly delivered to the carrier; but

(ii) if it does require delivery at a particular destination and the goods are there duly tendered while in the possession of the carrier, the risk of loss passes to the lessee when the goods are there duly so tendered as to enable the lessee to take delivery.

(b) If the goods are held by a bailee to be delivered without being moved, the risk of loss passes to the lessee on acknowledgment by the bailee of the lessee's right to possession of the goods.

(c) In any case not within subsection (a) or (b), the risk of loss passes to the lessee on the lessee's receipt of the goods if the lessor, or, in the case of a finance lease, the supplier, is a merchant; otherwise the risk passes to the lessee on tender of delivery.

§ 2A–220. Effect of Default on Risk of Loss.

(1) Where risk of loss is to pass to the lessee and the time of passage is not stated:

(a) If a tender or delivery of goods so fails to conform to the lease contract as to give a right of rejection, the risk of their loss remains with the lessor, or, in the case of a finance lease, the supplier, until cure or acceptance.

(b) If the lessee rightfully revokes acceptance, he [or she], to the extent of any deficiency in his [or her] effective insurance coverage, may treat the risk of loss as having remained with the lessor from the beginning.

(2) Whether or not risk of loss is to pass to the lessee, if the lessee as to conforming goods already identified to a lease contract repudiates or is otherwise in default under the lease contract, the lessor, or, in the case of a finance lease, the supplier, to the

extent of any deficiency in his [or her] effective insurance coverage may treat the risk of loss as resting on the lessee for a commercially reasonable time.

§ 2A–221. Casualty to Identified Goods.

If a lease contract requires goods identified when the lease contract is made, and the goods suffer casualty without fault of the lessee, the lessor or the supplier before delivery, or the goods suffer casualty before risk of loss passes to the lessee pursuant to the lease agreement or Section 2A–219, then:

(a) if the loss is total, the lease contract is avoided; and

(b) if the loss is partial or the goods have so deteriorated as to no longer conform to the lease contract, the lessee may nevertheless demand inspection and at his [or her] option either treat the lease contract as avoided or, except in a finance lease that is not a consumer lease, accept the goods with due allowance from the rent payable for the balance of the lease term for the deterioration or the deficiency in quantity but without further right against the lessor.

PART 3 Effect of Lease Contract

§ 2A–301. Enforceability of Lease Contract.

Except as otherwise provided in this Article, a lease contract is effective and enforceable according to its terms between the parties, against purchasers of the goods and against creditors of the parties.

§ 2A–302. Title to and Possession of Goods.

Except as otherwise provided in this Article, each provision of this Article applies whether the lessor or a third party has title to the goods, and whether the lessor, the lessee, or a third party has possession of the goods, notwithstanding any statute or rule of law that possession or the absence of possession is fraudulent.

§ 2A–303. Alienability of Party's Interest Under Lease Contract or of Lessor's Residual Interest in Goods; Delegation of Performance; Transfer of Rights.

(1) As used in this section, "creation of a security interest" includes the sale of a lease contract that is subject to Article 9, Secured Transactions, by reason of Section 9–102(1)(b).

(2) Except as provided in subsections (3) and (4), a provision in a lease agreement which (i) prohibits the voluntary or involuntary transfer, including a transfer by sale, sublease, creation or enforcement of a security interest, or attachment, levy, or other judicial process, of an interest of a party under the lease contract or of the lessor's residual interest in the goods, or (ii) makes such a transfer an event of default, gives rise to the rights and remedies provided in subsection (5), but a transfer that is prohibited or is an event of default under the lease agreement is otherwise effective.

(3) A provision in a lease agreement which (i) prohibits the creation or enforcement of a security interest in an interest of a party under the lease contract or in the lessor's residual interest in the goods, or (ii) makes such a transfer an event of default, is not enforceable unless, and then only to the extent that, there is an actual transfer by the lessee of the lessee's right of possession or use of the goods in violation of the provision or an actual delegation of a material performance of either party to the lease contract in violation of the provision. Neither the granting nor the enforcement of a security interest in (i) the lessor's interest under the lease contract or (ii) the lessor's residual interest in the goods is a transfer that materially impairs the prospect of obtaining return performance by, materially changes the duty of, or materially increases the burden or risk imposed on, the lessee within the purview of subsection (5) unless, and then only to the extent that, there is an actual delegation of a material performance of the lessor.

(4) A provision in a lease agreement which (i) prohibits a transfer of a right to damages for default with respect to the whole lease contract or of a right to payment arising out of the transferor's due performance of the transferor's entire obligation, or (ii) makes such a transfer an event of default, is not enforceable, and such a transfer is not a transfer that materially impairs the prospect of obtaining return performance by, materially changes the duty of, or materially increases the burden or risk imposed on, the other party to the lease contract within the purview of subsection (5).

(5) Subject to subsections (3) and (4):

(a) if a transfer is made which is made an event of default under a lease agreement, the party to the lease contract not making the transfer, unless that party waives the default or otherwise agrees, has the rights and remedies described in Section 2A–501(2);

(b) if paragraph (a) is not applicable and if a transfer is made that (i) is prohibited under a lease agreement or (ii) materially impairs the prospect of obtaining return performance by, materially changes the duty of, or materially increases the burden or risk imposed on, the other party to the lease contract, unless the party not making the transfer agrees at any time to the transfer in the lease contract or otherwise, then, except as limited by contract, (i) the transferor is liable to the party not making the transfer for damages caused by the transfer to the extent that the damages could not reasonably be prevented by the party not making the transfer and (ii) a court having jurisdiction may grant other appropriate relief, including cancellation of the lease contract or an injunction against the transfer.

(6) A transfer of "the lease" or of "all my rights under the lease", or a transfer in similar general terms, is a transfer of rights and, unless the language or the circumstances, as in a transfer for security, indicate the contrary, the transfer is a delegation of duties by the transferor to the transferee. Acceptance by the transferee constitutes a promise by the transferee to perform those duties. The promise is enforceable by either the transferor or the other party to the lease contract.

(7) Unless otherwise agreed by the lessor and the lessee, a delegation of performance does not relieve the transferor as against the other party of any duty to perform or of any liability for default.

(8) In a consumer lease, to prohibit the transfer of an interest of a party under the lease contract or to make a transfer an event of default, the language must be specific, by a writing, and conspicuous.

As amended in 1990.

§ 2A–304. Subsequent Lease of Goods by Lessor.

(1) Subject to Section 2A–303, a subsequent lessee from a lessor of goods under an existing lease contract obtains, to the extent of the leasehold interest transferred, the leasehold interest in the goods that the lessor had or had power to transfer, and except as provided in subsection (2) and Section 2A–527(4), takes subject to the existing lease contract. A lessor with voidable title has power to transfer a good leasehold interest to a good faith subse-

quent lessee for value, but only to the extent set forth in the preceding sentence. If goods have been delivered under a transaction of purchase, the lessor has that power even though:

(a) the lessor's transferor was deceived as to the identity of the lessor;

(b) the delivery was in exchange for a check which is later dishonored;

(c) it was agreed that the transaction was to be a "cash sale"; or

(d) the delivery was procured through fraud punishable as larcenous under the criminal law.

(2) A subsequent lessee in the ordinary course of business from a lessor who is a merchant dealing in goods of that kind to whom the goods were entrusted by the existing lessee of that lessor before the interest of the subsequent lessee became enforceable against that lessor obtains, to the extent of the leasehold interest transferred, all of that lessor's and the existing lessee's rights to the goods, and takes free of the existing lease contract.

(3) A subsequent lessee from the lessor of goods that are subject to an existing lease contract and are covered by a certificate of title issued under a statute of this State or of another jurisdiction takes no greater rights than those provided both by this section and by the certificate of title statute.

As amended in 1990.

§ 2A–305. Sale or Sublease of Goods by Lessee.

(1) Subject to the provisions of Section 2A–303, a buyer or sublessee from the lessee of goods under an existing lease contract obtains, to the extent of the interest transferred, the leasehold interest in the goods that the lessee had or had power to transfer, and except as provided in subsection (2) and Section 2A–511(4), takes subject to the existing lease contract. A lessee with a voidable leasehold interest has power to transfer a good leasehold interest to a good faith buyer for value or a good faith sublessee for value, but only to the extent set forth in the preceding sentence. When goods have been delivered under a transaction of lease the lessee has that power even though:

(a) the lessor was deceived as to the identity of the lessee;

(b) the delivery was in exchange for a check which is later dishonored; or

(c) the delivery was procured through fraud punishable as larcenous under the criminal law.

(2) A buyer in the ordinary course of business or a sublessee in the ordinary course of business from a lessee who is a merchant dealing in goods of that kind to whom the goods were entrusted by the lessor obtains, to the extent of the interest transferred, all of the lessor's and lessee's rights to the goods, and takes free of the existing lease contract.

(3) A buyer or sublessee from the lessee of goods that are subject to an existing lease contract and are covered by a certificate of title issued under a statute of this State or of another jurisdiction takes no greater rights than those provided both by this section and by the certificate of title statute.

§ 2A–306. Priority of Certain Liens Arising by Operation of Law.

If a person in the ordinary course of his [or her] business furnishes services or materials with respect to goods subject to a lease contract, a lien upon those goods in the possession of that person given by statute or rule of law for those materials or services takes priority over any interest of the lessor or lessee under the lease contract or this Article unless the lien is created by statute and the statute provides otherwise or unless the lien is created by rule of law and the rule of law provides otherwise.

§ 2A–307. Priority of Liens Arising by Attachment or Levy on, Security Interests in, and Other Claims to Goods.

(1) Except as otherwise provided in Section 2A–306, a creditor of a lessee takes subject to the lease contract.

(2) Except as otherwise provided in subsections (3) and (4) and in Sections 2A–306 and 2A–308, a creditor of a lessor takes subject to the lease contract unless:

(a) the creditor holds a lien that attached to the goods before the lease contract became enforceable;

(b) the creditor holds a security interest in the goods and the lessee did not give value and receive delivery of the goods without knowledge of the security interest; or

(c) the creditor holds a security interest in the goods which was perfected (Section 9–303) before the lease contract became enforceable.

(3) A lessee in the ordinary course of business takes the leasehold interest free of a security interest in the goods created by the lessor even though the security interest is perfected (Section 9–303) and the lessee knows of its existence.

(4) A lessee other than a lessee in the ordinary course of business takes the leasehold interest free of a security interest to the extent that it secures future advances made after the secured party acquires knowledge of the lease or more than 45 days after the lease contract becomes enforceable, whichever first occurs, unless the future advances are made pursuant to a commitment entered into without knowledge of the lease and before the expiration of the 45-day period.

As amended in 1990.

§ 2A–308. Special Rights of Creditors.

(1) A creditor of a lessor in possession of goods subject to a lease contract may treat the lease contract as void if as against the creditor retention of possession by the lessor is fraudulent under any statute or rule of law, but retention of possession in good faith and current course of trade by the lessor for a commercially reasonable time after the lease contract becomes enforceable is not fraudulent.

(2) Nothing in this Article impairs the rights of creditors of a lessor if the lease contract (a) becomes enforceable, not in current course of trade but in satisfaction of or as security for a pre-existing claim for money, security, or the like, and (b) is made under circumstances which under any statute or rule of law apart from this Article would constitute the transaction a fraudulent transfer or voidable preference.

(3) A creditor of a seller may treat a sale or an identification of goods to a contract for sale as void if as against the creditor retention of possession by the seller is fraudulent under any statute or rule of law, but retention of possession of the goods pursuant to a lease contract entered into by the seller as lessee and the buyer as lessor in connection with the sale or identification of the goods is not fraudulent if the buyer bought for value and in good faith.

§ 2A–309. Lessor's and Lessee's Rights When Goods Become Fixtures.

(1) In this section:

(a) goods are "fixtures" when they become so related to particular real estate that an interest in them arises under real estate law;

(b) a "fixture filing" is the filing, in the office where a mortgage on the real estate would be filed or recorded, of a financing statement covering goods that are or are to become fixtures and conforming to the requirements of Section 9–402(5);

(c) a lease is a "purchase money lease" unless the lessee has possession or use of the goods or the right to possession or use of the goods before the lease agreement is enforceable;

(d) a mortgage is a "construction mortgage" to the extent it secures an obligation incurred for the construction of an improvement on land including the acquisition cost of the land, if the recorded writing so indicates; and

(e) "encumbrance" includes real estate mortgages and other liens on real estate and all other rights in real estate that are not ownership interests.

(2) Under this Article a lease may be of goods that are fixtures or may continue in goods that become fixtures, but no lease exists under this Article of ordinary building materials incorporated into an improvement on land.

(3) This Article does not prevent creation of a lease of fixtures pursuant to real estate law.

(4) The perfected interest of a lessor of fixtures has priority over a conflicting interest of an encumbrancer or owner of the real estate if:

(a) the lease is a purchase money lease, the conflicting interest of the encumbrancer or owner arises before the goods become fixtures, the interest of the lessor is perfected by a fixture filing before the goods become fixtures or within ten days thereafter, and the lessee has an interest of record in the real estate or is in possession of the real estate; or

(b) the interest of the lessor is perfected by a fixture filing before the interest of the encumbrancer or owner is of record, the lessor's interest has priority over any conflicting interest of a predecessor in title of the encumbrancer or owner, and the lessee has an interest of record in the real estate or is in possession of the real estate.

(5) The interest of a lessor of fixtures, whether or not perfected, has priority over the conflicting interest of an encumbrancer or owner of the real estate if:

(a) the fixtures are readily removable factory or office machines, readily removable equipment that is not primarily used or leased for use in the operation of the real estate, or readily removable replacements of domestic appliances that are goods subject to a consumer lease, and before the goods become fixtures the lease contract is enforceable; or

(b) the conflicting interest is a lien on the real estate obtained by legal or equitable proceedings after the lease contract is enforceable; or

(c) the encumbrancer or owner has consented in writing to the lease or has disclaimed an interest in the goods as fixtures; or

(d) the lessee has a right to remove the goods as against the encumbrancer or owner. If the lessee's right to remove terminates, the priority of the interest of the lessor continues for a reasonable time.

(6) Notwithstanding subsection (4)(a) but otherwise subject to subsections (4) and (5), the interest of a lessor of fixtures, including the lessor's residual interest, is subordinate to the conflicting interest of an encumbrancer of the real estate under a construction mortgage recorded before the goods become fixtures if the goods become fixtures before the completion of the construction. To the extent given to refinance a construction mortgage, the conflicting interest of an encumbrancer of the real estate under a mortgage has this priority to the same extent as the encumbrancer of the real estate under the construction mortgage.

(7) In cases not within the preceding subsections, priority between the interest of a lessor of fixtures, including the lessor's residual interest, and the conflicting interest of an encumbrancer or owner of the real estate who is not the lessee is determined by the priority rules governing conflicting interests in real estate.

(8) If the interest of a lessor of fixtures, including the lessor's residual interest, has priority over all conflicting interests of all owners and encumbrancers of the real estate, the lessor or the lessee may (i) on default, expiration, termination, or cancellation of the lease agreement but subject to the agreement and this Article, or (ii) if necessary to enforce other rights and remedies of the lessor or lessee under this Article, remove the goods from the real estate, free and clear of all conflicting interests of all owners and encumbrancers of the real estate, but the lessor or lessee must reimburse any encumbrancer or owner of the real estate who is not the lessee and who has not otherwise agreed for the cost of repair of any physical injury, but not for any diminution in value of the real estate caused by the absence of the goods removed or by any necessity of replacing them. A person entitled to reimbursement may refuse permission to remove until the party seeking removal gives adequate security for the performance of this obligation.

(9) Even though the lease agreement does not create a security interest, the interest of a lessor of fixtures, including the lessor's residual interest, is perfected by filing a financing statement as a fixture filing for leased goods that are or are to become fixtures in accordance with the relevant provisions of the Article on Secured Transactions (Article 9).

As amended in 1990.

§ 2A–310. Lessor's and Lessee's Rights When Goods Become Accessions.

(1) Goods are "accessions" when they are installed in or affixed to other goods.

(2) The interest of a lessor or a lessee under a lease contract entered into before the goods became accessions is superior to all interests in the whole except as stated in subsection (4).

(3) The interest of a lessor or a lessee under a lease contract entered into at the time or after the goods became accessions is superior to all subsequently acquired interests in the whole except as stated in subsection (4) but is subordinate to interests in the whole existing at the time the lease contract was made unless the holders of such interests in the whole have in writing consented to the lease or disclaimed an interest in the goods as part of the whole.

(4) The interest of a lessor or a lessee under a lease contract described in subsection (2) or (3) is subordinate to the interest of

(a) a buyer in the ordinary course of business or a lessee in the ordinary course of business of any interest in the whole acquired after the goods became accessions; or

(b) a creditor with a security interest in the whole perfected before the lease contract was made to the extent that the creditor makes subsequent advances without knowledge of the lease contract.

(5) When under subsections (2) or (3) and (4) a lessor or a lessee of accessions holds an interest that is superior to all interests in

the whole, the lessor or the lessee may (a) on default, expiration, termination, or cancellation of the lease contract by the other party but subject to the provisions of the lease contract and this Article, or (b) if necessary to enforce his [or her] other rights and remedies under this Article, remove the goods from the whole, free and clear of all interests in the whole, but he [or she] must reimburse any holder of an interest in the whole who is not the lessee and who has not otherwise agreed for the cost of repair of any physical injury but not for any diminution in value of the whole caused by the absence of the goods removed or by any necessity for replacing them. A person entitled to reimbursement may refuse permission to remove until the party seeking removal gives adequate security for the performance of this obligation.

§ 2A–311. Priority Subject to Subordination.

Nothing in this Article prevents subordination by agreement by any person entitled to priority.

As added in 1990.

PART 4 Performance of Lease Contract: Repudiated, Substituted and Excused

§ 2A–401. Insecurity: Adequate Assurance of Performance.

(1) A lease contract imposes an obligation on each party that the other's expectation of receiving due performance will not be impaired.

(2) If reasonable grounds for insecurity arise with respect to the performance of either party, the insecure party may demand in writing adequate assurance of due performance. Until the insecure party receives that assurance, if commercially reasonable the insecure party may suspend any performance for which he [or she] has not already received the agreed return.

(3) A repudiation of the lease contract occurs if assurance of due performance adequate under the circumstances of the particular case is not provided to the insecure party within a reasonable time, not to exceed 30 days after receipt of a demand by the other party.

(4) Between merchants, the reasonableness of grounds for insecurity and the adequacy of any assurance offered must be determined according to commercial standards.

(5) Acceptance of any nonconforming delivery or payment does not prejudice the aggrieved party's right to demand adequate assurance of future performance.

§ 2A–402. Anticipatory Repudiation.

If either party repudiates a lease contract with respect to a performance not yet due under the lease contract, the loss of which performance will substantially impair the value of the lease contract to the other, the aggrieved party may:

(a) for a commercially reasonable time, await retraction of repudiation and performance by the repudiating party;

(b) make demand pursuant to Section 2A–401 and await assurance of future performance adequate under the circumstances of the particular case; or

(c) resort to any right or remedy upon default under the lease contract or this Article, even though the aggrieved party has notified the repudiating party that the aggrieved party would await the repudiating party's performance and assurance and has urged retraction. In addition, whether or not the aggrieved party is pursuing one of the foregoing remedies, the aggrieved party may suspend performance or, if the aggrieved party is the lessor, proceed in accordance with the provisions of this Article on the lessor's right to identify goods to the lease contract notwithstanding default or to salvage unfinished goods (Section 2A–524).

§ 2A–403. Retraction of Anticipatory Repudiation.

(1) Until the repudiating party's next performance is due, the repudiating party can retract the repudiation unless, since the repudiation, the aggrieved party has cancelled the lease contract or materially changed the aggrieved party's position or otherwise indicated that the aggrieved party considers the repudiation final.

(2) Retraction may be by any method that clearly indicates to the aggrieved party that the repudiating party intends to perform under the lease contract and includes any assurance demanded under Section 2A–401.

(3) Retraction reinstates a repudiating party's rights under a lease contract with due excuse and allowance to the aggrieved party for any delay occasioned by the repudiation.

§ 2A–404. Substituted Performance.

(1) If without fault of the lessee, the lessor and the supplier, the agreed berthing, loading, or unloading facilities fail or the agreed type of carrier becomes unavailable or the agreed manner of delivery otherwise becomes commercially impracticable, but a commercially reasonable substitute is available, the substitute performance must be tendered and accepted.

(2) If the agreed means or manner of payment fails because of domestic or foreign governmental regulation:

(a) the lessor may withhold or stop delivery or cause the supplier to withhold or stop delivery unless the lessee provides a means or manner of payment that is commercially a substantial equivalent; and

(b) if delivery has already been taken, payment by the means or in the manner provided by the regulation discharges the lessee's obligation unless the regulation is discriminatory, oppressive, or predatory.

§ 2A–405. Excused Performance.

Subject to Section 2A–404 on substituted performance, the following rules apply:

(a) Delay in delivery or nondelivery in whole or in part by a lessor or a supplier who complies with paragraphs (b) and (c) is not a default under the lease contract if performance as agreed has been made impracticable by the occurrence of a contingency the nonoccurrence of which was a basic assumption on which the lease contract was made or by compliance in good faith with any applicable foreign or domestic governmental regulation or order, whether or not the regulation or order later proves to be invalid.

(b) If the causes mentioned in paragraph (a) affect only part of the lessor's or the supplier's capacity to perform, he [or she] shall allocate production and deliveries among his [or her] customers but at his [or her] option may include regular customers not then under contract for sale or lease as well as his [or her] own requirements for further manufacture. He [or she] may so allocate in any manner that is fair and reasonable.

(c) The lessor seasonably shall notify the lessee and in the case of a finance lease the supplier seasonably shall notify the lessor and the lessee, if known, that there will be delay or nondelivery and, if allocation is required under paragraph (b), of the estimated quota thus made available for the lessee.

§ 2A–406. Procedure on Excused Performance.

(1) If the lessee receives notification of a material or indefinite delay or an allocation justified under Section 2A–405, the lessee may by written notification to the lessor as to any goods involved, and with respect to all of the goods if under an installment lease contract the value of the whole lease contract is substantially impaired (Section 2A–510):

(a) terminate the lease contract (Section 2A–505(2)); or

(b) except in a finance lease that is not a consumer lease, modify the lease contract by accepting the available quota in substitution, with due allowance from the rent payable for the balance of the lease term for the deficiency but without further right against the lessor.

(2) If, after receipt of a notification from the lessor under Section 2A–405, the lessee fails so to modify the lease agreement within a reasonable time not exceeding 30 days, the lease contract lapses with respect to any deliveries affected.

§ 2A–407. Irrevocable Promises: Finance Leases.

(1) In the case of a finance lease that is not a consumer lease the lessee's promises under the lease contract become irrevocable and independent upon the lessee's acceptance of the goods.

(2) A promise that has become irrevocable and independent under subsection (1):

(a) is effective and enforceable between the parties, and by or against third parties including assignees of the parties; and

(b) is not subject to cancellation, termination, modification, repudiation, excuse, or substitution without the consent of the party to whom the promise runs.

(3) This section does not affect the validity under any other law of a covenant in any lease contract making the lessee's promises irrevocable and independent upon the lessee's acceptance of the goods.

As amended in 1990.

PART 5 Default

A. In General

§ 2A–501. Default: Procedure.

(1) Whether the lessor or the lessee is in default under a lease contract is determined by the lease agreement and this Article.

(2) If the lessor or the lessee is in default under the lease contract, the party seeking enforcement has rights and remedies as provided in this Article and, except as limited by this Article, as provided in the lease agreement.

(3) If the lessor or the lessee is in default under the lease contract, the party seeking enforcement may reduce the party's claim to judgment, or otherwise enforce the lease contract by self-help or any available judicial procedure or nonjudicial procedure, including administrative proceeding, arbitration, or the like, in accordance with this Article.

(4) Except as otherwise provided in Section 1–106(1) or this Article or the lease agreement, the rights and remedies referred to in subsections (2) and (3) are cumulative.

(5) If the lease agreement covers both real property and goods, the party seeking enforcement may proceed under this Part as to the goods, or under other applicable law as to both the real property and the goods in accordance with that party's rights and remedies in respect of the real property, in which case this Part does not apply.

As amended in 1990.

§ 2A–502. Notice After Default.

Except as otherwise provided in this Article or the lease agreement, the lessor or lessee in default under the lease contract is not entitled to notice of default or notice of enforcement from the other party to the lease agreement.

§ 2A–503. Modification or Impairment of Rights and Remedies.

(1) Except as otherwise provided in this Article, the lease agreement may include rights and remedies for default in addition to or in substitution for those provided in this Article and may limit or alter the measure of damages recoverable under this Article.

(2) Resort to a remedy provided under this Article or in the lease agreement is optional unless the remedy is expressly agreed to be exclusive. If circumstances cause an exclusive or limited remedy to fail of its essential purpose, or provision for an exclusive remedy is unconscionable, remedy may be had as provided in this Article.

(3) Consequential damages may be liquidated under Section 2A–504, or may otherwise be limited, altered, or excluded unless the limitation, alteration, or exclusion is unconscionable. Limitation, alteration, or exclusion of consequential damages for injury to the person in the case of consumer goods is prima facie unconscionable but limitation, alteration, or exclusion of damages where the loss is commercial is not prima facie unconscionable.

(4) Rights and remedies on default by the lessor or the lessee with respect to any obligation or promise collateral or ancillary to the lease contract are not impaired by this Article.

As amended in 1990.

§ 2A–504. Liquidation of Damages.

(1) Damages payable by either party for default, or any other act or omission, including indemnity for loss or diminution of anticipated tax benefits or loss or damage to lessor's residual interest, may be liquidated in the lease agreement but only at an amount or by a formula that is reasonable in light of the then anticipated harm caused by the default or other act or omission.

(2) If the lease agreement provides for liquidation of damages, and such provision does not comply with subsection (1), or such provision is an exclusive or limited remedy that circumstances cause to fail of its essential purpose, remedy may be had as provided in this Article.

(3) If the lessor justifiably withholds or stops delivery of goods because of the lessee's default or insolvency (Section 2A–525 or 2A–526), the lessee is entitled to restitution of any amount by which the sum of his [or her] payments exceeds:

(a) the amount to which the lessor is entitled by virtue of terms liquidating the lessor's damages in accordance with subsection (1); or

(b) in the absence of those terms, 20 percent of the then present value of the total rent the lessee was obligated to pay for the balance of the lease term, or, in the case of a consumer lease, the lesser of such amount or $500.

(4) A lessee's right to restitution under subsection (3) is subject to offset to the extent the lessor establishes:

(a) a right to recover damages under the provisions of this Article other than subsection (1); and

(b) the amount or value of any benefits received by the lessee directly or indirectly by reason of the lease contract.

§ 2A–505. Cancellation and Termination and Effect of Cancellation, Termination, Rescission, or Fraud on Rights and Remedies.

(1) On cancellation of the lease contract, all obligations that are still executory on both sides are discharged, but any right based on prior default or performance survives, and the cancelling party also retains any remedy for default of the whole lease contract or any unperformed balance.

(2) On termination of the lease contract, all obligations that are still executory on both sides are discharged but any right based on prior default or performance survives.

(3) Unless the contrary intention clearly appears, expressions of "cancellation," "rescission," or the like of the lease contract may not be construed as a renunciation or discharge of any claim in damages for an antecedent default.

(4) Rights and remedies for material misrepresentation or fraud include all rights and remedies available under this Article for default.

(5) Neither rescission nor a claim for rescission of the lease contract nor rejection or return of the goods may bar or be deemed inconsistent with a claim for damages or other right or remedy.

§ 2A–506. Statute of Limitations.

(1) An action for default under a lease contract, including breach of warranty or indemnity, must be commenced within 4 years after the cause of action accrued. By the original lease contract the parties may reduce the period of limitation to not less than one year.

(2) A cause of action for default accrues when the act or omission on which the default or breach of warranty is based is or should have been discovered by the aggrieved party, or when the default occurs, whichever is later. A cause of action for indemnity accrues when the act or omission on which the claim for indemnity is based is or should have been discovered by the indemnified party, whichever is later.

(3) If an action commenced within the time limited by subsection (1) is so terminated as to leave available a remedy by another action for the same default or breach of warranty or indemnity, the other action may be commenced after the expiration of the time limited and within 6 months after the termination of the first action unless the termination resulted from voluntary discontinuance or from dismissal for failure or neglect to prosecute.

(4) This section does not alter the law on tolling of the statute of limitations nor does it apply to causes of action that have accrued before this Article becomes effective.

§ 2A–507. Proof of Market Rent: Time and Place.

(1) Damages based on market rent (Section 2A–519 or 2A–528) are determined according to the rent for the use of the goods concerned for a lease term identical to the remaining lease term of the original lease agreement and prevailing at the times specified in Sections 2A–519 and 2A–528.

(2) If evidence of rent for the use of the goods concerned for a lease term identical to the remaining lease term of the original lease agreement and prevailing at the times or places described in this Article is not readily available, the rent prevailing within any reasonable time before or after the time described or at any other place or for a different lease term which in commercial judgment or under usage of trade would serve as a reasonable substitute for the one described may be used, making any proper allowance for the difference, including the cost of transporting the goods to or from the other place.

(3) Evidence of a relevant rent prevailing at a time or place or for a lease term other than the one described in this Article offered by one party is not admissible unless and until he [or she] has given the other party notice the court finds sufficient to prevent unfair surprise.

(4) If the prevailing rent or value of any goods regularly leased in any established market is in issue, reports in official publications or trade journals or in newspapers or periodicals of general circulation published as the reports of that market are admissible in evidence. The circumstances of the preparation of the report may be shown to affect its weight but not its admissibility.

As amended in 1990.

B. Default by Lessor

§ 2A–508. Lessee's Remedies.

(1) If a lessor fails to deliver the goods in conformity to the lease contract (Section 2A–509) or repudiates the lease contract (Section 2A–402), or a lessee rightfully rejects the goods (Section 2A–509) or justifiably revokes acceptance of the goods (Section 2A–517), then with respect to any goods involved, and with respect to all of the goods if under an installment lease contract the value of the whole lease contract is substantially impaired (Section 2A–510), the lessor is in default under the lease contract and the lessee may:

(a) cancel the lease contract (Section 2A–505(1));

(b) recover so much of the rent and security as has been paid and is just under the circumstances;

(c) cover and recover damages as to all goods affected whether or not they have been identified to the lease contract (Sections 2A–518 and 2A–520), or recover damages for nondelivery (Sections 2A–519 and 2A–520);

(d) exercise any other rights or pursue any other remedies provided in the lease contract.

(2) If a lessor fails to deliver the goods in conformity to the lease contract or repudiates the lease contract, the lessee may also:

(a) if the goods have been identified, recover them (Section 2A–522); or

(b) in a proper case, obtain specific performance or replevy the goods (Section 2A–521).

(3) If a lessor is otherwise in default under a lease contract, the lessee may exercise the rights and pursue the remedies provided in the lease contract, which may include a right to cancel the lease, and in Section 2A–519(3).

(4) If a lessor has breached a warranty, whether express or implied, the lessee may recover damages (Section 2A–519(4)).

(5) On rightful rejection or justifiable revocation of acceptance, a lessee has a security interest in goods in the lessee's possession or control for any rent and security that has been paid and any expenses reasonably incurred in their inspection, receipt, transportation, and care and custody and may hold those goods and dispose of them in good faith and in a commercially reasonable manner, subject to Section 2A–527(5).

(6) Subject to the provisions of Section 2A–407, a lessee, on notifying the lessor of the lessee's intention to do so, may deduct all or any part of the damages resulting from any default under the lease contract from any part of the rent still due under the same lease contract.

As amended in 1990.

§ 2A–509. Lessee's Rights on Improper Delivery; Rightful Rejection.

(1) Subject to the provisions of Section 2A–510 on default in installment lease contracts, if the goods or the tender or delivery fail in any respect to conform to the lease contract, the lessee may reject or accept the goods or accept any commercial unit or units and reject the rest of the goods.

(2) Rejection of goods is ineffective unless it is within a reasonable time after tender or delivery of the goods and the lessee seasonably notifies the lessor.

§ 2A–510. Installment Lease Contracts: Rejection and Default.

(1) Under an installment lease contract a lessee may reject any delivery that is nonconforming if the nonconformity substantially impairs the value of that delivery and cannot be cured or the nonconformity is a defect in the required documents; but if the nonconformity does not fall within subsection (2) and the lessor or the supplier gives adequate assurance of its cure, the lessee must accept that delivery.

(2) Whenever nonconformity or default with respect to one or more deliveries substantially impairs the value of the installment lease contract as a whole there is a default with respect to the whole. But, the aggrieved party reinstates the installment lease contract as a whole if the aggrieved party accepts a nonconforming delivery without seasonably notifying of cancellation or brings an action with respect only to past deliveries or demands performance as to future deliveries.

§ 2A–511. Merchant Lessee's Duties as to Rightfully Rejected Goods.

(1) Subject to any security interest of a lessee (Section 2A–508(5)), if a lessor or a supplier has no agent or place of business at the market of rejection, a merchant lessee, after rejection of goods in his [or her] possession or control, shall follow any reasonable instructions received from the lessor or the supplier with respect to the goods. In the absence of those instructions, a merchant lessee shall make reasonable efforts to sell, lease, or otherwise dispose of the goods for the lessor's account if they threaten to decline in value speedily. Instructions are not reasonable if on demand indemnity for expenses is not forthcoming.

(2) If a merchant lessee (subsection (1)) or any other lessee (Section 2A–512) disposes of goods, he [or she] is entitled to reimbursement either from the lessor or the supplier or out of the proceeds for reasonable expenses of caring for and disposing of the goods and, if the expenses include no disposition commission, to such commission as is usual in the trade, or if there is none, to a reasonable sum not exceeding 10 percent of the gross proceeds.

(3) In complying with this section or Section 2A–512, the lessee is held only to good faith. Good faith conduct hereunder is neither acceptance or conversion nor the basis of an action for damages.

(4) A purchaser who purchases in good faith from a lessee pursuant to this section or Section 2A–512 takes the goods free of any rights of the lessor and the supplier even though the lessee fails to comply with one or more of the requirements of this Article.

§ 2A–512. Lessee's Duties as to Rightfully Rejected Goods.

(1) Except as otherwise provided with respect to goods that threaten to decline in value speedily (Section 2A–511) and subject to any security interest of a lessee (Section 2A–508(5)):

(a) the lessee, after rejection of goods in the lessee's possession, shall hold them with reasonable care at the lessor's or the supplier's disposition for a reasonable time after the lessee's seasonable notification of rejection;

(b) if the lessor or the supplier gives no instructions within a reasonable time after notification of rejection, the lessee may store the rejected goods for the lessor's or the supplier's account or ship them to the lessor or the supplier or dispose of them for the lessor's or the supplier's account with reimbursement in the manner provided in Section 2A–511; but

(c) the lessee has no further obligations with regard to goods rightfully rejected.

(2) Action by the lessee pursuant to subsection (1) is not acceptance or conversion.

§ 2A–513. Cure by Lessor of Improper Tender or Delivery; Replacement.

(1) If any tender or delivery by the lessor or the supplier is rejected because nonconforming and the time for performance has not yet expired, the lessor or the supplier may seasonably notify the lessee of the lessor's or the supplier's intention to cure and may then make a conforming delivery within the time provided in the lease contract.

(2) If the lessee rejects a nonconforming tender that the lessor or the supplier had reasonable grounds to believe would be acceptable with or without money allowance, the lessor or the supplier may have a further reasonable time to substitute a conforming tender if he [or she] seasonably notifies the lessee.

§ 2A–514. Waiver of Lessee's Objections.

(1) In rejecting goods, a lessee's failure to state a particular defect that is ascertainable by reasonable inspection precludes the lessee from relying on the defect to justify rejection or to establish default:

(a) if, stated seasonably, the lessor or the supplier could have cured it (Section 2A–513); or

(b) between merchants if the lessor or the supplier after rejection has made a request in writing for a full and final written statement of all defects on which the lessee proposes to rely.

(2) A lessee's failure to reserve rights when paying rent or other consideration against documents precludes recovery of the payment for defects apparent on the face of the documents.

§ 2A–515. Acceptance of Goods.

(1) Acceptance of goods occurs after the lessee has had a reasonable opportunity to inspect the goods and

(a) the lessee signifies or acts with respect to the goods in a manner that signifies to the lessor or the supplier that the goods are conforming or that the lessee will take or retain them in spite of their nonconformity; or

(b) the lessee fails to make an effective rejection of the goods (Section 2A–509(2)).

(2) Acceptance of a part of any commercial unit is acceptance of that entire unit.

§ 2A–516. Effect of Acceptance of Goods; Notice of Default; Burden of Establishing Default After Acceptance; Notice of Claim or Litigation to Person Answerable Over.

(1) A lessee must pay rent for any goods accepted in accordance with the lease contract, with due allowance for goods rightfully rejected or not delivered.

(2) A lessee's acceptance of goods precludes rejection of the goods accepted. In the case of a finance lease, if made with knowledge of a nonconformity, acceptance cannot be revoked because of it. In any other case, if made with knowledge of a nonconformity, acceptance cannot be revoked because of it unless the acceptance was on the reasonable assumption that the nonconformity would be seasonably cured. Acceptance does not of itself impair any other remedy provided by this Article or the lease agreement for nonconformity.

(3) If a tender has been accepted:

(a) within a reasonable time after the lessee discovers or should have discovered any default, the lessee shall notify the lessor and the supplier, if any, or be barred from any remedy against the party not notified;

(b) except in the case of a consumer lease, within a reasonable time after the lessee receives notice of litigation for infringement or the like (Section 2A–211) the lessee shall notify the lessor or be barred from any remedy over for liability established by the litigation; and

(c) the burden is on the lessee to establish any default.

(4) If a lessee is sued for breach of a warranty or other obligation for which a lessor or a supplier is answerable over the following apply:

(a) The lessee may give the lessor or the supplier, or both, written notice of the litigation. If the notice states that the person notified may come in and defend and that if the person notified does not do so that person will be bound in any action against that person by the lessee by any determination of fact common to the two litigations, then unless the person notified after seasonable receipt of the notice does come in and defend that person is so bound.

(b) The lessor or the supplier may demand in writing that the lessee turn over control of the litigation including settlement if the claim is one for infringement or the like (Section 2A–211) or else be barred from any remedy over. If the demand states that the lessor or the supplier agrees to bear all expense and to satisfy any adverse judgment, then unless the lessee after seasonable receipt of the demand does turn over control the lessee is so barred.

(5) Subsections (3) and (4) apply to any obligation of a lessee to hold the lessor or the supplier harmless against infringement or the like (Section 2A–211).

As amended in 1990.

§ 2A–517. Revocation of Acceptance of Goods.

(1) A lessee may revoke acceptance of a lot or commercial unit whose nonconformity substantially impairs its value to the lessee if the lessee has accepted it:

(a) except in the case of a finance lease, on the reasonable assumption that its nonconformity would be cured and it has not been seasonably cured; or

(b) without discovery of the nonconformity if the lessee's acceptance was reasonably induced either by the lessor's assurances or, except in the case of a finance lease, by the difficulty of discovery before acceptance.

(2) Except in the case of a finance lease that is not a consumer lease, a lessee may revoke acceptance of a lot or commercial unit if the lessor defaults under the lease contract and the default substantially impairs the value of that lot or commercial unit to the lessee.

(3) If the lease agreement so provides, the lessee may revoke acceptance of a lot or commercial unit because of other defaults by the lessor.

(4) Revocation of acceptance must occur within a reasonable time after the lessee discovers or should have discovered the ground for it and before any substantial change in condition of the goods which is not caused by the nonconformity. Revocation is not effective until the lessee notifies the lessor.

(5) A lessee who so revokes has the same rights and duties with regard to the goods involved as if the lessee had rejected them.

As amended in 1990.

§ 2A–518. Cover; Substitute Goods.

(1) After a default by a lessor under the lease contract of the type described in Section 2A–508(1), or, if agreed, after other default by the lessor, the lessee may cover by making any purchase or lease of or contract to purchase or lease goods in substitution for those due from the lessor.

(2) Except as otherwise provided with respect to damages liquidated in the lease agreement (Section 2A–504) or otherwise determined pursuant to agreement of the parties (Sections 1–102(3) and 2A–503), if a lessee's cover is by a lease agreement substantially similar to the original lease agreement and the new lease agreement is made in good faith and in a commercially reasonable manner, the lessee may recover from the lessor as damages (i) the present value, as of the date of the commencement of the term of the new lease agreement, of the rent under the new lease agreement applicable to that period of the new lease term which is comparable to the then remaining term of the original lease agreement minus the present value as of the same date of the total rent for the then remaining lease term of the original lease agreement, and (ii) any incidental or consequential damages, less expenses saved in consequence of the lessor's default.

(3) If a lessee's cover is by lease agreement that for any reason does not qualify for treatment under subsection (2), or is by purchase or otherwise, the lessee may recover from the lessor as if the lessee had elected not to cover and Section 2A–519 governs.

As amended in 1990.

§ 2A–519. Lessee's Damages for Non-delivery, Repudiation, Default, and Breach of Warranty in Regard to Accepted Goods.

(1) Except as otherwise provided with respect to damages liquidated in the lease agreement (Section 2A–504) or otherwise determined pursuant to agreement of the parties (Sections 1–102(3) and 2A–503), if a lessee elects not to cover or a lessee elects to cover and the cover is by lease agreement that for any reason does not qualify for treatment under Section 2A–518(2), or is by purchase or otherwise, the measure of damages for non-delivery or repudiation by the lessor or for rejection or revocation of acceptance by the lessee is the present value, as of the date of the default, of the then market rent minus the present value as of the same date of the original rent, computed for the remaining lease term of the original lease agreement, together with incidental and consequential damages, less expenses saved in consequence of the lessor's default.

(2) Market rent is to be determined as of the place for tender or, in cases of rejection after arrival or revocation of acceptance, as of the place of arrival.

(3) Except as otherwise agreed, if the lessee has accepted goods and given notification (Section 2A–516(3)), the measure of damages for non-conforming tender or delivery or other default by a lessor is the loss resulting in the ordinary course of events from the lessor's default as determined in any manner that is reasonable together with incidental and consequential damages, less expenses saved in consequence of the lessor's default.

(4) Except as otherwise agreed, the measure of damages for breach of warranty is the present value at the time and place of acceptance of the difference between the value of the use of the goods accepted and the value if they had been as warranted for the lease term, unless special circumstances show proximate damages of a different amount, together with incidental and consequential damages, less expenses saved in consequence of the lessor's default or breach of warranty.

As amended in 1990.

§ 2A–520. Lessee's Incidental and Consequential Damages.

(1) Incidental damages resulting from a lessor's default include expenses reasonably incurred in inspection, receipt, transportation, and care and custody of goods rightfully rejected or goods the acceptance of which is justifiably revoked, any commercially reasonable charges, expenses or commissions in connection with effecting cover, and any other reasonable expense incident to the default.

(2) Consequential damages resulting from a lessor's default include:

(a) any loss resulting from general or particular requirements and needs of which the lessor at the time of contracting had reason to know and which could not reasonably be prevented by cover or otherwise; and

(b) injury to person or property proximately resulting from any breach of warranty.

§ 2A–521. Lessee's Right to Specific Performance or Replevin.

(1) Specific performance may be decreed if the goods are unique or in other proper circumstances.

(2) A decree for specific performance may include any terms and conditions as to payment of the rent, damages, or other relief that the court deems just.

(3) A lessee has a right of replevin, detinue, sequestration, claim and delivery, or the like for goods identified to the lease contract if after reasonable effort the lessee is unable to effect cover for those goods or the circumstances reasonably indicate that the effort will be unavailing.

§ 2A–522. Lessee's Right to Goods on Lessor's Insolvency.

(1) Subject to subsection (2) and even though the goods have not been shipped, a lessee who has paid a part or all of the rent and security for goods identified to a lease contract (Section 2A–217) on making and keeping good a tender of any unpaid portion of the rent and security due under the lease contract may recover the goods identified from the lessor if the lessor becomes insolvent within 10 days after receipt of the first installment of rent and security.

(2) A lessee acquires the right to recover goods identified to a lease contract only if they conform to the lease contract.

C. Default by Lessee

§ 2A–523. Lessor's Remedies.

(1) If a lessee wrongfully rejects or revokes acceptance of goods or fails to make a payment when due or repudiates with respect to a part or the whole, then, with respect to any goods involved, and with respect to all of the goods if under an installment lease contract the value of the whole lease contract is substantially impaired (Section 2A–510), the lessee is in default under the lease contract and the lessor may:

(a) cancel the lease contract (Section 2A–505(1));

(b) proceed respecting goods not identified to the lease contract (Section 2A–524);

(c) withhold delivery of the goods and take possession of goods previously delivered (Section 2A–525);

(d) stop delivery of the goods by any bailee (Section 2A–526);

(e) dispose of the goods and recover damages (Section 2A–527), or retain the goods and recover damages (Section 2A–528), or in a proper case recover rent (Section 2A–529);

(f) exercise any other rights or pursue any other remedies provided in the lease contract.

(2) If a lessor does not fully exercise a right or obtain a remedy to which the lessor is entitled under subsection (1), the lessor may recover the loss resulting in the ordinary course of events from the lessee's default as determined in any reasonable manner, together with incidental damages, less expenses saved in consequence of the lessee's default.

(3) If a lessee is otherwise in default under a lease contract, the lessor may exercise the rights and pursue the remedies provided in the lease contract, which may include a right to cancel the lease. In addition, unless otherwise provided in the lease contract:

(a) if the default substantially impairs the value of the lease contract to the lessor, the lessor may exercise the rights and pursue the remedies provided in subsections (1) or (2); or

(b) if the default does not substantially impair the value of the lease contract to the lessor, the lessor may recover as provided in subsection (2).

As amended in 1990.

§ 2A–524. Lessor's Right to Identify Goods to Lease Contract.

(1) After default by the lessee under the lease contract of the type described in Section 2A–523(1) or 2A–523(3)(a) or, if agreed, after other default by the lessee, the lessor may:

(a) identify to the lease contract conforming goods not already identified if at the time the lessor learned of the default they were in the lessor's or the supplier's possession or control; and

(b) dispose of goods (Section 2A–527(1)) that demonstrably have been intended for the particular lease contract even though those goods are unfinished.

(2) If the goods are unfinished, in the exercise of reasonable commercial judgment for the purposes of avoiding loss and of effective realization, an aggrieved lessor or the supplier may either complete manufacture and wholly identify the goods to the lease contract or cease manufacture and lease, sell, or otherwise dispose of the goods for scrap or salvage value or proceed in any other reasonable manner.

As amended in 1990.

§ 2A–525. Lessor's Right to Possession of Goods.

(1) If a lessor discovers the lessee to be insolvent, the lessor may refuse to deliver the goods.

(2) After a default by the lessee under the lease contract of the type described in Section 2A–523(1) or 2A–523(3)(a) or, if agreed, after other default by the lessee, the lessor has the right to take possession of the goods. If the lease contract so provides, the lessor may require the lessee to assemble the goods and make them available to the lessor at a place to be designated by the lessor which is reasonably convenient to both parties. Without removal, the lessor may render unusable any goods employed in trade or business, and may dispose of goods on the lessee's premises (Section 2A–527).

(3) The lessor may proceed under subsection (2) without judicial process if it can be done without breach of the peace or the lessor may proceed by action.

As amended in 1990.

§ 2A–526. Lessor's Stoppage of Delivery in Transit or Otherwise.

(1) A lessor may stop delivery of goods in the possession of a carrier or other bailee if the lessor discovers the lessee to be insolvent and may stop delivery of carload, truckload, planeload, or larger shipments of express or freight if the lessee repudiates or fails to make a payment due before delivery, whether for rent, security or otherwise under the lease contract, or for any other reason the lessor has a right to withhold or take possession of the goods.

(2) In pursuing its remedies under subsection (1), the lessor may stop delivery until

(a) receipt of the goods by the lessee;

(b) acknowledgment to the lessee by any bailee of the goods, except a carrier, that the bailee holds the goods for the lessee; or

(c) such an acknowledgment to the lessee by a carrier via reshipment or as warehouseman.

(3) (a) To stop delivery, a lessor shall so notify as to enable the bailee by reasonable diligence to prevent delivery of the goods.

(b) After notification, the bailee shall hold and deliver the goods according to the directions of the lessor, but the lessor is liable to the bailee for any ensuing charges or damages.

(c) A carrier who has issued a nonnegotiable bill of lading is not obliged to obey a notification to stop received from a person other than the consignor.

§ 2A–527. Lessor's Rights to Dispose of Goods.

(1) After a default by a lessee under the lease contract of the type described in Section 2A–523(1) or 2A–523(3)(a) or after the lessor refuses to deliver or takes possession of goods (Section 2A–525 or 2A–526), or, if agreed, after other default by a lessee, the lessor may dispose of the goods concerned or the undelivered balance thereof by lease, sale, or otherwise.

(2) Except as otherwise provided with respect to damages liquidated in the lease agreement (Section 2A–504) or otherwise determined pursuant to agreement of the parties (Sections 1–102(3) and 2A–503), if the disposition is by lease agreement substantially similar to the original lease agreement and the new lease agreement is made in good faith and in a commercially reasonable manner, the lessor may recover from the lessee as damages (i) accrued and unpaid rent as of the date of the commencement of the term of the new lease agreement, (ii) the present value, as of the same date, of the total rent for the then remaining lease term of the original lease agreement minus the present value, as of the same date, of the rent under the new lease agreement applicable to that period of the new lease term which is comparable to the then remaining term of the original lease agreement, and (iii) any incidental damages allowed under Section 2A–530, less expenses saved in consequence of the lessee's default.

(3) If the lessor's disposition is by lease agreement that for any reason does not qualify for treatment under subsection (2), or is by sale or otherwise, the lessor may recover from the lessee as if the lessor had elected not to dispose of the goods and Section 2A–528 governs.

(4) A subsequent buyer or lessee who buys or leases from the lessor in good faith for value as a result of a disposition under this section takes the goods free of the original lease contract and any rights of the original lessee even though the lessor fails to comply with one or more of the requirements of this Article.

(5) The lessor is not accountable to the lessee for any profit made on any disposition. A lessee who has rightfully rejected or justifiably revoked acceptance shall account to the lessor for any excess over the amount of the lessee's security interest (Section 2A–508(5)).

As amended in 1990.

§ 2A–528. Lessor's Damages for Non-acceptance, Failure to Pay, Repudiation, or Other Default.

(1) Except as otherwise provided with respect to damages liquidated in the lease agreement (Section 2A–504) or otherwise determined pursuant to agreement of the parties (Sections 1–102(3) and 2A–503), if a lessor elects to retain the goods or a lessor elects to dispose of the goods and the disposition is by lease agreement that for any reason does not qualify for treatment under Section 2A–527(2), or is by sale or otherwise, the lessor may recover from the lessee as damages for a default of the type described in Section 2A–523(1) or 2A–523(3)(a), or, if agreed, for other default of the lessee, (i) accrued and unpaid rent as of the date of default if the lessee has never taken possession of the goods, or, if the lessee has taken possession of the goods, as of the date the lessor repossesses the goods or an earlier date on which the lessee makes a tender of the goods to the lessor, (ii) the present value as of the date determined under clause (i) of the total rent for the then remaining lease term of the original lease agreement minus the present value as of the same date of the market rent at the place where the goods are located computed for the same lease term, and (iii) any incidental damages allowed under Section 2A–530, less expenses saved in consequence of the lessee's default.

(2) If the measure of damages provided in subsection (1) is inadequate to put a lessor in as good a position as performance would have, the measure of damages is the present value of the profit, including reasonable overhead, the lessor would have made from full performance by the lessee, together with any incidental damages allowed under Section 2A–530, due allowance for costs reasonably incurred and due credit for payments or proceeds of disposition.

As amended in 1990.

§ 2A–529. Lessor's Action for the Rent.

(1) After default by the lessee under the lease contract of the type described in Section 2A–523(1) or 2A–523(3)(a) or, if agreed, after other default by the lessee, if the lessor complies with subsection (2), the lessor may recover from the lessee as damages:

(a) for goods accepted by the lessee and not repossessed by or tendered to the lessor, and for conforming goods lost or damaged within a commercially reasonable time after risk of loss passes to the lessee (Section 2A–219), (i) accrued and unpaid rent as of the date of entry of judgment in favor of the lessor, (ii) the present value as of the same date of the rent for the then remaining lease term of the lease agreement, and (iii) any incidental damages allowed under Section 2A–530, less expenses saved in consequence of the lessee's default; and

(b) for goods identified to the lease contract if the lessor is unable after reasonable effort to dispose of them at a reasonable price or the circumstances reasonably indicate that effort will be unavailing, (i) accrued and unpaid rent as of the date of entry of judgment in favor of the lessor, (ii) the present value as of the same date of the rent for the then remaining lease term of the lease agreement, and (iii) any incidental damages allowed under Section 2A–530, less expenses saved in consequence of the lessee's default.

(2) Except as provided in subsection (3), the lessor shall hold for the lessee for the remaining lease term of the lease agreement any goods that have been identified to the lease contract and are in the lessor's control.

(3) The lessor may dispose of the goods at any time before collection of the judgment for damages obtained pursuant to subsection (1). If the disposition is before the end of the remaining lease term of the lease agreement, the lessor's recovery against the lessee for damages is governed by Section 2A–527 or Section 2A–528, and the lessor will cause an appropriate credit to be provided against a judgment for damages to the extent that the amount of the judgment exceeds the recovery available pursuant to Section 2A–527 or 2A–528.

(4) Payment of the judgment for damages obtained pursuant to subsection (1) entitles the lessee to the use and possession of the goods not then disposed of for the remaining lease term of and in accordance with the lease agreement.

(5) After default by the lessee under the lease contract of the type described in Section 2A–523(1) or Section 2A–523(3)(a) or, if agreed, after other default by the lessee, a lessor who is held not entitled to rent under this section must nevertheless be awarded damages for non-acceptance under Section 2A–527 or Section 2A–528.

As amended in 1990.

§ 2A–530. Lessor's Incidental Damages.

Incidental damages to an aggrieved lessor include any commercially reasonable charges, expenses, or commissions incurred in stopping delivery, in the transportation, care and custody of goods after the lessee's default, in connection with return or disposition of the goods, or otherwise resulting from the default.

§ 2A–531. Standing to Sue Third Parties for Injury to Goods.

(1) If a third party so deals with goods that have been identified to a lease contract as to cause actionable injury to a party to the lease contract (a) the lessor has a right of action against the third party, and (b) the lessee also has a right of action against the third party if the lessee:

(i) has a security interest in the goods;

(ii) has an insurable interest in the goods; or

(iii) bears the risk of loss under the lease contract or has since the injury assumed that risk as against the lessor and the goods have been converted or destroyed.

(2) If at the time of the injury the party plaintiff did not bear the risk of loss as against the other party to the lease contract and there is no arrangement between them for disposition of the recovery, his [or her] suit or settlement, subject to his [or her] own interest, is as a fiduciary for the other party to the lease contract.

(3) Either party with the consent of the other may sue for the benefit of whom it may concern.

§ 2A–532. Lessor's Rights to Residual Interest.

In addition to any other recovery permitted by this Article or other law, the lessor may recover from the lessee an amount that will fully compensate the lessor for any loss of or damage to the lessor's residual interest in the goods caused by the default of the lessee.

As added in 1990.

ARTICLE 3

NEGOTIABLE INSTRUMENTS

PART 1 General Provisions and Definitions

§ 3–101. Short Title.

This Article may be cited as Uniform Commercial Code—Negotiable Instruments.

§ 3–102. Subject Matter.

(a) This Article applies to negotiable instruments. It does not apply to money or to payment orders governed by Article 4A. A negotiable instrument that is also a certificated security under Section 8–102(1)(a) is subject to Article 8 and to this Article.

(b) In the event of conflict between the provisions of this Article and those of Article 4, Article 8, or Article 9, the provisions of Article 4, Article 8 and Article 9 prevail over those of this Article.

(c) Regulations of the Board of Governors of the Federal Reserve System and operating circulars of the Federal Reserve Banks supersede any inconsistent provision of this Article to the extent of the inconsistency.

§ 3–103. Definitions.

(a) In this Article:

(1) "Acceptor" means a drawee that has accepted a draft.

(2) "Drawee" means a person ordered in a draft to make payment.

(3) "Drawer" means a person that signs a draft as a person ordering payment.

(4) "Good faith" means honesty in fact and the observance of reasonable commercial standards of fair dealing.

(5) "Maker" means a person that signs a note as promisor of payment.

(6) "Order" means a written instruction to pay money signed by the person giving the instruction. The instruction may be addressed to any person, including the person giving the

instruction, or to one or more persons jointly or in the alternative but not in succession. An authorization to pay is not an order unless the person authorized to pay is also instructed to pay.

(7) "Ordinary care" in the case of a person engaged in business means observance of reasonable commercial standards, prevailing in the area in which that person is located, with respect to the business in which that person is engaged. In the case of a bank that takes an instrument for processing for collection or payment by automated means, reasonable commercial standards do not require the bank to examine the instrument if the failure to examine does not violate the bank's prescribed procedures and the bank's procedures do not vary unreasonably from general banking usage not disapproved by this Article or Article 4.

(8) "Party" means party to an instrument.

(9) "Promise" means a written undertaking to pay money signed by the person undertaking to pay. An acknowledgment of an obligation by the obligor is not a promise unless the obligor also undertakes to pay the obligation.

(10) "Prove" with respect to a fact means to meet the burden of establishing the fact (Section 1–201(8)).

(11) "Remitter" means a person that purchases an instrument from its issuer if the instrument is payable to an identified person other than the purchaser.

(b) Other definitions applying to this Article and the sections in which they appear are:

"Acceptance" Section 3–409.
"Accommodated party" Section 3–419.
"Accommodation indorsement" Section 3–205.
"Accommodation party" Section 3–419.
"Alteration" Section 3–407.
"Blank indorsement" Section 3–205.
"Cashier's check" Section 3–104.
"Certificate of deposit" Section 3–104.
"Certified check" Section 3–409.
"Check" Section 3–104.
"Consideration" Section 3–303.
"Draft" Section 3–104.
"Fiduciary" Section 3–307.
"Guarantor" Section 3–417.
"Holder in due course" Section 3–302.
"Incomplete instrument" Section 3–115.
"Indorsement" Section 3–204.
"Indorser" Section 3–204.
"Instrument" Section 3–104.
"Issue" Section 3–105.
"Issuer" Section 3–105.
"Negotiable instrument" Section 3–104.
"Negotiation" Section 3–201.
"Note" Section 3–104.
"Payable at a definite time" Section 3–108.
"Payable on demand" Section 3–108.
"Payable to bearer" Section 3–109.
"Payable to order" Section 3–110.
"Payment" Section 3–603.
"Person entitled to enforce" Section 3–301.
"Presentment" Section 3–501.
"Reacquisition" Section 3–207.
"Represented person" Section 3–307.
"Special indorsement" Section 3–205.
"Teller's check" Section 3–104.
"Traveler's check" Section 3–104.
"Value" Section 3–303.

(c) The following definitions in other Articles apply to this Article:

"Bank" Section 4–105.
"Banking day" Section 4–104.
"Clearing house" Section 4–104.
"Collecting bank" Section 4–105.
"Customer" Section 4–104.
"Depositary bank" Section 4–105.
"Documentary draft" Section 4–104.
"Intermediary bank" Section 4–105.
"Item" Section 4–104.
"Midnight deadline" Section 4–104.
"Payor bank" Section 4–105.
"Suspends payments" Section 4–104.

(d) In addition, Article 1 contains general definitions and principles of construction and interpretation applicable throughout this Article.

§ 3–104. Negotiable Instrument.

(a) "Negotiable instrument" means an unconditional promise or order to pay a fixed amount of money, with or without interest or other charges described in the promise or order, if it:

(1) is payable to bearer or to order at the time it is issued or first comes into possession of a holder;

(2) is payable on demand or at a definite time; and

(3) does not state any other undertaking or instruction by the person promising or ordering payment to do any act in addition to the payment of money except that the promise or order may contain (i) an undertaking or power to give, maintain, or protect collateral to secure payment, (ii) an authorization or power to the holder to confess judgment or realize on or dispose of collateral, or (iii) a waiver of the benefit of any law intended for the advantage or protection of any obligor.

(b) "Instrument" means negotiable instrument.

(c) An order that meets all of the requirements of subsection (a) except subparagraph (1) and otherwise falls within the definition of "check" in subsection (f) is a negotiable instrument and a check.

(d) Notwithstanding subsection (a), a promise or order other than a check is not an instrument if, at the time it is issued or first comes into possession of a holder, it contains a conspicuous statement, however expressed, indicating that the writing is not an instrument governed by this Article.

(e) An instrument is a "note" if it is a promise, and is a "draft" if it is an order. If an instrument falls within the definition of both "note" and "draft," the person entitled to enforce the instrument may treat it as either.

(f) "Check" means (i) a draft, other than a documentary draft, payable on demand and drawn on a bank or (ii) a cashier's check or teller's check. An instrument may be a check even though it is described on its face by another term such as "money order."

(g) "Cashier's check" means a draft with respect to which the drawer and drawee are the same bank or branches of the same bank.

(h) "Teller's check" means a draft drawn by a bank (i) on another bank, or (ii) payable at or through a bank.

(i) "Traveler's check" means an instrument that (i) is payable on demand, (ii) is drawn on or payable at or through a bank, (iii) is designated by the term "traveler's check" or by a substantially similar term, and (iv) requires, as a condition to payment, a countersignature by a person whose specimen signature appears on the instrument.

(j) "Certificate of deposit" means an instrument containing an acknowledgment by a bank that a sum of money has been received by the bank, and a promise by the bank to repay the sum of money. A certificate of deposit is a note of the bank.

§ 3–105. Issue of Instrument.

(a) "Issue" means the first delivery of an instrument by the maker or drawer, whether to a holder or nonholder, for the purpose of giving rights on the instrument to any person.

(b) An unissued instrument, or an unissued incomplete instrument (Section 3–115) that is completed, is binding on the maker or drawer, but nonissuance is a defense. An instrument that is conditionally issued or is issued for a special purpose is binding on the maker or drawer, but failure of the condition or special purpose to be fulfilled is a defense.

(c) "Issuer" applies to issued and unissued instruments and means any person that signs an instrument as maker or drawer.

§ 3–106. Unconditional Promise or Order.

(a) Except as provided in subsections (b) and (c), for the purposes of Section 3–104(a), a promise or order is unconditional unless it states (i) an express condition to payment or (ii) that the promise or order is subject to or governed by another writing, or that rights or obligations with respect to the promise or order are stated in another writing; however, a mere reference to another writing does not make the promise or order conditional.

(b) A promise or order is not made conditional (i) by a reference to another writing for a statement of rights with respect to collateral, prepayment, or acceleration, or (ii) because payment is limited to resort to a particular fund or source.

(c) If a promise or order requires, as a condition to payment, a countersignature by a person whose specimen signature appears on the promise or order, the condition does not make the promise or order conditional for the purposes of Section 3–104(a). If the person whose specimen signature appears on an instrument fails to countersign the instrument, the failure to countersign is a defense to the obligation of the issuer, but the failure does not prevent a transferee of the instrument from becoming a holder of the instrument.

(d) If a promise or order at the time it is issued or first comes into possession of a holder contains a statement, required by applicable statutory or administrative law, to the effect that the rights of a holder or transferee are subject to claims or defenses that the issuer could assert against the original payee, the promise or order is not thereby made conditional for the purposes of Section 3–104(a), but there cannot be a holder in due course of the promise or order.

§ 3–107. Instrument Payable in Foreign Money.

Unless the instrument otherwise provides, an instrument that states the amount payable in foreign money may be paid in the foreign money or in an equivalent amount in dollars calculated by using the current bank-offered spot rate at the place of payment for the purchase of dollars on the day on which the instrument is paid.

§ 3–108. Payable on Demand or at a Definite Time.

(a) A promise or order is "payable on demand" if (i) it states that it is payable on demand or at sight, or otherwise indicates that it is payable at the will of the holder, or (ii) it does not state any time of payment.

(b) A promise or order is "payable at a definite time" if it is payable on elapse of a definite period of time after sight or acceptance or at a fixed date or dates or at a time or times readily ascertainable at the time the promise or order is issued, subject to rights of (i) prepayment, (ii) acceleration, or (iii) extension at the option of the holder or (iv) extension to a further definite time at the option of the maker or acceptor or automatically upon or after a specified act or event.

(c) If an instrument, payable at a fixed date, is also payable upon demand made before the fixed date, the instrument is payable on demand until the fixed date and, if demand for payment is not made before that date, becomes payable at a definite time on the fixed date.

§ 3–109. Payable to Bearer or to Order.

(a) A promise or order is payable to bearer if it:

(1) states that it is payable to bearer or to the order of bearer or otherwise indicates that the person in possession of the promise or order is entitled to payment,

(2) does not state a payee, or

(3) states that it is payable to or to the order of cash or otherwise indicates that it is not payable to an identified person.

(b) A promise or order that is not payable to bearer is payable to order if it is payable (i) to the order of an identified person or (ii) to an identified person or order. A promise or order that is payable to order is payable to the identified person.

(c) An instrument payable to bearer may become payable to an identified person if it is specially indorsed as stated in Section 3–205(a). An instrument payable to an identified person may become payable to bearer if it is indorsed in blank as stated in Section 3–205(b).

§ 3–110. Identification of Person to Whom Instrument Is Payable.

(a) A person to whom an instrument is payable is determined by the intent of the person, whether or not authorized, signing as, or in the name or behalf of, the maker or drawer. The instrument is payable to the person intended by the signer even if that person is identified in the instrument by a name or other identification that is not that of the intended person. If more than one person signs in the name or behalf of the maker or drawer and all the signers do not intend the same person as payee, the instrument is payable to any person intended by one or more of the signers.

(b) If the signature of the maker or drawer of an instrument is made by automated means such as a check-writing machine, the payee of the instrument is determined by the intent of the person who supplied the name or identification of the payee, whether or not authorized to do so.

(c) A person to whom an instrument is payable may be identified in any way including by name, identifying number, office, or account number. For the purpose of determining the holder of an instrument, the following rules apply:

(1) If an instrument is payable to an account and the account is identified only by number, the instrument is payable to the person to whom the account is payable. If an instrument is payable to an account identified by number and by the name of a person, the instrument is payable to the named person, whether or not that person is the owner of the account identified by number.

(2) If an instrument is payable to:

(i) a trust, estate, or a person described as trustee or representative of a trust or estate, the instrument is payable to the trustee, the representative, or a successor of either, whether or not the beneficiary or estate is also named;

(ii) a person described as agent or similar representative of a named or identified person, the instrument is payable either to the represented person, the representative, or a successor of the representative;

(iii) a fund or organization that is not a legal entity, the instrument is payable to a representative of the members of the fund or organization; or

(iv) an office or to a person described as holding an office, the instrument is payable to the named person, the incumbent of the office, or a successor to the incumbent.

(d) If an instrument is payable to two or more persons alternatively, it is payable to any of them and may be negotiated, discharged, or enforced by any of them in possession of the instrument. If an instrument is payable to two or more persons not alternatively, it is payable to all of them and may be negotiated, discharged, or enforced only by all of them. If an instrument payable to two or more persons is ambiguous as to whether it is payable to the persons alternatively, the instrument is payable to the persons alternatively.

§ 3–111. Place of Payment.

Except as otherwise provided for items in Article 4, an instrument is payable at the place of payment stated in the instrument. If no place of payment is stated, an instrument is payable at the address of the drawee or maker stated in the instrument. If no address is stated, the place of payment is the place of business of the drawee or maker. If a drawee or maker has more than one place of business, the place of payment is any place of business of the drawee or maker chosen by the person entitled to enforce the instrument. If the drawee or maker has no place of business, the place of payment is the residence of the drawee or maker.

§ 3–112. Interest.

(a) Unless otherwise provided in the instrument, (i) an instrument is not payable with interest, and (ii) interest on an interest-bearing instrument is payable from the date of the instrument.

(b) Interest may be stated in an instrument as a fixed or variable amount of money or it may be expressed as a fixed or variable rate or rates. The amount or rate of interest may be stated or described in the instrument in any manner and may require reference to information not contained in the instrument. If an instrument provides for interest but the amount of interest payable cannot be ascertained from the description, interest is payable at the judgment rate in effect at the place of payment of the instrument and at the time interest first accrues.

§ 3–113. Date of Instrument.

(a) An instrument may be antedated or postdated. The date stated determines the time of payment if the instrument is payable at a fixed period after date. Except as provided in Section 4–401(3), an instrument payable on demand is not payable before the date of the instrument.

(b) If an instrument is undated, its date is the date of its issue or, in the case of an unissued instrument, the date it first comes into possession of a holder.

§ 3–114. Contradictory Terms of Instrument.

If an instrument contains contradictory terms, typewritten terms prevail over printed terms, handwritten terms prevail over both, and words prevail over numbers.

§ 3–115. Incomplete Instrument.

(a) "Incomplete instrument" means a signed writing, whether or not issued by the signer, the contents of which show at the time of signing that it is incomplete but that the signer intended it to be completed by the addition of words or numbers.

(b) Subject to subsection (c), if an incomplete instrument is an instrument under Section 3–104, it may be enforced (i) according to its terms if it is not completed, or (ii) according to its terms as augmented by completion. If an incomplete instrument is not an instrument under Section 3–104 but, after completion, the requirements of Section 3–104 are met, the instrument may be enforced according to its terms as augmented by completion.

(c) If words or numbers are added to an incomplete instrument without authority of the signer, there is an alteration of the incomplete instrument governed by Section 3–407.

(d) The burden of establishing that words or numbers were added to an incomplete instrument without authority of the signer is on the person asserting the lack of authority.

§ 3–116. Joint and Several Liability; Contribution.

(a) Except as otherwise provided in the instrument, two or more persons who have the same liability on an instrument as makers, drawers, acceptors, indorsers who are indorsing joint payees, or anomalous indorsers, are jointly and severally liable in the capacity in which they sign.

(b) Except as provided in Section 3–417(e) or by agreement of the affected parties, a party with joint and several liability that pays the instrument is entitled to receive from any party with the same joint and several liability contribution in accordance with applicable law.

(c) Discharge of one party with joint and several liability by a person entitled to enforce the instrument does not affect the right under subsection (b) of a party with the same joint and several liability to receive contribution from the party discharged.

§ 3–117. Other Agreements Affecting an Instrument.

Subject to applicable law regarding exclusion of proof of contemporaneous or prior agreements, the obligation of a party to an instrument to pay the instrument may be modified, supplemented, or nullified by a separate agreement of the obligor and a person entitled to enforce the instrument if the instrument is issued or the obligation is incurred in reliance on the agreement or as part of the same transaction giving rise to the agreement. To the extent an obligation is modified, supplemented, or nullified by an agreement under this section, the agreement is a defense to the obligation.

§ 3–118. Statute of Limitations.

(a) Except as provided in subsection (e), an action to enforce the obligation of a party to pay a note payable at a definite time must be commenced within six years after the payment date or dates stated in the note or, if a payment date is accelerated, within six years after the accelerated payment date.

(b) Except as provided in subsection (d) or (e), if demand for payment is made to the maker of a note payable on demand, an action to enforce the obligation of a party to pay the note must be commenced within six years after the demand. If no demand for payment is made to the maker, an action to enforce the note is barred if neither principal nor interest on the note has been paid for a continuous period of 10 years.

(c) Except as provided in subsection (d), an action to enforce the obligation of a party to an unaccepted draft to pay the draft must be commenced within six years after dishonor of the draft or 10 years after the date of the draft, whichever period expires first.

(d) An action to enforce the obligation of the acceptor of a certified check or the issuer of a teller's check, cashier's check, or traveler's check must be commenced within six years after demand for payment is made to the acceptor or issuer, as the case may be.

(e) An action to enforce the obligation of a party to a certificate of deposit to pay the instrument must be commenced within six years after demand for payment is made to the maker, but if the instrument states a maturity date and the maker is not required to pay before that date, the six-year period begins when a demand for payment is in effect and the maturity date has passed.

(f) This subsection applies to an action to enforce the obligation of a party to pay an accepted draft, other than a certified check. If the obligation of the acceptor is payable at a definite time, the action must be commenced within six years after the payment date or dates stated in the draft or acceptance. If the obligation of the acceptor is payable on demand, the action must be commenced within six years after the date of the acceptance.

(g) Unless governed by other law regarding claims for indemnity or contribution, an action (i) for conversion of an instrument, for money had and received, or like action based on conversion, (ii) for breach of warranty, or (iii) to enforce an obligation, duty, or right arising under this Article and not governed by this section must be commenced within three years after the cause of action accrues.

§ 3–119. Notice of Right to Defend Action.

In an action for breach of an obligation for which a third person is answerable over pursuant to this Article or Article 4, the defendant may give the third person written notice of the litigation, and the person notified may then give similar notice to any other person who is answerable over. If the notice states (i) that the person notified may come in and defend and (ii) that failure to do so will bind the person notified in an action later brought by the person giving the notice as to any determination of fact common to the two litigations, the person notified is so bound unless after seasonable receipt of the notice the person notified does come in and defend.

PART 2 Negotiation, Transfer and Indorsement

§ 3–201. Negotiation.

(a) "Negotiation" means a transfer of possession, whether voluntary or involuntary, of an instrument to a person who thereby becomes its holder if possession is obtained from a person other than the issuer of the instrument.

(b) Except for a negotiation by a remitter, if an instrument is payable to an identified person, negotiation requires transfer of possession of the instrument and its indorsement by the holder. If an instrument is payable to bearer, it may be negotiated by transfer of possession alone.

§ 3–202. Negotiation Subject to Rescission.

(a) Negotiation is effective even if obtained (i) from an infant, a corporation exceeding its powers, or a person without capacity, or (ii) by fraud, duress, or mistake, or in breach of duty or as part of an illegal transaction.

(b) To the extent permitted by law, negotiation may be rescinded or may be subject to other remedies, but those remedies may not be asserted against a subsequent holder in due course or a person paying the instrument in good faith and without knowledge of facts that are a basis for rescission or other remedy.

§ 3–203. Rights Acquired by Transfer.

(a) An instrument is transferred when it is delivered by a person other than its issuer for the purpose of giving to the person receiving delivery the right to enforce the instrument.

(b) Transfer of an instrument, regardless of whether the transfer is a negotiation, vests in the transferee any right of the transferor to enforce the instrument, including any right as a holder in due course, but the transferee cannot acquire rights of a holder in due course by a transfer, directly or indirectly, from a holder in due course if the purchaser engaged in fraud or illegality affecting the instrument.

(c) Unless otherwise agreed, if an instrument is transferred for value and the transferee does not become a holder because of lack of indorsement by the transferor, the transferee has a specifically enforceable right to the unqualified indorsement of the transferor, but negotiation of the instrument does not occur until the indorsement is made.

(d) If a transferor purports to transfer less than the entire instrument, negotiation of the instrument does not occur. The transferee obtains no rights under this Article and has only the rights of a partial assignee.

§ 3–204. Indorsement.

(a) "Indorsement" means a signature, other than that of a maker, drawer, or acceptor, that alone or accompanied by other words, is made on an instrument for the purpose of (i) negotiating the instrument, (ii) restricting payment of the instrument, or (iii) incurring indorser's liability on the instrument, but regardless of the intent of the signer, a signature and its accompanying words is an indorsement unless the accompanying words, the terms of the instrument, the place of the signature, or other circumstances unambiguously indicate that the signature was made for a purpose other than indorsement. For the purpose of determining whether a signature is made on an instrument, a paper affixed to the instrument is a part of the instrument.

(b) "Indorser" means a person who makes an indorsement.

(c) For the purpose of determining whether the transferee of an instrument is a holder, an indorsement that transfers a security interest in the instrument is effective as an unqualified indorsement of the instrument.

(d) If an instrument is payable to a holder under a name that is not the name of the holder, indorsement may be made by the holder in the name stated in the instrument or in the holder's name or both, but signature in both names may be required by a person paying or taking the instrument for value or collection.

§ 3–205. Special Indorsement; Blank Indorsement; Anomalous Indorsement.

(a) If an indorsement is made by the holder of an instrument, whether payable to an identified person or payable to bearer, and the indorsement identifies a person to whom it makes the instrument payable, it is a "special indorsement." When specially indorsed, an instrument becomes payable to the identified person and may be negotiated only by the indorsement of that person. The principles stated in Section 3–110 apply to special indorsements.

(b) If an indorsement is made by the holder of an instrument and it is not a special indorsement, it is a "blank indorsement." When indorsed in blank, an instrument becomes payable to bearer and may be negotiated by transfer of possession alone until specially indorsed.

(c) The holder may convert a blank indorsement that consists only of a signature into a special indorsement by writing, above the signature of the indorser, words identifying the person to whom the instrument is made payable.

(d) "Anomalous indorsement" means an indorsement made by a person that is not the holder of the instrument. An anomalous indorsement does not affect the manner in which the instrument may be negotiated.

§ 3–206. Restrictive Indorsement.

(a) An indorsement limiting payment to a particular person or otherwise prohibiting further transfer or negotiation of the instrument is not effective to prevent further transfer or negotiation of the instrument.

(b) An indorsement stating a condition to the right of the indorsee to receive payment does not affect the right of the indorsee to enforce the instrument. A person paying the instrument or taking it for value or collection may disregard the condition, and the rights and liabilities of that person are not affected by whether the condition has been fulfilled.

(c) The following rules apply to an instrument bearing an indorsement (i) described in Section 4–201(2), or (ii) in blank or to a particular bank using the words "for deposit," "for collection," or other words indicating a purpose of having the instrument collected for the indorser or for a particular account:

(1) A person, other than a bank, that purchases the instrument when so indorsed converts the instrument unless the proceeds of the instrument are received by the indorser or are applied consistently with the indorsement.

(2) A depositary bank that purchases the instrument or takes it for collection when so indorsed converts the instrument unless the proceeds of the instrument are received by the indorser or applied consistently with the indorsement.

(3) A payor bank that is also the depositary bank or that takes the instrument for immediate payment over the counter from a person other than a collecting bank converts the instrument unless the proceeds of the instrument are received by the indorser or applied consistently with the indorsement.

(4) Except as otherwise provided in paragraph (3), a payor bank or intermediary bank may disregard the indorsement and is not liable if the proceeds of the instrument are not received by the indorser or applied consistently with the indorsement.

(d) Except for an indorsement covered by subsection (c), the following rules apply to an instrument bearing an indorsement using words to the effect that payment is to be made to the indorsee as agent, trustee, or other fiduciary for the benefit of the indorser or another person:

(1) Unless there is notice of breach of fiduciary duty as provided in Section 3–307, a person that purchases the instrument from the indorsee or takes the instrument from the indorsee for collection or payment may pay the proceeds of payment or the value given for the instrument to the indorsee without regard to whether the indorsee violates a fiduciary duty to the indorser.

(2) A later transferee of the instrument or person that pays the instrument is neither given notice nor otherwise affected by the restriction in the indorsement unless the transferee or payor knows that the fiduciary dealt with the instrument or its proceeds in breach of fiduciary duty.

(e) Purchase of an instrument bearing an indorsement to which this section applies does not prevent the purchaser from becoming a holder in due course of the instrument unless the purchaser is a converter under subsection (c).

(f) In an action to enforce the obligation of a party to pay the instrument, the obligor has a defense if payment would violate an indorsement to which this section applies and the payment is not permitted by this section.

§ 3–207. Reacquisition.

Reacquisition of an instrument occurs if it is transferred, by negotiation or otherwise, to a former holder. A former holder that reacquires the instrument may cancel indorsements made after the reacquirer first became a holder of the instrument. If the cancellation causes the instrument to be payable to the reacquirer or to bearer, the reacquirer may negotiate the instrument. An indorser whose indorsement is canceled is discharged, and the discharge is effective against any later holder.

PART 3 Enforcement of Instruments

§ 3–301. Person Entitled to Enforce Instrument.

"Person entitled to enforce" an instrument means (i) the holder of the instrument, (ii) a nonholder in possession of the instrument who has the rights of a holder, or (iii) a person not in possession of the instrument who is entitled to enforce the instrument pursuant to Section 3–309. A person may be a person entitled to enforce the instrument even though the person is not the owner of the instrument or is in wrongful possession of the instrument.

§ 3–302. Holder in Due Course.

(a) Subject to subsection (c) and Section 3–106(d), "holder in due course" means the holder of an instrument if:

(1) the instrument when issued or negotiated to the holder does not bear such apparent evidence of forgery or alteration or is not otherwise so irregular or incomplete as to call into question its authenticity, and

(2) the holder took the instrument (i) for value, (ii) in good faith, (iii) without notice that the instrument is overdue or has been dishonored or that there is an uncured default with respect to payment of another instrument issued as part of the same series, (iv) without notice that the instrument contains an unauthorized signature or has been altered, (v) without notice of any claim to the instrument stated in Section 3–306, and (vi) without notice that any party to the instrument has any defense or claim in recoupment stated in Section 3–305(a).

(b) Notice of discharge of a party to the instrument, other than discharge in an insolvency proceeding, is not notice of a defense under subsection (a), but discharge is effective against a person who became a holder in due course with notice of the discharge. Public filing or recording of a document does not of itself constitute notice of a defense, claim in recoupment, or claim to the instrument.

(c) Except to the extent a transferor or predecessor in interest has rights as a holder in due course, a person does not acquire rights of a holder in due course of an instrument taken (i) by legal process or by purchase at an execution, bankruptcy, or creditor's sale or similar proceeding, (ii) by purchase as part of a bulk transaction not in ordinary course of business of the transferor, or (iii) as the successor in interest to an estate or other organization.

(d) If, under Section 3–303(a)(1), the promise of performance that is the consideration for an instrument has been partially performed, the holder may assert rights as a holder in due course of the instrument only to the fraction of the amount payable under the instrument equal to the value of the partial performance divided by the value of the promised performance.

(e) If (i) the person entitled to enforce an instrument has only a security interest in the instrument and (ii) the person obliged to pay the instrument has a defense, claim in recoupment or claim to the instrument that may be asserted against the person who granted the security interest, the person entitled to enforce the instrument may assert rights as a holder in due course only to an amount payable under the instrument which, at the time of enforcement of the instrument, does not exceed the amount of the unpaid obligation secured.

(f) To be effective, notice must be received at such time and in such manner as to give a reasonable opportunity to act on it.

(g) This section is subject to any law limiting status as a holder in due course in particular classes of transactions.

§ 3–303. Value and Consideration.

(a) An instrument is issued or transferred for value if:

(1) the instrument is issued or transferred for a promise of performance, to the extent the promise has been performed;

(2) the transferee acquires a security interest or other lien in the instrument other than a lien obtained by judicial proceedings;

(3) the instrument is issued or transferred as payment of, or as security for, an existing obligation of any person, whether or not the obligation is due;

(4) the instrument is issued or transferred in exchange for a negotiable instrument; or

(5) the instrument is issued or transferred in exchange for the incurring of an irrevocable obligation to a third party by the person taking the instrument.

(b) "Consideration" means any consideration sufficient to support a simple contract. The drawer or maker of an instrument has a defense if the instrument is issued without consideration. If an instrument is issued for a promise of performance, the drawer or maker has a defense to the extent performance of the promise is due and the promise has not been performed. If an instrument is issued for value as stated in subsection (a), the instrument is also issued for consideration.

§ 3–304. Overdue Instrument.

(a) An instrument payable on demand becomes overdue at the earliest of the following times:

(1) on the day after the day demand for payment is duly made;

(2) if the instrument is a check, 90 days after its date; or

(3) if the instrument is not a check, when the instrument has been outstanding for a period of time after its date which is unreasonably long under the circumstances of the particular case in light of the nature of the instrument and trade usage.

(b) With respect to an instrument payable at a definite time the following rules apply: (1) If the principal is payable in installments and a due date has not been accelerated, the instrument becomes overdue upon default under the instrument for nonpayment of an installment, and the instrument remains overdue until the default is cured. (2) If the principal is not payable in installments and the due date has not been accelerated, the instrument becomes overdue on the day after the due date. (3) If a due date with respect to principal has been accelerated, the instrument becomes overdue on the day after the accelerated due date.

(c) Unless the due date of principal has been accelerated, an instrument does not become overdue if there is default in payment of interest but no default in payment of principal.

§ 3–305. Defenses and Claims in Recoupment.

(a) Except as stated in subsection (b), the right to enforce the obligation of a party to pay the instrument is subject to the following:

(1) A defense of the obligor based on (i) infancy of the obligor to the extent it is a defense to a simple contract, (ii) duress, lack of legal capacity, or illegality of the transaction that nullifies the obligation of the obligor, (iii) fraud that induced the obligor to sign the instrument with neither knowledge nor reasonable opportunity to learn of its character or its essential terms, or (iv) discharge of the obligor in insolvency proceedings.

(2) A defense of the obligor stated in another section of this Article or a defense of the obligor that would be available if the person entitled to enforce the instrument were enforcing a right to payment under a simple contract.

(3) A claim in recoupment of the obligor against the original payee of the instrument if the claim arose from the transaction that gave rise to the instrument. The claim of the obligor may be asserted against a transferee of the instrument only to reduce the amount owing on the instrument at the time the action is brought.

(b) The right of a holder in due course to enforce the obligation of a party to pay the instrument is subject to defenses of the obligor stated in subsection (a)(1), but is not subject to defenses of the obligor stated in subsection (a)(2) or claims in recoupment stated in subsection (a)(3) against a person other than the holder.

(c) Except as stated in subsection (d), in an action to enforce the obligation of a party to pay the instrument, the obligor may not assert against the person entitled to enforce the instrument a defense, claim in recoupment, or claim to the instrument (Section 3–306) of another person, but the other person's claim to the instrument may be asserted by the obligor if the other person is joined in the action and personally asserts the claim against the person entitled to enforce the instrument. An obligor is not obliged to pay the instrument if the person seeking enforcement of the instrument does not have rights of a holder in due course and the obligor proves that the instrument is a lost or stolen instrument.

(d) In an action to enforce the obligation of an accommodation party to pay an instrument, the accommodation party may assert against the person entitled to enforce the instrument any defense or claim in recoupment under subsection (a) that the accommodated party could assert against the person entitled to enforce the instrument, except the defenses of discharge in insolvency proceedings, infancy, or lack of legal capacity.

§ 3–306. Claims to an Instrument.

A person taking an instrument, other than a person having rights of a holder in due course, is subject to a claim of a property or possessory right in the instrument or its proceeds, including a claim to rescind a negotiation and to recover the instrument or its proceeds. A person having rights of a holder in due course takes free of the claim to the instrument.

§ 3–307. Notice of Breach of Fiduciary Duty.

(a) This section applies if (i) an instrument is taken from a fiduciary for payment or collection or for value, (ii) the taker has knowledge of the fiduciary status of the fiduciary, and (iii) the represented person makes a claim to the instrument or its proceeds on the basis that the transaction of the fiduciary is a breach of fiduciary duty. Notice of breach of fiduciary duty by the fiduciary is notice of the claim of the represented person. "Fiduciary" means an agent, trustee, partner, corporation officer or director, or other representative owing a fiduciary duty with respect to the instrument. "Represented person" means the principal, beneficiary, partnership, corporation, or other person to whom the duty is owed.

(b) If the instrument is payable to the fiduciary, as such, or to the represented person, the taker has notice of the breach of fiduciary duty if the instrument is (i) taken in payment of or as security for a debt known by the taker to be the personal debt of the fiduciary, (ii) taken in a transaction known by the taker to be for the personal benefit of the fiduciary, or (iii) deposited to an account other than an account of the fiduciary, as such, or an account of the represented person.

(c) If the instrument is made or drawn by the fiduciary, as such, payable to the fiduciary personally, the taker does not have notice of the breach of fiduciary duty unless the taker knows of the breach of fiduciary duty.

(d) If the instrument is made or drawn by or on behalf of the represented person to the taker as payee, the taker has notice of the breach of fiduciary duty if the instrument is (i) taken in payment of or as security for a debt known by the taker to be the personal debt of the fiduciary, (ii) taken in a transaction known by the taker to be for the personal benefit of the fiduciary, or (iii) deposited to an account other than an account of the fiduciary, as such, or an account of the represented person.

§ 3–308. Proof of Signatures and Status as Holder in Due Course.

(a) In an action with respect to an instrument, the authenticity of, and authority to make, each signature on the instrument is admitted unless specifically denied in the pleadings. If the validity of a signature is denied in the pleadings, the burden of establishing validity is on the person claiming validity, but the signature is presumed to be authentic and authorized unless the action is to enforce the liability of the purported signer and the signer is dead or incompetent at the time of trial of the issue of validity of the signature. If an action to enforce the instrument is brought against a person as the undisclosed principal of a person who signed the instrument as a party to the instrument, the plaintiff has the burden of establishing that the defendant is liable on the instrument as a represented person pursuant to Section 3–402(a).

(b) If the validity of signatures is admitted or proved and there is compliance with subsection (a), a plaintiff producing the instrument is entitled to payment if the plaintiff proves entitlement to enforce the instrument under Section 3–301, unless the defendant proves a defense or claim in recoupment. If a defense or claim in recoupment is proved, the right to payment of the plaintiff is subject to the defense or claim except to the extent the plaintiff proves that the plaintiff has rights of a holder in due course which are not subject to the defense or claim.

§ 3–309. Enforcement of Lost, Destroyed, or Stolen Instrument.

(a) A person not in possession of an instrument is entitled to enforce the instrument if (i) that person was in rightful possession of the instrument and entitled to enforce it when loss of possession occurred, (ii) the loss of possession was not the result of a voluntary transfer by that person or a lawful seizure, and (iii) that person cannot reasonably obtain possession of the instrument because the instrument was destroyed, its whereabouts cannot be determined, or it is in the wrongful possession of an unknown person or a person that cannot be found or is not amenable to service of process.

(b) A person seeking enforcement of an instrument pursuant to subsection (a) must prove the terms of the instrument and the person's right to enforce the instrument. If that proof is made, Section 3-308 applies to the case as though the person seeking enforcement had produced the instrument. The court may not enter judgment in favor of the person seeking enforcement unless it finds that the person required to pay the instrument is adequately protected against loss that might occur by reason of a claim by another person to enforce the instrument. Adequate protection may be provided by any reasonable means.

§ 3–310. Effect of Instrument on Obligation for Which Taken.

(a) Unless otherwise agreed, if a certified check, cashier's check, or teller's check is taken for an obligation, the obligation is discharged to the same extent discharge would result if an amount of money equal to the amount of the instrument were taken in payment of the obligation. Discharge of the obligation does not affect any liability that the obligor may have as an indorser of the instrument.

(b) Unless otherwise agreed and except as provided in subsection (a), if a note or an uncertified check is taken for an obligation, the obligation is suspended to the same extent the obligation would be discharged if an amount of money equal to the amount of the instrument were taken.

(1) In the case of an uncertified check, suspension of the obligation continues until dishonor of the check or until it is paid or certified. Payment or certification of the check results in discharge of the obligation to the extent of the amount of the check.

(2) In the case of a note, suspension of the obligation continues until dishonor of the note or until it is paid. Payment of the note results in discharge of the obligation to the extent of the payment.

(3) If the check or note is dishonored and the obligee of the obligation for which the instrument was taken has possession of the instrument, the obligee may enforce either the instrument or the obligation. In the case of an instrument of a third person which is negotiated to the obligee by the obligor, discharge of the obligor on the instrument also discharges the obligation.

(4) If the person entitled to enforce the instrument taken for an obligation is a person other than the obligee, the obligee may not enforce the obligation to the extent the obligation is suspended. If the obligee is the person entitled to enforce the instrument but no longer has possession of it because it was lost, stolen, or destroyed, the obligation may not be enforced to the extent of the amount payable on the instrument, and to that extent the obligee's rights against the obligor are limited to enforcement of the instrument.

(c) If an instrument other than one described in subsection (a) or (b) is taken for an obligation, the effect is (i) that stated in subsection (a) if the instrument is one on which a bank is liable as maker or acceptor, or (ii) that stated in subsection (b) in any other case.

§ 3–311. Accord and Satisfaction by Use of Instrument.

(a) This section applies if a person against whom a claim is asserted proves that (i) that person in good faith tendered an instrument to the claimant as full satisfaction of the claim, (ii) the amount of the claim was unliquidated or subject to a bona fide dispute, and (iii) the claimant obtained payment of the instrument.

(b) Unless subsection (c) applies, the claim is discharged if the person against whom the claim is asserted proves that the instrument or an accompanying written communication contained a conspicuous statement to the effect that the instrument was tendered as full satisfaction of the claim.

(c) Subject to subsection (d), a claim is not discharged under subsection (b) if the claimant is an organization and proves that within a reasonable time before the tender, the claimant sent a conspicuous statement to the person against whom the claim is asserted that communications concerning disputed debts, including an instrument tendered as full satisfaction of a debt, are to be sent to a designated person, office or place, and the instrument or accompanying communication was not received by that designated person, office, or place.

(d) Notwithstanding subsection (c), a claim is discharged under subsection (b) if the person against whom the claim is asserted proves that within a reasonable time before collection of the instrument was initiated, an agent of the claimant having direct responsibility with respect to the disputed obligation knew that the instrument was tendered in full satisfaction of the claim, or received the instrument and any accompanying written communication.

PART 4 Liability of Parties

§ 3–401. Signature.

(a) A person is not liable on an instrument unless (i) the person signed the instrument, or (ii) the person is represented by an agent or representative who signed the instrument and the signature is binding on the represented person under Section 3–402.

(b) A signature may be made (i) manually or by means of a device or machine, and (ii) by the use of any name, including any trade or assumed name, or by any word, mark, or symbol executed or adopted by a person with present intention to authenticate a writing.

§ 3–402. Signature by Representative.

(a) If a person acting, or purporting to act, as a representative signs an instrument by signing either the name of the represented person or the name of the signer, the represented person is bound by the signature to the same extent the represented person would be bound if the signature were on a simple contract. If the represented person is bound, the signature of the representative is the "authorized signature of the represented person" and the represented person is liable on the instrument, whether or not identified in the instrument.

(b) If a representative signs the name of the representative to an instrument and that signature is an authorized signature of the represented person, the following rules apply:

(1) If the form of the signature shows unambiguously that the signature is made on behalf of the represented person who is identified in the instrument, the representative is not liable on the instrument.

(2) Subject to subsection (c), if (i) the form of the signature does not show unambiguously that the signature is made in a representative capacity or (ii) the represented person is not identified in the instrument, the representative is liable on the instrument to a holder in due course that took the instrument without notice that the representative was not intended to be liable on the instrument. With respect to any other person, the representative is liable on the instrument unless the representative proves that the original parties to the instrument did not intend the representative to be liable on the instrument.

(c) If a representative signs the name of the representative as drawer of a check without indication of the representative status and the check is payable from an account of the represented person who is identified on the check, the signer is not liable on the check if the signature is an authorized signature of the represented person.

§ 3–403. Unauthorized Signature.

(a) Except as otherwise provided in this Article, an unauthorized signature is ineffective except as the signature of the unauthorized signer in favor of a person who in good faith pays the instrument or takes it for value. An unauthorized signature may be ratified for all purposes of this Article.

(b) If the signature of more than one person is required to constitute the authorized signature of an organization, the signature of the organization is unauthorized if one of the required signatures is missing.

(c) The civil or criminal liability of a person who makes an unauthorized signature is not affected by any provision of this Article that makes the unauthorized signature effective for the purposes of this Article.

§ 3–404. Impostors; Fictitious Payees.

(a) If an impostor by use of the mails or otherwise induces the maker or drawer of an instrument to issue the instrument to the impostor, or to a person acting in concert with the impostor, by impersonating the payee of the instrument or a person authorized to act for the payee, an indorsement of the instrument by any person in the name of the payee is effective as the indorsement of the payee in favor of any person that in good faith pays the instrument or takes it for value or for collection.

(b) If (i) a person whose intent determines to whom an instrument is payable (Section 3–110(a) or (b)) does not intend the person identified as payee to have any interest in the instrument, or (ii) the person identified as payee of the instrument is a fictitious person, the following rules apply until the instrument is negotiated by special indorsement:

(1) Any person in possession of the instrument is its holder.

(2) An indorsement by any person in the name of the payee stated in the instrument is effective as the indorsement of the payee in favor of any person that in good faith pays the instrument or takes it for value or for collection.

(c) Under subsection (a) or (b) an indorsement is made in the name of a payee if (i) it is made in a name substantially similar to that of the payee or (ii) the instrument, whether or not indorsed, is deposited in a depositary bank to an account in a name substantially similar to that of the payee.

(d) With respect to an instrument to which subsection (a) or (b) applies, if a person paying the instrument or taking it for value or for collection fails to exercise ordinary care in paying or taking the instrument and that failure substantially contributes to loss resulting from payment of the instrument, the person bearing the loss may recover from the person failing to exercise ordinary care to the extent the failure to exercise ordinary care contributed to the loss.

§ 3–405. Employer Responsibility for Fraudulent Indorsement by Employee.

(a) This section applies to fraudulent indorsements of instruments with respect to which an employer has entrusted an employee with responsibility as part of the employee's duties. The following definitions apply to this section:

(1) "Employee" includes, in addition to an employee of an employer, an independent contractor and employee of an independent contractor retained by the employer.

(2) "Fraudulent indorsement" means (i) in the case of an instrument payable to the employer, a forged indorsement purporting to be that of the employer, or (ii) in the case of an instrument with respect to which the employer is drawer or maker, a forged indorsement purporting to be that of the person identified as payee.

(3) "Responsibility" with respect to instruments means authority (i) to sign or indorse instruments on behalf of the employer, (ii) to process instruments received by the employer for bookkeeping purposes, for deposit to an account, or for other disposition, (iii) to prepare or process instruments for issue in the name of the employer, (iv) to supply information determining the names or addresses of payees of instruments to be issued in the name of the employer, (v) to control the disposition of instruments to be issued in the name of the employer, or (vi) to otherwise act with respect to instruments in a responsible capacity. "Responsibility" does not include the assignment of duties that merely allow an employee to have access to instruments or blank or incomplete instrument forms that are being stored or transported or are part of incoming or outgoing mail, or similar access.

(b) For the purpose of determining the rights and liabilities of a person who, in good faith, pays an instrument or takes it for value or for collection, if an employee entrusted with responsibility with respect to the instrument or a person acting in concert with the employee makes a fraudulent indorsement to the instrument, the indorsement is effective as the indorsement of the person to whom the instrument is payable if it is made in the name of that person. If the person paying the instrument or taking it for value or for collection fails to exercise ordinary care in paying or taking the instrument and that failure substantially contributes to loss resulting from the fraud, the person bearing the loss may recover from the person failing to exercise ordinary care to the extent the failure to exercise ordinary care contributed to the loss.

(c) Under subsection (b) an indorsement is made in the name of the person to whom an instrument is payable if (i) it is made in a name substantially similar to the name of that person or (ii) the instrument, whether or not indorsed, is deposited in a depositary bank to an account in a name substantially similar to the name of that person.

§ 3–406. Negligence Contributing to Forged Signature or Alteration of Instrument.

(a) A person whose failure to exercise ordinary care substantially contributes to an alteration of an instrument or to the making of a forged signature on an instrument is precluded from asserting the alteration or the forgery against a person that, in good faith, pays the instrument or takes it for value.

(b) If the person asserting the preclusion fails to exercise ordinary care in paying or taking the instrument and that failure substantially contributes to loss, the loss is allocated between the person precluded and the person asserting the preclusion according to the extent to which the failure of each to exercise ordinary care contributed to the loss.

(c) Under subsection (a) the burden of proving failure to exercise ordinary care is on the person asserting the preclusion. Under subsection (b) the burden of proving failure to exercise ordinary care is on the person precluded.

§ 3–407. Alteration.

(a) "Alteration" means (i) an unauthorized change in an instrument that purports to modify in any respect the obligation of a party to the instrument, or (ii) an unauthorized addition of words or numbers or other change to an incomplete instrument relating to the obligation of any party to the instrument.

(b) Except as provided in subsection (c), an alteration fraudulently made by the holder discharges any party to whose obligation the alteration applies unless that party assents or is precluded from asserting the alteration. No other alteration discharges any party, and the instrument may be enforced according to its original terms.

(c) If an instrument that has been fraudulently altered is acquired by a person having rights of a holder in due course, it may be enforced by that person according to its original terms. If an incomplete instrument is completed and is then acquired by a person having rights of a holder in due course, it may be enforced by that person as completed, whether or not the completion is a fraudulent alteration.

§ 3–408. Drawee Not Liable on Unaccepted Draft.

A check or other draft does not of itself operate as an assignment of funds in the hands of the drawee available for its payment, and the drawee is not liable on the instrument until the drawee accepts it.

§ 3–409. Acceptance of Draft; Certified Check.

(a) "Acceptance" means the drawee's signed agreement to pay a draft as presented. It must be written on the draft and may consist of the drawee's signature alone. Acceptance may be made at any time and becomes effective when notification pursuant to instructions is given or the accepted draft is delivered for the purpose of giving rights on the acceptance to any person.

(b) A draft may be accepted although it has not been signed by the drawer, is otherwise incomplete, is overdue, or has been dishonored.

(c) If a draft is payable at a fixed period after sight and the acceptor fails to date the acceptance, the holder may complete the acceptance by supplying a date in good faith.

(d) "Certified check" means a check accepted by the bank on which it is drawn. Acceptance may be made as stated in subsection (a) or by a writing on the check which indicates that the check is certified. The drawee of a check has no obligation to certify the check, and refusal to certify is not dishonor of the check.

§ 3–410. Acceptance Varying Draft.

(a) If the terms of a drawee's acceptance vary from the terms of the draft as presented, the holder may refuse the acceptance and treat the draft as dishonored. In that case, the drawee may cancel the acceptance.

(b) The terms of a draft are not varied by an acceptance to pay at a particular bank or place in the United States, unless the acceptance states that the draft is to be paid only at that bank or place.

(c) If the holder assents to an acceptance varying the terms of a draft, the obligation of each drawer and indorser that does not expressly assent to the acceptance is discharged.

§ 3–411. Refusal to Pay Cashier's Checks, Teller's Checks, and Certified Checks.

(a) In this section, "obligated bank" means the acceptor of a certified check or the issuer of a cashier's check or teller's check bought from the issuer.

(b) If the obligated bank wrongfully (i) refuses to pay a cashier's check or certified check, (ii) stops payment of a teller's check, or (iii) refuses to pay a dishonored teller's check, the person asserting the right to enforce the check is entitled to compensation for expenses and loss of interest resulting from the nonpayment and may recover consequential damages if the obligated bank refused to pay after receiving notice of particular circumstances giving rise to the damages.

(c) Expenses or consequential damages under subsection (b) are not recoverable if the refusal of the obligated bank to pay occurs because (i) the bank suspends payments, (ii) the obligated bank is asserting a claim or defense of the bank that it has reasonable grounds to believe is available against the person entitled to enforce the instrument, (iii) the obligated bank has a reasonable doubt whether the person demanding payment is the person entitled to enforce the instrument, or (iv) payment is prohibited by law.

§ 3–412. Obligation of Maker.

A maker of a note is obliged to pay the note (i) according to its terms at the time it was issued or, if not issued, at the time it first came into possession of a holder, or (ii) if the maker signed an incomplete instrument, according to its terms when completed as stated in Sections 3–115 and 3–407. The obligation is owed to a person entitled to enforce the note or to an indorser that paid the note pursuant to Section 3–415.

§ 3–413. Obligation of Acceptor.

(a) An acceptor of a draft is obliged to pay the draft (i) according to its terms at the time it was accepted, even though the acceptance states that the draft is payable "as originally drawn" or equivalent terms, (ii) if the acceptance varies the terms of the draft, according to the terms of the draft as varied, or (iii) if the acceptance is of a draft that is an incomplete instrument, according to its terms when completed as stated in Sections 3–115 and 3–407. The obligation is owed to a person entitled to enforce the draft or to the drawer or an indorser that paid the draft pursuant to Section 3–414 or 3–415.

(b) If the certification of a check or other acceptance of a draft states the amount certified or accepted, the obligation of the acceptor is that amount. If (i) the certification or acceptance does not state an amount, (ii) the instrument is subsequently altered by raising its amount, and (iii) the instrument is then negotiated to a holder in due course, the obligation of the acceptor is the amount of the instrument at the time it was negotiated to the holder in due course.

§ 3–414. Obligation of Drawer.

(a) If an unaccepted draft is dishonored, the drawer is obliged to pay the draft (i) according to its terms at the time it was issued or, if not issued, at the time it first came into possession of a holder, or (ii) if the drawer signed an incomplete instrument, according to its terms when completed as stated in Sections 3–115 and 3–407. The obligation is owed to a person entitled to enforce the draft or to an indorser that paid the draft pursuant to Section 3–415.

(b) If a draft is accepted by a bank and the acceptor dishonors the draft, the drawer has no obligation to pay the draft because of the dishonor, regardless of when or by whom acceptance was obtained.

(c) If a draft is accepted and the acceptor is not a bank, the obligation of the drawer to pay the draft if the draft is dishonored by the acceptor is the same as the obligation of an indorser stated in Section 3–415(a) and (c).

(d) Words in a draft indicating that the draft is drawn without recourse are effective to disclaim all liability of the drawer to pay the draft if the draft is not a check or a teller's check, but they are not effective to disclaim the obligation stated in subsection (a) if the draft is a check or a teller's check.

(e) If (i) a check is not presented for payment or given to a depositary bank for collection within 30 days after its date, (ii) the drawee suspends payments after expiration of the 30-day period without paying the check, and (iii) because of the suspension of payments the drawer is deprived of funds maintained with the drawee to cover payment of the check, the drawer to the extent deprived of funds may discharge its obligation to pay the check by assigning to the person entitled to enforce the check the rights of the drawer against the drawee with respect to the funds.

§ 3–415. Obligation of Indorser.

(a) Subject to subsections (b), (c) and (d) and to Section 3–419(d), if an instrument is dishonored, an indorser is obliged to pay the amount due on the instrument (i) according to the terms of the instrument at the time it was indorsed, or (ii) if the indorser indorsed an incomplete instrument, according to its terms when completed as stated in Sections 3–115 and 3–407. The obligation of the indorser is owed to a person entitled to enforce the instrument or to a subsequent indorser that paid the instrument pursuant to this section.

(b) If an indorsement states that it is made "without recourse" or otherwise disclaims liability of the indorser, the indorser is not liable under subsection (a) to pay the instrument.

(c) If notice of dishonor of an instrument is required by Section 3–503 and notice of dishonor complying with that section is not given to an indorser, the liability of the indorser under subsection (a) is discharged.

(d) If a draft is accepted by a bank after an indorsement was made and the acceptor dishonors the draft, the indorser is not liable under subsection (a) to pay the instrument.

(e) If an indorser of a check is liable under subsection (a) and the check is not presented for payment, or given to a depositary bank for collection, within 30 days after the day the indorsement was made, the liability of the indorser under subsection (a) is discharged.

§ 3–416. Transfer Warranties.

(a) A person that transfers an instrument for consideration warrants to the transferee and, if the transfer is by indorsement, to any subsequent transferee that:

(1) the warrantor is a person entitled to enforce the instrument,

(2) all signatures on the instrument are authentic and authorized,

(3) the instrument has not been altered,

(4) the instrument is not subject to a defense or claim in recoupment stated in Section 3–305(a) of any party that can be asserted against the warrantor, and

(5) the warrantor has no knowledge of any insolvency proceeding commenced with respect to the maker or acceptor or, in the case of an unaccepted draft, the drawer.

(b) A person to whom the warranties under subsection (a) are made and who took the instrument in good faith may recover from the warrantor as damages for breach of warranty an amount equal to the loss suffered as a result of the breach, but not more than the amount of the instrument plus expenses and loss of interest incurred as a result of the breach.

(c) The warranties stated in subsection (a) cannot be disclaimed with respect to checks. Unless notice of a claim for breach of warranty is given to the warrantor within 30 days after the claimant has reason to know of the breach and the identity of the warrantor, the warrantor is discharged to the extent of any loss caused by the delay in giving notice of the claim.

(d) A cause of action for breach of warranty under this section accrues when the claimant has reason to know of the breach.

§ 3–417. Presentment Warranties.

(a) If an unaccepted draft is presented to the drawee for payment or acceptance and the drawee pays or accepts the draft, (i) the person obtaining payment or acceptance, at the time of presentment, and (ii) a previous transferor of the draft, at the time of transfer, warrant to the drawee making payment or accepting the draft in good faith that:

(1) the warrantor is or was, at the time the warrantor transferred the draft, a person entitled to enforce the draft or authorized to obtain payment or acceptance of the draft on behalf of a person entitled to enforce the draft;

(2) the draft has not been altered; and

(3) the warrantor has no knowledge that the signature of the purported drawer of the draft is unauthorized.

(b) A drawee making payment may recover from any warrantor damages for breach of warranty equal to the amount paid by the drawee less the amount the drawee received or is entitled to receive from the drawer because of payment of the draft. In addition the drawee is entitled to compensation for expenses and loss of interest resulting from the breach. The right of the drawee to recover damages under this subsection is not affected by any failure of the drawee to exercise ordinary care in making payment. If the drawee accepts the draft (i) breach of warranty is a defense to the obligation of the acceptor, and (ii) if the acceptor makes payment with respect to the draft, the acceptor is entitled to recover from any warrantor for breach of warranty the amounts stated in the first two sentences of this subsection.

(c) If a drawee asserts a claim for breach of warranty under subsection (a) based on an unauthorized indorsement of the draft or an alteration of the draft, the warrantor may defend by proving that the indorsement is effective under Section 3–404 or 3–405 or the drawer is precluded under Section 3–406 or 4–406 from asserting against the drawee the unauthorized indorsement or alteration.

(d) This subsection applies if (i) a dishonored draft is presented for payment to the drawer or an indorser or (ii) any other instrument is presented for payment to a party obliged to pay the instrument, and payment is received. The person obtaining payment and a prior transferor of the instrument warrant to the person making payment in good faith that the warrantor is or was, at the time the warrantor transferred the instrument, a person entitled to enforce the instrument or authorized to obtain payment on behalf of a person entitled to enforce the instrument. The person making payment may recover from any warrantor for breach of warranty an amount equal to the amount paid plus expenses and loss of interest resulting from the breach.

(e) The warranties stated in subsections (a) and (d) cannot be disclaimed with respect to checks. Unless notice of a claim for breach of warranty is given to the warrantor within 30 days after the claimant has reason to know of the breach and the identity of the warrantor, the warrantor is discharged to the extent of any loss caused by the delay in giving notice of the claim.

(f) A cause of action for breach of warranty under this section accrues when the claimant has reason to know of the breach.

§ 3–418. Payment or Acceptance by Mistake.

(a) Except as provided in subsection (c), if the drawee of a draft pays or accepts the draft and the drawee acted on the mistaken belief that (i) payment of the draft had not been stopped under Section 4–403, (ii) the signature of the purported drawer of the draft was authorized, or (iii) the balance in the drawer's account with the drawee represented available funds, the drawee may recover the amount paid from the person to whom or for whose benefit payment was made or, in the case of acceptance, may revoke the acceptance. Rights of the drawee under this subsection are not affected by failure of the drawee to exercise ordinary care in paying or accepting the draft.

(b) Except as provided in subsection (c), if an instrument has been paid or accepted by mistake and the case is not covered by subsection (a), the person paying or accepting may recover the amount paid or revoke acceptance to the extent allowed by the law governing mistake and restitution.

(c) The remedies provided by subsection (a) or (b) may not be asserted against a person who took the instrument in good faith and for value. This subsection does not limit remedies provided by Section 3–417 for breach of warranty.

§ 3–419. Instruments Signed for Accommodation.

(a) If an instrument is issued for value given for the benefit of a party to the instrument ("accommodated party") and another party to the instrument ("accommodation party") signs the instrument for the purpose of incurring liability on the instrument without being a direct beneficiary of the value given for the instrument, the instrument is signed by the accommodation party "for accommodation."

(b) An accommodation party may sign the instrument as maker, drawer, acceptor, or indorser and, subject to subsection (d), is obliged to pay the instrument in the capacity in which the accommodation party signs. The obligation of an accommodation party may be enforced notwithstanding any statute of frauds and regardless of whether the accommodation party receives consideration for the accommodation.

(c) A person signing an instrument is presumed to be an accommodation party and there is notice that the instrument is signed for accommodation if the signature is an anomalous indorsement or is accompanied by words indicating that the signer is acting as surety or guarantor with respect to the obligation of another party to the instrument. Except as provided in Section 3–606, the obligation of an accommodation party to pay the instrument is not affected by the fact that the person enforcing the obligation had notice when the instrument was taken by that person that the accommodation party signed the instrument for accommodation.

(d) If the signature of a party to an instrument is accompanied by words indicating unambiguously that the party is guaranteeing collection rather than payment of the obligation of another party to the instrument, the signer is obliged to pay the amount due on the instrument to a person entitled to enforce the instrument only if (i) execution of judgment against the other party has been returned unsatisfied, (ii) the other party is insolvent or in an insolvency proceeding, (iii) the other party cannot be served with process, or (iv) it is otherwise apparent that payment cannot be obtained from the party whose obligation is guaranteed.

(e) An accommodation party that pays the instrument is entitled to reimbursement from the accommodated party and is entitled to enforce the instrument against the accommodated party. An accommodated party that pays the instrument has no right of recourse against, and is not entitled to contribution from, an accommodation party.

§ 3–420. Conversion of Instrument.

(a) The law applicable to conversion of personal property applies to instruments. An instrument is also converted if the instrument lacks an indorsement necessary for negotiation and it is purchased or taken for collection or the drawee takes the instrument and makes payment to a person not entitled to receive payment. An action for conversion of an instrument may not be brought by (i) the maker, drawer, or acceptor of the instrument or (ii) a payee or indorsee who did not receive delivery of the instrument either directly or through delivery to an agent or a co-payee.

(b) In an action under subsection (a), the measure of liability is presumed to be the amount payable on the instrument, but recovery may not exceed the amount of the plaintiff's interest in the instrument.

(c) A representative, other than a depositary bank, that has in good faith dealt with an instrument or its proceeds on behalf of one who was not the person entitled to enforce the instrument is not liable in conversion to that person beyond the amount of any proceeds that it has not paid out.

PART 5 Dishonor

§ 3–501. Presentment.

(a) "Presentment" means a demand (i) to pay an instrument made to the maker, drawee, or acceptor or, in the case of a note or accepted draft payable at a bank, to the bank, or (ii) to accept a draft made to the drawee, by a person entitled to enforce the instrument.

(b) Subject to Article 4, agreement of the parties, clearing house rules and the like,

(1) presentment may be made at the place of payment of the instrument and must be made at the place of payment if the instrument is payable at a bank in the United States; may be made by any commercially reasonable means, including an oral, written, or electronic communication; is effective when the demand for payment or acceptance is received by the person to whom presentment is made; is effective if made to any one of two or more makers, acceptors, drawees or other payors; and

(2) without dishonoring the instrument, the party to whom presentment is made may (i) treat presentment as occurring on the next business day after the day of presentment if the party to whom presentment is made has established a cut-off hour not earlier than 2 p.m. for the receipt and processing of instruments presented for payment or acceptance and presentment is made after the cut-off hour, (ii) require exhibition of the instrument, (iii) require reasonable identification of the person making presentment and evidence of authority to make it if made on behalf of another person, (iv) require a signed receipt on the instrument for any payment made or surrender of the instrument if full payment is made, (v) return the instrument for lack of a necessary indorsement, or (vi) refuse payment or acceptance for failure of the presentment to comply with the terms of the instrument, an agreement of the parties, or other law or applicable rule.

§ 3–502. Dishonor.

(a) Dishonor of a note is governed by the following rules:

(1) If the note is payable on demand, the note is dishonored if presentment is duly made and the note is not paid on the day of presentment.

(2) If the note is not payable on demand and is payable at or through a bank or the terms of the note require presentment, the note is dishonored if presentment is duly made and the note is not paid on the day it becomes payable or the day of presentment, whichever is later.

(3) If the note is not payable on demand and subparagraph (2) does not apply, the note is dishonored if it is not paid on the day it becomes payable.

(b) Dishonor of an unaccepted draft other than a documentary draft is governed by the following rules:

(1) If a check is presented for payment otherwise than for immediate payment over the counter, the check is dishonored if the payor bank makes timely return of the check or sends timely notice of dishonor or nonpayment under Section 4–301 or 4–302,

or becomes accountable for the amount of the check under Section 4–302.

(2) If the draft is payable on demand and subparagraph (1) does not apply, the draft is dishonored if presentment for payment is duly made and the draft is not paid on the day of presentment.

(3) If the draft is payable on a date stated in the draft, the draft is dishonored if (i) presentment for payment is duly made and payment is not made on the day the draft becomes payable or the day of presentment, whichever is later, or (ii) presentment for acceptance is duly made before the day the draft becomes payable and the draft is not accepted on the day of presentment.

(4) If the draft is payable on elapse of a period of time after sight or acceptance, the draft is dishonored if presentment for acceptance is duly made and the draft is not accepted on the day of presentment.

(c) Dishonor of an unaccepted documentary draft occurs according to the rules stated in subparagraphs (2), (3), and (4) of subsection (b) except that payment or acceptance may be delayed without dishonor until no later than the close of the third business day of the drawee following the day on which payment or acceptance is required by those subparagraphs.

(d) Dishonor of an accepted draft is governed by the following rules:

(1) If the draft is payable on demand, the draft is dishonored if presentment for payment is duly made and the draft is not paid on the day of presentment.

(2) If the draft is not payable on demand, the draft is dishonored if presentment for payment is duly made and payment is not made on the day it becomes payable or the day of presentment, whichever is later.

(e) In any case in which presentment is otherwise required for dishonor under this section and presentment is excused under Section 3–504, dishonor occurs without presentment if the instrument is not duly accepted or paid.

(f) If a draft is dishonored because timely acceptance of the draft was not made and the person entitled to demand acceptance consents to a late acceptance, from the time of acceptance the draft is treated as never having been dishonored.

§ 3–503. Notice of Dishonor.

(a) The obligation of an indorser stated in Section 3–415(a) and the obligation of a drawer stated in Section 3–414(c) may not be enforced unless (i) the indorser or drawer is given notice of dishonor of the instrument complying with this section or (ii) notice of dishonor is excused under Section 3–504(c).

(b) Notice of dishonor may be given by any person; may be given by any commercially reasonable means including an oral, written, or electronic communication; is sufficient if it reasonably identifies the instrument and indicates that the instrument has been dishonored or has not been paid or accepted. Return of an instrument given to a bank for collection is a sufficient notice of dishonor.

(c) Subject to Section 3-504(d), with respect to an instrument taken for collection by a collecting bank, notice of dishonor must be given (i) by the bank before midnight of the next banking day following the banking day on which the bank receives notice of dishonor of the instrument, and (ii) by any other person within 30 days following the day on which the person receives notice of dishonor. With respect to any other instrument, notice of dishonor must be given within 30 days following the day on which dishonor occurs.

§ 3–504. Excused Presentment and Notice of Dishonor.

(a) Presentment for payment or acceptance of an instrument is excused if (i) the person entitled to present the instrument cannot with reasonable diligence make presentment, (ii) the maker or acceptor has repudiated an obligation to pay the instrument or is dead or in insolvency proceedings, (iii) by the terms of the instrument presentment is not necessary to enforce the obligation of indorsers or the drawer, or (iv) the drawer or indorser whose obligation is being enforced waived presentment or otherwise had no reason to expect or right to require that the instrument be paid or accepted.

(b) Presentment for payment or acceptance of a draft is also excused if the drawer instructed the drawee not to pay or accept the draft or the drawee was not obligated to the drawer to pay the draft.

(c) Notice of dishonor is excused if (i) by the terms of the instrument notice of dishonor is not necessary to enforce the obligation of a party to pay the instrument, or (ii) the party whose obligation is being enforced waived notice of dishonor. A waiver of presentment is also a waiver of notice of dishonor.

(d) Delay in giving notice of dishonor is excused if the delay was caused by circumstances beyond the control of the person giving the notice and the person giving the notice exercised reasonable diligence after the cause of the delay ceased to operate.

§ 3–505. Evidence of Dishonor.

(a) The following are admissible as evidence and create a presumption of dishonor and of any notice of dishonor stated:

(1) a document regular in form as provided in subsection (b) which purports to be a protest;

(2) a purported stamp or writing of the drawee, payor bank, or presenting bank on or accompanying the instrument stating that acceptance or payment has been refused unless reasons for the refusal are stated and the reasons are not consistent with dishonor;

(3) a book or record of the drawee, payor bank, or collecting bank, kept in the usual course of business which shows dishonor, even if there is no evidence of who made the entry.

(b) A protest is a certificate of dishonor made by a United States consul or vice consul, or a notary public or other person authorized to administer oaths by the law of the place where dishonor occurs. It may be made upon information satisfactory to that person. The protest must identify the instrument and certify either that presentment has been made or, if not made, the reason why it was not made, and that the instrument has been dishonored by nonacceptance or nonpayment. The protest may also certify that notice of dishonor has been given to some or all parties.

PART 6 Discharge and Payment

§ 3–601. Discharge and Effect of Discharge.

(a) The obligation of a party to pay the instrument is discharged as stated in this Article or by an act or agreement with the party which would discharge an obligation to pay money under a simple contract.

(b) Discharge of the obligation of a party is not effective against a person acquiring rights of a holder in due course of the instrument without notice of the discharge.

§ 3–602. Payment.

(a) Subject to subsection (b), an instrument is paid to the extent payment is made (i) by or on behalf of a party obliged to pay the instrument, and (ii) to a person entitled to enforce the instrument. To the extent of the payment, the obligation of the party obliged to pay the instrument is discharged even though payment is made with knowledge of a claim to the instrument under Section 3–306 by another person.

(b) The obligation of a party to pay the instrument is not discharged under subsection (a) if:

(1) a claim to the instrument under Section 3–306 is enforceable against the party receiving payment and (i) payment is made with knowledge by the payor that payment is prohibited by injunction or similar process of a court of competent jurisdiction, or (ii) in the case of an instrument other than a cashier's check, teller's check, or certified check, the party making payment accepted, from the person having a claim to the instrument, indemnity against loss resulting from refusal to pay the person entitled to enforce the instrument, or

(2) the person making payment knows that the instrument is a stolen instrument and pays a person that it knows is in wrongful possession of the instrument.

§ 3–603. Tender of Payment.

(a) If tender of payment of an obligation of a party to an instrument is made to a person entitled to enforce the obligation, the effect of tender is governed by principles of law applicable to tender of payment of an obligation under a simple contract.

(b) If tender of payment of an obligation to pay the instrument is made to a person entitled to enforce the instrument and the tender is refused, there is discharge, to the extent of the amount of the tender, of the obligation of an indorser or accommodation party having a right of recourse against the obligor making the tender.

(c) If tender of payment of an amount due on an instrument is made by or on behalf of the obligor to the person entitled to enforce the instrument, the obligation of the obligor to pay interest after the due date on the amount tendered is discharged. If presentment is required with respect to an instrument and the obligor is able and ready to pay on the due date at every place of payment stated in the instrument, the obligor is deemed to have made tender of payment on the due date to the person entitled to enforce the instrument.

§ 3–604. Discharge by Cancellation or Renunciation.

(a) A person entitled to enforce an instrument may, with or without consideration, discharge the obligation of a party to pay the instrument (i) by an intentional voluntary act such as surrender of the instrument to the party, destruction, mutilation, or cancellation of the instrument, cancellation or striking out of the party's signature, or the addition of words to the instrument indicating discharge, or (ii) by agreeing not to sue or otherwise renouncing rights against the party by a signed writing.

(b) Cancellation or striking out of an indorsement pursuant to subsection (a) does not affect the status and rights of a party derived from the indorsement.

§ 3–605. Discharge of Indorsers and Accommodation Parties.

(a) For the purposes of this section, the term "indorser" includes a drawer having the obligation stated in Section 3–414(c).

(b) Discharge of the obligation of a party to the instrument under Section 3–605 does not discharge the obligation of an indorser or accommodation party having a right of recourse against the discharged party.

(c) If a person entitled to enforce an instrument agrees, with or without consideration, to a material modification of the obligation of a party to the instrument, including an extension of the due date, there is discharge of the obligation of an indorser or accommodation party having a right of recourse against the person whose obligation is modified to the extent the modification causes loss to the indorser or accommodation party with respect to the right of recourse. The indorser or accommodation party is deemed to have suffered loss as a result of the modification equal to the amount of the right of recourse unless the person enforcing the instrument proves that no loss was caused by the modification or that the loss caused by the modification was less than the amount of the right of recourse.

(d) If the obligation of a party to an instrument is secured by an interest in collateral and impairment of the value of the interest is caused by a person entitled to enforce the instrument, there is discharge of the obligation of an indorser or accommodation party having a right of recourse against the obligor to the extent of the impairment. The value of an interest in collateral is impaired to the extent (i) the value of the interest is reduced to an amount less than the amount of the right of recourse of the party asserting discharge, or (ii) the reduction in value of the interest causes an increase in the amount by which the amount of the right of recourse exceeds the value of the interest. The burden of proving impairment is on the party asserting discharge.

(e) If the obligation of a party to an instrument is secured by an interest in collateral not provided by an accommodation party and the value of the interest is impaired by a person entitled to enforce the instrument, the obligation of any party who is jointly and severally liable with respect to the secured obligation is discharged to the extent the impairment causes the party asserting discharge to pay more than that party would have been obliged to pay, taking into account rights of contribution, if impairment had not occurred. If the party asserting discharge is an accommodation party not entitled to discharge under subsection (d), the party is deemed to have a right to contribution based on joint and several liability rather than a right to reimbursement. The burden of proving impairment is on the party asserting discharge.

(f) Under subsection (d) or (e) causation of impairment includes (i) failure to obtain or maintain perfection or recordation of the interest in collateral, (ii) release of collateral without substitution of collateral of equal value, (iii) failure to perform a duty to preserve the value of collateral owed, under Article 9 or other law, to a debtor or surety or other person secondarily liable, or (iv) failure to comply with applicable law in disposing of collateral.

(g) An accommodation party is not discharged under subsection (c) or (d) unless the person agreeing to the modification or causing the impairment knows of the accommodation or has notice under Section 3–419(c) that the instrument was signed for accommodation. There is no discharge of any party under subsection (c), (d), or (e) if (i) the party asserting discharge consents to the event or conduct that is the basis of the discharge, or (ii) the instrument or a separate agreement of the party provides for waiver of discharge under this section either specifically or by general language indicating that parties to the instrument waive defenses based on suretyship or impairment of collateral.

ARTICLE 4
BANK DEPOSITS AND COLLECTIONS

PART 1 General Provisions and Definitions

§ 4–101. Short Title.

This Article may be cited as Uniform Commercial Code—Bank Deposits and Collections.

§ 4–102. Applicability.

(a) To the extent that items within this Article are also within Articles 3 and 8, they are subject to those Articles. If there is conflict, this Article governs Article 3, but Article 8 governs this Article.

(b) The liability of a bank for action or non-action with respect to an item handled by it for purposes of presentment, payment, or collection is governed by the law of the place where the bank is located. In the case of action or non-action by or at a branch or separate office of a bank, its liability is governed by the law of the place where the branch or separate office is located.

§ 4–103. Variation by Agreement; Measure of Damages; Action Constituting Ordinary Care.

(a) The effect of the provisions of this Article may be varied by agreement, but the parties to the agreement cannot disclaim a bank's responsibility for its lack of good faith or failure to exercise ordinary care or limit the measure of damages for the lack or failure. However, the parties may determine by agreement the standards by which the bank's responsibility is to be measured if those standards are not manifestly unreasonable.

(b) Federal Reserve regulations and operating circulars, clearing-house rules, and the like have the effect of agreements under subsection (a), whether or not specifically assented to by all parties interested in items handled.

(c) Action or non-action approved by this Article or pursuant to Federal Reserve regulations or operating circulars is the exercise of ordinary care and, in the absence of special instructions, action or non-action consistent with clearing-house rules and the like or with a general banking usage not disapproved by this Article, is prima facie the exercise of ordinary care.

(d) The specification or approval of certain procedures by this Article is not disapproval of other procedures that may be reasonable under the circumstances.

(e) The measure of damages for failure to exercise ordinary care in handling an item is the amount of the item reduced by an amount that could not have been realized by the exercise of ordinary care. If there is also bad faith it includes any other damages the party suffered as a proximate consequence.

§ 4–104. Definitions and Index of Definitions.

(a) In this Article, unless the context otherwise requires:

(1) "Account" means any deposit or credit account with a bank, including a demand, time, savings, passbook, share draft, or like account, other than an account evidenced by a certificate of deposit;

(2) "Afternoon" means the period of a day between noon and midnight;

(3) "Banking day" means the part of a day on which a bank is open to the public for carrying on substantially all of its banking functions;

(4) "Clearing house" means an association of banks or other payors regularly clearing items;

(5) "Customer" means a person having an account with a bank or for whom a bank has agreed to collect items, including a bank that maintains an account at another bank;

(6) "Documentary draft" means a draft to be presented for acceptance or payment if specified documents, certificated securities (Section 8–102) or instructions for uncertificated securities (Section 8–102), or other certificates, statements, or the like are to be received by the drawee or other payor before acceptance or payment of the draft;

(7) "Draft" means a draft as defined in Section 3–104 or an item, other than an instrument, that is an order;

(8) "Drawee" means a person ordered in a draft to make payment;

(9) "Item" means an instrument or a promise or order to pay money handled by a bank for collection or payment. The term does not include a payment order governed by Article 4A or a credit or debit card slip;

(10) "Midnight deadline" with respect to a bank is midnight on its next banking day following the banking day on which it receives the relevant item or notice or from which the time for taking action commences to run, whichever is later;

(11) "Settle" means to pay in cash, by clearing-house settlement, in a charge or credit or by remittance, or otherwise as agreed. A settlement may be either provisional or final;

(12) "Suspends payments" with respect to a bank means that it has been closed by order of the supervisory authorities, that a public officer has been appointed to take it over, or that it ceases or refuses to make payments in the ordinary course of business.

(b) Other definitions applying to this Article and the sections in which they appear are:

"Agreement for electronic presentment" Section 4–110.
"Bank" Section 4–105.
"Collecting bank" Section 4–105.
"Depository bank" Section 4–105.
"Intermediary bank" Section 4–105.
"Payor bank" Section 4–105.
"Presenting bank" Section 4–105.
"Presentment notice" Section 4–110.

(c) The following definitions in other Articles apply to this Article:

"Acceptance" Section 3–409.
"Alteration" Section 3–407.
"Cashier's check" Section 3–104.
"Certificate of deposit" Section 3–104.
"Certified check" Section 3–109.
"Check" Section 3–104.
"Good faith" Section 3–103.
"Holder in due course" Section 3–302.
"Instrument" Section 3–104.
"Notice of dishonor" Section 3–503.
"Order" Section 3–103.
"Ordinary care" Section 3–103.
"Person entitled to enforce" Section 3–301.
"Presentment" Section 3–501.

"Promise" Section 3–103.

"Prove" Section 3–103.

"Teller's check" Section 3–104.

"Unauthorized signature" Section 3–403.

(d) In addition, Article 1 contains general definitions and principles of construction and interpretation applicable throughout this Article.

As amended in 1990 and 1994.

§ 4–105. "Bank"; "Depositary Bank"; "Payor Bank"; "Intermediary Bank"; "Collecting Bank"; "Presenting Bank".

In this Article:

(1) "Bank" means a person engaged in the business of banking, including a savings bank, savings and loan association, credit union, or trust company;

(2) "Depositary bank" means the first bank to take an item even though it is also the payor bank, unless the item is presented for immediate payment over the counter;

(3) "Payor bank" means a bank that is the drawee of a draft;

(4) "Intermediary bank" means a bank to which an item is transferred in course of collection except the depositary or payor bank;

(5) "Collecting bank" means a bank handling an item for collection except the payor bank;

(6) "Presenting bank" means a bank presenting an item except a payor bank.

§ 4–106. Payable Through or Payable at Bank: Collecting Bank.

(a) If an item states that it is "payable through" a bank identified in the item, (i) the item designates the bank as a collecting bank and does not by itself authorize the bank to pay the item, and (ii) the item may be presented for payment only by or through the bank.

Alternative A

(b) If an item states that it is "payable at" a bank identified in the item, the item is equivalent to a draft drawn on the bank.

Alternative B

(b) If an item states that it is "payable at" a bank identified in the item, (i) the item designates the bank as a collecting bank and does not by itself authorize the bank to pay the item, and (ii) the item may be presented for payment only by or through the bank.

(c) If a draft names a nonbank drawee and it is unclear whether a bank named in the draft is a co-drawee or a collecting bank, the bank is a collecting bank.

§ 4–107. Separate Office of Bank.

A branch or separate office of a bank is a separate bank for the purpose of computing the time within which and determining the place at or to which action may be taken or notices or orders shall be given under this Article and under Article 3.

§ 4–108. Time of Receipt of Items.

(a) For the purpose of allowing time to process items, prove balances, and make the necessary entries on its books to determine its position for the day, a bank may fix an afternoon hour of 2 P.M. or later as a cutoff hour for the handling of money and items and the making of entries on its books.

(b) An item or deposit of money received on any day after a cutoff hour so fixed or after the close of the banking day may be treated as being received at the opening of the next banking day.

§ 4–109. Delays.

(a) Unless otherwise instructed, a collecting bank in a good faith effort to secure payment of a specific item drawn on a payor other than a bank, and with or without the approval of any person involved, may waive, modify, or extend time limits imposed or permitted by this [Act] for a period not exceeding two additional banking days without discharge of drawers or indorsers or liability to its transferor or a prior party.

(b) Delay by a collecting bank or payor bank beyond time limits prescribed or permitted by this [Act] or by instructions is excused if (i) the delay is caused by interruption of communication or computer facilities, suspension of payments by another bank, war, emergency conditions, failure of equipment, or other circumstances beyond the control of the bank, and (ii) the bank exercises such diligence as the circumstances require.

§ 4–110. Electronic Presentment.

(a) "Agreement for electronic presentment" means an agreement, clearing-house rule, or Federal Reserve regulation or operating circular, providing that presentment of an item may be made by transmission of an image of an item or information describing the item ("presentment notice") rather than delivery of the item itself. The agreement may provide for procedures governing retention, presentment, payment, dishonor, and other matters concerning items subject to the agreement.

(b) Presentment of an item pursuant to an agreement for presentment is made when the presentment notice is received.

(c) If presentment is made by presentment notice, a reference to "item" or "check" in this Article means the presentment notice unless the context otherwise indicates.

§ 4–111. Statute of Limitations.

An action to enforce an obligation, duty, or right arising under this Article must be commenced within three years after the [cause of action] accrues.

PART 2 Collection of Items: Depositary and Collecting Banks

§ 4–201. Status of Collecting Bank as Agent and Provisional Status of Credits; Applicability of Article; Item Indorsed "Pay Any Bank".

(a) Unless a contrary intent clearly appears and before the time that a settlement given by a collecting bank for an item is or becomes final, the bank, with respect to an item, is an agent or sub-agent of the owner of the item and any settlement given for the item is provisional. This provision applies regardless of the form of indorsement or lack of indorsement and even though credit given for the item is subject to immediate withdrawal as of right or is in fact withdrawn; but the continuance of ownership of an item by its owner and any rights of the owner to proceeds of the item are subject to rights of a collecting bank, such as those resulting from outstanding advances on the item and rights of recoupment or setoff. If an item is handled by banks for purposes of presentment, payment, collection, or return, the relevant provisions of this Article apply even though action of the parties clearly establishes that a particular bank has purchased the item and is the owner of it.

(b) After an item has been indorsed with the words "pay any bank" or the like, only a bank may acquire the rights of a holder until the item has been:

(1) returned to the customer initiating collection; or

(2) specially indorsed by a bank to a person who is not a bank.

§ 4–202. Responsibility for Collection or Return; When Action Timely.

(a) A collecting bank must exercise ordinary care in:

(1) presenting an item or sending it for presentment;

(2) sending notice of dishonor or nonpayment or returning an item other than a documentary draft to the bank's transferor after learning that the item has not been paid or accepted, as the case may be;

(3) settling for an item when the bank receives final settlement; and

(4) notifying its transferor of any loss or delay in transit within a reasonable time after discovery thereof.

(b) A collecting bank exercises ordinary care under subsection (a) by taking proper action before its midnight deadline following receipt of an item, notice, or settlement. Taking proper action within a reasonably longer time may constitute the exercise of ordinary care, but the bank has the burden of establishing timeliness.

(c) Subject to subsection (a)(1), a bank is not liable for the insolvency, neglect, misconduct, mistake, or default of another bank or person or for loss or destruction of an item in the possession of others or in transit.

§ 4–203. Effect of Instructions.

Subject to Article 3 concerning conversion of instruments (Section 3–420) and restrictive indorsements (Section 3–206), only a collecting bank's transferor can give instructions that affect the bank or constitute notice to it, and a collecting bank is not liable to prior parties for any action taken pursuant to the instructions or in accordance with any agreement with its transferor.

§ 4–204. Methods of Sending and Presenting; Sending Directly to Payor Bank.

(a) A collecting bank shall send items by a reasonably prompt method, taking into consideration relevant instructions, the nature of the item, the number of those items on hand, the cost of collection involved, and the method generally used by it or others to present those items.

(b) A collecting bank may send:

(1) an item directly to the payor bank;

(2) an item to a nonbank payor if authorized by its transferor; and

(3) an item other than documentary drafts to a nonbank payor, if authorized by Federal Reserve regulation or operating circular, clearing-house rule, or the like.

(c) Presentment may be made by a presenting bank at a place where the payor bank or other payor has requested that presentment be made.

§ 4–205. Depositary Bank Holder of Unindorsed Item.

If a customer delivers an item to a depositary bank for collection:

(1) the depositary bank becomes a holder of the item at the time it receives the item for collection if the customer at the time of delivery was a holder of the item, whether or not the customer indorses the item, and, if the bank satisfies the other requirements of Section 3–302, it is a holder in due course; and

(2) the depositary bank warrants to collecting banks, the payor bank or other payor, and the drawer that the amount of the item was paid to the customer or deposited to the customer's account.

§ 4–206. Transfer Between Banks.

Any agreed method that identifies the transferor bank is sufficient for the item's further transfer to another bank.

§ 4–207. Transfer Warranties.

(a) A customer or collecting bank that transfers an item and receives a settlement or other consideration warrants to the transferee and to any subsequent collecting bank that:

(1) the warrantor is a person entitled to enforce the item;

(2) all signatures on the item are authentic and authorized;

(3) the item has not been altered;

(4) the item is not subject to a defense or claim in recoupment (Section 3–305(a)) of any party that can be asserted against the warrantor; and

(5) the warrantor has no knowledge of any insolvency proceeding commenced with respect to the maker or acceptor or, in the case of an unaccepted draft, the drawer.

(b) If an item is dishonored, a customer or collecting bank transferring the item and receiving settlement or other consideration is obliged to pay the amount due on the item (i) according to the terms of the item at the time it was transferred, or (ii) if the transfer was of an incomplete item, according to its terms when completed as stated in Sections 3–115 and 3–407. The obligation of a transferor is owed to the transferee and to any subsequent collecting bank that takes the item in good faith. A transferor cannot disclaim its obligation under this subsection by an indorsement stating that it is made "without recourse" or otherwise disclaiming liability.

(c) A person to whom the warranties under subsection (a) are made and who took the item in good faith may recover from the warrantor as damages for breach of warranty an amount equal to the loss suffered as a result of the breach, but not more than the amount of the item plus expenses and loss of interest incurred as a result of the breach.

(d) The warranties stated in subsection (a) cannot be disclaimed with respect to checks. Unless notice of a claim for breach of warranty is given to the warrantor within 30 days after the claimant has reason to know of the breach and the identity of the warrantor, the warrantor is discharged to the extent of any loss caused by the delay in giving notice of the claim.

(e) A cause of action for breach of warranty under this section accrues when the claimant has reason to know of the breach.

§ 4–208. Presentment Warranties.

(a) If an unaccepted draft is presented to the drawee for payment or acceptance and the drawee pays or accepts the draft, (i) the person obtaining payment or acceptance, at the time of presentment, and (ii) a previous transferor of the draft, at the time of transfer, warrant to the drawee that pays or accepts the draft in good faith that:

(1) the warrantor is, or was, at the time the warrantor transferred the draft, a person entitled to enforce the draft or authorized to obtain payment or acceptance of the draft on behalf of a person entitled to enforce the draft;

(2) the draft has not been altered; and

(3) the warrantor has no knowledge that the signature of the purported drawer of the draft is unauthorized.

(b) A drawee making payment may recover from a warrantor damages for breach of warranty equal to the amount paid by the drawee less the amount the drawee received or is entitled to receive from the drawer because of the payment. In addition, the drawee is entitled to compensation for expenses and loss of interest resulting from the breach. The right of the drawee to recover damages under this subsection is not affected by any failure of the drawee to exercise ordinary care in making payment. If the drawee accepts the draft (i) breach of warranty is a defense to the obligation of the acceptor, and (ii) if the acceptor makes payment with respect to the draft, the acceptor is entitled to recover from a warrantor for breach of warranty the amounts stated in this subsection.

(c) If a drawee asserts a claim for breach of warranty under subsection (a) based on an unauthorized indorsement of the draft or an alteration of the draft, the warrantor may defend by proving that the indorsement is effective under Section 3–404 or 3–405 or the drawer is precluded under Section 3–406 or 4–406 from asserting against the drawee the unauthorized indorsement or alteration.

(d) If (i) a dishonored draft is presented for payment to the drawer or an indorser or (ii) any other item is presented for payment to a party obliged to pay the item, and the item is paid, the person obtaining payment and a prior transferor of the item warrant to the person making payment in good faith that the warrantor is, or was, at the time the warrantor transferred the item, a person entitled to enforce the item or authorized to obtain payment on behalf of a person entitled to enforce the item. The person making payment may recover from any warrantor for breach of warranty an amount equal to the amount paid plus expenses and loss of interest resulting from the breach.

(e) The warranties stated in subsections (a) and (d) cannot be disclaimed with respect to checks. Unless notice of a claim for breach of warranty is given to the warrantor within 30 days after the claimant has reason to know of the breach and the identity of the warrantor, the warrantor is discharged to the extent of any loss caused by the delay in giving notice of the claim.

(f) A cause of action for breach of warranty under this section accrues when the claimant has reason to know of the breach.

§ 4–209. Encoding and Retention Warranties.

(a) A person who encodes information on or with respect to an item after issue warrants to any subsequent collecting bank and to the payor bank or other payor that the information is correctly encoded. If the customer of a depositary bank encodes, that bank also makes the warranty.

(b) A person who undertakes to retain an item pursuant to an agreement for electronic presentment warrants to any subsequent collecting bank and to the payor bank or other payor that retention and presentment of the item comply with the agreement. If a customer of a depositary bank undertakes to retain an item, that bank also makes this warranty.

(c) A person to whom warranties are made under this section and who took the item in good faith may recover from the warrantor as damages for breach of warranty an amount equal to the loss suffered as a result of the breach, plus expenses and loss of interest incurred as a result of the breach.

§ 4–210. Security Interest of Collecting Bank in Items, Accompanying Documents and Proceeds.

(a) A collecting bank has a security interest in an item and any accompanying documents or the proceeds of either:

(1) in case of an item deposited in an account, to the extent to which credit given for the item has been withdrawn or applied;

(2) in case of an item for which it has given credit available for withdrawal as of right, to the extent of the credit given, whether or not the credit is drawn upon or there is a right of charge-back; or

(3) if it makes an advance on or against the item.

(b) If credit given for several items received at one time or pursuant to a single agreement is withdrawn or applied in part, the security interest remains upon all the items, any accompanying documents or the proceeds of either. For the purpose of this section, credits first given are first withdrawn.

(c) Receipt by a collecting bank of a final settlement for an item is a realization on its security interest in the item, accompanying documents, and proceeds. So long as the bank does not receive final settlement for the item or give up possession of the item or accompanying documents for purposes other than collection, the security interest continues to that extent and is subject to Article 9, but:

(1) no security agreement is necessary to make the security interest enforceable (Section 9–203 (1)(a));

(2) no filing is required to perfect the security interest; and

(3) the security interest has priority over conflicting perfected security interests in the item, accompanying documents, or proceeds.

§ 4–211. When Bank Gives Value for Purposes of Holder in Due Course.

For purposes of determining its status as a holder in due course, a bank has given value to the extent it has a security interest in an item, if the bank otherwise complies with the requirements of Section 3–302 on what constitutes a holder in due course.

§ 4–212. Presentment by Notice of Item Not Payable by, Through, or at Bank; Liability of Drawer or Indorser.

(a) Unless otherwise instructed, a collecting bank may present an item not payable by, through, or at a bank by sending to the party to accept or pay a written notice that the bank holds the item for acceptance or payment. The notice must be sent in time to be received on or before the day when presentment is due and the bank must meet any requirements of the party to accept or pay under Section 3–501 by the close of the bank's next banking day after it knows of the requirement.

(b) If presentment is made by notice and payment, acceptance, or request for compliance with a requirement under Section

3–501 is not received by the close of business on the day after maturity or, in the case of demand items, by the close of business on the third banking day after notice was sent, the presenting bank may treat the item as dishonored and charge any drawer or indorser by sending it notice of the facts.

§ 4–213. Medium and Time of Settlement by Bank.

(a) With respect to settlement by a bank, the medium and time of settlement may be prescribed by Federal Reserve regulations or circulars, clearing-house rules, and the like, or agreement. In the absence of such prescription:

(1) the medium of settlement is cash or credit to an account in a Federal Reserve bank of or specified by the person to receive settlement; and

(2) the time of settlement, is:

(i) with respect to tender of settlement by cash, a cashier's check, or teller's check, when the cash or check is sent or delivered;

(ii) with respect to tender of settlement by credit in an account in a Federal Reserve Bank, when the credit is made;

(iii) with respect to tender of settlement by a credit or debit to an account in a bank, when the credit or debit is made or, in the case of tender of settlement by authority to charge an account, when the authority is sent or delivered; or

(iv) with respect to tender of settlement by a funds transfer, when payment is made pursuant to Section 4A–406(a) to the person receiving settlement.

(b) If the tender of settlement is not by a medium authorized by subsection (a) or the time of settlement is not fixed by subsection (a), no settlement occurs until the tender of settlement is accepted by the person receiving settlement.

(c) If settlement for an item is made by cashier's check or teller's check and the person receiving settlement, before its midnight deadline:

(1) presents or forwards the check for collection, settlement is final when the check is finally paid; or

(2) fails to present or forward the check for collection, settlement is final at the midnight deadline of the person receiving settlement.

(d) If settlement for an item is made by giving authority to charge the account of the bank giving settlement in the bank receiving settlement, settlement is final when the charge is made by the bank receiving settlement if there are funds available in the account for the amount of the item.

§ 4–214. Right of Charge—Back or Refund; Liability of Collecting Bank: Return of Item.

(a) If a collecting bank has made provisional settlement with its customer for an item and fails by reason of dishonor, suspension of payments by a bank, or otherwise to receive settlement for the item which is or becomes final, the bank may revoke the settlement given by it, charge back the amount of any credit given for the item to its customer's account, or obtain refund from its customer, whether or not it is able to return the item, if by its midnight deadline or within a longer reasonable time after it learns the facts it returns the item or sends notification of the facts. If the return or notice is delayed beyond the bank's midnight deadline or a longer reasonable time after it learns the facts, the bank may revoke the settlement, charge back the credit, or obtain refund from its customer, but it is liable for any loss resulting from the delay. These rights to revoke, charge back, and obtain refund terminate if and when a settlement for the item received by the bank is or becomes final.

(b) A collecting bank returns an item when it is sent or delivered to the bank's customer or transferor or pursuant to its instructions.

(c) A depositary bank that is also the payor may charge back the amount of an item to its customer's account or obtain refund in accordance with the section governing return of an item received by a payor bank for credit on its books (Section 4–301).

(d) The right to charge back is not affected by:

(1) previous use of a credit given for the item; or

(2) failure by any bank to exercise ordinary care with respect to the item, but a bank so failing remains liable.

(e) A failure to charge back or claim refund does not affect other rights of the bank against the customer or any other party.

(f) If credit is given in dollars as the equivalent of the value of an item payable in foreign money, the dollar amount of any charge-back or refund must be calculated on the basis of the bank-offered spot rate for the foreign money prevailing on the day when the person entitled to the charge-back or refund learns that it will not receive payment in ordinary course.

As amended in 1990.

§ 4–215. Final Payment of Item by Payor Bank; When Provisional Debits and Credits Become Final; When Certain Credits Become Available for Withdrawal.

(a) An item is finally paid by a payor bank when the bank has first done any of the following:

(1) paid the item in cash;

(2) settled for the item without having a right to revoke the settlement under statute, clearing-house rule, or agreement; or

(3) made a provisional settlement for the item and failed to revoke the settlement in the time and manner permitted by statute, clearing-house rule, or agreement.

(b) If provisional settlement for an item does not become final, the item is not finally paid.

(c) If provisional settlement for an item between the presenting and payor banks is made through a clearing house or by debits or credits in an account between them, then to the extent that provisional debits or credits for the item are entered in accounts between the presenting and payor banks or between the presenting and successive prior collecting banks seriatim, they become final upon final payment of the item by the payor bank.

(d) If a collecting bank receives a settlement for an item which is or becomes final, the bank is accountable to its customer for the amount of the item and any provisional credit given for the item in an account with its customer becomes final.

(e) Subject to (i) applicable law stating a time for availability of funds and (ii) any right of the bank to apply the credit to an obligation of the customer, credit given by a bank for an item in a customer's account becomes available for withdrawal as of right:

(1) if the bank has received a provisional settlement for the item, when the settlement becomes final and the bank has had a reasonable time to receive return of the item and the item has not been received within that time;

(2) if the bank is both the depositary bank and the payor bank, and the item is finally paid, at the opening of the bank's second banking day following receipt of the item.

(f) Subject to applicable law stating a time for availability of funds and any right of a bank to apply a deposit to an obligation of the depositor, a deposit of money becomes available for withdrawal as of right at the opening of the bank's next banking day after receipt of the deposit.

§ 4–216. Insolvency and Preference.

(a) If an item is in or comes into the possession of a payor or collecting bank that suspends payment and the item has not been finally paid, the item must be returned by the receiver, trustee, or agent in charge of the closed bank to the presenting bank or the closed bank's customer.

(b) If a payor bank finally pays an item and suspends payments without making a settlement for the item with its customer or the presenting bank which settlement is or becomes final, the owner of the item has a preferred claim against the payor bank.

(c) If a payor bank gives or a collecting bank gives or receives a provisional settlement for an item and thereafter suspends payments, the suspension does not prevent or interfere with the settlement's becoming final if the finality occurs automatically upon the lapse of certain time or the happening of certain events.

(d) If a collecting bank receives from subsequent parties settlement for an item, which settlement is or becomes final and the bank suspends payments without making a settlement for the item with its customer which settlement is or becomes final, the owner of the item has a preferred claim against the collecting bank.

PART 3 Collection of Items: Payor Banks

§ 4–301. Deferred Posting; Recovery of Payment by Return of Items; Time of Dishonor; Return of Items by Payor Bank.

(a) If a payor bank settles for a demand item other than a documentary draft presented otherwise than for immediate payment over the counter before midnight of the banking day of receipt, the payor bank may revoke the settlement and recover the settlement if, before it has made final payment and before its midnight deadline, it

(1) returns the item; or

(2) sends written notice of dishonor or nonpayment if the item is unavailable for return.

(b) If a demand item is received by a payor bank for credit on its books, it may return the item or send notice of dishonor and may revoke any credit given or recover the amount thereof withdrawn by its customer, if it acts within the time limit and in the manner specified in subsection (a).

(c) Unless previous notice of dishonor has been sent, an item is dishonored at the time when for purposes of dishonor it is returned or notice sent in accordance with this section.

(d) An item is returned:

(1) as to an item presented through a clearing house, when it is delivered to the presenting or last collecting bank or to the clearing house or is sent or delivered in accordance with clearing-house rules; or

(2) in all other cases, when it is sent or delivered to the bank's customer or transferor or pursuant to instructions.

§ 4–302. Payor Bank's Responsibility for Late Return of Item.

(a) If an item is presented to and received by a payor bank, the bank is accountable for the amount of:

(1) a demand item, other than a documentary draft, whether properly payable or not, if the bank, in any case in which it is not also the depositary bank, retains the item beyond midnight of the banking day of receipt without settling for it or, whether or not it is also the depositary bank, does not pay or return the item or send notice of dishonor until after its midnight deadline; or

(2) any other properly payable item unless, within the time allowed for acceptance or payment of that item, the bank either accepts or pays the item or returns it and accompanying documents.

(b) The liability of a payor bank to pay an item pursuant to subsection (a) is subject to defenses based on breach of a presentment warranty (Section 4–208) or proof that the person seeking enforcement of the liability presented or transferred the item for the purpose of defrauding the payor bank.

§ 4–303. When Items Subject to Notice, Stop-Payment Order, Legal Process, or Setoff; Order in Which Items May Be Charged or Certified.

(a) Any knowledge, notice, or stop-payment order received by, legal process served upon, or setoff exercised by a payor bank comes too late to terminate, suspend, or modify the bank's right or duty to pay an item or to charge its customer's account for the item if the knowledge, notice, stop-payment order, or legal process is received or served and a reasonable time for the bank to act thereon expires or the setoff is exercised after the earliest of the following:

(1) the bank accepts or certifies the item;

(2) the bank pays the item in cash;

(3) the bank settles for the item without having a right to revoke the settlement under statute, clearing-house rule, or agreement;

(4) the bank becomes accountable for the amount of the item under Section 4–302 dealing with the payor bank's responsibility for late return of items; or

(5) with respect to checks, a cutoff hour no earlier than one hour after the opening of the next banking day after the banking day on which the bank received the check and no later than the close of that next banking day or, if no cutoff hour is fixed, the close of the next banking day after the banking day on which the bank received the check.

(b) Subject to subsection (a), items may be accepted, paid, certified, or charged to the indicated account of its customer in any order.

PART 4 Relationship Between Payor Bank and Its Customer

§ 4–401. When Bank May Charge Customer's Account.

(a) A bank may charge against the account of a customer an item that is properly payable from the account even though the charge creates an overdraft. An item is properly payable if it is authorized by the customer and is in accordance with any agreement between the customer and bank.

(b) A customer is not liable for the amount of an overdraft if the customer neither signed the item nor benefited from the proceeds of the item.

(c) A bank may charge against the account of a customer a check that is otherwise properly payable from the account, even though payment was made before the date of the check, unless the customer has given notice to the bank of the postdating describing the check with reasonable certainty. The notice is effective for the period stated in Section 4–403(b) for stop-payment orders, and must be received at such time and in such manner as to afford the bank a reasonable opportunity to act on it before the bank takes any action with respect to the check described in Section 4–303. If a bank charges against the account of a customer a check before the date stated in the notice of post-dating, the bank is liable for damages for the loss resulting from its act. The loss may include damages for dishonor of subsequent items under Section 4–402.

(d) A bank that in good faith makes payment to a holder may charge the indicated account of its customer according to:

(1) the original terms of the altered item; or

(2) the terms of the completed item, even though the bank knows the item has been completed unless the bank has notice that the completion was improper.

§4–402. Bank's Liability to Customer for Wrongful Dishonor; Time of Determining Insufficiency of Account.

(a) Except as otherwise provided in this Article, a payor bank wrongfully dishonors an item if it dishonors an item that is properly payable, but a bank may dishonor an item that would create an overdraft unless it has agreed to pay the overdraft.

(b) A payor bank is liable to its customer for damages proximately caused by the wrongful dishonor of an item. Liability is limited to actual damages proved and may include damages for an arrest or prosecution of the customer or other consequential damages. Whether any consequential damages are proximately caused by the wrongful dishonor is a question of fact to be determined in each case.

(c) A payor bank's determination of the customer's account balance on which a decision to dishonor for insufficiency of available funds is based may be made at any time between the time the item is received by the payor bank and the time that the payor bank returns the item or gives notice in lieu of return, and no more than one determination need be made. If, at the election of the payor bank, a subsequent balance determination is made for the purpose of reevaluating the bank's decision to dishonor the item, the account balance at that time is determinative of whether a dishonor for insufficiency of available funds is wrongful.

As amended in 1990.

See Appendix IX for material relating to changes made in text in 1990.

§ 4–403. Customer's Right to Stop Payment; Burden of Proof of Loss.

(a) A customer or any person authorized to draw on the account if there is more than one person may stop payment of any item drawn on the customer's account or close the account by an order to the bank describing the item or account with reasonable certainty received at a time and in a manner that affords the bank a reasonable opportunity to act on it before any action by the bank with respect to the item described in Section 4–303. If the signature of more than one person is required to draw on an account, any of these persons may stop payment or close the account.

(b) A stop-payment order is effective for six months, but it lapses after 14 calendar days if the original order was oral and was not confirmed in writing within that period. A stop-payment order may be renewed for additional six-month periods by a writing given to the bank within a period during which the stop-payment order is effective.

(c) The burden of establishing the fact and amount of loss resulting from the payment of an item contrary to a stop-payment order or order to close an account is on the customer. The loss from payment of an item contrary to a stop-payment order may include damages for dishonor of subsequent items under Section 4–402.

§ 4–404. Bank Not Obliged to Pay Check More Than Six Months Old.

A bank is under no obligation to a customer having a checking account to pay a check, other than a certified check, which is presented more than six months after its date, but it may charge its customer's account for a payment made thereafter in good faith.

§ 4–405. Death or Incompetence of Customer.

(a) A payor or collecting bank's authority to accept, pay, or collect an item or to account for proceeds of its collection, if otherwise effective, is not rendered ineffective by incompetence of a customer of either bank existing at the time the item is issued or its collection is undertaken if the bank does not know of an adjudication of incompetence. Neither death nor incompetence of a customer revokes the authority to accept, pay, collect, or account until the bank knows of the fact of death or of an adjudication of incompetence and has reasonable opportunity to act on it.

(b) Even with knowledge, a bank may for 10 days after the date of death pay or certify checks drawn on or before that date unless ordered to stop payment by a person claiming an interest in the account.

§ 4–406. Customer's Duty to Discover and Report Unauthorized Signature or Alteration.

(a) A bank that sends or makes available to a customer a statement of account showing payment of items for the account shall either return or make available to the customer the items paid or provide information in the statement of account sufficient to allow the customer reasonably to identify the items paid. The statement of account provides sufficient information if the item is described by item number, amount, and date of payment.

(b) If the items are not returned to the customer, the person retaining the items shall either retain the items or, if the items are destroyed, maintain the capacity to furnish legible copies of the items until the expiration of seven years after receipt of the items. A customer may request an item from the bank that paid the item, and that bank must provide in a reasonable time either the item or, if the item has been destroyed or is not otherwise obtainable, a legible copy of the item.

(c) If a bank sends or makes available a statement of account or items pursuant to subsection (a), the customer must exercise reasonable promptness in examining the statement or the items to determine whether any payment was not authorized because of an alteration of an item or because a purported signature by or on behalf of the customer was not authorized. If, based on the statement or items provided, the customer should reasonably have discovered the unauthorized payment, the customer must promptly notify the bank of the relevant facts.

(d) If the bank proves that the customer failed, with respect to an item, to comply with the duties imposed on the customer by subsection (c), the customer is precluded from asserting against the bank:

(1) the customer's unauthorized signature or any alteration on the item, if the bank also proves that it suffered a loss by reason of the failure; and

(2) the customer's unauthorized signature or alteration by the same wrong-doer on any other item paid in good faith by the bank if the payment was made before the bank received notice from the customer of the unauthorized signature or alteration and after the customer had been afforded a reasonable period of time, not exceeding 30 days, in which to examine the item or statement of account and notify the bank.

(e) If subsection (d) applies and the customer proves that the bank failed to exercise ordinary care in paying the item and that the failure substantially contributed to loss, the loss is allocated between the customer precluded and the bank asserting the preclusion according to the extent to which the failure of the customer to comply with subsection (c) and the failure of the bank to exercise ordinary care contributed to the loss. If the customer proves that the bank did not pay the item in good faith, the preclusion under subsection (d) does not apply.

(f) Without regard to care or lack of care of either the customer or the bank, a customer who does not within one year after the statement or items are made available to the customer (subsection (a)) discover and report the customer's unauthorized signature on or any alteration on the item is precluded from asserting against the bank the unauthorized signature or alteration. If there is a preclusion under this subsection, the payor bank may not recover for breach or warranty under Section 4–208 with respect to the unauthorized signature or alteration to which the preclusion applies.

§ 4–407. Payor Bank's Right to Subrogation on Improper Payment.

If a payor bank has paid an item over the order of the drawer or maker to stop payment, or after an account has been closed, or otherwise under circumstances giving a basis for objection by the drawer or maker, to prevent unjust enrichment and only to the extent necessary to prevent loss to the bank by reason of its payment of the item, the payor bank is subrogated to the rights

(1) of any holder in due course on the item against the drawer or maker;

(2) of the payee or any other holder of the item against the drawer or maker either on the item or under the transaction out of which the item arose; and

(3) of the drawer or maker against the payee or any other holder of the item with respect to the transaction out of which the item arose.

PART 5 Collection of Documentary Drafts

§ 4–501. Handling of Documentary Drafts; Duty to Send for Presentment and to Notify Customer of Dishonor.

A bank that takes a documentary draft for collection shall present or send the draft and accompanying documents for presentment and, upon learning that the draft has not been paid or accepted in due course, shall seasonably notify its customer of the fact even though it may have discounted or bought the draft or extended credit available for withdrawal as of right.

§ 4–502. Presentment of "On Arrival" Drafts.

If a draft or the relevant instructions require presentment "on arrival", "when goods arrive" or the like, the collecting bank need not present until in its judgment a reasonable time for arrival of the goods has expired. Refusal to pay or accept because the goods have not arrived is not dishonor; the bank must notify its transferor of the refusal but need not present the draft again until it is instructed to do so or learns of the arrival of the goods.

§ 4–503. Responsibility of Presenting Bank for Documents and Goods; Report of Reasons for Dishonor; Referee in Case of Need.

Unless otherwise instructed and except as provided in Article 5, a bank presenting a documentary draft:

(1) must deliver the documents to the drawee on acceptance of the draft if it is payable more than three days after presentment; otherwise, only on payment; and

(2) upon dishonor, either in the case of presentment for acceptance or presentment for payment, may seek and follow instructions from any referee in case of need designated in the draft or, if the presenting bank does not choose to utilize the referee's services, it must use diligence and good faith to ascertain the reason for dishonor, must notify its transferor of the dishonor and of the results of its effort to ascertain the reasons therefor, and must request instructions.

However the presenting bank is under no obligation with respect to goods represented by the documents except to follow any reasonable instructions seasonably received; it has a right to reimbursement for any expense incurred in following instructions and to prepayment of or indemnity for those expenses.

§ 4–504. Privilege of Presenting Bank to Deal With Goods; Security Interest for Expenses.

(a) A presenting bank that, following the dishonor of a documentary draft, has seasonably requested instructions but does not receive them within a reasonable time may store, sell, or otherwise deal with the goods in any reasonable manner.

(b) For its reasonable expenses incurred by action under subsection (a) the presenting bank has a lien upon the goods or their proceeds, which may be foreclosed in the same manner as an unpaid seller's lien.

ARTICLE 4A
FUNDS TRANSFERS

PART 1 Subject Matter and Definitions

§ 4A–101. Short Title.

This Article may be cited as Uniform Commercial Code— Funds Transfers.

§ 4A–102. Subject Matter.

Except as otherwise provided in Section 4A–108, this Article applies to funds transfers defined in Section 4A–104.

§ 4A–103. Payment Order—Definitions.

(a) In this Article:

(1) "Payment order" means an instruction of a sender to a receiving bank, transmitted orally, electronically, or in writing, to pay, or to cause another bank to pay, a fixed or determinable amount of money to a beneficiary if:

(i) the instruction does not state a condition to payment to the beneficiary other than time of payment,

(ii) the receiving bank is to be reimbursed by debiting an account of, or otherwise receiving payment from, the sender, and

(iii) the instruction is transmitted by the sender directly to the receiving bank or to an agent, funds-transfer system, or communication system for transmittal to the receiving bank.

(2) "Beneficiary" means the person to be paid by the beneficiary's bank.

(3) "Beneficiary's bank" means the bank identified in a payment order in which an account of the beneficiary is to be credited pursuant to the order or which otherwise is to make payment to the beneficiary if the order does not provide for payment to an account.

(4) "Receiving bank" means the bank to which the sender's instruction is addressed.

(5) "Sender" means the person giving the instruction to the receiving bank.

(b) If an instruction complying with subsection (a)(1) is to make more than one payment to a beneficiary, the instruction is a separate payment order with respect to each payment.

(c) A payment order is issued when it is sent to the receiving bank.

§ 4A–104. Funds Transfer—Definitions.

In this Article:

(a) "Funds transfer" means the series of transactions, beginning with the originator's payment order, made for the purpose of making payment to the beneficiary of the order. The term includes any payment order issued by the originator's bank or an intermediary bank intended to carry out the originator's payment order. A funds transfer is completed by acceptance by the beneficiary's bank of a payment order for the benefit of the beneficiary of the originator's payment order.

(b) "Intermediary bank" means a receiving bank other than the originator's bank or the beneficiary's bank.

(c) "Originator" means the sender of the first payment order in a funds transfer.

(d) "Originator's bank" means (i) the receiving bank to which the payment order of the originator is issued if the originator is not a bank, or (ii) the originator if the originator is a bank.

§ 4A–105. Other Definitions.

(a) In this Article:

(1) "Authorized account" means a deposit account of a customer in a bank designated by the customer as a source of payment orders issued by the customer to the bank. If a customer does not so designate an account, any account of the customer is an authorized account if payment of a payment order from that account is not inconsistent with a restriction on the use of that account.

(2) "Bank" means a person engaged in the business of banking and includes a savings bank, savings and loan association, credit union, and trust company. A branch or separate office of a bank is a separate bank for purposes of this Article.

(3) "Customer" means a person, including a bank, having an account with a bank or from whom a bank has agreed to receive payment orders.

(4) "Funds-transfer business day" of a receiving bank means the part of a day during which the receiving bank is open for the receipt, processing, and transmittal of payment orders and cancellations and amendments of payment orders.

(5) "Funds-transfer system" means a wire transfer network, automated clearing house, or other communication system of a clearing house or other association of banks through which a payment order by a bank may be transmitted to the bank to which the order is addressed.

(6) "Good faith" means honesty in fact and the observance of reasonable commercial standards of fair dealing.

(7) "Prove" with respect to a fact means to meet the burden of establishing the fact (Section 1–201(8)).

(b) Other definitions applying to this Article and the sections in which they appear are:

"Acceptance" Section 4A–209
"Beneficiary" Section 4A–103
"Beneficiary's bank" Section 4A–103
"Executed" Section 4A–301
"Execution date" Section 4A–301
"Funds transfer" Section 4A–104
"Funds-transfer system rule" Section 4A–501
"Intermediary bank" Section 4A–104
"Originator" Section 4A–104
"Originator's bank" Section 4A–104
"Payment by beneficiary's bank to beneficiary" Section 4A–405
"Payment by originator to beneficiary" Section 4A–406
"Payment by sender to receiving bank" Section 4A–403
"Payment date" Section 4A–401
"Payment order" Section 4A–103
"Receiving bank" Section 4A–103
"Security procedure" Section 4A–201
"Sender" Section 4A–103

(c) The following definitions in Article 4 apply to this Article:

"Clearing house" Section 4–104
"Item" Section 4–104
"Suspends payments" Section 4–104

(d) In addition Article 1 contains general definitions and principles of construction and interpretation applicable throughout this Article.

§ 4A–106. Time Payment Order Is Received.

(a) The time of receipt of a payment order or communication cancelling or amending a payment order is determined by the rules applicable to receipt of a notice stated in Section 1–201(27). A receiving bank may fix a cut-off time or times on a funds-transfer business day for the receipt and processing of payment orders and communications cancelling or amending payment orders. Different cut-off times may apply to payment orders, cancellations, or amendments, or to different categories of payment orders, cancellations, or amendments. A cut-off time may apply to senders generally or different cut-off times may apply to different senders or categories of payment orders. If a payment order or communication cancelling or amending a payment order is received after the close of a funds-transfer business day or after the appropriate cut-off time on a funds-transfer business day, the receiving bank may treat the payment order or communication as received at the opening of the next funds-transfer business day.

(b) If this Article refers to an execution date or payment date or states a day on which a receiving bank is required to take action, and the date or day does not fall on a funds-transfer business day, the next day that is a funds-transfer business day is treated as the date or day stated, unless the contrary is stated in this Article.

§ 4A–107. Federal Reserve Regulations and Operating Circulars.

Regulations of the Board of Governors of the Federal Reserve System and operating circulars of the Federal Reserve Banks supersede any inconsistent provision of this Article to the extent of the inconsistency.

§ 4A–108. Exclusion of Consumer Transactions Governed by Federal Law.

This Article does not apply to a funds transfer any part of which is governed by the Electronic Fund Transfer Act of 1978 (Title XX, Public Law 95–630, 92 Stat. 3728, 15 U.S.C. § 1693 et seq.) as amended from time to time.

PART 2 Issue and Acceptance of Payment Order

§ 4A–201. Security Procedure.

"Security procedure" means a procedure established by agreement of a customer and a receiving bank for the purpose of (i) verifying that a payment order or communication amending or cancelling a payment order is that of the customer, or (ii) detecting error in the transmission or the content of the payment order or communication. A security procedure may require the use of algorithms or other codes, identifying words or numbers, encryption, callback procedures, or similar security devices. Comparison of a signature on a payment order or communication with an authorized specimen signature of the customer is not by itself a security procedure.

§ 4A–202. Authorized and Verified Payment Orders.

(a) A payment order received by the receiving bank is the authorized order of the person identified as sender if that person authorized the order or is otherwise bound by it under the law of agency.

(b) If a bank and its customer have agreed that the authenticity of payment orders issued to the bank in the name of the customer as sender will be verified pursuant to a security procedure, a payment order received by the receiving bank is effective as the order of the customer, whether or not authorized, if (i) the security procedure is a commercially reasonable method of providing security against unauthorized payment orders, and (ii) the bank proves that it accepted the payment order in good faith and in compliance with the security procedure and any written agreement or instruction of the customer restricting acceptance of payment orders issued in the name of the customer. The bank is not required to follow an instruction that violates a written agreement with the customer or notice of which is not received at a time and in a manner affording the bank a reasonable opportunity to act on it before the payment order is accepted.

(c) Commercial reasonableness of a security procedure is a question of law to be determined by considering the wishes of the customer expressed to the bank, the circumstances of the customer known to the bank, including the size, type, and frequency of payment orders normally issued by the customer to the bank, alternative security procedures offered to the customer, and security procedures in general use by customers and receiving banks similarly situated. A security procedure is deemed to be commercially reasonable if (i) the security procedure was chosen by the customer after the bank offered, and the customer refused, a security procedure that was commercially reasonable for that customer, and (ii) the customer expressly agreed in writing to be bound by any payment order, whether or not authorized, issued in its name and accepted by the bank in compliance with the security procedure chosen by the customer.

(d) The term "sender" in this Article includes the customer in whose name a payment order is issued if the order is the authorized order of the customer under subsection (a), or it is effective as the order of the customer under subsection (b).

(e) This section applies to amendments and cancellations of payment orders to the same extent it applies to payment orders.

(f) Except as provided in this section and in Section 4A–203(a)(1), rights and obligations arising under this section or Section 4A–203 may not be varied by agreement.

§ 4A–203. Unenforceability of Certain Verified Payment Orders.

(a) If an accepted payment order is not, under Section 4A–202(a), an authorized order of a customer identified as sender, but is effective as an order of the customer pursuant to Section 4A–202(b), the following rules apply:

(1) By express written agreement, the receiving bank may limit the extent to which it is entitled to enforce or retain payment of the payment order.

(2) The receiving bank is not entitled to enforce or retain payment of the payment order if the customer proves that the order was not caused, directly or indirectly, by a person (i) entrusted at any time with duties to act for the customer with respect to payment orders or the security procedure, or (ii) who obtained access to transmitting facilities of the customer or who obtained, from a source controlled by the customer and without authority of the receiving bank, information facilitating breach of the security procedure, regardless of how the information was obtained or whether the customer was at fault. Information includes any access device, computer software, or the like.

(b) This section applies to amendments of payment orders to the same extent it applies to payment orders.

§ 4A–204. Refund of Payment and Duty of Customer to Report with Respect to Unauthorized Payment Order.

(a) If a receiving bank accepts a payment order issued in the name of its customer as sender which is (i) not authorized and not effective as the order of the customer under Section 4A–202, or (ii) not enforceable, in whole or in part, against the customer under Section 4A–203, the bank shall refund any payment of the payment order received from the customer to the extent the bank is not entitled to enforce payment and shall pay interest on the refundable amount calculated from the date the bank received payment to the date of the refund. However, the customer is not entitled to interest from the bank on the amount to be refunded if the customer fails to exercise ordinary care to determine that the order was not authorized by the customer and to notify the bank of the relevant facts within a reasonable time not exceeding 90 days after the date the customer received notification from the bank that the order was accepted or that the customer's account was debited with respect to the order. The bank is not entitled to any recovery from the customer on account of a failure by the customer to give notification as stated in this section.

(b) Reasonable time under subsection (a) may be fixed by agreement as stated in Section 1–204(1), but the obligation of a receiving bank to refund payment as stated in subsection (a) may not otherwise be varied by agreement.

§ 4A–205. Erroneous Payment Orders.

(a) If an accepted payment order was transmitted pursuant to a security procedure for the detection of error and the payment order (i) erroneously instructed payment to a beneficiary not intended by the sender, (ii) erroneously instructed payment in an amount greater than the amount intended by the sender, or (iii) was an erroneously transmitted duplicate of a payment order previously sent by the sender, the following rules apply:

(1) If the sender proves that the sender or a person acting on behalf of the sender pursuant to Section 4A–206 complied with the security procedure and that the error would have been detected if the receiving bank had also complied, the sender is not obliged to pay the order to the extent stated in paragraphs (2) and (3).

(2) If the funds transfer is completed on the basis of an erroneous payment order described in clause (i) or (iii) of subsection (a), the sender is not obliged to pay the order and the receiving bank is entitled to recover from the beneficiary any amount paid to the beneficiary to the extent allowed by the law governing mistake and restitution.

(3) If the funds transfer is completed on the basis of a payment order described in clause (ii) of subsection (a), the sender is not obliged to pay the order to the extent the amount received by the beneficiary is greater than the amount intended by the sender. In that case, the receiving bank is entitled to recover from the beneficiary the excess amount received to the extent allowed by the law governing mistake and restitution.

(b) If (i) the sender of an erroneous payment order described in subsection (a) is not obliged to pay all or part of the order, and (ii) the sender receives notification from the receiving bank that the order was accepted by the bank or that the sender's account was debited with respect to the order, the sender has a duty to exercise ordinary care, on the basis of information available to the sender, to discover the error with respect to the order and to advise the bank of the relevant facts within a reasonable time, not exceeding 90 days, after the bank's notification was received by the sender. If the bank proves that the sender failed to perform that duty, the sender is liable to the bank for the loss the bank proves it incurred as a result of the failure, but the liability of the sender may not exceed the amount of the sender's order.

(c) This section applies to amendments to payment orders to the same extent it applies to payment orders.

§ 4A–206. Transmission of Payment Order Through Funds-Transfer or Other Communication System.

(a) If a payment order addressed to a receiving bank is transmitted to a funds-transfer system or other third-party communication system for transmittal to the bank, the system is deemed to be an agent of the sender for the purpose of transmitting the payment order to the bank. If there is a discrepancy between the terms of the payment order transmitted to the system and the terms of the payment order transmitted by the system to the bank, the terms of the payment order of the sender are those transmitted by the system. This section does not apply to a funds-transfer system of the Federal Reserve Banks.

(b) This section applies to cancellations and amendments of payment orders to the same extent it applies to payment orders.

§ 4A–207. Misdescription of Beneficiary.

(a) Subject to subsection (b), if, in a payment order received by the beneficiary's bank, the name, bank account number, or other identification of the beneficiary refers to a nonexistent or unidentifiable person or account, no person has rights as a beneficiary of the order and acceptance of the order cannot occur.

(b) If a payment order received by the beneficiary's bank identifies the beneficiary both by name and by an identifying or bank account number and the name and number identify different persons, the following rules apply:

(1) Except as otherwise provided in subsection (c), if the beneficiary's bank does not know that the name and number refer to different persons, it may rely on the number as the proper identification of the beneficiary of the order. The beneficiary's bank need not determine whether the name and number refer to the same person.

(2) If the beneficiary's bank pays the person identified by name or knows that the name and number identify different persons, no person has rights as beneficiary except the person paid by the beneficiary's bank if that person was entitled to receive payment from the originator of the funds transfer. If no person has rights as beneficiary, acceptance of the order cannot occur.

(c) If (i) a payment order described in subsection (b) is accepted, (ii) the originator's payment order described the beneficiary inconsistently by name and number, and (ii) the beneficiary's bank pays the person identified by number as permitted by subsection (b)(1), the following rules apply:

(1) If the originator is a bank, the originator is obliged to pay its order.

(2) If the originator is not a bank and proves that the person identified by number was not entitled to receive payment from the originator, the originator is not obliged to pay its order unless the originator's bank proves that the originator, before acceptance of the originator's order, had notice that payment of a payment order issued by the originator might be made by the beneficiary's bank on the basis of an identifying or bank account number even if it identifies a person different from the named beneficiary. Proof of notice may be made by any admissible evidence. The originator's bank satisfies the burden of proof if it proves that the originator, before the payment order was accepted, signed a writing stating the information to which the notice relates.

(d) In a case governed by subsection (b)(1), if the beneficiary's bank rightfully pays the person identified by number and that person was not entitled to receive payment from the originator, the amount paid may be recovered from that person to the extent allowed by the law governing mistake and restitution as follows:

(1) If the originator is obliged to pay its payment order as stated in subsection (c), the originator has the right to recover.

(2) If the originator is not a bank and is not obliged to pay its payment order, the originator's bank has the right to recover.

§ 4A–208. Misdescription of Intermediary Bank or Beneficiary's Bank.

(a) This subsection applies to a payment order identifying an intermediary bank or the beneficiary's bank only by an identifying number.

(1) The receiving bank may rely on the number as the proper identification of the intermediary or beneficiary's bank and need not determine whether the number identifies a bank.

(2) The sender is obliged to compensate the receiving bank for any loss and expenses incurred by the receiving bank as a result of its reliance on the number in executing or attempting to execute the order.

(b) This subsection applies to a payment order identifying an intermediary bank or the beneficiary's bank both by name and an identifying number if the name and number identify different persons.

(1) If the sender is a bank, the receiving bank may rely on the number as the proper identification of the intermediary or beneficiary's bank if the receiving bank, when it executes the sender's order, does not know that the name and number identify different persons. The receiving bank need not determine whether the name and number refer to the same person or whether the name refers to a bank. The sender is obliged to compensate the receiving bank for any loss and expenses incurred by the receiving bank as a result of its reliance on the number in executing or attempting to execute the order.

(2) If the sender is not a bank and the receiving bank proves that the sender, before the payment order was accepted, had notice that the receiving bank might rely on the number as the proper identification of the intermediary or beneficiary's bank even if it identifies a person different from the bank identified by name, the rights and obligations of the sender and the receiving bank are governed by subsection (b)(1), as though the sender were a bank. Proof of notice may be made by any admissible evidence. The receiving bank satisfies the burden of proof if it proves that the sender, before the payment order was accepted, signed a writing stating the information to which the notice relates.

(3) Regardless of whether the sender is a bank, the receiving bank may rely on the name as the proper identification of the intermediary or beneficiary's bank if the receiving bank, at the time it executes the sender's order, does not know that the name and number identify different persons. The receiving bank need not determine whether the name and number refer to the same person.

(4) If the receiving bank knows that the name and number identify different persons, reliance on either the name or the number in executing the sender's payment order is a breach of the obligation stated in Section 4A–302(a)(1).

§ 4A–209. Acceptance of Payment Order.

(a) Subject to subsection (d), a receiving bank other than the beneficiary's bank accepts a payment order when it executes the order.

(b) Subject to subsections (c) and (d), a beneficiary's bank accepts a payment order at the earliest of the following times:

(1) when the bank (i) pays the beneficiary as stated in Section 4A–405(a) or 4A–405(b), or (ii) notifies the beneficiary of receipt of the order or that the account of the beneficiary has been credited with respect to the order unless the notice indicates that the bank is rejecting the order or that funds with respect to the order may not be withdrawn or used until receipt of payment from the sender of the order;

(2) when the bank receives payment of the entire amount of the sender's order pursuant to Section 4A–403(a)(1) or 4A–403(a)(2); or

(3) the opening of the next funds-transfer business day of the bank following the payment date of the order if, at that time, the amount of the sender's order is fully covered by a withdrawable credit balance in an authorized account of the sender or the bank has otherwise received full payment from the sender, unless the order was rejected before that time or is rejected within (i) one hour after that time, or (ii) one hour after the opening of the next business day of the sender following the payment date if that time is later. If notice of rejection is received by the sender after the payment date and the authorized account of the sender does not bear interest, the bank is obliged to pay interest to the sender on the amount of the order for the number of days elapsing after the payment date to the day the sender receives notice or learns that the order was not accepted, counting that day as an elapsed day. If the withdrawable credit balance during that period falls below the amount of the order, the amount of interest payable is reduced accordingly.

(c) Acceptance of a payment order cannot occur before the order is received by the receiving bank. Acceptance does not occur under subsection (b)(2) or (b)(3) if the beneficiary of the payment order does not have an account with the receiving bank, the account has been closed, or the receiving bank is not permitted by law to receive credits for the beneficiary's account.

(d) A payment order issued to the originator's bank cannot be accepted until the payment date if the bank is the beneficiary's bank, or the execution date if the bank is not the beneficiary's bank. If the originator's bank executes the originator's payment order before the execution date or pays the beneficiary of the originator's payment order before the payment date and the payment order is subsequently canceled pursuant to Section 4A–211(b), the bank may recover from the beneficiary any payment received to the extent allowed by the law governing mistake and restitution.

§ 4A–210. Rejection of Payment Order.

(a) A payment order is rejected by the receiving bank by a notice of rejection transmitted to the sender orally, electronically, or in writing. A notice of rejection need not use any particular words and is sufficient if it indicates that the receiving bank is rejecting the order or will not execute or pay the order. Rejection is effective when the notice is given if transmission is by a means that is reasonable in the circumstances. If notice of rejection is given by a means that is not reasonable, rejection is effective when the notice is received. If an agreement of the sender and receiving bank establishes the means to be used to reject a payment order, (i) any means complying with the agreement is reasonable and (ii) any means not complying is not reasonable unless no significant delay in receipt of the notice resulted from the use of the noncomplying means.

(b) This subsection applies if a receiving bank other than the beneficiary's bank fails to execute a payment order despite the existence on the execution date of a withdrawable credit balance in an authorized account of the sender sufficient to cover the order. If the sender does not receive notice of rejection of the order on the execution date and the authorized account of the sender does not bear interest, the bank is obliged to pay interest to the sender on the amount of the order for the number of days elapsing after the execution date to the earlier of the day the order is canceled pursuant to Section 4A–211(d) or the day the sender receives notice or learns that the order was not executed, counting the final day of the period as an elapsed day. If the withdrawable credit balance during that period falls below the amount of the order, the amount of interest is reduced accordingly.

(c) If a receiving bank suspends payments, all unaccepted payment orders issued to it are deemed rejected at the time the bank suspends payments.

(d) Acceptance of a payment order precludes a later rejection of the order. Rejection of a payment order precludes a later acceptance of the order.

§ 4A–211. Cancellation and Amendment of Payment Order.

(a) A communication of the sender of a payment order cancelling or amending the order may be transmitted to the receiving bank orally, electronically, or in writing. If a security procedure is in effect between the sender and the receiving bank, the communication is not effective to cancel or amend the order unless the communication is verified pursuant to the security procedure or the bank agrees to the cancellation or amendment.

(b) Subject to subsection (a), a communication by the sender cancelling or amending a payment order is effective to cancel or amend the order if notice of the communication is received at a time and in a manner affording the receiving bank a reasonable opportunity to act on the communication before the bank accepts the payment order.

(c) After a payment order has been accepted, cancellation or amendment of the order is not effective unless the receiving bank agrees or a funds-transfer system rule allows cancellation or amendment without agreement of the bank.

(1) With respect to a payment order accepted by a receiving bank other than the beneficiary's bank, cancellation or amendment is not effective unless a conforming cancellation or amendment of the payment order issued by the receiving bank is also made.

(2) With respect to a payment order accepted by the beneficiary's bank, cancellation or amendment is not effective unless the order was issued in execution of an unauthorized payment order, or because of a mistake by a sender in the funds transfer which resulted in the issuance of a payment order (i) that is a duplicate of a payment order previously issued by the sender, (ii) that orders payment to a beneficiary not entitled to receive payment from the originator, or (iii) that orders payment in an amount greater than the amount the beneficiary was entitled to receive from the originator. If the payment order is canceled or amended, the beneficiary's bank is entitled to recover from the beneficiary any amount paid to the beneficiary to the extent allowed by the law governing mistake and restitution.

(d) An unaccepted payment order is canceled by operation of law at the close of the fifth funds-transfer business day of the receiving bank after the execution date or payment date of the order.

(e) A canceled payment order cannot be accepted. If an accepted payment order is canceled, the acceptance is nullified and no person has any right or obligation based on the acceptance. Amendment of a payment order is deemed to be cancellation of the original order at the time of amendment and issue of a new payment order in the amended form at the same time.

(f) Unless otherwise provided in an agreement of the parties or in a funds-transfer system rule, if the receiving bank, after accepting a payment order, agrees to cancellation or amendment of the order by the sender or is bound by a funds-transfer system rule allowing cancellation or amendment without the bank's agreement, the sender, whether or not cancellation or amendment is effective, is liable to the bank for any loss and expenses, including reasonable attorney's fees, incurred by the bank as a result of the cancellation or amendment or attempted cancellation or amendment.

(g) A payment order is not revoked by the death or legal incapacity of the sender unless the receiving bank knows of the death or of an adjudication of incapacity by a court of competent jurisdiction and has reasonable opportunity to act before acceptance of the order.

(h) A funds-transfer system rule is not effective to the extent it conflicts with subsection (c)(2).

§ 4A–212. Liability and Duty of Receiving Bank Regarding Unaccepted Payment Order.

If a receiving bank fails to accept a payment order that it is obliged by express agreement to accept, the bank is liable for breach of the agreement to the extent provided in the agreement or in this Article, but does not otherwise have any duty to accept a payment order or, before acceptance, to take any action, or refrain from taking action, with respect to the order except as provided in this Article or by express agreement. Liability based on acceptance arises only when acceptance occurs as stated in Section 4A–209, and liability is limited to that provided in this Article. A receiving bank is not the agent of the sender or beneficiary of the payment order it accepts, or of any other party to the funds transfer, and the bank owes no duty to any party to the funds transfer except as provided in this Article or by express agreement.

PART 3 Execution of Sender's Payment Order by Receiving Bank

§ 4A–301. Execution and Execution Date.

(a) A payment order is "executed" by the receiving bank when it issues a payment order intended to carry out the payment order received by the bank. A payment order received by the beneficiary's bank can be accepted but cannot be executed.

(b) "Execution date" of a payment order means the day on which the receiving bank may properly issue a payment order in execution of the sender's order. The execution date may be determined by instruction of the sender but cannot be earlier than the day the order is received and, unless otherwise determined, is the day the order is received. If the sender's instruction states a payment date, the execution date is the payment date or an earlier date on which execution is reasonably necessary to allow payment to the beneficiary on the payment date.

§ 4A–302. Obligations of Receiving Bank in Execution of Payment Order.

(a) Except as provided in subsections (b) through (d), if the receiving bank accepts a payment order pursuant to Section 4A–209(a), the bank has the following obligations in executing the order:

(1) The receiving bank is obliged to issue, on the execution date, a payment order complying with the sender's order and to follow the sender's instructions concerning (i) any intermediary bank or funds-transfer system to be used in carrying out the funds transfer, or (ii) the means by which payment orders are to be transmitted in the funds transfer. If the originator's bank issues a payment order to an intermediary bank, the originator's bank is obliged to instruct the intermediary bank according to the instruction of the originator. An intermediary bank in the funds transfer is similarly bound by an instruction given to it by the sender of the payment order it accepts.

(2) If the sender's instruction states that the funds transfer is to be carried out telephonically or by wire transfer or otherwise indicates that the funds transfer is to be carried out by the most expeditious means, the receiving bank is obliged to transmit its payment order by the most expeditious available means, and to instruct any intermediary bank accordingly. If a sender's instruction states a payment date, the receiving bank is obliged to transmit its payment order at a time and by means reasonably necessary to allow payment to the beneficiary on the payment date or as soon thereafter as is feasible.

(b) Unless otherwise instructed, a receiving bank executing a payment order may (i) use any funds-transfer system if use of that system is reasonable in the circumstances, and (ii) issue a payment order to the beneficiary's bank or to an intermediary bank through which a payment order conforming to the sender's order can expeditiously be issued to the beneficiary's bank if the receiving bank exercises ordinary care in the selection of the intermediary bank. A receiving bank is not required to follow an instruction of the sender designating a funds-transfer system to be used in carrying out the funds transfer if the receiving bank, in good faith, determines that it is not feasible to follow the instruction or that following the instruction would unduly delay completion of the funds transfer.

(c) Unless subsection (a)(2) applies or the receiving bank is otherwise instructed, the bank may execute a payment order by transmitting its payment order by first class mail or by any means reasonable in the circumstances. If the receiving bank is instructed to execute the sender's order by transmitting its payment order by a particular means, the receiving bank may issue its payment order by the means stated or by any means as expeditious as the means stated.

(d) Unless instructed by the sender, (i) the receiving bank may not obtain payment of its charges for services and expenses in connection with the execution of the sender's order by issuing a payment order in an amount equal to the amount of the sender's order less the amount of the charges, and (ii) may not instruct a subsequent receiving bank to obtain payment of its charges in the same manner.

§ 4A–303. Erroneous Execution of Payment Order.

(a) A receiving bank that (i) executes the payment order of the sender by issuing a payment order in an amount greater than the amount of the sender's order, or (ii) issues a payment order in execution of the sender's order and then issues a duplicate order, is entitled to payment of the amount of the sender's order under Section 4A–402(c) if that subsection is otherwise satisfied. The bank is entitled to recover from the beneficiary of the erroneous order the excess payment received to the extent allowed by the law governing mistake and restitution.

(b) A receiving bank that executes the payment order of the sender by issuing a payment order in an amount less than the amount of the sender's order is entitled to payment of the amount of the sender's order under Section 4A–402(c) if (i) that subsection is otherwise satisfied and (ii) the bank corrects its mistake by issuing an additional payment order for the benefit of the beneficiary of the sender's order. If the error is not corrected, the issuer of the erroneous order is entitled to receive or retain payment from the sender of the order it accepted only to the extent of the amount of the erroneous order. This subsection does not apply if the receiving bank executes the sender's payment order by issuing a payment order in an amount less than the amount of the sender's order for the purpose of obtaining payment of its charges for services and expenses pursuant to instruction of the sender.

(c) If a receiving bank executes the payment order of the sender by issuing a payment order to a beneficiary different from the beneficiary of the sender's order and the funds transfer is completed on the basis of that error, the sender of the payment order that was erroneously executed and all previous senders in the funds transfer are not obliged to pay the payment orders they issued. The issuer of the erroneous order is entitled to recover from the beneficiary of the order the payment received to the extent allowed by the law governing mistake and restitution.

§ 4A–304. Duty of Sender to Report Erroneously Executed Payment Order.

If the sender of a payment order that is erroneously executed as stated in Section 4A–303 receives notification from the receiving bank that the order was executed or that the sender's account was debited with respect to the order, the sender has a duty to exercise ordinary care to determine, on the basis of information available to the sender, that the order was erroneously executed and to notify the bank of the relevant facts within a reasonable time not exceeding 90 days after the notification from the bank was received by the sender. If the sender fails to perform that duty, the bank is not obliged to pay interest on any amount refundable to the sender under Section 4A–402(d) for the period before the bank learns of the execution error. The bank is not entitled to any recovery from the sender on account of a failure by the sender to perform the duty stated in this section.

§ 4A–305. Liability for Late or Improper Execution or Failure to Execute Payment Order.

(a) If a funds transfer is completed but execution of a payment order by the receiving bank in breach of Section 4A–302 results in delay in payment to the beneficiary, the bank is obliged to pay interest to either the originator or the beneficiary of the funds transfer for the period of delay caused by the improper execution. Except as provided in subsection (c), additional damages are not recoverable.

(b) If execution of a payment order by a receiving bank in breach of Section 4A–302 results in (i) noncompletion of the funds transfer, (ii) failure to use an intermediary bank designated by the originator, or (iii) issuance of a payment order that does not comply with the terms of the payment order of the originator, the bank is liable to the originator for its expenses in the funds transfer and for incidental expenses and interest losses, to the extent not covered by subsection (a), resulting from the improper execution. Except as provided in subsection (c), additional damages are not recoverable.

(c) In addition to the amounts payable under subsections (a) and (b), damages, including consequential damages, are recoverable to the extent provided in an express written agreement of the receiving bank.

(d) If a receiving bank fails to execute a payment order it was obliged by express agreement to execute, the receiving bank is liable to the sender for its expenses in the transaction and for incidental expenses and interest losses resulting from the failure to execute. Additional damages, including consequential damages, are recoverable to the extent provided in an express written agreement of the receiving bank, but are not otherwise recoverable.

(e) Reasonable attorney's fees are recoverable if demand for compensation under subsection (a) or (b) is made and refused before an action is brought on the claim. If a claim is made for breach of an agreement under subsection (d) and the agreement does not provide for damages, reasonable attorney's fees are recoverable if demand for compensation under subsection (d) is made and refused before an action is brought on the claim.

(f) Except as stated in this section, the liability of a receiving bank under subsections (a) and (b) may not be varied by agreement.

PART 4 Payment

§ 4A–401. Payment Date.

"Payment date" of a payment order means the day on which the amount of the order is payable to the beneficiary by the beneficiary's bank. The payment date may be determined by instruction of the sender but cannot be earlier than the day the order is received by the beneficiary's bank and, unless otherwise determined, is the day the order is received by the beneficiary's bank.

§ 4A–402. Obligation of Sender to Pay Receiving Bank.

(a) This section is subject to Sections 4A–205 and 4A–207.

(b) With respect to a payment order issued to the beneficiary's bank, acceptance of the order by the bank obliges the sender to pay the bank the amount of the order, but payment is not due until the payment date of the order.

(c) This subsection is subject to subsection (e) and to Section 4A–303. With respect to a payment order issued to a receiving bank other than the beneficiary's bank, acceptance of the order by the receiving bank obliges the sender to pay the bank the amount of the sender's order. Payment by the sender is not due until the execution date of the sender's order. The obligation of that sender to pay its payment order is excused if the funds transfer is not completed by acceptance by the beneficiary's bank of a payment order instructing payment to the beneficiary of that sender's payment order.

(d) If the sender of a payment order pays the order and was not obliged to pay all or part of the amount paid, the bank receiving payment is obliged to refund payment to the extent the sender was not obliged to pay. Except as provided in Sections 4A–204 and 4A–304, interest is payable on the refundable amount from the date of payment.

(e) If a funds transfer is not completed as stated in subsection (c) and an intermediary bank is obliged to refund payment as stated in subsection (d) but is unable to do so because not permitted by applicable law or because the bank suspends payments, a sender in the funds transfer that executed a payment order in compliance with an instruction, as stated in Section 4A–302(a)(1), to route the funds transfer through that intermediary bank is entitled to receive or retain payment from the sender of the payment order that it accepted. The first sender in the funds transfer that issued an instruction requiring routing through that intermediary bank is subrogated to the right of the bank that paid the intermediary bank to refund as stated in subsection (d).

(f) The right of the sender of a payment order to be excused from the obligation to pay the order as stated in subsection (c) or to receive refund under subsection (d) may not be varied by agreement.

§ 4A–403. Payment by Sender to Receiving Bank.

(a) Payment of the sender's obligation under Section 4A–402 to pay the receiving bank occurs as follows:

(1) If the sender is a bank, payment occurs when the receiving bank receives final settlement of the obligation through a Federal Reserve Bank or through a funds-transfer system.

(2) If the sender is a bank and the sender (i) credited an account of the receiving bank with the sender, or (ii) caused an account of the receiving bank in another bank to be credited, payment occurs when the credit is withdrawn or, if not withdrawn, at midnight of the day on which the credit is withdrawable and the receiving bank learns of that fact.

(3) If the receiving bank debits an account of the sender with the receiving bank, payment occurs when the debit is made to the extent the debit is covered by a withdrawable credit balance in the account.

(b) If the sender and receiving bank are members of a funds-transfer system that nets obligations multilaterally among participants, the receiving bank receives final settlement when settlement is complete in accordance with the rules of the system. The obligation of the sender to pay the amount of a payment order transmitted through the funds-transfer system may be satisfied, to the extent permitted by the rules of the system, by setting off and applying against the sender's obligation the right of the sender to receive payment from the receiving bank of the amount of any other payment order transmitted to the sender by the receiving bank through the funds-transfer system. The aggregate balance of obligations owed by each sender to each receiving bank in the funds-transfer system may be satisfied, to the extent permitted by the rules of the system, by setting off and applying against that balance the aggregate balance of obligations owed to the sender by other members of the system. The aggregate balance is determined after the right of setoff stated in the second sentence of this subsection has been exercised.

(c) If two banks transmit payment orders to each other under an agreement that settlement of the obligations of each bank to the other under Section 4A–402 will be made at the end of the day or other period, the total amount owed with respect to all orders transmitted by one bank shall be set off against the total amount owed with respect to all orders transmitted by the other bank. To the extent of the setoff, each bank has made payment to the other.

(d) In a case not covered by subsection (a), the time when payment of the sender's obligation under Section 4A–402(b) or 4A–402(c) occurs is governed by applicable principles of law that determine when an obligation is satisfied.

§ 4A–404. Obligation of Beneficiary's Bank to Pay and Give Notice to Beneficiary.

(a) Subject to Sections 4A–211(e), 4A–405(d), and 4A–405(e), if a beneficiary's bank accepts a payment order, the bank is obliged to pay the amount of the order to the beneficiary of the order. Payment is due on the payment date of the order, but if acceptance occurs on the payment date after the close of the funds-transfer business day of the bank, payment is due on the next funds-transfer business day. If the bank refuses to pay after demand by the beneficiary and receipt of notice of particular circumstances that will give rise to consequential damages as a result of nonpayment, the beneficiary may recover damages resulting from the refusal to pay to the extent the bank had notice of the damages, unless the bank proves that it did not pay because of a reasonable doubt concerning the right of the beneficiary to payment.

(b) If a payment order accepted by the beneficiary's bank instructs payment to an account of the beneficiary, the bank is obliged to notify the beneficiary of receipt of the order before midnight of the next funds-transfer business day following the payment date. If the payment order does not instruct payment to an account of the beneficiary, the bank is required to notify the beneficiary only if notice is required by the order. Notice may be given by first class mail or any other means reasonable in the circumstances. If the bank fails to give the required notice, the bank is obliged to pay interest to the beneficiary on the amount of the payment order from the day notice should have been given until the day the beneficiary learned of receipt of the payment order by the bank. No other damages are recoverable. Reasonable attorney's fees are also recoverable if demand for interest is made and refused before an action is brought on the claim.

(c) The right of a beneficiary to receive payment and damages as stated in subsection (a) may not be varied by agreement or a funds-transfer system rule. The right of a beneficiary to be notified as stated in subsection (b) may be varied by agreement of the beneficiary or by a funds-transfer system rule if the beneficiary is notified of the rule before initiation of the funds transfer.

§ 4A–405. Payment by Beneficiary's Bank to Beneficiary.

(a) If the beneficiary's bank credits an account of the beneficiary of a payment order, payment of the bank's obligation under Section 4A–404(a) occurs when and to the extent (i) the beneficiary is notified of the right to withdraw the credit, (ii) the bank lawfully applies the credit to a debt of the beneficiary, or (iii) funds with respect to the order are otherwise made available to the beneficiary by the bank.

(b) If the beneficiary's bank does not credit an account of the beneficiary of a payment order, the time when payment of the bank's obligation under Section 4A–404(a) occurs is governed by principles of law that determine when an obligation is satisfied.

(c) Except as stated in subsections (d) and (e), if the beneficiary's bank pays the beneficiary of a payment order under a condition to payment or agreement of the beneficiary giving the bank the right to recover payment from the beneficiary if the bank does not receive payment of the order, the condition to payment or agreement is not enforceable.

(d) A funds-transfer system rule may provide that payments made to beneficiaries of funds transfers made through the system are provisional until receipt of payment by the beneficiary's bank of the payment order it accepted. A beneficiary's bank that makes a payment that is provisional under the rule is entitled to refund from the beneficiary if (i) the rule requires that both the beneficiary and the originator be given notice of the provisional nature of the payment before the funds transfer is initiated, (ii) the beneficiary, the beneficiary's bank and the originator's bank agreed to be bound by the rule, and (iii) the beneficiary's bank did not receive payment of the payment order that it accepted. If the beneficiary is obliged to refund payment to the beneficiary's bank, acceptance of the payment order by the beneficiary's bank is nullified and no payment by the originator of the funds transfer to the beneficiary occurs under Section 4A–406.

(e) This subsection applies to a funds transfer that includes a payment order transmitted over a funds-transfer system that (i) nets obligations multilaterally among participants, and (ii) has in effect a loss-sharing agreement among participants for the purpose of providing funds necessary to complete settlement of the obligations of one or more participants that do not meet their settlement obligations. If the beneficiary's bank in the funds transfer accepts a payment order and the system fails to complete settlement pursuant to its rules with respect to any payment order in the funds transfer, (i) the acceptance by the beneficiary's bank is nullified and no person has any right or obligation based on the acceptance, (ii) the beneficiary's bank is entitled to recover payment from the beneficiary, (iii) no payment by the originator to the beneficiary occurs under Section 4A–406, and (iv) subject to Section 4A–402(e), each sender in the funds transfer is excused from its obligation to pay its payment order under Section 4A–402(c) because the funds transfer has not been completed.

§ 4A–406. Payment by Originator to Beneficiary; Discharge of Underlying Obligation.

(a) Subject to Sections 4A–211(e), 4A–405(d), and 4A–405(e), the originator of a funds transfer pays the beneficiary of the originator's payment order (i) at the time a payment order for the benefit of the beneficiary is accepted by the beneficiary's bank in the funds transfer and (ii) in an amount equal to the amount of the order accepted by the beneficiary's bank, but not more than the amount of the originator's order.

(b) If payment under subsection (a) is made to satisfy an obligation, the obligation is discharged to the same extent discharge would result from payment to the beneficiary of the same amount in money, unless (i) the payment under subsection (a) was made by a means prohibited by the contract of the beneficiary with respect to the obligation, (ii) the beneficiary, within a reasonable time after receiving notice of receipt of the order by the beneficiary's bank, notified the originator of the beneficiary's refusal of the payment, (iii) funds with respect to the order were not withdrawn by the beneficiary or applied to a debt of the beneficiary, and (iv) the beneficiary would suffer a loss that could reasonably have been avoided if payment had been made by a means complying with the contract. If payment by the originator does not result in discharge under this section, the originator is subrogated to the rights of the beneficiary to receive payment from the beneficiary's bank under Section 4A–404(a).

(c) For the purpose of determining whether discharge of an obligation occurs under subsection (b), if the beneficiary's bank accepts a payment order in an amount equal to the amount of the originator's payment order less charges of one or more receiving banks in the funds transfer, payment to the beneficiary is deemed to be in the amount of the originator's order unless upon demand by the beneficiary the originator does not pay the beneficiary the amount of the deducted charges.

(d) Rights of the originator or of the beneficiary of a funds transfer under this section may be varied only by agreement of the originator and the beneficiary.

PART 5 Miscellaneous Provisions

§ 4A–501. Variation by Agreement and Effect of Funds-Transfer System Rule.

(a) Except as otherwise provided in this Article, the rights and obligations of a party to a funds transfer may be varied by agreement of the affected party.

(b) "Funds-transfer system rule" means a rule of an association of banks (i) governing transmission of payment orders by means of a funds-transfer system of the association or rights and obligations with respect to those orders, or (ii) to the extent the rule governs rights and obligations between banks that are parties to a funds transfer in which a Federal Reserve Bank, acting as an intermediary bank, sends a payment order to the beneficiary's bank. Except as otherwise provided in this Article, a funds-transfer system rule governing rights and obligations between participating banks using the system may be effective even if the rule conflicts with this Article and indirectly affects another party to the funds transfer who does not consent to the rule. A funds-transfer system rule may also govern rights and obligations of parties other than participating banks using the system to the extent stated in Sections 4A–404(c), 4A–405(d), and 4A–507(c).

§ 4A–502. Creditor Process Served on Receiving Bank; Setoff by Beneficiary's Bank.

(a) As used in this section, "creditor process" means levy, attachment, garnishment, notice of lien, sequestration, or similar process issued by or on behalf of a creditor or other claimant with respect to an account.

(b) This subsection applies to creditor process with respect to an authorized account of the sender of a payment order if the creditor process is served on the receiving bank. For the purpose of determining rights with respect to the creditor process, if the receiving bank accepts the payment order the balance in the authorized account is deemed to be reduced by the amount of the payment order to the extent the bank did not otherwise receive payment of the order, unless the creditor process is served at a time and in a manner affording the bank a reasonable opportunity to act on it before the bank accepts the payment order.

(c) If a beneficiary's bank has received a payment order for payment to the beneficiary's account in the bank, the following rules apply:

(1) The bank may credit the beneficiary's account. The amount credited may be set off against an obligation owed by the beneficiary to the bank or may be applied to satisfy creditor process served on the bank with respect to the account.

(2) The bank may credit the beneficiary's account and allow withdrawal of the amount credited unless creditor process with respect to the account is served at a time and in a manner affording the bank a reasonable opportunity to act to prevent withdrawal.

(3) If creditor process with respect to the beneficiary's account has been served and the bank has had a reasonable opportunity to act on it, the bank may not reject the payment order except for a reason unrelated to the service of process.

(d) Creditor process with respect to a payment by the originator to the beneficiary pursuant to a funds transfer may be served only on the beneficiary's bank with respect to the debt owed by that bank to the beneficiary. Any other bank served with the creditor process is not obliged to act with respect to the process.

§ 4A–503. Injunction or Restraining Order With Respect to Funds Transfer.

For proper cause and in compliance with applicable law, a court may restrain (i) a person from issuing a payment order to initiate a funds transfer, (ii) an originator's bank from executing the payment order of the originator, or (iii) the beneficiary's bank from releasing funds to the beneficiary or the beneficiary from withdrawing the funds. A court may not otherwise restrain a person from issuing a payment order, paying or receiving payment of a payment order, or otherwise acting with respect to a funds transfer.

§ 4A–504. Order in Which Items and Payment Orders May Be Charged to Account; Order of Withdrawals From Account.

(a) If a receiving bank has received more than one payment order of the sender or one or more payment orders and other items that are payable from the sender's account, the bank may charge the sender's account with respect to the various orders and items in any sequence.

(b) In determining whether a credit to an account has been withdrawn by the holder of the account or applied to a debt of the holder of the account, credits first made to the account are first withdrawn or applied.

§ 4A–505. Preclusion of Objection to Debit of Customer's Account.

If a receiving bank has received payment from its customer with respect to a payment order issued in the name of the customer as sender and accepted by the bank, and the customer received notification reasonably identifying the order, the customer is precluded from asserting that the bank is not entitled to retain the payment unless the customer notifies the bank of the customer's objection to the payment within one year after the notification was received by the customer.

§ 4A–506. Rate of Interest.

(a) If, under this Article, a receiving bank is obliged to pay interest with respect to a payment order issued to the bank, the amount payable may be determined (i) by agreement of the sender and receiving bank, or (ii) by a funds-transfer system rule if the payment order is transmitted through a funds-transfer system.

(b) If the amount of interest is not determined by an agreement or rule as stated in subsection (a), the amount is calculated by multiplying the applicable Federal Funds rate by the amount on which interest is payable, and then multiplying the product by the number of days for which interest is payable. The applicable Federal Funds rate is the average of the Federal Funds rates published by the Federal Reserve Bank of New York for each of the days for which interest is payable divided by 360. The Federal Funds rate for any day on which a published rate is not available is the same as the published rate for the next preceding day for which there is a published rate. If a receiving bank that accepted a payment order is required to refund payment to the sender of the order because the funds transfer was not completed, but the failure to complete was not due to any fault by the bank, the interest payable is reduced by a percentage equal to the reserve requirement on deposits of the receiving bank.

§ 4A–507. Choice of Law.

(a) The following rules apply unless the affected parties otherwise agree or subsection (c) applies:

(1) The rights and obligations between the sender of a payment order and the receiving bank are governed by the law of the jurisdiction in which the receiving bank is located.

(2) The rights and obligations between the beneficiary's bank and the beneficiary are governed by the law of the jurisdiction in which the beneficiary's bank is located.

(3) The issue of when payment is made pursuant to a funds transfer by the originator to the beneficiary is governed by the law of the jurisdiction in which the beneficiary's bank is located.

(b) If the parties described in each paragraph of subsection (a) have made an agreement selecting the law of a particular jurisdiction to govern rights and obligations between each other, the law of that jurisdiction governs those rights and obligations, whether or not the payment order or the funds transfer bears a reasonable relation to that jurisdiction.

(c) A funds-transfer system rule may select the law of a particular jurisdiction to govern (i) rights and obligations between participating banks with respect to payment orders transmitted or processed through the system, or (ii) the rights and obligations of some or all parties to a funds transfer any part of which is carried out by means of the system. A choice of law made pursuant to clause (i) is binding on participating banks. A choice of law made pursuant to clause (ii) is binding on the originator, other sender, or a receiving bank having notice that the funds-transfer system might be used in the funds transfer and of the choice of law by the system when the originator, other sender, or receiving bank issued or accepted a payment order. The beneficiary of a funds transfer is bound by the choice of law if, when the funds transfer is initiated, the beneficiary has notice that the funds-transfer system might be used in the funds transfer and of the choice of law by the system. The law of a jurisdiction selected pursuant to this subsection may govern, whether or not that law bears a reasonable relation to the matter in issue.

(d) In the event of inconsistency between an agreement under subsection (b) and a choice-of-law rule under subsection (c), the agreement under subsection (b) prevails.

(e) If a funds transfer is made by use of more than one funds-transfer system and there is inconsistency between choice-of-law rules of the systems, the matter in issue is governed by the law of the selected jurisdiction that has the most significant relationship to the matter in issue.

ARTICLE 5

LETTERS OF CREDIT

§ 5–101. Short Title.

This Article shall be known and may be cited as Uniform Commercial Code—Letters of Credit.

§ 5–102. Scope.

(1) This Article applies

(a) to a credit issued by a bank if the credit requires a documentary draft or a documentary demand for payment; and

(b) to a credit issued by a person other than a bank if the credit requires that the draft or demand for payment be accompanied by a document of title; and

(c) to a credit issued by a bank or other person if the credit is not within subparagraphs (a) or (b) but conspicuously states that it is a letter of credit or is conspicuously so entitled.

(2) Unless the engagement meets the requirements of subsection (1), this Article does not apply to engagements to make advances or to honor drafts or demands for payment, to authorities to pay or purchase, to guarantees or to general agreements.

(3) This Article deals with some but not all of the rules and concepts of letters of credit as such rules or concepts have developed prior to this act or may hereafter develop. The fact that this Article states a rule does not by itself require, imply or negate application of the same or a converse rule to a situation not provided for or to a person not specified by this Article.

§ 5–103. Definitions.

(1) In this Article unless the context otherwise requires

(a) "Credit" or "letter of credit" means an engagement by a bank or other person made at the request of a customer and of a kind within the scope of this Article (Section 5–102) that the issuer will honor drafts or other demands for payment upon compliance with the conditions specified in the credit. A credit may be either revocable or irrevocable. The engagement may be either an agreement to honor or a statement that the bank or other person is authorized to honor.

(b) A "documentary draft" or a "documentary demand for payment" is one honor of which is conditioned upon the presentation of a document or documents. "Document" means any paper including document of title, security, invoice, certificate, notice of default and the like.

(c) An "issuer" is a bank or other person issuing a credit.

(d) A "beneficiary" of a credit is a person who is entitled under its terms to draw or demand payment.

(e) An "advising bank" is a bank which gives notification of the issuance of a credit by another bank.

(f) A "confirming bank" is a bank which engages either that it will itself honor a credit already issued by another bank or that such a credit will be honored by the issuer or a third bank.

(g) A "customer" is a buyer or other person who causes an issuer to issue a credit. The term also includes a bank which procures issuance or confirmation on behalf of that bank's customer.

(2) Other definitions applying to this Article and the sections in which they appear are:

"Notation of Credit". Section 5–108.
"Presenter". Section 5–112(3).

(3) Definitions in other Articles applying to this Article and the sections in which they appear are:

"Accept" or "Acceptance". Section 3–409.
"Contract for sale". Section 2–106.
"Draft". Section 3–104.
"Holder in due course". Section 3–302.
"Midnight deadline". Section 4–104.
"Security". Section 8–102.

(4) In addition, Article 1 contains general definitions and principles of construction and interpretation applicable throughout this Article.

§ 5–104. Formal Requirements; Signing.

(1) Except as otherwise required in subsection (1)(c) of Section 5–102 on scope, no particular form of phrasing is required for a

credit. A credit must be in writing and signed by the issuer and a confirmation must be in writing and signed by the confirming bank. A modification of the terms of a credit or confirmation must be signed by the issuer or confirming bank.

(2) A telegram may be a sufficient signed writing if it identifies its sender by an authorized authentication. The authentication may be in code and the authorized naming of the issuer in an advice of credit is a sufficient signing.

§ 5–105. Consideration.

No consideration is necessary to establish a credit or to enlarge or otherwise modify its terms.

§ 5–106. Time and Effect of Establishment of Credit.

(1) Unless otherwise agreed a credit is established.

(a) as regards the customer as soon as a letter of credit is sent to him or the letter of credit or an authorized written advice of its issuance is sent to the beneficiary; and

(b) as regards the beneficiary when he receives a letter of credit or an authorized written advice of its issuance.

(2) Unless otherwise agreed once an irrevocable credit is established as regards the customer it can be modified or revoked only with the consent of the customer and once it is established as regards the beneficiary it can be modified or revoked only with his consent.

(3) Unless otherwise agreed after a revocable credit is established it may be modified or revoked by the issuer without notice to or consent from the customer or beneficiary.

(4) Notwithstanding any modification or revocation of a revocable credit any person authorized to honor or negotiate under the terms of the original credit is entitled to reimbursement for or honor of any draft or demand for payment duly honored or negotiated before receipt of notice of the modification or revocation and the issuer in turn is entitled to reimbursement from its customer.

§ 5–107. Advice of Credit; Confirmation; Error in Statement of Terms.

(1) Unless otherwise specified an advising bank by advising a credit issued by another bank does not assume any obligation to honor drafts drawn or demands for payment made under the credit but it does assume obligation for the accuracy of its own statement.

(2) A confirming bank by confirming a credit becomes directly obligated on the credit to the extent of its confirmation as though it were its issuer and acquires the rights of an issuer.

(3) Even though an advising bank incorrectly advises the terms of a credit it has been authorized to advise the credit is established as against the issuer to the extent of its original terms.

(4) Unless otherwise specified the customer bears as against the issuer all risks of transmission and reasonable translation or interpretation of any message relating to a credit.

§ 5–108. "Notation Credit"; Exhaustion of Credit.

(1) A credit which specifies that any person purchasing or paying drafts drawn or demands for payment made under it must note the amount of the draft or demand on the letter or advice of credit is a "notation credit".

(2) Under a notation credit

(a) a person paying the beneficiary or purchasing a draft or demand for payment from him acquires a right to honor only if the appropriate notation is made and by transferring or forwarding for honor the documents under the credit such a person warrants to the issuer that the notation has been made; and

(b) unless the credit or a signed statement that an appropriate notation has been made accompanies the draft or demand for payment the issuer may delay honor until evidence of notation has been procured which is satisfactory to it but its obligation and that of its customer continue for a reasonable time not exceeding thirty days to obtain such evidence.

(3) If the credit is not a notation credit

(a) the issuer may honor complying drafts or demands for payment presented to it in the order in which they are presented and is discharged pro tanto by honor of any such draft or demand;

(b) as between competing good faith purchasers of complying drafts or demands the person first purchasing has priority over a subsequent purchaser even though the later purchased draft or demand has been first honored.

§ 5–109. Issuer's Obligation to Its Customer.

(1) An issuer's obligation to its customer includes good faith and observance of any general banking usage but unless otherwise agreed does not include liability or responsibility

(a) for performance of the underlying contract for sale or other transaction between the customer and the beneficiary; or

(b) for any act or omission of any person other than itself or its own branch or for loss or destruction of a draft, demand or document in transit or in the possession of others; or

(c) based on knowledge or lack of knowledge of any usage of any particular trade.

(2) An issuer must examine documents with care so as to ascertain that on their face they appear to comply with the terms of the credit but unless otherwise agreed assumes no liability or responsibility for the genuineness, falsification or effect of any document which appears on such examination to be regular on its face.

(3) A non-bank issuer is not bound by any banking usage of which it has no knowledge.

§ 5–110. Availability of Credit in Portions; Presenter's Reservation of Lien or Claim.

(1) Unless otherwise specified a credit may be used in portions in the discretion of the beneficiary.

(2) Unless otherwise specified a person by presenting a documentary draft or demand for payment under a credit relinquishes upon its honor all claims to the documents and a person by transferring such draft or demand or causing such presentment authorizes such relinquishment. An explicit reservation of claim makes the draft or demand non-complying.

§ 5–111. Warranties on Transfer and Presentment.

(1) Unless otherwise agreed the beneficiary by transferring or presenting a documentary draft or demand for payment warrants to all interested parties that the necessary conditions of the credit have been complied with. This is in addition to any warranties arising under Articles 3, 4, 7 and 8.

(2) Unless otherwise agreed a negotiating, advising, confirming, collecting or issuing bank presenting or transferring a draft

or demand for payment under a credit warrants only the matters warranted by a collecting bank under Article 4 and any such bank transferring a document warrants only the matters warranted by an intermediary under Articles 7 and 8.

§ 5–112. Time Allowed for Honor or Rejection; Withholding Honor or Rejection by Consent; "Presenter".

(1) A bank to which a documentary draft or demand for payment is presented under a credit may without dishonor of the draft, demand or credit

(a) defer honor until the close of the third banking day following receipt of the documents; and

(b) further defer honor if the presenter has expressly or impliedly consented thereto.

Failure to honor within the time here specified constitutes dishonor of the draft or demand and of the credit [except as otherwise provided in subsection (4) of Section 5–114 on conditional payment].

Note: The bracketed language in the last sentence of subsection (1) should be included only if the optional provisions of Section 5–114(4) and (5) are included.

(2) Upon dishonor the bank may unless otherwise instructed fulfill its duty to return the draft or demand and the documents by holding them at the disposal of the presenter and sending him an advice to that effect.

(3) "Presenter" means any person presenting a draft or demand for payment for honor under a credit even though that person is a confirming bank or other correspondent which is acting under an issuer's authorization.

§ 5–113. Indemnities.

(1) A bank seeking to obtain (whether for itself or another) honor, negotiation or reimbursement under a credit may give an indemnity to induce such honor, negotiation or reimbursement.

(2) An indemnity agreement inducing honor, negotiation or reimbursement

(a) unless otherwise explicitly agreed applies to defects in the documents but not in the goods; and

(b) unless a longer time is explicitly agreed expires at the end of ten business days following receipt of the documents by the ultimate customer unless notice of objection is sent before such expiration date. The ultimate customer may send notice of objection to the person from whom he received the documents and any bank receiving such notice is under a duty to send notice to its transferor before its midnight deadline.

§ 5–114. Issuer's Duty and Privilege to Honor; Right to Reimbursement.

(1) An issuer must honor a draft or demand for payment which complies with the terms of the relevant credit regardless of whether the goods or documents conform to the underlying contract for sale or other contract between the customer and the beneficiary. The issuer is not excused from honor of such a draft or demand by reason of an additional general term that all documents must be satisfactory to the issuer, but an issuer may require that specified documents must be satisfactory to it.

(2) Unless otherwise agreed when documents appear on their face to comply with the terms of a credit but a required document does not in fact conform to the warranties made on negotiation or transfer of a document of title (Section 7–507) or of a certificated security (Section 8–306) or is forged or fraudulent or there is fraud in the transaction:

(a) the issuer must honor the draft or demand for payment if honor is demanded by a negotiating bank or other holder of the draft or demand which has taken the draft or demand under the credit and under circumstances which would make it a holder in due course (Section 3–302) and in an appropriate case would make it a person to whom a document of title has been duly negotiated (Section 7–502) or a bona fide purchaser of a certificated security (Section 8–302); and

(b) in all other cases as against its customer, an issuer acting in good faith may honor the draft or demand for payment despite notification from the customer of fraud, forgery or other defect not apparent on the face of the documents but a court of appropriate jurisdiction may enjoin such honor.

(3) Unless otherwise agreed an issuer which has duly honored a draft or demand for payment is entitled to immediate reimbursement of any payment made under the credit and to be put in effectively available funds not later than the day before maturity of any acceptance made under the credit.

[(4) When a credit provides for payment by the issuer on receipt of notice that the required documents are in the possession of a correspondent or other agent of the issuer

(a) any payment made on receipt of such notice is conditional; and

(b) the issuer may reject documents which do not comply with the credit if it does so within three banking days following its receipt of the documents; and

(c) in the event of such rejection, the issuer is entitled by charge back or otherwise to return of the payment made.]

[(5) In the case covered by subsection (4) failure to reject documents within the time specified in sub-paragraph (b) constitutes acceptance of the documents and makes the payment final in favor of the beneficiary.]

Amended in 1977.

Note: *Subsections (4) and (5) are bracketed as optional. If they are included the bracketed language in the last sentence of Section 5–112(1) should also be included.*

§ 5–115. Remedy for Improper Dishonor or Anticipatory Repudiation.

(1) When an issuer wrongfully dishonors a draft or demand for payment presented under a credit the person entitled to honor has with respect to any documents the rights of a person in the position of a seller (Section 2–707) and may recover from the issuer the face amount of the draft or demand together with incidental damages under Section 2–710 on seller's incidental damages and interest but less any amount realized by resale or other use or disposition of the subject matter of the transaction. In the event no resale or other utilization is made the documents, goods or other subject matter involved in the transaction must be turned over to the issuer on payment of judgment.

(2) When an issuer wrongfully cancels or otherwise repudiates a credit before presentment of a draft or demand for payment drawn under it the beneficiary has the rights of a seller after anticipatory repudiation by the buyer under Section 2–610 if he learns of the repudiation in time reasonably to avoid procurement of the required documents. Otherwise the beneficiary has an immediate right of action for wrongful dishonor.

§ 5–116. Transfer and Assignment.

(1) The right to draw under a credit can be transferred or assigned only when the credit is expressly designated as transferable or assignable.

(2) Even though the credit specifically states that it is nontransferable or nonassignable the beneficiary may before performance of the conditions of the credit assign his right to proceeds. Such an assignment is an assignment of an account under Article 9 on Secured Transactions and is governed by that Article except that

(a) the assignment is ineffective until the letter of credit or advice of credit is delivered to the assignee which delivery constitutes perfection of the security interest under Article 9; and

(b) the issuer may honor drafts or demands for payment drawn under the credit until it receives a notification of the assignment signed by the beneficiary which reasonably identifies the credit involved in the assignment and contains a request to pay the assignee; and

(c) after what reasonably appears to be such a notification has been received the issuer may without dishonor refuse to accept or pay even to a person otherwise entitled to honor until the letter of credit or advice of credit is exhibited to the issuer.

(3) Except where the beneficiary has effectively assigned his right to draw or his right to proceeds, nothing in this section limits his right to transfer or negotiate drafts or demands drawn under the credit.

§ 5–117. Insolvency of Bank Holding Funds for Documentary Credit.

(1) Where an issuer or an advising or confirming bank or a bank which has for a customer procured issuance of a credit by another bank becomes insolvent before final payment under the credit and the credit is one to which this Article is made applicable by paragraphs (a) or (b) of Section 5–102(1) on scope, the receipt or allocation of funds or collateral to secure or meet obligations under the credit shall have the following results:

(a) to the extent of any funds or collateral turned over after or before the insolvency as indemnity against or specifically for the purpose of payment of drafts or demands for payment drawn under the designated credit, the drafts or demands are entitled to payment in preference over depositors or other general creditors of the issuer or bank; and

(b) on expiration of the credit or surrender of the beneficiary's rights under it unused any person who has given such funds or collateral is similarly entitled to return thereof; and

(c) a charge to a general or current account with a bank if specifically consented to for the purpose of indemnity against or payment of drafts or demands for payment drawn under the designated credit falls under the same rules as if the funds had been drawn out in cash and then turned over with specific instructions.

(2) After honor or reimbursement under this section the customer or other person for whose account the insolvent bank has acted is entitled to receive the documents involved.

ARTICLE 6
BULK TRANSFERS

§ 6–101. Short Title.

This Article shall be known and may be cited as Uniform Commercial Code—Bulk Transfers.

§ 6–102. "Bulk Transfer"; Transfers of Equipment; Enterprises Subject to This Article; Bulk Transfers Subject to This Article.

(1) A "bulk transfer" is any transfer in bulk and not in the ordinary course of the transferor's business of a major part of the materials, supplies, merchandise or other inventory (Section 9–109) of an enterprise subject to this Article.

(2) A transfer of a substantial part of the equipment (Section 9–109) of such an enterprise is a bulk transfer if it is made in connection with a bulk transfer of inventory, but not otherwise.

(3) The enterprises subject to this Article are all those whose principal business is the sale of merchandise from stock, including those who manufacture what they sell.

(4) Except as limited by the following section all bulk transfers of goods located within this state are subject to this Article.

§ 6–103. Transfers Excepted From This Article.

The following transfers are not subject to this Article:

(1) Those made to give security for the performance of an obligation;

(2) General assignments for the benefit of all the creditors of the transferor, and subsequent transfers by the assignee thereunder;

(3) Transfers in settlement or realization of a lien or other security interest;

(4) Sales by executors, administrators, receivers, trustees in bankruptcy, or any public officer under judicial process;

(5) Sales made in the course of judicial or administrative proceedings for the dissolution or reorganization of a corporation and of which notice is sent to the creditors of the corporation pursuant to order of the court or administrative agency;

(6) Transfers to a person maintaining a known place of business in this State who becomes bound to pay the debts of the transferor in full and gives public notice of that fact, and who is solvent after becoming so bound;

(7) A transfer to a new business enterprise organized to take over and continue the business, if public notice of the transaction is given and the new enterprise assumes the debts of the transferor and he receives nothing from the transaction except an interest in the new enterprise junior to the claims of creditors;

(8) Transfers of property which is exempt from execution.

Public notice under subsection (6) or subsection (7) may be given by publishing once a week for two consecutive weeks in a newspaper of general circulation where the transferor had its principal place of business in this state an advertisement including the names and addresses of the transferor and transferee and the effective date of the transfer.

§ 6–104. Schedule of Property, List of Creditors.

(1) Except as provided with respect to auction sales (Section 6–108), a bulk transfer subject to this Article is ineffective against any creditor of the transferor unless:

(a) The transferee requires the transferor to furnish a list of his existing creditors prepared as stated in this section; and

(b) The parties prepare a schedule of the property transferred sufficient to identify it; and

(c) The transferee preserves the list and schedule for six months next following the transfer and permits inspection of either or both and copying therefrom at all reasonable hours by any creditor of the transferor, or files the list and schedule in*(a public office to be here identified).*

(2) The list of creditors must be signed and sworn to or affirmed by the transferor or his agent. It must contain the names and business addresses of all creditors of the transferor, with the amounts when known, and also the names of all persons who are known to the transferor to assert claims against him even though such claims are disputed. If the transferor is the obligor of an outstanding issue of bonds, debentures or the like as to which there is an indenture trustee, the list of creditors need include only the name and address of the indenture trustee and the aggregate outstanding principal amount of the issue.

(3) Responsibility for the completeness and accuracy of the list of creditors rests on the transferor, and the transfer is not rendered ineffective by errors or omissions therein unless the transferee is shown to have had knowledge.

§ 6–105. Notice to Creditors.

In addition to the requirements of the preceding section, any bulk transfer subject to this Article except one made by auction sale (Section 6–108) is ineffective against any creditor of the transferor unless at least ten days before he takes possession of the goods or pays for them, whichever happens first, the transferee gives notice of the transfer in the manner and to the persons hereafter provided (Section 6–107).

[§ 6–106. Application of the Proceeds]

In addition to the requirements of the two preceding sections:

(1) Upon every bulk transfer subject to this Article for which new consideration becomes payable except those made by sale at auction it is the duty of the transferee to assure that such consideration is applied so far as necessary to pay those debts of the transferor which are either shown on the list furnished by the transferor (Section 6–104) or filed in writing in the place stated in the notice (Section 6–107) within thirty days after the mailing of such notice. This duty of the transferee runs to all the holders of such debts, and may be enforced by any of them for the benefit of all.

(2) If any of said debts are in dispute the necessary sum may be withheld from distribution until the dispute is settled or adjudicated.

(3) If the consideration payable is not enough to pay all of the said debts in full distribution shall be made pro rata.]

Note: This section is bracketed to indicate division of opinion as to whether or not it is a wise provision, and to suggest that this is a point on which State enactments may differ without serious damage to the principal of uniformity. In any State where this section is omitted, the following parts of sections, also bracketed in the text, should also be omitted, namely:

Section 6–107(2)(e).

6–108(3)(c).

6–109(2).

In any State where this section is enacted, these other provisions should be also.

Optional Subsection (4)

[(4) The transferee may within ten days after he takes possession of the goods pay the consideration into the (specify court) in the county where the transferor had its principal place of business in this state and thereafter may discharge his duty under this section by giving notice by registered or certified mail to all the persons to whom the duty runs that the consideration has been paid into that court and that they should file their claims there. On motion of any interested party, the court may order the distribution of the consideration to the persons entitled to it.]

Note: Optional subsection (4) is recommended for those states which do not have a general statute providing for payment of money into court.

§ 6–107. The Notice.

(1) The notice to creditors (Section 6–105) shall state:

(a) that a bulk transfer is about to be made; and

(b) the names and business addresses of the transferor and transferee, and all other business names and addresses used by the transferor within three years last past so far as known to the transferee; and

(c) whether or not all the debts of the transferor are to be paid in full as they fall due as a result of the transaction, and if so, the address to which creditors should send their bills.

(2) If the debts of the transferor are not to be paid in full as they fall due or if the transferee is in doubt on that point then the notice shall state further:

(a) the location and general description of the property to be transferred and the estimated total of the transferor's debts;

(b) the address where the schedule of property and list of creditors (Section 6–104) may be inspected;

(c) whether the transfer is to pay existing debts and if so the amount of such debts and to whom owing;

(d) whether the transfer is for new consideration and if so the amount of such consideration and the time and place of payment; [and]

[(e) if for new consideration the time and place where creditors of the transferor are to file their claims.]

(3) The notice in any case shall be delivered personally or sent by registered or certified mail to all the persons shown on the list of creditors furnished by the transferor (Section 6–104) and to all other persons who are known to the transferee to hold or assert claims against the transferor.

§ 6–108. Auction Sales; "Auctioneer".

(1) A bulk transfer is subject to this Article even though it is by sale at auction, but only in the manner and with the results stated in this section.

(2) The transferor shall furnish a list of his creditors and assist in the preparation of a schedule of the property to be sold, both prepared as before stated (Section 6–104).

(3) The person or persons other than the transferor who direct, control or are responsible for the auction are collectively called the "auctioneer". The auctioneer shall:

(a) receive and retain the list of creditors and prepare and retain the schedule of property for the period stated in this Article (Section 6–104);

(b) give notice of the auction personally or by registered or certified mail at least ten days before it occurs to all persons shown on the list of creditors and to all other persons who are known to him to hold or assert claims against the transferor; [and]

[(c) assure that the net proceeds of the auction are applied as provided in this Article (Section 6–106).]

(4) Failure of the auctioneer to perform any of these duties does not affect the validity of the sale or the title of the purchasers, but if the auctioneer knows that the auction constitutes a bulk transfer such failure renders the auctioneer liable to the creditors of the transferor as a class for the sums owing to them from the transferor up to but not exceeding the net proceeds of the auction. If the auctioneer consists of several persons their liability is joint and several.

§ 6–109. What Creditors Protected; [Credit for Payment to Particular Creditors].

(1) The creditors of the transferor mentioned in this Article are those holding claims based on transactions or events occurring before the bulk transfer, but creditors who become such after notice to creditors is given (Sections 6–105 and 6–107) are not entitled to notice.

[(2) Against the aggregate obligation imposed by the provisions of this Article concerning the application of the proceeds (Section 6–106 and subsection (3)(c) of 6–108) the transferee or auctioneer is entitled to credit for sums paid to particular creditors of the transferor, not exceeding the sums believed in good faith at the time of the payment to be properly payable to such creditors.]

§ 6–110. Subsequent Transfers.

When the title of a transferee to property is subject to a defect by reason of his non-compliance with the requirements of this Article, then:

(1) a purchaser of any such property from such transferee who pays no value or who takes with notice of such noncompliance takes subject to such defect, but

(2) a purchaser for value in good faith and without such notice takes free of such defect.

§ 6–111. Limitation of Actions and Levies.

No action under this Article shall be brought nor levy made more than six months after the date on which the transferee took possession of the goods unless the transfer has been concealed. If the transfer has been concealed, actions may be brought or levies made within six months after its discovery.

Note to Article 6: Section 6–106 is bracketed to indicate division of opinion as to whether or not it is a wise provision, and to suggest that this is a point on which State enactments may differ without serious damage to the principle of uniformity. In any State where Section 6–106 is not enacted, the following parts of sections, also bracketed in the text, should also be omitted, namely:

Sec. 6–107(2)(e).

6–108(3)(c).

6–109(2).

In any State where Section 6–106 is enacted, these other provisions should be also.

ARTICLE 7

WAREHOUSE RECEIPTS, BILLS OF LADING AND OTHER DOCUMENTS OF TITLE

PART 1 General

§ 7–101. Short Title.

This Article shall be known and may be cited as Uniform Commercial Code—Documents of Title.

§ 7–102. Definitions and Index of Definitions.

(1) In this Article, unless the context otherwise requires:

(a) "Bailee" means the person who by a warehouse receipt, bill of lading or other document of title acknowledges possession of goods and contracts to deliver them.

(b) "Consignee" means the person named in a bill to whom or to whose order the bill promises delivery.

(c) "Consignor" means the person named in a bill as the person from whom the goods have been received for shipment.

(d) "Delivery order" means a written order to deliver goods directed to a warehouseman, carrier or other person who in the ordinary course of business issues warehouse receipts or bills of lading.

(e) "Document" means document of title as defined in the general definitions in Article 1 (Section 1–201).

(f) "Goods" means all things which are treated as movable for the purposes of a contract of storage or transportation.

(g) "Issuer" means a bailee who issues a document except that in relation to an unaccepted delivery order it means the person who orders the possessor of goods to deliver. Issuer includes any person for whom an agent or employee purports to act in issuing a document if the agent or employee has real or apparent authority to issue documents, notwithstanding that the issuer received no goods or that the goods were misdescribed or that in any other respect the agent or employee violated his instructions.

(h) "Warehouseman" is a person engaged in the business of storing goods for hire.

(2) Other definitions applying to this Article or to specified Parts thereof, and the sections in which they appear are:

"Duly negotiate". Section 7–501.

"Person entitled under the document". Section 7–403(4).

(3) Definitions in other Articles applying to this Article and the sections in which they appear are:

"Contract for sale". Section 2–106.

"Overseas". Section 2–323.

"Receipt" of goods. Section 2–103.

(4) In addition Article 1 contains general definitions and principles of construction and interpretation applicable throughout this Article.

§ 7–103. Relation of Article to Treaty, Statute, Tariff, Classification or Regulation.

To the extent that any treaty or statute of the United States, regulatory statute of this State or tariff, classification or regulation filed or issued pursuant thereto is applicable, the provisions of this Article are subject thereto.

§ 7–104. Negotiable and Non-Negotiable Warehouse Receipt, Bill of Lading or Other Document of Title.

(1) A warehouse receipt, bill of lading or other document of title is negotiable

(a) if by its terms the goods are to be delivered to bearer or to the order of a named person; or

(b) where recognized in overseas trade, if it runs to a named person or assigns.

(2) Any other document is non-negotiable. A bill of lading in which it is stated that the goods are consigned to a named person is not made negotiable by a provision that the goods are to be delivered only against a written order signed by the same or another named person.

§ 7–105. Construction Against Negative Implication.

The omission from either Part 2 or Part 3 of this Article of a provision corresponding to a provision made in the other Part does not imply that a corresponding rule of law is not applicable.

PART 2 Warehouse Receipts: Special Provisions

§ 7–201. Who May Issue a Warehouse Receipt; Storage Under Government Bond.

(1) A warehouse receipt may be issued by any warehouseman.

(2) Where goods including distilled spirits and agricultural commodities are stored under a statute requiring a bond against withdrawal or a license for the issuance of receipts in the nature of warehouse receipts, a receipt issued for the goods has like effect as a warehouse receipt even though issued by a person who is the owner of the goods and is not a warehouseman.

§ 7–202. Form of Warehouse Receipt; Essential Terms; Optional Terms.

(1) A warehouse receipt need not be in any particular form.

(2) Unless a warehouse receipt embodies within its written or printed terms each of the following, the warehouseman is liable for damages caused by the omission to a person injured thereby:

(a) the location of the warehouse where the goods are stored;

(b) the date of issue of the receipt;

(c) the consecutive number of the receipt;

(d) a statement whether the goods received will be delivered to the bearer, to a specified person, or to a specified person or his order;

(e) the rate of storage and handling charges, except that where goods are stored under a field warehousing arrangement a statement of that fact is sufficient on a non-negotiable receipt;

(f) a description of the goods or of the packages containing them;

(g) the signature of the warehouseman, which may be made by his authorized agent;

(h) if the receipt is issued for goods of which the warehouseman is owner, either solely or jointly or in common with others, the fact of such ownership; and

(i) a statement of the amount of advances made and of liabilities incurred for which the warehouseman claims a lien or security interest (Section 7–209). If the precise amount of such advances made or of such liabilities incurred is, at the time of the issue of the receipt, unknown to the warehouseman or to his agent who issues it, a statement of the fact that advances have been made or liabilities incurred and the purpose thereof is sufficient.

(3) A warehouseman may insert in his receipt any other terms which are not contrary to the provisions of this Act and do not impair his obligation of delivery (Section 7–403) or his duty of care (Section 7–204). Any contrary provisions shall be ineffective.

§ 7–203. Liability for Non-Receipt or Misdescription.

A party to or purchaser for value in good faith of a document of title other than a bill of lading relying in either case upon the description therein of the goods may recover from the issuer damages caused by the non-receipt or misdescription of the goods, except to the extent that the document conspicuously indicates that the issuer does not know whether any part or all of the goods in fact were received or conform to the description, as where the description is in terms of marks or labels or kind, quantity or condition, or the receipt or description is qualified by "contents, condition and quality unknown", "said to contain" or the like, if such indication be true, or the party or purchaser otherwise has notice.

§ 7–204. Duty of Care; Contractual Limitation of Warehouseman's Liability.

(1) A warehouseman is liable for damages for loss of or injury to the goods caused by his failure to exercise such care in regard to them as a reasonably careful man would exercise under like circumstances but unless otherwise agreed he is not liable for damages which could not have been avoided by the exercise of such care.

(2) Damages may be limited by a term in the warehouse receipt or storage agreement limiting the amount of liability in case of loss or damage, and setting forth a specific liability per article or item, or value per unit of weight, beyond which the warehouseman shall not be liable; provided, however, that such liability may on written request of the bailor at the time of signing such storage agreement or within a reasonable time after receipt of the warehouse receipt be increased on part or all of the goods thereunder, in which event increased rates may be charged based on such increased valuation, but that no such increase shall be permitted contrary to a lawful limitation of liability contained in the warehouseman's tariff, if any. No such limitation is effective with respect to the warehouseman's liability for conversion to his own use.

(3) Reasonable provisions as to the time and manner of presenting claims and instituting actions based on the bailment may be included in the warehouse receipt or tariff.

(4) This section does not impair or repeal...

Note: Insert in subsection (4) a reference to any statute which imposes a higher responsibility upon the warehouseman or invalidates contractual limitations which would be permissible under this Article.

§ 7–205. Title Under Warehouse Receipt Defeated in Certain Cases.

A buyer in the ordinary course of business of fungible goods sold and delivered by a warehouseman who is also in the business of buying and selling such goods takes free of any claim under a warehouse receipt even though it has been duly negotiated.

§ 7–206. Termination of Storage at Warehouseman's Option.

(1) A warehouseman may on notifying the person on whose account the goods are held and any other person known to claim an interest in the goods require payment of any charges and removal of the goods from the warehouse at the termination of the period of storage fixed by the document, or, if no period is fixed, within a stated period not less than thirty days after the notification. If the goods are not removed before the date specified in the notification, the warehouseman may sell them in accordance with the provisions of the section on enforcement of a warehouseman's lien (Section 7–210).

(2) If a warehouseman in good faith believes that the goods are about to deteriorate or decline in value to less than the amount of his lien within the time prescribed in subsection (1) for notification, advertisement and sale, the warehouseman may specify in the notification any reasonable shorter time for removal of the goods and in case the goods are not removed, may sell them at public sale held not less than one week after a single advertisement or posting.

(3) If as a result of a quality or condition of the goods of which the warehouseman had no notice at the time of deposit the goods are a hazard to other property or to the warehouse or to persons, the warehouseman may sell the goods at public or private sale without advertisement on reasonable notification to all persons known to claim an interest in the goods. If the warehouseman after a reasonable effort is unable to sell the goods he may dispose of them in any lawful manner and shall incur no liability by reason of such disposition.

(4) The warehouseman must deliver the goods to any person entitled to them under this Article upon due demand made at any time prior to sale or other disposition under this section.

(5) The warehouseman may satisfy his lien from the proceeds of any sale or disposition under this section but must hold the balance for delivery on the demand of any person to whom he would have been bound to deliver the goods.

§ 7–207. Goods Must Be Kept Separate; Fungible Goods.

(1) Unless the warehouse receipt otherwise provides, a warehouseman must keep separate the goods covered by each receipt so as to permit at all times identification and delivery of those goods except that different lots of fungible goods may be commingled.

(2) Fungible goods so commingled are owned in common by the persons entitled thereto and the warehouseman is severally liable to each owner for that owner's share. Where because of overissue a mass of fungible goods is insufficient to meet all the receipts which the warehouseman has issued against it, the persons entitled include all holders to whom overissued receipts have been duly negotiated.

§ 7–208. Altered Warehouse Receipts.

Where a blank in a negotiable warehouse receipt has been filled in without authority, a purchaser for value and without notice of the want of authority may treat the insertion as authorized. Any other unauthorized alteration leaves any receipt enforceable against the issuer according to its original tenor.

§ 7–209. Lien of Warehouseman.

(1) A warehouseman has a lien against the bailor on the goods covered by a warehouse receipt or on the proceeds thereof in his possession for charges for storage or transportation (including demurrage and terminal charges), insurance, labor, or charges present or future in relation to the goods, and for expenses necessary for preservation of the goods or reasonably incurred in their sale pursuant to law. If the person on whose account the goods are held is liable for like charges or expenses in relation to other goods whenever deposited and it is stated in the receipt that a lien is claimed for charges and expenses in relation to other goods, the warehouseman also has a lien against him for such charges and expenses whether or not the other goods have been delivered by the warehouseman. But against a person to whom a negotiable warehouse receipt is duly negotiated a warehouseman's lien is limited to charges in an amount or at a rate specified on the receipt or if no charges are so specified then to a reasonable charge for storage of the goods covered by the receipt subsequent to the date of the receipt.

(2) The warehouseman may also reserve a security interest against the bailor for a maximum amount specified on the receipt for charges other than those specified in subsection (1), such as for money advanced and interest. Such a security interest is governed by the Article on Secured Transactions (Article 9).

(3) (a) A warehouseman's lien for charges and expenses under subsection (1) or a security interest under subsection (2) is also effective against any person who so entrusted the bailor with possession of the goods that a pledge of them by him to a good faith purchaser for value would have been valid but is not effective against a person as to whom the document confers no right in the goods covered by it under Section 7–503.

(b) A warehouseman's lien on household goods for charges and expenses in relation to the goods under subsection (1) is also effective against all persons if the depositor was a legal possessor of the goods at the time of deposit. "Household goods" means furniture, furnishings and personal effects used by the depositor in a dwelling.

(4) A warehouseman loses his lien on any goods which he voluntarily delivers or which he unjustifiably refuses to deliver.

§ 7–210. Enforcement of Warehouseman's Lien.

(1) Except as provided in subsection (2), a warehouseman's lien may be enforced by public or private sale of the goods in bloc or in parcels, at any time or place and on any terms which are commercially reasonable, after notifying all persons known to claim an interest in the goods. Such notification must include a statement of the amount due, the nature of the proposed sale and the time and place of any public sale. The fact that a better price could have been obtained by a sale at a different time or in a different method from that selected by the warehouseman is not of itself sufficient to establish that the sale was not made in a commercially reasonable manner. If the warehouseman either sells the goods in the usual manner in any recognized market therefor, or if he sells at the price current in such market at the time of his sale, or if he has otherwise sold in conformity with commercially reasonable practices among dealers in the type of goods sold, he has sold in a commercially reasonable manner. A sale of more goods than apparently necessary to be offered to insure satisfaction of the obligation is not commercially reasonable except in cases covered by the preceding sentence.

(2) A warehouseman's lien on goods other than goods stored by a merchant in the course of his business may be enforced only as follows:

(a) All persons known to claim an interest in the goods must be notified.

(b) The notification must be delivered in person or sent by registered or certified letter to the last known address of any person to be notified.

(c) The notification must include an itemized statement of the claim, a description of the goods subject to the lien, a demand for payment within a specified time not less than ten days after receipt of the notification, and a conspicuous statement that unless the claim is paid within the time the goods will be advertised for sale and sold by auction at a specified time and place.

(d) The sale must conform to the terms of the notification.

(e) The sale must be held at the nearest suitable place to that where the goods are held or stored.

(f) After the expiration of the time given in the notification, an advertisement of the sale must be published once a week for two weeks consecutively in a newspaper of general circulation where the sale is to be held. The advertisement must include a description of the goods, the name of the person on whose account they are being held, and the time and place of the sale. The sale must take place at least fifteen days after the first publication. If there is no newspaper of general circulation where the sale is to be held, the advertisement must be posted at least ten days before the sale in not less than six conspicuous places in the neighborhood of the proposed sale.

(3) Before any sale pursuant to this section any person claiming a right in the goods may pay the amount necessary to satisfy the lien and the reasonable expenses incurred under this section. In that event the goods must not be sold, but must be retained by the warehouseman subject to the terms of the receipt and this Article.

(4) The warehouseman may buy at any public sale pursuant to this section.

(5) A purchaser in good faith of goods sold to enforce a warehouseman's lien takes the goods free of any rights of persons against whom the lien was valid, despite noncompliance by the warehouseman with the requirements of this section.

(6) The warehouseman may satisfy his lien from the proceeds of any sale pursuant to this section but must hold the balance, if any, for delivery on demand to any person to whom he would have been bound to deliver the goods.

(7) The rights provided by this section shall be in addition to all other rights allowed by law to a creditor against his debtor.

(8) Where a lien is on goods stored by a merchant in the course of his business the lien may be enforced in accordance with either subsection (1) or (2).

(9) The warehouseman is liable for damages caused by failure to comply with the requirements for sale under this section and in case of willful violation is liable for conversion.

PART 3 Bills of Lading: Special Provisions

§ 7–301. Liability for Non-Receipt or Misdescription; "Said to Contain"; "Shipper's Load and Count"; Improper Handling.

(1) A consignee of a non-negotiable bill who has given value in good faith or a holder to whom a negotiable bill has been duly negotiated relying in either case upon the description therein of the goods, or upon the date therein shown, may recover from the issuer damages caused by the misdating of the bill or the non-receipt or misdescription of the goods, except to the extent that the document indicates that the issuer does not know whether any part of all of the goods in fact were received or conform to the description, as where the description is in terms of marks or labels or kind, quantity, or condition or the receipt or description is qualified by "contents or condition of contents of packages unknown", "said to contain", "shipper's weight, load and count" or the like, if such indication be true.

(2) When goods are loaded by an issuer who is a common carrier, the issuer must count the packages of goods if package freight and ascertain the kind and quantity if bulk freight. In such cases "shipper's weight, load and count" or other words indicating that the description was made by the shipper are ineffective except as to freight concealed by packages.

(3) When bulk freight is loaded by a shipper who makes available to the issuer adequate facilities for weighing such freight, an issuer who is a common carrier must ascertain the kind and quantity within a reasonable time after receiving the written request of the shipper to do so. In such cases "shipper's weight" or other words of like purport are ineffective.

(4) The issuer may by inserting in the bill the words "shipper's weight, load and count" or other words of like purport indicate that the goods were loaded by the shipper; and if such statement be true the issuer shall not be liable for damages caused by the improper loading. But their omission does not imply liability for such damages.

(5) The shipper shall be deemed to have guaranteed to the issuer the accuracy at the time of shipment of the description, marks, labels, number, kind, quantity, condition and weight, as furnished by him; and the shipper shall indemnify the issuer against damage caused by inaccuracies in such particulars. The right of the issuer to such indemnity shall in no way limit his responsibility and liability under the contract of carriage to any person other than the shipper.

§ 7–302. Through Bills of Lading and Similar Documents.

(1) The issuer of a through bill of lading or other document embodying an undertaking to be performed in part by persons acting as its agents or by connecting carriers is liable to anyone entitled to recover on the document for any breach by such other persons or by a connecting carrier of its obligation under the document but to the extent that the bill covers an undertaking to be performed overseas or in territory not contiguous to the continental United States or an undertaking including matters other than transportation this liability may be varied by agreement of the parties.

(2) Where goods covered by a through bill of lading or other document embodying an undertaking to be performed in part by persons other than the issuer are received by any such person, he is subject with respect to his own performance while the goods are in his possession to the obligation of the issuer. His obligation is discharged by delivery of the goods to another such person pursuant to the document, and does not include liability for breach by any other such persons or by the issuer.

(3) The issuer of such through bill of lading or other document shall be entitled to recover from the connecting carrier or such other person in possession of the goods when the breach of the

obligation under the document occurred, the amount it may be required to pay to anyone entitled to recover on the document therefor, as may be evidenced by any receipt, judgment, or transcript thereof, and the amount of any expense reasonably incurred by it in defending any action brought by anyone entitled to recover on the document therefor.

§ 7–303. Diversion; Reconsignment; Change of Instructions.

(1) Unless the bill of lading otherwise provides, the carrier may deliver the goods to a person or destination other than that stated in the bill or may otherwise dispose of the goods on instructions from

(a) the holder of a negotiable bill; or

(b) the consignor on a non-negotiable bill notwithstanding contrary instructions from the consignee; or

(c) the consignee on a non-negotiable bill in the absence of contrary instructions from the consignor, if the goods have arrived at the billed destination or if the consignee is in possession of the bill; or

(d) the consignee on a non-negotiable bill if he is entitled as against the consignor to dispose of them.

(2) Unless such instructions are noted on a negotiable bill of lading, a person to whom the bill is duly negotiated can hold the bailee according to the original terms.

§ 7–304. Bills of Lading in a Set.

(1) Except where customary in overseas transportation, a bill of lading must not be issued in a set of parts. The issuer is liable for damages caused by violation of this subsection.

(2) Where a bill of lading is lawfully drawn in a set of parts, each of which is numbered and expressed to be valid only if the goods have not been delivered against any other part, the whole of the parts constitute one bill.

(3) Where a bill of lading is lawfully issued in a set of parts and different parts are negotiated to different persons, the title of the holder to whom the first due negotiation is made prevails as to both the document and the goods even though any later holder may have received the goods from the carrier in good faith and discharged the carrier's obligation by surrender of his part.

(4) Any person who negotiates or transfers a single part of a bill of lading drawn in a set is liable to holders of that part as if it were the whole set.

(5) The bailee is obliged to deliver in accordance with Part 4 of this Article against the first presented part of a bill of lading lawfully drawn in a set. Such delivery discharges the bailee's obligation on the whole bill.

§ 7–305. Destination Bills.

(1) Instead of issuing a bill of lading to the consignor at the place of shipment a carrier may at the request of the consignor procure the bill to be issued at destination or at any other place designated in the request.

(2) Upon request of anyone entitled as against the carrier to control the goods while in transit and on surrender of any outstanding bill of lading or other receipt covering such goods, the issuer may procure a substitute bill to be issued at any place designated in the request.

§ 7–306. Altered Bills of Lading.

An unauthorized alteration or filling in of a blank in a bill of lading leaves the bill enforceable according to its original tenor.

§ 7–307. Lien of Carrier.

(1) A carrier has a lien on the goods covered by a bill of lading for charges subsequent to the date of its receipt of the goods for storage or transportation (including demurrage and terminal charges) and for expenses necessary for preservation of the goods incident to their transportation or reasonably incurred in their sale pursuant to law. But against a purchaser for value of a negotiable bill of lading a carrier's lien is limited to charges stated in the bill or the applicable tariffs, or if no charges are stated then to a reasonable charge.

(2) A lien for charges and expenses under subsection (1) on goods which the carrier was required by law to receive for transportation is effective against the consignor or any person entitled to the goods unless the carrier had notice that the consignor lacked authority to subject the goods to such charges and expenses. Any other lien under subsection (1) is effective against the consignor and any person who permitted the bailor to have control or possession of the goods unless the carrier had notice that the bailor lacked such authority.

(3) A carrier loses his lien on any goods which he voluntarily delivers or which he unjustifiably refuses to deliver.

§ 7–308. Enforcement of Carrier's Lien.

(1) A carrier's lien may be enforced by public or private sale of the goods, in bloc or in parcels, at any time or place and on any terms which are commercially reasonable, after notifying all persons known to claim an interest in the goods. Such notification must include a statement of the amount due, the nature of the proposed sale and the time and place of any public sale. The fact that a better price could have been obtained by a sale at a different time or in a different method from that selected by the carrier is not of itself sufficient to establish that the sale was not made in a commercially reasonable manner. If the carrier either sells the goods in the usual manner in any recognized market therefor or if he sells at the price current in such market at the time of his sale or if he has otherwise sold in conformity with commercially reasonable practices among dealers in the type of goods sold he has sold in a commercially reasonable manner. A sale of more goods than apparently necessary to be offered to ensure satisfaction of the obligation is not commercially reasonable except in cases covered by the preceding sentence.

(2) Before any sale pursuant to this section any person claiming a right in the goods may pay the amount necessary to satisfy the lien and the reasonable expenses incurred under this section. In that event the goods must not be sold, but must be retained by the carrier subject to the terms of the bill and this Article.

(3) The carrier may buy at any public sale pursuant to this section.

(4) A purchaser in good faith of goods sold to enforce a carrier's lien takes the goods free of any rights of persons against whom the lien was valid, despite noncompliance by the carrier with the requirements of this section.

(5) The carrier may satisfy his lien from the proceeds of any sale pursuant to this section but must hold the balance, if any, for delivery on demand to any person to whom he would have been bound to deliver the goods.

(6) The rights provided by this section shall be in addition to all other rights allowed by law to a creditor against his debtor.

(7) A carrier's lien may be enforced in accordance with either subsection (1) or the procedure set forth in subsection (2) of Section 7–210.

(8) The carrier is liable for damages caused by failure to comply with the requirements for sale under this section and in case of willful violation is liable for conversion.

§ 7–309. Duty of Care; Contractual Limitation of Carrier's Liability.

(1) A carrier who issues a bill of lading whether negotiable or non-negotiable must exercise the degree of care in relation to the goods which a reasonably careful man would exercise under like circumstances. This subsection does not repeal or change any law or rule of law which imposes liability upon a common carrier for damages not caused by its negligence.

(2) Damages may be limited by a provision that the carrier's liability shall not exceed a value stated in the document if the carrier's rates are dependent upon value and the consignor by the carrier's tariff is afforded an opportunity to declare a higher value or a value as lawfully provided in the tariff, or where no tariff is filed he is otherwise advised of such opportunity; but no such limitation is effective with respect to the carrier's liability for conversion to its own use.

(3) Reasonable provisions as to the time and manner of presenting claims and instituting actions based on the shipment may be included in a bill of lading or tariff.

PART 4 Warehouse Receipts and Bills of Lading: General Obligations

§ 7–401. Irregularities in Issue of Receipt or Bill or Conduct of Issuer.

The obligations imposed by this Article on an issuer apply to a document of title regardless of the fact that

(a) the document may not comply with the requirements of this Article or of any other law or regulation regarding its issue, form or content; or

(b) the issuer may have violated laws regulating the conduct of his business; or

(c) the goods covered by the document were owned by the bailee at the time the document was issued; or

(d) the person issuing the document does not come within the definition of warehouseman if it purports to be a warehouse receipt.

§ 7–402. Duplicate Receipt or Bill; Overissue.

Neither a duplicate nor any other document of title purporting to cover goods already represented by an outstanding document of the same issuer confers any right in the goods, except as provided in the case of bills in a set, overissue of documents for fungible goods and substitutes for lost, stolen or destroyed documents. But the issuer is liable for damages caused by his overissue or failure to identify a duplicate document as such by conspicuous notation on its face.

§ 7–403. Obligation of Warehouseman or Carrier to Deliver; Excuse.

(1) The bailee must deliver the goods to a person entitled under the document who complies with subsections (2) and (3), unless and to the extent that the bailee establishes any of the following:

(a) delivery of the goods to a person whose receipt was rightful as against the claimant;

(b) damage to or delay, loss or destruction of the goods for which the bailee is not liable [, but the burden of establishing negligence in such cases is on the person entitled under the document];

Note: *The brackets in (1)(b) indicate that State enactments may differ on this point without serious damage to the principle of uniformity.*

(c) previous sale or other disposition of the goods in lawful enforcement of a lien or on warehouseman's lawful termination of storage;

(d) the exercise by a seller of his right to stop delivery pursuant to the provisions of the Article on Sales (Section 2–705);

(e) a diversion, reconsignment or other disposition pursuant to the provisions of this Article (Section 7–303) or tariff regulating such right;

(f) release, satisfaction or any other fact affording a personal defense against the claimant;

(g) any other lawful excuse.

(2) A person claiming goods covered by a document of title must satisfy the bailee's lien where the bailee so requests or where the bailee is prohibited by law from delivering the goods until the charges are paid.

(3) Unless the person claiming is one against whom the document confers no right under Sec. 7–503(1), he must surrender for cancellation or notation of partial deliveries any outstanding negotiable document covering the goods, and the bailee must cancel the document or conspicuously note the partial delivery thereon or be liable to any person to whom the document is duly negotiated.

(4) "Person entitled under the document" means holder in the case of a negotiable document, or the person to whom delivery is to be made by the terms of or pursuant to written instructions under a non-negotiable document.

§ 7–404. No Liability for Good Faith Delivery Pursuant to Receipt or Bill.

A bailee who in good faith including observance of reasonable commercial standards has received goods and delivered or otherwise disposed of them according to the terms of the document of title or pursuant to this Article is not liable therefor. This rule applies even though the person from whom he received the goods had no authority to procure the document or to dispose of the goods and even though the person to whom he delivered the goods had no authority to receive them.

PART 5 Warehouse Receipts and Bills of Lading: Negotiation and Transfer

§ 7–501. Form of Negotiation and Requirements of "Due Negotiation".

(1) A negotiable document of title running to the order of a named person is negotiated by his indorsement and delivery. After his indorsement in blank or to bearer any person can negotiate it by delivery alone.

(2) (a) A negotiable document of title is also negotiated by delivery alone when by its original terms it runs to bearer.

(b) When a document running to the order of a named person is delivered to him the effect is the same as if the document had been negotiated.

(3) Negotiation of a negotiable document of title after it has been indorsed to a specified person requires indorsement by the special indorsee as well as delivery.

(4) A negotiable document of title is "duly negotiated" when it is negotiated in the manner stated in this section to a holder who purchases it in good faith without notice of any defense against or claim to it on the part of any person and for value, unless it is established that the negotiation is not in the regular course of business or financing or involves receiving the document in settlement or payment of a money obligation.

(5) Indorsement of a non-negotiable document neither makes it negotiable nor adds to the transferee's rights.

(6) The naming in a negotiable bill of a person to be notified of the arrival of the goods does not limit the negotiability of the bill nor constitute notice to a purchaser thereof of any interest of such person in the goods.

§ 7–502. Rights Acquired by Due Negotiation.

(1) Subject to the following section and to the provisions of Section 7–205 on fungible goods, a holder to whom a negotiable document of title has been duly negotiated acquires thereby:

(a) title to the document;

(b) title to the goods;

(c) all rights accruing under the law of agency or estoppel, including rights to goods delivered to the bailee after the document was issued; and

(d) the direct obligation of the issuer to hold or deliver the goods according to the terms of the document free of any defense or claim by him except those arising under the terms of the document or under this Article. In the case of a delivery order the bailee's obligation accrues only upon acceptance and the obligation acquired by the holder is that the issuer and any indorser will procure the acceptance of the bailee.

(2) Subject to the following section, title and rights so acquired are not defeated by any stoppage of the goods represented by the document or by surrender of such goods by the bailee, and are not impaired even though the negotiation or any prior negotiation constituted a breach of duty or even though any person has been deprived of possession of the document by misrepresentation, fraud, accident, mistake, duress, loss, theft or conversion, or even though a previous sale or other transfer of the goods or document has been made to a third person.

§ 7–503. Document of Title to Goods Defeated in Certain Cases.

(1) A document of title confers no right in goods against a person who before issuance of the document had a legal interest or a perfected security interest in them and who neither

(a) delivered or entrusted them or any document of title covering them to the bailor or his nominee with actual or apparent authority to ship, store or sell or with power to obtain delivery under this Article (Section 7–403) or with power of disposition under this Act (Sections 2–403 and 9–307) or other statute or rule of law; nor

(b) acquiesced in the procurement by the bailor or his nominee of any document of title.

(2) Title to goods based upon an unaccepted delivery order is subject to the rights of anyone to whom a negotiable warehouse receipt or bill of lading covering the goods has been duly negotiated. Such a title may be defeated under the next section to the same extent as the rights of the issuer or a transferee from the issuer.

(3) Title to goods based upon a bill of lading issued to a freight forwarder is subject to the rights of anyone to whom a bill issued by the freight forwarder is duly negotiated; but delivery by the carrier in accordance with Part 4 of this Article pursuant to its own bill of lading discharges the carrier's obligation to deliver.

§ 7–504. Rights Acquired in the Absence of Due Negotiation; Effect of Diversion; Seller's Stoppage of Delivery.

(1) A transferee of a document, whether negotiable or non-negotiable, to whom the document has been delivered but not duly negotiated, acquires the title and rights which his transferor had or had actual authority to convey.

(2) In the case of a non-negotiable document, until but not after the bailee receives notification of the transfer, the rights of the transferee may be defeated

(a) by those creditors of the transferor who could treat the sale as void under Section 2–402; or

(b) by a buyer from the transferor in ordinary course of business if the bailee has delivered the goods to the buyer or received notification of his rights; or

(c) as against the bailee by good faith dealings of the bailee with the transferor.

(3) A diversion or other change of shipping instructions by the consignor in a non-negotiable bill of lading which causes the bailee not to deliver to the consignee defeats the consignee's title to the goods if they have been delivered to a buyer in ordinary course of business and in any event defeats the consignee's rights against the bailee.

(4) Delivery pursuant to a non-negotiable document may be stopped by a seller under Section 2–705, and subject to the requirement of due notification there provided. A bailee honoring the seller's instructions is entitled to be indemnified by the seller against any resulting loss or expense.

§ 7–505. Indorser Not a Guarantor for Other Parties.

The indorsement of a document of title issued by a bailee does not make the indorser liable for any default by the bailee or by previous indorsers.

§ 7–506. Delivery Without Indorsement: Right to Compel Indorsement.

The transferee of a negotiable document of title has a specifically enforceable right to have his transferor supply any necessary indorsement but the transfer becomes a negotiation only as of the time the indorsement is supplied.

§ 7–507. Warranties on Negotiation or Transfer of Receipt or Bill.

Where a person negotiates or transfers a document of title for value otherwise than as a mere intermediary under the next following section, then unless otherwise agreed he warrants to his immediate purchaser only in addition to any warranty made in selling the goods

(a) that the document is genuine; and

(b) that he has no knowledge of any fact which would impair its validity or worth; and

(c) that his negotiation or transfer is rightful and fully effective with respect to the title to the document and the goods it represents.

§ 7–508. Warranties of Collecting Bank as to Documents.

A collecting bank or other intermediary known to be entrusted with documents on behalf of another or with collection of a draft of other claim against delivery of documents warrants by such delivery of the documents only its own good faith and authority. This rule applies even though the intermediary has purchased or made advances against the claim or draft to be collected.

§ 7–509. Receipt or Bill: When Adequate Compliance With Commercial Contract.

The question whether a document is adequate to fulfill the obligations of a contract for sale or the conditions of a credit is governed by the Articles on Sales (Article 2) and on Letters of Credit (Article 5).

PART 6 Warehouse Receipts and Bills of Lading: Miscellaneous Provisions

§ 7–601. Lost and Missing Documents.

(1) If a document has been lost, stolen or destroyed, a court may order delivery of the goods or issuance of a substitute document and the bailee may without liability to any person comply with such order. If the document was negotiable the claimant must post security approved by the court to indemnify any person who may suffer loss as a result of non-surrender of the document. If the document was not negotiable, such security may be required at the discretion of the court. The court may also in its discretion order payment of the bailee's reasonable costs and counsel fees.

(2) A bailee who without court order delivers goods to a person claiming under a missing negotiable document is liable to any person injured thereby, and if the delivery is not in good faith becomes liable for conversion. Delivery in good faith is not conversion if made in accordance with a filed classification or tariff or, where no classification or tariff is filed, if the claimant posts security with the bailee in an amount at least double the value of the goods at the time of posting to indemnify any person injured by the delivery who files a notice of claim within one year after the delivery.

§ 7–602. Attachment of Goods Covered by a Negotiable Document.

Except where the document was originally issued upon delivery of the goods by a person who had no power to dispose of them, no lien attaches by virtue of any judicial process to goods in the possession of a bailee for which a negotiable document of title is outstanding unless the document be first surrendered to the bailee or its negotiation enjoined, and the bailee shall not be compelled to deliver the goods pursuant to process until the document is surrendered to him or impounded by the court. One who purchases the document for value without notice of the process or injunction takes free of the lien imposed by judicial process.

§ 7–603. Conflicting Claims; Interpleader.

If more than one person claims title or possession of the goods, the bailee is excused from delivery until he has had a reasonable time to ascertain the validity of the adverse claims or to bring an action to compel all claimants to interplead and may compel such interpleader, either in defending an action for non-delivery of the goods, or by original action, whichever is appropriate.

ARTICLE 8

REVISED (1994) INVESTMENT SECURITIES

PART 1 Short Title and General Matters

§ 8–101. Short Title.

This Article may be cited as Uniform Commercial Code—Investment Securities.

§ 8–102. Definitions.

(a) In this Article:

(1) "Adverse claim" means a claim that a claimant has a property interest in a financial asset and that it is a violation of the rights of the claimant for another person to hold, transfer, or deal with the financial asset.

(2) "Bearer form," as applied to a certificated security, means a form in which the security is payable to the bearer of the security certificate according to its terms but not by reason of an indorsement.

(3) "Broker" means a person defined as a broker or dealer under the federal securities laws, but without excluding a bank acting in that capacity.

(4) "Certificated security" means a security that is represented by a certificate.

(5) "Clearing corporation" means:

(i) a person that is registered as a "clearing agency" under the federal securities laws;

(ii) a federal reserve bank; or

(iii) any other person that provides clearance or settlement services with respect to financial assets that would require it to register as a clearing agency under the federal securities laws but for an exclusion or exemption from the registration requirement, if its activities as a clearing corporation, including promulgation of rules, are subject to regulation by a federal or state governmental authority.

(6) "Communicate" means to:

(i) send a signed writing; or

(ii) transmit information by any mechanism agreed upon by the persons transmitting and receiving the information.

(7) "Entitlement holder" means a person identified in the records of a securities intermediary as the person having a security entitlement against the securities intermediary. If a person acquires a security entitlement by virtue of Section 8–501(b)(2) or (3), that person is the entitlement holder.

(8) "Entitlement order" means a notification communicated to a securities intermediary directing transfer or redemption of a financial asset to which the entitlement holder has a security entitlement.

(9) "Financial asset," except as otherwise provided in Section 8–103, means:

(i) a security;

(ii) an obligation of a person or a share, participation, or other interest in a person or in property or an enterprise of a person, which is, or is of a type, dealt in or traded on financial markets, or which is recognized in any area in which it is issued or dealt in as a medium for investment; or

(iii) any property that is held by a securities intermediary for another person in a securities account if the securities intermediary has expressly agreed with the other person that the property is to be treated as a financial asset under this Article.

As context requires, the term means either the interest itself or the means by which a person's claim to it is evidenced, including a certificated or uncertificated security, a security certificate, or a security entitlement.

(10) "Good faith," for purposes of the obligation of good faith in the performance or enforcement of contracts or duties within this Article, means honesty in fact and the observance of reasonable commercial standards of fair dealing.

(11) "Indorsement" means a signature that alone or accompanied by other words is made on a security certificate in registered form or on a separate document for the purpose of assigning, transferring, or redeeming the security or granting a power to assign, transfer, or redeem it.

(12) "Instruction" means a notification communicated to the issuer of an uncertificated security which directs that the transfer of the security be registered or that the security be redeemed.

(13) "Registered form," as applied to a certificated security, means a form in which:

(i) the security certificate specifies a person entitled to the security; and

(ii) a transfer of the security may be registered upon books maintained for that purpose by or on behalf of the issuer, or the security certificate so states.

(14) "Securities intermediary" means:

(i) a clearing corporation; or

(ii) a person, including a bank or broker, that in the ordinary course of its business maintains securities accounts for others and is acting in that capacity.

(15) "Security," except as otherwise provided in Section 8–103, means an obligation of an issuer or a share, participation, or other interest in an issuer or in property or an enterprise of an issuer:

(i) which is represented by a security certificate in bearer or registered form, or the transfer of which may be registered upon books maintained for that purpose by or on behalf of the issuer;

(ii) which is one of a class or series or by its terms is divisible into a class or series of shares, participations, interests, or obligations; and

(iii) which:

(A) is, or is of a type, dealt in or traded on securities exchanges or securities markets; or

(B) is a medium for investment and by its terms expressly provides that it is a security governed by this Article.

(16) "Security certificate" means a certificate representing a security.

(17) "Security entitlement" means the rights and property interest of an entitlement holder with respect to a financial asset specified in Part 5.

(18) "Uncertificated security" means a security that is not represented by a certificate.

(b) Other definitions applying to this Article and the sections in which they appear are:

Appropriate person Section 8–107
Control Section 8–106
Delivery Section 8–301
Investment company security Section 8–103
Issuer Section 8–201
Overissue Section 8–210
Protected purchaser Section 8–303
Securities account Section 8–501

(c) In addition, Article 1 contains general definitions and principles of construction and interpretation applicable throughout this Article.

(d) The characterization of a person, business, or transaction for purposes of this Article does not determine the characterization of the person, business, or transaction for purposes of any other law, regulation, or rule.

§ 8–103. Rules for Determining Whether Certain Obligations and Interests Are Securities or Financial Assets.

(a) A share or similar equity interest issued by a corporation, business trust, joint stock company, or similar entity is a security.

(b) An "investment company security" is a security. "Investment company security" means a share or similar equity interest issued by an entity that is registered as an investment company under the federal investment company laws, an interest in a unit investment trust that is so registered, or a face-amount certificate issued by a face-amount certificate company that is so registered. Investment company security does not include an insurance policy or endowment policy or annuity contract issued by an insurance company.

(c) An interest in a partnership or limited liability company is not a security unless it is dealt in or traded on securities exchanges or in securities markets, its terms expressly provide that it is a security governed by this Article, or it is an investment company security. However, an interest in a partnership or limited liability company is a financial asset if it is held in a securities account.

(d) A writing that is a security certificate is governed by this Article and not by Article 3, even though it also meets the requirements of that Article. However, a negotiable instrument governed by Article 3 is a financial asset if it is held in a securities account.

(e) An option or similar obligation issued by a clearing corporation to its participants is not a security, but is a financial asset.

(f) A commodity contract, as defined in Section 9-115, is not a security or a financial asset.

§ 8–104. Acquisition of Security or Financial Asset or Interest Therein.

(a) A person acquires a security or an interest therein, under this Article, if:

(1) the person is a purchaser to whom a security is delivered pursuant to Section 8–301; or

(2) the person acquires a security entitlement to the security pursuant to Section 8–501.

(b) A person acquires a financial asset, other than a security, or an interest therein, under this Article, if the person acquires a security entitlement to the financial asset.

(c) A person who acquires a security entitlement to a security or other financial asset has the rights specified in Part 5, but is a purchaser of any security, security entitlement, or other financial asset held by the securities intermediary only to the extent provided in Section 8–503.

(d) Unless the context shows that a different meaning is intended, a person who is required by other law, regulation, rule, or agreement to transfer, deliver, present, surrender, exchange, or otherwise put in the possession of another person a security or financial asset satisfies that requirement by causing the other person to acquire an interest in the security or financial asset pursuant to subsection (a) or (b).

§ 8–105. Notice of Adverse Claim.

(a) A person has notice of an adverse claim if:

(1) the person knows of the adverse claim;

(2) the person is aware of facts sufficient to indicate that there is a significant probability that the adverse claim exists and deliberately avoids information that would establish the existence of the adverse claim; or

(3) the person has a duty, imposed by statute or regulation, to investigate whether an adverse claim exists, and the investigation so required would establish the existence of the adverse claim.

(b) Having knowledge that a financial asset or interest therein is or has been transferred by a representative imposes no duty of inquiry into the rightfulness of a transaction and is not notice of an adverse claim. However, a person who knows that a representative has transferred a financial asset or interest therein in a transaction that is, or whose proceeds are being used, for the individual benefit of the representative or otherwise in breach of duty has notice of an adverse claim.

(c) An act or event that creates a right to immediate performance of the principal obligation represented by a security certificate or sets a date on or after which the certificate is to be presented or surrendered for redemption or exchange does not itself constitute notice of an adverse claim except in the case of a transfer more than:

(1) one year after a date set for presentment or surrender for redemption or exchange; or

(2) six months after a date set for payment of money against presentation or surrender of the certificate, if money was available for payment on that date.

(d) A purchaser of a certificated security has notice of an adverse claim if the security certificate:

(1) whether in bearer or registered form, has been indorsed "for collection" or "for surrender" or for some other purpose not involving transfer; or

(2) is in bearer form and has on it an unambiguous statement that it is the property of a person other than the transferor, but the mere writing of a name on the certificate is not such a statement.

(e) Filing of a financing statement under Article 9 is not notice of an adverse claim to a financial asset.

§ 8–106. Control.

(a) A purchaser has "control" of a certificated security in bearer form if the certificated security is delivered to the purchaser.

(b) A purchaser has "control" of a certificated security in registered form if the certificated security is delivered to the purchaser, and:

(1) the certificate is indorsed to the purchaser or in blank by an effective indorsement; or

(2) the certificate is registered in the name of the purchaser, upon original issue or registration of transfer by the issuer.

(c) A purchaser has "control" of an uncertificated security if:

(1) the uncertificated security is delivered to the purchaser; or

(2) the issuer has agreed that it will comply with instructions originated by the purchaser without further consent by the registered owner.

(d) A purchaser has "control" of a security entitlement if:

(1) the purchaser becomes the entitlement holder; or

(2) the securities intermediary has agreed that it will comply with entitlement orders originated by the purchaser without further consent by the entitlement holder.

(e) If an interest in a security entitlement is granted by the entitlement holder to the entitlement holder's own securities intermediary, the securities intermediary has control.

(f) A purchaser who has satisfied the requirements of subsection (c)(2) or (d)(2) has control even if the registered owner in the case of subsection (c)(2) or the entitlement holder in the case of subsection (d)(2) retains the right to make substitutions for the uncertificated security or security entitlement, to originate instructions or entitlement orders to the issuer or securities intermediary, or otherwise to deal with the uncertificated security or security entitlement.

(g) An issuer or a securities intermediary may not enter into an agreement of the kind described in subsection (c)(2) or (d)(2) without the consent of the registered owner or entitlement holder, but an issuer or a securities intermediary is not required to enter into such an agreement even though the registered owner or entitlement holder so directs. An issuer or securities intermediary that has entered into such an agreement is not required to confirm the existence of the agreement to another party unless requested to do so by the registered owner or entitlement holder.

§ 8–107. Whether Indorsement, Instruction, or Entitlement Order Is Effective.

(a) "Appropriate person" means:

(1) with respect to an indorsement, the person specified by a security certificate or by an effective special indorsement to be entitled to the security;

(2) with respect to an instruction, the registered owner of an uncertificated security;

(3) with respect to an entitlement order, the entitlement holder;

(4) if the person designated in paragraph (1), (2), or (3) is deceased, the designated person's successor taking under other law or the designated person's personal representative acting for the estate of the decedent; or

(5) if the person designated in paragraph (1), (2), or (3) lacks capacity, the designated person's guardian, conservator, or other similar representative who has power under other law to transfer the security or financial asset.

(b) An indorsement, instruction, or entitlement order is effective if:

(1) it is made by the appropriate person;

(2) it is made by a person who has power under the law of agency to transfer the security or financial asset on behalf of the appropriate person, including, in the case of an instruction or entitlement order, a person who has control under Section 8–106(c)(2) or (d)(2); or

(3) the appropriate person has ratified it or is otherwise precluded from asserting its ineffectiveness.

(c) An indorsement, instruction, or entitlement order made by a representative is effective even if:

(1) the representative has failed to comply with a controlling instrument or with the law of the State having jurisdiction of the representative relationship, including any law requiring the representative to obtain court approval of the transaction; or

(2) the representative's action in making the indorsement, instruction, or entitlement order or using the proceeds of the transaction is otherwise a breach of duty.

(d) If a security is registered in the name of or specially indorsed to a person described as a representative, or if a securities account is maintained in the name of a person described as a representative, an indorsement, instruction, or entitlement order made by the person is effective even though the person is no longer serving in the described capacity.

(e) Effectiveness of an indorsement, instruction, or entitlement order is determined as of the date the indorsement, instruction, or entitlement order is made, and an indorsement, instruction, or entitlement order does not become ineffective by reason of any later change of circumstances.

§ 8–108. Warranties in Direct Holding.

(a) A person who transfers a certificated security to a purchaser for value warrants to the purchaser, and an indorser, if the transfer is by indorsement, warrants to any subsequent purchaser, that:

(1) the certificate is genuine and has not been materially altered;

(2) the transferor or indorser does not know of any fact that might impair the validity of the security;

(3) there is no adverse claim to the security;

(4) the transfer does not violate any restriction on transfer;

(5) if the transfer is by indorsement, the indorsement is made by an appropriate person, or if the indorsement is by an agent, the agent has actual authority to act on behalf of the appropriate person; and

(6) the transfer is otherwise effective and rightful.

(b) A person who originates an instruction for registration of transfer of an uncertificated security to a purchaser for value warrants to the purchaser that:

(1) the instruction is made by an appropriate person, or if the instruction is by an agent, the agent has actual authority to act on behalf of the appropriate person;

(2) the security is valid;

(3) there is no adverse claim to the security; and

(4) at the time the instruction is presented to the issuer:

(i) the purchaser will be entitled to the registration of transfer;

(ii) the transfer will be registered by the issuer free from all liens, security interests, restrictions, and claims other than those specified in the instruction;

(iii) the transfer will not violate any restriction on transfer; and

(iv) the requested transfer will otherwise be effective and rightful.

(c) A person who transfers an uncertificated security to a purchaser for value and does not originate an instruction in connection with the transfer warrants that:

(1) the uncertificated security is valid;

(2) there is no adverse claim to the security;

(3) the transfer does not violate any restriction on transfer; and

(4) the transfer is otherwise effective and rightful.

(d) A person who indorses a security certificate warrants to the issuer that:

(1) there is no adverse claim to the security; and

(2) the indorsement is effective.

(e) A person who originates an instruction for registration of transfer of an uncertificated security warrants to the issuer that:

(1) the instruction is effective; and

(2) at the time the instruction is presented to the issuer the purchaser will be entitled to the registration of transfer.

(f) A person who presents a certificated security for registration of transfer or for payment or exchange warrants to the issuer that the person is entitled to the registration, payment, or exchange, but a purchaser for value and without notice of adverse claims to whom transfer is registered warrants only that the person has no knowledge of any unauthorized signature in a necessary indorsement.

(g) If a person acts as agent of another in delivering a certificated security to a purchaser, the identity of the principal was known to the person to whom the certificate was delivered, and the certificate delivered by the agent was received by the agent from the principal or received by the agent from another person at the direction of the principal, the person delivering the security certificate warrants only that the delivering person has authority to act for the principal and does not know of any adverse claim to the certificated security.

(h) A secured party who redelivers a security certificate received, or after payment and on order of the debtor delivers the security certificate to another person, makes only the warranties of an agent under subsection (g).

(i) Except as otherwise provided in subsection (g), a broker acting for a customer makes to the issuer and a purchaser the warranties provided in subsections (a) through (f). A broker that delivers a security certificate to its customer, or causes its customer to be registered as the owner of an uncertificated security, makes to the customer the warranties provided in subsection (a) or (b), and has the rights and privileges of a purchaser under this section. The warranties of and in favor of the broker acting as an agent are in addition to applicable warranties given by and in favor of the customer.

§ 8–109. Warranties in Indirect Holding.

(a) A person who originates an entitlement order to a securities intermediary warrants to the securities intermediary that:

(1) the entitlement order is made by an appropriate person, or if the entitlement order is by an agent, the agent has actual authority to act on behalf of the appropriate person; and

(2) there is no adverse claim to the security entitlement.

(b) A person who delivers a security certificate to a securities intermediary for credit to a securities account or originates an instruction with respect to an uncertificated security directing that the uncertificated security be credited to a securities account makes to the securities intermediary the warranties specified in Section 8–108(a) or (b).

(c) If a securities intermediary delivers a security certificate to its entitlement holder or causes its entitlement holder to be registered as the owner of an uncertificated security, the securities intermediary makes to the entitlement holder the warranties specified in Section 8–108(a) or (b).

§ 8–110. Applicability; Choice of Law.

(a) The local law of the issuer's jurisdiction, as specified in subsection (d), governs:

(1) the validity of a security;

(2) the rights and duties of the issuer with respect to registration of transfer;

(3) the effectiveness of registration of transfer by the issuer;

(4) whether the issuer owes any duties to an adverse claimant to a security; and

(5) whether an adverse claim can be asserted against a person to whom transfer of a certificated or uncertificated security is registered or a person who obtains control of an uncertificated security.

(b) The local law of the securities intermediary's jurisdiction, as specified in subsection (e), governs:

(1) acquisition of a security entitlement from the securities intermediary;

(2) the rights and duties of the securities intermediary and entitlement holder arising out of a security entitlement;

(3) whether the securities intermediary owes any duties to an adverse claimant to a security entitlement; and

(4) whether an adverse claim can be asserted against a person who acquires a security entitlement from the securities intermediary or a person who purchases a security entitlement or interest therein from an entitlement holder.

(c) The local law of the jurisdiction in which a security certificate is located at the time of delivery governs whether an adverse claim can be asserted against a person to whom the security certificate is delivered.

(d) "Issuer's jurisdiction" means the jurisdiction under which the issuer of the security is organized or, if permitted by the law of that jurisdiction, the law of another jurisdiction specified by the issuer. An issuer organized under the law of this State may specify the law of another jurisdiction as the law governing the matters specified in subsection (a)(2) through (5).

(e) The following rules determine a "securities intermediary's jurisdiction" for purposes of this section:

(1) If an agreement between the securities intermediary and its entitlement holder specifies that it is governed by the law of a particular jurisdiction, that jurisdiction is the securities intermediary's jurisdiction.

(2) If an agreement between the securities intermediary and its entitlement holder does not specify the governing law as provided in paragraph (1), but expressly specifies that the securities account is maintained at an office in a particular jurisdiction, that jurisdiction is the securities intermediary's jurisdiction.

(3) If an agreement between the securities intermediary and its entitlement holder does not specify a jurisdiction as provided in paragraph (1) or (2), the securities intermediary's jurisdiction is the jurisdiction in which is located the office identified in an account statement as the office serving the entitlement holder's account.

(4) If an agreement between the securities intermediary and its entitlement holder does not specify a jurisdiction as provided in paragraph (1) or (2) and an account statement does not identify an office serving the entitlement holder's account as provided in paragraph (3), the securities intermediary's jurisdiction is the jurisdiction in which is located the chief executive office of the securities intermediary.

(f) A securities intermediary's jurisdiction is not determined by the physical location of certificates representing financial assets, or by the jurisdiction in which is organized the issuer of the financial asset with respect to which an entitlement holder has a security entitlement, or by the location of facilities for data processing or other record keeping concerning the account.

§ 8–111. Clearing Corporation Rules.

A rule adopted by a clearing corporation governing rights and obligations among the clearing corporation and its participants in the clearing corporation is effective even if the rule conflicts with this [Act] and affects another party who does not consent to the rule.

§ 8–112. Creditor's Legal Process.

(a) The interest of a debtor in a certificated security may be reached by a creditor only by actual seizure of the security certificate by the officer making the attachment or levy, except as otherwise provided in subsection (d). However, a certificated security for which the certificate has been surrendered to the issuer may be reached by a creditor by legal process upon the issuer.

(b) The interest of a debtor in an uncertificated security may be reached by a creditor only by legal process upon the issuer at its chief executive office in the United States, except as otherwise provided in subsection (d).

(c) The interest of a debtor in a security entitlement may be reached by a creditor only by legal process upon the securities intermediary with whom the debtor's securities account is maintained, except as otherwise provided in subsection (d).

(d) The interest of a debtor in a certificated security for which the certificate is in the possession of a secured party, or in an uncertificated security registered in the name of a secured party, or a security entitlement maintained in the name of a secured party, may be reached by a creditor by legal process upon the secured party.

(e) A creditor whose debtor is the owner of a certificated security, uncertificated security, or security entitlement is entitled to aid from a court of competent jurisdiction, by injunction or otherwise, in reaching the certificated security, uncertificated security, or security entitlement or in satisfying the claim by means allowed at law or in equity in regard to property that cannot readily be reached by other legal process.

§ 8–113. Statute of Frauds Inapplicable.

A contract or modification of a contract for the sale or purchase of a security is enforceable whether or not there is a writing signed or record authenticated by a party against whom enforcement is sought, even if the contract or modification is not capable of performance within one year of its making.

§ 8–114. Evidentiary Rules Concerning Certificated Securities.

The following rules apply in an action on a certificated security against the issuer:

(1) Unless specifically denied in the pleadings, each signature on a security certificate or in a necessary indorsement is admitted.

(2) If the effectiveness of a signature is put in issue, the burden of establishing effectiveness is on the party claiming under the signature, but the signature is presumed to be genuine or authorized.

(3) If signatures on a security certificate are admitted or established, production of the certificate entitles a holder to recover on it unless the defendant establishes a defense or a defect going to the validity of the security.

(4) If it is shown that a defense or defect exists, the plaintiff has the burden of establishing that the plaintiff or some person under whom the plaintiff claims is a person against whom the defense or defect cannot be asserted.

§ 8–115. Securities Intermediary and Others Not Liable to Adverse Claimant.

A securities intermediary that has transferred a financial asset pursuant to an effective entitlement order, or a broker or other agent or bailee that has dealt with a financial asset at the direction of its customer or principal, is not liable to a person having an adverse claim to the financial asset, unless the securities intermediary, or broker or other agent or bailee:

(1) took the action after it had been served with an injunction, restraining order, or other legal process enjoining it from doing so, issued by a court of competent jurisdiction, and had a reasonable opportunity to act on the injunction, restraining order, or other legal process; or

(2) acted in collusion with the wrongdoer in violating the rights of the adverse claimant; or

(3) in the case of a security certificate that has been stolen, acted with notice of the adverse claim.

§ 8–116. Securities Intermediary as Purchaser for Value.

A securities intermediary that receives a financial asset and establishes a security entitlement to the financial asset in favor of an entitlement holder is a purchaser for value of the financial asset. A securities intermediary that acquires a security entitlement to a financial asset from another securities intermediary acquires the security entitlement for value if the securities intermediary acquiring the security entitlement establishes a security entitlement to the financial asset in favor of an entitlement holder.

PART 2 Issue and Issuer

§ 8–201. Issuer.

(a) With respect to an obligation on or a defense to a security, an "issuer" includes a person that:

(1) places or authorizes the placing of its name on a security certificate, other than as authenticating trustee, registrar, transfer agent, or the like, to evidence a share, participation, or other interest in its property or in an enterprise, or to evidence its duty to perform an obligation represented by the certificate;

(2) creates a share, participation, or other interest in its property or in an enterprise, or undertakes an obligation, that is an uncertificated security;

(3) directly or indirectly creates a fractional interest in its rights or property, if the fractional interest is represented by a security certificate; or

(4) becomes responsible for, or in place of, another person described as an issuer in this section.

(b) With respect to an obligation on or defense to a security, a guarantor is an issuer to the extent of its guaranty, whether or not its obligation is noted on a security certificate.

(c) With respect to a registration of a transfer, issuer means a person on whose behalf transfer books are maintained.

§ 8–202. Issuer's Responsibility and Defenses; Notice of Defect or Defense.

(a) Even against a purchaser for value and without notice, the terms of a certificated security include terms stated on the certificate and terms made part of the security by reference on the certificate to another instrument, indenture, or document or to a constitution, statute, ordinance, rule, regulation, order, or the like, to the extent the terms referred to do not conflict with terms stated on the certificate. A reference under this subsection does not of itself charge a purchaser for value with notice of a defect going to the validity of the security, even if the certificate expressly states that a person accepting it admits notice. The terms of an uncertificated security include those stated in any instrument, indenture, or document or in a constitution, statute, ordinance, rule, regulation, order, or the like, pursuant to which the security is issued.

(b) The following rules apply if an issuer asserts that a security is not valid:

(1) A security other than one issued by a government or governmental subdivision, agency, or instrumentality, even though issued with a defect going to its validity, is valid in the hands of a purchaser for value and without notice of the particular defect unless the defect involves a violation of a constitutional provision. In that case, the security is valid in the hands of a purchaser for value and without notice of the defect, other than one who takes by original issue.

(2) Paragraph (1) applies to an issuer that is a government or governmental subdivision, agency, or instrumentality only if there has been substantial compliance with the legal requirements governing the issue or the issuer has received a substantial consideration for the issue as a whole or for the particular security and a stated purpose of the issue is one for which the issuer has power to borrow money or issue the security.

(c) Except as otherwise provided in Section 8–205, lack of genuineness of a certificated security is a complete defense, even against a purchaser for value and without notice.

(d) All other defenses of the issuer of a security, including nondelivery and conditional delivery of a certificated security, are ineffective against a purchaser for value who has taken the certificated security without notice of the particular defense.

(e) This section does not affect the right of a party to cancel a contract for a security "when, as and if issued" or "when distributed" in the event of a material change in the character of the security that is the subject of the contract or in the plan or arrangement pursuant to which the security is to be issued or distributed.

(f) If a security is held by a securities intermediary against whom an entitlement holder has a security entitlement with respect to the security, the issuer may not assert any defense that the issuer could not assert if the entitlement holder held the security directly.

§ 8–203. Staleness as Notice of Defect or Defense.

After an act or event, other than a call that has been revoked, creating a right to immediate performance of the principal obligation represented by a certificated security or setting a date on or after which the security is to be presented or surrendered for redemption or exchange, a purchaser is charged with notice of any defect in its issue or defense of the issuer, if the act or event:

(1) requires the payment of money, the delivery of a certificated security, the registration of transfer of an uncertificated security, or any of them on presentation or surrender of the security certificate, the money or security is available on the date set for payment or exchange, and the purchaser takes the security more than one year after that date; or

(2) is not covered by paragraph (1) and the purchaser takes the security more than two years after the date set for surrender or presentation or the date on which performance became due.

§ 8–204. Effect of Issuer's Restriction on Transfer.

A restriction on transfer of a security imposed by the issuer, even if otherwise lawful, is ineffective against a person without knowledge of the restriction unless:

(1) the security is certificated and the restriction is noted conspicuously on the security certificate; or

(2) the security is uncertificated and the registered owner has been notified of the restriction.

§ 8–205. Effect of Unauthorized Signature on Security Certificate.

An unauthorized signature placed on a security certificate before or in the course of issue is ineffective, but the signature is effective in favor of a purchaser for value of the certificated security if the purchaser is without notice of the lack of authority and the signing has been done by:

(1) an authenticating trustee, registrar, transfer agent, or other person entrusted by the issuer with the signing of the security certificate or of similar security certificates, or the immediate preparation for signing of any of them; or

(2) an employee of the issuer, or of any of the persons listed in paragraph (1), entrusted with responsible handling of the security certificate.

§ 8–206. Completion or Alteration of Security Certificate.

(a) If a security certificate contains the signatures necessary to its issue or transfer but is incomplete in any other respect:

(1) any person may complete it by filling in the blanks as authorized; and

(2) even if the blanks are incorrectly filled in, the security certificate as completed is enforceable by a purchaser who took it for value and without notice of the incorrectness.

(b) A complete security certificate that has been improperly altered, even if fraudulently, remains enforceable, but only according to its original terms.

§ 8–207. Rights and Duties of Issuer With Respect to Registered Owners.

(a) Before due presentment for registration of transfer of a certificated security in registered form or of an instruction requesting registration of transfer of an uncertificated security, the issuer or indenture trustee may treat the registered owner as the person exclusively entitled to vote, receive notifications, and otherwise exercise all the rights and powers of an owner.

(b) This Article does not affect the liability of the registered owner of a security for a call, assessment, or the like.

§ 8–208. Effect of Signature of Authenticating Trustee, Registrar, or Transfer Agent.

(a) A person signing a security certificate as authenticating trustee, registrar, transfer agent, or the like, warrants to a purchaser for value of the certificated security, if the purchaser is without notice of a particular defect, that:

(1) the certificate is genuine;

(2) the person's own participation in the issue of the security is within the person's capacity and within the scope of the authority received by the person from the issuer; and

(3) the person has reasonable grounds to believe that the certificated security is in the form and within the amount the issuer is authorized to issue.

(b) Unless otherwise agreed, a person signing under subsection (a) does not assume responsibility for the validity of the security in other respects.

§ 8–209. Issuer's Lien.

A lien in favor of an issuer upon a certificated security is valid against a purchaser only if the right of the issuer to the lien is noted conspicuously on the security certificate.

§ 8–210. Overissue.

(a) In this section, "overissue" means the issue of securities in excess of the amount the issuer has corporate power to issue, but an overissue does not occur if appropriate action has cured the overissue.

(b) Except as otherwise provided in subsections (c) and (d), the provisions of this Article which validate a security or compel its issue or reissue do not apply to the extent that validation, issue, or reissue would result in overissue.

(c) If an identical security not constituting an overissue is reasonably available for purchase, a person entitled to issue or validation may compel the issuer to purchase the security and deliver it if certificated or register its transfer if uncertificated, against surrender of any security certificate the person holds.

(d) If a security is not reasonably available for purchase, a person entitled to issue or validation may recover from the issuer the price the person or the last purchaser for value paid for it with interest from the date of the person's demand.

PART 3 Transfer of Certificated and Uncertificated Securities

§ 8–301. Delivery.

(a) Delivery of a certificated security to a purchaser occurs when:

(1) the purchaser acquires possession of the security certificate;

(2) another person, other than a securities intermediary, either acquires possession of the security certificate on behalf of the purchaser or, having previously acquired possession of the certificate, acknowledges that it holds for the purchaser; or

(3) a securities intermediary acting on behalf of the purchaser acquires possession of the security certificate, only if the certificate is in registered form and has been specially indorsed to the purchaser by an effective indorsement.

(b) Delivery of an uncertificated security to a purchaser occurs when:

(1) the issuer registers the purchaser as the registered owner, upon original issue or registration of transfer; or

(2) another person, other than a securities intermediary, either becomes the registered owner of the uncertificated security on behalf of the purchaser or, having previously become the registered owner, acknowledges that it holds for the purchaser.

§ 8–302. Rights of Purchaser.

(a) Except as otherwise provided in subsections (b) and (c), upon delivery of a certificated or uncertificated security to a purchaser, the purchaser acquires all rights in the security that the transferor had or had power to transfer.

(b) A purchaser of a limited interest acquires rights only to the extent of the interest purchased.

(c) A purchaser of a certificated security who as a previous holder had notice of an adverse claim does not improve its position by taking from a protected purchaser.

§ 8–303. Protected Purchaser.

(a) "Protected purchaser" means a purchaser of a certificated or uncertificated security, or of an interest therein, who:

(1) gives value;

(2) does not have notice of any adverse claim to the security; and

(3) obtains control of the certificated or uncertificated security.

(b) In addition to acquiring the rights of a purchaser, a protected purchaser also acquires its interest in the security free of any adverse claim.

§ 8–304. Indorsement.

(a) An indorsement may be in blank or special. An indorsement in blank includes an indorsement to bearer. A special indorsement specifies to whom a security is to be transferred or who has power to transfer it. A holder may convert a blank indorsement to a special indorsement.

(b) An indorsement purporting to be only of part of a security certificate representing units intended by the issuer to be separately transferable is effective to the extent of the indorsement.

(c) An indorsement, whether special or in blank, does not constitute a transfer until delivery of the certificate on which it appears or, if the indorsement is on a separate document, until delivery of both the document and the certificate.

(d) If a security certificate in registered form has been delivered to a purchaser without a necessary indorsement, the purchaser may become a protected purchaser only when the indorsement is supplied. However, against a transferor, a transfer is complete upon delivery and the purchaser has a specifically enforceable right to have any necessary indorsement supplied.

(e) An indorsement of a security certificate in bearer form may give notice of an adverse claim to the certificate, but it does not otherwise affect a right to registration that the holder possesses.

(f) Unless otherwise agreed, a person making an indorsement assumes only the obligations provided in Section 8–108 and not an obligation that the security will be honored by the issuer.

§ 8–305. Instruction.

(a) If an instruction has been originated by an appropriate person but is incomplete in any other respect, any person may complete it as authorized and the issuer may rely on it as completed, even though it has been completed incorrectly.

(b) Unless otherwise agreed, a person initiating an instruction assumes only the obligations imposed by Section 8–108 and not an obligation that the security will be honored by the issuer.

§ 8–306. Effect of Guaranteeing Signature, Indorsement, or Instruction.

(a) A person who guarantees a signature of an indorser of a security certificate warrants that at the time of signing:

(1) the signature was genuine;

(2) the signer was an appropriate person to indorse, or if the signature is by an agent, the agent had actual authority to act on behalf of the appropriate person; and

(3) the signer had legal capacity to sign.

(b) A person who guarantees a signature of the originator of an instruction warrants that at the time of signing:

(1) the signature was genuine;

(2) the signer was an appropriate person to originate the instruction, or if the signature is by an agent, the agent had actual authority to act on behalf of the appropriate person, if the person specified in the instruction as the registered owner was, in fact, the registered owner, as to which fact the signature guarantor does not make a warranty; and

(3) the signer had legal capacity to sign.

(c) A person who specially guarantees the signature of an originator of an instruction makes the warranties of a signature guarantor under subsection (b) and also warrants that at the time the instruction is presented to the issuer:

(1) the person specified in the instruction as the registered owner of the uncertificated security will be the registered owner; and

(2) the transfer of the uncertificated security requested in the instruction will be registered by the issuer free from all liens, security interests, restrictions, and claims other than those specified in the instruction.

(d) A guarantor under subsections (a) and (b) or a special guarantor under subsection (c) does not otherwise warrant the rightfulness of the transfer.

(e) A person who guarantees an indorsement of a security certificate makes the warranties of a signature guarantor under subsection (a) and also warrants the rightfulness of the transfer in all respects.

(f) A person who guarantees an instruction requesting the transfer of an uncertificated security makes the warranties of a special signature guarantor under subsection (c) and also warrants the rightfulness of the transfer in all respects.

(g) An issuer may not require a special guaranty of signature, a guaranty of indorsement, or a guaranty of instruction as a condition to registration of transfer.

(h) The warranties under this section are made to a person taking or dealing with the security in reliance on the guaranty, and the guarantor is liable to the person for loss resulting from their breach. An indorser or originator of an instruction whose signature, indorsement, or instruction has been guaranteed is liable to a guarantor for any loss suffered by the guarantor as a result of breach of the warranties of the guarantor.

§ 8–307. Purchaser's Right to Requisites for Registration of Transfer.

Unless otherwise agreed, the transferor of a security on due demand shall supply the purchaser with proof of authority to transfer or with any other requisite necessary to obtain registration of the transfer of the security, but if the transfer is not for value, a transferor need not comply unless the purchaser pays the necessary expenses. If the transferor fails within a reasonable time to comply with the demand, the purchaser may reject or rescind the transfer.

PART 4 Registration

§ 8–401. Duty of Issuer to Register Transfer.

(a) If a certificated security in registered form is presented to an issuer with a request to register transfer or an instruction is presented to an issuer with a request to register transfer of an uncertificated security, the issuer shall register the transfer as requested if:

(1) under the terms of the security the person seeking registration of transfer is eligible to have the security registered in its name;

(2) the indorsement or instruction is made by the appropriate person or by an agent who has actual authority to act on behalf of the appropriate person;

(3) reasonable assurance is given that the indorsement or instruction is genuine and authorized (Section 8–402);

(4) any applicable law relating to the collection of taxes has been complied with;

(5) the transfer does not violate any restriction on transfer imposed by the issuer in accordance with Section 8–204;

(6) a demand that the issuer not register transfer has not become effective under Section 8–403, or the issuer has complied with Section 8–403(b) but no legal process or indemnity bond is obtained as provided in Section 8–403(d); and

(7) the transfer is in fact rightful or is to a protected purchaser.

(b) If an issuer is under a duty to register a transfer of a security, the issuer is liable to a person presenting a certificated security or an instruction for registration or to the person's principal for loss resulting from unreasonable delay in registration or failure or refusal to register the transfer.

§ 8–402. Assurance That Indorsement or Instruction Is Effective.

(a) An issuer may require the following assurance that each necessary indorsement or each instruction is genuine and authorized:

(1) in all cases, a guaranty of the signature of the person making an indorsement or originating an instruction including, in the case of an instruction, reasonable assurance of identity;

(2) if the indorsement is made or the instruction is originated by an agent, appropriate assurance of actual authority to sign;

(3) if the indorsement is made or the instruction is originated by a fiduciary pursuant to Section 8–107(a)(4) or (a)(5), appropriate evidence of appointment or incumbency;

(4) if there is more than one fiduciary, reasonable assurance that all who are required to sign have done so; and

(5) if the indorsement is made or the instruction is originated by a person not covered by another provision of this subsection, assurance appropriate to the case corresponding as nearly as may be to the provisions of this subsection.

(b) An issuer may elect to require reasonable assurance beyond that specified in this section.

(c) In this section:

(1) "Guaranty of the signature" means a guaranty signed by or on behalf of a person reasonably believed by the issuer to be responsible. An issuer may adopt standards with respect to responsibility if they are not manifestly unreasonable.

(2) "Appropriate evidence of appointment or incumbency" means:

(i) in the case of a fiduciary appointed or qualified by a court, a certificate issued by or under the direction or supervision of the court or an officer thereof and dated within 60 days before the date of presentation for transfer; or

(ii) in any other case, a copy of a document showing the appointment or a certificate issued by or on behalf of a person reasonably believed by an issuer to be responsible or, in the absence of that document or certificate, other evidence the issuer reasonably considers appropriate.

§ 8–403. Demand That Issuer Not Register Transfer.

(a) A person who is an appropriate person to make an indorsement or originate an instruction may demand that the issuer not register transfer of a security by communicating to the issuer a notification that identifies the registered owner and the issue of which the security is a part and provides an address for communications directed to the person making the demand. The demand is effective only if it is received by the issuer at a time and in a manner affording the issuer reasonable opportunity to act on it.

(b) If a certificated security in registered form is presented to an issuer with a request to register transfer or an instruction is presented to an issuer with a request to register transfer of an uncertificated security after a demand that the issuer not register transfer has become effective, the issuer shall promptly communicate to (i) the person who initiated the demand at the address provided in the demand and (ii) the person who presented the security for registration of transfer or initiated the instruction requesting registration of transfer a notification stating that:

(1) the certificated security has been presented for registration of transfer or the instruction for registration of transfer of the uncertificated security has been received;

(2) a demand that the issuer not register transfer had previously been received; and

(3) the issuer will withhold registration of transfer for a period of time stated in the notification in order to provide the person who initiated the demand an opportunity to obtain legal process or an indemnity bond.

(c) The period described in subsection (b)(3) may not exceed 30 days after the date of communication of the notification. A shorter period may be specified by the issuer if it is not manifestly unreasonable.

(d) An issuer is not liable to a person who initiated a demand that the issuer not register transfer for any loss the person suffers as a result of registration of a transfer pursuant to an effective indorsement or instruction if the person who initiated the demand does not, within the time stated in the issuer's communication, either:

(1) obtain an appropriate restraining order, injunction, or other process from a court of competent jurisdiction enjoining the issuer from registering the transfer; or

(2) file with the issuer an indemnity bond, sufficient in the issuer's judgment to protect the issuer and any transfer agent, registrar, or other agent of the issuer involved from any loss it or they may suffer by refusing to register the transfer.

(e) This section does not relieve an issuer from liability for registering transfer pursuant to an indorsement or instruction that was not effective.

§ 8–404. Wrongful Registration.

(a) Except as otherwise provided in Section 8–406, an issuer is liable for wrongful registration of transfer if the issuer has registered a transfer of a security to a person not entitled to it, and the transfer was registered:

(1) pursuant to an ineffective indorsement or instruction;

(2) after a demand that the issuer not register transfer became effective under Section 8–403(a) and the issuer did not comply with Section 8–403(b);

(3) after the issuer had been served with an injunction, restraining order, or other legal process enjoining it from registering the transfer, issued by a court of competent jurisdiction, and the issuer had a reasonable opportunity to act on the injunction, restraining order, or other legal process; or

(4) by an issuer acting in collusion with the wrongdoer.

(b) An issuer that is liable for wrongful registration of transfer under subsection (a) on demand shall provide the person entitled to the security with a like certificated or uncertificated security, and any payments or distributions that the person did not receive as a result of the wrongful registration. If an overissue would result, the issuer's liability to provide the person with a like security is governed by Section 8–210.

(c) Except as otherwise provided in subsection (a) or in a law relating to the collection of taxes, an issuer is not liable to an owner or other person suffering loss as a result of the registration of a transfer of a security if registration was made pursuant to an effective indorsement or instruction.

§ 8–405. Replacement of Lost, Destroyed, or Wrongfully Taken Security Certificate.

(a) If an owner of a certificated security, whether in registered or bearer form, claims that the certificate has been lost, destroyed, or wrongfully taken, the issuer shall issue a new certificate if the owner:

(1) so requests before the issuer has notice that the certificate has been acquired by a protected purchaser;

(2) files with the issuer a sufficient indemnity bond; and

(3) satisfies other reasonable requirements imposed by the issuer.

(b) If, after the issue of a new security certificate, a protected purchaser of the original certificate presents it for registration of transfer, the issuer shall register the transfer unless an overissue would result. In that case, the issuer's liability is governed by Section 8–210. In addition to any rights on the indemnity bond, an issuer may recover the new certificate from a person to whom it was issued or any person taking under that person, except a protected purchaser.

§ 8–406. Obligation to Notify Issuer of Lost, Destroyed, or Wrongfully Taken Security Certificate.

If a security certificate has been lost, apparently destroyed, or wrongfully taken, and the owner fails to notify the issuer of that fact within a reasonable time after the owner has notice of it and the issuer registers a transfer of the security before receiving notification, the owner may not assert against the issuer a claim for registering the transfer under Section 8–404 or a claim to a new security certificate under Section 8–405.

§ 8–407. Authenticating Trustee, Transfer Agent, and Registrar.

A person acting as authenticating trustee, transfer agent, registrar, or other agent for an issuer in the registration of a transfer of its securities, in the issue of new security certificates or uncertificated securities, or in the cancellation of surrendered security certificates has the same obligation to the holder or owner of a certificated or uncertificated security with regard to the particular functions performed as the issuer has in regard to those functions.

PART 5 Security Entitlements

§ 8–501. Securities Account; Acquisition of Security Entitlement From Securities Intermediary.

(a) "Securities account" means an account to which a financial asset is or may be credited in accordance with an agreement under which the person maintaining the account undertakes to treat the person for whom the account is maintained as entitled to exercise the rights that comprise the financial asset.

(b) Except as otherwise provided in subsections (d) and (e), a person acquires a security entitlement if a securities intermediary:

(1) indicates by book entry that a financial asset has been credited to the person's securities account;

(2) receives a financial asset from the person or acquires a financial asset for the person and, in either case, accepts it for credit to the person's securities account; or

(3) becomes obligated under other law, regulation, or rule to credit a financial asset to the person's securities account.

(c) If a condition of subsection (b) has been met, a person has a security entitlement even though the securities intermediary does not itself hold the financial asset.

(d) If a securities intermediary holds a financial asset for another person, and the financial asset is registered in the name of, payable to the order of, or specially indorsed to the other person, and has not been indorsed to the securities intermediary or in blank, the other person is treated as holding the financial asset directly rather than as having a security entitlement with respect to the financial asset.

(e) Issuance of a security is not establishment of a security entitlement.

§ 8–502. Assertion of Adverse Claim Against Entitlement Holder.

An action based on an adverse claim to a financial asset, whether framed in conversion, replevin, constructive trust, equitable lien, or other theory, may not be asserted against a person who acquires a security entitlement under Section 8–501 for value and without notice of the adverse claim.

§ 8–503. Property Interest of Entitlement Holder in Financial Asset Held by Securities Intermediary.

(a) To the extent necessary for a securities intermediary to satisfy all security entitlements with respect to a particular financial asset, all interests in that financial asset held by the securities intermediary are held by the securities intermediary for the entitlement holders, are not property of the securities intermediary, and are not subject to claims of creditors of the securities intermediary, except as otherwise provided in Section 8–511.

(b) An entitlement holder's property interest with respect to a particular financial asset under subsection (a) is a pro rata property interest in all interests in that financial asset held by the securities intermediary, without regard to the time the entitlement holder acquired the security entitlement or the time the securities intermediary acquired the interest in that financial asset.

(c) An entitlement holder's property interest with respect to a particular financial asset under subsection (a) may be enforced against the securities intermediary only by exercise of the entitlement holder's rights under Sections 8–505 through 8–508.

(d) An entitlement holder's property interest with respect to a particular financial asset under subsection (a) may be enforced against a purchaser of the financial asset or interest therein only if:

(1) insolvency proceedings have been initiated by or against the securities intermediary;

(2) the securities intermediary does not have sufficient interests in the financial asset to satisfy the security entitlements of all of its entitlement holders to that financial asset;

(3) the securities intermediary violated its obligations under Section 8–504 by transferring the financial asset or interest therein to the purchaser; and

(4) the purchaser is not protected under subsection (e).

The trustee or other liquidator, acting on behalf of all entitlement holders having security entitlements with respect to a particular financial asset, may recover the financial asset, or interest therein, from the purchaser. If the trustee or other liquidator elects not to pursue that right, an entitlement holder whose security entitlement remains unsatisfied has the right to recover its interest in the financial asset from the purchaser.

(e) An action based on the entitlement holder's property interest with respect to a particular financial asset under subsection (a), whether framed in conversion, replevin, constructive trust, equitable lien, or other theory, may not be asserted against any purchaser of a financial asset or interest therein who gives value, obtains control, and does not act in collusion with the securities intermediary in violating the securities intermediary's obligations under Section 8–504.

§ 8–504. Duty of Securities Intermediary to Maintain Financial Asset.

(a) A securities intermediary shall promptly obtain and thereafter maintain a financial asset in a quantity corresponding to the aggregate of all security entitlements it has established in favor of its entitlement holders with respect to that financial asset. The securities intermediary may maintain those financial assets directly or through one or more other securities intermediaries.

(b) Except to the extent otherwise agreed by its entitlement holder, a securities intermediary may not grant any security interests in a financial asset it is obligated to maintain pursuant to subsection (a).

(c) A securities intermediary satisfies the duty in subsection (a) if:

(1) the securities intermediary acts with respect to the duty as agreed upon by the entitlement holder and the securities intermediary; or

(2) in the absence of agreement, the securities intermediary exercises due care in accordance with reasonable commercial standards to obtain and maintain the financial asset.

(d) This section does not apply to a clearing corporation that is itself the obligor of an option or similar obligation to which its entitlement holders have security entitlements.

§ 8–505. Duty of Securities Intermediary With Respect to Payments and Distributions.

(a) A securities intermediary shall take action to obtain a payment or distribution made by the issuer of a financial asset. A securities intermediary satisfies the duty if:

(1) the securities intermediary acts with respect to the duty as agreed upon by the entitlement holder and the securities intermediary; or

(2) in the absence of agreement, the securities intermediary exercises due care in accordance with reasonable commercial standards to attempt to obtain the payment or distribution.

(b) A securities intermediary is obligated to its entitlement holder for a payment or distribution made by the issuer of a financial asset if the payment or distribution is received by the securities intermediary.

§ 8–506. Duty of Securities Intermediary to Exercise Rights as Directed by Entitlement Holder.

A securities intermediary shall exercise rights with respect to a financial asset if directed to do so by an entitlement holder. A securities intermediary satisfies the duty if:

(1) the securities intermediary acts with respect to the duty as agreed upon by the entitlement holder and the securities intermediary; or

(2) in the absence of agreement, the securities intermediary either places the entitlement holder in a position to exercise the rights directly or exercises due care in accordance with reasonable commercial standards to follow the direction of the entitlement holder.

§ 8–507. Duty of Securities Intermediary to Comply With Entitlement Order.

(a) A securities intermediary shall comply with an entitlement order if the entitlement order is originated by the appropriate person, the securities intermediary has had reasonable opportunity to assure itself that the entitlement order is genuine and authorized, and the securities intermediary has had reasonable opportunity to comply with the entitlement order. A securities intermediary satisfies the duty if:

(1) the securities intermediary acts with respect to the duty as agreed upon by the entitlement holder and the securities intermediary; or

(2) in the absence of agreement, the securities intermediary exercises due care in accordance with reasonable commercial standards to comply with the entitlement order.

(b) If a securities intermediary transfers a financial asset pursuant to an ineffective entitlement order, the securities intermediary shall reestablish a security entitlement in favor of the person entitled to it, and pay or credit any payments or distributions that the person did not receive as a result of the wrongful transfer. If the securities intermediary does not reestablish a security entitlement, the securities intermediary is liable to the entitlement holder for damages.

§ 8–508. Duty of Securities Intermediary to Change Entitlement Holder's Position to Other Form of Security Holding.

A securities intermediary shall act at the direction of an entitlement holder to change a security entitlement into another available form of holding for which the entitlement holder is eligible, or to cause the financial asset to be transferred to a securities account of the entitlement holder with another securities intermediary. A securities intermediary satisfies the duty if:

(1) the securities intermediary acts as agreed upon by the entitlement holder and the securities intermediary; or

(2) in the absence of agreement, the securities intermediary exercises due care in accordance with reasonable commercial standards to follow the direction of the entitlement holder.

§ 8–509. Specification of Duties of Securities Intermediary by Other Statute or Regulation; Manner of Performance of Duties of Securities Intermediary and Exercise of Rights of Entitlement Holder.

(a) If the substance of a duty imposed upon a securities intermediary by Sections 8–504 through 8–508 is the subject of other statute, regulation, or rule, compliance with that statute, regulation, or rule satisfies the duty.

(b) To the extent that specific standards for the performance of the duties of a securities intermediary or the exercise of the rights of an entitlement holder are not specified by other statute, regulation, or rule or by agreement between the securities intermediary and entitlement holder, the securities intermediary shall perform its duties and the entitlement holder shall exercise its rights in a commercially reasonable manner.

(c) The obligation of a securities intermediary to perform the duties imposed by Sections 8–504 through 8–508 is subject to:

(1) rights of the securities intermediary arising out of a security interest under a security agreement with the entitlement holder or otherwise; and

(2) rights of the securities intermediary under other law, regulation, rule, or agreement to withhold performance of its duties as a result of unfulfilled obligations of the entitlement holder to the securities intermediary.

(d) Sections 8–504 through 8–508 do not require a securities intermediary to take any action that is prohibited by other statute, regulation, or rule.

§ 8–510. Rights of Purchaser of Security Entitlement From Entitlement Holder.

(a) An action based on an adverse claim to a financial asset or security entitlement, whether framed in conversion, replevin, constructive trust, equitable lien, or other theory, may not be asserted against a person who purchases a security entitlement, or an interest therein, from an entitlement holder if the purchaser gives value, does not have notice of the adverse claim, and obtains control.

(b) If an adverse claim could not have been asserted against an entitlement holder under Section 8–502, the adverse claim cannot be asserted against a person who purchases a security entitlement, or an interest therein, from the entitlement holder.

(c) In a case not covered by the priority rules in Article 9, a purchaser for value of a security entitlement, or an interest therein, who obtains control has priority over a purchaser of a security entitlement, or an interest therein, who does not obtain control. Purchasers who have control rank equally, except that a securities intermediary as purchaser has priority over a conflicting purchaser who has control unless otherwise agreed by the securities intermediary.

§ 8–511. Priority Among Security Interests and Entitlement Holders.

(a) Except as otherwise provided in subsections (b) and (c), if a securities intermediary does not have sufficient interests in a particular financial asset to satisfy both its obligations to entitlement holders who have security entitlements to that financial asset and its obligation to a creditor of the securities intermediary who has a security interest in that financial asset, the claims of entitlement holders, other than the creditor, have priority over the claim of the creditor.

(b) A claim of a creditor of a securities intermediary who has a security interest in a financial asset held by a securities intermediary has priority over claims of the securities intermediary's entitlement holders who have security entitlements with respect to that financial asset if the creditor has control over the financial asset.

(c) If a clearing corporation does not have sufficient financial assets to satisfy both its obligations to entitlement holders who have security entitlements with respect to a financial asset and its obligation to a creditor of the clearing corporation who has a security interest in that financial asset, the claim of the creditor has priority over the claims of entitlement holders.

PART 6 Transition Provisions for Revised Article 8

§ 8–601. Effective Date.

This [Act] takes effect ....

§ 8–602. Repeals.

This [Act] repeals ....

§ 8–603. Savings Clause.

(a) This [Act] does not affect an action or proceeding commenced before this [Act] takes effect.

(b) If a security interest in a security is perfected at the date this [Act] takes effect, and the action by which the security interest was perfected would suffice to perfect a security interest under this [Act], no further action is required to continue perfection. If a security interest in a security is perfected at the date this [Act] takes effect but the action by which the security interest was perfected would not suffice to perfect a security interest under this [Act], the security interest remains perfected for a period of four months after the effective date and continues perfected thereafter if appropriate action to perfect under this [Act] is taken within that period. If a security interest is perfected at the date this [Act] takes effect and the security interest can be perfected by filing under this [Act], a financing statement signed by the secured party instead of the debtor may be filed within that period to continue perfection or thereafter to perfect.

ARTICLE 9

SECURED TRANSACTIONS; SALES OF ACCOUNTS AND CHATTEL PAPER

Note: The adoption of this Article should be accompanied by the repeal of existing statutes dealing with conditional sales, trust receipts, factor's liens where the factor is given a non-possessory lien, chattel mortgages, crop mortgages, mortgages on railroad equipment, assignment of accounts and generally statutes regulating security interests in personal property.

Where the state has a retail installment selling act or small loan act, that legislation should be carefully examined to determine what changes in those acts are needed to conform them to this Article. This Article primarily sets out rules defining rights of a secured party against persons dealing with the debtor; it does not prescribe regulations and controls which may be necessary to curb abuses arising in the small loan business or in the financing of consumer purchases on credit. Accordingly there is no intention to repeal existing regulatory acts in those fields by enactment or re-enactment of Article 9. See Section 9–203(4) and the Note thereto.

PART 1 Short Title, Applicability and Definitions

§ 9–101. Short Title.

This Article shall be known and may be cited as Uniform Commercial Code—Secured Transactions.

§ 9–102. Policy and Subject Matter of Article.

(1) Except as otherwise provided in Section 9–104 on excluded transactions, this Article applies

(a) to any transaction (regardless of its form) which is intended to create a security interest in personal property or fixtures including goods, documents, instruments, general intangibles, chattel paper or accounts; and also

(b) to any sale of accounts or chattel paper.

(2) This Article applies to security interests created by contract including pledge, assignment, chattel mortgage, chattel trust,

trust deed, factor's lien, equipment trust, conditional sale, trust receipt, other lien or title retention contract and lease or consignment intended as security. This Article does not apply to statutory liens except as provided in Section 9–310.

(3) The application of this Article to a security interest in a secured obligation is not affected by the fact that the obligation is itself secured by a transaction or interest to which this Article does not apply.

§ 9–103. Perfection of Security Interest in Multiple State Transactions.

(1) Documents, instruments and ordinary goods.

(a) This subsection applies to documents and instruments and to goods other than those covered by a certificate of title described in subsection (2), mobile goods described in subsection (3), and minerals described in subsection (5).

(b) Except as otherwise provided in this subsection, perfection and the effect of perfection or non-perfection of a security interest in collateral are governed by the law of the jurisdiction where the collateral is when the last event occurs on which is based the assertion that the security interest is perfected or unperfected.

(c) If the parties to a transaction creating a purchase money security interest in goods in one jurisdiction understand at the time that the security interest attaches that the goods will be kept in another jurisdiction, then the law of the other jurisdiction governs the perfection and the effect of perfection or non-perfection of the security interest from the time it attaches until thirty days after the debtor receives possession of the goods and thereafter if the goods are taken to the other jurisdiction before the end of the thirty-day period.

(d) When collateral is brought into and kept in this state while subject to a security interest perfected under the law of the jurisdiction from which the collateral was removed, the security interest remains perfected, but if action is required by Part 3 of this Article to perfect the security interest,

(i) if the action is not taken before the expiration of the period of perfection in the other jurisdiction or the end of four months after the collateral is brought into this state, whichever period first expires, the security interest becomes unperfected at the end of that period and is thereafter deemed to have been unperfected as against a person who became a purchaser after removal;

(ii) if the action is taken before the expiration of the period specified in subparagraph (i), the security interest continues perfected thereafter;

(iii) for the purpose of priority over a buyer of consumer goods (subsection (2) of Section 9–307), the period of the effectiveness of a filing in the jurisdiction from which the collateral is removed is governed by the rules with respect to perfection in subparagraphs (i) and (ii).

(2) Certificate of title.

(a) This subsection applies to goods covered by a certificate of title issued under a statute of this state or of another jurisdiction under the law of which indication of a security interest on the certificate is required as a condition of perfection.

(b) Except as otherwise provided in this subsection, perfection and the effect of perfection or non-perfection of the security interest are governed by the law (including the conflict of laws rules) of the jurisdiction issuing the certificate until four months after the goods are removed from that jurisdiction and thereafter until the goods are registered in another jurisdiction, but in any event not beyond surrender of the certificate. After the expiration of that period, the goods are not covered by the certificate of title within the meaning of this section.

(c) Except with respect to the rights of a buyer described in the next paragraph, a security interest, perfected in another jurisdiction otherwise than by notation on a certificate of title, in goods brought into this state and thereafter covered by a certificate of title issued by this state is subject to the rules stated in paragraph (d) of subsection (1).

(d) If goods are brought into this state while a security interest therein is perfected in any manner under the law of the jurisdiction from which the goods are removed and a certificate of title is issued by this state and the certificate does not show that the goods are subject to the security interest or that they may be subject to security interests not shown on the certificate, the security interest is subordinate to the rights of a buyer of the goods who is not in the business of selling goods of that kind to the extent that he gives value and receives delivery of the goods after issuance of the certificate and without knowledge of the security interest.

(3) Accounts, general intangibles and mobile goods.

(a) This subsection applies to accounts (other than an account described in subsection (5) on minerals) and general intangibles (other than uncertificated securities) and to goods which are mobile and which are of a type normally used in more than one jurisdiction, such as motor vehicles, trailers, rolling stock, airplanes, shipping containers, road building and construction machinery and commercial harvesting machinery and the like, if the goods are equipment or are inventory leased or held for lease by the debtor to others, and are not covered by a certificate of title described in subsection (2).

(b) The law (including the conflict of laws rules) of the jurisdiction in which the debtor is located governs the perfection and the effect of perfection or non-perfection of the security interest.

(c) If, however, the debtor is located in a jurisdiction which is not a part of the United States, and which does not provide for perfection of the security interest by filing or recording in that jurisdiction, the law of the jurisdiction in the United States in which the debtor has its major executive office in the United States governs the perfection and the effect of perfection or non-perfection of the security interest through filing. In the alternative, if the debtor is located in a jurisdiction which is not a part of the United States or Canada and the collateral is accounts or general intangibles for money due or to become due, the security interest may be perfected by notification to the account debtor. As used in this paragraph, "United States" includes its territories and possessions and the Commonwealth of Puerto Rico.

(d) A debtor shall be deemed located at his place of business if he has one, at his chief executive office if he has more than one place of business, otherwise at his residence. If, however, the debtor is a foreign air carrier under the Federal Aviation Act of 1958, as amended, it shall be deemed located at the designated office of the agent upon whom service of process may be made on behalf of the foreign air carrier.

(e) A security interest perfected under the law of the jurisdiction of the location of the debtor is perfected until the expiration of four months after a change of the debtor's location to another jurisdiction, or until perfection would have ceased by the law of the first jurisdiction, whichever period first expires. Unless perfected in the new jurisdiction before the end of that period, it becomes unperfected thereafter and is deemed to have been unperfected as against a person who became a purchaser after the change.

(4) Chattel paper.

The rules stated for goods in subsection (1) apply to a possessory security interest in chattel paper. The rules stated for accounts in subsection (3) apply to a non-possessory security interest in chattel paper, but the security interest may not be perfected by notification to the account debtor.

(5) Minerals.

Perfection and the effect of perfection or non-perfection of a security interest which is created by a debtor who has an interest in minerals or the like (including oil and gas) before extraction and which attaches thereto as extracted, or which attaches to an account resulting from the sale thereof at the wellhead or minehead are governed by the law (including the conflict of laws rules) of the jurisdiction wherein the wellhead or minehead is located.

(6) Uncertificated securities.

The law (including the conflict of laws rules) of the jurisdiction of organization of the issuer governs the perfection and the effect of perfection or non-perfection of a security interest in uncertificated securities.

§ 9–104. Transactions Excluded From Article.

This Article does not apply

(a) to a security interest subject to any statute of the United States, to the extent that such statute governs the rights of parties to and third parties affected by transactions in particular types of property; or

(b) to a landlord's lien; or

(c) to a lien given by statute or other rule of law for services or materials except as provided in Section 9–310 on priority of such liens; or

(d) to a transfer of a claim for wages, salary or other compensation of an employee; or

(e) to a transfer by a government or governmental subdivision or agency; or

(f) to a sale of accounts or chattel paper as part of a sale of the business out of which they arose, or an assignment of accounts or chattel paper which is for the purpose of collection only, or a transfer of a right to payment under a contract to an assignee who is also to do the performance under the contract or a transfer of a single account to an assignee in whole or partial satisfaction of a preexisting indebtedness; or

(g) to a transfer of an interest in or claim in or under any policy of insurance, except as provided with respect to proceeds (Section 9–306) and priorities in proceeds (Section 9–312); or

(h) to a right represented by a judgment (other than a judgment taken on a right to payment which was collateral); or

(i) to any right of set-off; or

(j) except to the extent that provision is made for fixtures in Section 9–313, to the creation or transfer of an interest in or lien on real estate, including a lease or rents thereunder; or

(k) to a transfer in whole or in part of any claim arising out of tort; or

(l) to a transfer of an interest in any deposit account (subsection (1) of Section 9–105), except as provided with respect to proceeds (Section 9–306) and priorities in proceeds (Section 9–312).

§ 9–105. Definitions and Index of Definitions.

(1) In this Article unless the context otherwise requires:

(a) "Account debtor" means the person who is obligated on an account, chattel paper or general intangible;

(b) "Chattel paper" means a writing or writings which evidence both a monetary obligation and a security interest in or a lease of specific goods, but a charter or other contract involving the use or hire of a vessel is not chattel paper. When a transaction is evidenced both by such a security agreement or a lease and by an instrument or a series of instruments, the group of writings taken together constitutes chattel paper;

(c) "Collateral" means the property subject to a security interest, and includes accounts and chattel paper which have been sold;

(d) "Debtor" means the person who owes payment or other performance of the obligation secured, whether or not he owns or has rights in the collateral, and includes the seller of accounts or chattel paper. Where the debtor and the owner of the collateral are not the same person, the term "debtor" means the owner of the collateral in any provision of the Article dealing with the collateral, the obligor in any provision dealing with the obligation, and may include both where the context so requires;

(e) "Deposit account" means a demand, time, savings, passbook or like account maintained with a bank, savings and loan association, credit union or like organization, other than an account evidenced by a certificate of deposit;

(f) "Document" means document of title as defined in the general definitions of Article 1 (Section 1–201), and a receipt of the kind described in subsection (2) of Section 7–201;

(g) "Encumbrance" includes real estate mortgages and other liens on real estate and all other rights in real estate that are not ownership interests;

(h) "Goods" includes all things which are movable at the time the security interest attaches or which are fixtures (Section 9–313), but does not include money, documents, instruments, accounts, chattel paper, general intangibles, or minerals or the like (including oil and gas) before extraction. "Goods" also includes standing timber which is to be cut and removed under a conveyance or contract for sale, the unborn young of animals, and growing crops;

(i) "Instrument" means a negotiable instrument (defined in Section 3–104), or a certificated security (defined in Section 8–102) or any other writing which evidences a right to the payment of money and is not itself a security agreement or lease and is of a type which is in ordinary course of business transferred by delivery with any necessary indorsement or assignment;

(j) "Mortgage" means a consensual interest created by a real estate mortgage, a trust deed on real estate, or the like;

(k) An advance is made "pursuant to commitment" if the secured party has bound himself to make it, whether or not a subsequent event of default or other event not within his control has relieved or may relieve him from his obligation;

(l) "Security agreement" means an agreement which creates or provides for a security interest;

(m) "Secured party" means a lender, seller or other person in whose favor there is a security interest, including a person to whom accounts or chattel paper have been sold. When the holders of obligations issued under an indenture of trust, equipment trust agreement or the like are represented by a trustee or other person, the representative is the secured party;

(n) "Transmitting utility" means any person primarily engaged in the railroad, street railway or trolley bus business, the electric or electronics communications transmission business, the transmission of goods by pipeline, or the transmission or the production and transmission of electricity, steam, gas or water, or the provision of sewer service.

(2) Other definitions applying to this Article and the sections in which they appear are:

"Account". Section 9–106.
"Attach". Section 9–203.
"Construction mortgage". Section 9–313(1).
"Consumer goods". Section 9–109(1).
"Equipment". Section 9–109(2).
"Farm products". Section 9–109(3).

"Fixture". Section 9–313(1).
"Fixture filing". Section 9–313(1).
"General intangibles". Section 9–106.
"Inventory". Section 9–109(4).
"Lien creditor". Section 9–301(3).
"Proceeds". Section 9–306(1).
"Purchase money security interest". Section 9–107.
"United States". Section 9–103.

(3) The following definitions in other Articles apply to this Article:

"Check". Section 3–104.
"Contract for sale". Section 2–106.
"Holder in due course". Section 3–302.
"Note". Section 3–104.
"Sale". Section 2–106.

(4) In addition Article 1 contains general definitions and principles of construction and interpretation applicable throughout this Article.

§ 9–106. Definitions: "Account"; "General Intangibles".

"Account" means any right to payment for goods sold or leased or for services rendered which is not evidenced by an instrument or chattel paper, whether or not it has been earned by performance. "General intangibles" means any personal property (including things in action) other than goods, accounts, chattel paper, documents, instruments, and money. All rights to payment earned or unearned under a charter or other contract involving the use or hire of a vessel and all rights incident to the charter or contract are accounts.

§ 9–107. Definitions: "Purchase Money Security Interest".

A security interest is a "purchase money security interest" to the extent that it is

(a) taken or retained by the seller of the collateral to secure all or part of its price; or

(b) taken by a person who by making advances or incurring an obligation gives value to enable the debtor to acquire rights in or the use of collateral if such value is in fact so used.

§ 9–108. When After-Acquired Collateral Not Security for Antecedent Debt.

Where a secured party makes an advance, incurs an obligation, releases a perfected security interest, or otherwise gives new value which is to be secured in whole or in part by after-acquired property his security interest in the after-acquired collateral shall be deemed to be taken for new value and not as security for an antecedent debt if the debtor acquires his rights in such collateral either in the ordinary course of his business or under a contract of purchase made pursuant to the security agreement within a reasonable time after new value is given.

§ 9–109. Classification of Goods; "Consumer Goods"; "Equipment"; "Farm Products"; "Inventory".

Goods are

(1) "consumer goods" if they are used or bought for use primarily for personal, family or household purposes;

(2) "equipment" if they are used or bought for use primarily in business (including farming or a profession) or by a debtor who is a non-profit organization or a governmental subdivision or agency or if the goods are not included in the definitions of inventory, farm products or consumer goods;

(3) "farm products" if they are crops or livestock or supplies used or produced in farming operations or if they are products of crops or livestock in their unmanufactured states (such as ginned cotton, wool-clip, maple syrup, milk and eggs), and if they are in the possession of a debtor engaged in raising, fattening, grazing or other farming operations. If goods are farm products they are neither equipment nor inventory;

(4) "inventory" if they are held by a person who holds them for sale or lease or to be furnished under contracts of service or if he has so furnished them, or if they are raw materials, work in process or materials used or consumed in a business. Inventory of a person is not to be classified as his equipment.

§ 9–110. Sufficiency of Description.

For purposes of this Article any description of personal property or real estate is sufficient whether or not it is specific if it reasonably identifies what is described.

§ 9–111. Applicability of Bulk Transfer Laws.

The creation of a security interest is not a bulk transfer under Article 6 (see Section 6–103).

§ 9–112. Where Collateral Is Not Owned by Debtor.

Unless otherwise agreed, when a secured party knows that collateral is owned by a person who is not the debtor, the owner of the collateral is entitled to receive from the secured party any surplus under Section 9–502(2) or under Section 9–504(1), and is not liable for the debt or for any deficiency after resale, and he has the same right as the debtor.

(a) to receive statements under Section 9–208;

(b) to receive notice of and to object to a secured party's proposal to retain the collateral in satisfaction of the indebtedness under Section 9–505;

(c) to redeem the collateral under Section 9–506;

(d) to obtain injunctive or other relief under Section 9–507(1); and

(e) to recover losses caused to him under Section 9–208(2).

§ 9–113. Security Interests Arising Under Article on Sales.

A security interest arising solely under the Article on Sales (Article 2) is subject to the provisions of this Article except that to the extent that and so long as the debtor does not have or does not lawfully obtain possession of the goods

(a) no security agreement is necessary to make the security interest enforceable; and

(b) no filing is required to perfect the security interest; and

(c) the rights of the secured party on default by the debtor are governed by the Article on Sales (Article 2).

§ 9–114. Consignment.

(1) A person who delivers goods under a consignment which is not a security interest and who would be required to file under this Article by paragraph (3)(c) of Section 2–326 has priority over a secured party who is or becomes a creditor of the consignee and who would have a perfected security interest in the goods if they were the property of the consignee, and also has priority with respect to identifiable cash proceeds received on or before delivery of the goods to a buyer, if

(a) the consignor complies with the filing provision of the Article on Sales with respect to consignments (paragraph (3)(c) of Section 2–326) before the consignee receives possession of the goods; and

(b) the consignor gives notification in writing to the holder of the security interest if the holder has filed a financing statement covering the same types of goods before the date of the filing made by the consignor; and

(c) the holder of the security interest receives the notification within five years before the consignee receives possession of the goods; and

(d) the notification states that the consignor expects to deliver goods on consignment to the consignee, describing the goods by item or type.

(2) In the case of a consignment which is not a security interest and in which the requirements of the preceding subsection have not been met, a person who delivers goods to another is subordinate to a person who would have a perfected security interest in the goods if they were the property of the debtor.

PART 2 Validity of Security Agreement and Rights of Parties Thereto

§ 9–201. General Validity of Security Agreement.

Except as otherwise provided by this Act a security agreement is effective according to its terms between the parties, against purchasers of the collateral and against creditors. Nothing in this Article validates any charge or practice illegal under any statute or regulation thereunder governing usury, small loans, retail installment sales, or the like, or extends the application of any such statute or regulation to any transaction not otherwise subject thereto.

§ 9–202. Title to Collateral Immaterial.

Each provision of this Article with regard to rights, obligations and remedies applies whether title to collateral is in the secured party or in the debtor.

§ 9–203. Attachment and Enforceability of Security Interest; Proceeds; Formal Requisites.

(1) Subject to the provisions of Section 4–210 on the security interest of a collecting bank, Section 8–321 on security interests in securities and Section 9–113 on a security interest arising under the Articles on Sales and Leases, a security interest is not enforceable against the debtor or third parties with respect to the collateral and does not attach unless:

(a) the collateral is in the possession of the secured party pursuant to agreement, or the debtor has signed a security agreement which contains a description of the collateral and in addition, when the security interest covers crops growing or to be grown or timber to be cut, a description of the land concerned;

(b) value has been given; and

(c) the debtor has rights in the collateral.

(2) A security interest attaches when it becomes enforceable against the debtor with respect to the collateral. Attachment occurs as soon as all of the events specified in subsection (1) have taken place unless explicit agreement postpones the time of attaching.

(3) Unless otherwise agreed a security agreement gives the secured party the rights to proceeds provided by Section 9–306.

(4) A transaction, although subject to this Article, is also subject to . . .*, and in the case of conflict between the provisions of this Article and any such statute, the provisions of such statute control. Failure to comply with any applicable statute has only the effect which is specified therein.

*Note: At * in subsection (4) insert reference to any local statute regulating small loans, retail installment sales and the like.*

The foregoing subsection (4) is designed to make it clear that certain transactions, although subject to this Article, must also comply with other applicable legislation.

This Article is designed to regulate all the "security" aspects of transactions within its scope. There is, however, much regulatory legislation, particularly in the consumer field, which supplements this Article and should not be repealed by its enactment. Examples are small loan acts, retail installment selling acts and the like. Such acts may provide for licensing and rate regulation and may prescribe particular forms of contract. Such provisions should remain in force despite the enactment of this Article. On the other hand if a retail installment selling act contains provisions on filing, rights on default, etc., such provisions should be repealed as inconsistent with this Article except that inconsistent provisions as to deficiencies, penalties, etc., in the Uniform Consumer Credit Code and other recent related legislation should remain because those statutes were drafted after the substantial enactment of the Article and with the intention of modifying certain provisions of this Article as to consumer credit.

§ 9–204. After-Acquired Property; Future Advances.

(1) Except as provided in subsection (2), a security agreement may provide that any or all obligations covered by the security agreement are to be secured by after-acquired collateral.

(2) No security interest attaches under an after-acquired property clause to consumer goods other than accessions (Section 9–314) when given as additional security unless the debtor acquires rights in them within ten days after the secured party gives value.

(3) Obligations covered by a security agreement may include future advances or other value whether or not the advances or value are given pursuant to commitment (subsection (1) of Section 9–105).

§ 9–205. Use or Disposition of Collateral Without Accounting Permissible.

A security interest is not invalid or fraudulent against creditors by reason of liberty in the debtor to use, commingle or dispose of all or part of the collateral (including returned or repossessed goods) or to collect or compromise accounts or chattel paper, or to accept the return of goods or make repossessions, or to use, commingle or dispose of proceeds, or by reason of the failure of the secured party to require the debtor to account for proceeds or replace collateral. This section does not relax the requirements of possession where perfection of a security interest depends upon possession of the collateral by the secured party or by a bailee.

§ 9–206. Agreement Not to Assert Defenses Against Assignee; Modification of Sales Warranties Where Security Agreement Exists.

(1) Subject to any statute or decision which establishes a different rule for buyers or lessees of consumer goods, an agreement by a buyer or lessee that he will not assert against an assignee any claim or defense which he may have against the seller or lessor is enforceable by an assignee who takes his assignment for value, in good faith and without notice of a claim or defense, except as to defenses of a type which may be asserted against a holder in due course of a negotiable instrument under the Article on Negotiable Instruments (Article 3). A buyer who as part of one transaction signs both a negotiable instrument and a security agreement makes such an agreement.

(2) When a seller retains a purchase money security interest in goods the Article on Sales (Article 2) governs the sale and any disclaimer, limitation or modification of the seller's warranties.

§ 9–207. Rights and Duties When Collateral Is in Secured Party's Possession.

(1) A secured party must use reasonable care in the custody and preservation of collateral in his possession. In the case of an instrument or chattel paper reasonable care includes taking necessary steps to preserve rights against prior parties unless otherwise agreed.

(2) Unless otherwise agreed, when collateral is in the secured party's possession

(a) reasonable expenses (including the cost of any insurance and payment of taxes or other charges) incurred in the custody, preservation, use or operation of the collateral are chargeable to the debtor and are secured by the collateral;

(b) the risk of accidental loss or damage is on the debtor to the extent of any deficiency in any effective insurance coverage;

(c) the secured party may hold as additional security any increase or profits (except money) received from the collateral, but money so received, unless remitted to the debtor, shall be applied in reduction of the secured obligation;

(d) the secured party must keep the collateral identifiable but fungible collateral may be commingled;

(e) the secured party may repledge the collateral upon terms which do not impair the debtor's right to redeem it.

(3) A secured party is liable for any loss caused by his failure to meet any obligation imposed by the preceding subsections but does not lose his security interest.

(4) A secured party may use or operate the collateral for the purpose of preserving the collateral or its value or pursuant to the order of a court of appropriate jurisdiction or, except in the case of consumer goods, in the manner and to the extent provided in the security agreement.

§ 9–208. Request for Statement of Account or List of Collateral.

(1) A debtor may sign a statement indicating what he believes to be the aggregate amount of unpaid indebtedness as of a specified date and may send it to the secured party with a request that the statement be approved or corrected and returned to the debtor. When the security agreement or any other record kept by the secured party identifies the collateral a debtor may similarly request the secured party to approve or correct a list of the collateral.

(2) The secured party must comply with such a request within two weeks after receipt by sending a written correction or approval. If the secured party claims a security interest in all of a particular type of collateral owned by the debtor he may indicate that fact in his reply and need not approve or correct an itemized list of such collateral. If the secured party without reasonable excuse fails to comply he is liable for any loss caused to the debtor thereby; and if the debtor has properly included in his request a good faith statement of the obligation or a list of the collateral or both the secured party may claim a security interest only as shown in the statement against persons misled by his failure to comply. If he no longer has an interest in the obligation or collateral at the time the request is received he must disclose the name and address of any successor in interest known to him and he is liable for any loss caused to the debtor as a result of failure to disclose. A successor in interest is not subject to this section until a request is received by him.

(3) A debtor is entitled to such a statement once every six months without charge. The secured party may require payment of a charge not exceeding $10 for each additional statement furnished.

PART 3 Rights of Third Parties; Perfected and Unperfected Security Interests; Rules of Priority

§ 9–301. Persons Who Take Priority Over Unperfected Security Interests; Rights of "Lien Creditor".

(1) Except as otherwise provided in subsection (2), an unperfected security interest is subordinate to the rights of

(a) persons entitled to priority under Section 9–312;

(b) a person who becomes a lien creditor before the security interest is perfected;

(c) in the case of goods, instruments, documents, and chattel paper, a person who is not a secured party and who is a transferee in bulk or other buyer not in ordinary course of business or is a buyer of farm products in ordinary course of business, to the extent that he gives value and receives delivery of the collateral without knowledge of the security interest and before it is perfected;

(d) in the case of accounts and general intangibles, a person who is not a secured party and who is a transferee to the extent that he gives value without knowledge of the security interest and before it is perfected.

(2) If the secured party files with respect to a purchase money security interest before or within ten days after the debtor receives possession of the collateral, he takes priority over the rights of a transferee in bulk or of a lien creditor which arise between the time the security interest attaches and the time of filing.

(3) A "lien creditor" means a creditor who has acquired a lien on the property involved by attachment, levy or the like and includes an assignee for benefit of creditors from the time of assignment, and a trustee in bankruptcy from the date of the filing of the petition or a receiver in equity from the time of appointment.

(4) A person who becomes a lien creditor while a security interest is perfected takes subject to the security interest only to the extent that it secures advances made before he becomes a lien creditor or within 45 days thereafter or made without knowledge of the lien or pursuant to a commitment entered into without knowledge of the lien.

§ 9–302. When Filing Is Required to Perfect Security Interest; Security Interests to Which Filing Provisions of This Article Do Not Apply.

(1) A financing statement must be filed to perfect all security interests except the following:

(a) a security interest in collateral in possession of the secured party under Section 9–305;

(b) a security interest temporarily perfected in instruments or documents without delivery under Section 9–304 or in proceeds for a 10 day period under Section 9–306;

(c) a security interest created by an assignment of a beneficial interest in a trust or a decedent's estate;

(d) a purchase money security interest in consumer goods; but filing is required for a motor vehicle required to be registered; and fixture filing is required for priority over conflicting interests in fixtures to the extent provided in Section 9–313;

(e) an assignment of accounts which does not alone or in conjunction with other assignments to the same assignee transfer a significant part of the outstanding accounts of the assignor;

(f) a security interest of a collecting bank (Section 4–210) or in securities (Section 8–321) or arising under the Articles on Sales and Leases (see Section 9–113) or covered in subsection (3) of this section;

(g) an assignment for the benefit of all the creditors of the transferor, and subsequent transfers by the assignee thereunder.

(2) If a secured party assigns a perfected security interest, no filing under this Article is required in order to continue the perfected status of the security interest against creditors of and transferees from the original debtor.

(3) The filing of a financing statement otherwise required by this Article is not necessary or effective to perfect a security interest in property subject to

(a) a statute or treaty of the United States which provides for a national or international registration or a national or international certificate of title or which specifies a place of filing different from that specified in this Article for filing of the security interest; or

(b) the following statutes of this state; [list any certificate of title statute covering automobiles, trailers, mobile homes, boats, farm tractors, or the like, and any central filing statute]; but during any period in which collateral is inventory held for sale by a person who is in the business of selling goods of that kind, the filing provisions of this Article (Part 4) apply to a security interest in that collateral created by him as debtor; or

(c) a certificate of title statute of another jurisdiction under the law of which indication of a security interest on the certificate is required as a condition of perfection (subsection (2) of Section 9–103).

(4) Compliance with a statute or treaty described in subsection (3) is equivalent to the filing of a financing statement under this Article, and a security interest in property subject to the statute or treaty can be perfected only by compliance therewith except as provided in Section 9–103 on multiple state transactions. Duration and renewal of perfection of a security interest perfected by compliance with the statute or treaty are governed by the provisions of the statute or treaty; in other respects the security interest is subject to this Article.

Amended in 1972 and 1977.

§ 9–303. When Security Interest Is Perfected; Continuity of Perfection.

(1) A security interest is perfected when it has attached and when all of the applicable steps required for perfection have been taken. Such steps are specified in Sections 9–302, 9–304, 9–305 and 9–306. If such steps are taken before the security interest attaches, it is perfected at the time when it attaches.

(2) If a security interest is originally perfected in any way permitted under this Article and is subsequently perfected in some other way under this Article, without an intermediate period when it was unperfected, the security interest shall be deemed to be perfected continuously for the purposes of this Article.

§ 9–304. Perfection of Security Interest in Instruments, Documents, and Goods Covered by Documents; Perfection by Permissive Filing; Temporary Perfection Without Filing or Transfer of Possession.

(1) A security interest in chattel paper or negotiable documents may be perfected by filing. A security interest in money or instruments (other than certificated securities or instruments which constitute part of chattel paper) can be perfected only by the secured party's taking possession, except as provided in subsections (4) and (5) of this section and subsections (2) and (3) of Section 9–306 on proceeds.

(2) During the period that goods are in the possession of the issuer of a negotiable document therefor, a security interest in the goods is perfected by perfecting a security interest in the document, and any security interest in the goods otherwise perfected during such period is subject thereto.

(3) A security interest in goods in the possession of a bailee other than one who has issued a negotiable document therefor is perfected by issuance of a document in the name of the secured party or by the bailee's receipt of notification of the secured party's interest or by filing as to the goods.

(4) A security interest in instruments (other than certificated securities) or negotiable documents is perfected without filing or the taking of possession for a period of 21 days from the time it attaches to the extent that it arises for new value given under a written security agreement.

(5) A security interest remains perfected for a period of 21 days without filing where a secured party having a perfected security interest in an instrument (other than a certificated security), a negotiable document or goods in possession of a bailee other than one who has issued a negotiable document therefor

(a) makes available to the debtor the goods or documents representing the goods for the purpose of ultimate sale or exchange or for the purpose of loading, unloading, storing, shipping, transshipping, manufacturing, processing or otherwise dealing with them in a manner preliminary to their sale or exchange, but priority between conflicting security interests in the goods is subject to subsection (3) of Section 9–312; or

(b) delivers the instrument to the debtor for the purpose of ultimate sale or exchange or of presentation, collection, renewal or registration of transfer.

(6) After the 21 day period in subsections (4) and (5) perfection depends upon compliance with applicable provisions of this Article.

§ 9–305. When Possession by Secured Party Perfects Security Interest Without Filing.

A security interest in letters of credit and advices of credit (subsection (2)(a) of Section 5–116), goods, instruments (other than certificated securities), money, negotiable documents, or chattel paper may be perfected by the secured party's taking possession of the collateral. If such collateral other than goods covered by a negotiable document is held by a bailee, the secured party is deemed to have possession from the time the bailee receives notification of the secured party's interest. A security interest is perfected by possession from the time possession is taken without a relation back and continues only so long as possession is retained, unless otherwise specified in this Article. The security interest may be otherwise perfected as provided in this Article before or after the period of possession by the secured party.

§ 9–306. "Proceeds"; Secured Party's Rights on Disposition of Collateral.

(1) "Proceeds" includes whatever is received upon the sale, exchange, collection or other disposition of collateral or pro-

ceeds. Insurance payable by reason of loss or damage to the collateral is proceeds, except to the extent that it is payable to a person other than a party to the security agreement. Money, checks, deposit accounts, and the like are "cash proceeds". All other proceeds are "non-cash proceeds".

(2) Except where this Article otherwise provides, a security interest continues in collateral notwithstanding sale, exchange or other disposition thereof unless the disposition was authorized by the secured party in the security agreement or otherwise, and also continues in any identifiable proceeds including collections received by the debtor.

(3) The security interest in proceeds is a continuously perfected security interest if the interest in the original collateral was perfected but it ceases to be a perfected security interest and becomes unperfected ten days after receipt of the proceeds by the debtor unless

(a) a filed financing statement covers the original collateral and the proceeds are collateral in which a security interest may be perfected by filing in the office or offices where the financing statement has been filed and, if the proceeds are acquired with cash proceeds, the description of collateral in the financing statement indicates the types of property constituting the proceeds; or

(b) a filed financing statement covers the original collateral and the proceeds are identifiable cash proceeds; or

(c) the security interest in the proceeds is perfected before the expiration of the ten day period.

Except as provided in this section, a security interest in proceeds can be perfected only by the methods or under the circumstances permitted in this Article for original collateral of the same type.

(4) In the event of insolvency proceedings instituted by or against a debtor, a secured party with a perfected security interest in proceeds has a perfected security interest only in the following proceeds:

(a) in identifiable non-cash proceeds and in separate deposit accounts containing only proceeds;

(b) in identifiable cash proceeds in the form of money which is neither commingled with other money nor deposited in a deposit account prior to the insolvency proceedings;

(c) in identifiable cash proceeds in the form of checks and the like which are not deposited in a deposit account prior to the insolvency proceedings; and

(d) in all cash and deposit accounts of the debtor in which proceeds have been commingled with other funds, but the perfected security interest under this paragraph (d) is

(i) subject to any right to set-off; and

(ii) limited to an amount not greater than the amount of any cash proceeds received by the debtor within ten days before the institution of the insolvency proceedings less the sum of (I) the payments to the secured party on account of cash proceeds received by the debtor during such period and (II) the cash proceeds received by the debtor during such period to which the secured party is entitled under paragraphs (a) through (c) of this subsection (4).

(5) If a sale of goods results in an account or chattel paper which is transferred by the seller to a secured party, and if the goods are returned to or are repossessed by the seller or the secured party, the following rules determine priorities:

(a) If the goods were collateral at the time of sale, for an indebtedness of the seller which is still unpaid, the original security interest attaches again to the goods and continues as a perfected security interest if it was perfected at the time when the goods were sold. If the security interest was originally perfected by a filing which is still effective, nothing further is required to continue the perfected status; in any other case, the secured party must take possession of the returned or repossessed goods or must file.

(b) An unpaid transferee of the chattel paper has a security interest in the goods against the transferor. Such security interest is prior to a security interest asserted under paragraph (a) to the extent that the transferee of the chattel paper was entitled to priority under Section 9–308.

(c) An unpaid transferee of the account has a security interest in the goods against the transferor. Such security interest is subordinate to a security interest asserted under paragraph (a).

(d) A security interest of an unpaid transferee asserted under paragraph (b) or (c) must be perfected for protection against creditors of the transferor and purchasers of the returned or repossessed goods.

§ 9–307. Protection of Buyers of Goods.

(1) A buyer in ordinary course of business (subsection (9) of Section 1–201) other than a person buying farm products from a person engaged in farming operations takes free of a security interest created by his seller even though the security interest is perfected and even though the buyer knows of its existence.

(2) In the case of consumer goods, a buyer takes free of a security interest even though perfected if he buys without knowledge of the security interest, for value and for his own personal, family or household purposes unless prior to the purchase the secured party has filed a financing statement covering such goods.

(3) A buyer other than a buyer in ordinary course of business (subsection (1) of this section) takes free of a security interest to the extent that it secures future advances made after the secured party acquires knowledge of the purchase, or more than 45 days after the purchase, whichever first occurs, unless made pursuant to a commitment entered into without knowledge of the purchase and before the expiration of the 45 day period.

§ 9–308. Purchase of Chattel Paper and Instruments.

A purchaser of chattel paper or an instrument who gives new value and takes possession of it in the ordinary course of his business has priority over a security interest in the chattel paper or instrument

(a) which is perfected under Section 9–304 (permissive filing and temporary perfection) or under Section 9–306 (perfection as to proceeds) if he acts without knowledge that the specific paper or instrument is subject to a security interest; or

(b) which is claimed merely as proceeds of inventory subject to a security interest (Section 9–306) even though he knows that the specific paper or instrument is subject to the security interest.

§ 9–309. Protection of Purchasers of Instruments, Documents and Securities.

Nothing in this Article limits the rights of a holder in due course of a negotiable instrument (Section 3–302) or a holder to whom a negotiable document of title has been duly negotiated (Section 7–501) or a bona fide purchaser of a security (Section 8–302) and the holders or purchasers take priority over an earlier security interest even though perfected. Filing under this Article does not constitute notice of the security interest to such holders or purchasers.

§ 9–310. Priority of Certain Liens Arising by Operation of Law.

When a person in the ordinary course of his business furnishes services or materials with respect to goods subject to a security interest, a lien upon goods in the possession of such person given by statute or rule of law for such materials or services takes priority over a perfected security interest unless the lien is statutory and the statute expressly provides otherwise.

§ 9–311. Alienability of Debtor's Rights: Judicial Process.

The debtor's rights in collateral may be voluntarily or involuntarily transferred (by way of sale, creation of a security interest, attachment, levy, garnishment or other judicial process) notwithstanding a provision in the security agreement prohibiting any transfer or making the transfer constitute a default.

§ 9–312. Priorities Among Conflicting Security Interests in the Same Collateral.

(1) The rules of priority stated in other sections of this Part and in the following sections shall govern when applicable: Section 4–208 with respect to the security interests of collecting banks in items being collected, accompanying documents and proceeds; Section 9–103 on security interests related to other jurisdictions; Section 9–114 on consignments.

(2) A perfected security interest in crops for new value given to enable the debtor to produce the crops during the production season and given not more than three months before the crops become growing crops by planting or otherwise takes priority over an earlier perfected security interest to the extent that such earlier interest secures obligations due more than six months before the crops become growing crops by planting or otherwise, even though the person giving new value had knowledge of the earlier security interest.

(3) A perfected purchase money security interest in inventory has priority over a conflicting security interest in the same inventory and also has priority in identifiable cash proceeds received on or before the delivery of the inventory to a buyer if

(a) the purchase money security interest is perfected at the time the debtor receives possession of the inventory; and

(b) the purchase money secured party gives notification in writing to the holder of the conflicting security interest if the holder had filed a financing statement covering the same types of inventory (i) before the date of the filing made by the purchase money secured party, or (ii) before the beginning of the 21 day period where the purchase money security interest is temporarily perfected without filing or possession (subsection (5) of Section 9–304); and

(c) the holder of the conflicting security interest receives the notification within five years before the debtor receives possession of the inventory; and

(d) the notification states that the person giving the notice has or expects to acquire a purchase money security interest in inventory of the debtor, describing such inventory by item or type.

(4) A purchase money security interest in collateral other than inventory has priority over a conflicting security interest in the same collateral or its proceeds if the purchase money security interest is perfected at the time the debtor receives possession of the collateral or within ten days thereafter.

(5) In all cases not governed by other rules stated in this section (including cases of purchase money security interests which do not qualify for the special priorities set forth in subsections (3) and (4) of this section), priority between conflicting security interests in the same collateral shall be determined according to the following rules:

(a) Conflicting security interests rank according to priority in time of filing or perfection. Priority dates from the time a filing is first made covering the collateral or the time the security interest is first perfected, whichever is earlier, provided that there is no period thereafter when there is neither filing nor perfection.

(b) So long as conflicting security interests are unperfected, the first to attach has priority.

(6) For the purposes of subsection (5) a date of filing or perfection as to collateral is also a date of filing or perfection as to proceeds.

(7) If future advances are made while a security interest is perfected by filing, the taking of possession, or under Section 8–321 on securities, the security interest has the same priority for the purposes of subsection (5) with respect to the future advances as it does with respect to the first advance. If a commitment is made before or while the security interest is so perfected, the security interest has the same priority with respect to advances made pursuant thereto. In other cases a perfected security interest has priority from the date the advance is made.

§ 9–313. Priority of Security Interests in Fixtures.

(1) In this section and in the provisions of Part 4 of this Article referring to fixture filing, unless the context otherwise requires

(a) goods are "fixtures" when they become so related to particular real estate that an interest in them arises under real estate law

(b) a "fixture filing" is the filing in the office where a mortgage on the real estate would be filed or recorded of a financing statement covering goods which are or are to become fixtures and conforming to the requirements of subsection (5) of Section 9–402

(c) a mortgage is a "construction mortgage" to the extent that it secures an obligation incurred for the construction of an improvement on land including the acquisition cost of the land, if the recorded writing so indicates.

(2) A security interest under this Article may be created in goods which are fixtures or may continue in goods which become fixtures, but no security interest exists under this Article in ordinary building materials incorporated into an improvement on land.

(3) This Article does not prevent creation of an encumbrance upon fixtures pursuant to real estate law.

(4) A perfected security interest in fixtures has priority over the conflicting interest of an encumbrancer or owner of the real estate where

(a) the security interest is a purchase money security interest, the interest of the encumbrancer or owner arises before the goods become fixtures, the security interest is perfected by a fixture filing before the goods become fixtures or within ten days thereafter, and the debtor has an interest of record in the real estate or is in possession of the real estate; or

(b) the security interest is perfected by a fixture filing before the interest of the encumbrancer or owner is of record, the security interest has priority over any conflicting interest of a predecessor in title of the encumbrancer or owner, and the debtor has an interest of record in the real estate or is in possession of the real estate; or

(c) the fixtures are readily removable factory or office machines or readily removable replacements of domestic appliances which are consumer goods, and before the goods become fixtures the security interest is perfected by any method permitted by this Article; or

(d) the conflicting interest is a lien on the real estate obtained by legal or equitable proceedings after the security interest was perfected by any method permitted by this Article.

(5) A security interest in fixtures, whether or not perfected, has priority over the conflicting interest of an encumbrancer or owner of the real estate where

(a) the encumbrancer or owner has consented in writing to the security interest or has disclaimed an interest in the goods as fixtures; or

(b) the debtor has a right to remove the goods as against the encumbrancer or owner. If the debtor's right terminates, the priority of the security interest continues for a reasonable time.

(6) Notwithstanding paragraph (a) of subsection (4) but otherwise subject to subsections (4) and (5), a security interest in fixtures is subordinate to a construction mortgage recorded before the goods become fixtures if the goods become fixtures before the completion of the construction. To the extent that it is given to refinance a construction mortgage, a mortgage has this priority to the same extent as the construction mortgage.

(7) In cases not within the preceding subsections, a security interest in fixtures is subordinate to the conflicting interest of an encumbrancer or owner of the related real estate who is not the debtor.

(8) When the secured party has priority over all owners and encumbrancers of the real estate, he may, on default, subject to the provisions of Part 5, remove his collateral from the real estate but he must reimburse any encumbrancer or owner of the real estate who is not the debtor and who has not otherwise agreed for the cost of repair of any physical injury, but not for any diminution in value of the real estate caused by the absence of the goods removed or by any necessity of replacing them. A person entitled to reimbursement may refuse permission to remove until the secured party gives adequate security for the performance of this obligation.

§ 9–314. Accessions.

(1) A security interest in goods which attaches before they are installed in or affixed to other goods takes priority as to the goods installed or affixed (called in this section "accessions") over the claims of all persons to the whole except as stated in subsection (3) and subject to Section 9–315(1).

(2) A security interest which attaches to goods after they become part of a whole is valid against all persons subsequently acquiring interests in the whole except as stated in subsection (3) but is invalid against any person with an interest in the whole at the time the security interest attaches to the goods who has not in writing consented to the security interest or disclaimed an interest in the goods as part of the whole.

(3) The security interests described in subsections (1) and (2) do not take priority over

(a) a subsequent purchaser for value of any interest in the whole; or

(b) a creditor with a lien on the whole subsequently obtained by judicial proceedings; or

(c) a creditor with a prior perfected security interest in the whole to the extent that he makes subsequent advances

if the subsequent purchase is made, the lien by judicial proceedings obtained or the subsequent advance under the prior perfected security interest is made or contracted for without knowledge of the security interest and before it is perfected. A purchaser of the whole at a foreclosure sale other than the holder of a perfected security interest purchasing at his own foreclosure sale is a subsequent purchaser within this section.

(4) When under subsections (1) or (2) and (3) a secured party has an interest in accessions which has priority over the claims of all persons who have interests in the whole, he may on default subject to the provisions of Part 5 remove his collateral from the whole but he must reimburse any encumbrancer or owner of the whole who is not the debtor and who has not otherwise agreed for the cost of repair of any physical injury but not for any diminution in value of the whole caused by the absence of the goods removed or by any necessity for replacing them. A person entitled to reimbursement may refuse permission to remove until the secured party gives adequate security for the performance of this obligation.

§ 9–315. Priority When Goods Are Commingled or Processed.

(1) If a security interest in goods was perfected and subsequently the goods or a part thereof have become part of a product or mass, the security interest continues in the product or mass if

(a) the goods are so manufactured, processed, assembled or commingled that their identity is lost in the product or mass; or

(b) a financing statement covering the original goods also covers the product into which the goods have been manufactured, processed or assembled.

In a case to which paragraph (b) applies, no separate security interest in that part of the original goods which has been manufactured, processed or assembled into the product may be claimed under Section 9–314.

(2) When under subsection (1) more than one security interest attaches to the product or mass, they rank equally according to the ratio that the cost of the goods to which each interest originally attached bears to the cost of the total product or mass.

§ 9–316. Priority Subject to Subordination.

Nothing in this Article prevents subordination by agreement by any person entitled to priority.

§ 9–317. Secured Party Not Obligated on Contract of Debtor.

The mere existence of a security interest or authority given to the debtor to dispose of or use collateral does not impose contract or tort liability upon the secured party for the debtor's acts or omissions.

§ 9–318. Defenses Against Assignee; Modification of Contract After Notification of Assignment; Term Prohibiting Assignment Ineffective; Identification and Proof of Assignment.

(1) Unless an account debtor has made an enforceable agreement not to assert defenses or claims arising out of a sale as provided in Section 9–206 the rights of an assignee are subject to

(a) all the terms of the contract between the account debtor and assignor and any defense or claim arising therefrom; and

(b) any other defense or claim of the account debtor against the assignor which accrues before the account debtor receives notification of the assignment.

(2) So far as the right to payment or a part thereof under an assigned contract has not been fully earned by performance, and notwithstanding notification of the assignment, any modification of or substitution for the contract made in good faith and in accordance with reasonable commercial standards is effective against an assignee unless the account debtor has otherwise agreed but the assignee acquires corresponding rights under the modified or substituted contract. The assignment may provide that such modification or substitution is a breach by the assignor.

(3) The account debtor is authorized to pay the assignor until the account debtor receives notification that the amount due or to become due has been assigned and that payment is to be made to the assignee. A notification which does not reasonably identify the rights assigned is ineffective. If requested by the account debtor, the assignee must seasonably furnish reasonable proof that the assignment has been made and unless he does so the account debtor may pay the assignor.

(4) A term in any contract between an account debtor and an assignor is ineffective if it prohibits assignment of an account or prohibits creation of a security interest in a general intangible for money due or to become due or requires the account debtor's consent to such assignment or security interest.

PART 4 Filing

§ 9–401. Place of Filing; Erroneous Filing; Removal of Collateral.

First Alternative Subsection (1)

(1) The proper place to file in order to perfect a security interest is as follows:

(a) when the collateral is timber to be cut or is minerals or the like (including oil and gas) or accounts subject to subsection (5) of Section 9–103, or when the financing statement is filed as a fixture filing (Section 9–313) and the collateral is goods which are or are to become fixtures, then in the office where a mortgage on the real estate would be filed or recorded;

(b) in all other cases, in the office of the [Secretary of State].

Second Alternative Subsection (1)

(1) The proper place to file in order to perfect a security interest is as follows:

(a) when the collateral is equipment used in farming operations, or farm products, or accounts or general intangibles arising from or relating to the sale of farm products by a farmer, or consumer goods, then in the office of the ____________ in the county of the debtor's residence or if the debtor is not a resident of this state then in the office of the ____________ in the county where the goods are kept, and in addition when the collateral is crops growing or to be grown in the office of the ____________ in the county where the land is located;

(b) when the collateral is timber to be cut or is minerals or the like (including oil and gas) or accounts subject to subsection (5) of Section 9–103, or when the financing statement is filed as a fixture filing (Section 9–313) and the collateral is goods which are or are to become fixtures, then in the office where a mortgage on the real estate would be filed or recorded;

(c) in all other cases, in the office of the [Secretary of State].

Third Alternative Subsection (1)

(1) The proper place to file in order to perfect a security interest is as follows:

(a) when the collateral is equipment used in farming operations, or farm products, or accounts or general intangibles arising from or relating to the sale of farm products by a farmer, or consumer goods, then in the office of the ____________ in the county of the debtor's residence or if the debtor is not a resident of this state then in the office of the ____________ in the county where the goods are kept, and in addition when the collateral is crops growing or to be grown in the office of the ____________ in the county where the land is located;

(b) when the collateral is timber to be cut or is minerals or the like (including oil and gas) or accounts subject to subsection (5) of Section 9–103, or when the financing statement is filed as a fixture filing (Section 9–313) and the collateral is goods which are or are to become fixtures, then in the office where a mortgage on the real estate would be filed or recorded;

(c) in all other cases, in the office of the [Secretary of State] and in addition, if the debtor has a place of business in only one county of this state, also in the office of ____________ of such county, or, if the debtor has no place of business in this state, but resides in the state, also in the office of ____________ of the county in which he resides.

Note: One of the three alternatives should be selected as subsection (1).

(2) A filing which is made in good faith in an improper place or not in all of the places required by this section is nevertheless effective with regard to any collateral as to which the filing complied with the requirements of this Article and is also effective with regard to collateral covered by the financing statement against any person who has knowledge of the contents of such financing statement.

(3) A filing which is made in the proper place in this state continues effective even though the debtor's residence or place of business or the location of the collateral or its use, whichever controlled the original filing, is thereafter changed.

Alternative Subsection (3)

[(3) A filing which is made in the proper county continues effective for four months after a change to another county of the debtor's residence or place of business or the location of the collateral, whichever controlled the original filing. It becomes ineffective thereafter unless a copy of the financing statement signed by the secured party is filed in the new county within said period. The security interest may also be perfected in the new county after the expiration of the four-month period; in such case perfection dates from the time of perfection in the new county. A change in the use of the collateral does not impair the effectiveness of the original filing.]

(4) The rules stated in Section 9–103 determine whether filing is necessary in this state.

(5) Notwithstanding the preceding subsections, and subject to subsection (3) of Section 9–302, the proper place to file in order to perfect a security interest in collateral, including fixtures, of a transmitting utility is the office of the [Secretary of State]. This filing constitutes a fixture filing (Section 9–313) as to the collateral described therein which is or is to become fixtures.

(6) For the purposes of this section, the residence of an organization is its place of business if it has one or its chief executive office if it has more than one place of business.

Note: *Subsection (6) should be used only if the state chooses the Second or Third Alternative Subsection (1).*

§ 9–402. Formal Requisites of Financing Statement; Amendments; Mortgage as Financing Statement.

(1) A financing statement is sufficient if it gives the names of the debtor and the secured party, is signed by the debtor, gives an address of the secured party from which information concerning the security interest may be obtained, gives a mailing address of the debtor and contains a statement indicating the types, or describing the items, of collateral. A financing statement may be filed before a security agreement is made or a security interest otherwise attaches. When the financing statement covers crops growing or to be grown, the statement must also contain a description of the real estate concerned. When the financing statement covers timber to be cut or covers minerals or the like (including oil and gas) or accounts subject to subsection (5) of Section 9–103, or when the financing statement is filed as a fixture filing (Section 9–313) and the collateral is goods which are or are to become fixtures, the statement must also comply with subsection (5). A copy of the security agreement is sufficient as a financing statement if it contains the above information and is signed by the debtor. A carbon, photographic or other reproduction of a security agreement or a financing statement is sufficient as a financing statement if the security agreement so provides or if the original has been filed in this state.

(2) A financing statement which otherwise complies with subsection (1) is sufficient when it is signed by the secured party instead of the debtor if it is filed to perfect a security interest in

(a) collateral already subject to a security interest in another jurisdiction when it is brought into this state, or when the debtor's location is changed to this state. Such a financing statement must state that the collateral was brought into this state or that the debtor's location was changed to this state under such circumstances; or

(b) proceeds under Section 9–306 if the security interest in the original collateral was perfected. Such a financing statement must describe the original collateral; or

(c) collateral as to which the filing has lapsed; or

(d) collateral acquired after a change of name, identity or corporate structure of the debtor (subsection (7)).

(3) A form substantially as follows is sufficient to comply with subsection (1):

Name of debtor (or assignor) ____________

Address ____________

Name of secured party (or assignee) ____________

Address ____________

1. This financing statement covers the following types (or items) of property:

(Describe) ____________

2. (If collateral is crops) The above described crops are growing or are to be grown on:

(Describe Real Estate) ____________

3. (If applicable) The above goods are to become fixtures on*

*Where appropriate substitute either "The above timber is standing on ____________" or "The above minerals or the like (including oil and gas) or accounts will be financed at the wellhead or minehead of the well or mine located on ____________"

(Describe Real Estate) ____________ and this financing statement is to be filed [for record] in the real estate records. (If the debtor does not have an interest of record) The name of a record owner is ____________

4. (If products of collateral are claimed) Products of the collateral are also covered.

(use	____________
whichever is	Signature of Debtor (or Assignor)
	____________
applicable)	Signature of Secured Party (or Assignee)

(4) A financing statement may be amended by filing a writing signed by both the debtor and the secured party. An amendment does not extend the period of effectiveness of a financing statement. If any amendment adds collateral, it is effective as to the added collateral only from the filing date of the amendment. In this Article, unless the context otherwise requires, the term "financing statement" means the original financing statement and any amendments.

(5) A financing statement covering timber to be cut or covering minerals or the like (including oil and gas) or accounts subject to subsection (5) of Section 9–103, or a financing statement filed as a fixture filing (Section 9–313) where the debtor is not a transmitting utility, must show that it covers this type of collateral, must recite that it is to be filed [for record] in the real estate records, and the financing statement must contain a description of the real estate [sufficient if it were contained in a mortgage of the real estate to give constructive notice of the mortgage under the law of this state]. If the debtor does not have an interest of record in the real estate, the financing statement must show the name of a record owner.

(6) A mortgage is effective as a financing statement filed as a fixture filing from the date of its recording if

(a) the goods are described in the mortgage by item or type; and

(b) the goods are or are to become fixtures related to the real estate described in the mortgage; and

(c) the mortgage complies with the requirements for a financing statement in this section other than a recital that it is to be filed in the real estate records; and

(d) the mortgage is duly recorded.

No fee with reference to the financing statement is required other than the regular recording and satisfaction fees with respect to the mortgage.

(7) A financing statement sufficiently shows the name of the debtor if it gives the individual, partnership or corporate name of the debtor, whether or not it adds other trade names or names of partners. Where the debtor so changes his name or in the case of an organization its name, identity or corporate structure that a filed financing statement becomes seriously misleading, the filing is not effective to perfect a security interest in collateral acquired by the debtor more than four months after the change, unless a new appropriate financing statement is filed before the expiration of that time. A filed financing statement remains effective with respect to collateral transferred by the debtor even though the secured party knows of or consents to the transfer.

(8) A financing statement substantially complying with the requirements of this section is effective even though it contains minor errors which are not seriously misleading.

Note: Language in brackets is optional.

Note: Where the state has any special recording system for real estate other than the usual grantor-grantee index (as, for instance, a tract system or a title registration or Torrens system) local adaptations of subsection (5) and Section 9–403(7) may be necessary. See Mass.Gen.Laws Chapter 106, Section 9–409.

§ 9–403. What Constitutes Filing; Duration of Filing; Effect of Lapsed Filing; Duties of Filing Officer.

(1) Presentation for filing of a financing statement and tender of the filing fee or acceptance of the statement by the filing officer constitutes filing under this Article.

(2) Except as provided in subsection (6) a filed financing statement is effective for a period of five years from the date of filing. The effectiveness of a filed financing statement lapses on the expiration of the five year period unless a continuation statement is filed prior to the lapse. If a security interest perfected by filing exists at the time insolvency proceedings are commenced by or against the debtor, the security interest remains perfected until termination of the insolvency proceedings and thereafter for a period of sixty days or until expiration of the five year period, whichever occurs later. Upon lapse the security interest becomes unperfected, unless it is perfected without filing. If the security interest becomes unperfected upon lapse, it is deemed to have been unperfected as against a person who became a purchaser or lien creditor before lapse.

(3) A continuation statement may be filed by the secured party within six months prior to the expiration of the five year period specified in subsection (2). Any such continuation statement must be signed by the secured party, identify the original statement by file number and state that the original statement is still effective. A continuation statement signed by a person other than the secured party of record must be accompanied by a separate written statement of assignment signed by the secured party of record and complying with subsection (2) of Section 9–405, including payment of the required fee. Upon timely filing of the continuation statement, the effectiveness of the original statement is continued for five years after the last date to which the filing was effective whereupon it lapses in the same manner as provided in subsection (2) unless another continuation statement is filed prior to such lapse. Succeeding continuation statements may be filed in the same manner to continue the effectiveness of the original statement. Unless a statute on disposition of public records provides otherwise, the filing officer may remove a lapsed statement from the files and destroy it immediately if he has retained a microfilm or other photographic record, or in other cases after one year after the lapse. The filing officer shall so arrange matters by physical annexation of financing statements to continuation statements or other related filings, or by other means, that if he physically destroys the financing statements of a period more than five years past, those which have been continued by a continuation statement or which are still effective under subsection (6) shall be retained.

(4) Except as provided in subsection (7) a filing officer shall mark each statement with a file number and with the date and hour of filing and shall hold the statement or a microfilm or other photographic copy thereof for public inspection. In addition the filing officer shall index the statement according to the name of the debtor and shall note in the index the file number and the address of the debtor given in the statement.

(5) The uniform fee for filing and indexing and for stamping a copy furnished by the secured party to show the date and place of filing for an original financing statement or for a continuation statement shall be $__________ if the statement is in the standard form prescribed by the [Secretary of State] and otherwise shall be $__________, plus in each case, if the financing statement is subject to subsection (5) of Section 9–402, $__________. The uniform fee for each name more than one required to be indexed shall be $__________. The secured party may at his option show a trade name for any person and an extra uniform indexing fee of $__________; shall be paid with respect thereto.

(6) If the debtor is a transmitting utility (subsection (5) of Section 9–401) and a filed financing statement so states, it is effective until a termination statement is filed. A real estate mortgage which is effective as a fixture filing under subsection (6) of Section 9–402 remains effective as a fixture filing until the mortgage is released or satisfied of record or its effectiveness otherwise terminates as to the real estate.

(7) When a financing statement covers timber to be cut or covers minerals or the like (including oil and gas) or accounts subject to subsection (5) of Section 9–103, or is filed as a fixture filing, [it shall be filed for record and] the filing officer shall index it under the names of the debtor and any owner of record shown on the financing statement in the same fashion as if they were the mortgagors in a mortgage of the real estate described, and, to the extent that the law of this state provides for indexing of mortgages under the name of the mortgagee, under the name of the secured party as if he were the mortgagee thereunder, or where indexing is by description in the same fashion as if the financing statement were a mortgage of the real estate described.

Note: In states in which writings will not appear in the real estate records and indices unless actually recorded the bracketed language in subsection (7) should be used.

§ 9–404. Termination Statement.

(1) If a financing statement covering consumer goods is filed on or after __________, then within one month or within ten days following written demand by the debtor after there is no outstanding secured obligation and no commitment to make advances, incur obligations or otherwise give value, the secured party must file with each filing officer with whom the financing statement was filed, a termination statement to the effect that he no longer claims a security interest under the financing statement, which shall be identified by file number. In other cases whenever there is no outstanding secured obligation and no commitment to make advances, incur obligations or otherwise give value, the secured party must on written demand by the debtor send the debtor, for each filing officer with whom the financing statement was filed, a termination statement to the effect that he no longer claims a security interest under the financing statement, which shall be identified by file number. A termination statement signed by a person other than the secured party of record must be accompanied by a separate written statement of assignment signed by the secured party of record complying with subsection (2) of Section 9–405, including payment of the required fee. If the affected secured party fails to file

such a termination statement as required by this subsection, or to send such a termination statement within ten days after proper demand therefor, he shall be liable to the debtor for one hundred dollars, and in addition for any loss caused to the debtor by such failure.

(2) On presentation to the filing officer of such a termination statement he must note it in the index. If he has received the termination statement in duplicate, he shall return one copy of the termination statement to the secured party stamped to show the time of receipt thereof. If the filing officer has a microfilm or other photographic record of the financing statement, and of any related continuation statement, statement of assignment and statement of release, he may remove the originals from the files at any time after receipt of the termination statement, or if he has no such record, he may remove them from the files at any time after one year after receipt of the termination statement.

(3) If the termination statement is in the standard form prescribed by the [Secretary of State], the uniform fee for filing and indexing the termination statement shall be $__________, and otherwise shall be $__________, plus in each case an additional fee of $__________ for each name more than one against which the termination statement is required to be indexed.

Note: *The date to be inserted should be the effective date of the revised Article 9.*

§ 9–405. Assignment of Security Interest; Duties of Filing Officer; Fees.

(1) A financing statement may disclose an assignment of a security interest in the collateral described in the financing statement by indication in the financing statement of the name and address of the assignee or by an assignment itself or a copy thereof on the face or back of the statement. On presentation to the filing officer of such a financing statement the filing officer shall mark the same as provided in Section 9–403(4). The uniform fee for filing, indexing and furnishing filing data for a financing statement so indicating an assignment shall be $__________ if the statement is in the standard form prescribed by the [Secretary of State] and otherwise shall be $__________, plus in each case an additional fee of $__________ for each name more than one against which the financing statement is required to be indexed.

(2) A secured party may assign of record all or part of his rights under a financing statement by the filing in the place where the original financing statement was filed of a separate written statement of assignment signed by the secured party of record and setting forth the name of the secured party of record and the debtor, the file number and the date of filing of the financing statement and the name and address of the assignee and containing a description of the collateral assigned. A copy of the assignment is sufficient as a separate statement if it complies with the preceding sentence. On presentation to the filing officer of such a separate statement, the filing officer shall mark such separate statement with the date and hour of the filing. He shall note the assignment on the index of the financing statement, or in the case of a fixture filing, or a filing covering timber to be cut, or covering minerals or the like (including oil and gas) or accounts subject to subsection (5) of Section 9–103, he shall index the assignment under the name of the assignor as grantor and, to the extent that the law of this state provides for indexing the assignment of a mortgage under the name of the assignee, he shall index the assignment of the financing statement under the name of the assignee. The uniform fee for filing, indexing and furnishing filing data about such a separate statement of assignment shall be $__________ if the statement is in the standard form prescribed by the [Secretary of State] and otherwise shall be $__________, plus in each case an additional fee of $__________; for each name more than one against which the statement of assignment is required to be indexed. Notwithstanding the provisions of this subsection, an assignment of record of a security interest in a fixture contained in a mortgage effective as a fixture filing (subsection (6) of Section 9–402) may be made only by an assignment of the mortgage in the manner provided by the law of this state other than this Act.

(3) After the disclosure or filing of an assignment under this section, the assignee is the secured party of record.

§ 9–406. Release of Collateral; Duties of Filing Officer; Fees.

A secured party of record may by his signed statement release all or a part of any collateral described in a filed financing statement. The statement of release is sufficient if it contains a description of the collateral being released, the name and address of the debtor, the name and address of the secured party, and the file number of the financing statement. A statement of release signed by a person other than the secured party of record must be accompanied by a separate written statement of assignment signed by the secured party of record and complying with subsection (2) of Section 9–405, including payment of the required fee. Upon presentation of such a statement of release to the filing officer he shall mark the statement with the hour and date of filing and shall note the same upon the margin of the index of the filing of the financing statement. The uniform fee for filing and noting such a statement of release shall be $__________ if the statement is in the standard form prescribed by the [Secretary of State] and otherwise shall be $__________, plus in each case an additional fee of $__________ for each name more than one against which the statement of release is required to be indexed.

[§ 9–407. Information From Filing Officer].

[(1) If the person filing any financing statement, termination statement, statement of assignment, or statement of release, furnishes the filing officer a copy thereof, the filing officer shall upon request note upon the copy the file number and date and hour of the filing of the original and deliver or send the copy to such person.]

[(2) Upon request of any person, the filing officer shall issue his certificate showing whether there is on file on the date and hour stated therein, any presently effective financing statement naming a particular debtor and any statement of assignment thereof and if there is, giving the date and hour of filing of each such statement and the names and addresses of each secured party therein. The uniform fee for such a certificate shall be $__________ if the request for the certificate is in the standard form prescribed by the [Secretary of State] and otherwise shall be $__________. Upon request the filing officer shall furnish a copy of any filed financing statement or statement of assignment for a uniform fee of $__________ per page.]

Note: This section is proposed as an optional provision to require filing officers to furnish certificates. Local law and practices should be consulted with regard to the advisability of adoption.

§ 9–408. Financing Statements Covering Consigned or Leased Goods.

A consignor or lessor of goods may file a financing statement using the terms "consignor," "consignee," "lessor," "lessee" or the like instead of the terms specified in Section 9–402. The provisions of this Part shall apply as appropriate to such a financing statement but its filing shall not of itself be a factor in determining whether or not the consignment or lease is intended as security (Section 1–201(37)). However, if it is determined for other reasons that the consignment or lease is so intended, a security interest of the consignor or lessor which attaches to the consigned or leased goods is perfected by such filing.

PART 5 Default

§ 9–501. Default; Procedure When Security Agreement Covers Both Real and Personal Property.

(1) When a debtor is in default under a security agreement, a secured party has the rights and remedies provided in this Part and except as limited by subsection (3) those provided in the security agreement. He may reduce his claim to judgment, foreclose or otherwise enforce the security interest by any available judicial procedure. If the collateral is documents the secured party may proceed either as to the documents or as to the goods covered thereby. A secured party in possession has the rights, remedies and duties provided in Section 9–207. The rights and remedies referred to in this subsection are cumulative.

(2) After default, the debtor has the rights and remedies provided in this Part, those provided in the security agreement and those provided in Section 9–207.

(3) To the extent that they give rights to the debtor and impose duties on the secured party, the rules stated in the subsections referred to below may not be waived or varied except as provided with respect to compulsory disposition of collateral (subsection (3) of Section 9–504 and Section 9–505) and with respect to redemption of collateral (Section 9–506) but the parties may by agreement determine the standards by which the fulfillment of these rights and duties is to be measured if such standards are not manifestly unreasonable:

(a) subsection (2) of Section 9–502 and subsection (2) of Section 9–504 insofar as they require accounting for surplus proceeds of collateral;

(b) subsection (3) of Section 9–504 and subsection (1) of Section 9–505 which deal with disposition of collateral;

(c) subsection (2) of Section 9–505 which deals with acceptance of collateral as discharge of obligation;

(d) Section 9–506 which deals with redemption of collateral; and

(e) subsection (1) of Section 9–507 which deals with the secured party's liability for failure to comply with this Part.

(4) If the security agreement covers both real and personal property, the secured party may proceed under this Part as to the personal property or he may proceed as to both the real and the personal property in accordance with his rights and remedies in respect of the real property in which case the provisions of this Part do not apply.

(5) When a secured party has reduced his claim to judgment the lien of any levy which may be made upon his collateral by virtue of any execution based upon the judgment shall relate back to the date of the perfection of the security interest in such collateral. A judicial sale, pursuant to such execution, is a foreclosure of the security interest by judicial procedure within the meaning of this section, and the secured party may purchase at the sale and thereafter hold the collateral free of any other requirements of this Article.

§ 9–502. Collection Rights of Secured Party.

(1) When so agreed and in any event on default the secured party is entitled to notify an account debtor or the obligor on an instrument to make payment to him whether or not the assignor was theretofore making collections on the collateral, and also to take control of any proceeds to which he is entitled under Section 9–306.

(2) A secured party who by agreement is entitled to charge back uncollected collateral or otherwise to full or limited recourse against the debtor and who undertakes to collect from the account debtors or obligors must proceed in a commercially reasonable manner and may deduct his reasonable expenses of realization from the collections. If the security agreement secures an indebtedness, the secured party must account to the debtor for any surplus, and unless otherwise agreed, the debtor is liable for any deficiency. But, if the underlying transaction was a sale of accounts or chattel paper, the debtor is entitled to any surplus or is liable for any deficiency only if the security agreement so provides.

§ 9–503. Secured Party's Right to Take Possession After Default.

Unless otherwise agreed a secured party has on default the right to take possession of the collateral. In taking possession a secured party may proceed without judicial process if this can be done without breach of the peace or may proceed by action. If the security agreement so provides the secured party may require the debtor to assemble the collateral and make it available to the secured party at a place to be designated by the secured party which is reasonably convenient to both parties. Without removal a secured party may render equipment unusable, and may dispose of collateral on the debtor's premises under Section 9–504.

§ 9–504. Secured Party's Right to Dispose of Collateral After Default; Effect of Disposition.

(1) A secured party after default may sell, lease or otherwise dispose of any or all of the collateral in its then condition or following any commercially reasonable preparation or processing. Any sale of goods is subject to the Article on Sales (Article 2). The proceeds of disposition shall be applied in the order following to

(a) the reasonable expenses of retaking, holding, preparing for sale or lease, selling, leasing and the like and, to the extent provided for in the agreement and not prohibited by law, the reasonable attorneys' fees and legal expenses incurred by the secured party;

(b) the satisfaction of indebtedness secured by the security interest under which the disposition is made;

(c) the satisfaction of indebtedness secured by any subordinate security interest in the collateral if written notification of demand therefor is received before distribution of the proceeds is completed. If requested by the secured party, the holder of a subordinate security interest must seasonably furnish reasonable proof of his interest, and unless he does so, the secured party need not comply with his demand.

(2) If the security interest secures an indebtedness, the secured party must account to the debtor for any surplus, and, unless otherwise agreed, the debtor is liable for any deficiency. But if the underlying transaction was a sale of accounts or chattel paper, the debtor is entitled to any surplus or is liable for any deficiency only if the security agreement so provides.

(3) Disposition of the collateral may be by public or private proceedings and may be made by way of one or more contracts. Sale or other disposition may be as a unit or in parcels and at any time and place and on any terms but every aspect of the disposition including the method, manner, time, place and terms must be commercially reasonable. Unless collateral is perishable or threatens to decline speedily in value or is of a type customarily sold on a recognized market, reasonable notification of the time and place of any public sale or reasonable notification of the time after which any private sale or other intended disposition is to be made shall be sent by the secured party to the debtor, if he has not signed after default a statement renouncing or modifying his right to notification of sale. In the case of consumer goods no other notification need be sent. In other cases notification shall be sent to any other secured party from whom the secured party has received (before sending his notification to the debtor or before the debtor's renunciation of his rights) written notice of a claim of an interest in the collateral. The secured party may buy at any public sale and if the collateral is of a type customarily sold in a recognized market or is of a type which is the subject of widely distributed standard price quotations he may buy at private sale.

(4) When collateral is disposed of by a secured party after default, the disposition transfers to a purchaser for value all of the debtor's rights therein, discharges the security interest under which it is made and any security interest or lien subordinate thereto. The purchaser takes free of all such rights and interests even though the secured party fails to comply with the requirements of this Part or of any judicial proceedings

(a) in the case of a public sale, if the purchaser has no knowledge of any defects in the sale and if he does not buy in collusion with the secured party, other bidders or the person conducting the sale; or

(b) in any other case, if the purchaser acts in good faith.

(5) A person who is liable to a secured party under a guaranty, indorsement, repurchase agreement or the like and who receives a transfer of collateral from the secured party or is subrogated to his rights has thereafter the rights and duties of the secured party. Such a transfer of collateral is not a sale or disposition of the collateral under this Article.

§ 9–505. Compulsory Disposition of Collateral; Acceptance of the Collateral as Discharge of Obligation.

(1) If the debtor has paid sixty per cent of the cash price in the case of a purchase money security interest in consumer goods or sixty per cent of the loan in the case of another security interest in consumer goods, and has not signed after default a statement renouncing or modifying his rights under this Part a secured party who has taken possession of collateral must dispose of it under Section 9–504 and if he fails to do so within ninety days after he takes possession the debtor at his option may recover in conversion or under Section 9–507(1) on secured party's liability.

(2) In any other case involving consumer goods or any other collateral a secured party in possession may, after default, propose to retain the collateral in satisfaction of the obligation. Written notice of such proposal shall be sent to the debtor if he has not signed after default a statement renouncing or modifying his rights under this subsection. In the case of consumer goods no other notice need be given. In other cases notice shall be sent to any other secured party from whom the secured party has received (before sending his notice to the debtor or before the debtor's renunciation of his rights) written notice of a claim of an interest in the collateral. If the secured party receives objection in writing from a person entitled to receive notification within twenty-one days after the notice was sent, the secured party must dispose of the collateral under Section 9–504. In the absence of such written objection the secured party may retain the collateral in satisfaction of the debtor's obligation.

§ 9–506. Debtor's Right to Redeem Collateral.

At any time before the secured party has disposed of collateral or entered into a contract for its disposition under Section 9–504 or before the obligation has been discharged under Section 9–505(2) the debtor or any other secured party may unless otherwise agreed in writing after default redeem the collateral by tendering fulfillment of all obligations secured by the collateral as well as the expenses reasonably incurred by the secured party in retaking, holding and preparing the collateral for disposition, in arranging for the sale, and to the extent provided in the agreement and not prohibited by law, his reasonable attorneys' fees and legal expenses.

§ 9–507. Secured Party's Liability for Failure to Comply With This Part.

(1) If it is established that the secured party is not proceeding in accordance with the provisions of this Part disposition may be ordered or restrained on appropriate terms and conditions. If the disposition has occurred the debtor or any person entitled to notification or whose security interest has been made known to the secured party prior to the disposition has a right to recover from the secured party any loss caused by a failure to comply with the provisions of this Part. If the collateral is consumer goods, the debtor has a right to recover in any event an amount not less than the credit service charge plus ten per cent of the principal amount of the debt or the time price differential plus 10 per cent of the cash price.

(2) The fact that a better price could have been obtained by a sale at a different time or in a different method from that selected by the secured party is not of itself sufficient to establish that the sale was not made in a commercially reasonable manner. If the secured party either sells the collateral in the usual manner in any recognized market therefor or if he sells at the price current in such market at the time of his sale or if he has otherwise sold in conformity with reasonable commercial practices among dealers in the type of property sold he has sold in a commercially reasonable manner. The principles stated in the two preceding sentences with respect to sales also apply as may be appropriate to other types of disposition. A disposition which has been approved in any judicial proceeding or by any bona fide creditors' committee or representative of creditors shall conclusively be deemed to be commercially reasonable, but this sen-

tence does not indicate that any such approval must be obtained in any case nor does it indicate that any disposition not so approved is not commercially reasonable.

ARTICLE 10
EFFECTIVE DATE AND REPEALER

§ 10–101. Effective Date.

This Act shall become effective at midnight on December 31st following its enactment. It applies to transactions entered into and events occurring after that date.

§ 10–102. Specific Repealer; Provision for Transition.

(1) The following acts and all other acts and parts of acts inconsistent herewith are hereby repealed: (Here should follow the acts to be specifically repealed including the following:

Uniform Negotiable Instruments Act
Uniform Warehouse Receipts Act
Uniform Sales Act
Uniform Bills of Lading Act
Uniform Stock Transfer Act
Uniform Conditional Sales Act
Uniform Trust Receipts Act
Also any acts regulating:
Bank collections
Bulk sales
Chattel mortgages
Conditional sales
Factor's lien acts
Farm storage of grain and similar acts
Assignment of accounts receivable)

(2) Transactions validly entered into before the effective date specified in Section 10–101 and the rights, duties and interests flowing from them remain valid thereafter and may be terminated, completed, consummated or enforced as required or permitted by any statute or other law amended or repealed by this Act as though such repeal or amendment had not occurred.

Note: *Subsection (1) should be separately prepared for each state. The foregoing is a list of statutes to be checked.*

§ 10–103. General Repealer.

Except as provided in the following section, all acts and parts of acts inconsistent with this Act are hereby repealed.

§ 10–104. Laws Not Repealed.

(1) The Article on Documents of Title (Article 7) does not repeal or modify any laws prescribing the form or contents of documents of title or the services or facilities to be afforded by bailees, or otherwise regulating bailees' businesses in respects not specifically dealt with herein; but the fact that such laws are violated does not affect the status of a document of title which otherwise complies with the definition of a document of title (Section 1–201).

[(2) This Act does not repeal ____________ *, cited as the Uniform Act for the Simplification of Fiduciary Security Transfers, and if in any respect there is any inconsistency between that Act and the Article of this Act on investment securities (Article 8) the provisions of the former Act shall control.]

Note: *At * in subsection (2) insert the statutory reference to the Uniform Act for the Simplification of Fiduciary Security Transfers if such Act has previously been enacted. If it has not been enacted, omit subsection (2).*

ARTICLE 11
(REPORTERS' DRAFT) EFFECTIVE DATE AND TRANSITION PROVISIONS

This material has been numbered Article 11 to distinguish it from Article 10, the transition provision of the 1962 Code, which may still remain in effect in some states to cover transition problems from pre-Code law to the original Uniform Commercial Code. Adaptation may be necessary in particular states. The terms "[old Code]" and "[new Code]" and "[old U.C.C.]" and "[new U.C.C.]" are used herein, and should be suitably changed in each state.

Note: This draft was prepared by the Reporters and has not been passed upon by the Review Committee, the Permanent Editorial Board, the American Law Institute, or the National Conference of Commissioners on Uniform State Laws. It is submitted as a working draft which may be adapted as appropriate in each state.

§ 11–101. Effective Date.

This Act shall become effective at 12:01 A.M. on ____________, 19 ____________.

§ 11–102. Preservation of Old Transition Provision.

The provisions of [here insert reference to the original transition provision in the particular state] shall continue to apply to [the new U.C.C.] and for this purpose the [old U.C.C. and new U.C.C.] shall be considered one continuous statute.

§ 11–103. Transition to [New Code]—General Rule.

Transactions validly entered into after [effective date of old U.C.C.] and before [effective date of new U.C.C.], and which were subject to the provisions of [old U.C.C.] and which would be subject to this Act as amended if they had been entered into after the effective date of [new U.C.C.] and the rights, duties and interests flowing from such transactions remain valid after the latter date and may be terminated, completed, consummated or enforced as required or permitted by the [new U.C.C.]. Security interests arising out of such transactions which are perfected when [new U.C.C.] becomes effective shall remain perfected until they lapse as provided in [new U.C.C.], and may be continued as permitted by [new U.C.C.], except as stated in Section 11–105.

§ 11–104. Transition Provision on Change of Requirement of Filing.

A security interest for the perfection of which filing or the taking of possession was required under [old U.C.C.] and which attached prior to the effective date of [new U.C.C.] but was not perfected shall be deemed perfected on the effective date of [new U.C.C.] if [new U.C.C.] permits perfection without filing or authorizes filing in the office or offices where a prior ineffective filing was made.

§ 11–105. Transition Provision on Change of Place of Filing.

(1) A financing statement or continuation statement filed prior to [effective date of new U.C.C.] which shall not have lapsed prior to [the effective date of new U.C.C.] which shall remain effective for the period provided in the [old Code], but not less than five years after the filing.

(2) With respect to any collateral acquired by the debtor subsequent to the effective date of [new U.C.C.], any effective financing statement or continuation statement described in this section shall apply only if the filing or filings are in the office or offices that would be appropriate to perfect the security interests in the new collateral under [new U.C.C.].

(3) The effectiveness of any financing statement or continuation statement filed prior to [effective date of new U.C.C.] may be continued by a continuation statement as permitted by [new U.C.C.], except that if [new U.C.C.] requires a filing in an office where there was no previous financing statement, a new financing statement conforming to Section 11–106 shall be filed in that office.

(4) If the record of a mortgage of real estate would have been effective as a fixture filing of goods described therein if [new U.C.C.] had been in effect on the date of recording the mortgage, the mortgage shall be deemed effective as a fixture filing as to such goods under subsection (6) of Section 9–402 of the [new U.C.C.] on the effective date of [new U.C.C.].

§ 11–106. Required Refilings.

(1) If a security interest is perfected or has priority when this Act takes effect as to all persons or as to certain persons without any filing or recording, and if the filing of a financing statement would be required for the perfection or priority of the security interest against those persons under [new U.C.C.], the perfection and priority rights of the security interest continue until 3 years after the effective date of [new U.C.C.]. The perfection will then lapse unless a financing statement is filed as provided in subsection (4) or unless the security interest is perfected otherwise than by filing.

(2) If a security interest is perfected when [new U.C.C.] takes effect under a law other than [U.C.C.] which requires no further filing, refiling or recording to continue its perfection, perfection continues until and will lapse 3 years after [new U.C.C.] takes effect, unless a financing statement is filed as provided in subsection (4) or unless the security interest is perfected otherwise than by filing, or unless under subsection (3) of Section 9–302 the other law continues to govern filing.

(3) If a security interest is perfected by a filing, refiling or recording under a law repealed by this Act which required further filing, refiling or recording to continue its perfection, perfection continues and will lapse on the date provided by the law so repealed for such further filing, refiling, or recording unless a financing statement is filed as provided in subsection (4) or unless the security interest is perfected otherwise than by filing.

(4) A financing statement may be filed within six months before the perfection of a security interest would otherwise lapse. Any such financing statement may be signed by either the debtor or the secured party. It must identify the security agreement, statement or notice (however denominated in any statute or other law repealed or modified by this Act), state the office where and the date when the last filing, refiling or recording, if any, was made with respect thereto, and the filing number, if any, or book and page, if any, of recording and further state that the security agreement, statement or notice, however denominated, in another filing office under the [U.C.C.] or under any statute or other law repealed or modified by this Act is still effective. Section 9–401 and Section 9–103 determine the proper place to file such a financing statement. Except as specified in this subsection, the provisions of Section 9–403(3) for continuation statements apply to such a financing statement.

§ 11–107. Transition Provisions as to Priorities.

Except as otherwise provided in [Article 11], [old U.C.C.] shall apply to any questions of priority if the positions of the parties were fixed prior to the effective date of [new U.C.C.]. In other cases questions of priority shall be determined by [new U.C.C.].

§ 11–108. Presumption that Rule of Law Continues Unchanged.

Unless a change in law has clearly been made, the provisions of [new U.C.C.] shall be deemed declaratory of the meaning of the [old U.C.C.].

GLOSSARY

Accepted check A check that the drawee bank has signed. This signature is a promise that the bank will pay the check out of its own funds. (Chapter 24)

Accession The use of labor and/or materials to add value to the personal property of another. (Chapter 47)

Accommodation party Someone who does not benefit from an instrument but agrees to guarantee its payment. (Chapter 24)

Accord and satisfaction An agreement to settle a debt for less than the sum claimed. (Chapter 12)

Accounts Any right to receive payment for goods sold or leased, other than rights covered by chattel paper or instruments. (Chapter 26)

Accredited investor Under the Securities Act of 1933, an accredited investor is an institution (such as a bank or insurance company) or any individual with a net worth of more than $1 million or an annual income of more than $200,000. (Chapter 38)

Acquit To find the defendant not guilty of the crime for which he was tried. (Chapter 7)

Act of State doctrine A rule requiring American courts to abstain from cases if a court order would interfere with the ability of the President or Congress to conduct foreign policy. (Chapter 8)

Actus reus The guilty act. The prosecution must show that a criminal defendant committed some proscribed act. In a murder prosecution, taking another person's life is the *actus reus*. (Chapter 7)

Adhesion contract A standard form contract prepared by one party and presented to the other on a "take it or leave it" basis. (Chapter 13)

Adjudicate To hold a formal hearing in a disputed matter and issue an official decision. (Chapter 3)

Administrative law Concerns all agencies, boards, commissions, and other entities created by a federal or state legislature and charged with investigating, regulating, and adjudicating a particular industry or issue. (Chapter 1)

Administrator A person appointed by the court to oversee the probate process for someone who has died intestate (that is, without a will). (Chapter 48)

Administratrix A female administrator. (Chapter 48)

Adverse possession A means of gaining ownership of land belonging to another by entering upon the property, openly and notoriously, and claiming exclusive use of it for a period of years. (Chapter 45)

Affidavit A written statement signed under oath. (Chapter 7)

Affirm A decision by an appellate court to uphold the judgment of a lower court. (Chapter 1)

Affirmative action A plan introduced in a workplace for the purpose of either remedying the effects of past discrimination or achieving equitable representation of minorities and women. (Chapter 30)

After-acquired property Items that a debtor obtains after making a security agreement with the secured party. (Chapter 26)

Agent A person who acts for a principal. (Chapter 7)

Alternative dispute resolution Any method of resolving a legal conflict other than litigation, such as: negotiation, arbitration, mediation, mini-trials, and summary jury trials. (Chapter 2)

Amendment Any addition to a legal document. The constitutional amendments, the first ten of which are known collectively as the Bill of Rights, secure numerous liberties and protections directly for the people. (Chapter 1)

Annual report Each year, public companies must send their shareholders an annual report that contains detailed financial data. (Chapter 37)

Answer The pleading, filed by the defendant in court and served on the plaintiff, which responds to each allegation in the plaintiff's complaint. (Chapter 2)

Apparent authority A situation in which conduct of a principal causes a third party to believe that the principal consents to have an act done on his behalf by a person purporting to act for him when, in fact, that person is not acting for the principal. (Chapter 29)

Appellant The party who appeals a lower court decision to a higher court. (Chapter 2)

Appellate court Any court in a state or federal system that reviews cases that have already been tried. (Chapter 2)

Appellee The party opposing an appeal from a lower court to a higher court. (Chapter 2)

Arbitration A form of alternative dispute resolution in which the parties hire a neutral third party to hear their respective arguments, receive evidence, and then make a binding decision. (Chapter 2)

Arson Malicious use of fire or explosives to damage or destroy real estate or personal property. (Chapter 7)

Assault An intentional act that causes the plaintiff to fear an imminent battery. (Chapter 5)

Assignee The party who receives an assignment of contract rights from a party to the contract. (Chapter 16)

Assignment The act by which a party transfers contract rights to a third person. (Chapter 16)

Assignor The party who assigns contract rights to a third person. (Chapter 16)

Attachment A court order seizing property of a party to a civil action, so that there will be sufficient assets available to pay the judgment. (Chapter 4)

Authorized and unissued stock Stock that has been approved by the corporation's charter, but has not yet been sold. (Chapter 35)

Authorized and issued stock Stock that has been approved by the corporation's charter and subsequently sold. (Chapter 35)

Bailee A person who rightfully possesses goods belonging to another. (Chapter 13)

Bailment Giving possession and control of personal property to another person. (Chapter 13)

Bailor One who creates a bailment by delivering goods to another. (Chapter 13)

Battery The intentional touching of another person in a way that is unwanted or offensive. (Chapter 5)

Bearer paper An instrument payable "to bearer." Any holder in due course can demand payment. (Chapter 23)

Bilateral contract A binding agreement in which each party has made a promise to the other. (Chapter 10)

Bill of lading A receipt for goods, given by a carrier such as a ship, that minutely describes the merchandise being shipped. A **negotiable** bill of lading may be transferred to other parties, and entitles any holder to collect the goods. (Chapter 8)

Bill of Rights The first ten amendments to the Constitution. (Chapter 4)

Bill A proposed statute that has been submitted for consideration to Congress or a state legislature. (Chapter 3)

Blue sky laws State securities laws. (Chapter 38)

Bona fide occupational qualification A job requirement that would otherwise be discriminatory is permitted in situations in which it is *essential* to the position in question. (Chapter 30)

Bona fide purchaser Someone who buys goods in good faith, for value, typically from a seller who has merely voidable title. (Chapter 20)

Bonds Long-term debt secured by some of the issuing company's assets. (Chapter 35)

Brief The written legal argument that an attorney files with an appeal court. (Chapter 2)

Bulk sale A transfer of most or all of a merchant's assets. (Chapter 20)

Burden of proof The allocation of which party must prove its case. In a civil case, the plaintiff has the burden of proof to persuade the factfinder of every element of her case. In a criminal case, the government has the burden of proof. (Chapter 2)

Business judgment rule A common law rule that protects managers from liability if they are acting without a conflict of interest, and make informed decisions that have a rational business purpose. (Chapter 36)

Buyer in ordinary course of business Someone who buys goods in good faith from a seller who routinely deals in such goods. (Chapter 26)

Bylaws A document that specifies the organizational rules of a corporation or other organization, such as the date of the annual meeting and the required number of directors. (Chapter 35)

Capacity The legal ability to enter into a contract. (Chapter 10)

Certificate of deposit An instrument issued by a bank which promises to repay a deposit, with interest, on a specified date. (Chapter 23)

Certified check A check that the drawee bank has signed. This signature is a promise that the bank will pay the check out of its own funds. (Chapter 24)

***Certiorari*, writ of** Formal notice from the United States Supreme Court that it will accept a case for review. (Chapter 2)

Challenge for cause An attorney's request, during *voir dire*, to excuse a prospective juror because of apparent bias. (Chapter 2)

Chancery, court of In medieval England, the court originally operated by the Chancellor. (Chapter 1)

Charging order A court order granting the creditor of a partner the right to receive that partner's share of partnership profits. (Chapter 34)

Chattel paper Any writing that indicates two things: (1) a debtor owes money and (2) a secured party has a security interest in specific goods. The most common chattel paper is a document indicating a consumer sale on credit. (Chapter 26)

Check An instrument in which the drawer orders the drawee bank to pay money to the payee. (Chapter 23)

Chicago School A theory of antitrust law first developed at the University of Chicago. Adherents to this theory believe that antitrust enforcement should focus on promoting efficiency and should not generally be concerned about the size or number of competitors in any market. (Chapter 40)

CISG *See* Convention on Contracts for the International Sale of Goods. (Chapter 11)

Civil law The large body of law concerning the rights and duties between parties. It is distinguished from criminal law, which concerns behavior outlawed by a government. (Chapter 1)

Class action A method of litigating a civil lawsuit in which one or more plaintiffs (or occasionally defendants) seek to represent an entire group of people with similar claims against a common opponent. (Chapter 2)

Classification The process by which the Customs Service decides what label to attach to imported merchandise, and therefore what level of tariff to impose. (Chapter 8)

Close corporation A corporation with a small number of shareholders. Its stock is not publicly traded. (Chapter 32)

Codicil An amendment to a will. (Chapter 48)

Collateral The property subject to a security interest. (Chapter 26)

Collateral promises A promise to pay the debt of another person, as a favor to the debtor. (Chapter 15)

Collective bargaining Contract negotiations between an employer and a union. (Chapter 31)

Collective bargaining unit The precisely defined group of employees who are represented by a particular union. (Chapter 31)

Comity A doctrine that requires a court to abstain from hearing a case out of respect for another court that also has jurisdiction. **International comity** demands that an American court refuse to hear a case in which a foreign court shares jurisdiction if there is a conflict between the laws and if it is more logical for the foreign court to take the case. (Chapter 8)

Commerce clause One of the powers granted by Article I, §8 of the Constitution, it gives Congress exclusive power to regulate international commerce and concurrent power with the states to regulate domestic commerce. (Chapter 4)

Commercial impracticability After the creation of a contract, an entirely unforeseen event occurs which makes enforcement of the contract extraordinarily unfair. (Chapter 17)

Commercial paper Instruments such as checks and promissory notes that contain a promise to pay money. Commercial paper includes both negotiable and non-negotiable instruments. (Chapter 23)

Commercial speech Communication, such as television advertisements, that has the dominant theme of proposing a commercial transaction. (Chapter 4)

Common carrier A transportation company that makes its services available on a regular basis to the general public. (Chapter 47)

Common law Judge-made law, that is, the body of all decisions made by appellate courts over the years. (Chapter 1)

Common stock Certificates that reflect ownership in a corporation. Owners of this equity security are last in line for corporate pay-outs such as dividends and liquidation proceeds. (Chapter 35)

Comparative negligence A rule of tort law that permits a plaintiff to recover even when the defendant can show that the plaintiff's own conduct contributed in some way to her harm. (Chapter 6)

Compensatory damages Those that flow directly from the contract. (Chapter 18)

Complaint A pleading, filed by the plaintiff, providing a short statement of the claim. (Chapter 2)

Concerted action Tactics, such as a strike, used by a union to gain a bargaining advantage. (Chapter 31)

Condition A condition is an event that must occur in order for a party to be obligated under a contract. (Chapter 17)

Condition precedent A condition that must occur before a particular contract duty arises. (Chapter 17)

Condition subsequent A condition that must occur after a particular contract duty arises, or the duty will be discharged. (Chapter 17)

Confiscation Expropriation without adequate compensation of property owned by foreigners. (Chapter 8)

Conforming goods Items that satisfy the contract terms. If a contract call for blue sailboats, then green sailboats are non-conforming. (Chapter 22)

Consent order An agreement entered into by a wrongdoer and an administrative agency (such as the Securities and Exchange Commission or the Federal Trade Commission) in which the wrongdoer agrees not to violate the law in the future. (Chapter 42)

Consequential damages Those resulting from the unique circumstances of *this injured party*. (Chapter 18)

Consideration In contract law, something of legal value that has been bargained for and given in exchange by the parties. (Chapter 12)

Constitution The supreme law of a political entity. The United States Constitution is the highest law in the country. (Chapter 1)

Constructive trust If someone wrongfully obtains ownership of property, he is deemed to be holding that property for the benefit of the real owner. (Chapter 48)

Contract A legally enforceable promise or set of promises. (Chapter 10)

Contract carrier A transportation company that does not make its services available to the general public but engages in continuing agreements with particular customers. (Chapter 47)

Contributory negligence A rule of tort law that permits a negligent defendant to escape liability if she can demonstrate that the plaintiff's own conduct contributed in any way to the plaintiff's harm. (Chapter 6)

Control security Stock owned by any officer or director of the issuer, or by any shareholder who holds more than 10 percent of a class of stock of the issuer. (Chapter 38)

Convention on Contracts for the International Sale of Goods A United Nations sponsored agreement that creates a neutral body of law for sale of goods contracts between companies from different countries. (Chapter 11)

Conversion A tort committed by taking or using someone else's personal property without his permission. (Chapter 5)

Copyright Under federal law, the holder of a copyright owns a particular expression of an idea, but not the idea itself. This ownership right applies to creative activities such as literature, music, drama, and software. (Chapter 44)

Corporation by estoppel Even if a corporation has not actually been formed, courts will sometimes enforce contracts entered into in the belief that the corporation did indeed exist. (Chapter 35)

Counter-claim A claim made by the defendant against the plaintiff. (Chapter 2)

Cover The buyer's right to obtain substitute goods when a seller has breached a contract. (Chapter 2)

Creditor beneficiary When one party to a contract intends to benefit a third party to whom he owes a debt, that third party is referred to as a creditor beneficiary. (Chapter 16)

Criminal law Rules that permit a government to punish certain behavior by fine or imprisonment. (Chapter 1)

Cross-examination During a hearing, for a lawyer to question an opposing witness. (Chapter 2)

Cure The seller's right to respond to a buyer's rejection of non-conforming goods; the seller accomplishes this by delivering conforming goods before the contract deadline. (Chapter 22)

Cy pres A doctrine that permits a court to change a trust's purpose if the original objective is no longer suitable, possible, or legal. (Chapter 48)

Damages (1) The harm that a plaintiff complains of at trial, such as an injury to her person, or money lost because of a contract breach. (2) Money awarded by a trial court for injury suffered. (Chapter 5)

***De facto* corporation** Occurs when a promoter makes a good faith effort to incorporate (although fails to complete the process entirely) and uses the corporation to conduct business. The state can challenge the validity of the corporation, but a third party cannot. (Chapter 35)

***De jure* corporation** The promoter of the corporation has substantially complied with the requirements for incorporation, but has made some minor error. No one has the right to challenge the validity of the corporation. (Chapter 35)

De novo The power of an appellate court or appellate agency to make a new decision in a matter under appeal, entirely ignoring the findings and conclusions of the lower court or agency official. (Chapter 3)

Debentures Long-term, unsecured debt, typically issued by a corporation. (Chapter 35)

Debtor A person who owes money or some other obligation to another party. (Chapter 26)

Decedent A person who has died. (Chapter 48)

Defamation The act of injuring someone's reputation by stating something false about her to a third person. *Libel* is defamation done either in writing or by broadcast. *Slander* is defamation done orally. (Chapter 5)

Default The failure to perform an obligation, such as the failure to pay money when due. (Chapter 26)

Default judgment Court order awarding one party everything it requested because the opposing party failed to respond in time. (Chapter 2)

Default rules Under the Uniform Partnership Act, these rules govern the relationship among the partners unless the partners explicitly make a different agreement. (Chapter 33)

Definiteness A doctrine holding that a contract will only be enforced if its terms are sufficiently precise that a court can determine what the parties meant. (Chapter 11)

Delegation The act by which a party to a contract transfers duties to a third person who is not a party to the contract. (Chapter 16)

Deponent The person being questioned in a deposition. (Chapter 2)

Deposition A form of discovery in which a party's attorney has the right to ask oral questions of the other party or of a witness. Answers are given under oath. (Chapter 2)

Derivative action A lawsuit brought by shareholders in the name of the corporation to enforce a right of the corporation. (Chapter 37)

Deterrence Using punishment, such as imprisonment, to discourage criminal behavior. (Chapter 7)

Devisee Someone who inherits under a will. (Chapter 48)

Direct examination During a hearing, for a lawyer to question his own witness. (Chapter 2)

Directed verdict The decision by a court to instruct a jury that it must find in favor of a particular party because, in the judge's opinion, no reasonable person could disagree on the outcome. (Chapter 2)

Disaffirmance The act of notifying the other party to a contract that the party giving the notice refuses to be bound by the agreement. (Chapter 14)

Discharge (1) A party to a contract has no more duties. (2) A party to an instrument is released from liability. (Chapter 17)

Disclaimer A statement that a particular warranty does not apply. (Chapter 21)

Discovery A stage in litigation, after all pleadings have been served, in which each party seeks as much relevant information as possible about the opposing party's case. (Chapter 2)

Dishonor An obligor refuses to pay an instrument that is due. (Chapter 24)

Dismiss To terminate a lawsuit, often on procedural grounds, without reaching the merits of the case. (Chapter 2)

Dissociation A dissociation occurs when a partner leaves a partnership. (Chapter 33)

Diversity jurisdiction One of the two main types of civil cases that a United States district court has the power to hear. It involves a lawsuit between citizens of different states, in which at least one party makes a claim for more than $50,000. (Chapter 2)

Domestic corporation A corporation is a domestic corporation in the state in which it was formed. (Chapter 35)

Donee A person who receives a gift. (Chapter 47)

Donee beneficiary When one party to a contract intends to make a gift to a third party, that third party is referred to as a donee beneficiary. (Chapter 16)

Donor A person who makes a gift to another. (Chapter 47)

Draft The drawer of this instrument orders someone else to pay money. Checks are the most common form of draft. The drawer of a check orders a bank to pay money. (Chapter 23)

Drawee The person who pays a draft. In the case of a check, the bank is the drawee. (Chapter 23)

Drawer The person who issues a draft. (Chapter 23)

Due Process Clause Part of the Fifth Amendment. *Procedural due process* ensures that before depriving anyone of liberty or property, the government must go through procedures which ensure that the deprivation is fair. *Substantive due process* holds that certain rights, such as privacy, are so fundamental that the government may not eliminate them. (Chapter 4)

Dumping Selling merchandise at one price in the domestic market and at a cheaper, unfair price in an international market. (Chapter 8)

Durable power of attorney An instrument that permits an attorney-in-fact to act for a principal. A durable power is effective until the principal revokes it or dies. It continues in effect even if the principal becomes incapacitated. (Chapter 48)

Duress (1) A criminal defense in which the defendant shows that she committed the wrongful act because a third person threatened her with imminent physical harm. (2) An improper threat made to force another party to enter into a contract. (Chapter 7)

Duty A tax imposed on imported items. (Chapter 8)

Easement The right to enter land belonging to another and make a limited use of it, without taking anything away. (Chapter 45)

Economic loss doctrine A common law rule holding that when an injury is purely economic, and arises from a contract made between two businesses, the injured party may only sue under the UCC. (Chapter 21)

Element A fact that a party to a lawsuit must prove in order to prevail. (Chapter 5)

Embezzlement Fraudulent conversion of property already in the defendant's possession. (Chapter 7)

Eminent domain The power of the government to take private property for public use. (Chapter 4)

Employee at will A worker whose job does not have a specified duration. (Chapter 30)

Enabling legislation A statute authorizing the creation of a new administrative agency and specifying its powers and duties. (Chapter 3)

Entrapment A criminal defense in which the defendant demonstrates that the government induced him to break the law. (Chapter 7)

Equal Protection Clause Part of the Fourteenth Amendment, it generally requires the government to treat equally situated people the same. (Chapter 4)

Equity The broad powers of a court to fashion a remedy where justice demands it and no common law remedy exists. An injunction is an example of an equitable remedy. (Chapter 1)

Error of law A mistake made by a trial judge that concerns a legal issue as opposed to a factual matter. Permitting too many leading questions is a legal error; choosing to believe one witness rather than another is a factual matter. (Chapter 2)

Estate The legal entity that holds title to assets after the owner dies and before the property is distributed. (Chapter 48)

Estoppel Out of fairness, a person is denied the right to assert a claim. (Chapter 29)

Evidence, rules of Law governing the proof offered during a trial or formal hearing. These rules limit the questions that may be asked of witnesses and the introduction of physical objects. (Chapter 2)

Exclusionary rule In a criminal trial, a ban on the use of evidence obtained in violation of the Constitution. (Chapter 7)

Exclusive dealing agreement A potential violation of §1 of the Sherman Act, in which a distributor or retailer agrees with a supplier not to carry the products of any other supplier. (Chapter 41)

Exculpatory clause A contract provision that attempts to release one party from liability in the event the other party is injured. (Chapter 13)

Executed contract A binding agreement in which all parties have fulfilled all obligations. (Chapter 10)

Executive agency An administrative agency within the executive branch of government. (Chapter 3)

Executive order An order by a president or governor, having the full force of law. (Chapter 1)

Executor A person chosen by the decedent to oversee the probate process. (Chapter 15)

Executory contract A binding agreement in which one or more of the parties has not fulfilled its obligations. (Chapter 10)

Executrix A female executor. (Chapter 48)

Exhaustion of remedies A principle of administrative law that no party may appeal an agency action to a court until she has utilized all available appeals within the agency itself. (Chapter 3)

Expectation interest A remedy in a contract case that puts the injured party in the position he would have been in had both sides fully performed. (Chapter 18)

Expert witness A witness in a court case who has special training or qualifications to discuss a specific issue, and who is generally permitted to state an opinion. (Chapter 2)

Express authority Conduct of a principal that, reasonably interpreted, causes the agent to believe that the principal desires him to do a specific act. (Chapter 29)

Express contract A binding agreement in which the parties explicitly state all important terms. (Chapter 10)

Express warranty A guarantee, created by the words or actions of the seller, that goods will meet certain standards. (Chapter 21)

Expropriation A government's seizure of property or companies owned by foreigners. (Chapter 8)

Factfinder The one responsible, during a trial, for deciding what occurred, that is, who did what to whom, when, how, and why. It is either the jury or, in a jury-waived case, the judge. (Chapter 4)

Fair representation, duty of The union's obligation to act on behalf of all members impartially and in good faith. (Chapter 31)

False imprisonment The intentional restraint of another person without reasonable cause and without her consent. (Chapter 5)

Federal question jurisdiction One of the two main types of civil cases that a United States district court has the power to hear. It involves a federal statute or a constitutional provision. (Chapter 2)

Federalism A form of national government in which power is shared between one central authority and numerous local authorities. (Chapter 1)

Fee simple absolute The greatest possible ownership right in real property, including the right to possess, use, and dispose of the property in any lawful manner. (Chapter 45)

Fee simple defeasible Ownership interest in real property that may terminate upon the occurrence of some limiting event. (Chapter 45)

Felony The most serious crimes, typically those for which the defendant could be imprisoned for more than a year. (Chapter 7)

Fiduciary duty An obligation to behave in a trustworthy and confidential fashion toward the object of that duty. (Chapter 28)

Financing statement A document that a secured party files to give the general public notice that the secured party has a secured interest in the collateral. (Chapter 26)

Firm offer A contract offer that cannot be withdrawn during a stated period. (Chapter 11)

Fixtures Goods that are attached to real estate. (Chapter 26)

Foreign corporation A corporation formed in another state. (Chapter 35)

Foreign Sovereign Immunity Act A federal statute that protects other nations from suit in courts of the

United States, except under specified circumstances. (Chapter 8)

Formal rulemaking The process whereby an administrative agency notifies the public of a proposed new rule and then permits a formal hearing, with opportunity for evidence and cross-examination, before promulgating the final rule. (Chapter 3)

Founding Fathers The authors of the United States Constitution, who participated in the Constitutional Convention in Philadelphia in 1787. (Chapter 1)

Framers *See* Founding Fathers. (Chapter 4)

Franchise An arrangement in which the franchisee buys from a franchiser the right to establish a business using the franchiser's trade name and selling the franchiser's products. Typically the franchiser also trains the franchisee in the proper operation of the business. (Chapter 32)

Fraud Deception of another person to obtain money or property from her. (Chapter 5)

Freedom of Information Act (FOIA) A federal statute giving private citizens and corporations access to many of the documents possessed by an administrative agency. (Chapter 3)

Freehold estate The present right to possess property and to use it in any lawful manner. (Chapter 45)

Frustration of purpose After the creation of a contract, an entirely unforeseen event occurs that eliminates the value of the contract for one of the parties. (Chapter 17)

Fully disclosed principal If the third party in an agency relationship knows the identity of the principal, that principal is fully disclosed. (Chapter 29)

Fundamental rights In constitutional law, those rights that are so basic that any governmental interference with them is suspect and likely to be unconstitutional. (Chapter 4)

GAAP Generally accepted accounting principles. Rules set by the Financial Accounting Standards Board to be used in preparing financial statements. (Chapter 39)

GAAS Generally accepted auditing standards. Rules set by the American Institute of Certified Public Accountants (AICPA) to be used in conducting audits. (Chapter 39)

GATT *See* General Agreement on Tariffs and Trade. (Chapter 8)

General Agreement on Tariffs and Trade (GATT) A massive international treaty, negotiated in stages between the 1940s and 1994 and signed by over 130 nations. (Chapter 8)

General deterrence *See* Deterrence. (Chapter 7)

General intangibles Potential sources of income such as copyrights, patents, trademarks, goodwill and certain other rights to payment. (Chapter 26)

Gift A voluntary transfer of property from one person to another without consideration. (Chapter 47)

Gift *causa mortis* A gift made in contemplation of approaching death. (Chapter 47)

Goods Anything movable, except for money, securities, and certain legal rights. (Chapter 26)

Grantee The person who receives property, or some interest in it, from the owner. (Chapter 45)

Grantor (1) An owner who conveys property, or some interest in it. (2) Someone who creates a trust. (Chapter 45)

Greenmail If a company is threatened with a hostile takeover, its board of directors may offer to buy the stock of the attacker at an above-market price with the hope that the attacker will take her profits and leave the company alone. (Chapter 36)

Harmless error A ruling made by a trial court which an appeals court determines was legally wrong but not fatal to the decision. (Chapter 2)

Heir Someone who inherits from a decedent who died intestate (that is, without a will). (Chapter 48)

Holder in due course Someone who has given value for an instrument, in good faith, without notice of outstanding claims or other defenses. (Chapter 23)

Holographic will A handwritten will that has not been witnessed. (Chapter 48)

Horizontal agreement or merger An agreement or merger between two potential competitors. (Chapter 40)

Hybrid rulemaking A method of administrative agency procedure incorporating some elements of formal and some elements of informal rulemaking, typically involving a limited public hearing with restricted rights of testimony and cross-examination. (Chapter 3)

Identify In sales law, to designate the specific goods that are the subject of a contract. (Chapter 22)

Illegal contract An agreement that is void because it violates a statute or public policy. (Chapter 13)

Illusory promise An apparent promise that is unenforceable because the promisor makes no firm commitment. (Chapter 12)

Implied authority When a principal directs an agent to undertake a transaction, the agent has the right to do acts that are incidental to it, usually accompany it, or are reasonably necessary to accomplish it. (Chapter 29)

Implied contract A binding agreement created not by explicit language but by the informal words and conduct of the parties. (Chapter 10)

Implied warranty Guarantees created by the Uniform Commercial Code and imposed on the seller of goods. (Chapter 21)

Implied warranty of habitability A landlord must meet all standards set by the local building code, or otherwise ensure that the premises are fit for human habitation. (Chapter 45)

Import To transport goods or services into a country. (Chapter 8)

In camera "In the judge's chambers," meaning that the judge does something out of view of the jury and the public. (Chapter 2)

Incidental damages The relatively minor costs, such as storage and advertising, that the injured party suffered when responding to a contract breach. (Chapter 18)

Incorporator The person who signs a corporate charter. (Chapter 35)

Indemnification A promise to pay someone else's obligations. (Chapter 28)

Independent agency An administrative agency outside the executive branch of government, such as the Interstate Commerce Commission. (Chapter 3)

Independent contractor Someone who undertakes tasks for others and whose work is not closely controlled. (Chapter 29)

Indictment The government's formal charge that a defendant has committed a crime. (Chapter 7)

Indorser Anyone, other than the issuer or acceptor, who signs an instrument. (Chapter 24)

Infliction of emotional distress A tort. It can be the *intentional infliction of emotional distress,* meaning that the defendant behaved outrageously and deliberately caused the plaintiff severe psychological injury, or it can be the *negligent infliction of emotional distress,* meaning that the defendant's conduct violated the rules of negligence. (Chapter 5)

Informal rulemaking The process whereby an administrative agency notifies the public of a proposed new rule and permits comment but is then free to promulgate the final rule without a public hearing. (Chapter 3)

Initial public offering (IPO) A company's first public sale of securities. (Chapter 38)

Injunction A court order that a person either do or stop doing something. (Chapter 1)

Instructions or charge The explanation given by a judge to a jury, outlining the jury's task in deciding a lawsuit and the underlying rules of law the jury should use in reaching its decision. (Chapter 2)

Instruments Drafts, checks, certificates of deposit and notes. (Chapter 26)

Insurable interest A person has an insurable interest if she would be harmed by the danger that she has insured against. (Chapter 13)

Insured A person whose loss is the subject of an insurance policy. (Chapter 49)

Insurer The person who issues an insurance policy. (Chapter 49)

Integrated contract A writing that the parties intend as the complete and final expression of their agreement. (Chapter 15)

Intentional tort An act deliberately performed that violates a legally imposed duty and injures someone. (Chapter 5)

***Inter vivos* gift** A gift made "during life," that is, when the donor is not under any fear of impending death. (Chapter 47)

***Inter vivos* trust** A trust established while the grantor is still living. (Chapter 47)

Interest A legal right in something, such as ownership or a mortgage or a tenancy. (Chapter 48)

Interference with a contract *See* Tortious interference with a contract. (Chapter 5)

Interference with a prospective advantage *See* Tortious interference with a prospective advantage. (Chapter 5)

Interpretive rules A formal statement by an administrative agency expressing its view of what existing statutes or regulations mean. (Chapter 3)

Interrogatory A form of discovery in which one party sends to an opposing party written questions that must be answered under oath. (Chapter 2)

Intestate Without a will. (Chapter 48)

Inventory Goods that the seller is holding for sale or lease in the ordinary course of its business. (Chapter 26)

Invitee Someone who has the right to be on property, such as a customer in a shop. (Chapter 6)

Issue All direct descendants such as children, grandchildren, and so on. (Chapter 1)

Issuer The maker of a promissory note or the drawer of a draft. (Chapter 23)

Joint and several liability All members of a group are liable. They can be sued as a group, or any one of them can be sued individually for the full amount owing. (Chapter 34)

Joint liability All members of a group are liable and must be sued together. (Chapter 34)

Joint venture A partnership for a limited purpose. (Chapter 32)

Judgment *non obstante verdicto* (n.o.v.) "Judgment notwithstanding the verdict." A trial judge overturns the verdict of the jury and enters a judgment in favor of the opposing party. (Chapter 2)

Judicial activism The willingness shown by certain courts (and not by others) to decide issues of public policy, such as constitutional questions (free speech, equal protection, etc.) and matters of contract fairness (promissory estoppel, unconscionability, etc.). (Chapter 4)

Judicial restraint A court's preference to abstain from adjudicating major social issues and to leave such matters to legislatures. (Chapter 4)

Judicial review The power of the judicial system to examine, interpret, and even nullify actions taken by another branch of government. (Chapter 3)

Jurisdiction The power of a court to hear a particular dispute, civil or criminal, and to make a binding decision. (Chapter 2)

Jurisprudence The study of the purposes and philosophies of the law, as opposed to particular provisions of the law. (Chapter 1)

Justification A criminal defense in which the defendant establishes that he broke the law to avoid a greater harm. (Chapter 7)

Larceny Taking personal property with the intention of preventing the owner from ever using it. (Chapter 7)

Law merchant The body of rules and customs developed by traders and businesspersons throughout Europe from roughly the fifteenth to the eighteenth century. (Chapter 19)

Lease A contract creating a landlord-tenant relationship. (Chapter 46)

Legal positivism The legal philosophy holding that law is what the sovereign says it is, regardless of its moral content. (Chapter 1)

Legal realism The legal philosophy holding that what really influences law is who makes and enforces it, not what is put in writing. (Chapter 1)

Legal remedy Generally, money damages. It is distinguished from equitable remedy, which includes injunctions and other non-monetary relief. (Chapter 18)

Legislative history Used by courts to interpret the meaning of a statute, this is the record of hearings, speeches, and explanations that accompanied a statute as it made its way from newly proposed bill to final law. (Chapter 3)

Legislative rules Regulations issued by an administrative agency. (Chapter 3)

Letter of credit A commercial device used to guarantee payment in international trade, usually between parties that have not previously worked together. (Chapter 8)

Libel *See* Defamation. (Chapter 5)

License To grant permission to another person (1) to make or sell something or (2) to enter on property. (Chapter 45)

Licensee A person who is on the property of another for her own purposes, but with the owner's permission. A social guest is a typical licensee. (Chapter 6)

Lien A security interest created by rule of law, often based on labor that the secured party has expended on the collateral. (Chapter 26)

Life estate An ownership interest in real property entitling the holder to use the property during his lifetime, but which terminates upon his death. (Chapter 45)

Limited liability company An organization that has the limited liability of a corporation but is not a taxable entity. (Chapter 32)

Limited liability limited partnership In a limited liability limited partnership, the general partner is not personally liable for the debts of the partnership. (Chapter 32)

Limited partnership A partnership with two types of partners: (1) limited partners who have no personal liability for the debts of the enterprise nor any right to manage the business, and (2) general partners who are responsible for management and personally liable for all debts. (Chapter 32)

Liquidated damages A contract clause specifying how much a party must pay upon breach. (Chapter 18)

Liquidated debt The amount of the indebtedness is not in dispute. (Chapter 12)

Litigation The process of resolving disputes through formal court proceedings. (Chapter 2)

Living trust A trust established while the grantor is alive. *See inter vivos* trust. (Chapter 48)

Living will An instrument that permits adults to refuse medical treatment. It can also appoint a health care proxy to make medical decisions for a person who has become incompetent. (Chapter 48)

Lockout A management tactic, designed to gain a bargaining advantage, in which the company refuses to allow union members to work (and hence deprives them of their pay). (Chapter 31)

Mailbox rule A contract doctrine holding that acceptance is effective upon dispatch, that is, when it is mailed or otherwise taken out of the control of the offeree. (Chapter 11)

Maker The issuer of a promissory note. (Chapter 23)

Material Important or significant. Information that would affect a person's decision if he knew it. (Chapter 14)

Mediation The process of using a neutral person to aid in the settlement of a legal dispute. A mediator's decision is non-binding. (Chapter 2)

Mens rea Guilty state of mind. (Chapter 7)

Merger An acquisition of one company by another. (Chapter 37)

Mini-trial A form of alternative dispute resolution in which the parties present short versions of their cases to a panel of three "judges." (Chapter 2)

Minor A person under the age of 18. (Chapter 14)

Minority shareholders Shareholders who do not own enough stock to control their corporation. (Chapter 37)

Minute book Records of shareholder meetings and directors's meetings are kept in the corporation's minute book. (Chapter 35)

Mirror image rule A contract doctrine that requires acceptance to be on exactly the same terms as the offer. (Chapter 11)

Misdemeanor A less serious crime, typically one for which the maximum penalty is incarceration for less than a year, often in a jail, as opposed to a prison. (Chapter 7)

Misrepresentation A factually incorrect statement made during contract negotiations. (Chapter 14)

Mitigation One party acts to minimize its losses when the other party breaches a contract. (Chapter 18)

Modify An appellate court order changing a lower court ruling. (Chapter 2)

Money laundering Taking the profits of criminal acts and either (1) using the money to promote more crime or (2) attempting to conceal the money's source. (Chapter 7)

Monopolization A company acquires or maintains a monopoly through the commission of unacceptably aggressive acts. A violation of §2 of the Sherman Act. (Chapter 40)

Mortgage A security interest in real property. (Chapter 26)

Mortgagee A creditor who obtains a security interest in real property, typically in exchange for money given to the mortgagor to buy the property. (Chapter 26)

Mortgagor A debtor who gives a mortgage (security interest) in real property to a creditor, typically in exchange for money used to buy the property. (Chapter 26)

Motion A formal request that a court take some specified step during litigation. A motion to compel discovery is a request that a trial judge order the other party to respond to discovery. (Chapter 2)

Motion to suppress A request that the court exclude evidence because it was obtained in violation of the Constitution. (Chapter 7)

Multinational enterprise A corporation that is doing business in more than one country simultaneously. (Chapter 8)

N

NAFTA *See* North American Free Trade Agreement. (Chapter 8)

National Labor Relations Board (NLRB) The administrative agency charged with overseeing labor law. (Chapter 3)

Nationalization A government's seizure of property or companies. (Chapter 8)

Natural law The theory that an unjust law is no law at all, and that a rule is only legitimate if based on an immutable morality. (Chapter 1)

Negative or dormant aspect of the Commerce Clause The doctrine that prohibits a state from any action that interferes with or discriminates against interstate commerce. (Chapter 4)

Negligence per se Violation of a standard of care set by statute. Driving while intoxicated is illegal; thus, if a drunk driver injures a pedestrian, he has committed negligence per se. (Chapter 6)

Negotiable instrument A type of commercial paper that is freely transferable. (Chapter 26)

Negotiation The transfer of an instrument. To be negotiated, order paper must be indorsed and then delivered to the transferee. For bearer paper, no indorsement is required—it must simply be delivered to the transferee. (Chapter 23)

Nominal damages A token sum, such as one dollar, given to an injured plaintiff who cannot prove damages. (Chapter 18)

Noncompetition agreement A contract in which one party agrees not to compete with another in a stated type of business. (Chapter 10)

North American Free Trade Agreement A commercial association among Canada, the United States, and Mexico designed to eliminate almost all trade barriers. (Chapter 8)

Note An unconditional, written promise that the maker of the instrument will pay a specific amount of money on demand or at a definite time. When issued by a corporation, a note refers to short-term debt, typically payable within five years. (Chapter 23)

Novation If there is an existing contract between *A* and *B*, a novation occurs when *A* agrees to release *B* from all liability on the contract in return for *C*'s willingness to accept *B*'s liability. (Chapter 16)

Nuncupative will An oral will. (Chapter 48)

O

Obligee The party to a contract who is entitled to receive performance from the other party. (Chapter 16)

Obligor The party to a contract who is required to do something for the benefit of the other party. (Chapter 16)

Obscenity Constitutional law doctrine holding that some works will receive no First Amendment protection because a court determines they depict sexual matters in an offensive way. (Chapter 4)

Offer In contract law, an act or statement that proposes definite terms and permits the other party to create a contract by accepting those terms. (Chapter 11)

Offeree The party in contract negotiations who receives the first offer. (Chapter 11)

Offeror The party in contract negotiations who makes the first offer. (Chapter 11)

Order paper An instrument that includes the words "pay to the order of" or their equivalent. (Chapter 23)

Output contract An agreement that obligates the seller of goods to sell everything he produces during a stated period to a particular buyer. (Chapter 11)

Override The power of Congress or a state legislature to pass legislation despite a veto by a president or governor. A congressional override requires a two-thirds vote in each house. (Chapter 3)

Parol evidence Written or oral evidence, outside the language of a contract, offered by one party to clarify interpretation of the agreement. (Chapter 15)

Parol evidence rule In the case of an integrated contract, neither party may use evidence outside the writing to contradict, vary, or add to its terms. (Chapter 15)

Part performance An exception to the statute of frauds permitting a buyer of real estate to enforce an oral contract if she paid part of the price, entered the property, and made improvements, with the owners's knowledge. (Chapter 15)

Partially disclosed principal If the third party in an agency relationship knows that the agent is acting for a principal, but does not know the identity of the principal, that principal is partially disclosed. (Chapter 29)

Partnership An association of two or more persons to carry on as co-owners a business for profit. (Chapter 32)

Partnership at will A partnership that has no fixed duration. A partner has the right to resign from the partnership at any time. (Chapter 33)

Partnership by estoppel If a person who is not a partner implies that he is a partner or does not object when other people imply it, he is liable as if he really were a partner. (Chapter 33)

Patent The right to the exclusive use of an invention for 20 years. (Chapter 44)

Payable on demand The holder of an instrument is entitled to be paid whenever she asks. (Chapter 23)

Payee Someone who is owed money under the terms of an instrument. (Chapter 23)

***Per se* violation of an antitrust law** An automatic breach. Courts will generally not consider mitigating factors. (Chapter 40)

Peremptory challenge During *voir dire*, a request by one attorney that a prospective juror be excused for an unstated reason. (Chapter 2)

Perfect tender rule A rule permitting the buyer to reject goods if they fail in any respect to conform to the contract. (Chapter 22)

Perfection A series of steps a secured party must take to protect its rights in collateral against people other than the debtor. (Chapter 26)

Personal property All property other than real property. (Chapter 47)

Plain meaning rule In statutory interpretation, the premise that words with an ordinary, everyday significance will be so interpreted, unless there is some apparent reason not to. (Chapter 3)

Pleadings The documents that begin a lawsuit: the complaint, the answer, the counter-claim and reply. (Chapter 2)

Positive aspect of the Commerce Clause The power granted to Congress to regulate commerce between the states. (Chapter 4)

Precedent An earlier case that decided the same legal issue as that presently in dispute, and which therefore will control the outcome of the current case. (Chapter 1)

Predatory pricing A violation of §2 of the Sherman Act in which a company lowers its prices below cost to drive competitors out of business. (Chapter 41)

Preemption The doctrine, based on the Supremacy Clause, by which any federal statute takes priority whenever (1) a state statute conflicts or (2) there is no conflict but Congress indicated an intention to control the issue involved. (Chapter 4)

Preferred stock Owners of preferred stock have a right to receive dividends and liquidation proceeds of the company before common shareholders. (Chapter 35)

Preponderance of the evidence The level of proof that a plaintiff must meet to prevail in a civil lawsuit. It means that the plaintiff must offer evidence that, in sum, is slightly more persuasive than the defendant's evidence. (Chapter 2)

Presentment A holder of an instrument makes a demand for payment. (Chapter 24)

Pretermitted child A child omitted from a parent's will. (Chapter 48)

Prima facie "At first sight." A fact or conclusion that is presumed to be true unless someone presents evidence to disprove it. (Chapter 30)

Principal In an agency relationship, the principal is the person for whom the agent is acting. (Chapter 28)

Privacy Act A federal statute prohibiting federal agencies from divulging to other agencies or organizations information about private citizens. (Chapter 3)

Privity The relationship that exists between two parties who make a contract, as opposed to a third party who, though affected by the contract, is not a party to it. (Chapter 21)

Probable cause In a search and seizure case, it means that the information available indicates that it is more likely than not that a search will uncover particular criminal evidence. (Chapter 7)

Probate The process of carrying out the terms of a will. (Chapter 48)

Procedural due process *See* Due Process Clause. (Chapter 4)

Procedural law The rules establishing how the legal system itself is to operate in a particular kind of case. (Chapter 1)

Proceeds Anything that a debtor obtains from the sale or disposition of collateral. Normally, proceeds refers to cash obtained from the sale of the secured property. (Chapter 26)

Production of documents and things A form of discovery in which one party demands that the other furnish original documents or physical things, relating to the suit, for inspection and copying. (Chapter 2)

Product liability The potential responsibility that a manufacturer or seller has for injuries caused by defective goods. (Chapter 21)

Professional corporation A form of organization that permits professionals (such as doctors, lawyers, and accountants) to incorporate. Shareholders are not personally liable for the torts of other shareholders, or for the contract debts of the organization. (Chapter 32)

Profit The right to enter land belonging to another and take something away, such as minerals or timber. (Chapter 45)

Promissory estoppel A doctrine in which a court may enforce a promise made by the defendant even when there is no contract, if the defendant knew that the plaintiff was likely to rely on the promise, the plaintiff did in fact rely, and enforcement of it is the only way to avoid injustice. (Chapter 10)

Promissory note The maker of the instrument promises to pay a specific amount of money. (Chapter 23)

Promoter The person who creates a corporation by raising capital and undertaking the legal steps necessary for formation. (Chapter 35)

Promulgate To issue a new rule. (Chapter 3)

Prosecution The government's attempt to convict a defendant of a crime by charging him, trying the case, and forcing him to defend himself. (Chapter 7)

Prospectus Under the Securities Act of 1933, an issuer must provide this document to anyone who purchases a security in a public transaction. The prospectus contains detailed information about the issuer and its business, a description of the stock, and audited financial statements. (Chapter 38)

Protective order A court order limiting one party's discovery. (Chapter 2)

Proxy (1) A person whom the shareholder designates to vote in his place. (2) The written form (typically a card) that the shareholder uses to appoint a designated voter. (Chapter 37)

Proxy statement When a public company seeks proxy votes from its shareholders, it must include a proxy statement. This statement contains information about the company, such as a detailed description of management compensation. (Chapter 37)

Publicly traded corporation A company that (1) has completed a public offering under the Securities Act of 1933, or (2) has securities traded on a national exchange, or (3) has 500 shareholders and $10 million in assets. (Chapter 36)

Punitive damages Money awarded at trial not to compensate the plaintiff for harm but to punish the defendant for conduct that the factfinder considers extreme and outrageous. (Chapter 5)

Purchase money security interest A security interest taken by the person who sells the collateral to the debtor, or by a person who advances money so that the debtor may buy the collateral. (Chapter 26)

Quantum meruit "As much as she deserves." The damages awarded in a quasi-contract case. (Chapter 10)

Quasi-contract A legal fiction in which, to avoid injustice, the court awards damages as if a contract had existed, although one did not. (Chapter 10)

Quid pro quo A Latin phrase meaning "this for that." It refers to a form of sexual harassment in which some aspect of a job is made contingent upon sexual activity. (Chapter 30)

Quiet enjoyment A tenant's right to use property without the interference of the landlord. (Chapter 46)

Quorum The number of voters that must be present for a meeting to count. (Chapter 37)

Ratification When someone accepts the benefit of an unauthorized transaction or fails to repudiate it once he has learned of it, he is then bound by it. (Chapter 29)

Real property Land, together with certain things associated with it, such as buildings, subsurface rights, air rights, plant life and fixtures. (Chapter 26)

Reasonable doubt The level of proof that the government must meet to convict the defendant in a criminal case. The factfinder must be persuaded to a very high degree of certainty that the defendant did what the government alleges. (Chapter 2)

Reciprocal dealing agreement An agreement under which Company *A* will purchase from Company *B* only if Company *B* also buys from Company *A*. These agreements are rule of reason violations of the Sherman Act. (Chapter 40)

Record date To vote at a shareholders meeting, a shareholder must own stock on the record date. (Chapter 37)

Red herring A preliminary prospectus. (Chapter 38)

Reformation The process by which a court rewrites a contract to ensure its accuracy or viability. (Chapter 18)

Refusal to deal An agreement among competitors that they will not trade with a particular supplier or buyer. Such an agreement is a rule of reason violation of the Sherman Act. (Chapter 40)

Registration statement A document filed with the Securities and Exchange Commission under the Securities Act of 1933 by an issuer seeking to sell securities in a public transaction. (Chapter 38)

Reliance interest A remedy in a contract case that puts the injured party in the position he would have been in had the parties never entered into a contract. (Chapter 18)

Remand The power of an appellate court to return a case to a lower court for additional action. (Chapter 2)

Reply A pleading, filed by the plaintiff in response to a defendant's counter-claim. (Chapter 2)

Repossess A secured party takes collateral because the debtor has defaulted on payments. (Chapter 26)

Repudiation An indication made by one contracting party to the other that it will not perform. (Chapter 22)

Request for admission A form of discovery in which one party demands that the opposing party either admit or deny particular factual or legal allegations. (Chapter 2)

Requirements contract An agreement that obligates a buyer of specified goods to purchase all of the goods she needs during a stated period from a particular seller. (Chapter 11)

Res ipsa loquitur A doctrine of tort law holding that the facts may imply negligence when the defendant had exclusive control of the thing that caused the harm, the accident would not normally have occurred without negligence, and the plaintiff played no role in causing the injury. (Chapter 6)

Resale price maintenance A *per se* violation of the Sherman Act in which a manufacturer enters into an agreement with retailers about the prices they will charge. (Chapter 41)

Rescind To cancel a contract. (Chapter 12)

Respondeat superior A rule of agency law holding that a principal is liable when a servant acting within the scope of employment commits a tort that causes physical harm to a person or property. (Chapter 29)

Restitution Restoring an injured party to its original position. (Chapter 14)

Restitution interest A remedy in a contract case that returns to the injured party a benefit that he has conferred on the other party, which it would be unjust to leave with that person. (Chapter 18)

Restricted security Any stock purchased in a private offering (such as one under Regulation D). (Chapter 38)

Resulting trust When a trust terminates before its assets are exhausted, the assets are returned to the grantor. (Chapter 48)

Retribution Giving a criminal defendant the punishment he deserves. (Chapter 7)

Reverse The power of an appellate court to overrule a lower court and grant judgment for the party that had lost in the lower court. (Chapter 2)

Revocation The act of disavowing a contract offer, so that the offeree no longer has the power to accept. (Chapter 11)

Rule of reason violation An action that breaches the antitrust laws only if it has an anticompetitive impact. (Chapter 40)

Rulemaking The power of an administrative agency to issue regulations. (Chapter 3)

S corporation A corporation that is not a taxable entity. (Chapter 32)

Sale on approval A transfer in which a buyer takes goods intending to use them herself, but has the right to return the goods to the seller. (Chapter 20)

Sale or return A transfer in which the buyer takes the goods intending to resell them, but has the right to return the goods to the original owner. (Chapter 20)

Scienter In a case of securities fraud, the plaintiff must prove that the defendant acted willfully, knowingly, or recklessly. (Chapter 38)

Secondary boycott Picketing, directed by a union against a company, designed to force that company to stop doing business with the union's employer. (Chapter 31)

Security Any purchase in which the buyer invests money in a common enterprise and expects to earn a profit predominantly from the efforts of others. (Chapter 38)

Security agreement A contract in which the debtor gives a security interest to the secured party. (Chapter 26)

Security interest An interest in personal property or fixtures that secures the performance of some obligation. (Chapter 26)

Separation of powers The principle, established by the first three articles of the Constitution, that authority should be divided among the legislative, executive, and judicial branches. (Chapter 4)

Servant An agent whose work is closely controlled by the principal. (Chapter 29)

Service mark A type of trademark used to identify services, not products. (Chapter 44)

Settlor Someone who creates a trust. (Chapter 48)

Sexual harassment Unwanted sexual advances, comments or touching, sufficiently severe to violate Title VII of the 1964 Civil Rights Act. (Chapter 30)

Short-swing trading Under §16 of the Securities Exchange Act, insiders must turn over to the corporation any profits they make from the purchase and sale or sale and purchase of company securities in a six-month period. (Chapter 38)

Signatory A person, company, or nation that has signed a legal document, such as a contract, agreement, or treaty. (Chapter 8)

Single recovery principle A rule of tort litigation that requires a plaintiff to claim all damages, present and future, at the time of trial, not afterwards. (Chapter 5)

Slander *See* Defamation. (Chapter 5)

Sole proprietorship An unincorporated business owned by a single person. (Chapter 32)

Sovereign immunity The right of a national government to be free of lawsuits brought in foreign courts. (Chapter 8)

Specific deterrence *See* Deterrence. (Chapter 7)

Specific performance A contract remedy requiring the breaching party to perform the contract, by conveying land or some unique asset, rather than by paying money damages. (Chapter 18)

Spendthrift trust A trust that prevents creditors from attaching a beneficiary's interest in it. (Chapter 48)

Stakeholders Anyone who is affected by the activities of a corporation, such as employees, customers, creditors, suppliers, shareholders, and neighbors. (Chapter 36)

Stale check A check presented more than six months after its due date. (Chapter 25)

Stare decisis "Let the decision stand." A basic principle of the common law, it means that precedent is usually binding. (Chapter 1)

Statute A law passed by a legislative body, such as Congress. (Chapter 1)

Statute of frauds This law provides that certain contracts are not enforceable unless in writing. (Chapter 15)

Statute of limitations A statute that determines the period within which a particular kind of lawsuit must be filed. (Chapter 17)

Statute of repose A law that places an absolute limit on when a lawsuit may be filed, regardless of when the defect was discovered. (Chapter 21)

Statutory interpretation A court's power to give meaning to new legislation by clarifying ambiguities, providing limits, and ultimately applying it to a specific fact pattern in litigation. (Chapter 3)

Strict liability A tort doctrine holding to a very high standard all those who engage in ultrahazardous activity (e.g., using explosives) or who manufacture certain products. (Chapter 6)

Strike The ultimate weapon of a labor union, it occurs when all or most employees of a particular plant or employer walk off the job and refuse to work. (Chapter 31)

Strike suit A lawsuit without merit that defendants sometimes settle simply to avoid the nuisance of litigation. (Chapter 37)

Subpoena An order to appear, issued by a court or government body. (Chapter 3)

Subpoena duces tecum An order to produce certain documents or things before a court or government body. (Chapter 3)

Subrogation The substitution of one person for another. For example, if an insurance company pays a claim, it acquires through subrogation whatever rights the insured had against any third parties. (Chapter 49)

Substantial performance The promisor performs contract duties well enough to be entitled to his full contract price, minus the value of any defects. (Chapter 17)

Substantive due process *See* Due Process Clause. (Chapter 4)

Substantive law Rules that establish the rights of parties. For example, the prohibition against slander is substantive law, as opposed to procedural law. (Chapter 1)

Summary judgment The power of a trial court to terminate a lawsuit before a trial has begun, on the grounds that no essential facts are in dispute. (Chapter 2)

Summary jury trial A form of alternative dispute resolution in which a small panel of jurors hears shortened, summarized versions of the evidence. (Chapter 2)

Supermajority voting Typically, shareholders can approve charter amendments by a majority vote. However, sometimes corporations require more than a majority of shareholders (e.g., 80 percent) to approve certain charter amendments, such as a merger. These provisions are designed to discourage hostile takeovers. (Chapter 36)

Superseding cause An event that interrupts the chain of causation and relieves a defendant from liability based on her own act. (Chapter 6)

Supremacy Clause From Article VI of the Constitution, it declares that federal statutes and treaties take priority over any state law, if there is a conflict between the two or, even absent a conflict, if Congress manifests an intent to preempt the field. (Chapter 4)

Surety Someone who promises to pay another person's obligations. (Chapter 49)

Takings Clause Part of the Fifth Amendment, it ensures that when any governmental unit takes private property for public use, it must compensate the owner. (Chapter 4)

Tariff A duty imposed on imported goods by the government of the importing nation. (Chapter 8)

Tenancy by the entirety A form of joint ownership available only to married couples. If one member of the couple dies, the property goes automatically to the survivor. Creditors cannot attach the property, nor can one owner sell the property without the other's permission. (Chapter 45)

Tender To make conforming goods available to the buyer. (Chapter 22)

Tender offer A public offer to buy a block of stock directly from shareholders. (Chapter 36)

Term partnership When the partners agree in advance on the duration of a partnership. (Chapter 33)

Testamentary trust A trust created by the grantor's will. (Chapter 48)

Testator Someone who dies having executed a will. (Chapter 48)

Testatrix A female testator. (Chapter 48)

Third party beneficiary Someone who stands to benefit from a contract to which she is not a party. An *intended* beneficiary may enforce such a contract; an *incidental* beneficiary may not. (Chapter 16)

Three-Fifths Clause A clause in Article 1, section 2 of the United States Constitution, now void and regarded as racist, which required that for purposes of taxation and representation, a slave should be counted as three-fifths of a person. (Chapter 4)

Tort A civil wrong, committed in violation of a duty that the law imposes. (Chapter 5)

Tortious interference with a contract A tort in which the defendant deliberately impedes an existing contract between the plaintiff and another. (Chapter 5)

Tortious interference with a prospective advantage A tort in which the defendant deliberately obstructs a developing venture or advantage that the plaintiff has created. (Chapter 5)

Totten trust A bank account held by the grantor in trust for someone else. (Chapter 48)

Trade acceptance A draft drawn by a seller of goods on the buyer and payable to the seller or some third party. (Chapter 23)

Trade secret A formula, device, process, method, or compilation of information that, when used in business, gives the owner an advantage over competitors who do not know it. (Chapter 44)

Trademark Any combination of words and symbols that a business uses to identify its products or services and that federal law will protect. (Chapter 44)

Treasury stock Stock that has been bought back by its issuing corporation. (Chapter 35)

Trespass A tort committed by intentionally entering land that belongs to someone else, or remaining on the land after being asked to leave. (Chapter 5)

Trial court Any court in a state or federal system that holds formal hearings to determine the facts in a civil or criminal case. (Chapter 2)

Trust An entity that separates legal and beneficial ownership. (Chapter 48)

Tying arrangement A violation of the Sherman and Clayton Acts in which a seller requires that two distinct products be purchased together. The seller uses its significant power in the market for the tying product to shut out a substantial part of the market for the tied product. (Chapter 41)

Ultra vires An activity that is not permitted by a corporation's charter. (Chapter 35)

Ultrahazardous activity Conduct that is lawful yet unusual and much more likely to cause injury than normal commercial activity. (Chapter 6)

Unconscionable contract An agreement that a court refuses to enforce because it is fundamentally unfair as a result of unequal bargaining power by one party. (Chapter 13)

Undisclosed principal If a third party in an agency relationship does not know that the agent is acting for a principal, that principal is undisclosed. (Chapter 29)

Undue influence One party so dominates the thinking of another party to a contract that the dominant party cannot truly consent to the agreement. (Chapter 14)

Unfair labor practice An act, committed by either a union or an employer, that violates the National Labor Relations Act, such as failing to bargain in good faith. (Chapter 31)

Unilateral contract A binding agreement in which one party has made an offer that the other can accept only by action, not words. (Chapter 10)

Unliquidated debt A claimed debt that is disputed, either because the parties disagree over whether there is in fact a debt or because they disagree over the amount. (Chapter 12)

Usury Charging interest at a rate that exceeds legal limits. (Chapter 13)

Valuation A process by which the Customs Service determines the fair value of goods being imported, for purposes of imposing a duty. (Chapter 8)

Verdict The decision of the factfinder in a case. (Chapter 2)

Vertical agreement or merger An agreement or merger between two companies at different stages of the production process, such as when a company acquires one of its suppliers or distributors. (Chapter 40)

Veto The power of the president to reject legislation passed by Congress, terminating the bill unless Congress votes by a ⅔ majority to override. (Chapter 3)

Void agreement An agreement that neither party may legally enforce, usually because the purpose of the bargain was illegal or because one of the parties lacked capacity to make it. (Chapter 10)

Voidable contract An agreement that, because of some defect, may be terminated by one party, such as a minor, but not by both parties. (Chapter 10)

Voir dire The process of selecting a jury. Attorneys for the parties and the judge may inquire of prospective jurors whether they are biased or incapable of rendering a fair and impartial verdict. (Chapter 2)

Warranty A guarantee that goods will meet certain standards. (Chapter 21)

Warranty of fitness for a particular purpose An assurance under the Uniform Commercial Code that the goods are fit for the special purpose for which the buyer intends them and of which the seller is aware. (Chapter 21)

Warranty of merchantability An assurance under the Uniform Commercial Code that the goods are fit for their ordinary purpose. (Chapter 21)

Whistleblower Someone who discloses wrongful behavior. (Chapter 30)

Winding up The process whereby the assets of a partnership are sold and the proceeds distributed. (Chapter 33)

Writ An order from a government compelling someone to do a particular thing. (Chapter 1)

ANSWERS TO PRACTICE TESTS*

CHAPTER 1

1. Yes. Whatever business you choose to engage in, courts and the general public alike will expect you to know what you are doing. This does not mean that you need to know everything a lawyer knows. It does mean that you must be able to anticipate legal problems. Sometimes you will know exactly what to do; other times you will know enough to call a lawyer. If you permit sexual harassment in your company, the company is liable whether you understood the law or not. If you casually agree to manufacture and sell a new product with a friend, you may have created a binding contract, an agency relationship, or a partnership. Courts will look at what you *did*, not what you understood.

3. The Securities Act of 1933 is a statute. A statute is any law passed by a legislative body. Voters elect members of Congress who, at least in theory, respond to demands from the electorate. Congress passes statutes (which are generally signed by the president), and those statutes then govern all of us. We all have a chance to affect the law, and we all are governed by the law.

5. The partners are indeed liable. *Bergh v. Mills*, 763 P.2d 214 (Wyo. 1998). That is the essence of a partnership: all partners are liable for the acts of any partner committed in the partnership's normal business. This is the general idea of collective responsibility. It relates to the "tithing" of English legal history, in which all tithing members were legally responsible for the conduct of the others.

7. Billie is relying on procedural law. Substantive law probably allows the OTS to get a court order barring her from spending assets. Rather than fight, and lose, on the substantive law, she is arguing that the notice was defective. The appeals court agreed. *Parker v. Ryan*, 960 F.2d 543, 1992 U.S. App. LEXIS 10488 (5th Cir. 1992). The OTS may try again, but this procedure was clearly defective.

9. Jack has a criminal law problem. He will be arrested by Katrina and prosecuted by the federal government. The local United States attorney will be in charge of the case, and he will try to obtain a verdict of guilty against Jack. Jack may be fined and/or sentenced to prison. Jill has a civil dispute with Freddy. Jill, the plaintiff, must file a lawsuit against Freddy, the defendant, seeking money damages of $500. Freddy will not go to jail.

11. Natural law should be a question in the back of our minds throughout the course, because it is a reminder of morality, and law without morality is despotism. Nonetheless, Stendhal is obviously correct that both strength and need help to create law. The important thing for this course is continually to apply moral principles to the rules we study, and make your own determinations about whether natural law really plays a role.

CHAPTER 2

1. Yes. Try blending ADR mechanisms. Have the ADR clause state that in the event of a dispute, the parties will negotiate it in good faith, and take no further steps for 30 days. If negotiation fails, an additional 30-day cooling off period follows. The next step could be a mini-trial in front of three people, two of whom represent the parties respectively and the third acts as a neutral mediator. Finally, if the mini-trial fails to produce a settlement, the parties will hire an arbitrator. You might require that the arbitrator be a national of neither Turkey nor the United States. You must specify the law to be applied and where the arbitration will take place. List any claims that are not arbitrable, such as antitrust or securities. This should preserve a working relationship while ensuring that disputes will be settled rapidly.

3. (a) The state trial court of general jurisdiction may hear the case. There is no federal court jurisdiction.

(b) The general trial court of Texas, only. There is no federal court diversity jurisdiction because the money sought is less than $50,000.

(c) Ohio's general trial court has jurisdiction. The United States district court has concurrent jurisdiction, based on diversity. The parties live in different states and the amount in question is over $50,000.

(d) The United States district court has federal question jurisdiction, based on the federal statutes at issue. The general trial court of Kansas has concurrent jurisdiction.

* Answers to the odd-numbered questions only.

5. The trial judge has broad discretion to protect the interests of both parties. When it hears a motion for protective orders, it will have to weigh the family's privacy needs versus the school's right to defend itself. One solution is to require the family to furnish the documents to the judge, who can inspect them in *camera*. If they are relevant, and helpful to the defense, he can then give them to the defense.

7. The purpose of a trial is to learn the facts and apply the law to them. Because the Anglo-American trial system is adversarial, both sides certainly need some opportunity to prepare. At some point, however, trial preparation may turn into the scripting and rehearsal of a "show," designed to manipulate the factfinder. In the American system, the greatest danger is that the trial attorneys, who know the law and understand how juries often react, will simply tell the witnesses what to say. Legally and ethically, they are not entitled to do so, but realistically there is a fine line between rehearsing direct examination and writing dialogue. The British system prevents the barristers from preparing the witnesses and may reduce the opportunity for dishonest "script writing." Advocates of the American system might respond that putting on effective direct examination is so difficult that the parties deserve every opportunity they can get to prepare a cohesive, comprehensible series of questions.

9. No. The court of appeals reversed and remanded for a new trial, stating that there was enough evidence for a jury reasonably to infer that age was a factor in Dace's demotion. If the case had gone to a jury and the jury had found for the defendant, that verdict would have been affirmed. But had they found for the plaintiff, that too would have been affirmed. *Dace v. ACF Industries*, 722 F.2d 374 (8th Cir. 1984).

11. No. The court of appeals held that the incorrect jury instruction was harmless error. *Williams v. U.S. Elevator Corp.*, 929 F.2d 1019 (D. C. Cir. 1990). The jury specifically found that the elevator company had committed no negligence in either the design or maintenance of the elevator. The incorrect instruction was insignificant.

CHAPTER 3

1. It appears that no state requires restaurant employees to furnish first aid to choking victims, because of the possibility that they could do more harm than good. But some states do require the restaurant to respond. The Wyoming court has ruled that a restaurant has a legal duty to summon aid for a choking victim but no duty to provide the aid itself or train the staff to do so. *Drew v. Lejay's Sportsman's Cafe*, 806 P.2d 301 (Wyo. 1991).

3. Virtually every state would refuse to enforce the clause, finding it unconscionable. An "unconscionable" clause is one that grossly and unfairly favors the party with more power. (See Unit 2, on contract law.) This is such a clause. But the problem with permitting this flexibility to enter into contract law is that we now are less certain of being able to enforce contracts generally. A party who wishes to get out of a contract may attempt a claim of unconscionability.

5. No. When the Supreme Court declares that the Constitution protects an activity, such as flag burning, that is the final word. This is different from the *Griggs–Wards Cove* dispute. There, the Court was simply interpreting a statute, the 1964 Civil Rights Act. Whenever Congress believes that the Court has misinterpreted a statute, it is free to pass a law correcting the interpretation. But Congress has no power to overrule the Court on a matter of constitutional rights.

7. "Promulgated" simply means "issued." The FAA used the informal process, meaning that it published its proposed rules, allowed interested parties an opportunity to comment in writing and oppose the rules if they wished, considered all comments, and then published the final rules with supporting reasons and explanations of why it rejected the opposing comments. There was no hearing.

9. No. Pursuant to the *Chevron* case, a court will look to see if there is clear congressional intent. If there is, it must be followed. If there is not, then the agency's interpretation will be followed if it is "permissible," meaning reasonable. In *Public Citizen v. FAA*, 988 F.2d 186, 1993 U.S. App. LEXIS 6024 (D.C. Cir. 1993), the court found that there *was* a clear congressional intent: to permit the ASIA to exempt additional information from public disclosure for purposes of airport security. The agency's view became irrelevant, but the plaintiffs lost anyway.

CHAPTER 4

1. The positive aspect of the Commerce Clause grants Congress the power to regulate interstate commerce. The negative, or dormant, aspect severely restricts the power of the states to do so: a state statute that discriminates against interstate commerce is invariably unconstitutional. The dormant aspect is designed to prevent the states from taxing goods and services produced in other states, and thus turning the nation into 50 competing sovereigns. In this case, the United States District Court and the Court of Appeals both found that Michigan's statute did not violate the Commerce Clause, but the Supreme Court reversed, finding a violation of the dormant aspect. There was no valid reason to limit the amount of waste that a landfill operator could accept from outside the county (and thus from outside the state) while placing no limit on locally created waste. *Fort Gratiot Landfill, Inc. v. Michigan Dept. of Natural Resources*, 504 U.S. 353, 112 S. Ct. 2019, 1992 U.S. LEXIS 3252 (1992).

3. The milk tax violates the dormant, or negative, aspect of the Commerce Clause. *West Lynn Creamery, Inc. v. Healy*, 114 S. Ct. 2205, 1994 U.S. LEXIS 4638 (1994). The Supreme Court found that this was a tax on interstate commerce. Although the tax is applied on all milk sales, it is redistributed to local producers. It is effectively a tax only on out-of-state producers, a major interference with interstate commerce.

5. The constitutional issue is judicial review. Since *Marbury v. Madison*, 5 U.S. 137 (1803), federal courts have insisted that they have the power to review acts of the other two branches. The Supreme Court ruled that while there was a limited executive privilege, it did not include the right to

withhold evidence in a criminal investigation. When the Supreme Court did in fact order Nixon to produce the tapes, he hesitated—but obeyed. The tapes he produced destroyed his credibility and his political base, and he became the first president to resign his office. But the principle of judicial review was affirmed.

7. It is a boring cliché, but there is no constitutional violation. The First Amendment protects your right to free speech, including symbolic speech such as buttons. But it only protects you from the government, not from a private party such as a corporation.

9. The Supreme Court said that it did not. *United States v. Edge Broadcasting*, 509 U.S. 418, 113 S. Ct. 2696, 1993 U.S. LEXIS 4402 (1993). This is commercial speech and receives a lower level of protection than other speech. In order for a restriction to survive a First Amendment test, it need only "be tailored in a reasonable manner to serve a substantial state interest" (*Edenfield v. Fane*, quoted in text). Here, the purpose of giving support to states that oppose lotteries is a substantial one, and this restriction reasonably serves that purpose.

11. His claim is based on the Takings Clause of the Fifth Amendment. The Supreme Court was unable to make a final ruling because certain facts were unclear from the record. But the Court stated that when the owner of real property has been called upon to sacrifice all economically beneficial uses in the name of the common good, he has suffered a taking and is entitled to compensation. It appears very likely that Lucas's property has lost all beneficial uses. If South Carolina can demonstrate some unexpected common law right to prohibit Lucas from building, such as nuisance, it may prevail. In all likelihood, though, South Carolina will end up paying "just compensation" for Lucas's land. *Lucas v. South Carolina Coastal Council*, 505 U.S. 1003, 112 S. Ct. 2886, 1992 U.S. LEXIS 4537 (1992).

CHAPTER 5

1. This is a suit for libel. (Broadcasting is considered libel, not slander, by most courts.) The Massachusetts high court ruled that Fleming could not maintain the action based on these words because a reasonable person would understand them to be opinion, ridicule, and mere pejorative rhetoric. They are not statements of fact because they could not be proven true or false. A statement like "dictators and Nazis" is not taken literally by anyone. *Fleming v. Benzaquin*, 390 Mass. 175, 454 N.E.2d 95 (1983).

3. Caldwell sued for false imprisonment. The jury found in her favor, and the court of appeals affirmed. *Caldwell v. K-Mart*, 306 S.C. 27, 410 S.E.2d 21, 1991 S.C. App. LEXIS 135 (S.C. Ct. App. 1991). From this evidence, a finder of fact could draw various inferences about whether K-Mart's actions in investigating were conducted for a reasonable time and in a reasonable manner. The initial stop in the parking lot was probably justified, but the actions of the guard in walking Caldwell through the store and continuing to accuse her of taking merchandise were not justified as part of a reasonable investigation.

5. The appeal court affirmed, stating: "The evidence here was sufficient to authorize the jury to find that the sum of $8 million was an amount necessary to deter Ford from repeating its conduct; that is, its conscious decisions to defer implementation of safety devices in order to protect its profits. One internal memo estimated that 'the total financial effect of the Fuel System Integrity program [would] reduce Company profits over the 1973–1976 cycle by $109 million,' and recommended that Ford defer adoption of the safety measures on all affected cars until 1976 to realize a design cost savings of $20.9 million compared to 1974.' Unless a jury verdict is palpably unreasonable or excessive, or the product of bias, it will not be disturbed on appeal.' *Ford Motor Co. v. Stubblefield*, 171 Ga. App. 331, 319 S.E.2d 470 (Ga. Ct. App. 1984). Clearly, a corporation is not obligated to manufacture a totally safe car, since such an automobile, if it could be built, would be prohibitively expensive. Most commentators would say that a car maker is morally—and legally—obligated to use all feasible initiatives to improve a car's safety.

7. The district court gave summary judgment for United, and the court of appeals affirmed. *Pacific Express, Inc. v. United Airlines, Inc.*, 959 F.2d 814, 1992 U.S. App. LEXIS 5139 (9th Cir. 1992). The primary issue was whether United was genuinely trying to compete, which it had the right to do or was simply out to destroy Pacific, which would be interference with a prospective advantage (as well as an antitrust violation). United officials testified that the expanded routes would generate new connecting traffic for other San Francisco flights. That is a competitive purpose, which is legitimate, and enough to defeat Pacific's claim.

9. Castrol's suit is based on §43 of the Lanham Act. Castrol sought an injunction to bar use of the commercial. Under the Act, a plaintiff must show either that the ad is literally false or, though literally true, likely to mislead consumers. Here Castrol claimed the ad was literally false. While Quaker State's oil did move more quickly, the evidence demonstrated that it did not accomplish what the ad claimed. The district court granted the injunction and the court of appeals affirmed. *Castrol v. Quaker State Corp.*, 977 F.2d 57, 1992 U.S. App. LEXIS 25726 (2d Cir. 1992).

CHAPTER 6

1. Irving loses. *Biakanja v. Irving*, 49 Cal. 2d 647, 320 P.2d 16 (1958). Although Irving was only working for Maroevich, he could easily foresee that Biakanja would be injured by an improper will, since it was precisely to benefit her that Maroevich had requested the will. Irving had a duty of care to Biakanja, and he is liable for negligence.

3. Harris was a trespasser, and as a result the railroad had no duty of due care to him. The railroad would be liable only if it caused Harris's death by reckless or intentional conduct. There was no evidence of either. The widow was not permitted to introduce evidence of negligence, because even if the railroad had been negligent, it would be not be liable. *Harris v. Mass. Bay Transit Authority*, (D. Mass. 1994), Mass. Lawyers Weekly, Feb. 7, 1994, p. 15.

5. The case was reversed and remanded for trial. *Powers v. Ryder Truck*, 625 So. 2d 979, 1993 Fla. App. LEXIS 10729 (Fla. Dist. Ct. App. 1993). Whether an event is a superseding cause is a jury question, unless it is so bizarre as to be entirely unforeseeable by the defendant. Here, even if Powers was negligent in attaching a nylon rope, that negligence was not so bizarre as to be unforeseeable by Ryder.

7. The AIDS phobia claims were dismissed. They were judged to be too speculative, without a showing that there was any real basis for the fear. *Hare v. State*, 143 Misc. 2d 281, 539 N.Y.S.2d 1018 (Ct. Claims 1989), *aff'd*, 173 A.D.2d 523 (2d Dept. 1991), *app. denied*, 78 N.Y.2d 859 (1991).

9. (b). Comparative negligence permits a plaintiff to recover damages even if she was partly at fault. Candy was 25 percent at fault and Zeke 75 percent, so Candy will recover 75 percent of her damages from Zeke. Under the older rule of contributory negligence, a plaintiff who was even slightly at fault for the harm caused could recover nothing from the defendant. In a contributory negligence state, Candy would lose.

11. The Supreme Court of Arkansas was unimpressed, and dismissed both claims. *Van Houten v. Pritchard*, 315 Ark. 688, 1994 Ark. LEXIS 70 (1994). The court said that an owner is strictly liable for an animal that is either (1) of a vicious species or (2) known to have dangerous tendencies. This cat was neither, and there is no strict liability. Further, domestic animals that normally cause no harm are permitted to roam freely in Arkansas. Because the owner could foresee no reason to anyone, he is not liable in negligence, either. Case dismissed.

CHAPTER 7

1. The different verdicts are due to different burdens of proof. The state had to prove Arnie's guilt *beyond a reasonable doubt*, and evidently could not do so. But that same evidence, used in the civil trial, might well prove *by a preponderance of the evidence* that Arnie caused the injury to Vickie's store.

3. The ruling appears to contradict the purpose of the insanity defense, which is to distinguish those who are not morally responsible for their actions from criminals deserving punishment. If the psychiatrists are correct that he is now sane and no danger, he should be released. The atrociousness of the killings is legally irrelevant because the original verdict was that he was not legally (or morally) responsible for them.

5. The government charged Hathcoat with embezzlement. The money was lawfully in her possession and she converted it to her use. She pleaded guilty to embezzlement and was sentenced. *United States v. Hathcoat*, 30 F.3d 913, 1994 U.S. App. LEXIS 19490 (7th Cir. 1994).

7. Yes. It is money laundering to take the proceeds of illegal acts and either conceal them or, as he did, use them to promote additional crimes.

9. In the United States, a police officer must give the four essential parts of the *Miranda* warnings: the right to remain silent; that anything said can be used in court; that the suspect is entitled to a lawyer; and that if he cannot afford one, the court will appoint one. The British warning puts additional pressure on a suspect. If the suspect remains silent at the time of arrest but then at trial states an alibi, the prosecution will be allowed to attack the alibi because it was not mentioned earlier. American reaction to the new British rule has been critical. Commentators claim that putting greater pressure on a suspect to speak increases the possibility of confused, forced explanations that will lead to wrongful convictions. The British government created the new practice because, it claimed, innocent suspects speak up freely but sophisticated criminals wait until later to concoct false defenses.

CHAPTER 8

1. The only items that the federal government may place on the list are exports that would (1) endanger national security, (2) harm foreign policy goals, or (3) drain scarce materials. Mandel cares very much whether these electronic goods appear on the list, because he has been charged with a criminal violation of the Export Administration Act of 1985. After failing to convince the court that the goods were wrongfully listed, he faces a prison term. *United States v. Mandel*, 696 F. Supp. 505, 1988 U.S. Dist. LEXIS 10781 (E.D. Cal. 1988). (This case was later reversed. 914 F2d 1215 (9th Cir.).)

3. Hector's idea is unethical and dumb. Hector should not make an apparent commitment, requiring the Italian exporter to tie up 30,000 parkas, if he doesn't plan to honor it. The commitment might seem clever to Hector as he makes it, but he would not be happy if someone pulled the ploy on him. Surely, he should behave toward others the way he would like to be treated. Hector's promise is also foolish. An oral contract for the sale of goods worth more than $500 is *generally* not binding in the United States, under the UCC. But sales of goods between Italy and the United States are governed by the Convention On Contracts For The International Sale of Goods (CISG) unless the parties specify otherwise. These parties have not specified any other law. The CISG does not require *any* contracts to be in writing, and will consider this a binding deal. Zoey and Hector are probably legally committed to the purchase.

5. Allied. The whole point of a letter of credit is that the issuer (Continental Bank) is making an independent promise to pay the beneficiary (Allied). Continental's concerns about Bill's financial health should have been resolved before issuing the letter of credit, not after all goes awry. *Eakin v. Continental Illinois National Bank & Trust Co.*, 875 F.2d 114, 1989 U.S. App. LEXIS 6951 (7th Cir. 1989).

7. The announcement of the end of repatriation taxes is good news. It means that for the first time a company that successfully invests in Kyrgyzstan can theoretically take out of the country any and all profits that it desires, without paying a penalty. But the announcement of the change in government demonstrates the instability of law in new republics. If the government can change by announcement, so can the law on repatriation. A company considering a major investment in the Kyrgyz Republic should obtain a guarantee from the government assuring it of unobstructed repatriation (and should also, on a related note, obtain expropriation insurance from OPIC).

9. Kirkpatrick is relying on the Act of State doctrine, which holds that an American court should withdraw from any case if its intervention would interfere with the ability of the president or Congress to carry on foreign diplomacy. Although the district court was persuaded to dismiss the case, the United States Supreme Court ultimately ruled that the Act of State doctrine did *not* require abstention. The Court held that Act of State controls only when a court might potentially rule that a foreign government's action was illegal and void. Such a ruling would interfere with proper foreign policy. But here, the Nigerian contract is valid and nothing in the trial can change that. Even if the court finds for Tectonics and declares that a Nigerian official accepted a bribe, this will not invalidate the contract (though Kirkpatrick may later go to jail under the FCPA). An official's motive is irrelevant to the Act of State doctrine. *W. S. Kirkpatrick & Co. v. Environmental Tectronics Corp.*, 493 U.S. 400, 110 S. Ct. 701, 1990 U.S. LEXIS 486 (1990).

11. Johnson and Reid were arrested and charged with violations of the Arms Export Control Act. A jury convicted them and they were sentenced to prison. *United States v. Johnson*, 952 F.2d 565, 1991 U.S. App. LEXIS 29747 (1st Cir. 1991).

CHAPTER 9

1. Jewett went home that night and prepared a short statement for the class about why she felt as if she had been raped the day before. Her friends talked her out of delivering the statement, but she has always regretted that she remained silent.

3. Employees were amazed to find that they had all received the same calls and were incensed when they realized what had happened. They vented their anger to a newspaper reporter, who wrote a front-page article about the company's lies and insensitivity. The company spent millions on an employee-relations campaign and a public-relations blitz but has yet to undo the damage. Steve Goldfarb, "Little White Lies," *Across the Board*, May 1992, vol. 29, no. 5, p. 53.

7. [No answer to this question.]

9. This was a true case (in which the names have been changed). In the event, Todd and David told the manager that they could not have lunch with him because Stacey was their friend and they did not feel comfortable excluding her. The manager was a little cold to them for some time afterwards, but eventually he seemed to get over it.

CHAPTER 10

1. Contracts are designed to control future events and thus to make business dealings more predictable and profitable.

3. Central Maine is obligated to pay because the parties created a unilateral contract. Central Maine's offer could be accepted only by performance. Motel Services accepted the offer by building the units with electrical heat. The contract is enforceable. *Motel Services, Inc. v. Central Maine Power Co.*, 394 A.2d 786 (Me. 1978).

5. Yes, they can recover under promissory estoppel. The Wisconsin Supreme Court found that Red Owl had made a promise knowing that the Hoffmans would rely; the Hoffmans did in fact rely on the promise, selling their businesses and purchasing a lot; and it would be unjust not to enforce the promise. The Hoffmans recovered about $20,000. *Hoffman v. Red Owl Stores*, 26 Wis. 2d 683, 133 N.W.2d 267 (1965).

7. The common law is the basis of all contract law and still governs agreements for services, employment, the sale of land, and certain other things. It varies from state to state. Article 2 of the UCC governs the sale of goods. The Restatement (Second) of Contracts is not the law anywhere, but it is influential and frequently cited by judges.

9. Honeywell is right. *Honeywell, Inc. v. Minolta Camera Co., Ltd.*, 1991 U.S. Dist. LEXIS 20743 (D.N.J. 1991). Whether the contract is for the sale of goods or for services is determined by the predominant purpose test. Although Honeywell delivered some goods to Minolta, the predominant purpose of the contract was the exchange of technical data, ideas, designs, and so forth. It was therefore a services contract and the UCC did not apply.

CHAPTER 11

1. No. The plaintiff must show that both sides intended to make a contract and that they agreed on definite terms. Here, there is no indication that Roberts intended to make a final deal. Merely handing out order forms is neither an offer nor an acceptance. Further, virtually no binding terms were discussed. *Arnold Pontiac-GMC, Inc. v. General Motors Co.*, 786 F.2d 564 (3d Cir. 1986).

3. (e). Kate will win nothing. The only thing Arturo obligated himself to do is pay $4.50 an hour while Kate worked. He did not promise her a year's employment. The statement about the bonus was too indefinite to be enforceable: there is no way to measure whether "business is good" or what a "healthy" bonus is.

5. The case is governed by UCC §2-207. Litronic offered to sell at a particular price, with a specified warranty. Northrop accepted, but provided a warranty with a different time limit. Yes, there is a contract. Pursuant to §2-207, Northrop intended to accept and create a contract, and the fact that it proposed a different warranty period does not prevent formation of a contract. The question then becomes, what is the warranty period? The conflicting warranty terms cancel each other out and will be replaced by the appropriate Code provision. In this case, the Code provides a "reasonable time" that applies (UCC §2-309). The court found that six months was within the reasonable time, and Northrop won. *Northrop Corp. v. Litronic Industries*, 29 F.3d 1173, 1994 U.S. App. LEXIS 17736 (7th Cir. 1994).

7. Yes. GE made a "firm offer," governed by UCC §2-205. When a merchant signs a written firm offer, the offer may not be revoked within that period or three months, whichever is less. Here the offer was for three months, so it is

irrevocable. *Consolidated Edison Co. v. General Electric*, 555 N.Y.S.2d 355, 1990 N.Y.App. LEXIS 5774 (N.Y. App. Div. 1990).

9. Not for contract, since the written contract excludes this accident. But he has a winning case under promissory estoppel. Wofford, understanding the type of loads that Brown carried, promised that he had full coverage. Wofford knew that Brown would rely on the promise, as he did. The only way to avoid injustice is to enforce Wofford's promise, which in this case nets Brown as much money as the policy itself would have provided. *Bill Brown Construction Co. v. Glens Falls Insurance Co.*, 818 S.W.2d 1, 1991 Tenn. LEXIS 426 (Tenn. 1991).

11. (e). Spike wins nothing. Although he used the phrase, "I accept," he included a counteroffer, which is a rejection of Rebecca's offer. She has no obligation to him.

CHAPTER 12

1. No. The parties never engaged in any bargaining or any exchange. The aunt did not seek anything from the boy in exchange for her promise, nor did the child promise or do anything. He gave no consideration to support her promise, and it is unenforceable. *Daugherty v. Salt*, 227 N.Y. 200, 125 N.E. 94 (1919).

3. (a). CPA Examination, November 1989, #10. There must be bargaining that leads to an exchange. Normally, a benefit to the promisor or a detriment to the promisee will support the promise.

5. Empire won over $3.2 million, and the appeals court affirmed. *Empire Gas Corp. v. American Bakeries Co.*, 840 F.2d 1333, 1988 U.S. App. LEXIS 2482 (7th Cir. 1988). Since this was a requirements contract for the sale of goods (the conversion units and the propane gas were the goods), it was governed by UCC §2-306. American Bakeries did have the right to reduce the number of conversions from the estimated 3,000. It could potentially reduce them even to zero, but any reduction had to be done *in good faith*, meaning that changed circumstances made a reduction important. Here, American Bakeries never offered any reason at all, and the jury verdict was reasonable.

7. Konitz need not pay. Tindall's work had already been performed, without any expectation of payment, when the parties signed the contract. Past consideration is no consideration, and the contract is void. *Tindall v. Konitz Contracting, Inc.*, 249 Mont. 345, 783 P.2d 1376, 1989 Mont. LEXIS 348 (1989).

9. Gintzler did, and should. The consideration to support Melnick's promise of repairs was Gintzler's acceptance of the defective foundation. He was under no obligation to accept a house in that condition. *Gintzler v. Melnick*, 116 N.H. 566, 364 A.2d 637 (1976).

CHAPTER 13

1. (d). Vicki will win nothing. She has no insurable interest in George's life, and her policy is therefore an unenforceable wagering contract.

3. Graham wins. Statutes that require contractors to be licensed are designed to protect the public. As a result, they are strictly enforced. Regardless of what Graham knew, Wagner cannot collect on this illegally earned debt. *Wagner v. Graham*, 296 S.C. 1, 370 S.E.2d 95, 1988 S.C. App. LEXIS 94 (S.C. Ct. App. 1988).

5. McElroy is right. The contract is usurious. By purchasing the property for only $80,000, but guaranteeing McElroy the right to quickly repurchase for $120,000, Grisham is charging $40,000 interest on an $80,000 loan. He would have been better to stay within the bounds of the usury laws: the court ruled that McElroy was entitled to receive *double* the interest he paid. *McElroy v. Grisham*, 306 Ark. 4, 810 S.W.2d 933, 1991 Ark. LEXIS 324 (1991).

7. No. The noncompete clause is unenforceable here because the two companies are not really in competition and Guyan therefore has no confidential information or customer lists to protect. *Voorhees v. Guyan Machinery Co.*, 191 W. Va. 450, 446 S.E.2d 672, 1994 W. Va. LEXIS 27 (1994).

9. It does matter. Because the exculpatory clause was negotiated and was reasonable, the New York Court of Appeals held that it was valid as to ordinary negligence. However, the clause was held invalid as to gross negligence. The court remanded the case to determine whether the dispatcher was grossly negligent. *Sommer v. Federal Signal Corp.*, 79 N.Y.2d 540, 593 N.E.2d 1365, 1992 N.Y. LEXIS 1305 (1992).

11. The danger is that the noncompete clause is overly broad and that a court will not enforce it. In the majority of states, a court will modify the agreement so that it is more reasonable. But in a minority of states, the court will strike the noncompete altogether, leaving the seller free to compete directly with the buyer. That is precisely what happened in *CAE Vanguard, Inc. v. Newman*, 246 Neb. 334, 518 N.W.2d 652, 1994 Neb. LEXIS 156 (1994).

CHAPTER 14

1. The contract is voidable by Barrows's family. Barrows suffered from a mental impairment, senility. The contract is completely one-sided, with almost no money as a down payment and no interest. This reinforces the impression that Barrows was impaired. The family was permitted to rescind. *Barrows v. Bowen*, 1994 Del. Ch. LEXIS 63 (Del. Ch. 1994).

3. You should reverse. The Utah Supreme Court did. There is strong evidence that Beck forced Andreini to sign under duress. The threat to withhold surgery was almost certainly improper, and Andreini probably had no reasonable alternative. *Andreini v. Hultgren*, 860 P.2d 916, 1993 Utah LEXIS 123 (Utah 1993).

5. Fletcher wins. Marshall's agreement to pay one-half was voidable since he was a minor when he signed the lease. But after turning 18 he moved into the apartment and began paying rent. These acts ratified the contract, and at that point it became fully enforceable against him. *Fletcher v. Marshall*, 260 Ill. App. 3d 673, 632 N.E.2d 1105, 1994 Ill. App. LEXIS 559 (Ill. App. Ct. 1994).

7. The Silvas are entitled to damages for fraud (saying the I-beam had been added merely for reinforcement) and

nondisclosure (not mentioning the problems). The jury awarded $21,000 damages and $15,000 punitive damages, and the state supreme court affirmed the verdict. *Silva v. Stevens*, 156 Vt. 94, 589 A.2d 852, 1991 Vt. LEXIS 42 (1991).

9. No. Newburn signed under economic duress. Treadwell had no right to hold the truck, Newburn had no reasonable alternative, and Treadwell's conduct caused economic distress. The release was invalid and Newburn was entitled to damages for his losses. *Newburn v. Dobbs Mobile Bay, Inc.*, 657 So. 2d 849, 1995 Ala. LEXIS 137 (Ala. 1995).

11. Yes. There was no fraud or misrepresentation because Conley knew nothing of the tanks. But there is mutual mistake: the parties were both in error about an important factual assumption, namely, the ground's condition. Morrell was permitted to rescind. *Morrell v. Conley Detective and Security Guard Agency, Inc.*, Michigan Lawyers Weekly No. 18079, Nov. 28, 1994 (Mich. Ct. App. 1994).

CHAPTER 15

1. (d). It *can* be completed within one year. CPA Examination, May 1989, #27.

3. Elmer successfully argued that his promise was a collateral promise, done as a favor to Donald. As an oral promise to pay the debt of another, it was unenforceable. *Waide v. Bingham*, 583 So. 2d 263, 1991 Ala. LEXIS 462 (Ala. 1992).

5. It makes no difference whether he said it or not. An oral promise in consideration of marriage is enforceable. Steven was not obligated to pay child support. *Byers v. Byers*, 618 P.2d 930 (Okla. 1980).

7. Hippen's claim fails. The purchase—or repurchase—of a house is the classic interest in land, and any such promise must be written to be enforceable. *Hippen v. First National Bank*, 1992 U.S. Dist. LEXIS 6029 (D. Kan. 1992).

9. The writing must contain all essential terms. This lease said nothing about duration, an essential part of a lease. The tenant lost. *Simon v. Simon*, Mass Lawyers Weekly No. 11-002-94 (Mass. App. Ct. 1994).

11. Bazak. This contract is for the sale of goods and thus is governed by UCC §2-201. Both parties are merchants. Under the merchants' exception, UCC §2-201(2), when Bazak sent a signed memo sufficient to hold it, Bazak, liable on the deal, Mast would *also* be held to the terms of the deal unless it objected within 10 days. Mast made no objection and Bazak won. *Bazak International Corp. v. Mast Industries*, 73 N.Y. 2d 113, 535 N.E.2d 633, 1989 N.Y. LEXIS 200 (1989).

CHAPTER 16

1. Raritan was hoping to be a third party beneficiary of the contract between IMC and Cherry, Bekaert. But the court was unpersuaded. It found that the accountants had no intention of benefiting anyone other than IMC, that they had no knowledge all of Raritan, and that Raritan had never even seen the original audit, but merely a report of the audit. The court declared that Raritan was an incidental beneficary and hence a loser. *Raritan River Steel Co. v. Cherry, Bekaert & Holland*, 329 N.C. 646, 407 S.E.2d 178, 1991 N.C. LEXIS 519 (1991).

3. (d). CPA Examination, November 1991, #24.

5. Rampart's motion was allowed. Gasket was merely an incidental beneficiary of the Rampart-Nationwide contract. Neither party intended to benefit Gasket, and Gasket thus had no right to enforce the contract. *Orion Group v. Nationwide Discount Sleep Center*, 1990 U.S. Dist. LEXIS 10197 (E.D. Pa. 1990).

7. (a). See UCC §2-210(2). CPA Examination, May 1991, #28.

9. The delegation was legal. Duties are generally delegable unless prohibited by contract, and this agreement was silent on the subject. Delegation is also illegal if the obligee has a substantial interest in personal service by the obligor. But installing and maintaining soft drink machines does not require the level of skill or judgment mandating personal service. Practically anyone can do it, and Virginia Coffee was free to delegate. *Macke Co. v. Pizza of Gaithersburg, Inc.*, 259 Md. 479, 270 A.2d 645 (1970).

11. Hayes loses. He had indeed delegated his duties, but that in itself does not remove his own contractual liability. To establish a novation, he had to demonstrate that the Brookses had explicitly agreed to look only to the subcontractors for performance. There was no such evidence, and no novation. Hayes remained liable. *Brooks v. Hayes*, 133 Wis. 2d 228, 395 N.W.2d 167 (1986).

CHAPTER 17

1. No. The requirement that Krogness introduced the buyer *directly* to Best Buy was a condition precedent to his earning a commission. The condition never occurred and he received nothing. *Krogness v. Best Buy Co.*, 524 N.W.2d 282, 1994 Minn. App. LEXIS 1190 (Minn. Ct. App. 1994).

3. This case creates an issue of substantial performance. The court held that the low garage ceiling was a minor problem and would not defeat substantial performance. But the cracked beams were very serious and might require major reconstruction. The water collecting in the patio could seep under the house and destroy the foundation. The freezing pipes posed a danger of bursting. The contractor had failed to substantially perform and was not entitled to his contract price. He was owed only the value of work completed, if any. *Evans & Associates v. Dyer*, 246 Ill. App. 3d 231, 615 N.E.2d 770, 1993 Ill. App. LEXIS 826 (Ill. App. Ct. 1993).

5. The bank won. Good faith in this setting requires that the bank honestly believe itself to be insecure and that there be *some basis* for the belief. The bank honestly did consider itself at risk of a default, and the combination of the drought and Ruda's refusal to sell land provided a basis for the belief. *Watseka First National Bank v. Ruda*, 135 Ill. 2d 140, 552 N.E.2d 775, 1990 Ill. LEXIS 20 (1990).

7. Loehmann's violated the lease by failing to pay common charges within 10 days of the default letter, regardless of whether 10 days is measured from the day of mailing or receipt. But the breach was trivial. It would be a "dangerous doctrine to permit forfeiture" for any breach, no matter how inconsequential. Loehmann's is still selling clothes at

the mall. *Foundation Development Corp. v. Loehmann's, Inc.*, 163 Ariz. 438, 788 P.2d 1189, 1990 Ariz. LEXIS 44 (1990).

9. (c). CPA Examination, November 1989, #19.

11. Power wins. Although it was impossible for Krug to complete its deal with Iraqi Airways, it was entirely possible for Krug to accept and pay for the gearbox. Defenses of commercial impracticability and frustration of purpose both fail because Power did not know that Krug intended to reship to Iraq. The international resale was not part of the Krug-Power contract, and its failure is no defense. *Power Engineering & Mfg. v. Krug International*, 501 N.W.2d 490, 1993 Iowa LEXIS 157 (Iowa 1993).

CHAPTER 18

1. The market price is relevant. The Beards are entitled to their expectation interest. They will get compensatory damages, representing the difference between the contract price and the market value of the house as it should have been built. If they can prove the value was $100,000 higher than the contract price, they get that sum. They are also entitled to the rental costs, which were consequential damages. S/E could foresee that the Beards would have to rent while waiting for the new house. *Beard v. S/E Joint Venture*, 321 Md. 126, 581 A.2d 1275, 1990 Md. LEXIS 174 (1990).

3. Twin Creeks' claim is dismissed. The Paramount losses are consequential damages. Under the UCC, a seller may not recover consequential damages for the sale of goods. *Twin Creeks Entertainment, Inc. v. U.S. JVC Corp.*, 1995 U.S. Dist. LEXIS 2413 (N.D. Cal. 1995).

5. He should, and did, seek restitution. Expectation damages will be unavailable since Racicky is bankrupt. Specific performance is impossible because Racicky does not own the land. Reformation is irrelevant. Simon gets restitution, since he has conferred a benefit on Racicky and it would be unjust for the defendant to keep it. *Racicky v. Simon*, 831 P.2d 241, 1992 Wyo. LEXIS 60 (Wyo. 1992).

7. A claim for punitive damages, based on Liberty Mutual's bad faith in discouraging Parkinson from filing a claim for money to which she was entitled. The court awarded her $2,000 for uninsured motorist coverage and $40,000 punitive damages. *Liberty Mutual Insurance Co. v. Parkinson*, 487 N.E.2d 162, *reh'g denied*, 491 N.E.2d 229 (Ind. Ct. App. 1986).

9. (d). CPA Examination, May 1992, #35.

11. It sued and obtained an injunction, based on a violation of the NFL's copyright in the broadcasts. The permanent injunction prohibited the bars from showing any blacked-out games without written permission. *NFL v. Rondor, Inc.*, 840 F. Supp. 1160, 1993 U.S. Dist. LEXIS 19599 (N.D. Ohio 1993).

CHAPTER 19

1. (a). CPA Examination, November 1989, #46.

3. The court granted summary judgment for Scotts, ruling that the clause was not unconscionable. The court noted that such clauses are seldom held unconscionable when the buyer is a corporation, as here. Further, the clause was clear and easy to understand, and it was reasonable for the seller to limit its losses when it had no way of gauging the potential consequential damages that a user might allege. *Jim Dan, Inc. v. O. M. Scott & Sons Co.*, 785 F. Supp. 1196, 1992 U.S. Dist. LEXIS 8325 (W.D. Pa. 1992).

5. The parties did create an enforceable agreement because they key is intention. When Mail Code notified Grauberger that it accepted him as a dealer, they had a contract. The question becomes, what are its terms? Under UCC §2-207, the forum selection clause is an *additional* term included in the acceptance. It will become part of the bargain *unless* (1) the offer insisted on its own terms, (2) the additional term materially alters the offer, or (3) the offeror promptly objects to the added term. Grauberger's offer did not insist on its own terms nor did Grauberger promptly object to the new clause. But the forum selection clause *did materially alter* the bargain because it strongly affected Grauberger's ability to enforce the deal. Therefore it *was not* part of the contract, and Grauberger was entitled to sue in Kansas. *M.K.C. Equipment Co. v. M.A.I.L. Code, Inc.*, 843 F. Supp. 679, 1994 U.S. Dist. LEXIS 1204 (D. Kan. 1994).

7. Probably. Under UCC §2-201(2), a signed memo between merchants that would be binding against the sender is sufficient to satisfy the statute of frauds against the recipient if he reads it and fails to object within 10 days.

9. (b). The automobile lease is governed by Article 2A.

CHAPTER 20

1. (d). CPA Examination, November 1989, #49.

3. First State gets it. UCC §2-326(3) creates a presumption in favor of creditors. When goods are delivered *to be sold*, the goods are subject to the creditors' claims unless the owner (Havelka) takes one of the statutory steps to protect himself, such as posting a sign indicating that he owns the merchandise. He did not do that here. The only issue is whether Havelka delivered the seed *to sell*. The court held that because Havelka and other farmers had used Miller to sell seed in the past, which the bank knew, and because the stored seed was indistinguishable from the seed for sale, the purpose of §2-326 would be accomplished by protecting the creditor. The bank had no way of knowing that some of the goods that Miller appeared to own really belonged to others. *First State Bank of Purdy v. Miller*, 119 Bankr. 660, 1990 U.S. Dist. LEXIS 12407 (W.D. Ark. 1990).

5. *In favor:* "Creditor" means anyone who has a right to require the merchant to fulfill an obligation. A monthly rent payment for the next few years is an important obligation, and the landlord may be a creditor with a major interest in the merchant's finances. There is no basis for distinguishing one creditor from another, and all should be protected from a slippery merchant who tries to skip town. See, e.g., *Stone's Pharmacy, Inc. v. Pharmacy Accounting Management, Inc.*, 812 F.2d 1063, 1987 U.S. App. LEXIS 2734 (8th Cir. 1987) (the term "creditor" is not restricted to any one class). *Opposed:* Article 6 seems to refer to normal trade creditors, that is, wholesalers who sell goods to a retailer, or banks that loan money. Those people may well extend security based on the assets of the merchant. But a merchant often will have no assets at the time she signs a lease, so the landlord is not relying on them the way other creditors do. And if the tenant is current with the rent, the landlord does not have a clearly calculable debt, the way, for example, a bank does when the debtor has defaulted. See, e.g., *Schlussel v. Emmanuel Roth Co.*, 270 N.J. Super. 628, 637 A.2d 944, 1994 N.J. Super. LEXIS 53 (N.J. Super. Ct. App. Div. 1994) (a landlord is *not* normally a creditor for Article 6 purposes).

7. Universal is right. UCC §2-401 provides that when goods are being moved, title passes to the buyer when the seller completes whatever transportation it is obligated to do. Pifcom completed its work by delivering to the trucking company, at which time title passed. *Pittsburgh Industrial Furnace Co. v. Universal Consolidated Companies, Inc.*, 789 F. Supp. 184, 1991 U.S. Dist. LEXIS 19936 (W.D. Pa. 1991).

9. (b). CPA Examination, May 1990 #47.

11. (d). CPA Examination, May 1994, #45.

CHAPTER 21

1. (a). CPA Examination, May 1994, #43.

3. The one-line description of the steel, in Callier's invoice, created an express warranty. Assuming that the steel delivered actually was inferior, Leighton would win its warranty claim, even if Callier had made no other warranty, oral or written. *Leighton Industries, Inc. v. Callier Steel Pipe & Tube, Inc.*, 991 U.S. Dist LEXIS 1749 (N.D. Ill. 1991).

5. Betty will win because the remedy limitation is unconscionable. Courts dislike the limitations when they apply to consumer goods, especially in cases of personal injury. See *Collins v. Uniroyal*, 64 N.J. 260, 315 A.2d 16 (1974) (tire blowout causes buyer's death; sales agreement limiting remedy to repair or replacement held unconscionable). But in commercial cases, where the loss is purely economic, the remedy limitation is enforceable, and Green will recover nothing. See, e.g., *Golden Reward Mining Co. v. Jervis B. Webb Co.*, 772 F. Supp. 1118, 1991 U.S. Dist. LEXIS 12601 (D.S. Dak. 1991) (exclusion of consequential damages is not unconscionable in commercial contract with purely economic loss).

7. Highland lost. The merchantability warranty requires that goods be fit "for their ordinary purpose." Brochures are not normally placed in contact with very hot pizza. Comark had no idea the brochure would be subjected to such heat and was entitled to its contract damages. *Comark Merchandising, Inc. v. Highland Group*, 932 F.2d 1196, 1991 U.S. App. LEXIS 10470 (7th Cir. 1991).

9. (a). CPA Examination, May 1992, #57.

CHAPTER 22

1. (b). CPA Examination, November 1993, #56.

3. Lost profits are consequential damages. Haddad is right that a buyer may not recover consequential damages that it could have prevented by cover. But Jewell-Rung offered legitimate reasons for not covering: the only Lakeland garments now available to it were those made by Olympic. Olympic would not sell a competitor the garments at reasonable prices. Further, Jewel-Rung could not rely on the quality of the garments manufactured by a different company. Jewell-Rung's failure to cover was reasonable, and the company was entitled to prove its lost profits. *Jewell-Rung Agency, Inc. v. Haddad Organization, Ltd.*, 814 F. Supp. 337, 1993 U.S. Dist. LEXIS 1923 (S.D.N.Y. 1993).

5. Storms has *repudiated* the contract, meaning that he has stated he will not perform. Cargill is entitled to wait for a reasonable time to see if Storms will still perform his obligations. Cargill is also entitled to resort immediately to any of the remedies the Code allows for actual *breach* of the contract. The most reasonable remedy is probably for Cargill to resell the seed elsewhere and sue Storms for any deficiency. *Cargill, Inc. v. Storms Agri Enterprises*, 46 Ark. App. 237, 878 S.W.2d 786, 1994 Ark. App. LEXIS 368 (Ark. Ct. App. 1994)

7. Allied recovers the entire purchase price for the 35,000 chips. Pulsar does have a right to cure its delivery of non-conforming goods, but Pulsar must pay the entire cost of curing, including testing. Its offer was not a true cure, and Allied gets its money back. *Allied Semi-Conductors International, Ltd. v. Pulsar Components International, Inc.*, 842 F. Supp. 653, 1993 U.S. Dist. LEXIS 19735 (E.D.N.Y. 1993).

9. (a). CPA Examination, May 1992, #56.

11. *Reversed.* The Association's members can potentially recover consequential damages for lost profits. The losses could represent lost sales of gasoline, lost sales of other items in the mini-mart, and lost goodwill. Gasoline is a legitimate lost profit because, under the agreement with ARCO, the owners could not cover by purchasing gasoline elsewhere. It is reasonable to assume that if gasoline sales dropped, there was a ripple effect on mini-mart sales. Finally, as long as the plaintiffs can provide a reasonable basis from which the jury can calculate goodwill damages, they may pursue that issue as well.

CHAPTER 23

1. For an instrument to be negotiable, it must be payable on demand or at a definite time. The certificate of deposit was not payable until the death of the owner, which was not a definite time. Therefore, it was not negotiable and did not require Wygant's indorsement. *West Greeley National Bank v. Wygant*, 650 P.2d 1339 (Colo. Ct. App. 1982).

3. (a). Because of the shelter rule. CPA Examination, May 1990, #38.

5. The court held that Parkhill was not a holder in due course. Parkhill's anticipated profit was so high, she should have suspected that the underlying transaction had a defect. *In re Nusor*, 23 Bankr. 55, 1991 Bankr. LEXIS 57 (9th Cir. 1991).

7. The lawyers could not be holders in due course unless they had given value for the note. The appeals court asked the trial court to determine the value of the legal services the lawyers had performed for the corporation at the time the note was given to them. *Fernandez v. Cunningham*, 268 So.2d 166 (Ct. App. Fla. 1972).

9. Yes. Even though the payment of the loan will discharge your obligation to the lender, such discharge is not effective upon a holder in due course without notice of the payment. Therefore, you should either require the return of the original promissory note or confirm that the original promissory note has been marked "satisfied" so that the promissory note cannot be sold to a holder in due course without notice. Christopher Combs, "Failure to Inspect Home Personally Isn't a Legal Reason to Cancel Sale," *Arizona Republic/Phoenix Gazette*, Dec. 4, 1993, p. AH4.

11. Littlegreen alleged the note was unenforceable because of duress. The court held that, to sustain a charge of duress, Littlegreen would have had to prove that Gardner could carry out his threat. Littlegreen was unable to show that Gardner could indeed have blocked the loan. Therefore, the note was enforceable. *Littlegreen v. Gardner*, 208 Ga. 523, 67 S.E.2d 713 (1951).

CHAPTER 24

1. The bank was held liable for conversion. *Lawyers' Fund v. Manufacturers Hanover Trust Co.*, 153 Misc. 2d 360, 581 N.Y.S.2d 133, 1992 N.Y. Misc. LEXIS 65 (N.Y. Sup. Ct. 1992).

3. (d). CPA Examination, November 1992, #41.

5. An unauthorized indorsement is the same as a forged indorsement. The court held that the bank was liable for the conversion of Phariss's check. *Phariss v. Eddy*, 478 N.W.2d 848, 1991 Iowa App. LEXIS 459 (IOWA Ct. App. 1991).

7. The court held that D-FW was not liable to Knopf because an indorser is only liable to the holder of an instrument and to other indorsers, not to the issuer of a check. *Knopf v. Dallas-Fort Worth Roofing Supply Co., Inc.*, 786 S.W.2d 37, 1990 Tex. App. LEXIS 708 (Tex. Ct. App. 1990).

9. To avoid personal liability, the two men were required to give the name of the principal and indicate that they were signing as agents. Under the parol evidence rule (discussed in Chapter 15), the court would not even admit evidence of the bank officer's promise. There is a moral to this story: never sign a contract that does not say what you mean. *Bostwick Banking Co. v. Arnold*, 227 Ga. 18, 178 S.E.2d 890 (1970).

11. The court found for the bank on the grounds that the owner of the company had been negligent in not reviewing his bank statements. If he had done so, he would have discovered the forgeries early in the game and limited his losses. *Winkie, Inc. v. Heritage Bank of Whitefish Bay*, 299 N.W.2d 829 (S.Ct. Wis. 1981).

CHAPTER 25

1. More than 90 days elapsed between Fischer's indorsement of the check and her receipt of notice of its dishonor. It is apparent that one of the several banks involved in the collection process violated its midnight deadline in giving notice of dishonor. Fischer's liability as an indorser was discharged when the violation of the midnight deadline by a bank, identity unknown, resulted in unreasonable delay in notice of dishonor. Nevada State Bank may look to the violator for its recovery. *Nevada State Bank v. Fischer*, 93 Nev. 317, 565 P.2d 332 (1997).

3. The UCC requires customers to examine a statement within a reasonable time to discover if payment has been made on a forged or altered instrument. That statute is not applicable to the situation in which a bank disregards a valid stop payment order. If the customer can prove a loss, the bank is liable on the stop payment order. The bank is liable. *Begg & Daigle, Inc. v. Chemical Bank*, 575 N.Y.S.2d 638, 1991 N.Y. Misc. LEXIS 605 (N.Y. Sup. Ct. 1991).

5. Once the bank paid the check, it became entitled to any claim arising out of the transaction that Woodhaven had against Ava or Ava had against Woodhaven. By its agreement to accept $5,000 from Ava, the bank relinquished its right to proceed in subrogation against Ava. The bank was still, however, subrogated to Ava's rights against Woodhaven and could proceed against Woodhaven. *Manufacturers Hanover Trust Co. v. Ava Industries, Inc.*, 414 N.Y.S. 2d 425 (N.Y. Sup. Ct. 1979).

7. If an unauthorized person withdraws money from a customer's account, the customer is liable only for $50, provided that she notifies the bank within 60 days of receiving the bank statement on which the unauthorized transfer is reported. Joanne Johnson, "High-Tech Caper Prompts Banks to Step Up Security," *Hartford Courant*, July 11, 1993, p. D1.

9. (c). If a customer uses a teller to deposit a government check in an account, she can write a check on those funds on the next business day. She can withdraw $400 in cash on the same day that funds are available for check writing. The next day, she can withdraw the balance. Harriet gets the apartment!

11. No, in executing a payment order, a bank may rely on the account number, instead of the name. First American had placed the money in the account that matched the number on the wire, so it was not liable even though the names did not match. *Shawmut Worcester Cty. Bank v. First American Bank & Trust*, 731 F. Supp. 57, 1990 U.S. Dist. LEXIS 2038 (1990).

CHAPTER 26

1. (b). CPA Examination, May 1994, #50.

3. Yes to both questions. The bank had a valid security interest in all of Able's equipment, including after-acquired equipment. After-required clauses are valid. The only question is whether the bank's security interest could *attach* to the backhoe. Attachment requires that the debtor has *rights* in the collateral. But this does not mean that the debtor must own the goods. Here, Ables had the lawful use and possession of the backhoe, based on his purchase agreement with Myers. He thus had rights in the backhoe, and as soon as he took possession of it, the bank's security interest attached. The bank gets the backhoe. *United States v. Ables*, 739 F. Supp. 1439, 1990 U.S. Dist. LEXIS 7064 (D. Kan. 1990).

5. The creditors were right, but they still lost. Gallatin had filed in the wrong county, but its interest had perfected automatically. Gallatin had taken a purchase money security interest in a consumer good, which perfects automatically. The bank had not needed to perfect anywhere. *In re Lockovich*, 124 Bankr. 660, 1991 U.S. Dist. LEXIS 8486 (W.D. Pa. 1991).

7. First of America gets the machine. A perfected security interest takes priority over an unperfected interest. *Barwell, Inc. v. First of America Bank-Laporte, N.A.*, 768 F. Supp. 1312, 1991 U.S. Dist. LEXIS 10222 (N.D. Ind. 1991).

9. (c). CPA Examination, May 1993, #46.

11. The legal answer: If the parties had a secured transaction governed by Article 9, GECC was obligated to give the Dannemans notice before selling the collateral. If they had a lease, there was no such requirement. The court ruled it was a secured transaction:

If you look at the situation in common sense terms without the legal veneer, it seems clear that this agreement is a financing arrangement with security. The "lessor" has retained no significant burdens of ownership and, for that matter, no significant burdens of a "seller." Indeed, this particular "lessor" holds the paper by assignment. In terms of simple justice, why should a Court bend this factual reality to permit repossession of the goods followed by a private sale, somewhat of a sweetheart arrangement back to the manufacturer, without notice to the one to be held ultimately responsible for the debt.

The ethical answer: Although we do not know exactly why the Dannemans misunderstood the documents they signed, we do know the documents were drafted by Kodak. Should Kodak have an obligation to make clear to its customers what they are signing? Whether the Dannemans behaved ethically depends on whether they legitimately had all of the problems they claimed, something we do not know. Kodak's behavior is troublesome because the company never made clear it was making a lease, and because it may well have been involved in a sweetheart deal, as the court points out. GECC not only violated Article 9 by failing to give notice, but it would seem to have resorted to an unfair scheme to keep Kodak happy while maximizing the Dannemans' deficiency. It is just that sort of conduct that Article 9 was designed to *prevent. G.E. Capital Corp. v. Danneman Associates, Inc.*, 1995 Del. Super. LEXIS 131 (Del. Super. 1995).

CHAPTER 27

1. The court refused to discharge the loans because the debtor had acted in bad faith. He pretended to his then wife and father-in-law that he was making an effort to stabilize his marriage, when in fact he was rendering it asunder. *In re Milbank*, 1 Bankr. 150 (Bankr. S.D.N.Y. 1979).

3. The court agreed with Hartley's argument that the $1 million debt is dischargeable because he did not intend to injure Jones when he threw the firecracker into the basement. *In re Hartley*, 869 F.2d 394, 1989 U.S. App. LEXIS 2711 (8th Cir. 1989). (This case was later vacated. 874 F.2d 1254.)

5. The court refused to approve the reaffirmation because the Credit Union's threats constituted duress. *In re Brown*, 95 Bankr. 35, 1989 Bankr. LEXIS 543 (Bankr. E.D. Va. 1989).

7. Under Chapter 7, fraud claims are not dischargeable. *In re Britton*, 950 F.2d 602, 1991 U.S. App. LEXIS 28487 (9th Cir. 1991).

9. (d). CPA Examination, May 1991, #29.

11. The court would not permit this debt to be discharged because Dr. Khan was not acting in good faith. *In re M. Ibrahim Khan, P.S.C.*, 34 Bankr. 574 (Bankr. W.D. Ky. 1983).

CHAPTER 28

1. A broker owes his principal a duty to exercise due care and to act in good faith. Gregory violated this duty when he failed even to follow Bache's own procedures. He was liable to Mrs. Thropp. *Thropp v. Bache Halsey Stuart Shields, Inc.*, 650 F.2d 817 (6th Cir. 1981).

3. A formal agreement, either written or oral, is not necessary to establish an agency relationship. Consent, control, and a fiduciary relationship are enough. *United States v. German-American Vocational League, Inc.*, 153 F.2d 860 (3rd Cir. 1946).

5. (c). CPA Examination, May 1992, #6.

7. Ingersoll violated his duty not to compete against his principal when he bid on the DOD contract while employed by RTV. *Radio TV Reports, Inc. v. Ingersoll*, 742 F. Supp. 19, 1990 U.S. Dist. LEXIS 10588 (D.D.C. 1990).

9. No. The Fellowship had no control over the trip to Perryville; therefore, no agency relationship. *Lafayette Bank & Trust Co. v. Price*, 440 N.E.2d 759 (Ind. Ct. App. 1982).

11. The court held that Western Pioneer was liable for Arlington's legal fees. Arlington acted in good faith within the scope of its authority. If Western Pioneer had paid the Wilson claim when due, Arlington would not have had to undergo the expense of defending itself at trial. *Wilson v. Arlington Auto Sales, Inc.*, 743 S.W.2d 923 (1987).

CHAPTER 29

1. Mr. Pommert had not ratified Mrs. Pommert's actions because he had not known all the material facts when he placed the Christmas decorations in his car. *Bryan v. Pommert*, 110 Ind. App. 61, 37 N.E.2d 720 (Ind. App. 1941).

3. Yes, the story is accurate. Under the theory of *respondeat superior*, a principal is liable when a servant acting within the scope of employment commits a negligent or intentional tort that causes physical harm to a person or property. Anthony DeStefano, "Wreck's 1st Legal Claim Seeks $10M for Injuries," *Newsday*, Aug. 29, 1991, p. 10.

5. The court held that the school district was not liable because the employee's actions were prompted wholly by personal motivation and were clearly not incidental to his duties as a custodian. Also, the act was not foreseeable because it was not "typical" of the enterprise undertaken by the employer. *Alma W. v. Oakland Unified School District*, 123 Cal. App. 3d 133, 176 Cal. Rptr. 287 (Cal. Ct. App. 1981).

7. Principals are liable for the torts of their independent contractors only if they have been negligent in hiring the contractors. Presumably, Gerulaitis's mother will try to prove that the Raynes were negligent in hiring the mechanic who installed the heater. Vivian S. Troy, "Gerulaitis's Mother Files Suit in Son's Carbon Monoxide Death," *New York Times*, June 1, 1995, p. B5.

9. The court held that the Assistant United States Attorney did indeed have implied authority to represent the U.S. government and, therefore, the INS could not deport Thomas. *Thomas v. INS*, 35 F.3d 1332, 1994 U.S. App. LEXIS 33649 (9th Cir. 1994).

11. Bennett alleged that the company was liable for the assault committed by its independent contractor because it had been negligent in hiring him. The appeals court held for Bennett on the grounds that she was entirely innocent, whereas T & F could have prevented the injury by being more careful during the hiring process. *Bennett v. T & F Distrib. Co.*, 117 N.J. Super. 439, 285 A.2d 59 (N.J. 1971).

CHAPTER 30

1. The court held that freedom of association is an important social right, and one that ordinarily should not dictate employment decisions. However, the right to associate with a nonspouse at an employer's convention without fear of termination is not a threat to public policy. Nor is discharge for being too successful. *Staats v. Ohio National Life Insurance Co.*, 620 F. Supp. 118 (W.D. Pa. 1985).

3. Ledbetter committed a wrongful discharge when he fired Delaney for refusing to commit the tort of defamation. *Delaney v. Taco Time International, Inc.*, 297 Or. 10, 681 P.2d 114 (1984).

5. The court held that "sexual discrimination that creates a hostile or abusive work environment is a violation of Title VII of the Civil Rights Act." The employer was liable because he knew about the harassment but did not stop it. The plaintiffs filed a claim with the EEOC and then commenced a lawsuit after the EEOC granted them a right-to-sue notice. *Hall v. Gus Construction Co.*, 842 F.2d 1010, 1988 U.S. App. LEXIS 3666 (8th Cir. 1988).

7. The court held that the company was liable for the intentional infliction of emotional distress. *Agis v. Howard Johnson*, 371 Mass. 140, 355 N.E.2d 315 (1976).

9. The Supreme Court held that Duke Power Company was in violation of Title VII because the job requirements did not measure job performance. The court stated that, "What Congress has commanded is that any tests used must measure the person for the job and not the person in the abstract." *Griggs v. Duke Power Co.*, 401 U.S. 24, 91 S.Ct. 849, 1971 U.S. LEXIS 134.

11. The court found the Postal Service liable on the grounds that Lussier had been dismissed solely because of his disability. *Lussier v. Runyon*, 1994 U.S. Dist. LEXIS 4668 (D. Maine 1994).

CHAPTER 31

1. Each of the acts described was an unfair labor practice in violation of §8 of the NLRA. Workers have the right to organize and join a union. Although management is entitled to advocate vigorously against unionization, it may not *threaten* employees or *interfere* with the organizing effort. The NLRB found the employer's interference to be extreme, and it issued a bargaining order. The court of appeals affirmed. *Power, Inc. v. NLRB*, 40 F.3d 409, 1994 U.S. App. LEXIS 32648 (D.C. Cir. 1994).

3. The union claimed that the company had committed numerous ULPs and asked for the exceptional remedy of a bargaining order, that is, an order to the company to begin bargaining without an election. The NLRB granted the order and the court of appeals affirmed. *NLRB v. Q-1 Motor Express, Inc.*, 25 F.3d 473, 1994 U.S. App. LEXIS 12283 (7th Cir. 1994).

5. The strike was initially over pay and was thus an economic strike. If the company committed a ULP by refusing to bargain until the validity of the strike was resolved, then it converted the dispute into a ULP strike. In that case, all striking workers would be entitled to their jobs back, even if it meant laying off replacement workers. But the court ruled that the company had *not* committed a ULP. Gibson claimed in good faith that the strike was illegal. The strike remained an economic one, and the striking workers were *not* guaranteed their jobs back (though they had to be rehired without discrimination if openings appeared). *Gibson Greetings v. NLRB*, 53 F.3d 385, 1995 U.S. App. LEXIS 11788 (D.C. Cir. 1995).

7. The union is correct. Eads *locked out* its employees by refusing to allow them back to work. A lockout is a legitimate weapon with which a company may apply economic pressure on a union to force agreement on a CBA. But the company must *notify* the union of the lockout before it begins, so that the union understands the position and may bargain or respond accordingly. Without such notice, the lockout doesn't serve to bring the parties together, which is the purpose of NLRA. *Eads Transfer, Inc. v. NLRB*, 989 F.2d 373, 1993 U.S. App. LEXIS 6872 (9th Cir. 1993).

9. The Board of Education committed a ULP by terminating the position. The Board has a continuing duty to bargain in good faith—even after a CBA has been signed. If issues arise that require bargaining, or a grievance under the CBA, the Board must act in good faith. Here, the Board terminated a position to evade an arbitrator's award made pursuant to the CBA. That is a ULP. The court ordered the Board of Education to restore the job to Schipul. *Board of Education of Thomaston v. State Board of Labor Relations*, 217 Conn. 110, 584 A.2d 1172, 1991 Conn. LEXIS 10 (1991).

11. Companies rely on two main arguments to justify subcontracting to a cheaper labor source, whether the work is sent to a less expensive part of the United States or overseas. First, companies have to survive to offer work to *anyone*. In a global economy, a firm that cannot compete with cheaper goods imported from another part of the country, or from a developing country, will go under. Second, sending work to a less prosperous area or country contributes to that local economy, raising the standard of living. All regions and nations have to go through the gradual development and rising standards that much of the industrialized world has already witnessed. Unions reply that it is madness to expect U.S. workers to compete with impoverished workers who live in squalor in countries that violently repress employees' rights to organize. Society is harmed, not helped, by taking work away from those who have achieved a liv-

able wage and giving it to those who will not be paid fairly. The proper solution is to refuse to trade with nations that force workers to live in poverty by refusing them the right to form unions.

CHAPTER 32

1. The court found for Hardee's. Although Hardee's personnel were irresponsible in providing sales figures for the Maumelle store and overstating the possibility of buying a company-owed store, the plaintiff should not have relied on these representations because they were not contained in the offering circular. *Hardee's of Maumelle v. Hardee's Food System*, 31 F.3d 573, 1994 U.S. App. LEXIS 20264 (7th Cir. 1994).

3. Although a limited liability company is a partnership for federal income tax purposes, an LLC is a separate legal entity (although not a taxable entity). The rights and interests of a member in an LLC are similar to those of shareholders in a corporation. Therefore, Fox Hollow Ventures must be represented by a lawyer in court. *Poore v. Fox Hollow Enterprises*, 1994 Del. Super. LEXIS 193 (Del. Super. Ct. 1994).

5. A sole proprietorship would not have worked because there was more than one owner. A partnership would have been a disaster because of the unlimited liability. An S corporation would probably have been the best choice because the owners could have deducted their losses on this investment from their (substantial) other income and still enjoyed limited liability. The owners would probably not have been troubled by the restraints of an S corporation—only one class of stock, for example. They could also have used a limited liability company. A limited partnership would have worked, too, but the owners would have wanted to form a corporation to serve as general partner.

7. Yes. The Biscuit Bakery was a sole proprietorship. No matter how Mrs. Meadows signed the contracts, she is still personally liable for the debts of the business.

9. It is unlawful to sell a franchise without providing the prospective franchisee with a copy of the offering circular at least seven days prior to the execution of a binding franchise. Any sale of a franchise in violation of the law is voidable at the election of the franchisee. The Germains were therefore entitled to rescind the franchises. *My Pie International, Inc. v. Debould, Inc.*, 687 F.2d 919 (7th Cir. 1982).

CHAPTER 33

1. The court held the Greiner was not a partner by estoppel because, before the accident, Perry did not know that Greiner had held himself out as a partner of Bryan Little's. Therefore, she did not rely on the existence of the partnership before parking her car at the airport. *Greiner v. Perry*, 13 Ohio L. Abs. 688 (Ct. App., Clark County 1933).

3. The court held that that the two men were partners in the dozer business because they were operating as co-owners. *Nolen v. Burnett*, 1992 Ark. App. LEXIS 54 (Ark. Ct. App. 1992).

5. The dissolution had no effect on the existing liabilities of the partnership. A partnership's legal existence continues during the winding up of its affairs, and the partnership can sue and be sued for the enforcement of the partnership's rights and obligations until the winding up is complete. *Baker v. Rushing*, 104 N.C. App. 240, 409 S.E.2d 108, 1991 N.C. App. LEXIS 1018 (N.C. Ct. App. 1991).

7. Gull was not entitled to share in fees from new business undertaken by Van Epps and Werth during the winding up of the partnership. He was, however, entitled to his share of fees for work in progress at the time of the dissolution. Likewise, Van Epps and Werth were entitled to a share of the fees earned by Gull during the winding up process on work that was in progress when he left the partnership. *Gull v. Van Epps*, 185 Wis. 2d 609, 517 N.W.2d 531, 1994 Wis. App. LEXIS 628 (Wis. Ct. App. 1994).

9. The partnership owes a total of $50,000. It sold the business for only $26,000. Each partner must contribute $8,000 toward the $24,000 deficit. Effectively, Professor Lawless will receive the $26,000 from the sale of the business. Then Lauren will pay both him and Megan $4,000. Kristen also will pay Megan $8,000.

11. (b).

CHAPTER 34

1. The trial court dismissed Cook's complaint on a motion for summary judgment. The Supreme Court of Texas overturned the dismissal on the grounds that Cook was entitled to a trial on the issue of whether Lyon had apparent authority for the firm when he offered Cook investment advice. *Cook v. Brundidge, Fountain, Elliott & Churchill*, 533 S.W.2d 751 (Tex. 1976).

3. Where the remaining partners in a firm expel a partner under a no-cause expulsion clause in a partnership agreement freely negotiated and entered into, the expelling partners act in good faith regardless of motivation as long as they do not wrongfully withhold money or property legally due the expelled partner. *Lawlis v. Kightlinger & Gray*, 562 N.E.2d 435, 1990 Ind. App. LEXIS 1450 (Ind. Ct. App. 1990).

5. The court denied David's request for compensation. There was no evidence that Jerome benefited from using the property as collateral. Nor was the partnership damaged, even potentially, by the listing of its property as collateral, because a partner's right in specific partnership property is not transferable and any attempt to transfer such property is void. *Schoenborn v. Schoenborn*, 402 N.W. 2d 212 (Minn. Ct. App. 1987).

7. Creditors with contract claims against a partnership must first exhaust partnership assets before proceeding directly against individual partners. *Seventy-Three Land v. Maxlar Partners*, 270 N.J. Super. 332, 637 A.2d. 202, 1994 N.J. Super. LEXIS 51 (N.J. Super. Ct. App. Div. 1994).

9. Yes. Bill and Heidi's vote was binding on the partnership and on all the partners. Dutch would not have been liable if he had dissolved the partnership by withdrawing before the loan was made.

11. Partnership property is owned by the partnership as an entity. An individual partner does not have the right to assign a specific item of partnership property without the consent of the other partners. Columbia's mortgage is void and unenforceable. *Columbia Mortg. Co. v. Hsieh*, 42 Wash. App. 114, 708 P.2d 1226 (Wash. 1985).

CHAPTER 35

1. The appeals court pierced the corporate veil and held the shareholder liable because the corporation had grossly inadequate capitalization and had disregarded corporate formalities, and the shareholder was also actively participating in the operation of the business. *Laya v. Erin Homes, Inc.*, 177 W. Va. 343, 352 S.E.2d 93 (1986).

3. Only an ethical obligation, not a legal one. The court held that the second contract was a novation that ended Wilkerson's obligations under the first contract. *Ajouelo v. Wilkerson*, 85 Ga. App. 397, 69 S.E.2d 375 (Ga. Ct. App. 1952).

5. The court dismissed the complaint because the defendants did not pretend to be acting for a corporation. Nor did any of the defendants sign contracts for the commission. *Shoreham Hotel L.P. v. Wilder*, 866 F. Supp. 1, 1994 U.S. Dist. LEXIS 15277 (D.D.C. 1994).

7. The court ruled that the directors' activities were *ultra vires* only if they had deliberately committed illegal acts themselves. *Resolution Trust Corp. v. Norris*, 830 F. Supp. 351, 1993 U.S. Dist. LEXIS 3902 (S.D.Tex. 1993).

9. Waltuch was not entitled to indemnification because he was not "successful on the merits or otherwise." Although Waltuch himself did not pay the individual plaintiffs, Conticommodity had paid for him. *Waltuch v. Conticommodity Servs.*, 833 F. Supp. 302, 1993 U.S. Dist. LEXIS 13066 (S.D.N.Y. 1993).

11. If Angelica incorporates in Delaware, she will have to qualify to do business in Arkansas. Given that she does not plan a multistate operation for some years, it probably does not make sense to incorporate in Delaware now and incur an extra set of fees. If, at some point, it turns out that Delaware (or some other state) offers significant advantages, she can always switch her state of incorporation then.

CHAPTER 36

1. The court prohibited the low-price sale of two divisions because the sale could not rationally be related to any benefit to the stockholders. Further, it held that when the breakup of the company became inevitable, the Revlon board had a duty to maximize the company's sale price. The board could not accept the lower offer. *Revlon, Inc. v. MacAndrews & Forbes Holdings*, 506 A.2d 173 (Del. 1986).

3. A shareholder of a company that has a staggered board must control the votes of more stock to elect a director than the shareholder of a company without a staggered board. The formula for cumulative voting is:

$$\text{Number of Shares to Elect One Director} = \frac{\text{Number of Shares Outstanding}}{\text{Number of Directors Being Elected} + 1} + 1$$

To review this formula, see Chapter 35, Life and Death of a Corporation. Under cumulative voting, if a company had 15 directors and 165,000,000 shares outstanding, without a staggered board, a shareholder would have to control

$$x = \left[\frac{165{,}000{,}000}{15 + 1}\right] + 1$$

$$x = 10{,}312{,}501 \text{ shares to elect a director.}$$

With a staggered board, only five directors would be up for election; in that case, the shareholder would have to control

$$x = \left[\frac{165{,}000{,}000}{5 + 1}\right] + 1$$

$$x = 27{,}500{,}001 \text{ shares to elect a director.}$$

5. The failure of the board of directors to obtain an updated appraisal of the subsidiary before agreeing to accept Burmah's offer violated the business judgment rule. The court granted an injunction against the sale until the value of the company could be determined. *Gimbel v. Signal Cos.*, 316 A.2d 599 (Del. Ch. 1974).

7. The directors would be liable only if they had actual knowledge of the illegal antitrust actions of the company's employees. Absent cause for suspicion, there is no duty upon the directors to install and operate a corporate system of espionage to ferret out wrongdoing that they have no reason to suspect exists. *Graham v. Allis-Chalmers Manufacturing Co.*, 41 Del. Ch. 78, 188 A.2d 125 (1963).

9. (c). (a) is a conflict of interest. (b) is a violation of the duty of loyalty. (d) could only be done with the approval of the entire board. CPA Examination, May 1991, #5.

11. The Paramount board had no right to turn down the high bidder on the grounds that it preferred the low-bidder's long-term strategy. No matter which bidder was successful, control of the company would change, and the current board would have no meaningful input into the company's future strategy. *Paramount Communications, Inc. v. QVC Network*, 637 A.2d 34, 1994 Del. LEXIS 57 (Del. 1994).

CHAPTER 37

1. A shareholder proposal is not binding on the company. Even if the shareholders approved NYSCRF's proposal, A & P would be under no obligation to carry it out. A bylaw amendment, on the other hand, would indeed be binding on the company.

3. The Supreme Judicial Court of Massachusetts held that "the defendants bear the burden of proving, first, that the merger was for a legitimate business purpose, and, sec-

ond, that, considering the totality of the circumstances, it was fair to the minority." Since the defendants could not meet that burden, the court declared the merger to be illegal. Ordinarily, the court would have rescinded the merger, but by then it was nearly 10 years old. Instead, the Supreme Judicial Court remanded the case to the trial court to determine appropriate monetary damages. *Coggins v. New England Patriots*, 397 Mass. 525, 492 N.E.2d 1112 (1986).

5. According to the Model Act, a company must seek shareholder approval before "a sale of assets other than in the regular course of business." Because a sale of most of Finalco's assets is not "in the regular course of business," Finalco would indeed need shareholder approval. Michael Abramowitz, "Feud Creates Foggy Future for Finalco; Company May Sell Assets—But Then, It May Not," *Washington Post*, Dec. 12, 1987, p. C1.

7. Fogel also notified shareholders that, under Maryland law, they were entitled to exercise "dissenters' rights." They could object to the buyout and have the value of their stock set by an appraiser appointed by the courts. Stan Hinden, "Waterbed Firm Taken Private after Sales Dry Up," *Washington Post*, Mar. 18, 1991, p. F33.

9. The court held that DuPont was not required to include the proposal because it dealt with a matter relating to the conduct of DuPont's ordinary business operations. *Roosevelt v. E. I. DuPont de Nemours & Co.*, 958 F.2d 416, 1992 U.S. App. LEXIS 3497 (D.C. Cir. 1992).

CHAPTER 38

1. The painting was not a security because there was no "common enterprise." The investors did not pool funds or share profits with other investors. Nor did Love share in any profits earned on Stenger's paintings. *Stenger v. R. H. Love Galleries, Inc.*, 741 F.2d 144 (7th Cir. 1984).

3. Fluor was not in violation because the company lacked *scienter*. Fluor had no intent to defraud investors; it was simply making a good faith effort to comply with the terms of its contract. *State Teachers Retirement Board v. Fluor Corp.*, 654 F.2d 843 (2d Cir. 1981).

5. This ice cream company is selling a security and must comply with both state and federal securities laws. Ellen Lahr, "Investor Milks Profits of Ice Cream Firm," *Boston Globe*, July 30, 1995, p. 38.

7. (b). The company is traded on a securities exchange. CPA Examination, May 1989, #41.

9. This is how *Investor's Business Daily, Inc.* answered: In this case, answer "(b)" shouldn't get you into trouble. But if that stranger happens to be talking to you and he's not a stranger at all, but a neighbor and XYZ's president, watch out. Geanne Perlman Rosenberg, "When a Tip Becomes a Trap," *Investor's Business Daily, Inc.*, June 14, 1995, p. A1.

11. A company cannot presume that all shareholders are able to access the annual report and proxy materials via an Internet Web site. Therefore, unless the company had consent from all of its shareholders, this posting would not meet SEC requirements. The company is not prohibited from putting the materials on the Web site, but it must also provide a paper version. Use of Electronic Media for Delivery Purposes Securities Act Release No. 7233, Exchange Act Release No. 36-345 (October 6, 1995).

CHAPTER 39

1. Krouse was not liable. *Toro Co. v. Krouse, Kern & Co.*, 827 F.2d 155, 1987 U.S. App. LEXIS 11186 (7th Cir. 1987).

3. The accountant was not liable. *Badische v. Caylor*, 356 S.E.2d 198 1987 Ga. LEXIS 768 (Ga. 1987).

5. Deloitte was not liable because GAAS did not require it to disclose the flaws. Furthermore, the internal controls functioned adequately at the time of the audit. *Monroe v. Hughes*, 31 F.2d 772, 1994 U.S. App. LEXIS 18003 (9th Cir. 1994).

7. Jackson has committed fraud and is liable to Hall. The negligence doctrine is irrelevant. In the case of fraud, an accountant is liable to any foreseeable user of the work product who justifiably relies on it. *Hall v. Edge*, 782 P.2d 122, 1989 Okla. LEXIS 173 (Okla. 1989).

9. Although, in theory, the accountant owns the working papers, he may not disclose confidential client information without the client's permission. Ian Burrell and Adrian Levy, "Venables to Sue BBC Chief over 'Stolen' Papers," *Sunday Times*, July 16, 1995, Home News section.

11. The court held that the doctors could file suit in either tort or contract. It was implied in the contract that Peat would act like a reasonably careful accountant under the circumstances. When Peat was negligent, it violated the contract. *Billings Clinic v. Peat Marwick Main & Co.*, 797 P.2d 899, 1990 Mont. LEXIS 241 (1990).

CHAPTER 40

1. Agreements between competitors to allocate territory are illegal under §1 of the Sherman Act. *Palmer v. BRG of Georgia*, 498 U.S. 46, 111 S. Ct. 401, 1990 U.S. LEXIS 5901 (1990).

3. The Department of Justice investigated these firms to determine if they had colluded to fix salaries for summer and first-year associates in violation of the Sherman Act. But similar pay does not alone constitute an antitrust violation. So-called parallel pricing is common when businesses are competing with each other. To build a case against the firms, the government would need to find evidence that the firms colluded to set prices through meetings, telephone calls, or other communication. In the end, the government dropped its investigation. Andrea Gerlin, "Law Firms Face Salary-Fixing Inquiry," *Wall Street Journal*, July 2, 1993, p. B4.

5. The first issue is whether Visa and the restaurants engaged in an illegal refusal to deal. Did the group organize a boycott? If there was a boycott, did it have an adverse impact on competition in the credit card business? The FTC investigated these charges, but ultimately decided not to take action. American Express might be in violation of a different provision of the antitrust laws—the Robinson-Patman Act. Is it illegally discriminating in price between large-volume and small-volume restaurants? To defend against such a charge,

American Express would have to show that the reduced charges to large restaurants were based on lower costs for servicing them. Johnnie L. Roberts, "FTC Probes American Express Restaurant Fee Revolt," *Wall Street Journal*, Apr. 26, 1991, p. B1.

7. The court found that Owens-Corning had not violated the Robinson-Patman Act because the company had lowered its prices to meet the competition. *Reserve Supply Corp. v. Owens-Corning Fiberglass Corp. and CertainTeed Corp.*, CCH ¶69,304 (DC N IL, Dec. 1990); BNA ATRR No. 1498 (Jan 10, 1991).

9. The Justice Department and the FTC have promised not to challenge a joint venture among hospitals to purchase expensive medical equipment if the joint venture includes only the number of hospitals whose participation is needed to support the equipment. A hospital or group of hospitals will be considered able to support high-technology or other expensive medical equipment if it can recover the acquiring, operating, and marketing costs of the equipment over its useful life. Charles J. Steele, "Antitrust Statements Are Too Cautious," *Health Care Competition Week*, vol. 10, no. 19, 1993.

11. The court held for MasterCard on the grounds that its action had a moral, not an economic basis. Nor did MasterCard seek any competitive advantage for itself. Moreover, there was no anticompetitive effect because all adult bookstores and similar businesses were treated the same. *Alpha-Sentura Business Services, Inc. v. Interbank Card Association*, 1979-2 Trade Cas. (CCH) ¶62,960.

CHAPTER 41

1. EPS agreed to open its system to new rivals to avoid prosecution by the Justice Department on charges of illegal monopolization. The Justice Department alleged that banks that had to use EPS's processing services paid higher prices—on average 10¢ per transaction. EPS might also have been guilty of imposing an illegal tying arrangement. Edmund L. Andrews, "A.T.M. Case on Monopoly Is Settled," *New York Times*, Apr. 22, 1994, p. D1.

3. Pilkington settled the case by agreeing to drop its rule that American companies cannot build factories outside the territories assigned in their licenses. The company also agreed that some of its technology would now be publicly available. The Justice Department conceded that this case had little to do with the glass market in the United States. Instead it was seeking to ensure that American companies could freely operate abroad. The Justice Department was, in essence, using antitrust law to advance U.S. trade policy. The settlement of the case was the first under a 1992 policy change that permitted the department to challenge foreign business conduct that harms the U.S. export trade. Keith Bradsher, "U.S. Sues British in Antitrust Case," *New York Times*, May 27, 1994, p. 1.

5. The FTC accused the doctors of an illegal tying arrangement. Because the doctors effectively controlled such a high percentage of the patients needing the service, other oxygen companies could not enter the market. To settle the FTC charges, the companies agreed that no more than 25 percent of the lung specialists in the area would be affiliated with the companies. Robert Pear, "Doctors Assailed in Antitrust Move," *New York Times*, November 3, 1993, p. A25.

7. The first question is whether the U.S. government has the authority to act against companies in Japan. The Sherman Act provides that the government may pursue any companies overseas whose actions have a direct, substantial, and reasonably foreseeable effect on U.S. export trade. As for specific sections of antitrust law, the Justice Department might consider:

Exclusive dealing. If the keiretsus prohibit their buyers from dealing in competing goods, they could be in violation of §1 of the Sherman Act and §3 of the Clayton Act, provided that the arrangement substantially lessens competition in a given market.

Reciprocal dealing. If a Japanese company required one of its suppliers also to purchase goods from the company, the arrangement could be a reciprocal deal that violates §§1 and 2 of the Sherman Act, again provided that the arrangement has an anticompetitive effect on the market.

Joel Davidow, "Keiretsu and U.S. Antitrust," *Law and Policy in International Business*, vol. 24, no. 104, June 22, 1993, p. 1035.

9. The plaintiffs alleged that this practice was an illegal tying arrangement under §1 of the Sherman Act and §3 of the Clayton Act. The courts, however, rejected this claim. In the case of a suit against the Buffalo Bills, for instance, the court ruled that the team has a monopoly over the presentation of football games in both the regular and the preseason. Thus, the Bills are not using their market power in the regular season to shut out a significant part of the market in preseason games because there are no other competitors in the preseason market. *Coniglio v. Highwood Services, Inc.*, 495 F.2d 1286 (2d Cir. 1974).

CHAPTER 42

1. Jenkins entered into a second mortgage that was not from the same bank as her first mortgage. Therefore, under the Truth in Lending Act, Jenkins had an automatic right to rescind for three business days. However, because the lender did not give the required forms to her at the closing, Jenkins could rescind for up to three years. *Jenkins v. Landmark Mortgage Corp.*, 696 F. Supp. 1089, 1988 U.S. Dist. LEXIS 11397 (W.D. Va. 1988).

3. The court held that the defendant did not have a claim because there was no evidence the manufacturer had knowingly violated a consumer product safety rule. *Curtis v. Pope & Talbot*, 1992 U.S. App. LEXIS 14917 (6th Cir. 1992).

5. Once Chilton received notice of the dispute, it was obligated to re-verify the accuracy of the information. It was not enough simply to ask Schmidt, because Chilton knew that Schmidt and Pinner had had a dispute. If no one else could verify the reports Chilton should have deleted it. Schmidt was not in violation because the information he provided was essentially true—Pinner's account at Sherwin-

Williams was delinquent. *Pinner v. Schmidt*, 805 F.2d 1258 (5th Cir. 1986).

7. Although Guimond was never denied credit, she had been deterred from even applying because of her concerns about the contents of her file. TransUnion was liable. *Guimond v. Trans Union Credit Info. Co.*, 45 F.3d 1329, 1995 U.S. App. LEXIS 917 (9th Cir. 1995).

9. It depends on whom you believe. If, as Universal alleged, the damage was caused by Waldock's unreasonable use, then the warranty was invalid. The jury believed Waldock, however, and found that Universal had violated the warranty. The jury awarded Waldock the fair market value of the car. *Universal Motors v. Waldock*, 719 P.2d 254 (Alaska 1986).

11. The Fair Credit Reporting Act required TNT to ask Drury's permission before requesting a consumer report. Then, before firing him, TNT was required to give him a copy of the report and a description of his rights under this statute. *Drury v. TNT Holland Motor Express, Inc.*, 885 F. Supp. 161, 1994 U.S. Dist. LEXIS 11583 (D.Ct. 1994).

CHAPTER 43

1. Boldt was found guilty of a criminal violation of the Clean Water Act. *United States v. Boldt*, 929 F.2d 35, 1991 U.S. App. LEXIS 5372 (1st Cir. 1991).

3. Both FMC and the U.S. government were liable for cleanup costs under the Comprehensive Environmental Response, Compensation, and Liability Act (CERCLA). *FMC Corp. v. Department of Commerce*, 29 F.3d 833, 1994 U.S. App. LEXIS 16514 (3rd Cir. 1994).

5. When setting standards, the EPA was obligated by law to provide an adequate margin of safety. Establishing a standard that prevented EP elevation achieved this goal. Under the Clean Air Act, the EPA was not permitted to consider the economic impact of its decisions. The court upheld the EPA's standards. *Lead Industries Assn. v. EPA*, 647 F.2d 1130 (D.C. Cir. 1980).

7. The factory was required to obtain a permit from the state of Indiana ensuring that, even with the increase in pollution, the area would still meet the national ambient air quality standards. *United States v. AM General Corp.*, 34 F.3d 472, 1994 U.S. App. LEXIS 23975 (7th Cir. 1994).

9. A 1990 amendment to the Clean Air Act allowed polluters to meet federal standards four ways: installing scrubbers, using low-sulfur coal, switching to alternative fuels, or trading emission allowances. Illinois did not want these large plants to use low-sulfur fuel from out-of-state. A federal appeals court overturned the Illinois law on the grounds that it violated the Commerce Clause of the U.S. Constitution by discriminating against out-of-state coal producers. *Alliance for Clean Coal v. Miller*, 44 F.3d 591, 1995 U.S. App. LEXIS 460 (7th Cir. 1995).

11. "Point source" means a physical structure such as a pipe, ditch, channel, or vessel—not a human being. Therefore, Villegas is not a point source and is not liable for violating the Clean Water Act. *United States v. Plaza Health Laboratories, Inc.*, 3 F.3d 63, 1993 U.S. App. LEXIS 22414 (2d Cir. 1993).

CHAPTER 44

1. Merriam-Webster alleged that Random House had violated its trade dress. The court found for Random House because the logos and the color of the type face were different. *Merriam-Webster, Inc. v. Random House*, 35 F.3d 65, 1994 U.S. App. LEXIS 24401 (2d Cir. 1994).

3. Mr. Foissey is a "fruit sleuth." His task is to make sure that no one grows fruit without paying royalties to those who have patented the plants.

5. The PTO patented these numbers because they were useful, had never been used before by anyone else, and their use for this particular technique was not obvious. Simson Garfinkel, "A Prime Argument in Patent Debate," *Boston Globe*, Apr. 6, 1995, p. 69.

7. Yes. The court held that Yardley could obtain both a patent and a copyright on this design. *In re Yardley*, 493 F.2d 1389 (C.C.P.A. 1974).

9. *Nation* alleged "fair use." The appeals court agreed, but the Supreme Court overturned the appeals court, holding that the article was not fair use because it had damaged the market for the work. *Harper & Row v. Nation Enterprises*, 471 U.S. 539, 105 S. Ct. 2218, 1985 U.S. LEXIS 17 (1985).

11. The court held that these customer lists were not trade secrets because New England had not made sufficient effort to keep them secret. *New England Ins. v. Miller*, 1991 Conn. Super. LEXIS 817 (1991).

CHAPTER 45

1. Yes, he was. The farmers who cut across Thayer's property for half a century established an easement by prescription. Page acquired the easement when he bought his farm. He was allowed to do whatever was reasonably necessary to make use of his easement, including grading the road and making it safer. *Page v. Bloom*, 223 Ill. App. 3d 18, 584 N.E.2d 813, 1991 Ill. App. LEXIS 2060 (Ill. App. Ct. 1991).

3. The trial court was wrong. The church held a fee simple defeasible. The moment the church ceased to use the property as a church, the land reverted automatically to Collins and his heirs. *Collins v. Church of God of Prophecy*, 304 Ark. 37, 800 S.W.2d 418, 1990 Ark. LEXIS 566 (1990).

5. Yes, Summey is liable. Regardless of what Summey did or did not explicitly promise, the law imposes an implied warranty of habitability on the builder of new property. The jury found Summey liable for $205,000, and the appellate court affirmed. *Tower South Property Owners Assn. v. Summey Building Systems*, 1995 U.S. App. LEXIS 2881 (4th Cir. 1995).

7. The Fagerstroms win and take title to the land by adverse possession. Their use, and their ancestors' use, was open and notorious, and adverse to the claim of the true owner. The owner of the land had many years in which it could have ejected the Fagerstroms, but failed to do so. Although the Fagerstroms used the land only in the summer, that is sufficient to obtain title when it is the normal use for land in the given area. *Nome 2000 v. Fagerstrom*, 799 P.2d 304, 1990 Alaska LEXIS 107 (Alaska 1990).

9. (d). CPA Examination, May 1993, #51.
11. (d). CPA Examination, November 1990, #56.

CHAPTER 46

1. (d). CPA Examination, November 1992, #53.

3. Although the tenant is obligated to pay rent for the entire lease period, the current trend is to require a landlord to mitigate damages for property the tenant abandons early. Here, Andreo did not make a serious effort to lease the space for about nine months. The court rejected his rent claim for that period. He recovered the full rental amount for all months during which he seriously attempted to lease the space. *Andreo v. Tropical Isle Pet Shop*, 1992 Conn. Super. LEXIS 3108 (Conn. Super. Ct. 1992).

5. The Putnams win. The common law imposes very limited liability on a landlord for injuries and no liability at all for harm caused by a tenant's dogs. Other states have moved away from the common law rule, but the Arkansas Supreme Court gave summary judgment to the landlords. *Bryant v. Putnam*, 322 Ark. 284, 908 S.W.2d 338, 1995 Ark. LEXIS 631 (1995).

7. Rowley loses. The contemporary trend, followed in Alabama, is to prohibit a landlord from unreasonably withholding permission to assign. But a landlord is allowed to consider the appropriateness of the assignee, including its financial stability and intended use. Mobile was unable to do that, since Rowley provided no information about the proposed assignee, and the city was within its rights to refuse assignment. *Rowley v. City of Mobile*, 1995 Ala. Civ. App. LEXIS 619 (Ala. Civ. App. 1995).

9. (b). CPA Examination, November 1991, #53.

11. The court held the defendant liable for $900 (treble damages) and an additional $900 in attorney's fees. The rationale for treble damages is that, historically, landlords often willfully refuse to refund security deposits, knowing that most tenants would not bother to sue. That was obviously unethical. By trebling the damages, state legislatures have given landlords a financial incentive to be fair. By permitting attorney's fees, such laws ensure that injured tenants have access to court and a remedy. *Preece v. Turman Realty Co. Inc.*, 228 Ga. App. 609, 492 S.E.2d 342, 1997 Ga. App. LEXIS 1216 (Ga. App. 1997).

CHAPTER 47

1. Ann does. A. T. Rylands made a valid *inter vivos* gift of the violin while Ann was still a student. He intended to transfer ownership to her immediately and made delivery by permitting her to pick up the violin. From that point on, Ann owned it. *Rylands v. Rylands*, 1993 Conn. Super. LEXIS 823 (Conn. Super. Ct. 1993).

3. The trial court held that this was a gratuitous bailment and that therefore the defendants were liable only for gross negligence. Because there was no gross negligence, the court found for the defendants. The appellate court reversed, holding that this bailment mutually benefited the parties. The benefit to the district was less congestion, and the court said the car owner received the same benefit indirectly: cleared streets and smoother traffic flow. As a result the defendants were obligated to use ordinary care. The court remanded for a determination of whether the defendants had used ordinary care. *First American Bank, N.A. v. District of Columbia*, 583 A.2d 993, 1990 D.C. App. LEXIS 302 (D.C. 1990).

5. (d). CPA Examination, May 1994 #60.

7. A common carrier is one that makes its services available on a regular basis to the general public. A common carrier is strictly liable for any loss to the goods, unless the carrier can demonstrate that the harm was caused by an act of God, an enemy of the state, a public authority, the shipper itself, or the nature of the goods themselves. Most such defenses fail. A contract carrier, however, is an ordinary bailee, who will escape liability if it used ordinary care. Here, Putman made its services available to the general public on a regular basis and was thus a common carrier. It was liable for the full value of the lost rugs. *Marjan International Corp. v. V. K. Putman, Inc.*, 1993 U.S. Dist. LEXIS 18243 (S.D.N.Y. 1993).

9. The finder of lost property must try to locate the owner. The purse contained a photo identification, and the police could easily have tracked down the owner had Francia made a slight attempt to find her. *People v. Francia*, 154 Misc. 2d 211, 585 N.Y.S.2d 157, 1992 N.Y. Misc. LEXIS 232 (N.Y. Crim. Ct. 1992).

11. You should know that the common law of bailment obligates a bailor to keep goods in serviceable condition and to notify the bailee of defects in the property bailed if you knew of them or should reasonably have known of them. In addition, Article 2A of the Uniform Commercial Code governs leases. As a rental agency, you are a merchant, as the Code defines one, in the business of renting goods. The goods you rent are subject to implied warranties of merchantability and fitness for a particular purpose.

CHAPTER 48

1. The court held that the handwritten notes were a codicil, not a new will, because they did not indicate an intent to revoke the prior will. The codicil was admissible even though it had not been witnessed because it was a holographic will (handwritten). *Gilbert v. Gilbert*, 652 S.W.2d 663 (Ky. Ct. App. 1983).

3. (d). CPA Examination, November 1992, #9.

5. After a six-month trial, the probate court issued a 113-page decision that refused to apply the *cy pres* doctrine to modify the Marin-only restriction. The court determined that all of the income could be spent in Marin County. *Estate of Buck* 29 Cal. App. 4th 1846, 35 Cal. Rptr. 2d 442, 1994 Cal. App. LEXIS 1151 (Cal. Ct. App. 1994).

7. The court determined that Kosmalski held the property in constructive trust for Sharp because she had used undue influence to obtain it. *Sharp v. Kosmalski*, 40 N.Y.2d 119, 386 N.Y.S.2d 72, 351 N.E.2d 721 (1976).

9. (d). It means dying without a will, which is happening more often these days. An estimated two-thirds of

U.S. residents don't have wills, perhaps because they consider themselves too young to think about it or believe their assets aren't great enough. But without a will, the state will dictate how your possessions are distributed. And dying intestate can complicate probate—the process of legally distributing your estate. Where there's a will, there's a way. Don Wascoe Jr., "Consumer Queries," *Minneapolis Star Tribune*, Dec. 26, 1993, p. D1.

11. The court held that the bank could attach the property in the spendthrift trust because Chang was the settlor. Spendthrift trusts do not protect against creditors when the settlor is also the beneficiary. *Security Pacific Bank Washington v. Chang*, 80 F.3d 1412, 1996 U.S. App. LEXIS 7460 (1996).

CHAPTER 49

1. (a). CPA Examination, November 1989, #21.

3. Farm Bureau could refuse coverage only if the misrepresentation was material. The test of materiality is whether the company would have issued the policy even if it had known about Mark's prior tickets. *Zulcosky v. Farm Bureau Life Insurance Co.*, 206 Mich. App. 95, 520 N.W.2d 366, 1994 Mich. App. LEXIS 308 (Mich. Ct. App. 1994).

5. Harvey sued Allstate for a violation of the covenant of good faith and fair dealing. A jury awarded her $94,000 plus attorney's fees. *Harvey v. Allstate Insurance Co.*, 1993 U.S. App. LEXIS 33865 (10th Cir. 1993).

7. The insurance company had the right to cancel the policy because Anderson had made material misstatements on the application. *Auto-Owners Insurance Co. v. Johnson*, 209 Mich. App. 61, 530 N.W.2d 485, 1995 Mich. App. LEXIS 66 (Mich. Ct. App. 1995).

9. T.F. may not have intended to transmit herpes, but his action was so careless as to be the equivalent of intent. He was not covered under this policy. *R.W. v. T.F.*, 528 N.W.2d 869, 1995 Minn. LEXIS 246 (Minn. 1995).

11. The court held for Prudential. The two Prudential sales managers were not authorized to execute policies, only the home office could. Nor did they have the right to determine if premiums could be waived on a policy. Moreover, the application form specifically stated: "No agent can make or change a contract, or waive any of Prudential's rights or needs." *Nichols v. Prudential*, 851 S.W.2d 657, 1993 Mo. App. LEXIS 338 (Mo., 1993).

TABLE OF CASES

INDEX

C

D

E

T

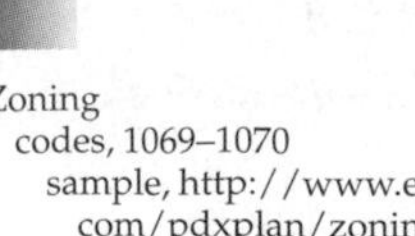

PHOTO CREDITS

6, © R. Sheridan/Ancient Art & Architecture; **30,** © *PhotoDisc, Inc;* **45,** © Susan Van Etten; **55,** © *PhotoDisc, Inc.;* **59,** © AP/Wide World Photo; **69,** © Susan Van Etten; **86,** © *PhotoDisc, Inc.;* **91,** © *Corbis/Bettmann;* **100,** © *Corbis/Annie Griffiths Belt;* **113,** © *PhotoDisc, Inc.;* **135,** © Susan Van Etten; **146,** © *PhotoDisc, Inc.;* **154,** © *PhotoDisc, Inc.;* **162,** © *PhotoDisc, Inc.;* **189,** © *Corbis/Neil Rabinowitz;* **202** © *Corbis/Jacques M. Chenet;* **209** © Corbis/Bettmann; **217,** © *Corbis/Lilly Lane;* **223,** © *Corbis/Stephanie Maze;* **235,** © *Corbis/National Gallery Collection, By kind permission;* **242,** © Susan Van Etten; **256,** © Corbis/Bettmann; **262,** © *PhotoDisc, Inc.;* **279,** © Susan Van Etten; **284,** © Susan Van Etten; **301,** © *Corbis/Gunter Marx;* **303,** © Susan Van Etten; **326,** © Susan Van Etten; **331,** © *PhotoDisc, Inc.;* **345,** © *Corbis/Julie Habel;* **349,** © *PhotoDisc, Inc.;* **367,** © *Corbis/Davis A. Northcott;* **371,** © *Corbis/Joseph Sohm; ChromoSohm Inc.;* **371,** © *Corbis/Morton Beebe, S.F.;* **386,** © *Corbis/Vince Streano;* **395,** © *PhotoDisc, Inc.;* **401,** © *Corbis/Mitchell Gerber;* **413,** © AP/Wide World Photos; **430,** © *PhotoDisc, Inc;* **436,** © *PhotoDisc, Inc.;* **451,** © *PhotoDisc, Inc.;* **459,** © Susan Van Etten; **462,** © Susan Van Etten; **488,** © *PhotoDisc, Inc.;* **500,** © Susan Van Etten; **512,** © *Corbis/The Purcell Team;* **522,** © Gamma Liaison International; **565,** © Susan Van Etten; **586,** © Susan Van Etten; **621,** © *Corbis/Paul A. Souders;* **633,** © *Corbis/John Garrett;* **635,** © *Corbis/Jim Zuckerman;* **659,** © Susan Van Etten; **668,** © *Corbis/Kelly-Moony Photography;* **683,** © *Corbis/Michael Yamashita;* **691,** © AP/Wide World Photos; **712,** Courtesy of the Library of Congress; **716,** © *PhotoDisc, Inc.;* **721,** © *Corbis/Hulton-Deutsch Collection;* **731,** © Susan Van Etten; **731,** © *PhotoDisc, Inc.;* **739,** © Susan Van Etten; **761,** Courtesy of the Montreal Expos Baseball; **772,** © *Corbis/Mitchell Gerber;* **781,** © *Corbis/Historical Picture Archive;* **786,** Corbis/Bettmann-UPI; **789,** Courtesy Colette Bohatch Mehle, Esq.; **811,** © Susan Van Etten; **825,** © Susan Van Etten; **836,** © *PhotoDisc, Inc.;* **848,** © *Corbis/Bill Rose;* **853,** © *Corbis/Amos Nachoum;* **862,** © Susan Van Etten; **870,** © Susan Van Etten; **887,** © *Corbis/Bettmann;* **895,** © Susan Van Etten; **895** © Susan Van Etten; **900,** © *Corbis/Bob Krist;* **920,** © *Corbis/Lynn Goldsmith;* **926,** © Corbis/Bettman-UPI; **947,** © Susan Van Etten; **947,** © Susan Van Etten; **966,** © Susan Van Etten; **969,** © Susan Van Etten; **977,** © Susan Van Etten; **987,** © Susan Van Etten; **1003,** © *Corbis/David Muench;* **1005,** © Susan Van Etten; **1010,** © Susan Van Etten; **1029,** © Susan Van Etten; **1038,** © Susan Van Etten; **1038,** © Susan Van Etten; **1056,** © *Corbis/Monika Smith; Cordaiy Photo Library Ltd.;* **1079,** © *Corbis/Catherine Karnow;* **1081,** © Susan Van Etten; **1108,** © *Corbis/Robert Maass;* **1111,** © *Corbis/Michael Yamamshita;* **1119** © Corbis/Reuters; **1135,** © *Corbis/Catherine Karnow;* **1142,** © Susan Van Etten; **1153,** © *PhotoDisc, Inc.*